Contents

Colour section 1–24

Introduction 6
Where to go 8
When to go 12
Things not to miss 14

Basics 25–80

Getting there 27
Getting around 35
Accommodation 45
Food and drink 50
The media 55
Sports and outdoor activities ... 59
Living in France 65
Culture and etiquette 67
Shopping 68
Travelling with children 69
Travel essentials 70

Guide 81–1264

1. Paris and around 83
2. The north 217
3. Alsace and Lorraine 293
4. Normandy 337
5. Brittany 407
6. The Loire 489
7. Burgundy 561
8. Poitou-Charentes and the Atlantic coast 615
9. The Dordogne, Limousin and Lot 679
10. The Pyrenees 755
11. Languedoc 839
12. The Massif Central 899
13. The Alps and Jura 957
14. The Rhône valley and Provence 1023
15. The Côte d'Azur 1119
16. Corsica 1201

Contexts 1265–1337

History 1267
Art 1291
Architecture 1305
Cinema 1313
Books and maps 1328

Language 1339–1355

Travel store 1357–1360

Small print & Index 1361–1384

Cafés, bistros and brasseries colour section following p.168

Walking in France colour section following p.808

Festive France colour section following p.1048

◀◀ Spectators at the Tour de France ◀ Driving through the dappling, Languedoc

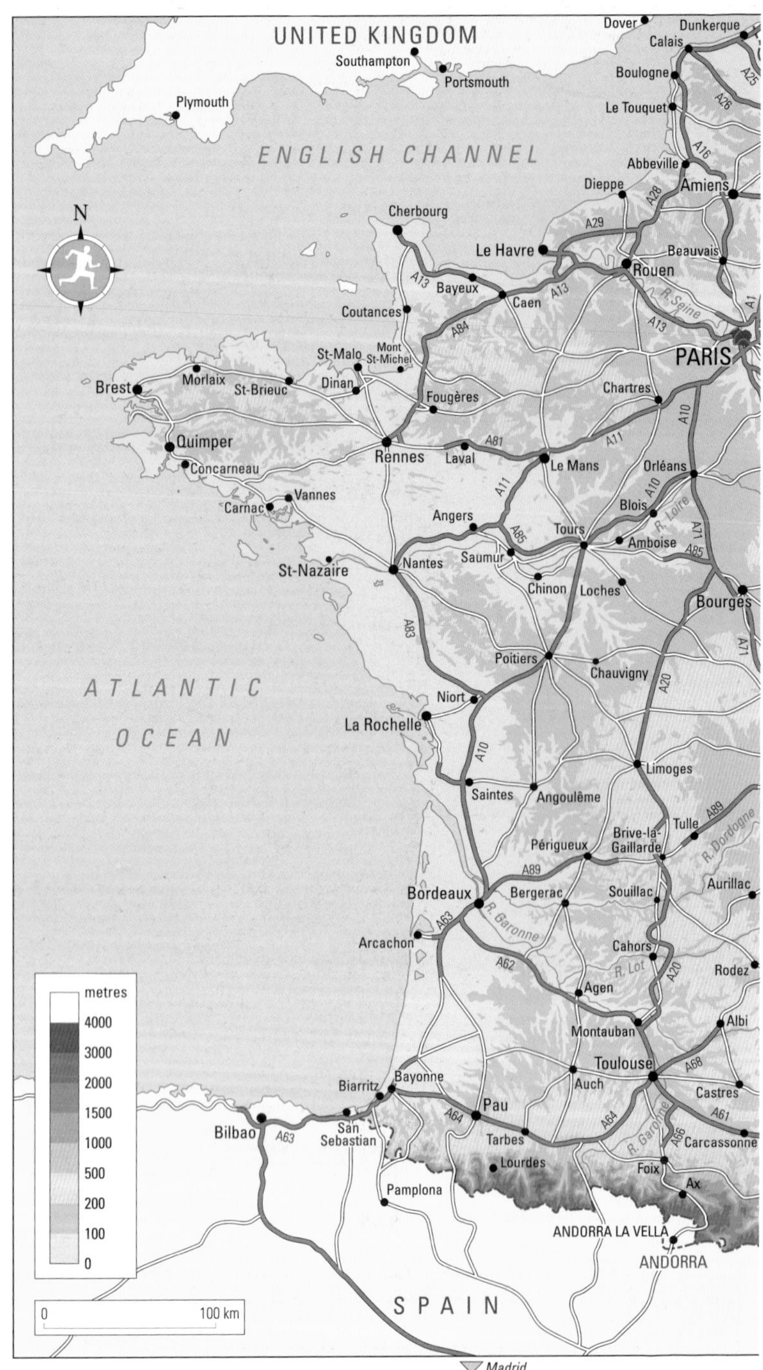
UNITED KINGDOM
ENGLISH CHANNEL
ATLANTIC OCEAN
SPAIN
ANDORRA
N
Dover
Dunkerque
Calais
Boulogne
Le Touquet
Abbeville
Amiens
Dieppe
Southampton
Portsmouth
Plymouth
Cherbourg
Le Havre
Rouen
Beauvais
Bayeux
Caen
Coutances
PARIS
R. Seine
St-Malo
Mont St-Michel
Dinan
Morlaix
St-Brieuc
Brest
Fougères
Chartres
Quimper
Concarneau
Rennes
Laval
Le Mans
Orléans
Vannes
Carnac
Blois
R. Loire
Angers
Tours
Amboise
Saumur
St-Nazaire
Nantes
Chinon
Loches
Bourges
Poitiers
Chauvigny
Niort
La Rochelle
Limoges
Saintes
Angoulême
Tulle
R. Dordogne
Périgueux
Brive-la-Gaillarde
Aurillac
Bordeaux
Bergerac
Souillac
R. Garonne
Arcachon
Cahors
R. Lot
Rodez
Agen
Montauban
Albi
Toulouse
Auch
Castres
Biarritz
Bayonne
Pau
Bilbao
San Sebastian
Tarbes
Carcassonne
Lourdes
Foix
Ax
Pamplona
ANDORRA LA VELLA
Madrid
A25
A26
A16
A28
A29
A13
A1
A84
A81
A11
A10
A85
A71
A83
A20
A89
A63
A62
A68
A64
A61
A66
metres
4000
3000
2000
1500
1000
500
200
100
0
0
100 km

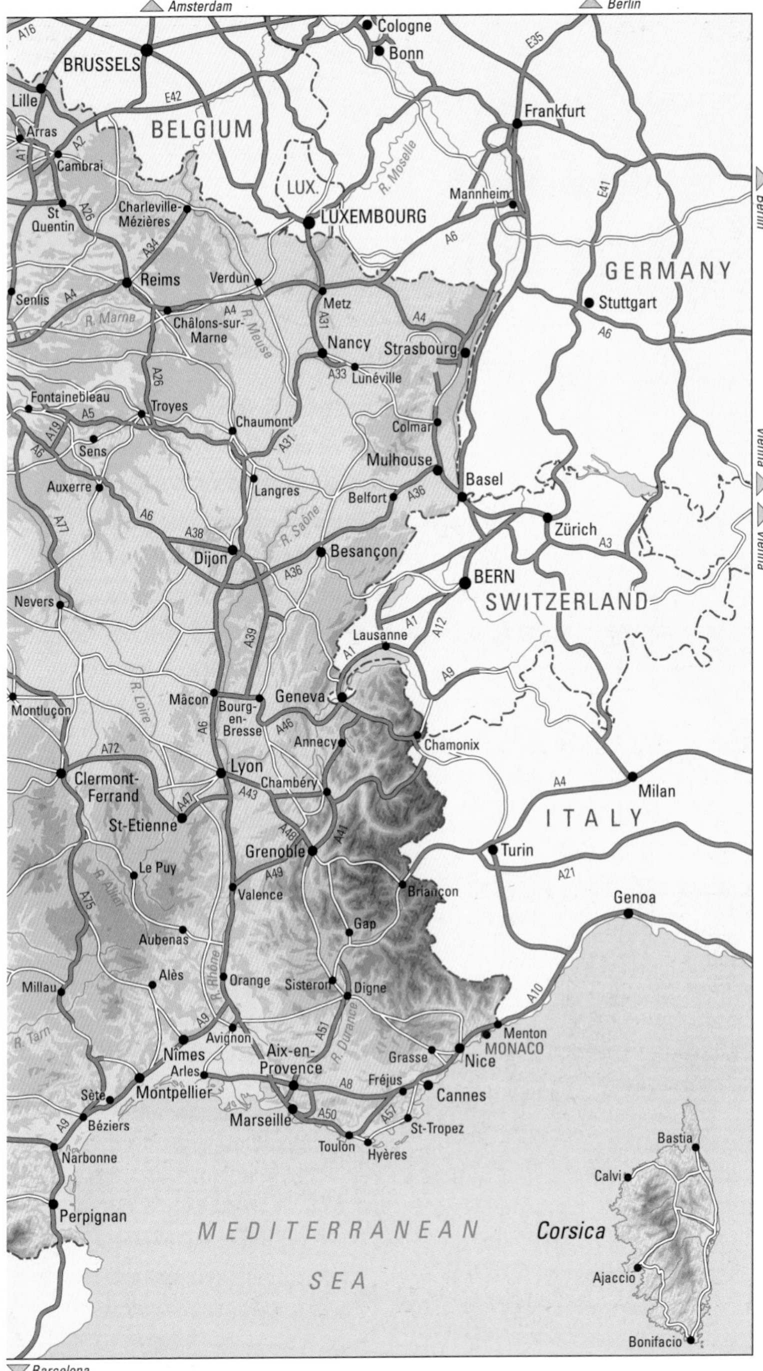
Amsterdam
Berlin
Cologne
Bonn
BRUSSELS
Lille
BELGIUM
Arras
Cambrai
LUX.
LUXEMBOURG
Frankfurt
Mannheim
R. Moselle
St Quentin
Charleville-Mézières
Reims
Verdun
Metz
GERMANY
Stuttgart
Senlis
R. Marne
Châlons-sur-Marne
R. Meuse
Nancy
Strasbourg
Lunéville
Fontainebleau
Troyes
Chaumont
Colmar
Sens
Mulhouse
Basel
Auxerre
Langres
Belfort
R. Saône
Zürich
Dijon
Besançon
BERN
SWITZERLAND
Nevers
Lausanne
Montluçon
R. Loire
Mâcon
Bourg-en-Bresse
Geneva
Annecy
Chamonix
Lyon
Clermont-Ferrand
Chambéry
Milan
ITALY
St-Etienne
Grenoble
Turin
Le Puy
R. Allier
Valence
Briançon
Genoa
Gap
Aubenas
Alès
R. Rhône
Orange
Sisteron
Digne
Millau
R. Durance
R. Tarn
Avignon
Menton
MONACO
Nîmes
Aix-en-Provence
Grasse
Nice
Arles
Fréjus
Cannes
Sète
Montpellier
Marseille
St-Tropez
Béziers
Toulon
Hyères
Bastia
Narbonne
Calvi
Perpignan
MEDITERRANEAN SEA
Corsica
Ajaccio
Bonifacio
Vienna
Barcelona
A16
E42
A2
A1
A26
A34
A4
A31
A33
A5
A19
A6
A77
A38
A36
A39
A12
A9
A46
A72
A47
A43
A48
A41
A49
A75
A51
A8
A50
A57
A10
A21
A3
E35
E41

Introduction to France

The sheer physical diversity of France would be hard to exhaust in a lifetime of visits. Landscapes range from the fretted coasts of Brittany and the limestone hills of Provence to the canyons of the Pyrenees and the half-moon bays of Corsica, and from the lushly wooded valleys of the Dordogne and the gentle meadows of the Loire valley to the glaciated peaks of the Alps. Each region looks and feels different, has its own style of architecture, its own characteristic food and often its own dialect. Though the French word *pays* is the term for a whole country, people frequently refer to their own region as *mon pays* – my country – and this strong sense of regional identity has persisted despite centuries of centralizing governments, from Louis XIV to de Gaulle.

Industrialization came relatively late to France, and for all the millions of French people that live in cities, the idea persists that theirs is a rural country. The importance of the land reverberates throughout French culture, manifesting itself in areas as diverse as regional pride in local cuisine and the state's fierce defence of Europe's agricultural subsidies. Perhaps the most striking feature of the French **countryside** is the sense of space. There are huge tracts of woodland and undeveloped land without a house in sight, and, away from the main urban centres, hundreds of towns and villages have changed only slowly and organically over the years, their old houses and streets intact, as much a part of the natural landscape as the rivers, hills and fields.

Despite this image of pastoral tranquillity, France's history is notable for its extraordinary vigour. For more than a thousand years the country has been in the vanguard of European development, and the accumulation of wealth and experience is evident everywhere in the astonishing variety of **things to see**, from the Dordogne's prehistoric cave-paintings and the Roman monuments of the south, to the Gothic cathedrals of the north, the châteaux of the Loire, and the cutting-edge architecture of the *grands projets* in Paris. This legacy of history and culture – **la patrimoine** – is so widely dispersed across the land that even the briefest of stays will leave the visitor with a powerful sense of France's past.

The importance of these traditions is felt deeply by the French state, which fights to preserve and develop its national **culture** perhaps harder than any other country in the world, and private companies, who also strive to maintain French traditions in arenas as diverse as *haute couture*, pottery and, of course, food. The fruits of these efforts are evident in the subsidized **arts**, notably the film industry, and in the lavishly endowed and innovative **museums and galleries**.

▲ Café, St-Germain, Paris

Fact file

- With a land area of 547,000 square kilometres, France is the **second largest country** in Europe; its population of around 60 million is less only than its European neighbours, Germany and the UK.
- Now in its Fifth Republic, France has a long **secular republican tradition** dating back to the Revolution of 1789. Yet the majority of the population is Roman Catholic – notionally, at least – and there's a substantial Muslim minority of around 5–10 percent.
- **The Government** consists of a directly elected president and a two-house parliament. As a nuclear power and G8-member, and with a permanent seat on the United Nations Security Council, France retains a strong international profile.
- **Annual GDP** per capita is around US$30,000, making France one of the world's richer countries, but unemployment is a persistent problem, at around 9 percent. Taxes are high, at around 45 percent of GDP, but so is social spending, at almost 30 percent.
- France remains by far the **most popular tourist destination** in the world, with some 75 million visitors each year.

◀ St-Cirque-Lapopie

From colonial history to fishing techniques, aeroplane design to textiles, and migrant shepherds to manicure, these collections can be found across the nation, but, inevitably, first place must go to the fabulous displays of fine art in Paris, a city which has nurtured more than its share of the finest creative artists of the last century and a half, both French – Monet and Matisse for example – and foreign, such as Picasso and Van Gogh.

There are all kinds of pegs on which to hang a holiday in France: a city, a region, a river, a mountain range, gastronomy, cathedrals, châteaux. All that open space means there's endless scope for outdoor activities – from walking, canoeing and cycling to skiing and sailing – but if you need more urban stimuli – clubs, shops, fashion, movies, music – then the great cities provide them in abundance.

Where to go

Travelling around France is easy. Restaurants and hotels proliferate, many of them relatively inexpensive when compared with other developed Western European countries. Train services are admirably efficient, as is the road network – especially the (toll-paying) autoroutes – and cyclists are much admired and encouraged. **Information** is highly organized and available from tourist offices across the country, as well as from specialist organizations for walkers, cyclists, campers and so on.

Hundreds of towns and villages have changed only slowly and organically over the years... as much a part of the natural landscape as the rivers, hills and fields.

As for specific destinations, **Paris**, of course, is the outstanding cultural centre, with its impressive buildings and atmospheric backstreets, its art, trendy nightlife and ethnic diversity, though the great **provincial cities** – Lyon, Bordeaux, Toulouse, Marseille – all now vie with the capital and each other for prestige in the arts, ascendancy in sport and innovation in attracting visitors.

For most people, however, it's the unique characters of the **regions** – and not least their cuisines – that will define a trip. Few holiday-makers stay long in the largely flat, industrial **north**, but there are some fine cathedrals and energetic cities to leaven the mix. The picture is similar in **Alsace-Lorraine** where Germanic influences are strong, notably in the food. On the northern Atlantic coast, **Normandy** has a rich heritage of cathedrals, castles, battlefields and beaches – and, with its cream-based sauces, an equally rich cuisine. To the west, **Brittany** is more renowned for its Celtic links, beautiful coastline, prehistoric sites and seafood, while the **Loire** valley, extending inland towards Paris, is famed for soft, fertile countryside and a marvellous parade of châteaux. Further east, the green valleys of **Burgundy** shelter a wealth of Romanesque churches, and the wines and food are among the finest in France. More Romanesque churches follow the

▲ Métro sign outside the Pompidou Centre, Paris

Food and drink

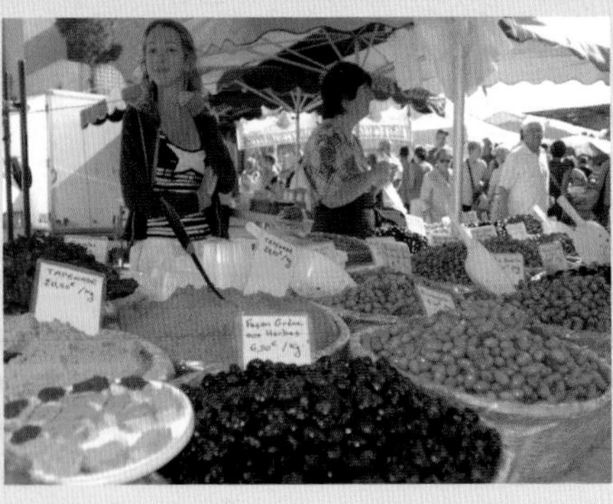

The power and influence of French culture is evident anywhere that people read, wear clothes, vote or go to the cinema, but nowhere is the country's contribution greater than in culinary affairs. In France, a picnic could be a simple crusty baguette with cheese, washed down by an inexpensive red wine, or a gourmet feast of cold meats and prepared salads, as available from practically any charcuterie; either way it's likely to be as good as you'll find anywhere in the world. The same is true of eating out, whether that means a perfect *steak-frites* at a railway-station brasserie, a lovingly prepared set menu in a provincial restaurant, featuring the homeliest of regional specialities, or the most exquisite refinements of a Parisian chef.

There's an endless variety of cheeses, cakes and pastries to match, as well as wines – and not just those from the renowned vineyards of Bordeaux, Burgundy and Champagne. Whether choosing a good local vintage or pondering some obscure regional speciality, never be afraid to ask advice – most French people are true enthusiasts, ever ready to convert the uninitiated.

pilgrim routes through rural **Poitou-Charentes** and down the Atlantic coast to **Bordeaux**, where the wines rival those of Burgundy. Inland from Bordeaux, visitors flock to the gorges, prehistoric sites and picturesque fortified villages of the **Dordogne** and neighbouring **Limousin**, drawn too by the truffles and duck and goose dishes of Périgord cuisine. To the south, the great mountain chain of the **Pyrenees** rears up along the Spanish border, running from the Basque country on the Atlantic to the Catalan lands of **Roussillon** on the Mediterranean; there's fine walking and skiing to be had, as well as beaches at either end. Further along the Mediterranean coast, **Languedoc** offers dramatic landscapes, medieval towns and Cathar castles, as well as more beaches, while the

▼ Horses in the Camargue

Massif Central, in the centre of the country, is undeveloped and little visited, but beautiful nonetheless, with its rivers, forests and the wild volcanic uplands of the **Auvergne**. The **Alps**, of course, are prime skiing territory, but a network of signposted paths makes walking a great way to explore too; to the north, the wooded mountains of the **Jura** provide further scope for outdoor pursuits. Stretching down from the Alps to the Mediterranean is **Provence**, which, as generations of travellers have discovered, seems to have everything: Roman ruins, picturesque villages, vineyards and lavender fields – and legions of visitors. Its cuisine is similarly diverse, encompassing fruit, olives, herbs, seafood, lamb and an unusual emphasis on vegetables. Along the Provençal coast, the beaches, towns and chic resorts of the **Côte d'Azur** form a giant smile extending from the down-at-heel but vibrant city of **Marseille** to the super-rich Riviera hotspots of Nice and Monaco. For truly fabulous beaches, however, head for the rugged island of **Corsica**, birthplace of Napoleon and home to an Italian-leaning culture and cuisine and some fascinating Neolithic sculptures.

The French

According to the clichés, the French are stylish, romantic and passionate. They also have a reputation for rudeness – and yet they are courteous with each other to the point of formality. It's common for someone entering a shop to wish customers and shopkeeper alike a general "good morning", and foreigners on business quickly learn the importance of shaking hands, asking the right questions and maintaining respectful eye contact. At the same time, if they want something, many French people can be direct in ways that are disconcerting for Anglo-Saxons. To foreigners stumbling over the language, never mind the cultural gap, this can seem like rudeness; it isn't. It's fairer to say that the French are proud. Opinions tend to be held and argued strongly – it's not for nothing that so many revolutions have shaken the political landscape. Culture, too, is a source of great pride, and artists, writers and thinkers are held in high esteem even beyond elite circles. And French people everywhere are proud of their locality. Whether it's for a village shopfront, a civic floral display or another landmark building for the French state, no effort is too great.

View over Nice

When to go

The single most important factor in deciding when to visit France is tourism itself. As most French people take their holidays in their own country, it's as well to consider avoiding the main **French holiday periods** – mid-July to the end of August. It's at this time that almost the entire country closes down, except for the tourist industry itself. You can easily walk a kilometre and more in Paris, for example, in search of an open boulangerie, and the city sometimes seems deserted by all except fellow tourists. Prices in the resorts rise to take full advantage and often you can't find a room for love nor money, and on the Côte d'Azur not even a space in the campsites. The seaside is the most crowded, but the mountains and popular regions like the Dordogne are not far behind. Easter, too, is a bad time for Paris: half of Europe's schoolchildren seem to descend on the city. For the same reasons, ski buffs should keep in mind the February school ski break. And no one who values life, limb, and sanity should ever be caught on the roads during the last weekend of July or August, and least of all on the weekend of August 15.

Generally speaking, **climate** needn't be a major consideration in planning when to go. If you're a skier, of course, you wouldn't choose the

The great provincial cities – Lyon, Bordeaux, Toulouse, Marseille – all now vie with the capital and each other for prestige in the arts, ascendancy in sport and innovation in attracting visitors.

mountains between May and November; and if you want a beach holiday, you wouldn't head for the seaside out of summer – except for the Mediterranean coast, which is at its most attractive in spring. **Northern France**, like nearby Britain, is wet and unpredictable. **Paris** has a marginally better climate than New York, rarely reaching the extremes of heat and cold of that city,

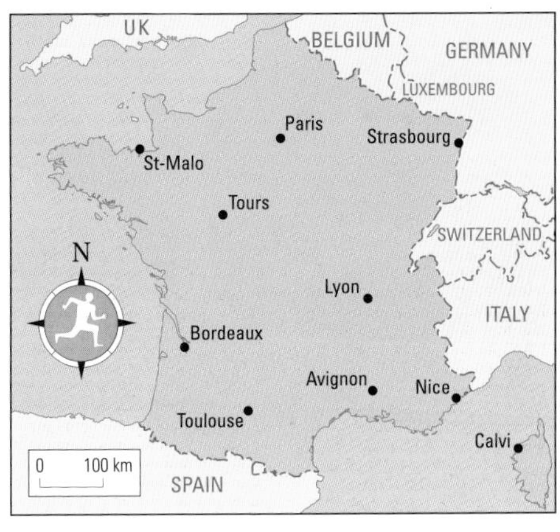

but only **south of the Loire** does the weather become significantly warmer. **West coast** weather, even in the south, is tempered by the proximity of the Atlantic, subject to violent storms and close thundery days even in summer. The **centre** and **east**, as you leave the coasts behind, have a more continental climate, with colder winters and hotter summers. The most reliable weather is along and behind the **Mediterranean** coastline and on **Corsica**, where winter is short and summer long and hot.

Average daily maximum temperatures

For a recorded weather forecast you can phone the main forecasting line on Ⓣ08.92.68.08.08, or check online at Ⓦwww.meteofrance.com. Temperatures below are given in degrees Celsius.

	Jan	Feb	Mar	Apr	May	Jun	Jul	Aug	Sep	Oct	Nov	Dec
Paris	7.5	7	10.2	15.7	16.6	23.4	25	25.6	21	16.5	11.7	7.8
Strasbourg	5.5	5.3	9.3	13.7	15.8	23	24	26.3	21	14.9	7.6	4.7
St-Malo	9	8.6	11	17	16	22.7	25	24	21.2	16.5	12	9.3
Tours	7.8	6.8	10.3	16	16.4	23.6	25.8	24.5	21	16.2	11.2	7
Lyon	7.4	6.7	10.8	15.8	17.3	25.6	27.6	27.6	23.5	16.5	10.4	7.8
Bordeaux	10	9.4	12.2	19.5	18	23.7	27	25.7	24	19.7	15.4	11
Toulouse	12.4	11.5	12.5	17.6	20	26.5	28.4	28	26	21	15.8	13.5
Avignon	12	12	14	18.5	20.8	26.6	28	28.4	25.2	22.2	16.8	14
Nice	12	12	14	18.5	20.8	26.6	28	28.4	25.2	22.2	16.8	14
Calvi	13	14	16	18	21	25	27	28	26	22	17	14

34 things not to miss

It's not possible to see everything that France has to offer in one trip – and we don't suggest you try. What follows is a selective taste of the country's highlights: natural wonders and outstanding sights, plus the best activities and experiences. They're arranged in five colour-coded categories, so you can browse through to find the very best things to see and do. All highlights have a page reference to take you straight into the guide, where you can find out more.

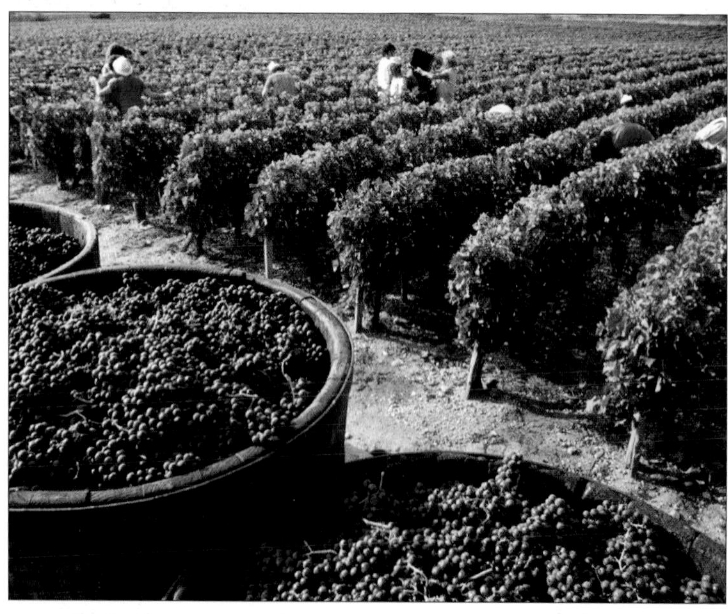

01 **Wine** Page **52** • French wines are unrivalled in the world for their sophistication, diversity and sheer excellence.

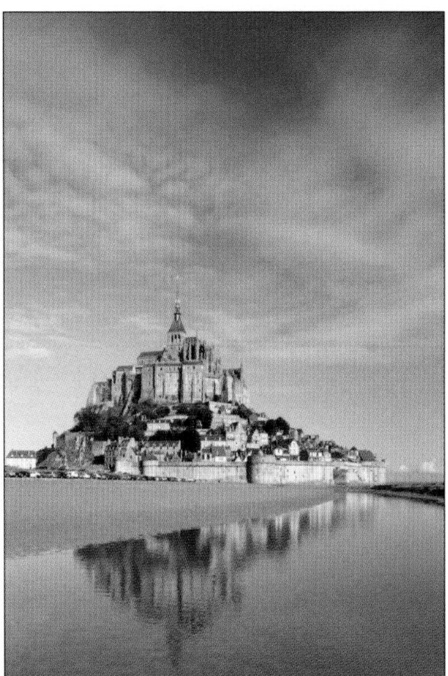

02 Mont St-Michel Page **389** • Second only to the Eiffel Tower as France's best-loved landmark, the *merveille* of Mont St-Michel is a splendid union of nature and architecture.

03 Bastille Day Page **56** & *Festive France* **colour section** • July 14 sees national celebrations commemorating the beginning of the French Revolution, with fireworks and parties across the whole country.

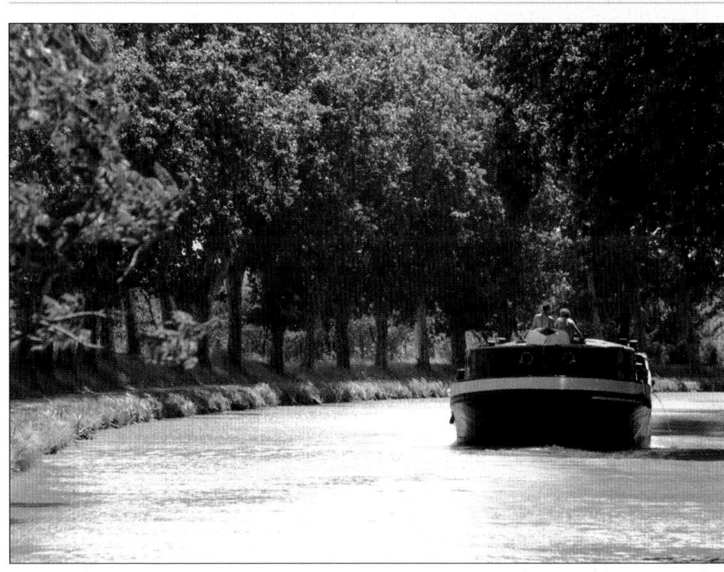

04 Canal du Midi Page **874** • A calm, watery avenue, stretching from beyond Toulouse to the Mediterranean. Cycling, walking or drifting along its tree-shaded course is the most atmospheric way of savouring France's southwest.

05 Avignon Page **1060** • Great city of the popes, and once one of France's artistic centres, picturesque Avignon offers spectacular monuments and museums, countless places to eat and drink, and a superb annual summer festival.

06 Carnac Page **472** • Archeologically, Brittany is one of the richest regions in the world and the alignments at Carnac rival Stonehenge.

07 Amiens cathedral Page **242** • The largest Gothic building in all France, this lofty cathedral has a clever evening light show that gives a vivid idea of how the west front would have looked when it rejoiced in coloured paint.

08 Tour de France Page **59** • One of the world's greatest sporting events, this gruelling, three-week bike race follows a different route around the country every year, always ending on the Champs-Élysées.

09 Beaches Page **1220** • France's coasts have many beautiful beaches with some of the best being found on Corsica, including the plage de Saleccia, with its soft white shell sand, turquoise water and not a building or road in sight.

10 The Issenheim altarpiece Page **317** • The village of Colmar might be excessively twee, but it's still worth a visit for Grünewald's amazing altarpiece, one of the most extraordinary works of art in the country.

11 Les Gorges du Verdon Page **1104** • The mighty gorges are Europe's answer to the Grand Canyon, and offer stunning views, a range of hikes, and colours and scents that are uniquely, gorgeously Provençal.

12 Cheese Page **52** • For serious cheese-lovers, France is paradise. Not so for politicans: as an exasperated de Gaulle once commented, "How can you govern a country that has 245 kinds of cheese?"

13 Châteaux of the Loire Page **500** • The River Loire is lined with gracious châteaux, of which Chambord is surely the most staggeringly impressive, both for its size and the double-spiral staircase designed by Leonardo da Vinci.

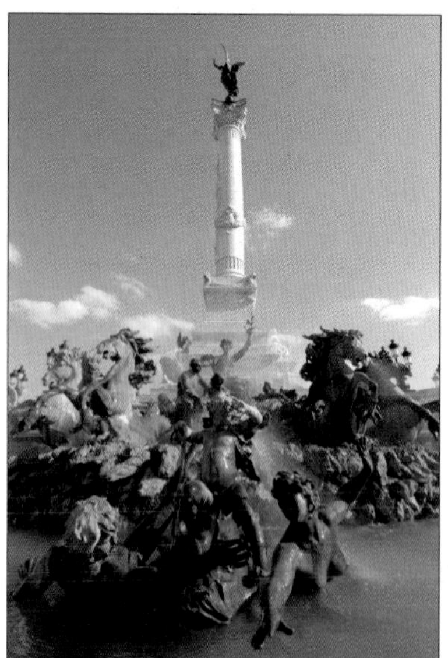

14 Bordeaux Page **657** •Stylish and lively Bordeaux became the principal English stronghold in France for three hundred years, and is still known for the refined red wines – claret – which the English popularized.

15 The GR20 Page **1226** & *Walking in France* **colour section** • Arguably France's most dramatic – and most demanding – long-distance footpath climbs through and over Corsica's precipitous mountains for some 170km.

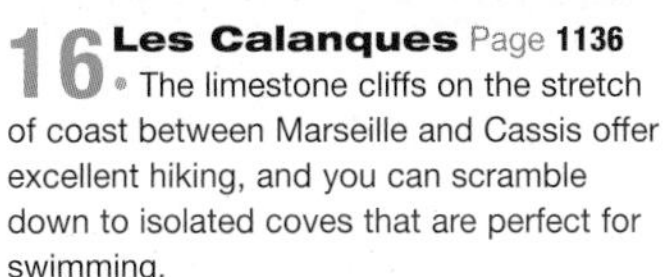

16 **Les Calanques** Page **1136** • The limestone cliffs on the stretch of coast between Marseille and Cassis offer excellent hiking, and you can scramble down to isolated coves that are perfect for swimming.

17 **Cafés** See *Cafés, bistros and brasseries* **colour section** • Taking your time over a glass of wine or cup of coffee in a café is a quintessentially French experience.

18 **War memorials** Page **263 & 375** • World Wars I and II left permanent scars on the French countryside – and on its psyche. The dead are remembered in solemn, sometimes overwhelming cemeteries, such as the one at Ryes in Normandy.

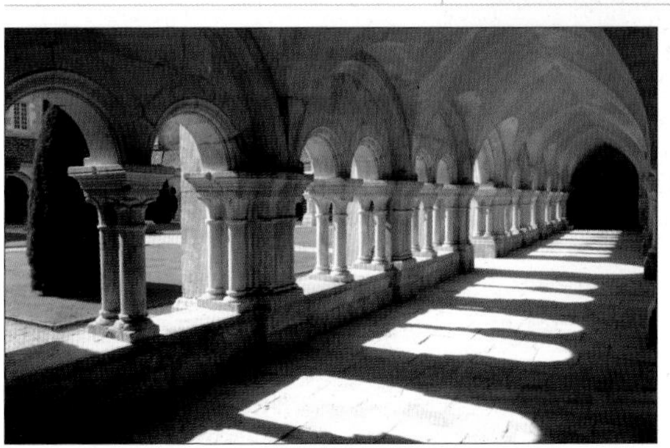

19 **Fontenay Abbey** Page **576** • One of the most complete monastic complexes anywhere, this Burgundian monastery has a serene setting in a stream-filled valley.

20 Bayeux Tapestry Page **379** • This 70-metre-long tapestry is an astonishingly detailed depiction of the 1066 Norman invasion of England, and one of the finest artistic works of the early medieval era.

21 Outdoor activities Page **61** • From surfing off Biarritz and skiing in Val d'Isère to climbing in the Pyrenees and canoeing on the Loire, France has energetic pursuits to suit everyone.

22 Medieval Provençal villages Page **1090** • Provence's hilltop villages attract visitors by the score. Though Gordes is one of the most famous, there are others less well known but equally beautiful.

23 **Bastide towns** Page **694** • Monpazier is one of the best preserved of the fortified towns – *bastides* – built in the Dordogne region during the turbulent medieval period when there was almost constant conflict between the French and English.

24 **Jardin du Luxembourg** Page **141** • Paris's most beautiful park, in the heart of the laid-back Left Bank, is the ideal spot for relaxing.

25 Aix-en-Provence Page **1094** • Marseille may be the biggest city in Provence, but aristocratic Aix is the region's capital, and it's a wonderful place to shop, eat and linger under the plane trees with a pastis.

26 Champagne tasting at Épernay Page **279** • Dom Pérignon might be the most famous, but there are plenty of other bubblies to try in the atmospheric cellars of Épernay's *maisons*.

27 Strasbourg cathedral Page **302** • Visible throughout Strasbourg is the magnificent filigree spire of the pink sandstone cathedral, dominating not just the city but much of Alsace.

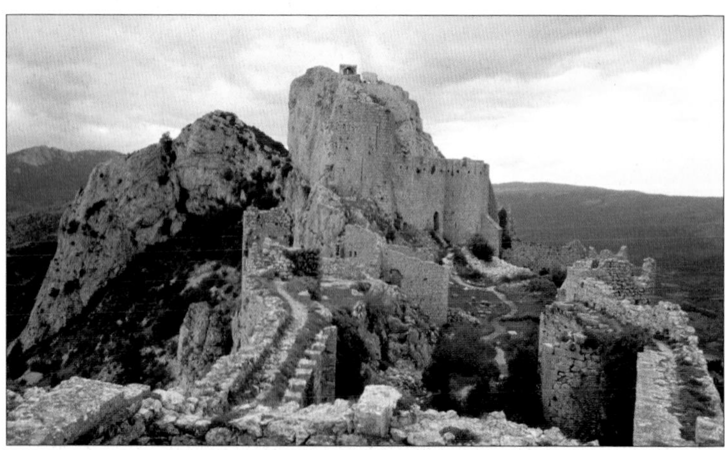

28 Cathar castles Page **821** • Languedoc's mountains are dotted with these gaunt fortresses, grim but fascinating relics of the brutal crusade launched by the Catholic church and northern French nobility against the heretic Cathars.

29 The Louvre Page **115** • The palace of the Louvre cuts a grand Classical swathe through the centre of Paris and houses what is nothing less than the gold standard of France's artistic tradition.

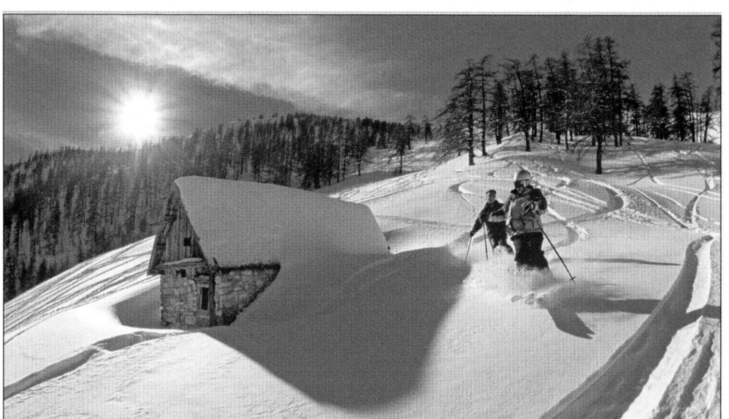

30 Winter sports in the Alps Page **981** • The French Alps are home to some of the world's most prestigious ski resorts, offering a wide range of winter sports.

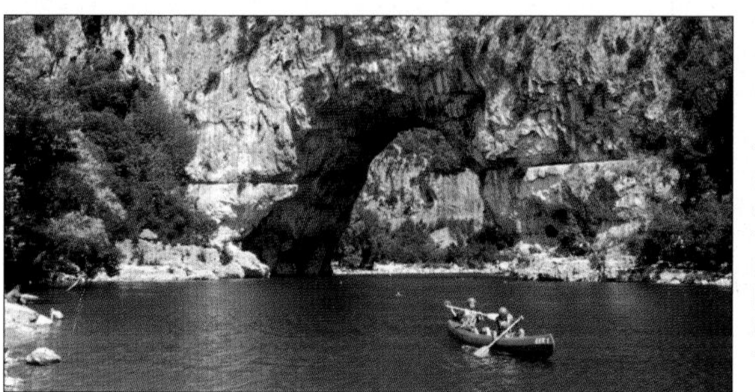

31 Gorges de l'Ardèche Page **947** • The fantastic gorges begin at the Pont d'Arc and cut their way through limestone cliffs before emptying into the Rhône valley.

32 Annecy Page **988** • One of the prettiest towns in the Alps, Annecy has a picture-postcard quality which even the crowds can't mar.

33 Prehistoric cave art Page **704** • Prehistoric art can be seen in several places around France, but perhaps the most impressive paintings are those at Lascaux in the Dordogne.

34 Carcassonne Page **872** • So atmospheric is this medieval fortress town, that it manages to resist even relentless commercialization and summer's throng of visitors.

Basics

Basics

Getting there 27

Getting around 35

Accommodation 45

Food and drink 50

The media 55

Sports and outdoor activities 59

Living in France 65

Culture and etiquette 67

Shopping 68

Travelling with children 69

Travel essentials 70

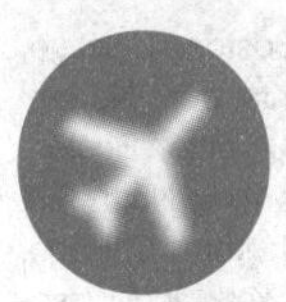

Getting there

The quickest way of reaching France from most parts of the United Kingdom and Ireland is by air. The budget airlines offer a vast array of flights to destinations all over the country, whilst the more traditional carriers such as British Airways and Air France also cover much of the country between them. From southeast England, however, the Channel Tunnel rail link provides a viable alternative, making the journey from London to Paris in just three hours. The Tunnel is the most flexible option if you want to take your car to France, though cross-Channel ferries are often cheaper. It's also worth bearing in mind that if you live west of London, or are heading to Brittany or to southwest France, the ferry services to Roscoff, St-Malo, Cherbourg, Caen and Le Havre can save a lot of driving time. From the US and Canada a number of airlines fly direct to Paris, from where you can pick up onward connections. You can also fly direct to Paris from South Africa, whilst the best fares from Australia and New Zealand are to be found if you fly via Asia.

Whether you are travelling by air, sea or rail, prices generally depend on the season, and are at their highest from around early June to the end of August, when the weather is best; fares drop during the "shoulder" seasons – roughly September to October and April to May – and are at their cheapest during the low season, November to March (excluding Christmas and New Year when prices are hiked up and seats are at a premium) and if you book well in advance. Note also that flying at weekends can be more expensive; price ranges quoted below assume midweek travel.

If you prefer to have everything organized for you, and especially if your visit is going to be geared around special interests, such as walking, cycling, art or wine, you may want to consider a **package tour** (see "Agents and operators" p.33). They may organize your entire trip for you or amount to no more than a flight plus car or train pass and accommodation. Taking a tour may work out cheaper than organizing the same arrangements on arrival in France and can help you make the most of your time if you're on a tight schedule.

Flights from the UK and Ireland

With the rapid increase in the number of **budget airlines** between the UK, Ireland and France, flying is becoming an ever cheaper and more attractive option, particularly if you're leaving from or heading to one of the regional airports. The largest of the budget airlines are bmibaby, easyJet, flyBE and Ryanair, which between them cover a total of thirty airports across France, including Avignon, Bergerac, Chambery, La Rochelle, Nantes, Pau, Rennes, Toulon and Tours, as well as more established hubs such as Paris, Lyon and Nice. Bear in mind though that routes and destinations change regularly, so it's wise to keep an eye on the airlines' websites (see p.32). It's also worth double-checking exactly where the airport is in relation to where you want to be; Ryanair claim to fly to Paris, for example, but in reality fly to the airport in Beauvais, a ninety-minute coach drive from the city centre. **Tickets** work on a quota system, and it's wise to book as early as possible for the really cheap seats, which can if you're lucky work out as little as a penny, with airport taxes and surcharges on top often coming to only £16–20/€25–30 each way. To keep costs down, be as flexible as possible – flying midweek at an ungodly hour will probably secure the cheapest tickets.

It's worth checking out the **traditional carriers**, such as Air France, British Airways, bmi and Aer Lingus, who have lowered their prices in recent years in the face of stiff competition from the budget airlines. The further ahead you book the better, but low-season return fares to Paris (including tax) start at around £70 from London, £110 from Edinburgh and €200 from Dublin; to Nice you'll pay upwards of £110, £160 and €300 respectively.

Air France, along with its partners, offers the widest regional coverage. It flies to Paris Charles-de-Gaulle (CDG) several times daily from London Heathrow, Dublin and regional airports such as Birmingham, Manchester, Southampton and Glasgow. It also operates flights from Heathrow and other UK airports direct to French regional airports such as Bordeaux, Lyon, Nantes, Nice and Strasbourg. Flights to Corsica – into Ajaccio, Bastia or Calvi – involve a change in Paris. **British Airways** has several flights a day to Paris CDG from London Gatwick and Heathrow and at least one daily from Birmingham, Manchester, Aberdeen, Edinburgh and Glasgow. BA also operates flights from London to Bordeaux, Lyon, Marseille, Montpellier, Nantes, Nice, Toulon and Toulouse. In Northern Ireland, BA flies directly from Belfast City Airport to Paris CDG on weekdays. **Bmi** flies from Heathrow to Paris CDG at least three times daily and to Nice twice daily; it also flies to Paris CDG at least once daily from Leeds-Bradford, and daily from Manchester to Toulouse. In Ireland, **Aer Lingus** offers direct flights from Dublin and Cork to Paris CDG, and from Dublin to Lyon, Nice and Toulouse.

In the summer months, **charter flights** represent the best value for getting to Ajaccio or Bastia in Corsica, with prices from £30 including tax one way. They are also worth bearing in mind during the ski season to hubs such as Grenoble, Geneva and Toulouse; one-way prices start at around £50 including tax.

Flights from the US and Canada

Most major airlines operate scheduled flights to Paris from the US and Canada. Air France has the most frequent service, with good onward regional connections, but their fares tend to be on the expensive side. Other airlines offering **nonstop** services to Paris from a variety of US cities include: American Airlines from New York, Boston, Chicago, Dallas and Miami; Continental from Newark and Houston; Delta from Atlanta, Boston, Cincinnati, Miami and New York; Northwest from Detroit; and United from Chicago, Boston, Philadelphia, New York and Washington DC. Air Canada offers nonstop services to Paris from Montréal and Toronto, while Air Transat offers good-value **charter flights** from a number of bases. Another option is to take one of the other European carriers, such as British Airways, bmi, Iberia, or Lufthansa, from the US or Canada to their home base and then continue on to Paris or a regional French airport. If you have a specific French destination in mind outside Paris and you're in a hurry – and are prepared to pay extra – it's possible to be ticketed straight through to any of more than a dozen regional airports. Most of these entail changing planes in Paris, and check to make sure there's no inconvenient transfer between the city's two main airports, Charles-de-Gaulle and Orly.

Thanks to intense competition, transatlantic **fares** to France are very reasonable. A typical return fare for a midweek flight to Paris is around US$650 from New York (7hr), US$750 from Los Angeles (13hr) and US$850 from Houston (8hr). From Canada, prices to Paris are in the region of CAN$850 from Montréal and Toronto (14hr), and CAN$1100 from Vancouver (16hr).

Flights from Australia, New Zealand and South Africa

Most travellers from **Australia and New Zealand** choose to fly to France via London, although the majority of airlines can add a Paris leg (or a flight to any other major French city) to an Australia/New Zealand–Europe ticket. Flights via Asia or the Middle East, with a transfer or overnight stop at the airline's home port, are generally the cheapest option; those routed through the US tend to be slightly pricier. Return **fares** start at around AUS$1500 from Sydney (30hr), AUS$1600 from Perth (25hr), AUS$1700 from Darwin (25hr) and NZ$1800 from Auckland (30hr).

From **South Africa**, Johannesburg is the best place to start, with Air France flying

Fly less – stay longer! Travel and climate change

Climate change is a serious threat to the ecosystems that humans rely upon, and air travel is among the fastest-growing contributors to the problem. Rough Guides regard travel, overall, as a global benefit, and feel strongly that the advantages to developing economies are important, as is the opportunity of greater contact and awareness among peoples. But we all have a responsibility to limit our personal impact on global warming, and that means giving thought to how often we fly, and what we can do to redress the harm that our trips create.

Flying and climate change

Pretty much every form of motorized travel generates CO_2 – the main cause of human-induced climate change – but planes also generate climate-warming contrails and cirrus clouds and emit oxides of nitrogen, which create ozone (another greenhouse gas) at flight levels. Furthermore, flying simply allows us to travel much further than we otherwise would do. The figures are frightening: one person taking a return flight between Europe and California produces the equivalent impact of 2.5 tonnes of CO_2 – similar to the yearly output of the average British car.

Fuel-cell and other less harmful types of plane may emerge eventually. But until then, there are really just two options for concerned travellers: to reduce the amount we spend travelling by air (take fewer trips – stay for longer!), and to make the trips we do take "climate neutral" via a carbon offset scheme.

Carbon offset schemes

Offset schemes run by ⓦclimatecare.org, ⓦcarbonneutral.com and others allow you to make up for some or all of the greenhouse gases that you are responsible for releasing. To do this, they provide "carbon calculators" for working out the global-warming contribution of a specific flight (or even your entire existence), and then let you contribute an appropriate amount of money to fund offsetting measures. These include rainforest reforestation and initiatives to reduce future energy demand – often run in conjunction with sustainable development schemes.

Rough Guides, together with Lonely Planet and other concerned partners in the travel industry, are supporting the carbon offset scheme run by **climatecare.org**. Please take the time to view our website and see how you can help to make your trip climate neutral.

ⓦwww.roughguides.com/climatechange

direct to Paris from around R6140 return; from Cape Town, they fly via Amsterdam and are more expensive at around R7600. BA, flying via London, are pricier still, with fares at around R10,000 from Cape Town and R8600 from Johannesburg. Other, though pricier options, are to fly via Frankfurt with Lufthansa, or via Dubai with Emirates. Flight times are around ten hours from Johannesburg to Paris, and 14 hours from Cape Town including a stopover in Amsterdam.

Trains

Eurostar operates high-speed passenger trains daily from Waterloo International to France via the **Channel Tunnel**; most but not all services stop at Ashford in Kent (40min from London). Services depart roughly every hour (from around 6am to 7.30pm) for Paris Gare du Nord (2hr 40min), a few of which stop at Calais (1hr 20min) and Lille (1hr 40min), where you can connect with TGV trains heading south to Bordeaux, Lyon and Nice. In addition, Eurostar runs direct trains from London to Disneyland Paris (daily; 2hr 40min), to Avignon (mid-July to mid-Sept daily Mon–Sat; mid-Sept to mid-July daily Mon–Fri; 6hr), and a special twice-weekly ski service to Moutiers, Aime-la-Plagne and Bourg-St-Maurice in the French Alps (Dec–March; around 8hr); skis are carried free.

Standard "Leisure" **fares** from London to Paris start at £59 (£55 to Lille and £99 to Avignon) for a non-refundable, non-exchangeable return purchased up to fourteen days before departure and including a Saturday night away. The next option is the changeable "Semi-flexible" ticket (from £125/£120/£189 respectively), which again must include a Saturday night. All these deals have limited availability, so it pays to plan ahead; tickets go on sale three months before the date of travel. Otherwise, you're looking at £298/£250/£250 for a fully refundable "Business" ticket with no restrictions. Return "Leisure" fares to Disneyland Paris start at £59 for adults (£44 for children aged 4–11) and those on the Eurostar ski train at £179 (£130 for children). Under-4s travel for free.

There is plentiful **parking** at Ashford station, just off the M20, at £9.50 per day; at Waterloo, Eurostar passengers pay £17 for 24 hours' parking. You can get through-ticketing from stations around Britain – including the tube journey across London to Waterloo – from Eurostar, many travel agents and mainline stations. InterRail and Eurail **rail passes** (see below for more) give discounts on Eurostar trains. For information about taking your bike on Eurostar, see p.43. For rail contacts, see p.34.

By car via the Channel Tunnel

The simplest way of taking your car across to France from the UK is to load it on one of the drive-on drive-off shuttle trains operated by **Eurotunnel** through the Channel Tunnel. The service runs continuously between Folkestone and Coquelles, near Calais, with up to four departures per hour (only 1 per hour midnight–6am) and takes 35 minutes (45 minutes for some night departures). It is possible to turn up and buy your ticket at the toll booths (exit the M20 at junction 11a), though at busy times booking is advisable; if you have a booking, you must arrive at least thirty minutes before departure. Inside the carriages, you can get out of your car to stretch your legs; there are toilets but no shops or refreshments. Note that Eurotunnel is not allowed to transport cars fitted with LPG or CNG tanks.

In general, the amount you pay depends on the time of year, time of day, length of stay, how long in advance you book and how flexible you need your ticket to be. Standard single, non-flexible **fares** start at £49, though to get the cheapest price, you have to travel early morning or late at night, and book well in advance. Alternatively, if you want to be fully flexible and refundable, a "standard" fare purchased on the spot can be as much as £330. There's a specially adapted carriage for **bicycles** that makes the crossing twice a day – it costs £32 return for a bike plus rider if you are staying more than five days, or £16 for a shorter stay.

Rail passes

There are a number of international rail passes useful for travel within France, many of which need to be bought in your home country (for details of railcards that you can buy in France, see "Discounts", p.38). **Rail Europe**, the umbrella company for all national and international rail purchases, is the most useful source of information on which rail passes are available, and have all the current prices. For information on where to buy InterRail, Eurail, and France Rail passes, see p.34.

InterRail Pass

InterRail Passes are only available to European residents, and you will be asked to provide proof of residency before being allowed to purchase one. They come in over-26 and (cheaper) under-26 versions, and cover 29 European countries, grouped together in zones, of which France is in zone E along with Belgium, Luxembourg and the Netherlands.

The passes are available for 16 days (one zone only; £145 for under-26s/£215 for over-26s), 22 days (two zones; £205/295) or one month (£285/405) for all zones. InterRail Passes do not include travel within your country of residence, though pass holders are eligible for discounts on rail fares to and from the border of the relevant zone as well as reductions on Eurostar and cross-Channel ferries.

Eurail Pass

A **Eurail Pass**, which is not available to European residents and must be purchased before arrival in Europe, is not likely to pay for itself if you're planning to stick to France alone. The pass allows unlimited free first-class train travel in France and seventeen other countries, and is available in increments of fifteen days, 21 days, one month, two months and three months. The pass comes in different forms, but the most useful is likely to be the **Eurailpass Youth**, which is valid for second-class travel for under-26s, and costs US$394 for 15 days, and up to US$1108 for three months.

France Rail Pass

Non-Europeans can buy the **France Rail Pass** before arriving in France. This entitles the holder to three days' unlimited train travel over a one-month period for US$238/AUS$300/NZ$350/R1670 (first class) or US$202/AUS$260/NZ$290/R1415 (second class), with the option of buying up to six additional days' travel at US$36/31, AUS$46/40, NZ$52/45 or R250/217 per day. There are discounts for travellers under 26, those over 60 and for two or more people travelling together.

Ferries

Though slower than travelling by plane or via the Channel Tunnel, the ferries and catamarans plying between Dover and Calais offer the most frequent services to France **from the UK** and are particularly convenient if you live in southeast England. Even if your starting point is west of London, it may still be worth heading to one of the south-coast ports and catching a ferry to Brittany or Normandy, though some routes have been cut following stiff competition from the Channel Tunnel. If you're coming from the north of England or Scotland, you could consider the overnight crossings from Hull (14hr) and Rosyth (18hr) to Zeebrugge in Belgium operated by P&O Ferries and Superfast Ferries respectively. Heading to southwest France, there's also the option of taking a ferry to Santander (with Brittany Ferries; 20hr) or Bilbao (P&O Ferries; 11hr) in northern Spain. From **Ireland**, putting the car on the ferry from Cork or Rosslare (near Wexford) to Cherbourg or Roscoff (13hr) in Brittany cuts out the drive across Britain to the Channel.

Ferry **prices** are seasonal and, for motorists, depend on the size of your vehicle. In general the further you book ahead, the cheaper the fare and it's well worth playing around with dates and times to find the best deals: midweek, midday sailings are usually cheapest. Return fares are now available for as little as £60 (if you book online) for a car and five passengers with SpeedFerries on the Dover–Boulogne route, while companies offering the Dover–Calais route charge in the region of £100. Return fares from Ireland (Cork–Roscoff) start at around €450.

Most ferry companies also offer fares for **foot passengers**, from £15 one way; accompanying bicycles can usually be carried free in low season, though there may be a small charge during peak periods.

Buses

Eurolines, a network of European bus companies, offers services from London Victoria to most major French cities, crossing the Channel by ferry or Eurotunnel depending on the time of day. Prices are lower than for the same journey by train, with standard adult return fares starting at around £44 to Paris, £52 to Lille and £66 each to Lyon, Bordeaux and Toulouse; there are discounts for return journeys booked a month in advance. Regional return fares from the rest of England and from Wales are available, as are student and youth discounts. Eurolines also offers a pass for Europe-wide travel, for fifteen or thirty days. Prices range from £135 for an adult fifteen-day pass in low season

Travelling with pets from the UK

If you wish to take your dog (or cat) to France, the **Pet Travel Scheme (PETS)** enables you to avoid putting it in quarantine when re-entering the UK as long as certain conditions are met. Current regulations are available on the Department for Environment, Food and Rural Affairs (DEFRA) website ⓦ www.defra.gov.uk/animalh/quarantine/index.htm or through the PETS Helpline (ⓣ 0870 241 1710).

(£115 for under-26s and over-60s) to £299 for a peak-season thirty-day pass (£245 for under-26s and over-60s).

Also worth investigating is **Busabout**, a hop-on, hop-off bus network which runs on three cross-continental circuits ("loops") between May and October. Loops depart from Paris every two to three days, heading north, south or west. The western loop covers Paris, Nice, Avignon, Bordeaux and Tours, taking in some of Switzerland and passing through Spain on its way. If you want to start in London, you can also add on a London–Paris link for £25 single, £39 return. Passes are valid for the entire season, and cost £275 for one loop, £450 for two, and £575 for all three. Alternatively, you can buy a flexipass which allows you to choose six stops for £225. See p.34 for contact details.

Airlines, agents and operators

There are a vast number of travel agents and tour operators offering holidays in France, with options varying from luxury, château-based breaks to adventure trips involving skiing and hiking. The following pages list the most useful contacts.

Online booking

Many airlines and discount travel websites offer you the opportunity to book your tickets, hotels and holiday packages online, cutting out the costs of agents and middlemen. These are worth investigating, as long as you don't mind the inflexibility of non-refundable, non-changeable deals. There are some bargains to be had on auction sites too, if you're prepared to bid keenly. Also, almost all airlines have their own websites (see below), offering tickets that can be just as cheap and which may be more flexible.

ⓦ www.expedia.co.uk (in UK), ⓦ www.expedia.com (in US), ⓦ www.expedia.ca (in Canada)
ⓦ www.lastminute.com (in UK), **ⓦ www.lastminute.com.au** (in Australia)
ⓦ www.opodo.co.uk (in UK)
ⓦ www.orbitz.com (in US)
ⓦ www.travelocity.co.uk (in UK), **ⓦ www.travelocity.com** (in US), **ⓦ www.travelocity.ca** (in Canada)
ⓦ www.zuji.com.au (in Australia),
ⓦ www.zuji.co.nz (in New Zealand)

Airlines

Aer Lingus UK ⓣ 0870 876 5000, Republic of Ireland ⓣ 0818/365 000, US and Canada ⓣ 1-800-IRISH-AIR; ⓦ www.aerlingus.com. Regular flights from Dublin and Cork to eight French destinations, plus direct flights to Dublin from Chicago, LA, New York and Boston.

Air Canada ⓣ 1-888-247-2262, ⓦ www.aircanada.com. Direct flights to Paris from Toronto and Montréal.

Air France UK ⓣ 0870 142 4343, US ⓣ 1-800-237-2747, Canada ⓣ 1-800-667-2747, Australia ⓣ 1300 390 190, South Africa ⓣ 0861 340 340; ⓦ www.airfrance.com. Flights from the UK, US, Canada, Australia, New Zealand and South Africa to airports across France.

Air Tahiti Nui US ⓣ 1-877-824-4846, Australia ⓣ 02/9244 2799, New Zealand ⓣ 09/308 3360; ⓦ www.airtahitinui-usa.com. Direct flights to Paris from New York and LA, and from Sydney and Auckland via the US.

Air Transat Canada ⓣ 1-877-872-6728, ⓦ www.airtransat.com. Charter flights from Montréal, Ottowa, Québec and Toronto to Paris, and from Montréal to six other French cities.

American Airlines US ⓣ 1-800-433-7300, Australia ⓣ 1300 650 7347, New Zealand ⓣ 0800 887 997; ⓦ www.aa.com. Flights from the US and Australasia to Paris.

Austrian Airlines US ⓣ 1-800-843-0002, Australia ⓣ 1800 642 438; ⓦ www.aua.com. From New York, Washington, Toronto, Melbourne and Sydney to Paris via Vienna.

bmi UK ⓣ 0870 607 0555, Republic of Ireland ⓣ 01/407 3036, US ⓣ 1-800-788-0555; ⓦ www.flybmi.com. Direct to Paris, Nice and Toulouse from the UK and Ireland, and from across the US via the UK.

bmibaby UK ⓣ 0870 264 2229, Republic of Ireland ⓣ 1890 340 122; ⓦ www.bmibaby.com. Budget flights from UK and Ireland to Paris, Lyon, Bordeaux, Toulouse, Nice and Perpignan.

British Airways UK ⓣ 0870 850 9850, Republic of Ireland ⓣ 1890 626 747, US and Canada ⓣ 1-800-AIRWAYS, Australia ⓣ 1300 767 177, New Zealand ⓣ 09/966 9777, South Africa ⓣ 011/441 8600; ⓦ www.ba.com. Direct flights from UK to France, with connections via London from the US, Canada, Australia, New Zealand and South Africa.

Cathay Pacific Australia ⓣ 13 1747, New Zealand ⓣ 09/379 0861; ⓦ www.cathaypacific.com. From Australia and New Zealand via Hong Kong to Paris.

Continental Airlines ⓣ 1-800-231-0856, ⓦ www.continental.com. Direct flights from New York JFK to Paris.

Delta US and Canada ⓣ1-800-221-1212, ⓦwww.delta.com. Direct flights to Paris from New York, LA, Boston and Chicago.

easyJet UK ⓦwww.easyjet.com. Budget flights to Bordeaux, Geneva, Grenoble, La Rochelle, Lyon, Marseille, Nice, Paris and Toulouse from across the UK.

Emirates Australia ⓣ02/9290 9700, New Zealand ⓣ09/968 2200, South Africa ⓣ0861/364 728; ⓦwww.emirates.com. From Johannesburg, Brisbane, Melbourne, Perth, Sydney, Auckland and Christchurch to Paris via Dubai.

flyBE UK ⓣ0870 889 0908, Republic of Ireland ⓣ1890/925 532; ⓦwww.flybe.com. Budget flights from across the UK to Angers, Avignon, Bergerac, Bordeaux, Brest, Chambéry, Geneva, Limoges, Nice, Paris, Perpignan, Rennes and Toulouse.

Gulf Air Australia ⓣ1300 366 337, South Africa ⓣ011/202 7626; ⓦwww.gulfairco.com. Sydney and Johannesburg to Paris via Bahrain or Muscat.

Iberia US ⓣ1-800-772-4642, ⓦwww.iberia.com. Flights from the US and Canada to airports across France via Madrid, Spain.

JAL (Japan Airlines) Australia ⓣ02/9272 1111, New Zealand ⓣ09/379 9906; ⓦwww.jal.com. From Australia and New Zealand to Paris via Japan.

Jet2 UK ⓣ0871 226 1737, ⓦwww.jet2.com. Budget flights to Paris, Nice and Chambéry from the north of England.

KLM Australia ⓣ1300 303 747, New Zealand ⓣ09/309 1782, South Africa ⓣ082/2345 747; ⓦwww.klm.com. Flights from Australia, New Zealand and South Africa via Amsterdam.

Korean Air Australia ⓣ02/9262 6000, New Zealand ⓣ09/914 2000; ⓦwww.koreanair.com. To Paris via Korea from Australia and New Zealand.

Lufthansa US ⓣ1-800-645-3880, Canada ⓣ1-800-563-5954, Australia ⓣ1300 655 727, New Zealand ⓣ09/303 1529, South Africa ⓣ0861/842538; ⓦwww.lufthansa.com. From major cities in the US, plus Australia, New Zealand and South Africa, to airports across France, all via Frankfurt.

Malaysia Airlines Australia ⓣ03/2979 9997, New Zealand ⓣ0800 777 747; ⓦwww.malaysia-airlines.com. From Australia and New Zealand to Paris via Kuala Lumpur.

MyTravelLite UK ⓣ0870 241 5333, ⓦwww.mytravellite.com. From across the UK to Grenoble for the ski season.

Northwest Airlines US ⓣ1-800-225-2525, ⓦwww.nwa.com. Flights from across the US to France via Amsterdam.

Qantas Australia ⓣ13 13 13, New Zealand ⓣ0800 808 767; ⓦwww.qantas.com. Airports across Australia to Paris via Singapore.

Ryanair UK ⓣ0871 246 0000, Republic of Ireland ⓣ0818 303 030; ⓦwww.ryanair.com. Budget flights to 18 French destinations from the UK and Ireland, including Biarritz, Carcassonne, Limoges, Lyon, Nantes, Paris and Rodez.

Singapore Airlines Australia ⓣ13 1011, New Zealand ⓣ0800 808 909; ⓦwww.singaporeair.com. From Australia and New Zealand to Paris via Singapore.

South African Airways South Africa ⓣ0861 359 722, ⓦwww.flysaa.com. Flights from South Africa to Paris, Lyon and Nice. Code shares with Lufthansa.

Thai Airways Australia ⓣ1300 651 960, New Zealand ⓣ09/377 3886; ⓦwww.thaiair.com. Paris via Bangkok from Australia and New Zealand.

Thomsonfly.com UK ⓣ0870 1900 737, Republic of Ireland ⓣ01247 77723; ⓦwww.thomsonfly.com. Budget flights from Doncaster and Coventry to Paris, and Coventry and Bournemouth to Grenoble.

United Airlines US ⓣ1-800-241-6522, ⓦwww.united.com. Nonstop to Paris from Chicago, Boston, Philadelphia, New York and Washington DC.

US Airways US and Canada ⓣ1-800-428-4322, ⓦwww.usair.com. Direct from Philadelphia to Paris.

Agents and operators

Belle France UK ⓣ0870 405 4056, ⓦwww.bellefrance.co.uk. Walking, cycling and boating holidays throughout France.

Bonnes Vacances Direct UK ⓣ0870 7607 071, ⓦwww.bvdirect.co.uk. Agent for property owners in France for self-catering and B&B accommodation.

Canvas Holidays UK ⓣ0870 192 1154, ⓦwww.canvas.co.uk. Tailor-made caravan and camping holidays.

Château to Château France ⓣ+33 (0)6.19.75.30.23, ⓦwww.chateautochateau.com. Upmarket wine and perfume tours, cycling holidays and spa and golfing breaks.

Chez Nous UK ⓣ0870 197 1000, ⓦwww.cheznous.com. Search over 4000 self-catering and B&B properties online.

Corsican Places UK ⓣ0845 330 2059, ⓦwww.corsica.co.uk. Corsica specialists.

Crown Blue Line UK ⓣ0870 160 5634, ⓦwww.crownblueline.com. Good-value self-drive canal holidays all over France.

Cycling for Softies UK ⓣ0161/2488 282, ⓦwww.cycling-for-softies.co.uk. Easy-going cycle holiday operator to rural France.

ebookers UK ⓣ0800/082 3000, Republic of Ireland ⓣ01/488 3507; ⓦwww.ebookers.com. Low fares on an extensive selection of scheduled flights and package deals.

Euro-Bike & Walking Tours US & Canada ⓣ1-800-321-6060, ⓦwww.eurobike.com. Good range of bike and walking tours all over France for family groups or solo travellers.
Eurocamp UK ⓣ0870 901 9410, ⓦwww.eurocamp.co.uk. Camping holidays with kids' activities and single-parent deals.
Fields Fairway France ⓣ+33 (0)3.21.33.65.64, ⓦwww.fieldsfairway.co.uk. British-run, France-based company offering all-inclusive golfing holidays.
France Afloat UK ⓣ0870 011 0538, ⓦwww.franceafloat.com. Canal and river cruises across France.
France Holiday Store ⓦwww.fr-holidaystore.co.uk. Wide range of holidays.
French Life Ski UK ⓣ0870 336 2886, ⓦwww.frenchlifeski.co.uk. Skiing package deals and accommodation across France.
French Travel Connection Australia ⓣ02/9966 1177, ⓦwww.frenchtravel.com.au. Offers large range of holidays to France.
Headwater UK ⓣ01606/720033, USA & Canada through Breakaway Adventures ⓣ1-800-567-6286, Australia & New Zealand through Adventure World, Australia ⓣ02/8913 0700, New Zealand ⓣ09/524 5118; ⓦwww.headwater.com. UK-based operator offering walking, cycling and canoeing tours throughout France.
Holiday France ⓦwww.holidayfrance.org.uk. Website that allows you to search for French tour operators by holiday type and location.
Keycamp Holidays UK ⓣ0870 700 0740, ⓦwww.keycamp.com. Caravan and camping holidays, including transport to France.
Locaboat France ⓣ+33 (0)3.86.91.72.72, ⓦwww.locaboat.com. France-based company specializing in holidays on *pénichettes* (scaled-down replicas of commercial barges).
North South Travel UK ⓣ01245/608 291, ⓦwww.northsouthtravel.co.uk. Friendly, competitive travel agency, offering discounted fares worldwide. Profits are used to support projects in the developing world, especially the promotion of sustainable tourism.
Rascals in Paradise US ⓣ415/921-7000, ⓦwww.rascalsinparadise.com. Customized itineraries built around activities for kids.
STA Travel UK ⓣ0870 1630 026, US ⓣ1-800-781-4040, Canada ⓣ1-888-427-5639, Australia ⓣ1300 733 035, New Zealand ⓣ0508/782 872, South Africa ⓣ0861/781 781; ⓦwww.statravel.com. Worldwide specialists in independent travel; also student IDs, travel insurance, car rental, rail passes, and more. Good discounts for students and under-26s.
Trailfinders UK ⓣ0845 058 5858, Republic of Ireland ⓣ01/677 7888, Australia ⓣ1300 780 212; ⓦwww.trailfinders.com. One of the best-informed and most efficient agents for independent travellers.
Winetrails UK ⓣ01306/712 111, ⓦwww.winetrails.co.uk. Walking, cycling and gourmet holidays in the main French wine regions.

Rail, Channel Tunnel and bus contacts

Busabout UK ⓣ020/7950 1661, ⓦwww.busabout.com. In the US, Busabout passes are available from STA Travel (see above).
Eurolines UK ⓣ0870 580 8080, Republic of Ireland ⓣ01/836 6111; ⓦwww.nationalexpress.com/eurolines. For all Eurolines tickets and passes.
European Rail UK ⓣ020/7387 0444, ⓦwww.europeanrail.com. Provides itineraries and booking for a £5 fee which you can redeem against any tickets you buy.
Eurostar UK ⓣ0870 160 6600, ⓦwww.eurostar.com.
Eurotunnel UK ⓣ0870 535 3535, ⓦwww.eurotunnel.com.
International Rail UK ⓣ0870 751 5000, ⓦwww.international-rail.com. Sell InterRail and France Rail Pass.
Rail Europe (SNCF French Railways) UK ⓣ0870 584 8848, ⓦwww.raileurope.co.uk; US ⓣ1-877-257-2887, Canada ⓣ1-800-361-RAIL, ⓦwww.raileurope.com. Discounted rail fares for under-26s; also agents for Eurostar, and sell InterRail (UK only), Eurail and France Rail Pass.
Rail Plus Australia ⓣ1300 555 003 or 03/9642 8644, ⓦwww.railplus.com.au. Sells Eurail passes and tickets.
Trainseurope UK ⓣ0900 195 0101, ⓦwww.trainseurope.co.uk. InterRail passes, as well as other train tickets.

Ferry contacts

Brittany Ferries UK ⓣ0870 366 5333, ⓦwww.brittanyferries.co.uk; Republic of Ireland ⓣ021/4277 801, ⓦwww.brittanyferries.ie. Plymouth to Roscoff, Cherbourg and St-Malo and Santander (March–Nov/Dec only); Poole to Cherbourg; Portsmouth to Caen, Cherbourg and St-Malo; and Cork to Roscoff (March–Oct only).
Condor Ferries UK ⓣ0870 243 5140, ⓦwww.condorferries.co.uk. Poole to Cherbourg and St-Malo (both May–Sept); Portsmouth to Cherbourg (May–Sept); and Weymouth to St-Malo via the Channel Islands.
EuroDrive UK ⓣ0870 423 5540, ⓦwww.eurodrive.co.uk. Cut-price fares for people taking their cars across the Channel.
Ferry Savers UK ⓣ0870 990 8492, ⓦwww.ferrysavers.com. Useful for price comparisons between operators.

Irish Ferries UK ⓣ0870 517 1717, Republic of Ireland ⓣ0818/300 400; ⓦwww.irishferries.com. Rosslare to Cherbourg and Roscoff (March–Sept).
Norfolkline UK ⓣ0870 870 1020, ⓦwww.norfolkline.com. Dover to Dunkerque.
P&O Ferries UK ⓣ0870 598 0333, ⓦwww.poferries.com. Dover to Calais and Portsmouth to Bilbao.
Sea France UK ⓣ0870 443 1653, ⓦwww.seafrance.com. Dover to Calais.
SpeedFerries UK ⓣ0870 220 0570, ⓦwww.speedferries.com. Dover to Boulogne.
Superfast Ferries UK ⓣ0870 234 0870, ⓦwww.superfast.com. Rosyth to Zeebrugge (Belgium).
Transmanche Ferries UK ⓣ0800 917 1201, ⓦwww.transmancheferries.com. Newhaven to Dieppe.

Getting around

With the most extensive train network in Western Europe, France is a great country in which to travel by rail. The nationally owned French train company, SNCF (Société Nationale des Chemins de Fer), runs fast, efficient trains between the main towns. Buses cover the rural areas, but services can be rather sporadic, with departures often at awkward times. If you really want to get off the beaten track, by far the best option is to have your own transport.

Flying within France has the obvious advantage of speed, but is only recommended for those with deep pockets who are short on time. Aside from Corsica, which can also be reached by air, France's islands are serviced only by **ferries**, some of which are seasonal and not all of which are equipped to carry vehicles.

For independent transport, by **car**, **motorbike** or **bicycle**, you'll need to be aware of a number of French road rules and peculiarities. The extensive network of inland waterways in France makes **boating** a very pleasant way of exploring the country. Long-distance walking is also extremely popular; for information on walking, canoeing and other similar activities, see "Sports and outdoor activities".

Approximate journey times and frequencies of the main train, bus, plane and ferry services can be found in the "Travel details" at the end of each chapter.

By train

SNCF (ⓣ08.92.35.35.35, ⓦwww.voyages-sncf.com) has pioneered one of the most efficient, comfortable and user-friendly railway systems in the world. Its staff are generally courteous and helpful, and its trains – for the most part, fast, clean and reliable – continue, in spite of the closure of some rural lines, to serve the vast part of the country.

Trains

Pride and joy of the French rail system is the high-speed **TGV** (*train à grande vitesse*), capable of speeds of over 300kph, and its offspring Eurostar. The continually expanding TGV network has its main hub at Paris, from where a main line heads north to Lille, and two other trunk routes head south: one down the east side of the country to Marseille and the Mediterranean, the other west to Tours, Bordeaux and the Spanish frontier. Spur lines service Brittany and Normandy, the Alps, Pyrenees and Jura, while from June 2007 a brand new line should be up and running east from Paris to Reims, Nancy and Strasbourg.

As well as the traditional TGV, a new style high-speed train, the **iDTGV** (ⓦwww.idtgv.com) was introduced in 2004 in order to compete with the budget airlines. The trains come with all mod cons, such as facililties to watch DVDs and play computer games

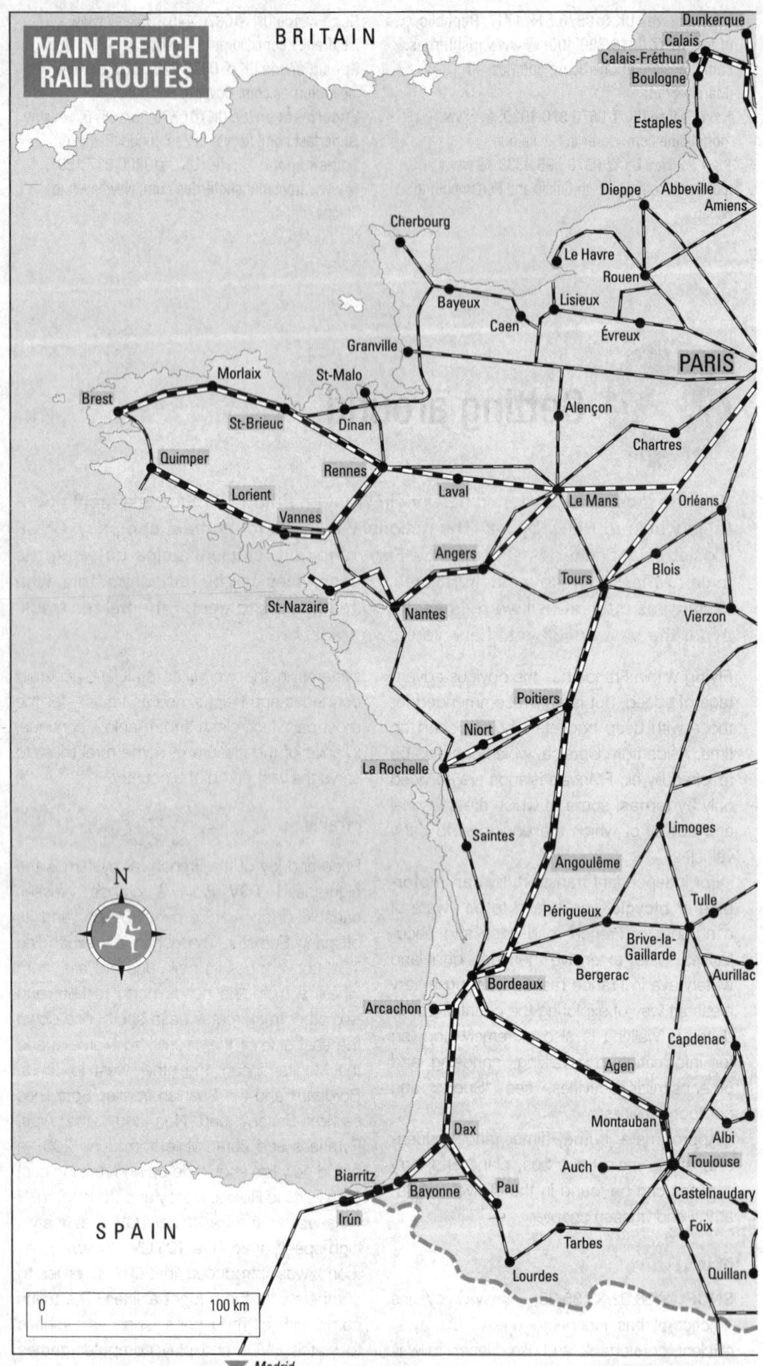
MAIN FRENCH RAIL ROUTES
BRITAIN
SPAIN
N
Dunkerque
Calais
Calais-Fréthun
Boulogne
Estaples
Abbeville
Dieppe
Amiens
Cherbourg
Le Havre
Rouen
Bayeux
Lisieux
Caen
Évreux
Granville
PARIS
Morlaix
St-Malo
Brest
Dinan
St-Brieuc
Alençon
Chartres
Quimper
Rennes
Laval
Lorient
Le Mans
Orléans
Vannes
Angers
Blois
Tours
St-Nazaire
Nantes
Vierzon
Poitiers
Niort
La Rochelle
Limoges
Saintes
Angoulême
Tulle
Périgueux
Brive-la-Gaillarde
Bergerac
Aurillac
Bordeaux
Arcachon
Capdenac
Agen
Montauban
Albi
Dax
Auch
Toulouse
Biarritz
Bayonne
Pau
Castelnaudary
Irún
Foix
Tarbes
Lourdes
Quillan
0
100 km
Madrid

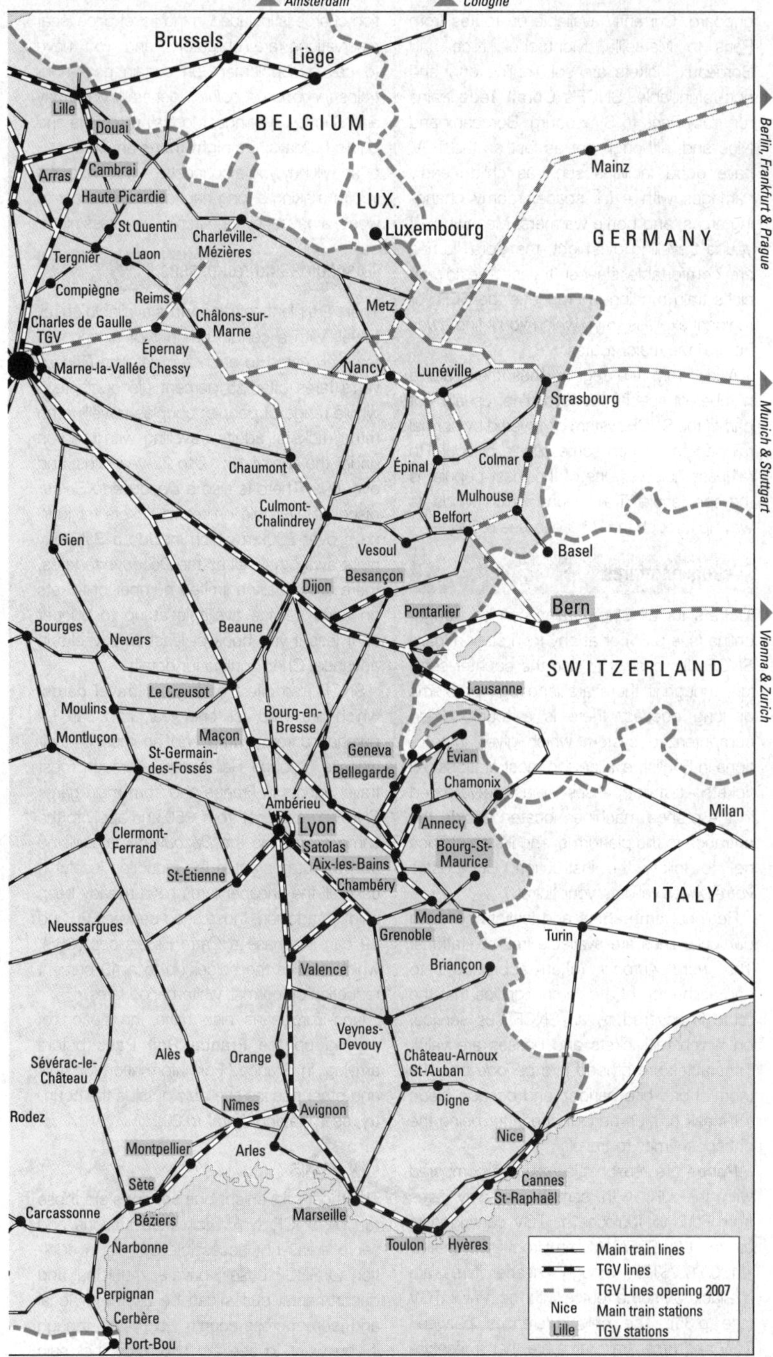

Amsterdam
Cologne
Brussels
Liège
BELGIUM
LUX.
Luxembourg
GERMANY
Mainz
SWITZERLAND
ITALY
Lille
Douai
Arras
Cambrai
Haute Picardie
St Quentin
Charleville-Mézières
Tergnier
Laon
Compiègne
Reims
Charles de Gaulle TGV
Châlons-sur-Marne
Épernay
Marne-la-Vallée Chessy
Metz
Nancy
Lunéville
Strasbourg
Colmar
Mulhouse
Basel
Épinal
Chaumont
Culmont-Chalindrey
Vesoul
Belfort
Gien
Dijon
Besançon
Pontarlier
Bern
Bourges
Nevers
Beaune
Lausanne
Le Creusot
Moulins
Bourg-en-Bresse
Montluçon
Maçon
Geneva
Évian
St-Germain-des-Fossés
Bellegarde
Chamonix
Ambérieu
Lyon
Annecy
Milan
Clermont-Ferrand
Satolas
Aix-les-Bains
Bourg-St-Maurice
St-Étienne
Chambéry
Modane
Neussargues
Grenoble
Turin
Valence
Briançon
Veynes-Devouy
Sévérac-le-Château
Alès
Orange
Château-Arnoux St-Auban
Digne
Rodez
Nîmes
Avignon
Nice
Montpellier
Arles
Cannes
Sète
St-Raphaël
Carcassonne
Béziers
Marseille
Toulon
Hyères
Narbonne
Perpignan
Cerbère
Port-Bou
Barcelona
Main train lines
TGV lines
TGV Lines opening 2007
Nice Main train stations
Lille TGV stations
Berlin, Frankfurt & Prague
Munich & Stuttgart
Vienna & Zurich

onboard. Currently available on routes from Paris to Marseille, Montpellier, Nice and Bordeaux, tickets are sold online only and non-refundable. SNCF's **Corail Téoz** trains run from Paris to Strasbourg, Bordeaux and Nice and, although not as fast as the TGV, have good facilities such as child-friendly carriages with extra space, roomy changing areas, and bottle warmers. Meanwhile, if you're travelling overnight, the Corail Lunéa are comfortable sleeper trains. The lowest class train running in France is the **TER**, or regional express train, which you'll find away from all the major routes.

Aside from the regular lines there are a number of special **tourist trains**, usually not part of the SNCF system or covered by normal rail passes, though some offer a discount to rail pass holders. One of the most popular is the spectacular Train Jaune which winds its way up through the Pyrenees (see p.836).

Tickets and fares

Tickets for all SNCF trains can be bought online (see p.35) or at any train station (*gare SNCF*). It's easiest to use the counter service, though if there are language problems or long queues, there is a touch-screen computerized system which gives instructions in English available in most stations. All tickets – but not passes – must be validated in the orange machines located beside the entrance to the platforms, and it's an offence not to follow the instruction, *Compostez votre billet* ("validate your ticket").

Regional **timetables** and leaflets covering particular lines are available free at stations. The word *Autocar* (often abbreviated to *car*) at the top of a column signifies that the route is covered by an SNCF bus service, on which rail tickets and passes are valid. Timetables are divided into *période blanche* (normal or white period), and *période bleue* (off-peak or blue period), the latter being the cheapest times to travel.

Prices are reasonable, at least compared with the UK, with sample one-way fares from Paris to Toulouse by TGV coming in at around €80/£55/$102, and from Paris to Nice €100/£69/$127, though cheaper fares are available on some routes with the new iDTGV (see p.35). The only differences between TGV and other train fares are that a reservation charge is included in the ticket price (seat reservations are obligatory) and you have to pay a supplement on certain peak-hour trains (*période de pointe*), generally on Friday and Sunday evenings, Monday mornings and public holidays. On **night trains** an extra €15 or so will buy you a couchette – well worth it if you're making a long haul and don't want to waste a day recovering from a sleepless night.

Discounts and rail passes

There are plenty of **discounts** available on rail travel, with a certain number of discounted fares allocated to each service. The *Découverte* fares offer 25 percent discounts to a whole range of people: couples travelling on return tickets; adults travelling with children under the age of 12; 12 to 25-year-olds; and over-60s. There is also a *Découverte Séjour* discount available on return tickets for journeys over 200km which include a Saturday night away. As well as the *Découverte* fares, there are usually a limited number of tickets on each service available at up to 50 per cent less if you book at least two weeks in advance. Check online for details.

SNCF also offers a range of **travel cards**, which are valid for one year, and can be purchased from a number of sources: on their website; through Rail Europe; through most travel agents in France and from main *gares SNCF*. These cost from €50 and apply to the same groups as the *Découverte* fares listed above, but guarantee the reduction (useful in case all the cheaper fares have already been sold). In addition, those aged between 26 and 59 can purchase a *Carte Escapades* (€85), which entitles the holder up to a 40 percent reduction on normal, white-period fares.

Non-Europeans also have the option of picking up the **France Rail Pass** before arriving in France. For information on this and other passes available outside the country, see "Getting there" (p.30).

By bus

The most convenient **bus services** are those run by SNCF, which join train stations and serve areas not accessible by rail. In addition to SNCF buses, private, municipal and departmental buses can be useful for local and some cross-country journeys, though if you want to see much outside the main towns be prepared for early starts and careful planning – the timetable is often constructed to suit working, market and school hours. As a rule, all buses are cheaper and slower than trains.

Larger towns usually have a *gare routière* (bus station), often next to the *gare SNCF*. However, the private bus companies don't always work together and you'll frequently find them leaving from an array of different points (the local tourist office should be able to help locate them).

In addition to the SNCF, Eurolines (see p.31) runs a number of routes through the country with prices starting at around €30.

By ferry

The majority of France's coastal islands, which are concentrated around Brittany and the Côte d'Azur, can only be reached by **ferry**. Small local companies run services, with timetables and prices varying according to season. Some routes have a reduced schedule or cease to operate completely in winter months, while in high season booking ahead is recommended on all but the most frequent services. Information on these local companies is listed in the Brittany and Normandy and Côte d'Azur chapters in the Guide. For details of ferry services from the mainland to Corsica, see p.1206.

By air

Unless you're travelling from the mainland to Corsica, you're unlikely to need to use any of France's domestic air services, though if you've come from outside Europe you may be able to get a good deal on add-on flights (see p.28). Air France operates the most routes within the country, although competition is hotting up, with the likes of easyJet running internal cut-price flights from Paris to Toulouse, Nice and Geneva. You may also be able to pick up an internal flight on some of the foreign airlines (such as Lufthansa) whose routes include intermediate stops within France. For details of airlines operating within France, see "Getting there" p.32.

By car

Driving in France can be a real pleasure, with a magnificent network of autoroutes which provide huge, sweeping views of the countryside. Happily, because of the size and shape of the country, congestion is rarely a problem. This is equally true of the older main roads, or *routes nationales* (marked RN116 or just N116, for example, on signs and maps), and the minor *routes départementales* or *itinéraire bis* (marked with a D). Do not shun these latter: you can often travel for kilometres across country, seeing few other cars, on a road as broad and well maintained as a major road. These alternative routes are usually signposted with special green "Bison Futé" road signs.

Of course, there are times when it's wiser not to drive: most obviously in big urban agglomerations; around major seaside resorts in high season; and at peak holiday migrations such as the beginning and end of the month-long August holiday, and the notoriously congested weekends nearest July 14 and August 15.

Practicalities

US, Canadian, Australian, New Zealand, South African and all EU **driving licences** are valid in France, though an International Driver's Licence makes life easier. The minimum driving age is 18 and you must hold a full (not a provisional) licence. Drivers are required to carry their licence with them when driving, and you should also have the insurance papers with you in the car. If the vehicle is rented, its registration document (*carte grise*) must also be carried.

All the major car manufacturers have garages and service stations in France, which can help if you run into mechanical difficulties. You can find them listed in the Yellow Pages of the phone book under "Garages d'automobiles"; for breakdowns, look under "Dépannages". If you have an accident or break-in, you should contact the local police – keeping a copy of their report – in order to make an insurance claim. Within Europe, most car insurance **policies** cover taking your own car to France; check with your insurer while planning your trip. However, you're advised to take out extra cover for motoring assistance in case your car breaks down.

Note that **petrol stations** in rural areas tend to be few and far between, and those

Driving distances (in km)

	Avignon	Biarritz	Bordeaux	Calais	Dijon	Grenoble	La Rochelle	Le Havre	Lyon
Avignon		630	576	990	424	220	751	889	235
Biarritz	630		203	174	851	830	387	887	846
Bordeaux	576	203		871	641	679	184	686	593
Calais	990	174	871		569	867	702	272	751
Dijon	424	851	641	569		274	568	504	187
Grenoble	220	830	679	867	274		658	742	108
La Rochelle	751	387	184	702	568	658		464	552
Le Havre	889	887	686	272	504	742	464		643
Lyon	235	846	593	751	187	108	552	643	
Marseille	118	702	645	1062	507	268	771	948	313
Montpellier	101	550	486	993	492	293	617	872	301
Nice	265	874	818	1144	598	322	934	1049	426
Paris	693	787	582	268	311	547	453	197	452
Perpignan	253	510	443	1098	635	431	610	964	448
Reims	715	938	730	262	274	554	597	327	461
St Malo	1034	730	539	506	633	807	321	240	695
Strasbourg	734	1146	948	591	310	514	843	637	441
Toulouse	334	312	253	937	617	521	409	768	471
Tours	713	551	344	476	394	530	232	285	427

that do exist usually open only during normal shop hours – don't count on being able to buy petrol at night and on Sunday. An increasing number of stations are equipped with automated 24-hour pumps, but many of these only work with French bank cards. Petrol **prices** have risen steadily in recent years and at the time of writing were around €1.29 a litre for unleaded (*sans plomb*), €1.25 a litre for four-star (*super*) and €1 a litre for diesel (*gazole* or *gasoil*); you'll find prices lowest at out-of-town hypermarkets.

Most autoroutes have **tolls**: rates vary, but to give you an idea, travelling only by motorway from Calais to Montpellier would cost you roughly €64; pay in cash or by credit card at the frequent tollgates (*péages*). You can work out routes and costs of both petrol and tolls online at the useful Ⓦwww.viamichelin.com.

Rules of the road

Since the French **drive on the right**, drivers of right-hand-drive British cars must adjust their headlights to dip to the right. This is most easily done by sticking on black glare deflectors, which can be bought at most motor accessory shops, and at the Channel ferry ports or the Eurostar terminal. It is more complicated if your car is fitted with modern High-Intensity Discharge (HID) or halogen-type lights; check with your dealer about how to adjust these well in advance.

It is a legal requirement that cars not fitted with flashing warning lights must carry a **red warning triangle** (and it's highly recommended to carry one in any case, since lights can fail or you might break down on a blind corner). You are also strongly advised to carry a spare set of bulbs, a fire extinguisher and a first-aid kit. Seat belts are compulsory and children under 10 years are not allowed to sit in the front of the car. It is illegal to use a hand-held **mobile phone** while driving.

The law of *priorité à droite* – giving way to traffic coming from your right, even when it is coming from a minor road – is being slowly phased out as it's a major cause of acci-

Marseille	Montpellier	Nice	Paris	Perpignan	Reims	St Malo	Strasbourg	Toulouse	Tours
118	101	265	693	253	715	1034	734	334	713
702	550	874	787	510	938	730	1146	312	551
645	486	818	582	443	730	539	948	253	344
1062	993	1144	268	1098	262	506	591	937	476
507	492	598	311	635	274	633	310	617	394
268	293	322	547	431	554	807	514	521	530
771	617	934	453	610	597	321	843	409	232
948	872	1049	197	964	327	240	637	768	285
313	301	426	452	448	461	695	441	471	427
	162	190	769	308	775	982	758	388	704
162		326	724	148	761	882	743	231	627
190	326		872	471	874	1131	740	558	857
769	724	872		823	147	370	441	660	228
308	148	471	823		883	931	890	197	682
775	761	874	147	883		501	327	789	367
982	882	1131	370	931	501		808	728	280
758	743	740	441	890	327	808		912	637
388	231	558	660	197	789	728	912		491
704	627	857	228	682	367	280	637	491	

dents. However, it still applies on some roads in built-up areas and the occasional roundabout, so it pays to be vigilant at junctions. A sign showing a yellow diamond on a white background indicates that you have right of way, while the same sign with a diagonal black slash across it warns you that vehicles emerging from the right have priority. Stop signs mean you must stop completely; *Cédez le passage* means "Give way".

If you have an **accident** while driving, you must fill in and sign a *constat d'accident* (declaration form) or, if another car is also involved, a *constat aimable* (jointly agreed declaration); these forms should be provided with the car's insurance documents. For minor driving offences such as speeding, the police can impose on-the-spot fines. For anything more serious, you could lose your licence.

Unless otherwise indicated **speed limits** are: 130kph (80mph) on autoroutes; 110kph (68mph) on dual carriageways; 90kph (55mph) on other roads; and 50kph (31mph) in towns. In wet weather, and for drivers with less than two years' experience, these limits are 110kph (68mph), 100kph (62mph) and 80kph (50mph) respectively; the town limit is the same. The police are cracking down hard on speeding in a bid to reduce the shock-

Road information

For up-to-the-minute information regarding traffic jams and road works on autoroutes throughout France, ring ⓣ08.92.68.10.77 (€0.34/min; French only) or consult the bilingual website ⓦwww.autoroutes.fr. Traffic information for other roads can be obtained from the Bison Futé recorded information service (ⓣ08.26.02.20.22; €0.15/min; French only) or their website ⓦwww.bison-fute.equipement.gouv.fr.

ingly high accident rate in France. Radars are being installed along main roads and there are stiff penalties for driving violations, which can mean **fines** of up to €9000 and a suspended licence. The standard fine for exceeding the speed limit by 20kph (12mph), for example, is €90; above 40kph (25mph) you will not only be fined but will also have to go to court. The **alcohol limit** is 0.05 percent (50 mg per litre of blood) and random breath tests are increasingly common.

Car rental

Car rental in France costs upwards of €70 a day and €250 for a week, but can be cheaper if arranged before you leave home or online. You'll find the big firms represented at airports and in most major towns and cities; addresses are detailed throughout the Guide. Renting from airports normally includes a surcharge. Local firms can be cheaper but most don't offer one-way rentals and you need to check the small print carefully.

The cost of car rental includes car **insurance**, though this will only cover the basic legal requirement. Under the standard contract you are liable for an excess (*franchise*) of around €500 (for the smallest car) for any damage to the vehicle – most firms accept a valid credit card rather than cash. You should return the car with a full tank of fuel to avoid paying an exorbitant fuel charge.

North Americans and Australians in particular should be forewarned that it's difficult to arrange the rental of a car with **automatic transmission**; if you can't drive a manual you should try to book an automatic well in advance, possibly before you leave home, and be prepared to pay a much higher price for it.

Most rental companies will only deal with people **over 25** unless an extra insurance premium, typically around €20–23 per day, is paid (and you still must be over 21 and have driven for at least one year). OTU Voyages (Ⓣ01.55.82.32.32, Ⓦwww.otu.fr), the student travel agency, can arrange car rental for drivers under 25, with prices beginning at €110 for a weekend.

Car rental agencies

Alamo US Ⓣ1-800-462-5266, Ⓦwww.alamo.com.
Apex New Zealand Ⓣ0800 939597 Ⓦwww.apexrentals.co.nz.
Auto Europe US and Canada Ⓣ1-888-223-5555, Ⓦwww.autoeurope.com.
Avis UK Ⓣ08706 060100, Republic of Ireland Ⓣ021/428 1111, US Ⓣ1-800-230-4898, Canada Ⓣ1-800-272-5871, Australia Ⓣ13 63 33 or 02/9353 9000, New Zealand Ⓣ09/526 2847 or 0800 655111, South Africa Ⓣ0861 113 748; Ⓦwww.avis.com.
Budget UK Ⓣ08701 565656, Republic of Ireland Ⓣ09/0662 7711, US Ⓣ1-800-527-0700, Canada Ⓣ1-800-268-8900, Australia Ⓣ1300 362 848, New Zealand Ⓣ0800 283438; Ⓦwww.budget.com.
Dollar US Ⓣ1-866-434-2226, Ⓦwww.dollar.com.
Enterprise Rent-a-Car US Ⓣ1-800-261-7331, Ⓦwww.enterprise.com.
Europcar UK Ⓣ08706 075000, Republic of Ireland Ⓣ01/614 2888, US & Canada Ⓣ1-877-940 6900, Australia Ⓣ1300 131 390; Ⓦwww.europcar.com.
Europe by Car US Ⓣ1-800-223-1516, Ⓦwww.europebycar.com.
Hertz UK Ⓣ020/7026 0077, Republic of Ireland Ⓣ01/870 5777, US Ⓣ1-800-654-3131, Canada Ⓣ1-800-263-0600, Australia Ⓣ08/9921 4052, New Zealand Ⓣ0800 654321, South Africa Ⓣ021 935 4800; Ⓦwww.hertz.com.
Holiday Autos UK Ⓣ0871 222 3200, Republic of Ireland Ⓣ01/872 9366, Australia Ⓣ1300 554 432, New Zealand Ⓣ0800 144040; Ⓦwww.holidayautos.co.uk.

Buy-back leasing schemes

If you are not resident in an EU country and will be touring France for between 17 days and six months, it's worth investigating the special **buy-back leasing schemes** operated by Peugeot ("Peugeot Open Europe") and Renault ("Renault Eurodrive"). Under these deals, you purchase a new car tax-free and the manufacturer guarantees to buy it back from you for an agreed price at the end of the period. In general, the difference between the purchase and repurchase price works out considerably less per day than the equivalent cost of car hire. Further details are available from Peugeot and Renault dealers and online at Ⓦwww.peugeot-openeurope.com and Ⓦwww.eurodrive.renault.com.

Canal and river trips

With over 7000km of navigable rivers and canals, **boating** can be one of the best and most relaxed ways of exploring France. Except on parts of the Moselle, there's no charge for use of the waterways, and you can travel without a permit for up to six months in a year. For information on maximum dimensions, documentation, regulations and so forth, contact Voies Navigables de France (VNF) (Ⓣ03.21.63.24.24, Ⓦwww.vnf.fr), which has information (in French) on boating throughout France, and details of firms that rent out boats. Expect to pay between €800 and €2000 per week, depending on the season and level of comfort, for a four- to six-person boat. Details of firms offering canal and river holidays can be found on p.33. For a full list of rental firms operating in France contact the Fédération des Industries Nautiques (Ⓣ01.44.37.04.00, Ⓦwww.france-nautic.com).

The **principal areas** for boating are Brittany, Burgundy, Picardy-Flanders, Alsace and Champagne. Brittany's canals join up with the Loire, but this is only navigable as far as Angers. Other waterways permit numerous permutations, including joining up via the Rhône and Saône with the Canal du Midi in Languedoc and then northwestwards to Bordeaux and the Atlantic. The eighteenth-century Canal de Bourgogne and 300-year-old Canal du Midi are fascinating examples of early canal engineering. The latter, together with its continuation the Canal du Sète à Rhône, passes within easy reach of several interesting areas.

The through-journey from the Channel to the Mediterranean requires some planning. The Canal de Bourgogne has an inordinate number of locks, while other waterways demand considerable skill and experience – the Rhône and Saône rivers, for example, have tricky currents. The most direct route is from Le Havre to just beyond Paris, then south along either Canal du Loing et de Briare or Canal du Nivernais to the Canal Latéral à la Loire, which you follow as far as Digoin in southern Burgundy, where it crosses the River Loire and meets the Canal du Centre. You follow the latter as far as Châlon, from where you continue south on the Saône and Rhône until you reach the Mediterranean at Port St-Louis in the Camargue.

National UK Ⓣ08704 004581, US Ⓣ1-800-CAR-RENT, Australia Ⓣ02/131045, New Zealand Ⓣ03/366 5574; Ⓦwww.nationalcar.com.
SIXT Republic of Ireland Ⓣ1850 206088, Ⓦwww.irishcarrentals.ie.
Suncars UK Ⓣ08705 005566, Republic of Ireland Ⓣ1850/201416; Ⓦwww.suncars.com.
Thrifty UK Ⓣ01494/751600, Republic of Ireland Ⓣ0800 2728728, US & Canada Ⓣ1-800-847-4389, Australia Ⓣ1300 367 227, New Zealand Ⓣ0800 737070; Ⓦwww.thrifty.com.

By bicycle

Bicycles (*vélos*) have high status in France, where cyclists are given respect both on the roads and as customers at restaurants and hotels. In addition, local authorities are actively promoting cycling, not only with city cycle lanes, but comprehensive networks linking rural areas (frequently utilizing disused railways). Most towns have well-stocked repair shops, where parts are normally cheaper than in Britain or the US. However, if you're using a foreign-made bike with non-standard metric wheels, it's a good idea to carry spare tyres.

The **train network** runs various schemes for cyclists, all of them covered by the free leaflet, *Train et Vélo*, available from most stations. A number of TGVs and other trains (marked with a bicycle in the timetable) allow you to take a bike free either in the dedicated bike racks or in the luggage van as long as there's space; in the latter case, it's a good idea to reserve a slot several days in advance during busy periods, though this will cost you €10. Otherwise, you can take your dismantled bike, packed in a carrier, on TGVs and other trains with sufficiently large luggage racks. Another option is to send your bike parcelled up as registered luggage for a fee of €39; delivery should take two days (though the service doesn't operate at weekends). Eurostar allows you to take your bicycle as part of your baggage allowance provided it's dismantled and packed in a bag no more than 120cm by 90cm (phone ⓣ08702 649899 for further details). If you're already travelling with more than two pieces of luggage, however, they encourage you to send your bike unaccompanied with their registered baggage service, Esprit Europe (ⓣ08705 850850, ⓦwww.espriteurope.co.uk), which costs £20 one way and has a guaranteed arrival time of 24 hours; you can register up to 24 hours before departure. Ferries usually take bikes free (though you may need to register first), as do airlines such as British Airways and Air France, though some no-frills airlines charge – remember to check when making your booking.

Bikes – usually mountain bikes (*vélos tout terrain* or VTT) – are often available to **rent** from campsites and hostels, as well as from specialist cycle shops and some tourist offices; they usually cost around €15 per day. The bikes are often not insured, however, and you will be presented with the bill for a replacement if it's stolen or damaged; check your travel insurance policy for cover.

As for **maps**, a minimum requirement is the IGN 1:100,000 series (see p.75) – the smallest scale that carries contours. The UK's national cyclists' association, the CTC (ⓣ08708 730060, ⓦwww.ctc.org.uk), can suggest routes and supply advice for members (£33 a year or £53 for a family of four, and £12 for under 26 years). They run a particularly good **insurance** scheme. Companies offering specialist bike touring holidays are listed on p.33.

By scooter and motorbike

Scooters are relatively easy to find and, though they're not built for long-distance travel, are ideal for pottering around local areas. Places that rent out bicycles often also rent out scooters; expect to pay in the region of €40 a day for a 50cc machine, less for longer periods. No licence is needed for bikes of 50cc and under, but for you'll need a valid motorbike licence for anything larger.

Rental prices for a **motorbike** are around €55 a day for a 125cc bike; expect to leave a hefty deposit by cash or credit card too – over €1000 is the norm – which you may lose in the event of damage or theft. Remember to take along your passport or some other form of photographic identity. Crash helmets are compulsory on all bikes, whatever the size, and the headlight must be switched on at all times. You are recommended to carry a first-aid kit and a set of spare bulbs.

French addresses

Addresses in France are pretty straightforward, beginning with the house name or number, street name and town, followed by region and postal code. Occasionally you'll come across the name of a town followed by the word *cedex*; this means simply that the recipient collects their mail from the post office rather than having it delivered. The terms *bis* and *ter* following a house number indicate a subdivision of the building, equivalent to A or B in the UK or the US.

Accommodation

At most times of the year, you can turn up in any French town and find a room or a place in a campsite. Booking a couple of nights in advance can be reassuring, however, as it saves you the effort of trudging round and ensures that you know what you'll be paying; many hoteliers, campsite managers and hostel managers speak at least a little English. In most places, you'll be able to get a simple double for €30 or so, though expect to pay around €45 for a reasonable level of comfort. Paris is more expensive, however, with equivalent rates of roughly €40 and €80. We've detailed a selection of hotels throughout the Guide, and given a price range for each (see box below); as a general rule the areas around train stations have the highest density of cheap hotels.

Problems may arise between mid-July and the end of August, when the French take their own vacations en masse. During this period, hotel and hostel accommodation can be hard to come by, particularly in the coastal resorts, and you may find yourself falling back on local tourist offices for help. In addition, big cities can be difficult throughout the year: we've given a greater range of possibilities for them in the Guide and very detailed accommodation listings for Paris, the worst case of all.

All **tourist offices** can provide lists of hotels, hostels, campsites and bed-and-breakfast possibilities, and some offer a booking service, though they can't guarantee rooms at a particular price. With campsites, you can be more relaxed about finding an empty space, unless you're touring with a caravan or camper van or looking for a place on the Côte d'Azur.

Hotels

Most French hotels are graded from zero to five stars. The price more or less corresponds to the number of stars, though the system is a little haphazard, having more to do with ratios of bathrooms per guest and

Accommodation price categories

All the hotels and guesthouses listed in this book have been price coded according to the scale below. The prices quoted are for the cheapest available double room in high season, including tax (7 percent), and without breakfast, although remember that many of the cheap places will also have more expensive rooms with en-suite facilities. For accommodation in the ❶ bracket, expect simple rooms, with communal (*dans le palier*) showers (*douches*) and toilets (WC or *toilettes*); there may also be a charge to use them. At ❷, rooms tend to come with their own bath or shower, though not necessarily a toilet, whilst ❸ will probably guarantee you a separate bathroom (*salle de bain*) and TV. At around ❹, accommodation will be comfortable and en suite, if not state-of-the-art; anything from ❺ upwards tends towards luxury, with all the mod cons you would expect, except in the larger cities, where luxury rooms tend to start at around ❻. Rooms from ❼ upwards will be increasingly plush, and there will be decent breakfast buffets. By the time they get to a ❾, sumptuous rooms will often be accompanied by a sauna, gym, swimming pool and many other services.

❶ Under €30
❷ €30–40
❸ €40–55
❹ €55–70
❺ €70–85
❻ €85–100
❼ €100–125
❽ €125–150
❾ Over €150

so forth than genuine quality, and some unclassified and single-star hotels can actually be very good. What you get for your money varies enormously between establishments; for a general guide see the box on p.45. Single rooms – if the hotel has any – are only marginally cheaper than doubles, so sharing always slashes costs, especially since most hotels willingly provide rooms with extra beds for three or more people at good discounts.

Big cities tend to have a good variety of cheap establishments; in small towns or villages, you may not be so lucky. Swanky resorts, particularly those on the Côte d'Azur, have very high **prices** in July and August, but even these are still cheaper than Paris, which is far more expensive than the rest of the country. If you're staying for more than three nights in a hotel it's often possible to negotiate a lower price, particularly out of season.

Breakfast, which is not normally included in the quoted price, will add between €5 and €15 per person to a bill, sometimes more – though there is no obligation to take it. The cost of eating **dinner** in a hotel's restaurant can be a more important factor to bear in mind when deciding where to stay. It's actually illegal for hotels to insist on your taking half board (*demi-pension*), though you'll come across some that do, especially during the summer peak. This is not always such a bad thing, however, since the food may be excellent and you can sometimes get a real bargain.

Note that many **family-run hotels** close for two or three weeks a year in low season. In smaller towns and villages they may also close for one or two nights a week, usually Sunday or Monday. Details are given where relevant in the Guide, but dates change from year to year and some places may decide to close for a few days in low season if they have no bookings. The best precaution is to phone ahead to be sure.

A very useful option, especially if you're driving and are looking for somewhere late at night, are the **chain hotels** located at motorway exits and on the outskirts of major towns. They may be soulless, but you can count on a decent and reliable standard. Among the cheapest (from around €26 for a three-person room with communal toilets and showers) and biggest is the one-star Formule 1 chain (Ⓣ08.92.68.56.85, Ⓦwww.hotelformule1.com). Other budget chains include B&B (Ⓣ08.92.78.29.29, Ⓦwww.hotel-bb.com), the slightly more comfortable Première Classe (Ⓣ08.25.00.30.03, Ⓦwww.premiereclasse.fr) and Etap Hôtel (Ⓣ08.92.68.89.00, Ⓦwww.etaphotel.com). More upmarket but still affordable chains are Ibis (Ⓣ08.92.68.66.86, Ⓦwww.ibishotel.com) and Campanile (Ⓣ01.64.62.46.00, Ⓦwww.campanile.fr), where en-suite rooms with satellite TV and direct-dial phones cost from around €40–50.

There are a number of well-respected **hotel federations** in France. The biggest and most useful of these is Logis de France (Ⓣ01.45.84.83.84, Ⓦwww.logis-de-france.fr), an association of over 3500 hotels nationwide. They produce a free annual guide, available in French tourist offices (see p.79), from Logis de France itself and from member hotels. Two other, more upmarket federations worth mentioning are Châteaux & Hôtels de France (Ⓣ01.72.72.92.02, Ⓦwww.chateauxhotels.com) and the Relais du Silence (Ⓣ01.44.49.90.00, Ⓦwww.silencehotel.com), both of which offer high-class accommodation in beautiful older properties, often in rural locations. Over thirty cities in France participate in the "Bon Weekend en Villes" programme, whereby you get two nights for the price of one at participating hotels. In most cases the offer is restricted to the winter period (Nov–March). Further details are available from tourist offices or online at Ⓦwww.bon-week-end-en-villes.com.

Bed and breakfast and self-catering

In country areas, in addition to standard hotels, you will come across **chambres d'hôtes** – bed-and-breakfast accommodation in someone's house, château or farm. Though the quality varies widely, on the whole standards have improved dramatically in recent years and the best can offer more character and greater value for money than an equivalently priced hotel. If you're lucky, the owners may also provide traditional home-cooking and a great insight into

French life. In general, prices range between €30 and €70 for two people including breakfast; payment is almost always expected in cash. Some offer meals on request (*tables d'hôtes*), usually evenings only.

If you're planning to stay a week or more in any one place it might be worth considering renting self-catering accommodation. This will generally consist of self-contained country cottages known as **gîtes**. Many *gîtes* are in converted barns or farm outbuildings, though some can be quite grand. "Gîtes Panda" are *gîtes* located in a national park or other protected area and are run on environmentally friendly lines.

You can get lists of both *gîtes* and *chambres d'hôtes* from the government-funded agency Gîtes de France (ⓣ01.49.70.75.75, ⓦwww.gites-de-france.fr); on the website you can search for accommodation by type or theme as well as by area (for example, you could select a *gîte* near fishing or riding opportunities). In addition, every year the organization publishes a number of national guides, such as *Nouveaux Gîtes Ruraux* (listing new addresses), *Chambres et Tables d'Hôtes* and *Chambres d'Hôtes de Charme*, all of which cost around €20, and more comprehensive departmental guides which include photos (around €10–20). All these guides are available online or from departmental offices of Gîtes de France, as well as from bookstores and tourist offices. Tourist offices will also have lists of places in their area which are not affiliated to Gîtes de France.

Hostels and student accommodation

At between €10 and €15 per night for a **dormitory bed**, sometimes with breakfast thrown in, youth hostels – *auberges de jeunesse* – are invaluable for single travellers of any age on a budget. Some now offer rooms, occasionally en suite, but they don't necessarily work out cheaper than hotels – particularly if you've had to pay a taxi fare to reach them. However, many allow you to cut costs by eating in the hostels' cheap canteens, while in a few you can prepare your own meals in the communal kitchens. In the Guide we have given exact prices for the cost of a dormitory bed.

In addition to those belonging to the two French hostelling associations listed below, there are now also several independent hostels, particularly in Paris. At these, dorm beds cost €15–20 with breakfast included, though these tend to be party places with an emphasis on good times rather than a good night's sleep.

A few large towns provide hostel accommodation in Foyers des Jeunes Travailleurs, **residential hostels** for young workers and students, where you can usually get a private room for upwards of €10. On the whole they are more luxurious than youth hostels and normally have a good cafeteria or canteen. These are listed in the Guide, or ask at local tourist offices. During July & August, there's also the possibility of staying in **student accommodation** in university towns and cities at prices similar to hostels. Contact CROUS (ⓣ01.40.51.55.55, ⓦwww.crous-paris.fr) for further information.

Youth hostel associations

Slightly confusingly, there are two rival **French hostelling associations** – the

Fédération Unie des Auberges de Jeunesse and the much smaller Ligue Française (see below). Normally, to stay at FUAJ or LFAJ hostels you must show a current Hostelling International (HI) **membership card**. It's usually cheaper and easier to join before you leave home, provided your national youth hostel association is a full member of HI. Alternatively, you can purchase an HI card in certain French hostels for €15.25 (€10.70 for those under 26), or buy individual "welcome stamps" at a rate of €2.90 per night; after six nights you are entitled to the HI card.

France

Fédération Unie des Auberges de Jeunesse (FUAJ) ⓣ01.44.89.87.27, ⓦwww.fuaj.org.
Ligue Française pour les Auberges de Jeunesse (LFAJ) ⓣ01.44.16.78.78, ⓦwww.auberges-de-jeunesse.com.

UK and Ireland

Youth Hostel Association (YHA) England and Wales ⓣ0870 770 8868, ⓦwww.yha.org.uk.
Scottish Youth Hostel Association ⓣ01786/891 400, ⓦwww.syha.org.uk.
Irish Youth Hostel Association Republic of Ireland ⓣ01/830 4555, ⓦwww.irelandyha.org.
Hostelling International Northern Ireland ⓣ028/9032 4733, ⓦwww.hini.org.uk.

US and Canada

Hostelling International-American Youth Hostels US ⓣ1-301-495-1240, ⓦwww.hiayh.org.
Hostelling International Canada ⓣ1-800-663-5777, ⓦwww.hihostels.ca.

Australia, New Zealand and South Africa

Australia Youth Hostels Association Australia ⓣ02/9565 1699, ⓦwww.yha.com.au.
Youth Hostelling Association New Zealand ⓣ0800 278 299 or 03/379 9970, ⓦwww.yha.co.nz.

Gîtes d'étape and refuges

In the countryside, an alternative hostel-style option exists in the form of **gîtes d'étape**. Aimed primarily at hikers and long-distance bikers, *gîtes d'étape* are often run by the local village or municipality and are less formal than hostels, providing bunk beds and primitive kitchen and washing facilities from around €10 per person. They are marked on the large-scale IGN walkers' maps and listed in the individual GR Topo-guides (see "Walking and climbing" p.61). In addition, mountain areas are well supplied with **refuge huts**, mostly run by the Club Alpin Français (CAF), or the Fédération Français des Clubs Alpins et de Montagne (FFCAM; ⓣ01.53.72.87.00, ⓦwww.ffcam.fr). These huts, generally only open in summer, offer dorm accommodation and meals, and are the only available shelter once you are above the villages. Costs range from €10 to €15 for the night, or half of this if you're a member of a climbing organization affiliated to FFCAM. Meals – invariably four courses – cost around €12, which is good value when you consider that in some cases supplies have to be brought up by mule or helicopter.

More information can be found either online or in the guides *Gîtes d'Étape et de Séjours* (€10), published by Gîtes de France (see opposite).

Camping

Practically every village and town in France has at least one **campsite** to cater for the thousands of people who spend their holiday under canvas. Most sites open from some time in April to September or October. The vast majority are graded into four categories, from one to four stars, by the local authority. One- and two-star sites are very basic, and tend to be quite crowded. There are usually toilets and showers (not necessarily with hot water) but little else, and standards of cleanliness are not always brilliant. At the other extreme, four-star sites are far more spacious, have hot-water showers and electrical hook-ups. Most will have a swimming pool (sometimes heated), washing machines, a shop and sports facilities, and will provide refreshments or meals in high season. At three-star sites you can expect a selection of these facilities and less spacious plots. A further designation, **Camping Qualité** (ⓦwww.campingqualite.com), has been introduced to indicate those campsites with particularly high standards of hygiene, service and privacy, while the **Clef Verte** (ⓦwww.laclefverte.org) label is awarded to sites run along environmentally friendly lines. For those who really like to get away from it all, camping **à la ferme** – on somebody's farm – is a good, simple option. Lists of sites are available at local tourist offices or from Gîtes de France (see p.48).

The Fédération Française de Camping et de Caravaning (ⓣ01.42.72.84.08, ⓦwww.ffcc.fr) publishes an annual **guide** (€16) covering 11,000 campsites, details of which can also be found online on the excellent Camping France website (ⓦwww.camping-france.com). If you'd rather have everything organized for you, a number of companies specialize in camping holidays; see "Getting there" p.33 for details.

Though **charging systems** vary, most places charge per site and per person, usually including a car, while others apply a global figure. As a rough guide, a family of four with a tent and car should expect to pay from €10 per day at a one-star site, rising to €30 or more at a four-star. In peak season it's wise to book ahead, and note that many of the big sites now have caravans and even chalet bungalows for rent.

If you're planning to do a lot of camping, buying an **international camping carnet** before you leave is a good investment. The carnet gives discounts at member sites and serves as useful identification. Many campsites will take it instead of making you surrender your passport during your stay, and it covers you for third-party insurance when camping. It costs £6.50/$18, and is available to members of the following; RAC (ⓦwww.rac.co.uk), the Camping and Caravanning Club (ⓣ0845 130 7631, ⓦwww.campingandcaravanningclub.co.uk), and members of the major motoring organizations in the US, Canada, Australia, New Zealand and South Africa.

Lastly, a word of caution: never **camp rough** (*camping sauvage*) on anyone's land without first asking permission. If the dogs don't get you, the guns might – farmers have been known to shoot first, and ask later. On the other hand, a politely phrased request for permission will as often as not get positive results. Camping on public land is not officially permitted, but is widely practised by the French, and if you're discreet you're unlikely to have problems. On beaches, it's best to camp out only where other people are doing so.

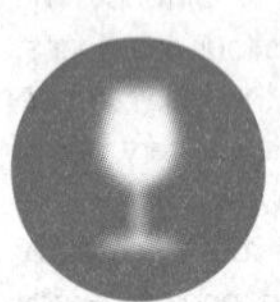

Food and drink

France is famous for producing some of the most sublime food in the world, whether you're talking about the rarefied delicacies of haute cuisine or the robust, no-nonsense fare served up at country inns. Nevertheless, French cuisine has taken a bit of a knocking in recent years. The wonderful ingredients are still there, as every town and village market testifies, but those little family restaurants serving classic dishes that celebrate the region's produce – and where the bill is less than €15 – are increasingly hard to find. Don't be afraid to ask locals for their recommendations; this will usually elicit strong views and sound advice. For more on where to eat in France, see the "Cafés, bistros and brasseries" colour section.

In the rarefied world of **haute cuisine**, where the top chefs are national celebrities, a battle has long been raging between traditionalists, determined to preserve the purity of French cuisine, and those who experiment with different flavours from around the world to create novel combinations. At this level, French food is still brilliant – in both camps – and the good news is that prices are continuing to come down.

Many gourmet places offer weekday lunchtime menus where you can sample culinary genius for under €40.

France is also a great place for **foreign cuisine**, in particular North African, Caribbean (known as Antillais) and Asiatic. Moroccan, Thai or Vietnamese restaurants are not necessarily cheap options but they are usually good value for money.

Breakfast and lunch

A croissant or *pain au chocolat* (a chocolate-filled, light pastry) in a café or bar, with tea, hot chocolate or coffee, is generally the best-value way to eat breakfast, costing around €4 to €5. If there are no croissants left, it's perfectly acceptable to go and buy your own at the nearest baker or patisserie. The standard hotel breakfast comprises bread and/or pastries, jam and a jug of coffee or tea, and orange juice if you're lucky, from around €5 or €6. More expensive places might offer a buffet comprising cereals, fruit, yoghurt and the works.

The main meal of the day is traditionally eaten at **lunchtime**, usually between noon and 2pm. Midday, and sometimes in the evening, you'll find places offering a *plat du jour* (daily special) for €8–12, or *formules*, limited menus typically offering a main dish and either a starter or a dessert for a set price. **Crêpes**, or pancakes with fillings, served up at ubiquitous crêperies, are popular lunchtime food. The savoury buckwheat variety (*galettes*) provide the main course; sweet, white-flour crêpes are dessert. They can be very tasty, but are generally poor value in comparison with a restaurant meal; you need at least three, normally at over €5 each (€3 for the sweet variety), to feel full. **Pizzerias**, usually *au feu du bois* (baked in wood-fired ovens), are also very common. They are somewhat better value than crêperies, but quality and quantity vary greatly.

For **picnics**, the local outdoor market or supermarket will provide you with almost everything you need from tomatoes and avocados to cheese and pâté. Cooked meat, prepared snacks, ready-made dishes and assorted salads can be bought at charcuteries (delicatessens), which you'll find even in most small villages, and at supermarket cold-food counters. You purchase by weight, or you can ask for *une tranche* (a slice), *une barquette* (a carton) or *une part* (a portion) as appropriate.

Snacks

Food snobs may say this is where French cuisine falls short, and where American-influenced fast food culture is creeping in. There is, however, a large range of choice when it comes to eating on the run, or snacking between meals. *Croques-monsieur* or *croques-madame* (variations on the toasted cheese-and-ham sandwich) are on sale at cafés, brasseries and many street stands, along with *frites* (potato fries), crêpes, *galettes*, *gauffres* (waffles), *glaces* (ice creams) and all kinds of fresh-filled baguettes (which usually cost between €3 and €5 to take away). For variety, in main towns and cities you can find Tunisian snacks like *brik à l'œuf* (a fried pastry with an egg inside), *merguez* (spicy North African sausage), Greek *souvlaki* (kebabs) and Middle Eastern falafel (deep-fried chickpea balls in flat bread with salad). Wine bars are good for regional sausages and cheese, usually served with brown bread (*pain de campagne*).

Regional dishes

French cooking is as varied as its landscape, and differs vastly from region to region. In **Provence**, in close proximity to Italy, local dishes make heavy use of olive oils, garlic and tomatoes, as well as Mediterranean vegetables such as aubergines (eggplant) and peppers. In keeping with its proximity to the sea, the region's most famous dish is without doubt *bouillabaisse*, a hearty fish stew from Marseille. To the southwest in **Languedoc** and **Pays Basque**, hearty *cassoulet* stews and heavier meals are in order, more in common with Spanish cuisine. **Alsace**, in the northeast, features Germanic influences in its cuisine, specializing in dishes such as *choucroute* (sauerkraut), and a hearty array of sausages. **Burgundy**, famous for its wines, is the home of what many people consider classic French dishes such as *coq au vin* and *boeuf bourguignon*. In the northwest, **Normandy** and **Brittany** are about the best places you could head for seafood, as well as for sweet and savoury crêpes and *galettes*. Finally, if you're in the **Dordogne**, make sure to sample its famous foie gras or pricey truffles (*truffes*).

For more on which regional dishes to try, see the boxes at the start of each chapter in the Guide.

Vegetarian food

On the whole, **vegetarians** can expect a somewhat lean time in France. Most cities now have at least one specifically vegetarian restaurant, but elsewhere your best bet will probably be a crêperie or pizzeria. Failing that you may have to fall back on an omelette or a plate of vegetables (often tinned) in an ordinary restaurant. Sometimes restaurants are willing to replace a meat dish on the fixed-price menu (*menu fixe*); at other times you'll have to pick your way through the *carte*. Remember the phrase *Je suis végétarien(ne); est-ce qu'il y a quelques plats sans viande?* ("I'm a vegetarian; are there any non-meat dishes?"). **Vegans**, however, should probably forget all about eating in restaurants and stick to self-catering.

Drink

Wherever you can eat you can invariably drink, and vice versa. Drinking is done at a leisurely pace whether it's a prelude to food (*apéritif*) or a sequel (*digestif*), and **café-bars** are the standard places to do it. By law the full price list, including service charges, must be clearly displayed. You normally pay when you leave, and it's perfectly acceptable to sit for hours over just one cup of coffee, though in this case a small tip will be appreciated.

Wine

French **wines** (*vin*), drunk at just about every meal or social occasion, are unrivalled in the world for their range, sophistication, diversity and status. With the exception of the north-west of the country and the mountains, wine is produced just about everywhere. The great wine-producing **regions** are Champagne, Bordeaux and Burgundy, closely followed by the Loire and Rhône valleys. Alsace also has some great wines, and there are some beautiful ones to be had in the lesser wine regions of Bergerac, Languedoc, Roussillon, Provence and Savoie. Even within each region, there's enormous diversity, with differences generated by the varying types of soil, the lie of the land, the type of grape grown – there are over sixty varieties – the ability of the wine to age, and the individual skills of the producer.

The **quality** of wine can also vary enor-

Cheese

Charles de Gaulle famously commented that "You can unite the French only through fear. You cannot simply bring together a country that has over 265 kinds of cheese". For serious **cheese**-lovers, France is the ultimate paradise. Other countries may produce individual cheeses which are as good as, or even better than, the best of the French, but no country offers a range that comes anywhere near them in terms of sheer inventiveness. In fact, there are officially over 300 types of French cheese, and the way they are made are jealously guarded secrets. Many cheese-makers have successfully protected their products by gaining the right to label their produce **AOC** (*appellation d'origine contrôlée*), covered by laws similar to those for wines, which – among other things – controls the amount of cheese that a particular area can produce. As a result, the subtle differences between French local cheeses have not been overwhelmed by the industrialized uniformity that has plagued other countries.

The best, or most traditional, restaurants offer a well-stocked *plateau de fromages* (cheeseboard), served at room temperature with bread, but not butter. Apart from the ubiquitous Brie, Camembert and numerous varieties of goat's cheese (*chèvre*), there will usually be one or two local cheeses on offer – these are the ones to go for. If you want to buy cheese, local markets are always the best bet, while in larger towns you'll generally find a *fromagerie*, a shop with perhaps 200 varieties or more to choose from. We've indicated the best regional cheeses throughout the Guide.

mously. *Vin de table* or *vin ordinaire* – table wine – is generally drinkable and always cheap, although it may be disguised and priced-up as the house wine, or *cuvée*. Local *vins de pays* can vary in quality but they are still exceptional for the price. The best-quality wines are denoted by the **AOC** (*appellation d'origine contrôlée*) label, which means that the wine comes from an area (known in this case as an *appellation*) where the amount of wine produced is strictly controlled. The **price** of AOC wines starts at around €4, and you can buy a very decent bottle in a shop for €6; €10 and over will get you something worth savouring. By the time restaurants have added their considerable mark-up, wine can constitute an alarming proportion of the bill. A glass of wine in a bar will typically cost around €3–6.

Choosing wine is an extremely complex business and it's hard not to feel intimidated by the seemingly innate expertise of all French people. Many individual wines and *appellations* are mentioned in the text, but trusting your own taste is the best way to go. Knowing the grape types that you particularly like (or dislike), whether you like wines very fruity, dry, light or heavy, is all useful when discussing your choice with a waiter, producer or wine merchant. The more interest you show, the more helpful advice you're likely to receive. The only thing the French cannot tolerate is people ordering Coke or the like to accompany a gourmet meal.

The best way of **buying wine** is directly from the producers (*vignerons*), either at vineyards, at Maisons or Syndicats du Vin (representing a group of wine-producers), or at Coopératifs Vinicoles (producers' co-ops) – at all these places you can usually sample the wines first. It's best to make clear at the start how much you want to buy (particularly if it's only one or two bottles) and you'll not be popular if you drink several glasses and then fail to buy at least one bottle. The most economical option is to buy *en vrac*, which you can also do at some wine shops (*caves*), filling an easily obtainable plastic five- or ten-litre container (usually sold on the premises) straight from the barrel. In cities, supermarkets are the best places to buy your wine, often at very competitive prices.

The basic wine terms are: *brut*, very dry; *sec*, dry; *demi-sec*, sweet; *doux*, very sweet; *mousseux*, sparkling; *méthode champenoise*, mature and sparkling.

Beer and spirits

Familiar light Belgian and German brands, plus French brands from Alsace, account for most of the **beer** you'll find. Draught beer (*à la pression*) – usually Kronenbourg – is the cheapest drink you can have next to coffee and wine; *un pression* or *un demi* (0.33 litre) will cost around €3. For a wider choice of draught and bottled beer you need to go to the special beer-drinking establishments such as the English- and Irish-style pubs found in larger towns and cities. A small bottle at one of these places can set you back double what you'd pay in an ordinary café-bar. In supermarkets, however, bottled or canned beer is exceptionally cheap.

Spirits, such as cognac and armagnac, and liqueurs are consumed at any time of day, though in far smaller quantities these days thanks to the clampdown on drink-driving. *Pastis* – the generic name of aniseed drinks such as Pernod and Ricard – is served diluted with water and ice (*glace* or *glaçons*). It's very refreshing and not expensive. Among less familiar names, try Poire William (pear brandy), or Marc (a spirit distilled from grape pulp). Measures are generous, but they don't come cheap: the same applies for imported spirits like whisky (*Scotch*). Two drinks designed to stimulate the appetite – *un apéritif* – are pineau (cognac and grape juice) and kir (white wine with a dash of Cassis – blackcurrant liqueur – or with champagne instead of wine for a Kir Royal). Cognac, armagnac and Chartreuse are among the many aids to digestion – *un digestif* – to relax over after a meal. Cocktails are served at most late-night bars, discos and clubs, as well as upmarket hotel bars and at every seaside promenade café; they usually cost at least €5.

Soft drinks, tea and coffee

You can buy cartons of unsweetened **fruit juice** in supermarkets, although in cafés the bottled (sweetened) nectars such as apricot (*jus d'abricot*) and blackcurrant (*cassis*) still hold sway. Fresh orange (*jus d'orange*) or lemon juice (*citron pressé*) are a much more refreshing choice on a hot day – for the latter, the juice is served in the bottom of a long ice-filled glass, with a jug of water and a sugar bowl to sweeten it to your taste. Other soft drinks to try are syrups (*sirops*) – mint or grenadine, for example, mixed with water. The standard fizzy drinks of lemonade (*limonade*), Coke (*coca*) and so forth are all available, and there's no shortage of bottled mineral **water** (*eau minérale*) or spring water (*eau de source*) – whether sparkling (*gazeuse*) or still (*plate*) – either, from the big brand names to the most obscure spa product. But there's not much wrong with the tap water (*l'eau de robinet*) which will always be brought free to your table if you ask for it. The only time you shouldn't drink the tap water, is if the tap is labelled *eau non potable*.

Coffee is invariably espresso – small, black and very strong. *Un café* or *un express* is the regular; *un crème* is with milk; *un grand café* or *un grand crème* are large versions. In the morning you could also ask for *un café au lait* – espresso in a large cup or bowl topped up with hot milk. *Un déca* is decaffeinated, now widely available. Ordinary **tea** (*thé*) – Lipton's nine times out of ten – is normally served black (*nature*) or with a slice of lemon (*limon*); to have milk with it, ask for *un peu de lait frais* (some fresh milk). *Chocolat chaud* – **hot chocolate** – unlike tea, lives up to the high standards of French food and drink and can be had in any café. After meals, herb teas (*infusions* or *tisanes*), offered by most restaurants, can be soothing. The more common ones are *verveine* (verbena), *tilleul* (lime blossom), *menthe* (mint) and *camomille* (camomile).

The media

French newspapers and magazines are available from any of the ubiquitous street-side kiosks, or *tabacs*, whilst TV, satellite and otherwise, is easy to track down in most forms of accommodation. Even if you can't read or speak French, you can still get your news fix by getting hold of an international edition of a British or American newspaper or an international news magazine to keep up with current events.

Newspapers and magazines

Of the French **national daily papers**, *Le Monde* (ⓦwww.lemonde.fr) is the most intellectual; it's widely respected, and somewhat austere, though it does now carry such frivolities as colour photos, Conservative, and at times controversial, *Le Figaro* (ⓦwww.lefigaro.fr) is the most respected of the more right-wing papers. *Libération* (ⓦwww.liberation.com), founded by Jean-Paul Sartre in the 1960s, is moderately left-wing, pro-European, independent and more colloquial, whilst rigorous left-wing criticism of the French government comes from *L'Humanité* (ⓦwww.humanite.presse.fr), the Communist Party paper. The other nationals are all **tabloids**; predictably more readable and a good source of news, is *Aujourd'hui* (published in Paris as *Le Parisien*), followed by the much troubled *France Soir*, whilst *L'Équipe* (ⓦwww.lequipe.fr) is dedicated to sports coverage. The widest circulations are enjoyed by the **regional dailies**, of which the most important is the Rennes-based *Ouest-France* (ⓦwww.ouest-france.fr). For visitors, these are mainly of interest for their listings.

Weekly **magazines** of the *Newsweek/Time* model include the wide-ranging and socialist-inclined *Le Nouvel Observateur* (ⓦwww.nouvelobs.com), its right-wing-counterpoint *L'Express* (ⓦwww.lexpress.fr) and the centrist with bite *Marianne* (ⓦwww.marianne-en-ligne.fr). Comprising mainly translated articles, *Courier International* (ⓦwww.courrierinternational.com) offers an overview of what's being discussed in media around the globe. The best investigative journalism is to be found in the weekly satirical paper *Le Canard Enchainé* (ⓦwww.lecanardenchaine.fr), while *Charlie Hebdo* is roughly equivalent to the UK's *Private Eye*. Monthlies include the young and trendy *Nova* (ⓦwww.novaplanet.com), which has excellent listings of cultural events. There are also, of course, the French versions of *Vogue*, *Elle* and *Marie-Claire*, and the relentlessly urban *Biba*, for women's fashion and lifestyle.

English-language newspapers, such as the *European*, *Washington Post*, *New York Times,* the *Guardian* and the *International Herald Tribune*, are on sale on the day of publication in the main cities and the day after elsewhere, although they tend to cost from around €3.

Moral censorship of the press is rare. On the newsstands you'll find pornography of every shade alongside knitting patterns and DIY. You'll also find French **comics** (*bandes dessinées*), many of which are aimed at the adult market, with wild and wonderful illustrations; they're considered to be quite an art form and whole museums are devoted to them.

Radio

The publicly-owned radio provider is **Radio France** (ⓦwww.radio-france.fr), which operates seven stations; these include France Bleu, its regional radio station network, France Culture for arts, France Info for news, and music channels France Musique and Le Mouv', which have wide-ranging playlists. Other major private stations include Europe 1 (ⓦwww.europe1.fr) for news, debate and sport. **English-language** broadcasts are available from the BBC (ⓦwww.bbc.co.uk/worldservice), Radio Canada (ⓦwww.rcinet.ca), and Voice of America (ⓦwww.voa.gov); see

Festivals

It's hard to beat the experience of arriving in a small French village, expecting no more than a bed for the night, to discover the streets decked out with flags and streamers, a band playing in the square and the entire population out celebrating the feast of their patron saint. As well as nationwide celebrations such as the Fête de la Musique (June 21, the summer solstice; ⓦwww.fetedelamusique.culture.fr), Bastille Day (July 14) and the Assumption of the Virgin Mary (August 15), there are any number of festivals – both traditional and of more recent origin – held in towns and villages throughout France. For a detailed account of some of the major ones, see the *Festive France* colour section. Below is a list of the main festivals; alternatively, see ⓦwww.culture.fr and ⓦwww.viafrance.com.

January

Nantes La Folle Journée (late Jan to early Feb; ⓦwww.follejournee.fr).

Nice Carnival (Jan–Feb; ⓦwww.nicecarnaval.com).

February to April

Menton Fête du Citron (two weeks following Mardi Gras, forty days before Easter); ⓦwww.feteducitron.com) Parades, concerts and fireworks.

Nîmes La Féria de Nîmes (Pentecost, seven weeks after Easter) Bullfights.

Orcival Procession of Notre-Dame d'Orcival (Ascension Day, forty days after Easter).

May

Cannes Festival de Cannes (ⓦwww.festival-cannes.com) International film festival.

Les Saintes-Maries-de-la-Mer Fête de Ste Sarah (May 24–25) Romany festival.

Paris Festival de St-Denis (May–June; ⓦwww.festival-saint-denis.fr) Classical music festival.

Angoulême Musiques Metisses (late May; ⓦwww.musiques-metisses.com) Afro-Caribbean and Latin American music.

June

Châlons-en-Campagne Festival Furies (early June; ⓦwww.festival-furies.com) Street theatre.

Lyon Les Nuits de Fourvière (early June to early Aug; ⓦwww.nuitsdefourviere.fr) Performance arts.

Paris Festival Django Reinhardt (ⓦwww.django.samois.free.fr) Jazz.

Strasbourg Festival de Musique de Strasbourg (ⓦwww.festival-strasbourg.com) Classical music.

Uzès Uzès Danse (ⓦwww.uzesdanse.fr) Contemporary dance.

Grenoble Rencontres du Jeune Théâtre Européen (late June) Contemporary theatre.

Bordeaux Fête le Vin (late June in even-numbered years; ⓦwww.bordeaux-fete-le-vin.com).

Paris La Marche des Fiertés Lesbienne, Gai, Bi & Trans (late June; ⓦwww.inter-lgbt.org).

Sotteville-lès-Rouen Viva Cité (late June) Street theatre.

Montpellier Montpellier Danse (late June to early July; ⓦwww.montpellierdanse.com).

Vienne Jazz à Vienne (late June to mid-July; ⓦwww.jazzavienne.com).

July

Alès Cratère/Surfaces (early July; ⓦwww.lecratere.fr) Street theatre.

Belfort Eurockéennes (early July; ⓦwww.eurockeennes.fr) Contemporary music.

Mont-de-Marsan Arte Flamenco (early July) Flamenco music.

(continued overleaf)

Reims Flâneries Musicales d'Été (early July to early Aug) Open-air concerts.

Beaune Festival International d'Opéra Baroque (early July to early Aug; ⓦwww.festivalbeaune.com).

La Rochelle Festival International du Film (early July; ⓦwww.festival-larochelle.org).

Rennes Les Tombées de la Nuit (early July; ⓦwww.lestdnuit.com) Concerts, cinema and performance arts.

Nice Jazz Festival (ⓦwww.nicejazzfest.com).

Aix-en-Provence Festival International d'Art Lyrique (ⓦwww.festival-aix.com) Classical music.

Avignon Festival d'Avignon (ⓦwww.festival-avignon.com) Contemporary dance and theatre.

Colmar Festival International de Colmar (ⓦwww.festival-colmar.com) Classical music.

Carhaix Festival des Vieilles Charrues (ⓦwww.vieillescharrues.asso.fr) Contemporary music festival.

Saintes Académies Musicales de Saintes (ⓦwww.festival-saintes.org) Classical music.

La Rochelle Francofolies (mid-July; ⓦwww.francofolies.fr) Contemporary French music.

La Roque d'Anthéron Festival International de Piano (mid-July to mid-Aug; ⓦwww.festival-piano.com).

Arles Les Suds à Arles (mid-July; ⓦwww.suds-arles.com). World music.

Juan-les-Pins Jazz à Juan (mid-July).

Vaison-la-Romaine Vaison Danse (mid-July; ⓦwww.vaison-festival.com) Contemporary dance.

Chalon-sur-Saône Chalon dans la Rue (third week July; ⓦwww.chalondanslarue.com) Street theatre.

Annecy Les Noctibules (late July) Street theatre.

Gannat (near Vichy) Les Cultures du Monde (late July; ⓦwww.gannat.com).

Aix-en-Provence Danse à Aix (late July/early Aug; ⓦwww.aix-en-provence.com/danse-a-aix).

Prades Festival Pablo Casals (late July to mid-Aug; ⓦwww.prades-festival-casals.com) Chamber music.

Orange Chorégies d'Orange (July–Aug; ⓦwww.choregies.asso.fr) Opera.

August

Aurillac Festival International de Théâtre de Rue (ⓦwww.aurillac.net) Street theatre.

Quimper Semaines Musicales (ⓦwww.semaines-musicales-quimper.org) Classical, jazz and folk music.

Lorient Festival Interceltique (early Aug; ⓦwww.festival-interceltique.com) Celtic folk festival.

Marciac Jazz in Marciac (early Aug; ⓦwww.jazzinmarciac.com).

Périgueux Mimos (early Aug; ⓦwww.mimos.fr) International mime festival.

Menton Festival de Musique de Chambre (ⓦwww.festivalmusiquementon.com) Chamber music.

St-Malo La Route du Rock (mid-Aug; ⓦwww.laroutedurock.com).

Mulhouse Festival du Jazz (mid- to late Aug; ⓦwww.jazz-mulhouse.org).

Paris Rock en Seine (late Aug; ⓦwww.rockenseine.com).

Festivals (continued)

September

Lyon Bienniale de la Dance (next in 2008; Ⓦwww.biennale-de-lyon.org).

Paris Biennial des Antiquaires (next in 2008) Antiques fair; Jazz à la Villette (Ⓦwww.villette.com); Festival d'Automne (mid-Sept to mid-Dec; Ⓦwww.festival-automne.com) Theatre, concerts, dance, films and exhibitions.

Puy-en-Velay Fête Renaissance du Roi de l'Oiseau (mid-Sept; Ⓦwww.roideloiseau.com) Historical pageants, fireworks and re-creations.

Perpignan Visa pour l'Image (mid-Sept; Ⓦwww.visapourlimage.com) International photojournalism.

Amiens Festival des Cathédrales de Picardie (Sept–Oct; Ⓦwww.festivaldescathedrales.com) Baroque and Renaissance music.

Strasbourg Musica (Sept–Oct; Ⓦwww.festival-musica.org) Contemporary music.

Limoges Les Francophonies en Limousin (end Sept to mid-Oct; Ⓦwww.lesfrancophonies.com) Contemporary theatre.

October

Nancy Jazz Pulsations (Ⓦwww.nancyjazzpulsations.com).

Paris Foire International d'Art Contemporain.

Bastia Les Musicales (Ⓦwww.musicales-de-bastia.com) Sacred and world music.

Montpellier Festival International Cinéma Méditerranéen (late Oct to early Nov; Ⓦwww.cinemed.tm.fr).

November to December

Strasbourg Jazz d'Or (Nov; Ⓦwww.jazzdoor.com).

Les Saintes-Maries-de-la-Mer Festival d'Abrivado (Nov 11) Bull-running.

Rennes Rencontres Transmusicales (early Dec; Ⓦwww.lestrans.com) Contemporary music.

their websites for local frequencies. In the Paris region, you can listen to the news in English on Radio France International (RFI, Ⓦwww.rfi.fr) at 7am, 2.30pm and 4.30pm on 738 kHz.

Television

French **terrestrial TV** has six channels: three public (France 2, France 3 and Arte/France 5); one subscription (Canal Plus – with some unencrypted programmes); and two commercial (TF1 and M6). Of these, TF1 and France 2 are the most popular channels: **TF1** is home to dubbed US comedies and the inevitable reality shows, while **France 2** has decent news coverage and a number of chat and debate shows. **M6** follows closely in the popularity stakes with a large range of American series. **Arte/France 5** (also known as La Cinquième) offers slightly more highbrow programming, including daily documentaries, art criticism, serious French and German movies and complete operas. During the daytime (7am–7pm), France 5 uses the frequency to broadcast educational programmes. **Canal Plus** is the main movie channel, with repeats of foreign films usually shown at least once a day in the original language. **France 3** is strong on regional news and more heavyweight movies, including a fair number of undubbed foreign films. The main French **news** broadcasts are at 8pm on France 2 and TF1.

In addition there are any number of **cable and satellite channels**, which include CNN, BBC World and BBC Prime, Eurosport, MTV, Planète, which specializes in documentaries, Ciné Première, and Canal Jimmy (*Friends* and the like in French). The main French-run music channel is MCM.

Sports and outdoor activities

France has a wide range of sports on offer, both for the spectator and the participant. It's not difficult to get tickets for domestic and international football and rugby matches, while the biggest event of all, the Tour de France, is free. And if you're interested in expending some energy yourself, there's a whole host of activities and adventure sports available.

Spectator sports

More than any of the cultural jamborees, it's **sporting events** that really excite the French – particularly cycling, football, rugby and tennis. In the south, bullfighting and the Basque game of pelota are also popular. At the local, everyday level, the rather less gripping game of *boules* is the sport of choice, played in every town and village.

Cycling

The sport the French are truly mad about is **cycling**. It was, after all, in Paris's Palais Royale gardens in 1791 that the precursor of the modern bicycle, the *célerifière*, was presented, and in the same city seventy years later that father and son team Pierre and Ernest Michaux constructed the *vélocipede* (from which comes the French term *vélo* for bicycle), the first really efficient bicycle. The French can also legitimately claim the sport of cycle racing as their own, with the first event, a 1200-metre sprint, held in Paris's Parc St-Cloud in 1868 – sadly for national pride, however, the first champion was an Englishman.

That most French of sporting events, and the world's premier cycling race, is the **Tour de France**, held in July. Covering around 3500 kilometres, the course of the three-week event changes every year, sometimes including foreign countries in its itinerary (Britain and Ireland, among others, have hosted stages). Wherever, it's held, some truly arduous mountain stages and some time trials are always part of the action. An aggregate of each rider's times is made daily, the overall leader wearing the coveted yellow jersey (*maillot jaune*). Huge crowds turn out to cheer on the cyclists on the Champs-Élysées, where the ultimate stage is completed. The French president himself presents the jersey to the overall winner, though the crowds have been waiting for a French cyclist to win the Tour since Bernard Hinault's victory in 1985.

Over recent years the event has been rocked by drug scandals, beginning in 1998 when evidence of systematic doping within the cycling teams came to light, and casting a shadow over the American rider Lance Armstrong's monumental achievement of becoming the first man to have won seven consecutive races. More recently, in 2006, fellow American Floyd Landis' spectacular win was brought into doubt when drugs testing revealed higher than normal amounts of testosterone in his system.

Other classic long-distance bike races include the **Paris–Roubaix**, instigated in 1896 and held in April, which is reputed to be the most exacting one-day race in the world, parts of it over cobblestones; the **Paris–Brussels** (Sept), held since 1893; and the rugged seven-day **Paris–Nice** event (March), covering over 1100km. The **Grand Prix des Nations** (Sept), which takes place in the Seine-Maritime *département*, is the world's foremost time trial; the Palais Omnisport de Bercy in Paris (see p.191) holds other time trials and cycling events. Details for all the above can be found at ⓦwww.letour.fr.

Football

In France, as in most countries, **football** is the number-one team sport. Football fever reached a pitch in the late 1990s, when the French team won the **1998 World Cup** in front of their home crowd and in 2000

Sporting calendar

January Monte Carlo Car Rally (ⓦwww.acm.mc).

February Six Nations rugby tournament (Paris; ⓦwww.6-nations-rugby.com).

April Paris Marathon (ⓦwww.parismarathon.com); Le Mans 24-hour motorcycle rally (ⓦwww.lemans.org).

May Roland Garros International Tennis Championship (Paris; ⓦwww.rolandgarros.com); Monaco Formula 1 Grand Prix (ⓦwww.monaco-formula1.com).

June Le Mans 24-hour car rally (ⓦwww.lemans.org).

July Tour de France; (ⓦwww.letour.fr); Nevers French Formula 1 Grand Prix (ⓦwww.magnyf1.com).

October Grand Prix de l'Arc de Triomphe (Paris; ⓦwww.france-galop.com).

became the first side ever to add a **European Championships** title to the world crown. Despite the occasional high point, the team has perhaps inevitably found it hard to live up to expectations since then, despite boasting some of the world's top players. A low point was the 2002 World Cup, when they were eliminated in the first round without scoring a single goal. They performed slightly better in the 2004 European Championships, but were unexpectedly knocked out by Greece, the eventual winner, in the quarter-finals. The **2006 World Cup**, hosted by Germany, saw the national team's fortunes improve dramatically. Despite a slow start, France advanced to the final, even beating tournament favourites Brazil, only to lose out to Italy on penalties. Sadly the game will probably be best remembered for national hero **Zinedine Zidane**, representing France for the last time, being sent from the pitch for headbutting an Italian defender.

Buoyed by the success of the national team, the **domestic game** has been on the up in recent years, and average attendances have improved. Almost all clubs now have sound financial backing, and the biggest clubs, such as Monaco, Marseille and Paris St-Germain (PSG), have all performed well in European competitions. For the latest information visit the website of the *Ligue de Football Professionel* at ⓦwww.lfp.fr.

Tickets to see domestic clubs are available either from specific club websites, or in the towns where they are playing; ask at local tourist offices. To watch the national team, you can get tickets online at ⓦwww.fff.fr (Fédération Française de Football), or try ⓦwww.francebillet.com. Prices tend to start at around €10–15.

Rugby

Although most popular in the southwest of the country, **rugby** enjoys a passionate following throughout France. The French have a rich rugby heritage and are renowned throughout the world for the flair with which they play the game. French rugby's greatest moment to date came in the semi-finals of the 1999 World Cup, when they stunned the world by trouncing favourites New Zealand, though they blew cold in the final, losing to an Australian side that never had to rouse itself out of second gear. In 2003 France made it as far as the semi-final, only to be thrashed by an England team en route to the podium. It remains to be seen what will happen when France plays host to the **2007 World Cup** (ⓦwww.rugbyworldcup.com).

More international fare is provided by the **Six Nations** tournament – the other five nations being England, Wales, Scotland, Ireland and Italy – which takes place every year between February and April. Matches are played alternately at home and away. Over the past few years, France has been the most consistent team, clinching Grand Slams in 2002 and 2004, and winning again in 2006, despite a surprise defeat to Scotland.

Domestically, the French clubs have ridden out rugby's occasionally fraught transition from amateur to professional status and look to be in good shape. Though France has lost some of its stars to predatory English clubs, unlike in football the majority of the national side still plays at home. Sides to watch for are Stade Français from Paris (winners of the French Championship in 2006), Toulouse, Perpignan and Brive (past winners of the Europe-wide Heineken Cup), Agen, and the Basque teams of Bayonne and Biarritz, which still retain their reputation as keepers of the game's soul, despite the latter's poor performances in recent years.

Tickets for local games can be bought through the clubs themselves, with prices starting around €10. For bigger domestic and international games, they are available online at Ⓦwww.francebillet.com; prices start at around €20. Information can be found on the Fédération Française de Rugby's website (Ⓦwww.ffr.fr).

Pelota

In the Basque country (and also in the nearby Landes), the main draw for crowds is the national ball game of **pelota**, a lethally (sometimes literally) fast variety of team handball or raquetball played in a walled court with a ball of solid wood. The most popular form today is played with bare hands in a two-walled court called a *fronton*. In other varieties wooden bats are used or wicker slings strapped to the players' arms. Ask at local tourist offices for details of where to see the game played.

Bullfighting

In and around the Camargue, the number-one sport is **bullfighting.** Different from the Spanish version, the *course camarguaise* involves variations on the theme of removing cockades from the base of the bull's horns, and it's generally the fighters, rather than the bulls, who get hurt. Further west, particularly in the Landes *département*, you'll come across the similar *courses landaises*, where men perform acrobatics with the by-no-means docile local cows.

Spanish bullfights, known as *corridas*, do take place – and draw capacity crowds – in southern France. The major events of the year are the Féria de Nîmes (see p.845) at Pentecost (Whitsun) and the Easter *féria* at Arles (p.1080). See the local press or ask at tourist offices for details of where to pick up tickets.

Boules

In every town or village square, particularly in the south, you'll see beret-clad men playing *boules* or its variant, *pétanque* (in which contestants must keep both feet on the ground when throwing). Although more women are taking up *boules*, at competition level it remains very male-dominated: there are café or village teams and endless championships. There's even talk – not all of it in jest – of getting *boules* recognized as an Olympic sport.

Outdoor activities

In addition to the perennial favourites – walking, cycling and skiing – France provides a fantastically wide range of outdoor activities. Most have a national federation (listed in the text where relevant), which can provide information on local clubs.

Walking and climbing

Long-distance **walkers** are well served in France by a network of some 60,000km of long-distance marked footpaths, known as *sentiers de grande randonnée* or, more commonly, simply as **GRs**. They're fully signposted and equipped with campsites, refuges and hostels (*gîtes d'étape*) along the way. Some are real marathons, like the GR5 from the coast of Holland to Nice, the trans-Pyrenean GR10, the Grande Traversée des Alpes (the GTA), and, best of all, the GR20 in Corsica (see box, pp.1226–27). Other famous hikes include the Chemin de St-Jacques (GR65), which follows the ancient pilgrim route from Le Puy in the Auvergne to the Spanish border above St-Jean-Pied-de-Port and on to the shrine of Santiago de Compostela, and the GR3, which traces the Loire from source to sea. There are also thousands of shorter *sentiers de promenade et de randonnée*, the **PRs**, as well as nature walks and many other local footpaths.

Each GR and many PRs are described in the **Topo-guide series** (available outside France in good travel bookshops), which give a detailed account of each route, including maps, campsites, refuges, sources of provisions, and so on. In France, the guides are available from bookshops and some tourist offices, or direct from the principal French walkers association, the Fédération Française de la Randonnée Pédestre (Ⓣ01.44.89.93.90, Ⓦwww.ffrandonnee.fr). In addition, many tourist offices can provide guides to local footpaths.

Climbing is possible all year round, although bear in mind that some higher routes will be snowbound until quite late in the year, and require special equipment such as crampons and ice axes; these shouldn't be attempted without experience or at least a local guide. No matter where you are walking, make sure you have your own water supplies, or find out locally if you'll be able to fill up your water bottles on the way. You'll also need decent footwear, waterproofs and a map, compass and possibly GPS system. Unless staying in mountain refuges (see "Accommodation", p.49) you'll also need warm clothes, a tent, sleeping bag and ground mat, not to mention supplies. Finally, especially if walking at high altitudes, don't forget sunblock, sunglasses and a hat.

In mountain areas there are associations of professional **mountain guides**, often located in the tourist office, who organize walking and climbing (*escalade*) expeditions for all levels of experience. For more information you could also contact the Fédération Française de la Montagne et de l'Escalade (Ⓣ01.40.18.75.50, Ⓦwww.ffme.fr).

Details of tour operators specializing in walking holidays are listed on p.33.

Cycling

Cyclists have around 50,000km of marked cycle paths (*pistes cyclables*) in France. Many towns and cities have established cycle lanes, while in the countryside there are an increasing number of specially designated mountain-bike tracks. Aquitaine, in southwest France, is particularly well provided for: there are extensive **routes** through the Landes forest and south to the Spanish border. The Fédération Française de Cyclisme (Ⓣ01.49.35.69.00, Ⓦwww.ffc.fr) produces a guide to mountain-biking sites, and tourist offices can provide details of local cycle ways; the Fédération Française de Cyclotourisme (Ⓣ01.56.20.88.88, Ⓦwww.ffct.org) provides links to local cycling clubs, and lists local trips. IGN's 1:100,000 maps are the best for cyclists (see p.75).

For information on the practicalities of cycling in France, see "Getting around", p.43. You'll find details of tour operators specializing in cycling holidays on p.33.

Skiing and snowboarding

Millions of visitors come to France to practise **skiing and snowboarding**; whether downhill, cross-country or mountaineering, it's also enthusiastically pursued by the French. It can be an expensive sport to practise independently, however, and the best deals are often to be had from package operators (see p.33). These can be arranged in France or before you leave (most travel agents sell all-in packages). Though it's possible to ski from early November through to the end of April at high altitudes, peak season is February and March.

The best skiing and boarding is generally to be had in the **Alps**. The higher the resort the longer the season, and the fewer the anxieties you'll have about there being enough snow. Resorts such as Tignes, Les Deux-Alpes or Val Thorens are almost all modern, with the very latest in lift technology. They're terrific for full-time skiing, but they lack the cachet, charm or the nightlife of the older, lower resorts such as Megève and Morzine. For a brief rundown of all the main Alpine skiing areas, see the box on p.981. The foothills of the Alps in **Provence** have the same mix of old and new on a smaller scale. The clientele are Riviera residents and prices are not cheap, though at least you can nip down to the coast when you're bored with snow. The **Pyrenees** are a friendlier range of mountains, less developed (though that can be a drawback if you want to get in as many different runs as possible per day) and warmer, which means a shorter season and less reliable snow.

Cross-country skiing (*ski de fond*) is being promoted hard, especially in the smaller ranges of the Jura and Massif Central. It's easier on the joints, but don't be fooled into thinking it's any less athletic a sport. For the really experienced and fit, though, it can be a good means of transport, using snowbound GR routes to discover villages still relatively uncommercialized. Several independent operators organize **ski-mountaineering courses** in the French mountains (see p.33).

Practicalities

Lift **passes** start at around €20 a day in most resorts, but can reach around €50 in the pricier spots; passes for a week will set you back anything from €80 to over €300. **Equipment** hire is available at most resorts, and comes in at around €20 per day all in, whilst a week's hire will set you back anything from €100. Although there are plenty of tour operators offering cheap all-in deals, don't forget to check out **local hotels** and B&Bs who offer independent ski deals; see the Guide for details.

The Fédération Française de Ski (ⓣ04.50.51.40.34, ⓦwww.ffs.fr) and the Association Française de Snowboard (ⓣ04.92.41.80.00, ⓦwww.afs-fr.com) can provide links to local clubs, whilst ⓦwww.skifrance.fr is a good overall source of **information**, with links to all the country's ski resorts.

Adventure sports

Hang-gliding and **paragliding** (a cross between parachuting and hang-gliding) are popular in the Hautes-Alpes of Provence, the Pyrenees and Corsica. Prices start at around €80 for a single trip; contact local tourist offices for more information.

Caving is popular in the limestone caverns of southwest France and in the gorges and ravines of the Pyrenees, the Alps and the Massif Central. You'll need to make an arrangement through a local club, which usually organize beginner courses as well as half- or full-day outings. For more information, contact the Fédération Française de Spéléologie (ⓣ04.72.56.09.63, ⓦwww.ffspeleo.fr).

As for all adventure sports, it is important to make sure that your **insurance** covers you for these rather more risky activities. See p.74 for details.

Horse riding

Horse riding is an excellent way to explore the French countryside. The most famous and romantic region for riding is the flat and windswept Camargue at the Rhône Delta, but practically every town has an equestrian centre (*centre équestre*) where you can ride with a guide or unaccompanied. **Mule-** and **donkey-trekking** are also increasingly popular, particularly along the trails of the Pyrenees and Alps. A day's horse- or donkey- trekking will cost upwards of €30.

Lists of **riding centres** and events are available in French only from the Comité National de Tourisme Équestre (ⓣ01.53.26.15.50, ⓦwww.tourisme-equestre.fr), or from local tourist offices.

Water sports and activities

France's extensive coastline has been well developed for recreational activities, especially in the south. Although in summer you can swim just about anywhere, from Normandy to the Mediterranean, the Côte d'Azur and Corsica are justly reputed as the best for beaches.

In the towns and resorts of the Mediterranean coast, you'll find every conceivable sort of beachside activity, including boating, sea-fishing and diving, and if you don't mind high prices and crowds, the too-blue waters and sandy coves are unbeatable. The wind-battered western Mediterranean is where **windsurfers** head to enjoy the calm of the broad saltwater inlets (*étangs*) that typify the area. The Atlantic coast is good for **sailing**, particularly around Brittany, while the best conditions for **surfing** (Fédération Française de Surfing; ⓦwww.surfingfrance.com) are to be found off Biarritz, something of a Mecca for the sport; north up the coast from Biarritz, Anglet, Hossegor and Lacanau are also excellent surf spots and regularly host international competitions. Corsica is the most popular destination for **diving** and snorkelling; contact the Fédération Française d'Études et de Sports Sous-Marins (ⓣ04.91.33.99.31, ⓦwww.ffessm.com) for more information.

Most towns have a **swimming pool** (*piscine*), though outdoor pools tend to open only in the height of summer. You may be requested to wear a bathing cap, so come prepared. You can also swim at many river beaches (usually signposted) and in the real and artificial lakes that pepper France. Many lakes have leisure centres (*bases de plein airs* or *centres de loisirs*) at which you can rent pedaloes, windsurfers and dinghies, as well as larger boats and, on the bigger reservoirs, jet-skis.

Canoeing (Fédération Française de Canoë-Kayak; ⓣ01.45.11.08.50, ⓦwww.ffck.org) is hugely popular in France, and in summer practically every navigable stretch of river has outfits renting boats and organizing excursions. The rivers of the southwest (the Dordogne, Vézère, Lot and Tarn) in particular offer tremendous variety.

Another relatively placid inland activity is **fishing** on permitted lakes and rivers. Brittany is one of the biggest areas for carp fishing; salmon and trout can be caught in several rivers in Brittany and Normandy, and in the River Loire, but by far the most varied – and scenic – salmon rivers are those of the western Pyrenees; and the rivers Lot, Tarn and Garonne, in the southwest, and the Saône are well stocked with bass. Local tourist offices and fishing shops will assist you in obtaining a licence. Sea-fishing in the Mediterranean or off the Atlantic coast offers grey mullet, bass, mackerel, bream or sardines as well as lobster, crayfish and scallops. Night-fishing expeditions are becoming increasingly popular.

For information on **canal-boating**, see the box on p.43 in "Getting around".

Practicalities

Tourist offices will be able to put you in touch with local companies to help you arrange activities, or contact the national federations listed in the text. For tour operators organizing holidays around these activities, see p.33.

Golf

France has over 500 **golf courses**, of which several are ranked among the world's best. At the top of this list is the challenging – and absolutely immaculate – Les Bordes course (ⓦwww.lesbordes.com), near Orléans, which boasts Europe's largest putting green and excellent practice facilities. Other first-class courses include Kempferhof (ⓦwww.golf-kempferhof.com), outside Strasbourg; Royal Park Evian (ⓦwww.royalparcevian.com), near Geneva and home to the Evian Masters women's tournament; and Spérone (ⓦwww.sperone.net) in Corsica. This last is a technically difficult course made even more demanding by strong winds, but boasting superb views – on a clear day you can see Sardinia. You'll find plenty more scenic courses in Provence and all along the Côte d'Azur, where the Monte-Carlo Golf Club (ⓣ04.93.41.09.11) stands out for its setting perched 800m up on the slopes of Mont Agel.

Down in the southwest, Pau Golf Club (ⓦwww.paugolfclub.com) was the first course to be opened in continental Europe, in 1856, followed three decades later by Biarritz Le Phare (ⓦwww.golf-biarritz.com); both are still excellent and challenging courses. Also near Biarritz, the Chiberta Golf Club (ⓣ05.59.52.51.10) is a traditional links, alternating between pine forest and seashore, which rates as one of the top ten in France. In fact, the whole area stretching north along the coast from Biarritz to Bordeaux is a golfer's paradise.

Practicalities

Green fees are usually in the range of €40 to €60. Alternatively, you can buy a "Golf Pass" which allows entry to several courses in a particular region at reduced rates. Contact the Fédération Française de Golf (ⓣ01.41.49.77.00, ⓦwww.ffg.org) or the departmental tourist office for further details. There are also plenty of tour operators specializing in golfing holidays, with prices starting at around £300/US$550 for a week's accommodation and green fees.

Living in France

Specialists aside, most non-EU citizens who manage to survive for long periods of time in France do it on luck, brazenness and willingness to live in pretty basic conditions. In the cities and larger towns, bar or club work, teaching English, translating or working as an au pair are some of the ways people scrape by; in the countryside, the options come down to seasonal fruit- or grape-picking, teaching English, busking or DIY oddjobbing. Remember that unemployment is high – the current rate stands at around nine percent and is on the rise.

EU citizens are free to work in France on the same basis as a French citizen. This means that you don't have to apply for a residence or work permit except in very rare cases – contact your nearest French consulate for further information (see "Entry requirements", p.72). **Non-EU citizens**, however, will need both a work permit (*autorisation de travail*) and a residence permit; again, contact your nearest French consulate or, if already in France, your local *mairie* or *préfecture* to check what rules apply in your particular situation.

When **looking for a job**, a good starting point is to get hold of one of the books on working abroad published by Vacation Work (Ⓦwww.vacationwork.co.uk). In France, check out the "Offres d'Emploi" (job offers) in *Le Monde*, *Le Figaro* and the *International Herald Tribune*; and try the youth information agency CIDJ (Ⓦwww.cidj.com), or CIJ (Centre d'Information Jeunesse) offices in main cities, which sometimes have information about temporary jobs for foreigners and produce all sorts of useful information about working in France. The national employment agency, ANPE (Agence Nationale pour l'Emploi; Ⓦwww.anpe.fr), with offices all over France, advertises temporary jobs in all fields and, in theory, offers a whole range of services to job-from all over the EU, but is not renowned for its helpfulness to foreigners. Non-EU citizens will have to show a work permit to apply for any of jobs they list. In Paris, it's worth looking out for the free English-language magazine, *FUSAC* (Ⓦwww.fusac.fr), published every two weeks, which carries ads for employment and housing among other things.

Teaching English

Applying for a job **teaching English** should be done in advance; late summer is usually the best time. You don't need fluent French to get a post, but a degree and a TEFL (Teaching English as a Foreign Language) or similar qualification are normally required. The British Council (Ⓣ0161/957 7755, Ⓦwww.britishcouncil.org.), which recruits and trains TEFL teachers for work abroad, is worth contacting. The annual *EL Gazette Guide to English Language Teaching Around the World* (Ⓦwww.elgazette.com) gives a thorough breakdown of TEFL courses available and provides all sorts of practical information, including lists of schools. Other useful resources are *Teaching English Abroad* published by Vacation Work and the TEFL website (Ⓦwww.tefl.com), with its database of English-teaching vacancies. If you apply for jobs from home, most schools will fix up the necessary papers for you.

It's just feasible to find a teaching job when you're in France, but you may have to accept semi-official status and no job security. You'll find more choice and better pay outside Paris and the main tourist centres; look under "Enseignement: Langues" in the local yellow pages (Ⓦwww.pagesjaunes.fr) for addresses of schools, or ask in the local Chambre de Commerce et d'Industrie (Chamber of Commerce). Offering private lessons (via university noticeboards or classified ads, for example), is always worth a try, though you'll have lots of competition.

Au pair work

Au pair work is usually arranged through an agency, who should sort out any necessary paperwork; you'll find agencies listed in *The Au Pair & Nanny's Guide to Working Abroad* published by Vacation Work (see p.65) and on the International Au Pair Association (IAPA) website, Ⓦwww.iapa.org. *The Lady* (Ⓦwww.lady.co.uk), published in Britain, is *the* magazine for classified adverts for au pairs.

Terms and conditions are never very generous, but should include board, lodging and pocket money. Prospective employers are required by law to provide a written job description, so there is protection on both sides. Even so, it's wise to have an escape route (such as a ticket home) in case you find the conditions intolerable and your employers insufferable.

Other work opportunities

The American/Irish/British **bars and restaurants** in the main cities and resorts sometimes have vacancies. You'll need to speak French, look smart and be prepared to work very long hours. Some people find jobs selling magazines on the street and **leafleting** by asking people already doing it for the agency address.

For temporary jobs in the **travel industry**, you should preferably write to tour operators in early spring, and have good French (and another European language will help). Jobs revolve around *courier* work – supervising and working on bus tours or summer campsites. The latter jobs are slightly easier to get, and usually involve putting up tents at the beginning of the season, taking them down again at the end and general maintenance and troubleshooting work in the months between; Canvas Holidays (see p.33) is often worth approaching. Travel magazines such as the reliable *Wanderlust* (Ⓦwww.wanderlust.co.uk) have a "Job Shop" section which often advertises job opportunities with tour companies.

Study programmes

It's relatively easy to be a **student** in France. Foreigners pay no more than French nationals to enrol for a course, and you'll be eligible for subsidized accommodation, meals and all the student reductions. In general, French universities are fairly informal, but there are strict entry requirements, including an exam in French, for undergraduate degrees (though not for postgraduate courses). For full details and prospectuses, contact the Cultural Service of any French embassy or consulate (see p.73).

Embassies and consulates can also provide details of **language courses** at French universities and colleges, which are often combined with lectures on French "civilization" and usually very costly. Alternatively, you can sign up to one of the hundreds of language-learning courses offered by private organizations – contact the tourist board for details. It's also worth noting that if you're a full-time non-EU student in France, you can get a non-EU **work permit** for the following summer so long as your visa is still valid.

Further contacts

American Institute for Foreign Study US Ⓣ1-800-727-2437, Ⓦwww.aifs.com. Language study and cultural immersion for the summer or school year.

Council on International Educational Exchange (CIEE) US Ⓣ1-800-40-STUDY, Ⓦwww.ciee.org. A non-profit organization with summer, semester and academic-year programmes in France.

Erasmus UK Ⓣ01227/762712, Ⓦwww.erasmus.ac.uk. EU-run student exchange programme enabling students at participating EU universities to study in another European member country. Mobility grants available from three months to a full academic year. Contact your university's international relations office for details.

Experiment in International Living US Ⓣ1-800-345-2929, Ⓦwww.usexperiment.org. Summer programmes for high-school students.

Culture and etiquette

With over 60 million inhabitants, France is a diverse country culturally as well as geographically. While you may find that money-minded Paris lives up to the French reputation for pride and stand-offishness, travel to the Alsatian east, the Celtic west, or the laid-back Catalan- or Italian-influenced south, and any preconceptions you've held will be turned on their heads. And even so, France has plenty to be proud of, from food to its fabled *patrimoine*, and wherever you decide to travel, a certain "Frenchness" pervades.

Social life and etiquette

If you're invited to someone's house for a **meal**, you should bring a gift of some kind, such as a decent bottle of wine or flowers. Mealtimes tend to be late, and slow, so allow yourself a good few hours even if meeting someone for lunch. At restaurants you only need to leave an additional cash **tip** if you feel you have received service out of the ordinary, since restaurant prices almost always include a service charge. It's customary to tip porters, tour guides, taxi drivers and hairdressers between one and two euros.

Smoking was banned (*fumer interdit*) in all public places, including public transport, stations and museums, in Febuary 2007. In 2008, it will also be made illegal in all cafés, restaurants and nightclubs. Surprisingly, in a country where it's estimated that about 40 percent of the population smoke, there's been a deal of support for the ban, although it remains unclear how it will work in practice. In the meantime, feel free to ask someone to stop smoking next to you, but don't expect to get much of a result.

What you **wear** will vary little from what you would wear at home. Do bear in mind though that in the swankier restaurants, people will dress up. On the beaches, especially on the Riviera, women young and old tend to go **topless**. Be sensitive though; if on the rare occasion you find you're the only one baring all on the beach, do cover up.

If you're looking for a **toilet**, ask for *les toilettes* or look for signs to the WC (pronounced "vay say"). Standards of cleanliness in public toilets are often poor and many tend not to have toilet paper. Toilets in railway stations and department stores are usually okay; most have an attendant and charge a small sum. You'll occasionally come across automated toilet booths in town centres; note that children under 10 aren't allowed in them on their own. Also, don't be surprised to come across squat toilets, even at busy tourist sites.

Greetings

Just a few words in French will do much to improve your standing even with the most grumpy of Parisian shopkeepers (see the Language section, pp.1339–1355, for vocabulary). When **meeting** someone for the first time, it's customary to shake hands. This often (usually only among women and between women and men) progresses quickly to kisses (*la bise*) on the cheek – a custom which can be quite complicated, and embarrassing, if you're not sure how many kisses to expect. As a rule, in Paris you should expect one on each side and no more. In the rest of the country, especially in the south, you can't be so sure, as three kisses are common, and four kisses are used among family members and close friends. In all but the south of the country, *la bise* is not common between men, and a handshake will usually suffice. Bear in mind too that the kiss isn't exactly a kiss, but more a touching of cheeks whilst kissing into the air. It's usually enough to follow the French person's lead, and accept that from time to time you're bound to make a mistake, though be aware that a single kiss on the cheek is deemed somewhat flirtatious.

Women

Despite a relatively strong feminist movement, France can still feel like a very male-dominated country, with the male population still in possession of a rather strong set of chauvinist ideas. Change is in the air, with female politicians starting to take a higher profile and giving the male ruling class a run for their money but for the moment, women very much suffer under the double burden of being housewife and earner.

French men tend to be on the predatory side, but are usually easily brushed off if you don't want the attention. It's not unusual, however, to be chatted up on a regular basis, or have men (more often boys) call at you from cars in the street, and make comments as they pass you. The best way to deal with this is simply to avoid making eye contact and fail to react, and they'll soon get the message.

Contraception

Condoms (*préservatifs*) are sold in all local pharmacies, and often in coin-operated dispensers in métro stations, outside pharmacies, and in bar and restaurant toilets. The pill (*la pilule*), and the morning-after pill (*la pilule du lendemain*) are also available over the counter from pharmacies.

Shopping

France in general is a paradise for shoppers. Even outside of Paris, which is crammed with international clothing chains, fashion boutiques and antique shops (see pp.194–195) most main towns have a range of excellent department stores, such as Printemps and Galeries Lafayette, as well as a host of independent shops which make superb targets for window-shopping (known as *lèche-vitrines*, or literally "window-licking" in French).

Food is a particular joy to shop for; well-stocked supermarkets are easy to find, whilst on the outskirts of most towns of any size you'll come across at least one *hypermarché*, enormous supermarkets selling everything from food to clothes and garden furniture. The most well-known chains include Carrefour, Leclerc and Casino. Every French town worth its salt holds at least one **market** (*marché*) a week; these are listed in the Guide, but asking locals or at tourist offices will also find them out. Markets tend to be vibrant, mostly morning affairs when local producers gather to sell speciality goods such as honey, cheese and alcohol, alongside excellent quality vegetable, meat and fish stalls. Boulangeries are the best places to buy bread. These usually open early in the morning, and again around 6pm, and sell freshly baked bread and pastries; some will also open at lunchtime for sandwiches.

Regional specialities are mostly of the edible kind. If you're travelling in Brittany, be sure to pick up some of the local cider (*cidre*), whilst Normandy is famous for its calvados, and the south for its pastis. Provence is well known for its superb olive oil (*huile d'olive*), and pricey truffles (*truffes*), as is the Dordogne. No matter where you go, each region will produce at least one local cheese (see p.52), and wine of course also varies from region to region (see p.52). Cognac (pp.651–53) and the Champagne region (pp.271–81) are also obvious stop-offs if you're looking to stock up.

Other items to look out for include **lace** (*dentelle*) in the north of the country, **pottery** in Brittany and **ceramics** in Limoges, whilst in Normandy, the small town of

Villedieu-les-Poêles (p.404) is well known for its **copperwork**. The northeast, especially Lorraine, is renowned for its **crystal** production, whilst Provence, particularly the town of Grasse (pp.1169–71), is *the* place in France to buy **perfume**.

Non-EU residents are able to claim back **VAT** (*TVA*) on purchases that come to over €175. To do this, make sure the shop you're buying from fills out the correct paperwork, and present this to customs before you check in at the airport for your return flight.

Travelling with children

France is a relatively easy country in which to travel with children. They're generally welcome everywhere and young children and babies in particular will be fussed over. There are masses of family-oriented theme parks and no end of leisure activities geared towards kids, while most public parks contain children's play areas.

Local **tourist offices** will have details of specific activities for children, which might include anything from farm visits, nature walks or treasure hunts to paintball and forest ropeways for older children. In summer most seaside resorts organize clubs for children on the beach, while bigger campsites put on extensive programmes of activities and entertainments. Children under 4 years travel free on trains and buses, while those between 4 and 12 pay half-fare. Museums and the like are generally free to under-12s and half-price up to the age of 18.

Hotels charge by the room, with a small supplement for an additional bed or cot, and family-run places will usually babysit or offer a listening service while you eat or go out. In addition, some youth hostels are now starting to offer family rooms. **Eating out** is easy enough, although you may be restricted by late meal times, and the children's menus that do exist tend to be of the steak-and-chips and ice cream variety. Disposable **nappies/diapers** (*couches à jeter*) are available at most pharmacies and supermarkets, as is **milk** powder, although this tends to be rich, and you'd be advised to bring enough of the brand you are used to at home. You'll also find a wide range of **baby foods** in the same outlets, though you should be aware that nearly all have added sugar and salt; again bring your own if this is likely to be a concern. Most **medicines** are available over the counter at pharmacies. Note that it is rare to see women **breastfeed** in public, and you may encourage disapproving stares if you try it.

One final thing to be aware of – not that you can do much about it – is the difficulty of negotiating a child's buggy over cobbled streets in the medieval town centres. Also, lawns in parks are often out of bounds, so sprawling on the grass with toddlers and napping babies is usually not an option; look out for signs saying *pelouse interdite*.

For details of tour operators specializing in travel with kids, see "Getting there" p.33.

Further information

Baby Centre ⓦ www.babycentre.co.uk/baby/travel. Covers everything you need to know about going on holiday with young babies, including the most family-friendly tour operators and airlines, and country-specific reports.

Family Travel ⓦ www.family-travel.co.uk. Excellent website covering all aspects of traveling with young children and babies. Includes information on where to go, health and what to pack.

Travel essentials

Costs

France is not an expensive place to visit, at least compared to other northern European countries, largely because of the relatively low cost of accommodation and eating out. When and where you go, however, will make a difference: in prime tourist spots hotel prices can go up by a third during July and August, while places like Paris and the Côte d'Azur are always more expensive than other regions.

For a reasonably comfortable existence – staying in hotels, eating lunch and dinner in restaurants, plus moving around, café stops and museum visits – you need to allow a **budget** of around £69/$127/€100 a day per person. By counting the pennies – staying at youth hostels or camping and being strong-willed about extra cups of coffee and doses of culture – you could manage on £35/$64/€50 a day, or even less if you're surviving on street snacks and market food.

Admission charges to museums and monuments can also eat into your budget, though many state-owned museums have one day of the week when they're free or half-price. Reductions are often available for those over 60 and under 18 (for which you'll need your passport as proof of age) and for students under 26 (see p.76), while many are free for children under 12, and almost always for kids under 4. Several towns and regions offer multi-entry tickets covering a number of sights (detailed in the Guide).

For more on costs see the "Getting around", "Accommodation" and "Food and drink" sections of Basics; for advice on **tipping**, see p.66.

Crime and personal safety

Theft

While violent crime involving tourists is rare in France, **petty theft** is endemic in all the big cities, along the Côte d'Azur, on beaches and at major tourist sights. In Paris, be especially wary of pickpockets at train stations and on the métro and RER lines; RER line B, serving Charles de Gaulle airport and Gare du Nord, and subway line number 1 are particularly notorious. Cars with foreign number-plates face a high risk of break-ins; vehicles are rarely stolen, but car radios and luggage – even if locked out of sight – make tempting targets. Motorbike thieves operate in big cities and along the Mediterranean coast, often stealing from cars at traffic lights or in jams; don't leave valuables on the seats and keep car windows shut and doors locked at all times.

It obviously makes sense to take the normal **precautions**: don't flash wads of notes or travellers' cheques around; carry your bag or wallet securely and be especially careful in crowds; never leave cameras and other valuables lying around; and park your car overnight in a monitored parking, garage or within sight of a police station. It's wise to keep a separate record of cheque and credit card numbers and the phone numbers for cancelling them (see p.76). Finally, make sure you have a good insurance policy (see p.74).

Contacting the police

There are two main types of **police** in France – the Police Nationale and the Gendarmerie Nationale. The former deals with all crime, parking and traffic affairs within large and mid-sized towns, where you'll find them in the Commissariat de Police, while the Gendarmerie Nationale covers the rural areas. In the Alps or Pyrenees, you may come across specialized mountaineering sections of the police force. These are unfailingly helpful, friendly and approachable, providing rescue services and guidance. Note that the police have the right to stop you at any time to ask for your ID and can also search you or your car without a warrant; if it happens to you, it's not worth being difficult.

If you need to **report a theft**, go to the local gendarmerie or Commissariat de Police (addresses are given in the Guide for the major cities), where they will fill out a *constat de vol*. The first thing they'll ask for is your passport, and vehicle documents if relevant. Although the police are not always as co-operative as they might be, it's their duty to assist you if you've lost your passport or all your money, and will usually be able to find someone who speaks English if they don't themselves.

Drugs

Drug use is just as prevalent in France as anywhere else in Europe – and just as risky. People caught smuggling or possessing drugs, even just a few grams of marijuana, are liable to find themselves in jail. Should you be arrested on any charge, you have the right to contact your consulate (addresses given in the Guide), though don't expect much sympathy.

Racism

Though the self-proclaimed home of "liberté, égalité, fraternité", France has an unfortunate reputation for **racism and anti-Semitism**. The majority of racist incidents are focused against the Arab community and occur largely, but by no means exclusively, within the cities. As a result, particularly Arab, but also black and Asian visitors may encounter an unwelcome degree of curiosity or suspicion from shopkeepers, hoteliers and the like. It is not unknown for hotels to claim they are fully booked when they're not, for example, and the police are far more likely to stop Arab and black people and demand to see their ID. In the worst cases, you might be unlucky enough to experience outright hostility. If you suffer a **racial assault**, contact the police, your consulate or one of the local anti-racism organizations (though they may not have English-speakers): SOS Racism (Ⓦwww.sos-racisme.org) and Mouvement contre le Racisme et pour l'Amitié entre les Peuples (MRAP; Ⓦwww.mrap.asso.fr) have offices in most regions of France. Alternatively, you could contact the **English-speaking** helpline SOS Help (Ⓣ01.46.21.46.46, daily 3–11pm; Ⓦwww.soshelpline.org). The service is manned by trained volunteers who not only provide a confidential listening service, but also offer practical information for foreigners facing problems in France.

Safety

Pedestrians should take great care when crossing roads. Although the authorities are trying to improve matters, French drivers pay little heed to pedestrian/zebra crossings. Never step out onto a crossing assuming that drivers will stop. Also be wary at traffic lights: check cars are not still speeding towards you even when the green man is showing.

Disabled travellers

The French authorities have been making a concerted effort to improve facilities for **disabled travellers**. Though haphazard parking habits and stepped village streets remain serious obstacles for anyone with mobility problems, ramps or other forms of access are gradually being added to hotels, museums and other public buildings. All but the oldest hotels are required to adapt at least one room to be wheelchair accessible and a number of theatres now display the text for the deaf and hard-of-hearing during certain performances.

For **getting to France**, Eurotunnel (see p.30) offers the simplest option for travellers from the UK, since you can remain in your car. Alternatively, Eurostar trains have

Emergency numbers

Police Ⓣ17
Medical emergencies/ambulance Ⓣ15
Fire brigade/paramedics Ⓣ18
Rape crisis (SOS Viol) Ⓣ08.00.05.95.95
All emergency numbers are toll-free.

a limited number of wheelchair spaces in first class for the price of the regular second-class fare; it's wise to reserve well in advance, when you might also like to enquire about the special assistance that Eurostar offers. If you're flying, it's worth noting that, while airlines are required to offer access to travellers with mobility problems, the level of service provided by some discount airlines may be fairly basic. All cross-Channel ferries have lifts for getting to and from the car deck, but moving between the different passenger decks may be more difficult.

Within France, most train stations now make provision for travellers with mobility problems. Spaces for wheelchairs are available in first-class carriages of all high-speed TGVs for the price of the regular second-class fare; note that these must be booked in advance. For other trains, a wheelchair symbol in the timetable indicates services offering special on-board facilities, though it's best to double check when booking. SNCF (see p.35) also produces a free guide, *Le Mémento du Voyageur Handicapé*, detailing all its services, which is available from main stations.

Drivers of **taxis** are legally obliged to help passengers in and out of the vehicle and to carry guide dogs. Specially adapted taxi services are available in some towns: contact the local tourist office for further information, or one of the organizations listed below. The big **car rental** agencies such as Hertz and Europcar provide automatic cars and cars with hand controls, but only in certain locations and you'll need to reserve well in advance.

As for finding suitable **accommodation**, guides produced by Logis de France (see p.47) and Gîtes de France (see p.48) indicate places with specially adapted rooms, though it's advisable to double-check when booking that the facilities meet your needs.

Up-to-date **information** about accessibility, special programmes and discounts is best obtained before you leave home from the organizations listed below. French readers might want to get hold of the *Handitourisme* guide, published by Petit Futé (www.petitfute.com), available online or from major bookstores. You should also visit the French tourist board website at www.franceguide.com.

Useful contacts

Association des Paralysés de France (APF) France ☎01.40.78.69.00, www.apf.asso.fr. National association which can answer general enquiries and put you in touch with their departmental offices.

Fédération Française Handisport France ☎01.40.31.45.00, www.handisport.org. Amongst other things, this federation provides information on sports and leisure facilities for people with disabilities.

Holiday Care UK ☎0845 124 9971, www.holidaycare.org.uk. Provides a comprehensive travel pack on France with details of facilities in hotels, resorts and so on.

Mobile en Ville France www.mobile-en-ville.com. Information on getting around Paris (French only).

Wheels Up! US ☎1-888-38-WHEELS, www.wheelsup.com. Provides discounted airfares, tours and cruises for disabled travellers; also publishes a free monthly newsletter.

Electricity

Voltage is almost always 220V, using **plugs** with two round pins. If you need a transformer, it's best to buy one before leaving home, though you can find them in big department stores in France.

Entry requirements

Citizens of **EU countries** can enter France freely, while those from many **non-EU countries**, including Australia, Canada, New Zealand and the United States, among other countries, do not need a visa for a stay of **up to ninety days**. South African citizens require a short-stay visa for up to ninety days, which should be applied for in advance, and costs €35. You'll need to have a return ticket, and provide evidence that you have accommodation in France, as well as family or private connections for a longer stay.

All non-EU citizens who wish to remain **longer than ninety days** must apply to the local *mairie* or town hall for a residence permit (a *titre de séjour*, also known as a *carte de séjour*), for which you will have to show proof of – among other things – a regular income or sufficient funds to support yourself, evidence of medical insurance and the appropriate visa (such as a business or study visa, if required). Be aware, however, that the situation can change and it's advisable to check with your nearest French embassy or consulate before departure. For further information about visa regulations consult the Ministry of Foreign Affairs website: ⓦwww.diplomatie.gouv.fr.

French embassies and consulates

Australia Canberra ⓣ02/6216 0100, Sydney ⓣ02/9261 5779; ⓦwww.ambafrance-au.org.
Britain London ⓣ020/7073 1200, ⓦwww.ambafrance-uk.org, Edinburgh ⓣ0131/220 6324; ⓦwww.consulfrance-edimbourg.org.
Canada Montréal ⓣ1-514/878 4385, ⓦwww.consulfrance-montreal.org; Québec ⓣ1-418/694 2294, ⓦwww.consulfrance-quebec.org; Toronto ⓣ1-416/925 8041, ⓦwww.consulfrance-toronto.org; Vancouver ⓣ1-604/681 4345, ⓦwww.consulfrance-vancouver.org.
Ireland Dublin ⓣ01/260 1666, ⓦwww.ambafrance-ie.org.
New Zealand Wellington ⓣ04/384 2555, ⓦwww.ambafrance-nz.org.
South Africa Johannesburg ⓣ011/778 5600, ⓦwww.consulfrance-jhb.org; Cape Town ⓣ21/423 1575, ⓦwww.consulfrance-lecap.org.
USA Atlanta ⓣ1-404/495 1660, ⓦwww.consulfrance-atlanta.org; Boston ⓣ1-617/542 7735, ⓦwww.consulfrance-boston.org; Chicago ⓣ1-312/787 5359, ⓦwww.consulfrance-chicago.org; Houston ⓣ1-713/572 2799, ⓦwww.consulfrance-houston.org; Los Angeles ⓣ1-310/235 3200, ⓦwww.consulfrance-losangeles.org; Miami ⓣ1-305/372 9798, ⓦwww.consulfrance-miami.org; New Orleans ⓣ1-504/523 5772, ⓦwww.consulfrance-nouvelleorleans.org; New York ⓣ1-212/606 3600, ⓦwww.consulfrance-newyork.org; San Francisco ⓣ1-415/616 4910, ⓦwww.consulfrance-sanfrancisco.org; Washington ⓣ1-202/944 6200, ⓦwww.ambafrance-us.org.

Gay and lesbian travellers

France is more liberal on **homosexuality** than most other European countries. The age of consent is 16, and same-sex couples have been able to form civil partnerships, called PACs, since 1999. Gay marriage, however, along with the right to adopt, remains illegal, despite the fact that the controversial mayor of Bègles, near Bordeaux, conducted the country's first and only gay marriage in 2004 (it was later declared invalid).

Gay male communities thrive, especially in Paris and southern towns such as Toulouse and Nice. Lesbian life is rather less upfront, although Toulouse has a particularly lively lesbian community. Nevertheless, gays tend to keep a low profile outside communities and specific gay venues, parades, and the prime gay areas of Paris and the coastal resorts. The biggest annual event is the Gay Pride march in Paris (ⓦwww.gaypride.fr), which takes place every June.

In **Corsica**, attitudes remain much more conservative than on the mainland. Women can get away with holding hands and walking with arms around each other, but gay men can expect hostile comments if they do the same. At the same time, the island has long been a popular destination for discreet gay couples and no one is likely to raise much more than an eyebrow when checking in to a hotel. Addresses of local gay and/or lesbian establishments are listed in the Guide. Also useful is the French tourist board website with their online magazine *Franceguide for the Gay Traveller*.

Useful contacts

Dykeplanet ⓦwww.dykeplanet.com. Sells *Le dykeGuide*, a guidebook listing lesbian-friendly places across France. Published annually, in French only, it's also available from FNAC and other bookstores.
Spartacus ⓦwww.spartacusworld.com. Site selling the English-language *Spartacus International Gay Guide*, which has an extensive section on France and contains some information for lesbians.
Têtu ⓦwww.tetu.com. Highly rated French gay/lesbian magazine with events listings and contact addresses; you can buy it in bookshops or through their website, which is also an excellent source of information.

Health

Visitors to France have little to worry about as far as health is concerned. No vaccinations are required, there are no nasty diseases to be wary of and tap water is safe to drink. The worst that's likely to happen to you is a case of sunburn or an upset stomach from eating too much rich food. If you do need treatment, however, you should be in good hands: the French healthcare system is rated one of the best in the world.

Under the French health system, all services, including doctors' consultations, prescribed medicines, hospital stays and ambulance call-outs, incur a charge which you have to pay upfront. **EU citizens** are entitled to a refund (usually between 70 and 100 percent) of medical and dental expenses, providing the doctor is government-registered (*un médecin conventionné*) and provided you have the correct documentation (the European Health Insurance Card – EHIC; application forms available from main post offices in the UK). This can still leave a hefty shortfall, however, especially after a stay in hospital, so you might want to take out some additional insurance. All **non-EU visitors** should ensure they have adequate medical insurance cover.

For minor complaints go to a **pharmacie**, signalled by an illuminated green cross. You'll find at least one in every small town and even some villages. They keep normal shop hours (roughly 9am–noon & 3–6pm), though some stay open late and in larger towns at least one (known as the *pharmacie de garde*) is open 24 hours according to a rota; details are displayed in all pharmacy windows, or the local police will have information.

For anything more serious you can get the name of a **doctor** from a pharmacy, local police station, tourist office or your hotel. Alternatively, look under "Médecins" in the Yellow Pages of the phone directory. The consultation fee is in the region of €20 to €25, and you'll be given a *Feuille de Soins* (Statement of Treatment) for later insurance claims. Any prescriptions will be fulfilled by the pharmacy and must be paid for; little price stickers (*vignettes*) from each medicine will be stuck on the *Feuille de Soins*.

In serious **emergencies** you will always be admitted to the nearest general hospital (*centre hospitalier*). Phone numbers and addresses of hospitals in all the main cities are given in the Guide. The national number for calling an ambulance is ⓣ15.

Insurance

Though EU citizens are entitled to healthcare privileges in France, even they would do well to take out an **insurance policy** before travelling in order to cover against theft, loss, illness or injury. Before paying for a new policy, however, it's worth checking whether you are already covered: some all-risks home insurance policies may cover your possessions when overseas, and many private medical schemes include cover when abroad. In Canada, provincial health plans usually provide partial cover for medical mishaps overseas, while holders of official student, teacher or youth cards in Canada and the US are entitled to meagre accident coverage and hospital in-patient benefits. **Students** will often find that their student health coverage extends during the vacations and for one term beyond the date of last enrolment.

After checking out the possibilities above, you might want to contact a **specialist travel insurance** company, or consider the travel insurance deal we offer (see below). A typical travel insurance policy usually provides cover for the loss of baggage, tickets and – up to a certain limit – cash or cheques, as well as cancellation or curtailment of your journey. Most of them exclude so-called **dangerous sports** unless an extra premium is paid; in France this can mean skiing, whitewater rafting, rock-climbing and potholing. Many policies can be chopped and changed to exclude coverage you don't need – for example, sickness and accident benefits can often be excluded or included at will.

If you do take **medical coverage**, ascertain whether benefits will be paid as treatment proceeds or only after you return home, and if there is a 24-hour medical emergency number. When securing **baggage cover**, make sure that the per-article limit – typically under £500/$750 and sometimes as little as £250/$400 – will cover your most valuable possession. If you need to **make a claim**, you should keep receipts for medicines and medical treatment, and in the event you have anything stolen, you must obtain an official statement from the police (called a *constat de vol*; see p.71).

Rough Guides has teamed up with Columbus Direct to offer you **travel insurance** that can be tailored to suit your needs. Products include a low-cost **backpacker** option for long stays; a **short break** option for city getaways; a typical **holiday package** option; and others. There are also annual **multi-trip** policies for those who travel regularly. Different sports and activities (trekking, skiing, etc) can be usually be covered if required.

See our website (Ⓦwww.roughguides insurance.com) for eligibility and purchasing options. Alternatively, UK residents should call Ⓣ08700 339988; US citizens should call Ⓣ1-800-749-4922; Australians should call Ⓣ1300 669 999. All other nationalities should call Ⓣ+44 870 890 2843.

Internet

Internet access is relatively easy to come by; you'll find Internet cafés in most towns and cities, as well as points (*point internet*) in hotels, hostels, and many of the larger post offices. Wifi is becoming more common in cafes and bars, and ISDN access is available in many hotels. Internet cafés tend to charge €4–10 per hour, whilst you'll pay around €8 an hour at a post office, and invariably more in your hotel.

Laundry

Laundries are common in French towns – just ask in your hotel or the tourist office, or look in the phone book under "Laveries automatiques" or "Laveries en libre-service". They are often unattended, so come armed with small change. Machines are graded for different wash sizes; a 7kg will cost in the region of €4–5. Most **hotels** forbid doing laundry in your room, though you should get away with just one or two items.

Mail

French **post offices**, known as La Poste and identified by bright yellow-and-blue signs, are generally open from around 8.30am to 6 or 7pm Monday to Friday, and 8.30am to noon on Saturday. However, these hours aren't set in stone: smaller branches tend to keep shorter hours and may close for an hour or so at lunch, while in Paris the main post office is open 24 hours.

You can **receive letters** using the poste restante system available at the central post office in every town. They should be addressed (preferably with the surname first and in capitals) "Poste Restante, Poste Centrale, Town x, post code". You'll need your passport to collect your mail and there'll be a charge of €0.50 per item. Items are usually only kept for fifteen days.

For **sending letters**, remember that you can buy stamps (*timbres*) with less queuing from *tabacs* and newsagents. Standard letters (20g or less) and postcards within France and to other European Union countries cost €0.53; to North America, Australia, New Zealand and South Africa they cost €0.90. Inside larger post offices you'll find rows of yellow-coloured *guichets automatiques* – automatic stamp machines with instructions available in English where you can weigh letters and packages and buy the appropriate stamps; sticky labels and tape are also dispensed. To post your letter on the street, look for the bright yellow postboxes.

Small **packages** (*paquet*) can be sent from any post office with relative ease, and you'll be able to buy the necessary boxes and envelopes on site. For large items you may be better off using the services of companies such as Fedex (Ⓦwww.fedex.com) who will pick up your package for you. Alternatively, if you're buying a large item that you wish to post back home, shops will often be able to ship it for you, though there will usually be a substantial charge.

For **further information** on postal rates, among other things, log on to the post office web site Ⓦwww.laposte.fr.

Maps

In addition to the maps in this guide and the various free town plans and regional maps you'll be offered along the way, the one extra map you might want is a good, up-to-date **road map** of France. Michelin (Ⓦwww.viamichelin.fr) and the Institut Géographique National (IGN; Ⓦwww.ign.fr) produce the best ones, both at a scale of 1:100,000. Both companies also issue good **regional maps** at 1:25,000, either as individual sheets or in one large spiral-bound *atlas routier*; Michelin's version is available in English as the *France Tourist & Motoring Atlas* (£13.99).

If **walking or cycling**, it's worth investing in the more detailed IGN maps. Their Carte de Randonnée series (1:25,000) is specifically designed for walkers, while the Carte de Promenade (1:25,000) is good for cyclists. See "Contexts" (p.1336) for details of walking guides.

Rough Guides also produces a national map of France, a city map of Paris, and regional maps of Brittany, Corsica and the Pyrenees.

Money

Currency

France's **currency** is the euro, which is divided into 100 cents (often still referred to as *centimes*). There are seven notes – in denominations of 5, 10, 20, 50, 100, 200 and 500 euros – and eight different coins – 1, 2, 5, 10, 20 and 50 cents, and 1 and 2 euros. At the time of writing, the **exchange rate** for the euro was around €1.49 to the pound sterling (or £0.66 to €1) and €1.30 to the dollar (or $0.77 to €1). See Ⓦwww.xe.com for current rates.

Currency exchange

Banks will have a sign outside if they offer currency exchange. Rates and commission vary from bank to bank, so it's worth shopping around; some will change travellers' cheques for "free" but then make up for it by offering a poor exchange rate, while others levy up to three percent commission, with a minimum charge that can go as high as €8 (or they may simply charge a flat rate whatever the amount). **Post offices** also change money and travellers' cheques, and sometimes offer a better rate of exchange.

There are **money-exchange counters** (*bureaux de change*) at French airports, major train stations and usually one or two in town centres as well. You'll occasionally also find them in tourist offices. These services are handy when the banks are closed though don't always offer the best exchange rates.

ATMs

By far the easiest way to access money in France is to use your credit or debit card to withdraw cash from an **ATM** (known as a *distributeur* or *point argent*); most machines give instructions in a variety of European languages. Note that there is often a transaction fee, so it's more efficient to take out a sizeable sum each time rather than making lots of small withdrawals.

Credit and debit cards

Credit and debit cards are also widely accepted in shops, hotels and restaurants, although some smaller establishments don't accept cards, or only for sums above a certain threshold. Visa – called Carte Bleue in France – is almost universally recognized, followed by MasterCard (also known as EuroCard). American Express ranks a bit lower. Be aware that French cards are equipped with a chip and require the user to provide a PIN when making a purchase. If your card is not a chip and pin, and you're asked to tap in a PIN or are told that your card has been rejected, you may need to explain that that yours is a *carte à piste* and not a *carte à puce*.

Another option is a **pre-paid debit card**; you load up the account with funds before you leave, and then just throw the card away when it's finished. In the US they are available through Travelex (Ⓣ1-877-394-2247, Ⓦwww.cashpassportcard.com) and in the UK through American Express (Ⓣ0870 600 1060, Ⓦwww.americanexpress.com/uk).

To cancel **lost or stolen cards**, call the following 24-hour numbers: American Express Ⓣ01.47.77.72.00; Diners' Club Ⓣ08.10.31.41.59; MasterCard Ⓣ01.45.67.84.84; Visa Ⓣ08.00.90.11.79.

Discount cards

Once obtained, various official and quasi-official youth/student ID cards soon pay for themselves in savings. Full-time students are eligible for the **International Student ID Card** (ISIC, Ⓦwww.isiccard.com, or Ⓦwww.isic.org in the US and Canada), which entitles the bearer to special air, rail and bus fares and discounts at museums, theatres and other attractions. For Americans there's also a health benefit, providing up to $3000 in emergency medical coverage and $100 a day for 60 days in the hospital, plus a 24-hour hotline to call in the event of a medical, legal or financial emergency. The card costs US$22 in the US; Can$16 in Canada; AUS$16.50 in Australia; NZ$21 in New Zealand; £7 in the UK; and €12.70 in the Republic of Ireland.

You only have to be 26 or younger to qualify for the **International Youth Travel Card**

(IYTC), which costs £7/US$22 and carries the same benefits. Teachers qualify for the **International Teacher Card (ITIC)**, offering similar discounts and costing US$22, Can$16, AUS$16.50 and NZ$21. See ⓦwww.istc.com or ⓦwww.isic.org for further details, and your nearest outlet. Several other travel organizations and accommodation groups also sell their own cards, good for various discounts. A **university photo ID** might open some doors, but is not always as easily recognizable as the above cards.

Most museums and other tourist sites give discounts to the **over-60s** (usually the same as the student reduction) while SNCF offers special deals on train tickets (see p.38), although proof of age will usually be required.

Opening hours and public holidays

Basic **hours of business** are Monday to Saturday 9am to noon and 2 to 6.30pm. In big cities, **shops** and other businesses stay open throughout the day, and in July and August most **tourist offices** and museums don't close for lunch. In rural areas and throughout southern France places tend to close for at least a couple of hours at lunchtime. Small food shops may not reopen till halfway through the afternoon, closing around 7.30 or 8pm, just before the evening meal. The standard **closing day** is Sunday, even in larger towns and cities, though some food shops and newsagents are open in the morning. Some shops and businesses, particularly in rural areas, also close on Mondays.

Core **banking hours** are Monday to Friday 9am to noon and 2 to 4.30pm. Some branches, especially those in rural areas, close on Monday, while those in big cities may remain open at midday and may also open on Saturday morning. All are closed on Sunday and public holidays.

Museums tend to open from 9 or 10am to noon and from 2 or 3pm to 5pm or 6pm, though in the big cities some stay open all day and opening hours tend to be longer in summer. Museum closing days are usually Monday or Tuesday, sometimes both. **Churches and cathedrals** are generally open from around 8am to dusk, but may close at lunchtime and are reserved for worshippers during services (times of which will be posted on the door). Country churches are increasingly kept locked; there will usually be a note on the door telling you where to get the key, usually from the priest's house (*presbytère*) or someone else living nearby.

France celebrates twelve **public holidays** (*jours fériés*), when most shops and businesses (though not necessarily restaurants), and some museums, are closed. May is a particularly busy month for holidays: as well as May Day and VE Day, Ascension Day normally falls then, as sometimes does Pentecost (Whitsun).

Phones

You can make domestic and international **phone calls** from any telephone box (*cabine*) and can also receive calls – look for

Public holidays

January 1 New Year's Day
Easter Sunday
Easter Monday
Ascension Day (forty days after Easter)
Pentecost or **Whitsun** (seventh Sunday after Easter)
May 1 Labour Day
May 8 Victory in Europe (VE) Day 1945
July 14 Bastille Day
August 15 Assumption of the Virgin Mary
November 1 All Saints' Day
November 11 Armistice Day
December 25 Christmas Day

the number in the top right-hand corner of the information panel. The vast majority of public phones require a phone card (*télécarte*), available from post offices, *tabacs*, newsagents and railway stations; they come in units of 50 and 120 units (€7.50 and €15 respectively). You can also use credit cards in many call boxes. Coin-operated phones have almost completely disappeared except in cafés and bars.

Calling within France

For **calls within France** – local or long distance – simply dial all ten digits of the number. Numbers beginning with ⓣ08.00 up to ⓣ08.05 are free-dial numbers; those beginning ⓣ08.10 and ⓣ08.11 are charged as a local call; anything else beginning ⓣ08 is premium-rated (typically €0.34 per minute). Note that none of these ⓣ08 numbers can be accessed from abroad. Calls to mobile phones (numbers starting with ⓣ06) are also charged at premium rates.

Calling home from France

One of the most convenient ways of phoning home from abroad is via a **telephone charge card** from your phone company back home. Using a PIN number, you can make calls from most hotel, public and private phones that will be charged to your account. Since most major charge cards are free to obtain, it's certainly worth getting one at least for emergencies; bear in mind though that rates aren't necessarily cheaper than calling from a public phone. In **the UK and Ireland**, British Telecom (ⓣ0800 345 144, ⓦwww.payphones.bt.com) will issue the BT Charge Card free to all customers. In the **US and Canada**, AT&T, MCI, Sprint, Canada Direct and other North American long-distance companies all enable their customers to make calls while overseas, billed to your home number. Call your company's customer service line to set up this service. In **Australia** and **New Zealand**, similar schemes are offered by Telstra, Optus, and Telecom NZ.

Another option is one of the **pre-paid phone cards** (*cartes à codes*) on sale at *tabacs*, newsagents and post offices which you can use with any public or private telephone. The €15 "L'Astuce Internationale" marketed by Tiscali (ⓦwww.prepaye.tiscali.fr), for example, gives you roughly three and a half hours to the UK, USA or Canada.

Mobile phones

If you want to use your **mobile/cell phone**, contact your phone provider to check whether it will work in France and what the call charges are – they tend to be pretty exorbitant, and remember you're likely to be charged extra for receiving calls. French mobile phones operate on the European GSM standard, so US cellphones won't work in France unless you have a tri-band phone.

If you are going to be in France for any length of time and will be making and receiving a lot of local calls, it may be worth your while buying a **French SIM card** (which will give you a local phone number) and pre-paid recharge cards (*mobicartes*). You can buy a SIM card from any of the big mobile providers (France Télécom's Orange, SFR and Boygues Telecom), all of which have high-street outlets. They cost from around €30,

Calling home from abroad

Note that the initial zero is omitted from the area code when dialling the UK, Ireland, Australia and New Zealand from abroad.

UK international access code + 44 + city code

Republic of Ireland international access code + 353 + city code.

US and Canada international access code + 1 + area code

Australia international access code + 61 + city code

New Zealand international access code + 64 + city code

South Africa international access code + 27 + city code.

and you'll need to have an address in France to register – that of your hotel or a friend will usually suffice.

Time

France is in the Central European Time Zone (GMT+1). This means it is one hour ahead of the UK, six hours ahead of Eastern Standard Time and nine hours ahead of Pacific Standard Time. Between March and October France is eight hours behind eastern Australia and ten hours behind New Zealand; from October to March it is ten hours behind southeastern Australia and twelve hours behind New Zealand. Daylight Saving Time (GMT+2) in France lasts from the last Sunday in March to the last Sunday in October.

Tourist information

The **French Government Tourist Office** (Maison de la France; Ⓦwww.franceguide.com) increasingly refers you to their website for information, though they still produce a useful practical guide for young travellers to France, and dispense items including maps and the Logis de France book (see "Accommodation" p.47). For more detailed information, such as hotels, campsites, activities and festivals in a specific location, it's best to contact the relevant regional or departmental tourist offices; contact details can be found online at Ⓦwww.fncrt.com and Ⓦwww.fncdt.net respectively.

In France itself you'll find a tourist office – usually an **Office du Tourisme** (OT) but sometimes a **Syndicat d'Initiative** (SI, run by local businesses) – in practically every town and many villages (addresses, contact details and opening hours are detailed in the Guide). All these offices provide specific local information, including hotel and restaurant listings, leisure activities, car and bike rental, bus times, laundries and countless other things; many can also book accommodation for you. If asked, most offices will provide a town plan (for which you may be charged a nominal fee), and will have maps and local walking guides on sale. In mountain regions they display daily meteorological information and often share premises with the local hiking and climbing organizations. In the big cities you can usually pick up free *What's On* guides.

Tourist offices and government sites

Australia Level 20, 25 Bligh St, Sydney, NSW 2000 Ⓣ02/9231 5244, Ⓦau.franceguide.com.
Britain 178 Piccadilly, London W1J 9AL Ⓣ09068 244123 (60p/min), Ⓦuk.franceguide.com.
Canada 1981 Ave McGill College, Suite 490, Montréal, QC H3A 2W9 Ⓣ1-514/288 2026, Ⓦca-en.franceguide.com.
Ireland Ⓣ1560 235 235, Ⓦie.franceguide.com.
New Zealand Contact the office in Australia.
South Africa Ⓣ11/880 8062, Ⓦza.franceguide.com.
USA 9454 Wilshire Blvd, Suite 715, Beverly Hills, CA 90212 Ⓣ1-514-288-1904; 444 Madison Avenue, New York, NY 10022 Ⓣ1-410-286-8310; Ⓦus.franceguide.com.

Other useful websites

Bibliothèque Pompidou Ⓦwww.bpi.fr. Good links to media and a very comprehensive list of arts and humanities sites for France. French-language only.
FNOTSI Ⓦwww.tourisme.fr. Searchable database run by the national association of tourist offices. Town listings have practical and cultural information, details of local tourist offices and links to local websites.
France 2 Ⓦwww.france2.fr. The latest news, weather and road conditions from the France 2 TV channel. Also provides an online translation service to/from various European languages.
Ministry of Culture Ⓦwww.culture.fr. Information (in French) on cultural events and a comprehensive list of links to organizations related to the whole gamut of artistic media.
Service-Public Ⓦwww.servicepublic.fr. Multilingual portal sight for the French civil service, containing news, information and masses of useful links.

Guide

Guide

1 Paris and around 83–216

2 The north 83–216

3 Alsace-Lorraine and the Jura Mountains 83–216

4 Normandy 83–216

5 Brittany 83–216

6 The Loire 83–216

7 Burgundy 83–216

8 Poitou Charentes and the Atlantic Coast 83–216

9 The Dordogne, Limousin and Lot 83–216

10 The Pyrenees 83–216

11 Languedoc 83–216

12 The Massif Central 83–216

13 The Alps 83–216

14 Provence 83–216

15 The Côte d'Azur 83–216

16 Corsica 83–216

1 Paris and around

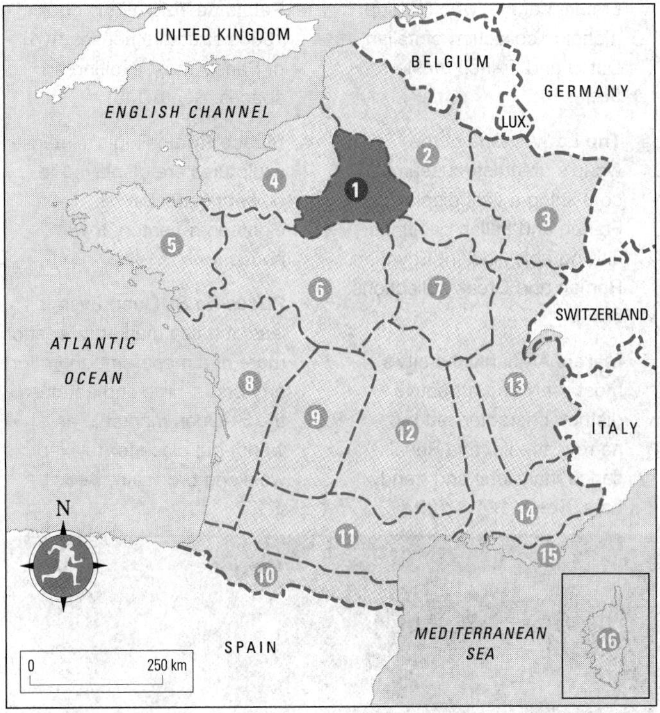
UNITED KINGDOM
ENGLISH CHANNEL
BELGIUM
GERMANY
LUX.
SWITZERLAND
ITALY
ATLANTIC OCEAN
SPAIN
MEDITERRANEAN SEA
N
0
250 km
1
2
3
4
5
6
7
8
9
10
11
12
13
14
15
16

CHAPTER 1 Highlights

* **Sainte-Chapelle** The stunning stained-glass windows of the Sainte-Chapelle rank among the finest achievements of French High Gothic. See p.108
* **Musée Jacquemart-André** One-time sumptuous residence of a wealthy Second-Empire couple, who built up a choice collection of Italian, Dutch and French masters. See p.112
* **The Louvre** One of the world's greatest museums, containing a vast display of French and Italian paintings and notable Ancient Egyptian, Roman and Greek collections. See p.115
* **Marais** Arguably the city's most lively and attractive district, characterized by narrow streets, fine Renaissance mansions and trendy bars. See p.124 & 168
* **Jardin du Luxembourg** The haunt of old men playing *boules*, children riding donkeys, students reading textbooks and couples kissing, these gardens capture Paris at its most warm-hearted. See p.141
* **Palais de Tokyo** This cool 1930s structure houses two of Paris's most exciting art spaces. See p.146
* **Musée Rodin** Rodin's intense sculptures are displayed to powerful effect in his eighteenth-century town house. See p.149
* **Puces de St-Ouen** Even if it's less of a flea market now, and more of a mega-emporium for arty bric-a-brac and antiques, the St-Ouen market is a wonderful place for relaxed weekend browsing. See p.157

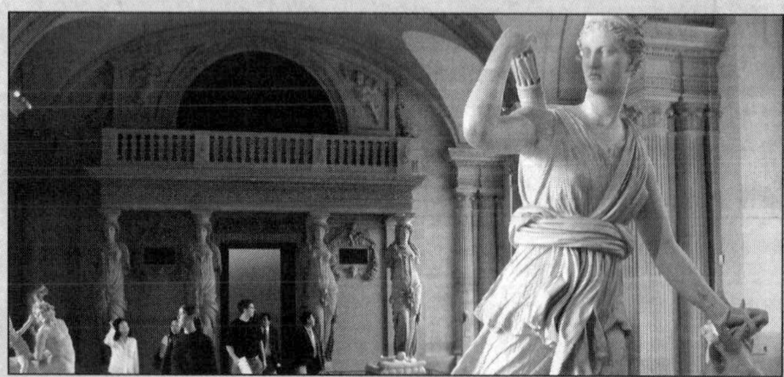

△ The Louvre

1

Paris and around

Long considered the paragon of style, **PARIS** is perhaps the most glamorous city in Europe. It is at once deeply traditional – a village-like metropolis whose inhabitants continue to be notorious for their hauteur – and famously cosmopolitan. The city's reputation as a magnet for writers, artists and dissidents lives on, and it remains at the forefront of Western intellectual, artistic and literary life. At the same time the cultural contributions of its large immigrant populations, particularly from Algeria and West and Central Africa, have sparked unprecedented social transformation in the past few decades. While such contradictions and contrasts may be the reality of any city, they are the makings of Paris: consider the tiny lanes and alleyways of the Quartier Latin or Montmartre against the monumental vistas of the Louvre and La Défense; the multiplicity of markets and old-fashioned pedestrian arcades against the giant underground commercial complexes of Montparnasse, the Louvre and Les Halles; or the obsession with refashioning old buildings and creating ground-breaking architecture against the old ladies who still iron sheets by hand in the laundries of Auteil.

The most tangible and immediate pleasures of Paris are to be found in its street life and along the banks and bridges of the River Seine. Few cities can compete with the cafés, bars and restaurants that line every street and boulevard, and the city's compactness makes it possible to experience the individual feel of the different *quartiers*. You can move easily, even on foot, from the calm, almost small-town atmosphere of **Montmartre** and parts of the **Quartier Latin** to the busy commercial centres of the **Bourse** and **Opéra-Garnier** or the aristocratic mansions of the **Marais**.

The city's lack of open space is redeemed by unexpected havens like the **Mosque**, **Arènes de Lutèce** and the **place des Vosges**, and courtyards of grand houses like the **Hôtel de Sully**. The gravelled paths and formal beauty of the **Tuileries** create the backdrop for the ultimate Parisian Sunday promenade, while the islands and quaysides of the Left and Right Banks of the **River Seine** and the Quartier Latin's two splendid parks, the **Luxembourg** and the **Jardin des Plantes**, make for a wonderful wander.

Paris's architectural spirit resides in the elegant streets and boulevards begun in the nineteenth century under Baron Haussmann. The mansion blocks that line them are at once grand and perfectly human in scale, a triumph in city planning proved by the fact that so many remain residential to this day. Rising above these harmonious buildings are the more arrogant monuments that define the French capital. For centuries, an imposing Classical style prevailed with great set pieces such as the **Louvre**, **Panthéon** and **Arc de Triomphe**, but the last hundred years or so has seen the architectural mould repeatedly broken in a succession

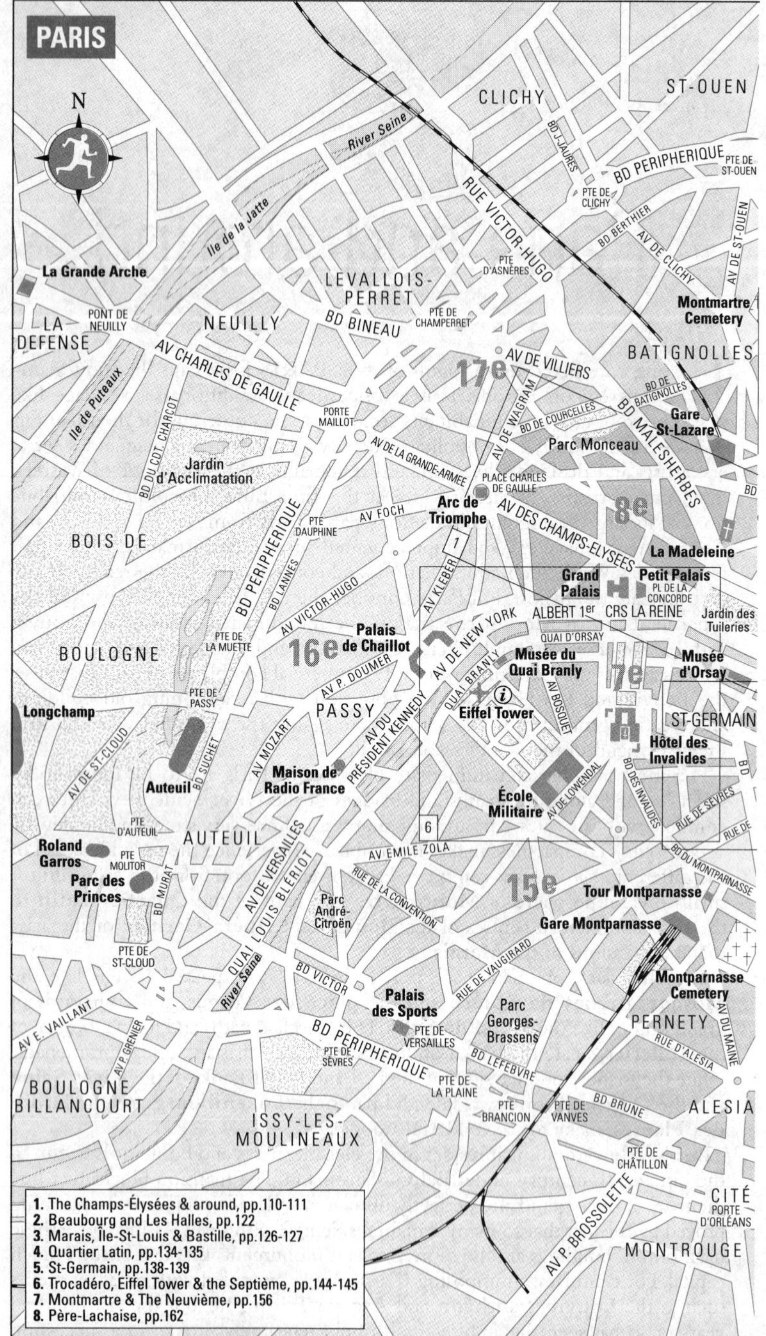
PARIS
N
CLICHY
ST-OUEN
River Seine
BD J-JAURES
RUE VICTOR-HUGO
BD PERIPHERIQUE
PTE DE ST-OUEN
PTE DE CLICHY
BD BERTHIER
AV DE CLICHY
AV DE ST-OUEN
Ile de la Jatte
La Grande Arche
LEVALLOIS-PERRET
PTE D'ASNIERES
Montmartre Cemetery
PONT DE NEUILLY
LA DEFENSE
NEUILLY
BD BINEAU
PTE DE CHAMPERRET
AV DE VILLIERS
BATIGNOLLES
AV CHARLES DE GAULLE
17e
BD DE BATIGNOLLES
Ile de Puteaux
BD DU CDT. CHARCOT
PORTE MAILLOT
AV DE WAGRAM
BD DE COURCELLES
BD MALESHERBES
Gare St-Lazare
Parc Monceau
Jardin d'Acclimatation
AV DE LA GRANDE-ARMEE
PLACE CHARLES DE GAULLE
Arc de Triomphe
AV DES CHAMPS-ELYSEES
8e
PTE DAUPHINE
AV FOCH
BD PERIPHERIQUE
BOIS DE
1
La Madeleine
BD LANNES
Grand Palais
Petit Palais
PL DE LA CONCORDE
AV KLEBER
AV VICTOR-HUGO
ALBERT 1er
CRS LA REINE
Jardin des Tuileries
PTE DE LA MUETTE
Palais de Chaillot
AV DE NEW YORK
QUAI D'ORSAY
BOULOGNE
16e
Musée du Quai Branly
Musée d'Orsay
AV P. DOUMER
QUAI BRANLY
7e
PTE DE PASSY
PASSY
AV DU PRÉSIDENT KENNEDY
Eiffel Tower
AV BOSQUET
ST-GERMAIN
Longchamp
AV MOZART
Hôtel des Invalides
AV DE ST-CLOUD
BD SUCHET
Maison de Radio France
Auteuil
AV DE LOWENDAL
BD DES INVALIDES
École Militaire
RUE DE SEVRES
PTE D'AUTEUIL
6
Roland Garros
AUTEUIL
AV DE VERSAILLES
AV EMILE ZOLA
BD DU MONTPARNASSE
PTE MOLITOR
RUE DE LA CONVENTION
Parc des Princes
15e
Tour Montparnasse
BD MURAT
LOUIS BLÉRIOT
Parc André-Citroën
Gare Montparnasse
PTE DE ST-CLOUD
QUAI
River Seine
RUE DE VAUGIRARD
BD VICTOR
Palais des Sports
Montparnasse Cemetery
AV E. VAILLANT
Parc Georges-Brassens
PERNETY
AV DU MAINE
BD PERIPHERIQUE
PTE DE VERSAILLES
RUE D'ALESIA
AV P. GRENIER
PTE DE SÈVRES
BD LEFEBVRE
BOULOGNE BILLANCOURT
PTE DE LA PLAINE
BD BRUNE
ALESIA
PTE BRANCION
PTE DE VANVES
ISSY-LES-MOULINEAUX
PTE DE CHÂTILLON
AV P. BROSSOLETTE
CITÉ
PORTE D'ORLÉANS
MONTROUGE
1. The Champs-Élysées & around, pp.110-111
2. Beaubourg and Les Halles, pp.122
3. Marais, Île-St-Louis & Bastille, pp.126-127
4. Quartier Latin, pp.134-135
5. St-Germain, pp.138-139
6. Trocadéro, Eiffel Tower & the Septième, pp.144-145
7. Montmartre & The Neuvième, pp.156
8. Père-Lachaise, pp.162

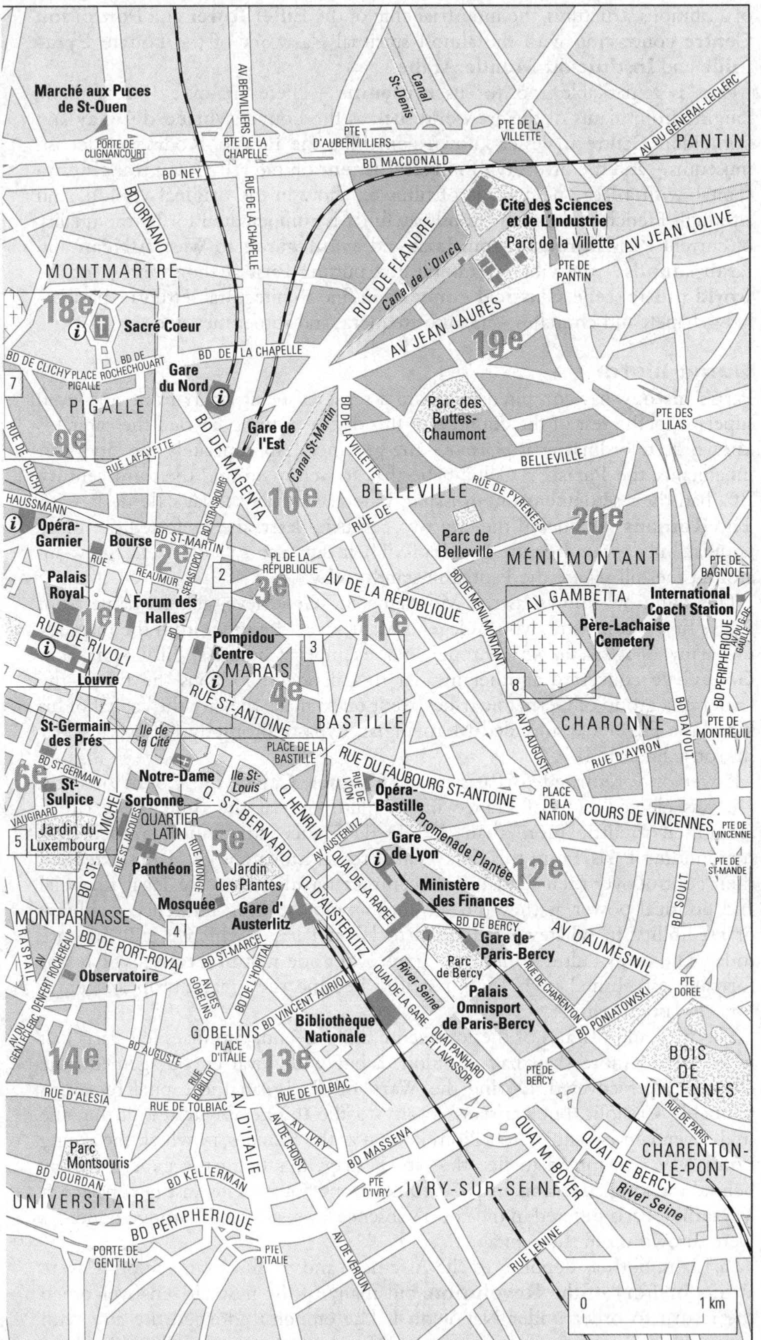
Marché aux Puces de St-Ouen
PORTE DE CLIGNANCOURT
PTE DE LA CHAPELLE
PTE D'AUBERVILLIERS
PTE DE LA VILLETTE
PANTIN
BD MACDONALD
BD NEY
Cite des Sciences et de L'Industrie
Parc de la Villette
AV JEAN LOLIVE
PTE DE PANTIN
MONTMARTRE
18e
Sacré Coeur
AV JEAN JAURES
19e
Gare du Nord
PIGALLE
9e
Gare de l'Est
Parc des Buttes-Chaumont
PTE DES LILAS
BELLEVILLE
10e
Opéra-Garnier
Bourse
2e
Parc de Belleville
20e
MÉNILMONTANT
PL DE LA RÉPUBLIQUE
Palais Royal
Forum des Halles
3e
AV DE LA REPUBLIQUE
AV GAMBETTA
International Coach Station
Père-Lachaise Cemetery
1er
RUE DE RIVOLI
Pompidou Centre
11e
MARAIS
Louvre
4e
RUE ST-ANTOINE
BASTILLE
CHARONNE
St-Germain des Prés
Ile de la Cité
PLACE DE LA BASTILLE
RUE DU FAUBOURG ST-ANTOINE
Notre-Dame
Ile St-Louis
Opéra-Bastille
6e
St-Sulpice
Sorbonne
PLACE DE LA NATION
COURS DE VINCENNES
Jardin du Luxembourg
QUARTIER LATIN
5e
Gare de Lyon
Promenade Plantée
12e
Panthéon
Jardin des Plantes
Ministère des Finances
Mosquée
Gare d' Austerlitz
MONTPARNASSE
AV DAUMESNIL
Gare de Paris-Bercy
Observatoire
Parc de Bercy
River Seine
Palais Omnisport de Paris-Bercy
Bibliothèque Nationale
GOBELINS
PLACE D'ITALIE
14e
13e
BOIS DE VINCENNES
RUE D'ALESIA
RUE DE TOLBIAC
AV D'ITALIE
CHARENTON-LE-PONT
Parc Montsouris
QUAI DE BERCY
UNIVERSITAIRE
IVRY-SUR-SEINE
BD PERIPHERIQUE
PORTE DE GENTILLY
PTE D'ITALIE
0
1 km

of ambitious structures, the industrial chic of the **Eiffel Tower** and **Pompidou Centre** contrasting with the almost spiritual glasswork of the Louvre **Pyramide** and **Institut du Monde Arabe**.

Paris is remarkable, too, for its **museums** – there are over 150 of them, ranging from giants of the art world such as the Louvre, **Musée d'Orsay** and Pompidou Centre to lesser-known gems like the Picasso, Rodin and Jewish museums – and the diversity of **entertainment** on offer. Paris is a real **cinema** capital, with a large percentage of films on show in the original version. And although French rock is notoriously awful, it is compensated for by the quality of current Parisian **music**, from **jazz** and **avant-garde** to **West African** and **Arab sounds** – the vibrant cultural mix putting Paris at the forefront of the **world music** scene. **Classical concerts** in fine architectural settings – particularly chapels and churches – are also frequent, and sometimes free.

Some history

Paris's **history** has conspired to create a sense of being apart from, and even superior to, the rest of the country. To this day, everything beyond the capital is known quite ordinarily as *province* – the provinces. Appropriately, the city's first inhabitants, the **Parisii**, a Celtic tribe that arrived in around the third century BC, had their settlement on an island: Lutetia, probably today's Île de la Cité. The **Romans** conquered the city two centuries later, and preferred the more familiar hilly ground of the Left Bank. Their city, also called Lutetia, grew up around the hill where the Panthéon stands today.

This hill, now known as the Montagne Ste-Geneviève, gets its name from Paris's first patron saint, who, as legend has it, saved the town from the marauding army of Attila in 451 through her exemplary holiness. Fifty years later **Geneviève** converted another invader to Christianity: Clovis the Frank, the leader of a group of Germanic tribes, went on to make the city the capital of his kingdom. His newly founded Merovingian dynasty promptly fell apart under his son Childéric II.

Power only returned to Paris under **Hugues Capet**, the Count of Paris. He was elected king of France in 987, although at the time his territory amounted to little more than the Île de France, the region immediately surrounding Paris. From this shaky start French monarchs gradually extended their control over their feudal rivals, centralizing administrative, legal, financial and political power as they did so, until anyone seeking influence, publicity or credibility, in whatever field, had to be in Paris – which is still the case today. The city's cultural influence grew alongside its **university**, which was formally established in 1215 and swiftly became the great European centre for scholastic learning.

The wars and plagues of the fourteenth and fifteenth centuries left Paris half in ruins and more than half abandoned, but with royal encouragement, the city steadily recovered. During the **Wars of Religion** the capital remained staunchly Catholic, but Parisians' loyalty to the throne was tested during the mid-seventeenth-century rebellions known as the Frondes, in which the young Louis XIV was forced to flee the city. Perhaps this traumatic experience lay behind the king's decision, in 1670, to move the court to his vast new palace at **Versailles**. Paris suffered in the court's absence, even as grand Baroque buildings were thrown up in the capital.

Parisians, both as deputies to the Assembly and mobs of sans-culottes, were at the forefront of the **Revolution**, but many of the new citizens welcomed the return to order under Napoleon I. The emperor adorned the city with many of its signature monuments, Neoclassical almost-follies designed to amplify his majesty: the Arc de Triomphe, Arc du Carrousel and the Madeleine. He also instituted the Grandes Écoles, super-universities for the nation's elite administrators, engineers and teachers. At the fall of the Empire, in 1814, Paris was saved from destruction by the arch-diplomat Talleyrand, who delivered the city to the Russians with hardly a shot fired. Nationalists grumbled that the occupation continued well into the Restoration regime, as the city once again became the playground of the rich of Europe, the ultimate tourist destination.

The greatest shocks to the fabric of the city came under Napoléon III. He finally completed the Louvre, rebuilding much of the facade in the process, but it was his Prefect of the Seine, **Baron Haussmann**, who truly transformed the city, smashing through the slums to create wide boulevards that could be easily controlled by rifle-toting troops – not that it succeeded in preventing the **1871 Commune**, the most determined insurrection since 1789. In the process of slum clearance, Haussmann created the uniquely Parisian aesthetic that survives today, of long geometrical boulevards lined with rows of grey bourgeois residences. It was down these boulevards that **Nazi troops** paraded in June 1940, followed – after a relatively uneventful war for many, if not all, Parisians – by the Allies, led by General Leclerc, in August 1944.

Although riotous street protests are still a feature of modern Parisian life – most famously in **May 1968**, when students burst onto the streets of the Quartier Latin – the traditional barricade-builders have long since been booted into the suburban factory-land or depressing satellite towns, alongside the under-served populations of immigrants and their descendants. Many Parisians see the economic and cultural integration of these communities as the greatest challenge facing the contemporary city, and there's a strong undercurrent of **racism** in Paris, as throughout France.

The city continues to expand outward, but offices are steadily elbowing out apartments in the centre, even in this most village-like of cities. **Housing** remains a problem – trying to find an apartment in Paris is a notoriously difficult affair – and yet the decaying parts of the city, especially in the east and north, are gradually being rebuilt, and grand-scale new developments such as La Défense and the Paris Rive Gauche area attest to the vitality of the city's commercial life.

The interests of business and the bourgeoisie – not to mention those of the mayor's family and friends – flourished under the rule of **Jacques Chirac**, Paris's mayor from 1977 to 1995, and his successor Jean Tiberi, but in March 2001, a socialist politician called Bertrand Delanoë took over. It was the first time the Left had controlled Paris since the 1871 Commune, and the first time that city had had an openly gay mayor – not that many Parisians seem to think it matters. Delanoë promised to restore life to Paris by taking on the traffic problem, creating new green spaces and fighting the "museumification" of the city. To date, however, the most visible projects have been more populist and superficial: "Paris Plages" sees a swathe of the Seine's *quais* converted into a beach every summer, while the "Nuit Blanche" keeps Parisians up all night with city-wide art and cultural events.

Arrival

Many British travellers to Paris arrive by Eurostar at the central **Gare du Nord train station**, while more far-flung visitors are likely to land at one of

Paris's two main airports: Charles de Gaulle and Orly. Trains from other parts of France or continental Europe draw in at one of the six central mainline stations. Almost all the **buses** coming into Paris – whether international or domestic – arrive at the main *gare routière* at 28 av du Général-de-Gaulle, Bagnolet, at the eastern edge of the city; métro Gallieni (line 3) links it to the centre. If you're **driving** in yourself, don't try to go straight across the city to your destination. Use the ring road – the *boulevard périphérique* – to get around to the nearest *porte*: it's much quicker, except at rush hour, and far easier to navigate, albeit pretty terrifying.

By air

The two main Paris airports that deal with international flights are **Roissy-Charles de Gaulle** and **Orly**, both well connected to the centre. Detailed information in English can be found online at Ⓦwww.adp.fr. The more distant **Beauvais** airport is used by some budget airlines, including Ryanair.

Roissy-Charles de Gaulle Airport

Roissy-Charles de Gaulle Airport (24hr information in English Ⓣ01.48.62.22.80), usually referred to as Charles de Gaulle and abbreviated to CDG or Paris CDG, is 23km northeast of the city. The airport has two main **terminals**, CDG 1 and CDG 2. A third terminal, CDG 3 (sometimes called CDG-T3), handles various low-cost airlines, including easyJet. Make sure you know which terminal your flight is departing from when it's time to leave Paris, so you take the correct bus or get off at the right train station. A TGV station links the airport (CDG 2) with Bordeaux, Brussels, Lille, Lyon, Nantes, Marseille and Rennes, among other places.

The least expensive and probably quickest way into the centre of Paris is to take the suburban train line **RER B3**, sometimes called Roissyrail, which runs every ten to fifteen minutes from 5am until midnight; the journey time is thirty minutes and tickets cost €8.10 one way (no return tickets). To get to the RER station from CDG 1 you have to take a free shuttle bus (*navette*) to the RER station, but from CDG 2 and CDG-T3 it's simpler to take the pedestrian walkway, though the station is also served by a shuttle bus. The RER train stops at stations including Gare du Nord, Châtelet–Les Halles and St-Michel, at all of which you can transfer to the ordinary métro system – your ticket is valid through to any métro station in central Paris.

Various bus companies provide services from the airport direct to various city-centre locations, but they're slightly more expensive than Roissyrail, and may take longer. A more useful alternative is the Blue Vans door-to-door **minibus** service (€65 one way for four people, or €58 return for two people on a shared basis; no extra charge for luggage). Bookings must be made at least 24 hours in advance on Ⓣ01.30.11.13.00 or, for the best rates, online at Ⓦwww.paris-blue-airport-shuttle.fr/.

Taxis into central Paris from CDG cost around €50 on the meter, plus a small luggage supplement (€0.90 per item), and should take between fifty minutes and one hour. Note that if your flight gets in after midnight your only means of transport is a taxi.

Orly Airport

Orly Airport (information in English daily 6am–11.30pm; Ⓣ01.49.75.15.15), 14km south of Paris, has **two terminals**, Orly Sud and Orly Ouest, linked by shuttle bus but easily walkable; Ouest (West) is used for domestic flights while Sud (South) handles international flights.

The easiest way into the centre is via Orlyval, a fast **train shuttle** link to the suburban RER station Antony, where you can pick up RER line B trains to the central RER/métro stations Denfert-Rochereau, St-Michel and Châtelet-Les Halles; Orlyval runs every four to eight minutes from 6.10am to 11pm (€9.10 one way; 35min to Châtelet). A useful alternative is the **Orlybus**: a shuttle bus takes you to direct to RER line B station Denfert-Rochereau, on the Left Bank, with good onward métro connections; Orlybus runs every fifteen to twenty minutes from roughly 6am to 11.20pm (€6 one way; total journey around 30min). **Taxis** take about 35 minutes to reach the centre of Paris and cost around €35.

Beauvais Airport

Ryanair passengers arrive at Beauvais Airport (Ⓣ08.92.68.20.66, Ⓦwww.aeroportbeauvais.com), some 65km northwest of Paris. **Coaches** (€13 one way) shuttle between the airport and Porte Maillot, at the northwestern edge of Paris, where you can pick up métro line 1 to the centre. Coaches take about an hour, and leave between fifteen and thirty minutes after the flight has arrived and about three hours before the flight departs on the way back. Tickets can be bought online via the airport's web address (see above), at Arrivals or from the Beauvais shop at 1 bd Pershing, near the Porte Maillot terminal.

By train

Paris has six mainline train stations. **Eurostar** (Ⓣ08.92.35.35.39, Ⓦwww.eurostar.com) terminates at the busy **Gare du Nord**, rue Dunkerque, in the northeast of the city. Coming off the train, turn left for the métro and the RER, and right for taxis (expect to pay around €10 to central Paris). Just short of the taxi exit, head down the escalators for left luggage (*consignes*) and the various car rental desks. Two bureaux de change (neither offer a good deal) allow you to change money at the station, or you can use your card in one of the ATM cash machines. The Gare du Nord is also the arrival point for trains from Calais and other north-European countries.

Nearby, the **Gare de l'Est** (place du 11-Novembre-1918, 10e) serves eastern France and central and eastern Europe. The **Gare St-Lazare** (place du Havre, 8e), serving the Normandy coast and Dieppe, is the most central, close to the Madeleine and the Opéra-Garnier. Still on the Right Bank but towards the southeast corner is the **Gare de Lyon** (place Louis-Armand, 12e), for trains to Italy and Switzerland and TGV lines to southeast France. South of the river, **Gare Montparnasse** (bd de Vaugirard, 15e) is the terminus for Chartres, Brittany, the Atlantic coast and TGV lines to Tours and southwest France. **Gare d'Austerlitz** (bd de l'Hôpital, 13e) serves the Loire Valley and the Dordogne. The **motorail station**, Gare de Paris-Bercy, is down the tracks from the Gare de Lyon on boulevard de Bercy, 12e.

All the stations are equipped with cafés, restaurants, *tabacs*, banks, left-luggage facilities and bureaux de change, and all are connected to the métro system; Gare du Nord and Gare de Lyon have **tourist offices** which book same-day accommodation (see p.92). For **information** on national train services and reservations, phone Ⓣ08.36.35.35.39 (if you dial extension 2 you should get through to an English-speaking operator) or consult the website Ⓦwww.sncf.fr. For information on suburban lines call Ⓣ01.53.90.20.20. You can buy tickets at any train station, online at the SNCF website and from travel agents.

Orientation

Finding your way around Paris is remarkably easy, as the centre is fairly small for a major capital city, and very **walkable**. The city proper is divided into twenty arrondissements, or districts. These are marked on the map on pp.86–87 and are included as an integral part of addresses throughout the chapter. Arrondissements are abbreviated as 1er (premier = first), 2e (deuxième = second), 3e, 4e and so on; the numbering is confusing until you work out that it spirals out from the centre.

The **Seine** flows in a downturned arc from east to west, cutting the city in two. In the middle of the Seine lie two islands, while north of the river is the busy, commercial **Right Bank**, or *rive droite*. Most of the city's sights are found here, within the historic central arrondissements (1er to 4e). South of the river is the relatively laid-back **Left Bank**, or *rive gauche* (5e to 7e). The outer arrondissements (8e to 20e) were mostly incorporated into the city in the nineteenth century. Generally speaking, those to the east accommodated the working classes while those to the west were, and still are, the addresses for the aristocracy and new rich. For a brief rundown of Paris's different quarters, see the introduction to the city on p.107.

Paris proper is encircled by the *boulevard périphérique* ring-road. The sprawling conurbation beyond is known as the **banlieue**, or suburbs. There are few sights for the tourist here, and only one of significant interest: St-Denis, with its historic cathedral.

Information

At Paris's **tourist offices** (Ⓣ08.92.68.30.00, Ⓦwww.parisinfo.com) you can pick up maps and information, book hotel accommodation and buy the Paris Museum Pass (see box below). The most usefully located branches are at 25 rue Pyramides, 1er (June–Oct daily 9am–7pm; Nov–May Mon–Sat 10am–7pm, Sun 11am–7pm; M° Pyramides), and in the Carrousel du Louvre, accessed from 99 rue de Rivoli, 1er (daily 10am–6pm; M° Palais Royal-Musée du Louvre). The last also has information on the region around Paris, the Île de France. There are smaller offices at the Gare du Nord (daily 8am–6pm) and Gare de

Reductions and the Museum Pass

The permanent collections at all municipal museums are free all year round, while all national museums (including the Louvre, Musée d'Orsay and Pompidou Centre) are free on the first Sunday of the month – see Ⓦwww.rmn.fr for a full list – and to under-18s. Elsewhere, the cut-off age for free admission varies between 18, 12 and 4. Reduced admission is usually available for 18 to 26-year-olds and for those over 60 or 65; you'll need to carry your passport or ID card around with you as proof of age. Some discounts are available for students with an ISIC Card (International Student Identity Card; Ⓦwww.isiccard.com). If you're planning to visit a great many museums in a short time, it might be worth buying the **Paris Museum Pass** (€30 two-day, €45 four-day, €60 six-day; Ⓦwww.parismuseumpass.fr). Available from the tourist office and participating museums, it's valid for 35 of the most important museums and monuments including the Louvre (but not special exhibitions) inside Paris, and allows you to bypass ticket queues (though not the security checkpoints).

Lyon (Mon–Sat 8am–6pm), and on place du Tertre, in Montmartre, 18e (daily 10am–6pm; M° Anvers).

For what's-on information it's worth buying one of Paris's inexpensive weekly **listings magazines** from a newsagent or kiosk. The best and glossiest is *Zurban* (Ⓦ www.zurban.com), although *Pariscope* has a comprehensive section on films. For more detail, French speakers should check out the monthly *Nova* magazine, while the free English-language monthly magazines *Paris Voice* (Ⓦ www.parisvoice.com) and *GoGo Paris* (Ⓦ gogoparis.com), available from Anglo bars and bookshops, have good listings and small ads.

If you feel the need for a separate **map**, the *Rough Guide Map: Paris* is detailed and produced on waterproof paper. For a comprehensive A–Z, your best bet is one of the pocket-sized "*L'indispensable*" series booklets, sold everywhere in Paris.

City transport

While walking is undoubtedly the best way to discover Paris, the city's integrated **public transport system** of bus, métro and trains – the RATP (Régie Autonome des Transports Parisiens) – is cheap, fast and meticulously signposted. Free métro and bus maps of varying sizes and detail are available at most stations, bus terminals and the tourist office: the largest and most useful is the *Grand Plan*

Tickets and passes

For a short stay in the city, **carnets** of ten tickets can be bought from any station or *tabac* (€10.90, as opposed to €1.40 for an individual ticket). The city's integrated transport system, the RATP (Ⓦ www.ratp.fr), is divided into **five zones**, and the métro system itself more or less fits into zones 1 and 2. The same tickets are valid for the buses (including the night bus), métro and, within the city limits and immediate suburbs (zones 1 and 2), the RER express rail lines, which also extend far out into the Île de France. Only one ticket is ever needed on the métro system, and within zones 1 and 2 for any RER or bus journey, but you can't switch between buses or between bus and métro/RER on the same ticket. For RER journeys beyond zones 1 and 2 you must buy an RER ticket. In order to get to La Défense on the RER rather than on the métro, for example, you need to buy a RER ticket, as La Défense is in zone 3. Children under 4 travel free and from ages 4 to 10 at half-price. Don't buy from the touts who hang round the main stations – you may pay well over the odds, quite often for a used ticket – and be sure to keep your ticket until the end of the journey as you'll be fined on the spot if you can't produce one.

If you're doing a fair number of journeys in one day, it might be worth getting a **Mobilis day pass** (from €5.50 for the city), which offers unlimited access to the métro, buses and, depending on which zones you choose, the RER. Other possibilities are the **Paris Visite** passes (Ⓦ www.parisvisite.com), one-, two-, three- and five-day visitors' passes at €8.50, €13.95, €18.60 and €27.20 for Paris and close suburbs, or €17.05, €27.15, €38.10 and €46.60 to include the airports, Versailles and Disneyland Paris (make sure you buy this one when you arrive at Roissy-Charles de Gaulle or Orly to get maximum value). A half-price child's version is also available. You can buy them from métro and RER stations, tourist offices and online from Ⓦ www.allofrance.co.uk. Paris Visite passes can begin on any day and entitle you to unlimited travel (in the zones you have chosen) on bus, métro, RER, SNCF and the Montmartre funicular; they also allow you discounts at certain monuments and museums.

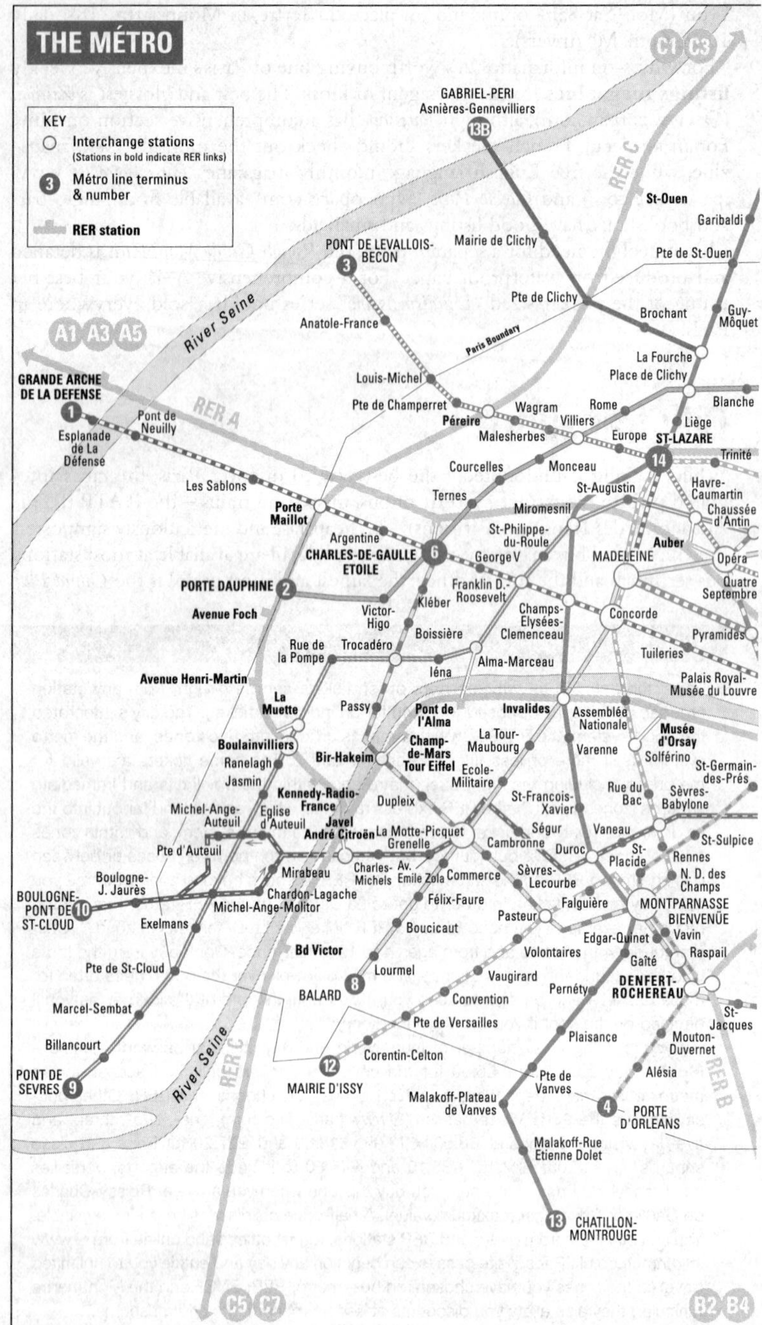
THE MÉTRO
KEY
Interchange stations
(Stations in bold indicate RER links)
Métro line terminus & number
RER station
GABRIEL-PERI
Asnières-Gennevilliers
PONT DE LEVALLOIS-BECON
GRANDE ARCHE DE LA DEFENSE
River Seine
RER A
RER C
RER B
Paris Boundary
St-Ouen
Garibaldi
Mairie de Clichy
Pte de St-Ouen
Pte de Clichy
Brochant
Guy-Môquet
Anatole-France
La Fourche
Place de Clichy
Louis-Michel
Pte de Champerret
Péreire
Wagram
Rome
Blanche
Villiers
Liège
Malesherbes
Europe
ST-LAZARE
Trinité
Pont de Neuilly
Esplanade de La Défense
Les Sablons
Courcelles
Monceau
Ternes
St-Augustin
Havre-Caumartin
Porte Maillot
Miromesnil
Chaussée d'Antin
Argentine
St-Philippe-du-Roule
Auber
CHARLES-DE-GAULLE ETOILE
George V
MADELEINE
Opéra
PORTE DAUPHINE
Franklin D.-Roosevelt
Quatre Septembre
Kléber
Victor-Higo
Champs-Elysées-Clemenceau
Concorde
Avenue Foch
Boissière
Pyramides
Rue de la Pompe
Trocadéro
Tuileries
Alma-Marceau
Iéna
Avenue Henri-Martin
Palais Royal-Musée du Louvre
La Muette
Passy
Pont de l'Alma
Invalides
Assemblée Nationale
Musée d'Orsay
Boulainvilliers
Champ-de-Mars Tour Eiffel
La Tour-Maubourg
Varenne
Solférino
Ranelagh
Bir-Hakeim
Ecole-Militaire
St-Germain-des-Prés
Jasmin
Kennedy-Radio-France
Rue du Bac
Sèvres-Babylone
Michel-Ange-Auteuil
Eglise d'Auteuil
Dupleix
St-Francois-Xavier
Javel André Citroën
La Motte-Picquet Grenelle
Ségur
Vaneau
St-Sulpice
Pte d'Auteuil
Cambronne
Duroc
St-Placide
Rennes
Mirabeau
Charles-Michels
Av. Emile Zola
Commerce
Sèvres-Lecourbe
N. D. des Champs
Boulogne-J. Jaurès
Chardon-Lagache
BOULOGNE-PONT DE ST-CLOUD
Michel-Ange-Molitor
Félix-Faure
Falguière
MONTPARNASSE BIENVENÜE
Pasteur
Exelmans
Boucicaut
Edgar-Quinet
Vavin
Bd Victor
Volontaires
Raspail
Pte de St-Cloud
Lourmel
Gaîté
Vaugirard
DENFERT-ROCHEREAU
BALARD
Pernéty
Convention
Marcel-Sembat
Pte de Versailles
St-Jacques
Plaisance
Mouton-Duvernet
Billancourt
Corentin-Celton
Alésia
PONT DE SEVRES
MAIRIE D'ISSY
Pte de Vanves
Malakoff-Plateau de Vanves
PORTE D'ORLEANS
Malakoff-Rue Etienne Dolet
CHATILLON-MONTROUGE

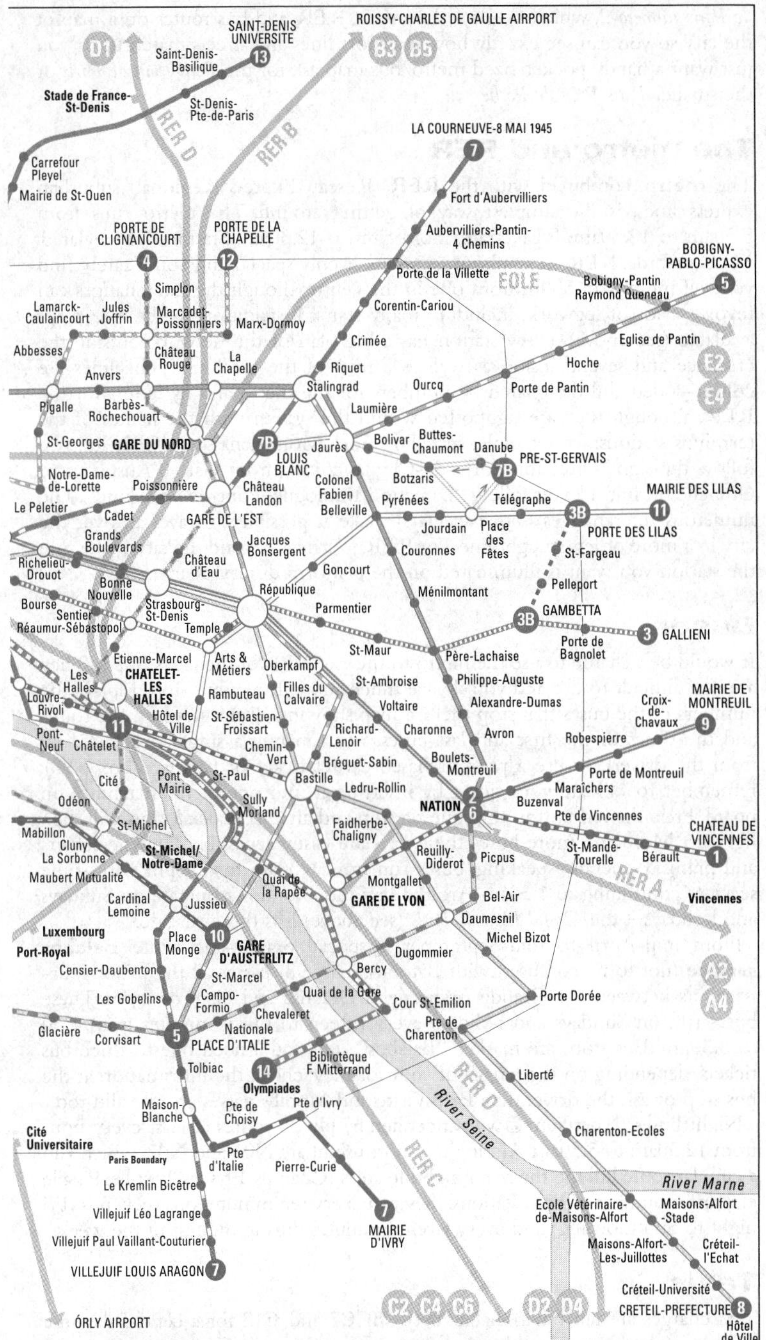

ROISSY-CHARLES DE GAULLE AIRPORT
SAINT-DENIS UNIVERSITE
13
D1
B3
B5
Saint-Denis-Basilique
Stade de France-St-Denis
St-Denis-Pte-de-Paris
RER D
RER B
Carrefour Pleyel
Mairie de St-Ouen
LA COURNEUVE-8 MAI 1945
7
Fort d'Aubervilliers
Aubervilliers-Pantin-4 Chemins
PORTE DE CLIGNANCOURT
4
PORTE DE LA CHAPELLE
12
BOBIGNY-PABLO-PICASSO
5
Porte de la Villette
EOLE
Bobigny-Pantin Raymond Queneau
Simplon
Corentin-Cariou
Lamarck-Caulaincourt
Jules Joffrin
Marcadet-Poissonniers
Marx-Dormoy
Eglise de Pantin
Crimée
Abbesses
Château Rouge
La Chapelle
Hoche
Riquet
E2
Anvers
Stalingrad
Ourcq
Porte de Pantin
E4
Pigalle
Barbès-Rochechouart
Laumière
St-Georges
GARE DU NORD
7B
Jaurès
Bolivar
Buttes-Chaumont
Danube
LOUIS BLANC
PRE-ST-GERVAIS
Notre-Dame-de-Lorette
Poissonnière
Château Landon
Colonel Fabien
Botzaris
7B
MAIRIE DES LILAS
Le Peletier
Cadet
GARE DE L'EST
Belleville
Pyrénées
Télégraphe
3B
11
Grands Boulevards
Jourdain
Place des Fêtes
PORTE DES LILAS
Richelieu-Drouot
Jacques Bonsergent
Château d'Eau
Couronnes
St-Fargeau
Bonne Nouvelle
Goncourt
Pelleport
Bourse
Sentier
Strasbourg-St-Denis
République
Ménilmontant
Réaumur-Sébastopol
Temple
Parmentier
3B
GAMBETTA
3
GALLIENI
Etienne-Marcel
Arts & Métiers
St-Maur
Porte de Bagnolet
Père-Lachaise
Les Halles
CHATELET-LES HALLES
Oberkampf
Louvre-Rivoli
Rambuteau
Filles du Calvaire
St-Ambroise
Philippe-Auguste
MAIRIE DE MONTREUIL
Alexandre-Dumas
Croix-de-Chavaux
9
11
Hôtel de Ville
St-Sébastien-Froissart
Voltaire
Pont-Neuf
Châtelet
Chemin-Vert
Richard-Lenoir
Charonne
Avron
Robespierre
Bréguet-Sabin
Boulets-Montreuil
Porte de Montreuil
Cité
Pont Mairie
St-Paul
Bastille
Ledru-Rollin
Maraîchers
2
NATION
6
Buzenval
Odéon
Sully Morland
Pte de Vincennes
Mabillon
St-Michel
Faidherbe-Chaligny
CHATEAU DE VINCENNES
Cluny La Sorbonne
St-Michel/Notre-Dame
Reuilly-Diderot
Picpus
St-Mandé-Tourelle
Bérault
1
Maubert Mutualité
Quai de la Rapée
RER A
Montgallet
Cardinal Lemoine
Jussieu
GARE DE LYON
Bel-Air
Vincennes
Daumesnil
Luxembourg
Place Monge
10
GARE D'AUSTERLITZ
Michel Bizot
Port-Royal
Dugommier
Censier-Daubenton
Bercy
A2
St-Marcel
Les Gobelins
Campo-Formio
Quai de la Gare
Cour St-Emilion
Porte Dorée
A4
Chevaleret
Glacière
Corvisart
5
PLACE D'ITALIE
Nationale
Pte de Charenton
Bibliotèque F. Mitterrand
14
Olympiades
Tolbiac
RER D
Liberté
River Seine
Maison-Blanche
Pte de Choisy
Pte d'Ivry
Cité Universitaire
Paris Boundary
Pte d'Italie
RER C
Charenton-Ecoles
Pierre-Curie
Le Kremlin Bicêtre
River Marne
Ecole Vétérinaire-de-Maisons-Alfort
Maisons-Alfort-Stade
Villejuif Léo Lagrange
7
MAIRIE D'IVRY
Villejuif Paul Vaillant-Couturier
Maisons-Alfort-Les-Juillottes
Créteil-l'Echat
VILLEJUIF LOUIS ARAGON
7
Créteil-Université
C2
C4
C6
D2
D4
CRETEIL-PREFECTURE
8
ÓRLY AIRPORT
Hôtel de Ville

de Paris numéro 2, which overlays the métro, RER and bus routes on a map of the city so you can see exactly how transport lines and streets match up. If you just want a handy pocket-sized métro/bus map ask for the *Petit Plan de Paris* or the smaller *Paris Plan de Poche*.

The métro and RER

The **métro**, combined with the **RER** (Réseau Express Régional) suburban express lines, is the simplest way of getting around. The métro runs from 5.30am to 12.30am, RER trains from 5am to 12.30am. Stations (abbreviated: M° Concorde, RER Luxembourg, etc) are evenly spaced and you'll rarely find yourself more than 500m from one in the centre, though the interchanges can involve a lot of legwork, including many stairs. In addition to the free maps available (see above), every station has a big plan of the network outside the entrance and several inside, as well as a map of the local area. The lines are colour-coded and designated by numbers for the métro and by letters for the RER, although they are signposted within the system with the names of the terminus stations: for example, travelling from Montparnasse to Châtelet, you follow the sign "Direction Porte-de-Clignancourt"; from Gare d'Austerlitz to Grenelle on line 10 you follow "Direction Boulogne–Pont-de-St-Cloud". The numerous interchanges (*correspondances*) make it possible to travel all over the city in a more or less straight line. For RER journeys beyond the city, make sure the station you want is illuminated on the platform display board.

Buses

It would be a shame to use the métro to the exclusion of the city's **buses**. They are not difficult to use and you do see much more. Every bus stop displays the numbers of the buses that stop there, a map showing all the stops on the route, and the times of the first and last buses. You can buy a single ticket (€1.40 from the driver), or use a pre-purchased carnet ticket or pass (see box p.93); remember to validate your ticket by inserting it into one of the machines on board. Press the red button to request a stop and an *arrêt demandé* sign will then light up. More and more buses these days are easily accessible for wheelchairs and prams. Generally speaking, buses run from 6.30am to 8.30pm with some services continuing to 1.30am. Around half the lines don't operate on Sundays and holidays – the *Grand Plan de Paris* (see above) lists those that do.

From mid-April to mid-September, a special orange-and-white **Balabus service** (not to be confused with Batobus, see p.98) passes all the major tourist sights between the Grande Arche de la Défense and Gare de Lyon. These buses run on Sundays and holidays every fifteen to thirty minutes from 1.30 to 8.30pm. Bus stops are marked "Balabus", and you'll need one to three bus tickets, depending on the length of your journey: check the information at the bus stop or ask the driver. The Paris Visite and Mobilis passes are all valid too.

Night buses (Noctilien; Ⓦwww.noctilien.fr) ply 35 routes at least every hour from 12.30am to 5.30am. Among the most useful are N01 and N02, which run a circular route linking the main nightlife areas (Champs-Élysées, Bastille, Pigalle etc) and a number of train stations; they run every ten minutes on weekends (Fri night to Sun morning) and every twenty minutes during the rest of the week.

Taxis

Taxi charges are fairly reasonable: between €7 and €12 for a central daytime journey, though considerably more if you call one out. Before you get into the taxi you can tell which of the **three rates** is operating from the three small indicator lights on its roof: "A" (passenger side; white) indicates the daytime rate (7am–7pm) for Paris within the *boulevard périphérique* (around €0.60 per km); "B" (orange) is the rate for Paris at night, on Sunday and on public holidays, and for the suburbs during the day (around €1 per km); "C" (blue) is the night rate for the suburbs (€1.25 per km). The minimum charge for a journey is €5.20; there's a time charge of around €25 an hour for when the car is stationary, an extra charge of €0.75 if you're picked up from a mainline train station, and a €0.90 charge for each piece of luggage carried. **Tipping** is not mandatory, but ten percent will be expected. Taxi drivers do not have to take more than three passengers (they don't like people sitting in the front); if a fourth passenger is accepted, an extra charge of €2.70 will be added.

Waiting at a **taxi rank** (*arrêt taxi* – there are around 470 of them) is usually more effective than hailing one from the street. The large white light signals the taxi is free; the orange light means it's in use. You can also call a taxi out directly: phone numbers are shown at the taxi ranks, or try Taxis Bleus (Ⓣ08.91.70.10.10, Ⓦwww.taxis-bleus.com), Alpha Taxis (Ⓣ01.45.85.85.85) or Artaxi (Ⓣ01.42.03.50.50). Taxis can, however, be rather thin on the ground at lunchtime and any time after 7pm.

Disabled travellers

If you're disabled, **taxis** are obliged by law to carry you and help you into the vehicle – and to carry your guide dog if you are blind or visually impaired. A number of taxi firms, such as G7 Taxis (Ⓣ01.47.39.00.91, Ⓦwww.taxisg7.fr), offer specially adapted taxis; many more are listed on the Paris tourist office website (Ⓦwww.parisinfo.com). For travel on the **buses**, **métro** or **RER**, the RATP offers accompanied journeys for disabled people not in wheelchairs (Les compagnons du voyage; Ⓦwww.compagnons.com), which is available daily from 6.30am until 8pm and costs €25 an hour. You have to book on Ⓣ01.53.11.12. (Mon–Fri 6am–7pm, Sat & Sun 9am–6pm) at least a day in advance. Blind and visually impaired passengers can request a free companion from the volunteer organization Auxiliaires des Aveugles (Ⓣ01.43.06.39.68). A **Braille métro map** costing €2.80 and a separate bus map are obtainable from L'Association Valentin Haûy (AVH), 5 rue Duroc, 7e (Ⓣ01.44.49.27.27, Ⓦwww.avh.asso.fr).

The new métro line 14 and an increasing number of RER and métro stations on other lines are readily accessible to **wheelchair** users. A detailed list of all accessible stations and routes is available from RATP ticket offices or on Ⓦwww.ratp.fr. More extensive information on getting around the city can be found on Ⓦwww.infomobi.com, in French only. A useful **publication**, *Access in Paris* by Gordon Couch and Ben Roberts, published in Britain by Quiller Press, is available for £6.95, though bear in mind that it was published in 1993 and some of the information will be out of date.

Driving and parking

Travelling around by **car** – in the daytime at least – is hardly worth it because of the difficulty of finding parking spaces. You're better off finding a motel-style place on the edge of the city and using public transport. But if you're determined to use the **pay-and-display** parking system you must first buy a Paris Carte (€10) from a *tabac*, then look for the blue "P" signs alongside grey parking meters. Put the card into the meter – in the centre you'll pay €3 an hour for a maximum of two hours. Covered car parks cost around €2.50 per hour.

△ The Seine

Whatever you do, don't park in a bus lane or the Axe Rouge **express routes** (marked with a red square). Should you be towed away, you'll find your car in the pound (*fourrière*) belonging to that particular arrondissement – check with the local *mairie* for the address.

In the event of a **breakdown**, call SOS Dépannage (Ⓣ01.47.07.99.99) for round-the-clock assistance. Alternatively, ask the police.

See p.199 for details of car rental.

Boats

There remains one final mode of transport, **Batobus** (Ⓦwww.batobus.com), which operates all year round, apart from January, stopping at eight points along the Seine, from the Eiffel Tower to the Jardin des Plantes. Boats run every 25

Boat trips

A less conventional way to see Paris is to take a **boat trip** on the Seine. The faithful old Bateaux-Mouches are the best-known operator. Their embarkation point is the Embarcadère du Pont de l'Alma on the Right Bank in the 8e (reservations and information ☎01.42.25.96.10; M° Alma-Marceau). The rides last one hour ten minutes, cost €8 (€4 for children and over-65s) and take you past the major Seine-side sights, such as Notre-Dame and the Louvre. Departures are at 11am, noon, 1pm, and every 45 minutes from 1.45 to 7pm, then every half an hour from 7 to 9.30pm; winter departures are less frequent. The night-time cruises use lights to illuminate the streetscapes that are so bright they almost blind passers-by – much more fun on board than off – and at all times a narration in several languages blares out. The outrageously priced lunch and dinner trips, for which "correct" dress is mandatory, are probably best avoided. Bateaux-Mouches has many competitors, all much of a muchness and detailed in *Pariscope* under "Croisières" in the "Visites et Promenades" section.

A more unusual way of seeing less-visited sights are the **canal boat trips** run by Canauxrama (reservations ☎01.42.39.15.00) between the Port de l'Arsenal, opposite 50 bd de la Bastille, 12e (M° Bastille), and the Bassin de la Villette, 13 quai de la Loire, 19e (M° Jaurès), on the Canal St-Martin. Departing daily at 9.45am and 2.45pm from the Bassin de la Villette and at 9.45am and 2.30pm from the Bastille, the ride lasts nearly three hours and costs €14 (children €8). A more stylish vessel for exploring the canal is the **catamaran** of Paris-Canal, which runs two-and-a-half-hour trips between the Musée d'Orsay, quai Anatole-France, 7e (M° Musée d'Orsay), and the Parc de la Villette ("Folie des Visites du Parc"; M° Porte-de-Pantin); boats operate in both directions daily from the end of March to mid-November, leaving the museum at 9.30am and the park at 2.30pm (reservations on ☎01.42.40.96.97; €16, children €9).

minutes (Jan to mid-March & Nov to early Jan 10.30am–4.30pm; mid-March to May, Sept & Oct 10am–7pm; June–Aug 10am–9pm). The total journey time from one end to the other is around thirty minutes and you can hop on and off as many times as you like – a day pass costs €11 (there are no single tickets).

Accommodation

Paris has some two thousand hotels offering a wide range of comfort, price and location. Hotels in the budget and mid-range category are reasonably priced and are cheaper than those in many other European capitals. By contrast, its four- and five-star hotels, some of them truly luxurious, are among Europe's most expensive. Smaller two-star hotels often charge between €55 and €85 (❸–❻) for a double room, though for something with a bit of style you'll probably have to pay upwards of €85 (❻), and €110 or more (❼) in swankier areas. However, it's possible to find a double room with a shower, in a decent central location, for around €45 (❸), and bargains exist in the 10e and 11e, especially around place de la République. You can get good deals in quieter areas further out, in the 13e and 14e, south of Montparnasse, and the 17e, around Place de Clichy.

If you want to secure a really good room it's worth booking a couple of months or more in advance, as even the nicer hotels often leave their pokiest rooms at the back for last-minute reservations, and the best places will sell out well in advance in all but the coldest months. If you find yourself stuck on arrival, the main tourist office at rue des Pyramides and the branches at the Gare de Lyon and Eiffel Tower will find you a room in a hotel or hostel free of charge.

Our hotel recommendations are divided by area (see map on pp.86–87). Prices are divided into nine categories: where there are only very few rooms in a hotel in the lower price categories, we show the complete price range on offer. Hostels and campsites are listed separately on pp.105–106.

The Champs-Élysées and around

See map, pp.110–111.

Brighton 218 rue de Rivoli, 1er ⓣ01.47.03.61.61, ⓔhotel.brighton@orange.fr; Mº Tuileries. An elegant hotel dating back to the late nineteenth century and affording magnificent views of the Tuileries gardens from the front-facing rooms on the upper floors. Most of the 65 rooms have recently been renovated; the standard of the others varies, though many retain period charm and ambience. ❽

Des Champs-Élysées 2 rue Artois, 8e ⓣ01.43.59.11.42, ⓕ01.45.61.00.61; Mº St-Philippe-du-Roule. The rooms at this two-star hotel are small but nicely decorated in warm colours and come with shower or bath, plus satellite TV, minibar, hairdryer and safe. Breakfast is served in a cool, relaxing converted stone cellar. ❼

Chopin 46 passage Jouffroy, entrance on bd Montmartre, near rue du Faubourg-Montmartre, 9e ⓣ01.47.70.58.10, ⓕ01.42.47.00.70; Mº Grands-Boulevards. A lovely period building hidden away at the end of an elegant *passage*, with quiet and pleasantly furnished rooms, though the cheaper ones are on the small side and a little dark. ❺

De L'Élysée 12 rue des Saussaies, 8e ⓣ01.42.65.29.25, ⓦwww.france-hotel-guide.com/h75008efsh.htm; M° Champs-Élysées-Clemenceau. This comfy three-star, a mere chandelier swing from the Élysée Palace, has sixty rooms decorated in traditional style, with *toile de jouy* wallpaper, solid mahogany furniture and jacquard bedspreads. ❽

Lancaster 7 rue de Berri, 8e ⓣ01.40.76.40.76, ⓦwww.hotel-lancaster.fr; Mº George-V. Once the pied-à-terre for the likes of Garbo, Dietrich and Sir Alec Guinness, this elegantly restored nineteenth-century town house is still a favourite hide-out today for those fleeing the paparazzi. The rooms retain original features and are chock-full of Louis XVI and rococo antiques, but with a touch of contemporary chic. To top it all off, there's a superlative restaurant and zen-style interior garden. Doubles start at €470. ❾

Pergolèse 3 rue Pergolèse, 16e ⓣ01.53.64.04.04, ⓦwww.hotelpergolese.com. A classy four-star boutique hotel in a tall, slender building on a quiet side street near the Arc de Triomphe. The decor is all contemporary – wood floors, cool colours, chic styling – but without chilliness: sofas and friendly service add a cosy touch. Plenty of special deals bring prices well below the advertised rate of €250 for a double. ❾

Relais St-Honoré 308 rue St-Honoré, 1er ⓣ01.42.96.06.06, ⓦsainthonore.free.fr; M° Tuileries. A snug little hotel set in a stylishly renovated seventeenth-century town house. The pretty wood-beamed rooms are decorated in warm colours and rich fabrics. Facilities include free broadband Internet access and flat-screen TVs. Doubles from €196. ❾

Vivienne 40 rue Vivienne, 2e ⓣ01.42.33.13.26, ⓔparis@hotel-vivienne.com; Mº Grands-Boulevards. Ideally located for the Opéra-Garnier and the Grands Boulevards, this is a friendly place, with good-sized, cheery rooms done up with rather nice woods and prints. ❺

Beaubourg and Les Halles

See map, p.122.

Agora 7 rue de la Cossonnerie, 1er ⓣ01.42.33.46.02, ⓦwww.123france.com/hotel-agora; Mº Châtelet-Les Halles. A well-located two-star on a pedestrianized street right in the heart of Les Halles. The thirty cosy en-suite rooms are all different and adorned with antique furnishings and floral wallpaper. ❻

Henri IV 25 place Dauphine, 1er ⓣ01.43.54.44.53; Mº Pont-Neuf/Cité. In an old building on handsome place Dauphine, right in the centre of Paris, this is arguably the best-located hotel in the city. It's also one of the cheapest, and for a reason: most of the rooms are pretty run-down and come with nothing more luxurious than a *cabinet de toilette*, with shared showers on the landing; a handful have been renovated, however, and have en-suite facilities. It's advisable to book well in advance. No credit cards. ❷–❹.

Marais, Île St-Louis & the Bastille

See map, pp.126–127.

Beaumarchais 3 rue Oberkampf, 11e ⓣ01.43.38.16.16, ⓦwww.hotelbeaumarchais.com; M° Filles-du-Calvaire/Oberkampf. A fashionable, gay-friendly hotel with personal service and colourful Fifties-inspired decor; all rooms are en suite with air conditioning, individual safes and cable TV. ❼

Caron de Beaumarchais 12 rue Vieille-du-Temple, 4e ⓣ01.42.72.34.12, ⓦwww.carondebeaumarchais.com; M° Hôtel-de-Ville. Named after the eighteenth-century French playwright Beaumarchais, who lived just up the road, this fine hotel has only nineteen rooms. Everything – down to the original engravings and Louis XVI-style furniture, not to mention the pianoforte in the foyer – evokes the refined tastes of high-society pre-Revolutionary Paris. Rooms overlooking the courtyard are small but cosy, while those on the street are more spacious, some with a balcony ❽–❾.

Grand Hôtel Jeanne d'Arc 3 rue de Jarente, 4e ⓣ01.48.87.62.11, ⓦwww.hoteljeannedarc.com; M° St-Paul. An excellent-value hotel in a Marais town house, just off pretty place du Marché Sainte-Catherine. The rooms are a decent size, with nice individual touches, plus cable TV. It's very popular, so booking well in advance is advised. ❺

Grand Hôtel du Loiret 8 rue des Mauvais Garçons, 4e ⓣ01.48.87.77.00, ⓦwww.hotel-loiret.fr; M° Hôtel-de-Ville. A budget hotel, grand in name only, though it has recently renovated its foyer and installed a lift. The rooms are essentially uneventful, but acceptable for the price; cheaper ones have washbasin only, all have TV and telephone. The two triples on the top floor have distant views of Sacré-Coeur. ❸

De Lutèce 65 rue St-Louis-en-l'Île, 4e ⓣ01.43.26.23.52, ⓦwww.paris-hotel-lutece.com; M° Pont-Marie. Twenty-three tiny but appealing rooms, recently renovated in contemporary style and equipped with sparkling-white bathrooms, are eked out of this old wood-beamed town house situated on the most desirable island in France. ❾

Marais Bastille 36 bd Richard-Lenoir, 11e ⓣ01.48.05.75.00, ⓦwww.paris-hotel-marais-bastille.com; M° Bréguet-Sabin. A pleasant three-star, part of the Best Western chain, located on a fairly quiet road near the Bastille. Rooms are equipped with minibar, TV and Internet point and are attractively furnished in light oak and pastel colours. ❽

De Nevers 53 rue de Malte, 11e ⓣ01.47.00.56.18, ⓦwww.hoteldenevers.com; M° République/Oberkampf. A hospitable one-star with simple but cheerfully decorated rooms – the best are the en-suite doubles at the front; courtyard-facing rooms are dark and poky. ❷

De Nice 42bis rue de Rivoli, 4e ⓣ01.42.78.55.29, ⓕ01.42.78.36.07, ⓦwww.hoteldenice.com; M° Hôtel-de-Ville. A delightful old-world atmosphere pervades this six-storey town house, its pretty rooms hung with old prints and furnished with deep-coloured fabrics and Indian-cotton bedspreads. Double-glazing helps block out the traffic on rue de Rivoli. ❼

Pavillon de la Reine 28 place des Vosges, 3e ⓣ01.40.29.19.19, ⓦwww.pavillon-de-la-reine.com; M° Bastille. A perfect honeymoon or romantic-weekend hotel in a beautiful ivy-covered mansion secreted away off the place des Vosges. It preserves an intimate ambience, with friendly, personable staff. The rooms mostly have a distinctly 1990s "hip hotel" feel, and could probably use another makeover. Doubles from €350. ❾

Du Petit Moulin 29–31 rue du Poitou, 3e ⓣ01.42.74.10.10, ⓦwww.paris-hotel-petitmoulin.com; M° Saint-Sébastien-Froissart/Filles du Calvaire. A stylish boutique hotel, set in an old bakery and designed top to bottom by Christian Lacroix. Each room bears the designer's hallmark flamboyancy and is a fusion of different styles, from elegant Baroque to Sixties kitsch. Doubles from €180. ❾

De Roubaix 6 rue Greneta, 3e ⓣ01.42.72.89.91, ⓦwww.hotel-de-roubaix.com; M° Réaumur-Sébastopol or M° Arts-et-Métiers. An old-fashioned two-star hotel run by a pleasant elderly couple, who don't speak much English. The 53 rooms are small and done out with floral wallpaper and rickety furniture, but they're pretty good value when you consider the location, just five minutes' walk from the Pompidou Centre. Breakfast (€4) – a hunk of crusty bread and a hot drink – is included in the price whether you want it or not. ❹

Quartier Latin

See map, pp.134–135.

Le Central 6 rue Descartes, 5e ⓣ01.46.33.57.93; M° Maubert-Mutualité/Cardinal-Lemoine. Plain but decent backpacker-oriented rooms in a typically Parisian house above a café-restaurant on the Montagne Ste-Geneviève. ❸

Du Commerce 14 rue de la Montagne-Ste-Geneviève, 5e ⓣ01.43.54.89.69, ⓦwww.commerce-paris-hotel.com; M° Maubert-Mutualité. Professionally run budget hotel in the heart of the Quartier Latin, with newly redecorated rooms. Rooms with en-suite showers cost €10 more (❹) than those just with a WC. ❸

Esmeralda 4 rue St-Julien-le-Pauvre, 5e ⓣ01.43.54.19.20, ⓕ01.40.51.00.68; M°

St-Michel/Maubert-Mutualité. Nestling in an ancient house on square Viviani, this ancient hotel has cosy and deeply unmodernized rooms, some with superb views of nearby Notre-Dame. A trio of faintly decrepit singles (€40) come with washbasin only. ❻

Familia 11 rue des Ecoles, 5e ⓣ01.43.54.55.27, ⓦwww.hotel-paris-familia.com; M° Cardinal-Lemoine/Maubert-Mutualité/Jussieu. Friendly, family-run hotel in the heart of the *quartier*. Rooms are small but full of character. Some have views of nearby Notre-Dame; others have their own balcony. The three-star *Minerva* next door has the same owners. ❻

Des Grandes Écoles 75 rue du Cardinal-Lemoine, 5e ⓣ01.43.26.79.23, ⓦwww.hotel-grandes-ecoles.com; M° Cardinal-Lemoine. This welcoming three-star in the heart of the Quartier Latin has an extraordinary setting around a peaceful courtyard garden. Rooms are bright, if rather heavy on the floral wallpaper. ❼

Marignan 13 rue du Sommerard, 5e ⓣ01.43.54.63.81, ⓦwww.hotel-marignan.com; M° Maubert-Mutualité. One of the best bargains in town, with a free breakfast thrown in. Totally sympathetic to the needs of rucksack-toting foreigners, with free laundry and ironing facilities, plus a room to eat your own food in – plates, fridge and microwave provided – and rooms for up to five people. ❹

Médicis 214 rue St-Jacques, 5e ⓣ01.43.54.14.66; RER Luxembourg. Basic, tatty old hotel, but the low prices make it very popular with hard-up backpackers. ❷

Select 1 place de la Sorbonne, 5e ⓣ01.46.34.14.80, ⓦwww.selecthotel.fr; RER Luxembourg/M° Cluny-La Sorbonne. This designer-styled but un-snooty three-star sits right on the *place*. Standard room prices begin at €150, but it's probably worth paying the extra thirty-odd euros for a *supérieure*. ❾

De la Sorbonne 6 rue Victor-Cousin, 5e ⓣ01.43.54.58.08, ⓦwww.hotelsorbonne.com; RER Luxembourg/M° Cluny-La Sorbonne. Housed in an attractive old building close to the Luxembourg gardens, this is a quiet, comfortable and professional hotel. ❻

St-Germain

See map, pp.138–139.

De l'Angleterre 44 rue Jacob, 6e ⓣ01.42.60.34.72, ⓦwww.hotel-dangleterre.com; M° St-Germain-des-Prés. Classy and elegant hotel, in a building that once housed the British Embassy and, later, Ernest Hemingway, although in those days he only paid three francs a night. The luxury rooms (€260) are huge, and many have beautiful original roof beams. Standard rooms start at €185. ❾

Bersoly's St-Germain 28 rue de Lille, 6e ⓣ01.42.60.73.79, ⓦwww.bersolyshotel.com; M° Rue-du-Bac. Small but exquisite rooms, each named after an artist. Impeccable service, and a good location near the shopping areas of St-Germain. ❼

Ferrandi St-Germain 92 rue du Cherche-Midi, 6e ⓣ01.42.22.97.40, ⓔhotel.ferrandi@orange.fr; M° Vaneau/St-Placide. Genteel, independent two-star with a distinctly old-fashioned feel, hidden away in a charming residential corner of St-Germain. Rooms are sunny, homely and fairly large by Parisian standards, but don't expect all mod cons. ❽

Du Globe 15 rue des Quatre-Vents, 6e ⓣ01.43.26.35.50, ⓦwww.hotel-du-globe.fr; M° Odéon. Welcoming hotel in a tall, narrow, seventeenth-century building decked out with four-posters, stone walls, roof beams and the like. ❽

Grand Hôtel des Balcons 3 rue Casimir-Delavigne, 6e ⓣ01.46.34.78.50, ⓦwww.balcons.com; M° Odéon. An attractive and comfortable hotel with a few Art Deco motifs in the modern rooms. Lovely location near the Odéon and Luxembourg gardens. ❼

L'Hôtel 13 rue des Beaux-Arts, 6e ⓣ01.44.41.99.00, ⓦwww.l-hotel.com; M° Mabillon/St-Germain-des-Prés. This extravagant four-star place is a destination in itself, with twenty sumptuously decorated, almost kitsch rooms. Prices start at €280 in high season and soar well above – notably for the room Oscar Wilde died in. ❾

Des Marronniers 21 rue Jacob, 6e ⓣ01.43.25.30.60, ⓦwww.hotel-marronniers.com; M° St-Germain-des-Prés. A romantic hotel, with small rooms swathed in expensive fabrics. The dining room looks out on a courtyard garden. ❽

De Nesle 7 rue de Nesle, 6e ⓣ01.43.54.62.41, ⓦwww.hoteldenesleparis.com; M° St-Michel. Friendly, offbeat hotel with themed rooms decorated with cartoon murals that you'll either love or hate. ❺

Récamier 3bis place St-Sulpice, 6e ⓣ01.43.26.04.89, ⓕ01.46.33.27.73; M° St-Sulpice/St-Germain-des-Prés. Comfortable, if plain and old-fashioned hotel in a fantastic situation on the corner of the square. ❽

Relais Christine 3 rue Christine, 6e ⓣ01.40.51.60.80, ⓦwww.relais-christine.com; M° Odéon. Deeply elegant four-star in a sixteenth-century building set around a deliciously hidden courtyard. Standard doubles cost €355, and you can sometimes find weekend offers for the gorgeous *supérieure* rooms for very little more. ❾

Relais Saint-Sulpice 3 rue Garancière, 6e ⓣ01.46.33.99.00, ⓦmonsite.orange.fr/relaisstsulpice; M° St-Sulpice. Set in an aristocratic town house immediately behind St-Sulpice, this is a discreet and classy three-star with well-furnished rooms. ❾

St-André-des-Arts 66 rue St-André-des-Arts, 6e ⓣ01.43.26.96.16, ⓔhsaintand@orange.fr; M° Odéon/St-Germain-des-Prés. Friendly, family-run hotel in the heart of St-Germain. Rooms are pleasantly decorated and preserve some features of the seventeenth-century building; the best are on the front, with big floor-to-ceiling windows. ❻

De l'Université 22 rue de l'Université, 6e ⓣ01.42.61.09.39, ⓦwww.hoteluniversite.com; M° Rue du Bac. Gorgeously cosy three-star with two-dozen rooms filled with antique details, including beamed ceilings and fireplaces in the larger rooms. Doubles from €165; €200 with a private terrace. ❾

Trocadéro, Eiffel Tower and the Septième

See map, pp.144–145.

Du Champs-de-Mars 7 rue du Champs-de-Mars, 7e ⓣ01.45.51.52.30, ⓦwww.hotel-du-champ-de-mars.com; M° École-Militaire. Spotless, prettily decorated and good-value rooms in a friendly hotel just off the rue Cler market. ❺

Grand Hôtel Lévèque 29 rue Cler, 7e ⓣ01.47.05.49.15, ⓦwww.hotel-leveque.com; M° École-Militaire/La Tour-Maubourg. Located smack in the middle of the posh rue Cler market, this is a large but decent place, run by a friendly family. Book a month ahead for one of the two brighter rooms on the rue Cler. ❻

Du Palais Bourbon 49 rue de Bourgogne, 7e ⓣ01.44.11.30.70, ⓦwww.hotel-palais-bourbon.com; M° Varenne. This handsome old two-star offers spacious and attractively furnished rooms. Family rooms are available, as well as one tiny but inexpensive double (€68) and some well-priced singles. The immediate area is a bit dead in terms of cafés and restaurants, but it's classy and very quiet. ❽

Saint Dominique 62 rue Saint-Dominique, 7e ⓣ01.47.05.51.44, ⓦwww.saintdominique.com; M° Invalides/La Tour-Maubourg. Welcoming, well-priced hotel in a classy quarter close to the Eiffel Tower with prettily wallpapered rooms arranged around a bright courtyard. ❻

De la Tulipe 33 rue Malar, 7e ⓣ01.45.51.67.21, ⓦwww.paris-hotel-tulipe.com; M° Invalides/La Tour-Maubourg. Attractively cottage-like three-star with exposed-stone walls and flagstones, and a small patio. You pay for the third star, and the location. ❾

Montmartre and the Neuvième

See map, p.156.

André Gill 4 rue André Gill, 18e ⓣ01.42.62.48.48, ⓔblounis@aol.com; M° Pigalle/Abbesses. This family-run hotel is set in a handsome and quiet cul-de-sac. Warm fabrics and good soundproofing make up for uninspiring furnishings. ❻

Bonséjour Montmartre 11 rue Burq, 18e ⓣ01.42.54.22.53, ⓦwww.hotel-bonsejour-montmartre.fr; M° Abbesses. Set in a marvellous location on a quiet untouristy street on the slopes of Montmartre, this hotel is run by friendly and conscientious owners, and the rooms, which are clean and spacious, are one of the city's best deals. Ask for a corner room (23, 33, 43 or 53), which have balconies. ❷

Caulaincourt 2 square Caulaincourt, by 63 rue Caulaincourt, 18e ⓣ01.46.06.46.06, ⓦwww.caulaincourt.com. An excellent, friendly budget hotel with well-kept, decent-value rooms – en suite or with shared facilities. From the larger dormitory room of the hostel section (€24 a night), the lucky backpackers get a fine view. ❸

Ermitage 24 rue Lamarck, 18e ⓣ01.42.64.79.22, ⓦwww.ermitagesacrecoeur.fr; M° Anvers. A discreet, welcoming hotel, hidden away behind Sacré-Coeur. Rooms are slightly chintzy in the classic French manner; some have views out across northern Paris. Approach via the funicular to avoid a steep climb. ❻

Langlois 63 rue St-Lazare, 9e ⓣ01.48.74.78.24, ⓦwww.hotel-langlois.com; M° Trinité. Superbly genteel hotel that's hardly changed in half a century, with antique furnishings and some unusually large rooms. ❼

Perfect 39 rue Rodier, 9e ⓣ01.42.81.18.86, ⓕ01.42.85.01.38; M° Anvers. Popular hotel on a lively street lined with restaurants. Simple, clean rooms – some very good value, with shared bathroom facilities – and a warm welcome. ❸

Regyns Montmartre 13 place des Abbesses, 18e ⓣ01.42.54.45.21, ⓦwww.paris-hotels-montmartre.com; M° Abbesses. Friendly, tidy rooms with country-style decor, a number of which give onto the quiet place des Abbesses. The more expensive top-floor rooms have grand views. ❺–❼

Timhotel Montmartre place Émile-Goudeau, 11 rue Ravignan, 18e ⓣ01.42.55.74.79, ⓦwww.timhotel.com; M° Abbesses. Rooms are modern and comfortable, if nondescript, but the location is the point – so book one of the more expensive rooms with a view. ❼

Eastern Paris

Gilden-Magenta 35 rue Yves Toudic, 10e ⓣ01.42.40.17.72, ⓦwww.multi-micro.com/hotel.gilden.magenta; M° République/Jacques-Bonsergent. Friendly hotel, with fresh, colourful decor; rooms 61 and 62, up in the attic, are the best and have views of the Canal St-Martin. Breakfast is served in a pleasant patio area. ❺

Jarry 6 rue de Jarry, 10e ⓣ01.47.70.70.38 ⓕ01.42.46.34.45; M° Gare-de-l'Est/Château-d'Eau. Simple, low-budget hotel in a lively immigrant quarter. Distinctly fresher than the cheap dives on the same street. ❷

Mondia 22 rue du Grand Prieuré, 10e ⓣ01.47.00.93.44, ⓦwww.hotel-mondia.com; M° République/Oberkampf. Pastel colours and floral prints hold sway in the simply furnished rooms of this budget hotel; the two attic hideaways (nos. 602 and 603) have a certain charm. For stays of three nights or more in quieter periods you'll get a ten-percent reduction on presentation of your Rough Guide. ❹

Nouvel Hôtel 24 av du Bel Air, 12e ⓣ01.43.43.01.81, ⓦwww.nouvel-hotel-paris.com. M° Nation. A quiet, family-run hotel, with a little garden and patio. The rooms, though tiny, are immaculate and prettily decorated in pastels and white-painted furniture; no. 9, opening directly onto the garden, is the one to go for. ❺

Port-Royal 8 bd Port-Royal, 5e ⓣ01.43.31.70.06, ⓦwww.hotelportroyal.fr; M° Gobelins. The rooms at this superb budget address are immaculately clean and attractive, though towards the southern edge of the quarter. Fifteen inexpensive rooms (around €55) are available with shared bathroom facilities, though showers cost €2.50. ❺

De la Porte Dorée 273 av Daumesnil, 12e ⓣ01.43.07.56.97.04, ⓦwww.paris-hotels-paris.com; M° Porte-Dorée. Traditional features such as ceiling mouldings, fireplaces and the elegant main staircase have been retained in this welcoming two-star and many of the furnishings are antique. The Bastille is seven mintues away by métro or a pleasant twenty-minute walk along the Promenade Plantée. ❹

Tamaris 14 rue des Maraîchers, 20e ⓣ01.43.72.85.48, ⓦwww.hotel-tamaris.fr; M° Porte-de-Vincennes. An old-fashioned, simply furnished, but clean and quiet hotel, run by nice people. The neighbourhood's a bit dull, but it's only four métro stops from the Bastille and close to the terminus of #26 bus route from Gare du Nord. ❸

Southern Paris

Celtic 15 rue d'Odessa, 14e ⓣ01.43.20.93.53, ⓕ01.43.20.66.07; M° Montparnasse-Bienvenüe/Edgar-Quinet. A garish paint job doesn't quite cover the tattier corners, but there's lots of old-fashioned one-star charm, with fireplaces and other period details in many rooms, and it's very close to Montparnasse. ❹

Istria 29 rue Campagne-Première, 14e ⓣ01.43.20.91.82, ⓔhotel.istria@orange.fr; M° Raspail. Smartly decorated and very comfortable hotel on a quiet side street near the cafés of Montparnasse. Comes with all mod cons and legendary artistic associations to boot – Duchamp, Man Ray, Aragon, Josephine Baker and Rilke all stayed here. ❻

De la Loire 39bis rue du Moulin Vert, 14e ⓣ01.45.40.89.07, ⓔhoteldelaloire@orange.fr; M° Pernety/Alésia. Behind the pretty blue shutters lies a delightful family hotel with a garden and a genuinely homely feel. Rooms all have charming personal touches and spotless bathrooms. ❸

Printemps 31 rue du Commerce, 15e ⓣ01.45.79.83.36, ⓔhotel.printemps.15e@yahoo.fr; M° La Motte-Picquet–Grenelle/Émile-Zola. Cheap furnishings and ageing decor don't stop this being a good backpacker choice for its neighbourhood location, welcome and low prices. ❷

Résidence Les Gobelins 9 rue des Gobelins, 13e ⓣ01.47.07.26.90, ⓦwww.hotelgobelins.com; M° Les Gobelins. This quiet and delightfully genteel establishment is well known, so book some time in advance. ❺

Tolbiac 122 rue de Tolbiac, 13e ⓣ01.44.24.25.54, ⓦwww.hotel-tolbiac.com; M° Tolbiac. Situated on a noisy junction, but all rooms are clean and decently furnished, and very inexpensive, especially those with shared showers. In July and Aug you can rent small studios by the week. ❷

Le Vert-Galant 41 rue Croulebarbe, 13e ⓣ01.44.08.83.50, ⓕ01.44.08.83.69; M° Les Gobelins. Set on a quiet, green square, with a large garden behind and the *Auberge Etchegorry* below (see p.177), this could be a family-run provincial hotel. Rooms are modern but pleasantly airy; the bigger ones give onto the garden and have kitchenettes. ❻

Des Voyageurs 22 rue Boulard, 14e ⓣ01.43.21.08. 02, ⓔhotel.des.voyageurs2@orange.fr; M° Denfert-Rochereau. A good-value Montparnasse establishment with an original, warm spirit. Rooms are comfortable and modern, with air conditioning and free Internet access. ❸

Northern Paris

Eldorado 18 rue des Dames, 17e ⓣ01.45.22.35.21, ⓦwww.eldoradohotel.fr; M° Rome/Place-de-Clichy. Idiosyncratic and charming hotel with bright colour schemes and an attractive annexe at the back of the courtyard garden. A few simple shared-bath rooms are also available. ❹

Savoy 21 rue des Dames, 17ᵉ ⓣ01.42.93.13.47; M° Place-de-Clichy/Rome. Basic but acceptable Paris cheapie. The reception is a bit musty but the rooms are clean and quite large, and the bathrooms recently refurbished. Some rooms have private showers (❷). ❶

Style Hôtel 8 rue Ganneron, 17ᵉ ⓣ01.45.22.37.59, ⓕ01.45.22.81.03; M° Place-de-Clichy. Wooden floors, marble fireplaces, a secluded internal courtyard, and nice people. Great value, especially the rooms with shared bathrooms (€35). ❸

Hostels, student accommodation and campsites

Paris is well supplied with **hostel** accommodation. You can book in advance for most hostels. The three main hostel groups, charging around €23 for a dorm bed, are the **Fédération Unie des Auberges de Jeunesse** (FUAJ; ⓦwww.fuaj.fr), for which you need Hostelling International (HI) membership (available on the spot, no age limit), and **UCRIF** (Union des Centres de Rencontres Internationaux de France; ⓦwww.ucrif.asso.fr). We've detailed only the most central of the UCRIF hostels, but a full list is available on their website, or you can contact their main office at 27 rue de Turbigo, 2ᵉ (Mon–Fri 10am–6pm; ⓣ01.40.26.57.64; M° Étienne-Marcel). A smaller group is the **MIJE** (Maison Internationale de la Jeunesse et des Étudiants; ⓦwww.mije.com), which runs three hostels in historic buildings in the Marais district, with dorm beds from €28. A handful of privately run hostels also exist, most of which cost around €15–20, depending on season. Except where indicated below, there is no effective age limit.

Single and double rooms, where available, generally cost five or ten euros extra. Most hostels impose a stay limit, which can be negotiable, depending on the season, and bear in mind, too, that some places have a curfew – usually around 11pm – though you may be given a key or entry code.

Student accommodation is let out during the summer vacation. Rooms are spartan, part of large modern university complexes, often complete with self-service kitchen facilities and shared bathrooms. Space tends to fill up quickly with international students, school groups and young travellers, so it's best to make plans well in advance. Expect to pay €15–30 per night for a room. The organization to contact for information and reservations is CROUS, Académie de Paris, 39 av Georges-Bernanos, 5ᵉ (Mon–Fri 9.15am–4.30pm; ⓣ01.40.51.55.55, ⓦwww.crous-paris.fr; M° Port-Royal).

The cheapest accommodation option of all is camping. There are three **campsites** on the outskirts of Paris, which, although pleasant enough, are a bit of a pain to get to on public transport.

Hostels

D'Artagnan 80 rue Vitruve, 20ᵉ ⓣ01.40.32.34.56; M° Porte-de-Bagnolet. Colourful, funky, modern HI hostel, with a fun atmosphere and lots of facilities including a small cinema, a restaurant and bar, and a local swimming pool nearby. It's located on the eastern edge of the city near Charonne, which has some good bars. You can reserve online at ⓦwww.fuaj.org. Beds cost €21.50 a night.

Auberge Internationale des Jeunes 10 rue Trousseau, 11ᵉ ⓣ01.47.00.62.00, ⓦwww.aijparis.com; M° Bastille/Ledru-Rollin; see map, pp.126-127. Despite the official-sounding name, this is a laid-back (though very noisy) independent hostel for under-25s in a great location five minutes' walk from the Bastille. It's clean and professionally run with 24hr reception, generous breakfast (included in the price) and free luggage storage. Rooms for 2, 3 and 4. €14 March–June, Sept & Oct €15, July & Aug €17, €13 Nov–Feb.

VJ Paris/Louvre 20 rue Jean-Jacques-Rousseau, 1ᵉʳ ⓣ01.53.00.90.90, ⓦwww.bvjhotel.com; M° Louvre/Châtelet-Les Halles; see map, pp.110–111. Clean, modern and efficiently run independent hostel for 18- to 35-year-olds. Bookings should be made by phone at least fifteen days prior to your stay. Accommodation ranges from single rooms to dorms sleeping eight. From €25 per person, including breakfast.

BVJ Paris Quartier Latin 44 rue des Bernardins, 5e ⓣ01.43.29.34.80, ⓦwww.bvjhotel.com; Mº Maubert-Mutualité; see map, pp.134–135. Typically institutional UCRIF hostel, but spick and span and in a good location. Dorm beds (€26), plus single or double rooms (€35 and €28 per person, respectively).

Le Fauconnier 11 rue du Fauconnier, 4e ⓣ01.42.74.23.45, ⓕ01.40.27.81.64; Mº St-Paul/Pont-Marie; see map, pp.126–127. A MIJE hostel in a superbly renovated seventeenth-century building with a courtyard. Dorms (€28 per person) sleep four to eight, and there are some single (€45) and double rooms (€33) with en-suite showers. Breakfast is included.

Le Fourcy 6 rue de Fourcy, 4e ⓣ01.42.74.23.45; Mº St-Paul; see map, pp.126–127. Another MIJE hostel (same prices as *Le Fauconnier*, above) housed in a beautiful mansion. This one has a small garden and an inexpensive restaurant. Doubles and triples are available as well as dorms.

Jules Ferry 8 bd Jules-Ferry, 11e ⓣ01.43.57.55.60, ⓕ01.43.14.82.09; Mº République. A fairly central HI hostel, in a lively area at the foot of the Belleville hill. You can't reserve in advance, but if you show up early in the morning you should get a place; if they're full they will help you find a bed elsewhere. Dorm beds cost €20.50, including breakfast.

Maubuisson 12 rue des Barres, 4e ⓣ01.42.74.23.45; Mº Pont-Marie/Hôtel-de-Ville; see map, pp.126–127. A MIJE hostel in a medieval timbered mansion on a quiet street. Accommodation is in dorms only, sleeping four (€28 per person). Breakfast is included.

Three Ducks Hostel 6 place Étienne-Pernet, 15e ⓣ01.48.42.04.05, ⓦwww.3ducks.fr; Mº Commerce/Félix-Faure. A private youth hostel with kitchen and Internet facilities, a cheap bar and no age limit. In high season, beds cost €23 in dorm rooms (four to ten people), and double rooms cost €26; there are discounts in winter. Book ahead between May and Oct. Lockout noon–4pm, curfew at 2am.

Le Village Hostel 20 rue d'Orsel, 18e ⓣ01.42.64.22.02, ⓦwww.villagehostel.fr; Mº Anvers. Attractive, brand-new hostel in a handsome old building, with good facilities such as phones in the rooms. There's a view of the Sacré-Coeur from the terrace. Dorms cost €23, twins €27 and triples €25 per person, including breakfast. Small discounts in winter.

Woodstock Hostel 48 rue Rodier, 9e ⓣ01.48.78.87.76, ⓦwww.woodstock.fr; Mº Anvers/St-Georges. Another reliable hostel in the *Three Ducks* stable, with its own bar, set in a great location on a pretty street not far from Montmartre. Dorm beds €18–21, twin rooms €21–24 per person. Book ahead.

Young and Happy Hostel 80 rue Mouffetard, 5e ⓣ01.47.07.47.07, ⓦwww.youngandhappy.fr; Mº Monge/Censier-Daubenton; see map, pp.134–135. Noisy, basic and studenty independent hostel in a lively location. Dorms, with shower, sleep four (€21–23 per person), and there are a few doubles (€23–26 per person). Curfew at 2am.

Campsites

Camping du Bois de Boulogne allée du Bord-de-l'Eau, 16e ⓣ01.45.24.30.00, ⓦwww.abccamping.com/boulogne.htm; Mº Porte-Maillot then bus #244 to Moulins Camping (bus runs 6am–9pm). Much the most central campsite, with space for 436 tents, next to the River Seine in the Bois de Boulogne, and usually booked up in summer. The ground is pebbly, but the site is well equipped and has a useful information office. Prices start at €11 for a tent with two people; there are also bungalows for four to six people, starting at €49 per night. An extra shuttle bus runs every morning from April to October between the campsite and Mº Porte-Maillot.

Camping la Colline rte de Lagny, Torcy ⓣ01.60.05.42.32, ⓦwww.camping-de-la-colline.com; RER line A4 to Torcy, then phone from the station and they will come and collect you, or take bus #421 to stop Le Clos. Pleasant wooded lakeside site to the east of the city near Disneyland (minibus shuttle to Disneyland costs €12.50 return), offering rental of anything from luxury tents to bungalows; erecting your own tent costs €25 per night for two people.

The City

Rather than slavishly following the boundaries of the official twenty arrondissements (see map pp.86–87 and p.92), this book divides Paris into several quarters, each with their own distinct identities. The account begins with the **Île de la Cité**, the ancient heart of Paris and home of the cathedral of **Notre-Dame**. Headings north onto the **Right Bank**, it takes in the Arc de Triomphe and follows the Voie Triomphale through the glamorous **Champs-Élysées** area to the Louvre palace. Immediately north is the expensive **Opéra district**, home of the shopping arcades of the *passages*, ritzy Place Vendôme and the tranquil gardens of the Palais Royal. East, the bustle and tacky shops of **Les Halles** and **Beaubourg** give way to the aristocratic and fashionable **Marais** and still-trendier **Bastille** quarters. Detouring via the Île St-Louis, Paris's second island, the chapter crosses the Seine onto the (southern) **Left Bank**, moving west from the studenty **Quartier Latin** through elegant and international **St-Germain** and into the aristocratic, museum-rich area around the **Eiffel Tower**, taking in the **Trocadéro** quarter, immediately across the river. The account then explores outlying areas of the city, visiting first **Montparnasse** and southern Paris, then heading out west to the wealthy **Beaux Quartiers**, the green space of the Bois de Boulogne and the outlying business district of La Défense. Lastly, it moves up to **Montmartre** and the northern arrondissements before finishing up in the working-class eastern end of the city, which incorporates the vast Père-Lachaise cemetery.

Île de la Cité

The **Île de la Cité** (see maps pp.126–127 and pp.134–135) is where Paris began. The earliest settlements were built here, followed by the small Gallic town of Lutetia, overrun by Julius Caesar's troops in 52 BC. A natural defensive site commanding a major east–west river trade route, it was an obvious candidate for a bright future. The Romans garrisoned it and laid out one of their standard military town plans. While they never attached any great political importance to the settlement, they endowed it with an administrative centre that became the stronghold of the Merovingian kings in 508, then of the counts of Paris who in 987 became kings of France.

The Frankish kings built themselves a splendid palace at the western tip of the island, of which the **Sainte-Chapelle** and **Conciergerie** survive today. At the other end of the island, they erected the great cathedral of **Notre-Dame**. By the early thirteenth century this tiny island had become the bustling heart of the capital, accommodating twelve parishes, not to mention numerous chapels and convents. It's hard to imagine this today: virtually the whole medieval city was erased by heavy-handed nineteenth-century demolition and much of it replaced by four vast edifices largely given over to housing the law. The warren of narrow streets around the cathedral was swept away and replaced with a huge, rather soulless square, known as the Parvis de Notre-Dame, but it does at least afford uncluttered views of the cathedral.

Pont-Neuf and the quais, Sainte-Chapelle and the Conciergerie

One of the most popular approaches to the island is via the graceful, twelve-arched **Pont-Neuf**, which despite its name is Paris's oldest surviving bridge, built in 1607 by Henri IV. It takes its name ("new") from the fact that it was the first in the city to be built of stone. Henri is commemorated with an equestrian statue halfway across, and also lends his nickname to the **square du Vert-Galant**, enclosed within the triangular stern of the island and reached via steps leading down behind the statue. "Vert-Galant", meaning a "green" or "lusty gentleman", is a reference to Henri's legendary amorous exploits, and he would no doubt have approved of this tranquil, tree-lined garden, a popular haunt of lovers.

Back on Pont-Neuf, opposite the square du Vert-Galant, red-bricked seventeenth-century houses flank the entrance to **place Dauphine**, one of the city's most appealing squares. Traffic noise recedes in favour of the gentle tap of *boules* being played in the shade of the chestnuts. At the further end looms the huge facade of the **Palais de Justice**, which swallowed up the palace that was home to the French kings until Étienne Marcel's bloody revolt in 1358 frightened them off to the greater security of the Louvre.

A survivor of the old palace complex is the magnificent **Sainte-Chapelle** (daily: March–Oct 9.30am–6pm; Nov–Feb 9am–5pm; €6.50, combined admission to the Conciergerie €9.50; M° Cité), accessed from the boulevard du Palais. It was built by Louis IX between 1242 and 1248 to house a collection of holy relics, including Christ's crown of thorns and a fragment of the True Cross, bought at extortionate rates from the bankrupt empire of Byzantium. Though much restored, the chapel remains one of the finest achievements of French High Gothic. Its most radical feature is its seeming fragility – created by reducing the structural masonry to a minimum to make way for a huge expanse of exquisite stained glass. The impression inside is of being enclosed within the wings of a myriad brilliant butterflies.

Further along boulevard du Palais is the entrance to the **Conciergerie** (same hours as Sainte-Chapelle; €6.50, combined ticket with Ste-Chapelle €9.50; M° Cité), Paris's oldest prison, where Marie-Antoinette and, in their turn, the leading figures of the Revolution were incarcerated before execution. Inside are several splendidly vaulted late-Gothic halls, vestiges of the old Capetian kings' palace. The most impressive is the Salle des Gens d'armes, originally the canteen and recreation room of the royal household staff. The far end, separated off by an iron grille, was reserved during the French Revolution for prisoners who couldn't afford to bribe a guard for their own cell and were known as the *pailleux* because all they had to sleep on was hay (*paille*). Beyond, a number of rooms and prisoners' cells have been reconstructed to show what they might have been like at the time of the Revolution. Among them is Marie-Antoinette's cell and the innocent-sounding *salle de toilette*, the room where the condemned had their hair cropped and shirt collars ripped in preparation for the guillotine.

Back outside, on the corner of boulevard du Palais, you'll see the **Tour de l'Horloge**, built around 1350, and so called because it displayed Paris's first public clock. The original was replaced in 1585 and survives to this day – an ornate affair flanked with classical figures representing Law and Justice. Heading east from here, along the north side of the island, you come to **place Lépine**, named after the police boss who gave Paris's cops their white truncheons and whistles. The police headquarters, better known as the Quai des Orfèvres to readers of Georges Simenon's Maigret novels, stands on one side of the square, while the other side is enlivened by an exuberant **flower market**, held daily and augmented by a chirruping bird market on Sundays.

Cathédrale de Notre-Dame

One of the masterpieces of the Gothic age, the **Cathédrale de Notre-Dame** (daily 7.45am–6.45pm; free; M° St-Michel/Cité) rears up from the Île de la Cité's southeast corner like a ship moored by huge flying buttresses. It was among the first of the great Gothic cathedrals built in northern France and one of the most ambitious, its nave reaching an uprecedented 33m.

Built on the site of the old Merovingian cathedral of Saint-Étienne, Notre-Dame was begun in 1160 under the auspices of Bishop de Sully and completed around 1345. In the seventeenth and eighteenth centuries it fell into decline, suffering its worst depredations during the French Revolution when the frieze of Old Testament kings on the facade was damaged by enthusiasts who mistook them for the kings of France. It was only in the 1820s that the cathedral was at last given a much-needed restoration, a task entrusted to the great architect-restorer, Viollet-le-Duc, who carried out a thorough – some would say too thorough – renovation, including remaking most of the statuary on the facade (the originals can be seen in the Musée National du Moyen-Âge, see p.133) – and adding the steeple and baleful-looking gargoyles, which you can see close up if you brave the ascent of the **towers** (daily: April–Sept 9.30am–7.30pm, till 11pm Sat & Sun June–Aug; Oct–March 10am–5.30pm; €7.50). Queues for the towers often start before they open, so it pays to get here early or to come in the evening, when it's often quieter. The same goes for visiting the cathedral itself.

The cathedral's **facade** is one of its most impressive exterior features; the Romanesque influence is still visible, not least in its solid H-shape, but the overriding impression is one of lightness and grace, created in part by the delicate filigree work of the central rose window and gallery above. Of the facade's magnificent **carvings**, the oldest, dating from the twelfth century, are those in the right portal, depicting the Virgin Enthroned, elegantly executed and displaying all the majesty of a royal procession.

The interior

Inside Notre-Dame, the immediately striking feature is the dramatic contrast between the darkness of the nave and the light falling on the first great clustered pillars of the choir. It's the end walls of the transepts that admit all this light: they are nearly two-thirds glass, including two magnificent rose windows coloured in imperial purple. These, the vaulting and the soaring columns, are all definite Gothic elements, though there remains a strong sense of Romanesque in the stout round pillars of the nave. Free guided tours (1hr–1hr 30min) take place in English on Wednesdays and Thursdays at 2pm and on Saturdays at 2.30pm; the gathering point is the welcome desk near the entrance. There are free organ concerts every Sunday, usually at 4.30pm, plus four Masses on Sunday morning and one at 6.30pm.

The kilomètre zéro and crypte archéologique

On the pavement by the west door of the cathedral is a spot known as **kilomètre zéro**, the symbolic heart of France, from which all main road distances in the country are calculated. At the far end of the *place* is the entrance to the atmospheric **crypte archéologique** (Tues–Sun 10am–6pm; €3.30), a large excavated area under the square revealing the remains of the original cathedral, as well as remnants of the streets and houses that once clustered around Notre-Dame: most are medieval, but some date as far back as Gallo-Roman times and include parts of a Roman hypocaust (heating system).

Le Mémorial de la Déportation

At the eastern tip of the island is the symbolic tomb of the 200,000 French who died in Nazi concentration camps during World War II – Resistance fighters, Jews and forced labourers among them. The stark and moving **Mémorial de la Déportation** (daily 10am–noon & 2–7pm, closes 5pm in winter; free) is scarcely visible above ground; stairs hardly shoulder-wide descend into a space like a prison yard and then into the crypt, off which is a long, narrow, stifling corridor, its wall covered in thousands of points of light representing the dead. Floor and ceiling are black, and it ends in a raw hole, with a single naked bulb hanging in the middle. Above the exit are the words "Pardonne, n'oublie pas" ("Forgive, do not forget").

The Champs-Élysées and around

Synonymous with Parisian glitz and glamour, the **Champs-Élysées** cuts through one of the city's most exclusive districts, studded with luxury hotels and top fashion boutiques. The avenue forms part of a grand, nine-kilometre axis that extends from the Louvre, at the heart of the city, to the Grande Arche de la Défense, in the west. Often referred to as the Voie Triomphale, or Triumphal Way, it offers impressive vistas all along its length and incorporates some of the city's most famous landmarks – the **Tuileries** gardens, **place de**

la Concorde, the **Champs-Élysées** avenue and the **Arc de Triomphe**. The whole ensemble is so regular and geometrical it looks as though it was laid out by a single town planner rather than by successive kings, emperors and presidents, all keen to add their stamp and promote French power and prestige.

The Arc de Triomphe

The best view of the Voie Triomphale is from the top of the **Arc de Triomphe** (daily: April–Sept 10am–11pm; Oct–March 10am–10.30pm; €8; M° Charles-de-Gaulle-Étoile), towering above the traffic in the middle of **place Charles-de-Gaulle**, better known as l'Étoile ("star") on account of the twelve avenues radiating out from it. Access is via underground stairs from the north corner of the Champs-Élysées. The arch was started by Napoleon as a homage to the armies of France and himself, but it wasn't actually finished until 1836 by Louis-Philippe, who dedicated it to the French army in general. The names of 660 generals and numerous French battles are engraved on the inside of the

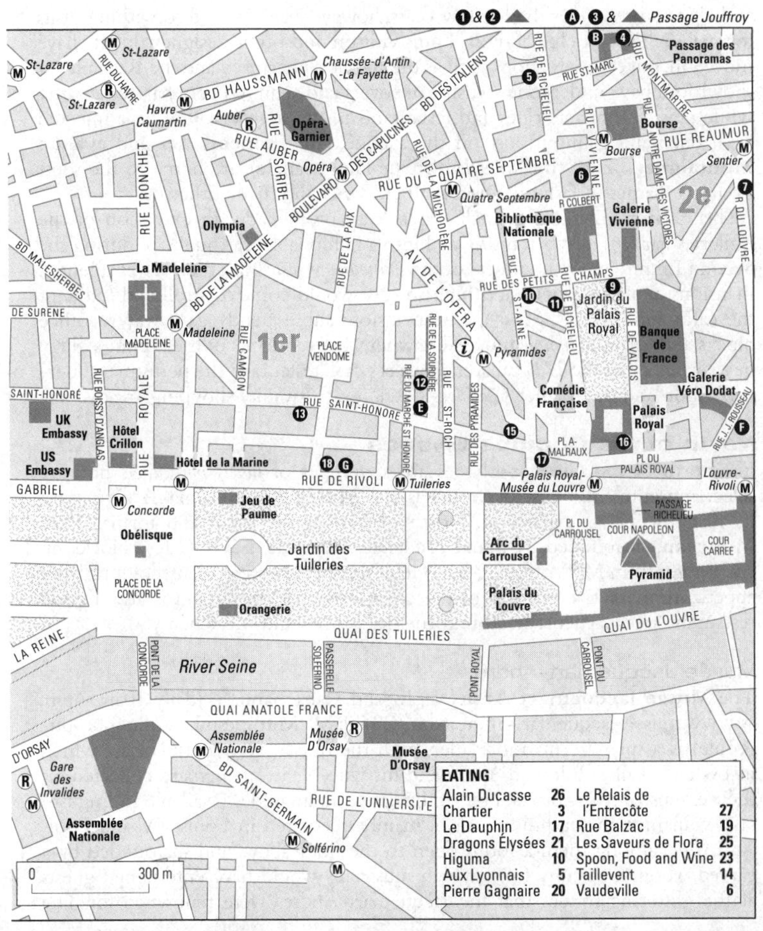

arch, and reliefs adorn the exterior: the best is François Rude's extraordinarily dramatic *Marseillaise*, in which an Amazon-type figure personifying the Revolution charges forward with a sword, her face contorted in a fierce rallying cry. A quiet reminder of the less glorious side of war is the **tomb of the unknown soldier** placed beneath the arch and marked by an eternal flame that is stoked up every evening at 6.30pm by war veterans. If you're up for climbing the 280 steps to the top you'll be amply rewarded by the panoramic views; the best time to come is towards dusk on a sunny day, when the marble of the Grande Arche de la Défense sparkles in the setting sun and the Louvre is bathed in warm light.

The Champs-Élysées

The celebrated **avenue des Champs-Élysées**, a popular rallying point at times of national crisis and the scene of big military parades on Bastille Day, sweeps down from the Arc de Triomphe towards the place de la Concorde. Seen from a distance it's an impressive sight, but close up can be a little disappointing, with its constant stream of traffic and fast-food outlets, airline offices and chain stores. Over the last few years, however, it's regained something of its former cachet as a chic address: Louis Vuitton and other designer outlets have moved in, once dowdy shops such as the Publicis pharmacy and the Renault car showroom have undergone stylish makeovers and acquired cool bar-restaurants, while new, fashionable cafés and restaurants in the streets around have injected fresh buzz and glamour. Just off the avenue, **rue Francois 1er** and **avenue Montaigne**, part of the "*triangle d'or*" (golden triangle), are home to the most exclusive names in fashion: Dior, Prada, Chanel and many others.

The Champs-Élysées began life as a leafy promenade, an extension of the Tuileries gardens. It was transformed into a fashionable thoroughfare during the Second Empire when members of the *haute bourgeoisie* built themselves splendid mansions along its length and high society would come to stroll and frequent the cafés and theatres. Most of the mansions subsequently gave way to office blocks and the *beau monde* moved elsewhere, but remnants of the avenue's glitzy heyday live on at the *Lido* cabaret, *Fouquet's* café-restaurant, the perfumier Guerlain's shop and the former *Claridges* hotel, now a swanky shopping arcade.

North of the Champs-Élysées

Just north of the Champs-Élysées are a number of *hôtels particuliers* housing select museums, the best of which is the **Musée Jacquemart-André**, with its magnificent art collection. North of here is the small and formal **Parc Monceau**, surrounded by grand residences. **Rue de Lévis** (a few blocks up rue Berger from M° Monceau) has one of the city's most strident, colourful and appetizing markets every day of the week except Monday, and is also a good restaurant area, particularly around rue des Dames and rue Cheroy.

Musée Jacquemart-André

The **Musée Jacquemart-André** at 158 bd Haussmann, 8e (daily 10am–6pm; Ⓦwww.musee-jacquemart-andre.com; €9.50; M° Miromesnil/St-Philippe-du-Roule) is a splendid mansion laden with the outstanding works of art which its owners, banker Édouard André and his wife Nélie Jacquemart, collected on their extensive trips abroad. Free, informative audioguides (available in English) take you through sumptuous *salons*, mainly decorated in Louis XV and Louis XVI style, among them a room open to the floor above and surrounded by a carved wooden balcony from which musicians would have entertained guests at the glittering soirees that the Jacquemart-Andrés were renowned for. The library is hung with a number of Van Dycks and three Rembrandts, though the pride of the couple's collection was their early Italian Renaissance paintings, on the upper floor. At the top of the stairs is a huge, animated fresco by Tiepolo depicting the French king Henri III being received by Frederigo Contarini in Venice. Other highlights are Uccello's *St George and the Dragon*, a haunting *Virgin and Child* by Mantegna, and another by Botticelli. An excellent way to finish off a visit is a reviving halt at the museum's **salon de thé**, with its lavish interior and ceiling frescoes by Tiepolo.

South of the Rond-Point des Champs-Élysées

The lower stretch of the Champs-Élysées, between the Rond-Point des Champs-Élysées and place de la Concorde, is bordered by chestnut trees and municipal flower beds and is the most pleasant part of the avenue for a stroll. The gigantic Neoclassical building with exuberant statuary rising above the greenery to the south is the **Grand Palais**, created with its neighbour, the Petit Palais, for the 1900 Exposition Universelle. The glass of the Grand Palais' dome – some 15,000 square metres – has recently been restored and the ironwork spruced up with a new coat of sea-green paint. Renovation work on the exterior will be fully complete in 2007; meanwhile the building's main exhibition hall, known as the *grand nef*, is gradually resuming its role as a cultural centre, hosting music festivals and art exhibitions as well as trade fairs and fashion shows. In the Grand Palais' north wing is the **Galeries nationales** (Ⓦwww.rmn.fr/galeriesnationalesdugrandpalais), the city's prime venue for blockbuster art exhibitions, while occupying the west wing is the **Palais de la Découverte**, avenue Franklin-D.-Roosevelt, 8ᵉ (Tues–Sat 9.30am–6pm, Sun & hols 10am–7pm; €6.50, combined ticket with planetarium €10; Ⓦwww.palais-decouverte.fr; M° Champs-Élysées–Clemenceau), a science museum with fun interactive exhibits and a planetarium.

The **Petit Palais**, facing the Grand Palais on avenue Winston-Churchill, is hardly "petit" but certainly palatial, with beautiful spiral wrought-iron staircases and a grand gallery on the lines of Versailles' Hall of Mirrors. A major renovation, completed in 2005, has returned the building to its original splendour, allowing more natural light to flood in and illuminate the restored stained-glass windows and ceiling frescoes. The revamp has freed up more space for the museum's extensive holdings of paintings, sculpture and decorative artworks, ranging from the ancient Greek and Roman period up to the early twentieth century. At first sight it looks like it's mopped up the leftovers after the other city's galleries have taken their pick, but there are some real gems here, such as Monet's *Sunset at Lavacourt* and Courbet's *Young Ladies on the Bank of the Seine*. There's also fantasy jewellery of the Art Nouveau period, Russian icons, effete eighteenth-century furniture and porcelain and a fine collection of seventeenth-century Dutch landscape painting. A newly installed café overlooks the interior garden.

On the other side of the avenue, to the north of place Clemenceau, combat police guard the high walls round the presidential **Palais de l'Élysée** and the line of ministries and embassies ending with the US in prime position on the corner of place de la Concorde. On Thursdays and at weekends you can see more national branding in the **postage-stamp market** at the corner of avenues Gabriel and Marigny.

Place de la Concorde and the Tuileries

At the lower end of the Champs is the vast **place de la Concorde**, where crazed traffic makes crossing over to the middle a death-defying task. As it

△ Jardin des Tuileries

happens, some 1300 people did die here between 1793 and 1795, beneath the Revolutionary guillotine – Louis XVI, Marie-Antoinette, Danton and Robespierre among them. The centrepiece of the square is a stunning gold-tipped **obelisk** from the temple of Luxor, offered as a favour-currying gesture by the viceroy of Egypt in 1829. From here there are sweeping vistas in all directions; the Champs–Élysées looks particularly impressive, and you can admire the alignment of the Assemblée Nationale in the south with the church of the Madeleine – sporting an identical Neoclassical facade – to the north (see p.120).

The symmetry continues beyond place de la Concorde in the formal layout of the **Jardin des Tuileries**, the formal French garden *par excellence*. It dates back to the 1570s, when Catherine de Médicis had the site cleared of the medieval warren of tilemakers (*tuileries*) to make way for a palace and grounds. One hundred years later, Louis XIV commissioned renowned landscape artist Le Nôtre to redesign them and the results are largely what you see today: straight avenues, formal flowerbeds and splendid vistas. Shady tree-lined paths flank the grand central alley, and ornamental ponds frame both ends. The much-sought-after chairs strewn around the ponds are a good spot from which to admire the landscaped surroundings and contemplate the superb statues executed by the likes of Coustou and Coysevox, many of them now replaced by copies, the originals transferred to the Louvre.

The two buildings flanking the garden at the Concorde end are the Orangerie, by the river, and the **Jeu de Paume** (Tues noon–9pm, Wed–Fri noon–7pm, Sat & Sun 10am–7pm; Ⓦwww.jeudepaume.org; €6; M° Concorde), by rue de Rivoli, once a royal tennis court. The Centre National de la Photographie now resides here and mounts major photographic exhibitions.

The **Orangerie** (daily except Tues 12.30–7pm, till 9pm Fri; groups only 9am–12.30pm; €6.50; Ⓦwww.musee-orangerie.fr), a private art collection including eight of Monet's giant water-lily paintings, reopened in 2006 after six years of renovations designed to bring Monet's masterpieces "back into the light". In the 1960s a concrete ceiling had been added to accommodate a new storey; this has now been removed and once again the natural light illumines the water-lilies – exactly how Monet wished them to be seen. These vast, mesmerizing canvases were executed in the last years of the artist's life, a period when he almost obsessively painted the pond in his garden at Giverny, attempting to capture the fleeting light and changing colours. On the lower floor of the museum is a fine collection of paintings by Monet's contemporaries Renoir, Matisse, Cézanne, Utrillo and Modigliani.

The Louvre

The palace of the **Louvre** cuts a grand Classical swathe right through the centre of the city, its stately ranks of carved pilasters, arches and pediments stretching west along the right bank of the Seine from the Île de la Cité towards the Voie Triomphale. Inside, the giant collection of the Louvre museum acts as nothing less than the gold standard of France's artistic tradition.

Before becoming a museum during the French Revolution, the Louvre was for centuries the home of the French court, and almost every French ruler with a taste for grandeur has built on the site, right down to President Mitterrand. The original fortress was begun by Philippe-Auguste in 1200 to store his scrolls, jewels and swords, while he himself lived on the Île de la Cité. Charles V was the first French king to make the castle his residence, but not until François I in the mid-sixteenth century were the beginnings of the palace laid and the fortress demolished. François' daughter-in-law, Catherine de Médicis, added the **Palais des Tuileries** some 500m to the west, and fifty years later Henri IV joined the two together with a long extension along the bank of the Seine. Louis XIV completed the square plan of the Cour Carré, but it wasn't until Napoléon III completed the Richelieu wing and remodelled all the facades of the Cour Napoléon in the 1860s that the Louvre and Tuileries palaces were finally united. It didn't last long – the Tuileries was razed during the Paris Commune of 1871 and the Louvre now opens out onto the lovely gardens (see opposite) that bear its name.

For all its many transformations, the palace remained a surprisingly harmonious building, with a grandeur, symmetry and Frenchness entirely suited to this most historic of Parisian edifices. Then came the controversial **Pyramide**, designed by I.M. Pei and opened in 1989, erupting from the centre of the Cour Napoléon like a visitor from another architectural planet.

As part of the same late 1980s makeover, Mitterrand managed to persuade the Finance Ministry to move out of the northern Richelieu wing, which then had its two main courtyards dramatically roofed over in glass. A public passageway, the **passage Richelieu**, cuts through from the Cour Napoléon, opposite the Pyramide, to the rue de Rivoli, outside; it also offers a better view of the sculptures in these courtyards than you get from inside the museum.

Napoleon's pink marble **Arc du Carrousel**, just east of place du Carrousel, which originally formed a gateway for the former Tuileries Palace, has always looked a bit out of place (though it sits precisely on the Voie Triomphale axis); now it's definitively and forlornly upstaged by the Pyramide.

Quite separate from the Louvre proper, but still within the palace, are three museums under the aegis of the **Union Centrale des Arts Décoratifs**, dedicated to fashion and textiles, decorative arts and advertising. The entrance to the **Musée de la Mode et du Textile**, the **Musée des Arts Décoratifs** and the **Musée de la Publicité** can be found at 107 rue de Rivoli.

The Musée du Louvre

It's easy to be put off by tales of long queues outside the Pyramide, miles of foot-wearying corridors or multilingual jostles in front of the *Mona Lisa*, but there are ways around such hassles – you can use a back entrance, stop at one of the cafés or make for a less well-known section – and ultimately, the draw of the mighty collections of the **Musée du Louvre** is irresistible.

Access and opening hours

The Pyramide is the main **entrance** to the Musée du Louvre, although the often lengthy lines can be avoided by using one of the alternative entrances: at the Porte des Lions, just east of the Pont Royal; at the Arc du Carrousel; at 99 rue de Rivoli; or directly from the métro station Palais Royal-Musée du Louvre (line 1 platform). If you've already got a ticket or a museum pass (see p.92) you can also enter from the passage Richelieu.

The permanent collection is open every day except Tuesday, from 9am to 6pm. On Wednesdays and Fridays, it stays open till 9.45pm – these "*nocturnes*" are an excellent time to visit. Some less popular parts of the museum are closed one day a week on a rotating basis, so if you're interested in a particular section it's worth checking the schedule at Ⓦwww.louvre.fr.

The usual **entry fee** is €8.50, reduced to €6 for the twice-weekly evening openings. Admission is free on the first Sunday of each month, and to under-18s at all times. Under-26s get in free on the Friday *nocturne*, ie after 6pm. For a surcharge of a little over €1, tickets can be bought in advance through Ticketnet (Ⓣ01.46.91.57.57, Ⓦwww.ticketnet.fr) or from FNAC (Ⓣ01.41.57.32.28, Ⓦlouvre. fnacspectacles.com; see p.195 for branches); the advantage is in being able to jump the entrance queue via the passage Richelieu. All tickets allow you to leave and re-enter as many times as you like throughout the day – handy if the crowds (or the artworks) get too much.

Orientation

The museum is divided into **three main wings**, Denon (south), Richelieu (north) and Sully (east, around the giant quadrangle of the Cour Carré). These wings are further subdivided into seven sections: **Antiquities** (Oriental, Egyptian and Classical); **Sculpture**; **Painting**; the **Medieval Louvre**; and **Objets d'art**. Some sections spread across two wings, or two floors of the same wing.

From the Hall Napoléon, under the Pyramide, stairs lead south into the **Denon wing**, which is by far the grandest and most popular area of the museum, with the must-see Italian masterpieces of the Grande Galerie, the famous nineteenth-century large-scale French paintings and the *Mona Lisa*, all on the first floor. Denon also houses Classical and Italian sculpture on the two palatial lower floors.

Serious lovers of French art will head north to the **Richelieu wing**, whose glazed-over courtyards contain a French sculpture collection. The grand chronology of French painting begins on the second floor, while the superb *objets d'art* collection on the first floor includes everything French that's not painting or sculpture – furniture, tapestries, crystal and jewels.

Richelieu also houses Middle Eastern antiquities and Islamic art (ground and lower ground floors), and northern European painting (second floor).

Rather fewer visitors begin with the **Sully wing**, although it's here that the story begins, with the foundations of Philippe-Auguste's twelfth-century fortress on the lower ground floor. The floors above mostly continue chronologies begun on other wings, with antiquities from Greece and the Levant (ground floor), and the seventeenth- and eighteenth-century periods from the Objets d'Art (first floor) and French painting (second floor) sections. The complete Pharaonic Egypt collection is here too.

With all that in mind, it's well worth picking up a **floor plan** from the information booth in the Hall Napoléon, or at one of the alternative entrances. This makes sense of it all by colour-coding the museum's seven main sections. A few of the best-known masterpieces are highlighted on the plan, and the whole system is surprisingly painless once you get to grips with it. The plan's only drawback is that it doesn't spotlight the magnificently decorated suites and rooms that give such a strong identity to certain sections of the museum.

You can always step outside for a break, but three moderately expensive **cafés** are enticing and open all day. *Café Richelieu* (first floor, Richelieu) is elegant and relatively quiet, and on sunny days you can sit outside on the terrace, with spectacular views of the pyramid. *Café Denon* (lower ground floor, Denon) is cosily romantic, while *Café Mollien* (first floor, Denon) has a summer terrace and some inexpensive snacks. The various cafés and restaurants under the Pyramide are mostly noisy and overpriced.

Antiquities

Oriental Antiquities covers the sculptures, stone-carved writings, pottery and other relics of the ancient Middle and Near East, including the Mesopotamian, Sumerian, Babylonian, Assyrian and Phoenician civilizations, plus the art of ancient Persia. The highlight of this section is the boldly sculpted stonework, much of it in relief. Watch out for the statues and busts depicting the young Sumerian prince Gudea, and the black, two-metre-high Code of Hammurabi, which dates from around 1800 BC. Standing erect like a warning finger, a series of royal precepts (the "code") is crowned with a stern depiction of the king meeting the sun god Shamash, dispenser of justice. The Cour Khorsabad, adjacent, is dominated by two giant Assyrian winged bulls that once acted as guardians to the palace of Sargon II, from which many treasures were brought to the Louvre by the French archeologist Paul-Emilie Botta, in the mid-nineteenth century. The refined **Arts of Islam** collection is next door.

Egyptian Antiquities contains jewellery, domestic objects, sandals, sarcophagi and dozens of examples of the delicate naturalism of Egyptian decorative technique, such as the wall tiles depicting a piebald calf galloping through fields of papyrus, and a duck taking off from a marsh. Among the major exhibits are the Great Sphinx, carved from a single block of pink granite, the polychrome Seated Scribe statue, the striking, life-size wooden statue of Chancellor Nakhti, a bust of Amenophis IV and a low-relief sculpture of Sethi I and the goddess Hathor.

The collection of **Greek and Roman Antiquities**, mostly statues, is one of the finest in the world. The biggest crowd-pullers in the museum, after the *Mona Lisa*, are here: the *Winged Victory of Samothrace*, at the top of Denon's great staircase, and the *Venus de Milo*. Venus is surrounded by hordes of antecedent Aphrodites, from the graceful marble head known as the "Kaufmann Head" and the delightful *Venus of Arles* – both early copies of the work of the great sculptor Praxiteles – to the strange *Dame d'Auxerre*. In the Roman section a sterner style takes over, but there are some very attractive mosaics from Asia Minor and luminous frescoes from Pompeii and Herculaneum.

Sculpture

The **French Sculpture** section is arranged on the lowest two levels of the Richelieu wing, with the more monumental pieces housed in two grand, glass-roofed courtyards: the four triumphal *Marly Horses* grace the Cour Marly, while Cour Puget has Puget's dynamic *Milon de Crotone* as its centrepiece. The surrounding rooms trace the development of sculpture in France from painful Romanesque Crucifixions to the lofty public works of David d'Angers. The startlingly realistic Gothic pieces – notably the Burgundian *Tomb of Philippe Pot*, complete with hooded mourners – and the experimental Mannerist works are particuarly rewarding, but towards the end of the course you may find yourself crying out for an end to all those gracefully perfect nudes and grandiose busts of noblemen. You'll have to leave the Louvre for Rodin, but an alternative antidote lies in the smaller, more intense **Italian and northern European** sections, on the lower two floors of Denon, where you'll find such bold masterpieces as two of Michelangelo's writhing *Slaves*, Duccio's virtuoso *Virgin and Child Surrounded by Angels*, and some severely Gothic Virgins from Flanders and Germany.

Objets d'Art

The vast **Objets d'Art** section presents the finest tapestries, ceramics, jewellery and furniture commissioned by France's most wealthy and influential patrons, beginning with an exquisite little equestrian sculpture of Charlemagne and continuing through eighty-one relentlessly superb rooms through to a salon decorated in the style of Louis-Philippe, the last king of France. Walking through the entire chronology is an enlightening experience, and the refined, opulent works give a powerful sense of the evolution of aesthetic taste. The exception is the Middle Ages section, which is of a more pious nature and includes carved ivories and Limoges enamels. Towards the end, the circuit passes through the breathtaking apartments of Napoléon III's Minister of State, full of plush upholstery, immense chandeliers, gilded putti and caryatids and dramatic ceiling frescoes in true Second Empire style.

Painting

The largest section by far is **Painting**. The main **French collection** begins on the second floor of the Richelieu wing, and continues right round the Cour Carré, which comprises the Sully wing. It traces the development of French painting from its beginnings as far as Corot, whose airy landscapes anticipate the Impressionists. Surprisingly few works predate the Renaissance, and the preliminary Richelieu section is chiefly of interest for the portraits of French kings, from the Sienese-style *Portrait of John the Good* to Jean Clouet's *François I*. As you turn the corner into Sully, look out for the strange Mannerist atmosphere of the two Schools of Fontainebleau, and the luminous paintings of Georges de la Tour and the Le Nain brothers, reminiscent of Caravaggio. It's not until Poussin breaks onto the scene that an obviously French style emerges, and you'll need a healthy appetite for Classical grandeur in the next suite of rooms, with large-scale works by the likes of Lorrain, Le Brun and Rigaud. The more intimate paintings of Watteau come as a relief, followed by Chardin's intense still lifes and the inspired Rococo sketches by Fragonard known as the *Figures of Fantasy*. From the southern wing of Sully to the end of this section, the chilly wind of Neoclassicism blows through the paintings of Gros, Gérard, Prud'hon, David and Ingres, contrasting with the more sentimental style that begins with Greuze and continues into the Romanticism of Géricault and Delacroix. The final set of rooms takes in Millet, Corot and the Barbizon school of painting.

The nineteenth century is most dramatically represented in the second area of the Louvre devoted to painting, on the first floor of the Denon wing. A pair of giant rooms is dedicated to Nationalism and Romanticism respectively, featuring some of France's best-known works including such gigantic, epic canvases as David's *Coronation of Napoleon in Notre Dame*, Géricault's *The Raft of the Medusa*, and Delacroix's *Liberty Leading the People*, the icon of nineteenth-century revolution.

Denon also houses the frankly staggering **Italian collection**. The high-ceilinged Salon Carré – which has been used to exhibit paintings since the first "salon" of the Royal Academy in 1725 – displays the so-called Primitives, with works by Giotto, Cimabue and Fra Angelico, as well as one of Uccello's bizarrely theoretical panels of the *Battle of San Romano*. To the west of the Salon, the famous Grande Galerie stretches into the distance, parading all the great names of the Italian Renaissance – Mantegna, Filippo Lippi, Leonardo da Vinci, Raphael, Coreggio, Titian. The playfully troubled Mannerists kick in about halfway along, but the second half of the Galerie dwindles in quality and representativeness as it moves towards the eighteenth century. Leonardo's *Mona Lisa*, along with Paolo Veronese's huge *Marriage at Cana*, hangs in the Salle des États, a room halfway along the Galerie between the two rooms of Nationalist and Romantic French art. If you want to catch *La Joconde* – as she's known to the French – without a swarm of admirers, go first or last thing in the day. At the far end of Denon, the relatively small but worthwhile **Spanish** collection has some notable Goya portraits.

The western end of Richelieu's second floor is given over to a more selective collection of **German**, **Flemish** and **Dutch** paintings, with a brilliant set of works by Rubens and twelve Rembrandts, including some powerful self-portraits. Interspersed throughout the painting section are rooms dedicated to the Louvre's impressive collection of **Prints and Drawings**, including prized sketches and preliminary drawings by Ingres and Rubens and some attributed to Leonardo. Because of their susceptibility to the light, however, they are exhibited in rotation.

Union Centrale des Arts Décoratifs

The other museums housed in the Louvre palace, under an umbrella organization with the snappy title of **Union Centrale des Arts Décoratifs** (entrance at 107 rue de Rivoli; Tues, Wed & Fri 11am–6pm, Thurs 11am–8pm; Sat & Sun 10am–6pm; €8 combined ticket for all three museums; Ⓦwww.ucad.fr) are often unjustly overlooked, yet their exhibitions can be among the city's most innovative.

The eclectic collection of art objects and superbly crafted furnishing at the **Musée des Arts Décoratifs** fits the Union Centrale's "design" theme. The works in the "historical" rooms, running from the medieval period through to Art Deco and Art Nouveau, may seem humble in comparison with those in the Louvre's airy Objets d'Art section, but most of those here were made to be lived with or actually used, and feel more accessible as a result. There are curiously shaped and beautifully carved chairs, dressers and tables, religious paintings, Venetian glass and some wonderful tapestries. A number of "period rooms" have been reconstituted top-to-toe in the style of different eras, giving a powerful flavour of the ethos behind design trends, while separate galleries focus on jewellery and toys. Perhaps the most exciting part of the museum is the brand-new contemporary section, on the topmost floors, with rooms dedicated to each decade from the 1940s through to the present day. There are brilliant works by French, Italian and Japanese designers, including some great examples from the prince of French design, Philippe Starck.

The **Musée de la Mode et du Textile** holds high-quality exhibitions demonstrating the most brilliant and cutting-edge of Paris fashions from all eras. Recent exhibitions have included Jackie Kennedy's famous 1960s dresses and the work of the couturier Balenciaga. Immediately above, the **Musée de la Publicité** shows off its collection of advertising posters through cleverly themed, temporary exhibitions. Designed by the French über-architect Jean Nouvel, the space is appropriately trendy: half exposed brickwork and steel panelling, half crumbling Louvre finery. There's even a bar and a dozen computers from which you can freely access the archive.

The Opéra district

Between the Louvre and **boulevards Haussmann**, **Montmartre**, **Poissonnière** and **Bonne-Nouvelle** to the north lies the city's main **commercial and**

financial district. Right at its heart stand the solid institutions of the Banque de France and the Bourse, while just to the north, beyond the glittering **Opéra-Garnier**, are the large department stores **Galeries Lafayette** and **Printemps**. More well-heeled shopping is concentrated on the rue **St-Honoré** in the west and the streets around aristocratic place Vendôme, lined with top couturiers, jewellers and art dealers. Scattered around the whole area are the delightful, secretive **passages** – nineteenth-century arcades that hark back to shopping from a different era.

The passages

Among the most attractive of the *passages* is the **Galerie Vivienne**, between rue Vivienne and rue des Petits-Champs, its decor of Grecian and marine motifs providing a suitably flamboyant backdrop for its smart shops, such as a branch of Jean-Paul Gaultier. But the most stylish examples are the three-storey **passage du Grand-Cerf**, between rue St-Denis and rue Dussoubs, and **Galerie Véro-Dodat**, between rue Croix-des-Petits-Champs and rue Jean-Jacques-Rousseau, named after the two pork butchers who set it up in 1824. This last is the most homogeneous and aristocratic *passage*, with painted ceilings and faux marble columns. North of rue St-Marc, the several arcades making up the **passage des Panoramas** are more workaday, although they do retain a great deal of character: there's an old brasserie with carved wood panelling (now a tea shop, *L'Arbre à Cannelle*, see p.165) and a printshop with its original 1867 fittings, as well as bric-a-brac shops, and stamp and secondhand postcard dealers. In **passage Jouffroy**, across boulevard Montmartre, a shop, Monsieur Segas, sells unusual walking canes and theatrical antiques opposite a shop with exquisite dolls' house furniture, while Paul Vulin spreads his secondhand books further down along the passageway, and Ciné-Doc appeals to cinephiles with its collection of old film posters.

The Madeleine and the Opéra-Garnier

Set back from the boulevard des Capucines and crowning the avenue de l'Opéra is the dazzling **Opéra-Garnier**, which was constructed from 1860 to 1875 as part of Napoléon III's new vision of Paris. The building's architect, Charles Garnier, whose golden bust by Carpeaux can be seen on the rue Auber side of his edifice, pulled out all the stops to provide a suitably grand space in which Second Empire high society could parade and be seen. The facade is a fabulous extravaganza of white, pink and green marble, colonnades, rearing horses, winged angels and niches holding gleaming gold busts of composers. You can look round the equally sumptuous **interior** (daily 10am–5pm; €7), including the plush auditorium – rehearsals permitting – the colourful ceiling of which is the work of Chagall, depicting scenes from well-known operas and ballets. The visit includes the **Bibliothèque-Musée de l'Opéra**, dedicated to the artists connected with the Opéra throughout its history, and containing model sets, dreadful nineteenth-century paintings and rather better temporary exhibitions on operatic themes.

West of the Opéra, occupying nearly the whole of the place de la Madeleine, the imperious-looking **Église de la Madeleine** is the parish church of the cream of Parisian high society. Modelled on a Greek classical temple, it's surrounded by 52 Corinthian columns and fronted by a huge pediment depicting the *Last Judgement*. Originally intended as a monument to Napoleon's army, it narrowly escaped being turned into a railway station before finally being consecrated to Mary Magdalene in 1845. Inside, a wonderfully theatrical sculpture of *Mary Magdalene Ascending to Heaven* draws your eye to the high altar. In the half-dome above, a fresco entitled *The History of Christianity* commemorates the concordat signed between the church and the state after the Revolution and depicts all the major figures in Christendom, with Napoleon centre-stage, naturally.

If the Madeleine caters to spiritual needs, the rest of the square is given over to nourishment of quite a different kind, for this is where Paris's top gourmet food stores Fauchon and Hédiard are located. Their remarkable displays are a feast for the eyes, and both have *salons de thé* where you can sample some of their epicurean treats. On the east side of the Madeleine church is one of the city's oldest **flower markets** dating back to 1832, open every day except Monday while, nearby, some rather fine Art Nouveau public toilets are definitely worth inspecting.

Place Vendôme

A short walk east of the Madeleine along ancient rue St-Honoré, a preserve of top fashion designers and art galleries, lies **place Vendôme**, one of the city's most impressive set pieces. Built by Versailles' architect Hardouin-Mansart, it's a pleasingly symmetrical, eight-sided *place*, enclosed by a harmonious ensemble of elegant mansions, graced with Corinthian pilasters, mascarons and steeply pitched roofs. Once the grand residences of tax collectors and financiers, they now house such luxury establishments as the *Ritz* hotel, Cartier, Bulgari and other top-flight jewellers, lending the square a decidedly exclusive air. No. 12, now occupied by Chaumet jewellers, is where Chopin died in 1849.

Somewhat out of proportion with the rest of the square, the centrepiece is a towering triumphal **column**, surmounted by a statue of Napoleon dressed as Caesar, raised in 1806 to celebrate the Battle of Austerlitz – bronze reliefs of scenes of the battle, cast from 1200 recycled Austro-Russian cannons, spiral their way up the column.

The Palais Royal and Bibliothèque Nationale

At the eastern end of rue St-Honoré stands the handsome, colonnaded **Palais Royal**, built for Cardinal Richelieu in 1624, though much modified and renovated since. The current building houses various governmental bodies and the **Comédie Française**, a long-standing venue for the classics of French theatre. To its rear lie gardens lined with stately three-storey houses built over arcades housing quirky antique and designer shops. It's an attractive and peaceful oasis, with avenues of limes, fountains and flowerbeds. You'd hardly guess that this was a site of gambling dens, brothels and funfair attractions until the Grands Boulevards took up the baton in the 1830s. Folly, some might say, has returned in the form of Daniel Buren's art installation, which consists of black and white striped pillars, rather like sticks of Brighton rock, all of varying heights, dotted about the palace's main courtyard.

The gardens are a handy short cut from the rue de Rivoli to the **Bibliothèque Nationale** (Tues–Sat 10am–7pm, Sun noon–7pm; Ⓦwww.bnf.fr) on the north side; you can enter free of charge and peer into the atmospheric reading rooms, though some look rather bereft, as many books have now been transferred to the new François Mitterrand site on the Left Bank. Visiting the library's temporary exhibitions (closed Mon) will give you access to the beautiful **Galerie Mazarine**, with its panelled ceilings painted by Romanelli (1617–1662). It's also worth calling into the **Cabinet des Monnaies, Médailles et Antiques** (daily 1–5/6pm; free), a permanent display of coins and ancient treasures built up by successive kings from Philippe-Auguste onwards; Charlemagne's ivory chess set is a particular highlight.

Les Halles and around

Les Halles was the city's main food market for over eight hundred years. It was moved out to the suburbs in 1969, despite widespread opposition, and replaced by a large underground shopping and leisure complex, known as the Forum des Halles, and an RER/métro interchange. Unsightly, run down, even unsavoury in parts, the complex is now widely acknowledged as an architectural disaster – so much so that steps are under way to give it a major facelift. The French architect David Mangin, who won the competition to redevelop the site, plans to suspend a **vast glass roof** over the forum, allowing light to flood in, while also redesigning the gardens and creating a wide promenade

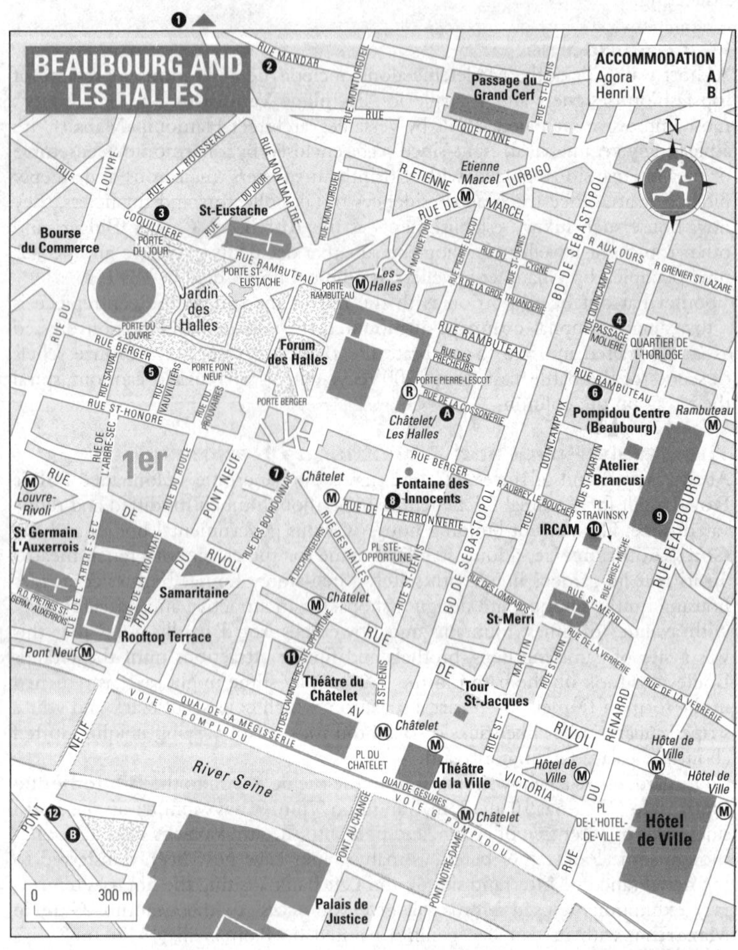

EATING				DRINKING			
Chez Dilan	2	À la Tour de Montlhéry (Chez Denise)	5	Banana Café	8	Le Triptyque	1
Georges	9	La Victoire Suprème du Coeur	7	Cafe Beaubourg	10		
Au Pied de Cochon	3	Au Vieux Molière	4	Le Petit Marcel	6		
La Robe et le Palais	11			Taverne Henri IV	12		

on the model of Barcelona's Ramblas. Work is due to start in 2007 and should be complete by 2012.

The **Forum des Halles** centre stretches underground from the Bourse du Commerce rotunda to rue Pierre-Lescot and is spread over four levels. The overground section comprises aquarium-like arcades of shops, arranged around a sunken patio, and landscaped gardens. The shops are mostly devoted to high-street fashion and there's also a large FNAC bookshop and the Forum des Créateurs, an outlet for young fashion designers. It's not all commerce, however: there's scope for various diversions including swimming, billiards and movie-going.

Although little now remains of the former working-class quarter, you can still catch a flavour of the old Les Halles atmosphere in some of the surrounding bars and bistros and on the lively market street of **rue Montorgueil** to the north, where traditional grocers, horse butchers and fishmongers still ply their trade.

At the foot of rue Montorgueil stands another survivor from the past, the beautiful, gracefully buttressed church of **St-Eustache**. Built between 1532 and 1637, it's a glorious fusion of Gothic and Renaissance styles, with soaring vaults, Corinthian pilasters and arcades. It was the scene of Molière's baptism, and Rameau and Marivaux are buried here.

Centre Georges Pompidou

The **Centre Georges Pompidou** (aka Beaubourg; Ⓦwww.centrepompidou.fr; M° Rambuteau/Hôtel-de-Ville), housing the Musée National d'Art Moderne, is one of the twentieth century's most radical buildings and its opening in 1977 gave rise to some violent reactions. Since then, however, it has won over critics and public alike, and has become one of the city's most recognizable landmarks. Architects Renzo Piano and Richard Rogers freed up maximum gallery space inside by placing all infrastructure outside: utility pipes and escalator tubes, all brightly colour-coded according to their function, climb around the exterior in crazy snakes-and-ladders fashion. The transparent escalator on the front of the building, giving access to the modern art museum, affords superb views over the city. Aside from the museum there are two cinemas, performance spaces and a library.

Tickets for the museum cost €10 and include entry to the Atelier Brancusi and temporary exhibitions. Under-18s get in free – pick up a pass at the ticket office. Admission to the museum and exhibitions is free for everyone on the first Sunday of the month.

Musée National d'Art Moderne

The superb **Musée National d'Art Moderne** (daily except Tues 11am–9pm; see above for admission) presides over the fourth and fifth floors of the Centre Pompidou, with the fifth floor usually covering 1905 to 1960 and the fourth 1960 to the present day. Thanks to an astute acquisitions policy and some generous gifts, the collection is a near-complete visual essay on the history of twentieth-century art and is so large that only a fraction of the 50,000 works are on display at any one time. The paintings are frequently rotated and rearranged.

The section covering the years **1905 to 1960** is a near-complete visual essay on the history of modern art: Fauvism, Cubism, Dada, abstract art, Surrealism and abstract expressionism are all well represented. There's a particularly rich collection of Matisses, ranging from early Fauvist works to his late masterpieces – a stand-out is his *Tristesse du Roi*, a moving meditation on old age and memory. Other highlights include a number of Picasso's and Braque's early Cubist paintings and a substantial collection of Kandinskys, including his pioneering abstract works *Avec l'arc noir* and *Composition à la tache rouge*. A whole room is usually devoted to the characteristically colourful paintings of Robert and Sonia Delaunay, contrasting with the darker mood of more unsettling works likely to be on display by Surrealists Magritte, Dalí and Ernst.

In the post-1960s section the works of Yves Klein are perhaps the most arresting, especially his luminous blue "body prints", made by covering female models in paint and using them as human paintbrushes. Established **contemporary artists** you're likely to come across include Claes Oldenburg, Christian Boltanski and Daniel Buren. Christian Boltanski is known for his large *mise-en-scène* installations, often containing veiled allusions to the Holocaust. Daniel Buren's works are easy to spot: they all bear his trademark stripes, exactly 8.7cm in width.

Atelier Brancusi

On the northern edge of the Pompidou Centre, down some steps off the sloping piazza, in a small separate one-level building, is the **Atelier Brancusi** (daily except Tues 2–6pm), the reconstructed home and studio of Constantin Brancusi. The sculptor bequeathed the contents of his workshop to the state on condition that the rooms be arranged exactly as he left them, and they provide a fascinating insight into how he lived and worked. Studios one and two are crowded with Brancusi's trademark abstract bird and column shapes in highly polished brass and marble, while studios three and four comprise the artist's private quarters.

Quartier Beaubourg and the Hôtel de Ville

The *quartier* around the Centre Pompidou, known as **Beaubourg**, is home to more contemporary art. Jean Tinguely and Niki de St-Phalle created the colourful moving sculptures and fountains in the pool in front of Église St-Merri on **place Igor Stravinsky**. This squirting waterworks pays homage to Stravinsky – each fountain corresponds to one of his compositions (*The Firebird*, *The Rite of Spring* and so on) – and shows scant respect for passers-by. On the west side of the square is the entrance to **IRCAM**, a research centre for contemporary music founded by the composer Pierre Boulez and an occasional venue for concerts; much of it is underground, with an overground extension by Renzo Piano. To the north are numerous commercial art galleries, occupying the attractive old *hôtels particuliers* on pedestrianized **rue Quincampoix**.

Heading back towards the river along rue Renard will bring you to the **Hôtel de Ville**, the seat of the city's government. It's a mansion of gargantuan proportions in florid neo-Renaissance style, modelled pretty much on the previous building burned down in the Commune. Those opposed to the establishments of kings and emperors created their alternative municipal governments on this spot in 1789, 1848 and 1870. But with the defeat of the Commune in 1871, the conservatives concluded that the Parisian municipal authority had to go if order was to be maintained and the working class kept in their place. Thereafter Paris was ruled directly by the ministry of the interior. Eventually, in 1977 the city was allowed to run its own affairs again and Jacques Chirac was elected mayor. In front of the Hôtel de Ville, the huge square – a notorious guillotine site in the French Revolution – becomes the location of a popular ice-skating rink from December to March (see p.192).

The Marais, the Île St-Louis and the Bastille

Jack Kerouac translated **rue des Francs-Bourgeois**, the Marais' main east–west axis along with rue Rivoli/rue St-Antoine, as "street of the outspoken middle classes", though the original owners of the mansions lining its length would not have taken kindly to such a slight on their blue-bloodedness. The name's origin is medieval and actually means "people exempt from tax" in reference to the penurious inmates of an almshouse that stood on the site of no. 34. It was not until the sixteenth and seventeenth centuries that the **Marais**, as the area between the Pompidou Centre and the Bastille is known, became a fashionable aristocratic district. After the Revolution it was abandoned to the masses, who, up until some fifty years ago, were living ten to a room on unserviced, squalid streets. Since then, gentrification has proceeded apace and the middle classes are finally ensconced – mostly media, arty or gay, and definitely outspoken.

The renovated **mansions**, their grandeur concealed by the narrow streets, have become museums, libraries, offices and chic apartments, flanked by trendy fashion outlets, interior design shops and art galleries. Though cornered by Haussmann's boulevards, the Marais itself was spared the baron's heavy touch and has been left pretty much unspoilt. This is Paris at its most seductive – old, secluded, as lively by night as it is by day, and with as many alluring shops, bars and places to eat as you could wish for.

Rue des Francs-Bourgeois

Rue des Francs-Bourgeois begins with the eighteenth-century magnificence of the **Palais Soubise**, which houses the Archives Nationales de France and the **Musée de l'Histoire de France**. The palace's fabulous rococo interiors are the setting for changing exhibitions (Mon & Wed–Fri 10am–12.30pm & 2–5.30pm, Sat & Sun 2–5.30pm; around €3) drawn from the archives. The adjacent Hôtel de Rohan is also occasionally used for exhibitions from the archives and has more sumptuous interiors, notably the charming Chinese-inspired Cabinet des Singes, whose walls are painted with monkeys acting out various aristocratic scenes.

Opposite, at the back of a driveway for the Crédit Municipal bank, stands a pepperpot tower which formed part of Philippe-Auguste's twelfth-century **city walls**. Further down the street are two of the grandest Marais *hôtels*, **Carnavalet** and **Lamoignon**, housing respectively the Musée Carnavalet and the Bibliothèque Historique de la Ville de Paris.

Musée Carnavalet

The **Musée Carnavalet**, whose entrance is off rue des Francs-Bourgeois at 23 rue de Sévigné (Tues–Sun 10am–6pm; free; M° St-Paul), presents the history of Paris from its origins up to the Belle Époque through an extraordinary collection of paintings, sculptures, decorative arts and archeological finds. The museum's setting in two beautiful Renaissance mansions, Hôtel Carnavalet and Hôtel Le Peletier, surrounded by attractive gardens, makes a visit worthwhile in itself. There are 140 rooms in all, impossible to visit in one go, so it's best to pick up a floor plan and decide which areas you'd like to concentrate on. The **collection** begins with nineteenth- and early twentieth-century shop and inn signs (beautiful objects in themselves) and fascinating models of Paris through the ages, along with maps and plans. Other highlights on the ground floor include the renovated orangery, which houses a significant collection of Neolithic finds such as wooden pirogues which were unearthed during the 1990s redevelopment of the Bercy riverside area.

On the **first floor** there are numerous Louis XV and Louis XVI salons and boudoirs rescued from buildings destroyed to make way for Haussmann's boulevards, and remounted here more or less intact. Rooms 128 to 148 are largely devoted to the Belle Époque, evoked through vivid paintings of the period

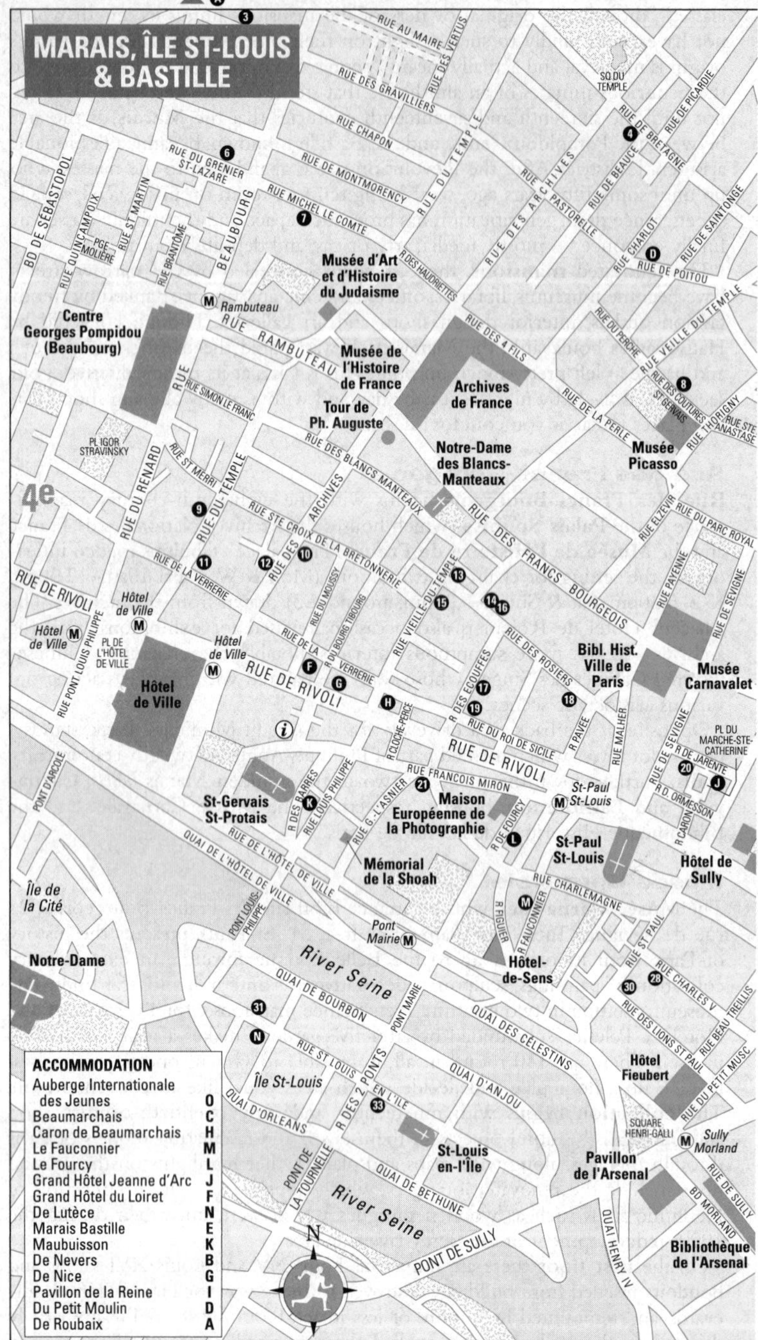
MARAIS, ÎLE ST-LOUIS & BASTILLE
ACCOMMODATION
Auberge Internationale des Jeunes O
Beaumarchais C
Caron de Beaumarchais H
Le Fauconnier M
Le Fourcy L
Grand Hôtel Jeanne d'Arc J
Grand Hôtel du Loiret F
De Lutèce N
Marais Bastille E
Maubuisson K
De Nevers B
De Nice G
Pavillon de la Reine I
Du Petit Moulin D
De Roubaix A
Centre Georges Pompidou (Beaubourg)
Musée d'Art et d'Histoire du Judaïsme
Musée de l'Histoire de France
Archives de France
Tour de Ph. Auguste
Notre-Dame des Blancs-Manteaux
Musée Picasso
Bibl. Hist. Ville de Paris
Musée Carnavalet
Hôtel de Ville
St-Gervais St-Protais
Maison Européenne de la Photographie
Mémorial de la Shoah
St-Paul St-Louis
Hôtel de Sully
Hôtel-de-Sens
Hôtel Fieubert
Pavillon de l'Arsenal
Bibliothèque de l'Arsenal
St-Louis en-l'Île
Notre-Dame
Île de la Cité
Île St-Louis
River Seine
4e
Rambuteau
Hôtel de Ville
St-Paul St-Louis
Pont Marie
Sully Morland
RUE AU MAIRE
RUE DES VERTUS
RUE DES GRAVILLIERS
RUE CHAPON
RUE DE MONTMORENCY
RUE DU GRENIER ST-LAZARE
RUE MICHEL LE COMTE
RUE DU TEMPLE
RUE DES ARCHIVES
RUE PASTORELLE
RUE DE BEAUCE
RUE DE BRETAGNE
RUE DE PICARDIE
RUE CHARLOT
RUE DE SAINTONGE
RUE DE POITOU
SQ DU TEMPLE
BD DE SÉBASTOPOL
RUE QUINCAMPOIX
RUE ST MARTIN
PGE MOLIÈRE
RUE BRANTÔME
BEAUBOURG
R DES HAUDRIETTES
RUE RAMBUTEAU
RUE DES 4 FILS
RUE DU PERCHE
RUE VIEILLE DU TEMPLE
RUE DES COUTURES ST GERVAIS
RUE DE LA PERLE
RUE THORIGNY
RUE STE ANASTASE
RUE SIMON LE FRANC
PL IGOR STRAVINSKY
RUE DU RENARD
RUE ST MERRI
RUE DU TEMPLE
RUE DES BLANCS MANTEAUX
RUE STE CROIX DE LA BRETONNERIE
RUE DES FRANCS BOURGEOIS
RUE ELZEVIR
RUE DU PARC ROYAL
RUE PAYENNE
RUE DE SÉVIGNÉ
RUE DE LA VERRERIE
RUE DU MOUSSY
R DU BOURG TIBOURG
RUE VIEILLE-DU-TEMPLE
RUE DES ROSIERS
R DES ÉCOUFFES
RUE DE RIVOLI
PL DE L'HÔTEL DE VILLE
RUE PONT LOUIS PHILIPPE
R CLOCHE-PERCE
RUE DU ROI DE SICILE
R PAVÉE
RUE MALHER
PL DU MARCHÉ-STE-CATHERINE
R DE JARENTE
R D. ORMESSON
R CARON
RUE FRANÇOIS MIRON
R DES BARRES
RUE LOUIS PHILIPPE
RUE G. L'ASNIER
R DE FOURCY
PONT D'ARCOLE
RUE DE L'HÔTEL DE VILLE
QUAI DE L'HÔTEL DE VILLE
RUE CHARLEMAGNE
R FIGUIER
R FAUCONNIER
RUE ST PAUL
RUE CHARLES V
RUE DES LIONS ST PAUL
RUE BEAUTREILLIS
RUE DU PETIT MUSC
PONT LOUIS-PHILIPPE
QUAI DE BOURBON
PONT MARIE
QUAI DES CÉLESTINS
QUAI D'ANJOU
RUE ST LOUIS EN L'ÎLE
R DES 2 PONTS
QUAI D'ORLÉANS
QUAI DE BÉTHUNE
PONT DE LA TOURNELLE
PONT DE SULLY
QUAI HENRY IV
SQUARE HENRI-GALLI
RUE DE SULLY
BD MORLAND
N

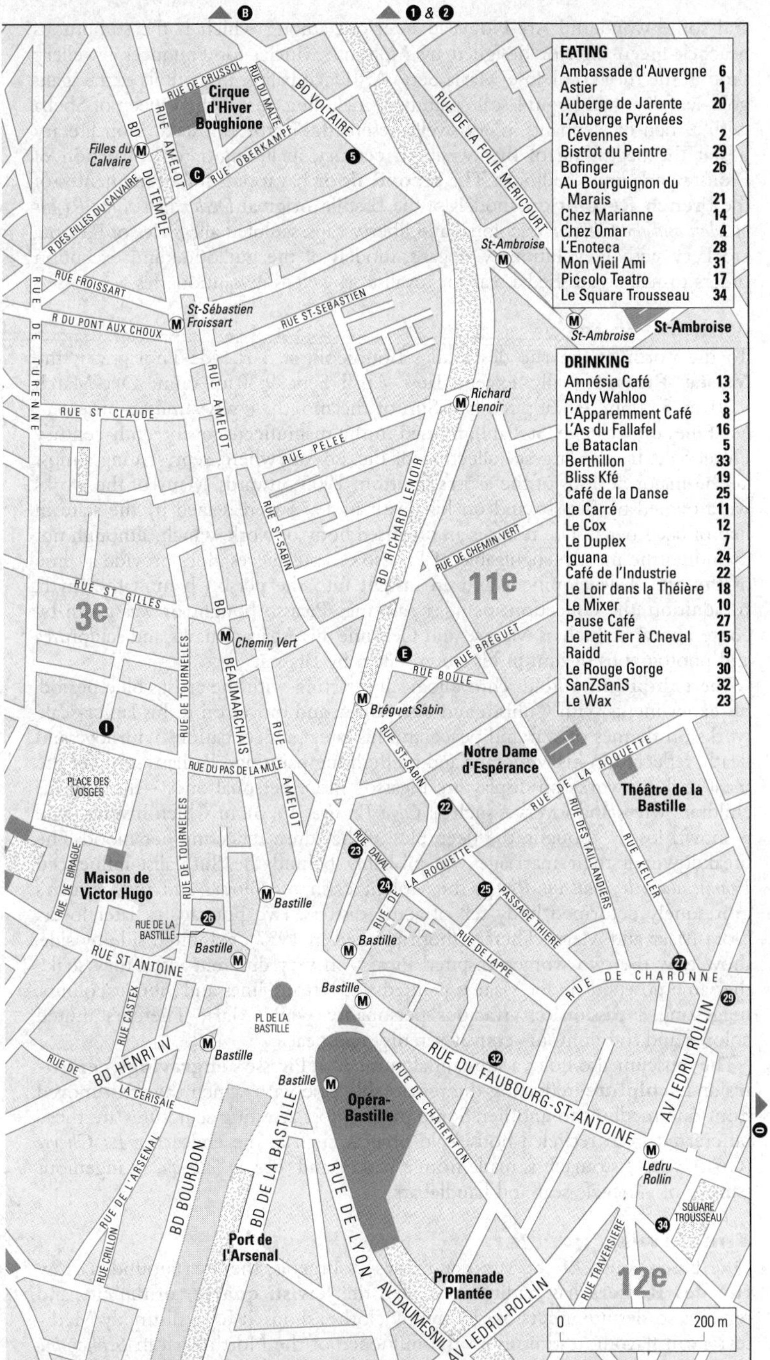
EATING
Ambassade d'Auvergne 6
Astier 1
Auberge de Jarente 20
L'Auberge Pyrénées Cévennes 2
Bistrot du Peintre 29
Bofinger 26
Au Bourguignon du Marais 21
Chez Marianne 14
Chez Omar 4
L'Enoteca 28
Mon Vieil Ami 31
Piccolo Teatro 17
Le Square Trousseau 34
DRINKING
Amnésia Café 13
Andy Wahloo 3
L'Apparemment Café 8
L'As du Fallafel 16
Le Bataclan 5
Berthillon 33
Bliss Kfé 19
Café de la Danse 25
Le Carré 11
Le Cox 12
Le Duplex 7
Iguana 24
Café de l'Industrie 22
Le Loir dans la Théière 18
Le Mixer 10
Pause Café 27
Le Petit Fer à Cheval 15
Raidd 9
Le Rouge Gorge 30
SanZSanS 32
Le Wax 23
Cirque d'Hiver Boughione
Filles du Calvaire
St-Ambroise
St-Sébastien Froissart
Richard Lenoir
Chemin Vert
Bréguet Sabin
Notre Dame d'Espérance
Théâtre de la Bastille
PLACE DES VOSGES
Maison de Victor Hugo
Bastille
PL DE LA BASTILLE
Opéra-Bastille
Ledru Rollin
SQUARE TROUSSEAU
Port de l'Arsenal
Promenade Plantée
3e
11e
12e
RUE DE CRUSSOL
RUE DU MALTE
BD VOLTAIRE
RUE DE LA FOLIE MERICOURT
RUE OBERKAMPF
RUE AMELOT
BD DU TEMPLE
R DES FILLES DU CALVAIRE
RUE FROISSART
R DU PONT AUX CHOUX
RUE ST-SEBASTIEN
RUE DE TURENNE
RUE ST CLAUDE
RUE PELEE
RUE ST-SABIN
BD RICHARD LENOIR
RUE DE CHEMIN VERT
RUE ST GILLES
BD BEAUMARCHAIS
RUE DE TOURNELLES
RUE BREGUET
RUE BOULE
RUE DU PAS DE LA MULE
RUE DE LA ROQUETTE
RUE DES TAILLANDIERS
RUE KELLER
RUE DAVAL
PASSAGE THIERE
RUE DE LAPPE
RUE DE CHARONNE
RUE DE BIRAGUE
RUE DE LA BASTILLE
RUE ST ANTOINE
RUE CASTEX
AV LEDRU ROLLIN
RUE DU FAUBOURG-ST-ANTOINE
RUE DE BD HENRI IV
LA CERISAIE
RUE DE CHARENTON
RUE DE L'ARSENAL
BD BOURDON
BD DE LA BASTILLE
RUE DE LYON
RUE CRILLON
AV DAUMESNIL
AV LEDRU-ROLLIN
RUE TRAVERSIERE
0
200 m

and some wonderful Art Nouveau interiors, among which is the sumptuous peacock-green interior designed by Alphonse Mucha for Fouquet's jewellery shop in the rue Royal. José-Maria Sert's Art Deco ballroom, with its extravagant gold-leaf decor and grand-scale paintings, including one of the Queen of Sheba with a train of elephants, is also well preserved. Nearby is a section on literary life at the beginning of the twentieth century, including a reconstruction of Proust's cork-lined bedroom. The **second floor** has rooms full of mementos of the **French Revolution**: models of the Bastille, original *Declaration of the Rights of Man and the Citizen*, tricolours and liberty caps, sculpted allegories of Reason, crockery with Revolutionary slogans, models of the guillotine and execution orders to make you shed a tear for royalists as well as revolutionaries.

Musée Picasso

To the north of the rue des Francs-Bourgeois, at 5 rue de Thorigny, is the **Musée Picasso** (daily except Tues: April–Sept 9.30am–6pm; Oct–March 9.30am–5.30pm; €6.50; free first Sun of the month; Ⓦ www.musee-picasso.fr; M° Filles du Calvaire/St-Paul), housed in the magnificent seventeenth-century Hôtel Salé. It's the largest collection of Picassos anywhere, representing almost all the major periods of the artist's life from 1905 onwards. Many of the works were owned by Picasso and on his death in 1973 were seized by the state in lieu of taxes owed. The result is an unedited body of work, which, although not including the most recognizable of Picasso's masterpieces, does provide a sense of the artist's development and an insight into the person behind the myth. In addition, the collection includes paintings Picasso bought or was given by contemporaries such as Matisse and Cézanne, his African masks and sculptures and photographs of him in his studio taken by Brassaï.

The **exhibition** unfolds chronologically, starting with the artist's blue period, his experiments with Cubism and Surrealism, and moves on to his larger-scale works on themes of war and peace and his later preoccupations with love and death, reflected in his Minotaur and bullfighting paintings. Perhaps some of the most striking works on display are Picasso's more personal ones – those of his children, wives and lovers – such as *Olga Pensive* (1923), in which his first wife is shown lost in thought, the deep blue of her dress reflecting her mood. The breakdown of their marriage was probably behind the Surrealist-influenced *Femme dans le Fauteuil Rouge*: the violent clash of colours and the woman's grotesquely deformed body tell of acute distress. Two portraits of later lovers Dora Maar and Marie-Thérèse (both painted in 1937), exhibited side by side, show how the two women inspired Picasso in very different ways: they strike the same pose, but Dora Maar is painted with strong lines and vibrant colours, suggesting a passionate, vivacious personality, while Marie-Thérèse's muted colours and soft contours convey serenity and peace.

The museum also holds a substantial number of Picasso's **engravings**, **ceramics** and **sculpture**, reflecting the remarkable ease with which the artist moved from one medium to another. Some of the most arresting sculptures are those he created from recycled household objects, such as the endearing *La Chèvre* (Goat), whose stomach is made from a basket, and *Tête de Taureau*, an ingenious pairing of a bicycle seat and handlebars.

The Jewish quarter

One block south of the rue des Francs-Bourgeois, the area around narrow **rue des Rosiers** has traditionally been the **Jewish quarter** of the city, and remains so, despite incursions by trendy clothes shops. It has a distinctly Mediterranean flavour, testimony to the influence of the North African *Sephardim*, who replenished Paris's Jewish population, depleted when its *Ashkenazim* were rounded up by the Nazis and the French police and transported to the concentration camps.

That fate befell some of the inhabitants who once lived in the Hôtel de St-Aignan, at 71 rue de Temple, just northeast of the Centre Pompidou, now fittingly home to the **Musée d'Art et d'Histoire du Judaisme** (Mon–Fri 11am–6pm, Sun 10am–6pm; €6.80, Ⓦwww.mahj.org; M° Rambuteau). The museum is a combination of the collections of the now closed Musée d'Art Juif in Montmartre, Isaac Strauss, conductor of the Paris Opera orchestra, and the Dreyfus archives, a gift to the museum from his grandchildren. Free audioguides in English are well worth picking up if you want to get the most out of your visit. The museum traces the culture, history and artistic endeavours of the Jewish people from the Middle Ages to the present day. The focus is on the history of Jews in France, but there are also many artefacts from the rest of Europe and North Africa. Some of the most notable exhibits are a Gothic-style Hanukkah lamp, one of the very few French Jewish artefacts to survive from the period before the expulsion of the Jews from France in 1394; an Italian gilded circumcision chair from the seventeenth century; and a completely intact late nineteenth-century Austrian *sukkah*, a brightly painted wooden hut built as a temporary dwelling for the celebration of the harvest. Other artefacts include Moroccan wedding garments, highly decorated marriage contracts from eighteenth-century Modena and gorgeous, almost whimsical, spice containers. One room, appropriately enough, is devoted to the **Dreyfus affair**, documented with letters, postcards and press clippings; you can read Émile Zola's famous letter "*J'accuse*" and the letters that Dreyfus sent to his wife from Devil's Island in which he talks of *épouvantable* ("terrible") suffering and loneliness. There's also a significant collection of paintings and sculpture by Jewish artists, such as Soutine and Chagall, who came to live in Paris at the beginning of the twentieth century. Events beyond the early twentieth century are taken up at the Mémorial de la Shoah's museum (see p.130).

Place des Vosges

A vast square of symmetrical pink brick and stone mansions built over arcades, the **place des Vosges**, at the eastern end of rue des Francs-Bourgeois, is a masterpiece of aristocratic elegance and the first example of planned development in the history of Paris. It was built by Henri IV and inaugurated in 1612 for the wedding of Louis XIII and Anne of Austria; Louis's statue – or, rather, a replica of it – stands hidden by chestnut trees in the middle of the grass and gravel gardens at the square's centre. The gardens are popular with families on weekends – children can run around on the grass (unusually for Paris the "pelouse" is not "interdite") and mess about in sandpits. Buskers often play under the arcades, serenading diners at the outside tables of restaurants and cafés, while well-heeled shoppers browse in the upmarket art, antique and fashion boutiques.

Through all the vicissitudes of history, the square has never lost its cachet as a smart address. Among the many celebrities who made their homes here was Victor Hugo: his house, at no. 6, where he wrote much of *Les Misérables*, is now a museum, the **Maison de Victor Hugo** (Tues–Sun 10am–6pm; closed hols; free; M° Chemin-Vert/Bastille); a whole room is devoted to posters of the various stage adaptations of his most famous novel. Hugo was multi-talented: as well as writing, he drew – many of his ink drawings are exhibited – and designed his own furniture; he even put together the extraordinary Chinese-style dining room on display here. That apart, the usual portraits, manuscripts

△ Place des Vosges

and memorabilia shed sparse light on the man and his work, particularly if you don't read French.

From the southwest corner of the square, a door leads through to the formal château garden, orangery and exquisite Renaissance facade of the **Hôtel de Sully**, the sister site to the Jeu de Paume (see p.114). Changing photographic exhibitions, usually with social, historical or anthropological themes, are mounted here (Tues–Fri noon–7pm, Sat & Sun 10am–7pm; €5), and there's a bookshop with an extensive collection of books on Paris, some in English.

South of rue de Rivoli

The southern section of the Marais, below rues de Rivoli and St-Antoine, is quieter than the northern part and has some atmospheric streets, such as cobbled rue des Barres, perfumed with the scent of roses from nearby gardens and the occasional waft of incense from the church of **St-Gervais-St-Protais**, a late Gothic construction that looks somewhat battered on the outside owing to a direct hit from a Big Bertha howitzer in 1918. Its interior contains some lovely stained glass, carved misericords and a seventeenth-century organ – Paris's oldest.

One block further east, at 17 rue Geoffroy-l'Asnier, is the **Mémorial de la Shoah** (Mon–Fri & Sun 10am–6pm, Thurs until 10pm; free). Since 1956 this has been the site of the Mémorial du Martyr Juif Inconnu (Memorial to an Unknown Jewish Martyr), a sombre crypt containing a large black marble star of David, with a candle at its centre. In 2005 President Chirac opened a new museum here and unveiled a Wall of Names: four giant slabs of marble engraved with the names of the 76,000 French Jews sent to death camps from 1942 to 1944. Their weight is overwhelming.

The museum gives an absorbing account of the history of Jews in France, especially Paris, during the German occupation. There are last letters from deportees to their families, videotaped testimony from survivors, numerous ID cards and photos.

A little further east, between rues Fourcy and François-Miron, the handsome Hôtel Hénault de Cantoube, with its two-storey crypt, has become the **Maison Européenne de la Photographie** (Wed–Sun 11am–8pm; €6, free Wed after 5pm; Ⓦwww.mep-fr.org; M° St-Paul/Pont-Marie) and hosts excellent exhibitions of contemporary photography; the entrance is at 5/7 rue du Fourcy.

The Île St-Louis

Often considered the most romantic part of Paris, the peaceful **Île St-Louis** is prime strolling territory. Unlike its larger neighbour, the Île de la Cité, the Île St-Louis has no heavyweight sights, just austerely handsome seventeenth-century houses on single-lane streets, tree-lined *quais*, a school, church, restaurants, cafés, interesting little shops, and the best sorbets in the world at *Berthillon*, 31 rue St-Louis-en-l'Île (see p.168). Unsurprisingly, the island is one of the most coveted of the city's addresses (Baron Guy de Rothschild has a house here). The island is particularly atmospheric in the evening, and an arm-in-arm wander along the *quais* is a must in any lover's itinerary.

The Bastille

The landmark column topped with the gilded "Spirit of Liberty" on **place de la Bastille** was erected not to commemorate the surrender in 1789 of the prison – whose only visible remains have been transported to square Henri-Galli at the end of boulevard Henri-IV – but the July Revolution of 1830 that replaced the autocratic Charles X with the "Citizen King" Louis-Philippe. When Louis-Philippe fled in the more significant 1848 Revolution, his throne was burnt beside the column and a new inscription added. Four months later, the workers again took to the streets. All of eastern Paris was barricaded, with the fiercest fighting on rue du Faubourg-St-Antoine, until the rebellion was quelled with the usual massacres and deportation of survivors. However, it is the events of July 14, 1789, symbol of the end of feudalism in Europe, that France celebrates every year on Bastille Day.

The Bicentennial in 1989 was marked by the inauguration of the **Opéra-Bastille** (see p.185), President Mitterrand's pet project. Filling almost the entire block between rues de Lyon, Charenton and Moreau, it has shifted the focus of place de la Bastille, so that the column is no longer the pivotal point; in fact, it's easy to miss it altogether when dazzled by the night-time glare of lights emanating from this "hippopotamus in a bathtub", as one critic dubbed the Opéra.

The building's construction destroyed no small amount of low-rent housing, but, as with most speculative developments, the pace of change is uneven, and cobblers and ironmongers still survive alongside cocktail haunts and sushi bars, making the **quartier de la Bastille** a simultaneously gritty and trendy quarter. **Place** and **rue d'Aligre**, east of square Trousseau, still have their raucous daily market and, on **rue de Lappe**, *Balajo* is one remnant of a very Parisian tradition: the *bals musettes*, or music halls of 1930s *gai Paris*, frequented between the wars by Piaf, Jean Gabin and Rita Hayworth. It was founded by one Jo de France, who introduced glitter and spectacle into what were then seedy gangster dives, and brought Parisians from the other side of the city to the rue de Lappe lowlife. Now the street is full of fun, cool bars, full to bursting at the weekends. Hip bars and cafés have also sprung up in the surrounding streets, especially on rue de **Charonne**, also home to fashion boutiques and whacky interior designers, while alternative, hippy outfits cluster on **rues Keller** and **de la Roquette.**

Just south of here you can find quiet havens in the courtyards of **rue du Faubourg-St-Antoine**. Since the fifteenth century, this has been the principal artisan and working-class *quartier* of Paris, the cradle of revolutions and mother of street-fighters. From its beginnings the principal trade associated with it has been **furniture-making**, and the maze of interconnecting yards and *passages* are still full of the workshops of the related trades: marquetry, stainers, polishers and inlayers.

Quartier Latin

South of the river, the **Rive Gauche** (Left Bank) has long maintained an "alternative" identity, opposed to the formal, businesslike ambience of the Right Bank – as much left wing as left bank. These days, this image is mostly kept up by the student population of the **Quartier Latin**, which first settled on the high ground of the Montagne Ste-Geneviève in the twelfth century. No one knows if it was the learned Latin of the medieval scholars or the ruins of the Roman city of Lutetia that gave the area its name. The pivotal point of this "Latin quarter" is **place St-Michel**, where the tree-lined **boulevard St-Michel** begins. The famous *boul' Mich* has long since changed from radical student heartland to busy commercial thoroughfare, but the universities on all sides maintain the area's traditions, and the cafés and shops are still jammed with people, mainly young and – in summer – largely foreign.

Around St-Séverin

The touristy scrum is at its ugliest around **rue de la Huchette**, just east of the place St-Michel. The Théâtre de la Huchette still shows Ionesco's *La Cantatrice Chauve* (*The Bald Prima Donna*) almost fifty years on, but it's a last bastion of the area's postwar heyday, and is now hemmed in by cheap bars and indifferent Greek restaurants. Connecting rue de la Huchette to the riverside is **rue du Chat-qui-Pêche**, a narrow slice of medieval Paris as it was before Haussmann got to work.

At the end of rue de la Huchette, **rue St-Jacques** is aligned on the main street of Roman Paris, and was the road up which millions of medieval pilgrims trudged at the start of their long march to Santiago de Compostela in Spain. One block south of rue de la Huchette, just west of rue St-Jacques, is the mainly fifteenth-century church of **St-Séverin**, whose entrance is on rue des Prêtres St-Séverin (Mon–Sat 11am–7.15pm, Sun 9am–8.30pm; M° St-Michel/ Cluny–La Sorbonne). It's one of the city's more intense churches, its flamboyant choir resting on a virtuoso spiralling central pillar and its windows filled with edgy stained glass by the modern French painter Jean Bazaine. East of rue St-Jacques, and back towards the river, **square Viviani** provides a perfect view of Notre-Dame and a pleasant patch of green. The mutilated church behind is **St-Julien-le-Pauvre** (daily 9.30am–12.30pm & 3–6.30pm; M° St-Michel/ Maubert Mutualité). The same age as Notre-Dame, it used to be the venue for university assemblies until rumbustious students tore it apart in 1524. Across rue Lagrange from the square, rue de la Bûcherie is the home of the celebrated English-language bookshop **Shakespeare and Co** (see p.195), which acts as an informal hostel for wannabe Hemingways. The still-more-famous original site – under Sylvia Beach, the first publisher of Joyce's *Ulysses* – was on rue de l'Odéon.

The riverbank and Institut du Monde Arabe

A short walk from square Viviani on the riverbank, you'll find old books, postcards and prints on sale from the **bouquinistes**, whose green boxes line the parapets of the **riverside quais**. It's a pleasant walk upstream to the **Pont de Sully** – which leads across to the Île St-Louis and offers a dramatic view of the apse and steeple of Notre-Dame – and the beginning of a sunny riverside garden dotted with interesting though worn pieces of modern sculpture.

Opposite the Pont de Sully, you can't miss the bold glass and aluminium mass of the **Institut du Monde Arabe** (Tues–Sun 10am–6pm; Ⓦ www.imarabe.org; M° Jussieu/Cardinal-Lemoine), a cultural centre built to further understanding of the Arab world. Designed by Paris's architect of the moment, Jean Nouvel, its broad southern facade comprises thousands of tiny shutters which modulate the light levels inside while simultaneously mimicking a *moucharabiyah*, or traditional Arab latticework balcony. Originally designed to be light-sensitive, they now simply open and shut on the hour every hour to show off the effect. Inside, a sleek **museum** (€5) winds down from the seventh floor as it traces the evolution of art in the Islamic world, with precious glass, rugs, ceramics, illuminated manuscripts, woodcarving, metalwork and scientific instruments. On other levels there's a library and multimedia centre for scholars, an auditorium for films and concerts, and a specialist bookshop with a very good selection of CDs from the Arab world. The **café-restaurant** on the ninth floor is a great place to enjoy a mint tea and the view towards the apse of Notre-Dame.

The Musée National du Moyen-Âge and the Sorbonne

The nearby area around the slopes of the **Montagne Ste-Geneviève**, the hill on which the Panthéon stands, is good for a stroll. The best approach is from **place Maubert** (which has a good market on Tues, Thurs & Sat mornings) or from the St-Michel/St-Germain crossroads, where the walls of the third-century **Roman baths** are visible in the garden of the **Hôtel de Cluny**, a sixteenth-century mansion built by the abbots of the powerful Cluny monastery as their Paris pied-à-terre. It now houses the **Musée National du Moyen-Âge**, 6 place Paul-Painlevé, off rue des Écoles (daily except Tues 9.15am–5.45pm; €6.50, €4.50 on Sun; Ⓦ www.musee-moyenage.fr; M° Cluny-La Sorbonne/St-Michel), a treasure house of medieval art. The vaults of the former *frigidarium* are intact – though temporarily protected by corrugated sheets, pending funds for restoration – and shelter two beautiful Roman capitals, as well as some fragments from the original west front of Notre-Dame, lopped off during the French Revolution. There's more medieval sculpture throughout, including the flamboyant Gothic chapel, with its vault splaying out from a central pillar, though the real beauties are the **tapestries**. Conjuring up scenes from the medieval world, there are depictions of a grape harvest, a woman embroidering while her servant patiently holds the threads for her, a lover making advances and a woman in a bath which overflows into a duck pond. But the greatest wonder of all is the truly stunning *La Dame à la Licorne* ("The Lady with the Unicorn"). Made in the late fifteenth century, probably in Brussels, the set depicts the five senses – along with the virtue in controlling them – in six richly coloured and detailed allegoric scenes, each featuring a beautiful woman flanked by a lion and a unicorn. Excellent hour-long sessions of medieval music are held on Friday lunchtimes (12.30pm) and Saturday afternoons (4pm), and there is a great programme of evening concerts.

The forbidding-looking buildings on the other side of rue des Écoles are the **Sorbonne**, **Collège de France** and **Lycée Louis-le-Grand**, which numbers Molière, Robespierre, Sartre and Victor Hugo among its pupils. A better aspect can be found if you head up rue de la Sorbonne to the traffic-free **place de la Sorbonne**, overlooked by the dramatic Counter-Reformation facade of the Sorbonne's chapel, built in the 1640s by the great Cardinal Richelieu, whose

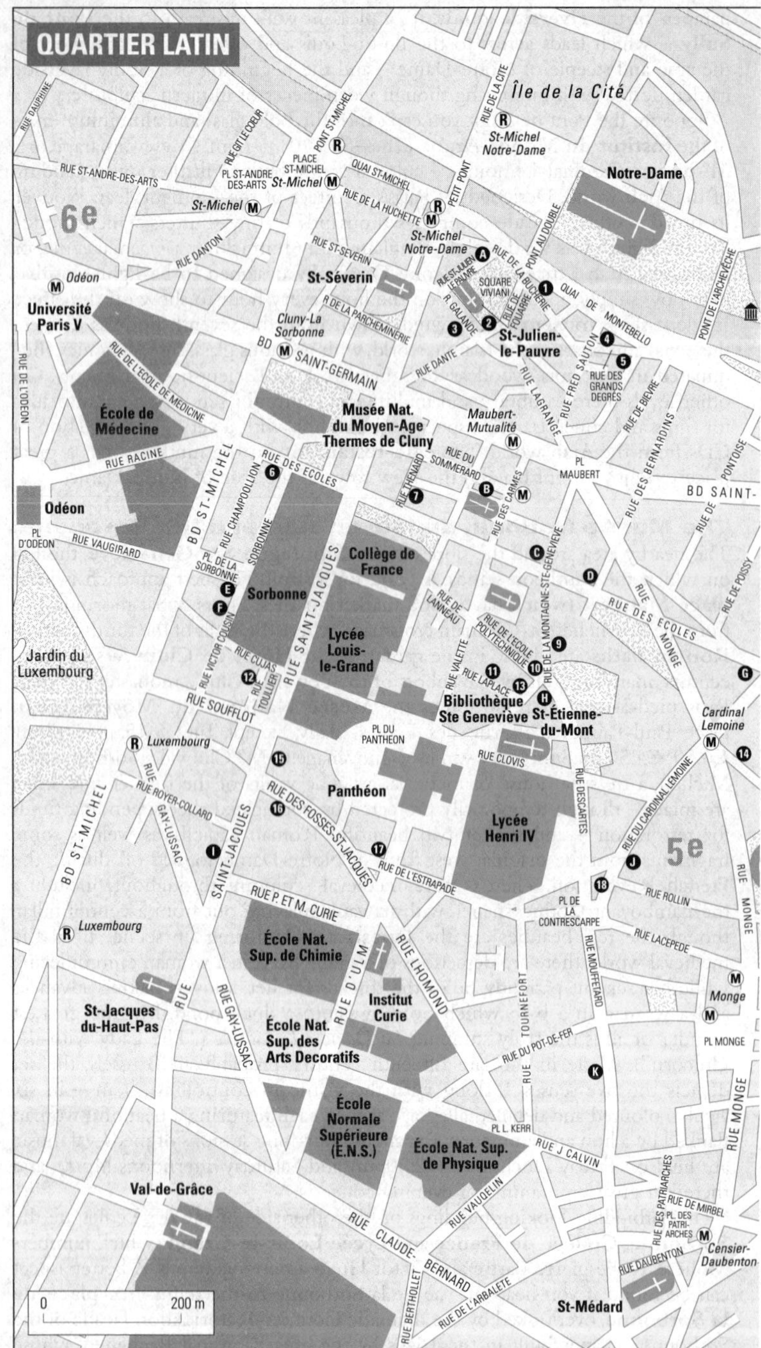
QUARTIER LATIN
Île de la Cité
Notre-Dame
St-Michel Notre-Dame
St-Michel
Odéon
Université Paris V
6e
5e
St-Séverin
Cluny-La Sorbonne
St-Julien-le-Pauvre
SQUARE VIVIANI
École de Médecine
Musée Nat. du Moyen-Age Thermes de Cluny
Maubert-Mutualité
Odéon
Collège de France
Sorbonne
Lycée Louis-le-Grand
Jardin du Luxembourg
Bibliothèque Ste Geneviève
St-Étienne-du-Mont
Cardinal Lemoine
Luxembourg
Panthéon
Lycée Henri IV
École Nat. Sup. de Chimie
Institut Curie
École Nat. Sup. des Arts Decoratifs
St-Jacques du-Haut-Pas
Monge
École Normale Supérieure (E.N.S.)
École Nat. Sup. de Physique
Val-de-Grâce
Censier-Daubenton
St-Médard
RUE DAUPHINE
RUE ST-ANDRE-DES-ARTS
PL ST-ANDRE DES-ARTS
PLACE ST-MICHEL
PONT ST-MICHEL
RUE GIT LE COEUR
QUAI ST-MICHEL
RUE DE LA HUCHETTE
PETIT PONT
RUE DE LA CITE
RUE DANTON
RUE ST-SEVERIN
RUE ST-JULIEN LE PAUVRE
R. GALANDE
RUE DE FOUARRE
RUE DE LA BUCHERIE
PONT AU DOUBLE
QUAI DE MONTEBELLO
PONT DE L'ARCHEVÊCHE
R DE LA PARCHEMINERIE
BD SAINT-GERMAIN
RUE DANTE
RUE FRED SAUTON
RUE DES GRANDS DEGRES
RUE DE BIEVRE
RUE LAGRANGE
RUE DE L'ODEON
RUE DE L'ECOLE DE MEDECINE
RUE RACINE
BD ST-MICHEL
RUE DES ECOLES
RUE DU SOMMERARD
RUE THENARD
RUE DES CARMES
PL MAUBERT
RUE DES BERNARDINS
RUE DE PONTOISE
BD SAINT-
PL D'ODEON
RUE VAUGIRARD
RUE CHAMPOLLION
SORBONNE
PL. DE LA SORBONNE
RUE SAINT-JACQUES
RUE DE LANNEAU
RUE DE LA MONTAGNE-STE-GENEVIEVE
RUE DE L'ECOLE POLYTECHNIQUE
RUE MONGE
RUE DE POISSY
RUE VICTOR COUSIN
RUE CUJAS
RUE TOULLIER
RUE VALETTE
RUE LAPLACE
RUE SOUFFLOT
PL DU PANTHEON
RUE CLOVIS
RUE DESCARTES
RUE DU CARDINAL LEMOINE
RUE ROYER-COLLARD
RUE GAY-LUSSAC
RUE DES FOSSES-ST-JACQUES
RUE DE L'ESTRAPADE
PL DE LA CONTRESCARPE
RUE ROLLIN
RUE P. ET M. CURIE
RUE D'ULM
RUE LHOMOND
RUE MOUFFETARD
RUE LACEPEDE
RUE TOURNEFORT
RUE DU POT-DE-FER
PL MONGE
PL L. KERR
RUE J CALVIN
RUE VAUQUELIN
RUE CLAUDE-BERNARD
RUE DES PATRIARCHES
RUE DE MIRBEL
PL. DES PATRIARCHES
RUE DAUBENTON
RUE BERTHOLLET
RUE DE L'ARBALETE
0 200 m

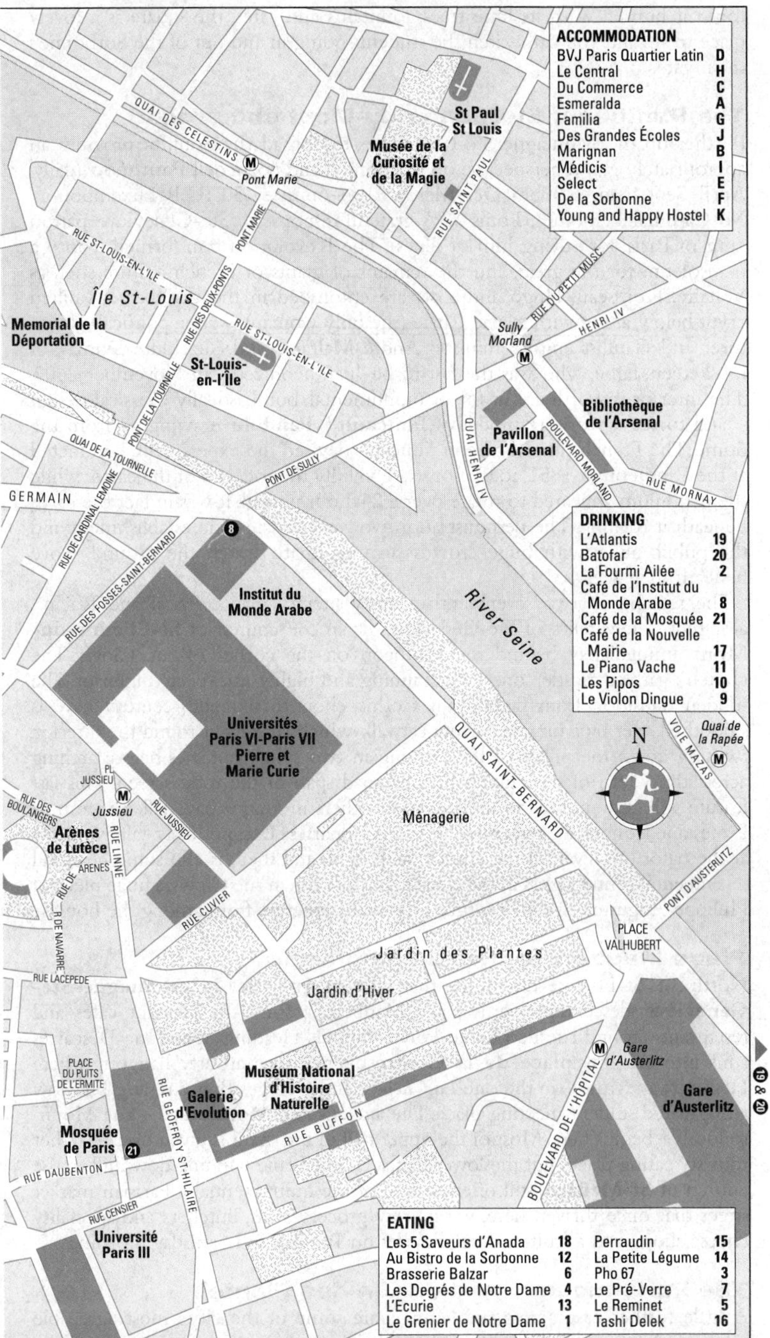
ACCOMMODATION
BVJ Paris Quartier Latin D
Le Central H
Du Commerce C
Esmeralda A
Familia G
Des Grandes Écoles J
Marignan B
Médicis I
Select E
De la Sorbonne F
Young and Happy Hostel K
DRINKING
L'Atlantis 19
Batofar 20
La Fourmi Ailée 2
Café de l'Institut du Monde Arabe 8
Café de la Mosquée 21
Café de la Nouvelle Mairie 17
Le Piano Vache 11
Les Pipos 10
Le Violon Dingue 9
EATING
Les 5 Saveurs d'Anada 18
Au Bistro de la Sorbonne 12
Brasserie Balzar 6
Les Degrés de Notre Dame 4
L'Ecurie 13
Le Grenier de Notre Dame 1
Perraudin 15
La Petite Légume 14
Pho 67 3
Le Pré-Verre 7
Le Reminet 5
Tashi Delek 16
QUAI DES CELESTINS
Pont Marie
PONT MARIE
St Paul St Louis
Musée de la Curiosité et de la Magie
RUE SAINT PAUL
RUE ST-LOUIS-EN-L'ILE
Île St-Louis
RUE DES DEUX-PONTS
Memorial de la Déportation
St-Louis-en-l'Île
RUE DU PETIT MUSC
HENRI IV
Sully Morland
Bibliothèque de l'Arsenal
Pavillon de l'Arsenal
QUAI HENRI IV
BOULEVARD MORLAND
RUE MORNAY
PONT DE LA TOURNELLE
QUAI DE LA TOURNELLE
PONT DE SULLY
GERMAIN
RUE DE CARDINAL LEMOINE
RUE DES FOSSES-SAINT-BERNARD
Institut du Monde Arabe
River Seine
Universités Paris VI-Paris VII Pierre et Marie Curie
PL JUSSIEU
Jussieu
RUE DES BOULANGERS
RUE JUSSIEU
Arènes de Lutèce
RUE LINNE
RUE DE ARENES
R DE NAVARRE
QUAI SAINT-BERNARD
VOIE MAZAS
Quai de la Rapée
N
Ménagerie
PONT D'AUSTERLITZ
RUE CUVIER
PLACE VALHUBERT
Jardin des Plantes
RUE LACEPEDE
Jardin d'Hiver
PLACE DU PUITS DE L'ERMITE
Muséum National d'Histoire Naturelle
Galerie d'Evolution
RUE GEOFFROY ST-HILAIRE
Mosquée de Paris
RUE BUFFON
Gare d'Austerlitz
BOULEVARD DE L'HÔPITAL
RUE DAUBENTON
RUE CENSIER
Université Paris III

19 & 20

tomb it houses. With its lime trees, fountains and cafés, the square is a lovely place to sit, and you can watch the students going in and out of the Sorbonne's main gate.

The Panthéon, St-Étienne-du-Mont and around

Further up the Montagne Ste-Geneviève, the broad rue Soufflot provides an appropriately grand perspective on the domed and porticoed **Panthéon** (daily: April–Sept 10am–6.30pm; Oct–March 10am–6pm; €7.50; RER Luxembourg/ M° Cardinal-Lemoine), Louis XV's grateful response to Ste-Geneviève, patron saint of Paris, for curing him of illness. The Revolution transformed it into a mausoleum for the great, and the remains of giants of French culture such as Voltaire, Rousseau, Hugo and Zola are entombed in the vast, barrel-vaulted crypt below, along with Marie Curie (the only woman), writer, political adventurer and Gaullist culture minister André Malraux, and Alexandre Dumas, of musketeers fame, who was the last to be "panthéonized", in November 2002. The interior is worth a visit for its monumental, bombastically Classical design – and to see a working model of **Foucault's Pendulum** swinging from the dome. The French physicist Léon Foucault devised the experiment, conducted at the Panthéon in 1851, to demonstrate vividly the rotation of the earth: while the pendulum appeared to rotate over a 24-hour period, it was in fact the earth beneath it turning. The demonstration wowed the scientific establishment and the public alike, with huge crowds turning up to watch the ground move beneath their feet.

The remains of two seventeenth-century literary giants, Pascal and Racine, alongside a few relics of Ste-Geneviève, lie in the church of **St-Étienne-du-Mont**, immediately behind the Panthéon on the corner of rue Clovis. The church's garbled facade conceals a stunning and highly unexpected interior. The sudden transition from flamboyant Gothic choir to sixteenth-century nave is smoothed over by a bizarre narrow catwalk which runs right round the interior, twisting down the pillars of the crossing in two spiral staircases before arching across the width of the church in the broad span of the rood screen. This last feature is highly unusual in itself, as most others in France have fallen victim to Protestant iconoclasts, reformers or revolutionaries. Exceptionally tall windows at the triforium level fill the church with light, and there is also some beautiful seventeenth-century glass in the cloister. Further down rue Clovis, a huge piece of Philippe-Auguste's twelfth-century **city walls** emerges from among the houses.

Place Maubert to the rue Mouffetard

North of St-Étienne-du-Mont, the villagey **rue de la Montagne-Ste-Geneviève** descends towards place Maubert, passing the pleasant cafés and restaurants around rue de l'École-Polytechnique. Heading uphill, rue Descartes runs into the tiny **place de la Contrescarpe**, once an arty hangout where Hemingway wrote – in the café *La Chope* – and Georges Brassens sang, but now a dog-eared student meeting-place. The ancient **rue Mouffetard** – rue Mouff' to locals – begins here. Most of the upper half of the street is given over to rather touristy eating places but the lower half, a cobbled lane winding downhill to the church of **St-Médard**, still offers a taste of the quintessentially Parisian market street that once thrived here, with a few grocers' stalls, butchers and speciality cheese shops, and a fruit-and-veg market on Tuesday and Saturday mornings.

The Paris mosque and Jardin des Plantes

A little further east, across rue Monge, are some of the city's most agreeable surprises. Just past place du Puits de l'Ermite stand the crenellated walls of the

Mosquée de Paris (daily except Fri & Muslim hols 9am–noon & 2–6pm; Ⓦwww.mosquee-de-paris.org; €3). You can walk in the sunken garden and patios with their polychrome tiles and carved ceilings, but not the prayer room. There's also a lovely, gardened **tearoom** (see p.170), which is open to all, and an atmospheric **hamam** (Turkish bath, see p.192): one of the most enjoyable things to do in this part of the city.

Behind the mosque is the **Jardin des Plantes** (daily: summer 8am–7.30pm; winter 8am–dusk; free; M° Austerlitz/Jussieu/Monge), which was founded as a medicinal herb garden in 1626 and gradually evolved into Paris's botanical gardens, with shady avenues of trees, lawns to sprawl on, hothouses, museums and a zoo. By the rue Cuvier exit is a fine Lebanon Cedar, planted in 1734, raised from a seed from the Oxford Botanical Gardens, and a slice of an American sequoia more than 2000 years old. In the nearby physics labs, Henri Becquerel discovered radioactivity in 1896, and two years later the Curies discovered radium.

Magnificent, varied floral beds make a fine approach to the collection of buildings which form the **Muséum National d'Histoire Naturelle** (Ⓦwww.mnhn.fr). These musty museums of palaeontology, anatomy, mineralogy, entomology and palaeobotany should, however, be sidestepped in favour of the **Grand Galerie de l'Évolution** (daily except Tues 10am–6pm; €8), housed in a dramatically restored nineteenth-century glass-domed building; the entrance is off rue Buffon. The museum tells the story of evolution and the relations between human beings and nature with the aid of a huge cast of life-size animals that parade across the central space. The wow-factor may initally grab children's attention, but you'll have to look out for the translation placards to make the most of the visit.

Real animals can be seen in the small **menagerie** across the park to the northeast near rue Cuvier (April–Sept Mon–Sat 9am–6.30pm, Sun 9am–5pm; Oct–March daily 9am–5pm; €7). Founded here just after the Revolution, it is France's oldest zoo – and looks it. The old-fashioned iron cages of the big cats' *fauverie*, the stinky vivarium and the unkempt, glazed-in primate house are frankly depressing, though these animals are at least spared the fate of their predecessors during the starvation months of the 1870 Prussian siege. Most of the zoo is pleasantly park-like, however, and given over to deer, antelope, goats, buffaloes and other marvellous beasts that seem happy enough in their outdoor enclosures. The **Microzoo** allows you to inspect headlice and other minuscule wonders.

A short distance away to the northwest, with entrances in rue de Navarre, rue des Arènes and through a passage on rue Monge, is the **Arènes de Lutèce**, an unexpected backwater hidden from the street, and, along with the Roman baths (see p.133), Paris's only Roman remains. Once an amphitheatre for ten thousand, a few ghostly rows of stone seats now look down on old men playing *boules* in the sand, and benches, gardens and a kids' playground stand behind.

St-Germain

The northern half of the 6e arrondissement, centred on **place St-Germain-des-Prés**, is one of the most attractive, lively and wealthy square kilometres in the city – and one of the best places to shop for clothes. The most dramatic approach is to cross the river from the Louvre by the footbridge, the **Pont des Arts**, from where there's a classic upstream view of the Île de la Cité, with barges moored at the quai de Conti, the Tour St-Jacques and Hôtel de Ville breaking the skyline of the Right Bank. The dome and pediment at the end of

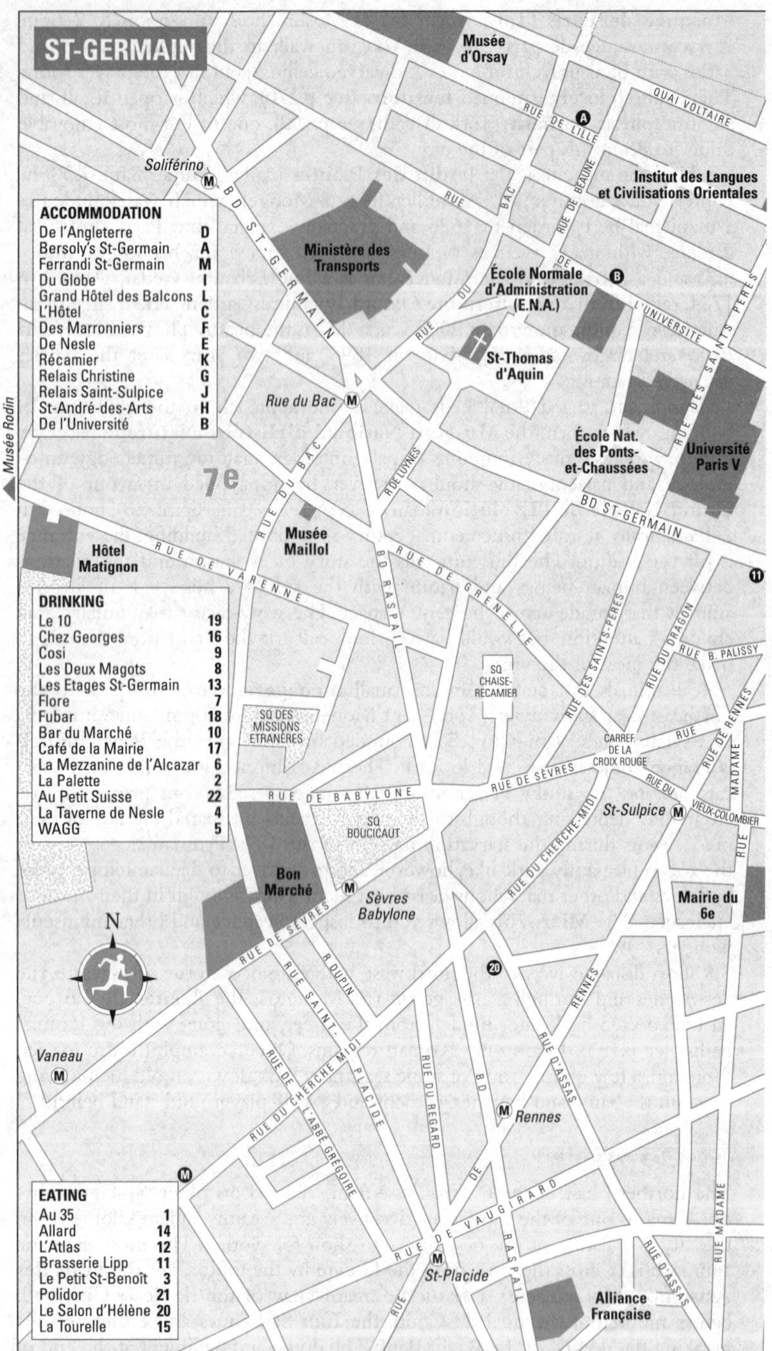
ST-GERMAIN
ACCOMMODATION
De l'Angleterre D
Bersoly's St-Germain A
Ferrandi St-Germain M
Du Globe I
Grand Hôtel des Balcons L
L'Hôtel C
Des Marronniers F
De Nesle E
Récamier K
Relais Christine G
Relais Saint-Sulpice J
St-André-des-Arts H
De l'Université B
DRINKING
Le 10 19
Chez Georges 16
Cosi 9
Les Deux Magots 8
Les Etages St-Germain 13
Flore 7
Fubar 18
Bar du Marché 10
Café de la Mairie 17
La Mezzanine de l'Alcazar 6
La Palette 2
Au Petit Suisse 22
La Taverne de Nesle 4
WAGG 5
EATING
Au 35 1
Allard 14
L'Atlas 12
Brasserie Lipp 11
Le Petit St-Benoît 3
Polidor 21
Le Salon d'Hélène 20
La Tourelle 15
Musée d'Orsay
Quai Voltaire
Rue de Lille
Institut des Langues et Civilisations Orientales
Solférino
BD St-Germain
Ministère des Transports
Rue du Bac
Rue de Beaune
École Normale d'Administration (E.N.A.)
Rue de l'Université
St-Thomas d'Aquin
Rue des Saints Pères
Rue du Bac
École Nat. des Ponts-et-Chaussées
Université Paris V
Musée Rodin
7e
R. de Luynes
Musée Maillol
Hôtel Matignon
Rue de Varenne
BD Raspail
Rue de Grenelle
Rue des Saints-Pères
Rue du Dragon
Rue B. Palissy
SQ Chaise-Récamier
SQ des Missions Etranères
Carref. de la Croix Rouge
Rue de Rennes
Rue de Sèvres
Rue du Vieux-Colombier
Rue Madame
St-Sulpice
Rue de Babylone
SQ Boucicaut
Rue du Cherche-Midi
Bon Marché
Sèvres Babylone
Mairie du 6e
N
Rue de Sèvres
R. Dupin
Rue Saint-Placide
Rennes
Rue d'Assas
Vaneau
Rue du Cherche Midi
Rue de l'Abbé Grégoire
Rue du Regard
BD
Rennes
Rue de Vaugirard
Raspail
Rue Madame
St-Placide
Rue d'Assas
Alliance Française
Gare Montparnasse

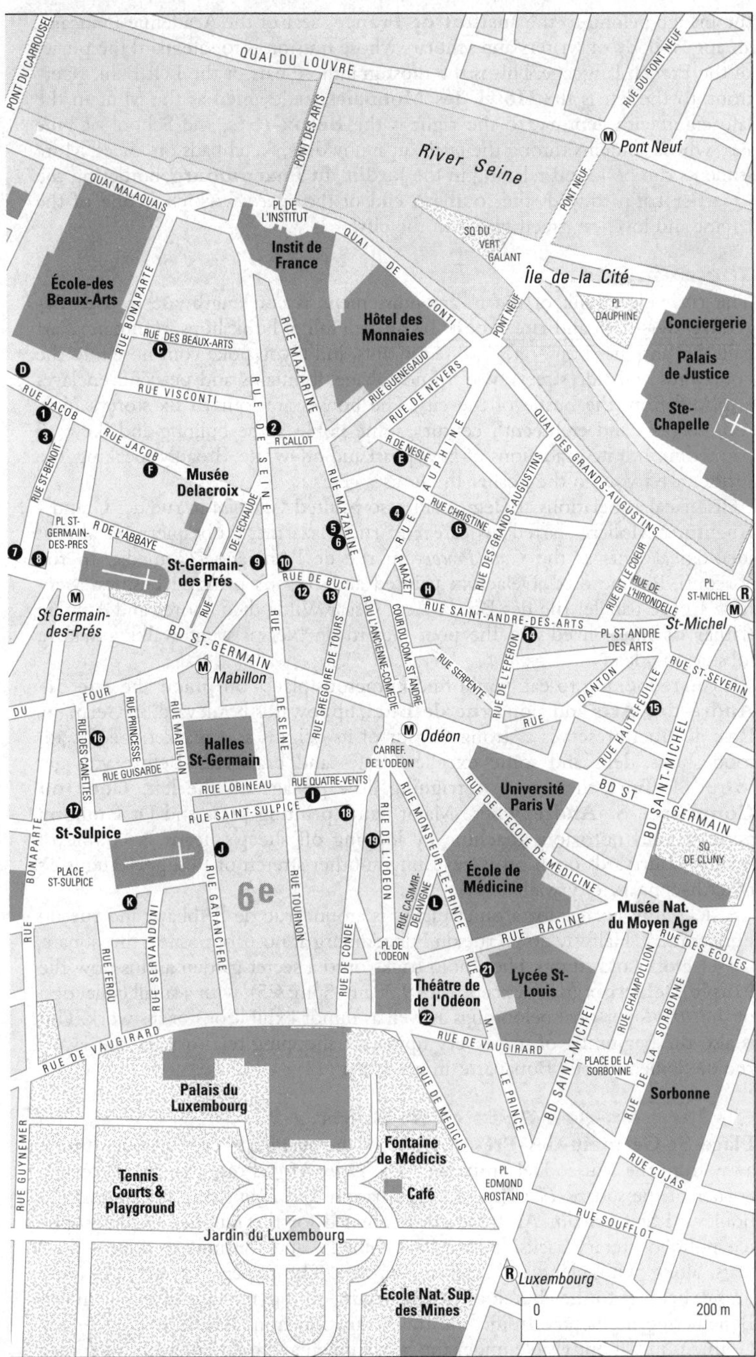
QUAI DU LOUVRE
PONT DU CARROUSEL
PONT DES ARTS
RUE DU PONT NEUF
Pont Neuf
River Seine
QUAI MALAQUAIS
PL DE L'INSTITUT
Instit de France
SQ DU VERT GALANT
PONT NEUF
QUAI DE CONTI
Île de la Cité
École-des Beaux-Arts
RUE BONAPARTE
Hôtel des Monnaies
PL DAUPHINE
Conciergerie
Palais de Justice
Ste-Chapelle
RUE DES BEAUX-ARTS
RUE MAZARINE
RUE GUENEGAUD
RUE DE NEVERS
RUE VISCONTI
RUE JACOB
RUE DE SEINE
R CALLOT
R DE NESLE
RUE DAUPHINE
QUAI DES GRANDS-AUGUSTINS
Musée Delacroix
RUE ST-BENOIT
RUE CHRISTINE
PL ST-GERMAIN-DES-PRES
R DE L'ABBAYE
RUE DE L'ECHAUDE
St-Germain-des Prés
R MAZET
RUE DES GRANDS-AUGUSTINS
RUE GIT LE COEUR
RUE DE L'HIRONDELLE
PL ST-MICHEL
RUE DE BUCI
St Germain-des-Prés
RUE SAINT-ANDRE-DES-ARTS
St-Michel
BD ST-GERMAIN
R DU L'ANCIENNE-COMEDIE
COUR DU COM. ST ANDRE
PL ST ANDRE DES ARTS
Mabillon
RUE SERPENTE
RUE DE L'EPERON
RUE ST-SEVERIN
RUE DU FOUR
RUE GREGOIRE DE TOURS
RUE DANTON
RUE HAUTEFEUILLE
RUE PRINCESSE
RUE MABILLON
RUE DES CANETTES
Halles St-Germain
Odéon
CARREF. DE L'ODEON
BD SAINT-MICHEL
RUE GUISARDE
RUE LOBINEAU
RUE QUATRE-VENTS
Université Paris V
BD ST GERMAIN
RUE SAINT-SULPICE
RUE DE L'ECOLE DE MEDICINE
St-Sulpice
RUE MONSIEUR-LE-PRINCE
RUE DE L'ODEON
SQ DE CLUNY
PLACE ST-SULPICE
RUE GARANCIERE
RUE TOURNON
École de Médicine
6e
RUE CASIMIR-DELAVIGNE
Musée Nat. du Moyen Age
RUE SERVANDONI
RUE RACINE
RUE DES ECOLES
RUE FEROU
RUE DE CONDE
PL DE L'ODEON
Lycée St-Louis
Théatre de de l'Odéon
RUE CHAMPOLLION
RUE DE VAUGIRARD
PLACE DE LA SORBONNE
RUE DE LA SORBONNE
Palais du Luxembourg
RUE DE MEDICIS
RUE LE PRINCE
Sorbonne
RUE GUYNEMER
Fontaine de Médicis
Tennis Courts & Playground
Café
PL EDMOND ROSTAND
RUE CUJAS
RUE SOUFFLOT
Jardin du Luxembourg
Luxembourg
École Nat. Sup. des Mines
0
200 m

the bridge belong to the **Institut de France**, seat of the Académie Française, an august body of writers and scholars whose mission is to safeguard the purity of the French language. This is the most grandiose part of the Left Bank riverfront: to the left is the **Hôtel des Monnaies**, redesigned as the Mint in the late eighteenth century; to the right is the **Beaux-Arts**, the School of Fine Art, whose students throng the *quais* on sunny days, sketchpads on knees. More students can be found relaxing in the **Jardin du Luxembourg**, bordering the Quartier Latin towards the southern end of the *sixième*, which is one of the largest and loveliest green spaces in the city.

The riverside

The riverside chunk of the 6e arrondissement is cut lengthwise by **rue St-André-des-Arts** and **rue Jacob**. It's an area full of bookshops, commercial art galleries, antique shops, cafés and restaurants, and if you poke your nose into the courtyards and side streets, you'll find foliage, fountains and peaceful enclaves removed from the bustle of the city. The houses are four to six storeys high, seventeenth- and eighteenth-century, some noble, some bulging and skew, all painted in infinite gradations of grey, pearl and off-white. Broadly speaking, the further west you go the posher the houses get.

Historical associations are legion: Picasso painted *Guernica* in rue des Grands-Augustins; Molière started his career in rue Mazarine; Robespierre et al split ideological hairs at the *Café Procope* in rue de l'Ancienne-Comédie. In rue Visconti, Racine died, Delacroix painted and Balzac's printing business went bust. In the parallel rue des Beaux-Arts, Oscar Wilde died, Corot and Ampère (father of amps) lived and the poet Gérard de Nerval went walking with a lobster on a lead.

If you're looking to eat, you'll find numerous places on **place** and **rue St-André-des-Arts** and along **rue de Buci**, up towards boulevard St-Germain. Rue de Buci preserves a strong flavour of its origins as a market street, with food shops, delis and some excellent cafés and brasseries. Before you get to rue de Buci, there is an intriguing little passage on the left, **Cour du Commerce St-André**, where Marat had a printing press and Dr Guillotin perfected his notorious machine by lopping off sheep's heads. A couple of smaller courtyards open off it, revealing another stretch of Philippe-Auguste's twelfth-century city wall.

A delightful corner for a quiet picnic is around rue de l'Abbaye and rue du Furstemberg. Halfway down rue du Furstemburg at no. 6, opposite a tiny square, is Delacroix's old studio. The studio backs onto a secret garden and is now the **Musée Delacroix** (daily except Tues 9.30am–5pm; €5), with a small collection of the artist's personal belongings as well as minor exhibitions of his work. This is also the beginning of some very upmarket shopping territory, in rue Jacob, rue de Seine and rue Bonaparte in particular.

St-Germain-des-Prés to St-Sulpice

Place St-Germain-des-Prés, the hub of the *quartier*, is only a stone's throw away from the Musée Delacroix, with the *Deux Magots* café (see p.171) on the corner of the square, *Flore* (see p.171) adjacent and *Lipp* (see p.172) across the boulevard St-Germain. All three are renowned for the number of philosophico-politico-literary backsides that have shined – and continue to shine – their seats, along with plenty of celebrity-hunters. The tower opposite the *Deux Magots* belongs to the church of **St-Germain**, all that remains of an enormous Benedictine monastery. Inside, the transformation from Romanesque to early Gothic is just about visible under the heavy green and gold nineteenth-century paintwork. The last chapel on the south side contains the tomb of the philosopher René Descartes.

South of boulevard St-Germain, the streets round St-Sulpice are calm and classy. **Rue Mabillon** is pretty, with a row of old houses set back below the level of the modern street. On the left are the shops of the **Halles St-Germain**, on the site of a fifteenth-century market. Rue St-Sulpice leads through to the front of the enormous, early eighteenth-century church of **St-Sulpice** (daily 7.30am–7.30pm), an austerely Classical building with a Doric colonnade surmounted by an Ionic, and Corinthian pilasters in the towers; uncut masonry blocks still protrude from the south tower, awaiting the sculptor's chisel. Three Delacroix murals, including one of St Michael slaying a dragon, can be seen in the first chapel on the right, but most visitors these days come to see the **gnomon**, a kind of solar clock whose origins and purpose were so compellingly garbled by *The Da Vinci Code*.

The main attractions of **place St-Sulpice** are the headquarters boutiques of Yves Saint Laurent Rive Gauche and agnès b, and the fashionable *Café de la Mairie*, with its outside tables on the sunny side of the square. All is expensive elegance in these parts, but if you're heading east towards boulevard St-Michel, the glitzy shops quickly fade into the worthy bookshops and inexpensive restaurants around the École de Médecine.

Jardin du Luxembourg

The **Palais du Luxembourg** fronts onto **rue de Vaugirard**, Paris's longest street. It was constructed for Marie de Médicis, Henri IV's widow, to remind her of the Palazzo Pitti and Giardino di Boboli of her native Florence. Today, it's the seat of the French Senate and its **gardens** are the chief lung of the Left Bank, with formal lawns among the floral parterres dotted with trees in giant pots that are taken inside in winter. Children rent toy yachts to sail on the central round pond, but the western side is the more active area, with tennis courts (open to all-comers, though you may have to wait), donkey rides, a children's playground, chess tables that are invariably packed out, and the inevitable sandy area for *boules*. The **puppet theatre** (€4.20; call ⓣ01.43.26.46.47 for timings – in French) has been in the same family for the best part of a century, and still puts on enthralling shows. The quieter, wooded southeast corner ends in a miniature orchard of elaborately espaliered pear trees. The gardens get crazily crowded on summer days, when the most contested spots are the shady **Fontaine de Médicis** in the northeast corner, and the lawns of the southernmost strip – the only area where you're allowed to lie out on the grass. Elsewhere, you're restricted to slumping on the heavy, sage-green metal chairs, which are liberally distributed around the gravel paths.

Musée d'Orsay

On the riverfront just west of the Beaux-Arts, in a former railway station whose stone facade disguises a stunning vault of steel and glass, is the **Musée-d'Orsay**, at 1 rue de la Légion d'Honneur (Tues–Sun 9.30am–6pm, Thurs till 9.45pm; €7.50, Sun after 4.15pm and Thurs after 8pm €5.50, free on first Sun of the month, free to under-18s; ⓦwww.musee-orsay.fr; M° Solférino/RER Musée-d'Orsay). Housing painting and sculpture from 1848 to 1914, and thus bridging the gap between the Louvre and Centre Pompidou, its highlights are the electrifying works of the **Impressionists** and so-called **Post-Impressionists**. You could spend half a day meandering through the numbered rooms in chronological order, but the layout makes it easy to confine your visit to a specific section, each of which has a very distinctive atmosphere.

The two **cafés** are fine – if pricey – places to take stock: the one on the upper level has a summer terrace and wonderful view of Montmartre through the giant railway clock, while the tearoom on the middle level is resplendently gilded in authentic period style.

The ground level

The **ground floor**, under the great glass arch, is devoted to pre-1870 work, with a double row of sculptures running down the central aisle like railway tracks, and paintings in the odd little bunkers on either side. The first set of rooms (1–3) is dedicated to Ingres, Delacroix – the bulk of whose work is in the Louvre – and the serious-minded works of the painters acceptable to the mid-nineteenth century salons; just beyond (rooms 11–13) are the relatively wacky works of Puvis de Chavannes, Gustave Moreau and the younger Degas. The influential **Barbizon school** and the **Realists** are showcased on the Seine side (rooms 4–7), with canvases by Daumier, Corot, Millet and Courbet. Just a few steps away, room 14 explodes with the early controversies of Monet's violently light-filled *Femmes au Jardin* (1867) and Manet's provocative *Olympia* (1863), which heralded the arrival of Impressionism.

The upper level

To continue chronologically you have to go straight to the **upper level**, done up like a suite of attic studios, where you pass first through the private collection donated by Étienne Moreau-Nélaton (room 29). An assiduous collector and art historian, his collection contains some of the most famous **Impressionist** images: Monet's *Poppies*, as well as Manet's *Déjeuner sur l'Herbe*, which sent the critics into apoplexies of rage and disgust when it appeared in 1863, and was refused for that year's Salon. From this point on, you'll have to fight off a persistent sense of familiarity or recognition – Degas' *L'Absinthe*, Renoir's *Bal du Moulin de la Galette*, Monet's *Femme à l'Ombrelle* – in order to appreciate Impressionism's vibrant, experimental vigour. There's a host of small-scale landscapes and outdoor scenes by Renoir, Sisley, Pissarro and Monet, paintings which owed much of their brilliance to the novel practice of setting up easels in the open to capture the light. Less typical works include Degas' ballet-dancers, which demonstrate his principal interest in movement and line as opposed to the more common Impressionist concern with light, and *Le Berceau* (1872), by Berthe Morisot, the first woman to join the early Impressionists. More heavyweight masterpieces can be found in rooms 34 and 39, devoted to **Monet** and **Renoir** in their middle and late periods – the development of Monet's obsession with light is shown with five of his Rouen Cathedral series, each painted in different light conditions. Room 35 is full of the fervid colours and disturbing rhythms of **Van Gogh**, while **Cézanne**, another step removed from the preoccupations of the mainstream Impressionists, is wonderfully represented in room 36: one of the canvases most revealing of his art is *Pommes et Oranges* (1895–1900), in which the background abandons perspective while the fruit has an extraordinary solidity.

Passing the **café** – with a summer terrace and a wonderful view of Montmartre through the giant railway clock – you arrive at a dimly lit, melancholy chamber (40) devoted to **pastels** by Redon, Manet, Mondrian and others. The next and final suite of rooms on this level is given over to the various offspring of Impressionism, and has an edgier, more modern feel, with a much greater emphasis on psychology. It begins with Rousseau's dreamlike *La Charmeuse de*

Serpent (1907) and continues past **Gauguin**'s ambivalent Tahitian paintings to **Pointillist** works by Seurat (the famous *Cirque*), Signac and others, ending with **Toulouse-Lautrec** at his caricaturial nightclubbing best.

The middle level

Don't miss the covetable little Kaganovitch collection (rooms 49 & 50) on your way down to the **middle level**, where the flow of the painting section continues with Vuillard and Bonnard (rooms 71 & 72), tucked away behind Pompon's irresistible sculpture of a polar bear on the rue de Lille side of the railway chamber. On the far side, in rooms 55 and 58 overlooking the Seine, you can see a less familiar side of late nineteenth-century painting, with epic, naturalist works such as Detaille's stirring *Le Rêve* (1888) and Cormon's *Caïn* (1880), as well as a troubling handful of **Symbolist** paintings from artists as diverse as Munch, Klimt and Odilon Redon (rooms 59 & 60). On the parallel sculpture terraces, nineteenth-century marbles on the Seine side face early twentieth-century pieces across the divide, while the **Rodin terrace** bridging the two puts almost everything else to shame. Those visitors with energy to spare should head straight for the last half-dozen rooms, which contain superb Art Nouveau furniture and *objets*.

The Trocadéro, Eiffel Tower and the Septième

As examples of landmark architecture, the **Palais de Tokyo** and **Palais de Chaillot** are hard to love. These twin white elephants have long given the heights of the Trocadéro, on the north bank of the river, a forlorn air, but in recent years some exciting new museums and galleries have brought both palaces back to life. You can also enjoy the splendid view of the **Eiffel Tower**, across the river. The area at the tower's feet, to the east, is the **septième** (7e) arrondissement, worth exploring for the classy, villagey shops and restaurants around the **rue Cler**. Much of the rest of the quarter is dominated by monumental military and government buildings, most domineeringly the **École Militaire** and **Hôtel des Invalides**. The latter houses an impressive war museum and, appropriately enough, the **tomb of Napoleon**. Tucked away in the streets to the east, towards St-Germain, the **Musée Rodin** and **Musée Maillol** show off the two sculptors' works in the intimate surroundings of handsome private houses.

The Palais de Chaillot and Palais de Tokyo

The stupendously ugly **Palais de Chaillot** was built in 1937, although on the strength of its bastardized Modernist-Classical architecture you'd think it dated from the height of Fascist occupation. An anthropologically themed **Musée de l'Homme** clings on in the west wing, along with the **Musée de la Marine** (daily except Tues 10am–6pm; €8, or €6.50 when there's no exhibition), which traces French naval history using models of ships and their accoutrements. The east wing of the palace is occupied by the Théâtre National de Chaillot, with a programme of popular theatre and contemporary dance. At the time of writing, it was about to be joined by the new **Cité de l'Architecture et du Patrimoine** (see Ⓦ www.citechaillot.org for opening hours), a combined institute, library and museum of architecture. The top floor of the museum focuses on the modern and contemporary, with models, designs and a reconstruction of an entire apartment from Le Corbusier's Cité Radieuse, in Marseille. On the vaulted level below, the Galerie des Moulages displays giant-sized plaster-casts taken from great French buildings at the end of the nineteenth century,

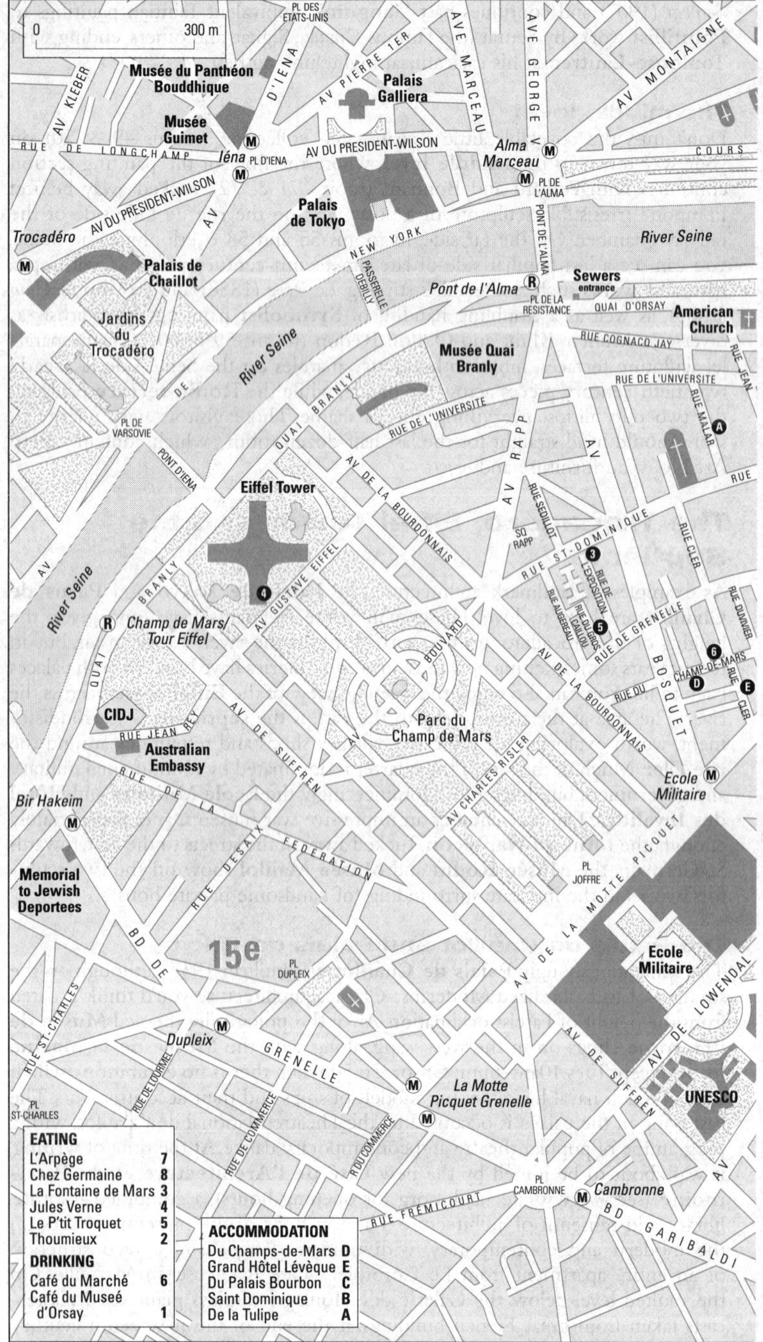
0 300 m
Musée du Panthéon Bouddhique
Musée Guimet
Palais Galliera
Palais de Tokyo
Palais de Chaillot
Jardins du Trocadéro
Trocadéro
Iéna
Alma Marceau
River Seine
Pont de l'Alma
Sewers entrance
American Church
Musée Quai Branly
Eiffel Tower
Champ de Mars/ Tour Eiffel
Parc du Champ de Mars
CIDJ
Australian Embassy
Bir Hakeim
Memorial to Jewish Deportees
Ecole Militaire
UNESCO
15e
Dupleix
La Motte Picquet Grenelle
Cambronne
AV KLEBER
RUE DE LONGCHAMP
AV DU PRESIDENT-WILSON
AV D'IENA
AV PIERRE 1ER
AVE MARCEAU
AVE GEORGE V
AV MONTAIGNE
COURS
NEW YORK
PASSERELLE DEBILLY
PONT DE L'ALMA
PL DE L'ALMA
PL DE LA RESISTANCE
QUAI D'ORSAY
RUE COGNACQ JAY
RUE DE L'UNIVERSITE
RUE MALAR
QUAI BRANLY
PL DE VARSOVIE
PONT D'IENA
AV DE LA BOURDONNAIS
AV RAPP
RUE SEDILLOT
SQ RAPP
RUE ST-DOMINIQUE
RUE CLER
RUE DE L'EXPOSITION
RUE AUGEREAU
RUE DU GROS CAILLOU
RUE DE GRENELLE
RUE DUVIVIER
RUE DU CHAMP-DE-MARS
AV BOSQUET
AV GUSTAVE EIFFEL
AV BOUVARD
AV DE SUFFREN
RUE JEAN REY
RUE DE LA FEDERATION
AV CHARLES RISLER
RUE DESAIX
AV DE LA MOTTE PICQUET
PL JOFFRE
AV DE LOWENDAL
BD DE GRENELLE
PL DUPLEIX
RUE ST-CHARLES
PL ST-CHARLES
RUE DE LOURMEL
RUE DE COMMERCE
R DU COMMERCE
RUE FRÉMICOURT
PL CAMBRONNE
BD GARIBALDI
PL DES ETATS-UNIS
PL D'IENA
EATING
L'Arpège 7
Chez Germaine 8
La Fontaine de Mars 3
Jules Verne 4
Le P'tit Troquet 5
Thoumieux 2
DRINKING
Café du Marché 6
Café du Musée d'Orsay 1
ACCOMMODATION
Du Champs-de-Mars D
Grand Hôtel Lévêque E
Du Palais Bourbon C
Saint Dominique B
De la Tulipe A

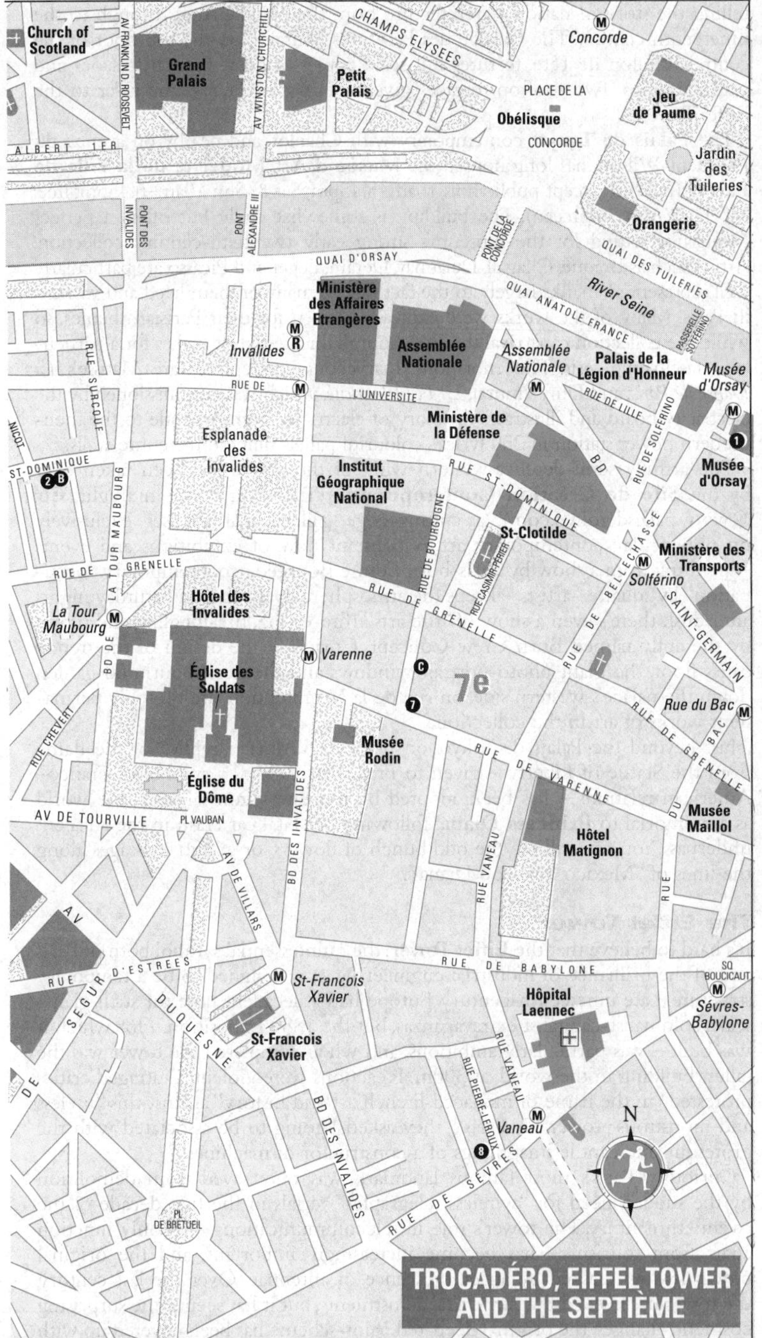
TROCADÉRO, EIFFEL TOWER AND THE SEPTIÈME
Church of Scotland
Grand Palais
Petit Palais
Champs Elysees
Concorde
Place de la Concorde
Obélisque
Jeu de Paume
Jardin des Tuileries
Orangerie
Av Franklin D. Roosevelt
Av Winston Churchill
Albert 1er
Pont des Invalides
Pont Alexandre III
Pont de la Concorde
Quai d'Orsay
Quai des Tuileries
River Seine
Quai Anatole France
Passerelle Solférino
Ministère des Affaires Etrangères
Invalides
Assemblée Nationale
Palais de la Légion d'Honneur
Musée d'Orsay
Rue Surcouf
Rue de l'Université
Rue de Lille
Ministère de la Défense
Esplanade des Invalides
Nicot
St-Dominique
Rue St-Dominique
Institut Géographique National
Bd de la Tour Maubourg
Rue de Bourgogne
St-Clotilde
Rue Casimir-Périer
Bd St-Germain
Rue de Solferino
Rue de Bellechasse
Ministère des Transports
Solférino
Rue de Grenelle
Hôtel des Invalides
La Tour Maubourg
Varenne
Église des Soldats
7e
Rue du Bac
Rue Chevert
Musée Rodin
Église du Dôme
Rue de Varenne
Musée Maillol
Av de Tourville
Pl Vauban
Av de Villars
Bd des Invalides
Rue Vaneau
Hôtel Matignon
Av de Segur
Rue d'Estrees
Rue de Babylone
Sq Boucicaut
Sévres-Babylone
St-Francois Xavier
Duquesne
Hôpital Laennec
Rue Pierre-Leroux
Vaneau
Rue de Sèvres
Pl de Breteuil
N

telling the story of national architecture from the Middle Ages through to the nineteenth century. The Galerie des Peintures Murales, on the top floor of the central Pavillon de Tête, features full-scale copies of great French frescoes and wall-paintings. Two rooftop terraces give superb views across the river to the Eiffel Tower.

The **Palais de Tokyo**, contemporary with Chaillot, and nearby on avenue du Président-Wilson, has long housed the **Musée d'Art Moderne de la Ville de Paris** (Tues–Fri except public hols 10am–5.45pm, Sat & Sun 10am–6.45pm; free; M° Iéna/Alma-Marceau). The building is somewhat chilly but offers a perfect Modernist setting for the museum's strong early twentieth-century collection. Artists such as Braque, Chagall, Delaunay, Derain, Léger and Picasso are particularly well represented, thanks largely to the fact that so many of them lived and worked in Paris. Many of the works were expressly chosen for their Parisian themes, so while the collection can't rival the Beaubourg's for prestige, it makes for a particularly fascinating visit. The enormous, marvellous centrepieces are Matisse's *La Danse de Paris*; and Dufy's mural, *La Fée Électricité*, which was commissioned by the electricity board and illustrates the story of electricity from Aristotle to the then-modern power station in 250 lyrical, colourful panels filling three entire walls.

The artfully semi-derelict western wing of the palace has been taken over by the **Site de Création Contemporaine** (Tues–Sun noon–midnight; €6; Ⓦwww.palaisdetokyo.com), a cutting-edge gallery that focuses exclusively on present-day contemporary art. A constant flow of exhibitions and events – anything from a show by Paris-born Louise Bourgeois to a temporary "occupation" by squatter-artists – keeps the atmosphere lively, and on Saturday nights after dusk there's even a show of "fire arts" (fire-eating, fire-juggling and more) by the aptly named Burn Crew Concept. Curiously, the design of the trendy café's floor, the giant photo-portrait windows and the neighbourhood garden down the palace's western side, on rue de la Manutention, are the only permanent works of art in the collection.

Just beyond the Palais de Tokyo, on place de l'Alma, a replica of the flame from the Statue of Liberty – given to France in 1987 as a symbol of Franco–American relations – has been adopted by mourners from all over the world as a memorial to **Princess Diana**, following her fatal car crash in the adjacent underpass. You can still see the odd bunch of flowers, or graffiti messages along the lines of "Mexico love you Diana".

The Eiffel Tower

It's hard to believe that the **Eiffel Tower**, the quintessential symbol both of Paris and of the brilliance of industrial engineering, was designed to be a temporary structure. Late nineteenth-century Europe had a decadent taste for such giant-scale, colonialist-capitalist extravaganzas, but the 1889 Exposition – for which it was built – was particularly ambitious, and when completed the tower was the tallest building in the world, at 300m. Reactions were violent. Outraged critics protested "in the name of menaced French art and history" against this "useless and monstrous" tower. "Is Paris", they asked, "going to be associated with the grotesque, mercantile imaginings of a constructor of machines?"

Curiously, Paris's most famous landmark was only saved from demolition by the sudden need for "wireless telegraphy" aerials in the first decade of the twentieth century. The tower's role in telecommunications – its only function apart from tourism – has become increasingly important, and the original crown is now masked by an efflorescence of antennae. Over the last century, the tower has needed few structural adjustments, but it has seen some surprising cosmetic changes: the original deep-red paint-scheme has been covered up with

△ The Eiffel Tower

a sombre, dusty-chocolate brown since the late 1960s – at least Paris is spared the canary yellow that covered the tower for some of the 1890s. In the 1980s the tower was given a new system of illumination from within its superstructure, and for the millennium celebrations a fireworks spectacular transformed it into a gargantuan space rocket. A giant searchlight, added at the same time, still sweeps the skies from the top of the tower, making it look like some monstrous urban lighthouse, and after dusk thousands of effervescent lights fizz maniacally all over the structure for the first ten minutes of every hour – an effect well worth seeing from a distant vantage point.

Going up (daily: mid-June to Aug 9am–12.45am; Sept to mid-June 9.30am–11.45pm) costs €11 for the top, €7.70 for the second level (or €3.80 by the stairs) and €4.20 for the first level. Note that access to the upward-bound lifts stops 45 minutes before closing time, and you'll need to arrive up to an hour and 45 minutes before closing time if you plan to make it all the way to the top level; note, too, that the stairs close at 6.30pm from September to mid-June. Paris looks surreally microscopic from the top, and the views are almost better from the second level, especially on hazier days, but there's something irresistible about taking the lift all the way.

Stretching back from the legs of the Eiffel Tower, the long rectangular gardens of the **Champs de Mars** lead to the eighteenth-century buildings of the **École Militaire**, originally founded in 1751 by Louis XV for the training of aristocratic army officers, and attended by Napoleon, among other fledgling leaders. The surrounding *quartier* may be expensive and sought after as an address, but it's mostly uninspiring to visit.

The riverside

A short distance upstream of the Eiffel Tower, on quai Branly, stands the gleamingly new **Musée du Quai Branly** (Tues, Wed & Fri–Sun 10am–6.30pm,

Thurs 10am–9.30pm; €8.50, free on first Sun of month; ⓦwww.quaibranly.fr). It brings together hundreds of thousands of non-European cultural or art objects bought or purloined by France at various times. The whole project is the child of President Chirac's passion for what he would no doubt call *arts primitifs* or *arts premiers* – though these terms were deemed too controversial to use in the museum's name. Presidential backing helped secure funding for the frankly princely museum building, a **futuristic glass edifice on stilts** by the French state's favourite architect, Jean Nouvel. Don't miss the huge terrace with its view of the Eiffel Tower, the garden or the unmistakeable "wall of vegetation". Setting aside the rather dubious politics of excluding Western art, the 3500 objects on display at any one time are as fascinating as they are beautiful, and the museum has gone to some length to explain their cultural, and often ritual, contexts. Four separate areas are devoted to Asia, Africa, the Americas and the Pacific ("Oceania").

Just beyond, opposite the Pont d'Alma on the northeast side of the busy junction of place de la Résistance, is the entrance to the **sewers**, or *les égouts* (Mon–Wed, Sat & Sun: May–Sept 11am–5pm; Oct–April 11am–4pm; €4). Once you're underground it's dark, damp and noisy from the gushing water, though the main exhibition, which runs along a gantry walk poised above a main sewer, turns the history of the city's water supply and waste management into a surprisingly fascinating topic. Children, however, may be disappointed to find that it's not all that smelly.

A little further upstream still, the **American Church** on quai d'Orsay, together with the American College nearby at 31 av Bosquet, is a focal point in the well-organized life of Paris's large American community. The noticeboard is usually plastered with job and accommodation offers and queries. Immediately to the south lies a chi chi, a villagey wedge of early nineteenth-century streets. This tiny neighbourhood, between rue St-Dominique and rue de Grenelle, is full of appealingly bijou shops, hotels and restaurants, with the lively market street of **rue Cler** at the centre of it all.

Les Invalides

The **Esplanade des Invalides**, striking due south from **Pont Alexandre III**, is a more attractive vista than the one from the Palais de Chaillot to the École Militaire. The proud dome and heavy facade of the **Hôtel des Invalides**, built as a home for soldiers on the orders of Louis XIV, looms at the further end of the Esplanade. Under the dome are two churches, one for the soldiers, the other intended as a mausoleum for the king but now containing the mortal remains of Napoleon.

Les Invalides today houses the vast **Musée de l'Armée** (daily except the first Mon of every month: April–Sept 10am–6pm, Oct–March 10am–5pm; €7.50 ticket also valid for the Église du Dôme and Musée des Plans-Reliefs), an enormous national war museum whose most interesting wing, reached via the south entrance beside the Église du Dôme, is devoted to Général de Gaulle and World War II. The battles, the resistance and the slow liberation are documented through imaginatively displayed war memorabilia combined with stirring reels of contemporary footage, most of which have an English-language option. One leaves with the distinct impression that de Gaulle was personally responsible for the liberation of France. The beautiful collection of medieval and Renaissance armour in the west wing of the royal courtyard is well worth admiring, but the core of the museum, dedicated to the history of the French army from Louis XIV up to the 1870s, is closed for restoration until at least 2008.

Up under the roof of the east wing, the super-scale models of French ports and fortified cities in the **Musée des Plans-Reliefs** (same hours and ticket as Musée de l'Armée, above), are crying out for a few miniature armies. Essentially giant three-dimensional maps, they were created to plan defences or plot potential artillery positions. The eerie green glow of their landscapes only just illuminates the long, tunnel-like attic; the effect is rather chilling.

The two Invalides churches have separate entrances. The lofty **Église des Soldats** (free; entrance from main courtyard of Les Invalides) is the spiritual home of the French army. The walls are hung with almost one hundred enemy standards captured on the battlefield, the rump of a collection of some three thousand that once adorned Notre-Dame. The proud simplicity of this "Soldiers' Church" stands in stark contrast to the lavish **Église du Dôme** (same hours and ticket as Musée de l'Armée above; entrance from south side of Les Invalides), which lies on the other side of a dividing glass wall – a design innovation that allowed worshippers to share the same high altar without the risk of coming into social contact. The domed "Royal church" is a supreme example of the architectural pomposity of Louis XIV's day, with grandiose frescoes and an abundance of Corinthian columns and pilasters. **Napoleon**, or rather his ashes, lies in a hole in the floor in a cold, smooth sarcophagus of red porphyry, installed there on December 14, 1840. Freshly returned from St Helena, his remains were carried through the streets from the newly completed Arc de Triomphe to the Invalides. As many as half a million people came out to watch the emperor's last journey, and Victor Hugo commented that "it felt as if the whole of Paris had been poured to one side of the city, like liquid in a vase which has been tilted".

Musée Rodin and Musée Maillol

Immediately east of Les Invalides is the **Musée Rodin**, on the corner of rue de Varenne (Tues–Sun: April–Sept 9.30am–5.45pm, garden closes 6.45pm; Oct–March 9.30am–4.45pm, garden closes 5pm; house and gardens €7, garden only €1; Ⓦwww.musee-rodin.fr; M° Varenne), elegantly presented in a beautiful eighteenth-century mansion which the sculptor leased from the state in return for the gift of all his work at his death. Major projects like *The Burghers of Calais*, *The Thinker*, *The Gate of Hell* and *Ugolini and Son* are exhibited in the garden – the latter forming the centrepiece of the ornamental pond. Indoors, which is usually very crowded, are well-loved works like *The Kiss* and *The Hand of God*. There's something particularly fascinating about works such as *Romeo and Juliet* and *The Centaur*, which seem only half-created, not wholly liberated from their raw blocks of stone.

The rest of rue de Varenne and the parallel rue de Grenelle is full of aristocratic mansions, including the **Hôtel Matignon**, the prime minister's residence. At 61 rue de Grenelle, a handsome eighteenth-century house has been turned into the **Musée Maillol** (daily except Tues 11am–6pm; €8; Ⓦwww.museemaillol.com; M° Rue-du-Bac), overstuffed with Aristide Maillol's endlessly buxom sculpted female nudes, copies of which can be seen to better effect in the Louvre's Jardin du Carrousel. His paintings follow a similar theme, and there are also minor works by contemporaries like Matisse, Dufy, Bonnard, Picasso, Degas, Gauguin and Kandinsky.

From here, **rue du Bac** leads south to rue de Sèvres, cutting across **rue de Babylone**, another of the *quartier*'s livelier streets, with the rich man's folly of **La Pagode** at no. 57bis. The building was brought over from Japan at the turn of the century and long used as an arts cinema; it has been recently renovated, with a café in the Japanese garden inside.

Montparnasse and southern Paris

The entertainment nexus of **Montparnasse** divides the well-heeled opinion-formers and powerbrokers of St-Germain and the 7e from the relatively anonymous populations to the south. The three arrondissements to the south have suffered from large-scale housing developments, most notably along the riverfronts to both east and west, but villagey areas such as **rue du Commerce** in the 15e, **Pernety** in the 14e and the **Buttes-aux-Cailles** in the 13e are well worth a foray. On the fringes of the city proper, hard up against the *périphérique* ring-road, are three fantastic parks: **André Citroën**, **Georges-Brassens** and **Montsouris**.

Like other Left Bank *quartiers*, Montparnasse trades on its association with the wild characters of the inter-war artistic and literary boom. Many were *habitués* of the cafés *Select*, *Coupole*, *Dôme*, *Rotonde* and *Closerie des Lilas*. The cafés are all still going strong on **boulevard du Montparnasse**, while the glitterati have mostly ended up in the nearby **Montparnasse cemetery**. The quarter's artistic traditions are maintained in a couple of second-tier, but fascinating, art museums, while elsewhere in Montparnasse you can ascend the **Tour Montparnasse**, Paris's first and ugliest skyscraper, and descend into the bone-lined **catacombs**.

Around Montparnasse station

Most of the life of the quarter is concentrated between the junction with boulevard Raspail, where Rodin's *Balzac* broods over the traffic, and at the station end of boulevard du Montparnasse, where the colossal **Tour du Montparnasse** has become one of the city's principal and most despised landmarks. Although central Paris is more distant, the view from the top is better than the one from the Eiffel Tower in that it includes the Eiffel Tower – and excludes the Tour du Montparnasse. It also costs less to ascend (April–Sept daily 9.30am–11pm; Oct–March Mon–Thurs & Sun 9.30am–10pm, Fri & Sat 9.30am–10.30pm; €9). Alternatively, you could sit down for an expensive drink in the 56th-storey bar, from where you get a tremendous view westwards.

One block northwest of the tower, on rue Antoine-Bourdelle, a garden of sculptures invites you into the **Musée Bourdelle** (Tues–Sun 10am–6pm; €4.50), which has been built around the sculptor's atmospheric old studio. As Rodin's pupil and Giacometti's teacher, Bourdelle's bronze and stone works move from a naturalistic style – as in the wonderful series of Beethoven busts – towards a more geometric, Modernist style, seen in his better-known, monumental sculptures.

Montparnasse station was once the great arrival and departure point for travellers heading across the Atlantic, a connection commemorated in the extraordinary **Jardin Atlantique**, a sizeable park that the city planners have actually suspended on top of the train tracks. Hemmed in by cliff-like high-rise apartment blocks, the park is a wonderful example of French design. There's a field of Atlantic-coast grasses, wave-like undulations in the lawns, a giant sundial and thermometer – which broke in the heatwave of 2003 when it exceeded its maximum – and a grid through which you can look down on the platforms below.

Montparnasse cemetery, the catacombs and the Observatoire

Just south of boulevard Edgar-Quinet (which has a good street market and cafés full of traders) is the main entrance to the **Montparnasse cemetery** (mid-March to Oct Mon–Fri 8am–6pm, Sat 8.30am–6pm, Sun 9am–6pm; Nov to mid-March closes at 5.30pm), a gloomy city of the dead, with ranks of miniature temples, dreary and bizarre, and plenty of illustrious names, from Baudelaire to Beckett and Gainsbourg to Saint-Saëns. The joint grave of Jean-Paul Sartre and Simone de Beauvoir lies immediately right of the main entrance. In the southwest corner is an old windmill, one of the seventeenth-century taverns frequented by the carousing, versifying students who caused the district to be named after Mount Parnassus, the legendary home of the muses of poetry and song, and of Bacchus's drunken revels. Hidden away in the northern corner of the cemetery, on the east side of rue Emile-Richard, a tomb is poignantly crowned with a version of Brancusi's sculpture, *The Kiss*.

If you're determined to spend time among the dead, you can also get down into the **catacombs** (Tues–Sun 10am–4pm; €5) in nearby **place Denfert-Rochereau**, formerly place d'Enfer (Hell Square). The catacombs are abandoned quarries stacked with millions of bones, which were cleared from overstocked charnel houses and cemeteries between 1785 and 1871. Lining the passageway, the long thigh bones are stacked end-on, forming a wall to keep in the smaller bones, which can just be seen heaped higgledy-piggledy behind. These high femoral walls are further inset with skulls and plaques carrying macabre quotations such as "happy is he who always has the hour of his death in front of his eyes, and readies himself every day to die". Older children often love the whole experience, but there are a good couple of kilometres to walk, and it can quickly become claustrophobic in the extreme, and cold.

Rue Schoelcher and boulevard Raspail, on the east side of the cemetery, have some interesting examples of twentieth-century architecture, from Art Nouveau to contemporary facades of glass in the **Cartier Foundation** at 259 bd Raspail (Tues–Sun noon–8pm; €6.50). Built in 1994 by Jean Nouvel, Parisian architect of the moment, this presents all kinds of contemporary art – installations, videos, multimedia – in high-quality temporary exhibitions. About 500m to the northeast, on avenue de l'Observatoire, the classical **Observatoire de Paris** sat on France's zero meridian line from the 1660s, when it was constructed, until 1884. After that date, they reluctantly agreed that 0° longitude should pass through a small village in Normandy that happens to be due south of Greenwich. You can see one of the bronze markers of the "Arago line" – which has nothing to do with any mystical "rose line", notwithstanding the claims of a certain best-selling conspiracy thriller – set into the cobbles of the observatory's courtyard.

The 15e arrondissement

The western edge of the 15e arrondissement fronts the Seine from the **Porte de Javel** to the Eiffel Tower. From Pont Mirabeau northwards, the riverbank is marred by a sort of mini-Défense development of half-cocked futuristic towers with pretentious galactic names, rising out of a litter-blown pedestrian platform some 10m above street level. Far pleasanter riverside strolling is to be had on the narrow midstream island, the **Allée des Cygnes**, which you can reach from the Pont de Grenelle. A scaled-down version of the **Statue of Liberty** stands at the downstream end. South of Pont Mirabeau, between rue Balard and the river, is the city's newest park, the hyper-designed **Parc André-Citroën** (M° Balard), so named because the site used to be the Citroën motor works. Its best features are the glasshouses full of exotic-smelling shrubs, the dancing fountains – which bolder park-goers run through on hot days – and the tethered **balloon** (fine days only: 9am to roughly one hour before dusk; Mon–Fri €10, Sat & Sun €12), which offers eye-wateringly spectacular views.

It was in the **rue du Commerce**, running down the middle of the arrondissement from M° La Motte Piquet-Grenelle, that George Orwell worked as a dishwasher, an experience described in *Down and Out in Paris and London*. These days it's a lively, old-fashioned high street full of small shops and peeling, shuttered houses, with one fine old brasserie, the *Café du Commerce* (see p.179). Towards the end of the street is place du Commerce, with a bandstand in the middle, a model of old-fashioned petit-bourgeois respectability.

The other park in the 15ᵉ, the **Parc Georges-Brassens**, lies in the south-east corner (M° Convention/Porte-de-Vanves). It's a delight, with a garden of scented herbs and shrubs (best in late spring) designed principally for blind and visually impaired visitors, puppets and rocks and merry-go-rounds for kids, a mountain stream with pine and birch trees, beehives and a tiny terraced vineyard. The corrugated pyramid with a helter-skelter-like spiral is the Silvia-Montfort theatre.

On the west side of the park, in a secluded garden in passage Dantzig, off rue Dantzig, stands an unusual polygonal building known as **La Ruche**. Home to Fernand Léger, Modigliani, Chagall, Soutine and many other artists at the start of the century, it's still used by creative types. In the sheds of the old horse market between the park and rue Brançion, a **book market** is held every Saturday and Sunday morning.

The 14ᵉ below Montparnasse

The jokey quasi-Classical Ricardo Bofill apartment complex around place de Catalogne gives way to a walkway along the old rue Vercingétorix and to the cosy district of **Pernety**, which was long an artists' haunt. Wandering around Cité Bauer, rue des Thermopyles and rue Didot reveals adorable houses, secluded courtyards and quiet mews, and on the corner of rue du Moulin Vert and rue Hippolyte-Maindron you'll find Giacometti's old ramshackle studio and home. There are more artistic associations south of rue d'Alésia near the junction with avenue Réné-Coty: Dalí, Lurcat, Miller and Durrell lived in the tiny cobbled street of **Villa Seurat** off rue de la Tombe-Issoire; Lenin and his wife lodged across the street at 4 rue Marie-Rose; Le Corbusier built the studio at 53 av Reille, close to the secretive and verdant square du Montsouris which links with rue Nansouty; and Georges Braque's home was in the cul-de-sac now named after him off this street.

All these characters would have taken strolls in **Parc Montsouris** (RER Cité-Universitaire). Along with a lake and waterfall, its more surprising features include a meteorological office, a marker of the old meridian line, near boulevard Jourdan, and, by the southwest entrance, a kiosk run by the French Astronomy Association. The strange array of buildings across the boulevard from the park form the **Cité Universitaire**, home to several thousand students from over one hundred different countries.

The 13ᵉ arrondissement

The 13ᵉ is one of the most disparate areas of the city. **Place d'Italie**, with the ornate *mairie* and vast new Gaumont cinema, is the hub, with each of the major roads radiating out into very different *quartiers*. Avenue des Gobelins, leading north, has the **Gobelins tapestry workshops** at no. 42 (guided visits in French only: Tues–Thurs at 2pm & 2.45pm; €8; ⓦ www.gobelins.fr; M° Les Gobelins), which have operated here for some four hundred years. Tapestries are still being made by the same painfully slow methods, but are now based on drawings by contemporary painters. Almost all of the dozen or so works completed each year are destined for French government offices.

Between boulevard Auguste-Blanqui and rue Bobillot is the lively hilltop quarter of the **Butte-aux-Cailles**. If you're looking for unpretentious, youthful and vaguely lefty restaurants and nightlife, it's well worth the short métro ride out from the centre. The easiest route is to walk up rue Bobillot from place d'Italie.

Over to the east, in the middle of a swathe of high-rise social housing, is the **Chinese quarter** of Paris. Avenues de Choisy and d'Ivry are full of Vietnamese, Chinese, Thai, Cambodian and Laotian restaurants and food shops, as is **Les Olympiades**, a weird semi-derelict pedestrian area seemingly suspended between giant tower blocks.

Following rue Tolbiac or boulevard Vincent-Auriol to the river, you reach the entirely new district of **Paris Rive Gauche**, whose star attraction is the **Bibliothèque Nationale de France**. Accessible from its northern and southern corners (M° Quai-de-la-Gare or Bibliothèque-François-Mitterrand), it has four enormous towers – intended to look like open books – framing a huge platform surrounding a sunken pine copse with glass walls that allow light to filter through to the underground library spaces. Architect Dominique Perrault's design attracted widespread derision after shutters had to be added to the towers to protect the books and manuscripts from sunlight. There are occasional small-scale exhibitions, and the reading rooms on the "haut-jardin" level are open to everyone over 16 (Tues–Sat 10am–8pm, Sun 1–7pm; €3.30 for a day pass; ⓦ www.bnf.fr); the garden level is reserved for accredited researchers only.

From the Bibliothèque Nationale down to the *boulevard périphérique*, almost every stick of street furniture and square metre of tarmac is shiny and new. The still-underpopulated cafés and apartment blocks give the area a futuristic frontier-town feel that's perfectly represented in the form of the **Passerelle Bercy-Tolbiac**, a €21-million footbridge that crosses the Seine in a hyper-modern double-ribbon structure. Between the bridge and the Pont de Tolbiac, several **barges** have made the area a nightlife attraction in its own right (see p.181). Just west of the library, near métro Chevaleret, a few small but cutting-edge art galleries have sprung up on and around **rue Louise Weiss**. Immediately south of rue Tolbiac, the giant, decaying warehouse of **Les Frigos** was once used for cold-storage of meat and fish destined for Les Halles, but was taken over immediately after the market's closure by artists and musicians. It has been run as an anarchic studio space ever since, with open-door exhibitions once or twice a year, a bar-restaurant for the artists and an on-site gallery.

The Beaux Quartiers and Bois de Boulogne

Commonly referred to as the **Beaux Quartiers**, Paris's well-manicured western arrondissements, the 16e and 17e, are mainly residential with few specific sights, the chief exception being the **Musée Marmottan**, with its dazzling collection of late Monets. The most rewarding areas for exploration are the old villages of Passy, whose tranquillity attracted writers and artists such as Balzac and Berthe Morisot, and **Auteuil**. Both were incorporated into the city in the late nineteenth century and soon became very desirable districts. Well-to-do Parisians commissioned houses here, and as a result, the area is rich in fine examples of architecture, notably by Hector Guimard and Le Corbusier. Bordering the area to the west is the **Bois de Boulogne**, with its trees, lakes, cycling trails and the beautiful floral displays of the Parc de Bagatelle. Further west, modern architecture comes bang up to date with the gleaming skyscrapers of the purpose-built commercial district of **La Défense**, dominated by the enormous Grande Arche.

Auteuil

The **Auteuil district** is now an integral part of the city, but there's still a village-like feel about its streets, and it has some attractive *villas* (leafy lanes of old houses, fronted with English-style gardens), not to mention fine Art Nouveau buildings by Hector Guimard – there's a concentration on rue de la Fontaine (M° Église-d'Auteuil), including the exuberantly decorated Castel Béranger at no. 14. If the bulgy curves of Art Nouveau aren't for you, head up rue du Dr-Blanche for the cool, rectilinear lines of Le Corbusier's first private houses (they date from 1923), in a cul-de-sac to the right, looked after by the Fondation Le Corbusier. You can visit one of the houses, the **Villa Roche** (Mon 1.30–6pm, Tues–Fri 10am–12.30pm & 1.30–6pm, till 5pm on Fri, Sat 10am–5pm; closed Aug; €2.50). Built in a very plain, strictly Cubist style with windows in bands, the only extravagance is the raising of one wing on piers and a curved frontage. The houses look commonplace enough from the outside, but were a big contrast to anything that had gone before and, once you're inside, the spatial play still seems ground-breaking.

After taking a left at the northern end of rue du Dr-Blanche, then right on boulevard Beauséjour, use the short cut immediately opposite rue du Ranelagh across the disused *Petite Ceinture* train line to reach avenue Raphaël, from where it's a pleasant walk along the shady trees of the pretty, green-lawned Jardin du Ranelagh to the **Musée Marmottan**, 2 rue Louis-Boilly (Tues–Sun 10am–6pm; €7; M° Muette), which showcases Impressionist works. There's a dazzling collection of canvases from Monet's last years at Giverny, including several *Nymphéas* (Water Lilies), as well as his canvas entitled *Impression, Soleil Levant* (Impression, Sunrise), an 1872 rendering of a misty sunrise over Le Havre, whose title the critics usurped to give the Impressionist movement its name. The collection also features some of his contemporaries – Manet, Renoir and Berthe Morisot.

Bois de Boulogne

The **Bois de Boulogne** (M° Porte-Maillot) is an area of extensive parkland running down the west side of the 16e. The "bois" of the name is somewhat deceptive, though it does contain some remnants of the once great Forêt de Rouvray. Once the playground of the wealthy, it also established a reputation as the site of the sex trade and its associated crime. The same is true today and you should avoid it at night. By day, however, the park is an extremely pleasant spot for a stroll.

The best, and wildest, part for walking is towards the southwest corner. **Bikes** are available for rent at the entrance to the Jardin d'Acclimatation adventure park (see p.193) and you can go **boating** on the Lac Inférieur. One of the main attractions is the **Parc de Bagatelle** (bus #244 from M° Porte-Maillot, or bus #43 from M° Pont-de-Neuilly), which features beautiful displays of tulips, hyacinths and daffodils in the first half of April, irises in May, water lilies and roses at the end of June.

La Défense

An impressive complex of gleaming skyscrapers, **La Défense** (M°/RER Grande-Arche-de-la-Défense) is Paris's prestige business district and a monument to late twentieth-century capitalism. Its most popular attraction is the huge **Grande Arche**, an astounding 112-metre hollow cube clad in white marble, standing 6km out from the Arc de Triomphe at the far end of the Voie Triomphale. Suspended within its hollow – which could enclose Notre-Dame with ease – are open lift shafts and a "cloud" canopy. You can take a lift up to the roof (daily 10am–7pm; €7.50) and, on a clear day, scan to the Louvre and beyond, though the view from the bottom of the arch is nearly as good.

Montmartre and northern Paris

Perched on Paris's highest hill, towards the northern edge of the city, **Montmartre** was famously the home and playground of artists such as Renoir, Degas, Picasso and Toulouse-Lautrec. The crown of the Butte Montmartre, around place du Tertre, is overrun with tourists these days, but the steep streets around **Abbesses** métro preserve an attractively festive, village-like atmosphere – and seem to become more gentrified and more fashionable every year. **Pigalle**, by contrast, at the southern foot of the Butte, remains brassy and seedy, while the **Goutte d'Or**, to the east, is vibrantly multi-ethnic. Out at the northern city limits, the mammoth **St-Ouen market** hawks everything from extravagant antiques to the cheapest flea-market hand-me-downs.

Place des Abbesses and up to the Butte

In spite of being one of the city's chief tourist attractions, the **Butte Montmartre** manages to retain the quiet, almost secretive, air of its rural origins. The most popular access route is via the rue de Steinkerque and the steps below the Sacré-Coeur (the funicular railway from place Suzanne-Valadon is covered by normal métro tickets). For a quieter approach, go up via place des Abbesses or rue Lepic.

Place des Abbesses is postcard-pretty, with one of the few complete surviving Guimard métro entrances. To the east, at the Chapelle des Auxiliatrices in rue Yvonne-Le-Tac, Ignatius Loyola founded the Jesuit movement in 1534. It's also supposed to be the place where St-Denis, the first bishop of Paris, had his head chopped off by the Romans around 250 AD. He is said to have carried it until he dropped, where the cathedral of St-Denis now stands north of the city. Today, the streets are full of trendy boutique clothes shops and laid-back restaurants.

Continuing from place des Abbesses to the top of the Butte, two quiet and attractive routes are up rue de la Vieuville and the stairs in rue Drevet to the minuscule **place du Calvaire**, with a lovely view back over the city, or up rue Tholozé, then right below the **Moulin de la Galette** – the last survivor of Montmartre's forty-odd windmills, immortalized by Renoir – into rue des Norvins.

Artistic associations abound hereabouts. Zola, Berlioz, Turgenev, Seurat, Degas and Van Gogh lived in the area. Picasso, Braque and Juan Gris invented Cubism in an old piano factory in place Émile-Goudeau, known as the **Bateau-Lavoir**, still serving as artists' studios, though the original building burnt down years ago. Toulouse-Lautrec's inspiration, the **Moulin Rouge**, survives too, albeit as a shadow of its former self, on the corner of boulevard de Clichy and place Blanche (see p.182).

The **Musée de Montmartre**, at 12 rue Cortot (Wed–Sun 10am–6pm; €5.50), just over the brow of the hill, tries to recapture something of the feel of those pioneering days, but it's a bit of a disappointment, except for the occasional temporary exhibition. The house itself, rented at various times by Renoir, Dufy, Suzanne Valadon and her alcoholic son Utrillo, is worth visiting for the view over the neat terraces of the tiny **Montmartre vineyard** – which produces some 1500 bottles a year – on the north side of the Butte. You can walk round to the vineyard, where the steep rue de Saules falls away past the cabaret club **Au Lapin Agile**. Famously painted and patronized by Picasso,

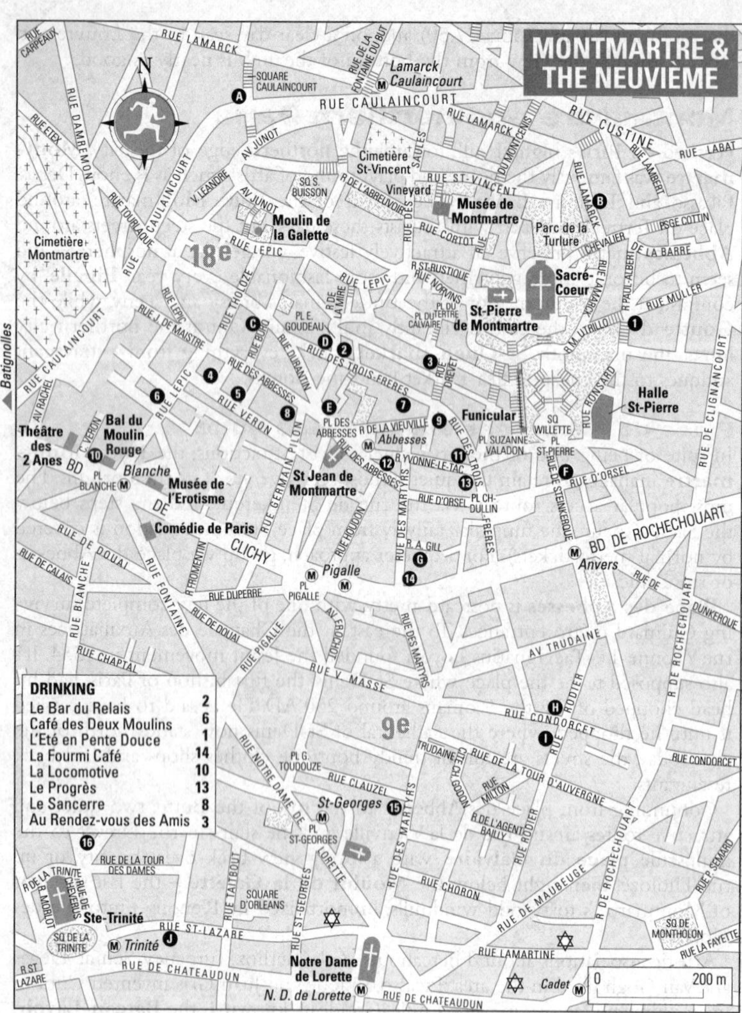

ACCOMMODATION

André Gill	G	Perfect	I
Bonséjour Montmartre	C	Regyns Montmartre	E
Caulaincourt	A	Timhotel Montmartre	D
Ermitage	B	Le Village Hostel	F
Langlois	J	Woodstock Hostel	H

EATING

Le Bistro des Deux-Théâtres	16	Haynes	15
Chez les Fondus	11	Le Mono	4
La Famille	7	Le Relais Gascon	12
Au Grain de Folie	9	Le Restaurant	5

Utrillo and other leading lights of the early twentieth-century Montmartre scene, it still puts on arty cabaret shows featuring French chanson and poetry (Tues–Sun 9pm–2am; €24).

Place du Tertre and Sacré-Coeur

The **place du Tertre** is the heart of Montmartre. It's photogenic but basically fraudulent, jammed with tourists, overpriced restaurants and "artists" knocking up garish paintings with their eyes shut. Between place du Tertre and the Sacré-Coeur, the old church of **St-Pierre** is all that remains of the Benedictine abbey that occupied the Butte Montmartre from the twelfth century on. Though much altered, it still retains its Romanesque and early Gothic feel. In it are four ancient columns, two by the door, two in the choir, leftovers from a Roman shrine that stood on the hill – *mons mercurii* (Mercury's Hill), the Romans called it.

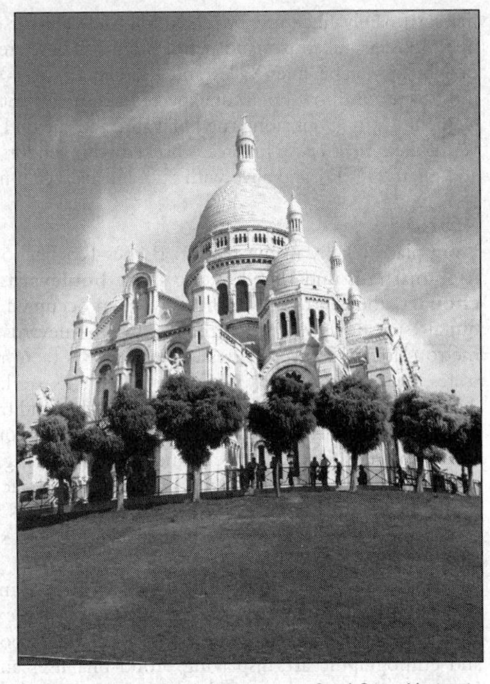

△ Sacré-Coeur, Montmartre

Crowning the Butte is the **Sacré-Coeur** (daily 6am–10.30pm), whose white tower and frothy, ice-cream-scoop dome are an essential part of the Paris skyline. Construction was started in the 1870s on the initiative of the Catholic Church to atone for the "crimes" of the Commune. **Square Willette**, the space at the foot of the monumental staircase, is named after the local artist who turned out on inauguration day to shout "Long live the devil!". The best thing about the church is the **view** from the top of the dome (daily: April–Sept 8.30am–7pm; Oct–March 9am–6pm; €5), which takes you almost as high as the Eiffel Tower; on bright days the best views are not to be had in the middle of the day, as Paris lies directly to the south

Montmartre cemetery

West of the Butte, near the beginning of rue Caulaincourt in place Clichy, lies the **Montmartre cemetery** (mid-March to Oct Mon–Fri 8am–6pm, Sat 8.30am–6pm, Sun 9am–6pm; Nov to mid-March closes 5.30pm; free). Ramshackle and peeling, on a tiny courtyard full of plants, it epitomizes the kind-hearted, instinctively arty, sepia-tinged Paris that every romantic visitor secretly cherishes. The cemetery is tucked down below street level in the hollow of an old quarry with its entrance on avenue Rachel under rue Caulaincourt. A tangle of trees and funereal pomposity, it holds the graves of Zola, Stendhal, Berlioz, Degas, Feydeau, Offenbach and Truffaut, among others.

St-Ouen flea market

Officially open Saturday to Monday 9am to 7pm – unofficially, from 5am – the **puces de St-Ouen** (M° Porte-de-Clignancourt) claims to be the largest flea market in the world, the name "flea" deriving from the state of the secondhand mattresses, clothes and other junk sold here when the market first operated outside the city walls. Nowadays it's predominantly a proper – and expensive – antiques market (mainly furniture, but including old café-bar counters, telephones, traffic lights, posters, jukeboxes and petrol pumps). There are twelve individual markets, of which Marché Jules-Vallès and Marché Lécuyer-Vallès are the cheapest and most likely to throw up an unexpected treasure. What is left of the rag-and-bone element is strung out along rue J.H. Fabre and rue du Dr-Babinski, under the flyover of the *périphérique*. This area is packed with vendors selling counterfeit clothing and pirated DVDs, and alive with cup-and-ball scam merchants and the like.

Pigalle

From place Clichy in the west to Barbès-Rochechouart in the east, the hill of Montmartre is underlined by the sleazy **boulevards of Clichy and Rochechouart**, the centre of the roadway often occupied by bumper-cars and other funfair sideshows. At the Barbès end of boulevard Rochechouart, where the métro clatters by on iron trestles, the crowds teem round the Tati department stores, the city's cheapest, while the pavements are lined with West and North African street vendors offering fabrics, watches and trinkets. At the place Clichy end, tour buses from all over Europe feed their contents into massive hotels. In the middle, between place Blanche and place Pigalle, **sex shows**, sex shops, tiny bars where hostesses lurk in complicated tackle, and street prostitutes (both male and female) coexist with one of Paris's most elegant private *villas* on avenue Frochot. The city's best specialist music shops can be found in the adjacent streets.

Perfectly placed amongst all the sex shops and shows is the **Musée de l'Erotisme** (daily 10am–2am; €8), which explores different cultures' approaches to sex. The ground floor and first floor are dedicated to sacred and ethnographic art, displaying proud phalluses and well-practised positions from Asia, Africa and pre-Colombian Latin America, plus a few more satirical European pieces. The rest of the floors upstairs are devoted to often fascinating temporary exhibitions.

The Goutte d'Or

Along the north side of boulevard de la Chapelle, between boulevard Barbès and the Gare du Nord rail lines, stretches the poetically named *quarter* of the **Goutte d'Or** ("Drop of Gold"), a name that derives from the medieval vineyard that occupied this site. It has gradually become an immigrant ghetto since World War I, when large numbers of North Africans were first imported to replenish the ranks of Frenchmen dying in the trenches. While the quartier remains poor, it is home to a host of mini-communities, now predominantly West African and Congolese, rather than North African, but with pockets of South Asian, Haitian, Turkish and other ethnicities as well. Countless shops can be found selling African music and fabrics, but the main sight for visitors is on rue Dejean, a few steps east of métro Château-Rouge, where the **Marché Dejean** (closed Sun afternoon and all day Mon) heaves with African groceries and thrums with shoppers. Another, more general market takes place in the mornings twice weekly (Wed & Sat) underneath the métro viaduct on the **boulevard de la Chapelle**.

Canal St-Martin and La Villette

The **Bassin de la Villette** and the **canals** at the northeastern gate of the city were for generations the centre of a densely populated working-class district. Most of the jobs were in the La Villette abattoirs and meat market or the related industries that spread around the waterways. The amusements were skating or swimming, betting on cockfights or eating at the many restaurants famed for their fresh meat. The abattoirs and meat market are gone, replaced by the huge complex of La Villette, a postmodern park of science and technology.

The whole Villette complex stands at the junction of the **Ourcq** and **St-Denis canals**. The first was built by Napoleon to bring fresh water into the city; the second is an extension of the Canal St-Martin built as a short cut to the great western loop of the Seine around Paris. The canals have undergone extensive renovation, and derelict sections of the *quais* are being made more appealing to cyclists, rollerbladers and pedestrians.

Canal St-Martin and place de Stalingrad

The **Canal St-Martin** runs underground at the Bastille to surface again in boulevard Jules-Ferry by rue du Faubourg-du-Temple. The canal still has a slightly industrial feel, especially along its upper stretch. The lower part is more attractive, with plane trees, cobbled *quais* and elegant, high-arched footbridges. In the last decade or so the area has been colonized by the new arty and media intelligentsia, bringing trendy bars, cafés and boutiques in their wake. The area is particularly lively on Sunday afternoons, when the *quais* are closed to traffic, pedestrians, cyclists and rollerbladers take over the streets and a young crowd hangs out along the canal's edge, nursing beers or softly strumming guitars. Inevitably, having acquired a certain cachet, the district has attracted property developers, and bland apartment blocks have elbowed in among traditional, solid, mid-nineteenth-century residences such as the **Hôtel du Nord** of Marcel Carné's film, at 102 quai de Jemappes – now a restaurant.

The canal disappears underground again further north at **place de Stalingrad**. To one side of the square stands the beautifully restored Rotonde de la Villette, one of Ledoux's tollhouses in Louis XVI's tax wall, where taxes were levied on all goods coming into the city – a major bone of contention in the lead-up to the 1789 Revolution.

Beyond the square is the renovated **Bassin de la Villette** dock, popular for Sunday strolls, fishing and canoeing. Recobbled, and with its dockside buildings converted into offices for canal boat trips, and a cinema (the MK2) with an attached waterfront brasserie, the Bassin has lost all vestiges of its former status as France's premier port. At rue de Crimée a unique hydraulic bridge marks the end of the dock and the beginning of the Canal de l'Ourcq. If you keep to the south bank on quai de la Marne, you can cross directly into the Parc de la Villette.

The Parc de la Villette

The **Parc de la Villette** (daily 6am–1am; free; Ⓦwww.villette.com) music, art and science complex, between avenues Corentin-Cariou and Jean-Jaurès, has so many disparate and disconnected elements that it's hard to know where to start. To help you get your bearings, there's an **information centre** at the entrance by M° Porte-de-Pantin, to the south.

The main attraction is the enormous **Cité des Sciences et de l'Industrie** (Tues–Sat 10am–6pm, Sun 10am–7pm; €7.50 or €10.50 with the planetarium; Ⓦwww.cite-sciences.fr; M° Porte-de-la-Villette). This high-tech museum devoted to science and all its applications is built into the concrete hulk of the abandoned abattoirs on the north side of the Canal de l'Ourcq. Four times the size of the Pompidou Centre, it's a colossal glass-walled building, surrounded by a moat. Inside are crow's-nests, cantilevered platforms, bridges and suspended walkways, the different levels linked by lifts and escalators around a huge central space open to the full forty-metre height of the roof. The permanent exhibition, called

Explora, covers subjects such as sound, robotics, energy, light, ecology, maths, medicine, space and language. As the name suggests, the emphasis is on exploring, encouraged through interactive computers, videos, holograms, animated models and games.

When all the interrogation and stimulation becomes too much, you can relax in cafés within Explora, before joining the queue for the **planetarium**. Back on the ground floor there's the **Louis-Lumière Cinema**, which shows 3-D films (included in Cité des Sciences et de l'Industrie ticket), and the **Cité des Enfants** for children (see p.193), as well as a whole programme of excellent **temporary exhibitions**.

In front of the complex floats the **Géode** (hourly shows Tues–Sat 10.30am–9.30pm, Sun 10.30am–7.30pm; €9), a bubble of reflecting steel that looks as though it's been dropped from an intergalactic *boules* game into a pool of water. Inside is a screen for Omnimax 180° films, not noted for their plots, but a great visual experience. There's also the **Cinaxe**, between the Cité and the Canal St-Denis (screenings every 15min Tues–Sun 11am–5pm; €5.40, or €4.80 with Explora ticket), combining 70mm film shot at thirty frames a second with seats that move. Beside the Géode is a real 1957 French **submarine**, the **Argonaute** (Tues–Sat 10am–6pm, Sun 10am–7pm; €3). South of the canal are bizarrely landscaped **themed gardens** of "mirrors", "mists", "winds and dunes" and "islands", and over to the east is the **Zénith** inflatable rock music venue. To the south, the largest of the old **market halls** is now a vast and brilliant exhibition space, the **Grande Salle**.

South of the Grande Salle stands the **Cité de la Musique** (Ⓦwww.cite-musique.fr), in two complexes to either side of the Porte-de-Pantin entrance. To the west is the national music academy, while to the east are a concert hall, the very chic *Café de la Musique*, a music and dance information centre and the excellent **Musée de la Musique** (Tues–Sat noon–6pm, Sun 10am–6pm; €7), presenting the history of music from the end of the Renaissance to the present day, both visually – a collection of 4500 instruments – and aurally, with headsets and interactive displays. The buildings' abstract designs are meant to evoke their function; the academy's windows are arranged in sequence like musical notation and the wavy roof, according to its architect Christian de Portzamparc, is like Gregorian chant, but could equally suggest the movement of a dancer or a conductor's baton.

Belleville, Ménilmontant and Père-Lachaise

Traditionally working class, with a history of radical and revolutionary activity, the gritty **eastern districts** of Paris, particularly the old villages of **Belleville** and **Ménilmontant**, are nowadays some of the most diverse and vibrant parts of the city, home to sizeable ethnic populations, as well as students and artists, attracted by the low rents. The main visitor attraction in the area is the **Père-Lachaise cemetery**, final resting place of many well-known artists and writers. Visiting the modern **Parc de Belleville** will reveal the area's other main asset – wonderful views of the city below. Excellent views of Sacré-Coeur are also to be had from the fairytale-like **Parc des Buttes-Chaumont**.

Parc des Buttes-Chaumont

At the northern end of the Belleville heights, a short walk from La Villette, is the **parc des Buttes-Chaumont** (M° Buttes-Chaumont/Botzaris), constructed by Haussmann in the 1860s to camouflage what until then had been a desolate warren of disused quarries and miserable shacks. Out of this rather unlikely setting a wonderfully romantic park was created – there'a a grotto with a cascade and artificial stalactites, and a picturesque lake from which a huge rock rises up topped with a delicate Corinthian temple. From the temple you get fine views of Sacré-Coeur and beyond. The park stays open all night and, equally rarely for Paris, you're not cautioned off the grass.

Belleville and Ménilmontant

The route from Buttes-Chaumont to Père-Lachaise will take you through the one-time villages of **Belleville** and **Ménilmontant**. Many of the old village lanes disappeared in the tower-block mania of the 1960s and 1970s, but others have now been opened up, and many of the newest buildings are imaginative infill, following the height and curves of their older neighbours. Dozens of cobbled and gardened *villas* (lanes) lined with houses remain intact: east of Buttes-Chaumont towards place Rhin-et-Danube, between rue Boyer (with a 1920s Soviet-style building at no. 25) and rue des Pyrénées just north of Père-Lachaise, and out to the east by Porte de Bagnolet, up the very picturesque steps from place Octave-Chanute.

The first main street you cross coming down from Buttes-Chaumont, **rue de Belleville**, is the Chinatown of Paris. Vietnamese and Chinese shops and restaurants have proliferated over the years, adding considerable visual and gastronomic cheer to the area. African and oriental fruits, spices, music and fabrics can be bought at the **boulevard de Belleville market** on Tuesdays and Fridays. Edith Piaf was abandoned on the steps of no. 72 rue de Belleville when just a few hours old, and there's a small **museum** dedicated to her at 5 rue Créspin-du-Gast (Mon–Thurs 1–6pm; closed Sept; by appointment on ⓣ01.43.55.52.72; donation; M° Ménilmontant/St-Maur).

You get fantastic views down onto the city centre from the higher reaches of Belleville and Ménilmontant: the best place to watch the sun set is the **Parc de Belleville** (M° Couronnes/Pyrénées), which descends in a series of terraces and waterfalls from rue Piat. And from **rue de Ménilmontant**, by rues de l'Ermitage and Boyer, you can look straight down to the Pompidou Centre. Large numbers of students and artists have moved into rue de Ménilmontant and its extension **rue Oberkampf** – the latter in particular has undergone quite a transformation as a result, with an explosion of trendsetting bars and cafés jostling for space alongside the ethnic bakeries, cheap goods stores and grocers.

Père-Lachaise cemetery

Père-Lachaise cemetery (Mon–Fri 8am–5.30pm, Sat 8.30am–5.30pm, Sun 9am–5.30pm; M° Gambetta/Père-Lachaise/Alexandre-Dumas/Phillipe-Auguste), final resting place of numerous notables, is an atmospheric, eerily beautiful haven, with little cobbled footpaths, terraced slopes and magnificent old trees which spread their branches over the tombs as though shading them from the outside world. The cemetery was opened in 1804, after an urgent stop had been put to further burials in the overflowing city cemeteries and churchyards. The civil authorities had Molière, La Fontaine, Abelard and Héloïse reburied here, and to be interred in Père-Lachaise quickly acquired cachet. A free **map** of the cemetery is available at all the entrances or you can buy a more detailed one for €2 at nearby newsagents and florists.

Among the most visited graves is that of **Chopin** (Division 11), often attended by Poles bearing red-and-white wreaths and flowers. Fans also flock to the ex-Doors lead singer **Jim Morrison** (Division 6), who died in Paris at the age of 27. You can tell when you're getting near his grave: messages in praise of love and drugs are scribbled on nearby trees and tombs.

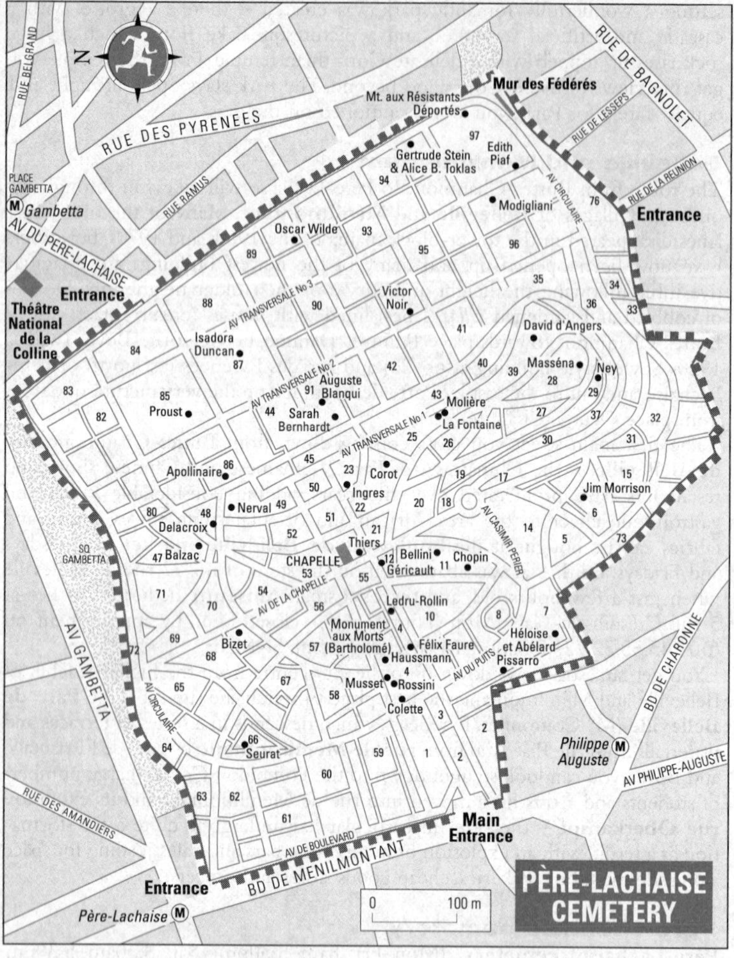

Femme fatale Colette's tomb, close to the main entrance in Division 4, is very plain, though always covered in flowers. The same holds true for those of Sarah Bernhardt (Division 44) and the great chanteuse Edith Piaf (Division 97). Marcel Proust lies in his family's black-marble, conventional tomb (Division 85).

Cutting a rather romantic figure, French president Félix Faure (Division 4), who died in the arms of his mistress in the Elysée palace in 1899, lies draped in a French flag, his head to one side. Corot (division 24) and Balzac (division 48) both have superb busts, while Géricault reclines on cushions of stone (division 12), paint palette in hand. One of the most impressive of the individual tombs is Oscar Wilde's (Division 89), topped with a sculpture by Jacob Epstein of a mysterious Pharaonic winged messenger (sadly vandalized of its once prominent member, last seen being used as a paperweight by the director of the cemetery). Nearby, in division 96, is the grave of **Modigliani** and his lover

Jeanne Herbuterne, who killed herself in crazed grief a few days after the artist died in agony from meningitis.

In Division 97 are the memorials to the victims of the Nazi concentration camps and executed Resistance fighters. The sculptures are relentless in their images of inhumanity, of people forced to collaborate in their own degradation and death. Marking one of the bloodiest episodes in French history is the Mur des Fédérés (Division 76), the wall where the last troops of the Paris Commune were lined up and shot in the final days of the battle in 1871. The man who ordered their execution, Adolphe Thiers, lies in the centre of the cemetery in division 55.

Bercy, the Promenade Plantée and Bois de Vincennes

The 12e arrondissement has seen a number of exciting urban regeneration projects in the last few years. Much of the development has taken place in the riverside **Bercy** *quartier*, which extends from the Gare de Lyon down to the *périphérique*. For centuries this was the site of warehouses where the capital's wine supplies were unloaded from river barges. Much of the area has now been turned into a welcome green space, the extensive **Parc de Bercy** (M° Bercy), cleverly incorporating elements of the old warehouse district such as disused railway tracks and cobbled lanes. The park has arbours, rose gardens, lily ponds, a huge stepped fountain set into one of the grassy banks and a Maison du Jardinage which holds exhibitions and provides information on all aspects of gardening.

The impressive building resembling a pack of falling cards that overlooks the east side of the park, at 51 rue de Bercy, was designed by Bilbao's Guggenheim architect Frank O. Gehry and houses the **Cinémathèque** (Ⓦwww.cinematheque.fr; M° Bercy), the repository for a huge archive of films dating back to the earliest days of cinema. Regular retrospectives of French and foreign films are screened in the four cinemas and it also has an engaging museum (Mon & Wed–Fri noon–7pm, Thurs till 10pm, Sat & Sun 10am–8pm; €4), with lots of early cinematic equipment and silent-film clips, as well as the dress that Vivien Leigh wore in *Gone with the Wind*.

Continuing eastwards through the Parc de Bercy, you come to **Bercy Village** (M° Cour Saint-Émilion), another new development, the main thoroughfare of which is the Cour Saint Émilion, a pedestrianized street lined with former wine warehouses converted into cafés, restaurants and shops. The ochre-coloured stone and the homogeneity of the buildings make for an attractive ensemble and it's an agreeable spot for a wander.

Even better for a stroll, especially if you feel like escaping from the bustle of the city for a bit, is the **Promenade Plantée** (M° Bastille/Ledru-Rollin), a stretch of disused railway line, much of it along a viaduct, that has been converted into an elevated walkway and planted with a profusion of trees and flowers – cherry trees, maples, limes, roses and lavender. The walkway starts near the beginning of avenue Daumesnil, just south of the Bastille opera house, and is reached via a flight of stone steps – or lifts – with a number of similar access points all the way along. It takes you to the Parc de Reuilly, then descends to ground level and continues nearly as far as the *périphérique*, from where you can follow signs to the Bois de Vincennes. The whole walk is around 4.5km long, but if you don't feel like doing the entire thing you could just walk the first part – along the viaduct – which also happens to be the most attractive stretch, running past venerable old mansion blocks and giving a bird's-eye view of the area below and of small architectural details not seen from street level. What's more, the arches of the viaduct itself have been ingeniously converted into spaces for artisans' ateliers and craftshops, collectively known as the **Viaduc des Arts**. There are 51 of them, including furniture restorers, interior designers, cabinet makers and fashion and jewellery boutiques; a full list and map is available from no. 23 av Daumesnil.

The Bois de Vincennes

The **Bois de Vincennes** is the city's only extensive green space besides the Bois de Boulogne. Unfortunately it's so crisscrossed with roads that countryside sensations don't stand much of a chance. There are some very pleasant corners though, including Paris's best gardens, the **Parc Floral** (daily Nov–Jan 9.30am–5pm; Feb & Oct 9.30am–6pm; March & April 9.30am–7pm; April–Sept 9.30am–8pm; €1; Ⓦwww.parcfloraldeparis.com; bus #112 or short walk from M° Château-de-Vincennes). Flowers are always in bloom in the Jardin des Quatres Saisons; you can picnic beneath pines, then wander through concentrations of camellias, cacti, ferns, irises and bonsai trees.

Elsewhere in the Bois de Vincennes, you can spend an afternoon boating on Lac Daumesnil, or you could visit the zoo, just north of the lake, at 53 av de St-Maurice (see p.194). On the northern edge of the *bois*, the **Château de Vincennes** (daily 10am–5/6pm; M° Château-de-Vincennes), royal medieval residence, then state prison, porcelain factory, weapons dump and military training school, can be visited on one of two guided tours (45min €5, or 1hr 15min €6.50). The highlight is the flamboyant Gothic **Chapelle Royale**, completed in the mid-sixteenth century and decorated with superb Renaissance stained-glass windows around the choir.

Eating and drinking

Eating and drinking are among the chief delights of Paris, as they are in France as a whole. An incredible number of restaurants remain defiantly traditional, offering the classic *cuisine bourgeoise* based on well-sauced meat dishes, but you can find a tremendous variety of foods, from Senegalese to Vietnamese, and from eastern European to North African. Regional French cuisines, notably from the southwest, are always popular, as is contemporary French gastronomy – spices and ingredients from the Asia-Pacific region are current fads. There is a huge diversity of places to eat: luxuriously hushed **restaurants** decked with crystal and white linen; noisy, elbow-to-elbow bench-and-trestle-table joints; intimate neighbourhood **bistros** with specials on the blackboard; grand seafood **brasseries** with splendid, historic interiors; and artfully distressed **cafés** serving dishes of the day. Relatively inexpensive offshoots of top restaurants are something of a fashion at the moment, as are the more commercial equivalents – the spin-off bistros of celebrity chefs like Alain Ducasse and Guy Savoy, often focusing on a speciality such as rôtisserie or Basque food.

Excluding top-flight restaurants, **costs** vary less than you might expect – though in terms of what the French call *rapport qualité-prix* it goes without saying that restaurants in tourist hotspots are usually best avoided. Fixed-price menus of two or three courses – called a *menu* in French, or sometimes a *formule* at lunchtime – often represent the least expensive way to eat. You'll pay as little as €10–15 at lunchtime; in the evening, €20–30 is fairly typical, though you can often easily pay less – and a lot more. Above that you should be getting some

Parisian dining

In general, prices fall as you move away from the centre – as does the proportion of foreign to Parisian diners. Paris has always been an international city, but if you're looking for a pungently Parisian experience, the best advice is to eat in one of the more outlying *quartiers*, and eat late. Given how closely packed tables tend to be, your neighbours can really make a difference to the atmosphere.

gourmet satisfaction, while for true, starred gastronomy you'll pay something in the region of €100–150 or more. The big boulevard cafés and brasseries are always more expensive than those a little further removed, and addresses in the smarter or more touristy arrondissements set prices soaring. A snack or drink on the Champs-Élysées or place St-Germain-des-Prés, for instance, will be double or triple the price of one in Belleville or Batignolles.

Drinking venues range from the many **cafés** that move seamlessly from coffees to cocktails as evening approaches, to the tiny, dedicated **wine bars** offering little-known vintages from every region of France. There are cavernous **beer cellars**, designer **bars** with DJ *soirées* at weekends and the ubiquitous Irish/British/Canadian **pubs**. You can take coffee and cakes in a chintzy **salon de thé**, in a bookshop or gallery, or even in the courtyard of a mosque. Many bars have happy hours, but prices can double after 10pm, and any clearly trendy, glitzy or stylish place is bound to be expensive.

The different **eating** and **drinking establishments** are listed here by arrondissement. They are divided into restaurants, including brasseries and bistros, and bars and cafés, a term used to incorporate anywhere you might go for a drink or a lighter meal – cafés, ice-cream parlours and *salons de thé*. You'll also find boxes listing vegetarian (see p.175), ethnic (see p.178) and late-night (see p.177) possibilities. Restaurant **opening times** are typically noon–2/2.30pm and 7.30–10.30/11pm; exceptions to this are noted in the text. Where possible, we have marked restaurants listed on the maps. It's best to **book ahead** for evening meals, especially from Thursday to Saturday; for most places it's usually enough to book on the day, though for the top gourmet restaurants you'll need to book at least two or three weeks in advance.

The Champs-Élysées and around

See map, pp.110–111.

Bars and cafés

Angelina 226 rue de Rivoli, 1er; Mº Tuileries. This elegant old *salon de thé*, with its murals, gilded stucco work and comfy leather armchairs, does the best hot chocolate in town – a generous jugful with whipped cream on the side costs around €6. Mon–Fri 8am–7pm, Sat & Sun 9am–7pm.

L'Arbre à Cannelle 57 passage des Panoramas, 2e; Mº Rue-Montmartre. Tucked away in an attractive *passage*, this *salon de thé* with exquisite wood panelling, frescoes and painted ceilings makes an excellent spot to treat yourself to salads and tarts both savoury and sweet. Mon–Sat 11.30am–6pm.

Aux Bons Crus 7 rue des Petits-Champs, 1er; Mº Palais-Royal. This relaxed, workaday place has been serving good wines and cheese, sausage and ham for over a century. A carafe costs from €6, a plate of cold meats from €13. Mon 9am–3pm, Tues–Sat 7.30am–11pm.

Bar Costes *Hotel Costes*, 239 rue St-Honoré, 8e; Mº Concorde/Tuileries. A favourite haunt of fashionistas and celebs, this is a romantic place for an aperitif or late-night drinks amid decadent nineteenth-century decor of red velvet, swags and columns, set around an Italianate courtyard. Cocktails around €15. Daily until 2am.

Juveniles 47 rue de Richelieu, 2e; Mº Palais-Royal. A very popular tiny wine bar run by a Scot. There are usually around ten different wines available by the glass (from €3); *plats du jour* cost €11, cheese plates and other light dishes €7. Tues–Sat 11am–11pm, Sun noon–2pm, Mon 7.30–11pm.

Ladurée 75 av des Champs-Élysées, 8e; M° George-V. This Champs-Élysées branch of the *Ladurée* tearooms, with its luxurious gold and green decor, is perfect for a shopping break. Try the delicious macaroons or the thick hot chocolate (€6.10). Daily 7.30am–11.30pm.

Musée Jacquemart-André 158 bd Haussmann, 8e ☎01.45.62.11.59; M° St-Philippe-du-Eoule/Miromesnil. Part of the Musée Jacquemart-André but with independent access, this is the most sumptuously appointed *salon de thé* in the city. Admire the ceiling frescoes by Tiepolo while savouring fine pastries or salads. Daily 11.30am–5.30pm.

Le Café Noir 65 rue Montmartre, 2e; M° Sentier. Despite the name, it's the colour red that predominates in this buzzy little corner bar, great for an aperitif or late-night drinks, when the music and ambience hot up and it's standing room only at the bar. Mon–Fri 8.30am–2am, Sat 4pm–2am.

Le Rubis 10 rue du Marché-St-Honoré, 1er; M° Pyramides. This very small and very crowded wine bar is one of the oldest in Paris, known for its excellent wines – mostly from the Beaujolais and Loire regions – and home-made *rillettes* (a kind of pork pâté). *Plats du jour* for around €10 are served at midday. Mon–Fri 7.30am–9pm, Sat 9am–3pm; closed mid-Aug.

Verlet 56 rue St-Honoré, 1er; M° Palais-Royal/Musée du Louvre. A heady aroma of coffee greets you as you enter this charming old-world coffee merchant's-cum-café. Wood furnishings, green-leather benches and caddies line one wall, the menu features 25 varieties of coffee and there's a selection of teas and light snacks, too. Mon–Sat 9am–7pm.

Restaurants

Alain Ducasse at the Plaza-Athénée *Hotel Plaza-Athénée*, 25 av Montaigne, 8e ☎01.53.67.65.00, ⓦwww.alain-ducasse.com; M° Alma-Marceau. One of Paris's top *haute cuisine* temples, run by star chef Alain Ducasse, whose sublime dishes, such as Brittany langoustines with Oscietra caviar, are likely to revive even the most jaded palate. The stylish decor features Louis XV-style chairs and Swarowski crystal chandeliers. Around €200 a head. Thurs & Fri 12.45–2.15pm & 7.45–10.15pm.

Chartier 7 rue du Faubourg-Montmartre, 9e ☎01.47.70.86.29; M° Montmartre. Dark-stained woodwork, brass hat-racks, mirrors, waiters in long aprons – this has the original decor of an early twentieth-century soup kitchen. Though crowded and rushed, it's worth a visit, and the food's not bad at all. Three courses for €16, and a bottle of wine from €6. Daily 11.30am–3pm & 6–10pm.

Le Dauphin 167 rue St-Honoré, 1er ☎01.42.60.40.11; M° Palais-Royal/Musée-du-Louvre. This old bistro, with original Art Deco stained glass, serves inventive southwestern dishes. Specialities are the *parilladas*, such as the *parillada du boucher* (€23) made up of steak, duck, chicken breast and sausage; veggies are catered for too with the *parillada de la terre* (tomatoes, courgette, aubergine, fennel, peppers and endives; €19). Daily.

Dragons Élysées 11 rue de Berri, 8e ☎01.42.89.85.10; M° George-V. The Chinese-Thai cuisine encompasses dim sum, curried seafood and baked mussels, but the overriding attraction is the extraordinary decor: beneath a floor of glass tiles water runs from pool to pool inhabited by exotic fish. Midweek lunchtime menu €14, otherwise count on around €35 a head. Daily.

Higuma 32bis rue St-Anne, 1er ☎01.47.03.38.59; M° Pyramides. Authentic Japanese canteen with cheap, filling ramen dishes and a good-value set menu at €10. Daily 11.30am–10pm.

Aux Lyonnais 32 rue St-Marc, 2e ☎01.42.96.65.04; M° Bourse/Richelieu-Drouot. This revamped old bistro, with lovely Belle Époque tiles and mirrored walls, serves up delicious Lyonnais fare – try the *quenelles* (light and delicate fish dumplings) followed by the heavenly Cointreau soufflé for dessert. Three-course set menu €28. Closed Sat lunch, Sun & Mon.

Pierre Gagnaire *Hôtel Balzac*, 6 rue Balzac, 8e ☎01.58.36.12.50, ⓦwww.pierre-gagnaire.com; M° George-V. Judged third-best restaurant in the world by Restaurant magazine in 2006, *Pierre Gagnaire* is a gastronomic adventure. The lunch menu costs €90, dinner at least €200. Mon–Fri noon–1.30pm & 7.30–9.30pm, Sun 7.30–9.30pm.

Le Relais de l'Entrecôte 15 rue Marbeuf, 8e; M° Franklin-D.-Roosevelt. No reservations are taken at this bustling diner, so you may have to queue for the single dish on the menu: steak and *frites*. This is no ordinary steak though – the secret is in the delicious, buttery sauce. Around €22 including a salad starter. Desserts at around €6 are excellent too. Daily; closed Aug.

Rue Balzac 3–5 rue Balzac, 8e ☎01.53.89.90.91; M° Charles-de-Gaulle. This ultra-stylish restaurant is the enterprise of rock singer Johnny Hallyday and chef Michel Rostang. The low lighting and subdued reds and yellows of the decor provide an atmospheric backdrop to classy cuisine, available in small or large servings ("petit modèle" and "grand modèle"). Around €60 a head. M° George-V. Closed lunch Sat & Sun, & Aug.

Les Saveurs de Flora 36 av George-V, 8e ☎01.40.70.10.49; M° George-V. A stylish, cosy restaurant, with an open fireplace and chandeliers, run by chef-owner Flora Mikula, who creates tasty, inventive dishes, drawing mainly on Mediterranean influences. The set menu at €36 is very good value, considering the high quality and upmarket location. Closed Sat lunch & Sun.

Spoon, Food and Wine 14 rue de Marignan, 8e ☎01.40.76.34.44; M° Franklin-D.-Roosevelt. Innovative world-food bistro headed up by top chef Alain Ducasse. The chic, minimalist decor and inventive cuisine, marrying unusual flavours and ingredients, attract a fashionable crowd. Count on around €65 a head. Closed Sat, Sun & mid-July to mid-Aug.

Taillevent 15 rue Lamennais, 8e ☎01.44.95.15.01; M° Charles-de-Gaulle. One of Paris's finest gourmet restaurants. The Provencal-influenced cuisine and wine list are exceptional, the decor classy and refined. There's a set menu for €70 at lunch only, otherwise reckon on an average of €150 a head, excluding wine, and book well in advance. Closed Sat, Sun & Aug.

Vaudeville 29 rue Vivienne, 2e ☎01.40.20.04.62; M° Bourse. There's often a queue to get a table at this lively late-night brasserie, attractively decorated with marble and mosaics. Dishes include grilled cod with truffle sauce and *belle tête de veau*. Lunchtime menu €22.90, dinner €29.90. Daily noon–3pm & 7pm–1am.

Beaubourg and Les Halles

See map, p.122.

Bars & cafés

Café Beaubourg 43 rue St-Merri, 4e; M° Rambuteau/Hôtel-de-Ville. Seats under the expansive awnings of this stylish café, bearing the trademark sweeping lines of designer Christian Portamparc, command frontline views of the Pompidou piazza and are great for people-watching. Drinks €5. It's also good for a relaxing Sunday brunch (from €15). Daily 8am–1am.

Le Petit Marcel 63 rue Rambuteau, 4e; M° Rambuteau. Speckled tabletops, mirrors and Art Nouveau tiles, a cracked and faded ceiling and about eight square metres of drinking space. There's a small dining area, too, where you can get cheap and filling dishes such as *frites* and omelette. Mon–Sat till 2am.

Taverne Henri IV 13 place du Pont-Neuf, Île de la Cité, 1er; M° Pont-Neuf. An old-style wine bar that's probably changed little since Yves Montand used to come here with Simone Signoret. It's especially lively at lunchtime when lawyers from the nearby Palais de Justice drop in for generous plates of meats and cheeses (for around €12) and *tartines* (with a choice of cheeses, hams, pâté and saucisson). Mon–Fri 11.30am–9.30pm, Sat noon–5pm; closed Sun & Aug.

Restaurants

Chez Dilan 13 rue Mandar, 2e ☎01.42.21.14.88; M° Les Halles/Sentier. An excellent-value Kurdish restaurant, strewn with kilims and playing taped Kurdish music. Starters include melt-in-your mouth *babaqunuc* (stuffed aubergines) and mains *beyti* (spiced minced beef wrapped in pastry, with yoghurt, tomato sauce and bulgar wheat). Around €18 for two courses; €9 for half a litre of Kurdish wine. Closed Sun.

Georges Centre Georges Pompidou, 4e ☎01.44.78.47.99; M° Rambuteau/Hôtel-de-Ville. On the top floor of the Pompidou Centre, this trendy minimalist restaurant with outdoor terrace commands stunning views over Paris and makes a stylish place for lunch or dinner. The French-Asian fusion cuisine is pretty good, if overpriced. Count on around €50 to €60 per head. Daily except Tues noon–midnight.

Au Pied de Cochon 6 rue Coquillière, 1er ☎01.40.13.77.00; M° Châtelet-Les Halles. A Les Halles institution, this is the place to go for extravagant middle-of-the-night pork chops, steak and, of course, pigs' trotters. Mains cost around €20. Daily 24hr.

La Robe et le Palais 13 rue des Lavandières St-Opportune, 1er ☎01.45.08.07.41; M° Châtelet. Small, busy *restaurant à vins* serving traditional cuisine and an excellent selection of wines, running to around 250 vintages. Typical main courses include sea bream, *boudin noir* (black pudding), *andouillette* (tripe sausage) and steak. The two-course lunch menu is good value at around €15. Closed Sun.

À la Tour de Montlhéry (Chez Denise) 5 rue des Prouvaires, 1er ☎01.42.36.21.82; M° Louvre-Rivoli/Châtelet. A quintessential old-style Parisian bistro, going back to the Les Halles market days. Diners sit elbow to elbow at long tables in a narrow, smoky dining room and tuck into filling meaty dishes, such as *andouillette* (tripe sausage), offal and steak, accompanied by perfectly cooked *frites*. Mains cost around €22. Mon–Fri noon–3pm & 7.30pm–5am. Closed mid-July to mid-Aug.

La Victoire Suprême du Coeur 41 rue des Bourdonnais, 1er ☎01.40.41.93.95; M° Louvre-Rivoli/Châtelet. While the interior – plastered with photos and drawings of Indian guru Sri Chimnoy – takes some getting used to, this restaurant does some of the best vegetarian food in Paris, including tasty salads, quiches and wholesome mains, such as mushroom roast with blackberry sauce. Two courses at lunch cost as little as €12.50, €15.30 for dinner. Mon–Sat 11.45am–10pm.

Au Vieux Molière passage Molière, 157 rue Saint-Martin, 3e ⓣ01.42.78.37.87, ⓦwww.vieux-moliere.com; M° Étienne-Marcel/Rambuteau/RER Châtelet. Tucked away down a small *passage*, this is an atmospheric restaurant, with French chansons playing softly in the background and prints of literary figures on the walls. The menu changes daily, but typical dishes are garlic-roasted chicken and mullet in saffron sauce. Reckon on around €35 for dinner. Closed Sat & Sun lunch.

Marais, Île St-Louis & Bastille

See map, pp.126–127.

Bars and cafés

Andy Wahloo 69 rue des Gravilliers, 3e ⓣ01.42.71.20.38; M° Arts-et-Métiers. A very popular bar decked out in original Pop Art-inspired Arabic decor. Yummy mezze appetizers are served until midnight and the bar serves a few original cocktails, including the Wahloo Special (rum, lime, ginger, banana and cinnamon; €9). DJs play a wide range of dance music. Mon–Sat 11am–2am.

L'Apparemment Café 18 rue des Coutures-St-Gervais, 3e; M° St-Sébastien-Froissart. A chic and cosy café resembling a series of comfortable sitting rooms, with quiet corners and deep sofas. The salads (from around €8), which you compose yourself by ticking off your chosen ingredients and handing your order to the waiter, are recommended. Mon–Fri noon–2am, Sat 4pm–2am, Sun 12.30pm–midnight.

L'As du Fallafel 34 rue des Rosiers, 4e ⓣ01.48.87.63.60; M° St-Paul. The best falafel shop in the Jewish quarter. Falafels to take away cost only €4; you can pay a bit more and sit in the little dining room. Daily noon–midnight; closed Fri eve & Sat.

Berthillon 31 rue St-Louis-en-l'Île, 4e; M° Pont-Marie. You may well have to queue for one of *Berthillon*'s exquisite ice creams or sorbets – arguably the best in Paris. Wed–Sun 10am–8pm.

Iguana 15 rue de la Roquette, cnr rue Daval, 11e; M° Bastille. A place to be seen in with a decor of trellises, colonial fans and a brushed bronze bar. By day, the clientele studies recherché art reviews over excellent coffee, while things hot up at night with a youngish, high-spirited crowd. DJ on Thurs. Cocktails around €9. Daily 9am–5am.

Café de l'Industrie 16 rue St-Sabin, 11e; M° Bastille. Rugs on the floor around solid old wooden tables, miscellaneous objects – from stuffed crocodiles to atmospheric black-and-white photos – on the walls, and a young, unpretentious crowd enjoying the comfortable absence of minimalism. One of the best Bastille cafés, packed out every evening. Daily 10–2am.

△ Dining at *Bofinger*

CAFÉS, BISTROS AND BRASSERIES

France is famous for its cuisine, of course, but how do you decide exactly where to eat it? What's the difference between a bistro and a brasserie? What does *gastronomique* mean and where can you get a simple sandwich? Read on. Just like anywhere in the world, France has its share of fast-food outlets and takeaways. But if you want to sit down to eat in reasonable comfort you'll be faced with an overwhelming variety of alluring establishments to choose from.

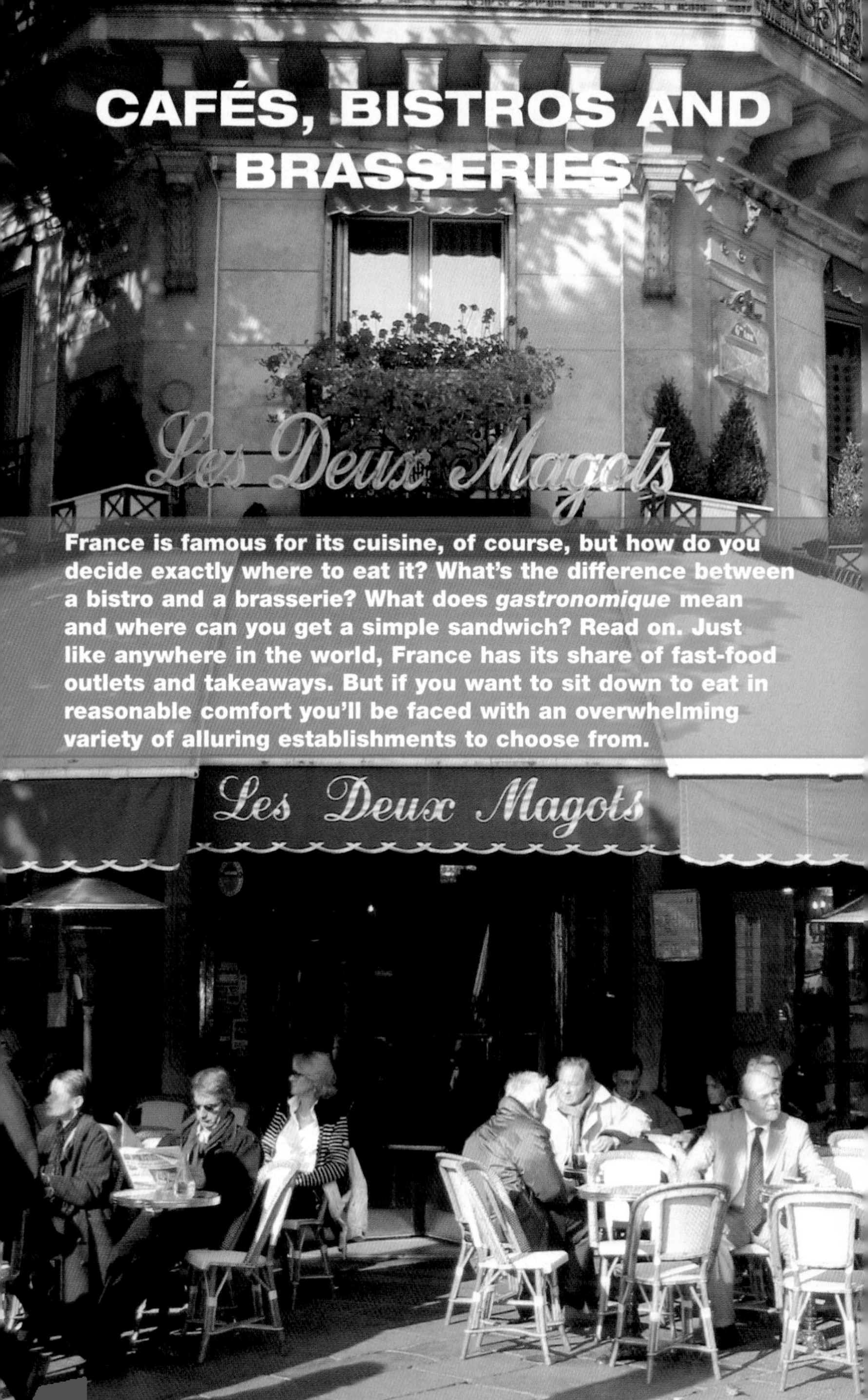

▲ *Polidor*, St-Germain, Paris

Cafés and wine bars

If you're looking for breakfast or a simple snack, your best bet is a **café-bar**, where you can lounge for hours, watching the world go by. In addition to an extensive drinks list, most cafés offer morning croissants and can rustle up filled baguettes, toasted sandwiches and the like at lunchtime, possibly all day. Some might run to more substantial fare, along the lines of a couple of *plats du jour*, maybe even a basic menu (see box overleaf), but nothing too elaborate.

For a more sophisticated, night-time feel, drop into a **wine bar**, which you'll generally find in larger towns and cities. At the top end, these can be very refined establishments catering to serious wine connoisseurs. Others are small and convivial. While the wine takes priority, you'll typically be offered cheese or cold meat platters to nibble on.

Brasseries vs Bistros

These are the quintessential urban French eateries. **Brasseries** are typically large and bustling, with lots of mirrors and brasswork, whereas **bistros** tend to be small, casual and inexpensive neighbourhood restaurants. Most bistros open for lunch and dinner; brasseries generally serve meals all day – a few city-centre places may keep going until midnight – and double as café-bars outside regular meal times. Standard brasserie fare consists of salads, omelettes, grills and a smattering of fish dishes, plus seafood platters at more upmarket places. Don't expect any fireworks, but the food should be quick and wholesome.

▼ *La Cigale*, Nantes

If it's something more homely you're after, you'll probably be better off in a bistro, where the daily dishes could be a selection of fuss-free classics, such as boeuf bourguignon or quiche and salad. Though most bistros still offer traditional fare, you'll find some now offering more contemporary, eye-catching cuisine, often with minimalist furnishings and upbeat colour schemes to match.

Farm feast

In country areas keep an eye out for **fermes auberges**. These farm restaurants provide a means for small farmers to supplement their income, the main criteria being that they produce the majority of ingredients themselves. They are often the best place to sample really traditional local cuisine. In southwest France, for example, you'll be treated to all manner of dishes prepared from goose or duck: rich slabs of foie gras followed by *magret* (breast) or *confit* (preserved duck or goose) served with potatoes – fried in the birds' fat, of course. Elsewhere it might be pork or lamb, but always at very reasonable prices; a four-course meal for between €15 and €35 is the norm, including an aperitif and wine. Reservations are a must.

All the restos

If it offers meals and doesn't fall into any of the above categories, it must be a **restaurant**. From the lowly truckers' *routiers* up through family-run country inns (usually called *auberges* or sometimes *relais*) and hotel dining rooms to Michelin-starred establishments serving the very highest *haute cuisine*, restaurants cover a broad range. In general, however, they're more formal than café-bars or brasseries and stick to the traditional meal times of noon–2pm, and 7–9pm, sometimes later in larger towns and during the summer months. The food could be traditional or modern, hearty home-cooking or classic and refined, international or resolutely French.

Top qualité?

Unfortunately, while eating at top-class establishments usually guarantees a certain excellence, elsewhere it can be a matter of luck. There's nothing to say you'll eat better in a smart-looking restaurant than in a simple café. In either the food could be inspired and inventive or come from the freezer via the microwave. The best rule of thumb is to avoid places that are half empty at peak times, use your nose and regard long menus with suspicion. Be cautious, too, of restaurants or menus professing to offer *gastronomique* cuisine. In theory, this means they use the best ingredients and blend texture and taste, colour and aroma to create an unbeatable eating experience. Sadly, the term is much overused and the food often doesn't live up to the hype – or the price tag.

▼ Dessert at *Astier*, Paris

Restaurant etiquette

Bread and tap water are provided free of charge in France. If there's no side-plate, just put your bread on the table. It's fine to tear it into pieces and also to mop your plate with it. Elbows on the table is fine, too. In fact, you should keep your hands visible at all times.

In touristy areas in high season, and for all the more upmarket places, it's wise to reserve. Prices, and what you get for them, must be posted outside. The vast majority include a service charge of 15 percent – in which case it should say *service compris* (*s.c.*) or *prix net*. Very occasionally you'll see *service non compris* (*s.n.c.*) or *servis en sus*, which means it's up to you whether you leave a tip or not.

▲ Parisian waiter

Menu primer

Plat du jour Reasonably priced "daily specials" commonly served at lunchtime.

Menu fixe or **menu du jour** Fixed-price menus – often referred to simply as menus – comprising a set number of courses and a limited choice. Lunchtime menus are cheaper than those at dinner and often represent excellent value.

Formule Usually available only at lunchtime, a *formule* is a trimmed-down menu, typically offering just two courses for a set price.

Carte Choosing from the *carte* (the full menu) naturally offers a greater choice – though you'll pay more for the privilege.

Menu carte Choose freely from the *carte* but pay a fixed price according to whether you opt for one, two or three courses.

Le Loir dans la Théière 3 rue des Rosiers, 4e; M° Saint-Paul. A laid-back *salon de thé* where you can sink into a battered sofa and feast on enormous portions of home-made cakes and vegetarian quiches. Come early for the popular Sunday brunch (€15). Mon–Fri 11am–7pm, Sat & Sun 10am–7pm.

Pause Café 41 rue de Charonne, cnr rue Keller, 11e; M° Ledru-Rollin. A traditional high-ceilinged, glass-fronted café with tiled floors. Its terrace is particularly prized in warmer weather. Tues–Sat 8am–2am, Sun to 9pm.

Le Petit Fer à Cheval 30 rue Vieille-du-Temple, 4e; M° St-Paul. A very attractive small drinking spot with original *fin-de-siècle* decor, including a marble-topped bar in the shape of a horseshoe (*fer à cheval*). You can snack on sandwiches or something more substantial in the little back room furnished with old wooden métro seats. Mon–Fri 9am–2am, Sat & Sun 11am–2am; food noon–midnight.

Le Rouge Gorge 8 rue St-Paul, 4e; M° St-Paul. Friendly wine bar and restaurant with bare stone walls and jazz or classical music playing in the background. Devoted to exploring a wide range of wines: one week it might be Corsica, the next Spain or the Loire, and the theme is taken up in the frequently changing menu. Mains cost around €16. Mon–Sat noon–11pm. Closed last fortnight in Aug.

SanZSanS 49 rue du Faubourg-St-Antoine, 11[e]; M° Bastille. Gothic getup of red velvet, oil paintings and chandeliers, popular with a young crowd, especially on Friday and Saturday evenings, when DJs play funk, Brazilian beats and house. Drinks are reasonably priced. Daily 9am–5am.

Le Wax 15 rue Daval, 11[e]; M° Bastille. A popular bar with great early 70s interior, full of happy locals and foreigners dancing to soul, house and electronica. Tues–Thurs till 2am, Fri & Sat till 5am.

Restaurants

Ambassade d'Auvergne 22 rue de Grenier St-Lazare, 3e ☎01.42.72.31.22; M° Rambuteau. Suited, mustachioed waiters serve scrumptious Auvergnat cuisine that would have made Vercingétorix proud. There's a set menu for €28, but you may well be tempted by some of the house specialities, like the roast guineafowl with garlic (€17). Daily noon–2pm & 7.30–10pm; closed last two weeks in Aug.

Astier 44 rue Jean-Pierre-Timbaud, 11e ☎01.43.57.16.35; M° Parmentier. Very popular restaurant with an unstuffy atmosphere and food renowned for its freshness and refinement. Outstanding selection of perfectly ripe cheeses and excellent wine list. It's essential to book; lunch is often less crowded (€21.50 menu) and just as enjoyable. Evening menu €26. Closed Sat & Sun, Aug & fortnight in May & at Christmas.

Auberge de Jarente 7 rue Jarente, 4e ☎01.42.77.49.35; M° St-Paul. This friendly Basque restaurant serves up hearty dishes of cassoulet, hare stew, *magret de canard*, *pipérade* and the like. Set menus at €21 and €30. Tues–Sat noon–2.30pm & 7.30–10.30pm; closed Aug.

L'Auberge Pyrénées Cévennes 106 rue de la Folie Méricourt, 11e ☎01.43.57.33.78; M° République. Make sure you come hungry to this homely little place serving hearty portions of country cuisine. The garlicky *moules marinières* and the wonderful cassoulet, served in its own copper pot, are highly recommended. Around €30 a head à la carte. Noon–2pm & 7–11pm, closed Sat lunch and all day Sun.

Bistrot du Peintre 116 av Ledru Rollin, 11e ☎01.47.00.34.39; M° Faidherbe-Chaligny. A traditional neighbourhood bistro, where small tables are jammed together beneath faded Art Nouveau frescoes and wood panelling. The emphasis is on hearty cuisine, with dishes such as beef tartare and *confit de canard* for around €14. Mon–Sat 7am–2am, Sun 10am–8pm.

Bofinger 7 rue de la Bastille, 4e ☎01.42.72.87.82; M° Bastille. Popular *fin-de-siècle* brasserie with its splendid original decor perfectly preserved. Specialities are sauerkraut and seafood and there's a set dinner menu for €29.90. Daily noon–3pm & 7pm–1am.

Au Bourguignon du Marais 52 rue François Miron, 4e ☎01.48.87.15.40; M° St-Paul. A warm, relaxed restaurant, with attractive contemporary decor and tables outside in summer, serving excellent Burgundian cuisine with carefully selected wines to match. Mains cost €15–25, wine starts at €20. Mon–Fri noon–3pm & 8–11pm; closed two weeks in Aug.

Chez Marianne 2 rue des Hospitalières-St-Gervais, 4e ☎01.42.72.18.86; M° St-Paul. You can eat very well and cheaply at this homely restaurant specializing in Middle Eastern and Jewish delicacies. A platter of mezzes that might include tabbouleh, aubergine purée, chopped liver and hummus starts from €12, and the wines are reasonably priced too. Daily noon–midnight.

Chez Omar 47 rue de Bretagne, 3e; M° Arts-et-Métiers. No reservations are taken at this popular North African couscous restaurant, but it's no hardship to wait at the bar for a table, taking in the handsome old brasserie decor and the buzzy atmosphere. Portions are copious and the couscous light and fluffy. The *merguez* (spicy sausage) costs €12, or go all out for the *royal* (€22). No credit cards. Daily except Sun lunch noon–2.30pm & 7–11.30pm.

L'Enoteca 25 rue Charles-V, 4e ☎01.42.78.91.44; M° St-Paul. A fashionable Italian *bistro à vins* in an old wood-beamed Marais building, with an impressive wine list running to 22 pages. Food doesn't take a back seat either: choose from an array of antipasti laid out enticingly in the middle of the room, fresh pasta or more substantial dishes such as *courgettes farcis à la viande de veau*. There's a two-course midweek lunchtime menu for €13, otherwise reckon on around €40 a head. Daily noon–11.30pm; closed one week in mid-Aug.

Mon Vieil Ami 69 rue St-Louis-en-l'Ile, 4e ☎01.40.46.01.35; M° Pont-Marie. Charming little bistro, with appealing contemporary decor of chocolate browns and frosted-glass panels. The excellent cuisine is bold and zesty, using seasonal ingredients, and the wine list includes some choice vintages. Three courses cost around €40. Daily 12.30–2.30pm & 7.30–10.30pm. Closed Jan & Aug.

Piccolo Teatro 6 rue des Ecouffes, 4e ☎01.42.72.17.79; M° St-Paul. A cosy vegetarian restaurant with low lighting, stone walls and wooden beams. The speciality is *gratins*, with poetic names such as *douceur et tendresse* (spinach, mint, mozzarella and Gruyère). Reckon on €15–20 without drinks. Closed Mon & Aug.

Le Square Trousseau 1 rue Antoine Vollon, 12e ☎01.43.43.06.00; M° Ledru-Rollin. Handsome *belle-époque* brasserie patronized by a chic but relaxed crowd. The regularly changing menu features excellent traditional cuisine. Lunch menu for €20; à la carte reckon on at least €40. Closed Sun & Aug.

Quartier Latin

See map, pp.134–135.

Bars and cafés

La Fourmi Ailée 8 rue du Fouarre, 5e; M° Maubert-Mutualité. This former feminist bookshop has been transformed into a *salon de thé* offering simple, light fare. A high ceiling painted with a lovely mural and a book-filled wall contribute to the unusual atmosphere. From noon to 3pm it's restaurant service only – count on around €10–15 for a *plat*. Daily noon–7pm.

Café de l'Institut du Monde Arabe 1, rue des Fossés St-Bernard, 5e; M° Jussieu/Cardinal-Lemoine. Rooftop café-restaurant where you can drink mint tea and nibble on cakes looking out on the Seine. Inside the building, the self-service cafeteria *Moucharabiyah* offers a decent plate of lunchtime couscous. Tues–Sun 10am–6pm.

Café de la Mosquée 39 rue Geoffroy-St-Hilaire, 5e; M° Monge. You can drink mint tea and eat sweet cakes beside a fountain and assorted fig trees in the courtyard of this Paris mosque – a delightful haven of calm. Meals are served in the adjoining restaurant for around €15 and up. Daily 9am–11pm.

Café de la Nouvelle Mairie 19 rue des Fossés-St-Jacques, 5e; M° Cluny-La Sorbonne/RER Luxembourg. Sleek café-wine bar with a relaxed feel generated by its older, university-based clientele. Serves inventive and reasonably priced mains, and you can drink at the outside tables on sunny days. Mon, Wed & Fri 9am–10pm, Tues & Thurs 9am–11pm.

Le Piano Vache 8 rue Laplace, 5e; M° Cardinal-Lemoine. Venerable bar crammed with students drinking at little tables, with cool music and a laid-back atmosphere. Mon–Fri noon–2am, Sat & Sun 9pm–2am.

Les Pipos 2 rue de l'École-Polytechnique, 5e; M° Maubert-Mutualité/Cardinal-Lemoine. Old, rustically wooden bar, serving inexpensive wines along with simple plates of charcuterie, cheese and the like. Mon–Sat 8am–1am; closed two weeks in Aug.

Le Violon Dingue 46 rue de la Montagne-Ste-Geneviève, 5e; M° Maubert-Mutualité. A long, dark student pub that's noisy, friendly and popular with young travellers. English-speaking bar staff and cheap drinks. The cellar bar stays open until 4.30am on busy nights. Daily 6pm–2.30am; happy hour 8–10pm.

Restaurants

Les 5 Saveurs d'Anada 72 rue Cardinal-Lemoine, 5e ☎01.43.29.58.54; M° Cardinal-Lemoine. Airy and informal restaurant serving delicious, reasonably priced organic vegetarian food. The salads are good, or you could try one of the creative meat-substitute dishes (around €12), such as tofu soufflé or seitan with celeriac and basil. Daily noon–2.30pm & 7.30–10.30pm.

Au Bistro de la Sorbonne 4 rue Toullier, 5e ☎01.43.54.41.49; RER Luxembourg. Traditional French and delicious North African food – tagines, couscous – served at reasonable prices to a crowd of locals and students. The interior is bright and attractively muralled. Closed Sun.

Brasserie Balzar 49 rue des Écoles, 5e ☎01.43.54.13.67; M° Maubert-Mutualité. Truly classic high-ceilinged, pot-plant-festooned brasserie, long frequented by the literary intelligentsia of the Quartier Latin, though it draws a more international crowd earlier on. À la carte around €30. Daily 8am–11.30pm.

Les Degrés de Notre Dame 10 rue des Grands Degrés, 5e ☎01.55.42.88.88; M° Maubet-Mutualité. Reliable, inexpensive and substantial French food served in a friendly, faintly rustic dining room. Good-value lunch menu. Closed Sun.

L'Ecurie 58 rue de la Montagne Ste-Geneviève, 5e ☎01.46.33.68.49; M° Maubert-Mutualité/Cardinal-Lemoine. Shoe-horned into a former stables, this family-run restaurant is bustling and very lovable. Expect well-cooked meat dishes served without flourishes – grilled with chips, mostly – for less than €15, and book ahead. Mon–Sat noon–3pm & 7pm–midnight, Sun 7pm–midnight.

Le Grenier de Notre Dame 18 rue de la Bûcherie, 5e ☎01.43.29.98.29; M° Maubert-Mutualité/St-Michel. Some people love the menu of unreconstructed veggie classics and the quiet, dimly lit, neighbourhood atmosphere; others find it dull. At around €20 for a meal, the prices aren't low. Mon–Fri noon–2.30pm & 7–11pm, Sat & Sun noon–11pm.

Perraudin 157 rue St-Jacques, 5e ☎01.46.33.15.75; RER Luxembourg. One of the classic bistros of the Left Bank.The atmosphere is thick with Parisian chatter and the tables brightly lit and tightly packed. Solid cooking, with moderately priced menus. No reservations. Closed Sat & Sun; closed two weeks in Aug.

La Petite Légume 36 rue Boulangers, 5e ☎01.40.46.06.85; M° Jussieu. A health-food grocery that doubles as a vegetarian restaurant and tearoom, serving homely, organic *plats* for €8–12, along with organic Loire wines. Closed Sun.

Pho 67 59 rue Galande, 5e ☎01.45.25.56.69; M° Maubert-Mutualité. Authentic Vietnamese, with dishes for around €6. Try the famous *pho* soup, in this case made with tender French steak.

Le Pré-Verre 8 rue Thénard, 5e ☎01.43.54.59.47; M° Maubert-Mutualité. This sleek, modern *bistro à vins* has a great wine list, while blackboard lists are dotted with unusual ingredients and spices – think swordfish on a bed of quinoa grain or wild boar ragout with quince. Evening menu at €25. Tues–Sat noon–2pm & 7.30–10.30pm; closed three weeks in Aug.

Le Reminet 3 rue des Grands Degrés, 5e ☎01.44.07.04.24; M° Maubert-Mutualité. This artful little bistro-restaurant shows its class through small touches: snowy-white tablecloths, fancy chandeliers and carefully considered and imaginative sauces. Gastronomic menu at €50, but you can get away with two courses à la carte for about half that. Closed Tues & Wed.

Tashi Delek 4 rue des Fossés-St-Jacques, 5e ☎01.43.26.55.55; RER Luxembourg. Elegantly styled Tibetan restaurant serving Himalayan dishes ranging from delicious broths to the addictive, ravioli-like *momok*. You can eat handsomely for under €20. Closed Sun & two weeks in Aug.

St-Germain

See map, pp.138–139.

Bars & cafés

Le 10 10 rue de l'Odéon, 6e; M° Odéon. Small, dark bar with Art Deco posters above and an atmospheric, studenty cellar bar below. Daily 6pm–2am.

Chez Georges 11 rue des Canettes, 6e; M° Mabillon. This tobacco-stained wine bar has its old shopfront still in place and oozes Left Bank character. The downstairs bar attracts a younger crowd that stays lively well into the small hours. Relatively inexpensive for the area, too. Tues–Sat noon–2am; closed Aug.

Cosi 54 rue de Seine, 6e; M° St-Germain-des-Prés. Great Italian deli sandwiches on home-made focaccia. You can eat in, with a glass of wine, enjoying the musical tastes of the opera-loving owner. Daily noon–midnight.

Les Deux Magots 170 bd St-Germain, 6e; M° St-Germain-des-Prés. Right on the corner of place St-Germain-des-Prés, this expensive café is the victim of its own reputation as the historic hangout of Left Bank intellectuals, but it's great for people-watching. It's worth arriving early for the breakfasts. Daily 7.30am–1am.

Les Étages St-Germain 5 rue de Buci, 6e; M° Mabillon. Outpost of boho trendiness at the edge of the rue de Buci market, with a certain trashy glamour. The downstairs café-bar is open to the street, and in the evenings you can lounge around upstairs with a cocktail. Daily 11am–2am.

Flore 172 bd St-Germain, 6e; M° St-Germain-des-Prés. The great rival and immediate neighbour of *Les Deux Magots*, with a very similar clientele. Sartre, De Beauvoir, Camus and Marcel Carné used to hang out here. Best for a late-afternoon coffee or after-dinner drink, preferably in the insiders' haunt upstairs. Daily 7am–1.30am.

Fubar 5 rue St-Sulpice, 6e; M° Odéon. Relaxed lounge bar with a young, international crowd drinking well past the last métro. The upstairs room is very cosy, with soft armchairs and deep red walls. Daily 5pm–2am.

Café de la Mairie Place St-Sulpice, 6e; M° St-Sulpice. Famous for the beautiful people sun-seeking on the outdoor *terrasse*, which looks onto the beautiful square. Mon–Sat 7am–2am.

Bar du Marché 75 rue de Seine, 6e; M° Mabillon. Humming café where the waiters are funkily kitted out in flat caps and bright aprons. It's great fun – in a self-consciously bohemian way – and perennially fashionable. You pay a little extra for the location near the rue de Buci market. Daily 7am–2am.

La Mezzanine de l'Alcazar 62 rue Mazarine, 6e; M° Odéon. The decor is *très design* at this cool cocktail bar, set on a mezzanine level overlooking Conran's *Alcazar* restaurant. Expensive but exquisite – much like the clientele. DJs Wed–Sat. Daily 7pm–2am.

La Palette 43 rue de Seine, 6e; M° Odéon. Once-famous Beaux-Arts student hangout, now frequented by art dealers and their customers. The decor is superb, including, of course, a large selection of colourful, used palettes. Mon–Sat 9am–2am.

Au Petit Suisse 16 rue de Vaugirard, 6e; RER Luxembourg/M° Cluny-La Sorbonne. Everything you'd need from a café: outdoor terrace, in-house *tabac*, two-hundred-year history, Art Deco interior, menu of sandwiches, salads and decent *plats du jour*, and a mezzanine level that's made for people-watching. Daily 6.30am–midnight.

La Taverne de Nesle 32 rue Dauphine, 6e; M° Odéon. Full of young, local night-birds fuelled up by happy hour cocktails and one or more of the vast selection of beers. DJs at weekends. Daily 6pm till around 4am.

Restaurants

Au 35 35 rue Jacob, 6e ☎01.42.60.23.24; M° St-Germain-des-Prés. Adorably intimate bistro, but the food's the thing – from a perfect duck breast to an exotic, rich pastilla of lamb with honey and spices. Around €30 without wine. Mon–Fri noon–2.30pm & 7.30–11pm, Sat 7.30–11pm.

Allard 41 rue St-André-des-Arts, 6e ☎01.43.26.48.23; M° Odéon. Proudly unreconstructed Parisian restaurant with a meaty, homely cuisine. If it wasn't for the international clientele, you could be dining in another century. From around €30. Closed Sun.

L'Atlas 11 rue de Buci, 6e ☎01.40.51.26.30; M° Mabillon. Unpretentious market brasserie serving good seafood, and simple, meaty main dishes at around €17. Daily 6.30am–1am.

Brasserie Lipp 151 bd St-Germain, 6e; M° St-Germain-des-Prés. One of the most celebrated of all the classic Paris brasseries, the haunt of the very successful and very famous, with a wonderful 1900s wood-and-glass interior. Decent *plats du jour*, including the famous sauerkraut, for under €20, but the full menu is expensive. No reservations, so be prepared to wait. Daily 9am–1am.

Le Petit St-Benoît 4 rue St-Benoît, 6e ☎01.42.60.27.92; M° St-Germain-des-Prés. Another tobacco-stained St-Germain institution, all rickety wooden tables and brass train-carriage-style coat racks. Serves the sort of meaty, comfort food your *grand-mère* would cook, at reasonable prices. Closed Sun.

Polidor 41 rue Monsieur-le-Prince, 6e ☎01.43.26.95.34; M° Odéon. A bright, noisy traditional bistro, open since 1845. Packed until late with regulars and tourists alike enjoying meaty Parisian classics on the good-value menus (€20 and €30, or just €12 for a weekday lunch). No bookings; just turn up and wait. Mon–Sat noon–2.30pm & 7pm–12.30am, Sun noon–2.30pm & 7–11.30pm.

Le Salon d'Hélène 4 rue d'Assas, 6e ☎01.42.22.00.11; M° St-Sulpice/Sèvres-Babylone. Underneath celebrity chef Hélène Darroze's gastronomic restaurant, the trendier and more relaxed ground-floor bistro bar offers superbly imaginative tapas-style dishes drawing on her native Basque cuisine. Book well in advance and bring upwards of €100 a head. Closed Tues lunch, Mon & Sun; closed Aug.

La Tourelle 5 rue Hautefeuille, 6e ☎01.46.33.12.47; M° St-Michel. This splendidly convivial, almost medieval-styled bistro offers fresh, simple and largely meaty cuisine. No bookings, so just turn up and wait. Closed Sat lunch & Sun; closed Aug.

Trocadéro, Eiffel Tower and the Septième

See map, pp.144–145.

Bars and cafés

Café du Marché 38 rue Cler, 7e ☎01.47.05.51.27; M° La Tour-Maubourg. This big, busy café-brasserie in the bustling heart of the rue Cler market serves inexpensive, market-fresh *plats du jour*. Mon–Sat noon–11pm.

Café du Museé d'Orsay 1 rue Bellechasse, 7e; RER Musée-d'Orsay/M° Solférino. Superb views through the giant clockface dominating the museum's rooftop café, which serves snacks and drinks. Tues–Sun 11am–5pm.

Restaurants

L'Arpège 84 rue de Varenne, 7e ☎01.45.05.09.06; M° Varenne. Elite chef Alain Passard shocked the gastronomic establishment at his Michelin-starred restaurant by making vegetables the centrepiece of his cuisine. Exhilarating cooking in a (relatively) relaxed, plain setting. Budget on €100 as a bare minimum, and book well in advance. Closed Sat & Sun.

Chez Germaine 30 rue Pierre-Leroux, 7e ☎01.42.73.28.34; M° Duroc/Vaneau. This tiny family-run restaurant packs them in for the inexpensive lunchtime menu of simple but perfectly cooked French food. Mon–Fri noon–2.30pm & 7–10pm, Sat noon–2.30pm; closed Aug.

La Fontaine de Mars 19 rue St-Dominique, 7e ☎01.47.05.46.44; M° École-Militaire/La Tour-Maubourg. Almost entirely decked out in genteel pinks – tablecloths, napkins, gingham café-curtains – this local restaurant is formal but friendly, and there's a wonderful summer *terrasse* under a stone arcade that's perfect for lunch (€16 menu). Daily noon–3pm & 7.30–11pm.

Jules Verne South Pillar, Eiffel Tower, 7e ☎01.45.55.61.44; M° Ecole Militaire. Genuinely *haute* cuisine – served on the second-floor of the Eiffel Tower. The decor feels a bit moodily 1980s, but there are lots of romantic corners and the food is truly gastronomic. Book three months in advance. Lunch menu at €49 (weekdays only), evening menus from €114. Daily 12.15–1.45pm & 7.15–9.45pm.

Le P'tit Troquet 28 rue de l'Exposition, 7e ☎01.47.05.80.39; M° École Militaire. Tiny, discreet restaurant done out like an elegant antiques shop, serving delicate and classy traditional cuisine to the diplomats and politicians of the *quartier*. Expect to pay upwards of €30. Mon 7.30–10pm, Tues–Sat 12.30–2.30pm & 7.30–10pm.

Thoumieux 79 rue St-Dominique, 7e ☎01.47.05.49.75; M° La Tour-Maubourg. Cavernous, bemirrored traditional brasserie, popular with a smart local clientele for reliable classics. The basic lunch menu is inexpensive, but you'll pay over €30 in the evening. Daily noon–3.30pm & 6.30pm–midnight.

Montmartre & le Neuvième

See map, p.156.

Bars and cafés

Le Bar du Relais 12 rue Ravignan, 18e; M° Abbesses. Quaint building in a beautiful spot just under the Butte, with tables out on the little square where Picasso's Beateau-Lavoir studio used to be. Quiet and atmospheric by day, youthful and bohemian by night, with an *electronique* playlist. Mon–Thurs 3pm–2am, Fri–Sun noon–2am.

Café des Deux Moulins 15 rue Lepic, 18e; M° Blanche. Having seen its heyday of fans on the trawl of *Amélie* lore (she waited tables here in the film), this diner-style café is back to its old self: a down-to-earth neighborhood hangout, preserved in a bright, charming 1950s interior. The Sunday brunch is popular. Daily 7am–2am.

L'Eté en Pente Douce 23 rue Muller, cnr rue Paul-Albert, 18e; M° Anvers/Château Rouge. Pure Montmartre atmosphere, with chairs and tables set out beside the long flight of steps that leads up to Sacré-Coeur from the eastern side. Serves good, fairly inexpensive traditional French *plats*. Daily noon–midnight.

La Fourmi Café 74 rue des Martyrs, 18e; M° Pigalle/Abbesses. Trendy, high-ceilinged café-bar, full of conscientiously beautiful young Parisians drinking coffee by day and cocktails at night to a retro-lounge soundtrack. Mon–Thurs 8am–2am, Fri & Sat 8am–4am, Sun 10am–2am.

Le Progrès 1 rue Yvonne Le Tac, 18e; M° Abbesses/Anvers. This café is something of a lighthouse for the young bobos (bohemian-bourgeoises) of Montmartre. By day a simple, relaxed café serving reasonably priced meals and salads (€12–15), at night it turns into a lively bar. Daily 9am–2am.

Le Sancerre 35 rue des Abbesses, 18e; M° Abbesses. A fashionable, sunny hangout under the southern slope of Montmartre, with a row of outside tables that's perfect for watching the world go by. The food can be disappointing. Daily 7am–2am.

Au Rendez-vous des Amis 23 rue Gabrielle, 18e; M° Abbesses. Halfway up the Butte, this small, ramshackle, smoky and community-spirited hangout is a magnet for Montmartre locals, especially the young, artsy and alternative. Daily 8.30am–2am.

Restaurants

Le Bistro des Deux-Théâtres 18 rue Blanche, cnr rue Pigalle, 9e ☎01.45.26.41.43; M° Trinité. Classic luvvie hangout serving particularly good *cuisine bourgeoise* in a long, plush dining room decorated with actors' photos. The €32 all-in menu includes an aperitif, half a bottle of wine and coffee. Daily noon–2.30pm & 7pm–12.30am.

Chez les Fondus 17 rue des Trois Frères, 18e ☎01.42.55.22.65; M° Abbesses. The €15 menu here gets you a hearty fondue – Bourguignonne (meat) or Savoyarde (cheese) – and your personal baby bottle of wine. It's unflaggingly popular with a raucous young Parisian crowd, who squeeze onto the banquette tables between the zanily graffitied walls. Daily 5pm–2am.

La Famille 41 rue des Trois-Frères, 18e ☎01.42.52.11.12; M° Abbesses. Customers at the laid-back *Famille* are trendy, local, thirty-somethings for the most part, and the decor is appropriately distressed, urban-designer in feel. The food is jokily retro but worryingly hit-and-miss – some think the "KFC-style" chicken very witty, for instance; others find it inedible. Menus for around €30. Meals served Tues–Sat 9–11.15pm, bar till around 2am; closed three weeks in Aug.

Au Grain de Folie 24 rue La Vieuville, 18e ☎01.42.58.15.57; M° Abbesses. Tiny, simple and colourfully dilapidated vegetarian place. All the food is inexpensive and organic and there's always a vegan option. Mon–Sat 12.30–2.30pm & 7–10.30pm, Sun 12.30–10.30pm.

Haynes 3 rue Clauzel, 9e ☎01.48.78.40.63; M° St-Georges. Classic black American soul-food restaurant with a jazz-cellar feel – and blues or jazz most nights from around 8pm. Around €40, with wine. Tues–Sat 7.30pm–12.30am.

Le Mono 40 rue Véron, 18e ☎01.46.06.99.20; M° Abbesses. Welcoming, family-run Togolese restaurant. The delicious mains (around €10) are mostly grilled fish or meats served with sour-sweet, hot sauces and rice or cassava on the side. There's a great atmosphere, with *soukous* (African rumba) on the stereo and Togolese carvings on the walls. Closed Wed.

Le Relais Gascon 6 rue des Abbesses, 18e ☎01.42.58.58.22; M° Abbesses. Serving filling and inexpensive meals all day, this noisy two-storey restaurant provides a welcome blast of Gascon heartiness. Offers enormous hot salads for €10.50. Daily 10am–2am.

Le Restaurant 32 rue Véron, 18e ☎01.42.23.06.22; M° Abbesses. The decor and clientele follow the fashion for distressed, arty chic but, while there are a few adventurous flavours, most of the food is surprisingly homely and robust. Two-course menu at around €20. Mon–Fri 12.30–2.30pm & 7.30pm–midnight, Sat 7.30–11.30pm.

Northern Paris

Bars and cafés

Le Dépanneur 27 rue Fontaine, 9e; M° Pigalle. Relaxed all-night bar just off place Pigalle. One to know about for winding down after clubbing. Open 24 hours.

Restaurants

Bistral 80 rue Lemercier, 17e ☎01.42.63.59.61; M° Place de Clichy. Imaginatively cooked food with superb ingredients in a relaxed, modern setting. The blackboard menu changes daily but you might find a delicious lamb loin with a shrimp crust or *andouille* in a pepper butter. Mon–Fri noon–2.30pm & 7.30–10.30pm, Sat 7.30–11pm.

Le Morosophe 83 rue Legendre, 17e ☎01.53.06.82.82; M° Brochant. Relaxed contemporary bistro serving unpretentious but well-cooked seasonal dishes. Lunchtime menu at €12, evenings at €27. Closed Sun.

Le Relais Savoyard 13 rue Rodier, cnr rue Agent-Bailly, 9e ☎01.45.26.17.48; M° Notre-Dame-de-Lorette/Anvers/Cadet. Generous helpings of inexpensive and hearty Savoyard cuisine in a little dining room at the back of a local bar. Closed Sun, Mon lunch & two weeks in Aug.

Wepler 14 place de Clichy, 17e ☎01.45.22.53.24; M° Place de Clichy. As palatial, historic brasseries go, *Wepler* has remained unashamedly unfussy. Serves honest brasserie fare (€18 for two courses, €25 for three). Daily noon–1am, café from 7am.

Eastern Paris

Bars and cafés

L'Atmosphère 49 rue Lucien-Sampaix, 10e; M° Gare-de-l'Est. Lively café-bar by the canal St-Martin, with an alternative flavour and occasional live music on Sundays. Tues–Fri 11am–2am, Sat 5.30pm–2am.

Le Baron Rouge 1 rue Théophile-Roussel, cnr place d'Aligre market, 12e; M° Ledru-Rollin. This traditional *bar à vins* is perfect for a light lunch or aperitif after shopping at the place d'Aligre market. If it's crowded inside, join the locals standing around the wine barrels on the pavement lunching on *saucisson* or mussels washed down with a glass of Muscadet. Tues–Sat 10am–2pm & 5–9.30pm, Sun 10am–2pm.

Café Charbon 109 rue Oberkampf, 11e; M° St-Maur/Parmentier. A very successful and attractive resuscitation of a *fin-de-siècle* café, packed in the evenings with a young and trendy clientele, quieter during the day and ideal for a leisurely breakfast or an aperitif in the early evening. Beer €2.30; full-blown meals (€20–25) also available noon–2.30pm & 8–11pm. Wed–Sat 9am–4am, Sun–Tues 9am–2am.

Chez Prune 36 rue Beaurepaire, 10e ☎01.42.41.30.47; M° Jacques-Bonsergent. A very friendly and laid-back café-bar with pleasant outdoor seating overlooking the canal. Creative *assiettes* (around €9) are guaranteed to tempt both meat-eaters and vegetarians, and it's a romantic place to sip a glass of wine or indulge in a dessert. Mon–Sat 7.30am–1.45am, Sun 10am–1.45am.

Lou Pascalou 14 rue des Panoyaux; 20e; M° Ménilmontant. This local boho hangout with a zinc bar is a great place for a relaxing evening drink. Be sure to try some of their delicious mint tea – over a game of chess if you fancy it. There's a wide range of beers, bottled and on tap, from €2 and cocktails from €5. Daily 9am–2am.

La Mère Lachaise 78 bd Ménilmontant, 20e ☎01.47.97.61.60; M° Père-Lachaise. The sunny terrace of this stylish bar-restaurant makes a good place for a drink after a visit to Père-Lachaise, while the cosy interior bar has a retro-chic decor of painted wood and wrought-iron lamps. Mon–Sat 8am–2am, Sun 9am–1am.

Café de la Musique 213 av Jean-Jaurès, M° Porte-de Pantin. Part of the Cité de la Musique, this café, with a popular terrace just inside the La Villette complex, was designed by the Cité architect Portzamparc and exudes sophistication, discretion and comfort, but be prepared to pay over the odds for a coffee. Daily till 2am.

Café Tribal cour des Petites-Écuries, 10e; M° Château-d'Eau. Tucked down an atmospheric side street, this North African-tinged café-bar pulls in the new bohemians of the quarter with loud music, cheap beer and mojitos, outside tables and free couscous on Friday and Saturday nights (or free *moules frites* on Wed and Thurs). Daily noon–2am.

Le Viaduc Café 43 av Daumesnil, 12e; M° Gare-de-Lyon. A stylish restaurant-bar in one of the Viaduc des Arts' converted railway arches, with seating outside in nice weather. Ideal for lunch (€17) or drinks after perusing the galleries or walking the Promenade Plantée. The three-course Sunday jazz brunch from noon to 4pm is especially popular. Daily 8am–2am.

De La Ville Café 34 bd de la Bonne Nouvelle, 10e; M° Bonne-Nouvelle. This ex-bordello, with grand staircase, gilded mosaics and marble columns, draws a fashionable crowd. On weekends, well-known DJs spin the disks till the early hours. Cocktails cost €8, a *demi* €3.50. Daily 11am–2am, Fri & Sat till 4am.

Restaurants

Les Allobroges 71 rue des Grands-Champs, 20e ☎01.43.73.40.00; M° Maraîchers. Charming neighbourhood restaurant, serving traditional French cuisine to consistently high standards. Count on around €35 a head. Closed Sun & Mon & Aug.

Flo 7 cour des Petites-Écuries, 10e ☎01.47.70.13.59; M° Château-d'Eau. Tucked away down a secret side alley, this is a dark, handsome and extremely atmospheric old-time brasserie. Fish and seafood are the specialities, but the food is generally excellent – if not cheap, at around €25 minimum. Daily 11am–1am.

Jacques-Mélac 42 rue Léon-Frot, 11e; M° Charonne. Some way off the beaten track (between Père-Lachaise and place Léon-Blum) but a highly respected and very popular *bistro à vins*, whose *patron* even makes his own wine – the solitary vine winds round the front of the shop. The food (*plats* around €12), wines and atmosphere are great; no bookings. Tues–Sat 9am–10.30pm; closed Aug.

Julien 16 rue du Faubourg-St-Denis, 10e ☎01.47.70.12.06; M° Strasbourg-St-Denis. Part of the same enterprise as *Flo* (see above), with an even more splendid decor of globe lamps, brass, murals, white linen and polished wood – if not such a romantic situation. Similar high-quality brasserie cuisine at the same prices. Daily until 1am.

Lao Siam 49 rue de Belleville, 19e ☎01.40.40.09.68; M° Belleville. The surroundings are nothing special, but the excellent Thai and Laotian food, popular with locals, makes up for it. From €20 a head. Mon–Fri noon–3pm & 6–11.30pm, Sat & Sun noon–12.30am.

La Mansouria 11 rue Faidherbe-Chaligny, 11e ☎01.43.71.00.16; M° Faidherbe-Chaligny. An

Paris for vegetarians

The chances of finding vegetarian main dishes on the menus of traditional French restaurants are not good, though these days some of the newer, more innovative restaurants will often have one or two on offer. It's also possible to put together a meal from vegetarian starters, omelettes and salads. Your other option is to go for a Middle Eastern or Indian restaurant or head for one of the city's handful of proper **vegetarian restaurants** – they do tend to be based on a healthy diet principle rather than *haute cuisine*, but at least you get a choice. All the establishments listed below are reviewed in the pages that follow, listed under the relevant map area.

Les 5 Saveurs d'Anada 72 rue du Cardinal-Lemoine, see p.170.
Aquarius 40 rue de Gergovie, see p.172.
L'Arpège 84 rue de Varenne, see p.171.
Au Grain de Folie 24 rue de la Vieuville, see opposite.
Le Grenier de Notre Dame 18 rue de la Bûcherie, see p.171.
La Petite Légume 36 rue Boulangers, see p.171.
Piccolo Teatro 6 rue des Ecouffes, see p.170.
La Victoire Suprème du Coeur 41 rue des Bourdonnais, see p.167.

excellent, elegant Moroccan restaurant, serving superb couscous and tagines. Set menu €29. Closed Sun eve & two weeks in Aug.

Pooja 91 passage Brady, 10e ⓣ01.48.24.00.83; M° Strasbourg-St-Denis/Château-d'Eau. Not quite London, let alone Bombay, but friendly and located in a glazed passage that is lined with Indian restaurants, all offering good if rather similar fare. Costs around €20 in the evening. Daily noon–3pm & 6–11pm; closed Mon lunchtime.

Terminus Nord 23 rue de Dunkerque, 10e ⓣ01.42.85.05.15; M° Gare-du-Nord. Another magnificent 1920s brasserie in the *Flo* family (same hours and prices; see p.175). The location right opposite the Gare du Nord draws a less local clientele, but it's a fine introduction – or farewell – to old-style Paris dining if you're travelling by Eurostar.

Le Train Bleu Gare de Lyon, 12e ⓣ01.43.43.09.06; M° Gare de Lyon. The sumptuous decor of what must be the world's most luxurious station buffet is straight out of a bygone golden era – everything drips with gilt, and chandeliers hang from high ceilings frescoed with scenes from the Paris–Lyon–Marseilles train route. The traditional French cuisine has a hard time living up to all this, but is still pretty good, if a tad overpriced. The set menu costs €45, including half a bottle of wine; for à la carte reckon on €70. Daily 11.30am–3pm & 7–11pm.

Waly Fay 6 rue Godefroy-Cavaignac, 11e ⓣ01.40.24.17.79; M° Charonne. A moderately priced West African restaurant with a cosy, stylish atmosphere, the dim lighting, rattan and old, faded photographs creating an intimate, faintly colonial ambience. Smart young black and white Parisians come here to dine on perfumed, richly spiced stews and other West African delicacies. Mon–Sat noon–2pm & 7.30–11pm, Sun 11am–5pm; closed last two weeks of Aug.

Le Zéphyr 1 rue Jourdain, 20e ⓣ01.46.36.65.81; M° Jourdain. Trendy but relaxed 1930s Art Deco-style bistro where you'll pay around €13 for lunch – double that in the evenings – for fine traditional cooking. Daily noon–3pm & 7–11pm, closed Aug.

Southern Paris

Bars and cafés

L'Entrepôt 7–9 rue Francis-de-Pressensé, 14e; M° Pernety. Arty cinema with a spacious, relaxed café, outside seating in the courtyard and frequent evening gigs. Offers a great Sunday brunch and *plats* for around €10–16. Mon–Sat noon–2am.

La Folie en Tête 33 rue Butte-aux-Cailles, 13e; M° Place-d'Italie/Corvisart. Alternative-spirited, laid-back and distinctly lefty bar. Cheap drinks and snacks in the daytime and a wide-ranging soundtrack at night. Mon–Sat 5pm–2am.

Le Merle Moqueur 11 rue Butte-aux-Cailles, 13e; M° Place-d'Italie/Corvisart. Tiny, noisy and ramshackle bar serving up home-made flavoured rums to young Parisians. Daily 5pm–2am.

Le Select 99 bd du Montparnasse, 14e; M° Vavin. Perhaps not quite as famous as its immediate neighbours – the *Dôme*, the *Rotonde* and the other Montparnasse cafés frequented by Picasso, Modigliani, Cocteau and the rest – but much less spoilt, distinctly less expensive and infinitely more satisfying. Perfect for a coffee or a cognac. Mon–Thurs & Sun till 3am, Fri & Sat till 4.30am.

Restaurants

Aquarius 40 rue de Gergovie, 14e ⓣ01.45.41.36.88; M° Pernety/Plaisance. Homely vegetarian restaurant serving wholesome if not spectacular meals from a tiny kitchen. Mexican chilli and lasagne cost around €12. Closed Sun and three weeks in Aug/Sept.

Student restaurants

Students of any age – with an ISIC card – are eligible to apply for meal tickets for university cafeterias and restaurants. The tickets, which cost €4.80, have to be obtained from the particular restaurant of your choice (opening hours generally 11.30am–2pm & 6–8pm). Though the food isn't wonderful, you can't complain about the price. The most central venues are all on the Left Bank, and some of the most usefully located include: *Châtelet*, 10 rue Jean-Calvin, 5e (M° Censier-Daubenton; closed Sat & Sun); *Mabillon*, 3 rue Mabillon, 6e (M° Mabillon); *Mazet*, rue André Mazet, 6e (M° Odéon; lunch only). Not all serve both midday and evening meals, and most are closed on the weekend and only operate during term-time; the exception is *Bullier*, 39 av Georges-Bernanos, 5e (M° Port-Royal), which is open every day, including during vacations. A full list of venues is available from ⓦwww.crous-paris.fr.

Late-night Paris

It's not at all unusual for bars and brasseries in Paris to stay open after midnight; the list below is of cafés and bars that remain open after 2am, and restaurants that are open beyond midnight – though not all of the latter will still serve food beyond that time. Note that the three Drugstores, at 133 av des Champs-Élysées and 1 av Matignon in the 8e, and 149 bd St-Germain in the 6e, stay open till 2am, with bars, restaurants, shops and *tabacs*. Each restaurant is listed under the relevant map area in the main listings.

Bars and cafés

Le Dépanneur 27 rue Fontaine, 9e. All-nighter, see p.174.

Fourmi Café 74 rue des Martyrs, 18e. Mon–Thurs & Sun till 2am, Fri & Sat till 4am, see p.173.

Iguana 15 rue de la Roquette, 11e. Daily till 5am, see p.168.

SanZSanS 49 rue du Faubourg-St-Antoine, 11e. Daily till 5am, see p.169.

La Taverne de Nesle 32 rue Dauphine, 6e. Mon–Thurs & Sun till 4am, Fri & Sat till 5am, see p.172.

De La Ville Café 34 bd de la Bonne Nouvelle, 10e. Daily 11am–2am, Fri & Sat till 4am, see p.175.

Le Wax 15 rue Daval, 11e. Tues–Thurs till 2am, Fri & Sat till 5am, see p.169.

Restaurants

L'Atlas 11 rue de Buci, 6e. Daily till 1am, see p.172.

Bofinger 7 rue de la Bastille, 4e. Daily till 1am, see p.169.

Brasserie Lipp 151 bd St-Germain, 6e. Daily till 1am, see p.172.

Chez Gladines 30 rue des Cinq-Diamants, 13e. Daily till 1am, see p.178.

Chez les Fondus 17 rue des Trois-Frères, 18e. Daily till 2am, see p.173.

La Coupole 102 bd du Montparnasse, 14e. Daily till 1am, see p.179.

L'Entrepôt 7–9 rue Francis-de-Pressensé, 14e. Mon–Sat till 2am, see opposite.

La Famille 41 rue des Trois-Frères, 18e. Daily till 2am, see p.173.

Flo 7 cours des Petites-Écuries, 10e. Daily till 1.30am, see p.175.

Haynes 3 rue Clauzel, 9e. Tues–Sat till 12.30am, see p.174.

Julien 16 rue du Faubourg-St-Denis, 10e. Daily till 1am, see p.175.

N'Zadette M'Foua 152 rue du Château, 14e. Daily till 2am, see p.179.

Au Pied de Cochon 6 rue Coquillière, 1er. All-nighter, see p.167.

Polidor 41 rue Monsieur-le-Prince, 6e. Mon–Sat till 12.30am, see p.172.

Le Relais Gascon 6 rue des Abbesses, 18e. Daily till 2am, see p.174.

Terminus Nord 23 rue de Dunkerque, 10e. Daily till 1am, see opposite.

À la Tour de Montlhéry (Chez Denise) 5 rue des Prouvaires, 1e. Mon–Fri till 5am, see p.167.

Vaudeville 29 rue Vivienne, 2e. Daily till 1am, see p.167.

Wepler 14 place de Clichy, 17e. Daily till 1am, see p.174.

Auberge Etchegorry 41 rue Croulebarbe, 13e ☎01.44.08.83.51; M° Gobelins. A former *guinguette* (dance hall) on the banks of the Bièvre, this Basque restaurant has an old-fashioned atmosphere of relaxed conviviality, and the food's good too. From around €35 a head. Closed Sun & Mon.

L'Avant Goût 37 rue Bobillot, 13e ☎01.45.81.14.06; M° Place d'Italie. Small neighbourhood restaurant with a big reputation for excitingly good modern French cuisine, and wines to match. Cool contemporary decor and presentation. The €15 lunch menu is one of the city's best deals; you'll pay upwards of €30 in the evening.

Ethnic restaurants of Paris

Our selection of Paris's ethnic restaurants only scratches the surface of what's available. North African places can be found just about everywhere, as can Indo-Chinese restaurants, with notable concentrations around avenue de la Porte-de-Choisy in the 13e and in the Belleville Chinatown. Indian restaurants are common in and around the passage Brady in the 10e. The Greeks, bunched together in rue de la Huchette, rue Xavier-Privas and along rue Mouffetard, all in the 5e, are for the most part disappointing and overpriced. Each restaurant is listed under the relevant map area in the main listings.

West African and North African

Chez Omar 47 rue de Bretagne, 11e, See p.169.
Café de l'Institut du Monde Arabe 1, rue des Fossés St-Bernard, 5e, See p.170.
La Mansouria 11 rue Faidherbe-Chaligny, 11e, See p.175.
Le Mono 40 rue Véron, 18e, See p.174.
N'Zadette M'Foua 152 rue du Château, 14e, See opposite.
Waly Fay 6 rue Godefroy-Cavaignac, 11e, See p.176.

Indian

Pooja 91 passage Brady, 10e, See p.176.

Indo-Chinese

Le Bambou 70 rue Baudricourt, 13e, see below.
Dragons Élysées 11 rue de Berri, 8e, see p.166.
Lao Siam 49 rue de Belleville, 20e, see p.175.
Lao-Thai 128 rue de Tolbiac; 13e, see opposite.
Pho 67 59 rue Galande, 5e, see p.171.
Tricotin 15 av de Choisy, 13e, see p.180.

Italian

L'Enoteca 25 rue Charles-V, 4e, see p.170.

Japanese

Higuma 32bis rue Sainte-Anne 2e, see p.166.

Jewish

L'As du Fallafel 34 rue des Rosiers, 4e, see p.168.
Chez Marianne 2 rue des Hospitalières-Saint-Gervais, 4e, see p.169.

Kurdish

Chez Dilan 13 rue Mandar, 2e, see p.167.

Tibetan

Tashi Delek 4 rue des Fossés-St-Jacques, 5e, see p.171.

Tues–Sat noon–2.30pm & 7.30–11pm; closed three weeks in Aug.

Le Bambou 70 rue Baudricourt, 13e ⓣ01.45.70.91.75; M° Tolbiac. Tiny bistro crammed with punters, French and Vietnamese alike, tucking into sublimely fresh-tasting Vietnamese food, including giant, strongly flavoured *pho* soups. Tues–Sun noon–3pm & 7–10.30pm.

Chez Gladines 30 rue des Cinq-Diamants, 13e ⓣ01.45.80.70.10; M° Corvisart. This excellent-value tiny corner bistro is always

Gourmet restaurants of Paris

It's worth budgeting for at least one meal in one of Paris's truly spectacular **gourmet restaurants**. One of the top rated is *Alain Ducasse at the Plaza-Athénée* hotel (see p.166). The first-ever chef to have been awarded six Michelin stars (shared between two restaurants), Ducasse swept like a tidal wave through the world of French cuisine in the early 1990s and hasn't looked back. Other greats include *Pierre Gagnaire* (see p.166), famed for its highly inventive cuisine, and *Taillevent* (see p.167), which concentrates on the great classics of French cooking, with a touch of the Mediterranean, and boasts a wine list out of this world. Relatively few gastronomic restaurants situate themselves on the Left Bank, but those that do tend to offer a surprise of some kind: *Hélène Darroz*, 4 rue d'Assas, 6e (Ⓣ01.42.22.00.11) breaks the mould by being run by a woman and offering bold combinations; Alain Passard at *L'Arpège* (see p.172) works principally with vegetables; the theatrical, rooftop *Le Tour d'Argent*, 15–17 quai de la Tournelle, 5e (Ⓦwww.letourdargent.com), is four hundred years old and obsessed with duck; while at *Jules Verne*, up on the top floor of the Eiffel Tower (see p.173), the surprise is that the cooking matches the view.

At almost all of these restaurants you'll need to dress smartly; most prefer men to wear a jacket and tie. Prices are often cheaper if you go at midday during the week, and some offer a set lunch menu for around €70–90. Otherwise count on €100 as a bare minimum – the top menus soar above €200, and there's no limit on the amount you can pay for wine. Recently, some of the star chefs have made their fine cuisine more accessible to a wider range of customers by opening up less expensive and more casual high-quality establishments. In addition to presiding over the *Plaza Athénée*, for example, Alain Ducasse also runs the cutting-edge bistro *Spoon, Food and Wine* (see p.167), while Hélène Darroze has her relatively relaxed *Salon d'Hélène* on the ground floor (see p.172).

welcoming, with a young clientele packed in on rickety tables. Serves hearty Basque and southwest dishes such as *magret de canard*, and giant warm salads. Mon & Tues noon–3pm & 7pm–midnight, Wed–Sun noon–3pm & 7pm–1am.

Le Café du Commerce 51 rue du Commerce, 15e Ⓣ01.45.75.03.27; M° Émile-Zola. This former workers' brasserie has a dramatic setting on three levels around a buzzing central atrium. The emphasis is on high-quality meat, with inexpensive lunch menus and evening meals for around €30–40, all-in. Daily noon–midnight.

La Coupole 102 bd du Montparnasse, 14e Ⓣ01.43.20.14.20; M° Vavin. The most enduringly famous arty-chic Parisian hangout, with noisy conversation filling the huge and splendid dining room. The menu runs from oysters to Welsh rarebit; the evening menu is €33.50, or two courses for €23.50 before 6pm and after 10pm. The downstairs club gets going from around 9.30pm. Daily 8am–1am.

Lao-Thai 128 rue de Tolbiac, 13e Ⓣ01.44.24.28.10; M° Tolbiac. Big glass-fronted place on a busy interchange, serving fine Thai and Laotian food. Inexpensive lunch menus, otherwise around €25 for two. Daily except Wed.

N'Zadette M'Foua 152 rue du Château, 14e Ⓣ01.43.22.00.16; M° Pernety. Small, cheerily tacky Congolese restaurant serving tasty dishes such as *maboké* (meat or fish baked in banana leaves). It's mostly meat in sauces, but there's a vegetarian menu. Count on €20-30 a head. Tues–Sun 7pm–2am.

L'Os à Moëlle 3 rue Vasco de Gama, 15e Ⓣ01.45.57.27.27; M° Lourmel. On the southwestern edge of the city, chef Thierry Faucher's relaxed neighbourhood bistro offers superb French cuisine at reasonable prices (the evening menu is €38). His *Cave de l'Os à Moelle* (Ⓣ01.45.57.28.88), across the road, is a friendly wine bar with communal tables groaning with excellent, homely food; for a mere €20 you just help yourself. Tues–Sat noon–2pm & 7pm–midnight; closed Aug.

La Régalade 49 av Jean-Moulin, 14e Ⓣ01.45.45.68.58; M° Alésia. Deceptively simple bistro whose utterly classic décor – tiled floor, plain old café furniture – matches the menu. But there's a surprise: the standard €30 *prix fixe* delivers a memorable meal in the best French tradition. Closed Mon lunch, Sat & Sun; closed Aug.

Le Temps des Cerises 18–20 rue Butte-aux-Cailles, 13e ⓣ01.45.89.69.48; M° Place-d'Italie/Corvisart. Welcoming restaurant – it's run as a workers' co-op – with elbow-to-elbow seating and a different daily choice of imaginative dishes. The lunch and evening menus are inexpensive, though there are opportunities to splash out a little too. Mon–Fri noon–2pm & 7.30–11.45pm, Sat 7.30pm–midnight.

Tricotin 15 av de Choisy, 13e ⓣ01.45.85.51.52 & ⓣ01.45.84.74.44; M° Porte-de-Choisy. Glazed in like a pair of overgrown fish tanks, the twin *Tricotin* restaurants are just set back from the broad av de Choisy, at the south end of Chinatown (next to the Chinese-signed McDonald's). Restaurant no. 1 (closed Tues) also specializes in Thai and grilled dishes, while no. 2 has a longer list of Vietnamese, Cambodian and steamed foods. Daily 9am–11.30pm.

Au Vin des Rues 21 rue Boulard, 14e ⓣ01.43.22.19.78. Charmingly old-fashioned bistro, with tiny tables and rickety wooden chairs serving solid French classics. Convivial atmosphere, especially on the rowdy accordion and *pot-au-feu* evenings (Thurs). Around €30 a head. Closed Sun lunch.

Music and nightlife

The strength of the Paris **music scene** is its diversity – a reputation gained mainly from its absorption of immigrant and exile populations. The city has no rival in Europe for the variety of **world music** to be discovered: Algerian, West and Central African, Caribbean and Latin American sounds are represented in force. You'll have to look out for individual gigs in one of the listings magazines (see map p.93), as most venues don't specialize but instead pursue eclectic programmes that might feature Congolese hip-hop cheek-by-jowl with home-grown pop-rock. For the quintessentially Parisian experience try to find a **chanson** night – the song style long associated with the city through wartime cabaret artists such as Edith Piaf, Maurice Chevalier and Charles Trenet and 1960s poet-musicians ranging from Georges Brassens to Serge Gainsbourg. **Jazz** fans are in for a treat, with all styles from New Orleans to current experimental to be heard, although in most clubs admission and drinks prices are a real drawback.

Nightlife recommendations for **clubs** are listed separately from live venues, though many clubs also showcase live acts on certain nights, and many concert venues hold DJ-led sessions after hours. Most clubs play *électro*, which covers anything from lounge to techno, though you'll also find some interesting Latin and African flavours, and rock music is once more on the up. Places that cater for a primarily **gay or lesbian** clientele are listed in the "Gay and lesbian Paris" section.

Classical music, as you might expect in this Neoclassical city, is in vibrant form. The **Paris Opéra**, with its two homes – the Opéra-Garnier and Opéra-Bastille – puts on a fine selection of opera and ballet. The need for advance reservations (except sometimes for the concerts held in churches) rather than the price is the major inhibiting factor here. On June 21 the **Fête de la Musique** sees live bands and free concerts of every kind of music throughout the city.

Information and tickets

See p.93 for **listings magazines**. The best places to get **tickets** for concerts, whether rock, jazz, chansons or classical, are branches of the FNAC chain, selling books and music: the main store is at Forum des Halles, 1–5 rue Pierre-Lescot, 1er (ⓣ01.40.41.40.00, ⓦwww.fnac.com; M° Chatelet-Les Halles), and there's one on the place de la Bastille (see p.198). Virgin Megastore (see p.198) also has a concerts booking agency.

Music venues

Most of the **music venues** listed below are also clubs, and some fall into many categories – the boundaries between world music and jazz, in particular, can be blurred. A few places have live music all week, but the majority host bands on just a couple of nights, usually Thursday to Saturday. **Admission prices** depend on who's playing, but you can expect to pay around €7–15 entry.

Rock and world music venues

Le Bataclan 50 bd Voltaire, 11e ⓣ01.43.14.00.30, ⓦwww.le-bataclan.com; M° Oberkampf; see map pp.124–125. Classic ex-music-hall venue with one of the best and most eclectic line-ups of any venue, covering anything from international and local dance and rock musicians – Francis Cabrel, Chemical Brothers, Khaled, Moby – to opera, comedy and techno nights.

La Cigale 120 bd de Rochechouart, 18e ⓣ01.49.25.81.75, ⓦwww.lacigale.fr; M° Pigalle. Formerly playing host to the likes of Mistinguett and Maurice Chevalier, since 1987 and a Philippe Starck renovation this historic, 1400-seater Pigalle theatre has become a leading venue for cutting-edge rock and indie acts, especially French and other continental European bands.

Café de la Danse 5 passage Louis-Philippe, 11e ⓣ01.47.00.57.59, ⓦwww.chez.com/cafedeladanse; M° Bastille; see map pp.124–125. Rock, pop, world and folk music played in an intimate and attractive space. Open nights of concerts only.

Le Divan du Monde 75 rue des Martyrs, 18e ⓣ01.40.05.06.99, ⓦwww.divandumonde.com; M° Pigalle. A youthful venue in a café whose regulars once included Toulouse-Lautrec. One of the city's most eclectic, exciting programmes, ranging from techno to Congolese rumba, with dancing till dawn on weekend nights.

Élysée Montmartre 72 bd de Rochechouart, 18e ⓣ01.55.07.06.00, ⓦwww.elyseemontmartre.com; M° Anvers. A historic Montmartre nightspot with a wonderful, vast arched-roof dance floor. Hosts frequent gigs midweek from up-and-coming and touring bands, plus regular club events (including fortnightly party night Le Bal, with live acts and DJs playing all those 1980s French pop tunes you never sang along to, but everyone around you clearly did).

La Flèche d'Or 102bis rue de Bagnolet 20e ⓣ01.44.64.01.02, ⓦwww.flechedor.com; M° Porte-de-Bagnolet. Friendly alternative venue set in a converted train station. Most nights from around 9pm there's a varied and inexpensive (often free) programme of indie, rock and club acts.

La Guinguette Pirate quai François Mauriac, 13e ⓣ01.44.06.96.45, ⓦwww.guinguettepirate.com; M° Quai-de-la-Gare. Beautiful Chinese barge, moored alongside the quay in front of the Bibliothèque Nationale, hosting relaxed but upbeat world music nights from Tuesday to Sunday, with occasional excursions into chanson and slam poetry. Moored adjacent, the radical *Péniche Alternat* (ⓦwww.alternat.org) and *Batofar* (see p.183) are excellent alternatives, with similarly adventurous programmes of gigs.

Maison des Cultures du Monde 101 bd Raspail, 6e ⓣ01.45.44.72.30, ⓦwww.mcm.asso.fr; M° Rennes. All the arts from all over the world, including music, art, dance and theatre. Runs its own world music label, Inedit, and holds a festival of world theatre and music in March.

Le Nouveau Casino 109 rue Oberkampf, 11e ⓣ01.43.57.57.40, ⓦwww.nouveaucasino.net. A sample month might include Swedish indie, Anglo-French electro-reggae, folk-hop and Belgian chanson. Turns into a club later on.

Olympia 28 bd des Capucines, 9e ⓣ08.92.68.33.68, ⓦwww.olympiahall.com; M° Madeleine/Opéra. The classic Paris venue, a renovated old-style music hall hosting top international rock and pop acts, with a good programme of domestic stars as well.

Trabendo Parc de la Villette, 19e ⓣ01.49.25.81.75, ⓦwww.trabendo.fr; M° Porte-de-Pantin. Despite its moderate size, this place attracts some big French and international names in the world, jazz and rock fields. Open on the nights of concerts only.

Zenith Parc de la Villette, 211 av Jean-Jaurès, 20e ⓣ01.42.08.60.00, ⓦwww.le-zenith.com/paris; M° Porte-de-Pantin. Seating for 6000 in a giant tent designed exclusively for rock and pop concerts, with a good programme including acts like Coldplay, Morcheeba and Paco de Lucia. Head for the concrete column with a descending red aeroplane.

Jazz venues

Le Baiser Salé 58 rue des Lombards, 1er ⓣ01.42.33.37.71, ⓦwww.lebaisersale.com; M° Châtelet. Small, crowded upstairs room with live music every night from 10pm – usually jazz, rhythm & blues, fusion, reggae or Brazilian. This is one of the less expensive jazz clubs, with free jam sessions on Mondays. The downstairs bar is great for just chilling out. Admission €5–18. Mon–Sat 5.30pm–6am.

Cabaret

Paris's **cabaret clubs** are still high-kicking along, but if you're looking for an atmosphere of sexy, bohemian exuberance you're better off in the gay bars of the Marais (see p.186) and if it's titillation you're after try the sex clubs of Pigalle. That said, the cabaret shows listed below provide a certain glitzy good time, and the dancers are superbly professional. Audiences are mostly groups of international tourists, paying top dollar. You can also choose to have dinner before the show, but you'll pay heavily for the privilege. To get away from the crowds, as long as you don't mind roughing it, you could visit the tiny transvestite cabaret on rue des Martyrs, just up from Pigalle métro.

Chez Michou 80 rue des Martyrs, 18e ⓣ01.46.06.16.04, ⓦwww.michou.com. At its best this is like a scene from an Almodóvar film, with transvestites masquerading as various female celebrities, lip-syncing to classic songs and teasing the audience – but you'll need to know your French pop culture to get the most out of it, and it can be rather desperate on a quiet night. Show €36, not including the various dinner menus.

Crazy Horse 12 av George-V, 8e ⓣ01.47.23.32.32, ⓦwww.lecrazyhorseparis.com; Mº George-V. At the sexier end of the scene, with lots of provocative "dancing". Two shows daily at 8.30pm and 11pm (or three shows squeezed in on Saturdays at 8pm, 10.15pm and 12.15am). €90 including two drinks, or €49 standing at the bar.

Le Lido 116bis av des Champs-Élysées, 8e ⓣ01.40.76.56.10, ⓦwww.lido.fr; Mº George-V. The most spectacular show, with expensive lighting and sound effects, lots of professional, Vegas-style glitz. Two shows daily at 9.30pm (€100) and 11.30pm (€80).

Le Moulin Rouge 82 bd de Clichy, 18e ⓣ01.53.09.82.82, ⓦwww.moulinrouge.fr; Mº Blanche. The traditional Paris show, with the serried ranks of the sixty Doriss Girls' frilly knickers as the highlight. Shows at 9pm (€97) and 11pm (Thurs–Sun only; €87). Book up to two months in advance at weekends.

Le Bilboquet 13 rue St-Benoît, 6e ⓣ01.45.48.81.84, ⓦjazzclub.bilboquet.free.fr; Mº St-Germain. Traditional jazz can be heard nightly at this smart, comfortable club founded in 1947 and once host to legendary greats such as Charlie Parker and Stéphane Grappelli. The music starts at 9.30pm, and food is served until 1am. Admission €18. Mon–Sat 9pm–dawn.

Caveau de la Huchette 5 rue de la Huchette, 5e ⓣ01.43.26.65.05, ⓦwww.caveaudelahuchette.fr; Mº St-Michel. One of the city's oldest jazz clubs dating back to the mid-1940s. Both Lionel Hampton and Sidney Bechet played here. Live jazz, usually trad and big band, to dance to on a floor surrounded by tiers of benches. Popular with students. Admission Sun–Thurs €11; Fri & Sat €13; drinks around €6. Daily 9.30pm–2am or later.

New Morning 7–9 rue des Petites-Écuries, 10e ⓣ01.45.23.51.41, ⓦwww.newmorning.com; Mº Château-d'Eau. This cavernous, somewhat spartan venue, an ex-printing press, is the place to hear the big international names on the circuit. It's often standing room only unless you get here early. Admission €16.50–20. Usually Mon–Sat 8pm–1.30am (concerts start around 9pm).

Le Petit Journal 71 bd St-Michel, 5e ⓣ01.43.26.28.59; RER Luxembourg. Small, smoky bar, with good, mainly French, traditional and mainstream sounds. These days rather middle-aged and tourist-prone. Admission, including first drink, €16, subsequent drinks €6; €43–48 including meal. Closed Aug.

Le Petit Journal Montparnasse 13 rue du Commandant-Mouchotte, 14e ⓣ01.43.21.56.70, ⓦwww.petitjournal-montparnasse.com; Mº Montparnasse. Under the *Hôtel Montparnasse*, and sister establishment to the above, with bigger visiting names, both French and international. Admission free, but first drink around €18. Mon–Sat 8.30pm–2am (concerts from 10pm). Closed mid-July to mid-Aug.

Le Petit Opportun 15 rue des Lavandières-Ste-Opportune, 1er ⓣ01.42.36.01.36; Mº Châtelet-Les Halles. Arrive early to get a seat for the live music in the dungeon-like cellar where the acoustics play strange tricks and you can't always see the musicians. Fairly eclectic policy and a crowd of genuine connoisseurs. Admission, including first drink, from €11, subsequent drinks €4. Tues–Sat 9pm–dawn, with first set starting at 10.30pm; closed Aug.

Le Sunside/Le Sunset 60 rue des Lombards, 1er ⓣ01.40.26.46.60, ⓦwww.sunset-sunside.com; M° Châtelet-Les Halles. Two clubs in one: *Le Sunside* on the ground floor features mostly traditional jazz, whereas the downstairs *Sunset* is a venue for electric and fusion jazz. The *Sunside* concert usually starts at 9 or 9.30pm and the *Sunset* at 10pm, so you can sample a bit of both. Admission €20–25. Daily 9pm–2.30am.

Utopia 79 rue de l'Ouest, 14e ⓣ01.43.22.79.66; M° Pernety. No genius here, but good French blues singers interspersed with jazz and blues records, with a mainly young, studenty audience and a pleasant atmosphere. Admission free; drinks from €8. Mon–Sat 10pm–dawn; closed Aug.

Chanson venues

Casino de Paris 16 rue de Clichy, 9e ⓣ01.49.95.99.99, ⓦwww.casinodeparis.fr; M° Trinité. This decaying, once-plush former casino in one of the seediest streets in Paris is a venue for all sorts of performances – including chansons, poetry combined with flamenco guitar and cabaret. Check the listings magazines under "Variétés" and "Chansons". Most performances start at 8.30pm. Tickets start at €20.

Au Limonaire 18 Cité Bergère, 9e ⓣ01.45.23.33.33, ⓦlimonaire.free.fr; M° Grands Boulevards. Tiny backstreet venue, perfect for Parisian chanson nights showcasing young singers and zany music/poetry/performance acts. Dinner beforehand – traditional, inexpensive, and fairly good – guarantees a seat for the show at 10pm (Tues–Sat) – otherwise you'll be crammed up against the bar, if you can get in at all.

La Locandiera 145 rue Oberkampf, 11e ⓣ01.56.98.12.18; M° Ménilmontant. Friendly Italian bar-restaurant with a vaulted basement that frequently features chanson acts (from 9pm) – both in the classic French manner and with pop, world and jazz inflections. Free.

Au Magique 42 rue de Gergovie, 14e ⓣ01.45.42.26.10, ⓦwww.aumagique.com; M° Pernety. A bar and "chanson cellar" with traditional French chanson performances by lesser-known stars during the week. At weekends the owner takes to the piano. Admission is free, payment for the show is at your own discretion, and drinks are very reasonably priced. Wed–Sat 8pm–2am.

Clubs

The **clubs** listed below are recommended as dance venues, although a few also put on live music gigs. It's worth remembering that most of the places listed under "Music venues" also function as clubs, and many gay and lesbian venues attract mixed crowds, often from the trendy end of the nightlife spectrum. Things rarely kick off before 1am, and at the most fashionable places you'll need to look good to avoid hanging around at the velvet rope. You'll have to keep your ear to the ground to find the very latest must-go *soirée* – check out the listings in *Zurban* magazine (see p.93), or try simply asking around in likely-looking bars or music shops. Most entry prices include one free drink, and vary according to when you turn up – usually anything from €10–12 on weekdays to €15–20 on Friday and Saturday after midnight; exceptions are noted below. Given the difficulty of finding a taxi after hours (see p.96), many Parisian clubbers just keep going until the métro starts running at around 5.30am.

L'Atlantis 32 quai d'Austerlitz, 13e ⓣ01.44.23.24.00; M° Gare d'Austerlitz. The number one black music club in Paris, and one of the biggest, most up-tempo and most hustly clubs of all. *Soirées* include African and Caribbean nights, but there's a backbone of hip-hop and R&B.

Batofar quai François Mauriac, 13e ⓣ01.56.29.10.00, ⓦwww.batofar.org. This old lighthouse boat moored at the foot of the Bibliothèque Nationale is a small but classic address. The programme is very eclectic: from dancehall to electroclash via contemporary Brazilian sounds. Entry is usually around €10. Tues–Thurs 8pm–2am, Fri 11pm–dawn, Sat 11pm–noon.

Le Cab 2 place du Palais-Royal, 1er ⓣ01.58.62.56.25; M° Palais-Royal; see map, pp.110–111. This miniature maze of a cellar club drags the beautiful people away from the Champs-Élysées – on weekend nights you'll need to look good to get in, though dining beforehand at the glitzy supper club certainly helps. Designer retro-meets-futuristic lounge decor, with a similar music policy. Mon–Sat 11.30pm–5am.

La Locomotive 90 bd de Clichy, 18e ⓣ08.36.69.69.28, ⓦwww.laloco.com; M° Blanche; see map, p.156. High-tech monster club with three dance floors, all playing variations on house. Tues–Sun 11pm–dawn.

Man Ray 34 rue Marbeuf, 8e ⓣ01.56.88.36.36, ⓦwww.manray.fr; see map, pp.110–111. Celebrity-designed, celebrity-patronized, and celebrity-owned (Johnny Depp is among the owners), this is Paris's A-list "gastro-club", set in a vast and very theatrical underground space. Dining tables are cleared away at midnight to reveal the dancefloor. Entry free, but drinks very expensive at around €15. Sun–Thurs 7pm–2am, Fri & Sat 7pm–5am.

Le Pulp 25 bd Poissonnière, 2e, ⓦwww.pulp-paris.com; M° Bonne-Nouvelle; see map, pp.110–111. Ultra-fashionable lesbian club with superb (and free) mixed nights Wed and Thurs. Wed–Sat midnight–6am.

Rex Club 5 bd Poissonnière, 2e ⓣ01.42.36.28.83; M° Grands-Boulevards; see map, pp.110–111. The clubbers' club: spacious and serious about its music, which is strictly electronic, notably techno. Attracts big-name DJs such as Laurent Garnier. Entry around €13. Thurs–Sat 11.30pm–6am; closed Aug.

Le Triptyque 142 rue Montmartre, 2e ⓣ01.40.28.05.55, ⓦwww.letriptyque.com; M° Palais de la Bourse; see map, p.122. Unpretentious club packed with anyone from local students to lounge lizards. For once, it's all about the music, with concerts earlier on, then themed DJ *soirées* which change nightly – everything from electro to jazz to hip-hop to ska. Entry is sometimes free on some nights; others rise to around €15. Open daily till 6am.

WAGG 62 rue Mazarine, 6e ⓣ01.55.42.22.00; M° Odéon; see map, pp.138–139 International St-Germain yuppie-types lounge around on designer furnishings in this intimate, Conran-designed cellar club. The music is UK-influenced house and disco-funk. Fri & Sat 11.30pm–dawn, Sun 5pm–midnight. Entry €15, free on Sun.

Classical music

Paris is a stimulating environment for **classical music**, both established and contemporary. The former is well represented in performances within churches – sometimes free or very cheap – and in an enormous choice of commercially promoted concerts held every day of the week. Contemporary and experimental computer-based work also flourishes.

Concert venues

Some of the city's most dynamic and eclectic programming is to be found at the **Cité de la Musique** at La Villette (ⓦwww.cite-musique.fr; M° Porte-de-Pantin). Ancient music, contemporary works, jazz, chanson and music from all over the world can be heard at the complex's two major concert venues: the **Conservatoire** (the national music academy) at 209 av Jean-Jaurès, 19e (ⓣ01.40.40.46.46); and the **Salle des Concerts** at 221 av Jean-Jaurès, 19e (ⓣ01.44.84.44.84).

These apart, the top **auditoriums** are: Salle Gaveau, 45 rue de la Boëtie, 8e (ⓣ01.49.53.05.07, ⓦwww.sallegaveau.com; M° Miromesnil); Théâtre des Champs-Élysées, 15 av Montaigne, 8e (ⓣ01.49.52.50.50, ⓦwww.theatrechampselysees.fr; M° Alma-Marceau); the Théâtre Musical de Paris (ⓦwww.chatelet-theatre.com; M° Châtelet) and the Salle Pleyel, 252 rue du Faubourg-St-Honoré, 8e (ⓣ08.25.00.02.52, ⓦwww.pleyel.com; M° Concorde). **Tickets** are best bought at the box offices, though for big names you may find overnight queues, and a large number of seats are always booked by subscribers. The price range is very reasonable.

Churches and **museums** are also good places to hear classical music. Regular concerts can be caught at the Église St-Séverin, 1 rue des Prêtres St-Séverin, 5e (ⓣ01.48.24.16.97; M° St-Michel); the Église St-Julien le Pauvre, 23 quai de Montebello, 5e (ⓣ01.42.26.00.00; M° St-Michel); and the Sainte-Chapelle, 4 bd du Palais, 1er (ⓣ01.42.77.65.65; M° Cité).

The Musée du Louvre (Ⓦwww.louvre.com) and the Musée d'Orsay (Ⓦwww.musee-orsay.fr) both host chamber music recitals in their auditoriums, while from time to time the Musée National du Moyen-Âge holds recitals of medieval music. Sometimes free classical concerts take place at **Radio France**, 166 av du Président-Kennedy, 16e (Ⓣ01.56.40.15.16, Ⓦradio-france.fr; M° Passy).

Opera

Despite the inevitable discussion about the acoustics of the new opera house, opened in 1989, the **Opéra-Bastille** orchestra is first-rate and nearly every performance is a sell-out. The current musical director, Belgian Gérard Mortier, has been pulling audiences in with some daring and unusual offerings. 2005 saw a sell-out performance of Wagner's *Tristan and Isolde*, directed by Peter Sellars and designed by the video artist Bill Viola. Tickets (€5–150) can be bought online (Ⓦwww.opera-de-paris.fr): the date that tickets go on sale varies with each production and is given on the site. You can also book by phone (Mon–Fri 9am–6pm, Saturday 9am–1pm; Ⓣ01.72.29.35.35, or at the ticket office (Mon–Sat 11am–6.30pm) within two weeks of the performance – the number of tickets available by this stage however is limited and for popular performances people start queuing at 9am, if not earlier. Unfilled seats are sold at a discount to students fifteen minutes before the curtain goes up, and 62 standing tickets at €5 are available for Opéra-Bastille performances one and a half hours before the curtain goes up.

The Opéra-Bastille enjoys a friendly rivalry with the **Théâtre du Châtelet**, 1 place du Châtelet, 1er (Ⓣ01.40.28.28.40; M° Châtelet), which also puts on large-scale productions. Operas are still staged at the old **Opéra-Garnier**, place de l'Opéra, 9e (Ⓣ08.92.89.90.90, Ⓦwww.opera-de-paris.fr; M° Opéra), though these days it hosts mostly ballets; the procedure for getting tickets for the latter is the same as for the Opéra-Bastille above. Operetta, as well as more daring modern operas, are performed at the **Opéra-Comique**, Salle Favart, 5 rue Favart, 2e (Ⓣ01.42.44.45.46, Ⓦwww.opera-comique.com; M° Richelieu-Drouot).

Festivals

Festivals are plentiful in all the diverse fields that come under the far too general term of "classical". The **Festival d'Art Sacré** consists mainly of concerts and recitals of early sacred music (end of Nov to mid-Dec; Ⓦwww.festivaldartsacre.new.fr); concerts feature in the general arts **Festival d'Automne** (mid-Sept to end Dec; Ⓦwww.festival-automne.com); and a **Festival Chopin** is held in the lovely setting of the Bois de Boulogne's Orangerie (mid-June to mid-July; Ⓦwww.frederic-chopin.com).

For details of these and more, the current year's **festival schedule** is available from tourist offices or their website (Ⓦwww.paris-info.com).

Gay and lesbian Paris

Paris is one of Europe's major centres for **gay men**, with numerous bars, clubs, restaurants, saunas and shops catering for a gay clientele. Its focal point is the **Marais**, whose central street, rue Sainte-Croix-de-la-Bretonnerie, has visibly gay commerces at almost every other address. **Lesbians** have many fewer dedicated addresses, but there are a handful of women-only places. The high spot of the calendar is the annual **Marche des Fiertés LGBT**, or gay pride march, which normally takes place on the last Saturday in June.

Information and contacts

The gay and lesbian community is well catered for by the media, the best source of information being *Têtu* (ⓦwww.tetu.com), France's main gay monthly magazine – the name means "headstrong". Alternatively, have a look at ⓦwww.paris-gay.com, a major portal for gay tourists visiting Paris.

Centre Gai et Lesbien de Paris 3 rue Keller, 11e ⓣ01.43.57.21.47 ⓦwww.cglparis.org; M° Ledru-Rollin/Bastille/Voltaire. The first port-of-call for information and advice – legal, social, psychological and medical, this also has a good library and puts on small exhibitions. Mon–Sat 4–8pm.

Maison des Femmes 163 rue de Charenton, 12e ⓣ01.43.43.41.13, ⓦmaisondesfemmes.free.fr; M° Reuilly-Diderot. Feminist campaigning centre that organizes occasional gay/straight lunches and social nights. Mon–Wed 9am–7pm, Thurs & Fri 9am–5pm.

Les Mots à la Bouche 6 rue Sainte-Croix-de-la-Bretonnerie, 4e ⓣ01.42.78.88.30, ⓦwww.motsbouche.com; M° Hôtel-de-Ville. The main gay and lesbian bookshop, with exhibition space, meeting rooms and lots of free maps, listings and club flyers to pick up. There is a selection of literature in English, and one of the helpful assistants usually speaks English too. Mon–Sat 11am–11pm, Sun 2–8pm.

Pharmacie du Village 26 rue du Temple, 4e ⓣ01.42.72.60.71; M° Hôtel-de-Ville. Gay-run pharmacy. Open Mon–Sat 8.30am–9.30pm, Sun 9am–8pm.

SOS Homophobie ⓣ01.48.06.42.41, ⓦwww.sos-homophobie.org. First-stop helpline for victims of homophobia. Lines open Mon–Fri & Sun 8–10pm, Sat 2–4pm.

Bars and clubs

In terms of nightlife, Paris is one of the world's great cities to be gay. The Marais area, especially, has a wide range of **gay venues** – the selection given below only scratches the surface – and although lesbians do not enjoy a wide selection of women-only places, they are welcome in some of the predominantly male

△ *Le Pulp*

clubs. The reputation of wild hedonism in gay clubs has spread outside the gay community and attracted heterosexuals in search of a good time. Consequently, heterosexuals are welcome in some gay establishments if in gay company – some gay clubs have all but abandoned a gay policy – while many of the more mainstream clubs have started doing gay nights. For a complete rundown, consult *Têtu* magazine's Agenda section.

Amnésia Café 42 rue Vieille-du-Temple, 4e; M° Hotel-de-Ville/St-Paul; see map, pp.126–127. Daily 10am–2am. One of the more relaxed and friendlier gay bars in the Marais, with a predominantly Parisian, fairly well-heeled clientele lounging around on the sofas. Low-lit, cosy and straight-friendly.
Banana Café 13 rue de la Ferronnerie, 1er ☎01.42.33.35.31; M° Châtelet; see map, p.122. Seriously hedonistic club-bar, packing in the punters with up-tempo clubby tunes. Daily 6pm–5am.
Bliss Kfé 30 rue du Roi de Sicile, 3e ☎01.42.78.49.36; M° St-Paul; see map, pp.126–127. Small, laid-back and faintly grungy bar with a good programme of DJ *soirées*, massage sessions and so on. Draws a friendly, fairly cool crowd of lesbians, straights and gay guys. At weekends, people spill down the stairs into the cellar bar later on. Daily 5pm–2am.
Le Carré 18 rue du Temple, 4e; M° Hotel-de-Ville; see map, pp.126–127. Big, stylish, designer café with good food, comfortable chairs, ultra-cool lighting and an excellent *terrasse* on the street. Mostly full of sophisticated, good-looking Parisians, with a loyal local gay clientele. Daily 10am–4am.
Le Cox 15 rue des Archives, 3e ☎01.42.72.08.00; M° Hôtel-de-Ville; see map, pp.126–127. Muscly, body-beautiful clientele up for a seriously good time. A good pre-club place, with DJs on weekend nights. Daily 1pm–2am.
Le Duplex 25 rue Michel-le-Comte, 3e ☎01.42.72.80.86; M° Rambuteau; see map, pp.126–127. Popular with trendy media types for its relatively sophisticated atmosphere, but still relaxed and friendly. Sun–Thurs 8pm–2am, Fri & Sat 8pm–4am.
Le Mixer 23 rue Sainte-Croix-de-la-Bretonnerie, 4e ☎01.48.87.55.44; M° Hôtel-de-Ville; see map, pp.126–127. Popular gay, lesbian and straight-friendly bar with a futuristic, Beaubourg-meets-Blade Runner decor. The small dancefloor is overlooked by a DJ on a giddy plinth, and there's a cosy mezzanine level. Daily 5pm–2am.
Le Pulp 25 bd Poissonnière, 2e ☎01.40.26.01.93, Ⓦwww.pulp-paris.com; M° Bonne-Nouvelle; see map, pp.110–111. Paris's lesbian club *par excellence*, especially on Fri and Sat nights, playing anything from techno to Madonna. Wed–Sat midnight–6am.
Raidd 23 rue du Temple, 4e; M° Hotel-de-Ville; see map, pp.126–127. The city's premier gay bar, famous for its sculpted topless waiters, go-go boys' shower shows and unabashed hedonism. Straights and non-beautiful people need not apply. Daily 5pm–2am.
Redlight 34 rue du Départ, 15e ☎01.42.79.94.53; M° Montparnasse-Bienvenüe. Gay flavour of the moment for its huge weekend club nights, which begin well after midnight and end around 10am, or noon on Sundays. Expect to hear a lot of house.
Le Tango 13 rue au-Maire, 3e ☎01.42.72.17.78; M° Arts-et-Métiers. Gay and lesbian club with a traditional Sunday afternoon *bal* from 5pm, featuring proper slow dances as well as tangos and camp 70s and 80s disco classics. Turns into a full-on club on Friday, Saturday and Sunday nights. Fri & Sat 10.30pm–dawn, Sun 5pm–5am.

Film, theatre and dance

Cinema-goers have a choice of around three hundred films showing in Paris in any one week. The city's plethora of little arts cinemas screen unrivalled programmes of classic and contemporary films, and you can find mainstream movies at almost any time of the day or night. The city also has a vibrant **theatre** scene. Several superstar directors are based here, including Peter Brook and Ariane Mnouchkine. **Dance** enjoys a high profile, enhanced by the recent opening of the Centre National de la Danse, Europe's largest dance academy.

The main **festivals** include the **Festival de Films des Femmes** (March; ☎01.49.80.38.98, Ⓦwww.filmsdefemmes.com) at the Maison des Arts in Créteil, just south east of Paris (M° Créteil-Préfecture); the **Festival Exit**

(March; Ⓦwww.maccreteil.com), which features international contemporary dance, performance and theatre, at the same venue; **Paris Quartier d'Été** (mid-July to mid-Aug; Ⓦwww.quartierdete.com), with music, theatre and cinema events around the city; the **Festival d'Automne** (Sept–Dec; Ⓦwww.festival-automne.com), with traditional and experimental theatrical, musical, dance and multimedia productions from all over the world; and the **Festival du Cinéma en Plein Air** (July to mid-Aug; Ⓦwww.cinema.arbo.com) at Parc de la Villette, showing free films in the park.

Information and tickets

The most comprehensive **film listings** are given in the inexpensive weeklies *Zurban* (Ⓦwww.zurban.com) and *Pariscope*. In *Pariscope*, watch out for the smaller Reprises section, where you'll usually find a number of British or American classics listed, though often enough these turn out to be one-off screenings at an unlikely hour of the afternoon. You rarely need to book in advance; programmes (*séances*) often start around midday and continue through to the early hours. The average price is around €8, but many smaller cinemas have lower rates on Monday or Wednesday and for earlier *séances*, and student reductions are available from Monday to Thursday. Almost all of the huge selection of foreign films will be shown at some cinemas in the original language – *version originale* or *v.o.* in the listings. Dubbed films will be listed as *v.f.* and English versions of co-productions as *version anglaise* or *v.a.*

Stage productions are detailed in *Pariscope* and *L'Officiel des Spectacles* with brief résumés or reviews. Ticket prices are often around €15–30, though you may pay less in smaller venues, and more for many commercial and major state productions (most closed Sun & Mon). Half-price previews are advertised in *Pariscope* and *L'Officiel des Spectacles*, and there are weekday student discounts. Tickets can be bought directly from the theatres, from FNAC shops and the Virgin Megastore (see p.198), or at the **ticket kiosks** on place de la Madeleine, 8e, opposite no. 15, and on the parvis of the Gare du Montparnasse, 15e (Tues–Sat 12.30–7.45pm, Sun 12.30–3.45pm). They sell half-price same-day tickets and charge a small commission, but be prepared to queue.

Film

Even though many of the smaller movie houses in obscure corners of the city have closed in recent years and the big chains, UGC and Gaumont, keep opening new multi-screen cinemas, you still have an unbeatable choice of non-mainstream **films** in Paris, covering every place and period. You can go and see Senegalese, Taiwanese, Brazilian or Finnish films, for example, that would never be shown in Britain or the US or watch your way through the entire careers of individual directors in the mini-festivals held at many of the independents.

The Quartier Latin, around the Sorbonne, has a particularly high concentration of arts cinemas showing an almost incredible repertoire of classic films, while the area around the Gare Montparnasse is chock-full with big-screen movie-houses offering the latest glossy releases. For the biggest screen of all, check out the Gaumont cinema on place de l'Italie.

Classic venues

L'Arlequin 76 rue des Rennes, 6e; Mº St-Suplice. The Quartier Latin's best cinephile's palace, offering special screenings of classics every Sunday at 11pm followed by debates in the café opposite.

Cinémathèque Française 51 rue de Bercy, 12e, Ⓦwww.cinematheque.fr; Mº Bercy. The chief institution of French cinema has, as you'd expect, a superb archive of art films – and, since 2005, a stunning Frank Gehry building in which to show them off. Films are shown throughout the afternoon and evening, with regular festivals.

L'Entrepôt 7–9 rue Francis-de-Pressensé, 14e ⓦwww.lentrepot.fr; Mº Pernety. One of the best alternative Paris cinemas, this has been keeping film addicts happy for years with three screens dedicated to the obscure, the subversive and the brilliant, as well as its bookshop and bar-restaurant.

Forum des Images 2 Grande Galerie, Porte St-Eustache, Forum des Halles, 1er ⓦwww.forumdesimages.net; RER Châtelet-Les Halles. The entirely renovated venue screens several films or projected videos daily, but also has a large library of newsreel footage, film clips, adverts, documentaries, etc – all connected with Paris – that you can access yourself from a computer terminal.

Grand Action and Action Écoles 5 & 23 rue des Écoles, 5e; Mº Cardinal-Lemoine/Maubert-Mutualité; Action Christine, 4 rue Christine, 6e; Mº Odéon/St-Michel. The Action chain specializes in new prints of ancient classics and screens contemporary films from different countries.

Le Grand Rex 1 bd Poissonnière, 2e; Mº Bonne-Nouvelle. Just as outrageous as La Pagode (see below), but in the kitsch line, with a Metropolis-style tower blazing its neon name, 2750 seats, a ceiling of stars and Moorish city skyline. Foreign films are always dubbed.

Max Linder Panorama 24 bd Poissonnière, 9e; Mº Bonne-Nouvelle. Opposite Le Grand Rex, and with almost as big a screen, this cinema always shows films in the original and has state-of-the-art sound and Art Deco decor.

MK2 Bibliothèque 128–162 av de France, 13e; Mº Bibliothèque/Quai de la Gare. Brand new, and right behind the Bibliothèque Nationale, this is an architecturally cutting-edge cinema with a very cool café, mini-sofas for couples, and fourteen screens showing a varied range of French films – mostly new, some classic – and *v.o.* foreign movies.

La Pagode 57bis rue de Babylone, 7e; Mº François-Xavier. The most beautiful of the city's cinemas, transplanted from Japan at the turn of the last century to be a rich Parisienne's party place. The wall panels of the Grande Salle auditorium are embroidered in silk, golden dragons and elephants hold up the candelabra and a battle between Japanese and Chinese warriors rages on the ceiling.

Reflet Medicis II and III, Quartier Latin and Le Champo 3 rue Champollion, 9 rue Champollion and 51 rue des Écoles, 5e; Mº Cluny-La-Sorbonne/Odéon. A cluster of inventive little cinemas, tirelessly offering up rare screenings and classics, including frequent retrospective cycles covering great directors, both French and international (always in *v.o.*). The small, all-black cinema café *Le Reflet*, on the other side of the street, is a little-known cult classic in itself.

Le Studio 28 10 rue de Tholozé, 18e; Mº Blanche/Abbesses. In its early days, after one of the first showings of Buñuel's *L'Âge d'Or*, this was done over by extreme right-wing Catholics who destroyed the screen and the paintings by Dalí and Ernst in the foyer. The cinema still hosts avant-garde premieres, followed occasionally by discussions with the director, as well as regular festivals.

UGC Ciné-Cité Les Halles 7 place de la Rotonde, Forum des Halles, 1er; Mº Châtelet-Les Halles. A nightmare to find – on the bottom level of the Forum des Halles complex, on the Porte Rambuteau side – but worth perservering for the frequent screenings of arthouse and *v.o.* films, for once on large screens backed by up-to-date sound. Expect to queue for tickets.

Theatre

Bourgeois farces, postwar classics, Shakespeare, Racine and Molière are all staged with the same range of talent or lack of it that you'd find in London or New York. What is rare are home-grown, socially concerned and realist dramas, though touring foreign companies make up for that. Exciting contemporary work is provided by the superstar breed of directors such as Peter Brook, Ariane Mnouchkine and Patrice Chéreau; spectacular and dazzling sensation tends to take precedence over speech in their productions, which often feature huge casts, extraordinary sets and overwhelming sound and light effects – an experience, even if you haven't understood a word.

Bouffes du Nord 37bis bd de la Chapelle, 10e ⓣ01.46.07.34.50, ⓦwww.bouffesdunord.com; Mº La Chapelle. Peter Brook resurrected the derelict Bouffes du Nord in 1974 and has been based there ever since. The theatre also hosts top-notch chamber music recitals.

Cartoucherie rte du Champ-de-Manoeuvre, 12e; Mº Château-de-Vincennes. Home to several interesting theatre companies including workers' co-op Théâtre du Soleil, set up by Ariane Mnouchkine (Ⓣ01.43.74.24.08, Ⓦwww.theatre-du-soleil.fr).

Comédie Française 2 rue de Richelieu, 1er Ⓣ01.44.58.15.15, Ⓦwww.comedie-francaise.fr; M° Palais-Royal. The national theatre, staging mainly Racine, Molière and other classics, but also twentieth-century greats such as Anouilh and Genet.

Odéon Théâtre de l'Europe 1 place Paul-Claudel, 6e Ⓣ01.44.41.36.36, Ⓦwww.theatre-odeon.fr; M° Odéon. Contemporary plays and foreign-language productions in the theatre that became an open parliament during May 1968.

Théâtre de la Huchette 23 rue de la Huchette, 5e Ⓣ01.43.26.38.99; M° Saint-Michel. Fifty years on, this small theatre is still showing Ionesco's *Cantatrice Chauve* (*The Bald Prima Donna*; 7pm) and *La Leçon* (8pm), two classics of the Theatre of the Absurd. Reserve by phone or at the door from 5pm; tickets €18 for one play or €28 for two.

Théâtre National de Chaillot Palais de Chaillot, place du Trocadéro, 16e Ⓣ01.53.65.30.00, Ⓦwww.theatre-chaillot.fr; M° Trocadéro. Puts on an exciting programme and regularly hosts foreign productions; Deborah Warner and Robert Lepage are regular visitors.

Théâtre National de la Colline 15 rue Malte-Brun, 20e Ⓣ01.44.62.52.52, Ⓦwww.colline.fr; M° Gambetta. Known for its modern and cutting-edge productions under director Alain Françon.

Dance

The status of dance in the capital received a major boost with the inauguration in 2004 of the **Centre National de la Danse**, a long overdue recognition of the importance of dance in a nation that boasts six hundred dance companies. A huge complex on the scale of the Pompidou, the CND is committed to promoting every possible dance form from classical to contemporary, and including ethnic traditions. Its creation also reflects an increased interest in the capital in dance, especially in contemporary dance, and while Paris itself has few homegrown companies (government subsidies go to regional companies expressly to decentralize the arts) it makes up for this by regularly hosting all the best contemporary practitioners. Names to look out for are Régine Chopinot's troupe from La Rochelle, Maguy Marin's from Rilleux-le-Pape and Angelin Preljocaj's from Aix-en-Provence. Plenty of space and critical attention are also given to tango, folk and to visiting traditional dance troupes from all over the world. As for ballet, the principal stage is at the Palais Garnier, home to the Ballet de l'Opéra National de Paris, directed by Brigitte Lefèvre. It still bears the influence of **Rudolf Nureyev**, its charismatic, if controversial, director from 1983 to 1989, and frequently revives his productions, such as *Swan Lake* and *La Bayadère*. Many of the venues listed above under "Theatre" also host dance productions.

Centre National de la Danse 1 rue Victor Hugo, Pantin Ⓣ01.41.83.27.27, Ⓦwww.cnd.fr; M° Hoche/RER Pantin. The capital's major new dance centre occupies an impressively large building, ingeniously converted from a disused 1970s monolith into an airy high-tech space. Though several of its eleven studios are used for performances, the main emphasis of the centre is to promote dance through training, workshops and exhibitions.

Centre Pompidou rue Beaubourg, 4e Ⓣ01.44.78.13.15, Ⓦwww.centrepompidou.fr; M° Rambuteau/RER Châtelet-Les Halles. The Grande Salle in the basement is used for dance performances by visiting companies.

Maison des Arts de Créteil place Salvador-Allende, Créteil Ⓣ01.45.13.19.19, Ⓦwww.maccreteil.com; M° Créteil-Préfecture. A lively suburban dance and theatre venue, hosting the acclaimed Festival Exit (see p.187) and home of the innovative dance troupe Compagnie Montalvo-Hervieu.

Opéra-Garnier place de l'Opéra, 9e Ⓣ08.36.69.78.68, Ⓦwww.opera-de-paris.fr; M° Opéra. Main home of the Ballet de l'Opéra National de Paris.

Théâtre des Abbesses 31 rue des Abbesses, 18e; M° Abbesses. The Théâtre de la Ville's sister company, where you'll find slightly more offbeat performances by the likes of provocative choreographers Robyn Orlin and Jan Fabre.

Théâtre Musical de Paris place du Châtelet, 4e Ⓣ01.40.28.28.40, Ⓦwww.chatelet-theatre.com;

M° Châtelet. A major ballet venue where, in 1910, Diaghilev put on the first season of Russian ballet. Though mainly used for classical concerts and opera, it also hosts top-notch visiting ballet companies such as the Mariinsky.

Théâtre de la Ville 2 place du Châtelet, 4e ⓣ01.42.74.22.77, ⓦwww.theatredelaville-paris.com; M° Châtelet. The height of success for contemporary dance productions is to end up here. Works by Karine Saporta, Maguy Marin and Pina Bausch are regularly featured, along with modern theatre classics, comedy and concerts.

Sports and activities

When it's cold and wet and you've had your fill of café vistas and peering at museums, monuments and the dripping panes of shopfronts, don't despair or retreat back to your hotel. As well as movies, Paris offers a whole host of pleasant ways to pass the time indoors – **skating**, **swimming**, **Turkish baths** – or outdoors, with a range of **popular sports** to watch or participate in.

Information

L'Officiel des Spectacles has the best listings of **sports facilities** (under "Activités sportives"). Information on municipal facilities is available from the town hall, the Mairie de Paris, place de l'Hôtel de Ville, 4e (ⓣ01.42.76.40.40, ⓦwww.paris.fr). For details of current **sporting events**, try daily sports paper *L'Équipe*. The Palais Omnisport Paris-Bercy (POPB), 8 bd Bercy, 12e (ⓣ01.46.91.57.57, ⓦwww.bercy.fr; M° Bercy) is a major venue for a wide range of sports, including athletics, cycling, show jumping, ice hockey, ballroom dancing, judo and motorcross.

Spectator sports

Cycling The biggest event of the French sporting year is the grand finale of the Tour de France on the Champs-Élysées in late July. Huge crowds turn out to cheer on the cyclists at the finishing line of the ultimate stage in the gruelling three-week 3500-odd-kilometre event, and the French president presents the yellow jersey (*maillot jaune*) to the overall winner. Races commencing in Paris include the Paris–Roubaix, instigated in 1896, which is reputed to be the most exacting one-day race in the world, and the rugged six-day Paris–Nice event, covering over 1100km. The Palais Omnisport (see above) holds other bike races and cycling events. For more information on the Tour de France and other cycling events, see Basics.

Football and rugby The Stade de France, on rue Francis de Pressensé in St-Denis (ⓣ01.55.93.00.00, ⓦwww.stadefrance.fr; RER Stade-de-France-St-Denis), is the venue for international football matches and rugby's Six Nations' Cup and other international matches. The Parc des Princes, 24 rue du Commandant-Guilbaud, 16e (ⓣ01.42.30.03.60, ⓦwww.bercy.fr; M° Porte-de-St-Cloud), is the home ground for the first-division football team Paris-St-Germain (PSG) plus the rugby team Le Racing.

Horse-racing The biggest races are the Prix de la République and the Grand Prix de l'Arc de Triomphe on the first and last Sunday in October at Auteuil and Longchamp, both in the Bois de Boulogne. Trotting races, with the jockeys in chariots, run from Aug to Sept in the Hippodrome de Vincennes, 2 rte de la Ferme (ⓦwww.cheval-francais.com), in the Bois de Vincennes. L'Humanité and Paris-Turf carry details of all races; admission charges are under €5. If you want to place a bet, any bar or café with the letters "PMU" will take your money on a three-horse bet, known as *le tiercé*.

Running The Paris Marathon is held in April over a route from place de la Concorde to Vincennes. Up-to-date information is available online at ⓦwww.parismarathon.com.

Tennis The French Open takes place in the last week of May and first week of June at Roland-Garros, 2 av Gordon-Bennett, 16e (ⓣ01.47.43.48.00, ⓦwww.frenchopen.org; M° Porte-d'Auteuil). Evening tickets are available at heavily reduced prices on the same day, from 5pm. Otherwise there's a fair chance of booking non-numbered tickets for the lower-profile matches on outside courts. Smaller tournaments, including November's Paris Open, take place throughout the year.

Activities

Boules The classic French game involving balls, *boules* (or *pétanque*), is best performed (if you have your own set or are prepared to make some new French friends) or watched at the Arènes de Lutèce (p.137) and the Bois de Vincennes (p.164). On balmy summer evenings it's a common sight in the city's parks and gardens.

Cycling Since 1996 the Mairie de Paris has made great efforts to introduce dedicated cycle lanes in Paris, which now add up to some 300km. You can pick up a free bike map, the *carte des voies cyclables*, from town halls, tourist offices and bike hire outlets (see p.199). If you prefer cycling in a more natural environment, the Bois de Boulogne and the Bois de Vincennes have extensive bike tracks. On Sundays cycling and rollerblading (see below) by the Seine is popular, when its central *quais* are closed to cars between 9am and 5pm; the *quais* along the Canal St-Martin are closed to cars from 10am to 6pm on Sundays. Excellent day and night bicycle tours are offered by Paris à Vélo C'est Sympa/Vélo Bastille, 22 rue Alphonse Baudin, 11e (ⓣ01.48.87.60.01, ⓦwww.parisvelosympa.com; M° Bastille) for around €35; Fat Tire Bike Tours, 24 rue Edgar Faure, 15e (ⓣ01.56.58.10.54, ⓦwww.FatTireBikeToursParis.com; M° Dupleix) offers tours on the Left Bank for around €25, as well as tours on Segway "human transporter" machines. For bike rental, see Listings, p.199.

Ice skating From Dec to March a small rink is set up in place Hôtel de Ville (daily 9am–10pm; M° Hôtel-de-Ville); skating is free and skates are available for hire for €5. The ice-rink on the first floor of the Eiffel Tower looks set to become a regular fixture; it's free, but you'll need a ticket for the tower to use it.

In-line skating Rollerblading has become so popular in Paris that it takes over the streets most Friday nights from 9.45pm, when expert skaters – over 10,000 on fine evenings – meet on the esplanade of the Gare Montparnasse in the 14e (M° Montparnasse) for a three-hour circuit of the city; check out ⓦwww.pari-roller.com for details. Three good places to find more information and rent rollerblades (around €7 for a half-day) are: Vertical Line, 4 rue de la Bastille, 4e (ⓣ01.42.74.70.00, ⓦwww.vertical-line.com; M° Bastille); Nomades, 37 bd Bourdon, 4e (ⓣ01.44.54.07.44, ⓦwww.nomadeshop.com; M° Bastille); and Ootini, 73 av de la République, 11e (ⓣ01.43.38.89.63, ⓦwww.ootini.com); Vertical Line and Nomades also hold their own roller events. The main outdoor in-line skating and skateboarding arena is the concourse of the Palais de Chaillot (M° Trocadéro). Les Halles (around the Fontaine des Innocents), the Pompidou Centre piazza and place du Palais-Royal are also very popular, as well as the central *quais* of the Seine on Sundays (see Cycling, above).

Swimming *L'Officiel des Spectacles* lists all the municipal pools (€2.60), of which the best are the brand-new and luxurious Josephine Baker, 13e which actually floats on the Seine beside the Bibliothèque Nationale (M° Bibliothèque François-Mitterrand/Quai de la Gare), and has a sliding roof; unchlorinated student hangout Jean Taris, 16 rue de Thouin, 5e (M° Cardinal-Lemoine); the 1930s-style, also studenty Piscine de Pointoise, 18 rue de Pointoise, 5e (M° Maubert-Mutualité); the Art Deco Butte aux Cailles, 5 place Verlaine, 13e (M° Place-d'Italie); and the 50-metre-long Piscine Susanne Berlioux/Les Halles, 10 place de la Rotonde, niveau 3, Porte du Jour, Forum des Halles, 1er (RER Châtelet-Les Halles). For something more spectacular, Aquaboulevard, 4 rue Louis-Armand (ⓣ01.40.60.10.00; M° Balard/Porte de Versailles), provides an array of pools, wave machines, jacuzzis and waterslides; for the €20 all-day ticket (€10 for children aged 3–11) you can use all the other fitness and sports facilities as well.

Tennis One of the nicest places to play tennis is on one of the six asphalt courts at the Jardins du Luxembourg (daily 8am–9pm; €6.50 per hour; RER Luxembourg/M° Notre-Dame-des-Champs). Addresses and opening hours of the other 41 courts in Paris can be found at ⓦwww.tennis.paris.fr, which also allows you to book in advance – though you have to set up a log-in in French. It may be simpler to call ⓣ01.71.71.70.70 or just turn up, book yourself in and wait – there'll usually be a place within an hour or so.

Turkish baths The most atmospheric hamam or Turkish baths is the Hamam de la Mosquée, 39 rue Geoffroy-St-Hilaire, 5e (ⓣ01.43.31.38.20; entry €15, towels and massage extra; M° Censier-Daubenton), with its vaulted cooling-off room and marble-lined steam chamber; times may change, so check first, but generally women on Mon, Wed, Thurs & Sat 10am–9pm, Fri 2–9pm, men Tues 2–9pm & Sun 10am–9pm. For a more upmarket, Parisian version of a hamam, head for Les Bains du Marais, 31–33 rue des Blancs Manteaux, 4e (ⓣ01.44.61.02.02, ⓦwww.lesbainsdumarais.com; sauna and steam room €35, massage €35 extra; M° Rambuteau); there are mixed sessions on Wednesday evenings (7–11pm), Saturdays (10am–8pm) and Sundays (11am–11pm) for which you have to bring a partner and a swimsuit.

Kids' Paris

For most **kids** the biggest attraction for miles around is **Disneyland Paris** (see p.207), though within the city there are plenty of less expensive and more educational possibilities for keeping them entertained. Wednesday afternoons, when primary school children have free time, and Saturdays are the big times for children's activities and entertainments; Wednesdays continue to be child-centred even during the school holidays. The tours around the **sewers** and the **catacombs** will delight some older children, while smaller ones can enjoy performances of **Guignol** (the equivalent of Punch and Judy) in the city's parks. Many of the **museums** and **amusements** already detailed will appeal, especially the **Cité des Sciences et de l'Industrie** (see p.159) and its special section for children, the **Cité des Enfants** (see below), in the Parc de la Villette. A number of museums have children's activities on Wednesdays and Saturdays, details of which are carried in the free booklet *Objectif Musée*, available from the museums. The Musée du Moyen-Âge, Musée d'Art Moderne de la Ville de Paris, Carnavalet, the Louvre, the Institut du Monde Arabe and the Musée d'Orsay have regular or special programmes but they will of course be conducted in French. Otherwise, the most useful **sources of information** for current shows, exhibitions and events are the special sections in the listings magazines ("Enfants" in *Pariscope*, and "Jeunes" in *L'Officiel des Spectacles*) and the Kiosque Paris-Jeunes at the Direction Jeunesse et Sports, 25 bd Bourdon, 4e (Mon–Fri noon–7pm; ⓣ01.42.76.22.60; M° Bastille), and at the CIDJ (Centre Information et Documentation Jeunesse), 101 quai Branley, 15e (Mon–Fri 9.30am–6pm, Sat 9.30am–1pm; ⓣ01.44.49.12.00; M° Bir-Hakeim). The tourist office also publishes a free booklet in French, *Paris-Île-de-France Avec Des Yeux Enfants*, with lots of ideas and contacts.

Cité des Enfants

The **Cité des Enfants,** with areas for 3 to 5 year olds and 6 to 12 year-olds, is a hugely engaging special section of the Cité des Sciences et de l'Industrie – detailed on p.159 – in the Parc de la Villette (Tues–Sat 10am–6pm, Sun 10am–7pm). The kids can touch, smell and feel things, play about with water, construct buildings on a miniature construction site, experiment with sound and light, manipulate robots, put together their own television news and race their own shadows. It's beautifully organized and managed, and if you haven't got a child it's worth borrowing one to get in here. Sessions run for an hour and a half (Tues, Thurs & Fri 11.30am, 1.30pm & 3.30pm; Wed, Sat, Sun & public hols 10.30am, 12.30pm, 2.30pm & 4.30pm; adults and children €5; children must be accompanied by at least one adult). It's worth booking in advance during busy holiday periods at the Cité des Sciences ticket office on ⓣ08.92.69.70.72.

The rest of the museum is also pretty good for kids, particularly the **planetarium**, the various film shows, the *Argonaute* submarine and the frequent temporary exhibitions designed for the young. And in the park, there's lots of green space, a dragon slide and seven themed gardens featuring mirrors, trampolines, water jets and spooky music.

Jardin d'Acclimatation

The **Jardin d'Acclimatation**, in the Bois de Boulogne by Porte des Sablons (daily: June–Sept 10am–7pm; Oct–May 10am–6pm; adults and children €2.70; ⓦwww.jardindacclimatation.fr; M° Les Sablons/Porte-Maillot) is a children's paradise: a cross between a funfair, zoo and amusement park. Temptations range from bumper cars, go-karts and pony and camel rides to sea lions, birds, bears and monkeys; plus there's a magical mini-canal ride (*la rivière enchantée*), distorting mirrors, scaled-down farm buildings and a puppet theatre. Rides do cost extra – around €2.50 a time, or you can buy a carnet of fifteen tickets for €30. The best way to get to the park is via the *petit train* (€5.20 return, including entrance fee) which leaves every fifteen minutes from behind the *L'Orée du Bois* restaurant near Porte Maillot métro station.

Parc Floral

Fun and games are always to be had at the **Parc Floral**, in the Bois de Vincennes, route de la Pyramide (M° Château-de-Vincennes, then a seven-minute walk past the Château de Vincennes, or bus #112; daily: March–Sept 9.30am–7pm, Oct–Feb 9.30am–5pm; €1, children €0.50 plus supplements for some activities, under-7s free; Ⓦwww.parcfloraldeparis.com). The excellent playground has slides, swings, ping-pong, pedal carts, miniature golf modelled on Paris monuments (from 2pm), an electric car circuit and a *petit train* touring all the gardens (April–Oct daily 1–5pm; €1). Tickets for the activities are sold at the playground between 2 and 5.30pm weekdays and until 7pm on weekends; activities stop fifteen minutes afterwards. Note that many of these activities are available from March/April to August only and on Wednesdays and weekends only in September and October. On Wednesdays at 2.30pm (May–Sept) there are free performances by clowns, puppets and magicians. Also in the park is a children's theatre, the **Théâtre Astral**, which puts on mime, clowns and other not-too-verbal shows for small children aged 3 to 8 (Wed, Sun & during school hols Mon–Fri 3pm; Ⓣ01.43.71.31.10; €6). There's also a series of pavilions with child-friendly educational exhibitions (free entry) which look at nature in Paris; the best is the **butterfly garden** (1.30–5.15pm).

Parc Zoologique

The top Paris **zoo** is in the Bois de Vincennes at 53 av de St-Maurice, 12ᵉ (April–Sept Mon–Sat 9am–6pm, Sun 9am–6.30pm; Oct–March closes one hour earlier; €5; M° Porte-Dorée). It was one of the first zoos in the world to get rid of cages and use landscaping to simulate a more natural environment.

Funfairs and the circus

The Tuileries gardens normally have a **funfair** in July, and there's usually a **merry-go-round** at the Forum des Halles and beneath Tour St-Jacques at Châtelet, with carousels for smaller children on place de la République and at the Rond-Point des Champs-Élysées, by avenue Matignon. Circus shows are put on from October to January at the **Cirque d'Hiver Bouglione**, 110 rue Amelot, 11ᵉ (M° Filles-du-Calvaire; details in *Pariscope* and *L'Officiel des Spectacles*).

Shopping

Even if you don't plan – or can't afford – to buy, browsing Paris's **shops and markets** is one of the chief delights of the city. Flair for style and design is as evident here as it is in other aspects of the city's life. Parisians' epicurean tendencies and fierce attachment to their small local traders has kept alive a wonderful variety of speciality shops, despite the pressures to concentrate consumption in gargantuan underground and multistorey complexes. Among specific areas, the square kilometre around **place St-Germain-des-Prés** is hard to beat, packed with books, antiques, gorgeous garments, artworks and playthings. But in every *quartier* you'll find enticing displays of all manner of consumables.

Bookshops

Books are not cheap in France – foreign books least of all – but don't let that stop you from browsing. The best areas are in the studenty Quartier Latin and along the Seine, where rows of **bouquinistes**' stalls are perched on the parapets of the *quais*. Here we've listed a few specialists and favourites.

Artcurial 9 av Matignon, 8e; M° Franklin-D.-Roosevelt. The best art bookshop in Paris, set in an elegant town house. Sells French and foreign editions, and there's also a gallery and café. Mon–Sat 10.30am–7pm; closed two weeks in Aug.

FNAC 74 av des Champs-Élysées, 8e; M° George-V; Forum des Halles, niveau 2, Porte Pierre-Lescot, 1er; M°/RER Châtelet-Les Halles; 136 rue de Rennes, 6e; M° Montparnasse; ⓦwww.fnac.com. Not the most congenial of bookshops, but it's the biggest and covers everything. Mon–Sat 10am–7.30pm; the Champs-Élysées branch is open till midnight daily.

Gibert Jeune 10 place St-Michel, 5e; M° St-Michel. The biggest of the Quartier Latin student/academic bookshops. No. 10 has the main English selection, and you can find almost any subject covered at the other branches on the *place*. An institution.

Parallèles 47 rue St-Honoré 1er; M° Châtelet-Les Halles. An alternative bookshop, with everything from anarchism to New Age. Good for info on current events and gigs. Mon–Sat 10am–7pm.

Shakespeare & Co 37 rue de la Bûcherie, 5e; M° Maubert-Mutualité. A cosy, famous literary haunt, staffed by American wannabe Hemingways, with the biggest selection of secondhand English books in town. Daily noon–midnight.

Village Voice 6 rue Princesse, 6e; M° Mabillon. Welcoming recreation of a neighbourhood bookstore, with a good selection of contemporary titles and a decent list of British and American classics. Mon 2–8pm, Tues–Sat 10am–8pm, Sun 2–7pm.

W.H. Smith 248 rue de Rivoli, 1e; M° Concorde. The Paris outlet of the British chain has a wide range of new books and newspapers. Daily 9.30am–7pm.

Clothes

The best places to start shopping for clothes are the **department stores**. Otherwise, all the main international **labels** can easily be found in and around the streets named below – as long as you can brave the intimidatingly chic assistants. We've listed only the most quintessentially Parisian names (for a more complete list, including all branches, see ⓦwww.modeaparis.com), plus a few particularly interesting one-off boutiques.

The different quarters of Paris cater for very different clientele. The streets around **St-Sulpice** métro – rues du Vieux Colombier, de Rennes, Madame, de Grenelle and du Cherche-Midi – are lined with clothing shops of all kinds, and the relatively compact size and relaxed, Left-Bank atmosphere makes this one of the most appealing of Paris's shopping quarters. For couture and seriously expensive designer wear, make for the wealthy, manicured streets around the **Champs-Élysées**, especially avenue François-1er, avenue Montaigne and **rue du Faubourg-St-Honoré**. In recent years, younger designers have begun colonizing the lower reaches of the latter street, between rue Cambon and rue des Pyramides. On the eastern side of the city, around the **Marais** and **Bastille**, the clothes, like the residents, are younger, cooler and less formal. Chic boutiques line the Marais' main shopping street, **rue des Francs-Bourgeois**, and young, trendy designers and hippie outfits congregate on Bastille streets **rue de Charonne** and **rue Keller**. At the more alternative end of the spectrum, there's a good concentration of one-off designer boutiques around **Abbesses** métro stop, at the foot of Montmartre – try rues des Martyrs, des Trois-Frères, de la Vieuville, Houdon and Durantin. For streetwise clothing, the **Forum des**

Halles and surrounding streets is a good place to browse – though there's a lot of inexpensive rubbish; in this area, **rue Étienne-Marcel** and pedestrianized **rue Tiquetonne** are best for young, trendy boutiques.

As long as there's a strong euro, visitors from outside the eurozone will find shopping relatively expensive. That said, the **sales** are officially held twice a year, beginning in mid-January and mid-July and lasting a month. Ends of lines and old stock of the couturiers are sold year round in "*stock*" **discount** shops, listed below, or out at the vast, American-style **La Vallée Village** mall, which lies inside the frontiers of Disneyland (Mon–Thurs 10am–7pm, Fri & Sat 10am–8pm, Sun 11am–7pm; Ⓦwww.lavalleevillage.com; RER Val d'Europe–Serris-Montévrain).

agnès b 6 rue du Jour, 1er (M° Châtelet-Les Halles), 6 & 10 rue du Vieux Colombier, 6e (M° St-Sulpice). The queen of classic understatement, for men and women of all persuasions. Relatively affordable for designer gear.

Anne Willi 13 rue Keller, 11e; M° Ledru-Rollin/Voltaire. Original pieces of clothing in gorgeous fabrics that respect classic French sartorial design. Prices from €60 upwards. Mon 2–8pm, Tues-Sat 11.30am–8pm.

APC 3 & 4 rue de Fleurus, 6e; M° St-Placide. Young and urban, but still effortlessly classic in that Parisian way. The men's and women's shops face each other across the road. Mon, Fri & Sat 11am–7pm, Tues–Thurs 9am–7.30pm.

Bonnie Cox 38 rue des Abbesses, 18e; M° Abbesses. Young fashion names such as Michiko, Custo and Xüly Bet at relatively uninflated prices – think €150 for a dress. Daily 11am–8pm.

Collections Privé 40 bd de la Tour Maubourg, 7e; M° La Tour-Maubourg. A kind of gallery for young, independent and very individualistic designers; most clothes fall in the €100-250 range. Tues, Wed, Fri & Sat 11am–7pm, Thurs 11am–9pm.

Comptoir des Cotonniers 30 rue de Buci & 58 rue Bonaparte, 6e; M° Mabillon/St-Germain-des-Prés. Utterly reliable little chain stocking well-cut women's basics that nod to contemporary fashions. Trousers, shirts and dresses for around €100. Has around twenty branches in Paris – two handy ones are at 29 rue du Jour (M° Les Halles) and 33 rue des Francs Bourgeois (M° St-Paul). Mon 11am–7pm, Tues–Sat 10am–7.30pm.

Dépôt-vente du 17e 109 rue de Courcelles, 17e; M° Courcelles. Big, chic shop whose speciality is heavily discounted ready-to-wear brands like Armani, Dior and Rykiel. Mon 2–7pm, Tues–Sat 10.30am–7pm.

Heaven 83 rue des Martyrs, 18e; M° Abbesses. Luxurious clothing for men and women; its sometimes brash, sometimes classically elegant. Tues-Sat 11am–7.30pm, Sun 2–7.30pm.

Isabel Marant 16 rue de Charonne, 11e; M° Bastille. Marant excels in feminine and flattering clothes in quality fabrics such as silk and cashmere. Prices are €90 upwards. Mon–Sat 10.30am–7.30pm.

Jacques Le Corre 193 rue Saint-Honoré, 1er; M° Tuileries. Creative, original hats, footwear and

Department stores

Le Bon Marché 38 rue de Sèvres, 7e, Ⓦwww.lebonmarche.fr; M° Sèvres-Babylone. Paris's oldest department store, founded in 1852, and currently one of the most highly regarded – and correspondingly expensive. Mon–Wed & Fri 9.30am–7pm, Thurs 10am–9pm, Sat 9.30am–8pm.

Galeries Lafayette 40 bd Haussmann, 9e, Ⓦwww.galerieslafayette.com; M° Havre-Caumartin. The store's forte is high fashion. Three floors are given over to the latest creations by leading designers for women, while an adjoining three-storey store is devoted to men's fashion. Then there's a huge *parfumerie* and a host of big names in men and women's accessories – all under a superb 1900 dome. It's also worth checking out Lafayette Maison, the huge and impressive home store just up the road at 35 bd Haussmann. Mon–Sat 9.30am–7.30pm, Thurs till 9pm.

Au Printemps 64 bd Haussmann 9e, Ⓦwww.printemps.com; M° Havre-Caumartin. Books, records, a *parfumerie* even bigger than that of rival Galeries Lafayette and excellent fashion for men and women. Mon–Sat 9.35am–7pm, Thurs till 10pm.

handbags. The stylish, unisex hats here come in interesting colours and shapes; Jacques is famed for his classic cotton *cloche*, perfecting the vagrant-chic look. Mon–Sat 11am–7pm.

Le Mouton à Cinq Pattes 19 rue Gregoire de Tours, 6e; M° Odéon. A classic bargain clothing address, with racks upon racks of end-of-line and reject clothing from designer names both great and small. You might find a shop-soiled Gaultier classic; you might find nothing. At these prices, it's worth the gamble. Another shop is at 138 bd St-Germain. Mon–Sat 10am–7pm.

Sabbia Rosa 71–73 rue des Saints-Pères, 6e; M° St-Germain-des-Prés. Supermodels' knickers – literally, they all shop here – at supermodel prices. Mon–Sat 10am–7pm.

Sonia/Sonia Rykiel 61 rue des Saints-Pères, 6e; M° Sèvres-Babylone. Sonia Rykiel has been a St-Germain institution since 1968; this is the younger, more exciting and less expensive offshoot. Mon–Sat 10.30am–7pm.

Spree 16 rue de la Vieuville, 18e; M° Abbesses. So fashionable it actually looks like an art gallery, with a collection led by individual designers such as Vanessa Bruno, Isabel Marant and Christian Wijnants. Mostly in the €100–250 range, though vintage pieces can run way higher. Mon 2–7pm, Tues–Sat 11am–7.30pm.

Vanessa Bruno 25 rue St-Sulpice, 6e; M° Odéon. Bright, breezy and effortlessly top-drawer women's fashions. Mon–Sat 10.30am–9.30pm.

YSL Rive Gauche men 6 place St-Sulpice, 6e (M° St-Sulpice/Mabillon), women 32–38 rue du Faubourg-Saint-Honoré, 8e (M° Concorde). Ready-to-wear spin-off from the designer label. Skinny monochrome chic remains the staple for men; the lines for women are more colourful but no less distinctively YSL.

Zadig & Voltaire 1 & 3 rue du Vieux Colombier, 6e; M° St-Sulpice. The women's clothes at this small, moderately expensive Parisian chain are pretty and feminine. In style it's not a million miles from agnès b. Mon–Sat 10am–7pm. Branches at 15 rue du Jour, 1er (M° Les Halles); 9 rue du 29 Juillet, 1er (M° Tuileries); 11 rue Montmartre, 1er (M° Les Halles); 36 rue de Sévigné, 4er (M° St-Paul).

Food and drink

You can, of course, find sumptuous food stores all over Paris: the listings below are for the **specialist places**, palaces of gluttony many of them, with prices to match. Economical food shopping is invariably best done at the **street markets** or **supermarkets**, though save your bread buying for the local boulangerie. The least expensive supermarket chain is Ed ("l'épicier"). Food markets are detailed at the end of this section.

Barthélémy 51 rue de Grenelle, 7e; M° Bac. Purveyors of cheeses to the rich and powerful. Tues–Sat 8am–1pm & 4–7.15pm; closed Aug.

Les Caves Augé 116 bd Haussmann, 8e; M° St-Augustin. This old-fasioned, wood-panelled shop is the oldest *cave* in Paris and not only sells fine wines, but also a wide selection of port, armagnac, cognac and champagne. Mon 1–7.30pm, Tues–Sat 9am–7.30pm.

Caves Michel Renaud 12 place de la Nation, 12e; M° Nation. Established in 1870, this wine shop sells superb-value French and Spanish wines, champagnes and Armagnac. Mon–Fri 9.30am–1pm & 2–8.30pm.

Comptoir du Saumon 60 rue François-Miron, 4e; M° St-Paul. This place specializes in salmon, but also sells eels, trout and all things fishy, as well as having a delightful little restaurant in which to taste the fare. Mon–Sat 10am–10pm.

Debauve and Gallais 30 rue des Sts-Pères, 7e; M° St-Germain-des-Prés/Sèvres-Babylone. A beautiful, ancient shop specializing in exquisite chocolates. Mon–Sat 9.30am–7pm; closed Aug.

Fauchon 26 place de la Madeleine, 8e; M° Madeleine. An amazing range of groceries and wine, all at exorbitant prices; there's a self-service counter for patisseries and *plats du jour*, and a *traiteur* which stays open until 9pm. Mon–Sat 9am–7pm.

Hédiard 21 place de la Madeleine, 8e; M° Madeleine. The aristocrat's grocer since 1850; there are several other branches throughout the city. Mon–Sat 9am–10pm.

La Maison de l'Escargot 79 rue Fondary, 15e; M° Dupleix. As the name suggests, this place specializes in snails: they even sauce and re-shell them while you wait. Tues–Sat 9.30am–7pm; closed Aug.

Mariage Frères 30 rue du Bourg-Tibourg, 4e; M° Hôtel-de-Ville. Hundreds of teas, neatly packed in tins, line the floor-to-ceiling shelves of this 100-year-old emporium. There's a *salon de thé* in the back with exquisite pastries (daily noon–7pm). Daily 10.30am–7.30pm.

Poilâne 8 rue du Cherche-Midi, 6e; M° Sèvres-Babylone. The source of the famous "Pain Poilâne" – a kind of sourdough bread. Mon–Sat 6.15am–8.15pm.

Rendez-Vous de la Nature 96 rue Mouffetard, 5e; Mº Cardinal-Lemoine. One of the city's most comprehensive health-food stores, with everything from fresh organic produce to herbal teas. Tues–Sat 11am–7pm.

Music

New **cassettes and CDs** are not particularly cheap in Paris, but there are plenty of secondhand bargains, and you may come across selections that are novel enough to tempt you. There are plentiful world music and jazz albums that would be specialist rarities in the UK or US.

Crocodisc 40–42 rue des Écoles, 5e, Ⓦwww.crocodisc.com; Mº Maubert-Mutualité. Folk, Oriental, Afro-Antillais, raï, funk, reggae, salsa, hip-hop, soul, country; Crocojazz is nearby at 64 rue de la Montagne-Ste-Geneviève, 5e. Offers new and secondhand music at some of the best prices in town. Tues–Sat 11am–7pm.

FNAC Musique 4 place de la Bastille, 12e; Mº Bastille. Extremely stylish shop in black, grey and chrome, with computerized catalogues, books, every variety of music and a concert booking agency. Mon–Sat 10am–8pm.

Paul Beuscher 15–29 bd Beaumarchais, 4e; Mº Bastille. A music department store that's been going strong for over 100 years, selling instruments, scores, books and recording equipment. Mon–Fri 9.45am–12.30pm & 2–7pm, Sat 9.45am–7pm.

Virgin Megastore 52–60 av des Champs-Élysées, 8e; Mº Franklin-D.-Roosevelt (Mon–Sat 10am–midnight, Sun noon–midnight) and 99 rue de Rivoli, 1er; Mº Palais-Royal (Wed–Sat 10am–10pm, Sun & Mon 10am–8pm). The biggest and trendiest of Paris's music shops, with a concert booking agency.

Sport and outdoor activities

Nomades 37 bd Bourdon, 4e; Mº Bastille. The place to buy and rent rollerblades and equipment, with its own bar out back. See also "In-line skating", p.192. Tues–Sat 11am–7pm, Sun noon–6pm.

Au Vieux Campeur 48 rue des Écoles, 5e Ⓦwww.au-vieux-campeur.fr; Mº Maubert-Mutualité. Giant outdoor activities shop with over a dozen well-stocked branches on the same block – you'll be directed to the right section for maps, boots, tents and so on. Times vary; generally 11am–7.30pm.

Markets

Paris's **markets**, like its shops, are grand spectacles. Mouthwatering arrays of **food** from half the countries of the globe, captivating in colour, shape and smell, assail the senses in even the drabbest parts of town. We've listed some of the most distinctive or specialized below; a full list is available online at Ⓦwww.paris.fr/fr/marches. Though all have semi-official opening and closing hours, many begin business in advance and drag on till dusk. Food markets usually start between 7am and 8am and tail off around 1pm, though a few stalls may carry on into the afternoon and evening. The covered markets have specific opening hours, detailed below.

Paris's well-organized **flea markets**, or *marchés aux puces*, are increasingly oriented towards genuine antiques, but you can still find some bargains among the more junk-like offerings typically sold around the fringes of the markets proper. Arrive early.

Flea markets

Place d'Aligre 12e; Mº Ledru-Rollin. A small flea market and the only one located in the city proper, peddling secondhand clothes and bric-a-brac – anything from old gramophone players to odd bits of crockery. Tues–Sun 7.30am–12.30pm.

Porte de Montreuil 20e; Mº Porte-de-Montreuil. The most junkyard-like of them all, and the best for secondhand clothes – it's cheapest on Mon when leftovers from the weekend are sold off. Also good for old furniture and household goods. Sat, Sun & Mon 7am–7.30pm.

Porte de Vanves 14e; Mº Porte-de-Vanves. One of the best for bric-a-brac and little Parisian knick-knacks. Professionals deal alongside weekend amateurs. Sat & Sun 7am–7.30pm.
St-Ouen/Porte de Clignancourt 18e; Mº Porte-de-Clignancourt. Huge collection of over a dozen antiques markets, with some collectable design items to be found, especially in Marchés Vernaison and Jules-Vallès. Marché Malik is good for second-hand/vintage clothes and bags. Stalls selling records, books and junk of all sorts can be found along rue Jean-Henri Fabre, between the market proper and the métro station. Mon, Sat & Sun 9am–6.30pm.

Food markets

Belleville bd de Belleville, 20e; Mº Belleville/Ménilmontant. Tues & Fri 7am–2pm.
Dejean place du Château-Rouge, 18e; Mº Château-Rouge. Africa central. Tues–Sun.
Enfants-Rouges 39 rue de Bretagne, 3e; Mº Filles-du-Calvaire. Tues–Sat 8am–1pm & 4–7pm, Sun 8am–2pm.
Maubert place Maubert, 5e; Mº Maubert-Mutualité. Tues, Thurs & Sat.
Montorgueil rue Montorgueil & rue Montmartre, 1er; Mº Châtelet-Les Halles/Sentier. Tues–Sat 8am–1pm & 4–7pm, Sun 9am–1pm.
Place d'Aligre 12e; Mº Ledru-Rollin. Tues–Sun until 12.30pm.
Porte-St-Martin rue du Château-d'Eau, 10e, Mº Château-d'Eau. Tues–Sat 8am–1pm & 4–7.30pm, Sun 8am–1pm.
Raspail bd Raspail, between rue du Cherche-Midi & rue de Rennes, 6e; Mº Rennes. Tues & Fri. Celebrated organic market on Sun.
Richard Lenoir bd Richard Lenoir, 11e; Mº Bastille/Richard Lenoir. Thurs & Sun.
Rue de Lévis 17e; Mº Villiers. Tues–Sun.
Tang Frères 48 av d'Ivry, 13e; Mº Porte-d'Ivry. More a supermarket yard than a market; a vast emporium of all things oriental. Tues–Sun 9am–7.30pm.
Ternes rue Lemercier, 17e; Mº Ternes. Specializes in flowers. Tues–Sun 8am–7.30pm.

Listings

Airlines Aer Lingus ⓣ01.70.20.00.72; Air Canada ⓣ08.25.88.08.81; Air France ⓣ08.20.82.08.20; British Airways ⓣ08.25.82.54.00; Bmibaby ⓣ08.90.71.00.81; Delta ⓣ08.00.30.13.01; easyJet ⓣ08.25.08.25.08; Qantas ⓣ08.11.98.00.02; Ryanair ⓣ08.92.23.23.75.
Banks and exchange Money-exchange bureaux and automatic exchange machines can be found at all airports and mainline train stations, along with ATM points. Beware of exchange bureaux, which may advertise the selling rather than buying rate and add on hefty commission fees. On the whole, you're better off in a bank, or by just using credit and debit cards in many cash machines.
Bike hire Charges start from about €15 a day; you'll need to show a picture ID, and you'll also be asked to pay a deposit of around €200–300, and/or leave a passport or credit card. If you want a bike for Sunday, when all of Paris takes to the *quais*, you'll need to book in advance. Try Paris-Vélo, 2 rue du Fer-à-Moulin, 5e (ⓣ01.43.37.59.22, ⓦwww.paris-velo-rent-a-bike.fr; Mº Censier-Daubenton), for 21-speed and mountain bikes; Paris à Vélo C'est Sympa, 22 rue Alphonse Baudin, 11e (ⓣ01.48.87.60.01, ⓦwww.parisvelosympa.com; Mº Bastille), who also offer enjoyable and well-run bicycle tours; or Fat Tire Bike Tours, 24 rue Edgar Faure, 15e (ⓣ01.56.58.10.54, ⓦwww.fattirebiketoursparis.com; Mº Dupleix), who offer a wide range of bikes, including tandems, childrens' bikes and bikes with child seats and run fun bike tours that are a good way to get to grips with the city. For more information about bike tours see p.192. In addition, RATP, the transport authority, has two bike rental offices (both daily 9am–7pm; ⓦwww.rouelibre.fr): at 1 passage Mondétour, opposite 120 de la rue Rambuteau, 1er (ⓣ01.44.76.86.43; Mº Les Halles), and at 37 bd Bourdon, 4e (ⓣ01.44.54.19.29; Mº Bastille). It also has a few Cyclobus mobile bike-rental vans parked near Notre-Dame, Porte d'Auteuil and Château de Vincennes (Esplanade St-Louis).
Buses For national and international buses, including Eurolines (ⓣ08.36.69.52.52), you can get information and tickets at the main terminus, 28 av du Général-de-Gaulle, Bagnolet (Mº Gallieni).
Car hire The big international car hire companies have offices at the airports, at the Gare du Nord – down the stairs near the Eurostar platform and taxi gate – and at various points around the city. Two reliable local firms are Buchard, 99 bd Auguste-Blanqui ⓣ01.45.88.28.38; and Locabest ⓣ01.48.31.77.05, ⓦwww.locabest.fr, with offices at 3 rue Abel (Mº Gare-de-Lyon) and at 104 bd Magenta, 10e (Mº Gare-du-Nord).

Dental treatment A useful (private) emergency service is SOS Dentaire, 87 bd Port-Royal, 5e ⓣ01.43.37.51.00; Mº Port-Royal.

Embassies/Consulates Australia, 4 rue Jean-Rey, 15e ⓣ01.40.59.33.00, ⓦwww.france.embassy.gov.fr; Mº Bir-Hakeim; Canada, 35 av Montaigne, 8e ⓣ01.44.43.29.00, ⓦwww.amb-canada.fr; Mº Franklin-D.-Roosevelt; Germany, 13–15 av Franklin D. Roosevelt, 8e ⓣ01.53.83.45.00, ⓦwww.amb-allemagne.fr, Mº Franklin-D.-Roosevelt; Ireland, 4 rue Rude, 16e ⓣ01.44.17.67.00, Mº Charles-de-Gaulle-Étoile; New Zealand, 7ter, rue Léonardo-de-Vinci, 16e ⓣ01.45.01.43.43; Mº Victor-Hugo; UK, 35 rue du Faubourg-St-Honoré, 8e ⓣ01.44.51.32.81, ⓦwww.amb-grande-bretagne.fr; Mº Concorde; US, 2 av Gabriel, 8e ⓣ01.43.12.22.22, ⓦwww.amb-usa.fr; Mº Concorde.

Emergencies Call the SAMU ambulance service on ⓣ15 (operators can put you through to an English-speaker) or the private association SOS-Médecins on ⓣ08.20.33.24.24 for 24hr medical help.

Festivals There are free concerts and street performers all over Paris for the Fête de la Musique, which coincides with the summer solstice (June 21; ⓦwww.fetedelamusique.culture.fr). Gay Pride follows swiftly afterwards, on the last Saturday of June. July 14 (Bastille Day) is celebrated with official pomp in parades of tanks down the Champs-Élysées, firework displays and concerts. For a month from this date, the *quais* are transformed into a beach along the Seine as part of the Paris Plages scheme. The Tour de France finishes along the Champs-Élysées on the third or fourth Sunday of July. In early October, the Nuit Blanche ("sleepless night") persuades Parisians to stay up all night for an energetic programme of arts events and parties all over the city. See Basics and the *Festive France* colour section for other music and religious festivals.

Hospitals In emergencies, call an ambulance on ⓣ15. If you require longer-term out-patient care, perhaps, or if you prefer not to avail yourself of France's superb healthcare system, then consider one of the English-speaking private, not-for-profit hospitals. These include the Hertford British Hospital, 3 rue Barbès, Levallois-Perret (ⓣ01.46.39.22.22, ⓦwww.british-hospital.org; Mº Anatole-France) and the American Hospital, 63 bd Victor-Hugo, Neuilly-sur-Seine (ⓣ01.46.41.25.25, ⓦwww.american-hospital.org; Mº Porte-Maillot then bus #82 to terminus).

Internet Internet access is everywhere in Paris – if it's not in your hotel it'll be in a café nearby, and there are lots of *points internet* around the city. Most post offices offer online access, too.

Language schools French lessons are available from the Alliance Française, 101 bd Raspail, 6e ⓣ01.42.84.90.00, ⓦwww.alliancefr.org, and numerous other establishments. A full list is obtainable from embassy cultural sections.

Laundries There's bound to be a self-service laundromat (*laverie self-service* or *libre-service*) somewhere near where you're staying – just ask locally. They're generally open from 7am to around 8pm.

Left luggage Lockers are available at all train stations.

Libraries The American Library in Paris, 10 rue du Général-Camou, 7e (Tues–Sat 10am–7pm; ⓣ01.53.59.12.60; ⓦwww.americanlibraryinparis.org; Mº École-Militaire), has American papers and a vast range of books; to use the library you'll need to get a day pass (€11). The Bibliothèque Publique d'Information, Pompidou Centre, 3e (Mon & Wed–Fri noon–10pm, Sat & Sun 11am–10pm; closed May 1; free; ⓦwww.bpi.fr; Mº Rambuteau), and the Bibliothèque Nationale François Mitterrand, 13e (see p.153) have vast collections, including all the foreign press.

Lost property Your first port of call should be the Commissariat de Police for the arrondissement where you think the loss took place; the next step is the central police Bureau des Objets Trouvés, 36 rue des Morillons, 15e (ⓣ08.21.00.25.25; Mº Convention; Mon–Thurs 8.30am–5pm, Fri 8.30am–4.30pm). For property lost on métro/RER and bus services, try the station where you might have lost it first, then call ⓣ08.92.68.77.14. If you lose your passport, report it to a police station and then your embassy.

Pharmacies 24hr service at: Dhery, 84 av des Champs-Élysées, 8e ⓣ01.45.62.02.41 (Mº George-V); 6 place Clichy, 9e ⓣ01.48.74.65.18. There's a British pharmacy, SNC, at 62 av des Champs-Élysées, 8e ⓣ01.43.59.22.52; it's open daily from 8am to midnight. All pharmacies, if closed, post the address of one nearby that stays open late (*pharmacie de garde*).

Police ⓣ17 (ⓣ112 from a mobile) for emergencies. To report a theft, go to the commissariat de police of the arrondissement in which the theft took place.

Post office Main office at 52 rue du Louvre 1er; Mº Châtelet-Les-Halles. Open daily 24hr for letters, poste restante, faxes, telegrams and phone calls. Other offices are usually open Mon–Fri 8am–7pm, Sat 8am–noon.

Telephones To call within Paris, even if you're already in the city, you need to dial the ⓣ01 code. ⓣ08.92 numbers cost €0.34 a minute from any (landline) phone in France; ⓣ08.21 numbers cost

€0.12; neither work from abroad. Public phones accept phonecards (*télécartes*), sold at *tabacs*, and sometimes credit cards – rarely coins. If you plan to make a lot of calls, consider buying a French phone using pre-paid charge-up cards (*mobicartes*); deals are often available for around €30 – less than the cost of just a few international calls on a foreign mobile. Note that France operates on the European GSM standard, so US cellphones won't work in France unless you've got a tri-band phone. Numbers for mobile phones (*portables*) begin ⓣ06.

Travel agencies OTU Voyages, 119 rue St-Martin, 4e, opposite the Pompidou Centre (ⓣ01.55.82.32.32, ⓦwww.otu.fr) is good for student and discount travel, as is Voyages Wasteels, 11 rue Dupuytren, 6e (ⓣ01.43.25.12.52, ⓦwww.wasteels.fr).

Around Paris

The region around the capital – the **Île de France** – and the borders of the neighbouring provinces are studded with large-scale **châteaux**. Many were royal or noble retreats for hunting and other leisured pursuits, while some – like **Versailles** – were for more serious state show. All are impressive, especially **Vaux-le-Vicomte** for its harmonious architecture and **Chantilly** for its masterpiece-studded art collection. If you have even the slightest curiosity about church buildings, make sure you visit the **cathedral of Chartres**, which more than fulfils expectations. Closer in, on the edge of Paris itself, **St-Denis** boasts a cathedral second only to Notre-Dame – a visit which can be combined

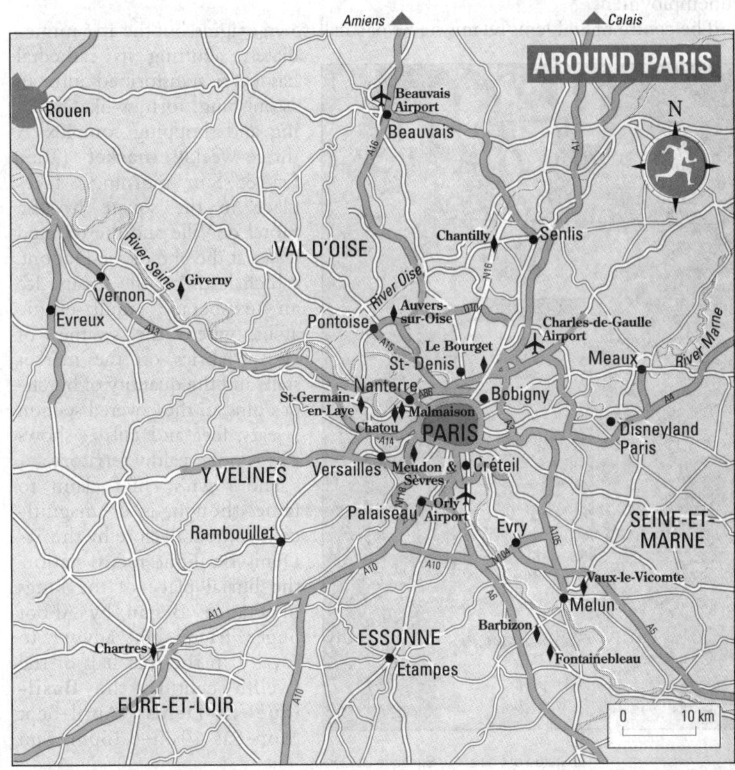

with a wander back into the centre of the city along the banks of the St-Denis canal. Other **waterside walks** include **Chatou** and the Marne-side towns, which were famously frequented by the carousing, carefree painters and musicians of the early 1900s, when these places were open countryside or small villages. **Auvers-Sur-Oise** is Van Gogh's final resting place, and has a museum that transports you back to Impressionist days and landscapes. Whether the various suburban museums deserve your attention will depend on your degree of interest in the subjects they represent – china at **Sèvres**, French prehistory at **St-Germain-en-Laye**, Napoleon at **Malmaison** or horses at **Chantilly**. The biggest pull for kids is without question **Disneyland Paris**, out beyond the bizarre satellite town of **Marne-la-Vallée**, but they might also like the air and space museum at **Le Bourget**.

All of the attractions listed in this section are easily accessible by the region's public transport links of train, RER, métro and bus. We have arranged the accounts geographically, moving in a clockwise direction around Paris from St-Denis in the north to Malmaison in the west.

St-Denis

ST-DENIS, 10km north of the centre of Paris and accessible by métro (M° St-Denis-Basilique) is home to one of the most heavily industrialized communities in France and has long been the stronghold of the Communist Party. Recession has, however, taken a heavy toll in the form of closed factories and unemployment.

The centre of St-Denis retains traces of small-town origins, but the area immediately abutting its cathedral has been transformed into an astonishing, fortress-like housing and shopping complex. A thrice-weekly **market** (Tues, Fri & Sun mornings) takes place in the square by the Hôtel de Ville and the covered *halles*, at the end of rue Dupont, which leads off the square. It's an exuberant, multi-ethnic affair, where the swathes of cheap fabrics on the market stalls and the quantity of butcher's offal in the covered section – ears, feet and tails – shows this is not wealthy territory.

△ Statue of Louis XVI, Basilique St-Denis

The town's chief claim to fame, though, is its magnificent cathedral, close by the St-Denis-Basilique métro station, the burial place of the kings of France. Begun by Abbot Suger, friend and adviser to royalty, in the first half of the twelfth century, the **Basilique St-Denis** (April–Sept Mon–Sat 10am–6.15pm, Sun

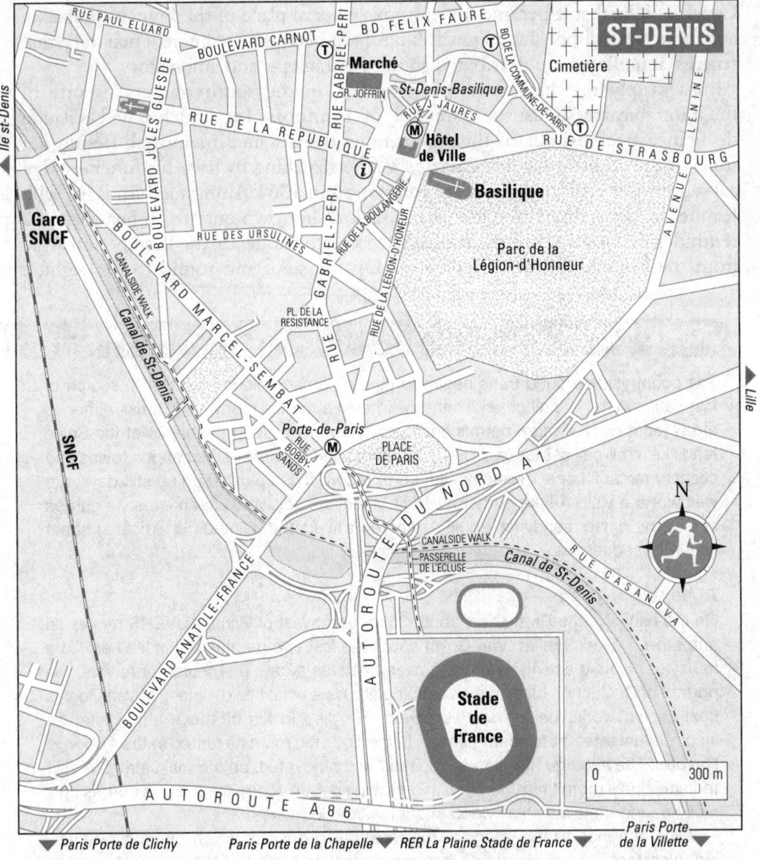

noon–6.15pm; Oct–March Mon–Sat 10am–5.15pm, Sun noon–5pm; tombs €6.50, closed during services) is generally regarded as the birthplace of the Gothic style in European architecture. The west front was the first ever to have a rose window, but it is in the choir that you best see the emergence of the new style: the slimness and lightness that comes with the use of the pointed arch, the ribbed vault and the long shafts of half-column rising from pillar to roof. It's a remarkably well-lit church, thanks to the transept windows – so big that they occupy their entire end walls – and the clerestory, which is almost one hundred percent glass – another first for St-Denis.

Legend holds that the first church here was founded by a mid-third-century Parisian bishop, later known as St-Denis. The story goes that after he was beheaded for his beliefs at Montmartre (Mount of the Martyr), he picked up his head and walked all the way to St-Denis, thereby establishing the abbey. It's not that far – just over five kilometres – though as a friend of Edward Gibbon's once remarked, "the distance is nothing, it's the first step that counts". The abbey maintained royal connections by holding the coronation of Pepin the Short, in 754, and appointing the king as its abbot during much of the Carolingian era. It was with Hugues

Capet, in 996, that it became the customary burial place of the French monarchs, and since then all but three French kings have been interred here. Their very fine **tombs** and effigies are distributed about the transepts and ambulatory.

Immediately on the left of the entrance, in the south transept, is one of the most bizarre sights: the bare feet of **François 1er** and his wife Claude de France peeking out of their enormous Renaissance memorial. Beside the steps to the ambulatory lies **Charles V**, the first king to have his funeral effigy carved from life, on the day of his coronation in 1364. Alongside him is his wife Jeanne de Bourbon, who clutches the sack of her own entrails to her chest – a reminder that royalty was traditionally eviscerated at death, the flesh boiled away from the bones and buried separately. Up the steps and round to the right, a

Artistic haunts

The countryside around Paris began to take a primary role for painters in search of inspiration in the late nineteenth century, when it attracted many a city artist, either on a day jaunt or on a more permanent basis. The towns along the banks of the Seine read like a roll-call of Musée d'Orsay paintings, and pockets of unchanged towns and scenery remain. Local museums, set up to record these pioneering artistic days, are well worth a visit. A little further afield is Monet's studio and Japanese-style garden at Giverny, in Normandy (see p.364), where he lived and painted his almost abstract water-lily sequences.

Auvers-Sur-Oise

On the banks of the River Oise, about 35km northwest of Paris, **AUVERS** makes an attractive rural excursion. **Van Gogh** spent the last two months of his life here, in a frenzy of painting activity, averaging over a canvas a day. The church at Auvers, the portrait of Dr Gachet, black crows flapping across a wheat field – many of Van Gogh's best-known works belong to this period. He died in his brother's arms, after an incompetent attempt to shoot himself, in the tiny attic room he rented in the **Auberge Ravoux**. The *auberge* still stands, repaired and renovated, on the main street. A visit to Van Gogh's room (mid-March to mid-Nov Wed–Sun 10am–6pm; €5) is surprisingly moving, and there's a short video about his time in Auvers.

At the entrance to the village is the **Château d'Auvers**, which offers a fascinating, high-tech tour of the world the Impressionists inhabited (April–Sept Tues–Sun 10.30am–6pm; Oct–March Tues–Fri 10.30am–4.30pm, Sat & Sun 10.30am–5.30pm; ⓦwww.chateau-auvers.fr; €10.50). Most evocative of all is a walk through the old part of the village, past the church and the red lane into the famous wheat field and up the hill to the cemetery where, against the far left wall in a humble ivy-covered grave, the Van Gogh brothers lie side by side.

Auvers boasts a further artistic connection in Van Gogh's predecessor, Daubigny – contemporary of Corot and Daumier. A small museum (Wed–Sun: April–Oct 2–6pm, Nov–March 2–5pm; €3.50), dedicated to him and his art, can be visited above the tourist office. His studio-house (April–Nov Thurs–Sun 2–6.30pm; €4.50), built to his own requirements, can also be visited at 61 rue Daubigny. From here, Daubigny would go off for weeks at a time, in his boat, to paint. This is represented by a boat sitting in the garden which is, in fact, a replica of a smaller boat once owned by Monet.

To reach Auvers you can take trains from Gare du Nord or Gare St-Lazare, changing at Pontoise.

Chatou

A long narrow island in the Seine, the **Île de Chatou** was once a rustic spot to which Parisians came on the newly opened train line in the mid-nineteenth century to row florid Louis XVI and busty **Marie-Antoinette** – often graced by bouquets of flowers – kneel in prayer. The mawkish scene was sculpted in 1830, long after their execution.

Most visitors to St-Denis, however, come for a match or concert at the **Stade de France**. At least €430 million was spent on the construction of this high-tech stadium, whose cosmic elliptic structure is best appreciated at night when lit up. If there isn't an event on, you can visit its grounds, facilities and small **museum** (daily 10am–6pm; €6).

To **walk back to Paris**, follow rue de la République from the Hôtel de Ville to the church of St-Denis-de-l'Estrée, then go down the left side of the church until you reach the canal bridge. If you turn left, you can walk practically all

on the river and dine and flirt at the *guinguettes* (dance halls). A favourite haunt of many artists was the **Maison Fournaise**, just below the Pont de Chatou road bridge, now a restaurant (closed Sun evening in winter; ⓣ01.30.71.41.91; menu €25), with a small museum of memorabilia (Wed–Sun 10am–6pm; €4). One of **Renoir**'s best-known canvases, *Le Déjeuner des Canotiers*, shows his friends lunching on the balcony, which is still shaded by a magnificent riverside plane tree. As well as many Impressionists, Vlaminck, Derain, Matisse and other members of the Fauve movement were *habitués*.

Access to the island is from the Rueil-Malmaison RER stop. Take the exit av Albert-1er, go left out of the station and right along the dual carriageway onto the bridge – a ten-minute walk. Bizarrely, the island hosts a twice-yearly **ham and antiques fair** (March & Sept), which is fun to check out.

Barbizon

The landscape and country life around Barbizon, 60km southeast of Paris and 10km from Fontainebleau, inspired painters such as **Rousseau** and **Millet** to set up camp here, initiating an artistic movement known as the Barbizon group. More painters followed, as well as writers and musicians, all attracted by the lifestyle and community. The **Auberge du Père Ganne**, on the main road, became the place to stay, not unrelated to the fact that the generous owner accepted the artists' decorations of his inn and furniture as payment. Now home to a museum (daily except Tues 10am–12.30pm & 2–5.30pm; €6), the Impressionist inn still contains the original painted furniture as well as many Barbizon paintings. To get to Barbizon, you'll need your own wheels; a summer bus service connects with Fontainebleau (see p.211), but it's fairly infrequent and limited to weekends.

Meudon

The tranquil suburb of Meudon, to the southwest of Paris, was where **Rodin** spent the last years of his life. In 1895, he acquired the **Villa des Brillants** at 19 av Rodin (April–Sept Fri–Sun 1–6pm; €2), installing his studio in the first room you encounter as you enter through the veranda. It was in this room that he used to dine with his companion, Rose Beuret, on summer evenings, and here that he married her, after fifty years together, just a fortnight before her death in February 1917. His own death followed in November, and they are buried together on the terrace below the house, beneath a version of *The Thinker*. The classical facade behind them masks an enormous pavilion containing plaster casts of many of his most famous works. To get there, you can take RER line C to Meudon-Val Fleury, from where it's a fifteen-minute walk along avenues Barbusse and Rodin. Alternatively, the tramway line T2 connects Meudon with La Défense and the ceramic museum at Sèvres (see p.210).

the way along the towpath (parts of the canalside are being rehabilitated and may necessitate a slight detour) – between an hour and a half and two hours – to Porte de la Villette. There are stretches where it looks as if you're probably not supposed to be there, but pay no attention and keep going. You pass peeling *villas* with unkempt gardens, patches of greenery, sand and gravel docks, and waste ground where larks rise above rusting bedsteads and doorless fridges. Decaying tenements and improvised shacks give way to lock-keepers' cottages with roses and vegetable gardens, then derelict factories and huge sheds where trundling gantries load bundles of steel rods onto Belgian barges.

Chantilly

CHANTILLY, a small town 40km north of Paris, is associated mainly with horses. Some 3000 thoroughbreds prance the forest rides of a morning, and two of the season's classiest flat races, the Jockey Club and the Prix de Diane, are held here. The old château stables are given over to a horse museum.

Trains take about thirty minutes from Paris's Gare du Nord to Chantilly. Occasional free buses pass from the station to the château, though it's only twenty or thirty minutes' walk away, on a pleasant, signposted path through the forest. **Footpaths** GR11 and 12 pass through the château park and its surrounding forest: following them makes a peaceful and leisurely way of exploring this bit of country.

The château and the Musée Vivant du Cheval

The Chantilly estate used to belong to two of the most powerful clans in France: first the Montmorencys, then, through marriage, to the Condés. The present **Château** (April–Oct daily except Tues 10am–6pm; Nov–March Mon & Wed–Fri 10.30am–12.45pm & 2–5pm, Sat & Sun 10.30am–5pm; €8; park open daily 10am–5/6pm, €4) was built in the late nineteenth century on the ruins of the Grand Château, built for the Grand Condé, who helped Louis XIV smash Spanish power in the mid-seventeenth century. It's a beautiful structure, graceful and romantic, surrounded by water and looking out over a formal arrangement of pools and pathways designed by Le Nôtre, Louis XIV's gardener.

The entrance is across a moat, past two realistic bronzes of hunting hounds. The visitable parts are mainly made up of an enormous collection of **paintings and drawings** owned by the Institut de France (see p.140). Stipulated to remain as organized by Henri d'Orléans (the donor of the château), the arrangement is haphazard by modern standards, but immensely satisfying. Some highlights can be found in the Rotunda of the picture gallery – Piero di Cosimo's *Simonetta Vespucci* and Raphael's *Madone de Lorette* – and in the so-called Sanctuary, with Raphael's *Three Graces* displayed alongside Filippo Lippi's *Esther et Assuerius* and forty miniatures from a fifteenth-century Book of Hours (an illuminated religious text) attributed to the great French Renaissance artist Jean Fouquet. Pass through the Galerie de Psyche, with its series of sepia stained glass illustrating Apuleius' *Golden Ass*, to the room known as the Tribune, where Italian art, including Botticelli's *Autumn*, takes up two walls, and Ingres and Delacroix have a wall each.

A guided tour (free) is the only way to access the apartments of the sixteenth-century wing known as the **Petit Château**. The first port of call is the well-stocked **library**, where a facsimile of the museum's single greatest treasure is on display, *Les Très Riches Heures du Duc de Berry*, the most celebrated of all the Books of Hours. The illuminated pages illustrate the months of the year with representative scenes from contemporary (early 1400s) rural life – harvesting, ploughing, sheep-shearing and pruning – and are richly coloured and drawn with a delicate naturalism. The remaining half-dozen rooms on the tour mostly show off superb furnishings, with exquisite *boisieries* panelling the walls of the Monkey Gallery, wittily painted with allegorical stories in a pseudo-Chinese style. A grand parade of canvases in the long gallery depicts the many battles won by the Grand Condé.

Five minutes' walk back towards town along the château drive, the colossal stable block has been transformed into a horse museum, the **Musée Vivant du Cheval** (April–Oct Mon & Wed–Fri 10.30am–5.30pm, Sat & Sun 10.30am–6pm; Nov–March Mon & Wed–Fri 2–5pm, Sat & Sun 10.30am–5.30pm; €8.50; Ⓦ www.museevivantducheval.fr). The building was erected at the beginning of the eighteenth century by the incumbent Condé prince, who believed he would be reincarnated as a horse and wished to provide fitting accommodation for 240 of his future relatives. In the vast main hall, horses of different breeds from around the world are stalled, with a central ring for **demonstrations** (April–Oct daily 11.30am, 3.30pm & 5.15pm; Nov–March weekends only; entry included in ticket).

Disneyland Paris

There are no two ways about it: children will love **Disneyland Paris**, 32km east of the capital, and the high-speed rides will thrill even the most jaded adult. The park takes its inspiration from (Disney) films as much as funfair rides, and the results are sometimes clever and high-tech, sometimes enjoyably old-fashioned. Commercialism is shrilly insistent, however – it would be hard to find sponsors less magical than Esso, McDonalds and Nestlé – and prices for food and drink are inflated. Bad weather can take the Florida shine off the outing, too, but it does have one advantage: on a wet and windy off-season weekday you can get round every ride you want. Otherwise, lines for the big rides are common, though you can reduce the wait at the most popular attractions by using the Fastpass scheme, where you turn up and reserve a time in advance – you then come back and walk right through.

The complex is divided into three areas: **Disneyland Park**, the original Magic Kingdom, with most of the big rides; **Walt Disney Studios Park**, a more technology-based attempt to recreate the world of cartoon film-making, with fake sets and virtual reality rides; and **Disney Village**, where you can eat overpriced, mostly American-style food. A clutch of (expensive) Disney hotels allow you to sleep locally if you're planning on making more than a day of it.

Disneyland Park

Since the opening of Space Mountain, **Disneyland Park** has provided a variety of good thrill rides, though the majority of attractions remain relatively sedate. The Magic Kingdom is divided into four "lands" radiating out from **Main Street USA**. **Fantasyland** appeals to the tinies, with Sleeping Beauty's Castle, Peter Pan's Flight, the Mad Hatter's Teacups and Alice's Curious Labyrinth among its attractions. **Adventureland** has the most outlandish sets and two of the best rides – Pirates of the Caribbean and Indiana Jones and the Temple of Peril: Backwards. **Frontierland** has the *Psycho*-inspired but insipid Phantom Manor and the hair-raising roller coaster Big Thunder Mountain, modelled on a runaway mine train. In **Discoveryland** there's a high-tech 3-D experience called "Honey, I Shrunk The Audience", a 360-degree Parisian exposé in Le Visionarium, the Nautilus submarine of *20,000*

Leagues Under the Sea and the terrifyingly fast Space Mountain roller coaster. The grand **parade** of floats representing all the top box-office Disney movies sallies down Main Street USA at 4pm every day (a good time to try for the more popular rides). Night-time Princess Parades and **firework displays** take place several times a week.

Walt Disney Studios Park

Other than the "Rock 'N' Roller Coaster Starring Aerosmith", a corkscrew-looping, metal-playing white-knuckler, the new **Walt Disney Studios Park** lacks the big, scary rides offered by its older neighbour. Yet in some ways it's a more satisfying affair, focusing on what Disney was and is still renowned for – animation. Cartoonists can be visited "at work", there are mock film and TV sets where you can be part of the audience, and the special effects and stunt shows are impressive, although probably not as impressive as your average film. The virtual-reality ride Armageddon is genuinely thrilling – your space-station is bombarded by meteors – and the tram tour's passage through the collapsing Catastrophe Canyon is good fun. A few minutes' walk away, you can book a two-hour football coaching session for 7- to 14-year-olds at the high-tech **Manchester United Soccer School**.

Arrival and information

To reach Disneyland from Paris, take RER line A from Châtelet-Les Halles to Marne-la-Vallée/Chessy station, which is opposite the main park gates. The journey takes around 45 minutes and costs €11.90 for a round-trip (children under 12 €5.94, under-3s free). If you're coming from Charles de Gaulle airport, you can take the TGV straight to the park in ten minutes (14 trains daily from roughly 9am–9pm; €13.80). From both CDG or Orly airports, shuttle buses run to individual hotels (times and frequencies change seasonally, but roughly every 20–30min 8.30am–7.45pm; €16, children aged 3-11 €13; Ⓦwww.vea.fr). Marne-la-Vallée/Chessy also has its own TGV train station, linked to Lille, Lyon – and London via special Eurostar trains. By car, the park is a 32-kilometre drive east of Paris along the A4: take the "Porte de Bercy" exit off the *périphérique*, then follow "direction Metz/Nancy", leaving at exit 14. From Calais follow the A26, changing to the A1, the A104 and finally the A4.

Admission charges for the "1-day/1-Park" ticket are €43 for an adult or €35 for a child (aged 3–11); the ticket allows entry to either the Disneyland Park or Walt Disney Studios Park, not both (though if you opt for the Studios you can visit the Disneyland Park after the Studios closes). One-day "Hopper" tickets, allowing access to both parks, cost €53/45; two-and three-day Hopper tickets are also available. **Opening hours** vary depending on the season and whether it's a weekend, and should be checked when you buy your ticket (which can be done online at Ⓦwww.disneylandparis.com) but they are usually 9/10am–8pm, or until 9pm or 11pm on weekends in high summer; Walt Disney Studios Park always closes at 6pm. You can buy admission passes and train tickets in Paris at all RER line A and B stations and in major métro stations.

Accommodation

Disney's six heavily themed **hotels** are a mixed bag, and only worth staying in as part of a multi-day package booked through an agent, or through Disneyland; otherwise they're incredibly expensive. From the UK, for example, you can get a three-day pass, with a return ticket on Eurostar and two nights' accommodation at the *Hotel Santa Fe* for around £300 per adult and £140 per child. For details look online or call Ⓣ00 33.1.60.30.60.81 from the US, Ⓣ0870 503

0303 in the UK ⓣ01.60.30.60.53 in France or from other countries. To really economize, you could camp at the nearby *Camping du Parc de la Colline*, route de Lagny, 77200 Torcy (ⓣ01.30.58.56.20), which is open all year and offers minibus shuttles to the park

Vaux-le-Vicomte

Of all the great mansions within reach of a day's outing from Paris, the classical **Château of Vaux-le-Vicomte** (end March to mid-Nov daily 10am–6pm; ⓦwww.vaux-le-vicomte.com; €12.50), 46km southeast of Paris, is the most architecturally harmonious and aesthetically pleasing – and the most human in scale.

To get there, take a train from Gare de Lyon (or RER line D from Châtelet) to Melun (40min), and pick up the *navette*, or shuttle bus (€7 return), though it only runs on weekends and you'll have to check the timetable on the château website. Otherwise, a taxi costs roughly €15 for the seven-kilometre ride to the château.

The château

Louis XIV's finance superintendent, Nicholas Fouquet, had the **château** built at colossal expense, using the top designers of the day – architect Le Vau, painter Le Brun and landscape gardener Le Nôtre. The result was magnificence and precision in perfect proportion, and a bill that could only be paid by someone who occasionally confused the state's accounts with his own. The house-warming party, to which the king was invited, was more extravagant than any royal event – a comparison which other finance ministers ensured that Louis took to heart. Within three weeks Fouquet was jailed for life on trumped-up charges, and the design team carted off to build the king's own gaudy piece of one-upmanship at Versailles.

Seen from the entrance, the château is a rather austere grey pile surrounded by an artificial moat, and it's only when you go through to the south side – where clipped box and yew, fountains and statuary stand in formal gardens – that you can look back and appreciate the very harmonious and very French combination of a steep, tall roof and a central dome with classical pediment and pilasters.

In terms of the interior, the main artistic interest lies in the work of Le Brun, who was responsible for the two fine **tapestries** in the entrance. These were made in the local workshops set up by Fouquet specifically to adorn his house (and subsequently removed by Louis XIV to become the famous Gobelins works in Paris). Le Brun's **painted ceilings** include Fouquet's Bedroom, the Salon des Muses, *Sleep* in the Cabinet des Jeux and the so-called King's Bedroom, whose decor is the first example of the style that became known as "Louis Quatorze".

Other points of interest are the **kitchens**, which have not been altered since construction, and a room displaying letters in the hand of Fouquet, Louis XIV and other notables. One, dated November 1794 (mid-Revolution), addresses the incumbent Duc de Choiseul-Praslin as *tu*. "Citizen," it says, "you've got a week to hand over one hundred thousand pounds …", and signs off with "Cheers and brotherhood". You can imagine the shock to the aristocratic system.

Every fine Saturday evening from May to mid-October, and every Friday for most of July and August, the **state rooms** and gardens are illuminated with two thousand candles between 8pm and midnight (€15.50 entrance) – as they

Museums around Paris

The **museums** in the general vicinity of Paris – **ceramics** at Sèvres, **prehistory** at St-Germain-en-Laye and **aviation** at Le Bourget – are excellent and shouldn't be missed if their subjects arouse interest.

Musée de l'Air et d'Espace

The French were always pioneering aviators and **LE BOURGET**, a short hop up the A1 motorway from St-Denis, is intimately connected with their earliest exploits. Lindbergh landed here after his epic first flight across the Atlantic and, until the development of Orly in the 1950s, this was Paris's principal airport. The **museum** (Tues–Sun: April–Sept 10am–6pm; Oct–March 10am–5pm; Ⓦwww.mae.org; €7) occupies the old airport buildings, and consists of five hangars and the Grande Galerie, all littered with real planes. The latter takes you from the earliest attempts of the Montgolfier brothers, with their devil-may-care **hot-air balloons**, to the quixotic aircraft of World War I. The dedicated World War II hangar shows off the finest aircraft from the era while the Hall Concorde, adjacent, houses the first, beautiful Concorde prototype. Other hangars focus on France's high-tech achievements since the 1950s, including space exploration and the super-sophisticated, best-selling Mirage fighters. **To get there**, take RER line B from Gare du Nord to Gare du Bourget, or métro line 7 to La Courneuve; bus #152 connects both station to the museum. Alternatively, take bus #350 from the Gare du Nord.

Musée National de la Céramique

The **Musée National de la Céramique** (daily except Tues 10am–5pm; €4.50; Ⓦwww.musee-ceramique-sevres.fr) in **SÈVRES** possesses one of the world's greatest collections of pottery and china. If you're interested in ceramics there's a vast quantity to savour here, including Islamic, Chinese, Italian, German, Dutch and English pieces. There is also, inevitably, a comprehensive collection of French Sèvres ware: the stuff is still made right here. Close by, overlooking the river, the **Parc de St-Cloud** is good for fresh air and has a geometrical sequence of pools and fountains delineating a route down to the river and across to the city. **Getting to Sèvres** from Paris is easy: take the métro to the Pont-de-Sèvres terminus, cross the bridge and spaghetti junction and the museum is the massive building facing the riverbank on your right. Alternatively, the new riverbank tramway line T2 now connects the museum directly with La Défense, via the Rodin museum at Meudon (see p.205).

Musée des Antiquités Nationales

ST-GERMAIN is a pleasant town, but the **Musée des Antiquités Nationales** (daily except Tues 9am–5.15pm; Ⓦwww.musee-antiquitesnationales.fr; €4.50, free first Sun of the month) is the main attraction. It's housed opposite St-Germain-en-Laye RER station in a renovated château that was one of the main residences of the French court before Versailles was built. The extensive Stone Age section includes mock-ups of several cave drawings and carvings, and a beautiful collection of decorative objects, tools and so forth. All ages of early French history are covered, from Celts and Romans to Franks. A great section on Alésia – where Vercingétorix found himself besieged by Caesar's army – shows how the battle was won. Outside the château, a **terrace** – Le Nôtre, again, was responsible – stretches for more than 2km above the Seine, with a view over the whole of Paris.

probably were on the occasion of Fouquet's fateful party. The **fountains** and other waterworks can be seen in action on the second and last Saturdays of each month in summer (April–Sept only; 3–6pm). In the stables, the **Musée des Équipages** comprises a collection of horse-drawn vehicles, including those used by Charles X fleeing Paris and the Duc de Rohan retreating from Moscow.

Fontainebleau

From the Gare de Lyon it's a fifty-minute train ride to **FONTAINEBLEAU**, famous for its vast, rambling **Château** (daily except Tues: June–Sept 9.30am–6pm; Oct–May 9.30am–5pm; €6.50, Ⓦ www.musee-chateau-fontainebleau.fr). The connecting buses #A and #B from Fontainebleau-Avon station take you to the château gates in fifteen minutes.

The château owes its existence to its situation in the middle of a magnificent forest, which made it the perfect base for royal hunting expeditions. A lodge was built here as early as the twelfth century, but it only began its transformation into a luxurious palace during the sixteenth on the initiative of François I, who imported a colony of Italian artists – most notably Rosso il Fiorentino and Niccolò dell'Abate – to carry out the decoration. They were responsible for the celebrated **Galerie François-1er** – which had a seminal influence on the subsequent development of French aristocratic art and design – the Salle de Bal, the Salon Louis XIII and the Salle du Conseil with its eighteenth-century decoration. The palace continued to enjoy royal favour well into the nineteenth century; Napoleon spent huge amounts of money on it, as did Louis-Philippe.

You can take various guided tours (all €3), of which the most interesting takes you round the Petits Appartements, which were fitted out for Napoleon and his first wife Josephine, and preserve their original decor. Of more recherché interest are the tours of the Chinese museum created for Eugénie, the wife of Napoléon III, and the Musée Napoléon 1er, which mostly attracts those nostalgic for the First Empire. For details of tour times, ring Ⓣ 01.60.71.50.70.

The **gardens** are equally luscious, but if you want to escape to the relative wilds, the surrounding **forest** of Fontainebleau is full of walking and cycling trails, all marked on Michelin map #196 (*Environs de Paris*).

Versailles

The **Palace of Versailles** (Tues–Sun: April–Oct 9am–6pm; Nov–March 9am–5pm; closed public hols; €13.50, Ⓦ www.chateauversailles.fr) is rightly one of the most visited monuments in France. The standard ticket gives you free access to the key rooms of the palace, but if you plan to visit the Trianons in the park (see p.213) and the "Grandes Eaux Musicales", or dancing fountains (see p.213), it's worth buying the "passport" (April–Oct Mon–Fri €20, Sat & Sun €25; Nov–March €16). All tickets allow you to come and go during the day. Don't set out to see all the palace in one visit – it's not possible.

To **get there**, take RER line C5 to Versailles-Rive Gauche (40min), turn right out of the station and immediately left to approach the palace.

The palace

The **palace** was inspired by the young Louis XIV's envy of his finance minister's château at Vaux-le-Vicomte (see p.209), which he was determined to outdo. He recruited the design team of Vaux-le-Vicomte architect Le Vau, painter Le Brun and gardener Le Nôtre and ordered something a hundred times the size. Versailles is the apotheosis of French regal indulgence and, even if its extravagant decor and the blatant propaganda of the Sun King are not to your liking, it will certainly leave an impression.

Construction began in 1664 and lasted virtually until Louis XIV's death in 1715. Second only to God, and the head of an immensely powerful state,

△ Hall of Mirrors, Versailles

Louis XIV was an institution rather than a private individual. His risings and sittings, comings and goings, were minutely regulated and rigidly encased in ceremony, attendance at which was an honour much sought after by courtiers. Versailles was the headquarters of every arm of the state. More than 20,000 people – nobles, administrative staff, merchants, soldiers and servants – lived in the palace in a state of unhygienic squalor, according to contemporary accounts.

Following Louis XIV's death, the château was abandoned for a few years before being reoccupied by Louis XV in 1722. It remained the residence of the royal family until the Revolution of 1789, when the furniture was sold and the pictures dispatched to the Louvre. Thereafter Versailles fell into ruin until Louis-Philippe established his giant museum of French Glory here – it still exists, though most is mothballed. In 1871, during the Paris Commune, the château became the seat of the nationalist government, and the French parliament continued to meet in Louis XV's opera building until 1879. Restoration only began in earnest between the two world wars, and since 2003, the palace has become the focus of one of Jacques Chirac's pet schemes, a grand restoration project to rival Mitterrand's Louvre, with a budget of €400 million. The château's management eagerly buys back its original furnishings every time they come up for auction. Intriguingly, it has chosen to restore the château as it appeared in the last days of the monarchy.

The most stunning room is the **Galerie des Glaces** – or Hall of Mirrors – where the Treaty of Versailles was signed to end World War I. Restoration works are expected to continue until 2008, but at least half the gallery will be visible at any one time; it's best viewed at the end of the day, when the crowds have departed and sunlight fills it from the west. Overdoses of gilding await you in the **grands appartements**, the state apartments of the king and queen, and the royal **chapel**, a grand structure that ranks among France's finest Baroque creations.

The park and Grand and Petit Trianons

You could spend the whole day just exploring the **park** at Versailles (April–Oct 7am–8.30pm; Nov–March 8am–6pm; free, except on "Grandes Eaux" days, see p.211). Studded around the park are various outcroppings of the royal mania for building. The Italianate **Grand Trianon** was designed by Hardouin-Mansart in 1687 as a "country retreat" for Louis XIV, while the delicious **Petit Trianon** was built by Gabriel in the 1760s for Louis XV's mistress, Mme de Pompadour. The quintessentially picturesque **Hameau de la Reine** was built in 1783 as a play farm for Marie-Antoinette, so she could indulge the fashionable, Rousseau-inspired fantasy of the natural life. Unless you have the "passport", a separate ticket is needed for all three buildings (daily noon–5/6pm; €9, or €5 after 4pm and from Nov to March). At weekends in summer, the various Louis XIV **fountains** are switched on, to the accompaniment of Baroque music; when this "Grandes Eaux Musicales" is in action, you have to pay extra to visit the park (€7), unless you have the "passport" ticket.

Distances in the park are considerable. If you can't manage them on foot, a *petit train* shuttles between the terrace in front of the château and the Trianons. There are **bikes** for hire at the Grille de la Reine, Porte St-Antoine and by the Grand Canal. **Boats** are for hire on the Grand Canal, within the Park.

Near the park entrance at the end of boulevard de la Reine is the **Hôtel Palais Trianon**, where the final negotiations for the Treaty of Versailles took place in 1919; the hotel has a wonderfully posh **tearoom**. The style of the *Trianon* is very much that of the town in general. The dominant population is aristocratic; those with pre-revolutionary titles are disdainful of those dating merely from the Napoleonic era. On Bastille Day, local conservatives like to show their colours, donning black ribbons and ties to mourn the passing of the *ancien régime*.

Chartres

About 80km southwest of Paris, **CHARTRES** is a modest but charming market town whose existence is almost entirely overshadowed by its extraordinary **cathedral** (daily: May–Oct 8am–8pm; Nov–April 8.30am–7.30pm; free). Built between 1194 and 1260, it was one of the quickest ever constructed and, as a result, preserves a uniquely harmonious design. The astounding size of the cathedral is entirely due to the presence of the Sancta Camisia – supposed to have been the robe Mary wore when she gave birth to Jesus. After an earlier Romanesque structure burnt down in 1194, the relic was discovered three days later, miraculously unharmed. It was a sign that the Virgin wanted her church lavishly rebuilt – at least, so said the canny **medieval fundraisers**. In the medieval heyday of the pilgrimage to Santiago de Compostela, hordes of pilgrims on their way south to Spain would stop here to venerate the relic – the sloping

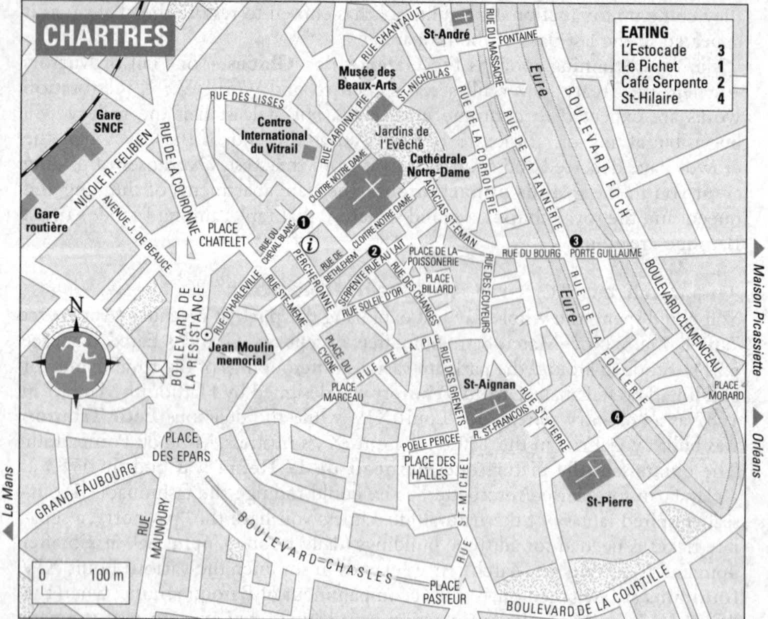

floor evident today allowed for it to be washed down more easily. The Sancta Camisia still exists, though after many years on open display it was recently rolled up and put into storage. It may yet be restored to the cathedral.

The geometry of Chartres is unique in being almost unaltered since its consecration, and virtually all of the magnificent **stained glass** is original thirteenth-century work. But if a group of medieval pilgrims suddenly found themselves here they would be deeply dismayed. The paint and gilt work that once brought the portal sculptures to life has vanished, while the walls have lost the whitewash that reflected the vivid colours of the stained-glass windows. Worse still, the high altar has been brought down into the body of the church, among the hoi polloi, and chairs usually cover up the thirteenth-century **labyrinth** on the floor of the nave. The cathedral's **stonework**, however, is still captivating, particularly the **choir screen**, which curves around the ambulatory. Outside, hosts of sculpted figures stand like guardians at each **entrance portal**. Like the south tower and spire which abuts it, the mid-twelfth-century **Royal Portal** actually survives from the earlier Romanesque church. You have to pay extra to visit the crypt and treasury, though these are relatively unimpressive. Crowds permitting, it's worth climbing the **north tower** for its bird's-eye view of the sculptures and structure of the cathedral (Mon–Sat 9am–12.30pm & 2–4.30pm, Sun 2–4.30pm; May–Aug open until 5.30pm; €4). There are **gardens** at the back from where you can contemplate the innovative flying buttresses.

In the former episcopal palace immediately behind the cathedral, the **Musée des Beaux-Arts** (Mon & Wed–Sat 10am–noon & 2–6pm (till 5pm Nov–April), Sun 2–6pm; €2.70, combined ticket with Maison Picassiette, opposite, €5.80), has some beautiful tapestries, a room full of works by Maurice de Vlaminck and an excellent *Sainte Lucie* by Zurbarán. Behind the museum, rue

Chantault leads past old town houses to the River Eure and Pont du Massacre. You can follow the river upstream, passing ancient wash-houses. A left turn at the end of rue de la Tannerie, then third right, will bring you to the **Maison Picassiette**, at 22 rue du Repos (April–Oct Mon & Wed–Sat 10am–noon & 2–6pm, Sun 2–6pm; €4.30). This house was entirely decorated with mosaics by a local road-mender and later cemetery-caretaker, Raymond Isidore, creating a strange yet moving folly – "I took the things that other people threw away", as he put it. Back at the end of rue de la Tannerie, the bridge over the river brings you back to the medieval town, where you can wander about spotting little details such as the sixteenth-century carved salmon that decorates a house at the eastern end of place de la Poissonnerie. A large food **market** takes place on place Billard and rue des Changes on Saturday morning, and there's a flower market on place du Cygne (Tues, Thurs & Sat).

At the edge of the old town, at the junction of boulevard de la Résistance and rue Collin-d'Arleville, stands a memorial to **Jean Moulin**, Prefect of Chartres until 1942. In 1940, he refused to sign a document claiming that Senegalese soldiers in the French army were responsible for Nazi atrocities. He later became de Gaulle's number-one man on the ground, coordinating the Resistance, but died at the hands of Klaus Barbie in 1943, on his way to a concentration camp in Germany.

Practicalities

Trains run from Paris's Gare du Montparnasse at least every hour on weekdays (1hr). From the **gare SNCF**, it's less than ten minutes' walk to the cathedral and **tourist office** (April–Sept Mon–Sat 9am–7pm, Sun 9.30am–5.30pm; Oct–March Mon–Sat 10am–6pm, Sun 10am–1pm & 2.30–4.30pm; ⓣ02.37.18.26.26). The latter can supply free maps and help with accommodation.

For a snack, there are lots of places with outside tables on rue Cloître-Notre-Dame, opposite the south side of the cathedral: try the *Café Serpente*. For a proper **restaurant** meal, *Le Pichet*, 19 rue de Cheval Blanc, almost under the northwest spire (ⓣ02.37.21.08.35; closed Wed, Tues & Sun eve), has a cosy interior full of gingham and bric-a-brac, and serves simple dishes like steak or Greek salads for around €10–14. The slightly more upmarket *L'Estocade*, 1 rue de la Porte Guillaume (ⓣ02.37.34.27.17; closed Mon, Sun evening & Nov–April), has a lovely situation down by the peaceful, canal-like River Eure. The *St-Hilaire*, 11 rue du Pont St-Hilaire (ⓣ02.37.30.97.57; closed Mon & Sun), serves refined regional cuisine (menus €25–40) in a sweet little upstairs dining room.

Malmaison

The **Château of Malmaison** (daily except Tues: April–Oct 10am–4.30pm; Nov–March 10am–noon & 1.30–5.15pm; €5; ⓦwww.chateau-malmaison.fr), set in the beautiful grounds of the **Bois-Préau**, about 15km west of central Paris, is a relatively small and enjoyable place to visit. It was the home of the Empress Josephine, and – during the 1800–1804 Consulate – of Napoleon, too. According to his secretary, "it was the only place next to the battlefield where he was truly himself". After their divorce, Josephine stayed on here, building up her superb rose garden and occasionally receiving visits from the emperor until her death in 1814. Tours of the château include the private and official apartments, some with original furnishings, as well as Josephine's clothes, china, glass and personal possessions. There are other Napoleonic bits in the adjacent **Bois-Préau museum** (same hours and ticket).

To get to Malmaison take the métro to Grande-Arche-de-la-Défense, then bus #258 to Malmaison-Château. Alternatively, if you'd like a walk, take the RER to Rueil-Malmaison and follow the GR11 footpath for about two kilometres from the Pont de Chatou along the left bank of the Seine and into the château park.

Travel details

Trains

Gare de'Austerlitz to: Tours (hourly; 2hr 30min).

Gare de l'Est to: Metz (10 daily; 2hr 50min); Nancy (12 daily; 2hr 50min–3hr 20min); Reims (15 daily; 1hr 40min–2hr 20min); Strasbourg (11 daily; 4hr).

Gare de Lyon to: Avignon (13 daily; 2hr 40min–3hr 30min); Besançon (8 daily; 2hr 30min–3hr); Dijon (hourly; 1hr 40min); Grenoble (13 daily; 2hr 50min–3hr 50min); Lyon (hourly; 2hr–2hr 30min); Marseille (hourly; 3hr 10min); Nice (7 daily; 5hr 30min–6hr 30min).

Gare Montparnasse to: Bayonne (6 daily; 4hr 45min–6hr 30min); Bordeaux (at least hourly; 3hr–3hr 30min); Brest (8 daily; 4hr 20min–5hr 20min); Nantes (11 daily; 2hr); Pau (7 daily; 5hr 15min–7hr 20min); Poitiers (14 daily; 1hr 40min); Rennes (at least hourly; 2hr 15min); Toulouse (10 daily; 5hr–6hr 30min); Tours (hourly; 1hr–1hr 30min).

Gare du Nord to: Amiens (at least hourly; 1hr 45min); Arras (roughly every 2hr; 50min); Boulogne (at least hourly; 2hr 10min); Lille (hourly; 1hr).

Gare St-Lazare to: Caen (hourly; 1hr 50min–2hr 30min); Cherbourg (roughly every 2hr; 3hr–3hr 30min); Dieppe (2 daily; 2hr 15min); Le Havre (every 2–3hr; 2hr–2hr 30min); Rouen (hourly; 1hr 15min).

2

The north

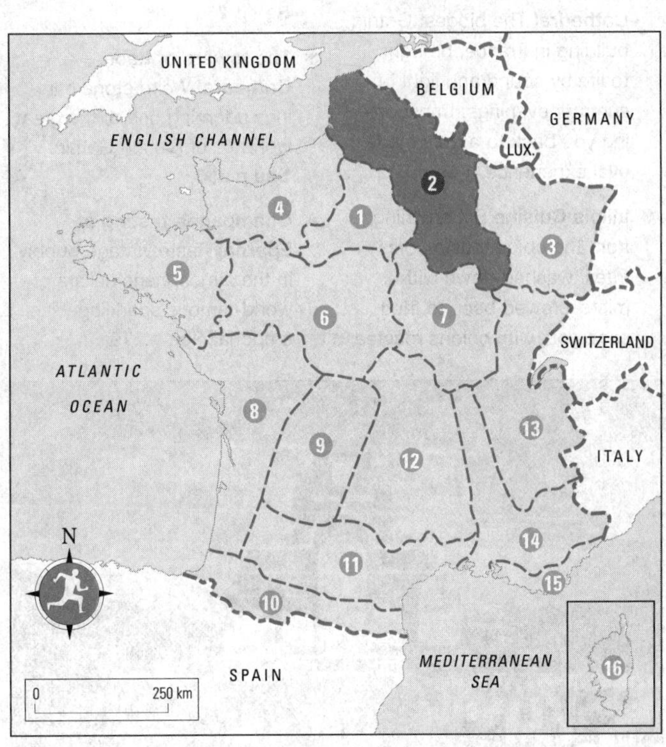
UNITED KINGDOM
BELGIUM
GERMANY
ENGLISH CHANNEL
LUX.
2
4
1
3
5
6
7
SWITZERLAND
ATLANTIC
OCEAN
8
9
12
13
ITALY
N
14
11
15
10
MEDITERRANEAN
SEA
SPAIN
16
0
250 km

CHAPTER 2 Highlights

* **Marquenterre Bird Sanctuary** From geese and godwits to storks and spoonbills, a huge variety of birds make their home amid briny meres and tamarisk-fringed dunes. See p.238

* **Son et Lumière at Amiens Cathedral** The biggest Gothic building in France, brought to life by sound and light on summer evenings, transporting you back to a truly medieval experience. See p.242

* **Lillois Cuisine** Eat anything from the ubiquitous *moules-frites*, washed down with micro-brewed beer, to fried *escargots* with onions roasted in lavender oil in the historic centre of Lille, the cultural capital of northern France. See p.251

* **World War I monuments in the Somme** Moving memorials by Lutyens and others to the victims of the trenches. See p.263

* **The towers of Laon Cathedral** Weird stone carvings adorning one of the great wonders of French Gothic. See p.266

* **Champagne tasting at Épernay** Taste vintage bubbly in the atmospheric cellars of world-famous sparkling wine emporia. See p.279

△ Lutyens' Memorial to the Missing, Thiepval

2

The north

When conjuring up exotic holiday locations, you're unlikely to light upon the **north** of France. Even among the French, the most enthusiastic tourists of their own country, it has few adherents. Largely flat Artois and Flanders include the most heavily industrialized parts of the country, these days hit by post-industrial depression, while across the wheat fields of the more sparsely populated regions of Picardy and Champagne a few drops of rain are all that is required for total gloom to descend. Coming from Britain it's likely, however, that you'll arrive and leave France via this region, and there are good reasons to stop within easy reach of Calais and the Channel Tunnel, even at **Boulogne**, whose attractive medieval quarter makes it by far the most appealing of the northern Channel ports. Just inland the delightful village of **Cassel** is a rare example of a Flemish hill settlement, while **St-Omer** and **Montreuil-sur-Mer** are also strong contenders in terms of charm and interest.

Northern France has been on the path of various invaders into the country, from northern Europe as well as from Britain, and the events that have taken place in Flanders, Artois and Picardy have shaped French and world history. The bloodiest battles were those of World War I, above all the **Battle of the Somme**, which took place north of Amiens, and **Vimy Ridge**, near Arras, where the trenches have been preserved in perpetuity; a visit to any of these is highly recommended to understand the sacrifice and futility of war.

On a more cheerful note, **Picardy** boasts some of France's finest cathedrals, including those at **Amiens**, **Beauvais** and **Laon**. Further south, the wineries, vineyards and world-famous produce of the **Champagne** region are the main draw, for which the best bases are **Épernay** and **Reims**, the latter with another fine cathedral. Other attractions include the bird sanctuary of **Marquenterre**; the wooded wilderness of the **Ardennes**; industrial archeology in the coalfields around **Douai**, where Zola's *Germinal* was set; the great medieval castle of **Coucy-le-Château**; and the battle sites of the Middle Ages – **Agincourt** and **Crécy** – familiar names in the long history of Anglo–French rivalry.

In city centres from **Lille** to **Troyes**, you'll find your fill of food, culture and entertainment in the company of locals similarly intent on having a good time. And in addition to the more obvious pleasures of the Champagne region, there's the possibility of finding relatively lucrative employment during the harvest season towards the end of September.

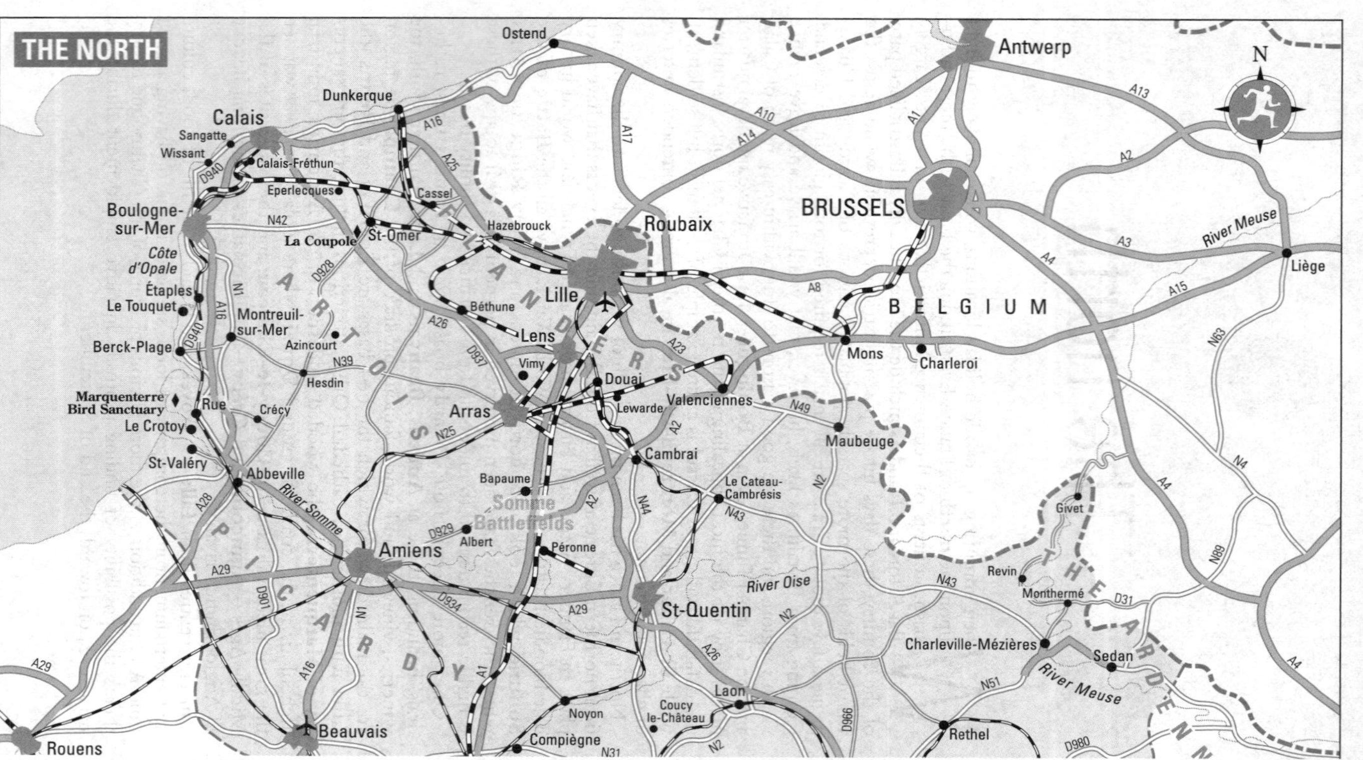
THE NORTH
N
Ostend
Antwerp
Dunkerque
Calais
Sangatte
Wissant
Calais-Fréthun
Eperlecques
Cassel
Boulogne-sur-Mer
N42
La Coupole
St-Omer
Hazebrouck
Roubaix
BRUSSELS
River Meuse
Liège
Côte d'Opale
Étaples
Le Touquet
Lille
Béthune
B E L G I U M
Montreuil-sur-Mer
Azincourt
Lens
Berck-Plage
Hesdin
Vimy
Mons
Charleroi
Douai
Marquenterre Bird Sanctuary
Rue
Crécy
Arras
Lewarde
Valenciennes
Le Crotoy
St-Valéry
Maubeuge
Cambrai
Abbeville
Bapaume
Le Cateau-Cambrésis
River Somme
Somme Battlefields
Givet
Albert
Péronne
Amiens
Revin
River Oise
Monthermé
St-Quentin
Charleville-Mézières
Sedan
River Meuse
Le Havre
Laon
Coucy le-Château
Noyon
Rethel
Beauvais
Compiègne
Rouens
F L A N D E R S
A R T O I S
P I C A R D Y
T H E A R D E N N
A1
A2
A3
A4
A8
A10
A13
A14
A15
A16
A17
A23
A25
A26
A28
A29
N1
N2
N4
N25
N31
N39
N43
N44
N49
N51
N63
N89
D31
D901
D928
D929
D934
D937
D940
D966
D980

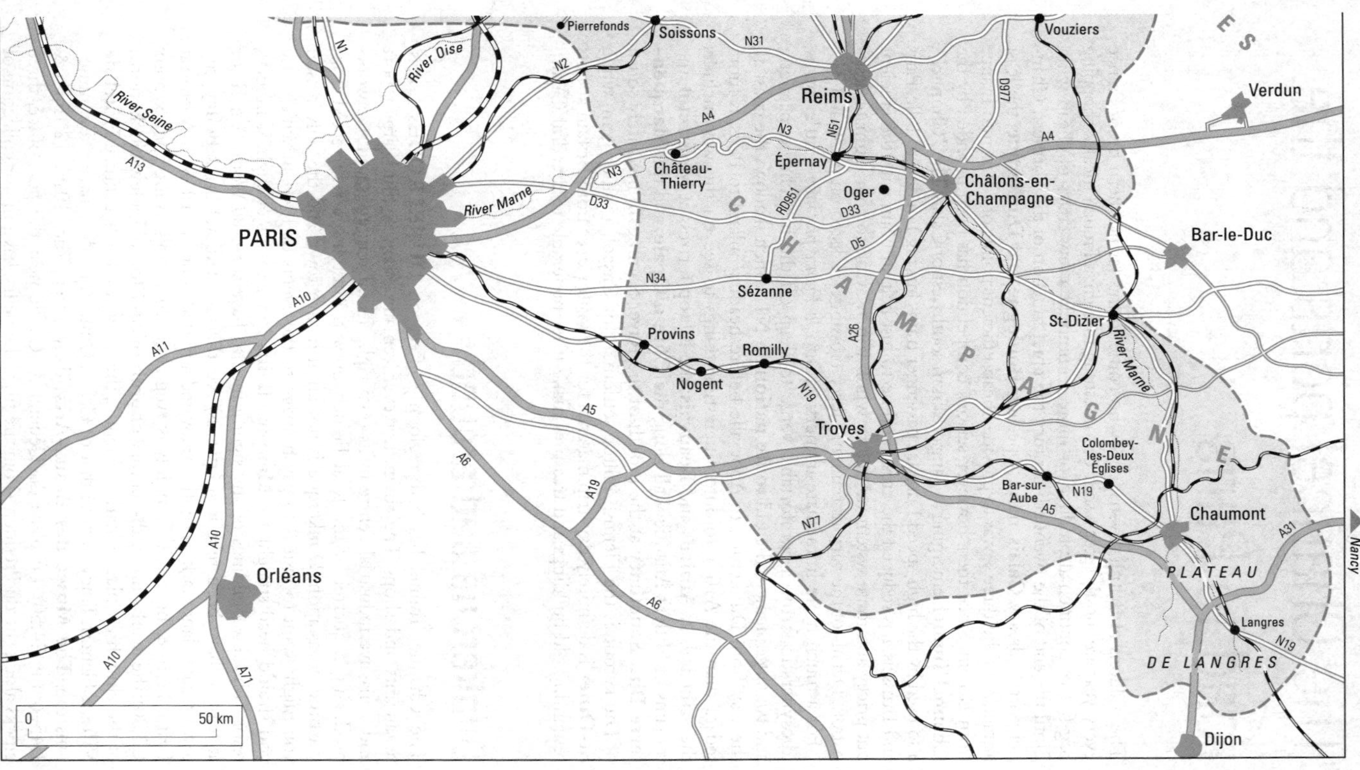
Pierrefonds
Soissons
Vouziers
Verdun
Reims
PARIS
Château-Thierry
Épernay
Oger
Châlons-en-Champagne
Bar-le-Duc
Sézanne
Provins
Nogent
Romilly
St-Dizier
Troyes
Colombey-les-Deux Églises
Bar-sur-Aube
Chaumont
Langres
Dijon
Orléans
Nancy
River Seine
River Oise
River Marne
C H A M P A G N E
PLATEAU DE LANGRES
A4
A5
A6
A10
A11
A13
A19
A26
A31
A71
N1
N2
N3
N19
N31
N34
N51
N77
D5
D33
D977
RD951
0
50 km

The Channel ports and the road to Paris

The millions of British day-trippers who come to this far northern tip of France every year are mostly after a sniff of something foreign: a French meal, a shopping bag full of continental produce, or more commonly a few crates of cheap wine. Until the end of the twentieth century the chief function of the northern Channel ports – dreary **Calais**, more appealing **Boulogne**, and **Dunkerque**, the least attractive of the three – was to provide cheap, efficient points of access into France from Britain. Since then, however, serious competition has been provided by the **Channel Tunnel**, emerging at Sangatte, 5km southwest of Calais. The "Chunnel", also used by the high-speed Eurostar passenger trains linking London to Lille, Paris and Brussels, has reduced the crossing time to just half an hour, with the efficient but pricey autoroute system waiting to whisk you away off to your ultimate destination. Details of the various train and ferry crossings are listed on pp.30 and 31.

For a much more immediate immersion into *la France profonde* – little towns, idiosyncratic farms, a comfortable verge to sleep off the first cheese, baguette and *vin rouge* picnic – the old **route nationale N1**, which shadows the coast all the way from Dunkerque to Abbeville before heading inland to Paris, is more sedate than the A16 autoroute. Interesting things to see on the way include: the cathedrals at **Amiens** and **Beauvais**; the hilltop fortress at **Montreuil**; the remains of Hitler's Atlantic Wall along the **Côte d'Opale**; and the **Marquenterre Bird Sanctuary** at the mouth of the River Somme. Immediately south of Dunkerque is the Flemish hilltop settlement of **Cassel**, a minor gem, while **St-Omer** is definitely day-trip material for the visitor over from Britain and its remaining old buildings and treasures make it far preferable to dreadful Calais.

Dunkerque and around

The Channel Tunnel has had a gloomy effect on **DUNKERQUE**'s hotels, restaurants and shops. The town, however, remains France's third largest port and a massive industrial centre in its own right, its oil refineries and steelworks producing a quarter of the total French output. Unstylishly resurrected from wartime devastation, Dunkerque is not an attractive town and the only reason you might want to visit is to pay homage to the events of 1940, in which case you should head straight for **Malo-les-Bains** is a pleasant enough, if modest, resort. The few buildings of any significance to have survived World War II (or at least to have been rebuilt afterwards) are: the tall medieval brick **belfry**, the town's chief landmark, recently renovated (guided tours: April–Sept Mon–Sat 10am, 11am & hourly 2–5pm; July & Aug also Sun & hols 11am, 2pm & 3pm; €2.80); the nearby fifteenth-century **church of St-Éloi**; and, a few blocks north of the church on place Charles-Valentin, the early twentieth-century **Hôtel de Ville**, a Flemish fancy to rival that of Calais. Dunkerque does have a few museums too. **The Musée des Beaux-Arts** (daily except Tues 10am–12.15pm & 1.45–6pm; €4.50), on place du Général-de-Gaulle near the post office, three blocks along rue du Président-Poincaré from the belfry, has a minor collection of

Dunkerque 1940

The evacuation of 350,000 Allied troops from the beaches of **Dunkerque** from May 27 to June 4, 1940, has become a wartime legend. However, the story conveniently conceals the fact that the Allies, through their own incompetence, almost lost their entire armed forces in the first few weeks of the war.

The German army had taken just ten days to reach the English Channel and could very easily have cut off the Allied armies. Unable to believe the ease with which he had overcome a numerically superior enemy, however, Hitler ordered his generals to halt their lightning advance, giving Allied forces trapped in the Pas-de-Calais enough time to organize **Operation Dynamo**, the largest wartime evacuation ever undertaken. Initially it was hoped that around 10,000 men would be saved, but thanks to low-lying cloud and the assistance of more than 1750 vessels – among them pleasure cruisers, fishing boats and river ferries – 140,000 French and more than 200,000 British soldiers were successfully shipped back to England. The heroism of the boatmen and the relief at having saved so many British soldiers were the cause of much national celebration.

In France, however, the ratio of British to French evacuees caused bitter resentment, since Churchill had promised that the two sides would go *bras dessus, bras dessous* ("arm in arm"). Meanwhile, the British media played up the "remarkable discipline" of the troops as they waited to embark, the "victory" of the RAF over the Luftwaffe and the "disintegration" of the French army all around. In fact, there was widespread indiscipline in the early stages as men fought for places on board; the battle for the skies was evenly matched; and the French fought long and hard to cover the whole operation, some 150,000 of them remaining behind to become prisoners of war. In addition, the Allies lost seven destroyers and 177 fighter planes and were forced to abandon more than 60,000 vehicles. After 1940 Dunkerque remained occupied by Germans until the bitter end of the war. It was the last French town to be liberated in 1945.

seventeenth- and eighteenth-century French, Dutch and Flemish paintings, with bits of natural history and a display on the May 1940 evacuations. The **LAAC (Lieu d'Art et Action Contemporaine)**, or Modern Art Museum (mid-May to mid-Oct: Tues, Wed & Fri 2–6.30pm; Thurs 2–8.30pm; Sat & Sun 10am–12.30pm; mid-Oct to mid-May: Tues, Wed & Fri 2–5.30pm; Thurs 2–8.30pm; Sat & Sun 10am–12.30pm & 2–5.30pm), in the middle of the sculpture park beside the canal on avenue des Bains, specializes in the period from 1950 to 1980 and features Andy Warhol, Pierre Soulages and César in its collection. More interesting, especially for children, is the **Musée Portuaire** (daily except Tues: July & Aug 10am–6pm; Sept–June 10am–12.45pm & 1.30–6pm; €4), at 9 quai de la Citadelle on the Bassin du Commerce, which illustrates the history of Dunkerque from its beginnings as a fishing hamlet, using models of boats and tools of the various trades associated with the port.

Practicalities

From Dunkerque's **gare SNCF** – where buses also stop – it's a short walk to the **tourist office** (July & Aug Mon–Sat 9.30am–6.30pm, Sun 10am–noon & 2–6pm; Sept–June Mon–Sat 9.30am–12.30pm & 1.30–6.30pm, Sun 10am–noon & 2–4pm; ⓣ03.28.66.79.21, ⓦwww.ot-dunkerque.fr) housed in the belfry itself. If you're looking to rent a **car**, there's a branch of Avis at the station (ⓣ03.28.66.67.95).

A reasonable **accommodation** option by the station on 22/27 place de la Gare is the comfortable two-star *Le Select* (ⓣ03.28.66.64.47, ⓦwww.leselect-hotel.fr.st; ❷). More salubrious hotels away from the station include the *Borel*, a

Regional food and drink

French Flanders has one of France's richest regional cuisines. Especially on the coast the **seafood** – oysters, shrimps and scallops – and **fish** – above all sole and turbot – are outstanding, while in Lille *moules-frites* are appreciated every bit as much as in neighbouring Belgium. Here, too, **beer** is the favourite drink, with pale and brown Pelforth the local brew. Traditional *estaminets* or brasseries also serve a range of dishes cooked in beer, most famously the *carbonades à la flamande*, a kind of beef stew; rabbit, chicken, game and fish may also be prepared *à la bière*. Other pot-cooked dishes include the *hochepot* (a meaty broth), *waterzooi* (chicken in a creamy sauce) and *potjevlesch* (various white meats in a rich sauce). In addition to the *boulette d'Avesnes*, the Flemish **cheese** *par excellence* is the strong-flavoured *maroilles*, used to make *flamiche*, a kind of open tart of cheese pastry, also made with leeks (*aux poireaux*). For the sweet toothed, *crêpes à la cassonade* (pancakes with muscovado sugar) are often on menus, but **waffles** (*gaufres*) are the local speciality and come in two basic varieties: the thick honeycomb type served with sugar or cream, or the wafer-like biscuit filled with jam or syrup. Charles de Gaulle, who was from Lille, was apparently particularly fond of the latter sort.

Champagne's cuisine is dominated by the famous **sparkling wine**, large quantities of which are sloshed in sauces or over sorbets. Otherwise the province's cooking is known for little apart from its **cheeses** – sharp-tasting, creamy white Chaource and orange skinned Langres – and Champagne's main contribution to French food, the **andouillette**, for which Troyes is famed. Translated euphemistically into English as "chitterling sausage", it is in actual fact an intestine crammed full of more intestines, all chopped up. An acquired taste (and texture), it's better than it sounds – look out for the notation AAAAA, a seal of approval awarded by the Association of Amateurs of the Authentic Andouillette. The **Ardennes** is another area that really lacks a distinctive repertoire (*à l'ardennaise* just means flavoured with juniper berries); game looms large on all menus, *pâté d'Ardennes* being the most famous dish.

modern three-star with well-set-up rooms overlooking the fishing boats of the Bassin du Commerce at 6 rue Hermitte (Ⓣ03.28.66.51.80, Ⓦwww.hotelborel.fr; ④), and the equally well-appointed but more old-fashioned *Europ'Hôtel*, close by at 13 rue Leughenaer (Ⓣ03.28.66.29.07, Ⓦwww.europ-hotel.com; ⑤). There's also a seafront **HI hostel** on place Paul Asseman, 2km east of the centre, practically at Malo-les-Bains (Ⓣ03.28.63.36.34; take blue bus #3 to Piscine, direction "Malo-les-Bains"; €12.20 including breakfast, plus €2.80 for sheets).

There are more enjoyable **eating** options in Malo-les-Bains, but if you're staying in Dunkerque, try *La Sirène*, 65 rue de l'Amiral-Ronarc'h, near the belfry, for good seafood (Ⓣ03.28.59.03.29; closed Sat & Sun; menus from €20); or *The Famous Tormore Pub* at 11 place Charles-Valentin near the town hall, which is better than its name suggests – it's a brasserie-cum-grill serving Flemish dishes and popular with locals (Ⓣ03.28.63.15.95; €15 or so à la carte, €12 lunch menu). At 6 quai de la Citadelle, *Le Corsaire* has menus from €25, as well as a view over the port and the *Duchesse Anne*, a 1901 German ship given to France as part of the war reparations in 1946. For a (non-alcoholic) drink, the *Café MEO'7*, at 6 Place du Beffroi, offers a wide range of organic coffees, teas and fruit juices.

Malo-les-Bains

MALO-LES-BAINS is a pleasant enough nineteenth-century seaside suburb on the east side of Dunkerque (buses #3 & #9), from whose vast sandy beach the Allied troops embarked in 1940 (see box, p.223). Digue des Alliés is the dirtier end of an extensive beachfront promenade lined with cafés and restaurants; at the cleaner end, Digue de Mer, the beach can almost seem pleasant when the sun comes out – as long as you avert your eyes from the industrial inferno to the west. However, the suburb actually reveals its *fin-de-siècle* charm away from the seafront, a few parallel blocks inland along avenue Faidherbe and its continuation avenue Kléber, with place Turenne sandwiched in between; around here you'll find some excellent patisseries, boulangeries and charcuteries.

A beachfront **campsite**, *La Licorne*, is at 1005 bd de l'Europe (ⓣ03.28.69.26.68, ⓔcampingdelalicorne@ville-dunkerque.fr). Other **places to stay** include the *Hirondelle*, 46/48 av Faidherbe (ⓣ03.28.63.17.65, ⓦwww.hotelhirondelle.com; ❹), a modern two-star in a great position; and the unassuming, less expensive *Au Bon Coin*, 49 av Kléber (ⓣ03.28.69.12.63, ⓕ03.28.69.64.03; ❸), whose cosy bar is good for a drink; both have well-regarded **restaurants** specializing in seafood with menus from around €14. Also on avenue Kléber are a few more exotic eateries, including a Vietnamese and a North African. Two popular beachfront brasseries, again focusing on seafood, are *L'Iguane*, 15 Digue des Alliés (towards Dunkerque), a down-to-earth establishment offering generous servings at €10 a *plat*, and the stylish but more expensive *Le Pavois*, at 175 Digue de Mer (menu €17).

Cassel

Barely 30km southeast of Dunkerque and just off the A25 autoroute towards Lille, is the tiny hilltop town of **CASSEL**. Hills are rare in Flanders, and consequently Cassel was much fought over from Roman times onwards. During World War I, Marshal Foch spent "some of the most distressing hours" of his life here, and it was supposedly up to the top of Cassel's hill that the "Grand Old Duke of York" marched his 10,000 men in 1793, though, as hinted at in the nursery rhyme, he failed to take the town.

Cassel boasts a very Flemish **Grand'Place**, lined with some magnificent mansions, from which narrow cobbled streets fan out to the ramparts. From the public gardens in the upper town, you have an unrivalled view over Flanders, with Belgium just 10km away. Here among the trees is eighteenth-century **Kasteel Meulen**, the last of Cassel's wooden windmills (April–Sept daily 10am–12.30pm & 2–6pm; Oct–March Sat, Sun & school hols; €2.80), which once numbered 29 across the town, pounding out flour and linseed oil for educational purposes.

Practicalities

There's no public transport into town from Cassel's **gare SNCF** (a regular service on the Dunkerque–Lille line), a full 3km west, so your own transport would come in handy. The town's useful **tourist office** is on the square (July & Aug Mon–Fri 9am–noon & 1.30–5.45pm, Sat 9am–noon & 2–5.45pm, Sun 2–6.30pm; Sept–June Mon–Fri 8.30am–noon & 1.30–5.30pm, Sat 9am–noon; ⓣ03.28.40.52.55, ⓦwww.ot-cassel.fr); they have a list of bed-and-breakfast *gîtes* and other **places to stay** in or near Cassel. An upmarket option is the very smart *Châtellerie de Schoebeque* at 32 rue Foch (ⓣ03.28.42.42.67, ⓦwww.schoebeque.com; ❾), which has fifteen individually designed rooms, and offers a free driver service in the evening to restaurants in the surrounding countryside.

On the southern side of the Grand'Place many of the cafés and restaurants have a fabulous view over the surrounding countryside, which is especially attractive on a sunny day. Of the numerous options, *La Taverne Flamande*, at no. 35 (closed Tues eve & Wed; from €16) specializes in Flemish cuisine, while *Le Sauvage*, no. 38 (☎03.28.42.40.88), is more for classic French food at similar prices. Up near the windmill at 8 rue St Nicolas, *'T Kasteel Hof* (☎03.28.40.59.29; menu €15) oozes local ambience and has a variety of beers to go with the simple cuisine, which includes a delicious *carbonade*; its popularity makes bookings advisable at weekends. Cassel is home to an annual international artisanal **beer festival** for a weekend at the end of September (☎03.28.42.45.35 or check with the tourist office for details).

Calais and around

CALAIS is less than 40km from Dover – the Channel's shortest crossing – and is by far the busiest French passenger port, though the new ferry service to Boulogne-sur-Mer (see p.232) is giving it a run for its money. The port and its accompanying petrochemical works dominate the town; in fact, there's not much else here. In World War II the British destroyed it to prevent it being used as a base for a German invasion, but the French still refer to it as "the most English town in France", an influence that began after the battle of Crécy in 1346, when Edward III seized it for use as a beachhead in the Hundred Years War. It remained in English hands for over two hundred years until 1558, when its loss caused Mary Tudor famously to say: "When I am dead and opened, you shall find Calais lying in

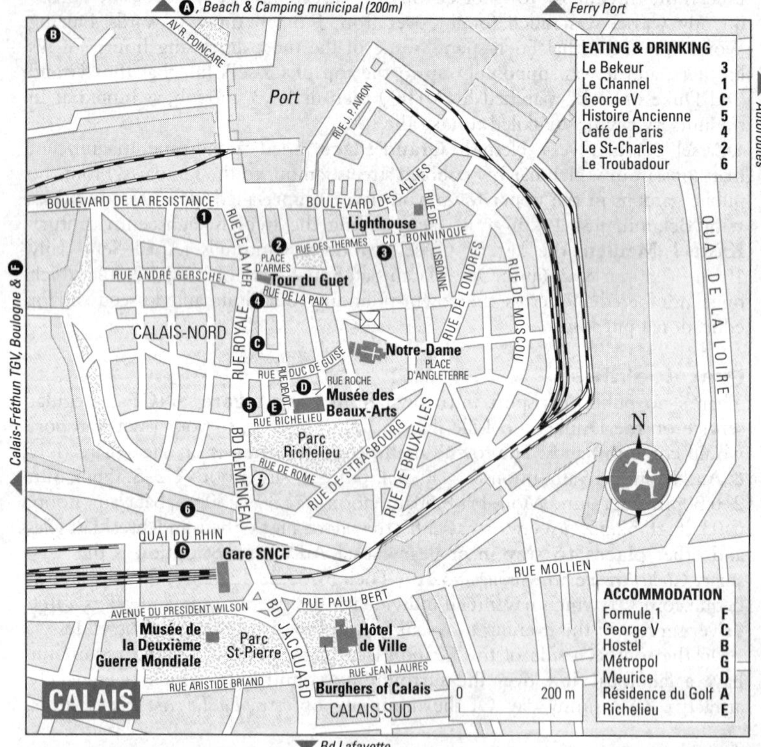

my heart." The association has been maintained by various Brits across the centuries: Lady Emma Hamilton, Lord Nelson's mistress; Oscar Wilde; Nottingham lacemakers who set up business in the early nineteenth century; and, nowadays, nine million British travellers per year, plus another million-odd day-trippers.

Arrival, information and accommodation

There's a free if infrequent daytime **bus** service from the ferry terminal to place d'Armes and the central Calais-Ville **gare SNCF**, in front of which is a **bus station**, with departures for Dunkerque, Boulogne and the out-of-city hypermarkets. To get to the outlying **gare TGV** ("Calais-Fréthun" is actually much further from Calais than the name suggests) for Eurostar trains to London and Paris, either take a bus (free on demonstration of a SNCF ticket) or one of the regular trains to Boulogne, checking first that it stops there (most do). If you're driving and intent on skipping Calais in favour of Paris, which would be understandable, take a left out of the ferry terminal – the new autoroute bypass begins almost immediately, leading to both the A26 and the N1. If you plan to **rent a car**, you could try Avis (Ⓣ03.21.34.66.50) or Budget (Ⓣ03.21.96.42.20), both located in place d'Armes and at the ferry terminal; a cheaper option, also at the ferry terminal, is National/Citer (Ⓣ03.21.34.58.45). For details of ferry crossings, see Basics.

If you decide to stay in Calais, plenty of **accommodation** is available, though it's wise to book ahead in the high season. The **tourist office** at 12 bd Clemenceau, the continuation of rue Royale (Mon–Sat 10am–1pm & 2–6.30pm; June–Sept also open Sun 10am–1pm; Ⓣ03.21.96.62.40, Ⓦwww.calais-cotedopale.com), has a free accommodation booking service as well as a list of *gîtes* in the region.

Hotels

Formule 1 av Charles-de-Gaulle, chemin de Bergnieulles, Coquelles Ⓣ08.92.68.56.85, Ⓦwww.hotelformule1.com. Just a ten-minute drive from the car ferry, this is a characterless but perfectly modern and clean option. ❷

George V 36 rue Royale Ⓣ03.21.97.68.00, Ⓦwww.legeorgev.com. Smart en-suite rooms and a traditional brasserie-restaurant. ❺

Métropol 43 quai du Rhin Ⓣ03.21.97.54.00, Ⓦwww.metropolhotel.com. Situated beside the canal right next to the train station, this is a comfortable and modern but nondescript hotel with small rooms. ❸

Meurice 5 rue Edmond-Roche Ⓣ03.21.34.57.03, Ⓦwww.hotel-meurice.fr. Comfortable three-star with a grand entrance, luxurious high beds and antique furniture in a quiet street behind the Musée des Beaux-Arts. ❺

Résidence du Golf 74 Digue G. Berthe Ⓣ03.21.96.88.99, Ⓦwww.hoteldugolf-calais.com. Neat, bright motel-style rooms which, although lacking in character, have the advantages of a kitchenette, a view of the water and proximity to both the beach and the centre of town. ❹

Richelieu 17 rue Richelieu Ⓣ03.21.34.61.60, Ⓦwww.hotelrichelieu-calais.com. Overlooking the park of the same name, this hotel has light and airy rooms, all equipped with shower, TV and toilet. ❸

Hostel and campsite

Hostel av du Maréchal-de-Lattre-de-Tassigny Ⓣ03.21.34.70.20, Ⓔadjcalais@orange.fr. Modern hostel located right at the seaward end of rue Royale, just one block from the beach. Double rooms, breakfast included. €14.50 with HI card, €16 without.

Camping municipal 26 av Raymond-Poincaré Ⓣ03.21.97.89.79. A large exposed site close to the beach, open all year. Right next door is a special short-term overnight parking area for cars; enquire at the campsite.

The Town

Calais divides in two with **Calais-Nord**, the old town rebuilt after the war with the drab place d'Armes and rue Royale as its focus, separated by canals from the sprawling "new town" or **Calais-Sud**, centred around the Hôtel de Ville and the main shopping streets, boulevards Lafayette and Jacquard – the latter named after the inventor of looms, who mechanized Calais' lacemaking industry.

Calais-Nord's charms, such as they are, soon wear thin. The **Tour du Guet**, on place d'Armes, is the only medieval building in the quarter to have survived wartime bombardment. From the Tour, rue de la Paix leads to the **church of Notre-Dame**, where Charles de Gaulle married local girl Yvonne Vendroux in 1921. Rather spuriously dubbed the only English Perpendicular church on the continent, it's not a particularly good example of the style, especially in its present state of dereliction. There is an unusual lacemaking exhibition, along with a small but interesting collection of sixteenth- to twentieth-century art, including paintings by Picasso and Dubuffet, and a Rodin sculpture, in the **Musée des Beaux-Arts et de la Dentelle** on rue Richelieu (Mon & Wed–Fri 10am–noon & 2–5.30pm, Sat 10am–noon & 2–6.30pm, Sun 2–6.30pm; €5, free Wed), which runs alongside the Parc Richelieu, at the other end of rue Royale from the place d'Armes. Continue in the other direction on rue Royale and you'll come to the city's **beach**, where the waters are chilly but swimmable, and from which on a fine day the English shore is visible; or take rue des Thermes to visit the 51-metre **lighthouse** at place Henri-Barbusse, with 271 steps to a panoramic view (June–Sept daily 10am–noon & 2–5.30pm; Oct–May Wed 2–5.30pm; €2.50).

Calais-Sud is scarcely more exciting. Just over the canal bridge, the town's landmark, the **Hôtel de Ville**, raises its belfry over 60m into the sky; this Flemish extravaganza was finished in 1926, and miraculously survived World War II. Somewhat dwarfed by the building, Rodin's famous bronze, the *Burghers of Calais*, records for ever the self-sacrifice of local dignitaries, who offered their lives to assuage the blood lust of the victor at Crécy, Edward III – only to be spared at the last minute by the intervention of Queen Philippa, Edward's wife. For a record of Calais' wartime travails you can consult the fascinating **Musée de la Deuxième Guerre Mondiale** (mid-Feb to April & Sept to mid-Nov daily except Tues 11am–5pm; May–Aug daily 10am–6pm; €6), installed in a

Shopping in Calais

For truly epic cross-the-border shopping it's best to head to the **hypermarkets**, or *grandes surfaces*, a few kilometres out of town. The best of these is the **Auchan** complex on the Boulogne road, the N1 (Mon–Sat 9am–9pm; bus #5; change given in sterling if you wish); this is closely followed by **Carrefour/Mi-Voix**, on the east side of town, on avenue Georges-Guynemer (daily 9am–9pm; bus #4). **Cité Europe**, a vast shopping complex by the Channel Tunnel terminal and just off the A16 in the direction of Boulogne (bus #7), offers you another large Carrefour (Mon–Fri 9am–10pm, Sat 8.30am–10pm) as well as high-street clothes shops and food shops (Mon–Thurs & Sat 10am–8pm, Fri 10am–9pm), all under one roof.

In Calais-Nord, **place d'Armes** and **rue Royale** are the main shopping arteries with a string of boutiques selling mainly clothes and chocolate; try La Maison du Fromage et des Vins (closed Mon & Tues but open Sun morning) for a good selection of cheeses and wine. Generally, however, the streets of Calais-Sud – particularly boulevards Jacquard and Lafayette – are a better bet. A new shopping mall or *centre commercial*, **Les 4 Boulevards** (Mon–Sat 7am–9pm), has recently opened on boulevard Jacquard and houses some thirty boutiques, many of them selling designer clothing. More colourful still are the markets around place d'Armes (Wed & Sat) and boulevard Lafayette (Thurs & Sat).

former German *Blockhaus* in the Parc St-Pierre across the street, with exhibits of uniforms, weapons and models from World War II and a small section devoted to World War I.

Eating and drinking

Calais is full of mediocre **eateries**, catering for its day-tripper trade – place d'Armes is full of such examples – and there are plenty of self-service and fast-food outlets near the beach. **Drinking** establishments are mainly of the Gaelic theme-pub variety and are in abundance on rue Royale and its continuation, rue de la Mer. *Le Troubadour* on quai du Rhin is a popular hangout for local music-heads, with lots of long hair around the games tables by day and bands by night. *Le Bekeur* is a **gay bar** close to the town centre at 40 rue de Thermes, playing French disco music for the over thirties; it opens until late and serves three-course menus from €12.

Le Channel 3 bd de la Résistance ⓣ03.21.34.42.30. Generous menus – ranging from €18 to €60 – and stylish decor. Beautifully prepared but safely unadventurous food, with a wide range of delicious desserts, and views over the yacht basin. Closed Sun eve & Tues; booking recommended.

George V 36 rue Royale ⓣ03.21.97.68.00. Brasserie-restaurant with immaculate white tablecloths and a classic menu (€22–44) or half menu (€17). Closed Sat lunch & Sun.

Histoire Ancienne 20 rue Royale ⓣ03.21.34.11.20. Greek-run brasserie with a charming interior, particularly its old bar; the good, mainly French menu includes the occasional Greek dish plus salads that will delight vegetarians. Menus from €11 for early lunch and dinner; otherwise from €17.50.

Café de Paris 72 rue Royale ⓣ03.21.34.76.84. The closest France gets to an American diner, this brasserie is popular with locals and tourists alike for its cheap fare; *plats du jour* from €9.30, menu at €12.50.

Le St-Charles 47 place d'Armes ⓣ03.21.96.02.96. By far the best option on the place d'Armes, and consequently often crowded. Menus consist of traditional French and Italian dishes and start from €11. Closed Tues and Sun eve.

Around Calais

Understandably, most tourists travel straight through the **Pas-de-Calais** – Calais' hinterland – but if you're on a short break from across the Channel, it's worth making the effort to venture inland to the likes of **St-Omer** and its surrounding World War II museums.

St-Omer

Away from the ports, the landscape becomes more rural and the roads straighter and quieter. The first stop inland for many visitors to France is **ST-OMER**, a quiet, attractive little town, 43km southeast of Calais. The Hôtel de Ville, and some of the recently restored mansions on rue Gambetta, display genuine flights of Flemish magnificence. The Gothic **Basilique Notre-Dame** (daily March–Sept 8.30am–6pm, Oct–Feb 8.30am–5pm) contains some fine statues and the fascinating **Musée de l'Hôtel Sandelin** at 14 rue Carnot (Wed–Sun 10am–noon & 2–6pm; €4.50) is worth a stop. The decor and artwork of each room is representative of a certain period and country, with some fine furniture, sculpture, and remarkable French, Dutch and Flemish paintings, all meticulously laid out. In the Flemish room you'll find a Breugel, while in the next room are two works by his son. The museum also contains some of the finest decorative art in France, including a glorious piece of medieval goldsmithing known as the *Pied de Croix de St-Bertin*.

It's also worth visiting the pleasant **public gardens** to the west of town and you can explore the nearby **marais**, a network of Flemish waterways cut between plots of land on reclaimed marshes east of town along the river. Boat trips, or *bateaux-promenade*, run by Isnor Location (Ⓣ03.21.39.15.15, Ⓦwww.isnor.fr) leave from the church in nearby Clairmarais (July & Aug daily 11am & hourly 2–5pm; Sept–June Sat & Sun hourly 2–5pm; €6.20). Round trips take about an hour, and include a commentary in French on the flora and fauna of the marshes, while longer trips also include a ride down the unique vertical boat-lift at Arques. For further information, including times, plus details of kayak and canoe rental, contact the tourist office (see below).

Practicalities

To get to the centre of town from the exuberant 1903 **gare SNCF**, cross over the canal and walk for ten minutes down rue F.-Ringot, past the post office and into rue Carnot. The **tourist office** is in the western end of town near the park at 4 rue Lion d'Or (Easter–Sept Mon–Sat 9am–6pm, Sun 10am–1pm; Oct–Easter Mon–Sat 9am–12.30pm & 2–6pm; Ⓣ03.21.98.08.51, Ⓦwww.tourisme-saintomer.com).

For **accommodation**, try the pretty, old, *Hôtel St-Louis* at 25 rue d'Arras (Ⓣ03.21.38.35.21, Ⓦwww.hotel-saintlouis.com; ❸; *Le Flaubert* restaurant from €16); the *Bretagne*, 2 place du Vainquai, near the train station (Ⓣ03.21.38.25.78, Ⓦwww.hotellebretagne.com; ❹; *Le Vainquai* restaurant from €18), or the *Au Vivier*, 22 rue Louis-Martel, on a small pedestrian street near the town hall (Ⓣ03.21.95.76.00, Ⓔlevivier@orange.fr; ❸; closed beginning of Jan), whose restaurant specializes in fish (closed Sun, menus from €16). The closest **campsite** is *Le Clair Marais* on rue du Romelaër near the Forêt de Clairmarais, 4.5km east of St-Omer (Ⓣ03.21.38.34.80, Ⓕ03.21.98.37.05; April–Oct), although there's no transport out there. For **places to eat** other than the hotels, try the establishments around place Maréchal-Foch: *Les Trois Caves*, at no. 18 has the best reputation and specializes in local dishes (menu €24; Ⓣ03.21.39.72.52; closed Mon lunch).

The Blockhaus at Eperlecques

In the Forêt d'Eperlecques, 12km north of St-Omer off the D300, you can visit the largest ever **Blockhaus**, or concrete bunker, built in 1943–44 by the Germans – or rather by 6000 of their half-starved prisoners of war (daily: March 2.15–6pm; April & Oct 10am–noon & 2.15–6pm; May–Sept 10am–7pm; Nov 2.15–5pm; €7, or dual ticket with La Coupole €13). It was designed to launch V2 rockets against London, but fortunately the RAF and French Resistance prevented it ever being ready for use by bombing it during construction – unfortunately killing many of the Allied prisoners at the same time. As well as the Blockhaus, you will also see remnants of many weapons that were used to attack (or were built with the purpose of attacking) London, including a 45-metre ramp for launching V1 rockets.

The Blockhaus is hard to reach without your own transport: it's a four-kilometre walk from the station at Watten, on the eastern edge of the forest, to which there are several trains daily from Calais.

La Coupole

Of all the converted World War II bunker museums, **La Coupole** (daily: July & Aug 10am–7pm; Sept–June 9am–6pm; closed for two weeks over Christmas and New Year; Ⓦwww.lacoupole.com; €9), 5km southwest of St-Omer, is the most modern and stimulating. As you walk around the site of an intended V2 rocket launch pad, you can listen on multilingual infrared headphones to a discussion of the occupation of northern France by the Nazis, the use of prisoners as slave labour, and the technology and ethics of the first liquid-fuelled rocket – advanced by Hitler and taken at the end of the war by the Soviets, the French and the Americans and developed in the space race. Visits last two and a half hours: films, models and photographs, all with accompanying text in four different languages, help to develop each theme. Getting there by car is easy: it's just off the D928 (A26 junctions 3 & 4), but there are only a few buses running from St-Omer train station (ring La Coupole or St-Omer tourist office for times).

The Côte d'Opale

The **Côte d'Opale** is the stretch of Channel coast between Calais and the mouth of the River Somme, characterized by huge, wild and windswept sandy beaches more attractive than anything to be found in any of the port cities. In the northern part, as far as Boulogne, the beaches are fringed, as on the English side of the Channel, by white chalk cliffs. Here, between the prominent headlands of **Cap Blanc-Nez** and **Cap Gris-Nez**, the D940 coast road winds high above the sea, allowing you to appreciate the "opal" in the name – the sea and sky merging in an opalescent, oyster-grey continuum. The southern part of the coast is flatter, and the beach, uninterrupted for 40km, is backed by a landscape of pine-anchored dunes and brackish tarns, punctuated every few hundred metres by solid German pillboxes now toppled on their noses by the shifting sand foundations. An organization called **Eden 62** publishes ten free leaflets detailing walks around the area (Ⓣ03.21.32.13.74, Ⓦwww.eden62.fr). It also offers six guided nature walks per month.

South from Calais: the Channel Tunnel and Wissant

Right on the southern outskirts of Calais, **Blériot-Plage** was thus named to commemorate Louis Blériot's epic first cross-Channel flight in 1909. Six kilometres further along the foreshore of well-conserved dunes, by the dreary village of Sangatte, the Channel Tunnel comes ashore; the actual terminal is 5km to the east outside the village of Fréthun. Thereafter, the D940 winds up onto the grassy windswept heights of **Cap Blanc-Nez**, topped by an obelisk commemorating the Dover Patrol, who kept the Channel free from U-boats during World War I. Just off the D940, opposite the turn-off to the Cap Blanc-Nez obelisk, is the **Musée du Transmanche** (April–June & Sept Tues–Sun 2–6pm; July & Aug daily 10am–6pm; €3.80), which offers an overall history of Channel Tunnel exploits; the museum is housed in the basement of *Le Thomé du Gamond*, a rather pricey restaurant with panoramic views (open all year from noon; menus from €15). From here, 130m above sea level, you can spot the Channel craft plying the water to the north, while to the south you look down on Wissant and its enormous beach between the capes from which Julius Caesar set sail in 55 BC for a first look at Britain. Before arriving in Wissant, you pass through the small beachside town of **Escalles**, where you can stay at the clean, modern, and appropriately named *Escale* (Ⓣ03.21.85.25.00, Ⓦwww.hotel-lescale.com; ❸; restaurant from €14).

WISSANT itself is a small and quietly attractive place, popular out of season with windsurfers and weekending Britons. The **tourist office** (May–Sept Mon–Sat 9am–noon & 2–6pm, Sun 10am–1pm & 3–6pm; Oct–April Mon–Sat 9am–noon & 2–6pm; Ⓣ03.21.82.48.00, Ⓦwww.ville-wissant.fr) is on place de la Mairie. The **hotels** here are expensive, which is not surprising given their proximity to the sea. First and foremost is the old, red-timbered *Hôtel de la Plage*, 1 place Edouard-Houssen (ⓣ03.21.35.91.87, ⓦwww.hotelplage-wissant.com; ❸; good restaurant from €14), whose rooms are arranged around a wide courtyard. Alternatively, the two-star *Bellevue*, 10 rue P. Crampel, is less expensive than some of the one-stars in town (ⓣ03.21.35.91.87, ⓦwww.wissant-hotel-bellevue.com; ❸). Wissant also has a **campsite**, *La Source* (ⓣ03.21.35.92.46; closed mid-Nov to March). The best place to **eat** in town is *L'Auberge de l'Amiral Benbow*, 7 rue Gambetta, where you can feast on oysters and *filet mignon* in the meticulously decorated rooms of an old house (menus from €25; ⓣ03.21.35.90.07, reserve; closed Jan & open Sat & Sun only in off season).

To Cap Gris-Nez and the Blockhaus at Audinghen

The GR du Littoral footpath passes through Wissant and continues up to **Cap Gris-Nez**, just 28km from the English coast. To get to the cape by road, take the turn-off north 1km outside **AUDINGHEN**, from which it's another three kilometres. Just after the Cap Gris-Nez turn-off beside the D940 is one of the many massive concrete **Blockhäuser** that stud the length of the Côte d'Opale though those with a real interest in the subject should visit the Blockhaus at Eperlecques (see p.230). The remainder of the drive along the D940 towards Boulogne-sur-Mer is lined with beautiful and undeveloped dunes with frequent turn-offs for **walking paths** to the shore, each of which is tempting on a fine day.

Boulogne-sur-Mer

BOULOGNE-SUR-MER is the most pleasant of the channel ports and although the **ville basse** is pretty unprepossessing, rising above the lower town is an attractive medieval quarter, the **ville haute**, contained within the old town walls and dominated by a grand, domed basilica that apes St Paul's in London. The basilica is a metaphor for the town itself, once grand but now in need of serious renovation.

Shopping in Boulogne

For the serious **hypermarkets**, catch bus #20 for the Leclerc or bus #8 for the huge Auchan complex, 8km along the N42 towards St-Omer – certainly the most convenient place for large-scale food and wine shopping. More fastidious foodies should stay in town and head for the **Grande-Rue** and streets leading off it, but be aware that most are closed all day Monday. For charcuterie, locals' favourite Bourgeois is at 1 Grande-Rue; for chocolates and other goodies, head for Timmerman at no. 40. Check out the fabulous fish displays at Aux Pêcheurs d'Étaples, at no. 31; you can also sample the seafood at the brasserie tucked behind. A shop definitely not to be missed is Philippe Olivier's famous *fromagerie*, just around the corner at 43 rue Thiers, which has a selection of over two hundred cheeses in various states of maturation. To go with it you'll find a great choice of wines at Les Vins de France, 10 rue Nationale, but for buying wine in bulk try Le Chais at 49 rue des Deux-Ponts, in the Bréquerecque district by the train station. On Wednesday and Saturday mornings place Dalton hosts a **market**, or for basic groceries and a cheap cafeteria head for the Centre Commercial Liane on the corner of boulevards Diderot and Daunou.

Arrival, information and accommodation

It is only a fifteen-minute walk across the river from the **ferry terminal** into town, though currently the service is not open to foot passengers; there is no bus service. The centre is a ten-minute walk from the **gare SNCF** (Boulogne-Ville), down boulevard Voltaire then right along boulevard Diderot. The **tourist office** (July & Aug Mon–Sat 9am–7pm, Sun 10.15am–1.15pm & 3–6pm; Sept–June Mon–Sat 9am–12.30pm & 1.30–6.30pm, Sun 10.15am–1.15pm; ⓣ03.21.10.88.10, ⓦwww.tourisme-boulognesurmer.com), at Pont Marguet, can advise on rooms – which, in summer, get taken early. There's plenty of inexpensive **accommodation** in Boulogne, plus a couple of upmarket places around the centre.

Hotels

Enclos de L'Evêché 6 rue de Pressy ⓣ03.91.90.05.90, ⓦwww.enclosdeleveche.com. Five individually designed rooms, in a fine town house in the heart of the medieval *ville haute*. 7

Faidherbe 12 rue Faidherbe ⓣ03.21.31.60.93, ⓕ03.21.87.01.14. Great value two-star near the water and shops, with elegant rooms and friendly proprietors. 3

Hamiot 1 rue Faidherbe at corner with bd Gambetta ⓣ03.21.31.44.20, ⓦwww.hotelhamiot.com. Harbour-side hotel over a popular bistro. The recently renovated rooms have bath and double-glazing. 4

La Matelote 70 bd Ste-Beuve ⓣ03.21.30.33.33, ⓦwww.la-matelote.com. Very smart rooms in a row of converted town houses along from the famed restaurant; minibar, a/c, cable TV and tasteful decor in all rooms. 6

Le Metropole 51 rue Thiers ⓣ03.21.31.54.30, ⓦwww.hotel-metropole-boulogne.com. A plush three-star with spacious rooms in the middle of a fashionable street; central but not noisy. 5

Hostel and campsite

Camping municipal *Les Sapins*, at La Capelle-lès-Boulogne, near the Auchan centre on the N42 ⓣ03.21.83.16.61. Closed mid-Sept to mid-April.

Hostel (HI) place Rouget-de-l'Îsle ⓣ03.21.99.15.30, ⓔboulogne-sur-mer@fuaj.org, opposite the *gare SNCF* in the middle of a housing estate. Friendly hostel with rooms for three to four people at €15.50 per person, breakfast included; €2.90 extra for non-members. En-suite double rooms 1.

The Town

Boulogne's number one attraction – and one of the most visited in northern France – is the Centre National de la Mer, or **Nausicaá**, on boulevard Ste-Beuve (daily: July & Aug 9.30am–7.30pm; Sept–June 9.30am–6.30pm, closed for 3 weeks in Jan; Ⓦwww.nausicaa.fr; €9.50–12.50, depending on time of year), though in May and June all of the floors are crawling with French and British school groups, and you may find it best to stay away altogether. With ultraviolet lighting and New Age music creating a suitably weird ambience, you wander from tank to tank while hammerhead sharks circle overhead, a shoal of tuna lurks in a diamond-shaped aquarium, and giant conger eels conceal themselves in rusty pipes. Compared with the startling colours of the tropical fish and the clownish antics of the sea lions at feeding time, some of the educational stuff (in French and English throughout – one in five visitors is British) is rather dull. Although little over a decade old, it's all beginning to look a bit tired and dated, though the 3D film show goes some way to alleviating the boredom. Environmental issues are touched on in some of the display materials but, perhaps, too timidly for some tastes. As you'd expect in France, the sea as a source of food is given a high level of importance – witness the chic *Bistrot de la Mer* where you can sample suitably fresh fish and wine, the latter probably a necessity for those adults who have lost their children several times in the labyrinthine five-storey layout.

The quiet cobbled streets of the **ville haute**, southeast of Nausicaá and uphill, make a pleasant respite from the noise and drabness of the *ville basse*. The most impressive sight here is the **medieval walls** themselves, which are decked out with rose beds, gravel paths and benches for picnicking, and provide impressive views of the city below; it takes about 45 minutes to complete the walk around them. Within the square walls, the domed **Basilique Notre-Dame** (summer 9am–noon & 2–6pm; winter 10am–noon 2–5pm) is an odd building – raised in the nineteenth century by the town's vicar without any architectural knowledge or advice – yet it seems to work. In the vast **crypt** (Tues–Sun 2–5pm; €2) you

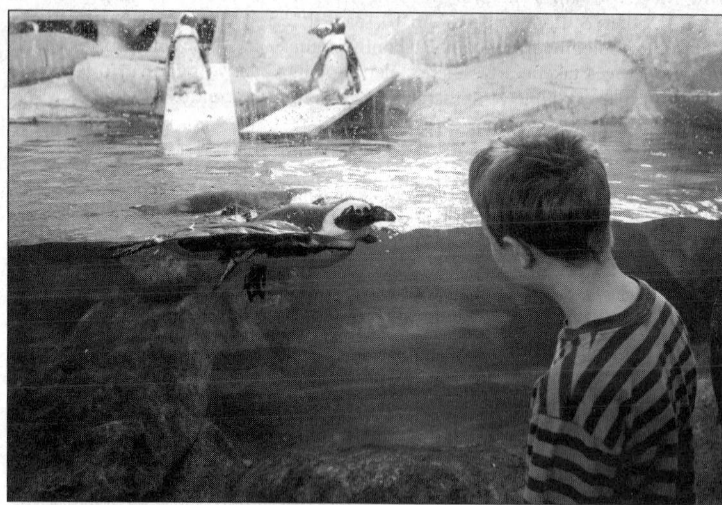

△Nausicaá, Boulogne

can see frescoed remains of the Romanesque building and relics of a Roman temple to Diana. In the main part of the church sits a bizarre white statue of the Virgin and Child on a boat-chariot, drawn here on its own wheels from Lourdes over the course of six years during a pilgrimage in the 1940s.

Nearby, the **Château Musée** (July & Aug Mon & Wed–Sat 10am–5pm, Sun 10am–5.30pm; Sept–June Mon & Wed–Sat 10am–12.30pm & 2–5pm, Sun 10am–12.30pm & 2–5.30pm; closed 3 weeks in Jan; €3.50) contains Egyptian funerary objects donated by a local-born Egyptologist, an unusual set of Eskimo masks and a sizeable collection of Greek pots. A short walk down the main tourist street, **rue de Lille**, will bring you to the **Hôtel de Ville**, whose twelfth-century belfry is the most ancient monument in the old town, but is only accessible by arranging a guided tour with the tourist office.

Three kilometres north of Boulogne on the N1 stands the **Colonne de la Grande Armée** where, in 1803, Napoleon is said to have changed his mind about invading Britain and turned his troops east towards Austria. The column was originally topped by a bronze figure of Napoleon symbolically clad in Roman garb – though his head, equally symbolically, was shot off by the British navy during World War II. It's now displayed in the Château Musée (see above).

Eating and drinking

As you might expect from a large fishing port, Boulogne is a good spot to **eat** fresh fish and seafood. With dozens of possibilities for eating around place Dalton and the *ville haute* (mostly the rue de Lille) bear in mind the day-tripper trade and be selective. If you're just after a **drink**, there is a concentration of bars in place Godefroy-de-Bouillon, opposite the Hôtel de Ville, and a raft of lively bars in place Dalton, with *Au Bureau* and the *Welsh Pub* being the most popular.

L'Étoile de Marrakech 228 rue Nationale. A friendly and well-regarded Moroccan restaurant; olives, bread and spicy sausage come as complimentary starters, and the servings of couscous (from €11) are incredibly generous. Closed Wed.

Bar Hamiot 1 rue Faidherbe. Under the hotel of the same name, this brasserie remains as popular as ever with locals and tourists alike, offering a large range of dishes from €7 omelettes and €10–16 fish dishes to €14–19 menus.

Chez Jules 8 place Dalton ⓣ03.21.31.54.12. On the square of the *ville basse* and a great place to watch the Wednesday and Saturday markets. Typical brasserie fare with menus from €23.

La Matelote 80 bd Ste-Beuve ⓣ03.21.30.17.97. The best restaurant near the water, located opposite Nausicaá, featuring a *dégustation* menu at €60. If you'd rather not spend that much, you could go for the €30 menu or à la carte fish from €19. Loving care is taken over the food and service, but it's not especially creative and rather snooty. Closed Sun eve.

La Poivrière 15 rue de Lille ⓣ03.21.80.18.18. Set in a parade of rather mediocre eateries in the prettiest part of the *haute ville*, offering traditional French cuisine starting with a very reasonable €15 menu. Closed Tues & Wed.

Les Terrasses de l'Enclos 2 Enclos de l'Evêché ⓣ03.91.90.05.90 is the smartest restaurant in the *ville haute* and probably the whole area. Having no freezer, the restaurant focuses on freshness, with an excellent seafood menu. Menus from €19.50. Closed Sun eve & Tues.

South to Amiens

South of Boulogne the coast is as wild and magnificent as the Côte d'Opale but without your own transport it's hard to get down to the beach: a band of unstable dunes forces the D940 coast road and the Calais–Paris railway to keep a few kilometres inland. With the exception of **Étaples**, the seaside towns are artificial resorts of twentieth-century creation – only of interest in that they provide access to the beach. That, however, really is worth getting to, and its eerie beauty is best experienced by walking the coastal GR path or any one of the several marked trails that the local tourist offices promote, or by visiting the **Marquenterre Bird Sanctuary**. For car-drivers, the D119 between Boulogne and just north of Dannes is closer to the water with turn-offs directly into the dunes.

The quickest route south is the A16 Boulogne–Abbeville autoroute, which continues all the way to Paris. More interesting, if you want to take in the battlefield of **Agincourt**, is a winding cross-country route exploring some of the English-looking side valleys on the north side of the River Canche – such as the Crequoise, Planquette and Ternoise – whose farms and hamlets have been largely bypassed by the onward march of French modernity. For more information on the region consult Ⓦwww.somme-tourisme.com.

Le Touquet and around

Situated among dunes and wind-flattened tamarisks and pines, **LE TOUQUET** (officially called Le Touquet-Paris-Plage) is a kind of French Hollywood on the Channel coast, with ambitious villas freed from the discipline of architectural fashion hidden away behind its trees. Now dully suburban, the town was the height of fashion in the 1920s and 1930s and for a spell after World War II, ranking alongside places on the Côte d'Azur. An affordable treat worth indulging in – especially if you've got kids – is Le Touquet's **Aqualud** swimming complex right on the beach (July & Aug €14.50, Sept–June €11.50), which boasts three giant water slides and a series of indoor and outdoor themed pools; there's also the vast **Bagatelle** amusement park, 10km south of town on the D940 (April to mid-Sept daily 10am–7pm; €19).

Practicalities

To get to Le Touquet, take the train from Boulogne to Étaples, from where a local bus covers the last four kilometres. Alternatively, you can take a bus (Mon–Sat only) directly from Boulogne (Ⓣ03.21.83.88.52 in Boulogne or Ⓣ03.21.05.09.43 in Le Touquet for times) from outside the ANPE office on boulevard Daunou; the bus heads on down the coast through Le Touquet to Berck-sur-Mer. Le Touquet's **tourist office** is in the Palais de l'Europe on place de l'Hermitage (Mon–Sat 9am–7pm, Sun 10am–6pm; Ⓣ03.21.06.72.00, Ⓦwww.letouquet.com), and can furnish you with a free map of the town.

If you're looking for somewhere reasonable to **stay**, try the hostel *Riva Bella* just 30m from the sandy beach at 12 rue Léon-Garet (Ⓣ03.21.05.08.22, Ⓦwww.rivabella-touquet.com; €15–23), or the two-star *Armide*, 56 rue Léon-Garet (Ⓣ03.21.05.21.76, Ⓕ03.21.05.97.77; half-board ③). If you fancy splashing out, you have the choice of several luxurious hotels, including the palatial *Le Manoir* on avenue du Golf (Ⓣ03.21.06.28.28, Ⓦwww.opengolfclub.com/mnh; ⑧) and *Le Westminster*, 5 av du Verger (Ⓣ03.21.05.48.48, Ⓦwww.westminster.fr; ⑧). There's also a **caravan site**, the *Stoneham* (Ⓣ03.21.05.16.55, Ⓕ03.21.05.06.48; closed late Nov to early Feb), on avenue François-Godin, 1km from the centre and 1km from the beach.

Places to **eat** are also generally expensive in Le Touquet. For a treat, visit *Le Café des Arts*, 80 rue de Paris, which specializes in fish dishes (menus from €16; Ⓣ03.21.05.21.55; closed Tues & Wed), or for more traditional cuisine try the *Auberge de la Dune aux Loups* on the avenue of the same name (menus from €20; Ⓣ03.21.05.42.54; closed Tues eve & Wed), where you can eat traditional French cuisine on the terrace. Less expensive than these is *Les Sports*, 22 rue St-Jean (ⓣ03.21.05.05.22), a classic brasserie with a menu at €15.

Étaples

On the other side of the River Canche is the much more workaday **ÉTAPLES**, a picturesque fishing port whose charm lies in its relaxed air. Between April and September **boat trips** departing from the port can be booked via the **tourist office** (Mon–Fri 9am–noon & 2–6pm, Sat 10am–noon & 3–6pm; ⓣ03.21.09.56.94) at Le Clos St-Victor on boulevard Bigot-Descelers. You can choose between a fifty-minute sea jaunt (€7) and a more rigorous twelve-hour fishing stint with experienced fishermen (€50). Étaples also boasts a good seafood **restaurant**, *Aux Pêcheurs d'Étaples*, situated upstairs from the bustling and well-stocked **fish market** on quai de la Canche (from €13; ⓣ03.21.94.06.90).

Montreuil-sur-Mer

Once a port, **MONTREUIL-SUR-MER** is now stranded 13km inland from the sea, owing to the silting up of the River Canche. Perched on a sharp little hilltop above the river and surrounded by ancient walls, it's an immediately appealing place. Quite compact, it's easily walkable, with its hilltop ramparts offering amazing views. Laurence Sterne spent a night here on his *Sentimental Journey*, and it was the scene of much of the action in Victor Hugo's *Les Misérables*, perhaps best evoked by the steep cobbled street of pavée St-Firmin, first left after the Porte de Boulogne, a short climb from the *gare SNCF*.

Two heavily damaged Gothic churches grace the main square: the **church of St-Saulve** and a tiny wood-panelled **chapelle** tucked into the side of the red-brick hospital, now a three-star hotel (see p.238). To the south there are numerous cobbled lanes to wander down, all lined with half-timbered artisan houses. In the northwestern corner of the walls lies Vauban's **Citadelle** (March to mid-Dec daily 10am–noon & 2–6pm; €2.50) – ruined, overgrown and, after dark, pretty atmospheric, with subterranean gun emplacements and a fourteenth-century tower that records the coats of arms of the French noblemen killed at Agincourt. A path following the top of the walls provides views out across the Canche estuary.

In the second half of August, Montreuil puts on a surprisingly lively mini-arts **festival** of opera, theatre and dance, Les Malins Plaisirs, while between September and June the theatre/cinema Passerelles (ⓣ03.21.81.57.78) on place St-Walloy puts on plays and dances, and shows old movies, with a special festival in May.

Practicalities

The **tourist office** is by the citadelle at 21 rue Carnot (April–Sept Mon–Sat 9.30am–12.30pm & 2–6pm, Sun 10am–1pm & 3–5pm; Oct–March Mon–Sat 9.30am–12.30pm & 2–5.30pm, Sun 10am–1pm; ⓣ03.21.06.04.27). For an **accommodation** treat, there's the classy and expensive *Château de Montreuil* (ⓣ03.21.81.53.04, ⓦwww.chateaudemontreuil.com; ❾; closed mid-Dec to Jan), which overlooks the citadelle and is popular with the English. It contains a top-class restaurant (closed Mon and out of season for lunch on Thurs), whose lunchtime menu is good value at €38. For delightful food and accommodation at more manageable prices, there's no beating *Le Darnétal*, in place Darnétal (ⓣ03.21.06.04.87; ❷; closed Mon eve, Tues & first two weeks in

July; restaurant from €18). Another good bet is the *Clos des Capucins* on the wide place de Gaulle, the shopping centre of the town (Ⓣ03.21.06.08.65, Ⓔclos-des-capucins@orange.fr; ❸; menu from €15). The former Hôtel Dieu on the main square now houses a large upmarket hotel, the *Hermitage* (Ⓣ03.21.06.74.74, Ⓦwww.hermitage-montreuil.com; ❺), with friendly and accommodating service and spacious if corporate-style rooms. There's also a newly renovated **HI hostel** (Ⓣ03.21.06.10.83; closed Nov–Feb; €7.70, plus extra for sheets and breakfast; reception open 2–6pm only), housed in one of the citadelle's outbuildings and giving access to the place long after the gates have been closed to the public. There's also a **campsite**, *La Fontaine des Clercs*, (Ⓣ03.21.06.07.28, Ⓕ03.21.86.15.10; open all year) below the walls, by the Canche on rue d'Église.

The Agincourt and Crécy battlefields

Agincourt and Crécy, two of the bloodiest Anglo–French battles of the Middle Ages, took place near the attractive little town of **HESDIN** on the River Canche (a town that will be familiar to Simenon fans from the TV series *Inspector Maigret*). Getting to either site is difficult without your own transport.

Twenty kilometres southwest of Hesdin, at the **Battle of Crécy**, Edward III inflicted the first of his many defeats of the French in 1346. This was the first appearance on the continent of the new English weapon, the six-foot longbow, and the first use in European history of gunpowder. There's not a lot to see today: just the **Moulin Édouard III** (now a watchtower), 1km northeast of the little town of **Crécy-en-Ponthieu** on the D111 to Wadicourt, site of the windmill from which Edward watched the hurly-burly of battle. Further south, on the D56 to Fontaine, the battered **croix de Bohème** marks the place where King John of Bohemia – fighting for the French – died, having insisted on leading his men into the fight in spite of his blindness.

Ten thousand more died in the heaviest defeat ever of France's feudal knighthood at the **Battle of Agincourt** on October 25, 1415. Forced by muddy conditions to fight on foot in their heavy armour, the French, though more than three times as strong in number, were sitting ducks to the lighter, mobile English archers. The rout took place near present-day **AZINCOURT**, about 12km northeast of Hesdin off the D928, and a colourful well-organized museum in the village, the **Centre Historique Médiéval Azincourt** (April–June & Sept–Oct daily 10am–6pm; July–Aug daily 9.30am–6.30pm; Nov–March daily 10am–5pm; €6.50) includes a short film about the battle. On the battle site itself notice boards are placed at strategic points to indicate the sequence of fighting. Just east of the village, by the crossroads of the D104 and the road to Maisoncelle, a cross marks the position of the original grave pits.

The Marquenterre Bird Sanctuary and around

Even if you know nothing about birds, the **Parc ornithologique du Marquenterre** (daily: Feb, March & Oct to mid-Nov 10am–6pm; April–Sept 10am–7.30pm; mid-Nov to Jan 10am–5pm; Ⓦwww.parcdumarquenterre.com; €9.90), situated 30km south of Étaples off the D940 between the estuaries of the rivers Canche and Somme, will still be a revelation. In terms of landscape, it's beautiful and strange: all dunes, tamarisks and pine forest, full of salty meres and ponds thick with water plants. This is "new" land, formed by the erosion of the Normandy coast and the silting of the Somme estuary, where thousands of cattle are grazed today to give their meat the much-prized flavour of the "salt meadows". One of only two bird sanctuaries in the whole of France, Marquenterre is a reserve in an area not known for valuing the fowl that pass through each year – though protected inside the park's tiny boundaries, almost all species are prey to local hunters, and between September and January the sound of gunshot is common.

Binoculars can be hired (€3.50); otherwise you can rely on the guides posted at some of the observation huts, who set up portable telescopes and will tell you about the nesting birds. Once inside, there's a choice of three itineraries – two longer, more interesting walks (2–3hr) and a shorter one (roughly 1hr 30min). The routes take you from resting area to resting area from where you can train your field glasses on dozens of species – ducks, geese, oyster-catchers, terns, egrets, redshanks, greenshanks, spoonbills, herons, storks, godwits – some of them residents, most taking a breather from their epic migratory flights. In April and May they head north, returning from the end of August to October, while in early summer the young nesting chicks can be seen learning to find food under the sharp eyes of their mothers.

Keen natural historians might also want to drop into the **Maison de l'Oiseau** on the other side of the bay, between St-Valéry-sur-Somme and Cayeux-sur-Mer, which has a display of stuffed birds, as well as live demonstrations with birds of prey (daily: April–Sept 10am–6pm; Oct–March 10am–5pm; ⓣ03.22.26.93.93 ⓦwww.maisondeloiseau.com; €6.20).

The nearest town of any size is **RUE**, 5km east of Marquenterre, one of a number of attractive former fishing villages in the area now stranded inland by the silting up of the Somme. It's worth a halt for the splendid Gothic vaulting and facade of the **Chapelle du St-Esprit** (April–Oct daily 9.30am–5.30pm). The best place to **eat** is the *Lion d'Or* on rue Barrière (menus €13–29; ⓣ03.22.25.74.18, ⓕ03.22.25.66.63; closed Sun eve & all day Mon); it also has simple **rooms** (❸). Only 7km to the south, near the tiny hamlet of **FAVIÈRES**, you'll find one of the area's finest restaurants, the *Clé des Champs* on place des Frères-Caudron (menus €13–37; ⓣ03.22.27.88.00); excellent country cooking is served in a beautiful white farmhouse, its walls decorated with plates and copper pans.

The Somme estuary

After Rue, the D940 meanders through yet more dry fishing hamlets, whose crouching cottages are reminders of their former poverty. Some, like **LE CROTOY**, have enough sea still to attract the yachties, and are enjoying the second-home boom. Le Crotoy's south-facing beach has attracted numerous writers and painters over the years: Jules Verne wrote *Twenty Thousand Leagues under the Sea* here, and Colette, Toulouse-Lautrec and Seurat were also frequent visitors. For **accommodation**, try the seaside *Hotel Les Tourelles*, 2–4 rue Pierre-Guerlain (ⓣ03.22.27.16.33, ⓦwww.lestourelles.com; ❹); or, for bed and breakfast in town, the *Les Abris-Côtiers* (ⓣ03.22.27.0945, ⓦwww.abris-cotiers.com; ❸) or *La Villa Marine*, 14 rue du Phare (ⓣ03.22.37.84.56, ⓦwww.villamarine.com; ❹).

At the mouth of the bay lies **ST-VALÉRY-SUR-SOMME**, accessible in summer by a **steam train** (Easter–June & Sept to mid-Oct Wed, Sat & Sun; July & Aug daily; ⓦwww.chemin-fer-baie-somme.asso.fr; €7–14) from Le Crotoy and Noyelles, and by two buses a day from Noyelles. This is the place from which William, Duke of Normandy, set sail to conquer England in 1066. With its walled and gated medieval citadelle still intact and its brightly painted quays,

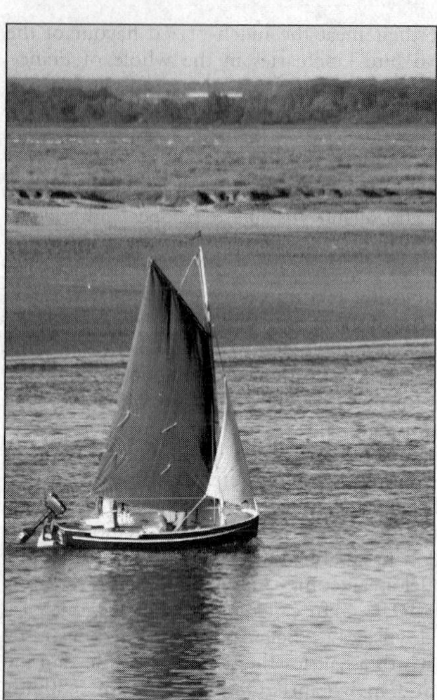

△ Boat at St-Valéry-sur-Somme

free of modern development, looking out over mud flats and tilting boats, St-Valéry is the jewel of the coast. The only notable sight is the **Écomusée Picarvie** at 5 quai du Romerel (April–Sept Mon & Wed–Sun 2–6.30pm; July & Aug also open Tues; €5), with its interesting collection of tools and artefacts relating to vanished trades and ways of life. Otherwise, there are plenty of **activities**, including boat trips from €9 (ⓣ03.22.60.74.68), cycling (bikes can be rented from €10; ⓣ03.22.26.96.80) and guided walks (ⓣ03.22.26.92.30). Digging for shellfish is also popular, but you have to be extremely careful about the tide. When it's high it reaches up to the quays, but withdraws 14km at low tide, creating a dangerous current; equally, it returns very suddenly, cutting off the unwary.

The town's **tourist office** (June–Aug daily 9.30am–noon & 2.30–6pm; Sept–May Tues–Sun 9.30am–noon & 2.30–5pm; ⓣ03.22.60.93.50) is situated on the quayside. There are two very attractive **hotels**, both with deservedly popular restaurants: the modest three-star *Hôtel du Port et des Bains* (ⓣ03.22.60.80.09; ⓦwww.hotelhpb.fr; ❹; restaurant menu from €28), right on the quayside after the tourist office as you drive in from Rue; and the grander two-star *Relais Guillaume de Normandie* (ⓣ03.22.60.82.36, ⓦwww.guillaumedenormandy.com; ❸; restaurant from €18, closed Tues) on the waterside promenade at the foot of the old town. Rue de la Ferté is lined with **seafood restaurants**; of these, *Les Pilotes* at no. 62 has over thirty different ways of serving mussels, with most options under €10.

About 9km to the east of St-Valéry, and 2km from the station in Noyelles-sur-Mer (served by the steam train) lies the hamlet of **NOLETTE**. This is home to one of the most unusual war graves in France: a **Chinese cemetery**, where 887 members of the Chinese Labour Corps are buried. Employed by the British army in World War I, most of them died of disease. Their neat headstones, sharing two or three rather perfunctory epitaphs, along with two lion statues donated by the Chinese, lie in a field just outside the village.

Abbeville

ABBEVILLE lies about halfway from Calais to Paris and makes a convenient stop-off on the N1. Until hit by a German air raid in May 1940, it was a very beautiful town. Nowadays, all that remain of its former glories are a superbly ornate Flemish-style **gare SNCF**; a **belfry**, reputedly the oldest in France; and the Gothic **church of St-Vulfran**, which was on a par with the cathedrals at Amiens and Beauvais. Restoration work on the church, which was badly scarred during the war, only finished in 1993. The western facade still bears superficial scars but the interior pillars have been replaced with exact copies and the keystones painted with their original colours. Also worth a visit is the eighteenth-century **Château de Bagatelle**, 2km south of town – not to be confused with the nearby amusement park of the same name – set in ten hectares of parkland (guided visits July & Aug daily except Tues 2–6pm; €8). When the château is closed you can sometimes visit the **gardens** (mid-May to mid-July & Sept to mid-Oct Mon–Fri 2–4.30pm; mid-July to Aug daily except Tues 2–6pm; €4), famed for their elaborate topiaries and rare species of tree.

The **tourist office** is at 1 place de l'Amiral-Courbet (Ⓣ03.22.24.27.92). It provides a free booking service and organizes guided visits to the church of St-Vulfran. For those who want to **stay** in style, two suites in the château are used for bed-and-breakfast accommodation (Ⓣ06.08.05.96.83, Ⓦwww.chateaudebagatelle.com; ❹). Otherwise, Abbeville has a chain **hotel** at every price level, but few establishments with individual charm. The most comfortable and central of the chains is the *Mercure Hôtel de France*, in place du Pilori in the town centre (Ⓣ03.22.24.00.42, Ⓕ03.22.24.26.15; ❺; menus from €16), while a very cheap local option is the neat but basic *Le Liberty*, 5 rue St-Catherine (Ⓣ & Ⓕ03.22.24.21.71; ❶). If you just want a **meal** then *L'Escale en Picardie*, at 15 rue des Teinturiers (menus from €20; Ⓣ03.22.24.21.51), is highly commendable, and specializes in fresh fish with crisp white wines, while the pizzeria *Le Céladon*, 30 place du Grand Marché, is pastel plush and full of locals, with pasta dishes from under €7.

Amiens and the route south

AMIENS was badly scarred during both world wars, but, unlike so many towns in this area, it has been intelligently restored and the centre is pleasingly car-free. **St-Leu**, the medieval quarter north of the cathedral with its network of canals, has been renovated; the town's university makes its presence felt; and within a few minutes' walk from the train station the *hortillonnages* (see p.243) transport you into a peaceful rural landscape. Although no hotel in the town exudes character, there are some good mid-range options and there is plenty of life in the evening to make it worth staying at least one night.

Arrival, information and accommodation

The main **gare SNCF** (Amiens-Nord) and **gare routière** are both on the rectangular place A.-Fiquet. A two-storey shopping complex, Amiens 2, is connected to the train station and is useful for its supermarket and public toilets. The **tourist office** is south of the cathedral, just off place Gambetta at 6bis rue Dusevel (April–Sept Mon–Sat 9.30am–7pm, Sun 10am–noon & 2–5pm; Oct–March Mon–Sat 9.30am–6pm, Sun 10am–noon & 2–5pm; Ⓣ03.22.71.60.50, Ⓦwww.amiens.com/tourisme).

Amiens has many two-star **hotels**, all with similar prices, which tend to fill up fairly fast. The best value of these is the fully renovated *Victor Hugo*, 2 rue de l'Oratoire, just a block from the cathedral, whose ten rooms resemble those of an attractive country bed and breakfast (Ⓣ03.22.91.57.91, Ⓕ03.22.92.74.02; ❷). Also near the cathedral is the slightly more upmarket *Le Prieuré*, 17 rue Porion (Ⓣ03.22.71.16.71, Ⓕ03.22.92.46.16; ❸). If the *Victor Hugo* is full, try one of the two hotels next door to each other on rue Alexandre-Fatton, one of the streets opposite the station: the *Spatial*,

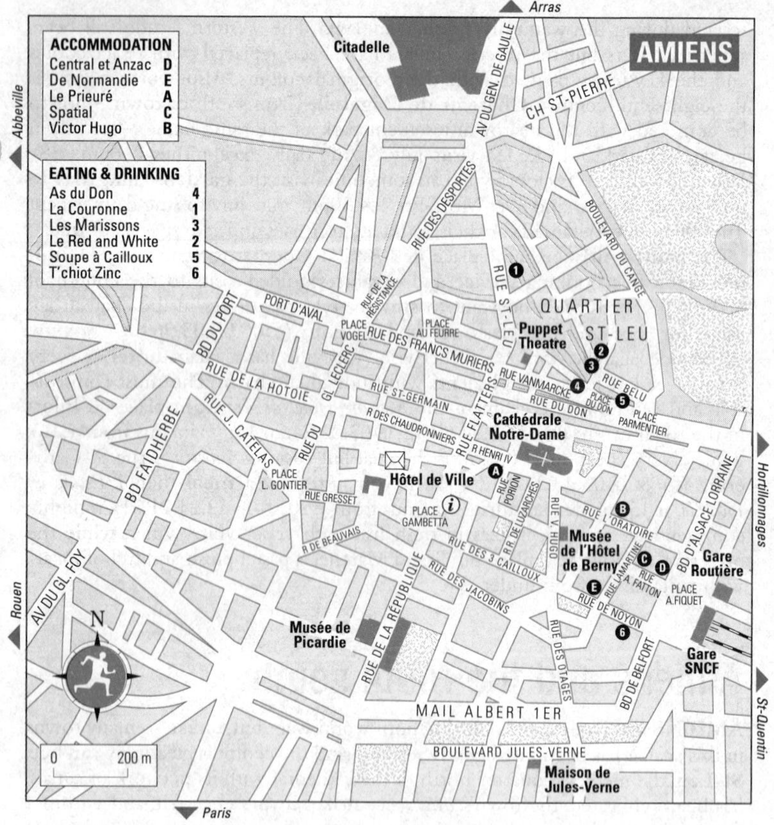

at no. 15 (Ⓣ03.22.91.53.23, Ⓦwww.hotelspatial.com; ❷), or, at no. 17, the *Central et Anzac* (Ⓣ03.22.91.34.08, Ⓦwww.hoteletcentralanzac.com; ❷); the former is less expensive and more comfortable than its neighbour. Another option just around the corner on rue Lamartine is the *Hôtel de Normandie* (Ⓣ03.22.91.74.99, Ⓦwww.hotelnormandie-80.com; ❷).

The City

The **Cathédrale Notre-Dame** (daily: April–Sept 8.30am–6.45pm; Oct–March 8.30am–noon & 2–5.30pm) provides the city's very obvious focus. First of all, it dominates by sheer size – it's the biggest Gothic building in France – but its appeal lies mainly in its unusual uniformity of style. Begun in 1220 under architect Robert de Luzarches, it was effectively finished by1269, and so the building escaped the influence of succeeding architectural fads that marred the "purity" of some of its more leisurely built sisters. A laser scrub, used on the west front, has revealed traces of the original polychrome exterior, in stark contrast to its sombre, grey modern appearance. An evening **light show** (daily: June 15–June 30 10.45pm, July 10.30pm, Aug 10pm, Sept 9.45pm, Dec 15–Jan 6 8pm; free) gives a vivid idea of how the west front would have looked when coloured, with music added to create atmosphere, and an explanation of the various statues on the facade first in French and then in English. By way of contrast, the interior is all vertical lines and no fuss: a light, calm and unaffected space. Ruskin thought the apse "not only the best, but the very first thing done perfectly in its manner by northern Christendom". The later embellishments, like the sixteenth-century choir stalls, are works of breathtaking virtuosity. The same goes for the sculpted panels depicting the life of St Firmin, Amiens' first bishop, on the right side of the choir screen. The choir itself can be visited at 3.30pm daily but is otherwise locked. Those with strong legs can mount the cathedral's front **towers** (Mon & Wed–Fri 3–4.30pm, Sat & Sun 2–5.15pm; €2.50). One of the most atmospheric ways of seeing the cathedral is to attend a Sunday morning Mass (10.15am), when there's sublime Gregorian chanting.

Just north of the cathedral is the **quartier St-Leu**, a very Flemish-looking network of canals and cottages that was once the centre of Amiens' thriving textile industry. The town still produces much of the country's velvet, but the factories moved out to the suburbs long ago, leaving St-Leu to rot away in peace – until, that is, the property developers moved in. The slums have been tastefully transformed into neat brick cottages on cobbled streets, and the waterfront has been colonized by restaurants and clubs.

On the edge of town, the canals still provide a useful function as waterways for the **hortillonnages** – a series of incredibly fertile market gardens, reclaimed from the marshes created by the very slow-flowing Somme. Farmers travel about them in black, high-prowed punts and a few still take their produce into the city by boat for the Saturday morning **market**, the *marché sur l'eau*, on the riverbank of place Parmentier. The best way to see the *hortillonnages* is from the water: the Association des Hortillonnages provides inexpensive **boat tours** from its office at 54 bd de Beauvillé (April–Oct daily 2–6pm, ticket office open from 1.30pm – best to arrive early; €5.50). They also provide free maps so that you can wander some of the footpaths around the water gardens on foot.

If you're interested in Picardy culture, you might take a look at Amiens' two regional museums. Five minutes' walk down rue de la République, south of central place Gambetta, an opulent nineteenth-century mansion houses the splendidly laid out **Musée de Picardie** (Tues–Sun 10am–12.30pm & 2–6pm; €4), whose star exhibits are the Puvis de Chavannes paintings on the main stairwell, the room created by Sol LeWitt, and a collection of rare sixteenth-century paintings on wood donated to the cathedral by a local literary society. Close by the cathedral, in the seventeenth-century **Musée de l'Hôtel de Berny** (May–Sept Thurs–Sun 2–6pm; Oct–April Sun 10am–12.30pm & 2–6pm; €2) is an annexe to the main museum, with *objets d'art* and local history collections, including a portrait of Choderlos de Laclos, author of *Les Liaisons Dangereuses*, who was born in Amiens in 1741. A third museum, at 2 rue Dubois, was once the **house of Jules Verne** (mid-April to mid-Oct Mon & Wed–Fri 10am–12.30pm & 2–6.30pm, Tues 2–6.30pm, Sat & Sun 11am–6.30pm; mid-Oct to mid-April Mon & Wed–Fri 10am–12.30pm & 2–6pm, Sat & Sun 2–6pm, closed Tues; €5). The author spent most of his life in Amiens, and died here. Although a historic and attractive building, with a romantic turret, the museum, which focuses on Verne's life, is worth the trip for fans only.

Just to the west of the city, at Tirancourt off the N1 to Abbeville, a large museum-cum-park, **Samara** (from Samarobriva, the Roman name for Amiens), recreates the life of prehistoric man in northern Europe with reconstructions of dwellings and displays illustrating the way of life, trades and so on (mid-March to April & Sept to mid-Nov Mon–Fri 9.30am–5.30pm, Sat & Sun 9.30am–6.30pm; May Mon–Fri 9.30am–5.30pm, Sat & Sun 10am–7.30pm;

June Mon–Fri 9.30am–5.30pm, Sat & Sun 9.30am–7.30pm; July & Aug daily 10am–7.30pm; Ⓦ www.samara.fr; €9).

Eating, drinking and entertainment

By far the most attractive area to eat is around **St-Leu**, where many of the **restaurants** have outdoor seating overlooking a canal, especially on the rue Belu. Two favourite places are in the pretty, cobbled place du Don directly below the cathedral, with room to sit outside in good weather: the *Soupe à Cailloux* serves delicious cuisine, including regional dishes, for a reasonable price (weekday lunch menu at €11, other times from €15; Ⓣ 03.22.91.92.70; closed Mon in winter), and is consequently very popular; and the equally attractive *As du Don*, across the square, does a *formule* for €18 and has a heated terrace. Just over the canal by the Pont de la Dodane is Amiens' best gourmet restaurant, *Les Marissons* (menus from €40, *carte* from around €50, €20 for lunch; Ⓣ 03.22.92.96.66; closed Sat lunch & Sun). Also try *La Couronne* at 64 rue St-Leu (€22–30; Ⓣ 03.22.91.88.57; closed Sat lunch & Sun dinner), where delicious food at reasonable prices is served in pleasantly sober surroundings. In the upper town, the handsome *T'chiot Zinc* (menu at €14, *plats* for €8; closed Mon lunch & Sun), conveniently located at 18 rue Noyon, opposite the station, serves traditional country fare. **Bars** and pubs abound in the area, especially on la rue des Bondes, and there is a trendy late-night gay bar *Le Red and White* at 9 rue de la Dodane.

For one week in late March, Amiens bursts into life for its annual international **jazz festival**; on the third weekend in June, the local costumes come out for the **Fête d'Amiens**, which is the best time of year to visit the *hortillonnages*. Traditional Picardy **marionette** (*cabotans*) performances take place (July & Aug Tues–Sun; Sept–June Wed & Sun) at the Théâtre de Chés Cabotans d'Amiens, 31 rue Edouard-David: contact Théâtre d'Animation Picard (Ⓣ 03.22.22.30.90, Ⓦ www.ches-cabotans-damiens.com) for reservations – tickets are around €10. To purchase or take a look at hand-made marionettes, visit the workshop of Jean-Pierre Facquier at 67 rue du Don.

Beauvais

As you head south from Amiens towards Paris, the countryside becomes broad and flat; **BEAUVAIS**, 60km south of Amiens, seems to fit into this landscape. Rebuilt, like Amiens, after World War II, it's a drab, neutral place redeemed slightly by its Gothic cathedral, the **Cathédrale St-Pierre** (daily: May–Oct 9am–12.15pm & 2–6.15pm, Nov–April 9am–12.15pm & 2–5.30pm), which rises above the town. It's a building that perhaps more than any other in northern France demonstrates the religious materialism of the Middle Ages – its main intention was to be taller and larger than its rivals. The choir, completed in 1272, was once 5m higher than that of Amiens, though only briefly, as it collapsed in 1284. Its replacement, only completed three centuries later, was raised by the sale of indulgences – a right granted to the local bishops by Pope Leo X. This, too, fell within a few years, and, the authorities having overreached themselves financially, the church remained unfinished, forlorn and mutilated. In some respects the cathedral has succeeded in its original ambitious aim – at over 155m high, the interior vaults are undeniably impressive, giving the impression that the cathedral is of a larger scale than at Amiens. The building's real beauty, however, lies in its glass, its sculpted doorways and the remnants of the so-called Basse-Oeuvre, a ninth-century Carolingian church incorporated into the structure. It also contains a couple of remarkable **clocks**: one, a 12m-high astronomical clock built in 1865, above which on the hour 68 figures mimic scenes from the Last Judgement; the other, a medieval clock that's been working for seven hundred years.

Though the cathedral is the town's only remarkable sight, the church of **St-Étienne**, a few blocks to the south of the cathedral on rue de Malherbe, is worth a look for yet more spectacular Renaissance stained-glass windows. There are also: the **Galerie Nationale de Tapisserie** behind the cathedral (April–Sept daily 9.30am–12.30pm & 2–6pm; Oct–March daily 10am–12.30pm & 2–5pm; free), a museum of the tapestry for which Beauvais was once renowned, housing a collection ranging from the fifteenth century to the present day; and the **Musée Départemental** (daily except Tues: July–Sept 10am–6pm, Oct–June 10am–noon & 2–6pm; €2), devoted to painting, local history and archeology, in the sharp, black-towered building opposite. The rousing statue in the central square is of local heroine Jeanne Hachette, a fighter and inspiration in the defence of the town in 1472 against Charles the Bold, duke of Burgundy.

Practicalities

Beauvais is just over an hour by train from Paris, and the **gare SNCF** is a short walk from the centre of town – take avenue de la République, then turn right up rue de Malherbe. Paris-Beauvais **airport** is just outside the town but there is no public transport into Beauvais (see p.91 for details of transport into Paris). The **tourist office** (Mon–Sat 9.30am–12.30pm & 1.30–6pm, Sun 10am–5pm; ⓣ03.44.15.30.30) is opposite the Galerie Nationale de Tapisserie, at 1 rue Beauregard.

If you want to **stay**, plump for the modest *Hôtel du Palais Bleu*, within sight of the cathedral at 9 rue St-Nicolas (ⓣ03.44.45.18.58, ⓕ03.44.15.06.94; ❸), or try *The Cygne*, 24 rue Carnot (ⓣ03.44.48.68.40, ⓦwww.hotelducygne-beauvais.com; ❷). There's a municipal **campsite** (ⓣ03.44.02.00.22; closed mid-Sept to mid-May) just out of town on the Paris road. For fine **food** on the square, call in at *Le Marignan*, 1 rue de Malherbe (ⓣ03.44.48.15.15), which has menus from €12 in the brasserie downstairs, and from €20 in the very good restaurant upstairs. Less expensive is the charming *L'Auberge de la Meule*, 8 rue du 27 Juin, which specializes in cheese-based dishes including fondues and cheesy salads, with *plats* at around €10.

The Flemish cities and world war battlefields

From the Middle Ages until the late twentieth century, great Flemish cities like Lille, **Roubaix**, **Douai** and **Cambrai** flourished, mainly thanks to their textile industries. The other dominating – though now all but extinct – presence in this part of northern France was the **coalfields** and related industries, which, at their peak in the nineteenth century, formed a continuous stretch from Béthune in the west to Valenciennes in the east. At **Lewarde** you can visit one of the pits, while in the region's big industrial cities you can see what the masters built with their profits: noble town houses, magnificent city halls, ornate churches and some of the country's finest art collections. **Lille** is now a major trans-European communications hub and, despite visible problems of post-industrial urban decay, has transformed itself into a city with a thriving centre of interest to locals and tourists alike.

On a more sombre note, Picardy, Artois and Flanders are littered with the monuments, battlefields and cemeteries of the two world wars, and nowhere as intensely as the region northeast of Amiens, between **Albert** and the appealing market town of **Arras** with its pair of handsome squares. It was here, among the fields and villages of the Somme, that the main battle lines of World War I were drawn. They can be visited most spectacularly at **Vimy Ridge**, just off the A26 north of Arras, where the trenches have been left *in situ*. Lesser sites, often more poignant, are dotted over the countryside around Albert and along the **Circuit de Souvenir**.

Lille and around

LILLE (Rijsel in Flemish), by far northern France's largest city, surprises many visitors with its impressive architecture, the winding streets of its tastefully restored old quarter (Vieux Lille), its plethora of excellent restaurants, and bustling nightlife scene. It boasts some vibrant and obviously prosperous commercial areas, modern residential squares, a large university, a new métro system, and a very serious attitude to culture, reflected in a busy music and arts scene and some great museums. At the same time, the city spreads far into the countryside in every direction, a mass of suburbs and largely abandoned factories, and for the French it remains the very symbol of the country's heavy industry and working-class politics. Lille is facing up to many of the tough issues of contemporary France: poverty and racial conflict, a crime rate similar to that of Paris and Marseille, and a certain regionalism – Lillois sprinkle their speech with a French-Flemish patois ("Ch'ti") and to some extent assert a Flemish identity. But Lille managed to scrub its streets, sights and monuments until they were squeaky clean for its stint as the European Capital of Culture in 2004, making itself worthy of its incredible location – it takes less than an hour to Paris and Brussels by train, and just an hour and forty minutes to London by Eurostar. While in the past Lille was unfamiliar as a tourist destination, today it is a deservedly popular place to spend a weekend.

Arrival, information and accommodation

The central Grand'Place is just a few minutes' walk from **Gare Lille-Flandres** (originally Paris's Gare du Nord, but brought here brick by brick in 1865), served by regional trains plus the hourly shuttle service to Paris. TGV and Eurostar services from London, Brussels and further afield stop at the modern **Lille-Europe** station, five minutes' walk further out from the centre, or one stop on the métro – check which station your train uses. If you arrive by air, a shuttle-bus service (Ⓣ03.20.90.79.79; €4.60 one way) whisks you to Euralille, just by Gare Lille-Flandres, in twenty minutes from **Lesquin airport**. Despite being the fifth-largest city in France, Lille's centre is small enough to walk round and, unless you choose to visit the modern art museum

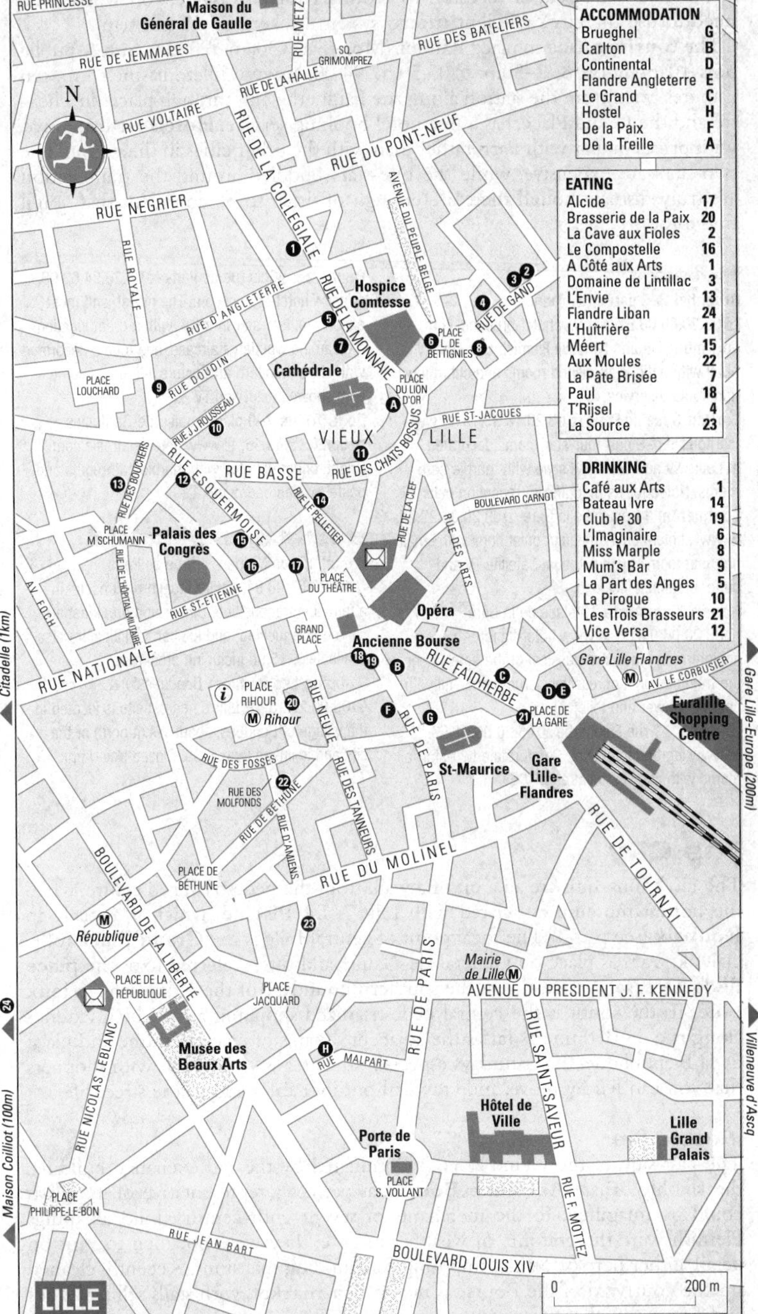
ACCOMMODATION
Brueghel G
Carlton B
Continental D
Flandre Angleterre E
Le Grand C
Hostel H
De la Paix F
De la Treille A
EATING
Alcide 17
Brasserie de la Paix 20
La Cave aux Fioles 2
Le Compostelle 16
A Côté aux Arts 1
Domaine de Lintillac 3
L'Envie 13
Flandre Liban 24
L'Huîtrière 11
Méert 15
Aux Moules 22
La Pâte Brisée 7
Paul 18
T'Rijsel 4
La Source 23
DRINKING
Café aux Arts 1
Bateau Ivre 14
Club le 30 19
L'Imaginaire 6
Miss Marple 8
Mum's Bar 9
La Part des Anges 5
La Pirogue 10
Les Trois Brasseurs 21
Vice Versa 12
Maison du Général de Gaulle
Hospice Comtesse
Cathédrale
VIEUX LILLE
Palais des Congrès
Opéra
Ancienne Bourse
St-Maurice
Gare Lille-Flandres
Gare Lille Flandres
Euralille Shopping Centre
Musée des Beaux Arts
Hôtel de Ville
Porte de Paris
Lille Grand Palais
Mairie de Lille
Rihour
République
Citadelle (1km)
Gare Lille-Europe (200m)
Villeneuve d'Ascq
Maison Coilliot (100m)
Musée d'Histoire Naturelle (50m)
LILLE
0 200 m

at Villeneuve-d'Ascq, or to travel to Roubaix for La Piscine, you won't even need to use the city's efficient **métro** system (tickets €1.15 per trip).

The **tourist office** in place Rihour (Mon–Sat 9.30am–6.30pm, Sun & public hols 10am–noon & 2–5pm; ⓣ03.59.57.94.00, ⓦwww.lilletourisme.com), ten minutes' walk from the station along rue Faidherbe and through place du Théâtre and the Grand'Place, has a free hotel booking service. **Hotels** are expensive, with prices on par with Paris rather than with the other cities in the region. The two-stars are expensive, while the one-stars huddled around the train station are truly dismal, though there are enough of them to be confident that you'll find a room.

Hotels

Brueghel 3–5 parvis St-Maurice ⓣ03.20.06.06.69, ⓦwww.hotel-brueghel.com. Very attractive and typically Flemish two-star hotel with antique-furnished rooms and charming, understated service. ⑤

Carlton 3 rue de Paris ⓣ03.20.13.33.13, ⓦwww.carltonlille.fr. Smart four-star rooms decorated in Louis XV and Louis XVI style with marble bathrooms. Noted for its magnificent reception halls. ⑨

Continental 11 place de la Gare ⓣ03.20.06.22.24, ⓦwww.hotel-continental.fr. A quiet hotel with small but neat rooms by the station. Satellite TV and buffet breakfast included. ④

Flandre Angleterre 13 place de la Gare ⓣ03.20.06.04.12, ⓦwww.hotel-flandre-angleterre.fr. Much the classiest of the hotels near the train station: impressively large rooms, all with bath or shower and toilet. ④

Le Grand 51 rue Faidherbe ⓣ03.20.06.31.57, ⓦwww.legrandhotel.com. Comfortable two-star; all rooms with shower, toilet and TV. ④

De la Paix 46bis rue de Paris ⓣ03.20.54.63.93, ⓦwww.hotel-la-paix.com. The nicest, and most expensive, two-star in town, with a great location, a gleaming wooden staircase, and rooms decorated with classy modern art posters. All rooms come with shower, toilet and TV. ⑤

De la Treille 7–9 place Louise-de-Bettignies ⓣ03.20.55.45.46, ⓦwww.hoteldelatreille.com. Bright, cheerful hotel, with marble bathrooms and pastel-walled bedrooms. ⑥

Hostel and campsite

Hostel 12 rue Malpart, off rue de Paris ⓣ03.20.57.08.94, ⓔlille@fuaj.org. HI hostel in a fairly central position. Dinner and breakfast are served if requested, and kitchen facilities are also available. €15.90 including breakfast.

Camping Les Ramiers Bondues ⓣ & ⓕ03.20.23.13.42. Lille's nearest site is located in the village of Bondues, about 10km north of the city and is linked by bus 35. Closed Nov–April.

The City

The city's museums are all a bit of a walk from the pedestrianized centre, while the hottest museum associated with Lille is **La Piscine**, which is actually in **Roubaix** (see p.253). The focal point of central Lille is the **Grand'Place** (officially known as place du Général-de-Gaulle and often referred to as the **place de la Déesse**), which marks the southern boundary of the old quarter, **Vieux Lille**. To the south is the central pedestrianized shopping area, which extends along rue de Béthune as far as the adjacent squares of place Béthune and place de la République. On Saturdays especially, the area is so jammed with shoppers that you can hardly move, and crowded outdoor cafés add to the street life.

Vieux Lille

The east side of the Grand'Place is dominated by the old exchange building, the lavishly ornate **Ancienne Bourse**, as perfect a representative of its age as could be imagined. To the merchants of seventeenth-century Lille, all things Flemish were the epitome of wealth and taste; they were not men to stint on detail, either here or on the imposing surrounding mansions. Recently cleaned up, the courtyard of the Bourse is now a **flea market**, with stalls selling books and flowers in the afternoons. A favourite Lillois pastime is lounging around the fountain at the centre of the square, in the middle of which is a **column** commemorating the city's resistance to the Austrian siege of 1792, topped by *La Déesse* (the goddess), modelled on the wife of the mayor at the time – hence the square's alternative moniker.

In the adjacent **place du Théâtre**, you can see how Flemish Renaissance architecture became assimilated and Frenchified in grand flights of Baroque extravagance. The superlative example of this style is the **Opéra**, (Ⓣ03.28.38.40.40, Ⓦwww.opera-lille.fr; closed July & Aug). It was built at the turn of the twentieth century by Louis Cordonnier, who also designed the extravagant **belfry** of the neighbouring Nouvelle Bourse – now the regional Chamber of Commerce – a small part of which is given over to the city's most central post office.

From the north side of these two squares, the smart shopping streets, rues Esquermoise and Lepelletier, lead towards the heart of **Vieux Lille**, a warren of red-brick terraces on cobbled lanes and passages. It's an area of great character and charm, successfully reclaimed and reintegrated into the mainstream of the city's life, having been for years a dilapidated North African ghetto. To experience the atmosphere of Vieux Lille, head up towards rue d'Angleterre, rue du Pont-Neuf and the Porte de Gand, rue de la Monnaie and place Lion-d'Or. Places to eat and drink are everywhere, interspersed with chic boutiques.

Vieux Lille's main sight is the **Hospice Comtesse** at 32 rue de la Monnaie. Twelfth century in origin, though much reconstructed in the eighteenth, it served as a hospital until as recently as 1945 and its medicinal garden, a riot of poppies and verbena, is a delight. The old ward, the Salle des Malades, often used for concerts, and the chapel can both be visited (Mon 2–6pm, Wed–Sun 10am–12.30pm & 2–6pm; €2.30).

Charles de Gaulle was born in this part of the town, at 9 rue Princesse, in 1890. His house is now a **museum** (Wed–Sun 10am–noon & 2–5pm; €5), which normally exhibits, amongst de Gaulle's effects, the bullet-riddled Citroën in which he was driving when the OAS attempted to assassinate him in 1962

△Grand'Place, Lille

(see Contexts, p.128). Another must for military buffs is the **citadelle** that overlooks the old town to the northwest, constructed in familiar star-shaped fashion by Vauban in the seventeenth century. Still in military hands, it can be visited on Sundays between May and August by guided tour (€7; tours depart from the citadelle's Porte Royale at 3pm). To get there, go along rue de la Barre from Vieux Lille.

Amid all the city's secular pomp, Lille's ecclesiastical architecture used to seem rather subdued. However, the facade of the cathedral, **Notre-Dame-de-la-Treille**, just off rue de la Monnaie, has broken the mould. The body of the cathedral is a fairly homogeneous though not unattractive Neo-Gothic construction begun in 1854; the new facade though, completed in 1999, is completely different – a translucent marble front supported by steel wires, best appreciated from inside, or at night when lit up from within. More traditional, but also impressive, is the **church of St-Maurice**, close to the station off place de la Gare, a classic red-brick Flemish Hallekerke, with the characteristic five aisles of the style.

South of the Grand'Place

Just south of the Grand'Place is **place Rihour**, a largely modern square flanked by brasseries and the remains of an old palace that now houses the tourist office, hidden behind an ugly war monument of gigantic proportions. Close by, the busiest shopping street, rue de Béthune, leads into place de Béthune, home to some excellent cafés, and beyond to the **Musée des Beaux-Arts** on place de la République (Mon 2–6pm, Wed–Sun 10am–6pm; €4.60). The late 1990s redesign is rather disappointing – too sleek and spacious to give any coherence to the collection – but the museum does contain some important works. Flemish painters form the core of the collection, from "primitives" like Dirck Bouts, through the northern Renaissance to Ruisdael, de Hooch and the seventeenth-century schools. Other works include Goya's interpretation of youth and old age, *Les Jeunes et Les Vieilles*, and a scattering of the nineteenth-century French greats including Renoir, Monet and Rodin. Look out for the temporary exhibitions, which cost more but can be worthwhile.

A few hundred metres to the south of the museum, near the green avenue Jean-Baptiste Lebas, is the **Musée d'Histoire Naturelle**, 19 rue de Bruxelles (Mon–Sat 9am–noon & 2–5pm, Sun 10am–5pm; €2.30). It's a small museum, a manageable size for children, with a lovely collection of dinosaur bones, fossils, and an impressive array of beautifully stuffed birds, including a dodo.

West of the Musée des Beaux-Arts, on rue de Fleurus, lies **Maison Coilliot**, one of the few houses built by Hector Guimard, who made his name designing the Art Nouveau entrances to the Paris métro – it's worth taking a look at the facade. Built at the height of the Art Nouveau movement, it's as striking today as it obviously was to the conservative burghers of Lille (there are no other such buildings in the city), but it also displays the somewhat muddled eclecticism of the style, coming over as half brick-faced mansion, half timber-framed cottage. East of the museum, near the triumphal arch of Porte de Paris, is the city's ugly but serviceable **Hôtel de Ville**, executed in a bizarre Flemish Art Deco style, with an extremely tall belfry.

Euralille

Thanks to Eurostar and the international extension of the TGV network, Lille has become the transport hub of northern Europe, a position it is trying to exploit to turn itself into an international business centre: hence **Euralille**, the burgeoning complex of buildings behind the old *gare SNCF*.

One definite architectural success is the new Lille-Europe station, composed of lots of props and struts and glass and sunscreens. It's lean, elegant and functional, a fitting setting for the magnificent TGV and Eurostar trains that use it. Some of the buildings in the complex are, however, less successful – for example, the boot-shaped tower treading on the roof of the new station, and the enormous shopping centre opposite with galvanized walkways, marbled malls and relentless muzak.

Villeneuve d'Ascq: the Musée d'Art Moderne

The suburb of Villeneuve d'Ascq is a mark of Lille's cultural ambition. Acres of parkland, an old windmill or two, and a whole series of mini-lakes form the setting for the **Musée d'Art Moderne** (daily except Tues 10am–6pm; €6.50), which houses an unusually good, if small, collection in its uninviting red-brick buildings. It's 8km from the city but accessible by public transport – to get there take the métro to Pont-de-Bois, then bus #41. The ground floor is generally given over to exhibitions of varying quality by contemporary French artists, while the permanent collection, on the first floor, contains canvases by Picasso, Braque, Modigliani, Miró and a whole room devoted to Fernand Léger and Georges Rouault. On the top floor, a small room – easy to miss but worth the search – contains graphics by many of the above. Meanwhile, outside on the grass, sculptures by Giacometti and Calder provide some playful picnic backdrops.

Eating, drinking and entertainment

A Flemish flavour and a taste for mussels characterize the city's traditional cuisine, with the main area for cafés, **brasseries** and **restaurants** around **place Rihour** and along rue de Béthune. But Lille is also gaining a reputation for gastronomic excellence, and for something more exotic, **rue Royale** has a selection of fairly pricey but generally very good options, ranging from Cambodian or Japanese to French with a twist. The best area for cheap restaurants is the **student quarter** along the rues Solférino and Masséna, while Vieux Lille in general is definitely fashionable, in particular the atmospheric **rue de Gand**. Foodies should also make a pilgrimage to Philippe Olivier's *fromagerie* with its 300 cheeses on 3 rue du Curé-St-Étienne.

The **cafés** around the Grand'Place and place Rihour are always buzzing with life. Rue de Paris has lots of tacky, loud, crushed **bars** raging at all hours, while up near the cathedral, rue Basse and place Louise-de-Bettignies have some trendier spots. West of place de la République, bars are thick on the ground in rues Solférino and Masséna, and attract a young crowd, while student bars, both trendy and friendly, fill up along the base of rue Royale. For **gay bars**, of which there are several, try *Mum's Bar* at 4 rue Doudin, *Vice Versa* on rue de la Barre, and, for lesbians, *Miss Marple* at 18 rue de Gand. Art and music events are always worth checking up on – there's a particularly lively **jazz** scene. Pick up a copy of the free weekly listings magazine, *Sortir*, from the tourist office, or look in the local paper, *La Voix du Nord*.

Restaurants and cafés

Alcide 5 rue Débris St-Étienne ⓣ03.20.12.06.95. A Lillois institution, an upmarket brasserie tucked down a narrow alleyway near the Grand'Place. Reliable, hearty fare (*flamiche*, fish, *crêpes à la cassonade*) and home-made ice creams served in a wood-panelled dining room. Menus from €20, half-menu €15. Open daily, closed Sunday eve and mid-July to mid-Aug.

Café aux Arts 1 place du Concert. Good old-fashioned café with wicker chairs on its terrace, in an unbeatable vantage point over the market.

Brasserie de la Paix 25 place Rihour ⓣ03.20.54.70.41. Sumptuous brasserie, unrelated

to its namesake hotel, specializing in mussels and seafood. Menus from €17.50. Closed Sun.
La Cave aux Fioles 39 rue de Gand ☎03.20.55.18.43. The jazz-related decor is backed by the music and mellow ambience. Food ranges from classics and Flemish specials to more adventurous fare. Menus from €33 or *plats* from €10. Closed Sat lunch & Sun.
Le Compostelle 4 rue St-Étienne ☎03.28.38.08.30. In a much renovated Knights Templar Renaissance palace, this airy restaurant with indoor trees offers refined versions of traditional French specialities, including vegetarian options. Menus from €27.
A Côté aux Arts 5 place du Concert ☎03.28.52.34.66. Friendly little brasserie serving dishes such as *andouillette*, stuffed pig's trotters, and *magret* of duck with fresh figs (€13–20 for main course). Closed Sun & Mon.
Domaine de Lintillac 43 rue de Gand ☎03.20.06.53.51. Unpretentious old-fashioned French cuisine specializing in foie gras, cassoulet and other *produits du terroir* from the owner's farm (the *produits* can also be purchased). Mains from €8. Closed Sun & Mon.
L'Envie 34 rue des Bouchers ☎03.20.15.29.39. Classically delicious French food served in creative ways in a small restaurant on a quiet street, but just steps away from the trendy bars on rue Royale. Menus from €13.50. Closed Sat lunch & Sun.
Flandre Liban 127 rue des Postes ☎03.20.57.28.69. Excellent, friendly Lebanese restaurant in a mainly North African and Middle Eastern quarter. Go for the meze menu at €18. Closed Sun eve.
L'Huîtrière 3 rue des Chats-Bossus ☎03.20.55.43.41. A wonderful shop (worth a visit just to look and the mosaics and stained glass) with an expensive, chandelier-hung restaurant at the back – acclaimed as Lille's best – specializing in fish and oysters at €30-plus a dish; there's an impressive €120 menu. Closed Sun eve, hols & late July to late Aug.
Méert 25–27 rue Esquermoise ☎03.20.57.07.44. Decorated with mirrors and chandeliers this is Lille's most famous (and expensive) *salon de thé* specializing in *gaufres* as well as excellent cakes and teas. Closed Mon morning. *Méert* also runs the restaurant at La Piscine in Roubaix (see p.254).
Aux Moules 34 rue de Béthune ☎03.20.57.12.46. The best place to eat mussels; it's been serving them since 1930 in its Art Deco-style interior. Nothing costs much over €10, including the other brasserie fare, and it's all excellent value. Daily noon–midnight.
La Pâte Brisée 63–65 rue de la Monnaie ☎03.20.74.29.00. Delicious quiches and tarts in a bright, modern decor. *Formules* from €8.10.
Paul place du Théâtre, cnr rue Faidherbe ☎03.20.78.20.78. *Paul* is an institution in Lille; though it's now becoming a bit of a chain, it started here with the boulangerie, patisserie and *salon de thé* all under one roof. Daily 7am–7.30pm.
T'Rijsel 25 rue de Gand ☎03.20.15.01.59. Traditional Flemish *estaminet*, open eve only, serving the whole gamut of regional dishes and over 40 beers. *Plats* from €10. Closed Sun & Mon.
La Source 13 rue du Plat ☎03.20.57.53.07. Vegetarian restaurant and healthfood store, best at lunchtime. From €8

Bars and clubs

Bateau Ivre 41 rue Lepelletier. Loud music ranging from house to soul in a pleasant street in the old quarter (the interior includes a seventeenth-century vaulted cellar), with a mainly young crowd. Sun–Fri 3pm–3am, Sat 11am–3am.
Club le 30 30 rue de Paris ☎03.20.30.15.54. One of Lille's many jazz venues, this one probably attracts the best artists. Open every eve except Mon.
L'Imaginaire place Louise-de-Bettignies, next door to the *Hôtel Treille*. Arty young bar with paintings adorning the walls. Mon–Sat 10pm–2am.
La Part des Anges 50 rue de la Monnaie. Trendy wine bar with an enviable cellar, serving simple meals and snacks to accompany the wine.
La Pirogue 16 rue J.-J.-Rousseau. Antilles-themed bar with reasonably priced cocktails, especially popular with local students.
Les Trois Brasseurs 22 place de la Gare. Dark, smoke-stained dining stalls surround copper cauldrons in this genuine brasserie that brews its own beer. Food is also served but it's the beer that's the main attraction.

Listings

Banks All the banks have big branches on rue Nationale, and you can guarantee to find one open until 4pm on Saturday.
Books Le Furet du Nord, 11 place Général-de-Gaulle, is a huge, seven-storey bookshop (it claims to be Europe's biggest) with a wide selection of books in English.
Car rental is mostly from the two train stations: ADA, Gare Europe ☎03.20.55.18.18; Avis, Gare Flandres ☎03.20.06.35.55,

Gare Europe ☎03.20.51.12.31; Hertz, Gare Flandres ☎03.28.36.28.70, Gare Europe ☎03.28.36.25.90.

Cinema Lille's two main cinemas, Le Majestic and UGC, are along the rue de Béthune; UGC at no. 40 shows blockbusters with usually at least one film in English, Le Majestic at nos. 54–56 is more arty and sometimes runs festivals. Le Métropole at 26 rue des Ponts-de-Comines normally shows original-language versions.

Doctors SOS Médecins ☎03.20.29.91.91.

Festivals The major festival of the year, the Grande Braderie, takes place over the first weekend of Sept, when a big street parade and vast flea market fill the streets of the old town by day, and the evenings see a *moules-frites* frenzy in all the restaurants, with empty mussel shells piled up in the streets.

Internet Cyber Office 20 place des Reignaux (open daily till late).

Laundry There are several outlets of Lavotec, the most central being at 72 rue Pierre-LeGrand, 57 rue des Postes and 137 rue Solférino, open daily 6am–9pm.

Markets The loud and colourful Wazemmes flea market, selling food and clothes, spills around place de la Nouvelle Aventure, to the west of central Lille. Main day Sun but also open Tues and Thurs (7am–2pm). A smaller food market takes place in Vieux Lille on place du Concert (Wed, Fri & Sun 7am–2pm).

Post office 8 place de la République (☎03.28.36.10.20) and 13–15 rue Nationale (☎03.28.38.18.40); both Mon–Fri 8am–6.30pm, Sat 8.30am–12.30pm.

Taxi Gare ☎03.20.06.64.00; Taxi Union ☎03.20.06.06.06.

Roubaix

Just 15km northeast of Lille, right up against the Belgian border, **ROUBAIX** is another great Flemish city whose former wealth was founded on the wool industry. Nowadays it's best known in France as the origin of mail-order clothes, and as the destination of the gruelling 250-kilometre Paris–Roubaix cycle race, held in mid-April. In the nineteenth century, however, the Industrial Revolution turned Roubaix into one of France's most prosperous cities. The population multiplied fifteen-fold between 1800 and World War I, and the city's prosperity was reflected in great textile mills, Art Nouveau houses, parks, hospitals, a sophisticated social welfare system and a flamboyant Hôtel de Ville, whose architect was also responsible for Gare d'Orsay in Paris. Coincidentally, the main attraction of present-day Roubaix is a disused Art Deco swimming pool, **La Piscine**, converted into an outstanding museum of fine art and industry by the same architect responsible for the conversion of the Paris station into the Musée d'Orsay. Another worthwhile museum is housed in a working textile factory, and a couple of manufacturer outlets in town offer a chance to snap up bargain-priced clothing.

Arrival and information

The best way to get to Roubaix is via the **métro** from Lille, which takes twenty minutes and stops at Roubaix Gare/Jean-Baptiste-Lebas, Grand'Place and Eurotélépor, the last of which, immediately to the east of Grand'Place, is also the terminus of the tramway from Lille's Eurostar station. The tram has the sightseeing advantage of being overground, though the journey takes ten minutes extra (fares are the same – €1.15 one way). The **gare SNCF** is at the western end of avenue Jean-Baptiste-Lebas, a five-minute walk along which leads to the central Grand'Place.

The Town

Modern Roubaix is not a beautiful place, owing to severe world war bombardment and decades of industrial decline. The **Grand'Place** has a desolate feel, not helped by the opulence of the Hôtel de Ville, built in 1911. But the city has been earnestly trying to overcome its difficulties in recent years, and nowhere is this more manifest than in **La Piscine**, or the **Musée d'Art et d'Industrie**

(Tues–Thurs 11am–6pm, Fri 11am–8pm, Sat & Sun 1–6pm; €3 for the permanent collection, plus €3 for temporary exhibitions, or €5 joint ticket), one of most original art museums in the country, halfway between the *gare SNCF* and the Grand'Place at 23 rue de l'Espérance. This fascinating, partly interactive museum opened its doors in 2001, after years of work to convert one of France's most beautiful swimming pools and water cure complexes. Originally built in the early 1930s by local architect Albert Baert, contemporary architect Paul Philippon retained various aspects of the baths – part of the pool, the shower-cubicles, the changing-rooms and the bathhouses – and used each part of the complex to display a splendid collection of mostly nineteenth- and early twentieth-century sculpture and painting, plus haute couture clothing, textiles and a collection of photographs of the swimming pool in its heyday. A fine set of sculptures is reflected in the water, and don't miss the water-filter machinery in the museum's excellent shop. Interesting temporary exhibitions are staged throughout the year.

A short way to the southeast of central Roubaix, at 25 rue de la Prudence, is the massive **La Manufacture des Flandres**, a working tapestry factory, where you'll find the **Musée du Jacquard** (Tues–Sun 1.30–5pm; €5). One-hour guided tours take you round an interesting collection of looms and other machinery, plus tapestries from the Middle Ages to the present day, and end up in a boutique selling the factory's wares.

Although the choice and range are nothing like as good as at Troyes (see p.281), there are some good deals to be had on designer-label clothing in Roubaix, with prices at up to fifty percent off normal shop prices. Two major **factory outlets** are worth investigating: L'Usine (Mon–Sat 10am–7pm), at 228 av Alfred-Motte, a short distance away from the centre; and McArthur Glen (same opening hours), at 44 Mail de Lannoy, right in the centre – Cacharel, Bruce Field, Adidas and Reebok are just a few names which may entice you.

Eating and drinking

There are plenty of **restaurants** in Roubaix, many serving regional specialities. One of the best is in the Piscine museum itself – a gastronomic restaurant and *salon du thé* run by *Méert*, the Lillois patisserie (Ⓣ03.20.57.07.44; open daily except Mon for lunch, Fri only for dinner). The *Grand Hôtel Mercure*, a nineteenth-century palace, offers a beautiful brasserie for a stylish lunch at 22 av J-B Lebas (Ⓣ03.20.73.40.00, menus from €18). Another establishment of high repute is the *Auberge de Beaumont*, 143 rue de Beaumont (Ⓣ03.20.75.43.28; closed Wed lunch, Sun & Mon eve; menus from €23), with appealingly rustic decor, while *Chez Charly*, 127 av J-B Lebas is an excellent place for lunch (Ⓣ03.20.70.78.58; closed eves and all day Sun; menus €17–29), serving classic food in a cosy wood-panelled dining room. For couscous and other North African fare head for *Les Hammadites*, 45 rue du Chemin de Fer, or for a **drink** there's *La Grande Brasserie de l'Impératrice Eugénie* at 22 place de la Liberté.

Douai and around

Right at the heart of mining country, 40km south of Lille, and badly damaged in both world wars, **DOUAI** is a surprisingly attractive and lively town, its handsome streets of eighteenth-century houses cut through by both the River Scarpe and a canal. Once a haven for English Catholics fleeing Protestant oppression in Tudor England, Douai later became the seat of

Flemish local government under Louis XIV, an aristocratic past evoked in the novels of Balzac.

The Town

Centre of activity is the **place d'Armes**, where life focuses around a fountain, while rue de la Mairie, leading west, is overlooked by the massive Gothic belfry of the **Hôtel de Ville** (guided tours: July & Aug daily 10am, 11am & hourly 2–6pm; Sept–June Mon 3pm, 4pm & 5pm Tues–Sun 11am, 3pm, 4pm & 5pm; €3.50), popularized by Victor Hugo and renowned for its carillon of 62 bells – the largest single collection in Europe. It rings every fifteen minutes, and there are hour-long concerts every Saturday at 11am, and on public holidays at 11.30am.

One block north of the town hall, on **rue Bellegambe**, is an outrageous Art Nouveau facade fronting a very ordinary haberdashery store. At the end of the street, rising above the old town, are the Baroque dome and tower of the **church of St-Pierre**, an immense, mainly eighteenth-century church with – among other treasures – a spectacular carved Baroque organ case. East of the place d'Armes, Douai's oldest church, the twelfth-century **church of Notre-Dame**, suffered badly in World War II but has been refreshingly modernized inside. Beyond the church is the better of the town's two surviving medieval gateways, the **Porte Valenciennes.** With the exception of the 1970s extension to the old Flemish Parliament building, the riverfront west of the town hall is pleasant to wander along. Between the river and the canal to the west, at 130 rue des Chartreux, the **Ancienne Chartreuse** has been converted into a wonderful **museum** (Mon & Wed–Sat 10am–noon & 2–5pm, Sun 10am–noon & 3–6pm; €3), with a fine collection of paintings by Flemish, Dutch and French masters, including Van Dyck, Jordaens, Rubens and Douai's own Jean Bellegambe. The adjacent chapel, shows off to full effect an array of sculptures including a poignant *Enfant prodige* by Rodin.

Practicalities

The **gare SNCF** is a five-minute walk from the centre – from the station head left down avenue Maréchal-Leclerc, then right onto the place d'Armes. The **tourist office** (April–Sept Mon–Sat 10am–1pm & 2–7pm Sun & public hols 3–6pm; Oct–March Mon–Sat 10am–12.30pm & 2–6.30pm; ⓣ03.27.88.26.79, ⓦwww.ville-douai.fr) is housed within the fifteenth-century Hôtel du Dauphin on the square.

For **accommodation** there's the central but shabby *Hôtel au Grand Balcon*, on 26 place Carnot (ⓣ03.27.88.91.07; ❷). A far classier option is *La Terrasse*, a swanky four-star in the narrow terrasse St-Pierre (ⓣ03.27.88.70.04, ⓦwww.laterrasse.fr; ❹), to one side of the church of St-Pierre; its restaurant is well regarded, with menus from €25.

Lewarde

A visit to the colliery at **LEWARDE**, 7km east of Douai, is a must for admirers of Zola's *Germinal*, perhaps the most electrifying "naturalistic" novel ever written. The bus from Douai heads east across the flat and featureless beet fields, down a road lined with poor brick dwellings that recall the company-owned housing of *Germinal*, intersected by streets named after Pablo Neruda, Jean-Jacques Rousseau, Georges Brassens and other luminaries of the French and international Left. This is the traditional heart of France's coal-mining country, always dispiriting and now depressed by closures and recession. Even the distinctive landmarks of slag heaps and winding gear are fast disappearing in the face of demolition and landscaping.

The bus puts you down at the main square, leaving a fifteen-minute walk down the D132 towards Erchin to get to the colliery. **The Centre Historique Minier** (guided tours: March–Oct daily 9am–5.30pm; Nov–Feb Mon–Sat 1–5pm, Sun 10am–5pm; 2hr; March–Oct €10.60, Nov–Feb €9.40) is on the left in the old Fosse Delloye, sited, like so many pits, amid woods and fields. Visits are guided by retired miners, many of whom are not French, but Polish, Italian or North African.

The main part of the tour – in addition to film shows and visits to the surface installations of winding gear, machine shops, cages, sorting areas and the rest – is the exploration of the pit-bottom roadways and faces, equipped to show the evolution of mining from the earliest times to today. These French pits were extremely deep and hot, with steeply inclined narrow seams that forced the miners to work on slopes of 55 degrees and more, just as Étienne and the Maheu family do in Zola's story. Accidents were a regular occurrence in the old days: the northern French pits had a particularly bad record in the last years of the nineteenth century. The worst mining disaster occurred at Courrières in 1906, when 1100 men were killed. Incredibly, despite the fact that the owners made little effort to search for survivors, thirteen men suddenly emerged after twenty days of wandering in the gas-filled tunnels without food, water or light. The first person they met thought that they were ghosts and fainted in fright. More incredible still, a fourteenth man surfaced alone after another four days.

Cambrai and around

Despite the tank battle of November 1917 (see box opposite) and the fact that the heavily defended Hindenburg Line ran through the town centre for most of World War I, **CAMBRAI** has kept enough of its character to make a passing visit worthwhile, though it is less attractive than either Douai, its sister town 27km to the north, or Arras to the northwest.

The huge, cobbled main square, **place Aristide-Briand**, is dominated by the Neoclassical Hôtel de Ville, and still suggests the town's former wealth, which was based on the textile and agricultural industries. Unlike most places, Cambrai's chief ecclesiastical treasure is not its cathedral – the medieval one was dismantled after the Revolution – but the **Church of St-Géry**, off rue St-Aubert west of the main square, worth a visit for a celebrated *Mise au Tombeau* by Rubens. The appealingly presented **Musée de Cambrai** (10am–noon & 2–6pm; €3, free first weekend of every month) at 15 rue de l'Épée, a short way south of the town square, is also worthwhile. Paintings by Velázquez, Utrillo and Ingres feature prominently alongside works by various Flemish old masters, plus great twentieth-century artists like Zadkine and Van Dongen. Don't turn down the audio-guided tour and don't leave out the archeological display in the basement, where you can see some fascinating exhibits including elegant statues rescued from the decimated cathedral. Look out for the *gourde eucharistique de Concevreux*, an amazingly well-preserved sixth-century bronze hipflask.

Cambrai's **tourist office** is housed in the Maison Espagnole on the corner of avenue de la Victoire at 48 rue de Noyon (Mon–Sat 10am–noon & 2–6pm, Sun 3–6pm; ⓣ03.27.78.36.15, ⓦwww.cambraiofficedetourisme.com). Central **accommodation** includes *Le Mouton Blanc*, 33 rue d'Alsace-Lorraine

Cambrai 1917

At dawn on November 20, 1917, the first full-scale **tank battle** in history began at Cambrai, when over 400 British tanks poured over the Hindenburg Line. In just 24 hours, the Royal Tank Corps and British Third Army made an advance that was further than any undertaken by either side since the trenches had first been dug in 1914. A fortnight later, however, casualties on both sides had reached 50,000, and the armies were back where they'd started.

Although in some respects the tanks were ahead of their time, they still relied on cavalry and plodding infantry as their back-up and runners for their lines of communication. And, before they even reached the "green fields beyond", most of them had broken down. World War I tanks were primitive machines, operated by a crew of eight who endured almost intolerable conditions – with no ventilation system, the temperature inside could rise to 48°C. The steering alone required three men, each on separate gearboxes, communicating by hand signals through the din of the tank's internal noise. Maximum speed (6kph) dropped to almost 1kph over rough terrain, and refuelling was necessary every 55km. Consequently, of the 179 tanks lost in the battle at Cambrai, very few were destroyed by the enemy; the majority broke down and were abandoned by their crews.

(Ⓣ03.27.81.30.16, Ⓦmouton-blanc.com; ④), a convenient and moderately priced hotel close to the station, with a posh **restaurant** inside (from €18; closed Sun eve & Mon, plus the eves of public hols & Aug 1–15). Alternatively, there is a small, family-oriented **hostel**, *L'Étape*, 1.5km southeast of the centre of town on Sentier de l'Église (Ⓣ03.27.37.80.80, Ⓔeducrotois@l-etape.asso.fr; €11.70). The nearest **campsite** is *Les Colombes* at Aubencheul-au-Bac (mid-March to mid-Oct; Ⓣ03.27.89.25.90), 10km away off the N43 to Douai. Crêperie *La Sarrazine* opposite the tourist office at 1 place St-Sépulcre is the best bet for an economical **meal** (closed Sun).

Le Cateau-Cambrésis

Twenty-two kilometres east of Cambrai along an old Roman road, the small town of **LE CATEAU-CAMBRÉSIS** is the birthplace of Henri Matisse (1869–1954), and as a gift to his home town, the artist bequeathed it a collection of his works. Some of them are displayed in the **Musée Matisse** (daily except Tues: June–Sept 10am–6pm; Oct–May 10am–noon & 2–6pm; €4.50, free first Sun of month), housed in Palais Fénelon in the centre of town. Although no major works are displayed, this is the third-largest Matisse collection in France, and the paintings here are no less attractive and interesting than the better-known ones exhibited elsewhere. The collection includes several studies for the chapel in Vence, plus a whole series of his characteristically simple pen-and-ink sketches. Also worth looking at is the work of local Cubist Auguste Herbin, particularly his psychedelic upright piano. For somewhere to **stay** and eat there's the simple but comfortable *Hostellerie du Marché* at 9 rue Landrecies (Ⓣ03.27.84.09.32, Ⓦwww.hostelleriedumarche.com; ②; menus €14 & €20).

Arras, Albert and the Somme battlefields

Around **Arras** and **Albert** some of the fiercest and most futile battles of World War I took place. The beautiful town of Arras, easily accessible from Paris and

Lille by TGV, is the best base for exploring the battlefields. Nearby to the north, at the moving **Vimy Ridge,** Canadians fell in their thousands, while at Notre-Dame de Lorette, the French suffered the same fate; the battlefields and cemeteries of the Somme lie to the south, around **Albert** and **Péronne**, home to a fascinating museum devoted to explaining and remembering the war.

Arras

ARRAS, with its fine old centre, is one of the prettiest towns in northern France. It was renowned for its tapestries in the Middle Ages, giving its name to the hangings behind which Shakespeare's Polonius was killed by Hamlet. Subsequently the town fell under Spanish control, and many of its citizens today claim that Spanish blood runs in their veins. Only in 1640 was Arras returned to the kingdom of France, with the help of Cyrano de Bergerac. During World War I, the British used it as a base, digging tunnels under the town to try to surprise the Germans to the northeast.

Although destroyed by the Germans in World War I, the town bears few obvious battle scars. Reconstruction here, particularly after World War II, has been careful and stylish, and two grand arcaded Flemish- and Dutch-style squares in the centre – **Grand'Place** and the smaller **Place des Héros** – preserve their historic, harmonious character, though both resemble large car parks today. On every side are restored seventeenth- and eighteenth-century mansions and, on place des Héros, there's a grandly ornate **Hôtel de Ville**, its entrance hall housing a photographic display documenting the wartime destruction of the town and sheltering a set of *géants* (festival giants) awaiting the city's next fête.

Also inside the town hall is the entrance to the **belfry** viewing platform, 150m high – to which a lift fortunately takes you up almost all the way (€2.60) – and **les souterrains** (or *les boves*) – cold, dark passageways and spacious vaults tunnelled since the Middle Ages, and completed by the British during World War I, beneath the centre of the city (frequent bilingual guided tours – ask for times in the tourist office; €4.60). Once down, you're escorted on a 40-minute tour and given an interesting survey of local history. The rooms – many of which have fine, tiled floors and lovely pillars and stairways – were used as a British barracks and hospital. Pictures from this period are on display, as is a bilingual newspaper published for the soldiers. In the spring, some of the rooms are converted into an underground garden.

Next to its enormous cathedral is Arras's other main sight, the **Benedictine Abbaye St-Vaast**, a grey-stone classical building – still pockmarked by wartime shrapnel – erected in the eighteenth century by Cardinal Rohen. The abbey now houses the **Musée des Beaux-Arts**, with its entrance at 22 rue Paul-Donnier (daily except Tues 9.30am–noon & 2–5.30pm; €4), which contains a motley collection of paintings, including a couple of Jordaens and Brueghels, plus fragments of sculpture and local porcelain. Only one of the tapestries or *arras* that made the town famous in medieval times survived the wartime bombardments. Figuring among the highlights are a pair of delicately sculpted thirteenth-century angels, the *Anges de Saudemont*, and a room on the first floor filled with vivid seventeenth-century paintings by Philippe de Champaigne and his contemporaries, including his own *Présentation de la Vierge au Temple*.

Nearby, on the small, dark rue Maximillien-Robespierre, opposite a ghostly mask and costume shop, is the **Maison Robespierre**, home between 1787 and 1789 to the revolutionary leader before his hands were stained with blood, and now a small museum (9.30am–noon & 2–5.30pm; free).

Thirty minutes away by foot on the mournful western edge of town, along boulevard Général-de-Gaulle from the Vauban barracks (which although a citadelle was monikered "*la belle inutile*" because it served no purpose in protecting the city, even when it was built in 1668), is a **war cemetery** and memorial by the British architect Sir Edwin Lutyens. It's a movingly elegiac, classical colonnade of ivy-covered brick and stone, commemorating 35,928 missing soldiers, the endless columns of their names inscribed on the walls. Around the back of the barracks, alongside an overgrown moat, is the **Mémorial des Fusillés**, a stark wall accessed via the avenue of the same name; its plaques commemorate two hundred Resistance fighters shot by firing squad in World War II – many of them of Polish descent, nearly all of them miners, and most of them Communists.

On a lighter note, if you are in Arras for the last Sunday of August, the town transforms itself into an open-air bistro for La Fête de l'Andouillette, with parades, colourful costumes and tasting of the sausage itself.

Practicalities

From the **gare SNCF** it's a ten-minute walk up rue Gambetta then rue Désiré-Delansorne, to the **tourist office**, located in the Hôtel de Ville on place des Héros (May–Sept Mon–Sat 9am–6.30pm, Sun 10am–1pm & 2.30–6.30pm; Oct–April Mon 10am–noon & 2–6pm, Tues–Sat 9am–noon & 2–6pm, Sun 10am–12.30pm & 2.30–6.30pm; ⓣ03.21.51.26.95, ⓦwww.ot-arras.fr); the tourist office is worth consulting for details of transport and tours of local battlefields (see "Vimy Ridge and around", p.260). To reach the Vimy memorial, you can also rent a car from Hertz, boulevard Carnot (ⓣ03.21.23.11.14), or Euroto, 15 av Paul-Michonneau (ⓣ03.21.55.05.05).

There are two good, inexpensive **hotels** on the beautiful squares in the centre: the *Diamant*, 5 place des Héros (ⓣ03.21.71.23.23, ⓦwww.arras-hotel-diamant.com; ❸), a comfortable, reliable two-star; and *Ostel Les Trois Luppars*, 47 Grand'Place (ⓣ03.21.60.02.03, ⓦwww.ostel-les-3luppars.com; ❸), a friendly family-run place with modern facilities in a characterful old building. For a more luxurious night, go to the *Univers*, a beautiful former monastery around a courtyard at 3 place de la Croix-Rouge, near the Abbaye St-Vaast (ⓣ03.21.71.34.01, ⓦwww.hotel-univers-arras.com; ❹; restaurant €20–42). Near the train station there are hotels in nearly every price range, including the shabby but inexpensive one-star, *Le Passe Temps* (ⓣ03.21.50.04.04, ⓕ03.21.50.33.78; ❶); and the top-of-the-range *Hotel d'Angleterre* (ⓣ03.21.51.51.16, ⓦwww.hotelangleterre.info; ❻). The newly modernized **hostel** is extremely well positioned at 59 Grand'Place (ⓣ03.21.22.70.02, ⓕ03.21.07.46.15; closed Dec & Jan; €11.70, HI cardholders only). The municipal **campsite** at 166 rue du Temple (ⓣ03.21.71.55.06; closed Feb & March) lies 1km out of town on the Bapaume road.

Restaurants worth trying include *La Rapière*, 44 Grand'Place (ⓣ03.21.55.09.92), with excellent regional food and menus from €14.50; and, for a splurge, the gourmet *La Faisanderie*, across the square at no. 45 (ⓣ03.21.48.20.76; from €23). Nearer the station at 26 bd de Strasbourg is an attractive, old-fashioned brasserie, *La Coupole*, where you'll find locals and tourists eating oysters and other fresh seafood, as well as traditional brasserie dishes (ⓣ03.21.71.88.44; €29 menu; closed Sat lunch).

There's a good *fromagerie*, Jean-Claude Leclercq, at 39 place des Héros (closed Mon). Saturdays are the best day for food and wine, when the squares are taken up with a morning **market**, and Resto Cave, an extensive sixteenth-century wine cellar run by the delightfully large and quirky proprietor of the *Trois Luppars*, is open for the sale of fine wines (10am–1pm & 3–8pm).

Vimy Ridge and around

Eight kilometres north of Arras on the D49, **Vimy Ridge**, or Hill 145, was the scene of some of the worst trench warfare of World War I: almost two full years of battle, culminating in its capture by the Canadian Corps in April 1917. It's

△ Vimy Ridge

a vast site, given in perpetuity to the Canadian people out of respect for their sacrifices, and the churned land has been preserved, in part, as it was during the conflict. You really need your own transport to get there as the nearest bus stop is 45 minutes' walk away (for details contact the tourist office in Arras). Alternatively, a private taxi tour can be booked in advance with Mr Ishak (Ⓣ06.16.20.34.38), whose father and grandfather fought with the Canadian forces. It is well worth the journey – of all the battlefields, it is perhaps easiest here to gain an impression of the lay of the land, and of how it may actually have felt to be part of a World War I battle.

There's an **information centre** (daily 10am–6pm; Ⓣ03.21.50.68.68) supervised by friendly, bilingual Canadian students, who run free guided **tours** (daily 10am–5.30pm; call to book, or check in at the office near the trenches upon arrival). Tours are run either of the "subway", the Canadian term for the series of interlinking underground tunnels used as secret passageways and to hoard ammunition and equipment, or of the cemeteries and battlefields. No children under 12 are allowed underground and it is advisable to have something warm to wear.

Near the information centre, long worms of neat, sanitized **trenches** meander over the now grassy ground, still heavily pitted by shell bursts beneath the planted pines. Grenades and shrapnel are still found here, and pedestrians are warned not to stray from the directed paths on to the grassy areas. Filled in by topsoil and grass, some of the craters have become smaller over time, but the ground remains sufficiently damaged and uneven, almost a hundred years later, to relay the impact of these battles. Beneath the ground lie some 11,000 bodies still unaccounted for and countless rounds of unexploded ammunition.

On the brow of the ridge to the north of the trenches, overlooking the slag-heap-dotted plain of Artois, a great white **monument** reaches for the heavens, inscribed with the names of 11,285 Canadians and Newfoundlanders whose bodies were never found. It must have been an unenviable task to design a fitting memorial to such slaughter, but this one, aided by its setting, succeeds with great drama. Nearby is a subdued but informative **museum** (same hours as the information centre; free), which illustrates the well-planned Canadian attack and and its importance for the Canadians. This was the first time that they were recognized as fighting separarately from the British, thus adding to their growing sense of nationhood.

Back from the ridge lies a memorial to the Moroccan Division who also fought at Vimy, and in the woods behind, on the headstones of another exquisitely maintained cemetery, you can read the names of half the counties of rural England.

La Targette, Neuville-St-Vaast and Notre-Dame de Lorette

At the crossroads (D937/D49) of **LA TARGETTE**, 8km north from the centre of Arras and accessible from there by bus, the **Musée de la Targette** (daily 9am–8pm; €3) contains an interesting collection of World War I and II artefacts. It's the private collection of one David Bardiaux, assembled with passion and meticulous attention to detail under the inspiration of tales told by his grandfather, a veteran of the 1916 Battle of Verdun. Its appeal lies in the absolute precision with which the thirty-odd mannequins of British, French, Canadian and German soldiers are dressed and equipped, down to their sweet and tobacco tins and such rarities as a 1915 British-issue cap with earflaps – very comfortable for the troops but withdrawn because the top brass thought it made their men look like yokels. All the exhibits have been under fire; some belonged to known individuals and are complete with stitched-up tears of old wounds.

More **cemeteries** lie a little to the south of La Targette, nominally at **NEUVILLE-ST-VAAST**, though the village is actually 1km away to the east. There's a small British cemetery, a huge French one, and an equally large and moving German cemetery, containing the remains of 44,833 Germans, four to a cross or singly under a Star of David. In the village itself a Polish memorial – among the Poles that died in action here was the sculptor Henri Gaudier-Brzeska, in 1915 – and a Czech cemetery face each other across the main street.

On a bleak hill a few kilometres to the northwest of Vimy Ridge (and 5km north of Neuville-St-Vaast) is the church of **Notre-Dame de Lorette**, scene of a costly French offensive in May 1915. The original church was blasted to bits during the war and rebuilt in grim Neo-Byzantine style in the 1920s, grey and dour on the outside but rich and bejewelled inside. It now stands at the centre of a vast graveyard with over 20,000 crosses laid out in pairs, back to back, each one separated by a cluster of roses. There are 20,000 more buried in the ossuary, and there's the small **Musée Vivant 1914–1918** (daily 9am–8pm; €3) behind the church, displaying photographs, uniforms and other military paraphernalia. You can reach Notre-Dame de Lorette by bus from Arras, direction "Lens".

Albert and around

The church at **ALBERT**, 40km south of Arras and 30km northeast of Amiens – now, with the rest of the town, completely rebuilt – was one of the minor landmarks of World War I. Its tall tower was hit by German bombing early on in the campaign, leaving the statue of the Madonna on top leaning at a precarious angle. The British, entrenched over three years in the region, came to know it as the "Leaning Virgin". Army superstition had it that when she fell the war would end, a myth inspiring frequent hopeful pot shots by disgruntled troops. Before

The Battle of the Somme

On July 1, 1916, the British and French launched the **Battle of the Somme** to relieve pressure on the French army defending Verdun. The front ran roughly northwest–southeast, 6km east of Albert across the valley of the Ancre and over the almost treeless high ground north of the Somme – huge hedgeless wheat fields now. These windy open hills had no intrinsic value, nor was there any long-term strategic objective – the region around Albert was the battle-site simply because it was where the two Allied armies met.

There were 57,000 British casualties on the first day alone, approximately 20,000 of them dead, making it the costliest defeat the British army has ever suffered. **Sir Douglas Haig** is the usual scapegoat for the Somme, yet he was only following the military thinking of the day, which is where the real problem lay. As historian A.J.P. Taylor put it, "Defence was mechanized: attack was not." Machine guns were efficient, barbed wire effective, and, most important of all, the rail lines could move defensive reserves far faster than the attacking army could march. The often ineffective heavy bombardment that presaged an advance was favoured by both sides but only made matters worse, since the shells forewarned the enemy of an offensive and churned the trenches into a giant muddy quagmire.

Despite the bloody disaster of the first day, the battle wore on until bad weather in November made further attacks impossible. The cost of this futile struggle was roughly 415,000 British, 195,000 French and 600,000 German casualties.

embarking on a visit of the region's battle sites and war cemeteries, otherwise known as the Circuit de Souvenir (see below), you might want to stop in at the **Musée "Somme 1916"** (daily: Feb–May & Oct to mid-Dec 9am–noon & 2–6pm; June–Sept 9am–6pm; €4), an underground museum which has re-enactments of fifteen different scenes from life in the trenches of the Somme in 1916. The mannequins look slightly too jolly and eager but it does go some way to bringing the props to life. The museum's final section recreates the actual battle scene, complete with flashing lights and the sound of exploding shells. Enthusiastically portrayed, some may find this a little tasteless, though to others it may in part succeed in explaining how soldiers, forced to live in these conditions for long periods, returned home with shell-shock.

As you arrive (trains from Amiens or Arras), the town's new tower, capped now by an equally improbably posed statue, is the first thing that catches your eye. The **tourist office** is close by at 9 rue Gambetta (April–Sept Mon–Sat 10am–noon & 2–6.30pm, Sun 9.30am–noon; Oct–March Mon–Sat 10am–noon & 3–5pm; Ⓣ03.22.75.16.42). Cobbers Tours (Ⓣ06.80.08.68.63, Ⓔcobbers@tiscali.fr) is based in Albert and specializes in offering an Australian accent to story of the battlefields. Of the town's **hotels**, *La Paix*, a friendly establishment with a decent restaurant, at 43 rue Victor-Hugo (Ⓣ03.22.75.01.64, Ⓕ03.22.75.44.17; ❸; menus from €14), is the only one that can be recommended.

The Circuit de Souvenir

Was it for this the clay grew tall?
O what made fatuous sunbeams toil
To break earth's sleep at all?

Wilfred Owen, *Futility*

The **Circuit de Souvenir** conducts you from graveyard to mine crater, trench to memorial. There's not a lot to see; certainly no evidence of the shocking atrocities and scenes of destruction that happened here less than a hundred years ago. Neither do you get much sense of movement or even of battle tactics. But you will find that, no matter what the level of your interest in the Great War, you have in fact embarked on a sort of pilgrimage, in which each successive step becomes more harrowing and oppressive.

The **cemeteries** are the most moving aspect of the region – beautiful, the grass perfectly mown, an individual bed of flowers at the foot of every gravestone. And there are tens of thousands of gravestones, all identical, with a man's name, if it's known (nearly half the British dead have never been found), and his rank and regiment. In the lanes between Albert and Bapaume you'll see the cemeteries everywhere: at the angle of copses, halfway across a wheat field, in the middle of a bluebell wood, terrible in their simple beauty.

Lying on minor roads, the circuit can be explored by either car or bicycle. Both Albert to the west and Péronne to the southeast (see p.264) make good starting points, the tourist offices and museums in either town are able to provide you with a free **map** of the circuit. Once en route, sights of interest are marked along the road by arrows and poppy symbols, with Commonwealth graves also indicated in English. It would be difficult to see all of the 400 British and Commonwealth cemeteries in the area, though getting off the beaten track to visit one or two small ones can be rewarding. What follows is necessarily just a selected handful of some of the better-known sites.

If you start from Albert the first town you'll reach is **BEAUMONT-HAMEL** (7km north), where the 51st Highland Division walked abreast to their deaths with their pipes playing. Here, on the hilltop where most of them died, a series of trenches, now grassed over and eroding, is preserved. Just across the river, towards the village of **THIEPVAL**, the 5000 Ulstermen who died in the Battle of the Somme are commemorated by the incongruously Celtic **Ulster Memorial**, a replica of Helen's Tower at Clandeboyne near Belfast (information bureau open Mon–Sat 11am–5pm; closed Dec & Jan). Probably the most famous of Edwin Lutyens' many memorials is south of Thiepval: the colossal **Memorial to the Missing**, in memory of the 73,357 British troops whose bodies were never recovered at the Somme.

Five kilometres east at **POZIÈRES** on the Albert–Bapaume road is perhaps the oddest memorial. Here, *Le Tommy* café has a permanent World War I exhibition (daily 9.30am–6pm; free) in its back garden, consisting mainly of a reconstructed section of trench and "equipped" with genuine battlefield relics, all accompanied by a recorded loop of patriotic British war songs. It's a bit amateurish, but worth a look if you're passing through. The French owner of the café had first collected objects from the battlefield as a boy to sell for pocket money. Farmers apparently still turn up several tonnes of shells every year – not surprising when you think the British alone fired one and a half million shells in the last week of June 1916.

Delville Wood, known as "**Devil's Wood**", lies another 5km to the east at **LONGUEVAL**. Here, thousands of **South Africans** lost their lives, and a memorial to the dead from both world wars has been erected, as well as a small **museum** (daily except Mon: April–Oct 10am–5.45pm, Nov & March 10am–3.45pm) relating not just the battle in France but also the longest march of the war, undertaken thousands of kilometres away, when South African troops walked 800km to drive the Germans out of East Africa (now Tanzania).

The most informative of all the World War I museums in the surrounding *départements* is at **PÉRONNE**, on the River Somme some 25km east of Albert – the **Historial de la Grande Guerre** (mid-Jan to mid-Dec 10am–6pm; €7.50). All kinds of exhibits – such as newsreel and film footage, newspapers, posters, commemorative plates, Otto Dix drawings and artificial limbs – combine with displays of hardware to provide a broad, modern view of the whole catastrophe. It also provides an excellent history of the complex political and cultural tensions that led to war, something that is lacking in most of the other sights.

There's a **TGV** station about 15km away from Péronne – the **Gare Haute Picardie** – which is thirty minutes from the Eurostar stop at Lille-Europe; for a taxi to or from the station, call Mouret (Ⓣ03.22.84.15.83) or Fouque (Ⓣ03.22.84.52.49). The **tourist office** is at 1 rue Louis XI, opposite the museum (June–Aug Mon–Sat 9am–noon & 2–6.30pm, Sun 10am–noon & 3–6pm; Sept–May closed Sun; Ⓣ03.22.84.42.38). **Accommodation** includes the old-fashioned *Hostellerie des Remparts*, on the opposite side of the main square at 23 rue Beaubois (Ⓣ03.22.84.01.22, Ⓕ03.22.84.38.96; ❸; restaurant from €16), or the modern *Campanile* (Ⓣ03.22.84.22.22, Ⓕ03.22.84.16.86; ❸), part of a chain, just out of town on the N17 to Roye and Paris.

To the southwest of the main circuit near **VILLERS-BRETONNEUX**, 18km southwest of Albert near the River Somme, stands another fine Lutyens memorial. As at Vimy, the landscaping of the **Australian Memorial** here is dramatic – for the full effect, climb up to the viewing platform of the stark white central tower. The monument was one of the last to be inaugurated, in July 1938, when the prospects for peace were again looking bleak.

Aisne and Oise

To the southeast of the Somme, away from the coast and the main Paris through-routes, the often rainwashed and dull province of Picardy becomes considerably more inviting. In the *départements* of **Aisne** and **Oise**, where the region merges with neighbouring Champagne, there are some real attractions amid the lush wooded hills. **Laon**, **Soissons** and **Noyon** all centre around handsome Gothic cathedrals, while at **Compiègne**, Napoleon Bonaparte and Napoléon III enjoyed the luxury of a magnificent château and embellished it to their hearts' content. The most rewarding overnight stop is off the beaten track in the tiny fortified town of **Coucy-le-Château-Auffrique**, in the forest and on a hill between Soissons and Laon. **Transport** is good, too, with a network of bus connections from Amiens and good train and bus links with Paris.

Laon

Looking out over the plains of Champagne and Picardy from the spine of a high narrow ridge, still protected by its gated medieval walls, **LAON** (pronounced "Lon") is one of the highlights of the region. Dominating the town, and visible for miles around, are the five great towers of one of the earliest and finest Gothic cathedrals in the country. Of all the cathedral towns in the Aisne, Laon is the one to head for.

Arrival, information and accommodation

Arriving by train or road, you'll find yourself in the disappointingly shabby and characterless lower town, or **ville basse**. To get to the upper town – **ville haute** – without your own transport, you can make the stiff climb up the steps at the end of avenue Carnot, or take the **Poma 2000** (Mon–Sat 7am–8pm every 3–6 min, irregularly on Sun 2.30–6pm in summer only; one-day return ticket €1), a fully automated, rubber-tyred, overland métro, Laon's pride and joy; you board next to the train station and alight by the town hall (Terminus "Hôtel de Ville") on place Général-Leclerc; from there a left turn down rue Sérurier brings you nose to nose with the cathedral.

The **tourist office** (daily 10am–1pm & 2–6pm; ⓣ03.23.20.28.62, ⓦwww.tourisme-paysdelaon.com) is right by the western end of the cathedral, housed within the impressive Gothic Hôtel-Dieu, built in 1209; ask for information about local *gîtes* and guesthouses. If you need **accommodation** in the *ville basse* (if you arrive too late to take the Poma), try *Hôtel Welcome* (ⓣ03.23.23.06.11, ⓔhotel-welcome.laon@orange.fr; ❶), at 2 av Carnot, straight in front of the *gare SNCF*. Otherwise, in the *ville haute*, *Hôtel de la Paix*, 52 rue St-Jean (ⓣ03.23.79.06.34; ❶; restaurant from €11, closed Sat & Sun), is inexpensive, though you'd do better at the charming and characterful old *Les Chevaliers*, at 3–5 rue Sérurier, near the Poma stop (ⓣ03.23.27.17.50, ⓔhotelchevaliers@aol.com; ❸). Laon's smartest accommodation is at the three-star *Hôtel de la Bannière de France*, 11 rue Franklin-Roosevelt (ⓣ03.23.23.21.44, ⓦwww.hoteldelabannieredefrance.com; ❹; decent traditional restaurant from

€20). *La Chênaie* (☎03.23.20.25.56; Jan–Sept), Laon's **campsite**, is on allée de la Chênaie, on the northwest side of town.

The Town

Laon really only has one attraction, its magnificent **Cathédrale Notre-Dame** (daily 9am–6.30pm; guided tours at 3pm from tourist office: July & Aug daily; Sept–June Sat, Sun & public hols only). Built in the second half of the twelfth century, the cathedral was a trendsetter in its day, elements of its design – the gabled porches, the imposing towers and the gallery of arcades above the west front – being repeated at Chartres, Reims and Notre-Dame in Paris. When wrapped in thick mist, the towers seem otherworldly. The creatures craning from the uppermost ledges, looking like reckless mountain goats borrowed from a medieval bestiary, are reputed to have been carved in memory of the valiant horned steers who lugged the cathedral's masonry up from the plains below. Inside, the effects are no less dramatic – the high white nave is lit by the dense ruby, sapphire and emerald tones of the stained glass, which at close range reveals the appealing scratchy, smoky quality of medieval glass.

Crowded in the cathedral's lee is a web of quiet, grey, eighteenth-century streets. One – rue Pourier – leads past the post office and onto the thirteenth-century Porte d'Ardon, which looks out over the southern part of the *ville basse*. A left turn at the post office along rue Ermant leads to the little twelfth-century octagonal **Chapelle des Templiers** – the Knights Templar – set in a secluded garden. Next door is the **Musée de Laon**, 32 rue Georges-Ermant (June–Sept Tues–Sun 11am–6pm; Oct–May Tues–Sun 2–6pm; €3.20), which contains a pitifully displayed collection of classical antiquities, albeit with some fine Grecian ceramics among them, and a jumble of furniture and paintings, including an acclaimed seventeenth-century work, *Le Concert*, by local lad Mathieu Le Nain. The rest of the *ville haute*, which rambles along the ridge to the west of the cathedral into the Le Bourg quarter around the early Gothic church of St-Martin, is enjoyable to wander round, with fine views from the **ramparts**.

Eating, drinking and entertainment

Simple **snacks** and basic meals can be had at the *Brasserie du Parvis*, which overlooks the west front of the cathedral (*plats* around €10); at *Crêperie L'Agora*, an inexpensive Breton place near the cathedral at 16 rue des Cordeliers (open until 1am; closed Sat lunch & Mon; menu €7.50); at *La Bonne Heure*, specializing in quiche-like *tourtinettes* (€6 each) at 53 rue Châtelaine; or at the lively *Brasserie les Chenizelles*, 1 rue du Bourg, the continuation of rue Châtelaine (menus from €13.50). Proper **restaurants** in Laon tend to be expensive: *La Petite Auberge*, the gourmets' favourite, at 45 bd Pierre-Brossolette in the *ville basse* near the station, falls into this category, serving traditional French cuisine using the freshest ingredients (menus from €23; ☎03.23.23.02.38, booking recommended; closed Sat lunch, Sun and Mon eve). They also own the bistro next door, which is slightly less pricey. There's also an excellent selection of wine shops, boulangeries and *fromageries* along pedestrianized rue Châtelaine, in the *ville haute*.

There's usually something going on at the **Maison des Arts de Laon** (MAL), based in a theatre on the place Aubry to the north of the cathedral – including a concentration of events during the Fêtes Médiévales de Laon held in late May. October sees a series of big-name classical concerts during the Festival de Laon, either in the cathedral or MAL venues (details from the tourist office), while for a week in June Laon plays host to hundreds of antique cars, which come and follow a circuit of the city and surrounding region (☎03.23.79.83.58 for details). *Le Welcome*, next door to MAL arts complex on the place, is an Irish-style **bar** and a good place for a drink.

Soissons and around

Half an hour by train, or 30km down the N2, southwest of Laon, **SOISSONS** can lay claim to a long and highly strategic history. Before the Romans arrived it was already a town, and in 486 AD it was here that the last Roman ruler, Syagrius, suffered a decisive defeat at the hands of Clovis the Frank, making Soissons one of the first real centres of the Frankish kingdom. Napoleon, too, considered it a crucial military base, a judgement borne out in the twentieth century by extensive war damage.

The town boasts the fine, if not well-known, **Cathédrale Notre-Dame** – thirteenth century for the most part with majestic glass and vaulting – at the west end of the main square, place F.-Marquigny. More impressive still is the ruined **Abbaye de St-Jean-des-Vignes**, to the south of the cathedral down rue Panleu and then right down rue St-Jean. The facade of the tremendous Gothic abbey church rises sheer and grand, impervious to the now empty space behind it. The rest of the complex, save for remnants of a **cloister** and **refectory** (free to visit), was dismantled in 1804. Near the *abbaye* is the impressive eighteenth-century **Hôtel de Ville** with its grand stone gate.

Practicalities

Soissons is relatively compact. From the **gare SNCF** (with good services to Laon and Paris) the main square is a fifteen-minute walk away along avenue du Général-de-Gaulle, which becomes rue St-Martin. The **gare routière** is closer to the centre by the river on Le Mail; buses leave for Compiègne early in the morning, at lunchtime and at the end of the afternoon. The **tourist office** is on place F.-Marquigny behind the cathedral (mid-June to mid-Sept Mon–Sat 9.30am–6.30pm, Sun 9.30am–12.30pm & 2–6pm; mid-Sept to mid-June Mon–Sat 9.30am–12.30pm & 2–6.30pm, Sun 9.30am–12.30pm & 2–6pm; ⓣ03.23.53.17.37).

The town is more of a place to stop en route than to **stay** but if you're keen to explore the nearby forest or are just stuck, try the reasonably priced two-star hotel *Terminus* by the station at 56 av du Général-de-Gaulle (ⓣ03.23.53.33.59; ❷; closed Sun & Aug), or the **campsite** (ⓣ03.23.74.52.69), 1km from the station on avenue du Mail. An excellent place for *galettes* is *La Galetière* (closed Mon) at 1 rue du Beffroi by the cathedral, and there's a good Tunisian **restaurant**, the *Sidi Bou*, at 4 rue de la Bannière down towards the river.

Coucy-le-Château-Auffrique

About 30km west of Laon, and just over 15km north of Soissons, in hilly countryside on the far side of the forest of St-Gobain, lie the straggling ruins of one of the greatest castles of the Middle Ages, **Coucy-le-Château** (daily: April & Sept 10am–12.30pm & 2–6pm; May–Aug 10am–12.30pm & 2–6.30pm; Oct–March Mon–Fri 10am–12.30pm & 2–5pm; €4.60). The castle's walls still stand, and encircle the attractive village of **COUCY-LE-CHÂTEAU-AUFFRIQUE**. In the past this was a seat of great power and the influence of its lords, the Sires de Coucy, rivalled and often even exceeded that of the king – "King I am not, neither Prince, Duke nor Count. I am the Sire of Coucy" was

Enguerrand III's proud boast. The retreating Germans capped the destruction of World War I battles by blowing up the castle's keep as they left in 1917, but enough remains, crowning a wooded spur, to be extremely evocative.

Enter the village through one of three original gates, squeezed between powerful, round flanking towers – there's a footpath all around the outside which is open even when the castle is closed. A small museum, the **Tour de Coucy Musée Panorama** (daily: May–Sept 2.30–6.30pm; Oct–April 2.30–6pm; free), in the tower at the **Porte de Soissons** on the south side of the walled part of town, has a display of photographs showing how it looked pre-1917, which can be compared with today's remains from the vantage point of the roof.

Practicalities

It's hard to get to Coucy-le-Château without a car, though several Laon–Soissons trains stop at Anizy-Pinon – which cuts the distance by about half and there is an infrequent bus to or from Soissons. The **tourist office** is in the central square (May–Aug Mon–Sat 9.30am–12.30pm & 2–6pm, Sun 2–6pm; Sept–April Mon–Sat 10am–12.30pm & 2–6pm; ⓣ03.23.52.44.55), just north of the Porte de Soissons. There are so many medieval spectacles offered in this magical non-Disney town that checking ⓦwww.coucy.com in advance of your visit to book some tickets is highly recommended.

Staying the night here, especially if you have children, is something special. For **accommodation**, try the *Hôtel Le Belle Vue* within the walls, although the bedrooms have seen better days (ⓣ03.23.52.69.70, ⓦwww.hotel-bellevue-coucy.com; ❷; closed last week Dec); its restaurant specializes in Picardy cuisine (menus from €20), and serves special "medieval" meals (€17) on certain summer nights, when medieval re-enactments are held across the city.

Compiègne and around

Thirty-eight kilometres west of Soissons lies **COMPIÈGNE**, whose reputation as a tourist centre rests on the presence of a vast royal palace, built at the edge of the Forêt de Compiègne in order that generations of French kings could play at "being peasants", in Louis XIV's words. Although the town itself is a bit of a one-horse place with a bland, Sunday-afternoon feel, it's worth a visit for the opulent palace interiors, and a good base for walks in the surrounding forest and a day-trip to the cathedral town of Noyon.

Arrival, information and accommodation

The **gares routière** and **SNCF** are adjacent to each other, just a few minutes' walk away from the centre of town: cross the wide River Oise and go up rue Solférino to place de l'Hôtel-de-Ville. The **tourist office** (April–Sept Mon–Sat 9.15am–12.15pm & 1.45–6.15pm, Sun 10am–12.15pm & 2.15–5pm; Oct–March Mon 1.45–5.15pm, Tues–Sat 9.15am–12.15pm & 1.45–5.15pm, Sun 10am–12.15pm & 2.15–5pm; ⓣ03.44.40.01.00) takes up part of the ornate Hôtel de Ville. It offers free hotel bookings, and will provide you with a plan of the town, on which is conveniently marked an exhaustive visitors' route, including the forest paths (see p.270).

As for **accommodation**, there are cheap rooms at the *Hôtel St-Antoine*, 17 rue de Paris (ⓣ03.44.23.22.27; ❶), concealed above a Chinese restaurant. A little more expensive but much more comfortable is the *Hôtel Vega*, 4 rue du Général-Leclerc (ⓣ03.44.23.32.17; ❷). *Hôtel de Flandre*, at 16 quai de la

République (Ⓣ03.44.83.24.40, Ⓦhoteldeflandre.com; ❶–❸), has some good-value, simple top-floor rooms with hall showers and is near the train station overlooking the river.

The Town

Compiègne itself is plain disappointing, though that shouldn't come as a surprise, as a platoon of German soldiers burnt it down in 1942 to provide their commander with evidence of a subjugated community. Fortunately, however, they spared the town's star attraction, the large and opulent **Palais National**, with its extensive gardens, which make excellent picnicking ground. The seventeenth-and eighteenth-century Palais stands two blocks east of the Hôtel de Ville (see below) on rue des Minimes, and for all its pompous excess, inspires a certain fascination, particularly its interior, which can only be visited on a guided tour (March–Oct 10am–6pm; Nov–Feb 10am–4.30pm; €4.50, €5.50 for combined ticket with the Musée de la Voiture). The lavishness of Marie-Antoinette's rooms, the sheer, vulgar sumptuousness of the First and Second Empire and the evidence of the unseemly haste with which Napoleon I moved in, scarcely a dozen years after the Revolution, are impressive. The palace also houses the Musée du Second Empire and the **Musée de la Voiture** (same hours as Palais National but closed on Tuesday; €4, €5.50 combined ticket), the latter containing a wonderful array of antique bicycles, tricycles and fancy aristocratic carriages, as well as the world's first steam coach. The **Théâtre Impérial**, planned (but never finished) by Napoléon III, was finally completed in 1991 at a cost of some thirty million francs. Originally designed with just two seats for Napoléon and his wife, it now seats 900 and is regularly used for concerts.

If you don't want to take the guided tour, a visit to the palace gardens or **petit parc** (daily: summer 7.30am–8pm; winter 8am–6.30pm) is a pleasant alternative. Much of the formal French-style gardens were replaced with a *jardin à l'Angleterre* during the first Empire, which explains the long, lightly landscaped avenue which extends far into the Forêt de Compiègne (see p.270) on the edge of town.

The centre of town is much less picturesque, though several half-timbered buildings remain on the pedestrianized rue Napoléon and rue des Lombards, south of the main place de l'Hôtel-de-Ville. The **Hôtel de Ville** itself – Louis XII Gothic – has ebullient nineteenth-century statuary including the image of Joan of Arc, who was captured in this town by the Burgundians before being handed to the English.

By the side of the town hall is the **Musée de la Figurine Historique** (Tues–Sat 9am–noon & 2–6pm, Sun 2–6pm; closes at 5pm in winter; €2), which features reputedly the world's largest collection of military figurines in mock-up battles from ancient Greece to World War II. Also of specialist interest is the **Musée Vivenel**, on rue d'Austerlitz (same hours and price), which has one of the best collections of Greek vases in the world, notably a series illustrating the Panathenaic Games from Italy; it's a a welcome dose of classical restraint and good taste compared with the palace. There's also a section on the flora and fauna of the Forêt de Compiègne, which includes a wild boar the size of an armoured car.

Eating and drinking

Compiègne lacks a wide variety of good places to **eat**. Notable places include: *Le Cordelier*, 1 rue des Cordeliers (from €14, Ⓣ03.44.40.23.38; closed all day Mon plus Sun and Tues eves), and *Le Bistrot de Flandre*, 2 rue d'Amiens, next to the hotel of the same name. Next to the *Hôtel des Beaux-Arts*, at 35 cours

Guynemer, is one of Compiègne's best restaurants, the *Bistrot des Arts*, serving traditional bistro food with a twist, accompanied by excellent wines, for around €25 a head (☎03.44.20.10.10; closed Sat lunch and Sun). *Le Saint Clair*, 6 rue des Lombards (☎03.44.40.58.18; from €12), guarantees a good meal, a comprehensive selection of Belgian beers and a warm welcome for gay travellers. There is an **Internet** café, *L'évasion* at 5 rue St-Martin. On Saturdays, there's a big all-day **market** in the square by place de l'Hôtel-de-Ville.

The Forêt de Compiègne and the Clairière de l'Armistice

Very ancient, and cut by a succession of hills, streams and valleys, the **Forêt de Compiègne**, with the GR12 running through it, is ideal for walkers and cyclists. East of Compiègne, some 6km into the forest and not far from the banks of the Aisne, is a green and sandy clearing guarded by cypress trees, known as the **Clairière de l'Armistice**. Here, in what was then a rail siding for rail-mounted artillery, World War I was brought to an end on November 11, 1918. A plaque commemorates the deed: "Here the criminal pride of the German empire was brought low, vanquished by the free peoples whom it had sought to enslave." To avenge this humiliation, Hitler had the French sign their capitulation on June 22, 1940, on the same spot, in the very same rail carriage. The original car was taken immediately to Berlin, then destroyed by fire in the last days of the war. Its replacement, housed in a small **museum** (daily except Tues: April–Sept 9am–12.30pm & 2–6pm; Oct–March 9am–noon & 2–5.30pm; €3), is similar, and the objects inside are the originals.

Vieux-Moulin and **St-Jean-aux-Bois** are picturesque villages worth heading for right in the heart of the forest, the latter retaining part of its twelfth-century fortifications; while 13km southeast of Compiègne at **PIERREFONDS** there's a classic medieval **château** (May–Aug 10am–6.30pm; Sept–April 10am–1pm 2–5.30pm; €6.50), built in the twelfth century, and heavily restored since, to make it into a model castle – a fantastic fairy-tale affair of turrets, towers and moat. The inside is unfurnished but displays some beautiful tapestries.

Noyon

Further up the Oise, and a possible day-trip from Compiègne, is **NOYON**, another of Picardy's cathedral towns. Its quiet provinciality belies a long, illustrious history, first as a Roman prefecture, then as seat of a bishopric from 531. Here, in 768, Charlemagne was crowned king of Neustria, largest of the Frankish kingdoms; in 987, Hugues Capet was crowned king of France; and John Calvin was born here in 1509.

Rowing along the Oise on his *Inland Journey* of 1876, Robert Louis Stevenson stopped briefly at Noyon, which he described as "a stack of brown roofs at the best, where I believe people live very respectably in a quiet way". It's still like that, though the **cathedral**, to which Stevenson warmed, is impressive, at least in passing. Spacious and a little stark, it successfully blends Romanesque and Gothic, and is flanked by the ruins of thirteenth-century cloisters and a strange, exquisitely shaped Renaissance library that contains a ninth-century illuminated Bible (only open to the public on the two days of the year, normally the third weekend of September, known as *journées du patrimoine*). On the south side of the cathedral, the old episcopal palace now houses the **Musée du Noyonnais** (Tues–Sun 10am–noon & 2–6pm; Nov–March closes 5pm; €2.50), a small, well-presented collection of local archeological finds and cathedral treasure. Close by, signs direct you to the **Musée Calvin** (same hours; €2.50), ostensibly on the site of the reformer's birthplace. The respectable citizens of Noyon were never among their local boy's adherents and tore down the original building long before its tourist potential was appreciated.

The **tourist office** is in the Hôtel de Ville on place Bertrand Labarre (Mon–Sat 9am–noon & 2–6.15pm, closed Mon morning; in summer also open Sun 10am–noon; ⓣ03.44.44.21.88, ⓦwww.noyon.com). The best **accommodation** option is *Le St Eloi*, at 81 bd Carnot (ⓣ03.44.44.01.49, ⓦwww.hotelsainteloi.fr; ❸; restaurant €23), just off the roundabout between the train station and the cathedral. The nearest **campsite**, *La Montagne* (ⓣ03.44.76.98.29, ⓕ03.44.76.98.29; open all year), is 5km out of town along the N32 to Compiègne. Local buses leave from outside the *gare SNCF*. Big days in Noyon are Saturday morning, when a colourful **market** spills out across place de l'Hôtel-de-Ville, and the first Tuesday of the month, when a livestock market takes over virtually the entire town centre.

Champagne and the Ardennes

The bubbly stuff is the reason why most people visit **Champagne**. The cultivation of vines was already well established in Roman times, when Reims was the capital of the Roman province of Belgae (Belgium), and by the seventeenth century still wines from the region had gained a considerable reputation. Contrary to popular myth, however, it was not Dom Pérignon, cellar master of the Abbaye de Hautvillers near Épernay, who then "invented" champagne. He was probably responsible for the innovation of mixing grapes from different vineyards but the wine's well-known tendency to re-ferment within the bottle was not controllable until eighteenth-century glass-moulding techniques (developed in Britain) produced sufficiently strong vessels to contain the natural effervescence.

Away from the vineyards with their serried ranks of vines, the region's rolling plains are an uninspiring sight, growing more wheat and cabbages per hectare than any other region of France, though it seems to bring the villages no great benefit. Some places look so run-down it looks like the shutters would fall off if you popped a paper bag.

At least the official capital of Champagne, the cathedral city of **Reims**, is worth a visit, and has a reasonably full cultural calendar. Some of the most extravagant champagne houses are found here, the *caves* beneath them notable for their vaulted ceilings and kilometres of bottles. **Épernay**, a smaller town surrounded by vineyards, is the scenic heart of the region. The champagne *maisons* here are not hidden among city streets but set aside on their own avenue, enabling visitors to float from one house to another like so many bubbles. Across the plains, neither **Châlons-en-Champagne** nor the smaller further-flung towns like **Chaumont** or **Langres**, dotted along the Marne towards its source, are much of an incentive to break your journey. The only real attraction in the rest of the region is the town of **Troyes**, some way off to the southwest. Smaller than Reims, it's a great place to stay to stroll through the cobbled streets, admire the city's ancient timbered houses, to sample some excellent food (though visitors won't find much in the way of sparkling wine here), and to buy inexpensive clothing.

Reims

Laid flat by the bombs of World War I, **REIMS** (pronounced like a nasal "Rance", and traditionally spelled Rheims in English) may give the first impression of being a large industrial centre with little to redeem it. Despite appearances however, the city centre is a walkable size, while lurking beneath its dull streets lie its real treasure – kilometre upon kilometre of bottles of fermenting champagne. Moreover,

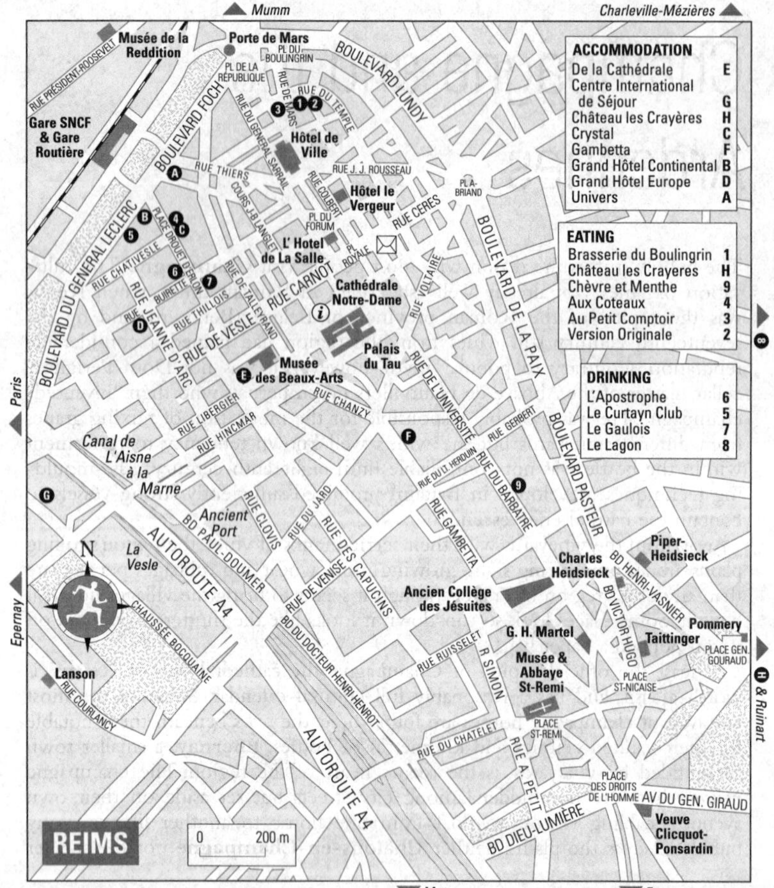

Champagne: the facts

Nowhere else in France, let alone the rest of the world, are you allowed to make a drink called **champagne**, though many people do all the same, calling it "champan", "shampanskoye" and all manner of variants. You can blend grape juice harvested from chalk-soil vineyards, double-ferment it, store the result for years at the requisite constant temperature and high humidity in sweating underground *caves*, turn and tilt the bottles little by little to clear the sediment, add some vintage liqueur, and finally produce a bubbling golden (or pink) liquid; but in accordance with national and international trade law you may refer to it only as the "*méthode champenoise*". It's perhaps an outrageous monopoly guarded to keep the region's sparkling wines in the luxury class, although the locals will tell you the difference comes from the squid fossils in the chalk, the lay of the land and its critical climate, the evolution of the grapes, the regulated pruning methods and the legally enforced quantity of juice pressed.

Three authorized **grape varieties** are used in champagne: chardonnay, the only white grape, growing best on the Côte des Blancs and contributing a light and elegant element; pinot noir, grown mainly on the Montagne de Reims slopes, giving body and long life; and pinot meunier, cultivated primarily in the Marne valley, adding flowery aromas.

The **vineyards** are owned either by *maisons*, who produce the *grande marque* champagne, or by small cultivators called *vignerons*, who sell the grapes to the *maisons*. The *vignerons* also make their own champagne and will happily offer you a glass and sell you a bottle at two-thirds the price of a *grande marque* (ask at any tourist office in the Champagne region for a list of addresses). The difference between the two comes down to capital. The *maisons* can afford to blend grapes from anything up to sixty different vineyards and to tie up their investment while their champagne matures for several years longer than the legal minimum (one year for non-vintage, three years vintage). So the wine they produce is undoubtedly superior – and not a lot cheaper here than in a good discount off-licence/liquor store in Britain or the US.

If you could visit the head offices of Cartier or Dior, the atmosphere would probably be similar to that in the champagne *maisons,* whose palaces are divided between Épernay and Reims. Visits to the handful of *maisons* that organize regular **guided tours** are not free, and some require appointments, but don't be put off – their staff all speak English and a generous *dégustation* is nearly always thrown in. Their audiovisuals and (cold) cellar tours are on the whole very informative, and do more than merely plug brand names. Local tourist offices can provide full lists of addresses and times of visits.

If you want to work on the **harvest**, contact any of the smaller *maisons* direct; the Agence Nationale pour l'Emploi, Cour de la Gare, Épernay (☎03.26.54.88.29), or 40 rue de Talleyrand, Reims (☎03.26.89.52.60); or try the **hostel** in Verzy, 22km from Reims, at 16 rue du Bassin (☎03.26.97.90.10), where casual workers are often recruited and work is advertised.

beyond its status as champagne capital of the world, Reims possesses one of the most impressive Gothic cathedrals in France – formerly the coronation church of dynasties of French monarchs going back to Clovis, first king of the Franks. For those interested in the field of education and/or Roman Catholicism, Reims is the birthplace of St Jean-Baptiste de la Salle, the patron saint of educators and home to the world's main museum on his life.

Arrival, information and accommodation

The cathedral is less than ten minutes' walk from the **gare SNCF** and **gare routière**. The **tourist office**, 2 rue Guillaume-de-Machault (Easter to mid-Oct Mon–Sat 9am–7pm, Sun 10am–6pm; mid-Oct to Easter Mon–Sat

Museum pass

If you're planning to visit more than one of Reims' museums, a **museum pass** (€3) from the tourist office gives entry to the Musée des Beaux-Arts, Musée St-Remi, Ancien Collège des Jésuites and the Musée de la Reddition. Alternatively €12 will buy you, in addition to the museum pass, a one-day bus pass, a visit and *dégustation* at one of the champagne houses, and a some *biscuits roses de Reims*, pink champagne biscuits traditionally dunked in a glass of bubbly. Private tours are offered by the tourist office and range in price from €5 to €15.

9am–6pm, Sun 10am–5pm; ⓣ03.26.77.45.00, ⓦwww.tourisme.fr/reims),, is located next door to the cathedral in a picturesque ruin. Reliable **Internet access** is available at *Clique et Croque*, a cybercafé serving snacks throughout the day, located in a shopping gallery at 27 rue de Vesle (Mon–Sat 10am–12.30am, Sun 2–9pm).

Rooms are at city sizes and prices in Reims, which is to say, smaller and more costly than anywhere in the surrounding region, but they are fairly easy to come by. Bear in mind too that Reims is an easy day-trip from Épernay or Paris, so it may not be necessary to stay at all.

Hotels

De la Cathédrale 20 rue Libergier ⓣ03.26.47.28.46, ⓔhoteldelacathedrale @orange.fr. Old-fashioned but comfortable two-star near, as the name suggests, the cathedral. ❸

Château Les Crayères 64 bd Henry-Vasnier ⓣ03.26.82.80.80, ⓦwww.gerardboyer.com. Ideal for a very special occasion, this refined hotel in a restored eighteenth-century château is a member of Relais & Châteaux. It has a beautiful garden, luxurious rooms and impeccable service, as well as one of the region's most sophisticated restaurants (see p.278). ❾

Crystal 86 place Drouet-d'Erlon ⓣ03.26.88.44.44, ⓦwww.hotel-crystal.fr. Small rooms, pleasant service and a small courtyard which blocks out much of noise from the lively street below. ❸

Gambetta 13 rue Gambetta ⓣ03.26.47.22.00, ⓕ03.26.47.22.43. Neat, well-designed, modern rooms, all with shower and toilet above an excellent restaurant, *Le Vonelly*. ❸

Grand Hôtel Continental 93 place Drouet-d'Erlon ⓣ03.26.40.39.35, ⓦwww.grandhotelcontinental.com. Well-situated hotel, with quiet rooms, all with bathroom and TV. ❹

Grand Hôtel Europe 29 rue Buirette ⓣ03.26.47.39.39, ⓦwww.hotel-europe-reims.com. A quiet *fin-de-siècle* four-storey three-star. ❺

Univers 41 bd Foch ⓣ03.26.88.68.08, ⓦwww .hotel-univers-reims.com Handsomely located on the tree-lined Hautes Promenades, this smart neo-Art Deco-style establishment, with double-glazing, is the best mid-range hotel in the city. ❺

Hostel

Centre International de Séjour 1 chaussée Bocquaine, Parc Léo Lagrange ⓣ03.26.40.52.60, ⓦwww.cis-reims.com. A large, well-run HI hostel with single (€28 with shower, €18 without) or double rooms (€16 per person with bath, €12 without). Either take bus H to "Pont de Gaulle", or it's a fifteen-minute walk from the station on the other side of the canal: cross over the big roundabout in front of the station, turn right down bd du Général-Leclerc to Pont de Vesle; chaussée Bocquaine is the first left after the bridge. Bike hire available.

The City

The old centre of Reims stretches from the **cathedral** and its adjacent episcopal palace north to place de la République's triumphal Roman arch, the **Porte de Mars**, punctuated by the grand squares of place Royale, place du Forum and place de l'Hôtel-de-Ville. To the south, about fifteen minutes' walk from the cathedral, is the other historical focus of the town, the **Abbaye St-Remi**, and nearby the Jesuits' College. To the east of here are most of the **champagne maisons** and, further east still, a museum of cars.

The cathedral and around

The thirteenth-century **Cathédrale Notre-Dame** (daily 7.30am–7.30pm) features prominently in French history: in 1429 Joan of Arc succeeded in getting the Dauphin crowned here as Charles VII – an act of immense significance when France was more or less wiped off the map by the English and their allies. In all, 26 kings of France were crowned in the Gothic glory of this edifice.

The lure of the cathedral's interior is the kaleidoscopic patterns in the stained glass, with fantastic Marc **Chagall** designs in the east chapel and champagne processes glorified in the south transept. But the greatest appeal is outside: an inexplicable joke runs around the restored but still badly mutilated statuary on the west front – the giggling angels who seem to be responsible for disseminating the prank are a delight. Not all the figures on the cathedral's west front are originals – some have been removed to spare them further erosion and are now at the former bishop's palace, the Palais du Tau. The **towers** of the cathedral are open to the public (April to Sept daily 10–11am & 2–5pm; Oct–March Sat & Sun 10–11am & 2–5pm; €4.60, or combined ticket with the Palais du Tau €7.50); as well as a walk round the transepts and chevet, you get to see inside the framework of the cathedral roof; tickets available from the Palais du Tau.

At the **Palais du Tau** (daily: May–Aug 9.30am–6.30pm; Sept–April 9.30am–12.30pm & 2–5.30pm; €6.10, or combined ticket with the towers €7.50), next door to the cathedral, you can appreciate the expressiveness of the statuary from close up – a view that would never have been possible in their intended monumental positions on the cathedral. Apart from the grinning angels, there is also a superb Eve, shiftily clutching the monster of sin, while embroidered tapestries of the Song of Songs line the walls. The palace also preserves, in a state of unlikely veneration, the paraphernalia of Charles X's coronation in 1824, right down to the dauphin's hat box.

Just west of the cathedral on rue Chanzy, the **Musée des Beaux-Arts** (daily except Tues & public hols 10am–noon & 2–6pm; €3) is the city's principal art museum, which, though ill-suited to its ancient building, effectively covers French art from the Renaissance to the present. Few of the works are among the particular artists' best but the collection does contain one of David's replicas of his famous Marat death scene, a set of 27 Corots, two great Gauguin still lifes, and some beautifully observed sixteenth-century German portraits.

Just north of the cathedral, **L'Hôtel de La Salle** (daily except Sun 9am–noon & 2.30–6pm; ⓣ03.26.47.73.21; 1hr guided tour), 4bis rue de l'Arbalète, was the birthplace in 1651 of St Jean-Baptiste de la Salle, the patron saint of teachers. Built in 1545, the building retains some original features and houses a private museum illuminating the revolutionary pedagogical methods of this inspirational educator, as well as some personal effects, including his cilice. De La Salle founded the first-ever teacher training college, and his educational ventures led to the foundation of the order known as the De La Salle Brothers, or Christian Brothers, today active in some 87 countries. Five minutes' north of the cathedral, there's another museum in the **Musée-Hôtel Le Vergeur**, 36 place du Forum (Tues–Sun 2–6pm; €3.90). It's a stuffed treasure house of all kinds of beautiful objects, including two sets of Dürer engravings – an *Apocalypse* and *Passion of Christ* – but you have to go through a long guided tour of the whole works. By the museum there's access to sections of the partly submerged arcades of the **crypto portique Gallo-Romain** (mid-June to mid-Sept Tues–Sun 2–5pm; free), which date back to 200 AD. Reims' other Roman monument, the quadruple-arched **Porte de Mars**, on place de la République, belongs to the same era.

West of the Porte, behind the station in rue Franklin-Roosevelt, is the **Musée de la Reddition** ("Museum of Surrender"; daily except Tues & public hols

10am–noon & 2–6pm; €3), based around an old schoolroom that served as Eisenhower's HQ from February 1945. In the early hours of May 7, 1945, General Jodl agreed to the unconditional surrender of the German army here, thus ending World War II in Europe. The room has been left exactly as it was (minus the ashtrays and carpet), with the Allies' battle maps on the walls. The visit includes a good documentary film and numerous photographs and press cuttings.

The Abbaye St-Remi, Jesuits' College and surrounding museums

Most of the early French kings were buried in Reims' oldest building, the eleventh-century **Basilique St-Remi**, fifteen minutes' walk from the cathedral on rue Simon (Mon–Wed, Fri & Sun 8am–dusk, Thurs & Sat 9am–dusk, closed

Champagne tasting in Reims

Tours of the Reims champagne houses and *caves* range from the Disney-esque to the extremely technical. A tour at an appointment-only house does not necessarily guarantee personal attention – central houses such as Pommery and Veuve Cliquot often host quite large groups. Those in the southern part of town near the Abbaye St-Remi tend to have the most impressive cellars – some have been carved in cathedral-esque formations from the Gallo-Roman quarries used to build the city, long before champagne was invented.

Non-appointment houses

G. H. Martel & Co 17 rue des Créneaux, near the Basilique St-Remi ⓣ03.26.82.70.67, ⓦwww.champagnemartel.com. At €4.50, this is the best-value tour, with a *dégustation* of three champagnes including a vintage and a rosé. Though the cellars are average, in the *caves* there is a display of the old tools used for each step of the process, and the tour can be truly informative as you're likely to have a small group. Open daily year round (10am–7pm), this is a good option when most other houses are closed (over lunch or after 5pm).

Mumm 34 rue du Champ-de-Mars ⓣ03.26.49.59.70, ⓦwww.mumm.com. Known by its red-slashed Cordon Rouge label, Mumm's un-French-sounding name is the legacy of its founders, affluent German wine-makers from the Rhine Valley who established the business in 1827. The tour is fairly informal – you can wander freely about its cellar museum and throw questions at the approachable guides – though you pick up the basics from a corny pre-tour video. It all ends with a generous glass of either Cordon Rouge, the populist choice; the sweeter Cordon Vert; or their Extra Dry. March–Oct daily 9–11am & 2–5pm; Nov–Feb by appointment only; tour 45min; €7.50–18 depending on what you taste.

Piper-Heidsieck 51 bd Henry-Vasnier ⓣ03.26.84.43.44, ⓦwww.piper-heidsieck.com. At twenty minutes, and complete with animated characters, this is something of a Mickey Mouse tour. Although founded in 1785, Piper is better known in the New World than the Old, having been the champagne of the American movie industry since first appearing – with Laurel and Hardy – in the 1934 classic *Sons of the Desert*. The only folk who'll get anything out of the tour – which ends up at a gallery of celebrity snaps – are confirmed film buffs and lovers of tackiness: the antique *caves* are toured in a five-seater shuttle resembling a ghost train; out of the darkness and timed to a cliché-ridden narration loom giant fibreglass grapes and life-size lumpy figures positioned as cellar masters. You emerge to a much-needed drink. March–Dec daily 9.30am–12.30pm & 2–6pm; tariff starts at €7.50 for one tasting.

Taittinger 9 place St-Niçaise ⓣ03.26.85.84.33, ⓦwww.taittinger.com. Similar to Mumm's tour, with information on the making of champagne and a stroll through the during services; music & light show July–Sept Sat 9.30pm; free), part of a former Benedictine abbey named after the 22-year-old bishop who baptized Clovis and 3000 of his warriors. An immensely spacious building, with aisles wide enough to drive a bus along, it preserves its Romanesque transept walls and ambulatory chapels, some of them with modern stained glass that works beautifully. The spectacular abbey buildings alongside the church house the **Musée St-Remi** (Mon–Fri 2–6.30pm, Sat & Sun 2–7pm; €1.50), the city's archeological and historical museum, whose eclectic collection includes some fine tapestries on St Remi's life, plus sixteenth-century weapons and armour. Its twelfth- to thirteenth-century chapter house has been listed as a UNESCO World Heritage site.

The **Ancien Collège des Jésuites** (tours daily 10am, 11am, 2.15pm, 3.30pm & 4.45pm, Tues afternoon hours only, Sat & Sun morning hours only; €3), a

ancient cellars, some of which have doodles and carvings added by more recent workers; there are also statues of St Vincent and St Jean, patron saints respectively of *vignerons* and cellar hands. Mid-March to mid-Nov daily 9.30am–1pm & 2–5.30pm; mid-Nov to mid-March Mon–Fri same hours, closed Sat & Sun; tour 1hr; €7.

Appointment-only houses

These houses prefer that you call or email a week in advance, but in summer you may often be able to walk right in, or at least just show up in the morning and reserve something for the afternoon. More upmarket hotels can make reservations, and some will offer discounts for tours as well. This is not a comprehensive list of all the *maisons* in the city, but includes the most visitor-friendly places. If the marque that's always on your table isn't listed here, it's worth looking the house up and calling – there's a good chance they'll be able to show you around.

Lanson 66 rue de Courlancy ⓣ03.26.78.50.50, ⓦwww.lanson.fr. It's worth the trip across the river to tour the factory of the champagne of Tesco and Waitrose. Small and in-depth, the tours here actually bring you into the factory, and demonstrate the mechanized day-to-day process of champagne making. On most days you'll be able to see the machines degorging the bottles, as well as labelling and filling them in preparation for the second fermentation. A refreshing change from those houses that just talk about the process and show their cellars. Mon–Fri only, closed Aug; €7.

Pommery 5 place du Général-Gouraud ⓣ03.26.61.62.56, ⓦwww.pommery.fr. The creator of the cute one-eighth size "Pop" bottles has excavated Roman quarries for its cellars – it claims to have been the first *maison* to do so. The tour descends a 116-step stairway into the cellars, which are a showcase for contemporary art and often a greater focus than the champagne itself. Tours 1hr–1hr 30min; €8.

Ruinart 4 rue des Crayères ⓣ03.26.77.51.51, ⓦwww.ruinart.com. The fanciest of the champagne houses, in a swanky mansion. Reserved and upmarket, the tours are nonetheless informative. €11–36, depending on number of tastings.

Veuve Clicquot-Ponsardin 1 place des Droits-de-l'Homme ⓣ03.26.89.54.41, ⓦwww.veuve-cliquot.com. In 1805 the prematurely widowed Mme Clicquot not only took over her husband's business – *veuve* means "widow" in French – but also later bequeathed it to her business manager rather than to her children, a radical break with tradition. She also took great interest not only in the business of champagne but in its fabrication, inventing the first riddling table – a method of settling sediment from the second fermentation in the bottles' necks that many houses still use. In keeping with its innovative past, the *maison* is one of the least pompous, and its *caves* some of the most spectacular, sited in ancient Gallo-Roman quarries, with high vaulted ceilings. Tours last 1hr 30min with tasting; from €7.50.

short walk north on rue du Grand-Cerf, was founded in Reims in 1606, and the building completed in 1678. Guided tours in French take you round the refectory, kitchens and, highlight of the visit, the beautifully ornate carved wooden fittings of the library. The books on the shelves are false and remain from the filming of *La Reine Margot,* for which they were made.

If you have even a passing interest in old cars you should make for the **Musée de l'Automobile**, 84 av Georges-Clemenceau (daily except Tues 10am–noon & 2–6pm; €6), fifteen minutes' walk southeast of the cathedral. All the vehicles are part of the private collection of Philippe Charbonneaux, designer of a number of the postwar classics on display. In addition to the full-scale cars, there's an impressive selection of models, antique toys and period posters.

Eating and drinking

Place Drouet-d'Erlon, a wide pedestrianized boulevard lined with **bars** and **restaurants**, is where you'll find most of the city's nightlife, such as it is. For self-catering, there's a big Wednesday and Saturday **market** in place du Boulingrin (6am–1pm).

Brasserie du Boulingrin 48 rue de Mars ⓣ03.26.40.96.22. Charming and good-value brasserie, dating back to 1925, famed for its seafood platters and *fondant au chocolat*. Weekday menus at €16 and €23, including wine. Open until midnight, closed Sun.

Château les Crayères 64 bd Henry-Vasnier ⓣ03.26.82.80.80. Reputed to be one of France's finest gastronomic restaurants – with prices and style to match. Closed Mon & Tues lunch ; menus from €140.

Chèvre et Menthe 63 rue de Barbâtre ⓣ03.26.05.17.03. A homely, inexpensive establishment recommended for vegetarians with a range of gourmet salads from €5.50. Daily *carte* dishes (some contain meat) might include moussaka (€7) as well as more traditional choices, plus the eponymous goat's cheese and fresh mint quiche. Closed Sun & Mon.

Aux Coteaux 86–88 place Drouet d'Erlon ⓣ03.26.47.08.79. The best of the many restaurants on this popular street, with a wide range of pizzas and salads from under €8. Closed Sun & Mon.

Au Petit Comptoir 17 rue de Mars ⓣ03.26.40.58.58. Close to the Marché du Boulingrin, with traditional and inventive dishes from €15 and a menu at €26, served in modern surroundings – a subtle grey decor with white leather chairs. Champagne by the glass. Closed Sun & Mon.

Version Originale 25bis rue du Temple ⓣ03.26.02.69.32. Creative, fresh menus with flavours from all over the world in a small restaurant with tasteful but informal decor. A great deal at lunchtime with menus at €14.50 and €17, à la carte only for dinner with mains from €14. Closed Sun.

Nightlife and entertainment

For **drinking** into the early hours there are plenty of large terrace cafés on place Drouet-d'Erlon; try *Le Gaulois*, at nos. 2–4, which serves excellent cocktails. One of the trendiest nightspots in town is *L'Apostrophe* at no. 59, for tapas, cocktails, special music nights and a designer decor. If you want to **dance**, try *Le Curtayn Club* at 7 bd Général-Leclerc (daily 10pm–4am ⓣ03.26.49.09.02) or *Le Lagon* at 1 rue de Nice (ⓣ03.26.07.61.34), the best **gay club** in Reims.

Azimuth Productions (ⓣ03.26.04.56.38) puts on a rock **festival**, Octob'Rock, every October, while the Opéra Cinema, 3 rue T.-Dubois (ⓣ03.26.47.29.36), shows undubbed films. From July 1 to mid-August, over a hundred classical concerts – many of them free – take place as part of **Les Flâneries Musicales d'Été**; pick up a leaflet at the tourist office.

Épernay and around

ÉPERNAY is 26km south of Reims and a more attractive place to stay, beautifully situated below rolling, vine-covered hills, with opulent tree-lined streets. It's a small town but contains some of the most famous champagne *maisons* as well as several smaller houses. Épernay also makes an excellent base for exploring the surrounding villages and vineyards.

Arrival, information and accommodation

Épernay's **gare SNCF** is a five-minute walk north of place de la République, down rue Jean-Moët. The **gare routière** is on the corner of rues Dr-Verron and Dr-Rousseau one block northeast from place de la République. The **tourist office** is at 7 av de Champagne (Easter to mid-Oct Mon–Sat 9.30am–12.30pm & 1.30–7pm, Sun 11am–4pm; mid-Oct to Easter Mon–Sat 9.30am–12.30pm & 1.30–5.30pm; Ⓣ03.26.53.33.00) and has information about a huge selection of guided tours ranging from minibuses to hot-air balloons. If you feel like roaming around the vineyards on a **mountain bike** (**VTT**), either independently or in an organized group, contact Bulleo, in Parc Roger Menu (Ⓣ03.26.53.35.60; from €10 per half day).

The best of the cheap **hotels** in Épernay is the excellent one-star *St-Pierre*, 1 rue Jeanne-d'Arc (Ⓣ03.26.54.40.80, Ⓕ03.26.57.88.68; ❶), in a quiet street away from the centre. More comfortable rooms are to be had at the excellent-value *Les Berceaux*, at 13 rue des Berceaux (Ⓣ03.26.55.28.84, Ⓦwww.lesberceaux.com; ❺), which also has one of the best restaurants in town (see p.280); or failing that the Best Western-run *Hôtel de Champagne*, 30 rue E.-Mercier (Ⓣ03.26.53.10.60, Ⓦwww.bw-hotel-champagne.com; ❺). Classiest of all in town is the elegant *Clos Raymi*, 3 rue Joseph-de-Venoge (Ⓣ03.26.51.00.58, Ⓦwww.closraymi-hotel.com; ❼), in a beautiful red-brick house once belonging to the Chandon family. For even more luxurious accommodation out of town, head for the *Royal Champagne*, 5km north on the N2051 to Champillon, (Ⓣ03.26.52.87.11, Ⓦwww.royalchampagne.com; ❾), which has luxurious rooms with vineyard views (see also p.280). At the opposite end of the scale, the local **campsite** is 2km to the north on route de Cumières in the Parc des Sports, on the south bank of the Marne (Ⓣ03.26.55.32.14; closed Oct–May).

The Town

The first place to head for in Épernay is the appropriately named **avenue de Champagne**, running east from the central place de la République. Dubbed "the most drinkable street in the world" by champagne-lover Winston Churchill, it's worth a stroll for its impressive eighteenth- and nineteenth-century mansions and champagne *maisons*.

The largest, and probably the most famous *maison* of all, though neither the most beautiful nor necessarily the most interesting to tour, is **Moët et Chandon**, 20 av de Champagne (9.30–11.30am & 2–4.30pm; mid-Nov to March closed Sat & Sun; €8 including *dégustation* of the brut Impérial); one of the keystones of the LVMH (Louis Vuitton, Moët and Hennessy) empire which owns Mercier, Veuve Clicquot, Krug and Ruinart, and a variety of other concerns, including Dior perfumes. The house is also the creator of the iconic **Dom Pérignon** label. The tour is rather generic, beginning with a mawkish video, followed by a walk through the cellars, which are adorned with mementos of Napoleon (a good friend of the original M. Moët), and concluding with a tasting of their truly excellent champagne.

Just next door at no. 26 is **Perrier Jouët** (Mon–Fri 9–11.15am & 2–4.15pm, tour with tasting of the cuvée Belle Époque €9; call or email in advance for more expensive vineyard tours ⓣ03.26.53.38.07; ⓦwww.perrier-jouet.com). Another upmarket brand, its *belle-époque* bottles are recognizable by the flowers painted on the exterior. The *maison* is beautiful, full of Art Nouveau furniture, paintings, and stained glass to match its bottles, while the tour here is much more personalized than at Moët et Chandon. At the other end of the scale, **Esterlin**, just across the street at 25 av de Champagne (daily 10am–noon & 2–5pm; free) will sit you down with a glass of free champagne in front of a ten-minute video, no questions asked.

Further up the street, **Mercier**, at 70 av de Champagne, runs a fairly rewarding tour around its cellars in an electric train (mid-March to mid-Nov 9.30–11.30am & 2–4.30pm; €6.50, including *dégustation*). Nowadays Mercier is known as the lower-end champagne of French supermarkets, showing that M. Mercier was successful in his goal: he founded the house, aged 20, in 1858 with a plan to make champagne more accessible to the French people. In 1889 he carted a giant barrel that held 200,000 bottles' worth to the Paris Exposition, with the help of 24 oxen – only to be upstaged by the Eiffel Tower. The barrel is on display in the lobby – you can drop in to see it without taking the tour.

Castellane, by the station at 57 rue de Verdun (March–Dec daily 10am–noon & 2–6pm; €7 including *dégustation*), provides Épernay with its chief landmark: a tower looking like a kind of Neoclassical signal box. As well as the inevitable cellars, the visit shows off the working assembly lines that fill the champagne bottles, and the huge vats that hold the grape juice prior to fermentation. After the tour you can wander the little museum freely and climb the tower, which reveals a great view of the surrounding vineyards.

Épernay has a few other *grandes maisons* that can be visited by appointment, but perhaps more worthwhile are the many smaller houses. Since these houses have fewer employees it's best to call or email well in advance. Two which offer tours with *dégustation*, as well as visits to their vineyards, are located on rue Chaude-Ruelle, west of avenue de Champagne, with views over the town: **Leclerc-Briant** is at no. 67 (ⓣ03.26.54.45.33, ⓦwww.leclercbriant.com). For €8 they give a tour of their presshouse, museum and cellars, as well as a tasting of three vintages and a souvenir champagne glass. **Janisson-Baradon** is across the street at no. 65 (ⓣ03.26.54.45.85, ⓦwww.champagne-janisson.com), and offers personalized tours and tastings for €7.

Eating and drinking

Restaurants in Épernay are not generally cheap but there is superb value to be had at *Les Berceaux*, 13 rue des Berceaux (ⓣ03.26.55.28.84; closed Mon, Tues & last two weeks of August; menus from €30), which also has a wine bar. *La Table Kobus*, 3 rue Dr-Rousseau, is highly recommended for its traditional French cuisine (ⓣ03.26.51.53.53; €25). There are several cheaper places on rue Gambetta, between the *gare* and place de la République: call in advance to squeeze into *La Cave à Champagne* at no. 16 (ⓣ03.26.55.50.70; from €15), or stop in for inexpensive Italian at *Le Rimini* across the street at no. 17. For a major blowout, the *Royal Champagne*, north of town (see p.279), serves a surprise *dégustation* menu at €95, weekday lunchtime menus from €25, and evening menus from €50.

Around Épernay

The villages in the appealing **vineyards** of the Montagne de Reims, Côte des Blancs and Vallée de la Marne which surround Épernay promote a range of curiosities: the world's largest champagne bottle and cork in **Mardeuil**; the world's largest champagne glass and an artisan chocolate producer in **Pierry**; a snail farm in **Olizy-Violaine**; a museum of marriage in Oger; and a traditional *vigneron*'s house and early twentieth-century school room at **Oeuilly**. Many of the villages have conserved their sleepy old stone charm: **Vertus**, 16km south of Épernay, is particularly pretty, and so too is **Hautvillers**, 6km north of town, where you can see the abbey of Dom Pérignon fame (though it is unfortunately closed to the public).

The best reason for taking yourself out into the countryside, though, is simply to view the vines and taste less well known but often delicious champagnes. One such house is Charlier & Fils, set in an attractive *maison* surrounded by flowers at 4 rue des Pervenches, **MONTIGNY-SOUS-CHATILLON**, 15km west of Épernay (ⓣ03.26.58.35.18, ⓦwww.champagne-charlier.com). For a champagne experience a bit more down-to-earth than Épernay, head to J. Desautels Père et Fils, 13 rue de la Côte, **OGER** (ⓣ03.26.57.54.75), where twelve generations of the Desautels family have passed the vineyard from father to son; Jérôme, the present "J", will personally show you how he turns the bottles and tell the story of how the big champagne houses depend on smaller growers such as he and his family. For a more upmarket tasting, make an appointment at the Château de Bligny, in the village of **BLIGNY** (ⓣ03.25.27.40.11) where you can even organize a private meal in their dining room.

For somewhere to **stay** that offers a real treat in an atmosphere of faded elegance, base yourself at *Château d'Etoges*, 4 rue Richebourg, **Etoges** (ⓣ03.26.59.30.08, ⓦwww.etoges.com; ⑧). This small château, which was regularly frequented by eighteenth-century French monarchs, offers twenty bedrooms full of individual character and a top-notch restaurant.

Troyes

It is easy to find charm in the leaning medieval half-timbered houses and many churches of **TROYES**, the ancient capital of the Champagne region. The town also offers top-quality museums and shopping outlets, and is the best place around to try the regional speciality, *andouillette* (see p.224).

Arrival, information and accommodation

The **gare SNCF** and **gare routière** are side by side off boulevard Carnot (part of the ring road). Not all buses use the main station, though, and if you're heading for the outlet stores or the countryside it's best to check first with the **tourist office** (ⓦwww.tourisme-troyes.com). There are two branches: the station branch is at 16 bd Carnot (Mon–Sat 9am–12.30pm & 2–6.30pm; ⓣ03.25.82.62.70); and the town-centre branch is on rue Mignard facing the Église St-Jean (April, May & mid-Sept to Oct Mon–Sat 9am–12.30pm & 2–6.30pm, Sun 10am–noon and 2–5pm; July to mid-Sept daily 10am–7pm; Nov–March closed; ⓣ03.25.73.36.88). For information concerning the Aube *département*, of which Troyes is the capital, consult ⓦwww.aube-champagne.com or visit the Aube tourist office on place de la Libération (Mon–Fri 9.30am–12.30pm & 1.30–6pm). If you want to **rent a car** try ADA at 2, rue Voltaire near the station (ⓣ03.25.73.41.68).

Places to stay around the station are plentiful, though for not much more you can find **accommodation** right in the centre of the old town. Outside term-time there may be room in the city's *foyers* for longer stays – the tourist office

△ Troyes

Museum pass

The museum pass (€12) to visit all of the city's museums is well worth the fee if you plan to visit the **Musée d'Art Moderne, La Maison de l'Outil et de la Pensée Ouvrière** and one other. It also includes a *dégustation* of two champagnes from a local shop, an hour's free parking, thirty minutes of Internet use, and discount vouchers for the factory outlets. It's only valid for one visit to each establishment, but can be used over the course of a year. Buy it from the tourist office or in any of the city's museums. It's worth noting as well that all the museums are free for those under 18 and for students under 26.

has details, along with information about *chambres d'hôtes* and places to stay in the wine villages around Troyes.

Hotels

Les Comptes de Champagne 54 rue de la Monnaie ⓣ03.25.73.11.70. Central and charming two-star in a twelfth-century house with slanted floors. Friendly proprietors and covered parking. ❷

Grand Hôtel/Patiotel 4 av Mal-Joffre ⓣ03.25.79.90.90, ⓦwww.grand-hotel-troyes.com. Right opposite the station, a big three-star hotel with swimming pool and garden; "Patiotel" rooms are less grand (only two-star) and accordingly cheaper. ❸–❹

La Maison de Rhodes 18 rue Linard-Gonthier ⓣ03.25.43.11.11, ⓦwww.maisonderhodes.com. A fine Renaissance house, with Templar links, near the cathedral, which has been transformed into a four-star boutique hotel with contemporary interior decor and an abundance of medieval wooden beams. The lovely internal courtyard is a tranquil place for a quality evening meal. ❼

Le Relais St-Jean 51 rue Paillot-de-Montabert ⓣ03.25.73.89.90, ⓦwww.relais-st-jean.com. Posh hotel in a half-timbered building on a narrow street right in the centre. ❺

Royal 22 bd Carnot ⓣ03.25.73.19.99, ⓦwww.royal-hotel-troyes-com. Decent, pleasantly restored hotel behind a stern facade near the station; spacious bathrooms and a copious breakfast. ❹

Splendid 44 bd Carnot ⓣ03.25.73.08.52, ⓕ03.25.73.41.04. The best of the cheap places near the station; rooms have shower and TV. ❷

Hostel and campsite

Camping municipal 7 rue Roger-Salengro, Pont Ste-Marie ⓣ & ⓕ03.25.81.02.64. Attractive grassy campsite, situated 5km out on the N60 to Châlons, on the left, with good facilities including washing machines and children's play area. Minimum two-night reservation, closed mid-Oct to March.

HI hostel chemin Ste-Scholastique, Rosières ⓣ03.25.82.00.65, ⓦwww.fuaj.org/aj/troyes. Decent hostel located in a former fourteenth-century priory, 5.5km out of town on the Dijon road; take bus #8 direction "Rosières", stop "Liberté". Opposite the sign saying "Vielaines", a path leads down to the priory. Open year round; HI card required. Beds in 5–6-person dorms €8.80, breakfast and bedding extra.

The Town

The central part of Troyes between the station and the cathedral is scattered with marvellous **churches**, four of which are open to the public. Leading the way, and the first you come to, on rue de Vauluisant, is the sumptuous, high-naved church of **St-Pantaléon** (daily 10am–noon & 2–5pm; July & Aug till 6pm), almost a museum of sculpture. A short walk to the north is Troyes' oldest remaining church, twelfth-century **Ste-Madeleine**, on the road of the same name (same hours as St-Pantaléon). It was considerably remodelled in the sixteenth century, when the delicate stonework rood screen (*jubé*) – used to keep the priest separate from the congregation – was added; it's one of the few left in France. A short way to the southeast, between rues Émile-Zola and Champeaux and opposite the municipal tourist office, is the church of **St-Jean-au-Marché**. It's historically important as the church where Henry V of England married Catherine of France after being recognized as heir to the French throne in the 1420 Treaty of Troyes, known to the French as the "shameful treaty". Between it and the cathedral is the elegant Gothic **Basilique St-Urbain**, on place Vernier (same hours as St-Pantaléon), its exterior dramatizing the Day of Judgement.

Across the Canal de la Haute Seine lies the city's most outstanding museum, the **Musée d'Art Moderne** (Tues–Sun 11am–6pm; €5, or part of the museum pass, see box p.283), magnificently housed in the old bishops' palace next to the cathedral on place St-Pierre. The museum displays part of an extraordinary private collection, particularly rich in Fauvist paintings by the likes of Vlaminck and Derain (including the famous paintings of Hyde Park and Big Ben) – along with other first-class works by Degas, Courbet, Gauguin, Bonnard, Braque, Modigliani, Rodin, Robert Delaunay and Ernst. One room is given over to a beautiful collection of African masks and other carvings. Belonging to Pierre and Denise Lévy, the collection is not just impressive for its breadth, but for its impeccable taste and its depth, with several rooms devoted entirely to a single artist.

This is the ancient **quartier de la Cité**, an area with many of the city's oldest buildings. These all huddle around the **Cathédrale St-Pierre-et-St-Paul** (daily: July to mid-Sept 10am–7pm; mid-Sept to June 9am–noon & 2–5pm), whose pale Gothic nave is stroked with reflections from the wonderful stained-glass windows. On the other side of the cathedral from the Musée d'Art Moderne, at 1 rue Chrétien-de-Troyes, the once glorious **Abbaye St-Loup** houses the **Musée des Beaux-Arts** (daily except Tues 10am–noon & 2–6pm; €4 or part of museum pass scheme, see box p.283), seemingly endless galleries of mostly French paintings, including a couple by Watteau, an impressive collection of medieval sculpture, and some dismally displayed natural history and archeological exhibits. Down rue de la Cité, but with its entrance round the corner on quai des Comtes de Champagne, is the **apothicairerie**, a richly decorated sixteenth-century pharmacy (Mon, Wed, Sat & Sun 10am–noon & 2–6pm; €4.60 or part of museum pass scheme, see box p.283) occupying one corner of the majestic eighteenth-century **Hôtel-Dieu-le-Comte**; rows of painted wooden "simple" boxes dating from the eighteenth century adorn its shelves.

Despite being raked by numerous fires since the Middle Ages, Troyes has retained many of its timber-framed buildings in the streets and alleyways of the old town, off the pedestrianized rue Champeaux, and around the maze of streets south of the main shopping thoroughfare, rue Émile-Zola. Indeed, the most famous fire, in 1524, led to a massive rebuilding scheme that resulted in Troyes' wealth of Renaissance palaces. An outstanding example, just to the east of the church of St Pantaléon, is the beautiful sixteenth-century Hôtel de Mauroy, 7 rue de la Trinité, once an orphanage, then a textile factory, but now occupied by the **Maison de l'Outil et de la Pensée Ouvrière** (10am–6pm; €6.50 or part of the museum pass scheme, see box p.283). Troyes' most original tourist attraction by far, this surprisingly fascinating museum of tools, with exhibits from the seventeenth, eighteenth and nineteenth centuries, provides a window into the world of workers who used them and the people who crafted them. State-of-the-art techniques somehow transform shoals of hammers and spanners, flocks of axes and chisels, and myriad implements used by coopers, wheelwrights and tile-makers into jewel-like treasures.

Clothes shopping in Troyes

Troyes made its name in the clothing trade, and today the industry still accounts for more than half of the town's employment. Buying clothes from **factory outlets** is one of the chief attractions: designer-label clothes can be picked up at two-thirds or less of the normal shop price**. Espace Belgrand** in rue Belgrand, off boulevard du 14-Juillet (Mon 2–7pm, Tues–Fri 10am–7pm, Sat 9am–7pm), has quite a range, while rues Émile-Zola and des Bas Trévois are also worth a wander. Better still you can go out to the manufacturers on the outskirts, where gigantic warehouse stores defy any preconceived notions about *petite* French boutiques. Dozens of factory shops sell clothes, shoes and leather goods designed for everyone, from Nike to Laura Ashley, Boss to Kenzo, and Yves St-Laurent to Jean-Paul Gaultier. The best array is in the four giant sheds of **Marques Avenue**, 114 bd de Dijon, St-Julien-les-Villas, a couple of kilometres south of the city on the N71 to Dijon or on bus #2 (Mon 2–7pm, Tues–Fri 10am–7pm, Sat 9.30am–7pm, plus some Sun; extended hours during sale periods; ⓦwww.marquesavenue.com); there's also a special "shed" for household goods a few blocks towards town, including luxury glass- and chinaware. At Pont-Ste-Marie, a short way to the northeast of Troyes along the D960 to Nancy, are **Marques City**, on rue Marc-Verdier (ⓦwww.marquescity.com), and **McArthur Glen**, on rue Danton (ⓦwww.mcarthurglen.fr), both with the same hours as Espace Belgrand. Buses for the outlets on the outskirts of town depart from the bus stops by Marché les Halles (ask at the tourist offices for details).

Nearby, along rue Brunneval, which is lined with another row of wooden houses (in varying states of repair), is Troyes' **synagogue**, inaugurated in the 1980s in memory of the Jewish scholar, Rachi (1040–1105). He was a member of the small Jewish community that flourished for a time during the eleventh and twelfth centuries under the protection of the counts of Champagne. His commentaries on both the Old Testament and the Talmud are still important to academics today: the Rachi University Institute opposite is devoted to studying his work.

As tourist pamphlets are at pains to point out, the ring of boulevards round the town is shaped like a champagne cork. In fact it also looks a bit like a sock – a shape that's just as suitable, since hosiery ("bonneterie") and woollens have been Troyes' most important industry since the late Middle Ages. In the seventeenth century Louis XIII decreed that charitable houses had to be self-supporting and the orphanage of the Hôpital de la Trinité (the Hôtel de Mauroy) set its charges to knitting stockings. Some of the old machines and products used for creating garments can be seen in the sixteenth-century palace, the **Hôtel de Vauluisant**, at 4 rue de Vauluisant, part of which houses the **Musée de la Bonneterie** (June–Sept daily except Tues 10am–1pm & 2–6pm; Oct–May Wed–Sun 10am–noon & 2–6pm; €3 or part of the museum pass scheme, see box p.283); well restored and visually appealing, it sets an example for all crafts museums with its respect for traditions and lack of sentimentality. The palace also houses the **Musée Historique de Troyes et de la Champagne Méridionale** (same hours and ticket), which contains some fascinating and original religious paintings on wooden shutters. The exteriors are painted in black and white trompe l'oeil, but when thrown open (as they have would been on holidays) reveal beautifully coloured paintings beneath. An impressively steep tower staircase leads to a cellar with a small exhibit of ceramic floor tiles.

Eating, drinking and entertainment

Self-caterers should head for the Marché les Halles, a daily (except Sun) covered **market** on the corner of rue Général-de-Gaulle and rue de la République, close to the Hôtel de Ville. Vegetarians and the health-conscious will think they're in heaven at Coopérative Hermès, 39 rue Général-Saussier, an excellent healthfood store. Central Troyes is packed with **places to eat**, mostly economical but unexciting. Along rue Champeaux there are several crêperies, and the restaurant *Le Gaulois* at no. 12 (Ⓣ03.25.43.90.27), where skewers of meat are grilled and served with bowls of sauces for €13. A great place to try the regional speciality of *andouillette* (see box on "Regional food and drink", p.224), along with delicious homestyle cooking, is the classic *Bistroquet* on place Langevin (Ⓣ03.25.73.65.65; closed Sun eve; menus from €16.50). *La Marinière*, 3 rue de la Trinité, behind the Musée d'Outil, has an oceanic theme and specializes in fish (Ⓣ03.25.73.77.29, closed Sun, from €11). Although the interior decor doesn't quite work, gastronomic delights from around the world at reasonable prices can be had at *Le Valentino*, 11 cours de la Rencontre (Ⓣ03.25.73.14.14, reservations essential; closed Mon & Sat lunch, Sun dinner & for 3 weeks in Aug & Sept; menus €22 for lunch, from €29 for dinner). Perhaps the best restaurant in town is *La Mignardise*, 1 ruelle des Chats (Ⓣ03.25.73.15.30; closed Sun eve and Mon during low season), set in a sixteenth-century building with a quiet courtyard and serving a traditional French menu from €22.

Le Tricasse is a perennially popular **bar**, with tables and the occasional live band, at 2 rue Charbonnet, on the corner with narrow rue Paillot-de-Montabert. You'll find a few more bars down this street, including the tiny and consistently packed-out *Bar des Bougnets des Pouilles*. A real delight for a relaxing, convivial evening is *Aux Crieurs de Vins*, at 4 place Jean-Jaurès, an uncomplicated wine bar (and shop), with a painted concrete floor and a jumble of different furniture. The accent is on good wine and simple but quality dishes to accompany it: plates cost from €8 (try the delicious pressed pigs' cheeks with gherkins if it's on the menu), and there's always a choice of different *andouillette* on offer.

From late June to mid-September, the city organizes a series of free **Ville en Lumière** concerts in outdoor venues around town – pick up a schedule at the tourist office.

The Plateau de Langres

The Seine, Marne, Aube and several other lesser rivers rise in the **Plateau de Langres** between Troyes and Dijon, with main routes from the former to the Burgundian capital skirting this area. To the east, the N19 (which the train follows) takes in **Chaumont** and **Langres**, two towns that could briefly slow your progress if you're in no hurry, and the home village of Charles de Gaulle, **Colombey-les-Deux-Églises**.

Chaumont

Situated on a steep ridge between the Marne and Suize valleys, **CHAUMONT** (Chaumont-en-Bassigny to give its full name), 93km east of Troyes, is best approached by train, which enables you to cross the town's stupendous mid-nineteenth-century viaduct, which took an average of 2500 labourers working night and day two years to construct. It's possible to walk across the viaduct, which gives you fine views of the Suize valley.

The town's most interesting historic building is the **Basilique St-Jean-Baptiste**. Though built with the same dour, grey stone of most Champagne churches, it has a wonderful Renaissance addition to the Gothic transept of balconies and turreted stairway. The decoration includes a fifteenth-century polychrome *Mise en Tombeau* with muddy tears but expressive faces, and an *Arbre de Jessé* of the early sixteenth-century Troyes school, in which all the characters are sitting in the tree, dressed in the style of the day.

You shouldn't leave without taking a look at **Les Silos**, 7–9 av Foch, near the *gare SNCF* (Tues, Thurs & Fri 2–7pm, Wed & Sat 10am–6pm; free), a 1930s agricultural co-op transformed into a graphic arts centre and *médiathèque*. As well as hosting temporary exhibitions, it's the main venue for Chaumont's international **poster festival** (Festival de l'Affiche), held every year from mid-May to mid-June. As for the rest of the old town, there's not much to do except admire the strange, bulging towers of the houses, through which the shapes of wide spiral staircases are visible.

The **tourist office** is on place du Général-Charles-de-Gaulle (Mon–Sat 9.30am–12.30pm, Sun 10am–noon & 2–5pm; ⓣ03.25.03.80.80). If you decide to stay, try *Le Terminus Reine*, on the *place* (ⓣ03.25.03.66.66, ⓦwww.grand-hotel-terminus-reine-chaumont.federal-hotel.com; ❹), an old-fashioned hotel with great charm; its restaurant, *La Chaufferie*, is the best place to eat. For a cheap room, there's a small **hostel** at 1 rue Carcassonne (ⓣ03.25.03.22.77; bus #2 from the *gare SNCF* to "La Suize"; €10–12 including breakfast).

Colombey-les-Deux-Églises

Twenty-seven kilometres northwest of Chaumont, on the N19 to Troyes, is **COLOMBEY-LES-DEUX ÉGLISES**, the village where Gaullist leaders come to pay their respects at the grave of **General Charles de Gaulle**. The former president's family home, **La Boisserie**, opens its ground floor to the public (Feb–Nov daily except Tues 10am–noon & 2–5.30pm; €4), but the most impressive memorial is the pink-granite **Cross of Lorraine**, symbol of the French Resistance movement, standing over 40m high on a hill just west of the village, signposted off the N19.

The best place to **stay** here is the splendid newly Michelin-starred *Hostellerie La Montagne*, ruelle des Charmilles (ⓣ03.25.01.51.69, ⓦwww.hostellerielamontagne.com; ❼; menus from €28), where the rooms are individually designed and truly top-notch. Run by a father and son team, it's really a restaurant with rooms: there are three intimate dining rooms, or, if you have a fascination with fine cuisine, you can take the table located in a private corner of the new third-of-a-million-euro kitchen and observe your dinner being cooked. A more modest option, with a simple country dining room and smartly renovated rooms with hi-tech bathrooms, is *La Grange du Relais* (ⓣ03.25.01.50.40; ❸; menus from €15.90) on the RN19 at the bottom of the town.

Langres

LANGRES, 35km south of Chaumont and just as spectacularly situated above the Marne, suffered very little damage during the war and retains its encirclement of gateways, towers and ramparts. Walking this circuit, which gives views east to the hills of Alsace and southwest across the Plateau de Langres, is the best thing to do if you're just stopping for an hour or so. Don't miss the **St-Ferjeux tower** with its beautiful metal sculpture, *Air and Dreams*. Wandering inside the walls is also rewarding – Renaissance houses and narrow streets give the feel of a place time has left behind, swathed in the mists of southern Champagne. Langres was home to the eighteenth-century Enlightenment philosopher **Diderot** for the first sixteen years of his life, and people like to make the point that, if he were to return to Langres today, he'd have no trouble finding his way around.

The **Hôtel du Breuil de St-Germain**, at 2 rue Chambrûlard, is one of the best of the town's sixteenth-century mansions, though it can only be viewed from the outside. The **Musée d'Art et Histoire** on place du Centenaire, near the cathedral (daily: April–Oct 10am–noon & 2–6pm; until 5pm in winter; free) has a section devoted to Diderot, with his encyclopedias and various other first editions of his works, a portrait by Van Loos and collections of local archeology. The highlight of the museum is the superbly restored Romanesque **chapel of St Didier** in the old wing, housing a fourteenth-century painted ivory *Annunciation*. Sets of dining knives, a craft for which this area was famous for several centuries, are also on display along with other decorative arts. Local faïence – glazed terracotta – is featured, though these nicely crafted pieces are upstaged by the sixteenth-century tiles from Rouen in one of the nave chapels of the **Cathédrale St-Mammès**. This grey-stone edifice has not been improved by the eighteenth-century addition of a new facade, but there's an amusing sixteenth-century relief of the Raising of Lazarus, in which the apostles watch, totally blasé, while other characters look like kids at a good horror movie.

Practicalities

The **tourist office** is just inside the town's main gate, the Porte des Moulins, on place Bel'Air (April & Oct Mon–Sat 9am–noon & 1.30–6pm; May–Sept Mon–Sat 9am–noon & 1.30–6.30pm, Sun 10am–noon & 2–6pm; Nov–March Mon–Sat 9am–noon & 1.30–5.30pm; Ⓣ03.25.87.67.67, Ⓦwww.tourisme-langres.com), on the other side of town from the **gare SNCF** (infrequent connections to Troyes and Dijon); staff can give you a useful map of the main sights in town, and also have information on the four lakes in the surrounding region. The **bus** timetable from the train station to the Porte des Moulins is loosely based on the train timetable; note though that the last bus leaves at 7pm Monday to Friday, 4pm on Saturday and there's no connection on Sunday.

For **accommodation**, there's a **hostel** close by the Porte des Moulins on place Bel'Air (Ⓣ03.25.87.09.69, Ⓕ03.25.87.76.74; book ahead for Sat & Sun as the reception closes at weekends; ❶, breakfast and bedding extra), and the reasonable *Auberge Jeanne d'Arc*, 26 rue Gambetta (Ⓣ03.25.86.87.88; ❷), in the centre of town. More comfortable rooms can be had at the characterful *Cheval Blanc*, in a converted church at 4 rue de l'Estrés (Ⓣ03.25.87.07.00, Ⓦwww.hotel-langres.com; ❹), or in the seventeenth-century, though rather less elegant, *Grand Hôtel de l'Europe*, 23–25 rue Diderot (Ⓣ03.25.87.10.88, Ⓕ03.25.87.60.65; ❸). For good but expensive **food**, try *Restaurant Diderot* at the *Cheval Blanc* (closed Tues eve & Wed lunch). Better value is to be had at the *Lion d'Or* (Ⓣ03.25.87.03.30), a restaurant and hotel just outside the town on the route de Vesoul with views of the surrounding lakes. Langres has its own highly flavourful, strong-smelling – and excellent – cheese, which you can buy at the Friday **market** on place Jenson.

The Ardennes

To the northeast of Reims, the scenery of the **Ardennes** region along the Meuse valley knocks spots off any landscape in Champagne. Most of the hills lie over the border in Belgium, but there's enough of interest on the French side to make it well worth exploring.

In war after war, the people of the Ardennes have been engaged in protracted last-ditch battles down the valley of the Meuse, which, once lost, gave invading armies a clear path to Paris. The rugged, hilly terrain and deep forests (frightening even to Julius Caesar's legionnaires) gave some advantage to World War II's Resistance fighters when the Ardennes was annexed to Germany, but even during peace time life has never been easy. The land is unsuitable for crops, and the slateworks and ironworks, which were the main source of employment during the nineteenth century, were closed in the 1980s. The only major investment in the region has been a nuclear power station in the loop of the Meuse at Chooz, to which locals responded by etching "Nuke the Élysée!" high on a half-cut cliff of slate just downstream.

This said, tourism, the main growth industry, is developing apace – there are walking and boating possibilities, plus good train and bus connections – though the eerie, isolated atmosphere of this region remains.

Charleville-Mézières

The twin towns of **CHARLEVILLE** and **MÉZIÈRES** provide a good starting point for exploring the northern part of the region, which spreads across the meandering Meuse before the valley closes in and the forests take over. Of the two, Charleville is the one to head for.

The seventeenth-century **place Ducale**, in the centre of Charleville, was the result of the local duke's envy of the contemporary place des Vosges in Paris. Despite the posh setting, the shops in the arcades remain very down-to-earth and the cafés charge reasonable prices to sit outside: a very good position on Tuesdays, Thursdays and Saturdays, when the **market** is held here. From 31 place Ducale you can reach the complex of old and new buildings that house the **Musée de l'Ardenne** (Tues–Sun 10am–noon & 2–6pm; €4, combined ticket with Musée Arthur Rimbaud, see below), which covers the different economic activities of the region over the ages through local paintings, prehistoric artefacts, legends, puppetry, weapons and coins. You need to keep up a good pace to get round all the rooms, but it's fun and informative.

The most famous person to emerge from the town was Arthur Rimbaud (1854–91), who ran away from Charleville four times before he was 17, so desperate was he to escape from its quiet provincialism. He is honoured in the **Musée Arthur Rimbaud**, housed in a very grand stone windmill – a contemporary of the place Ducale – on quai Arthur-Rimbaud, two blocks north of the main square (Tues–Sun 10am–noon & 2–6pm; €4 combined ticket with Musée de l'Ardenne, see above). It contains a host of pictures of him and people he hung out with, including his lover Verlaine, as well as facsimiles of his writings and related documents. A few steps down the quayside is the spot where he composed his most famous poem, *Le Bateau Ivre*. After penning poetry in Paris, journeying to the Far East and trading in Ethiopia and Yemen, Rimbaud died in a Marseille hospital. His body was brought back to his home town – probably the last place he would have wanted to be buried – and true Rimbaud fanatics can visit his **tomb** in the cemetery west of the place Ducale at the end of avenue Charles Boutet.

Charleville is also a major international puppetry centre (its school is justly famous), and every three years it hosts one of the largest puppet festivals in the world, the **Festival Mondial des Théâtres de Marionnettes** (Ⓦwww.marionnette.com). As many as 150 professional troupes – some from as far away as Mali and Burma – put on something like fifty shows a day on the streets and in every available space in town. Tickets are cheap, and there are shows for adults as well as the usual stuff aimed at kids. If you miss the festival you can still catch one of the puppet performances in the summer months every year (Ⓣ03.24.33.72.50 for booking and information; tickets around €12), or if you're passing by the **Institut de la Marionnette** between 10am and 9pm, you can see one of the automated episodes of the *Four Sons of Aymon* enacted on the facade's clock every hour, or all twelve scenes on Saturday at 9.15am.

Practicalities

From the **gare SNCF**, place Ducale is a five-minute ride away on buses #1, #3 or #5; the **gare routière** is a couple of blocks northeast of the square, between rues du Daga and Noël. The **regional tourist office** for the Ardennes is at 22 place Ducale (July & Aug Mon–Sat 9am–7pm, Sun 10am–7pm; Sept–June Mon–Sat 9am–12.30pm & 1.30–7pm, Sun 2–7pm; Ⓣ03.24.56.06.08), with Charleville-Mézières' **tourist office** at no. 4 (July & Aug Mon–Fri 9.30am–noon & 1.30–7pm, Sat & Sun 9.30am–noon & 1.30–6pm; Sept–June Mon–Sat 9.30am–noon & 1.30–6pm; Ⓣ03.24.55.69.90, Ⓦwww.charleville-mezieres.org).

Three fairly central **hotels** that are worth trying are: the *Hôtel de Paris*, 24 av G.-Corneau, which offers free Internet access, though make sure to ask for a newly renovated room in the main building (Ⓣ03.24.33.34.38, Ⓦwww.hoteldeparis08.fr; ❷); the *Central*, 23 av du Maréchal-Leclerc (Ⓣ03.24.33.33.69, Ⓕ03.24.59.38.25; ❸); and *Le Relais du Square*, 3 place de la Gare (Ⓣ03.24.33.38.76, Ⓦwww.hotel-charleville-mezieres.com; ❸), a two-star hotel in a tree-filled square near the station. The town's **campsite**, *Camping du Mont Olympe* (Ⓣ03.24.33.23.60, Ⓔcamping-charlevillemezieres@orange.fr; open May to mid-Oct), is north of place Ducale, over the river and left along rue des Paquis. There are plenty of places to **eat and drink**. For something a bit special, *La Côte à l'Os*, at 11 cours Aristide-Briand (Ⓣ03.24.59.20.16), specializes in *fruits de mer* and local cuisine; daily menus start at €13.50. *La Cigogne*, at 40 rue Dubois-Crancé (Ⓣ03.24.33.25.39; closed Sun eve, Mon & first week Aug), also serves good regional dishes, with menus from €15. At 33 rue du Moulin, *La Clef des Champs* (Ⓣ03.24.56.17.50) offers menus from €15 and is known for family cooking.

North of Charleville

George Sand wrote of the stretch of the Meuse that winds through the Ardennes that "its high wooded cliffs, strangely solid and compact, are like some inexorable destiny that encloses, pushes and twists the river without permitting it a single whim or any escape". What all the tourist literature emphasizes, however, are the legends of medieval struggles between Good and Evil whose characters have given names to some of the curious rocks and crests. The grandest of these, where the schist formations have taken the most peculiar turns, is the **Roc de la Tour**, also known as the "Devil's Castle", up a path off the D31, 3.5km out of Monthermé. **MONTHERMÉ** itself is a slate-roofed little town with nothing of great interest except a twelfth-century church with late medieval frescoes.

The journey through this frontier country should ideally be done on foot or skis, or **by boat**. The alternatives for the latter are: good old *bateau-mouche*-type cruises (RDTA; April–June & Sept–Oct weekends only; July & Aug Tues–Sun; ⓣ03.24.33.77.70), which depart from the Vieux Moulin (Musée Rimbaud) in Charleville-Mézières and the quai des Paquis in Monthermé; or live-in pleasure boats – not wildly expensive if you can split the cost four or six ways. These can be rented out, with bikes on board, from Ardennes Plaisance in Charleville-Mézières, 76 rue des Forges-St-Charles (ⓣ03.24.56.47.61), and Ardennes Nautisme in **SEDAN**, 16 rue du Château (ⓣ03.24.27.05.15, ⓦwww.ardennes-nautisme.com), the next town downstream from Charleville. The latter moor their boats just east of Dom-Le-Mesnil on the D764 at the junction of the Meuse and the Canal des Ardennes. The regional tourist office at Charleville (see opposite) can provide information on hiking, canoeing, biking or riding. For **public transport** from Charleville, trains follow the Meuse into Belgium, and a few buses run up to Monthermé and **LES HAUTES-RIVIÈRES**, the latter on the River Semoy.

The **GR12** is a good walking route, circling the **Lac des Vieilles Forges**, 17km northwest of Charleville, then meeting the Meuse at Bogny and crossing over to Hautes-Rivières in the even more sinuous **Semoy Valley**. There are plenty of other tracks, too, though beware of *chasse* (hunting) signs – French hunters tend to hack through the undergrowth with their safety catches off and are notoriously trigger-happy. Wild boar are the main quarry being hunted – they are nowhere near as dangerous as their pursuers, and would seem to be more intelligent, too, rooting about near the crosses of the Resistance memorial near **REVIN**, while hunters stalk the forest. A good place to stay, overlooking the river at Revin, is the *Hôtel François-1er*, 46 quai Camille-Desmoulins (ⓣ03.24.40.15.88, ⓦwww.francois1.fr; ❸), which rents out bikes and canoes, and gives good advice on walks.

The abundance of wild boar is partly explained when you rummage around on the forest floor yourself and discover, between the trees to either side of the river, an astonishing variety of mushrooms, and, in late summer, wild strawberries and bilberries. For a quaint insight into life in the forest, stop at the **Musée de la Forêt**, situated right on the edge of the Ardennes, 2km north of **Renwez** on the D40 (ⓣ03.24.54.82.66, March–May & mid-Sept to mid-Nov daily 9am–noon & 2–5pm; June to mid-Sept daily 9am–7pm; mid-Nov to Feb Mon–Fri 9am–noon & 2–5pm; €8). All manner of woodcutting, gathering and transporting is enacted by wooden dummies along with displays of utensils and flora and fauna of the forest; it's also a tranquil spot for a picnic.

Travel details

Trains

Amiens to: Arras (10 daily; 40–50min); Compiègne (5 daily; 1hr 20min); Laon (6 daily; 1hr 40min); Lille (frequent; 1hr 20min); Paris (hourly; 1hr 20min);
Arras to: Albert (10 daily; 25min); Douai (very frequent; 15–30min); Lille (several daily; 1hr); Paris (frequent; 50min).
Beauvais to: Paris (hourly; 1hr 10min).
Boulogne-Ville to: Amiens (8 daily; 1hr 15min); Arras (4 daily; 2hr–2hr 30min); Calais-Ville (very frequent; 30min); Étaples-Le Touquet (hourly; 20min); Montreuil-sur-Mer (7 daily; 30–40min); Paris (8 daily; 2hr 40min; very frequent connections to Calais for TGV; 2hr 10min).
Calais-Ville to: Boulogne-Ville (very frequent; 30min); Étaples-Le Touquet (9 daily; 1hr); Lille, via the Calais-Fréthun Eurostar station (3 daily; 30min,

otherwise frequent; 1hr–1hr 50min); Paris (TGV 6 daily; 1hr 30min).
Compiègne to: Paris (frequent; 40–50min).
Dunkerque to: Arras (10 daily; 1hr 20min); Calais-Ville (frequent; 1hr–1hr 15min via Hazebrouck); Paris (TGV frequent; 2hr 20min via Arras).
Laon to: Paris (8 daily; 1hr 40min–2hr); Reims (10 daily; 40min); Soissons (1 hourly; 30min).
Lille to: Arras (TGV frequent; 40min; otherwise very frequent; 40min–1hr); Brussels (TGV 6 daily; 40min); Cambrai (frequent, mostly via Douai; 1hr); Douai (very frequent; 20–30min); Lyon (TGV 7 daily; 3hr–3hr 30min; or 4hr via Paris); Marseille (TGV several daily; 4hr 50min–6hr, sometimes via Lyon); Paris (TGV 1 hourly; 1hr).
Reims to: Charleville-Mézières (almost hourly; 50min); Épernay (frequent; 30min); Paris (frequent; 1hr 30min–2hr).
Troyes to: Chaumont (hourly; 50min); Langres (6 daily; 1hr 15min); Paris (frequent; 1hr 30min).

Buses

Amiens to: Abbeville (2 daily; 1hr 30min); Albert (4 daily; 40min); Arras (2 daily; 2hr); Beauvais (4 daily; 1hr 15min).
Boulogne to: Calais (4 daily; 1hr); Le Touquet (4 daily; 1hr).
Calais to: Boulogne (4 daily; 1hr); Le Touquet (4 daily; 2hr).
Dunkerque to: Calais (2–9 daily; 30min).
Reims to: Troyes (1–3 daily; 2hr 30min).

Alsace and Lorraine

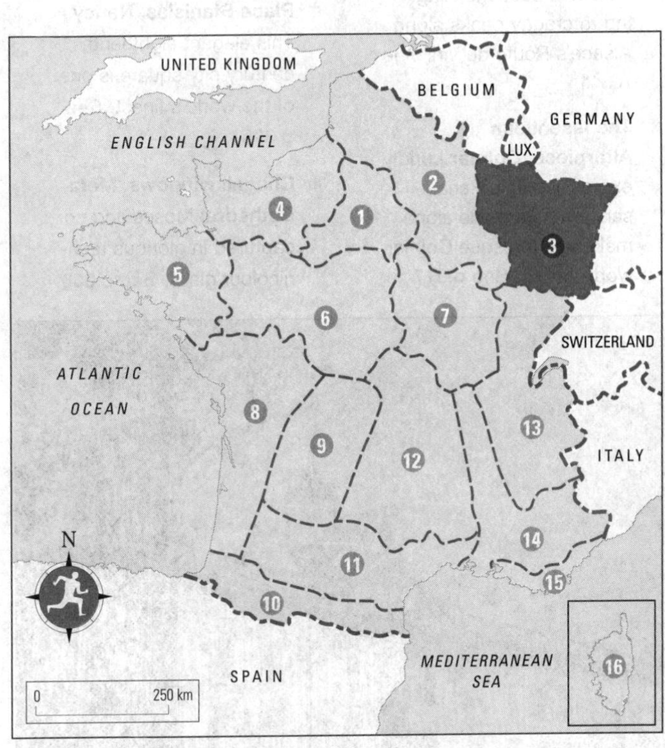

CHAPTER 3

Highlights

* **Spire of Strasbourg Cathedral** This Gothic steeple soars over the city like some medieval Chrysler building. See p.302
* **Vineyards and castles in the Vosges** Eyrie-like forts and bastions clinging to craggy peaks along Alsace's Route du Vin. See p.311
* **The Issenheim Altarpiece, Colmar** Luridly expressive, this Renaissance masterpiece alone makes picturesque Colmar worth a visit. See p.317
* **Bugattis at Mulhouse's Cité de l'Automobile** A unique collection of vintage motors in the city where the French car industry was set in motion. See p.321
* **Place Stanislas, Nancy** This elegant eighteenth-century city square is one of the world's finest. See p.325
* **Chagall windows, Metz Cathedral** Moses and co. captured in glorious technicolour glass. See p.330

△ Hôtel de Ville, Nancy

3

Alsace and Lorraine

France's easternmost provinces, Alsace and Lorraine, are invariably coupled together, at times even hyphenated, in part because they share a tumultuous history. Disputed throughout the Middle Ages by the French kings and the princes of the Holy Roman Empire, more recently they were involved in a tug-of-war between France and Germany, culminating in some of the worst conflicts of both world wars. This has bequeathed a mixed legacy: alongside splendid palaces built for powerful bishops and magical hill-top fortresses, you will find massive war cemeteries, solemn memorials and France's only Nazi concentration camp.

On the ground, there are more contrasts than similarities. The introverted people of **Alsace**, many of whom converse in Elsässisch, a Germanic dialect, tend to display a Mitteleuropa taste for Hansel-and-Gretel-type decoration – oriel windows, carved timberwork and Toytown gables. Buildings are maintained in pristine condition and window-boxes overflow with geraniums. The combination of French and German influences makes for a distinct culture and atmosphere seen at its most vivid in the numerous wine villages that punctuate the **Route du Vin**, along the eastern margin of the tree-clad Vosges mountains. The crisp white wines that give this route its name are an attraction in themselves; giving rise to no end of harvest festivities, they accompany a cuisine that mostly revolves around pork, cabbage and pungent cheese. The handsome regional (and European Union) capital, **Strasbourg**, and smaller, more postcardish **Colmar**, are home to some of France's finest art and architecture, with outstanding museums and churches, and winding streets lined with half-timbered houses. Conservative yet cosmopolitan, and known for a strong musical tradition, Alsace is a noticeably wealthy province, whose productive industries churn out cars, textiles, machine tools and telephones, plus half the beer in France.

Alsace's long-time (but much less prosperous) rival, **Lorraine**, sharing borders with Luxembourg, Germany and Belgium, is part farmland, part rust belt. Though not a province packed with unmissable sights, it's well worth visiting for its elegant former capital, **Nancy**, home to a major school of Art Nouveau; **Metz**, the green cathedral city and current capital; and the morbid World War I battlefields near **Verdun**, as impressive as they are horrific. While it is gastronomically less renowned than other French provinces, it has given the world one of its most popular savoury pies, the *quiche lorraine*. Although the Lorrains also have their own Germanic dialect, it is little used and the people have more in common with the Walloons, across the border in Belgium, when it comes to lifestyle and aesthetics.

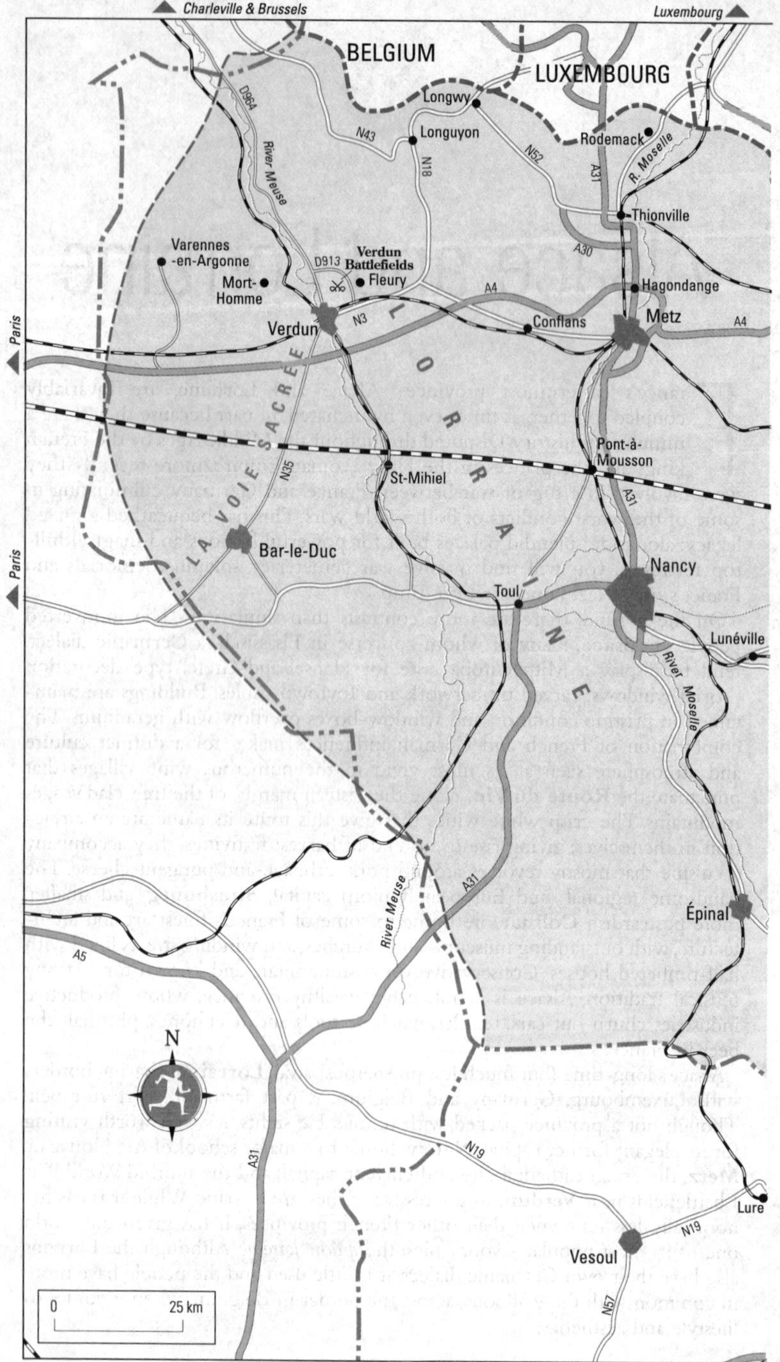
Charleville & Brussels
Luxembourg
BELGIUM
LUXEMBOURG
Longwy
Longuyon
Rodemack
R. Moselle
D964
N43
N18
N52
A31
River Meuse
Thionville
A30
Varennes
-en-Argonne
Verdun
Battlefields
D913
Mort-
Homme
Fleury
Hagondange
A4
Verdun
N3
Conflans
Metz
A4
Paris
LA VOIE SACREE
LORRAINE
N35
St-Mihiel
Pont-à-
Mousson
A31
Bar-le-Duc
Paris
Nancy
Toul
Lunéville
River Moselle
Épinal
A31
River Meuse
A5
N
N19
A31
Lure
N19
Vesoul
N57
0
25 km

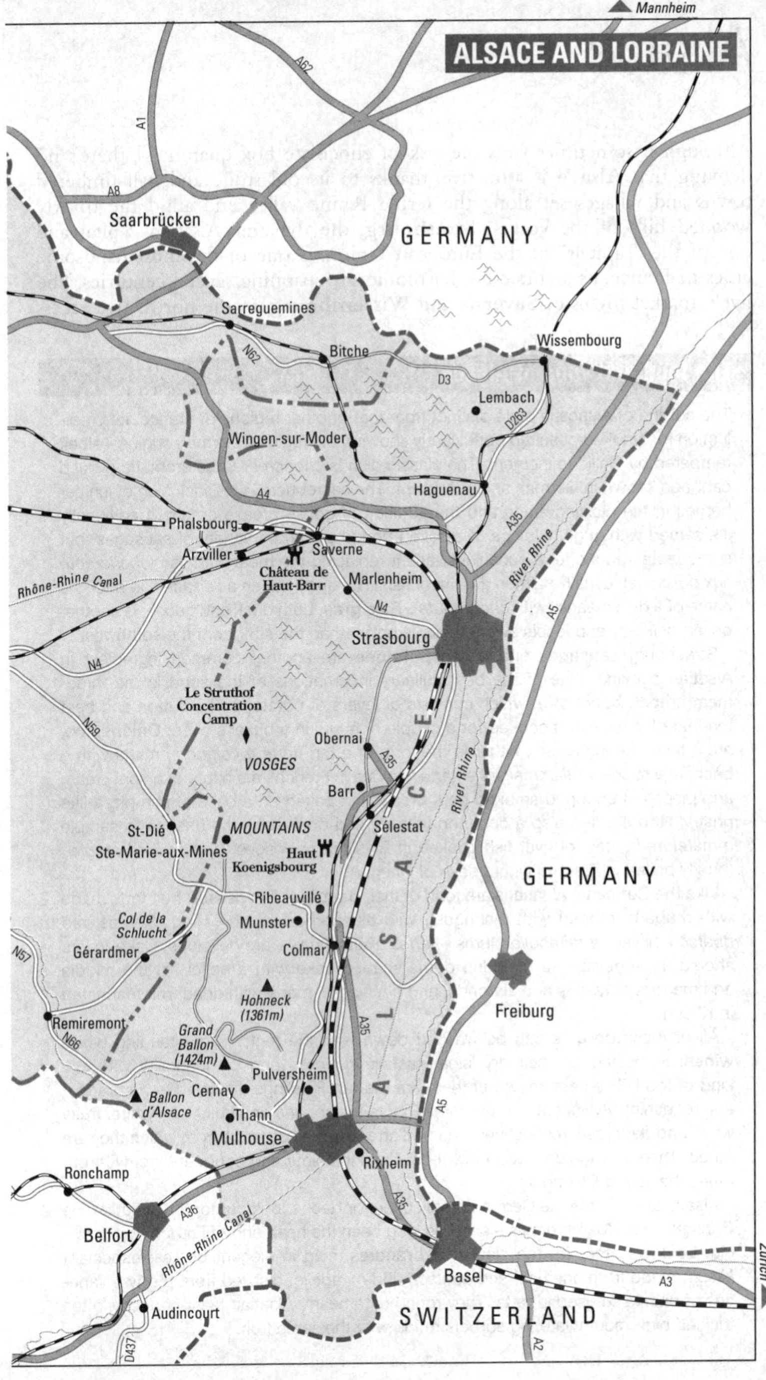
ALSACE AND LORRAINE
Mannheim
A62
A1
A8
Saarbrücken
GERMANY
Sarreguemines
N62
Bitche
Wissembourg
D3
Lembach
D263
Wingen-sur-Moder
Haguenau
A4
A35
River Rhine
Phalsbourg
Saverne
Arzviller
Château de
Haut-Barr
Rhône-Rhine Canal
Marlenheim
N4
A5
Strasbourg
N4
Le Struthof
Concentration
Camp
N59
Obernai
A35
VOSGES
Barr
River Rhine
St-Dié
MOUNTAINS
Sélestat
Ste-Marie-aux-Mines
Haut
Koenigsbourg
GERMANY
Ribeauvillé
Col de la
Schlucht
Munster
Colmar
N57
Gérardmer
Freiburg
Hohneck
(1361m)
Remiremont
N66
Grand
Ballon
(1424m)
A35
Pulversheim
Cernay
Ballon
d'Alsace
Thann
A5
Mulhouse
Rixheim
Ronchamp
A36
A35
Belfort
Rhône-Rhine Canal
Basel
Zurich
A3
Audincourt
SWITZERLAND
D437
A2
ALSACE

Alsace

Although it sometimes runs the risk of chocolate-box quaintness, there's no denying that **Alsace** is attractive, thanks to its old stone and half-timbered towns and villages set along the fertile Rhine valley and amid the thickly wooded hills of the Vosges. **Strasbourg**, the dynamic Alsatian capital and one of the "capitals" of the European Union, is one of the most handsome cities in France, its architecture harmoniously spanning several centuries. The lively market towns of **Saverne** and **Wissembourg**, to the north, give access

The food and wine of Alsace

The cuisine of Alsace is quite distinct from that of other regions of France, its predilection for smoked or salted pork clearly showing the region's German origins – albeit tempered by Gallic refinement. The classic dish is *choucroute*, the aromatic pickled cabbage known in German as **sauerkraut**. The secret here is the inclusion of juniper berries in the pickling stage and the addition of goose grease or lard. Traditionally it's served with large helpings of smoked pork, ham and a variety of sausages, but some restaurants offer a succulent variant replacing the meat with fish (*choucroute aux poissons*), usually salmon and monkfish. The qualification *à l'alsacienne* after the name of a dish means "with *choucroute*". **Foie gras**, both duck and goose, is another prized delicacy and locals swear theirs is better than the stuff from the southwest.

Strasbourg **sausages** and boiled **potatoes** are another common ingredient in Alsatian cooking. One of the best culinary incarnations of the spud is the three-meat hotpot, **baeckoffe**, which consists of layers of potato, pork, mutton and beef marinated in wine and cooked for a couple of hours in a baker's oven. **Onions**, too, are a favourite ingredient, either in the form of a tart (*tarte à l'oignon*), made with a béchamel sauce, or *flammeküche* (*tarte flambée* in French), a mixture of onion, cream and pieces of chopped smoked pork breast and baked on a base of thin pizza-like pastry. **Noodles** are also a common feature, and don't miss the chance to sample a *matelote* (a stew of river fish cooked in Riesling) or Vosges trout cooked *au bleu* (briefly boiled in Riesling with a dash of vinegar).

Like the Germans, Alsatians are fond of their **pastries**. The dessert fruit tarts made with rhubarb (topped with meringue), wild blueberries, apple or red cherries, red *quetsch* or yellow *mirabelle* plums – *tartes alsaciennes* – are delicious. Cake-lovers should try *kugelhopf*, a moulded dome-shaped cake with a hollow in the middle and made with raisins and almonds, and *birewecks*, made with dried fruit marinated in Kirsch.

All of these delights can be washed down with the region's outstanding **white wines**, renowned for their dry, clean-tasting fruitiness and compatibility with any kind of food. The best known of them are the tart Rieslings, flowery Gewürztraminers, refreshing Sylvaners and the three Pinots (blanc, gris and noir – dry white, fruity white and dark rosé, respectively), named after the type of grape from which they are made. There are, incidentally, a few reds – light in colour and bouquet – from Ottrott, Marlenheim and Cleebourg.

Alsace also shares the German predilection for **beer** – look out for the flavoursome Christmas and March brews – and has long been the heartland of French hop-growing. Look out, too, for the clear fruit **brandies**, sold in elegant bottles, especially *kirsch*, made from cherries, and *quetsch* and *mirabelle*, distilled from the two varieties of plum also used in tarts. They round off a hearty Alsatian feast perfectly, often trickled over mouthwatering sorbets made with the same fruit.

to some spectacular ruined castles in the **northern Vosges,** while south of Strasbourg, along the **Route du Vin** there are countless picturesque medieval hamlets and yet more ruined fortresses. A very different, horribly sobering experience is the concentration camp of **Le Struthof**, hidden away near the wine village of Barr.

Pretty **Colmar**, parts of which are admittedly twee, is well worth a visit, in particular for Grünewald's amazing Issenheim altarpiece, one of the most spectacular works of art in the whole country. By contrast, **Mulhouse** is thoroughly industrial but boasts some wonderful museums devoted to subjects as varied as cars, trains, wallpaper and printed fabric.

Every town has a **tourist office** (Ⓦwww.tourisme-alsace.com), which is often housed in the *mairie* or Hôtel de Ville in smaller places. Special tourist maps are on sale, but free maps containing a reasonable amount of information are always available too.

Strasbourg

STRASBOURG owes both its Germanic name – "the City of the Roads" – and its wealth to its strategic position on the west bank of the Rhine, long one of the great natural transport arteries of Europe. Self-styled *le Carrefour de l'Europe* ("Europe's Crossroads"), it lies at the very heart of Western Europe, closer to Frankfurt, Zurich and even Milan than to Paris, although the much awaited TGV has recently halved the four-hour train journey from the French capital. The city's medieval commercial pre-eminence was damaged by its involvement in the religious struggles of the sixteenth and seventeenth centuries, but recovered with the absorption into France in 1681. Along with the rest of Alsace, Strasbourg was annexed by Germany from 1871 to the end of World War I and again from 1940 to 1944.

Today old animosities have been submerged in the European Union, with Strasbourg the seat of the Council of Europe, the European Court of Human Rights and the European Parliament. Prosperous, beautiful and easy to get around, with an orderliness that is more Teutonic than Gallic, the city is big enough – with a population of over a quarter of a million people – to have a metropolitan air without being overwhelming. It has one of the loveliest cathedrals in France and one of the oldest and most active universities: that, plus the great variety of museums, the considerable range of cultural activities and a host of excellent restaurants make it a leading destination in its own right.

Arrival and information

The **gare SNCF** lies on the west side of the city centre, barely fifteen minutes' walk from the cathedral along rue du Maire-Kuss and rue du 22-Novembre. The **airport shuttle bus** (*navette*), departing Entzheim international airport every twenty minutes (5.30am–11pm), drops off at Baggersee, south of the centre, from where you can catch the very convenient and futuristic tram into central Strasbourg (€5.10 combined ticket).

The main **tourist office** is at 17 place de la Cathédrale (daily 9am–7pm; Ⓣ03.88.52.28.28, Ⓦwww.strasbourg.com), with the regional office for the Bas-Rhin *département* (northern Alsace) nearby at 9 rue du Dôme (Mon–Fri 9am–noon & 1.30–5pm; Ⓣ03.88.15.45.85/88). The tourist office can provide you with a map (€1 for one with museums and sights marked on it; free otherwise), though not all street names are marked. There's also a tourist office in the

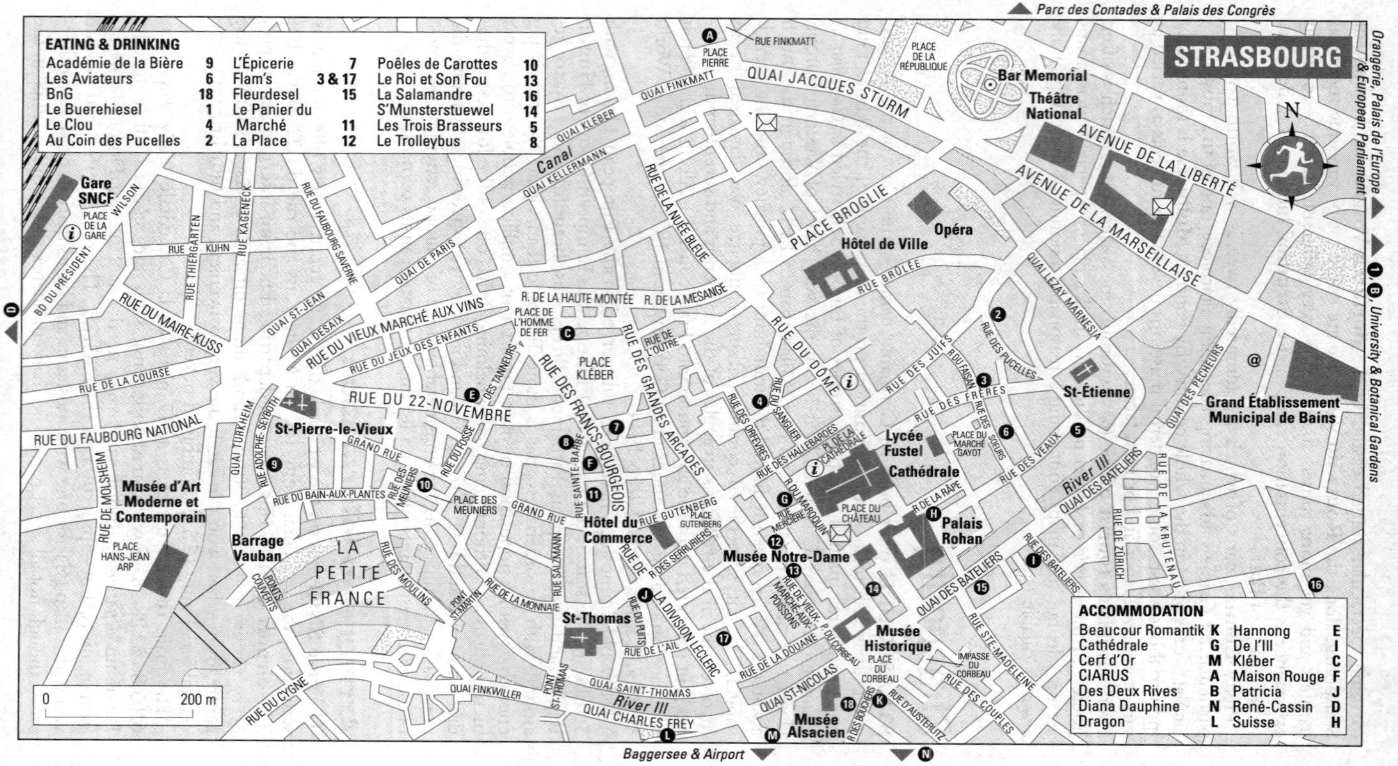

STRASBOURG

EATING & DRINKING

Académie de la Bière	9	L'Épicerie	7	Poêles de Carottes	10
Les Aviateurs	6	Flam's	3 & 17	Le Roi et Son Fou	13
BnG	18	Fleurdesel	15	La Salamandre	16
Le Buerehiesel	1	Le Panier du Marché	11	S'Munsterstuewel	14
Le Clou	4	La Place	12	Les Trois Brasseurs	5
Au Coin des Pucelles	2			Le Trolleybus	8

ACCOMMODATION

Beaucour Romantik	K	Hannong	E
Cathédrale	G	De l'Ill	I
Cerf d'Or	M	Kléber	C
CIARUS	A	Maison Rouge	F
Des Deux Rives	B	Patricia	J
Diana Dauphine	N	René-Cassin	D
Dragon	L	Suisse	H

Parc des Contades & Palais des Congrès
Orangerie, Palais de l'Europe & European Parliament
1, B, University & Botanical Gardens
Baggersee & Airport
N
D
0 200 m

Gare SNCF
Place de la Gare
Bar Memorial
Théâtre National
Place de la République
Opéra
Hôtel de Ville
Place Broglie
Place Kléber
Place Pierre
Place de l'Homme de Fer
St-Étienne
Grand Établissement Municipal de Bains
Lycée Fustel
Cathédrale
Place du Château
Place du Marché Gayot
Palais Rohan
Musée Notre-Dame
Musée Historique
Place du Corbeau
Musée Alsacien
Hôtel du Commerce
Place Gutenberg
St-Thomas
St-Pierre-le-Vieux
Musée d'Art Moderne et Contemporain
Place Hans-Jean Arp
Barrage Vauban
Ponts Couverts
La Petite France
Place des Meuniers
Canal
River Ill

Quai Jacques Sturm
Quai Finkmatt
Rue Finkmatt
Quai Kléber
Quai Kellermann
Avenue de la Liberté
Avenue de la Marseillaise
Quai Lezay Marnesia
Quai des Pêcheurs
Rue de la Krutenau
Rue de Zürich
Quai des Bateliers
Rue des Bateliers
Rue Ste-Madeleine
Impasse du Corbeau
Rue des Couples
Rue d'Austerlitz
Rue des Bouchers
Quai St-Nicolas
Rue de la Douane
P. du Corbeau
Rue de Vieux-Marché-aux-Poissons
Rue du Maroquin
Rue Mercière
R. de la Râpe
Pl. de la Cathédrale
Rue des Hallebardes
Rue des Orfèvres
Rue du Sanglier
Rue du Dôme
Rue Brûlée
Rue des Juifs
R. du Faisan
Rue des Pucelles
Rue des Frères
Rue des Sœurs
Rue des Veaux
Rue de la Nuée Bleue
R. de la Mésange
R. de la Haute Montée
Rue de l'Outre
Rue des Grandes Arcades
Rue des Francs-Bourgeois
Rue Sainte-Barbe
Rue Gutenberg
Rue des Serruriers
Rue de la Division Leclerc
Rue du Puits
Rue de l'Ail
Quai Saint-Thomas
Pont St-Thomas
Quai Charles Frey
Quai Finkwiller
Rue Salzmann
Grand Rue
Rue de la Monnaie
Pont St-Martin
Rue des Moulins
Rue des Meuniers
Rue du Bain-aux-Plantes
Rue du Fossé
Rue des Tanneurs
Rue du 22-Novembre
Rue du Jeux des Enfants
Rue du Vieux Marché aux Vins
Quai Desaix
Quai St-Jean
Quai de Paris
Rue du Faubourg Saverne
Rue Kageneck
Rue Kuhn
Rue Thiergarten
Wilson
Bd du Président
Rue du Maire-Kuss
Rue de la Course
Rue du Faubourg National
Quai Turkheim
Rue Adolphe-Seyboth
Rue de Molsheim
Rue du Cygne

new underground shopping complex just in front of the train station (Mon–Sat 9am–7pm, Sun 9am–6pm), and another at the airport (daily 8.30am–12.30pm & 1.15–5pm). It may be worth investing in a **Strasbourg Pass** (€10.90), which entitles you to one free museum entry, one half-price museum entry, a boat tour, a full day of bike hire and the cathedral tower and clock.

With much of the city centre now pedestrian-only, several car parks (Ⓦwww.parcus.com) cater for those who are **driving** into town; those on the outskirts of the city are either free or include tram tickets for the journey into the town centre. Strasbourg must be a strong contender for France's most **bicycle**-friendly city; 300km of bicycle lanes and particularly inexpensive bicycle hire (see "Listings", p.307) make cycling a tempting option.

Accommodation

When looking for a place to **stay**, bear in mind that once a month (except August, but twice in October) the European Parliament is in session for the best part of a week, bringing hundreds of MEPs and their numerous entourages into town. This puts all the city's facilities under pressure, especially hotel accommodation, which gets block-booked months ahead. The **hostels**, at least, are less affected, though even they play host to one or two MEPs. To find out in advance when the parliament is sitting, contact the main tourist office. The station area has the usual clutch of hotels – useful, if occasionally seedy, standbys.

Hotels

Beaucour Romantik 5 rue des Bouchers Ⓣ03.88.76.72.00, Ⓦwww.hotel-beaucour.com. Very central but rather overpriced boutique hotel, just off place du Corbeau, in a handsome old house with its own courtyard. ❽

Cathédrale 12–13 place de la Cathédrale Ⓣ03.88.22.12.12, Ⓦwww.hotel-cathedrale.fr. Extremely smart rooms, some of which offer stunning views of the cathedral; breakfast is served in the stylish bar. ❼

Cerf d'Or 6 place de l'Hôpital Ⓣ03.88.36.20.05, Ⓕ03.88.36.68.67. Attractive sixteenth-century hotel with its own bar and smart restaurant (menu from €19–24; closed most of July) on the south side of the River Ill. Closed mid-Dec to mid-Jan. ❺

Diana Dauphine 30 rue de la 1er-Armée Ⓣ03.88.36.26.61, Ⓦwww.hotel-diana-dauphine.com. This welcome newcomer a few hundred metres south of the Ill is the city's first conscious attempt at an accessible boutique hotel, with plush, sleek designer furniture and fittings, albeit it in a you-wouldn't-look-at-twice building. ❻

Dragon 2 rue de l'Écarlate Ⓣ03.88.35.79.80, Ⓦwww.dragon.fr. Fully modernized luxury hotel popular with European Parliament employees. Closed Christmas. ❺

Hannong 15 rue du 22-Novembre Ⓣ03.88.32.16.22, Ⓦwww.hotel-hannong.com. Beautiful parquet floors and tasteful furnishings in the rooms go some way to justifying the room rates; the cocktail bar is open late and serves snacks till midnight. ❼

De l'Ill 8 rue des Bateliers Ⓣ03.88.36.20.01, Ⓦwww.hotel-ill.com. The best bargain in Strasbourg; a quiet, comfortable, family-run place just 50m from the river, in sight of the cathedral. Closed end of Dec to mid-Jan. ❹

Kléber 29 place Kléber Ⓣ03.88.32.50.41, Ⓦwww.hotel-kleber.com. Comfortably modern, designer-furnished, no-smoking hotel right at the heart of the city, whose bijou rooms – with names like gourmet ice-cream flavours – are done out in different fabrics and colours. ❹

Maison Rouge 4 rue des Francs-Bourgeois Ⓣ03.88.32.08.60, Ⓦwww.maison-rouge.com. Lavishly decorated hotel with a sitting-room on every floor and comfortable bedrooms. ❽

Patricia 1a rue du Puits Ⓣ03.88.32.14.60, Ⓕ03.88.32.19.08. Decent rooms in a great location in the backstreets of the old town not far from place Gutenberg. ❸

Suisse 2–4 rue de la Râpe Ⓣ03.88.35.22.11, Ⓦwww.hotel-suisse.com. The rooms are cramped but the location, just underneath the mass of the lofty cathedral, is impressive. ❺

Hostels and campsite

CIARUS 7 rue Finkmatt Ⓣ03.88.15.27.88/90, Ⓦwww.ciarus.com. Protestant-run hostel near the Palais de Justice, just north of the centre. Bus #10 or #20 from the station to place Pierre. €17 including breakfast, or double rooms (③).

Des Deux Rives rue des Cavaliers ⓣ03.88.45.54.20, ⓕ03.88.45.54.21. Large HI hostel set in a park on the banks of the Rhine close to the Pont de l'Europe over the Rhine to Germany. Bus #21 from place Gutenberg, direction "Kehl", stop "Parc du Rhin". €19 including breakfast, for cardholders.

La Montagne-Verte 2 rue Robert-Forrer ⓣ03.88.30.25.46. A well-equipped campsite, located behind the *René-Cassin* hostel. Mar–Oct.

René-Cassin 9 rue de l'Auberge-de-Jeunesse ⓣ03.88.30.26.46, ⓔstrasbourg.rene-cassin@fuaj.org. Large and fully equipped HI hostel 3km southwest of the city centre. Bus #3, #23 from Homme de Fer, stop "Auberge de Jeunesse". €18 including breakfast, for cardholders.

The City

It isn't difficult to find your way around Strasbourg on foot, as the flat city centre is concentrated on a small island encircled by the **River Ill** and an old canal. The magnificent filigree spire of the pink-sandstone **cathedral** is visible throughout the city. It dominates not just Strasbourg but much of Alsace, though its silhouette at the time of writing was deformed by scaffolding likely to be in place for some time, owing to urgent restoration work. Immediately south of this building are the best of the museums, while to the northwest, unappealing **place Kléber** lies at the heart of the commercial district. To the south, the more intimate **place Gutenberg** is nominally the main square. About a ten-minute walk west, on the tip of the island, is picturesque **La Petite France**, where timber-framed houses and gently flowing canals hark back to the city's medieval trades of tanning and dyeing. Across the canal to the east of the centre is the late nineteenth-century **German quarter** and the city's European institutions, including the European Parliament building.

The cathedral and place Gutenberg

The **Cathédrale de Notre-Dame** (daily 7–11.30am & 12.40–7pm; closed during services) soars out of the close huddle of medieval houses at its feet with a single spire of such delicate, flaky lightness that it seems the work of confectioners rather than masons. It's worth slogging up the 332 steps to the

The Alsatian language

Travelling through the province, you might well mistake the language being spoken in the shops and streets for German. In fact, it is **Elsässisch**, or Alsatian, a High German dialect known to philologists as Alemannic. To confuse matters further, there are two versions, High and Low Alemannic, plus an obscure Frankish dialect spoken in the Wissembourg region and a Romance one called *Welche* from the valleys around Orbey. You'll hear a different version spoken in almost every town.

In many ways, it's a miracle that the language has survived. During the French Revolution, it was suppressed in favour of French for nationalistic reasons, only to be ousted by German when the Prussians annexed the region in 1870. On its return to French rule, all things Germanic were disdained, and many Alsatians began to speak French once more ... until the Nazi occupation brought in laws that made the speaking of French and even the wearing of berets imprisonable offences.

Nowadays, most daily transactions are conducted in French, and Elsässisch has still not made it onto the school curriculum. Yet it remains a living language, with a rich medieval literary legacy, and is still spoken by young and old throughout Alsace – especially in rural areas – and even parts of Lorraine. A renaissance of regional identity has meant that Elsässisch is also beginning to reappear on signs and to be spoken at official level too.

spire's **viewing platform** (daily: March & Oct 9am–5.30pm; April–June & Sept 9am–6.30pm; July & Aug 8.30am–7pm; Nov–Feb 9am–4.30pm; €4.40) for the superb view of the old town, and, in the distance, the Vosges to the west and the Black Forest to the east.

The **interior**, too, is magnificent, the high nave a model of proportion enhanced by a glorious sequence of stained-glass windows. The finest are in the south aisle next to the door, depicting the life of Christ and the Creation, but all are beautiful, including, in the apse, the modern glass designed in 1956 by Max Ingrand to commemorate the first European institutions in the city. On the left of the nave, the cathedral's organ perches precariously above one of the arches, like a giant gilded eagle, while further down on the same side is the late fifteenth-century pulpit, a masterpiece of intricacy in stone by the aptly named Hans Hammer.

In the south transept are the cathedral's two most popular sights. The **Pilier des Anges** is a slender triple-tiered central column, decorated with some of the most graceful and expressive statuary of the thirteenth century. The huge and enormously complicated **astrological clock** (tickets can be bought from the postcard stand 9am–11.30am, then at the cash desk at the south door 11.50am–12.20pm; €0.80, children free) was built by Schwilgué of Strasbourg in 1842. It is a favourite with the tour-group operators, whose customers roll up in droves to witness the clock's crowning performance of the day, striking the hour of noon, which it does with unerring accuracy at 12.30pm – that being 12 o'clock "Strasbourg time", as the city lies well east of the Greenwich meridian. Death strikes the chimes; the apostles parade in front of Christ, who occupies the highest storey of the clock and gives each one his blessing.

Narrow rue Mercière, busy with drinkers, shoppers and cathedral-gazers, funnels west to **place Gutenberg**, with its steep-pitched roofs and brightly painted facades. It was named after the printer and pioneer of moveable type who lived in the city in the early fifteenth century and whose statue occupies the middle of the square. On the west side stands the sixteenth-century **Hôtel de Commerce**, where the writer Arthur Young watched the destruction of the magistrates' records during the Revolution; excellent art exhibitions are often held on the ground floor.

South of the cathedral

Most of Strasbourg's **museums** lie to the south of the cathedral, between the tree-lined place du Château and the river. Check with the tourist office for museum passes/discounts (see p.299) if you're planning to visit them all.

Right next to the cathedral, place du Château is enclosed to the east by the Lycée Fustel and to the south by the imposing **Palais Rohan**, both eighteenth-century buildings; the latter was designed for the immensely powerful Rohan family, who, for several generations in a row, cornered the market in cardinals' hats. There are three museums in the Palais Rohan itself (daily except Tues 10am–6pm; closed public hols; €4 each): the **Musée des Arts Décoratifs**; the **Musée des Beaux-Arts**, which has a decent collection of European paintings from Giotto to the nineteenth century; and the rather specialist **Musée Archéologique**. Of the three collections, the Arts Décoratifs, with its eighteenth-century faïence tiles crafted in the city by Paul Hannong, stands out. The rooms of the palace are vast and ostentatious but not especially interesting.

Next door, in the mansion lived in by the cathedral architects, the excellent **Musée de l'Oeuvre Notre-Dame** (daily except Tues 10am–6pm; €4) houses the original sculptures from the cathedral exterior, damaged in the Revolution and replaced today by copies; both sets are worth seeing. Other treasures here include: glass from the city's original Romanesque cathedral; the eleventh-century Wissembourg Christ, said to be the oldest representation of a human figure in stained glass; and the architect's original parchment drawings for the statuary, done in fascinating detail down to the expressions on each figure's face.

Past the picturesque place du Marché-aux-Cochons-de-Lait and the much restored **Musée Historique** (closed for lengthy renovation at time of writing; reopening scheduled for late 2007) and across the river, in a typically Alsatian house at quai St-Nicolas, is the charming **Musée Alsacien** (daily except Tues 10am–6pm; €4), which contains elaborately painted furniture and other quaint local artefacts.

Musée d'Art Moderne et Contemporain

The latest addition to Strasbourg's museums is the **Musée d'Art Moderne et Contemporain** (Tues, Wed & Fri–Sun 11am–7pm; Thurs noon–10pm; €5), 1 place Hans-Jean Arp, housed in a mega-budget, purpose-built, glass-fronted building overlooking the river and Vauban's dam (see below) to the west of the centre. It's a light and airy space and its collection is well presented, making up for its shortcomings by acknowledging the importance of some lesser-known artists. The ground floor confronts the themes and roots of modern European art from the late nineteenth century through to the 1950s by way of the Impressionists, Symbolists and a good section on Surrealism, with plenty of folkloric, mystical paintings by Brauner, plus a room devoted to the voluptuous curves sculpted by Strasbourg's own Arp. The chronology continues upstairs with conceptual art and Arte Povera, and finishes up with stripey creations by Daniel Buren and video art by Bill Viola. The temporary exhibitions – devoted to the likes of Le Corbusier and Picasso – have been reliably good.

La Petite France and the rest of the old city

On the south side of the Pont du Corbeau, the medieval street, **Impasse du Corbeau**, still looks much as it must have done in the fourteenth century. Downstream, to the east, the **quai des Bateliers** was part of the old business quarter, and the streets leading off it – rue Ste-Madeleine, rue de la Krutenau and rue de Zürich – are still worth a wander.

Two bridges upstream, the Pont St-Thomas leads to the **church of St-Thomas** (Jan & Feb Sat & Sun 2–5pm; March, Nov & Dec daily 10am–noon & 2–5pm; April–Oct daily 10am–noon & 2–6pm; closed Sun morning for services; ⓣ03.88.32.14.46), with a Romanesque facade and Gothic towers. Strasbourg was a bastion of the Reformation and since 1549 it has been the principal Protestant church of the city; one of its leaders, Martin Bucer, preached here. The amazing piece of sculpture behind the altar is Jean-Baptiste Pigalle's **tomb of the Maréchal de Saxe**, a French military commander active against the Duke of Cumberland in the War of the Austrian Succession in the middle of the eighteenth century.

From here, it's a short walk upstream to the Pont St-Martin, which marks the beginning of the district known as **La Petite France**, where the city's millers, tanners and fishermen used to live. At the far end of a series of canals are the so-called **Ponts Couverts** (they are in fact no longer covered), built as part of the fourteenth-century city fortifications and still punctuated by watchtowers. Just beyond is a **dam** built by Vauban (daily 9am–7.30pm; mid-March to mid-Oct till 8pm; free) to protect the city from waterborne assault. The whole area is picture-postcard pretty, with winding streets – most notably rue du Bain-aux-Plantes – bordered by sixteenth- and seventeenth-century houses adorned with flowers and elaborately carved woodwork.

The area east of the cathedral, where rue des Frères leads to place St-Étienne, is good for a stroll, too. **Place du Marché-Gayot**, off rue des Frères behind the cathedral, is very lively, almost southern in feel, with a row of trendy studenty cafés on the north side and a mixed bunch of eateries opposite. From the north side of the cathedral, rue du Dôme leads to the eighteenth-century **place Broglie**, with the Hôtel de Ville, the bijou **Opéra** and some imposing eighteenth-century mansions. It was at 4 place Broglie in 1792 that Rouget de l'Isle first sang what later became known as the *Marseillaise* for the mayor of Strasbourg, who had challenged him to compose a rousing song for the troops of the army of the Rhine.

The German quarter (Neustadt) and the European institutions

Across the canal from place Broglie, **place de la République** is surrounded by vast German Neo-Gothic edifices erected during the post-1870 Imperial Prussian occupation, one example being the main **post office** on avenue de la Marsellaise. At the centre of the square, amid the magnolias, is a **war memorial** showing a mother holding two dead sons in her arms, neither of which, unusually for such monuments, wears a military uniform. This testifies to the horrific family divisions faced by Alsatian families, whose members often found themselves fighting on opposing sides in World War II. At the other end of avenue de la Liberté, across the confluence of the Ill and Aar, is the city's **university**, where Goethe studied. Adjacent, at the beginning of boulevard de la Victoire, are the splendidly Teutonic municipal baths, the **Grand Établissement Municipal de Bains**, where you can take a sauna or Turkish bath (€11.50) or just swim (consult the complicated opening hours on the board outside).

From in front of the university, the wide, straight alleé de la Robertsau, flanked by confident *fin-de-siècle* bourgeois residences and beautiful early twentieth-century buildings including some Art Nouveau masterpieces, leads to the headquarters of three major European institutions: the bunker-like **Palais de l'Europe**, 1970s-built home of the 44-member Council of Europe; the glass and steel curvilinear **European Parliament building**, opened in 1999; and Richard Rogers' **European Court of Human Rights**, completed in 1995, which incorporates a curving glass entrance and silver towers that rise to a boat-like superstructure overlooking a sweep of canal. To visit the European Parliament (ⓣ03.88.17.20.07; free) or the European Court of Human Rights and the Council of Europe, which are visited together (ⓣ03.90.21.49.40; free), you have to book.

Opposite the Palais, the **Orangerie** is Strasbourg's best bit of greenery, and hosts a variety of exhibitions and free concerts. Here the storks, to be seen perching on many buildings in the town, have their main nesting site. There's also a zoo with small animals, such as monkeys, and exotic birds including flamingos.

Eating and drinking

For the classic Strasbourg (and Alsatian) eating experience, you should go to a **winstub**, loosely translated as a "wine bar", a cosy establishment with bare beams, panels and benches, and a noisy, convivial atmosphere. In the classic version there is a special table, a *Stammtisch*, set aside for the *patron*'s friends and regulars. The food revolves around the Alsatian classics, all accompanied by local wines (or, especially in a *bierstub*, beer), though the more sophisticated ones offer interesting variations on these themes. Traffic-free place du Marché-Gayot

△ Bierstub, Strasbourg

("PMG") near the cathedral is one of the best spots for **cafés**, most of which open until late, while there is a good selection of less touristy **restaurants** in rue du Faubourg Saverne. The city and rest of the region have more than their fair share of gastronomic awards; some of the best (for which you'll have to book ahead) are listed among the options below.

Restaurants

Le Buerehiesel 4 parc de l'Orangerie ⓣ03.88.45.56.65, ⓦwww.buerehiesel.com. This outstanding and prestigious restaurant, delightfully housed in a farmhouse in the Parc de l'Orangerie, is the ideal place for an extravagant bout of self-pampering. Menus €60–150.

Le Clou 32 rue du Chaudron ⓣ03.88.32.11.67. This has become the most reliable, traditional *winstub* in the city centre, making reservations a must; the liver dumplings are unbeatable, as are the desserts. Closed Wed & Sun.

Au Coin des Pucelles 12 rue des Pucelles ⓣ03.88.35.35.14. Reasonably priced *winstub* popular with theatre-goers because of its late opening hours, serving traditional fare with an original twist and reliable wines. Closed Tues & Sun.

Flam's 1 rue de l'Épine, with another at the corner of rues des Frères and du Faisan. A good place to sample the local speciality, *tarte flambée* (the Alsatian equivalent of pizza), with an €11 all-you-can-eat *tarte flambée* menu (includes dessert). Meals from €6.

Fleurdesel 22 quai des Bateliers ⓣ03.88.36.01.54. Trendy place serving adventurous food with an emphasis on exotic flavourings and combinations, such as the prawn and pineapple brochettes for starters. Main dishes are €15, the lunchtime menu is €25. Closed Sun & Mon.

Le Panier du Marché 15 rue Sainte-Barbe ⓣ03.88.32.04.07. Stylish gourmet restaurant with a young clientele and fixed menu (€27 without drinks) for which seasonal ingredients are used to compose meals of outstanding quality. Closed Sat & Sun.

La Place 3 place des Tripiers ⓣ03.88.22.22.20. Ultra-trendy brasserie that is now one of the places to be. Surprisingly, the well-prepared, delicious bistro-style food is not overpriced, and comes in copious helpings, with half-portions on offer. Open daily till late and has a very popular summer terrace.

Poêles de Carottes 2 place des Meuniers ⓣ03.88.32.33.23. The best vegetarian, organic restaurant in town, in a quiet square tucked away near picturesque Petite France. Lunch €10, dinner €17. Closed Sun.

S'Munsterstuewel 8 place du Marché-aux-Cochons-de-Lait ⓣ03.88.32.17.63, ⓔmunsterstuewel@orange.fr. A very special *winstub* on one of the city's most attractive squares, this serves both traditional and more unusual dishes till late, with excellent wines to match. Closed Sun & Mon. Meals around €45.

Les Trois Brasseurs 22 rue des Veaux. Wonderful *bierstub*, which brews its own beer: the enormous copper brewing equipment is part of the decor. *Tarte flambée* starts at €5, and other Alsatian specialities are available. Happy hour 5–7pm.

Cafés and bars

Académie de la Bière 17 rue Adolphe-Seyboth. Strasbourg's most famous *bierstub*, open daily till very late.

Les Aviateurs 12 rue des Soeurs. "*Les Aviat*", as it's known locally, is regularly packed with Strasbourg's fashionable intelligentsia sipping cocktails or draught Guinness until the early hours.

BnG 6 rue des Bouchers. A new "modern bar", as its publicity states, run by friendly management, with chill-out music, cocktails and a tiny terrace for the warmer months.

L'Épicerie 6 rue du Vieux Seigle. Tucked away in the labyrinthine side streets, this appealing little reconstruction of an old-fashioned grocer's dishes up a wide variety of *tartines* (open sandwiches), along with a range of beers, ciders and soft drinks.

Le Roi et Son Fou 37 rue du Vieil-Hôpital. Friendly brasserie with a sunny terrace looking on to a quiet square, popular with locals for its low-priced lunchtime specials, decent breakfasts and daytime drinks and coffees.

La Salamandre 3 rue Paul-Janet ⓣ03.88.25.79.42. A popular bar-disco (free entrance) famous for its rock concerts (tickets €10–25) and theme nights (€5).

Le Trolleybus 14 rue Sainte-Barbe. Much-frequented focal point in this stretch of newly pedestrianized backstreet – where crowds are drawn by an Irish pub, a Lebanese restaurant, a sushi bar and a couple of other trendy joints; in the warmer months, you can drink and people-watch outside, and there's occasionally live music playing too.

Entertainment

Strasbourg usually has lots going on, particularly when it comes to music. Pick up free monthly magazine *Spectacles à Strasbourg et alentours* (ⓦwww.spectacles-publications.com), with entertainment info and practical **listings** and, in summer months, the free *Saison d'Été* listings leaflet, both available from the tourist offices. If you're here during university term-time, you might want to check the notice boards at the university as well. **Free concerts** are held regularly in the Parc des Contades and Parc de l'Orangerie, which also boasts a bowling alley.

The best of the annual **festivals** focus on classical music in mid-June, jazz in July, and "contemporary classical" music – Musica – from mid-September to early October. In addition, there's **Les Nuits de Strasbourg**, a firework, light and music display at the Ponts Couverts during July and August, and an impressive illumination of the cathedral facade every summer evening. At the Christkindelsmärik or **Marché de Noël** (late Nov to Dec 24), an increasingly commercial event dating back over 400 years, central Strasbourg is taken over by wooden stalls selling mulled wine, crafts of varying quality and spicy Christmas cookies known as *bredele*.

Listings

Bike rental Bicycles can be hired from 4 rue du Maire Kuss, Parking Ste-Aurélie, place du Château and Impasse de la Grande Écluse (near the Ponts Couverts) for €5 a day.

Boat trips Strasbourg Fluvial (ⓣ03.88.84.13.13, ⓦwww.strasbourg.port.fr) runs cruises on the Ill all year round. Cruises depart from the landing stage in front of the Palais Rohan (daily: April–Nov every 30min 9.30am–9pm; Dec–March four departures 10.30am–4pm). The itinerary includes Petite-France, the Vauban dam and the Palais de l'Europe. Evening cruises depart at 9.30 and 10pm May to September only. The trip costs €7, half-price for students and children (€7.40 for evening cruises) and lasts 1hr 10min.

Books FNAC, 22 place Kléber, for a huge selection of books, records and concert tickets; Librairie Internationale Kléber, 1 rue des Francs-Bourgeois,

sells new books, some in English; La Librocase, 2 quai des Pêcheurs, sells secondhand books; Quai des Brumes, 120 Grand'Rue, has a very good range; Bookworm, 4 rue de Pâques, is a small English bookshop with new and used books, plus greetings cards.
Buses Eurolines has an office at 5 rue des Frères (☎03.88.22.73.74). Some out-of-town buses leave from place des Halles.
Car rental Europcar, airport ☎03.88.68.95.55; 15 place de la Gare ☎03.88.15.55.66; Avis, Galérie Marchande, place de la Gare ☎03.88.32.30.44; Hertz, 6 bd de Metz by the *gare SNCF* ☎03.88.32.57.62.
Cinemas Le Star, 27 rue du Jeu-des-Enfants (☎03.88.22.73.20) and Le Star St Exupéry, 18 rue du 22-novembre (☎03.88.22.28.79); L'Odyssée, 3 rue des Francs-Bourgeois (☎03.88.75.10.47), a sumptuous restored cinema with red velvet seats, shows a combination of classic and contemporary films, many in *v.o.*
Internet NET SUR COUR, 18 quai des Pêcheurs.
Markets The city's biggest fruit and vegetable market takes place every Tues and Sat morning on bd de la Marne; mostly organic local produce, including foie gras and honey, is sold on the small square next to the forecourt of the Palais Rohan every Sat morning; the Marché aux Puces (Wed & Sat) is on rue du Vieil-Hôpital (near the cathedral).
Post offices 5 av de la Marseillaise and place de la Cathédrale.
Taxis Novotaxi ☎03.88.75.19.19; Taxis 13 ☎03.88.36.13.13.

The northern Vosges

The **northern Vosges** begin at the Saverne gap northwest of Strasbourg and run up to the German border, where they continue as the Pfälzerwald. They don't reach the same heights as the southern Vosges (see p.311), nor do they boast particularly photogenic villages or famous vineyards but, as a result, they're spared the mass tourism of the southern range. Much of the region comes under the auspices of the Parc Régional des Vosges du Nord, and there are numerous hiking possibilities, plus a couple of attractive towns – **Saverne** and **Wissembourg** – built in the characteristic red sandstone of the area.

Transport here is erratic, as elsewhere in Alsace, though not hopeless. SNCF buses wind their way through the villages and apple orchards around Haguenau, and the Strasbourg–Sarreguemines and Hagenau–Bitche train lines cut across the range. Saverne and Wissembourg are also linked to Strasbourg by rail. Even so, the ideal way to explore the region is with your own transport – hilly but rewarding work, if it's a bike.

Saverne and around

SAVERNE, seat of the exiled Catholic prince-bishops of Strasbourg during the Reformation, commands the only easy route across the Vosges into Alsace, at a point where the hills are pinched to a narrow waist. The best launch pad from which to explore the northern Vosges, it's a small and friendly town, with plenty of the region's characteristic steep-pitched roofs and window boxes full of geraniums.

One of the sights worth visiting is the vast red-sandstone Château des Rohan, on place de Gaulle, built in rather austere classical style by one of the Rohans who was prince-bishop at the time, and now housing the **Musée Rohan** (March–June & Sept–Nov daily except Tues 2–5pm; July & Aug daily except Tues 10am–noon & 2–6pm; Dec–March Sun only 2–5pm; €2.70) and hostel. A feature of the museum is the collection of local Resistance journalist Louise Weiss. The River Zorn and the Marne–Rhine canal both weave their way through the town, the latter framing the château's formal gardens in a graceful right-angle bend. Alongside the château, the **church of Notre-Dame-de-la-Nativité** contains another finely carved pulpit by Hans Hammer. Horticultural distraction can be found in the town's famed rose garden, **La Roseraie** (June–Sept daily 10am–7pm; ⓣ03.88.71.83.33; ⓦwww.roseraie-saverne.fr; €2.50), to the west of the centre by the river, which boasts over four hundred varieties, and the **botanical gardens**, 3km out of town off the N4 Metz–Nancy road (May, June & first two weeks in Sept Mon–Fri 9am–5pm, Sun 2–6pm; July & Aug Mon–Fri 9am–5pm, Sat & Sun 2–7pm; €2.50).

There are several relatively easy **walks** around Saverne (the tourist office can give details), the most popular taking in the ruined **Château du Haut-Barr**, which takes about two hours there and back. Follow rue du Haut-Barr southeast along the canal past the leafy suburban villas until you reach the woods, where a signboard indicates the various walks possible. Take the path marked "Haut-Barr" through woods of chestnut, beech and larch, and you'll see the castle standing dramatically on a narrow sandstone ridge, with fearsome drops on both sides and views across the wooded hills and eastward over the plain towards Strasbourg. Approaching by road you'll pass the reconstruction of a late eighteenth-century **relay tower** (July & Aug Wed–Sun 1–6pm; €1.50) that was part of the optical telegraph link between Paris and Strasbourg until the middle of the nineteenth century. An audio-visual presentation inside explains the pioneering system invented by Claude Chappe in 1794.

If you're driving, you can easily get to the beautiful small towns and villages around Saverne, in particular Bouxwiller, Neuwiller, Pfaffenhoffen and Ingwiller, from where an alternative road to Bitche leads through the densely wooded heart of the northern Vosges. A short way outside Ingwiller, the much-restored **Château of Lichtenburg** (March & Nov Mon–Sat 1–4pm, Sun 10am–7pm; April, May, Sept & Oct Mon 1.30–6pm, Tues–Sat 10am–noon & 1.30–4pm, Sun & hols 10am–7pm; June–Aug Mon 1.30–6pm, Tues–Sat 10am–6pm, Sun & hols 10am–7pm; €2.50) dates back to the thirteenth century.

Practicalities

The **tourist office** is at 37 Grand' Rue (Mon–Sat 9am–12.30pm & 2–7pm; May–Oct also open Sun 10am–12.30pm & 2–5pm; ⓣ03.88.91.80.47, ⓦwww.ot-saverne.fr); they can provide a map of walks in the area published by the Saverne Centre de Randonnées Pedestres (part of the Club Vosgien). For **accommodation** in town, try the *Europe*, at 7 rue de la Gare (ⓣ03.88.71.12.07, ⓦwww.hotel-europe-fr.com; ❺), with bright, modern rooms. Alternatively, the *Hotel/Restaurant Chez Jean*, 3 rue de la Gare (ⓣ03.88.91.10.19, ⓦwww.chez-jean.com; ❺), has a restaurant with good Alsatian food (menus €17–45). A less expensive option is the *National*, 2 Grand' Rue (ⓣ03.88.91.14.54, ⓦwww.hotel-national-saverne.com; ❹); more reasonable still is the friendly **HI hostel** in the Château Rohan, on place de Gaulle (ⓣ03.88.91.14.84, ⓔsaverne@fuaj.org; reception open 8–10am & 5–10pm; cardholders only). There's also a **campsite** about 1km from town, below the Château du Haut-Barr on rue du Père-Liebermann (ⓣ03.88.91.35.65; April–Sept).

As for **food**, gourmets will appreciate the *Taverne Katz* on the main street, 80 Grand' Rue (ⓣ03.88.71.16.56; closed Tues eve & Wed; menu €15–25): a beautiful old house with an ornately carved facade and plush decor within, it offers excellent traditional cuisine, with very good *baeckoffe* and divine sorbets. *Restaurant Staeffele*, 1 rue Poincaré (ⓣ03.88.91.63.94; closed Wed, Thurs lunch & Sun eve; menus €35–50), is also worth a visit for impeccably prepared Alsatian fare in stylish surroundings. More modest and with a local ambience, the *Restaurant de la Marne*, 5 rue du Griffon (ⓣ03.88.91.19.18; closed Mon), overlooks the Marne–Rhine canal in the centre of town and serves copious salads amongst a varied menu. There's also a restaurant specializing in foie gras at the Château du Haut-Barr (see p.309; ⓣ03.88.91.17.61; closed all day Mon and Thurs dinner; menus €18–40).

Wissembourg

WISSEMBOURG, 60km north of Strasbourg and right on the German border, is a small town of cobbled and higgledy-piggledy prettiness, largely given over to moneyed German weekenders. The townspeople have a curious linguistic anomaly; they speak an ancient dialect derived from Frankish, unlike their fellow Alsatians whose language is closer to modern German.

At the end of rue Nationale, the town's main commercial street, stands the imposing Gothic **church of St-Paul-et-St-Pierre**, with a Romanesque belfry and some fine twelfth- and thirteenth-century stained glass, once attached to the town's abbey. Beneath the apse, the meandering River Lauter flows under the Pont du Sel beside the town's most striking secular building and first hospital, the **Maison du Sel** (1450), in a part of town dubbed **la Petite Venise** (Little Venice). A few minutes' walk away, at 3 rue du Musée on the northern edge of town, another fine old building, with beautifully carved woodwork round its windows, contains the town's folk museum, the **Musée Westercamp** (closed for renovation at the time of writing). Along the southern edge of town, following the riverbank from the Tour des Husgenossen in the western corner, a long section of the **medieval walls** survives intact, built – like the houses – in the local red sandstone.

Practicalities

Wissembourg's **tourist office** is at 9 place de la République (May–Sept Mon–Sat 9am–12.30pm & 2–6pm, Sun 2–5.30pm; Oct–April Mon–Sat 9am–noon & 2–5.30pm; ⓣ03.88.94.10.11, ⓦwww.ot-wissembourg.fr). From the **gare SNCF** the "Office du Tourisme" signs are for cars – if you're on foot the quickest route is to turn left out of the station and walk to the roundabout, where you'll see signs of café life. Turn right and you're in town.

For **accommodation**, the most attractive hotel is the *Hôtel du Cygne*, 3 rue du Sel, next to the town hall on the central place de la République (ⓣ03.88.94.00.16, ⓕ03.88.54.38.28; ❸; closed two weeks in Feb & two weeks in July; restaurant €20–54). The friendly *Hôtel de la Gare*, opposite the train station (ⓣ03.88.94.13.67, ⓕ03.88.94.06.88; ❸), has a well-priced restaurant (closed Sun; menu at €14–27). In the main street, the hotel-restaurant *L'Escargot*, 40 rue Nationale (ⓣ03.88.94.90.29, ⓕ03.88.94.90.29; ❸; closed Sun; menu at €11.50–23), has a restaurant that serves traditional Alsatian cuisine.

In addition to the hotel restaurants above there are some reasonable **places to eat** on the main rue Nationale, such as *Au Petit Dominicain*, 36 rue Nationale (ⓣ03.88.94.90.87; closed Mon and Tues; menu at €9–20), which serves traditional Alsatian food. A much fancier establishment, with a chef who serves his own inventive variations on the traditional regional cuisine, is *À l'Ange*, 2 rue de la République (ⓣ03.88.94.12.11; closed Tues eve, Wed & last two weeks in Feb), in a beautiful old house by the stream next to place du Marché-aux-Choux; the cheapest menu is the lunchtime €28, otherwise you're looking at twice that. For simple *tartes flambées* (from €6), *Au Saumon*, behind the Maison du Sel, has a delightful garden and outdoor oven. *La Mirabelle*, 3 rue Général-Leclerc, is an agreeable outdoor café for summer meals, also from €6.

The southern Vosges

The major attractions of the **southern Vosges**, which stretch all the way down to Belfort (see p.961), are conveniently located along the **Route du Vin** ("Wine Route"). Every turn in the road, which follows the foot of the mountains along the western edge of the wide and flat Rhine valley, reveals yet another exquisitely preserved medieval town or village. Many of these, such as **Colmar**, the main centre for the route, suffer from an overdose of visitors, so to escape from the crowds, you need to head for the hills proper, along the **Route des Crêtes**, which traces the central ridge of the Vosges to the west.

The Route du Vin

Set against the "blue line of the Vosges", the **Route du Vin** winds from Marlenheim, west of Strasbourg, to Thann, near Mulhouse, through endless terraced vineyards which produce the region's famous white wines. Opportunities for tasting the local produce are plentiful, with free *dégustations* along the roadside and in the *caveaux* of most villages (though you're expected to buy at least a couple of bottles), and also at the region's countless wine festivals – mostly coinciding with the October harvest. For a closer look at the vines themselves you can follow various *sentiers vinicoles* (vineyard paths); Strasbourg and local tourist offices have details. In the midst of this sea of vines are dozens of typically picturesque Alsatian villages, which outdo each other to have the biggest display of window-box geraniums. Many are dominated from the nearby craggy heights by an extraordinary number of ancient ruined castles, testimony to the province's turbulent past.

The Route du Vin is deceptively hilly work on a bike, but **getting around** is definitely easier with your own transport. Otherwise you're dependent either on the train, which narrowly misses some of the best villages, or the region's so-so bus service. In summer and autumn there's a **food or wine festival** each weekend in a different town or village, with wine-tastings, *tarte flambée* and other local delicacies, arts and crafts and, if you're unlucky, traditional Alsatian music.

Obernai and around

Picturesque little **OBERNAI**, on the D422, is the first place most people head for when travelling south along the route from Strasbourg. Miraculously unscathed by the last two world wars, Obernai has retained almost its entire **rampart system**, including no fewer than fifteen towers, along with street after street of carefully maintained medieval houses. Not surprisingly, it also gets more than its fair share of visitors; this shouldn't put you off as the town is just about big enough to absorb the crowds, but do try to come on a weekday in the summer. The **tourist office**, on place du Beffroi (May–Oct Mon–Sat 9.30am–12.30pm & 2–7pm, Sun 9am–12.30pm & 2–5.30pm; Nov–April Mon–Sat 9am–noon & 2–5pm; ⓣ03.88.95.64.13), has lots of useful information about wine and easy-to-follow routes for exploring the region. There are a couple of moderately priced **hotels**, the *Maison du Vin*, 1 rue de la Paille (ⓣ03.88.95.46.82, ⓕ03.88.95.54.00; ❸), whose pretty rooms are above a wine shop; and *La Diligence*, 23 place de la Mairie (ⓣ03.88.95.55.69, ⓦwww.hotel-diligence.com; ❸), with a charming and reasonably priced *salon de thé* serving *petits plats* all day. For something more special, you could try the appealing boutique hotel *Le Colombier* (ⓣ03.88.47.63.33, ⓦwww.hotel-colombier.com; ❻), at 6–8 rue Dietrich. *La Halle au Blé* is a good **café** for a hot chocolate after a hard day's hiking in the Vosges.

ROSHEIM, 7km north of Obernai and up in the hills a little to the west of the D422, is relatively off the beaten track. Its two main sights are the Romanesque **church of St-Pierre-et-St-Paul**, whose roof is peppered with comical sculptured figures contemporary with the building, and the twelfth-century **Heidenhüs**, at 24 rue de la Principale, thought to be the oldest building in Alsace. The simple, clean, friendly family-run *Hôtel Alpina*, 39 rue du Lion (Ⓣ03.88.50.49.30, Ⓕ03.88.49.25.75; ❸), with an attractive terrace and breakfast room, is a great place to stay. **Rosenwiller**, a couple of kilometres up the hill among the vineyards, has a prettily sited and atmospherically overgrown **Jewish cemetery** at the edge of the woods, testimony to Alsace's once flourishing Jewish community.

From Rosheim's *gare SNCF*, 1.5km northeast of the village, a **steam train** runs up the valley on Sundays and holidays to **Ottrott**, which produces one of the few red wines of Alsace. An elegantly restored and modernized village house at 11 rue des Châteaux has been transformed into a rather luxurious **hotel**, the *Hostellerie des Châteaux* (Ⓣ03.88.48.14.14, Ⓦwww.hostellerie-chateaux.fr; ❽), with a sauna, swimming pool and overpriced restaurant.

Ottrott brings you within hiking distance – 6km – of **Mont Ste-Odile** (763m), whose summit is surrounded by a mysterious prehistoric wall (known as the **Mur Païen**, or Pagan Wall), originally built in the tenth century BC. The wall is almost 10km in length and in parts reaches a height of 3.5m. St Odilia herself is buried in the small **chapel** on top of the hill, a pilgrimage site even today. According to tradition, she was cast out by her father at birth on account of her blindness, but miraculously regained her sight during childhood and returned to found the convent on Mont Ste-Odile, where she cured thousands of cases of blindness and leprosy.

Barr

For some reason, **BARR**, west of the main road, is overlooked by mass tourism. Every bit as charming as Obernai, it's easy to while away a couple of hours wandering its twisting cobbled streets, at their busiest during the mid-July **wine festival** and on Sundays when the vintners come to ply their wines. The town has just one specific sight, **La Folie Marco**, at 30 rue du Docteur-Sultzer (June & Oct Sat & Sun 10am–noon & 2–6pm; July–Sept daily except Tues 10am–noon & 2–6pm; Ⓣ03.88.08.94.72; €3), an unusually large eighteenth-century house on the outskirts of town along the road to Obernai, which has displays of period French and Alsatian furniture. There are regular *dégustations* in the garden cellar, and a festival of dance and waltz at the end of May. There's also a **restaurant** serving Alsatian specialities (menus €17–24, *tarte flambée* €7). Some interesting walks begin behind the Hôtel de Ville, including one to Mont Ste-Odile (14km; 3–4 hours).

The nearest **gare SNCF** is in the neighbouring village of Gertwiller, 1km to the east. The nicest **place to stay** in Barr is the superb *Hôtel Le Manoir*, 11 rue St-Marc (Ⓣ03.88.08.03.40, Ⓕ03.88.08.53.71; ❹), on the edge of town, with light, spacious rooms and a splendid buffet breakfast. Alternatively, there are two **campsites**: the *Camping St-Martin*, at rue de l'Ill, near the Catholic church (Ⓣ03.88.08.00.45; June to mid-Oct), and municipal **campsite**, *Ste-Odile "Wepfermatt"*, 3km out of town at 137 rue de la Vallée (Ⓣ03.88.08.02.38; May–Oct). St-Pierre, 3km south of Barr, also has a campsite – the *Beau Séjour* (Ⓣ03.88.08.52.24 or 03.88.08.90.79; mid-May to Sept). For a really good *tarte flambée* in a **restaurant** with great atmosphere, try *Les Caveau des Tanneurs*, 32 rue Neuve (Ⓣ03.88.08.91.50; *tarte flambée* from €6; Wed–Sun dinner only): the Munster (a pungent kind of cheese) with cumin seeds is particularly good.

Winstub S'Barrer Stubbel, 5 place de l'Hôtel-de-Ville (Ⓣ03.88.08.57.44), also serves good local specialities at reasonable prices.

Le Struthof concentration camp

Deep in the forests and hills of the Vosges, over 20km west of Barr, **Le Struthof-Natzwiller** (daily: March, April & mid-Sept to Dec 10am–5pm; May to mid-Sept 9am–6pm; closed Jan & Feb; Ⓣ03.88.97.04.49, Ⓦwww.struthof.fr; €5) was the only Nazi concentration camp to be built on French soil (though at the time, of course, it was part of the Greater German Reich). The site is almost perversely beautiful, its stepped terraces cut into steep hillside, giving fantastic views across the Bruche valley. Set up shortly after Hitler's occupation of Alsace-Lorraine in 1940, it is thought that over 10,000 people died here. When the Allies liberated the camp on November 23, 1944, they found it empty – the remaining prisoners had already been transported to Dachau.

The barbed wire and watchtowers are as they were, though only two of the prisoners' barracks remain, one of which is now a **museum** of the deportations. An arson attack on the museum by neo-Nazis in 1976 only served to underline the need for such displays; captions are in French only, but the pictures suffice to tell the story. At the foot of the camp is the crematorium with its ovens still intact, while a couple of kilometres down the road to the west, towards Schirmeck, the Germans built a gas chamber – proof that Le Struthof was a fully integrated part of the Nazi killing machine. To the east, the two main granite quarries worked by the internees still survive, clearly signposted from the main road.

Sélestat and around

Back on the Route du Vin, **SÉLESTAT**, midway between Strasbourg and Colmar, is a delightful old town, and a good base for exploring the central and most popular section of the route. The choice of reasonable accommodation is better than average, and the town itself contains a couple of interesting churches and a great museum for bibliophiles.

The oldest and finest of the two churches is the **church of Ste-Foy**. Built by the monks of Conques, it has been much restored since but its clean, austerely Romanesque lines have not been entirely wiped out. Close by, to the north, the much larger Gothic **church of St-Georges** sports spectacularly multicoloured roof tiles and some very fine stained glass. For a brief period in the late fifteenth and early sixteenth centuries, Sélestat was the intellectual centre of Alsace, owing mainly to its Latin School, which attracted a group of humanists led by Beatus Rhenanus, whose personal library was one of the most impressive collections of its time. At the **Bibliothèque Humaniste**, founded in the fifteenth century and housed in the town's former corn exchange just by St-Georges (July & Aug Mon & Wed–Fri 9am–noon & 2–6pm, Sat 9am–noon & 2–5pm, Sun 2–5pm; Sept–June Mon & Wed–Fri 9am–noon & 2–6pm, Sat 9am–noon; €3.70), Rhenanus' collection is now on display along with some unusual and very rare books and manuscripts from as far back as the seventh century. A highlight for many is the 1507 manuscript *Cosmographiae Introductio*, the first document ever to use the word "America".

Sélestat is comparatively well served transport-wise, with frequent train connections to Strasbourg and Colmar; the **gare SNCF** is west of the town centre down avenue de la Liberté. Information is available from the **tourist office** by the ring road on boulevard du Général-Leclerc (May–Sept Mon–Fri 9am–12.30pm & 1.30–7pm, Sat 9am–noon & 2–5pm, Sun 9am–3pm; Oct–April Mon–Fri 8.30am–noon & 1.30–6pm, Sat 9am–noon & 2–5pm;

Ⓣ03.88.58.87.20, Ⓦwww.selestat-tourisme.com). For a **place to stay**, there's none better than the comfortable, friendly *Auberge des Alliés*, 39 rue des Chevaliers, in the middle of town (Ⓣ03.88.92.09.34, Ⓦwww.auberge-des-allies.com; ❹; closed Sun eve & Mon); its restaurant is good value and worth a look for its splendid tiled stove (menus €18–40). A modern alternative is the *Vaillant* on place de la République (Ⓣ03.88.92.09.46, Ⓦwww.hotel-vaillant.com; ❹; restaurant €17–37). There's a **campsite**, *Les Cigognes* (Ⓣ03.88.92.03.98; May to mid-Oct), south of the centre behind Vauban's remaining ramparts.

Castles around Sélestat

Within easy range of Sélestat is a whole host of **ruined castles**. Seven kilometres north, and accessible by train, the village of **DAMBACH-LA-VILLE**, with its walls and three fortified gates all intact, is one of the highlights of the route. A thirty-minute climb west of the village is the formidable **Castle of Bernstein**. This is a typically Germanic mountain keep: tall and narrow with few openings and little use for everyday living. Around it are residential buildings enclosed within an outer wall, the masonry cut into protruding knobs giving it a curious pimpled texture. You can also go on a mini-train **tour** of the town and local vineyards (July & Aug Mon, Thurs & Sat 5pm; €5), leaving from the main town square. Dambach has an inexpensive municipal **campsite** (Ⓣ03.88.92.48.60; mid-May to mid-Oct), 1km east on the D210, and a small but most attractive and inexpensive restaurant, *À la Couronne*, 13 place du Marché (Ⓣ03.88.92.40.85; closed Thurs, Feb 12 to March 1 & Nov 15–30; menus €11–23).

The best cluster of castles, though, is southwest of Sélestat. Four kilometres from the village, **KINTZHEIM** boasts a small but wonderful ruined castle built around a cylindrical refuge-tower. Today it's an aviary, the **Volerie des Aigles**, for birds of prey, with magnificent displays of aerial prowess by eagles and vultures (April–Nov; Ⓣ03.88.92.84.33 for details of afternoon demonstrations, Ⓦwww.voleriedesaigles.com; adults €9, children under 15 €6). If watching Barbary apes at play in the Vosgian jungle takes your fancy, you can do just that a couple of kilometres further west at the **Montagne des Singes** (daily: April, Oct & Nov 10am–noon & 1–5pm; May, June & Sept 10am–noon & 1–6pm; July & Aug 10am–6pm; Ⓦwww.montagnedessinges.com; €7.50, children €4.50).

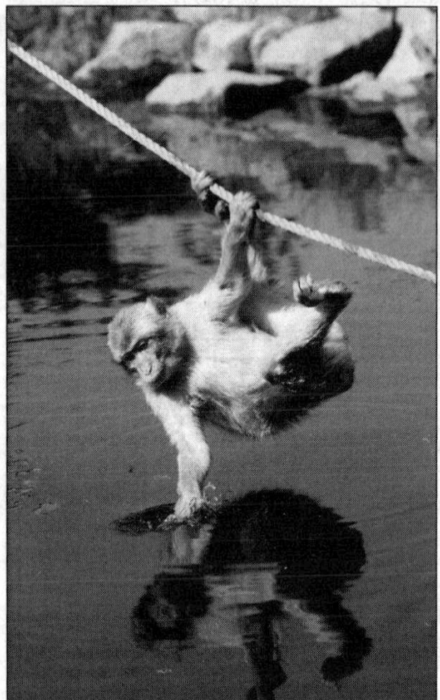

△ Barbary apes at the Montagne des Singes

Another 5km on from Kintzheim, the ruins of **Oudenbourg Castle**, its sizeable hall preserved among the trees, are dwarfed by the massive **Haut-Koenigsbourg** (daily: March & Oct 9.45am–5pm; April, May & Sept 9.30am–5.30pm; June, July & Aug 9.30am–6.30pm; Nov–Feb

9.45am–noon & 1–5pm; ⓣ03.88.82.50.60, ⓦwww.haut-koenigsbourg.net; €7.50, free for children and on first Sun of month Oct–March), one of the biggest, most visited castles in Alsace, and – astride its 757-metre bluff – by far the highest. Ruined after an assault in 1633, it was heavily restored in the early years of the twentieth century for Kaiser Wilhelm II. It's easy to criticize some of the detail of the restoration, but it's an enjoyable experience and a remarkably convincing re-creation of a castle-palace of the period. There are guided tours, but it's best explored on your own, taking in the fantastic views. There's a winding road down to Bergheim from here (see below), if you'd rather not retrace your tracks to Sélestat.

Ribeauvillé and around

RIBEAUVILLÉ is the largest town between Sélestat and Colmar – not as pretty as some of its immediate neighbours, but right at the foot of the mountains and well placed for exploring the many castles and villages that surround it. If you wish to **stay**, you could try the fancy but friendly little *Hôtel de la Tour*, in a converted winery at 1 rue de la Mairie (ⓣ03.89.73.72.73, ⓦwww.hotel-la-tour.com; ④; closed Jan to mid-March), with a Turkish bath and a *winstub*. Two local **campsites** are *Camping des Trois Châteaux* (ⓣ03.89.73.20.00; July & Aug), to the north of Ribeauvillé, and the much plusher *Pierre-de-Courbertin* site (ⓣ03.89.73.66.71; March–Nov) to the south.

Nearby are the romantic ruins of a trio of fortresses built by the counts of Ribeaupierre, all open to the public, free of charge: **St-Ulrich**, an hour's haul up a marked path; just north of it the smaller **Girsberg**, balanced on a pinnacle which somehow provides room for a bailey, two towers and other buildings; and, further on, the ruins of the **Château du Haut-Ribeaupierre**, whose keep is inaccessible for safety reasons.

BERGHEIM, 3.5km northeast of Ribeauvillé, retains a good part of its old fortifications, with three towers still surviving – despite being one of the most beautiful Alsatian villages, it rarely attracts the attentions of the tour groups. Also within easy walking range of Ribeauvillé, this time to the south, the village of **HUNAWIHR** is another beguiling hamlet, with a fourteenth-century walled church standing out amid the green vines. Hunawihr is at the forefront of the Alsatian ecological movement aimed at protecting the stork – the *cigogne* – of the region, and there's a **reserve** for them plus otters (*loutres*) and other fishing mammals to the east of the village, the **Centre de Réintroduction des Cigognes et des Loutres** (April, May & Sept to mid-Nov daily 10am–noon & 2–6pm; June–Aug daily 10am–6pm; call to check show times, ⓣ03.89.73.72.62, ⓦwww.cigogne-loutre.com; €8).

Lastly, nearer to the hub of Colmar are a couple of very busy tourist targets, which are best visited midweek or out of season. A couple of kilometres south of Hunawihr, the walled village of **RIQUEWIHR** is exceptionally well preserved, with plenty of medieval houses and a château containing a **postal museum**, the Musée d'Histoire des PTT d'Alsace (April–Oct & Dec daily except Tues 10am–5.30pm; €4); consequently it suffers more visitors per annum than any other village along the route. **KAYSERSBERG**, still further southwest, boasts a fortified **bridge** and a handsome sixteenth-century wooden altarpiece in the main **church**. But the town's principal renown is as the birthplace of theologian, philosopher and Nobel Peace Prize-winner Albert Schweitzer, who spent most of his extremely active, and not always peaceful, life at the leprosy hospital he founded at Lambaréné in French Equatorial Africa, now Gabon. He is honoured with the **Centre Culturel Albert Schweitzer**, 126 rue du Général-de-Gaulle (Easter & May–Oct daily 9am–noon & 2–6pm; €2).

Colmar

The old centre of **COLMAR**, a fifty-minute train ride south of Strasbourg, is totally *echt* Alsatian, with crooked houses, half-timbered and painted, on crooked lanes – all extremely picturesque, and very busy with tourists virtually year round. Colmar is also the proud home to one of the most extraordinary of all Gothic paintings – the altarpiece for St Anthony's monastery at Issenheim, painted by Mathias Grünewald.

Arrival, information and accommodation

From the **gare SNCF** it's a ten-minute walk down avenue de la République to the **tourist office** on place d'Unterlinden (April–June, Sept & Oct Mon–Sat 9am–6pm, Sun 10am–2pm; July & Aug Mon–Sat 9am–7pm, Sun 9.30am–2pm; Nov–March Mon–Sat 9am–noon & 2–6pm, Sun 10am–2pm; ⓣ03.89.20.68.92, ⓦwww.ot-colmar.fr). Besides selling Club Vosgien hiking maps and a booklet of day walks in the hills behind the town, they'll also give you details of the **buses** to the towns and villages of the Route du Vin, which leave from outside the *gare SNCF*. **Bikes** can be rented from a number of outlets in town.

Accommodation is not as overpriced as you might expect, with a wide range of places to stay, including an excellent boutique hotel, plus a popular youth hostel. You could also ask at the tourist office for a list of recommended *chambres d'hôtes* and *fermes auberges* (farms with guest rooms) in and near the city.

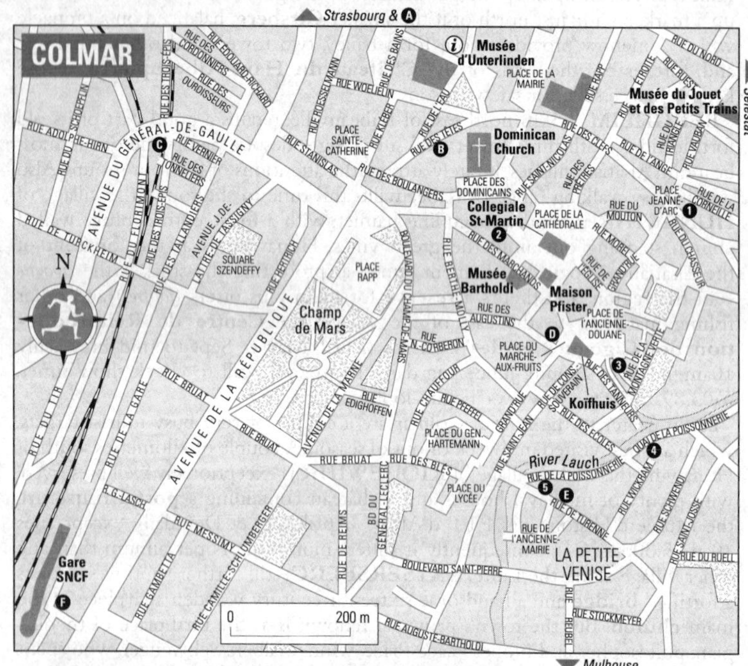

ACCOMMODATION

Auberge de Jeunesse Mittelhardt	A	Grand Hôtel Bristol	F
Colbert	C	St Martin	D
Le Colombier	E	Les Têtes	B

EATING

Le Restaurant du Marché	2	À la Ville de Paris	1
Le Petit Gourmand	4	Winstub Brenner	5
Le Streusel	3		

Hotels

Colbert 2 rue des Trois-Épis ⓣ03.89.41.31.05, ⓕ03.89.23.66.75. A plain, run-of-the-mill place but quiet, comfortable and conveniently located. ②

Le Colombier 7 rue Turenne ⓣ03.89.23.96.00, ⓦwww.hotel-le-colombier.fr. Colmar's only boutique hotel, right in the heart of the Petite Venise quarter, has charming air-conditioned rooms and a garage. ⑦

Grand Hôtel Bristol 7 place de la Gare ⓣ03.89.23.59.59, ⓦwww.grand-hotel-bristol.fr. Directly opposite the station exit, this relic of the grand old prewar days of tourism is now comfortably refurbished and part of a chain. ⑥

St-Martin 38 Grand'Rue, ⓣ03.89.24.11.51, ⓦwww.hotel-saint-martin.com. Chintzy furnishings with a riot of checks, flowers and flounces but this impeccably maintained hotel is still unbeatable for its central location. ⑤

Les Têtes 19 rue des Têtes ⓣ03.89.24.43.43, ⓦwww.ila-chateau.com/tetes. Like its gourmet restaurant set in the atmospheric courtyard, this well-appointed hotel in a historic building is a touch old-fashioned, verging on the starchy, but still an obvious choice for a special visit. ⑥

Hostel and campsite

Auberge de Jeunesse Mittelhardt 2 rue Pasteur ⓣ03.89.80.57.39, ⓕ03.89.80.76.16. The town's only youth hostel is perfectly decent but gets extremely busy in summer with teenagers. Take bus #4 from the station or rue d'Unterlinden, stop "Lycée Technique".

Camping Colmar-Horbourg-Wihr rte de Neuf-Brisach ⓣ03.89.41.15.94. Acceptable campsite, the nearest to the town centre, 2km away. Take bus #1 from the station, direction "Wihr", stop "Plage de l'Ill". March–Dec.

The Town

The *pièce de résistance* of the unmissable **Musée d'Unterlinden**, housed in a former Dominican convent at 1 rue d'Unterlinden (May–Oct daily 9am–6pm; Nov–April daily except Tues 9am–noon & 2–5pm; closed public hols; €7; ⓦwww.musee-unterlinden.com) is the **Issenheim altarpiece**. Originally designed as a single piece, on the front was the Crucifixion, almost luridly expressive: a tortured Christ with stretched ribcage and outsize hands turned upwards, fingers splayed in pain, flanked by his pale, fainting mother and saints John and Mary Magdalene. Then it unfolded, relative to its function on feast days, Sundays and weekdays, to reveal an Annunciation, Resurrection, Virgin and Child, and finally a sculpted panel depicting saints Anthony, Augustine and Jerome. Completed in 1515, the painting is affected by Renaissance innovations in light and perspective while still rooted in the medieval spirit, and visitors are invariably struck by the "modern" appearance of some details. Also worth a look is the collection of modern paintings in the basement, which includes works by Picasso, Léger and Vasarély.

A short walk away, the austere **Dominican church** on rue des Serruriers (April–Dec daily 10am–1pm & 3–6pm; €1.50) has some fine glass and, above all, a radiantly beautiful altarpiece known as *The Virgin in a Bower of Roses*, painted in 1473 by Martin Schongauer, who is also represented in the Musée d'Unterlinden. At the other end of the street you come to the **Collégiale St-Martin** on a busy café-lined square. Known locally as "the cathedral", it's worth a quick peek for its stonework and stained glass, as is the sixteenth-century **Maison Pfister**, on the south side of the church, for its external painted panels. Frédéric Auguste Bartholdi, the nineteenth-century sculptor responsible for New York's Statue of Liberty, was born at 30 rue des Marchands. This has been turned into the **Musée Bartholdi** (March–Dec daily except Tues 10am–noon & 2–6pm; closed public hols; €4.10), containing Bartholdi's personal effects, plus the original designs for the statue, along with sundry Colmarabilia.

Rue des Marchands continues south to the Ancienne Douane or **Koïfhus**, its gaily painted roof tiles loudly proclaiming the city's medieval prosperity. This is the heart of Colmar's old town, a short step away from the archly picturesque quarter down the Grand'Rue, cut through by the River Lauch and known as

La Petite Venise (Little Venice). The dolly-mixture colours of the old fishing cottages on quai de la Poissonnerie, contrast with the much taller, black-and-white, half-timbered tanners' houses on **rue des Tanneurs**, which leads off from the Koïfhus. The openings on the top floor were designed for drying hides. A stroll through the old town also takes you to the **Musée Animé du Jouet et des Petits Trains**, 40 rue Vauban (July–Sept daily 9am–6pm; Oct–June daily except Tues 10am–noon & 2–6pm; €4), whose collection of toys and toy trains is great fun for children.

Eating and drinking

There is no lack of **cafés** and tearooms in Colmar, dotted all around the central streets and squares, but **restaurants** are generally overpriced, particularly the Alsatian ones located along the tourist trail. A tempting alternative is to amass a sumptuous picnic from the town's patisseries, charcuteries, and fruit and vegetable **markets** (every Thursday around the Koïfhus; every Saturday on place St-Joseph).

Le Restaurant du Marché 20 place de la Cathédrale. More sophisticated cuisine than elsewhere – the chef occasionally wields a wok – based on French cordon bleu, making a change from the pig-based local fare but at a price: main courses €17–24. Closed Wed & Sun.

Le Petit Gourmand quai de la Poissonnerie ⓣ03.89.41.09.32. Unassuming little Alsatian restaurant with a delightful little waterside terrace. Closed Mon and Tues eve.

Le Streusel 4 passage de l'Ancienne Douane. Slightly hidden away, despite being close to the touristy Grand'Rue and near the Petite Venise. Excellent salads and other vegetarian dishes are served, in addition to traditional *choucroute* and the like, and first-class pastries for afternoon tea and coffee.

À la Ville de Paris 4 place Jeanne-d'Arc. This atmospheric little *winstub* is a preferred haunt of locals; ham, pork and river fish main courses €12–16, or from €27 à la carte. Closed Tues.

Winstub Brenner 1 rue Turenne. Traditional mainstay Petite Venise *winstub* serving delicious, generous meals, with a lovely summertime waterside terrace; menu €22. Closed Tues & Wed.

Munster and the Route des Crêtes

MUNSTER owes its existence and its name to a band of Irish monks who founded a monastery here in the seventh century, some 19km west of Colmar up the narrowing valley of the River Fecht, and overlooked by Le Petit Ballon (1267m) and Le Hohneck (1362m), among the highest peaks of the Vosges. Its name today is particularly associated with a rich, creamy and exceedingly smelly **cheese**, the crowning glory of many an Alsatian meal. The town makes a peaceful and verdant base either for exploring further into the mountain range, much of which lies within the Parc Régional des Ballons des Vosges, or for visiting Colmar and other places along the Route du Vin. It also holds a reputed **jazz festival** in early May each year (ⓔjazzalsace@aol.com).

Munster is accessible by **train** from Colmar. The **tourist office**, 1 rue du Couvnet (July & Aug Mon–Sat 9.30am–12.30pm & 1.30–6.30pm; Sept–June Mon–Fri 9.30am–12.30pm & 2–6pm, Sat 10am–noon & 2–6pm; ⓣ03.89.77.31.80), has lots of information about hiking in the Munster valley and the *parc régional*. However, the Maison du Parc, 1 cour de l'Abbaye (May–Sept daily except Mon 9am–noon & 2–6pm; Oct–April Mon–Fri 10am–noon & 2–6pm; ⓣ03.89.77.90.20), is the best place to get information about the park.

If you want to **stay**, you could try the large, modern *Hôtel Verte-Vallée*, 10 rue Alfred-Hartmann (ⓣ03.89.77.15.15, ⓦwww.verte-vallee.com; ❻), in the depths of the wooded valley, which, with its spa, squeaky-clean atmosphere and pastel colours, makes a perfect haven for a day or two. It has a good restaurant specializing

Hiking in the southern Vosges

There's no shortage of waymarked paths in the **southern Vosges**. Six **GRs** cross the Vosges and are a good way to see the less-frequented castles.

GR7: Ballon d'Alsace to Remiremont.

GR53: Wissembourg to Belfort (part of the route coincides with GR5).

GR59: Ballon d'Alsace to Besançon.

GR531: Wissembourg to the Ballon d'Alsace.

GR532: Soultz-sous-Forêts to Belfort.

GR533: Sarrebourg to Belfort, along the west flank of the Vosges.

There are five treks of between five and eleven days' duration described in *Les Grandes Traversées des Vosges*, published by the Office Départemental du Tourisme du Bas-Rhin, 9 rue du Dôme, 67000 Strasbourg (Ⓣ03.88.15.45.80), with details of accommodation, access and so on. Another useful contact for information is the Association Départmentale du Tourisme du Haut-Rhin, 1 rue Schlumberger, 68006 Colmar (Ⓣ03.89.20.10.62/68, Ⓦwww.tourisme68.asso.fr).

Organized walks, involving guides or luggage transport or both, are arranged by tourist offices and a handful of companies, the most reliable of which is Horizons d'Alsace, 7 Grand' Rue, Kientzheim (Ⓣ03.89.78.35.20, Ⓦwww.horizons-alsace.com). Three- to six-night walks, with emphasis on wine-tasting and gourmet cuisine, cost on average €400–600 per person, meals included.

Belfort, in Franche-Comté (see p.961), is another good place to base a hiking trip in the southern Vosges. The Ballon d'Alsace, in the centre of the Parc Régional des Ballons des Vosges, is the meeting point of the GR5, GR7 and GR59, and a discovery trail has been marked out around the summit. A number of PR trails (rambles) begin from here. The Malsaucy lake along the GR5 trail is another popular hiking area. Contact the Belfort tourist office for maps and information.

in traditional French dishes, with a terrace overlooking the stream (closed most of Jan; menu €18–52, *carte* from €33). Munster's **campsite**, *Camping municipal du Parc de la Fecht*, is on the route de Gunsbach (Ⓣ03.89.77.31.08; May to mid-Sept).

The Route des Crêtes

Above Munster the main road west to Gérardmer crosses the mountains by the principal pass, the Col de la Schlucht, where it intersects the "Route des Crêtes", built for strategic purposes during World War I. It's a spectacular trail, traversing thick forest and open pasture, where the herds of cows that produce the Munster cheese graze in summer; in winter it becomes one long cross-country ski route. Starting in **Cernay**, 15km west of Mulhouse, it follows the main ridge of the Vosges, including the highest peak of the range, the Grand Ballon (1424m), north as far as **Ste-Marie-aux-Mines**, 20km west of Sélestat, once at the heart of a silver-mining district. From Munster it's also accessible by a twisting minor road through Hohrodberg, which takes you past beautiful glacial lakes, the Lac Blanc and the Lac Noir, and the eerie World War I battlefield of **Linge**, where the French and German trenches, once separated by just a few metres, are still clearly visible.

Mulhouse and around

A large sprawling industrial city 35km south of Colmar, **MULHOUSE** was Swiss until 1798 when, at the peak of its prosperity (based on printed cotton fabrics and allied trades), it voted to become part of France. Even now many people who live here work in Basel, Switzerland. It's also the birthplace of Alfred Dreyfus, the unfortunate Jewish army officer who was wrongly convicted of espionage in 1894 (see "Contexts", p.1278). Not having much of an old town, it is not ideal for strollers, but there are a handful of outstanding – and rather unusual – museums in and around the town that delve into the region's manufacturing past: wallpaper and printed fabrics, locomotives and automobiles are all given their platform, along with some even quirkier themes. The **jazz festival** in August is a good time to be out partying, with concerts in the museums, the schools, the streets, the cafés and the bars.

The Town

Close to the *gare SNCF*, just along the canal to the right, is the interesting **Musée de l'Impression sur Étoffes**, 14 rue Jean-Jacques-Henner (daily except Mon 10am–noon & 2–6pm; €6, combined with the Musée du Papier-Peint in Rixheim, €10; ⓦwww.musee-impression.com). Its vast collection of the most beautiful fabrics imaginable, including the eighteenth-century Indian and Persian imports that revolutionized the European ready-to-wear market in their time and made Mulhouse a prosperous manufacturing centre, is mostly displayed in temporary exhibitions lasting several months; there are also shows dedicated to related art forms such as patchwork quilts. Try and coincide with one of the demonstrations – consult the website for details. Also in the centre, the **Hôtel de Ville** on central place de la Réunion contains a beautifully presented history of the city and its hinterland in the **Musée Historique** (daily except Tues: July & Aug 10am–noon & 2–6.30pm; Sept–June 10am–noon & 2–6pm; free), which also exhibits seventeenth- and eighteenth-century furnishings.

Some way to the west of the centre, in the direction of the A36 autoroute, is the recently revamped **Cité du Train – Musée Français du Chemin de Fer**, 2 rue Alfred-de-Glehn (daily 10am–5/6pm, Jan closed weekday mornings; €10, combined ticket with Cité de l'Automobile, €15.50; take bus #20 from *gare SNCF* to stop "Musées"; ⓦwww.citedutrain.com). Slicker and more interactive than ever after an early millennium makeover, including the introduction of info about the TGV, its main attractions remain the impressive railway rolling stock on display, including Napoléon III's aide-de-camp's drawing room, decorated by Viollet-le-Duc in 1856, and a luxuriously appointed 1926 diner from the *Golden Arrow*. There are cranes, stations, signals

△Bugatti at the Cité de l'Automobile, Mulhouse

and related artefacts, but the stars of the show are the big locomotive engines with brightly painted boilers, gleaming wheels and pistons, and tangles of brass and copper piping – real works of art.

A couple of kilometres north of the city centre, with a shining new entrance showing off some hi-tech displays, the **Cité de l'Automobile, Musée National-Collection Schlumpf**, 192 av de Colmar (daily 10am–5/6pm, Jan closed weekday mornings; €10.50, combined ticket with Cité du Train, €15.50; take tram #1 from *gare SNCF* or place Porte-Jeune to stop "Musée Auto"; Ⓦwww.collection-schlumpf.com), houses an overwhelming collection of over six hundred cars, originally the private collection of local Schlumpf brothers. Lined up in endless row after endless row under massive hangars, the impeccably preserved vehicles range from the industry's earliest attempts, like the extraordinary wooden-wheeled Jacquot steam "car" of 1878, to 1968 Porsche racing vehicles and contemporary factory prototypes. The largest group is that of locally made Bugatti models: dozens of alluringly displayed, glorious racing cars, coupés and limousines, the pride of them being the two Bugatti Royales, out of only seven that were constructed – one of them Ettore Bugatti's own, with bodywork designed by his son. Car freaks will want to spend hours (there is a restaurant and a café-bar).

Practicalities

Relatively picturesque place de la Réunion is five minutes' walk north of the **gare SNCF**. The **tourist office** is on the ground floor of the Musée Historique, in the brightly painted Hôtel de Ville (July, Aug & Dec daily 10am–7pm, Jan–June & Sept–Nov Mon–Sat 10am–6pm, Sun and public holidays 10am–noon & 2–6pm; Ⓣ03.89.66.93.13, Ⓦwww.tourisme-mulhouse.com). The city's public **transport** network has been revolutionized by the two new tram lines – for details of them and new bus routes consult Ⓦwww.solea.info.

As for **accommodation**, rooms are generally overpriced in Mulhouse, but the three following hotels are all central, comfortable and affordable: *St-Bernard*, 3 rue des Fleurs (Ⓣ03.89.45.82.32, Ⓦwww.hotel-saint-bernard.com; ❸), with Internet access in the "library" in the foyer; *Schoenberg*, 14 rue Schoenberg, behind the station (Ⓣ03.89.44.19.41, Ⓕ03.89.44.49.80; ❸); and *Central*, 15–17 passage Central (Ⓣ03.89.46.18.84, Ⓕ03.89.56.31.66; ❸). For something more luxurious there's the stylish *Hôtel du Parc* (Ⓣ03.89.66.12.22, Ⓦwww.hotelduparc-mulhouse.com; ❽), with spacious rooms, some overlooking a shady garden, at 26 rue de la Sinne. The **HI hostel** is some way to the west of the centre at 37 rue de l'Illberg (Ⓣ03.89.42.63.28, Ⓕ03.89.59.74.95; tram #2, stop "Palais des Sports"; closed mid-Dec to mid-Jan; €13), and also has facilities for camping. Otherwise there's another pleasant **campsite**, *Camping de l'Ill*, at 1 rue Pierre-de-Coubertin, near the suburb of Dornach, 4km from the city centre on the banks of the River Ill (Ⓣ03.89.06.20.66; closed Oct–March); take a bus from place Porte-Jeune.

Mulhouse's Alsatian **restaurants** can get very busy, but there are plenty of them, some aimed at tourists to judge by the multilingual menus. One of the best, in a pleasantly tranquil street off the place de la Réunion – where tables are put outside, weather permitting – is the *Winstub Henriette* at 9 rue Henriette, with all the usual dishes, such as *pot-au-feu*, for €11–19. The *Crêperie Crampous Mad*, 14 impasse des Tondeurs (menu €9–17; closed Sun), due north of the *place*, is a good standby, while superb seafood is served at *Le Bistrot à Huîtres*, to the southwest of the *gare SNCF* at 2 rue Moenschberg (Ⓣ03.89.64.01.60; menus from €24; closed Sun & Mon). You can drown your sorrows at *Gambrinus*, 5 rue des Franciscains, northwest of place de la Réunion (menu €8–27; closed Sun & Mon), which boasts over thirty **beers** on tap and offers simple dishes to help keep you sober.

At the beginning of August you can see some of the vintage cars from the Musée de l'Automobile in gear as part of a **Grande Parade**, and in late August, Mulhouse hosts the region's hottest **jazz festival** (festival dates and information ⓣ03.89.45.63.95). To find out what's going on throughout the year, get hold of a copy of *Spectacles*, the free regional **listings** monthly, or *L'Echo Mulhousien*, also free but focused on events in the city; the tourist office stocks both.

Rixheim and Ungersheim

In the village of **RIXHEIM**, 6km east of Mulhouse, the **Musée du Papier-Peint**, 28 rue Zuber (10am–noon & 2–6pm, Oct–May closed Tues; €6, combined ticket with Musée de l'Impression sur Étoffes, €10; ⓦwww.museepapierpeint.org), is housed in the splendid former headquarters of the Teutonic Knights, a branch of the medieval crusaders. A wallpaper museum may not be everyone's idea of a fun afternoon out, but this space contains a stunning cornucopia of antique painted wallpaper, notably in a series of luxuriant panoramas, as well as impressive antique machinery. The thematic temporary exhibitions are often excellent, and the frequent printing demonstrations (June–Sept Tues, Thurs & Sat at 3.30pm) bring the place to life. Rixheim can be reached from Mulhouse either by train or on bus #10, direction "Commanderie", stop "Centre Europe".

Just past Pulversheim, 10km northwest of Mulhouse off the D430 at **Ungersheim**, the **Écomusée d'Alsace** (daily: March–June & Sept 10am–6pm; July & Aug 9.30am–7pm; Oct–Feb 10am–5pm; €12.50–15, children €7–9.50, depending on time of year; ⓣ03.89.74.44.74, ⓦwww.ecomusee-alsace.com) is an open-air museum presenting regional traditions and customs. It's plenty of fun for adults and kids, with over fifty traditional Alsatian buildings spanning the centuries, plus on-site craft workers doing their various things. A regional bus runs frequent services Monday to Saturday from Mulhouse's *gare SNCF*, direction "Guebwiller" (€7 one way).

Lorraine

Lorraine derives its name from the Latin, *Lotharii regnum*, "the kingdom of Lothar", one of the three grandsons of Charlemagne, among whom his empire was divided in 843 AD. Much of the province is a rolling, windswept plateau of dull farmland; that said, the focal point of the city of **Nancy**, its smart former capital, is a harmoniously proportioned Neoclassical square regarded by many as the finest in France. The Ecole de Nancy, a prominent branch of Art Nouveau, added to the city's attractions with some sumptuous paintings, furniture and glassware, which are displayed in a set of outstanding museums. North of Nancy, the handsome present-day capital of **Metz** is justly famed for its magnificent cathedral; beyond, the province's northern reaches peter out into moribund coalfields and heavy industrial wastelands along the Belgian and German frontiers.

West of Metz, several sites connected with the province's bloody history make an interesting detour. During World War II, when de Gaulle and the Free French chose Lorraine's double-barred cross as their emblem, they were making a powerful point. For over a thousand years Lorraine has been the principal route of invasion from the German lands across the Rhine, even though the trench-like valleys of the rivers Meuse and Moselle form a main line of defence. Joan of Arc was born in 1412 at Domrémy-la-Pucelle on the Meuse, when Lorraine was disputed by the dukes of Burgundy and the kings of France – it only finally became part of the kingdom of France in 1766. In 1870 Napoléon III's armies suffered a humiliating defeat at the hands of the Prussians on the heights above Metz. Then, in the twentieth century, the two world wars saw terrible fighting in the area, both ultimately involving Allied troops alongside the French armies. Of all the killing fields, the bloodiest was **Verdun**, due west from Metz, where the French army fought one of the most costly and protracted battles of all time from 1916 to 1918. Poignant **memorials** to these horrors built at or near the **battlefields** draw many visitors, not least relatives of the myriad victims.

Nancy

The city of **NANCY**, on the River Meurthe, is justly famed for the magnificent place Stanislas, cited as a paragon of eighteenth-century Neoclassical urban planning, but also has on offer some of the most impressive examples of Art Nouveau furniture and glassware you are likely to see anywhere. Unlike much of Lorraine, the city was not occupied by the Prussians after 1870, and its centre, largely unaffected by the undistinguished modern sprawl that blights the valley sides, is simply spectacular. For this, it has the last of the independent dukes of Lorraine to thank, the dethroned king of Poland and father-in-law of Louis XV, Stanislas Leszczynski. During the twenty-odd years of his office in the mid-eighteenth century, he ordered some of the most successful construction of the period in all France.

Arrival, information and accommodation

The part of Nancy you're likely to want to see extends to no more than a ten- or fifteen-minute walk either side of **rue Stanislas**, the main axis and shopping street connecting the **gare SNCF** and the principal **place Stanislas**. The **tourist office**, on the south side of place Stanislas in the Hôtel de Ville (April–Oct Mon–Sat 9am–7pm, Sun & hols 10am–5pm; Nov–March Mon–Sat 9am–6pm, Sun 10am–1pm; Ⓣ03.83.35.22.41, Ⓦwww.ot-nancy.fr), is well stocked with information about both the city and region, and organizes the *petit train touristique*, a frequent 45-minute **guided tour** of the town (May–Sept; €6; departure from place de la Carrière), along with several other themed visits of the town. Regional **buses** depart from rue de l'Île de Corse and boulevard d'Austrasie, both on the eastern side of town. **Internet** access is available at the excellent e-café, 11 rue des Quatre-Églises.

Reasonable **accommodation** is not hard to find in Nancy. There are plenty of hotels visible from the station, and signs directing you to most of the others – all are within ten to fifteen minutes' walk of the station. For somewhere special out of town, try the *Château d'Adoménil* near Lunéville, 37km southeast by the A33 autoroute (Ⓣ03.83.74.04.81, Ⓦwww.relaischateaux.fr/adomenil; ⑨; closed Sun out of season); it has seven beautifully furnished rooms overlooking water, orchards and a home farm, and its small restaurant is highly rated (cheapest menu €40; *carte* upwards of €70).

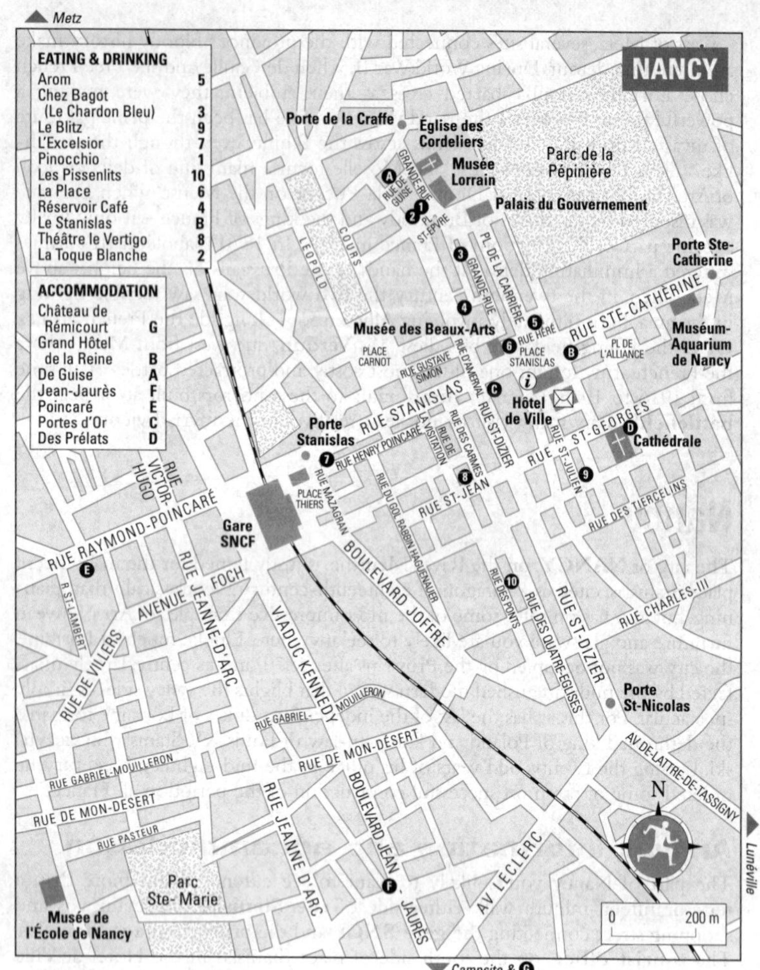

Hotels

Grand Hôtel de la Reine 2 place Stanislas ⓣ03.83.35.03.01, ⓦwww.concorde-hotels.com. The grandest hotel in town, for both location and luxury. The same goes for its chic restaurant, *Le Stanislas*, featuring a succulent business lunch at €31 and an extravagant dinner menu including pigeon, lamb and all kinds of fish at €62. ❽

De Guise rue de Guise, just off Grande-Rue ⓣ03.83.32.24.68, ⓦwww.hoteldeguise.com. Atmospherically furnished with antiques, this hotel is located in the old part of Nancy, and is the former residence of the countess of Bressy. All rooms en suite. ❺

Jean-Jaurès 14 bd Jean-Jaurès ⓣ03.83.27.74.14, ⓦwww.hotel-jeanjaures.fr. Slightly weary and worn, but a friendly place in a pretty location. ❸

Poincaré 81 rue Raymond-Poincaré ⓣ03.83.40.25.99. Pleasant and clean, with a special bargain rate at weekends: stay Friday and Saturday night, and you get Sunday night for free. ❷

Portes d'Or 21 rue Stanislas ⓣ03.83.35.42.34, ⓦwww.hotel-lesportesdor.com. Double glazing protects you from city-centre noise at this place whose location and home-from-home comfort make this an unbeatable choice. ❹

Des Prélats 56 place du Monseigneur-Ruch ⓣ03.83.30.20.20, ⓦwww.hoteldesprelats.com. Welcome newcomer in a neatly converted seventeenth-century house that belonged to the primate of Lorraine – comfortable rooms, some with four-poster beds, and all mod cons, including air-con and Wi-Fi. ❻

Hostel and campsite

Camping de Brabois ⓣ03.83.27.18.28. Set in a large park near the hostel. To get there take bus #26 direction "Villers Clairlieu", stop "Camping". April to mid-Oct.

Château de Rémicourt 149 rue de Vandoeuvre ⓣ03.83.27.73.67, ⓔaubergeremicourt@mairie-nancy.fr. Spacious and pretty hostel, set in a sixteenth-century castle, but a fair distance from the centre in the suburb of Villers-lès-Nancy, to the southwest off the N74 Dijon road/av Général-Leclerc, near the Rond-Point du Vélodrome. To get there, take bus #16 on rue des Carmes, to the end of the line, "Villers-Lycée Stanislas", or the #26, direction "Villers Clairlieu", stop "Fiacre". €14 including breakfast in dorm; ❷ in double room.

The Town

Pride of place in Nancy must go to the beautiful **place Stanislas**, the middle of which belongs to the solitary statue of its inspirer, the portly Stanislas himself, who was responsible for laying out the square in the 1750s. On the south side stands the imposing **Hôtel de Ville**, its roof-line topped by a balustrade ornamented with florid urns and *amorini*, while along its walls lozenge-shaped lanterns dangle from the beaks of gilded cockerels; similar motifs adorn the other buildings bordering the square – look out for the fake, two-dimensional replacements. Its entrances are closed by magnificent wrought-iron gates, with the best work of all in the railings of the northeastern and northwestern corners, which frame glorious fountains dominated by statues of Neptune and Amphitrite. Since 2005, when the square was given a complete makeover, with much improved illuminations, it has been totally pedestrianized.

In the corner where rue Stanislas joins the square, the **Musée des Beaux-Arts** (daily except Tues 10.30am–6pm; €6) has an excellent presentation of French nineteenth- and twentieth-century art on the ground floor, with a good selection of paintings by Émile Friant and Nancy's own Victor Prouvé, together with a Manet, a Matisse and a Picasso. The rest of the collection upstairs, encompassing Italian, German, northern European and more French painting, is less interesting. Time is better spent in the basement, where works from Nancy's glass company, Daum, are beautifully lit in black rooms. The layout of the basement follows the shape of fortifications constructed from

Stanislas Leszczynski

Stanislas Leszczynski, born in the Polish-Ukrainian city of Lemberg (now Lviv) in 1677, lasted just five years as the elected king of Poland before being forced into exile by the Russian Tsar Peter the Great. For the next twenty-odd years he lived on a French pension in Wissembourg, along with a motley entourage of Polish expats. After fifteen years of relatively humdrum existence in the town's Ancien Hôpital, south of the main church, Stanislas' luck changed when he managed, against all odds, to get his daughter, Marie, betrothed to the 15-year-old king of France, **Louis XV**. Marie was not quite so fortunate: married by proxy in Strasbourg Cathedral, and having never even set eyes on the groom, she subsequently had a total of ten children, only to be ultimately rejected by Louis, who preferred hunting and the company of his two more powerful mistresses, Mme de Pompadour and Mme du Barry. Bolstered by his daughter's marriage, Stanislas had another brief spell on the Polish throne from 1733 to 1736, but eventually gave it up in favour of the comfortable dukedom of Barr and Lorraine. He lived out his final years in true aristocratic style in the capital, Nancy, which he transformed into one of France's most beautiful towns.

the fifteenth century through to Vauban's seventeenth-century alterations, which were found during the museum's 1990s renovation. For a glimpse of Daum's contemporary creations you can visit their shop, also on place Stanislas. A short walk east of the square is the excellent **Muséum-Aquarium de Nancy**, at 34 rue Ste-Cathérine (daily 10am–noon & 2–6pm; €3.80). Upstairs is a colossal collection of stuffed animals and birds, while downstairs is a startling aquarium of exotic fish whose colours surpass even the daring of Matisse.

On its north side, place Stanislas opens into the long, tree-lined **place de la Carrière**, a handsome eighteenth-century transformation of what was originally a jousting ground. Its far end is closed by the classical colonnades of the **Palais du Gouvernement**, former residence of the governor of Lorraine. Behind it, housed in the fifteenth-century Palais Ducal and entered through a handsome doorway surmounted by an equestrian statue of one of the dukes, is the **Musée Lorrain**, 64 Grande-Rue (daily except Tues 10am–12.30pm & 2–6pm, closed public hols; €3.10, €4.60 combined ticket with the Musée des Cordeliers). Dedicated to the history and traditions of Lorraine, it contains, among other treasures, a room full of superb etchings by the Nancy-born seventeenth-century artist, Jacques Callot, whose concern with social issues, evident in series such as *The Miseries of War* and *Les Gueux* (or *The Beggars*), presaged much nineteenth- and twentieth-century art. Next door, in the Église des Cordeliers et Chapelle Ducale, is the **Musée des Cordeliers** (same hours as Musée Lorrain; €3.10, €4.60 combined ticket with the Musée Lorrain), where rural life in the region in days gone by is illustrated. On the other side of the Palais du Gouvernement, you can play crazy golf, admire the deer or just collapse with exhaustion on the green grass of the **Parc de la Pépinière**, a sort of cross between a formal French garden and an English park. There's also a free zoo.

A half-hour walk southwest of the train station, the **Musée de l'École de Nancy**, 36 rue Sergent-Blandan (Wed–Sun 10.30am–6pm; €6), is housed in a 1909 villa built for the Corbin family, founders of the Magasins Réunis chain of department stores. Even if you're not into Art Nouveau, this collection is exciting. Although not all of it belonged to the Corbins, the museum is arranged as if it were a private house. The furniture is outstanding – all swirling curvilinear forms – and the standards of workmanship are superlative, with a fair sprinkling of Gallé's work on display, too. The beautiful **gardens** are worth exploring – they're planted with irises, magnolias, saxifrages and all kinds of other plants that inspired the School of Nancy's creations.

Eating and drinking

There are plenty of places to eat and drink in Nancy, led by the excellent *Le Stanislas* restaurant in the *Grand Hôtel de la Reine*. Good streets for **restaurants** include Grande-Rue, rue des Maréchaux ("gourmet row") and rue des Ponts. Place Stanislas is a good place to start an evening, and perfect for a coffee, day or night. There are several bar-cafés that make good vantage points to watch Nancy go by: *Grand Café du Commerce*, *Jean Lamour*, new *Le Cinq* and, restored to its original splendour, the sumptuous *Grand Café Foy*. Later on you should head up the Grande-Rue or down the rue des Ponts and their parallels/offshoots, where you will certainly find a late-night bar – possibly not on Sunday, though, when most are closed. A good website to consult is Ⓦwww.nancybynight.com.

Restaurants

Arom 26 rue Héré. One of several restaurants with see-and-be-seen terraces along this stumpy street, offering a vantage point of place Stanislas. The food, served on square glass plates, is modish but delicious all the same. Closed Sun eve & Wed.

Chez Bagot (Le Chardon Bleu) 45 Grande-Rue ⓣ03.83.37.42.43. Fresh fish dishes cooked to Breton recipes served up in an appropriately decorated restaurant. Menus from €14. Closed Sun eve, Mon, & Tues lunch.

L'Excelsior 50 rue Henri-Poincaré, opposite the train station. A *fin-de-siècle* Art Nouveau brasserie, frequented by everyone who aspires to be anyone in Nancy. Now part of the *Flo* brasserie chain but managing to retain its superb interior and good classic food (menus at €20 and €27). It's also the best daytime stop for coffee.

Les Pissenlits 25bis rue des Ponts. Real old-fashioned bistro fare on a menu at €15, with an appealing atmosphere. Closed Sun & Mon.

La Toque Blanche 1 rue Mgr-Trouillet, just off place St-Epvre ⓣ03.83.30.17.20. One of the finest gourmet restaurants in Nancy. The €22 menu is a bargain; à la carte costs €60 and more. Closed Sun eve & Mon.

Cafés and bars

Le Blitz 76 rue St-Julien. One of several lively bars along this street, with danceable music and a trendy clientele.

Pinocchio 9 place St-Epvre. Features stylish wooden interior furnishings and a terrace facing the church of St-Epvre; good for drinks at all hours.

La Place 7 place Stanislas. Extravagant decor and varied music attracts a mixed crowd of drinkers, boppers and general revellers.

Réservoir Café 13 rue Callot. Leather armchairs and mellow music add to the cosiness of this fashionable café-bar known for its stiff cocktails.

Théâtre le Vertigo 29 rue de la Visitation. Post-modern gargoyles contribute to its interesting theatrical atmosphere. Bands and other performances regularly.

Metz and around

METZ (pronounced "Mess"), the capital of Lorraine, lies on the east bank of the River Moselle, close to the Autoroute de l'Est, linking Paris and Strasbourg, and the main Strasbourg–Brussels train line. Its origins go back at least to Roman times, when, as now, it stood astride major trade routes. On the death of Charlemagne it became the capital of Lothar's portion of his empire, managing to maintain its prosperity in spite of the dynastic wars that followed. By the Middle Ages it had sufficient wealth and strength to proclaim itself an independent republic, which it remained until its absorption into France in 1552. A frontier town caught between warring influences, Metz has endured more than its share of historical hand-changing. In 1870, when Napoléon III's defeated armies were forced to surrender to Kaiser Wilhelm I, it was ceded to Germany. It recovered its liberty at the end of World War I in 1918, only to be re-annexed by Hitler in 1940 before being liberated again by Allied troops in 1944.

Although its only really important sight is the magnificent **cathedral**, beautifully lit at night, Metz is not at all the dour place you might expect from its northern geography and industrial background – indeed it deserves its self-styled title of *Ville jardin* or Garden City, with impeccable flower-beds, the warm hues of mustard-yellow stone buildings and the waters of the Moselle all making for an appealing cityscape. The university founded here in the 1970s is at least partly responsible for its liveliness.

Arrival, information and accommodation

The huge granite **gare SNCF** stands opposite the **post office** at the end of rue Gambetta. The **gare routière** is east of the train station and on the other side of the railway tracks on avenue de l'Amphithéâtre. The **tourist office** (July & Aug

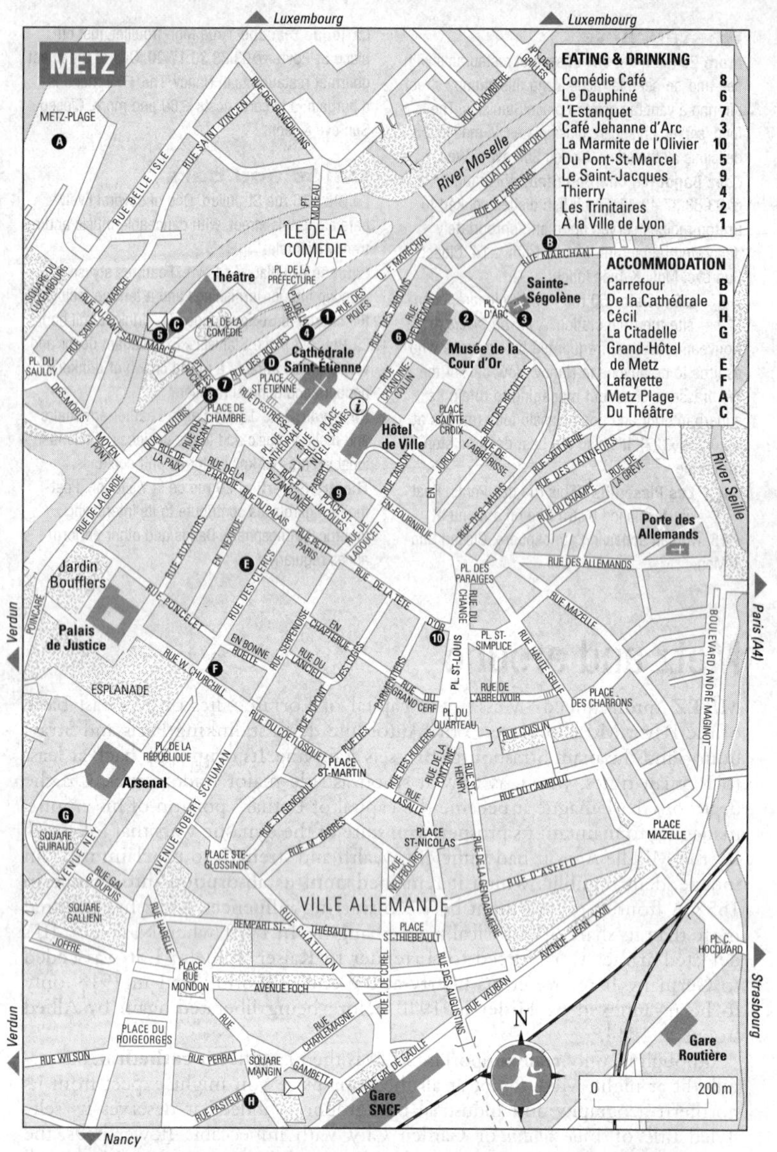

Mon–Sat 9am–9pm, Sun 10am–1pm & 3–5pm; Sept–June Mon–Sat 9am–7pm, Sun 10am–1pm & 3–5pm; ⓣ03.87.55.53.76, ⓦwww.ot-metz.fr) is located by the side of the Hôtel de Ville on place d'Armes in the old town. Almost any bus from the station will take you there.

Metz offers a fair range of hotels and budget **accommodation**, including an HI hostel, *foyer* (the tourist office has information about other *foyers* available in summer) and campsite, plus a couple of ritzy establishments.

Hotels

De la Cathédrale 25 place de Chambre ⓣ03.87.75.00.02, ⓦwww.hotelcathedrale-metz.fr. Charming, wonderfully located hotel with original beams and stained-glass windows. ❺

Cécil 14 rue Pasteur ⓣ03.87.66.66.13, ⓦwww.cecilhotel-metz.com. Extremely welcoming hotel whose functional rooms are spacious, as are its bathrooms, and done out in eye-catching pink and yellow shades; there is also a garage. ❹

La Citadelle 5 av Ney ⓣ03.87.17.17.17, ⓦwww.citadelle-metz.com. Recently opened and Impressively smart hotel housed in an impeccably converted fifteenth-century military building. Every detail in the rooms is state-of-the-art design, and the pricey restaurant (menus from €49 to €82) has already earned prestigious awards. ❾

Grand-Hôtel de Metz 3 rue des Clercs ⓣ03.87.36.16.33, ⓦwww.grandhotelmetz.com. A characterful old establishment, with friendly staff; the decor is on the prissy side, though. ❹

Lafayette 24 rue des Clercs ⓣ03.87.75.21.09. Cheap and cheerful place – but be warned, the street can get noisy. ❷

Du Théâtre 3 rue du Pont-St-Marcel ⓣ03.87.31.10.10, ⓦwww.port-saint-marcel.com. Smart hotel with pastel-hued decor, in a prime riverside location with cathedral vistas. Facilities include a swimming pool. ❼

Hostels and campsite

Camping municipal allée de Metz-Plage ⓣ03.87.68.26.48, ⓕ03.87.38.03.39. Quiet, grassy campsite right next door to *Metz Plage* (see below). May–Sept.

Carrefour 6 rue Marchant ⓣ03.87.75.07.26, ⓔascarrefour@orange.fr. Friendly HI hostel (membership compulsory), with double rooms (❷) and dorms (€10.20 per person), located in an atmospheric district near lively bars. Internet access available.

Metz Plage 1 allée de Metz-Plage ⓣ03.87.30.44.02, ⓕ03.87.33.19.80. Clean, friendly hostel on the picturesque Île Chambière. Bus #3 or #11 (stop "Pontiffroy") from the *gare SNCF*. Around €15 including breakfast.

The City

Metz in effect is two towns: the original French quarters, gathered round the cathedral, and the *ville allemande*, undertaken as part of a once-and-for-all process of Germanification after the Prussian occupation in 1870. To the south the

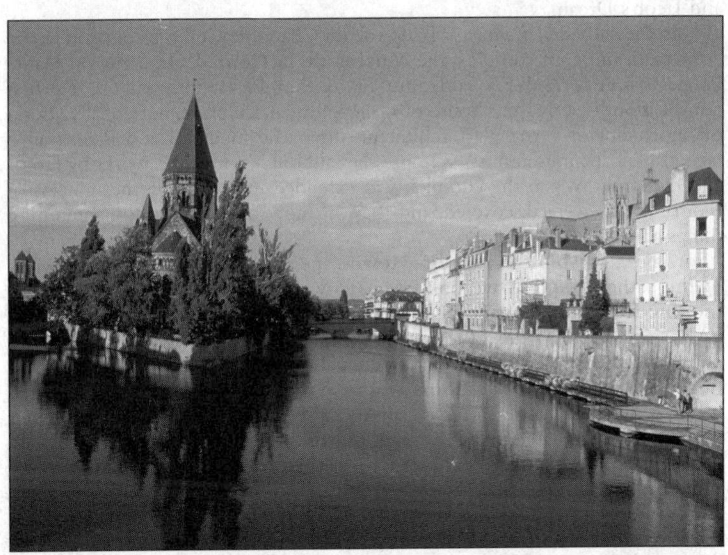

△ The Moselle at Metz

latter, unmistakably Teutonic in style, has considerable elegance and grandeur. The **gare SNCF** sets the tone, a vast and splendid granite structure of 1870 in Rhenish Romanesque, a bizarre cross between a Scottish laird's hunting lodge and a dungeon. Its gigantic dimensions reflect the Germans' long-term strategic intention to use it as the fulcrum of their military transport system in subsequent wars against the French. It's matched in style by the **post office** opposite and by some imposing bourgeois apartment buildings in the surrounding streets, some of them in an attractive Art Nouveau style. The whole quarter was meant to serve as a model of superior town planning, in contrast to the squalid Latin hugger-mugger of the old French neighbourhoods a short way to the north.

The place de la République is a major parking area, bounded on the east side by shops and cafés, with army barracks to the south and the formal gardens of the **Esplanade**, overlooking the Moselle, to the west. To the right, as you look down the esplanade from the square, is the handsome classical **Palais de Justice** in the city's characteristic yellow stone. To the left, a gravel drive leads past the old arsenal, now converted into a prestigious concert hall (**L'Arsenal**) by the postmodernist architect Ricardo Bofill.

From the north side of place de la République, **rue des Clercs** cuts through the attractive, bustling and largely pedestrianized heart of the old city, where most of the shops are located. Past the **place St-Jacques**, with its numerous outdoor cafés, you come to the eighteenth-century **place d'Armes**, where the lofty Gothic **Cathedral of St-Étienne** towers above the pedimented and colonnaded classical facade of the Hôtel de Ville. Its nave is the tallest in France – after Beauvais and Amiens cathedrals – but its best feature is without doubt the stained glass (*vitraux*), both medieval and modern, including windows dating from the thirteenth century. Pride of place, however, goes to **Chagall**'s 1963 masterpiece in the western wall of the north transept, representing the Garden of Eden, while his slightly earlier works in the ambulatory vividly depict Old Testament scenes – Moses and David, Abraham's Sacrifice and Jacob's Dream.

From the cathedral, a short walk up rue du Chanoine Collin brings you to the city's main museum complex, the **Musées de la Cour d'Or**, 2 rue du Haut-Poirier (Mon & Wed–Fri 9am–5pm, Sat & Sun 10am–5pm; €4.60, free first Sun of month), a treasure house of Gallo-Roman sculpture, but equally strong on mock-ups of vernacular architecture from the medieval and Renaissance periods. The art museum is less impressive, although it includes works by Corot and Delacroix. When the complex was extended in the 1930s, the remains of Roman baths were discovered, and they are now one of the most interesting things about the museums.

For the city's most compelling townscape, plus the most dramatic view of the cathedral, you have only to go down to the riverbank and cross to the tiny **Île de la Comédie**, dominated by its classical eighteenth-century square and theatre (the oldest in France) and a rather striking Protestant church erected under the German occupation. An older and equally beautiful square is the **place St-Louis** with its Gothic arcades some ten minutes' walk to the east of the cathedral along En-Fournirue. On the way, wander up into the Italianate streets climbing the **hill of Sainte-Croix** to your left, the legacy of the Lombard bankers who came to run the city's finances in the thirteenth century. It's also worth continuing east from the place des Paraiges, at the end of En-Fournirue, down the rue des Allemands to have a look at the **Porte des Allemands** – a massive, fortified double gate that once barred the eastern entrances to the medieval city.

Eating and drinking

Finding somewhere **to eat** is not difficult in Metz, but the food on offer is much of a muchness, with few places straying from staple fare such as *quiche lorraine* or suckling-pig with *mirabelle* plums. The many cafés on place St-Jacques are popular with locals and tourists, while late-night **drinking** is mostly focused on place Jeanne-d'Arc.

Restaurants

Le Dauphiné 8 rue du Chanoine-Collin. Spruce little place in a handy location, popular for its reasonable lunchtime menus (€10–22), the more expensive ones featuring delicacies such as frogs' legs and duck breast. Closed Sun & Mon–Thurs eve.

L'Estanquet 27 rue des Roches. Riverside wine-bar offering a wide selection of keenly priced salads and snacks, especially pleasant in the summer months when there is a large terrace. Closed Sun.

La Marmite de l'Olivier 9 place Saint-Louis. Both cosy interior and the outdoor tables under the arches get packed, especially at lunchtime, for expertly prepared traditional fare (dishes €11–19), including the inevitable pork and plums favourite. Closed Sun.

Du Pont-St-Marcel 1 rue du Pont-St-Marcel ⓣ03.87.30.12.29. A seventeenth-century establishment, distinctive for its excellent regional cuisine and staff dressed in regional costume. Menus at €18 and €28, including eel and suckling-pig, and wines from the French Moselle. Closed Sun eve & Mon.

Thierry 5 rue des Piques ⓣ03.87.36.64.51. Modern decor and a charming patio combine with some of the most adventurous cuisine in the city (a fusion of North African, southeast Asian and traditional French, with lots of fresh coriander thrown in) and an intelligent wine-list to make this a place that needs advance booking. Menu €22; closed Sun & Wed.

À la Ville de Lyon 7 rue des Piques ⓣ03.87.74.01.23. A rather formal restaurant, a couple of doors along from *Thierry*, specializing in the best traditional cooking, including dishes from Lyon (as the name suggests), such as *quenelles* and *saucisson*. From €35; closed Sun eve, Mon & during Aug.

Cafés and bars

Comédie Café quai Vautris. Rather poky but atmospheric, studenty bar/café with games, jukebox and TV. Open daily.

Café Jehanne d'Arc place Jeanne-d'Arc. Medieval beams and frescoes inside, and an attractive balmy-weather terrace on the square, dominated by the lofty towers of Ste-Ségolène church. There are free jazz concerts outside every Thurs evening in summer.

Le Saint-Jacques 10 place Saint-Jacques. Open daily till late, this is one of the busiest of the many bars on this lively square – and doubles up as a cybercafé.

Les Trinitaires 10–12 rue des Trinitaires ⓣ03.87.20.03.03, ⓦwww.lestrinitaires.com. The place to go for serious jazz, rock, folk and chanson, enhanced by the Gothic cellars. Live music some days at 9pm. Closed Sun & Mon.

The Amnéville complex

Most people heading north from Metz whizz along the A31 autoroute towards Luxembourg and Belgium to avoid numbingly dull towns like Thionville. But that means missing out on the attractions in the **Bois de Coulange**, 3km south of the industrial town of **Amnéville**.

At the top of most people's list of the complex's attractions is the **Musée de la Moto et du Vélo** (Tues, Thurs & Fri 1.30–6pm; Wed, Sat & Sun 10am–noon & 1.30–6pm; €5). Monsieur Chapleur started collecting bikes and motorbikes in the 1930s when he was a mechanic at Citroën, and the museum has over 200 models of different origins on display, all overhauled and in working order. And they are beauties – works of art in copper, brass, chrome and steel, with some of the bicycles dating back to 1865, and the motorbikes from 1900 to 1940. A unique object to look out for is the 1906 René Gillet 4.5hp belt-driven tandem.

But the complex has other draws as well. At **Thermapolis** (Mon–Wed 10am–10pm, Thurs 9am–10pm, Fri & Sat 10am–midnight, Sun 9am–8pm; closed Sept, Christmas and New Year; €10.50 for two hours), you can soak away pains or just relax in a series of pools fed by a ferruginous spring; kitsch decor adorns the saunas, hammams and rest areas. There's also a zoo, an aquarium and all kinds of other curiosities, plus a multiplex cinema.

For more information about all tourist attractions contact the tourist office (☎03.87.70.10.40, Ⓦwww.amneville.com). The Amnéville complex can be reached from Metz by a combination of local train, several times a day, to Hagondange, and shuttle bus (*navette*), more frequent at weekends.

Verdun and the battlefield

The small country town of **VERDUN** lies in a bend of the River Meuse, some 70km west of Metz. Of no great interest in itself, what makes it remarkable is its association with the ghastly battle that took place on the bleak uplands to its north between 1916 and 1918.

In the aftermath of German victory in the 1870–71 war, Verdun and its environs became the most heavily fortified military region in France, the lynch-pin of its northeastern defences. For this reason, and in order to break the stalemate of trench warfare, the German General Erich von Falkenhayn chose it as the target for an offensive that, in 1916, was the most devastating ever launched in the annals of war (see opposite). He advanced to within 5km of the town, but never succeeded in taking it. Gradually the French clawed back the lost ground, but final victory came only in the last months of the war in 1918 and then only with the aid of US troops under the command of General Pershing. Hundreds of thousands of men died in the battle, both French and German, but it was particularly devastating for the French: the battle was fought on their native soil against the enemy who had humiliated them so badly in 1870, and it decimated the country's young male population. Most of the names inscribed on the thousands of sad memorials that stand in every village, hamlet and town of France belong to men who died at Verdun.

The Town

Given the pounding it received in World War I and the bomb damage of World War II, Verdun is not as grim as you might expect. The liveliest part lies between the river and the steep little hill dominated by the cathedral, along rues St-Paul and Mazel. Near the railway station, the **Rodin memorial**, a suitably disturbing statue of a winged Victory, stands beside a handsome eighteenth-century gateway at the northern end of rue St-Paul, where it joins avenue Garibaldi. Nearby is a simple engraving listing all the years between 450 and 1916 that Verdun has been involved in bloody conflict. Another fine gate, the fourteenth-century **Porte Chaussée**, guards the river-crossing in the middle of town. Beyond it, further along rue Mazel, a flight of steps climbs up to the **Monument de la Victoire**, where a helmeted warrior leans on his sword in commemoration of the 1916 battle, while in the crypt below a roll is kept of all the soldiers, French and American, who took part. Beyond the monument, on rue de la Belle Vierge, lies the **Musée de la Princerie** (April–Oct daily except Tues 9.30am–noon & 2–6pm; €3), a small museum housed in a sixteenth-century town house exhibiting ceramics, furniture and paintings from Verdun's ancient and religious history.

The rue de la Belle Vierge leads round to the **Cathedral of Notre-Dame**, whose outward characteristics are Gothic: its earlier Romanesque origins were only uncovered by shell damage in 1916. The superbly sober crypt was subsequently dug out, revealing some of the original carved capitals; the new replacements show scenes from the World War I fighting. The rather beautiful **bishop's palace** behind it has been converted into a **Centre Mondial de la Paix et des Droits de l'Homme** (Feb–May & Sept–Dec daily except Mon 9.30am–noon & 2–6pm; June–Aug daily 9.30am–7pm; €3), hosting exhibitions and conferences about peacekeeping and human rights.

Rue du Rû, the continuation of rue Mazel, takes you to the underground galleries of the **Citadelle** (daily 9am–12.30pm & 1.30–6pm; €6), used as shelter and hospital for thousands of soldiers during the battle. The Unknown Soldier, whose remains now lie under the Arc de Triomphe in Paris, was chosen from among the dead who lie here.

Practicalities

The **gare SNCF** and the **bus station** are both on avenue Garibaldi. The **tourist office** (May–Sept Mon–Sat 8.30am–6.30pm, Sun 9am–5pm; Oct–April Mon–Sat 9am–noon & 2–5.30pm, Sun 10am–1pm; Ⓣ03.29.86.14.18, Ⓦwww.verdun-tourisme.com) lies just across the River Meuse from the Porte Chaussée opposite the end of the bridge. Staff run daily four-hour minibus **tours of the battlefield** (in French only: May–Sept 2pm; €25.50); they're not exactly cheap, but the guides are interesting and the experience is not one that you're likely to repeat. Call ahead to try and arrange an English-speaking guide if your French is not up to it.

As for **accommodation**, there's much more to choose from in Metz or Nancy. However, if you do need to spend the night in Verdun, head for the very friendly *Hôtel St-Paul*, 12 place St-Paul (Ⓣ & Ⓕ03.29.86.02.16; ❸; closed Dec 7–Jan 7), close to the Rodin memorial. Decent and inexpensive alternatives are *Hôtel Montaulbain*, 4 rue de la Vieille-Prison (Ⓣ03.29.86.00.47; ❷), and the *Auberge de Jeunesse* (Ⓣ03.29.86.28.28, Ⓕ03.29.86.28.82; ❶; closed Jan), located between the cathedral and Centre Mondial, with a fantastic view over the town and its surroundings.

You shouldn't have trouble finding somewhere to **eat**: there are plenty of brasseries and crêperies along the river, and *Hôtel St-Paul* (see above) has a good traditional restaurant with menus from €16. For **drinking**, *L'Estaminet*, on rue des Rouyers, has a great selection of beers and a pleasant terrace, and is open until 3am.

The battlefield

The **Battle of Verdun** opened on the morning of February 21, 1916, with a German artillery barrage that lasted ten hours and expended two million shells. It concentrated on the forts of Vaux and Douaumont, which the French had built after the 1870 Franco-Prussian War. By the time the main battle ended ten months later, nine villages had been pounded to nothing. Not a single trace of them is detectable in aerial photos taken at the time. The heavy artillery shells ploughed the ground to a depth of 8m and, although much of it is now reforested, there are parts even today that steadfastly refuse anchorage to any but the coarsest vegetation.

The most visited part of the battlefield extends along the hills north of Verdun, but the fighting also spread well to the west of the Meuse, to the hills of Mort-Homme and Hill 304, to Vauquois and the Argonne, and south along

The Maginot Line

Like the Séré de Rivières forts constructed along the line of the rivers Meuse and Moselle after the 1870–71 war, the **Maginot Line** was designed to keep the Germans out. Constructed between 1930 and 1940, it was the brainchild of the French Minister of War (1929–31), André Maginot. Spanning the entire length of the French–German border – plus a section of the French–Belgian border – it comprised a complete system of defence in depth. There were advance posts equipped with anti-tank weapons and machine guns. There were fortified police stations close to the frontier. But the main line consisted of a continuous chain of underground strong points linked by anti-tank obstacles and equipped with state-of-the-art machinery. It was of course hugely expensive and, when put to the test in 1940, proved to be worse than useless: the Germans simply violated Belgian neutrality and drove round the other end of the Line.

One of the largest forts, the **Fort de Fermont**, situated about 50km north of Verdun near the small town of Longuyon, is open to the public (guided visits: April, May & Sept Sat & Sun 2pm & 3.30pm; June–Aug Mon–Fri 3pm, Sat & Sun 2pm & 3.30pm; ☎03.82.39.21.21; €6; times are susceptible to change so check in advance). The entrance is hidden in woodland and nothing shows above ground but the scarcely noticeable cupolas of the gun turrets. Armed with nine fire points, it was served by 6km of underground tunnels and a garrison of six hundred. The tunnels are equipped with power plants, electric trains, monorails, elevators and all the other technological paraphernalia necessary to support such a lunatic enterprise. The place has the feel of a nuclear bunker.

Getting there without your own transport is not easy. There are trains to Longuyon from Metz and Verdun (change at Conflans), but you'll have to hitch or walk the last 5km to the fort.

the Meuse to St-Mihiel, where the Germans held an important salient until dislodged by US forces in 1918. The only really effective way to explore the area is with your own transport. The main sights are reached via two minor roads that snake through the battlefields, forming a crossroads northeast of Verdun: the D913 and D112.

The monument to André Maginot and the Fort de Souville

The D913 branches left from the main N3 to Metz, 5km east of Verdun; the D112 leaves the same N3 opposite the Cimetière du Faubourg-Pavé on the eastern outskirts of Verdun and is soon enclosed by appropriately gloomy conifer plantations. If you take the D112, on the right you pass a **monument to André Maginot**, who was himself wounded in the battle and under whose later stewardship at the Ministry of War the famous Maginot Line (see box above) was built.

Shortly afterwards, a sign points out a forest ride to the **Fort de Souville**, the furthest point of the German advance in 1916. The site is not on the main tourist beat, and is a very moving, if rather frightening, twenty-minute walk over ground absolutely shattered by artillery fire, with pools of black water standing in the now grassy shell-holes. The fort itself lies half-hidden among the scrub, the armoured gun turrets still louring in their pits, the tunnels to their control rooms dank and dangerous with collapse. A little way beyond the fort, where the D112 intersects the D913, a **stone lion** marks the precise spot at which the German advance was checked. To the left the D913 continues to Fleury, 1km from the crossroads, and on to Douaumont, before curling back round to the D964.

Fleury and the Fort de Vaux

The horrifying story of the battle is graphically documented at **FLEURY**, in the **Musée-Memorial de Fleury** (daily: Feb, March & mid-Nov to mid-Dec 9am–noon & 2–5pm; April to mid-Sept 9am–6pm; mid-Sept to mid-Nov 9am–noon & 2–6pm; €5), which is included in the Verdun tourist office's guided tour. Contemporary newsreels and photos present the stark truth, and in the well of the museum, a section of the shell-torn terrain that was once the village of Fleury has been reconstructed as the battle left it.

Another major monument is the **Fort de Vaux**, 4km east of Fleury (Feb to Dec 23 daily 9am–5pm; €3), where, after six days' hand-to-hand combat in the confined, gas-filled tunnels, the French garrison were left with no alternative but surrender. On the exterior wall of the fort a plaque commemorates the last messenger pigeon sent to the command post in Verdun vainly asking for reinforcements. Having safely delivered its message, the pigeon expired as a result of flying through the gas-filled air above the battlefield. It was posthumously awarded the Légion d'Honneur.

Douaumont

The principal memorial to the carnage stands in the middle of the battlefield a short distance along the D913 beyond Fleury. It is the **Ossuaire de Douaumont** (daily: March & Oct 9am–noon & 2–5.30pm; April 9am–6pm; May–Aug 9am–6.30pm; Sept 9am–noon & 2–6pm; Nov 9am–noon & 2–5pm; €3.50), a vast and surreal structure with the stark simplicity of a Romanesque crypt or a Carolingian sarcophagus, from which rises a central tower shaped like a projectile aimed at the heavens. Its vaults contain the bones of thousands upon thousands of unidentified soldiers, French and German, some of them visible through windows set in the base of the building. When the battle ended in 1918, the ground was covered in fragments of corpses; 120,000 French bodies were identified, perhaps a third of the total killed.

Across the road, a **cemetery** contains the graves of 15,000 men who died more or less whole – Christians commemorated by rows of identical crosses, Muslims of the French colonial regiments by gravestones aligned in the direction of Mecca. Nearby, a wall commemorates the Jewish dead, beneath a treeless ridge-top on whose tortured, pitted ground around the remains of the Fort de Thiaumont some of them must have died.

The **Fort de Douaumont** (daily: Feb, March & Oct–Dec 10am–1pm & 2–5pm; April–June & Sept 10am–6pm; July & Aug 10am–7pm; closed Jan;

St-Mihiel and the Voie Sacrée

In an attempt to cut Verdun off as early as 1914, the Germans captured the town of **St-Mihiel** on the River Meuse to the south, which gave them control of the main supply route into Verdun. The only route left open to the French – and that far from safe – was the N35, winding north from Bar-le-Duc over the open hills and wheat fields. In memory of all those who kept the supplies going, the road is called **La Voie Sacrée** (The Sacred Way) and marked with milestones capped with the helmet of the *poilu* (the slang term for the French infantryman). In St-Mihiel itself, the **Église St-Michel** contains the **Sépulcre** or *Entombment of Christ*, by local sculptor **Ligier Richier** – a set of thirteen stone figures, carved in the mid-sixteeenth century and regarded as one of the masterpieces of the French Renaissance. Just beyond the town to the east, on the Butte de Montsec, is a **memorial** to the Americans who died here in 1918 and a US **cemetery** at Thiancourt on the main road.

€3.50) is 900m down the road from the cemetery. Completed in 1912 and commanding the highest point of land, it was the strongest of the 38 forts built to defend Verdun. In one of those inexplicable aberrations of military top brass, however, the armament of these forts was greatly reduced in 1915, and when the Germans attacked in 1916, twenty men were enough to overrun the garrison of 57 French territorials. The fort is on three levels, two of them underground, and its claustrophobic, dungeon-like galleries are hung with stalactites. The Germans, who held it for eight months, had 3000 men housed in its cramped quarters with no toilets – continuously under siege, its ventilation ducts blocked for protection against gas, infested with fleas and lice and plagued by rats that attacked the sleeping and the dead indiscriminately.

Travel details

Trains

Colmar to: Mulhouse (every 30min; 20min); Munster (hourly; 30min).
Metz to: Amnéville (hourly, 20min); Hagondange (for Thermapolis; 4 hourly; 15min); Nancy (hourly; 1hr); Paris-Est (TGV 10 daily; 1hr 30min); Strasbourg (every 2hr; 1hr 30min).
Nancy to: Paris-Est (TGV 10 daily; 1hr 30min); Saverne (3 daily; 1hr); Strasbourg (every 2hr; 1hr 20 min).
Sélestat to: Ste-Marie-aux-Mines (hourly; 35min).
Strasbourg to: Barr (9 daily; 55min); Basel (hourly; 1hr 30min–2hr); Colmar (every 40min; 40–50min); Dambach (9 daily; 1hr); Dole (10 daily; 3hr 30min); Kehl, Germany (hourly; 10min); Mulhouse (hourly; 1hr); Obernai (9 daily; 40min); Paris-Est (TGV 10 daily; 2hr 20min); Rosheim (9 daily; 25min); Sélestat (every 40min; 30min); Wissembourg (direct, hourly; 1hr).
Verdun to: Metz (4 daily; 1hr–1hr 15min); Nancy (2 daily; 1hr 40min); Paris-Est (up to 5 daily; 3hr).

Buses

Colmar to: Mulhouse (at least 1 hourly; 1hr); Sélestat (hourly; 1hr).
Metz to: Verdun (5 daily Mon–Sat; 2hr).
Saverne to: Molsheim (2 daily; 1hr).

4

Normandy

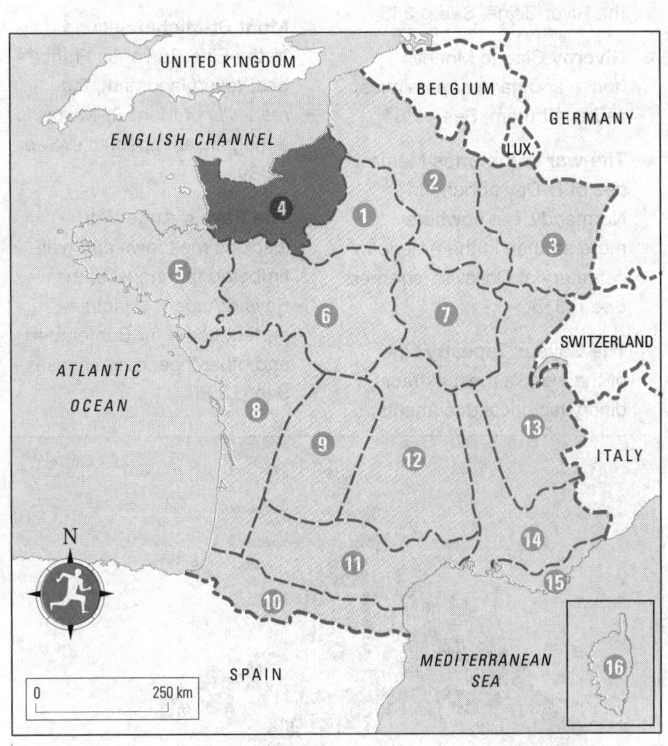
UNITED KINGDOM
BELGIUM
GERMANY
LUX.
ENGLISH CHANNEL
SWITZERLAND
ATLANTIC OCEAN
ITALY
N
SPAIN
MEDITERRANEAN SEA
0
250 km
1
2
3
4
5
6
7
8
9
10
11
12
13
14
15
16

CHAPTER 4

Highlights

* **Rouen** This fine old medieval city would still seem familiar to Joan of Arc, whose life came to a tragic end in its main square. See p.355
* **Château Gaillard** Richard the Lionheart's sturdy fortress commands superb views of the River Seine. See p.363
* **Giverny** Claude Monet's house and garden remain just as he left them. See p.364
* **The war cemeteries** Memories of D-Day abound in Normandy, but nowhere more so than in the American cemetery at Colleville-sur-mer. See p.375
* **The Bayeux Tapestry** One of the world's most extraordinary historical documents, embroidering the saga of William the Conqueror in every colourful detail. See p.379
* **Barfleur** This beautiful ancient port makes a great last-night stop for ferry passengers returning to England. See p.385
* **Mont St-Michel** Second only to the Eiffel Tower as France's best-loved landmark, the *merveille* of Mont St-Michel is a magnificent spectacle. See p.389
* **The Pays d'Auge** With luscious meadows and half-timbered farmhouses, the Pays d'Auge is a picture-perfect home for Camembert and other legendary cheeses. See p.395

△ Mont St-Michel

4

Normandy

Though firmly incorporated into the French mainstream, the seaboard province of **Normandy** has a history of prosperous independence as one of the crucial powers of medieval Europe. Colonized by Scandinavian Vikings (or Norsemen) from the ninth century onwards, it in turn began to colonize during the eleventh and twelfth centuries, with military expeditions conquering not only England but as far afield as Sicily and areas of the Near East. Later, as part of France, it was instrumental in the settlement of Canada.

Normandy has always had large ports: **Rouen**, on the Seine, is the nearest navigable point to Paris, while **Dieppe**, **Le Havre** and **Cherbourg** have important transatlantic trade. Inland, it is overwhelmingly agricultural – a fertile belt of tranquil pastureland, where the chief interest for most visitors will be the groaning restaurant tables of regions such as the **Pays d'Auge**. Significant portions of the seaside are overdeveloped, whether because of industry, as with the huge sprawl of Le Havre, or tourism – in the second half of the nineteenth century, the last French emperor created a "Norman Riviera" around **Trouville** and **Deauville**, and an air of pretension still hangs about their elegant promenades. However, more ancient harbours such as **Honfleur** and **Barfleur** remain visually irresistible, and there are numerous seaside villages with few crowds or affectations. The banks of the Seine, too, hold several delightful little communities, including Caudebec and Jumièges.

Normandy also boasts extraordinary Romanesque and Gothic architectural treasures, although only the much-restored capital, Rouen, retains a complete medieval centre. Elsewhere, the attractions are more often single buildings than entire towns. Most famous of all is the spectacular *merveille* on the island of **Mont St-Michel**, but there are also the monasteries at **Jumièges** and **Caen**, the cathedrals of **Bayeux** and **Coutances** and Richard the Lionheart's castle above the Seine at **Les Andelys**. In addition, **Bayeux** has its vivid and astonishing tapestry, while among more recent creations are Monet's garden at **Giverny** and, at Le Havre, a fabulous collection of paintings by Dufy and Boudin, as well as other Impressionists. Furthermore, Normandy's vernacular architecture makes it well worth exploring inland – the back roads through the countryside are lined with splendid centuries-old half-timbered manor houses. It's remarkable how much has survived – or, less surprisingly, been restored – since the Allied landings in 1944 and the subsequent **Battle of Normandy**, which has its own legacy in a series of war museums, memorials and cemeteries.

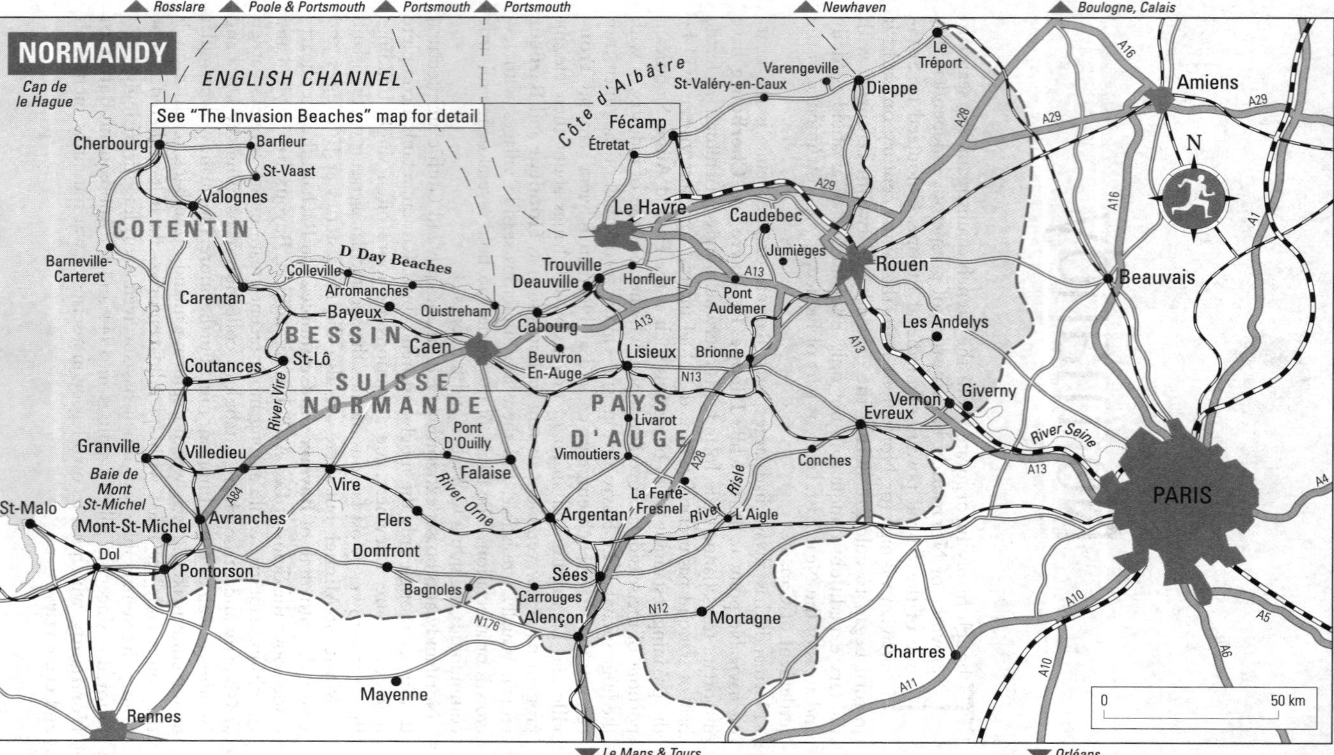
Rosslare
Poole & Portsmouth
Portsmouth
Portsmouth
Newhaven
Boulogne, Calais
NORMANDY
ENGLISH CHANNEL
Cap de
le Hague
See "The Invasion Beaches" map for detail
Côte d'Albâtre
Cherbourg
Barfleur
St-Vaast
Valognes
COTENTIN
Barneville-
Carteret
Carentan
Colleville
D Day Beaches
Arromanches
Bayeux
Ouistreham
BESSIN
Caen
St-Lô
Coutances
SUISSE
NORMANDE
River Vire
Granville
Villedieu
Baie de
Mont
St-Michel
St-Malo
Mont-St-Michel
Avranches
A84
Dol
Pontorson
Rennes
Vire
Flers
River Orne
Pont
D'Ouilly
Falaise
Domfront
Bagnoles
Carrouges
N176
Mayenne
Fécamp
Étretat
Le Havre
Trouville
Deauville
Honfleur
Cabourg
Beuvron
En-Auge
Lisieux
PAYS
D'AUGE
Livarot
Vimoutiers
Argentan
Sées
Alençon
N12
Mortagne
La Ferté-
Fresnel
River Risle
L'Aigle
A28
Pont
Audemer
A13
Brionne
N13
Caudebec
Jumièges
St-Valéry-en-Caux
Varengeville
Dieppe
Le
Tréport
Rouen
A29
Les Andelys
Vernon
Giverny
Evreux
Conches
River Seine
Amiens
A16
N
Beauvais
A1
PARIS
A4
A5
A6
A10
A11
Chartres
0
50 km
Le Mans & Tours
Orléans

The food of Normandy

The **food of Normandy** owes its most distinctive characteristic – its gut-bursting, heart-pounding richness – to the lush orchards and dairy herds of its agricultural heartland, and most especially the area southeast of Caen known as the Pays d'Auge. Menus abound in **meat** such as veal (*veau*) cooked in *vallée d'Auge* style, which consists largely of the profligate addition of cream and butter. Many dishes also feature orchard fruit, either in its natural state or in successively more alcoholic forms – either as apple or pear cider, or perhaps further distilled to produce brandies.

Normans have a great propensity for blood and guts. In addition to gamier meat and fowl such as rabbit and duck (a speciality in Rouen, where the birds are strangled to ensure that all their blood gets into the sauce), they enjoy such intestinal preparations as *andouilles*, the sausages known in English as chitterlings, and *tripes*, stewed for hours *à la mode de Caen*. A full blowout at a country restaurant in one of the small towns of inland Normandy – places like Conches, Vire and the Suisse Normande – will also traditionally entail one or two pauses between courses for the *trou normand*: a glass of the apple brandy Calvados that lets you catch your breath before struggling on with the feast.

Normandy's long coastline ensures that it is also a wonderful region for **seafood**. Many of the larger ports and resorts have long waterfront lines of restaurants competing for attention, each with its "*copieuse*" *assiette de fruits de mer*. **Honfleur** is probably the most enjoyable of these, but **Dieppe**, **Étretat** and **Cherbourg** also offer endless eating opportunities. The menus tend to be much the same as those on offer in Brittany, if perhaps slightly more expensive.

The most famous products of Normandy's meadow-munching cows are, of course, their **cheeses**. The tradition of cheese-making in the Pays d'Auge is thought to have started in the monasteries during the Dark Ages. By the eleventh century the local products were already well defined; in 1236, the *Roman de la Rose* referred to Angelot cheese, identified with a small coin depicting a young angel killing a dragon. The principal modern varieties began to emerge in the seventeenth century – Pont l'Evêque, which is square with a washed crust, soft but not runny and Livarot, which is round, thick and firm, and has a stronger flavour. Although Marie Herel is generally credited with having invented Camembert in the 1790s, a smaller and stodgier version of that cheese had already existed for some time. A priest fleeing the Revolution seems to have stayed in Mme Herel's farmhouse at Camembert, and suggested modifications in her cheese-making in line with the techniques he'd seen employed to manufacture Brie de Meaux – a slower process, gentler on the curd and with more thorough drainage. The rich full cheese thus created was an instant success in the market at Vimoutiers, and the development of the railways (and the invention of the chipboard cheesebox in 1880) helped to give it a worldwide popularity.

To the French, at least, the essence of Normandy is its produce. This is the land of Camembert and Calvados, cider and seafood, and a butter- and cream-based cuisine with a proud disdain for most things *nouvelle*. Economically, however, the richness of the dairy pastures has been Normandy's downfall in recent years. EU milk quotas have liquidated many small farms, and stringent sanitary regulations have forced many small-scale traditional cheese factories to close. Parts of inland Normandy are now among the most depressed in the whole country, and in the forested areas to the south, where life has never been easy, things have not improved.

Seine Maritime

The *département* of Seine Maritime comprises three very distinct sections: Normandy's dramatic **northern coastline**, home not only to major ports like Dieppe and Le Havre but also to such delightful resorts as **Étretat**; the meandering course of the **River Seine**, where unchanged villages stand both up- and downstream of the provincial capital of Rouen; and the flat chalky **Caux plateau**, which makes for pleasant cycling country but holds little of note to detain visitors.

Dieppe in particular offers a much more appealing introduction to France than its counterparts further north in Picardy, and with the impressive white cliffs of the aptly named **Côte d'Albâtre** (Alabaster Coast) stretching away to either side it could easily serve as the base for a long stay. The most direct route to Rouen from here is simply to head due south, but it's well worth tracing the shore all the way west to **Le Havre**, and then following the Seine inland.

Driving along the D982 along the northern bank of the Seine, you'll often find your course paralleled by mighty tankers and container ships out on the water. Potential stops en route include the medieval abbeys of **Jumièges** and **St-Wandrille**, but **Rouen** itself is the prime destination, its association with the execution of Joan of Arc merely the most compelling episode in its fascinating and conspicuous history. Further upstream, Monet's wonderful house and garden at **Giverny** and the redoubtable English frontier stronghold of Château Gaillard at **Les Andelys** also justify taking a slow route into Paris.

Dieppe

Squeezed between high cliff headlands, **DIEPPE** is an enjoyably small-scale port that used to be more of a resort. During the nineteenth century, Parisians came here by train to take the sea air, promenading along the front while the English colony indulged in the peculiar pastime of swimming. These days, it's not a place many travellers go out of their way to visit, but it's one of the nicer ferry ports in northern France, and you're unlikely to regret spending an afternoon or evening here before or after a Channel crossing. With kids in tow, the aquariums of the **Cité de la Mer** are the obvious attraction; otherwise, you could settle for admiring the cliffs and the castle as you stroll the extravagant seafront lawns. The business of the port goes on as ever, with Dieppe's commercial docks unloading half the bananas of the Antilles and forty percent of all shellfish destined to slither down French throats. The markets sell fish right off the boats, displayed with the usual Gallic flair, and the sole, scallops and turbot available in profusion at the restaurants may well tempt you to stay.

Arrival and information

Dieppe's **tourist office** is on the pont Ango, which separates the ferry harbour from the pleasure port (May, June & Sept Mon–Sat 9am–1pm & 2–7pm, Sun 10am–1pm & 3–6pm; July & Aug Mon–Sat 9am–7pm, Sun 10am–1pm & 3–6pm; Oct–April Mon–Sat 9am–noon & 2–6pm; ⓣ02.32.14.40.60, ⓦwww.dieppetourisme.com). **Bicycles** can be rented very cheaply from Vélo Service, just across the bridge (ⓣ06.24.56.06.27). The main **post office** is at 2 bd

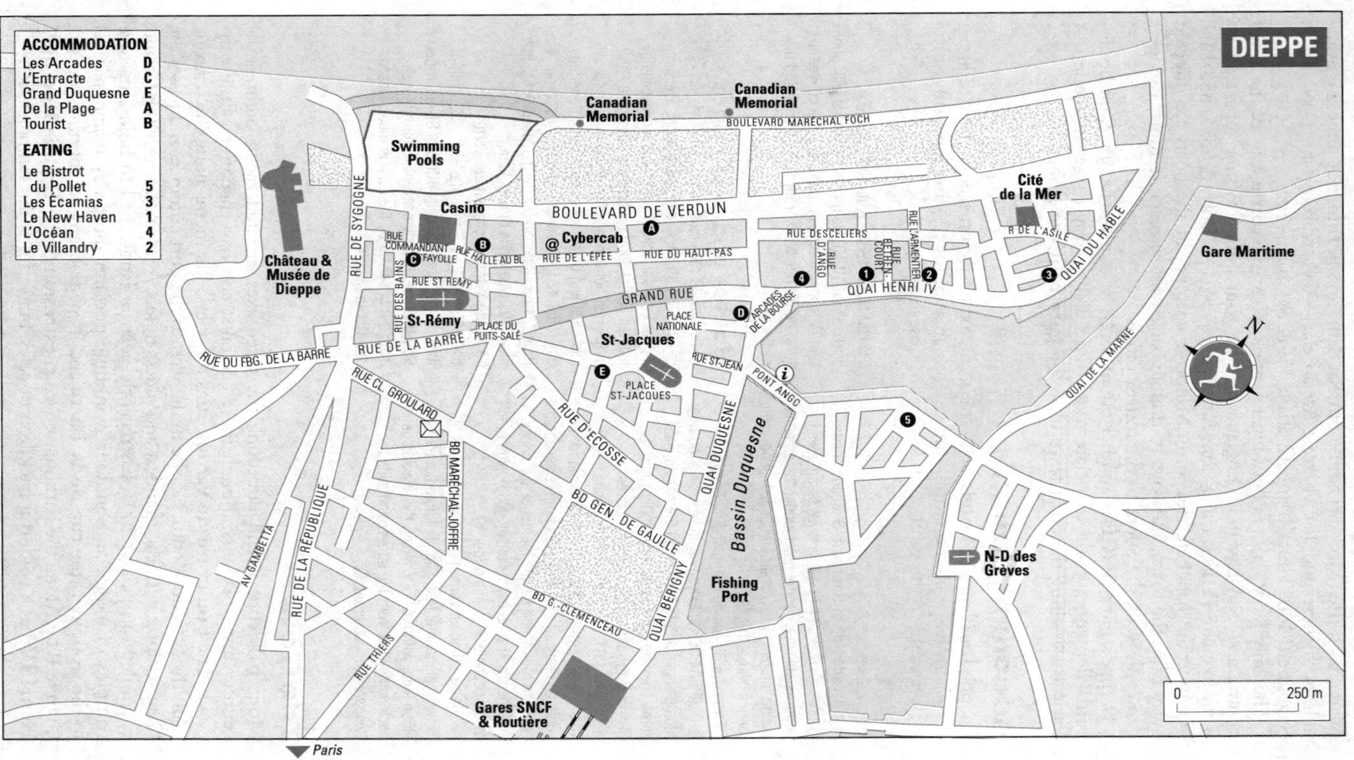
DIEPPE
ACCOMMODATION
Les Arcades D
L'Entracte C
Grand Duquesne E
De la Plage A
Tourist B
EATING
Le Bistrot du Pollet 5
Les Écamias 3
Le New Haven 1
L'Océan 4
Le Villandry 2
Canadian Memorial
Canadian Memorial
BOULEVARD MARÉCHAL FOCH
Swimming Pools
Casino
BOULEVARD DE VERDUN
Cité de la Mer
Gare Maritime
Château & Musée de Dieppe
RUE DE SYGOGNE
RUE COMMANDANT FAYOLLE
RUE HALLE AU BL
@ Cybercab
RUE DE L'ÉPÉE
RUE DU HAUT-PAS
RUE DESCELIERS
RUE D'ANGO
RUE BETHENCOURT
RUE L'ARMENTIER
R DE L'ASILE
QUAI DU HABLE
QUAI HENRI IV
RUE DES BAINS
RUE ST RÉMY
St-Rémy
PLACE DU PUITS-SALÉ
GRAND RUE
PLACE NATIONALE
ARCADES DE LA BOURSE
St-Jacques
RUE DU FBG. DE LA BARRE
RUE DE LA BARRE
RUE ST-JEAN
PONT ANGO
PLACE ST-JACQUES
QUAI DE LA MARNE
RUE CL. GROULARD
RUE D'ECOSSE
QUAI DUQUESNE
Bassin Duquesne
BD MARÉCHAL-JOFFRE
BD GEN. DE GAULLE
N-D des Grèves
Fishing Port
AV GAMBETTA
RUE DE LA RÉPUBLIQUE
BD G.-CLEMENCEAU
QUAI BERIGNY
RUE THIERS
Gares SNCF & Routière
Pourville & Varengeville
Paris
0 250 m
N

Maréchal-Joffre (Mon–Fri 8am–6pm, Sat 8am–noon); **Internet access** is available both there, and at Cybercafé Art au Bar – Cybercab for short, 19 rue de Sygogne (Mon–Thurs 10am–12.30am, Fri & Sat 10am–2pm).

The only ferry services between Dieppe's **gare maritime**, east of the town centre, and Newhaven in England are the four-hour crossings operated by Transmanche Ferries, using conventional vessels (1–4 daily; ⓣ08.00.65.01.00, ⓦwww.transmancheferries.com). Motorists coming off the boats are directed away from the town, and have to double back west to reach it; foot passengers can easily walk the 500m to the tourist office.

Dieppe's **gare SNCF** is another 500m south of the tourist office, on boulevard Clemenceau, and trains are much the quickest way to get to Rouen or Paris. Buses along the coast leave from the **gare routière** alongside.

Accommodation

Dieppe has plenty of **hotels**, with the more expensive ones concentrated along the seafront – which is among the quietest areas of town – and especially at the western end of the boulevard de Verdun, closest to the castle.

Hotels

Les Arcades de la Bourse 1–3 arcades de la Bourse ⓣ02.35.84.14.12, ⓦwww.lesarcades.fr. Long-established central hotel, under the arcades facing the port. The restaurant has full, good-value menus from €18. ❹

L'Entracte 39 rue du Commandant Fayolle ⓣ02.35.84.26.45. Extremely inexpensive, no-frills rooms above a little bar behind the casino, plus some en-suite ones at slightly higher rates. ❶

Grand Duquesne 15 place St-Jacques ⓣ02.32.14.61.10, ⓦaugrandduquesne.free.fr. This small, central hotel is unusually plain for the Logis de France organization, but offers acceptable en-suite rooms and simple menus at low prices, and there's also an exceptionally good-value family room, capable of sleeping four. ❸

La Plage 20 bd de Verdun ⓣ02.35.84.18.28, ⓦwww.plagehotel.fr.st. Slightly upmarket rooms, all en suite with cable TV, facing the sea and set back somewhat from the street, alongside the *Windsor*. No restaurant. ❹

Tourist Hôtel 16 rue de la Halle au Blé ⓣ02.35.06.10.10. Plain en-suite rooms with phone and TV, above a Turkish restaurant in a converted town house one block from the beach behind the casino. ❸

Hostel and campsite

HI hostel 48 rue Louis-Fromager ⓣ02.35.84.85.73, ⓔdieppe@fuaj.org. Welcoming and comfortable, if somewhat inconveniently located hostel, 2km southwest of the *gare SNCF* in the quartier Janval, offering dorm beds for €8 (not including breakfast or bed linen). Served by bus route #2 from the tourist office (direction "Val Druel", stop "Château Michel"). Closed Oct to late May, plus weekends during June.

Camping Vitamin chemin des Vertus ⓣ02.35.82.11.11. Three-star site, well south of town in an unremarkable setting in St-Aubin-sur-Scie that's really only convenient for motorists, even if it is served by the #2 bus route. Closed mid-Oct to March.

The Town

Modern Dieppe is laid out along the three axes dictated by its eighteenth-century town planners, though these central streets have become a little run-down. The **boulevard de Verdun** runs for over a kilometre along the seafront, from the fifteenth-century castle in the west to the port entrance, and passes the Casino, along with the grandest and oldest hotels. A large area near the Casino, scheduled to open in 2007, has recently been re-landscaped to hold a massive complex of indoor and outdoor swimming pools. A short way inland, parallel to the seafront, is the **rue de la Barre** and its pedestrianized continuation, the Grande Rue. Along the harbour's edge, an extension of the **Grande Rue**, **quai Henri IV** has a colourful backdrop of cafés, brasseries and restaurants.

The **place du Puits Salé**, at the centre of the old town, is dominated by the huge, restored **Café des Tribunaux**, built as an inn towards the end of the seventeenth century. Two hundred years later, it was favoured by painters and writers such as Renoir, Monet, Sickert, Whistler and Pissarro. For English visitors, its most evocative association is with the exiled and unhappy Oscar Wilde, who drank here regularly. It's now a cavernous café, popular with college students and open until after midnight.

As for monuments, the obvious place to start is the medieval **castle** overlooking the seafront from the west, home of the **Musée de Dieppe** and two showpiece collections (June–Sept daily 10am–noon & 2–6pm; Oct–May daily except Tues 10am–noon & 2–5pm; €3). The first collection is a group of carved ivories – virtuoso pieces of sawing, filing and chipping of the plundered riches of Africa, shipped back to the town by early Dieppe explorers. The other permanent exhibition is made up of a hundred or so prints by the co-founder of **Cubism**, Georges Braque, who went to school in Le Havre, spent summers in Dieppe and is buried just west of the town at Varengeville-sur-Mer. Other galleries upstairs hold paintings of local scenes by the likes of Pissarro, Renoir, Dufy, Sickert and Boudin, while a separate, much newer wing of the castle stages temporary exhibitions.

An exit from the western side of the castle takes you out onto a path up to the **cliffs**. On the other side, a flight of steps leads down to the **square du Canada**, originally named in commemoration of the role played by Dieppe sailors in the colonization of Canada. Now a small plaque is dedicated to the Canadian soldiers who died in the suicidal 1942 raid on Dieppe, justified later as a trial run for the 1944 Normandy landings.

Cité de la Mer

On the eastern end of town just back from the harbour, the **Cité de la Mer**, at 37 rue de l'Asile-Thomas, sets out simultaneously to entertain children and to serve as a centre for scientific research, and succeeds in both without being all that interesting for the casual adult visitor (daily 10am–noon & 2–6pm; Ⓦestrancitedelamer.free.fr; €5). Kids are certain to enjoy learning the principles of navigation by operating radio-controlled boats. Thereafter, the museum traces the history of seagoing vessels, featuring a Viking *drakkar* under construction, following methods depicted in the Bayeux Tapestry. Next comes a very detailed geological exhibition covering the formation of the local cliffs, in which you learn how to convert shingle into sandpaper. Visits culminate with large **aquariums** filled with the marine life of the Channel: flat fish with bulbous eyes and twisted faces, retiring octopuses, battling lobsters and hermaphrodite scallops (the white part is male, the orange female). A lack of sentimentality means that jars of fish soup, whose exact provenance is not made explicit, are on sale at the exit.

Eating and drinking

The most promising area to look for **restaurants** in Dieppe is along the quai Henri IV, which makes a lovely place to stroll and compare menus of a summer's evening.

The beach itself holds no formal restaurants, but it does have a couple of open-air cafés selling mussels, salads and so on, and plenty of crêpe stands. As well as the daily spectacle of the fish on sale in the **fishing port**, there's an all-day open-air **market** in the place Nationale and Grande Rue on Saturday. The largest of several hypermarkets in the area is Auchan (Mon–Sat 8.30am–10pm), out of town at the Centre Commercial du Belvédère on the route de Rouen (RN 27), and reached by free courtesy buses from the tourist office.

Le Bistrot du Pollet 23 rue du Tête du Boeuf ⓣ02.35.84.68.57. Little local restaurant just east of Pont Ango, especially cosy on a winter's evening, which sells fresh seafood at low prices. Closed Mon, Sun, two weeks in March & all Aug.

Les Écamias 129 quai Henri IV ⓣ02.35.84.67.67. Small, friendly traditional French restaurant at the quieter seaward end of the main quay, offering dishes such as skate with capers; the €15.50 option includes *moules marinières*. Closed Mon.

Le New Haven 53 quai Henri IV ⓣ02.35.84.89.72. Reliable seafood specialist, towards the quieter end of the quayside, with good menus from €16. The €21 *menu de la Jetée* is fine if you hanker after fish livers, while €19 buys you a *choucroute de la mer* (seafood sauerkraut). Closed Tues eve, plus Mon & Wed in winter.

L'Océan 23 quai Henri IV ⓣ02.32.90.97.80. Big, sprawling quayside bistro that's ideal for a large group; its long menu combines a wide variety of meat, fish and shellfish, with set menus from €10 to €30 and good-value *formules* besides.

Le Villandry 85 quai Henri IV ⓣ02.35.82.55.49. Harbourfront restaurant that has an indoor dining room, but is at its best in summer, when tables spread onto its large, uncovered pavement patio. The €16.50 menu features oysters and mussels, followed by solid fish courses and basic desserts.

The Côte d'Albâtre

The shoreline of the Côte d'Albâtre is eroding at a ferocious rate, and it's conceivable that the small resorts here, tucked in among the cliffs at the ends of a succession of valleys, may not last more than another century or so. For the moment, however, they are quietly prospering, with casinos, sports centres and yacht marinas ensuring a modest but steady summer trade. To the east of Dieppe **Le Tréport** is pleasant enough, but the obvious direction to head is west, where you can take your pick of **St-Valéry**, **Fécamp** and the best of the bunch, **Étretat**.

Le Tréport

Thirty kilometres east of Dieppe, on the border with Picardy, **LE TRÉPORT** is a seaside resort that has clearly seen better days. It was already something of a bathing station when the railways arrived in 1873 and promoted this as "the prettiest beach in Europe, just three hours from Paris". It remained the capital's favoured resort until the 1950s – and is still served by around five trains daily – but it can't ever have been that pretty, and these days its charms are definitely fading.

Le Tréport divides into three sections: the flat wedge-shaped **seafront** area, bounded on one side by the Channel, on another by the harbour at the mouth of the River Bresle, and on the third by imposing 100-metre-high white chalk cliffs; the **old town**, higher up the slopes on safer ground; and the **modern town** further inland. Only the parts closest to the shore are of any interest to visitors. The seafront itself is entirely taken up by a hideous pink-and-orange concrete apartment block, with one or two snack bars but no other sign of life, facing the Casino and a drab grey shingle beach. The more sheltered harbourside quai François-1er around the corner holds most of the action, lined with restaurants, souvenir shops and cafés. The assorted stone jetties and wooden piers around the harbour make an enjoyable stroll, watching the comings and goings of the fishing boats.

Climbing up from the *quai*, you come to the heavily nautical **Église St-Jacques**, built in the fifteenth century to replace an eleventh-century original that crumbled into the sea, along with the cliff on which it stood. Nearby, next to the fortified former town hall that is now the local library, successive flights of steps, 365 of them in all, climb to the top of the cliffs.

Practicalities

Trains and **buses** arrive in Le Tréport on the far side of the harbour, a short walk from the main *quai*. Turning left as you hit the main drag will bring you to the **tourist office**, on quai Sadi-Carnot (April–June & Sept Mon–Thurs 10am–noon & 3–6pm, Fri & Sat 10am–12.30pm & 2.30–7pm, Sun 10am–1pm & 3–5pm; July & Aug daily 10am–7pm; Oct–March Mon–Sat 10am–noon & 3–6pm; ⓣ02.35.86.05.69, ⓦwww.ville-le-treport.fr). Of the **hotels**, the best in terms of a sea view and good-quality food is the *Richelieu* at 50–51 quai François-1er (ⓣ02.35.86.26.55; ❸), which has comfortable, colourful rooms with showers and a wide range of menus starting at €15 for a "bistro" meal. The *St-Louis*, 43 quai François le Premier (ⓣ02.35.86.20.70), is a quayside seafood **restaurant** with a high gourmet reputation.

Varengeville

If the museum in Dieppe (see p.345) awakened your interest in Georges Braque, you may be interested in visiting his grave in the clifftop church some way further up the coast of **VARENGEVILLE**, 8km west of Dieppe (25min ride on bus #311 or #312, afternoon only). Braque's marble **tomb** is topped by a sadly decaying mosaic of a white dove in flight. More impressive is his vivid blue *Tree of Jesse* stained-glass window inside the church, through which the sun rises in summer.

Back along the road towards Dieppe from the church, the house at the **Bois des Moutiers**, built for Guillaume Mallet from 1898 onwards and un-French in almost every respect, was one of architect Edwin Lutyens' first commissions. Lutyens, then aged just 29, was at the start of a career that was to culminate during the 1920s when he laid out most of the city of New Delhi. The real reason to visit, however, is to enjoy the magnificent **gardens**, designed by Mallet in conjunction with Gertrude Jekyll, which are at their most spectacular in the second half of May (house open mid-March to mid-Nov daily 10am–noon & 2–6pm; gardens open April–Oct 10am–8pm; €8 entry to house & gardens during May & June, otherwise €7). Enthusiastic guides lead you through the highly innovative engineering of the house and grounds, full of quirks and games – you must take the tour of the house, but can walk freely through the gardens. The colours of the tapestry by British painter Edward Burne-Jones hanging in the stairwell were copied from Renaissance cloth in William Morris's studio; the rhododendrons were chosen from similar samples. Outside, paths lead through vistas based on paintings by Poussin, Lorrain and other seventeenth-century artists.

While the village of Varengeville offers little choice of **accommodation**, its one available option is absolutely irresistible – the lovely ★ *Hôtel de la Terrasse*, a Logis set amid the pines on the route de Vastérival, (ⓣ02.35.85.12.54, ⓦwww.hotel-restaurant-la-terrasse.com; closed mid-Oct to mid-March; ❸). Reached via a right turn off the main highway as you head west of town, it's perched high above the cliffs, with great sea views. Fish menus in its panoramic dining room cost from €20, and you can follow footpaths down through narrow cracks in the cliffs to reach the rocky beach below.

St-Valéry-en-Caux

The first sizeable community west of Dieppe is **ST-VALÉRY-EN-CAUX**, a rebuilt town that is the clearest reminder of the fighting – and massive destruction

– of the Allied retreat of 1940. A monument on the western cliffs pays tribute to the French cavalry division who faced Rommel's tanks on horseback, brandishing their sabres with hopeless heroism, while beside the ruins of a German artillery emplacement on the opposite cliffs another commemorates a Scottish division, rounded up while trying to fight their way back to Le Havre and the boats home.

Much the most attractive house to survive in St-Valéry, the Renaissance Maison Henri-IV on the quai d'Aval serves as the **tourist office** (Feb–March & Oct–Dec 11am–1pm & 2.30–6pm; April–May Sat & Sun 11am–1pm & 3–7pm; June & Sept Wed–Sun 11am–1pm & 3–7pm; July & Aug daily 10.30am–1pm & 3–7pm; Ⓣ02.35.97.00.63, Ⓦwww.ville-saint-valery-en-caux.fr). The only **hotel** facing the sea is at 22 rue le Perrey; formerly known as the *Terrasse*, it should have reopened by mid-2007 as *La Maison des Galets*, with a contemporary-style refurbishment (Ⓣ02.35.97.11.22; phone hotel for details), and have a tearoom but not a restaurant. Several other hotels surround the main market square, including the *Eden*, above a brasserie at 21 place du Marché (Ⓣ02.35.97.11.44; ❶–❸; closed Mon & Sun eve in low season), where not all rooms are en suite, while in high season the 149 comfortable if characterless rooms of the *Hôtel du Casino*, 500m back from the seafront at 14 av Clemenceau (Ⓣ02.35.57.88.00, Ⓦwww.hotel-casino-saintvalery.com; ❺), can be a godsend. There are also two **campsites**: the large four-star *D'Etennemare* (Ⓣ02.35.97.15.79), set back from the sea southwest of the harbour and open year round, and the one-star *Falaise d'Amont* (Ⓣ02.35.97.05.07; closed mid-Nov to mid-March), on the eastern cliffs. The *Restaurant du Port*, overlooking the harbour at 18 quai d'Amont (Ⓣ02.35.97.08.93; closed Mon, plus Sun eve in low season), serves a delicious €21 seafood menu.

Fécamp

FÉCAMP, just over halfway from Dieppe to Le Havre, is a serious fishing port with an attractive seafront promenade. One compelling reason to pay a brief visit is to see the **Benedictine Distillery** on rue Alexandre-le-Grand, in the narrow strip of streets running parallel to the port towards the town centre. Tours (daily: early Feb to March & Oct–Dec 10.30–11.45am & 2–5pm; April to early July & early Sept to Oct 10am–noon & 2–5.30pm; early July to early Sept 10am–6pm; admission by 90 min guided tours only; €5.80) start with a small **museum**, set firmly in the Middle Ages with props of manuscripts, locks, testaments, lamps and religious paintings beneath a nightmarish mock-Gothic roof. The first whiff of Benedictine – a sweet herby liqueur often combined with brandy – comes in the grim rust-and-grey-coloured Salle des Abbés, and at this point the script abruptly changes – from mysterious monks to PR for an exclusive product. The boxes of ingredients are a rare treat for the nose (take it easy with the myrrh), and there's further theatricality in the old distillery, where boxes of herbs are flung with gusto into copper vats and alembics, though commercial production has long since moved to an out-of-town site. Finally you're offered a *dégustation* in their bar across the road – neat, in a cocktail, or on crêpes; make sure you hold onto your ticket to qualify.

If your aesthetic sensibilities need soothing after this, head for the soaring medieval nave and Renaissance carved screens of the **church of the Trinité**, up in the town centre, or the modern **Musée des Terres-Neuvas et de la Pêche**, on the seafront at 27 bd Albert 1er (July & Aug daily 10am–7pm; Sept–June daily except Tues 10am–noon & 2–5.30pm; €3). Spreading across two floors, with lots of miniature model boats and amateur paintings, it focuses on the long tradition whereby the fishermen of Fécamp decamp en masse each year to catch cod in the cold, foggy waters off Newfoundland. Sailing vessels continued to make the trek from the sixteenth century right up until 1931; today vast refrigerated container ships have taken their place.

Practicalities

Fécamp's main **tourist office** is opposite the distillery at 113 rue Alexandre-le-Grand (Sept–March Mon–Fri 9am–6pm, Sat 9.30am–12.30pm & 2–6pm; April–June Mon–Fri 9am–6pm, Sat & Sun 10am–6.30pm; July & Aug daily 9am–6.30pm; ⓣ02.35.28.51.01, ⓦwww.fecamptourisme.com). Most of the **hotels** are set back away from the sea on odd side streets, but there are a couple of good options near the waterfront, well worth booking in advance. Only the higher rooms at the smarter of the two, the rather genteel *Hôtel de la Plage*, 87 rue de la Plage (ⓣ02.35.29.76.51, ❷), have sea views, but almost all have been well refurbished and the location is quiet. The *De la Mer*, on the seafront at 89 bd Albert 1er (ⓣ02.35.28.24.64, ⓦwww.hotel-dela-mer.com; ❷), is good value, and nicer inside than it looks from the outside. There's also a superb **campsite,** the *Camping de Renneville* (ⓣ02.35.28.20.97, ⓦwww.campingdereneville.com; closed mid-Nov to mid-March), five minutes' walk up from the seafront, in a dramatic location on the western cliffs, with magnificent views but plenty of shade if you need it.

There are a number of well-priced fish **restaurants**: *La Marée*, 75 quai Bérigny (ⓣ02.35.29.39.15; closed Sun eve & Mon), is attached to a fish shop and offers menus from €18; and the friendly little *Marine*, 23 quai de la Vicomté (ⓣ02.35.28.15.94), is open daily for €15 lunches and serves a great *choucroute de la mer*.

Étretat

Here the alabaster cliffs are at their most spectacular – their arches, tunnels and the solitary "needle" will doubtless be familiar from tourist brochures – and the town itself has grown up simply as a pleasure resort. There isn't even a port of any kind: the seafront consists of a sweeping unbroken curve of concrete above a shingle beach.

Thanks partly to its superb setting, and the lovely architectural ensemble that surrounds its central **place Foch**, Étretat is a very pretty little place. The old wooden market *halles* still dominate the main square, the ground floor now converted into souvenir shops, but the beams of the balcony and roof are bare and ancient. As soon as you step onto the beach you'll see the cliff formations to either side. To the west, on the **Falaise**

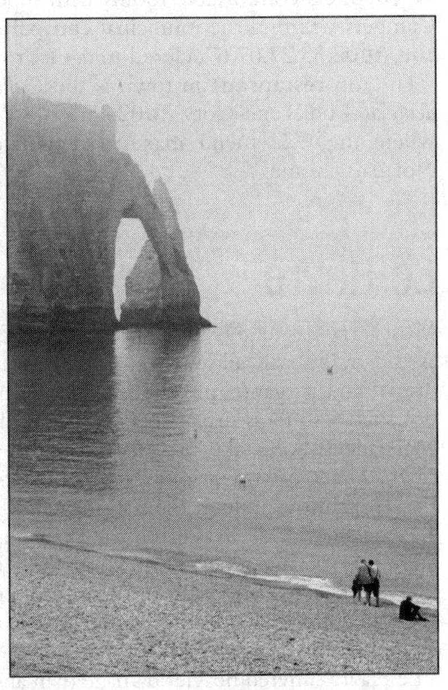

△ Étretat

d'Aval, a straightforward walk – made unnerving by the scary drops nearby – leads up the crumbling side of the cliff, with lush lawns and pastures to the inland side and German fortifications on the shore side extending to the point where the turf abruptly stops, occasionally ripped by the latest rock fall. From the windswept top you can see further rock formations and sometimes even glimpse Le Havre, but the views back to the town sheltered in the valley, and the **Falaise d'Amont** – which Maupassant compared to an elephant dipping its trunk into the ocean – on its eastern side, are what stick in the memory. The cliff itself presents an idyllic rural scene, with a gentle footpath winding up the green hillside to the little chapel of Notre-Dame.

Practicalities

Étretat's **tourist office** is alongside the main road through the centre of town, on place M. Guillard (mid-March to mid-June & mid-Sept to mid-Nov Mon–Sat 10am–noon & 2–6pm; mid-June to mid-Sept daily 10am–7pm; mid-Nov to mid-March Fri & Sat 10am–noon & 2–6pm ⓣ02.35.27.05.21, ⓦwww.etretat.net). Of the four well-priced **hotels** that crowd the corners of place Foch, the *Hôtel la Résidence*, 4 bd René-Coty (ⓣ02.35.27.02.87; ❷–❼), is most picturesque, a dramatic half-timbered old mansion with beautiful wooden carvings decorating its every nook and cranny – the quality of rooms, however, is variable, and few are as elegant as the facade. The *Hôtel des Falaises*, opposite at 1 bd René-Coty (ⓣ02.35.27.02.77; ❸), is more reliable – in fact from its modernized rooms you get a better view of the *Résidence* than if you're actually staying there. *L'Escale*, on place Foch itself (ⓣ02.35.27.03.69; ❸), has simple but pleasant rooms, and a snack restaurant downstairs specializing in *moules-frites* and crêpes. The grand, modern *Dormy House*, perched above town on the coastal route du Havre to the west (ⓣ02.35.27.07.88, ⓦwww.dormy-house.com; ❺–❾), offers comfortable rooms with superlative views, and a good restaurant. Campers will find the municipal **campsite** 1km out on rue Guy-de-Maupassant (ⓣ02.35.27.07.67; closed mid-Oct to mid-March).

The top **restaurant** in town is the *Galion*, distinct from the adjoining *Résidence* at 4 bd René-Coty (ⓣ02.35.29.48.74; closed Tues & Wed in low season), where the €22 menu makes a definitive introduction to all that's best in Norman cuisine.

Le Havre

Most ferry passengers head straight out of the port of **LE HAVRE** as quickly as the traffic will allow to escape a city that guidebooks tend to dismiss as dismal and gargantuan. While it's hardly picturesque or tranquil, however, it's not such a soulless urban sprawl, even if the port – the largest in France after Marseille – does take up half the Seine estuary, extending way beyond the town. The city was originally built in 1517 to replace the ancient ports of Harfleur and Honfleur, then silting up. Under the simple name of Le Havre – "The Harbour", it became the principal trading post of France's northern coast, prospering especially during the American War of Independence and thereafter, importing cotton, sugar and tobacco. In the years before 1939, it was the European home of the great luxury liners such as the *Normandie*, *Île de France* and *France*.

Le Havre suffered heavier damage than any other port in Europe during World War II. Following its near-total destruction, it was rebuilt to the specifications of

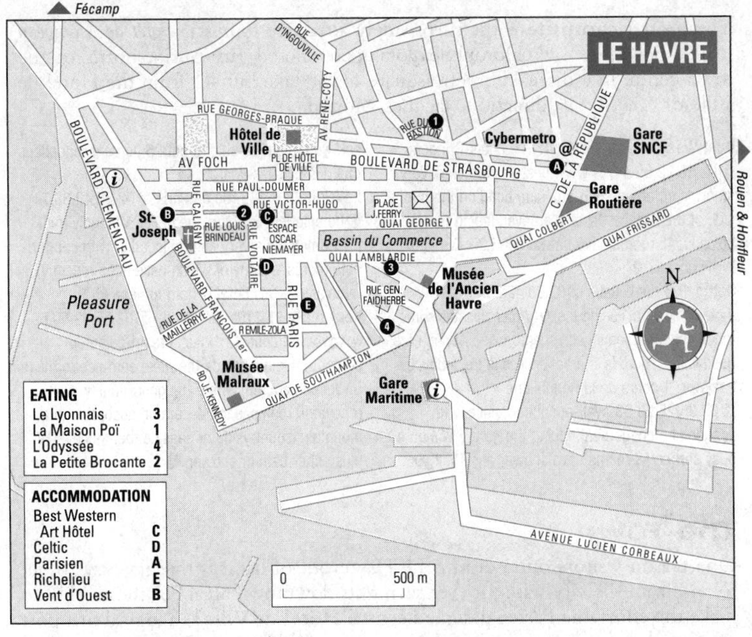

a single architect, **Auguste Perret**, between 1946 and 1964, an enterprise visibly circumscribed by constraints of time and money. The sheer sense of space can be exhilarating: the showpiece monuments have a winning self-confidence, and the few surviving relics of the old city have been sensitively integrated into the whole. Admittedly, the endless mundane residential blocks can be dispiriting, but with the sea visible at the end of almost every street and open public space and expanses of water at every turn, even those visitors who fail to agree with Perret's famous dictum that "concrete is beautiful" should enjoy a stroll around his city.

Arrival and information

P&O having discontinued its service, **ferries** to Le Havre have dwindled to just one sailing daily from either England or Ireland. Operated from Portsmouth by LD Lines (Ⓣ08.25.30.43.04, Ⓦwww.ldlines.co.uk), these arrive at the **Terminal de Grande Bretagne**, not far from the train and bus stations in the Bassin de la Citadelle (Ⓣ08.25.01.30.13).

Le Havre's rather inconspicuous and not very central **tourist office** is on the main seafront drag, at 186 bd Clemenceau (May–Oct Mon–Sat 9am–7pm, Sun 10am–12.30pm & 2.30–6pm; Nov–April Mon–Fri 9am–6.30pm, Sat 9am–12.30pm & 2–6.30pm, Sun 10am–1pm; Ⓣ02.32.74.04.04, Ⓦwww.lehavretourisme.com). The **post office** at 62 rue Jules-Siegfried (Mon–Fri 8am–7pm, Sat 8am–noon) offers **Internet** access, as does Cybermetro, facing the **gare SNCF** at 15 cours de la République (Mon–Sat 7am–midnight; Ⓣ02.32.73.04.28).

Accommodation

Le Havre holds two main concentrations of **hotels**: one group faces the *gare SNCF*, while most of the rest lie within walking distance of the ferry terminal.

The nearest **campsite** is the surprisingly attractive four-star *Forêt de Montgeon* (ⓣ02.35.46.48.84, ⓔchlorophile@orange.fr; closed Jan–April), north of the town centre in a three-kilometre square forest; take bus #1 from the Hôtel de Ville or *gare SNCF*, direction "Jacques-Monod".

Best Western Art Hôtel 147 rue Louis-Brindeau ⓣ02.35.22.69.44, ⓦwww.bestwestern.com. Very smart, comfortable non-smoking hotel on the north side of the Espace Oscar Niemeyer, facing the Volcano. All rooms have flat-screen LCD TVs and Wi-Fi access. ❻

Celtic 106 rue Voltaire ⓣ02.35.42.39.77, ⓦwww.hotelceltic.com. Facing the *Art Hôtel*, this has some much cheaper rooms (with shared toilets), which are good value. There is Internet access in the lobby. ❷

Parisien 1 cours de la République ⓣ02.35.25.23.83. Well-appointed place, with congenial management, facing the *gare SNCF* on a busy corner. All rooms have shower and TV. If you ask, you might be able to get 25 percent reductions on Fri & Sat Dec–March. ❸

Le Richelieu 135 rue de Paris ⓣ02.35.42.38.71, ⓔhotel.lerichelieu@orange.fr. For a friendly mid-priced hotel in a very central location with comfortable rooms – many of which have been recently renovated – this hotel is hard to beat. ❸

Vent d'Ouest 4 rue de Caligny ⓣ02.35.42.50.69, ⓦwww.ventdouest.fr. Plain, cream-coloured cement building, beside the main entrance to the St-Joseph church, where the good-quality, well-renovated rooms, each decorated according to a mountain, countryside or seaside theme, have TV plus either bath or shower. ❼

The Town

One reason visitors often dismiss Le Havre out of hand is that it's easy to get to and from the city without ever seeing its downtown area. For those who do make the effort, the Perret-designed central **Hôtel de Ville** is a logical first port of call, a long, low, flat-roofed building topped by a seventeen-storey concrete tower. Surrounded by pergola walkways, flower beds and flowing water from an array of fountains, it's an attractive, lively place with a high-tech feel, and is often the venue for imaginative exhibitions.

Perret's other major creation, clearly visible southwest of the town hall, is the **church of St-Joseph**, built on a cross of which all four arms are equally short. From the outside it's a plain mass of speckled concrete, the main doors thrown open to hint at dark interior spaces within. When you get inside it all makes sense: the altar is right in the centre, with the hundred-metre bell tower rising directly above it. Very simple patterns of stained glass, all around the church and right the way up the tower, create a bright interplay of coloured light, focusing on the altar.

Le Havre's boldest specimen of modern architecture is even newer – the cultural centre known as the **Volcano** (or less reverentially as the "yoghurt pot"), dominating the Espace Oscar Niemeyer. Niemeyer, a Brazilian architect, is best known for overseeing the construction of Brasilia, and was still hard at work – at the age of 98 – when this book when to press. He designed this slightly asymmetrical smooth gleaming white cone during the 1970s; it's cut off abruptly just above the level of the surrounding buildings, so that its curving planes are undisturbed by doors or windows.

The **Bassin du Commerce**, which stretches away from the complex, is of minimal commercial significance. Kayaks and rowing boats can be rented to explore its regular contours, and a couple of larger boats are moored permanently to serve as clubs or restaurants – it's all disconcertingly quiet, serving mainly as an appropriate stretch of water for the graceful white footbridge of the Passarelle du Commerce to cross.

Overlooking the harbour entrance, the modern **Musée Malraux & Ancien Havre** (Mon & Wed–Fri 11am–6pm, Sat & Sun 11am–7pm; €5) ranks among the best-designed art galleries in France, making full use of natural light to display an enjoyable assortment of nineteenth- and twentieth-century French paintings. Its principal highlights are over two hundred canvases by Eugène Boudin, including greyish landscapes produced all along the Norman coastline with views of Trouville, Honfleur and Étretat, as well as an entire wall of miniature cows and a lovely set of works by Raoul Dufy (1877–1953), which make Le Havre seem positively radiant, whatever the weather outside.

If you have the time to spare, you might like to see what old Le Havre looked like in the prewar days when Jean-Paul Sartre wrote *La Nausée* here. He taught philosophy for five years during the 1930s in a local school, and his almost transcendent disgust with the place cannot obscure the fascination he felt in exploring the seedy dockside quarter of St-François, in those spare moments when he wasn't visiting Simone de Beauvoir in Rouen. Little survives of the city Sartre knew, but pictures and artefacts gathered from the rubble are on display in one of the few buildings that escaped World War II intact, the **Musée de l'Ancien Havre** at 1 rue Jérôme-Bellarmato, just south of the Bassin du Commerce (Wed–Sun 10am–noon & 2–6pm; €1.50).

Eating and drinking

Few of the **restaurants** in Le Havre are worth making a fuss about. There are, however, lots of **bars**, **cafés** and **brasseries** around the *gare SNCF*, and all sorts of crêperies and ethnic alternatives in the backstreets of the St-François district. If you're shopping for food to take home, try the central **market**, just west of place Gambetta, or two Auchan **hypermarkets** (both Mon–Sat 8.30am–10pm): the larger, at the Mont Gaillard Centre Commercial, is reached by following cours de la République beyond the *gare SNCF*; the other, at Montivilliers, is signposted off the Tancarville road.

Le Lyonnais 7–9 rue de Bretagne ⓣ02.35.22.07.31. Small, cosy restaurant with chequered tablecloths and an English-speaking owner (hence the menu translated into English). The house speciality is baked fish, though dishes from Lyon, such as *andouillettes*, are also available on menus from €12.50 for lunch, €16 for dinner. Closed Sun.

La Maison Poï 25 rue du Bastion ⓣ02.35.22.99.45. Trendy, Parisian-style "café-brunch" place where fixed menus are replaced by *poïchonas de Poï* – fried snacks equivalent to tapas – and some good salads for around €12. It's also a good place for an evening. Closed Sun & Mon. In summer, another branch on the Promenade de la Plage, facing the beach, is open daily until 2am.

L'Odyssée 41 rue Général-Faidherbe ⓣ02.35.21.31.42. First-rate seafood restaurant close to the ferry terminal in the old town, serving a reliable €21 weekday lunch menu and a more adventurous €27 dinner option. Closed Sat lunch, Sun eve, Mon & first three weeks in Aug.

La Petite Brocante 75 rue Louis-Brindeau ⓣ02.35.21.42.20. Lively central bistro, where the set menus are a little pricey at €25 and up. There's always a good-value *plat du jour*, though, as often as not fresh fish. Closed Sun & first three weeks in Aug.

Along the Seine to Rouen

Until relatively recently, no bridges crossed the Seine any lower than Rouen, which made the river an all but impassable barrier for motorists heading between Upper and Lower Normandy. Since 1995, however, the enormous **Pont de Normandie** has spanned the rivermouth, enabling motorists to zip across from Le Havre to Honfleur (for a hefty €5 toll), while further inland the immense **Tancarville** suspension bridge and magnificent **Pont de Brotonne**, just upstream from Caudebec, offer alternative routes across the river. If Rouen is your destination from Le Havre, however, it makes much more sense to stick to the north bank of the river. A succession of quiet roads follow the Seine's every loop, leading through sleepy towns such as **Caudebec-en-Caux** and past intriguing ruins like the abbey of **Jumièges**.

Caudebec-en-Caux

The first town of any size on the right bank of the Seine is **CAUDEBEC-EN-CAUX**. Most traces of its long past were destroyed by fire in the last war, after which it was rebuilt. The damage – and previous local history – is recorded in the thirteenth-century **Maison des Templiers**, one of the few buildings to be spared (hours variable: notionally summer Wed & Fri 3–6pm, Sat 10am–12.30pm & 3.30–6.30pm; €5). A more specific and contemporary look at the role of the Seine in Norman history – the river's tidal swell still threatens at this narrow point to swamp unwary promenaders – is taken by the **Musée de la Marine de Seine**, avenue Winston-Churchill (daily: April–Sept 2–6.30pm; Oct–March 2–5.30pm; €3.25). A **market** has been held every Saturday since 1390 in the main square.

Caudebec's **tourist office** is slightly south of the centre, in place Charles-de-Gaulle (April–Nov daily 10am–12.30pm & 1.30–6.30pm; Dec–March Mon–Sat 3–6pm, Sun 10am–noon & 3–6pm; ⓣ02.32.70.46.32, ⓦwww.caudebec-en-caux.com). Two indistinguishable Logis de France face the river side by side from quai Guilbaud, with similar room rates: the *Normotel La Marine* at no. 18 (ⓣ02.35.96.20.11, ⓦwww.normotel-lamarine.fr; ❹; restaurant closed Fri eve, Sat lunch & Sun eve), and the *Normandie* at no. 19 (ⓣ02.35.96.25.11, ⓦwww.le-normandie.fr; ❹; restaurant closed Sun eve). There's also a riverside **campsite** to the north, the *Barre Y Va* (ⓣ02.35.96.26.38; closed Nov–March).

Abbaye de St-Wandrille

Just beyond the Pont de Brotonne as you continue towards Rouen, the medieval abbey in **ST-WANDRILLE** was founded – so legend has it – by a seventh-century count who, with his wife, renounced all earthly pleasures on the day of their wedding. The abbey's buildings make an attractive if curious architectural ensemble: part ruin, part restoration and, in the case of the main buildings, part transplant – a fifteenth-century barn brought in a few years ago from another Norman village miles away.

St-Wandrille remains an active monastery, home to fifty Benedictine monks who in addition to their spiritual duties turn their hands to money-making tasks that range from candle-making to running a reprographic studio; they also show visitors around the abbey on **guided tours** (Easter–Oct Mon & Wed–Sat 3.30pm, Sun 11.30am & 3.30pm; Nov–Easter Sun 11.30am; €3.50; ⓦwww.st-wandrille.com). You can wander through the **grounds** (daily 5.15am–1pm & 2–9.15pm) for no charge, and you can also listen to the monks' **Gregorian chanting** in their new church (Mon–Sat 5.25am, 7.30am, 9.45am, 12.45pm, 2.15pm, 5.30pm & 8.35pm; Sun 5.25am, 7.30am, 10am, 12.45pm, 2.30pm, 5pm & 8.35pm).

There's a crêperie opposite the abbey, and, a few doors along in the place de l'Église, the more upmarket *Deux Coronnes* **restaurant** (ⓣ02.35.96.11.44; closed Sun evening & Mon), a seventeenth-century inn – half-timbered, naturally – serving delicious menus priced at €15 for lunch and €25 for dinner.

Abbaye de Jumièges

In the next loop of the Seine, 12km on from St-Wandrille, comes the highlight of the Seine valley: the majestic **abbey** in **JUMIÈGES** (mid-April to June and first fortnight of Sept Mon–Fri 9.30am–1pm & 2.30–6.30pm, Sat & Sun 9.30am–6.30pm; July Mon–Fri & Sun 9.30am–6.30pm, Sat 9.30am–6.30pm & 10.30pm–12.30am; Aug Mon–Fri & Sun 9.30am–6.30pm, Sat 9.30am–6.30pm & 9.30pm–12.30am; mid-Sept to mid-April daily 9.30am–1pm & 2.30–5.30pm; €5), said to have been founded by St Philibert in 654 AD, just five years after St-Wandrille. A haunting ruin, the abbey was burned by marauding Vikings in 841, rebuilt a century later, then destroyed again – as a deliberate act – during the Revolution. Its main surviving outline, as far as it can still be discerned, dates from the eleventh century – William the Conqueror himself attended its re-consecration in 1067. The twin towers, 52m high, are still standing, as is one arch of the roofless nave, while a one-sided yew tree stands in the centre of what were once the cloisters. The *Auberge des Ruines*, across from the abbey at 17 place de la Mairie (ⓣ02.35.37.24.05; closed Sun eve, Tues eve, Wed and over Christmas and New Year), is a truly superb **restaurant**, with outdoor seating on a shaded terrace. Its menus start at €18 for lunch and go up to €55 for a gastronomic evening feast.

Rouen

ROUEN, the capital of Upper Normandy, is one of France's most ancient cities. Standing on the site of Roman Rotomagus, the lowest point on the river then capable of being bridged, it was laid out by the Viking Rollo shortly after he became Duke of Normandy in 911. Captured by the English in 1419, it was the stage in 1431 for the trial and execution of Joan of Arc, and returned to French control in 1449.

Over the centuries, Rouen has suffered repeated devastation; there were 45 major fires in the first half of the thirteenth century alone. It has had to be almost entirely rebuilt during the last sixty years, and now you could spend a whole day wandering around the city without realizing that the Seine ran through its centre. Wartime bombs destroyed all its bridges, the area between the cathedral and the *quais*, and much of the industrial quarter. The riverside area has never been adequately restored, and what you might expect to be the most beautiful part of the city is in fact something of an abomination.

Enormous sums have, however, been lavished on an upmarket restoration job on the streets a few hundred metres north of the river, which turned the centre into the closest approximation to a medieval city that modern imaginations could come up with. The suggestion that for historical authenticity the houses should be painted in bright, clashing colours was not deemed appropriate, but so far as it goes, the whole of this inner core can be very seductive, and its churches are impressive by any standards.

Outside the renovated quarters, things are rather different. While Rouen proper is home to a population of 100,000, the metropolitan area holds four times that number. The city spreads deep into the loop of the Seine, with its docks and industrial infrastructure stretching endlessly away to the south, and it is increasingly expanding up into the hills to the north as well. As the nearest point that large container ships can get to Paris, this remains the fourth-largest port in the country; it's also the biggest exporter of foodstuffs in the European Union, and the biggest in the world for wheat.

Arrival

Rouen is currently a difficult and unpleasant city to **drive** into, with all traffic funnelled into the hideous multi-lane highways that line both banks of the

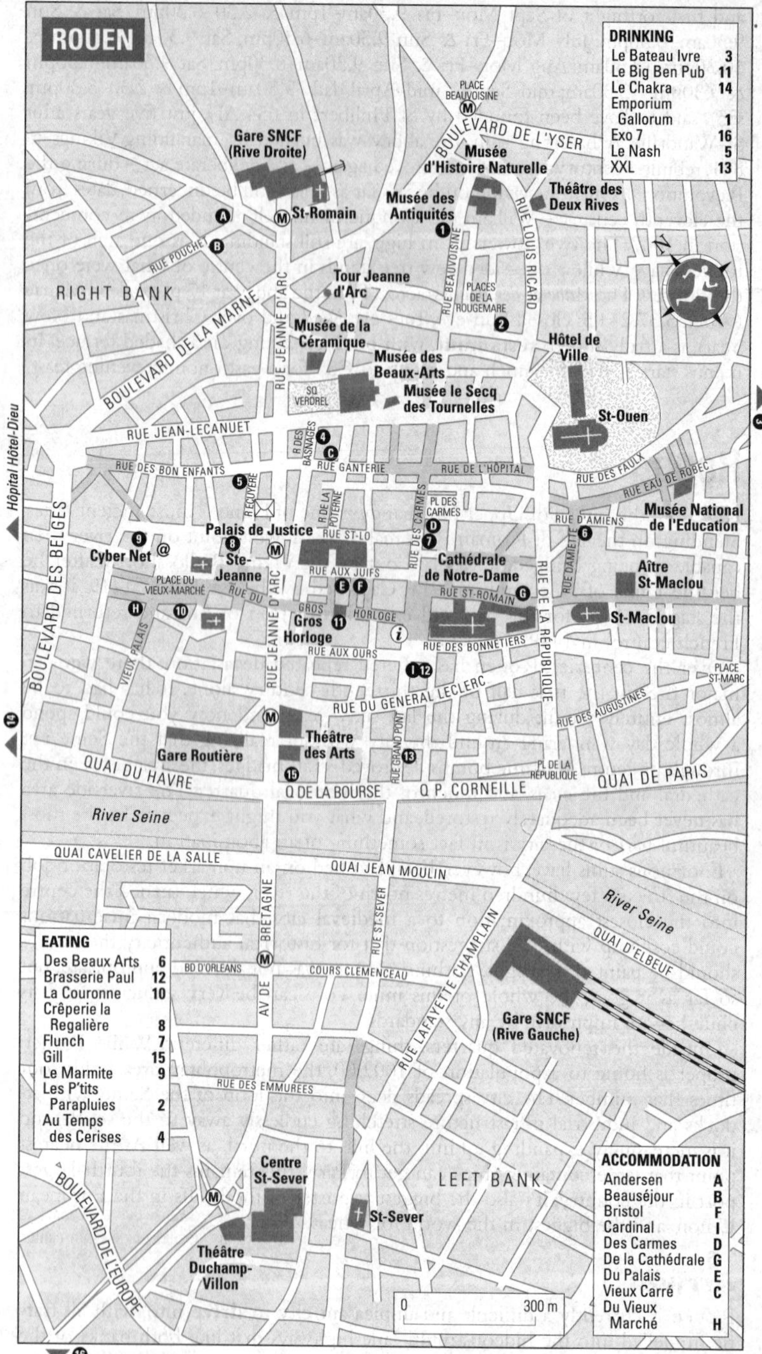
ROUEN
DRINKING
Le Bateau Ivre 3
Le Big Ben Pub 11
Le Chakra 14
Emporium Gallorum 1
Exo 7 16
Le Nash 5
XXL 13
EATING
Des Beaux Arts 6
Brasserie Paul 12
La Couronne 10
Crêperie la Regalière 8
Flunch 7
Gill 15
Le Marmite 9
Les P'tits Parapluies 2
Au Temps des Cerises 4
ACCOMMODATION
Andersen A
Beauséjour B
Bristol F
Cardinal I
Des Carmes D
De la Cathédrale G
Du Palais E
Vieux Carré C
Du Vieux Marché H
Gare SNCF (Rive Droite)
St-Romain
Place Beauvoisine
Boulevard de l'Yser
Musée d'Histoire Naturelle
Musée des Antiquités
Théatre des Deux Rives
Rue Louis Ricard
Rue Beauvoisine
Rue Pouchet
Right Bank
Tour Jeanne d'Arc
Places de la Rougemare
Boulevard de la Marne
Rue Jeanne d'Arc
Musée de la Céramique
Musée des Beaux-Arts
Musée le Secq des Tournelles
Sq Verdrel
Hôtel de Ville
St-Ouen
Rue Jean-Lecanuet
R des Basnages
Rue Ganterie
Rue de l'Hôpital
Rue des Faulx
Rue Eau de Robec
Rue des Bon Enfants
Rue Écuyère
R de la Poterne
Pl des Carmes
Rue des Carmes
Rue d'Amiens
Musée National de l'Education
Hôpital Hôtel-Dieu
Boulevard des Belges
Palais de Justice
Rue St-Lo
Cyber Net
Ste-Jeanne
Place du Vieux-Marché
Cathédrale de Notre-Dame
Rue Damiette
Aître St-Maclou
Rue aux Juifs
Rue du Gros Horloge
Rue St-Romain
Rue de la République
St-Maclou
Gros Horloge
Vieux Palais
Rue des Bonnetiers
Rue aux Ours
Place St-Marc
Rue du General Leclerc
Rue des Augustines
Théatre des Arts
Gare Routière
Rue Grand Pont
Pl de la République
Quai du Havre
Q de la Bourse
Q P. Corneille
Quai de Paris
River Seine
Quai Cavelier de la Salle
Quai Jean Moulin
Rue St-Sever
Av de Bretagne
Rue Lafayette Champlain
Quai d'Elbeuf
Bd d'Orleans
Cours Clemenceau
Gare SNCF (Rive Gauche)
Rue des Emmurees
Centre St-Sever
Left Bank
Boulevard de l'Europe
St-Sever
Théatre Duchamp-Villon
0
300 m

river. The city's sixth and largest bridge across the Seine, designed to connect the motorways just west of the city, was due to be completed in 2007 and may ease things considerably. Many of the central streets, north of the river, have in any case been pedestrianized, so it's best to park as soon as you can – there are plenty of central underground **car parks**, especially near the cathedral and the place du Vieux-Marché – and explore the city on foot.

The main *gare SNCF*, Gare Rive Droite, stands at the north end of rue Jeanne-d'Arc. It's connected to the centre by a **métro** system, which follows the line of the rue Jeanne-d'Arc, making two stops before it resurfaces to cross the river by bridge. Individual journeys cost €1.30 and a book is €10.40. All **buses** from the *gare SNCF* except #2A run down rue Jeanne-d'Arc to the centre, which takes five minutes. From the fifth stop, the "Théâtre des Arts" by the river, the **gare routière** is one block west in rue des Charettes, tucked away behind the riverfront buildings (ⓣ02.35.52.92.00).

Information

Rouen's **tourist office** stands opposite the cathedral at 25 place de la Cathédrale (May–Sept Mon–Sat 9am–7pm, Sun 9.30am–12.30pm & 2–6pm; Oct–April Mon–Sat 9am–6pm, Sun 10am–1pm; ⓣ02.32.08.32.40, ⓦwww.rouentourisme.com). It serves as the starting point for daily two-hour, French-language **walking tours** of the city, departing at 2pm, while a tour in English leaves on Fridays at 5pm. Both cost €6.50. For more sedate visitors, a motorized **petit train** makes a forty-minute-loop tour from the tourist office at regular intervals (April–Oct daily 10am, 11am and hourly 2–5pm; €6).

You can rent **bicycles** from Rouen Cycles, 45 rue St-Éloi (Tues–Sat 9am–noon & 2–7pm; ⓣ02.35.71.34.30). The **post office** is at 45 rue Jeanne-d'Arc, in the centre of town (Mon–Fri 8am–7pm, Sat 8am–noon). For **Internet** access, head to the café-style *Cyber Net*, 47 place du Vieux-Marché (daily 10am–11pm).

Accommodation

With over three thousand **hotel** rooms in town, there should be no difficulty in finding appropriate accommodation in Rouen, even at the busiest times. Few of the hotels have restaurants, chiefly because there's such a wide choice of places to eat all over town.

Hotels

Andersen 4 rue Pouchet ⓣ02.35.71.88.51, ⓦwww.hotelandersen.com. Very friendly place with plenty of character, a short walk to the right as you come out from the Gare Rive Droite, set behind a small gravel yard. Rooms are large, light and colourful – the cheaper ones share showers. ❸

Beauséjour 9 rue Pouchet ⓣ02.35.71.93.47, ⓦwww.hotel-beausejour.com. Good-value place near the station (turn right as you come out), though, beyond the orange facade and nice garden courtyard, the rooms are on the plain side. Almost all have TV, phone and en-suite facilities; there's one cheaper single without its own shower. Closed second half of July. ❷

Bristol 45 rue aux Juifs ⓣ02.35.71.54.21. Clean, pretty nine-room hotel, above its own little brasserie (ⓣ02.35.71.66.35) in a half-timbered house overlooking the Palais de Justice. All rooms are en suite, and have TV. Closed Sun, plus 3 weeks in Aug. ❷

Cardinal 1 place de la Cathédrale ⓣ02.35.70.24.42, ⓦwww.cardinal-hotel.fr. Very well-priced hotel in a stunning location facing the cathedral; the rooms have excellent en-suite facilities (the higher ones have cathedral-view balconies), and ample buffet breakfasts are served for €7. ❹

Des Carmes 33 place des Carmes ⓣ02.35.71.92.31, ⓦwww.hoteldescarmes.fr.st. Twelve-room hotel in a beautiful nineteenth-century house on a quiet central square, a short walk north from the cathedral. The rooms are on the small side, but have benefited from recent renovation. "Normandy" breakfasts are €6.90. ❸

De la Cathédrale 12 rue St-Romain ⓣ02.35.71.57.95, ⓦwww.hotel-de-la-cathedrale.fr. Attractive, conveniently located hotel, alongside the cathedral and archbishop's palace, though the plain rooms themselves don't live up to the appealing facade and quaint old flower-filled courtyard. Set in a quiet pedestrianized street – it costs €5 to use the public car park nearby – lined with fourteenth-century timber-framed houses. Buffet breakfasts €7.50. ❹

Du Palais 12 rue du Tambour ⓣ02.35.71.41.40. Very inexpensive central hotel, tucked away just north of the Gros Horloge, offering stylish though not fancy rooms at unbeatable prices. All rooms have showers, while an in-room toilet costs just €2 extra. ❷

Vieux Carré 34 rue Ganterie ⓣ02.35.71.67.70, ⓦwww.vieux-carre.fr. Small, pleasant rooms in a half-timbered house in a pedestrianized central street. The nice little tea shop below doubles as the breakfast room. ❹

Du Vieux Marché 15 rue de la Pie ⓣ02.35.71.00.88, ⓦwww.hotelduvieuxmarche.com. Very modern place, set around a venerable old courtyard, just a few steps from the place du Vieux-Marché. A high standard of comfort has quickly made this the most popular upmarket hotel in town. ❼

Campsites

Camping de l'Aubette 23 Vert Buisson in St-Léger du Bourg-Denis ⓣ02.35.08.47.69. Basic site in a more rural, but much less accessible setting than the *Camping municipal*, 4km east of town on bus route #8.

Camping municipal rue Jules-Ferry in Déville-lès-Rouen ⓣ02.35.74.07.59. Surprisingly small site, 4km northwest of town, that's geared towards caravans rather than tents; bus #2.

The Town

Rouen has traditionally spent a bigger slice of its civic budget on monuments than any other provincial town, which maddens many a Rouennais. As a tourist, however, your one complaint may be the lack of time to visit them all.

The place du Vieux-Marché to the cathedral

The obvious place to start sightseeing is the **place du Vieux-Marché**, where a small plaque and a huge cross (nearly 20m high) mark the spot on which Joan of Arc (see box opposite) was burnt to death on May 30, 1431. A modern memorial **church** to the saint was dedicated in the square in 1979 (Mon–Sat 10am–12.30pm & 2–6pm, Sun 2–6pm): it's a wacky, spiky-looking thing and an architectural triumph, incorporating some sixteenth-century stained glass and said to represent either an upturned boat or the flames that consumed Joan. It forms part of an ensemble that manages to incorporate a covered food market in similar style. The theme of the church's fish-shaped windows is continued in the scaly tiles that adorn its roof, which is elongated to form a walkway across the square. The outline of its vanished predecessor's foundations is visible on the adjacent lawns, which also mark the precise spot of Joan's martyrdom. The square itself is surrounded by fine old brown-and-white half-timbered houses, many of those on the south side now serving as restaurants. The private **Musée Jeanne d'Arc**, tucked in among them in an ancient cellar in the back of a gift shop, draws large crowds to its collection of tawdry waxworks and facsimile manuscripts (daily: mid-April to mid-Sept 9.30am–7pm; mid-Sept to mid-April 10am–noon & 2–6.30pm; €5).

From place du Vieux-Marché, **rue du Gros-Horloge** leads east towards the cathedral. Just across the intersection with rue Jeanne-d'Arc you come to the **Gros Horloge** itself, due – after ten years of renovation – to be unveiled in 2007. A colourful one-handed clock, it used to be on the adjacent Gothic **belfry** until it was moved down by popular demand in 1529, so that people could see it better.

Despite the addition of all sorts of different towers, spires and vertical extensions, the **Cathédrale de Notre-Dame** (Mon 2–7pm, Tues–Sat 7.30am–7pm, Sun 8am–6pm) remains at heart the Gothic masterpiece that was built in the

Joan of Arc

When the 17-year-old peasant girl known to history as **Joan of Arc** (Jeanne d'Arc in French) arrived at the French court early in 1429, the Hundred Years War had already dragged on for over ninety years. Most of northern France was in the grip of an Anglo-Burgundian alliance, but Joan, who had been hearing voices since 1425, was certain she could save the country, and came to present her case to the as-yet-uncrowned Dauphin. Partly through recognizing him despite a simple disguise he wore to fool her at their first meeting, she convinced him of her divine guidance; and after a remarkable three-week examination by a tribunal of the French *parlement*, she went on to secure command of the armies of France. In a whirlwind **campaign**, which culminated in the raising of the siege of Orléans on May 8, 1429, she broke the English hold on the Loire Valley. She then escorted the Dauphin deep into enemy territory so that, in accordance with ancient tradition, he could be crowned King Charles VII of France in the cathedral at Reims, on July 17.

Within a year of her greatest triumph, Joan was **captured** by the Burgundian army at Compiègne in May 1430, and held to ransom. Chivalry dictated that any offer of payment from the vacillating Charles must be accepted, but in the absence of such an offer Joan was handed over to the English for 10,000 ducats. On Christmas Day 1430, she was imprisoned in the château of Philippe-Auguste at Rouen.

Charged with heresy, on account of her "false and diabolical" visions and refusal not to wear men's clothing, Joan was put on trial for her life on February 21, 1431. For three months, a changing panel of 131 assessors – only eight of whom were English-born – heard the evidence against her. Condemned, inevitably, to death, Joan recanted on the scaffold in St-Ouen cemetery on May 24, and her sentence was commuted to life imprisonment. The presiding judge, Bishop Pierre Cauchon of Beauvais, reassured disappointed English representatives that "we will get her yet". The next Sunday, Joan was tricked into breaking her vow and putting on male clothing, and taken to the archbishop's chapel in rue St-Romain to be condemned to death for the second time. On May 30, 1431, she was burned at the stake in the place du Vieux-Marché; her ashes, together with her unburned heart, were thrown into the Seine.

Joan passed into legend, until the discovery and publication of the full transcript of her trial in the 1840s. The forbearance and devout humility she displayed throughout her ordeal added to her status as France's greatest religious heroine. She was canonized as recently as 1920, and soon afterwards became the country's patron saint.

twelfth and thirteenth centuries. The west facade of the cathedral, intricately sculpted like the rest of the exterior, was Monet's subject for over thirty studies of changing light, which now hang in the Musée d'Orsay in Paris. Monet might not recognize it now, however – in the last few years, it's been scrubbed a gleaming white, free from the centuries of accreted dirt he so carefully recorded. In recent summers, the town has laid on a thirty-minute light show, **La Cathédrale de Monet aux Pixels** (daily: late June to mid-Sept 10.45pm; free), whereby colours inspired by Monet's cathedral paintings are projected onto the church's facade, transforming it quite magnificently into a series of giant Monet-esque canvases.

Inside the cathedral, the carvings of the misericords in the choir provide a study of fifteenth-century life – in secular scenes of work and habits along with the usual mythical beasts. The **ambulatory** and **crypt** – closed on Sundays and during services – hold the assorted tombs of various recumbent royalty, stretching back as far as Duke Rollo, who died "enfeebled by toil" in 933 AD, and the actual heart of Richard the Lionheart.

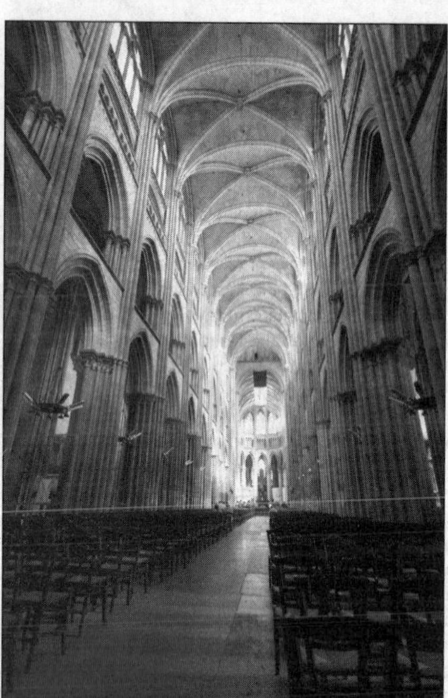

△ Rouen Cathedral

St-Ouen and around

The **church of St-Ouen**, next to the Hôtel de Ville (which itself occupies buildings that were once part of the abbey), is larger than the cathedral and has far less decoration, so from the outside there's nothing to diminish the instant impact of its vast Gothic proportions and the purity of its lines. Inside (mid-Jan to mid-March and Nov to mid-Dec Tues, Sat & Sun 10am–noon & 2–5pm; mid-March to Oct Tues–Sat 10am–12.15pm & 2–6pm, Sun 9am–12.15pm & 2–6pm), it holds some stunning fourteenth-century stained glass, though much was destroyed during the Revolution. The world that produced it – and, nearer the end of the era, the light and grace of the **church of St-Maclou** not far to the south – was one of mass death from the plague: thus the **Aître St-Maclou** immediately to the east, a cemetery for the victims, was an integral part of the St-Maclou complex (daily: mid-March to Oct 8am–8pm; Nov to mid-March 8am–7pm; entrance between 184 & 186 rue Martainville; free). It's now the tranquil garden courtyard of the Fine Arts school, but if you examine the one open lower storey of the surrounding buildings you'll discover the original deathly decorations and a mummified cat. In the square outside are several good antique bookshops, and a few art shops.

The **rue Eau de Robec**, which runs east from rue Damiette just south of St-Ouen, was described by one of Flaubert's characters in an earlier age as a "degraded little Venice". It's now a textbook example of how Rouen has been restored. Where once a shallow stream flowed beneath the raised doorsteps of venerable half-timbered houses, a thin trickle now makes its way along a stylized cement bed crossed by concrete walkways. In a fine old mansion at no. 185, the **Musée National de l'Éducation** (Mon & Wed–Fri 10am–12.30pm & 1.30–6pm, Sat & Sun 2–6pm; €3) tells the story of the last five centuries of schooling in France, with photos, paintings, ancient textbooks and a mocked-up schoolroom. Unless you read French well, however, it's unlikely to hold your interest, and you're better off heading north past the Hôtel de Ville to the **Musée des Antiquités**, which occupies a seventeenth-century convent on rue Beauvoisine (Mon & Wed–Sat 10am–12.15pm & 1.30–5.30pm, Sun 2–6pm; €3): its tapestries and medieval collection are particularly good.

The Musée des Beaux-Arts and around

Rouen's imposing **Musée des Beaux-Arts** commands the square Verdrel from just east of the central rue Jeanne-d'Arc (daily except Tues 10am–6pm; €3).

Even this grand edifice is not quite large enough to display some of its medieval tapestries, which trail inelegantly along the floor, but the collection as a whole is consistently absorbing. Unexpected highlights include dazzling Russian icons from the sixteenth century onwards, and an entertaining three-dimensional eighteenth-century *Nativity* from Naples. Many of the biggest names among the painters – Caravaggio (the centrepiece *Flagellation of Christ*), Velázquez, Rubens – tend to be represented by a single minor work, but there are several Modiglianis and a couple of Monets: *Rouen Cathedral* (1894), and the *Vue Générale de Rouen*. The central sculpture court, roofed over but very light, is dominated by a wonderful three-part mural of the course of the Seine from Paris to Le Havre, prepared by Raoul Dufy in 1937 for the Palais de Chaillot in Paris.

Rouen's history as a centre for *faïencerie*, or earthenware pottery, is recorded in the **Musée de la Céramique**, facing the Beaux-Arts from the north (daily except Tues 10am–1pm & 2–6pm; €2.30). A series of beautiful rooms, some of which incorporate sixteenth-century wood panelling rescued from a demolished nunnery of St-Amand, display specimens from the 1600s onwards. Assorted tiles and plates reflect the eighteenth-century craze for *chinoiserie*, although the genuine Chinese and Japanese pieces nearby possess a sophistication contemporary French craftsmen could only dream of emulating. The mood changes abruptly in the Revolutionary era, as witnessed by plates bearing slogans from both sides of the political fence.

Behind the Beaux-Arts, housed in the old, barely altered church of St-Laurent on rue Jacques-Villon, the **Musée Le Secq des Tournelles** (daily except Tues 10am–1pm & 2–6pm; €2.30) consists of a gloriously eccentric and uncategorizable collection of wrought-iron objects of all dates and descriptions, among them nutcrackers and door knockers, spiral staircases that lead nowhere and hideous implements of torture.

The Tour Jeanne d'Arc

The pencil-thin **Tour Jeanne d'Arc** (April–Sept Mon & Wed–Sat 10am–12.30pm & 2–6pm, Sun 2–6.30pm; Oct–March Mon & Wed–Sat 10am–12.30pm & 2–5pm, Sun 2–5.30pm; €1.50), a short way southeast of the *gare SNCF*, is all that remains of the castle of Philippe-Auguste, built in 1205 and scene of the imprisonment and trial of Joan of Arc. It served as the castle's keep and entrance-way, and was itself fully surrounded by a moat. It was not, however, Joan's actual prison – that was the Tour de la Pucelle, demolished in 1809 – while the trial took place first of all in the castle's St-Romain chapel, and then later in its great central hall, both of which were destroyed in 1590. The tall, sharp-pointed tower was bought by public subscription in 1860, and restored to its present state. After seeing a small collection of Joan-related memorabilia, you can climb a steep spiral staircase to the very top, but you can't see out over the city, let alone step outside into the open air.

Eating, drinking and nightlife

Unlike the hotels, which sometimes have cheaper weekend rates, Rouen's upmarket **restaurants** tend to charge more over weekends, when families eat out. The greatest concentration of restaurants is in place du Vieux-Marché, where there's a daily **food market**, while the area just north is full of Tunisian **takeaways**, **crêperies** and so forth. Some of Rouen's most agreeable **bars** are in the maze of streets between rue Thiers and place du Vieux-Marché. Incoming sailors used to head straight for this area of the city, and the small bars are still there even if the sailors aren't.

Restaurants

Des Beaux Arts 34 rue Damiette ⓣ02.35.70.17.15. Very good-value Algerian cuisine, on a pretty pedestrianized street north of St-Maclou church: couscous from €8 or tajine from €10, with all kinds of sausages and assorted meats. Closed Mon & Tues eve.

Brasserie Paul 1 place de la Cathédrale ⓣ02.35.71.86.07. The definitive address for Rouen's definitive bistro, an attractive *belle-époque* place with seating both indoors and on a terrace in full view of the cathedral. Daily lunch specials, such as the goats' cheese and smoked duck salad that was Simone de Beauvoir's favourite in the 1930s, cost around €11.

La Couronne 31 place du Vieux-Marché ⓣ02.35.71.40.90. Claiming to be the oldest *auberge* in France, serving food since 1345, this is definitely the eatery of choice on the place du Vieux-Marché. If you find the interior a little too stuffy and formal, there are a few tables on the square itself. Menus range from €23 for lunch and €29 or €45 for dinner.

Crêprie la Regalière 12 rue Massacre ⓣ02.35.15.33.33. This inexpensive but quality crêperie, with some outdoor seating just off the place du Vieux-Marché, is one of central Rouen's best bargains, with menus at €8 and €12. Closed Sun.

Flunch 60 rue des Carmes ⓣ02.35.71.81.81. Efficient, popular self-service on a street running north from the cathedral, with many fresh dishes, starters and desserts, and a €5.60 daily *formule*. Unlimited vegetables with any hot dish, or an all-you-can-eat salad for €4.40.

Gill 9 quai de la Bourse ⓣ02.35.71.16.14. Absolutely definitive French restaurant with specialities such as lobster grilled with asparagus and pigeon baked in puff pastry. Weekday lunch menus start at €40 (not bad value considering the quality), while the most expensive dinner menu will set you back €85. Closed Sun & Mon, plus three weeks in Aug.

Le Marmite 3 rue de Florence ⓣ02.35.71.75.55. Romantic little place just west of the place du Vieux-Marché, offering beautiful, elegantly presented gourmet dishes as part of well-priced menus at €25, €35 (featuring hot foie gras) and €50. Closed Sun eve, Mon, & Tues lunch.

Les P'tits Parapluies 46 rue Bourg l'Abbé, place de la Rougemare ⓣ02.35.88.55.26. Elegant, secluded half-timbered restaurant not far north of the Hôtel de Ville. Counting your calories is not really an option here; the trio of menus, some of which change weekly, start at €25 and include such delights as foie gras and oysters, and come with two glasses of wine. Closed Sat lunch, Sun eve & Mon.

Au Temps des Cerises 4–6 rue des Basnages ⓣ02.35.89.98.00. If you've come to Normandy for the cheeses, this trendy, if slightly overstyled restaurant is the place to get it all out of your system, with turkey breast in Camembert, goats' cheese crêpes and, above all, fondues of every description. Lunch menus from €13, dinners from €16. Closed Mon & Sat lunches & all Sun.

Bars and clubs

Le Bateau Ivre 17 rue des Sapins ⓣ02.35.70.09.05. This low-key but atmospheric hangout a long way northeast of the centre puts on a rock-oriented programme of music and performance, with an open-mic night on Thursdays. Tues & Wed 10pm–2am, Thurs–Sat 10pm–4am. Closed Sun, Mon & all Aug.

Big Ben Pub 95 rue du Gros-Horloge ⓣ02.35.88.44.50. Right under the big clock, this busy pub in a splendid half-timbered house has the air of a medieval tavern, even if it does feature karaoke on Thurs, Fri and Sat evenings (except during summer). There are two floors inside and some tables on the busy street outside. Mon 6pm–2am, Tues–Sat noon–2am.

Le Chakra 4 bd Ferdinand-de-Lesseps ⓣ02.32.10.12.02. Busy, sweaty club beside the Seine, a couple of kilometres west of the centre, where big-name DJs play house and techno to a predominantly young crowd. Fri 11pm–4am, Sat 5–9pm & 11pm–4am, Sun 5–9pm.

Emporium Gallorum 151 rue Beauvoisine ⓣ02.35.71.76.95. Busy half-timbered bar, a short walk north of the centre, that's especially popular with students, which often puts on small-scale gigs and theatrical productions. Tues & Wed 8pm–2am, Thurs–Sat 6pm–4am. Closed Aug.

Exo 7 13 place des Chartreux ⓣ02.35.03.32.30, ⓦwww.exo7.net. Traditionally the centre of Rouen's heavy-rock scene, a long way south of the centre, the *Exo 7* (pronounced "Exocet") is nowadays a bit more eclectic, with varied gigs and dance nights as well. Fri & Sat 11pm–5am. Closed first 3 weeks of Aug.

Le Nash 97 rue Écuyère ⓣ02.35.98.25.24. Relaxed bar popular with locals. With its moody lighting and zebra-striped upholstery, the interior has a lounge-like feel, while the outdoor terrace is much more akin to a classic French café and serves light snacks. Music ranges from ambient to Latin. Mon–Fri 11.30am–2pm & 6pm–2am, Sat 6pm–2am.

XXL 25–27 rue de la Savonnerie ⓣ02.35.88.84.00. Well-known gay (male) bar near the river, just south of the cathedral, which has regular theme nights and a small dance floor in the basement. Although unambiguously geared to men looking for men, women will not be turned away. Tues & Wed 9pm–2am, Thurs–Sat 9pm–4am, Sun 10pm–2am.

Entertainment

As you would expect in a conurbation of 400,000, there's always plenty going on in Rouen, from classical concerts in churches to alternative events in community and commercial centres. The city has several **theatres**, which mainly work to winter seasons. The most highbrow venue for big spectacles is the **Théâtre des Arts**, 7 rue de Dr-Rambert (Tues–Sat 1–8pm; ⓣ08.10.81.11.16, ⓦwww.operaderouen.com), which puts on opera, ballet and concerts. The more adventurous repertory company of the **Théâtre des Deux Rives** (ⓣ02.35.70.22.82), based opposite the Antiquités museum at the junction of rue Louis-Ricard and rue de Joyeuse, presents work by playwrights such as Beaumarchais, Shakespeare, Beckett and Gorky.

Major **concerts** often take place in the **Théâtre Duchamp-Villon** in the St-Sever complex (ⓣ02.32.18.28.10, ⓦwww.theatreduchampvillon.com), accessible by métro (stop "St-Sever"). Also south of the river and on the métro (direction "Georges Braque"), albeit a long way further out, is the **Théâtre Charles Dullin**, allée des Arcades, Grand Quévilly (ⓣ02.35.69.51.18, ⓦwww.theatre-charles-dullin.com). There are two multi-screen **cinemas** just north of the river (at 28 rue de la République and 75 rue du Général-Leclerc, and another to the south in the St-Sever complex.

Upstream from Rouen

Upstream from Rouen towards Paris, high cliffs on the north bank of the Seine imitate the coast, looking down on waves of green and scattered river islands. By the time you reach **Les Andelys**, 25km southeast of Rouen, you're within 100km of the capital, meaning that accommodation and eating prices tend to be geared towards affluent weekend and day-trippers. Large country estates abound in this agreeable countryside, and public transport is minimal. However, infrequent buses run from Rouen to Les Andelys, and trains from Rouen call at **Vernon**, just across the river from one of Normandy's most visited tourist attractions, the village of **Giverny**.

Les Andelys

The most dramatic sight anywhere along the Seine has to be Richard the Lionheart's **Château Gaillard**, perched high above **LES ANDELYS**. Constructed in a position of impregnable power, it looked down over any movement on the river at the frontier of the English king's domains. Built in less than a year (1196–97), the castle might have survived intact had Henri IV not ordered its destruction in 1603 in the aftermath of the War of Religion between Catholics and Protestants. As it is, the dominant outline remains. Visits to the château are permitted between mid-March and mid-November only (daily except Tues 10am–1pm & 2–6pm; €3). On foot, you can make the steep climb up via a path that leads off rue Richard-Coeur-de-Lion in Petit Andely. The only route for motorists is extraordinarily convoluted, following a long-winded one-way system that starts opposite the church in Grand Andely.

The **tourist office** for Les Andelys is in Petit Andely, at 24 rue Philippe-Auguste (Oct–May Mon–Fri 2–6pm, Sat & Sun 10am–noon & 2–5pm; June–Sept Mon–Fri 10am–noon & 2–6pm, Sat & Sun 10am–noon & 2–7pm; ⓣ02.32.54.41.93, ⓦwww.ville-andelys.fr). One of the nicest **hotels** is the eighteenth-century *Chaîne d'Or*, on the banks of the Seine opposite the thirteenth-century church of St-Sauveur at 27 rue Grande (ⓣ02.32.54.00.31, ⓦwww.hotel-lachainedor.com; ❺; restaurant closed in winter all Mon & Tues lunch). Some of the gorgeous large modernized rooms overlook the river and are undeniably well priced; the one drawback is that though the food in its **restaurant** is utterly wonderful, the very cheapest dinner menu costs €44, and even breakfast costs €14. There's also a lovely riverside **campsite**, far below the château, the *Île des Trois Rois* (ⓣ02.32.54.23.79, ⓦwww.camping-troisrois.fr; closed mid-Nov to mid-March).

Giverny

Roughly 15km south of the ancient fortifications of Les Andelys, on the north bank of the river, you come to **Monet's house and gardens** – complete with water-lily pond – at **GIVERNY** (gardens and house April–Oct Tues–Sun 9.30am–6pm; last entrance 5.30pm, no advance sales; ⓣ02.32.51.28.21, ⓦwww.fondation-monet.com; €5.50 house and gardens, €4 gardens only). Monet lived here from 1883 till his death in 1926, and the gardens that he laid out were considered by many of his friends to be his masterpiece. In fact art lovers who make the pilgrimage here tend to be outnumbered by garden enthusiasts. None of Monet's original paintings is on display – most are in the Orangerie and Musée d'Orsay in Paris – whereas the gardens are still lovingly tended in all their glory.

You enter the house through the huge studio, built in 1915, where Monet painted the last and largest of his canvases depicting water lilies (in French, *nymphéas*). It now serves as a well-stocked book and gift shop. A gravel footpath leads to the actual house, a long two-storey structure facing down to the river. Monet's bedroom is bedecked with family photos and paintings by friends and family, while his salon holds further washed-out reproductions. All other main rooms are crammed floor-to-ceiling with his collection of Japanese prints, especially works by Hokusai and Hiroshige. Most of the original furnishings are gone, but you do get a real sense of how the dining room used to be, with all its walls and fittings painted a glorious bright yellow; Monet designed his own yellow crockery to harmonize with the surroundings. By contrast, the stairs and upstairs rooms are a pale blue.

Colourful flower gardens, with trellised walkways and shady bowers, stretch down from the house. At the bottom, a dank underpass beneath the road leads to the *jardin d'eau*, focused around the narrow **water-lily pond**. Footpaths around the perimeter and arching Japanese footbridges offer differing views of the water lilies themselves, nurtured by gardeners in rowing boats. May and June, when the rhododendrons flower around the pond and the wisteria that winds over the Japanese bridge is in bloom, are the best times to visit. Whenever you come, however, you'll have to contend with camera-happy crowds jostling to capture their own impressions of the water lilies.

A few minutes' walk up Giverny's village street, the **Musée d'Art Américain** is an unattractive edifice that hides a spacious and well-lit gallery devoted to American artists resident in France between 1865 and 1915 (April–Oct Tues–Sun 10am–6pm; ⓦwww.maag.org; €5.50, free first Sun of each month). Some took their admiration of Monet to a point that now seems embarrassing, painting many of the same scenes, but there are some interesting works by John Singer Sargent, Winslow Homer and, especially, Mary Cassatt.

Giverny's one **hotel**, the *Musardière*, stands not far beyond Monet's house at 123 rue Claude-Monet (ⓣ02.32.21.03.18, ⓔiraymonde@aol.com; ❹); dinner menus in its restaurant start at €26. The nearest inexpensive accommodation is the *Hôtel d'Évreux*, 11 place d'Évreux (☎02.32.21.16.12; Ⓦwww.hoteldevreux.fr; ❷), across the river in the heart of the town of **VERNON**. Connecting buses from Vernon's **gare SNCF** run to the gardens in Giverny.

Basse Normandie

As you head west along the coast of Basse Normandie from Le Havre, a succession of somewhat exclusive resorts – of which only **Honfleur** is especially memorable – is followed first by the beaches where the Allied armies landed in 1944, and then by the wilder, and in places deserted, shore around the **Cotentin Peninsula**. There are two absolutely unmissable sights along this stretch – the glorious island abbey of **Mont St-Michel** and the **Bayeux Tapestry**.

The Norman Riviera

The only section of the Norman coast to have serious delusions of grandeur is the stretch that lies immediately west of the mouth of the Seine. The **Pont de Normandie** across the river estuary from Le Havre has made such places as **Trouville** and **Deauville** too hectic for comfort, though only **Honfleur** could be said to have had all that much to lose.

Honfleur

HONFLEUR, the best preserved of the old ports of Normandy and the most easterly on the Calvados coast, is a near-perfect seaside town that lacks only a beach. It used to have one, but with the accumulation of silt from the Seine the sea has steadily withdrawn, leaving the eighteenth-century waterfront houses of **boulevard Charles-V** stranded and a little surreal. The ancient port, however, still functions – the channel to the beautiful Vieux Bassin is kept open by regular dredging – and though only pleasure craft now use the moorings in the harbour basin, fishing boats tie up alongside the pier nearby, and you can usually buy fish either directly from the boats or from stands on the pier, still by right run by fishermen's wives.

Honfleur is highly picturesque, and has moved significantly upmarket since the opening of the Pont de Normandie. Despite now being just a few minutes' drive from Le Havre, the old port has strong echoes of the fishing village that appealed so greatly to artists in the second half of the nineteenth century.

Arrival and information

Honfleur's **gare routière**, just to the east of the Vieux Bassin, is served by over a dozen direct daily **buses** from Caen (#20), and up to eight express services from Le Havre (Bus Verts; ☎08.01.21.42.14, Ⓦwww.busverts.fr). The nearest **gare SNCF** is at Pont l'Evêque, connected to Honfleur by the Lisieux bus (#50) – a twenty-minute ride.

The **tourist office** adjoins the glass-fronted Mediathèque on quai Le Paulmier, between the Vieux Bassin and the *gare routière* (Easter–June & Sept Mon–Sat 10am–12.30pm & 2–6.30pm, Sun 10am–5pm; July & Aug Mon–Sat 10am–7pm, Sun 10am–5pm; Oct–Easter Mon–Sat 10am–12.30pm & 2–6pm ; ⓣ02.31.89.23.30, ⓦwww.ot-honfleur.fr). Ask about their summer programme of **guided tours** of the town, which range from two-hour walkabouts to full-day excursions including meals.

Accommodation

If finding budget **accommodation** is one of your main priorities, it probably makes sense for you not to stay in Honfleur at all, and simply to visit for the day. On summer weekends especially, so many visitors turn up that even the most ordinary hotel can get away with charging rates well above the average for Normandy. No hotels overlook the harbour itself, while the two-star **Camping du Phare** (ⓣ02.31.89.10.26; closed Oct–March) is on place Jean-de-Vienne at the western end of boulevard Charles-V.

Belvédère 36 rte Emile-Renouf ⓣ02.31.89.08.13, ⓦwww.hotel-belvedere-honfleur.com. Peaceful, traditional Logis de France, with garden and terrace, roughly ten minutes' walk east of (and up from) the harbour. All nine rooms are en suite; some are in a cottage in the grounds that has views of the Pont de Normandie, and there's a good restaurant, with menus from €16.90. Closed Jan. ❹

Cascades 17 place Thiers ⓣ02.31.89.05.83. Seventeen-room hotel-restaurant opening onto both place Thiers and the cobbled rue de la Ville behind. Slightly noisy rooms upstairs, and a good-value if not particularly exciting restaurant with outdoor seating on both sides; menus start at €13; more expensive options featuring dishes such as *fruits de mer* are from €30. Closed Mon & Tues in low season (restaurant), plus mid-Nov to early Feb (hotel and restaurant). ❷

Des Loges 18 rue Brûlée ⓣ02.31.89.38.26, ⓦwww.hoteldesloges.com. Brightly refurbished hotel with chic, elegant decor on a quiet cobbled street just 100m inland from Ste-Catherine church. It's decked out with flowers, is run by helpful staff, and offers a high standard of expensive accommodation. Baby-sitting available. ❼

Monet Charrière du Puits ⓣ02.31.89.00.90, ⓦwww.motelmonet.fr. This old ivy-covered house is in a very quiet location ten minutes' walk up a moderately steep hill from the centre and offers modern, en-suite rooms and plenty of courtyard parking. ❹

Tilbury 30 place Hamelin ⓣ02.31.98.83.33, ⓦwww.hotel-tilbury.com. Very central, a stone's throw from the Lieutenance, with well-equipped and comfortable rooms, all with baths, above a crêperie. There are three suites suitable for families. ❹

The Town

Visitors to Honfleur inevitably gravitate towards the old centre, around the **Vieux Bassin**. At the *bassin*, slate-fronted houses, each of them one or two storeys higher than seems possible, harmonize – despite their tottering and ill-matched forms – into a backdrop that is only excelled by the **Lieutenance** at the harbour entrance. The latter was the dwelling of the King's Lieutenant, and has been the gateway to the inner town since at least 1608, when Samuel Champlain sailed from Honfleur to found Québec. The **church of St-Étienne** nearby is now the **Musée de la Marine**, which combines a collection of model ships with several rooms of antique Norman furnishings (mid-Feb to March & Oct to mid-Nov Tues–Fri 2.30–5.30pm, Sat & Sun 10am–noon; April–Sept Tues–Sun 10am–noon & 2–6.30pm; €3.10, or €4.30 with Musée de Vieux Honfleur). Just behind it, two seventeenth-century **salt stores** that used to contain the precious commodity during the days of the much-hated *gabelle*, or salt tax, now serve as the **Musée du Vieux Honfleur** (same hours and entrance fee), filled with everyday artefacts from old Honfleur.

The town's artistic past – and its present concentration of galleries and painters – owes most to Eugène Boudin, forerunner of Impressionism. He was born and worked in the town, trained the 18-year-old Monet and was joined for various periods by Pissarro, Renoir and Cézanne. Boudin was among the founders of what's now the **Musée Eugène Boudin** (mid-March to Sept daily except Tues 10am–noon & 2–6pm; Oct to mid-March Mon & Wed–Fri 2.30–5pm, Sat & Sun 10am–noon & 2.30–5pm; €5.20), west of the port on place Erik-Satie, and left 53 works to it after his death in 1898. His pastel seascapes and sunsets in particular are quite appealing here in context, and they're accompanied by changing temporary exhibitions and a few ethnographic displays.

Admission to the museum also gives you access to the detached belfry of the **church of Ste-Catherine** (daily 9am–6pm). Both church and belfry are built almost entirely of wood – supposedly owing to economic restraints after the Hundred Years War. The church itself makes a change from the usual Norman stone constructions, and has the added peculiarity of being divided into twin naves, with one balcony running around both. From **rue de l'Homme-de-Bois** behind you can see yacht masts through the houses overlooking the *bassin* and, in the distance, the huge industrial panorama of Le Havre's docks.

Just down the hill from the Musée Boudin, at 67 bd Charles-V, is **Les Maisons Satie** (daily except Tues: May–Sept 10am–7pm; mid-Feb to April & Oct–Dec 11am–6pm; last entrance 60min before closing time; €5.10), the red-timbered house of Erik Satie. From the outside it looks unchanged since the composer was born there in 1866. Step inside, however, and you'll find yourself in Normandy's most unusual and enjoyable museum. As befits a close associate of the Surrealists, Satie is commemorated by all sorts of weird and wonderful interactive surprises. It would be a shame to give too many of them away here; suffice it to say that you're immediately confronted by a giant pear, bouncing into the air on huge wings to the strains of his best-known piano piece, *Gymnopédies*. You also get to see a filmed reconstruction of *Parade*, a ballet on which Satie collaborated with Picasso, Stravinsky and Cocteau, which created a furore in Paris in 1917.

Eating

With its abundance of day-trippers and hotel guests, Honfleur supports an astonishing number of **restaurants**, most specializing in seafood. Few face onto the harbour itself; the narrow buildings around the edge seem to be better suited to being snack bars, crêperies, cafés and ice-cream parlours.

L'Absinthe 10 quai de la Quarantaine ☎02.31.89.39.00. This eighteenth-century mansion houses the most imaginative and gastronomic of the row of five restaurants that stand just around the corner from the *bassin*, with dishes such as smoked salmon *carpaccio* or foie gras in ginger on menus ranging from €30 up to a seven-course €60 extravaganza. Closed mid-Nov to mid-Dec.

Le Bouillon Normand 7 rue de la Ville ☎02.31.89.02.41. Old-fashioned bistro, with indoor and outdoor seating, set just back from the basin behind St-Étienne church. Fish, cider and cheese are prominent on simple, good-value menus at €16 and €23. Closed Wed, Sun eve, & Jan.

Au P'tit Mareyeur 4 rue Haute ☎02.31.98.84.23. No distance from the centre, but all the seating is indoors and there are no views. Very good fish dishes such as red crab soup with garlic, plus plenty of creamy Pays d'Auge sauces and superb desserts. The "Menu Carte" is great value at €21, while *bouillabaisse* costs €19. Closed Mon, Tues & Jan.

La Tortue 36 rue de l'Homme de Bois ☎02.31.89.04.93. A welcoming place near the Musée Boudin, where €16 buys a great-value five-course meal. There's even a €12 vegetarian menu, consisting of apple soup, a couple of salads, vegetables and dessert. Closed Mon eve & Tues, Oct–March only.

Le Vieux Honfleur 13 quai St-Étienne ☎02.31.89.15.31. The best of the restaurants around the harbour itself, with spacious alfresco dining – in shade at lunchtime – on its pedestrianized eastern side. Simple menus, but the seafood is very good, as befits prices starting at €29. The only other set menu, at €49.50, offers lobster or turbot, with no meat options other than foie gras.

Trouville and Deauville

Heading west along the corniche from Honfleur, green fields and fruit trees lull the land's edge, and cliffs rise from sandy beaches all the way to Trouville, 15km away. The resorts aren't exactly cheap but they're relatively undeveloped, and if you want to stop along the coast this is the place to do it. The next stretch, from Trouville to Cabourg, is what you might call the Riviera of Normandy: with Trouville as "Nice" and Deauville as "Cannes" within a stone's throw of each other.

TROUVILLE retains some semblance of a real town, with a constant population and industries other than tourism. But it is still a resort, with a tangle of busy pedestrian streets just back from the beach that are alive with restaurants and hotels. It's been a chic destination ever since Napoléon III started bringing his court here every summer in the 1860s. One of his dukes, looking across the river, saw, instead of marshlands, money – and lots of it, in the form of a racetrack. His vision materialized, and villas appeared between the racetrack and the sea to become **DEAUVILLE**, which likes to style itself the "21st arrondissement" of Paris. Now you can lose money on the horses, cross five streets and lose more in the casino, then lose yourself across 200m of sports and "cure" facilities and private swimming huts before reaching the *planches*, 500m of boardwalk, beyond which rows of primary-coloured parasols obscure the view of the sea.

Deauville's **American Film Festival** (Ⓦwww.festival-deauville.com), held in the first week of September, is the antithesis of Cannes, with public admission to a wide selection of previews.

Practicalities

Trouville and Deauville share their **gare SNCF** and **gare routière**, located in between the two just south of the marina. Each day, thirteen of the hourly buses from Caen continue along the coast to Honfleur. The usual lavish brochures can be found at the **tourist office** on place de la Mairie in Deauville (May & June Mon–Fri 9am–12.30pm & 2–6.30pm, Sat 9am–6.30pm, Sun 10am–1pm & 2–5pm; July & Aug Mon–Sat 9am–7pm, Sun 10am–1pm & 3–6pm; Sept–April Mon–Sat 9am–12.30pm & 2–6.30pm, Sun 10am–1pm & 2–5pm; Ⓣ02.31.14.40.00, Ⓦwww.deauville.org), or the one at 32 quai F. Moureaux in Trouville (April–June, Sept & Oct Mon–Sat 9.30am–noon & 2–6.30pm, Sun 10am–1pm; July & Aug Mon–Sat 9.30am–7pm, Sun 10am–4pm; Nov–March Mon–Sat 9.30am–noon & 1.30–6.30pm, Sun 10am–1pm; Ⓣ02.31.14.60.70, Ⓦwww.trouvillesurmer.org).

As you might imagine, **hotels** here tend to be luxurious, overpriced or both. If you fancy staying right on the seafront, it's hard to beat the *Flaubert*, rue Gustave-Flaubert (Ⓣ02.31.88.37.23, Ⓦwww.flaubert.fr; ❺), a grand, faux-timbered mansion at the start of Trouville's boardwalk that's home to the excellent *Le Vivier* restaurant. Cheaper options include the *Hôtel des Sports*, behind Deauville's fish market at 27 rue Gambetta (Ⓣ02.31.88.22.67; ❸; closed Feb & Nov, plus Sun in winter), is among the least expensive, and Trouville's closest equivalent, *Le Trouville*, 50m from the beach at 1 rue Thiers (Ⓣ02.31.98.45.48, Ⓦwww.hotelletrouville.com; ❸; closed Jan). Deauville, meanwhile, has a **campsite**, *La Vallée de Deauville*, 3km from the centre on route de Beaumont-en-Auge in St-Arnoult (Ⓣ02.31.88.58.17; Ⓦwww.camping-deauville.com; closed Nov–March).

A good **place to eat** in Deauville is *Chez Miocque* at 81 rue Eugène-Colas (ⓣ02.31.88.09.52; closed Tues in winter, plus all Jan), a top-quality Parisian-style bistro where a full meal costs around €40. Trouville also has its fair share of good fish restaurants, including *Les Vapeurs* at 160 bd F.-Moureaux (ⓣ02.31.88.15.24) – one of several lively brasseries opposite the attractive old half-timbered fish market – and *La Petite Auberge*, 7 rue Carnot (ⓣ02.31.88.11.07; closed Tues all year, plus Wed except in Aug), though both get very crowded at weekends.

Houlgate

A hundred years ago, **HOULGATE**, 15km west of Deauville, was every bit as glamorous and sophisticated a destination as its immediate neighbours. What makes it different today is that it has barely changed since then. Its long straight beach remains lined with a stately procession of nineteenth-century villas, while the town's handful of commercial enterprises are confined to the narrow parallel street, the **rue des Bains**, fifty metres inland. As a result, Houlgate is the most relaxed of the local resorts, ideal if you're looking for a peaceful family break where the only stress is deciding whether to paddle or play mini-golf.

The **tourist office** is well back from the sea on boulevard des Belges (April–June Sept & Oct Mon–Sat 10am–1pm & 2–6pm, Sun 10.30am–1pm & 2–4pm; July & Aug daily 10am–1pm & 2–6.30pm; Nov–March Mon–Sat 10am–1pm & 2–6pm; ⓣ02.31.24.34.79, ⓦwww.ville-houlgate.fr). The *Hostellerie Normande*, just off the rue des Bains at 11 rue E.-Deschanel (ⓣ02.31.24.85.50; ❹), is a pretty but rather impersonal little **hotel** covered with ivy and creeping flowers, with a €14 lunch menu on which you can follow fish soup with a plate of *moules-frites* or tripe. Above the Vaches Noires ("Black Cows") cliffs on the corniche road east of town, *La Ferme Auberge des Aulnettes* (ⓣ02.31.28.00.28; ❸; closed Dec & Jan), is a lovely half-timbered country house in pleasant gardens, where the cheapest rooms have a shower but share a WC. A good restaurant with outdoor seating serves menus from €17. The best **campsite** in the area, the four-star *Les Falaises* (ⓣ02.31.24.81.09, ⓦwww.lesfalaises.com; closed mid-Oct to March), is not far away.

Dives and Cabourg

DIVES, the port from which William the Conqueror sailed for Hastings, is another 3km west from Houlgate, though like Honfleur it's now pushed well back from the sea. A lively Saturday **market** focuses around the ancient oak *halles*, whose steep tiled roof stretches far above its walls; on market days, it's crammed with mouthwatering delicacies and Norman specialities. Dives is home to a large, inexpensive *Étap* **hotel**, on voie nouvelle de Port-Guillaume (ⓣ08.92.68.08.54; ❷).

At the much newer town of **CABOURG**, across the mouth of the Dives River, the *fin-de-siècle* streets of the town centre fan out in perfect symmetry from what is almost certainly the straightest promenade in France, with semicircular avenues linking them together. The resort, contemporary with Deauville, seems to be stuck in the nineteenth century – immobilized by memories of Proust, perhaps, who wrote for a while in the **Grand Hôtel**, one of an outrageously ostentatious ensemble of buildings around the **Jardins du Casino**. The **tourist office** in the Jardins du Casino has full details on hotels (April–June & Sept–Oct Mon–Sat 10am–12.30pm & 2–5.30pm; July & Aug daily 9.30am–7pm; Sun 10am–noon & 2–4pm; Nov–March Mon & Wed–Sat 10am–12.30pm & 2–5.30pm, Sun 10am–noon & 2–4pm; ⓣ02.31.91.20.00,

Ⓦwww.cabourg.net). A pleasant place to **stay** and eat is the *Oie qui Fume*, 18 av de la Brèche-Buhot (Ⓣ02.31.91.27.79, Ⓦwww.cabourg-hotel.fr; ④), 100m back from the sea on a quiet road half a dozen streets west of the centre; its €24 menu features goose (*oie*) as either starter or main course.

Caen

CAEN, capital and largest city of Basse Normandie, may well not be a place where you'll want to spend much time: in the months of fighting in 1944, it was devastated. Nonetheless, the city that nine hundred years ago was the favoured residence of William the Conqueror remains impressive in parts.

Its central feature is a ring of ramparts that no longer have a castle to protect, and, though there are the scattered spires and buttresses of two abbeys and eight old churches, roads and roundabouts fill the wide spaces where prewar houses stood. Approaches are along thunderous dual carriageways through industrial suburbs, now prospering once more following an influx of high-tech newcomers.

Arrival and information

Caen's small, modern **airport**, 7km west just outside **Carpiquet** (Ⓣ02.31.71.20.10), is served by **buses** (€1.20) connecting with all services, taking 25 minutes to run to and from the Tour-le-Roi stop in place

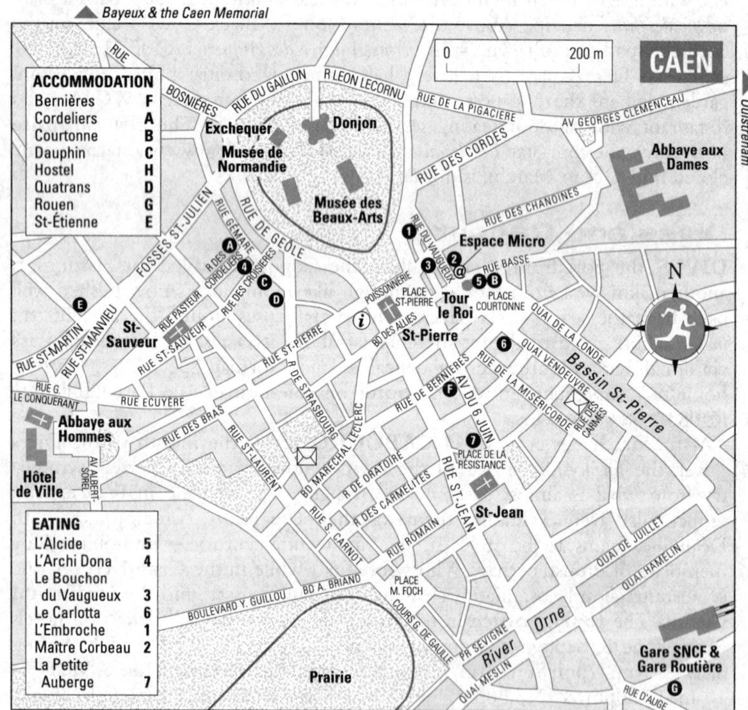

Courtonne. Avis (Ⓣ02.31.34.88.89), Budget (Ⓣ02.31.83.70.47) and Rent A Car (Ⓣ02.31.84.10.10) provide **car hire** both in the terminal and in town.

The **gare SNCF** (Ⓣ08.36.35.35.35) is a rather dull kilometre's walk south of the town centre across the river, with the **gare routière** alongside. An extensive network of local **buses** and **trams** is run by TWISTO (Ⓣ02.31.15.55.55, Ⓦwww.twisto.fr), which has ticket and information centres at 15 rue de Geôle (just north of the tourist office), and on boulevard Maréchal-Leclerc. The main tram route connects the southern and northern suburbs, running through the heart of the city from the *gare SNCF* up avenue de 6-Juin to the university and beyond.

Caen's **tourist office** is on place St-Pierre across from the church of St-Pierre (April–June & Sept Mon–Sat 9.30am–1pm & 2–6.30pm, Sun 10am–1pm; July & Aug Mon–Sat 9am–7pm, Sun 10am–1pm & 2–5pm; Oct–March Mon–Sat 9.30am–1pm & 2–6pm, Sun 10am–1pm; Ⓣ02.31.27.14.14, Ⓦwww.caen.fr/tourisme). You can go **online** at Espace Micro, on place Courtonne at 1 rue Basse (Mon–Thurs 10am–11pm, Fri & Sat 10am–1am, Sun 10am–1pm & 3–9pm; Ⓣ02.31.53.68.68), or the main **post office** on place Gambetta (Mon–Fri 8am–7pm, Sat 8am–noon).

Accommodation

Caen has a great number of **hotels**, though, as ever in the rebuilt bomb-damaged cities of Normandy, few could be called attractive. They're not particularly concentrated in any one area either, though you'll find clusters just west of the castle and tourist office – a convenient location for motorists heading to or from the ferry – as well as around the pleasure port, and a handful facing the *gare SNCF*. With plenty of dedicated restaurants in town, few hotels bother to provide food.

Hotels

Bernières 50 rue de Bernières Ⓣ02.31.86.01.26, Ⓦwww.hotelbernieres.com. This bright, central hotel offers appealing en-suite rooms above a brasserie halfway between the churches of St-Pierre and St-Jean. ❸

Cordeliers 4 rue des Cordeliers Ⓣ02.31.86.37.15. Friendly hotel, centred on a fine eighteenth-century house in a small side street near the castle. The very cheapest rooms have showers but no toilet, but fully en-suite ones are not much more expensive. ❷

Courtonne 5 rue des Prairies St-Gilles Ⓣ02.31.93.47.83, Ⓦwww.hotel-courtonne.com. This very welcoming modernized hotel overlooks place Courtonne and the pleasure port, though the building is so narrow it's easy to miss. All rooms have bath or shower, phone and TV. ❹

Dauphin 29 rue Gémare Ⓣ02.31.86.22.26, Ⓦwww.le-dauphin-normandie.com. Upmarket hotel, tucked away behind the tourist office. Part of it was a priory during the eighteenth century, not that you'd guess. The public areas are impressive, while the rooms are comfortable without being exciting in any way, and there's a sauna and fitness centre. Grand restaurant, with an €19 weekday dinner menu; weekend menus €30 and €52 (restaurant closed Sat lunch & Sun all year, and open for dinner only June–Sept). ❺

Quatrans 17 rue Gémare Ⓣ02.31.86.25.57, Ⓦwww.hotel-des-quatrans.com. Fully renovated hotel in an anonymous modern setting, a very short walk from the tourist office and château. The pastel theme of the facade continues inside; some might find it cloying, but the service is friendly, and everything works well. All rooms en suite. ❹

Rouen 8 place de la Gare Ⓣ02.31.34.06.03. Reasonably smart budget option, furthest to the west (right) in the parade that faces you as you exit the *gare SNCF*, and offering rooms with and without en-suite facilities. Worth considering if there is no room at the more central hotels. ❸

St-Étienne 2 rue de l'Académie Ⓣ02.31.86.35.82, Ⓦwww.hotel-saint-etienne.com. Friendly budget hotel in an old stone house in the characterful St-Martin district, not far from the Abbaye des Hommes. The cheaper rooms have no showers, but en-suite ones cost little more. ❷

Hostel

HI hostel Foyer Robert-Remé, 68bis rue E.-Restout, Grâce-de-Dieu Ⓣ02.31.52.19.96. Lively and welcoming hostel, situated in an otherwise sleepy area about 500m southwest of the *gare SNCF*. Beds in both four-bed dorms or two-bed private rooms cost €11 per person. Take tram #B from the town centre or *gare SNCF*, direction "Grace de Dieu". Reception open 5–9pm. Closed Oct–May.

The Town

A virtue was made of the postwar necessity of clearing away the rubble of Caen's medieval houses, which formerly pressed up against its ancient **château ramparts**. The resulting open green space means that those walls are now fully visible for the first time in centuries. In turn, walking the circuit of the ramparts gives a good overview of the city, with a particularly fine prospect of the reconstructed fourteenth-century facade of the nearby **church of St-Pierre**. Some magnificent Renaissance stonework has survived intact at the church's east end.

Most of the centre of Caen is taken up with busy new shopping developments and pedestrian precincts, where the cafés are distinguished by names such as Fast Food Glamour Vault. Outlets of the big Parisian stores – and of the aristocrats' grocers, Hédiard, in the cours des Halles – are here, along with good local rivals. The main city **market** takes place on Friday, spreading along both sides of Fosse St-Julien, and there's also a Sunday market in place Courtonne. The **Bassin St-Pierre**, the pleasure port at the end of the canal that links Caen to the sea, is where most life goes on, at least in summer.

Castle grounds

Within the castle walls, it's possible to visit the former **Exchequer** – which dates from shortly after the Norman conquest of England, and was the scene of a banquet thrown by Richard the Lionheart en route to the Crusades – and inspect a garden that has been replanted with the herbs and medicinal plants that were cultivated here during the Middle Ages. Also inside the precinct, though not in original structures, are two museums. Most visitors will prefer the **Musée des Beaux-Arts** (daily except Tues 9.30am–6pm; permanent collection free, special exhibitions €3 or €5), which traces a potted history of European art from Renaissance Italy through such Dutch masters as Brueghel the Younger up to grand portraits from eighteenth-century France in the upstairs galleries. Downstairs brings things up to date with some powerful twentieth-century art, though there are few big-name works. The other museum, the **Musée de Normandie** (June–Sept daily 9.30am–6pm, Oct–March daily except Tues 9.30am–6pm; permanent collection free, special exhibitions €3), provides a cursory overview of Norman history, ranging from archeological finds like stone tools from the region's megalithic period and glass jewellery from Gallo-Roman Rouen up to the impact of the Industrial Revolution. It also hosts two or three temporary exhibitions per year, covering particular themes in much greater detail.

Abbaye aux Hommes

The **Abbaye aux Hommes**, at the west end of rue St-Pierre, was founded by William the Conqueror and designed to hold his tomb within the huge, austere Romanesque church of St-Étienne (Mon–Sat 8.30am–12.30pm & 1.30–7pm, Sun 8.30am–12.30pm & 2.30–7pm; free; 1hr 15min guided tours leave adjacent Hôtel de Ville daily 9.30am, 11am, 2.30pm & 4pm; tours in English mid-July to Aug only, daily 11am, 1.30pm & 4pm; €2, free on Sun). However, his burial here, in 1087, was hopelessly undignified. The funeral procession first caught fire and was then held to ransom, as various factions squabbled over his rotting corpse for any spoils they could grab. A further interruption came when a man halted the service to object that the grave had been constructed without compensation on the site of his family house, and the assembled nobles had to pay him off before William could be laid to rest. During the Revolution the tomb was again ransacked, and it now holds a solitary thighbone rescued from the river. Still, the building itself is a wonderful Romanesque monument. Adjoining the church are the abbey buildings, designed during the eighteenth century and now housing the Hôtel de Ville.

Abbaye aux Dames

At the other end of the town centre, at the end of rue des Chanoines, is the **Abbaye aux Dames**, commissioned by William's wife Matilda in the hope of saving her soul after committing the godless sin of marrying her cousin. Her monument – the **church of La Trinité** – is even more starkly impressive than her husband's, with a gloomy pillared crypt, wonderful stained glass behind the altar and odd sculptural details like the fish curled up in the holy-water stoup. The convent buildings today house the regional council but are open to the public (daily 2–5.30pm; guided tours 2.30pm & 4pm; free).

The Caen Memorial

Just north of Caen, at the end of avenue Marshal-Montgomery in the Folie Couvrechef area, the **Caen Memorial** (late Jan to mid-Feb, and early Nov to early Jan daily except Mon 9.30am–6pm; mid-Feb to mid-July & late Aug to early Nov daily 9am–7pm; mid-July to late Aug daily 9am–8pm; closed three weeks in Jan; last entry 1hr 15min before closing; ⓣ02.31.06.06.44, ⓦwww.memorial-caen.fr; March–Sept €17.50; Oct–Feb €16.50), which describes itself as a "museum for peace", stands on a plateau named after General Eisenhower on a clifftop beneath which the Germans had their HQ in June and July 1944. Funds and material for it came from the US, Britain, Canada, Germany, Poland, Czechoslovakia, the USSR and France.

The museum is a typically French high-tech, novel-architecture conception, with excellent displays divided into several distinct sections; allow two hours at the very least for a visit. The first section deals with the rise of fascism in Germany, another with resistance and collaboration in France, while a third charts all the major battles of World War II. Most of the captions, though not always the written exhibits themselves, are translated into English. Further areas examine the course of the Cold War and the prospects for global peace, with the former German bunkers below housing the Nobel Peace Prize Winners' Gallery. Portraits and short essays commemorate each recipient in turn, placing their achievements in context. There's also a good-value self-service restaurant upstairs. The memorial is served by bus #2 from the "Tour le Roi" stop in the centre of town.

Eating

Caen's town centre offers two major areas for **eating**: with cosmopolitan restaurants in the pedestrianized **quartier Vaugueux** and more traditional French restaurants on the streets off **rue de Geôle**, near the western ramparts, particularly rue des Croisiers and rue Gémare.

L'Alcide 1 place Courtonne ⓣ02.31.44.18.06. Large, rather anonymous-looking bistro-style place, which serves classic rich French dishes cooked with great attention to detail. Menus from €15.20 up to €23.50. Closed Sat.

L'Archi Dona 8 rue des Croisiers ⓣ02.31.85.30.30. This atmospheric restaurant belies its stately setting by serving delightfully fresh and zestful Mediterranean-influenced cuisine, ranging from simple entrée-plus-dessert meals at

€12 up to the €32 "seduction" menu. Closed Sun, Mon & three weeks in Aug.

Le Bouchon du Vaugueux 12 rue du Graindorge ⓣ02.31.44.26.26. Intimate little brasserie in the Vaugueux quarter, offering two menus: one at €17 featuring steak tartare and another at €22 where you can choose from veal, duck or roast pork. Closed Mon, Wed & Sun, plus first three weeks of Aug.

Le Carlotta 16 quai Vendeuvre ⓣ02.31.86.68.99 ⓦwww.lecarlotta.fr. Busy and fashionable Paris-style brasserie beside the pleasure port, which serves good Norman cooking both à la carte and on menus from €22. Closed Sun.

L'Embroche 17 rue Porte au Berger ⓣ02.31.93.71.31. Cosy little place in a busy restaurant district, where the open kitchen whips up simple regional specialities in full view of appreciative diners, with lunch from €18 and dinner from €22. Closed Sat lunch, Sun & Mon lunch.

Maître Corbeau 8 rue Buquet ⓣ02.31.93.93.00. Fondue is the speciality in this eccentric little place, and they won't let you forget it, festooning the whole place with cheesy iconography. A typical fondue costs around €14, while non-fondue menus start from €16. Closed Sat lunch, Sun, Mon lunch & three weeks in Aug.

La Petite Auberge 17 rue des Équipes-d'Urgence ⓣ02.31.86.43.30. Plain and simple restaurant, with a nice view of the St-Jean church. Very well-priced Norman specialities served on a €12 menu (daily except Sat eve) that doesn't force you to eat tripe, or a wide-ranging €19 one. Closed Sun, Mon & first three weeks of Aug.

The D-Day beaches

Despite the best efforts of Steven Spielberg, it's all but impossible now to picture the scene at dawn on **D-Day**, June 6, 1944, when Allied troops landed along the Norman coast between the mouth of the Orne and Les Dunes de Varneville on the Cotentin Peninsula. For the most part, these are innocuous beaches backed by gentle dunes, and yet this foothold in Europe was won at the cost of 100,000 soldiers' lives. That the invasion happened here and not nearer to Germany was partly a result of the disastrous Canadian raid on Dieppe in 1942, which showed the perils of attacking fortified positions without strong air and artillery support. The ensuing **Battle of Normandy** killed thousands of civilians and reduced nearly six hundred towns and villages to rubble but, within a week of its eventual conclusion, Paris was liberated.

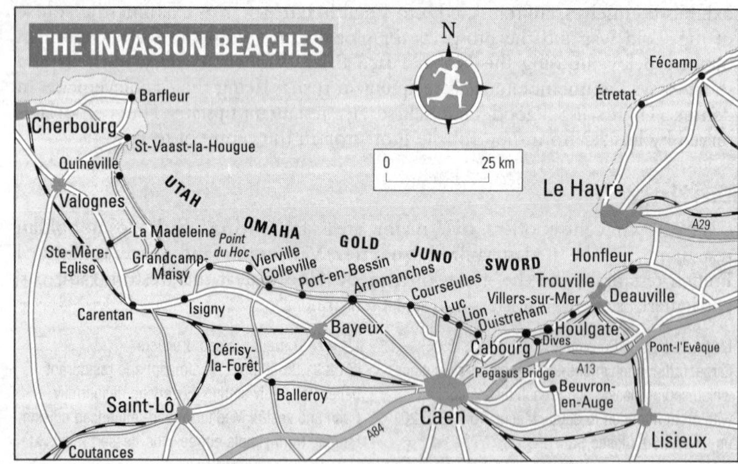

The war cemeteries

The **World War II** cemeteries that dot the Norman countryside are filled with foreigners – most of the French dead are buried in the churchyards of their home towns. After the war, some felt that the soldiers should remain buried in the original makeshift graves that were dug where they fell. Instead, commissions gathered the remains into purpose-built cemeteries devoted to the separate warring nations.

△ US Military Cemetery, Colleville-sur-Mer

The **British** and **Commonwealth** cemeteries are magnificently maintained. They tend not to be screened off with hedges or walls, or to be forbidding expanses of manicured lawn, but are instead intimate, punctuated with bright flowers. The family of each soldier was invited to suggest an inscription for his tomb, making each grave very personal, and yet part of a common attempt to bring meaning to the carnage. Some epitaphs are questioning – "One day we will understand"; some are accepting – "Our lad at rest"; some matter-of-fact, simply giving the home address; some patriotic, quoting the "corner of a foreign field that is forever England". And interspersed among them all is the chilling refrain of the anonymous "A soldier ... known unto God". Thus the cemetery at **Ryes**, where so many of the graves bear the date of D-Day, and so many of the victims are under 20, remains immediate and accessible – each grave clearly contains a unique individual. Even the monumental sculpture is subdued, a very British sort of fumbling for the decent thing to say. The understatement of the memorial at **Bayeux**, with its painfully contrived Latin epigram commemorating the return as liberators of "those whom William conquered", conveys an entirely appropriate humility and deep sadness.

An even more eloquent testimony to the futility of war is afforded by the **German** cemeteries, filled with soldiers who served a cause so despicable as to render any talk of "nobility" or "sacrifice" obscene. What such cemeteries might have been like had the Nazis won doesn't bear contemplation. As it is, they are sombre places, inconspicuous to minimize the bitterness they still arouse. At **Orglandes** ten thousand are buried, three to each of the plain headstones set in the long flat lawn, almost hidden behind an anonymous wall. There are no noble slogans and the plain entrance is without a dedicatory monument. At the superb site of **Mont d'Huisnes** near Mont St-Michel, the circular mausoleum holds another ten thousand, filed away in cold concrete tiers. Though no attempt is made to defend the indefensible, there's still an overpowering sense of sorrow – that there is nothing to be said in such a place bitterly underlines the sheer waste and stupidity.

The largest **American** cemetery, at **Colleville-sur-mer** near the Pointe du Hoc, may already be familiar from the opening sequences of *Saving Private Ryan*. Here, by contrast, neat rows of crosses cover the tranquil clifftop lawns, with no individual epitaphs, just gold lettering for a few exceptional warriors. At one end, a muscular giant dominates a huge array of battlefield plans and diagrams, covered with surging arrows and pincer movements.

The **beaches** are still often referred to by their wartime code names: from east to west, Sword, Juno, Gold, Omaha and Utah. Substantial traces of the fighting are rare, the most remarkable being the remains of the astounding **Mulberry Harbour** at **Arromanches**, 10km northeast of Bayeux. Further west, at **Pointe du Hoc** on Omaha Beach, the cliff heights are deeply pitted with German bunkers and shell holes, while the church at **Ste-Mère-Église**, from whose steeple the US paratrooper dangled during heavy fighting throughout *The Longest Day*, still stands, and now has a model parachute permanently fastened to the roof. Note that **Utah Beach**, the westernmost of the Invasion Beaches, is on the Cotentin Peninsula, and covered on p.386 onwards.

Just about every coastal town has its **war museum**. These tend as a rule to shy away from the unbearable reality of war in favour of *Boy's Own*-style heroics, but the wealth of incidental human detail can nonetheless be overpowering. Veterans and their descendants apart, visitors these days come to this stretch of coast for its **seaside**: sand and seafood (the best oysters are at Courseulles), plenty of campsites and no Deauville chic.

Bus Verts (Ⓣ08.10.21.42.14, Ⓦwww.busverts.fr) run all along this coast. From Bayeux, bus #75 goes to Arromanches, Courseulles, and Ouistreham, and bus #70 to the Pointe du Hoc, the US cemetery at Colleville-sur-mer, and Port-en-Bessin. From Caen, bus #30 runs inland to Isigny via Bayeux, express bus #1 to Ouistreham, and express bus #3 to Courseulles. In July and August, Bus Verts' special **D-Day Line** departs daily from Caen's *gare routière* (9.20pm) and place Courtonne (9.35am), calling at Courseulles, Arromanches, the German gun emplacements at Longues-sur-mer, the US cemetery and the Pointe du Hoc, before returning to Caen at around 6pm (€14 flat fare).

In addition, the Caen Memorial (see p.373) organizes expensive, informative bilingual **guided tours** of the beaches in groups of around eight people, with four or five hours on the road and a visit to the Memorial at your own pace (mid-Jan to March & Oct–Dec daily 1pm; April–Sept daily 9am & 2pm; Ⓣ02.31.06.06.45, Ⓦwww.memorial-caen.fr; €67.50).

Ouistreham and around

The small community of **OUISTREHAM**, on the coast 15km north of Caen and connected to it by a fast dual carriageway, gives the impression that it can barely believe its luck at having become a major ferry port. Brittany Ferries started their service here in 1986, and the easternmost of the D-Day resorts has developed an extensive array of reasonable hotels and restaurants.

If, instead of setting off for Caen, you head directly west along the coast from the ferry terminal, after a few hundred metres you come to the long straight main drag of beach – the **Riva Bella** itself. This is progressively shedding its run-down image; the large casino has been remodelled as a 1930s passenger liner, housing an expensive restaurant and cocktail bar, and even the old-fashioned bathing huts have had a fresh lick of paint.

Nearby, the **Musée du Mur de l'Atlantique** (daily: Feb, March & Oct to mid-Nov 10am–6pm; April–Sept 9am–7pm; €6.50) is housed in a lofty bunker – hence its alternative name, the Grand Bunker. This was the headquarters of the several German batteries that defended the mouth of the River Orne; after brief resistance, it fell to Allied forces on June 9, 1944. Inside the heavily restored bunker, displays re-create living conditions, with newspapers, cutlery and packets of cigarettes adding a welcome human touch to the moderately interesting explanations of the workings of the generators, gas filters and radio room.

The **tourist office**, alongside the casino on the beach (April–June & Sept daily 10am–12.30pm & 2–6.30pm; July & Aug daily 10am–1pm & 2–7pm; Oct–March Mon–Sat 10am–12.30pm & 2.30–6pm, Sun 10am–12.30pm; ⓣ02.31.97.18.63, ⓦwww.ville-ouistreham.fr), provides **Internet access** at €0.10 per min. Several cafés and brasseries in the place Courbonne, immediately outside the *gare maritime*, are eager to liberate passengers from their spare change, while *Le Channel*, just around the corner at 79 av Michel-Cabieu (ⓣ02.31.96.51.69; ❷), is the best value for both **eating and sleeping**: menus start with the €10.50 *menu pêcheur*, while the many higher priced options increase in splendour; guest rooms are in a separate building across the street. The smart *Le Normandie*, a few doors down at 71 av Michel-Cabieu (ⓣ02.31.97.19.57, ⓦwww.lenormandie.com; ❹; closed mid-Dec to mid-Jan, plus Sun eve & Mon Nov–March), has pleasant, quiet rooms. Its "Régional" menu at €21 features *boudin noir*, while the €37 "Gourmand" option makes an excellent last-night blowout.

Pegasus Bridge

Roughly 5km south of Ouistreham, the main road towards Caen passes close by the site now known as **Pegasus Bridge**. On the night before D-Day, the twin bridges here that cross the Caen canal and the River Orne were a crucial Allied objective, and were the target of a daring but successful glider assault just after midnight. The original bridge was replaced in 1994, but is now the focus of the **Mémorial Pegasus** immediately to the east (daily: Feb–March & Oct–Nov 10am–1pm & 2–5pm; April–Sept 9.30am–6.30pm; ⓦwww.normandy1944.com; €5.50). This vaguely glider-shaped museum holds the expected array of helmets, goggles, medals and other memorabilia, most captioned in English, as well as various model bridges used in planning the attack.

Arromanches

At **ARROMANCHES**, 10km northeast of Bayeux, an artificial **Mulberry harbour**, "Port Winston", protected the landings of 2,500,000 men and 500,000 vehicles during the invasion. Two of these prefab concrete constructions were built in Britain, while "doodlebugs" blitzed overhead; they were then submerged in rivers away from the prying eyes of German aircraft, and finally towed across the Channel at 6kph as the invasion began. The seafront **Musée du Débarquement**, in Arromanches' main square (Feb–April & Oct–Dec daily 9/10am–12.30pm, 1.30-5/6pm; May–Sept daily 9/10am–6/7pm; €6.50; ⓦwww.normandy1944.com), recounts the whole story by means of models, machinery and movies. A huge picture window runs the length of the museum, enabling you to look straight out to where the bulky remains of the harbour, whose sheer scale is impossible to appreciate at this distance, make a strange intrusion on the beach and shallow sea bed (the other one, slightly further west on Omaha Beach, was destroyed by a ferocious storm within a few weeks). There are war memorials throughout Arromanches, and statues of Jesus and Mary high up on the cliffs above the invasion site.

Nonetheless, Arromanches somehow manages to be quite a cheerful place to stay, with a lively pedestrian street of **bars** and **brasseries**, and a long expanse of sand where you can rent windsurfing boards. *La Marine* at 2 quai Canada (ⓣ02.31.22.34.19, ⓦwww.hotel-de-la-marine.fr; closed mid-Nov to mid-Feb; ❹), is a slightly expensive **hotel**, with an excellent sea-view restaurant serving fishy menus from €22. Across the main square stands the *Arromanches*, 2 rue du Colonel-René-Michel (ⓣ02.31.22.36.26, ⓦwww.hoteldarromanches.fr; restaurant closed Tues & Wed in low season; whole place closed Jan to mid-Feb;

④), whose restaurant has menus at €16.50 and €26.50, while nearby at 5 place du 6-Juin is the cheaper but perfectly adequate *Normandie* (☎02.31.22.34.32; ③). The spacious three-star municipal **campsite** is 200m back from the seafront (☎02.31.22.36.78; closed Nov–March).

Bayeux and around

BAYEUX, with its perfectly preserved medieval ensemble, magnificent cathedral and world-famous tapestry, is 23km west of Caen – a mere twenty-minute train ride. It's a smaller and much more intimate city, and, despite the large crowds of summer tourists, a far more enjoyable place to visit.

Arrival and information

The **gare SNCF** is fifteen minutes' walk south of the town centre, just outside the ring road, while the **gare routière** is on the north side of place St-Patrice. For information on local **buses**, contact Bus Verts du Calvados (☎08.10.21.42.14, ⓦwww.busverts.fr), whose services stop at both the *gare SNCF* and the *gare routière*. Travellers without cars who plan to visit the landing beaches and/or the war cemeteries are better advised to join a

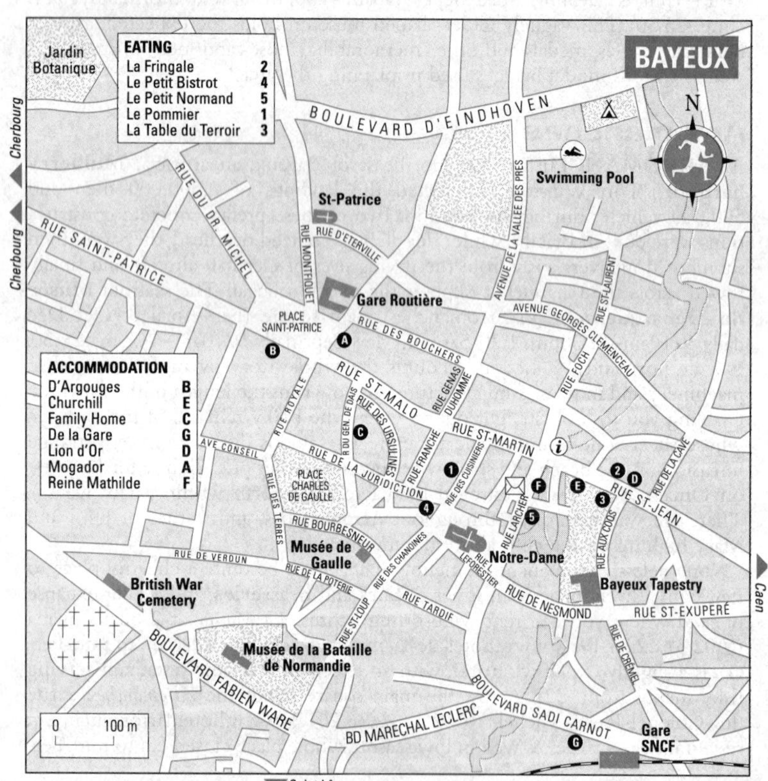

minibus trip with a local operator such as Normandy Sightseeing Tours (Ⓣ02.31.51.70.52, Ⓦwww.d-daybeaches.com) or Normandy Tours, 26 place de la Gare (Ⓣ02.31.92.10.70, Ⓦwww.normandy-landing-tour.com). Prices for half-day tours start from €40. Bayeux's **tourist office** stands in the centre of town, on the arched Pont St-Jean (Jan–March & Nov–Dec Mon–Sat 9.30am–12.30pm & 2–5.30pm; April–May & Sept–Oct daily 9.30am–12.30pm & 2–6pm; June–Aug Mon–Sat 9am–7pm, Sun 9am–1pm & 2–6pm; Ⓣ02.31.51.28.28, Ⓦwww.bayeux-bessin-tourism.com).

Accommodation

As one of Normandy's most important tourist destinations, Bayeux is well equipped with **accommodation**. On the whole, however, the hotels are more expensive than usual. There's a large three-star **campsite** on boulevard d'Eindhoven (Ⓣ02.31.92.08.43; closed Oct–April), on the northern ring road (RN13) near the river.

D'Argouges 21 rue St-Patrice Ⓣ02.31.92.88.86, Ⓦwww.hotel-dargouges.com. Quiet, central and very stylish eighteenth-century building, with an imposing courtyard entered via an archway on the west side of place St-Patrice and a well-kept garden around the back. Several rooms are very grand, with magnificent exposed wooden beams; all have bath plus shower, and the rates are very reasonable for what you get. No restaurant. ❹

Churchill 14–16 rue St-Jean Ⓣ02.31.21.31.80, Ⓦwww.hotel-churchill.fr. Relatively large, completely renovated 32-room hotel, which often has rooms when elsewhere is full, and whose size does not preclude personal and friendly service. Perfectly situated in the heart of the town centre, with free parking directly behind the hotel. Closed mid-Nov to mid-Feb. ❺

Family Home 39 rue du Général-de-Dias Ⓣ02.31.92.15.22. This hostel is conveniently central, in a seventeenth-century house, but travellers remain divided as to its merits: some are put off by the staff's often minimal English, while others say you couldn't hope to find a friendlier atmosphere. Its prices are a little high – dorm beds cost €18 for members, €20 for non-members, while private doubles are €30 – but rates include breakfast. Communal dinners, served at 7.30pm nightly at a long table, cost €12 per person. They also offer bike hire and can find you a bed in their other property, about 1km from the centre, if the *Family Home* is full – which it often is during summer. ❶

De la Gare 26 place de la Gare Ⓣ02.31.92.10.70. Old but perfectly adequate basic hotel, with a simple brasserie, beside the station, on the ring road fifteen minutes' walk from the cathedral. ❶

Lion d'Or 71 rue St-Jean Ⓣ02.31.92.06.90, Ⓦwww.liondor-bayeux.fr. Grand old coaching inn, dating from 1734 and affiliated to the quiet "Relais du Silence" organization, that's set back behind a courtyard just beyond the pedestrianized section of rue St-Jean, opposite the Halles des Grains (now the assembly rooms). The rooms themselves are brighter and newer than the exterior suggests. Closed mid-Dec to late Jan. Menus from €26. ❻

Mogodor 20 rue Chartier Ⓣ02.31.92.24.58, Ⓔhotel.mogador@orange.fr. Friendly little hotel facing Bayeux's main square; the rooms are simple but very presentable, with the quieter ones overlooking the inner courtyard. ❸

Reine Mathilde 23 rue Larcher Ⓣ02.31.92.08.13, Ⓦwww.hotel-reinemathilde.com. Simple but well-equipped rooms – all have showers and TV – backing onto the canal, between the tapestry and the cathedral. The nice open-air, lunch-only brasserie downstairs, *Le Guillaume* (closed Tues), has menus from €10. Closed mid-Nov to mid-Feb. ❸

The Town

Housed in an impressive eighteenth-century seminary on rue de Nesmond, the **Bayeux Tapestry** (daily: mid-March to April & Sept–Oct 9am–6.30pm; May–Aug 9am–7pm; Nov to mid-March 9.30am–12.30pm & 2–6pm; last admission 45min before closing; €7.60) – also known to the French as the Tapisserie de la Reine Mathilde – is a seventy-metre strip of embroidered linen that recounts the story of the Norman conquest of England. Although created over nine centuries ago, the brilliance of its coloured wools has barely faded, and the tale is enlivened throughout with parallel scenes of medieval life, popular fables and mythical beasts; the skill of its draughtsmanship, and the sheer vigour and detail, are stunning. The work is thought to have been carried out by monks or nuns in England, commissioned by Bishop Odo, William's half-brother, in time for the inauguration of Bayeux cathedral in 1077.

Visits are well planned and highly atmospheric, if somewhat exhausting. First comes a slide show, projected onto billowing sheets of canvas; you then pass along a photographic replica of the tapestry, with enlargements and detailed commentaries. After an optional film show, you finally approach the real thing, to find that it has a strong three-dimensional presence you might not expect from all the flat reproductions. The tapestry looks – and reads – like a modern comic strip. Harold is every inch the villain, with his dastardly little moustache and shifty eyes. He looks extremely self-satisfied as he breaks his oath to accept William as king of England and seizes the throne for himself, but his comeuppance swiftly follows, as William, the noble hero, crosses the Channel and defeats the English armies at Hastings.

The **Cathédrale Notre-Dame** (daily: Jan–March 9am–5pm; April–June 8am–6pm; July–Sept 8.30am–7pm; Oct–Dec 8.30am–6pm) was the first home of the tapestry and is just a short walk away from its latest resting-place. Despite such eighteenth-century vandalism as the monstrous fungoid baldachin (canopy) that flanks the pulpit, the original Romanesque plan of the building is still intact, although only the crypt and towers date from the original work of 1077. The crypt is a beauty, its columns graced with frescoes of angels playing trumpets and bagpipes, looking exhausted by their performance for eternity. On the southern side of the cathedral, the **Musée Baron Gerard** on rue Lambert-Forestier displays a large collection of beautifully decorated porcelain and intricate lacework, donated by local families over the centuries to the archbishops of Bayeux (daily: July & Aug 10am–12.30pm & 2–7pm; Sept–June 10am–12.30pm & 2–6pm; €2.60, free with ticket for the tapestry).

Although the **Musée-Mémorial Général de Gaulle**, at 10 rue de Bourbesneur near place de Gaulle (March–May & Sept–Nov 10am–12.30pm & 2–6pm, June–Aug daily 9.30am–12.30pm & 2–6.30pm; €3.50), is aimed squarely at French devotees of the great man, it does make an interesting detour for foreign visitors. The sheer obsessiveness of the displays, which focus on the three separate day-trips De Gaulle made to Bayeux during the course of his long life, somehow illuminates the extent to which he came to epitomize the very essence of a certain kind of Frenchness, which seems scarcely removed from self-parody.

Set behind massive guns next to the ring road on the southwest side of town, Bayeux's **Musée de la Bataille de Normandie** (daily: May to mid-Sept 9.30am–6.30pm; mid-Sept to April 10am–12.30pm & 2–6pm; €6.50) is one of the old school of war museums, with its emphasis firmly on hardware rather than humans. By way of contrast, the understated and touching **British War Cemetery** stands immediately across the road (see box, p.375).

Eating

Some of Bayeux's hotels have good dining rooms, while most **restaurants** are in the rue St-Jean leading east from the river; on Sundays most places are shut.

La Fringale 43 rue St-Jean ⓣ02.31.21.34.40. The nicest of the many pavement restaurants along rue St-Jean, offering lunch menus from €14.50, generous salads and snacks and more formal fish dinners. Closed Wed, plus mid-Dec to mid-Feb.

Le Petit Bistrot 2 rue Bienvenue ⓣ02.31.51.85.40. Tiny old place opposite the cathedral, where the menus from €25 upwards boast a fine assortment of terrines and foie gras. Closed Sun & Mon.

Le Petit Normand 35 rue Larcher ⓣ02.31.22.88.66. Below the cathedral, offering good traditional cooking, with seafood specialities and local cider. Lunch menus from €11, dinner from €19. Closed mid-Dec to Jan.

Le Pommier 38–40 rue des Cuisiniers ⓣ02.31.21.52.10. Popular traditional restaurant near the cathedral, with a tiny terrace. Meat- and dairy-rich Norman cuisine on menus from €12.50 (lunch only) up to €28.50, including an €18.50 vegetarian option. Closed mid-Dec to mid-Jan, plus Tues & Wed in low season.

La Table du Terroir 42 rue St-Jean ⓣ02.31.92.05.53. A rendezvous for closet meat freaks, tucked away behind a butcher's shop and serving the freshest, bloodiest flesh on a well-judged triplet of menus, at €16, €21 and €26. Seating is at communal tables. Closed Sun eve in low season.

Cerisy and Balleroy

Heading southwest from Bayeux towards St-Lô, you pass close to the remarkable Romanesque **Abbaye de Cerisy-la-Forêt** (access to church Easter–Oct daily 9am–6.30pm; €2; guided tours Easter–Sept daily 10.30am–12.30pm & 2.30–6.30pm; Oct Sat & Sun 10.30am–noon & 2.30–6pm; €4), halfway along the D572 and 5km to the north of it. Its triple tiers of windows and arches and the delicate workmanship of its nave and choir are testimony to the breathtaking skills of medieval Norman masons.

No less notable is the **Château de Balleroy** (château and museum mid-March to mid-Oct daily 10am–6pm; mid-Oct to mid-March daily 10am–noon & 2–5pm; ⓦwww.chateau-balleroy.com; château €5.35, museum €4.27, both €6.86), 3km southeast of the same junction, where you switch to an era when architects ruled over craftsmen. The main street of the village leads straight to the brick-and-stone château, a masterpiece of François Mansart, the celebrated seventeenth-century architect, which stands like a faultlessly reasoned and dogmatic argument for the power of its owners and their class. It belongs to the family of the late American press magnate Malcolm Forbes, owner of *Forbes* magazine, keen balloonist and pal of Nixon, Ford and Nancy Reagan. His is the enlarged colour photograph sharing the stairwell with Dutch still lifes, and he left his mark on most other aspects of the house, too – only the salon remains in its original state of glory, with brilliant portraits of the (then) royal family by Mignard. Admission also includes a **hot-air balloon museum**.

The Cotentin Peninsula

Hard against the frontier with Brittany, and cut off from the rest of Normandy by difficult marshy terrain, the **Cotentin Peninsula** has traditionally been seen as something of a backwater, far removed from the French mainstream. It nonetheless makes a surprisingly rewarding goal for travellers, and one that by sea at least is very easily accessible. Regular ferries from both England and Ireland dock at the peninsula's major port, **Cherbourg**, a city turned resolutely seaward. Nearby are a plethora of attractive little villages, such as **Barfleur** and **St-Vaast**, nestled amid the hills to the east, and the handsome landscapes of heather-clad cliffs and stone-wall-divided patchwork fields to be found in La Hague to the west.

For many visitors the Cotentin's long western flank, with its flat beaches, serves primarily as a prelude to **Mont St-Michel**, with hill towns such as **Coutances** and **Avranches** cherishing architectural and historical relics associated with the abbey. Halfway down, however, the walled port of **Granville**, an extremely popular destination with French holiday-makers, is a sort of small-scale mirror-image of Brittany's St-Malo.

Cherbourg

If you are arriving from Britain or Ireland, **CHERBOURG** may well be your port of arrival. Many people head straight out and on, yet the town offers a busy network of pedestrian streets lined with appealing stone facades, the labyrinth of alleyways known as *boëls*, some lively bars, and an impressive maritime museum in a converted Art Deco station. In addition there are some extremely appealing destinations a short distance to either side, not least the varied landscapes of La Hague. Napoleon inaugurated the transformation of

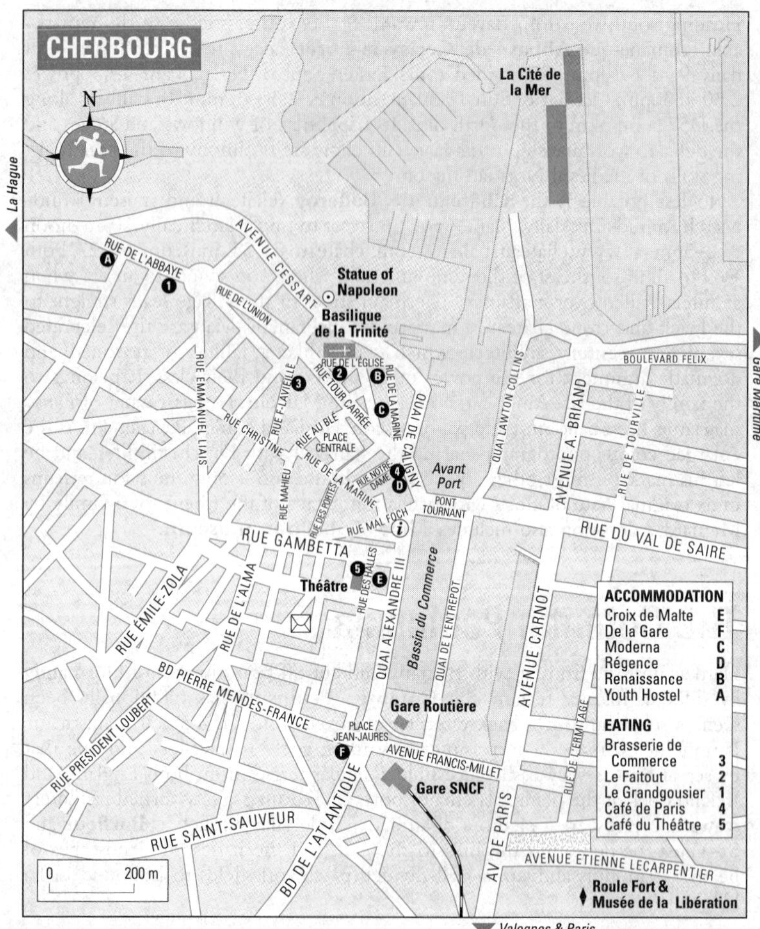

what had been a rather poor, but perfectly situated, natural harbour into a major transatlantic port, by means of massive artificial breakwaters. An equestrian statue commemorates his boast that in Cherbourg he would "recreate the wonders of Egypt"; although there are as yet no pyramids nearer than the Louvre, he succeeded in providing the city with one of the biggest fortified harbours in the world.

Arrival and information

The days of the great transatlantic liners may be over, but cross-Channel ferries still sail into Cherbourg's **gare maritime** (daily 5.30am–11.30pm; ⓣ02.33.44.20.13), not far east of the town centre. Brittany Ferries ⓣ08.03.82.88.28, ⓦwww.brittany-ferries.com) operate services from both Portsmouth (1–2 daily; May–Oct high-speed 3hr, otherwise 5–7hr) and Poole (1–3 daily; some high-speed in summer, 2hr 15min, otherwise 4hr 15min–5hr 30min). Irish Ferries also sail to Cherbourg, from Rosslare (3–4 weekly; ⓣ02.33.23.44.44, ⓦwww.irishferries.com). Regular €1 shuttle buses connect the terminal with the tourist office and **gare SNCF**.

Cherbourg's **tourist office** is at 2 quai Alexandre III (June Mon–Sat 9am–12.30pm & 2–6.30pm; July & Aug Mon–Sat 9am–6.30pm, Sun 10am–12.30pm; Sept–May Mon–Fri 9am–noon & 2–6pm Sat 9am–12.30pm & 2–6pm; ⓣ02.33.93.52.02, ⓦwww.ot-cherbourg-cotentin.fr). The **gare SNCF**, on avenue François-Miller/place Jean-Jaurès, is served by regular trains to Paris, Bayeux and Caen. Tourisme Verney (ⓣ02.33.44.32.22) run buses to Barfleur, Valognes, Coutances, St-Lô, Granville and other destinations from the **gare routière** opposite.

Accommodation

By usual Norman standards, **room rates** in Cherbourg are very reasonable and there's no reason for ferry passengers to avoid spending a night here, though traffic and the lack of parking space can be problematic. Few hotels maintain their own restaurants, but there are plenty of independent eateries to choose from.

Hotels

Croix de Malte 5 rue des Halles ⓣ02.33.43.19.16, ⓔhotel.croix.malte@orange.fr. Simple hotel on three upstairs floors, one block back from the harbour and around the corner from the theatre. Clean renovated rooms – all have TV and at least a shower – with the cheapest rates being for the perfectly acceptable, windowless ones in the attic. ❷

De la Gare 10 place Jean-Jaurès ⓣ02.33.43.06.81, ⓔluc-fleury@orange.fr. Very convenient for the *gares SNCF* and *routière*, if not exactly stunning in itself. The cheapest rooms have a shower but no toilet. ❷

Moderna 28 rue de la Marine ⓣ02.33.43.05.30, ⓦwww.moderna-hotel.com. Reasonable, very well-priced rooms, slightly back from the harbour; the cheapest have only sinks, while the pricier ones have phones, good showers and cable TV. ❶

Régence 42–44 quai de Caligny ⓣ02.33.43.05.16, ⓦwww.laregence.com. Small, neat rooms overlooking the harbour, in a Logis de France just around the corner from the tourist office. The restaurant downstairs starts with a reasonable €17 menu, and ranges up to €31, but it's not the best along the *quai*. ❹

Renaissance 4 rue de l'Église ⓣ02.33.43.23.90, ⓦwww. hotel-renaissance-cherbourg.com. Nicely refurbished rooms, all en suite and some with sea views, in a friendly hotel facing the port in the most appealing quarter of town. The "Église" of the address is the attractive Trinité. ❸

Hostel and campsite

Camping de Collignon Tourlaville ⓣ02.33.20.16.88, ⓦwww.mairie-tourlaville.fr. Three-star campsite, 3km east towards Barfleur, that's the closest to the ferry terminal. Closed Oct–April.

Youth Hostel 55 rue de l'Abbaye ⓣ02.33.78.15.15, ⓔcherbourg@fuaj.org. Well-equipped red-brick hostel, 15min walk west of the centre, offering dorm beds for €16.40 (members) or €19.50 (non-members), including breakfast and bicycle hire. Two bedrooms are designed for visitors with limited mobility. Check-in 9am–1pm or 6–11pm, closed Jan.

The Town

Cherbourg's best, and newest, attraction is **La Cité de la Mer** (daily: May, June & Sept 9.30am–6pm; July & Aug 9.30am–7pm; Oct–Dec & Feb–April 10am–6pm, with irregular closures on certain Mondays; closed Jan; last entry 1hr before closing; April–Sept €14, Oct–March €12.50; Ⓦ www.citedelamer.com). The museum combines often quite technical displays, explained in both French and English, on every aspect of the sea – myths and legends, environmental issues including climatic change, economic activities and, above all, exploration of the seabed – with aquariums and a visitable nuclear submarine. You enter through the grand former Transatlantic ferry terminal, a fabulously restored Art Deco treasure, housing the ticket offices, a cafeteria, an excellent restaurant unsurprisingly specializing in seafood, a mediathèque and temporary exhibits. Frequently interactive displays in a new building behind tell the story of underwater exploration in history and fiction, moving swiftly via Jules Verne and H.P. Lovecraft to Jacques Cousteau, pictured with a diving saucer shaped, as the museum claims, "like a giant lentil" in 1959. Separate fish tanks hold giant crabs, sharks, eels, jellyfish, seahorses, and large (though sadly not giant) squid, while at different levels you can peer into a vast cylindrical aquarium where shoals of vivid fish offer a colourful spectacle – all with an educational emphasis on aspects such as how marine creatures move and survive.

The overarching idea is to show how human submarine technology was inspired by the wonders of nature, preparing the visitor for the main attraction: in a dry dock alongside stands the dark cigar-shaped hulk of *Le Redoutable*, France's first ballistic missile submarine. Armed with an audio-commentary you can scramble through its labyrinth of tube-like corridors and control rooms, though as the miniature nuclear power station that once powered it has been removed, there's a cavernous empty space at its heart. The cramped crew quarters will feel very familiar if you've just shared a cabin on an overnight ferry crossing, while the plush carpeting and moulded chairs in the living room are remarkably reminiscent of Elvis's Graceland.

Otherwise, if you're waiting for a boat, the best way to kill time is to settle into a café or restaurant or do some last-minute shopping. Try the excellent Thursday **market**, held on and off rue des Halles, near the majestic theatre with its *belle-époque* facade, or the tempting array of small shops and boutiques clustered round the place Centrale – including a place to buy the city's most famous product, the genuine **Cherbourg umbrella**, at 30 rue des Portes.

As for walking off lunch, the only area in the centre that really encourages a ramble is over by the **Basilique de la Trinité**, worth a quick look inside for its English alabaster decorations dating from the Hundred Years War, and the former town **beach**, now grassed over to form the "Plage Verte". Over to the south, you could alternatively climb up to **Roule Fort** for an impressive view of the whole port. The fort itself contains a **Musée de la Libération** (June–Sept Mon & Sun 2–6pm, Tues–Sat 10am–noon & 2–6pm; Oct–May Wed–Sun 2–6pm; €3), with the usual dry maps and diagrams but plenty of contemporary newsreel – much of it, for once, in English – commemorating the period in 1944 when Cherbourg was briefly the busiest port in the world.

Eating

Restaurants in Cherbourg divide readily into the glass-fronted seafood places along the quai de Caligny, each with its "copious" *assiette de fruits de mer*, and the more varied, more adventurous and less expensive little places tucked away in the pedestrianized streets and alleyways of the old town. This is also where you'll find some animated **bars**, especially along rue de l'Union.

Brasserie de Commerce 42 rue François-la-Vieille ☎02.33.53.18.20. If you're tired of white tablecloths and over-attentive service, this in-town brasserie, much large than it looks from the outside, serves huge portions of good food from 11am until late, with cheap menus from €13 and plenty of à la carte options. The home-made pâté is particularly good. Closed Sun.

Le Faitout 25 rue Tour-Carrée ☎02.33.04.25.04. Shopping-district restaurant that offers traditional French cuisine, including bowls of mussels, prepared with celery, apples and the like, generally for under €10. Most dishes are à la carte with meat and fish dishes priced around €10–13. Closed Sun & Mon.

Le Grandgousier 21 rue de l'Abbaye ☎02.33.53.19.43. Formal, definitive French fish restaurant, well worth the walk to its unprepossessing location at the west end of town. Menus start at €16, but this is a place to expect to spend a lot and dine well, with lobster, for example, featuring on the €38 option. Closed Sun eve & Mon.

Café de Paris 40 quai de Caligny ☎02.33.43.12.36. Work your way up through the ranks of *assiettes de fruits de mer*, from the €18.50 *Matelot* to the *Amiral* at €110 for two; there's also a selection of menus from €21, featuring a few meat dishes along with the predominately fishy selection. Closed Sun eve, plus Mon lunch in low season.

Café du Théâtre 8 place de Gaulle ☎02.33.43.01.49. Attractive setup adjoining the theatre, with a café behind plate-glass windows on the ground floor and a full-scale brasserie upstairs, arranged on three sides of the central opening. It's a place used by the community as a whole rather than a typical tourist restaurant. The varied menus, from €13.50, offer more than just seafood; the €24 one features snails. Closed Sun.

Around the Cotentin

Once you get away from the industrial harbour city of Cherbourg, the largely rural Cotentin Peninsula is geographically an area of transition. Little ports such as **Barfleur** on the indented northern headland presage the rocky Breton coast, while inland the meadows resemble the farmlands of the Bocage and the Bessin. **La Hague** is a little-explored gem – many people are put off by its associations with a nuclear reprocessing plant – where all manner of activities, from sailing and diving to riding and rambling, can be practised. In any case, the temptation to race south towards Mont St-Michel is likely to be thwarted by slow traffic on the peninsula's narrow roads, though the Cherbourg–St-Lô route is now mostly four-lane, so you might as well stop off in your pick of the towns and resorts that line its western shore, such as **Coutances**, **Granville** and **Avranches**.

Barfleur

The pleasant little harbour village of **BARFLEUR**, 25km east of Cherbourg, was the biggest port in Normandy seven centuries ago. The population has since dwindled from nine thousand to six hundred, and fortunes have diminished – most recently through the invasion of a strain of plankton that poisoned all the mussels. It's now a surprisingly low-key place, where the sweeping crescent of the grey-granite quayside sees little tourist activity. Near the town, about a thirty-minute walk away, the Gatteville lighthouse is the second tallest in France (daily: March, May–Aug & Oct 10am–noon & 2–7pm; April & Sept 10am–noon & 2–6pm; Feb, first two weeks in Nov & last two weeks in Dec 10am–noon & 2–4pm; closed mid-Nov to mid-Dec & all Jan; €2). It guards the rocks on which William, son and heir of Henry I of England, was drowned in 1120, together with three hundred of his nobles.

Barfleur has two fine **hotels**. *Le Conquérant* stands a short distance back from the sea at 16–18 rue St-Thomas-à-Becket (02.33.54.00.82; closed mid-Nov to mid-March; 4); behind its stern stone facade lies a gorgeous, rambling and very welcoming old town house, where the nicest rooms face onto a lovely garden, and there's a summer-only crêperie. *Le Moderne* is tucked away south of the main road at 1 place de Gaulle (02.33.23.12.44; closed Tues eve & Wed mid-Sept to mid-July, plus all Jan to mid-Feb; 3); some of the rooms are very inexpensive, while the restaurant is superb, with the €25 menu featuring a fish-shaped *feuilleton* (pastry) of seafood. The house speciality is oysters, stuffed or raw. A nice, albeit basic **campsite** stands a couple of kilometres north of town in Le Crabec. *La Ferme du Bord du Mer* (02.33.54.01.77), true to its name, is a farm beside the sea, where grassy meadows hold donkeys as well as tents and caravans, and there's a scruffy flat beach.

Surprisingly, no hotels, and barely any bars or other businesses, face the harbour itself, but there is another excellent restaurant on the waterfront, the friendly and very charming *Comptoir de la Presqu'île*, 30 quai Henri-Chardon 02.33.20.37.51), which as well as its outdoor tables has an upstairs dining room with good views of the port. The cuisine is all à la carte, and is dominated by fish, with a deliciously simple whole grilled bream costing the amazing price of €9.20.

St-Vaast

Pretty **ST-VAAST-LA-HOUGUE**, 11km south of Barfleur, is more of a resort, with lots of tiny Channel-crossing yachts moored in the bay where Edward III landed on his way to Crécy and a string of fortifications from Vauban's time. The *Hôtel de France et des Fuchsias*, just back from the sea at 18 rue du Maréchal-Foch (02.33.54.42.26, www.france-fuchsias.com; closed Jan–Feb, plus Mon in winter; 3–7) has splendid gardens and an excellent restaurant and is an ideal stopover for ferry passengers – in fact both it and the annexe at the end of the garden are packed throughout the season with British visitors.

Utah Beach

The westernmost of the main Invasion Beaches, **Utah Beach** stretches for approximately thirty kilometres south from St-Vaast. From 6.30am onwards on D-Day, 23,000 men and 1700 vehicles landed here. A minor coast road, the D241, traces the edge of the dunes and enables visitors to follow the course of the fighting, though in truth there's precious little to see these days. Ships deliberately sunk to create artificial breakwaters are still visible at low tide, while markers along the seafront commemorate individual fallen heroes.

Two museums now tell the story: the **Mémorial de la Liberté** in **QUINÉVILLE** (April to mid-Nov daily 10am–7pm; www.memorial-quineville.com; €6), which focuses on everyday life for the people of Normandy under Nazi occupation, and the much more comprehensive **Musée du Débarquement d'Utah-Beach** in **STE-MARIE-DU-MONT** (Feb, March & first two weeks of Nov daily 10am–12.30pm & 2–5.30pm; April, May & Oct daily 10am–6pm; June–Sept daily 9.30am–7pm; mid-Nov–Dec Sat, Sun & hols 10am–12.30pm & 2–5.30pm; closed Jan; www.utah-beach.com; €5), which explains the operations in exhaustive detail, with huge sea-view windows to lend immediacy to the copious models, maps, films and diagrams.

La Hague

If you go west from Cherbourg to **La Hague**, the northern tip of the peninsula, you'll find wild and isolated countryside where you can lean into the wind, watch waves smashing against rocks in secluded inlets or sunbathe amid a spring profusion of wild flowers, while a whole range of activities are on offer. The area's main **tourist office**, at 45 rue Jallot in the village of Beaumont-Hague, 14km out of Cherbourg on the D901, can supply the details (June Mon–Sat 9am–12.30pm & 2–6.30pm; July–Aug Mon–Sat 9am–6.30pm, Sun 10am–12.30pm; Sept–May Mon–Sat 9am–12.30pm & 2–6pm; ⓣ02.33.52.74.94, ⓦwww.lahague.org).

Attractions on the cape include some of the highest cliffs in Europe at the **Nez de Jobourg**, reachable by the Sentier des Douaniers, a well-marked ramblers' path that hugs the coast for 43km between Urville-Nacqueville, on the north coast, to the dunes at Biville, in the far south of the region. Crêperies, bars and little restaurants dot the headland, as do *gîtes-rurales* (information also from the tourist office), many in the area's handsome, immaculately kept stone cottages, with their slate roofs and pretty gardens.

Art and poetry fans might like to visit the houses where Jean-François Millet and Jacques Prévert were born and died respectively. The painter of poster-favourite *Les Glaneuses* was born at Hameau Gruchy (daily April & May 2–6pm, June & Sept 11am–6pm, July & Aug 11am–7pm; €4), at **GRÉVILLE-HAGUE**, where temporary exhibitions are held, while the great twentieth-century writer's workshop and garden at the home he retired to in the 1970s can be visited at Le Val, **OMONVILLE-LA-PETITE** (same opening hours and fee as the Millet house). Two other interests, star-gazing and botany, are catered for at the Ludiver planetarium at the village of **TONNEVILLE**, in the east of the promontory (July & Aug daily 10am–7pm; Sept–June Mon–Fri 9am–12.30pm & 2–5.30pm, Sun & public holidays 2–6pm, closed Sat; see website for schedules of planetarium shows; tour €3.50, tour and show €7; ⓦwww.ludiver.com), and at the tropical-looking garden at the Château de Vauville, in the especially picturesque village of **VAUVILLE** to the west (May, June & Sept Tues & Fri–Sun 2–6pm; July & Aug daily 2–6pm; access free, tours €6; ⓦwww.jardin-vauville.fr); it is famed for its huge palm-grove, a sign of the area's mild microclimate.

South of La Hague a great curve of sand – some of it military training ground – takes the land's edge to **Flamanville** and another nuclear installation. But the next two sweeps of beach down to **Carteret**, with sand dunes like mini-mountain ranges, are probably the best beaches in Normandy: there are no resorts, no hotels and just two campsites – at **Le Rozel** (*Le Ranch*; ⓣ02.33.10.07.10, ⓦwww.camping-leranch.com; closed Oct–March) and **Surtainville** (*Les Mielles*; ⓣ02.33.04.31.04, ⓦwww.surtainville.new.fr).

Coutances

The old hill town of **COUTANCES**, 65km south of Cherbourg, confined by its site to just one main street, has on its summit a landmark for all the surrounding countryside, the **Cathédrale de Notre-Dame**. Essentially Gothic, it is still very Norman in its unconventional blending of architectural traditions, and the octagonal lantern crowning the crossing in the nave is nothing short of divinely inspired. The son et lumière on Sunday evenings and throughout the summer is for once a true complement to the light stone building. Also illuminated on summer nights (and left open) are the formal fountained **public gardens**.

Coutances' **gare SNCF**, about 1.5km southeast of the town centre (at the bottom of the hill), also serves as the stop for **buses** heading north and south. The local **tourist office** is housed behind the Hôtel de Ville in place Georges-Léclerc (July & Aug Mon–Fri 9.30am–6pm, Sat 10am–noon & 2–6pm, Sun 10am–1pm; Sept–June Mon–Wed & Fri 9.30am–12.30pm & 2–6pm, Thurs 9.30am–6pm, Sat 10am–12.30pm & 2–5pm; Ⓣ02.33.19.08.10, Ⓦwww.ville-coutances.fr). Central Coutances is very short of **hotels**. In the cathedral square, the *Hôtel du Parvis* (Ⓣ02.33.45.13.55; ❸; restaurant closed Sun), has unexciting but adequate rooms, above a reasonable brasserie. A more comfortable alternative is the large *Cositel* (Ⓣ02.33.19.15.00; Ⓦwww.hotelcositel.com; ❸), halfway up the hill west of town that's climbed by the D44 towards Agon. That stands next to an excellent year-round municipal **campsite**, *Les Vignettes* (Ⓣ02.33.45.43.13).

Granville

From Coutances, the D971 runs down to the coast at **GRANVILLE**, the Norman equivalent of Brittany's St-Malo, with a history of piracy and the severe citadel of the **haute ville** guarding the approaches to the bay of Mont St-Michel. Thanks in part to the long beach that stretches away north of town, and disappears almost completely at low tide, it's the most lively town and most popular resort in the area. However, with its nightmarish traffic and hordes of tourists milling around in summer in the vain hope of finding some way of amusing themselves, it simply doesn't match the appeal of its Breton rival.

The great difference between Granville and St-Malo is that in Granville the fortified citadel contains little of interest, just three or four long, narrow, parallel streets of forbidding grey-granite eighteenth-century houses, although the views up and down the coast, across to Mont St-Michel and out to the Îles Chausey, whose granite was quarried for the Mont St-Michel buildings, are dramatic. In pride of place at the inland end of the haute ville is the **Musée d'Art Moderne Richard Anacréon** (April–Sept daily except Mon 11am–6pm, Oct–March Wed–Sun 2–6pm; €2.60), housing art accumulated by a Parisian bookseller from 1940 onwards. Filled with sketches and autographs from the likes of Jean Cocteau and André Derain, it's not all that compelling, but the gallery itself is impressive, and hosts interesting temporary exhibitions.

The **tourist office** is below the citadel at 4 cours Jonville (July & Aug Mon–Sat 9am–1pm & 2–7pm, Sun 10am–1pm; Sept–June Mon–Sat 9am–noon & 2–6pm; Ⓣ02.33.91.30.03, Ⓦwww.ville-granville.fr). Trains between Paris and Cherbourg arrive well to the east at the **gare SNCF** on avenue Maréchal-Leclerc, which also serves as the **gare routière**. **Ferries** run from Granville to the Channel Islands and the Îles Chausey.

With so many visitors in summer, it's well worth booking **accommodation** in advance, most of it concentrated in the new town that sprawls below the citadel, either beneath the walls on the seaward side, or near the station. The *Michelet*, 5 rue Jules-Michelet (Ⓣ02.33.50.06.55; ❶), is well equipped but characterless; the *Des Bains*, closer to the tourist office at 19 rue G-Clemenceau (Ⓣ02.33.50.17.31; ❸), has a reasonable restaurant. An option nearer the station is the *Terminus* at 5 place de la Gare (Ⓣ02.33.50.02.05, Ⓦwww.hotel-granville-france.com; ❷). The modern, oceanfront *Centre Régional de Nautisme* (Ⓣ02.33.91.22.62, Ⓦwww.crng.asso.fr; closed Sat & Sun Nov–Feb; €12.50 per dorm bed), a kilometre south of the station in the town centre, serves as Granville's **hostel**.

Where Granville really does excel is in its waterfront **restaurants**, hard below the citadel walls, though be warned that the views here are of a gritty commercial port rather than a delightful harbour. The best are the *Restaurant du Port*, 19 rue du Port (Ⓣ02.33.50.00.55; closed Sun eve, plus Mon in low season), with its mouthwatering assortment of very fishy menus, and the *Phare*, nearby at no. 11

(Ⓣ02.33.50.12.94; closed Tues & Wed), which has the standard mussels and *panaché de poissons* on its €18.50 menu, and a superb *assiette des fruits de mer* on the €29.50 equivalent. Up in the old town, *L'Échauguette*, 24 rue St-Jean (Ⓣ02.33.50.51.87), serves good crêpes and simple meals, cooked over an open fire.

St-Jean-le-Thomas and Gênets

South of Granville the crowded towns and small resorts compete for views and proximity to Mont St-Michel. **ST-JEAN-LE-THOMAS** is the first point from which you can walk at low tide across the bay to the abbey, although it's not a walk to take on a drunken impulse. The tide, as they like to tell you, comes up faster than galloping horses. You can join a **guided walk** from the beach at **GÊNETS** with Chemins de la Baie (most days mid-April to Oct, depending on tides; Ⓣ02.33.89.80.88, Ⓦwww.cheminsdelabaie.com; €5.50–20).

Avranches

AVRANCHES is the nearest large town to Mont St-Michel, and it has always had close connections with the abbey. The Mont's original church was founded by a bishop of Avranches, spurred on by the Archangel Michael, who supposedly became so impatient with the lack of progress that he prodded a hole in the bishop's skull – still to be seen in Avranches' **St-Gervais basilica**. Robert of Torigny, a subsequent abbot of St-Michel, played host in the town on several occasions to Henry II of England, the most memorable being when Henry was obliged, barefoot and bareheaded, to do public penance for the murder of Thomas Becket, on May 22, 1172. The arena for this act of contrition was Avranches cathedral, designed, most inexpertly, by de Torigny himself: the cathedral swiftly "crumbled and fell for want of proper support", and all that marks the site today is a fenced-off platform – the *plate-forme*.

A more vivid evocation of the area's medieval splendours comes from the illuminated manuscripts, mostly created on the Mont, on display in a state-of-the-art new museum in the place d'Estouteville, the **Scriptorial d'Avranches** (Feb–April & Oct–Dec Tues–Fri 10am–12.30pm & 2–5pm, Sat & Sun 10am–12.30pm & 2–6pm; May, June & Sept daily except Mon 10am–6pm; July & Aug daily 10–7pm; closed Jan; €7). Additional exhibits trace the history of Avranches, and bring the story up to date by covering modern book-production techniques.

The **gare SNCF** is about a mile downhill from the town centre. In high summer, one bus per day runs to Mont St-Michel from the **tourist office** on place Général-de-Gaulle (July & Aug Mon–Sat 9.30am–12.30pm & 2–7pm, Sun 9.30am–12.30pm & 2–6pm; Sept–June Mon–Fri 9.30am–12.30pm & 2–6pm, Sat 10am–12.30pm & 2–6pm; Ⓣ02.33.58.00.22, Ⓦwww.ot-avranches.com). The nicest **hotel** has to be the gloriously old-fashioned *Croix d'Or*, near the Patton monument at 83 rue de la Constitution (Ⓣ02.33.58.04.88, Ⓦwww.hoteldelacroixdor.fr; closed Jan, plus Sun eve in winter; ④), which boasts beautiful hydrangea-filled gardens and absolutely the best **restaurant** in town. Reasonable alternatives include *Le Jardin des Plantes*, across town at 10 place Carnot (Ⓣ02.33.58.03.68; Ⓦwww.le-jardin-des-plantes.fr; ④), where the restaurant is more basic but still good value.

Mont St-Michel

The island of **MONT ST-MICHEL** was once known as the "Mount in Peril from the Sea", as many pilgrims in medieval times drowned or were sucked

Visiting Mont St-Michel

Access to the island of Mont St-Michel is free and unrestricted, although there's a €4 fee to park on either the causeway or the sands below it (which are submerged by the tides). If you're visiting by car in summer, you might prefer to park on the mainland well short of the Mont, both to enjoy the walk across the causeway and to avoid the dense traffic jams.

Between May and August, the **abbey** is open daily from 9am to 7pm, with last admission at 6pm; from September to April, it's open daily from 9.30am until 6pm, last admission at 5pm. It's closed on Jan 1, May 1 and Dec 25. The same **admission fee** (adults €8, ages 18–25 €4.50, under-18s free) is charged whether you choose to wander the generally accessible areas on your own, or to join an expert-led **guided tour**. The tours last 45 minutes between mid-June and mid-Sept, and a full hour the rest of the year, and are available in French and English year round, as well as other languages in summer; the daily schedule for each language is displayed at the entrance to the abbey and at the tourist office. There are also a number of more detailed two-hour tours, in French only, which take you both higher and deeper (July & Aug daily 10.30am, 11.30am, 2pm & 4pm; Sept–June Sat & Sun 10.30am & 2pm; €4 extra).

In some recent years, the Mont has stayed open **after hours** during July and August, both in the early evening when visitors can stroll freely in the gardens, and at night when the abbey itself has reopened for musical and video installations. Whether it does so in any particular year seems to be unpredictable, however; contact the tourist office or access Ⓦwww.monum.fr for the latest information.

under by quicksand while trying to cross the bay to the eighty-metre-high rocky outcrop. The Archangel Michael was its vigorous protector, the most militant spirit of the Church Militant, with a marked tendency to leap from rock to rock in titanic struggles against Paganism and Evil. The abbey dates back to the eighth century, when the archangel supposedly appeared to a bishop of Avranches, Aubert, who duly founded a monastery on the island poking out of the Baie du Mont St-Michel. Since the eleventh century – when work on the sturdy church at the peak commenced – new buildings have been grafted onto the island to produce a fortified hotchpotch of Romanesque and Gothic buildings clambering to the pinnacle of the graceful church, forming probably the most recognizable silhouette in France after the Eiffel Tower.

Although it was such a prominent **religious community**, there were never more than forty monks resident on the Mont up to the time of the Revolution, when it was converted into a prison. In 1966, exactly a thousand years after Duke Richard the First originally brought the order to the Mont, the Benedictines were invited to return, but they departed again in 2001, having found that the present-day island does not exactly lend itself to a life of quiet contemplation. In their place, a dozen nuns and monks from the Monastic Fraternity of Jerusalem now maintain a presence.

For many years, the Mont has not, strictly speaking, been an island – the causeway (*digue*) that leads to it is never submerged, and is continuing to silt up to either side. Current plans envisage that the causeway will soon be cut away and replaced by a bridge, with a tram service to spare visitors the two-kilometre walk from the mainland. Currently scheduled for completion in 2010, this should not only make tourist numbers easier to control but also enable the sea to wash away much of the accumulated silt. For the latest news on the project, contact Ⓦwww.projetmontsaintmichel.org.

The abbey

The **abbey**, an architectural ensemble incorporating the high-spired, archangel-topped church and the magnificent Gothic buildings known since 1228 as the **Merveille** ("The Marvel") – which in turn includes the entire north face, with the cloister, Knights' Hall, Refectory, Guest Hall and cellars – is visible from all around the bay, but it becomes if anything more awe-inspiring the closer you approach. In Maupassant's words:

> I reached the huge pile of rocks which bears the little city dominated by the great church. Climbing the steep narrow street, I entered the most wonderful Gothic dwelling ever made for God on this earth, a building as vast as a town, full of low rooms under oppressive ceilings and lofty galleries supported by frail pillars. I entered that gigantic granite jewel, which is as delicate as a piece of lacework, thronged with towers and slender belfries which thrust into the blue sky of day and the black sky of night their strange heads bristling with chimeras, devils, fantastic beasts and monstrous flowers, and which are linked together by carved arches of intricate design.

The Mont's rock comes to a sharp point just below what is now the transept of the **church**, a building where the transition from Romanesque to Gothic is only too evident in the vaulting of the nave. In order to lay out the church's ground plan in the traditional shape of the cross, supporting crypts had to be built up from the surrounding hillside, and in all construction work the Chausey granite has had to be sculpted to match the exact contours of the hill. Space was always limited, and yet the building has grown through the centuries, with an architectural ingenuity that constantly surprises in its geometry – witness the shock of emerging into the light of the cloisters from the sombre Great Hall.

Not surprisingly, the building of the **monastery** was no smooth progression: the original church, choir, nave and tower all had to be replaced after collapsing. The style of decoration has varied, too, along with the architecture. That you now walk through halls of plain grey stone is a reflection of modern taste. In the Middle Ages, the walls of public areas such as the refectory would have been festooned with tapestries and frescoes, while the original coloured tiles of the cloisters have long since been stripped away to reveal bare walls.

To get a clearer sense of the abbey's historical development, be sure to take a look at the intriguing scale models in the reception area, which depict it during four different epochs.

The rest of the island

The base of Mont St-Michel rests on a primeval slime of sand and mud. Just above that, you pass through the heavily fortified **Porte du Roi** onto the narrow **Grande Rue**, climbing steadily around the base of the rock and lined with medieval gabled houses and a jumble of overpriced postcard and souvenir shops, maintaining the ancient tradition of prising pilgrims from their money. A plaque near the main staircase records that Jacques Cartier was presented to King François I here on May 8, 1532, and charged with exploring the shores of Canada.

The rather dry **Musée Maritime** offers an insight into the island's ties with the sea, while the Archangel Michael manages in just fifteen minutes to lead visitors on a voyage through space and time in the **Archéoscope**, with the full majestic panoply of multimedia mumbo jumbo. Further along the Grande Rue and up the steps towards the abbey church, next door to the eleventh-century **church of St-Pierre**, the absurd **Musée Grévin** contains such edifying specimens as a wax model of a woman drowning in a sea of mud (open Feb to mid-Nov daily 9am–6pm; €15 for all, or €7 each one).

Large crowds gather each day at the **North Tower**, to watch the tide sweep in across the bay. Seagulls wheel away in alarm, and those foolish enough to be wandering too late on the sands have to sprint to safety.

Practicalities

Mont St-Michel has its own **tourist office**, in the lowest gateway (April–June & Sept Mon–Sat 9am–12.30pm & 2–6.30pm, Sun 9am–noon & 2–6pm; July & Aug daily 9am–7pm; Oct–March Mon–Sat 9am–noon & 2–6pm, Sun 10am–noon & 2–5pm; ⓣ02.33.60.14.30, ⓦwww.ot-montsaintmichel.com). Regular buses connect it with the SNCF stations at Pontorson (see below), Rennes and St-Malo.

The island holds a surprising number of **hotels** and **restaurants**, albeit nothing like enough to cope with the sheer number of visitors. Most are predictably expensive, though virtually all seem to keep a few cheaper rooms. The most famous hotel, *La Mère Poulard* (ⓣ02.33.89.68.68, ⓦwww.mere-poulard.com; ❼–❾), uses the time-honoured legend of its fluffy omelettes, as enjoyed by Leon Trotsky and Margaret Thatcher (not simultaneously), to justify extortionate charges. Higher up the Mont, room prices fall to more realistic levels. The cheapest option is the *Du Guesclin* (ⓣ02.33.60.14.10, ⓔhotel.duguesclin@orange.fr; closed Nov–March; ❹), a Logis de France where all the rooms have been reasonably spruced up, and five have sea views; the nicest is the *Hôtel La Croix Blanche* (ⓣ02.33.60.14.04; closed mid-Nov to mid-Feb; ❻), with its small but exquisite rooms; and the *Mouton Blanc* (ⓣ02.33.60.14.08, ⓦwww.lemoutonblanc.com; ❺) falls somewhere in between.

Sadly, **restaurants** on the Mont are consistently worse than almost anywhere in France; it's impossible to make any confident recommendations other than to eat elsewhere. In addition, the main approach road to the island, the D976, is lined shortly before the causeway by around a dozen large and virtually indistinguishable hotels and motels, each with its own brasserie or restaurant. Typical among these are the *Motel Vert* (ⓣ02.33.60.09.33, ⓦwww.le-mont-saint-michel.com; closed mid-Nov to early Feb; ❸), the *Hôtel Formule Verte* (ⓣ02.33.60.14.13, ⓦwww.le-mont-saint-michel.com; closed mid-Nov to mid-Feb; ❸), and the *Hôtel de la Digue* (ⓣ02.33.60.14.02, ⓦwww.ladigue.fr; closed Dec–Feb; ❹). The three-star, 350-pitch *Camping du Mont-St-Michel* (ⓣ02.33.60.22.10; closed mid-Nov to mid-Feb) is also on the mainland just short of the causeway.

Many visitors to Mont St-Michel choose instead to stay at **PONTORSON**, 6km inland, which has the nearest **gare SNCF**, connected to the Mont by a bus service (€5 return). The **hotels** here are not especially interesting, but both the *Montgomery*, in a fine old ivy-covered mansion at 13 rue du Couesnon (ⓣ02.33.60.00.09, ⓦwww.hotel-montgomery.fr; closed two weeks in Feb & Nov; ❹), and the *Tour Brette*, 8 rue du Couesnon (ⓣ02.33.60.10.69, ⓦwww.latourbrette.fr.st; ❷; restaurant closed Wed in low season), have good restaurants.

Inland Normandy

Seeking out specific highlights is not really the point when you're exploring **inland Normandy**. The pleasure of a visit lies not so much in show-stopping sights or individual towns as in the feel of the landscape – the lush meadows, orchards and forests of the Norman countryside. **Gastronomy** is, of course, a major motivation for coming here. The cheeses, creams, apple and pear brandies and ciders for which the region is famous are at their best in the **Pays d'Auge**, south of Lisieux, and the **Vire Valley** to the west. The **Suisse Normande** is canoeing and rock-climbing country, and there are endless good walks in the stretch along the southern border of the province designated as the **Parc Naturel Régional de Normandie-Maine**. Of the towns, **Conches** is the most charming, **Falaise** has William the Conqueror as a constant fall-back attraction, and **Lisieux** has its religious significance.

South of the Seine

Heading south from the Seine you can follow the River Risle from the estuary just east of Honfleur, or the Eure and its tributaries from upstream of Rouen. Between the two stretches the long featureless **Neubourg Plain**. The lowest major crossing point over the Risle is at **PONT-AUDEMER**, where medieval houses lean out at alarming angles over the crisscrossing roads, rivers and canals. From here, perfect cycling roads lined with timbered farmhouses follow the river south.

Le Bec-Hellouin

The size and tranquillity of the **Abbaye de Bec-Hellouin**, upstream from Pont-Audemer just before Brionne, give a monastic feel to the whole Risle valley. Bells echo across the water and white-robed monks go soberly about their business. From the eleventh century onwards, the abbey was one of the most important centres of intellectual learning in the Christian world; the philosopher Anselm was abbot here before becoming Archbishop of Canterbury in 1093. Owing to the Revolution, most of the monastery buildings are recent – the monks only returned in 1948 – but there are some survivors and appealing clusters of stone ruins, including the fifteenth-century **bell tower of St-Nicholas** and the cloister. Recent archbishops of Canterbury have maintained tradition by coming here on retreat. Visitors are welcome to wander through the grounds for no charge, though you can also join regular **guided tours** (June–Sept Mon & Wed–Sat 10.30am, 3pm, 4pm & 5pm, Sun & hols noon, 3pm & 4pm; Oct–May Mon & Wed–Sat 10.30am, 3pm & 4pm, Sun & hols noon, 3pm & 4pm; €4.60; Ⓦwww.abbayedubec.com).

The tiny and rather twee adjacent village of **Bec-Hellouin** is home to **riding stables**, the Centre Equestre du Bec-Hellouin, where horses can be booked by the hour or the day (Ⓣ02.32.44.86.31). There are also a couple of **restaurants**; the ivy-covered *Canterbury* (Ⓣ02.32.44.14.59; closed Sun & Tues eves, Wed & all Feb), which serves regional specialities on menus from €18 up to €38, and the rather cheaper *Restaurant de la Tour* on place Guillaume-le-Conquérant

(Ⓣ02.32.44.86.15; closed Wed eve & Thurs, plus two weeks in Nov), which has some outdoor tables.

Brionne and Beaumont-le-Roger

BRIONNE, on the Rouen–Lisieux rail line, is a small town with large regional markets on Thursday and Sunday. The fish hall is on the left bank, the rest by the church on the right bank. Above them both, with panoramic views, is an excellent example of a Norman *donjon* (keep). If you decide to **stay**, try the lovely old half-timbered *Auberge du Vieux Donjon*, 19 rue Soie (Ⓣ02.32.44.80.62, Ⓦwww.auberge-vieux-donjon.com; ❸; closed Mon, plus Sun eve & Thurs eve Oct–May), which has a good restaurant.

The River Charentonne joins the Risle near Serquigny. The town is also the meeting point of rail lines and main roads and the banks are clogged with fuming industrial conglomerations. But 7km upstream, at **BEAUMONT-LE-ROGER**, you are back in pastoral tranquillity. The ruins of a thirteenth-century **priory church** slowly crumble to the ground, the slow restoration of one or two arches unable to keep pace. In the village, little happens beyond the hammering of the church bell next door to the abbey by a nodding musketeer. The next riverside village, **LA FERRIÈRE-SUR-RISLE**, has an especially beautiful **church**, with some interesting sculpture, and a fourteenth-century covered **market hall**. Paddocks and meadows lead down to the river and a small and inviting **hotel**, the *Vieux-Marché* (Ⓣ02.32.30.25.93; ❷).

Conches-en-Ouche

Fourteen kilometres east of La Ferrière across the wild and open woodland of the **Forêt de Conches**, standing above the River Rouloir on an abrupt and narrow spur, is **CONCHES-EN-OUCHE**, many a Norman's favourite heartland town. At the highest point, in the middle of a row of medieval houses, is the **church of Ste-Foy**, its windows a stunning sequence of Renaissance stained glass. Behind are the gardens of the **Hôtel de Ville**, where a robust, if anatomically odd stone boar gazes proudly out over a spectacular view. Next to that, you can scramble up the slippery steps of the ruined twelfth-century **castle**. Conches is given a certain edge over other towns with historic relics by the pieces of modern sculpture that seem to lie around every other corner.

The town's **tourist office** is close to the castle, 200m south of the church in place Aristide-Briand (July & Aug Tues–Sat 10am–12.30pm & 2–6pm, Sun 10am–noon; Sept–June Tues–Sat 10am–12.30pm & 2–6pm; Ⓣ02.32.30.76.42, Ⓦwww.conches-en-ouche.fr) and hire out mountain bikes. The best **accommodation** option is *Le Cygne*, a Logis de France at 2 rue Paul-Guilbaud at the north end of town (Ⓣ02.32.30.20.60, Ⓦwww.lecygne.fr; ❸; closed Sun eve & Mon), which has a good restaurant where menus start at €17. There's also a two-star municipal **campsite**, *La Forêt* (Ⓣ02.32.30.22.49; closed Oct–March), while on Thursday the whole town is taken up by a **market**.

Évreux

If you're heading south to Conches from Rouen, you follow first the River Eure, and then its tributary the Iton, passing through **ÉVREUX**, capital of the Eure *département*. It's hardly an exciting place, but an afternoon's wander in the vicinity of the **cathedral** – a minor classic with flamboyant exterior decoration and original fourteenth-century windows – and the ramparts alongside the Iton river bank is pleasant. Évreux's **tourist office** is right in the heart of town, 300 metres north of the cathedral at 1 place de Gaulle (June–Sept Mon–Sat 9.30am–12.30pm & 1.30–6.15pm, Sun 10am–12.30pm; Oct–May Mon–Sat same hours, closed Sun; ⓣ02.32.24.04.43, ⓦwww.ot-pays-evreux.fr). The *Hôtel de France*, 200m northwest at 29 rue St-Thomas (ⓣ02.32.39.09.25, ⓦwww.hoteldefrance-evreux.com; ❸; restaurant closed Sat lunch, Sun eve & Mon), offers large, smart **rooms** and a top-notch dining room.

Lisieux and the Pays d'Auge

The rolling hills and green twisting valleys of the **Pays d'Auge** stretch south of the cathedral town of **Lisieux** and are scattered with magnificent manor houses. The pastures here are the lushest in the province, their produce the world-famous cheeses of Camembert, Livarot and Pont L'Evêque. They are intermingled with hectares of orchards, which yield the best of Norman ciders, both apple and pear (*poiré*), as well as Calvados apple brandy.

Lisieux

LISIEUX, 35 minutes by train from Caen, is the main town of the Pays d'Auge, and the large street **market** on Wednesday and Saturday is a good place to get to know its cheeses and ciders. Most people, however, come to Lisieux in pilgrimage. St Thérèse, the most popular French spiritual figure of the last hundred years, was born in 1873 and lived just 24 years. Passivity, self-effacement and a self-denial that verged on masochism were her trademarks, and she is honoured by the gaudy and gigantic **Basilique de Ste-Thérèse**, completed in 1954 on a slope to the southwest of the town centre. The huge modern mosaics that decorate the nave are undeniably impressive, but the overall impression is of a quasi-medieval hagiography. The faithful can ride on a white, flag-bedecked fairground train around the holiest sites, which include the infinitely restrained and sober **Cathédrale St-Pierre**.

Lisieux's **tourist office**, 11 rue d'Alençon, is the best place to gather information on the rural areas further inland (June–Sept Mon–Sat 8.30am–6.30pm, Sun 10am–12.30pm & 2–5pm; Oct–May Mon–Sat 8.30am–noon & 1.30–6pm; ⓣ02.31.48.18.10, ⓦwww.lisieux-tourisme.com). The quantity of pilgrims means the town is full of good-value **hotels**, such as the *Terrasse*, near the basilica at 25 av Ste-Thérèse (ⓣ02.31.62.17.65; ❷; closed mid-Jan to mid-Feb, plus Mon in winter), and the smart, central *Azur Hôtel*, just north of the Église St-Jacques at 15 rue au Char (ⓣ02.31.62.09.14, ⓦwww.azur-hotel.com; ❹; closed mid-Dec to mid-Jan). There's also a large two-star **campsite**, *de la Vallée* (ⓣ02.31.62.00.40; closed early Oct to early April), but campers would probably be better off somewhere more rural, such as Livarot or Orbec.

Into the Pays d'Auge

Though the tourist authorities responsible for the Pays d'Auge have laid out a **Route du Fromage** and a **Route du Cidre**, you won't be missing out if you don't follow these itineraries. For really good solid Norman cooking this is the perfect area to look out for *fermes auberges*, working farms which welcome paying visitors to share their meals. Local tourist offices can provide copious lists of these and of local producers from whom you can buy your cheese and booze.

Crèvecoeur-en-Auge

While it's always fun to stumble across dilapidated old half-timbered farms in the Pays d'Auge, here and there it's possible to visit prime specimens that have been beautifully restored and preserved. An especially fine assortment has been gathered just west of **CRÈVECOEUR-EN-AUGE**, 17km west of Lisieux on the N14, in the grounds of a small twelfth-century **château** (April–June & Sept daily 11am–6pm; July & Aug daily 11am–7pm; Oct Sun 2–6pm; guided tours July & Aug Sun 2.30–4.30pm; Ⓦwww.chateau-de-crevecoeur.com; €5). Around the pristine lawns of a re-created village green, circled by a shallow moat, this photogenic group of golden adobe structures includes a manor house, a barn and a tall thin dovecote that date from the fifteenth century. The little twelfth-century chapel that adjoins the château holds a fascinating exhibition on the music and instruments of the Middle Ages, although almost all the explanatory captions are in French.

Beuvron-en-Auge

By far the prettiest of the Pays d'Auge villages is **BEUVRON-EN-AUGE**, 7km north of the N13 halfway between Lisieux and Caen. It consists of an oval central square, ringed by a glorious ensemble of multicoloured half-timbered houses, including the yellow-and-brown sixteenth-century Vieux Manoir. The very centre of the square is taken up by the *Pavé d'Auge* restaurant

△ Grocery Beuvron-en-Auge

(Ⓣ02.31.79.26.71; closed Mon, plus Tues Sept–June), where regularly changing menus start at €29.50.

Orbec and Livarot

The town of **ORBEC**, 19km southeast of Lisieux, epitomizes the simple pleasures of the Pays d'Auge. Along the rue Grande, you'll see several houses in which the gaps between the timbers are filled with intricate patterns of coloured tiles and bricks. Debussy composed *Jardin sous la Pluie* in one of these, and the oldest and prettiest of the lot – a tanner's house dating back to 1568, known as the **Vieux Manoir** – holds a museum of local history. On the whole, though, it's more fun just to walk down behind the church to the river, and its watermill and paddocks.

The centre of the cheese country is the old town of **LIVAROT**, with the appealing **hotel** and restaurant *Du Vivier* in its heart (Ⓣ02.31.32.04.10, Ⓦwww.hotel-du-vivier.com; ❸; Oct–May, restaurant closed Fri eve, Sun eve & Mon lunch). The **Fromagerie Graindorge** on the route de Vimoutiers (Mon–Fri 9.30am–noon & 1.30–5pm, Sat 9.30am–noon; free), gives you a closer look at how Livarot's eponymous cheese is made, with free samples doled out at the end of each visit. For the best views of the valley, climb up to the thirteenth-century church of **St-Michel de Livet**, just above the town.

Vimoutiers and Camembert

VIMOUTIERS, due south of Livarot, contains yet another **cheese museum**, at 10 av Général-de-Gaulle (April–Sept Mon 2.30–6pm, Tues–Sat 9am–noon & 2–6pm, Sun 10am–noon & 2–6pm; Nov–March Mon 2–5.30pm, Tues–Sat 10am–noon & 2–5.30pm; €3). This one specializes in labels – the cheeses underneath are mostly polystyrene.

A statue in the town's main square honours Marie Harel, who, at the nearby village of Camembert, developed the original cheese early in the nineteenth century, promoting it with a skilful campaign that included sending free samples to Napoleon. Marie is confronted across the main street by what might be called the statue of the Unknown Cow.

Vimoutiers is the venue of a **market** on Monday afternoons. Its **tourist office**, in the cheese museum (same hours; Ⓣ02.33.39.30.29, Ⓦwww.mairie-vimoutiers.fr), has piles of information on local cheese-related attractions. Of its **hotels**, the central *Soleil d'Or*, 3 rue de Chatelet (Ⓣ02.33.39.07.15; ❷; hotel closed two weeks in Feb & two weeks in Oct; restaurant closed Fri eve & Sun eve), has a reasonable €17 menu and a better €23 one.

A short way south of Vimoutiers, en route to Camembert, the beautifully sited lake known as the **Escale du Vitou** offers everything you need for windsurfing, swimming and horse-riding, as well as its own comfortable, rural **hotel**, *L' Escale du Vitou* (Ⓣ02.33.39.12.04, Ⓦgite-normandie.ifrance.com/hotel.htm; ❷). There's also a clean and very cheap **campsite** nearby on boulevard Docteur-Dentu, the two-star *La Campière* (Ⓣ02.33.39.18.86; closed Nov–Feb).

CAMEMBERT itself, 3km southeast of Vimoutiers, is tiny, hilly and very rural, home to far more cows than humans. On one side of its little central square, the largest local cheese producers, **La Ferme Président**, run their own eleven-room cheese museum (March–May, Sept & Oct Wed–Sun 10am–noon & 2–5.30pm; June–Aug Wed–Sun 10am–noon & 2–6pm; Ⓦwww.fermepresident.com; €5), where the forty-minute tour, threading through assorted farm buildings, adds little to anything you may have learned in Vimoutiers. On the other side, the rival **Le Maison du Camembert** is a British-run cheese and souvenir stall with an equally ramshackle free museum (Feb–April & Sept Wed–Sun 10am–6pm, May–Aug daily 10am–6pm; Ⓦ www.maisonducamembert.com).

La Ferté-Fresnel

For some truly wonderful rural lodging, it's well worth heading thirty kilometres east of Vimoutiers on the D12 to the little hamlet of **LA FERTÉ-FRESNEL**. The massive nineteenth-century *Château de la Ferté-Fresnel* here has been converted into an opulent **B&B** (Ⓣ 02.33.24.23.23, Ⓦ chateau.fertefresnel .free.fr; ⑤). Standing at the end of a majestic avenue of trees, the château is set in superb formal grounds, while its huge, high-ceilinged guest rooms are reached via a graceful curving double staircase.

Falaise

William the Conqueror, or William the Bastard as he is more commonly known here, was born in **FALAISE**, 40km southwest of Lisieux. His mother, Arlette, a laundrywoman, was spotted by his father, Duke Robert of Normandy, at the washing place below the château. She was a shrewd woman, scorning secrecy in her eventual assignation by riding publicly through the main entrance to meet him. During her pregnancy, she is said to have dreamed of bearing a mighty tree that cast its shade over Normandy and England.

Falaise's **castle** keep, firmly planted on the massive rocks of the cliff (*falaise*) that gave the town its name, and towering over the **Fontaine d'Arlette** down by the river, is one of the most evocative historic sights imaginable. Nonetheless, it was so heavily damaged during the war that it took over fifty years to reopen for regular visits (Feb–June & Sept–Dec daily 10am–6pm; July & Aug daily 10am–7pm; English-language tours daily 11.30am, with another at 3.30pm in July & Aug; Ⓦ www.chateau-guillaume-leconquerant.fr; €6). Huge resources have been lavished on restoring the central **donjon**, reminiscent of the Tower of London with its cream-coloured Caen stone. A guiding principle was to avoid any possible confusion as to what is original and authentic and what is new. Rest assured you'll be in no doubt whatever. Steel slabs, concrete blocks, glass floors and tent-like canvas awnings have been slapped down atop the bare ruins, and metal staircases squeezed into the wall cavities. The raw structure of the keep, down to its very foundations, lies exposed to view, while the newly created rooms are used for changing exhibitions that focus on the castle's fascinating past.

The whole of Falaise was devastated in the struggle to close the "Falaise Gap" in August 1944 – the climax of the **Battle of Normandy**, as the Allied armies sought to encircle the Germans and cut off their retreat. By the time the Canadians entered the town on August 17, they could no longer tell where the roads had been and had to bulldoze a new four-metre strip straight through the middle. The full bloody story is told in horrific detail at the **Musée Août 44**, beyond the château in a former cheese factory that resembles nothing so much as a giant cheesebox, on the chemin des Rochers (early April to mid-Nov 10am–noon & 2–6pm; €5.50).

Practicalities

The **tourist office** can be found on the boulevard de la Libération (May to mid-June Mon–Sat 9.30am–12.30pm & 1.30–6.30pm; mid-June to Sept same hours plus Sun 10am–noon & 3–5pm; Oct–April Mon–Sat 9.30am–12.30pm & 1.30–5.30pm; Ⓣ 02.31.90.17.26, Ⓦ www.otsifalaise.com). Most of Falaise's few **hotels** stand along the main Caen–Argentan road, which can make them rather noisy. The *Poste*, not far from the tourist office at 38 rue Georges-Clemenceau (Ⓣ02.31.90.13.14, Ⓔhotel.delaposte@orange.fr; ❸; hotel closed Jan, restaurant closed Jan, Sun eve & Mon) serves good food on menus from €15, while rooms and meals at the *Hôtel de la Place*, next to the church at 1 place St-Gervais (Ⓣ02.31.40.19.00; ❷; closed Sun eve & Wed), are significantly cheaper. The three-star **campsite**, *Camping du Château* (Ⓣ02.31.90.16.55; closed Oct–April), next to Arlette's fountain and the municipal swimming pool, is in a much better location.

The Suisse Normande

The area known as the **Suisse Normande** lies roughly 25km south of Caen, along the gorge of the River Orne, between Thury-Harcourt and Putanges. While the name is a little far-fetched – there are certainly no mountains – it is quite distinctive, with cliffs and crags and wooded hills at every turn. There are plenty of opportunities for outdoor pursuits: you can race along the Orne in canoes and kayaks, cruise more sedately on pedaloes or a bizarre species of inflatable rubber tractor, or dangle on ropes from the sheer rock-faces high above. For mere walkers the Orne can be frustrating: footpaths along the river are few and far between, and often entirely overgrown.

The Suisse Normande is usually approached from Caen or Falaise and contrasts dramatically with the prairie-like expanse of wheat fields en route. On wheels, the best access is via the D235 from Caen (signed to Falaise then right through Ifs). Bus Verts #34 will take you to **Thury-Harcourt** or **Clécy** on its way to Flers, and there are occasional special summer train excursions from Caen.

Thury-Harcourt and Clécy

At **THURY-HARCOURT**, the **tourist office** on place St-Sauveur (Jan–April & Oct–Dec Mon 2.30–5pm, Tues–Fri 10am–12.30pm & 2.30–5pm, Sat 10am–12.30pm; May, June–Sept Tues–Sat 10am–12.30pm & 2.30–6.30pm, Sun 10am–12.30pm; July & Aug also open Mon 10am–12.30pm & 2.30–6.30pm; Ⓣ02.31.79.70.45, Ⓦwww.suisse-normande.com) can suggest walks, rides and *gîtes d'étape* throughout the Suisse Normande. Hotels are for the most part overpriced, but there is an attractive four-star **campsite**, the *Vallée du Traspy* (Ⓣ02.31.79.61.80; closed Oct–March), beside the river on the rue du Pont-Benoit.

CLÉCY, 10km to the south, is a slightly better bet for finding a room, although visitors outnumber residents in peak season. The **hotel** facing the church in the village centre, *Au Site Normand*, 1 rue des Châtelets (Ⓣ02.31.69.71.05, Ⓦwww.ausitenormand-clecy.com; ❸; closed mid-Dec to mid-Feb), consists of an old-fashioned and good-value dining room in the main timber-framed building and a cluster of newer units around the back. The river is a kilometre away, down the hill. En route, in the Parc des Loisirs, is a **Musée du Chemin de Fer Miniature** (March to mid-April Sun 2–5.30pm; mid-April to mid-June daily 10am–noon & 2–6pm; second half of June & all Sept daily except Mon 10am–noon & 2–6pm; July & Aug daily 10am–noon & 2–6.30pm; Oct to early Nov Sun 2–5pm; €5), featuring a gigantic model railway certain to appeal to children. Set in spacious grounds on the far bank of the river, the *Moulin du Vey* (Ⓣ02.31.69.71.08, Ⓦwww.moulinduvey.com; ❺; hotel closed Dec, restaurant closed Sun in winter) is a beautifully positioned, luxuriously appointed hotel that takes its name from the restored watermill right by the bridge, which is itself, confusingly, now a restaurant. The western riverbank continues in a brief splurge of restaurants, takeaways and snack bars as far as the two-star municipal **campsite** (Ⓣ02.31.69.70.36, Ⓦwww.campings.com/campingclecy; closed mid-Oct to March).

Pont d'Ouilly

If you're planning on walking or cycling, a good central spot in which to base yourself is **PONT D'OUILLY**, at the point where the main road from Vire to Falaise crosses the river. It's a small town, with a few basic shops, an old covered market hall and a promenade (with bar) slightly upstream alongside the weir. Continuing upstream, a pleasant walk leads for 3.5km alongside the river to the pretty little village of Le Mesnil Villement.

As well as a **campsite** overlooking the river (Ⓣ02.31.69.46.12; closed Oct–Easter), Pont d'Ouilly offers an attractive **hotel**, the *Du Commerce* (Ⓣ02.31.69.80.16; ❷; closed Sun eve & Mon), the quintessential French village hotel, with a friendly welcome and attentive service. Its **restaurant** is very popular with local families, serving superb, definitive Norman cooking, with plenty of creamy Pays d'Auge sauces, on menus that start at €16. About a kilometre north, the more upmarket *Auberge St-Christophe* (Ⓣ02.31.69.81.23; ❸; closed Sun eve, Mon & three weeks in Feb) stands, covered with ivy and geraniums, in a beautiful setting on the right bank of the Orne.

A short distance south of Pont-d'Ouilly is the **Roche d'Oëtre**, a high rock with a tremendous view into the deep and totally wooded gorge of the Rouvre, a tributary of the Orne. The river widens soon afterwards into the **Lac du Rabodanges**, formed by the many-arched Rabodanges Dam.

Southern Normandy

As an alternative to following the more northerly routes across Normandy, motorists heading west from Paris towards Brittany may prefer to cut directly across the province by following the line of the N12 through **Alençon** and then heading northwest on the N176. Much of the terrain along Normandy's southern border is taken up by the dense woodlands of the **Forêt d'Écouves** and the **Forêt des Andaines**, so there's plenty of good walking to be had, while the hill towns of **Carrouges** and **Domfront** make great stopovers.

Alençon and around

ALENÇON, a fair-sized and busy town, is known for its traditional – and now pretty much defunct – lacemaking industry. The **Musée des Beaux-Arts et de la Dentelle** (July & Aug daily 10am–noon & 2–6pm; Sept–June daily except Mon 10am–noon & 2–6pm; €3) is housed in a former Jesuit school and has all the best trappings of a modern museum. The highly informative history of lacemaking upstairs, with examples of numerous different techniques, can, however, be tedious for anyone not already riveted by the subject. It also contains an unexpected collection of gruesome Cambodian artefacts like spears and lances, tiger skulls and elephants' feet, gathered by a militant socialist French governor at the end of the nineteenth century. The paintings in the adjoining Beaux-Arts section are nondescript, except for a few works by Courbet and Géricault. The **Château des Ducs**, the old town castle close by the museum, looks impressive but doesn't encourage visitors: it's now a prison, and people in Alençon have nightmarish memories of its use by the Gestapo during the war. Wandering around the town might also take you to St Thérèse's birthplace on rue St-Blaise, just in front of the **gare routière**.

The **Forêt d'Écouves**, north of Alençon and inaccessible by public transport, is a dense mixture of spruce, pine, oak and beech, unfortunately a favoured spot of the military – and, in autumn, deer hunters, too. You can usually ramble along the cool paths, happening on wild mushrooms and even the odd wild boar.

Practicalities

The **tourist office** is housed in the fifteenth-century Maison d'Ozé on place La Magdelaine (July & Aug Mon–Sat 9.30am–7pm, Sun 10am–12.30pm & 2–5pm; Sept–June Mon–Sat 9.30am–noon & 2–6pm; ⓣ02.33.80.66.33, ⓦwww.paysdalencontourisme.com). The **gare routière** and the **gare SNCF** are both northeast of the centre, in an area that holds Alençon's prime concentration of **hotels**. The *Hôtel de Paris* here, above a bar at 26 rue de Denis-Papin (ⓣ02.33.29.01.64; ❶), offers simple rooms at very good rates. A Logis de France, *Le Grand Cerf*, occupies a Neoclassical town house a few hundred yards closer to the centre at 21 rue St-Blaise (ⓣ02.33.26.00.51, ⓦwww.hotelgrandcerf-61.com; ❹; hotel closed Sun) and has large comfortable rooms and a top-quality restaurant, with garden seating in summer. Alençon has good shops and **cafés** in a few pedestrianized streets at the heart of its abysmal one-way traffic system. A good place to sample the thriving local **bar** scene is the half-timbered *Café des Sept Colonnes* at 2 rue du Château.

Carrouges

An alternative base to Alençon, at the western end of the Forêt d'Écouves, is the hill town of **CARROUGES**, with its fine old-style **château** set in spacious grounds at the foot of the hill (daily: April to mid-June & Sept 10am–noon & 2–6pm; mid-June to Aug 9.30am–noon & 2–6.30pm; Oct–March 10am–noon & 2–5pm; €6.10). Its two highlights are a superb restored brick staircase and a room containing portraits of fourteen successive generations of the Le Veneur family, an extraordinary illustration of the processes of heredity. On the narrow rue Ste-Marguerite that runs through the heart of Carrouges – a noisier location than it might look – the *Hôtel du Nord* (ⓣ02.33.27.20.14; ❶; closed mid-Dec to mid-Jan, plus Fri eve & Sun eve Sept–June) offers a handful of reasonably large en-suite **rooms** at low rates, and delicious local cuisine on menus that start at €10.10.

Bagnoles-de-l'Orne

West of Carrouges, the spa town of **BAGNOLES-DE-L'ORNE** is quite unlike anywhere else in this part of the world, attracting the moneyed sick and convalescent from all over France to its thermal baths. The layout is formal and spacious, centring on a lake with gardens, from where horse-drawn *calèches* take the clients to an enormous casino. With so many visitors to keep entertained, and spending money, there are also innumerable cultural events of a restrained and stressless nature, such as tea dances and stage shows.

Whether you'd actually want to spend time in Bagnoles depends on your disposable income as well as your health. Furthermore, the town as a whole operates to a season that lasts roughly from early April to the end of October; arrive in winter, and you may find everything shut. The numerous hotels are expensive and sedate places, in which it's possible to be too late for dinner at seven o'clock and locked out altogether at nine, and the three-star **campsite**, *De la Vée* (Ⓣ02.33.37.87.45; closed Nov to mid-March), south of town, is rather forlorn.

The **tourist office** on place du Marché (April–Oct Mon–Sat 9.30am–12.30pm & 2–6pm, Sun 10am–12.30pm & 2.30–6.30pm; Nov–March Mon–Sat 9.30am–12.30pm & 2–6pm; Ⓣ02.33.37.85.66, Ⓦwww.bagnolesdelorne.com) will give details on accommodation in Bagnoles and its less exclusive sister town of **TESSE-MADELEINE**. Among the cheaper options in Bagnoles proper is the *Bagnôles Hotel*, on the central roundabout at 6 place de la République (Ⓣ02.33.37.86.79; ❸; closed Nov–March), while the *Celtic*, in Tesse at 14 rue du Dr P-Noal (Ⓣ02.33.37.92.91; ❸; closed mid-Jan to early March), has excellent menus from €18. Despite its ugly would-be-Deco exterior, the *Hôtel du Béryl*, on rue des Casinos (Ⓣ02.33.38.44.44, Ⓦwww.groupe-emeraude.com; ❺), is the biggest and probably the best of the crop, bedecked with balconies and terraces overlooking the lake.

Domfront

The road through the forest from Bagnoles, the D335 and then the D908, climbs above the lush woodlands and progressively narrows to a hog's back before entering **DOMFRONT**. Less happens here than at Bagnoles, but the countryside is prettier.

A public park, near the long-abandoned former train station, leads up to some redoubtable castle ruins perched on an isolated rock. Eleanor of Aquitaine was born in this **castle** in October 1162, and Thomas à Becket came to stay for Christmas 1166, saying Mass in the **Notre-Dame-sur-l'Eau** church down by the river, which has sadly been ruined by vandals. The views from the flower-filled gardens that surround the mangled keep are spectacular, including a very graphic panorama of the ascent you've made to get up. A slender footbridge connects the castle with the narrow little village itself, which boasts an abundance of half-timbered houses. Near its sweet central square, the modern **St Julien church**, constructed out of concrete segments during the 1920s, is bursting with exciting mosaics.

On summer afternoons (July & Aug Tues & Thurs 4.30pm), free **guided tours** (in French) of old Domfront leave from the **tourist office**, facing the castle entrance at 12 place de la Roirie (Mon–Sat 9.30am–12.30pm & 2.30–6pm; Ⓣ02.33.38.53.97, Ⓦwww.domfront.com). Domfront's **hotels**, clustered together at the foot of the hill below the old town, make useful and very pleasant stopovers. Two Logis de France stand side by side: the *Relais St-Michel*, 5 rue du Mont-St-Michel (Ⓣ02.33.38.64.99, Ⓦwww.hotellerelaisstmichel.com; ❶–❸; closed Fri & Sun eve), has rooms with and without en-suite facilities, plus menus from €15, while the similarly priced *Hôtel de France*, 7 rue du Mont-St-Michel (Ⓣ02.33.38.51.44, Ⓦwww.hoteldefrance-fr.com; ❷), has a nice bar and garden. Campers should note that the two-star local **campsite**, *du Champs Passais* (Ⓣ02.33.37.37.66; closed Oct–March), is exceptionally small.

The Bocage

The region that centres on **St-Lô**, just south of the Cotentin, is known as the **Bocage**, from a word that refers to a type of cultivated countryside common in the west of France, where fields are cut by tight hedgerows rooted into walls of earth well over a metre high. An effective form of smallhold farming in pre-industrial days, it also proved to be a perfect system of anti-tank barricades. When the Allied troops tried to advance through the region in 1944, it was almost impenetrable – certainly bearing no resemblance to the East Anglian plains where they had trained. The war here was hand-to-hand slaughter, and the destruction of villages was often wholesale.

St-Lô

The city of **ST-LÔ**, 60km south of Cherbourg and 36km southwest of Bayeux, is still known as the "Capital of the Ruins". Memorial sites are everywhere and what is new speaks as tellingly of the destruction as the ruins that have been preserved. In the main square, the gate of the old prison commemorates Resistance members executed by the Nazis, people deported east to the concentration camps and soldiers killed in action. When the bombardment of St-Lô was at its fiercest, the Germans refused to take any measures to protect the prisoners and the gate was all that survived. Samuel Beckett was here during and after the battle, working for the Irish Red Cross as interpreter, driver and provision-seeker – for such things as rat poison for the maternity hospitals. He said he took away with him a "time-honoured conception of humanity in ruins".

All the trees in the city are the same height, all planted to replace the battle's mutilated stumps. But the most visible – and brilliant – reconstruction is the **Cathédrale de Notre-Dame**. Its main body, with a strange southward-veering nave, has been conventionally repaired and rebuilt. But the shattered west front and the base of the collapsed north tower have been joined by a startling sheer wall of icy green stone that makes no attempt to mask the destruction.

By way of contrast, a lighthouse-like 1950s folly spirals to nowhere on the main square. Should you feel the urge, you can climb its staircase and make your way into the new and even more pointless labyrinth of glass at its feet for a €1.50 admission fee. More compelling, around behind the Mairie, is the **Musée des Beaux-Arts** (Wed–Sun 10am–noon & 2–6pm; €2), which is full of treasures: a Boudin sunset; a Lurçat tapestry of his dog, *Nadir and the Pirates*; works by Corot, van Loo, Moreau; a Léger watercolour; a fine series of unfaded sixteenth-century Flemish tapestries on the lives of two peasants; and sad bombardment relics of the town.

St-Lô's **tourist office** adjoins the "lighthouse" on the main square (July & Aug Mon–Sat 9am–6pm; Sept–June Mon 2–6pm, Tues–Fri 10am–12.30pm & 2–6pm, Sat 10am–1pm; ⓣ02.33.77.60.35, ⓦwww.mairie-saint-lo.fr). Most of the **hotels**, restaurants and bars are across the river, near the **gare SNCF**. Overlooking the river from the brow of a ridge beside the station, the upmarket Logis *Hôtel des Voyageurs*, 5–7 av Briovère (ⓣ02.33.05.08.63; ❹) is home to the *Tocqueville* **restaurant**, which has menus from €19. If you'd rather be up in town, *La Crémaillère*, at 8 rue de la Chancellerie (ⓣ02.33.57.14.68; ❷; closed Fri eve & Sat in low season), has a good restaurant where all the menus, which start at €9.50 for lunch and €12.50 for dinner, include a buffet of hors d'oeuvres.

The Vire Valley

Once St-Lô was taken in the Battle of Normandy, the armies speedily moved on southwestwards for their next confrontation. The **Vire Valley**, trailing south from St-Lô, saw little action – and its towns and villages seem to have been rarely touched by any historic or cultural mainstream. The motivation in coming to this landscape of rolling hills and occasional gorges is essentially to consume the region's cider, Calvados apple brandy (much of it bootleg), fruit pastries and sausages made from pigs' intestines.

From St-Lô to Tessy-sur-Vire

The best section of the valley is south of St-Lô through the Roches de Ham to Tessy-sur-Vire. The **Roches de Ham** are a pair of sheer rocky promontories high above the river. Though these are promoted as "viewing tables", the pleasure lies as much in the walk up, through lanes lined with blackberries, hazelnuts and rich orchards. Downstream from the Roches at **LA CHAPELLE-SUR-VIRE**, the church that towers majestically above the river has been an object of pilgrimage since the twelfth century. According to legend, in the Middle Ages a shepherd tending his flock noticed a lamb rooted to the spot; after digging he unearthed a statue of the Virgin Mary, since revered as a miraculous relic.

Five kilometres northeast of La Chapelle, **TORIGNI-SUR-VIRE** was the base of the Grimaldi family before they achieved quasi-royal status upon moving on to the principality of Monaco. A spacious country town, it boasts a few grand buildings and an attractive **campsite**, *Camping du Lac* (Ⓣ02.33.56.91.74). The *Auberge de l'Orangerie*, 3 rue Victor-Hugo (Ⓣ02.33.56.70.64, Ⓦwww.auberge-orangerie.abcsalles.com; hotel closed mid-Nov to mid-Feb; restaurant closed Sun eve & Mon; ❷), is a good **restaurant**, with menus starting at €15, and also offers five rooms.

At the eastern end of the sinuous Vire gorge, 10km north of Vire, the former railway viaduct of **Le Viaduc de la Souleuvre** was designed by Gustave Eiffel. A wooden boardwalk has been laid across half the span of the bridge, on which visitors can cross to the deepest part of the gorge. Once there, 61m up, they are expected to jump off – this is A.J. Hackett's **bungy-jumping** centre (hours vary, but open daily mid-June to mid-Sept; late March to late June and mid-Sept to mid-Nov Sat, Sun & hols only; reservations essential Ⓣ02.31.66.31.66, Ⓦwww.ajhackett.fr). Jumpers have to be aged at least 13, and for one to three people to make a single jump each costs €79 per person; you also have to pay €3 for the privilege of parking in the adjacent field.

Vire

VIRE itself is worth visiting specifically for the **food**; the one problem is what to do when you're not eating. The town is best known for its dreaded, offal-based *andouille* sausages, but you can gorge yourself on salmon or trout fresh from the river instead, accompanied by local *poiré*. It makes sense to choose a **hotel** with a good dining room. At the central *Hôtel de France*, 4 rue d'Aignaux (Ⓣ02.31.68.00.35, Ⓦwww.hoteldefrancevire.com; ❸), the €28 *menu Virois* is packed with local specialities, including *andouillettes*. The *Hôtel des Voyageurs*, at the bottom of avenue de la Gare (Ⓣ02.31.68.01.16; ❷), serves sumptuous buffets of hors d'oeuvres and desserts; you can sample both for €15.

Villedieu-les-Poêles

VILLEDIEU-LES-POÊLES – literally "City of God the Frying Pans" – is a lively though touristy place, 28km west of Vire. Copper souvenirs and kitchen utensils gleam from its rows of shops, and the tourist office has lists of dozens of local ateliers for more direct purchases, plus details of the copperwork museum.

All of this can seem a bit obsessive, though there is more authentic interest at the **Fonderie de Cloches** at 13 rue du Pont-Chignon, one of the twelve remaining bell foundries in Europe. Work here is only part time as demand is limited, but you may find the forge lit (mid-Feb to early July & Sept to mid-Nov Tues–Sat 10am–12.30pm & 2–5.30pm; early July to Aug daily 9am–12.30pm

& 2–6pm; Ⓦwww.cornille-havard.com; €4.30) for visits. Expert craftsmen will show you the moulds, composed of an unpleasant-looking combination of clay, goat's hair and horse manure.

The local **tourist office** is on place des Costils (April–June & Sept Mon–Sat 9am–12.30pm & 2–6.30pm; July & Aug daily 9am–6.30pm; Oct–March Mon–Sat 9am–noon & 2–6pm; Ⓣ02.33.61.05.69, Ⓦwww.ot-villedieu.fr). If you're charmed into staying, the welcoming Logis *Hôtel St-Pierre et St-Michel*, 12 place de la République (Ⓣ02.33.61.00.11, Ⓦwww.st-pierre-hotel.com; ❸; closed mid-Jan to mid-Feb), houses the stylish *Le Sourdin* restaurant, where the €34 menu is seriously gastronomic. There's also a three-star **campsite** by the river, *Jean-Louis Bougord* (Ⓣ02.33.61.02.44; closed late Sept to Easter).

Travel details

Trains

Through services to Paris connect with ferries at Dieppe, Le Havre and Cherbourg: if you're doing this journey, it's easiest to buy a combined rail–ferry–rail ticket at your point of departure.

Alençon to: Caen (6 daily; 1hr 20min), via Sées (13min) and Argentan (30min); Tours (1 daily; 2hr 10min); Le Mans (10 daily; 50min).

Caen to: Cherbourg (10 daily; 1hr 15min), via Bayeux (20min) and Valognes (1hr); Lisieux (hourly; 30min); Le Mans (5 daily; 2hr), via Argentan (45min) and Alençon (1hr 15min); Paris-St-Lazare (at least hourly; 2hr 10min); Rennes (4 daily; 3hr), via Bayeux (20min), St-Lô (50min), Coutances (1hr 15min) and Pontorson (2hr); Rouen (6 daily; 2hr); Tours (1 daily; 3hr).

Cherbourg to: Paris (8 daily; 3hr), via Valognes (15min) and Caen (1hr 15min).

Dieppe to: Paris-St-Lazare (19 daily; 2hr 10min), via Rouen (50min).

Granville to: Coutances (7 daily; 30min).

Le Havre to: Paris (11 daily; 2hr 15min); Rouen (15 daily; 1hr).

Rouen to: Caen (6 daily; 2hr); Paris-St-Lazare (19 daily; 1hr 15min); Vernon (12 daily; 30min).

St-Lô to: Caen (4 daily; 50min), via Bayeux (30min); Rennes (4 daily; 2hr 10min), via Coutances (20min) and Pontorson (1hr 15min).

Trouville-Deauville to: Lisieux (6 daily in winter, much more frequently in summer; 20min); Paris (6 daily in winter, much more frequently in summer; 2hr).

Buses

Alençon to: Bagnoles (3 daily; 1hr); Bellême (1–2 daily; 1hr); Évreux (1 daily; 2hr), via L'Aigle (1hr 40min); Mortagne (1–3 daily; 1hr); Vimoutiers (1–3 daily; 1hr 30min), via Sées (30min).

Bayeux to: Arromanches (4 daily; 30min); Ouistreham (3 daily; 1hr 15min).

Caen to: Arromanches (1 daily; 1hr 10min); Bayeux (3 daily; 50min); Clécy (4 daily; 50min); Falaise (7 daily; 1hr); Honfleur (13 daily; 2hr), via Cabourg (50min), Houlgate (55min) and Deauville (1hr 5min), of which 5 continue to Le Havre (2hr 30min); Le Havre (2 daily bus #80 express services; 1hr 25min), via Honfleur (1hr); Ouistreham (20 daily; 30min); Pont L'Evêque (3 daily; 1hr 10min); Thury-Harcourt (5 daily; 40min).

Cherbourg to: St-Lô (3 daily; 1hr 45min); St-Vaast (3 daily; 50min) via Barfleur (30min).

Dieppe to: Fécamp (4 daily; 2hr 20min); Le Tréport (4 daily; 30min); St-Valery (5 daily; 1hr).

Le Havre to: Caen (2 daily express services; 1hr 25min); Étretat (9 daily; 50min); Fécamp (8 daily; 1hr 30min); Honfleur (7 daily; 30min).

Mont St-Michel to: Rennes (5 daily; 1hr 20min); St-Malo (4 daily; 1hr 30min).

Rouen to: Clères (6 daily; 45min); Évreux (hourly; 1hr); Le Havre (hourly; 2hr 45min), via Jumièges and Caudebec; Lisieux (2 daily; 2hr 30min).

St-Lô to: Bayeux (8 daily; 30min); Cherbourg (3 daily; 1hr 45min); Coutances (5 daily; 30min).

Travel details

5

Brittany

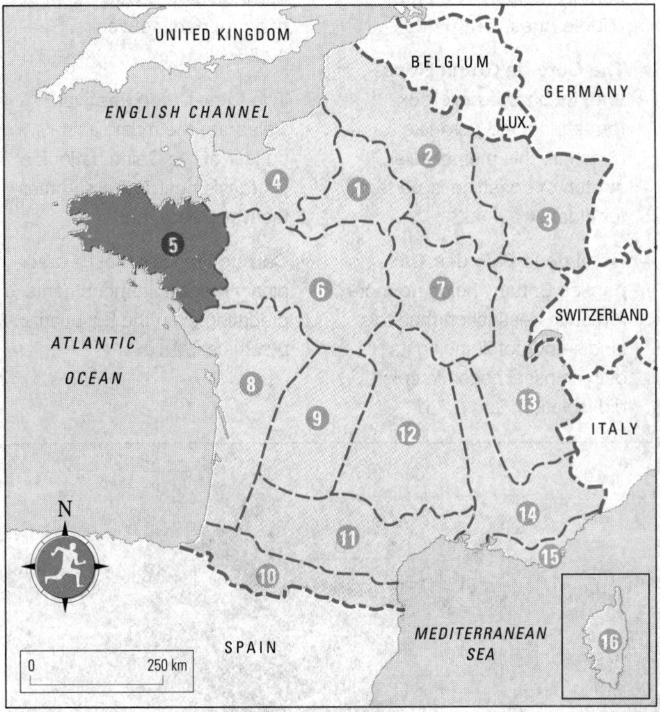
UNITED KINGDOM
BELGIUM
GERMANY
LUX.
ENGLISH CHANNEL
1
2
3
4
5
6
7
8
9
10
11
12
13
14
15
16
SWITZERLAND
ATLANTIC
OCEAN
ITALY
N
SPAIN
MEDITERRANEAN
SEA
0
250 km

CHAPTER 5 Highlights

* **Cancale** If you love oysters, the stalls and restaurants in Cancale's little harbour will have you in raptures. See p.425

* **Dinan** Gorgeously preserved walled town, with its own riverfront port, that feels barely changed since the Middle Ages. See p.425

* **The Côte de Granit Rose** With its bizarre pink rock formations and gem-like beaches, this memorable stretch of coastline is perfect for kids. See p.433

* **Hôtel de la Baie des Tréspassés** Brittany holds no more romantic destination than this land's-end hotel, facing its own colossal beach in splendid isolation. See p.451

* **Île de Sein** Misty and mysterious island, barely rising from the Atlantic, that makes a great day-trip from western Finistère. See p.453

* **Faïence de Quimper** For centuries the craft-workers of Quimper have been producing hand-painted ceramics, which make perfect souvenirs. See p.456

* **The Inter-Celtic Festival** Celebrate the music and culture of the Celtic nations at Brittany's best-loved summer festival. See p.468

* **Carnac** France's most extraordinary megalithic monuments, predating even the Egyptian pyramids. See p.474

△ Le Gouffre, near Plougrescant, Côte de Granit Rose

Brittany

No one area – and certainly no one city or town – in **Brittany** encapsulates the character of the province; that lies in its people and in its geographical unity. For generations Bretons risked their lives fishing and trading on the violent seas and struggled with the arid soil of the interior. This toughness and resilience is tinged with **Celtic** culture: mystical, musical, sometimes morbid and defeatist, sometimes vital and inspired.

Though archeologically Brittany is one of the richest regions in the world – the alignments at **Carnac** rival Stonehenge – its first appearance in recorded history is as the quasi-mythical "Little Britain" of Arthurian legend. In the days when to travel by sea was safer and easier than by land, it was intimately connected with "Great Britain" across the water. Settlements such as St-Malo, St-Pol and Quimper were founded by Welsh and Irish missionary "saints" whose names are not to be found in any official breviary. Brittany remained **independent** until the sixteenth century, its last ruler, Duchess Anne, only managing to protect the province's autonomy through marriage to two consecutive French monarchs. After her death, in 1532, François I took her daughter and lands, and sealed the **union with France** with an act supposedly enshrining certain privileges. These included a veto over taxes by the local *parlement* and the people's right to be tried, or conscripted to fight, only in their province. The successive violations of this treaty by Paris, and subsequent revolts, form the core of Breton history since the Middle Ages.

As their language has been steadily eradicated, and the interior of the province severely depopulated, many Bretons continue to treat France as a separate country. Few, however, actively support Breton nationalism (which it's a criminal offence to advocate) much beyond putting *Breizh* (Breton for "Brittany") stickers on their cars. But there have been many successes in reviving the language, and the economic resurgence of the last three decades, helped partly by summer tourism, has largely been due to local initiatives, like Brittany Ferries re-establishing an old trading link, carrying produce and passengers across to Britain and Ireland. At the same time a Celtic artistic identity has consciously been revived, and local festivals – above all August's **Inter-Celtic Festival** at Lorient – celebrate traditional Breton music, poetry and dance, with fellow Celts treated as comrades.

If you're looking for traditional Breton fun, and you can't make the Lorient festival (or the smaller *Quinzaine Celtique* at Nantes in June/July), look out for gatherings organized by **Celtic folklore groups** – *Circles* or *Bagadou*. You may also be interested by the **pardons**, pilgrimage festivals commemorating local saints, which guidebooks (and tourist offices) tend to promote as exciting spectacles. In truth, unlike most French festivals, these are not phoney affairs kept alive for tourists, but deeply serious and rather gloomy religious occasions.

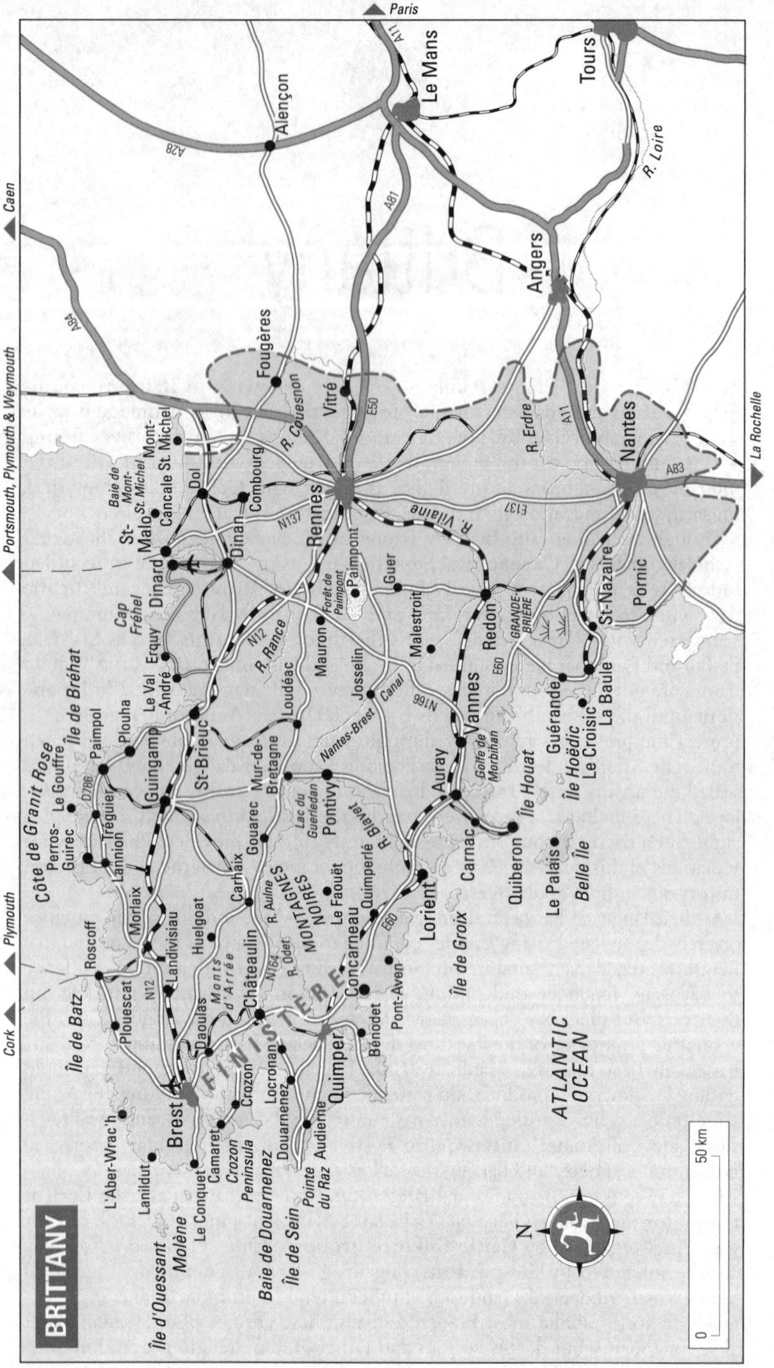

BRITTANY

Cork
Plymouth
Portsmouth, Plymouth & Weymouth
Caen
Côte de Granit Rose
Perros-Guirec
Le Gouffre
Île de Bréhat
Île de Batz
Roscoff
D786
Paimpol
L'Aber-Wrac'h
Plouescat
Lannion
Tréguier
Plouha
Morlaix
N12
Lanildut
Cap Fréhel
St-Malo
Baie de Mont-St. Michel
Mont-St. Michel
Cancale
Île d'Ouessant
Molène
Brest
Landivisiau
Guingamp
Le Val-André
Erquy
Dinard
Dol
Le Conquet
Daoulas
Huelgoat
St-Brieuc
Camaret
Monts d'Arrée
Crozon Peninsula
Crozon
FINISTÈRE
Carhaix
Dinan
Combourg
Châteaulin
Gouarec
Mur-de-Bretagne
Fougères
Alençon
Baie de Douarnenez
Locronan
N164
R. Aulne
R. Rance
N137
R. Couesnon
Douarnenez
R. Odet
MONTAGNES NOIRES
Loudéac
Île de Sein
Pointe du Raz
Audierne
Lac du Guerledan
Rennes
Quimper
Le Faouët
Pontivy
Mauron
Forêt de Paimpont
Vitré
Concarneau
Nantes-Brest Canal
Paimpont
Quimperlé
Josselin
Bénodet
R. Blavet
E50
Pont-Aven
E60
Guer
A81
Paris
A11
Lorient
N166
Malestroit
R. Vilaine
Le Mans
Auray
Île de Groix
Carnac
Vannes
Golfe de Morbihan
Redon
E60
GRANDE-BRIÈRE
E137
Quiberon
Île Houat
R. Erdre
Angers
Le Palais
Guérande
ATLANTIC OCEAN
Île Hoëdic
Belle Île
Le Croisic
A11
La Baule
St-Nazaire
Tours
Nantes
Pornic
R. Loire
A83
A84
A28
N
0
50 km
La Rochelle

Food in Brittany

Brittany's proudest addition to the great cuisines of the world has to be the **crêpe** and its savoury equivalent the **galette**; crêperies throughout the region attempt to pass them off as satisfying meals, serving them with every imaginable filling. However, few people plan their holidays specifically around eating pancakes, and gourmets are more likely to be enticed to Brittany by its magnificent array of **seafood.** Restaurants in resorts such as St-Malo and Quiberon jostle tp attract fish connoisseurs, while some smaller towns – like Cancale, which specializes in oysters (*huîtres*), and Erquy, with its scallops (*coquilles St-Jacques*) – depend wholly on one specific mollusc for their livelihood.

Although they can't claim to be uniquely Breton, two appetizers feature on every self-respecting menu. These are **moules marinières**, giant bowls of succulent orange mussels steamed in a combination of white wine, shallots and parsley (and perhaps enriched with cream or crème fraîche to become *moules à la crème*), and **soupe de poissons** (fish soup), traditionally served with a pot of the garlicky mayonnaise known as *rouille* (coloured with pulverized sweet red pepper), a mound of grated *gruyère*, and a bowl of croutons. Jars of fresh *soupe de poissons* – or even crab or lobster – are always on sale in seaside *poissonneries*, and make an ideal way to take a taste of France home with you. Paying a bit more in a restaurant – typically on menus costing €25 or more – brings you into the realm of the **assiette de fruits de mer**, a mountainous heap of langoustines, crabs, oysters, mussels, clams, whelks and cockles, most raw and all delicious. **Main courses** tend to be plainer than in Normandy, with fresh local fish being prepared with relatively simple sauces. Skate served with capers, or salmon baked with a mustard or cheese sauce, are typical dishes, while even the **cotriade**, a stew containing sole, turbot or bass, as well as shellfish, is distinctly less rich than its Mediterranean equivalent, the *bouillabaisse*. Brittany is also better than much of France in maintaining its respect for fresh **vegetables**, thanks to the extensive local production of peas, cauliflowers, artichokes and the like. Only with the **desserts** can things get a little heavy; **far Breton**, considered a great delicacy, is a baked concoction of sponge and custard dotted with chopped plums, while *îles flottantes* are soft meringue icebergs adrift in a sea of *crème anglaise*, a light egg custard.

Strictly speaking, no **wine** is produced in Brittany. However, along the lower Loire valley, the *département* of Loire-Atlantique, centred on Nantes, is still generally regarded as "belonging" to Brittany – and is treated as such in this chapter. Vineyards here are responsible for the dry white Muscadet – normally used in *moules marinières* – and the even drier Gros-Plant.

For most visitors, however, the Breton **coast** is the dominant feature. Apart from the Côte d'Azur, this is the most popular resort area in France, for both French and foreign tourists. Its attractions are obvious: warm white-sand beaches, towering cliffs, rock formations and offshore islands and islets, and everywhere the stone dolmens and menhirs of a prehistoric past. The most frequented areas are the **Côte d'Émeraude** around **St-Malo**; the **Côte de Granit Rose** in the north; the **Crozon peninsula** in far western **Finistère**; the family resorts such as **Bénodet** just to the south; and the **Morbihan coast** below **Vannes**. Accommodation and campsites here are plentiful, if pushed to their limits from mid-June to the end of August. Be aware, though, that out of season, many of the coastal resorts close down completely.

Whenever you come, don't leave Brittany without visiting one of its scores of **islands** – such as the **Île de Bréhat**, the **Île de Sein**, or **Belle-Île** – or taking in cities like **Quimper** or **Morlaix**, testimony to the riches of the medieval duchy. Allow time, too, to leave the coast and explore the interior, even if the price you pay for the solitude is sketchy transport and a shortage of hotels and campsites.

Eastern Brittany and the north coast

All roads in Brittany curl eventually inland to **Rennes**, the capital, which lies a short way northeast of the legendary **Forêt de Paimpont**. East of Rennes, the fortified citadels of **Fougères** and **Vitré** protected the eastern approaches to medieval Brittany, which vigorously defended its independence against incursors. Along the north coast, west of Normandy's Mont St-Michel, stand some of Brittany's finest old towns. A spectacular introduction to the province greets ferry passengers from Portsmouth: the **River Rance**,

A Breton glossary

Estimates of the number of **Breton-speakers** range from 400,000 to 800,000. You may well encounter it spoken as a first, day-to-day language by the very old and the young in parts of Finistère and the Morbihan. Learning Breton is not really a viable prospect for visitors without a grounding in Welsh, Gaelic or some other Celtic language. However, as you travel through the province, it's interesting to note the roots of Breton place names, many of which have a simple meaning in the language. Below are some of the most common:

aber	estuary	*lann*	heath
argoat	land	*lech*	flat stone
armor	sea	*mario*	dead
avel	wind	*men*	stone
bihan	little	*menez*	(rounded) mountain
bran	hill	*menhir*	long stone
braz	big	*meur*	big
coat	forest	*nevez*	new
cromlech	stone circle	*parc*	field
dol	table	*penn*	end, head
dolmen	stone table	*plou*	parish
du	black	*pors*	port, farmyard
enez	island	*roc'h*	ridge
goaz	stream	*ster*	river
gwenn	white	*stivel*	fountain, spring
hir	long	*traez henn*	beach
ker	village or house	*trou*	valley
kozh	old	*ty*	house
lan	holy place	*wrach*	witch

guarded by magnificently preserved **St-Malo** on its estuary, and beautiful medieval **Dinan** 20km upstream. Further west stretches a varied coastline that culminates in the seductive **Île de Bréhat**, and the colourful chaos of the **Côte de Granit Rose**.

Rennes

For a city that has been the capital and power centre of Brittany since the 1532 union with France, **Rennes** is – outwardly at least – uncharacteristic of the province, with its Neoclassical layout and pompous major buildings. What potential it had to be a picturesque tourist spot was destroyed in 1720, when a drunken carpenter managed to set light to virtually the whole city. Only the area known as **Les Lices**, at the junction of the canalized Ille and the River Vilaine, was undamaged. The remodelling of the rest of the city was handed over to Parisian architects, not in deference to the capital but in an attempt to rival it. The result, on the north side of the river at any rate, is something of a

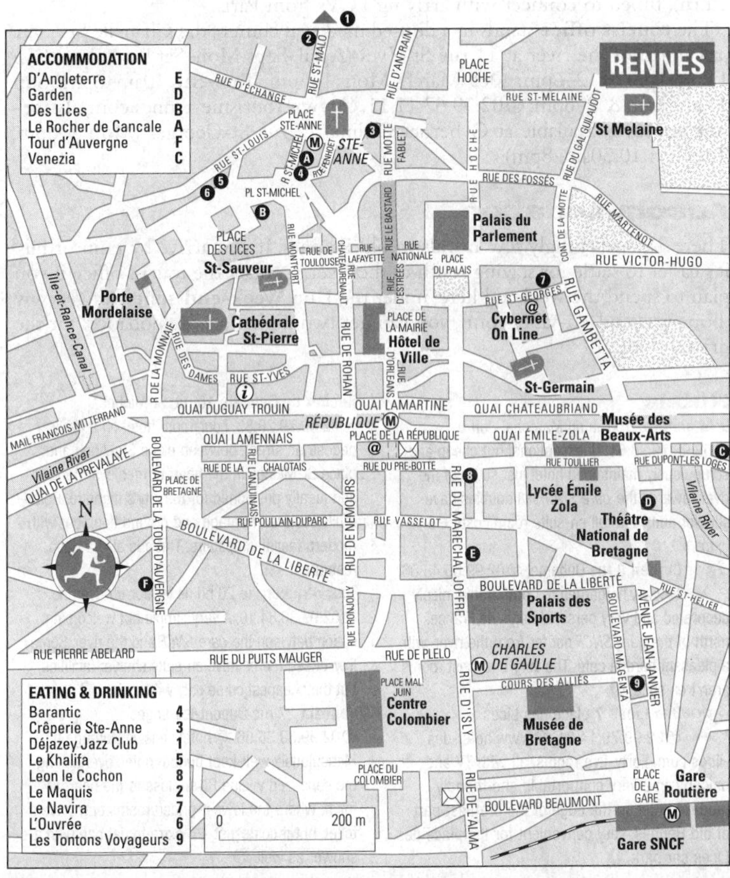

patchwork quilt, consisting of grand eighteenth-century public squares interspersed with intimate little alleys of half-timbered houses. It's quite a pleasant city to stroll around for half a day, but it lacks a cohesive personality.

Arrival and information

Rennes' **gare SNCF** (ⓣ08.36.35.35.35) is south of the Vilaine, twenty minutes' walk from the tourist office and a little more from the medieval quarter. A fast, efficient and ultra-clean **métro** system (Mon–Sat 5am–12.45am, Sun 7.15am–12.45am); connects the *gare SNCF*, the place de la République and the place Ste-Anne, as well as other destinations of less interest to visitors. Any one-way journey costs €1.10, or you can ride all day for €3.20.

Although the **gare routière** stands alongside the *gare SNCF* on boulevard Solferino, most local **buses** start and finish by the canal in the heart of town, on or near place de la République. Rennes is a busy junction, with direct services to St-Malo (TIV; ⓣ02.99.30.87.80), and Dinan and Dinard (Armor Express or TAE; ⓣ02.99.26.16.00, ⓦwww.illenoo.fr). Les Courriers Bretons (ⓣ02.99.19.70.80, ⓦwww.lescourriersbretons.com) run regular services to Mont St-Michel (departing Rennes' *gare routière* up to five times daily; €25return), timed to connect with arriving TGVs from Paris.

The **tourist office** stands in a disused medieval church, the Chapelle St-Yves, just north of the river at 11 rue St-Yves (April–Sept Mon–Sat 9am–7pm, Sun 11am–1pm & 2–6pm; Oct–March Mon 1–6pm, Tues–Sat 10am–6pm, Sun 11am–1pm & 2–6pm; ⓣ02.99.67.11.11, ⓦwww.tourisme-rennes.com). **Internet access** is available at Cybernet Online, 22 rue St-Georges (Mon 2–8pm, Tues–Fri 10.30am–8pm).

Accommodation

There are surprisingly few **hotels** in old Rennes. If you arrive by train or bus, it's easier to settle for staying south of the river. Contact the tourist office if you plan to spend the weekend here; under the **Bon Week-end scheme** (ⓦwww.bon-weekend-en-villes.com), you can get two nights' accommodation for the price of one.

Hotels

D'Angleterre 19 rue du Maréchal-Joffre ⓣ02.99.79.38.61. Unexceptional but cheap and scrupulously maintained hotel just south of the river towards the *gare SNCF*; all doubles have shower and TV, a full en-suite room costs €6 extra. ❷

Garden 3 rue Duhamel ⓣ02.99.65.45.06, ⓦwww.hotgarden.fr. Comfortable, nicely decorated and very personal Logis de France, north of the *gare SNCF* not far from the river, with a pleasant garden café. The very cheapest rooms aren't en suite. ❹

Des Lices 7 place des Lices ⓣ02.99.79.14.81, ⓦwww.hotel-des-lices.com. Forty-five rooms, all with TV and balcony, in a very comfortable and friendly modern hotel on the edge of the prettiest part of old Rennes, very convenient for the place des Lices car park. ❹

Rocher de Cancale 10 rue St-Michel ⓣ02.99.79.20.83. Four-room hotel on a lively pedestrian street, between place Ste-Anne and place St-Michel, in the heart of medieval Rennes and ideally positioned for the city's nightlife. Beautifully restored frontage and ground floor, but with modern facilities upstairs. There is also a good restaurant. ❸

Tour d'Auvergne 20 bd de la Tour-d'Auvergne ⓣ02.99.30.84.16. A very simple but welcoming option between the *gare SNCF* and the river. Some low-priced rooms have en-suite shower facilities, but the cheapest come only with a sink. ❶

Venezia 27 rue Dupont-les-Loges ⓣ02.99.30.36.56, ⓔhotel.venezia@orange.fr. Meticulously well-kept budget hotel, overlooking the canalized Vilaine River close to the heart of town, where the lowest-priced rooms only have a toilet, but it costs just €6 extra to get one with a shower as well. ❷

Hostel and campsite

Centre International de Séjour 10–12 Canal St-Martin ⓣ02.99.33.22.33, ⓔrennes@fuaj.org. Welcoming, attractively positioned HI hostel, 3km north of the centre beside the Canal d'Ille et Rance. Charging €16 per person per night for a dorm bed, it has a cafeteria and a laundry, and operates a 1am curfew; membership of a hostelling association is compulsory. Bus #18 runs there from the place Ste-Anne métro station, direction "St-Gregoire". Open all year.

Camping Municipal des Gayeulles, rue de Professeur-Maurice-Audin ⓣ02.99.36.91.22. An appealingly verdant site 1km east of central Rennes; take bus #3. Closed Nov–March.

The City

Rennes' surviving **medieval quarter**, bordered by the canal to the west and the river to the south, radiates from **Porte Mordelaise**, the old ceremonial entrance to the city. Just to the northeast of the *porte*, the **place des Lices** is dominated by two usually empty market halls but comes alive every Saturday for one of France's largest **street markets**. The place was originally the venue for jousting tournaments, and it was on this spot in 1337 that the hitherto unknown Bertrand du Guesclin, then aged 17, fought and defeated several older opponents. This set him on his career as a soldier, during which he was to save Rennes when it was under siege by the English. However, after the Bretons were defeated at Auray in 1364, he fought for the French, and twice invaded Brittany.

The one central building to escape the 1720 fire was the **Palais du Parlement** on rue Hoche downtown. Ironically, however, the Palais was all but ruined by a mysterious conflagration in 1994, thought to have been sparked by a flare during a demonstration by Breton fishermen. Since then, the entire structure has been rebuilt and restored, and is once more topped by an impressive array of gleaming gilded statues. Inside, its lobby stages temporary exhibitions.

If you head south from the Palais, you'll soon reach the **River Vilaine**, which flows through the centre of Rennes, narrowly confined into a steep-sided channel. The south bank is every bit as busy as, if not busier than, the north, with the **Musée des Beaux-Arts** at 20 quai Émile-Zola (daily except Mon 10am–noon & 2–6pm; €5.30). Unfortunately many of its finest artworks – which include drawings by Leonardo da Vinci, Botticelli, Fra Lippo Lippi and Dürer – are not usually on public display. Instead you'll find indifferent Impressionist views of Normandy by the likes of Boudin and Sisley, interspersed with the occasional treasure.

The showpiece **Musée de Bretagne**, housed in the new edifice Champs Libres, 500 metres south on the cours des Alliés, provides a high-tech overview of Breton history and culture (Tues noon–9pm, Wed–Fri noon–7pm, Sat & Sun 2–7pm; €4, or €7 for museum and Éspace des Sciences; ⓦwww.musee-bretagne.fr). It starts at the very beginning, with a hearth used by humans in a Finistère seacave half a million years ago that ranks among the oldest signs of fire in the world. From there on, a quick, entertaining skate through regional history covers the dolmens and menhirs of the megalith builders, some magnificent jadeite axes and Bronze Age swords, and the arrival of first the Celts, next the Romans, and later still the spread of Christianity from the fifth century onwards. With labels in English as well as French and Breton, it makes a good introduction to the region, but unless some compelling temporary exhibition is on it's not really unmissable. Under the same roof, and sharing the same hours and entrance fees, the **Éspace des Sciences** is a peculiar sort of scaly volcano that contains two floors of rather dry scientific displays, this time with no English captions.

Eating and drinking

Most of Rennes' more interesting bars and **restaurants** are in the streets just south of the **place Ste-Anne**, towards the place des Lices, with rues St-Michel and Penhoët, each with a fine assemblage of ancient wooden buildings, as the epicentre. Ethnic alternatives are concentrated along **rue St-Malo** just to the north, and also on **rue St-Georges** near the place du Palais. Rue Vasselot is the nearest equivalent south of the river.

One of the city's favourite **bars** is the *Barantic* at 4 rue St-Michel, which puts on occasional live music for a mixed crowd of Breton nationalists and boisterous students; if you don't like the look of it, or it's too full, there are half a dozen similar alternatives within spitting distance. Live **jazz** and other gigs take place at *Déjazey Jazz Club*, 54 rue St-Malo (ⓣ02.99.38.70.72; closed Sun).

Crêperie Ste-Anne 5 place Ste-Anne ⓣ02.99.79.22.72. Appealing crêperie on the place Ste-Anne opposite the church, with plenty of outdoor seating and a good selection of *galettes* for around €5. Closed Sun.

Le Khalifa 20 haut de la place des Lices ⓣ02.99.30.87.30. Assorted Moroccan dishes, served outside or in an atmospheric dining room. Couscous and *brochettes* from €9.95, tagine €11.50, as well as various set *formules*. Closed all Mon, & Tues lunch.

Leon le Cochon 1 rue Maréchal-Joffre ⓣ02.99.79.37.54. Tasteful, contemporary but classically French restaurant, where the simple lunch menu costs just €11.50, but it's best to reserve to enjoy dinner menus that range up to €37. Closed Sun in July & Aug.

Le Maquis 13 rue St-Malo ⓣ02.99.63.83.06. Very lively, friendly African restaurant, serving lots of Senegalese marinated chicken and fish dishes for around €9, plus a €16.50 vegetarian set menu. Dinner only. Closed Mon.

Le Navira 39 rue St-Georges ⓣ02.99.38.88.90. Simple, welcoming French restaurant with outdoor seating on a busy semi-pedestrian alley east of the Palais du Parlement, offering good-value lunch (€14.60) and dinner (€19.10) menus. Closed Sun & Mon.

L'Ouvrée 18 place des Lices ⓣ02.99.30.16.38. Formal but very friendly gourmet restaurant, spread through two dining rooms decorated in warm reds and yellows. Menus range from €14.50 to €32, and feature small but tasty portions with an emphasis on fish, as for example with the *flan de langoustines*, plus wonderful desserts. Closed Sat lunch, Sun eve & Mon.

Les Tontons Voyageurs 4 av Janvier ⓣ02.99.30.09.20. Lively, eclectic place that incorporates a piano bar and a cigar room, and puts on live music, while also serving inexpensive, high-quality brasserie lunches, and dinner menus up to €29.50. Closed Sat lunch, all Sun, & Mon eve.

Festivals and theatre

Rennes is at its best in the first ten days of July, when the **Festival des Tombées de la Nuit** celebrates Breton culture with music, theatre, film, mime and poetry (ⓣ02.99.32.56.56, ⓦwww.lestdnuit.com). In the first week of December, the **Transmusicales** rock festival attracts big-name acts from all over France and the world at large, while retaining a Breton emphasis (ⓣ02.99.31.12.10, ⓦwww.lestrans.com). The **Théâtre National de Bretagne**, 1 rue St-Helier (ⓣ02.99.31.12.31, ⓦwww.t-n-b.fr), puts on varied events throughout the year, except in August. All year round, in a different auditorium on the same premises, *Club Ubu* (ⓣ02.99.31.12.00, ⓦwww.ubu-rennes.com) puts on large-scale gigs.

The Forêt de Paimpont

Thirty kilometres west of Rennes, the **Forêt de Paimpont**, known also by its ancient name of Brocéliande, is – according to song and legend – the forest of the wizard Merlin. Medieval Breton minstrels, like their Welsh counterparts, set the tales of King Arthur and the Holy Grail both in Grande Bretagne and here in Petite Bretagne. For all the magic of these shared legends, however, and a succession of likely sites, few people come out here.

Roaming around for a day is easy, with **MAURON**, reachable by bus from Rennes, making a good place to start. From the hamlet of Folle Pensée, just south, a circuitous but enjoyable twenty-minute walk leads to **La Fontaine de Barenton** – Merlin's spring. The path leads off from the end of the road at Folle Pensée, turning to the right, running through pines and gorse to a junction of forest tracks: here, take the track straight ahead for about 100m, where an unobvious path to the left goes into the woods and turns back north to the spring – walled, and filled by the most delicious water imaginable. After drinking, stroke the great stone slab beside the spring to call up a storm, roaring lions and a horseman in black armour. Here Merlin first set eyes on Vivianne, who bound him willingly in a prison of air.

The Fountain of Eternal Youth is hidden nearby and accessible only to the pure in heart. Another forest walk, more scenic but without a goal, is the **Val sans Retour** (the Valley of No Return), off the GR37 from Tréhorenteuc to La Guette. The path to follow leads out from the D141 just south of Tréhorenteuc to a steep valley from which exits are barred by thickets of gorse and giant furze on the rocks above; at one point it skirts an overgrown table of rock, the **Rocher des Faux Amants** (Rock of the False Lovers), from which the seductress Morgane le Fay supposedly enticed unwary boys.

Practicalities

The **bus** from Rennes to Guer runs twice a day past the southern edge of the forest, stopping at Forges-les-Paimpont, while another bus runs around the north corner to Mauron – again twice a day. Information on the forest can be picked up from the **tourist office** next to the lakeside abbey in the little market village of **PAIMPONT** (Feb–June & Sept–Dec Tues–Sat 10am–noon & 2–5pm; July & Aug daily 10am–noon & 2–6pm; Ⓣ02.99.07.84.23). Paimpont makes the most obvious base for explorations: it's right at the centre of the woods, and has some excellent **accommodation**. At the *Relais de Brocéliande* in town, 7 rue des Forges (Ⓣ02.99.07.84.94, Ⓦwww.le-relais-de-broceliande.fr; ④), a flower-bedecked delight, you can fill up for €26.50, or much more, in the restaurant under the gaze of stuffed animal heads. There's also a two-star municipal **campsite** on the edge of the village (Ⓣ02.97.07.89.16; closed Oct–April). Other accommodation in the forest includes a *gîte d'étape*-cum-*chambre d'hôte* in tiny Trudeau on the D40 (Ⓣ02.99.07.81.40; dorm beds €9.70, B&B ③) and a lovely **hostel**, at Le Choucan-en-Brocéliande, 5km out on the Concoret road (Ⓣ02.97.22.76.75; dorm beds €9.70; closed mid-Sept to May).

The frontier towns

If you're entering Brittany by road from Normandy, Maine or Le Mans, you're likely to pass through or close to **Fougères**, **Vitré and Dol-de-Bretagne**, all of which were, at one time or another, heavily fortified strategic sites.

Fougères and its forest

The topography of **FOUGÈRES**, which lies on the main Caen–Rennes road, is impossible to grasp from a map; streets that look a few metres long turn out to be precipitous plunges down the escarpments of its split-levelled site, and lanes collapse into flights of steps. The dominant feature is the town's robust **château**, built well below the level of the main part of town, on a low spit of land that separates, and is towered over by, two mighty rock faces. Its massive and seemingly impregnable bulk is protected by great curtain walls growing out of the rock, and encircled by a hacked-out moat full of weirs and waterfalls – none of which prevented its repeated capture by such medieval adventurers as du Guesclin.

The best approach to the castle is from place des Arbres beside St-Léonard's church off the main street of the old fortified town. Footpaths, ramps and stairways drop down through formal gardens, offering magnificent views of the ramparts along the way, to reach the meadows beside the River Nançon, which you cross beside a little cluster of medieval houses. Sadly, however, the interior of the château fails to live up to its compelling exterior; instead the hourly **château tours** place a rather deadening emphasis on the local shoe industry (daily: April to mid-June & last two weeks of Sept 9.30am–noon & 2–6pm; mid-June to mid-Sept 9am–7pm; Oct–Dec, Feb & March 10am–noon & 2–5pm; €3.60).

Fougères' **tourist office**, at 1 place Aristide-Briand, provides copious information on all aspects of the town and local countryside (Easter–June, Sept & Oct Mon–Sat 9.30am–12.30pm & 2–6pm, Sun 1.30–5.30pm; July & Aug Mon–Sat 9am–7pm, Sun 10am–noon & 2–4pm; Nov–Easter Mon 2–6pm, Tues–Sat 10am–12.30pm & 2–6pm; ⓣ02.99.94.12.20, ⓦwww.ot-fougeres.fr). The *Hôtel des Voyageurs*, nearby at 10 place Gambetta (ⓣ02.99.99.08.20, ⓦwww.hotel-voyageurs-fougeres.com; ❸; closed second fortnight in Aug), is a rambling old town house with some good, comfortable rooms, and has a separate but excellent **restaurant** downstairs (closed Sat lunch & Sun dinner). There are no hotels in the immediate vicinity of the château, but the squares on all sides are crammed with an abundance of appealing **bars** and **crêperies**. At *Le Medieval* (ⓣ02.99.94.92.59), which has lots of outdoor seating beside the moat, you can snack on *moules-frites* or crêpes, or get a full dinner from €17.

Vitré

VITRÉ, just north of the Le Mans–Rennes motorway, 30km east of Rennes, rivals Dinan as the best-preserved medieval town in Brittany. While its walls are not quite complete, the thickets of medieval stone cottages that lie outside them have hardly changed. The towers of the **castle**, which dominates the western end of the ramparts, have pointed slate-grey roofs in best fairy-tale fashion, looking like freshly sharpened pencils, but sadly the municipal offices and **museum** of shells, birds, bugs and local history inside are not exactly thrilling (May–Sept daily 10am–12.45pm & 2–6pm; Oct–April Mon & Wed–Sat 10am–12.15pm & 2–5.30pm, Sun 2–5.30pm; €4).

Vitré is a market town rather than an industrial centre, with its principal **market** held on Mondays in the square in front of **Notre-Dame church**. The old city is full of twisting streets of half-timbered houses, a good proportion of which are bars – **rue Beaudrairie** in particular has a fine selection.

The local **gare SNCF** is on the southern edge of the centre, where the ramparts have disappeared and the town blends into its newer sectors. Just across the square from the station you'll find the **tourist office** (July & Aug daily 10am–12.30pm & 2–7pm; Sept–June Mon 2.30–6pm, Tues–Fri 9.30am–12.30pm & 2.30–6pm, Sat 10am–12.30pm & 3–5pm; ⓣ02.99.75.04.46, ⓦwww.ot-vitre.fr). Most of the **hotels** are nearby. The *Petit Billot*, 5bis place du Général-Leclerc (ⓣ02.99.75.02.10, ⓦwww.petit-billot.com; ❸), is good value, while rooms on the higher floors of the *Hôtel du Château*, 5 rue Rallon (Ⓣ02.99.74.58.59; ❸; closed Sun in low season), on a quiet road just below the castle, have views of the ramparts. Of the **restaurants**, *Le St-Yves*, immediately below the castle at 1 place St-Yves (Ⓣ02.99.74.68.76; closed all Mon eve, plus Tues, Thurs & Sun eves), serves menus from €17 to €28, while *La Soupe aux Choux*, a little higher up at 32 rue Notre-Dame (Ⓣ02.99.75.10.86; closed Sat lunch, plus Sun in low season), prepares simple but classic French food, with a duo of frogs' legs and pork for example costing €12.

Dol-de-Bretagne and around

During the Middle Ages, **DOL-DE-BRETAGNE**, 30km west of Mont St-Michel, was an important bishopric. It no longer has a bishop, though its huge granite **cathedral** endures, with its strange, squat, tiled towers. The ambitious **CathédralOscope** (April–Oct daily 10am–7pm; rest of the year consult tourist office; €7.50), in the cathedral square, sets out to explain the construction and significance of medieval cathedrals in general, but for all its high-tech presentation and flair, non-French-speakers may well find it rather heavy going.

Dol still has a few streets packed with venerable buildings, most notably its central axis, the pretty **Grande-Rue**, where one Romanesque edifice dates back as far as the eleventh century, alongside an assortment of 500-year-old half-timbered houses that look down on the bustle of shoppers below.

All approaches to Dol from the bay are guarded by the former island of **Mont Dol**, now eight rather marshy kilometres in from the sea. This abrupt granite outcrop was the legendary site of a battle between the Archangel Michael and the Devil. Fancifully named indentations in the rock, such as the "Devil's Claw", testify to the savagery of their encounter, which as usual the Devil lost. The site has been occupied since prehistoric times – flint implements have been unearthed alongside the bones of mammoths, sabre-toothed tigers and even rhinoceroses. Later on, it appears to have been used for worship by the druids, before becoming, like Mont St-Michel, an island monastery, all traces of which have long vanished. You can drive to the top from the attractive little village at the foot of the hill, or it makes a pleasant climb on foot. Just below the summit, the lawns of a crêperie-cum-bar hold crowds of summer day-trippers. A little further up, there's a tiny chapel, while the peak itself is crowned by a granite tower topped by a white statue of the Madonna and child. Ascending the 55 tight little spiral steps within brings you to a platform commanding immense views across the surrounding pancake-flat plains.

There's not a great deal to keep casual visitors in Dol. However, the **tourist office**, at 3 Grande-Rue (June & Sept Mon 2–6pm, Tues–Sat 10am–12.30pm & 2–6pm; July & Aug Mon–Fri 9.30am–7pm, Sat & Sun 9.30am–1pm & 2–7pm; Oct–May Tues–Sat 10am–12.30pm & 2–6pm; Ⓣ02.99.48.15.37, Ⓦwww.pays-de-dol.com), can direct you eastwards to a reasonable **hotel**, the *Bretagne*, next to the market at 17 place Chateaubriand (Ⓣ02.99.48.02.03; ❷; closed Oct), where rooms at the back look out across a vestige of ramparts towards Mont Dol; menus vary from €11.50 to €28. The best **campsite** in the area is the luxurious *Castel-Camping des Ormes* (Ⓣ02.99.73.53.00, Ⓦwww.lesormes.com; closed mid-Sept to mid-May), set around a lake 6km south towards Combourg on the N795, which offers horse-riding, golf and even cricket.

A couple of nice **fish restaurants** stand opposite each other in the ancient houses on rue Ceinte, as it winds its way from Grande-Rue to the Cathedral: *Le Porche au Pain* at no. 1 (Ⓣ02.99.48.37.57; closed Wed in low season), and *La Grabotais* at no. 4 (Ⓣ02.99.48.19.89; closed Mon, plus Sun eve in low season).

St-Malo and around

Walled and built with the same grey granite stone as Mont St-Michel, **ST-MALO** was originally a fortified island at the mouth of the Rance, controlling not only the estuary but the open sea beyond. Now inseparably attached to the mainland, it's the most visited place in Brittany – thanks more to its superb

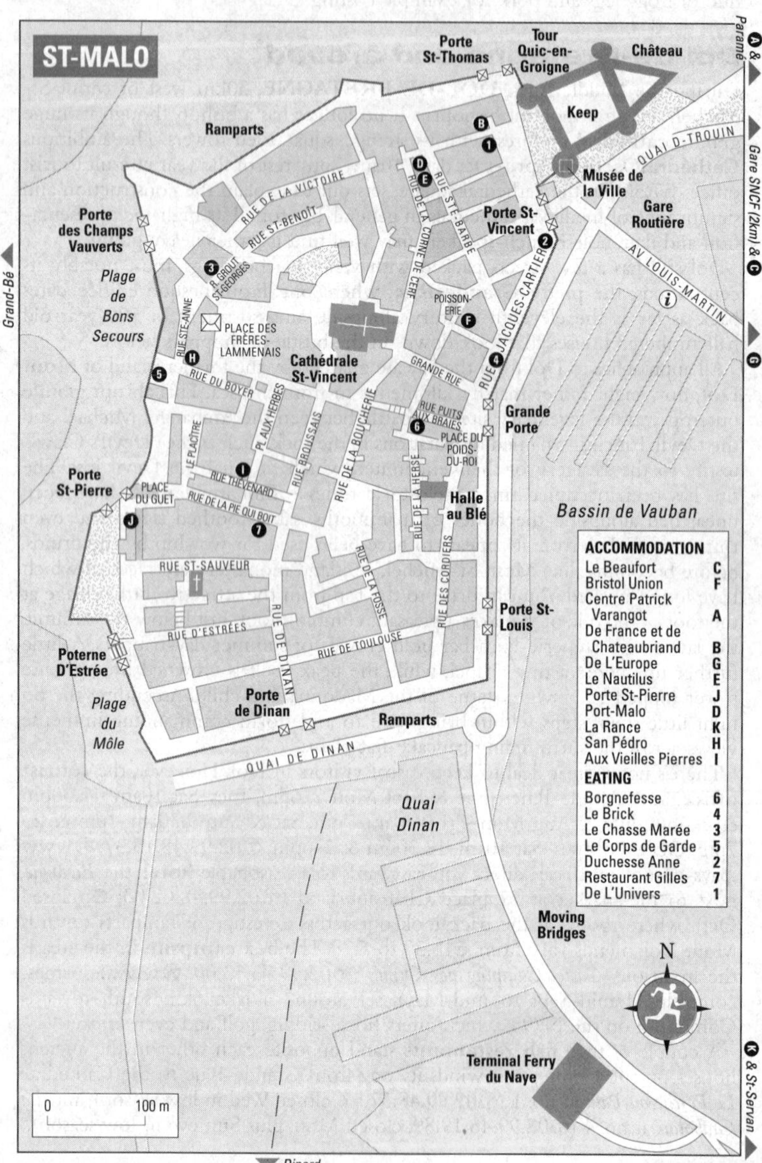

old citadelle than to the ferry terminal that's tucked into the harbour behind. From outside the walls, the dignified ensemble of the old city might seem stern and forbidding, but passing through into the *intra-muros* ("within the walls") streets brings you into a busy, lively and very characterful town, packed with hotels, restaurants, bars and shops. Yes, the summer crowds can be oppressive, but even then a stroll atop the ramparts should restore your equilibrium, while the presence of vast, clean beaches right on the city's doorstep is a very big bonus if you're travelling with kids in tow. Having to spend a night here before or after a ferry crossing is a positive pleasure – so long as you take the trouble to reserve accommodation in advance.

Arrival and information

St-Malo is always busy with **boats**. From the **Terminal Ferry du Naye**, Brittany Ferries (Ⓣ02.99.40.64.41, Ⓦwww.brittanyferries.com) sails to Portsmouth, while Condor Ferries (Ⓣ02.99.20.03.00, Ⓦwww.condorferries.co.uk) connects with both Weymouth (via Jersey or Guernsey) and Poole during spring and summer; for details, see p.31. Between April and early November, regular passenger **ferries to Dinard** operate from the **quai Dinan**, just outside the westernmost point of the ramparts (Compagnie Corsaire; Ⓣ08.25.13.80.35, Ⓦwww.compagniecorsaire.com; €4 single, €6 return, bikes €4.50 or €7.50 return); the trip across the estuary takes an all-too-short ten minutes.

Though almost all St-Malo buses, whether local or long-distance, coincide also with trains at the **gare SNCF** – 2km out from the citadelle, set back from square Jean-Coquelin, and convenient neither for the old town nor the ferry – the **gare routière** is officially an expanse of concrete right in front of the city walls, beside the Bassin Duguay-Trouin in the Port des Yachts. The two main regional bus companies both have ticket offices here. Tourisme Verney act as agents for the Compagnie de Transport d'Ille et Vilaine (TIV; Ⓣ02.99.82.26.26), which run services to Dinard, Dinan, Cancale, Combourg (not in July and August) and Rennes. Les Courriers Bretons (Ⓣ02.99.19.70.80, Ⓦwww.lescourriersbretons.com), go to Cancale, Mont St-Michel, Dol and Fougères. In summer, they also operate a complicated schedule of day-trips and half-day trips to destinations including **Mont St-Michel**, Dinan, Cap Fréhel and the Île de Bréhat.

St-Malo's helpful **tourist office** is alongside the *gare routière* (April–June & Sept Mon–Sat 9am–12.30pm & 1.30–6.30pm, Sun 10am–12.30pm & 2.30–6pm; July & Aug Mon–Sat 9am–7.30pm, Sun 10am–6pm; Oct–March Mon–Sat 9am–12.30pm & 1.30–6pm; Ⓣ08.25.13.52.00, Ⓦwww.saint-malo-tourisme.com). For **Internet access**, head to Cop' Imprim, just west of the *gare SNCF* at 29bis bd des Talards (Mon–Fri 9am–7pm, Sat 9am–noon; Ⓣ02.99.56.05.83; Ⓦwww.cybermalo.com).

Bicycles can be rented from Les Velos Bleus, 19 rue Alphonse-Thébault (Ⓣ02.99.40.31.63, Ⓦwww.velos-bleus.fr), or Espace Nicole, 11–13 rue Robert-Schuman, Paramé (Ⓣ02.99.56.11.06, Ⓦwww.cyclesnicole.com).

Accommodation

St-Malo boasts over a hundred **hotels**, including the seaside boarding houses just off the beach, along with several **campsites** and a **hostel** – in high season it needs every one of them. If you plan to stay the night before catching a summer ferry, it's best to make a reservation well in advance.

You pay a premium to stay within the city walls, since that's where any night-life takes place, and it's a fair walk in through the docks from the surrounding suburbs. Unfortunately, the *intra-muros* hotels tend to take advantage of high summer demand by insisting that you eat in their own restaurants. Cheaper rates can be found by the *gare SNCF*, or in suburban Paramé (bus #2 or #5), but it's hardly worth being away from the citadelle for the sake of saving a few euros. The hostel is notoriously busy, while the four municipal campsites also tend to be full in July and August.

Hotels in the citadelle

Bristol Union 4 place de la Poissonnerie ⓣ02.99.40.83.36, ⓦwww.hotel-bristol-union.com. Tall hotel, equipped with a lift, in a quiet little square facing the former fish market, just off the Grande Rue, which offers unexciting but acceptable modernized rooms, some very small. ④

De France et de Chateaubriand place Chateaubriand ⓣ02.99.56.66.52, ⓦwww. hotel-fr-chateaubriand.com. Elegant rooms at surprisingly reasonable prices in the imposing birthplace of the writer Chateaubriand, approached via a courtyard from the main square. Higher rooms have sea views; breakfast is €10 and parking €12. ⑥

Le Nautilus 9 rue de la Corne de Cerf ⓣ02.99.40.42.27, ⓦwww.lenautilus.com. Colourfully refitted, totally non-smoking hotel (with a lift) not far in from the Porte St-Vincent, offering small but good-value and bright rooms, all with shower and TV. ④

Port-Malo 15 rue Ste-Barbe ⓣ02.99.20.52.99. Eleven small but clean and en-suite rooms – above a nice old-fashioned bar, so go for the higher floors – with friendly and helpful management. No restaurant. ③

Porte St-Pierre 2 place du Guet ⓣ02.99.40.91.27. Comfortable Logis de France, peeping out to sea over the walls of the citadelle, near the small Porte St-Pierre. There's one cheaper single room, with no shower. Predominantly fish-based dinner menus, in the separate restaurant across the alley (closed Thurs lunch & all Tues), run from €26 upwards. Closed mid-Nov to Jan. ④

San Pédro 1 rue Ste-Anne ⓣ02.99.40.88.57, ⓦwww.sanpedro-hotel.com. Twelve compact but stylishly refurbished rooms in a nice quiet setting, just inside the walls in the north of the citadelle. Rooms on the higher floors (reached via a minuscule lift) enjoy sea views, and cost around €10 extra. No smoking. Closed mid-Nov to mid-Feb. ④

Aux Vieilles Pierres 9 rue Thévenard ⓣ02.99.56.46.80. Six-room hotel, near place aux Herbes, which remains one of the better bargains within the walls, even if a room with a shower costs €16 extra. Menus at the restaurant cost €24 or €32. Open all year. ②–③

Hotels outside the walls

Le Beaufort 25 chaussée du Sillon, Coutoisville ⓣ02.99.40.99.99, ⓦwww.hotel-beaufort.com. Grand sea-view hotel, 30min walk from the citadelle, with beautifully restored rooms – some with lovely balconies – and a good restaurant. ⑤–⑨

De l'Europe 44 bd de la République ⓣ02.99.56.13.42, ⓦwww.hotels-st-malo.com/europe. Year-round cheap but clean rooms (the cheaper ones don't have en-suite facilities) in a genuinely friendly (if noisy) hotel near the *gare SNCF*, with a cosy café serving breakfast for €5.50. ①–③

La Rance 15 quai Sébastopol, St-Servan ⓣ02.99.81.78.63, ⓦwww.larancehotel.com. Small, tasteful option in sight of the Tour Solidor, with eleven spacious rooms and a much more tranquil atmosphere than St-Malo itself. ④

Hostel and campsites

Centre Patrick Varangot 37 av du Père-Umbricht, Paramé ⓣ02.99.40.29.80, ⓦwww.centrevarangot.com. Dominated as a rule by lively young travellers, this is one of France's busiest hostels, 2km northeast of the *gare SNCF* in the suburb of Paramé, not far from the beach. Dorm beds from €16.20 including breakfast April–Sept, €15.25 Oct–March; hostelling association membership required. Rates include breakfast, and there's also a cut-price cafeteria, as well as kitchen facilities and tennis courts. No curfew, open all year.

La Cité d'Aleth allée Gaston Buy, St-Servan ⓣ02.99.81.60.91. By far the nearest campsite to the citadelle, in a dramatic location on the headland southwest of St-Malo, overlooking the city from within the wartime German fortified stronghold. Closed Nov–April.

Les Ilôts av de la Guimorais, Rothéneuf ⓣ02.99.56.98.72. Green little site, located five minutes' walk inland from either of two crescent beaches, roughly 5km east of the citadelle. Closed Sept–June.

Le Nicet av de la Varde, Rothéneuf ⓣ02.99.40.26.32. Right on the coast, by the Pointe de Nicet, just beyond the headland that marks the eastern limit of Paramé. Closed Oct–May.

Les Nielles av John-Kennedy, Paramé ⓣ02.99.40.26.35. On the beach at the smaller of Paramé's strands, the plage du Minhic, just a short walk from the town's facilities. Closed Sept–June.

The Town

The **citadelle** of St-Malo, very much the prime destination for visitors, was for many years joined to the mainland only by a long causeway, before the original line of the coast was hidden for ever by the construction of the harbour basin. Although its streets of restored seventeenth- and eighteenth-century houses can be crowded to the point of absurdity in summer, away from the more popular thoroughfares random exploration is fun.

Owing to the limitations of space, **buildings** within the walls tend to be higher-rise than you might expect. Ancient as they look, they are almost entirely reconstructed; following the two-week bombardment that forced the German surrender in 1944, eighty percent of the city had to be lovingly and precisely rebuilt, stone by stone. Beneath grey skies, the narrow lanes can appear sombre, even grim, but in high summer or at sunset they become light and almost unreal. In any case, you can always surface on the **ramparts** – first erected in the fourteenth century – to enjoy wonderful all-round views.

Besides the prominent **Grande Porte**, the main gate of the citadelle is the **Porte St-Vincent**. To the right is the town's **castle**, which houses the **Musée de la Ville** (April–Sept daily 10am–12.30pm & 2–6pm; Oct–March Tues–Sun 10am–noon & 2–6pm; €5). The museum is something of a hymn of praise to the "prodigious prosperity" enjoyed by St-Malo during its days of piracy, colonialism and slave trading. Climbing the 169 steps of the castle keep, you pass a fascinating mixture of maps, diagrams and exhibits – chilling handbills from the Nazi occupation, accounts of the "infernal machine" used by the English to blow up the port in 1693, and savage four-pronged *chausse-trappes* (a kind of early version of barbed wire), thrown by pirates onto the decks of ships being boarded to immobilize their crews.

You can pass under the ramparts at several points to reach the open shore, where a huge **beach** stretches away east beyond the rather featureless resort-suburb of **Paramé**. When the tide is low, it's safe to walk out to the small island of **Grand-Bé** – the walk is so popular that sometimes you even need to queue to get onto the short causeway. Solemn warnings are posted of the dangers of attempting to return from the island when the tide has risen too far – if you're caught there, there you have to stay. The island's "sight" is the tomb of the nineteenth-century writer-politician **Chateaubriand** (1768–1848).

The **St-Servan** district, within walking distance along the corniche south of the citadelle, was the city's original settlement, converted to Christianity by St Malou (or Maclou) in the sixth century; later, in the twelfth century, the townspeople moved to the impregnable island now called St-Malo. St-Servan curves round several small inlets and beaches to face the river. It's dominated by the distinctive **Tour Solidor**, which consists of three linked towers built in 1382, and in cross-section looks just like an ace of clubs. Originally known in Breton as the *Steir Dor*, or "gate of the river", it now holds a **museum** of Cape Horn clipper ships, open for ninety-minute guided visits (April–Sept daily 10am–12.30pm & 2–6pm; Oct–March Tues–Sun 10am–noon & 2–6pm; €5). Most of the great European explorers of the Pacific are covered, from Magellan onwards, but naturally the emphasis is on French heroes like Bougainville. Tours culminate with a superb view from the topmost ramparts.

If you follow the main road due south from St-Servan, ignoring signs for the Barrage de la Rance – or take bus #5 from the *gare SNCF* – you'll come to the **Grand Aquarium**, on a roundabout high above town (daily: April–June & Sept 10am–7pm; first two weeks in July & second two weeks in Aug 9.30am–8pm; mid-July to mid-Aug 9.30am–10pm; Oct–March 10am–6pm as a rule, but wide variations day by day, with some closures Nov–Jan; last admission one hour before closing; €13.90, under-18s €9.90; ⓣ02.99.21.19.00, ⓦwww.aquarium-st-malo.com). The postmodern aquarium itself can be bewildering at first, but it's an entertaining place where you can either learn interesting facts about slimy monsters of the deep or simply pull faces back at them. Its eight distinct fish tanks include one shaped so that visitors stand in the hole in the middle as myriad fish whirl around them. St-Malo's other aquarium, the logically named **Petit Aquarium**, set into the walls of the old city, is much less interesting.

For last-minute **shopping**, St-Malo's citadelle contains a few specialists, and there's a Carrefour **hypermarket** near the aquarium on the southern outskirts of town. **Markets** are held in the Halle au Blé within the walls of St-Malo on Tuesdays and Fridays, in St-Servan on Mondays and Fridays, and in Paramé on Wednesdays and Saturdays.

Eating

Intra-muros St-Malo boasts even more **restaurants** than hotels, with a long crescent lining the inside of the ramparts between the Porte St-Vincent and the Grande Porte. Prices are probably higher than anywhere else in Brittany, however, especially on the open café terraces – the demand is inflated by day-trippers and ferry passengers having last-night blowouts. Bear in mind that most of the crêperies also serve *moules* and similar quasi-snacks. All the restaurants listed below are in the citadelle.

Borgnefesse 10 rue du Puits aux Braies ⓣ02.99.40.05.05. This pirate-themed place offers good solid French cooking, even though it feels more like the tavern it used to be than a restaurant. A two-course meal costs €18, a three-course one €22. Closed Sun all day & Mon lunch.

Le Brick 5 rue Jacques-Cartier ⓣ02.99.40.18.88. Perhaps the best of the many seafood restaurants set into the walls near the Grande Porte, with a €14.50 menu that offers fish soup or "big size winkles" followed by skate, and more lavish options up to €33. Closed Mon.

Le Chasse Marée 4 rue Grout de St-Georges ⓣ02.99.40.85.10. Nautical decor and haute cuisine, just round the corner from the post office, with a few tables out on the quiet street and more upstairs. For €16 you get a simple lunch, for €22 a rich fish soup followed by a choice of entrees, and for €35 an opulent fish menu featuring scallops with langoustines. Closed Sat lunch, all Sun, & Mon lunch.

Le Corps de Garde 3 montée Notre-Dame ⓣ02.99.40.91.46. The only restaurant that's right up on St-Malo's ramparts is unfortunately an ordinary crêperie, serving standard €3.50–8.50 crêpes. However, the views from its large open-air terrace are sensational, looking out over the beach to the myriad little islets.

Duchesse Anne 5–7 place Guy-la-Chambre ⓣ02.99.40.85.33. Situated right next to the Porte St-Vincent, the best known of St-Malo's upmarket restaurants continues to work hard to keep up its reputation – and its prices. The only set menu is a €70 lobster option; you might manage to get a lunch for under €20, but dinner will cost well over twice that. Whole baked fish is the main speciality, with an entire *turbotin* costing €131 for four diners. Closed Wed & Mon lunch, Sun eve in low season, plus all Dec & Jan.

Restaurant Gilles 2 rue de la Pie-qui-Boit ⓣ02.99.40.97.25. Bright, modern, good-value restaurant, just off the central pedestrian axis. The basic €19.20 menu is fine; alternatively, €22.50 brings you oysters or mussel soup and a rabbit *cuissot* with cider. Closed Wed.

Hôtel-Restaurant de l'Univers 10 place Chateaubriand ⓣ02.99.40.89.52. At this hotel restaurant, which offers the option of eating at tables out on the square opposite the château, you can have mussels followed by a cheese and ham crêpe for just €9, or get a full vegetarian menu for €16.50.

The Pointe du Grouin and Cancale

Along the coast east of St-Malo is the **Pointe du Grouin**, a perilous and windy height which offers spectacular views of the pinnacle of Mont St-Michel and

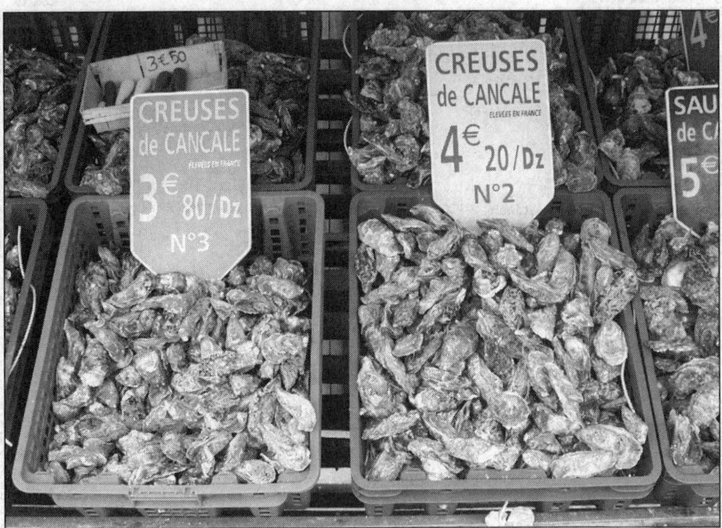

△ Oysters, Cancale

the bird sanctuary of the **Îles des Landes** to the east. Just south of the *pointe*, and less than 15km from St-Malo across the peninsula, **CANCALE** is renowned for its **oysters**. In the old church of St-Méen at the top of the hill, the town's obsession is documented with meticulous precision by the small **Musée des Arts et Traditions Populaires** (June & Sept Mon & Fri–Sun 2.30–6.30pm; July & Aug Mon 2.30–6.30pm, Tues–Sun 10am–noon & 2.30–6.30pm; €4). Cancale oysters were found in the camps of Julius Caesar, taken daily to Versailles for Louis XIV and even accompanied Napoleon on the march to Moscow.

From the rue des Parcs next to the jetty of the port, you can see at low tide the *parcs* where the oysters are grown. The rocks of the cliff behind are streaked and shiny like mother-of-pearl; underfoot the beach is littered with countless generations of empty shells. The port area is very pretty and very smart, with a long line of upmarket glass-fronted hotels and restaurants. Cancale's **hotels** mostly insist that you eat in if you want to stay; among the best value are *La Houle*, with its highly desirable balconies overlooking the middle of the port at 18 quai Gambetta (Ⓣ02.99.89.62.38; ❷), and *Le Phare*, above its own restaurant at 6 quai Thomas (Ⓣ02.99.89.60.24; ❸; closed mid-Nov to mid-Feb, restaurant closed Wed, plus Thurs in low season). Budget travellers can head instead for the **hostel** 2km north of town at Port Picain (Ⓣ02.99.89.62.62, Ⓔcancale@fuaj.org; closed Jan), where a dorm bed costs €12.50. *Au Pied de Cheval*, 10 quai Gambetta (Ⓣ02.99.89.76.95), is a ramshackle, gloriously atmospheric little place to sample a few oysters, with great baskets of them spread across its wooden quayside tables. A dozen raw oysters on a bed of seaweed can cost just €5.

Dinan

The wonderful citadel of **DINAN** has preserved almost intact its three-kilometre encirclement of protective masonry, with street upon colourful street of

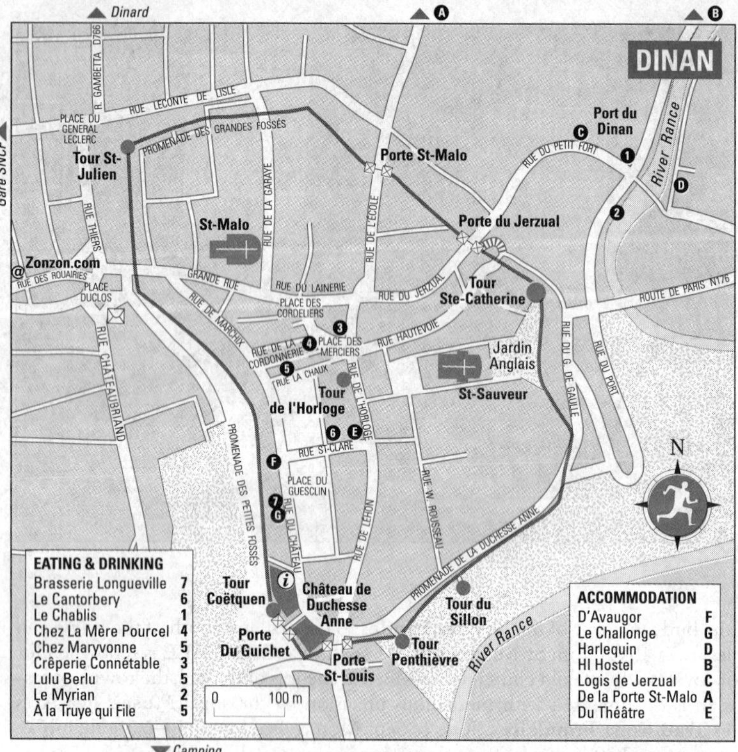

late medieval houses within. Like St-Malo, just 25km to the north, it's best seen when arriving by boat up the River Rance, which allows you to appreciate its castle and fortifications to their best advantage. Behind the houses on the left bank quay where the boats tie up, a steep and cobbled street with fields and bramble thickets on either side climbs up to the thirteenth-century ramparts, partly hidden by trees.

Arrival, information and accommodation

Both the Art Deco **gare SNCF** and the **gare routière** (Ⓣ02.96.39.21.05) are in the rather gloomy modern quarter, on place du 11-Novembre, ten minutes' walk west of the walled town. The **tourist office** can be found at the southwest corner of the place du Guesclin, at 9 rue du Château (mid-June to mid-Sept Mon–Sat 9am–7pm, Sun 10am–12.30pm & 2.30–6pm; mid-Sept to mid-June Mon–Sat 9am–12.30pm & 2–6pm; Ⓣ02.96.87.69.76, Ⓦwww.dinan-tourisme.com). **Internet access** is available at Zonzon.com, just outside the walled town at 9 rue des Rouairies (Ⓣ02.96.87.95.86, Ⓦwww.zonzon.com.fr).

Between mid-April and late September, **boats** along the Rance sail between the port downstream and Dinard and St-Malo. The trip takes two hours 45 minutes, with the exact schedule varying according to the tides (adults €20, under-13s €12). It's only possible to do a day return by boat (adults €26, under-13s €15.50) if you start from St-Malo or Dinard; starting from Dinan, you'd have to come back by bus or train. For details, contact

Compagnie Corsaire on the quai de la Rance (ⓣ08.25.13.81.20, ⓦwww.compagniecorsaire.com).

Dinan has a surprising shortage of the kind of welcoming mid-range hotel-restaurant **accommodation** that characterizes so many Breton towns, so if that's what you're looking for you might do best to visit only as a day-trip. There are, however, plenty of budget options including a hostel, and a couple of boutique hotels if you're after something a little classier.

Hotels and B&Bs

D'Avaugour 1 place du Champ ⓣ02.96.39.07.49, ⓦwww.avaugourhotel.com. Smart, elegant hotel, entered from the main square but backing onto the ramparts, with very tasteful renovated rooms and lovely gardens. ❼

Le Challonge 29 place du Guesclin ⓣ02.96.87.16.30, ⓦwww.lechallonge.fr.st. Modernized rooms, many with balconies, above a good brasserie (see p.428) and overlooking Dinan's main square. ❹

Harlequin 8 rue du quai Talard ⓣ02.96.39.68.68. Distinguished old building in a lovely setting just across the Rance, offering pleasant rooms with and without en-suite facilities, including some very well-priced family suites. They also serve reasonable French cooking on a terrace overlooking the river, for €14.50 and up. ❷–❺

Logis de Jerzual 25–27 rue du Petit Fort ⓣ02.96.85.46.54, ⓦwww.logis-du-jerzual.com. *Chambres d'hôtes* halfway up the exquisite little lane that leads from the port. The five rooms have wonderful character, with four-poster beds, modern bathrooms and romantic views over the rooftops. The house is surrounded by a lovely garden terrace and the friendly owner serves tasty breakfasts. ❺

De la Porte St-Malo 35 rue St-Malo ⓣ02.96.39.19.76, ⓦwww.hotelportemalo.com. Very comfortable rooms in a tasteful small hotel just outside the walls, beyond the Porte St-Malo. ❸

Du Théâtre 2 rue Ste-Claire ⓣ02.96.39.06.91. Nine basic rooms above a bar, right by the Théâtre des Jacobins; the cheapest come only with a sink, but even those with en-suite bathrooms still cost under €30. Run by the same efficient management as the nearby *Restaurant Cantorbery* (see below). ❶

Hostel and campsite

HI hostel Moulin de Méen, Vallée de la Fontaine-des-Eaux ⓣ02.96.39.10.83, ⓔdinan@fuaj.org. Attractive, rural hostel, set in green fields below the town centre. Unfortunately it's not on any bus route: to walk there, follow the quay downstream from the port on the town side. Dorm bed €11.50, and camping is permitted in the grounds. Closed Jan.

Camping Municipal 103 rue Châteaubriand ⓣ02.96.39.11.96. Just outside the western ramparts. Closed late Sept to late May.

The Town

For all its slightly unreal perfection, Dinan is not excessively overrun with tourists. There are no great museums; the monument is the town itself, and time is best spent wandering from crêperie to café, admiring overhanging houses along the way. Unfortunately, you can only walk along one small stretch of the **ramparts**, from the Jardin Anglais behind St-Sauveur church to a point just short of Tour Sillon overlooking the river. You can get a good general overview from the **Tour de l'Horloge**, dating from the end of the fifteenth century (daily: April–June & Sept 2–6pm; July & Aug 10am–6.30pm; €2.75).

St-Sauveur church, very much the town's focus, is a real mixture of ages, with a Romanesque porch and an eighteenth-century steeple. Even its nine Gothic chapels feature five different patterns of vaulting in no symmetrical order, and the most complex pair, in the centre, would make any spider proud. A cenotaph contains the heart of Bertrand du Guesclin, the fourteenth-century Breton warrior (and later Constable of France), who fought and won a single combat with the English knight Thomas of Canterbury, in what is now place du Guesclin, to settle the outcome of the siege of Dinan in 1364.

North of the church, rue du Jerzual leads down to the gate of the same name and on down (as rue du Petit-Fort) to the lovely **port du Dinan**. Here the river is sufficiently narrow to be spanned by a small but majestic old stone bridge, and artisans' shops and restaurants line the quay.

As you might guess from its blending of two separate towers, the fourteenth-century keep that once protected the town's southern approach was built by Estienne Le Tour, architect of St-Malo's Tour Solidor (see p.423). Now known as the **Château de Duchesse Anne**, it offers visitors access to both towers (daily: June–Sept 10am–6.30pm; Oct–Dec & Feb–May 1.30–5.30pm; €4.20). The keep itself, or donjon, consists of four storeys, each of which holds an unexpected hotch-potch of items, including two big old looms and assorted Greek and Etruscan perfume jars; at ground level, well below the walls, there's a slender, closed drawbridge. Nearby, the ancient **Tour Coëtquen** is all but empty, though if you descend the spiral staircase to its waterlogged bottom floor, you'll find a group of stone fifteenth-century notables resembling some medieval time capsule, about to depetrify at any moment.

On the third weekend of July, every other (even-numbered) year, the **Fête des Remparts** is celebrated with medieval-style jousting, banquets, fairs and processions, culminating in an immense fireworks display. There's a **market** every Thursday in the places du Champ and du Guesclin (the original medieval fairground).

Eating and drinking

All sorts of specialist **restaurants**, including several ethnic alternatives, are tucked away in the old streets of Dinan. Stroll of an evening through the town and down to the port, and you'll pass at least twenty places. For **bars**, explore the series of tiny parallel alleyways between place des Merciers and rue de Marchix. Along rue de la Cordonnerie, the busiest of the lot, the various hang-outs define themselves by their taste in music: *À la Truye qui File* at no. 14 is a contemporary folky Breton dive, while *Lulu Berlu*, next door at no. 12 (closed Sun & Mon), and *Chez Maryvonne* at no. 7, are considerably more raucous.

Brasserie Longueville 29 place du Guesclin ☎02.96.87.16.39. Sizeable brasserie adjoining the *Challonge* hotel (see p.426) with lots of open-air tables facing the main square. A good two-course lunch costs just €9.20, while full menus go up to €32.

Le Cantorbery 6 rue Ste-Claire ☎02.96.39.02.52. Reasonable food served in an old stone house with rafters, a spiral staircase and a real wood fire. Lunch from €12, while traditional dinner menus start with a good €24 option that includes fish soup and roast lamb. Closed Sun eve & Wed in low season.

Le Chablis 7 rue du Quai, port du Dinan ☎02.96.39.40.17. Large but attractive waterfront restaurant down by the port, which serves a wide range of traditional French cuisine; menus start with an €15.50 option that offers oysters followed by mussels or bream. They also have great seafood platters, and their own wine bar. Closed Sun eve & Mon.

Chez La Mère Pourcel 3 place des Merciers ☎02.96.39.03.80. Beautiful half-timbered fifteenth-century house in the central square. Good à la carte options are served all day, while the dinner menus (€18–33) are gourmet class. Closed Sun eve & Mon in low season.

Crêperie Connetable 1 rue de l'Apport. Magnificent old house, opposite the *Mère Pourcel* beside the place des Merciers, with crêpes for around €5 and snacks. The perfect spot for people-watching.

Le Myrian 3 rue du Port ☎02.96.87.93.36. Attractive and inexpensive pizzeria in a waterfront cottage down by the port, serving €7–12 pizzas, plus assorted salads and wine by the carafe, on its shady terrace.

The north coast from Dinard to Lannion

The coast that stretches from the resort town of **Dinard** to Finistère at the far western end of Brittany is divided into two distinct regions, either side of the bay of **St-Brieuc**. Between Dinard and St-Brieuc are the exposed green headlands of the **Côte d'Émeraude**, while beyond St-Brieuc, along the **Côte de Goëlo**, the shore becomes more extravagantly indented, with a succession of secluded little bays and an increasing proliferation of huge pink-granite boulders, seen at their best on the **Côte de Granit Rose** near Perros-Guirec.

Dinard

The former fishing village of **DINARD** sprawls around the western approaches to the Rance estuary, just across from St-Malo but a good twenty minutes away by road. While it might not feel out of place on the Côte d'Azur, with its casino, spacious villas and social calendar of regattas and ballet, here in Brittany it's a little incongruous. Its nineteenth-century metamorphosis was largely thanks to the tastes of the affluent English and Americans. Although Dinard is a hilly town, undulating over a succession of pretty little coastal inlets, it attracts great numbers of older visitors; as a result, prices tend to be high, and pleasures sedate.

Central Dinard faces north to the open sea, across the curving bay that holds the attractive **plage de l'Écluse**. As so often, the buildings that line the waterfront are – with the exception of the casino in the middle – venerable Victorian villas rather than hotels or shops, and so the beach itself has a low-key atmosphere, despite the summer crowds. An unexpected statue of **Alfred Hitchcock** dominates its main access point. Standing on a giant egg, with a ferocious-looking bird perched on each shoulder, he was placed here to commemorate the town's annual festival of English-language films.

Enjoyable **coastal footpaths** lead off in either direction from the principal beach, enlivened by notice boards holding reproductions of paintings produced at points along the way. It may well come as a surprise to see that Pablo Picasso's *Deux Femmes Courants sur la Plage* and *Baigneuses sur la Plage*, both of which look quintessentially Mediterranean with their blue skies and golden sands, were in fact painted here in Dinard during his annual summer visits throughout the 1920s. The path that heads east leads up to the Pointe du Moulinet for views over to St-Malo, and then as the **Promenade du Clair de Lune** continues past the tiny and now-exclusive port, and down to the estuary beach, the plage du Prieuré.

Practicalities

Dinard's small **airport**, 4km southeast of the town centre, off the D168 near **Pleurtuit**, is served by Ryanair flights from London Stansted. The connecting TIV bus #990 runs via Dinard's tourist office to St-Malo for a €4 flat fare. Many visitors simply come over for the day on one of the regular Émeraude Lines **boats** from St-Malo; tickets can be bought in Dinard at 27 av George-V, above the pleasure port. A couple of hundred metres west is the **tourist office**, in the centre at 2 bd Féart (Easter–June & Sept Mon–Sat 9am–12.15pm & 2–7pm; July & Aug daily 9.30am–7.30pm; Oct–Easter Mon–Sat 9am–12.15pm & 2–6pm; ⓣ02.99.46.94.12, ⓦwww.ot-dinard.com).

Dinard tends to be an expensive place to stay, but it does have a wide selection of **hotels** to choose from, many of which can be found at ⓦwww.dinard-hotel-plus.com. Options include two nice places near the pleasure port: the *Hôtel-Restaurant Printania*, 5 av George-V (ⓣ02.99.46.13.07, ⓦwww.printaniahotel.com; ❹; closed mid-Nov to mid-March), on a quiet street as it drops down to the port with a magnificent terrace restaurant looking towards St-Malo; and the *Hôtel-Restaurant de la Vallée*, 6 av George-V (ⓣ02.99.46.94.00, ⓦwww.hoteldelavallee.com; ❺), though unfortunately it faces the wrong way for views of St-Malo, its most basic rooms looking straight onto a bare cliff. The best local **campsite** is the municipal *Port Blanc*, also near the plage du Port-Blanc, on rue du Sergent-Boulanger (Ⓣ02.99.46.10.74; closed Oct–March).

The Côte d'Émeraude

To the west of the Rance, beyond Dinard, begins the green of the **Côte d'Émeraude**. Though composed mainly of developed family resorts, it also offers wonderful camping, at its best around the heather-backed beaches near **Cap Fréhel**, a high, warm expanse of heath and cliffs with views extending on good days as far as Jersey and the Île de Bréhat – camping is, however, forbidden within 5km of the headland itself. The **Fort la Latte**, to the east, is used regularly as a film set. Its tower, containing a cannonball factory, is accessible only over two drawbridges, and can only be visited on guided tours (early July to late Aug daily 10am–7pm; April to early July, and late Aug to Sept daily 10am–12.30pm & 2–6pm; Oct–March Sat, Sun & hols 2–6pm; €4.30; Ⓣ02.99.30.38.84, Ⓦwww.castlelalatte.com).

The nearest places to stay are the ideal, isolated **campsite** at Pléherel, the *Camping des Grèves d'En Bas* (Ⓣ02.96.41.43.34, Ⓔmairie.cap.frehel@orange.fr; closed Oct–May), and a basic **hostel** on the D16 just outside Plévenon en route towards the cape at Kérivet-en-Fréhel, *La Ville Hardrieux* (Ⓣ02.96.41.48.98, Ⓔcapfrehel@fuaj.org; dorm beds €8; closed Oct–March) – which also offers horse-riding and rents out bicycles.

Erquy

Further round the headland, the perfect crescent of beach at **ERQUY** curves through more than 180 degrees. At low tide, the sea disappears way beyond the harbour entrance, leaving gentle ripples of paddling sand. Equipped with suitable boots, you can walk right across its mouth, from the grassy wooded headland on the left side over to the picturesque little lighthouse at the end of the jetty on the right.

Erquy's **tourist office** on the boulevard de la Mer (July & Aug Mon–Sat 9.30am–1pm & 2–7pm, Sun 10am–1pm & 4–6pm; May–June & Sept 9.30am–12.30pm & 2–6pm; Oct–April Mon–Sat 9.30am–12.30pm & 2–5pm; Ⓣ02.96.72.30.12, Ⓦwww.erquy-tourisme.com) co-ordinates information for the surrounding area. The stately ★ *Hôtel Beauséjour*, perching at 21 rue de la Corniche (Ⓣ02.96.72.30.39, Ⓦwww.beausejour-erquy.com; ❸; closed Sun eve, plus Mon & Thurs eve in low season), has a good view of the bay, and excellent fish dinners from €18.50, while the more upmarket **restaurant** *l'Escurial* (Ⓣ02.96.72.31.56; closed Sun evening & Mon) by the seafront serves a five-course menu that consists entirely of **scallops**, the town's speciality. There are several **campsites** on the promontory (dotted with tiny coves) that leads to the Cap d'Erquy north of town, including the three-star *St-Pabu* (Ⓣ02.96.72.24.65, Ⓦwww.saintpabu.com; closed mid-Oct to March) right beside the sea.

St-Brieuc

The major city on the Côte d'Émeraude, **ST-BRIEUC** is far too busy being the industrial centre of northern Brittany to concern itself with entertaining tourists. It's an odd-looking city, with two very deep wooded valleys spanned by viaducts at its core, and it's almost impossible to bypass. The streets are hectic, with the town centre cut in two by a virtual motorway and unrelieved by any public parks. Motorists and cyclists, unfortunately, have little choice but to plough straight through rather than attempting to negotiate the backroads and steep hills around. Apart from the sturdy-looking **cathedral of St Stephen**, the fine views of the valley from **Tertre Aubé** and a handful of half-timbered houses in the streets around place au Lin, there's nothing to keep you here.

Trains between Paris and Brest stop at the **gare SNCF**, around 1km south of the centre, and regular **buses** run to the nearby resorts. If you decide to use the city as a base, the best place to **stay** is the central *Champ-de-Mars*, 13 rue du Général-Leclerc (ⓣ02.96.33.60.99, ⓔhoteldemars@orange.fr; ❸), above an old-fashioned, green-painted brasserie. St-Brieuc also has a **hostel**, two kilometres out, in the magnificent fifteenth-century Manoir de la Ville-Guyomard (ⓣ02.96.78.70.70, ⓔsaint-brieuc@fuaj.org; €13.75), on bus route #3. Some of the nicest **eating** options in town are in the old quarter, behind the cathedral. *La Cuisine du Marché*, 4–6 rue des Trois-Frères-Merlin (ⓣ02.96.61.70.94), is a friendly bistro serving impeccable classic French dishes, with a €9 lunchtime *plat* and dinner menus for €18 and €23.

The Côte de Goëlo

Moving northwest towards Paimpol along the **Côte de Goëlo**, the shoreline becomes wilder and harsher and the seaside towns tend to be crammed into narrow rocky inlets or set well back in river estuaries. **BINIC** is a narrow port surrounded by meadows, with a huge beach – at low tide, anyway – and the newly renovated *Hôtel Benhuyc*, 1 quai Jean-Bart (ⓣ02.96.73.39.00, ⓦwww.benhuyc.com; ❺). A little further on at the sedate family resort of **ST-QUAY-PORTRIEUX**, the *Gerbot d'Avoine* beside the beach is the best place to stay (ⓣ02.96.70.40.09, ⓦwww.gerbotdavoine.com; ❸; closed Jan & mid-Nov to mid-Dec).

After St-Quay, the coastal road shifts inland, through **PLOUHA**, the traditional boundary between French-speaking and Breton-speaking Brittany. A worthwhile diversion is the village of **KERMARIA-AN-ISQUIT**, signposted off the D21 from Plouha, with the extraordinary medieval frescoes of a *Danse Macabre* in its thirteenth-century **chapel** (Easter–Sept Mon–Sat 10am–noon & 2–6pm, Sun 3–6pm; donation). They show Ankou, who is death or death's assistant, leading representatives of every social class in a Dance of Death. An encounter between three living nobles out hunting and three philosophical corpses is also depicted, and there's a statue of the infant Jesus refusing milk from Mary's proffered breast.

Paimpol and around

Back on the coast, **PAIMPOL** is an attractive town with a tangle of cobbled alleyways and fine grey-granite houses, even if it has lost something in its transition from working fishing port to pleasure harbour. It was once the centre of a cod and whaling fleet, which sailed to Iceland each February after being sent off with a ceremony marked by a famous *pardon*. From then until September the town would be empty of its young men.

Thanks to naval shipyards and the like, the open sea is not visible from Paimpol; a maze of waterways leads to its two separate **harbours**. Both are usually filled with the high masts of yachts, but are still also used by the fishing vessels that keep a fish market and a plethora of *poissonneries* busy. This is doubtless a very pleasant place to arrive by boat, threading through the rocks, but from close quarters the tiny port area is a little disappointing, very much rebuilt and quite plain. Nonetheless, it's always lively in summer.

A couple of kilometres short of town, in a superbly romantic setting, the D786 passes the substantial ruins of the **Abbaye de Beauport** (daily: mid-June to mid-Sept 10am–7pm, with regular 1hr 30min guided tours; mid-Sept to mid-June 10am–noon & 2–5pm; Ⓦwww.abbaye-beauport.com; €4.50), established in 1202 by Count Alain de Goëlo. Its stone walls are covered with wild flowers and ivy, the central cloisters are engulfed by a huge tree, and birds fly everywhere. The Norman Gothic chapterhouse is the most noteworthy building to survive, but its roofless halls hold relics from all periods of its history. Footpaths lead down through the salt meadows, where the monks raised their sheep, to the sea. In summer, the abbey reopens for late-night visits, with imaginative lighting effects (July & Aug Wed & Sun 10pm–1am; €8), and also hosts weekly Breton music concerts (mid-July to mid-Aug Thurs 9pm; €12).

Places to **stay** in Paimpol include the grand old *Repaire de Kerroc'h*, overlooking the small-boat harbour from 29 quai Morand (Ⓣ02.96.20.50.13, Ⓔrepaire2kerroch@orange.fr; ❻), which though not quite as luxurious as it looks, offers comfortable en-suite rooms, great views, and a really good restaurant; the very hospitable *Hôtel Berthelot* at 1 rue du Port (Ⓣ02.96.20.88.66; ❶–❸); and the plainer *Hôtel Origano*, just back from the front at 7bis rue du Quai (Ⓣ02.96.22.05.49; ❸; closed mid-Nov to March). As for **restaurants**, *La Cotriade*, on the far side of the harbour on the quai Armand-Dayot (Ⓣ02.96.20.81.08; closed all day Mon, Fri eve & Sat lunch), is the best bet for authentic fish dishes, with menus from €21.

The Île de Bréhat

Two kilometres off the coast at Pointe de l'Arcouest, 6km northwest of Paimpol, the **ÎLE DE BRÉHAT** – in reality two islands joined by a tiny bridge – gives the appearance of spanning great latitudes. On its north side are windswept meadows of hemlock and yarrow, sloping down to chaotic erosions of rock; on the south, you're in the midst of palm trees, mimosa and eucalyptus. All around is a multitude of little islets – some accessible at low tide, others *propriété privée*, most just pink-orange rocks. All in all, it is one of the most beautiful places in Brittany, renowned as a sanctuary not only for rare species of wild flowers, but also for birds of all kinds. Individual private gardens are also meticulously tended, so you can always anticipate a magnificent display of colour, in summer, for example, from the erupting blue acanthus.

All boats to Bréhat (see below) arrive at the small harbour of **PORT-CLOS**, though depending on the tide passengers may have to walk several hundred metres before setting foot on terra firma. No **cars** are permitted on the island, so many visitors rent **bikes** at the port, for €15 per day. However, it's easy enough to explore the whole place on foot; walking from one end to the other takes less than an hour.

Each batch of new arrivals heads first to Bréhat's village, **LE BOURG**, five hundred metres up from the port. As well as a handful of hotels, restaurants and bars, it also holds a limited array of shops, a post office, a bank and an ATM, and hosts a small **market** most days. In high season, the attractive central square tends to be packed fit to burst, with exasperated holiday-home owners pushing their little hand-wagons through the throngs of day-trippers.

Continue a short distance north of Le Bourg, however, and you'll soon cross over the slender **Pont ar Prat bridge** to the northern island, where the crowds thin out, and countless little coves offer opportunities to sprawl on the tough grass or clamber across the rugged boulders. Though the coastal footpath around this northern half offers the most attractive walking on the island, the best **beaches** line the southern shores, with the **Grève du Guerzido** at its southeastern corner, being the pick of the crop.

Practicalities

Bréhat is connected regularly by **ferry** from the Pointe de l'Arcouest, 6km northwest of Paimpol, and served by summer buses from the *gare SNCF* there. Roughly speaking, sailings, with Les Vedettes de Bréhat (Ⓣ02.96.55.79.50, Ⓦwww.vedettesdebrehat.com), are half-hourly in July & Aug, hourly between April and June and in September, and every 1hr 30min otherwise, with the first boat out to Bréhat at 8.30am in summer, and the last boat back at 7.45pm. The return trip costs €8 (bikes, €15 extra, are only allowed outside peak crossing times). The same company also operates boats in summer from Erquy, Dahouët, Binic and St-Quay-Portrieux.

Bréhat's **tourist office** is in the main square in Le Bourg (July & Aug Mon–Sat 9am–4.30pm; rest of the year open three days a week, call for current hours; Ⓣ02.96.20.04.15. All three of its **hotels** tend to be booked through the summer, and close for at least part of the winter. Both the *Bellevue* in Port-Clos (Ⓣ02.96.20.00.05, Ⓦwww.hotel-bellevue-brehat.com; ❻; closed mid-Nov to mid-Feb), and the *Vieille Auberge*, on your left as you enter Le Bourg (Ⓣ02.96.20.00.24; ❻; closed Dec–Easter), insist on *demi-pension* in high season. The smaller *Aux Pêcheurs* (Ⓣ02.96.20.00.14; ❸; closed Jan), on the main square in Le Bourg, has a nice little garden terrace. There's also a wonderful **campsite** in the woods high above the sea west of the port (Ⓣ02.96.20.00.36; closed mid-Sept to mid-June).

The Côte de Granit Rose

The entire northernmost stretch of the Breton coast, from Bréhat to **Trégastel**, has loosely come to be known as the **Côte de Granit Rose**. There are indeed great granite boulders scattered in the sea around the island of Bréhat, and at the various headlands to the west, but the most memorable stretch of coast lies around **Perros-Guirec**, where the pink-granite rocks are eroded into fantastic shapes.

△Côte de Granit Rose

Tréguier

The D786 turns west from Paimpol, passing over a green *ria* on the bridge outside Lézardrieux before arriving at **TRÉGUIER**, one of the very few hill-towns in Brittany. Its central feature is the **Cathédrale de St-Tugdual**, which contains the tomb of St Yves, a native of the town who died in 1303 and – for his incorruptibility – became the patron saint of lawyers. Attempts to bribe him continue to this day; his tomb is surrounded by marble plaques and an inferno of candles invoking his aid.

It's best to **stay** down by the port, at either the fancy new *Hôtel Aigue-Marine*, close to the bridge (Ⓣ02.96.92.97.00, Ⓦwww.aiguemarine.fr; ❻), or the much more basic *Hôtel-Restaurant d'Estuaire* (Ⓣ02.96.92.30.25; ❶), which has great views from its upstairs dining room and serves a reasonable €13 menu. At the *Poissonnerie Moulinet*, above a fish shop just below the cathedral at 2 rue Ernest-Renan (Ⓣ02.96.92.30.27), you can buy superb seafood platters at low prices, to take away and eat in the square. During the **market** each Wednesday, clothes are spread out in the square by the cathedral, with food and fresh fish down by the port.

Plougrescant

Perhaps the best-known photographic image of Brittany is of a small seafront cottage somehow squeezed between two mighty pink-granite boulders. Surprisingly few visitors, however, manage to see the house in real life. It stands 10km north of Tréguier, 2km out from the village of **PLOUGRESCANT**. The precise spot tends to be marked on regional maps as either **Le Gouffre** or Le Gouffre du Castel-Meur, and is signposted off the coastal road a short way west of the Pointe du Château. Although you can't visit the cottage itself, which actually faces inland across a small sheltered bay, the shoreline nearby offers superb short walks, and there's a little summer-only café selling snacks and ice creams.

Château de la Roche-Jagu

About 10km inland from Tréguier, on a heavily wooded slope above the Trieux River, stands the fifteenth-century **Château de la Roche-Jagu** (daily: mid-June to mid-Sept 10am–7pm; mid-Sept to Nov & Feb to mid-June 10.30am–12.30pm & 2–6pm; park access free, château €3, or more during special exhibitions). It's a gorgeous building – a harmonious combination of fortress and home – and plays host to lavish annual exhibitions, usually on some sort of Celtic theme. The rooms within are bare, but if you climb to the top, you can admire the beautiful woodwork of the restored eaves, and walk the two long indoor galleries, offering tremendous views over the river.

Perros-Guirec and Ploumanac'h

PERROS-GUIREC is the most popular resort along this coast, though not perhaps the most exciting, consisting largely of a network of tree-lined avenues of suburban villas. It does stand, however, at one end of the long **Sentier des Douaniers** pathway, which winds round the clifftops to the tiny resort of **PLOUMANAC'H** past an astonishing succession of deformed and water-sculpted rocks. Birds wheel overhead towards the offshore bird sanctuary of **Sept-Îles**, and battered boats shelter in the narrow inlets or bob uncontrollably out on the waves. There are patches and brief causeways of grass, clumps of purple heather and yellow gorse.

Perros-Guirec's extremely efficient **tourist office** is at 21 place de l'Hôtel-de-Ville (July & Aug Mon–Sat 9am–7.30pm, Sun 10am–12.30pm & 4–7pm;

Sept–June Mon–Sat 9am–12.30pm & 2–6.30pm; ⓣ02.96.23.21.15; ⓦwww.perros-guirec.com). **Hotels** in Perros-Guirec itself include the old-fashioned *Les Violettes*, 19 rue du Calvaire (ⓣ02.96.23.21.33; ❸), which has a seriously cheap restaurant, and two places with sea views: the *Gulf Stream*, high on the hillside at 26 rue des Sept-Îles (ⓣ02.96.23.21.86, ⓦwww.gulf-stream-hotel-bretagne.com; ❺; closed mid-Jan to mid-Feb), and the *Bon Accueil*, 11 rue de Landerval (ⓣ02.96.23.25.77, ⓦwww.au-bon-accueil.com; ❹), home to a gourmet restaurant. Ploumanac'h offers the *St-Guirec et de la Plage* (ⓣ02.96.91.40.89, ⓦwww.hotelsaint-guirec.com; ❸–❺; closed Nov–March), which has some lovely sea-view rooms at bargain rates; eat either at the adjoining *Coste-Mor* (ⓣ02.96.91.65.55) – where good menus starting at €14, with a lovely seafood *pot au feu* on the €26 one, and the terrace is right above the beach – or the simpler, cheaper dining room reserved for *pensionnaire* guests. Immediately across the road, with an equally superb prospect of the beach, the *Castel Beau Site*, plage du St-Guirec (ⓣ02.96.91.40.87, ⓦwww.castelbeausite.com; ❻), is a much more lavish alternative, with a more expensive restaurant into the bargain. The nicest place to **camp** is the four-star *Le Ranolien* (ⓣ02.96.91.65.65, ⓦwww.leranolien.com; closed mid-Nov to March), in a superb position backing onto the Sentier des Douaniers near a little beach about halfway round, but directly accessible on the other side by road, and boasting a great array of swimming pools and waterslides.

Trégastel and Trébeurden

Of the smaller villages further round the coast to the west, **TRÉGASTEL**, with a couple of campsites, including the *Tourony* by the beach (ⓣ02.96.23.86.61, ⓦwww.camping-tourony.com; closed Oct–Easter), and **TRÉBEURDEN**, with the lovely seafront **hostel**, *Le Toëno*, 2km north of town at 60 rte de la Corniche (ⓣ02.96.23.52.22, ⓔtrebeurden@fuaj.org; dorm beds €11; closed Nov–Feb), make reasonable stopovers. Trégastel has managed to squeeze in an **aquarium** under a massive pile of boulders, and has a couple of huge lumps of pink granite slap in the middle of its fine beach.

The strangest sight along this coast, however, outdoing anything the erosions can manage, is just south of Trégastel on the **route de Calvaire**, where an old stone saint halfway up a high calvary raises his arm to bless or harangue the gleaming white discs and puffball dome of **the Pleumier-Bodou Telecommunications Centre**. When it opened in 1962, this was the first receiving station to pick up signals from the US Telstar satellite. No longer operational, the centre has been re-modelled as a **Musée de Télécommunications** also known as Cosmopolis (Feb Mon–Fri & Sun 2–6pm; April & Sept Mon–Fri 11am–6pm, Sat & Sun 2–6pm; May & June daily 11am–6pm; July & Aug daily 11am–7pm; March & Oct–Dec by appointment only; €7; ⓦwww.leradome.com). Inside the **Radôme**, the golf-ball itself, frequent spectacular son et lumière shows explain the history of the whole ensemble, and there's also a smaller **planetarium** alongside.

The Bay of Lannion

Despite being set significantly back from the sea on the estuary of the River Léguer, **Lannion** gives its name to the next bay west along the Breton coast – and it's the bay rather than the town that is most likely to impress visitors. One enormous beach stretches from **St-Michel-en-Grève**, which is little more than a bend in the road, as far as **Locquirec**; at low tide you can walk hundreds of metres out on the sands.

Lannion

LANNION, set amid plummeting hills and stairways, is a historic city with streets of medieval housing and a couple of interesting old churches – but it's also a centre for a burgeoning and extremely high-tech telecommunications industry, and one of modern Brittany's real success stories. Hence its rather self-satisfied nickname, *ville heureuse* or "happy town". In addition to admiring the half-timbered houses around the **place de Général-Leclerc** and along **rue des Chapeliers**, it's well worth climbing from the town up the 142 granite steps which lead to the twelfth-century Templar **Église de Brélévenez**. The views from its terrace are quite stupendous.

Lannion's **tourist office** is at 2 quai d'Aiguillon (July & Aug Mon–Sat 9am–7pm, Sun 10am–1pm; Sept–June Mon–Sat 9.30am–12.30pm & 2–6pm; ⓣ02.96.46.41.00, ⓦwww.ot-lannion.fr). The only **accommodation** in the centre is the *Ibis*, opposite the station at 30 av de Général-de-Gaulle (ⓣ02.96.37.03.67; ❹), which has modern rooms, but no restaurant; you can eat good cheap seafood cuisine at *La Flambée*, 67 rue Georges-Pompidou (ⓣ02.96.48.04.85; closed Mon). There's also a year-round **hostel**, *Les Korrigans*, near the town centre at 6 rue du 73e-Territorial (ⓣ02.96.37.91.28, ⓔlannion@fuaj.org; dorm beds €14 including breakfast). Its friendly management do not operate a curfew, and they arrange birdwatching and similar expeditions and rent out bikes.

The Cairn du Barnenez

In a glorious position at the mouth of the Morlaix estuary, 13km north of Morlaix itself, the prehistoric stone **Cairn du Barnenez** surveys the waters from the summit of a hill (May–Aug daily 10am–6.30pm; Sept–April Tues–Sun 10am–12.30pm & 2–5.30pm; €5). As on the island of Gavrinis in the Morbihan, its ancient masonry has been laid bare by recent excavations, and provides a stunning sense of the architectural prowess of the megalith builders. Radiocarbon testing has shown the work here to date back to around 4500 BC, which makes this one of the oldest large-scale monuments in the world.

The ensemble consists of two distinct stepped pyramids. Each rises in successive tiers, built of large flat stones chinked with pebbles; the second was added onto the side of the first, and the two are encircled by a series of terraces and ramps. The whole thing measures roughly 70m long by 15–25m wide and 6m high. Both pyramids were long buried under the same eighty-metre-long earthen mound. While the actual cairns are completely exposed to view, most of the passages and chambers that lie within them are sealed off. The two minor corridors that are open simply cut through the edifice from one side to the other, and were exposed by quarrying activities around thirty years ago; visitors are not permitted to pass through. Local tradition has it that one tunnel runs right through this "home of the fairies", and continues out deep under the sea.

Finistère

It's hard to resist the appeal of the **Finistère coast**, with its ocean-fronting cliffs and headlands. Summer crowds may detract from the best parts of the **Crozon**

peninsula and the **Pointe de Raz**, but there are many kilometres of coast where you can enjoy near solitude. If you have transport, explore the semi-wilderness of the **northern stretches** beyond Brest and the little fishing village of **Le Conquet**, or take a ferry trip to the misty offshore islands of **Ouessant**, **Molène** and **Sein**. From the top of **Ménez-Hom** you can admire the anarchic limits of western France, while the cities of **Morlaix** and **Quimper** display modern Breton life as well as ancient splendours, and the **parish closes** south of Morlaix reveal much about the beliefs of the past.

Léon

Memories of the days when Brittany was "Petite Bretagne", as opposed to "Grande Bretagne" across the water, linger in the names of Finistère's two main areas, **Léon** (once Lyonesse), the northern peninsula, and its southern neighbour Cornouaille (Cornwall). Both feature prominently in Arthurian legend. In the north of Léon, the ragged **coastline** is the prime attraction, indented with a succession of estuaries or **abers**, each of which shelters its own tiny harbour: heading west from either the thriving historic town of **Morlaix** or the appealing little Channel port of **Roscoff**, there are possible stopping places all the way to **Le Conquet**. From Le Conquet, you can reach the islands of **Ouessant** and **Molène** across a treacherous stretch of ocean. Inland, by contrast, the ornate medieval village churches known as **parish closes** hold some of Brittany's finest religious architecture.

Morlaix

MORLAIX, one of the great old Breton ports, thrived on trade with England in between wars during the "Golden Period" of the late Middle Ages. Built up the slopes of a steep valley with sober stone houses, the town was originally protected by an eleventh-century castle and a circuit of walls. Little is left of either, but the old centre remains in part medieval with its cobbled streets and half-timbered houses. The present grandeur comes from the pink-granite **viaduct** carrying trains from Paris to Brest way above the town centre. Coming by road from the north, the opening view is of shiny yacht masts paralleling the pillars of the viaduct.

On her way from Roscoff to Paris, Mary Queen of Scots passed through Morlaix in 1548 and stayed at the **Jacobin convent** that fronts place des Jacobins. She was at the time just 5 years old, and a contemporary account records that the crush to catch a glimpse of the infant was so great that the inner town's "gates were thrown off their hinges and the chains from all the bridges were broken down". The convent now houses the **Musée de Morlaix**, a reasonably entertaining assortment of Roman wine jars, bits that have fallen off medieval churches, cannons and kitchen utensils, and a few modern paintings (April, May & Sept Mon & Wed–Sat 10am–noon & 2–6pm, Sun 2–6pm; July & Aug daily 10am–12.30pm & 2–6.30pm; Oct–March & June Mon & Wed–Sat 10am–noon & 2–5pm; €4.10). The same ticket entitles you to a guided tour of the fabulously restored, sixteenth-century **Maison à Pondalez**, at 9 Grand-Rue (same hours).

Anne, Duchess of Brittany and Queen of France, visited Morlaix in 1506. She is reputed to have stayed at the **Maison de la Reine Anne** (May & June Mon–Sat 11am–6pm; July & Aug Mon–Sat 11am–6.30pm; Sept Mon–Sat 11am–5pm; €1.60), 33 rue du Mur, which, although much restored, does indeed date from the sixteenth century. Look out for the intricate external carvings, and the lantern roof and splendid Renaissance staircase inside; each of the house's storeys overhangs the square below by a few more centimetres.

Practicalities

The **tourist office** in Morlaix is in a solitary but central one-storey building, almost under the viaduct in place des Otages (July & Aug Mon–Sat 9am–12.30pm & 1.30–7pm, Sun 10.30am–12.30pm; Sept–June Mon 9.30am–12.30pm & 2–6pm, Tues–Sat 9am–12.30pm & 2–6pm; ⓣ02.98.62.14.94, ⓦwww.morlaixtoursime.fr). All **buses** conveniently depart from place Cornic, right under the viaduct, but the **gare SNCF** is on rue Armand-Rousseau, high above the town at the western end of the viaduct. To reach it on foot, you have to climb the steep steps of Venelle de la Roche.

On the whole, Morlaix's **hotels** are fairly uninspiring, but the eccentric old *De l'Europe*, above a simple but good brasserie at 1 rue d'Aiguillon (ⓣ02.98.62.11.99, ⓦwww.hotel-europe-com.fr; ❺), holds well-equipped modern rooms. Less expensive options include the *Hôtel de la Gare*, 25 place St-Martin close to the *gare SNCF* (ⓣ02.98.88.03.29; ❸).

The best hunting ground for **restaurants** is to be found between St-Melaine church and place des Jacobins. Choices include *La Marée Bleue*, 3 rampe Ste-Mélaine (ⓣ02.98.63.24.21; closed Oct, plus Sun eve & Mon), a well-respected seafood restaurant a minute's walk up from the tourist office – the €14 menu is a bit limited, but €27 ensures you a superb *assiette de fruits de mer*, and €36.50 buys a five-course feast – and the *Brocéliande*, 5 rue des Bouchers (ⓣ02.98.88.73.78; closed Mon & Tues), in the southeast of town, which offers elegant evening-only dining in a *fin-de-siècle* atmosphere.

The parish closes

Morlaix makes an excellent base for visiting the countryside towards Brest, where **parish closes**, or *enclos paroissiaux* (walled churchyards incorporating cemetery, calvary and ossuary), celebrate the distinctive character of Breton Catholicism – closer to the Celtic past than to Rome – in elaborately sculpted scenes. Stone calvaries are covered in detailed scenes of the Crucifixion above a crowd of saints, Gospel stories and legends; in richer parishes, a high stone arch leads into the churchyard, adjoining an equally majestic ossuary, where bones would be taken when the tiny cemeteries filled up. Most of the parish closes date from the two centuries either side of the union with France in 1532, Brittany's wealthiest period.

The most famous *enclos* are in three neighbouring parishes off the N12 between Morlaix and Landivisiau, on a clearly signposted route that's served by an SNCF bus. At **ST-THÉGONNEC**, the church **pulpit**, carved by two brothers in 1683, is the acknowledged masterpiece, albeit so swamped with detail – symbolic saints, sibyls and arcane figures – that it is almost too intricate to take in. At the pretty flower-filled village of **GUIMILIAU**, 6km southwest, the **calvary** is an incredible ensemble of over two hundred granite figures, depicting scenes from the life of Christ and rendered all the more dramatic by being covered with what has been called "secular lichen". A uniquely Breton illustration, just above the Last Supper, depicts the unfortunate Katell Gollet – Katherine the Damned, a figure from local myth who stole consecrated wafers to give to her lover, who naturally turned out to be the Devil – being torn to shreds by demons. At **LAMPAUL-GUIMILIAU**, the painted wooden baptistry, the dragons on the beams and the suitably wicked faces of the robbers on the calvary are the key components.

Katell Gollet is said to have lived in the ruined castle above the Elhorn estuary at **LA ROCHE-MAURICE**, 15km on towards Brest. In legend, she danced all her suitors to death until the reaper-figure Ankou stepped in to whirl her to eternal damnation; Ankou is depicted on the ossuary of the nearby church with the inscription "I kill you all". Another five-kilometre detour southeast brings further variations at **LA MARTYRE** (where Ankou clutches his disembodied head) and its adjoining parish **PLOUDIRY**, the sculpting of its ossuary affirming the equality of social classes – in the eyes of Ankou.

In St-Thégonnec the *Auberge de St-Thégonnec*, 6 place de la Mairie (T 02.98.79.61.18, W www.aubergesaintthegonnec.com; 6; closed Sat lunch, Sun eve & Mon lunch in July & Aug; Sun, Mon lunch & Sat lunch Sept–June, plus all Jan), is a surprisingly smart **hotel** for such a small village, and has a superb **restaurant**.

Roscoff

The opening of the deep-water port at **ROSCOFF** in 1973 was part of a general attempt to revitalize the Breton economy. The **ferry services** to Plymouth and to Cork aim not just to bring tourists, but also to revive the traditional trading links between the Celtic nations of Brittany, Ireland and southwest England. In fact, Roscoff had already long been a significant port. Mary Queen of Scots landed here in 1548 on her way to Paris to be engaged to François, the son of Henri II of France, as did Bonnie Prince Charlie, the Young Pretender, in 1746, after his defeat at Culloden.

Arrival and information

Boats from Plymouth, Cork and Rosslare dock at the Port de Bloscon, a couple of kilometres to the east (and just out of sight) of Roscoff. In summer, a direct **bus** service to Morlaix and Quimper leaves from the ferry terminal (Tues, Wed, Fri & Sat 7.30am, Mon, Thurs & Sun 3.30pm; CAT; T 02.98.44.46.73). From the **gare SNCF**, a few hundred metres south of the town proper, a restricted rail service (often replaced by buses) runs to Morlaix. Most **local buses** also go from here, including a direct service to Brest run by Bihan Voyages (T 02.98.83.45.80, W www.bihan.com).

The **tourist office** is at 46 rue Gambetta in town (July & Aug Mon–Sat 9am–12.30pm & 1.30–7pm, Sun 10am–12.30pm; Sept–June Mon–Sat 9am–noon & 2–6pm; T 02.98.61.12.13, W www.roscoff-tourisme.com).

Accommodation

For a small town, Roscoff is well equipped with **hotels**, which are accustomed to late-night arrivals from the ferries. Most, however, are relatively expensive and close for some or all of the winter. There's also a **hostel** on the Île de Batz (see below), and a two-star **campsite**, the beachfront *Aux Quatres Saisons*, 2km west in Perharidy, just off the route de Santec (T 02.98.69.70.86; E camping-perharidy@orange.fr; closed mid-Oct to March).

Armen Le Triton rue du Docteur Bagot T 02.98.61.24.44, W www.hotel-letriton.com. Peaceful hotel, with a pleasant garden, in a residential neighbourhood a short walk from the centre, with bright rooms on three floors. Closed Jan–Feb. 4

Du Centre 5 rue Gambetta T 02.98.61.24.25, W www.chezjanie.com. Family hotel above the café-bar *Chez Janie*, entered via the main street but looking out on the port. The rooms are modern and tastefully furnished; those with sea views cost €19 extra. Closed mid-Dec to mid-Feb. 5

Les Chardons Bleus 4 rue Amiral-Réveillère ⓣ02.98.69.72.03, ⓦwww.chardonsbleus.fr.st. Very friendly and helpful hotel in the heart of the old town, with a good restaurant (closed Thurs & Sun eve Sept–June) where dinner menus start at €19. Closed mid-Feb to mid-March. ❹

Grand Hôtel Talabardon 27 place Lacaze-Duthiers ⓣ02.98.61.24.95, ⓦwww.talabardon.fr. Imposing old stone building in the main square, facing the church on the inland side but with big sea-view balconies attached to several rooms. Seafood menus range from €27 to €49. Closed mid-Nov to Feb. ❺

Le Temps de Vivre 19 place Lacaze-Duthiers ⓣ02.98.19.33.19, ⓦwww.letempsdevivre.net, This gorgeously decorated newcomer to Roscoff's hotel scene, near the Notre-Dame church in the heart of town, offers luxuriously spacious rooms with designer bathrooms, and wonderful sea views. Off-season rates are significantly lower. ❽

The Town

Roscoff itself, nonetheless, remains a small resort, where almost all activity is confined to **rue Gambetta** and to the old port – the rest of the roads are residential backstreets full of retirement homes and institutions. The town's sixteenth-century church, **Notre-Dame-de-Croas-Batz**, at the far end of rue Gambetta, is embellished with an ornate Renaissance belfry, complete with sculpted ships and a protruding stone cannon. From the side, rows of bells can be seen hanging in galleries, one above the other like a wedding cake created by Walt Disney. Some way beyond is the grand **Thalassotherapy Institute** of Rock Roum, while a kilometre further on is Roscoff's best **beach**, at Laber, surrounded by expensive hotels and apartments.

The old **harbour** is livelier, mixing an economy based on fishing with relatively low-key pleasure trips to the **Île de Batz**. The island looks almost walkable; a narrow pier stretches over 300m towards it before abruptly plunging into deep rocky waters. The Pointe de Bloscon and the fishermen's white chapel, the **Chapelle Ste-Barbe**, make a good vantage point, particularly when the tide is in.

In 1828, Henri Ollivier took **onions** to England from Roscoff, thereby founding a trade that flourished until the 1930s. The story of the "Johnnies" – that classic French image of men in black berets with strings of onions hanging over the handlebars of their bicycles – is told at **La Maison des Johnnies et de l'Oignon Rosé de Roscoff**, 48 rue Brizeux, near the *gare SNCF* (mid-June to mid-Sept Mon–Fri 11am, 2pm, 3.30pm & 5pm, Sun 2pm, 3.30pm & 5pm; mid-Feb to mid-June & mid-Sept to Dec Mon, Tues, Thurs, Fri & Sun 2.30pm; €4).

Eating

The obvious places to **eat** in Roscoff are the dining rooms of the hotels themselves – *Le Temps de Vivre* is especially recommended – but the town does hold a few specialist **restaurants** as well, plus a bunch of appealing crêperies around the old harbour. If you're arriving on an evening ferry out of season, be aware that it can be difficult to find a restaurant still serving any later than 9.15pm.

Crêperie de la Poste 12 rue Gambetta ⓣ02.98.69.72.81. Central crêperie, open from 11.30am until late, where an à la carte meal of sweet and savoury pancakes should work out inexpensive; more exotic seafood options cost up to €8.50. They also serve fish soup, mussels and other simple meals. Closed Wed Sept–June, or Tues July & Aug.

L'Écume des Jours quai d'Auxerre ⓣ02.98.61.22.83. Cosy restaurant in a grand old house facing the port, offering good-value set lunches for €12.50 on weekdays, plus dinner menus from €20, featuring such delights as braised oysters or scallops with local pink onions. Closed Dec & Jan, and Tues & Wed in low season.

The Île de Batz

The long, narrow **ÎLE DE BATZ** (pronounced "Ba") mirrors Roscoff across the water, separated from it by a sea channel that's barely 200m wide at low tide but perhaps five times that when the tide is high. Appearances from the mainland are somewhat deceptive: the island's old town, home to a thousand or so farmers and fishermen, fills much of its southern shoreline, but those parts of Batz not visible from Roscoff are much wilder and more windswept. With no cars permitted, and some great expanses of sandy beach, it makes a wonderfully quiet retreat for families in particular, whether you're camping or staying in one of its two old-fashioned little hotels.

Ferries from Roscoff arrive at the quayside of the old town. There's a nice small beach along the edge of the harbour, though the sea withdraws so far at low tide that the port turns into a morass of slimy seaweed. You may well spot the island's best beach from the boat – it's the white-sand **Grève Blanche** towards its eastern end. Walking in that direction also brings you to the hostel (see below), and the 44-metre lighthouse that stands on the island's peak, all of 23m above sea level (second half of June daily except Wed 2–5pm; July to mid-Sept daily 1–5.30pm; €1.70).

Three different companies operate fifteen-minute **ferry** services to the Île de Batz from Roscoff's long pier. Between late June and mid-September, the service is pretty much nonstop between 8am and 8pm daily, while at other times of year there are eight to ten trips daily between 8.30am and 7pm. The return fare is €7, with a €5 charge for bikes.

The island's nicest **hotel**, at the centre of the harbour, is the ⛹ *Grand Hôtel Morvan* (Ⓣ02.98.61.78.06, Ⓦwww.grand-hotel-morvan.com; ❸; closed Dec to mid-March), which serves good meals on its large seafront terraces. There's a **hostel** in a beautiful setting by the beach at the evocatively named Creach ar Bolloc'h (Ⓣ02.98.61.77.69, Ⓦwww.aj-iledebatz.org; closed Nov–March; €11.90).

St-Pol-de-Léon

The main road south from Roscoff passes by fields of the famous Breton artichokes before arriving after 6km at **ST-POL-DE-LÉON**. It's not an exciting place but – assuming you've got your own transport – its two churches at least merit a pause. The **cathédrale**, in the main town square, was rebuilt towards the end of the thirteenth century along the lines of Coutances – a quiet classic of unified Norman architecture. The remains of St Pol are inside, alongside a large bell, rung over the heads of pilgrims during his *pardon* on March 12 in the unlikely hope of curing headaches and ear diseases. Just downhill is the original **Kreisker Chapel**, with access to the top of its sharp-pointed soaring granite belfry (now coated in yellow moss).

The abers

The coast west of Roscoff is among the most dramatic in Brittany, a jagged series of **abers** – deep, narrow estuaries – that hold a succession of small, isolated resorts. It's a little on the bracing side, especially if you're making use of the numerous **campsites**, but that just has to be counted as part of the appeal. In summer, at least, the temperatures are mild enough, and things get progressively more sheltered as you move around towards Le Conquet and Brest.

Around the abers

If you're dependent on public transport, bear in mind that the only stop on the Roscoff–Brest bus before it turns inland is **PLOUESCAT**. It's not quite on the sea itself, but there are campsites nearby on each of three adjacent beaches; of the **hotels**, best value is the *Roc'h-Ar-Mor*, right on the beach at Porsmeur (ⓣ02.98.69.63.01, ⓔroch.ar.mor@orange.fr; ❷; closed Oct–Easter).

BRIGNOGAN-PLAGE, on the next *aber*, has a small natural harbour, once the lair of wreckers, with beaches and weather-beaten rocks to either side, as well as its own menhir. The two high-season **campsites** are the central municipal site at Kéravezan, the *Côte des Legendes* (ⓣ02.98.83.41.65, ⓦwww.camping-cote-des-legendes.com; closed Nov–Easter) and the *Du Phare*, east of town (ⓣ02.98.83.45.06 ⓦwww.camping-du-phare.com; closed Oct–March), while the *Castel Regis* **hotel** (ⓣ02.98.83.40.22, ⓦwww.castelregis.com; ❺; closed Oct–April), is expensive but beautifully sited among the rocks, right at the headland. There are also schools of sailing and riding.

The *aber* between Plouguerneau and **L'ABER-WRAC'H** has a stepping-stone crossing just upstream from the bridge at Llanellis, built in Gallo-Roman times, and its long cut stones still cross the three channels of water (access off the D28 signposted "Rascoll"). L'Aber-Wrac'h itself is a promising place to spend a little time. It's an attractive, modest-sized resort within easy reach of a whole range of sandy beaches and a couple of worthwhile excursions. Beyond the town's little strip of bars and restaurants, the Baie des Anges stretches away towards the Atlantic, with the only sound the cry of seagulls feasting on the oyster beds. At the start of the bay, commanding stunning views out to sea, the elegant and irresistible *Hôtel la Baie des Anges*, 350 route des Anges (ⓣ02.98.04.90.04, ⓦwww.baie-des-anges.com; ❻; closed Jan), makes a peaceful and exceptionally comfortable place to **stay**. It has no dining room, but there's a classy bar with a small waterfront terrace, reserved for guests only. The best local **restaurant**, *Le Brennig* (ⓣ02.98.04.81.12; closed Tues & Nov–Feb), is back at the other end of town.

At the small harbour of **PORTSALL**, 5km along the coast from the far side of the next *aber*, l'Aber-Benoît, a defining moment in local history is commemorated by the **Espace Amoco Cadiz** (July & Aug Tues–Sun 2.30–6.30pm; Sept–June Sat & Sun 2.30–6.30pm; free). On March 17, 1978, the sinking of the *Amoco Cadiz* supertanker resulted in an oil spill that devastated 350km of the Breton coastline, and threatened to ruin the local economy. Displays and films document not only the immense task of cleaning up the mess, but also the long legal battle to obtain compensation from the "multinational monster" responsible.

Five kilometres west of Portsall is **TRÉMAZAN**, whose ruined castle was the point of arrival in Brittany for Tristan and Iseult. From here a beautiful corniche road leads further along the coast. Odd little chapels dot the route, and the views of sea and rocks are unhindered before turning inland just before Le Conquet.

Le Conquet

LE CONQUET, at the far western tip of Brittany 24km beyond Brest, is a wonderful place, scarcely developed, with a long beach of clean white sand, protected from the winds by the narrow spit of the Kermorvan peninsula. It's very much a working fishing village, with grey-stone houses leading down to the stone jetties of a cramped harbour. It occasionally floods, causing great amusement to locals who watch the waves wash over cars left there by tourists taking the ferry out to Ouessant and Molène. A good walk 5km south brings you to the lighthouse at **Pointe St-Mathieu**, looking out to the islands from its site among the ruins of a Benedictine abbey. A small exhibition explains the abbey's history, including the legend that it holds the skull of St Matthew, brought here from Ethiopia by local seafarers (April & May Wed, Sat & Sun 2.30–6.30pm; June & Sept Wed–Mon 2.30–6.30pm; July & Aug Wed–Sat & Mon 10am–12.30pm & 2–7pm, Sun 2–7pm; Oct–March Wed & Sat 2.30–6.30pm; €1.50).

The *Relais du Vieux Port*, 1 quai Drellac'h (Ⓣ02.98.89.15.91; ❷; closed Jan), offers inexpensive but attractive **rooms** right by the jetty in Le Conquet, and has a simple crêperie downstairs. Above, overlooking the harbour, the larger *Pointe Ste-Barbe* (Ⓣ02.98.89.00.26, Ⓦwww.hotelpointesaintebarbe.com; ❷–❼; hotel closed mid-Nov to mid-Dec, restaurant closed Mon in low season) may look like a concrete monstrosity, but once you're inside the location is truly superb. Guests in the more expensive rooms enjoy amazing sea views, and there's a great restaurant downstairs, where menus start with a good €19 option. There's also a well-equipped two-star **campsite** over on the Kermorvan peninsula, *Les Blancs Sablon*, (Ⓣ02.98.89.06.90, Ⓦwww.lescledelles.com; closed mid-Nov to mid-March).

The Îles d'Ouessant and de Molène

The **Île d'Ouessant** ("Ushant" to the English) lies 30km northwest of Le Conquet, and its lighthouse at **Creac'h** (said to be the strongest in the world) is regarded as the entrance to the English Channel.The island is the last in a chain of smaller islands and half-submerged granite rocks. Most are uninhabited, or like Beniguet the preserve only of rabbits, but the **Île de Molène**, midway, has a village and can be visited. Both Molène and Ouessant are served by at least one ferry each day from Le Conquet and Brest; however, it's not practicable to visit more than one in a single day.

Getting to Ouessant and Molène

Penn Ar Bed (Ⓣ02.98.80.80.80, Ⓦwww.pennarbed.fr) sail to Ouessant and Molène all year, with one to six daily departures from **Le Conquet** (first sailing at 8am daily early July to late Aug, 9am May to early July and late Aug to mid-Sept, 9.45am otherwise; Ouessant return €26.60, to Molène €23.40), and one to three daily from **Brest**, always including one at 8.30am, which is the only one that stops at Molène (Ouessant return €30.70; Molène return €27.50). They also depart from **Camaret** to Ouessant at 8.40am on Wednesday from early April until mid-Sept, and daily at 8.40am from early July until the end of Aug (return €27.50). Only on Fridays between early July and late Aug is it possible to sail from Camaret to Molène, at 8.40am (return €23.40).

Finist'Mer (Ⓣ08.25.13.52.35, Ⓦwww.finist-mer.fr) operate high-speed ferries to Ouessant in summer only. From **Le Conquet**, they offer two to four departures daily between April and September, with the first one being at 9am from early July until late August, and 9.30am otherwise (€26 return). Between early July and late August, they also sail to Ouessant **from** Brest, at 8.45am daily (€30.50 return), and from **Lanildut**, 25km northwest of Brest, with the first departure from Le Conquet calling there at 9.30am (€27.50 return). From **Camaret**, they sail on Thursdays only for the first three weeks of June, at 8.45pm; then offer a daily departure from late June until early July, and again from late August until mid-September, at 8.45am; between early July and late August, the boat leaves daily at 9.25am (€27 return).

In addition, you can **fly** to Ouessant with **Finist'Air** (Ⓣ02.98.84.64.87, Ⓦwww.finistair.fr). The fifteen-minute flights leave Brest's Guipavas airport daily at 8.30am and 4.45pm, with an adult one-way fare of €64 and groups of three or more adults costing €53 each.

Île d'Ouessant

You arrive on the **Île d'Ouessant** at the modern **harbour** in the ominous-sounding Baie du Stiff. There's a scattering of houses here and dotted around the island, but the single town – with the only hotels and restaurants – is 4km away at **LAMPAUL**. Everybody from the boat heads there, either by the bus that meets each ferry or on bicycles rented from one of the many waiting entrepreneurs – a good idea, as the island is a bit too big to explore on foot.

There's not a lot to Lampaul. The best beaches are sprawled around its bay, and, in case you should forget the perils of the sea, the town cemetery's **war memorial** lists all the ships in which townsfolk were lost, alongside graves of unknown sailors washed ashore and a chapel of wax "*proëlla* crosses" symbolizing the many islanders who never returned.

At **NIOU**, 1km northwest, the Maison du Niou is actually two houses and a few outbuildings, which jointly form the **Éco-Musée d'Ouessant** (Easter–Sept Tues–Sun 10.30am–6.30pm; Oct–Easter Tues–Sun 1.30–5.30pm; €3.30, or €6.50 for combined admission with the Musée des Phares et Balises). One house contains a museum of island history, detailing how boys from the age of 11 used to embark on sea voyages of up to three years' duration, while the women were responsible for growing crops back home. The other is a reconstruction of a traditional island house, almost entirely filled by massive "box-beds".

Another kilometre west, the **Creac'h lighthouse** was in 1939 the most powerful in the world, with a 500-million-candlepower beam capable of being seen from England's Cape Lizard. You can't visit the lighthouse tower itself, but the complex at its base holds the **Musée des Phares et Balises** (same hours as the Éco-Musée; €4.10 or €6.50 for both museums), a large museum about lighthouses and buoys. As well as providing a history of lighthouses from the Pharos of Alexandria and Roman examples, it's crammed with assorted lenses and mirrors, and has detailed displays on shipwrecks in the vicinity. None of the information is in English, however, and photography is not permitted.

The Creac'h lighthouse makes a good starting point from which to set out along the barren and exposed rocks of the north coast. Particularly in September and other times of migration, it's a remarkable spot for birdwatching, frequented by puffins, storm petrels and cormorants.

General information is available from Lampaul's central **tourist office** (Mon–Sat 10am–noon & 1.30–6pm, Sun 10am–noon; Ⓣ02.98.48.85.83, Ⓦwww.ot-ouessant.fr). The town boasts a small **hostel**, *La Croix Rouge*, north towards Niou (Ⓣ02.98.48.84.53, Ⓔajouessant@club-internet.fr; closed Jan), where a dorm bed plus breakfast costs €15. Lampaul also holds two **hotels**. Only one, the more attractive *Roch Ar Mor*, offers sea views, though not from all rooms (Ⓣ02.98.48.80.19, Ⓦperso.orange.fr/rocharmor; ❹; closed Jan to mid-Feb & late Nov to mid-Dec). Its restaurant too enjoys a fine prospect of the beach, but the food there is more expensive and less good than at the rival *Fromveur*, just up the street near the church (Ⓣ02.98.48.81.30; ❸; closed mid-Nov to Jan), where the rooms have been reasonably renovated, and the traditional island cooking is pretty good. Expect to pay around €20 for a set lunch. There's also a small official **campsite**, the *Penn ar Bed*, just outside town (Ⓣ02.98.48.84.65; closed Oct–March).

Île de Molène

The **Île de Molène** is quite well populated for a sparse strip of sand. Its inhabitants make their money from seaweed collecting and drying – and to an extent from crabbing and from crayfish, which they gather on foot, canoe or even tractor at low tide. The tides here are more than usually dramatic, halving or doubling the island's territory at a stroke – it's not called "the bald isle" for nothing. Few people do more than look at Molène as an afternoon's excursion from Le Conquet, but it's possible to stay too. There are **rooms** – very chilly in winter – at *Kastell An Doal* (Ⓣ02.98.07.39.11; ❸; closed mid-Jan to mid-Feb), one of the old buildings by the port.

Brest

Set in a magnificent natural harbour, known as the Rade de Brest, the city of **BREST** is doubly sheltered from ocean storms by the bulk of Léon to the north and by the Crozon peninsula to the south. It has always played an important role in war, and in trade whenever peace allowed. Today it is the base of the French Atlantic Fleet with a dry dock that can accommodate ships of up to 500,000 tonnes; as a ship repair centre, Brest ranks sixth in the world.

During World War II, Brest was continually bombed to prevent the Germans from using it as a submarine base. When the Americans liberated it on September 18, 1944 after a six-week siege, they found the town devastated beyond recognition. The architecture of the postwar town is raw and bleak and though there have been attempts to green the city, it has proved too windswept to respond.

Arrival and information

The **gare SNCF** and **gare routière** (Ⓣ02.98.44.46.73) stand shoulder-to-shoulder in place du 19ème RI at the bottom of avenue Clemenceau. Though right at the end of the railway system, Brest is just four hours away from Paris by TGV. **Bus** services include those to Plouescat and Roscoff, the Crozon peninsula via Le Faou, and to Le Conquet.

Brest's **airport** (Ⓣ02.98.32.01.00), 9km northeast of the centre at Guipavas, is served by flights from London Luton on Ryanair (Ⓦwww.ryanair.com), and from Birmingham, Edinburgh, Exeter and Southampton on British European (Ⓦwww.flybe.com), and also offers local connections to Ouessant (see p.443). An **airport shuttle** bus runs from the *gare SNCF* and the tourist office (6–11 daily; 25min; Ⓣ02.98.32.01.00). All the major international **car rental** chains are represented at the airport.

As well as the sailings to Ouessant, detailed on p.443, in summer **boats** make the 25-minute crossing from Brest's Port de Commerce to Le Fret on the Crozon peninsula (Société Azenor; July–Sept 2–4 daily; €15 return; Ⓣ02.98.41.46.23, Ⓦwww.azenor.com). The same company also sails to Camaret (July & Aug daily except Sat 2 daily; €15 return), as well as offering excursions, along with other operators, around the harbour and the Rade de Brest (1hr 30min; usually around €15).

Brest's **tourist office** on avenue Clemenceau faces place de la Liberté (July & Aug Mon–Sat 9.30am–7pm, Sun 10am–noon; Sept–June Mon–Sat 9.30am–12.30pm & 2–6pm; Ⓣ02.98.44.24.96, Ⓦwww.brest-metropole-tourisme.fr).

Accommodation

The vast majority of Brest's **hotels** remain open throughout the year; only a few, however, bother to maintain their own restaurants. Several lie within easy walking distance of the stations, near the central place de la Liberté. The year-round

hostel, at 5 rue de Kerbriant, Port de Plaisance du Moulin-Blanc, also serves inexpensive meals (Ⓣ02.98.41.90.41, Ⓦwww.aj-brest.org; €12.90 including breakfast). It's 3km east of the *gare SNCF* – take bus #7.

Hotels

Astoria 9 rue Traverse Ⓣ02.98.80.19.10, Ⓦwww.hotel-astoria-brest.com. Peaceful central hotel with a cheerful ambience and decor, not far up from the port. Some rooms have sea views, while the four cheapest only have a sink. Closed 3 weeks Dec–Jan. ❶–❸

Citôtel de la Gare 4 bd Gambetta Ⓣ02.98.44.47.01, Ⓦwww.hotelgare.com. En-suite rooms opposite the stations; you can pay a little extra for an uninterrupted view of the Rade de Brest from the upper storeys. Internet access for guests. ❸

Continental place de la Tour d'Auvergne Ⓣ02.98.80.50.40, Ⓦwww.hotel-sofibra.com. Grand luxury hotel, not far from the tourist office, with helpful staff and spotlessly clean rooms, several of them with fine Art Deco features; rooms on the fourth floor have large balconies. ❼

Océania Brest Centre 82 rue de Siam Ⓣ02.98.80.66.66, Ⓦwww.hotel-sofibra.com. Good-quality upmarket hotel, offering large, attractively fitted rooms on the town's principal thoroughfare, plus a classy restaurant. ❺

Pasteur 29 rue Louis-Pasteur Ⓣ02.98.46.08.73. Clean, good-value budget hotel, offering plain if potentially noisy en-suite rooms above a bar near the St-Louis church. ❷

The Town

For the casual tourist, Brest has little to offer, and few relics of the past remain. The fifteenth-century **castle** looks impressive on its headland and offers a superb panorama of the city, but inside it's not especially interesting. Three of its towers house part of the collection of the **Musée National de la Marine** (daily: April to mid-Sept 10am–6.30pm; mid-Sept to March 10am–noon & 2–6pm; €5; Ⓦwww.musee-marine.fr). The fourteenth-century **Tour Tanguy** on the opposite bank of the River Penfeld, with its conical slate roof, serves as a history museum of Brest before 1939 (June–Sept daily 10am–noon & 2–7pm; Oct–May Wed & Thurs 2–5pm, Sat & Sun 2–6pm; free).

Brest's most up-to-the-minute attraction is **Océanopolis**, a couple of kilometres east of the city centre beside the Port de Plaisance du Moulin-Blanc (daily: April to early Sept 9am–6pm; early Sept to March Tues–Sat 10am–5pm, Sun 10am–6pm; €15.40; Ⓦwww.oceanopolis.com). This futuristic complex currently consists of three distinct aquariums and a 3-D cinema. The aquarium in the main white dome, known as the Temperate Pavilion, focuses on the Breton littoral and Finistère's fishing industry, holding all kinds of fish, seals, molluscs, seaweed and sea anemones. The emphasis is very much on the edible, with the displays on the life-cycle of a scallop, for example, culminating in a detailed recipe. That's complemented by a Tropical Pavilion, with a tankful of ferocious-looking sharks plus a myriad of rainbow-hued smaller fish that populate a highly convincing coral reef, and a Polar Pavilion, complete with polar bears and penguins. Everything's very high-tech, and at times a little earnest, but it's possible to spend an entertaining day here – especially if you take the assorted restaurants, snack bars and gift stores into consideration.

Eating

As well as several low-priced places near the stations, Brest offers a wide assortment of **restaurants**. Rue Jean-Jaurès, climbing east from the place de la Liberté, holds plenty of bistros and bars, while place Guérin to the north is the centre of the student-dominated quartier St-Martin.

Le Bistro de Gaëtan 3 place Maurice-Gillet ⓣ02.98.43.44.10. Much-loved local restaurant in the St-Martin district, which serves a great-value €7.50 lunch menu but is most renowned for its many variations on the classic *kig ha farz* Breton stew, starting at €12.90. Closed Sun eve & Mon.

La Maison de l'Océan 2 quai de la Douane ⓣ02.98.80.44.84. Blue-hued fish restaurant down by the port, open daily for lunch and dinner, and serving top-quality seafood menus from €14.50.

Ma Petite Folie plage du Moulin-Blanc ⓣ02.98.42.44.42. Converted fishing boat, moored in the pleasure port, which serves a wonderfully fishy €20 set menu and also offers a wide range of à la carte dishes and daily specials.

Le Ruffé 1 rue Yves-Collet ⓣ02.98.46.07.70. An attractive place between the *gare SNCF* and the tourist office, open late, that prides itself on good, traditional French seafood dishes, served on menus costing €17.50 and upwards. Closed Sun eve & Mon.

The Crozon peninsula

The **Crozon peninsula**, a craggy outcrop of land shaped like a long-robed giant, arms outstretched to defend bay and roadstead, is the central feature of Finistère's torn chaos of estuaries and promontories. Much the easiest way for cyclists and travellers relying on public transport to reach the peninsula from Brest is via the **ferries** to Le Fret (see p.445).

As you approach the Crozon peninsula, it's well worth making a slight detour to climb the hill of **Ménez-Hom**, "at the giant's feet", for a fabulous view of the land and water alternating out to the ocean. Getting down to the coastal headlands themselves can be a bit of a disappointment after this vision: those extremities that don't house military installations tend to be too crowded. But it is the cliffs that tourists head for here, and some of the **beaches**, like **La Palue** on the southern arm, are almost deserted.

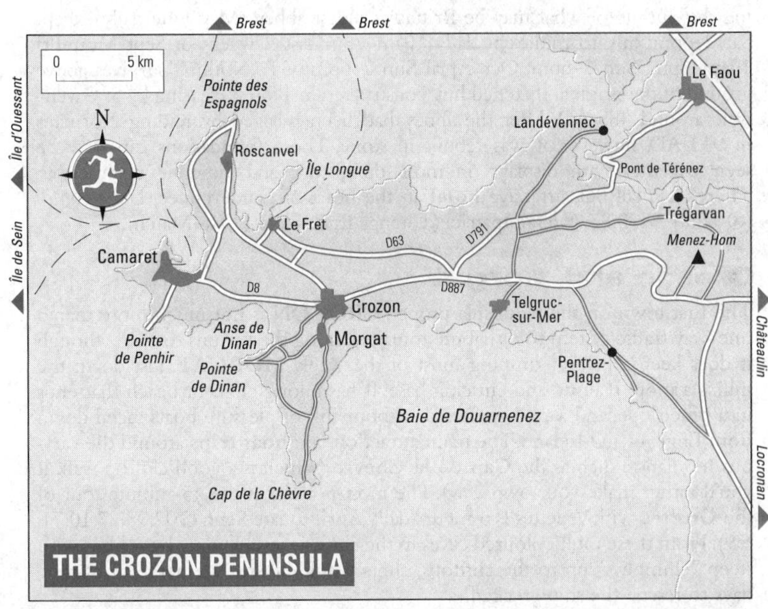

Daoulas and Le Faou

Ten kilometres beyond Plougastel-Daoulas, the **abbey** at **DAOULAS** holds Brittany's only Romanesque cloister. It now stands beautiful and isolated at the edge of cool monastery gardens, since its surrounding buildings were destroyed during the Revolution. Since 1984 it has been used as a cultural centre for Finistère, which stages ambitious historical exhibitions lasting for around six months at a time (daily 10.30am–6.30pm; ⓣ02.98.25.84.39, ⓦwww.abbaye-daoulas.com; €6 for the abbey, gardens and exhibition).

From Daoulas the motorway and railway cut down to Châteaulin and Quimper. For Crozon, you'll need to veer west at **LE FAOU**, a tiny medieval port, still boasting a few sixteenth-century gabled houses and set on its own individual estuary. From beside the pretty little village church, a sheltered corniche follows the river to the sea, where there are sailing and windsurfing facilities.

Le Faou holds two good and very similar **hotels**, both Logis de France with top-class restaurants – the *Relais de la Place*, 7 place aux Foires (ⓣ02.98.81.91.19; ❸; closed Sat & all of Jan), which serves a particularly good €25 *Menu du Terroir*, and the *Hôtel de Beauvoir* (ⓣ02.98.81.90.31, ⓦwww.hotel-beauvoir.com; ❹; closed Mon & Tues lunch mid-June to mid-Oct, Mon lunch & Sun eve mid-Oct to mid-June), where the cheapest menu is €27.50. The one snag is that they're not in the most attractive part of town, near the river, but a few hundred metres south.

Landévennec

Nine kilometres west of Le Faou, by way of a beautiful shoreline road, the **Pont de Térénez** spans the Aulne – outlet for the Nantes–Brest canal – to the Crozon peninsula. Doubling back to the right as soon as you cross the bridge brings you after a further 5km to **LANDÉVENNEC**, where archeologists are uncovering the outline of what may be Brittany's oldest abbey (May, June daily except Sat 2–6pm; July to mid-Sept daily 10am–7pm; last 2 weeks of Sept Mon–Fri 10am–6pm, Sun 2–6pm; Oct–April Sun 2–6pm; €4). Nothing survives above ground of the original thatched hut, constructed in a forest clearing by St Gwennolé around 485 AD. After the abbey had been pillaged by raiding Normans in 913 AD, however, it was rebuilt in stone. Those foundations can now be seen, together with displays on monastic history and facsimile manuscripts. There's a small but attractive **hotel** in the heart of Landévennec, *Le St-Patrick* (ⓣ02.98.27.70.83, ⓔlesaintpatrick@orange.fr; ❷; closed Oct–March).

Crozon and Morgat

The first town on the peninsula proper, **CROZON** is not much more than a one-way traffic system to distribute tourists among the various resorts – though it does keep a market running most of the week. **MORGAT**, just down the hill, is a more realistic and enticing base. It has a long crescent beach that ends in a pine slope, and a well-sheltered harbour full of pleasure boats raced down from England and Ireland. The main attractions are **boat trips** around the various headlands, such as the **Cap de la Chèvre** (which is a good clifftop walk if you'd rather make your own way). The most popular is the 45-minute tour of the **Grottes** with Vedettes Rosmeur (daily April to late Sept; ⓣ02.98.27.10.71; €9). From these multicoloured caves in the cliffs, accessible only by sea but with steep "chimneys" up to the clifftops, saints would allegedly emerge in bygone days to rescue the shipwrecked.

The **tourist office** for the whole peninsula is in the *gare routière* at Crozon (June & Sept Mon–Fri 9.15am–noon & 2–5.30pm, Sat 9.15am–noon & 2–5pm; July & Aug Mon–Sat 9.15am–7pm, Sun 10am–1pm; Oct–March Mon–Sat 9.15am–noon & 2–5.30pm; ⓣ02.98.27.07.92, ⓦwww.crozon.com).

Appealing **hotels** in Morgat include the imposing 1930s *Grand Hôtel de la Mer*, at the eastern end of the beach (ⓣ02.98.27.02.09, ⓔthierry.vignier@vvf-vacances.fr; ❹; closed mid-Oct to March), and the quieter *Julia*, 400m from the beach at 43 rue de Tréflez (ⓣ02.98.27.05.89, ⓦwww.hoteljulia.fr; ❹; closed Nov–Feb except Christmas). With around nine hundred pitches available, **campers** are spoilt for choice: the best options are the three-star sites at *Plage de Goulien* (ⓣ02.98.26.23.16, ⓔcamping.delaplage.degoulien@presquile-crozon.com; closed mid-Sept to mid-June) and *Les Pins*, towards the pointe de Dinan (ⓣ02.98.26.23.16, ⓔcamping.lespins@presquile-crozon.com; closed Nov–Easter).

A flowery stone cottage near the port at 24 quai du Kador holds *Au Pied du Port* (ⓣ02.98.26.12.63; closed Oct–Easter), Morgat's best **restaurant**, which serves refined menus from €24; what's on offer very much depends on the day's catch, but the E36 *Menu Tentation* is consistently wonderful.

Camaret

At **CAMARET** – another sheltered port, at the very tip of the peninsula – the most prominent building is the pink-orange **château de Vauban**, standing foursquare at the end of the long jetty that runs back parallel to the main town waterfront. Walled, moated, and accessible via a little gatehouse reached by means of a drawbridge, it was built in 1689 to guard the approaches to Brest; these days it guards no more than a motley assortment of decaying half-submerged fishing boats, abandoned to rot beside the jetty. There are two beaches nearby – a small one to the north and another, larger and more attractive, in the low-lying (and rather marshy) Anse de Dinan. In summer, **ferries** run from Camaret to the islands of Ouessant (see p.443) and Sein see p.443).

Camaret has its own little **tourist office** at 15 quai Kleber (July & Aug Mon–Sat 9am–7pm, Sun 10am–1pm; Sept–June Mon–Sat 9am–noon & 2–6pm; ⓣ02.98.27.93.60, ⓦwww.camaret-sur-mer.com). A little walk away from the centre, around the port towards the protective jetty, the quai du Styvel contains a row of excellent **hotels**. Both the *Vauban* (ⓣ02.98.27.91.36; ❷; closed Dec & Jan) and *Du Styvel* (ⓣ02.98.27.92.74; ❷; closed Jan) are exceptionally hospitable, with rooms that look right out across the bay, but only the *Styvel* has a restaurant. There are also several **campsites** nearby, such as the four-star *Grand Large* (ⓣ02.98.27.91.41, ⓦwww.campinglegrandlarge.com; closed Oct–March) and the two-star municipal *Lannic* (ⓣ02.98.27.91.31; closed Oct–March).

Back along the quayside in the centre of town, the quai Toudouze, you'll find a succession of excellent **fish restaurants**, including *Les Frères de la Côte* at no. 11 (ⓣ02.98.27.95.42; closed late Sept to April), and the *Côté Mer* at no. 12 (ⓣ02.98.27.93.79; closed Wed & Thurs in low season).

South towards Quimper

Moving south of the Crozon peninsula, you soon enter the ancient kingdom of **Cornouaille**. The most direct route to the region's principal city, **Quimper**, leaves the sea behind and heads due south, passing close to the unchanged medieval village of **Locronan**. However, if you can spare the time, it's worth following the supremely isolated coastline instead around the Baie de Douarnenez to the **Pointe du Raz**, the western tip of Finistère. With a few exceptions – most notably its "land's end" capes – this stretch of coast has kept out of the tourist mainstream, and nowhere does that hold more true than on the remarkable, remote **Île de Sein**.

Locronan

LOCRONAN, a short way from the sea on the minor road that leads down from the Crozon peninsula, is a prime example of a Breton town that has remained frozen in its ancient form by more recent economic decline. From 1469 through to the seventeenth century, it was a successful centre for woven linen, supplying sails to the French, English and Spanish navies. It was first rivalled by Vitré and Rennes, before suffering the "agony and ruin" so graphically described in its small **museum** (Feb–June & Sept Mon–Fri 10am–noon & 2–6pm; July & Aug Mon–Sat 10am–1pm & 2–7pm, Sun 2–7pm; €2). As a result, the rich medieval houses of the town centre have never been superseded or surrounded by modern development. Film directors love its authenticity, even if Roman Polanski, filming *Tess*, deemed it necessary to change all the porches, put new windows on the Renaissance houses, and bury the main square in mud to make it all look a bit more English.

Today Locronan, thanks to tourism, is once more prosperous, but this commercialization shouldn't put you off making at least a passing visit, for the town itself is genuinely remarkable, centred around the focal **Église St-Ronan**. Be sure to take the time to walk down the hill of the **rue Moal**, to the lovely little stone chapel of Nôtre-Dame de Bonne Nouvelle.

The **tourist office** is next to the museum (same hours; Ⓣ02.98.91.70.14, Ⓦwww.locronan.org). The one **hotel**, *du Prieuré*, at 11 rue du Prieuré on the main approach street (Ⓣ02.98.91.70.89, Ⓦwww.hotel-le-prieure.com; ❹; closed Feb, plus Fri eve & Sat lunch in low season) is not particularly attractive, but offers well-equipped rooms and possesses a good restaurant.

Douarnenez

Sufficient quantities of tuna, sardines and assorted crustaceans are still landed at the port of **DOUARNENEZ**, in the superbly sheltered Baie de Douarnenez, south of the Crozon peninsula, to keep the largest fish canneries in Europe busy. However, the catch has been declining ever since 1923, when eight hundred fishing boats brought in 100 million sardines during the six-month season. Over the last twenty years or so, Douarnenez has therefore set out – at phenomenal expense, the subject of considerable local controversy – to redefine itself as a living museum of all matters maritime.

Since 1993, **Port-Rhû**, on the west side of town, has been designated as the **Port-Musée**, with its entire waterfront taken up with fishing and other vessels gathered from throughout northern Europe. Its centrepiece, the **Musée du Bateau** (Boat Museum) in place de l'Enfer (April to mid-June & mid-Sept to early Nov daily except Mon 10am–12.30pm & 2–6pm; mid-June to mid-Sept daily 10am–7pm; €6.20) houses slightly smaller vessels than those found in the port, including a *moliceiro* from Portugal and coracles from Wales and Ireland, with exhaustive explanations on boat construction techniques and a strong emphasis on fishing. The most appealing part of the museum visit, however, is back at the waterfront, where you can roam in and out of five boats, peering into their oily metallic-smelling engine rooms and cramped sleeping quarters.

Of the three separate harbour areas still in operation, by far the most appealing is the rough-and-ready **port du Rosmeur**, on the east side, which is nominally the fishing port used by the smaller local craft. Its quayside – which is far from totally commercialized, but holds a reasonable number of cafés and restaurants – curves between a pristine wooded promontory to the right and the fish canneries to the left, which continue around the north of the headland.

Although the various **beaches** around town look pretty enough, the sea here is dangerous for swimming. They have, however, become very popular with **surfers** in recent years.

The **tourist office** in Douarnenez is at 2 rue du Dr-Mével (July & Aug Mon–Sat 10am–noon & 2–7pm; Sept–June Mon–Sat 10am–noon & 2–5.30pm; ⓣ02.98.92.13.35, ⓦwww.douarnenez-tourisme.com), a short walk up from the Port-Musée. Among good-value **hotels** are *Le Bretagne*, nearby at 23 rue Duguay-Trouin (ⓣ02.98.92.30.44, ⓦwww.le-bretagne.fr; ❸), above a restaurant serving reasonable Tex-Mex dishes for around €12, and the more upmarket *De France*, also nearby, on the main street at 4 rue Jean-Jaurès (ⓣ02.98.92.00.02, ⓔhotel.de.france.dz@orange.fr; ❹; closed Mon, Sat lunch & Sun eve), which has a good restaurant. Close by on the bay, at Tréboul/Les Sables Blancs, there's a two-star **campsite**, *Croas Men* (ⓣ02.98.74.00.18, ⓦwww.croas-men.com; closed Oct–March). In addition to the hotel **restaurants**, *Les Bigorneaux Amoureux*, 2 bd Richepin (ⓣ02.98.92.35.55; closed Mon), is a good seafood place which has a terrace overlooking the plage des Dames.

The Baie des Trépassés and the Pointe du Raz

The **Baie des Trépassés** (Bay of the Dead), 30km west of Douarnenez, gets its grim name from the shipwrecked bodies that used to be washed up there, and is a possible site of the lost city of Ys (see p.454). However, it's actually a very attractive spot; green meadows, too exposed to support trees, end abruptly on the low cliffs to either side; there's a huge expanse of flat sand (in fact little else at low tide); and out in the crashing waves surfers and windsurfers get thrashed to within an inch of their lives. Beyond them, you can usually make out the white-painted houses along the harbour on the Île de Sein, while the various uninhabited rocks in between hold a veritable forest of lighthouses.

In total, less than half a dozen scattered buildings intrude upon the emptiness, including two **hotels**, both with tremendous views. Right in the middle is the pink *Hôtel de la Baie des Trépassés* (ⓣ02.98.70.61.34, ⓦwww.baiedestrepasses.com; ❷–❸; closed mid-Nov to mid-Feb), which has a handful of cheaper rooms without en-suite facilities, and serves menus of wonderfully fresh seafood from €21. The larger *Relais de la Pointe du Van*, run by the same management, is slightly higher up, to the right (ⓣ02.98.70.62.79, same website; ❸; closed Oct–March).

The Pointe du Raz

The **Pointe du Raz** – the Land's End of both Finistère and France – is designated as a "Grand Site National", and makes a magnificent spectacle. Don't expect to have the place to yourself; with a million visitors every year, they've had to build a huge car park 1km short of the actual headland (€5 cars, €3

△ Pointe du Raz

motorcycles), alongside a new information complex (April–June & Sept daily 10.30am–6pm; July & Aug daily 9.30am–7pm; ⓣ02.98.70.67.18, ⓦwww.pointeduraz.com).

To reach the *pointe*, catch one of the frequent free shuttle buses (and check the time of the last one back); walk the most direct route, along an undulating, arrow-straight, track; or take a longer stroll along the footpath that skirts the top of the cliffs. You'll be glad of strong-gripping shoes as you teeter above the plummeting fissures of the *pointe*, filling and draining with a deafening surf-roar. The winds are often as fierce as the waves, buffeting the thousands of seabirds that make this their home.

Audierne

Though on the whole the exposed southwestern extremities of Brittany are not areas you'd immediately associate with a classic summer sun-and-sand holiday, **AUDIERNE**, 25km west of Douarnenez on the Baie d'Audierne, is an exception. An active fishing port, specializing in prawns and crayfish, it spreads along the northern shore of the Goyen estuary a short way back from the sea. From the town centre, the road continues just over 1km to the long, curving and surprisingly sheltered **beach** of Ste-Evette.

At the inland end of town, an **aquarium** called L'Aquashow (April–Sept daily 10am–7pm; Oct Sun–Thurs 2–5pm; Nov–March school holidays only 2–5pm; €11.50) holds tankfuls of mostly local fish, captioned as ever with the stress on gastronomy – "the flesh is firm and much enjoyed" – and captive cormorants and gulls put on regular aerobatic displays.

Audierne's **tourist office** is on the main square in the heart of town, at 8 rue Victor-Hugo (July & Aug Mon–Sat 10am–7pm; Sept–June Mon–Fri 9am–noon & 2–5pm, Sat 9am–1pm; Ⓣ02.98.70.12.20, Ⓦwww.audierne-tourisme.com). On the seaward side of the road, in a superb position right at Ste-Evette beach, stands the **hotel** *Au Roi Gradlon*, 3 bd Manu-Brusq (Ⓣ02.98.70.04.51, Ⓦwww.auroigradlon.com; ❸). Its unusual design means that its high-quality street-level dining room is in fact on the top storey, with several further floors, concealed from the road, dropping down below it to the beach.

The Île de Sein

Of all the Breton islands, the tiny **Île de Sein**, just 8km off the end of the Pointe du Raz, has to be the most extraordinary. Its very grip on existence seems so tenuous that it's hard to believe anyone could truly survive here; nowhere does it rise more than six metres above the surrounding ocean, and for much of its 2.5-kilometre length it's barely broader than the breakwater wall of bricks that serves as its central spine.

In fact, the island has been inhabited since prehistoric times, and it was reputed to have been the very last refuge of the druids in Brittany. It also became famous during World War II, when its entire male population answered General de Gaulle's call to join him in exile in England. Today, over three hundred islanders continue to make their living from the sea, gathering rainwater and seaweed, and fishing for scallops, lobster and crayfish.

Setting off to reach the island on a misty morning feels as though you're sailing off the edge of the world. There are no cars here, and even bicycles are not permitted. Depending on the tide, boats pull in at one or other of the two adjoining harbours that constitute Sein's one tight-knit village, in front of which a little beach appears at low tide. The village also holds a **museum** of local history (June & Sept daily 10am–noon & 2–4pm, July & Aug daily 10am–noon & 2–6pm; €2.50), packed with black-and-white photos and press clippings, and displaying a long list of shipwrecks from 1476 onwards. The basic activity for visitors, however, is to take a bracing walk.

The principal departure point for **boats** to Sein is Ste-Evette beach, just outside **Audierne** (see above); the crossing takes around an hour. Services are operated by Vedette-Biniou (early July to late Aug, daily 10am, 1.30pm & 5pm; Ⓣ02.98.70.21.15, Ⓦwww.vedette-biniou.fr.st; €25 return), and Penn Ar Bed (daily: early July to late Aug 9am, 11.30am & 4.50pm; late Aug to early July 9.30am; Ⓣ02.98.70.70.70, Ⓦwww.pennarbed.fr; €23.40 return). On Sundays from late June to early September, Penn Ar Bed also run trips to Sein from

Brest (departs 8am; 1hr 30min; €30.70 return) via **Camaret** (8.40am; 1hr; €27.50 return).

Sein is hardly bursting with facilities, but it does hold two **hotels**: the *Trois Dauphins*, looking out over the beach from the middle of the port (Ⓣ02.98.70.92.09; ❷, sea view ❸), and the *Hôtel-Restaurant d'Armen* (Ⓣ02.98.70.90.77, Ⓦwww.hotel-armen.net; ❸), the very last building you come to as you walk west out of town – all its rooms face the sea as there's ocean on both sides, and it serves good food.

Quimper

QUIMPER, capital of the ancient diocese, kingdom and later duchy of Cornouaille, is the oldest Breton city. According to legend, the first bishop of Quimper, St Corentin, came with the first Bretons across the Channel to the place they named Little Britain. He lived by eating a regenerating and immortal fish, and was made bishop by one King Gradlon, whose life he later saved when the sea-bed city of **Ys** was destroyed. Gradlon had built Ys in the Baie de Douarnenez, protected from the water by gates and locks to which only he and his daughter had keys. However, St Corentin suspected her of evil doings, and was proven right: at the urging of the Devil, the princess unlocked the gates, the city flooded and Gradlon escaped only by obeying Corentin and throwing his daughter into the sea. Back on dry land and in need of a new capital, Gradlon founded Quimper. Ys remains on the sea floor; it will rise again when Paris ("*Par-Ys*", "equal to Ys") sinks. According to tradition, on feast days sailors can still hear church bells and hymns under the water.

A relaxed kind of place, modern Quimper is still active enough to have the bars – and the atmosphere – to make it worth going out café-crawling. "The charming little place" known to Flaubert takes at most half an hour to cross on foot. The town's name comes from "kemper", denoting the junction of the two rivers, the Steir and the Odet, around which cram the cobbled streets (now mainly pedestrianized) of the **medieval quarter**, dominated by the cathedral nearby. As the Odet curves from east to southwest it's crossed by numerous low, flat bridges, bedecked with geraniums and chrysanthemums in autumn. You can stroll along the boulevards on both banks of the river, where several ultramodern edifices blend in a surprisingly harmonious way with their ancient – and attractive – surroundings. Overlooking all are the wooded slopes of **Mont Frugy**. There's no great pressure in Quimper to rush around monuments or museums, and the most enjoyable option may be to take a boat and drift down "the prettiest river in France" to the open sea at Bénodet.

Arrival and information

The **gare SNCF** and **gare routière** (Ⓣ02.98.90.88.89) are next to each other on avenue de la Gare, 1km east of the town centre. Both are connected to the centre by bus #6, and all city buses pass the tourist office, via either place de la Résistance or along rue du Parc on the other side of the river, depending on which direction you are going. If you want to use public transport to get to the coast anywhere in the immediate vicinity, the **bus** is your only option. The most useful local operator is the Compagnie Amoricaine de Transport, or CAT, 10 rue Jules-Verne (Ⓣ02.98.90.88.89), who run services to Bénodet, leaving from the *gare routière* or place de la Résistance; to Audierne and Pointe du Raz,

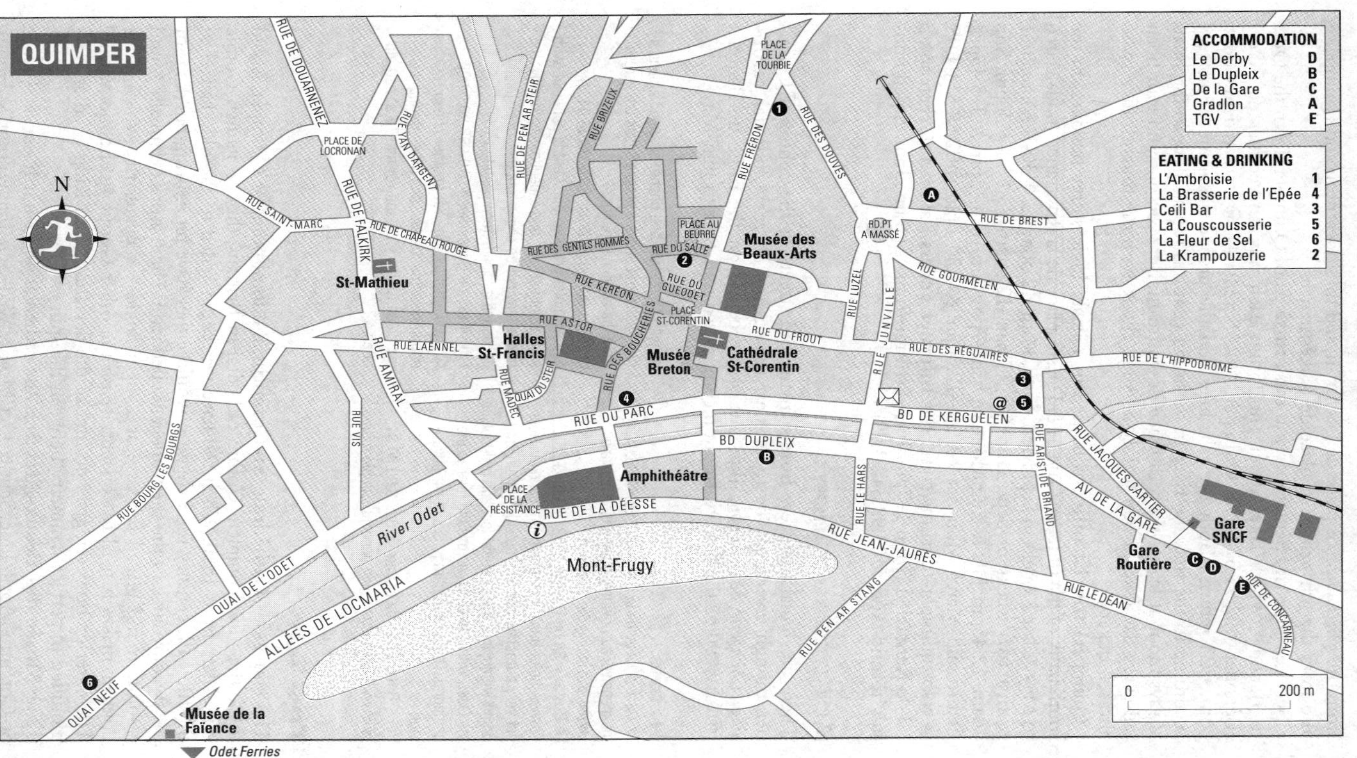
QUIMPER
ACCOMMODATION
Le Derby D
Le Dupleix B
De la Gare C
Gradlon A
TGV E
EATING & DRINKING
L'Ambroisie 1
La Brasserie de l'Epée 4
Ceili Bar 3
La Couscousserie 5
La Fleur de Sel 6
La Krampouzerie 2
Musée des Beaux-Arts
Cathédrale St-Corentin
Musée Breton
Halles St-Francis
St-Mathieu
Amphithéâtre
Mont-Frugy
River Odet
Gare SNCF
Gare Routière
Musée de la Faïence
Odet Ferries
Place de la Tourbie
Place de Locronan
Place au Beurre
Place St-Corentin
Place de la Résistance
Rd.Pt A Massé
Rue de Douarnenez
Rue Yan Dargent
Rue de Pen ar Steir
Rue Brizeux
Rue Fréron
Rue des Douves
Rue de Brest
Rue Saint-Marc
Rue de Falkirk
Rue de Chapeau Rouge
Rue des Gentils Hommes
Rue du Sallé
Rue Kéréon
Rue du Guéodet
Rue Astor
Rue des Boucheries
Rue Laënnel
Rue Amiral
Rue Madec
Quai du Steir
Rue du Frout
Rue Luzel
Rue Junville
Rue Gourmelen
Rue des Réguaires
Rue de l'Hippodrome
Rue du Parc
Bd de Kerguélen
Bd Dupleix
Rue Vis
Rue Bourg les Bourgs
Rue de la Déesse
Rue Jean-Jaurès
Rue Le Hars
Rue Aristide Briand
Rue Jacques Cartier
Av de la Gare
Rue Le Déan
Rue de Concarneau
Rue Pen ar Stang
Quai de l'Odet
Allées de Locmaria
Quai Neuf
0 200 m
N

from the *gare routière* or place de Locronan; and to Concarneau and Quimperlé, also from the *gare routière* or place de la Résistance.

Between June and September you can **cruise** from Quimper down the Odet to Bénodet, which takes about 1hr 15min each way, on Vedettes de l'Odet (Bénodet ⓣ02.98.57.00.58, Quimper ⓣ02.98.52.98.41, ⓦwww.vedettes-odet.com; €23 return). Both the schedules and the precise departure point vary according to the tide; the river in the town centre is too shallow, so the boats always moor at least a short distance downstream. Between one and four boats sail every day (except Sun in July & Aug); check with the tourist office (who also sell tickets).

Quimper's **tourist office** is housed in a small single-storey building on the south bank of the Odet at 7 rue de la Déesse, place de la Résistance (mid-March to May & last 2 weeks in Sept Mon–Sat 9.30am–12.30pm & 1.30–6.30pm; June & first two weeks of Sept Mon–Sat 9.30am–12.30pm & 1.30–6.30pm, Sun 10am–12.45pm; July & Aug Mon–Sat 9am–7pm, Sun 10am–1pm & 3–5.45pm; Oct to mid-March Mon–Sat 9.30am–12.30pm & 1.30–6pm; ⓣ02.98.53.04.05, ⓦwww.quimper-tourisme.com). For **Internet access**, call in at Cybercopy, 3 bd de Kerguélen (Mon 1–7pm, Tues–Fri 9am–7pm, Sat 9am–3pm, closed mid-July to mid-Aug; ⓣ02.98.64.33.99).

Accommodation

There are remarkably few **hotels** in the old streets in the centre of Quimper, though several can be found near the station. There's a four-star **campsite**, *Orangerie de Lannion*, 4km out of the centre on the route de Bénodet (ⓣ02.98.90.62.02; ⓦwww.lanniron.com; closed mid-Sept to mid-May).

Hotels

Le Derby 13 av de la Gare ⓣ02.98.52.06.91. Inexpensive, surprisingly quiet option above a corner bar facing the station. ❷

Le Dupleix 34 bd Dupleix ⓣ02.98.90.53.35, ⓦwww.hotel-dupleix.com. Modern concrete hotel, not very attractive from the outside but airy and bright within, in a good central location overlooking the Odet, with fine views across the river to the cathedral. The private garage is a major advantage. ❺

De la Gare 17 av de la Gare ⓣ02.98.90.00.81, ⓦwww.hoteldelagarequimper.com. Simple rooms, all with TV, shower and phone, arranged around a quiet patio and above a simple snack bar across from the station. Parking. ❸

Gradlon 30 rue du Brest ⓣ02.98.95.04.39, ⓦwww.hotel-gradlon.com. Central but quiet (with a pleasant garden), and exceptionally friendly. The rooms may not be cheap, but they're tastefully decorated in clean, fresh pastels. ❺

TGV 4 rue de Concarneau ⓣ02.98.90.54.00, ⓦwww.hoteltgv.com. Yet another cheap option near the station, this time offering plain but clean rooms with shower and TV at bargain rates. ❷

The Town

The enormous **Cathédrale St-Corentin**, the focal point of Quimper, is said to be the most complete Gothic cathedral in Brittany, though its neo-Gothic spires date from 1856. When the nave was being added to the old chancel in the fifteenth century, the extension would either have hit existing buildings or the swampy edge of the then-unchannelled river. The masons eventually found a solution and placed the nave at a slight angle – a peculiarity which, once noticed, makes it hard to concentrate on the other Gothic splendours within. The exterior, however, gives no hint of the deviation, with King Gradlon now mounted in perfect symmetry between the spires.

The **Musée des Beaux-Arts** faces the cathedral on its north side, at 4 place St-Corentin (April–June, Sept & Oct Mon & Wed–Sun 10am–noon & 2–6pm;

July & Aug daily 10am–7pm; Nov–March Mon & Wed–Sat 10am–noon & 2–6pm, Sun 2–6pm; €4.50). Refurbished to very classy effect, with new floors and suspended walkways, it focuses especially on an amazing assemblage of drawings by Max Jacob – who was born in Quimper – and his contemporaries. Jean-Julien Lemordant's vibrant murals of Breton scenes, commissioned in 1907 for Quimper's *Hôtel de l'Epée* (which closed in 1974) get a room to themselves, and there's also quite a selection of nineteenth- and twentieth-century paintings from the Pont-Aven school, though you'd hardly notice the only Gauguin, a goose he painted on the door of Marie Henry's inn in Pont-Aven itself.

The heart of **old Quimper** lies in and to the west of place St-Corentin, in front of the cathedral. This is where you'll find the liveliest shops and cafés, housed in old half-timbered buildings, such as the Breton Keltia-Musique record shop at 1 place au Beurre, and the Celtic shop, Ar Bed Keltiek, between the cathedral and the river at 2 rue du Roi-Gradlon. The light and spacious marketplace, the **Halles St-Francis**, on rue Astor, is quite a delight, not just for the food, but for the view past the upturned boat rafters through the roof to the cathedral's twin spires. It's open from Monday to Saturday, with an extra-large market spreading into the surrounding streets on Saturdays.

South of the covered market, on the opposite bank of the Odet at 14 rue Jean-Baptiste-Bosquet, is the excellent **Musée de la Faïence Jules Verlinque** (mid-April to mid-Oct Mon–Sat 10am–6pm; €4; ⓦwww.quimper-faiences.com). The museum tells the story of Quimper's long association with **faïence** – tin-glazed earthenware – which has been made in and around the town since 1690, and demonstrates that little has changed in the Breton pottery business since some unknown artisan hit on the idea of painting ceramic ware with naive "folk" designs. That was in around 1875, when the coming of the railways brought the first influx of tourists, and a consequent demand for souvenirs.

As you walk through the town, it's impossible to ignore faïence – you're invited to look and to buy on every corner. On weekdays, it's also possible to visit the major atelier **H.-B. Henriot**, in the allées de Locmaria just behind the museum (July & Aug Mon–Sat 9.15–11.15am & 1.30–4.15pm; Sept–June Mon–Fri 9.15–11.15am & 2–4.15pm; ⓣ02.98.90.09.36, ⓦwww.hb-henriot.com; €3.50). H.-B. Henriot maintain two bright, modern **gift shops** alongside; the prices, even for the seconds, are similar to those on offer everywhere else, but the selection is superb.

Eating and drinking

Although the pedestrian streets west of the cathedral are unexpectedly short on places to eat, there are quite a few **restaurants** further east on the north side of the river, en route towards the *gare SNCF*. Rue Aristide-Briand here also contains a lively Celtic **bar**, the *Ceili* at no 4. For crêperies, the place au Beurre, a short walk northwest of the cathedral, is a good bet.

L'Ambroisie 49 rue Élie-Fréron ⓣ02.98.95.00.02. Upmarket French restaurant a short climb north from the cathedral, featuring lots of fine seafood (including tuna) and meat dishes on menus from €22. Closed Mon, plus Sun eve in winter.

La Brasserie de l'Epée 14 rue du Parc ⓣ02.98.95.28.97. Lovely Art Nouveau brasserie, facing the river not far from the cathedral, which serves good-value menus in all price ranges, and stays open late – you can still get a meal at 11pm, which is rare indeed for Brittany. Closed Sun & Mon.

La Couscousserie 1 bd de Kerguélen ⓣ02.98.95.46.50. Plush, enjoyable Middle Eastern restaurant by the river, serving couscous platters at €11–22, and *tagines* for around €15, in two Arabian Nights-themed rooms decked out with hookahs and the like. Closed Aug.

La Fleur de Sel 1 quai Neuf ⓣ02.98.55.04.71. Gourmet French cooking not far west of the town centre opposite the Musée de la Faïence on the north bank of the river, with menus ranging from €19.50 to €26.50 that are strong on fish and

seafood, but do also have some meat. Closed Sat lunch & all Sun.
La Krampouzerie 9 rue du Sallé ⓣ02.98.95.13.08. One of the best of Quimper's many crêperies, with some outdoor seating on the place au Beurre. Most crêpes, such as the one with Roscoff onions and seaweed, cost around €3.50, though a wholewheat *galette* with smoked salmon and cream cheese is €5.80. Closed Sun, plus Mon in winter.

Entertainment

Quimper's **Festival de Cornouaille** started in 1923 and has gone from strength to strength since. This great jamboree of Breton music, costumes, theatre and dance is held in the week before the fourth Sunday in July, attracting guest performers from the other Celtic countries and a scattering of other, sometimes highly unusual, ethnic-cultural ensembles. The whole thing culminates in an incredible Sunday parade through the town. The official programme does not appear until July, but you can get provisional details in advance from the tourist office or at ⓦwww.festival-cornouaille.com. Accommodation is at a premium in Quimper while the festival is on.

Not so widely known are the **Semaines Musicales** (ⓦwww.semaines-musicales-quimper.org), which breathe life into the rather stuffy nineteenth-century theatre on boulevard Dupleix during the first three weeks of August. The music is predominantly classical and tends to favour French composers such as Berlioz, Debussy, Bizet and Poulenc.

South from Quimper

More tourists flock to Finistère's southern coast than to any other part of the region, with the busiest segment of all in summer centring on the family-friendly resort of **Bénodet**. The beaches between here and **La Forêt-Fouesnant** to the east rank among the finest in Brittany. A little further along the coast, the walled, sea-circled town of **Concarneau** makes a perfect day-trip destination, though a prettier place to spend a night or two would be the flowery village of **Pont-Aven**, immortalized by Paul Gauguin, slightly further to the east still.

Bénodet and around

Once out of its city channel, the Odet takes on the shape of most Breton inlets, spreading out to lake proportions then turning narrow corners between gorges. The family resort of **BÉNODET** at the mouth of the river (reachable by boat from Quimper) has a long, sheltered beach on the ocean side, with amusements for children and beachside nurseries. One of the nicest **hotels** in Bénodet is *Les Bains de Mer*, 11 rue du Kerguélen (ⓣ02.98.57.03.41, ⓦwww.lesbainsdemer.com; ❺; closed Jan), which has comfortable rooms, is close to the port and beach and has the added attraction of an outdoor heated swimming pool. Nearby *Ker Vennaïk*, 45 av de la Plage (ⓣ02.98.57.15.40; ❹; closed Nov–Easter), is a reasonable lower-priced alternative, where some rooms have balconies. Bénodet also has several large **campsites** – if anything, rather too many of them – such as the enormous four-star *Du Letty*, southeast of the village by plage du Letty on rue du Canvez (ⓣ02.98.57.04.69, ⓦwww.campingduletty.com; closed early Sept to mid-June). Recommended **restaurants** include *Le Spi*, at 3 av de la Plage (ⓣ02.98.57.19.50), which serves a fantastic €25 menu. You'll also find a sprinkling of decent crêperies across town.

The coast that continues east of Bénodet is rocky and repeatedly cut by deep valleys. Not so much a town as a loose conglomeration of villages, **FOUESNANT**, 9km along, is coming to rival its neighbour as a prime destination for family holidays. While Fouesnant itself is renowned for its cider-makers, and holds a pretty little Romanesque church, most local tourist amenities are gathered in its sister community of **LA FORÊT-FOUESNANT**, 3km further east. Clustered along the waterfront at the foot of a hill so steep that caravans are banned from even approaching, it holds an assortment of attractive hotels such as the *Hôtel de l'Espérance*, place de l'Église (ⓣ02.98.56.96.58, ⓦwww.hotel-esperance.org; ❷; closed mid-Nov to March) and the pricier *Aux Cerisiers*, 3 rue des Cerisiers (ⓣ02.98.56.97.24, ⓦwww.auxcerisiers.com; ❸; closed all day Sat and Sun eve, plus mid-Dec to mid-Jan).

Concarneau

The first sizeable town you come to east of Bénodet is **CONCARNEAU**, where the third most important fishing port in France does a reasonable job of passing itself off as a holiday resort. Its greatest asset is its **ville close**, the small and very well-fortified old city located a few metres offshore on an irregular rocky island in the bay, connected to the mainland by a narrow bridge. This can get too crowded for comfort in high summer, but otherwise it's a real delight.

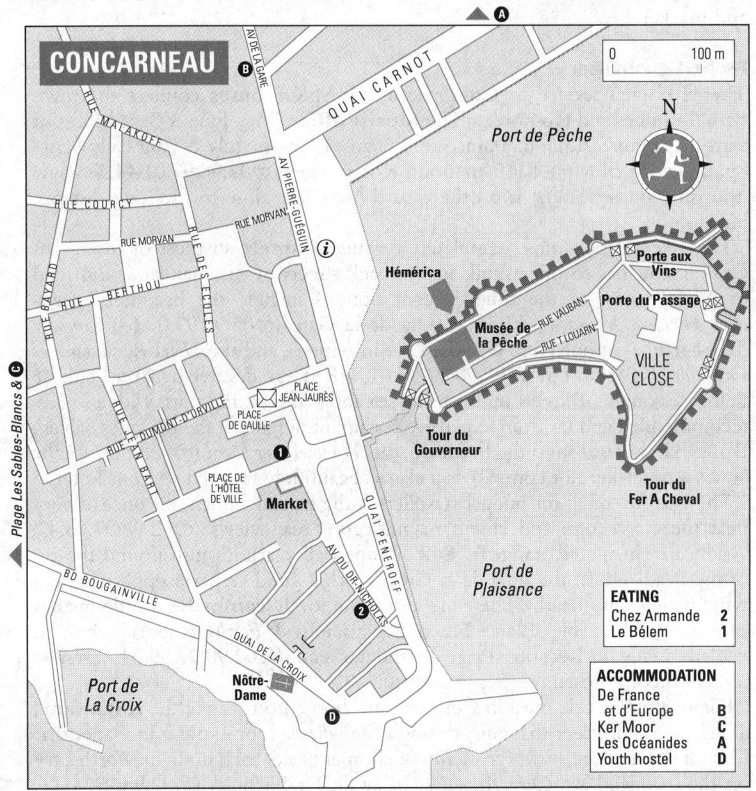

5 BRITTANY | South from Quimper

Like those of the citadelle at Le Palais on Belle-Île, its ramparts were completed by Vauban in the seventeenth century. The island itself, however, had been inhabited for at least a thousand years before that, and is first recorded as the site of a priory founded by King Gradlon of Quimper.

Concarneau boasts that it is a *ville fleurie*, and the flowers are most in evidence inside the walls, where climbing roses and clematis swarm all over the various gift shops, restaurants and crêperies. Walk the central pedestrianized street to the far end, and you can pass through a gateway to the shoreline to watch the fishing boats go by. The best views of all come from the (incomplete) promenade on top of the **ramparts** (daily 9am–7.30pm; mid-June to mid-Sept €1; mid-Sept to mid-June free). The absence of a railing means it's unsafe for children.

By exploring the history of fishing all over the world, the **Musée de la Pêche**, immediately inside the *ville close* (daily: July & Aug 9.30am–8pm; June & Sept 10am–6pm; Oct–May 10am–noon & 2–6pm; €6), provides an insight into the traditional life Concarneau shared with so many other Breton ports. Oddities on show include a three-thousand-year-old anchor from Crete; the swords of swordfish and the saws of sawfish; a Japanese giant crab; photos of bearded old lifeboatmen; cases full of sardine and tuna cans; and a live aquarium, where the lobsters little realize they are in no immediate danger of being eaten. Passing through the city walls at the rear of the museum, you can also tour a genuine trawler moored alongside. Back in the museum shop, you can buy diagrams and models of ships, and stock up on tinned sardines and mackerel.

Practicalities

There's no rail service to Concarneau, but SNCF **buses** connect the town with Quimper and Rosporden. The **tourist office** (May, June & Sept Mon–Sat 9am–12.30pm & 1.45–6.30pm, Sun 9.30am–12.30pm; July & Aug daily 9am–8pm; Oct–April Mon–Sat 9am–noon & 2–6.30pm; Ⓣ02.98.97.01.44, Ⓦwww.tourismeconcarneau.fr) is on the quai d'Aiguillon, close to the long-distance bus stop.

The *ville close* is almost completely devoid of **hotels**, so most of those that Concarneau has to offer skulk in the back streets of the mainland, and tend to be full most of the time. Decent options include the bright, modernized *Hôtel de France et d'Europe*, 9 av de la Gare (Ⓣ02.98.97.00.64, Ⓦwww.hotel-france-europe.com; ❺; closed Sat in winter), and the *Hôtel-Restaurant les Océanides*, 3 rue du Lin (Ⓣ02.98.97.08.61, Ⓦlesoceanides.free.fr; ❸), a Logis de France a couple of streets up from the sea above the fishing port, with a highly recommended and far from expensive restaurant. Right on the plage les Sables-Blancs, 2km west round the headland, the *Hôtel Ker Moor* (Ⓣ02.98.97.02.96, Ⓦwww.hotel-kermor.com; ❻), is a classic, beautifully restored seafront hotel.

The best bet of all for budget travellers is the **hostel**, which, for once, is very near the city centre and enjoys magnificent ocean views (Ⓣ02.98.97.03.47, Ⓔconcarneau.aj.cis@orange.fr; €12.30; open all year); it's just around the tip of the headland on the quai de la Croix, with a good crêperie opposite and a windsurfing shop nearby. There are also some lovely **campsites** a little further on, close to the Sables-Blancs beach; the spacious *Prés Verts* spreads through verdant fields at Kernous Plage at the far end (Ⓣ02.98.97.09.74, Ⓦwww.presverts.com; closed late Sept to April).

For an atmospheric meal in Concarneau, choose from any of the **restaurants** along the main street that runs through the *ville close*, or explore the lanes that lead off it. There are, however, plenty of cheaper places back in town. Worth a try on the mainland are *Chez Armande*, 15 av du Dr-Nicholas (Ⓣ02.98.97.00.76;

closed Wed all year, plus Tues in winter), an excellent seafood restaurant not far south of the market, and *Le Bélem*, place Jean-Jaurès (Ⓣ02.98.97.02.78; closed Wed), a pretty little indoor restaurant, next to the market, serving mussels for €9 and good seafood menus from €17.

Pont-Aven

PONT-AVEN, 14km east of Concarneau and just inland from the tip of the Aven estuary, is a small port packed with art galleries – and tourists. This was where Gauguin came to paint in the 1880s before he left for Tahiti. Though Gauguin inspired the **Pont-Aven School** of fellow artists, including Émile Bernard, for all the local hype the town has no permanent collection of his work. The **Musée Municipal** (daily: Feb, March, Nov & Dec 10am–12.30pm & 2–6pm; April–June, Sept & Oct 10am–12.30pm & 2–6.30pm; July & Aug 10am–7pm; €4) in the *mairie* holds changing exhibitions of the school and other artists active during the same period, but you can't count on paintings by the man himself.

Gauguin aside, Pont-Aven is pleasant in its own right. Just upstream of the little granite bridge at the heart of town, the **promenade Xavier-Grall** criss-crosses the tiny river itself on landscaped walkways, offering glimpses of the backs of venerable mansions, dripping with ivy, and a little "chaos" of rocks in the stream itself. A longer walk – allow an hour – leads into the romantically named **Bois d'Amour**, wooded gardens which have long provided inspiration to painters, poets and musicians.

Pont-Aven's **tourist office**, 5 place de l'Hôtel-de-Ville (April–June & Sept Mon–Sat 10am–12.30pm & 2–6pm, Sun 3–6pm; July & Aug Mon–Sat 9.30am–7pm, Sun 10am–1pm & 3–6pm; Oct–March Mon–Sat 10am–12.30pm & 2–6pm; Ⓣ02.98.06.04.70, Ⓦwww.pontaven.com), sells an excellent English-language booklet on the town that includes route maps of local walks. Much the best of the three relatively expensive **hotels** is the central *Hôtel des Ajoncs d'Or*, 1 place de l'Hôtel-de-Ville (Ⓣ02.98.06.02.06; ❸; closed Jan, plus Mon & Sun eve in low season), where gourmet menus start at €23. The nicest of the local **campsites** is the four-star *Domaine de Kerlann* (Ⓣ02.98.06.01.77, Ⓦwww.camping-kerlann.fr; closed Oct–March), set in a large wooded park with a swimming pool, tennis courts and mini-golf.

Inland Brittany: the Nantes–Brest Canal

The **Nantes–Brest canal** is a meandering chain of waterways from Finistère to the Loire, interweaving rivers with stretches of canal built at Napoleon's instigation to bypass the belligerent English fleets off the coast. Finally completed in 1836, it came into its own at the end of the nineteenth century as a coal, slate and fertilizer route. The building of the dam at **Lac Guerlédan** in the 1920s chopped the canal in two, leaving a whole section unnavigable by barge. Road transport had by then already superseded water haulage, but modern tourism has breathed life back into the canal.

En route the canal passes through riverside towns, such as **Josselin** and **Malestroit**, that long predate its construction; commercial ports and junctions – **Pontivy**, most notably – that developed in the nineteenth century because of it; the old port of **Redon**, a patchwork of water, where the canal crosses the River Vilaine; and a sequence of scenic splendours, including the string of lakes around the **Barrage de Guerlédan**, near Mur-de-Bretagne. As a focus for exploring **inland Brittany**, whether by barge, bike, foot, or all three, the canal is ideal. Not every stretch is accessible, but there are detours to be made away from it, such as into the wild and desolate **Monts d'Arrée** to the north of the canal in Finistère.

The Finistère stretch

As late as the 1920s, steamers would make their way across the Rade de Brest and down the Aulne River to **Châteaulin**, the first real town on the canal route. If you're walking the canal seriously, **Pont-Coblant** and **Pleyben** are just 10km further away on the map, but be warned that the meanders make it a several-hour hike. Pick your side of the water, too: there are no bridges between Châteaulin and Pont-Coblant.

Châteaulin

CHÂTEAULIN is a quiet place, where the main reason to stay is the canal itself – or river, as it is here. Most bars sell permits for local salmon and trout **fishing** (as do fishing shops, some of which rent out tackle). You should have little difficulty finding a room at the **hotel** *Le Christmas*, 33 Grande-Rue (Ⓣ02.98.86.01.24, Ⓔle-chrismas@orange.fr; ❸), which serves excellent food. Within a couple of minutes' walk upstream from the statue to Jean Moulin – the Resistance leader who was *sous-préfet* here from 1930 to 1933 – and the town centre, you'll find yourself on towpaths full of rabbits and squirrels and overhung by trees full of birds.

Carhaix

CARHAIX, a further 25km east of Châteaulin, is a road junction that dates back to the Romans. It has cafés and shops to replenish supplies, but other than for the third weekend of July, when it hosts the massive four-day **rock festival** des Vieilles Charrues (Ⓦwww.vieillescharrues.asso.fr), there's little reason to visit. The most interesting building in town is the granite Renaissance **Maison de Sénéchal** on rue Brisieux, which houses the **tourist office** (July & Aug Mon–Sat 9am–12.30pm & 1.30–7pm, Sun 10am–1pm; June & Sept Mon–Sat 9am–noon & 2–6pm; Oct–May Mon 2–6pm, Wed–Sat 10am–noon & 2–5.30pm; Ⓣ02.98.93.04.42, Ⓦwww.poher.com).

Huelgoat and its forest

HUELGOAT, next to its own small **lake** halfway between Morlaix and Carhaix on the minor road D769, makes a pleasant overnight stop. Spreading north and east from the village is the **Forêt de Huelgoat**, a landscape of trees, giant boulders and waterfalls tangled together in primeval chaos. Various paths lead into the depths of the woods, allowing for long walks amid spectacularly wild scenery.

The *Hôtel du Lac*, beside the lake at 9 rue du Général-de-Gaulle (☎02.98.99.71.14; ❸; closed Mon Sept–June, plus mid-Jan to mid-Feb), offers well-refurbished rooms and good food. Also beside the lake, on the road towards Brest, the two-star *Camping du Lac* (☎02.98.99.78.80; closed Sept–June) comes complete with swimming pool.

Le Faouët and Kernascléden

Thirty kilometres south of Carhaix on the D769, the secluded town of **LE FAOUËT** is served by neither buses nor trains but is distinguished mainly by its large old **market hall**. Above a floor of mud and straw, still used by local traders, rises an intricate latticework of ancient wood, propped on granite pillars and topped by a little clock tower.

The ornate and gargoyle-coated church at **KERNASCLÉDEN**, 15km southeast along the D782, holds some splendidly gruesome frescoes. On the damp-infested wall of a side chapel, horned devils stoke the fires beneath a vast cauldron filled with the souls of the damned, and there's also a Dance of Death, a faded cousin to that at Kermaria.

The central stretch

Although the canal is limited to canoeists between Carhaix and Pontivy, it's worth some effort to follow on land, particularly for the scenery around the long, narrow **Lac de Guerlédan**, created by the construction of a dam near **Mur-de-Bretagne**. Approaching by road, the canal path is most easily joined at **Gouarec**, served by five daily buses between Carhaix and Loudéac.

Quénécan Forest

For the 15km between Gouarec and Mur-de-Bretagne, the N164 skirts the edge of **Quénécan Forest**, within which is a series of artificial lakes created when the **Barrage de Guerlédan** was completed in 1928. It's a beautiful stretch of river, peaceful enough despite the summer influx of campers and caravans.

The best places to stay are just off the road, past the villages of **ST-GELVEN** and Caurel. At the former, the ravishing *Les Jardins de l'Abbaye* (☎02.96.24.95.77; ❸; closed Tues evening & Wed in low season) is an absolutely irresistible inexpensive **hotel-restaurant**, nestling beside the water at the end of an impressive avenue of ancient trees, and housed in the intact outbuildings of a twelfth-century Cistercian abbey. Porthole-like windows pierce the thick slate walls of its six cosy guest rooms, to look out across extensive riverfront grounds to the dramatic wooded slopes beyond.

From just before **CAUREL**, the brief loop of the D111 leads to tiny sandy beaches. At the spot known, justifiably, as **BEAU RIVAGE** (beautiful bank), a lavish holiday complex features the *Nautic International* campsite (☎02.96.28.57.94, ⓦcampingnautic.free.fr; closed Oct to mid-May), and the *Hôtel Beau Rivage* (☎02.96.28.52.15; ❸; closed Mon evening & Tues in low season), plus a restaurant, a snack bar and a 140-seat glass-topped cruise boat.

Pontivy

Today you can again take **barges** all the way to the Loire from **PONTIVY**, the central junction of the Nantes–Brest canal, where the course of the canal breaks off once more from the Blavet. When the waterway opened, the small medieval centre of the town was expanded, redesigned and given broad avenues to fit its new role. It was even briefly renamed Napoléonville, in honour of the man responsible for its new prosperity.

These days, Pontivy is a bright market town, its twisting old streets contrasting with the stately riverside promenades. At its northern end, on a commanding hillside site, is the **Château de Rohan**, built by the lord of Josselin in the fifteenth century (July & Aug daily 10.30am–6.30pm; April–June & Sept Wed–Sun 10am–noon & 2–6pm; Oct–Nov & Feb–March Wed–Sun 2–6pm; €4.60). Used in summer for low-key cultural events and temporary exhibitions, the castle still belongs to the Josselin family, who are slowly restoring it. At the moment, one impressive facade, complete with deep moat and two forbidding towers, looks out over the river – behind that, the structure rather peters out.

Pontivy's **tourist office** is just below the castle, on place de Gaulle (Mon–Sat 10am–noon & 2–6pm; ⓣ02.97.25.04.10, ⓦwww.pontivy.fr). Among local hotels are the *Porhoët*, nearby at 41 rue du Général-de-Gaulle (ⓣ02.97.25.34.88, ⓔduporhoet@orange.fr; ❸), and the grander *De l'Europe*, 12 rue François-Mitterrand (ⓣ02.97.25.11.14, ⓦwww.hotellerieurope.com; ❺), which has a good restaurant. In addition, the local **hostel**, 2km from the *gare SNCF* on the Île des Récollets (ⓣ02.97.25.58.27; €11.50), is in good condition and serves cheap meals, but may be closed at weekends out of season.

Josselin

About 30km further along the canal from Pontivy, you come to the three Rapunzel towers embedded in a vast sheet of stone of the **château** in **JOSSELIN**. The Rohan family used to own a third of Brittany, but the present duke contents himself with the position of local mayor. The pompous apartments of his residence

△ Château de Josselin

are not very interesting, even if they do contain the table on which the Edict of Nantes was signed in 1598. But the duchess's collection of dolls, housed in the **Musée des Poupées**, behind the castle, is something special (château & doll museum open April, May & Oct Sat, Sun & hols 2–6pm; June to mid-July & Sept daily 2–6pm; mid-July to Aug daily 10am–6pm; each €7, combined ticket €12).

The town is full of medieval splendours, from the gargoyles of the **basilica**, Notre-Dame-du-Roncier, to the castle **ramparts**, and the half-timbered houses in between. **Notre-Dame-du-Roncier** is built on the spot where, in the ninth century, a peasant supposedly found a statue of the Virgin under a bramble bush. The statue was burnt during the Revolution, but an important *pardon* is held each year on September 8.

Josselin's **tourist office** is in a superb old house on the place de la Congrégation, up in town next to the castle entrance (April–June & Sept Mon–Sat 10am–noon & 2–6pm, Sun 2–6pm; July & Aug daily 10am–6.30pm; Oct–March Mon–Thurs 10am–noon & 2–6pm, Sat 10am–noon; ⓣ02.97.22.36.43, ⓦwww.josselin.com). The lovely *Hôtel du Chateau*, a Logis de France facing the castle from across the river at 1 rue du Général-de-Gaulle (ⓣ02.97.22.20.11, ⓦwww.hotel-chateau.com; ❹; closed Feb), makes a perfect place to **stay**. Rooms with views of the château are slightly more expensive, but worth it, and the food, with dinner menus from €15, is first-rate. The nearest good campsite is the three-star *Bas de la Lande* (ⓣ02.97.22.22.20, ⓔcampingbassedelalande@orange.fr; closed Nov–March), half an hour's walk from the castle, south of the river and west of town.

Malestroit and around

Though not a lot happens in the thousand-year-old town of **MALESTROIT**, 25km southeast of Josselin, it's full of unexpected and enjoyable corners. As you come into the main square, the **place du Bouffay** in front of the church, the houses are covered with unlikely carvings – an anxious bagpipe-playing hare looking over its shoulder at a dragon's head on one beam, an oblivious sow in a blue buckled belt threading her distaff on another. The **church** itself is decorated with drunkards and acrobats outside, torturing demons and erupting towers within.

Two kilometres west of Malestroit (there is no bus connection), the village of **ST-MARCEL** hosts a **Musée de la Résistance Bretonne** (April to mid-June daily 10am–noon & 2–6pm; mid-June to mid-Sept daily 10am–7pm; mid-Sept to March daily except Tues 10am–noon & 2–6pm; ⓦwww.resistance-bretonne.com; €6.50). The museum stands on the site of a June 1944 battle in which the Breton *maquis* (guerrilla Resistance fighters), joined by Free French forces parachuted in from England, successfully diverted the local German troops from the main Normandy invasion movements.

If you arrive in Malestroit by barge (this is a good stretch to travel), you'll moor very near the town centre. The local **tourist office** stands at the edge of the main square at 17 place du Bouffay (mid-June to mid-Sept Mon–Sat 9am–7pm, Sun 10am–4pm; mid-Sept to mid-June Mon–Sat 9.30am–12.30pm & 2.30–6.30pm; ⓣ02.97.75.14.57, ⓦwww.malestroit.com). Sadly, Malestroit no longer has a hotel, but there's a two-star **campsite**, *La Daufresne* (ⓣ02.97.75.13.33; closed mid-Sept to April), down below the bridge in the Impasse d'Abattoir next to the swimming pool.

Rochefort-en-Terre

ROCHEFORT-EN-TERRE, commanding a high eminence 17km south of Malestroit, may be a prettified and polished version of its neighbour, but it ranks nonetheless among the most delightful villages in Brittany. Every available stone surface, from the window ledges to the picturesque wishing well, is festooned with colourful geraniums, a tradition that originated with the painter Alfred Klots, who was born in France to a wealthy American family in 1875, and bought Rochefort's ruined **château** in 1907. Perched on the town's highest point, the castle is now open for guided tours (April & May Sat & Sun 2–6.30pm; June & Sept daily 2–6.30pm; July & Aug daily 10am–6.30pm; €4), though not until you go through its dramatic gateway do you find out that in fact that gateway is all that survives of the original fifteenth-century structure.

Rochefort's **tourist office**, in the central place du Puits ((mid-June to mid-Sept Mon–Fri 10am–12.30pm & 2–6.30pm, Sat & Sun 2–6.30pm; mid-Sept to mid-June Mon–Fri 10am–12.30pm & 2–6pm; ⓣ02.97.43.33.57, ⓦwww.rochefort-en-terre.com), displays a list of *chambres d'hôte* in the neighbourhood, and operates the three-star municipal **campsite**, *Le Moulin Neuf*, in the chemin de Bogeais (ⓣ02.97.43.37.52; closed mid-Sept to mid-May). The one **hotel** stands in the place des Halles: *Le Pélican* (ⓣ02.97.43.38.48; ❹; closed mid-Jan to mid-Feb) offers reasonable rooms and good food, with dinner menus starting at around €16.50.

Redon

Thirty-four kilometres east of Malestroit, at the junction not only of the rivers Oust and Vilaine and the canal, but also of the train lines to Rennes, Vannes and Nantes, and of six major roads, **REDON** is not easy to avoid. And you shouldn't try to, either. A wonderful grouping of water and locks, it's a town with history, charm and life.

Until World War I, Redon was the seaport for Rennes. Its industrial docks – or what remains of them – are therefore on the Vilaine, while the canal, even in the very centre of town, is almost totally rural, its towpaths shaded avenues. Shipowners' houses from the seventeenth and eighteenth centuries can be seen along quai Jean-Bart by the *bassin* and quai Duguay-Truin next to the river. A rusted wrought-iron workbridge, equipped with a gantry, still crosses the river, but the main users of the port now are cruise ships heading down the Vilaine to La Roche-Bernard.

Redon was once also a religious centre, its first abbey founded in 832 by St Conwoion. The most prominent church today is **St-Sauveur**. Its unique four-storeyed Romanesque belfry is squat, almost obscured by later roofs and the high choir, and best seen from the adjacent cloisters; the Gothic tower was entirely separated from the main building by a fire. In the crypt, you'll find the tomb of the judge who tried the legendary Bluebeard – Joan of Arc's friend, Gilles de Rais.

Redon's **gare SNCF** is five minutes' walk west from the **tourist office** in the place de la République (July & Aug Mon–Sat 9am–7pm, Sun 10am–1pm & 4–6pm; Sept–June Mon & Wed–Fri 9.30am–noon & 2–6pm, Tues 2–6pm, Sat 10am–12.30pm & 3–5pm; ⓣ02.99.71.06.04, ⓦwww.tourisme-pays-redon.com), north across the railway tracks from the town centre. Most of the **hotels** are concentrated in town and near the *gare SNCF* rather than in the port area. The off-white *Hôtel le France* looks down on the canal from 30 rue Duguesclin (ⓣ02.99.71.06.11, ⓦhttp://lefrance.chez-alice.fr; ❷); its renovated rooms, nearly all of which have en-suite bathrooms, offer a considerable degree of comfort for the price. Nearer the station, the *Hôtel Chandouineau*, 1 rue Thiers (ⓣ02.99.71.02.04; ❺; closed Sat & Sun eve), is an upmarket establishment with just seven bedrooms, where the restaurant serves gourmet menus from €23.

The southern coast

Brittany's **southern coast** is best known for the province's – and indeed mainland Europe's – most famous prehistoric site, the alignments of **Carnac**, with the associated megaliths of the beautiful, island-studded **Golfe de Morbihan**. The beaches are not as spectacular as in Finistère, but there are more safe places to swim and the water is warmer. Of the cities, **Lorient** has Brittany's most compelling **festival** and **Vannes** has one of the liveliest medieval town centres. Further east, **La Baule** does a good impression of a Breton St-Tropez, and you can escape to the islands of **Belle-Île**, **Hoëdic** and **Houat**. Inevitably it's popular, and in summer you can be hard-pressed to find a room, but if you're prepared to make reservations, or you're camping, there shouldn't be much problem.

Lorient and around

LORIENT, Brittany's fourth largest city, lies on an immense natural harbour protected from the ocean by the Île de Groix and strategically located at the junction of the rivers Scorff, Ter and Blavet. A functional, rather depressing port today, it was once a key base for French colonialism, and was founded in the mid-seventeenth century for trading operations by the Compagnie des Indes, an equivalent of the Dutch and English East India Companies. Apart from the name, little else remains to suggest the plundered wealth that once arrived here. During the last war, Lorient was a major target for the Allies, but the Germans held out until the very end, and by the time they surrendered in May 1945 the city was almost completely destroyed. The only substantial remains were the U-boat pens, which have subsequently been expanded by the French for their nuclear submarines.

A former fishing trawler moored in the pleasure port, **La Thalassa**, now serves as an interactive museum of the ocean-going experience (July & Aug daily 9am–7pm; Sept–June Mon & Sun 2–6pm, Tues–Fri 9am–12.30pm & 2–6pm; €6.60). Different areas of its various decks aim to illustrate the lives of the ship's captain, those responsible for sailing it and fishing from it, and also of an scientific oceanographer.

Across the estuary in **Port-Louis**, the **Musée de la Compagnie des Indes** is a pretty dismal temple to imperialism (Feb–March daily except Tues 2–6pm; April to mid-May daily except Tues 10am–1pm & 2–6.30pm; mid-May to Aug daily 10am–6.30pm; Sept to mid-Dec daily except Tues 1.30–6pm; €5.50; ⓣ02.97.82.19.13; ⓦwww.lorient.com/musee). Time would be more enjoyably spent on a boat trip, either up the estuary towards **Hennebont** or out to the **Île de Groix**. This eight-kilometre-long steep-sided rock is a somewhat smaller version of Belle-Île, and holds some gorgeous beaches to encourage day-trippers.

Lorient's **tourist office**, beside the pleasure port on the quai de Rohan (mid-May to mid-July and late Aug to late Sept, Mon–Fri 10am–noon & 2–6pm, Sat 10am–noon & 2–5pm; mid-July to late Aug Mon–Sat 9.30am–1pm & 2–7pm, Sun 10am–1pm, except during festival, when it's daily 9am–8pm; late Sept to mid-May Mon–Fri 10am–noon & 2–5pm, Sat 10am–1pm; ⓣ02.97.21.07.84,

The Inter-Celtic Festival

The overriding reason people come to Lorient is for the **Inter-Celtic Festival**, held for ten days from the first Friday to the second Sunday in August. This is the biggest Celtic event in Brittany, or anywhere else for that matter, with representation from all the Celtic nations of Europe – Brittany, Ireland, Scotland, Wales, Cornwall, the Isle of Man, Asturias and Galicia. In a genuine celebration of cultural solidarity, well over a quarter of a million people come to more than a hundred different shows, five languages mingle, and Scotch and Guinness flow with French and Spanish wines and ciders. There is a certain competitive element, with championships in various categories, but the feeling of mutual enthusiasm and conviviality is paramount. Most of the activities – embracing music, dance and literature – take place around the central place Jules-Ferry, and this is where most people end up sleeping, too, as accommodation is stretched to the limit.

For **schedules** of the festival, and further details of temporary accommodation, contact the Festival Interceltique de Lorient, 2 rue Paul-Bert, 56100 Lorient (Ⓣ02.97.21.24.29, Ⓦwww.festival-interceltique.com), bearing in mind that the festival programme is not finalized until May each year. For certain events you need to reserve tickets well in advance.

Ⓦwww.lorient-tourisme.fr), can provide full details on local boat trips and organizes some excursions itself. Unless you arrive during the festival (see box), there's a huge choice of **hotels**. Among reasonable, fairly central options are two on rue Lazare-Carnot as it curves away south of the tourist office: the *Victor Hugo Hôtel* at no. 36 (Ⓣ02.97.21.16.24; ❸), which offers an action-packed €18 menu; and the *Hôtel d'Arvor* at no. 104 (Ⓣ02.97.21.07.55; ❷), also with a good-value restaurant. There's also an appealing (if noisy) **hostel** (Ⓣ02.97.37.11.65, Ⓔlorient@fuaj.org; €11.50), next to the River Ter at 41 rue Victor-Schoelcher, 3km out on bus line C1 from the *gare SNCF*, which has space for **camping** as well in summer. Good central **restaurants** include *Yesterday's*, 1 cours de la Bôve (Ⓣ02.97.84.85.07), a brasserie near the town hall that serves an excellent €18 menu, and *Le Café Leffe* (Ⓣ02.97.21.21.30; closed Jan), in the same building as the tourist office, facing the port, which is particularly strong on seafood.

The Presqu'île de Quiberon

The **Presqu'île de Quiberon**, south of Carnac, is well worth visiting on its own merits; **Quiberon** is quite a lively port, and you can get boats out to the islands or walk the shores of this narrow peninsula. The ocean-facing shore, known as the **Côte Sauvage**, is a wild and highly unswimmable stretch, where the stormy seas look like flashing scenes of snowy mountain tops. The sheltered eastern side has safe and calm sandy beaches, and plenty of campsites.

Quiberon

Much of the peninsula has become built up over the years, but it still holds only one true town, **QUIBERON**, at its southern tip. Its most active area, **Port-Maria**, is home to the **gare maritime** for the islands of Belle-Île, Houat and Hoëdic, and also holds a fishing harbour that was once famous for its sardines. Stretching away to the east is a long curve of fine sandy beach, lined for several hundred yards with bars, cafés and restaurants. At its centre is a busy little park and miniature golf course, but few of the streets further back hold anything of great interest. The exception is the little hill that leads down to the port from the **gare SNCF**, where browsing around is rewarded with some surprisingly good clothes and antique shops.

Practicalities

In July and August, the special Tire Bouchon train links Quiberon's *gare SNCF*, which is a short way above the town proper, with Auray. Bus #1 (TIM; ⓣ02.97.24.26.20) runs right to the *gare maritime* from Vannes, via Auray and Carnac.

The **tourist office** at 14 rue de Verdun (July & Aug Mon–Sat 9am–7.30pm, Sun 10am–1pm & 2–7pm; Sept–June Mon–Sat 9.30am–12.30pm & 2–6pm; ⓣ08.25.13.56.00, ⓦwww.quiberon.com), downhill from the *gare SNCF*, has a 24hr computer terminal outside showing which hotels are full, hour by hour.

Accommodation

For most of the year, it's hard to get a **room** in Quiberon. In July and August, the whole peninsula is packed, while in winter it's so quiet that virtually all its facilities close down. The nicest area to stay is along the seafront in **Port-Maria**, where several good hotel-restaurants face the Belle-Île ferry terminal. The local **hostel**, the spartan *Filets Bleus*, inland at 45 rue du Roc'h-Priol (ⓣ02.97.50.15.54, ⓔquiberon@fuaj.org; €9.70; closed Oct–March), 1.5km southeast of the *gare SNCF*, also provides space for camping.

Bellevue rue de Tiviec ⓣ02.97.50.16.28, ⓦwww.bellevuequiberon.com. Relatively quiet Logis de France, set slightly back from the sea near the casino and 500m east of the port. Has its own pool and a restaurant where menus cost €20 and up. Closed Oct–March. ❺

Au Bon Accueil 6 quai de Houat ⓣ02.97.50.07.92. Seafront hotel that's Port-Maria's best option for budget travellers. The rooms are basic but inexpensive, and there's a good restaurant downstairs. Closed mid-Nov to mid-Feb. ❸

Le Neptune 4 quai de Houat ⓣ02.97.50.09.62. Very close to *Au Bon Accueil*, and significantly more luxurious; if you're happy to pay that bit extra, it's the best value around. All the rooms have either sea or garden views – some with private balconies – and there's a very good restaurant (see below). Closed Jan & Mon in low season. ❹

L'Océan 7 quai de l'Océan ⓣ02.97.50.07.58, ⓦwww.hotel-de-locean.com. Attractive little hotel in the port, with multicoloured pastel shutters; no restaurant, but reasonably priced rooms. Closed Oct–March. ❷–❹

Eating and drinking

The most appealing area to browse the menus is along the waterfront in Port-Maria, where a line of seafood **restaurants** compete to attract ferry passengers. For **cafés**, those by the long bathing beach are the most enjoyable, along with the old-fashioned *Café du Marché* next to the PTT.

La Chaumine 36 place de Manémeur ⓣ02.97.50.17.67. Manémeur is technically a separate village to Quiberon, though it's not too far to walk around the headland west of the port. Set close to the menhir in the main square, this lovely little fish restaurant serves menus from €14 to €45, with an €23.50 option featuring salmon braised in champagne. Closed Sun eve & Mon, plus mid-Nov to March.

De la Criée 11 quai de l'Océan ⓣ02.97.30.53.09. A truly superb local fish restaurant, serving changing fish specialities every day, fresh from the morning's catch; make your choice from the baskets arrayed along the front. For €16 you get either the one set menu, which may include ling and sea bass, for example, and fish smoked on the premises, or a great seafood cous-cous. Closed Sun eve & Mon in low season, plus Jan.

Le Neptune 4 quai de Houat ⓣ02.97.50.09.62. Hotel dining room that serves exceptionally good seafood menus at €18 and €27. The portions are small, but the food is exquisite. Closed Jan & Mon in low season.

Belle-Île

The island of **BELLE-ÎLE**, 45 minutes by ferry from Quiberon, has its own Côte Sauvage on its Atlantic coast, while the landward side is fertile, cultivated ground, interrupted by deep estuaries with tiny ports. To appreciate the island's contrasts, some form of transport is advisable – you can **rent bikes** at the port and main town of **LE PALAIS**, and if you're in a small car the ferry fare is relatively low.

The island once belonged to the monks of Redon, then to the ambitious Nicolas Fouquet, Louis XIV's minister, and later to the English, who in 1761 swapped it for Menorca in an unrepeatable bargain deal. Docking at Le Palais, the abrupt star-shaped fortifications of the **citadelle** are the first thing you see (daily: April–June, Sept & Oct 9.30am–6pm; July & Aug 9am–7pm; Nov–March 9.30am–noon & 2–5pm; €6.10). Built along stylish and ordered lines by the great fortress-builder, Vauban, it is startling in size – filled with doorways leading to mysterious cellars and underground passages, endless sequences of rooms, dungeons and deserted cells. It only ceased being a prison in 1961, having numbered a succession of state enemies and revolutionaries among its inmates, including Ben Bella of Algeria. Less involuntarily, painters such as Monet and Matisse, the writers Flaubert and Proust and the actress Sarah Bernhardt all spent time on the island. And presumably Alexandre Dumas, too, as Porthos's death, in *The Three Musketeers*, takes place here. A **museum** documents the island's history, in fiction as much as in fact.

As for exploring the island, it's far too large to walk round, but a coastal footpath does run on bare soil for the length of the **Côte Sauvage**. Near the west end you'll find the **Grotte de l'Apothicairerie**, so called because it was once full of cormorants' nests, arranged like the jars on a pharmacist's shelves. Inland, on the D25 back towards Le Palais, you pass the two **menhirs**, Jean and Jeanne, said to be lovers petrified as punishment for wanting to meet before their marriage. Another larger menhir used to lie near these two; it was broken up to help construct the road that separates them.

Belle-Île's second town, **SAUZON**, is a beautiful little village arrayed along one side of a long estuary, 6km west of Le Palais. If you're staying any length of time, and you've got transport, it's a nicer place to base yourself.

Getting to Belle-Île

Throughout the year, the Société Morbihannaise et Nantaise de Navigation (ⓣ08.20.05.60.00, or, if you're calling from outside France, ⓣ02.97.35.02.00, ⓦwww.smn-navigation.fr) sends at least five **ferries** daily from **Port-Maria**, on the Quiberon peninsula, to **Le Palais**. The first departure each day is almost always at 8am, and the crossing normally takes 45 minutes, though between May and September the high-speed *Locmaria 56* makes three daily crossings in just 20 minutes. The standard adult return fare is €24.62, rising to €27.24 for the high-speed trip; under-25s pay €14.86 or €16.49; and over-60s €16.83 or €17.59. Small cars can be taken on the slower crossings only, for €116.28 return, while bikes cost €14.46 return.

Between early July and the end of August, the same company also sends the *Locmaria 56* on one daily return trip to **Sauzon** from **Lorient**, departing at 8.20am from Lorient's *gare maritime* and taking 1 hour to get there. Adults pay

€28.52 return, under-25s €19.96; there are no reductions for over-60s, and no vehicles can be taken.

During the summer, for similar fares, Compagnie des Îles (ⓣ02.97.46.18.19 ⓦwww.compagniedesiles.com) sails direct to **Le Palais** from **La Turballe**, with connecting services from **Le Croisic** as well, while Navix (ⓣ02.97.46.60.00, ⓦwww.navix.fr) also operate day-trips to the island from **Vannes**, **Port-Navalo** and **La Trinité**.

Belle-Île practicalities

The island's **tourist office** is next to the **gare maritime** in Le Palais (July & Aug Mon–Sat 8.45am–7.30pm, Sun 8.45am–1pm; Sept–June Mon–Sat 9am–12.30pm & 2–6pm; ⓣ02.97.31.81.93, ⓦwww.belle-ile.com).

Accommodation in Le Palais includes the simple *Frégate*, above a nice little bar on the quayside (ⓣ02.97.31.54.16; ❷; closed mid-Nov to March), and a couple of more expensive options: the *Hôtel-Restaurant de Bretagne* (ⓣ02.97.31.80.14, ⓦwww.hotel-de-bretagne.fr; ❹), and the *Atlantique* (ⓣ02.97.31.80.11, ⓦwww.hotel-atlantique.com; ❹), both of which have excellent sea-view **restaurants**. There are also three **campsites**, including the three-star *Camping de l'Océan* (ⓣ02.97.31.83.86, ⓦwww.camping-ocean-belle-ile.com; closed mid-Nov to March), and a **hostel** (ⓣ02.97.31.81.33, ⓔbelle-ile@fuaj.org; €11.50; closed Oct) which, despite holding almost a hundred beds, is always wildly oversubscribed; it's located a short way out of town along the clifftops from the citadelle at Haute-Boulogne.

Sauzon has one good hotel in a magnificent setting, the *Du Phare* (ⓣ02.97.31.60.36; ❸; closed Oct–March), where guests must eat its delicious fish dinners, and two two-star **campsites**, *Pen Prad* (ⓣ02.97.31.64.82, ⓔmariedesauzon@orange.fr; closed Oct–March) and *La Source* (ⓣ02.97.31.60.95, ⓦwww.belleile-lasource.com; closed late Sept to March).

Houat and Hoëdic

The islands of **Houat** and **Hoëdic** can also be reached by ferry from Quiberon-Port-Maria with the Société Morbihannaise et Nantaise de Navigation (1–6 sailings daily depending on the season; ⓣ08.20.05.60.00, or, from outside France, ⓣ02.97.35.02.00, ⓦwww.smn-navigation.fr; around €25 return). The crossing to Houat takes forty minutes, to Hoëdic another 25. Alternatively, Compagnie des Iles (ⓣ08.25.13.41.00, ⓦwww.compagniedesiles.com; €26.50 return) run similar trips from Vannes, Port-Navalo and Locmariaquer from April to September, and from Le Croisic and La Turballe in July and August; times vary. Finally, Navix (ⓣ02.97.46.60.00, ⓦwww.navix.fr; €26.50 return) run day-trips to Houat from **La Trinité** on most days between mid-July and late August.

You can't take your car to these two very much smaller versions of Belle-Île, and both have a feeling of being left behind by the passing centuries, although the younger fishermen of Houat have revived the island's fortunes by establishing a successful fishing co-operative. Houat in particular has excellent **beaches** – as ever on its sheltered (eastern) side – that fill up with campers in the summer even though camping is not strictly legal. Hoëdic on the other hand has a large municipal **campsite**, overlooking the port (ⓣ02.97.52.48.88; closed Sept–June). There are a couple of small **hotels** on Houat – *L'Ezenn* (ⓣ02.97.30.69.73; ❸; closed Feb) and the pricier *Hôtel-Restaurant des Îles* (ⓣ02.97.30.68.02; ❹; closed Nov–Easter) – and one on Hoëdic, *Les Cardinaux* (ⓣ02.97.52.37.27, ⓔlescardinaux@aol.com; ❹; closed Sun pm & Mon in winter).

Carnac and around

The **alignments** at **CARNAC** – rows of 2000 or so menhirs, or standing stones, stretching for over 4km to the north of the village – constitute the most important prehistoric site in Europe, long predating Knossos, the Pyramids, Stonehenge or the great Egyptian temples of the same name at Karnak. Mercifully, they now stand a few kilometres in from the sea, meaning you can combine a reasonably tranquil visit to the stones with a stay in the popular, modern seaside resort, pretty hectic by Brittany's mild standards.

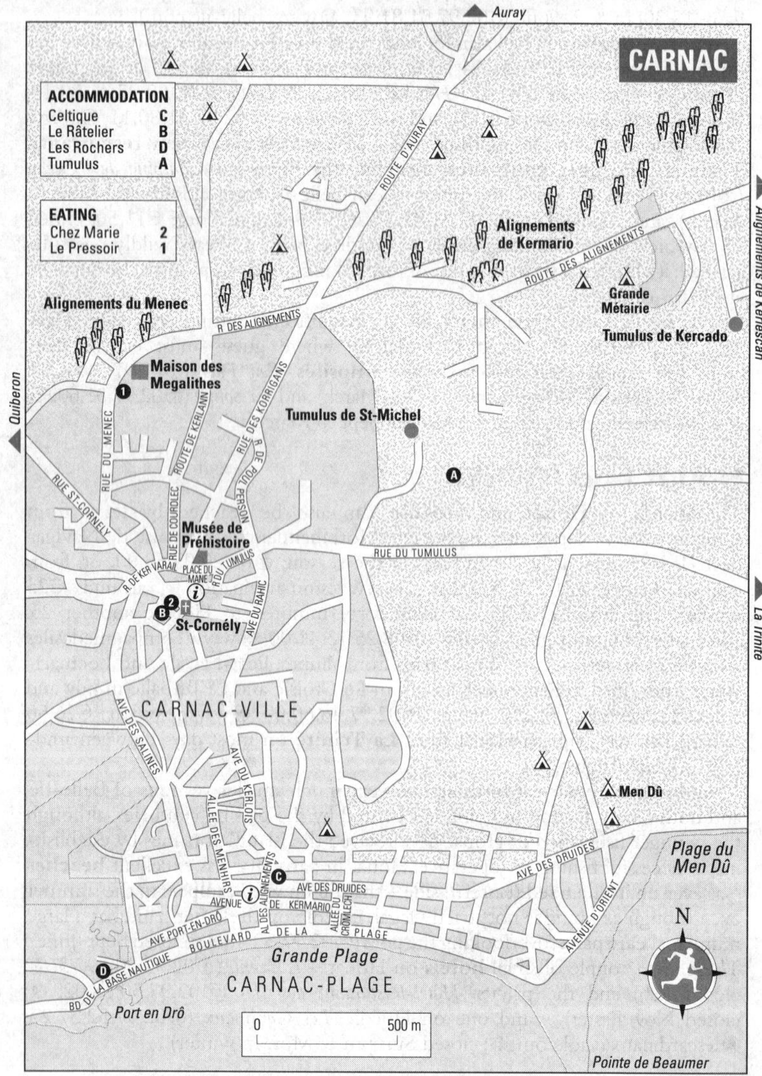

The alignments

The **megaliths** of Carnac make up three distinct major alignments, running roughly in the same northeast–southwest direction, but each with a slightly separate orientation. These are the **Alignements de Menec**, "the place of stones" or "place of remembrance", with 1169 stones in eleven rows; the **Alignements de Kermario**, "the place of the dead", with 1029 stones in ten rows; and the **Alignements de Kerlescan**, "the place of burning", with 555 stones in thirteen lines. All three are sited parallel to the sea alongside the **Route des Alignements**, 1km or so to the north of Carnac-Ville.

Thanks to increasing numbers of visitors (and despite vehement local opposition), the principal alignments are currently fenced off. The long-term plan is to allow the area to revegetate at a natural pace, but there's no predicting how long that process will take, and even when it's complete the chances are that access will still be restricted. Currently you are allowed to walk freely around the best-preserved sites from October to March (daily 10am–5pm); between April and September access is on guided tours only (€4), some of which are in English. To pick up the schedule of tours, examine a model of the entire site, and buy books and maps, call in at the official visitor centre, known as the **Maison des Mégalithes**, across the road from the Alignements de Menec (daily: May–Aug 9am–7pm; Sept–April 10am–5.15pm; ⓣ02.97.52.29.81).

The stones themselves are clearly visible behind the fences, though thanks to their destruction and displacement by generations of meddling humans, and several millennia of Breton winters, many look like no more than stumps in the heather. It has become hard to see any real consistency in the size or the shape of individual stones, or enough regularity in the lines to pinpoint their direction.

There are several distinct types of megalithic monuments. **Menhirs**, or "standing stones", range in size from mere stumps to five-metre-high blocks; some stand alone, others in circles known as **cromlechs**, or in approximate lines. In addition there are **dolmens**, groups of standing stones roofed with further stones laid across the top, which are generally assumed to be burial chambers.

Carnac's **Musée de Préhistoire**, at 10 place de la Chapelle in town (July & Aug Mon, Tues & Thurs–Sun 10am–6pm, Wed 1.30–6pm; May, June & Sept Mon & Thurs–Sun 10am–12.30pm & 2–6pm, Wed 2–6pm; Oct–April Mon & Thurs–Sun 10am–12.30pm & 2–5pm, Wed 2–5pm; €5; ⓦwww.museedecarnac.com), is a disappointingly dry museum of archeology that's likely to leave anyone whose command of French is less than perfect almost completely in the dark as to what all the fuss is about. It traces the history of the area from earliest times, starting with 450,000-year-old chipping tools and leading by way of the Neanderthals to the megalith builders and beyond. As well as authentic physical relics, it holds reproductions and casts of the carvings at Locmariaquer, a scale model of the Alignements de Menec and diagrams of how the stones may have been moved into place.

The Town

Carnac itself, divided between the original **Carnac-Ville** and the seaside resort of **Carnac-Plage**, is extremely popular and swarms with holiday-makers in July and August. For most of these, the alignments are, if anything, only a sideshow. But, as a holiday centre, Carnac has a special charm, especially in late spring and early autumn when it is less crowded – and cheaper. The town and seafront remain well wooded, and the tree-lined avenues and gardens are a delight, the climate being mild enough for evergreen oak and Mediterranean mimosa to grow alongside native stone pine and cypress.

The megaliths of Brittany

Megalithic sites can be found all around the Mediterranean, notably in Malta and Sardinia, and along the Atlantic seaboard from Spain to Scandinavia. Among the most significant are Newgrange in Ireland, Stonehenge in England and the Ring of Brodgar in the Orkneys. However, the megalith-building culture did not necessarily originate in the Mediterranean and spread to the "barbarian" outposts of Europe. In fact, the tumuli, alignments and single standing stones of Brittany are of pre-eminent importance.

Archeological evidence suggests that late **Stone Age settlements** existed along the Breton coast by around 6000 BC. Soon afterwards, the culture responsible either evolved to become the megalith builders, or was displaced by megalith-building newcomers. Dated at 5700 BC, the tumulus of Kercado at Carnac appears to be the earliest stone construction in Europe.

Each megalithic centre had its own distinct styles and traditions. Brittany has relatively few stone circles, and a greater proportion of free-standing stones; fewer burials, and more evidence of ritual fires; different styles of carving; and, uniquely, the sheer complexity of the Carnac alignments. Little is known of the people who erected the megaliths. Only rarely have skeletons been found in the graves, but what few there have been seem to indicate a short, dark, hairy race with a life expectancy of no more than the mid-thirties. What is certain is that the civilization was a long-lasting one; the earliest and the latest constructions at Carnac are over five thousand years apart.

As for the actual **purpose** of the megaliths, the most fashionable theory these days sees them as part of a vast system of astronomical measurement, record-keeping, and prediction. In Brittany, the argument goes, the now fallen Grand Menhir of Locmariaquer served as a "universal lunar foresight", its alignments with eight other sites corresponding to the eight extreme points of the rising and setting of the moon during its 18.61-year cycle. The Golfe de Morbihan made an ideal location for such a marking stone, set on a lagoon surrounded by low peninsulas. Once the need for the Grand Menhir was decided upon, it would have taken hundreds of years of careful observation of the moon to fix the exact spot for it. It's thought that this was done by lighting fires on the top of high poles at trial points on the crucial nights every nine years. The alignments of Carnac are thus explained as the graph paper on which the lunar movements were plotted.

However, this has been hotly disputed. Controversy rages as to whether the Grand Menhir ever stood at all, or, even if it did, whether it fell or was broken up before the eight supposedly associated sites came into being; moreover, sceptics say, these measurements ignore the fact that the sea level in southern Brittany 6600 years ago was 10m lower than it is today.

In any case, the stones at Carnac have been so greatly eroded that perhaps it's little more than wishful thinking to imagine that their original size, shape and orientation can be accurately determined. They have been knocked down by farmers seeking to cultivate the land; quarried for use in making roads; removed by landowners angry at the trespass of tourists and scientists; and shifted and re-erected by nineteenth-century pseudo-scientists.

An alternative approach places greater emphasis on sociological factors. This argues that the stones date from the period of transition when humankind was changing from a predatory role to a productive one, and that they can only have been put in place by the co-ordinated efforts of a large and stable **community**. It's possible that the megaliths were erected by Neolithic settlers, who generation by generation advanced across Europe from the east bringing advances in agriculture. As they came into conflict with existing Stone Age groups, they may have set up menhirs as territorial markers.

It also makes sense to imagine setting up a menhir as serving a valuable social purpose, both as an achievement in its own right and as a celebration of some other event. The annual or occasional setting-up of a new stone is easier to envisage than the vast effort required to erect them all at once – in which case the fact that they were arranged in lines, mounds and circles might have been of peripheral importance.

The town's five **beaches** extend for nearly 3km in total. The two most attractive beaches, usually counted as one of the five, are **plages Men Dû** and **Beaumer**, which lie to the east towards La Trinité beyond Pointe Churchill. They're especially popular these days with **kite surfers**.

Practicalities

Buses to Auray, Quiberon and Vannes stop near the tourist office on avenue des Druides, and on rue St-Cornély in Carnac-Ville. In July and August, when the Tire Bouchon **rail** link runs between Auray and Quiberon, trains call at Plouharnel, 4km northwest of Carnac. Carnac's main **tourist office** is slightly back from the main beach at 74 av des Druides (July & Aug Mon & Sat 9am–7pm, Tues–Fri 9am–1pm & 2–7pm, Sun 3–7pm; Sept–June Mon–Sat 9.30am–12.30pm & 2–6pm; ⓣ02.97.52.13.52, ⓦwww.carnac.fr). An annexe in the place de l'Église in town is open in summer (April–Sept Mon–Sat 9.30am–12.30pm & 2–6pm). **Bicycles** can be rented from several local campsites, or from Le Randonneur, 20 av des Druides, Carnac-Plage (ⓣ02.97.52.02.55). The *Grande Métairie* site (see below) also arranges horseback tours. There's a **market** in Carnac-Ville on Wednesday and Sunday mornings.

Hotels in Carnac are at a premium in July and August, when you can expect higher prices and intense pressure to take half-board (*demi-pension*). In **Carnac-Ville**, the old stone, ivy-clad *Hôtel le Râtelier*, 4 chemin de Douët (ⓣ02.97.52.05.04, ⓦwww.le-ratelier.com; ❸–❹; restaurant closed Tues & Wed Oct–March), has rooms of varying standards, not all en suite, and top-quality food on menus that start from €17; the fancier *Hôtel Tumulus*, east of town on the Chemin du Tumulus (ⓣ02.97.52.08.21, ⓦwww.hotel-tumulus.com; ❾; closed Jan–March), has a heated pool and another fine restaurant. The *Hôtel Celtique*, at 82 av des Druides in **Carnac-Plage** (ⓣ02.97.52.14.15, ⓦwww.hotel-celtique.com; ❺), is similarly luxurious, while several rooms at *Les Rochers*, 6 bd de la Base Nautique (ⓣ02.97.52.10.09, ⓦwww.les-rochers.com; ❻; closed Nov–Easter), have sea-view balconies. As befits such a family-oriented place, Carnac features as many as twenty **campsites**. Among the best are the two-star *Men Dû* (ⓣ02.97.52.04.23, ⓦwww.camping-mendu.fr; closed Oct–March) near the sea, inland from the plage du Men Dû, and the more expensive four-star *Grande Métairie* (ⓣ02.97.52.24.01, ⓦwww.lagrandemetairie.com; closed early Sept to March), near the Kercado tumulus. Most of the **restaurants** worth recommending are in the hotels, as described above, but *Chez Marie*, facing St-Cornély church at 3 place de l'Église (ⓣ02.97.52.07.93; closed Nov–Easter), and the *Pressoir* by the Ménec *alignements* (ⓣ02.97.52.01.86; closed Sept–Easter) are worthwhile crêperies.

Locmariaquer

With its complex patterning, the stone of the roof on Gavrinis (see p.479) has been identified as part of the same piece as the dolmen known as the **Table des Marchands** at **LOCMARIAQUER**, 12km east of Carnac. Locmariaquer also has the **Grand Menhir Brisé**, supposedly the crucial central point of the megalithic observatory of Carnac. Thought to have been toppled deliberately around the time the Table des Marchands was erected, it was by far the largest known menhir – 22m high and weighing more than a full jumbo jet at 347 tonnes. It now lies on the ground in four pieces, with a possible fifth missing, and is visited in conjunction with the Table des Marchands (daily: May–Sept

10am–7pm; Sept–April 10am–12.30pm & 2–5.15pm; €5, under-18s free; €7 with tour of Carnac).

Locmariaquer boasts a couple of reasonable small **hotels**, both with good restaurants: *L'Escale* (Ⓣ02.97.57.32.51; ❸; closed mid-Sept to mid-April), is right on the waterfront, with a great view from its terrace, while the *Lautram* is set slightly back from the sea, facing the church (Ⓣ02.97.57.31.32; ❸; closed Oct–March). **Campsites** include the excellent *Ferme Fleurie* (Ⓣ02.97.57.34.06; closed Dec–Jan), 1km towards Kerinis, and the *Lann Brick* (Ⓣ02.97.57.32.79, Ⓦwww.camping-lannbrick.com; closed Nov to mid-March), 1.5km further on, nearer the beach. Both are two-stars.

Vannes

Thanks to its position at the head of the Golfe de Morbihan, **VANNES**, 20km east of Auray, is southern Brittany's major tourist town. Modern Vannes is such a large and thriving community that the small size of the old walled town at its core, **Vieux Vannes**, may well come as a surprise. Its focal point, the old gateway of the **Porte St-Vincent**, commands a busy little square at the northern end of the long canalized port that provides access to the gulf itself. Once inside the ramparts, the old centre of chaotic streets – crammed around the cathedral, and enclosed by gardens and a tiny stream – is largely pedestrianized, in refreshing contrast to the somewhat insane road system beyond.

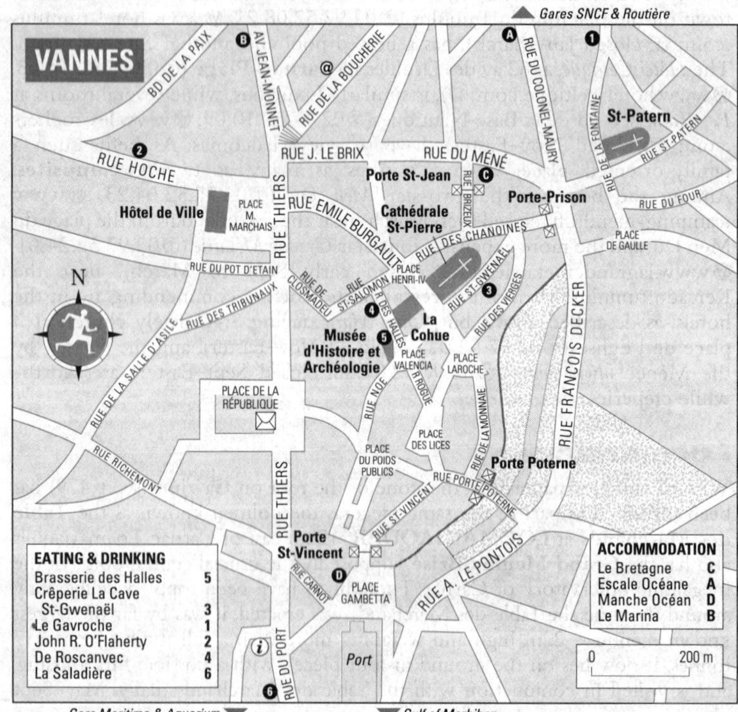

Arrival, information and accommodation

Vannes' **gare SNCF** is 25 minutes' walk north of the town centre. Buses to Auray, Carnac, Quiberon and other destinations leave from the **gare routière** alongside. The **tourist office** is at 1 rue Thiers (July & Aug Mon–Sat 9am–7pm, Sun 10am–6pm; Sept–June Mon–Sat 9.30am–12.30pm & 2–6pm; ⓣ08.25.13.56.10, ⓦwww.tourisme-vannes.com), near place Gambetta. **Internet access** is available at Futur I-Media, 14 rue de la Boucherie (Mon–Fri noon–1am, Sat & Sun 2pm–1am; ⓣ02.97.01.84.09; €4 per hr).

In peak season, Vannes can get claustrophobic, but it offers a better choice of **hotels** than anywhere else around the gulf. The town also has a **hostel**, 4km southeast of the town centre in Séné (ⓣ02.97.66.94.25, ⓔcis.sene@orange.fr; dorm bed €10.50; closed July & Aug), on bus route #4 from place de la République. The nearest **campsite** is the three-star *Camping Conleau* at the far end of avenue du Maréchal-Juin, alongside the gulf beyond the aquarium (ⓣ02.97.63.13.88, ⓔcamping@mairie-vannes.fr; closed Oct–March).

Hotels

Le Bretagne 36 rue du Méné ⓣ02.97.47.20.21, ⓔhotel-lebretagne@free.fr. Reasonable hotel just outside the walls, around the corner from the Porte-Prison. The rooms aren't fancy, but all have showers or bath plus TV. ❷

Escale Océane av Jean-Monnet ⓣ02.97.47.59.60, ⓦwww.hotel-sofibra.com. Functional upscale hotel a short walk northwest of the walled town, formerly known as the *Mascotte*, and offering 65 soundproofed, en-suite and air-conditioned rooms, plus an adequate restaurant. ❺

Manche Océan 31 rue du Col-Maury ⓣ02.97.47.26.46, ⓦwww.manche-ocean.com. Ordinary but perfectly acceptable modern rooms between the station and the walled town, used mainly by tour groups. Small-scale buffet breakfasts for €8. ❻

Le Marina 4 place Gambetta ⓣ02.97.47.00.10, ⓔlemarinahotel@aol.com. Fifteen pleasantly refurbished rooms – and a downstairs bar – right by the port, with sea views and morning sun. En-suite facilities cost €5 extra. ❸

The Town

Modern Vannes centres on **place de la République**; the focus was shifted outside the medieval city in the nineteenth-century craze for urbanization. The grandest of the public buildings here, guarded by a pair of sleek and dignified bronze lions, is the **Hôtel de Ville** at the top of rue Thiers. By day, however, the streets of the old city, with their overhanging, witch-hatted houses and busy commercial life, are the chief source of pleasure. **Place Henri-IV** in particular is stunning, as are the views from it down the narrow side streets.

La Cohue, a building that fills a block between rue des Halles and place St-Pierre, has served over the past 750 years as High Court and assembly room, prison, Revolutionary tribunal, theatre and marketplace, and was where the Breton *États* assembled in 1532 to ratify the Act of Union with France. It currently houses the **Musée des Beaux-Arts** (daily: July–Sept 10am–6pm; Oct–June 1.30–6pm; €4, or €6 with history museum). Upstairs there's a dull collection of paintings and engravings, heavy on worthy Breton artists such as J.-F. Boucher and Jean Frélaut, while the main gallery downstairs is the venue for different temporary exhibitions.

Opposite La Cohue, the **Cathédrale St-Pierre** is a rather forbidding place, with a stern main altar almost imprisoned by four solemn grey pillars. The light – purple through new stained glass – illuminates the desiccated finger of the Blessed Pierre Rogue, who was guillotined on the main square in 1796. For a small fee, in summer you can examine the assorted treasures in the chapterhouse, which include a twelfth-century wedding chest, brightly decorated with enigmatic scenes of romantic chivalry.

A sombre fifteenth-century private mansion at 2 rue Noé holds Vannes' **Musée d'Histoire et Archéologie** (mid-May to mid-June daily 1.30–6pm, mid-June to Sept daily 10am–6pm; otherwise by appointment only, ⓣ02.97.01.63.00; €4, or €6 with Beaux-Arts museum). Until recently, it was solely an archeological museum, focused on what's said to be one of the world's finest collections of prehistoric artefacts. However, although it certainly holds some elegant stone axes, for example, they're simply arrayed in formal patterns in glass cases, and the upper floors of the museum, designed to illustrate daily life in the Middle Ages, are more entertaining.

Vannes' modern **aquarium** (daily: April–June & Sept 10am–noon & 2–6pm; July & Aug 9am–7pm; Oct–March 2–6pm, except school hols 10am–noon & 2–6pm; adults €8.90, under-12s €5.90; ⓣ08.10.40.69.01, ⓦwww.aquarium-du-golfe.com), in the **Parc du Golfe**, 500m south of place Gambetta, claims to have the best collection of tropical fish in Europe. Certainly it holds some pretty extraordinary specimens, including four-eyed fish from Venezuela that can see simultaneously above and below the water, and are also divided into four sexes for good measure; cave fish from Mexico that by contrast have no eyes at all; and *arowana* from Guyana, which jump two metres out of the water to catch birds. A Nile crocodile found in the Paris sewers in 1984 shares its tank with a group of piranhas. Alongside, the separate **Jardin aux Papillons**, or Butterfly Garden, consists of a huge glass dome containing hundreds of free-flying butterflies (same hours; adults €7.50, under-12s €5.50, or €13 and €9 respectively for combined ticket with aquarium).

Eating, drinking and entertainment

Dining out in old Vannes can be an expensive experience, whether you eat in the intimate little restaurants along the rue des Halles, or down by the port. If you're just looking for a snack, try the area outside the walls in the northeast, towards the *gare SNCF*. The leading venue for **live music** is the *John R. O'Flaherty*, at 22 rue Hoche (ⓣ02.97.42.40.11; closed Sun), which has traditional Irish music on Fridays. At the end of July, the open-air concerts of the **Vannes Jazz Festival** take place in the Théâtre de Verdure.

Brasserie des Halles 9 rue des Halles ⓣ02.97.54.08.34. Inexpensive brasserie, open until midnight, which manages to squeeze a few tables out onto the pavement. For €9 you can get a bowl of mussels, for €17.50 a seafood *choucroute*, and there's a wide range of mainly fishy dishes at similar prices. Closed Sat lunch & Sun eve.

Crêperie La Cave St-Gwenaël 23 rue St-Gwenaël ⓣ02.97.47.47.94. Atmospheric, good-value crêperie in the cellar of a lovely old house, facing the cathedral. Closed Sun, plus Mon Sept–June, & all Jan.

Le Gavroche 17 rue de la Fontaine Pasteur ⓣ02.97.54.03.54. A true godsend for meat-lovers, where you can feast on excellent meat-packed menus starting at a mere €13.75. The steaks are cooked to perfection, while starters such as pig's trotters will put hairs on your chest. Closed Sun, Mon & Wed eve.

De Roscanvec 17 rue des Halles ⓣ02.97.47.15.96. Absolutely superb formal gourmet restaurant, in a lovely half-timbered house in the old town, with dining on two levels and also outdoors. Lunch at €17 is a bargain, while even the cheapest dinner menu, at €24, features unusual dishes such as *carbonara d'huîtres*, beautifully prepared and presented. Menus go all the way up to €74 for a lobster special. Closed Sun in summer, Sun eve & all Mon Sept–June.

La Saladière 36 rue du Port ⓣ02.97.42.52.10. Tasty, healthy fresh-made salads, in an inexpensive restaurant a short way down from the tourist office, with views towards the port. Closed Sun & Wed eve in low season.

The Golfe de Morbihan

It comes as rather a surprise to discover that Vannes is on the sea. Its harbour is a channelled inlet of the ragged-edged **Golfe de Morbihan** – *mor bihan* means "little sea" in Breton – which lets in the tides through a narrow gap between the peninsulas of **Rhuys** and **Locmariaquer**. By popular tradition the **islands** scattered around this enclosure used to number the days of the year, though for centuries the waters have been rising and there are now fewer than one for each week. Of these, thirty are owned by film stars and the like, while two – the **Île aux Moines** and **Île d'Arz** – have regular populations and ferry services and end up extremely crowded in summer. The rest are the best, and a **boat tour** around them, or at least a trip out to **Gavrinis** near the mouth of the gulf, is a compelling attraction. As the boats thread their way through the baffling muddle of channels, you lose track of what is island and what is mainland; and everywhere there are megalithic ruins, stone circles disappearing beneath the water and solitary menhirs on small hillocks.

Gavrinis

The reason to visit the island of **Gavrinis**, which can only be reached on guided boat tours from Larmor-Baden, is its **megalithic site**. The most impressive and

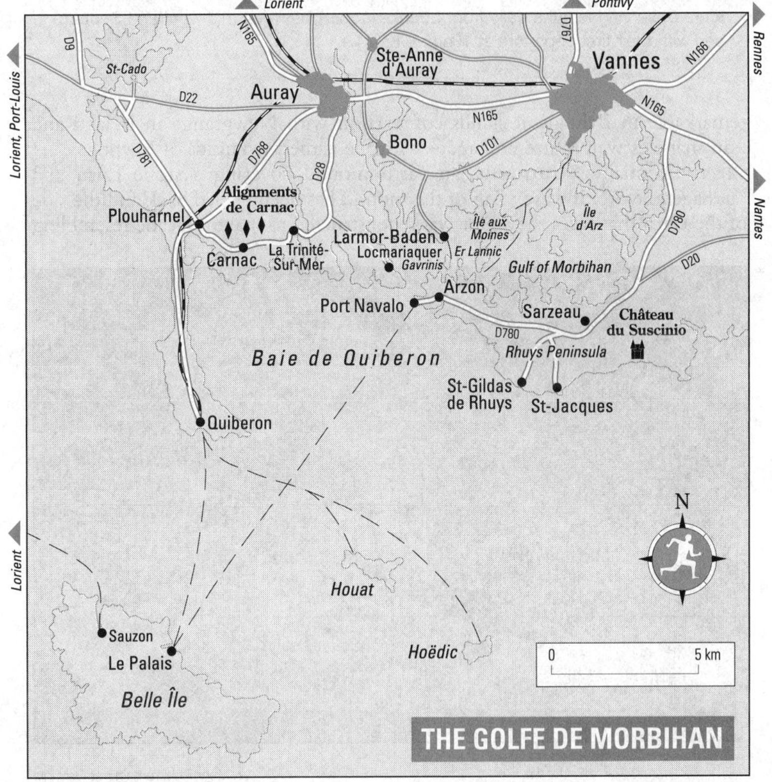

Gulf tours

In season, dozens of boats leave on **gulf tours** each day from Vannes, Port Navalo, La Trinité, Locmariaquer, Auray, Le Bono and Larmor-Baden. These are among the options:

Navix Ⓦ www.navix.fr. Up to six deluxe half-day (€21) and full-day (€28) tours around the gulf from Vannes (Ⓣ08.25.13.21.00) every day between mid-April and September. From mid-April until late June the first boat sails each day at 8.45am; it's at 9am until late Aug, and then at 10am until the end of Sept. They also offer lunch and dinner cruises to varying schedules. During the same period, similar tours also depart from Port Navalo (Ⓣ08.25.13.21.20) and Locmariaquer (Ⓣ08.25.13.21.30), while trips leave from Auray or Le Bono (Ⓣ08.25.13.21.50), and La Trinité (Ⓣ08.25.13.21.50) between early July and late August only.

Compagnie des Îles Ⓦ www.compagniedesiles.com. At least three gulf tours daily from **Vannes** between April and October (Ⓣ08.25.13.41.00; €15–28), plus slightly more limited schedules from Port Navalo (Ⓣ08.25.13.41.20; mid-April to Sept; €15–28); Locmariaquer (Ⓣ08.25.13.41.30; April–Oct €13.50–23); and Port Haliguen in Quiberon (Ⓣ08.25.13.41.40; April–Sept; €13.50–28).

Izenah Croisières Ⓣ02.97.57.23.24 or 02.97.26.31.45, Ⓦ www.izenah-croisieres.com. Gulf tours from Port Blanc at Baden in summer (April–Sept; €14–22) and a year-round ferry service, with departures every half-hour, to the Île aux Moines (daily: July & Aug 7am–10pm, Sept–June 7am–7.30pm; €3.80 return).

Vedettes Angelus Ⓣ02.97.57.30.29, Ⓦ www.vedettes-angelus.com. Up to five gulf tours of varying lengths daily from **Locmariaquer**, between mid-April and September, with their first departure at 10am; €12–24.

remarkable in Brittany, it stands comparison with Newgrange in Ireland and – in shape as well as size and age – with the earliest pyramids of Egypt.

It is essentially a **tumulus**, an earth mound covering a stone cairn and "passage grave". However, half of the mound has been peeled back and the side of the cairn that faces the water was reconstructed to make a facade resembling

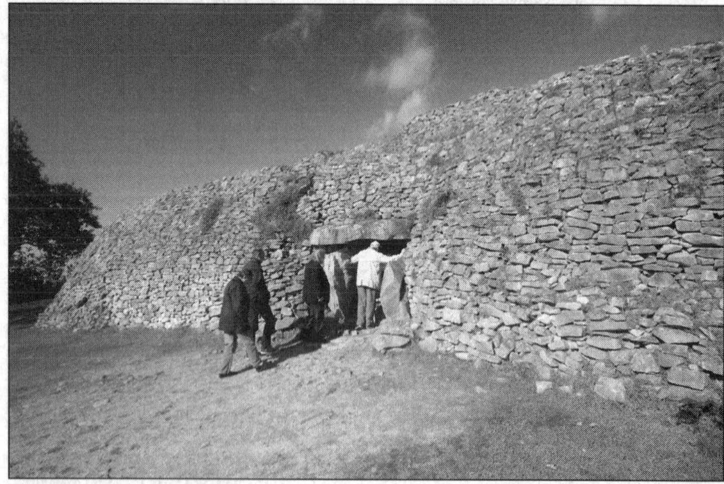

△ Megalithic remains at Gavrinis

a step-pyramid. Inside, every stone of both passage and chamber is covered in carvings, with a restricted "alphabet" of fingerprint whorls, axe-heads and other conventional signs, including the spirals familiar in Ireland but seen only here in Brittany.

Gavrinis can be reached between March and November only. Tides permitting, **ferries** leave Larmor-Baden at half-hourly intervals, and the cost includes a guided tour of the cairn (April, June & Sept daily 9.30am–12.30pm & 1.30–6.30pm; May Mon–Fri 1.30–6.30pm, Sat & Sun 9.30am–12.30pm & 1.30–6.30pm; July & Aug daily 9.30am–12.30pm & 1.30–7pm; March, Oct & Nov daily except Wed 1.30–5pm; ⓣ02.97.57.19.38; €10). The last boat of the morning leaves Larmor-Baden at noon in July & Aug, and at 11am otherwise; the last afternoon boat leaves at 3pm or 3.30pm daily, depending on how busy things are.

The Presqu'île de Rhuys

The tip of the Presqu'île de Locmariaquer is only a few hundred metres away from Port Navalo and the **Presqu'île de Rhuys**. This peninsula has a micro-climate of its own – warm enough for pomegranates, figs, bougainvillea and the only Breton vineyards. Oysters are cultivated on the muddy gulf shores, but the currents of the gulf make this no place for swimming. The ocean beaches are the ones to head for: east from St-Gildas-de-Rhuys is the most enticing and least crowded stretch, with glittering gold- and silver-coloured rocks. For details on the whole peninsula, call in at the **information centre** just off the main road as you come into Sarzeau (Feb–June, Sept & Oct Mon–Sat 9.15am–12.15pm & 2–6pm, Sun 2–5.30pm; July & Aug daily 9am–7pm; Nov–Jan Mon–Sat 9.15am–12.15pm & 2–6pm; ⓣ02.97.26.45.26, ⓦwww.rhuys.com).

Near **SARZEAU**, the impressive fourteenth-century **Château de Suscinio** is a completely moated castle that was once a hunting lodge of the dukes of Brittany, set in marshland at the edge of a tiny village and holding a sagging but still vivid mosaic floor. You can take a precarious stroll around its high ramparts (April–Sept daily 10am–7pm; Oct & Feb–March daily except Wed 10am–noon & 2–6pm; Nov–Jan daily except Wed 10am–noon & 2–5pm; €5). At the beautifully positioned little *Hôtel Bar du Port* in **ST-JACQUES**, 6km south, (ⓣ02.97.41.93.51; ④), all seven rooms have balconies that look out across the port to the gulf.

South to the Loire

When you cross the **Vilaine** on the way south, you're not only leaving the Morbihan *département* but also technically leaving Brittany itself. The roads veer firmly east and west – to Nantes or **La Baule**, avoiding the marshes of the **Grande-Brière**. For centuries these 20,000 acres of peat bog have been deemed to be the common property of all who lived in them. The scattered population, the *Brièrois*, still make their living by fishing for eels in the streams, gathering reeds and – on the nine days permitted each year – cutting peat. Tourism has arrived relatively recently, and is resented. The touted attraction is renting a punt to get yourself lost for a few hours with your pole tangled in the rushes.

Guérande

On the edge of the marshes of the Grande-Brière, just before you come to the sea, stands the tiny, gorgeous walled town of **GUÉRANDE**. It gave its name to this peninsula, and derived its fortune from controlling the salt pans that form a chequerboard across the surrounding inlets. This "white country" is composed of bizarre-looking *oeillets*, each 70 to 80 square metres in extent, in which sea water has been collected and evaporated since Roman times.

Guérande today is still entirely enclosed by its stout fifteenth-century ramparts. Although you can't walk along them, a spacious promenade leads right the way around the outside, passing four fortified gateways; for half its length the broad old moat remains filled with water. The main entrance, the **Porte St-Michel** on the east side of town, now holds a small **museum** of local history (April–Sept Mon 2.30–7pm, Tues–Sun 10am–12.30pm & 2.30–7pm; Oct Mon 2–6pm, Tues–Sun 10am–noon & 2–6pm; €3.50).

Guérande's **tourist office** is just outside the Porte St-Michel at 1 place du Marché au Bois (June & Sept Mon–Sat 9.30am–12.30pm & 1.30–6pm, Sun 10am–1pm & 3–5pm; July & Aug Mon–Sat 9.30am–7pm, Sun 10am–1pm & 3–5pm; Oct–May Mon–Sat 9.30am–12.30pm & 1.30–6pm; ⓣ02.40.24.96.71, ⓦwww.ot-guerande.fr). Tucked out of sight behind the market, the pretty *Roc-Maria*, 1 rue des Halles (ⓣ02.40.24.90.51, ⓦwww.hotelcreperierocmaria.com; ④; closed Mon in low season), offers cosy **rooms** above a crêperie in a fifteenth-century town house. To the north, opposite the Porte Vannetoise and the most impressive stretch of ramparts, the *Hôtel des Voyageurs*, 1 place du 8 Mai 1945 (ⓣ02.40.24.90.13; ④; closed late Dec to late Jan, plus Sun eve & Mon), is a Logis serving good menus from €12.

La Baule

There is something very surreal about emerging from the Brière to the coast at **LA BAULE** – an imposing, moneyed landscape where the dunes are no longer bonded together with scrub and pines, but with massive apartment buildings and luxury hotels. Sited on the long stretch of dunes that links the former island of Le Croisic to the mainland, it owes its existence to a storm in 1779 that engulfed the old town of Escoublac in silt from the Loire, and thereby created a wonderful crescent of sandy beach.

Neither La Baule's permanence nor its affluence seems in any doubt these days. It's a resort that very firmly imagines itself in the south of France: around the crab-shaped bay, bronzed nymphettes and would-be Clint Eastwoods ride across the sands into the sunset against a backdrop of cruising lifeguards, horse-dung removers and fantastically priced cocktails. It can be fun if you feel like a break from the more subdued Breton attractions – and the beach is undeniably impressive. But it's not a place to enjoy strolling around in search of hidden charms; the backstreets have an oddly rural feel, but hold nothing of any interest.

La Baule has two **gare SNCF**s, the barely used La-Baule-les-Pins, and the main La-Baule-Escoublac near the tourist office on place Rhin-et-Danube, where the TGVs from Paris arrive. The **gare routière** is away from the seafront, at 4 place de la Victoire (ⓣ08.25.24.34.44), while the **tourist office** is nearby at 8 place de la Victoire (July & Aug daily 9.30am–7.30pm; Sept–June Mon & Wed–Sat 9.15am–12.30pm & 2–6pm, Tues 10.15am–12.30pm & 2–6pm, Sun 10am–1pm; ⓣ02.40.24.34.44, ⓦwww.labaule.fr).

Few of the **hotels** are at all cheap, particularly in high season, and in low season more than half are closed. Relatively lower-priced options near the main *gare SNCF* include the comfortable *Marini*, 22 av Clemenceau (ⓣ02.40.60.23.29, ⓦwww.hotel-marini.com; ⑤), while the *Mascotte*, 26 av Marie-Louise (ⓣ02.40.60.26.55, ⓦwww.la-mascotte.fr; ⑤; closed Dec–Feb), is a quieter and classier option less than 100m back from the beach. The finest of the many local **campsites**, 2km from the sea, is the four-star *La Roseraie*, 20 av Sohier (Ⓣ02.40.60.46.66, Ⓦwww.laroseraie.com; closed Oct–March).

Le Croisic

The small port of **LE CROISIC**, sheltering from the ocean around the corner of the headland, but stretching right across the peninsula, is a more attractive place to stay than La Baule. These days it's basically a pleasure port, but fishing boats do still sail from its harbour, near the very slender mouth of the bay, and there's a modern **fish market** near the long Tréhic jetty, where you can watch the day's catch being auctioned. The hills on either side of the harbour, Mont Lenigo and Mont Esprit, are not natural; they were formed from the ballast left by the ships of the salt trade. If you're staying, choose between the **hotels** *Castel Moor*, 500m beyond the town centre towards the end of the headland, on the sheltered side (Ⓣ02.40.23.24.18, Ⓦwww.castel-moor.com; ❹; closed Jan), or *Les Nids*, set slightly back from the ocean side of the peninsula at 15 rue Pasteur (Ⓣ02.40.23.00.63, Ⓦwww.hotellesnids.com; ❺; closed mid-Nov to early April), which has its own small indoor swimming pool. Both have good restaurants.

Close by, all around the rocky sea coast known as the **Grande Côte**, are a range of **campsites**, including the *Océan* (Ⓣ02.40.23.07.69, Ⓦwww.camping-ocean.com; closed Oct–March). For equally good beaches and a chance of cheaper hotel accommodation, you could go east past La Baule to **Pornichet** (though preferably keeping away from the plush marina) or to the tiny **St-Marc**, where in 1953 Jacques Tati filmed *Monsieur Hulot's Holiday*.

Nantes

NANTES, the former capital of Brittany, is no longer officially part of the province: it was transferred to the Pays de la Loire in 1962 when the modern administrative regions were established. Nonetheless, such bureaucracy is not taken too seriously in a city whose history is so intimately bound up with Breton fortunes. A considerable medieval centre, it later achieved great wealth from colonial expeditions, the slave trade and shipbuilding – activities in turn surpassed by more recent industrial growth. Although much of the former provincial character of the city has been lost, thanks to such recent accretions as the tower blocks masking the Loire and motorways tearing past the city, it remains to its inhabitants an integral part of Brittany.

Arrival and information

Nantes' **gare SNCF**, a little way east of the centre, is served by a dozen TGVs daily from Paris (just two hours away). It has two exits; for most facilities (tramway, buses, hotels) use Accès Nord. There are two main **bus** stations. The one just south of the centre on allée Baco, near place Ricordeau, is used by buses heading south and southwest, while the one where the cours des 50 Ôtages meets rue de l'Hôtel de Ville serves routes that stay north of the river. Modern rubber-wheeled **trams** run along the old riverfront, past the *gare SNCF* and the two bus stations. Flat-fare tickets, at €1.50, are valid for one hour, rather than just a single journey, though one-day tickets are also available for €3.50.

Nantes' **tourist office** is between the medieval city and the nineteenth-century town at 3 cours Olivier-de-Clisson (Mon, Tues & Wed–Sun 10am–6pm; Thurs

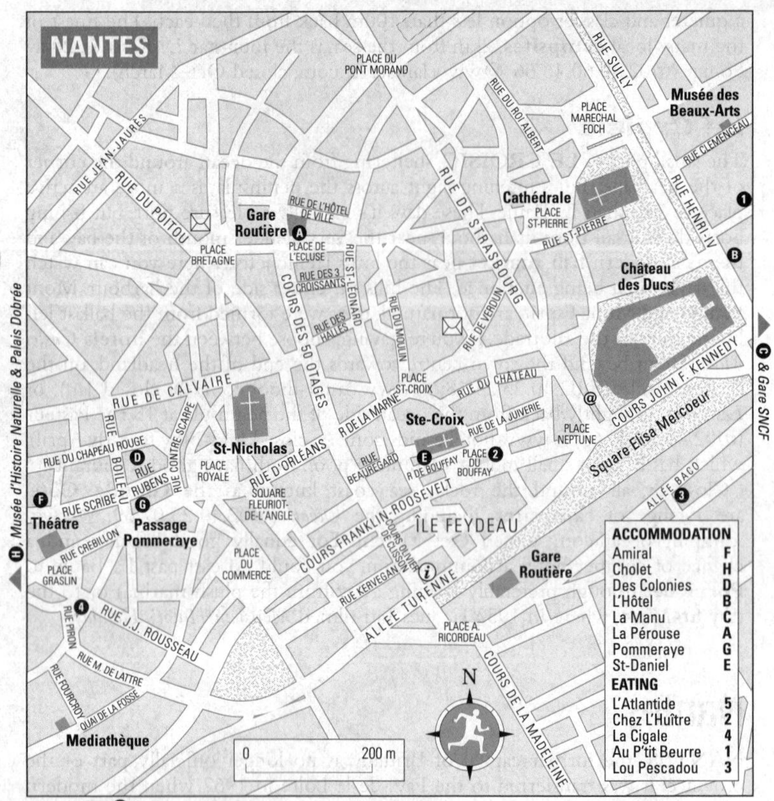

10.30am–6pm; ⓣ08.92.46.40.44, ⓦwww.nantes-tourisme.com); it provides free book-size guides to local hotels and restaurants, and runs various guided tours of the city. It also sells the **Pass Nantes**, available in 24-hour (€14), 48-hour (€24) and 72-hour (€30) versions, which grants unrestricted use of local transport, including river cruises, and free admission to a wide range of museums. Cyber Cité, 14 rue de Strasbourg, offers **Internet access** (daily 1pm–1am; ⓣ02.40.89.57.92; €4 per hr).

Accommodation

Although it holds plenty of **hotels** to suit all budgets, Nantes is one of those cities where you won't necessarily stumble upon a suitable place just by walking or driving around at whim. Instead, there are two main concentrations: one, as ever, in the immediate vicinity of the *gare SNCF*, and the other in the narrow streets around the place Greslin. The tourist office runs a booking service (ⓣ08.92.46.40.44, ⓦwww.resanantes.com), while at weekends you can get two nights for the price of one (ⓦwww.bon-week-end-en-villes.com).

The **hostel**, *La Manu*, in a postmodern former tobacco factory at 2 place de la Manufacture (ⓣ02.40.29.29.20, ⓔnanteslamanu@fuaj.org; €14.90 per night), is a few hundred metres east of the *gare SNCF*, and accessible by taking tramway #1 towards Malachère.

Hotels

Amiral 26bis rue Scribe ⓣ02.40.69.20.21, ⓦwww.hotel-nantes.fr. Well-maintained little hotel on a lively pedestrianized street just north of place Graslin. All rooms have TV, bath and double-glazing. Mon–Fri ④, Sat & Sun ③

Cholet 10 rue Gresset ⓣ02.40.73.31.04, ⓦwww.hotelcholet-nantes.com. Quiet, friendly option very close to place Graslin, with a wide assortment of rooms, all with en-suite facilities. Mon–Fri ④, Sat & Sun ③

Des Colonies 5 rue du Chapeau Rouge ⓣ02.40.48.79.76, ⓦwww.hoteldescolonies.fr. Spruce, good-value hotel a couple of blocks up from place Graslin, within walking distance of everything. The lobby doubles as an art gallery, and one entire floor is reserved for non-smokers. Discounts at weekends. No restaurant. ④

L'Hôtel 6 rue Henri-IV ⓣ02.40.29.30.31, ⓦwww.nanteshotel.com. An insouciant name for one of the city's finest options, a very grand modern edifice facing the château with a high standard of comfort. Buffet breakfasts cost €8.50; parking is €8. ⑤

La Pérouse 3 allée Duquesne ⓣ02.40.89.75.00, ⓦwww.hotel-laperouse.fr. Superb contemporary building ingeniously integrated with the older architecture that surrounds it. The interior is decorated with 1930s furniture, stucco walls and ultramodern touches such as high-tech TVs and wireless Internet access in the rooms. An original, comfortable and friendly place to stay, with excellent breakfasts to boot. Mon–Fri ⑥, Sat & Sun ⑤

Pommeraye 2 rue Boileau ⓣ02.40.48.78.79, ⓦwww.hotel-pommeraye.com. Extremely good-value modern boutique hotel with large, designer-decor rooms, beautiful bathrooms and free parking; good buffet breakfast. Mon–Fri ⑤, Sat & Sun ④

St-Daniel 4 rue du Bouffay ⓣ02.40.47.41.25, ⓦwww.hotel-saintdaniel.com. These simple but pleasant and well-lit rooms, on a cobbled street just off the place du Bouffay in the very heart of the old city, are much in demand in summer. Paying €5 extra secures a TV and en-suite toilet. ②

The City

The Loire, the source of Nantes' riches, has dwindled from the centre. As recently as the 1930s, the river crossed the city in seven separate channels, but German labour as part of reparations for World War I filled in five. What are still called "islands" in the centre are now surrounded and isolated, not by water, but by hectic dual carriageways. These are not easy to cross, but they do at least mean that Nantes is separated into a series of discernible districts: the older **medieval city** is concentrated around the cathedral, with the château prominent in its southeast corner, while the elegant **nineteenth-century town** lies to the west, across the cours des 50-Otages.

The old town

Though no longer on the waterfront, the **Château des Ducs** still preserves the form in which it was built by two of the last rulers of independent Brittany, François II, and his daughter Duchess Anne, born here in 1477. The list of famous people who have been guests or prisoners, defenders or belligerents, of the castle includes Gilles de Rais (Bluebeard), publicly executed in 1440; Machiavelli, in 1498; John Knox as a galley-slave from 1547–49; and Bonnie Prince Charlie preparing for Culloden in 1745. In addition, the **Edict of Nantes** was signed here in 1598 by Henri IV, ending the Wars of Religion by

At the time this book went to press, the tourist office in Nantes was promising that a remarkable new attraction would open in the city in the summer of 2007. The plan is for a **giant artificial elephant** to carry thirty passengers at a time through the streets, for €6 per person. Tours of the workshop responsible for constructing the preposterous pachyderm, on the Île de Nantes, will also be available.

granting a degree of toleration to the Protestants. It had far more crucial consequences when it was revoked, by Louis XIV, in 1685.

The stout **ramparts** of the château remain pretty much intact, and most of the encircling moat is filled with water, surrounded by well-tended lawns that make a popular spot for lunchtime picnics. Within the walls stand a rather incongruous potpourri of buildings added in differing styles over the years. At the time of writing the entire château complex had for many years been in the process of a major facelift, which made it impossible to visit. Assuming it has finally reopened when you read this, it should hold a new museum covering the history of Nantes, and it should also be possible to walk the complete circuit of the ramparts.

In 1800 the Spaniards Tower, the castle's arsenal, exploded, shattering the stained glass of the **Cathédrale de St-Pierre-et-St-Paul** over 200m away. This was just one of many disasters that have befallen the church. It was used as a barn during the Revolution, bombed during World War II, and damaged by fire in 1972. Restored and finally reopened, its soaring height and lightness are emphasized by its clean white stone. It contains the tomb of François II and his wife Margaret – with somewhat grating symbols of Power, Strength and Justice for him and Fidelity, Prudence and Temperance for her.

Nantes' **Musée des Beaux-Arts**, east of the cathedral on rue Clemenceau, has a respectable collection of paintings displayed in excellent modern galleries, and plays host to a high standard of temporary exhibitions (Mon, Wed & Fri–Sun 10am–6pm, Thurs 10am–8pm; €3.50, €2 after 4.30pm). Not all its Renaissance and contemporary works are on display at any one time, but you should be able to take in canvases ranging from a gorgeous *David Triumphant* by Delaunay to Chagall's *Le Cheval Rouge* and Monet's *Nymphéas*.

The nineteenth-century town

The financier Graslin took charge of the development of the western part of the city in the 1780s, when Nantes' prosperity was at a high due to the sugar and slave trades. **Place Royale**, with its distinctive fountain, was first laid out in the closing years of the eighteenth century, and has been rebuilt since it was bombed in 1943; the 1780s also produced the nearby **place Graslin**, named after its creator, with the elaborately styled **Grand Théâtre**, whose Corinthian portico contrasts with the 1895 Art Nouveau of the not-to-be-missed *La Cigale* brasserie (see opposite) on the corner.

West of the place Royale on rue Crebillon, a spectacular nineteenth-century multi-level shopping centre mentioned by Flaubert, the **Passage Pommeraye**, drops down three flights of stairs towards the place du Commerce. The attention to detail lavished upon it is on a scale undreamt of in modern malls, giving a glimpse of early consumerism; each of the gas lamps that light the central area is held by an individually crafted marble cherub.

Rue Voltaire runs west of the place Graslin, leading to the **Musée d'Histoire Naturelle** at no. 12 (daily except Tues 10am–6pm, Ⓦwww.museum.nantes.fr; €3.50). This holds an eccentric assortment of oddities, including tatty stuffed specimens of virtually every bird and animal imaginable, plus rhinoceros toenails, a coelecanth, an aepyornis egg and an Egyptian mummy. There's even a complete tanned human skin, taken in 1793 from the body of a soldier whose dying wish was to be made into a drum. Further along is Viollet-le-Duc's **Palais Dobrée** (Tues–Fri 1.30–5.30pm, Sat & Sun 2.30–5.30pm; €3, free on Sun), a nineteenth-century mansion given over to two museums, one of which claims to feature Duchess Anne's heart in a box.

Eating

Restaurants fill the winding lanes of the old city and it shouldn't take long to come up with something if you wander the pedestrian streets in the centre. Nantes is big enough to have all sorts of ethnic alternatives as well, with Algerian, Italian, Chinese, Vietnamese and Indian places in addition to those listed here.

L'Atlantide Centre des Salorges, 16 quai Ernest-Renaud ☎02.40.73.23.23. Designer restaurant, with big views from the fourth floor of a modern block, that serves the contemporary French cuisine of chef Jean-Yves Gueho. Fish is the speciality, but expect quirky twists like the bananas braised in beer. Menus at €28 and €70. Closed Sat lunch & all Sun, plus first 3 weeks of Aug.

Chez L'Huître 5 rue des Petites-Écuries ☎02.51.82.02.02. Much as the name suggests, this lovely little restaurant specializes in oysters of all sizes and provenance, priced from €7.80 to €15 per half-dozen. The "*apérihuître*" consists of six oysters and a glass of Muscadet for €8.50; you can also get smoked fish, fish soup and other simple dishes. Open until late nightly, closed Sun lunch.

La Cigale 4 place Graslin ☎02.51.84.94.94. Fabulous late nineteenth-century brasserie, offering fine meals in opulent surroundings, with seating at terrace tables or in a more formal indoor dining room. Fish is a speciality, with lunch options like the €16.90 *tartare de thon.*The €11.90 and €22.90 menus are served until midnight.

Au P'tit Beurre 18 rue de Richebourg ☎02.40.74.11.61. Friendly little place with outdoor seating near the château, that serves good-value local food. The €14 weekday lunch menu is good value; dinner menus range up to €30. Closed Sat lunch, Sun eve & Mon.

Lou Pescadou 8 allée Baco ☎02.40.35.29.50. Despite being somewhat off the beaten track, near the *gare routière*, this is Nantes' most fashionable venue for fresh fish, with menus from €14. Closed Mon eve, Sat lunch & Sun.

Travel details

Trains

Brest to: Le Mans (1 daily; 3hr 40min); Morlaix (16 daily; 35min); Paris-Montparnasse (7 TGVs daily; 4hr 20min); Quimper (7 daily; 1hr 15min); Rennes (8 daily; 2hr 15min).

Guingamp to: Paimpol (June–Sept only, 4–5 daily; 45min).

Quimper to: Lorient (5 daily; 40min); Nantes (3 daily; 2hr 30min); Redon (6 daily; 1hr 40min); Vannes (8 daily; 1hr 10min).

Rennes to: Brest (5 TGVs daily; 2hr 15min, plus 6 daily slower services, 2hr 40min); Caen (4 daily; 3hr) via Dol (35min) and Pontorson (1hr); Morlaix (10 daily; 1hr 45min), via Lamballe (40min), St-Brieuc (50min); Nantes (5 daily; 1hr 30min); Paris-Montparnasse (10 TGVs daily; 2hr 10min); Quimper (9 daily; 2hr 30min); Vannes (6 daily; 1hr); Vitré (10 daily; 35min).

Roscoff to: Morlaix (4 daily; 35min).

St-Malo to: Rennes (6 daily; 50min; connections for Paris on TGV). All trains pass through Dol (20min).

Buses

Brest to: Brignogan (7 daily; 1hr); (Camaret (5 daily; 1hr 10min); Le Conquet (7 daily; 40min); Le Faou (7 daily; 30min); Quimper (5 daily; 1hr 15min); Roscoff (3 daily; 1hr 50min).

Quimper to: Audierne (10 daily; 50min); Beg-Meil (8 daily; 50min); Bénodet (3–8 daily; 30min); Camaret (3 daily; 1hr 20min); Concarneau (7 daily; 30min); Crozon (3 daily; 1hr 10min); Douarnenez (10 daily; 40min); Fouesnant (8 daily; 30min); Locronan (3 daily; 20min); Pointe du Raz (5 daily; 1hr 30 min); Roscoff (1 daily; 2hr 30min).

Rennes to: Dinan (6 daily; 1hr 20min); Dinard (5 daily; 1hr 40min); Fougères (10 daily; 1hr); Mont St-Michel (5 daily; 1hr 20min).

Roscoff to: Brest (3 daily; 2hr); Morlaix (5 daily; 1hr); Quimper (1 daily; 2hr 30min).

St-Malo to: Cancale (4 daily; 45min); Combourg (2 daily; 1hr); Dinan (4 daily; 45min); Dinard (8 daily; 30min); Fougères (3 daily; 2hr 15min); Mont St-Michel (4 daily; 1hr 30min); Pontorson (4 daily; 1hr 15min); Rennes (3 daily; 1hr 30min).

Vannes to: Arzon (4 daily; 50min); Auray (8 daily; 30min); Carnac (7 daily; 1hr 20min); Quiberon (7 daily; 2hr); Pontivy (9 daily; 1hr 10min); Malestroit (3 daily; 50min).

Ferries

For details of ferries to Ouessant & Molène, see p.443; to Bréhat, see p.433; to Batz, see p.441; to Sein, see p.453; to Belle-Île, see p.470; and for tours of the Gulf of Morbihan see p.480.

6

The Loire

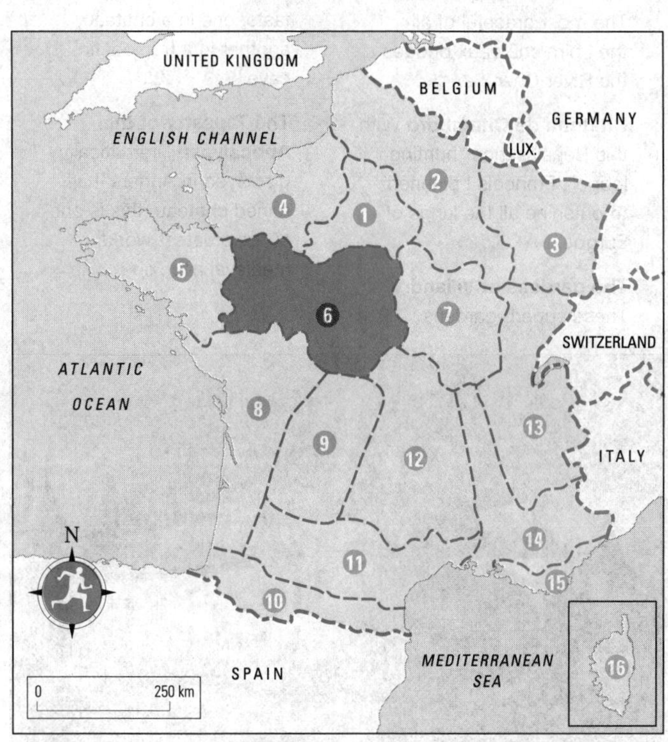
UNITED KINGDOM
BELGIUM
GERMANY
LUX.
ENGLISH CHANNEL
SWITZERLAND
ATLANTIC
OCEAN
ITALY
SPAIN
MEDITERRANEAN
SEA
N
0
250 km
1
2
3
4
5
6
7
8
9
10
11
12
13
14
15
16

CHAPTER 6

Highlights

* **Stained glass at Bourges cathedral** Some of France's finest stained-glass windows are preserved in Bourges' extravagant Gothic cathedral. See p.510

* **Château de Chenonceau** The most graceful of all the Loire châteaux bridges the River Cher. See p.512

* **Château de Chambord** With this Renaissance "hunting lodge", François I planned to outshine all the kings of Europe. See p.525

* **The gardens at Villandry** These superb gardens are home to allegorical Renaissance hedge-work and a world-beating vegetable plot. See p.537

* **Bed and breakfast in Azay-le-Rideau** This tiny but pretty town has two unusual bed and breakfasts: one in a château, another in a troglodytic cave. See p.539

* **The Tapestry of the Apocalypse** Dramatically displayed in Angers' half-ruined château, this is one of the greatest works of medieval art. See p.551

△ Château du Plessis-Bourré

6

The Loire

When the **Loire** reaches its halfway point and finally turns west towards the Atlantic, locals say that it ceases to be a mere *rivière*, it becomes a *fleuve* – which is something altogether grander. In this proudest stretch, from the hills of Sancerre to the city of Angers, it flows past an extraordinary parade of castles, palaces and fine mansions – a relic of late medieval times, when the Loire was the favoured region of the French royal family and the chief hunting and pleasure ground of the aristocracy. In fact, the Loire valley is so densely populated with these châteaux that when it came to choosing which should be awarded the title of World Heritage Site, UNESCO just bestowed the label on the entire valley. The roll call can be intimidating for the visitor, but if you pick your châteaux carefully, rid yourself of a sense of duty to guided tours and spend days on riverbanks with supplies of local cheese, fruit and wines, the Loire can be the most beguiling of all French regions.

The region's heartland **Touraine**, long known as "the garden of France", has some of the best wines, the tastiest goat's cheese, the most regal history and, it's argued, the purest French accent in the land. It also has one of the finest châteaux in **Chenonceau** and by far the most developed tourist industry to match. But Touraine also takes in three of the Loire's pleasantest tributaries: the **Cher**, **Indre** and **Vienne**, each of which can be explored at a slower, more intimate pace. If you have just a week to spare for the region, then these are the parts to concentrate on. The attractive towns of **Blois** and **Amboise**, each with their own exceptional châteaux, make good bases for visiting the area upstream of Tours. Numerous grand châteaux dot the wooded country immediately south and east of Blois, including **Chambord**, the grandest of them all, while the wild and watery region of the **Sologne** stretches away further to the south-east. Downstream of Tours, around handsome **Saumur**, fascinating troglodyte dwellings have been carved out of the rock faces.

As well as the many châteaux, the region has a few unexpected sights, most compelling of which are the gardens at **Villandry**, outside Tours; the abbey at

Château and monument pass

The handy **Passeport Val de Loire** "la clef des temps" (€25, free to under-18s) allows you to visit ten national monuments in the Loire valley over the course of a year. You can purchase it at any participating site, including the châteaux at Angers, Azay-le-Rideau, Chambord and Chaumont, the Cloître de la Psalette at Tours cathedral, and the Abbaye de Fontevraud.

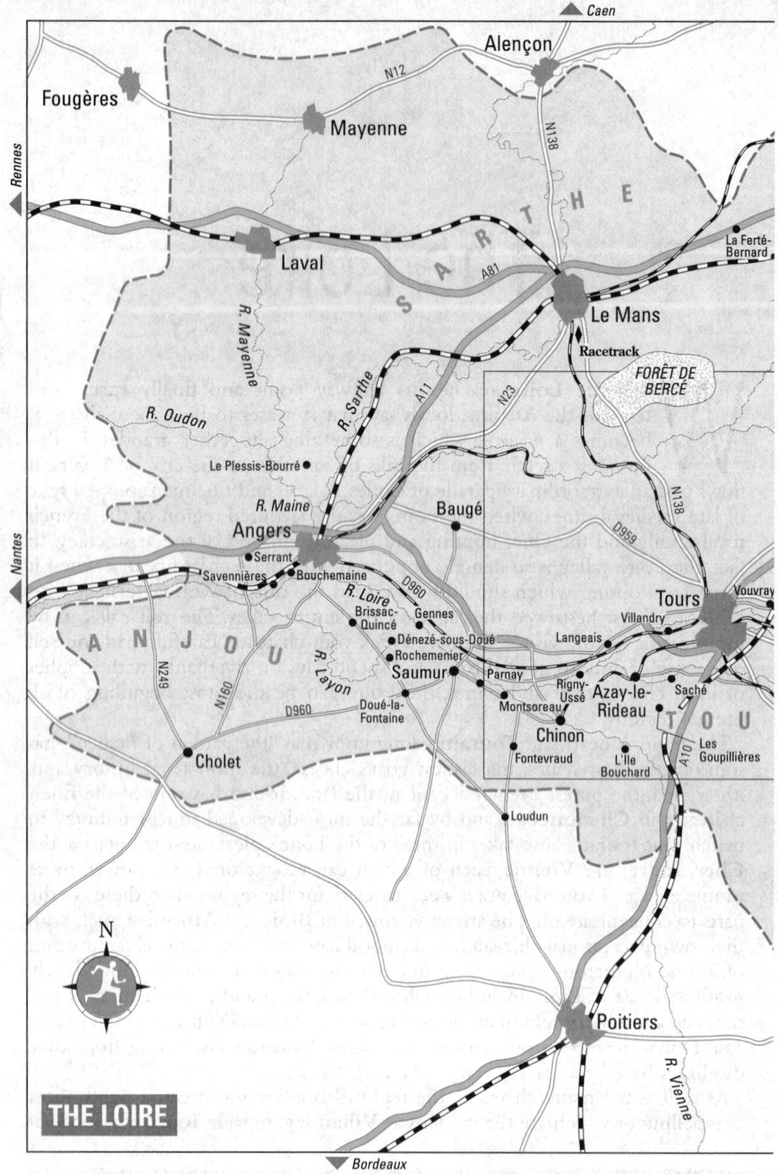

Fontevraud; and the apocalyptic tapestry sequence in **Angers**, capital of the ancient wine-producing county of **Anjou**. Of the three main cities, **Tours** and Angers provide the best urban bases, though **Orléans** has its own charm. Each city has its distinctive cathedral, though none is as impressive as the hybrid Romanesque-Gothic cathedral of busy, modern **Le Mans**, located some way north of the Loire valley in the topographically uninspiring *département* of

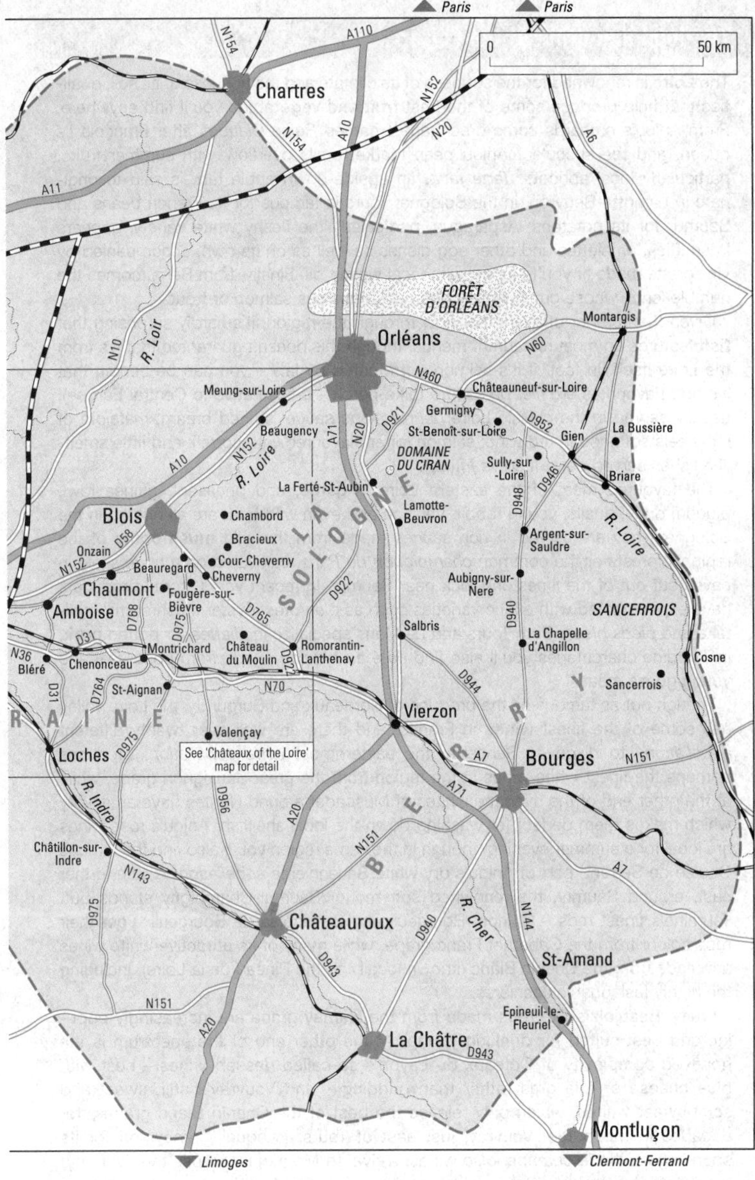

Sarthe, or the stunningly glazed Gothic fantasy of medieval **Bourges**, which lies well south of the Loire, in the marshy farmland of the **Berry**.

The Loire itself is often called the last wild river in France, mostly because unpredictable currents and shallow water brought an end to commercial river traffic as soon as the railways arrived, and the many quays remain largely forgotten, except by the occasional tour boat. The river's wildness also takes shape

The food and drink of the Loire

The **Loire** is renowned for the softness of its climate and the richness of its soil, qualities that help produce some of the best **fruit** and **vegetables** you'll find anywhere. From Anjou's orchards come greengages, named *Reine Claudes* after François I's queen, and the succulent Anjou pear. Market stalls overflow with summer fruits, particularly local apricots. *Tarte tatin*, an upside-down apple tart, is said to originate in Lamotte-Beuvron, in the Sologne. Tours is famous for its French beans and Saumur for its potatoes. Asparagus, particularly the fleshy white variety, appears in soufflés, omelettes and other egg dishes as well as on its own, accompanied by vinaigrette made (if you're lucky) with local walnut oil. Finally, from Berry, comes the humble lentil, whose green variety often accompanies salmon or trout.

Given the number of rivers that flow through the region, it's hardly surprising that **fish** features on most restaurant menus, though this doesn't guarantee that it's from the Loire itself. In fact, if it's salmon – protected by law – you can be certain that it's not. Favourites are *filet de sandre* (pike-perch – a fish native to Central Europe), usually served in the classic Loire *beurre blanc* sauce; stuffed bream; *matelote* of local eels softened in red wine; salmon (often flavoured with sorrel); and little smelt-like fishes served deep-fried (*la friture*).

The favoured meat of the eastern Loire is **game**, and pheasant, guinea fowl, pigeon, duck, quails, young rabbit, venison and even wild boar are all hunted in the Sologne. They are served in rich sauces made from the wild **mushrooms** of the region's forests or the common *champignon de Paris*, cultivated on a huge scale in caves cut out of the limestone rock near Saumur. In recent years, some producers have experimented with exotic varieties such as *pleurotes* (oyster mushrooms), shiitake and *pieds bleus*. Both Tours and Le Mans specialize in *rillettes*, or potted **pork**; in Touraine charcuteries you'll also find *pâté au biquion*, made from pork, veal and young goat's meat.

Though not as famous as the produce of Bordeaux and Burgundy, the Loire valley has some of the finest **wines** in France, and there are well over twenty different *appellations* to discover. Sancerre, the easternmost Loire *appellation*, produces perhaps the finest white wines in the region from the great Sauvignon grape, while at the other end of the river, the whites of Muscadet around Nantes have an acidity which makes them perfect for washing down the local shellfish. Anjou's rosé wines are ideal for a summer evening, though in the same region you'll also find the famous Coulée de Serrant, part of Anjou's dry white Savennières *appellation*. A little further east, around Saumur, the renowned soft red of Saumur-Champigny stands out. Touraine's finest reds – Chinon, Bourgeuil and St-Nicolas de Bourgeuil – get their ruby colour from the Cabernet Franc grape, while many of its attractive white wines are made from the Chenin Blanc (known locally as the Pineau de la Loire), including the highly fashionable Jasnières.

Fruity, Beaujolais-like reds made from the Gamay grape are increasingly popular, and best suited for drinking young. At the other end of the spectrum is the honeyed complexity of Côteaux du Layon's so-called dessert wines – best with blue cheese or foie gras rather than pudding – and Vouvray's still, sweet and semi-sweet whites, which only release the best of the Chenin Blanc grape after decades in the bottle. Vouvray, just east of Tours, is equally renowned for its sparkling *méthode champenoise* wines, a rival to Montlouis, across the river, and the full, fruity sparkling Saumur – a good example of which is a serious match for most Champagnes.

Touraine makes something of a cult of its **goat's cheese**, and a local *chèvre fermier* (farm-produced goat's cheese) can be a revelation. Four named cheeses are found on most boards: Ste-Maure is a long cylinder with a piece of straw running through the middle; Pouligny-St-Pierre and Valençay are pyramid-shaped; and Selles-sur-Cher is flat and round.

The Loire by bike

Thanks to the **Loire à Vélo** scheme (Ⓦwww.loire-a-velo.fr), the Loire valley is now one of the loveliest and safest – not to mention flattest – places in the world to have a cycling holiday or take a day out on a hired bike. A mix of dedicated cycle paths and meticulously signposted routes along minor roads now runs all the way along the Loire from Orléans to beyond Angers – a distance of more than 300km. Or almost all the way: a single gap upstream of Tours means you'll have to follow ordinary roads for 50km between Tours and Candé-sur-Beuvron, 14km downstream of Blois – or work out a much lengthier route on back roads. Work is now under way to fill this gap, however, and to extend the network further up- and downstream. The region around Blois offers an additional, 300-kilometre network, **Châteaux à vélo** (Ⓦwww.chateauxavelo.com; see p.522). These routes thread inland among the forests, linking the area's many châteaux.

Tourist offices can provide detailed maps and other information, and you can download most details, including maps, online. French villages are well accustomed to cyclists parading round in garish gear, and all larger towns have at least one hire agency. Bikes can also be hired at many hotels, campsites, tourist offices, train stations and even restaurants along the way. Many have signed up to the admirable **Détours de Loire scheme** (Ⓣ02.47.61.22.23, Ⓦwww.locationdevelos.com), which allows you to pick up a bike in one place and drop it off in another, paying inexpensive drop-off costs per zone crossed – on top of the bike rental charge, of course.

in dramatic floods, but for most of the year it meanders gently past its shifting sandbanks, shaded by reeds and willows, and punctuated by long, sandy islands beloved by birds. The dangers of collapsing sandbanks and strong currents mean that swimmers should confine themselves to one of the many tributaries, though it's possible to rent a kayak in many places.

In general, this is a region where rental cars and bus tours are the norm. Yet train lines run along the river towards Nantes and Brittany and up through Tours to Paris, and most sites are accessible by **public transport**. If you're exploring on your own, however, it's a good idea to hire some means of transport, at least for occasional forays, because bus schedules can be skeletal and mostly geared to commuters and schoolchildren, and trains too limiting. Hiring a bike is perhaps the most enjoyable option of all: this is wonderful and easy **cycling** country, best of all on the flood banks, or levees, of the river itself, on the quiet country backroads, and on the dedicated cycle routes that make up the new Loire à Vélo network (see box above).

Orléans and around

ORLÉANS is the northernmost city on the Loire, sitting at the apex of a huge arc in the river as it switches direction and starts to flow southwest. Its proximity to Paris, just over 100km away, has always shaped this ancient city. Goods and passengers sailing up the Loire would disembark at Orléans for the overland journey on to the capital, and it became an important port. The city's glory may have faded in the late nineteenth century along with the fortunes of the river, but recent years have seen an economic renaissance. High-speed train and motorway links to the capital and a rash of cosmetics factories set up in the suburbs have brought new jobs and prosperity. The ancient riverside quays have been redeveloped and ultramodern trams have been introduced

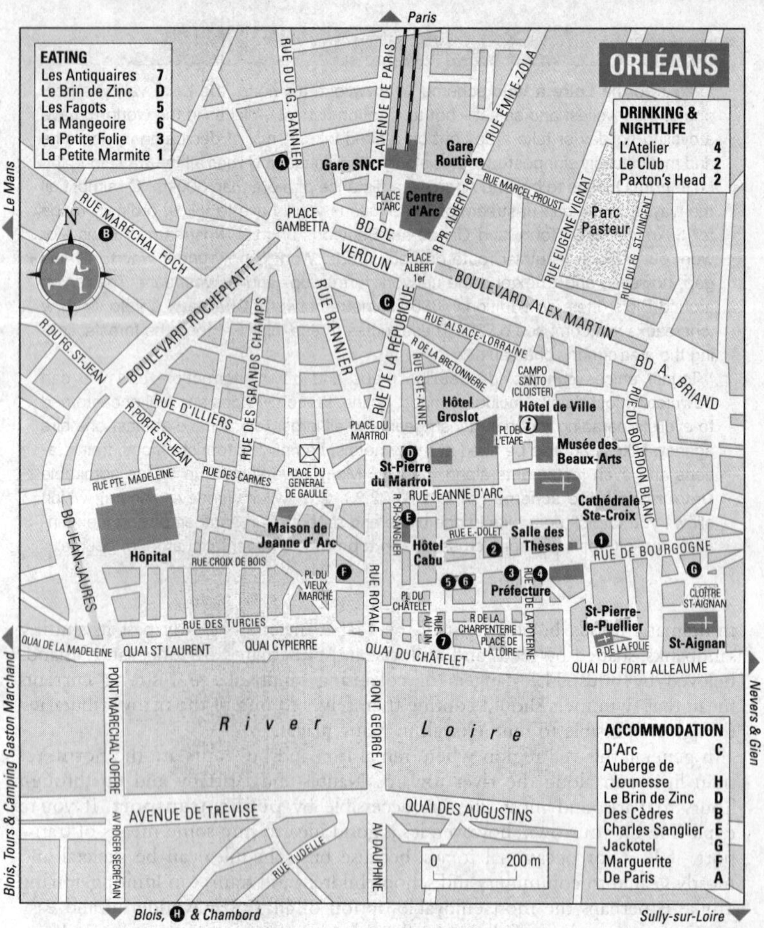

– a perfect foil to the handsome eighteenth- and nineteenth-century streets of the old centre.

Despite a rich early history of being a centre of revolt against Julius Caesar in 52 BC (for which it was burnt to the ground), besieged by Attila the Hun in the mid-fifth century, and elevated to the position of temporary capital of the Frankish kingdom in 498, it's **Joan of Arc**'s deliverance of the city in May 1429 that the town feels bound to commemorate. This was the turning point in the Hundred Years War (1339–1453), when Paris had been captured by the English and Orléans, as the key city in central France, was under siege. Joan, a 17-year-old peasant girl in men's clothing, had talked her way into meeting Charles, the heir to the French throne, and persuaded him to reconquer his kingdom. Her role in the week-long battle that lifted the siege was probably slighter than is usually claimed, but her standard and sheer conviction certainly inspired the troops to victory. Less than three years later she was captured in battle, tried as a heretic, and burnt at the stake. Today, the Maid of Orléans is honoured everywhere; in museums, in civic statues and most memorably, in the stained glass of the vast Neo-Gothic cathedral. One of the best times to visit is the evening before and the day of May 8 (**Joan of Arc Day**), when the city is filled with parades, fireworks and a medieval fair.

Arrival, information and accommodation

The **gare SNCF** leads straight into the modern shopping centre on place d'Arc, which fronts onto a huge swathe of busy roads; the old town centre lies on the far side of the traffic. The **gare routière**, on rue Marcel-Proust, is just north of place d'Arc. The main **tourist office**, 2 place de l'Étape (April & May Mon–Sat 9.30am–1pm & 2–6.30pm; June & Sept Mon–Sat 9am–1pm & 2–7pm; July & Aug Mon–Sat 9am–7pm, Sun 10am–1pm; Oct–March Mon–Sat 10am–1pm & 2–6pm; Ⓣ02.38.24.05.05), is in the old centre, opposite the cathedral.

Accommodation in Orléans is mostly uninspiring. A few inexpensive central hotels stand out from the rest and there are plenty of fall-back choices near the station.

Hotels

D'Arc 37 rue de la République Ⓣ02.38.53.10.94, Ⓦwww.hoteldarc.fr. This long-established Art Nouveau hotel has touches of grandeur. The most attractive rooms have small balconies with window boxes, looking down onto the tramlines and pedestrianized street below. 6

Le Brin de Zinc 62 rue Ste-Catherine Ⓣ02.38.53.88.77, Ⓦwww.brindezinc.fr. Half a dozen sparsely furnished but pleasant and well-maintained rooms in an old building above a popular and very central restaurant. 2

Des Cèdres 17 rue Maréchal-Foch Ⓣ02.38.62.22.92, Ⓦwww.hoteldescedres.com. Welcoming, newly renovated three-star with a garden in a peaceful quarter of town. The interconnecting rooms are useful for families. 5

Charles Sanglier 8 rue Charles-Sanglier Ⓣ02.38.53.38.50, Ⓔhotelsanglier@wanadoo.fr. Very central, so tends to get booked up. The modern building is unprepossessing, and the rooms are small and a little shabby, but it's a friendly place, and comfortable enough. 3

Jackotel 18 Cloître-St-Aignan Ⓣ02.38.54.48.48, Ⓕ02.38.77.17.59. Unrivalled location overlooking the church of St-Aignan across a shaded square, but the decor is anonymous 1980s-style. 4

Marguerite 14 place du Vieux-Marché Ⓣ02.38.53.74.32, Ⓔhotel.marguerite@wanadoo.fr. Central, friendly and well run. The large, immaculate rooms are painted in cheery modern colours – a few unrenovated rooms are cheaper. 4

De Paris 29 Faubourg-Bannier Ⓣ02.38.53.39.58. Old-fashioned but clean rooms above a very ordinary bar, near the train station. Extremely friendly and helpful management. 1

Hostel and campsite

Auberge de Jeunesse d'Orléans-La Source Stade Omnisports, 7 av Beaumarchais Ⓣ02.38.53.60.06, Ⓔauberge.crjs@wanadoo.fr. Good hostel, with friendly management and very modern rooms and facilities. The major downside is the suburban location, underneath a stand of Orléans' stadium: take tram A from the train station, get off at "Université l'Indien" (30min), then walk 500m east down av du Président-Kennedy. Reception Mon–Fri 8am–7pm; €9 per night with HI membership.

Camping Gaston Marchand chemin de la Roche, St-Jean-de-la-Ruelle Ⓣ02.38.88.39.39. The municipal campsite, and the closest to Orléans, 3km away out on the Blois road, beside the Loire; bus #26, stop "Petite Espère". Closed Sept–June.

The City

St Joan turns up all over town. In pride of place in the large, central **place du Martroi**, a mostly pedestrianized square at the end of rue de la République, rises a bulky mid-nineteenth-century likeness of her on horseback. Just beyond place du Martroi, the grand nineteenth-century boulevard of rue Jeanne-d'Arc marches arrow-straight up to the doors of the **Cathédrale Sainte-Croix** (daily 9.15am–noon & 2–6pm), where Joan celebrated her victory over the English – although the uniformly Gothic structure actually dates from well after her death. Huguenot iconoclasts destroyed the transepts in 1568, and in 1601 Henri IV inaugurated a rebuilding programme which lasted until the nineteenth century. The lofty towers of the west front, which culminate in a delicate stone palisade, were only completed at the time of the Revolution. Inside, skeletal columns of stone extend in a single vertical sweep from the cathedral floor to the vault. Joan's canonization in 1920 is marked by a garish monumental altar next to the north transept, supported by two jagged and golden leopards that represent the English. In the nave, the late nineteenth-century stained-glass windows tell the story of her life, starting from the north transept. In a series of cartoon-like images, *L'Anglois Perfide*, or perfidious Albion, gets a rough ride, while the role of the Burgundians in her capture and the French clergy in her trial is rather brushed over. Across place d'Étape from the cathedral, outside the red-brick Renaissance **Hôtel Groslot**, the old Hôtel de Ville, Joan appears again, in pensive mood, her skirt now shredded by World War II bullets.

You're spared the Maid in the cavernous **Musée des Beaux-Arts**, opposite the Hôtel Groslot (Tues–Sat 10am–12.15pm & 1.30–5.45pm, Sun 2–6.30pm, €3), where the highlights of the main French collection on the first floor include Claude Deruet's *Four Elements*, the Le Nain brothers' dream-like and compelling *Bacchus Discovering Ariane on Naxos*, and the exquisite collection of eighteenth-century pastel portraits in room eight. The suite of rooms on the mezzanine level leads from nineteenth-century Neoclassicism through Romanticism and on to a large chamber devoted to the early Realists, dominated by Antigna's taut, melodramatic *The Fire*. Foreign art, mainly Flemish and Italian sixteenth- and seventeenth-century works, is on the second floor – look out for Coreggio's renowned *Holy Family* (1522) and Velázquez's *St Thomas*. Twentieth-century art lurks in the basement, where the big names include Picasso and Gauguin; a small inner chamber has a number of African-influenced sculptures by Henri Gaudier-Brzeska (1891–1915), who was born just outside Orléans at St-Jean-de-Braye.

If you follow rue Jeanne-d'Arc east from the cathedral and turn left down rue Charles-Sanglier, you'll find the ornate **Hôtel Cabu** (May, June & Sept Tues–Sat 1.30–5.45pm, Sun 2–6.30pm; July & Aug Tues–Sat 9.30am–12.15pm & 1.30–5.45pm, Sun 2–6.30pm; Oct–April Wed & Sat 1.30–5.45pm, Sun 2–5.45pm; same ticket as Musée des Beaux-Arts), whose three tiers faithfully follow the three main classical orders in strict Renaissance style. Inside, a small historical and archeological museum houses the extraordinary **Treasure of Neuvy-en-Sullias**, a collection of bronze animals and figurines found near Orléans in 1861. The cache was probably buried in the second half of the third century AD, either to protect it from Germanic invaders or to stop it being melted down for coinage at a time of rampant inflation, and possibly represents the last flourishing of Celtic religion at the end of the Gallo-Roman period. The floors above house various medieval oddities and Joan-related pieces, as well as exhibits on the history of Orléans. The entrance is on square Abbé-Desnoyers.

At the end of rue Jeanne-d'Arc, on place Général-de-Gaulle, is the semi-timbered **Maison de Jeanne d'Arc** (Tues–Sun: May–Oct 10am–12.30pm & 1.30–6pm; Nov–April 1.30–6pm; €2), a 1960s reconstruction of the house where Joan stayed. Its contents are fun, most of all for children, with good models and displays of the breaking of the Orléans siege. Despite the consistency in artists' renderings of the saint, it seems the pageboy haircut and demure little face are part of the myth – there is no contemporary portrait of her, save for a clerk's doodle in the margin of her trial proceedings, kept in the National Archives in Paris.

The riverfront and around

The scattered vestiges of the old city are on the east, down towards the river. **Rue de Bourgogne** was the Gallo-Roman main street, and is now lined with lively bars and restaurants. The **Salles des Thèses** is all that remains of the medieval university of Orléans where the hardline Reformation theologian Calvin studied Roman law. A short distance west on rue de Bourgogne, the circular Greek Revival-style **Protestant chapel** dates from the 1830s.

To the south, the attractive narrow streets of the old industrial area slope gently down towards the river. Once semi-derelict, it is now the focus of a campaign to make the riverfront once more the focus of the city. On the **place de la Loire**, which slopes down to the river from a nine-screen cinema complex, the flagstones are inset with a pattern that's supposed to suggest waves. At least two of the quarter's churches are on the list of precious monuments: the remains of **St-Aignan** and its well-preserved eleventh-century crypt; and the Romanesque **St-Pierre-le-Puellier**, a former university church now used for concerts and exhibitions. St-Aignan was destroyed during the English siege, rebuilt by the Dauphin and extended into one of the greatest churches in France by Louis XII. More sieges of the city during the Wars of Religion took their toll, leaving just the choir and transepts standing. Tours of the **crypt**, which was built in the early eleventh century to house the relics of St-Aignan, are occasionally conducted by the tourist office.

Eating and drinking

Rue de Bourgogne is the main street for **restaurants** and **nightlife**. You can choose from among French, Spanish, North African, Middle Eastern, Indian and Asian cuisines, all of which can be sampled at very reasonable prices. For buying your own provisions there are the covered **market halls** on place du Châtelet, near the river.

Restaurants

Les Antiquaires 2 & 4 rue au Lin ⓣ02.38.53.52.35. Run by a renowned chef, Philippe Bardau, this is Orléans' best restaurant and must be booked in advance. Lobster consommé, wild turbot with girolle mushrooms and pike-perch steak are some of its delights. Menus begin at €46, but there's an excellent €38 menu (not available Sat eve or Sun) which includes selected wines. Closed Sun eve & Mon.

Le Brin de Zinc 62 rue Ste-Catherine. Bustling bistro just off place du Martroi in hotel of the same name. The outside tables are packed with a noisy crowd tucking into huge seafood platters (€14–28) and *plats du jour* (€7.40).

Les Fagots 32 rue du Poirier ⓣ02.38.62.22.79. Wonderfully convivial place that looks like it has been crammed into someone's grandmother's kitchen. Traditional main courses and grilled meats feature on the €11 and €15 menus. Closed Sun & Mon.

La Mangeoire 28 rue du Poirier ⓣ02.38.68.15.38. This homely, brightly lit bistro is packed full of locals enjoying straightforward pasta, salads and French standards, with starters at €5 and mains from €10–15. Closed Sun.

La Petite Folie 223 rue de Bourgogne ⓣ02.38.53.39.87. Youthful, designer bar-restaurant serving fresh, light and exciting food – you might have asparagus flan, chicken with *sauce Canadienne*, then strawberry soup with wine – all for around €20. Closed Sun; closed at lunchtime Oct–April.

La Petite Marmite 178 rue de Bourgogne ⓣ02.38.54.23.83. The most highly regarded restaurant on this busy street combines a stylish but homely feel with excellent regional cuisine. The excellent €20 *menu du terroir* features local products such as rabbit and guinea fowl from the Sologne. Closed Tues & Wed.

Bars and nightlife

L'Atelier 203 rue de Bourgogne. Arty, studenty place, with regular concerts and exhibitions. The mood is cosily friendly rather than pretentious and drinks are reasonably priced.

Le Club 266 rue de Bourgogne. Cellar club-bar with a tiny dance floor overlooked by a little mezzanine seating level. Nothing special but a friendly choice if you're out late at the weekend and want to push on past 2am. Entry €10 with a drink.

Paxton's Head 264–266 rue de Bourgogne. English pub with a club in the cellars that's popular with a trendy, 20-something crowd, with occasional karaoke or live music. Daily 3pm–3am.

Listings

Bike hire The only central option is CAD, 95 rue Faubourg-Bannier ⓣ02.38.81.23.00. Otherwise, try Kit Loisirs, 1720 rue Marcel-Belot (ⓣ02.38.63.44.34, ⓦwww.kitloisirs.com), out in the suburb of Olivet.
Car rental Avis, *Gare SNCF* ⓣ02.38.62.27.04; Rent-a-Car, 3 rue Sansonnières ⓣ02.38.62.22.44; Europcar, 17 av de Paris ⓣ02.38.73.00.40.
Cinemas Le Select, 45 rue Jeanne-d'Arc, often shows good art-house movies in the original language; Cinema Multiplex Pathé, 45 rue des Halles, place de la Loire, sometimes shows Hollywood blockbusters in English. Programme info for both on ⓣ08.92.68.69.25, ⓦwww.cinemaspathe.com.
Festivals Fête de Jeanne d'Arc is a series of period-costume parades held on April 29, May 1

Which châteaux?

Choosing which Loire châteaux to visit can be a bewildering business, and trying to pack in the maximum can quickly blunt your sensibilities. The most famous sites usually justify the crowds they draw, but it's often wise to time your visit for lunchtime, or first and last thing. Visiting one of the lower-key sites, particularly if you have the place practically to yourself, is something special.

Of the most famous, **Azay-le-Rideau** (see p.539) and **Chenonceau** (see p.512) both belong exclusively to the Renaissance period, and their settings in the middle of moat and river respectively are very beautiful, rivalled only by the wonderful Renaissance gardens of **Villandry** (see p.537). **Blois** (see p.520), with its four wings representing four distinct eras, is extremely impressive, as is the monstrously huge **Chambord** (see p.525), the triumph of François I's Renaissance. At **Valençay** (see p.516), the interior of the Renaissance château is Napoleonic, while **Cheverny** (see p.523) is the prime example of seventeenth-century magnificence.

Many châteaux that started life as serious military defences were turned into luxurious residences by their royal or ducal owners: good examples are **Brissac** (see p.555), **Chaumont** (see p.523), with its nineteenth-century stables, and **Ussé** (see p.540), the most fairy-tale of them all. **Le Plessis-Bourré** (see p.553) is a fine example of late fifteenth-century elegant residence and strong defences combined, while **Sully** (see p.504) projects the power of its most famous owner, the Duc de Sully. Other feudal fortresses have preserved their medieval feel, among them: the ruined **Chinon** (see p.543); **Langeais** (see p.538), beautifully furnished in fifteenth-century style; **Meung-sur-Loire** (see opposite), with its dungeons; **Fougères-sur-Bièvre** (see p.524), whose towers and staircases you can explore on your own; and **Amboise** (see p.535), which rears above the Loire like a cliff. For an evocation of medieval times, the citadel of **Loches** (see p.517) is hard to beat.

Other châteaux are more compelling for their contents than for their architecture: **Beauregard** (see p.524) is most famous for its portrait gallery while **La Bussière** (see p.506) for its obsessive nineteenth-century decoration, entirely dedicated to freshwater fishing, and **La Ferté-St-Aubin** is a living aristocratic home. At **Saumur** (see p.546), a museum on horses rivals the attraction of the castle itself, while at **Angers** (see p.551) the stark, largely ruined medieval castle houses the Tapestry of the Apocalypse, the greatest work of art in the Loire valley.

Entry prices are pretty steep, particularly for the châteaux that have remained in private hands – and there are a surprising number of French aristocrats still living the fine life in the region. There is no consistency in concessions offered, and children rarely go free. If you're over 65, under 25, a student or still at school, check for any reductions and make sure you've got proof of age or a student card with you.

and May 7–8, with the big set-pieces occurring in front of the cathedral on the night of the 7th and morning of the 8th May. The Festival de Jazz d'Orléans is held right through June, culminating in concerts held in the Campo Santo (Ⓦwww.ville-orleans.fr/orleansjazz). Every Sept in odd years, the Loire Festival takes place, with five days of concerts and shows beside the Châtelet quay.

Internet Leader Best Phone, 196 rue de Bourgogne (July & Aug 9.30am–11.30pm; Sept–June 11am–11.30pm; €3 per hour).
Medical assistance Centre Hospitalier, 1 rue Porte-Madeleine ⓣ02.38.51.44.44; emergencies ⓣ15.
Police 63 rue du Faubourg-St-Jean ⓣ02.38.24.30.00; emergencies ⓣ17.
Taxis Taxi Radio d'Orléans ⓣ02.38.53.11.11.

Château de Meung

Little streams known as *les mauves* flow between the houses in the village of **MEUNG-SUR-LOIRE**, 14km southwest of Orléans on the Blois rail line. During the summer months they leave slimy green high-water marks, but the sound of water is always pleasant, and Meung is an agreeable place to spend an afternoon, having also accumulated a number of literary associations over the centuries.

In the late thirteenth century, Jean de Meun, or de Meung, added 18,000 lines to the already 4000-line-long *Roman de la Rose*, a poetic hymn to sexuality written half a century earlier (by Guillaume de Lorris, from the town of the same name in the nearby Forêt d'Orléans). Inspired by the philosophical spirit of the times, de Meun transformed the poem into a finely argued disquisition on the nature of love, and inspired generations of European writers. Most recently, the town featured in the works of Georges Simenon – his fictional hero, Maigret, takes his holidays here.

Looming at the western edge of the old town centre, the **Château de Meung** (March–Oct daily 10am–7pm; Nov–Feb Sat & Sun 2–6pm; €7, Ⓦwww.chateaudemeung.com) remained in the hands of the bishops of Orléans from its construction in the twelfth century right up to the Revolution, since when it has passed through seven or eight private hands. The exterior of the château on the side facing the old drawbridge looks grimly defensive, retaining its thirteenth-century pepper-pot towers, while the side facing the park presents a much warmer facade, its eighteenth-century windows framed by salmon-pink stucco. You can explore the older part on your own, even poking around under the roof but most of this pleasantly shambolic section of the building was remodelled in the nineteenth century, and little sense of the building's history remains. More impressive is the eighteenth-century wing, where the bishops entertained their guests in relative comfort. Below here are the **cellars** where criminals condemned by the Episcopal courts were imprisoned. The most famous of the detainees was the poet François Villon, who was kept under lock and key between May and October 1461.

Beaugency

Six kilometres southwest of Meung along the Loire, **BEAUGENCY** is a pretty little town, which, in contrast to its innocuous appearance today, played its part in the conniving games of early medieval politics. In 1152 the marriage of Louis VII of France and Eleanor of Aquitaine was annulled by the Council of Beaugency in the church of Notre-Dame, allowing Eleanor to marry Henry Plantagenet, the future Henry II of England. Her huge land holdings in southwest France thus passed to the English crown – which already controlled Normandy, Maine, Anjou and Touraine – and the struggles between the French and English kings over their claims to these territories, and to the French throne itself, lasted for centuries.

Liberated by the indefatigable Joan of Arc on her way to Orléans in 1429, Beaugency was a constant battleground in the Hundred Years War due to its strategic significance as the only bridge-crossing point of the Loire between Orléans and Blois. Remarkably, the 26-arch **bridge** still stands and gives an excellent view of the once heavily fortified medieval heart of the town, which clusters tightly around a handful of central squares. **Place St-Firmin**, with its statue of Joan, is overlooked by a tower of a church destroyed during the Revolution, while **place Dunois** is bordered by the massive eleventh-century **Tour de César**, formerly part of the rather plain, fifteenth-century **Château Dunois**, which is closed to visitors for major structural works, probably until 2009. The square is completed by the rather severe Romanesque **abbey church of Notre-Dame**, the venue for the council's fateful matrimonial decision in 1152. Shady place du Docteur-Hyvernaud, two blocks north of place Dunois, is dominated by the elaborate sixteenth-century facade of the **Hôtel de Ville**. Inside, the main council chamber is graced by eight fine **embroidered wall hangings** from the era of Louis XIII, but you'll have to ask at the tourist office (on the same square) to be allowed inside to have a look. One set illustrates the four continents as perceived in the seventeenth century, with the rest dramatizing pagan rites such as gathering mistletoe and sacrificing animals.

Practicalities

A small **tourist office** (May–Sept 10am–12.30pm & 2.30–6.30pm, Sun 10am–noon; Oct–April Mon–Sat 9.30am–noon & 2.30–6pm; ⓣ02.38.44.54.42, ⓦwww.beaugency.fr) is on place Docteur-Hyvernaud. Two rather lovely **hotels** make the most of Beaugency's atmosphere of genteel charm: the *Hôtel de l'Abbaye*, 2 quai de l'Abbaye (ⓣ02.38.44.67.35, www.hotel-abbaye-beaugency.com; ❼), is set in a beautiful seventeenth-century abbey with painted ceilings and beds on raised platforms; while the small, delightful *Hôtel de la Sologne*, 6 place St-Firmin (ⓣ02.38.44.50.27, ⓦwww.hoteldelasologne.com; ❹; closed Dec 20–Jan 15) has some rooms with views of the Tour de César. The family-run *Relais de Templiers*, 68 rue du Pont (ⓣ02.38.44.53.78, ⓦwww.hotelrelaistempliers.com; ❸) is relatively inexpensive, but it's cosy, characterful and very welcoming. There's also a good **HI hostel** in the suburb of Vernon at 152 rte de Châteaudun, 2km north off the main Orléans–Blois road from the east side of town (ⓣ02.38.44.61.31; closed Jan), and a riverside **campsite** (ⓣ02.38.44.50.39; closed Oct–Easter), on the opposite bank from town.

Le Relais du Château, 8 rue du Pont (ⓣ02.38.44.55.10; closed Wed), is a decent, traditional **restaurant** with menus from €14; alternatively, *Le P'tit Bateau*, 54 rue du Pont (ⓣ02.38.44.56.38; closed Mon), has a pleasant terrace and slightly more elevated gastronomic ambitions, with menus from €20 upwards. Midway between the two, *La Crep'zeria*, 32 rue du Pont, serves decent pizzas and crêpes on its sunny terrace.

Château de la Ferté-St-Aubin and around

The **Château de la Ferté-St-Aubin** lies 20km south of Orléans (mid-Feb to mid-Nov daily 10am–7pm; €7, children aged 4–15 €4.50; ⓦwww.chateau-ferte-st-aubin.com), at the north end of the village of the same name. The late sixteenth- and early seventeenth-century building presents an enticing combination of salmon-coloured brick, creamy limestone and dark roof slates, while the interior is a real nineteenth-century home – and you are invited to treat it as such. You can wander freely into almost every room, playing billiards or the piano, picking up the old telephone, sitting on the worn armchairs or washing your hands in a porcelain sink; only the rather fancier grand salon, with its *boiseries* painted with views of the château and its antique furnishings, is cordoned off. Roughly every hour there are demonstrations down in the kitchens of how to make Madeleine cakes – the sweet spongy biscuit that so inspired Proust. At the rear of the château, also enclosed by the moat, there's a play fort with sponge balls supplied for storming it, little cabins with dummies acting out fairy tales, and a toy farm. Older children and adults can explore the adjacent reconstructed 1930s railway station building, with its original *Compagnie des Wagons Lits* (Orient Express) carriages pulled up outside.

The **gare SNCF** is roughly 200m southwest of the village square; around nine trains arrive daily from Orléans and continue south to Vierzon and Bourges. For **eating**, an inexpensive option is the *Auberge Solognote*, at 50 rue des Poulies (closed Tues eve & Wed), behind the covered market on La Ferté's main square.

Six kilometres east of La Ferté-St-Aubin, halfway between Ménestreau-en-Villette and Marcilly-en-Villette, just off the D108, is the little hamlet of **CIRAN**, where you can explore the 300 hectares of the **Domaine de Ciran** (daily 10am–sunset; €5). Its working farm is a typical Sologne setup where the principal activities are deer breeding, keeping goats and making *chèvre*, but the main reason to come is to explore the forested parts of the *domaine*, where you may well catch a glimpse of wild deer, as well as herons and geese around the ponds and sometimes even coypus. It's also possible to come across wild boar, so be careful, though they are not very threatening unless they're with their young. The six-kilometre signed walk – for which waterproof footwear is advisable – gives a good taste of the different landscapes of the region.

East to the Burgundy border

Upstream from Orléans, the rambling Forêt d'Orléans spreads to the north. Beyond it, a bland, treeless wheat plain stretches to Paris, and the immediate countryside to the south is similarly drab: sticking to the Loire itself is the best advice. Along the river are plenty of lesser-known attractions, most notably the **abbey at St-Benoît**, the **château at Sully-sur-Loire**, the small town of **Gien**, the **aqueduct at Briare** and the hilltop town of **Sancerre**, right on the Burgundy border, which makes some of the best dry whites in France.

Germigny-des-Près and St-Benoît-sur-Loire

Heading east of Orléans on the D960, you pass through **Châteauneuf-sur-Loire** – whose château has very pleasant gardens of rhododendrons and magnolias and a small museum of traditional Loire shipping – en route to **GERMIGNY-DES-PRÈS**, 30km from the city. It's a pleasant afternoon's bike ride. The small, plain **church** at Germigny (daily: April–Oct 8.30am–7.30pm; Nov–March 8.30am–6pm; €2 coin needed for lighting) incorporates at its east end one of the few surviving buildings from the Carolingian Renaissance, a tiny, perfectly formed church in the shape of a Greek cross. It was built in 806 as a private oratory for Theodulf, who was one of Charlemagne's counsellors as well as bishop of Orléans and abbot of St-Benoît. The chapel's horseshoe arches suggest the Arabic form but in fact reflect Theodulf's Visigothic origins, while the chapel itself is a typically Carolingian design, rationally planned and drawing on Classical design. The oratory's sheer antiquity is spoiled by too-perfect restoration work, but the unique gold and silver mosaic on the dome of the eastern chapel preserves all its rare beauty. Covered by distemper, it was only discovered by accident in the middle of the nineteenth century when children were found playing with coloured glass cubes in the church.

Five kilometres further upstream, along the D60, **ST-BENOÎT-SUR-LOIRE** offers a more impressive edifice, the Romanesque **Abbaye de Fleury** (daily: April–Oct 7am–9pm; Nov–March 9am–7pm; Ⓦwww.abbaye-fleury.com). In around 672, monks from Fleury returned home from a daring expedition to Monte Cassino in Lombard-occupied Italy with the remains of St-Benoît (St Benedict), the sixth-century founder of the reforming Benedictine order. The presence of the relics secured a prestigious future for the abbey, and over the course of the next 1100 years its abbots included many familiar names from French and Loire history, including the Cardinal of Guise, murdered in the château at Blois, and the great Cardinal Richelieu, who received the title of abbot as a political reward in 1621. For all its importance, the abbey stagnated as often as it flourished, and its population had dwindled to ten monks at the time of the Revolution, after which it was abandoned and dismantled. But the church itself survived, and Benedictine monks returned in 1944. The community now numbers some forty brothers, who still observe the original Rule – poverty, chastity and obedience – and can be heard singing Gregorian chant at the daily midday mass (11am on Sun).

Built in warm, cream-coloured stone between 1020 and 1218, the church dates from the abbey's greatest epoch. The oldest part, the porch tower, illustrates St John's vision of the New Jerusalem in Revelation – foursquare, with open gates on each side. The fantastically sculpted capitals of the heavy pillars are alive with acanthus leaves, birds and exotic animals. Three of them depict scenes from the Apocalypse, while another shows Mary's flight into Egypt. Inside, the choir is split into two levels: above, a marble mosaic of Roman origin covers the chancel floor; below, in the ancient crypt, the relics of St-Benoît lie buried at the very root of the church's forest of columns and arches. You can leave by the north door, where an unfinished Romanesque frieze, discovered only in 1996, shows the progress of sculpture from blind block of stone to finished work.

Sully-sur-Loire and around

SULLY-SUR-LOIRE lies on the south bank of the Loire, 7km east of St-Benoît and accessible by bus from Orléans. The grand **château** here is pure fantasy, despite savage wartime bombing that twice destroyed the nearby Loire bridge and caused incidental damage to the château itself. From the outside, rising massively out of its gigantic moat, it has all the picture-book requirements of pointed towers, machicolations and drawbridge. The interior is slowly being refurnished by its owners – the *département* of the Loiret – and is expected to reopen to visitors in July 2007.

The castle originally belonged to one of Charles VII's favourites, Georges de la Trémoïlle, who infuriated Joan of Arc by encouraging the Dauphin to devote himself to idle hunting in the forests around Sully, and by pursuing a pacifying, diplomatic solution to the wars. After Joan's failure to liberate Paris in 1430, de la Trémoïlle virtually imprisoned her in the castle. She escaped, but was captured less than two months later at the disastrous battle of Compiègne. The castle changed hands in 1602, this time being snapped up by Henri IV's minister, the Duke of Sully, who added the moat and park. After Henri's death, the duke was forced into retirement, which he spent writing in his castle. In the eighteenth century young Voltaire, exiled from Paris for libellous political verse, also spent time at the château. Sully's **International Music Festival**

(Ⓦwww.festival-sully.com) runs right through June, featuring classical concerts held in a huge marquee in the château grounds.

The **village** of Sully itself is brick-built and fairly humdrum, but the quiet riverbank roads are worth exploring by bike, or you can venture north into the Forêt d'Orléans, on the far bank. From the village of **Les Bordes**, 6km north of Sully on the D948/D961, a seven-kilometre forest road will take you due east to the Carrefour de la Résistance, a crossroads in the heart of the wood surrounded by stands of giant oaks and sequoias.

Practicalities

The **gare SNCF**, on the Bourges–Étampes line, is 500m from the centre of the village, where the **tourist office** can be found on place de Gaulle (May–Sept Mon–Sat 9.45am–12.15pm & 2.30–6.30pm, Sun 10.30am–1pm; Oct–April Mon 10am–noon, Tues, Wed, Fri & Sat 10am–noon & 2–6pm, Thurs 2–6pm; Ⓣ02.38.36.23.70). Bikes can be hired from Passion Deux Roues, 10 rue des Epinettes (Ⓣ02.38.35.13.13).

Two decent **hotels** stand around the central marketplace: the *Hostellerie du Grand Sully*, 10 bd du Champ-de-Foire (Ⓣ02.38.36.27.56, Ⓦwww.grandsully.com; ❸; closed Sun eve & Mon) is a reliable choice with a swish restaurant (menus from €27); while the rambling *Hôtel de la Tour*, above a bar at 21 rue Porte de Sologne (Ⓣ02.38.36.21.72, Ⓕ02.38.36.37.63; ❸), has simple rooms freshly done up in a modern style. For camping, *Camping Hortus* (Ⓣ02.38.36.35.94, Ⓦwww.camping-hortus.com; closed Nov–April) is on the opposite side of the Loire. For **eating** out, *Côtes et Jardin*, 8 rue du Grand Sully (Ⓣ02.38.36.35.89; closed Sun & Tues eves, Wed & last 2 weeks in Sept), on the château side of the village, is a distinctly classy affair, with an exceptionally good-value lunchtime menu for €13.

Gien and around

The pretty town of **GIEN** has been restored to its late fifteenth-century quaintness after extensive wartime bombing, and the sixteenth-century stone **bridge** spanning the river gives excellent views as you approach from the south. Looking downstream, the huge cooling towers of the nuclear power station at Dampierre-en-Burly, can be seen emitting streaming clouds of water vapour. The fifteenth-century **château** in the town centre – where the young Louis XIV and his mother, Anne of Austria, hid during the revolts against taxation known as the *Frondes* (see p.1273) – has been turned over to the **Musée International de la Chasse et de la Nature** (Feb, March & Oct–Dec daily except Tues 10am–noon &

△ Along the river at Gien

2–5pm; (April–June & Sept daily except Tues 10am–6pm; July & Aug daily 10am–6pm; closed Jan; €5). Numerous exhibits venerating *la chasse* – hunting horns, tapestries, exquisite watercolours of horseback hunts, guns and falconers' gear – rather outweigh *la nature*. The château itself is modest, but unusual in its brick construction, a pattern of dark red interrupted by geometric inlays of grey; the interior is similarly striking, with its warm combination of brick and timber. Although the exhibits here are dominated by depictions of royal and aristocratic hunting as a sport, it's worth remembering that one of the significant consequences of the French Revolution for rural people was the right to hunt; a right jealously guarded today, particularly in the nearby Sologne.

Gien has also long been known in France for its fine china, and a large factory employs more than two hundred people today. You can buy the ordinary tableware, some of it attractive enough, in the **factory shop** on place de la Victoire, 1km west of the château and bridge, and the hand-worked, arty stuff either in the shops all over town, or direct from the **Musée de la Faïencerie**, immediately adjacent to the factory shop (Jan & Feb Mon–Fri 2–6pm, Sat 9am–noon & 2–6pm; March–Dec Mon–Sat 9am–noon & 2–6pm, Sun 10am–noon & 2–6pm; €3.50), which displays the more extravagant ceramic knick-knacks produced over the last 180-odd years, ranging from exquisitely worked vases to some monstrously pretentious *objets d'art*. A video shows current fabrication techniques, which you can sometimes see for real in the **factory** (by appointment only; closed July, Aug & Dec; ⓣ02.38.67.44.92).

Practicalities

Gien's **tourist office** is on place Jean-Jaurès, between the château and the river (June & Sept Mon–Sat 9am–12.30pm & 2–6.30pm; July & Aug Mon–Sat 9.30am–6.30pm, Sun 10am–noon; Oct–May Mon–Sat 9.30am–noon & 2–6pm; ⓣ02.38.67.25.28). **Bus** #3, which runs between Briare and Orléans, stops at place Leclerc, at the north end of the bridge. For **accommodation**, *La Poularde*, 13 quai de Nice (ⓣ02.38.67.36.05, ⓔlapoularde2@wanadoo.fr; ❸), on the way out of town on the road to Briare, has some lovely rooms looking out onto the river, and an excellent restaurant (menus €29–50). If they're full, try the rather ugly, modern *Sanotel* (ⓣ02.38.67.61.46, ⓦwww.sanotel.fr; ❷), which is just about redeemed by the views from the river-facing rooms. Adjacent is the **campsite** (ⓣ02.38.67.12.50, ⓦwww.camping-gien.com; closed mid-Nov to Feb), which has a swimming pool and lays on outdoor activities, including bike hire and canoe trips. For an alternative to the **restaurant** at *La Poularde*, make for the small strip of decent places on quai Lenoir, by the bridge; the pick of the bunch is the *Restaurant de la Loire*, at no. 18 (ⓣ02.38.67.00.75; closed Mon), which is a refined place serving a wide variety of fish on menus from €18.50.

La Bussière

Twelve kilometres northeast of Gien is another château dedicated to catching your own dinner – this time by fishing. The so-called **Château des Pêcheurs** at **LA BUSSIÈRE** is moored like a ship on its enormous, six-hectare fishpond, connected to a formal arrangement on its mainland of gardens and huge outbuildings (April–June & Sept to mid-Nov Mon & Wed–Sat 10am–noon & 2–6pm; July & Aug daily 10am–6pm; €7). Initially a fortress, the château was turned into a luxurious residence at the end of the sixteenth century, but only the gateway and one pepper-pot tower are recognizably medieval. Guided tours are available, but you're free to wander around, soaking up the genteel atmosphere evoked by the handsome, largely nineteenth-century furnishings and the eccentrically huge collection of freshwater fishing memorabilia bequeathed by Count Henri de Chasseval, whose widow lives in an apartment in one of the outbuildings. Paintings, models, stuffed fish, engravings, flies and rods are scattered throughout the house, while a huge coelacanth (a giant prehistoric relic discovered in the Comoros islands) lurks in a formaldehyde tank in the basement, next to the well-preserved kitchens and laundry.

Briare

The small town of **BRIARE**, 10km southeast of Gien on the Orléans–Nevers road and the Paris–Nevers rail line, centres on its *belle-époque* iron aqueduct, the **Pont Canal**, linking the Canal de Briare to the north with the Canal Lateral à la Loire, which runs south to the Saône. The design of the Pont Canal came from the workshops of Gustav Eiffel (of Tower fame), but parts of the canal scheme date back to the early seventeenth century, when internal waterways linking the Mediterranean, Atlantic and Channel coasts were devised. Poised high above the Loire, you can walk along the aqueduct's extraordinary 625-metre span, with its wrought-iron crested lamps and railings, hopefully without a *bâteau-mouche* spoiling the effect.

On the opposite side of town from the canal, at the northern end, the tiny **Maison des Deux Marines** (daily: March–Sept 10am–12.30pm & 2–6.30pm; Oct to mid-Nov 2–6pm; €5, or €8 with Musée de la Mosaïque) is dedicated to the rival boatmen who plied the Loire and the Canal Lateral; its basement houses a modest aquarium of Loire species. Just across the street, the **Musée de la Mosaïque et des Emaux** (daily: Feb–Sept 10am–6.30pm; Oct–Dec 2–6pm; €5), has a small collection of reproduction and contemporary mosaics made using locally manufactured tiles – Briare's wares adorn sites as prestigious and varied as the mosque at Medina and Paris's RER stations.

The **tourist office**, 1 place Charles-de-Gaulle (April–Sept Mon–Sat 10am–noon & 2–6pm, Sun 10am–noon; Oct–March Mon 2–5pm, Tues–Sat 10am–noon & 2–5pm; ⓣ02.38.31.24.51, ⓦwww.briare-le-canal.com), can provide details of canal boats and canoe rental as well as maps of footpaths, towpaths and the locks (the one at Chatillon-sur-Loire, 4km upstream, is particularly appealing). For **accommodation**, the modern *Auberge du Pont Canal* at 19 rue du Pont-Canal (ⓣ02.38.31.24.24, ⓔnicolas.rou@wanadoo.fr; ❷) is right next to the bridge.

Sancerre and around

Huddled at the top of a steep, round hill with the vineyards below, **SANCERRE** could almost be in Tuscany. The village trades heavily on its famous wines – there are endless *caves* offering tastings – rather than any particular sights or attractions, but it's certainly picturesque and the rolling hills of the Sancerrois, to the northwest, make an attractive venue for walks and cycle rides. First port of call for wine enthusiasts should be the **Maison de Sancerre**, 3 rue du Méridien (April, May, Oct & Nov 10am–6pm, June–Sept 10am–7pm; €5; ⓦwww.maison-des-sancerre.com), which has an elaborate permanent exhibition on winemaking in Sancerre, and a garden of aromatic plants that represent the sixty key flavours found in Sancerre wines. The building itself is a fine fourteenth-century town house, the top of whose tower offers a great view over the rolling, vine-clad hills around.

Wine outlets in the village itself tend to belong to the most famous names, with prices to match, but the informative Aronde Sancerroise, at 4 rue de la Tour, just off the central Nouvelle Place (ⓣ02.48.78.05.72) offers excellent, free tastings as well as tours of local vineyards. The **tourist office**, on Nouvelle Place (daily: June–Sept 10am–6pm; Oct–May 10am–12.30pm & 2.30–5.30pm; ⓣ02.48.54.08.21, ⓦwww.sancerre.fr) can supply lists of *vignerons*; most are small-scale, traditional winemakers and welcome visitors on at least six days of the week. The Daumy family, based in Crézancy-en-Sancerre (ⓣ02.48.79.05.75), has been making excellent organic wines for three generations, including the wonderful but much less commonly made red Sancerre. For a more unusual buy than the well-known white Sancerre, it's well worth exploring the neighbouring areas of Menetou-Salon and Pouilly-Fumé. Well suited to the wines is the local crottin de Chavignol, a goat's cheese named after the neighbouring village in which it's made; signs in Chavignol direct you to **fromageries** open to visitors.

The stretch of the Loire upstream of Sancerre is particularly lovely, and **kayaks** are available to hire (April–Oct 7.30am–9pm; ⓣ02.48.78.00.34) from a shop at the campsite in **St-Satur**, the town at the foot of the hill below Sancerre. The owner, Yvan Thibaudat, is something of a naturalist, and his guided kayak expeditions (€14 for a half day) are fascinating, even if you don't speak French.

Practicalities

The choice of **hotels** in Sancerre is surprisingly poor, but two charming *chambres d'hôtes* more than make up for it: *Le Logis du Grillon*, 3 rue du Chantre (ⓣ02.48.78.09.45; ❹); and *La Belle Époque*, rue St-André (ⓣ02.48.78.00.04; ❸). The two-star *St-Martin*, rue St-Martin (ⓣ02.48.54.21.11; ❸), is comfortable enough, but you're better off down by the river in St-Satur, at the antique-furnished *Hôtel de la Loire*, 2 quai de la Loire (ⓣ02.48.78.22.22, ⓦwww.hotel-de-la-loire.com; ❹) or the welcoming *Auberge de St-Thibault*, 37 rue J.-Combes (ⓣ02.48.78.04.10; ❶), a block away from the river, which has five simple and exceptional-value rooms. An excellent **campsite** (ⓣ02.48.54.04.67; closed Oct–April) is found a little further along the quay, beyond the kayak shop.

There are two fine **restaurants** in Sancerre: *La Pomme d'Or*, 1 rue de la Panneterie (ⓣ02.48.54.13.30; closed Tues & Wed eve); and the more formal *La Tour*, 31 place de la Halle (ⓣ02.48.54.00.81), both with reasonably priced as well as more showy menus. The *Auberge Joseph Mellot*, Nouvelle Place (ⓣ02.48.54.20.53; closed Sun, Tues eve & all Wed) serves good, simple meals that are designed to complement its own top notch wines.

Bourges

BOURGES, the chief town of the rather bland region of Berry, is some way from the Loire valley proper but linked to it historically. The miserable Dauphin (later Charles VII), mockingly dubbed "King of Bourges" by the English, retreated to the city after Henry V's victory at Agincourt had put all of northern France under English control. The presence of one of the finest Gothic cathedrals in France, rising gloriously out of the unpretentious and handsome medieval quarter, provides reason enough for making a detour, but the city also offers an impressive mansion belonging to the Dauphin's financial advisor, Jacques Coeur. Sadly, the citizens of Bourges aren't called "Bourgeois" but instead, "Berruyer".

Bourges's **festival** programme is excellent. Les Printemps de Bourges (ⓦwww.printemps-bourges.com) features hundreds of contemporary music acts from rock to rap, and lasts for one week during the French Easter holidays. More esoteric are the Festival Synthèse, an electronic and acoustic music bash during the first week of June, and Un Été à Bourges (late June to late Sept), a line-up of free, outdoor performances of anything from local organ music to Chinese jazz. Atmospheric ambient lighting transforms the streets of the old town every evening in July and August (and from Thurs to Sat in May, June and Sept).

Arrival, information and accommodation

The **gare routière** is west of the city beyond boulevard Juranville on rue du Prado. The **gare SNCF** lies 1km north of the centre; it's a straightforward-enough walk along avenues Henri Lauder and Jean-Jaurès to place Planchat, from where rue du Commerce connects with the main street, **rue Moyenne**. The **tourist office** is just off the top end of rue Moyenne, at 21 rue Victor-Hugo, facing the south facade of the cathedral (April–Sept Mon–Sat 9am–7pm, Sun 10am–7pm; Oct–March Mon–Sat 9am–6pm, Sun 2–5pm; ⓣ02.48.23.02.60, ⓦwww.bourges-tourisme.com). The old medieval quarter falls away to the east, below the cathedral.

Accommodation in Bourges mostly fails to make the best of the old city, the only attractive options being two three-star hotels and a superb *chambre d'hôte*.

Hotels and chambres d'hôtes

D'Angleterre place des Quatre-Piliers ⓣ02.48.24.68.51, ⓦwww.bestwestern-angleterre-bourges.com. This is the old, traditional town-centre hotel, with an excellent location right next to the Palais de Jacques-Coeur. It has a degree of old-fashioned charm though a recent refurbishment has made it conform to Best Western three-star standards. The less expensive rooms are very small for the price. 6–7

Les Bonnets Rouges 3 rue de la Thaumassière ⓣ02.48.65.79.92, ⓦbonnets-rouges.bourges.net. Five beautifully furnished *chambres d'hôtes* in a striking seventeenth-century house with views of the cathedral from the attic rooms. 5

De Bourbon bd de la République ⓣ02.48.70.70.00, ⓦhoteldebourbon.fr. Between the town centre and the railway station, this is a luxurious hotel converted from a seventeenth-century abbey, though inside it's standard luxury-hotel-chain fare. 7

Le Central 6 rue du Docteur-Témoin ⓣ02.48.24.10.25. Tiny, inexpensive and deeply old-fashioned rooms above a friendly bar just off rue Moyenne. 7

Le Christina 5 rue de la Halle ⓣ02.48.70.56.50, ⓦwww.le-christina.com. The six-storey modern exterior is uninspiring, but inside you'll find a friendly, professionally run hotel with seventy cheerfully decorated rooms, some with a/c. Good value and close to the old centre. 3

Hostel and campsite

HI hostel 22 rue Henri-Sellier ⓣ02.48.24.58.09, ⓔbourges@fuaj.org. Hostel located a short way southwest of the centre, overlooking the River Auron. Bus #1 from the station towards "Golf", stop "Europe"; or a 10min walk from the cathedral or *gare routière*. Open mid-Jan to mid-Dec daily 8am–noon & 6–10pm. HI membership required.

Camping Robinson 26 bd de l'Industrie ⓣ02.48.20.16.85. Decent-sized three-star site located south of the HI hostel. Bus #1 from place Cujas, stop "Joffre", or a 10min walk from the *gare routière*. Closed mid-Nov to mid-March.

The City

The centre of **Bourges** sits on a hill rising from the marshes of the River Yèvre, in the shadow of its main attraction, the magnificent early Gothic cathedral. Having seen the cathedral, many people move straight on, but the rest of the city is worth at least a couple of hours of wandering, with a number of ancient *hôtels* and burghers' houses displaying the wealth of a place that was built to rival the ruling provincial city of Dijon.

The cathedral

The exterior of the twelfth-century **Cathédrale St-Étienne** (daily: April–June & Sept 8.30am–7.15pm; July & Aug 8.30am–7.45pm; Oct–March 9am–5.45pm) is characterized by the delicate, almost skeletal appearance of flying buttresses supporting an entire nave that has no transepts to break up its bulk. A much-vaunted example of Gothic architecture, it's modelled on Notre-Dame in Paris but incorporates improvements on the latter's design, such as the astonishing height of the inner aisles.

The **tympanum** above the main door of the west portal could engross you for hours with its tableau of the Last Judgement, featuring carved, naked figures with bodies full of movement and faces alive with expression. Thirteenth-century imagination has been given full rein in the depiction of the devils, complete with snakes' tails and winged bottoms and faces appearing from below the waist, symbolic of the soul in the service of sinful appetites.

The interior's best feature is the twelfth- to thirteenth-century **stained glass**. There are geometric designs in the main body of the cathedral, but the most glorious windows, with astonishing deep colours, are around the choir, all created between 1215 and 1225. You can follow the stories of the Prodigal Son, the Rich Man and Lazarus, the life of Mary, Joseph in Egypt, the Good Samaritan, Christ's Crucifixion, the Last Judgement and the Apocalypse – binoculars come in handy for picking up the exquisite detail. On either side of the central absidal chapel, polychrome figures kneel in prayer; these are **Jean de Berry**, the great artistic patron of late fourteenth-century Bourges, and his wife. The painted decoration of the **astronomical clock** in the nave celebrates the wedding of Charles VII, who married Marie d'Anjou here on April 22, 1422.

On the northwest side of the nave aisle is the door to the **Tour de Beurre** (daily except Sun morning: April & Sept 9.45–11.45am & 2–5.30pm; May & June 9.30–11.30am & 2–6pm; July & Aug 9.30am–6.15pm; Oct–March 9.30–11.30am & 2–4.45pm; €5, or €9 with the crypt and Palais de Jacques-Coeur), which you can climb unsupervised for fantastic views over the old city, the marshes and the countryside beyond. You can also join a guided tour of the **crypt** (same hours and ticket; tours roughly every hour), where you can see the alabaster statue of a puggish Jean de Berry, a small bear, symbol of strength, lying asleep at his feet. Alongside are fragments of the cathedral's original rood screen, which survived the Protestant siege of 1562 but not the modernizers of the mid-eighteenth century, while a wonderful polychrome *Entombment* from the 1530s adorns the dark centre of the crypt. The same ticket allows you to climb unsupervised to the top of the north **tower**, rebuilt in flamboyant style after the original collapsed in 1506.

Next to the cathedral in place E.-Dolet, the **Musée des Meilleurs Ouvriers de France** (Tues–Sat 10am–noon & 2–5pm, Sun 2–5pm; free) displays show-off pieces by French artisans. The theme changes each year, and recent features have included glassblowing, woodwork and pastry-making.

The rest of the city

Bourges's museums may be modest, but they are housed in some beautiful medieval buildings, the finest of which are all within a stone's throw of the north end of rue Moyenne. Rue Bourbonnoux, parallel to rue Moyenne to the east of the cathedral, is worth a wander for the early Renaissance **Hôtel Lallemant**, richly decorated in an Italianate style. It houses the **Musée des Arts Décoratifs** (Tues–Sat 10am–noon & 2–5pm, Sun 2–5pm; free), a diverting enough museum of paintings, tapestries, furniture and *objets d'art*, including works by the Berrichon artist Jean Boucher (1575–1633). The coffered ceiling of the oratory is carved with alchemical symbols. Halfway along the street, you can take a narrow passage up to the remains of the Gallo-Roman town **ramparts**, lined with old houses and trees. On rue Edouard-Branly, you'll find the fifteenth-century **Hôtel des Échevins**, home to the **Musée de Maurice Estève** (Mon & Wed–Sat 10am–noon & 2–5pm, Sun 2–5pm; free), dedicated to the highly coloured, mostly abstract paintings and tapestries by the locally born artist, who died in 2001.

The continuation of rue Edouard-Branly, **rue Jacques-Coeur**, was the site of the head office, stock exchange, dealing rooms, bank safes and home of Charles VII's finance minister, Jacques Coeur (1400–56), a medieval shipping magnate, moneylender and arms dealer who dominates Bourges as Joan of Arc does Orléans – Charles VII just doesn't get a look-in. The **Palais de Jacques-Coeur** (daily: May & June 9.45–11am & 2–5.15pm; July & Aug 9.45–11.30am & 2–5.45pm; Sept–April 9.45–11am & 2–4.15pm; €6.10; guided tours every 30min–1hr, depending on the season) is one of the most remarkable examples of fifteenth-century domestic architecture in France. The visit starts with the fake windows on the entrance front from which two realistically sculpted half-figures look down. There are hardly any furnishings, but much of the decoration of the house's stonework recalls the man who had it built, including a pair of bas-reliefs on the courtyard tower that may represent Jacques and his wife, and numerous hearts and scallop shells inside that playfully allude to his name. On the first floor, a wonderful bas-relief of a *galleasse*, with its oars and sails spread, symbolizes Jacques' trading empire. The house is unusually modern for its time, with latrines, a steam room, and a rationally planned design that predates the symmetries of French Renaissance architecture. A reconstruction of the tomb of Jean de Berry dominates one of the rooms on the upper floor.

Steps lead down beside the palace to rue des Arènes, where the sixteenth-century **Hôtel Cujas** houses the **Musée du Berry** (Mon & Wed–Sat 10am–noon & 2–5pm, Sun 2–5pm; free), which has an interesting collection of local artefacts, most notably ten of the forty *pleurants* that survived the breaking up of Jean de Berry's tomb; Rodin considered these weeping statues so beautiful that he paid 6000 francs for one shortly before his death. Etruscan bronzes and Roman funerary monuments bear witness to Bourges's ancient history, while an exhibition on the theme of traditional rural life occupies the first floor. Close by is the pleasant **place Notre-Dame**, with its church clearly showing the shift from Gothic to Renaissance.

Eating and drinking

Bourges's main centre for **eating** is along rue Bourbonnoux, which runs between place Gordaine and the cathedral. *D'Antan Sancerrois*, at 50 rue Bourbonnoux (Ⓣ02.48.65.96.26; closed Sun & Mon lunch), features excellent local dishes (à la carte mains around €18), while the friendly *Bourbonnoux*, at no. 44 (Ⓣ02.48.24.14.76; closed Sat lunch, Fri & Sun eve out of season) has some ambitious regional menus (€13–30); *La Crêperie des Remparts*, at no. 59, (Ⓣ02.48.24.55.44; closed Sun & Mon lunch) has a better-than-usual range of crêpes and salads. Just off rue Borbonnoux, the deliciously refined tea room *Cak't*, promenade des Remparts (Ⓣ02.48.24.94.60; closed Sun & Mon) serves home-made quiches and tarts at lunchtime and afternoon tea.

Just off attractive, medieval place Gordaine, the smart Bourges institution *Au Sénat*, 8 rue de la Poissonnerie (Ⓣ02.48.24.02.56; closed Wed & Thurs) cooks excellent traditional dishes, and has tables out on the street (menus €17–33). *Le Louis XI*, 200m down from the cathedral at 11 rue Porte Jaune

(Ⓣ02.48.70.92.14; closed Sun), serves impeccable steaks and chargrilled meats in a small, informal dining room (menus €17–26). For a complete change, the friendly *Margouillat*, at 53 rue Edouard Vaillant, beyond place Gordaine (Ⓣ02.48.24.08.13; closed Sun, plus Sat & Mon lunch) offers delicious, reasonably priced food from Réunion such as giant prawns or pork and beans served with hot dips, plus delicious tropical desserts and cocktails.

Those with a sweet tooth should head for the excellent **patisserie**, Aux Trois Flûtes, on the corner of rues Joyeuse and Bourbonnoux; for chocolates and the local sweet speciality of *fourrées au praliné*, try the imposing Maison Forestines, on place Cujas, at the foot of rue Porte Jaune. On warm nights, place Cujas is also a great spot for a **drink**; the bar *Le Cujas* has plenty of outside seating.

The Cher and upper Indre

Of all the Loire's many tributaries, the slow-moving **Cher** and **Indre** are closest to the heart of the region, watering a host of châteaux as they flow northwest from the little-visited region to the south. Twenty kilometres southeast of Tours, spanning the Cher, the **Château de Chenonceau** is perhaps the best of all the Loire châteaux for its architecture, site, contents and atmosphere. Further upstream, **Montrichard** and **St-Aignan** make quieter diversions from the endless stream of castle tours. To the south is the château of **Valençay**, with its exquisite Empire interiors. A short drive west of here, on the River Indre itself, **Loches** possesses the most magnificent medieval citadel in the region.

Château de Chenonceau

Unlike the Loire, the gentle River Cher flows so slowly and passively between the exquisite arches of the **Château de Chenonceau** (daily: first 2 weeks Feb & first 2 weeks Nov 9am–5pm; last 2 weeks Feb & last 2 weeks Oct 9am–5.30pm; first 2 weeks March & first 2 weeks Oct 9am–6pm; mid-March to mid-Sept 9am–7pm; last 2 weeks Sept 9am–6.30pm; Nov 16 to Jan 9am–4.30pm; €9; Ⓦwww.chenonceau.com) that you're almost always assured of a perfect reflection. The château is not visible from the road so you have to pay before even getting a peek at the residence. While the tree-lined path to the front door is dramatic, for a more intimate approach, head through the **gardens**, which were laid out under Diane de Poitiers, mistress of Henri II.

The building of Chenonceau was always controlled by women. Catherine Briçonnet – whose husband Thomas Bohier bought the site on the proceeds from embezzling from his master, François I – hired the first architects in 1515 and had them begin building on the foundations of an old mill that stood on the granite bed of the Cher. The château's most characteristic feature, the set of **arches** spanning the River Cher, was begun later in the century by Diane de Poitiers and completed by the indomitable Catherine de Médicis (wife of Henri II), after she had evicted Diane and forced her to hand over the château in return for Chaumont (see p.523). Mary, Queen of Scots, child bride of François II, also spent time here until her husband's early death. Then, after a long period of disuse, one Madame Dupin brought eighteenth-century life to this gorgeous residence, along with her guests Voltaire, Montesquieu and Rousseau, whom she hired as tutor to her son. Restoration back to the sixteenth-century designs was completed by another woman, Madame Pelouze, in the late nineteenth century. It's now a profitable business, owned and run by the Menier chocolate family firm.

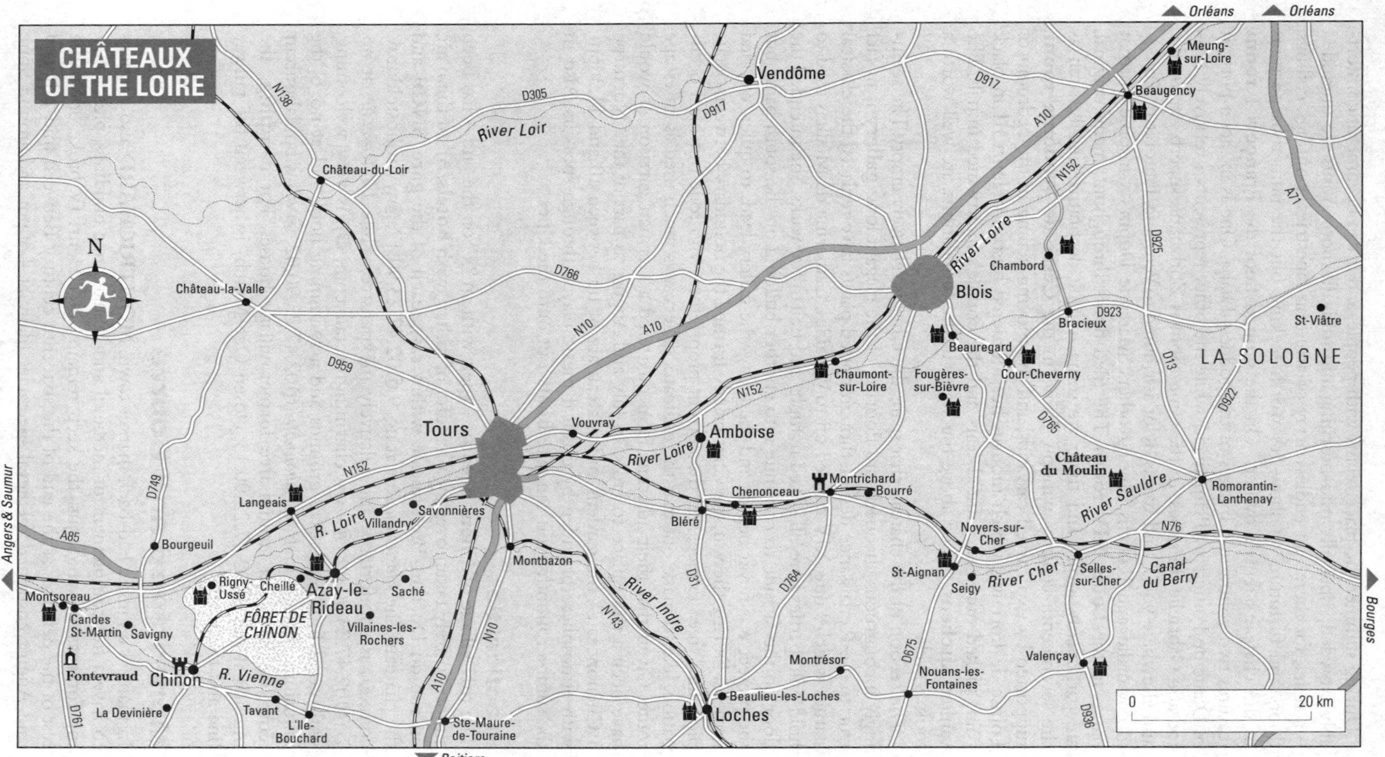
CHÂTEAUX OF THE LOIRE
Orléans
Orléans
Bourges
Poitiers
Angers & Saumur
N
0
20 km
LA SOLOGNE
Vendôme
Meung-sur-Loire
Beaugency
Château-du-Loir
Château-la-Valle
Chambord
Blois
St-Viâtre
Bracieux
Beauregard
Cour-Cheverny
Chaumont-sur-Loire
Fougères-sur-Bièvre
Tours
Vouvray
Amboise
Château du Moulin
Montrichard
Bourré
Chenonceau
Romorantin-Lanthenay
Langeais
Savonnières
Villandry
Bléré
Noyers-sur-Cher
Bourgeuil
Montbazon
St-Aignan
Seigy
Selles-sur-Cher
Canal du Berry
Montsoreau
Rigny-Ussé
Cheillé
Azay-le-Rideau
Saché
Candes St-Martin
Savigny
FÔRET DE CHINON
Villaines-les-Rochers
Montrésor
Valençay
Fontevraud
Chinon
R. Vienne
Nouans-les-Fontaines
Beaulieu-les-Loches
La Devinière
Tavant
L'Ile-Bouchard
Loches
Ste-Maure-de-Touraine
River Loir
River Loire
River Loire
R. Loire
River Sauldre
River Cher
River Indre
N138
D305
D917
D917
A10
N152
A71
D925
D766
N10
A10
D923
D959
D13
N152
D922
D765
N152
D749
A85
N76
D31
D764
N143
N10
D675
A10
D761
D936

During summer the place teems with people, and it can become uncomfortably crowded, especially mid-morning and mid-afternoon. Visits are unguided – a relief, for there's an endless array of arresting tapestries, paintings, ceilings, floors and furniture on show. It's worth seeking out the numerous portraits of the château's female owners. On the ground floor the **François I room** features two contrasting images of the goddess Diana. One is in fact a portrait of Diane de Poitiers by Primaticcio while the other represents a relatively aristocratic Gabrielle d'Estrées. In the same room is Zurbarán's superb *Archimedes*, and elsewhere you'll find works by or attributed to Veronese, Tintoretto, Coreggio, Murillo and Rubens, among others; Madame Dupin's winsome portrait hangs in the **Louis XIV room**. The tiled floors throughout, many original, are particularly lovely, and there are some unique decorative details, such as the seventeenth-century window-frame in the **César de Vendôme room**, supported by two carved caryatids, and the moving ceiling in the bedroom of Louise de Lorraine, which mourns her murdered husband Henri III in black paint picked out with painted tears and the couple's intertwined initials. The vaulted **kitchens**, poised above the water in the foundations, are well worth a look as well.

The section of the château that spans the Cher is relatively empty. The seemingly incongruous chequerboard flooring of the elegant long **gallery** is in fact true to the Renaissance design, though potted plants have replaced the classical statues which Louis XIV carried off to Versailles. Catherine de Médicis used to hold wild parties here, all naked nymphs and Italian fireworks. She intended the door on the far side to continue into another building on the south bank, but the project was never begun, and these days the gallery leads to quiet, wooded gardens. During the war, the Cher briefly formed the boundary between occupied and "free" France, and the current proprietors, who rode out Nazi occupation, like to make out that the château's gallery was much used as an escape route. Given that their adjacent farm quartered a German garrison, it would have been a risky place to cross. In July and August, as part of the "Nocturne à Chenonceau", the gardens and château are lit up between 10 and 11.30pm, with atmosphere provided by classical music played through speakers. Also in the summer months, you can take **boats** out onto the Cher.

Practicalities

The tiny village of **Chenonceaux** – spelt with an "x" on the end – has been almost entirely taken over by a handful of rather swish **hotels**. All of them are on rue du Docteur-Bretonneau, within easy reach of the **gare SNCF** and the château. The *Hostel du Roy* at no. 9 ⓣ02.47.23.90.17, ⓦwww.hostelduroy.com; ❸) is comfortable and relatively inexpensive; while *La Roseraie*, at no. 7 (ⓣ02.47.23.90.09, ⓦwww.charmingroseraie.com; ❹), is very welcoming, with good food, extensive grounds and a swimming pool; and at no. 6, the luxurious *Auberge du Bon Laboureur* (ⓣ02.47.23.90.02, ⓦwww.bonlaboureur.com; ❼) is spread around five former village houses. For **camping**, the municipal site (ⓣ02.47.23.90.13; closed Oct–March) is between the railway line and the river.

Montrichard and Bourré

In many ways just a laid-back market town, **MONTRICHARD** also happens to have a full complement of medieval and Renaissance buildings, plus a hilltop **fortress**, of which just the keep remains after Henri IV broke down the rest of the defences at the end of the sixteenth century. Between mid-July and mid-August costumed medieval spectacles (daily at 4.30pm and around 9pm;

€15) in the former château grounds entertain mostly children. At any time, you can climb up the hill for the view of the Cher – though the keep itself is out of bounds. Montrichard's Romanesque **church** was where the disabled 12-year-old princess, Jeanne de Valois, who would never be able to have children, married her cousin the Duc d'Orléans. When he became King Louis XII, after the unlikely death of Charles VIII at Amboise, politics dictated that he marry Charles VIII's widow, Anne of Brittany. Poor Jeanne was divorced and sent off to govern Bourges, where she founded a new religious order and eventually took the veil herself, before dying in 1505. It's not all gloom: in summer, you can rent pedalos and **kayaks** (Ⓣ02.54.71.49.48; closed Sept–June) at the pleasant artificial **beach** on the opposite bank of the Cher. Some hardy locals swim from here, but be sure to seek advice before entering the water.

Three kilometres to the east of Montrichard, the hills around **BOURRÉ** are riddled with enormous, cave-like quarries, dug deep to get at the famous château-building stone that gets whiter as it weathers. Some of the caves are now used to cultivate mushrooms – big business in the Loire – a peculiar process that you can witness at the **Caves Champignonnières**, 40 rte des Roches (guided visits daily: Easter to mid-Nov 10am, 11am, 2pm, 3pm, 4pm & 5pm; €6; Ⓦwww.le-champignon.com). A second tour takes you to a "subterranean city" (€6, or €10 for both tours) sculpted in recent years as a tourist attraction, and there's an excellent shop including rare varieties of mushroom and various mushroom products. You can visit a fascinating troglodyte dwelling at **La Magnanerie**, 4 chemin de la Croix-Bardin (guided visits only: Easter–Aug daily except Tues at 11am, 3pm, 4pm & 5pm; Sept Sun–Thurs at 3pm, 4pm & 5pm; Oct Fri–Sun at 4pm; €6). The owner demonstrates how his family and their ancestors lived a troglodyte life here, quarrying the soft stone using huge saws, and producing silk in a chamber riddled with pigeonhole-like niches and stocked with living silkworms.

Practicalities

Montrichard's **tourist office** is in the Maison Ave Maria (April–Sept Mon–Sat 9am–noon & 2–6pm, Sun 10am–noon; Ⓣ02.54.32.05.10, Ⓦwww.officetourisme-montrichard.com), an ancient house with saints and beasties sculpted down its beams, on rue du Pont. The only enticing **hotel** is *La Tête Noir*, 24 rue de Tours (Ⓣ02.54.32.05.55, Ⓔg.galimard@wanadoo.fr; ❹), with its terrace on the river, though the atmospheric *Manoir de la Salle du Roc*, 69 rte de Vierzon (Ⓣ02.54.32.73.54, Ⓦmanoirdelasalleduroc.monsite.wanadoo.fr; ❺), offers grand *chambres d'hôtes* set in an ancient manor house above the main road leading west from Bourré. There's also a **campsite**, *L'Étourneau* (Ⓣ02.54.32.10.16; closed mid-Sept to May), right in town, on the banks of the Cher. Decent meals can be had at *Les Tuffeaux*, a straightforward brasserie on Montrichard's main square, place Bartélémy-Gilbert.

St-Aignan

ST-AIGNAN, 15km southeast of Montrichard, is a small town comprising a cluster of houses below a huge Romanesque collegiate church and sixteenth-century private château. The lofty **Collégiale de St-Aignan** (Mon–Sat 9am–7pm, Sun 1–7pm) features some fine capitals carved in the twelfth century, though many more are nineteenth-century recreations. The crypt is renowned for its remarkably preserved, brightly coloured twelfth- and thirteenth-century frescoes, some of which show the beginnings of naturalistic Gothic tendencies. A flight of 144 steps climbs from the *collégiale* to a grand gravelled terrace of the

château, enclosed on one side by the L-shape of the Renaissance *logis*, and on the other by the remnants of the eleventh-century fortress. Private ownership means it's closed to visitors, but you're free to stroll around – the far corner of the terrace leads through to a great **view** of the river, and you can continue down some steep steps to the river. You can ask at the tourist office for details of **boat trips** on the Cher, or hire windsurfers, canoes and sail boats at the lake a couple of kilometres upstream, in **Seigy.** The Maison du Vin, on place Wilson (July & Aug daily 10am–noon & 3–6pm; Sept–June Tues & Thurs 8am–noon), is open for tastings and sales of Côteaux du Cher wines.

One of the region's biggest tourist attractions is the excellent **Zoo Parc Beauval** (daily: 9am–dusk; €17, children aged 3–12 €12; Ⓦwww.zoobeauval.com), 2km to the south of town on the D675. The space given to the animals is ample, and it's part of a Europe-wide programme for breeding threatened species in captivity. Sumptuous flower-beds give way to little streams and lakes where islands provide natural enclosures for some of the monkeys. Two hothouses with tropical flowers and greenery are home to an extraordinary collection of birds as well as a large group of chimpanzees and two families of orang-utans.

Practicalities

The **tourist office**, 60 rue Constant-Ragot (June & Sept Mon–Sat 10am–12.30pm & 2–6.30pm, Sun 10am–noon & 3–6pm; July & Aug Mon–Sat 9.30am–12.30pm & 2–6.30pm, Sun 10am–noon & 3–6pm; Oct–May Mon–Sat 10am–12.30pm & 2–6pm; Ⓣ02.54.75.22.85, Ⓦwww.tourisme-valdecher-staignan.com) is just off the car park-like place Président-Wilson, in the upper part of town. The only two **hotels** are both alongside the river, on either side of the bridge: *Hôtel du Moulin*, 7 rue Novilliers (Ⓣ02.54.75.15.54; ❷; closed Sun), is fairly basic but friendly; while *Le Grand Hôtel St-Aignan*, 7–9 quai J.-J.-Delorme Ⓣ02.54.75.18.04, Ⓔgrand.hotel.st.aignan@wanadoo.fr; ❸) is a hushed, well-furnished affair, with a good restaurant (menus €13–36). St-Aignan has an excellent **campsite** on the bank of the river near Seigy, the *Camping des Cochards* (Ⓣ02.54.75.15.59; closed mid-Oct to March). For an alternative to the hotel **restaurants**, the *Mange-Grenouille*, 10 rue Paul-Boncour (Ⓣ02.54.71.74.91; closed Tues eve & Wed; menus €14–28) has a delightful sixteenth-century decor and outside seating in its courtyard. The welcoming *L'Amarena*, place de la Paix (Ⓣ02.54.75.47.98, closed Mon lunch), serves inexpensive Italian food on an attractive square.

Château de Valençay

There is nothing medieval about the fittings and furnishings of the **Château de Valençay**, 20km southeast of St-Aignan on the main Blois–Châteauroux road (daily: April, May & Sept 10.30am–6pm; June 9.30am–6pm; July & Aug 9.30am–7.30pm; Oct 10.30am–5.30pm; €9; Ⓦwww.chateau-valencay.com), for all its huge pepper-pot towers and turreted, decorated keep. This refined castle was originally built to show off the wealth of a sixteenth-century financier, but the lasting impression of a visit today is the imperial legacy of its greatest owner, the **Prince de Talleyrand**.

One of the great political operators and survivors, Talleyrand owes his greatest fame to his post as Napoleon's foreign minister. A bishop before the Revolution, with a reputation for having the most desirable mistresses, he proposed the nationalization of church property, renounced his bishopric, escaped to America during the Terror, backed Napoleon and continued to serve the state under the restored Bourbons. One of his tasks for the emperor was keeping Ferdinand VII of Spain entertained for six years here after the king had been forced to abdicate in favour of Napoleon's brother Joseph. The Treaty of Valençay, signed in the château in 1813, put an end to Ferdinand's forced guest status, giving him back his throne. The interior consequently is largely First Empire: elaborately embroidered chairs, Chinese vases, ornate inlays to all the tables, faux-Egyptian details, finicky clocks and chandeliers. A single discordant note is struck by the leg-brace and shoe displayed in a glass cabinet along with Talleyrand's uniforms – the statesman's deformed foot was concealed in every painting of the man, including the one displayed in the portrait gallery that runs the length of the graceful Neoclassical wing.

The château **park** (same hours as above) keeps a collection of unhappy-looking camels, zebras, llamas and goats, and there's a small, imaginative maze. In the village, about 100m from the château gates, a **car museum** (daily: April–June, Sept & Oct 10am–12.30pm & 1.30–6pm; July & Aug closes 7.30pm; €3) houses an excellent collection of sixty-odd mostly prewar cars.

Loches and around

LOCHES, 42km southeast of Tours, is the obvious place to head for in the Indre valley. Its walled **citadel** is by far the most impressive of the Loire valley fortresses, with its unbreached ramparts and the Renaissance houses below still partly enclosed by the outer wall of the medieval town. Tours is only an hour away by bus, but Loches makes for a quiet, relatively untouristy base for exploring the Cher valley, or the much lesser-known country south, up the Indre.

The **old town** is dominated by the Tour St-Antoine belfry, close to the handsome place du Marché, which links rue St-Antoine with Grande Rue. Two fifteenth-century gates to the old town still stand: the **Porte des Cordeliers**, by the river at the end of Grande Rue, and the **Porte Picois** to the west, at the end of rue St-Antoine. Rue du Château, lined with Renaissance buildings, leads to the twelfth-century towers of **Porte Royale**, the main entrance to the citadel.

The citadel

Behind the Porte Royale, the **Musée Lansyer** occupies the house of local nineteenth-century landscape painter Emmanuel Lansyer, done up in period style (April–Oct daily except Tues 10.30am–12.30pm & 2.30–5pm; €3). Straight ahead is the Romanesque church, the **Collégiale de St-Ours**, with its distinctively odd roofline – the nave bays are capped by two octagonal stone pyramids, sandwiched between two more conventional spires. The porch has some entertaining twelfth-century monster carvings, and the stoup, or basin for holy water, is a Gallo-Roman altar. But the church's highlight is the shining white **tomb of Agnès Sorel**, the mistress of the Dauphin Charles VII. It's a beautiful recumbent figure tenderly watched over by angels. The alabaster is rather more pristine than it should be, as it had to be restored after anticlerical revolutionary soldiers mistook her for a saint – an easy error to make.

The northern end of the citadel is taken up by the **Logis Royal**, or Royal Lodgings, of Charles VII and his three successors (daily: Jan–March & Oct–Dec 9.30am–5pm; April–Sept 9am–7pm; €5, €7 including the donjon). It has two distinct halves, similar at first glance, but separated by a century in which the medieval need for defence began to give way to a more courtly, luxurious lifestyle. The first section was built in the late fourteenth century as a kind of pleasure palace for the Dauphin Charles and Agnès Sorel. A copy of Charles's portrait by Fouquet can be seen in the antechamber to the Grande Salle, where the Dauphin met the second woman of importance in his life between June 3 and June 5, 1429 – Joan of Arc, who came here victorious from Orléans to give the defeatist Dauphin another pep talk about coronations.

From the Logis Royal, cobbled streets overlooked by handsome town houses wind through to the far end of the elevated citadel, where the **donjon** (same hours and ticket as Logis Royal) begun by Foulques Nerra, the eleventh-century count of Anjou, stands in grim ruin. Vertiginous gantry stairways climb up through the empty shell of the massive keep to its very top, but the main interest lies in the dungeons and lesser towers. The Tour Ronde was built under Louis XI to provide a platform for artillery and also served as a prison for his adviser, Cardinal Balue, who was kept locked up in a wooden cage in one of the upper rooms. Perhaps he was kept in the extraordinary graffiti chamber on the second floor, which is decorated with an enigmatic series of deeply carved, soldier-like figures that may date from the thirteenth century. From the courtyard, steps lead down into the bowels of the Martelet, which became the home of a more famous prisoner: Ludovico "Il Moro" Sforza, duke of Milan, patron of Leonardo da Vinci and captive of Louis XII. In the four years he was imprisoned here, from 1500, he found time to decorate his cave-like cell with ruddy wall-paintings, still faintly visible. The dungeons peter out into quarried-out galleries which produced the stone for the keep.

Practicalities

From Tours, trains and buses alike arrive at the **gare SNCF** on the east side of the Indre, just up from place de la Marne, where the **tourist office** is housed in a little wooden chalet (April–June & Sept Mon–Sat 9.30am–12.30pm & 1.30–6.30pm, Sun 10am–12.30pm & 1.30–6pm; July & Aug Mon–Sat 9am–7pm, Sun 10am–12.30pm & 1.30–6pm; Oct–March Mon–Sat 10am–12.30pm & 2.30–6pm; Ⓣ02.47.91.82.82, Ⓦwww.loches-tourainecotesud.com).

The best **accommodation** option is the old-fashioned and characterful *Hôtel de France*, 6 rue Picois (Ⓣ02.47.59.00.32, Ⓦwww.hoteldefranceloches.com; ❸), which has a good restaurant. The *Hôtel George Sand*, 37 rue Quintefol (Ⓣ02.47.59.39.74, Ⓦwww.hotelrestaurant-georgesand.com; ❺), just below the eastern ramparts, has its best rooms at the back, looking onto the river; its restaurant has a lovely terrace overlooking the Indre. Inexpensive rooms can be found at the charmingly tumbledown *Hôtel de Beaulieu*, 3 rue Foulques-Nerra (Ⓣ02.47.91.60.80; ❷), right next to the abbey in Beaulieu-les-Loches, 1km across the river (see below). The municipal **campsite** *La Citadelle* (Ⓣ02.47.59.05.91; closed mid-Oct to mid-March) is between two branches of the Indre by the swimming pool and stadium.

For an alternative to the hotel **restaurants**, *L'Entracte*, 4 Grande-Rue (Ⓣ02.47.94.05.70, closed Sun; menus from €10) does hearty and generous bistro food, and has a lovely courtyard out back. The recreations of medieval recipes at *Le Vicariat*, next to the château on place Charles-VII (Ⓣ02.47.59.08.79; closed Mon & Sun eve; menus €19–43), can be fun, and there is a great outside terrace. The best option of all is to stock up at the superb **market**, held in the winding streets just above the château gate on Wednesday and Saturday mornings.

Beaulieu-les-Loches

Just across the Indre from Loches is the village of **BEAULIEU-LES-LOCHES** – a little-known place, thoroughly medieval in appearance, with its parish church built into the spectacular ruins of an abbey contemporary with Loches' grisly donjon. Its other church, St-Pierre, holds the bones of Foulques Nerra, the eleventh-century count of Anjou responsible for the donjon.

Blois and around

The château at **BLOIS**, the handsome former seat of the dukes of Orléans, is one of the most stately and historic of them all. Its great facade rises above the modern town like an Italianate cliff, with the dramatic esplanade and courtyard behind and the rooms within steeped in, sometimes bloody, history. The town itself is unexceptional but makes a good base for getting out into the countryside, with several stretches of woodland within striking distance including the **Forêt de Blois** to the west of the town on the north bank of the Loire, and the **Parc de Chambord** and **Forêt de Boulogne**, further upstream. To the south and east, the forested, watery, game-rich area known as the **Sologne** lies between the Loire and Cher, stretching beyond Orléans almost as far as Gien. And if you haven't yet tired of **châteaux**, some of the grandest of all, as well as some of the most intimate, are within cycling distance.

Arrival, information and accommodation

Blois is easy to get around: avenue Jean-Laigret is the main street leading south from the **gare SNCF** to place Victor-Hugo and the château, and past it to the town centre. The **gare routière** is directly in front of the *gare SNCF*, with **buses** leaving up to three times a day for Cheverny and Chambord. The **tourist office**, 23 place du Château, the château esplanade (May–Sept Mon & Sun 10am–7pm, Tues–Sat 9am–7pm; Oct–April Mon–Sat 9am–12.30pm & 2–6pm, Sun 9.30am–12.30pm; ⓣ02.54.90.41.41, ⓦwww.loiredeschateaux.com), organizes hotel rooms for a small fee and has information on day coach tours of Chambord and Cheverny. It also sells a combined ticket (€15) to the château, son et lumière and Maison de la Magie. Regional information is available online at ⓦwww.chambordcountry.com. **Bikes** can be hired from Cycles Leblond, 44 levée des Tuileries (ⓣ02.54.74.30.13, ⓦcycles.leblond.free.fr), and Bike in Blois, 8 rue Henri Drussy (ⓣ02.54.56.07.73, ⓦwww.locationdevelos.com). The hotels in Blois are decent but none are outstanding.

Hotels

Du Bellay 12 rue des Minimes ⓣ02.54.78.23.62, ⓦhoteldubellay.free.fr. Comfortable budget option with twelve well-worn but clean little rooms, much cheered up by pictures of local sights and the odd wooden beam. Good location at the top of the hill, above the town centre. ❷

Côté Loire 2 place de la Grève ⓣ02.54.78.07.86, ⓦwww.coteloire.com. Charming boutique hotel, tucked away in a quiet corner by the river. Rooms have antique furnishings and brand-new bathrooms – those on the front have views of the river. ❹

De France et de Guise 3 rue Gallois ⓣ02.54.78.00.53, ⓦannedebretagne.free.fr. Grand, comfortable old hotel on a busy road just below the château. Formerly the Guise's town house, though little evidence remains. Some rooms have balconies with views of the château's loggia. ❸

Mercure 28 quai St-Jean ⓣ02.54.56.66.66, ⓦwww.mercure.com. No character whatsoever, but it certainly offers *tout confort* – all mod cons, including a pool. Overlooks the river to the east of the town centre. ❼

Le Monarque 61 rue Porte Chartraine ⓣ02.54.78.02.35, ⓦannedebretagne.free.fr. Professional and energetically managed hotel with rooms cheerfully renovated in a modern style. Usefully located at the top end of town. ❸

Le Savoie 6 rue du Ducoux ⓣ02.54.74.32.21, ⓦwww.hotel-blois.com. Unexceptional but nonetheless likeable hotel near the train station, with pretty little rooms. Run by a friendly young couple. ❸

Hostel and campsite

HI Hostel 18 rue de l'Hôtel-Pasquier ⓣ02.54.78.27.21, ⓔblois@fuaj.org. Five km downstream from Blois, between the Forêt de Blois and the river. Bus #4 runs at least once an hour, but stops at around 7pm, so you'll need wheels. Closed mid-Nov to Feb.

Camping Rives de Loire Vineuil ⓣ08.00.30.04.10. On the south bank of the river, 4km from the town centre. Bus #3C (stop "Mairie Vineuil") only runs four times daily, but the campsite offers bike hire. Closed Oct–May.

The château

The six great kings of the sixteenth century all spent time at the **Château de Blois** (daily: April–Oct 9am–6.30pm; Nov–March 9am–12.30pm & 2–5.30pm; €6.50), and the ones who didn't build here left their mark on its history instead. From the plateau-like esplanade in front of the château, you step into the courtyard, where the extraordinary clash of architectural styles has only been slightly muted by time. The relatively plain stone of the Gothic Salle des États, the manorial assembly hall, juts forward in the near right-hand corner, while immediately to the left, the graceful lines and inspired Italianate stonework of

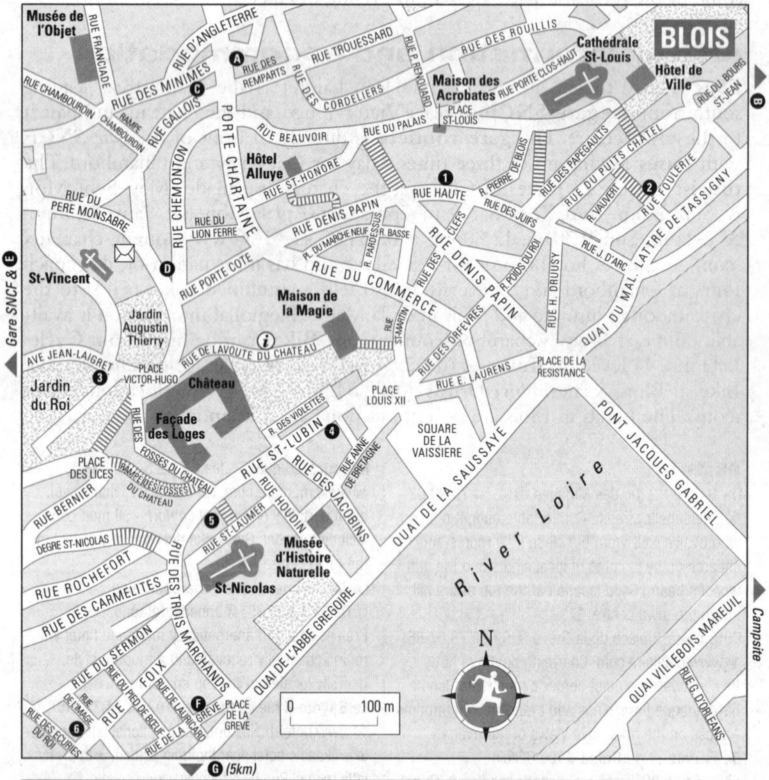

BLOIS

EATING & DRINKING				ACCOMMODATION			
Les Banquettes Rouges	5	Le St-James	2	Du Bellay	C	Mercure	B
Le Castelet	4	Velvet Jazz Lounge	1	Côté Loire	F	Le Monarque	A
L'Orangerie du Château	3			De France et de Guise	D	Le Savoie	E
Au Rendez-Vous des Pêcheurs	6			Hostel	G		

François I's Renaissance north wing is interrupted by a superb spiral staircase. Ahead, the grandly Classical west wing was built in the 1630s by François Mansart for Gaston d'Orléans, the brother of Louis XIII. Turning to the south side you return 140-odd years to Louis XII's St-Calais chapel, which contrasts with the more exuberant brickwork of his flamboyant Gothic east wing.

The signposts point you straight ahead and up Mansart's breathtaking staircase, which leads you round to the **François I wing**. The garish decor dates from Félix Duban's mid-nineteenth-century efforts to turn an empty barn of a château into a showcase for sixteenth-century decorative motifs. One of the largest rooms is given over to paintings of the notorious murder of the Duke of Guise and his brother, the Cardinal of Lorraine, by Henri III. As leaders of the radical Catholic League, the Guises were responsible for the summary execution of Huguenots at Amboise. The king had summoned the States-General to a meeting in the Grande Salle, only to find that an overwhelming majority supported the Duke, along with the stringing up of Protestants, and aristocratic rather than royal power. Henri had the duke summoned to his bedroom in the palace, where he was ambushed and hacked to death, and the cardinal was murdered in prison the next day. Their deaths were avenged a year later when a monk assassinated the king himself.

The château was also home to Henri III's mother and manipulator, Catherine de Médicis, who died here a few days after the murders in 1589. The most famous of her suite of rooms is the study, where, according to Alexandre Dumas' novel, *La Reine Margot*, she kept poison hidden in secret caches in the skirting boards and behind some of the 237 narrow carved wooden panels; they now contain small Renaissance *objets d'art*. In the nineteenth century, revolutionaries were tried in the Grande Salle for conspiring to assassinate Napoléon III, a year before the Paris Commune of 1870. You can return to the courtyard via the vast space of the Salle des États, where the arches, pillars and fireplaces are another riot of nineteenth-century colour.

The Louis XII wing houses an undistinguished **Musée des Beaux-Arts**, with portraits from the gallery at Beauregard and a tapestry collection. If you're still not flagging, you can head back across the courtyard to the ground floor of the François I wing, where an **archeological museum** displays original stonework from the staircase and dormer windows, as well as carved details rescued from other châteaux.

French-speakers may want to take the two-hour guided **visite privilégiée** (July & Aug daily at 3pm; €7.50), which explores parts of the château you won't normally see, such as the roof and cellars. You can usually just turn up at the gate for the **son et lumière** (mid-April to mid-Sept daily; €6.50, or €10 including château entrance; in English on Wed), which takes place at dusk on summer evenings. It's one of the best in the region, rising above the usual mix of melodrama, light and musical effects by making the most of the château's fascinating history and lovely courtyard setting.

The rest of the town

Just below the château on rue St-Laumen, the **church of St Nicholas** (daily 9am–6.30pm) once belonged to an abbey, and the choir is a handsome example of the humble Benedictine treatment of the Romanesque style. Children are unlikely to be convinced by the rather shoddy optical illusions housed in the cavernous **Maison de la Magie**, facing the château on the far side of the esplanade (April–Sept daily 10am–12.30pm & 2–6pm; €7.50 or €12 with château entry; Ⓦwww.maisondelamagie.fr); the afternoon magic shows are in mime, so at least there's no need to understand French. More instructive is the **Musée d'Histoire Naturelle**, rue Anne-de-Bretagne (daily except Mon 2–6pm; €2.50), with some good dioramas showing the different environments of the region, and the birds and animals that live in them.

At the top of town, the superb **Musée de l'Objet**, 6 rue Franciade (March–June & Sept–Nov Sat & Sun 1.30–6.30pm; July & Aug Wed–Sun 1.30–6.30pm; €4), celebrates modern sculptures created from found objects rather than traditional materials. A forest of hammers hanging from the staircase ceiling gradually morphs into handbags, and the two long, spacious galleries are filled with similarly witty or alarming artworks, including some by major figures in modern art.

At the east end of town, on the handsome **place St-Louis**, look out for the half-timbered and sculpted facade of the **Maison des Acrobates**. The Gothic **cathédrale St-Louis** (daily 7.30am–6pm), at the west end of the square, leans against a weighty bell tower whose lowest storey is twelfth-century. The interior is fairly bare, but the most interesting feature is the modern **stained-glass windows**, completed in 2003 by the Dutch artist Jan Dibbets. Leading off place St-Louis, rue du Palais traverses above the town centre, passing the long stairs at the head of rue Denis-Papin and leading into rue St-Honoré. At no. 8, the elaborate **Hôtel Alluye**, the private house of the royal treasurer Florimond Robertet, is a rare survival of Blois' golden years under Louis XII.

Eating and drinking

Most of Blois' traditional **restaurants** can be found on or around rue Saint-Lubin, between the château and the river. *Le Castelet*, 40 rue Saint-Lubin (Ⓣ02.54.74.66.09; closed Wed & Sun; meals from €15) specializes in homely Loire cuisine, using regional produce. A little further along the same street, *Les Banquettes Rouges*, 16 rue des Trois Marchands (Ⓣ02.54.78.74.92; closed Sun & Mon), serves modern French, Mediterranean-influenced food, with evening menus from €21. The best gastronomic experience in town is unquestionably *Au Rendez-Vous des Pêcheurs*, 27 rue du Foix (Ⓣ02.54.74.67.48; closed Mon lunch, Sun and 3 weeks in Aug), with elaborate fish dishes on the eight-course, €74 *menu découverte*. There is also a week-night menu at €28. The elaborate and sprawling *L'Orangerie du Château*, 1 av Jean-Laigret (Ⓣ02.54.78.05.36; menus €30–68) is also excellent, though the atmosphere can suffer from the group banqueting factor.

The small square at the end of rue Vauvert, on the east side of town, has a number of crêperies and pizzerias with tables set out under the trees. Immediately below, rue de la Foulerie is the best place for ethnic food – Portuguese, Moroccan and Indian – and for late-night **bars** as well. The cocktail bar *Le St-James*, 50 rue de la Foulerie, is a good bet, as is the *Velvet Jazz Lounge*, nearby at 15bis rue Haute.

Around Blois

On the south bank of the river, within a 20km radius south and east of Blois, is a cluster of impressive and easily visited **châteaux**. By car you could call at all of them in a couple of days, but they also make ideal cycling or walking targets if you arm yourself with a map and strike out along minor roads and woodland rides. A new 300-kilometre-long network of tranquil cycle routes and dedicated cycle paths takes advantage of the mostly flat forest alleys and wooded back roads. Chaumont has frequent daily trains from Blois (make for Onzain, on the north side of the river, then cross the bridge), but otherwise **public**

transport in the area is very poor, with even the main routes served by only a couple of commuter buses a day. Note, however, that the local bus company TLC (ⓣ02.54.58.55.55, ⓦwww.tlcinfo.net) runs **coach trips** to Chambord and Cheverny, with two morning and one lunchtime departure from Blois' *gare SNCF* (mid-May to Aug; €10.75). Check exact times when you buy your ticket – from the tourist office. Staff may also be able to find places on a chartered taxi or minibus tour.

Château de Chaumont

Catherine de Médicis forced Diane de Poitiers to hand over Chenonceau in return for the **Château de Chaumont** (daily: April & late Sept 10.30am–5.30pm; May to mid-Sept 9.30am–6.30pm; Oct–March 10am–12.30pm & 1.30–5pm; €6.10; grounds open daily 9.30am–dusk; free), 20km downstream from Blois. Diane got a bad deal but this is still one of the lovelier châteaux.

The original fortress was destroyed by Louis XI in the mid-fifteenth century in revenge for the part its owner, Pierre d'Amboise, played in the "League of Public Weal", an alliance of powerful nobles against the ever-increasing power of the monarch. But Pierre found his way back into the king's favour, and with his son Charles I, built much of the quintessentially medieval castle that stands today. Proto-Renaissance design is more obvious in the courtyard, which today forms three sides of a square, the fourth side having been demolished in 1739 to improve views over the river, which are spectacular. Inside, the heavy nineteenth-century decor of the ground-floor rooms dates from the ownership of the Broglie family, but a few rooms on the first floor have been remodelled in the Renaissance style. The large council chamber is particularly fine, with seventeenth-century majolica tiles on the floor and its walls adorned with wonderfully busy sixteenth-century tapestries showing the gods of each of the seven planets known at the time.

The Broglie family also transformed the 21-hectare landscaped **park** into the fashionable English style and built the remarkable *belle époque* **stables**, with their porcelain troughs and elegant electric lamps for the benefit of the horses at a time before the château itself was wired – let alone the rest of the country. A corner of the château grounds now plays host to an annual **Festival des Jardins** (May to mid-Oct daily 9.30am to dusk; €8.50, or €11 with château entry), which shows off the extravagant efforts of contemporary garden designers.

On weekends in summer, you can secure the best view of the château from the deck of a traditional Loire boat. Contact the Association Millière Raboton (ⓣ06.88.76.57.14, ⓦwww.milliere-raboton.net), whose **boat trips** (€12–15) leave from the quay immediately below the château, and last roughly an hour and a half. Best for wildlife are the regular dawn excursions, and you can organize longer trips – even camping out overnight on an island sandbank.

Château de Cheverny

Fifteen kilometres southeast of Blois, the **Château de Cheverny** (daily: April–June & Sept 9.15am–6.15pm; July & Aug 9.15am–6.45pm; Oct–March 9.45am–5pm; ⓦwww.chateau-cheverny.fr; €6.50) is the perfect example of a seventeenth-century château. Built between 1604 and 1634 and never altered, it presents an immaculate picture of symmetry, harmony and the aristocratic good life – descendants of the first owners still own, live in and go hunting from Cheverny today. Its stone, from Bourré on the River Cher, lightens with age, and the château gleams like a great white brick in its acres of rolling parkland. The interior decoration has only been added to, never destroyed, and the extravagant display of

Tintin in the Loire

Cheverny's architecture, minus the outermost towers, was used by Hergé as a model for Marlinspike Hall (Moulinsart in French), the ancestral home of Tintin's nautical friend Captain Haddock. The connection is milked dry in the slick exhibition, **Les Secrets de Moulinsart**, housed in the outbuilding next to the main gate (daily 9.30am–6.45pm; adults €11.50 with château ticket, children aged 7–14 €6.40 with château ticket), which retells various stories of the Belgian fictional hero in rooms dressed up in the style of the cartoon, enlivened by audiovisual effects and film clips.

paintings, furniture, tapestries and armour against the gilded, sculpted and carved walls and ceilings is extremely impressive. The most precious objects are hard to pick out from the sumptuous whole, but some highlights are the painted wall panels in the dining room telling stories from *Don Quixote*; the vibrant, unfaded colours of the Gobelin tapestry in the arms room; and the three rare family portraits by François I's court painter, François Clouet, in the gallery.

You can explore the elegant **grounds** on foot, or take a sedate tour by golf buggy and boat (April to mid-Nov; €11.20 including château entry). The **kennels** near the main entrance are certainly worth a look: a hundred lithe hounds mill and loll about while they wait for the next stag; feeding time (5pm) is something to be seen. Cheverny's hunt culls around thirty deer a year, a figure set by the National Forestry Office.

You can **stay** in the rustic *Hôtel des Trois Marchands* (Ⓣ02.54.79.96.44, Ⓦwww.hoteldes3marchands.com; ❸), in **COUR-CHEVERNY**, Cheverny's larger neighbour, 1km north. The hotel's restaurant is rather smart, or there's the inexpensive bar and grill next door.

Château de Fougères

The proudly defensive **Château de Fougères** (mid-May to mid-Sept daily 9.30am–12.30pm & 2–6.30pm; mid-Sept to mid-May daily except Tues 10am–12.30pm & 2–5pm; €4.60) provides a good contrast to Cheverny. It lies in the village of **FOUGÈRES-SUR-BIÈVRE**, 10km southwest of Cheverny, and was built in 1470 by Louis XI's chancellor, who was clearly sceptical about long-term peace. It is a veritable fortress, turned tightly in on its internal courtyard, and you can scurry freely about the many corridors, rooms and spiral staircases, even clambering under the roof and strolling along the guard's walk. There are rarely other visitors to interfere with the medieval fantasy, though various exhibits along the way explain medieval building techniques. You'll need fairly good French to appreciate the explanations.

Château de Beauregard

An easy cycle ride from Blois, the little-visited **Château de Beauregard**, 7km south of Blois on the D956 to Contres (Feb 8 to end March, Oct, Nov & Dec 20 to end Dec daily except Wed 9.30am–noon & 2–5pm; April–June & Sept daily 9.30am–noon & 2–7.30pm; July & Aug daily 9.30am–6.30pm; €6.50; Ⓦwww.beauregard-loire.com), lies amid the Forêt de Russy. It was – like Chambord – one of François I's hunting lodges, but its transformation in the sixteenth century involved beautification rather than aggrandizement. It was added to in the seventeenth century and the result is sober and serene, very much at ease in its manicured geometric park.

The highlight of the château is a richly decorated, long **portrait gallery**, whose floor of Delft tiling depicts an army on the march. The walls are entirely panelled with 327 portraits of kings, queens and great nobles, including European celebrities such as Francis Drake, Anne Boleyn and Charles V of Spain. All of France's kings are represented from Philippe VI (1328–50), who precipitated the Hundred Years War, to Louis XIII (1610–43), who occupied the throne when the gallery was created. Kings, nobles and executed wives alike are given equal billing – except for Louis XIII, whose portrait is exactly nine times the size of any other. It's worth strolling down through the grounds to the sunken **Jardin des Portraits**, a Renaissance-influenced creation by contemporary landscaper Gilles Clément, who was responsible for Paris's futuristic Parc André Citroën. It could be better tended, but the garden's formal arrangement – by colour of flower and foliage – is fascinating.

Château de Chambord

The **Château de Chambord**, François I's little "hunting lodge", is the largest and most popular of the Loire châteaux (daily: April to mid-July & mid-Aug to end Sept 9am–6.15pm; mid-July to mid-Aug 9am–7.30pm; Oct–March 9am–5.15pm; July & Aug €9.50, Sept–June €8.50; Ⓦ www.chambord.org) and one of the most extravagant commissions of its age. Its patron's principal object – to outshine the Holy Roman Emperor Charles V – would, he claimed, leave him renowned as "one of the greatest builders in the universe".

Before you even get close, the sheer gargantuan scale of the place is awe-inspiring: there are more than 440 rooms and 85 staircases, and a petrified forest of 365 chimneys runs wild on the roof. In architectural terms, the mixture of styles is as outrageous as the size. The Italian architect Domenico da Cortona was chosen to design the château in 1519 in an effort to establish prestigious Italian Renaissance art forms in France, though the labour was supplied by French masons. The château's plan (attributed by some to da Vinci) is pure Renaissance: rational, symmetrical and totally designed to express a single idea – the central power of its owner. Four hallways run crossways through the central keep, at the heart of which the Great Staircase rises up in two unconnected spirals before opening out into the great lantern tower, which draws together the confusion on the roof like a great crown.

The cold, draughty size of the château made it unpopular as an actual residence – François I himself stayed there for just 42 days in total – and Chambord's role in history is slight. A number of rooms on the first floor were fitted out by Louis XIV and his son, the Comte de Chambord, and as reconstructed today they feel like separate apartments within the unmanageable whole. You can explore them freely, along with the adjacent eighteenth-century apartments, where the château was made habitable by lowering ceilings, building small fireplaces within the larger ones, and cladding the walls with the fashionable wooden panelling known as *boiseries*. The second floor houses a rambling **Museum of Hunting** where, among the endless guns and paintings that glorify hunting, are two superb seventeenth-century tapestry cycles: one depicts Diana, goddess of the hunt; another, based on cartoons by Lebrun, tells the story of Meleager, the heroic huntsman from Ovid's *Metamorphoses*. Children love playing on the double spiral staircase that leads up to the airy rooftop, where you can get a good feel for the contrasting and occasionally discordant architectural styles.

The **events and festivals** calendar is a busy one, with evening lighting displays, guided nature walks, cycle rides and jeep tours in the forest, costumed tours for children and a twice-daily dressage display, among other attractions. A free leaflet available at the château gives details, or you can call Ⓣ 02.54.50.50.00.

The **Parc de Chambord** around the château is an enormous walled game reserve – the largest in Europe. Wild boars roam freely, though red deer are the

△ Cycling near Chambord

beasts you're most likely to spot. You can explore on foot, or by bike or boat – both rentable from the jetty where the Cosson passes alongside the main facade of the château.

Accommodation in the village of **Chambord** itself can be found opposite the château (and beside the cafeterias and postcard stalls) at the *Hôtel du Grand St-Michel* (Ⓣ02.54.20.31.31; Ⓦwww.saintmichel-chambord.com; ③–⑥). Taking in the sight of Chambord after the crowds have left is very satisfying, but the hotel is otherwise unexceptional. In **BRACIEUX**, a small village just beyond the southern wall of the Parc de Chambord, 8km from the château, the *Hôtel de la Bonnheure*, 9bis rue R.-Masson (Ⓣ02.54.46.41.57, Ⓦwww.hoteldelabonnheur.com; ④) has various rooms and apartments set around floral gardens. Bracieux also has a top-flight **restaurant**, *Le Relais de Bracieux* (Ⓣ02.54.46.41.22; €38–140; closed Tues & Wed), and a large **campsite** (Ⓣ02.54.46.41.84; closed Nov to mid-March) with a summer-only pool.

The Sologne

Stretching southeast of Blois, **the Sologne** is one of those traditionally rural regions of France that help keep alive the national self-image. Depending on the weather and the season, it can be one of the most dismal areas in central France: damp, flat, featureless and foggy. But at other times its forests, lakes, ponds and marshes have a quiet magic – in summer, for example, when the heather is in bloom and the ponds are full of water lilies, or in early autumn when you can collect mushrooms. Wild boar and deer roam here, not to mention the ducks, geese, quails and pheasants, who far outnumber the small human population. The Sologne remains the refuge of the French aristocracy, along with the descendants of rich industrialists who bought land and built châteaux here in the latter part of the nineteenth century. Hunting is the thing, not tourism, and much of the region is out of bounds or simply physically impenetrable.

La Fête Étrange

There is much dispute as to where the magical party in **Alain-Fournier's novel** *Le Grand Meaulnes* was set, despite the fact that it was clearly an imaginary mixture of many places. Fournier was born in La Chapelle d'Angillon, 34km north of Bourges. He spent much of his childhood in the château there, but went to school in Épineuil-le-Fleurial (the Ste-Agathe of the novel) well beyond the Sologne and Bourges, some 25km south of St-Armand-Montrond (turn right off the Montluçon road from Bourges to cross the Cher at Meaulne). Albicoco's 1967 film of the book was shot around Épineuil, where the elementary school described in the book now houses a small museum. But the "domain with no name" where the *fête étrange* takes place is certainly in the Sologne: "In the whole of the Sologne," he wrote, "it would have been hard to find a more desolate spots".

Two *grandes randonnées* lead through the Sologne, both variants of the main GR3 along the Loire. The northern **GR3C** runs through Chambord and east mostly along forest roads to Thoury and La Ferté-St-Cyr, where it rejoins the southern branch, the **GR31**, which has taken a more attractive route through Bracieux and along footpaths through the southern part of the Forêt de Chambord. There are numerous other well-signposted paths, and tourist offices in most of Sologne's towns and villages can provide maps and details of bike rental or horse riding, as well as accommodation details. If you're exploring the Sologne during the hunting season (Oct 1–March 1), don't stray from the marked paths: there are endless stories of people being accidentally shot.

Romorantin-Lanthenay

ROMORANTIN-LANTHENAY, 67km south of Orléans, is the biggest town in the Sologne and best visited in the last weekend in October for the **Journées Gastronomiques**, a major food festival when every restaurant and hundreds of street stalls tempt you with traditional and novel dishes centred on game, wild mushrooms, apples and pumpkins. The rest of the year the only sight of interest is the **Musée de Sologne**, in the old mills in the centre of Romorantin (daily: Mon & Wed–Sat 10am–noon & 2–6pm, Sun 2–6pm; €4.50; ⓦwww.museedesologne.com), which presents the history, ecology and traditions of the area.

For information on walking routes in the Sologne, as well as bike hire, contact the **tourist office** on place de la Paix (Mon 10am–12.15pm & 2–6.30pm, Tues–Sat 8.45am–12.15pm & 1.30–6.30pm; July & Aug also Sun 10am–noon; ⓣ02.54.76.43.89, ⓦwww.tourisme-romorantin.com). If you fancy a splurge, head for *Grand Hôtel du Lion d'Or*, 69 rue G.-Clemenceau (ⓣ02.54.94.15.15, ⓦwww.hotel-liondor.fr; ⑧), an old manor house, with a fabulous courtyard garden, sixteen well-appointed **rooms** and a stellar **restaurant** (meals more than €100).

Château du Moulin

Built almost entirely of brick, surrounded by water, and standing in romantic isolation at the end of a long avenue of oak trees, the **château du Moulin** (April–Sept daily except Wed 10am–11.30pm & 2–5.30pm; €7.50) is the quintessential Sologne château. It lies just outside the village of **LASSAY-SUR-CROISNE**, 10km west of Romorantin-Lanthenay, and is still occupied by its elderly owner, Mme de Marchéville, whose family bought it off the du Moulins in 1901. The original builder, Philippe du Moulin, earned the right to set himself up as a nobleman with a fortified château after saving Charles VIII's life at the 1495 Battle of Fornova. The château's brickwork is striking, curving smoothly around the various towers, the pink tint offset by an inlaid lozenge pattern in dark grey and the window frames of white tufa stone. Guided visits of the **interior**, on which you're shown half a dozen beautifully furnished rooms in the main keep section, take place roughly every half-hour.

St-Viâtre and Lamotte-Beuvron

Deep in the Sologne, the tiny village of **ST-VIÂTRE** is ringed by the *étangs*, or artificial lakes that characterize swathes of the Sologne. A panel in the centre of the village details circular walks in the locality, but the best place for information is the **Maison des Étangs**, 2 rue de la Poste (April–Oct 10am–noon & 2–6pm; rest of year call ⓣ02.54.88.23.00; ⓦwww.maison-des-etangs.com). It occupies a half-timbered house in the centre of St-Viâtre and has an excellent exhibition on local social and natural history (€4.50). The handsome village **church** houses a sixteenth-century **polyptych** of eight richly coloured and superbly realized panels, painted in the Flemish style.

Bikes can be hired from the flowershop, La Malle aux Raboliots (ⓣ02.54.88.43.75). A splendidly unreconstructed French meal – along with a decent room for the night – can be had at the *Auberge le Creusard*, 6 place de l'Église (ⓣ02.54.88.91.33, ⓕ02.54.96.18.06; ③), but gastro-tourists should make the pilgrimage 15km northeast to the modest town of **LAMOTTE-BEUVRON**, where the large, well-to-do *Hôtel Tatin*, 5 av de Vierzon (ⓣ02.54.88.00.03, ⓦwww.hotel-tatin.com; ④; closed first week in Aug), is the original home of *tarte Tatin* – supposedly created by accident by the Tatin sisters, who once ran the hotel. It serves the tart all day long, along with refined cuisine (menus €21–51).

Tours and around

Straddling a spit of land between the rivers Loire and Cher, the ancient cathedral city of **TOURS** is the chief town of the Loire valley. It has long had a reputation as a staid, bourgeois place, the home of lawyers and administrators rather than, say, artists or factory workers. However, the city's proximity to Paris – less than an hour away on the TGV line – has always tempered its nature, ensuring that Tours is indefinably more switched on than other French provincial cities, and in recent years an influx of smart commuters has perceptibly modified its conservative feel.

There are scores of bustling bars and cafés, an active if limited nightlife, and some fine restaurants – among the best in the region. It has a prettified and animated **old quarter**, some unusual **museums** – of wine, crafts, stained glass and an above-average Beaux-Arts museum – and a great many fine buildings, not least **St Gatien cathedral**. If you don't have your own transport, it's the obvious Touraine base, with both bus and train connections to some of the most notable châteaux – **Villandry**, **Langeais**, **Azay-le-Rideau** and **Amboise**.

Arrival, information and accommodation

The **gare routière** and **gare SNCF** are situated a short way southeast of the cathedral district, facing the futuristic Centre de Congrès Vinci. Most TGVs stop at **St-Pierre-des-Corps** station, in an industrial estate outside the city, but frequent shuttles (or sometimes buses) provide a link to the main station.

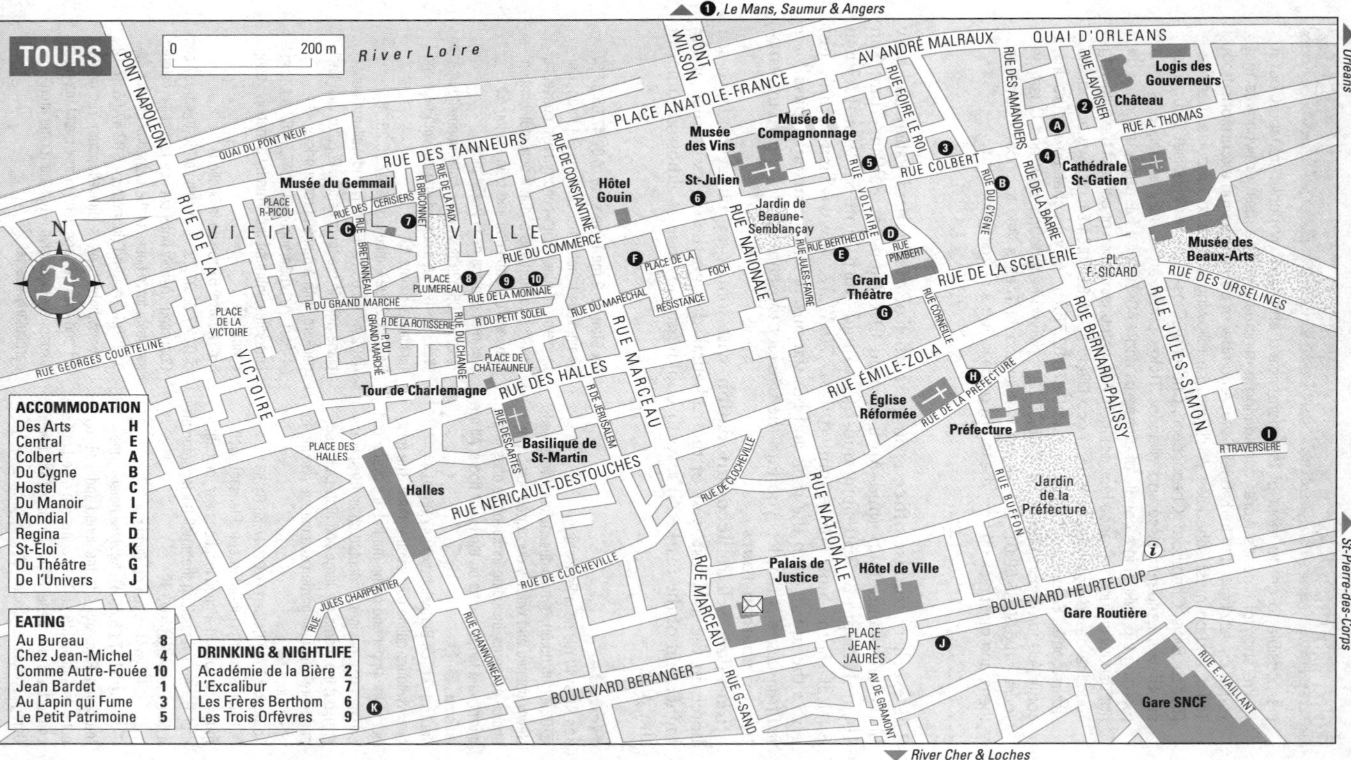

ACCOMMODATION	
Des Arts	H
Central	E
Colbert	A
Du Cygne	B
Hostel	C
Du Manoir	I
Mondial	F
Regina	D
St-Éloi	K
Du Théâtre	G
De l'Univers	J

EATING	
Au Bureau	8
Chez Jean-Michel	4
Comme Autre-Fouée	10
Jean Bardet	1
Au Lapin qui Fume	3
Le Petit Patrimoine	5

DRINKING & NIGHTLIFE	
Académie de la Bière	2
L'Excalibur	7
Les Frères Berthom	6
Les Trois Orfèvres	9

Château tours

It's possible to get to most of the more-visited châteaux by public transport but if you're short of time it's worth considering a minibus trip. The main drawback is that you're usually limited to fairly brief visits. A number of companies run **excursions** from Tours, and on most schedules you'll find the following châteaux: Amboise, Azay-le-Rideau, Blois, Chambord, Chenonceau, Cheverny, Clos-Lucé (in Amboise), Fougères-sur-Bièvre, Langeais, Ussé and Villandry. **Ticket** prices are usually around €19 for a morning trip, taking in a couple of châteaux, and €40–50 for a full-day tour; prices do not usually include entrance fees or lunch. Ask at tourist offices or contact the following Touraine-based **agencies** directly: Acco Dispo (ⓣ06.82.00.64.51, ⓦwww.accodispo-tours.com); Saint-Eloi Excursions (ⓣ06.70.82.78.75, ⓦwww.chateauxexcursions.com); Alienor Excursions (ⓣ06.10.85.35.39, ⓦwww.alienortours.com); and Quart de Tours (ⓣ06.30.65.52.01, ⓦwww.quartdetours.com.) There's little to choose between them, and most pick up from the tourist office in Tours or from your hotel.

The excellent **tourist office** is on the corner of rue Bernard-Palissy and busy boulevard Heurteloup (mid-April to mid-Oct Mon–Sat 8.30am–7pm, Sun 10am–12.30pm & 2.30–5pm; mid-Oct to mid-April Mon–Sat 9am–12.30pm & 1.30–6pm, Sun 10am–1pm; ⓣ02.47.70.37.37, ⓦwww.ligeris.com), just across the square from the train and bus stations. It sells a **museum pass** (*carte multi-visites*; €7) that lets you into the five city museums, and can give information on **château tours**.

Tours does well for **accommodation**, with some great budget and two-star hotels in the area just west of the cathedral, though there's less choice at the higher end of the market. It's worth booking in advance at almost all times of the year.

Hotels

Des Arts 40 rue de la Préfecture ⓣ02.47.05.05.00, ⓔhoteldesartstours@orange.fr. Newly opened and warmly decorated hotel with a choice of rooms, including inexpensive ones in the garret, and larger rooms on the lower floors. All are en suite. ❷–❸

Central 21 rue Berthelot ⓣ02.47.05.46.44, ⓦwww.tours-online.com/central-hotel. The best bet at the upper end of the market. It's overpriced and part of a business-oriented chain (Best Western), but the rooms are large and high-ceilinged, and there's a small garden and garage parking for €9 a night. ❻

Colbert 78 rue Colbert ⓣ02.47.66.61.56, ⓔhotel-colbert@club-internet.fr. Pleasant, well-furnished hotel in a good location near the cathedral. Rooms overlooking the small back garden are a little more expensive. ❸

Du Cygne 6 rue du Cygne ⓣ02.47.66.66.41, ⓦwww.hotel-cygne-tours.com. Pleasantly old-fashioned and well-run hotel on a quiet street. The rooms are dated but comfortable and preserve the flavour of the house. Garage parking available. ❹

Du Manoir 2 rue Traversière ⓣ02.47.05.37.37, ⓦsite.voila.fr/hotel.manoir.tours. Set in an over-modernized nineteenth-century town house, but friendly, comfortable and in a peaceful location between the cathedral and train station. ❸

Mondial 3 place de la Résistance ⓣ02.47.05.62.68, ⓦwww.hotelmondialtours.com. Well situated on a central square, with new and functional rooms. ❸

Regina 2 rue Pimbert ⓣ02.47.05.25.36, ⓕ02.47.66.08.72. Friendly and well-run budget place right in the town centre. Popular with backpackers, with a range of room prices. ❶

St-Éloi 79 bd Béranger ⓣ02.47.37.67.34. Excellent-value, intimate hotel run by a friendly young couple. ❷

Du Théâtre 57 rue de la Scellerie ⓣ02.47.05.31.29, ⓦwww.hotel-du-theatre37.com. Charming, friendly hotel set in a tastefully restored medieval town house in the cathedral quarter. ❹

De l'Univers 5 bd Heurteloup ⓣ02.47.05.37.12, ⓦwww.hotel-univers-loirevalley.com. The grandest and most historic hotel in town, and the most luxuriously expensive – but the rooms aren't particularly special. ❾

Hostel

HI Hostel 5 rue Bretonneau ⓣ02.47.37.81.58, ⓔtours@fuaj.org. Large, modern youth hostel with an excellent central location near place Plumereau. Singles or twin-bed rooms available. Bicycles are hired out inexpensively, too. Reception 8am–noon & 6–11pm.

The City

The centre of Tours lies between the Loire and its tributary, the Cher, but the city has spread far across both banks, with industrial Tours north of the Loire. Neither river is a particular feature of the town, though there are parks on islands in both and an attractive new footbridge leads across the Loire from the site of the old castle on quai d'Orléans. The city's two distinct old quarters lie on either side of **rue Nationale**, which forms the town's main axis. The quieter of the areas lies around the **cathedral**, while the more developed, touristy zone around picturesque **place Plumereau**, some 600m to the west, was once a major pilgrimage site.

The cathedral quarter

The great west towers of the **Cathédrale St-Gatien**, standing on the square of the same name, are visible all over the city. Their surfaces crawl with decorated stone in the flamboyant Gothic style, and even the Renaissance belfries that cap them share the same spirit of refined exuberance. Inside, the style moves back in time, ending with relatively severe High Gothic east end – built in the thirteenth century – and its glorious stained-glass windows. Just beyond the south transept stands the tomb of the sons of Charles VIII and Anne de Bretagne. After their deaths, and the accidental death of their father, the Valois line proper came to an end, and Anne was obliged by law to marry Charles's cousin, Louis XII.

A door in the north aisle leads to the **Cloître de la Psalette** (April–Sept Mon–Sat 9.30am–12.30pm & 2–6pm, Sun 2–6pm; Oct–March Wed–Sun closes 5pm; €2.30), which has an unfinished air, with the great foot of a flying buttress planted in the southeast corner and the missing south arcade – lost when a road was driven through in 1802 by the same progressive, anticlerical prefect who destroyed the basilica of St-Martin. The area behind the cathedral and museum, to the east, is good for a short stroll. There's a fine view of the spidery buttresses supporting the cathedral's painfully thin-walled apse from **place Grégoire de Tours**. Overlooking the square is the oldest wing of the **archbishop's palace**, whose end wall is a mongrel of Romanesque and eighteenth-century work, with an early sixteenth-century projecting balcony once used by clerics to address their flock.

Just south of the cathedral, the **Musée des Beaux-Arts** (daily except Tues 9am–12.45pm & 2–6pm; €4) is housed in the former archbishop's palace. Other than Mantegna's intense, unmissable *Agony in the Garden* (1457–59), in the basement, there are few celebrity works in the large collection. Even Rembrandt's much-advertised *Flight into Egypt* is a small oil study rather than a finished work. But the stately, loosely chronological progression of palatial seventeenth- and eighteenth-century rooms, each furnished and decorated to match the era of the paintings it displays, is extremely attractive. Local gems include Boulanger's portrait of Balzac, and engravings of *The Five Senses* by the locally born Abraham Bosse, which have been interpreted as full-size canvases in the handsome Louis XIII room.

On the other side of the cathedral, between rue Albert-Thomas and the river, just two towers remain of the ancient royal **château** of Tours. You can get inside when an exhibition is being held but there's nothing much left of the interior. In the fifteenth-century **Logis des Gouverneurs** alongside (Wed & Sat 2–6pm, sometimes closed during school holidays; free), across the remnants of the city's Gallo-Roman wall, there's an exhibition of historical artefacts called "Vivre à Tours" (Life in Tours) that gives a good sense of how the city has developed over the centuries.

The old quarter

To the west, the pulse of the city quickens as you approach **place Plumereau** – or place Plum' as it's known locally. The square's tightly clustered, ancient houses have been carefully restored as the city's showpiece, transforming what was once a slum into a vibrant and wealthy quarter. On sunny days, the square is packed almost end to end with café tables, and students and families drink and dine out until late in the evening. One of the less brash places on the square is the *Café du Vieux Mûrier*, so named for the large **mulberry tree** outside, a reminder of the days when Tours' silkworms used to feed on mulberries planted in their thousands in and around the city.

To escape the maelstrom, slip down **rue Briçonnet** into a miniature maze of quiet, ancient streets. Opposite an oddly Venetian-looking, fourteenth-century house, at no. 41 rue Briçonnet, a passageway leads past a palm tree and an ancient outdoor staircase to the quiet and insulated **Jardin de St-Pierre-le-Puellier**, laid out around the dug-out ruins of a conventual church. Further down rue Briçonnet, at no. 16, just before the heavily modernized riverfront, is the Gothic **Maison de Tristan**.

Off rue Briçonnet at 7 rue du Mûrier, the **Musée du Gemmail** (April to mid-Oct Tues–Sun 10am–noon & 2–6pm; mid-Oct to March Sat & Sun 10am–noon & 2–6pm; €5.40) is dedicated to an obscure, locally invented modern art form that uses fragments of backlit stained glass as a medium. Although some of the works are signed by such luminaries as Dufy, Modigliani and Picasso – who was particularly enamoured of the technique – the actual execution is by professional technicians working from a design.

To the south lay the pilgrim city once known as **Martinopolis** after St Martin, the ex-soldier who became bishop of Tours in the fourth century and went on to be a key figure in the spread of Christianity through France. Among Catholics he is usually remembered for giving half his cloak to a beggar, an image repeated on capitals and in stained-glass windows all over the region. The Romanesque **basilica** stretched along rue des Halles from rue des Trois-Pavées-Ronds almost to place de Châteauneuf: the outline is traced out in the street, but only the north tower, the Tour de Charlemagne, and the western clock tower survived the iconoclastic Huguenot riots of 1562. The new **Basilique de St-Martin**, on rue Descartes, is a late nineteenth-century neo-Byzantine affair built to honour the relics of St Martin, rediscovered in 1860. They are now housed in the crypt, watched over by hundreds of votive prayers carved into the walls. St Martin's day, 11 November, is still celebrated. A short distance away, down rue des Halles, lies the huge, modern **Halles**, or covered market – an excellent place to browse for a picnic in the morning.

Around rue Nationale

At the head of **rue Nationale**, Tours' main street, statues of Descartes and Rabelais – both Touraine-born – overlook the scruffy walkways that run along the bank of the Loire. A short walk back from the river and you come to the Benedictine **church of St Julien**, whose old monastic buildings are home to two museums. The dry-as-dust **Musée des Vins**, 16 rue Nationale (daily except Tues 9am–noon & 2–6pm; €4.20), is only worth visiting for its location in the barn-like twelfth-century cellars of the abbey, though if your French is up to it, there's a comprehensive display on the history, mythology and production of wine. Behind the museum, a Gallo-Roman winepress from Cheillé sits in the former cloisters of the church. The **Musée de Compagnonnage**, at 8 rue Nationale (mid-June to mid-Sept daily 9am–noon & 2–6pm; mid-Sept to mid-June closed Tues; €4) is housed in the eleventh-century guesthouse and sixteenth-century monks' dormitory. It honours the peculiarly French cult of the artisan, displaying the "masterpieces" that craftsmen had to create in order to join their guild (*compagnonnage*) as a master craftsman. The skills are unquestionable but many of these showpieces are breathtakingly vulgar, displaying arts as diverse as cake-making, carpentry, clog-making and cooperage.

A few steps west of rue Nationale, the **Hôtel Gouin**, 25 rue du Commerce, has a Renaissance facade to stop you in your tracks, but the **museum** inside (Tues–Sun 10am–1pm & 2–6pm; €4.50) is a dull collection of archeological oddities and the remnants of a private scientific laboratory from Chenonceau – more rich man's toys than cutting-edge research tools.

At the southern end of rue Nationale, the huge, traffic-ridden place Jean-Jaurès is the site of the grandiose Hôtel de Ville and Palais de Justice. To the west of place Jean-Jaurès, a giant **flower market** takes over boulevard Béranger on Wednesdays and Saturdays, lasting from 8am into the early evening.

St-Cosme

In May, when the roses are in full bloom, the **Prieuré de St-Cosme**, 3km west of the centre (mid-March to April & Sept to mid-Oct daily 10am–6pm; May–Aug daily 10am–7pm; mid-Oct to mid-March daily except Tues 10am–12.30pm & 2–5pm; €4.50), is one of the loveliest sights in Touraine even if it is hemmed in by suburbs and barred off from the nearby Loire by a trunk road. Once an island priory, now a semi-ruin, it was here that Pierre de Ronsard – arguably France's greatest poet – lived as prior from 1565 until his death in 1585. Vestiges of many monastic buildings survive but the most affecting sight is the lovingly tended garden of roses, which has some 2000 rose bushes, and 250 varieties – including the tightly rounded, pink rose called "Pierre de Ronsard". To get there by public transport, take **bus** #7 from immediately outside the Palais de Justice, on place Jean-Jaurès, towards La Riche-Petit Plessis, getting off at the La Pléiade stop.

Eating

The streets around place Plumereau, especially rue du Grand-Marché, are overrun with cafés, bars and **bistros**, and if you're looking for pizza, pasta or *steak-frites*, and don't mind paying a little extra for the bustling atmosphere and an outside table, this is the area to head for. On the cathedral side of rue Nationale, rue Colbert is lined with much less touristy bars and ethnic eateries, as well as a few good restaurants serving regional cuisine. For a drink or a **snack**, make for the pleasant café-patisserie *Aux Délices de Michel Colombe*, 1 place François-Sicard, near the cathedral, or *Scarlett*, a relaxed tearoom at 70 rue Colbert.

Au Bureau place Plumereau. One of a number of places serving pizzas and simple dishes on the square but worth recommending for its decent *plats du jour*, late-night service and outside tables.

Chez Jean-Michel 123 rue Colbert ☎02.47.20.80.20. Intimate wine bar and restaurant that manages to be elegant and relaxed at the same time. Serves good regional dishes to go along with the excellent local wines. Main courses at around €15. Closed Sat & Sun.

Comme Autre-Fouée 11 rue de la Monnaie ☎02.47.05.94.78. Something of a gimmick, in that the food is a revival of the archaic *fouace* (or *fouée*) breads praised by Rabelais, served hot and heavily garnished with local titbits. Good fun and inexpensive. Closed Sun, Mon & Tues lunch.

Jean Bardet 57 rue Groison ⓣ02.47.41.41.11, ⓦwww.jeanbardet.com. Tours' top restaurant, on the north side of the Loire. Extremely sophisticated, healthy food with rare herbs and old varieties of vegetables straight from the hotel's renowned vegetable garden. Menus €60–165, and an unmissable all-vegetable menu at €69. Closed Tues, plus Mon & Sat lunch.

Au Lapin qui Fume 90 rue Colbert ⓣ02.47.66.95.49. Tiny, relaxed but elegant restaurant serving a good menu that's half Loire and half south of France. Lots of *lapin* (rabbit) – it comes as a terrine, as a fricassée with rosemary, or *confit* – but it's not obligatory. Evening menus around the €20 mark.

Le Petit Patrimoine 58 rue Colbert ⓣ02.47.66.05.81. Romantic little place serving rich, lovingly prepared Loire dishes and good Loire wines. Menus €14–26.

Drinking and nightlife

Packed with tables and chairs, place Plumereau is *the* place to start the evening with an open-air aperitif and to finish it with a coffee. Giant Irish **pubs**, pizzerias and branded ice cream parlours are slowly making inroads into the area, but there are plenty of less commercial places to be found in the streets around, with some good **café-bars** on rue du Commerce – try *Les Frères Berthom*, which has lots of outside tables. In the cathedral quarter, the bars on rue Colbert are mostly strip-lit local affairs, but the *Académie de la Bière*, just up from the cathedral at 43 rue Lavoisier, is a lively, student-friendly place, though dead when school's out.

Even in summer, when local students are away, the **nightclubs** just off place Plumereau fill up with backpackers, locals and language students, though things don't usually get going until past midnight. Try *Les Trois Orfèvres*, 6 rue des Orfèvres, or *L'Excalibur*, which has a medieval theme. For details of **classical music** concerts, ask at the tourist office which provides a free monthly magazine of exhibitions, concerts and events in Touraine, *Détours et des nuits*.

Listings

Airport Aéroport Tours Val de Loire ⓣ02.47.49.37.00, ⓦwww.tours-aeroport.com.

Bike hire Store Trek, 31 bd Heurteloup, opposite the tourist office ⓣ02.47.61.22.35, ⓦwww.locationdevelos.com. Runs the Détours de Loire scheme (see p.495), which allows you to drop off the bike at various locations along the river, for a small extra charge.

Car hire Avis, gare de Tours ⓣ02.47.20.53.27; Budget, 194 av André-Maginot ⓣ02.47.88.00.50; Europcar, 76 rue Bernard-Palissy ⓣ02.47.64.47.76; Hertz, 57 rue Marcel-Tribut ⓣ02.47.75.50.00. All offer pick up and drop off at Tours airport, at St-Pierre-des-Corps TGV station or near the *gare SNCF* in Tours.

Cinema Les Studios, 2 rue des Urselines (ⓣ02.47.20.27.00, ⓦwww.studiocine.com), shows arty, obscure and old favourites in their original language.

Emergencies Ambulance ⓣ15; different hospital departments are spread around the city – call ⓣ02.47.47.47.47 to check where to head, or ask at the tourist office; late-night pharmacy, phone police (see below) for address.

Internet Alliance Arena, 32bis rue Briçonnet (Mon–Sat 11am–7pm; Sun 1–8pm), is good value. Otherwise try L'Alexandra, 106 rue du Commerce (daily 3pm–1am or 2am); or Globilis Communication, 30 rue Michelet (Mon–Sat 9am–11pm, Sun 2–11pm).

Laundries In the old quarter: 20 rue Bretonneau, 45 rue Georges-Courteline and 17 place du Grand-Marché. Just west of the train station: 88 rue Michelet.

Police Commisariat Général 70–72 rue Marceau ⓣ02.47.70.88.88.

Taxis Groupement Taxis Radio Tours ⓣ02.47.20.30.40.

Amboise

Twenty kilometres upstream of Tours, **AMBOISE** is a prim little riverside town trading on long-gone splendours, notably its impressive but disappointingly empty **château** and Leonardo da Vinci's peaceful residence of **Clos-Lucé**, with its exhibition of the great man's inventions. Amboise draws a busy tourist trade that may detract from the quieter pleasures of strolling around town, but makes it a good destination for children. In July and August, **son et lumière** shows are held around 10pm at the château (Wed & Sat; adults from €12, children 6–14 from €6; Ⓦwww.renaissance-amboise.com), with Leonardo images projected on the walls and costumed actors prancing about to loud Renaissance-style music. The one concession to modern art in Amboise is a twentieth-century **fountain** by Max Ernst of a turtle topped by a teddy bear figure, standing in front of the spot where the **market** takes place every Saturday and Sunday morning by the riverside.

Arrival, information and accommodation

The **gare SNCF** is on the north bank of the river, at the end of rue Jules-Ferry, about 1km from the château. There are good connections to Tours and Blois. Information on Amboise and its environs, including the vineyards of the Touraine-Amboise *appellation*, is available at the **tourist office** on quai du Général-de-Gaulle, on the riverfront (June & Sept Mon–Sat 9.30am–1pm & 2–6.30pm, Sun 10am–1pm & 3–6pm; July & Aug Mon–Sat 9am–8pm, Sun 10am–6pm; Oct–May Mon–Sat 10am–1pm & 2–6pm; Ⓣ02.47.57.09.28, Ⓦwww.amboise-valdeloire.com).

Bikes can be hired from Cycles Richard, 2 rue Nazelles, near the station (Ⓣ02.47.57.01.79), or Locacycle, on rue Jean-Jacques-Rousseau (April–Oct; Ⓣ02.47.57.00.28). **Canoes** are available from the Club de Canoë-Kayak, at the Base de l'Île d'Or (Ⓣ02.47.23.26.52, Ⓦwww.loire-aventure.com), which also runs guided trips.

Hotels

Café des Arts place Michel-Debré Ⓣ02.47.57.25.04. Simple but friendly backpacker-oriented place – think pine bunkbeds and hard-wearing carpet – set up above an inexpensive café. ❶

Le Belle Vue 12 quai Charles-Guinot Ⓣ02.47.57.02.26, Ⓔbellevuehotel.amboise@wanadoo.fr. Long-established Logis de France three-star just below the château, with comfortable, old-fashioned bedrooms. Some rooms at the front overlook the Loire – and the main road. Closed mid-Nov to mid-March. ❹

Le Blason 11 place Richelieu Ⓣ02.47.23.22.41, Ⓦwww.leblason.fr. Very smartly kept but homely hotel in a quiet corner. The furnishings are modern, but all rooms have pretty, exposed beams. Triples and quads available. Parking and Internet access free. ❸

Le Chaptal 13 rue Chaptal Ⓣ02.47.57.14.46. The rooms are plain and rather Spartan, and the welcome not exactly effusive, but it's inexpensive, perfectly decent and all rooms are equipped with bathrooms and TVs. ❷

Le Choiseul 36 quai Charles-Guinot Ⓣ02.47.30.45.45, Ⓦwww.le-choiseul.com. Serious luxury, set in an eighteenth-century riverside mansion. Rooms have heavy curtains, thick carpets and fresh flowers – the best have views over the river. Open-air swimming pool in summer. ❾

Le Vieux Manoir 13 rue Rabelais Ⓣ02.47.30.41.27, Ⓦwww.le-vieux-manoir.com. Eighteenth-century mini-manor house converted for use as a luxury bed and breakfast, with antique furniture coupled with a/c and brand new fittings. Closed mid-Nov to mid-Feb. ❽

Hostel and campsite

Camping de l'Île d'Or Île d'Or Ⓣ02.47.57.23.37. Pleasant, leafy campsite alongside the hostel, with access to the pool. Closed Oct–March.

Centre Charles Péguy Île d'Or Ⓣ02.47.30.60.90, Ⓔcis.amboise@wanadoo.fr. Ordinary but recently done-up hostel in a pleasant location on the midstream island, halfway across the town bridge, with a small summer swimming pool. Reception is open Mon–Fri 3–8pm, but it's best to reserve in advance. Prices vary, but beds cost no more than €11.50 a night.

Château d'Amboise

Rising above the river is the remains of the **château** (daily: Feb to mid-March 9am–noon & 1.30–5.30pm; last 2 weeks March & Sept to mid-Nov 9am–6pm; April–June 9am–6.30pm; July & Aug 9am–7pm; mid-Nov to Jan 9am–noon & 2–4.45pm; €8, Ⓦwww.chateau-amboise.com), once five times its present size, but much reduced by wars and lack of finance. It was in the late fifteenth century, following his marriage to Anne of Brittany at Langeais that Charles VIII decided to turn the old castle of his childhood days into an extravagant palace, adding the flamboyant Gothic wing that overlooks the river and the **chapelle de St-Hubert**, which perches incongruously atop a buttress of the defensive walls. But not long after the work was completed, he managed to hit his head, fatally, on a door frame. He left the kingdom to his cousin, Louis XII, who spent most of his time at Blois but built a new wing at Amboise (at right angles to the main body) to house his nearest male relative, the young François d'Angoulême, thereby keeping him within easy reach. When the young heir acceded to the throne as François I he didn't forget his childhood home. He embellished it with classical stonework (visible on the east facade of the Louis XII wing), invited Leonardo da Vinci to work in Amboise under his protection, and eventually died in the château's collegiate church.

Henri II continued to add to the château, but it was during the reign of his sickly son, François II, that it achieved notoriety. The Tumult of Amboise was one of the first skirmishes in the Wars of Religion. Persecuted by the young king's powerful advisors, the Guise brothers, Huguenot conspirators set out for Amboise in 1560 to "rescue" their king and establish a more tolerant monarchy under their tutelage. But they were ambushed by royal troops in woods outside the town, rounded up and summarily tried in the Salle des Conseils. Some were drowned in the Loire below the château, some were beheaded in the grounds, and others were hung from the château's balconies.

After such a history, the interior of the château is a letdown, though there's a fairly atmospheric progression of large rooms hung with tapestries. The last French king, Louis-Philippe, also stayed in the château, hence the abrupt switch from the solid Gothic furnishings of the ground floor to the 1830s post-First Empire style of the first-floor apartments. The **Tour des Minimes**, the original fifteenth-century entrance, is architecturally the most exciting part of the castle. With its massive internal ramp, it was designed for the maximum number of fully armoured men on horseback to get in and out as quickly as possible. These days it leads down to the pleasant gardens which in turn lead to the exit.

Clos-Lucé

Following his campaigns in Lombardy, François I decided that the best way to bring back the ideas of the Italian Renaissance was to import one of the finest exponents of the new arts. In 1516, **Leonardo da Vinci** ventured across the Alps in response to the royal invitation, carrying with him the *Mona Lisa* among other paintings. For three years before his death in 1519, he made his home at the **Clos-Lucé**, at the end of rue Victor-Hugo (daily: Jan 10am–5pm; Feb, March, Nov & Dec 9am–6pm; April–June, Sept & Oct 9am–7pm; July & Aug 9am–8pm; April–Oct €12, Nov–March €9). Leonardo seems to have enjoyed a semi-retirement at Amboise, devoting himself to inventions of varying brilliance and impracticability, and enjoying conversations with his royal patron. The house – an attractive brick mansion with Italianate details added by Charles VIII – is now a museum to Leonardo, and if you can ignore the persistently piped Renaissance music it's interesting to browse through the forty models of his mechanical inventions. From the suspension bridge to the paddle-wheel boat and turbine, they are all meticulously constructed according to Leonardo's plans and sketches.

Beyond the town centre

If you take the main road south out of Amboise and turn right just before the junction with the D31, you'll come to an unlikely looking eighteenth-century **pagoda**, once part of the enormous but now demolished château of Chanteloup. You can climb to the top for an expansive view and explore the grounds of the surrounding park (April Mon–Fri 10am–noon & 2–6pm, Sat & Sun 10am–6pm; May & Sept daily 10am–6.30pm; June daily 10am–7pm; July & Aug daily 9.30am–7.30pm; Oct to mid-Nov Sat & Sun 10am–5pm; €6.90). Just south of town on the D751 to Chenonceaux, near the pagoda, the park **Mini-Châteaux** (daily: April–June, Sept & Oct 10am–6pm, July & Aug closes 7pm; €12, children 4–15 years €8) houses more than forty surprisingly good scale models of the chief Loire châteaux.

At Lussault, 5km west towards Tours, the mammoth **Aquarium du Val de Loire** (daily: July & Aug 10am–7pm; Sept–June 10am–6pm, closed last 2 weeks Jan & last 2 weeks Nov; adults €12, children 4–15 years €8; Ⓦwww.aquariumduvaldeloire.com) boasts 10,000 fish, along with turtles, alligators and a tunnel through a large shark tank.

Eating and drinking

For a real blowout **meal**, make for Pascal Bouvier's Michelin-starred dining room at the hotel *Le Choiseul* (Ⓣ02.47.30.45.45; menus at €59 & €90). *L'Épicerie*, 46 place Michel-Debré (Ⓣ02.47.57.08.94; menus €11–37; closed Mon & Tues except July & Aug), is overlooked by the chapelle St-Hubert and serves good country cuisine, while *L'Alliance,* 14 rue Joyeuse (Ⓣ02.47.30.52.13; menus €18–43; closed Wed & Jan), serves mainly fish; in summer, both need to be booked in advance. *Chez Hippeau*, 1 rue François-I (Ⓣ02.47.57.26.30; menus €11–30), is a bustling brasserie next to the Hôtel de Ville, with good lunchtime menus and pleasant outdoor seating out back. If you fancy a late drink, head over to the Île d'Or, where you'll find the cocktail **bar** *Le Shaker* (6pm–2am; closed Mon), whose outside terrace has great views across to the château.

Château de Villandry

Even if gardens aren't your thing, those at the **Château de Villandry** (gardens open daily: Jan, Nov & Dec 9am–5pm; Feb 9am–5.30pm; March 9am–6pm; April–June & Sept 9am–7pm; July & Aug 9am–7.30pm; Oct 9am–6.30pm; château closes 30min–1hr earlier, plus mid-Nov to mid-Dec; €8 château and gardens, €5.50 gardens only; Ⓦwww.chateauvillandry.com) are definitely worth a visit. Thirteen kilometres west of Tours along the Cher – a delightful bike trip along the Loire on the cycle path – this recreated Renaissance garden is as much symbolic as ornamental or practical. At the topmost level and in the elevated Classical spirit is a large, formal water garden. Next down, beside the château itself, is the ornamental garden, which features geometrical arrangements of box hedges symbolizing different kinds of love: tender, passionate, fickle and tragic. But the highlight, spread out at the lowest level across 12,500 square metres, is the potager, or Renaissance kitchen garden. Carrots, cabbages and aubergines are arranged into intricate patterns, while rose bowers and miniature box hedges form a kind of frame. Even in winter, there is almost always something to see, as the entire area is replanted twice a year. At the far end of

△ Villandry gardens

the garden, overlooked by the squat tower of the village church, beautiful vine-shaded paths run past the medieval herb garden and the maze.

The elegant **château** was erected in the 1530s by one of François I's royal financiers, Jean le Breton, though the keep – from which there's a fine view of the gardens – dates back to a twelfth-century feudal castle. Le Breton's Renaissance structure is arranged around three sides of a *cour d'honneur*, the fourth wing having been demolished in the eighteenth century. In summer you can take a **minibus** directly from Tours (ⓣ02.47.70.37.37); the service leaves from the tourist office at 10am and 2.30pm and costs €16 return.

There are some top-class options for **eating** out in and around Villandry. In the centre of the tiny village, just down from the château, the wine bar, deli and restaurant, *L'Épicerie Gourmande* (ⓣ02.47.43.37.49) matches Loire wines with delicious delicatessen specialities, served all day. For something hearty, head 1km down the D121 towards Druye, where you'll find a hearty farmhouse restaurant, the *Étape Gourmande* at the Domaine de la Giraudière (ⓣ02.47.50.08.60; menus €15–30; closed mid-Nov to mid-March); its courtyard throngs with families enjoying honest home-cooked fare, with the farm's own goat's cheese featuring prominently. Right beside the Loire in Berthenay, a tiny village across the Cher from Villandry – you have to make a 7km round trip via Savonnières – *Au Bout du Monde* (ⓣ02.47.43.51.50; evening menus €28–52; closed Sun eve, Mon eve & Tues) serves fresh, light, imaginative cuisine in a lovely garden setting.

Château de Langeais

Twenty-three kilometres west of Tours, the small riverside town of **LANGEAIS** huddles in the shadow of its forbidding **château** (daily: Feb–June & Sept to mid-Nov; July & Aug 9am–7pm; mid-Nov to Jan 10am–5pm; €7.20), which was built to stop any incursions up the Loire by the Bretons. This threat ended with the marriage of Charles VIII and Duchess Anne of Brittany in 1491, which was celebrated in the castle, and a diptych of the couple portrays them looking less than joyous at their union – Anne had little choice in giving up her independence. The event is also recreated in waxworks in the chapel.

Few châteaux have such a good collection of furnishings, and the ones here are mostly fifteenth century, to match the building. There are fascinating tapestries, some rare paintings, cots and beds, a number of *chaires*, or seigneurial chairs, and in the huge marriage chamber, the gilded and bejewelled wedding coffer of Charles and Anne, carved with a miniature scene of the Annunciation and figures of the apostles, the wise and foolish virgins depicted on the lid.

Langeais has a pleasant **hotel**, the *Errard-Hosten*, 2 rue Gambetta (ⓣ02.47.96.82.12, ⓦwww.errard.com; ❺), with a good but expensive restaurant. The *Anne de Bretagne*, 27 rue Anne de Bretagne (ⓣ02.47.96.08.52; ❸), offers some exceptional *chambres d'hôtes* in a restored early nineteenth-century home. Sixteen kilometres north along the D57, just outside the village of Hommes, the *Vieux Château d'Hommes*, (ⓣ02.47.24.95.13, ⓦwww.le-vieux-chateau-de-hommes.com; ❼) offers well-furnished rooms in a fifteenth-century outhouse of the main château.

Azay-le-Rideau and around

Even without its **château** (daily: April–June & Sept 9.30am–6pm; July & Aug 9.30am–7pm; Oct–March 10am–12.30pm & 2–5.30pm; €7.50), the quiet village of **AZAY-LE-RIDEAU** would bask in its serene setting, complete with an old mill by the bridge and curious, doll-like Carolingian statues embedded in the facade of the church of St Symphorien. On its little island in the Indre, the château is one of the loveliest in the Loire: perfect turreted early Renaissance, pure in style right down to the blood-red paint of its window frames. Visiting the interior, furnished in mostly period style, doesn't add much to the experience although the grand staircase is worth seeing, and it's fun to look out through the mullioned windows across the moat and park and imagine yourself the *seigneur*. In summer, the château's grounds are the setting for a restrained and rather lovely **son et lumière** (July & Aug daily; early Sept Fri & Sat only; €9, or €12 with daytime château entry).

Practicalities

Azay's **tourist office** sits just off the village's main square, place de la République (May, June & Sept Mon–Sat 9am–1pm & 2–6pm, Sun 10am–1pm & 2–5pm; July & Aug Mon–Sat 9am–7pm, Sun 10am–6pm; Oct–April Mon–Sat 9am–1pm & 2–6pm; ⓣ02.47.45.44.40, ⓦwww.ot-paysazaylerideau.fr). The **bus stop** is next to the tourist office on the main road, but the **gare SNCF** is awkwardly situated a fifteen-minute walk west of the centre, along avenue Adélaïde-Riché – trains from Tours call at Azay-le-Rideau on their way to Chinon roughly every two hours (some services are replaced by SNCF buses). You can hire **bikes** from Cycles Leprovost, 13 rue Carnot (ⓣ02.47.45.40.94), and in summer **canoes** can be hired from beside the bridge on the road out towards Chinon (daily 11am–7pm; ⓣ06.61.21.80.29).

Azay-le-Rideau has some of the best **accommodation** in the area, with two very pleasant hotels on or just off the main square. The *Hôtel de Biencourt*, 7 rue Balzac (ⓣ02.47.45.20.75, ⓦwww.hotelbiencourt.com; ❸; closed mid-Nov to Feb) is attractive and friendly, while *Le Grand Monarque*, 3 place de la République (ⓣ02.47.45.40.08, ⓦwww.legrandmonarque.com; ❹–❾) is indeed rather grand, and has a wide range of rooms. But the best options are all *chambres d'hôtes*: the welcoming *Manoir de la Rémonière*, 1km from Azay on the opposite side of the Indre, on the road to Saché (ⓣ02.47.45.24.88;

ⓦwww.manoirdelaremoniere.com; ❼–❾) was once the château's fifteenth-century hunting lodge; *Le Clos Philippa*, 10 rue Pineau (ⓣ02.47.45.26.49; ❹) occupies an elegant old town house; while the two rooms offered by *M. et Mme Sarrazin*, 9 chemin des Caves Mecquelines (ⓣ02.47.45.31.25, ⓦwww.troglododo.com; ❹) are both in troglodyte chambers hollowed out of the rock. Upstream from the château is a large **campsite**, the *Camping du Sabot* (ⓣ02.47.45.42.72; closed Nov–March), signposted off the D84 to Saché.

For **restaurants**, *La Ridelloise*, 24 rue Nationale (ⓣ02.47.45.46.53; menus €11–33), has a family atmosphere and inexpensive but decent cooking. In summer, *L'Aigle d'Or*, 10 av Adélaïde-Riché (ⓣ02.47.45.24.58; closed Wed & Sun evening), serves elegant cuisine in its delightful garden, with menus from €24 to 60. At the relatively touristy *Les Grottes*, 23ter rue Pineau (ⓣ02.47.45.21.04; menus from €16), you can eat good regional specialities in a troglodyte cave.

Château d'Ussé

Fourteen kilometres west of Azay-le-Rideau, as the Indre approaches its confluence with the Loire, is the **Château d'Ussé** in **RIGNY-USSÉ** (daily: mid-Feb to March & Oct to mid-Nov 10am–noon & 2–5pm; April–Sept 9.30am–6.30pm; €9.80). With its shimmering white towers and terraced gardens, this is the ultimate fairy-tale château – so much so that it's supposed to have inspired Charles Perrault's classic retelling of the Sleeping Beauty myth. The exterior is a beautiful, late fifteenth-century vision of white turrets and machicolations largely built by Antoine de Bueil, comte de Sancerre, who married the illegitimate daughter of Charles VII and Agnès Sorel. The inner courtyard was once closed by a fourth wing, demolished in the seventeenth century to improve the picturesque view. Going inside for the **guided tour** isn't half as compelling as you'd expect, but the **gardens**, designed by Le Nôtre, are pleasant to wander, and children may enjoy climbing the tall **round tower** whose theatrical attic rooms are populated by dressed-up dummies illustrating the story of Sleeping Beauty. The loveliest feature of all is the Renaissance **chapel** in the grounds, shaded by ancient cedars.

The tiny village of Rigny-Ussé has a welcoming, family-run **hotel-restaurant**, *Le Clos d'Ussé* (ⓣ & ⓕ02.47.95.55.47; ❸), with eight simple rooms. Behind the château, in a tranquil, wooded fold of the valley, the *Domaine de la Juranvillerie*, 15 rue des Fougères (ⓣ02.47.95.57.85, ⓦwww.lajuranvillerie.com; ❸), is a charming little group of cottages, one housing a simple, attractive *chambres d'hôtes*. The friendly owners are enthusiastic naturalists and can advise on walks in the Forêt de Chinon.

Les Goupillières

As the D84 back road passes out of Azay-le-Rideau, heading east, it's overshadowed on the left by low, creamy cliffs riddled with **caves** used as storehouses, wine *caves* and even homes. These are the modern-day remnants of the region's fascinating troglodyte (cave dwellers) traditions, which can be explored at the fascinating complex of **Les Goupillières**, 3km from Azay-le-Rideau (April–Nov Mon–Fri 10am–7pm, Sat & Sun 2–7pm; €4; ⓦwww.troglodytedesgoupillieres.fr). The "troglodyte valley" is actually a paddock-like area depressed below the level of the surrounding farmland, its outer edges burrowed away to create cave-farmhouses, cave-barns, cave-grain silos and even a cave-rabbit hutch. The whole "village" was hacked out of the soft tufa rock by hand, over hundreds of years. It was gradually abandoned around a hundred years ago, but has been rediscovered and re-excavated by a knowledgeable local family, who now run the guided tours with infectious enthusiasm.

Chinon and around

CHINON lies on the north bank of the Vienne, 12km from its confluence with the Loire, and is surrounded by some of the best vineyards in the Loire valley. The spectacular line of towers and ramparts on the high ridge to the east of the town look as if they must enclose one of the best of this region's châteaux, but all is ruined within, and the town's dedication to tourism detracts from its charm.

Arrival, information and accommodation

The **gare SNCF** lies to the east of the town, from where rue du Dr-P.-Labussière and rue du 11-Novembre lead to the **gare routière** on place Jeanne-d'Arc, where Joan is sculptured in mid-battle charge. Keep heading west, either along the riverbank or across place Mirabeau into rue Rabelais, and you'll soon reach the old quarter. The **tourist office** is on place d'Hofheim, on the central rue Jean-Jacques-Rousseau (May–Sept daily 10am–7pm; Oct–April Mon–Sat 10am–noon & 2–6pm; ⓣ02.47.93.17.85, ⓦwww.chinon.com), and can provide addresses of local vineyards where you can taste Chinon's famous red wine. Just beside the campsite, Chinon Loisirs Activités Nature (ⓣ06.23.82.96.33) hires out **canoes** and kayaks, and runs half-day and full-day guided trips in summer.

Hotels

Agnès Sorel 4 quai Pasteur ⓣ02.47.93.04.37, ⓦwww.agnes-sorel.com. The situation down by the main road, at the western edge of the old town, lacks atmosphere and is awkward for the train station, but it's very clean and welcoming inside. Bikes are rented to all-comers. ❸

Château de Danzay near Avoine, 5km north of Chinon ⓣ02.47.98.44.51, ⓦwww.chateaudedanzay.com. The seven rooms at this miniature medieval castle have rich, medieval-stye colour schemes, stone walls, huge fireplaces, four-poster beds tucked under the roof beams and lots of luxurious little touches. Heated swimming pool and manicured gardens. Prices begin at €180. Closed Oct–April. ❾

Diderot 7 rue Diderot ⓣ02.47.93.18.87, ⓦwww.hoteldiderot.com. Solidly bourgeois hotel with an old-fashioned welcome in a venerable town house. Has some grand old rooms with antique furnishings in the main building, and some brighter modern ones in the annexe. ❸–❹

De France 47–49 place du Général-de-Gaulle ⓣ02.47.93.33.91, ⓦwww.bestwestern.com/fr/hoteldefrancechinon. Historic hotel overlooking the leafy main square. Rooms are attractive and cosy, with big comfy beds, beams and exposed stone walls. ❹

Le Plantagenêt 12 place Jeanne-d'Arc ⓣ02.47.93.36.92, ⓦwww.hotel-plantagenet.com. Decent, welcoming two-star hotel on the large market square on the eastern edge of town. Rooms in the main, nineteenth-century house are pleasantly decorated; those in the garden annexe are characterless but have a/c. Family rooms available. ❸

Le Tennessee 11 rue Voltaire ⓣ02.47.93.02.85. Three basic but acceptable rooms above a central Tex-Mex bar and restaurant. ❷

La Treille 4 place Jeanne-d'Arc ⓣ02.47.93.07.71. Tiny, Spartan and full of character, with four basic rooms shoe-horned into an ancient building. ❷

Campsite

Camping de l'Île Auger ⓣ02.47.93.08.35. Overlooks the old town and château from the south bank of the Vienne; turn right from the bridge along quai Danton. Closed mid-Oct to mid-March.

The Town

A fortress of one kind or another existed at Chinon from the Stone Age until the time of Louis XIV, the age of the most recent of its ruins. It was a favourite residence of Henry Plantagenet, who held title to it long before he inherited the throne of England. He added a new castle to the first medieval fortress on

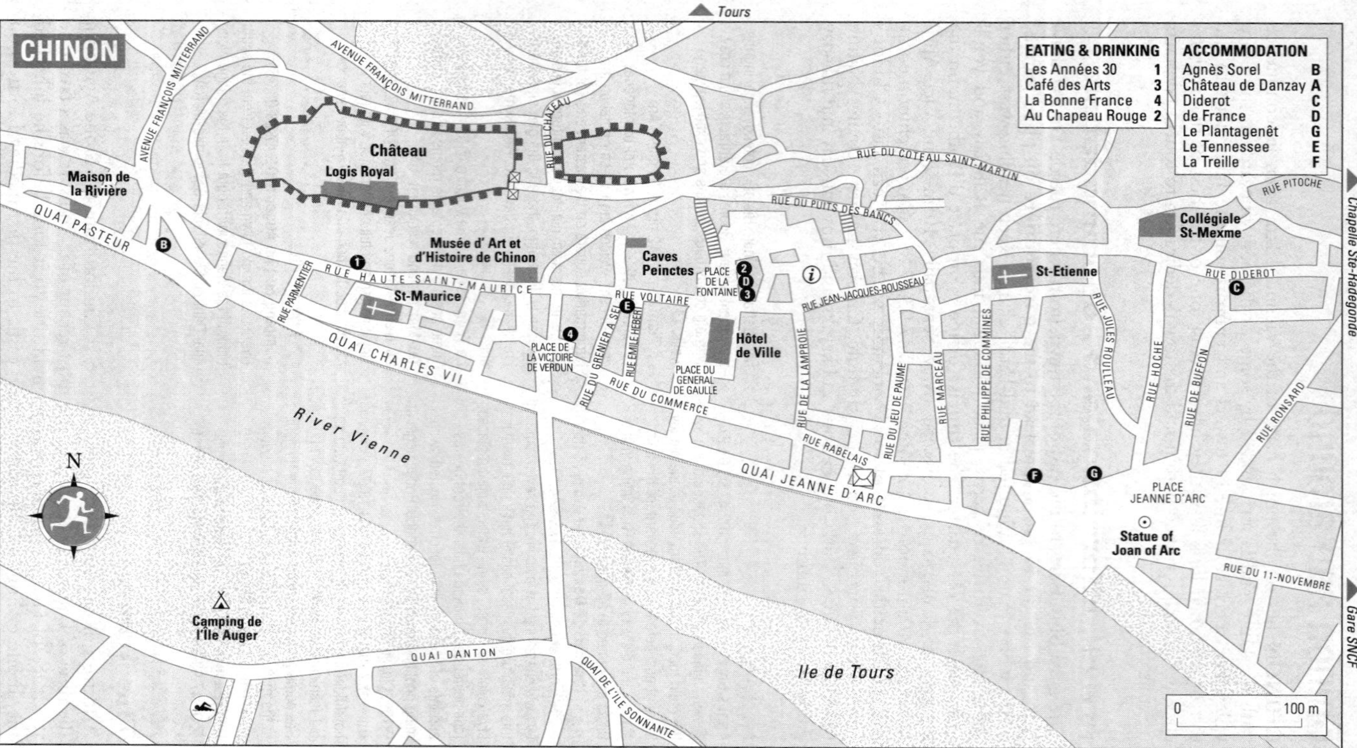
CHINON
EATING & DRINKING
Les Années 30 1
Café des Arts 3
La Bonne France 4
Au Chapeau Rouge 2
ACCOMMODATION
Agnès Sorel B
Château de Danzay A
Diderot C
de France D
Le Plantagenêt G
Le Tennessee E
La Treille F
Tours
Chapelle Ste-Radegonde
Gare SNCF
A
Château
Logis Royal
Maison de la Rivière
Musée d' Art et d'Histoire de Chinon
St-Maurice
Caves Peinctes
PLACE DE LA FONTAINE
Hôtel de Ville
PLACE DU GENERAL DE GAULLE
PLACE DE LA VICTOIRE DE VERDUN
St-Etienne
Collégiale St-Mexme
PLACE JEANNE D'ARC
Statue of Joan of Arc
River Vienne
Ile de Tours
Camping de l'Ile Auger
N
0 100 m
AVENUE FRANÇOIS MITTERRAND
RUE DU CHATEAU
RUE DU COTEAU SAINT-MARTIN
RUE PITOCHE
RUE DU PUITS DES BANCS
QUAI PASTEUR
RUE HAUTE SAINT-MAURICE
RUE PARMENTIER
QUAI CHARLES VII
RUE VOLTAIRE
RUE DU GRENIER A SEL
RUE EMILE HEBERT
RUE DU COMMERCE
RUE JEAN-JACQUES-ROUSSEAU
RUE DE LA LAMPROIE
RUE RABELAIS
RUE DU JEU DE PAUME
RUE MARCEAU
RUE PHILIPPE DE COMMINES
RUE JULES ROULLEAU
RUE HOCHE
RUE DE BUFFON
RUE RONSARD
RUE DIDEROT
QUAI JEANNE D'ARC
RUE DU 11-NOVEMBRE
QUAI DANTON
QUAI DE L'ILE SONNANTE

the site, built by his ancestor Foulques Nerra, and died here, crying vengeance on his son Richard, who had treacherously allied himself with the French king Philippe-Auguste. Henry's youngest son, John, with no English inheritance, stayed in Chinon off and on but after a year's siege in 1204–05, Philippe-Auguste finally took the castle and put an end to the Plantagenet rule over Touraine and Anjou.

Over two hundred years later, Chinon was one of the few places where the Dauphin Charles, later Charles VII, could safely stay while Henry V of England held Paris and the title to the French throne. Charles's situation changed with the arrival here in 1429 of Joan of Arc from Domrémy in Lorraine, who was able to talk her way into meeting him. The usual story – as depicted in a tapestry on display on the site – is that as Joan entered the great hall, the Dauphin remained hidden anonymously among the assembled nobles, as a test, but that Joan picked him out straight away. Joan herself told a different story, claiming that an angel had appeared before the court, bearing a crown. Either way, it is clear that she begged him to allow her to rally his army against the English. To the horror of the courtiers, Charles said yes.

Today, the **château** (currently daily, though times may vary during ongoing works: April–Sept 9am–7pm; Oct–March 9.30–11.30am & 2–5.30pm; €3) is little more than a ring of tumbledown walls and broken towers. The scene of Joan's encounter, the **Logis Royal**, is being partially rebuilt under a new roof, with works expected to continue at least until the end of 2008. Access will be permitted throughout, so you will be able to watch traditional artisans at work, and an exhibition will explain the techniques involved.

Below, the medieval streets with their half-timbered and sculpted town houses are pleasant enough to wander through, or you could duck into one of the town's low-key museums – but avoid the tacky wine- and barrel-making museum. The **Musée d'Art et d'Histoire de Chinon**, 44 rue Haute St-Maurice (June–Sept daily 10.30am–12.30pm & 2–6pm; Oct–May Mon–Fri 2.15–6pm; €3), has some diverting oddments of sculpture, pottery and paintings related to the town's history. The **Maison de la Rivière**, on the riverbank at 12 quai Pasteur (July & Aug Tues–Fri 10am–12.30pm & 2–5.30pm, Sat & Sun 3–5.30pm; €3; ⓣ02.47.93.21.34, ⓦwww.cpie-val-de-loire.org), displays models of the many kinds of Loire river vessels, and on weekend afternoons in summer you can take a short river trip on a traditional *fûtreau* or *toue* (€6); staff also lead regular guided nature walks. Though it's better with a good meal, if you want to try a glass of Chinon you could visit the **Caves Peinctes**, off rue Voltaire, a deep cellar carved out of the rock where a fancy

The troglodyte saint

A rewarding excursion out of Chinon starts along the road that leads east through town from rue Jean-Jacques-Rousseau, passing the Romanesque church of **St-Mexme** and then continuing along the cliffs past numerous **troglodyte dwellings**, some of which are still inhabited. After a kilometre or so the path runs out at the **Chapelle Ste-Radegonde**, a rock-cut church which is part of a complex of cave dwellings in which St Radegonde lived with her followers. The sixth-century German princess renounced the world and her husband – probably not a great sacrifice, since he eventually murdered her brother – in order to devote her life to God. The chapel's guardian has lived in the troglodyte home next door for nearly thirty years and often takes visitors into the chapel and caves behind – check with the tourist office in advance, or ask politely.

local winegrowers' guild runs **tastings** (July to mid-Sept daily except Mon 11am, 3pm, 4.30pm & 6pm; €3). The name of the *cave* supposedly derives from Rabelais, the author of the sixteenth-century satirical romps *Gargantua* and *Pantagruel*. Rabelais was born at the manor farm of **La Devinière**, 6km southwest of town, where there's a good but rather dry museum. An antiques and flea market takes place every third Sunday of the month, while regular **market day** is Thursday.

Eating and drinking

Chinon's main square, place du Général-de-Gaulle, is enticingly filled with outdoor tables. Among the **restaurants** on the square, *Au Chapeau Rouge* (Ⓣ02.47.98.08.08), serves top-quality regional cuisine with menus from €26, while the *Café des Arts* offers reliable and reasonably priced brasserie fare. A more intimate square a short walk west, place de la Victoire de Verdun, conceals a good, homely restaurant, *La Bonne France* (Ⓣ02.47.98.01.34; closed Thurs eve & Wed). The cosy and old-fashioned *Les Années 30*, 78 rue Voltaire (Ⓣ02.47.93.37.18) has some adventurous dishes on its menus (€23 and €36).

Forêt de Chinon

Northeast of Chinon, the elevated terrain of the *landes* is covered by the ancient **Forêt de Chinon**, crisscrossed by roads and forest alleys that make for delightful cycling or walking – the GR3 long-distance footpath runs right through from Chinon to Azay-le-Rideau (see p.539). If you want to **stay** in the area, there's a good *chambres d'hôtes* near Rigny-Ussé (see p.540). Just outside St-Benoît-la-Forêt, the village in the heart of the forest, is a woodland adventure park, **Saint-Benoît Aventure** (Easter school holidays daily 1.30–7pm; May & June Sat & Sun 10am–7pm; July & Aug daily 10am–8pm; Sept & Oct Sat & Sun 1.30–7pm; adults €18, children aged 5–8 €8, aged 9–12 €12, aged 13–15 €15; Ⓣ06.89.07.18.96, Ⓦwww.stbenoitaventure.new.fr). It offers a chance to let kids off the leash – or rather attach them to it, in the form of an alarming aerial ropeway assault course that threads its way through the trees. There's also a mountain bike circuit and a nature walk.

Tavant

Sixteen kilometres southeast of Chinon, the village of **TAVANT** hides a little jewel-box of a church, **St-Nicolas** (March–Nov Wed–Sun 10am–12.30pm & 1.30–6pm, closed first Sun of every month; €3). The exterior is unremarkable, but the twelfth-century, Romanesque **wall paintings** in its **crypt** rank among the finest in Europe. It's not clear why this crypt was so richly painted, as it hasn't been identified with any major relic cult or tomb. It's thought that the entire structure, inside and out, would once have been painted in bright colours, but today just fragments survive in the upper church, as well as a giant figure of Christ in Majesty on the half-dome of the apse. If the chapel isn't open when you arrive, ask for the guardian at the nearby *mairie*.

Saumur and around

Of all the Loire's comfortable towns, **SAUMUR** is perhaps the most elegantly bourgeois, with its graceful château lording it over the handsome town houses spread out below on both banks of the river and on the large island midstream. The town's 250-year association with the military, as home to the French Cavalry Academy and its successor, the Armoured Corps Academy, has only further elevated its pretensions. Even the local sparkling wines are renowned for their charm.

The stretch of the Loire from Chinon to Angers, which passes through Saumur, is particularly lovely, with the bizarre added draw of **troglodyte dwellings** carved out of the cliffs. The land on the south bank, under grapes and sunflowers, gradually rises away from the river, with long-inactive windmills still standing. Across the water cows graze in wooded pastures. For **transport** to Angers, you can either take the train, bus #5 along the south bank or bus #11 crossing to the north bank halfway at Gennes.

Arrival, information and accommodation

Saumur spreads along both banks of the Loire and over the small Île d'Offard in the middle of the river too. Arriving at the **gare SNCF**, you'll find yourself on the north bank: turn right onto avenue David-d'Angers and either take bus #30 to the centre or cross the bridge to the island on foot. From the island the old **Pont Cessart** leads across to the main part of the town on the south bank, where you'll find the **gare routière**, a couple of blocks west of the bridge on place St-Nicolas, and the **tourist office**, next to the bridge on place de la Bilange (mid-May to mid-Oct Mon–Sat 9.15am–7pm, Sun 10.30am–5.30pm; mid-Oct to mid-May Mon–Sat 9.15am–12.30pm & 2–6pm, Sun 10am–noon; ⓣ02.41.40.20.60, ⓦwww.saumur-tourisme.com). The **old quarter**, around St-Pierre and the castle, lies immediately behind the Hôtel de Ville, on the riverbank 100m east of the bridge.

Accommodation in Saumur is mostly upmarket and overpriced, but there are a number of very attractive hotels.

Hotels

Anne d'Anjou 32 quai Mayaud ⓣ02.41.67.30.30, ⓦwww.hotel-anneanjou.com. Comfortable hotel, with a wide range of attractively decorated rooms in a grand, eighteenth-century listed building. ⑤

La Bouère-Salée rue Grange-Couronne ⓣ02.41.67.38.85, ⓦwww.ifrance.com/labouere. Delightful bed and breakfast in a handsome nineteenth-century town house, though it's two blocks north of the train station, on the far side of the river from the historic centre. ③

Cristal 10–12 place de la République ⓣ02.41.51.09.54, ⓦwww.cristal-hotel.fr. One of the nicer hotels in town, with a great situation on the riverfront, and friendly proprietors. Rooms on the side street can be noisy, but those with river or château views are usually fine. Some inexpensive attic rooms are also available. ②–③

De Londres ⓣ02.41.51.23.98, ⓦwww.lelondres.com. This sprawling but comfortable old town-centre hotel has been spotlessly renovated in recent years, but retains some period charm. ③

St-Pierre 3 rue Haute-St-Pierre ⓣ02.41.50.33.00, ⓦwww.saintpierresaumur.com. Hushed boutique hotel with ancient beams and a stone spiral staircase. The rooms are a little fussy and overpriced, though the tiny, cheaper garret rooms are relatively inexpensive. ⑤–⑦

Le Volney 1 rue Volney ⓣ02.41.51.25.41, ⓦwww.levolney.com. This simple, budget hotel on the south side of town is a bit tired round the edges, but has friendly management and some inexpensive but cosy little rooms under the roof. ②

Hostel and campsite

Hostel rue de Verden, Île d'Offard ⓣ02.41.40.30.00, ⓦwww.hebergement-international-saumur.com. Large hostel at the east end of the island with laundry facilities, swimming-pool access and views of the château. Reception 9am–noon & 2–7pm. Boat and bike hire available. Closed Nov–Feb.

Camping de l'Île d'Offard rue de Verden, Île d'Offard ⓣ02.41.40.30.00, ⓦwww.cvtloisirs.com. Big, well-run site right next door to the hostel.

The Town

Set high above town, Saumur's airy, gleaming white fantasy of a **château** (interior closed for restoration works; exterior daily except Tues 10am–1pm & 2–5.30pm; €2), may seem oddly familiar, but then its famous depiction in *Les Très Riches Heures du Duc de Berry*, the most celebrated of all the medieval illuminated prayer books, is reproduced all over the region. It was largely built in the latter half of the fourteenth century by Louis I, Duc d'Anjou, who wanted to compete with his brothers Jean de Berry and Charles V. The threat of marauding bands of English soldiers made the masons work flat out – they weren't even allowed to stop for feast days. The château's serenely impregnable image took a knock in April 2001, when a huge chunk of the star-shaped outer fortifications collapsed down the hill towards the river. In the aftermath, the alarmed authorities decided to embark on a major renovation programme, which looks likely to continue until 2008. Until works are complete, large parts of the interior will remain closed to visitors, including the formerly excellent Musée des Arts Décoratifs and Musée du Cheval.

Down by the public gardens south of the château, Saumur's oldest church, **Notre-Dame de Nantilly** (daily 9am–6pm), houses a large tapestry collection in its Romanesque nave. The original Gothic **church of St Pierre**, in the centre of the old town (daily 9am–noon & 2–5pm), hides behind a Counter-Reformation facade built as part of the church's efforts to overawe its persistently Protestant population – Louise de Bourbon, abbess of Fontevraud, called the town a "second Geneva", horrified at the thought that Saumur might become a similarly radical Calvinist power-base. Meanwhile, the theological college at **Notre-Dame des Ardilliers**, down by the river on the eastern edge of town (daily 8am–noon & 2–6.30pm) is dominated by the tremendous dome of its classical rotunda, rebuilt after bombing in June 1940.

For relief from military and ecclesiastical history, try a glass of the famous Saumur *méthode champenoise* wines at the **Maison du Vin** on quai Lucien-Gautier (April–Sept Mon 2–7pm, Tues–Sat 9am–1pm & 2–7pm, Sun 9.30am–1pm; Oct–March Tues–Sat 10.30am–12.30pm & 2–6pm; Ⓦwww.interloire.com), which can also provide addresses of wine-growers and *caves* that you can visit. Alternatively, make for the Caves des Vignerons at St-Cyr-en-Bourg (Ⓣ02.41.53.06.06), a short train hop south of Saumur and near the station, where there are kilometres of cellars.

△ Saumur market

Beyond the town centre

Saumur's cavalry traditions are displayed most proudly at the **École Nationale d'Équitation**, in St-Hilaire-St-Florent, a suburb to the east of the centre (if you don't have your own transport, take bus #31 from the south end of rue Franklin-Roosevelt to the "Alouette" stop, then continue down the route de Marson, turning right at the signpost; it's a walk of a little over 1km). The Riding School (April–Sept Mon 2–6pm, Tues–Fri 9am–6pm, Sat 9am–12.30pm; €7.50) provides guided tours in which you can watch training sessions (mornings are best) and view the stables. Displays of dressage and anachronistic battle manoeuvres by the crackshot Cadre Noir, the former cavalry trainers, are regular events (programme details from the tourist office or online at Ⓦwww.cadrenoir.fr). The history of the tank – traditionally considered as cavalry not infantry – is covered in the separate **Musée des Blindés**, at 1043 rue Fricotelle, to the southeast of the centre (daily: May–Sept 9.30am–6.30pm; Oct–April 10am–5pm; €6).

The main activity in St-Hilaire-St-Florent, especially along the main stretch of the riverside road, along rue Ackerman and rue Leopold-Palustre, is making **sparkling wine**. You can visit the impressive rock-carved cellars of any of Ackerman-Laurance, Bouvet-Ladubay, Langlois-Château, Gratien & Meyer, Louis de Grenelle and Veuve Amiot. Choosing between them is a matter of personal taste, and possibly a question of opening hours, though most are open all day every day throughout the warmer months (generally 10am–6pm, though most close for a couple of hours at lunchtime out of season).

Eating and drinking

There are several reasonably inexpensive places around place St-Pierre, many of which offer a chance to enjoy a glass of sparkling Saumur brut at an outside table. There's nothing much to do after hours except seek out a café or "pub" that's still serving.

Les Ardilliers 35 rue Rabelais ⓣ02.41.67.12.86. Relaxed, contemporary bistro-restaurant on the way out towards Notre-Dame des Ardilliers. There's a sleek bar area, a pleasant summer terrace and some modern twists on the classic dishes – three fish and three meat, every day. Menus €15–30; closed Tues lunch, Sun eve & Mon.

Auberge Reine de Sicile 71 rue Waldeck-Rousseau Île d'Offard. ⓣ02.41.67.30.48. Over the bridge, on the Île d'Offard, with an atmospherically ancient dining room. The food is delicious, with fish dishes grilled in front of you in the old chimney place. Menus at €19 and €33; closed Mon & Sun eve, plus for the last week in Aug and first week in Sept.

Les Forges de St-Pierre 1 place St-Pierre ⓣ02.41.38.21.79. Specializing in grilled meats, this is one of the busy, slightly touristy but ultimately enjoyable restaurants on the atmospheric old square. Steaks around €10–15; closed Tues eve & Sun.

Le Grand Bleu 6 rue du Marché ⓣ02.41.67.41.83. Specializes in sea fish – Brittany is, after all, not so far away. Pleasant situation on a miniature square, with outside seating in summer. Menus from €14–26; closed Wed.

Les Ménéstrels At the *Hôtel Anne d'Anjou*, 32 quai Mayaud ⓣ02.41.67.71.10. Saumur's best place for serious, formal gastronomy, though the stone walls and exposed beams add a note of rustic relaxation. The set lunch menu is a bargain at €19, but expect to pay at least twice that for an evening meal.

Troglodyte dwellings around Saumur

The "falun" or soft shellstone found in the Loire valley lends itself to **troglodyte dwellings** – homes carved out of rocky outcrops, of which there are more in this area (between Saumur and Angers) than anywhere else in France. It's reckoned that in the twelfth century half the local population lived in homes carved out of the rock. Today, some of the rock dwellings have surprising uses, along with the more predictable "Troglo" bars and restaurants.

Away from the Loire cliffs on the plains to the south, troglodyte villages were built by digging holes like large craters and then carving out the walls. The best example is at **ROCHEMENIER**, northwest of Doué-la-Fontaine and about

20km west of Saumur, where an underground village housed a small farming community with its own underground chapel (daily: April–Nov 9.30am–7pm; €4.70), and was only abandoned in the 1930s. The visit includes a typical troglodyte dwelling, along with a museum of domestic items, including wine and oil presses. Just 3km north, at **DÉNEZÉ-SOUS-DOUÉ**, there are underground carvings thought to have been sculpted by a secret sixteenth-century sect of libertarians. The cartoon-style figures mock religion, morality, the state and the ruling class, with scenes of sex, strange deformities and inverted Christian imagery (April–Oct Tues–Sun 10.30am–1pm & 2–6.30pm; €4).

East of Saumur, the sunny microclimate and rocky soil provides the ideal conditions for making red wine, which is produced under the renowned *appellation* of Saumur-Champigny. You can visit numerous wine-growers' caves in the pretty villages around **PARNAY**. Set well back from the Loire's floodplain in the shelter of the tufa escarpment, the sandy stone walls of its ancient houses are hardly distinguishable from the surrounding natural rock. Just beyond, in **LE VAL-HULIN**, are the last producers of the once common Saumurois dried whole apples, known as *pommes tapées* – each apple, after drying, is given a little expert tap to check its readiness for bottling. At the **Troglo des Pommes Tapées** (hours and price vary; ask at the tourist office in Saumur), you're taken through the apple drying and tapping process, before rounding off the visit with a tasting. **TURQUANT**, a few hundred metres beyond Le-Val-Hulin, is the starting point for a **sentier d'interprétation**, a two-hour circular walk around the village following signposts describing the local flora and fauna set up by the regional Parc Naturel.

From a distance, the **château de Brézé**, 10km southeast of Saumur (Feb to mid-April & Oct–Dec Tues–Fri 2–6pm, Sat & Sun 10am–6pm; mid-April to Sept daily 10am–6.30pm; tunnels €8.15, château and tunnels €14), looks like a typically noble sixteenth-century château built in creamy-white tufa. Get up close, however, and the eighteen-metre-deep dry moat – one of the largest in Europe – reveals itself. The guided tour of the château's refined interior isn't particularly gripping, but exploring the moat and the medieval tunnels hacked out of the soft rock beneath the château is very enjoyable.

The Abbaye de Fontevraud

At the heart of the stunning Romanesque complex of the **Abbaye de Fontevraud**, 13km southeast of Saumur, are the tombs of the Plantagenet royal family, eerily lifelike works of funereal art that powerfully evoke the historical bonds between England and France (daily: June–Sept 9am–6.30pm; Oct–May 10am–5.30pm; €6.50). A religious community was established in around 1100 as both a nunnery and a monastery with an abbess in charge – an unconventional move, even if the post was filled solely by queens and princesses. The remaining buildings date from the twelfth century and are immense, built as they were to house and separate not only the nuns and monks but also the sick, lepers and repentant prostitutes. There were originally five separate institutions, of which three still stand in graceful Romanesque solidity. Used as a prison from the Revolution until 1963, it was an inspiration for the writer Jean Genet, whose book *Miracle of the Rose* was partly based on the recollections of a prisoner incarcerated here.

The **abbey church** is an awe-inspiring space, not least for the four tombstone effigies: Henry II, his wife Eleanor of Aquitaine, who died here, their son Richard the Lionheart and daughter-in-law Isabelle of Angoulême, King John's queen. Carved as they were at the time of their deaths, the figures are eerily lifelike. The strange domed roof, the great cream-coloured columns of the choir and the graceful capitals of the nave add to the atmosphere. Elsewhere in the complex you can explore the magnificent **cloisters**, the **chapterhouse**, decorated with sixteenth-century murals, and the vast **refectory**. All the cooking for the religious community, which would have numbered several hundred, was done in the – now perfectly restored – Romanesque **kitchen**, an octagonal building as extraordinary from the outside (with its 21 spiky chimneys) as it is from within.

The abbey is now the **Centre Culturel de l'Ouest** (CCO), the cultural centre for western France, and one of Europe's most important centres of medieval archeology, and is used for a great many activities, from concerts to lectures, art exhibitions and theatre. Programme details are available at the abbey (Ⓣ02.41.51.73.52, Ⓦwww.abbaye-fontevraud.com) or from the Saumur tourist office. **Bus** #1 runs from Saumur to Fontevraud, but it's not a frequent service and the timetable varies throughout the year, so check with the tourist office in advance.

Candes St-Martin and Montsoreau

The ancient village of **CANDES-ST-MARTIN**, on the Loire 5km north of Fontevraud, gets part of its name from the renowned local saint, Martin, who died here in around 400 while trying to settle a dispute between squabbling monks. This is a beautiful corner of the region, the village set under a rocky bluff overlooking the confluence of the Loire and Vienne. The principal sight is the airy *collégiale*, notably its elaborately sculpted porch. The oldest part of the church, though heavily restored, is the chapelle St-Martin, on the left of the choir, where you can trace the life of the saint in nineteenth-century stained-glass windows. From the quay below the village, you can take trips in an old-fashioned **Loire riverboat**, *L'Amarante* (mid-June to mid-Sept; Ⓣ02.47.95.80.85 or 06.33.34.57.16; from €12 per person). You can extend the cruise to include barbecues or breakfasts, or even sleeping out overnight.

The fifteenth-century **château de Montsoreau**, 1km downstream (Feb–April & Oct to mid-Nov 2–6pm; May–Sept daily 10am–7pm; €8.10), is one of the most photogenic châteaux of them all, its north side rising cliff-like almost straight out of the river. The interior has been turned into an elaborately presented museum dedicated to the river trade and the history of the castle, and there's a panoramic view from the open-air battlements.

Right beside the Candes-St-Martin's church in a venerable building is an excellent, relaxed local **restaurant**, the *Auberge de la Route d'Or* (Ⓣ02.47.95.81.10; closed Tues & Wed). In Montsoreau, the welcoming and well-run *Hôtel le Bussy*, 4 rue Jeanne-d'Arc (Ⓣ02.41.38.11.11, Ⓦwww.hotel-lebussy.fr; ❹), is a tranquil place to spend the night.

Angers and around

ANGERS, capital of the ancient county of Anjou, stands majestically on the banks of the Maine, which feeds the Loire just south of the city with the waters of the Mayenne, Sarthe and Loire rivers. Long known as "Black Angers" from the gloomy-coloured slate and stone quarried here since the ninth century, it is actually a very pretty, friendly town, with a lively atmosphere. The overriding reason for coming here is to see its two stunning **tapestry** series, the fourteenth-century *Apocalypse* and the twentieth-century *Le Chant du Monde*.

Arrival, information and accommodation

The **gare SNCF** is south of the centre. Bus #6 (#25 on Sun) makes the one-kilometre journey to the tourist office and château, while buses #1 and #16 will take you to central place du Raillement, which is roughly twice as far away; a flat-rate **bus** ticket, which you can buy on board, costs €1.10. The **gare routière** is down by the river, just past the Pont de Verdun on place Molière. The main **tourist office** is on place Kennedy, facing the château (May–Sept Mon–Sat 9am–7pm, Sun 10am–6pm; Oct–April Mon 2–6pm, Tues–Sat 9am–6pm, Sun 10am–1pm; ⓣ02.41.23.50.00, ⓦwww.angersloiretourisme.com); it sells a **city pass** (€14 for 24 hours, €21 for 48), which allows access to the tapestries as well as the city's museums and galleries.

There's a wide range of **accommodation** on offer, and finding a room shouldn't present too many problems, though it's still wise to book ahead in summer.

Hotels

Centre 12 rue St-Laud ⓣ02.41.87.45.07. Recently renovated hotel above a lively bar. Double-glazing keeps out the worst of the street noise. ❸

Continental 12–14 rue Louis-de-Romain ⓣ02.41.86.94.94, ⓦwww.hotellecontinental.com. Well-equipped and well-run hotel with good service and a/c. Gets busy during the week with a business crowd. ❹

Des Lices 25 rue des Lices ⓣ02.41.87.44.10. A real bargain in a balustraded town house on a distinctly posh, town-centre street. Closed August 1–15. ❷

Du Mail 8 rue des Ursules ⓣ02.41.25.05.25, ⓦwww.hotel-du-mail.com. Old-fashioned and extremely attractive two-star, with courtyard, pleasant rooms and a great location in a quiet corner of the centre. Parking available. ❹

St-Julien 9 place du Ralliement ⓣ02.41.88.41.62, ⓦwww.hotelsaintjulien.com. Large hotel right in the centre of the city, offering a good spread of modernized rooms. Some of the pretty little ones under the roof have views over town. ❹

Hostel and campsite

Centre d'Accueil du Lac de Maine 49 av du Lac de Maine ⓣ02.41.22.32.10, ⓦwww.lacdemaine.fr. Rather swish hostel-style accommodation, complete with extensive sports facilities, a 20min ride southwest of the town; bus #6 (bus #11 from 7.30pm–midnight, bus #26 on Sun) either from the train station or bd Général-de-Gaulle. Single rooms €35, dorms €17. You can rent canoes at the Base Nautique in the complex. There's also a campsite here (ⓣ02.41.73.05.03, ⓔcamping@lacedemaine.fr; closed Oct–March), agreeably situated next to the lake.

The City

Your lasting impression of Angers will be of the **château**, an impressive, sturdy fortress by the river, its moat now filled with striking formal flower arrangements and softened by trees. From here, it's just a fifteen-minute stroll east to the **cathedral** and its entourage of several smaller churches and museums.

Across the pont Verdun from the château is the suburb of **La Doutre**, where the **Hôpital St-Jean** houses the modern response to the castle's Apocalypse tapestry, *Le Chant du Monde*. Further out in the suburbs is a rash of interesting museums, easily reached by bus, exalting everything from early aeroplanes to Cointreau and communication methods.

The château and Apocalypse tapestry

The **Château d'Angers** (daily: May–Aug 9.30am–6.30pm; Sept–April 10am–5.30pm; €7.50) is a formidable early medieval fortress. The sense of impregnability is accentuated by its dark stone, the purple-brown schist characteristic of western Anjou. The château's mighty kilometre-long curtain wall is reinforced by seventeen circular towers, their brooding stone offset by decorative bands of pale tufa. Inside are a few miscellaneous remains of the counts' royal lodgings and chapels, but the chief focus is the astonishing **Tapestry of the Apocalypse**. Woven between 1373 and 1382 for Louis I of Anjou, it was originally 140m long, of which 100m now survives. From the start, it was treated as a masterpiece, and only brought out to decorate the cathedral of Angers on major festival days. The sheer grandeur of the conception is overwhelming but the tapestry's reputation rests as much on its superb detail and stunning colours, preserved today by the very low light levels in the long viewing hall. These reds and greens and golds were once even more vivid – as you can see if you buy the handy English-language booklet (€5.30), which uses photographs of the tapestry's unfaded reverse side – astonishingly, this is a perfectly finished mirror-image of the front. If you plan to follow the apocalypse story right through, the booklet comes in handy but a Bible would be even better. In brief: the Day of Judgement is signalled by the breaking of the seven seals – note the four horsemen – and the seven angels blowing their trumpets. As the battle of Armageddon rages, Satan appears first as a seven-headed red dragon, then as the seven-headed lion-like Beast. The holy forces break the seven vials of plagues, whereupon the Whore of Babylon appears mounted on the Beast. She is challenged by the Word of God, seen riding a galloping horse, who chases the hordes of Satan into the lake of fire, allowing the establishment of the heavenly Jerusalem.

Those feeling in need of a drink can head straight out of the castle and into the **Maison du Vin de l'Anjou**, 5bis place Kennedy (May–Sept Tues–Sat 9am–1pm & 3–6.30pm, Sun 9am–1pm; Oct–April Tues–Sat 9.30am–1pm & 3–6.30pm), where the helpful staff will offer you wine to taste before you buy, and can provide lists of wine-growers to visit.

The cathedral and around

The most dramatic approach to the **Cathédrale St-Maurice** is via the quayside, from where a long flight of steps leads straight up to the mid-twelfth-century portal – which shows another version of the apocalypse. Built in the 1150s and 1160s, the cathedral exemplifies the Plantagenet style – in fact, it's probably the earliest example in France of this influential architectural development. The three aisle-less bays of the nave span a distance of over 16m, the dome-like Plantagenet or Angevin vaulting creating structural strength as well as a faintly Byzantine feel. The fifteenth-century rose windows in the transepts are particularly impressive.

In front of the cathedral, on place Sainte-Croix, is the town's favourite carpentry detail, the unlikely genitals of one of the carved characters on the medieval **Maison d'Adam**. Heading northeast from place Sainte-Croix, you pass **place du Ralliement**, hub of modern Angers and site of the nineteenth-century **Théâtre Municipal**. From here, proceed into rue Lenepveu, the main shopping street, where the turreted facade of the **Hôtel Pincé**, at no. 32, crawls with Italianate decoration. The museum of antiquities formerly inside – mostly ceramics from Greece, China and Japan, with a few Japanese caricatures of actors – looks set to be closed for restoration for the foreseeable future.

Arguably the greatest stoneworks in Angers are the creations of the famous local sculptor David d'Angers (1788–1856), whose Calvary adorns the cathedral. His great civic commissions can be seen all over France, but these large-scale marbles and bronzes are almost all copies of the smaller plaster of Paris works created by the artist himself. It's mostly these plaster originals that are exhibited in the **Galerie David d'Angers**, 37bis rue Toussaint (June–Sept daily 10am–7pm; Oct–May Tues–Sun 10am–noon & 2–6pm; €4), set impressively in the glazed-over nave of a ruined thirteenth-century church, the **Église Toussaint**.

The **Musée des Beaux-Arts**, at 10 rue du Musée (June–Sept daily 10am–7pm; Oct–May Tues–Sun 1–6pm; €4), is housed in the **Logis Barrault**, a proudly decorated mansion built by a wealthy late fifteenth-century mayor. Years of extensive restoration have cleaned up – and in some places entirely remade – the flamboyant Gothic stone carving. Eighteenth- and nineteenth-century paintings dominate the collection, with works by Watteau, Chardin and Fragonard, as well as Ingres' operatic *Paolo et Francesca* – the same subject depicted by Rodin in *The Kiss* – and a small collection devoted to Boucher's *Génie des Arts*.

La Doutre

The district facing the château across the Maine is known as **La Doutre** (literally, "the other side"), and still has a few mansions and houses dating from the medieval period, despite redevelopment over the years.

In the north of the area, a short way from the Pont de la Haute-Chaine (and just under 2km from the château), the **Hôpital St-Jean**, at 4 bd Arago, was built by Henry Plantagenet in 1174 as a hospital for the poor, a function it continued to fulfil until 1854. Today it houses the **Musée Jean Lurçat et de la Tapisserie Contemporaine** (June–Sept daily 10am–7pm; Oct–May Tues–Sun 10am–noon & 2–6pm; €4), which contains the city's great twentieth-century tapestry, **Le Chant du Monde**. The tapestry sequence was designed by Jean Lurçat in 1957 in response to the Apocalypse tapestry, though he died nine years later before its completion. It hangs in a vast vaulted space, the original ward for the sick, or Salle des Malades. The first four tapestries deal with *La Grande Menace*, the threat of nuclear war: first the bomb itself; then *Hiroshima Man*, flayed and burnt with the broken symbols of belief dropping from him; then the collective massacre of the *Great Charnel House*; and the last dying rose falling with the post-Holocaust ash through black space – the *End of Everything*. From then on, the tapestries celebrate the joys of life: *Man in Glory in Peace*; *Water and Fire*; *Champagne* – "that blissful ejaculation", according to Lurçat; *Conquest of Space*; *Poetry*; and *Sacred Ornaments*. Subject matter and treatment are intense, and the setting helps: it's a huge echoey space, with rows of columns supporting soaring Angevin vaulting. The artist's own commentary is available in English. The Romanesque cloisters at the back, with their graceful double columns, are also worth a peek.

There are more modern tapestries in the building adjoining the Salle des Malades, where the collection is built up around the donation by Lurçat's widow of several of his paintings, ceramics and tapestries, along with the highly tactile but more muted abstract tapestries of Thomas Gleb, who died in Angers in 1991, and Josep Grau Garriga. With four local ateliers, Angers is a leading centre for contemporary tapestry, and the neighbouring **Centre Régional d'Art Textile**, 3 bd Daviers (Mon–Fri 10am–noon & 2–4pm), can put you in touch with local artists and let you know where to find private exhibitions.

South of the Hôpital St-Jean, on La Doutre's central square, place de la Laiterie, the ancient buildings of the **Abbaye de Ronceray** are now occupied by one of France's elite *grandes écoles*, the **École des Arts et Métiers**, which trains the leading students of aerospace technology, among others. The abbey church is used to mount art exhibitions, worth visiting just to see the Romanesque galleries of the old abbey and admire their beautiful murals. When there's no exhibition, you can only visit as part of the tourist office's weekly tour of La Doutre. Inside the adjacent twelfth-century **Église de la Trinité**, an exquisite Renaissance wooden spiral staircase fails to mask a great piece of medieval bodging used to fit the wall of the church around a part of the abbey that juts into it.

Musée de l'Ardoise

The **Musée de l'Ardoise** (July to mid-Sept daily except Mon 2–6pm; mid-Feb to June & mid-Sept to Nov Sun 2–6pm; demonstrations at 3pm; €5.50; Ⓦwww.lemuseedelardoise.fr) is rather lost in the industrial satellite village of Trelaze, 2km southeast of the centre – take bus #2 to stop "Ludovic Ménard". It's not a museum as such, rather a demonstration of traditional slate-mining techniques by former miners, on the site of a shut-down open-cast slate mine. Just watching a sexagenarian split a giant block of schist into millimetre-perfect, size-graded slates using a big wooden hammer and a pair of outsize clogs is fairly astounding, even if you don't understand the commentary.

Eating

The streets around place du Ralliement and place Romain have a wide variety of **cafés** and **restaurants**, many of them very inexpensive.

Le 14 14 rue Bodinier ⓣ02.41.20.15.20. Eccentrically decorated bistro crammed with chattering diners tucking into the speciality bruschetta (€9–13). Closed Sun, Mon & first two weeks of July.

La Cantina 9 rue de l'Oisellerie ⓣ02.41.87.36.34. Relaxed café-bistro serving southwestern dishes such as *magret de canard* (duck steak). Good value for lunch, with straightforward fish and meat *plats* and salads for around €15. Closed Mon.

Les Caves du Ralliement 9 place du Ralliement ⓣ02.41.88.47.77. Busy brasserie underneath the posh and well-regarded *Provence Caffè*. Good for inexpensive *moules-* or *steak-frites* at lunchtime, and oysters or eels with a glass of wine in the evening, sitting at an outside table on the square. Closed Mon evening.

Le Grandgousier 7 rue St-Laud ⓣ02.41.87.81.47. Serves meats grilled on the wood fire, complemented by local wines, which are included in the price of the €15 and €24 menus. Closed Sun.

Papagayo 44 bd Ayrault ⓣ02.41.87.03.35. Friendly bar-bistro near the university campus, with a great atmosphere during term-time and a conservatory room for summer. Serves decent, inexpensive traditional French food. Closed Mon lunch, Sat lunch & Sun.

Le Soufflerie 8 place Pilori ⓣ02.41.87.45.32. Popular café specializing in soufflés, both large and savoury (at around €11) and small and sweet (around €8). Closed Sun, Mon & 4 weeks in July/Aug.

Villa Toussaint 43 rue Toussaint ⓣ02.41.88.15.64. Fashionable, ultra-contemporary bar-restaurant serving high quality seafood (platters from €14), with sushi featuring on some menus. The leafy terrace is a lovely spot in summer. Closed Sun.

Drinking and nightlife

Late-opening **bars** congregate around rue St-Laud: *Bar du Centre*, below *Hôtel Centre* is full of young Angevins, and there's a cluster of popular Irish-type places at the bottom end of the road, around place Romain. Just beyond the square, *Safari*, 23 rue du Mail (closed Mon), is a trendy bar with DJs playing salsa, reggae or hip-hop. Over in La Doutre, *La Descente de la Marine*, at 28 quai des Carmes, is an old-time bar with a strong nautical flavour, attracting lots of students and young people who come down for an outdoor, early evening *apéro* on the quay. Among Angers' numerous **clubs**, *Boléro*, 38 rue St-Laud, is popular and central, with an unpretentious, sometimes cheesy music policy. *Le Mid'Star*, 25 quai Félix-Faure, is the biggest and best-known clubbing venue, with a more serious playlist. *Chabada*, 56 bd du Doyenné, in the Monplaisir quarter just north of St-Serge (take a taxi) puts on live music.

Listings

Bike hire A desk in the tourist office hires out bikes.

Boat hire Numerous companies hire out canoes and run guided kayak trips on the five rivers in the vicinity of Angers. Try: Canoe Kayak Club d'Angers, 75 av du lac de Maine (on the Maine and Lac de Maine) ⓣ02.41.72.07.04, ⓦckcac.free.fr; Club Nautique d'Écouflant, rue de l'île St-Aubin, Écouflant (Sarthe, Mayenne, Loire, Maine) ⓣ02.41.34.56.38, ⓦwww.kayakecouflant.com; and Club de Canoe Kayak les Ponts de Cé, 30 rue Maximin-Gelineau, Les Ponts de Cé (on the Loire) ⓣ02.41.44.65.15, ⓦwww.canoelespontsdece.new.fr. The tourist office has details of more sedate trips on sightseeing boats.

Car hire Budget 14 rue Denis-Papin ⓣ02.41.24.96.18; Anjou Auto Location, 100 av Victor-Chatenay ⓣ02.41.18.59.18; Europcar, 10 rue Fulton ⓣ02.41.24.05.89; Hertz, place de la Gare ⓣ02.41.88.15.16.

Emergencies Ambulance ⓣ15; Centre Hospitalier, 4 rue Larrey (ⓣ02.41.35.36.37); for late-night pharmacies, phone the police on ⓣ02.41.57.52.00.

Festivals At the end of May, the Tour de Scènes festival (ⓦwww.tourdescenes.com) brings rock and world music acts to the city centre for four days of concerts. The Festival Angers l'Été features jazz and world music gigs in the atmospheric Cloître Toussaint, the cloisters behind the Galerie David d'Angers, on Tuesday and Thursday evenings throughout July and August; book through the tourist office. In early September, the festival Les Accroche Coeurs brings a host of theatrical companies, musicians and street-performers for three days of surreal entertainment.

Internet Go online at 48 rue Plantagenêt, near Les Halles; 37 rue Bressigny, near bd Foch; and 25 rue de la Roë, just east of place de la République.

Laundries 9 place Hérault; 17 rue Marceau; 15 rue Plantagenêt; 5 place de la Visitation.

Market There are a number of markets Tues–Sat throughout the city including a flower market on place Leclerc on Sat – Anjou is a major flower-growing region – and an organic produce market on rue Saint-Laud on Sat.

Police Commissariat, 15 rue Dupetit-Thouars ⓣ02.41.66.86.35.

Taxis Accueil Taxi Angevin ⓣ02.41.34.96.52; Allo Anjou Taxi ⓣ02.41.87.65.00.

Around Angers

Lazing around the Loire and its tributaries between visits to vineyards can fill a good summer week around Angers, as long as you have your own transport, and you can easily reach a couple more châteaux in these parts: **Brissac-Quincé**, 20km south of the town (also bus #9), and **Le Plessis-Bourré** near Ecuillé (impossible to get to by public transport), 17km to the north. For a more accessible glimpse of a real monster of a mansion, head for the **Château de Serrant**, just outside St-Georges-sur-Loire, on bus routes #7 and #18 from Angers.

Château de Brissac

The giant **Château de Brissac** at **BRISSAC-QUINCÉ** (guided tours only: April–June, Sept & Oct daily except Tues 10.15am–12.15pm & 2–6pm; July & Aug daily 10am–6.30pm; €8.50; Ⓦwww.brissac.net) has been owned since 1502 by the same line of dukes. It boasts of its status as the tallest in France but it's by no means the most handsome, looking like an ugly duckling frozen halfway through its transformation into a swan. On the main west front, two round towers survive from an earlier, fifteenth-century fortress, with the château's ill-proportioned seventeenth-century facade awkwardly wedged in between them. Under the original rebuilding plan, the old fortified towers were to be pulled down, but the death of Duke Charles II in 1621 brought the project to a standstill. The interior is a riot of opulent taste, with some beautiful ceilings and tapestries, and lots of priceless furnishings; the guided tours supplies various family anecdotes. The château has had a **vineyard** since 1515, with its own label, and a wine tasting – with opportunity to buy, of course – concludes the tour. There are also some extravagantly wonderful **chambres d'hôtes** – at €390 per room.

Château du Plessis-Bourré

Five years' work at the end of the fifteenth century produced the fortress of **Le Plessis-Bourré** (guided tours only: mid-Feb to end March, Oct & Nov daily except Wed 2–6pm; April–June & Sept Mon, Tues & Fri–Sun 10am–noon & 2–6pm, Thurs 2–6pm; July & Aug daily 10am–6pm; closed Jan to mid-Feb & Dec; €9; Ⓦwww.plessis-bourre.com), 17km north of Angers, between the Sarthe and Mayenne rivers. Despite the vast, full moat, spanned by an arched bridge with a still-functioning drawbridge, it was built as a luxurious residence rather than a defensive castle. The treasurer of France at the time, Jean Bourré, received important visitors here, among them Louis XI and Charles VIII.

Given the powerful, medieval exterior, the first three rooms on the ground floor are a surprise, being beautifully decorated and furnished in the Louis XVI, XV and Régence styles respectively, though things revert to type in the Gothic Salle du Parlement. The highlight of the tour comes in the Salle des Gardes, just above, where the original, deeply coffered ceiling stems from Bourré's fashionable interest in alchemy. Every inch is painted with allegorical scenes: sixteen panels depict alchemical symbols such as the phoenix, the pregnant siren and the donkey singing Mass, while eight cartoon-like paintings come with morals attached – look out for "Chicheface", the hungry wolf that only eats faithful women, whose victim is supposed to be Jean Bourré's wife.

Château de Serrant

At the **Château de Serrant**, 15km west of Angers beside the N23 near **ST-GEORGES-SUR-LOIRE**, the combination of dark-brown schist and creamy tufa give a rather pleasant cake-like effect to the outside (guided tours only, departing on the hour; mid-March to June & Sept to mid-Nov daily except Tues 9.45am–noon & 2–5.15pm; July & Aug daily 9.45am–5.15pm; €9.50; Ⓦwww.chateau-serrant.net). But with its heavy slate bell-shaped cupolas pressing down on massive towers, the exterior is grandiose rather than graceful. The building was begun in the sixteenth century and added to up until the eighteenth century. In 1755 it belonged to an Irishman, Francis Walsh, to whom Louis XV had given the title Count of Serrant as a reward for Walsh's help against the old enemy, the English. The Walsh family married into the ancient La Trémoille clan, whose descendants – via a Belgian offshoot – still own the château. The massive rooms of the interior are packed with all the trappings of old wealth. Much of the decor dates from the late nineteenth and early twentieth centuries, but it's tastefully – and expensively – done, and you are also shown the Renaissance staircase, the sombre private chapel designed by Mansart, a bedroom prepared for Napoleon (who only stopped here for a couple of hours), and the attractive vaulted kitchens.

Le Mans and around

LE MANS, the historic capital of the Maine region, is taken over by car fanatics in the middle of June for the famous 24-hour race, but during the rest of the year it's a fascinating and unusually peaceful place to visit. As a large, industrial and traditionally left-wing city, its atmosphere could hardly be more different from the bourgeois Loire valley proper, 80km to the south, but it shares a good deal of history: Le Mans was the favourite home of the Plantagenet family, the counts of Anjou, Touraine and Maine. The old quarter, in the shadow of the magnificent cathedral, is unusually well preserved, while outside town you can visit the serene Cistercian abbey of Epau and, of course, the racetrack.

Arrival, information and accommodation

The hub of Le Mans today is **place de la République**, beneath which, in the underground shopping centre, is the city **bus terminal**. At the time of writing, bus #16 ran between here and the **gare SNCF** via avenue Général-Leclerc, where the **gare routière** is located – but expect disruption to traffic and bus routes in the town centre until at least the end of 2008, when a new tram system is expected to be up and running. From place de la République, rue Bolton leads east into rue de l'Étoile, where you'll find the **tourist office** (July & Aug Mon–Sat 9am–6pm, Sun 10am–12.30pm & 2.30–5pm; Sept–June same hours except closed Sat noon–2pm and all day Sun; Ⓣ02.43.28.17.22, Ⓦwww.lemanstourisme.com). To hire a **bike,** make your way to the northern suburb of La-Chapelle-St-Aubin, where you'll find Veloland at 1 rue du Moulin-aux-Moines (Ⓣ02.43.51.16.00, Ⓦwww.veloland.com) – take bus #8 to its terminus, "Moulin aux Moines".

Unless your visit coincides with one of the big **racing events** during April, June or September – when hotel rates can quadruple – you should be able to find **accommodation** easily without having to book, though there's nothing in the old quarter.

Hotels

Chantecler 50 rue de la Pelouse Ⓣ02.43.14.40.00, Ⓦwww.hotelchantecler.fr. Quiet, professionally run hotel, offering dull but well-fitted-out rooms and parking. ⑤

Levasseur 5–7 bd René-Levasseur Ⓣ02.43.39.61.61, Ⓔhotellevasseur@wanadoo.fr. Well located just off place de la République, if rambling and functional in feel. Closed Aug. ④

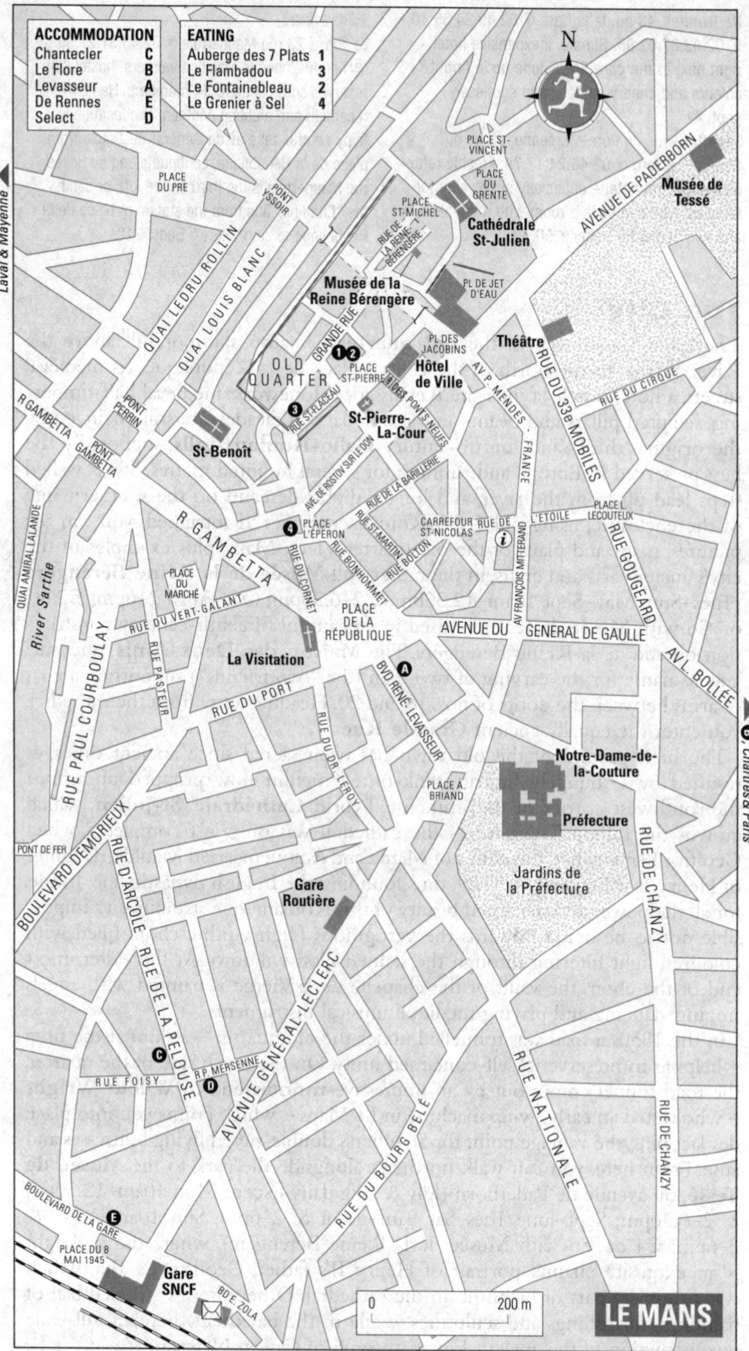
ACCOMMODATION
Chantecler C
Le Flore B
Levasseur A
De Rennes E
Select D
EATING
Auberge des 7 Plats 1
Le Flambadou 3
Le Fontainebleau 2
Le Grenier à Sel 4
N
Laval & Mayenne
Cathédrale St-Julien
Musée de Tessé
Musée de la Reine Bérengère
OLD QUARTER
Hôtel de Ville
Théâtre
St-Pierre-La-Cour
St-Benoît
La Visitation
Notre-Dame-de-la-Couture
Préfecture
Jardins de la Préfecture
Gare Routière
Gare SNCF
River Sarthe
B, Chartres & Paris
Tours & Racing Circuits
0 200 m
LE MANS

De Rennes 43 bd de la Gare ⓣ02.43.24.86.40, ⓕ02.43.87.02.95. Simple, inexpensive hotel right next to the *gare SNCF* done up in bright colours and cheery pastels, and spotlessly kept. ❷

Select 13 rue du Père-Mersenne, off av du Général-Leclerc ⓣ02.43.24.17.74. Freshly refurbished budget hotel – especially good value for families, who can have a room with a double bed and two bunks for under €50. ❷

Hostel

Le Flore 23 rue Maupertuis ⓣ02.43.81.27.55, ⓔflorefjt@noos.fr. Mainly a workers' hostel, but reserves some beds for HI members. Has 24hr reception and a cheap canteen. The location is fairly central: take av du Général-de-Gaulle from place de la République, continue along av Bollée; rue Maupertuis is the third on the left; or catch the "Citadine" bus from the station or place de la République to stop "Flore". Beds €12.

The City

The complicated web of the **old quarter** lies atop a minor hill above the River Sarthe, to the north of the central place de la République. Its medieval streets, a hotchpotch of intricate Renaissance stonework, medieval half-timbering, sculpted pillars and beams and grand classical facades, are still encircled by the original third- and fourth-century **Gallo-Roman walls**, supposedly the best preserved in Europe and running for several hundred metres. Steep, walled steps lead up from the river, and longer flights descend on the southern side of the enclosure, using old Gallo-Roman entrances. If intrigued, you can see pictures, maps and plans of the old quarter, Vieux Mans, plus examples of the city's ancient arts and crafts, in the rather dull **Musée de la Reine Bérengère** (Tues–Sun: May–Sept 10am–12.30pm & 2–6.30pm; Oct–April 2–6pm; €2.80, or €6 with Musée de Tessé), housed in a beautiful fifteenth-century construction on rue de la Reine-Bérengère. The **Maison des Deux-Amis**, opposite, gets its name for the carving of two men (the "two friends") supporting a coat of arms between the doors of nos. 18 and 20. Heading away from the cathedral, you enter the equally ancient **Grande Rue**.

The high ground of the old town has been sacred since ancient times, as testified by a strangely human, pink-tinted menhir now propped up against the southwest corner of the immense, hybrid **Cathédrale St-Julien**, which crowns the hilltop. The nave of the cathedral was only just completed when Geoffroi Plantagenet, the count of Maine and Anjou, married Matilda, daughter of Henry I of England, in 1129, thus founding the English dynastic line. Inside, for all the power and measured beauty of this Romanesque structure, it's impossible not to be drawn towards the vertiginous High Gothic choir, filled with coloured light filtering through the stained-glass windows. At the easternmost end of the choir, the vault of the chapelle de la Vierge is painted with angels singing, dancing and playing medieval musical instruments.

In the 1850s a road was tunnelled under the old quarter – a slum at the time – helping to preserve its self-contained unity. On the north side of the quarter, the road tunnel comes out by an impressive **monument to Wilbur Wright** – who tested an early flying machine in Le Mans – which points you into place des Jacobins, the vantage point for St-Julien's double-tiered flying buttresses and apse. From here, you can walk northeast alongside the park to the **Musée de Tessé**, on avenue de Paderborn (July & Aug daily except Mon 10am–12.30pm & 2–6.30pm; Sept–June Tues–Sat 9am–noon & 2–6pm, Sun 10am–noon & 2–6pm; €4 or €6 with Musée de la Reine Bérengère), where the highlight is an exquisite enamel portrait of Henry II's father, Geoffroi Le Bel, which was originally part of his tomb in the cathedral. Otherwise it's a mixed bag of paintings, furnishings and sculptures, while in the basement there's a full-scale reconstruction of the ancient Egyptian tomb of Queen Nefertari.

The modern centre of Le Mans is place de la République, bordered by a mixture of *belle-époque* buildings and more modern office blocks, and the Baroque bulk of the **church of the Visitation**, built in 1730, with a balustrade inside designed by one of the sisters of the order.

On summer nights, the cathedral and various other buildings in the old town are illuminated in Le Mans' **son et lumière** show, called *La Nuit des Chimères*. The displays are free and take place daily, starting at 11pm in July and 10.30pm in August. The highlight is a parade of mythical monsters projected along the length of the Gallo-Roman walls.

Eating and drinking

In the centre of town, the **cafés** and **brasseries** on place de la République stay open till late, while on nearby place l'Éperon there's a very good, if expensive, **restaurant**, *Le Grenier à Sel* (ⓣ02.43.23.26.30; closed Sun & Mon; menus from €18). The most atmospheric restaurants, however, are located in the old quarter. The *Auberge des 7 Plats*, 79 Grande-Rue (ⓣ02.43.24.57.77; closed Sun & Mon), does a good range of good-value *plats* and menus. For a special occasion make for the rustically styled *Le Flambadou*, 14bis rue St-Flaceau (ⓣ02.43.24.88.38; closed Sat lunch & Sun), which offers a very meaty menu from Périgord and the Landes with mains from around €15. Nearby on place St-Pierre, *Le Fontainebleau* (ⓣ02.43.14.25.74; closed Mon & Tues) has pleasant outside seating facing the Hôtel de Ville and serves moderately priced classic French cuisine. There's a daily **market** in the covered halls on place du Marché, plus a bric-a-brac market on Wednesday, Friday (when there's also food) and Sunday mornings on place du Jet-d'Eau, below the cathedral on the new town side.

The racetrack and car museum

The first big race at Le Mans was in 1906, and two years later aviator **Wilbur Wright** took off here, remaining in the air for a record-breaking one hour and 31 minutes and 30 seconds. The first 24-hour car race was run as early as 1923, on the present 13.6-kilometre Sarthe circuit, with average speeds of 92kph (57mph) – these days, the drivers average around 210kph (130mph). The Sarthe circuit, on which the now world-renowned **24 Heures du Mans** car race takes place every year in mid-June, stretches south from the outskirts of the city, along ordinary roads. During the race weekend, you'll need a ticket to get anywhere near the circuit. These can be bought direct from the organizers at ⓦwww.lemans.org, or via the tourist office, and cost €61 for all three days, €25 for trial days (Fri & Sat), and €39 for race day, which is always on a Sunday. You'll need a separate ticket (€61–102) to get access to the grandstands, and be sure to book well in advance. Many enthusiasts' clubs and ticket agencies offer tour packages including accommodation – otherwise impossible to find at race times – and the crucial parking passes; try ⓦwww.clubarnage.com or ⓦwww.pageandmoy.com, or look through the adverts in a motor-sports magazine. True petrol-heads book themselves a place at one of the circuit-side campsites.

At other times of year, you can watch practice sessions, or there's the bikers' **24 Heures Moto** in early April or the **Le Mans Classic** in September. Outside race days, the simplest way to get a taste of the action is just to take the main road south of the city towards Tours, a stretch of ordinary highway which follows the famous **Mulsanne straight** for 5.7km – a distance that saw race cars reach speeds of up to 375kph, until two chicanes were introduced in 1989. Alternatively, visit the **Musée de l'Automobile** (daily: Feb–May & Oct–Dec 10am–6pm; June–Sept 10am–7pm; €7), on the edge of the Bugatti circuit – the dedicated track section of the main Sarthe circuit, where the race starts and finishes. It parades some 150 vehicles, ranging from the humble 2CV to classic Lotus and Porsche race cars.

The Abbaye de L'Epau

If car racing holds no romance, there's another outing from Le Mans of a much quieter nature, to the Cistercian **Abbaye de l'Epau** (daily 9.30–11.30am & 2–5.30pm; opening hours may vary in summer to accommodate exhibitions; ⓣ02.43.84.22.29; €3), 4km out of town off the Chartres–Paris road (bus #14 from place de la République in Le Mans, stop "Pologne", then a walk of some 500 metres). The abbey was founded in 1229 by Queen Berengaria, consort of Richard the Lionheart, and it stands in a rural setting on the outskirts of the Bois de Changé more or less unaltered since its fifteenth-century restoration after a fire. The visit includes the dormitory, with the remains of a fourteenth-century fresco, the abbey church and the scriptorium, or writing room. The church contains the recumbent figure of Queen Berengaria over her tomb.

Travel details

Trains

Angers to: Le Mans (frequent; 40min–1hr 20min); Nantes (frequent; 45min); Paris (frequent; 1hr 40min); Saumur (frequent; 20–30min); Tours (frequent; 1hr–1hr 30min).
Bourges to: Nevers (8–12 daily; 50min); Orléans (9 daily; 1hr–1hr 40min); Tours (12 daily; 1hr 40min).
Le Mans to: Angers (frequent, 40min–1hr 20min); Nantes (frequent, 55min–1hr 45min); Paris (frequent; 1hr); Rennes (frequent; 2hr); Saumur (3 daily; 2hr); Tours (frequent; 1hr).
Orléans to: Beaugency (frequent; 20min); Blois (frequent; 40min); La Ferté-St-Aubin (frequent; 15–25min); Meung-sur-Loire (frequent; 15min); Paris (at least hourly; 1hr); Romorantin-Lanthenay (change at Salbris; 7 daily; 1hr 30min); Tours (frequent; 1hr–1hr 30min).
Tours to: Amboise (frequent; 20min); Azay-le-Rideau (7 daily; 30min); Blois (frequent; 40min); Chenonceaux (6 daily; 35min); Chinon (7 daily; 45min); Langeais (8 daily; 25min); Le Mans (7 daily; 1hr); Montrichard (10 daily; 30min); Orléans (frequent; 1hr–1hr 30min); Paris (hourly; 2hr 30min, TGVs via St-Pierre-des-Corps 1hr); Saumur (frequent; 45min).

Buses

Angers to: Brissac-Quincé (5–7 daily; 30min).
Blois to: Chambord (1–3 daily; 45min); Cour-Cheverny (3 daily; 35min); Romorantin-Lanthenay (3 daily; 1hr); St-Aignan (2–3 daily; 1hr 10min); Valençay (3 daily; 1hr 30min).
Bourges to: Sancerre (1–3 daily; 1hr 15min).
Orléans to: Beaugency (4–6 daily; 45min); Chartres (9 daily; 1hr 10min–1hr 45min); Germigny-des-Près (3 daily; 1hr); Gien (3 daily; 1hr 50min); Meung-sur-Loire (8 daily; 35min); St-Benoît-sur-Loire (3 daily; 1hr); Sully-sur-Loire (2–3 daily; 45min–1hr 20min).
Saumur to: Fontevraud (4–6 daily; 35min).
Tours to: Amboise (7 daily; 50min); Azay-le-Rideau (2 daily; 50min); Chinon (2 daily; 1hr 10min); Loches (12 daily; 40min); Richelieu (1–4 daily; 1hr 50min).

Burgundy

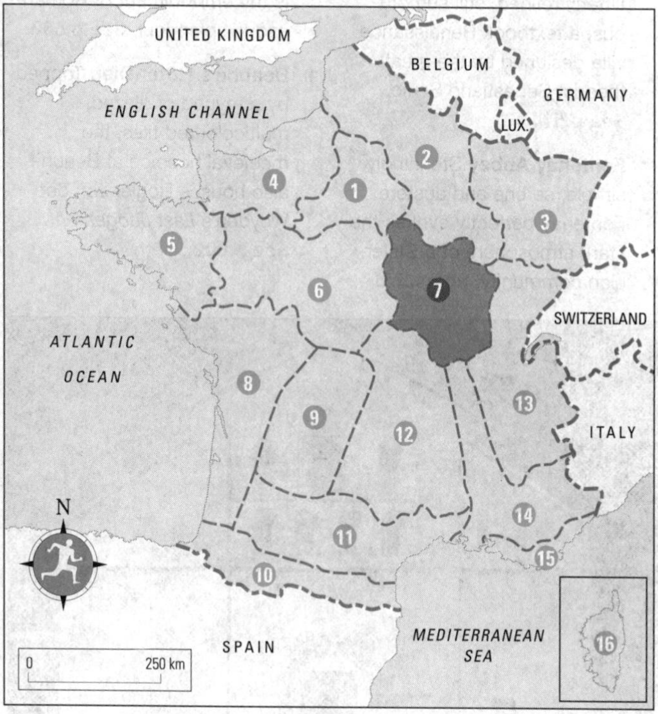

UNITED KINGDOM
BELGIUM
GERMANY
LUX.
ENGLISH CHANNEL
SWITZERLAND
ATLANTIC OCEAN
ITALY
SPAIN
MEDITERRANEAN SEA
N
0 250 km
1 2 3 4 5 6 7 8 9 10 11 12 13 14 15 16

CHAPTER 7

Highlights

* **à la bourguignonne** Voluptuaries, prepare to indulge – Burgundy's ambrosial sauces are based on its full-flavoured red wines. Snails meanwhile are stewed in dry, white Chablis. See opposite

* **Château d'Ancy-le-Franc** Utterly refined, still sumptuous; a textbook Renaissance villa designed by the great theorist Sebastiano Serlio. See p.574

* **Fontenay Abbey** Stunningly simple, serene and austere Fontenay perfectly evokes the stark atmosphere of a Cistercian community. See p.576

* **Semur-en-Auxois** Almost impossibly beautiful, this postcard-perfect market town perches above the lovely River Armançon. See p.578

* **Vézelay** An intensely atmospheric pilgrim destination, the Basilica of La Madeleine is the embodiment of Romanesque splendour. See p.582

* **Beaune's Hôtel-Dieu** Topped by a myriad of glazed, multicoloured tiles, the medieval hospice at Beaune also houses Rogier van der Weyden's *Last Judgement*. See p.602

△ Fontenay Abbey

7

Burgundy

Peaceful, rural **Burgundy** is one of the most prosperous regions in modern France, but for centuries its powerful dukes remained independent of the French crown. During the Hundred Years War, they even sided with the English, selling them the captured Joan of Arc. By the fifteenth century their power extended over all of Franche-Comté, Alsace and Lorraine, Belgium, Holland, Picardy and Flanders, and their state was the best organized and richest in Europe, its revenues equalled only by Venice. It finally fell to the French kings only when Duke Charles le Téméraire (the Bold) was killed besieging Nancy in 1477.

There's evidence everywhere of this former wealth and power, both secular and religious: in the dukes' capital of **Dijon**, in the great abbeys of **Vézelay** and **Fontenay**, in the ruins of the monastery of **Cluny** (whose abbots' influence was second only to the pope's), and in the châteaux of **Tanlay** and **Ancy**.

The food of Burgundy

The **cuisine** of Burgundy is known for its richness, due in large part to two factors: the region's heavy red wines and its possession of one of the world's finest breeds of beef cattle, the Charollais. The **wines** are used in the preparation of the sauces which earn a dish the designation of *à la bourguignonne*. Essentially, this means cooked in a red wine sauce to which baby onions, mushrooms and *lardons* (pieces of bacon) are added. The classic Burgundy dishes cooked in this manner are *bœuf bourguignon* and *coq au vin*. Another term which frequently appears on menus is *meurette*, also a red wine sauce but made without mushrooms and flambéed with a touch of marc brandy. It's used with eggs, fish and poultry as well as red meat.

Snails (*escargots*) are hard to avoid in Burgundy, and the local style of cooking them involves stewing for several hours in the white wine of Chablis with shallots, carrots and onions, then stuffing them with a butter of garlic and parsley and finishing them off in the oven. **Other specialities** include the parsley-flavoured ham (*jambon persillé*); hams from the Morvan hills cooked in a cream *saupiquet* sauce; calf's head (*tête de veau*, or *sansiot*); a *pauchouse* of river fish (that is, poached in white wine with onions, butter, garlic and *lardons*); a *poussin* (tender chicken) from Bresse; a saddle of hare (*rable de lièvre à la Piron*); and a *potée bourguignonne*, or soup of vegetables cooked in the juices of long-simmered bacon and pork bits.

Like other regions of France, Burgundy produces a variety of **cheeses.** The best known are the creamy white Chaource, the soft St-Florentin from the Yonne valley, the orange-skinned Époisses and the delicious goat's cheeses from the Morvan. And then there is *gougère*, a kind of cheesecake, best eaten warm with a glass of Chablis.

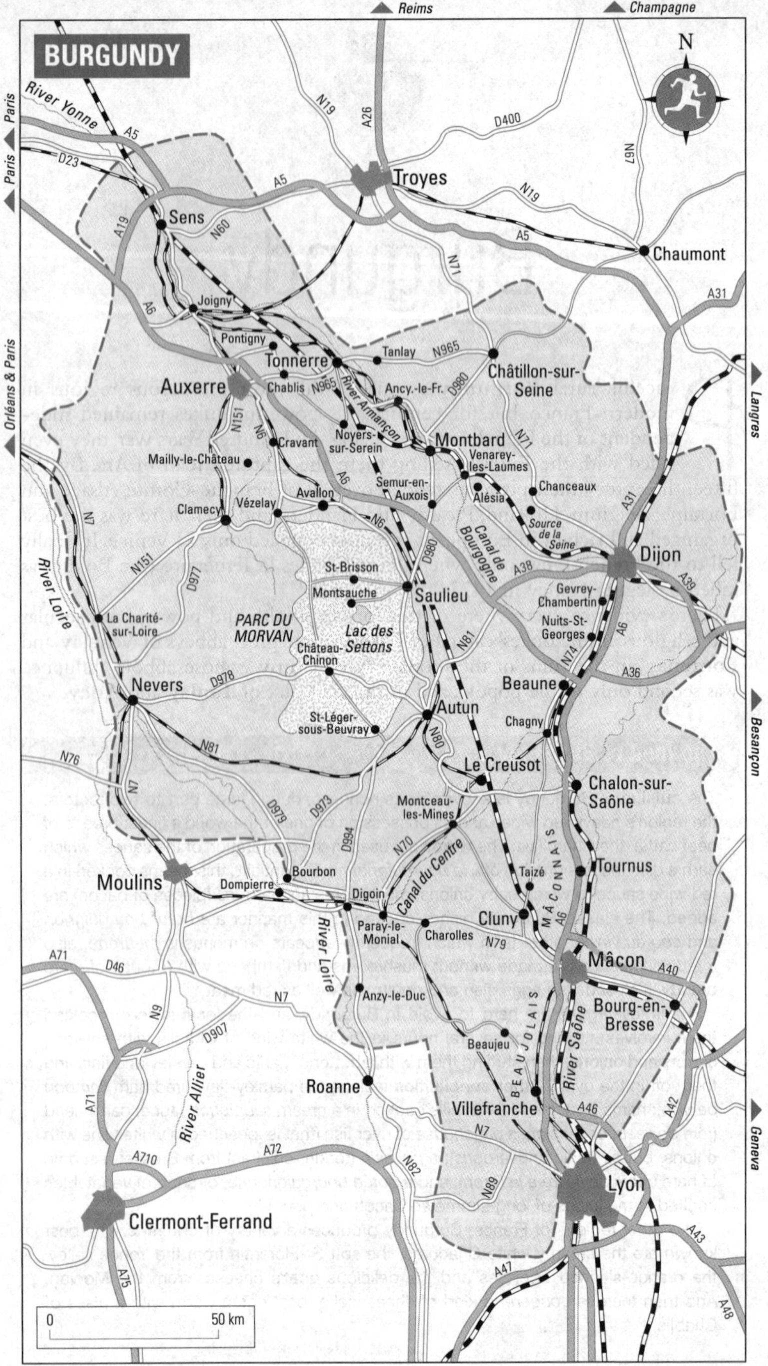
BURGUNDY
N
Reims
Champagne
Paris
Paris
Orléans & Paris
Langres
Besançon
Geneva
River Yonne
River Loire
River Loire
River Allier
River Armançon
River Saône
Canal de Bourgogne
Canal du Centre
PARC DU MORVAN
Lac des Settons
MÂCONNAIS
BEAUJOLAIS
Troyes
Sens
Joigny
Pontigny
Tonnerre
Tanlay
Auxerre
Chablis
Châtillon-sur-Seine
Ancy.-le-Fr.
Noyers-sur-Serein
Montbard
Venarey-les-Laumes
Cravant
Mailly-le-Château
Semur-en-Auxois
Alésia
Chanceaux
Source de la Seine
Clamecy
Vézelay
Avallon
Dijon
St-Brisson
Montsauche
Saulieu
Gevrey-Chambertin
Nuits-St-Georges
La Charité-sur-Loire
Château-Chinon
Beaune
Nevers
Autun
St-Léger-sous-Beuvray
Chagny
Le Creusot
Chalon-sur-Saône
Montceau-les-Mines
Tournus
Moulins
Bourbon
Dompierre
Taizé
Digoin
Cluny
Paray-le-Monial
Charolles
Mâcon
Bourg-en-Bresse
Anzy-le-Duc
Beaujeu
Roanne
Villefranche
Lyon
Clermont-Ferrand
Chaumont
A5
A6
A19
A26
A31
A36
A38
A39
A40
A42
A43
A46
A47
A48
A71
A72
A75
A710
N6
N7
N9
N19
N60
N67
N70
N71
N74
N76
N79
N80
N81
N82
N89
N151
N965
D23
D46
D400
D907
D973
D977
D978
D979
D980
D994
0
50 km

Because of its monastic foundations, Burgundy became – along with Poitou and Provence – one of the great church-building areas in the Middle Ages. Practically every village has its Romanesque church, especially in the country around Cluny and Paray-le-Monial, and where the Catholic Church built, so had the Romans before; with their legacy hugely visible in the substantial Roman remains at **Autun**. And the history goes back further: **Bibracte**, on the vast, windswept hill of Mont-Beuvray, was an important Gallic capital, and **Alésia** was the scene of Julius Caesar's epic victory over the Gauls in 52 BC. In more modern times the rustic backwater of **Le Creusot** became a powerhouse of the Industrial Revolution, with the manufacture of railway engines, artillery pieces and latterly nuclear boilers – using the ample forests and iron-ore deposits to fuel the forges.

For voluptuaries, **wine** is, of course, the region's most obvious attraction, and devotees head straight for the great **vineyards**, whose produce has played the key role in the local economy since Louis XIV's doctor prescribed wine as a palliative for the royal dyspepsia. If you lack the funds to indulge your taste for expensive drink, go in September or October when the *vignerons* are recruiting harvesters.

Between bouts of gastronomic indulgence, you can engage in some moderate activity: for **walkers** there's a wide range of hikes, from the gentle to the relatively demanding, in the **Parc Régional du Morvan** and the **Côte d'Or**. There are also several long-distance canal paths, which make great **bike** trips. As for the waterways themselves, aficionados rate most highly the **Canal de Bourgogne** and the **Canal du Nivernais**, both of which can be cruised by rented barge; contact the Comité Régional du Tourisme de Bourgogne (ⓣ03.80.28.02.80, ⓦwww.burgundy–tourism.com/fleuve).

The road to Dijon

The old **road to Dijon**, the Nationale 6, runs from Paris down to the Côte d'Azur, the route taken by the National Guardsmen of Marseille when they marched on Paris singing the *Marseillaise* in 1792. It enters the province of Burgundy just south of Fontainebleau, near where the River Yonne joins the Seine, and follows the Yonne valley through the historic towns of **Sens**, **Joigny** and **Auxerre**. Scattered in a broad corridor to the west and east of the road, in the valleys of the Yonne's tributaries, the Armançon, Serein, Cure and Cousin rivers, is a fascinating collection of abbeys, châteaux, towns, villages and other sites as ancient as the history of France. It makes for a route far more interesting, albeit slower, than speeding around the bland curves of its modern replacement, the **Autoroute du Soleil** (A6), entrance to which requires a modest toll payment.

Sens

The name of **SENS**, the northernmost town in Burgundy, commemorates the Senones, the Gallic tribe whose shaggy troops all but captured Rome in 390

BC; they were only thwarted by the Capitoline geese cackling and waking the garrison. Its heyday as a major ecclesiastical centre was in the twelfth and thirteenth centuries, but it lost its pre-eminence in the ensuing centuries largely through damage caused by the Hundred Years War and the Wars of Religion. Nowadays, it is a quiet, relaxed place on the banks of the River Yonne – although the cathedral, its treasury and the adjacent museum make a stop worthwhile.

The Town

Contained within a ring of tree-lined boulevards where the city walls once stood, the town's ancient centre is still dominated by the **Cathédrale St-Étienne** (daily: April–Oct 7.30am–7pm; Nov–March 8am–6pm, reserved for mass Sun morning) close to the intersection of Grande-Rue and rue de la République, which, together with their prolongations, neatly quarter the town centre. Begun around 1130, it was the first of the great French Gothic cathedrals, and having been built without flying buttresses – these were added later for stability – its profile is relatively wide and squat. The architect who completed it, William of Sens, went on to rebuild the choir of Canterbury Cathedral in England – the link being Thomas Becket, who had previously spent several years in exile around Sens. The story of Thomas's murder is told in the twelfth-century windows in the north aisle of the choir. The **treasury**, which can be entered either from the cathedral or the museum (see below for times), is also uncommonly rich, containing Islamic, Byzantine and French vestments – including those belonging to Thomas Becket – jewels and embroideries.

Next door is the thirteenth-century **Palais Synodal**, with its roof of Burgundian glazed tiles restored by the nineteenth-century "purist" Viollet-le-Duc, as were those of so many other buildings in this region. Its vaulted halls, originally designed to accommodate the ecclesiastical courts, now house the excellent **Musée de Sens** (June–Sept Wed–Mon 10am–noon & 2–6pm; Oct–May Wed, Sat & Sun 10am–noon & 2–6pm, Mon, Thurs & Fri 2–6pm; €5), which makes use of all available space to display a prize collection of artifacts found locally, including statuary from the cathedral and Gallo-Roman mosaics. Prize exhibits include the Villethierry treasure, which consists of 867 items of bronze jewellery in a jar which are thought to be a craftsman's hoard. The vaults of the building – partly constituting the remains of a Gallo-Roman building, including baths heated through the pavement – have also been incorporated into the museum. There are guided tours of the cathedral, treasury and museum each afternoon in July and August.

Facing the cathedral across the central place de la République are fine wood and iron *halles*, where a **market** is held on Monday, Friday and Saturday mornings. Near by, **rue de la République** and **Grande-Rue** are lined with old houses now converted into shops, and mainly reserved for pedestrians. There are three particularly finely carved and timbered houses on the corner of rue Jean-Cousin one block south of the square: the **Maison d'Abraham** and the **Maison du Pilier**, with **Maison Jean Cousin** on rue du Général-Alix.

Practicalities

From the **gare SNCF**, Grande-Rue crosses over the two broad arms of the River Yonne and leads straight to the place de la République and the cathedral – about fifteen minutes' walk. The **tourist office** is an octagonal building in place Jean-Jaurès (July & Aug Mon–Sat 9am–12.30pm & 1.30–7pm, Sun 10am–12.30pm & 2–5.30pm; Sept–June Mon–Fri 9am–noon &

1.30–6.15pm, Sat 9am–noon & 1.30–5.15pm; ⓣ03.86.65.19.49, ⓦwww.office-de-tourisme-sens.com), just north of the Hôtel de Ville, where rue de la République becomes rue Leclerc.

For central **places to stay**, try the simple but spotless *Esplanade*, (ⓣ03.86.83.14.70, ⓕ03.86.83.14.71; closed Sun & Aug; ❷), 2 bd du Mail, above a bar at the east end of place Jean-Jaurès. Just round the corner at 21 rue de Trois Croissants, is the *Hôtel Brennus* (ⓣ03.86.64.04.40, ⓦwww.hotel-brennus.fr; ❸), where rooms have more character, some with crooked angles and painted beams. Close to the cathedral is the old-time-feel *Hôtel de Paris et de la Poste* (ⓣ03.86.65.17.43, ⓦwww.hotel-paris-poste.com; ❼), at 97 rue de la République. Here the halls and stairways are lined with polished wood and tapestries but the bedrooms tend to be more anonymous. The hotel also has an excellent restaurant specializing in traditional country cuisine (menus €20–30). The local **campsite**, *Entre-deux-Vannes*, is at 191 av de Sénigallia (ⓣ03.86.65.64.71, ⓔespacesverts@mairie-sens.fr; June to late Sept), twenty minutes' walk south of town.

For **eating**, you'll find pizza, Mexican and French food on place de la République, which is also the place for a coffee or drink. In the same area – almost on the doorstep of the cathedral – is the friendly, bustling crêperie *Au P'tit Creux*, at 3 rue de Brennus, where you can enjoy excellent home-made desserts. Superb seafood can be had at *Le Soleil Levant*, 51 rue Emile-Zola (ⓣ03.86.65.71.82; closed Wed, Sun eve & Aug; menus €15–35), near the train station.

Joigny

As you travel from Sens towards Auxerre, the next place of any size on the Yonne is the modest town of **JOIGNY**, its elegant old houses ranged up the slope above the river. The first fort was constructed here at the end of the tenth century, with houses built beneath it, though much of the original settlement was destroyed by a fire in 1530. The town is not worth a prolonged visit, but makes a pleasant rest stop, particularly on market days (Wed & Sat). Buildings worthy of attention are the **Château des Gondi**, built by Cardinal Gondi in the sixteenth century and wilfully Classical, and the remains of the twelfth-century **ramparts** on Chemin de la Guimbard. A few half-timbered houses that somehow escaped the 1530 fire can be seen on **rue Montant-au-Palais**, the street leading up to the church of St-Jean, including the best known, **Maison du Pilori**, combining Gothic and Renaissance styles, with some carvings strangely reminiscent of crocodile heads. On place Jean de Joigny, the main beam supporting the **Maison de l'Arbre de Jessé** illustrates Christ's family tree, with worn, tendril-like branches adorned with figures from the Old Testament.

The helpful **tourist office** is by the bridge at 4 quai Henri Ragobert (July & Aug Mon–Sat 9am–12.30pm & 2–7pm, Sun 10am–1pm; Sept–June Tues–Sat 9am–noon & 2–5/6pm, Mon 2–5/6pm; ⓣ03.86.62.11.05, ⓦwww.tourisme-joigny.fr.fm) by the **gare routière**. There are no hotels in the old town itself but *Le Rive Gauche* (ⓣ03.86.91.46.66, ⓦwww.hotel-le-rive-gauche.fr; menus €27–35; ❹), at Chemin du Port au Bois, has a view of it and a terrace overlooking the water. In a less picturesque, but very handy, location the *Hôtel Paris-Nice* (ⓣ03.86.62.06.72, ⓔparisnice@orange.fr; ❸) at Rond Point de la Résistance, is two minutes walk from the train station. But the nicest place, both to stay and eat, is 6km west of town, along the D182 towards St-Julien-du-Sault.

Le P'tit Claridge (☎03.86.63.10.92, Ⓕ03.86.63.01.34; ❸; closed Jan & Feb) in Thèmes, has rooms full of charm and a restaurant offering a very good-value menu at €16 (closed Sun evening & Mon).

An interesting side trip from Joigny, located about 45 minutes away by car, is the village of **ST-SAUVEUR-EN-PUISAYE** and the birthplace, in 1873, of the French writer Colette. The **Musée Colette** is in the château (April–Oct daily except Tues 10am–6pm; Nov–March Sat & Sun 2–6pm; €5) and includes a reconstruction of her apartment in Paris, as well as personal items and original manuscripts.

Auxerre and around

A pretty old town of narrow lanes and unexpected open squares, **AUXERRE** stands on a hill a further 15km up the Yonne from Joigny. It looks its best from Pont Paul-Bert and the riverside **quais**, where houseboats and barges moor, its churches soaring dramatically and harmoniously above the surrounding rooftops.

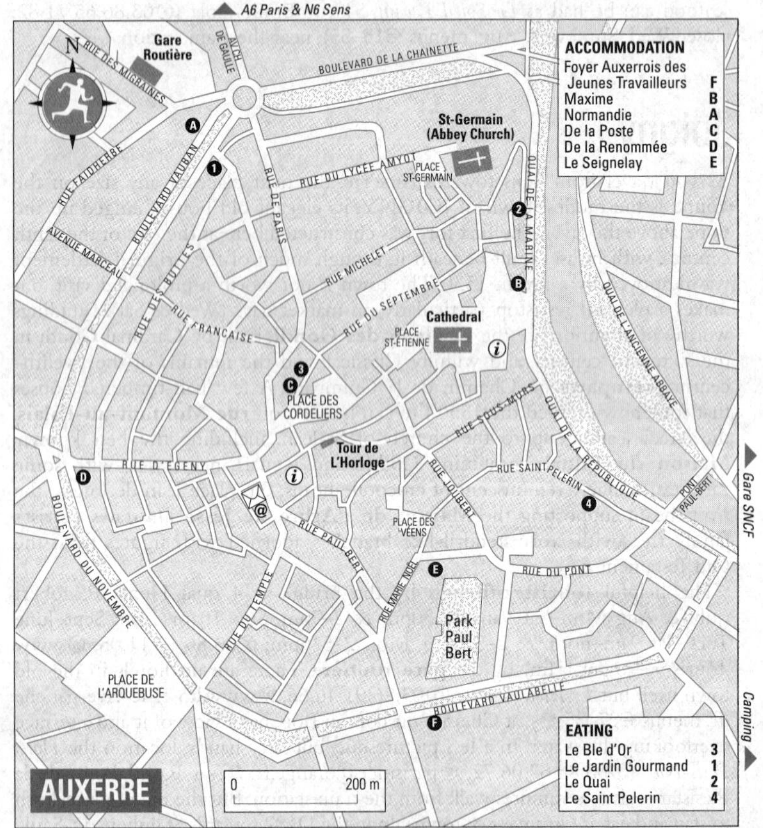

Arrival, information and accommodation

The **gare SNCF** in rue Paul-Doumer, is across the river from the town: follow signs for the *centre ville*, crossing Pont Paul-Bert. The **tourist office** sits by the river at 2 quai de la République (mid-June to mid-Sept Mon-Fri 9am–1pm & 2–7pm, Sun 9.30am–1pm & 3–6.30pm; mid-Sept to mid-June Mon–Sat 9.30am–12.30pm & 2–6pm, Sun 10am–1pm; ⓣ03.86.52.06.19, ⓦwww.ot-auxerre.fr), with an annexe in rue de Fourbisseurs near the clock tower in summer. They can advise about **bike** rental (€3 per hour), cycle routes and **boat cruises** (€7.40 per hour). The **gare routière** lies in place des Migraines off the *boulevard périphérique*. To enjoy some local colour, and local produce, try the **market** in place de l'Arquebuse (Tues & Fri morning). The post office, just south of place des Cordeliers, has **Internet access**.

Hotels

Maxime 2 quai de la Marine ⓣ03.86.52.14.19, ⓦwww.lemaxime.com. An elegant option sandwiched between the old town and the river, with tall ceilings, modern furnishings and old wooden wine-making machinery dotted about the place. Ask for a room with river views as they are not necessarily more expensive; instead it's the size that matters here. There's also an excellent €33 menu in the restaurant, or go for the €60 option – including a glass of wine with each course. Closed mid-Dec to Jan. ❺

Normandie 41 bd Vauban ⓣ03.86.52.57.80, ⓦwww.hotelnormandie.fr. Just outside the old town centre, this fairly luxurious, creeper-covered chain hotel occupies a former nineteenth-century country house. Its airy rooms are tastefully decorated, the staff are welcoming and it's also good for nocturnal sauna and billiards – should you require them, these amenities are available 24hr. ❹

De la Poste 9 rue d'Orbandelle ⓣ03.86.52.12.02, ⓕ03.86.51.68.61. To enter this hotel is to enter a world of bizarre decor. In the corridors burgundy coconut-matting-clad walls meet a burgundy-check-carpeted floor. But they lead, surprisingly, to charmingly decorated, modern rooms. A great, central location and a good mid-range choice. ❹

De la Renommée 27 rue d'Egleny ⓣ03.86.51.31.45. A reasonable family-run, budget option. It's also a good half-hour uphill walk from the train station, sitting just inside the western ring-road. The restaurant has menus from €11. Closed Sun & three weeks in Aug. ❷

Le Seignelay 2 rue du Pont ⓣ03.86.52.03.48, ⓦwww.leseignelay.com. Very well placed – just a few minutes walk from the old town centre – the rooms can be a bit dingy. Friendly staff, a hearty buffet breakfast and a good little restaurant (closed Sun & Mon) in its courtyard. Closed Feb. ❷–❸

Hostel and campsite

Foyer Auxerrois des Jeunes Travailleurs 16 bd Vaulabelle ⓣ03.86.52.45.38. Hard to find (it's at the back of the courtyard of the Citroën garage and isn't signed) this hostel is a strange place. Downstairs are old wood and upholstered benches whilst upstairs is reminiscent of a run-down block of flats. Rooms are very bare bones and rather depressing – but then it is cheap; €15.20 including breakfast.

Camping Municipal D'Auxerre 8 rte de Vaux ⓣ03.86.52.11.15, ⓔcamping.marie@auxerre.com. Next to the riverside football ground, a pleasant site on the south side of town. Open April–Sept.

The Town

The most interesting of Auxerre's many churches is the disused abbey church of **St Germain**, now a museum (daily except Tues: June–Sept 10am–12.30pm & 2–6pm; Oct–May 10am–noon & 2–6pm; €4.30 or €6 combined ticket with the Musée Leblanc-Duvernoy, see below), at the opposite end of rue Cauchois from the cathedral. Partial demolition has left its belfry detached from the body of the building, but what gives it special interest is the **crypt**, one of the few surviving examples of Carolingian architecture, with its plain barrel vaults still resting on their thousand-year-old oak beams. Deep inside, the faded ochre frescoes of St Stephen (St-Étienne) are among the most ancient in France, dating back to around 850 AD.

The **cathedral** itself (daily: April–Oct 7.30am–6pm; Nov–March 7.30am–5pm; Sunday mornings reserved for Mass) still remains unfinished, despite the fact that its construction was drawn out over more than three centuries from 1215 to 1560: the southernmost of the two west front towers has never been completed. Look out for the richly detailed sculpture of the porches and the glorious colours of the original thirteenth-century glass that still fills the windows of the choir, despite the savagery of the Wars of Religion and the Revolution. There has been a church on the site since about 400 AD, though nothing visible survives earlier than the eleventh-century **crypt** (€2.80). Among its frescoes is a unique depiction of a warrior Christ mounted on a white charger, accompanied by four mounted angels.

From in front of the cathedral, rue Fourier leads to place des Cordeliers and off left to the Hôtel de Ville and the old city gateway known as the **Tour de l'Horloge**, with its fifteenth-century coloured clock face. The whole quarter, from place Surugue through rue Joubert and down to the river, is full of attractive old houses.

Eating

Le Ble d'or 5 rue d'Orbandelle ☎03.86.48.16.84. A good little crêperie, slightly light on atmosphere, but excellent, filling, tasty food at fair prices (€4–8).

Le Jardin Gourmand 56 bd Vauban ☎03.86.51.53.52. Polished glass, crisp linen and immaculate décor; this is truly fine dining. Beef with *foie gras*, roast turbot risotto with *langoustines* – the least expensive menu comes in at €40 (though they do give you a lot of food for your money). Or sample the range of their culinary skills and go for the *menu dégustation* (5 *petits plats*, cheese and desserts) for €85 including wine. Closed Tues & Wed.

Le Quai place St-Nicholas ☎03.86.51.66.67. The perfect lazy-lunch spot, its rows of tables line up in the very pretty place St-Nicholas, beside the river. At lunchtime its *plats du jour* are around €12.

Le Saint Pelerin 56 rue St-Pélerin ☎03.86.52.77.05. Near the Pont Paul-Bert, this intimate restaurant has an excellent traditional menu at €25. Choices include eggs cooked in the wonderfully rich Burgundy wine sauce, local duck and roasted pig's trotters. Closed Sun, Mon & three weeks in Aug.

Around Auxerre

On or close to the D965 and the Paris–Dijon train route in the open, rolling country east of Auxerre lie several minor attractions, ranging from Greek treasures to Cistercian abbeys and Renaissance châteaux. The valley of the aptly named Serein River is the location of the villages of **Pontigny**, of monastic origin, **Chablis**, famed for its excellent vineyards, and the time-locked **Noyers-sur-Serein**; while to the south, a string of villages along the **upper valley of the Yonne** provides a glimpse of a gentler, more secluded countryside.

Pontigny

The ravages of time – in particular the 1789 Revolution – have destroyed most of the great monastic buildings of the Cistercian order of monks. Their rigorous insistence on simplicity and manual labour under their most influential twelfth-century leader, St Bernard, was a revolutionary response to the worldliness and luxury of the Benedictine abbots of Cluny. The only places in Burgundy where you can get an idea of how Cistercian ideas translated into bricks and mortar are at Pontigny and Fontenay.

PONTIGNY lies 18km northeast of Auxerre, and its beautifully preserved twelfth-century **abbey church** stands on the edge of the village, where its functional mass rises from the meadows. There's no tower, no stained glass and no statuary to distract from its austere, harmonious lines, though the effect is marred by the seventeenth-century choir that occupies much of the nave. Built through the 1100s, it spans the transition between the old Romanesque and the new Gothic, and was much copied in the country round about – in Chablis, for example.

Three Englishmen played a major role in the abbey's early history, all of them archbishops of Canterbury: Thomas Becket took refuge from Henry II in the abbey in 1164, Stephen Langton similarly hid here during an argument over his eligibility for the primacy from 1207 to 1213, and Edmund Rich retired here in 1240 after unsuccessfully trying to stand up to Henry III. The abbey was also the origin of an attraction with which a nearby village is more often associated: the famous **Chablis wine**. It was the monks of Pontigny who originally developed and refined the variety, and the village and its unassuming neighbouring hamlets are better places to sample the wine than in the expensive bars of Chablis itself.

There's a simple **hotel–restaurant** in Pontigny: the *Relais de Pontigny* on the N77 (ⓣ03.86.47.96.74; ❷), but, with more cash, it's better to go for the comfortable *Relais St-Vincent* (ⓣ03.86.47.53.38, ⓔrelais.saint.vincent@libertysurf.fr; ❸; menus from €13), 14 Grande-Rue in nearby **Ligny-le-Chatel**, 4km along the D91. Ligny also has a **campsite** by the Serein off the D8 Auxerre road (mid-May to Sept).

Chablis

Sixteen kilometres to the south of Pontigny on winding, rural D965, the pretty red-roofed village of **CHABLIS** is the home of the region's famous light dry white wines. It lies in the valley of the River Serein between the wide and mainly treeless upland wheat fields typical of this corner of Burgundy. As you head into town you'll notice rows of vines etching the hills, interspersed by the yellow splashes of fields full of sunflowers. While wandering around the village you could take a look at the side door of the **church of St-Martin**, decorated with ancient horseshoes and other bits of rustic ironwork left as *ex votos* by visiting pilgrims. Legend has it that Joan of Arc was one of them.

If you're using public transport the summer bus service from Auxerre and Tonnerre is "on demand" and has to be booked before 5pm the day before you want to travel – pick up a leaflet at a tourist office or train station. Chablis **tourist office** (Maison de la Vigne et du Vin) is just over the Serein bridge at 1 rue du Maréchal de Lattre de Tassigny (daily 10am–12.30pm & 1.30–6pm; Dec–March closed Sun; ⓣ03.86.42.80.80, ⓦwww.chablis.net). If you want to **stay** the night, a superb choice is the nearby *Relais de la Belle Etoile* (ⓣ03.86.18.96.08, ⓦwww.chablis-france.fr; ❺; closed mid-Dec to mid-Jan) at 4 rue des Moulins, a charming bed-and-breakfast-style hotel, its rooms are beautifully and individually decorated. Meanwhile the *Hostellerie des Clos* (ⓣ03.86.42.10.63, ⓦwww.hostellerie-des-clos.fr; ❹) in rue Jules-Rathier, is impeccably presented and undeniably luxurious though also more formulaic. It offers mini-apartments for up to €183 and has an excellent restaurant (menus €38–73). If you're camping there's an attractive **campsite**, the *Camping de Chablis* (ⓣ03.86.42.44.39, ⓕ03.86.42.49.71; June–Sept), beside the river just outside the village. For **food**, *À vins du Domaine Laroche*, 18 rue des Moulins (ⓣ03.86.42.47.30), is a good, stylish restaurant (*plats* €13–20) where they'll happily advise you on a choice of wine. Alternatively, *Bistro des Grand Clus* (ⓣ03.86.42.19.41), 8 rue Jules-Rathier, has a very affordable *plat*-plus-wine menu at €9.50, with three courses for €20.

Chablis: the wine

The neatly staked **Chablis** vineyards, originally planted by the monks of Pontigny (see p.570), cover the sunny, well-drained, stony slopes on both sides of the valley. The grape is the chardonnay, which is to white wine what the pinot noir is to red: raw material of all the greatest Burgundies. To taste the wines, avoid Chablis itself: the town milks its product for all it's worth. Overpriced wine bars and stuffy restaurants abound, meaning you don't get the opportunity to taste the cheaper varieties, and there's haughty disapproval if you hope to spend less than €15 a bottle. You'd be better off walking ten minutes south from the centre to the co-operative, **La Chablisienne**, 8 bd Pasteur (July & Aug daily 9am–7pm, Sept–June 9am–noon & 2–6pm; Ⓣ03.86.42.89.98, Ⓦwww.chablisienne.com), which offers maximum variety in a casual environment – better still, drink in one of the other villages like Pontigny or Maligny. If you want to buy a good wine, go for one with an *appellation*; the seven distinguished *grands crus*, from the northern slopes of the valley, are the best, with the *premiers crus*, made from more widely planted grapes, next in line.

Noyers-sur-Serein

Twenty-three kilometres to the southeast of Chablis, you come to the beautiful little town of **NOYERS-SUR-SEREIN.** With no public transport, it's sealed from the modern world in a medieval time warp. Half-timbered and arcaded houses, ornamented with rustic carvings – particularly those on place de la Petite-Étape-aux-Vins and round place de l'Hôtel-de-Ville – are corralled inside a loop of the river and the town walls, and pleasant hours can be passed wandering the path between the river and the irregular walls, with their robust towers. The Serein here is as pretty as in Chablis, but Noyers, being remarkably free of commercialism, has more charm.

The town's main sight is the **Musée de Noyers** (Feb–May & Oct–Dec Sat & Sun 2.30–6.30pm; June–Sept Wed–Mon 11am–6.30pm; €4), comprising the remarkable collection of art historian Jacques Yankel. The Naive painters had no formal training and were often workers lacking academic education (one, Augustine Lesage, worked as a miner for sixty years before he started painting). Some star exhibits include Gérard Lattier's morbid comic-strip-style work, the excellent collages of Louis Quilici and dreamy early twentieth-century paintings of Jacques Lagrange. If you're in shape, you might want to attempt the hike up to the **Chateau Vieux** after visiting the museum. The ruins of the twelfth-century castle are in the midst of a slow restoration, but the site offers a beautiful panorama over the town. To reach the dilapidated castle, turn right just before the town entrance archway.

The best place to **stay** is the ivy-covered seventeenth-century *Hôtel de la Vieille Tour* (Ⓣ03.86.82.87.69, Ⓕ03.86.82.66.04; ④) in place du Grenier-à-Sel in the town centre. The Dutch-owned establishment offers ten beautifully furnished rooms rife with personality and views across the gardens to the river. Their restaurant, run by the son, does excellent *table d'hôte* meals for €15 – reservations are essential for dinner. If you can't get in there, try *L'Étape Nucerienne* (Ⓣ03.86.82.60.92), which is a few doors down from the tourist office at 27 place de la Petite-Étape-aux-Vins.

The valley of the Yonne

If you're travelling south from Auxerre and want a break from the main roads, head along the D163, a twisting minor road which follows the course of the **River Yonne** through a score of peaceful rural villages. Several have places both to stay and eat, making for a much more restful overnight stop than the towns.

VAUX and **ESCOLIVES-STE-CAMILLE**, the first villages you come to, both have attractive Romanesque churches. **VINCELOTTES** and **IRANCY**, on the opposite bank of the river, are flower-decked and picturesque: Irancy produces the only red wine in this area, much loved by Louis XIV, while Vincelottes was the port for shipping it.

A nice **place to stay** hereabouts is *Le Castel* (Ⓣ03.86.81.43.06, Ⓦwww.lecastelmailly.com; ④), a *chambre d'hôte* on place de l'Église in **MAILLY-LE-CHÂTEAU**, a further 10km along the river which offers an excellent *table d'hôte* for €32, including wine. The main part of the village is on high ground above the river, but there's also a lovely riverside quarter, with ancient houses huddling under cliffs.

The Canal de Bourgogne

From Migennes near Joigny on the N6, the River Armançon, in tandem with the **Canal de Bourgogne**, branches off to the north of the River Yonne. Along or close to its valley are several places of real interest: the Renaissance châteaux of **Ancy-le-Franc** and **Tanlay**, **Fontenay Abbey**, and the site of Julius Caesar's victory over the Gauls at **Alésia**. Just east of the Canal, perched above the River Armançon as it flows through a miniature gorge, is the exquisitely picturesque town of **Semur-en-Auxois**.

Further east the Canal encompasses the upper reaches of the River Seine: at **Châtillon-sur-Seine** is the famous Celtic Treasure of Vix, and you can trace the river south as far as its source.

Tonnerre and around

On the Paris–Sens–Dijon TGV train route, **TONNERRE** is a useful, though not that inspiring, starting point for exploring this corner of the region. A run-down little town, it clearly has not enjoyed the same prosperity as its neighbour Chablis.

In the centre of town the principal sight is the vast and well-conserved medieval hospital, the **Hôtel-Dieu** (entrance via the tourist office, same hours – see p.574; €4.50). The late thirteenth-century building is dominated by the staggering curve of a huge boat's-keel roof in pale oak, but it's otherwise mostly empty, apart from occasional exhibitions. A gnomon, or meridian line, traced on the floor allowed the calculation of astronomic time, but the real draw lurks in the small chapel at the far end, where there's an expressive and realistic *Entombment of Christ* in the Burgundian style pioneered by Claus Sluter.

A couple of blocks from the hospital, the **Hôtel d'Uzès** saw the birth of Tonnerre's quirkiest claim to fame, an eighteenth-century gentleman with the fittingly excessive moniker Charles-Geneviève-Louis-Auguste-André-Timothé Déon de Beaumont (b.1728). He tickled his contemporaries' prurience by going about his important diplomatic missions for King Louis XV dressed in women's clothes. His act was so convincing that while he was in London bookmakers took bets on his real sex. Interestingly he was also a fearsome swordsman, though history does not relate what he wore to fight in. When he died, the results of the autopsy were eagerly awaited by the gossip columnists of the day.

Despite all this architecture, Tonnerre's big draw is a natural feature on the hill tucked under the Église Saint Pierre. The **Fosse Dionne** is a fascinating

– and more than slightly spooky – blue-green pool encircled by an eighteenth-century *lavoir*, or washing place. A number of legends are attached to the spring (the name derives from Divona, Celtic goddess of water), one of which holds that it was the lair of a ferocious serpent slain by a local saint – a tale which may refer to the draining of the malarial marshes. The dark, alarming hole at the bottom is popularly supposed to lead to hell, and divers have penetrated 360m along a narrow underwater passageway with no end in sight. Further exploration is now banned as three divers have died in exploration attempts.

The **tourist office** is next to the old hospital at 12 rue François-Mitterrand (April–Oct Mon–Sat 9am–12.30pm & 2–6.30pm, Sun 10am–noon & 2–5pm; Nov–March closed Sun; ⓣ03.86.55.14.48, ⓦwww.tonnerre.fr). You can hire bikes here, and pick up an interesting, free, town history-trail leaflet. Directly opposite is the least expensive **accommodation** in town; the *Hôtel du Centre* (ⓣ03.86.55.10.56, ⓕ03.86.55.10.53; ❷), 65 rue de l'Hôpital, a relaxed, old-fashioned provincial hotel with a reasonable little restaurant (menus from €14). For the pinnacle of luxury, try *L'Abbaye Saint Michel* (ⓣ03.86.55.05.99, ⓦwww.abbayesaintmichel.com; ❾), at montée St-Michel, which sits impossibly gorgeous and super-chic atop the town in an orchard of green serenity. Here suites will set you back €200–400. More centrally, in fact directly overlooking the spring, the *Ferme de la Fosse Dionne*, 11 rue de la Fosse Dionne (ⓣ03.86.54.82.62, ⓦwww.fermefossedionne.com; ❹; breakfast included) is a tiny, sensitively restored former farm, with lovely rooms in bright colours and a beamed, covered balcony overlooking a small courtyard. The local **campsite**, *La Cascade* (ⓣ03.86.55.15.44; June–Oct), is between the River Armançon and the Canal de Bourgogne. For **eating**, *Ankara*, a popular local hangout on rue de l'Hôpital in the centre, has decent kebabs for €3.50, while just round the corner *Les Vieux Volets* (closed Mon & Sun eve), on the rue de l'Hôtel-de-Ville, is an excellent crêperie.

The châteaux of Ancy-le-Franc and Tanlay

Close to Tonnerre are two of the finest, though least-known and least-visited, châteaux in France: Ancy-le-Franc and Tanlay. The former has the edge for architectural purity, the latter for romantic appeal. There's no longer any public transport from Tonnerre, but if you turn up at the *gare SNCF* 24 hours in advance you can **book a taxi** for the same price per kilometre as for a train journey of equivalent length.

The **Château d'Ancy-le-Franc** (guided tours only, April to mid-Nov Tues–Sun hourly at 10.30am, 11.30am & 2–4pm; plus July & Aug 9.30am and April–Sept 5pm; €8; ⓦwww.chateau-ancy.com) is 25km from Tonnerre and was built in the mid-sixteenth century for the brother-in-law of the notorious Diane de Poitiers, mistress of Henri II. More Italian than French, with its textbook classical countenance, it is the only accepted work of the Italian Sebastiano Serlio, one of the most important architectural theorists of the Renaissance, who was brought to France in 1540 by François I to work on his palace at Fontainebleau. The exterior is rather austere and forbidding, but the inner courtyard is an utterly refined embodiment of the principles of classical architecture. Some of the apartments are sumptuous, decorated by the Italian artists Primaticcio and Niccolò dell'Abbate, who also worked at Fontainebleau. If you're visiting in August or October, its worth asking if they're staging one of their night-time openings, complete with candlelit tours, costumed guides and sixteenth-century singing.

Ancy has a small **hotel**, the modernized *Hostellerie du Centre*, 34 Grande-Rue (ⓣ03.86.75.15.11, ⓦwww.diaphora.com/hostellerieducentre; ❸; good restaurant from €15), which has a tiny indoor heated swimming pool. The brasserie at *Bar du Chateau*, 12 Place Clermont Tonnerre, serves a *plat du jour* for €10.

The **Château de Tanlay** (April to mid-Nov, guided tours daily except Tues: 10 & 11.30am, 2.15 & 5.15pm, July & Aug also 5.45pm; €8), is some 8km from Tonnerre. This 1559 construction, very French in feel and full of ambience is only slightly later in date than its near-neighbour, but those extra few years were enough for the purer Italian influences visible in Ancy to have become Frenchified. Encircling the château are water-filled moats and standing guard over the entrance to the first grassy courtyard is the grand lodge, from where you enter the château proper across a stone drawbridge. Domed and lanterned turrets terminate the wings of the *cour d'honneur* and urns line the ridge of the roof, from whose slates project carved and pedimented dormers. The round, white stone medieval towers, leftovers from the original fortress, add to the irregularity and charm. To get here cheaply by taxi you can follow the same procedure as for the Château d'Ancy-le-Franc, or cover the distance by walking or cycling alongside the Canal de Bourgogne.

For a bite to **eat**, *Le Bonheur Gourmand* (Ⓣ03.86.75.82.18; €15–23), just next to the château entrance, has ample menus.

Châtillon-sur-Seine

For those interested in pre-Roman France, there is one compelling reason for going to **CHÂTILLON-SUR-SEINE**: the so-called **Treasure of Vix**. Housed in the town's **museum** in the Maison Philandrier, 7 rue du Bourg, close to the centre (July & Aug daily 10am–6pm; Sept–June daily except Tues 9.30am–noon & 2–5pm; €4.50), it consists of the finds from the sixth-century BC tomb of a Celtic princess buried in a four-wheeled chariot at **Vix**, 6km northwest of Châtillon. In addition to pieces of the chariot, the finds include exquisite jewellery and Etruscan bowls. But the best objects on show are the starkly beautiful heavy gold torc that she was wearing and the largest bronze vase (*krater*) of Greek origin known from antiquity. It stands an incredible 1.64m high on triple tripod legs, and around its rim is a superbly modelled high-relief frieze depicting naked hoplites and horse-drawn chariots, with Gorgons' heads for handles. The village of Vix is the highest navigable point on the Seine, and it's thought the Celtic chieftains who controlled it received these foreign treasures as gifts possibly from traders in Cornish tin shipped south from Britain via here on its way to the Adriatic. It is an indication of the Princess' status that items of such value were buried with her.

Archaeology aside, Châtillon makes for a very picturesque stop. Here the Seine embarks on gloriously complex series of tangents and S-bends; many spanned by ancient, flower-decked bridges crying out to be photographed. Set against this – on the rocky bluff overlooking the steep-pitched roofs of the old quarter – are the ruins of a **castle** and the beautifully spare, early Romanesque **church of St Vorles**. At its foot in a luxuriantly verdant spot, a **spring** swells out of the rock forming an enchanting pool before tumbling off to join the infant Seine.

The **tourist office** is off place Marmont (Mon–Sat 9am–noon & 2–6pm, plus June–Sept Sun 10am–noon; Ⓣ03.80.91.13.19), and can provide an English-language town history-trail leaflet. If you decide to **stay**, try *Sylvia* (Ⓣ03.80.91.02.44, Ⓦwww.sylvia-hotel.fr; ❷–❸), north of the centre at 9 av de la Gare – here you'll find charming rooms and great breakfasts, which includes home-made cake on Sundays. In the middle of town at 2 rue Charles-Ronot there's the *Hôtel de la Côte d'Or* (Ⓣ03.80.91.13.29, Ⓕ03.80.91.29.15; ❸; closed Jan & Feb), a wonderfully atmospheric old post-house, complete with hunting trophies on the walls. It also has a very good **restaurant** (from €17). Otherwise the *Grill-Creperie O Chapo ron* (☎03.80.91.32.41), 21 rue de la Liberation, is a great little place, with a large (heated if necessary) terrace and a blazing cooking fire (*plats* €8). Or you can kick back with a pint of Belgian draught and scoff down a baguette (€3) along the banks of the river at *Pub le Splendide*, on quai de Seine by the bridge.

Fontenay Abbey

Six kilometres east of the small industrial town of Montbard, and accessible from the GR213 footpath is the privately owned **Abbey of Fontenay** (ⓦwww.abbayedefontenay.com; daily: April to mid-Nov 10am–6pm; mid-Nov to March 10am–noon & 2–5pm; €8.90). Founded in 1118, it's the only Burgundian monastery to survive intact, despite conversion to a paper mill in the early nineteenth century. It was restored in the early 1900s to its original form and is one of the world's most complete monastic complexes, comprising caretaker's lodge, guesthouse and chapel, dormitory, hospital, prison, bakery, kennels, dovecote and abbot's house, as well as a church, cloister, chapterhouse and even a forge.

On top of all this, the abbey's physical setting, at the head of a quiet stream-filled valley enclosed by woods of pine, fir, sycamore and beech, is superb. There's a bucolic calm about the place, particularly in the graceful cloister, and in these surroundings the spartan simplicity of Cistercian life seems utterly attractive. Hardly a scrap of decoration softens the church: even the carving on the capitals is reduced to the barest-bones outline of an acanthus leaf – the motherly statue of the Virgin arrived after St Bernard's death. There's no direct lighting in the nave, just an other-worldly glow from the square-ended apse. The effect is beautiful but daunting, the perfect structural embodiment of St Bernard's ascetic principles.

Alésia and around

One train stop south of Montbard (or three hours on the GR213) brings you to the dull little industrial town of **VENAREY-LES-LAUMES**. It was here, or rather behind and above the town, on the flat-topped hill of Mont Auxois, that the Gauls, united for once under the leadership of Vercingétorix, made their last stand against the military might of Rome at the **Battle of Alésia** in 52 BC. Julius Caesar himself commanded the Roman army, surrounding the hilltop town with a huge double ditch and earthworks and starving the Gauls out, bloodily defeating any and all attempts at escape. Vercingétorix surrendered to save his people, was imprisoned in Rome for six years until Caesar's formal triumph and then strangled. The battle was a fundamental turning point in the fortunes of the region. Thereafter, Gaul remained under Roman rule for four hundred years.

The **site** of Alésia (March–June, Oct & Nov 10am–6pm; daily: July–Sept 10am–7pm; €3), treeless and exposed, is back along the ridge 3km from the modern village of **ALISE-STE-REINE**, which overlooks Venarey from the top of Mont Auxois. At the site you can re-create the scenes of the battle in your mind's eye as well as visit the excavations of the town, including the theatre and a Gallo-Roman house. In town it's worth checking to see if the small archaeological **museum** has re-opened after renovations – its home to a plethora of artifacts found locally.

On the first weekend of September the martyrdom of St Reine is celebrated in a **costume procession** through the village, a custom that goes back to the year 866. St Reine was a young Christian girl who was put to death in 263 for refusing to marry the proconsul of the Gauls, Olibrius. The year of her martyrdom is held to mark the advent of Christianity in Alésia.

Directly above Alise-Ste-Reine, steps climb up to a great bronze **statue of Vercingétorix**. Erected by Napoléon III, whose influence popularized the rediscovery of France's pre-Roman roots, the statue represents Vercingétorix as a romantic Celt, half virginal Christ, half long-haired 1970s matinee idol. On the plinth is inscribed a quotation from Vercingétorix's address to the Gauls as imagined by Julius Caesar: "United and forming a single nation inspired by a single ideal, Gaul can defy the world". Napoléon signs his dedication, "Emperor of the French", inspired by a vain desire to gain legitimacy by linking his own name to that of a "legendary" Celt.

Practicalities

There's a **tourist office** in Venarey at place de Bingerbrûck (April–Sept Mon–Sat 9.30am–12.30pm & 2–7pm, Sun 10am–noon; Oct–March Mon–Sat 10am–noon & 3–6pm, Sun 10am–noon; ⓣ03.80.96.89.13, ⓦwww.alesia-tourisme.net), which can direct you to **accommodation**. The most attractive local stopover is three kilometres away up in Alise-Ste-Reine, where the *Hôtel-Restaurant Alésia* (ⓣ03.80.96.19.67; ❷) at 16 rue du Miroir is a welcoming, family-run hotel with a simple restaurant; all rooms have shared baths. A little further up the street at no. 9, *L'Auberge du Cheval Blanc* (ⓣ03.80.96.01.55; closed Mon & Tues) serves excellent regional cuisine, with wonderful menus at €17–40 (choices include snails, rabbit or *foie gras de canard*). In Venarey, *L'Orient Express*, a popular pizza-and-kebab locale by the *gare*, serves great, inexpensive food.

The Château de Bussy-Rabutin

Eight kilometres east of Alésia, on the D954, stands the handsome **Château de Bussy-Rabutin** (guided tours only, Tues–Sun: mid-May to mid-Sept 9.15am–noon & 2–6pm; mid-Sept to mid-May 9.15am–noon & 2–5pm; €6.50). It was built for Roger de Rabutin, a member of the Academy in the reign of Louis XIV and a notorious womanizer. The scurrilous tales of life at the royal court told in his book *Histoires Amoureuses des Gaules* earned him a spell in the Bastille, followed by years of exile in this château, which contains some interesting portraits of great characters of the time, including the famous female beauties of the age, each underlined by an acerbic little comment such as: "The most beautiful woman of her day, less renowned for her beauty than the uses she put it to".

The source of the Seine

You'll need your own car to get to the **source of the Seine**, which lies some 15km southeast of Alésia, or be prepared to hitch to the hamlet of **COURCEAU**. From there, by road, take the D103 through the upland hamlet of St-Germain, all crumbling stone farms and barns; or, better still, because rides are unlikely, pick up the GR2 at the bridge in Courceau for a two-hour walk.

The Seine, no more than a trickle here, rises in a tight little vale of beech woods. The spring is now covered by an artificial grotto complete with a languid nymph, Sequana, spirit of the Seine. In Celtic times it was a place of worship, as is clear from the numerous votive offerings discovered there, including a neat bronze of Sequana standing in a bird-shaped boat, now in the Dijon archaeological museum.

Semur-en-Auxois

Extraordinarily beautiful, the small fortress town of **SEMUR-EN-AUXOIS** sits on a rocky bluff – a place of cobbled lanes, medieval gateways and ancient gardens tumbling down to the River Armançon. Thirteen kilometres west of Alésia, all roads here lead to place Notre-Dame, a handsome square dominated by the large thirteenth-century **church of Notre-Dame** (another Viollet-le-Duc restoration) characterized by its huge entrance porch and the narrowness of its nave. The best view is from the east in place de l'Ancienne-Comédie, past the finely sculpted north transept door (depicting the Life of Doubting Thomas), with a couple of Burgundy snails, symbol of the region's culinary traditions, carved on the flanking columns. Inside, the windows of the second chapel on the left commemorates the dead of World War I – Semur was the general headquarters of the American 78th division, and the battlefields were not far away.

Down the street in front of the church you come to the four sturdy towers of Semur's once-powerful **castle**, all that is left after the body of the fortress was dismantled in 1602 because of its utility to enemies of the French crown. You can explore the winding streets around the castle – there's scarcely a lane in town without some building of note – and continue down to the delightful stretch of river between the Pont des Minimes and the Pont Joly, from where there's a dramatic view of town. The **museum** on rue J.-J.-Collenot (April–Sept daily except Tues 2–6pm; Oct–March Mon & Wed–Fri 2–5pm; €3.25) is a very old-fashioned affair – and retains a deal of charm because of it; featuring an almost overwhelming ammonite collection, although the pickled snakes will be an exhibit too far for some. It also has a tiny but good section on the Middle Ages. In the same complex is the town **library** (☎03.80.97.20.43), if you have time, call ahead to try and arrange to see their fantastic collection of illuminated manuscripts and early printed books.

Cheese connoisseurs might like to take a twelve-kilometre hop **further** west on the Avallon road to **ÉPOISSES**, not just for its village and château (July &

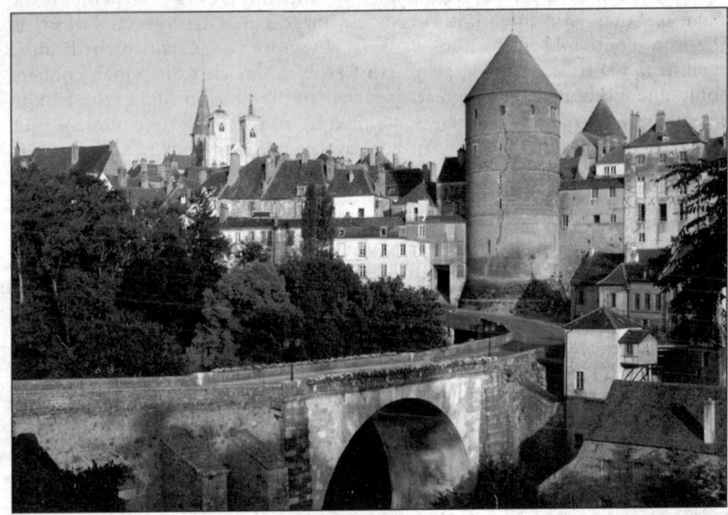

△ Semur-en-Auxois

Aug daily except Tues 10am–noon & 3–6pm; €6), but for its distinctive soft orange-skinned cheeses washed in *marc de Bourgogne*.

Practicalities

Semur's **tourist office** is on the small place Gaveau (July & Aug 9.30am–1pm & 1.45–7pm; Sept–June 9am–noon & 2–6pm; ⓣ03.80.97.05.96, ⓦwww.ville-semur-en-auxois.fr), at the junction of rues de l'Ancienne-Comédie, de la Liberté and Buffon, where the medieval Porte Sauvigny and Porte Guillier combine to form a single long, covered gateway. Cyber Kfé, next to the hotel *Le Commerce*, has **Internet** access (Mon–Sat 7.30am–1pm & 4.30–8pm; €4 per hour), although it's opening hours can be a little erratic.

The least expensive **hotel** rooms in town are at 19 rue de la Liberté at *Le Commerce* (ⓣ03.80.96.64.40, ⓔcyber21@free.fr; ❷), a basic but friendly and acceptable affair. However, the *Hôtel des Gourmets* (ⓣ03.80.97.09.41, ⓦwww.hotellesgourmets.tk; ❷), inside the medieval city proper at 4 rue de Varenne, is a better bet. Simple, but with much more homespun appeal, its been in the same family for three generations and the engaging owners take great pride in the locally sourced delights prepared for their courtyard restaurant (menus €22). A few minutes away the *Hôtel des Cymaises* (ⓣ03.80.97.21.44, ⓦwww.hotelcymaises.com; ❹; closed Nov & Feb), is tucked away off a winding back-street at 7 rue du Renaudot. It provides a degree of old-world charm, with decent rooms in a grand old mansion house. The local **campsite** is at Lac-de-Pont, 3km south of town.

Decent *plats du jour* and grills can be had at *Le Saint-Vernier* (ⓣ03.80.97.32.96) at 13 rue Févret – including a filling *menu de jour* for €10.70. For something special, it is well worth wandering down to the river and the Pont des Minimes, where the *Maison Dieu Les Minimes* (ⓣ03.80.97.26.86; menus €16–27; closed Sun eve & Mon) is a great find: excellent food, a warm atmosphere and an extremely good price – look out for their great-value recommended wines. In the heart of the old town, the patisserie-**chocolaterie** at 14 rue Buffon (closed Mon) specializes in local *semurettes*, addictive little nuggets of chocolate made without butter.

The Morvan to the Loire

The **Morvan** region lies smack in the middle of Burgundy between the valleys of the Loire and the Saône, stretching roughly from **Clamecy**, **Vézelay** and **Avallon** in the north to **Autun** and **Le Creusot** in the south. It's a land of wooded hills, close and rounded rather than mountainous, although they rise to 900m above Autun. With poor soil and pastures only good for a few cattle, villages and farms are few and far between. In the old days, wood was the main business – supplying firewood and charcoal to Paris – and large tracts of hillside are now covered in coniferous plantations. But the region's chief export has been its escaping young, helping it earn a reputation as one of the poorest and most backward regions in the country, with few resources to trade on and little inspiration for outside investment.

The creation of a **parc naturel régional** in 1970 did something to promote the area as a place for outdoor activities and refuge from commuterdom, but more than anything it was the election of François Mitterrand, local politician and mayor of **Château-Chinon** for years, as president of the Republic that rescued the Morvan from oblivion. In addition to lending it some of the glamour of his office, he took concrete steps to beef up the local economy. Plentiful local information can be found **online** at Ⓦwww.morvan.com.

West of the Morvan, the landscape softens as it descends towards the River Loire and the fine medieval town of **Nevers**, on Burgundy's western border.

Avallon

Approaching **AVALLON** along the N6 from the north, you wouldn't give the place a second look. That though, would be a mistake; the southern aspect is altogether more promising, clustered high on a ridge above the wooded valley of the River Cousin, looking out over the hilly, sparsely populated country of the Morvan regional park. Once a staging post on the Romans' *Via Agrippa* from Lyon to Boulogne, it's a small and ancient town of stone facades and sleepy cobbled streets.

The Town

Bisceting the town north to south, the narrow **Grande-Rue-Aristide-Briand** leads under the straddling arch of the fifteenth-century **Tour de l'Horloge** – the spire of which dominates the town – to the pilgrim **church of St Lazare**, on whose battered Romanesque facade you can still decipher the graceful carvings of signs of the zodiac. Almost opposite, in a fifteenth-century house, is the tourist office, with the municipal **museum** (May–Oct daily except Tues 2–6pm; free) behind it. Exhibits include a room of modern silverware, designed by local boy Jean Despres, and a second-century mosaic from a Gallo-Roman villa. There is also the **Musée du Costume** at 6 rue Belgrand (April–Nov daily 10.30am–12.30pm & 1.30–5.30pm; €4), just off Grande-Rue, with a collection of regional dress.

Continuing from St-Lazare down what's now called rue Bocquillot brings you to the lime-shaded **Promenade de la Petite Porte**, with precipitous views across the plunging valley of the Cousin. You can walk from here around the outside of the **walls**. From the **Parc des Chaumes**, on the east side of town, there's a great view back to the old quarter, snug within its walls, with garden terraces descending on the slope beneath.

Practicalities

The **tourist office** is at 6 rue Bocquillot (April, May & Oct–March Mon 2.30–6pm, Tues–Sat 10am–12.30pm & 2.30–6pm, June–Sept daily 10am–1pm & 2.30–7pm; Ⓣ03.86.34.14.19, Ⓦwww.avallonnais-tourisme.com), between the clock tower and the church and has **Internet access**. **Bikes** can be hired from Loisirs en Morvan, 40 rue de Lyon (Ⓣ03.86.31.90.10; €23 per day).

For **accommodation**, *Les Capucins* (Ⓣ03.86.34.06.52, Ⓦwww.avallonlescapucins.com; ❸), at 6 av du Paul Doumer, is a few minutes' walk from the train station and is a delightful mid-range choice with its tree-shaded terrace. About 1km from the town centre on the busy 119 rue de Lyon – not

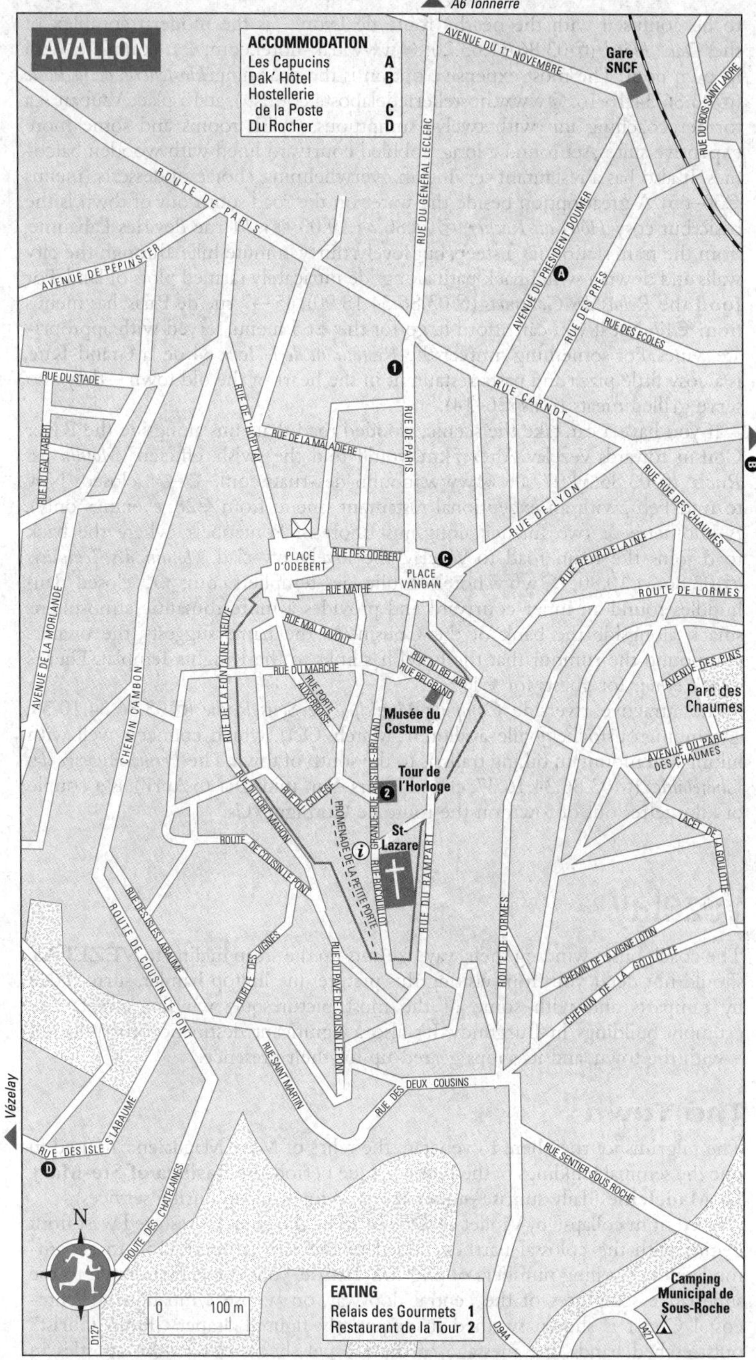

7

BURGUNDY | Avallon

to be confused with the nearby route de Lyon – is the modern complex of the *Dak' Hôtel* (ⓣ03.86.31.63.20, ⓦwww.dak-hotel.com; ④), complete with its own pool. The most expensive option is the charming *Hostellerie de la Poste* (ⓣ03.86.34.16.16, ⓦwww.hostelleriedelaposte.com; ⑧), at 13 place Vauban – a former coaching inn with twelve sumptuous, stylish rooms and some more expensive suites, set round a long, cobbled courtyard lined with wooden balconies. It also has a restaurant serving an overwhelming choice of desserts (menus €30–65). A great option beside the water on the road south out of town is the basic but cosy *Hôtel du Rocher* (ⓣ03.86.34.19.03; ①), 11 rue des Îles Labaume; from the train station it's a steep, but lovely, thirty-minute hike, through the city walls and down a switchback path alongside intricately farmed plots of land. For **food** the *Relais des Gourmets* (ⓣ03.86.34.18.90), 45–47 rue de Paris, has menus from €17, but if you can afford it, go for the €65 menu, served with appropriate wines. For something simpler the *Restaurant de la Tour*, 84 de la Grand-Rue, is a cosy little pizza and pasta restaurant in the heart of the old town – they also serve grilled meats (*plats* €6–14).

If you have a car, take the scenic, wooded road that runs alongside the River Cousin towards Vézelay. After 5km, you'll find the swish, efficient *Moulin des Ruats* (ⓣ03.86.34.97.00, ⓦwww.moulin-des-ruats.com; ⑤–⑧; closed Nov to mid-Feb), with an exceptional restaurant (menu from €28; evenings only). A kilometre or two further along, just short of Pontaubert, where the back road joins the main road to Vézelay, the lovely, ivy-clad *Moulin des Templiers* (ⓣ03.86.34.10.80, ⓦwww.hotel-moulin-des-templiers.com; ③; closed Jan) huddles round an inner courtyard and provides a more romantic atmosphere, smack alongside the bank of the Cousin. As the name suggests, the owners compound the rumour that the hotel has links to the Knights Templar. There's a *table d'hôte* for guests for €17.

The attractive, riverside *Camping Municipal de Sous-Roche* (ⓣ03.86.34.10.39; ⓔcampingsousroche@ville-avallon.fr; March–Oct), which connects well with hiking and mountain biking trails, is to the south of town. The *Ferme-Auberge des Chatelaines* (ⓣ03.86.34.16.37; closed Thurs–Sun mid-Oct to April), is a couple of kilometres out of town on the route de Corbigny/Us.

Vézelay

The coach buses winding their way like ants up the steep incline to **VÉZELAY** should not deter you from visiting this picturesque hilltop hamlet, surrounded by ramparts and with some of the most picturesque, winding streets and crumbly buildings in Burgundy. It's also a significant destination for pilgrims – with the town, and its shops geared-up for their presence.

The Town

The pilgrims journey here to venerate the relics of Mary Magdalene, housed in one the seminal buildings of the Romanesque period, the **Basilica of Ste-Mary La Madeleine** (daily sunrise–sunset, reserved for worship during services).

Saved from collapse by Viollet-le-Duc in 1840, the church's restored west front begins with the colossal narthex, added to the nave around 1150 to accommodate the swelling numbers of pilgrims. **Inside**, your eye is first drawn to the superlative sculptures of the central doorway, on whose tympanum a Pentecostal Christ is shown swathed in exquisitely figured drapery. From Christ's outstretched hands, the message of the Gospel shoots out to the apostles in the form of beams of fire, while the frieze below depicts the converted and the pagan peoples – among those featured are giants, pygmies (one mounting his horse with a ladder), a man with breasts and huge ears, and dog-headed heathens. Better preserved are the charming small-scale medallions of zodiacal signs and the labours of the months in the outermost arch.

From this great doorway you look down the long body of the church, vaulted by arches of alternating black and white stone, to a **choir** of pure early Gothic (completed in 1215), with a delicacy in sharp contrast to the more measured Romanesque nave. Its arches and arcades are edged with fretted mouldings, and the supporting pillars are crowned with 99 finely cut capitals, depicting scenes from the Bible, classical mythology, allegories and morality stories. One of the more famous is "The Mystic Mill" at the end of the fourth bay on the right, showing Moses pouring grain (Old Testament Law) through a mill (Christ), the flour (New Testament) being gathered by St Paul. St Bernard preached the Second Crusade at Vézelay in 1146. Because the church was too small, he preached in the open, down the hill to the north, where a **commemorative cross** marks the spot. Richard the Lionheart and Philippe-Auguste, king of France, also made their rendezvous here before setting off on the Third Crusade in 1190. But by the mid-thirteenth century the abbey was in decline, the final blow coming in 1279 when rumours spread that Mary Magdalene's bones were false relics. The monastery's surviving buildings were pillaged by Protestants in the sixteenth-century Wars of Religion, and much of the complex was dismantled during the Revolution. Today, a significant Franciscan community has been re-established, and pilgrims stream here to view different relics of Mary Magdalene, given to Vézelay in the 1870s, at an intensely atmospheric shrine in the crypt.

Before moving on, be sure to take a look at the beautiful Gothic **church** in the village of **ST-PÈRE**, a half-hour walk from the abbey at the southern foot of the hill. The village is also home to one of the greatest **restaurants** in the land, *L'Espérance* (Ⓣ03.86.33.39.10, Ⓦwww.marc-meneau-esperance.com; lunch menus from €90, dinner €160), and where you can also sleep amid antiques in the exquisite luxury of the adjoining **hotel** (❾).

Practicalities

Most visitors arrive by bus, car or coach party, but **cycling** is a pleasant way of covering the 20km from Avallon to Vézelay, despite the final ascent. Another option is a **taxi** (Ⓣ03.86.32.31.88; €20) from the train station at Sermizelles, 10km from Vézelay on the Auxerre–Avallon line. There's **Internet access** at Vézelay's small **tourist office** (daily 10am–1pm & 2–6pm; Nov to mid-June closed Thurs; Ⓣ03.86.33.23.69, Ⓦwww.vezelaytourisme.com) which is on the right of rue St-Pierre as you go up towards the abbey; ask for a brochure listing the numerous summer concerts and art exhibitions.

For **accommodation**, you'll need to book far in advance at weekends and in high season. In a beautiful old building above an art gallery on the main street the delightful *Au Porc Épic* (Ⓣ03.86.33.32.16, Ⓦwww.le-porc-epic.com; ❸), at 80 rue St-Pierre, is a delightful choice. Exposed stone, wood and tapestry line lovely rooms and there's also a raised courtyard-terrace for the excellent breakfast, which is included in the price. Further up the road, *La Terrasse* (Ⓣ03.86.33.25.50; ❸; closed March & Tues except July & Aug) has four reasonably priced rooms, and the location right outside the basilica is excellent.

Most of the town hotels cluster round the bustling place Champ-du-Foire, just outside the walls at the foot of town and still a very pleasant location. *Le Cheval Blanc* (Ⓣ03.86.33.22.12, Ⓕ03.86.33.34.29; ❸) offers simple, old-fashioned accommodation with shared facilities, and has a popular restaurant downstairs. If you can though, opt for their neighbour *Le Compostelle* (ⓣ03.86.33.28.63, ⓕ03.86.33.34.34; ❸–❹) which has a lovely garden, and nicer, all en-suite, rooms – you can pay more for one with a balcony overlooking the gorgeously wide sweep of the valley. There are also some pilgrims' hostels, run by religious orders and very much designed for those visiting Vézelay for spiritual reasons. One, the *Centre Ste-Madeleine* (ⓣ03.86.33.22.14; ❶), is on rue St-Pierre. The inexpensive youth hostel is about 1km along the route de l'Étang (ⓣ03.86.33.24.18; closed Jan); it also offers camping space (closed Nov–March).

Vézelay's **restaurants** can be rather touristy and overpriced. One great option is *Auberge de la Coquille* (ⓣ03.86.33.35.57), 81 rue St-Pierre. Deservedly popular with a lovely courtyard, they serve a huge range of dishes from crêpes to delicious Burgundian specialties. Their *menu de jour* (€14.50) is a good bet – but their five-course *menu gastronomique* (€26) is certainly worth the extra euros. Lower down the main street at no. 28, *Le Bougainville* (ⓣ03.86.33.27.57; closed Tues, Wed, Dec & Jan; menus €19–26), serves good regional cuisine in a genteel dining room.

Clamecy

In sharp contrast to its rustic neighbours, **CLAMECY**, 23km to the west of Vézelay on the banks of the River Yonne, has a distinctly industrial feel. It was the centre of the Morvan's logging trade from the sixteenth century to the completion of the Canal du Nivernais in 1834. Individual woodcutting gangs working in the hills floated their logs down the Yonne and its tributaries as far as Clamecy, where they were made up into great rafts for shipment on to Paris. This contact with the capital – and cradle of new egalitarian political ideas – led to the early spread of revolutionary thoughts among the workers and peasantry of the Morvan, who staged a number of violent insurrections even before 1789. The history of the logging trade is documented in the **museum** on rue de la Mirandole (daily: 10am–noon & 2–6pm, June–Sept closed Tues & Sun mornings, Oct–May closed Sun, Mon & Tues mornings; €3).

There's nothing special to see in town, apart from the many fifteenth- to eighteenth-century buildings in the centre, but it does have an interesting history and a bizarre connection with Bethlehem. In 1168 William IV, crusading Count of Nevers, died in Palestine, bequeathing one of his properties in Clamecy to the bishopric of Bethlehem, to serve as a sanctuary in the case of Palestine falling into the hands of what he perceived to be the infidel. When the Latin Kingdom of Jerusalem fell, the first bishop arrived to claim his legacy, and from 1225 until the Revolution fifty bishops of Bethlehem succeeded each other in Clamecy, honouring the little town with the title of bishopric. A curious little **chapel** by the bridge, built in 1927 in reinforced concrete, commemorates the connection.

The **tourist office** is at 24 rue du Grand-Marché (Tues–Sat 9.30am–12.30pm & 2–6/7pm, plus June–Sept Sun 10am–1pm; ⓣ03.86.27.02.51). For places to **stay**, try the lovely, old-fashioned *Hostellerie de la Poste*, on place Émile-Zola not far from the bridge (ⓣ03.86.27.01.55, ⓦwww.hostelleriedelaposte.fr; ❸; restaurant from €20). Or just across the river on the road to Auxerre at 5 place Bethléem, there's the excellent-value *Auberge de la Chapelle* (ⓣ03.86.27.11.55, ⓕ03.86.27.06.21; ❷), where you can dine in unusual surroundings – an atmospheric renovated thirteenth-century chapel. There's also a good riverside

campsite on the edge of town on the route de Chevroches (ⓣ03.86.27.05.97; May–Sept). If you're travelling south towards Nevers, the *Ferme-Auberge du Vieux Château* (ⓣ03.86.68.06.77, ⓦwww.vieuxchateau.com; ❹ with breakfast; dinner at €17) is 20km from Clamecy near the village of Oulon and just off the D977. It makes an ideal place to taste the good life, Burgundy-style, amid bucolic luxury and beautiful surroundings; meals are served exclusively with ingredients from the château's garden and farm.

Saulieu

SAULIEU suffered something of a decline with both the depopulation of the Morvan and then the construction of the A6 autoroute that took away the traffic from the old N6. These days however, it's a highly engaging old market town, with a reputation for its gastronomy. Every year the town waits hungrily for its Charollais **festival** on the third weekend of August – a super-gourmet festival featuring mountains of meat and other local produce, and there's a festival of produce from the Morvan on the Ascension Day weekend. Saulieu is also a good springboard for the cycling, hiking and riding possibilities of the Parc du Morvan (see p.586).

The old town – on the west side of the N6 – is pretty enough and perfect for an after-dinner stroll. Its main sight is the twelfth-century **Basilique St-Andoche**, noted for its lovely capitals (probably carved by a disciple of Gislebertus, the master sculptor of Autun), but little else. Next door, the **Musée François-Pompon** (Mon 10.30–noon, Wed–Sat 10am–12.30pm & 2–5.30pm, Sun 10.30am–noon & 2.30–5pm; closed Jan & Feb; €4) is surprisingly interesting, with good local folklore displays and a large collection of the works of the local nineteenth-century animal sculptor, François Pompon.

The **tourist office** (mid-June to mid-Sept Mon–Sat 9am–12.30pm & 2–7pm, Sun 9am–12.30pm & 2–5pm; mid-Sept to mid-June Tues–Sat 9am–noon & 2–5/6pm; ⓣ03.80.64.00.21, ⓦwww.saulieu.fr) is on the N6 near the hospital. The **gare SNCF** is straight up avenue de la Gare opposite the marketplace/car park.

You may want to **stay** the night if you've been tempted by the menus and wine lists at some of the restaurants (Saulieu makes for an excellent stopping point, halfway between Paris and Lyon). A good nine or ten hotel-restaurants are ranged along the N6, which zooms past the old town walls; luckily, most have very quiet rooms facing peaceful gardens at the back. Amongst the best is *La Borne Imperiale*, 14–16 rue d'Argentine (ⓣ03.80.64.19.76, ⓦwww.borne-imperiale.com; ❷; restaurant from €18, closed Wed evening & Thurs). Run by a charming couple, it has a fantastic atmosphere, a great restaurant with an attractive terrace and rooms with garden views. A few minutes walk away on rue Courtépée, *Le Bourgogne* (ⓣ03.80.64.08.41, ⓔhotelbourgog@orange.fr; ❸; restaurant from €15, closed Sun) has a warm, old-fashioned feel and some rooms overlooking a vine-covered courtyard. Should your trust fund mature while in Saulieu, head for 2 rue d'Argentine and *Le Relais Bernard Loiseau* (ⓣ03.80.90.53.53, ⓦwww.bernard-loiseau.com; ❽), which also bears the sign of its former name: *La Côte d'Or*). This hotel-restaurant-spa was created by the famed chef Bernard Loiseau (and made even more famous after his suicide in 2003 following a long bout with depression). It is an enchanting, elegant, beyond-luxurious place of rich woods, stone arches and plush furnishings which exudes wealth. Unfortunately it'll also drain yours; menus *start* at €145, rooms at €150 and suites go up to €470. Alternatively, there are also a couple of *gîtes d'étape* (Easter–Nov) and a **campsite** (ⓣ03.80.64.16.19, ⓔcamping .saulieu@orange.fr; April–Sept), 1km out along the Paris road.

The Parc du Morvan

Carpeted with forest and etched by cascading streams, the **Parc Régional du Morvan** was only officially designated in 1970, when 170,000 hectares of hilly countryside were set aside in an attempt to protect the local cultural and physical environment with a series of nature trails, animal reserves, museums and local craft shops. The Maison du Parc, its official **information centre** (April to early Nov Mon–Sat 9.30am–12.30pm & 2–5pm, Sun 10am–1pm & 3–5.30pm; early Nov to March Mon–Fri 9.30am–12.30pm; ⓣ03.86.78.79.57, ⓦwww .parcdumorvan.org), is located 13km from Saulieu in beautiful grounds about a kilometre outside **ST-BRISSON** on the D6. There's no public transport to get you there, but if you're walking or cycling it's a good place to head for, as they have all available information on routes and facilities in the park. There's also a small **museum** (April to mid-Nov daily 10am–1pm & 2–6pm; €4; ⓣ03.86.78.72.99), devoted to the region's World War II **Resistance** movement, which was particularly active in this hard-to-patrol forested backwater. The museum closes on odd Tuesdays, so if you're making a special detour, call to check it'll be open.

A map, *Saulieu Vélo Tout-Terrain en Morvan*, marks cycling and walking routes. For **walkers** the most challenging trip is the three-to four-day hike along the **GR13** footpath, crossing the park from Vézelay to Mont Beuvray and taking in the major lakes, which are among the park's most developed attractions. There are also hosts of less strenuous possibilities (ask at any of the local tourist offices for suggestions) including the four-kilometre walk from Saulieu to Lac Chamboux. **Riding** is a fairly popular way of seeing the park, and numerous *gîtes d'étape* offer pony-trekking facilities – again tourist offices can advise.

Every other village in the park seems to have its own **campsite** (most of which are open from April or May to Sept), and the larger ones often have a couple of simple **hotels** as well. There are several campsites and small, beach-resortish hotels round the large, wooded **Lac des Settons**, which basks at the heart of the park and makes for a good break from more strenuous activities with its watersports, café-restaurants and small beach areas. The plain, modern village of **MONTSAUCHE**, 4km to the northwest of the lake, is a good bet for provisions, including camping gas, and has a municipal campsite; **MOUX**, a similar distance to the southeast, can provide the same facilities, and also has a couple of decent hotels. **Bikes** are available from most campsites in the area: for a complete list ask at any tourist office, or check online for VTT (mountain bikes) at ⓦwww.morvan.com.

Château-Chinon

The most substantial community in the park – approximately 2500 residents – and accessible by bus from Autun, is the rather ugly village of **CHÂTEAU-CHINON**. It nestles though in contrastingly beautiful countryside dotted with evergreens, lakes and limestone deposits. President Mitterrand was mayor here from 1959 to 1981, and the town was the home base of his political life for half a century. Thanks largely to him, it now boasts a major hosiery factory and military printing works, both of which have provided much needed employment to an isolated and often forgotten region.

Atop the town in the **Musée du Septennat** (July & Aug daily 10am–1pm & 2–7pm; Sept–June Wed–Mon 10am–noon & 2–6pm; €4), you can see the extraordinary variety of gifts Mitterrand received as head of state: carpets from the Middle East, ivory from Togo, Japanese puppets, beaded spears from Burundi and the bizarre table decorated with butterfly wings. Another of the town's attractions is the **Musée du Costume**, 4 rue du Château (April–June & Sept Wed–Mon 10am–1pm & 2–6pm; July & Aug 10am–1pm & 2–7pm; €4), featuring a collection of over five thousand articles, the biggest in France.

Mitterrand's preferred **hotel** was the *Au Vieux Morvan* (ⓣ03.86.85.05.01, ⓦwww.auvieuxmorvan.com; ❸; closed mid-Dec to Jan), just past the main drag at 8 place Gudin, with a nice restaurant (from €18). Cheaper is the cosy and comfortable *Lion d'Or* (ⓣ03.86.85.13.56, ⓕ03.86.79.42.22; ❶; restaurant from €12, closed Sun evening & Mon) at 10 rue des Fossés; be sure to ask for one of the rooms with views to the hillside surrounding Château-Chinon. There's also a **campsite** here, *Le Perthuy d'Oiseau* (ⓣ03.86.85.08.17; May–Sept).

Autun

With its Gothic spire rising against a backdrop of Morvan hills, **AUTUN**, even today, is scarcely bigger than the circumference of its medieval **walls**, which in turn follow the line of earlier Roman fortifications. The emperor Augustus founded the town in about 10 BC as part of a massive and, in the long term, highly successful campaign to pacify and Romanize the brooding Celts of defeated Vercingétorix. Augustodunum, as it was called, was designed to eclipse by its splendour the memory of **Bibracte** (see p.590), the neighbouring capital of the powerful tribe of the Aedui. And it did indeed become one of the leading cities of Roman Gaul.

The Town

This city's Roman past is still present – and very tangible. Two of its four Roman gates survive: **Porte St-André**, spanning rue de la Croix-Blanche in the northeast, and **Porte d'Arroux** in Faubourg d'Arroux in the northwest. In a field just across the River Arroux stands a lofty section of wall known as the **Temple of Janus**, which was probably part of the sanctuary of a Gallic deity, while on the east side of the town, on avenue du 2ème-Dragon just off the Dijon road, you can see the remains of what was the largest **Roman theatre** in Gaul, with a capacity of fifteen thousand – in itself a measure of Autun's importance at that time. It's not a totally evocative site – the remaining seats now overlook a football pitch – but in July and August its authenticity is enhanced by the performances of a play in which six hundred locals, dressed in period costume, reconstruct the Gallo-Roman past of the town. An artificial lake below the football pitch, the **Plan d'eau du Vallon**, provides the usual watersports.

The most enigmatic of the Gallo-Roman remains in the region is the **Pierre de Couhard**, off Faubourg St-Pancrace to the southeast of the town. It's a 27-metre-tall stone pyramid situated on the site of one of the city's necropolises, thought to date from the first century, and most probably either a tomb or a cenotaph.

The Cathédrale St-Lazare and around

Autun's great twelfth-century **Cathédrale St-Lazare** was built nearly a thousand years after the Romans had gone and stands in the highest and best-fortified

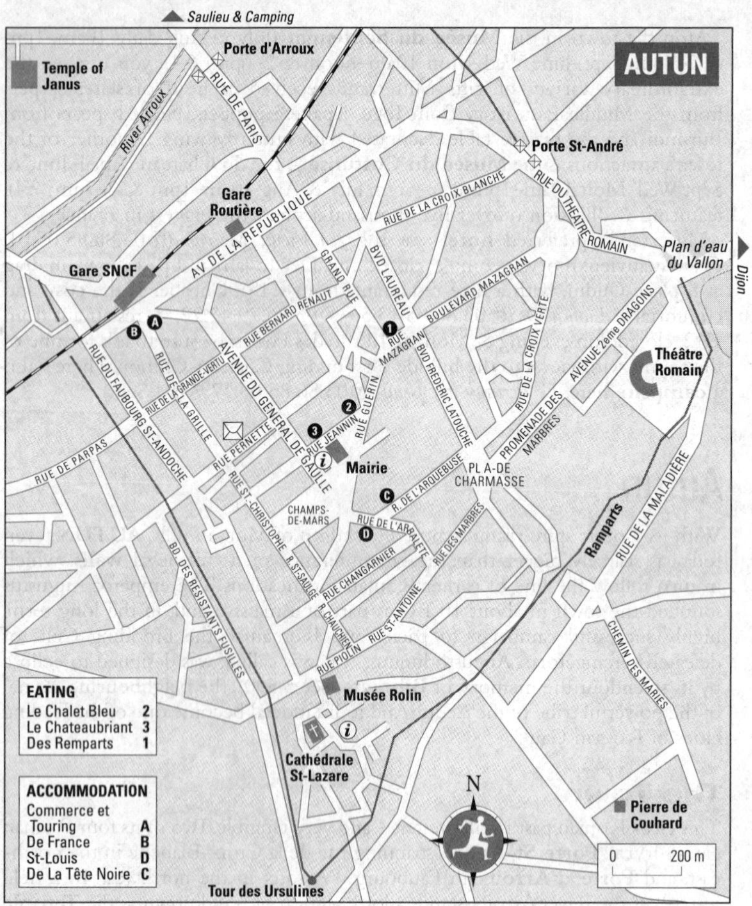

corner of the town. Its greatest claim to artistic fame lies in its sculptures, the work of Gislebertus, generally accepted as one of the greatest Romanesque sculptors.

The tympanum of the **Last Judgement** above the west door bears his signature – *Gislebertus hoc fecit* ("Gislebertus made this") – beneath the feet of Christ. To his left are depicted the Virgin Mary, the saints and the apostles, with the saved rejoicing below them; to the right the Archangel Michael disputes souls with Satan, who tries to cheat by leaning on the scales, while the damned despair beneath. During the eighteenth century the local clergy decided the tympanum was an inferior work and plastered it over, saving it from almost certain destruction during the Revolution. The head of Christ, however, had been hacked off, and was only rediscovered – hiding anonymously in the collection of the Musée Rolin – in 1948.

The interior of the cathedral, whose pilasters and arcading were modelled on the Roman architecture of the city's gates, was also decorated by Gislebertus, who carved most of the capitals himself. Conveniently for anyone wanting a close look, some of the finest are now exhibited in the old chapter library, up the stairs on the right of the choir, among them a beautiful *Flight into Egypt* and *Adoration of the Magi*.

Just outside the cathedral on rue des Bancs, the **Musée Rolin** (April–Sept Wed–Mon 9.30am–noon & 1.30–6pm, Oct–March Wed–Mon 10am–noon & 2.30–5pm; €3) occupies a Renaissance *hôtel* built by Nicolas Rolin, chancellor of Philippe le Bon. In addition to interesting Gallo-Roman pieces, the star attractions are Gislebertus's representation of Eve as an unashamedly sensual nude, and the Maître de Moulins' brilliantly coloured *Nativity*.

Practicalities

Whether you arrive at the **gare SNCF** or **gare routière** down the road, you'll find yourself on avenue de la République, which in turn leads to the wide square of the Champs-de-Mars and into the old town. The main **tourist office** is at 2 av de Charles-de-Gaulle (June to mid-Oct 9am–7pm; mid-Oct to May 9am–noon & 2–7pm; ⓣ03.85.86.80.38, ⓦwww.autun-tourisme.com), with an information point opposite the cathedral, at place du Terreau (June to mid-Oct 9am–7pm; ⓣ03.85.52.56.03). **Bikes** can be rented at the campsite, below, and at the Plan d'eau du Vallon (ⓣ03.85.86.95.80).

There's a good choice of **accommodation** in Autun. The inexpensive options are all on the main road opposite the station: the *Hôtel de France* (ⓣ03.85.52.14.00, ⓕ03.85.86.14.52; ❶–❸), 18 av de la République, is solid and traditional, and the *Commerce et Touring* (ⓣ03.85.52.17.90, ⓕ03.85.52.37.63; ❷; closed Jan; reasonable restaurant from €11), 20 av de la République, is also perfectly decent. For something a bit more quiet and classy, try one of the old coaching inns just off the Champs-de-Mars. Napoleon twice slept at the now slightly faded but once magnificent *St-Louis* (ⓣ03.85.52.01.01, ⓦwww.hotelsaintlouis.net; ❹), 6 rue de l'Arbalète. He obviously knew how to travel in style – he had his own suite installed (now a mini-museum) before he arrived; these days a suite will cost you up to €300. The comfortable but bland *Hôtel de La Tête Noire* is opposite at 3 rue de l'Arquebuse (ⓣ03.85.86.59.99, ⓦwww.hoteltetenoire.fr; ❹; restaurant from €22). There's also a **campsite** just across the river on the road to Saulieu, *Camping Pont d'Arroux* (ⓣ03.85.52.10.82, ⓦwww.camping-autun.com; closed Oct–Easter).

As well as the hotel **restaurants**, there are a couple of brasseries on the Champs-de-Mars, but the best options are in the street behind the Hôtel de Ville: *Le Chalet Bleu*, 3 rue Jeannin (ⓣ03.85.86.27.30; menus €16–48; closed Mon evening, Tues & most of Feb) is innovative and distinctly stylish, while *Le Chateaubriant*, 14 rue Jeannin (ⓣ03.85.52.21.58; menu from €14; closed Sun evening, Mon & most of July) offers a more traditional menu. Slightly north of the centre, at 17 rue Mazagran, is the *Restaurant des Remparts* (ⓣ03.85.52.54.02; menu €15.50–36; closed Mon): the kind of place where everyone seems to know everyone else – there's much kissing of cheeks, and the food is good too.

Mont-Beuvray and Bibracte

The base for the climb up Mont-Beuvray to the 2000-year-old site of the Gallic capital of Bibracte is **ST-LÉGER-SOUS-BEUVRAY**, about 26km southwest of Autun and reached along the N81 and D61 through typical Morvan countryside of wooded hills and scattered farms, coarse marshy pastures and brown streams. There's a morning and an afternoon bus from Autun to St-Léger. If you want to stay the *Hôtel-Restaurant du Morvan* (ⓣ03.85.82.51.06, ⓦwww.hoteldumorvan71.com; ❷), at place de la Marie, has old-fashioned but decent rooms, and serves local food menus at €16–22.

From St-Léger, it's the best part of a two-hour walk, or 8km by road, to the ancient site of **BIBRACTE** on top of the hill, at an altitude of 800m. If you want to recapture a pre-Roman mood, it's worth doing it on foot along the path winding up through woods of conifer and beech. The settlement of Bibracte, the lines of which you can still follow through the trees, was inhabited from 5000 BC. In 52 BC it was the scene of an assembly of all the Gallic tribes, which resulted in the election of Vercingétorix as their commander-in-chief, in one last desperate attempt to fight off Roman imperialism. Although it is two millennia since Bibracte was abandoned – probably on Roman orders – memories of its significance were preserved in the folk tales of the Morvan and a fair was held on the summit every May until the beginning of World War I. Close to the fortified earthwork that surrounds the site, great ceremonial stones like the **Pierre de la Wivre** are still standing. The Bibracte **Musée de la Civilisation Celtique** (mid-March to mid-Nov 10am–6pm, until 7pm in July & Aug; €5.75 museum entry, €9.50 with guided tour of the archeological site; ⓣ03.85.86.52.35 for bookings) is a fascinating state-of-the-art museum displaying the many Celtic coins, jugs, platters and pieces of statues unearthed from the neighbouring site – and a café, intriguingly, serving "Gaulish cuisine".

Le Creusot

LE CREUSOT (not to be confused with Le Creuset, the northern French town of cast-iron cookware fame) means one thing to French ears: the **Schneider iron and steelworks**, maker of the first French locomotive in 1838, the first steamship in 1839, the 75mm field gun – mainstay of World War I artillery – and the ironwork of the Pont Alexandre-III and the Gare d'Austerlitz in Paris. The last Schneider died in 1960, whereupon the company was broken up, and a number of different firms now carry on the tradition: Creusot-Loire manufactures specialized steels for the French military and nuclear industry, while Alstom manufactures parts of the TGV.

The town's main attraction is the **Écomusée le Creusot-Montceau** in the Château de la Verrerie on place Schneider (June to mid-Sept Mon–Fri 10am–noon & 1–6pm, Sat & Sun 2.30–7pm; mid-Sept to May Mon–Fri 11am–12.30pm & 3–6pm, Sat & Sun 2.30–6pm; €6). Built as a glassworks in 1786–87 – Louis XVI was a shareholder before losing his head – the château was sold to the Schneider family in 1838 and transformed into their private home and the administrative centre of their business empire. The Schneiders were paternalistic but despotic employers, providing housing, schools and health care for their workers, but expecting "gratitude and obedience" in return.

Today, the château houses a museum dedicated to the iron and steel industry, with paintings of various Schneiders, mock-ups of workers' quarters, and giant model trains. The peculiar cone-shaped constructions in the courtyard of the château were glass furnaces; one of them was transformed into a tiny Neoclassical theatre where plays were put on to entertain the Schneiders' wealthy and influential guests, and can be visited on regular tours.

A more recent development in town is the huge **Parc Touristique des Combes**, which boasts a narrow-gauge steam train (April–Oct 11am–7pm; Nov–March 2–7pm; €6), a karting track, a 435-metre-long dry luge piste (April–Oct; €2.50) and an unusual panorama. From the top of the Combe des Mineurs the view takes in the modern steelworks, the gleaming white Château de la Verrerie and the terraces of old workers' houses, all set against the northeastern bulwark of the Massif Central.

Practicalities

The **tourist office**, in the gatehouse of the Château de la Verrerie (Mon–Fri 10am–12.30pm & 1.30–6pm, Sat & Sun 2–6.30pm; ⓣ03.85.55.02.46, ⓦwww.creusot.net), can provide information about a mining museum in nearby Blanzy, and can direct you to tours of the modern ironworks. Frequent buses connect Le Creusot town with its **TGV station** 6km away in Montchanin, in turn connecting with Paris. If you need to **stay** overnight, head for *La Belle Époque* (ⓣ03.85.73.00.00, ⓕ03.85.73.00.10; ❸), 9 place Schneider, featuring a decent restaurant and rooms decked out in peach, orange and blue pastel. Or if on a budget, try *Le Bodsonn* (ⓣ03.85.55.03.34, ⓕ03.85.55.63.96; ❶), 26 rue de l'Yser, above a café-bar a bit out of the centre but with comfy rooms. On the more expensive side the curiously characterless *Le Petite Verrerie*, 4 rue Jules Guesde (ⓣ03.85.73.97.97, ⓦwww.hotelfp-lecreusot.com; ❺), has modern decor, a stylish restaurant and courtyard dining (menus €23).

Nevers

Some sixty kilometres west of the Parc du Morvan, at the western confines of Burgundy, **NEVERS** is a small provincial city on the confluence of the rivers Loire and Nièvre. In France it's known for its *nougatine* sweets and fine porcelain, hand-painted with a deep blue colour known as *bleue de Nevers*. **Faïence**, as it's called, has been a hallmark of Nevers since the seventeenth century and is now something of a growth industry, with six small artisans' workshops in town, all of which sell their wares in elegant, expensive shops called *faïenceries*. Parts of the **old town** date back to the twelfth century and make for a relaxed stroll away from the busier centre. Best viewed from the bridge over the Loire, the town is not necessarily a destination in itself, but with its open-air summer concert programme and some lively bars and restaurants it makes a pleasant stopover.

The Town

Nevers centres on **place Carnot**, close to the fifteenth-century **Palais Ducal**, former home of the dukes of Nevers, with octagonal turrets and an elegant central tower. Nearby, opposite the Hôtel de Ville, the stunning **Cathédrale de St-Cyr**, with its wonderful display of jutting gargoyles, reveals a sort of wall display of French architectural styles from the tenth to the sixteenth centuries; it even manages to have two opposite apses, one Gothic, the other Romanesque. Even more interesting and aesthetically satisfying is the late eleventh-century **church of St-Étienne**, on the east side of the town centre. Behind its plain exterior lies one of the prototype pilgrim churches, with galleries above the aisles, ambulatory and three radiating chapels around the apse.

On the north side of **Parc Roger-Salengro** is the **convent of St-Gildard**, where Bernadette of Lourdes ended her days. A steady flow of pilgrims come to visit her tiny, embalmed body, displayed in a glass-fronted **shrine** (daily 7am–noon & 1.30–7pm) in the convent chapel. Next door a small but very engaging, free museum displays some of her belongings and correspondence.

By place Mossé and the bridge over the Loire, there's a section of the old town walls and the eleventh-century **Tour Goguin**. The **Porte de Croux** is nearby; a cream stone tower with intact machicolations and a steep tiled roof. The **archeology museum** inside is due to reopen in 2007 but until then, some of the main pieces can be viewed in the basement of the Palais Ducal. Nearby, rue du 14-Juillet has a number of *faïencerie* shops where you can see the pieces being painted by hand.

To the north of the ducal palace on the way out of town towards Orléans, **Porte de Paris**, a triumphal arch, straddles rue des Ardilliers. It commemorates one of Europe's major conflicts, the battle of Fontenoy, fought out between Charlemagne's sons in 841 AD. The stakes were Charlemagne's empire, and the outcome the division of his lands east and west of the Rhine, which formed the basis of modern France and Germany.

Practicalities

The **gare SNCF** and **gare routière** are on rue du Chemin-de-Fer. The **tourist office**, in the foyer of the Palais Ducal (Mon–Sat 9am–6.30pm, Sun 10am–6pm; Nov & Feb closed Sun; Ⓣ03.86.68.46.00, Ⓦwww.nevers-tourisme.com), provides maps and information on the summer music festival, and can help arrange trips on the Loire. **Bike** and **canoe** rental is available from Eaux Mélées Randonnées (Ⓣ03.86.57.69.76). **Internet** access can be found at the Forum shopping centre on rue Nievre.

There aren't many **hotels** in the old centre, but the *Hôtel de Cleves*, 8 rue St Didier (Ⓣ03.86.61.15.87, Ⓕ03.86.57.13.80; ❸) is comfortable and well located just off place Carnot. Here the welcome is slightly eccentric but very warm; the owners have both perfected a vigorous handshake, and delight in speaking English. The likeable *Beauséjour*, 5 rue St-Gildard (Ⓣ03.86.61.20.84, Ⓦwww.hotel-beausejour-nevers.com; ❷), is almost opposite the church of Ste-Bernadette and has small rooms and a tiny outdoor garden for breakfast. The one star *Hôtel Thermidor* (Ⓣ03.86.57.15.47, Ⓔhotel.thermidor@9business.fr; ❶), is within a few minutes of the train station: turn left then almost immediately right down the narrow side street rue Claude-Tillier (number 14). The municipal **campsite** (Ⓣ06.84.98.69.79, Ⓦwww.campingnevers.com; mid-March to mid-Oct) is just across the Pont de Loire, beside the river at rue de la Jonction.

Avenue de-Gaulle has a few inexpensive **restaurants** and **cafés**, such as *La Mange'oir*, 24 av de-Gaulle (Ⓣ03.86.57.28.61; lunch menu €11.50, dinner €22; closed Sat & Sun lunch, & all day Mon), and some more upmarket places too, such as *Gambrinus*, 37 av de-Gaulle (Ⓣ03.86.57.19.48; closed Mon & Sat lunch, & all day Sun; menu from €21), and the excellent *Aux Chœurs de Bacchus*, 25 av de-Gaulle (Ⓣ03.86.36.72.70; closed Mon & Sat lunch, & all day Sun), which has a good menu at €15.10 and a wine-tasting version at €22.30. *Le Goemon*, 9 rue du 14-Juillet (closed Sun & Mon eve), is a wonderful, atmospheric crêperie with high-quality salads, and live jazz on Saturday nights. *Donald's Pub*, on rue François Mitterand near the river, is a good place for a drink.

Dijon and southern Burgundy

If the much-touted image of "rural Burgundy" has conjured up an image of slightly ramshackle rustic charm in your mind, you'll have to do some adjusting when you encounter the slick prosperity of **Dijon** and the wine-producing country to the south, known as the **Côte d'Or**. It may look peacefully pastoral, but there's nothing medieval about the methods or the profits made in today's wine business. For any trace of the older traditions you have to head into the southwestern corner of the region, into the wine-producing regions of the **Mâconnais** and **Beaujolais**, and the cattle country of the **Charollais**.

Dijon

DIJON owes its origins to its strategic position in Celtic times on the tin merchants' route from Britain up the Seine and across the Alps to the Adriatic. It became the capital of the dukes of Burgundy around 1000 AD, but its golden age occurred in the fourteenth and fifteenth centuries under the auspices of dukes Philippe le Hardi (the Bold), who as a boy had fought the English at Poitiers and been taken prisoner, Jean sans Peur (the Fearless), Philippe le Bon (the Good), who sold Joan of Arc to the English, and Charles le Téméraire (also the Bold). They used their tremendous wealth and power – especially their control of Flanders, the dominant manufacturing region of the age – to make Dijon one of the greatest centres of art, learning and science in Europe. It lost its capital status on incorporation into the kingdom of France in 1477, but has remained one of the country's pre-eminent provincial cities, especially since the rail and industrial booms of the mid-nineteenth century. Today, it's smart, modern and young, especially when the students are around.

Arrival, information and accommodation

Dijon is not an enormous city and the part you'll want to see is neatly confined to the eminently walkable centre. Whether you arrive by road or rail from either Paris and the north or Lyon and the south, you find yourself almost inevitably at the **gare SNCF** – the **gare routière** is next door.

From the stations a five-minute walk down avenue Maréchal-Foch takes you to place Darcy, and the **tourist office** (daily: May to mid-Oct 9am–7pm; mid-Oct to April 10am–6pm; ⓣ08.92.70.05.58, ⓦwww.dijon-tourism.com). There's also a smaller office at 34 rue des Forges (Mon–Sat 9am–noon & 2–6pm). Both offer services such as hotel booking, money changing and guided tours of the city. They also sell the "Dijon card" which allows access to all the museums listed below, and includes free guided tours and public transport; you can buy it in 24-hour (€10), 48-hour (€15) or 72-hour (€20) versions.

Dijon has no shortage of reasonably priced **hotels** in the centre of town, but it's worth booking at least a week in advance if you plan to stay in the busy months of May, June, September and October. The city's **hostel** is inconveniently located on the northeast side of the city.

Hotels

Le Chambellan 92 rue Vannerie ⓣ03.80.67.12.67, ⓔhotelchambellan@aol.com. Charming, old-fashioned hotel with friendly owners just east of the ducal palace. ❷

Hostellerie du Sauvage 64 rue Monge ⓣ03.80.41.31.21, ⓔhoteldusauvage@free.fr. Delightful and atmospheric, this former coaching inn has some rooms overlooking a vine-draped courtyard. There's also fine al fresco dining in its open-grill restaurant. Quiet, despite being in the liveliest quarter of town. Paid garage access. ❸

Le Jacquemart 32 rue Verrerie ⓣ03.80.60.09.60, ⓦwww.hotel-lejacquemart.fr. Elegant, high-ceilinged rooms, full of comfortable antique-style furniture. Close to the dukes' palace and cathedral, it offers rooms with or without bathrooms. ❷–❹

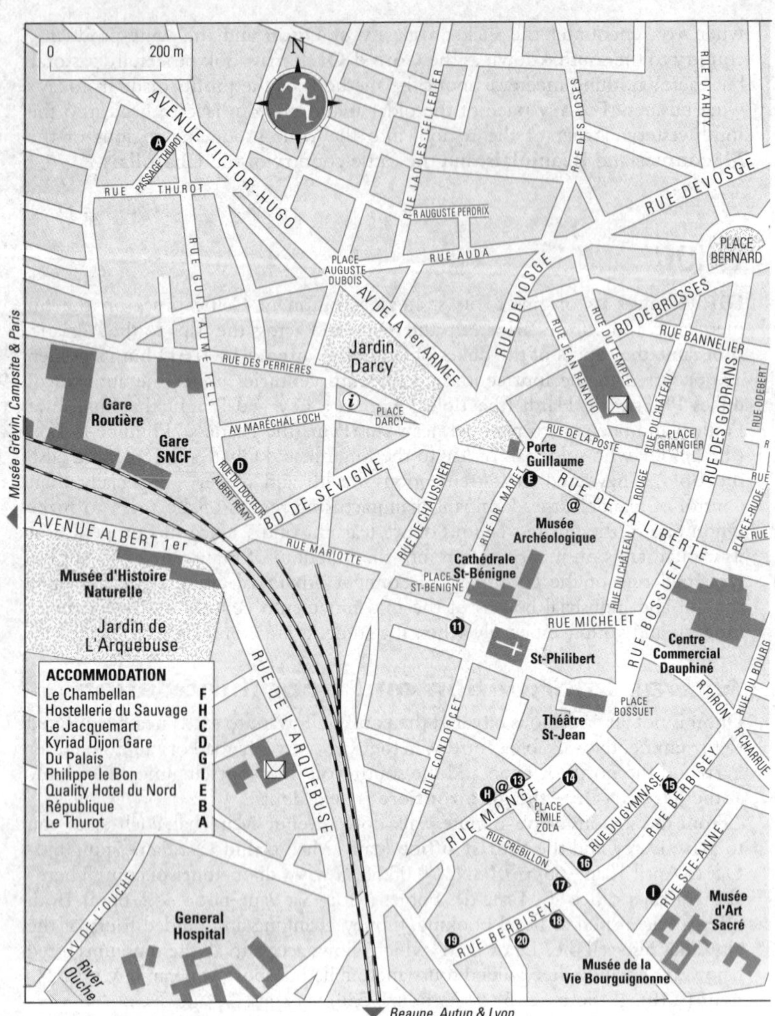

Kyriad Dijon Gare 7 rue Albert Remy ⓣ03.80.53.10.10, ⓦwww.kyriaddijon.com. Swish, stylish and carefully modernized by the huge Kyriad group but the bedrooms still feel like a chain hotel. Gorgeous indoor pool and sauna, wi-fi, garage and all the mod cons. Handy but unappealing location across the street from the train station, they have a sister hotel round the corner. ❹

Quality Hotel du Nord place Darcy ⓣ03.80.50.80.50, ⓦwww.hotel-nord.fr. Housed in a lovely old building, this is one of Dijon's more upscale places, but has modern, slightly anonymous bedrooms. Central with a decent restaurant downstairs. ❻

Du Palais 23 rue du Palais ⓣ03.80.67.16.26, ⓔhoteldupalais-dijon@orange.fr. Comfortable, high-ceilinged rooms have been carved out of this pleasant eighteenth-century townhouse, which stands on a quiet corner just south of the ducal palace. Friendly, polyglot owner. ❸

Philippe le Bon 18 rue Sainte Anne ⓣ03.80.30.73.52, ⓦwww.hotelphilippelebon.com. A grand, elegant old building set in an agreeable garden next to the Musée da la vie Bourguignonne and just outside of the city's hustle and bustle. The most expensive rooms are stunning; full of character and beautifully

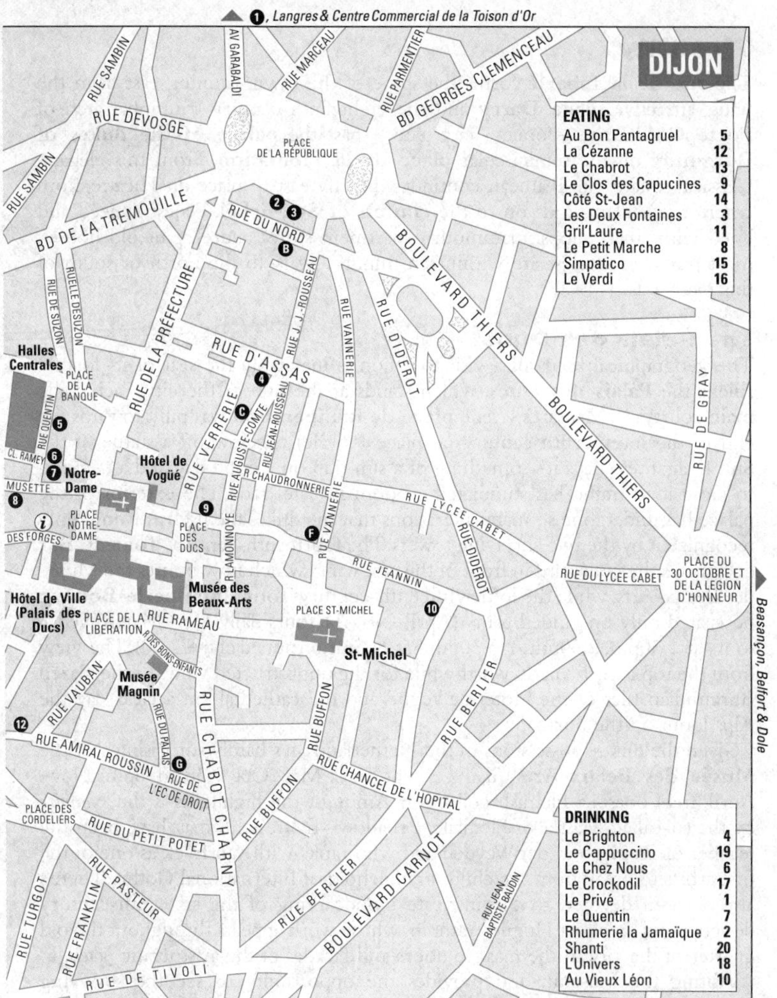

restored, the others are plush but a little bland in comparison. 8–9

République 3 rue du Nord ⓣ03.80.73.36.76, ⓕ03.80.72.46.04. A pleasant hotel near place de la République with a skylit foyer, friendly staff and clean rooms. On a quiet side street. 4

Le Thurot 4–6 passage Thurot ⓣ03.80.43.57.46, ⓦwww.hotel-thurot.com. Calm, simple and modern hotel ten minutes' walk from the train station. Convenient car park. 3

Hostel and campsite

Camping du Lac Kir 3 bd Chanoine Kir, ⓣ03.80.43.54.72, ⓦwww.camping-dijon.com. Appealing and popular site with a wealth of activities. Its about 1km out of town near Lake Kir: follow the signs for Paris, or take bus #3 from the train station, direction "Fontaine d'Ouche".

Centre de Rencontres Internationales 1 bd Champollion ⓣ03.80.72.95.20, ⓦwww.cri-dijon.com. An HI hostel in a modern complex 2km from the centre, with well-kept dorm rooms, a self-service canteen and sports facilities next door. Often teeming with adolescent school groups. Take bus #4, direction "Épirey", from rue des Godrans. The last bus back is at 9pm.

The City

The **rue de la Liberté** forms the spine of the town, running east from the wide, attractive **place Darcy** and the eighteenth-century triumphal arch of **Porte Guillaume** – once a city gate – past the **palace of the dukes of Burgundy** on the semicircular **place de la Libération**. From this elegant, Classical square, rue Rameau continues directly east to place du Théâtre, from where rue Vaillant leads on to the **church of St Michel**. Pedestrianized and lined with smart shops, mammoth department stores and elegant old houses, most places of interest are within ten minutes' walk to the north or south of this main axis.

The Palais des Ducs

The geographical focus of a visit to Dijon is inevitably the seat of its former rulers, the **Palais des Ducs**, which stands at the hub of the city. Facing the main courtyard, Mansart's serene **place de la Libération** was built towards the end of the seventeenth century (as place Royale) to show off a statue of the Sun King; these days it's something of a sun trap on a good day, and a decision to close it to traffic has stimulated a boom in café trade. The exterior of the palace has undergone so many alterations that the dukes themselves would only recognize it by the two surviving towers. The fourteenth-century **Tour de Bar** dominates the courtyard in front of the east wing, which now houses the Musée des Beaux-Arts, while the loftier, fifteenth-century **Tour Philippe-le-Bon** can be visited only on guided tours (April–Nov 11 tours daily, Dec–March Wed 3 tours at 1.30pm, 2.30pm & 3.30pm Sat & Sun 6 tours daily; €2.30). The view from the top is particularly worthwhile for the unobstructed views of the glazed Burgundian tiles of the Hôtel de Vogüé and the cathedral; on a clear day the Alps loom on the horizon.

Given the dukes' possessions in the Netherlands, it's hardly surprising that the **Musée des Beaux-Arts** (daily except Tues: May–Oct 9.30am–6pm; Nov–April, free) boasts a Flemish collection. Amongst the highlights is the *Nativity* by the so-called Master of Flémalle, a shadowy figure who may have been the teacher of Rogier van der Weyden and who ranks with van Eyck as one of the first artists to break from the chilly stranglehold of International Gothic. There's also a room devoted to the intricate woodcarving of the sixteenth-century designer and architect Hugues Sambin, whose work appears throughout the old quarter of the city in the massive doors and facades of the aristocratic *hôtels*.

Visiting the museum also provides the opportunity to see the surviving portions of the original ducal palace, including the vast **kitchen** and the magnificent **Salle des Gardes**, richly appointed with panelling, tapestries and a minstrels' gallery. Here are displayed the lavish, almost decadent **tombs** from the Chartreuse de Champmol of Philippe le Hardi and Jean sans Peur and his wife, Marguerite de Bavière, with their startling, painted effigies of the dead, surrounded by gold-plated angels.

The Quartier Notre-Dame

Architecturally more interesting than the palace, and much more suggestive of the city's former glories, are the lavish townhouses of its rich burghers. These abound in the streets behind the palace: rue Verrerie, rue Vannerie, rue des Forges, rue Chaudronnière (look out for no. 28, **Maison des Cariatides**). Some are half-timbered, with storeys projecting over the street, others are in more formal and imposing Renaissance stone. Particularly fine are the Renaissance **Hôtel de Vogüe**, 12 rue de la Chouette, and at no. 34, the **Hôtel**

Chambellan (1490), housing one of Dijon's tourist offices. For a glimpse of what must be nearly genuine medieval character, take a walk in the cobbled alleys by the **Tour St-Nicholas**, off rue Jean-Jacques-Rousseau.

Also in this quarter behind the dukes' palace, in the angle between rue de la Chouette and rue de la Préfecture, is the **church of Notre-Dame**, built in the early thirteenth century in the Burgundian Gothic style. In the south transept

△ Church of Notre-Dame, Dijon

there is a ninth-century wooden "black" Virgin, one of the oldest in France. Known as "Our Lady of Good Hope", she receives prayers for health and happiness written into the open book on a lectern in front of the altar. Outside on rue de la Chouette, in the north wall of the church, is a small sculpted owl – *chouette* – polished by the hands of passers-by who for centuries have touched it for luck and which gives the street its name.

From here rue de la Musette leads west, passing just south of the **market square** and the covered *halles*. The whole area is full of sumptuous displays of food and attractive cafés and restaurants, and is often thronged with people. Opening at 6am, the market operates on Tuesday and Friday mornings, and all day on Saturday; it spills over into the surrounding streets, with bric-a-brac in rue de Soissons on the north side and clothes in the beautiful little **place François-Rude,** named after the sculptor, and a favourite hangout, with its cafés and fountain graced by the bronze figure of a grape harvester.

South of the place de la Libération

On the south side of the place Darcy–church of St-Michel axis, and especially in the *quartier* behind place de la Libération, there's a concentration of magnificent *hôtels* from the seventeenth and eighteenth centuries. These were built for the most part by men who had bought themselves offices and privileges with the Parliament of Burgundy, established by Louis XI in 1477 after the death of Duke Charles le Téméraire (the Bold) as a concession designed to win the compliance of this newly acquired frontier province. One of them, 4 rue des Bons-Enfants, houses the **Musée Magnin** (Tues–Sun 10am–noon & 2–6pm; €3.50), the building – a seventeenth-century *hôtel particulier* – complete with its original furnishings, is more interesting than the exhibition of paintings by good but lesser-known artists. Other noteworthy houses are to be found nearby in rue Vauban, some showing the marks of Hugues Sambin's influence in their decorative details (lions' heads, garlands of fruit, tendrils of ivy and his famous *chou bourguignon*, or "Burgundy cabbage"), notably, nos. 3, 12, 21 and 23.

Continuing south from Musée Magnin, rue Ste-Anne, near place des Cordeliers, contains two museums. The **Musée de la Vie Bourguignonne** at no. 17 (daily except Tues: May–Sept 9am–6pm; Oct–April 9am–noon & 2–6pm; free) is all about nineteenth-century Burgundian life, featuring costumes, furniture and domestic industries like butter-, cheese- and bread-making, along with a reconstructed kitchen. Practically next door at no. 15, the **Musée d'Art Sacré** (same hours Musée de la Vie Bourguignonne; free) contains an important collection of church treasures, including a seventeenth-century statue of St Paul, the first in the world to be restored using an extraordinary technique that involves injecting the stone with resin and then solidifying the resulting compound using gamma rays. Formerly crumbling to dust, the guinea-pig saint is now completely firm.

A little further to the west, the **cathedral** – the once great abbey church of St-Bénigne – is no longer of very great interest, although its garishly tiled roof and nineteenth-century spire dominate the skyline impressively enough. In a chestnut-shaded garden next to the cathedral, the **Musée Archéologique**, 5 rue Dr-Maret (Wed–Sun: mid-May to Sept 9am–6pm; Oct to mid-May 9am–12.30pm & 1.30–6pm; free), has some extremely interesting finds from the Gallo-Roman period, especially funerary bas-reliefs and a collection of *ex votos* from the source of the Seine, among them the little bronze of the goddess

Sequana (Seine) upright in her bird-prowed boat. Also on show is Sluter's bust of Christ from the Chartreuse.

Eating, drinking and entertainment

Dijon has an inordinate number of **patisseries**, full of high-quality, tempting confectionery in which marzipan and fruit feature prominently. Some also promote the Dijon specialities: *pain d'épices*, a gingerbread made with honey and spices and eaten with butter or jam (from Mulot et Petitjean, 13 place Bossuet and other branches all over town), and *cassissines* – blackcurrant candies. **Chocolate**, best made on the premises, is another speciality – try Au Parrain Généreux, 21 rue du Bourg, southwest of the Palais. You can hardly forget that Dijon is also the high temple of **mustard** – there's the shop of leading producer Maille at 30 rue de la Liberté, selling a range from mild to cauterizing. To buy good but affordable **wine**: first and foremost, there's Nicot, 48 rue Jean-Jacques-Rousseau, where you can taste, seek advice or take courses; alternatively, try La Cave du Clos, 3 rue Jeannin, or Nicolas, 6 rue François-Rude.

There are a large number of excellent **restaurants** in town. Lively rue Berbisey, rue Monge and place Émile Zola hold the most promise for both eating and drinking options. The nearby **Théâtre du Parvis St-Jean** (Mon–Fri 9am–noon & 2–6pm; ⓣ03.80.30.63.53), has innovative programmes of dance, theatre and performance art.

Restaurants

Au Bon Pantagruel place du Marché, 20 rue Quentin ⓣ03.80.30.68.69. A popular, lively bistro alongside the market, with a good range of regional specialities on a menu that changes with healthy frequency. Menus at €20, set lunch €11.50. Closed Sun.

La Cézanne 38 rue Amiral Roussin ⓣ03.80.58.91.92. One of a string of tiny restaurants whose tables are crammed into a narrow, atmospheric old street, with a Provençal-influenced menu (€17–46). Hugely popular. If that doesn't suit, then there's Italian, classic French and crêpes very close to hand. Closed Mon lunch, Sun & last two weeks of Aug.

Le Chabrot 36 rue Monge ⓣ03.80.30.69.61. Atmospheric, friendly restaurant with hundreds of wine bottles lining the walls. On the west side of place Émile-Zola it has a staunchly Burgundian menu at €21.50 and a more refined offering at €32. Doubles as a wine bar-cum-cellar; the superb wine list offers lots of help for amateurs. Closed second week in Aug.

Le Clos des Capucines 3 rue Jeannin, at the end of rue Jean-Jacques-Rousseau ⓣ03.80.65.83.03. Housed in a beautiful medieval building, this restaurant serves very good traditional, rich Burgundy cuisine (*jambon persillé, escargots, boeuf bourguignon*) at very reasonable prices. Menus at €14–45. Closed Sun, Sat & first two weeks in August.

Côté St-Jean 13 rue Monge ⓣ03.80.50.11.77. Elegant restaurant offering such delights as veal with chanterelle mushrooms and tarragon-scented chocolate cake. Menus €27.50–39, with good-value lunch menus: two courses for €12, three for €15.50. Closed Wed & Sat lunch, Tues & mid-July to mid-Aug.

Les Deux Fontaines 16 place de la République ⓣ03.80.60.86.45. A short walk from the centre, in the northeast corner of the old town, but worth it for the airy, garden-like atmosphere and fresh, Mediterranean-influenced daily specials (menu €14, *plats* €13–15).

Gril'Laure 8 place St-Bénigne ⓣ03.80.41.86.76. Popular with the business lunch crowd for its convenient cathedral-side location, and pizzas, pasta and grilled dishes hot out of the wood-fired oven. Menu at €18, *plats* €13.

Le Petit Marche 27 rue Musette ⓣ03.80.30.15.10. Serves home-made vegetarian and organic dishes. Reasonably priced with menus from €10 to €14. Closed Sun.

Simpatico 30 rue Berbisey ⓣ03.80.30.53.53. Excellent Italian restaurant with funky decor and an almost defiantly Italian wine list. Lunch menus at €11.40, dinners à la carte from around €20. Closed Sun, Mon & Aug.

Le Verdi 24 place Émile Zola ⓣ03.80.30.25.88. Wildly popular lunch menu (€10), and the outdoor seating on the square gets busy in the evening too. Menu includes grills, pizza, fish and good inexpensive *escargots*. Dinners in the €20–25 range. Closed Sun.

Cafés, bars and nightclubs

Dijon is an important university city as well as one of France's main conference centres, so **nightspots** and cultural centres at both ends of the range are worth exploring. Place Émile Zola and rue Berbisey are good places to start a night out. The English/Irish theme pubs are predictably popular, but there are plenty of alternatives. For **information** on bands and DJs, pick up a free *Mag de la Nuit* (Ⓦwww.magdelanuit.net) at the tourist office or various establishments around the city.

Le Brighton 33 rue Auguste-Comte. English pub with 200 different kinds of beer, and dancing. Daily till around 3am or later.

Le Cappuccino 132 rue Berbisey. Speciality beers in a youthful, slightly bohemian bar. Daily till around 1.30am.

Le Chez Nous just behind rue Quentin. Tucked down a tiny alleyway just off rue Quentin, an authentic community bar with a proudly alternative ethos and a genuine atmosphere. Strip lighting, mismatched old tables, exhibitions and impromptu performances. Opening times and days vary, but usually daily till around 1am.

Le Crockodil 88 rue Berbisey. Pub-cum-café characterized by distressed chic. A good place for an afternoon coffee leading into an early evening drink. Mon–Sat till 2am.

Le Privé av Garibaldi. Large, traditional disco and pick-up joint, just off place de la République. Two rooms: one mainstream Euro-house, the other more retro. Wed–Sat till 5am.

Le Quentin rue Quentin. Relaxed café-bar on the southeast corner of the market square that's popular for its cheap bottles of wine, drunk early evening as an aperitif mixed with *sirop de violettes* – or any of a host of other *sirop* flavours.

Rhumerie la Jamaïque 14 place de la République. Popular with a trendy late-twenties/early-thirties crowd for its pricey cocktails and rock-opera decor; they have live bands on the weekend playing Caribbean music. Daily except Sun 3pm–3am. For something more Latin-based, traverse the square to *Salsapelpa* on rue Marceau, open daily until 2am.

Shanti 69 rue Berbisey. Great little hookah joint, decked out with divans in transcendental South Asian decor, serving delicious teas and flavoured *sheesha* (€7 for a tobacco pipe). Open until 2am.

L'Univers 47 rue Berbisey. Trendy and dark, this popular pub-bar has frequent blues, jazz and rock concerts in the cellar. Open till midnight and later.

Au Vieux Léon 52 rue Jeannin. Tiny, noisy, friendly little bar that's positively jumping with students. Decorated like an old-fashioned French café on acid.

Listings

Cinemas L'Eldorado, 21 rue Alfred-de-Musset (Ⓣ03.80.66.12.34; Ⓦwww.cinema-eldorado.com), is a three-screen arts cinema showing all films in original language with a concentration of foreign films. Devosge, 6 rue Devosge (Ⓣ03.80.30.74.79), shows some films in the original, and tries to deviate from the obvious classics.

Festivals The city has a good summer music season, with classical concerts throughout June in its Été Musical programme. L'Estivade, which takes place at various locations around the city between late June and mid-Aug, puts on endless music, dance and street theatre performances. The Fête de la Vigne, in the last week of Aug, is a traditional costume/folklore jamboree; while the Foire gastronomique, during the first two weeks of Nov, celebrates all things edible.

Internet Cybersp@ce21 (46 rue Monge; Mon–Sat 11am–midnight, Sun 2pm–midnight; €4/hr) is a good option in the centre of the old town.

Laundry 41 rue Auguste-Comte; daily 6am–9pm.

Markets From 6am Tues, Thurs (Les Halles only) & Fri mornings, and all day Sat along the four streets surrounding the covered market – rue Bannelier, rue Quentin, rue C. Ramey and rue Odebert.

Pharmacy Junction of rue Berbisey and rue Charrue Mon–Sat 8.45am–7pm.

Swimming pool Oxygène-Parc Aquatique, Centre Commercial de la Toison d'Or (closed Nov–March; Ⓣ03.80.74.16.16; adults €9, children €7.50; bus #16). Has a wave machine, Jacuzzi and water slides.

The Côte d'Or

South of Dijon, the attractive countryside of the **Côte d'Or** is characterized by the steep scarp of the *côte*, wooded along the top and cut by sheer little valleys called *combes*, where local rock climbers hone their skills (footpaths **GR7** and **GR76** run the whole length of the wine country as far south as Lyon). Spring is a good time to visit this region, when you avoid the crowds and the landscape is a dramatic symphony of browns – trees, earth and vines, along with millions of bone-coloured vine stakes wheeling past as you travel through, like crosses in a vast war cemetery.

The place names that line the N74 – Gevrey-Chambertin, Vougeot, Vosne-Romanée, Nuits-St-Georges, Pommard, Volnay, Meursault Beaune – are music to the ears of wine buffs. But apart from the busy tourist centre of **Beaune**, they turn out to be sleepy, dull though exceedingly prosperous villages, full of houses inhabited by well-heeled *vignerons*. You can make a very good living on a patch of four or five hectares, the average-sized plot, the proof being that none is ever up for sale.

There are numerous **caves** where you can taste (usually for a charge of €4.50–6) and buy the local elixir, but remember that the former is meant to be a prelude to the latter. And there's no such thing as a cheap wine here, red

The wines of Burgundy

Burgundy farmers have been growing grapes since Roman times, and their rulers, the dukes, frequently put their **wines** to effective use as a tool of diplomacy. Today they have never had it so good, which is why they're reticent about the quirks of soil and climate and the tricks of pruning and spraying that make their wines so special. **Vines** are temperamental: frost on the wrong day, sun at the wrong time, too much water or poor drainage, and they won't come up with the goods. And they like a slope, which is why so many wines are called "Côte [hill] de" somewhere. Burgundy's best wines come from a narrow strip of hillside called the **Côte d'Or** that runs southwest from Dijon to Santenay, and is divided into two regions, Côte de Nuits and Côte de Beaune. With few exceptions the reds of the Côte de Nuits are considered the best: they are richer, age better and cost more. Côte de Beaune is known particularly for its whites: Meursault, Montrachet and Puligny.

The single most important factor determining the "character" of wines is the **soil**. In the Côte d'Or, the relative mixture of chalk, flint and clay varies over very short distances, making for an enormous variety of taste. Chalky soil makes a wine *virile* or *corsé*, in other words "heady" – *il y a de la mâche*, they say, "something to bite on" – while clay makes it *féminin*, more *agréable*.

These and other more extravagant judgements are made after the hallowed procedure of **tasting**: in order to do it properly, by one account, you have to "introduce a draft of wine into your mouth, swill it across the tongue, roll it around the palate, churn it around, emitting the gargling sound so beloved of tasters, which is produced by slowly inhaling air through the centre of your mouth, and finally eject it". The ejection is what has to be learnt.

For an **apéritif** in Burgundy, you should try *kir*, named after the man who was both mayor and MP for Dijon for many years after World War II – two parts dry white wine, traditionally *aligoté*, and one part *cassis* or blackcurrant liqueur. To round the evening off there are many **liqueurs** to choose from, but Burgundy is particularly famous for its marcs, of which the best are matured for years in oak casks.

or white, €15–18 being the minimum price you'll pay for a bottle. The Hautes Côtes (Nuits and Beaune) – wines from the top of the slope – are cheaper, but they lack the connoisseur cachet of the big names.

Beaune

BEAUNE, the principal town of the Côte d'Or, manages to maintain its attractively ancient air, despite a near constant stream of tourists and rampant commercialism – this must be one of the few towns in France where most of the shops stay open at lunchtime. Narrow cobbled streets and sunny squares dotted with cafés make it a lovely spot to sample the region's wine, though you may find it cheaper and easier to use Dijon as a base for getting around in the area, as there are good connections by train and Transco buses, which service all the villages down the N74.

Beaune's town centre is a tightly clustered, rampart-enclosed *vieille ville*, and its chief attraction is the fifteenth-century hospital, the **Hôtel-Dieu** (daily: April to mid-Nov 9am–6.30pm; mid-Nov to March 9–11.30am & 2–5.30pm; €5.60), on the corner of place de la Halle. Here a cobbled courtyard is surrounded by a wooden gallery overhung by a massive roof patterned with diamonds of gaudy tiles – green, burnt sienna, black and yellow – and similarly multicoloured steep-pitched dormers and turrets. Inside is a vast paved hall with a glorious arched timber roof, the Grande Salle des Malades, which preserves

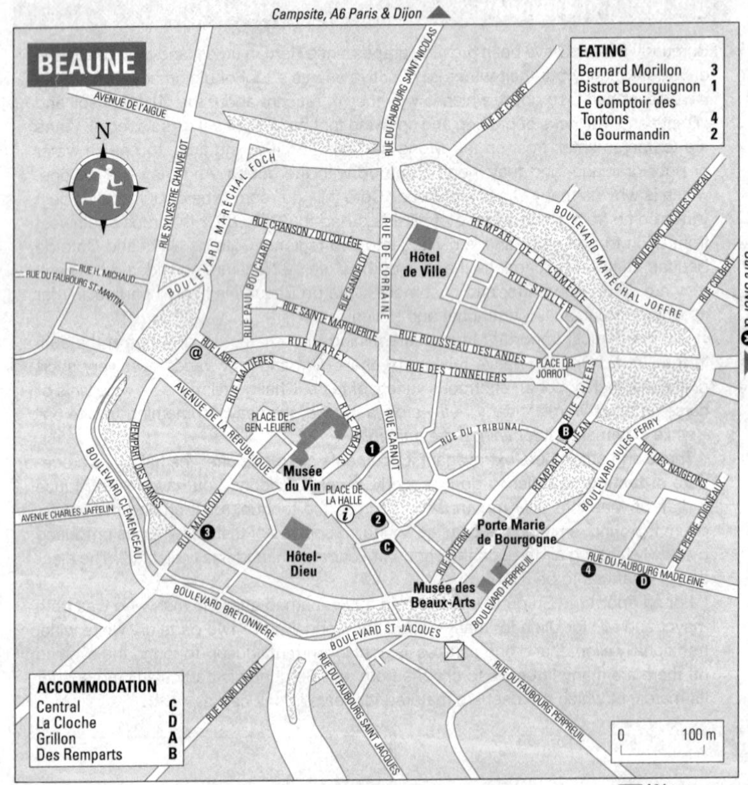

the heavy, enclosed wooden beds used in the nineteenth century and beyond – patients were treated here up until 1971. Passing through two smaller, furnished wards, the kitchen and the pharmacy, you reach a dark chamber housing the splendid fifteenth-century altarpiece of the *Last Judgement* by Rogier van der Weyden. The painting was commissioned by Nicolas Rolin, who also founded the hospital in 1443 (King Louis XI commented: "It was only fair that a man who had made so many people poor during his life should create an asylum for them before his death"). A major wine auction takes place here during the annual Trois Glorieuses festival (see p.604), the prices paid setting the pattern for the season.

The private residence of the dukes of Burgundy on rue d'Enfer now contains the **Musée du Vin** (April–Nov daily 9.30am–6pm; Dec–March daily except Tues 9.30am–5pm; €4.50), with giant winepresses, a collection of traditional tools of the trade and a relief map of the vineyards that begins to make sense of it all. If you feel like visiting three museums in one day, a **combined ticket** into the Musée du Vin, the Hôtel-Dieu and the town's **Musée de Beaux-Arts** costs €9.60.

It's worth checking at the tourist office to see if the **Musée Marey**, in the **Hôtel de Ville** which is devoted to early movie photography, has re-opened after renovations.

Practicalities

Beaune's **gare SNCF** is five minutes' walk away from the old walls to the east of the centre on avenue du 8-Septembre, buses into town also stop there. The **tourist office**, 1 rue de l'Hôtel-Dieu (March–Nov daily 9/10am–noon & 1–6/7pm; ⓣ03.80.26.21.30, ⓦwww.ot-beaune.fr), is opposite the Hôtel-Dieu, staff can advise on touring the region and tasting its wines. You can rent **bikes** from Bourgogne Randonnées at avenue de 8 Septembre by the *gare* (€3 per hour, €15 per day). For **Internet**, you'll need to head to the *bibliothèque municipale* at 11 place Marey (€2 per hour).

If you're going to **stay** in Beaune, be prepared to book well in advance and pay at least €40. There are only five hotels within the town walls: one of the less extravagantly priced is the bright and modern *Central*, right in the middle of things at 2 rue Victor-Millot (ⓣ03.80.24.77.24, ⓔhotel.central.beaune@orange.fr; ❺), with a good restaurant. The delightful *Hôtel des Remparts*, at 48 rue Thiers (ⓣ03.80.24.94.94, ⓦwww.webstore.fr/hotel-remparts; ❺–❽), is a wonderful place, sensitively restored and full of old beams and ancient stone. You can still see the ramparts that give it its name in some of the (admittedly more expensive) rooms. Set round a small cobbled courtyard it also has parking and Internet access in the rooms. Most of Beaune's hotels are found just outside the town walls to the southeast, around rue du Faubourg Madeleine and place Madeleine; *La Cloche*, at 40 rue du Faubourg Madeleine (ⓣ03.80.24.66.33, ⓦwww.hotel-cloche-beaune.com; ❹), with solid furnishings and an inner courtyard, is pleasant and reliable. Further out, *Hôtel Grillon*, 21 rte de Seurre, (ⓣ03.80.22.44.25, ⓦwww.hotel-grillon.fr; ❸) is set in gardens about 1km east of town, and has a small heated swimming pool. The pretty *Les Cent Vignes* **campsite**, 10 rue Auguste Dubois (ⓣ03.80.22.03.91; mid-March to Oct), is about 1km north out of town, off rue du Faubourg-St-Nicolas (the N74 to Dijon), before the bridge over the autoroute; booking is advisable.

Eating out is an expensive business here, although there are simple but excellent *plats* such as steaks and salads to be had at the *Bistrot Bourguignon*, on the *peotonal* at 8 rue Monge (ⓣ03.80.22.23.24; *plats* €14, midweek lunch menu €13), as well as a good range of wines by the glass. For something more sophisticated, try *Le Gourmandin*, 8 place Carnot (Ⓣ03.80.24.07.88, Ⓦwww.hotellegourmandin.com), with good menus at €28 and €32 and lunch at €11. Here a creaky spiral staircase leads up to two ultramodern, boutique-chic rooms (❼). There's also the decidedly upscale *Bernard Morillon*, 31 rue Maufoux (Ⓣ03.80.24.12.06; closed Mon & Tues lunch; *plats* from €36, menus €20–77), with high ceilings, beams and a delightful courtyard. Here they'll nestle your *langoustines* on walnuts, aubergine and tagliatelle. Just outside the town walls, *Le Comptoir des Tontons,* at 22 rue du Faubourg Madeleine (Ⓣ03.80.24.19.64; closed Sun & Mon), is stylish and unpretentious, with menus at €18–25.

Château du Clos-de-Vougeot

If you find French wine culture fascinating, it's worth visiting the **Château du Clos-de-Vougeot** to see the wine-making process (daily: April–Sept 9am–6.30pm; Oct–March 9–11.30am & 2–5.30pm, Sat closes 5pm; €3.60), 21km north of Beaune between Gévry-Chambertin and Nuits-St-Georges. Mammoth thirteenth-century winepresses installed by the Cistercian monks to whom these vineyards belonged for nearly 700 years until the Revolution, are still here. The château today is the home of a chivalrous order founded in 1934, the Confrèrie des Chevaliers du Tastevin. Chivalrous or not, the new monks continue the good wine work. After you've seen how it's made, you can taste it nearby on the N74 at La Grand Cave à Vougeot (9am–7pm). There's a three-day wine **festival**, Les Trois Glorieuses, on the third Saturday in November, starting in Vougeot and continuing in Beaune and Meursault.

The Saône valley

The **Saône valley** is prosperous and modern, nourished by the autoroute, tourism, industry and the wine trade. But turn your back on the river and head west and immediately you enter a different Burgundy: of hilly pasture and woodland, utterly rural and more populated by cattle than people. This is the hinterland – the Deep South – of Burgundy, where every village clusters under the tower of a Romanesque church, spawned by the influence of Cluny in the 1000s and 1100s. It is only when you reach the Loire and encounter the main traffic routes again that you re-enter the modern world.

Its beautiful country for **cycling**, though there are few places from which to actually rent a bike. There are, however, plenty of bus and train connections.

Chalon-sur-Saône

CHALON, a sizeable port and bustling industrial centre on a broad meander of the Saône, is not normally worth a stop in itself, though its old riverside quarter does have an easy charm, and it makes a good base for exploring the more expensive areas of the Côte d'Or. You may be tempted to stay, though by the pre-Lent carnival (February or March) which features a parade of giant masks and a confetti battle, and the national festival of street artists and theatre in July.

The **old town** is just back from the river around Grande-Rue and rue du Châtelet, with several fifteenth-century timber-framed houses. Nearby, 200m to the west on place de l'Hôtel-de-Ville, is the **Musée Denon** (daily except Tues 9.30am–noon & 2–5.30pm; €3.10, free on Wed & first Sun of the month), whose most vaunted exhibit is the 18,000-year-old Volgu flint, rated one of the finest stone tools yet discovered. Look out too for the local furniture and a painting by Vuillard.

Your ticket also gets you into the more unusual **Musée Niépce**, 28 quai des Messageries (daily except Tues: July & Aug 10am–12.30pm & 1.30–6pm; Sept–June 9.30–11.45am & 2–5.45pm; €3.10, free on Wed & first Sun of the month), just downstream from Pont St-Laurent. Nicéphore Niépce, who was born in Chalon, is credited with inventing photography in 1816 – though he named it "heliography". The museum possesses a fascinating range of cameras, from the first machine ever to the Apollo moon mission's equipment, plus a number of 007-type spy-camera devices, all attractively displayed.

The other interesting target in town is the **Maison des Vins** on Promenade Ste-Marie (Mon–Sat 9am–7pm), where you can taste and buy Côte Chalonnaise wines, chosen from the wines of 44 local villages by a choice committee of professional wine tasters.

Practicalities

The **tourist office** is just off the pedestrian walkway at boulevard de la République (July & Aug Mon–Sat 9.30am–7pm, Sun 10am–noon & 4–7pm; Sept–June Mon–Sat 9.30am–12.30pm & 2–6.30pm; ⓣ03.85.48.37.97, ⓦwww.chalon-sur-saone.net), and gives out excellent listings. The **gare SNCF** is five minutes' walk away at the end of avenue Jean-Jaurès; the **bus** to Cluny leaves from behind platform one.

The most attractive **hotel** in town is undoubtedly the lovely, airy *St-Jean*, right on the riverbank at 24 quai Gambetta (ⓣ03.85.48.45.65, ⓕ03.85.93.62.69; ④), with classical-style rooms. The family run *Hôtel de la Colombiere* (ⓣ03.85.48.07.31; ⓦwww.hotelcolombiere.com; ②) at 7 av Boucicaut, is five minutes' walk from the train station down avenue Jean-Jaurès. Chalon's *Hôtel Kyriad* (ⓣ03.85.90.08.00, ⓦwww.kyriad.com; ④) is comfortable, friendly and in the centre of town at 35 place de Beaune. If you're looking for dirt-cheap without the dirt, you could walk twenty minutes east out of town to the *Residences Chalon Jeunes* at 18 av Pierre Nugue (ⓣ03.85.46.44.90, ⓦwww.etudiant-chalon.com), which has rooms for €16.50 a night and a cafeteria-style restaurant. *Camping du Pont de Bourgogne* (ⓣ03.85.48.26.86; ⓔcampingchalon71@orange.fr), 2km out of town on the south bank of the Saône in St-Marcel, is accessible on bus #5 during the summer; if you're walking, cross either Pont St-Laurent or Pont J.-Richard and head east.

Rue de Strasbourg, across Pont St-Laurent on the so-called *île aux restos*, is lined with excellent **places to eat**. *Chez Jules* at no. 11 (ⓣ03.85.48.08.34, menus €18; closed Sat lunch and Sun) is one of the more refined choices. Also worthwhile is the bright and elegant *L'air du Temps* at no. 7 (ⓣ03.85.93.39.01, closed Sun & Mon), which does standard French fare including the obligatory *escargots* – menus €17–33. Nearby at no. 31 there's the tiny *Le Bistrot* (ⓣ03.85.93.22.01; closed July & Aug & weekends) which offers a traditional evening menu from €27. Or if by now you crave Italian cusine, *da Nunzio*, at no. 3 (ⓣ03.85.48.39.83, closed Tues and Sat lunch), has fresh pasta menus from €12 at lunchtime, €27 in the evening. A handful of late-night **bars** can be found just off rue de Strasbourg, including the *Boogie Blues Bar* (Mon–Thurs till 2am, Fri & Sat till 3am) in the cross-street, rue d'Uxelles. In the centre, the place for cafés is place St-Vincent, with its lovely half-timbered houses. There are food **markets** on rue aux Fèvres and place St-Vincent between 8am and noon on Friday and Sunday.

Tournus

Graced by ancient, golden buildings **TOURNUS** is a beautiful little town on the banks of the Saône. 27km south of Chalon, 30km north of Mâcon and squeezed between the N6 and the river – the narrow huddled streets have the inward-looking, self-protecting feel of a Mediterranean town, belying a prosperous past when commercial traffic thronged the busy riverside quays. Those quays are quiet today, and Tournus's modern prosperity is based on agriculture, light industry and, increasingly, tourism.

Coming from the N6 you enter the town through a **gateway** flanked by medieval towers and are confronted by the old **abbey church of St-Philibert**, one of the earliest and most influential Romanesque buildings in Burgundy. The first construction dates back to around 900 AD and the foundation of the monastic community by monks fleeing Norman raids on their home community of Noirmoutier off the Atlantic coast. The present building dates to the first half of the eleventh century.

The facade of the church, with its powerful towers and simple decoration of Lombard arcading, has the massive qualities and clean, pared-down lines more associated with a fortress. A narrow staircase opposite the main entrance in the west front leads up to a **high chapel** that looks down into the body of the church, a vestige of the Carolingian tradition of church building which doubled as a defensive feature. The chapel's main arch is inset with two extraordinary sculptures that may represent the abbot responsible for the rebuilding (on the right, holding a hammer and giving a blessing) and possibly the sculptor himself (on the left, full-face), who may even be the "Gerlamus" of the inscription – in which case this may be one of the earliest self-portraits of the medieval period. The nave and transept below are surprisingly light and graceful for such an early church with three exquisitely carved arches at the far end of the choir. Steps in the north transept lead down to the crypt, where a well plunges down to the level of the Saône – useful in times of siege.

To the south of town the **Hôtel Dieu** (April–Oct daily except Tues 10am–6pm; €5.25) is one of the region's many charity hospitals, and one of the best preserved. The sisters of Saint Martha, an order established in the fifteenth century to serve the hospital in Beaune, worked as ward nurses from the hospital's inception in 1674 right up until it closed in 1978, tending to patients in the ordered rows of closed oak beds, set in high-ceilinged wards to allow the noxious air to circulate. It's worth visiting for the elaborate dispensary alone, complete with a host of faïence pots and hand-blown glass jars.

Practicalities

The **gare SNCF** is on avenue Gambetta, across the road from the old town and a ten-minute walk from the **tourist office** at 2 place de l'Abbaye (June–Sept daily 10am–7pm; Oct–May Tues–Sat 9am–noon & 2–6pm; ⓣ03.85.27.00.20, ⓦwww.tournugeois.fr), opposite the west front of the abbey church.

At the southern end of the old town is the established, slightly uniform, *Hôtel aux Terrasses*, 18 av du 23-Janvier (ⓣ03.85.51.01.74, ⓦwww.aux-terrasses.com; ❹; closed Jan). It also has an excellent restaurant with menus at €27–56 (closed Jan, Sun eve through to Tues lunch). A stone's throw from the abbey church and right in the atmospheric heart of town *Hôtel Gras*, 2 rue Fénelon (ⓣ03.85.51.07.25; ❶; restaurant €13.50), is undeniably basic but also traditional, friendly and serves excellent home-cooked meals in the café-bar downstairs. Alternatively, up a couple of price brackets, the *Hôtel de la Paix* (ⓣ03.85.51.01.85, ⓦwww.hotel-de-la-paix.fr; ❸) at 9 rue Jean-Jaurès, is fairly central and well kept if a little bland. On the other side of the river the *Hôtel-Restaurant de Saône* (ⓣ03.85.51.20.65, ⓕ03.85.51.20.45; ❸), has cheerful, modern, if small, rooms in a splendidly tranquil riverside location. **Campers** should head for *Camping Municipal en Bagatelle* on rue des Canes (ⓣ03.85.51.16.58, ⓔcampingtournus@aol.com; May–Sept), a fifteen-minute walk north out of town, up rue René-Cassin.

For further **eating** possibilities outside of the hotels, there are a number of cafés and brasseries in and around place de l'Hôtel-de-Ville. For something more elegant try the very plush *Hôtel de Greuze* (ⓣ03.85.51.13.42; rooms ❾) – not to be confused with the very different *Hôtel Gras* – which blends traditional and contemporary styles and where menus start at €92, *plats* from €42.

Mâcon and around

MÂCON is a lively, prosperous place on the banks of the River Saône, 58km south of Chalon and 68km north of Lyon, with excellent transport connections between the two. It has no great sights, but despite being a centre for the wine trade does have a surprisingly sunny southern seaside feel, thanks to its long café-lined **riverbank** and free outdoor jazz concerts in late July–early August.

Lamartine, the nineteenth-century French Romantic poet (see box below), was born here in 1790 and his name is much in evidence. He is remembered in the handsome eighteenth-century mansion, the Hôtel Senecé, 41 rue Sigorgne, which houses the **Musée Lamartine** (Tues–Sat 10am–noon & 2–6pm, Sun 2–6pm; €2.50), part of which is dedicated to documents and other memorabilia to do with his personal, political and poetic lives. Nearby, on the corner of place des Herbes where a summertime fruit and veg market is held, stands the town's main tourist curiosity, an incredibly elaborate wooden house built around 1500 and known as the **Maison du Bois Doré**, with a wonderful bar/café downstairs that serves cocktails until 2 or 3am. The town also has a medieval art and Gallo-Roman archeological museum, the **Musée des Ursulines**, at 5 rue des Ursulines (Tues–Sat 10am–noon & 2–6pm, Sun 2–6pm; €2.50), housed in a seventeenth-century convent.

The most enjoyable way to bone up on the Mâcon, Beaujolais and Chalonnais **wines** is to head off on one of the much-signposted wine roads (ⓦwww.bourgogne-tourisme.com), which extend north into the Maconnais, and south into the Beaujolais, sampling as you go. If you don't have a car or a bike, however, you'll have to fall back on tasting with your meal. Alternatively,

Alphonse Lamartine (1790–1869)

Often referred to as the French Byron, **Alphonse Lamartine** is one of the best-known of the French Romantic poets. He was born and grew up in Milly, about 15km west of Mâcon, and published his first poetic work, *Méditations poétiques*, in 1820. In 1825 he published *Le Dernier Chant du Pélérinage d'Harold* as a tribute to Byron.

After the 1830 Revolution in Paris, he became involved in politics, being elected to the Chambre des Députés in 1833 and quickly acquiring a reputation as a powerful orator on the weighty questions of the day, like the abolition of slavery and capital punishment. His finest hour was as the leading figure in the provisional government of the Second Republic, which was proclaimed from the Hôtel de Ville in Paris on February 23, 1848. He withdrew from politics when reactionary forces, under the leadership of General Cavaignac, let the army loose on the protesting workers of Paris and Marseille in June 1848, after which he retired to St-Point, continuing to write and publish until his death in 1869.

the **Maison Mâconnaise des Vins**, 484 av Lattre-de-Tassigny (ⓣ03.85.22.91.18; daily 9am–7pm), can be found where the N6 comes into town along the riverside from Chalon – a ten-minute walk from the centre of town. It's little more than an outlet for a big producer, but they will arrange tastings of four wines for around €3.

Practicalities

The **gare SNCF** (adjacent to the **gare routière**) lies on rue Bigonnet at the southern end of rue Victor-Hugo, but TGV trains leave from Mâcon-Loché station 6km out of town – you'll have to make the connection by taxi. The **tourist office**, 1 place St Pierre (June–Sept Mon–Sat 10am–7pm, Sun 3–7pm; Oct–May Mon–Sat 10am–noon & 2–6pm; ⓣ03.85.21.07.07, ⓦwww.macon-tourism.com), has good maps and brochures covering the city and surrounding region.

There should be no difficulty finding a **place to stay**. Across the Pont de St-Laurent the *Hôtel du Beaujolais*, at 86 place République (ⓣ03.85.38.42.06, ⓕ03.85.38.78.02; ❸), has very clean, simple rooms. For a touch of only-slightly-faded grandeur try the *Hôtel d'Europe et d'Angleterre*, on the river at 92 quai Jean-Jaurès (ⓣ03.85.38.27.94, ⓦwww.hotel-europeangleterre-macon.com; ❸). It once played host to Queen Victoria and has the feel of former times – high ceilings, marble staircases and impossibly tall windows. It's also not as pricey as you might think and the rooms are tasteful and comfortable. Nearer the station, the *Inter-Hôtel de Bourgogne*, on the north side of place de la Barre at 6 rue Victor-Hugo (ⓣ03.85.21.10.23, ⓦwww.hoteldebourgogne.com; ❺; restaurant from €22), has retained some character and a lively atmosphere despite being part of a chain. For more of a budget place, try *La Promenade*, 266 quai Lamartine (ⓣ03.85.38.10.98; ❷), which looks right onto the Saône and houses a decent restaurant, *Le Carline*, with menus at €10–25. There's a **campsite** 3km north out of town on the N6 (ⓣ03.85.38.16.22; closed Nov to mid-March).

Mâcon has no shortage of good **restaurants** to choose from. For cheap eats, head for the river: the pleasant *Lamartine*, 266 quai Lamartine (closed Mon eve through to Wed lunch), is popular for both meals and drinks, while the *St Laurent*, on quai Bouchacourt, just over the Pont de St-Laurent, has great views and menus from €17. *Au Rocher de Cancale*, 393 quai Jean-Jaurés (ⓣ03.85.38.07.50; closed Sun eve & Mon), is a traditional restaurant serving excellent snails and Bresse chicken (menus €16–38). While the stylish *Pierre*, 7–9 rue Joseph Dufour (ⓣ03.85.38.14.23; closed Sun eve, Mon & Tues afternoon, plus first three weeks in July), is well worth a splurge, not least for its *menu gastronomique*, which is strong on truffles (menus €33–72).

Brou and Bourg-en-Bresse

BROU is an uninteresting suburban village outside Bourg-en-Bresse, 32km east of Mâcon, which happens to have an early sixteenth-century **church** (daily; €6.50). If you're heading east to Geneva or the Alps, take a look, but don't lose a lift or miss a train for it. Aldous Huxley found it "a horrible little architectural nightmare", its monuments "positively and piercingly vulgar". Certainly, it was a very rich woman's expensive folly, crammed with virtuoso craftsmanship from the dying moments of the Gothic style; it was undertaken by Margaret of Austria after the death of her husband, Philibert, Duke of Savoy, as a mausoleum for the two of them and Philibert's mother. No longer a place of worship, it's interesting to see, but soulless, without a trace of vision or inspiration.

BOURG-EN-BRESSE is the place to base yourself if you want to visit Brou's church, just a short bus ride away (#5; every 30min), leaving from place Carriat. The **tourist office** (Mon–Sat 8.30am–noon & 2–6.30pm; Ⓣ04.74.22.49.40, Ⓦwww.bourg-en-bresse.org) is in Centre Albert-Camus, 6 av Alsace-Lorraine, with an annexe by Brou church in summer. Wednesday is the local **market** day, held in Champ de Foire or if you want a real slice of French rural life try the livestock market, held every Tuesday afternoon at nearby Saint Denis Les Bourg. For somewhere to **stay** a good choice is the *Logis de Brou* (Ⓣ04.74.22.11.55, Ⓦwww.logisdebrou.com; ❹) at 132 bd de Brouw; here there's genteel charm, cheery rooms and a terrace for breakfast. The municipal **campsite** (Ⓣ04.74.45.37.21; April to mid-Oct) is at 5 allée du Centre Nautiqué – the N83 northeast of town heading for Lons-le-Saunier.

The Mâconnais, Beaujolais and Charollais

West of the valley of the Saône lies a tract of hilly country that is best known for its produce: the white wines of the **Mâconnais** are justly renowned, while the fashion for drinking the young red wine of **Beaujolais** has spread far beyond France. Further west still, the handsome white cattle that luxuriate in the green fields of the **Charollais** are an obvious sign that this is serious beef country.

In the past, however, the region was famed for its religion, and many large and powerful abbeys were established in the eleventh and twelfth centuries under the influence of the great monastery at Cluny. Few monks remain, and **Cluny** itself is largely destroyed, but Romanesque churches are almost as thick on the ground as cattle, and few are more impressive than the great basilica at **Paray-le-Monial**.

The Mâconnais

The **Mâconnais** wine-producing country lies to the west of the Saône, a strip hardly 20km wide, stretching from Mâcon to Tournus. The land rises sharply into steep little hills and valleys, at its prettiest in the south, where the region's best white wines come from, around the villages of **POUILLY**, **VINZELLES**, **PRISSÉ** and **FUISSÉ**, at the last of which, should you yearn for rustic rest, the *Hôtel La Vigne Blanche* (Ⓣ03.85.35.60.50, Ⓦwww.vigne-blanche.com; ❸), will provide just the setting you're looking for, with simple rooms, good regional cooking (menus from €13) and of course the chance to sample some of the local wines.

Directly above these villages rises the distinctive and precipitous 500-metre rock of **Solutré**, which in prehistoric times – around 20,000 BC – served as an ambush site for hunters after migrating animals: the bones of 100,000 horses have been found in the soil beneath the rock, along with mammoth, bison and reindeer carcasses. The history and results of the excavations are displayed in a museum at the foot of the rock, the **Musée Départemental de Préhistoire** (daily: Fe, March, Oct & Nov 10am–noon & 2–5pm; April–Sept 10am–6pm; €3.50). A steep path climbs to the top of the rock, where you get a superb view as far as Mont Blanc and the Matterhorn on a clear day, as well as looking down on the huddled roofs of **SOLUTRÉ-POUILLY**, the slopes beneath you covered with the vines of the Chardonnay grape that makes the exquisite greenish Pouilly-Fuissé wine. The area is at its most enchanting in early spring when the earth still shows its *terre-cuite* colours, punctuated by bursts of white cherry blossom and the blue drift of bonfire smoke from prunings amid the neatly staked rows of vines.

Aside from the sheer pleasure of wandering about in such reposeful landscapes – not so, however, if you're trying to tackle this very hilly country on a bike – there are some specific places to make for. One such is the sleepy hamlet of **ST-POINT**, where the poet Lamartine (see box on p.607) spent much of his life in the little medieval **Château de St-Point**, now a museum dedicated to his memory (Ⓣ03.85.50.50.30; phone to arrange a visit; €5), next to the Romanesque church where he's buried. If you continue up the road behind the château you come to an utterly rural farm where you can buy goat's cheese. There is a well-equipped **campsite** by the Lac St-Point (Ⓣ03.85.50.52.31; April–Oct).

Cluny and around

The abbey of **CLUNY** is the major tourist destination of the region. The voice of its abbot once made monarchs tremble, as his power in the Christian world was second only to that of the pope. The monastery was founded in 910 in response to the corruption of the existing church, and it took only a couple of vigorous early abbots to build the power of Cluny into a veritable empire. Gradually its spiritual influence declined, and Cluny became a royal gift. Both Richelieu and Mazarin did stints in the monastery as abbot.

Now, although the reputation of the place still pulls in the tourist coaches, little remains apart from the very attractive village. Hugues de Semur's vast and influential eleventh-century **church**, the largest building in Christendom until the construction of St Peter's in Rome, was dismantled in the destruction that followed the Revolution. Now what you see of the former **abbey** (daily: May–Aug 9.30am–6.30pm; Sept–April 9.30am–noon & 1.30–5pm; €6.50 combined ticket with museum) is an octagonal belfry and the huge south transept. Standing amid this fragment of a huge construction gives a tangible and poignant insight into the Revolution's enormous powers of transformation. Access to the belfry leads through the Grand École des Ingénieurs, one of France's elite higher-education institutions, and you can often see the students in their gowns decorated with cabalistic signs. At the back of the abbey is one of France's national stud farms, **Haras de Cluny** (Ⓣ06.22.94.52.69; July & Aug Tues–Sun 2, 3.30 & 5pm; Sept–June phone to book; €5), which you can visit but only on a guided tour. The **Musée d'Art et d'Archaeologie** (same hours and ticket as abbey), in the fifteenth-century palace of the last freely elected abbot, helps to flesh out the ruins with reconstructions and fragments of sculpture, while from the top of the **Tour des Fromages** (entrance through the tourist office; €1.25) you can picture it in the landscape below.

The **tourist office** is beside the Tours des Fromages, at 6 rue Mercière (April–June & Sept 10am–12.30pm & 2.30–6.45pm; July & Aug 10am–6.45pm; Oct–March 10am–12.30pm & 2.30–5pm; Ⓣ03.85.59.05.34, Ⓦwww.cluny-tourisme.com). **Bicycles** can be rented at Ludisport, by the platform of the abandoned railway station, on the southeast edge of town. For **accommodation**, the *Hôtel de Bourgogne*, place de l'Abbaye (Ⓣ03.85.59.00.58, Ⓦwww.hotel-cluny.com; ❺; closed Dec & Jan), is beautifully furnished and has an irresistible location in what must have been the north aisle of the church. Packed full of history and charm the excellent-value *Le Potin Gourmand*, at 4 place du Champ de Foire (Ⓣ03.85.59.02.06, Ⓦwww.potingourmand.com; ❸;

closed Jan & Feb) is a five-minute walk west from the centre. Arranged around a flower-filled courtyard, each of its seven beguiling rooms somehow manages to blend French rustic with nuances of a different style, from four-poster medieval to Byzantine. A much more prosaic option is the reasonably central *Hôtel du Commerce*, 8 place du Commerce (Ⓣ03.85.59.03.09, Ⓦwww.hotelducommerce-cluny.com; ❷–❸), where the cheaper rooms have shared facilities; do be sure to call ahead as they are given to closing early. The municipal **hostel**, *Cluny Séjour*, is right by the town bus stop at 22 rue Porte-de-Paris (Ⓣ03.85.59.08.83; Ⓔcluny.sejour@orange.fr; closed Dec to mid-Jan), and occupies some of the former buildings of the Benedictine monastery. There's also a municipal **campsite**, *St-Vital* (Ⓣ03.85.59.08.34; May to mid-Sept) across Pont de la Levée in the direction of Tournus.

For **meals**, there's good country cooking to be had at *Le Potin Gourmand* (evenings only, closed Sun; menus €23–30), while the *Brasserie du Nord*, right in the heart of things on the place de l'Abbaye, serves simple classics, with menus at €12–22. The bustling *Café du Centre* in rue Municipale, in a side street leading to the Abbey, is popular with students and serves excellent *plats* from €7.

Taizé

Another powerful attraction for the faithful might be the modern ecumenical community at **TAIZÉ**, 10km north of Cluny. It was founded in 1940 by the Swiss pastor Roger Schutz and centres around a restored Romanesque church and the new Church of Reconciliation. Hordes of youngsters come to take part in discussion groups and camp out. If you're seriously interested – and it's not likely to be to the taste of the merely curious – phone Ⓣ03.85.50.30.02, write to The Taizé Community, 71250 Taizé, France or visit the website (Ⓦwww.taize.fr), which gives full details. If you're passing through, you're more than welcome to visit the popular gift shop, where the brothers sell their wares, which include glazed dishware and musical recordings and writings translated into twenty languages.

The Beaujolais

Imperceptibly, as you continue south, the Mâconnais becomes the **Beaujolais**, a larger area of terraced hills producing lighter, fruity red wines, which it is now fashionable to drink very early. The Beaujolais grape is the Gamay, which, in contrast to other parts of Burgundy, thrives here on this granite soil. Of the four *appellations* of Beaujolais, the best are the *crus*, including Morgon and Fleurie, which come from the northern part of the region between St-Amour (the northernmost *cru*), and Brouilly in the south. If you have transport, you can follow the *cru* trail south from Mâcon by turning right at Crêches-sur-Saône up the D31 to St-Amour, and then south along the D68. Beaujolais Villages, which produces the most highly regarded *nouveau*, comes from the middle of the Beaujolais region, south of the *cru* belt, while plain Beaujolais and Beaujolais Supérieur are produced in the vineyards southwest of Villefranche.

The well-marked **route de Beaujolais** winds down through the wine villages to **VILLEFRANCHE**, not far from Lyon and a good base for the route. Here, the **tourist office** at 290 rue de Thizy (July & Aug daily 9.15am–12.15pm & 2–5.45pm; Sept–June Mon–Sat 9am–noon & 1.30–5.30pm; Ⓣ04.74.07.27.40) has information about *caves*, visits and wine tours. There are numerous cheap **hotels**, almost all near the **gare SNCF**. One great option is *Moulin à Vent* at 81 rue d'Anse, just across from the *gare* (Ⓣ04.74.68.36.13, Ⓕ04.74.65.09.70; ❷), which has a five simple but pleasant, en-suite rooms branching off from a spiral staircase above a bustling café-bar. With less character, *Hôtel Mercure* (ⓣ04.74.62.01.04; ⓦwww.accorhotels.com; ❺) at 146 rue de la Sous-Préfecture is part of a chain and offers reliable, central accommodation. Most of the **cafés** on rue Nationale are good for snacks or cheap menus. If you want something more substantial *Le Saladier* (ⓣ04.74.62.34.19; menus €15–29) at 579 rue Nationale is a good cafeteria-style restaurant with a courtyard terrace, while *L'Epicerie* (ⓣ04.74.62.04.04, closed Sun) at 55 rue Thizy offers traditional menus at €12–23.

Paray-le-Monial

Fifty kilometres west of Cluny, across countryside that becomes ever gentler and flatter as you approach the broad valley of the Loire, is **PARAY-LE-MONIAL**, whose major attraction is its **Basilique du Sacré-Coeur** (daily 9am–7pm). Not only is it an exquisite building in its own right, with a marvellously satisfying arrangement of apses and chapels stacking up in sturdy symmetry to its fine octagonal belfry, it's the best place to get an idea of what the abbey of Cluny looked like, as it was built shortly afterwards in devoted imitation of the mother church.

The town itself is steeped in religion and straddles the slow waters of the River Bourbince and the Canal du Centre. The only thing that disturbs its calm is the arrival of pilgrims of the Sacré-Coeur, or "Sacred Heart", a movement which originated here with Marguerite-Marie Alacoque, a local nun who received revelations advocating the worship of the sacred heart – and was later adopted by the entire Roman Catholic Church. The first pilgrimage took place in 1873, encouraged as a means of combating the socialist ideas espoused by the Paris Commune, and it raised the money to construct the church of the Sacré-Coeur on the hill of Montmartre in Paris. Paray is now second only to Lourdes as a pilgrim centre.

One secular building definitely worth a look, aside from just browsing down the main street – rue de la République/rue des Deux-Ponts/rue Victor-Hugo – is the highly ornamented **Maison Jayet**, now the Hôtel de Ville on place Guignaud, built in the 1520s.

Practicalities

The **tourist office** is on avenue Jean-Paul-II (July & Aug daily 9/10am–7pm; Sept–June Mon–Sat 10am–noon & 2.30–6pm; also Sun April–June & Sept–Oct; ⓣ03.85.81.10.92). You can rent **bikes** here and from Cycles Kaikinger, 24 rue de la République (ⓣ03.85.88.85.15).

For **accommodation**, try the *Hostellerie des Trois Pigeons*, 2 rue Daugard, just beyond the Hôtel de Ville (ⓣ03.85.81.03.77, ⓔ3p7103@inter–hotel.com; ❸; closed Dec–Feb; restaurant from €14), where comfortable furnishings mix well with old exposed stonework. There's also the less plush *Hôtel aux Vendanges de Bourgogne*, 5 rue Denis-Papin (ⓣ03.85.81.13.43, ⓦwww.auxvendangesdebourgogne.fr; ❸; closed mid-Nov to late Dec) with its popular, good-value restaurant (menu €14.50), on the south side of the Canal du Centre. The most attractive option, however, is the pleasantly old-fashioned yet well-appointed *Grand Hôtel de la Basilique*, 18 rue de la Visitation (ⓣ03.85.81.11.13, ⓦwww.hotelbasilique.com; ❸; closed Nov to April; restaurant from €13), with some rooms overlooking the basilica after which it's named. If you want to immerse yourself in the religious atmosphere of this town try the cavernous *Au Foyer de Sacré Coeur* next door at 14 rue de la Visitation (ⓣ03.85.81.11.01, ⓦwww.chez.com/fsc; ❷). It's bang opposite the chapel that stands on the spot where Ste Marguerite had her revelations, and is consequently occupied almost solely by pilgrims, who don't seem to mind the institutional albeit very friendly atmosphere. The *Mambré* **campsite** is on route du Gué-Léger (☎03.85.88.89.20; May to late Sept). For **food** as well as the hotel-restaurants above, rue Victor Hugo and place Guignault provide options for light meals.

To explore the little villages throughout the Mâconnais, there's no better base than the Merle family's organic farm at Vitry-en-Charollais (☎03.85.81.30.62; €40 with breakfast for two, dinner has to be booked ahead), with delicious home cooking, about 6km southwest of Paray.

The Charollais

The **Charollais** is cattle country, taking its name from the pretty little water-enclosed market town of **CHAROLLES**, with its 32 bridges, on the main N79 road, and in turn giving its name to one of the world's most illustrious breeds of cattle: the white, curly-haired, stocky Charollais, bred for its lean meat. Throughout this landscape, scattered across the rich farmland along the River Arconce, are dozens of small villages, all with more or less remarkable Romanesque churches, offspring of Cluny in its vigorous youth.

ANZY-LE-DUC, about 15km south of Paray off the main D982 to Roanne, boasts an exquisite complex of buildings: a perfect Romanesque church with jackdaw chatter echoing off the octagonal belfry, side by side with the remains of the old priory incorporated into a sort of fortified farm looking out over the Arconce valley, the whole built in a rich, warm stone. **MONTCEAUX-L'ÉTOILE**, a little nearer to Paray, has its special charm too: a quiet, worn church with beautiful sculptures adorning the porch, standing likewise above the Arconce valley, and, a little way down the village street, a curious tower-like house where a Marquis of Vichy is said to have practised alchemy with the notorious Italian wizard, Cagliostro.

Travel details

Trains

Autun to: Avallon (Mon–Sat 1–3 daily; 1hr 45min); Chalon-sur-Saône (1–2 daily; 1hr 10min–1hr 50min); Le Creusot-Ville (Mon–Sat 1–2 daily; 45min); Saulieu (2–6 daily; 50min).
Auxerre to: Avallon (4–6 daily; 1hr); Dijon (8–10 daily; 1hr 50min–2hr 20min); Joigny (9–11 daily; 35min); Paris (6–8 daily; 1hr 50min–2hr 30min); Sens (6–8 daily; 1hr).
Avallon to: Autun (1–2 daily; 1hr 45min); Auxerre (5–8 daily; 1hr 5min); Dijon (3 daily; 1hr 45min); Saulieu (4 daily; 50min–1hr).
Beaune to: Dijon (frequent; 25min); Lyon (10–12 daily; 1hr 50min–2hr 10min).
Bourg-en-Bresse to: Dijon (4–7 daily; 1hr 30min–2hr 10min); Lyon (frequent; 45min–1hr 30min); Mâcon (10 daily; 30–50min).
Dijon to: Auxerre (8–11 daily; 1hr 50min–2hr 20min); Beaune (frequent; 25min); Chalon-sur-Saône (frequent; 40min); Les Laumes-Alésia (frequent; 30–50min); Lyon (10–15 daily; 1hr 35min–2hr 10min); Mâcon (frequent; 1hr–1hr 20min); Montbard (8–11 daily; 30min); Nevers (3–6 daily; 2hr 10min–2hr 50min); Nuits-St-Georges (frequent; 15min); Paris (frequent; 1hr 40min–3hr 15min); Sens (6–9 daily; 1hr 45min–2hr 10min); Tonnerre (8–11 daily; 1hr–1hr 30min); Tournus (10 daily; 1hr); Villefranche (Mon–Sat frequent, Sun 5; 1hr 40min–2hr).
Mâcon to: Bourg-en-Bresse (10 daily; 30–50min); Dijon (frequent; 1hr–1hr 20min); Geneva (8–12 daily; 2hr 30min–3hr 30min); Lyon (frequent; 30min–1hr).
Nevers to: Autun (2–4 daily; 1hr 40min–2hr 20min); Chalon-sur-Saône (3 daily; 2hr 45min);

Clermont-Ferrand (7–8 daily; 1hr 30min–2hr 10min); Le Creusot (5–7 daily; 1hr 30min); Dijon (5–7 daily; 2hr 30min); Paris (frequent; 2–3hr).
Paray-le-Monial to: Chalon-sur-Saône (4–5 daily; 1hr 40min); Dijon (2–6 daily; 2hr 15min); Le Creusot (4 daily; 40min); Lyon (2–3 daily; 2hr); Moulins (3–5 daily; 1hr).
Sens to: Auxerre (4–6 daily; 30min–1hr 10min); Avallon (2–4 daily; 2hr); Dijon (9 daily; 1hr 50min–2hr 30min); Joigny (7–10 daily; 20min); Paris (9 daily; 1hr–1hr 30min); Tonnerre (9 daily; 1hr).
Tournus to: Chalon-sur-Saône (11–14 daily; 15min); Dijon (10 daily; 1hr); Mâcon (10 daily; 15min).

Buses

Autun to: Beaune (Mon–Fri 1 daily; 1hr 10min); Chalon-sur-Saône (2 daily; 1hr 30min); Château-Chinon (1–2 daily; 1hr); Le Creusot (3–5; 45min).
Auxerre to Clamecy (Mon–Sat 1–3; 1hr 15min).
Avallon to: Dijon (1–3 daily; 2hr–2hr 30min); Montbard (1–3 daily; 50min); Vézelay (summer only 1 daily; 30min).
Chablis to: Auxerre (winter Mon–Sat 1 daily, summer has to be booked 35min); Tonnerre (winter 1–2 daily, summer has to be booked; 1hr).
Châtillon-sur-Seine to: Dijon (3 daily; 1hr 30min–2hr); Montbard (3–6 daily; 40min).
Cluny to: Chalon-sur-Saône (2–4 daily; 1hr 30min); Charolles (2–5 daily; 45min); Mâcon (2–7 daily; 45min); Paray-le-Monial (1–5 daily; 1hr); Taizé (1–7 daily; 15min).
Dijon to: Autun (1 daily; 2hr 30min); Avallon (2–3 daily; 2hr 30min); Beaune (3–7 daily; 30min–1hr 30min); Châtillon-sur-Seine (2–4 daily; 1hr 30min–2hr); Saulieu (3 daily; 1hr 30min).
Mâcon to: Chalon-sur-Saône (4–7 daily; 2hr 15min); Charolles (2–5 daily; 2hr); Cluny (2–7 daily; 45min); Paray-le-Monial (2–5 daily; 2hr 20min).
Semur-en-Auxois to: Montbard (2–8 daily; 30min); Saulieu (2–6 daily; 35min); Venarey-les-Laumes for Alésia (Mon–Sat 3–11 daily; 20–30min).
Sens to: Joigny (1 daily; 1hr 10min); Troyes (3 daily; 1hr 45min).

8

Poitou-Charentes and the Atlantic coast

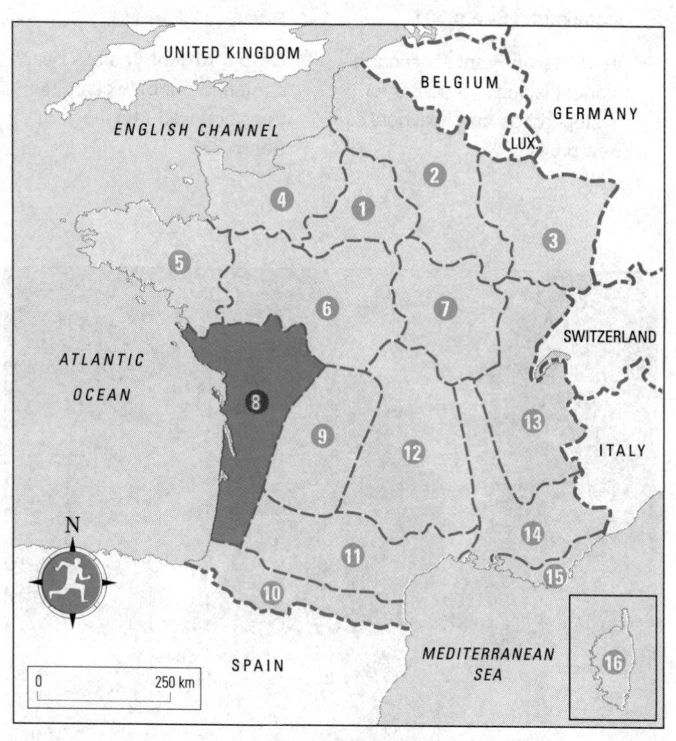

CHAPTER 8

Highlights

✱ **Marais Poitevin** The "green Venice", an intricate network of land and water that's perfect to explore by bike. See p.628

✱ **La Rochelle** This charming and unspoilt port town is the jewel of the west coast, with a well-preserved historic centre and some exquisite seafood restaurants. See p.631

✱ **Île d'Oléron** France's second biggest island is a centre for oysters, birds and hollyhocks. See p.644

✱ **Angoulême** Wholly underrated, this enchanting old-school town hosts an animated nightlife and rightfully lays claim to some of the best restaurants in the region. See p.653

✱ **Bordeaux** Lively, stylish city surrounded by some of the world's best vineyards. See p.657

✱ **Côte d'Argent** Endless beach stretched out between pine trees and wild Atlantic surf. See p.675

△ The River Sèvres at Coulon, Marais Poitevin

8

Poitou-Charentes and the Atlantic coast

Newsstands selling *Sud-Ouest* remind you where you are: this is not the Mediterranean, certainly, but in summer the quality of the light, the warm air, the fields of sunflowers and the shuttered siesta-silence of the farmhouses give you the first exciting promises of the south. The coast, on the other hand, remains unmistakably Atlantic – dunes, pine forest, reclaimed marshland and misty mud flats. While it has great charm in places, particularly out of season on the islands of **Noirmoutier**, **Ré** and **Oléron**, it's a family, camper-caravanner seaside, lacking the glamour and excitement of the Côte d'Azur. The principal port in the north, **La Rochelle**, is one of the prettiest and most distinctive towns in France. The sandy beaches are beautiful everywhere, though can occasionally be disappointing, especially the northern stretches, where the water is murky and shallow for a long way out. On the dune-backed **Côte d'Argent**, south of Bordeaux, however, the sea can be outright dangerous.

Inland, the valley of the slow and green **River Charente** epitomizes blue-overalled, Gauloise-smoking, peasant France. The towpath is accessible for long stretches, on foot or mountain bike, and there are boat trips from **Saintes** and **Cognac**. The **Marais Poitevin**, too, with its groves of poplars and island fields reticulated by countless canals and ditches, is both an unusual landscape and easy-going walking or cycling country.

But perhaps the most memorable aspect of the countryside – and indeed of towns like **Poitiers** and **Angoulême** – is the presence of exquisite Romanesque churches. This region formed a significant stretch of the medieval pilgrim routes across France and from Britain and northern Europe to the shrine of St Jacques (St James, or Santiago as the Spanish know him) at Compostela in northwest Spain, and was well endowed by its followers. The finest of the churches, among the best in all of France, are to be found in the countryside around Saintes and Poitiers: informal, highly individual and so integrated with their landscape they often seem as rooted as the trees.

Lastly, of course, remember that this is a region of seafood – fresh and cheap in every market for miles inland – and, around the modern, charismatic urban centre that is **Bordeaux**, some of the world's top vineyards.

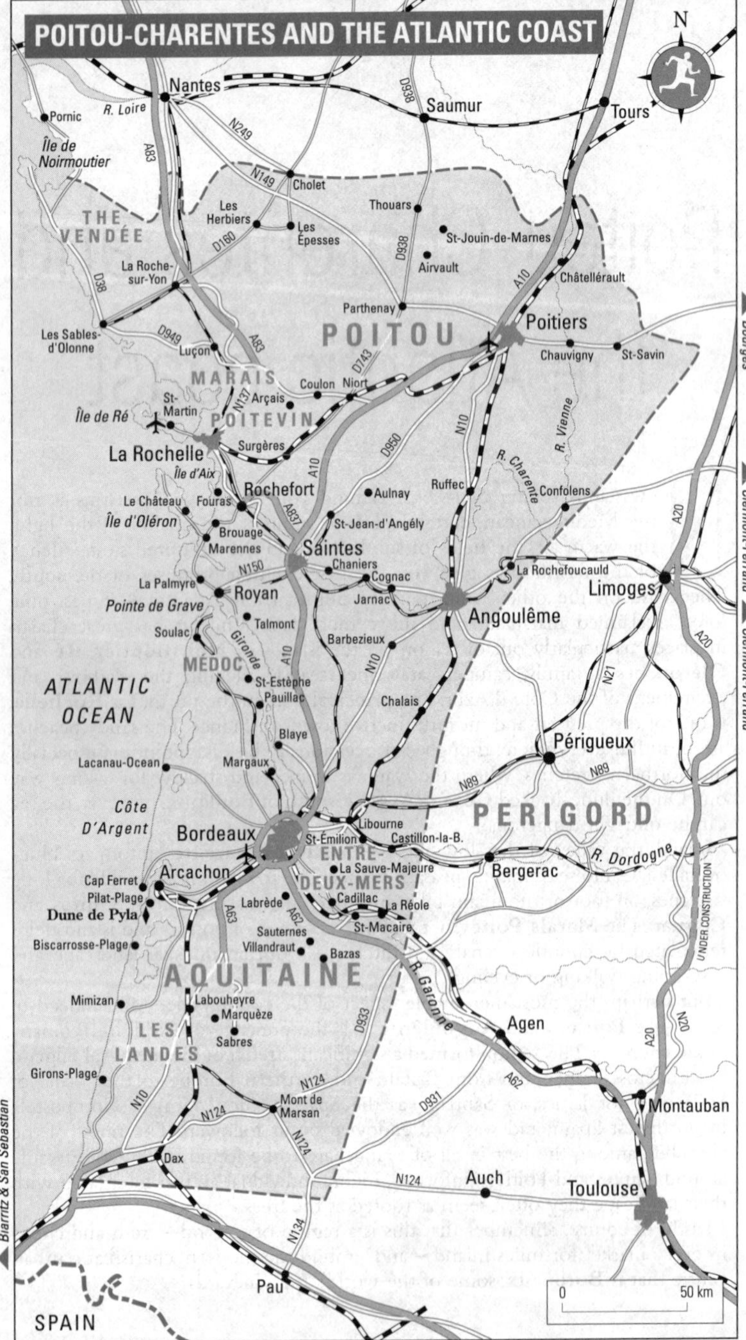
POITOU-CHARENTES AND THE ATLANTIC COAST
N
Nantes
R. Loire
Pornic
Île de Noirmoutier
A83
N249
D938
Saumur
Tours
N149
Cholet
THE VENDÉE
Les Herbiers
Les Épesses
D160
Thouars
St-Jouin-de-Marnes
Airvault
La Roche-sur-Yon
D38
Châtellérault
A10
Parthenay
Les Sables-d'Olonne
D949
Luçon
POITOU
Poitiers
Chauvigny
St-Savin
Bourges
MARAIS POITEVIN
D743
Coulon
Niort
Arçais
N137
St-Martin
Île de Ré
La Rochelle
Surgères
D950
N10
R. Vienne
R. Charente
Île d'Aix
Rochefort
Aulnay
Ruffec
Confolens
Clermont-Ferrand
Le Château
Fouras
Île d'Oléron
A837
St-Jean-d'Angély
Brouage
Marennes
Saintes
Chaniers
N150
Cognac
La Rochefoucauld
Limoges
A20
La Palmyre
Royan
Jarnac
Angoulême
Pointe de Grave
Talmont
Soulac
Gironde
Barbezieux
MÉDOC
St-Estèphe
Pauillac
N21
ATLANTIC OCEAN
Chalais
Blaye
Périgueux
Lacanau-Ocean
Margaux
N89
Côte D'Argent
PERIGORD
Libourne
Bordeaux
St-Émilion
Castillon-la-B.
ENTRE-DEUX-MERS
Bergerac
R. Dordogne
Cap Ferret
Arcachon
La Sauve-Majeure
Pilat-Plage
Dune de Pyla
Labrède
Cadillac
La Réole
A63
A62
St-Macaire
Biscarrosse-Plage
Sauternes
Villandraut
Bazas
UNDER CONSTRUCTION
AQUITAINE
R. Garonne
Mimizan
Labouheyre
Marquèze
D933
LES LANDES
Sabres
Agen
N20
Girons-Plage
N124
D931
Montauban
Mont de Marsan
Dax
Auch
Toulouse
N134
Biarritz & San Sebastian
Pau
0
50 km
SPAIN

Poitou

Most of the old province of **Poitou** comprises a huge expanse of rolling wheat fields and sunflower and maize plantations where the combines crawl and giant sprinklers shoot great arcs of white water over the fields in summertime, and villages are strung out along the valley floors. Heartland of the domains of Eleanor, Duchess of Aquitaine, whose marriage to King Henry II in 1152 brought the whole of southwest France under English control for 300 years, it is also the northern limit of the *langue d'oc*-speaking part of the country, whose Occitan dialect survives among the older generations even today.

West of **Poitiers** the open landscape of the Poitou plain gradually gives way to *bocages* – small fields enclosed by hedges and trees. The local farmers' co-operatives say that digging up woodland and creating vast windswept acreages in the name of efficiency and productivity is going out of fashion. And not just for aesthetic reasons: wind erosion has left scarcely 15cm of topsoil.

Poitiers

Heading south from Tours on the Autoroute de l'Aquitaine, you'd hardly be tempted by the cluster of towers and office blocks rising from the plain, which is all you see of **POITIERS**. But draw nearer and things look very different. Sitting on a hilltop overlooking two rivers, Poitiers is a country town with a unique charm that comes from a long and sometimes influential history – as the seat of the dukes of Aquitaine, for instance – discernible in the winding lines of the streets and the breadth of civic, domestic and ecclesiastical architectural fashions represented in its buildings. Its pedestrian precincts and wonderful central gardens make for comfortable sightseeing, while the large student population ensures a lively atmosphere in the restaurants and pavement cafés.

Arrival, information and accommodation

It's a short taxi ride (around €7) into the centre from Poitiers-Biard **airport**, located to the west of town, while the **gare SNCF** is on boulevard du Grand Cerf, part of the ring-road system that encircles the base of the hill on which Poitiers is built. There is no *gare routière*: out-of-town **buses**, run by Rapides de Poitou (Ⓣ05.49.46.27.45), leave from the train station. The **tourist office** is a fifteen-minute walk away at 45 place Charles-de-Gaulle (mid-June to mid-Sept daily 10am–10pm; mid-Sept to mid-June Mon–Sat 10am–6pm; Ⓣ05.49.41.21.24, Ⓦwww.ot-poitiers.fr), and can supply **walkers** and cyclists with various guides to the regional opportunities: the GR364 sets out from here, reaching the Vendée coast via Parthenay.

Bikes can be rented from Cyclamen, 60 bd Pont-Achard (Ⓣ05.49.88.13.25), **cars** from outlets near the train station on boulevard du Grand Cerf, such as National/Citer at no. 48 (Ⓣ05.49.58.51.58). If you can hear yourself think over the hordes of teens playing computer games, you'll enjoy the fast **Internet** connection at Cybercorner at 18 rue Charles-Gide, just off rue Carnot (daily 10am–4am; €2 per hr). The art house and independent **films** featured at Le Théâtre, place du Maréchal-Leclerc (Ⓦwww.letheatre-poitiers.com), are shown in their original language with French subtitles.

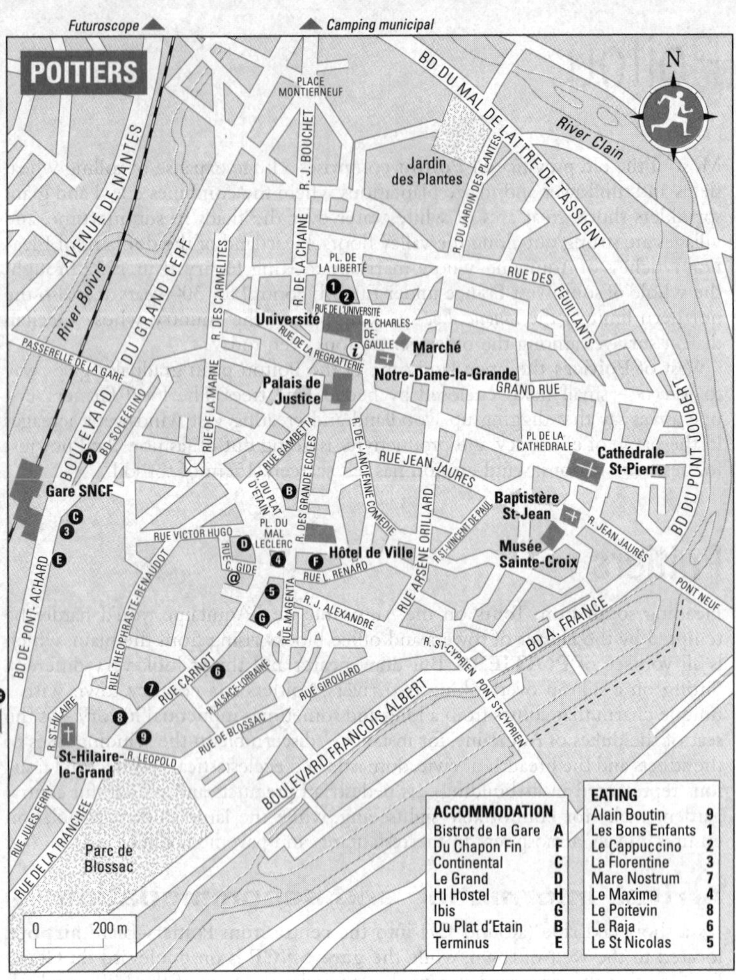

ACCOMMODATION	
Bistrot de la Gare	A
Du Chapon Fin	F
Continental	C
Le Grand	D
HI Hostel	H
Ibis	G
Du Plat d'Etain	B
Terminus	E

EATING	
Alain Boutin	9
Les Bons Enfants	1
Le Cappuccino	2
La Florentine	3
Mare Nostrum	7
Le Maxime	4
Le Poitevin	8
Le Raja	6
Le St Nicolas	5

There are plenty of **hotels** along boulevard du Grand Cerf by the train station, but the area is not particularly salubrious and at night streetwalkers are not uncommon; for more agreeable surroundings it's only a short uphill walk – boulevard Solférino, then to the right up the steep steps – to the town centre on place du Maréchal-Leclerc.

Hotels

Bistrot de la Gare 131 bd du Grand Cerf ⓣ05.49.58.56.30. Cheapest of the station hotels, with decent and reasonably priced rooms, though sometimes noisy. ❶

Du Chapon Fin 11 rue Lebascles ⓣ05.49.88.02.97, ⓦwww.hotel-chaponfin.com. Very central location – some rooms look out onto place Maréchal-Leclerc. All are clean and spacious with en-suite showers. Closed mid-Dec to mid-Jan. ❸

Continental 2 bd Solférino ⓣ05.49.37.93.93, ⓦwww.continental-poitiers.com. Comfortable two-star opposite the train station, whose soundproofed rooms all have bath or shower and TV. ❸

Le Grand 28 rue Carnot ⓣ05.49.60.90.60, ⓦwww.grandhotelpoitiers.fr. The classiest hotel in Poitiers, with Art Deco-style furnishings and a swanky bar complete with sun terrace. The large rooms all have TV and minibar; some are air-conditioned. ❺
Ibis 15 rue du Petit Bonneveau ⓣ05.49.88.30.42, ⓦwww.ibishotel.com. One of the better deals in town, a central chain hotel with comfortable rooms. It fills up with businesspeople on week nights. ❹
Du Plat d'Étain 7 rue du Plat d'Étain ⓣ05.49.41.04.80, ⓔhotelduplatdetain@orange.fr. An attractive, well-run hotel in a central quiet street just off the main shopping precinct. Closed mid-Dec to early Jan. ❸
Terminus 3 bd Pont-Achard ⓣ05.49.62.92.30, ⓕ05.49.62.92.40. One of the better hotels around the train station. Rooms are very clean, modern and soundproofed. Worthwhile reductions available for students. ❷

Hostel and campsite

HI Hostel 1 allée Roger-Tagault ⓣ05.49.30.09.70, ⓕ05.49.30.09.79. Large, modern hostel next to a swimming pool, often overrun with school groups. Take bus #7 from the *gare SNCF* to "Bellejouanne", 3km away. Well signposted, it's to the right off the N10 Angoulême road.
Camping municipal rue du Porteau ⓣ05.49.41.44.88. Grassy site with clean facilities situated 2km north of town; bus #7 towards Le Porteau. June–Sept.

The Town

The two poles of communal life in Poitiers are the tree-lined **place du Maréchal-Leclerc**, with its popular cafés and lively outdoor culture, and **place Charles-de-Gaulle** to the north, where a big and bustling food and clothes **market** takes place daily (7am–1pm). Between the two is a warren of prosperous streets – as far along as the half-timbered medieval houses of **rue de la Chaine**. Rue Gambetta cuts north past the old **Palais de Justice** (Mon–Fri 9am–6pm; free), whose nineteenth-century facade hides a much older core, including the magnificent thirteenth-century Gothic grand hall.

The church of Notre-Dame-la-Grande

The Palais de Justice looks down upon one of the greatest and most idiosyncratic churches in France, **Notre-Dame-la-Grande** (daily 8.30am–7pm), begun in the twelfth-century reign of Eleanor and renovated most recently in the mid-nineties, due to concerns about the salt from the market stalls of fishmongers and salt merchants seeping into the ground and up into the church's facade.

The weirdest and most spectacular thing about the church is the west front, which is wonderfully transformed in a display of coloured lights at 11pm every evening in summer. You can't call the facade beautiful, at least not in a conventional sense, squat and loaded as it is with detail to a degree that the modern eye could regard as fussy. And yet it's this detail which is enthralling, ranging from the domestic to the disturbingly anarchic: in the blind arch to the right of the door, a woman sits in the keystone with her hair blowing out from her head; in the frieze above, Mary places her hand familiarly on Elizabeth's pregnant belly. You see the newborn Jesus admired by a couple of daft-looking sheep and gurgling in his bathtub. Higher still are images of the apostles, and at the apex, where the eye is carried deliberately and inevitably, Christ in Majesty in an almond-shaped inset. Such elaborate sculpted facades – and domes like pine cones on turret and belfry – are the hallmarks of the Poitou brand of Romanesque. The interior, which is crudely overlaid with nineteenth-century frescoes, is not nearly as interesting.

The cathedral and around

At the eastern edge of the old town stands the **Cathédrale St-Pierre** (daily: May–Sept 8am–7.30pm; Oct–April 8am–6pm), an enormous building on whose broad, pale facade pigeons roost and plants take root. Some of the stained glass dates from the twelfth century, notably the Crucifixion in the central window of the apse, in which the features of Henry II and Eleanor are supposedly discernible. The choir stalls, too, are full of characteristic medieval detail: a coquettish Mary and Child, a peasant killing a boar, the architect at work with his dividers, a baker with a basket of loaves. But it's the grand eighteenth-century organ, the Orgue Clicquot, which is the cathedral's most striking feature, often playing deafening tunes, with organized concerts in the summer.

Opposite – literally in the middle of rue Jean-Jaurès – you come upon a chunky, square edifice with the air of a second-rate Roman temple. It's actually the mid-fourth-century **Baptistère St-Jean** (April–Sept 10.30am–12.30pm & 3–6pm; Oct–March 2.30–4.30pm; closed Tues except July & Aug; €1), reputedly the oldest Christian building in France and, until the seventeenth century, the only place in town you could have a proper baptism. The "font" was the octagonal pool sunk into the floor. Water pipes uncovered in the bottom show the water could not have been more than 30–40cm deep, which casts doubt upon the popular belief that early Christian baptism was by total immersion. There are also some very ancient and faded frescoes on the walls, including one of the emperor Constantine on horseback, and a collection of Merovingian sarcophagi. Striking a post-modern note between the cathedral and baptistry is the small domed shape of **Espace Mendès-France** (daily 2–6pm; closed Mon July & Aug; closed Sun Sept–June; €5; Ⓦ www.maison-des-sciences.org), which presents exhibitions on science and technology mainly aimed at kids and contains a state-of-the-art planetarium (€6).

Next to the baptistry is the town museum, the **Musée Sainte-Croix**, 3bis rue Jean-Jaurès (June–Sept Mon 2–6pm, Tues–Sun 10am–noon & 2–6pm; Oct–May Tues–Fri 10am–noon & 1.15–5pm, Sat–Mon 1.15–5pm; €3.70, free on Tues and 1st Sun of the month; Ⓦ www.musees-poitiers.org), featuring an interesting collection of farming implements. There's also a good Gallo-Roman section with some handsome glass, pottery and sculpture, notably a white marble Minerva of the first century. Another possibility is to take a more relaxed walk along the **riverside path** – on the right across Pont Neuf – upstream to Pont St-Cyprien. On the far bank, you'll see a characteristic feature of every French provincial town: neat, well-manured *potagers* – vegetable gardens – coming down to the water's edge with a little mud quay at the end and a moored punt.

The Parc de Blossac and St-Hilaire

Towards the southern tip of the old town, where the hump of the hill narrows to a point, the **Parc de Blossac** is a great spot to sit among the clipped limes and gravelled walks, to watch the *boules* and munch a baguette. Nearby is a UNESCO world heritage site, the eleventh-century **church of St-Hilaire-le-Grand** on rue du Doyenné, which unbelievably was pruned of part of its nave in the nineteenth century, though the chevet from the outside is still a fine sight; the apse has a particularly beautiful group of chapels surrounding it.

Eating and drinking

Poitiers offers good opportunities for fine **food** whatever your culinary persuasions – there's a good range of ethnic options to try if you're bored with French cuisine. If you're really keen to make your money last, you can ask about student/youth offers at the Centre Information Jeunesse (CIJ), 64 rue Gambetta (Ⓣ 05.49.60.68.78). The town's **nightlife** is best around the university, particularly in the bars along rue Carnot and on place de la Liberté, and posters announcing live music and dancing are easy to spot throughout town.

Alain Boutin 65 rue Carnot ⓣ05.49.88.25.53. A good bet for regional dishes like *cailles au pineau* (quails cooked in a brandy liqueur), with a small, carefully chosen selection; menus from €21. Closed Sat & Mon lunch, all Sun & first half of Jan.

Les Bons Enfants 11bis rue Cloche Perse ⓣ05.49.41.49.82. Good value for money: serves lunchtime menu at €9 on weekdays, evenings from €18. Try the scrumptious house speciality of *escargots* melted in a parsley-buttered baked potato. Closed Sun evening & Mon.

Le Cappuccino 5 rue de l'Université ⓣ05.49.88.27.39. One of a number of Italian restaurants in this area, with menus starting at €16.50 and a wide range of ice cream. Closed Sun & Mon.

La Florentine 1 bd Pont-Achard ⓣ05.49.58.27.95. This smart Italian restaurant offers good pizza and pasta at decent prices. A solid choice if you're staying near the station and don't fancy the walk up the hill.

Mare Nostrum 74 rue Carnot ⓣ05.49.41.58.80. Mediterranean specialities including *moussaka* and *kawage*, a baked ratatouille-style dish with aubergine and *haricots verts*. Closed Sat & Sun lunch.

Le Maxime 4 rue St-Nicolas ⓣ05.49.41.09.55. *Gastronomique* cuisine at its finest : delicious dishes served in an elegant setting. Lunch here is popular with the well-to-do business crowd. Evening menus at €31 and €50. Closed Sat and Sun.

Le Poitevin 76 rue Carnot ⓣ05.49.88.35.04. Seasonal, local food at decent prices, in an attractive interior with log fire in winter. Menus from €22. Closed Sun evening.

Le Raja 49 rue Carnot ⓣ05.49.39.24.57. A good-value Indian restaurant with lunchtime menus from €12 and a good range of vegetarian options. Closed Sun evening.

Le St Nicolas 7 rue Carnot ⓣ05.49.41.44.48. Actually located on a small traffic-free lane off rue Carnot, meaning you can eat outside peacefully. Traditional food with a contemporary feel. Menus €16 & €20. Closed Wed & Sun lunch.

Around Poitiers

The area immediately surrounding Poitiers is dominated by the post-modern cinema theme park **Futuroscope**, to the north, though more traditional attractions can be found at nearby **Chauvigny** and **St-Savin**, which boast medieval centres and two fine Romanesque churches, with some great sculpture and frescoes. Less inspired are the small town of **Parthenay** and the larger city of **Niort**, neither of which is worth a special trip, though both make useful stopovers for provisions before you head further west into the verdant marshes of the **Marais Poitevin**.

Futuroscope

Poitiers' best-known attraction is the giant high-tech film theme park called **Futuroscope: Le Parc Européen de l'Image** (ⓦwww.futuroscope.com), 8km north of the city, a collection of virtual-reality rides which draw onlookers into the action on screen, with the result that you feel you're being flung around or catapulted through the solar system in a vertigo-inducing 3-D nightmare. Futuroscope opens new attractions every year, and recent additions include various opportunities to interact with robots, taking the park a step beyond the virtual-reality films.

The futuristic **cinema pavilions** are set in several acres of greenery around a series of undulating lakes, and the 24 attractions take some getting around, with plenty of walking between them, so it's wise to arrive early to beat the huge queues. To see everything in the park in one day, with time off for lunch, takes about ten exhausting hours, and as well as taking in the screen entertainment, you should give yourself time to ride the oversized floating bicycles on

Futuroscope practicalities and attractions

The Paris Montparnasse–Poitiers TGV stops at Futuroscope; there are also regular buses (line #9; €1.20 return) from Poitiers' Hôtel de Ville or *gare SNCF*. The park is open all year apart from January, from 10am until shortly after sunset, when the laser show has finished. **Tickets** are valid for one or two days (adult one-day pass €31, child aged 5–16 €24; adult two-day pass €59, child €44) and in the summer you can get a ticket just for the evening laser show (adult €15, child €10). To avoid queues at the park, purchase tickets in advance from the Maison de Tourisme (the tourist office for the Vienne region) at 33 place Charles-de-Gaulle in Poitiers (Ⓣ05.49.37.48.48, Ⓦwww.tourisme-vienne.com). **Food** is predictably expensive inside, and a picnic lunch can cut costs substantially. There are various deals available that include admission plus a wide selection of accommodation on site, the cheapest of which costs €74 per adult in a four-bed room.

Attractions

Le Cinéma 360° Spain's contribution to Seville Expo '92 is now housed here permanently.

Cyber Avenue 72 multimedia kiosks with virtual games and video games.

Danse avec les Robots Brush up on your dance-floor moves, surrounded by robots showing you how it's done.

Le Défi d'Atlantis A virtual race through the underwater streets and houses of the lost city.

Destination Cosmos A vast planetarium brings the universe to life using images from the Hubble telescope.

Imax Solido An enormous screen, measuring 540 square metres, in conjunction with 3-D vision glasses brings you face to face with dinosaurs, animals or stunning landscapes – depending on what film is showing.

Zoo des Robots Six giant robotic animals parade around, allowing children to pet them and, apparently, learn more about the natural world.

the park's lakes. To orientate yourself, head first for **La Gyrotour** where a lift takes you to the top of the high rotating tower and you can get the full effect of the futuristic scenario.

All the films are in French, with English commentaries on headphones often available, but as these are not very effective, and as it's the visual impact that's most important anyway, it's better to do without. Apart from the films and robots, there's a **laser show**, "La Forêt des Rêves", a display of music, colour and effects focused on the park's dancing fountains (shows start daily just after sunset).

Chauvigny

Twenty-three kilometres east of Poitiers, **CHAUVIGNY** is a busy market town on the banks of the Vienne with half a dozen porcelain factories and lumber mills providing work for the area. Overlooking the bustling *ville basse*, the old town boasts five **medieval castles** whose imposing ruins stand atop a precipitous rock spur, but its pride and joy are the sculpted capitals in the Romanesque **church of St-Pierre**. If you take rue du Château, which winds up the spur from the central place de la Poste, you'll pass the ruins of the Château Baronnial, which belonged to the bishops of Poitiers and now hosts displays by birds of prey, then the better-preserved Château d'Harcourt, before coming to the attractive and unusual east end of St-Pierre. A short walk away on the place du Donjon, there's an interesting **Musée d'Archéologie** (Mon–Fri 10am–12.30pm & 2.30–6.30pm, Sat & Sun 2.30–6.30pm; €4.60), displaying well-preserved tools and pottery. The same ticket gets you into the twelfth-century tower, the **Donjon de Gouzon** (same hours as the museum) which has a stunning 360-degree panorama out over the town.

Inside, the church of St-Pierre is damp and a little shabby, but the choir capitals are a visual treat. Each one is different, evoking a terrifying, nightmarish world. Graphically illustrated monsters – bearded, moustached, winged, scaly, human-headed with manes of flame – grab hapless mortals – naked, upside-down and puny – ripping their bowels out and crunching their heads. The only escape offered is in the naively serene events of the Nativity. On the second capital on the south side of the choir, for instance, the Angel Gabriel announces Christ's birth to the shepherds while just around the corner the Archangel Michael weighs souls in hand-held scales and a devil tries to grab one for his dinner.

Coinciding your visit with the Saturday or Thursday **market** gives an extra dimension to a day-trip here. Held between the church of Notre-Dame and the river, it offers a mouthwatering selection of food – oysters, prawns, crayfish, cheeses galore and pâtés in aspic. The cafés are fun, too, bursting with noisy wine-flushed farmers.

There are five **buses** a day from Poitiers to Chauvigny, which will drop you in the *ville basse*. The **tourist office** is located in the old town at 5 rue St-Pierre (June & Sept Tues–Sun 10am–12.30pm & 2–6.30pm; July & Aug daily 10am–1pm & 2–7pm; Oct–March Tues–Fri 2–6pm, Sat 9am–noon – in the winter months the tourist office moves to a small booth on the arcade in front of the *mairie*; ⓣ05.49.46.39.01, ⓦwww.chauvigny.cg86.fr). If you want to **stay** overnight, your best bet is *Le Lion d'Or*, 8 rue du Marché (ⓣ05.49.46.30.28, ⓕ05.49.47.74.28; ❸) which also has a restaurant with menus from €11. Chauvigny's municipal **campsite** is just east of the centre on rue de la Fontaine (ⓣ05.49.46.31.94; ⓕ05.49.46.40.60; May–Sept). To **eat**, step down into *La Bigorne*, on place du Donjon next to the church; resembling a hobbit watering-hole, it serves excellent crêpes and omelettes.

St-Savin

You need to get an early start from Poitiers if you want to make a single day-trip by public transport to see both Chauvigny and **ST-SAVIN**, which is scarcely more than a hamlet in comparison with bustling Chauvigny.

The bus sets you down beside the abbey near the modern bridge over the poplar-lined River Gartempe; walk downstream a little way to the medieval bridge for a perfect view of the **abbey church**, now listed as a UNESCO monument of universal importance. Built in the eleventh century, possibly on the site of a church founded by Charlemagne, it rises strong and severe above the gazebos, vegetable gardens and lichened tile roofs of the houses at its feet. Inside, steps descend to the narthex and from there to the floor of the nave, stretching out to the raised choir: high, narrow, barrel-vaulted and flanked by bare round columns, their capitals deeply carved with interlacing foliage. The entire vault is covered with paintings, and, though colours are few, they're full of light and grace, depicting scenes from the stories of Genesis and Exodus. Some are instantly recognizable: Noah's three-decked ark, or Pharaoh's horses rearing at the engulfing waves of the Red Sea. Attached to the abbey is a fascinating multimedia **museum** of Romanesque art history with a number of innovative exhibits about medieval monastic life and architecture (Feb & March daily 1.30–5pm; April–June & Sept–Dec Mon–Sat 10am–12.30pm & 2–6pm, Sun

2–6pm; July & Aug daily 10am–7pm; Ⓦwww.pays-montmorillonnais.com). Be warned, though, it is all in French.

You'll find **rooms** at the squeaky-clean *Hôtel de France*, 38 place de la République (Ⓣ05.49.48.19.03, Ⓔhotel-saint-savin@orange.fr; ❸), which has a good restaurant serving menus from €17 (closed Sun eve & Mon except in July & Aug). There's a municipal **campsite**, too (Ⓣ05.49.48.18.02; mid-May to mid-Sept).

Parthenay and around

Directly west of Poitiers, and served by regular SNCF buses, the attractive small town of **PARTHENAY** was once an important stop on the pilgrim routes to Compostela and is now the site of a major cattle market every Wednesday. It's not a place to make a special detour for, but it's worth a stopover if you're heading north to Brittany or west to the sea.

Parthenay's medieval heart is well worth a look, even if nothing extraordinary stands out. Rue Jean-Jaurès and rue de la Saunerie cut in through the largely pedestrian shopping precinct to the Gothic **Porte de l'Horloge**, the fortified gateway to the old citadelle on a steep-sided neck of land above a loop of the River Thouet.

Through the gateway, on rue de la Citadelle, the attractively simple Romanesque **church of Sainte-Croix** faces the *mairie* across a small garden, which offers views over the ramparts and the **gully of St-Jacques**, with its medieval houses and vegetable plots climbing the opposite slope. Further along rue de la Citadelle is a handsome but badly damaged Romanesque door, all that remains of the castle chapel of **Notre-Dame-de-la-Couldre**. Of the castle itself, practically nothing is left, but from the tip of the spur where it once stood you can look down on the twin-towered **gateway** and the **Pont St-Jacques**, a thirteenth-century bridge through which the nightly flocks of pilgrims poured into the town for shelter and security. To reach it, turn left under the Tour de l'Horloge and down the medieval lane known as **Vaux St-Jacques**. The lane is highly evocative of that period, with crooked half-timbered dwellings crowding up to the bridge.

Practicalities

Finding your way around Parthenay is easy. From the **gare SNCF**, avenue de Gaulle leads directly west to the central square, the place du Drapeau, from where you can follow rue Jean-Jaurès to the medieval centre. The **tourist office** (Mon–Fri 8.30am–12.30pm & 2–6pm, Sat 2.30–6.30pm; Ⓣ05.49.64.24.24, Ⓦwww.cc-parthenay.fr) is on the far side of the citadelle at 8 rue de la Vau Saint-Jaques, right next to the old bridge.

If you're after **accommodation**, you'll find the smart two-star *Hôtel du Nord*, 86 av de Gaulle, opposite the station (Ⓣ05.49.94.29.11; ❸; restaurant from €14, closed Sat), or there is the newly renovated and very comfortable *Saint Jacques*, av de 114ème RI (Ⓣ05.49.64.33.33, Ⓔhotel-saint-jaques@district-parthenay.fr; ❸). A **hostel** sits some way from the centre at 16 rue Blaise-Pascal (Ⓣ05.49.95.46.89), with a central annexe at 115 bd Meilleraye: phone first and they will let you into the annexe. **Campers** have to head to the four-star site at *Le Bois Vert* (Ⓣ05.49.64.78.43, Ⓔbois-vert@orange.fr; April–Sept), part of the huge Base de Loisirs riverbank recreation area, about 3km west of Parthenay on the D949.

As for **eating**, Parthenay has the usual range of restaurants for a provincial town: Italian, Tunisian and Chinese, as well as traditional French. Best of the latter is *Le Fin Gourmet*, 28 rue Ganne (Ⓣ05.49.64.04.53; closed Sun eve, Mon & Wed lunch), where high-quality cuisine combines with a jovial atmosphere; menus range from €33 to €38. *L'Esplanade*, by the main square at 85 bd Meilleraye (Ⓣ05.49.64.00.16; closed Sat evening & Sun out of season) has good inexpensive menus from €9, which can be enjoyed sitting outside in the square.

Around Parthenay

There are three more beautiful **Romanesque churches** within easy reach of Parthenay. One – with a sculpted facade depicting a mounted knight hawking – is only a twenty-minute walk away on the Niort road, at **Parthenay-le-Vieux**. The others are at **Airvault**, 20km northeast of Parthenay and easily accessible on the Parthenay–Thouars SNCF bus route, and **St-Jouin-de-Marnes**, 9km northeast of Airvault (no public transport). A trip to St-Jouin can easily be combined with a visit to the sixteenth-century **Château d'Oiron**, 8.5km to the northwest. Alternatively, you could go on north to **Thouars**, 21km from Airvault or 16km from St-Jouin, to see the abbey church of St-Laon; here there are accommodation options in the form of cheap hotels and a municipal **campsite**.

Niort

NIORT, 50km southwest of Poitiers, and connected to it by regular trains, makes a useful stopover if your goal is the Marais Poitevin. The town itself has enough of interest to fill a pleasant morning's stroll, and it's the last place before the marshes to get a really wide choice of provisions. The most interesting part of the town is the mainly pedestrian area around **rue Victor-Hugo** and **rue St-Jean**, full of stone-fronted or half-timbered medieval houses. Coming from the *gare SNCF*, take rue de la Gare as far as avenue de Verdun, with the post office on the corner, then turn right into place de la Brèche. Rue Ricard leaves the square on the left; rue Victor-Hugo is its continuation, following the line of the medieval market in a gully separating the two small hills on which Niort is built. Up to the left, opposite the end of rue St-Jean, is the old **town hall**, a triangular building of the early sixteenth century with lantern, belfry and ornamental machicolations, perhaps capable of repelling drunken revellers but no match for catapult or sledgehammer.

At the end of the street is the river, the **Sèvre Niortaise**, with gardens and trees along the bank and, over the bridge, the ruins of a glove factory, the last vestige of Niort's once thriving leather industry. At the time of the Revolution, it kept more than thirty cavalry regiments in breeches. Today Niort's biggest industry is insurance: the most bourgeois town in France, so it's said, because of the prosperity brought by the large number of major insurance firms making their headquarters here. Accordingly, restaurants are usually packed at lunchtime, and well-heeled shoppers throng the pedestrianized streets, giving it a fairly lively, affluent feel.

Just downstream, opposite a riverside car park, is the **market hall** (with a café doing a good cheap lunch) and, beyond, vast and unmistakable on a slight rise, the keep of a **castle** (currently closed) begun by Henry II of England.

If you want to see the surrounding Marais area, the most pleasurable way is by bike – it's completely flat and small enough to cover pretty well in three days.

Practicalities

The **gare SNCF** is on rue Mazagran, with the **gare routière** just next door – though in reality it's no larger than a bus shelter, and local buses all leave from place de la Brèche anyway. The excellent **tourist office** at 16 rue de Petit St-Jean (July & Aug Mon–Fri 9.30am–7pm, Sat 10am–5pm, Sun 10am–1pm; Sept–June Mon–Fri 9.30am–6.30pm, Sat 9.30am–12.30pm & 1.30–6.30pm; ⓣ05.49.24.18.79, ⓦwww.niortourisme.com) has plenty of information about walking itineraries around the Marais and can help with reserving hotel rooms; for more rustic accommodation in the Marais itself, contact Gîtes de France, at 15 rue Thiers (ⓣ05.49.24.00.42). You can rent cars at any of the agencies that line rue de la Gare by the station, for example Avis at no. 89 (ⓣ05.49.24.36.98). Annoyingly, there is nowhere to rent **bikes** in Niort, but you'll find several options in the Marais Poitevin (see below). **Internet** access is available at Médi@clic, 8 rue Porte St-Jean (Mon–Sat 2–7pm, €3 per hour).

Restaurants to head for include *L'Atelier de Mets,* on 247 av de la Rochelle (ⓣ05.49.79.41.06; closed Sun), for traditional Marais Poitevin specialities (menus from €16), and, for lunches, *Sucrée Salée*, at 2 rue du Temple (ⓣ05.49.24.77.16), which specializes in tarts and crumbles *à l'anglaise*; menus from €10.

Accommodation

There's the usual crop of **hotels** close to the station, while more upmarket options are located on avenue de Paris, just off place de Verdun.

Ambassadeur 82 rue de la Gare ⓣ05.49.24.00.38, ⓦwww.ambassadeur-hotel.com. A good deal, with quite luxurious rooms and a pleasant, simply furnished bar to relax in. ❸

Grand 32 av de Paris ⓣ05.49.24.22.21, ⓦwww.grandhotel-niort.com. A sparkling, newly renovated hotel, whose higher rooms look out over the town centre. Each room has been decorated with its own individual colour scheme. ❺

De la Paix 107 rue de la Gare ⓣ05.49.24.17.90. A cheap option, right outside the train station, with comfortable rooms for the price – all have TV. ❷

Le Paris 12 av de Paris ⓣ05.49.24.93.78, ⓦwww.hotelparis79.com. A smart, well-run hotel, part of the Citotel chain. It has its own bar, and is in a handy location for various restaurant options. ❸

Saint Jean 21 av St-Jean-d'Angély ⓣ05.49.79.20.76, ⓕ05.49.35.03.27. Run by an extremely friendly and helpful couple, and offering simple rooms with TV. Showers and toilets on the landing are very clean, and it's closer to the centre than the other options. ❶

The Marais Poitevin

The **Marais Poitevin** is a strange, lazy landscape of fens and meadows, shielded by poplar trees and crisscrossed by an elaborate system of canals, dykes and slow-flowing rivers. Recently declared a regional park, it is known as "La Venise Verte" – the Green Venice – and indeed, farmers in this area frequently travel through the marshes in flat-bottomed punts as their fields lack dry-land access. A tourist industry of sorts has been developing around the villages, so it's best to avoid weekends, when evidence of the transformation is all too clear.

Access to the eastern edge of the marsh is easiest at the whitewashed village of **COULON**, on the River Sèvre, just 11km from Niort. The two or three buses per day set you down outside the **tourist office** on rue Gabriel-Auchier (July & Aug daily 10am–1pm & 2–6pm; Sept–June Mon–Sat 10am–1pm & 2–5.30pm; ⓣ05.49.35.99.29, ⓦwww.marais-poitevin.fr). From there it's a short walk to the central place de L'Eglise where **punts** can be rented, with or without a guide, from La Trigale (ⓣ05.49.35.14.14, ⓦwww.lemaraispoitevin.com), and **bikes**, tandems and pedal-powered family vehicles are all available from La Libellule (ⓣ05.49.35.83.42, ⓦwww.lalibellule.com).

There are two **hotels** in the village, both likely to be full in season: the family-run *Central*, 4 rue d'Autremont (ⓣ05.49.35.90.20, ⓦwww.hotel-lecentral-coulon.com; ❹; closed Sun & Mon, and mid-Jan to early Feb), and the nicely situated *Au Marais*, 46–48 quai Louis-Tardiy (ⓣ05.49.35.90.43,

Ⓦwww.hotel-aumarais.com; ❺; closed mid-Dec to late Jan). If you're **camping**, head for the attractively sited *Camping Venise Verte* (Ⓣ05.49.35.90.36; open April–Oct), in a meadow about 2km downstream (a 25-minute walk), or the municipal campsite *La Niquière* (Ⓣ05.49.35.81.19; May–Sept), north of Coulon on the road to Benet. The best eating option in Coulon is the regional cuisine served up at *Le Central*'s characterful **restaurant**; with generous servings, a well-deserved reputation and a menu from €17.50, it's wise to book.

An excellent place to rent **bikes** is La Bicyclette Verte (Ⓣ05.49.35.42.56, Ⓦwww.bicyclette-verte.com; €9 per day), on route de St Hilaire-la-Palud in the village of **ARÇAIS**, 10km west of Coulon; they also have children's bikes and tandems. If you're walking the marshes, it's best to stick to the lanes, since cross-country routes tend to end in fields surrounded by water, and you have to backtrack continually. Once you're away from the riverside road from Coulon to Arçais, there's practically no traffic, just meadows and cows. At the seaward end of the marsh – the area south of **LUÇON** – the landscape changes, becoming all straight lines and open fields of wheat and sunflowers. The villages cap low mounds that were once islands.

The Vendée

The northwest of the Poitou region falls within the rural *département* of the **Vendée**, whose main attraction is the eighty-kilometre stretch of coast between chic **Les Sables-d'Olonne** and the northernmost tip of the scenic **Île de Noirmoutier**. Inland, there is little of interest, aside from a marvellous summertime *spectacle* at **Les Épesses**.

Les Sables-d'Olonne

The area around **LES SABLES-D'OLONNE** and northwards has been heavily developed with Costa-style apartment blocks. If you're passing through, though, it's worth having a look at the surprisingly good modern art section in the **Musée de l'Abbaye Sainte-Croix** on rue Verdun (mid-June to Sept Tues–Sun 10am–noon & 2.30–6.30pm; Oct to mid-June Tues–Sun 2.30–5.30pm; €4.60) and the collection of 150 classic autos and other vehicles at the **Musée d'Automobile**, 8km southeast of town on the road to Talmont (April, May, Sept & Oct daily 9.30am–noon & 2–6.30pm; June–Aug daily 9.30am–7pm; Ⓦwww.musee-auto-vendee.com; €7.80). The main reason to stay, though, is the town's vast curve of clean, beautiful **beach**, which lures hordes in the summer.

Hotels get booked up well in advance for July and August, but you could try *Hôtel Antoine*, 60 rue Napoléon (Ⓣ02.51.95.08.36, Ⓦwww.antoinehotel.com; open April–Oct; ❹), with spacious, comfortable rooms. *La Vague*, a few blocks from the beach at 8 rue des Escoliers (Ⓣ & Ⓕ02.51.32.05.29; ❷) is the cheapest stay in town and open year round. For a bit more money and comfort, try the *Arundel* (Ⓣ02.51.32.03.77, Ⓦwww.arundel-hotel.fr; ❻–❽) at 8 bd Franklin-Roosevelt just behind the tourist office; the more expensive rooms have Jacuzzi baths and (partial) views of the water; prices drop by up to forty percent out of season. The municipal **campsite** (Ⓣ02.51.95.10.42, Ⓦwww.chadotel.com; April–Oct) is on rue des Roses, 400m from the beach; there are several more campsites in the Pironnière district, 3km south of town on the D949. For more accommodation options, ask at the **tourist office** on 1 promenade Joffre (July & Aug daily 9am–7pm; Sept–June Mon–Sat 9am–12.30pm & 2–6pm, Sun

10.30am–noon; ⓣ02.51.96.85.85, ⓦwww.lessablesdolonne-tourisme.com). The greatest selection of **restaurants** is on quai des Boucanniers, reached via the shuttle ferry which crosses the port channel (daily 6am–midnight; €0.85). There's **Internet** access at Mediafun 85, 52 av de Gaulle just next to the train station (Mon 2.30–7pm, Tues–Sat 9.30am–noon & 2–7pm; €3 per hour).

The Île de Noirmoutier

The twenty-kilometre-long **Île de Noirmoutier**, 60km north of Les Sables-d'Olonne on the D38, was an early monastic settlement of the seventh century; now it has bowed to pilgrims of a different type, serving as a relatively plush tourist resort. Although tourism is the island's main economy, it doesn't dominate everything. Salt marshes here are still worked, spring potatoes sown and fishes fished. The island can be reached in three hours by bus from Les Sables, and is connected to the shore by both bridge and the *passage de gois,* a channel across which you can drive your car when the tides are low.

Noirmoutier-en-L'Île

The island town, **NOIRMOUTIER-EN-L'ÎLE**, is a low-key place but has a twelfth-century **castle**, a **church** with a Romanesque crypt, an excellent **market** (Tues, Fri & Sun) in place de la République and most of the island's **nightlife** in the form of piano bars with longer-than-usual café hours. Campsites are dotted around the island – maps are available from the **tourist office** (July & Aug Mon–Sat 9am–1.30pm & 2.30–6.30pm, Sun 9am–1pm; Sept–June Mon–Sat 9am–12.30pm & 2–6pm,; ⓣ02.51.39.80.71, ⓦwww.ile-noirmoutier.com) on the main road from the bridge at Barbatre. **Bikes** can be rented from Vel-hop, 55 av Joseph-Pineau in Noirmoutier (ⓣ02.51.39.01.34).

Food options are pretty easy to come by, with a number of **restaurants** in the centre. Some good people-watching can be had on place St-Louis at *Le Blé Noir*, which serves excellent crêpes and *galettes* starting at €4.

Hotels

Bois de la Chaise 23 av de la Victoire ⓣ02.51.39.04.62, ⓕ02.51.39.11.89. A modern hotel with pleasant rooms, all with shower and TV. ❹

Chez Bébert 37 av Joseph-Pineau ⓣ02.51.39.08.97. The place to head if you're on a tight budget. Rooms are small but clean and adequate. ❶

Les Capucines 38 av de la Victoire ⓣ02.51.39.06.82, ⓔcapucineshotel@aol.com. An elegant option, just down the road from Bois de la Chaise. Rooms have all the trimmings and there's a good restaurant with menus from €23. ❺

Fleur de Sel rue des Saulniers ⓣ02.51.39.09.07, ⓦwww.fleurdesel.fr. The most upmarket hotel on the island, all rooms are luxurious, and the more expensive ones have private terraces. ❼–❽

The rest of the island

As for exploring the island, the western coast, with its great curves of sand, resembles the mainland, while the northern side dips in and out of little bays with rocky promontories between. Inland, were it not for the saltwater dykes, the horizon would suggest that you were far away from the sea. The more southerly resorts, though built up, have not been the main targets for developers; for accommodation in this part of the island, head for the village of Barbatre; *Le Goéland*, 15 rte du Gois (ⓣ02.51.39.68.66, ⓦwww.hotel-legoeland.fr.st; ❹), is just 300m from the beach and has its own private outside terrace. In the village centres there are still the one-storey houses that you see throughout La Vendée and southern Brittany – whitewashed and ochre-tiled with decorative brick-work around the windows and S- or Z-shaped coloured bars on the shutters.

During the spring, the weather is fickle – sunny one moment, stormy the next – and the heat of the summer cultivates a vicious mosquito population.

Les Épesses

Some 80km inland from Les Sables (on the N160 if you're driving), at the ruined **Château du Puy du Fou** in the village of **LES ÉPESSES**, a remarkable lakeside extravaganza takes place during the summer months (June–Sept Fri & Sat 10.30pm; 1hr 45min; booking essential, ⓣ02.51.64.11.11, ⓦwww.puydufou.com; €23). It's a weird affair: the enactment of the life of a local peasant from the Middle Ages to World War II, complete with fireworks, lasers, dances on the lake and Comédie Française voice-overs. The story, available in English through a headset translation (€7) is interesting but incidental – the massive spectacle itself is the real attraction, and all proceeds from the event go to charity.

To get to Les Épesses by public **transport**, you'll need to venture to **Cholet** (connected by train from Nantes) and take a bus south from there; Puy du Fou itself is 2.5km from Les Épesses on the D27 to Chambretaud. The tourist office in Cholet (ⓣ02.41.49.80.00) can provide information about transport. There is one reasonably priced **hotel** in Les Épesses, *La Crémaillère*, 2 rue de la Libération (ⓣ & ⓕ02.51.57.30.01; ❷), and further accommodation options 10km west in **Les Herbiers**.

The coast around La Rochelle

The coast around **La Rochelle** – especially the **islands** – is great for young families, with miles of safe sandy beaches and shallow water. Be aware, however, that in August, unless you're camping or book in advance, accommodation is a near-insuperable problem. Out of season you can't rely on sunny weather, but that shouldn't deter you since the quiet misty seascapes and working fishing ports have a melancholy romance all their own. La Rochelle and **Royan** in the south are the best bases, and are both served by train. Away from these centres – if you're not driving – you'll have to take pot luck with the rather quirky bus routes.

La Rochelle and around

LA ROCHELLE is the most attractive and unspoilt seaside town in France. Thanks to the foresight of 1970s mayor Michel Crépeau, its historic seventeenth- to eighteenth-century centre and waterfront were plucked from the clutches of the developers and its streets freed of traffic for the delectation of

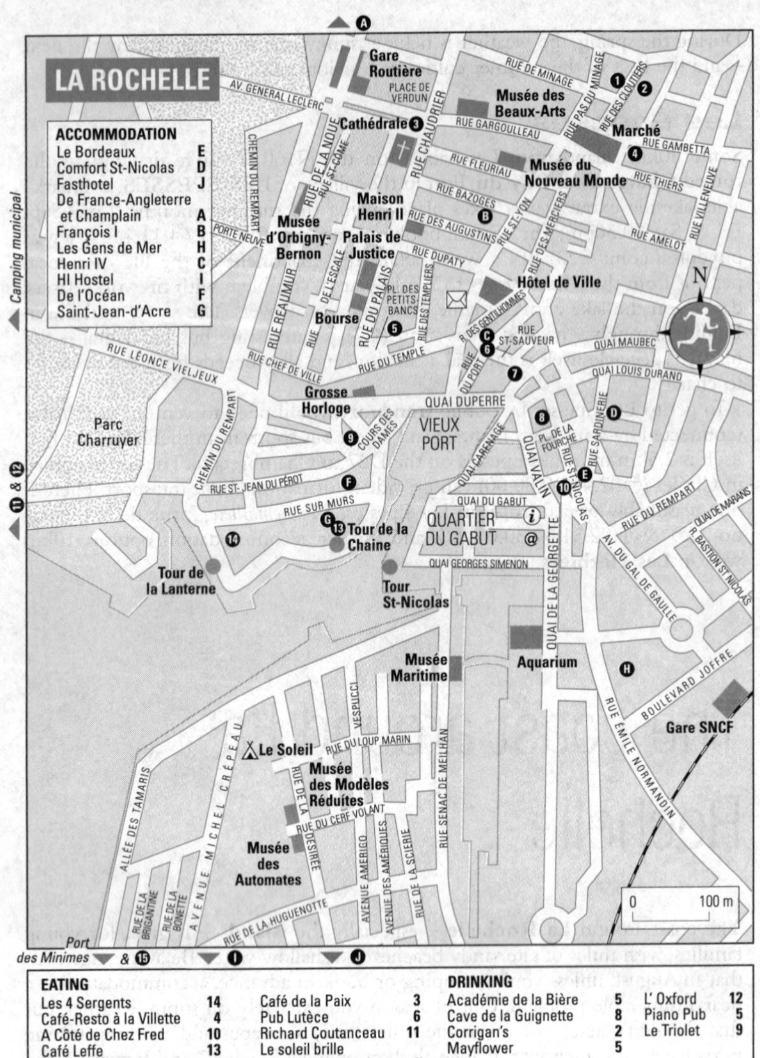

pedestrians. A real shock-horror outrage at the time, the policy has become standard practice for preserving old town centres across the country – more successful than Crépeau's picturesque yellow bicycle plan, designed to relieve the traffic problem.

La Rochelle has a long history, as you would expect of such a sheltered Atlantic port. Eleanor of Aquitaine gave it a charter in 1199, which released it from its feudal obligations, and it rapidly became a port of major importance, trading in salt and wine and skilfully exploiting the Anglo–French quarrels. The Wars of Religion, however, were particularly destructive for La Rochelle. It

△ Vieux Port, La Rochelle

turned Protestant and, because of its strategic importance, drew the remorseless enmity of Cardinal Richelieu, who laid siege to it in 1627. To the dismay of the townspeople, who reasoned that no one could effectively blockade seasoned mariners like themselves, he succeeded in sealing the harbour approaches with a dyke. The English dispatched the Duke of Buckingham to their aid, but he was caught napping on the Île de Ré and badly defeated. By the end of 1628 Richelieu had starved the city into submission. Out of the pre-siege population of 28,000, only 5000 survived. The walls were demolished and the city's privileges revoked. La Rochelle later became the principal port for trade with the French colonies in the Caribbean Antilles and Canada. Indeed, many of the settlers, especially in Canada, came from this part of France.

Arrival, information and transport

Ryanair now runs daily flights here from London's Stansted airport, which accounts for the large number of Brits who visit. Bus #7 runs every twenty minutes between the **airport** and town centre (Mon–Sat 7am–7.20pm; €1.20; 10min) Once in town, finding your way around La Rochelle is very straightforward. Arriving by train at the elaborate **gare SNCF** on boulevard Joffre, take avenue de Gaulle opposite to reach the town centre; on the left as you reach the waterfront you'll see the efficient **tourist office**, on quai du Gabut (April–June & Sept Mon–Sat 9am–6pm, Sun 10.30am–5.30pm; July & Aug Mon–Sat 9am–8pm, Sun 10.30am–5.30pm; Oct–March Mon–Sat 10am–12.30pm & 1.30–6pm, Sun 10am–1pm; ⓣ05.46.41.14.68, ⓦwww.larochelle-tourisme.com), which has excellent maps and a €6.60 **museum pass** covering the Nouveau

Monde, the Orbigny-Bernon and the Beaux-Arts. The office also leads morning **walking tours** of the old town (July & Aug Mon–Sat 10.30am, Sept–June Tues, Sat & Sun 10.30am; €6), and rather more fun two-hour evening tours of the city, led by a local donning medieval garb (mid-June to mid-Sept Thurs 8.30pm; €8). In addition, the **CDIJ Youth Centre**, 2 rue des Gentilshommes (Ⓣ05.46.41.16.36), has an information service for young people. Most things you'll want to see are in the area behind the waterfront; in effect, between the harbour and the place de Verdun, where the **gare routière** is situated. If you need an **Internet** connection, head to Akromicro, rue de l'Aimable Nanette (10am–midnight; €3 per hour).

Transport

The bus terminal for the town's efficient **public transport** system is also located on place de Verdun, and once you've stowed your luggage at your hotel, you can use **bikes** to get around: there are two free municipal **bike parks**, heir to Michel Crépeau's original pick-up-and-leave scheme: one in place de Verdun by the *gare routière* (Mon–Sat 7.30am–7pm, Sun 1.15–7pm), the other on quai Valin near the tourist office (May–Sept only 9am–12.30pm & 1.30–7pm). You get two hours of free bike time after handing over ID; after this it's a generous €1 per hour. **Car rental** is available from Ada, 19 av de Gaulle (Ⓣ05.46.41.02.17), and Rent-a-car, 29 av de Gaulle (Ⓣ05.46.27.27.27). There is a nifty, fixed-rate **taxi** system, but it's only available to residents of La Rochelle; visitors who need a taxi should call Ⓣ05.46.41.22.22 or 05.46.41.55.55. All town transport is coordinated by RTCR (Ⓣ05.46.34.02.22, Ⓦwww.rtcr.fr).

La Rochelle is the area's hub for **maritime transport**, with boat tours of the town as well as services to the Île de Ré, Île d'Oléron, Île d'Aix and Fort Boyard. Companies with departures from the port here include Navipromer (Ⓣ05.46.01.52.96) and Interîles (Ⓣ08.25.13.55.00, Ⓦwww.inter-iles.com); times and prices vary seasonally, and weather and tides may affect crossings.

Accommodation

Accommodation in La Rochelle can be a bit of a problem, so you should be sure to book in advance from May until well into autumn, even if you're camping. In general you can expect to pay resort prices at most establishments, especially in season. Alternatively, you might try the **self-catering apartments** that abound, particularly around Les Minimes and its Village Informatique. The tourist office has a handy board of rented accommodation and is able to reserve hotel rooms for a small fee.

Hotels

Le Bordeaux 43 rue St-Nicolas Ⓣ05.46.41.31.22, Ⓦwww.hotel-bordeaux-fr.com. Comfortable, friendly hotel in a characterful pedestrianized street between the train station and the port. Closed Dec. ❹

Comfort St-Nicolas 13 rue Sardinerie Ⓣ05.46.41.71.55, Ⓦwww.comforthotel-larochelle.com. A very attractive, modernized hotel in a pretty street 2min from the harbour. All rooms have air a/c and flat-screen TVs. ❻

Fasthotel 20 rue Alfred-Kastler, Les Minimes Ⓣ05.46.45.46.00, Ⓦwww.3y.fr/larochelle. Small, quiet hotel made up of modern bungalows, fifteen minutes from the port des Minimes and the beach. Larger rooms are available for families. ❹

De France-Angleterre et Champlain 20 rue Rambaud Ⓣ05.46.41.23.99, Ⓦwww.bw-fa-champlain.com. This chain hotel offers one of the best deals in town. The foyer is grand and elegant, with a marble staircase, and all rooms are luxurious and nicely decorated with paintings and drawings on the walls. ❹–❻

François I 15 rue Bazoges Ⓣ05.46.41.28.46, Ⓦwww.hotelfrancois1er.fr. Well-maintained hotel in a historic building with a walled courtyard. It's been modernized since François himself used to stop off here – there's an Internet access terminal for guests, and all rooms have bath, TV and phone. Prices drop by up to 40 percent in the off season. Closed Dec. 6

Les Gens de Mer 20 av du Général-de-Gaulle ⓣ05.46.41.26.24, ⓦwww.lesgensdemer.fr. One of the cheaper options in town, right next to the train station. Modern, comfortable rooms, all with shower and TV. 3

Henri IV 31 rue des Gentilhommes ⓣ05.46.41.25.79, ⓔhenri-iv@orange.fr. Recently renovated, this popular hotel has sparkling rooms right in the town centre on place de la Caille, a short stroll from the harbour front. 5

De l'Océan 36 cours des Dames ⓣ05.46.41.31.97, ⓦwww.hotel-ocean-larochelle.com. Comfortable two-star hotel in an enviable location, with air-conditioned rooms – many with views of the port. 3

Saint-Jean-d'Acre 4 place de la Chaine ⓣ05.46.41.73.33, ⓦwww.hotel-la-rochelle.com. This modern, luxurious Inter-hôtel offers good-sized rooms with probably the city's best views of the towers and harbour. 6

Hostel and campsites

HI Hostel av des Minimes ⓣ05.46.44.43.11, ⓦwww.fuaj-aj-larochelle.fr.st. A big modern hostel overlooking the marina at Port des Minimes, a 10min walk from the beach, shops and restaurants, and with a self-service restaurant and bar. Shared dorm-style rooms here cost around €14. Catch bus #10 from place de Verdun to Les Minimes, or walk from the train station, following the signs to the left.

Camping municipal de Port-Neuf on the north-west side of town ⓣ05.46.43.81.20. Well-kept and shaded campsite about 40min walk from the town centre. Take bus #20 from place Verdun, direction "Port-Neuf". Open all year.

Camping Le Soleil av Michel Crépeau ⓣ05.46.44.42.53. In a great location near the hostel and close to the beaches, this site is often crowded with raucous young holiday-makers. Take bus #10 from place Verdun to Les Minimes. Open late June to late Sept.

The Town

The **Vieux Port** is very much the focus of the town, with pleasure boats moored in serried ranks in front of the two impressive towers guarding the entrance to the port. Leading north from the **Porte de la Grosse Horloge**, the **rue du Palais** runs towards the cathedral and several of the museums on rue Thiers. Between the harbour and the **Port des Minimes**, a new marina development 2km south of the town centre, there are several excellent museums for children and a large frigate (permanently moored) providing some insight into the town's sea-going past.

The Vieux Port

Dominating the inner harbour, the heavy Gothic gateway of the **Porte de la Grosse Horloge** straddles the entrance to the old town. The quays in front of it are too full of traffic to encourage loitering; for that, it's best to head out along the tree-lined cours des Dames towards the fourteenth-century **Tour de la Chaine** (May–Sept daily 10am–12.30pm & 2–6.30pm; Oct–April daily except Mon 10am–12.30pm & 2–5.30pm; €5, or €10.50 for entry to all three towers), so called because of the heavy chain that was slung from here across to the opposite tower, **Tour St-Nicolas**, to close the harbour at night. Today the only night-time intruders are likely to be yachties from across the Channel, whose craft far outnumber the working boats – mainly garishly painted trawlers. Beyond the tower, steps climb up to rue Sur-les-Murs, which follows the top of the old sea wall to a third tower, the **Tour de la Lanterne** or Tour des Quatre Sergents, named after four sergeants imprisoned and executed for defying the Restoration monarchy in 1822 (same times and prices as at Tour de la Chaine). There's a way up onto what's left of the **city walls**, planted with unkempt greenery. Beyond is the beach, backed by a casino, hot-dog stands and amusement booths, along with an extensive, truly beautiful belt of park that continues up the western edge of the town centre and along the avenue du Mail behind the beach, where the first seaside village was built by the Rochelais rich.

The rue du Palais and around

The real charm of La Rochelle lies on the city's main shopping street, **rue du Palais**, leading up from the Vieux Port to place de Verdun. Lining the street are eighteenth-century houses, some grey-stone, some half-timbered, with distinctive Rochelais-style slates overlapped like fish scales, while the shopfronts are set back beneath the ground-floor arcades. Among the finest are the **Hôtel de la Bourse** – actually the Chamber of Commerce – and the **Palais de Justice** with its colonnaded facade, both on the left-hand side. A few metres further on, in **rue des Augustins**, there is another grandiose affair built for a wealthy Rochelais in 1555, the so-called **Maison Henri II**, complete with loggia, gallery and slated turrets, where the regional tourist board has its offices. Place de Verdun itself is dull and characterless, with an uninspiring, humpbacked, eighteenth-century classical **cathedral** on the corner. Its only redeeming feature is the marvellously opulent *belle-époque Café de la Paix* (see p. 638).

To the west of rue du Palais, especially in **rue de l'Escale**, paved with granite setts brought back from Canada as ballast in the Rochelais cargo vessels, you get the discreet residences of the eighteenth-century shipowners and chandlers, veiling their wealth with high walls and classical restraint. A rather less modest gentleman once installed himself on the corner of **rue Fromentin**: a seventeenth-century doctor who adorned his house front with the statues of famous medical men – Hippocrates, Galen and others. In rue St-Côme closer to the town walls is the **Musée d'Orbigny-Bernon** (April–Sept Mon & Wed–Fri 10am–12.30pm & 2.30–6pm, Sat & Sun 2.30–6pm; Oct–March Mon & Wed–Fri 9.30am–12.30pm & 1.30–5pm, Sat & Sun 2.30–6pm; €3.50, or part of the museum pass, see p.633), with an extensive section on local history, important collections of local faïence, porcelain from China and Japan and some handsome furniture.

East of rue du Palais, and starting out from place des Petits-Bancs, rue du Temple takes you up alongside the **Hôtel de Ville** (guided tours daily 3pm; €3.50), protected by a decorative but seriously fortified wall. It was begun around 1600 in the reign of Henri IV, whose initials, intertwined with those of Marie de Médicis, are carved on the ground-floor gallery. It's a beautiful specimen of Frenchified Italian taste, adorned with niches and statues and coffered ceilings, all done in a stone the colour of ripe barley. For quiet contemplation of these seemingly more gracious times, try the terrace of the *Café de la Poste*, in the small, traffic-free square outside. For more relaxed vernacular architecture nearly as ancient, carry on up rue des Merciers, the other main shopping area, to the cramped and noisy **market square**, where a food market takes place every morning, close to which you'll find the **Musée du Nouveau Monde** (same opening times and price as Musée d'Orbigny-Bernon, see above; included in the museum pass, see p.633), whose entrance is in rue Fleuriau. This museum occupies the former residence of the Fleuriau family, rich shipowners and traders who, like many of their fellow Rochelais, made fortunes out of the slave trade and Caribbean sugar, spices and coffee. There's a fine collection of prints, paintings and photos of the old West Indian plantations; seventeenth- and eighteenth-century maps of America; and an interesting display of aquatint illustrations for Marmontel's novel *Les Incas* – an amazing mixture of sentimentality and coy salaciousness. Nearby in rue Gargoulleau is the **Musée des Beaux-Arts** (opening times and prices as Musée d'Orbigny-Bernon; included in the museum pass, see p.633), whose works are centred around a few Rochelais artists and illustrate the history of art from the primitives to the present day.

Back towards the port, rue St-Nicolas and place de la Fourche boast several antique dealers and bookshops, and also share a **flea market** on Saturdays.

The quartier du Gabut and south to the Port des Minimes

On the east side of the old harbour behind the Tour St-Nicolas is the **quartier du Gabut**, the one-time fishermen's quarter of wooden cabins and sheds, now converted into bars, shops and eating places. Beyond it lies an extensive dock and the market and service buildings of the old fishing port. Right on the quayside is the spectacular **aquarium** (daily: April–June & Sept 9am–8pm; July & Aug 9am–11pm; Oct–March 10am–8pm; Ⓦwww.aquarium-larochelle.com; adults €12.50, children €9.50), whose pride and joy is an enormous shark tank containing twenty specimens. Opposite the aquarium is the **Musée Maritime** (Ⓦwww.museemaritimelarochelle.fr), consisting of two ships: an old weather station and a trawler whose working days are behind it. Both vessels were due for an overhaul at the time of writing, with the museum expected to reopen by mid-2007; check at the tourist office for opening hours and prices.

A further ten-minute walk brings you to the **Musée des Automates** (daily: July & Aug 9.30am–7pm; Sept–June 10am–noon & 2–6pm; adults €7.50, children €5, or joint ticket with Musée des Modèles Réduits, adults €11, children €6.50; Ⓦwww.museedesautomates.com) on rue de la Désirée, a fascinating collection of three hundred automated puppets, drawing you into an irresistible fantasy world. Some of the puppets are interesting from a historical angle; others, like one that writes the name "Pierrot", from a mechanical viewpoint. Further down the same street is the **Musée des Modèles Réduits** (same hours and ticket prices as the Automates). The prices may be a bit prohibitive for families – especially considering the whole tour takes barely half an hour – but this does combine well with a visit to the neighbouring Musée des Automates. Scale models of every variety and era are on show, starting with cars and including models of a submerged shipwreck and La Rochelle train station.

The **Port des Minimes** is a large modern marina development with mooring for thousands of yachts, about 2km south of the old harbour. Bus #10 from place Verdun will get you there, as will the more entertaining **bus de mer**, a small boat which runs from the old port to Port des Minimes, (April–June & Sept hourly 10am–7pm except 1pm; July & Aug half-hourly 9am–11.30pm; Oct–March Sat & Sun hourly 10am–6pm except 1pm ; €1.50 one way), otherwise it's a thirty-minute walk along the waterfront. There are shops, restaurants, bars and apartments, and the young and gorgeous flock out here at weekends and on summer evenings to parade on the beautiful **plage des Minimes**.

Eating

For eating, try the rue du Port/rue St-Sauveur area just off the waterfront, or the attractive rue St-Jean-du-Pérot, which has everything from crêperies and pizzerias to expensive gourmet restaurants and several ethnic eateries including Indian and Chinese places. Particularly worth seeking out are the town's many excellent **fish restaurants**. *Ernest Le Glacier*, 15 rue du Port, and *Olivier Glacier*, 21 rue St-Jean-du-Pérot, both serve excellent **ice cream** well into the evening.

Les 4 Sergents 49 rue St-Jean-du-Pérot Ⓣ05.46.41.35.80. Despite its smart appearance, the food here is not quite *haute cuisine*, but it's tasty nonetheless, and the restaurant has its own wine *cave* two doors down. Closed Mon lunch.

Café-Resto à la Villette 4 rue de la Forme, behind the market. Tiny, authentic place popular with locals; good *plats du jour* from €7.70. Closed Sun.

A Côté de Chez Fred 30–32 rue St-Nicolas ⓣ05.46.41.65.76. A characterful corner restaurant decorated with watercolours of seaside scenes. A blackboard *carte* changes depending on what's in at Fred the fishmonger's next door. Fish and oyster dishes from €9; around €17 for a full meal. Booking advisable. Closed Sun.

Café Leffe 48 cours des Dames. Brilliantly situated next to the Tour de la Chaine, this brasserie is popular from breakfast through to late evening, serving sandwiches and ice cream all day.

La Marie-Galante 35 av des Minimes ⓣ05.46.44.05.54. Pretty blue awnings over the outdoor seating overlooking the yacht basin at Les Minimes. Fish of the day is €10; generous menus from €11 at lunch. Its three neighbours are also good value.

La Moulinière 24 rue St-Sauveur ⓣ05.46.41.18.16. This is the place to come for mussels, which are served no fewer than twelve different ways. The creative maritime decor makes it a pleasant place to eat as well. Menus from €15. Closed Sun, and Mon evening out of season.

Café de la Paix place de Verdun. All mirrors, gilt and plush, La Rochelle's ladies of means come here to sip lemon tea and nibble daintily at sticky cakes – and there is a tempting charcuterie and seafood shop next door.

Pub Lutèce 1bis rue St-Sauveur. Reasonably priced brasserie with outdoor tables smack in the middle of all the action. Serves crêpes all day long.

Richard Coutanceau plage de la Concurrence ⓣ05.46.41.48.19. Located on the seafront just to the west of the old harbour, with a perfect view out over the beach and sea, this place is a veritable palace of gastronomic excellence, renowned for its fish and seafood and specialities. Menus €45–85.

Le soleil brille pour tout le monde 13 rue des Cloutiers ⓣ05.46.41.11.42. Cheerful and colourful food in agreeable surroundings. The *tartes* (€7.50) are outstanding and, like almost everything else here, are made from fresh organic ingredients from the market down the road. Mostly vegetarian, though seafood and meat sometimes feature on the *plats du jour*. Very popular, so book or get here early. Closed Sun & Mon.

Bars, nightlife and entertainment

As well as the numerous brasseries round the old harbour, a popular daytime **bar** to hang out at is the dark and down-to-earth wine bar *Cave de la Guignette* at 8 rue St-Nicolas, offering great pitchers of sangria. For a bit more local colour, head away from the waterfront to the area around the market, which is less crowded and has some great establishments. By far the most authentic of La Rochelle's numerous **Irish pubs** is *Corrigan's* at 20 rue des Cloutiers, which has a relaxed and familiar atmosphere, enjoyed by a mainly local clientele. Barry, the affable owner, organizes regular live music, including Irish folk evenings most Sundays. Check out ⓦwww.corrigans.fr for more details.

To find out **what's on**, try the monthly magazine *Sortir*, available at the tourist office, with theatre, cinema and mainstream and classical music listings. For **nightlife**, head for the rue St-Nicolas: many bars line the streets, some offering **live music** and most with a lively atmosphere. An older crowd heads for the more relaxed atmosphere of rue des Templiers, where you'll find the *Piano Pub*, the *Mayflower* and the *Académie de la Bière*. **Nightclubs** worth checking out include *L'Oxford*, plage de la Concurrence (ⓣ05.46.41.51.81), and *Le Triolet*, 8 rue des Carmes (ⓣ05.46.41.03.58). La Rochelle is also host to the major **festival** of French-language music, Les Francofolies (ⓦwww.francofolies.fr), in mid-July, which features musicians from overseas as well as France and attracts the best part of 100,000 fans to the city.

The Île de Ré

A half-hour drive west from La Rochelle, the **Île de Ré** is a low, narrow island some 30km long, fringed by sandy beaches to the southwest and salt marshes and oyster beds to the northeast, with the interior a motley mix of small-scale vine, asparagus and wheat cultivation. All the buildings on Ré must abide by height restrictions and incorporate the typical local features of whitewashed walls, curly orange tiles and green-painted shutters, which gives the island villages a southern holiday atmosphere but unfortunately also makes them look nearly identical.

Out of season the island has a slow, misty charm, and life in its little ports revolves exclusively around the cultivation of oysters and mussels. In season, though, it's extraordinarily crowded, with upwards of 400,000 visitors passing through. The crowds mainly head for the **southern beaches**; those to the northeast are covered in rocks and seaweed, and the sea is too shallow for bathing.

The island is connected to the mainland at **LA PALLICE**, a suburb of La Rochelle, by a three-kilometre-long toll bridge (€16.50 round trip per car in high season, €9 in low season). La Pallice was once a big commercial port with important shipyards, and although it still serves as a naval base, times have changed. As you drive past, you'll notice some colossal weather-stained concrete sheds, submarine pens built by the Germans to service their Atlantic U-boat fleet during World War II. Too difficult to demolish, they are still in use. As an alternative to the toll-bridge connection, Interîles, 14 cours des Dames, La Rochelle (Ⓦwww.inter-iles.com), also runs a passenger boat service to Sablonceaux on Ré (€15 return), and combined trips to the Îles de Ré and Oléron.

ST-MARTIN, the island's capital, is an atmospheric north-coast fishing port with whitewashed houses clustered around the stone quays of a well-protected harbour, from where trawlers and flat-bottomed oyster boats, piled high with cage-like devices used for "growing" oysters, slip out every morning on the muddy tide.

The military adventures of the Duke of Buckingham, who attacked the island unsuccessfully in 1627, are now only recalled by signs to the backstreet nightclub *Le Boucquingam*. However, to the east of the harbour, you can walk along the almost perfectly preserved **fortifications** – redesigned by Vauban in the late seventeenth century after Buckingham's attentions – to the citadelle, long used as a prison. From 1860 until 1938, it served as departure point for the *bagnards* – prisoners sentenced to hard labour in the penal colonies of French Guiana and New Caledonia. Most were headed for swift death and oblivion; one who wasn't was Henri Charrière, aka "Papillon", who floated away from Devil's Island on a sack of coconuts after nine escape attempts and thirteen years in the colonies, and went on to write a bestseller about it.

Practicalities

Rébus runs **bus services** all over the island from La Rochelle, leaving regularly from place Verdun via the train station; crossing to **Sablonceaux** just across the bridge costs €2.90. For frequent travelling, ten-trip cards are better value: La Rochelle–Sablonceaux costs €23.10, La Rochelle–St-Martin €43.20, La Rochelle to anywhere on the island €61.20, but the timetable can be awkward if you want to tour the island.

A great way to explore the island is on the excellent network of cycle paths which crisscross it. **Bikes** can be rented from Cyclosurf (Ⓣ05.46.30.19.51, Ⓦwww.cyclo-surf.fr) or Cycland (Ⓣ05.46.09.08.66, Ⓦwww.cycland.fr), who both have shops in all the towns on Ré and charge around €10 per day. Your best bet for **Internet** access is *CybeRése@u* at 15 cours Pasteur in St-Martin (Mon–Sat 11am–1pm & 3–6.30pm, longer hours in summer; €4 per hour).

Hotels are plentiful in all the island's villages, though packed in July and August. Most reasonably priced are the one-star *Le Sénéchal*, 6 rue Gambetta in Ars-en-Ré, in a protected bay on the western side of the island

(Ⓣ05.46.29.40.42, Ⓦwww.hotel-le-senechal.com; ❸; closed Jan); *L'Océan*, 172 rue St-Martin in Le-Bois-Plage (Ⓣ05.46.09.23.07, Ⓦwww.re-hotel-ocean.com; ❹; closed Jan); and, in La Flotte, *Le Français*, 1 cours Félix-Faure (Ⓣ05.46.09.60.06, Ⓦwww.lefrancais.com; ❸; closed mid-Nov to March), with its own restaurant. For more pampering, try the very stylish but not-quite-luxury *La Jetée* on the quayside in St-Martin (Ⓣ05.46.09.36.36, Ⓦwww.hotel-lajetee.com; ❻).

There are even more **campsites** on the island than there are hotels, and it shouldn't be difficult finding a place, except perhaps in desirable locations near the southern beaches at the height of the summer. A few names, if you want to book ahead, are the *Camp du Soleil* in Ars-en-Ré (Ⓣ05.46.29.40.62, Ⓦwww.campdusoleil.com; mid-March to mid-Nov); *L'Océan*, 50 route d'Ars in La Couarde (Ⓣ05.46.29.87.70, Ⓦwww.campingocean.com; April–Sept); and *L'Île Blanche* in La Flotte (Ⓣ05.46.09.52.43, Ⓦwww.ileblanche.com; April–Sept), with an outdoor heated pool and restaurant. Other options are listed at Ⓦwww.campings-ile-de-re.com.

Good-value **food** is available on the quayside in St-Martin at *La Merine*, 31 quai de la Poitheviniere (Ⓣ05.46.09.20.39), with outdoor heated seating and seafood menus starting at €18.50 all day long. The airy *La Salicorne*, 16 rue de l'Olivette in La Couarde (Ⓣ05.46.29.82.37), has a high standard of cuisine starting at €16 for lunchtime menus, as does *Le Bistrot de Bernard*, 1 quai de la Criée, in Ars-en-Ré. Though not quite local cuisine, *Le Bar Basque*, on the port in La Flotte, serves excellent seafood and Basque dishes from as little as €5, best accompanied by a glass of their sangria.

Rochefort and around

ROCHEFORT dates from the seventeenth century, when it was created by Colbert, Louis XIII's navy minister, to protect the coast from English raids. It remained an important naval base until modern times with its shipyards, sail-makers, munitions factories and hospital. Built on a grid plan with regular ranks of identical houses, the town is a monument to the tidiness of the military mind, but is not without charm for all that. The central **place Colbert** is very pretty and nearby **rue Courbet** is exactly as the seventeenth century left it, complete with lime trees, and cobblestones brought from Canada as ships' ballast. There are some sights worth making a special effort for, including the Centre International de la Mer, located in the seventeenth-century royal arsenal and ropeworks.

Various bus companies run services to the main towns along this stretch of coast, the main ones being Océcars (Ⓣ05.46.00.95.15), Aunis Saintonge (Ⓣ05.46.97.52.08) and Kéolis Littoral (Ⓣ05.46.82.31.30), but the timetables are far from convenient for sightseeing. To explore the area around Rochefort effectively you really need your own transport, or a good supply of patience.

Arrival, information and accommodation

The **gare SNCF** is located at the northern end of avenue du Président-Wilson, about a fifteen-minute walk from the centre of town. The efficient **tourist office** (mid-June to mid-Sept Mon–Sat 9.30am–7pm, till 7.30pm in July & Aug; mid-Sept to mid-June Mon–Sat 9.30am–12.30pm & 2–6pm; Ⓣ05.46.99.08.60) is on avenue Sadi-Carnot off rue du Dr-Peltier, two blocks north of the **gare routière**; the staff will reserve rooms for a small charge.

The municipal **campsite** (Ⓣ05.46.82.67.70; March–Nov) is a long haul if you've arrived at the *gare SNCF*: take avenue du Président-Wilson and keep going straight, until you reach the bottom of rue Toufaire, where you turn right, then left – about half an hour all the way. **Internet** access is available at Cybernet Copy 17, 38 rue du Dr-Peltier (Mon–Sat 9am–noon & 2–6pm; €3 per hour). In July and August, **bikes** can be hired from the train station for a generous €1 per hour.

Hotels

Caravelle 34 rue Jaurès Ⓣ05.46.99.02.53, Ⓦwww.hotel-lacaravelle-rochefort.com. This central hotel offers brightly coloured comfortable rooms, all equipped with TV and shower. ❸

La Corderie Royale rue Audebert Ⓣ05.46.99.35.35, Ⓦwww.corderieroyale.com. The smartest hotel in Rochefort, with luxurious rooms and its own swimming pool. It's situated in the lovely grounds of the ropeworks, a stone's throw from the banks of the Charente. Closed Feb. ❼

Lafayette 10 av Lafayette Ⓣ05.46.99.03.31, Ⓦwww.hotel-lafayette.fr. Excellent value – all the rooms are newly renovated, with soundproofed walls, TV and Internet points. Significantly larger rooms are available for families. ❸

Le Welcome place Françoise-Dorléac Ⓣ05.46.99.00.90, Ⓦwww.le-welcome-rochefort.com. The cheapest rooms in town, but still very acceptable; all have TV. There's also a garden and a good brasserie. ❶

Hostel

HI Hostel 20 rue de la République Ⓣ05.46.99.74.62. A basic hostel with clean rooms, communal kitchen and a pleasant garden area; no breakfast though. Dorm beds cost €13.

The Town

If you have a taste for the bizarre, then there's one good reason for visiting Rochefort – the house of the novelist Julien Viaud (1850–1923), alias Pierre Loti. Forty years a naval officer, he wrote numerous bestselling romances with exotic oriental settings and characters. The **Maison Pierre Loti**, at 141 rue Pierre-Loti (guided tours: July to mid-Sept daily every 30min from 10am; mid-Sept to June Mon & Wed–Sat 10.30am, 11.30am, 2pm, 3pm & 4pm; closed Tues Jan & public hols; €7.80; Ⓣ05.46.99.16.88, reservations essential), is part of a row of modestly proportioned grey-stone houses, outwardly a model of petit-bourgeois conformity and respectability, inside an outrageous and fantastical series of rooms decorated to exotic themes. There's a medieval banqueting hall complete with Gothic fireplace and Gobelin tapestries; a monastery refectory with windows pinched from a ruined abbey; a Damascus mosque; and a Turkish room, with kilim wall-hangings and a ceiling made from an Alhambra mould. To suit the mood of the place, Loti used to throw extravagant parties: a medieval banquet with swan's meat and hedgehog and a *fête chinoise* with the guests in costumes he had brought back from China, where he took part in the suppression of the Boxer rebellion.

Also worth a quick look is the **Centre International de la Mer** (April–Sept 9am–7pm; Oct–March 10am–6pm; €5; Ⓦwww.corderie-royale.com) situated in the Corderie Royale, or the royal ropeworks, off rue Toufaire. At 372m, the Corderie is the longest building in France and a rare and splendid example of seventeenth-century industrial architecture, substantially restored after damage in World War II. From 1660 until the Revolution, it furnished the entire French navy with rope, and the building now houses an appropriate exhibition on ropes and rope-making, including machinery from the nineteenth century. If you don't fancy visiting the museum, it's definitely worth a wander around the extensive building and its lawns along the River Charente, whose reed-fringed banks support a garden made up of plants brought back from long-forgotten expeditions overseas. One such, financed by Michel Bégon, quartermaster of

Rochefort in 1688, brought back the flower we know as the begonia. The small harbour, the **Bassin Laperouse**, next to the Corderie, is also worth a stroll.

Eating and drinking

Strolling through Rochefort, you should have no trouble finding somewhere to **eat**, though few establishments are culinary standouts. For inexpensive meals head to rue Toufaire, where there's *Le Galion*, which offers high-quality menus from €13 to enjoy on a quiet terrace by the arsenal; or try the more than adequate Vietnamese/Chinese, *L'Asie*, at no. 45. Probably the most upmarket restaurant in Rochefort is *Les Quatres Saisons*, 76 rue Grimaux (Ⓣ05.46.83.95.12; closed Sun & Mon), with menus from €23. On place Colbert, *Le Comptoir des Îles* serves good **beer** and brasserie fare, while the *Garden Ice Café* on the corner of rue de la République is the liveliest of the bars later in the evening.

Fouras and the Île d'Aix

FOURAS, some 30km south of La Rochelle and accessible by regular Océcar and Kéolis Littoral buses, is the main embarkation point for the tiny Île d'Aix (see below), where Napoleon spent his last days in Europe. It's an uninspiring town, redeemed only by a clutch of popular beaches and the *presqu'île*, the peninsula that extends 3km out to sea from the town centre, terminating at the ferry dock, **Pointe de la Fumée**. The peninsula is bordered by oyster beds, and off its westernmost tip at low tide can be seen the *bouchots à moules*, lines of mussel-encrusted stumps of wood. At high tide this is a popular place to fish for *crevettes* (shrimp). The finger of land is hemmed by sea-dashed fortresses, originally intended to protect the Charente, and particularly La Rochelle, against Norman attack, and later employed against the Dutch in the seventeenth century and English in the eighteenth. The seventeenth-century **Fort Vauban** (daily 10am–7pm) now houses a small local history museum (€2.50), but its esplanade offers a magnificent panorama of neighbouring forts and islands, including the lesser visited **Île Madame**, which is accessible at low tide from Port des Barques, via the Passe aux Boeufs causeway.

Fouras's **tourist office**, which also serves the Île d'Aix, is situated on avenue du Bois Vert on the peninsula (mid-June to mid-Sept Mon–Sat 9am–12.30pm & 1.30–6.30pm, Sun 9am–noon & 2–6pm; mid-Sept to mid-June Mon–Sat 9am–noon & 2–6pm; Ⓣ05.46.84.60.69). As for places to stay, Fouras has a posse of overpriced **hotels**, many of which can be contacted online at Ⓦwww.fouras.net, but first options should be the good-value *Roseraie*, at 2 rue Eric-Tabarly (Ⓣ05.46.84.64.89; ❹), and the comfortable *Grand Hotel des Bains*, 15 rue Général-Brüncher (Ⓣ05.46.84.03.44, Ⓦwww.grandhotel-desbains.com; ❸), housed in an old post office with a lovely courtyard and a snazzy restaurant (menus €11.50–34). There are also three **campsites** around the town, the nicest off which is the three-star *Cadoret*, near plage Nord on boulevard de Chaterny (Ⓣ05.46.82.19.19), with a swimming pool and miniature golf course. The best-value **food** in town is probably from *Restaurant La Jetée* at Pointe de la Fumée (Ⓣ05.46.84.60.43; closed Dec & Tues out of season), which serves excellent seafood at affordable prices (menus €18.50–38).

Île d'Aix

Less frequented than the bigger islands, the crescent-shaped **Île d'Aix** (pronounced 'eel-dex') is small enough – just 2km long – to be walked around in about three hours, giving a greater sense of its island status than is felt on the Île de Ré.

The island is well defended, with a pair of forts and ramparts around its southern tip; the whole island, particularly **Fort Liédot**, served as a prison for members of the Paris Commune and later held prisoners of war in the Crimean and First World Wars. There's a **museum** (June–Sept daily, Oct–May daily except Tues: 9.30am–12.30pm & 2–6pm; €4.50; Ⓦwww.musees-nationaux-napoleoniens.org) in the house constructed to Napoleon's orders. He lived in it for a week in 1815 while he was planning his escape to America, only to find himself en route to St Helena and exile, via Portsmouth. Extensive displays fill ten rooms with the emperor's works of art, clothing, portraits and arms. The white dromedary from which he conducted his Egyptian campaign is lodged nearby in the **Musée Africain**, with its entire collection devoted to African wildlife (same hours and prices as Musée Napoléon).

Access is by frequent ferry (half-hourly in season, according to tide schedule) from Pointe de la Fumée (Ⓣ05.46.84.26.77), or with Interîles from La Rochelle (May–Sept 2–4 daily). The only **hotel** on the island is the overpriced but somewhat charming *Napoléon* on rue Gourgaud (closed Dec & Jan, Ⓣ05.46.84.66.02, Ⓦwww.hotelnapoleon-aix.com; ⑥), where you're obliged to pay for half-board. There's also a **campsite**, the *Fort de la Rade* (Ⓣ05.46.84.28.28; May–Sept).

Brouage and Marennes

Eighteen kilometres southwest of Rochefort, **BROUAGE** is another seventeenth-century military base, this time created by Richelieu after the siege of La Rochelle.

The way into Brouage is through the **Porte Royale** in the north wall of the mid-seventeenth-century fortifications, which remain totally intact. Locked within its 400 square metres, the town now seems abandoned and somnolent; even the sea has retreated, and all that's left of the harbour are the partly freshwater pools, or *claires*, where oysters are fattened in the last stage of their rearing (see box).

Within the walls, the streets are laid out on a grid pattern, lined with low two-storey houses. On the second cross-street to the right is a **memorial** to Samuel de Champlain, the local boy who founded the French colony of Québec in 1608. In the same century, Brouage witnessed the last painful pangs of a royal romance: here, Cardinal Mazarin, successor to Richelieu, locked up his niece, Marie

Oysters

Marennes' speciality is fattening the **oysters** known as *creuses*. It's a lucrative but precarious business, extremely vulnerable to storm damage, changes of temperature or salinity in the water, the ravages of starfish and umpteen other improbable natural disasters.

Oysters begin life as minuscule larvae, which are "born" about three times a year. When a birth happens, the oystermen are alerted by a special radio service, and they all rush out to place their "collectors" – usually arrangements of roofing tiles – for the larvae to cling to. There the immature oysters remain for eight or nine months, after which they are scraped off and moved to *parcs* in the tidal waters of the sea: sometimes covered, sometimes uncovered. Their last move is to the *claires* – shallow rectangular pools where they are kept permanently covered by water less salty than normal sea water. Here they fatten up and acquire the greenish colour the market expects. With "improved" modern oysters, the whole cycle takes about two years, as opposed to four or five with the old varieties.

Mancini, to keep her from her youthful sweetheart, Louis XIV. The politics of the time made the Infanta of Spain a more suitable consort for the King of France than his daughter – in his own judgement. Louis gave in, while Marie pined and sighed on the walls of Brouage. Returning from his marriage in St-Jean-de-Luz, Louis dodged his escort and stole away to see her. Finding her gone, he slept in her room and paced the walls in her footsteps.

Half a dozen kilometres south, on a narrow, drier spit of land, past the graceful eighteenth-century **Château de la Gataudière** with its unique interior and original furnishings (April–Oct Tues–Sun 10am–noon & 2–5pm; €6) – built by the man who introduced rubber to France – you come to the village of **MARENNES**. This is the centre of oyster production for an area that supplies over sixty percent of France's requirements. If you want to visit the oyster beds and see how the business works, you can do so here; just ask at the **tourist office** on place Chasseloup-Laubat (April–June & Sept Tues–Sat 9.30am–noon & 2–5pm; July & Aug Mon–Sat 9.30am–6.30pm; Oct–March Tues–Sat 10am–noon & 2–4pm; ⓣ05.46.85.04.36) – visits cost from around €6.

For **accommodation** in Marennes, try the inexpensive *Hôtel du Commerce* at 9 rue de la République (ⓣ05.46.85.00.09; ❶), with a restaurant where you can eat generously and well from €14. A good alternative for **eating** is *La Verte Ostréa* at the end of the pier at La Cayenne, where oysters and shellfish form the basis of every menu (from €12).

The Île d'Oléron

The **Île d'Oléron** is France's largest island after Corsica and a favourite of day-trippers and families in the summer months for its beautiful sandy beaches. It's up the road from Marennes, joined to the mainland by a bridge. There are a couple of buses per day from Saintes, but the timings make a day-trip awkward. You're better off going from Rochefort on one of the five daily Kéolis Littoral buses; alternatively, take a guided excursion from La Rochelle.

Flat and more wooded than the Île de Ré, Oléron has plenty of greenery, with the extensive pine-studded **Forêt des Saumonards** in the northeast of the island; here you can eyeball a dazzling panorama of the surrounding *parcs à huîtres* and the mighty **Fort Boyard** stranded in the midst of the sea between Oléron and the Île d'Aix to the northeast. At the island's southern tip, the larger **Forêt de St-Trojan** creeps up the western coast along **La Grande Plage**, a popular spot but far enough from the main towns not to be too crowded. The island interior is pretty and distinctive. Waterways wind right into the land, their gleaming muddy banks overhung by round fishing nets suspended from ranks of piers. There are so many oyster *claires* that, from above, the island must look like an Afghan mirrored cushion; the stretch from Boyardville to St-Pierre – with its pines, tamarisks and woods of evergreen oak – is the most attractive.

The island's most interesting attraction is off the D126 between St-Pierre and Dolus, right in the middle of the island. The bird park of **Le Marais aux Oiseaux** (daily: April–June & Sept 10am–1pm & 2–6pm; July–Aug 10am–7pm; ⓦwww.centre-sauvegarde-oleron.com; €4.50) was originally established as a hospital for injured birds found in the wild, but is now a breeding centre with many examples of rare or endangered species. Some 300 to 400 types of bird are given the freedom of twenty hectares of beautiful countryside, while sixty species are caged for observation alongside public walkways.

Most of the little towns on the island have inevitably been ruined by the development of hundreds of holiday homes – and it can be a real battle in the summer season to find a place to stay. There are a few places that still retain some amount of charm, however, not least of which is the main town in the south of the island, **LE CHÂTEAU**, named after the **citadel** that still stands, along with some seventeenth-century **fortifications**. The town thrives on its traditional oyster farming and boat-building, and there's a lively **market** in place de la République every morning. The chief town in the north – and most picturesque of the island's settlements – is **ST-PIERRE**, whose market square has an unusual thirteenth-century monument, **La Lanterne des Morts**. A few kilometres to the northeast, **BOYARDVILLE** has no interest except for the ranks of *bouchots* – stakes for growing mussels – along the shore. It's tempting to help yourself, but these are private property and you'll be in trouble if someone sees you. Instead, head to the major attraction around here: the superb stretch of sandy beach at **LA BRÉE-LES-BAINS**. Halfway down the west coast is the pretty fishing port of **LA COTINIÈRE**, with a daily morning fish market (except Sun), Criée aux Poissons, where the fishermen traditionally cry out their wares.

Practicalities

The main **tourist office** is on place de la République in Le Château (July–Aug Mon–Sat 9.30am–12.30pm & 2.30–7pm, Sun 10am–12.30pm; Sept–June closed Sun; ⓣ05.46.47.60.51, ⓦwww.oleron.org), also the location of a couple of affordable restaurants. St-Pierre's tourist office is on place Gambetta (June–Aug Mon–Sat 9am–7pm, Sun 10am–1pm; Sept–May Tues–Sat 9.15am–12.30pm & 2–6pm; ⓣ05.46.75.32.84). **Bikes** can be rented from Vélos 17 (ⓣ05.46.47.14.05, ⓦwww.velos17loisirs.com), which has outlets in all the towns on the island.

Well-priced **accommodation** on the Île d'Oléron can be had at the modestly outfitted *Hôtel de la Petite Plage* at Domino, rue de l'Océan, St-Georges (ⓣ05.46.76.52.28; ❸); and smack on the rocky shore at *L'Albatros*, 11 bd du Dr-Pineau, St-Trojan-les-Bains (ⓣ05.46.76.00.08, ⓦwww.albatros-hotel-oleron.com; ❹; closed Oct–Feb), both offering restaurant service. For some extreme luxury, venture out to the *Novotel Thalassa Oléron*, Plage de Gatseau in St-Trojan-les-Bains (ⓣ05.46.76.02.46, ⓦwww.accorthalassa.com; ❾), a hotel-cum-spa offering every amenity under the sun to pacify body and mind. There are **campsites** all over the island: at La Brée, where the best beaches are, there's *Pertuis d'Antioche* (ⓣ05.46.47.92.00; April–Sept), 150m from the beach off the D273. Further down the east coast, *Signol* at Boyardville (ⓣ05.46.47.01.22, ⓦwww.signol.com; April–Sept) is pleasantly sited near pine forests. If you want to stay a week or so, you could rent a **holiday apartment**, easy enough outside of July and August: ask for a list at any of the tourist offices, or contact the Agence Centrale Oléronaise (ⓣ05.46.75.32.53).

Places to **eat** abound on the island, and St-Pierre has the greatest choice of restaurants and brasseries. One place worth mentioning is in La Cotinière: at *L'Écailler*, 65 rue du Port (ⓣ05.46.47.10.31; closed Dec & Jan), you can have a slap-up, super-fresh seafood meal facing the port from €18.50.

Royan and around

Before World War II, **ROYAN**, at the mouth of the Gironde, was a fashionable resort for the bourgeoisie. It's still popular, if no longer exclusive, but the modern town has lost its elegance to the dreary rationalism of 1950s town planning: broad boulevards, car parks, shopping centres, planned greenery.

Ironically, the occasion for this planners' romp was provided by Allied bombing, an attempt to dislodge a large contingent of German troops who had withdrawn into the area after the D-Day landings. But the **beaches** – the most elegant and fashionable of which is in the suburb of **Pontaillac** to the northwest (reached by a regular bus service from place Charles-de-Gaulle) – are beautiful: fine pale sand, meticulously harrowed and raked near town, and wild, pine-backed and pounded by the Atlantic to the north.

Arrival, information and accommodation

The **gare routière** and **gare SNCF** are located on cours de l'Europe. The nearby **tourist office** (mid-June to Aug Mon–Sat 9am–7.30pm, Sun 10am–1pm & 3–6pm; Sept to mid-June Mon–Sat 9am–12.30pm & 2–6pm; ⓣ05.46.05.04.71, ⓦwww.royan-tourisme.com) and **PTT** lie close to the Rond-Point-de-la-Poste at the east end of the seafront. You can rent **bikes** from Royan Bicycles at 1 Galerie Botton (ⓣ05.46.06.08.18); **car rental** is available from either Ada, 7 place du Dr-Gantier (ⓣ05.46.02.88.88), or Avis, 75 av de Pontaillac (ⓣ05.46.38.48.48).

Accommodation in Royan is expensive and in short supply in season, when your best bet is to camp up the coast to the north or visit for the day from Saintes or Rochefort. There are a number of **campsites** in the region and around Royan itself, including the *Clairefontaine* (ⓣ05.46.39.08.11, ⓦwww.camping-clairefontaine.com; June to mid-Sept), a fairly pricey site at 6 rue du Colonel-Lachaud, and the municipal *La Triloterie* (ⓣ05.46.05.26.91, ⓕ05.46.39.07.92) off avenue d'Aquitaine – the road to Bordeaux.

Hotels

Les Bleuets 21 façade de Foncillon ⓣ05.46.38.51.79, ⓦwww.hotel-les-bleuets.com. An attractive, nautically themed hotel right on the seafront. All rooms have shower and TV, while for a little more money you can have a small balcony with a sea view. ❹

La Colinette 16 av de la Grande Plage, Saint-Georges de Didonne ⓣ05.46.05.15.75, ⓔinfo@colinette.fr. Situated 100m from the sea 3km southeast of Royan. It has its own restaurant and in summer, the owners may expect all guests to take meals here. ❺

Le Crystal 1 bd Aristide-Briand ⓣ05.46.05.00.64, ⓕ05.46.05.32.41. A basic but satisfactory option right in the town centre, near the market and place de Gaulle. Showers are on the landing and cost €3. ❶

Miramar 173 av de Pontaillac ⓣ05.46.39.03.64, ⓦwww.miramar-pontaillac.com. Right opposite the beach, this well-run hotel has large, comfortable and sparkling rooms, while downstairs are an attractive bar and a breakfast terrace looking out over the sea. ❺

De la Plage 26 Front de Mer ⓣ05.46.05.10.27, ⓕ05.46.38.37.79. Located centrally, the rooms are a bit drab but a good size for the price – and all have TV and shower. There is a restaurant downstairs which serves mainly seafood, menus from €13.50. ❷

The Town

One sight worth seeing in Royan is the 1950s **church of Notre-Dame**, designed by Gillet and Hébrard, in a tatty square behind the main waterfront. Though the concrete has weathered badly, the overall effect is dramatic and surprising. Tall V-sectioned columns rise dramatically to culminate in a 65-metre bell tower, like the prow of a giant vessel. The interior is even more striking: using uncompromisingly modern materials and designs, the architects have succeeded in out-Gothicking Gothic. The stained-glass panels, in each of which a different tone predominates, borrow their colours from the local seascapes – oyster, sea, mist and murk – before a sudden explosion of colour in the Christ figure above the altar.

The most attractive area in Royan is around **boulevard Garnier**, which leads southeast from Rond-Point-de-la-Poste along the beach, and once housed Parisian high society in purpose-built, *belle-époque* holiday villas. Some of these have survived, including **Le Rêve**, 58 bd Garnier, where Émile Zola lived and wrote; **Kosiki**, 100 av du Parc (running parallel to bd Garnier), a nineteenth-century folly of Japanese inspiration; and **Tanagra**, 34 av du Parc, whose facade is covered in sculptures and balconies.

Various **cruises** are organized from Royan in season, including one to the **Cordouan lighthouse**, erected by Edward III's son, the Black Prince, and commanding the mouth of the Gironde River. There's a frequent thirty-minute **ferry** crossing (one way: pedestrians €3.10, bikes €1.50, motorbikes €9.50, cars €21.20) to the headland on the other side of the Gironde, the **Pointe de Grave**, from where a **bicycle trail** and the **GR8** head down the coast through the pines and dunes to the bay of Arcachon.

Eating, drinking and nightlife

The best **restaurant** possibilities are all located near the seafront, whilst self-caterers should head to the large covered market (daily except Mon out of season) at the end of boulevard Aristide-Briand. **Nightlife** has sadly all but died in Royan, but various bars along the waterfront are lively until reasonably late, especially in summer. Some of the restaurants have music, although even then not very often.

Restaurants

Le Bistrot Marin 6 bd de la Grandière ⓣ05.46.05.04.90. A smart restaurant, with good-value meat and fish dishes starting at €9. Their speciality is lobsters, which spend their last hours displayed in a tank in the middle of the restaurant.

Les Filets Bleus 14 rue Notre-Dame ⓣ05.46.05.74.00. Near the cathedral, this place serves up French specialities including seafood and foie gras; the decor has a muted maritime feel. A treat for all budgets, with menus from €16 to €58. Closed Sat lunch and Mon.

Le Régent Front de Mer ⓣ05.46.06.27.70. The best of the brasseries which line the waterfront. They serve menus from €10, often involving oysters, and if you're lucky there might be some live jazz as entertainment.

Le Relais de la Mairie 1 rue du Chay ⓣ05.46.39.03.15. A bit of a walk from town off av de Pontaillac, this restaurant offers imaginative mussel and oyster dishes, with menus starting at €12. Closed in the evenings Sun, Mon & Thurs.

Le Tiki You can't miss this huge establishment right on the beach by the tourist office. It is divided into different sections: a pizzeria, a brasserie and a more traditional restaurant, offering a higher level of gastronomic experience with menus from €16.

La Palmyre and Talmont

It's worth knowing about the **zoo park** in **La PALMYRE** (daily: April–Sept 9am–7pm; Oct–March 9am–6pm; ⓦwww.zoo-palmyre.fr; €13), 10km northwest of Royan up the D25 coast road, especially if you're travelling with children; an exciting range of exotic species belies the slightly tacky advertising. To reach it, there are **buses** all day from Royan's *gare routière* and the place Charles-de-Gaulle.

An ideal bicycle or picnic excursion just over an hour's ride from Royan is to **TALMONT**, 16km up the Gironde on the GR360 – apart from a few ups and downs through the woods outside Royan, it's all level terrain. The low-crouching village clusters about the twelfth-century **church of Ste-Radegonde**, standing at the edge of a cliff above the Gironde. With gabled transepts, a squat tower and an apse simply but elegantly decorated with blind arcading – all in weathered tawny stone and pocked like a sponge – it stands magnificently against the forlorn browny-grey seascapes typical of the Gironde. The entrance is through the north transept, where the rings of carving in the arched doorway depict acrobats standing on each other's shoulders and, in the outer braid, two tug-of-war teams hauling roped lions up the arch. The inside is as unpretentiously beautiful as the exterior.

The Charente

It's hard to believe that the tranquil fertile valley of the **River Charente** was once a busy industrial waterway, bringing armaments from **Angoulême** to the naval shipyards at Rochefort. Today peaceful, low, ochre-coloured farms crown the valley slopes, with green swathes of vineyard sweeping up to the walls, and the graceful turrets of minor châteaux – properties of wealthy cognac-producers – poke up from out of the woods. The towns and villages may look old-fashioned, but the prosperous shops and classy new villas are proof that where the grape grows, money and modernity are not far behind.

The **valley** itself is easy to travel as the main road and train lines to Limoges run this way. North and south, Poitiers, Périgueux (for the Dordogne) and Bordeaux are also easily reached by train. Otherwise, for cross-country journeys, you're heavily reliant on your own transport.

Saintes and around

SAINTES was formerly much more important than its present size suggests. Today a busy market town for the surrounding region, it was capital of the old province of Saintonge and a major administrative and cultural centre in Roman times. It still retains some impressive remains from that period, as well as two beautiful Romanesque pilgrim churches and an attractive centre of narrow lanes and medieval houses. It also has the doubtful distinction of being the birthplace of Dr Guillotin, whose instrument of decapitation came into its own during the Revolution.

The Town

The abbey church, the **Abbaye aux Dames** (daily: April–Sept 10am–12.30pm & 2–7pm; Oct–March 1–6pm; entry €2, guided tour €3), is as quirky as

Pineau des Charentes

Roadside signs throughout the Charente advertise **Pineau des Charentes**, a sweet liqueur that's a blending of grape juice stopped in its fermentation by adding cognac from the same vineyard. It's best drunk chilled as an aperitif; the locals also like it with oysters and love cooking with it. Favourite dishes include *moules au Pineau* (mussels cooked with tomatoes, Pineau, garlic and parsley) and *lapin à la saintongeaise* (rabbit casseroled with Pineau rosé, shallots, garlic, tomatoes, thyme and bay leaves).

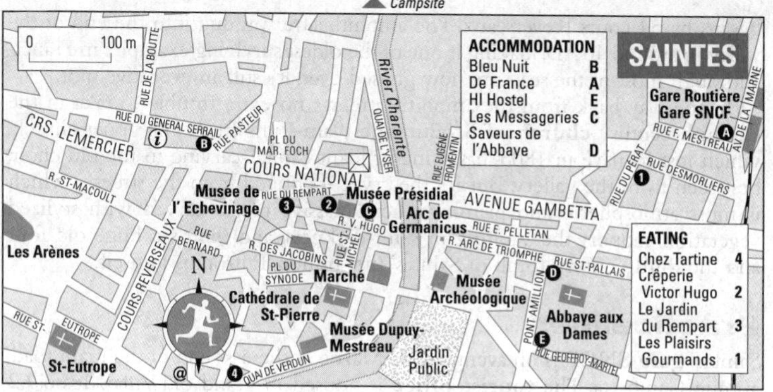

Notre-Dame in Poitiers. It stands back from the street on rue St-Pallais, in a sandy courtyard behind the smaller Romanesque church of St-Pallais. An elaborately sculpted doorway conceals the plain, domed interior. Its rarest feature is the eleventh-century tower, by turns square, octagonal and lantern-shaped, flanked with pinnacles and capped with the Poitou pine cone.

From here rue Arc de Triomphe brings you out on the riverbank beside an imposing Roman arch – the **Arc de Germanicus** – which originally stood on the bridge until 1843, when it was demolished to make way for the modern crossing and rebuilt here. The arch was dedicated to the emperor Tiberius, his son Drusus and nephew Germanicus in 19 AD. In a stone building next door is an **archeological museum** (June–Sept Mon–Sat 10am–6pm, Sun 1.30–6pm; Oct–May Mon–Sat 10am–5pm, Sun 1.30–5pm; €1.60), with a great many more Roman bits and pieces strewn about, mostly rescued from the fifth-century city walls into which they had been incorporated. This whole area comes alive on the first Monday of every month when a sprawling **market** extends from the abbey right through here and up most of avenue Gambetta.

A footbridge crosses from the archeological museum to the covered market on the west bank of the river and place du Marché at the foot of the rather uninspiring **Cathédrale de St-Pierre** (daily 9am–7pm), which began life as a Romanesque church but was significantly altered in the aftermath of damage inflicted during the Wars of Religion, when Saintes was a Huguenot stronghold. Its enormous, heavily buttressed tower, capped by a hat-like dome instead of the intended spire, is the town's chief landmark. North of the cathedral, an early seventeenth-century mansion on rue Victor-Hugo houses the **Musée Présidial** (June–Sept Tues–Sun 1.30–6pm; Oct–May Tues–Sun 1.30–5pm; €1.60), containing a collection of local pottery and some decent fifteenth- to eighteenth-century paintings. Just down the road is the **Musée de l'Echevinage** (same opening times), with nineteenth- and twentieth-century paintings, mainly by local artists of the Saintongaise and Bordelaise schools. A ticket costing €4.20 will get you into both galleries, the archeological museum and the **Musée Dupuy-Mestreau** down on the riverbank, which houses a vast personal collection of turn-of-the-century objects ranging from model ships to headdresses.

Saintes' Roman heritage is best seen at **Les Arènes** (June–Sept daily 10am–8pm; Oct–May Mon–Sat 10am–5pm, Sun 1.30–5pm; €2), an amphitheatre whose ruins lie at the head of a leafy little valley reached by a footpath which begins by 54 cours Reverseaux. The amphitheatre was dug into the end of the valley in around 40 AD, making it one of the oldest surviving examples in France. Although most of the seats are now grassed over, it's still an evocative spot.

On the way back from the amphitheatre, it's no extra trouble to take in the eleventh-century **church of St-Eutrope** (9am–7pm; free). The upper church, which lost its nave in 1803, has some brilliant capital-carving in the old choir, best seen from the gallery. But it's the crypt – entered from the street – which is most atmospheric and primitive: here massive pillars carved with stylized vegetation support the vaulting in semi-darkness, and there's a huge old font and the third-century tomb of Saintes' first bishop, Eutropius himself.

Practicalities

Saintes' **gare SNCF** is on avenue de la Marne at the east end of the main road, avenue Gambetta. The **tourist office** is housed in grand old Villa Musso, 62 cours National (July & Aug Mon–Sat 9am–1pm & 2–7pm; Sept–June Mon–Sat 9.30am–12.30pm & 2–5.30pm; Ⓣ05.46.74.23.82, Ⓦwww.ot-saintes.fr), and organizes **boat trips** on the Charente during the summer. **Internet** access is available until late into the evening at Le Satellite, 45 rue Berthonnière for a mere €1 per hour.

The municipal **campsite** (Ⓣ05.46.93.08.00; mid-April to mid-Oct) is to the right (if you are coming from the Arc de Germanicus) immediately after the bridge, along quai de l'Yser.

For eating, there's a good **restaurant**, the *Chez Tartine* (Ⓣ05.46.74.16.38; closed Sun dinner & Mon), by the river on place Blair, and the popular *Crêperie de Victor Hugo*, at 20 rue Victor-Hugo, off rue Alsace-Lorraine, the pedestrianized shopping street. *Le Jardin du Rempart*, 36 rue du Rempart (Ⓣ05.46.93.37.66; closed Tues dinner & Wed), serves top-value menus from €13.50, including salads, seafood and grills, while *Les Plaisirs Gourmands* (Ⓣ05.46.98.16.28; closed Sun & Mon) is another good bet with popular menus from €11.50. Out of town, the *Restaurant de la Charente* (Ⓣ05.46.91.03.17; closed Sun), 10km upstream at **Chaniers**, is the Sunday haunt of prosperous locals and makes a more expensive but fulfilling gastronomic experience.

Hotels

Bleu Nuit 1 rue Pasteur Ⓣ05.46.93.01.72, Ⓔau-bleu-nuit@t3a.com. A short walk from the town centre, the rooms here are well soundproofed and all have TV. ❸

De France 56 rue Frédéric-Mestreau Ⓣ05.46.93.01.16, Ⓕ05.46.74.37.90. The best of the options near the train station, rooms are comfortable and come at various prices; you pay more for a larger room and a bath. ❷

Les Messageries rue des Messageries Ⓣ05.46.93.64.99, Ⓦwww.hotel-des-messageries.com. A good place for more comfort: most rooms are air-conditioned and all have TV and minibar. The location is great – very central but set back from the main street on its own quiet courtyard. ❹

Saveurs de l'Abbaye 1 place St-Pallais Ⓣ05.46.94.17.91. A stylish and modern hotel with quiet and very comfortable rooms, all with TV, shower and warm, bright decor. There is an excellent restaurant downstairs as well, which serves stylish menus from €17.30. ❸

Hostel

HI Hostel 2 place Geoffroy-Martel Ⓣ05.46.92.14.92, Ⓕ05.46.92.97.82. In a superb position in behind the Abbaye aux Dames, the facilities are modern and breakfast is included. Dorm beds are €13.

Around Saintes

If you have a car, you could explore several of the marvellous Romanesque churches within easy reach of Saintes. In **FENIOUX**, 29km to the north towards St-Jean-d'Angély, there's superb St-Eutrope with its mighty spire, while the church at **RIOUX**, 12km to the south, is well worth visiting for its detailed facade. There's also the fine **Château of Roche-Courbon**, 18km northwest off the Rochefort road – once described by Pierre Loti (see p.641) as the Sleeping Beauty's castle – with some stylish interiors and gardens.

One place worth any amount of trouble to get to is the twelfth-century pilgrim **church of St-Pierre** at **AULNAY**, 37km northeast of Saintes, and sadly not served by public transport, though you can get the bus as far as St-Jean-d'Angély. Aulnay church's finest sculpture is on the west front, the south transept and apse, with some more fine work inside. On the building's main facade, two blind arches flank the central portal. The tympanum of the right depicts Christ in Majesty; the left, St Peter, crucified upside down with two extraordinarily lithe and graceful soldiers balancing on the arms of his cross to get a better swing at the nails in his feet. The apse, too, is a beauty, framed by five slender columns and lit by three perfectly arched windows, the centre one enclosed by figures wrapped in the finest twining foliage. Inside, there is more extraordinary carving: capitals depicting Delilah cutting Samson's hair, devils pulling a man's beard, human-eared elephants bearing the Latin inscription *Hic sunt elephants* – "Here are elephants" – presumably for the edification of ignorant locals.

You might also like to visit **Nuaillé-sur-Boutonne**, 9km west of Aulnay, which boasts another remarkable church; and, even nearer just down the D129 east of Aulnay, you can walk to **Salles-les-Aulnay** (20min), or **St-Mandé** (1hr), with humbler churches of the same period.

Cognac and around

Anyone who does not already know what **COGNAC** is about will quickly nose its quintessential air as they stroll about the medieval lanes of the town's

△ Cognac distillery

riverside quarter. For here is the greatest concentration of *chais* (warehouses), where the high-quality brandy is matured, its fumes blackening the walls with tiny fungi. Cognac *is* cognac, from the tractor driver and pruning-knife wielder to the manufacturer of corks, bottles and cartons. Untouched by recession (eighty percent of production is exported), it is likely to thrive as long as the world has sorrows to drown – a sunny, prosperous, respectable, self-satisfied little place.

The Town

Cognac has a number of medieval stone and half-timbered buildings in the narrow streets of the old town, of which rue Saulnier and rue de l'Îsle-d'Or make atmospheric backdrops for a stroll, and picturesque **Grande-Rue** winds through the heart of the old quarter to the *chais*. On the right is all that remains of the **castle** where King François I was born in 1494.

To the left are the *chais* and offices of the **Hennessy Cognac Company** (daily: March–Dec 10am–5pm; €7 for guided tour), a seventh-generation family firm and widely thought the best of the houses to visit. The first Hennessy, an officer in the Irish brigade serving with the French army, hailed from Ballymacnoy in County Cork and gave up soldiering in 1765 to set up a little business here. The visit begins with a film explaining what's what in the world of cognac. Only an *eau de vie* distilled from grapes grown in a strictly defined area can be called cognac, and this stretches from the coast at La Rochelle and Royan to Angoulême. It's all carefully graded according to soil properties – chalk essentially. The inner circle, from which the finest cognac comes – Grand Champagne and Petit Champagne (not to be confused with bubbly) – lies mainly south of the River Charente. Hennessy alone keeps 180,000 barrels in stock; the most attention-grabbing moment of the tour is a glimpse of the safeguarded barrels containing vintages from the late 1800s. All barrels are regularly checked and various *coupages* (blendings) made, of which only the best are kept – depending on the well-honed taste buds of the sober *maître du chais*.

Practicalities

From the very industrial **gare SNCF**, to get to the central place François-I, go down rue Mousnier, right on rue Bayard, past the PTT and up rue du 14-Juillet. The square is dominated by an equestrian statue of the king rising from a bed of begonias; in fine weather the cafés here teem with locals. The **tourist office** is on rue du 14-Juillet at no. 16 (July & Aug Mon—Sat 9am–7pm, Sun 10am–4pm; Sept–June Mon–Sat 10am–5pm; ⓣ05.45.82.10.71, ⓦwww.tourism-cognac.com), where you can ask about visiting the various *chais*, as well as get information on river trips. The town **campsite** (ⓣ05.45.32.13.32; May–Oct) is next to the river on boulevard de Chatenay, while **Internet access** is available at Cyber@salle, 24 allée de la Corderie (€3 per hour).

For **eating** out, relaxed *La Bonne Goule*, 42 allée de la Corderie (from €11; ⓣ05.45.82.06.37; closed Sun evening), serves up excellent Charentais specialities at low prices, and there's a good list of local wines. Another possibility is *Le Patio*, 42 av Victor-Hugo (ⓣ05.45.32.40.50; closed Sun & Mon), with a range of steak and duck dishes and a menu for €14.50. There's also good brasserie fare to be had at the *Coq d'Or* on the central place François-1er (ⓣ05.45.82.02.56), which has huge seafood platters for €22.80.

Hotels

Le Cheval Blanc 6 place Bayard ⓣ05.45.82.09.55, ⓦwww.hotel-chevalblanc.fr. A simple, good-value hotel close to the town centre. Rooms are clean and soundproofed, if a little unimaginatively furnished. ❸

Héritage 25 rue d'Angoulême ⓣ05.45.82.01.26, ⓦwww.hheritage.com. A creative hotel, with each room decorated according to a different theme; African, Chinese, pink and so on. It is very comfortable and has wireless Internet throughout. The restaurant features menus from €17.50 and the bar is open until midnight. ❹

L'Oliveraie 6 place de la Gare ⓣ05.45.82.04.15, ⓦwww.oliveraie-cognac.com. Right outside the train station, this family-run hotel has large rooms for the price, and most are air-conditioned. ❷

Les Pigeons Blancs 110 rue Jules-Brisson ⓣ05.45.82.16.36, ⓦwww.chateauxhotels.com/pigeonsblancs. Twenty minutes' walk from the town centre, set in lovely open grounds on top of a hill. Rooms are spacious and luxurious and there is a high-quality restaurant. ❺

La Résidence 25 av Victor-Hugo ⓣ05.45.36.62.40, ⓦwww.hotellaresidence-cognac.com. Good-value, large rooms with shower or bath and TV. A nice feature is the family rooms, which are partially divided to give parents some space from children. ❸

Around Cognac

The area around Cognac is gentle enough for some restful walks, taking in some pretty little Charentais villages. The best is the towpath or *chemin de halage* that follows the south bank of the Charente upstream to Pont de la Trâche, then on along a track to the village of **BOURG-CHARENTE**, with an excellent **restaurant** called *La Ribaudière* (ⓣ05.45.81.30.54, ⓦwww.laribaudiere.com; closed Sun evening, Mon & Tues lunch; menus €35–70), where you should most definitely try their speciality, *matelote d'anguilles* – eels cooked in wine sauce. From there, you can amble to the village's interesting castle and Romanesque church; the walk takes about three hours in all. A byroad leads back to **ST-BRICE** on the other bank, past sleepy farms and acres of shoulder-high vines. From there, another lane winds 3km up the hill and over to the ruined **abbaie de La Châtre**, abandoned amid brambles and fields. Alternatively, at the hamlet of **RICHEMONT**, 5km northwest of Cognac, you can swim in the pools of the tiny River Antenne below an ancient church on a steep bluff lost in the woods.

Further afield, 18km northwest of Cognac between the villages of Migron and Authon, there's the fascinating **Écomusée du Cognac** (mid-June to mid-Sept daily 10am–12.30pm & 2.30–6.30pm; rest of year by reservation; ⓣ05.46.94.91.16; free), which illustrates the history of the distillation process and the various tools involved, finishing off with a tasting of cognacs, liqueurs and cocktails; follow the D731 to St-Jean-d'Angély for 13km as far as Burie, then turn right onto the D131, 4km from Migron.

A particularly beautiful excursion is upstream to **JARNAC**, from where you can take boat trips on the Charente from €7, arranged by the tourist office (ⓦwww.jarnac-tourisme.com). In the town, the late President Mitterrand's modest grave has become a place of pilgrimage for elderly left-wingers, and you can also visit the **Musée François-Mitterrand**, 10 quai de l'Orangerie (July & Aug daily 10am–12.30pm & 2.30–6.30pm; Sept–June Wed–Sun 2–6pm; ⓣ05.45.81.38.88; €3.50), which houses a permanent exhibition on the public works carried out during Mitterrand's two terms of office.

Angoulême and around

The charming cathedral city of **ANGOULÊME** used to be dominated by paper mills that employed thousands of workers and bolstered the city's prosperity. The

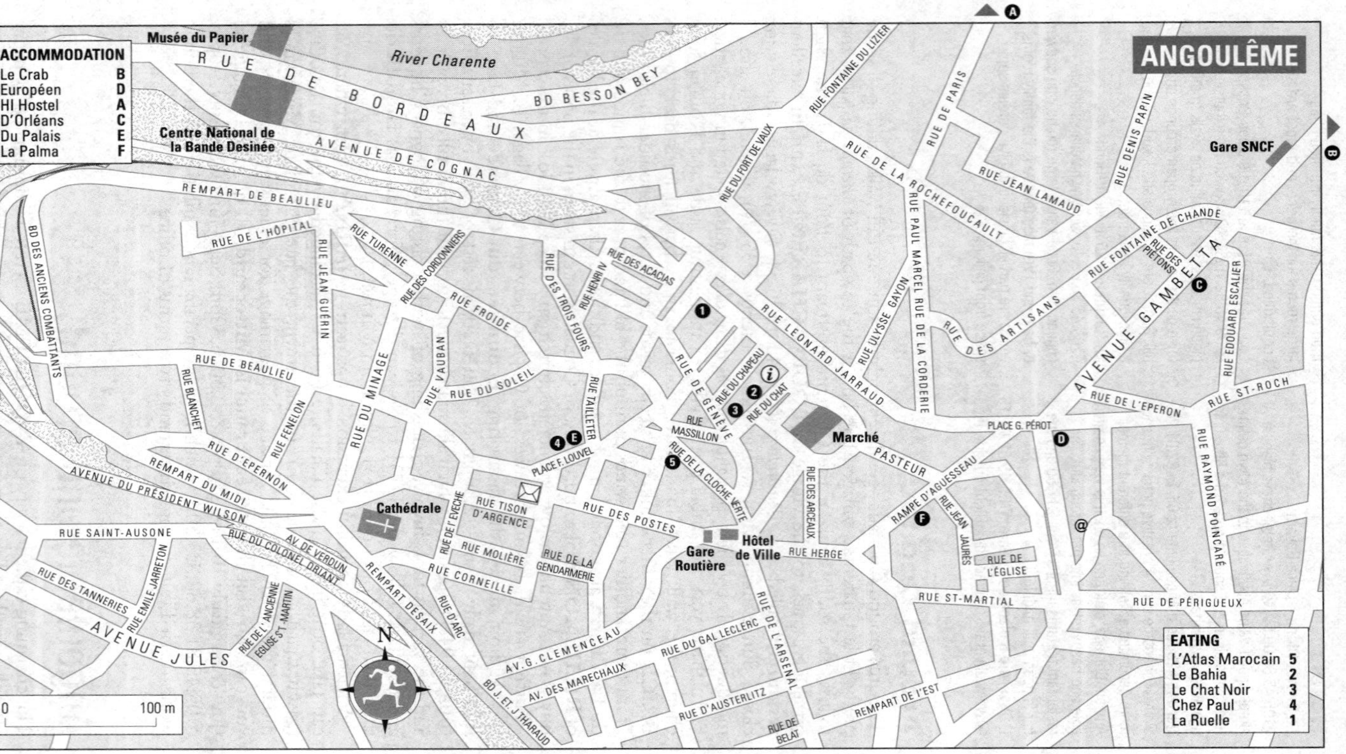
ANGOULÊME
ACCOMMODATION
Le Crab B
Européen D
HI Hostel A
D'Orléans C
Du Palais E
La Palma F
EATING
L'Atlas Marocain 5
Le Bahia 2
Le Chat Noir 3
Chez Paul 4
La Ruelle 1
Musée du Papier
River Charente
Centre National de la Bande Desinée
Gare SNCF
Marché
Cathédrale
Gare Routière
Hôtel de Ville
Place G. Pérot
Place F. Louvel
Rue de Bordeaux
Bd Besson Bey
Avenue de Cognac
Rempart de Beaulieu
Rue de l'Hôpital
Bd des Anciens Combattants
Rue Jean Guérin
Rue Turenne
Rue des Cordonniers
Rue Froide
Rue des Trois Fours
Rue Henri IV
Rue des Acacias
Rue du Fort de Vaux
Rue Fontaine du Lizier
Rue de Paris
Rue de la Rochefoucault
Rue Jean Lamaud
Rue Denis Papin
Rue Fontaine de Chande
Rue des Piétons
Avenue Gambetta
Rue Edouard Escalier
Rue des Artisans
Rue Ulysse Gayon
Rue Paul Marcel Rue de la Corderie
Rue Leonard Jarraud
Rue de l'Eperon
Rue St-Roch
Rue Raymond Poincaré
Rue de Beaulieu
Rue Blanchet
Rue Fenelon
Rue du Minage
Rue Vauban
Rue du Soleil
Rue Tailleter
Rue de Genève
Rue du Chapeau
Rue du Chat
Rue Massillon
Rue de la Cloche Verte
Pasteur
Rampe d'Aguesseau
Rue Jean Jaurès
Rue de l'Église
Rue des Arceaux
Rue Herge
Rue St-Martial
Rue de Périgueux
Rue d'Epernon
Rempart du Midi
Avenue du Président Wilson
Rue Saint-Ausone
Rue du Colonel Driant
Av. de Verdun
Rue de l'Eveche
Rue Tison d'Argence
Rue Molière
Rue de la Gendarmerie
Rue Corneille
Rue des Postes
Rempart Desaix
Rue d'Arc
Rue des Tanneries
Rue Emile Jarreton
Rue de l'Ancienne Église St-Martin
Avenue Jules
Av. G. Clemenceau
Av. des Marechaux
Bd J. et J Tharaud
Rue du Gal Leclerc
Rue de l'Arsenal
Rue d'Austerlitz
Rue de Belat
Rempart de l'Est
N
0 100 m

industry collapsed in the 1980s, and today only a couple of small, specialized mills still function. Since then the economy has picked up again, especially the tourist industry, and it's now a moderately prosperous place.

In the past, however, the former capital of the Angoumois province was a much-coveted city politically, being heavily fought over during the fourteenth-century Anglo–French squabbles and again in the sixteenth century during the Wars of Religion, when it was a Protestant stronghold. After the revocation of the Edict of Nantes, a good proportion of its citizens – among them many of its skilled papermakers – emigrated to Holland, never to return.

Arrival information and accommodation

Angoulême is easily accessible by **train** from Cognac, Limoges and Poitiers. From the **gare SNCF**, avenue Gambetta, with several cheap hotels, leads uphill to the town centre through place Pérot, a fifteen-minute walk. The **gare routière** is at the top of the hill on place Bouillaud, while the **tourist office**, 7 rue du Chat (July & Aug Mon–Sat 9.30am–7pm, Sun 10am–1pm & 2–5pm; Sept–June Mon–Fri 9am–12.30pm & 1.30–6pm, Sat 10am–noon & 2–5pm; Ⓣ05.45.95.16.84, Ⓦwww.angouleme-toursime.com), is on place des Halles, opposite the large covered market. For information on **walking** in the area contact the Centre Info Rando on boulevard de Bury (Ⓦwww.lacharente.com). **Internet** access is available at 24 rue de Montmoreau for a reasonable €3 per hour.

The tourist office can help with **accommodation**; but if you go it alone you'll find a clutch of cheap hotels around the station and some more attractive options nearer the town centre.

Hotels

Le Crab 27 rue Kléber Ⓣ05.45.93.02.93, Ⓔlecrab.angouleme@orange.fr. The nicest of the hotels around the station, with clean and comfortable rooms, all with TV. The downstairs restaurant has menus from €10. ❸

Européen 1 place G.-Pérot Ⓣ05.45.92.06.42, Ⓦwww.europeenhotel.com. An upmarket option, with soundproofed air-conditioned rooms, all with cable TV and minibar. It's in a good position for exploring the town. ❹

D'Orléans 133 av Gambetta Ⓣ05.45.92.07.53, Ⓦwww.hotel-orleans16.com. The cheapest stay in town, and right opposite the train station. Rooms have TV and are acceptable for the price. ❶

Du Palais 4 place Francis-Louvel Ⓣ05.45.92.54.11, Ⓔhoteldupalais.angouleme@orange.fr. A charming hotel in an elegantly preserved former convent. Most rooms are old-style, with wooden floorboards, but decorated with bright colours. Higher-floor rooms have balconies which look out onto the central square. ❺

La Palma 4 rampe d'Aguesseau Ⓣ05.45.95.22.89, Ⓦwww.restaurant-hotel-palma.com. Newly decorated, featuring large rooms with a/c. There's a small rooftop terrace for sunbathing, and an extremely popular restaurant with menus from €11.50. ❹

HI Hostel parc des Bourgines Ⓣ05.45.92.45.80, Ⓕ05.45.95.90.71. A basic hostel with breakfast but no kitchens, situated on an island in the Charente. Take bus #7 from the town centre. Dorm beds €12.

The Town

The **old town** occupies a high steep-sided plateau overlooking a bend in the Charente, a natural fortress. It has many charms, if few notable sights. The labyrinthine streets to the north of the delightful **place Louvel** and the massive Hôtel de Ville have been largely restored and pedestrianized. It's here that the restaurants and bars are concentrated, while the eastern section, down rue Marango and rue St-Martial, has become the main commercial centre. On the southern edge of the plateau stands the **cathedral**, whose west front – like Notre-Dame at Poitiers – is a fascinating display board for some expressive and lively twelfth-century

sculpture, culminating in a Risen Christ with angels and clouds about his head, framed in the usual blaze of a halo. The lively frieze beneath the tympanum to the right of the west door commemorates the recapture of Spanish Zaragoza from the Moors, showing a bishop transfixing a Moorish giant with his lance and Roland killing the Moorish king.

From the front of the cathedral, you can walk all around the **ramparts** encircling the plateau, with long views over the surrounding country, now largely filled with urban sprawl. There are **public gardens** below the parapet at the far end of the fortifications, and a gravelly esplanade by the *lycée* where locals gather to play *boules*.

Angoulême's most fascinating museum lies just below the city walls on the north side close to the River Charente: the **Centre National de la Bande Dessinée**, 121 rue de Bordeaux (Tues–Fri 10am–6pm, Sat & Sun 2–6pm; €5; bus #3 or #5; Ⓦwww.cnbdi.fr), devoted entirely to comic strips. Housed in a hundred-year-old brewery, with contemporary high-rise and glass additions, the museum gets across the message that comics ("BD") – from politics to pornography – are regarded as a serious art form in France. The museum owns a collection of some four thousand original drawings, which it displays in rotating exhibitions of about three hundred at a time. They range from the earliest stories with pictures and captions, the nineteenth-century *images d'Épinal*, through the introduction of the speech bubble in the 1920s to some of the darker contemporary productions. Astérix, Peanuts, Tintin and many other characters and artists are represented. There's also a vast library, much of it in English, where you're welcome to relax on cushions and flick through the comics.

Another riverfront museum close by is the **Musée du Papier**, 134 rue de Bordeaux (July & Aug noon–6.30pm; Sept–June Tues–Sun 2–6pm; free), located in a disused cigarette-paper factory – a fitting tribute to the declining Charentais paper industry. While exhibits get into the history and technicalities of paper-making, temporary exhibitions display paper's more artistic usages.

Eating

Angoulême has some wonderful **restaurants,** the best areas being rue de Genève, offering both traditional French and international options, and the narrow, pedestrianized rue Massillon.

L'Atlas Marocain 25 rue de la Cloche Verte Ⓣ05.45.94.95.30. Serves menus including a glass of wine for €10 in the evening. Couscous is a speciality, and you'll be offered a second helping.

Le Bahia 13 place des Halles Ⓣ05.45.95.94.55. A South American-themed brasserie opposite the market. Sangria and bottled Mexican beers are on offer, as are menus for around €16. There are salsa nights every Thursday out of season, and live music in summer. Closed Sun.

Le Chat Noir 24 rue de Genève Ⓣ05.45.95.26.27. Popular for its great-value salads and omelettes at lunchtime, and for its prize bruschetta and relaxed atmosphere in the evenings. On Thursday nights in summer it shares live music with *Le Bahia* next door. Closed Sun.

Chez Paul 8 place Francis-Louvel Ⓣ05.45.90.04.61. A high-class restaurant serving mainly seafood, with a large terrace and garden. Inside there is a rather trendy bar which stays open until midnight.

La Ruelle 6 rue 3 Notre-Dame Ⓣ05.45.95.15.19. A really fine restaurant, with impeccable service and some of the best food to be found in the region. Menus from €22, closed Sun & Mon.

Around Angoulême

LA ROCHEFOUCAULD, 22km east of Angoulême, is the site of a huge Renaissance **château** on the banks of the River Tardoire, which still belongs to the family that gave its name to the town a thousand years ago. The stately pile, although still lived in, opens its elaborate portals to the public (Easter–Nov daily 10am–7pm; €6.10). In August it stages a massive son et lumière with a brigade-sized cast. If you want to **stay**, try the lovely old *Auberge de la Carpe d'Or* at 1 rue de Vitrac (ⓣ05.45.62.02.72, ⓕ05.45.63.01.88; ❷). There's also a municipal **campsite** on rue des Flots beneath the château.

Further east, the country becomes hillier and more wooded, with buttercup pastures grazed by liver-coloured Limousin cattle. A good way to see it is to drive up the back roads along the River Vienne to the beautiful, if now rather touristy little town of **CONFOLENS**, about 40km northeast of La Rochefoucauld. Its ancient houses are stacked up a hillside above a broad brown sweep of the river, here crossed by a long narrow medieval bridge. The town's chief claim to fame today is the huge **International Folklore Festival**, held every year in the second week of August, when, of course, it's impossible to find anywhere to stay (festival information ⓣ05.45.84.00.77, ⓦwww.festivaldeconfolens.com). There is a municipal **campsite** by the tributary River Goire.

Having come this far, it's worth continuing the extra 6km to the minuscule village of **ST-GERMAIN-DE-CONFOLENS**, huddled by the riverside beneath the romantic towers of its ruined castle, where you can eat good country fare at the *Auberge de la Tour* (closed Mon except in July & Aug) for as little as €11.50.

Aquitaine

In Roman times, **Bordeaux** was capital of the province of Aquitania Secunda. With the marriage of Eleanor of Aquitaine and King Henry II of England in 1152, it quickly became the principal English foothold for their three-hundred-year Aquitanian adventure, and it was to their presence, and particularly their taste for its red wines – imported back to England and termed "claret" – that the region owed its first great economic boom. The second boom, which financed the building of the gracious eighteenth-century centre of Bordeaux, came with the expansion of colonial trade.

The surrounding countryside is more notable for its wines and **vineyards** than its scenery, though the hills of **Entre-Deux-Mers** and the pretty town of **St-Émilion** are worth visiting in their own right. More interesting is the vast pine-covered expanse of **Les Landes** and the huge, wild Atlantic beaches of the **Côte d'Argent** to the south, but it's not a landscape that charms. Its appeal is more in its size and uniqueness – and you definitely need your own transport to explore it.

Bordeaux

The city of **BORDEAUX** is stunning when approached from the south along the river. It's big, with a population of over half a million, and obviously rich – as it has been since the Romans set up a lively trading centre here; even today

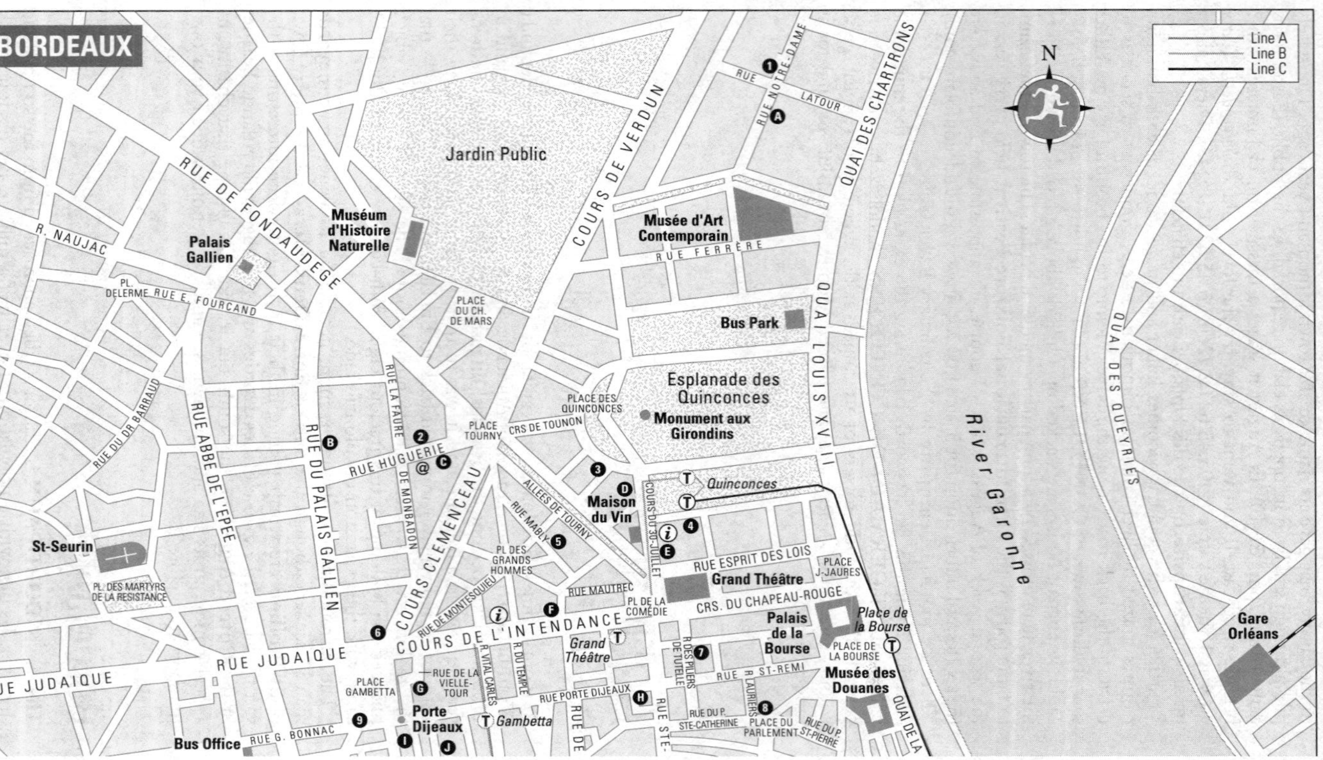
BORDEAUX
Line A
Line B
Line C
N
Jardin Public
Muséum d'Histoire Naturelle
Palais Gallien
Musée d'Art Contemporain
Bus Park
Esplanade des Quinconces
Monument aux Girondins
Maison du Vin
Grand Théâtre
Palais de la Bourse
Place de la Bourse
Musée des Douanes
Gare Orléans
St-Seurin
Porte Dijeaux
Bus Office
River Garonne
QUAI DES QUEYRIES
QUAI DES CHARTRONS
QUAI LOUIS XVIII
QUAI DE LA
COURS DE VERDUN
RUE DE FONDAUDEGE
R. NAUJAC
RUE NOTRE-DAME
RUE LATOUR
RUE FERRÈRE
PL. DELERME
RUE E. FOURCAND
PLACE DU CH. DE MARS
PLACE DES QUINCONCES
PLACE TOURNY
CRS DE TOUNON
RUE LA FAURE
RUE HUGUERIE
DE MONBADON
RUE DU PALAIS GALLIEN
RUE ABBE DE L'EPEE
RUE DU DR BARRAUD
PL. DES MARTYRS DE LA RESISTANCE
COURS CLEMENCEAU
ALLEES DE TOURNY
RUE MABLY
PL DES GRANDS HOMMES
RUE DE MONTESQUIEU
RUE MAUTREC
COURS DU 30-JUILLET
RUE ESPRIT DES LOIS
PLACE J-JAURES
PL DE LA COMÉDIE
CRS. DU CHAPEAU-ROUGE
COURS DE L'INTENDANCE
Grand Théâtre
Quinconces
Gambetta
RUE JUDAIQUE
PLACE GAMBETTA
RUE DE LA VIELLE-TOUR
R. VITAL CARLES
R. DU TEMPLE
RUE PORTE DIJEAUX
RUE DE
RUE STE-
R DES PILIERS DE TUTELLE
RUE ST-REMI
R LAURIERS
RUE DU P. STE-CATHERINE
PLACE DU PARLEMENT
RUE DU P. ST-PIERRE
PLACE DE LA BOURSE
RUE G. BONNAC

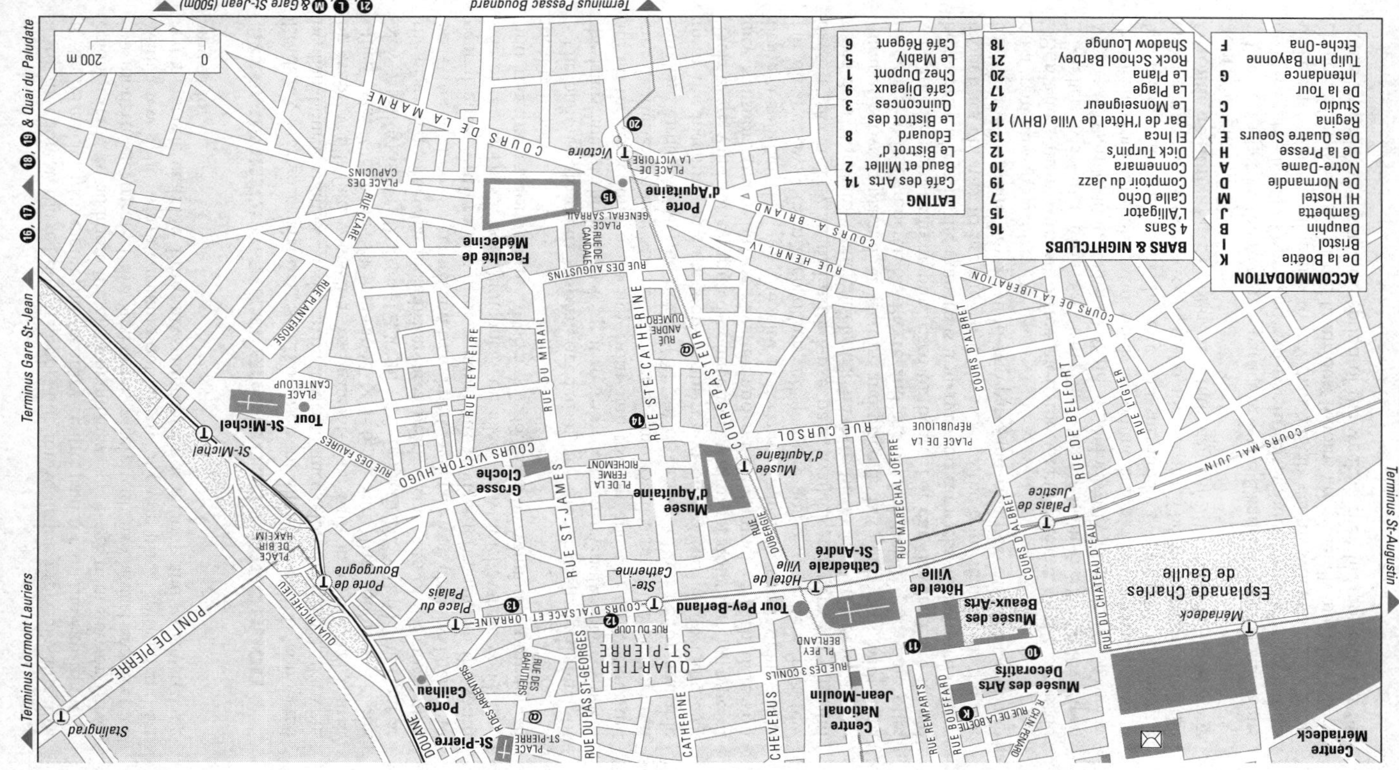

ACCOMMODATION
De la Boétie K
Bristol I
Dauphin B
Gambetta J
HI Hostel M
De Normandie D
Notre-Dame A
De la Presse H
Des Quatre Soeurs E
Regina L
Studio C
De la Tour
Intendance G
Tulip Inn Bayonne
Etche-Ona F
BARS & NIGHTCLUBS
4 Sans 16
L'Alligator 15
Calle Ocho 7
Comptoir du Jazz 19
Connemara 10
Dick Turpin's 12
El Inca 13
Bar de l'Hôtel de Ville (BHV) 11
Le Monseigneur 4
La Plage 17
Le Plana 20
Rock School Barbey 21
Shadow Lounge 18
EATING
Café des Arts 14
Baud et Millet 2
Le Bistrot d' Edouard 8
Le Bistrot des Quinconces 3
Café Dijeaux 9
Chez Dupont 1
Le Mably 5
Café Régent 6
Terminus Lormont Lauriers
Terminus Gare St-Jean
16, 17, 18, 19 & Quai du Paludate
21, L, M & Gare St-Jean (500m)
Terminus Pessac Bougnard
Terminus St-Augustin
0 200 m
Stalingrad
PONT DE PIERRE
QUAI RICHELIEU
PLACE DE BIR HAKEIM
St-Michel
Tour St-Michel
PLACE CANTELOUP
RUE PLANTEROSE
RUE CLARE
PLACE DES CAPUCINS
COURS DE LA MARNE
Porte de Bourgogne
RUE DES FAURES
COURS VICTOR-HUGO
DOUANE
Porte Cailhau
St-Pierre
PLACE ST-PIERRE
R DES ARGENTIERS
RUE DES BAHUTIERS
Place du Palais
COURS D'ALSACE ET LORRAINE
RUE LEYTEIRE
Grosse Cloche
RUE DU MIRAIL
Faculté de Médecine
RUE ST-JAMES
RUE DU PAS ST-GEORGES
QUARTIER ST-PIERRE
RUE DU LOUP
Ste-Catherine
PL DE LA FERME RICHEMONT
RUE DES AUGUSTINS
RUE DE CANDALE
PLACE GENERAL SARRAIL
Victoire
PLACE DE LA VICTOIRE
RUE STE-CATHERINE
RUE ANDRE DUMERC
CATHERINE
Tour Pey-Berland
Musée d'Aquitaine
COURS PASTEUR
Porte d'Aquitaine
CHEVERUS
RUE DES 3 CONILS
PL PEY BERLAND
Hôtel de Ville
RUE DUBERGIE
RUE CURSOL
RUE HENRI IV
COURS A. BRIAND
Centre National Jean-Moulin
Cathédrale St-André
RUE MARECHAL JOFFRE
PLACE DE LA RÉPUBLIQUE
RUE REMPARTS
RUE BOUFFARD
RUE DE LA BOETIE
R. CHN. PENARD
Musée des Arts Décoratifs
Musée des Beaux-Arts
Hôtel de Ville
COURS D'ALBRET
Palais de Justice
RUE DE BELFORT
COURS DE LA LIBERATION
RUE DU CHATEAU D'EAU
RUE LIGIER
Mériadeck
Esplanade Charles de Gaulle
COURS MAL JUIN
Centre Mériadeck

it still functions as the regional transport hub for Aquitaine. Especially attractive is the relatively small eighteenth-century centre, paid for by the expansion of colonial trade. In addition, the city's brand-new space-age tram network gives it a modern, electric feel that juxtaposes nicely with its classical architecture. With a few sights worth checking out, plenty of cheap places to sleep and eat and a fantastic nightlife, Bordeaux's atmosphere is inviting and worth sticking around for.

Arrival, information and accommodation

Bordeaux-Mérignac **airport** is 12km west of the city and is connected by half-hourly shuttles to the main tourist office (45min; €6.50). Arriving by **train**, you'll find yourself at the gare St-Jean, with its own small tourist office (May–Oct Mon–Sat 9am–noon & 1–6pm, Sun 10am–noon & 1–3pm; Nov–April Mon–Fri 9.30am–12.30pm & 2–6pm; ⓣ05.56.91.64.70), right at the heart of a somewhat insalubrious area, nearly 3km south of the city centre; bus #16 runs into the centre, and tram line C will take you close by. There's no central **gare routière**, but most regional bus services terminate on the south side of the esplanade des Quinconces, on allées de Munich, where you'll also find the information centre (ⓣ05.57.57.88.88, ⓦwww.infotbc.com) for all local transport.

The billion-euro **tram system**, opened in late 2003, has changed much of the landscape of the city, making it more pedestrian-friendly. Services operate on the three lines frequently from 5am to 1am, and run throughout the city centre, extending several kilometres into Bordeaux's suburbs. You can purchase either single-ride tickets (€1.30) or carnets of ten (€10), available from the machines at tram stops (coins only) or at *tabacs* all over the city. Tickets are valid for unlimited connections within an hour on any type of city transport (tram, bus or navette), and must be punched each time you begin a journey. Though the city is certainly walkable, some sights are a fair distance away from each other, and if you're going to be here for a few days, it pays to buy an **unlimited-use pass**, available for between one and seven days. Bordeaux's efficient electric **navette buses** run daily every 10–15 minutes between place de la Victoire and place de la Quinconces, with stops in between at Gambetta, St.-Pierre and St.-Michel; tickets (the same ones used for the trams) can be purchased on board. For **car** drivers, there should be ample parking in the numerous underground car parks in the town centre, though it's cheaper to use the car parks next to the tram stations on the east bank of the Garonne: buy a round-trip park-and-ride ticket (€2.60), and hop on a tram into the centre.

Bordeaux's main **tourist office**, near the Grand Théâtre on 12 cours du 30-Juillet (May–Oct Mon–Sat 9am–7pm, Sun 9.30am–6.30pm; Nov–April Mon–Sat 9am–6.30pm, Sun 9.45am–4.30pm; ⓣ05.56.00.66.00, ⓦwww.bordeaux-tourisme.com), can book accommodation free of charge, and it has useful information on the city and surrounding vineyards, to which it also arranges tours (see box on p.668 for details). The tourist office for the **Gironde region** is at 21 cours de l'Intendance (ⓣ05.56.52.61.40, ⓦwww.tourisme-gironde.fr).

The area right by the station – particularly rue Charles-Domercq and cours de la Marne – is full of one- and two-star **hotels**, though the dodgy shopfronts make this a less appealing area to stay than the city centre, where there's a good choice, from the basic to the luxurious. Rooms are generally not difficult to come by, with the notable exception of the week of the Vinexpo trade fair (in odd-numbered years) and Fête du Vin (in even-numbered years) in June, when Bordeaux is packed to the gunnels.

Hotels

De la Boétie 4 rue de la Boétie ⓣ05.56.81.76.68, ⓕ05.56.51.24.72. A good bargain, with shower and TV in all rooms, this cheap and central one-star hotel is on a quiet backstreet. Owned by the *Bristol* (see below), it shares its reception. ❶

Bristol 4 rue Bouffard ⓣ05.56.81.85.01, ⓔbristol@hotel-bordeaux.com. Comfortable, relaxed two-star hotel just south of place Gambetta; its well-equipped, en-suite rooms are decently sized and stylishly decorated. ❷

Dauphin 82 rue du Palais Gallien ⓣ05.56.52.24.62, ⓔdauphinhotel@orange.fr. Though a little out of the action, this fabulously decorated, old-fashioned hotel is justifiably popular; its recent renovation has added parquet floors and snazzy paint jobs in nearly all the rooms. The more spacious, top-price rooms, with their huge windows and high ceilings, offer best value for money. ❸

Gambetta 66 rue Porte-Dijeaux ⓣ05.56.51.21.83, ⓔhotgambetta@aol.com. Brilliantly positioned for exploring the old town, just off place Gambetta. All rooms have TV, phone and bathroom, and there is also a living room area for guests. ❸

De Normandie 7 cours du 30-Juillet ⓣ05.56.52.16.80, ⓦwww.hotel-de-normandie-bordeaux.com. Large, nicely furnished rooms with minibar, wireless Internet and all other mod cons. The top-floor rooms boast private balconies with unbeatable views of the city. ❻

Notre-Dame 36 rue Notre-Dame ⓣ05.56.52.88.24, ⓦwww.hotelnotredame.free.fr. Quiet, refined establishment in an interesting area of old streets just north of esplanade des Quinconces. A/c comes as standard, and for inspiration, rooms are decorated with posters of Bordeaux. Especially good rates available for families; they will put two rooms together for just €70. ❸

De la Presse 6–8 rue Porte Dijeaux ⓣ05.56.48.53.88, ⓦwww.hoteldelapresse.com. With very friendly staff, this well-kept family-run hotel in the pedestrian heart of Bordeaux is excellent value. Its light, bright rooms are well proportioned, with big beds to match, and provide three-star comforts such as minibar, air conditioning, and Internet access in the rooms. Closed one week at Christmas. ❺

Des Quatre Soeurs 6 cours du 30-Juillet ⓣ05.57.81.19.20, ⓦ4soeurs.free.fr. Popular, efficient and friendly hotel in an ideal spot next to the tourist office. The rooms are cheerfully coloured, though some are a touch boxy for the price. ❺

Regina 34 rue Charles-Domercq ⓣ05.56.91.66.07, ⓦwww.hotelreginabordeaux.com. The best option near the train station, the *Regina* offers simple, spruce rooms of a good size. The cheapest have a shower but no toilet and, while all rooms are equipped with phones, only some have TVs. Ask for a quieter room at the back. ❷

Studio 26 rue Huguerie ⓣ05.56.48.00.14, ⓔstudio@hotel-bordeaux.com. Easily the best deal in town, offering simple single rooms with bath and TV for a paltry €18, so very popular with backpackers. There's not much soundproofing though, so your night's sleep is slightly pot-luck. ❶

De la Tour Intendance 14–16 rue de la Vieille-Tour ⓣ05.56.44.56.56, ⓦwww.hotel-tour-intendance.com. Located just off place Gambetta, the rooms here are large and cool, with wooden paneling and simple decoration, while the reception area and breakfast room are also particularly attractive. They have a garage for parking overnight (€8). ❻

Tulip Inn Bayonne Etche-Ona 15 cours de l'Intendance ⓣ05.56.48.00.88, ⓦwww.bordeaux-hotel.com. Occupying two large buildings on quiet streets in behind the main road, this Best Western hotel has all the luxury you would expect, including CD players and flat-screen TVs in all rooms. They also have a suite available. ❼

Hostel

Hostel 22 cours Barbey ⓣ05.56.91.59.51. Situated off cours de la Marne, the hostel is a 10min walk from gare St-Jean, or take bus #16. Kitchen and laundry facilities, breakfast included. Dorm beds are €21.40, but note that it's not usually possible to reserve in advance.

The City

Bordeaux is reasonably spread out along the western side of the River Garonne, with the eighteenth-century **old town** lying between the place de la Comédie to the north, the imposing buildings of the riverbank and the cathedral to the west. North of the centre is the vast open square of the **esplanade des Quinconces**, and further still, the **Jardin Public**, containing some very scant remains of Bordeaux's Roman past.

Vieux Bordeaux

The elegant, eighteenth-century city centres on the **quartier St-Pierre** and stretches up to the Grand Théâtre to the north, the cathedral to the west and the cours Victor-Hugo to the south. The narrow streets are lined with grand mansions from Bordeaux's glory days, and much of the area has been done up over recent years, though some of the streets remain seedy in anticipation of the restorer's touch.

The social hub of the eighteenth-century city was the impeccably classical **Grand Théâtre** on **place de la Comédie** at the northern end of rue Ste-Catherine. Built on the site of a Roman temple by the architect Victor Louis in 1780, this lofty building is faced with an immense colonnaded portico topped by twelve Muses and Graces. Inside, the interior is likewise opulently decorated with trompe l'oeil paintings; the best way to see it is to attend one of the operas or ballets staged throughout the year, with seats in the gods from as little as €8 (☎05.56.00.85.95 for info & bookings), or ask at the tourist office about the guided tours they offer (July & Aug Mon–Sat 11am; €5.50). Smart streets radiate from here: the city's main shopping street, **rue Ste-Catherine**, running south and partially pedestrianized to ease the consumer flow; the ritzy cours de l'Intendance running west; and the sandy, tree-lined allées de Tourny running northwest, commemorating the Marquis Louis Aubert de Tourny – the eighteenth-century administrator who was prime mover of the city's "Golden Age" and supervised much of the rebuilding. Back in the narrow streets of the old town, the harmonious **place du Parlement** and **place St-Pierre** are both lined with typical Bordelais mansions and peppered with wrought-iron balconies and arcading, making impressive examples of town planning.

The riverfront was also given the once-over by early eighteenth-century planners, with the imposing **place de la Bourse** creating a focal point on the quayside. The impressive bulk of the old customs house of 1733 contains the **Musée des Douanes** (Tues–Sun 10am–6pm; €3), which gives a rundown on Bordeaux's port and seafaring past and retraces the history of the administration and work of French Customs. The square is balanced by the **Palais de la Bourse** (stock exchange) looking out over the quayside and the broad River Garonne. Further south along the riverbank, the fifteenth-century **Porte Cailhau** takes its name from the stones (*cailloux* – *cailhaux* in dialect) unloaded on the neighbouring quay to be used as ballast for boats. Crossing the river just south of here, the only testimony to a nobler past is the impressive **Pont de Pierre** – "Stone Bridge", though in fact it's mostly brick – built at Napoleon's command during the Spanish campaigns, with seventeen arches in honour of his victories. The views of the river and quays from here are memorable, particularly when floodlit at night.

Place Gambetta, the cathedral and around

Cours de l'Intendance, a street lined with chic shops, links place de la Comédie with café-lined **place Gambetta**, a pivotal square for the city's museums, shops and the cathedral. In the middle of place Gambetta's arcaded house fronts, a valiant attempt at an English garden adds some welcome relief, belying the fact that the guillotine lopped three hundred heads off here at the time of the Revolution. In one corner stands the eighteenth-century arch of the **Porte Dijeaux**, an old city gate.

South of place Gambetta is the **Cathédrale St-André** (Mon–Sat 7.30–11.30am & 2–6/6.30pm), whose most eye-catching feature is the great upward sweep of the twin steeples over the north transept, an effect heightened by the adjacent but separate bell tower, the fifteenth-century **Tour Pey-Berland** (June–Sept daily 10am–6pm; Oct–May Tues–Sun 10am–noon & 2–5pm; €5). The interior of the cathedral, begun in the twelfth century, is vast and impressive, even if there's not much of artistic interest apart from the choir, which provides one of the few complete examples of the florid late Gothic style known as Rayonnant, and the north transept door and the Porte Royale to the right, which feature some fine carving.

The cream of Bordeaux's museums is to be found scattered in the streets around the cathedral. Directly behind the classical Hôtel de Ville, formerly Archbishop Rohan's palace, the **Musée des Beaux-Arts** (daily except Tues 11am–6pm; permanent museum free; temporary exhibitions €5) has a small but worthy selection of European fine art, featuring works by Reynolds, Titian, Rubens, Matisse and Marquet (a native of the city), as well as Delacroix's superb painting of *La Grèce sur les ruines de Missolonghi*. More engaging, however, is the **Musée des Arts Décoratifs** (daily except Tues 2–6pm; same price system), two blocks north on rue Bouffard and housed in a handsome eighteenth-century house. The extensive collection includes some beautiful, mainly French, porcelain and faïence, period furniture, glass, miniatures, Barye animal sculptures and prints of the city in its maritime heyday.

Continuing to circle clockwise round the cathedral, you'll pass the **Centre National Jean-Moulin** (Tues–Sun 2–6pm; free), an interesting museum dedicated to the local Resistance, featuring a history of the occupation of Bordeaux and a harrowing permanant exhibit of Holocaust-inspired paintings by French artist J.J. Morran, before reaching the imaginatively laid-out **Musée d'Aquitaine**, on cours Pasteur (Tues–Sun 11am–6pm; temporary exhibitions €5), one of the city's best museums. A stimulating variety of objects and types of display emphasizes regional ethnography, and drawings and writings reveal the maritime, commercial and agricultural prowess of eighteenth-century Bordeaux. It's also worth taking a look at the section on the wine trade before venturing off on a vineyard tour in the region. A couple of blocks east, rue St-James is straddled by a heavy Gothic tower, the fifteenth-century **Grosse Cloche**, originally part of the medieval town hall.

North of the centre

North of the Grand Théâtre, cours du 30-Juillet leads into the bare, gravelly – and frankly unattractive – expanse of the **esplanade des Quinconces**, said to be Europe's largest municipal square. At the quayside end are two tall columns, erected in 1829 and topped by allegorical statues of Commerce and Navigation; at the opposite end of the esplanade is the **Monument aux Girondins**, a glorious *fin-de-siècle* ensemble of statues and fountains built in honour of the influential local deputies to the 1789 Revolutionary Assembly, later purged by Robespierre as moderates and counter-revolutionaries. During World War II, in a fit of anti-French spite, the occupying Germans made plans to melt the monument down, only to be foiled by the local Resistance, who got there first and, under cover of darkness, dismantled it piece by piece and hid it in a barn in the Médoc for the duration of the war.

To the northwest is the beautiful formal park, the **Jardin Public** (daily April–Oct 7am–8/9pm; Nov–March 7am–6pm; free), containing the city's botanical gardens as well as a small **natural history museum** (Mon & Wed–Fri 11am–6pm, Sat & Sun 2–6pm; temporary exhibitions €5). Behind it, to the west and north, lies a quiet, provincial quarter of two-storey stone houses. Concealed among the narrow streets, on rue du Dr-Albert-Barraud, is a large chunk of brick and stone masonry, the so-called **Palais Gallien**, in fact a

△ Place du Parlement, Bordeaux

third-century arena that's all that remains of Burdigala, Aquitaine's Roman capital. Nearby, on place Delerme, the unusual round **market hall** makes a focus for a stroll through the quarter. To the east of the gardens, closer to the river, the **Musée d'Art Contemporain** on rue Ferrère (Tues & Thurs–Sun 11am–6pm, Wed 11am–8pm; €5) occupies a converted nineteenth-century warehouse for colonial imports. The vast, arcaded hall provides a magnificent setting for the mostly post-1960 sculpture and installation-based work by artists such as Richard Long, Daniel Buren and Sol LeWitt. Few pieces from the permanent collection are on display at any one time, the main space being filled by temporary exhibitions, so it's hit and miss as to whether you'll like what's on offer. However, there's a superb collection of glossy art books in the library and an elegant café-restaurant on the roof (lunch only).

Eating and drinking

Bordeaux is packed with numerous **restaurants**, many of them top-notch, and due to its position close to the Atlantic coast, fresh seafood features prominently on many a Bordelais menu. The best place to look for restaurants is around place du Parlement and place St-Pierre, where you'll find something to satisfy all tastes and budgets. There are numerous sandwich bars and fast-food outlets all along rue Ste-Catherine and spilling into studenty place de la Victoire. In the summer, *guinguettes* – open-air **riverside stalls** selling shrimps, king prawns and other seafood snacks – set up along the quai des Chartrons. For **picnic fodder**, there's a marvellous, round **market** in the place des Grands-Hommes, and on rue de Montesquieu, just off the square, Jean d'Alos runs the city's best *fromagerie*, with dozens of farm-produced cheeses.

The student population ensures a collection of young, lively **bars**, a host of which are found on and around place de la Victoire. Several offer live music and all are packed on Thursday nights. There's also a clutch of English, Irish and antipodean **pubs** now in Bordeaux and a low-key **gay scene** concentrated at the south end of rue des Remparts and around the town hall.

Cafés and restaurants

Café des Arts 138 cours Victor-Hugo. This café-brasserie on the corner of rue Ste-Catherine is one of the city's few old-style cafés, its unique ambience created from faded relics of the 1940s. The food is good, too, with a *plat du jour* for around €9, and the kitchens stay open till 1am.

Baud et Millet 19 rue Huguerie ⓣ05.56.79.05.77. The ultimate cheese-and-wine feast consumed around a few tables at the back of a wine shop where you choose your own bottle from the shelves. Portions are generous and the food rich, so one dish goes a long way. You can have a cheese and salad buffet for €19.50, and *raclette* is another option. Closed Sun.

Le Bistrot d'Édouard 16 place du Parlement. ⓣ05.56.81.48.87. In a great position on a lovely square, with outdoor seating in summer, this is as good value as you'll find anywhere. There is a three-course menu for €12, with lots of choice – their salads are particularly worth trying.

Le Bistrot des Quinconces 4 place des Quinconces ⓣ05.56.52.84.56. Lively daytime and evening bistro. In fine weather locals vie for the outdoor tables, in a great spot facing the fountains. The modern, eclectic *carte* includes oysters and steak tartare, as well as a three-course weekday lunch menu at €15.

Café Dijeaux 14 place Gambetta. A great place to sit and watch the world go by, in the shadow of the city gate. Food is available all day and very reasonably priced.

Chez Dupont 45 rue de Notre-Dame ⓣ05.56.81.49.59. Bustling, old-fashioned restaurant in the Chartrons district, with wooden floors, old posters and waiters sporting colourful waistcoats. Prices are very reasonable, with main courses costing €12–18. The house sangria is also recommended.

Le Mably 12 rue Mably ⓣ05.56.44.30.10. Informal, friendly and popular restaurant with a warm, homely atmosphere. The food is of excellent quality and very traditional, most dishes featuring either duck or rabbit. Menus from €22. Closed Sun, Mon & three weeks in August.

Café Régent 46 place Gambetta. The place to be seen in Bordeaux, with plush leather seats and crimson upholstery. The bar is open for drinks all day, or you can get three courses for €15 at lunch or dinner.

Bars

L'Alligator 3 place du Général-Sarrail. Out of season, this bar is full to the rafters with student-types enjoying a party atmosphere, with a dance-floor downstairs. In summer, it's more chilled out; the music gets turned down a few notches and the terrace is a great place to enjoy a drink in the sun.

Calle Ocho 24 rue des Piliers-de-Tutelle ⓣ05.56.48.08.68. Bordeaux's best-known salsa bar has an unrivalled party atmosphere and is packed out most nights till 2am. They serve real Cuban rum and *mojitos*, and the self-inebriating barstaff frequently showers the crowds with water sprayed from the bar tap.

Connemara 18 cours d'Albret. For the homesick pining for a pint of Guinness, this is Bordeaux's liveliest Irish pub, with free concerts or some other event most nights, plus cheap bar snacks, such as fish and chips, beef and Guinness pie and apple crumble. Happy hour is 6–8pm daily.

Dick Turpin's 72 rue du Loup. Opposite the wisteria-filled courtyard of the municipal archives, this is a pretty good rendition of an English town pub with a quiet, relaxed atmosphere and an international clientele. There's the standard range of beers – Guinness, Bass and Newcastle Brown. Happy hour 5.30–8.30pm.

Bar de l'Hôtel de Ville (BHV) 4 rue de l'Hôtel-de-Ville. Friendly little gay café-bar which stages a variety of free events every other Sunday (10.30pm).

Le Plana 22 place de la Victoire. One of the more relaxed student hangouts around the square, though, like everywhere else, it's jumping on Thursday nights. Free live music on Sun (jazz), Mon & Tues (various).

Nightlife and entertainment

Since Bordeaux's **dance clubs** are constantly changing it's best to ask around for the latest hotspots. There are one or two discos in the city centre, such as *Le Monseigneur*, at 42 allées d'Orléans, next to the tourist office (ⓣ05.56.44.29.91), but the majority of clubs are spread out along southerly quai du Paludate, where things don't really get going until one in the morning and continue till closing time at four. Bear in mind that there isn't always the most welcoming atmosphere down at the quayside, and it can be hard to get in to some clubs if the bouncers don't recognize you. The places to head for are *La Plage* at no. 40, a fun disco in a tropical-beach setting, and the wonderfully Baroque *Shadow*

Lounge, 5 rue Cabannac, which plays house and techno. For alternative music from reggae to hip-hop, your best bet is *4 Sans* at 40 rue d'Armagnac, which often hosts good DJs.

To find out the latest **events and happenings** in and around Bordeaux, get hold of a copy of the regional newspaper *Sud-Ouest*. Alternatively there are the free *Bordeaux Plus* and *Clubs & Concerts*, detailing the city's current favourite clubs. The tourist office issues *Bordeaux Magazine*, a free monthly in French with coverage of more highbrow cultural events around town. To buy **tickets** for city and regional events, contact the venue direct or head for the box office (ⓣ05.56.48.26.26) in the nineteenth-century Galerie Bordelaise arcade, wedged between rue Ste-Catherine and rue des Piliers-de-Tutelle. Virgin Megastore (ⓣ05.56.56.05.55) on place Gambetta also has a ticket outlet, as does the FNAC on rue Ste-Catherine (ⓣ05.56.00.21.30).

Jazz and blues fans should head south down the river to the respected *Comptoir du Jazz*, 57 quai de Paludate (ⓣ05.56.85.98.85); entry is free but you're expected to buy at least one drink. The *Café des Arts* (see p.665) is also worth a try. There's no shortage of more **contemporary music**, either. Bordeaux's home of rock music is the *Rock School Barbey*, 18 cours Barbey (ⓣ05.56.33.66.00) which hosts recognized international bands quite regularly. Another place to check out is the more central *El Inca*, 28 rue Ste-Colombe, which has live rock or jazz most evenings.

Listings

Airlines Air France ⓣ08.20.82.08.20; British Airways ⓣ08.25.82.54.00.

Bike rental Yser Cyclo (ⓣ05.56.92.77.18; closed Sat & Sun) at 104 cours d'Yser has the best value of the various possibilities; town bikes are just €6 per day and €26 per week. Just down the road at 48 cours d'Yser, Station Vélo Services (ⓣ05.57.95.64.21) rents bikes out from €9 per day, and is also the place to go if you need any repairs done.

Books and newspapers Presse Gambetta, on place Gambetta, sells all the main English-language papers in addition to some regional guides and maps, while Bordeaux's largest bookstore, Mollat, 15 rue Vital Carles, has a better selection. They also stock a few English-language titles, though there's more choice at helpful Bradley's Bookshop, 8 cours d'Albret.

Car rental Numerous rental firms are located in and around the train station, including Avis ⓣ08.20.61.16.74; Budget ⓣ05.56.91.41.70; Europcar ⓣ05.56.33.87.40; Hertz ⓣ05.57.59.05.95; and National/Citer ⓣ05.56.92.19.62. They all have outlets at the airport as well.

Cinema You're most likely to find original-language (*version originale*, or *v.o.*) films at the wonderful art-house cinema Utopia, 5 place Camille-Jullian (ⓣ05.56.52.00.03, ⓦwww.cinemas-utopia.org), in a converted church. Other good options include Trianon-Jean Vigo, 6 rue Franklin, near place des Grands-Hommes (ⓣ05.56.44.35.17, ⓦwww.jeanvigo.com), and UGC Cinécité, 13–15 rue Georges-Bonnac (ⓣ08.92.70.00.00, ⓦwww.ugc.fr). For more standard fare, there's the vast, seventeen-screen Megarama (ⓣ08.92.69.33.17, ⓦwww.megarama.fr) across the Pont de Pierre in the old Gare d'Orléans.

Consulates UK, 353 bd du Président-Wilson ⓣ05.57.22.21.10. USA, 10 place de la Bourse ⓣ05.56.48.63.80.

Emergencies To call an ambulance, phone SAMU on ⓣ15.

Hospital Centre Hospitalier Pellegrin-Tripode, place Amélie-Raba-Léon (ⓣ05.56.79.56.79), to the west of central Bordeaux.

Internet Cyberstation, 23 cours Pasteur is a friendly and helpful cybercafé with rates from €2 per hour (before 2pm), while Artobas, 7 rue Maucoudinat just off the place St-Pierre, is more expensive but has a faster connection (Mon–Sat 11am–midnight; €3 per hour). The gare St-Jean claims to have a free Wi-Fi connection, but it seems about as reliable as the wind.

Money exchange American Express, 11 cours de l'Intendance (Mon–Fri 9.30am–5.55pm), handles most travellers' cheques and foreign currencies. The main banks along cours de l'Intendance also offer exchange facilities and 24hr ATMs.

Police Commissariat Central, 23 rue François-de-Sourdis (ⓣ05.57.85.77.77 or ⓣ17 in emergencies).

The Bordeaux wine region

Touring the **vineyards** and sampling a few local wines is one of the great pleasures of the Bordeaux region. The wine-producing districts lie in a great semicircle around the city, starting with the **Médoc** in the north, then skirting east through **St-Émilion**, before finishing south of the city among the vineyards of the **Sauternes**. In between, the less prestigious districts are also worth investigating, notably those of **Blaye**, to the north of Bordeaux, and **Entre-Deux-Mers**, to the east.

There's more to the region than its wine, however. Many of the Médoc's eighteenth-century châteaux are striking buildings in their own right, while the town of Blaye is dominated by a vast fortress, and there's a far older, more ruined castle at Villandraut on the edge of the Sauternes. St-Émilion is by far the prettiest of the wine towns, and has the unexpected bonus of a cavernous underground church. For scenic views, however, you can't beat the green, gentle hills of Entre-Deux-Mers and its ruined abbey, **La Sauve-Majeur**.

All these places are relatively well served by **public transport**. There are train lines from Bordeaux running north through the Médoc to Margaux and Pauillac, and south along the Garonne valley to St-Macaire and La Réole. St-Émilion, meanwhile, lies on the Bordeaux–Sarlat line, but the station is a couple of kilometres out of town. In addition, there's a very comprehensive regional bus network, with connections from Bordeaux to most of the towns mentioned below – you can pick up a route map from the office on allées de Munich in Bordeaux. Buses are operated by several different companies, the largest being Citram Aquitaine (ⓣ05.56.43.68.43), which runs to nearly everywhere around the city. **Cycling** is yet another option, as many of the towns are interconnected by well-marked, clean, blacktop footpaths that wend their way through the woods.

The Médoc

The landscape of **the Médoc**, a slice of land northwest of Bordeaux wedged between the forests bordering the Atlantic coast and the Gironde estuary, is itself rather monotonous: its gravel plains, occupying the west bank of the brown, island-spotted estuary, rarely swell into anything resembling a hill. Paradoxically, however, this poor soil is ideal for viticulture – vines root more deeply if they don't find the sustenance they need in the topsoil and, firmly rooted, they are less subject to drought and flooding. The region's eight *appellations* produce only red wines, from the grape varieties of Cabernet Sauvignon, Cabernet Franc, Merlot and, to a lesser degree, Petit Verdot. Cabernet Sauvignon gives body, bouquet, colour and maturing potential to the wine, while Merlot gives it its "animal" quality, making it rounder and softer. The D2 wine road, heading off the N15 from Bordeaux, passes through Margaux, St-Julien, Pauillac and St-Estèphe and, while the scenery might not be stunning, the many famous – albeit mostly inaccessible – châteaux are.

The problem of accommodation is much worse in the Médoc than in the rest of the wine region, but it's possible to visit the area on a day-trip from Bordeaux. Considering it's one of the most prestigious wine-growing areas in Bordeaux, it's surprisingly unwelcoming to visitors, with places to eat, and particularly affordable ones, also in short supply. There are regular bus and train services to Pauillac and Margaux, but it's worth considering car rental (see Bordeaux "Listings" opposite).

The wines of Bordeaux

With Burgundy and Champagne, the **wines of Bordeaux** form the "Holy Trinity" of French viticulture. Despite producing as many whites as reds, it is the latter – known as claret to the British – that have graced the tables of the discerning for centuries. The countryside that produces them encircles the city, enjoying near-perfect climatic conditions and soils ranging from limestone to sand and pebbles. It's the largest quality wine district in the world, turning out around 500 million bottles a year – over half the country's quality wine output and ten percent, by value, of the world's wine trade.

The Gironde estuary, fed by the Garonne and the Dordogne, determines the lie of the land. The **Médoc** lies northwest of Bordeaux between the Atlantic coast and the River Gironde, with its vines deeply rooted in poor, gravelly soil, producing good, full-bodied red wines; the region's **eight appellations** are Médoc, Haut Médoc, St-Estèphe, Pauillac, St-Julien, Moulis en Médoc, Listrac-Médoc and Margaux. Southwest of Bordeaux are the vast vineyards of **Graves**, producing the best of the region's dry white wines, along with some punchy reds, from some of the most prestigious communes in France – Pessac, Talence, Martillac and Villenave d'Ornon amongst them. They spread down to Langon and envelop the areas of **Sauternes** and **Barsac**, whose extremely sweet white dessert wines are considered among the world's best.

On the east side of the Gironde estuary and the Dordogne, the **Côtes de Blaye** feature some good-quality white table wines, mostly dry, and a smaller quantity of reds. The **Côtes de Bourg** specialize in solid whites and reds, spreading down to the renowned **St-Émilion** area. Here, there are a dozen producers who have earned the accolade of *Premiers Grands Crus Classés*, and their output is a full, rich red wine that doesn't have to be kept as long as the Médoc wines. Lesser-known neighbouring areas include the vineyards of **Pomerol**, **Lalande** and **Côtes de Francs**, all producing reds similar to St-Émilion but at more affordable prices.

Between the Garonne and the Dordogne is **Entre-Deux-Mers**, an area which yields large quantities of inexpensive, drinkable table whites, mainly from the Sauvignon grape. The less important sweet whites of **Sainte-Croix du Mont** come out of the area south of **Cadillac**. Stretching along the north bank of the Garonne, the vineyards of the **Côtes de Bordeaux** feature fruity reds and a smaller number of dry and sweet whites.

The **classification** of Bordeaux wines is an extremely complex affair. Apart from the usual *appellation d'origine contrôlée* (AOC) labelling – guaranteeing origin but not quality – the wines of the Médoc châteaux are graded into five *crus*, or growths. These were established as long ago as 1855, based on the prices the wines had fetched over the previous hundred years. Four were voted the best or *Premiers Grands Crus Classés*: Margaux, Lafitte, Latour and Haut-Brion. With the exception of Château Mouton-Rothschild, which moved up a class in 1973 to become the fifth *Premier Grand Cru Classé*, there have been no official changes, so divisions between the *crus* should not be taken too seriously. Since then, additional categories have been devised, for instance *Crus Bourgeois*, which has three categories of its own. The wines of Sauternes were also classified in 1855. If you're interested in **buying wines**, it's possible to find bargains at some of the châteaux. Advantages of buying at source include the opportunity to sample before purchasing and to receive expert advice about different vintages. In Bordeaux, the best place to go is La Vinotèque (Mon–Sat 10am–7.30pm), next to the tourist office. There's a growing fashion for organic methods and "green" wines, already available on many good labels.

To **visit the châteaux**, ask at the Maison du Vin in each wine-producing village; they will provide information on which châteaux accept visitors. In Bordeaux itself, this service is offered by the tourist office, which also organizes its own half-day **guided tours**, covering a different area each day (May–Oct daily 1.15pm; Nov–April Wed & Sat 1.15pm; €28). Generally interesting and informative, the guide translates into English the wine-maker's commentary and answers any questions. Tastings are generous, and expert tuition on how to go about it is part of the deal.

Château Margaux and Fort Médoc

Easily the prettiest of the Bordeaux châteaux, **Château Margaux** is an eighteenth-century villa in extensive, sculpture-dotted gardens close to the west bank of the Gironde, some 20km north of Bordeaux. Its wine, a classified *Premier Grand Cru* and world-famous in the 1940s and 1950s, went through a rough patch in the two succeeding decades but improved in the 1980s after the estate was bought by a Greek family. The château (by appointment only Mon–Fri 10am–noon & 2–4pm; closed Aug and during harvest; ⓣ05.57.88.83.83, ⓦwww.chateau-margaux.com; free) is not included in any tours, and it's best to book at least two weeks in advance.

In the small village of **MARGAUX** itself, there's an unusually friendly **Maison du Vin** (June–Sept Mon–Sat 10am–7pm, Sun 11am–4pm; Oct–May 3 days only per week; ⓣ05.57.88.70.82, ⓔsyndicat.margaux@orange.fr) that can help find accommodation and advise on visits to the *appellation*'s châteaux. At the other end of the village, the enterprising and inviting cellar La Cave d'Ulysse provides free tastings from a variety of Margaux châteaux, giving you a chance to try and buy (and ship, if you need) some very good wines. Prices range from a €5 run-of-the-mill Médoc to €2400 for a delicate, rare 1990 Petrus. Margaux has a somewhat expensive but very comfortable **hotel**, *Le Pavillon de Margaux* (ⓣ05.57.88.77.54, ⓦwww.marojallia.com; ❺), with a fine restaurant (menus from €28). Otherwise, try the *chambre d'hôte* (contact M. Péry ⓣ & ⓕ05.56.58.24.80; ❸; closed Christmas & New Year) at **Castelnau-de-Médoc**, 10km to the west. Besides the hotel, you can **eat** at Margaux's *Auberge de Savoie* (ⓣ05.57.88.31.76; closed Sun & Mon evenings), next to the Maison du Vin, with excellent traditional food on menus from €26.

The seventeenth-century **Fort Médoc**, off the D2 road between Margaux and St-Julien by the banks of the estuary, is a good place to tuck into a few purchases between châteaux. It was designed by the prolific military architect Vauban to defend the Gironde estuary against the British. The remains of the fort are scant but scrambleable, and in summer its Toytown aspect has a leafy charm, marred only by the view of a nuclear power station across the river to the north of Blaye. Since 1990, the annual Fort Médoc **jazz festival**, with big-name international acts, has been held here in mid-July (ⓣ05.56.94.43.43 for details).

A couple of kilometres south, **LAMARQUE** is a very pretty village, full of flowers and with a sweet church. It's a pleasant place to stop for lunch, with a very agreeable restaurant, *L'Escale* (menus from €10; closed Tues & evenings off season), down by the port. From here at least four ferries (one way: passengers €3.10, cycles €1.60, cars €12.60) cross the muddy Gironde daily to Blaye, another place fortified by Vauban, and an important, though less well-known, Bordeaux wine-growing centre.

Pauillac and around

PAUILLAC is the largest town in the Médoc region and central to the most important vineyards of Bordeaux: no fewer than three of the top five *Grands Crus* come from around here. It has grown rapidly in recent years and, while its little harbour and riverfront are pretty enough, they can't counteract the presence of the nuclear power plant across the Gironde.

Pauillac has a huge **Maison du Tourisme et du Vin** along the waterfront (July & Aug Mon–Sat 9.30am–7pm, Sun 10am–1pm & 2–6pm; Sept–June Mon–Sat 9.30am–12.30pm & 2–6pm, Sun 10.30am–12.30pm & 3.00–6pm; ⓣ05.56.59.03.08, ⓦwww.pauillac-medoc.com). It can provide you with a list of *gîtes* and make appointments for you to visit the surrounding châteaux

(€3.80 per château). To explore the area by **bike**, head to Sport Nature, 6 rue Joffre (Ⓣ05.57.75.22.60), which has decent rates for full-or half-day rental, though it's best to reserve in advance. Pauillac itself is not a great **place to stay**, but should you wish to, try the *Hôtel de France et d'Angleterre*, opposite the little harbour (Ⓣ05.56.59.01.20, Ⓦwww.hoteldefrance-angleterre.com; ❹; closed Christmas & New Year), with a good restaurant serving menus from €19.50 (closed Sun & Mon off season), or the welcoming riverfront **campsite** further south on route de la Rivière (Ⓣ05.56.59.10.03; April–Oct). Campsites are rare in the Médoc: the only other alternative is the two-star *Camping Le Paradis* at **ST-LAURENT-DE-MÉDOC** (Ⓣ05.56.59.42.15; April–Sept). Alternatively, there's an excellent *chambre d'hôte* about 8km northwest near the village of **CISSAC**: *Château Gugès* (Ⓣ05.56.59.58.04, Ⓦwww.chateau-guges.com; ❹), in a large eighteenth-century house attached to a vineyard on the road to Gunes.

The most famous of the **Médoc châteaux** – Château Lafite-Rothschild (Ⓣ05.56.73.18.18), Château Latour (Ⓣ05.56.73.19.80) and Château Mouton-Rothschild (Ⓣ05.56.73.21.29) – can be visited by appointment only, either direct (all have English-speaking staff) or through the Maison du Vin. Their vineyards occupy larger single tracts of land than elsewhere in the Médoc, and consequently neighbouring wines can differ markedly: a good vintage Lafite is perfumed and refined, whereas a Mouton-Rothschild is strong and dark and should be kept for at least ten years. **Château Mouton-Rothschild** and its wine **museum** (which can only be visited as part of the tour; €5) is the most absorbing of the big houses: as well as the viticultural stuff, you also get to see the Rothschilds' amazing collection of art treasures, all loosely connected with wine.

St-Estèphe

North of Pauillac, the wine commune of **ST-ESTÈPHE** is Médoc's largest *appellation*, consisting predominantly of *crus bourgeois* properties and growers belonging to the local *cave coopérative*, **Marquis de St-Estèphe**, on the D2 towards Pauillac (tastings July & Aug daily 10am–noon & 2–6pm; Sept–June by appointment, Ⓣ05.56.73.35.30). One of the *appellation*'s five *crus classés* is the distinctive **Château Cos d'Estournel**, with its over-the-top nineteenth-century French version of a pagoda; the *chais* (warehouses) can be visited by appointment (Ⓣ05.56.73.15.50; English spoken). The village of St-Estèphe itself is a sleepy affair dominated by its landmark, the eighteenth-century **church of St-Étienne**, with its highly decorative interior. The small, home-spun **Maison du Vin** (May & Oct Mon–Fri 10am–12.30pm & 1.30–5pm; June & Sept Mon–Fri 10am–5pm, Sat 1.30–5.30pm; July & Aug Mon–Sat 10am–7pm; Ⓣ05.56.59.30.59) is hidden in the church square.

For an elegant place to **stay**, head for *Château Pomys* (Ⓣ05.56.59.73.44, Ⓦwww.chateaupomys.com; ❺), just south of the village, a mansion set in its own park. There are also several good *chambres d'hôte* in the area, including *Clos de Puyzac* in Pez village (Ⓣ & Ⓕ05.56.59.35.28; ❸) and, further along the same road near Vertheuil-en-Médoc, the hacienda-style *Cantemerle* (Ⓣ05.56.41.96.24, Ⓦwww.bab-medoc.com; ❹), both with *tables d'hôte*.

Blaye

The green slopes north of the Garonne, the **Côtes de Bourg** and **Côtes de Blaye**, were home to wine production long before the Médoc was planted. The wine is a rather heavier, plummier red, and cheaper than anything found on the opposite side of the river, and the **Maison du Vin des Premières Côtes de**

Blaye on cours Vauban (Mon–Sat 8.45am–12.30pm & 2–6.30pm), the main street of the pretty little town of **BLAYE**, serves up a representative selection of the local produce, with some ridiculously inexpensive wines – you can get a good bottle for around €5.

Blaye has long played a strategic role defending Bordeaux, and was fortified by Vauban in the seventeenth century. The **citadelle** deserves a wander: people still live here, and it's a strange combination of peaceful village and tourist attraction. A beautiful spot, it has grass, trees, birds and a spectacular view over the Gironde estuary. Blaye is also the last resting place of the heroic paladin **Roland**, whose body was brought here in 778 after the battle of Roncevaux. However, his mausoleum is now no more than a heap of rocks.

The **tourist office**, at 33 allées Marines (Mon–Sat 9.30am–12.30pm & 2–5.30pm; ⓣ05.57.42.12.09; ⓦwww.tourisme-blaye.com), is really helpful and can reserve rooms (€1 per call) and give out details on wine tasting. If you fancy **staying** here, try the *Auberge du Porche*, 5 rue Ernest-Régnier (ⓣ05.57.42.22.69, ⓦwww.auberge-du-porche.com; ❸; closed one week in March & one week in Oct), a pleasant two-star south along the riverfront with a good-value restaurant (closed Sun evening & Mon; from €15). Alternatively, there's the more expensive *Hôtel La Citadelle* within the old fort with views over the Garonne (ⓣ05.57.42.17.10, ⓦwww.hotel-la-citadelle.com; ❺; restaurant from €22; half-board required July & Aug). Finally, there's a small municipal **campsite** within the citadelle (ⓣ05.57.42.00.20; May–Sept).

St-Émilion

ST-ÉMILION, 35km east of Bordeaux, and a short train trip, is well worth a visit. The old grey houses of this fortified medieval town straggle down the south-hanging slope of a low hill, with the green froth of the summer's vines crawling over its walls. Many of the growers still keep up the old tradition of planting roses at the ends of the rows, which in pre-pesticide days served as an early-warning system against infection, the idea being that the commonest bug, *oidium*, went for the roses first, giving three days' notice of its intentions.

The Town

The town's **belfry** belongs to the rock-hewn subterranean **Église Monolithe** beneath it, which can be visited only on a **guided tour** from the tourist office (daily every 45 min 10.45am–5pm; €6). The tour starts in a dark hole in someone's backyard, supposedly the cave where St Émilion lived a hermit's life in the eighth century. A rough-hewn ledge served as his bed and a carved seat as his chair, where infertile women reputedly still come to sit in the hope of getting pregnant.

Above is the half-ruined thirteenth-century **Trinity Chapel**, which was built in honour of St Émilion and converted into a cooperage during the Revolution; fragments of frescoes are still visible, including a kneeling figure who is thought to be the saint himself. On the other side of the yard, a passage tunnels beneath the belfry to the **catacombs**, where three chambers dug out of the soft limestone were used as ossuary and cemetery from the eighth to the eleventh centuries. In the innermost chamber – discovered by a neighbour enlarging his cellar some fifty years ago – an eleventh-century tombstone bears the inscription: "Aulius is buried between saints Valéry, Émilion and Avic", St Valéry being the patron saint of local wine-growers.

The ninth- and twelfth-century **church** itself is an incredible place. Simple and huge, the entire structure – barrel-vaulting, great square piers and all – has been hacked out of the rock. The impact has been somewhat diminished, however, by the installation of massive concrete supports after cracks were discovered in the bell tower above in 1990. The whole interior was painted once, but only faint traces survived the Revolution, when a gunpowder factory was installed here. These days, every June, the wine council – *La Jurade* – assembles in the church in distinctive red robes to evaluate the previous season's wine and decide whether each *viticulteur*'s produce deserves the *appellation contrôlée* rating.

Behind the tourist office, the town comes to an abrupt end with a grand view of the **moat** and old **walls**. To the right is the twelfth-century **collegiate church**, with a handsome but badly mutilated doorway and a lovely fourteenth-century **cloister**, accessed via the tourist office (same hours; free).

You should take advantage of the produce of this well-respected wine region, whose most famous wine originates at **Château Ausone**, immediately south of St-Émilion (not open to the public). If you're interested in visiting local vineyards, ask at the tourist office, which has detailed lists of those that are open, or at the **Maison du Vin** (Mon–Sat 9.30am–12.30pm & 2–6.30pm, Sun 10am–12.30pm & 2.30–6.30pm; ⓣ05.57.55.50.55), also at the top of the hill by the belfry.

Practicalities

The super-efficient **tourist office** on place des Créneaux by the belfry (daily: June–Sept 9.30am–7/8pm; Oct–May 9.30am–12.30pm & 1.45–6/6.30pm; ⓣ05.57.55.28.28, ⓦwww.saint-emilion-tourisme.com) is a good source of information and organizes bilingual (French and English) vineyard tours in season (May–Sept; €9.60). They also have **bikes** for rent (€14 per day).

If you're short of funds or without your own transport, St-Émilion is best seen as a day-trip from Bordeaux, as there's a chronic shortage of budget **accommodation** within the town. However, the tourist office can furnish you with an extensive list of *chambres d'hôte* in the area, many of which are very reasonably priced. Within the town itself, the two-star *Auberge de la Commanderie* on rue des Cordeliers (ⓣ05.57.24.70.19, ⓦwww.aubergedelacommanderie.com; ❹; closed mid-Dec to mid-Feb) offers the cheapest option. Two kilometres northwest on the road to Montagne, there's a fantastic three-star campsite, *La Barbanne* (ⓣ05.57.24.75.80; April–Sept), with several heated swimming pools.

You should try the town's speciality while you're here: **macaroons** were devised here by the Ursuline sisters in 1620, and the one authentic place to buy them is at Blanchez, 9 rue Gaudet, where the tiny melt-in-the-mouth biscuits are baked to the original recipe. An excellent place for a **meal** is the relaxed contemporary-style bistro *L'Envers du Décor* (closed Sun Nov–April) on rue du Clocher, with *plats du jour* for €12 and local wine by the glass, which you can accompany with omelettes, cheese, salads and light snacks.

Entre-Deux-Mers

The landscape of **Entre-Deux-Mers** (literally "between two seas") – so called because it's sandwiched between the tidal waters of the Dordogne and Garonne – is the prettiest of the Bordeaux wine regions, with its gentle hills and scattered medieval villages. Its wines, including the *Premières Côtes de Bordeaux*, are mainly dry whites produced by over forty *caves coopératives*, and are regarded as good but inferior to the Médocs or super-dry Graves to the south. It's also a region which can be explored, at least in part, by public transport, should you feel like avoiding the tourist office tour.

La Sauve-Majeure

The one place you should really try to see is the ruined **Abbey** (June–Sept daily 10am–6pm; Oct–May Tues–Sun 10am–1pm & 2.30–5.30pm; €4.60) at **LA SAUVE-MAJEURE**, some 25km east of Bordeaux, an important stop for pilgrims en route to Santiago de Compostela in Spain. Once it was all forest here, the abbey's name being a corruption of the Latin *silva major* (big wood). It was founded in 1079, and the treasures of what remains are the twelfth-century Romanesque apse and apsidal chapels and the outstanding sculpted capitals in the chancel. The finest are the ones illustrating stories from the Old and New Testaments (Daniel in the lions' den, Delilah shearing Samson's hair and so on), while others show fabulous beasts and decorative motifs. There is a small **museum** at the entrance, with some excellent photos of the ruins, along with keystones from the fallen roofs. But what makes the visit so worthwhile is not just the capitals themselves, but the remote, undisturbed nature of the site.

St-Macaire and La Réole

If you're heading south through Entre-Deux-Mers, Langon is the first town of any size you come to. But **ST-MACAIRE**, across the Garonne from Langon, is far better for a rest or food stop. The village still has its original **gates** and **battlements** and a beautiful medieval church, the **Église-Prieuré**. The **tourist office**, 8 rue Canton (June–Sept daily 10am–1pm & 3–7pm; April & May same hours, closed Mon; March & Oct Tues–Fri 2–6pm, Sat & Sun 10am–noon & 2–6pm; Nov–Feb same hours, also closed Tues; ⓣ05.56.63.32.14), doubles as a Maison du Pays, promoting regional produce, which here means honey and wine. Staff can help arrange visits to the *chais*, and in season (July & Aug daily) they organize tastings hosted by various local wine-makers. Opposite is a good **hotel**, *Les Feuilles d'Acanthe* (ⓣ05.56.62.33.75, ⓦwww.feuilles-dacanthe.fr; closed Dec; ❹) with good-sized rooms and a roof solarium and Jacuzzi. A cheaper option, *Les Tilleuls* (ⓣ05.56.76.83.79; ❸), is located just outside the medieval city next to the Hôtel de Ville; their restaurant, *Le Médiéval*, has menus from €14.50. There's another good restaurant on rue de Canton, *Le Macarien* (ⓣ05.56.76.83.79, closed Wed & Sun eve), which serves extremely popular, traditional menus from €13.50 while also offering pizza and omelettes.

LA RÉOLE, on the north bank 18km further east, boasts a wealth of medieval architecture along a well-signposted walk through its narrow, hilly streets. France's oldest **town hall**, constructed for Richard the Lionheart in the twelfth century, and the well-preserved simple **Abbaye des Bénédictins** – with a fantastic view over the River Garonne and the surrounding countryside – reward a stroll through the town, although little remains of the fortified **castle**.

La Réole's **tourist office** is on place Richard-Coeur-de-Lion (June–Sept Mon 3–6pm, Tues–Sat 9.30am–12.30pm & 3–6pm, Sun 9.30am–12.30pm; Oct–May closed Sun; ⓣ05.56.61.13.55, ⓦwww.entredeuxmers.com), and it conducts tours of the sights in July and August, though only for groups of ten or more (€5 per person). The only **hotel** in town is the cheap and cheerful *Auberge Réolaise* on the N113 just east of the centre (ⓣ & ⓕ05.56.61.01.33; ❶), though there's also a campsite (June–Sept), in a nice location just over the bridge on the south bank of the Garonne. A good **restaurant** is *Aux Fontaines* on rue du Verdun (closed Sun & Wed evenings & all day Mon, also two weeks in Feb & Nov), serving classic French cuisine, albeit with a modern touch, and several menus from €16.50; in the summer you can eat outside in their thatched roof terrace. A lively Saturday **market** on the esplanade des Quais along the Garonne provides good picnic provisions.

Sauternes and around

The **Sauternes** region, which extends southeast from Bordeaux for 40km along the left bank of the Garonne, is an ancient wine-making area, originally planted during the Roman occupation. The distinctive golden wine of the area is certainly sweet, but also round, full-bodied and spicy, with a long aftertaste. It's not necessarily a dessert wine, either: try it with some Roquefort cheese. Gravelly terraces with a limestone subsoil help create the delicious taste, but mostly it's due to a peculiar microclimate of morning autumn mists and afternoons of sun and heat which causes *Botrytis cinerea* fungus, or "noble rot", to flourish on the grapes, letting the sugar concentrate and introducing some intense flavours. When they're picked, they're not a pretty sight: carefully selected by hand, only the most shrivelled, rotting bunches are taken. The wines of Sauternes make up some of the most highly sought-after in the world, with bottles of Château d'Yquem, in particular, fetching thousands of euros.

SAUTERNES itself is a fairly quiet little village surrounded by vines and dominated by the **Maison du Sauternes** (Mon–Fri 9am–7pm, Sat & Sun 10am–7pm; ⓣ05.56.76.69.83, ⓦwww.maisondusauternes.com) at one end of the village, with a pretty church at the other. The *maison* is a room full of treasures, the golden bottles with white and gold labels being quite beautiful objects in themselves. It is a non-profit organization, so although staff can offer tastings, they're understandably reluctant about it unless you look like you're going to buy.

For a luxurious place to **stay**, try the sumptuous *Relais du Château d'Arche*, on the D125 just outside of Sauternes heading north (ⓣ05.56.76.66.55, ⓦwww.chateaudarche-sauternes.com; ❼). The seventeenth-century estate was recently restored to its original lustre and has been refurbished with near-period styling and paraphernalia; rooms are large and plush and many look directly onto the vineyard. There are two good places to **eat** in Sauternes. By the church, the *Auberge Les Vignes* (ⓣ05.56.76.60.06; closed Sun & Mon evening & Feb) is a typical country restaurant with regional specialities like *grillades aux Sauternes* (meats grilled over vine clippings), a great wine list and a lunch menu at €12. The other option is the more refined *Le Saprien* (ⓣ05.56.76.60.87; closed Christmas & Feb, also Sun & Wed evening), opposite the tourist office, combining regional-style elements with modern eclectic additions and featuring menus from €25.

Ten kilometres south of Sauternes, the ruinous curtain walls and corner towers of a colossal moated **château** (July & Aug daily 10am–7pm; June & Sept daily 2–6pm; Oct–May Sat & Sun 2–6pm; €3.50) still dominate **VILLANDRAUT**. Purchasing a ticket to the château gets you a complimentary tasting at the town's friendly Maison des Vins, on the central square a block from the castle (Mon–Sat 9.30am–12.30pm & 3–7.30pm). The castle itself was built by Pope Clement V, a native of the area who caused a schism by moving the papacy to Avignon in the fourteenth century. You can visit his tomb in the even smaller village of **UZESTE** en route to **BAZAS**, 15km east, which has a laid-back, southern air. Bazas' most attractive feature is the wide, arcaded place de la Cathédrale, overlooked by the grey, lichen-covered **Cathédrale St-Jean-Baptiste**, which displays a harmonious blend of Romanesque, Gothic and classical styles in its west front.

For places to **stay** in Bazas try the cheap, friendly *Hostellerie St-Sauveur*, 14 cours du Général-de-Gaulle (ⓣ05.56.25.12.18; ❸; closed early Oct), or the plush *Domaine de Fompeyre*, on the southern edge of town (ⓣ05.56.25.98.00, ⓦwww.domainedefompeyre.fr; ❺), which has a restaurant (closed Sun eve Oct–March;

from €33). The best place to **eat** is *Bistrot St-Jean* (☎05.56.25.18.53), under the colonnades on place de la Cathédrale. It has great lunch menus for €10 with generous helpings and friendly service (closed evenings except weekends in summer). Another good bet is *Les Remparts* (☎05.56.25.25.52; closed Sun eve and Mon), opposite, which has a good view from its terrace and a menu for €23. Many towns around this area offer *chambres d'hotes* from around €35 upwards: enquire at Villandraut's **tourist office** (☎05.56.25.31.39), located on place de la Mairie, for more information.

The Côte d'Argent

The **Côte d'Argent** is the long stretch of coast from the mouth of the Gironde estuary to Biarritz, which – at over 200km – is the longest, straightest and sandiest in Europe. The endless beaches are backed by high sand dunes, while behind lies the largest forest in western Europe, **Les Landes**. Despite these attractions, the lack of conventional tourist sights means that outside July and August the coast gets comparatively few visitors, and away from the main resorts it's still possible to find deserted stretches of coastline.

Arcachon

On summer weekends, the Bordelais escape en masse to **ARCACHON**, the oldest resort on the Côte d'Argent and a forty-minute train ride across flat, sandy forest from Bordeaux. The beaches of white sand are magnificent but can be crowded, and its central jetties, Thiers and Eyrac, are busy with boats going off on an array of cruises.

The town itself is a sprawl of villas great and small, the most exclusive area being the **ville d'hiver** (winter town), whose wide shady streets are full of fanciful Second Empire mansions overlooking the seaside **ville d'été** (summer town). Well worth a wander, the area can be reached by following the lively pedestrianized and restaurant-filled rue de Maréchal-de-Lattre-de-Tassigny, running perpendicular to the seafront boulevard de la Plage; at the end of this mouthful of a street, a lift (daily: July & Aug 7am–10pm; Sept–June 8am–7.30pm) carries you up to the flower-filled, wooded **Parc Mauresque** (same hours; free), with the *ville d'hiver* beyond it. From the park, there are fine views over the seafront.

Practicalities

A well-stocked **tourist office**, esplanade Georges-Pompidou (April–June & Sept Mon–Sat 9am–6pm, Sun 10am–1pm & 2–5pm; July & Aug daily 9am–7pm; Oct–March Mon–Fri 9am–6pm, Sat 9am–5pm; ☎05.57.52.97.97; Ⓦwww.arcachon.com), can be reached by following avenue Gambetta back from seafront place Thiers. In summer, boats leave the jetties of Thiers and Eyrac on various **cruises**, including the Île aux Oiseaux (1hr 45min; €13.50), and an exploration of the Arcachon basin with a look at the Dune de Pyla (2hr 30min; €18.50). There's also a regular boat service from here to Cap Ferret on the opposite peninsula (30min; €11 return). Discounted tickets can be purchased for all excursions at the tourist office.

You'll be hard-pushed to find an inexpensive **hotel** in summer, but the best value is probably at the *St-Christaud*, 8 allée de la Chapelle (☎05.56.83.38.53; ③), a short walk from the centre. Up the hill in the *ville d'hiver*, your only option is the *Marinette*, 15 allée José-Maria-de-Hérédia (Ⓣ05.56.83.06.67, Ⓦwww.hotel-marinette.com; ❹; closed Oct to mid-March), with pleasant rooms in a shady, villa-style building. For a luxury stay in the heart of the action, try the *Grand Hôtel Richelieu* at 185 bd de la Plage (Ⓣ05.56.83.16.50, Ⓦwww.grand-hotel-richelieu.com; ❻), where some of the rooms have balconies with sea views. Alternatively, the tourist office can give you a list of the many **holiday apartments** available to rent. **Camping** is another option, with plenty of sites around the Arcachon basin, though only the three-star *Le Camping Club*, allée de la Galaxie (Ⓣ05.56.83.24.15, Ⓦwww.camping-arcachon.com), is actually within the town; set in an expanse of bird-filled woodland beyond the *ville d'hiver*, it's worth the high summer prices.

For something approximating *gastronomique* **eating**, you're best off at *Chez Yvette*, 59 bd de Général-Leclerc, which offers traditional menus from €19 or immense platters of seafood for €30.

Cap Ferret and the north coast

The Atlantic coast between the Bassin d'Arcachon and the Gironde has a wild, undeveloped feel and despite its proximity to Bordeaux and Arcachon, is seldom crowded. No motorable road follows the coast for most of the way, which contributes to the relaxed nature of the place; instead a cycle path, built at the end of World War II, winds through more than 75km of pine-forested dunes from the low-key holiday village of **Cap Ferret** to the resort of Soulac in the north, from where trains run through the Médoc vineyards to Bordeaux or to the Pointe de Grave and Verdon for the ferry to Royan. Apart from the occasional surf shack or beach restaurant, the only settlement of any size is Lacanau-Ocean, 30km north of Cap Ferret, best avoided unless you're into overpriced hotels and golf courses. Cap Ferret can be reached by boat from Arcachon. There are a few places to **stay**, including the small, basic **HI hostel** at 87 av de Bordeaux (Ⓣ05.56.60.64.62; July & Aug only) and the characterful *Hotel des Pins* at 23 rue des Fauvettes (Ⓣ05.56.60.60.11, Ⓕ05.56.60.67.41; March to mid-Nov; ❹), overlooking the ocean and still decorated in the spirit of the 1920s, when it was built. It also has a restaurant with menus for €24. Some 10km to the north there's a **campsite** at Grand Crohot, Bremontier (Ⓣ05.56.60.03.99; May to mid-Sept). For more information contact the **tourist office** in Cap Ferret at 1 av du Général-de-Gaulle (Ⓣ05.56.03.94.49, Ⓦwww.lege-capferret.com).

The Dune du Pyla and Le Teich

The Côte d'Argent's chief curiosity is the **Dune du Pyla**. At over 100m it's the highest sand dune in Europe – a veritable mountain of wind-carved sand, about 12km south of Arcachon. Bus #611 leaves from the *gare SNCF* every hour in July and August – two to five a day at other times. From the end of the line the road continues straight on uphill for about fifteen minutes – if you're driving, it costs €2.30–3.05 to use the obligatory car park, though to save a few euros you could park closer to the station for free and make the hike up. There's the inevitable group of stands selling ice cream, *galettes* and junk, but from the top you get a superb view over the bay of Arcachon and the forest of the Landes stretching away to the south. It's a great sandy slide down to the sea (the sides are as steep as an Olympic ski-jump) and a long haul back up but well worth the effort.

At **LE TEICH**, about 14km east of Arcachon in the southeast corner of the Bassin d'Arcachon, one of the most important expanses of wetlands remaining in France has been converted into a bird sanctuary, the **Parc Ornithologique du Teich** (daily 10am–6pm; €6.40; Ⓦ www.parc-ornithologique-du-teich.com), one of only two in the country. There's no **accommodation** in Le Teich beyond a couple of **campsites**, but you can easily come here on a day-trip by train from Arcachon or Bordeaux.

Les Landes

Travelling south from Bordeaux by road or rail, you pass for what seems like hours through an unremitting, flat, sandy pine forest known as **Les Landes**. Until the nineteenth century it was a vast, infertile swamp, badly drained because of the impermeable layer of grit deposited by the glaciers of the quaternary age and steadily encroached upon by the shifting sand dunes of the coast. Today it supports nearly 10,000 square kilometres of trees and since 1970 has been designated a *parc naturel régional.*

Mont de Marsan

The administrative centre of Les Landes, **MONT DE MARSAN**, 100km south of Bordeaux and served by regular trains, makes a good base for exploring the region. The **tourist office** on place du Général-Leclerc (daily except Sun: July & Aug 9am–6pm; Sept–June 9am–12.30pm & 1.30–6pm; Ⓣ 05.58.05.87.37) can provide you with large-scale maps for walking and cycling in the area (€1.50 each). The town itself boasts various medieval remnants, most notably a **twelfth-century keep** which now contains a collection of work by two local sculptors (daily except Tues 10am–noon & 2–6pm; €3.40). By far the most attractive part of the centre is the **Parc Jean Rameau**, on the north bank of the river Douze, where immaculately kept lawns and blooming flowerbeds, interwoven with shady paths, make a great spot to spend a hot afternoon watching the locals play *boules*.

If you're lucky enough to be in the area at the right time in summer, you should definitely make the effort to see the **festival** for which Mont de Marsan is best known. Les Fêtes Madeleines (mid-July) consists of a week of parades, sports and carnival atmosphere, when the town's Basque identity is most tangible, with flamenco dancing and bullfighting playing a major role.

Apart from this period, **accommodation** shouldn't be hard to come by. The nicest place to stay is *Le Renaissance*, 225 av de Villeneuve (Ⓣ 05.58.51.51.51, Ⓦ www.le-renaissance.com; ❹) with its own outdoor swimming pool, plush bar and restaurant (menus from €18). Various cheaper and more central options are also available, another good bet being *Le Richelieu,* 3 rue Wlérick (Ⓣ 05.58.06.10.20, Ⓔ le.richelieu@orange.fr; ❸), which has comfortable rooms, some with air conditioning. For **eating**, there are several good-value brasseries along rue Gambetta, while the *Crêperie la Floralie* on rue Wlérick serves up a slice of Brittany for as little as €8.

The Écomusée de Marquèze

At **SABRES**, 30km north of Mont de Marsan on the N134, you can take a restored steam train to the excellent **Écomusée de Marquèze** (trains depart every 40min April–May & mid-Sept to Oct Mon–Sat 2–4.40pm, Sun 10am–4.40pm; June to mid-Sept daily 10am–5.20pm; €9.50 including entrance; Ⓦ www.parc-landes-de-gascogne.fr), set up by the park authorities to illustrate the traditional *landais* way of life, when shepherds used to clomp around the scrub on long stilts.

Travel details

Trains

Angoulême to: Bordeaux (20 daily; 1hr–1hr 30min); Limoges (6 daily; 1hr 30min–2hr); Poitiers (23 daily; 40min–1hr 10min); Royan (4 daily; 2hr).
Bordeaux to: Angoulême (17 daily; 1hr–1hr 30min); Arcachon (frequently; 40–45min); Bayonne (10–12 daily; 1hr 40min–2hr 10min); Bergerac (6–10 daily; 50min–1hr 30min); Biarritz (6–12 daily; 2hr–2hr 45min); Brive (1–2 daily; 2hr 15min); La Rochelle (6–8 daily; 2hr 20min); Lourdes (4–6 daily; 2hr 30min–3hr); Marseille (5–6 daily; 6–7hr); Mont de Marsan (4 daily; 1hr 30min) Nice (4 daily; 9–10hr); Paris-Montparnasse (8–10 daily; 3hr–3hr 30min); Périgueux (10–12 daily; 1hr–1hr 25min); Pointe de Grave (5 daily, 1hr 45min); Poitiers (8–15 daily; 1hr 45min); Saintes (7–14 daily; 1hr 30min); Sarlat (3–4 daily; 3hr); St-Jean-de-Luz (8–12 daily; 2hr–2hr 40min); Toulouse (10–17 daily; 2hr–2hr 40min).
La Rochelle to: Bordeaux (6 daily; 2hr 20min); La Roche-sur-Yon (5 daily; 1hr); Nantes (4 daily; 1hr 50min); Rochefort (12 daily; 20min); Paris-Montparnasse (8 daily; 3hr 10min); Saintes (9 daily; 50min–1hr).
La Roche-sur-Yon to: Les Sables-d'Olonne (4 daily; 30min).
Les Sables-d'Olonne to: Nantes (8 daily; 1hr 30min).
Poitiers to: Angoulême (17 daily; 1hr); Bordeaux (3–15 daily; 1hr 45min); Châtellérault (12 daily; 20min); Dax (2–3 daily; 3–4hr); Hendaye (3 daily; 4–5hr); Irun (2 daily; 4–5hr); La Rochelle (12 daily; 1hr 45min); Limoges (4–6 daily; 2hr); Niort (4–12 daily; 45min); Paris-Montparnasse (frequently; 1hr 45min); Surgères (10 daily; 1hr).
Royan to: Angoulême (3–4 daily; 2hr); Cognac (3–4 daily; 1hr); Saintes (3–4 daily; 30min).
Saintes to: Angoulême (9 daily; 1hr); Cognac (9 daily; 20min); Rochefort (9 daily; 30min).

Buses

Bordeaux to: Blaye (4–10 daily; 1hr 30min); Cap Ferret (4–10 daily; 2hr); Lacanau (2 daily; 1hr 15min); La Sauve-Majeure (2–4 daily; 40min); Margaux (2–8 daily; 45min–1hr); Pauillac (2–8 daily; 1hr–1hr 20min).
La Rochelle to: St-Martin de Ré (6–16 daily; 1hr)
Les Sables-d'Olonne to: Luçon (4 daily; 2hr); Nantes (4 daily; 5hr 30min).
Parthenay to: Airvault (several daily; 25min); Niort (8 daily; 50min); Thouars (at least 10 daily; 1hr).
Poitiers to: Châteauroux (3–5 daily; 3hr); Chauvigny (3–5 daily; 45min); Le Blanc (3–5 daily; 1hr 25min); Limoges (daily; 3hr); Parthenay (6–10 daily; 1hr 30min); Ruffec (daily; 2hr 30min); St-Savin (3–5 daily; 1hr).
Rochefort to: Château d'Oléron (4–6 daily; 1hr); La Fumée-Île d'Aix (6–8 daily; 30min).
Saintes to: Rochefort (2 daily; 1hr 20min); St-Pierre d'Oléron (2 daily; 2hr).

9

The Dordogne, Limousin and Lot

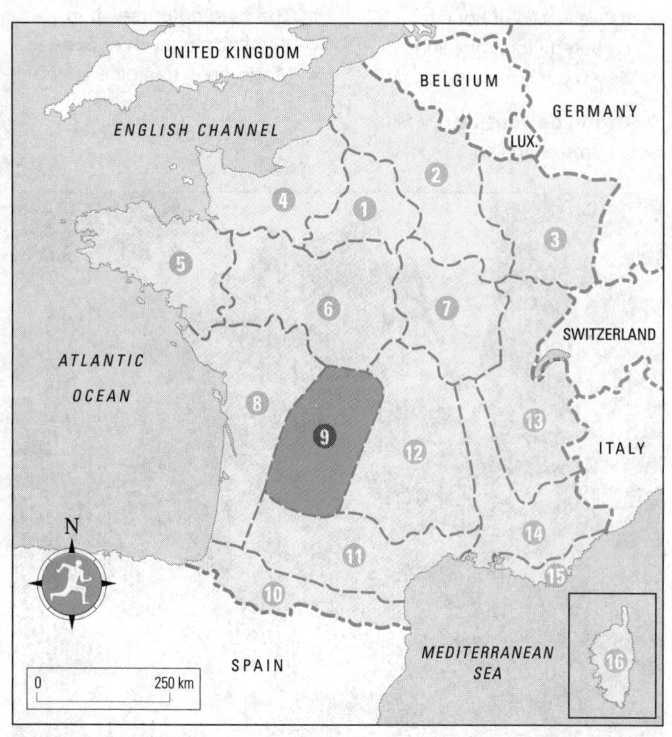

CHAPTER 9 Highlights

* **Cuisine** The Dordogne is the place to sample French country cooking at its best. See p.684
* **Monpazier** An almost perfectly preserved *bastide* (fortified town). See p.694
* **Sarlat** Wander the narrow lanes of this archetypal medieval town, with its *vielle ville* of honey-coloured stone buildings. See p.697
* **Grotte de Font-de-Gaume** Stunning examples of prehistoric cave-art, including the spectacular frieze of five bison. See p.701
* **Châteaux of Beynac and Castelnaud** Two of the region's most majestic castles eye each other across the Dordogne valley. See p.707
* **The carving of Isaiah in Souillac's church of Ste-Marie** An extraordinary masterpiece of Romanesque art. See p.710

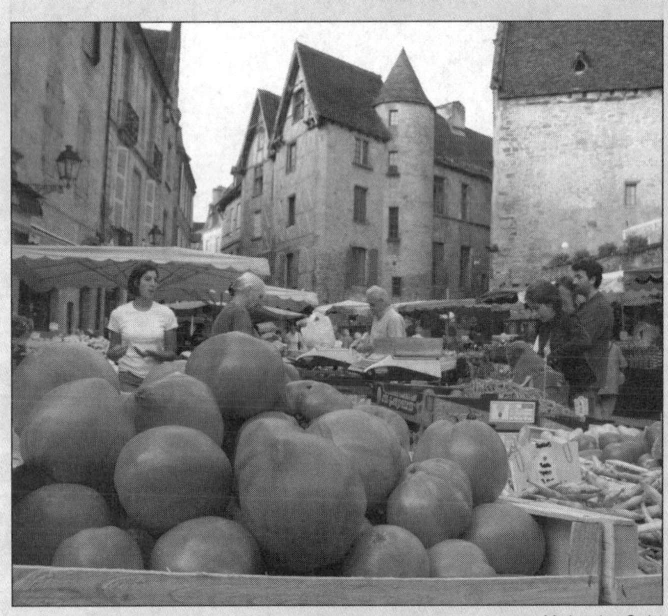

△ Market day, Sarlat

9

The Dordogne, Limousin and Lot

The land covered in this chapter forms a rough oval bordered to the east by the uplands of the Massif Central and to the west by the Atlantic plains. It's the area which was most in dispute between the English and the French during the Hundred Years War and which has been most in demand among English visitors and second-home buyers in more recent times. Although it doesn't coincide exactly with either the modern French administrative boundaries or the old provinces of Périgord and Quercy, which constitute the core of the region, the land has a physical and geographical homogeneity thanks to its great rivers: the **Dordogne**, the **Lot** and the **Aveyron**, all of which drain westwards from the Massif Central into the mighty **Garonne**, which forms the southern limit covered by this chapter.

There are no great cities in the area: its charm lies in the landscapes and the dozens of harmonious small towns and villages. Some, like **Sarlat** and **Rocamadour**, are so well known that they are overrun with tourists. Others, like **Figeac**, **Villefranche-de-Rouergue**, **Gourdon**, **Montauban**, **Monflanquin** and the many *bastides* (fortified towns) that pepper the area between the Lot and Dordogne, boast no single notable sight but are perfect organic ensembles.

The landscapes are surprisingly homogenous, too. From **Limoges** in the province of Limousin in the north to Montauban in the south towards Toulouse, the country is gently hilly, full of lush hidden valleys and miles of woodland, mainly oak. **Limousin**, at the north of this area, is slightly greener and wetter, the south more open and arid. But you can travel a long way without seeing a radical shift, except in the uplands of the **Plateau de Millevaches**, where the rivers plunge into gorges and the woods are beech, chestnut and conifer plantations. The other characteristic landscape is the *causses*, the dry scrubby limestone plateaux like the **Causse de Gramat** between the Dordogne and the Lot and the **Causse de Limogne** between the Lot and Aveyron. Where the rivers have cut their way through the limestone, the valleys are walled with overhanging cliffs, riddled with fissures, underground stream-beds and caves. And in these caves – especially in the valley of the Vézère around **Les Eyzies** – are some of the most awe-inspiring **prehistoric paintings** and reliefs to be found anywhere in the world.

The other great artistic legacy of the area is the Romanesque sculpture, most notably adorning the churches at **Souillac** and **Beaulieu-sur-Dordogne**, but

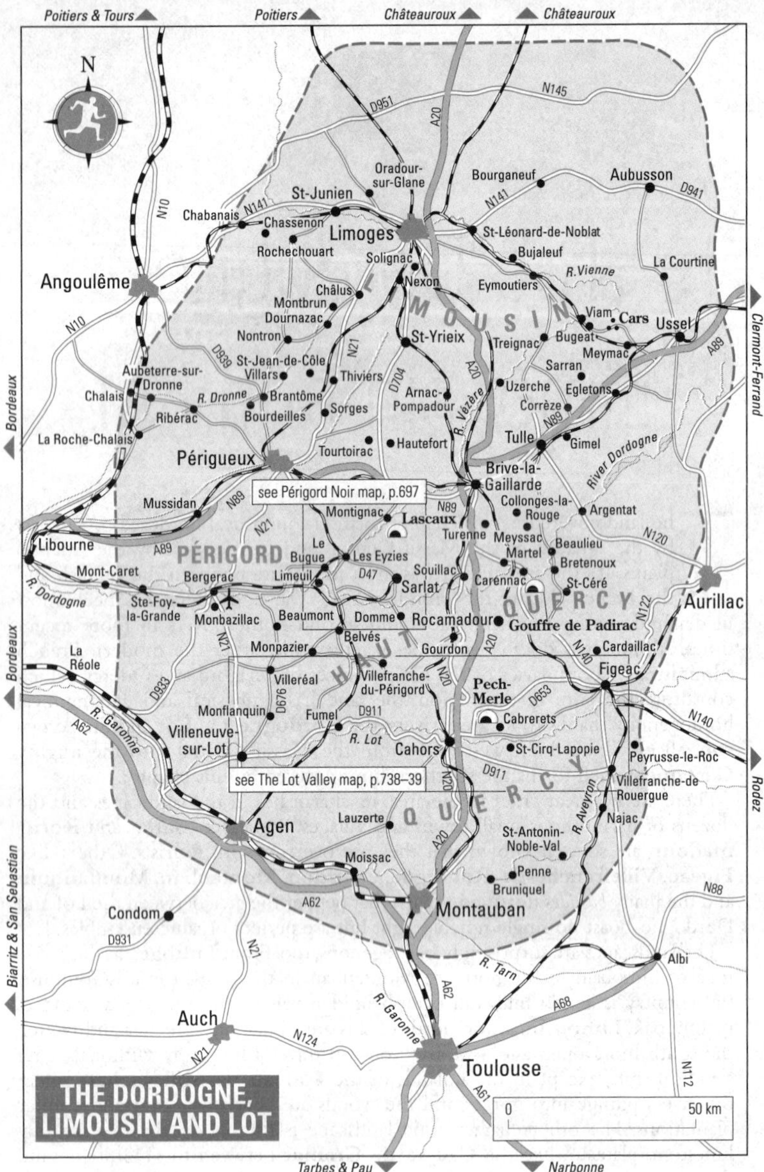

all modelled on the supreme example of the cloister of St-Pierre in **Moissac**. And the dearth of luxurious châteaux is compensated for by the numerous splendid **fortresses** of purely military design, such as **Bonaguil**, **Najac**, **Biron**, **Beynac** and **Castelnaud**.

The wartime Resistance was very active in these out-of-the-way regions, and the roadsides are dotted with tiny memorials to those killed in ambushes or shot in reprisals. There is also one monstrous monument to wartime atrocity: the ruined village of **Oradour-sur-Glane**, still as the Nazis left it after massacring the population and setting fire to the houses.

The Dordogne

To the French, the **Dordogne** is a river. To the British, it is a much looser term, covering a vast area roughly equivalent to what the French call Périgord. This starts south of Limoges and includes the Vézère and Dordogne valleys. The Dordogne is also a *département*, with fixed boundaries that pay no heed to either definition. The central part of the *département*, around Périgueux and the River Isle, is known as **Périgord Blanc**, after the light, white colour of its rock outcrops; the southeastern half around Sarlat as **Périgord Noir**, said to be darker in aspect than the Blanc because of the preponderance of oak woods. To confuse matters further, the tourist authorities have added another two colours to the Périgord patchwork: **Périgord Vert**, the far north of the *département*, so called because of the green of its woods and pastureland; and **Périgord Pourpre** in the southwest, purple because it includes the wine-growing area around Bergerac. This southern region is also known for its **bastides** – fortified towns – built during the turbulent medieval period when there was almost constant conflict between the French and English. In the reaches of the **upper Dordogne**, the colour scheme breaks down, but the villages and scenery in this less travelled backwater still rival anything the rest of the region has to offer.

Périgord Vert and Périgord Blanc

The close green valleys of **Périgord Vert** are very rural, with plenty of space and few people, large tracts of woodland and uncultivated land. Less well known than the much-frequented Périgord Noir, its largely granite landscape bears a closer resemblance to the neighbouring Limousin than to the rest of the Périgord. It's partly for this reason that in 1998 the most northerly tip, together with the southwestern part of the Haute-Vienne, was designated as the **Parc Naturel Régional Périgord-Limousin** – to give it a sense of identity and draw attention to its natural assets – in an attempt to promote "green" tourism in this economically fragile and depopulated area.

Périgueux, in the centre of **Périgord Blanc**, is interesting for its domed cathedral and its Roman remains, whose existence is a reminder of how long these parts have been civilized. But it's in the countryside that the region's finest monuments lie. One of the loveliest stretches is the **valley of the Dronne**, from **Aubeterre** on the Charente border through **Brantôme** to the marvellous Renaissance château of **Puyguilhem** and the picture-postcard village of **St-Jean-de-Côle**, and on to the Limousin border, where the scenery becomes higher and less intimate. Truffle-lovers might like to take a look at **Sorges**, where there's a nature trail through truffle country and a museum to explain it all.

The food and wine of Périgord

The two great stars of Périgord cuisine are **foie gras** and **truffles** (*truffes*). Foie gras is best eaten either chilled in succulent, buttery slabs, or lightly fried and served with a fruit compote to provide contrasting sweetness and acidity. Truffle is often dished up in omelettes and the rich *périgourdin* sauces which accompany many local meat dishes, but to really appreciate the delicate earthy flavour to the full, you really need to eat truffle on its own, with just a salad and some coarse, country bread.

The other mainstay of Périgord cuisine is the grey Toulouse **goose**, whose fat is used in the cooking of everything, including the flavourful potato dish, *pommes sarladaises*. The goose fattens well: *gavé* or crammed with corn, it goes from six to ten kilos in weight in three weeks, with its liver alone weighing nearly a kilo. Though some may find the process off-putting, small local producers are very careful not to harm their birds, if for no other reason than that stress ruins the liver. Geese are also raised for their meat alone, which is cooked and preserved in its own thick yellow grease as *confits d'oie*, which you can either eat on its own or use in the preparation of other dishes, like cassoulet. **Duck** is used in the same way, both for foie gras and *confits*. *Magret de canard*, or duck-breast fillet, is one of the favourite ways of eating duck and appears on practically every restaurant menu.

Another common goose delicacy is *cou d'oie farci* – goose neck stuffed with sausage meat, duck liver and truffles; a favourite salad throughout the region is made with warm *gésiers* or goose gizzards. Try not to be put off by fare such as this, or your palate will miss out on some delicious experiences – like *tripoux*, sheep's stomach stuffed with tripe, trotters, pork and garlic, which is really an Auvergnat dish but is quite often served in neighbouring areas like the Rouergue. Other less challenging specialities include stuffed *cèpes*, or wild mushrooms; *ballottines*, fillets of poultry stuffed, rolled and poached; the little flat discs of goat's cheese known as *cabécou* or *rocamadour*; and, for dessert there's *pastis*, a light apple tart topped with crinkled, wafer-thin pastry laced with armagnac.

The **wines** should not be scorned either. There are the fine, dark, almost peppery reds from Cahors, and both reds and whites from the vineyards of Bergerac, of which the sweet, white Monbazillac is the most famous. Pécharmant is the fanciest of the reds, but there are some very drinkable Côtes de Bergerac, much like the neighbouring Bordeaux and far cheaper. The same goes for the wines of Duras, Marmande and Buzet. If you're thinking of taking a stock of wine home, you could do much worse than make some enquiries in Bergerac itself, Ste-Foy, or any of the villages in the vineyard areas.

Périgueux

PÉRIGUEUX, capital of the *département* of the Dordogne and a central base for exploring the countryside of Périgord Blanc, is a small, busy and not particularly attractive market town for a province made rich by tourism and specialized farming. Its name derives from the Petrocorii, the local Gallic tribe, but it was the Romans who transformed it into an important settlement. A few Roman remains, as well as a medieval *vieille ville*, survive to this day.

Arrival, information and accommodation

The busiest and most interesting part of Périgueux is the square formed by the river, the allées Tourny, boulevard Montaigne and cours Fénelon. At the junction of the latter two is place Francheville, a wide, open square presently being redeveloped as a shopping and cinema complex, on the east side of which you'll find the **tourist office** (June–Sept Mon–Sat 9am–6pm,

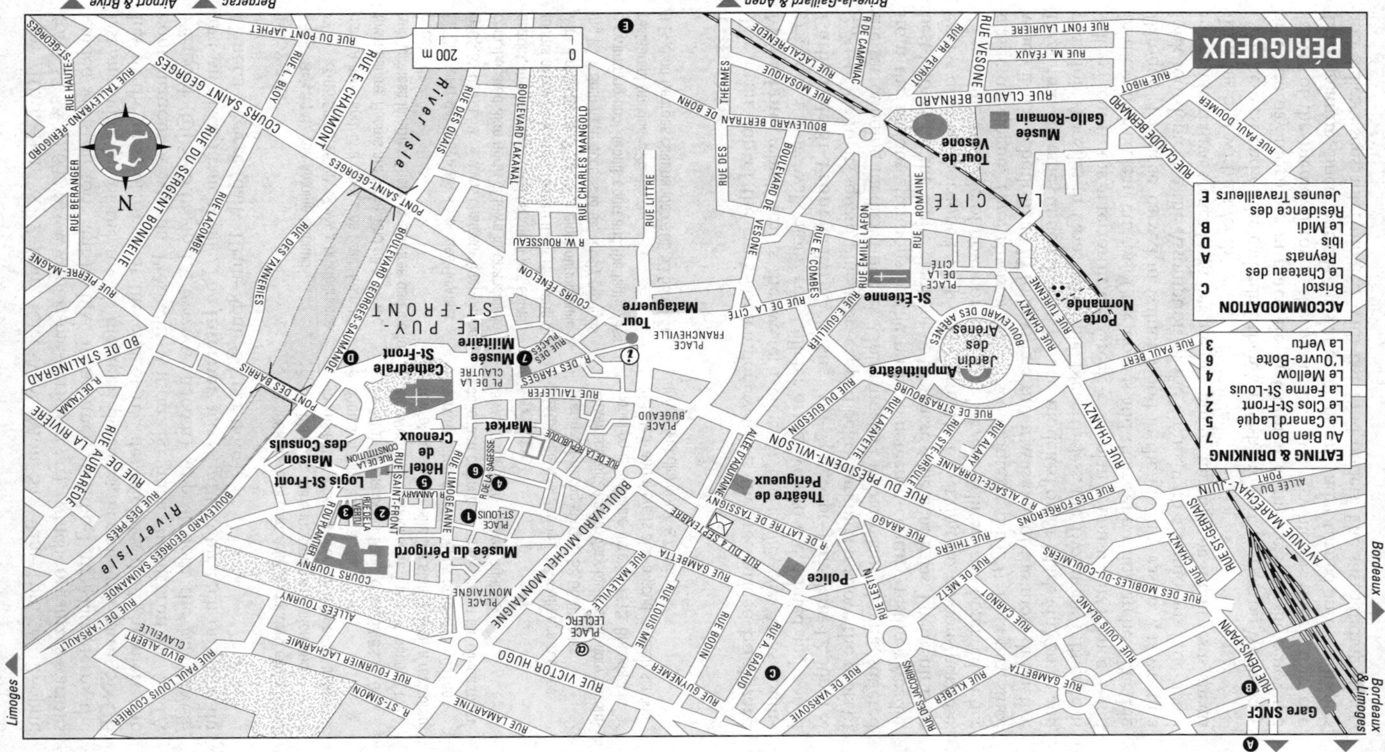
PÉRIGUEUX
EATING & DRINKING
Au Bien Bon 7
Le Canard Laqué 5
Le Clos St-Front 2
La Ferme St-Louis 1
Le Mellow 4
L'Ouvre-Boîte 6
La Vertu 3
ACCOMMODATION
Bristol C
Le Chateau des Reynats A
Ibis D
Le Midi B
Résidence des Jeunes Travailleurs E
0 200 m
N
Limoges
Bordeaux
Bordeaux & Limoges
Brive-la-Gaillard & Agen
Bergerac
Airport & Brive
Gare SNCF
River Isle
LE PUY-ST-FRONT
LA CITÉ
Musée du Périgord
Logis St-Front
Maison des Consuls
Hôtel de Crenoux
Cathédrale St-Front
Market
Musée Militaire
Tour Mataguerre
Théâtre de Périgueux
Police
Amphithéâtre
Jardin des Arènes
St-Étienne
Porte Normande
Tour de Vésone
Musée Gallo-Romain
Place Montaigne
Place St-Louis
Place Leclerc
Place Bugeaud
Place Francheville
Pl de la Clautre
Place de la Cité
Boulevard Michel Montaigne
Cours Tourny
Allées Tourny
Rue Victor Hugo
Rue du Président-Wilson
Cours Saint Georges
Pont des Barris
Pont Saint-Georges
Boulevard Georges-Saumande
Rue Chanzy
Rue Claude Bernard
Avenue Maréchal-Juin
Rue Denis-Papin

Sun 10am–1pm & 2–6pm; Oct–May Mon–Sat 9am–1pm & 2–6pm; ⓣ05.53.53.10.63, ⓦwww.tourisme-perigueux.fr), which organizes various guided visits on foot and by bike in summer, and the Tour Mataguerre, the last surviving bit of the town's medieval defences. Périgueux's **gare SNCF** lies to the west of town at the end of rue des Mobiles-du-Coulmiers, the continuation of rue du Président-Wilson. Regional **buses** run by CFTA Périgord (ⓣ05.53.08.43.13, ⓦwww.cftaco.fr) stop at both the *gare SNCF* and on place Francheville. For **Internet** access go to Ouratech on place du Général-Leclerc (daily 10am–8pm; €3 per hour).

Hotels

Bristol 37 rue Antoine Gadaud ⓣ05.53.08.75.90, ⓦwww.bristolfrance.com. A good find, in a quiet area 2min from the town centre. Rooms are large, and all have a/c and wireless Internet. There is also free parking for guests. ④

Le Château des Reynats 15 av des Reynats ⓣ05.53.03.53.59, ⓦwww.chateau-hotel-perigord.com. Located 3km north of town in Chancelade district, this luxurious establishment has some rooms available in the château itself (⑧), and more with three-star facilities in a neighbouring building (④). Both have access to the lovely grounds, a swimming pool, tennis court and the high-class restaurant (menus €26–65).

Ibis 8 bd Georges-Saumande ⓣ05.53.53.64.58, ⓔh0636@accor.com. A fairly standard chain hotel, but it's good value in terms of comfort and location; rooms either look out over the river or up to the domes of the cathedral. ④

Le Midi 18 rue Denis-Papin ⓣ05.53.53.41.06, ⓦwww.hotel-du-midi.com. The best value of the row of hotels opposite the station, with a restaurant serving three-course menus from €13.50. The collection of toy cars on display in the dining room is worth a visit in its own right. ②

Hostel

Résidence des Jeunes Travailleurs rue des Thermes-Prolongés ⓣ05.53.06.81.40, ⓔcontact@fjt24.com. Very basic dormitory accommodation is available here for €12. Breakfast is included, and there is also a good canteen serving lunch and dinner for €7 each.

The City

The main hub of the city's contemporary life is the tree-shaded **boulevard Montaigne**, which marks the western edge of the *vieille ville*. At its southern end, a short walk along rue Taillefer brings you to the domed and coned **Cathédrale St-Front** (daily: July & Aug 8am–7pm; Sept–June 8am–12.30pm & 2.30–6.30pm), its square, pineapple-capped belfry surging far above the roofs of the surrounding medieval houses. Unfortunately, it's no beauty, having suffered from the zealous attentions of the purist nineteenth-century restorer Abadie, best known for the white elephant of the Sacré-Coeur in Paris. The result is an excess of ill-proportioned, nipple-like projections serving no obvious purpose: "a supreme example of how not to restore", Freda White tartly observed in her classic travelogue, *Three Rivers of France* (see Contexts, p.1329). It's a pity, since when it was rebuilt in 1173 following a fire, it was one of the most distinctive Byzantine churches undertaken in France, modelled on St Mark's in Venice and the Holy Apostles in Constantinople. Nevertheless, the Byzantine influence is still evident in the interior in the Greek-cross plan – unusual in France – and in the massive clean curves of the domes and their supporting arches. The big Baroque altarpiece, carved in walnut wood in the gloomy east bay, is worth a look too, depicting the Assumption of the Virgin, with a humorous little detail in the illustrative scenes from her life of a puppy tugging the infant Jesus' sheets from his bed with its teeth.

At the west end of the cathedral, there's a fresh produce market on Wednesday and Saturday mornings in **place de la Clautre**, at the heart of the renovated streets of the medieval town, the most attractive of which is the narrow **rue Limogeanne**, lined with Renaissance mansions, now turned into boutiques and delicatessens, intermingled with fast-food outlets. The surrounding streets are also scattered with fine Renaissance houses: particularly handsome are the **Logis St-Front**, 7 rue de la Constitution, and the more sedate **Hôtel de Crenoux** at no. 3. Another striking building is at 17 rue de l'Éguillerie, on the corner of the attractive **place St-Louis**, where a turreted watchtower leans out over the street. There are other old houses down along the river by the Pont des Barris, notably the fifteenth-century **Maison des Consuls**.

At the northern end of rue Limogeanne, out on the broad tree-lined cours Tourny, the **Musée du Périgord** (Mon & Wed–Fri 10.30am–5.30pm, Sat & Sun 1–6pm; €4; Ⓦ musee-perigord.museum.com) is best known for its extensive and important prehistoric collection and some beautiful Gallo-Roman mosaics. Exhibits include copies of a 70,000-year-old skeleton, the oldest yet found in France, and a beautiful engraving of a bison's head. More lively but of less general interest is the **Musée Militaire**, near the cathedral at 32 rue des Farges (Jan–March Wed & Sat 2–6pm; April–Sept Mon–Sat 1–6pm; Oct–Dec Mon–Sat 2–6pm; €4), which contains some unusual exhibits, particularly relating to the French colonial wars in Vietnam.

Roman Périgueux

Roman Périgueux, known as **La Cité**, lies to the west of the town centre towards the *gare SNCF*. The most prominent vestige is the high brick **Tour de Vésone**, the last remains of a temple to the city's guardian goddess, standing in a public garden just south of the train tracks. Beside the tower, the foundations of an exceptionally well-preserved Roman villa form the basis of the new **Musée Gallo-Romain** (Feb, March & Oct–Dec Tues–Sun 10am–12.30pm & 2–5.30pm, April–June & Sept Tues–Sun 10am–6pm, July & Aug daily 10am–7pm; €5.50; Ⓦ www.semitour.com). This was no humble abode: the villa, complete with under-floor heating, thermal baths and colonnaded walkways around the central garden with its cooling pond and fountains, boasted at least sixty rooms. Around the walls you can see the remains of first-century murals of river and marine life, the colours still amazingly vibrant, and here and there, graffiti of hunting scenes, gladiatorial combat and even an ostrich – no doubt the work of some bored Roman urchin.

A short hop across the train tracks, the atmospheric ruins of the city's **amphitheatre** are concealed in the Jardin des Arènes, while further remains of fourth-century Roman defences are visible around the nearby Porte Normande off rue Turenne. The rather mutilated church in this neighbourhood – the result of Huguenot anger in 1577 – is the former cathedral, the church of **St-Étienne**, condemned to life as a traffic island in place de la Cité.

Eating and drinking

Surprisingly, there's no great abundance of good **restaurants** in Périgueux, but the best place to look is in the *vieille ville*, particularly around place St-Louis. For the best of Périgueux's limited **nightlife**, you'd be wise to head for rue de la Sagesse, where you'll find *Le Mellow* and *L'Ouvre-Boîte*, both lively bars with music and cocktails.

Restaurants

Au Bien Bon 15 rue des Places ⓣ05.53.09.69.91. A good lunch spot on a quiet square. Menus for €10 at midday, featuring traditional, regional food served in a rustic interior. Closed Sat lunch, Sun & Mon eve.

Le Canard Laqué 2 rue de Lanmary ⓣ05.53.09.15.61. If you fancy a change from the local fare, this restaurant offers Chinese, Thai, Vietnamese and Cambodian dishes. Their speciality is a duck, mushroom and bamboo soup. Closed Sun.

Le Clos St-Front 5 rue de la Vertu ⓣ05.53.46.78.58. High-quality menus served in a spacious, leafy, walled courtyard. You can eat for €24, but for €52 you get the best of the best and wine included. Closed Sun eve & Mon out of season.

La Ferme St-Louis place St-Louis ☎05.53.53.82.77. The best of the many restaurants on the square, it has a small terrace and a homely, stone-walled interior. Food wise, you can't get much more Périgordian than the duck breast in a truffle-based sauce. Closed Sun & Mon.

La Vertu 11 rue Notre-Dame. A lively bar and restaurant, serving tapas and menus for €11 at lunch and dinner. It only opens in summer, when the salsa music and pitchers of sangria go down best.

Brantôme and the valley of the Dronne

Although **Brantôme** itself is very much on the tourist trail, the country to both the west and east of the town along the **River Dronne** remains largely undisturbed. It's tranquil and very beautiful, and best savoured at a gentle pace, perhaps by bike or even by canoeing along the river.

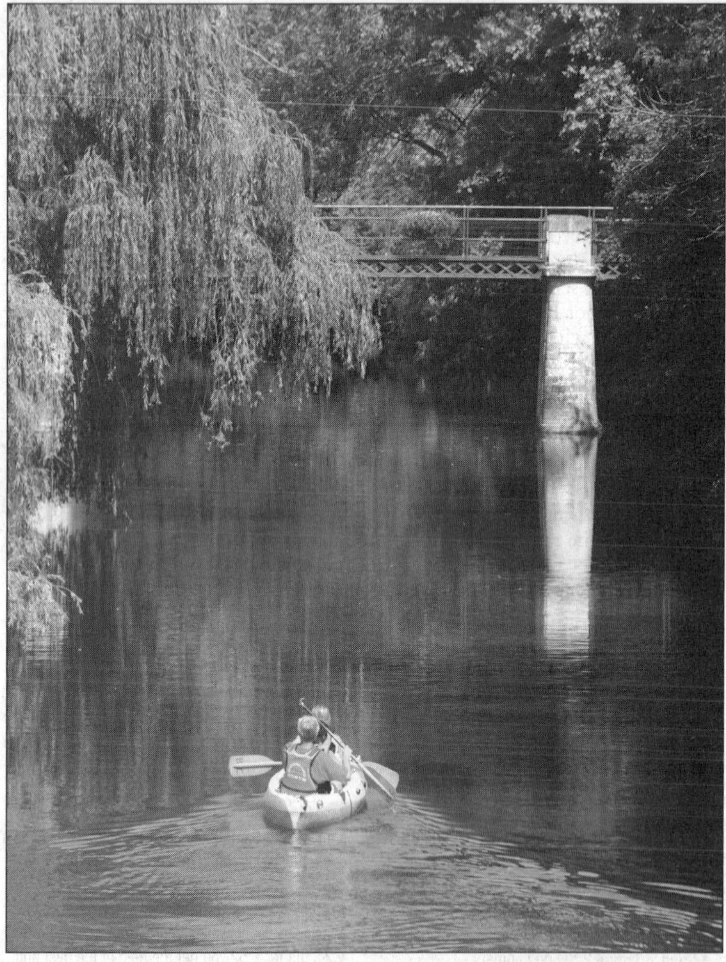

△ River Dronne at Brantôme

Brantôme

BRANTÔME, 27km north of Périgueux on the Angoulême road and beloved of British tourists, sits on an island in the River Dronne, whose still, water-lilied surface mirrors the limes and weeping willows of the riverside gardens. On the north bank of the river are the church and convent buildings of the former **Benedictine abbey** that has been Brantôme's focus ever since it was founded, possibly by Charlemagne. The other big name associated with the abbey is that of its most notorious abbot, Pierre de Bourdeilles, the sixteenth-century author of scurrilous tales of life at the royal court. It's worth taking a look inside the abbey church for the palm-frond vaulting of the chapterhouse and the font made from a carved and grounded pillar capital. Brantôme's best architectural feature, however, is the Limousin-style Romanesque **belfry**, built into the cliff-face behind the church and only accessible on a guided tour arranged by the tourist office (€6).

There are more pleasant views to be had wandering the nearby **gardens** and the balustraded riverbanks, while in summer you can take a leisurely **boat trip** on the river (Easter to mid-Oct; €7).

Four days a week (Mon, Wed, Fri & Sun), **buses** connect Brantôme with Périgueux and the TGV in Angoulême. The **tourist office** (Feb, March & Oct–Dec daily except Tues 10am–noon & 2–5pm; April–June & Sept daily except Tues 10am–12.30pm & 2–6pm; July & Aug daily 10am–7pm; ⓣ05.53.05.80.52, ⓦwww.ville-brantome.fr) is next to the abbey church. From April to September you can rent **canoes** from Brantôme Canoë (ⓣ05.53.05.77.24, ⓦwww.brantome-canoe.com), just over the bridge on the road to Thiviers, while **bikes** are available at *Spadzone*, 2 av des Martyrs (ⓣ05.53.08.02.65, ⓦwww.spadzone.com).

The cheapest **accommodation** is to be found at the friendly *Hôtel Versaveau*, 8 place de Gaulle, at the north end of town (ⓣ05.53.05.71.42; ❶–❷; restaurant from €12; closed three weeks in Nov & Christmas/New Year), though prettier and much more comfortable rooms are available at *Hôtel Chabrol* across the river (ⓣ05.53.05.70.15, ⓦwww.logis-de-france.fr; ❹; closed Feb & mid-Nov to mid-Dec), whose restaurant, *Les Frères Charbonnel*, is in the gourmet class, with its cheapest menu at €26 (closed Sun eve & Mon Oct–June). A lovely place to stay is the *Maison Fleurie*, an English-owned *chambre d'hôte* at 54 rue Gambetta (ⓣ05.53.35.17.04, ⓦwww.maisonfleurie.net; ❸), with a pool and quiet courtyard garden. Good **eating** options include *Les Jardins de Brantôme*, with an attractive garden, a short walk north of town at 33 rue Pierre-de-Mareuil (closed Wed & lunch Mon & Thurs; menus €18.50–26), and *Au Fil de l'Eau*, on quai Bertin, which specializes in not too expensive fish dishes (closed mid-Oct to Easter; menus from €24) and spreads along the riverbank in fine weather. Campers should head for the *Le Peyrelevade* **campsite** just east of Brantôme on the D78 Thiviers road (ⓣ05.53.05.75.24, ⓦwww.campingterreoceane.com; May to mid-Sept).

Bourdeilles

BOURDEILLES, 16km down the Dronne from Brantôme by a beautiful back road, is relatively hard to reach – perhaps the most appealing way is by canoe. It's a sleepy backwater, an ancient village clustering round its **château** (Feb, March, Nov & Dec Mon, Wed, Thurs & Sun 10am–12.30pm & 2–5.30pm; April–June, Sept & Oct daily except Tues 10am–12.30pm & 2–6pm; July & Aug daily 10am–7pm; €5.50; ⓦwww.semitour.com) on a rocky spur above the river. The château consists of two buildings: one a thirteenth-century fortress, the other an elegant Renaissance residence begun by the lady of the house as a piece of unsuccessful favour-currying with Catherine de Médicis – unsuccessful because Catherine never came to stay and the château remained unfinished. If you climb the octagonal keep, there's a good view over the town's clustered roofs and along the valley of the Dronne.

The château is now home to an exceptional collection of **furniture** and **religious statuary** bequeathed to the state by its former owners. Among the more notable pieces are some splendid Spanish dowry chests and a sixteenth-century Rhenish Entombment with life-sized statues, embodying the very image of the serious, self-satisfied medieval burgher. The *salon doré*, the room in which Catherine de Médicis was supposed to sleep, has also been preserved.

Lesser mortals wanting to **stay** the night could try the appealing *Hostellerie le Donjon* (ⓣ05.53.04.82.81, ⓦwww.hostellerie-ledonjon.fr; ❸; menus €12–25; closed mid-Nov to mid-Dec, Jan & March), on the main street, or the more upmarket *Hostellerie Les Griffons* (ⓣ05.53.45.45.35, ⓦwww.griffons.fr; ❼; closed Nov–Easter) in a sixteenth-century house beside the old bridge, with a restaurant serving top-notch regional cuisine (three courses from €32).

Ribérac

Surrounded by an intimate, hilly countryside of woods and hay meadows and drowsy hilltop villages, **RIBÉRAC**, 30km downstream from Bourdeilles, is a pleasant if unremarkable town whose greatest claim to fame is its major Friday **market**, which brings in producers and wholesalers from all around. It makes an agreeable base from which to explore the quiet, lush Dronne landscape, especially if you stay at the attractive and excellent-value *De France* on the north side of the central square at 3 rue Marc-Dufraisse (ⓣ05.53.90.00.61, ⓦwww.hoteldefranceriberac.com; ❸; closed Mon, also mid-Nov to mid-Dec & Jan), with a terrace garden and a locally renowned restaurant serving original cuisine (closed Mon, Tues lunch & Sat; menu at €23). There's also a riverside municipal **campsite** just outside Ribérac on the Angoulême road (ⓣ05.53.90.50.08; June to mid-Sept).

For further ideas about *chambres d'hôtes* in the surrounding country, Ribérac's **tourist office** on place de Gaulle is the place to ask (July & Aug Mon–Fri 9am–7pm, Sat 9am–noon & 2–6pm, Sun 10am–noon; Sept–June Mon–Sat 9am–noon & 2–5pm; ⓣ05.53.90.03.10, ⓦwww.riberac.fr); they can also provide information about the numerous Romanesque churches in outlying villages that could provide a focus for leisurely wandering. **Bikes** can be rented from Cycle Cum's, 35 rue du 26-Mars-1944 (ⓣ05.53.90.33.23).

Aubeterre-sur-Dronne and around

Rather touristy, but very beautiful with its ancient galleried and turreted houses, **AUBETERRE-SUR-DRONNE** hangs on a steep hillside above the river some 30km downstream of Ribérac. Its principal curiosity is the cavernous **Église Monolithe** (daily 9.30am–12.30pm & 2–6pm; €4), carved out of the soft rock of the cliff face in the twelfth century, with its rock-hewn tombs going back to the sixth. A (blocked-off) tunnel connects with the **château** on the bluff overhead. There's also the extremely beautiful church of **St-Jacques**, with an eleventh-century facade sculpted and decorated in the richly carved Poitiers style on the street leading uphill from the square.

The **tourist office** is beside the main car park (April–June, Sept & Oct Mon 2–6pm, Tues–Sat 10am–noon & 2–6pm; July & Aug Mon 2–7pm, Tues–Sun 10am–noon & 2–7pm; Nov–March Mon–Sat 2–6pm; ⓣ05.45.98.57.18, ⓦaubeterresurdronne.free.fr), round the corner from the simple, rather faded *Hôtel de France* (ⓣ05.45.98.50.43, ⓦwww.hoteldefrance-aubeterre.com; ❷;

restaurant from €13) on the central square. Alternatively, you'll find more comfortable **accommodation** and a fine restaurant just below the village at the *Hostellerie du Périgord*, beside the bridge (ⓣ05.45.98.50.46, ⓦwww.hostellerie-perigord.com; ❸; menus €16.50–28). There's also a **campsite** (ⓣ05.45.98.60.17; June–Sept) across the other side of the river. An early-morning **bus** runs to Angoulême (Mon–Sat), while Chalais, which is on the Angoulême train line, is only 12km away.

South of Aubeterre the country gradually changes. Farmland gives way to an extensive forest of oak and sweet chestnut, bracken and broom, interspersed with sour, marshy pasture, very sparsely populated. It's ideal cycling and picnicking country.

St-Jean-de-Côle and around

Twenty kilometres northeast of Brantôme, **ST-JEAN-DE-CÔLE** ranks as one of the loveliest villages in the Dordogne. Its ancient houses huddle together in typical medieval fashion around a wide sandy square dominated by the charmingly ill-proportioned eleventh-century **church of St-Jean-Baptiste** and the rugged-looking **Château de la Marthonie** (not open to the public). The château, which dates from the twelfth century, has acquired various additions in a pleasingly organic fashion.

The **tourist office** (July & Aug Mon–Fri 9am–noon & 2–7pm, Sat & Sun 2–7pm; Sept–June daily except Wed 2–5.30pm; ⓣ05.53.62.14.15, ⓦwww.ville-saint-jean-de-cole.fr) is also on the square, as well as a couple of **restaurants**. However, for good traditional fare like truffle omelette you can't beat the wisteria-covered *Hôtel St-Jean* (ⓣ05.53.52.23.20, ⓔlesaintjean@ville-saint-jean-de-cole.fr; ❷; menus from €12, closed Wed out of season) on the main road through the village; it also offers a few simple but clean and comfortable **rooms**.

Around 10km west of St-Jean, just outside the village of **VILLARS**, the **Château de Puyguilhem** (daily: July & Aug 10am–7pm; Sept–June 10am–12.30pm & 2–6pm; €5.50; ⓦwww.semitour.com) sits on the edge of a valley backed by oak woods. The building you see today was erected at the beginning of the sixteenth century on the site of an earlier military fortress. With its octagonal tower, broad spiral staircase, steep roofs, magnificent fireplaces and false dormer windows, it's a perfect example of French Renaissance architecture. From the gallery at the top of the stairs you get a close-up of the roof and window decoration, as well as a view down the valley, which once was filled by an ornamental lake.

In the next valley south, the ruined Cistercian **Boschaud abbey** merits a quick visit while you're in the area. Standing on the edge of the woods and reached by a lane not much wider than a farm track, its charm lies as much in the fact that it is – for once – unfenced, unpampered and free, as in the pure, stark lines of its twelfth-century architecture.

A short distance north of Villars, local cavers discovered an extensive cave system in 1958, part of which is open to the public. While the **Grotte de Villars** (daily: April–June & Sept 10am–noon & 2–7pm; July & Aug 10am–7pm; Oct 2–6.30pm; €6.50; ⓦwww.grotte-villars.com) boasts a few prehistoric paintings – notably of horses and a still unexplained scene of a man and a bison – the main reason for coming here is the impressive array of stalactites and stalagmites.

Thiviers and Sorges

If you're heading along the main N21 Périgueux–Limoges road, it's worth stopping off at the small market town of **THIVIERS**, which styles itself as the foie gras capital of the region. Its well-stocked **tourist office**, on the central square (May–Sept Mon–Sat 10am–1pm & 2–6pm, Sun 2–6pm; Oct–June closed Sun & Mon afternoon; ⓣ05.53.55.12.50, ⓦwww.thiviers.fr), makes the most of this with a small **museum** dedicated to the history and production of foie gras (same hours; €1.50). A particularly welcoming place to **stay** is the attractive and characterful *Hôtel de France et de Russie*, 51 rue du Général-Lamy (ⓣ05.53.55.17.80, ⓦwww.thiviers-hotel.com; ③), between the tourist office and the **gare SNCF**.

SORGES, closer to Périgueux and strung out along the road, has less to offer aesthetically than Thiviers. However, the **tourist office** (July & Aug daily 9.30am–12.30pm & 2.30–6.30pm; Sept–June Tues–Sun 10am–noon & 2–5pm; ⓣ05.53.05.90.11, ⓦwww.truffe-sorges.org) contains an informative **truffle museum** (same hours; €4), and staff can also direct you to a nature trail that gives an idea of how and where truffles grow. There's a very reasonable **hotel** here, too, the *Auberge de la Truffe* on the main road (ⓣ05.53.05.02.05, ⓦwww.auberge-de-la-truffe.com; ④), with an excellent restaurant (menus €16–70, closed for lunch Mon & Tues).

The Château de Hautefort

Forty kilometres east of Périgueux, the **Château de Hautefort** (daily: Feb, March, Oct & Nov Sat & Sun 2–6pm; April & May daily 10am–12.30pm & 2–6.30pm; June–Sept daily 9.30am–7pm; €8.50; ⓦwww.chateau-hautefort.com) enjoys a majestic position at the end of a wooded spur above its feudal village. A magnificent example of good living on a grand scale, the castle has an elegance that is out of step with the usual rough stone fortresses of Périgord. The approach is across a wide esplanade flanked by formal gardens, over the moat by a drawbridge, and into a stylish Renaissance courtyard, opening to the south. Once the property of well-known troubadour Bertrand de Born, it passed into the hands of the Hautefort family in the seventeenth century and was extensively remodelled. In 1968 a fire gutted the castle, but it has since been meticulously restored using traditional techniques; it's all unmistakably new, but the quality of the craftsmanship is superb.

Hautefort has a very pleasant **hotel**, the *Auberge du Parc* (ⓣ05.53.50.88.98, ⓕ05.53.51.61.72; ③; closed mid-Dec to mid-March; restaurant from €16, closed Sun eve & Wed), just beneath the castle walls. By car, the most attractive route from Périgueux is on the D5 along the River Auvézère via Cubjac and Tourtoirac.

Périgord Pourpre

The area known as the **Périgord Pourpre** takes its name from the wine-growing region concentrated in the southwest corner of the Dordogne *département*, most famous for the sweet white wines produced around **Monbazillac**. The only town of any size is **Bergerac**, which makes a good base for visiting the Roman remains at **Montcaret** and the nearby **Château de Montaigne**, home of the famous sixteenth-century philosopher. The uplands south of Bergerac are peppered with *bastides*, medieval fortified towns (see box on p.695), such as the beautifully preserved **Monpazier**, and here also you'll find the **Château de Biron**, which dominates the countryside for miles around.

Bergerac and around

BERGERAC, "capital" of Périgord Pourpre, lies on the riverbank in the wide plain of the Dordogne. Once a flourishing port for the wine trade, it is still the main market centre for the surrounding maize, vine and tobacco farms. Devastated in the Wars of Religion, when most of its Protestant population fled overseas, Bergerac is now essentially a modern town with some interesting and attractive reminders of the past.

The **vieille ville** is a calm and pleasant area to wander through, with numerous late medieval houses and some beautiful squares. In rue de l'Ancien-Pont, the splendid seventeenth-century Maison Peyrarède houses an informative **Musée du Tabac** (Feb–Dec daily except Sun morning & Mon 10am–noon & 2–6pm; €3.50), detailing the history of the weed, with collections of pipes and tools of the trade.

Bergerac has a couple of other museums, the best of which is the small **Musée Régional du Vin et de la Batellerie** in rue des Conférences in the heart of the old town (Tues–Fri 10am–noon & 2–5.30pm, Sat 10am–noon; April–Oct also Sun 2.30–6.30pm; €2.50), with displays on viticulture, barrel-making and the town's once-bustling river-trading past. Nearby, on the very picturesque place de la Myrpe, is a statue in honour of **Cyrano de Bergerac**, the town's most famous association, on whom a 1990 film starring Gérard Dépardieu was based. The big-nosed lead character in Edmond Rostand's play, though fictional, was inspired by the seventeenth-century philosopher of the same name, who, sadly, had nothing to do with the town.

Wine-lovers should make a beeline for the **Maison des Vins**, down by the river on quai Salvette (Feb–June & Sept–Dec Tues–Sun 10.30am–12.30pm & 2–6pm; July & Aug daily 10am–7pm), which offers free tastings and sells a selection of local wines, as well as providing information about the surrounding vineyards.

Practicalities

The **gare SNCF** is at the end of cours Alsace-Lorraine, ten minutes' walk north from the old town, while the **airport** (Ⓣ05.53.22.25.25) lies 5km southeast of Bergerac (roughly €12 by taxi). The main **tourist office** is at 97 rue Neuve-d'Argenson, two minutes' walk northeast of the old town (July & Aug Mon–Sat 9.30am–7.30pm; Sept–June Mon–Sat 9.30am–1pm & 2–7pm; Ⓣ05.53.57.03.11, Ⓦwww.bergerac-tourisme.com), and a second office opens in summer in the heart of the old town at the Cloître des Récollets (July & Aug daily 10.30am–1pm & 2–6.30pm). You can rent anything with wheels – **cars,** mopeds and **bicycles** – from Ucar at 31 bd Victor-Hugo (Ⓣ05.53.61.08.16, Ⓦwww.ucar-location.com), which also offers airport pick-ups. A vast **market** takes place on Wednesday and Saturday mornings in the covered *halles* in the old town centre and around Notre-Dame church; **Internet** access costs €2 per hour at phonebox 24, opposite the train station.

There's a decent range of **accommodation** to choose from. The best budget option is *Le Moderne*, opposite the station (Ⓣ05.53.57.19.62, Ⓕ05.53.61.80.50; ❶; closed two weeks in Oct), a welcoming, well-kept place with a brasserie restaurant (closed Sun; menus from €16). For something more comfortable, try one of the three-star hotels on place Gambetta between the station and the old town: the *De France* (Ⓣ05.53.57.11.61, Ⓦwww.hoteldefrance-bergerac.com; ❹), where the more expensive rooms have balconies and a/c, or the *De Bordeaux* (Ⓣ05.53.57.12.83, Ⓦwww.hotel-bordeaux-bergerac.com; ❹), with a marginally larger swimming pool. There's also a municipal **campsite**, *La Pelouse* (Ⓣ & Ⓕ05.53.57.06.67; mid-Feb to Oct), on the south bank of the river.

If you should find yourself here in July, don't miss the magnificent **food festival** called La Table de Cyrano in the week of July 14. Classical music concerts also take place throughout the month, with jazz on Wednesday evenings throughout July and August. Bergerac is well off for **restaurants**, the best area to look being the square around the market hall.

Restaurants

La Blanche Hermine place du Marché-Couvert ☎05.53.57.53.42. A popular crêperie, which also serves a range of salads – all at very reasonable prices. It's endearingly decorated with bright, if not exactly sophisticated, children's artwork. Closed Sun & Mon.

Aux Cèpes Enchantés rue de l'Ancien Pont ☎05.53.57.24.90. An excellent spot in summer, with plenty of outside seating and light regional menus from €14.50. There's also a good local wine list to complement the food. April–Sept only.

La Cocotte des Halles ☎05.53.24.10.00. In the covered market itself, this characterful restaurant offers very affordable lunches, with omelettes from €5 and huge plates of salad from €8.

L'Imparfait 8 rue des Fontaines ☎05.53.57.47.92. The most upmarket restaurant in Bergerac: tables surrounded by potted foliage spill out into an attractive pedestrian street. Gastronomic menus from €26. Closed Dec & Sun.

Les Jardins d'Epicure place du Marché-Couvert ☎05.53.57.80.90. A friendly restaurant offering the standard regional dishes, to be enjoyed on the tree-lined pavement. Menus start at €17.

Château de Monbazillac

Half a dozen kilometres south of Bergerac, looking out over the gentle slopes of its long-favoured vineyards, stands the handsome Renaissance **Château de Monbazillac** (Feb, March, Nov & Dec Tues–Sun 10am–noon & 2–5pm; April daily 10am–noon & 2–6pm; May & Oct daily 10am–12.30pm & 2–5pm; June–Sept daily 10am–7pm; €6), part residence and part fortress, with its corners reinforced by four sturdy towers. Inside is a moderately interesting **museum** of local traditions and crafts; most engaging are the wine-related displays in the cellar. You can taste – and buy – the velvety sweet white Monbazillac **wine** here, too; it's generally consumed with desserts or chilled as an aperitif.

Montcaret

West of Bergerac, the main place of interest is **MONTCARET**, whose biggest draw is a fourth-century **Gallo-Roman villa** (June–Sept daily 9.45am–12.30pm & 2–6.30pm; Oct–May daily except Sat 10am–12.30pm & 2–5.30pm; €5) with superb mosaics and baths plus an adjoining museum displaying the many objects exhumed on the site. It's another 3.5km to the **Château de Montaigne** (Feb–April & Nov–Dec Wed–Sun 10am–noon & 2–5.30pm; May, June, Sept & Oct Wed–Sun 10am–noon & 2–6.30pm; July & Aug daily 10am–6.30pm; €5.50 entry to château; €2.50 just for the gardens), where Michel de Montaigne wrote many of his chatty, digressive essays on the nature of life and humankind. All that remains of the original building is Montaigne's tower-study, its beams inscribed with his maxims; the rest of the château was rebuilt in pseudo-Renaissance style after a fire in 1885.

Monpazier and around

MONPAZIER, founded in 1284 by King Edward I of England (who was also Duke of Aquitaine), is one of the most complete of the surviving *bastides*, and still relatively free of the commercialism that suffocates a place like Domme. Picturesque and placid though it is today, the village has a hard and bitter history, being twice – in 1594 and 1637 – the centre of peasant rebellions provoked by the misery that followed the Wars of Religion. Both uprisings were brutally suppressed: the 1637 peasants' leader was broken on the wheel in the square. Sully, the Protestant general, describes a rare moment of light relief in the

Bastides

From the Occitan word *bastida*, meaning a group of buildings, ***bastides*** were the new towns of the thirteenth and fourteenth centuries. Although they are found all over southwest France, from the Dordogne to the foothills of the Pyrenees, there is a particularly high concentration in the area between the Dordogne and Lot rivers, which at that time formed the disputed "frontier" region between English-held Aquitaine and Capetian France.

That said, the earliest *bastides* were founded largely for economic and political reasons. They were a means of bringing new land into production – this was a period of rapid population growth and technological innovation – and thus extending the power of the local lord. But as tensions between the French and English forces intensified during the late thirteenth century, so the motive became increasingly military. The *bastides* now provided a handy way of securing the land along the frontier, and it was generally at this point that they were fortified.

As an incentive, anyone who was prepared to build, inhabit and defend the *bastide* was granted various perks and concessions in a founding charter. All new residents were allocated a building plot, garden and cultivable land outside the town. The charter might also offer asylum to certain types of criminal or grant exemption from military service, and would allow the election of consuls charged with day-to-day administration – a measure of self-government remarkable in feudal times. Taxes and judicial affairs, meanwhile, remained the preserve of the representative of the king or local lord under whose ultimate authority the *bastide* lay.

The other defining feature of a *bastide* is its layout. They are nearly always square or rectangular in shape, depending on the nature of the terrain, and are divided by streets at right angles to each other to produce a chequerboard pattern. The focal point is the market square, often missing its covered *halle* nowadays, but generally still surrounded by arcades, while the church is relegated to one side, or may even form part of the town walls.

The busiest *bastide* founders were Alphonse de Poitiers (1249–1271), on behalf of the French crown, after he became Count of Toulouse in 1249, and King Edward I of England (1272–1307), who wished to consolidate his hold on the northern borders of his Duchy of Aquitaine. The former chalked up a total of 57 *bastides*, including **Villeneuve-sur-Lot** (1251), **Monflanquin** (1252) and **Ste-Foy-la-Grande** (1255), while Edward was responsible for **Beaumont** (1272) and **Monpazier** (1284) amongst others. While many *bastides* retain no more than vestiges of their original aspect, both Monpazier and Monflanquin have survived almost entirely intact.

terrible wars, when the men of the Catholic *bastide* of Villefranche-du-Périgord planned to capture Monpazier on the same night as the men of Monpazier planned to capture Villefranche. By chance, both sides took different routes, met no resistance, looted to their hearts' content and returned home congratulating themselves on their luck and skill, only to find in the morning that things were rather different. The peace terms were that everyone should return everything to its proper place.

Monpazier follows the typical *bastide* layout, with a grid of streets built around a gem of a central square – sunny, still and slightly menacing. Deep, shady arcades pass under all the houses, which are separated from each other by a small gap to reduce fire risk; at the corners the buttresses are cut away to allow the passage of laden pack animals. There's also an ancient *lavoir* where women used to wash clothes, and a much altered church.

The well-organized **tourist office** is on the central square (daily: Jan & Dec 10.30am–12.30pm & 2.30–5.30pm; Feb–June & Sept–Nov 10am–12.30pm

& 2–6.30pm; July & Aug 10am–7pm; ⓣ05.53.22.68.59, ⓦwww.pays-des-bastides.com), where you'll also find reasonable **accommodation** at the *Hôtel de France*, 21 rue St-Jacques (ⓣ05.53.22.60.06, ⓕ05.53.22.07.27; ❸; closed Nov–March; restaurant from €18.50, closed Tues eve & Wed out of season). A more extravagant option is the *Hôtel Edward 1er* (ⓣ05.53.22.44.00, ⓦwww.hoteledward1er.com; ❻) at 5 rue St-Pierre, a few minutes' walk from the main square, with its own swimming pool and a restaurant from €27. When it comes to **eating** though, you can't beat *La Bastide*, at 52 rue St-Jacques (ⓣ05.53.22.60.59; closed Mon & Feb; menus €13.50–48), for traditional atmosphere and classic, regional cooking. The best of the **campsites** in the vicinity is the luxurious *Moulin de David*, roughly 3km to the south on the road to Villeréal (ⓣ05.53.22.65.25, ⓦwww.moulin-de-david.com; mid-May to mid-Sept).

The Château de Biron

Eight kilometres south of Monpazier, the vast **Château de Biron** (daily: July & Aug 10am–7pm; Sept–June 10am–12.30pm & 2–6pm; €5.50; ⓦwww.semitour.com) was begun in the eleventh century and added to piecemeal afterwards. You can take a guided tour (in French only), but better to borrow the English-language translation and wander at will around the rooms and the grassy courtyard, where there is a restored Renaissance chapel and guardhouse with tremendous views over the roofs of the feudal village below.

A single street runs through the village of **BIRON**, past a covered **market** on timber supports iron-hard with age, and out under an arched gateway, where well-manured vegetable plots interspersed with iris, lily and Iceland poppies lie under the tumbledown walls. At the bottom of the hill, another group of houses stands on a small square with a well in front of the village **church**, its Romanesque origins hidden by motley alterations. The *Auberge du Château*, back near the market hall, makes a perfect lunch spot (ⓣ05.53.63.13.33; closed Sat lunch & Mon, also Dec & Jan).

Périgord Noir

Périgord Noir encompasses the central part of the valley of the Dordogne, and the valley of the Vézère. This is the distinctive Dordogne country: deep-cut valleys enclosed by the water-smooth cliffs their rivers have eroded, with fields of maize in the alluvial bottoms and dense oak woods on the heights, interspersed with patches of not very fertile farmland. Plantations of walnut trees (cultivated for their oil), flocks of low-slung grey geese (their livers enlarged for foie gras) and prehistoric-looking stone huts called *bories* are all hallmarks of Périgord Noir.

The well-preserved medieval architecture of **Sarlat**, the wealth of prehistory and the staggering cave paintings of the **Vézère valley**, and the stunning beauty of the château-studded **Dordogne** have all contributed to making this one of the most heavily touristed inland areas of France, with all the concomitant problems of crowds, high prices and tack. If possible, it's worth coming out of season, but if you can't, seek accommodation away from the main centres, and always drive along the back roads – the smaller the better – even when there is a more direct route available.

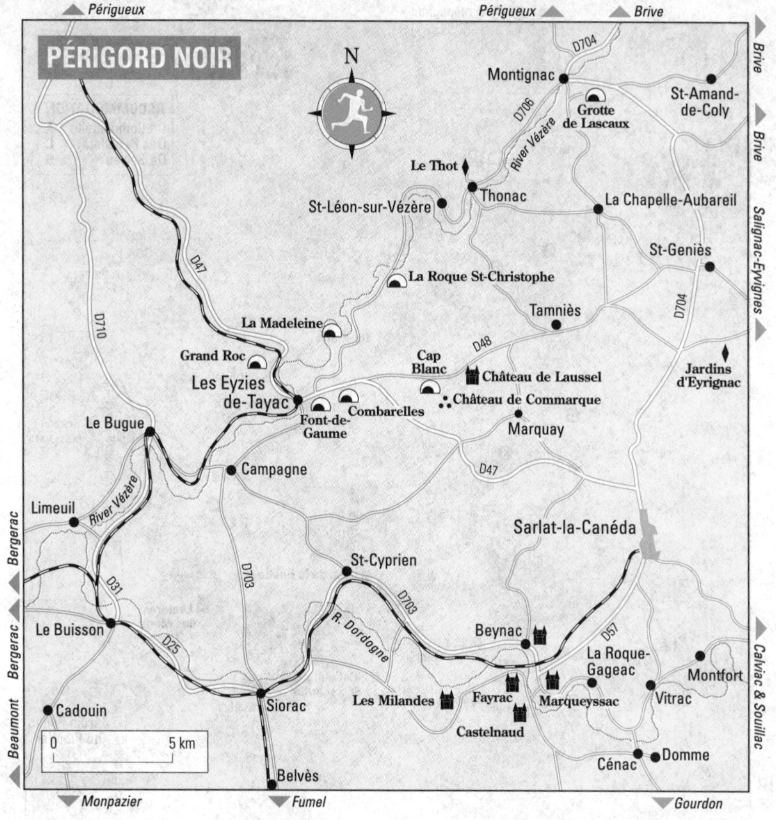

Sarlat and around

SARLAT-LA-CANÉDA, capital of Périgord Noir, lies in a hollow between hills 10km or so back from the Dordogne River. You hardly notice the modern town, as it's the mainly fifteenth- and sixteenth-century houses of the *vieille ville* in mellow, honey-coloured stone that draw the attention.

The **vieille ville** is an excellent example of medieval organic urban growth. The first town centre to benefit from culture minister André Malraux's law of 1962 which created the concept of the *secteur sauvegardé* (protected area), it boasts no fewer than 65 protected buildings and monuments. The old centre is violated only by the straight swath of the rue de la République which cuts through its middle. The west side remains relatively un-chic; the east side is where most people wander. As you approach the old town from the station, turn right down rue Lakanal which leads to the large and unexciting **Cathédrale St-Sacerdos**, mostly dating from its seventeenth-century renovation. Opposite stands the town's finest house, the **Maison de La Boétie** (not open to the public) once the home of Montaigne's friend Étienne de La Boétie, with its gabled tiers of windows and characteristic steep roof stacked with heavy limestone tiles (*lauzes*).

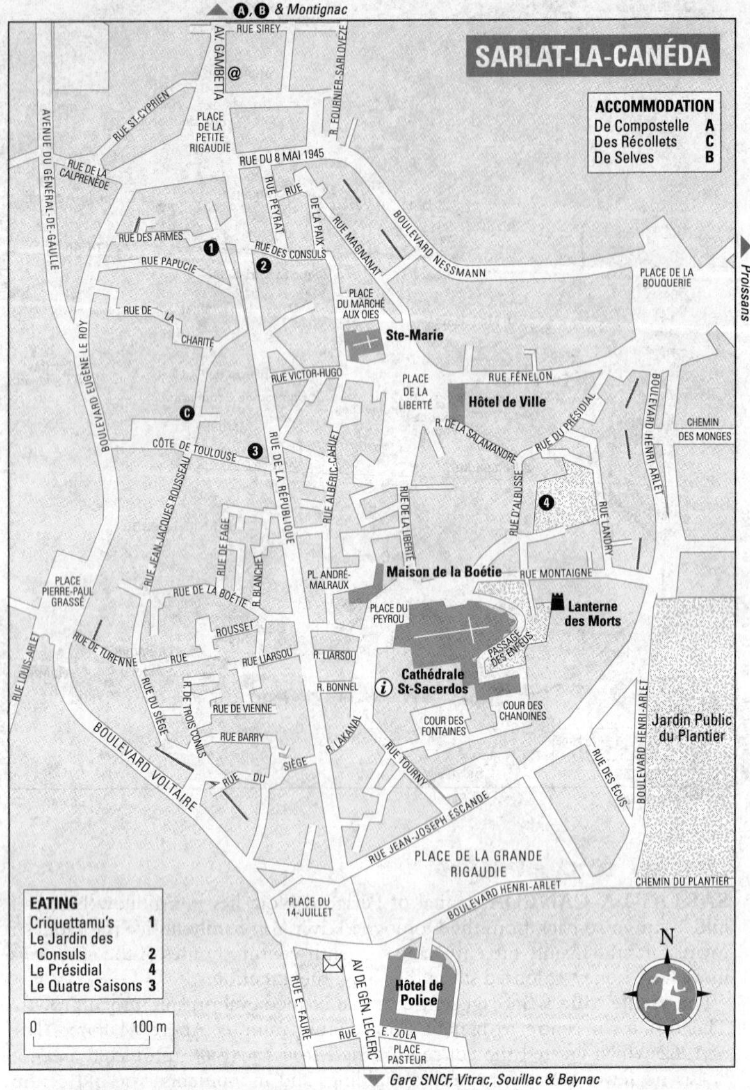

For a better sense of the medieval town, wander through the cool, shady lanes and courtyards – **cour des Fontaines** and **cour des Chanoines** – around the back of the cathedral. On a slope directly behind the cathedral stands the curious twelfth-century coned tower, the **Lanterne des Morts**, whose exact function has escaped historians, though the most popular theory is that it was built to commemorate St Bernard, who performed various miracles when he visited the town in 1147.

There are more wonderful old houses in the streets to the north, especially **rue des Consuls**, and up the slopes to the east. Eventually, though, Sarlat's labyrinthine lanes will lead you back to the central **place de la Liberté**, where the big Saturday **market** spreads its stands bearing foie gras, truffles, walnuts and mushrooms according to the season, and where various people try to make a living from the hordes who hit Sarlat in the summer.

Practicalities

The **gare SNCF** is just over 1km south of the old town, where on rue Tourny you'll find the **tourist office** (July & Aug Mon–Sat 9am–7pm, Sun 10am–noon & 2–6pm; June & Sept Mon–Sat 9am–1pm & 2–7pm; Oct–May Mon–Sat 9am–noon & 2–6pm; ⓣ05.53.31.45.45, ⓦwww.ot-sarlat-perigord.fr). For a small fee, they'll help find accommodation, though it can be extremely difficult in high season. You can rent **bicycles** and scooters from Cycles Sarladais, avenue A.-Briand (ⓣ05.53.28.51.87, ⓔcycles.sarladais@wanadoo.fr), while there is **Internet** access at Easy Planet, 17 av Gambetta – though at €6 per hour, it's daylight robbery.

The nicest and most reasonable **place to stay** in Sarlat is the *Hôtel des Récollets*, 4 rue J.-J.-Rousseau (ⓣ05.53.31.36.00, ⓦwww.hotel-recollets-sarlat.com; ❸), with comfortable rooms around an attractive patio. The modern, a/c *Hôtel de Compostelle* at 64 av de Selves, the northern extension of rue de la République (ⓣ05.53.59.08.53, ⓦwww.hotel-compostelle-sarlat.com; ❹; closed mid-Nov to Feb), is also good value, while the more upmarket *Hôtel de Selves*, 93 av de Selves, has a pool and small garden (ⓣ05.53.31.50.00, ⓦwww.selves-sarlat.com; ❺; closed mid-Jan to mid-Feb). The nearest **campsite**, *Les Périères*, on Sarlat's northern outskirts (ⓣ05.53.59.05.84, ⓦwww.lesperieres.com; April–Sept), is very well equipped but costs almost as much as a hotel; much better to try *Les Terrasses du Périgord*, about 2.5km north of Sarlat near Proissans village (ⓣ05.53.59.02.25, ⓦwww.terrasses-du-perigord.com; May–Sept).

Restaurants tend to be overpriced in Sarlat, particularly those that open only in summer. Two nice choices are *Criquettamu's*, 5 rue des Armes (menus €16–32; ⓣ05.53.59.48.10; closed Mon & Nov–March), serving up platters of local delicacies in a lovely fourteenth-century corner house, and *Le Jardin des Consuls*, 4 rue des Consuls (menus from €13; ⓣ05.53.59.18.77), which has its own terrace back from the street. For something a bit special try *Le Quatre Saisons*, 2 Côte de Toulouse (menus €18–34; ⓣ05.53.29.48.59; closed Tues & Wed out of season), with an interior courtyard, or splash out at *Le Présidial*, 6 rue Landry (menus €26–40; ⓣ05.53.28.92.47; closed Sun, Mon lunch & Nov–March), in a lovely seventeenth-century mansion and its walled garden.

Not far away there are some very pleasant alternatives to staying – or eating – in Sarlat. On the banks of the Dordogne at **VITRAC**, about 7km south of Sarlat, the *Hôtel La Treille* (ⓣ05.53.28.33.19, ⓦwww.latreille-perigord,com; ❸–❹; closed Feb, also Mon & Tues out of season) is great value, with large rooms and an excellent restaurant (menus from €16.50; closed Mon lunch) in a vine-covered building with a sunny terrace. Some 5km to the east, just outside the village of **CARSAC,** the *Hôtel la Villa Romaine* (ⓣ05.53.28.52.07, ⓦwww.lavillaromaine.com; ❽; closed Feb & 2 weeks in Nov) offers extreme pampering in a cluster of attractive former farm buildings around a swimming pool. One more good choice is the little hilltop hamlet of **MARQUAY** about halfway to Les Eyzies, where the *Hôtel des Bories* (ⓣ05.53.29.67.02; ❸; closed Nov–March) offers a marvellous view, pool and attached restaurant, *L'Esterel* (menus from €14), for which it's vital to book several months in advance for July and August.

Les Jardins d'Eyrignac

The *manoir* of **Eyrignac,** 13km northeast of Sarlat, is a very lovely seventeenth-century example of what in English would be called a country house. Its great glory is its **garden**, which is remarkable for its sculpted bushes and geometric arrangement (guided tours daily: April & May 10am–12.30pm & 2–7pm; June–Sept 9.30am–7pm; Oct–March 10.30am–12.30pm & 2.30pm–dusk; €8; house closed to the public). The original formal garden was the work of an eighteenth-century Italian architect, but it was later converted to an English romantic garden as the owners – still the same family – followed subsequent fashions. Today it is a combination of Italian and French styles, with practically no flowers but lines of evergreens – mainly box, hornbeam, cypress and yew – clipped and arranged in formal patterns of alleys and parterres. A work of art in its own right, it's now classified as a national monument.

The Vézère valley

The **valley of the Vézère** River between **Limeuil** and **St-Amand-de-Coly** justifiably styles itself as the prehistory capital of the world. The high, rocky outcrops which overlook acres of thick forest are riddled with caves which have provided shelter for humans for tens of thousands of years. It was here that the first skeletons of Cro-Magnon people – the first Homo sapiens, tall and muscular with a large skull – were unearthed in 1868 by labourers digging out the Périgueux–Agen train line. Since then, an incomparable wealth of archeological and artistic evidence about the life of late Stone Age people has been revealed in the area, most famously in the breathtakingly sophisticated cave paintings of **Lascaux** and **Font de Gaume**.

Away from the throngs of visitors at the caves, there is much to appreciate in the peace and quiet of the Vézère valley. It's best enjoyed from a **canoe**, where you'll often find yourself alone in a bend of the river, rather than part of a vast armada, as tends to be the case on the Dordogne.

Limeuil

Built into the steep slope at the confluence of the Dordogne and Vézère rivers, the beautiful village of **LIMEUIL** is a picturesque place to while away a couple of hours. From the riverbank – an ideal picnic spot, with a pebbly beach for those who fancy a dip – the narrow, cobbled rue du Port leads steeply uphill, winding in between the medieval houses and through the old gateways. At the top, the best views out over the village and surrounding countryside have been monopolized by the **Parc Panoramique** (April–June & Sept Mon–Sat 2.30–6pm, Sun 10am–6.30pm; July & Aug daily 10am–7pm; €5), a wilderness of trees, shrubs and crumbling stone walls which provide some welcome shade from which to enjoy the scenery.

Canoes can be rented for trips on either river down by the water, where there are also a couple of cafés. For **eating** though, by far the best option is up the hill at *Au Bon Accueil* (Ⓣ05.53.63.30.97, Ⓦwww.au-bon-accueil-limeuil.com; closed Nov–March; ❷), which serves quality regional menus at €16–37 and also has comfortable **rooms**.

Les Eyzies

The main base for visiting many of the prehistoric painted caves is **LES EYZIES-DE-TAYAC**, a one-street village completely dedicated to tourism. While you're here, though, visit the **Musée National de Préhistoire** (June & Sept daily except Tues 9.30am–6pm; July & Aug daily 9.30am–6.30pm;

Oct–May daily except Tues 9.30am–12.30pm & 2–5.30pm; €5; Ⓦwww.musee-prehistoire-eyzies.fr), at long last in its marvellous new home, which contains all the most important prehistoric artefacts found in the various caves in the region. Look out for the oil lamp from Lascaux and the exhibits from La Madeleine, to the north of Les Eyzies, including a superb bas-relief of a bison licking its flank.

The **tourist office**, on Les Eyzies' one street (June & Sept Mon–Sat 9am–noon & 2–6pm, Sun 10am–noon & 2–5pm; July & Aug Mon–Sat 9am–7pm, Sun 10am–noon & 2–6pm; Oct–May Mon–Sat 9am–noon & 2–6pm; Ⓣ05.53.06.97.05, Ⓦwww.leseyzies.com) offers **bike** rental, **Internet** access and information on local *chambres d'hôtes* and *gîtes d'étape*.

Hotels are pricey and may require half-board in high season. The cheapest is the friendly *Les Falaises*, in the main street (Ⓣ05.53.06.97.35, Ⓔhotel-des-falaises@wanadoo.fr; ❷; closed Dec), but the slightly more expensive *La Rivière*, about 1km away on the Périgueux road, has more comfortable rooms (Ⓣ05.53.06.97.14, Ⓦwww.lariviereleseyzies.com; ❷; closed Nov–March; simple meals from €12). There is also a **campsite** here (April–Oct), under the same management. Moving up a notch, the ivy-covered *Hostellerie du Passeur*, by the tourist office (Ⓣ05.53.06.97.13, Ⓦwww.hostellerie-du-passeur.com; ❹; closed Nov–Jan; restaurant €26–65), has small but very comfortable rooms, while just east of the centre, in a lovely spot by a millrace, *Le Moulin de la Beune* (Ⓣ05.53.06.94.33, Ⓦwww.moulindelabeune.com; ❹; closed Nov–March) has well-priced rooms and an excellent restaurant (closed Tues lunch, Wed & Sat lunch; menus €29–55). Alternatively, you could stay in **CAMPAGNE**, a pretty village 6km downstream, where you'll find big, bright rooms and regional menus at the *Hôtel du Château* (Ⓣ05.53.07.23.50, Ⓔhotduchateau@aol.com; ❸; closed mid-Oct to Easter; restaurant from €18).

Apart from the hotel **restaurants**, one place worth trying in Les Eyzies is *Le Chateaubriant* (Ⓣ05.53.35.06.11; closed Jan & Feb, Wed & Sun eve out of season), which has an attractive terrace and good-value menus from €11.

Around Les Eyzies

There are more **prehistoric caves** around Les Eyzies than you could possibly hope to visit in one day. Besides, the compulsory guided tours are tiring, so it's best to select just a couple of the ones listed below.

Most of these caves were not used as permanent homes, and there are various theories as to the purpose of such inaccessible spots. Most agree that they were sanctuaries and, if not actually places of worship, at least had religious significance. One suggestion is that making images of animals that were commonly hunted – like reindeer and bison – or feared – like bears and mammoths – was a kind of sympathetic magic intended to help men either catch or evade these animals. Another is that they were part of a fertility cult: sexual images of women with pendulous breasts and protuberant behinds are common. Others argue that these cave paintings served educational purposes, making parallels with Australian aborigines who used similar images to teach their young vital survival information as well as the history and mythological origins of their people. But much remains unexplained – the abstract signs that appear in so many caves, for example, and the arrows which clearly cannot be arrows, since Stone Age arrowheads looked different from these representations.

Grotte de Font-de-Gaume

Since its discovery in 1901, dozens of polychrome paintings have been found in the tunnel-like **Grotte de Font-de-Gaume** (daily except Sat: mid-May to mid-Sept 9.30am–5.30pm; mid-Sept to mid-May 9.30am–12.30pm & 2–5.30pm; €6.10; ⓣ05.53.06.86.00, ⓕ05.53.35.26.18), 1.5km along the D47 to Sarlat. Be aware that only 180 people are allowed to visit the cave each day and tickets sell out fast. You are advised to book (by phone or fax) at least a month ahead in high season and well in advance at other times. However, if you want to chance it, fifty tickets are sold on the spot each day; start queuing early.

The **cave** was first settled by Stone Age people during the last Ice Age – about 25,000 BC – when the Dordogne was the domain of roaming bison, reindeer and mammoths. The cave mouth is no more than a fissure concealed by rocks and trees above a small lush valley, while inside it's a narrow twisting passage of irregular height in which you quickly lose your bearings in the dark. The first painting you see is a frieze of bison, at about eye level: reddish-brown in colour, massive, full of movement, and very far from the primitive representations you might expect. Further on comes the most miraculous image of all, a **frieze** of five bison discovered in 1966 during cleaning operations. The colour, remarkably sharp and vivid, is preserved by a protective layer of calcite. Shading under the belly and down the thighs is used to give three-dimensionality with a sophistication that seems utterly modern. Another panel consists of superimposed drawings, a fairly common phenomenon in cave painting, sometimes the result of work by successive generations, but here an obviously deliberate technique. A reindeer in the foreground shares legs with a large bison behind to indicate perspective.

Stocks of **artists' materials** have also been found: kilos of prepared pigments; palettes – stones stained with ground-up earth pigments; and wooden painting sticks. Painting was clearly a specialized, perhaps professional, business, reproduced in dozens and dozens of caves located in the central Pyrenees and areas of northern Spain.

Grotte des Combarelles

The **Grotte des Combarelles** (same hours as Font-de-Gaume; €6.10; maximum six people per tour), 2km along the D47 towards Sarlat, was discovered in 1910. The innermost part of the cave is covered with **engravings** from the Magdalenian period (about 12,000 years ago). Drawn over a period of 2000 years, many are superimposed one upon another, and include horses, reindeer, mammoths and stylized human figures – among the finest are the heads of a horse and a lioness.

As with Font-de-Gaume, pre-booking is essential, especially in peak season (same phone and fax); collect tickets from Font-de-Gaume.

Abri du Cap Blanc and the Château de Commarque

Not a cave but a natural rock shelter, the **Abri du Cap Blanc** lies on a steep wooded hillside about 7km east of Les Eyzies (turn left onto the D48 shortly after Les Combarelles). At the time of writing it had just come under new ownership and was expected to be open year round – check at Les Eyzies' tourist office for exact opening hours. The shelter contains a **sculpted frieze** of horses and bison dating from the Middle Magdalenian period, about 14,000 years ago. Of only ten surviving prehistoric sculptures in France, this is undoubtedly the best. The design is deliberate, with the sculptures polished and set off against a pockmarked background. But what makes this place extraordinary is not just the large scale, but the high relief of some of the sculptures. This was only possible in places where light reached in, which in turn brought the danger of destruction by exposure to the air. Cro-Magnon people actually lived in this shelter, and a female skeleton has been found that is some 2000 years younger than the frieze.

For a non-cave detour, continue a little further up the heavily wooded Beune valley from Cap Blanc, to the elegant sixteenth-century **Château de Laussel** (closed to the public). On the opposite side of the valley stand the romantic ruins of the **Château de Commarque** (daily: April 10am–6pm; May, June & Sept 10am–7pm; July & Aug 10am–8pm; €5.60; Ⓦwww.commarque.com). Dating from the twelfth century, it was originally a **castrum**, a fortified village made up of six separate fortresses, each belonging to a different noble family. The ruins have now been made structurally sound and it's possible once again to climb the thirty-metre-high tower for views over the surrounding countryside. The easiest way to reach the château is by a footpath starting below Cap Blanc. Cars have to approach from the south, following signs from the D47 Sarlat road.

Grotte du Grand Roc

As well as prehistoric cave paintings, you can see some truly spectacular **stalactites** and **stalagmites** in the area around Les Eyzies. Some of the best examples are off the D47 towards Périgueux, 2km north of Les Eyzies, in the **Grotte du Grand Roc** (daily: April–June, Sept–Nov & Christmas holidays 10am–6pm; July & Aug 9.30am–7pm; €7; Ⓦwww.grandroc.com), whose entrance is high up in the cliffs that line much of the Vézère valley. There's a great view from the mouth of the cave and, inside, along some 80m of tunnel, a fantastic array of rock formations.

La Roque St-Christophe

The enormous prehistoric dwelling site, **La Roque St-Christophe** (daily: March–June, Sept & Oct 10am–6.30pm; July & Aug 10am–7pm; Nov–Feb 11am–5pm; €6.80; Ⓦwww.roque-st-christophe.com), 9km northeast of Les Eyzies along the D706 to Montignac, is made up of about one hundred **rock shelters** on five levels, hollowed out of the limestone cliffs. The whole complex is nearly a kilometre long and about 80m above ground-level, where the River Vézère once flowed. The earliest traces of occupation go back over 50,000 years. The view is pretty good, and the French guided tour instructive, but most of the finds are on display at the Musée National de Préhistoire in Les Eyzies (see p.700).

Montignac

Some 26km up the Vézère valley, **MONTIGNAC** is the main base for visiting the Lascaux caves. It's a more attractive place than Les Eyzies, with several wooden-balconied houses leaning appealingly over the river, a good **market** (Wed & Sat) and a lively annual **arts festival** in late July, featuring international folk groups. The **tourist office** is on place Bertran-de-Born (March–June, Sept & Oct Mon–Sat 9am–noon & 2–6pm; July & Aug daily 9am–7pm; Nov–Feb Mon–Sat 10am–noon & 2–5pm; Ⓣ05.53.51.82.60, Ⓦwww.bienvenue-montignac.com) and can provide a list of local *chambres d'hôtes*.

Hotels, as everywhere around here, get booked up quickly in summer. The *Hôtel de la Grotte*, on rue du 4-Septembre (Ⓣ05.53.51.80.48, Ⓔhoteldelagrotte@wanadoo.fr; ❸; restaurant from €19.50), is a good, reasonably priced option, with a pleasant garden beside a stream, but the cheapest rooms on offer are at *Le P'tit Monde*, just round the corner on the road to Sarlat (Ⓣ05.53.51.32.76, Ⓦwww.le-petit-monde.com; ❷; restaurant from €12, closed Sun). Then it's a big leap up to the three-star *Soleil d'Or*, also on the main rue du 4-Septembre (Ⓣ05.53.51.80.22, Ⓦwww.le-soleil-dor.com; ❺; closed Feb), with its own pool and restaurant (menus from €24). If you fancy some real luxury, you can stay in the pretty period rooms of the ivy- and wisteria-clad *Hostellerie de la Roseraie*, across the river in quiet place d'Armes (ⓣ05.53.50.53.92, ⓦwww.laroseraie-hotel.com; ❻; closed mid-Nov to March; restaurant from €19). And finally there's a well-tended three-star **campsite**, *Le Moulin Bleufond* (ⓣ05.53.51.83.95, ⓦwww.bleufond.com; April–Oct), on the riverbank 500m downstream.

There are other interesting restaurant and accommodation options in the area. If you book ahead, you're in for a feast at *Le Bareil*, a farm restaurant near **LA CHAPELLE-AUBAREIL**, a few kilometres beyond the Lascaux caves (ⓣ05.53.50.74.28; closed Mon), which serves traditional home cooking (menus from €22). A particularly good spot for campers in search of luxury is the four-star *Le Paradis* site (ⓣ05.53.50.72.64, ⓦwww.le-paradis.com; April–Oct) near the exquisite riverside village of **ST-LÉON-SUR-VÉZÈRE**, some 9km south of Montignac. Further south again at **TAMNIÈS**, midway between Montignac and Sarlat, the *Hôtel Laborderie* (ⓣ05.53.29.68.59, ⓦwww.hotel-laborderie.com; ❸; closed Nov–March) offers comfortable accommodation and good food (menus from €19).

Grotte de Lascaux and Lascaux II

The **Grotte de Lascaux** was discovered in 1940 by four boys who were, according to popular myth, looking for their dog and fell into a deep cavern decorated with marvellously preserved **paintings** of animals. Executed by Cro-Magnon people 17,000 years ago, the paintings are among the finest examples of prehistoric art in existence. There are five or six identifiable styles, and subjects include the bison, mammoth and horse, plus the biggest known prehistoric drawing, of a 5.5-metre bull with astonishingly expressive head and face. In 1948, the cave was opened to the public, and over the course of the next fifteen years more than a million tourists came to Lascaux. Sadly, because of deterioration from the body heat and breath of visitors, the cave had to be closed in 1963; now you have to be content with the replica known as **Lascaux II**, 2km south of Montignac on the D704 (Feb, March & Oct–Dec Tues–Sun 10am–12.30pm & 2–5.30pm; April–June & Sept daily 9am–6pm; July & Aug daily 9am–7pm; closed Jan; €8, combined ticket with Le Thot €10; ⓦwww.semitour.com). There are 2000 tickets on sale each day but these go fast in peak season; you can buy them in person a day or so in advance, while telephone bookings are accepted only in July and August (ⓣ05.53.51.96.23). Note also that in winter (Oct–March) tickets are normally on sale at the site, while in summer (April–Sept) they are only available from an office beside Montignac tourist office – the system and opening times are somewhat fickle, however, so it's safest to check in Montignac before heading up to the cave.

Opened in 1983, Lascaux II was the result of eleven years' painstaking work by twenty artists and sculptors, using the same methods and materials as the original cave painters. While the visit can't offer the excitement of a real cave, the reconstruction rarely disappoints the thousands who trek here every year. The guided tour lasts forty minutes (commentary in French or English). If you have bought the joint ticket to include entry into **Le Thot prehistoric theme park** (same opening times as Lascaux II; €5.50 for Le Thot alone, €10 for joint ticket; ⓦwww.semitour.com), 5km down the Vézère near **THONAC**, it's best to visit the park first for an enhanced appreciation of the cave itself, particularly if you have kids. The video showing the construction of Lascaux II is particularly interesting, and there are Disneyesque mock-ups of prehistoric scenes and live examples of some of the animals that feature in the paintings:

European bison, long-horned cattle and Przewalski's horses, rare and beautiful animals from Mongolia believed to resemble the prehistoric wild horse – notice the erect mane.

St-Amand-de-Coly

Nine kilometres east of Montignac, the village of **ST-AMAND-DE-COLY** boasts a superbly beautiful fortified Romanesque church, a magical venue for concerts in the summer. Despite its bristling military architecture, the twelfth-century church manages to combine great delicacy and spirituality, with its purity of line and simple decoration most evocative in the low sun of late afternoon or early evening. Its defences left nothing to chance: the walls are 4m thick, a ditch runs all the way round, and a passage once skirted the eaves, with numerous positions for archers to rain down arrows and blind stairways to mislead attackers. Near the church, the simple *Hôtel Gardette* (Ⓣ05.53.51.68.50, Ⓦwww.hotel-gardette.com; ❷; restaurant from €16, closed Oct–Easter) makes it possible to stay overnight in this tiny, idyllic place.

The Dordogne valley

The most familiar images of the River Dordogne are of the stretch around **Beynac** and **La Roque-Gageac**, when the scenery is at its most spectacular, with clifftop châteaux facing each other across the valley. The most imposing of these date from the Hundred Years War, when the river marked the frontier between French-held land to the north and English territory to the south. Further upstream, the hilltop *bastide* village of **Domme** offers stunning views, but is as crowded as Sarlat in summer.

Just south of the river, the **Abbaye de Cadouin** lies tucked out of harm's way in a fold of the landscape, hiding a lovely Gothic cloister. The train line from Bergerac to Sarlat runs along the river for this stretch, offering some wonderful views but unfortunately not stopping anywhere very useful; to appreciate the villages covered here, you need your own transport or, better still, a canoe.

The Abbaye de Cadouin

Before setting off up the Dordogne, it's worth taking a detour about 6km south of **Le Buisson** to the twelfth-century Cistercian **Abbaye de Cadouin**. For eight hundred years until 1935 it drew flocks of pilgrims to wonder at a piece of cloth first mentioned by Simon de Montfort in 1214 and thought to be part of Christ's shroud. In 1935 the two bands of embroidery at either end of the cloth were shown to contain an Arabic text from around the eleventh century. Since then the main attraction has been the finely sculpted but badly damaged capitals of the flamboyant Gothic **cloister** (Feb–June & Sept–Dec Mon, Wed, Thurs & Sun 10am–12.30pm & 2–6pm; July & Aug daily except Tues 10am–7pm; €5.50; Ⓦwww.semitour.com). Beside it stands a Romanesque **church** with a stark, bold front and wooden belfry roofed with chestnut shingles (chestnut trees abound around here – their timber was used in furniture-making and their nuts ground for flour during the formerly frequent famines). Inside the church, the nave is slightly out of alignment; this is thought to be deliberate and perhaps a vestige of pagan attachments, as the three windows are aligned so that at the winter and summer solstices the sun shines through all three in a single shaft.

You can **stay** across the road from the abbey at the *Restaurant de l'Abbaye* (Ⓣ05.53.63.40.93, Ⓕ05.53.63.40.28; ❷; closed Sun eve & Mon), which has four simple en-suite rooms and serves reasonably priced meals (menus from €13), or in the monks' dormitories themselves, now an excellent HI **youth**

hostel (Ⓣ05.53.73.28.78, Ⓔcadouin@fuaj.org; closed mid-Dec to Jan). There's also a small **campsite** in the village, *Les Jardins de l'Abbaye* (Ⓣ05.53.61.89.30, Ⓔjardins-abbaye@wanadoo.fr; April–Oct).

Another possibility is to stay in the hilltop town of **BELVÈS**, some 15km further east along the D54. The *Hôtel Le Home*, on the through road at the top of the hill, provides good cheap **accommodation** and food (Ⓣ05.53.29.01.65, Ⓦwww.lehomedebelves.fr; ❶; closed Sun & two weeks at Christmas; restaurant from €10). Next door is the more upmarket *Belvédère* (Ⓣ05.53.31.51.41, Ⓦwww.belvedere-perigord.com; ❸; closed two weeks in Nov, and Wed & Thurs out of season; restaurant €19–28). The nearest **campsite** is the three-star *Les Nauves* (Ⓣ05.53.29.12.64, Ⓦwww.lesnauves.com; April–Sept), 4.5km off the Monpazier road.

The châteaux of Les Milandes, Fayrac and Castelnaud

The first of the string of châteaux that line the Dordogne east of Le Buisson is **Les Milandes** (daily April–June, Sept & Oct 10am–6.15pm; July & Aug 9.30am–7.30pm; €7.80; Ⓦwww.milandes.com), perched high on the south bank. Built in 1489, it was the property of the de Caumont family until the

Josephine Baker and the Rainbow Tribe

Born on June 3, 1906, in the black ghetto of East St Louis, Illinois, **Josephine Baker** was one of the most remarkable women of the twentieth century. Her mother washed clothes for a living, her father was a drummer who soon deserted his family, yet by the late 1920s Josephine was the most celebrated cabaret star in France, primarily due to her role in the legendary Folies Bergères show in Paris. On her first night, de Gaulle, Hemingway, Piaf and Stravinsky were among the audience, and her notoriety was further enhanced by her long line of illustrious husbands and lovers, which included the Crown Prince of Sweden and the crime novelist Georges Simenon. She also mixed with the likes of Le Corbusier and Adolf Loos, and kept a pet cheetah called Mildred, with whom she used to walk around Paris. During the war, she was active in the Resistance, for which she won the Croix de Guerre. Later on, she became involved in the civil rights movement in North America, where she insisted on playing to non-segregated audiences, a stance which got her arrested in Canada and tailed by the FBI in the US.

By far her most bizarre project was the château of **Les Milandes**, which she rented from 1936 and then bought in 1947, after her marriage to the French orchestra leader Jo Bouillon. Having equipped the place with two hotels, three restaurants, a mini-golf course, tennis court and an autobiographical wax museum, she opened the château to the general public as a model multicultural community, popularly dubbed the "village du monde". In the course of the 1950s, she adopted babies (mostly orphans) of different ethnic and religious backgrounds from around the world, and by the end of the decade, she had brought twelve children to Les Milandes, including a black Catholic Colombian and a Buddhist Korean, along with her mother, brother and sister from East St Louis.

Over 300,000 people a year visited the château in the 1950s, but the conservative local population were never very happy about Les Milandes and what Josephine dubbed her "Rainbow Tribe". In the 1960s, Baker's financial problems, divorce and two heart attacks spelled the end for the project, and despite a sit-in protest by Baker herself (by then in her sixties), the château was sold off in 1968. Josephine died of a stroke in 1975 and was given a grand state funeral at La Madeleine in Paris, mourned by thousands of her adopted countryfolk.

Revolution, but its most famous owner was the Folies Bergères star, Josephine Baker (see box opposite), who lived here from 1936 to 1968. The stories surrounding the place are more intriguing than the château itself, which contains a motley collection of Ms Baker's effects. The garden, meanwhile, hosts daily displays by birds of prey.

Further along on the same side of the river, the **Château de Fayrac** was an English forward position in the Hundred Years War, built to watch over Beynac, on the opposite bank, where the French were holed up. All slated pepper-pot towers, it's unfortunately closed to the public, but you can visit the partially ruined **Château de Castelnaud** (daily: Feb–April & Oct to mid-Nov 10am–6pm; May, June & Sept 10am–7pm; July & Aug 9am–8pm; mid-Nov to Jan 2–5pm; €7, or €12.40 for a joint ticket with Marqueyssac; Ⓦ www.castelnaud.com), a little to the south of Fayrac and the true rival to Beynac in terms of impregnability – although it was successfully captured by the bellicose Simon de Montfort as early as 1214. The English held it for much of the Hundred Years War, and it wasn't until the Revolution that it was finally abandoned. Fairly heavily restored in the last two decades, it now houses a highly informative **museum of medieval warfare**. Its core is an extensive collection of original weaponry, including all sorts of bizarre contraptions, and a fine assortment of armour.

Beynac

Clearly visible on an impregnable cliff edge on the north bank of the river, the eye-catching village and castle of **BEYNAC-ET-CAZENAC** (generally shortened to Beynac) was built in the days when the river was the only route open to traders and invaders. By road, it's 3km to the **château** (daily: 10am–6pm; €7) but a steep lane leads up through the village and takes only fifteen minutes by foot. It's protected on the landward side by a double wall; elsewhere the sheer drop of almost 200m does the job. The flat terrace at the base of the keep, which was added by the English, conceals the remains of the houses where the beleaguered villagers lived; one of the houses has been partly excavated. Richard the Lionheart held the place for a time, until a gangrenous wound received while besieging the castle of Châlus, north of Périgueux ended his term of blood-letting.

Originally, to facilitate defence, the rooms inside the keep were only connected by a narrow spiral staircase – in stone, not wood as in the reconstruction, because of the danger of fire. The division of domestic space into dining rooms and so forth only came about when the advent of artillery made these old châteaux-forts militarily obsolete. From the roof there's a stupendous – and vertiginous – view upriver to the **Château de Marqueyssac**, whose beautiful seventeenth- and nineteenth-century **gardens** extend along the ridge (same hours as Castelnaud; €6.80, or €12.40 for a joint ticket with Castelnaud).

The best of Beynac's **hotels** are the *Hôtel du Château* (Ⓣ 05.53.29.19.20, Ⓦ www.hotelduchateau-dordogne.com; ④), with a small swimming pool and a restaurant from €20 (closed Dec), and the *Hôtel Bonnet* (Ⓣ 05.53.29.50.01, Ⓦ www.hotelbonnet.com; closed Nov–Feb; ④), which has attractively furnished rooms and a terrace overlooking the river. Both hotels are on the main road running along the river, where a little further east there's also a **campsite**, *Le Capeyrou* (Ⓣ 05.53.29.54.95, Ⓦ www.campinglecapeyrou.com; April–Sept).

La Roque-Gageac

The village of **LA ROQUE-GAGEAC** is almost too perfect, its ochre-coloured houses sheltering under dramatically overhanging cliffs. Regular

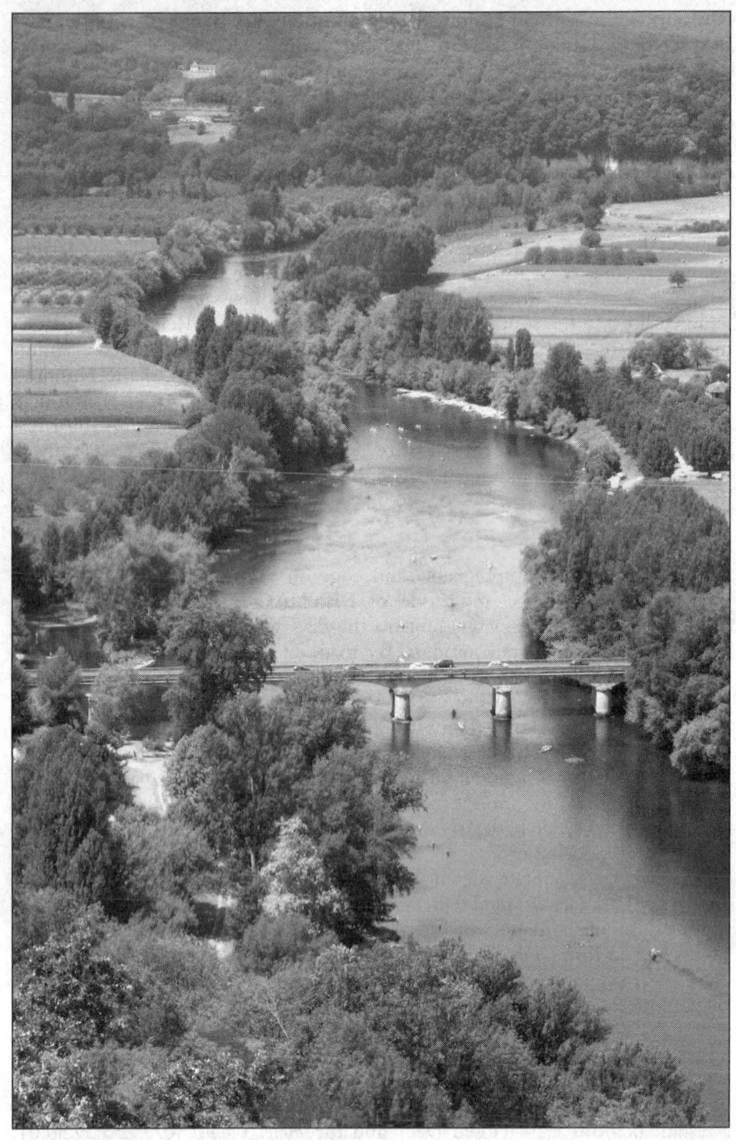

△ River Dordogne at Domme

winner of France's prettiest village contest, it inevitably pulls in the tourist buses, and since the main road separates the village from the river, the noise and fumes of the traffic can become oppressive. The best way to escape is to slip away through the lanes and alleyways that wind up through the terraced houses towards the ruins of some twelfth-century fortifications built into the cliff face (April–Oct daily 10.30am–6pm; €5). The other option is to rent a canoe and

Canoeing on the Dordogne and Vézère

Canoeing is hugely popular in the Dordogne, especially during the summer months when the Vézère and Dordogne rivers are shallow and slow-flowing – ideal for beginners. There are rental outlets at just about every twist in both rivers, and although it's possible to rent one-person kayaks or two-person canoes by the hour, it's best to take at least a half-day or longer, and simply cruise downstream. The company you book through will either take you to your departure point or send a minibus to pick you up from your final destination. **Prices** vary according to what's on offer; expect to pay around €18–22 per day. Most places function daily in July and August, on demand in May, June and September, and are closed the rest of the year. All companies are obliged to equip you with life jackets (*gilets*) and teach you basic safety procedures, most importantly how to capsize and get out without drowning. You must be able to swim. Below are just a handful of the choices on offer.

River Dordogne

Canoë Dordogne La Roque-Gageac ⓣ05.53.29.58.50, ⓦwww.canoe-dordogne.fr. Hourly rental to enjoy the view from the other side of the river, or distances of 9km, 16km or 25km paddling downstream past Beynac and Castelnaud to finish at the base in La Roque-Gageac.

Canoë Loisirs Vitrac ⓣ05.53.28.23.43, ⓦwww.canoes-loisirs.com. Trips start at Vitrac or Carsac, to be picked up at Castelnaud or Beynac.

Copeyre Canoë Souillac ⓣ05.65.37.33.51, ⓦwww.copeyre.com. Twelve bases from Argentat to Beynac; choose your own day-trip or longer outings of up to seven days. Many of their bases also rent out bikes.

Randonnée Dordogne Cénac ⓣ05.53.28.22.01, ⓦwww.euroriviere.com. Possibilities along the full length of the river, from 10km to seven-day trips.

Safaraid Vayrac ⓣ05.65.37.44.87, ⓦwww.canoe-kayak-dordogne.com. Eight bases from Argentat to Souillac; choose your own route, with rental available by the hour, day, week or longer.

River Vézère

Animations Vézère Canoë Kayak Les Eyzies ⓣ05.53.06.92.92, ⓦwww.canoes-loisirs.com. Various distances available between Montignac and Le Bugue.

Canoës Les 7 Rives Montignac ⓣ05.53.50.19.26, ⓔbernau@wanadoo.fr. Choice of distances downstream to Thonac, St-Léon or La Roque St-Christophe.

Canoës Rivières Loisirs Limeuil ⓣ05.53.63.38.73, ⓦwww.canoes-rivieres-loisirs.com. Day-trips from one to eight hours on either river, always finishing back in Limeuil.

paddle over to the opposite bank, where you can picnic and enjoy a great view of the village, at its best in the burnt-orange glow of the evening sun.

Most people just come here for the afternoon, so there's usually space if you want to **stay** the night, most pleasantly at *La Belle Étoile* ⓣ05.53.29.51.44, ⓔhotel.belle-etoile@wanadoo.fr; ③; closed Nov–March), whose restaurant serves good traditional cuisine (from €25, closed Mon & lunch Wed), and whose more expensive rooms have lovely views out over the river. Of the many **campsites** in the vicinity, *Le Beau Rivage* (ⓣ05.53.28.32.05, ⓦwww.camping-beau-rivage.com; March–Sept), on the D703 towards Sarlat, offers the greatest luxury.

Domme

High on the scarp on the south bank of the river, **DOMME** is one of the best preserved of the *bastides*, although it's now wholly given over to tourism. Its attractions, in addition to its position, include three original thirteenth-century **gateways** and a section of the old **walls**. From the northern edge of the village, marked by a drop so precipitous that fortifications were deemed unnecessary, you look out over a wide sweep of river country. Beneath the village is a warren of **caves** (Feb, Nov & Dec Mon–Fri 10am–12.30pm & 1.30–4pm; March–June, Sept & Oct daily 10am–noon & 2–6pm; July & Aug daily 10am–7pm; €6.50) in which the townspeople took refuge in times of danger. Their main interest lies in an impressive and pretty array of stalactites, stalagmites and other rock formations, which are all explained by the French guided tour. The entrance to the complex is on the main square, opposite the **tourist office** (same hours as the caves; ⓣ05.53.31.71.00, ⓦwww.ot-domme.com).

The smartest **hotel** in town is *L'Esplanade*, right on the cliff edge (ⓣ05.53.28.31.41, ⓦwww.esplanade-perigord.com; ❻; closed Nov–March), with a fine restaurant (menus €30–85); note that rooms with a view are premium-rated. A cheaper alternative is *Le Nouvel Hôtel*, at the top of the Grand'rue (ⓣ05.53.28.38.67, ⓦwww.domme-nouvel-hotel.com; ❸; closed Sun eve & Mon, also mid-Nov to Easter), which has several simple, reasonably priced rooms above a restaurant (menus €16–35). The closest **campsite** is the municipal site (ⓣ05.53.28.31.91, ⓕ05.53.31.41.32; mid-June to mid-Sept) down by the river at **Cénac**.

The upper Dordogne

East of Sarlat and Domme, you leave the crowds of Périgord Noir behind, but the Dordogne valley retains all of its beauty and interest. **Martel** and **Carennac** are wonderfully preserved medieval villages, and there are exceptional examples of Romanesque sculpture in the churches at **Souillac** and **Beaulieu**. Travel is difficult without a car, but Souillac is reachable by train and has bus routes to Sarlat and Martel.

Souillac

The first place of any size east of Sarlat is **SOUILLAC**, at the confluence of the Borrèze and Dordogne rivers and on a major road junction. Virginia Woolf stayed here in 1937, and was pleased to meet "no tourists ... England seems like a chocolate box bursting with trippers afterward". There are still few tourists, since Souillac's only real point of interest is the twelfth-century **church of Ste-Marie** (daily 8.30am–6pm), just off the main road. Roofed with massive domes like the cathedrals of Périgueux and Cahors, its spacious interior creates just the atmosphere for cool reflection on a summer's day. On the inside of the west door are some of the most wonderful Romanesque sculptures, including a seething mass of beasts devouring each other. The greatest piece of craftsmanship, though, is a **bas-relief of Isaiah**, fluid and supple, thought to be by one of the artists who worked at Moissac. Next to the church, the **Musée de l'Automate** (April, May & Oct Tues–Sun 10am–noon & 3–6pm; June & Sept daily 10am–noon & 3–6pm; July & Aug daily 10am–7pm; Nov–March Wed–Sun 2.30–5.30pm; €5) contains an impressive collection of nineteenth- and twentieth-century mechanical dolls and animals, which dance, sing and perform magical tricks; look out for the irresistible laughing man.

The **tourist office** (July & Aug Mon–Sat 9.30am–12.30pm & 2–7pm, Sun 10am–noon & 3–6pm; Sept–June Mon–Sat 10am–noon & 2–6pm; ⓣ05.65.37.81.56, ⓦwww.tourisme-souillac.com) is on the main boulevard

Louis-Jean-Malvy. For **accommodation,** head to the old quarter, where you'll find good-value rooms in the characterful *Auberge du Puits*, in the pretty place du Puits (Ⓣ05.65.37.80.32, Ⓦwww.auberge-du-puits.fr; ❶; closed Jan & Feb), with a good restaurant (menus from €15.90; closed Sat lunch, Sun eve and Mon), or, alternatively, more upmarket lodgings in *La Vieille Auberge*, 1 rue de la Recège (Ⓣ05.65.32.79.43, Ⓦwww.la-vieille-auberge.com; ❺; closed mid-Nov to mid-Dec; restaurant from €20, closed Sun eve & Mon), which has a pool, Jacuzzi and sauna and will arrange cycling and canoeing trips for you. There's also a large riverside **campsite**, *Les Ondines* (Ⓣ05.65.37.86.44; Easter–Sept). You can rent **bicycles and canoes** from Copeyre Canoë (Ⓣ05.65.32.72.61), next to the campsite.

Martel

About 15km east of Souillac and set back even further from the river, **MARTEL** is a minor medieval masterpiece, built in a pale, almost white, stone, offset by warm reddish-brown roofs. A Turenne-administered town (see p.726), its heyday came during the thirteenth and fourteenth centuries, when the viscounts established a court of appeal here.

The main square, **place des Consuls**, is mostly taken up by the eighteenth-century **market hall**, but on every side there are reminders of the town's illustrious past, most notably in the superb Gothic **Hôtel de la Raymondie**. Begun in 1280, it served as the Turenne law courts, though it doubled as the town's refuge, hence the distinctive corner turrets. Facing the hôtel is the **Tour des Pénitents**, one of the many medieval towers which gave the town its epithet, *la ville aux sept tours* ("the town with seven towers"). The Young King Henry, son of Henry II (see box below) died in the striking building in the southeast corner of the square, the **Maison Fabri**. One block south, rue Droite leads east to the town's main **church**, St-Maur, built in a fiercely defensive, mostly Gothic style, with a finely carved Romanesque tympanum depicting the Last Judgement above the west door.

If you'd rather **stay** here than in Souillac, head for the *Auberge des 7 Tours* (Ⓣ05.65.37.30.16, Ⓦwww.auberge7tours.com; ❷; restaurant from €13, closed for lunch Sat & Mon), or treat yourself to the luxurious rooms at the *Relais*

The tale of Young King Henry

At the end of the twelfth century, Martel was the stage for one of the tragic events in the internecine conflicts of the Plantagenet family. When Henry Plantagenet (King Henry II of England) imprisoned his estranged wife Eleanor of Aquitaine, his sons took up arms against their father. The eldest son, also Henry (nicknamed the Young King since he was crowned while his father was still on the throne), even went so far as to plunder the viscountcy of Turenne and Quercy. Furious, Henry II immediately stopped his allowance and handed over his lands to the third son, Richard the Lionheart. Financially insecure, and with a considerable army of soldiers to feed and clothe, Young King Henry began looting the treasures of every abbey and shrine in the region. Finally, he decided to sack the shrine at Rocamadour, making off with various artefacts, including Roland's famous sword, Durandal. This last act was to be his downfall, for shortly afterwards he fled to Martel and fell ill with a fever. Guilt-ridden and afraid for his life, he confessed his crimes and asked his father for forgiveness. Henry II was busy besieging Limoges, but sent a messenger to pardon him. On the messenger's arrival in Martel, young Henry died, and Richard the Lionheart became heir to the English throne.

Ste-Anne (Ⓣ05.65.36.40.56, Ⓦwww.relais-sainte-anne.com; ❺; closed mid-Nov to mid-March), in the ivy-covered buildings of a former religious school, surrounded by attractive gardens with a small pool. There's a basic municipal **campsite**, *La Callopie* (Ⓣ05.65.37.30.03, Ⓔmairiedemartel@wanadoo.fr; May–Sept), on the northern edge of town, and the more attractive riverside *Camping les Falaises* (Ⓣ05.65.37.37.78, Ⓕ05.65.41.05.32; May–Sept), 5km away in the village of **Gluges**, where you can also rent **canoes and bikes** from Copeyre Canoë down by the water (see box, p.709).

Railway enthusiasts might be interested in the **steam tourist trains** (April–Sept; Ⓣ05.65.37.35.81, Ⓦwww.trainduhautquercy.info), which run on the recently restored line between Martel and St-Denis. The return trip (€9.50) lasts about an hour and takes in some good scenery, the train puffing along the edges of the cliffs which overlook the river valley.

Carennac and Castelnau-Bretenoux

CARENNAC is without doubt one of the most beautiful villages along this part of the Dordogne River. Elevated just above the south bank of the river, 13km or so east of Martel, it's best known for its typical Quercy architecture, its Romanesque priory, where the French writer Fénelon spent the best years of his life, and for its greengages.

Carennac's feature, as so often in these parts, is the Romanesque tympanum – in the Moissac style – above the west door of its church, the **Église St-Pierre**. Christ sits in majesty with the Book of Judgement in his left hand, with the apostles and adoring angels below him. Next to the church, you can gain access to the old **cloisters and chapterhouse** (July & Aug daily 10am–1pm & 2–7pm; Sept–June Mon–Sat 10am–noon & 2–5pm; €2.50), which contain an exceptionally expressive life-size *Entombment of Christ*.

There are two comfortable and reasonably priced **hotels** in the village, both with good **restaurants** specializing in traditional regional cuisine: the *Auberge du Vieux Quercy*, to the south of the church (Ⓣ05.65.10.96.59, Ⓦwww.vieuxquercy.com; ❹; closed mid-Nov to March), whose restaurant offers menus from €20 (closed for lunch Tues & Wed); and the more rustic *Hostellerie Fénelon* on the main street, with views over the river (Ⓣ05.65.10.96.46, Ⓦwww.hotel-fenelon.com; ❸; closed Jan & Feb; restaurant from €15, closed Mon lunch & Fri). There's also a **campsite**, *L'Eau Vive*, 1km east of Carennac (Ⓣ05.65.10.97.39, Ⓦwww.dordogne-soleil.com; May–Sept).

Another 10km further upstream, the sturdy towers and machicolated red-brown walls of the eleventh-century **Château de Castelnau-Bretenoux** (May & June daily 9.30am–12.30pm & 2–6.30pm; July & Aug daily 9.30am–7pm; Sept–April daily except Tues 10am–12.30pm & 2–5.30pm; €6.50; Ⓦwww.monum.fr) dominate a sharp knoll above the Dordogne. Most of it has now been restored and refurnished. Below, on the banks of the River Cère, you come to the graceful little *bastide* of **BRETENOUX**, with two sides of its cobbled and arcaded square still intact.

Beaulieu-sur-Dordogne

Beautifully situated on the banks of the Dordogne, 8km upriver from Castelnau-Bretenoux, **BEAULIEU-SUR-DORDOGNE** boasts another of the great masterpieces of Romanesque sculpture on the porch of the **church of St-Pierre** in the centre of town. This doorway is unusually deep-set, with a tympanum presided over by an oriental-looking Christ with one arm extended to welcome the chosen. All around him is a complicated pattern of angels and apostles, executed in characteristic "dancing" style, similar to that at Carennac. The dead raise the lids of their coffins hopefully, while underneath a frieze depicts monsters crunching heads. Take the opportunity also to wander north along rue de la Chapelle past some handsome sculpted facades and down to the river.

The most appealing **hotel** is *Le Turenne* (Ⓣ05.55.91.10.16, Ⓦwww.hotelleturenne.com; ❸; closed Nov; menus €13–30), in a former abbey on place Marbot. The twelfth-century stone spiral staircase is still in use, and rooms have retained a lot of character, with fireplaces left in some. Another nice option is the riverside *Les Charmilles* (Ⓣ05.55.91.29.29, Ⓦwww.auberge-charmilles.com; ❹; restaurant from €18). The welcoming HI **hostel** is at the far end of rue de la Chapelle in a magnificent half-timbered and turreted building, with surprisingly modern rooms inside (Ⓣ05.55.91.13.82, Ⓔbeaulieu@fuaj.org; closed Nov–March). There are river-bathing and canoeing possibilities and a good riverside **campsite**, *Camping des Îles*, close by (Ⓣ05.55.91.02.65, Ⓦwww.camping-des-iles.net; mid-April to mid-Oct).

The Limousin

The **Limousin** – the country around **Limoges** – is hilly, wooded, wet and not particularly fertile: ideal pasture for the famous Limousin breed of cattle. This is herdsman's country, from where – presumably – the widespread use of the shepherd's cape known as a limousine gave its name to the big, wraparound, covered twentieth-century car.

The modern Limousin region stretches south to the Dordogne valley to include **Brive** and **Tulle**. But while these places, together with Limoges itself, are not without interest, the star of the show is the countryside – especially in the east on the **Plateau de Millevaches** round **Eymoutiers**, **Meymac** and **La Courtine**. Walkers, cyclists and other outdoor sports enthusiasts are well catered for and there are plenty of small hotels, *gîtes* and campsites to accommodate the wanderer. Although the region is remote and sparsely populated, a mountain rail line still survives, connecting Limoges and **Ussel**.

Limoges

LIMOGES is a pleasant city, if not one that calls for a long stay. Its main draws are a magnificent Art Deco train station and the craft industries that made the city a household name: enamel in the Middle Ages and, since the eighteenth century, china, including some of the finest ever produced. If these appeal, then the city's unique museum collections – and its Gothic cathedral – will reward a visit. But it has to be said that the industry today seems a spent tradition, hard hit by recession and changing tastes among the rich. The local *kaolin* (china clay) mines that gave Limoges china its special quality are exhausted, and the workshops survive mainly on the tourist trade.

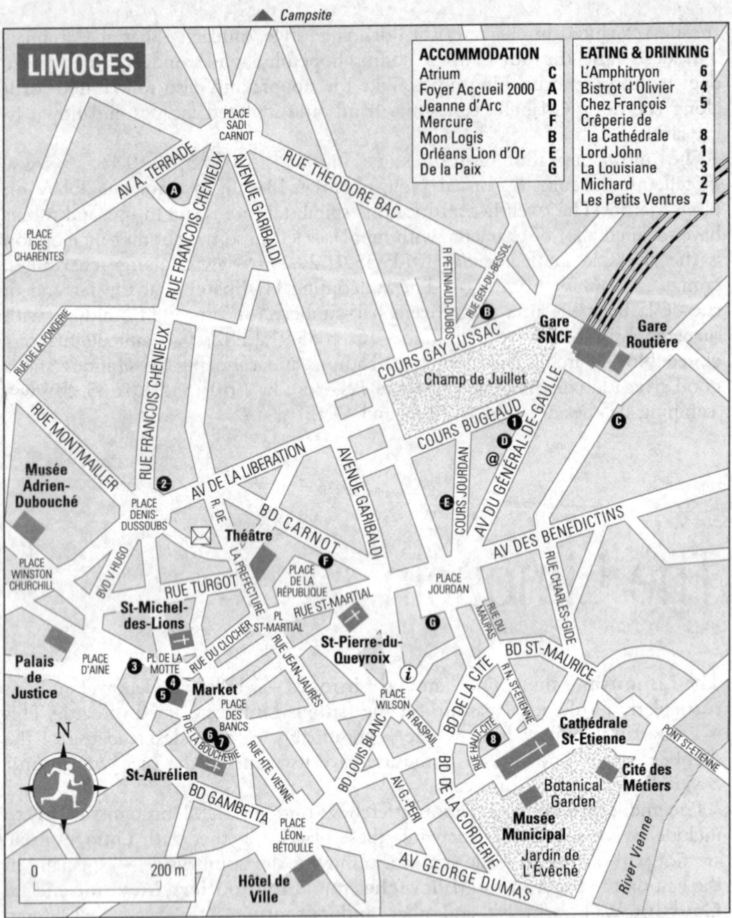

Arrival, information and accommodation

The town is built on high ground overlooking the River Vienne, with a small, attractive city centre enclosed by modern boulevards. The cathedral stands directly above the river, with the main commercial streets behind it. The magnificent **gare des Bénédictins** and neighbouring **gare routière** (ⓣ05.55.45.10.72) lie slightly off to the northeast, connected to the chestnut-shaded place Jourdan by avenue de-Gaulle, which has several outlets offering **car rental**, like ADA at no. 27 (ⓣ05.55.79.61.12). The **tourist office** is on place Wilson (April to mid-June & mid-Sept to Oct Mon–Sat 9.30am–7pm; mid-June to mid-Sept Mon–Sat 9am–7pm, Sun 10am–6pm; Nov–March Mon–Sat 9.30am–6pm; ⓣ05.55.34.46.87, ⓦwww.tourismelimoges.com). You can get a cheap, fast **Internet** connection at Pointcyber, 7 av de-Gaulle (Mon–Sat 9.30am–midnight, Sun 2pm–midnight; €3.40 per hour).

Hotels

Atrium Parc du Ciel – Gare des Bénédictins ⓣ05.55.10.75.75, ⓦwww.interhotel-atrium.com. The location is good for catching trains, but not great from any other point of view, with car park, train tracks and ring road to cross before you approach the town centre. Rooms are new, and have all the three-star comforts you would expect. ⑤

Jeanne d'Arc 17 av de-Gaulle ⓣ05.55.77.67.77, ⓦwww.hoteljeannedarc-limoges.fr. By far the most attractive upmarket option, with tastefully decorated rooms and an extremely grand breakfast hall. All rooms have wireless Internet, and there is off-street parking available. Closed Christmas. ⑤

Mercure place de la République ⓣ05.55.34.65.30, ⓦwww.mercure.com. The most central option, with rooms looking out over the cafés on the square. The building itself is an unattractive, concrete affair though, and only the most expensive rooms offer real luxury standards. A display of porcelain in the lobby makes some attempt to connect with the city's traditions. ⑥

Mon Logis 16 rue du Général-du-Bessol ⓣ05.55.77.41.43, ⓦwww.hotel-limoges-monlogis.com. A perfectly acceptable budget option on a quietish street near the station. The rooms are all bare, with uniform white walls, but you can have your own bathroom and a TV for quite a low price. Closed weekends Dec–Feb. ①–②

Orléans Lion d'Or 11 cours Jourdan ⓣ05.55.77.49.71, ⓦwww.orleansliondor.com. Bright, comfortable rooms and a friendly management make this a good choice. They can also put adjoining rooms together, creating a good solution for families. Closed Christmas. ③

De la Paix 25 place Jourdan ⓣ05.55.34.36.00, ⓕ05.55.32.37.06. A wonderful little hotel, doubling as a museum of gramophones, which decorate the breakfast room in all shapes and sizes. Bedrooms are equally characterful: large and nicely furnished for the price. ③

Hostel and campsite

Foyer Accueil 2000 20 rue Encombe-Vineuse ⓣ05.55.77.63.97, ⓔfjt.accueil-2000@wanadoo.fr. A bit of a hike out on the north side of town, but you still need to book well ahead. The €16 per night fee includes breakfast, and there is also a communal kitchen.

Camping municipal d'Uzurat ⓣ05.55.38.49.43, ⓕ05.55.37.32.78. About 5km out of town in Limoges' northern suburbs; take bus #20 from place Jourdan. March–Oct.

The City

The **Cathédrale St-Étienne** (Mon–Sat 10am–noon & 2.30–5.30pm; Sun 2.30–6.30pm; free), a landmark for miles around, was begun in 1273 and planned on the model of the cathedral of Amiens, though only the choir, completed in the early thirteenth century, is pure Gothic. The rest of the building was added piecemeal over the centuries, the western part of the nave not until 1876. The most striking external feature is the sixteenth-century facade of the north transept, built in full flamboyant style with elongated arches, clusters of pinnacles and delicate tracery in window and gallery. At the west end of the nave, the tower, erected on a Romanesque base that had to be massively reinforced to bear the weight, has octagonal upper storeys, in common with most churches in the region. It once stood as a separate campanile and probably looked the better for it. Inside, the effects are much more pleasing, and the rose stone looks warmer than on the weathered exterior. The sense of soaring height is accentuated by all the upward-reaching lines of the pillars, the net of vaulting ribs, the curling, flame-like lines repeated in the arcading of the side chapels and the rose window, and, above all, as you look down the nave, by the narrower and more pointed arches of the choir.

The best of the city's museums – with its showpiece collections of enamelware dating back as far as the twelfth century – is the **Musée Municipal de l'Évêché** (July–Sept daily 10am–noon & 2–6pm; Oct–June daily except Tues 10am–noon & 2–5pm; free) in the old bishop's palace next to the cathedral. There's an interesting progression to be observed in the museum, from the simple, sober, Byzantine-influenced *champlevé* (copper filled with enamel), to the later, especially seventeenth- and eighteenth-century work that used a far greater range of colours and indulged in elaborate virtuoso portraiture. By the nineteenth century, however, the spirit and vigour had dissipated, and although there are contemporary artisans in the city using the medium, their work, too – judging from this display – is not much more successful. There's also an **exhibition** of the wartime Resistance (same hours, but closed mornings Oct–May; free) housed in an outbuilding opposite the museum's main entrance.

Outside, the well-laid-out and interesting **botanical garden** (daily sunrise to sunset; free) is an inviting prospect, descending gracefully towards the River Vienne. In the garden's northern corner an old refectory now houses the excellent **Cité des Métiers et des Arts** (Easter–June, Sept & Oct Wed, Sat & Sun 2–6pm; July & Aug daily 10.30am–1pm & 2.30–7pm; €5) displaying pieces – mostly carpentry – by France's top crafts' guild members.

The best areas for a relaxed stroll are the network of pedestrianized streets just north of the cathedral, and, over to the west, the partly renovated **old quarter** of the town, where you'll find rue de la Boucherie, for a thousand years the domain of the butchers' guild. The dark, cluttered **chapel of St-Aurélien**, with a delicate fourteenth-century cross outside, belongs to them, while one of their former shophouses makes an interesting little museum, the **Maison de la Boucherie**, at no. 36 (July–Sept daily 10am–1pm & 2.30–7pm; free). At the top of the street is the **market** in place de la Motte and, to the right, partly hidden by adjoining houses, the fourteenth- and fifteenth-century **church of St-Michel-des-Lions**, named after the two badly weathered Celtic lions guarding the south door and topped by one of the best towers and spires in the region. The inside is dark and atmospheric, with two beautiful, densely coloured fifteenth-century windows either side of the choir.

Further east, the concrete swathes of place de la République conceal the fourth-century crypt of the long-vanished **Abbey of St-Martial** (July–Sept daily 10am–12.30pm & 2–7pm; free), containing the saint's massive sarcophagus, discovered during building operations in the 1960s. Nearby is the **church of St-Pierre-du-Queyroix** under another typically Limousin belfry. The interior, partly twelfth-century, has the same slightly pink granite glow as the cathedral. There's more fine stained glass here, including an eye-catching window at the end of the south aisle depicting the Dormition of the Virgin, signed by the great enamel artist Jean Pénicault in 1510.

Limoges' renowned **porcelain** is best displayed in the **Musée Adrien-Dubouché** (daily except Tues: July & Aug 10am–5.45pm; Sept–June 10am–12.30pm & 2–5.45pm; €4.50; Ⓦwww.musee-adriendubouche.fr), west of the old quarter on place Winston-Churchill. The well-presented collection is more interesting than you might expect, including samples of the local product and china displays from around the world, as well as various celebrity services ordered for the likes of Napoleon Bonaparte, Charles and Di, and sundry French royals.

Eating, drinking and festivals

Limoges has an abundance of good and not too expensive **places to eat**. For **drinks** at any time of the day, people sit out in the not very attractive place de la République; a nicer option is lively place Denis-Dussoubs, a short walk further west, where you'll find fine beers on tap at the *Michard* micro-brewery (closed Sun). Over on the other side of town, the *Lord John* pub on avenue de-Gaulle – complete with darts – is a low-key hangout, good for a quiet drink.

Cafés and restaurants

L'Amphitryon 26 rue de la Boucherie ⓣ05.55.33.36.39. There's no better place than this for a real treat of subtle and sophisticated cuisine. Veal, pigeon and tuna steak are all on the menu, combined with light, Mediterranean touches like fresh figs in olive oil. Lunch menus start at €19, while for €60 you get six courses of the chef's finest work. Closed Sun, Mon & three weeks in Aug/Sept.

Bistrot d'Olivier place de la Motte. Another characterful, lunch-only place in the market hall, with communal tables and wooden benches. It also has a bar, providing a sustaining midday tipple for the market workers. Menus from €9. Closed Sun & Mon; also July.

Chez François place de la Motte. For a good-value lunch and a lively atmosphere, head straight to the central market hall to join the locals round communal tables. The dining room is brightened up by colourful pictures of life around the market. Menus €9 & €16. Closed Sun & Aug.

Crêperie de la Cathédrale 3 rue Haute-Cité. One of a cluster of brasseries with outside seating on this attractive pedestrian street by the cathedral. It's good value at lunchtime, with a *plat du jour*, dessert and wine for €9.

La Louisiane place d'Aine. Elegant *salon de thé* serving salads, quiches and other light lunches, with great pastries to follow. Open noon–2pm only. Closed Sun & Mon.

Les Petits Ventres 20 rue de la Boucherie ⓣ05.55.34.22.90. This restaurant will delight lovers of brain, brawn, tongue and other unmentionable cuts – though they also do more everyday dishes and even a vegetarian platter. Menus from €14.50. Closed Nov–Feb, Sun & Mon.

Festivals

In late September, there's an interesting and important gathering of writers, dramatists and musicians from other French-speaking countries at the **Festival International des Théâtres Francophones** (ⓦwww.lesfrancophonies.com). Gourmets of a certain persuasion should make sure their visit coincide with the third Friday in October for the **Frairie des Petits Ventres**, when the entire population turns out to gorge on everything from pig's trotters to sheep's testicles in the rue de la Boucherie. Otherwise, there's **Urbaka**, a festival of street theatre held at the end of June, and the **Danse Émoi** contemporary dance festival every two years in January, the next one being in 2009.

Around Limoges

There's a clutch of villages within a day's reach of Limoges. A route linking places of interest on the south bank of the Vienne, like the **châteaux** of **Rochechouart**, **Châlus**, **Montbrun** and **Nexon** is detailed in the *Route Richard-Coeur-de-Lion* leaflet (available at local tourist offices), so called because of its associations with the English king. The route also takes you near the Roman baths at **Chassenon** and **Solignac**'s abbey church, close by which the **Château de Châlucet** is now reduced to atmospheric ruins. North of the Vienne, the charred walls of **Oradour-sur-Glane** stand testimony to a World War II massacre, while east of Limoges, beyond the attractive market town of **St-Léonard-de-Noblat**, the master weavers of **Aubusson** have been producing tapestries for more than six hundred years.

Visiting all these places really requires a car, but some at least are accessible by a combination of public transport, walking and patient hitching.

Oradour-sur-Glane

Twenty-five kilometres northwest of Limoges and a few kilometres north of the N141 road to Angoulême, the village of **ORADOUR-SUR-GLANE** stands just as the soldiers of the SS left it on June 10, 1944, after killing 642 of the inhabitants in reprisal for attacks by French *maquisards*. The village has been preserved both as a shrine and a chilling reminder of human brutality.

Before entering the village, the **Centre de la Mémoire**, immediately southeast of Oradour on the Limoges road (daily: Feb & Nov–Dec 19 9am–5pm; March to mid-May & mid-Sept to Oct 9am–6pm; May 15–Sept 15 9am–7pm; entry to village free, exhibition €6; Ⓦwww.oradour.org), sets the historical context and attempts to answer some of the questions. From here an underground passage leads into the village itself, where a sign admonishes *Souviens-toi* ("Remember"), and the main street leads past roofless houses gutted by fire. Telephone poles, iron bedsteads and gutters are fixed in tormented attitudes where the fire's heat left them; prewar cars rust in the garages; cooking pots hang over empty grates; last year's grapes hang wizened on a vine whose trellis has long rotted away.

To the north of the village a dolmen-like slab on a shallow plinth covers a crypt containing relics of the dead, and the awful list of names, while to the southeast, by the stream, stands the church where the women and children – five hundred of them – were burnt to death. The modern village of Oradour has been constructed beside the old, with a 1950s concrete church that tries to be impressive but struggles with the task of commemorating what happened here.

There are **buses** from Limoges to Oradour, or alternatively you can take the train to **ST-JUNIEN** and pick up a bus there. The *Relais de Comodoliac*, 22 av Sadi-Carnot (Ⓣ05.55.02.27.26, Ⓦwww.comodoliac.com; ④), about 1km northwest of the train station, with a garden and a popular restaurant (menus €15–36), makes a decent **place to stay** in St-Junien. There's also a **hostel**, 13 rue de St-Amand (Ⓣ & Ⓕ05.55.02.22.79), in an old abbey 500m further west along rue Henriette-Perucaud.

Rochechouart and Chassenon

ROCHECHOUART, a beautiful little walled town roughly 45km west of Limoges, has two claims to fame. Two hundred million years ago it was the site of impact of one of the largest **meteorites** ever to hit earth, a monster 1.5km in diameter and some 6000 million tonnes in weight. The traces of this cosmic calamity still attract the curiosity of astronomers, though the only evidence that a layman might notice is the unusual-looking breccia stone many of the region's older buildings are made of: the squashed, shattered, heat-transformed and reconstituted result of the collision. A small museum in town, the **Espace Meteorite**, 16 rue Jean Parvy (July, Aug & during school holidays Mon–Fri 10am–12.30pm & 1.30–6pm, Sat & Sun 2–6pm; rest of year Mon–Fri 2–6pm; €3) attempts to uncover the history of the meteorite with artists' impressions, but there are plans afoot to make the museum a more high-tech, interactive experience in the near future.

One building using the stone from the impact is Rochechouart's other source of pride: the handsome **château** that stands at the town's edge. It started life as a rough fortress before 1000 AD, was "modernized" in the thirteenth century (the sawn-off keep and entrance survive from this period) and civilized with Renaissance decoration and additions in the fifteenth. Until it was acquired as the *mairie* in 1832, it had belonged to the de Rochechouart family for 800 years. Today it houses not only the town hall, but also the very well-regarded and adventurous **Musée Départemental d'Art Contemporain** (daily except Tues: March–Sept 10am–12.30pm & 1.30–6pm; Oct to mid-Dec 10am–12.30pm & 2–5pm; €4.60), with an important collection of works by the Dadaist Raoul Haussmanh who died in Limoges in 1971. In another room decorated with its original sixteenth-century frescoes of the Labours of Hercules, the British artist, Richard Long, has made a special installation of white stones, while in the garden Guiseppe Penone's metal sculpture grapples with a tree.

The Rochechouart **tourist office** is at 6 rue Victor-Hugo (July & Aug daily 10am–12.30pm & 2.30–6pm; Sept–June Mon–Sat 10am–noon & 2.30–5.30pm; ⓣ05.55.03.72.73). Should you wish to **stay**, the *Hôtel de France*, on place Octave-Marquet (ⓣ05.55.03.77.40, ⓦwww.logis-de-france.fr; ❷–❸), provides brand-new, spick-and-span lodgings and interesting food served in an attractive dining room (closed Sun eve; menus from €12).

One side trip worth making if you have come this far is to the Roman baths 5km along the Chabanais road at **CHASSENON** (daily guided tours: April, May & mid-Sept to mid-Nov 2–5.30pm; June to mid-Sept 10am–noon & 2–7pm; €5; ⓦamis.chassenon.free.fr). The site, known as Cassinomagus in Gallo-Roman times, stood at an important crossroads on the Via Agrippa, the Roman road that connected Lyon to Saintes. A grand temple and theatre were destroyed for their breccia stone, but the baths alone are ample testimony to the magnificence of the place. There are hot and cold pools with some of the original floor tiles in places, and waterproof plastering, boiler rooms and elaborate hypocaust piping systems; you can even see the marks of the shuttering used to make the vaults in some of the subterranean passages.

Châlus and Nexon

The small town of **CHÂLUS**, 35km southwest of Limoges, is dominated by the ruined **Château de Châlus-Chabrol** (not open to the public), where in 1199 Richard the Lionheart was mortally wounded by an archer shooting from the still-extant keep. Richard, son of Eleanor of Aquitaine and as much French as English, was campaigning to suppress a local rebellion against English rule. On capturing the castle, Richard – by now on his deathbed – ordered all the rebels hanged save the archer, whom he pardoned. It was a short-lived reprieve; as soon as Richard was dead, the archer was flayed alive by the captain of the English troops.

Of several other castles around Châlus, the most rewarding is the medieval **Château de Montbrun** (July & Aug daily 11am–6pm; Sept–June Sat & Sun 2.30–4.30pm; €12; ⓦwww.montbrun.com), 8km to the southwest. The château, now a private home, has been beautifully restored and furnished, though its best attribute is perhaps its fairy-tale lakeside location – even more spectacular when floodlit at night. It also offers luxury *chambres d'hôtes* **accommodation** (ⓣ05.55.78.65.26, ⓔmontbrun@montbrun.com; ❺), and one of the outhouses has been converted into an equally atmospheric restaurant, *La Taverne* (closed Tues & Wed; menus from €15), which has live music on Friday evenings. Otherwise, you can stay in Châlus itself at the simple but reasonably comfortable *Auberge Richard Coeur de Lion*, 29 av Jean-Jaurès (ⓣ & ⓕ05.55.78.43.42; ❷), with menus from €9.50 in its restaurant.

Eighteen kilometres east in the village of **NEXON** you'll find a fine, heavily restored seventeenth-century **château** (now the *mairie*), whose gardens now host a summer **festival of circus arts** (ⓦwww.cirquenexon.com).

Châlucet and Solignac

A dozen kilometres south of Limoges in the lovely wooded valley of the Briance, the Château de Châlucet and the church of **SOLIGNAC** make the most attractive day's outing from the city. There are **buses** and **trains** to Solignac-Le Vigen station, a few minutes away on the Limoges–Brive line, and occasional buses to Solignac itself, but beware that in school holidays no combination allows you to see Solignac and get back in one day. You could stay the night at the comfortable **hotel** opposite the church, *Le St-Éloi* (Ⓣ05.55.00.44.52, Ⓦwww.lesainteloi.fr; ❸; closed three weeks in Jan & two in Sept; restaurant from €21; closed Sat lunch, Sun eve & Mon).

Approaching from Le Vigen you can see Solignac's Romanesque **abbey church** ahead of you, with the tiled roofs of its octagonal apse and neat little brood of radiating chapels. The twelfth-century facade is plain with just a little sculpture, as the granite from which it is built is too hard to permit intricate carving. Inside it's beautiful, a flight of steps leading down into the nave with a dramatic view of the length of the church. There are no aisles, just a single space roofed with three big domes, and no ambulatory either – an absolutely plain Latin cross in design. It's a simple, sturdy church, with the same feel of plain robust Christianity as the crypt of St-Eutrope in Saintes.

The **Château de Châlucet** is a good five-kilometre walk up the valley of the Briance in the other direction – uphill quite a lot of the way along the D32 and D32a. After about 45 minutes, at the highest point of the climb, there is a dramatic view across the valley to the romantic, ruined keep of the castle, rising above the woods. It's a further kilometre down to the bridge on the Briance, where a path follows the riverbank before climbing steeply up again into the woods. Built in the twelfth century, the château was in English hands during the Hundred Years War and, in the lawless aftermath, became the lair of a notorious local brigand, Perrot le Béarnais. Dismantled in 1593 for harbouring Protestants, it has recently been acquired by the local authorities who are in the middle of major restoration works, including an archeological dig. It's still possible to visit, though you are restricted to safe areas along fenced-off paths. You can borrow an explanatory guide from the visitors' centre (daily: mid-March to mid-June & mid-Sept to mid-Nov 9.30am–12.30pm & 1.30–6pm; mid-June to mid-Sept 9.30am–6.30pm) on the path up to the ruins.

St-Léonard-de-Noblat

ST-LÉONARD-DE-NOBLAT, twenty minutes by train from Limoges or 35 minutes by bus, is an appealing little market town of narrow streets and medieval houses with jutting eaves and corbelled turrets. There's a very lovely eleventh- and twelfth-century church, with a six-storey tower, high dome and simple, barrel-vaulted interior – the whole in grey granite. A couple of kilometres northwest of town on the banks of the Vienne, demonstrations of papermaking and printing are on offer at a lovingly restored fifteenth-century paper mill, the **Moulin du Got** (Tues–Sat: Feb–June & Sept–Dec 2.30–4pm; July & Aug 2–5pm; €5.50; Ⓦwww.moulindugot.com). In the town centre, the **railway museum**, on rue de Beaufort (July & Aug Mon–Fri 10am–noon & 2–6pm; €4.50; Ⓦwww.historail.com), is also good fun, with some excellent, working model railways.

The **tourist office** on place du Champs-de-Mars (July & Aug Mon–Sat 10am–1pm & 2.30–6.30pm, Sun 10am–12.30pm; Sept–June Mon–Sat 9.30am–12.30pm & 2.30–5pm; Ⓣ05.55.56.25.06) offers ideas for local walks and will point you to *chambre d'hôte* possibilities round about. A good **place to stay** is the *Relais St-Jacques* on the boulevard encircling the old town (Ⓣ05.55.56.00.25, Ⓔrelaisstjacques@aol.com; ❸; closed Sun eve & Mon Oct–May; restaurant from €15), and you can **eat** well just round the corner at the welcoming *Le Gay Lussac*, 18 rue Victor-Hugo (Ⓣ05.55.56.98.45; closed Sun), which offers great-value, imaginative menus from €12 at lunch on weekdays and €18 in the evening. There's a municipal **campsite**, the *Camping de Beaufort* (Ⓣ05.55.56.02.79, Ⓔcamping.beaufort@wanadoo.fr; mid-June to mid-Sept), beside the river a couple of kilometres out of town on the D39.

Aubusson

AUBUSSON is 90km east of Limoges and served by regular buses and trains. A neat grey-stone town in the bottom of a ravine formed by the River Creuse, it's of no great interest in itself. What makes it unique is its reputation as a centre for weaving **tapestries**, second only to the Gobelins in Paris. If you're interested, you should aim for the **Musée Départemental de la Tapisserie** in avenue des Lissiers (July & Aug Mon & Wed–Sun 10am–6pm, Tues 2–6pm; Sept–June daily except Tues 9.30am–noon & 2–6pm; €4), which traces the history of Aubusson tapestries over six centuries, up to the modern-day works of Jean Lurçat (see p.731). The **Maison du Tapissier** next to the tourist office (same hours as tourist office; €5) is also worth a quick look for its broad overview of weaving techniques and local history displayed in the sixteenth-century home of a master weaver.

For information about further exhibitions and workshop visits, ask at the **tourist office** in pedestrianized rue Vieille (July & Aug Mon–Sat 9.30am–6.30pm, Sun 10am–noon & 2.30–5.30pm; Sept–June Mon–Sat 9.30am–12.30pm & 2–6pm, Sun 10am–noon & 2.30–5.30pm; Ⓣ05.55.66.32.12, Ⓦwww.ot-aubusson.fr). The smartest **hotel** in town is the two-star *De France* at 6 rue des Déportés (Ⓣ05.55.66.10.22, Ⓦwww.lefrance-aubusson.com; ❹), with elegant rooms and a decent restaurant (menus €25–65). A good budget place is *Chapitre*, on the main Grande-Rue above a bar at no. 53 (Ⓣ05.55.66.18.54, Ⓦwww.hotellechapitre.com; ❷). The town's *La Croix Blanche* **campsite** (Ⓣ05.55.66.18.00; April–Sept), is by the river on the Felletin road.

The Plateau de Millevaches

Millevaches, the plateau of a thousand springs, is undulating upland country 800–900m in altitude, a sort of step on the northern edge of the Massif Central, with a wild and sparsely populated landscape and villages few and far between. Those that do exist appear small, grey and sturdy, inured like their mainly elderly inhabitants to the buffeting of upland weather. It's a country of conifer plantations and natural woodland – of beech, birch and chestnut – interspersed with reed-fringed tarns, dam-created lakes and pasture grazed by sheep and cows, where you still find people haymaking with rake and pitchfork.

Steam trains on Millevaches

From June to August every year **steam trains** potter along the beautiful Limoges-Ussel mountain line. Trips cost in the range of €8–40 (adults) and €5–18 (children), according to the length of the journey. There are various options, including Limoges–Meymac, Limoges–Eymoutiers, Eymoutiers–Bujaleuf, Meymac–Ussel and (on a different line) Limoges–Pompadour. For dates and times, consult the brochure *Train Touristiques à Vapeur en Limousin*, the website Ⓦwww.trainvapeur.com or the tourist offices in any of the towns above.

The small towns, like **Eymoutiers** and **Meymac**, have a primitive architectural beauty and an old-world charm largely untouched by modern development. It's an area to walk or cycle in, or at least savour at a gentle pace, and there's a surprisingly large number of attractive old-fashioned hotels.

Obviously, getting around by car is easiest, but there is access by public transport. **Ussel**, the largest town, is on the main road and rail link between Brive and Clermont-Ferrand, and is also connected by a cross-country line through Meymac and Eymoutiers to Limoges.

Ussel

On the southeastern edge of the plateau is **USSEL**, some 100km southeast of Limoges and 60km northeast of Tulle, where the land begins its gradual descent to the uppermost reaches of the Dordogne valley, thickly wooded and cut by deep tributary valleys. It's not a place with much to see, though the town is pleasant enough, with some attractive sixteenth- and seventeenth-century houses scattered about the central part, while a giant battered granite eagle on the place Voltaire stands as the sole reminder of a Roman settlement hereabouts.

One building worth a look is the house of the local lords, the **Maison Ducal des Ventadour**, who moved here from their draughty fortress in the hills to the south (see opposite). On the north side of place de la République, behind the church, it has a very provincial and rather amateurish Renaissance grandeur, perhaps aping their rich metropolitan cousins. Also of interest is the local **Musée du Pays d'Ussel** (July & Aug daily 10am–noon & 2–7pm; free), which is dedicated to traditional crafts and trades of the region and has a surprisingly good collection of tapestries. It's located in the eighteenth-century Hôtel Bonnot de Bay on rue Michelet, on the west side of town.

The **tourist office** is nearby on the wide place Voltaire (July & Aug Mon–Sat 10am–12.30pm & 3–6.30pm; Sept–June Mon–Fri 9am–noon & 2–5pm; Ⓣ05.55.72.11.50, Ⓦwww.ot-ussel.fr), immediately southwest of the old centre, while the **gare SNCF** is to the north along avenue Carnot.

The most comfortable **place to stay** is the striking 1970s *Les Gravades* (Ⓣ05.55.46.06.00, Ⓕ05.55.46.06.10; ❸; closed Christmas holidays; restaurant from €15; closed weekends), a couple of kilometres east of Ussel on the N89 and set in its own grounds. A pair of cheaper options are to be found opposite the station. There's also a municipal **campsite**, the *Camping du Ponty* (Ⓣ05.55.72.30.05, Ⓕ05.55.72.95.19; mid-June to mid-Sept), just off the road to Tulle. Ussel's best **restaurant** is 1km to the north of the centre, out by the railway tracks: *Le Chateau de la Borde*, rue des Buis (Ⓣ05.55.72.56.27; closed Sat lunch & Mon), offers *grillades* and local specialities on menus from a very reasonable €15.

Meymac and around

Pepper-pot turrets and steep slate roofs adorn the ancient grey houses of **MEYMAC**, 17km west of Ussel. The village is packed tightly around its Romanesque church, whose porch is flanked by striking pink capitals. Adjoining it are the remains of the original Benedictine **abbey**, whose foundation a thousand years ago brought the town into being. Part of the abbey now houses the innovative **Centre National d'Art Contemporain** (daily except Mon: July & Aug 10am–1pm & 2–7pm; Sept–June 2–6pm; closed Jan; €4), featuring changing exhibitions of young, local artists as well as big-name retrospectives. It's also worth popping into the adjacent **Musée de la Fondation Marius**

Vazeilles (daily except Tues: May, June, Sept & Oct 2.30–6.30pm; July & Aug 10am–noon & 2.30–6.30pm; €2.90) to learn about the history and traditions of the plateau.

Grande-Rue, the main street, ends in steps that climb past the round **bell tower**, the town's landmark, to the lime-shaded square in front of the town hall. The **tourist office** (June 15–Sept 15 Mon–Sat 10am–12.30pm & 2–6.30pm, Sun 10am–12.30pm; Sept 16–June 14 Mon–Fri 10am–noon & 2–4.30pm; ⓣ05.55.95.18.43, ⓦwww.ot-meymac.visit.org) is opposite the other side of a pretty fountain, and has plenty of information on hiking amongst other things.

There's a reasonable two-star **hotel** on the main road, the *Limousin*, 76 av Limousine (ⓣ05.55.46.12.11, ⓦwww.logis-de-france.fr; ❸; closed Sat off season & Sun eve all year; restaurant from €20), but better to book ahead for one of the four rooms at *Chez Françoise*, up the hill from the tourist office (ⓣ05.55.95.10.63, ⓕ05.55.95.40.22; ❹; closed Jan). They also run a well-respected **restaurant** serving local specialities (closed Sun eve & Mon out of season; menus €15–35) and a wonderful, old-fashioned cheese and wine shop. Finally, there's a municipal **campsite**, *La Garenne* (ⓣ05.55.95.22.80, ⓔmairie .meymac@wanadoo.fr; mid-June to mid-Sept), close at hand on the Sornac road.

One notable sight in the area is a ruined second-century **temple** and, a short walk through the woods, a **Gallo-Roman villa** at **CARS**, about 20km northwest of Meymac. Although there's nothing very spectacular to see, the very presence of Roman influence in such a remote location on the very edge of the Massif Central is interesting. If you want to **stay**, the simple, old-fashioned *Hôtel des Touristes* is just a few kilometres away in the village of **PÉROLS-SUR-VÉZÈRE** (ⓣ05.55.95.51.71, ⓔhotel-des-touristes@wanadoo.fr; ❷; closed mid-Dec to Jan), serving up tasty home cooking from €12. A few kilometres further west, just outside **BUGEAT**, there's also a well-run riverside **campsite**, the *Camping des 3 Ponts* (ⓣ05.55.95.50.34, ⓕ05.55.95.47.26; closed Oct–April).

Five kilometres northwest of Bugeat, the hamlet of **VIAM** perches prettily on the shores of an artificial lake, its houses clustered around an exquisite and proportionately minute, lopsided church. There's a municipal **campsite** down by the lake (ⓣ05.55.95.52.05, ⓔviam.mairie@wanadoo.fr; mid-June to Sept), but the nearest **hotel** is 15km southwest, just outside **TREIGNAC**, where the *Du Lac* (ⓣ05.55.98.00.44, ⓦwww.hotel-lac-vezere.com; ❸; closed Jan, and Mon & Tues out of season) offers bright, modern rooms overlooking a lake, and a well-rated **restaurant** (closed Mon & lunch Tues; menus from €10).

Egletons and around

Some 20km southwest of Meymac, the ancient market town of **EGLETONS** flourished during medieval times under the powerful dukes of Ventadour, whose twelfth-century **château** is now a magnificent ruin on the tip of a narrow spur about 6km southeast of Egletons near the hamlet of Moustier. The celebrated troubadour Bernard de Ventadour was born here, child of a castle servant. The site is now undergoing lengthy restoration work to make it safe; you can get quite close but the ruins themselves are fenced off.

By way of contrast, the area's other main sight is the **Musée du Président Jacques Chirac** (Jan & Feb Sat & Sun 10am–12.30pm & 1.30–6pm; March–June & Sept–Dec Tues–Sun 10am–12.30pm & 1.30–6pm; July & Aug daily 10am–12.30pm & 1.30–6pm; €4; ⓦwww.museepresidentjchirac.fr) at

SARRAN, in the depths of the country around 10km west of Egletons. This quirky, ultramodern and ever-expanding museum is a showcase of the gifts given to the president during state visits and other official duties. Look out for the natty cowboy boots (from then US President Bill Clinton), the stuffed coelacanth (a gift from the Comoros Islands for the man who has everything) and the delightful South African chess set in which the pieces are caricatures of Mandela, de Klerk, Archbishop Tutu and other famous personalities.

Egletons has a clutch of **hotels**, of which the smartest is the *Ibis* on the main road 1.5km east of town (Ⓣ05.55.93.25.16, Ⓦwww.ibishotel.com; ❸; restaurant from €16). A simpler option is the *Borie* in the centre of town on avenue Charles-de-Gaulle (Ⓣ05.55.93.12.00, Ⓦwww.hotelrestaurantborie.com; ❷; restaurant from €11, closed Sun eve). When it comes to **eating**, try *Le Jardin de Ventadour*, immediately north of the centre on place du Marchadial, which serves a range of imaginative dishes (closed Sun eve; menus €15–52).

Eymoutiers

EYMOUTIERS, in the north of the Plateau de Millevaches, 45km southeast of Limoges, is another upland town of tall, narrow stone houses crowding round a much-altered Romanesque **church**. Not interesting enough for a prolonged stay, it nonetheless makes another agreeable stopover, especially for campers, as it has a simple but magnificently sited municipal **campsite**, the *Château St-Pierre* (Ⓣ05.55.69.27.81, Ⓦwww.mairie-eymoutiers.fr; closed Oct–May), on a hill 2km southeast of town off the Treignac–Tulle road. If you prefer a **hotel**, you'll find simple rooms and excellent food at *Le Ranch des Lacs* (Ⓣ05.55.69.15.66, Ⓦwww.le-ranch-des-lacs.com; ❸; menus €12–35) about 7km northeast of Eymoutier, signposted off the Bujaleuf road.

Brive-la-Gaillarde and around

BRIVE-LA-GAILLARDE is a major rail junction and the nearest thing to an industrial centre for miles around, but it makes an agreeable base for exploring the Corrèze *département* and its beautiful villages, as well as the upper reaches of the Vézère and Dordogne rivers.

Though it has no commanding sights, Brive-la-Gaillarde does have a few distractions. Right in the middle of town is the much-restored **church of St-Martin**, originally Romanesque in style, though only the transept, apse and a few comically carved capitals survive from that era. St Martin himself, a Spanish aristocrat, arrived in pagan Brive in 407 AD on the feast of Saturnus, smashed various idols and was promptly stoned to death by the outraged onlookers.

Numerous streets fan out from the surrounding square, place du Général-de-Gaulle, with a number of turreted and towered houses, some dating back to the thirteenth century. The most impressive is the sixteenth-century **Hôtel de Labenche** on boulevard Jules-Ferry, now housing the town's archeological finds as well as a collection of seventeenth-century tapestries in the **Musée Labenche** (daily except Tues: April–Oct 10am–6.30pm; Nov–March 1.30–6pm; €4.70; Ⓦwww.musee-labenche.com). There's also the **Centre National d'Études Edmond Michelet** at 4 rue Champanatier (Mon–Sat 10am–noon & 2–6pm; free; Ⓦwww.centremichelet.org), based in the former house of this minister of de Gaulle, and one of the town's leading *résistants*, with exhibitions portraying the occupation and Resistance through photographs, posters and objects of the time.

From the **gare SNCF**, it's a five-minute walk north along avenue Jean-Jaurès to the boulevard ringing the old town. A right turn here brings you to place de Lattre-de-Tassigny and the **post office**. The **tourist office** is outside the ring road to the north on place 14-Juillet (May, June & Sept Mon–Sat 9am–12.30pm & 1.30–6.30pm; July & Aug Mon–Sat 9am–7pm, Sun 10am–4pm; Oct–April Mon–Sat 9am–noon & 2–6pm; ⓣ05.55.24.08.80, ⓦwww.brive-tourisme.com), where you'll also find a large car park, the modern market hall and the **gare routière** with a bus information office. The best place to go for **Internet** access is Le Mulot, on the ring road at 4 bd du Général-Koenig, (closed Thurs pm & Sun; €2.50 per hour).

For alternative **places to eat**, try *Le Corrèze* at 3 rue de Corrèze for its good-value regional cooking (closed Sun & two weeks in Sept; menus from €8), or the slightly smarter *Viviers St-Martin*, at 4 rue Traversière (closed two weeks each in March & Oct; menus from €11), tucked down an alley near St-Martin; both places offer a wide range of menus. Though it doesn't look much from the outside, *Le Boulevard* at 8 bd Jules-Ferry (ⓣ05.55.23.07.13) hides a cosy dining room where locals come for dishes such as duck breast with mustard (closed Sun eve & Mon; menus from €12).

Accommodation

Brive has no **hotels** right in its heart, but there are some nice options two minutes' walk away around the ring road, as well as several cheap dives near the station.

L'Andrea 39 av Jean-Jaurès ⓣ05.55.74.11.84, ⓦwww.landrea.com. The nicest of the station hotels, with pleasant rooms, each decorated differently. There's also a friendly bar downstairs serving a good house sangria. ❷

Le Chapon Fin 1 place de Lattre de Tassigny ⓣ05.55.74.23.40, ⓦwww.chaponfin-brive.com. Almost all the rooms here have been renovated in the last year, and they're large for the price, too. You'll get a friendly welcome from the proprietress who speaks excellent English, as well as most other major languages. ❷–❸

Le Collonges 3 place Winston-Churchill ⓣ05.55.74.09.58, ⓦwww.hotel-le-collonges.com. A smart, well-run hotel, also on the ring road. Rooms are light, with large windows and all the standard comforts. Free wireless Internet is thrown in as well. ❸

HI Hostel 56 av du Maréchal-Bugeaud ⓣ05.55.24.34.00, ⓔaj.brive@wanadoo.fr. East of town, a 25min walk from the station, this is a decent hostel with a kitchen for guests. Beds are €11.50 per night.

La Truffe Noire 22 bd Anatole-France ⓣ05.55.92.45.00, ⓦwww.la-truffe-noire.com. Brive's grandest hotel has an impressive lobby, with an enormous hearth. The rooms are disappointingly ordinary in comparison, but they're new, comfortable and air-conditioned. ❻

Uzerche and Arnac-Pompadour

A half-hour train ride north of Brive along the course of the bubbling River Vézère, the town of **UZERCHE** is impressively located above a loop in the river's course. It's worth a passing visit as the town has several fine old buildings. The **tourist office** (mid-June to mid-Sept 15 daily 10am–12.30pm & 2.30–6.30pm; school holidays Mon–Fri 10am–noon & 2.30–5pm, Sat 10am–noon; rest of year Mon–Fri 10am–noon; ⓣ05.55.73.15.71, ⓦwww.pays-uzerche.com), behind the main church, provides a suggested walking route, but the place is so small you can easily find your own way around. If you need a **place to stay**, the *Hôtel Teyssier*, down by the river (ⓣ05.55.73.10.05, ⓦwww.hotel-teyssier.com; closed Tues & Wed out of season; ❸; restaurant €19–35) is the nicest option. There's also a three-star municipal **campsite** (ⓣ05.55.73.12.75, ⓦwww.uzerche.fr; May–Sept) at the Minoterie leisure centre, 2km south along the river, from where you can rent **canoes** and **bikes** (Ⓣ05.55.73.02.84, Ⓦwww.vezerepassion.com).

Roughly 20km west of Uzerche (40min by train, on a different line, from Brive) is **ARNAC-POMPADOUR**. It's a town dominated by its grey, turreted château, presented in 1745 by Louis XV to his mistress, Madame de Pompadour, though she never actually visited it. Set in the green countryside of southern Limousin – reminiscent of parts of Ireland – the **château** is home to one of France's best-known **stud farms** (*haras*), created by Louis XV in 1761, where Anglo-Arabs were first bred. Only the château gardens are open to the public (guided visits only: April & Sept daily at 10am, 3pm & 5pm; May & June daily 10am & hourly 2–5pm; July & Aug daily 10am, 11am & half-hourly 2–6pm; Oct Tues–Sun 3pm; Nov Wed–Sun 3pm; Dec–March Tues–Sat 3pm; €4), but it's more interesting to visit the *dépôt des étalons* where the stallions are kept (visits: Jan–March Tues–Sat 2pm & 4pm; April–June & Sept daily 11am, 2pm & 4pm; July & Aug daily 10am, 11am & half-hourly 2–6pm; Oct Tues–Sun 2pm; Nov Wed–Sun 2pm & 4pm; Dec Tues–Sat 2pm; €6), across the square from the château. The mares live in the Jumenterie de la Rivière (visits: April–June daily hourly 2–5pm; July & Aug Tues, Thurs & Sat hourly 2–5pm; €5), 4km away near the village of Beyssac. All visits are organized by the château, and they may occasionally be cancelled; call Ⓣ05.55.98.51.10 to be safe. In spring the fields around are full of mares and foals, the best being kept for breeding, the rest sold worldwide as 2-year-olds. From March to October there are frequent race meetings on the magnificent track in front of the château, plus events and open days, the biggest of which is the **Fête du Cheval** on August 15; there's even a special day for donkeys on July 14.

The **gare SNCF** is 500m southeast of the old town along the main D7 Vigeois road. There's a reasonable **place to stay** and **eat**, the *Hôtel du Parc* (Ⓣ05.55.73.30.54, Ⓦwww.logis-de-france.fr; ❸; closed Christmas to mid-Jan; restaurant from €15), behind the château. Or you could try the modern *Auberge de la Mandrie*, 4km west on the D7, with chalet rooms around a heated pool (Ⓣ05.55.73.37.14, Ⓦwww.la-mandrie.com; ❸; restaurant from €12, closed Sun eve).

Turenne

TURENNE, just 16km south of Brive, is one of two very picturesque villages close to the town. Capital of the viscountcy of Turenne, whose most illustrious seigneur was Henri de la Tour d'Auvergne – the "Grand Turenne", whom Napoleon rated the finest tactician of modern times – the village today would still seem familiar to him. The same mellow stone houses crowd in the lee of the sharp bluff on whose summit sprout the towers of the castle, one forming part of someone's house. The other, known as **La Tour de César**, can be visited (April–June, Sept & Oct daily 10am–noon & 2–6pm; July & Aug daily 10am–7pm; Nov–March Sun 2–5pm; €3.50; Ⓦwww.chateau-turenne.com), and it's worth climbing for vertiginous views away over the ridges and valleys to the mountains of Cantal.

Collonges-la-Rouge

COLLONGES-LA-ROUGE, 7km east of Turenne, is the epitome of rustic charm with its red-sandstone houses, pepper-pot towers and pink-candled chestnut trees, although you need to time your visit carefully, as the village is now very much on the tourist bus circuit. Though small-scale, there's a grandeur about the place, as if the resident Turenne administrators were aping, within their means, the grandiloquence of their superiors. On the main square a twelfth-century **church** testifies to the imbecility of shedding blood over religious differences: here, side by side, Protestant and Catholic conducted their services simultaneously. Outside, the covered **market hall** still retains its old-fashioned baker's oven.

If you want to **stay** somewhere nearby, it's best to head downhill a few minutes to **MEYSSAC**, a town built in the same red sandstone, though less grandly, to the very pleasant *Relais du Quercy* (Ⓣ05.55.25.40.31, Ⓦwww.relaisduquercy.com.fr; ❸; closed two weeks in Feb; restaurant from €12), or the **campsite**, *Moulin de la Valanne* (Ⓣ05.55.25.41.59, Ⓦwww.meyssac.fr; May–Sept).

On weekdays it's possible to get to Collonges by **bus** from Brive, and with an early start you can see the town and return by the late-afternoon service. The prettiest route on foot from Turenne is along the back lanes through meadow and walnut orchards via **SAILLAC** (3hr), whose Romanesque church sports an elaborately carved tympanum upheld by a column of spiralling animal motifs.

Tulle

Seen from a distance, **TULLE**, 29km east of Brive, is a strange, unattractive-looking place. Strung out along the bottom of the narrow and deep valley of the Corrèze, it looks grey, run-down and industrial. But once you get down to the riverside and the area around the cathedral, it reveals itself to be full of fascinating winding lanes and stairways bordered by very handsome houses – many as old as the fourteenth century – with an imposing **Hôtel de Ville** at the end of rue du Trech, the main commercial street. If not worth a prolonged stay, Tulle certainly makes an interesting stopover.

The **Cathédrale Notre-Dame**, whose construction was drawn out from the Romanesque to Gothic periods, stands on the riverside quays in place Émile-Zola. The cloister beside it has a small **museum** (daily 9am–noon & 2–5pm, closed Wed & Sat afternoons; €2.50), containing a mishmash of exhibits ranging from archeology to accordions, with a large contingent of firearms, along with lace, once one of the town's major industries. Around the block, at 2 quai Edmond-Perrier, is a collection of documents to do with the Resistance at the **Musée Départemental de la Résistance et de la Déportation** (Mon–Fri 9am–noon & 2–6pm; free), particularly the terrible reprisals wreaked by the Germans when they recaptured the town from the Resistance on June 8, 1944, and hanged 99 people. It presents a more balanced view than many Resistance museums, though, and has some interesting examples of Vichy propaganda.

Practicalities

The **tourist office** is opposite the cathedral at 2 place Émile-Zola (July & Aug Mon–Fri 9am–7pm, Sat 9am–6pm, Sun 10.30am–12.30pm; Sept–June Mon–Sat 9am–noon & 2–6pm; Ⓣ05.55.26.59.61, Ⓦwww.paysdetulle-developpement.com), while the **bus** and **train stations** are side by side on the southwest edge of the town on avenue Winston-Churchill. The **market** takes place on Wednesday and Saturday mornings by the cathedral.

By far the nicest budget **hotel** is *Le Bon Accueil*, 10 rue du Canton (Ⓣ & Ⓕ05.55.26.70.57; ❷; closed two weeks at Christmas; restaurant from €12.50), in an old beamed house with stone mullion windows, across the river from the cathedral. A smarter option, by the train station, is the *Hôtel de la Gare* (Ⓣ05.55.20.04.04, Ⓦwww.hotel-restaurant-delagare-farjounel.com; ❸; closed two weeks in Aug/Sept; restaurant from €14). There are also a few reasonable, old-fashioned rooms at *La Toque Blanche*, 29 rue Jean-Jaurès (Ⓣ05.55.26.75.41,

Ⓦwww.hotel-latoqueblanche.com; ❸; closed Sun), only five minutes from the cathedral, but its real draw is a renowned **restaurant**, with an affordable menu at €24 (closed Sun eve & Mon). The municipal **campsite** is by the river on the Ussel side of town (Ⓣ & Ⓕ05.55.26.75.97; July & Aug only).

Gimel

If you're travelling by car, you might consider staying in one of the villages in the hilly wooded country northeast of Tulle. **GIMEL-LES-CASCADES**, in particular, is very beautiful and, out of season at least, very quiet. It is a minute hamlet, about 10km away and clinging to the edge of a steep valley beside a spectacular **waterfall**, which has sadly been turned into a paying "sight" (March–Oct daily 10am–6pm; until 7pm in July & Aug; €4). There's also a superb twelfth-century **reliquary**, known as the Chasse de St-Étienne, in the treasury of the local church.

The attractive *Hostellerie de la Vallée* (Ⓣ05.55.21.40.60, Ⓔhotel_de_la_vallee@hotmail.com; ❸) in the village has a few simple rooms and a good restaurant from €19. There's also a good three-star **campsite** (Ⓣ05.55.21.26.65; May–Sept) northeast of Gimel by a small but beautiful lake, the Étang de Ruffaud.

The Lot

The core of this section is formed by the old provinces of **Haut Quercy** and **Quercy**: the land between the Dordogne and the Lot and between the Lot and the Garonne, Aveyron and Tarn. We have extended it slightly eastwards to include the gorges of the River **Aveyron** and Villefranche-de-Rouergue on the edge of the province of Rouergue.

The area is hotter, drier, less well known and, with few exceptions, less crowded than the Dordogne, though no less interesting. The cave paintings at **Pech-Merle** are on a par with those at Les Eyzies. **Najac**, **Penne** and **Peyrusse** have ruined castles to rival those of the Dordogne. Towns like **Figeac** and **Villefranche-de-Rouergue** are without equal, as are villages like **St-Antonin-Noble-Val**, and stretches of country like that below **Gourdon**, around **Les Arques** where Osip Zadkine had his studio, and the **Célé valley**.

Again, without transport, many places are out of reach. Some consolation, however, is the existence of the Brive–Toulouse train line that makes Figeac, Villefranche-de-Rouergue and Najac accessible, while **Agen**, **Moissac** and **Montauban** are on the Bordeaux–Toulouse line.

Rocamadour and around

Halfway up a cliff in the deep and abrupt canyon of the Alzou stream, the spectacular setting of **ROCAMADOUR** is hard to beat; the town itself must have been beautiful once, too, but for centuries it has been inundated by religious pilgrims and, latterly, more secular-minded tourists. The constant stream has turned the

△ Rocamadour

place into something of a nightmare in high season, with every house displaying mountains of unbelievable junk. The reason for its popularity since medieval times is the supposed miraculous ability of the cathedral's Black Madonna. Nowadays, pilgrims are outnumbered by tourists, who come here to wonder at the sheer audacity of its location, built almost vertically into its rocky backdrop.

Legend has it that the history of Rocamadour began with the arrival of **Zacchaeus**, husband of St Veronica, who fled to France to escape religious persecution and lived out his last years here as a hermit. When in 1166 a perfectly preserved body was found in a grave high up on the rock, it was declared to be Zacchaeus, known in France as **St Amadour**. Rocamadour soon became a major pilgrimage site and a staging post on the road to Santiago de Compostela in Spain. St Bernard, numerous kings of England and France and thousands of others crawled up the chapel steps on their knees to pay their respects and seek cures for their illnesses. Young King Henry, son of Henry II of England (see box, p.711), was the first to plunder the shrine, but he was easily outclassed by the Huguenots, who tried in vain to burn the saint's corpse and finally resigned themselves simply to hacking it to bits. A reconstruction was produced in the nineteenth century, in an attempt to revive the flagging pilgrimage.

The area's other main sight is the **Gouffre de Padirac**, with its vast underground river system, which lies across open country to the northeast of Rocamadour. Further east again, the town of **St-Céré** is an attractive spot, best known for its museum dedicated to the twentieth-century artist Jean Lurçat.

The Town

Rocamadour is easy enough to find your way around. There's just one street, rue de la Couronnerie, strung out between two medieval gateways. Above it, the steep hillside supports no fewer than seven churches. There's a lift dug into the rock-face (€3 return), but it's far better to climb the 223 steps of the Via Sancta, up which the devout drag themselves on their knees to the smoke-blackened and votive-packed **Chapelle Notre-Dame** where the miracle-working twelfth-century Black Madonna resides. The tiny, macabre statue of walnut wood is appropriately lit in the mysterious half-light of her protective black cage, but the rest of the chapel is unremarkable. High up in the rock above the entrance to the chapel is a sword, supposedly Roland's legendary blade, Durandal.

There's no relief for the non-religious in the neighbouring **Musée d'Art Sacré** (Ⓦwww.relaisdesremparts.com), which contains sacred art treasures, reliquaries and various historical documents. It's dedicated to the French composer Francis Poulenc (1899–1963), whose music was inspired by a visit to the shrine. The museum was closed at the time of writing, but expected to re-open soon – check at the tourist office for times. The same goes for the ancient **ramparts** (usually open daily; €3) higher above Rocamadour in **L'Hospitalet**, reachable via a winding shady path, La Calvarie, past the Stations of the Cross, with stunning views across the valley, or else in another lift (€4 return).

There are two different **wildlife centres** worth visiting in L'Hospitalet: the **Rocher des Aigles** (April to mid-July & Sept daily 1.30–6pm; mid-July to Aug daily 11am–7.30pm; Oct to mid-Nov Tues–Sun 1.30–6pm; €7.50, Ⓦwww.rocherdesaigles.com), a breeding centre for birds of prey – don't miss the demonstrations of the birds in flight; and the **Forêt des Singes**, off the D673 (April–June & first two weeks Sept daily 10am–noon & 1–5.30pm; July & Aug daily 9.30am–6.30pm; mid-Sept to Oct Mon–Fri 1–5.30pm, Sat & Sun 10am–noon & 1–5.30pm; €7; Ⓦwww.la-foret-des-singes.com), where more than a hundred Barbary apes roam the plateau in relative freedom.

Practicalities

Getting to Rocamadour without your own transport is awkward, unless you're prepared to walk or take a taxi the 4km from the Rocamadour-Padirac **gare SNCF** on the Brive–Capdenac line. If you arrive by car, you'll have to park in L'Hospitalet, on the hilltop above Rocamadour (which has the best view of the town), or else in the car park several hundred metres below the town. There are two **tourist offices**: the main one in l'Hospitalet (Ⓣ05.65.33.22.00, Ⓦwww.rocamadour.com), and a second next to the Hôtel de Ville, on the main street. Inconveniently, the distribution of hours between the two offices changes significantly most years, though you're assured that at least one will be open on any given day.

Rocamadour's **hotels** are not too expensive but they're closed for the winter months, and you need to ring ahead in summer. There's good value at the *Lion d'Or*, on rue de la Couronnerie (Ⓣ05.65.33.62.04, Ⓦwww.liondor-rocamadour.com; ❷; closed Nov–March; restaurant from €12), and *Le Terminus des Pèlerins*, at the bottom of the Via Sancta, with fine views of the valley (Ⓣ05.65.33.62.14, Ⓦwww.terminus-des-pelerins.com; ❸; closed Nov–March; restaurant from €15). For a night of luxury, try the *Beau Site*, also on rue de la Couronnerie (Ⓣ05.65.33.63.08, Ⓦwww.bestwestern-beausite.com; ❹; closed mid-Nov to early Feb), which also has an excellent restaurant, the *Jehan de Valon* (menus from €23). Up in L'Hospitalet, the *Bellevue* (Ⓣ05.65.33.62.10, Ⓕ05.65.33.65.61; ❷–❸; menus from €14) enjoys prime positioning and has pleasant rooms. **Campers** should head for the three-star site nearby, *Les Cigales* (Ⓣ05.65.33.64.44, Ⓦwww.camping-cigales.com; April–Sept). The nicest **place to eat** is the genuine and homely *Chez Anne-Marie,* on rue de la Couronnerie (Ⓣ05.65.33.65.81), which has good-value menus for €14.50 at lunchtime.

Gouffre de Padirac

The **Gouffre de Padirac** (daily guided tours: April to mid-July, Sept & Oct 9am–noon & 2–6pm; last two weeks July 9am–6pm; Aug 8.30am–6.30pm;

€8.50; ⓦ www.gouffre-de-padirac.com) is about 20km east of Rocamadour on the other side of the main Brive–Figeac road. An enormous limestone sinkhole, about 100m deep and over 100m wide, it contains some spectacular formations of stalactites and waterfalls created by the accumulation of lime, and beautiful underground lakes, but is very, very popular. There is no system for reservations, so you're advised to avoid weekends and afternoons in summer, or you'll wait an age for tickets. Visits are partly on foot, partly by boat, and the guided tours last an hour and a half. In wet weather you'll need a waterproof jacket. If you have no car, the nearest **gare SNCF** is Rocamadour-Padirac, more than 10km to the west; the only alternative is walking or hitching.

St-Céré

East of Padirac and about 9km from Bretenoux on the River Bave, a minor tributary of the Dordogne, you come to the medieval town of **ST-CÉRÉ**, full of ancient houses crowding around place du Mercadial, and dominated by the brooding ruins of the **Château de St-Laurent-les-Tours,** whose two powerful keeps were once part of a fortress belonging to the Turennes. During World War II, the artist Jean Lurçat operated a secret Resistance radio post here; after the war he turned it into a studio, and it's now a marvellous **museum** of his work, mainly huge tapestries but also sketches, paintings and pottery (mid-July to Sept daily 9.30am–noon & 2.30–6.30pm; also open two weeks at Easter; ⓣ 05.65.38.28.21; €2.50). At over 200m altitude, the site is spectacular, with stunning views all around.

St-Céré has one very pleasant and reasonable **place to stay**: the *Hôtel Victor-Hugo*, avenue Victor-Hugo, by the river (ⓣ 05.65.38.16.15, ⓦ www.hotel-victor-hugo.fr; ③; closed two weeks in Feb & two in Nov; restaurant from €15, closed Sun eve and Mon). Otherwise, there's *Le Soulhol* riverside **campsite** (ⓣ 05.65.38.12.37, ⓦ www.campinglesoulhol.com; May–Sept) nearby.

Bikes can be rented from 45 rue Faidherbe (ⓣ 05.65.38.03.23; closed Sun & Mon) – one of the best trips you could do is to the extremely pretty little village of **AUTOIRE**, in a tight side valley about 10km to the west of St-Céré. Much hillier but glorious country lies to the east along the road to Aurillac via Sousceyrac and Laroquebrou.

Gourdon and around

GOURDON lies between Sarlat and Cahors, conveniently served by the Brive–Toulouse train line, and makes a quiet, pleasant base for visiting some of the major places in this part of the Dordogne and Lot. It's 17km south of the River Dordogne and pretty much at the eastern limit of the luxuriant woods and valleys of Périgord, which give way quite suddenly, at the line of the N20, to the arid limestone landscape of the **Causse de Gramat**.

In the Middle Ages, Gourdon was an important place, deriving wealth and influence from the presence of four monasteries. It was besieged and captured in 1189 by Richard the Lionheart, who promptly murdered its feudal lords. Legend has it that the archer who fired the fatal shot at Richard during the siege of Châlus was the last surviving member of this family. But more than anything it was the devastation of the Wars of Religion that dispatched the place into centuries of oblivion.

Gourdon is a beautiful town, its medieval centre of yellow-stone houses attached like a swarm of bees to a prominent hilltop, neatly ringed by modern boulevards containing all the shops. The main street through the old town, with a fortified **gateway** at one end, is rue du Majou. It's lined all the way up with splendid stone houses, some, like the **Maison d'Anglars** at no. 17, dating as far back as the thirteenth century. At its upper end, rue du Majou leads into a lovely square in front of the massive but not particularly interesting fourteenth-century **church of St-Pierre**, where in summer there's a farmers' market on Thursday mornings. From the square, steps climb to the top of the hill, where the castle once stood and from where there is a superb view over the Dordogne valley and surroundings.

A couple of kilometres along the Sarlat road in the direction of Cougnac from Gourdon, is a very interesting cave, the **Grottes de Cougnac**, discovered in 1949 (April–June & Sept daily 10–11.30am & 2.30–5pm; July & Aug daily 10am–6pm; Oct Mon–Sat 2–4pm; €6). It has beautiful rock formations as well as some fine prehistoric paintings rather similar to those at Pech-Merle and, intriguingly, sharing some of the same unexplained symbols.

Practicalities

Gourdon's **train station** is located roughly 1km northeast of the town centre; from the station, walk south on avenue de la Gare, then turn right on to avenue Gambetta to reach the boulevard encircling the old town. Turn left here to find rue du Majou and the **tourist office** at no. 24 (March–June, Sept & Oct Mon–Sat 10am–noon & 2–6pm; July & Aug Mon–Sat 10am–7pm, Sun 10am–noon; Nov–Feb Mon–Sat 10am–noon & 2–5pm; ⓣ05.65.27.52.50, ⓦwww.gourdon.fr), which has lists of B&B options in the area. **Bikes** can be rented from Nature Évasion, 73 av Cavignac (ⓣ05.65.37.65.12), out on the west side of town.

For an overnight **stay**, the *Hôtel de la Promenade*, on the northwestern side of the ring road at 48 bd Galiot-de-Genouillac (ⓣ05.65.41.41.44, ⓦwww.lapromenadegourdon.fr; ③; restaurant closed Sat lunch & Sun, menus from €16), is a cheerful place with pleasant, themed rooms, though you have to put up with the horrendous clutter of English-pub-style tack downstairs. On the opposite side of town, near the post office, is the agreeable *Bissonnier*, 51 bd des Martyrs (ⓣ05.65.41.02.48, ⓦwww.hotelbissonnier.com; ③), with a restaurant serving international fare such as spaghetti bolognese as well as the more local *salade de gésiers* (menus from €11 lunch, €20 dinner). There's a well-equipped municipal **campsite**, *Écoute s'il Pleut* (ⓣ05.65.41.06.19, ⓕ05.65.41.09.88; mid-June to mid-Sept), 1km north on the Sarlat road.

In addition to the hotels above, you'll find cafés and **restaurants** scattered along the main boulevard – the Tour-de-Ville – which encircles the old town.

Les Arques

Twenty-five kilometres southwest of Gourdon on the Fumel road, you come to a pretty but not remarkable *bastide* called **Cazals**. A left turn here takes you along the bottom of the valley of the Masse and up its left flank to the exquisite hamlet of **LES ARQUES**. This is quiet, remote, small-scale farming country, emptied of people by the slaughter of rustic sons in World War I and by migration to the towns in search of jobs and money.

Les Arques' main claim to fame is the Russian Cubist/Expressionist sculptor Osip Zadkine, who bought the old house by the church here in 1934. Some of his sculptures adorn the space outside the church as well as its lovely interior, and there's also a **museum** with a number of his other works (daily: April–Sept 10am–1pm & 2–7pm; Oct–March 2–5pm; €2.50).

The other reason to come here is the old village school, now transformed into a most unusual **restaurant**, *La Récréation* (☎05.65.22.88.08; closed Wed & Thurs, also Dec–March except Christmas hols), where you get a copious and delicious meal to eat beneath the chestnut trees of the school yard for €17, including wine, at midday in July and August, or otherwise for €29. On a summer night, with the swifts flying overhead, it's idyllic.

On the other side of the valley and well signposted, the tiny Romanesque **chapel of St-André-des-Arques** has some very lovely fifteenth-century frescoes discovered by Zadkine; get the key from the museum in Les Arques (see opposite).

Cahors and around

CAHORS, on the River Lot, was the capital of the old province of Quercy. In its time, it has been a Gallic settlement; a Roman town; a briefly held Moorish possession; a town under English rule; a bastion of Catholicism in the Wars of Religion, sacked in consequence by Henri IV; a university town for four hundred years; and birthplace of the politician Léon Gambetta (1838–82), after whom so many French streets and squares are named. Modern Cahors is a sunny southern backwater, with two interesting sights in its **cathedral** and the remarkable **Pont Valentré**.

While you're in the Cahors area, don't miss out on the local **wine**, heady and black but dry to the taste and not at all plummy like the Gironde wines from Blaye and Bourg, which use the same Malbec grape.

Arrival, information and accommodation

The **gare SNCF** is at the end of avenue Jean-Jaurès off rue du Président-Wilson. For further information on the area, make for the **tourist office** (Sept–June Mon–Sat 9am–12.30pm & 1.30–6pm; July & Aug, also Sun 10am–1pm; ☎05.65.53.20.65, Ⓦwww.mairie-cahors.fr/tourisme) on place François-Mitterrand, close to the cathedral. You can surf the **Internet** at INIT, 100 rue Jean-Vidal (€2.50 per hour). The nearest place to rent **bikes** is Antinéa Loisirs (☎05.65.30.95.79, Ⓦwww.antinea-loisirs.com), some 12km downstream in Douelle; for **canoes**, head to the base at St-Cirq-Lapopie (see p.736). A leisurely way to enjoy some of the Lot's scenery is through the **cruises** run by Croisières Fénelon (☎05.65.30.16.55, Ⓔbateaufenelon@wanadoo.fr). They offer day-trips from around €30 in July and August, for example to St-Cirq, where the boat moors to allow you time to explore the village.

Cahors boasts several attractive, mid-range hotel options, but there's less choice for those on a really tight budget. For campers, there is a riverside site, *Camping Rivière de Cabessut* (☎05.65.30.06.30, Ⓦwww.cabessut.com; April–Sept) across the Pont de Cabessut.

Hotels

La Chartreuse St-Georges ☎05.65.35.17.37, Ⓦwww.hotel-la-chartreuse.com. In a nice spot on the south bank, over the river from the town centre, this chain hotel has a small pool, a restaurant (menus from €14.50) and a bar with a billiard table. Ask for a room overlooking the river. ❹

Jean XXII or **L'Escargot** 5 bd Gambetta ☎05.65.35.07.66, Ⓦwww.hotel-escargot.com. Situated in the fourteenth-century buildings of the Palais Duèze, this hotel offers both charm and comfort. The rooms are recently renovated, and most have a/c. ❸

De la Paix 30 place St-Maurice ☎05.65.35.03.40, Ⓦwww.hoteldelapaix-cahors.com. Right in the thick of the action, opposite the covered market. The rooms are brand-new and sparkling clean, while downstairs is a popular café and bar, *The Blue Angel*. ❸

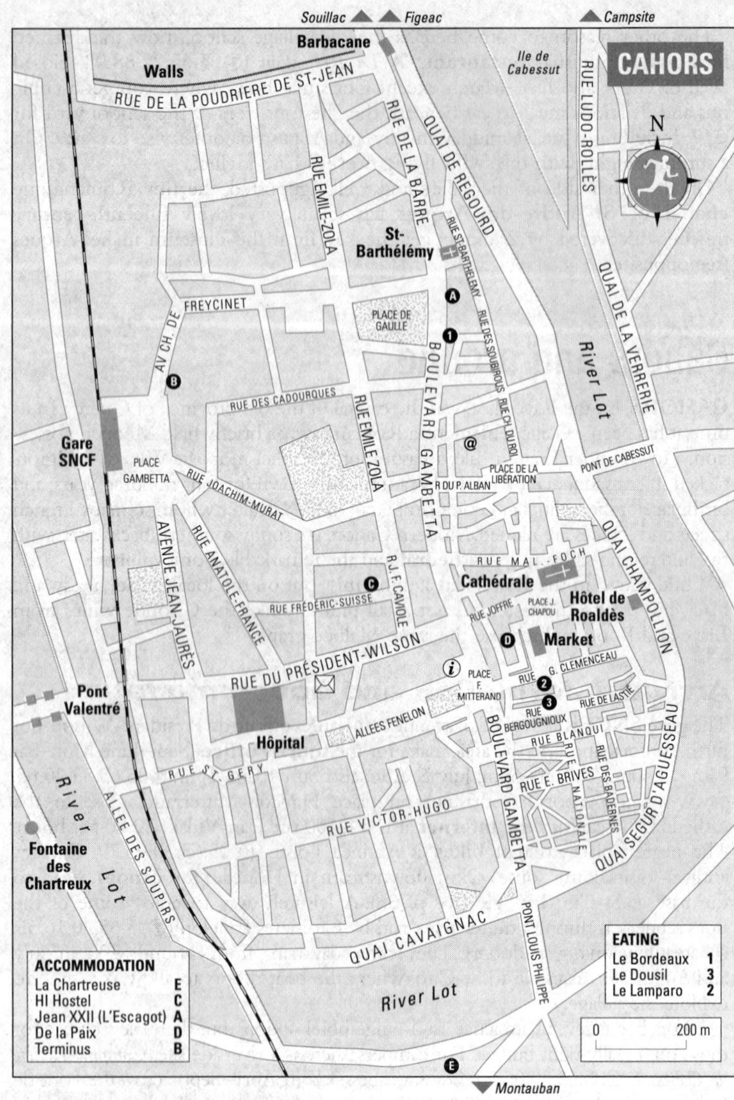

Terminus 5 av Charles-de-Freycinet ⓣ05.65.53.32.00, ⓦwww.balandre.com. In a grand old house opposite the station, you'll find large, comfortable and attractive rooms here. The restaurant, *Le Balandre*, is also outstanding (closed Sun & Mon; menus €40–85). ❹

Hostel

HI Hostel 20 rue Frédéric-Suisse ⓣ05.65.53.97.02, ⓔfjt46@wanadoo.fr. An extremely basic hostel in a fairly dilapidated building. It's central, though, and has a helpful reception and a canteen serving evening meals for €9 – the same price as a bed for the night.

The Town

Small and easily walkable, the town squats on a peninsula formed by a tight loop in the River Lot, and is protected on the northern side by a rank of fourteenth-century **fortifications**, with the **Barbacane de St-Jean** making a breach in the walls.

Right in the middle of the town is the **cathedral** which, consecrated in 1119, is the oldest and simplest in plan of the Périgord-style churches. The exterior is not exciting: a heavy square tower dominates the plain west front, whose best feature is the elaborately decorated portal in the street on the north side, where a Christ in Majesty dominates the tympanum, surrounded by angels and apostles, while cherubim fly out of the clouds to relieve him of his halo. Side panels show scenes from the life of St Stephen. The outer ring over the portal shows a line of naked figures being stabbed in the behind and hacked with axes.

Inside, the cathedral is much like St-Front at Périgueux, with a nave lacking aisles and transepts, roofed with two big domes; in the first are fourteenth-century frescoes of the stoning of St Stephen. The Gothic choir and apse are extensively but crudely painted, while to their right a door opens into a delicate **cloister** in the flamboyant style, still retaining some intricate, though damaged, carving. On the northwest corner pillar the Virgin is portrayed as a graceful girl with broad brow and ringlets to her waist. In the cloister's northeast corner St Gaubert's chapel holds the Holy Coif, a cloth said to have covered Christ's head in the tomb, which according to legend was brought back from the Holy Land in the twelfth century by Bishop Géraud de Cardaillac.

The area between the cathedral and the river is filled by a warren of narrow lanes and alleys, most of them handsomely restored during the last ten years. Many of the houses, turreted and built of flat, thin, southern brick, date from the fourteenth and fifteenth centuries. Rue Nationale, rue Bergougnioux and rue de Lastié are particularly interesting, along with rue du Château-du-Roi and its extension, rue des Soubirous, to the north. It's worth taking a look at the impressive, though now rather crumbly, **Hôtel d'Issale** in rue Bergougnioux and the **Hôtel de Roaldès** in place Henri-IV; also of interest are the **Hôpital Grossia** in rue des Soubirous and the **Palais Duèze**, further north opposite

△Pont Valentré, Cahors

the church of St-Barthélémy, built for the brothers of Pope John XXII in the fourteenth century.

Immediately south of the cathedral, the lime-bordered **place Jean-Jacques-Chapou** commemorates a local trade unionist and Resistance leader, killed in a German ambush on July 17, 1944. Next to it is the covered **market** and a building still bearing the name Gambetta, where the family of the famous deputy of Belleville in Paris had their grocery shop.

The reason most people venture to Cahors is the dramatic fourteenth-century **Pont Valentré**. Its three powerful towers, originally closed by portcullises and gates, made it effectively an independent fortress, guarding the river crossing on the west side of town. One of the finest surviving bridges of its time, it is, rightly, one of the most photographed monuments in France. Just upstream from the bridge is a resurgent river known as the **Fontaine des Chartreux**, flowing from the valley side. The Roman town was named Divona Carducorum after it, and it still supplies Cahors with drinking water.

Eating

In addition to the hotel **restaurants** mentioned on p.733–734, there's a lively brasserie, *Le Bordeaux*, at the top end of boulevard Gambetta (with menus from €11) while *Le Lamparo* (ⓣ05.65.35.25.93; evening menus from €22; closed Sun) on the south side of the market square, is equally popular for its varied menus and generous portions. *Le Dousil*, a wine bar just round the corner on rue Nationale (closed Sun & Mon), is a great venue to sample the local reds – and it dishes up good food, too: salads, open-sandwiches and cheese and charcuterie platters from around €10.

St-Cirq-Lapopie

If you have your own transport you could easily make a side trip from Cahors to the cliff-edge village of **ST-CIRQ-LAPOPIE**, 30km to the east, perched high above the south bank of the Lot. The village was saved from ruin when poet André Breton came to live here in the early twentieth century, and though it's now an irresistible draw for the tour buses with its cobbled lanes, half-timbered houses and gardens, it's still worth the trouble, especially if early or late in the day.

Public transport in the form of an SNCF bus will get you from Cahors to Gare-St-Cirq in the valley bottom at Tour-de-Faure, from where there's no alternative but to leg it up the steep hill for the final two kilometres. For **accommodation**, there's the pretty *Auberge du Sombral* on the central square (ⓣ05.65.31.26.08, ⓕ05.65.30.26.37; ❹; closed mid-Nov to March), with attractive, wooden furnishings, or *La Pélissaria* (ⓣ05.65.31.25.14, ⓦperso.orange.fr/hoteldelapelissaria; ❺; closed Nov–April), in a sixteenth-century house perched on the cliff at the eastern entrance to St-Cirq. There's also a very comfortable *gîte d'étape* in the village centre (ⓣ05.65.31.21.51, ⓔmaisonfourdonne@wanadoo.fr; closed Nov to mid-April), and two well-run **campsites**: *Camping de la Plage* (ⓣ05.65.30.29.51, ⓦwww.campingplage.com; open all year), down by the river with swimming and canoeing possibilities, and *La Truffière* (ⓣ05.65.30.20.22, ⓦwww.camping-truffiere.com; closed Oct–March), 3km to the southeast over the rim of the valley, with a heated swimming pool.

When it comes to **restaurants**, you can eat very well at *L'Oustal* (ⓣ05.65.31.20.17; closed Mon & Nov–March; menus from €9.50 at lunch, €17 evenings), tucked into a corner of rue de la Pélissaria just south of the church. At the top of the village, with views from its terrace over jumbled roofs, *Lou Bolat* serves a varied menu of crêpes, salads and regional dishes like *Cassoulet Campagnard* (closed mid-Nov to Feb & Tues; menu €17). For **canoeing** possibilities, from hourly rental to week-long expeditions on the Lot and Célé rivers, ask at Kalapca Loisirs (ⓣ05.65.30.29.51, ⓦwww.kalapca.com; open daily July & Aug, on reservation Sept–June), on the riverbank opposite Tour-de-Faure.

Downstream from Cahors

West of Cahors the vine-cloaked banks of the Lot are dotted with small and ancient villages. The first of these, **Luzech** and the dramatic **Puy-l'Évêque**, are served by an SNCF bus that threads along the valley from Cahors via Fumel to Monsempron-Libos, on the Agen–Périgueux train line. You'll need your own transport, however, to reach the splendid **Château de Bonaguil**, in the hills northwest of Puy-l'Évêque, worth the effort for its elaborate fortifications and spectacular position. From here on the Lot valley starts to get ugly and industrial, though **Villeneuve-sur-Lot** hides a surprisingly attractive old centre and provides a base for exploring the villages around. Prettiest are **Pujols**, to the south, which also boasts a number of excellent restaurants, and **Penne-d'Agenais**, overlooking the Lot to the east. **Monflanquin**, to the north of Villeneuve, is also well worth a visit for its hilltop location and almost perfect arcaded central square.

Luzech, Puy-l'Évêque and the Château de Bonaguil

Twenty kilometres downriver from Cahors you come to **LUZECH**, with scant Gaulish and Roman remains of the town of L'Impernal, and the **Chapelle de Notre-Dame-de-l'Île**, dedicated to the medieval boatmen who transported Cahors wines to Bordeaux. The town stands in a huge river loop, overlooked by a thirteenth-century keep, with some picturesque alleys and dwellings in the quarter opposite place du Canal.

Several bends in the river later – 22km by road – **PUY-L'ÉVÊQUE** is probably the prettiest village in the entire valley, with many grand houses built in honey-coloured stone and overlooked by both a **church** and the **castle** of the bishops of Cahors. The best view is from the bridge which crosses the Lot. For an overnight **stay**, the classy *Bellevue* (ⓣ05.65.36.06.60, ⓦwww.lothotel-bellevue.com; ❺; closed 2 weeks in Nov and 4 weeks in Jan/Feb), perched on the cliff edge, has stylish rooms and a good restaurant (from €25, or €12 in the brasserie; closed Sun & Mon). For something cheaper, at the bottom of the town, the *Henry* has excellent-value, a/c rooms (ⓣ05.65.21.32.24, ⓕ05.65.30.85.18; ❷), and there's a well-tended **campsite**, *Camping Les Vignes* (ⓣ05.65.30.81.72, ⓔlesvignes46700@aol.fr; closed Oct–March), 3km south by the river.

With your own transport, follow the Lot as far as Duravel and then cut across country via the picturesque hamlet of St-Martin-le-Redon to reach the **Château de Bonaguil** (Feb–May & Sept–Oct daily 11am–1pm & 2.30–5.30pm; June–Aug daily 10am–6pm; Nov Sun only 11am–1pm & 2.30–5pm; Christmas hols 2.30–5pm; €6) some 15km later. It's spectacularly perched at the end of a wooden spur commanding two valleys, about 8km northeast of Fumel. Dating largely from the fifteenth and sixteenth centuries with a double

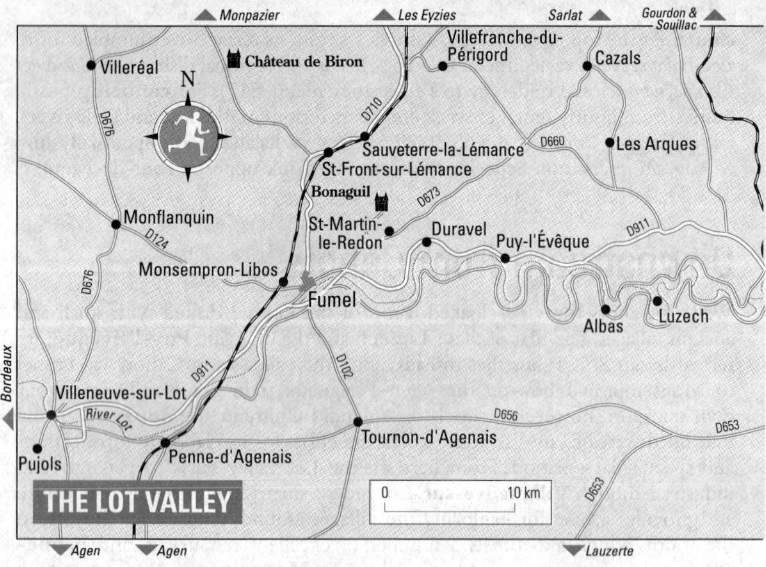

ring of walls, five huge towers and a narrow boat-shaped keep designed to resist artillery, it was the last of a dying breed, completed just when military architects were abandoning such elaborate fortifications.

Villeneuve-sur-Lot and around

VILLENEUVE-SUR-LOT, 75km west and downstream from Cahors, is a pleasant, workaday sort of town but otherwise does not have a great deal to commend it: there are no very interesting sights, though the handful of attractive timbered houses in the old town and the arcaded central square go some way to compensate. If you're reliant on public transport note that there's no train station in Villeneuve itself, but SNCF runs regular bus services to Agen, which is on the Bordeaux–Toulouse line.

The town's most striking landmark is the red-brick tower of the **church of Ste-Catherine**, completed as late as 1937 in typically dramatic neo-Byzantine style, but rather unusually built on a north–south axis; inside, the church retains some attractive stained glass from the previous fourteenth-century building. In the streets around the main square, **place La Fayette**, a couple of towers alone survive from the fortifications of this originally *bastide* town, and to the south the main avenue, rue des Cieutats, crosses thirteenth-century **Pont des Cieutat**, resembling the Pont Valentré in Cahors but devoid of its towers.

The **tourist office**, 3 place de la Libération (July & Aug Mon–Sat 9am–12.30pm & 2–7pm, Sun 10am–1pm; Sept–June Mon–Sat 9am–noon & 2–6pm; Ⓣ05.53.36.17.30, Ⓦwww.tourisme-villeneuve-sur-lot.com), lies just outside the town's northern gate. The best place to look for **accommodation** is around the former train station, now the **gare routière**, five minutes' walk south of centre, where the friendly *La Résidence*, 17 av Lazare-Carnot (Ⓣ05.53.40.17.03, Ⓔhotel.laresidence@wanadoo.fr; ❶–❸; closed 15 days in Nov), offers unbeatable value for money. Closer to the centre, *Les Platanes*, 40 bd de la Marine (Ⓣ05.53.40.11.40,Ⓦwww.hoteldesplatanes.com; ❸; restaurant from €13), offers attractive, individually decorated rooms. For campers, there's

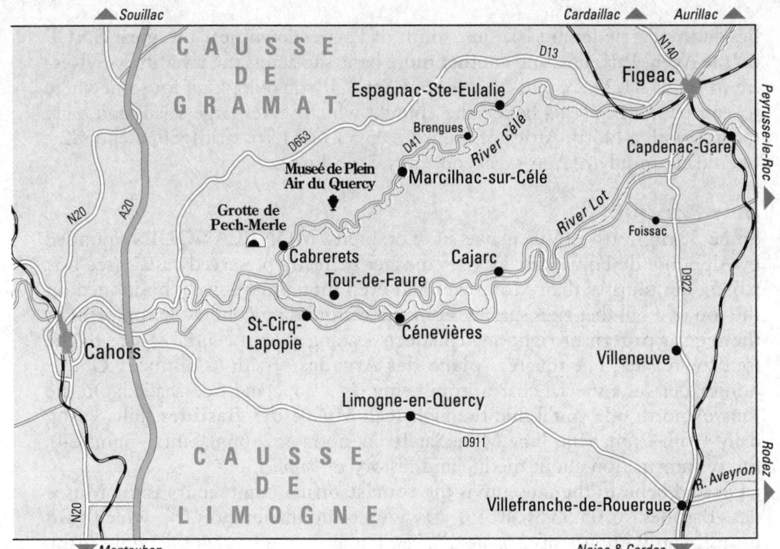

the *Camping du Rooy*, signed off the Agen road 1.5km south of the centre (☎05.53.70.24.18; mid-April to Sept).

When it comes to **eating**, *Chez Câline* in rue Notre-Dame (☎05.53.70.42.08; closed Sun; menus from €15.50), near the Pont des Cieutat, is a pretty little place offering traditional cuisine, with a tiny balcony jutting out over the river. Otherwise you could try *L'Entracte* at 30 bd de la Marine (closed Wed & Thurs; menus from €19), where you can sit out under the plane trees. The nearby *La Galerie*, 38 bd de la Marine (☎05.53.71.52.12; closed Mon & Tues), is the place to go for a bit more luxury and classic cuisine; menus start at €14. Alternatively, head south to Pujols (see below).

Pujols and Penne-d'Agenais

Three kilometres south of Villeneuve the tiny hilltop village of **PUJOLS** makes a popular excursion, partly to see the faded Romanesque frescoes in the **church of Ste-Foy** and partly for the views over the surrounding country. But the main reason locals come here is for the quality of its **restaurants**. Top of the list is the excellent but expensive *La Toque Blanche* (☎05.53.49.00.30, Ⓦwww.la-toque-blanche.com; closed Sun eve, Mon & Tues eve; menus €25–78), just south of Pujols with views back to the village. The panorama is even better, however, from their less formal outlet, *Lou Calel*, overlooking the Lot valley in Pujols itself, where you can sample some beautifully cooked traditional but light menus (☎05.53.70.46.14; closed Tues eve, Wed & lunch Thurs; menus from €18).

Another side trip could be to the beautiful but touristy old fortress town of **PENNE-D'AGENAIS**, 8km upstream on a steep hill also on the south bank of the Lot, with remains of a thirteenth-century castle teetering on a cliff edge. The **tourist office**, in rue du 14-Juillet just inside the old town gate (June–Sept Mon–Sat 9am–12.30pm & 2–7pm, Sun 2–7pm; Oct–May Mon–Sat 9am–12.30pm & 2–6pm, Sun 2–6pm; ☎05.53.41.37.80, Ⓦwww.penne-tourisme.com), can supply comprehensive lists of B&Bs and *gîtes* in the area. There's a good municipal **campsite** (☎05.53.41.30.97; mid-June to Aug) beside the Ferrié leisure lake just south of Penne, down near the **gare SNCF** on the Agen–Paris line, and another more basic site across the river in St-Sylvestre (Ⓣ05.53.41.22.23; mid-May to mid-Sept). If you're looking for somewhere to **eat**, try *Le Bombecul*, beside the church, which serves large salads and daily specials with a North African flavour (Ⓣ05.53.71.11.76; salads €9, menu €20; open daily in July & Aug, weekends only Sept–June).

Monflanquin

Some 30km north of Villeneuve-sur-Lot, pretty **MONFLANQUIN**, founded by Alphonse de Poitiers in 1256, is another perfectly preserved *bastide* (see box p.695), less touristy than Monpazier and even more impressively positioned on the top of a hill that rises sharply from the surrounding country. It conforms to the regular pattern of right-angled streets leading from a central square to the four town gates. The square – **place des Arcades** – with its distinctly Gothic houses, derives a special charm from being on a slope and tree-shaded. On the square's north side you'll find the high-tech **Musée des Bastides** (July & Aug daily 10am–7pm; Sept–June Mon–Sat 10am–noon & 2–6pm, Sun 3–5pm; €4), full of information about the life and history of *bastides*.

Located beneath the museum is the **tourist office** (same hours as the Musée des Bastides; Ⓣ05.53.36.40.19, Ⓦwww.cc-monflanquinois.fr), which can furnish you with lists of *chambres d'hôtes*. The best hotel in Monflanquin is the modern and slightly soulless *Monform*, just west of town (Ⓣ05.53.49.85.85, Ⓦwww.espace-forme-47.com; ❸; closed Feb), which doubles as a health centre with heated pool, sauna and gym. **Campers** are better served by the four-star *Camping des Bastides* (Ⓣ05.53.40.83.09, Ⓦwww.campingdesbastides.com; May–Aug), 10km east of Monflanquin, near the village of Salles. If you're looking for somewhere to eat, try one of the **cafés** and **restaurants** on place des Arcades: the *Bistrot du Prince Noir* (open daily July & Aug; Sept–June closed Tues & Wed; lunch menus from €12, evenings from €25) offers traditional dishes and more unusual specialities like chicken with caramelized raisins.

Figeac and around

FIGEAC lies on the River Célé, 71km east of Cahors and some 8km north of the Lot. It's a beautiful town with an unspoilt medieval centre not too encumbered by tourism. Like many other provincial towns hereabouts, it owes its beginnings to the foundation of an abbey in the early days of Christianity in France, one which quickly became wealthy because of its position on the pilgrim routes to both Rocamadour and Compostela. In the Middle Ages it became a centre of tanning, which partly accounts for the many houses whose top floors have *solelhos*, or open-sided wooden galleries used for drying skins and other produce. Again, as so often, it was the Wars of Religion that pushed it into eclipse, for Figeac threw in its lot with the nearby Protestant stronghold of Montauban and suffered the same punishing reprisals by the victorious royalists in 1662.

Roads and train line both funnel you automatically into the town centre, where the **Hôtel de la Monnaie** surveys place Vival. It's a splendid building whose origins go back to the thirteenth century, when the city's mint was located in this district. In the streets radiating off to the north of the square – Caviale, République, Gambetta and their cross-streets – there's a delightful range of houses of the medieval and classical periods, both stone and half-timbered with brick noggings, adorned with carvings and colonnettes, ogees, and interesting bits of ironwork. At the end of these streets are the two small squares of **place Carnot** and **place Champollion**, both of great charm. The former is the site of the old *halles*, under whose awning cafés now spread their tables.

Jean-François Champollion, who cracked Egyptian hieroglyphics by deciphering the triple text of the Rosetta Stone, was born in a house at 4 impasse Champollion, off the square, and the building now houses a **museum** dedicated to his life and work. At the time of writing, the museum was being extended to include coverage of ancient and modern alphabets from all over the world. Nearby, a larger-than-life reproduction of the Rosetta Stone forms the floor of the tiny **place des Écritures**, above which is a little garden planted with tufts of papyrus.

On the other side of place Champollion, rue Boutaric leads up to the cedar-shaded **church of Notre-Dame-du-Puy**, from where you get views over the roofs of the town. More interesting is the **church of St-Sauveur** off place des Herbes near the tourist office, with its lovely Gothic chapterhouse decorated with heavily gilded but dramatically realistic seventeenth-century carved wood panels illustrating the life of Christ.

Practicalities

The **gare SNCF** is a few minutes' walk to the south of place Vival across the river at the end of rue de la Gare and avenue des Poilus. SNCF **buses** leave from the train station, and others from the **gare routière** on avenue Maréchal-Joffre, a few minutes' walk west of place Vival. You'll find the **tourist office** in the Hôtel de la Monnaie on place Vival (May, June & Sept Mon–Sat 10am–12.30pm & 2.30–6pm, Sun 10am–1pm; July & Aug daily 10am–7.30pm; Oct–April Mon–Sat 10am–noon & 2.30–6pm; ⓣ05.65.34.06.25, ⓦwww.tourisme-figeac.com). For an **Internet** connection, the most reliable place is Dragoon at 1 av Émile-Bouyssou (closed Sun & Mon), south of the river.

Figeac boasts some excellent **restaurants**. *La Table de Marinette*, south of the river at 51 allées Victor-Hugo, has a well-deserved reputation for its traditional Quercy dishes (ⓣ05.65.50.06.07; menus €16–43; closed Fri & Sat lunch, also mid-Nov to mid-Dec & two weeks in Jan), while the elegant *La Cuisine du Marché*, 15 rue Clermont, just north of St-Sauveur church, offers a select range of well-prepared local dishes in menus that range from €12 to €36 (ⓣ05.65.50.18.55; closed Sun). For a lighter meal, head for the bars, cafés and crêperies around place Carnot and place Champollion.

The tourist office can recommend *chambres d'hôtes*, and there's a well-equipped riverside **campsite**, *Les Rives du Célé* (ⓣ05.65.34.59.00, ⓦwww.domainedesurgie.com; April–Sept), just east of town, with **bike** and **canoe** rental next door.

Hotels

Des Bains 1 rue du Griffoul ⓣ05.65.34.10.89, ⓦwww.hoteldesbains.fr. In a lovely spot on the riverbank, just across from the old town. Bright, airy rooms, Internet connection and a/c. Nov–Feb closed Fri–Sun. ❸

Champollion 3 place Champollion ⓣ05.65.34.04.37, ⓕ05.65.34.61.69. As central as you can get, located above a lively bar and café. Rooms are simple, but clean and comfortable, with a/c throughout. ❸

Chateau du Viguier du Roi rue Émile-Zola ⓣ05.65.50.05.05, ⓦwww.chateau-viguier-figeac.com. Surely the most luxurious hotel in the region. Set in the buildings and gardens of a fourteenth-century château just off place Champollion, rooms have four-poster beds and all four-star comforts. There is also an amazing series of exquisite, aristocratic drawing rooms, and a small swimming pool. May–Sept only. ❾

Du Faubourg 59 faubourg du Pin, ⓣ05.65.34.21.82, ⓕ05.65.34.24.19. An excellent budget option with quiet and spotless rooms, 2min walk east of the centre. The cheapest just have a washbasin, but for a little more money you get shower, toilet and TV. ❶

Le Pont d'Or 2 av Jean-Jaurès ⓣ05.65.50.95.00, ⓦwww.hotelpontdor.com. A smart chain hotel with sauna, gym and rooftop pool. The riverside rooms also have pleasant balconies, looking across to the church of St-Sauveur. Restaurant from €11.50. ❺

Cardaillac

Home of one of the great families of Quercy in the Middle Ages, the old part of the village of **CARDAILLAC**, about 10km to the north of Figeac off the N140, is gathered on the tip of a steep ridge above wild wooded valleys, an organic pile of houses, primitive machinery and crumbling fortifications of such antiquity you wonder how they're still there. The village has created what they call a **musée éclaté**, consisting of a tour of several old houses, giving an insight into the lifestyle and practices of yore, like bread-making, drying chestnuts and preparing prunes (tours in French daily except Sat: July 1–13 & Aug 26–Sept 15 3pm; July 14–Aug 25 3pm & 4.30pm; Sept 16–June by appointment on ⓣ05.65.40.10.63 or 05.65.40.15.65; donation expected). A handful of tours are offered in English in summer – check times at Figeac's tourist office, or phone the *musée* itself. An additional plus point to Cardaillac is the delightfully simple **hotel** *Chez Marcel*, on the through road (ⓣ05.65.40.11.16, ⓕ05.65.40.49.08; ❶; closed Sun–Thurs Jan–March, also closed two weeks in Oct), with a first-rate **restaurant** which works with locally grown produce to offer such delights as duck breast in a raspberry and honey sauce (menus from €13; closed Sun eve & Mon). They also run a *boutique* next door, where you can sample and purchase all manner of local specialities from small-scale producers.

Foissac and Peyrusse-le-Roc

Coming out of Figeac on the road to Villefranche-de-Rouerge, keep an eye out on the right for one of the **aiguilles**, or stone needles, that used to ring Figeac. They are 8m high and date from the 1100s; no one knows whether they were milestones, boundary markers for the abbey, or something completely different.

Some 20km further south, and west of the road to Villeneuve, is the village of **FOISSAC**, which has given its name to a local **cave** (April, May & Oct daily except Sat 2–6pm; June & Sept daily 10–11.30am & 2–6pm; July & Aug daily 10am–6pm; €7.20; ⓦwww.grotte-de-foissac.com). In addition to a variety of weird and wonderful formations, you'll see an unusual prehistoric **potter's workshop** dating from about 4000 BC.

To the east of Foissac, about 20km by a beautiful lane across the *causse*, you happen upon one of the most remarkable old villages in this corner of France, **PEYRUSSE-LE-ROC**. The "modern" village sits astride a ridge above a narrow wooded valley: a tiny huddle of long-eaved, half-timbered houses gathered round a seventeenth-century church. On the slopes below, hidden in the steep woods, lie the remains of a medieval stronghold, abandoned around 1700, that once stood guard over the silver-rich country round about, and which has only recently begun to be excavated. Cobbled paths connect the ruins of a Gothic church, a synagogue and a hospital, while a vertiginous ladder gives access to the twin towers of the old fort. The site is gradually being tidied up and some of the buildings restored, but for the moment at least, it remains a moving and atmospheric place.

The valley of the Célé

For the last stretch of its course from Figeac to Conduché, where it joins the Lot, the **River Célé** flows through a luxuriant canyon-like valley cut into the limestone uplands of the Causse de Gramat. A twisting minor road follows the river here: a silent backwater of a place, hot in summer, frequented mainly by canoeists (with any number of opportunities to rent craft). The **GR651** follows the same route, sometimes close to the river, sometimes on the edge of the *causse* on the north bank.

Espagnac-Ste-Eulalie and Marcilhac-sur-Célé

Travelling downstream from Figeac, two villages in particular are worth a stop. The first is **ESPAGNAC-STE-EULALIE**, about 18km west of Figeac. It's a tiny and beautiful hamlet reached across an old stone bridge on the south bank of the river, under the limestone outcrops of the *causse*. An eye-catching octagonal lantern crowns the belfry of the **church** (guided visits: daily 10.30am, 4pm & 5.30pm by appointment, call Mme Bonzani on ⓣ05.65.40.06.17; €2), and under a weathered tower next door, an ancient gateway now houses a *gîte d'étape* (ⓣ05.65.11.42.66; closed early Nov to Feb). There are two quiet riverside **campsites** in the next hamlet, **Brengues**: *Le Moulin Vieux* (ⓣ05.65.40.00.41, ⓔblasquez.a@wanadoo.fr; April–Sept), and the smaller municipal site (ⓣ05.65.40.06.82, ⓕ05.65.40.05.71; May–Sept).

The second village of real interest is **MARCILHAC-SUR-CÉLÉ**, 9km downstream of Brengues, whose partially ruined **abbey** (visits possible 1.30–5pm; call ⓣ05.65.40.65.52 to arrange one; €3), with its gaping walls and broken columns, conjures a strongly romantic atmosphere. Very early and rather primitive ninth-century Carolingian sculpture decorates the lintel, and there are some handsome Romanesque capitals in the chapterhouse. In the damp interior are frescoes from around 1500 and old coats of arms of the local nobility, testimony to Marcilhac's once mighty power, when even Rocamadour was under its sway. During World War II, it was the scene of one of the maquis' first theatrical gestures of turning the tables on the occupier: on November 11, 1943 – Armistice Day – Jean-Jacques Chapou's group (see p.736) briefly occupied the village and laid a wreath at the war memorial.

There's a *gîte d'étape* in the abbey (ⓣ05.65.40.61.43, ⓔsecretariat.mairie-de-marcilhac@wanadoo.fr; closed Nov–April), as well as the *Pré de Monsieur* **campsite** just outside the village (ⓣ & ⓕ05.65.40.77.88; April to mid-Oct).

Musée de Plein Air du Quercy

Set back from the north side of the River Célé, about 13km from Marcilhac, near **Cuzals**, the **Musée de Plein Air du Quercy** (May, June & Sept Wed–Sun 2–6pm; July & Aug daily 11am–7pm; €4; ⓦwww.patrimoine-lot.com) is one of the better open-air museums, and was set up in the 1980s to preserve the distinctive rural architecture of France. Reconstructions that range from a half-timbered eighteenth-century farmhouse to a garage from the 1920s are scattered around the site, which is centred around a twentieth-century château burnt down by the Nazis in the last war. It's best on Sundays in summer (June–Aug), when many traditional activities like milling, haymaking and blacksmithing are demonstrated. The information is dished out with an appealing blend of humour and didactics, and the whole place is less blatantly commercial than many other *écomusées*.

Grotte de Pech-Merle

Discovered in 1922, the **Grotte de Pech-Merle** (mid-Jan to March and Nov to mid-Dec by group reservation only; April–Oct daily 9.30am–noon &

1.30–5pm; ⓣ05.65.31.27.05, ⓦwww.pechmerle.com; €7) is less accessible than the caves at Les Eyzies but still attracts sufficient visitors to warrant restricting numbers to 700 per day; it's advisable to book at least three or four days ahead in July and August. The cave is well hidden on the scrubby hillsides above Cabrerets, which lies 15km from Marcilhac and 4km from Conduché. The cave itself is far more beautiful than those at Padirac or Les Eyzies, with galleries full of the most spectacular stalactites and stalagmites – structures tiered like wedding cakes, hanging like curtains, or shaped like whale baffles, discs or cave pearls. On the downside, the cave is wired for electric light and the guides make sure you're processed through in the scheduled time.

The first **drawings** you come to are in the so-called Chapelle des Mammouths, executed on a white calcite panel that looks as if it's been specially prepared for the purpose. There are horses, bison – charging head down with tiny rumps and arched tails – and tusked, whiskery mammoths. You then pass into a vast chamber where the glorious horse panel is visible on a lower level; it's a remarkable example of the way in which the artist used the contour and relief of the rock to do the work, producing an utterly convincing mammoth by just two strokes of black. The cave ceiling is covered with finger marks, preserved in the soft clay. You pass the skeleton of a cave hyena that has been lying there for 20,000 years – wild animals used these caves for shelter and sometimes, unable to find their way out, starved to death in them. And finally, the most spine-tingling experience at Pech-Merle: the footprints of an adolescent preserved in a muddy pool.

The admission charge includes an excellent film and **museum**, where prehistory is illustrated by colourful and intelligible charts, a selection of objects (rather than the usual 10,000 flints), skulls and beautiful slides displayed in wall panels.

There's a **campsite**, *Le Cantal* (ⓣ05.65.31.26.61, ⓕ05.65.31.20.47; May–Oct), close by at **CABRERETS**, a tiny place which also boasts a pair of two-star **hotels**: the *Auberge de la Sagne*, 1km outside the village on the road to Pech-Merle (ⓣ05.65.31.26.62, ⓔhotel.auberge.cabrerets@wanadoo.fr; ❸; closed mid-Sept to mid-May), which has a pool and a good restaurant (evening only; menus €15 & €23); and the riverside *Les Grottes* (ⓣ05.65.31.27.02, ⓦwww.hoteldesgrottes.com; ❷; closed Nov–Easter), also with a decent restaurant attached (menus from €11.50).

The valley of the Aveyron

Thirty-seven kilometres south of Figeac, **Villefranche-de-Rouergue** lies on a bend in the River Aveyron, clustered around its perfectly preserved, arcaded market square. From Villefranche the Aveyron flows south through increasingly deep, thickly wooded valleys, past the hilltop village of **Najac** and then turns abruptly west as it enters the **Gorges de l'Aveyron**. The most impressive stretch of this defile begins not far east of **St-Antonin-de-Noble-Val**, an ancient village caught between soaring limestone cliffs, and continues downstream to the villages of **Penne** and **Bruniquel**, perched beside their crumbling castles. Bruniquel marks the end of the gorges, as you suddenly break out into flat alluvial plains where the Aveyron joins the great rivers of the Tarn and Garonne.

Villefranche-de-Rouergue

No medieval junketing, not a craft shop in sight, **VILLEFRANCHE-DE-ROUERGUE** must be as close as you can get to what a French provincial town used to be like, though it is now starting to feature on more tourists' itineraries. It's a small town, lying on a bend in the Aveyron, 35km due south of Figeac and 61km east of Cahors across the **Causse de Limogne**. Built as a *bastide* by Alphonse de Poitiers in 1252 as part of the royal policy of extending control over the recalcitrant lands of the south, the town became rich on copper from the surrounding mines and its privilege of minting coins. From the fifteenth to the eighteenth centuries, its wealthy men built the magnificent houses that grace the cobbled streets to this day.

Rue du Sergent-Bories and rue de la République, the main commercial street, are both very attractive, but they are no preparation for **place Notre-Dame**, the loveliest *bastide* central square in the region. It's built on a slope, so the uphill houses are much higher than the downhill, and you enter at the corners underneath the buildings. All the houses are arcaded at ground-floor level, providing for a **market** (Thurs morning) where local merchants and farmers spread out their weekly produce – the quintessential Villefranche experience. The houses are unusually tall and some are very elaborately decorated, notably the so-called **Maison du Président Raynal** on the lower side at the top of rue de la République.

The east side of the square is dominated by the **church of Notre-Dame** with its colossal porch and bell tower, nearly 60m high. The interior has some fine late fifteenth-century stained glass, carved choir stalls and misericords.

On the boulevard that forms the northern limit of the old town, the seventeenth-century **Chapelle des Pénitents-Noirs** (July–Sept daily 10am–noon & 2–6pm; €3.50) boasts a splendidly Baroque painted ceiling and an enormous gilded retable. Another ecclesiastical building worth the slight detour is the **Chartreuse St-Sauveur** (same hours; €3.50), about 1km out of town on the Gaillac road. It was completed in the space of ten years from 1450, giving it a singular architectural harmony, and has a very beautiful cloister and choir stalls by the same master as Notre-Dame in Villefranche, which, by contrast, took nearly 300 years to complete.

Aside from the pleasing details of many of the houses you notice as you explore the side streets, the town reserves one other most unexpected surprise. The **Médiathèque**, on rue Sénéchal, includes an amazing collection of jazz records, books, papers, recordings and documents belonging to the late Hugues Panassié, famous French jazz critic and one of the founders of the Hot Club de France. Much of the material is unrecorded or unobtainable elsewhere; if you ring ahead (ⓣ05.65.81.27.36) you can peruse it and get some expert insights from the current curator.

Practicalities

The **gare SNCF** is located a couple of minutes' walk south across the Aveyron from the old town. For information about buses, contact the **tourist office** just north of the river on promenade du Guiraudet (May–June & Sept Mon–Fri 9am–noon & 2–7pm, Sat 9am–noon & 2–6pm; July & Aug also open Sun 10am–12.30pm; Oct–April Mon–Fri 9am–noon & 2–6pm, Sat 9am–noon; ⓣ05.65.45.13.18, ⓦwww.villefranche.com), beside the bridge. They also lay on guided tours of the town in summer, and can provide you with an audio-guide out of season.

The best **hotels** in town are *L'Univers*, 2 place de la République at the end of the bridge opposite the tourist office (ⓣ05.65.45.15.63, ⓔuniverhotel bourdy@wanadoo.fr; ❸; restaurant from €16), which has slightly dated but classically French decor, complete with acquired-taste wallpaper; and, nearby, the more modest *Bellevue*, 3 av du Ségala (ⓣ05.65.45.23.17, ⓕ05.65.45.11.19; ❷;

closed school hols in Feb & Nov, also Sun & Mon out of season), with a highly rated restaurant (menus €14–32). In a rather unpromising location, 3km out on the Figeac road, *Le Relais de Farrou* (Ⓣ05.65.45.18.11, Ⓦwww.relaisdefarrou.com; ③–④; restaurant from €15) offers more luxurious surroundings and good food. For cheaper accommodation, there's an excellent *Foyer de Jeunes Travailleurs* **HI hostel** (Ⓣ05.65.45.09.68, Ⓔfjt.villefranche@wanadoo.fr), next to the *gare SNCF*. There's also a *gîte d'étape* by the river at La Gasse (Ⓣ05.65.45.10.80; closed Nov–April), 3km out of town on the D269 back road to La Bastide-L'Évêque, at the start of GR62b, plus a **campsite**, the *Camping du Rouergue* (Ⓣ05.65.45.16.24, Ⓦwww.villefranche.com/camping; mid-April to Sept), 1.5km to the south on the D47 to Monteil.

For **eating**, the *Globe*, a bustling modern brasserie across the river from the tourist office, has a good range of dishes from around €8–10. For more refined cuisine, try *L'Epicurien* (Ⓣ05.65.45.01.12; menus €14–37), avenue Raymond-St-Gilles opposite the *Bellevue*, which is highly praised by the locals.

Najac

NAJAC occupies an extraordinary site on a conical hill isolated in a wide bend in the deep valley of the Aveyron, 25km south of Villefranche-de-Rouergue and on the Aurillac–Toulouse train line. Its photogenic castle, which graces many a travel poster, sits right on the peak of the hill, while the half-timbered and stone-tiled village houses tail out in a single street along the narrow back of the spur that joins the hill to the valley side.

The **château** (April, May & Sept daily 10am–12.30pm & 3–5.30pm; June daily 10am–12.30pm & 3–6.30pm; July & Aug daily 10am–1pm & 3–7pm; Oct Sun only 10am–12.30pm & 3–5.30pm; last entry 30min before closing; €4) is a model of medieval defensive architecture and was endlessly fought over because of its commanding and impregnable position in a region once rich in silver and copper mines. You can clearly see all the devices for restricting an attacker once he was inside the castle: the covered passages and stairs within the thickness of the walls, the multistorey positions for archers and, of course, the most magnificent all-round view from the top of the keep. In one of the chambers of the keep you can see the stone portraits of St Louis, king of France, his brother Alphonse de Poitiers and Jeanne, the daughter of the count of Toulouse, whose marriage to Alphonse was arranged in 1229 to end the Cathar wars by bringing the domains of Count Raymond and his allies under royal control. It was Alphonse who "modernized" the castle and made the place we see today – a fine model in one of the turrets shows his fortifications as they were in the castle's prime in 1253. Signatures of the masons who worked here are clearly visible on many stones.

Below the rather dull central square stretches the **faubourg**, a sort of elongated square bordered by houses raised on pillars as in the central square of a *bastide*, which reduces to a narrow waist of a street overlooked by more ancient houses and leading past a fountain to the castle gate. At the foot of the castle, in the centre of what was the medieval village, stands the very solid-looking **church of St-Jean** (daily 10am–noon & 2–6pm; free), which the villagers of Najac were forced by the Inquisition to build at their own expense in 1258 as a punishment for their conversion to Catharism. In addition to a collection of reliquaries and an extraordinary iron cage for holding candles, the church has one architectural oddity: its windows are solid panels of stone from which the lights have been cut out in trefoil form. Below the church, by a derelict farm, a surviving stretch of **Roman road** leads downhill to where a thirteenth-century bridge spans the Aveyron.

The **tourist office** is on the faubourg (April–June & Sept Mon–Sat 9am–noon & 2.30–6pm; July & Aug Mon–Sat 9am–noon & 2–6.30pm, Sun 10am–noon; Oct–March Mon–Fri 9am–noon & 2.30–6pm, Sat 9am–noon; ⓣ05.65.29.72.05). At the eastern entrance to the faubourg, you'll find a very comfortable **hotel**, *L'Oustal del Barry* (ⓣ05.65.29.74.32, ⓦwww.oustaldelbarry.com; ❺; closed mid-Nov to March), whose restaurant is renowned for its subtle and inventive cuisine (closed Mon & Tues lunch except July & Aug; menus €15–40). Below Najac is a four-star **campsite**, *Le Païsserou* (ⓣ05.65.29.73.96, or 02.40.82.41.48 off season, ⓔcledelles.najac@wanadoo.fr; April–Sept), with a *gîte d'étape* (same contact details; open all year).

St-Antonin-Noble-Val

One of the finest and most substantial towns in the valley is **ST-ANTONIN-NOBLE-VAL**, 30km southwest of Najac. It sits on the bank of the Aveyron beneath the beetling cliffs of the Roc d'Anglars, and has endured all the vicissitudes of the old towns of the southwest: it went Cathar, then Protestant and each time was walloped by the alien power of the kings from the north. Yet, in spite of all this, it recovered its prosperity, manufacturing cloth and leather goods, endowed by its wealthy merchants with a marvellous heritage of medieval houses in all the streets leading out from the lovely **place de la Halle**.

There's a café most conveniently and picturesquely placed next to the ancient *halle*, with a view of the town's finest building, the **Maison des Consuls**, whose origins go back to 1120. It now houses the town museum, **Musée du Vieux St-Antonin** (July & Aug daily except Tues 10am–1pm & 3–6pm; Sept–June apply to the tourist office; €2.50), with collections of objects to do with the former life of the place, as well as a section on local prehistoric sites.

The **tourist office** is in the "new" town hall next to the church (Jan & Feb Mon–Sat 2–5pm; March–June, Sept & Oct daily 10am–12.30pm & 2–5pm; July & Aug daily 9.30am–12.30pm & 2–7pm; Nov & Dec Tues–Sat 10am–12.30pm & 2–5pm; ⓣ05.63.30.63.47, ⓦwww.saint-antonin-noble-val.com), and will supply information about B&Bs, canoeing on the Aveyron and walks in the region. The only **hotel** in the village is the newly renovated *Du Commerce*, at 58 av Paul-Benet (ⓣ05.63.30.62.25; ❷) with five simple rooms and a bar, while the closest of several **camping** options is the municipal site 500m from the centre (ⓣ05.63.28.21.13; May–Sept).

Penne and Bruniquel

Twenty kilometres downstream of St-Antonin you come to the beautiful ridge-top village of **PENNE**, once a Cathar stronghold, with its ruined castle impossibly perched on an airy crag. Everything is old and leaning and bulging, but holding together nonetheless, with a harmony that would be impossible to create purposely.

BRUNIQUEL, a few kilometres further on, is another hilltop village clustered round its **castle** (daily: April–June, Sept & Oct 10am–12.30pm & 2–6pm; July & Aug 10am–7pm; €2.50, or €3.50 including guided visit; ⓦwww.bruniquel.org). You can also visit a handsome house in the village, the aristocratic **Maison des Comtes de Payrol** (April–Oct daily 10am–6pm; €3). If you want to **stay**, Marc de Badouin runs a good *chambre d'hôte* to the right of the church (ⓣ05.63.67.26.16, ⓦwww.chambres-bruniquel.fr; ❸; meals around €20); he's also a keen mountain-biker and can advise on local trails and footpaths. There's also a small two-star **campsite**, *Le Payssel* (ⓣ05.63.67.25.95, ⓔju2@free.fr; June–Sept), about 700m south on the D964 to Albi.

Montauban and around

MONTAUBAN today is a prosperous middle-sized provincial city, capital of the largely agricultural *département* of Tarn-et-Garonne. It lies on the banks of the River Tarn, 53km from Toulouse, close to its junction with the Aveyron and their joint confluence with the Garonne. It is also, conveniently, right on the main road and railway between Toulouse and Bordeaux.

The city's **history** goes back to 1144, when the count of Toulouse decided to create a *bastide* here as a bulwark against English and French royal power. In fact, it's generally regarded as the first *bastide*, the model for those rationally laid-out medieval new towns, and that plan is still clearly evident in the beautiful town centre.

Montauban has enjoyed various periods of great prosperity, as one can guess from the proliferation of fine town houses. The first followed the suppression of the Cathar heresy and the final submission of the counts of Toulouse in 1229, and was greatly enhanced by the building of the Pont-Vieux in 1335, making it the best crossing-point on the Tarn for miles around. The Hundred Years War did its share of damage, as did Montauban's opting for the Protestant cause in the Wars of Religion, but by the time of the Revolution it had become once more one of the richest cities in the southwest, particularly successful in the manufacture of cloth.

Arrival, information and accommodation

At Montauban's centre lies the exquisite **place Nationale**, with the cathedral five minutes' walk to the south on the unattractive **place Roosevelt** (where, if driving, you'll find the most convenient parking). From here, rue de l'Hôtel-de-Ville leads directly to the Pont-Vieux and across the river to avenue de Mayenne, at the end of which is the **gare SNCF**. There's no central *gare routière*, so you'll need to ask for bus information at the **tourist office**, on the northern corner of boulevard Midi-Pyrénées (July & Aug Mon–Sat 9.30am–6.30pm, Sun 10am–12.30pm; Sept–June Mon–Sat 9.30am–12.30pm & 2–6.30pm; Ⓣ05.63.63.60.60, Ⓦwww.montauban-tourisme.com). **Internet** access is available at Difintel Micro, 4 rue de la République, and **car rental** near the station at Europcar, 21 rue Salengro (Ⓣ05.63.20.29.00).

Montauban has a limited choice of **hotels**. The best deal is the attractive *Du Commerce*, 9 place Roosevelt (Ⓣ05.63.66.31.32, Ⓦwww.hotel-commerce-montauban.com; ❸), near the cathedral. Meanwhile the *Mercure*, opposite at 12 rue Notre-Dame (Ⓣ05.63.63.17.23, Ⓦwww.mercure.com; ❻; restaurant from €14), offers larger rooms and greater comfort, but has less character. A cheaper stay is possible out by the station at the dingy but adequate *Le Lion* d'Or (Ⓣ05.63.20.04.04, Ⓕ05.63.66.77.39; closed July; ❷), which has especially cheap single rooms, and a surprisingly decent restaurant (closed weekends; menus from €13.50).

The Town

Montauban couldn't be easier to find your way around. The greatest delight is simply to wander the streets of the city centre, with their lovely pink brick houses; the town is only a ten- or fifteen-minute stroll from end to end. The visitable part is the small kernel of central streets based on the original *bastide*, and is enclosed within an inner ring of boulevards between boulevard Midi-Pyrénées on the east and the river on the west. The finest point of all is the **place Nationale**, rebuilt after a fire in the seventeenth century and surrounded on all sides by exquisite double-vaulted arcades with the octagonal belfry of

St-Jacques showing above the western rooftops.

The adjacent **place du Coq** on rue de la République is also pretty, and if you follow the street down it brings you out by the **church of St-Jacques** (first built in the thirteenth century on the pilgrim route to Compostela) and the end of the **Pont-Vieux** with a wide view of the river. At the near end of the bridge, the former bishop's residence is a massive half-palace, half-fortress, begun by the Black Prince in 1363 but never finished because the English lost control of the town. It's now the **Musée Ingres** (July & Aug daily 10am–6pm; Sept–June Tues–Sat 10am–noon & 2–6pm, Sun 2–6pm; €6), so called because it houses drawings and paintings that artist Jean-Auguste-Dominique Ingres, a native of Montauban, left to the city on his death. It's a collection the city is very proud of, though his supremely realistic, luminous portraits won't be to everyone's taste. The museum also contains a substantial collection of sculptures by another native, Émile-Antoine Bourdelle, and hosts special exhibitions every summer.

The **Cathédrale Notre-Dame**, ten minutes' walk up rue de l'Hôtel-de-Ville, is a cold fish: an austere and unsympathetic building erected just before 1700 as part of the triumphalist campaign to reassert the glories of the Catholic faith after the cruel defeat and repression of the Protestants. Apart from being a rare example of a French cathedral built in the classical style, its most interesting features are the statues of the four evangelists which triumphantly adorn the facade. Those on show now are recent copies, but the weather-beaten originals can be seen just inside.

Eating and drinking

The **place Nationale** is the hub of all Montauban's evening life, but there are many good possibilities in the streets nearby.

Restaurants and bars

Bistro du Faubourg 111 faubourg Lacapelle ⓣ05.63.63.49.89. An excellent-value, old fashioned place with lunch menus from €12. Closed Sat & Sun.

Brasserie des Arts 4 place Nationale ⓣ05.63.20.20.90. One of the best spots on the central square. Tables are out under the colonnades and *plats du jour* are around €7.50, as are various pizza and pasta dishes.

Le Couvert des Drapiers 27 place Nationale ⓣ05.63.92.91.03. Great location, offering standard brasserie fare, with well-priced omelettes, large salads and an evening menu for €18. Closed Mon eve.

Le Flamand 8 rue de la République. With over 80 bottled beers and a long list of cocktails, there should be something to suit everybody's palate here. There's also a brasserie at lunch and dinner. Closed Sun.

Le Raymond 5 place Maréchal-Foch. A popular place to eat at lunchtime, with decent portions for €6. Come the evening, though, the food stops and there's music until 2am.

Le Santa Maria 2 square Léon-Bourjade ⓣ05.63.91.99.09. Owned by a former Russian rugby captain, this is a truly multicultural place. While specializing in their house paella and Mexican tapas, they also have an astonishing selection of vodkas. There's a great atmosphere, with Latino tunes until 2am, when the nightclub opens downstairs. Closed Sun & Mon.

Les Saveurs d'Ingres 13 rue de l'Hôtel de Ville ⓣ05.63.91.26.42. A small, simple interior masks the highly sophisticated dishes on offer, like salmon smoked over vine clippings. Menus €23–45, closed Sun & Mon.

Le Ventadour 23 quai Villebourbon ⓣ05.63.63.34.58. Magnificently sited in an old house on the riverbank, the ceiling is vaulted with the same pink brick as the Pont-Vieux outside. The food is good too, with pigeon and lobster on offer, as well as the ubiquitous duck. Closed Sat lunch, Sun & Mon.

Lauzerte

As you head north from Montauban towards Cahors, leaving the wide flat valleys of the Tarn and Garonne behind you, the land rises gradually to gently undulating country, green and woody, cut obliquely by parallel valleys running down to meet the Garonne and planted with vines and sunflowers, maize, and apple and plum orchards. It's a very soft landscape, and villages are small and widely scattered. The pace of life seems about equal with that of a turning sunflower.

Should you find yourself taking this route, then the place to make a halt is **LAUZERTE**, one of Raymond of Toulouse's *bastides* and once of great military importance as it commanded the road to Cahors. The town is short on sights, but there are some old houses, a pretty arcaded central square and a good Baroque altarpiece in the church, as well as views of the countryside round about.

You'll find a very pleasant **hotel** at the entrance to the village: *Le Quercy* (Ⓣ05.63.94.66.36, Ⓕ05.63.39.06.56; ❷; closed Sun eve & Mon), which also serves superb food, with lunch menus from €10.50 and dinner from €25. There's also a **campsite** nearby, *Le Melvin* (Ⓣ & Ⓕ05.63.94.75.60; May–Oct), and a *gîte d'étape* in the village for walkers on the GR65 (Ⓣ05.63.94.61.94, Ⓔlauzerte.tourisme@quercy-blanc.net; open March–Oct).

Moissac

There's nothing very memorable about the modern town of **MOISSAC**, 30km northwest of Montauban, largely because of the terrible damage done by the flood of March 1930, when the Tarn, swollen by a sudden thaw in the Massif Central, burst its banks, destroying 617 houses and killing 120 people.

Luckily, the one thing that makes Moissac a household name in the history of art survived: the cloister and porch of the **abbey church of St-Pierre**, a

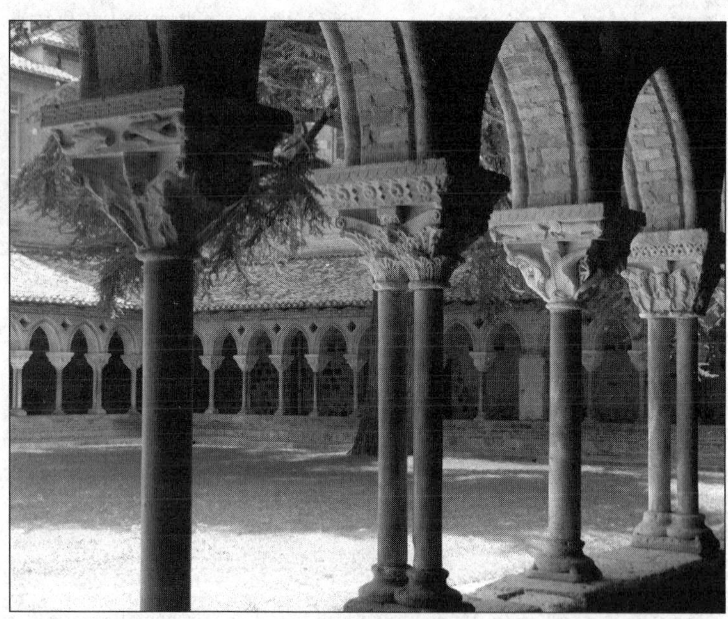

△ Cloister, abbey church of St-Pierre, Moissac

masterpiece of Romanesque sculpture and the model for hundreds of churches and buildings elsewhere. Indeed, the fact that it has survived countless wars, including siege and sack by Simon de Montfort senior in 1212 during the crusade against the Cathars, is something of a miracle. During the Revolution it was used as a gunpowder factory and billet for soldiers, who damaged many of the sculptures. In the 1830s it only escaped demolition to make way for the Bordeaux–Toulouse train line by a whisker.

Legend has it that Clovis the Frank first founded a monastery here, though it seems more probable that its origins belong a hundred years or so later in the seventh century, which saw the foundation of so many monasteries throughout Aquitaine. The first Romanesque church on the site was consecrated in 1063 and enlarged in the following century. The famous south **porch**, with its magnificent tympanum and curious wavy door jambs and pillars, dates from this second phase of building, and its influence can be seen in the decoration of porches on countless churches across the south of France. It depicts Christ in Majesty, right hand raised in benediction, the Book of Life in his hand, surrounded by the evangelists and the elders of the Apocalypse as described by St John in the Book of Revelation. There's more fine carving in the capitals inside the porch, and the interior of the church, which was remodelled in the fifteenth century, is interesting too, especially for some of the wood and stone statuary it contains.

The adjoining **cloister** (same hours as tourist office – see below; €5) is entered through the tourist office, and is most peaceful first thing in the morning. The cloister surrounds a garden shaded by a majestic cedar, and its pantile roof is supported by 76 alternating single and double marble columns. Each column supports a single inverted wedge-shaped block of stone, on which are carved with extraordinary delicacy all manner of animals and plant motifs, as well as scenes from Bible stories and the lives of the saints. An inscription on the middle pillar on the west side explains that the cloister was made in the time of Abbot Ansquitil in the year of Our Lord 1100.

Practicalities

The **tourist office** (April–June, Sept & Oct Mon–Fri 9am–noon & 2–6pm, Sat & Sun 10am–noon & 2–6pm; July & Aug daily 9am–7pm; Nov–March Mon–Fri 10am–noon & 2–5pm, Sat & Sun 2–5pm; ⓣ05.63.04.01.85, ⓦwww.moissac.fr) is next to the cloister, with the **gare SNCF** further west along avenue Pierre-Chabrié. There's a weekend **market** in place des Récollets at the end of rue de la République, which leads away from the abbey, a marvel of colour and temptation.

The *Moulin de Moissac* (ⓣ05.63.32.88.88, ⓦwww.lemoulindemoissac.com; ❹; restaurant from €28), occupying a former mill on the riverfront, rates as the top **hotel** in town; the building is large and not particularly attractive, but the interior has been beautifully refurbished. Between the river and the abbey church, *Le Chapon Fin* on place des Récollets (ⓣ05.63.04.04.22, ⓦwww.lechaponfin-moissac.com; ❹) also makes a pleasant place to stay, with a stylish restaurant from €20. For **campers**, there's a shady site across the river on a little island, the *Île du Bidounet* (ⓣ05.63.32.52.52, ⓔcamping-bidounet@moissac.fr; April–Sept), and for walkers a *gîte d'étape* at 5 sente du Calvaire (ⓣ05.63.04.62.21, ⓔaccueil.cafmoissac@wanadoo.fr) on the hill above town. The nicest **place to eat** is the magnolia-shaded *Auberge du Cloître* (ⓣ05.63.04.37.50; closed Mon & eves on Wed & Sun; menus €21–25), beside the tourist office.

Agen

AGEN, capital of the Lot-et-Garonne *département*, is a more pleasant town than it first appears. It was quartered by modern boulevards in the nineteenth century in its own version of a Haussmann clean-up, and it's down these roads that you're funnelled into the town, with the result that you see nothing of interest.

The town lies on the broad, powerful River Garonne halfway between Bordeaux and Toulouse, and lived through the Middle Ages racked by war with England and internecine strife between Catholics and Protestants. But it was able to extract some advantage from disputes as it seesawed between the English and French, gaining more and more privileges of independence as the price of its loyalty – a tradition that it maintained during and after the Revolution by being staunchly republican (the churches still bear the legend: *Liberté, Fraternité, Égalité*).

Its pre-Revolutionary wealth derived from the manufacture of various kinds of cloth and its thriving port on the Garonne, which in those days was alive with river traffic. But the Industrial Revolution put paid to all of that. Agen's prosperity now is based on agriculture – in particular, its famous prunes and plums, said to have been brought back from Syria during the Crusades.

The interesting part of Agen centres on **place Goya**, where boulevard de la République, leading to the river, crosses boulevard du Président-Carnot. The main shopping area is just to the south around place Wilson and rue Garonne, a left turn at the end of which brings you to the wide place du Dr-Esquirol and an exuberant *fin-de-siècle* municipal **theatre**; opposite this is the **Musée Municipal des Beaux-Arts** (daily except Tues: May–Sept 10am–6pm; Oct–March 10am–12.30pm & 1.30–6pm; €3.80), magnificently housed in four adjacent sixteenth- and seventeeth-century mansions. The collections include a rich variety of archeological finds, Roman and medieval, and some fine paintings – among them five Goyas and a Tintoretto rediscovered in the museum basement during an inventory in 1997. Not far from the museum, in place du Bourg at the end of rue des Droits-de-l'Homme, the cute little thirteenth-century **church of Notre-Dame** is also worth a look.

South of the theatre, rue Beauville, with heavily restored but beautiful medieval houses, leads to rue Richard-Coeur-de-Lion and the **Église des Jacobins**. The barn-like interior of this big, brick Dominican church of the thirteenth century, is divided by a single centre row of pillars, very like its counterpart in Toulouse; the deconsecrated church is now an annexe of the Musée des Beaux-Arts and hosts temporary exhibitions. Beyond lie the river and the public gardens of **Le Gravier**, where a **market** is held every Saturday morning; there's a footbridge across the Garonne, from where you can see a canal bridge dating from 1839 further downstream.

Opposite place Wilson on the north side of boulevard de la République, the arcaded rue Cornières leads through to the **Cathédrale St-Caprais**, somewhat misshapen but with a finely proportioned Romanesque apse and radiating chapels still surviving. There's a piece of the original fortifications still showing in rue des Augustins close by – the **Tour du Chapelet** – dating from around 1100. Again nearby, in rue du Puits-du-Saumon, is one of the finest houses in town, the fourteenth-century **Maison du Sénéchal**, with an elaborate open loggia on the first floor.

Practicalities

From the central place Goya, boulevard du Président-Carnot leads to the **gares SNCF** and **routière**. The **tourist office** is at 107 bd Carnot (July & Aug Mon–Sat 9am–7pm, Sun 9.30am–12.30pm; Sept–June Mon–Sat 9am–12.30pm & 2–6.30pm; ⓣ05.53.47.36.09, ⓦwww.ot-agen.org).

There are several reasonable **hotel** options in Agen. Best value, though a bit out of the way, is *Des Îles* (ⓣ05.53.47.11.33, ⓕ05.53.66.19.25; ❷) at 25 rue Baudin, with nicely furnished a/c rooms. More central is the friendly, simple and spotless *Des Ambans*, 59 rue des Ambans (ⓣ05.53.66.28.60, ⓕ05.53.87.94.01; ❶), near place Goya. A more comfortable alternative, *Le Provence*, 22 cours du 14-Juillet (ⓣ05.53.47.39.11, ⓦwww.hotel-leprovence.com; ❹) has individually and attractively decorated rooms, but for four-star luxury and buckets of atmosphere, head for the *Château des Jacobins*, in an elegant nineteenth-century town house beside the Jacobins church (ⓣ05.53.47.03.31, ⓦwww.chateau-des-jacobins.com; ❻).

As far as **restaurants** are concerned, *L'Atelier*, 14 rue du Jeu-de-Paume (ⓣ05.53.87.89.22; closed Sat & Sun; menus €20–28), is the place to go for home cooking with local produce and a friendly atmosphere, though *Les Mignardises*, 40 rue Camille-Desmoulins (closed Sat lunch, Sun eve & Mon), is good value at lunchtime, with menus from €11.50. More formal is the excellent *Mariottat*, 25 rue Louis-Vivent to the south of the Jacobins church, in a nice stately house and garden (ⓣ05.53.77.99.77; closed Sun eve, Mon & lunch Sat; menus €25–60).

Travel details

Trains

Agen to: Belvès (2–4 daily; 1hr); Bordeaux (hourly; 1hr 10min–1hr 50min); Le Buisson (2–4 daily; 1hr 10min–1hr 40min); Les Eyzies (2–4 daily; 1hr 40min); Moissac (6 daily; 25min); Monsempron-Libos (6–8 daily; 40min); Montauban (12 daily; 40–50min); Périgueux (2–4 daily; 2hr–2hr 20min); Toulouse (12 daily; 1hr–1hr 20min).

Bergerac to: Bordeaux (8–12 daily; 1hr 10min–1hr 30min); Montcaret (1–3 daily; 30–40min); St-Émilion (2–5 daily; 55min); Ste-Foy-la-Grande (7–12 daily; 20min); Sarlat (3–5 daily; 1hr–1hr 30min).

Brive to: Bordeaux (1–2 daily; 2hr 15min–2hr 45min); Cahors (6–8 daily; 1hr 10min); Figeac (4–5 daily; 1hr 15min–1hr 30min); Gourdon (6 daily; 40min); Limoges (10–15 daily; 1hr–1hr 15min); Meymac (2–6 daily; 1hr 30min); Montauban (6 daily; 1hr 50min); Paris-Austerlitz (9–14 daily; 4hr–4hr 45min); Périgueux (3–5 daily; 50min–1hr); Pompadour (3 daily; 35 min); Rocamadour-Padirac (3–5 daily; 40–50min); Souillac (6–8 daily; 25min); Toulouse (5–8 daily; 2hr–2hr 30min); Uzerche (6–8 daily; 30–45min); Villefranche-de-Rouergue (1 daily; 2hr–2hr 20min).

Cahors to: Brive (8 daily; 1hr–1hr 10min); Montauban (8–10 daily; 45min); Toulouse (6–8 daily; 1hr–1hr 20min).

Figeac to: Brive (5–6 daily; 1hr 30min); Najac (4–5 daily; 1hr); Rodez (4–6 daily; 1hr 20min–2hr); Toulouse (5–7 daily; 2hr 30min); Villefranche-de-Rouergue (6 daily; 40min).

Limoges to: Angoulême (6–8 daily; 2hr); Bordeaux (4 daily; 2hr 30min); Brive (10–15 daily; 1hr–1hr 50min); Eymoutiers (4–7 daily; 45min); Meymac (3–6 daily; 1hr 40min); Nexon (10 daily; 15min); Paris-Austerlitz (10–14 daily; 3hr–3hr 30min); Périgueux (8–15 daily; 1hr–1hr 20min); Poitiers (3–5 daily; 2hr); Pompadour (1–2 daily; 1hr 10min); St-Junien (3–10 daily; 40min); St-Léonard (3–4 daily; 20min); Solignac-Le Vigen (1–3 daily; 10min); Thiviers (6–10 daily; 40–50min); Ussel (3–6 daily; 1hr 35min–2hr).

Montauban to: Agen (10–15 daily; 40–50min); Bordeaux (hourly; 1hr 30min–2hr); Moissac (2–8 daily; 20min); Toulouse (1–2 hourly; 25–35min).

Périgueux to: Agen (2–5 daily; 2hr–2hr 20min); Belvès (2–4 daily; 1hr–1hr 20min); Bordeaux (8–13 daily; 1hr–1hr 40min); Brive (3–6 daily; 50min–1hr); Le Buisson (2–6 daily; 50min); Les Eyzies

(2–6 daily; 35min); Limoges (8–10 daily; 1hr–1hr 30min); Monsempron-Libos (2–4 daily; 1hr 30min).
Sarlat to: Bergerac (4–7 daily; 1hr–1hr 30min); Bordeaux (3–6 daily; 2hr 15min); Le Buisson (4–7 daily; 30–40min); Ste-Foy-la-Grande (4–6 daily; 1hr 20min–1hr 50min).

Buses

Agen to: Auch (6–8 daily; 1hr 20min); Condom (3 daily Mon–Sat; 45min); Villeneuve-sur-Lot (5–10 daily; 45min).
Argentat to: Beaulieu-sur-Dordogne (July & Aug Mon–Sat 3 daily; 1hr 20min); Tulle (1–3 daily; 40min).
Bergerac to: Marmande (Mon–Sat 1 daily; 2hr); Villeneuve-sur-Lot (Mon–Fri 1–2 daily; 1hr 15min).
Brive to: Argentat (Mon–Sat 2–4 daily; 1hr 40min); Arnac-Pompadour (Mon–Sat 1–2 daily; 2hr); Collonges-la-Rouge (Mon–Sat 2–4 daily; 30min); Meyssac (Mon–Sat 1–4 daily; 35min); Montignac (school term Mon–Sat 1–2 daily; 1hr 30min); Sarlat (school term Mon–Sat 1 daily; 1hr 50min); Tulle (Mon–Sat 1–4 daily; 50min); Turenne (Mon–Fri 1–2 daily; 20min); Uzerche (Mon–Sat 2–4 daily; 1hr 10min–1hr 30min); Vayrac (Mon–Sat 1–2 daily; 45min).
Cahors to: Cajarc (2–6 daily; 1hr); Figeac (2–6 daily; 1hr 35min); Fumel (5–6 daily; 1hr 10min); Luzech (6 daily; 20min); Monsempron-Libos (4–6 daily; 1hr 20min); Puy-l'Évêque (4–6 daily; 45min); Tour-de-Faure (4–6 daily; 35mins).
Limoges to: Aubusson (1–3 daily; 1hr 40min); Châlus (Mon–Sat 1–2 daily; 1hr); Nexon (Mon–Sat 1–3 daily; 50min); Oradour-sur-Glane (Mon–Sat 2–5 daily; 30–40min); Rochechouart (July & Aug only, Mon–Sat 2–4 daily; 1hr 10min); St-Junien (Mon–Sat 1–4 daily; 1hr); St-Léonard (3–4 daily; 35min); Solignac (Mon–Sat 1 daily; 30min); Le Vigen (Mon–Sat 2–3 daily; 20–30min).
Périgueux to: Angoulême (Mon, Wed, Fri & Sun 1–2 daily; 1hr 45min); Bergerac (Mon–Fri 3–5 daily; 1hr–1hr 30min); Brantôme (Mon, Wed, Fri & Sun 1–2 daily; 40min); Ribérac (Mon–Fri 3–5 daily; 1hr).
Souillac to: Martel (1–3 daily; 20min); Sarlat (2–3 daily; 50min).

10

The Pyrenees

CHAPTER 10 **Highlights**

* **Cesta punta** This variant of the Basque region's favourite sport of pelota is the fastest ball-game in the world. See it most reliably in St-Jean-de-Luz. See pp.759 & 767

* **Surfing the Côte Basque** Catch a wave at Biarritz or Anglet, Europe's top destination for both boogie-boarders and classic surfers. See pp.764 & 767

* **Cauterets** Several lake-spangled valleys above this agreeable spa offer superb trekking, whether modest day-loops or more ambitious multi-day traverses. See p.797

* **The Cirque de Gavarnie** A vast alpine amphitheatre with wind-blown cascades and traces of glacier, best enjoyed off-peak when the crowds subside. See p.801

* **Niaux cave** The upper Ariège valley hosts a cluster of prehistoric caves painted by Cro-Magnon humans over 10,000 years ago; Niaux contains the best preserved and most vivid of these images. See p.811

* **Cathar castles** The imposing castles of the upper Aude and Corbières region testify to southwestern Languedoc's era of independence. See p.821

* **Petit Train Jaune** Travel up the dramatic, winding Têt valley of Roussillon in an open-car, narrow-gauge train. See p.836

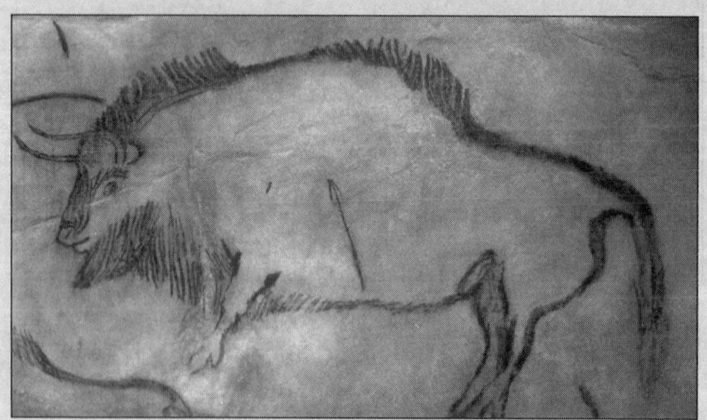

△ Niaux cave

The Pyrenees

Basque-speaking, wet and green in the west; craggy, snowy, Gascon-influenced in the middle; dry, Mediterranean and Catalan-speaking in the east – the **Pyrenees** are physically beautiful, culturally varied and considerably less developed than the Alps. The whole range is marvellous walkers' country, especially the central region around the **Parc National des Pyrénées**, with its 3000-metre-high peaks, streams, forests and wildlife. If you're a committed **hiker**, it's possible to traverse these mountains, usually from the Atlantic to the Mediterranean, along the **GR10** or the higher, more difficult **Haute Randonnée Pyrénéenne** (HRP). There are numerous alpine spa resorts as well – **Cauterets, Luz-St-Sauveur**, **Barèges, Ax-les-Thermes** – with shorter hikes to suit all temperaments and abilities, as well as skiing opportunities in winter.

As for the more conventional of the tourist attractions, the **Côte Basque** is lovely, sandy but very popular, suffering from seaside sprawl and a surfeit of caravan-colonized campsites. **St-Jean-de-Luz** is arguably the prettiest of the resorts, while once-elitist **Biarritz** is now enjoying a renaissance. **Bayonne**, just inland, is an attractive, if heavily touristed medieval town at the confluence of two broad rivers. The foothill towns are on the whole rather dull, although **Pau** merits at least a day, while **Lourdes** is such a monster of kitsch that it just has to be seen. Catalan-speaking **Roussillon** in the east, focused on busy **Perpignan**, has beaches every bit as popular as those of the Côte Basque, nestled into the compact coves of its rocky coast, while its interior consists of craggy terrain split by spectacular canyons, sprouting a crop of fine Romanesque abbeys – of which **St-Michel-de-Cuixà**, **St-Martin-de-Canigou** and **Serrabona** are the most dramatic – and a landscape bathed in Mediterranean heat and light. Finally, the sun-drenched foothills just to the northwest are home to the famous **Cathar castles**, legacies of the once-independent and ever-rebellious inhabitants of southwestern Languedoc.

Hiking in the Pyrenees

There are plenty of walkers' **guidebooks** to the area in both French and English (see p.1337), and two series of widely available **maps**. The most detailed of the latter are the French IGN 1:25,000 "TOP 25" series (Ⓦwww.ign.fr); #1547OT, #1647ET, #1647OT, #1748ET and #1748OT cover the Parc National des Pyrénées, whilst #1848OT covers the ever-popular Luchon area. Less demanding walkers can make do with Rando Éditions' *Cartes de Randonnées*, which covers the range at 1:50,000 in eleven sheets numbered from west to east (though #9 is out of print).

The **walking season** usually lasts from mid-June until late September; earlier in the year, few staffed refuges function, and you'll often find snow on parts of

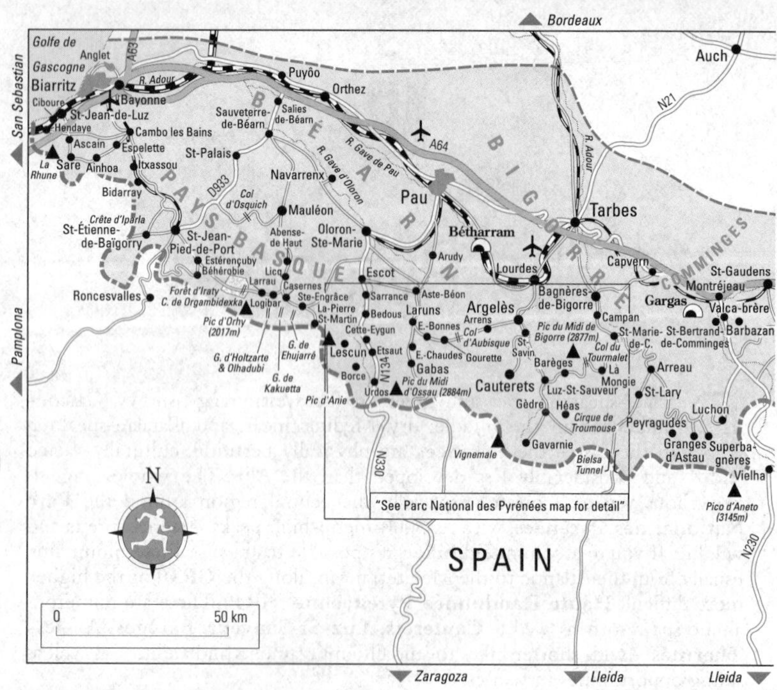

the GR10 (let alone the HRP) until early July. Remember that these are big mountains to be treated with respect: tackling any of the main walks means **proper preparation** and equipment. Before taking to the peaks, check weather forecasts – always posted at the local tourist office – and be properly equipped and provisioned. Above all, don't take chances: mountain conditions change very quickly, and sunny, warm weather in the valley doesn't necessarily mean it will be the same higher up, three hours later. If you don't have any mountain-walking experience, it's probably best not to embark on anything other than a well-frequented path unless you're accompanied by someone who does.

One kilometre in twelve minutes (5kph) is a rather brisk average **walking pace** for level ground; if you're going uphill, allow an hour for every 350m in elevation gained. If you're out of condition, or have a heavy pack, the same climb will take longer. Much terrain is so steep, and trail surface so uneven, that going downhill isn't any faster. Be mindful of the punishment your knees will take – bring or buy locally telescopic walking poles or a traditional walking stick.

The Pays Basque

The three **Basque provinces** – Labourd (Lapurdi), Basse Navarre (Behe Nafarroa) and Soule (Zuberoa) – share with their Spanish neighbours a

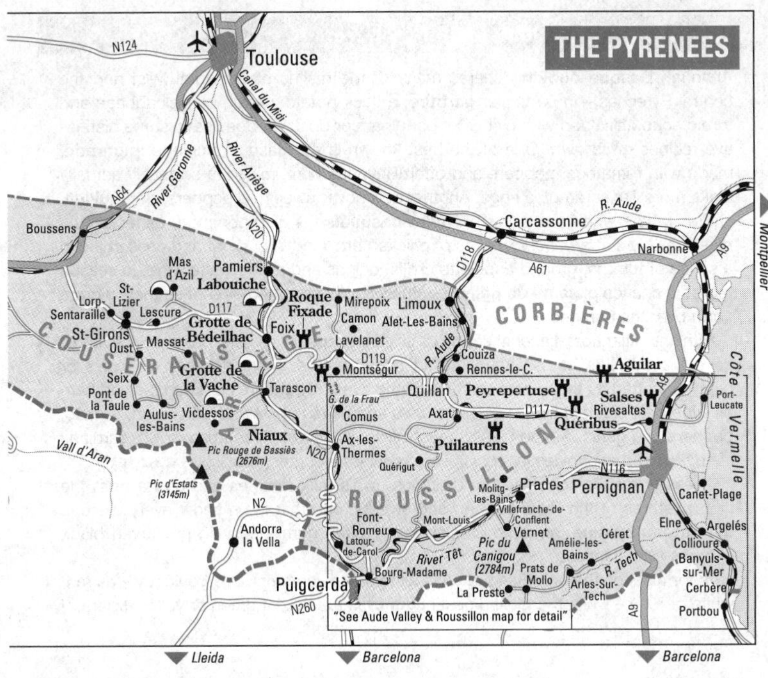

common language – Euskera – and a strong sense of separate identity. The language is widely spoken, and Basques refer to their country as Euskal-herri (or, across the border in Spain, Euskadi). You'll see bilingual French/Euskera signage and events posters throughout the region (sometimes only in Euskera), so in this section we have given the Euskera for all locations in brackets after the French. Unlike some of their Spanish counterparts, few French Basques favour an independent state or secession from France, though a Basque *département* has been mooted (see below). For decades the French authorities turned a blind eye to the Spanish Basque terrorist organization ETA, which used the region as a safe haven and organizational base. Since the millennium, however, as France has extradited suspected terrorists to Spain, incidents of violence and vandalism associated with nationalists have increased, notably around Bayonne and Pau. Such events, however, are so exceptional as to not concern visitors.

Administratively, the three French Basque provinces were organized together with the county of Béarn in the single *département* of Basses-Pyrénées (now Pyrénées-Atlantiques) at the time of the 1789 Revolution, when the Basques' thousand-year-old *fors* (customary privileges) were abolished. It was a move designed to curtail their nationalism, but ironically has probably been responsible for preserving their unity. Of late there have been proposals for the creation of a Pays-Basque *département*, hived off from the Pyrénées-Atlantiques, with its capital at Bayonne – a notion greeted with horror in the capital of such a centralized nation, but not so inconceivable now in an EU that gives increasing power to regions.

Apart from the language and the traditional broad beret, the most obvious manifestations of Basque national identity are the ubiquitous *trinquets* (enclosed) or *frontons* (open), the huge concrete courts in which the national game of

The food of the Basque Country

Although **Basque cooking** shares many of the dishes of the southwest and the central Pyrenees – in particular **garbure**, a thick potato, carrot, bean, cabbage and turnip soup enlivened with pieces of pork, ham or duck – it does have some distinctive recipes of its own. One of the best known is the Basque omelette, **pipérade**, made with tomatoes, peppers and often Bayonne ham, mixed in so that it actually looks more like scrambled eggs. Another delicacy is sweet red peppers, or **piquillos**, stuffed whole with *morue* (cod). **Poulet basquaise** is also common, especially as takeaway food at a *traiteur*: pieces of chicken browned in pork fat and casseroled in a sauce of tomato, ground Espelette chillis, onions and a little white wine. In season there's a chance of **salmí de palombe**, the wild doves netted or shot as they migrate north over the Pyrenees.

With the Atlantic adjacent, **seafood** is also a speciality. The Basques inevitably have their version of fish soup, called *ttoro*. Another great delicacy is **elvers** or *piballes*, netted as they come up the Atlantic rivers. **Squid** are common, served here as *txiperons*, either in their own ink, stuffed and baked or stewed with onion, tomato, peppers and garlic. All the locally caught fish – tuna (*thon*), sea bass (*bor*), sardines (*sardines*) and anchovies (*anchois*) – are regular favourites, too.

Cheeses mainly comprise the delicious ewe's-milk *tommes* and *gasna* from the high pastures of the Pyrenees. Among sweets, one that is on show everywhere is the **gâteau basque**, an almond-custard pie often garnished with preserved black cherries from Itxassou.

As for alcohol, the only Basque AOC **wine** is the very drinkable Irouléguy – as red, white or rosé – while the local digestif **liqueur** is the potent green or yellow Izzara.

pelota is played. Pairs of players wallop a hard leather-covered ball, either with their bare hands or a long basket-work extension of the hand called a *chistera* (in the variation known as *cesta punta*), against a high wall blocking one end of the court. It's extraordinarily dangerous – the ball travels at speeds of up to 200kph – and knockouts or worse are not uncommon. Trials of strength (*force Basque*), rather like Scottish Highland games, are also popular, including tugs-of-war, lifting heavy weights, turning massive carts and sawing or axing giant tree trunks.

The Côte Basque

Barely 30km long from the Spanish frontier to the mouth of the Adour, the **Basque coast** is easily accessible by air, bus and train, and reasonably priced accommodation is not difficult to find – except from mid-July through August, when space should be reserved at least six weeks in advance. **Bayonne**, slightly inland, is the cultural focus and only town with some life apart from tourism. **Biarritz**, the most prestigious and varied resort, is flanked by magnificent beaches but proves a rather noisy, congested place to stay in high season. Families manifestly prefer **St-Jean-de-Luz** to the south – an attractive and more manageable town in any case – or distinctly suburban **Anglet** just to the north, with even better beaches which attract surfers from near and far. At the border, **Hendaye** itself is rather dull but has another superb beach at the mouth of the Bidas(s)oa River.

Bayonne (Baïona)

BAYONNE stands back some 5km from the Atlantic, a position that until recently protected it from any real touristy exploitation. It bestrides the

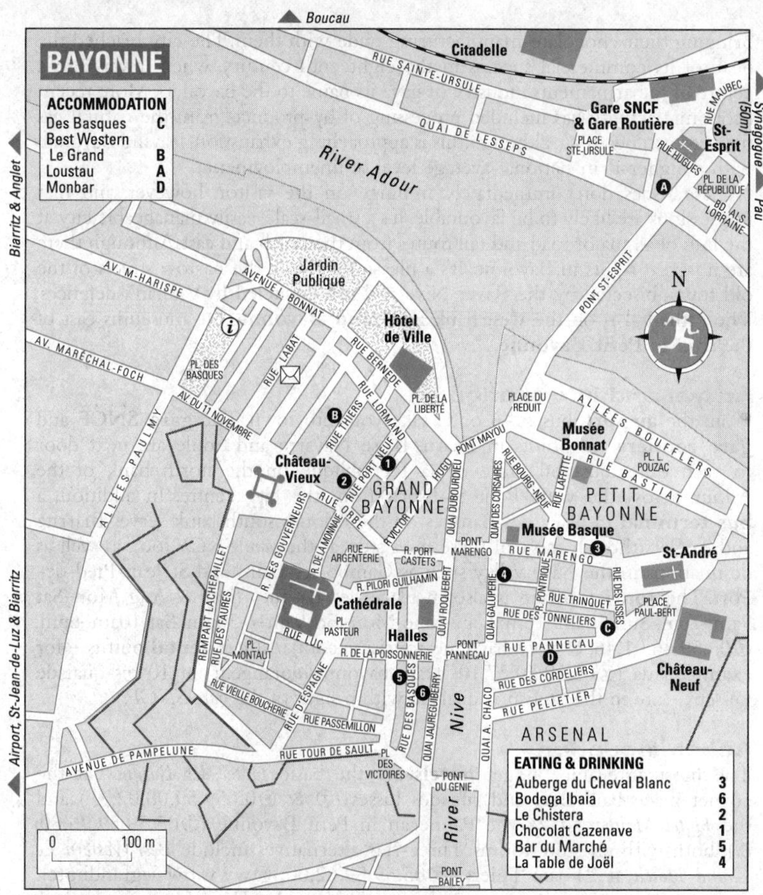

confluence of the River Adour, which rises in the region of the Pic du Midi d'Ossau, and the much smaller Nive, whose source is the Basque Pyrenees above St-Jean-Pied-de-Port. Although purists dispute whether it's truly a Basque rather than a Gascon city, Bayonne is effectively the economic and political capital of the Pays Basque. To the lay person, at least, its Basque flavour predominates, with tall half-timbered dwellings and woodwork painted in the specifically Basque hues of green and red. Here, too, Basques in flight from Franco's Spain came without hesitation to seek refuge amongst their own. For many years the Petit Bayonne quarter on the right bank of the Nive was a hotbed of violent Basque nationalism, until the French government clamped down on such dangerous tendencies.

The city's origins go back to the Lapurdum of Roman times; this Latin name, corrupted to Labourd (Lapurdi), was subsequently extended to cover the whole of this westernmost of the three Basque provinces. For three centuries until 1453 and the end of the Hundred Years War, it enjoyed prosperity and security under English domination, and this wealth was consolidated when, in the sixteenth century, Sephardic Jews fleeing the Portuguese Inquisition arrived, bringing their chocolate-manufacturing trade with them. The city reached the peak of its commercial success in the eighteenth century, when it was also a centre of the armaments industry (it gave its name to the bayonet). More recent economic activity has included processing of by-products from the natural gas field at Lacq near Pau, although this is approaching exhaustion, leaving Bayonne with a higher-than-national-average level of unemployment.

These issues don't immediately impinge on the visitor, however, and first impressions are likely to be favourable. It's a small-scale, easily manageable city, at the hub of all major road and rail routes from the north and east. Although there are no great sights in Bayonne, it's a pleasure to walk the narrow streets of the old town, bisected by the River Nive and still encircled by Vauban's defences. The cathedral is on the west bank in **Grand Bayonne**, the museums east of the river in **Petit Bayonne**.

Arrival and information

From the **airport**, buses #6 or C take you into town. The **gare SNCF** and **gare routière** for points in Béarn, Basse Navarre and Soule are next door to each other, just off place de la République on the north bank of the Adour, across the wide Pont St-Esprit from the city centre. In addition, a **bus terminal** in place des Basques on the Adour's south bank serves Biarritz and Anglet (though most of these lines stop at the *gare SNCF* too), as well as destinations in the Nive valley, such as Cambo-les-Bains and St-Jean-Pied-de-Port. The **tourist office** is also in place des Basques (July & Aug Mon–Sat 9am–7pm, Sun 10am–1pm; Sept–June Mon–Fri 9am–6.30pm, Sat 10am–6pm; Ⓣ05.59.46.01.46, Ⓦwww.bayonne-tourisme.com). All **car rental** outfits – for example Ada (Ⓣ05.59.50.37.10, Ⓔada.bayonne@orange.fr) at 10 bis quai de Lesseps – are in the St-Esprit quarter, within sight of the *gare SNCF*.

Accommodation

The most agreeable budget **hotels** are the basic *Hôtel des Basques*, at the corner place Paul-Bert and rue des Lisses (Ⓣ & Ⓕ05.59.59.08.02; ❷) and the *Hôtel Monbar*, at 24 rue Pannecau in Petit Bayonne (Ⓣ05.59.59.26.80; ❷), both with en-suite rooms. Three-star alternatives include *Best Western Le Grand Hôtel*, at 21 rue Thiers (Ⓣ05.59.59.62.00, Ⓦwww.bw-legrandhotel.com; ❹–❼), set in a gorgeous old mansion, and the *Hôtel Loustau*, on place de la République (Ⓣ05.59.55.08.08, Ⓦwww.hotel-loustau.com; ❺–❼), overlooking the river beside Pont St-Esprit; both have affordable attached restaurants. Hostellers can head for the **HI hostel** at 19 rte des Vignes in Anglet, 6km west of town on the Biarritz road; buses #4 or C from the centre of Bayonne stop right outside.

Grand Bayonne

In Grand Bayonne, just up the avenue from the tourist office, stands the town's fourteenth-century **castle** (closed to the public). The oldest part, the Château-Vieux, is a genuine example of no-nonsense late-medieval fortification; a plaque on the east wall lists some of the more famous willing or unwilling guests, including the Black Prince, King Pedro the Cruel of Castile, and the notorious mercenary Bertrand de Guescelin. The **Jardin Botanique** (mid-April to mid-Oct daily 9am–noon & 2–6pm; free) lies just west of the château – an enormous, well-designed garden with plants labelled in French, Basque and Latin.

Just around the corner on the magnolia-shaded place Pasteur, the **Cathédrale Ste-Marie** (Mon–Sat 10–11.45am & 3–5.45pm, Sun 3.30–6pm), with its twin towers and steeple rising with airy grace above the houses, is best seen from across the grassy expanse of its own **cloister** (daily 9am–12.30pm & 2–5/6pm) on its south side. Up close, the yellowish stone reveals bad weathering, with most of the decorative detail lost. Inside, its most impressive features are the height of the nave and some sixteenth-century glass (restored in 2002), set off by the prevailing gloom. Like other southern Gothic cathedrals of the period (around 1260), it was based on more famous northern models, in this case Soissons and Reims.

The smartest, most commercial streets in town extend northeast from the cathedral: **rue Thiers** leading to the Hôtel de Ville, and **rue de la Monnaie**, leading into **rue Port-Neuf**, with its aromatic chocolate *confiseries*. South and west of the cathedral, along **rue des Faures**, **rue d'Espagne**, and other streets closest to the old walls, there's a more Iberian feel, with washing strung at the windows, ethnic restaurants and quirky bars.

Petit Bayonne and St-Esprit

East of the cathedral, the riverside **quays** of the Nive are the city's most picturesque focus, with sixteenth-century arcaded houses on the Petit Bayonne side, one of which at 37 quai des Corsaires contains the worthwhile Basque ethnographic museum, the **Musée Basque** (May–Oct Tues–Sun 10am–6.30pm, also Mon July–Aug; Nov–April Tues–Sun 10am–12.30pm & 2–6pm; €5.50, €9 with Musée Bonnat). Its exhibits illustrate Basque life through the centuries, and include farm implements such as solid-wheeled oxcarts and field rollers, as well as *makhilak* – innocent-looking carved, wooden walking sticks with a concealed steel spear tip at one end, used by pilgrims and shepherds for self-protection if need be. The seafaring gallery features a superb rudder handle carved as a sea-monster, a wood-hulled fishing boat, and a model of Bayonne's naval shipyards ca. 1805; Columbus's skipper was a Basque, as was Juan Sebastián de Elakano, who completed the first global circumnavigation in 1522.

The city's second museum, the **Musée Bonnat**, close by at 5 rue Jacques-Lafitte (daily except Tues & hols: May–Oct 10am–6.30pm; Nov–April 10am–12.30pm & 2–6pm; €5.50, €9 with Musée Basque; Ⓦ www.musee-bonnat.com;), provides an unexpected treasury of art. Thirteenth- and fourteenth-century Italian painting is well represented, as are most periods before Impressionism. Highlights include Goya's *Self-Portrait* and *Portrait of Don Francisco de Borja*, Rubens' powerful *Apollo and Daphne* and *The Triumph of Venus*, plus works by Murrillo, El Greco and Ingrès. A whole gallery is devoted to high-society portraits by Léon Bonnat (1833–1922), whose personal collection formed the original core of the museum. There are also frequent temporary exhibits in the annexe at 9 rue Fredéric-Bastiat, well worth catching.

Apart from savouring the wide river skies, there is little to draw you to the northern bank of the Adour. A deliberately inconspicuous, early nineteenth-century **synagogue** at 33 rue Maubec serves as a reminder that Bayonne's Jewish community first settled here in France on arrival from Portugal during the sixteenth century. St-Esprit in effect became their ghetto after an expulsion order in 1602, when Grand Bayonne was consecrated to the Virgin and off-limits to unbelievers. The **church of St-Esprit**, opposite the station, is all that remains of a hostel that once ministered to the sore feet and other ailments of Chemin de St-Jacques pilgrims – it's worth a peek inside for a fine fifteenth-century wood sculpture of *The Flight into Egypt*. Just above the station is Vauban's massive **citadelle**; built in 1680 to defend the town against Spanish attack, it actually saw little action until the Napoleonic wars, when its garrison resisted a siege by Wellington for four months in 1813 before falling the next year.

Eating, drinking and entertainment

The best area for **eating** and **drinking** is along the Nive quays between Pont Marengo and Pont Pannecau and in the backstreets to either side of the river, especially in Petit Bayonne or the area south and west of the *halles*. Two of the best **restaurants** in Petit Bayonne are the seafood-strong, Michelin-starred *Auberge du Cheval Blanc*, 68 rue Bourg-Neuf (Ⓣ05.59.59.01.33; closed Sun eve & Mon except Aug; weekday lunch menu €35, but assume €90 expenditure; booking essential), and *La Table de Joël*, 28 quai Galuperie (closed Mon lunch & Sun; menu €17, à la carte €28–32), serving mostly meat but a few monkfish and cod dishes, plus creative desserts, at a riverside terrace. In Grand Bayonne, *Le Chistera*, 42 rue Port-Neuf (closed Mon, part May & Tues & Wed eves except July & Aug; menu €15, à la carte €19–25), is with its pelota decor a worthy option, dishing up hearty Bayonnais specialities based on fish, pork and tripe, best ordered off the daily-specials board.

For **bar** snacks, head for *Bar du Marché*, 39 rue des Basques in Grand Bayonne (closed all eves & all Sun), decorated with posters for the San Fermín bull-running at Pamplona. It begins serving food and drink – including good beer on tap – at 5am to market sellers and continues with good-value *plats du jour* at lunchtime. Nearby is *Bodega Ibaia*, 49 quai Jauréguiberry (closed Sun & Mon Sept–June), a lively, well-loved bar, with *plats du jour* for €7–12 at lunchtime. Bayonne duly honours its chocolate tradition with several outlets on, or just off, rue du Port-Neuf; *Chocolat Cazenave* at no. 19 serves hot whipped chocolate and cold cocoa-based desserts at tables under the arcade or in its Art Nouveau interior.

As far as **festivals** go, Bayonne's biggest annual bash is the Fêtes de Bayonne, which usually starts on the first Wednesday in August and consists of five days and nights of continuous boozing and entertainment. There are *corridas* (bullfights) the last two days, plus a few more in the run-up to August 15. A well-established jazz festival, La Ruee au Jazz, takes place in mid-July, and every October there's Les Translatines, a Franco-Spanish theatre festival.

Biarritz (Miarritze)

A few minutes by rail or road from Bayonne, **BIARRITZ** was, until the 1950s, the Monte Carlo of the Atlantic coast, transformed by Napoléon III during the

△ Surfers, Biarritz

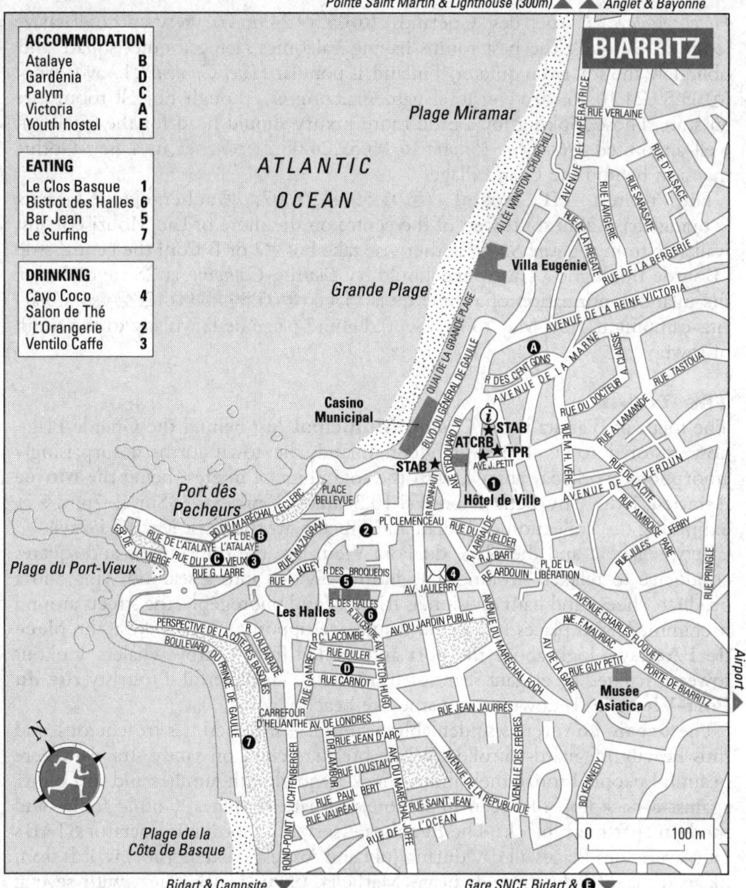

mid-nineteenth century into a playground for monarchs, aristos and glitterati. With the rise of the Côte d'Azur during the 1960s, however, the place went into seemingly terminal decline. But since the 1990s, Biarritz has been rediscovered by Parisian yuppies, the international surfing fraternity and a slightly alternative family clientele, who together have put the place back on the map.

Arrival, information and accommodation

The **gare SNCF** is 3km southeast of the centre at the end of avenue Foch/ avenue Kennedy in the *quartier* known as La Négresse (STAB bus #2 or B from or to square d'Ixelles). The **tourist office** is on square d'Ixelles (daily: July & Aug 8am–8pm; Sept–June Mon–Sat 10am–6pm, Sun 10am–5pm; ⓣ05.59.22.37.00, ⓦwww.biarritz.fr), also selling tickets for local events and spectacles.

Accommodation is booked out weeks in advance during July and August, especially the more affordable choices. *Hôtel Palym* at 7 rue du Port-Vieux (ⓣ05.59.24.16.56, ⓦwww.le-palmarium.com; ❷–❸), with a variety of old-fashioned rooms and a ground-floor bar-restaurant, is a solid budget option a stone's throw from plage du Port-Vieux. Nearby stands completely en-suite

Hôtel Atalaye, 6 rue des Goélands (Ⓣ05.59.24.06.76, Ⓦwww.hotelatalaye.com; ❸–❹), with the best rooms having balconies facing a quiet square and, obliquely, the sea. Even quieter, if inland, is popular *Hôtel Gardénia*, 19 av Carnot (Ⓣ05.59.24.10.46, Ⓦwww.hotel-gardenia.com; ❸), though not all rooms are en suite. Those looking for a little more luxury should head for the small but well-appointed *Hostellerie Victoria* (Ⓣ05.59.24.08.21; ❻), set in a neo-Gothic mansion behind the Grand Plage.

The nearest **HI hostel** (Ⓣ05.59.41.76.07, Ⓔaubergejeune.biarritz@orange.fr) is 2km southwest of the centre on the shore of Lac Mouriscot, just walkable from the *gare SNCF*; otherwise take bus #2 or B from the centre, stop "Bois de Boulogne". **Campers** should try *Biarritz-Camping*, at 28 rte d'Harcet, the inland continuation of avenue de la Plage (Ⓣ05.59.23.00.12, Ⓦwww.biarritz-camping.fr; mid-May to late Sept), behind plage de la Milady to the south of town.

The Town

The focus of Biarritz is the **Casino Municipal**, just behind the Grande Plage, now restored to its 1930s grandeur. Inland, the town forms a surprisingly amorphous, workaday sprawl, with the sole point of interest being the **Musée Asiatica**, 1 rue Guy-Petit (Mon–Fri 10.30am–6.30pm, Sat & Sun 2–7pm; €7), exhibiting the collection of Indian and Tibetan art specialist Michel Postel.

Between here and the plage du Port-Vieux are the only streets and squares conducive to relaxed strolling. The **halles**, divided into a seafood wing and a produce, cheese and ham division, is friendly and photogenic, the streets around it crammed with places to eat and drink (see opposite). To the west, the **place de l'Atalaye**, high above the port and named for a nearby whalers' lookout tower, is fringed by elegant mansions; just below, characterful if touristy **rue du Port-Vieux** leads down to its namesake beach.

The **ocean**, however, is undeniably beautiful – if sometimes treacherous, and thus heavily lifeguard-patrolled. White breakers crash on sandy strands, where beautiful people bronze their limbs cheek by jowl with families and surf bums, against a backdrop of ocean-liner hotels, ornate churches, Gothic follies and modern apartment blocks. The **beaches** – served by local bus operator STAB's La Navette des Plages all day during July and August – extend northwards from plage de la Milady through plage Marbella, Côte des Basques (with several surfing schools), plage du Port-Vieux, Grande Plage and plage Miramar to the Pointe St-Martin with its lighthouse. Most of the action takes place between the plage du Port-Vieux and the plage Miramar, overlooked by the huge **Hôtel du Palais** (formerly the Villa Eugénie), built by Napoléon III in the mid-nineteenth century for his wife, whom he met and courted in Biarritz.

Just beside the **plage du Port-Vieux**, the most sheltered and intimate of the beaches – you'll share it with scuba-divers and kayakers at times – a rocky promontory sticks out into the sea, ending in the **Rocher de la Vierge**, an offshore rock topped by a white statue of the Virgin, and linked to the mainland by an Eiffel-built iron catwalk. Around it are scattered other rocky islets where the swell heaves and combs. On the bluff above the Virgin stands the **Musée de la Mer** (daily: June & Sept 9.30am–7pm; July & Aug 9.30am–midnight; Oct–May 9.30am–12.30pm & 2–6pm; €7.50), which contains interesting displays on the fishing industry and the region's birds, and an aquarium of North Atlantic fish as well as the obligatory seal tank with twice-daily feedings.

Just below is the picturesque **Port des Pêcheurs**, most easily approached by a switchback pedestrian lane. The fishermen are long gone, replaced by pleasure boats, two scuba outfitters and pricey seafood restaurants. To the northeast lies the **Grande Plage**, an immaculate sweep of sand once dubbed the "Plage des Fous" after the 1850s practice of taking mental patients to bathe here as a primitive form of thalassotherapy.

Eating, drinking and nightlife

It's possible to eat well for an affordable price, away from the touristy snack bars on rue du Port-Vieux, especially near the *halles*. Two of the best options around the market are *Bar Jean*, at 5 rue Halles, a semi-subterranean Spanish-theme outfit with tapas or full seafood meals for about €21, or *Bistrot des Halles* (☎05.59.24.21.22), at 1 rue du Centre, which serves generously portioned, tasty fish or meat-under-sauce dishes (menu €13, lunch only, allow €28–32 à la carte; closed Sun eve except school hols). *Le Clos Basque* at 12 rue Louis-Barthou is another favourite bistro with meaty, hearty fare (☎05.59.24.24.96; menu €25; closed Sun eve & some Mon). For a sea view with your meal, *Le Surfing*, behind plage de Côte des Basques and festooned with antique boards, serves decent seafood grills and *frites*, while the *Littoral Café* at 3 esplanade du Port-Vieux does well-presented brasserie grub, strong on *moules*, *galettes* and big steins of beer.

More formal **nightlife** in the town centre includes *Cayo Coco*, a Cuban theme bar at 5 rue Jaulerry offering free salsa dance lessons Thursday nights, and *Ventilo Caffe* on rue du Port-Vieux, the favourite haunt of Parisian thirtysomethings. Whether you've slept the night before or not, have a good start to the day at *Salon de Thé l'Orangerie* (closed Wed) at 1 rue Gambetta, serving forty varieties of tea and a reasonably copious breakfast.

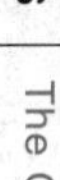

Anglet (Angelu)

Immediately north of Biarritz, suburban **ANGLET** sprawls up the coast from the Pointe St-Martin to the mouth of the Adour at La Barre. There's nothing to see except a half-dozen contiguous, superb beaches, broader and wilder than any at Biarritz. The most frequented are **Chambre d'Amour**, so named for two lovers trapped in their trysting place by the tide, and adjacent **Sables d'Or** and **Marinella**, both much favoured by the surfers and with schools operating in season.

The summertime Navette des Plages calls here too from the central stops in Biarritz, or you can walk the distance in about thirty minutes, along avenue de l'Impératrice, avenue MacCroskey, then second left down to the seaside boulevard des Plages. Anglet has a **HI hostel** at 19 rte des Vignes (☎05.59.58.70.00, ⓔanglet@fuaj.org; mid-Feb to mid-Nov; stop "Les Corsaires" on Navette des Plages or STAB bus #4 or C, from Biarritz). For **eating and drinking**, the most notable seaside establishments are the *Havana Café* at Chambre d'Amour, a permanently crowded bar that serves *plats du jour* at lunch for about €9, and the nearby *Café Bleu*, more of a proper restaurant with a menu for €16 (closed Wed Sept–June). Inland in the Chiberta neighbourhood near the pine forest, the popular *La Fleur de Sel*, 5 av de la Forêt (closed lunch Mon–Wed; menu €28.50, otherwise €34-plus), serving more *nouvelle Basquaise* fare.

St-Jean-de-Luz (Donibane Lohitzun)

With its fine sandy bay and magnificent old quarter speckled with half-timbered mansions, **ST-JEAN-DE-LUZ** remains the most attractive resort on the Basque coast, despite being fairly overrun by large families in peak season. As the only natural harbour between Arcachon and Spain, it has been a major port for centuries, with whaling and cod fishing the traditional preoccupations of its fleets. Even now, St-Jean remains one of the busiest fishing ports in France, and the principal one for landing anchovy and tuna.

Arrival, information and accommodation

St-Jean's **gare SNCF** is on the southern edge of the town centre, 500m from the beach, while **buses** operated by the Conseil Général arrive at the *halte routière* just opposite. The **tourist office** (April–June & Sept Mon–Sat 9am–12.30pm & 2–7pm, Sun 10am–1pm; July & Aug Mon–Sat 9am–7.30pm, Sun 10am–1pm & 3–7pm; Oct–March Mon–Sat 9am–12.30pm & 1.30–6.30pm, Sun 10am–1pm; ⓣ05.59.26.03.16, ⓦwww.saint-jean-de-luz.com) stands just behind place des Corsaires. **Bikes** can be rented at Luz Evasion on place Maurice-Ravel and ADO on avenue Labrouche, as well as at the *gare SNCF*, where ADA **car** rental (ⓣ05.59.26.26.22) is also based.

Opposite the train station, on and around avenue Verdun, are a few inexpensive (for St-Jean) if uninspiringly located **hotels**, among them the en-suite, well-kept *Hôtel de Paris*, 1 bd du Commandant-Passicot, corner avenue Labrouche (ⓣ05.59.85.20.20, ⓦwww.hoteldeparis-stjeandeluz.fr; ❸). Slightly more expensive, and better placed, are the *Hôtel Ohartzia* (ⓣ05.59.26.00.06, ⓦwww.hotel-ohartzia.com; ❹–❺), just inland from the beach at 28 rue Garat, with rear rooms overlooking the garden where breakfast is served, and the *Lafayette* (ⓣ05.59.26.17.74, ⓦwww.hotelpaysbasque.com; ❹–❺) at pedestrianized 18–20 rue de la République, the best rooms with balconies. Three-star comfort means either beachfront *Hôtel de la Plage* (ⓣ05.59.51.03.44, ⓦwww.hoteldelaplage.com; ❺–❼; closed mid-Nov to Easter), which has its own (paying) car park, Wi-Fi access and a ground-floor brasserie, or quietly set *Les Goëlands* at 4–6 av d'Etcheverry (ⓣ05.59.26.10.05, ⓦwww.hotel-lesgoelands.com; ❺; all year), consisting of two 2004-renovated *belle-époque* villas, with easy parking and a full-service restaurant (April–Oct) in one wing (HB at ❽–❾ obligatory mid-July to early Sept). There are numerous **campsites**, all east of town in Erromardie and Acotz districts, seaward of the N10 between St-Jean and Guéthary.

The Town

The wealth and vigour of St-Jean's seafaring past is evident in the town's surviving seventeenth- and eighteenth-century houses of the merchants and shipowners. One of the finest, adjacent to the Hôtel de Ville on the plane-tree-studded place Louis-XIV, is the turreted **Maison Louis XIV** (guided tours: June & Sept Mon–Sat 10.30am–noon & 2.30–5.30pm; July & Aug Mon–Sat 10.30am–noon & 2.30–6.30pm; €5), built for the Lohobiague family in 1635, but renamed after the young King Louis stayed here for a month in 1660 during the preparations for his marriage to Maria Teresa, Infanta of Castile. She lodged in the equally impressive pink Italianate villa known as the **Maison de l'Infante** (mid-June to mid-Oct 11am–12.30pm & 2.30–6.30pm; €3), overlooking the harbour on the eponymous quay. The corner house on rue Mazarin, nearby, was the Duke of Wellington's HQ during the 1813–14 winter campaign against Maréchal Soult.

The wedding of King Louis and Maria Teresa was *the* major event in local history, overshadowing the Spanish destruction of the town in 1558. The couple's sumptuous, not to say extravagant, wedding took place in the **church of St-Jean-Baptiste** on pedestrianized **rue Gambetta**, the main shopping-and-tourism street today. Cardinal Mazarin alone presented the new queen with twelve thousand pounds of pearls and diamonds, a gold dinner service and a pair of carriages drawn by teams of six horses – all paid for by money made in the service of France. The door through which they left the church – on the right of the existing entrance – has been sealed up ever since. Even without this curiosity, the church deserves a look inside: the largest French Basque church, it has a barn-like nave roofed in wood and lined on three sides with tiers of dark oak galleries accessed by wrought-iron stairways. These are a distinctive feature of Basque churches, and were reserved for the men, while the women sat at ground level. Equally Basque is the elaborate gilded retable of tiered angels, saints and prophets behind the altar. Hanging from the ceiling is an ex voto model of the Empress Eugénie's paddle-steamer, the *Eagle*, which narrowly escaped being wrecked outside St-Jean in 1867.

Ciboure (Ziburu), the harbour and Urrugne (Urruña)

On the other side of the harbour and Nivelle river mouth, **CIBOURE** seems a continuation of St-Jean but is in fact a separate community, terminating in the little fortress of Socoa (Sokoa), today home to a sailing/windsurfing club. Its streets are prettier (and emptier) than its neighbour's, especially waterfront **quai Maurice-Ravel** (the composer was born at no. 12) and the parallel **rue Pocolette** just inland, an exquisite terrace of wide-fronted, half-timbered, balconied Labourdian town houses gaily painted in typical Basque colours. The octagonal tower protruding above the houses belongs to the sixteenth-century **church of St-Vincent**, where you'll find more characteristic Basque galleries, a Baroque altarpiece and yet another ex-voto model ship; the entrance is in rue Pocolette through a paved courtyard with gravestones embedded in it.

From either side of the Nivelle or the Pont Charles-de-Gaulle linking St-Jean and Ciboure, the **fishing harbour** dominates proceedings to seaward, with most working tuna boats tied up on the quai de l'Infante or Ciboure's quai Pascal-Elisalt, cheek by jowl with a pleasure-craft harbour.

Also worth considering is a visit to the **Château d'Urtubie** (guided tours mid-March to early Nov 10.30am–12.30pm & 2–6.30pm; €6; Ⓦwww.chateaudurtubie.net) at **URRUGNE**, just outside Ciboure, 3km southwest of St-Jean-de-Luz, which has belonged to the same family since its construction as a fortified château in 1341. It was enlarged and gentrified during the sixteenth and eighteenth centuries, and provided hospitality for the French King Louis XI, as well as for Soult and later Wellington during the Napoleonic Wars. If you fancy following in their footsteps, it's also a very upmarket **hotel** (Ⓣ05.59.54.31.15, Ⓦwww.chateaudurtubie.net; ⑧) with dinner preferentially for guests and only by prior arrangement; otherwise just visit and take tea in the salon afterwards for an extra fee.

Eating and drinking

Leading off place Louis-XIV – with its cafés, sidewalk artists and **free summertime concerts** in the bandstand (Tues–Sun 10pm) – rue de la République has several **restaurants**, poshest being *Le Kaiku* at no. 17 (supper only, allow €40 à la carte), with noted seafood; less expensive alternatives on the same lane include cheap and cheerful *La Ruelle* (closed Mon, also Tues low season) at no. 19, with three seafood menus (€18–25), though service is "relaxed" and drinks stiffly priced. The next street east, rue Tourasse, also offers possibilities, including durable *La Vieille Auberge* at no. 22 (closed Weds, & Tues lunch), with four menus. Less scenically set but equally popular is friendly *Le Buvette des Halles* (lunch only to 3pm, closed Mon off season), on the corner of the market hall on boulevard Victor-Hugo, which serves impeccably fresh tuna, crab and sardines, plus *pipérade*, drink and dessert for around €22 (three courses), though portions could be more generous.

Hendaye (Hendaïa) and the Spanish frontier

HENDAYE, 15km southwest of St-Jean-de-Luz, is the last town in France before the Spanish frontier. Neither the town itself, **Hendaye-Ville**, nor the seaside quarter, **Hendaye-Plage**, is of much intrinsic interest, though the latter has a fine, safe beach popular with Spaniards in particular, who reckon it better than anything on their side until reaching San Sebastián.

The town, served by both the Paris–Bordeaux–Irún and Toulouse–Irún train lines, lies on the estuary of the River Bida(s)soa, which forms the border with Spain at this point. Just upstream, a tiny wooded island known as the **Île des Faisans** was once used as a meeting place for the monarchs of the two countries. François I, taken prisoner at the battle of Pavia in 1525, was ransomed here. In 1659 it was the scene of the signature of the Treaty of the Pyrenees, and in the following year of the marriage contract between Louis XIV and Maria Teresa. The painter Velázquez, responsible for the decor of the negotiations chamber, apparently caught the cold here which resulted in his death. Another interesting encounter was the meeting between Hitler and Franco at Hendaye train station on October 23, 1940. The version promulgated by Franco and his publicists, long believed even by his enemies, had "El Caudillo" preserving Spanish neutrality by parrying the Führer's threats to annexe Spain; in fact, Franco, dazzled by Hitler's early victories and the prospect of a greatly enlarged Spanish Morocco at the expense of France, begged to allowed to fight alongside Germany. But Hitler – mindful of how much assistance the Spanish Nationalists had needed to win their civil war, and aware of Spain's dire economic state – considered the proposed alliance a liability and was having none of it.

The main local sight is the **Château d'Abbadie** (Ⓦwww.academie-sciences.fr/abbadia.htm), home of nineteenth-century Dublin-born explorer Antoine d'Abbadie, on the headland closing off Hendaye-Plage on the east, just off the route de la Corniche (Feb–May & Oct to mid-Dec Tues–Sat guided visits only 2–5pm; June–Sept Mon–Fri guided visits 10–11.30am & 2–6pm, without guide 12.30–2pm; Sat & Sun visit without guide 2–6pm; €5.50–6.50). After expeditions in Ethiopia and Egypt, d'Abbadie had the neo-Gothic château built between 1860 and 1870; the architect was Eugène Viollet-le-Duc, the result a bizarre Franco-Hibernian folly, with Arabian boudoirs, Ethiopian frescoes, and inscriptions over the doors and lintels inside in Irish, Basque, Arabic and Ethiopian. It's also filled with objects collected by d'Abbadie on his travels.

Hendaye's **tourist office** is at 12 rue des Aubépines in Hendaye-Plage (April–June & Sept–Oct Mon–Sat 9am–12.30pm & 2–6pm, July & Aug Mon–Sat 9am–7.30pm, Sun 10.30am–1pm; Nov–March Mon–Sat 9am–12.30pm & 2–5pm; Ⓣ05.59.20.00.34, Ⓦwww.hendaye.com). Ten local **campsites** are all found east of Hendaye-Plage, just off the Route de la Corniche; one of the more tent-friendly, and closest to the beach, is *Alturan* (Ⓣ05.59.20.04.55; June–Sept), on rue de la Côte. Hendaye-Ville hotels are generally pretty grim, with proximity to the *gare SNCF* their only selling point; the most cheerful is *Hôtel La Palombe Bleue* at 38 rue du Commerce (Ⓣ05.59.20.43.80; March–Dec; ❷–❹). Most people stay down in Hendaye-Plage, where affordable, well-set choices include *Hôtel La Fon* at 99 bd de la Mer (Ⓣ05.59.20.04.67; April–Oct; ❹), a rambling, old-fashioned beachfront place with restaurant; *Hôtel Uhainak* at no. 3 (Ⓣ05.59.20.33.63, Ⓦwww.hotel-uhainak.com; Feb–Nov; ❹), again with some rooms overlooking the beach; and the friendly *Hôtel Bergeret-Sport* inland at 4 rue des Clématites (Ⓣ05.59.20.00.78, Ⓦwww.hotel-bergeret-sort.com; June–Sept except by arrangement; ❹, HB at ❽ obligatory July & Aug), with a well-regarded restaurant. Independent **restaurants** are overwhelmingly fishy if not too numerous; cheap (because prosaically set by a car park) and popular is *La Petite Marée* at 2 av des Mimosas. For a sea view, head west a few blocks to the yacht and fishing port, where *La Cabane du Pêcheur* (closed Sun eve & Mon) does full seafood meals (menus €15–24). Just around the corner at 4 rue des Orangers, *Le Parc à Huîtres* (closed Tues, also Mon eve low season) is a superb oyster-bar-cum-takeaway-deli with seating outdoors and in; make a meal of it with salad, assorted tapas, desserts and oyster-compatible wines in every conceivable measure.

Around Hendaye: up the coast and inland

Perhaps the best thing about Hendaye is arriving there, since the stretch of **coast** from St-Jean southwest has remained miraculously unspoilt, despite being traced by the D912. Drivers will enjoy this route, which is also served by Line 26-1 of the Conseil Général bus service between Hendaye and St-Jean. Behind the Château d'Abbadie stretches a vast nature reserve culminating in the **Pointe Ste-Anne** promontory; its dramatic shoreline is accessible from the **Sentier du Littoral** footpath from Hendaye-Plage.

Both trans-Pyrenean walking routes – the **GR10** and **HRP** – officially begin their course in Hendaye-Plage at the former casino on the beach. The first, two-hour stage inland is dull and gives no sense of the glories that lie ahead; if you're not concerned about the romance and purism of starting at the very beginning, splash out on a taxi to **BIRIATOU** (Biriatu, 7km away), where the walking starts to get interesting. A short steep section leads to a **church** with a collection of weather-worn typically Basque "keyhole" tombstones, next door to the pretty *Auberge Hirribarren*, a temporary haven for many escaping Allied soldiers during World War II. From here the main footpaths and a number of local variations rise rapidly to semi-isolation, where only the buzzing power lines (soon left behind) and the occasional rambler disturb the peace.

Inland: Labourd (Lapurdi) and Basse Navarre (Behe Nafarroa)

If you don't have your own transport, the simplest forays into the soft, seductive landscapes of the Basque hinterland are along the **St-Jean-de-Luz–Sare bus route** or the **Bayonne–St-Jean-Pied-de-Port train line**. Both give a representative sample of the area.

La Rhune (Larrun), Ascain (Azkaine), Sare (Sara) and Ainhoa

The 900-metre cone of **La Rhune**, straddling the frontier with Spain, is the westernmost skyward thrust of the Pyrenees before they decline into the Atlantic. As the landmark of Labourd, in spite of its unsightly multi-purpose antennae, and duly equipped with a rack-and-pinion rail service, it is predictably popular as a vantage point, offering fine vistas way up the Basque coast and east along the Pyrenees. Two or three **buses** a day (July & Aug Mon–Sat; Sept–June Mon–Fri), run by Le Basque Bondissant, ply the route from the *halte routière* in St-Jean-de-Luz, stopping at Ascain, Col de St-Ignace and Sare.

ASCAIN, where Pierre Loti wrote his romantic novel *Ramuntcho*, is like so many Labourdan villages – postcard-perfect and in danger of caricaturing itself, with its galleried church, *fronton* and polychrome, half-timbered houses. Loti's house on place du Fronton is now the **hotel-restaurant** *De la Rhune* (Ⓣ05.59.54.00.04, Ⓔhoteldelarhune@orange.fr; ❺) with a garden at the back, one of several accommodation options in the village.

You could walk up La Rhune from here in about two and a half hours, or take the little tourist train from **Col de St-Ignace** (mid-March to early Nov, minimum 2 departures daily 9 or 10am & 3pm, extra according to demand and weather conditions; every 35min July/Aug from 8.30am; €12 return; book on Ⓣ05.59.54.20.26, Ⓦwww.rhune.com). The ascent takes thirty minutes, but you should allow up to two hours for the round trip. Be warned: it's massively popular in peak season, with long waits and two snack bars near the base station taking full advantage of a captive clientele.

With or without the bus, it's worth continuing to **SARE**, another perfectly proportioned Basque knoll-top village ringed by satellite hamlets. You can either walk on the **GR10** from the intermediate station below the summit of La Rhune in about an hour and a quarter, or follow 3km of road from St-Ignace in rather less time. The village's several **hotels** make for a more attractive overnight than Ascain; most central – and poshest – choice is the three-star *Arraya* on the village square (Ⓣ05.59.54.20.46, Ⓦwww.arraya.com; April–Oct; ❼), a former hospice on the Santiago pilgrimage route. More affordable are the *Baratxartea*, 1km northeast in Ihalar hamlet (Ⓣ05.59.54.20.48, Ⓦwww.hotel-baratxartea.com; ❹), or for the impecunious the no-star, non-en-suite *Hôtel de la Poste* opposite the *Arraya* (Ⓣ05.59.54.20.06; ❸). The only independent **restaurant** is the popular *Lastiry* next door, offering *nouvelle Basquaise* cuisine under the arcade (menus €21–28). The more consistently open of two **campsites** just south of the village is *La Petite Rhune* (Ⓣ05.59.54.23.97; May–Sept).

Instead of going back to St-Jean-de-Luz from Sare, an easy three- to four-hour stint on the GR10 takes you on to **AINHOA**, another gem of a village. It consists of little more than a single street lined with substantial, mainly seventeenth-century houses, whose lintel plaques offer mini-genealogies as well as foundation dates. Take a look at the bulky towered **church** with its extravagant Baroque altarpiece of prophets and apostles in niches, framed by Corinthian columns. For **accommodation**, try the comfortable, good-value *Hôtel Oppoca* (Ⓣ05.59.29.90.72, Ⓦwww.opopoca.com; closed mid-Nov to mid-Dec and most of Jan; ❸) with a good restaurant (closed Mon; four menus €18–45). **Campers** should head for *Camping Harazpy* near the village centre (Ⓣ05.59.29.89.38; mid-June to mid-Sept).

The valley of the Nive

The valley of the **River Nive** is the only public transport corridor southeast into the Basque hinterland, with up to five trains a day making the riverside journey from Bayonne to St-Jean-Pied-de-Port, The luminous green landscape on the approach to the mountains is scattered with peaceful villages untouched by speculative development.

Cambo-les-Bains (Kambo)

The first major stop is **CAMBO-LES-BAINS**, an old spa town whose favourable microclimate made it an ideal centre for the treatment of tuberculosis in the nineteenth century; it's an attractive town, green and open, but suffers from the usual genteel stuffiness of spas. The "new" town, with its ornate houses and hotels, radiates out from the baths over the heights above the River Nive, while the old quarter of Bas Cambo, typically Basque with its whitewashed houses and galleried church, lies beside the river and *gare SNCF*.

The main local sight is the **Villa Arnaga**, 1.5km northwest of town on the Bayonne road (guided visits: April–June & Sept 10am–12.30pm & 2.30–7pm; March Sat & Sun 2.30–6pm; July & Aug 10am–7pm; Oct Sat 2.30–7pm; €5), built for Edmond Rostand, author of *Cyrano de Bergerac*, who came here to cure his pleurisy in 1903. This larger-than-life Basque house, painted in red trim, overlooks an almost surreal formal garden with discs and rectangles of water and segments of grass punctuated by blobs, cubes and cones of box, lined by lindens and blue cedars, with a distant view of green hills. Inside, it's very kitsch, with a minstrels' gallery, fake pilasters, allegorical frescoes, chandeliers, numerous portraits and various memorabilia.

The **tourist office** is in the Parc St-Joseph in the upper town centre (mid-July to Aug Mon–Fri 8.30am–6.30pm, Sat 8.30am–noon & 2–5.30pm, Sun 10am–12.30pm; Sept to mid-July Mon–Fri 8.30am–12.30pm & 2–6.30pm, Sat 8.30am–noon & 2–5.30pm; ⓣ05.59.29.70.25). For an overnight **stay**, try the *Auberge de Tante Ursule* in Bas Cambo by the pelota court (ⓣ05.59.29.78.23, ⓔchez.tante.ursule@orange.fr; ❸), with rooms in a modern annexe, plus an excellent **restaurant** in an older adjacent building offering menus featuring offal from €15–35. The nearest year-round **campsite** is *Ur-Hégia* on route des Sept-Chênes (ⓣ05.59.29.72.03), also in Bas Cambo.

Espelette (Ezpeleta) and Itxassou (Itsasu)

Buses cover the 5km southwest from Cambo to **ESPELETTE**, a somewhat busy village of wide-eaved houses, with a **church** notable for its heavy square tower, painted ceiling and keyhole-shaped gravestones. The village's principal source of renown is its dark red **chilli peppers** – much used in Basque cuisine, hung to dry in summer on many housefronts – and its **pottok** markets. *Pottoks* are an ancient Basque breed of stocky pony, once favoured for work in British coal mines but now reared mainly for meat and riding. The annual sales take place on the last Tuesday and Wednesday in January; the pepper jamboree takes place on the last Sunday in October. There's a very good **hotel-restaurant** in Espelette, the *Euzkadi* on the main street at the northeast edge of the village (ⓣ05.59.93.91.88, ⓔhotel.euzkadi@orange.fr; ❸; restaurant closed Mon, also Tues low season), with calmer rear rooms and three menus (€23–31) featuring hearty Basque country cooking.

About the same distance south from Cambo-les-Bains, next stop up the train line (though only one train a day stops here), is the delightful village of **ITXASSOU**, quieter than most of the others in the area, and surrounded by green wooded hills. The main point of interest is the little seventeenth-century **church of St-Fructueux**, about 1km out on the minor D349 road towards Pas de Roland and Laxia hamlet, its vast cemetery harbouring a significant collection of both modern and ancient keyhole-shaped gravestones; inside, its three-tiered wooden galleries and sumptuous retable are worth a quick look. Itxassou is a great base for a gentle recharge of the batteries, with about a half-dozen **hotel-restaurants** scattered locally. Best and quietest of these are – next to St-Fructueux – the excellent-value *Hôtel du Chêne* (ⓣ05.59.29.75.01, ⓕ05.59.29.27.39; closed Jan–Feb; ❸), with large, bright rooms and an equally well-kept restaurant (closed Mon, also Tues low season) where €23 gets a menu with *pipérade*, salad, game and dessert, and – at bucolic Laxia – the *Hôtel Ondoria* (ⓣ05.59.29.75.39, ⓕ05.59.29.25.99; closed Nov 15–Jan & Mon; ❸), where meals are taken at a wisteria-festooned terrace overlooking the river, swimmable here on hot days.

Bidarray (Bidarrai) and St-Étienne-de-Baïgorry (Baigorri)

The GR10 from Ainhoa, as well as the train line (station Pont-Noblia) and a perilously narrow road beyond Laxia, all converge at **BIDARRAY**, which at first glance seems restricted to a few houses clustered around its medieval bridge over the Nive, the **Pont d'Enfer**. Further investigation, however, reveals the upper village, scattered appealingly on a ridge with superb views. On the way into the village on the GR10 is a *gîte d'étape* spread over two buildings, the *Auñamendi* (Ⓣ05.59.37.71.34; €10pp), while the central place de l'Église is flanked by the characterful *Hôtel Barberaenea* (Ⓣ05.59.37.74.86, Ⓦwww.hotel-barberaenea.fr; closed mid-Nov to mid-Dec), with a mix of sink-only rooms (❷) and en-suites (❹). There's also a creditable **restaurant**, but lately the best eating in Bidarray is at *Auberge Iparla*, next to the shop and *fronton*, with €22 menus served in the wood-trim salon or on the shaded terrace. Another good staying/eating option down in the riverbank quarter is welcoming *Hôtel-Restaurant du Pont d'Enfer* (Ⓣ05.59.37.70.88, Ⓦwww.hotel-restaurant-du-pont-enfer.com; closed Jan–Feb; ❹), also known as *Chez Anny* after the owner, which has good-sized rooms and a restaurant serving several menus on a river-view terrace in summer. A short walk east, equidistant from upper and riverside quarters, lies tent-only *Camping Errekaldia* (Ⓣ05.59.37.72.36).

Bidarray is the preferred starting point for the classic **ridge-trek** of the Basque country, the section of the GR10 running roughly south along the **Crête d'Iparla**, then descending east to St-Étienne-de-Baïgorry. It's seven hours' walking one way, and should only be attempted in settled conditions – when bad weather closes in, you won't get its famous views and close-range sightings of vultures, and you'll be at risk from lightning strikes or falling from the mist-shrouded brink, both of which kill hikers here regularly. Consult current SNCF schedules before setting out so that you coincide with one of the afternoon **rail-buses** that cover the eight kilometres between St-Étienne and the actual train station of Ossès-St-Martin-d'Arrossa, one stop above Pont-Noblia.

Like most other Basque villages, **ST-ÉTIENNE-DE-BAÏGORRY** is divided into quite distinct quarters, more like separate hamlets than a unified settlement. A prosperous, sleek place, its business is still predominantly agriculture rather than tourism, with the Pays Basque's only vineyards scattered around, producing the Irouléguy (Irulegi) wine named after the village 5km east; the vintner's shop on the D15 road offers *dégustation* and sales. There's little to see here, other than a seventeenth-century, barrel-vaulted **church** with a fine organ over the southwest door in addition to the usual galleries and altarpiece, plus a picturesque medieval bridge posing against a backdrop of the romantic Château de Etchauz and distant hills.

The **tourist office** is opposite the church (May–Sept Mon–Sat 9am–noon & 2–6pm, Sun 10am–1pm; Oct–April Mon–Sat 9am–noon & 2–6pm; Ⓣ05.59.37.47.28). For budget **accommodation**, there's only the municipal **campsite** *Irouléguy* (Ⓣ05.59.37.43.96; April to mid-Dec), opposite the swimming pool on the St-Jean road, now that the local *gîte d'étape* has closed, plus *Hôtel-Restaurant Juantorena* on the through road in Bourg quarter (Ⓣ05.59.37.40.78, Ⓔrestaurant.juantorena@orange.fr; ❸), with a pleasant terrace and parking in the back. With transport, head for the tranquil, streamside *Hôtel-Restaurant Manechenea*, 5km north in the hamlet of Urdos (Urdoze)

(Ⓣ05.59.37.41.68, Ⓔhotel-manechenea@orange.fr; ③; closed Nov–Feb), with a decent restaurant (menu from €16).

St-Jean-Pied-de-Port (Donibane Garazi)

The old capital of Basse Navarre, **ST-JEAN-PIED-DE-PORT** lies in a circle of hills at the foot of the Bentarte pass into Spain. It owes its name to its position "at the foot of the *port*" – a Pyrenean word for "pass". Only part of France since the 1659 Treaty of the Pyrenees, it was an important centre for the **pilgrimage to Santiago de Compostela** in the Middle Ages. The routes from Paris, Vézelay and Le Puy converged just northeast of here at Ostabat, and it was the pilgrims' last port of call before struggling over the pass to the Spanish monastery of Roncesvalles (Roncevaux in French).

The town straddles the young River Nive, the old quarter enclosed by walls of pinky-red sandstone. Above it rises a wooded hill crowned by the Richelieu–Vauban **Citadelle**, while to the east a further defensive system guards the road to Spain. The pleasant but unremarkable modern town spreads down across the

The GR65 south from St-Jean – and the Chanson de Roland

The final French leg of the **GR65** pilgrim route starts from St-Jean and follows the line of the old Roman road across to Roncesvalles in Spanish Navarra, a full day's walk of 27km or at least seven hours. Follow characteristic star-ray yellow-on-blue signs south from the Porte d'Espagne, soon adopting the one-lane D428 with which you will stay for more than half the route; the typical yellow waymarks of the Chemin de St-Jacques show the way, as do newer red-and-white ones. Though the climb is initially dull, on tarmac, there are attractive farmhouses to look at, with immensely broad roofs – one side short, the other long enough to cover space for stalls and tools – plus long views out across the valleys east and west.

After about ninety minutes you'll reach the tiny hamlet of **HONTO**, which for late starters in particular offers excellent *chambres d'hôte* (as well as cheaper dorm beds at €12) and hearty evening meals at *Ferme Ithurburia* (Ⓣ05.59.37.11.17; ③; year round). Beyond Honto, the grade sharpens, but there's only one brief path short cut from the D428 before you arrive, an hour further along, at the well-sited *Refuge-Auberge Orisson* (Ⓣ06.81.49.79.56, Ⓔrefuge.orisson@orange.fr; 18 bunks; April–Oct; €14pp), your last chance for meals (€14) and shelter before Roncesvalles. After passing a pennant-festooned altar, you'll finally leave the D428 for a proper trail at Pic Urdanarré (1240m), some four hours along and just before the frontier and spring at Col de Bentarte (ca.1340m). The Chemin de St-Jacques was rerouted through the Col de Bentarte some years back, diverted from the Puerto de Ibañeta well inside Spain, to the probable annoyance of purists who were committed to the latter as the locale for the events related in the medieval **Chanson de Roland** (though Bentarte is just as likely a venue). Roland, the hero of the tale, was a historical character, warden of the Breton marches, who in 778 accompanied Emperor Charlemagne on a campaign to support the Muslim ruler of Zaragoza in his war against the Emir of Córdoba. The mission degenerated into raids for booty, and on their way home the Franks sacked the Navarrese capital of Pamplona. In revenge, local Basques ambushed and massacred Charlemagne's rearguard, commanded by Roland, as it withdrew up the slopes beyond Roncevaux/Roncesvalles. The medieval romance describes how Roland sounded his horn for aid in vain, and "hewed and smote" various and sundry with his magical sword Durandal – and also labels the dastardly foe as infidel Saracens rather than fellow Christians. This bit of propaganda was concocted four hundred years later during the Crusades, in order to demonize the contemporary Muslim foe.

main road onto lower ground. In season, all of it – except for the further reaches of the new quarters – is packed to the gills with visitors.

The old town consists essentially of a single cobbled street, first as **rue de la Citadelle**, running downhill from the fifteenth-century **Porte St-Jacques** – so named because it was the gate by which pilgrims entered the town, St Jacques being French for Santiago – to the **Porte d'Espagne**, commanding the bridge over the Nive, with a constantly photographed view of balconied houses overlooking the stream. A fourteenth-century Gothic church, **Notre-Dame-du-Bout-du-Pont**, stands just inside the Porte Notre-Dame and, opposite, short rue de l'Église leads through the **Porte de Navarre** to place du Général-de-Gaulle and the modern road; south of the Nive the same main thoroughfare continues, as **rue d'Espagne**, to the southerly **Porte d'Espagne**.

Practicalities

The **tourist office** is at 14 place du Général-de-Gaulle (July & Aug Mon–Sat 9am–7pm, Sun 9.30am–1pm & 2.30–5pm; Sept–June Mon–Sat 9am–noon & 2–6pm; ⓣ05.59.37.03.57, ⓦwww.terre-basque.com), while a handful of newsagents and bookstores sell guides and IGN maps. The **gare SNCF** lies a ten-minute walk away at the end of avenue Renaud, on the northern edge of the centre, while Cycles Garazi at 32bis av du Jaï Alaï rents everything from bikes up to 600cc motorcycles.

Amongst **hotels**, budget choices include the relatively quiet *Les Remparts*, 16 place Floquet (ⓣ05.59.37.13.79, ⓦwww.touradour.com/hotel-remparts.htm; ❸; closed Nov & Dec), just before you cross the Nive coming into town on the Bayonne road, and the *Itzalpea*, 5 place du Trinquet (ⓣ05.59.37.03.66, ⓔitzalpea@orange.fr; closed Sat; ❹). More comfortable are the *Ramuntcho*, just inside the city walls at 1 rue de France (ⓣ05.59.37.03.91, ⓕ05.59.37.35.17; ❺; closed mid-Nov to mid-Dec, Wed, & Tues low season), with a popular restaurant (menus €13–17.50), and the posh *Central* on place du Général-de-Gaulle (ⓣ05.59.37.00.22, ⓕ05.59.37.27.79; ❺; closed Dec–Feb; menu €18–42), with some river-view rooms and free parking.

There are also a few **dormitory lodgings** for pilgrims and hikers, among them the twelve-bunk, helpful *Gîte d'Étape Etchegoin* at 9 rte d'Uhart, on the Bayonne road (ⓣ05.59.37.12.08; €10pp), and Dutch-volunteer-run *L'Esprit du Chemin*, 40 rue de la Citadelle (ⓣ05.59.37.24.68, ⓦwww.espritduchemin.org, April–Sept; €20 HB pp; 14 bunks), offering sound advice and moral support to walkers and Santiago pilgrims. The municipal **campsite**, *Plaza Berri* (ⓣ05.59.37.11.19; Easter–early November), is on the south bank of the Nive, just off avenue du Fronton.

Independent **restaurants** are apt to be slapdash bistros and "café-snacks" aimed squarely at the day-tripper trade. Two exceptions are popular *Paxkal Oillarburu* at 8 rue de l'Église just inside the Porte de Navarre (closed Tues low season, book on ⓣ05.59.37.06.44 in summer), with a €20.50 menu whose portions aren't huge but *garbure* or *frites* are refilled free and quality is high, and *Hurrup Eta Klik* at 3bis rue de la Citadelle (ⓣ05.59.37.09.18; closed Wed), just inside the Porte Notre-Dame and serving country cooking and abundant measures of cider.

Estérençuby, Béhérobie and the source of the Nive

From St-Jean, the D301 follows the deepening valley of the Nive to the southeast, past small red- and green-shuttered farms and attractive villages, while the GR10 stays well northeast of the river, first on paved lanes and then on track or trail along Handiamendi ridge. Both routes converge at **ESTÉRENÇUBY**

(Ezterenzubi), 8km from St-Jean and an attractive spot, well supplied with **accommodation** within sight of the *fronton*. The budget option is hikers' hangout *Auberge Carricaburu* (ⓣ05.59.37.09.77; closed Feb, also Tues/Wed low season; ❷), where all rooms are en suite and some look to the river, with a decent restaurant (€13–18 menu) and the lively village bar. Alternatively, try the larger *Hôtel Andreinia-Larramendy* over the bridge (ⓣ05.59.37.09.70, ⓦwww.hotel-andreinia.com; closed mid-Nov to mid-Dec, Wed low season; ❸), with 2005-remodelled bathrooms and a more elaborate restaurant; they also run a 19-bunk *gîte d'étape* (€12pp).

Beyond Estérençuby the valley-floor D428 road continues alongside the Nive, now no more than a mountain stream, tumbling down between steep green slopes, covered in hay and bracken. Some 4km from Estérençuby the road reaches tiny **Béhérobie** (Beherobia) before climbing up to the border by the Col de Bentarte and looping back to St-Jean – an excellent bike-ride or drive. At Béhérobie the *Hôtel de la Source de la Nive* (ⓣ05.59.37.10.57, ⓔsource.nive@orange.fr; ❷; closed Jan and Tues out of season, booked out in Oct for the pigeon shooting season), beside the stream, is ideal for a quiet stay, with a restaurant where frog's legs, trout, eel and pigeon feature on menus (€14–30).

Just before the bridge at Béhérobie, a lane leads to the left, signposted to "**Source de la Nive**". With a car, you can drive 400m to the end of the asphalt, then continue on foot along the dirt track going left, not the one going over the bridge. After fifteen minutes, you'll reach the springs, where water percolates a thousand metres down through the karstic slopes to well up as surging rapids. Hidden in dense beech woods, it's a magic spot in any weather, with a faint mist often rising from the surface of the water.

Haute Soule

East of the Nive valley, you enter largely uninhabited country, the old Basque county known as the **Haute Soule**, threaded only by the GR10 and a couple of minor roads. The border between Basse Navarre and Soule skims the

Transhumance in the Pyrenees

Like other shepherds in south European or Mediterranean climes, the Basques are forced to take their flocks to high **mountain pastures** in summer in search of better grazing. A few shepherds still live with a couple of dogs out on the treeless slopes in stone-hut sheepfolds called *cayolars*, milking the ewes twice a day and making cheese, the *fromage de brébis*, whose soft and hard versions are a speciality throughout the pastoral Pyrenees. Most of the pastures today are accessible by pick-up or 4WD jeep, at least at the gentler Basque end of the Pyrenees, so a shepherd's life is not as harsh and isolated as it used to be – though there are still places accessible only by mule or pony. A measure of the pre-eminence of sheep in the Basque economy is the Basque word for "rich", *aberats*, the literal meaning of which is "he who owns large flocks".

Much of the grazing land is owned in common by various *communes*, who over the centuries have made elaborate agreements (*faceries*) to ensure a fair share of the best pasture and avoid disputes. One of the oldest of these, concluded by the inhabitants of Spanish Roncal and French Barétous in 1326, is still in force and renewed each July 13 at the frontier **Col de la-Pierre-St-Martin** on symbolic payment of three white heifers.

western edge of the **Forêt d'Iraty**, one of Europe's largest surviving beech woods, a popular summer retreat and winter cross-country skiing area. There are no shops or proper hotels until you reach **Larrau**, the only real village in these mountains, though the scattered hamlet of **Ste-Engrâce** in the east of the district has some facilities, as does **Licq** and **Abense-de-Haut**, foothill settlements some way down the valley. There's even a downhill ski resort, the westernmost in the Pyrenees, at **La-Pierre-St-Martin**, technically just over the border in Béarn but included here for convenience.

Haute Soule is a land of open skies, where griffon vultures turn on the thermals high above countless flocks of sheep (their occasional corpses providing sustenance for the vultures), with three vast gorges to explore. Although the overall distance from the Nive valley to Béarn is not great, the slowness of the roads (there's no public transport) or the GR10 – it's two days' hiking from Estérençuby to Larrau – and the grandeur of the scenery seem to magnify it.

The Forêt d'Iraty (Irati)

To drive to the **Forêt d'Iraty**, follow the D301 east out of the Nive valley from the junction on the D428, where the forest is signposted. The road is steep, narrow and full of tight hairpins and ambling cows, sheep or ponies – it's best avoided at night or in misty conditions – but as you climb up the steep spurs and around the heads of labyrinthine gullies, ever more spectacular views open beneath you. You can see way back over the valley of the Nive, St-Jean and the hills beyond. Beech copses fill the gullies, shadowing the lighter grass whose green is so intense it seems almost theatrical – an effect produced by a backdrop of purplish rock outcrops.

Once past the north flank of **Occabé** (Okabe; 1456m), you're in Soule, and from here the road loops down to meet the D18 on the **plateau d'Iraty**, with its small lake, clutch of snack bars and flat ground to camp on. A minor road, soon a jeep track, leads south towards Ochagavia in Spain via *Chalet Pedro* (1km), a hikers' *gîte* (Ⓣ05.59.28.55.98, Ⓦwww.iraty.chaletpedro.com; 8 places, mid-June to Sept 1; €27pp HB) also incorporating the best **restaurant** in the area. At this point the GR10 emerges from its descent of flat-topped Occabé (75min up from here), with its Iron Age **stone circle** and views across the forest. Continuing east from the plateau, the D18 road enters the densest part of the forest, climbing past another small lake and a **campsite** half hidden in the magnificent beeches, to a collection of nine wooden chalets and a *gîte d'étape* at the **Col de Bargagiak**. An **information** office at the col (open all year; Ⓣ05.59.28.51.29) takes bookings for the chalets and the *gîte* ; across the car park is a small shop and inexpensive restaurant. From here you descend slightly to the nearby **Col d'Orgambidexka**, which is one of the prime viewing fields for the autumn bird migrations. As you emerge into the open beyond Bargagiak, the ground drops sharply away on the left into the **Valleé de Larrau**, 600m lower. To the right, the brilliant grassy swards of the **Pic d'Orhy** (2017m; allow 5hr return hike) culminate in swirling strata of rock below the summit, barring the way to Spain.

Larrau (Larraiñe) to La-Pierre-St-Martin

The first thing you notice coming into **LARRAU** from the west is how different the architecture is. In contrast to the painted, half-timbered facades and tiled roofs of Labourd and Basse Navarre, the houses here are grey and stuccoed, with steep-pitched slate roofs to shed heavy snow – much more like Béarnais houses, in fact. And, although it's the biggest place since St-Jean, it's nonetheless very quiet – almost dead out of season. There are two friendly **hotels**: the simple, old-fashioned *Hôtel Despouey* (ⓣ05.59.28.60.82; ❷–❸; closed mid-Nov to Easter), with a mix of showers and tubs in the baths plus the local shop on the ground floor, and the much fancier *Hôtel-Restaurant Etchémaïté* (ⓣ05.59.28.61.45, ⓦwww.hotel-etchemaite.fr; ❸–❹, HB urged; closed Jan & late Nov), with state-of-the-art rooms and excellent restaurant serving such treats as eels, *cèpes*, pigeon and decadent desserts in small portions (closed Sun eve & Mon low season; menus €18–34).

There's one **campsite** in Larrau, the *Ixtila* (ⓣ05.59.28.63.09; April to mid-Nov), and the *Auberge Logibar*, a *gîte d'étape* with a bar-restaurant 3km away at **LOGIBAR** (ⓣ05.59.28.61.14; 30 places; €12pp restaurant closed Dec–Feb), close to the mouth of the **Gorges d'Holzarte**. This gorge is one of several in the region, cutting deep into northern slopes of the ridge that forms the frontier with Spain. A short track leads from Logibar across a lively, chilly stream to a car park, from where a steep, usually very busy path – a variant of the GR10 – climbs through the beech woods to the junction of the Holzarte gorge with the **Gorges d'Olhadubi** in about 45 minutes. Slung across the mouth of the latter is a spectacular Himalayan-style **suspension bridge**, the *passerelle*, which bounces and swings alarmingly as you walk out over the 180-metre drop. You can continue along the **GR10** to Ste-Engrâce in seven hours, or down to the beginning of the Gorges de Kakuetta in about six; less ambitiously, the car-bound can fashion a very satisfying four-hour loop-hike taking in the entire Gorges d'Olhadubi by using the old GR10, which takes you over the *passerelle*, up along the west flank of the *gorges*, and then crosses it at the Pont d'Olhadubi before returning to Logibar. The route is obviously marked on *Carte de Randonnées* no. 2, "Pays Basque Est".

Licq and Abense-de-Haut

The Gave (Stream) de Larrau and the Gave de Ste-Engrâce unite downstream from Logibar to form the Saison, the major river of Haute Soule. About 2km below this junction on the D26, the pleasant village of **LICQ** (Licq-Atherey on old maps; Ligi in Euskera) offers **accommodation** which, given the scarcity of indoor facilities in the area, might come in handy at high season, especially for those with transport: the rambling, old-style *Hôtel des Touristes-Bouchet* (ⓣ05.59.28.61.01; closed Dec & Jan; ❹), with the best balconied rooms on the first floor and a grassy camping area down by the river. The restaurant is competent but surprisingly pricey; half-board taking in the *menu du soir* eases the pain. Just under 6km north in **ABENSE-DE-HAUT**, *Hôtel Restaurant Ühaltia-Le Pont d'Abense* (ⓣ05.59.28.54.60, ⓔuhaltia@orange.fr; closed early Dec & Jan; ❸) offers better value especially on half-board, with an accomplished restaurant drawing clientele from some distance; the best two rooms have terraces, and the small town of Tardets-Sorholus, with shops and bank ATMs, lies just 800m north.

The Gorges de Kakuetta and Gorges d'Ehujarré

Fifteen kilometres by road east of Larrau, well beyond the turning for Licq and Abense-de-Haut, you reach the **Gorges de Kakuetta** (mid-March to mid-Nov daily 8am–nightfall; €4), having veered off the D26 and onto the D113. About 4km along the latter, the minuscule hamlet of **CASERNES** offers a food shop opposite the *mairie*, and an attractive riverside **campsite**, the *Ibarra* (ⓣ05.59.28.73.59; Easter–Oct).

Kakuetta gorge is truly dramatic and, outside peak season, not crowded at all; allow ninety minutes to two hours for the visit. It pays to be well shod – the metal catwalk or narrow path, by turns, are slippery in places and provided with safety cables where needed. The walls of the gorge are up to 300m high and scarcely more than 5m apart in spots, such that little sunlight penetrates except at midday from May to July. The air hangs heavy with mist produced by the dozens of seeps and tiny waterfalls, nurturing tenacious ferns, moss and other vegetation that thrives in the hothouse atmosphere. The path continues for about an hour up to a small cave beyond which only technical climbers need apply; just before it a twenty-metre waterfall (which you can walk behind) gushes out of a hole in the rock.

There's another, scarcely visited gorge, the **Gorges d'Ehujarré**, a short distance east at Senta, the easternmost of the three hamlets that comprise Ste-Engrâce (see below). It's a straightforward walk up – the route has been used for centuries for moving sheep up to the pastures of Pic Lakhoura – and then down along the gorge floor, but involves a five-hour round trip.

Ste-Engrâce and La-Pierre-St-Martin

Le bout du monde – "the end of the earth" – is what they used to call the tiny settlement of **STE-ENGRÂCE**, locked in its cul-de-sac valley beneath the Spanish frontier at the easternmost extremity of the Basque country. And, although a road now runs through it to Béarb and La-Pierre-St-Martin, the place remains beautifully remote and peaceful. Life is not so idyllic for the locals – there's no work and the young won't stay – but for an outsider not caught in the rural poverty trap, it has great charm.

Ste-Engrâce's hallmark is the eleventh-century Romanesque **church** in the hamlet of **SENTA**, which features in most coffee-table books about the Pyrenees. Focus of a popular festival the last two Sundays in July, it stands with its heavily buttressed walls, belfry and assymetrical roof, a sharply defined and angular assertion of humanity against the often mist-shrouded bulwarks of the mountains behind. Inside, it has some excellent carved column capitals depicting among other things the *Adoration of the Magi*, lions devouring Christians, and King Solomon copulating with the Queen of Sheba. There's a 30-bunk **gîte d'étape** opposite the church, the *Auberge Elichalt* (Ⓣ05.59.28.61.63; €10), with a few *chambres d'hôtes* (❸), a back garden to pitch a tent and a café-bar that serves light meals.

The road up to the ski resort of **LA-PIERRE-ST-MARTIN** (Arette-la-Pierre on old maps) gives fabulous views of the valley of Ste-Engrâce, through magnificent forests of pine and beech, though if the cloud is down, which it often is, you'll be lucky to see much at all. At a little col with a three-way junction, you're just inside the ancient county of Béarn, and can glimpse the descent east into the Vallée d'Aspe. The upper, right-hand turning leads into La-Pierre, an ugly ski resort with eighteen pistes (some very long), and the excellent *Refuge Jeandel* (Ⓣ05.59.66.14.46; Ⓦwww.refugejeandel.com; May–Sept; €10.50 in 3- to 6-bunk dorms), mostly serving trekkers on the GR10, with enthusiastic management and meals. The skiing here is better than you'd imagine at the modest altitude (2153m top point), owing to moist Atlantic exposure and some quite long runs for beginners and intermediates. There are also two nordic skiing areas nearby.

The Central Pyrenees

The **Central Pyrenees**, immediately east of the Pays Basque, hosts the range's highest mountain peaks, with the most spectacular southernmost

The Parc National des Pyrénées

The **Parc National des Pyrénées** was created in 1967 to protect at least part of the high Pyrenees from the development engendered by modern tourism – ski resorts, roads, mountain-top restaurants, car parks and other inappropriate amenities. It runs for more than 100km along the Spanish border from Pic de Laraille (2147m), south of Lescun, in the west, to beyond Pic de la Munia (3133m), almost to the Aragnouet–Bielsa tunnel. Varying in altitude between 1070m and 3298m at the Pic de Vignemale, south of Cauterets, the park takes in the spectacular cirques of Gavarnie and Troumouse, as well as over two hundred lakes, more than a dozen valleys and about 400km of marked walking routes.

Through the **banning of hunting** and all dogs and vehicles (except local herders), the park has also provided sanctuary for many rare and endangered species of birds and mammals. Among them are chamois, marmots, ermines, genets, griffon vultures, golden eagles, eagle owls and capercaillies, to say nothing of the rich and varied flora. The most celebrated animal – extinct as of 2004 – is the Pyrenean **brown bear**, whose prewar numbers ran to as many as two hundred; the dozen specimens are all descended from introduced Slovenian brown bears. Although largely herbivorous, these bears will take sheep or cows when given the opportunity, and the mountain shepherds are their remorseless enemies. To appease them, local authorities pay prompt and generous compensation for any losses – the restocking programme remains highly controversial, with pro- and anti-graffitti prominent on the road approaches to the park, and troublesome animals being shot illegally by aggrieved farmers or herders on a regular basis.

The **GR10** runs through the entire park on its 700-kilometre journey from coast to coast, starting at Argelès-sur-Mer on the Mediterranean and ending up at Hendaye-Plage on the Atlantic shore; the tougher **Haute Randonnée Pyrénéenne** (HRP) also finishes its course in Hendaye-Plage and runs roughly parallel to the GR10, but takes in much more rugged, alpine terrain. Hikers following either route are strongly advised to heed the warnings on p.758. Though the Pyrenees have a modest maximum altitude by world-mountain standards, their climate can be as extreme as ranges twice their height.

There are **Maisons du Parc** (park information centres) in Etsaut, Cauterets, Luz-St-Sauveur, Gavarnie, Laruns and Arrens-Marsous, giving information about the park's wildlife and vegetation, lists of accommodation options and the best walks. There are over a dozen wardened refuges in *parc* territory and plenty of hotels, campsites and *gîtes* just outside it, listed in the text of this chapter or highlighted on the map on p.792. Backcountry camping (*camping sauvage*) is forbidden in many areas, except for emergency bivouacs above 2000m elevation which must be disassembled by 9am. For an update on weather conditions in the *département* of Hautes-Pyrénées, telephone ⓣ08.92.68.02.65, or ⓣ3250, option 4.

section by the border protected within the **Parc National des Pyrénées**. Getting here by public transport is straightforward, at least as far as the foothill towns, served by frequent trains on the Bayonne–Toulouse line. But travelling uphill, and around once there, can be very slow. Buses – and most other traffic – keep mainly to the north–south valleys, making it difficult to switch from one valley system to the next without having to come all the way out of the mountains each time. The **GR10** provides a good lateral link if you're prepared to walk, and it's possible to hitch across the main passes such as the **Col d'Aubisque** and **Col du Tourmalet**, though you'll often get left on the top by drivers who come up for the view and go back the same way.

Highlights – apart from the lakes, torrents, forests and 3000-metre peaks around **Cauterets** – are the cirques of **Lescun**, **Gavarnie** and **Troumouse**, each with its distinctive character. And for less *sportif* interests, there's many a flower-starred mountain meadow accessible by car, especially near **Barèges** and **Luchon**, in which to picnic. The only real urban centres are **Pau**, a probable entry point to the area, dull **Tarbes** and the tacky pilgrimage target of **Lourdes**. Great monuments of the bricks-and-mortar kind – with the exception of the fortified churches at **Luz-St-Sauveur**, **St-Savin** and **St-Bertrand-de-Comminges** – are equally scarce, though there are also wonderful Romanesque carvings on smaller churches at **Oloron-Ste-Marie**, **St-Aventin** and **Valcabrère**.

Pau and around

From humble beginnings as a crossing on the Gave de Pau (*gave* is "mountain river" in Gascon dialect), **PAU** became the capital of the ancient viscountcy of Béarn in 1464, and of the French part of the kingdom of Navarre in 1512. In 1567 its sovereign, Henri d'Albret, married the sister of French King François I, Marguerite d'Angoulême, friend and protector of artists and intellectuals and

herself the author of a celebrated Boccaccio-like tale (the *Heptameron*), who transformed the town into a centre of the arts and nonconformist thinking.

Their daughter was Jeanne d'Albret, a philistine Protestant, whose zeal offended her own subjects as well as attracting the wrath of the Catholic king of France, Charles X, thus embroiling Béarn in the Wars of Religion – whose resolution, albeit only temporary, had to await the accession to the French throne of her own son, Henri III of Navarre, in 1589. An adroit politician, he renounced his faith to facilitate his transformation into Henri IV of France, quipping that "Paris is worth a Mass" and then appeasing the regional sensibilities of his Béarnais subjects by announcing that he was giving France to Béarn rather than Béarn to France. He did not incorporate Béarn into the French state; that was left to his heir and successor, Louis XIII, in 1620. As Pau's most famous son, Henri acquired a suitably colourful reputation. He was baptized in traditional Béarnais style with the local Jurançon wine, and his infant lips were rubbed with garlic. In his adult life he was known as the *vert-galant* for his prowess as a lover. He also gave France one of its more famous recipes, *poulet au pot* – chicken stuffed and boiled with vegetables: he reputedly said that he did not want anyone in his realm to be so poor as not to be able to afford a *poulet* in the *pot* once a week.

The least-expected thing about Pau is its English connection, which dates from the arrival of Wellington and his troops after the defeat of Maréchal Soult at Orthez in 1814. Seduced by its climate and persuaded (mistakenly) of its curative powers by the Scottish doctor Alexander Taylor, the English flocked to Pau throughout the nineteenth century, bringing along their peculiar cultural obsessions – fox-hunting, horse-racing, polo, croquet, cricket, golf (the first eighteen-hole course in continental Europe in 1860 and the first to admit women), tea salons and parks. When the railway arrived here in 1866, the French came, too: writers like Victor Hugo, Stendhal and Lamartine, as well as the socialites. The first French rugby club opened here in 1902, after which the sport spread throughout the southwest. During the 1950s, natural gas was discovered at nearby Lacq, bringing new jobs and subsidiary industries, as well as massive sulphur-dioxide-based pollution, now reduced by filtration – and the steady depletion of the gas fields. In addition, there's a well-respected university, founded in 1972, whose 15,000 students give the town a youthful buzz.

Pau lies within easy reach of numerous small, picturesque villages in **northwest Béarn**, as well as the GR65 footpath that runs some 60km down to the Spanish border.

Arrival and information

Pau's **airport** (Ⓣ05.59.33.33.00, Ⓦwww.pau.aeroport.fr), is increasingly busy, with Ryanair arrivals from London (Stansted) exceeding those at Biarritz and four flights weekly on Transavia from Amsterdam. Regular *navettes* run to the city centre (€5 one way), as well as to Lourdes and Tarbes (€6), but a taxi to town will cost about €20. The town lies on the A64 Autoroute Pyrénéenne and on the main east–west rail route, with connections to Bayonne and Biarritz to the west, and Lourdes, Tarbes and Toulouse to the east, as well as to Bordeaux and Paris. The **gare SNCF**, for both trains and SNCF buses, is on the southern edge of the city centre by the riverside. TPR buses leave from a terminal at 4 rue Lapouble, near place de Verdun, whilst CITRAM buses leave from a stop at the west end of the Parc Beaumont. Services run south down the Vallée d'Ossau and to Oloron-Ste-Marie, with onward connections from there to the Vallée d'Aspe. **Parking** is predictably difficult; there are a few free spaces at the far west end of boulevard des Pyrénées and on place de Verdun, otherwise shell out for kerbside meters or use the giant underground car park at place Georges-Clemenceau.

A **free funicular** (out of service indefinitely) used to carry you up from the train station to the boulevard des Pyrénées, opposite place Royale; until it's repaired, pedestrian rampways help tackle the grade. At the far end of the place is the **tourist office** (July & Aug daily 9am–6pm; Sept–June Mon–Sat 9am–6pm, Sun 9.30am–1pm; ⓣ05.59.27.27.08, ⓦwww.pau.fr). Librairie des Pyrénées at 14 rue St-Louis stocks a wide range of books and maps on the mountains.

Accommodation

For a friendly, clean and quiet budget **hotel**, try the *Hôtel le Matisse*, 17 rue Mathieu-Lalanne, opposite the Musée des Beaux-Arts (ⓣ05.59.27.73.80; ❷), all rooms with showers, some with toilets. Mid-range options include the excellent-value *Central*, 15 rue Léon-Daran (ⓣ05.59.27.33.28, ⓦwww.hotelcentralpau.com; ❸–❹), with unusually tasteful room decor and Wi-Fi connection throughout, or the *Postillon* at 10 Cours Camou behind place de Verdun (ⓣ05.59.72.83.00, ⓦwww.hotel-le-postillon.fr; ❸), an old coaching inn arrayed around its own courtyard, with parking possible on the *place*. Amongst a half-dozen three-star contenders, most stylish is 2005-renovated *Le Montpensier* (ⓣ05.59.27.42.72, ⓔhotel.montpensier-pau@orange.fr; ❹), at 36 rue Montpensier, an eighteenth-century building with private parking, non-smoking rooms and Internet access.

There is a **hostel** at 30 rue Michel-Hounau (ⓣ05.59.11.05.05, ⓦwww.ldjpau.org), and a single surviving municipal **campsite**, *La Plaine des Sports* on boulevard du Cami-Salié, off avenue Sallenave towards the autoroute, on the northern edge of town (ⓣ05.59.02.30.49; May to late Sept).

The Town

Pau has no must-see sights or museums, enabling you to enjoy its relaxed and friendly elegance without any sense of guilt. The parts to wander are the streets behind the **boulevard des Pyrénées**, especially the western end, which stretches along the rim of the scarp above the Gave de Pau, from the castle to the Palais Beaumont, now a convention centre, in the English-style **Parc Beaumont**. On a (rare) clear day, the view from the boulevard encompasses a hundred-kilometre sweep of the highest Pyrenean peaks, with the distinctive Pic du Midi d'Ossau slap in front of you.

In the narrow streets around the castle and down in the gully of the chemin du Hédas are numerous cafés, restaurants, bars and boutiques, with the main **market** in the *halles* just northeast on place de la République each Saturday morning. The **château** itself (exterior gardens free, unenclosed) is very much a landmark building, though not much remains of its original appearance beyond the southeasterly brick keep built by Gaston Fébus in 1370. The handsome Renaissance windows and other details on the inner courtyard were added by Henri d'Albret. Louis-Philippe renovated it in the nineteenth century after it had stood empty for two hundred years, and Napoléon III and Eugénie titivated it further with stellar vaulting, chandeliers and coffered ceilings to make it suitable for weekend house parties. The **Musée National** inside is visitable by a skull-thumpingly boring, French-only, one-hour guided tour (daily: mid-June to mid-Sept 9am–12.15pm & 1.30–5.45pm, mid-Sept to mid-June 9.30–11.45am & 2–5pm, €5 except €3.50 Sun), but this is the only way to see the vivid eighteenth-century tapestries with their wonderfully observed scenes of rural life, or Henri IV memorabilia like the giant turtle shell that allegedly served as his cradle.

A short distance northeast of the château, the mildly interesting **Musée Bernadotte**, 6 rue Tran (Tues–Sun 10am–noon & 2–6pm; €3), is the birthplace of the man who, having served as one of Napoleon's commanders, went on to become Charles XIV of Sweden. As well as fine pieces of traditional Béarnais furniture, the house contains some valuable works of art collected over his lifetime. Pau's other museum, the **Musée des Beaux-Arts** in rue Mathieu-Lalanne (daily except Tues 10am–noon & 2–6pm; €3), has an eclectic collection of little-known works from various European schools spanning the fourteenth to twentieth centuries; the only really world-class items are Rubens' *The Last Judgement* and Degas' *The Cotton Exchange*, a slice of finely observed *belle-époque* New Orleans life.

Eating and drinking

Pau's smarter **restaurants** are concentrated in the pedestrianized lanes around the château, on place Royal or in rue du Hédas, though there are a few choices elsewhere. **Bars**, many themed (Australia, rugby and so on), cluster immediately around the crescent of boulevard Aragon, about halfway along boulevard des Pyrénées.

Le Berry rue Gachet, near corner rue Louis-Barthou. Less than brilliant siting, by the "rabbit hole" of the subterranean car park, but compensated for by the excellent brasserie grub (*magret de canard*, Chateaubriand steaks). Expect a wait for interior tables; service until 11pm; budget €20–28 à la carte.

Le Champagne 5 place Royale. A newish, popular, upscale brasserie with *carte* or five *formules* at €11–22; there's a lovely interior with swirling fans, or eat out on the *place* in fine weather. Service barely copes with the crush, however.

Chez Maman 6 rue de Château. Simple but palatable crêperie/*cidrerie* right opposite the castle, which doesn't unduly abuse its unbeatable position; a good option for vegetarians, with big salads – for two courses and a bit of cider you'll have change from a €20 note. Tues–Sun 11am–midnight.

Au Fin Gourmet, 24 av Gaston-Lacoste, opposite the *gare SNCF*. Trim, modern place with a few game-oriented lunch menus (pigeon, rabbit) from €17, but best allow €35-plus à la carte. Closed Sun eve & Mon, plus 2 weeks in mid-summer.

O'Gascon 13 rue du Château. The most popular and reasonable of the four non-pizzerias on this little *place*; their €27 *menu tradition* – big salad, stuffed quail, free dessert choice – is excellent. Supper only except Sun lunch.

La Table d'Hôte 1 rue du Hédas. Elegant bare-brick restaurant in a former warehouse, one of the first to colonize this trendy area and relying on the backbone of traditional French cooking: duck, pork, foie gras, lamb. Affordable menus at €23–29; service can be leisurely. Closed all Sun, Mon lunch.

Around Pau

One excursion worth making from Pau, particularly for families, is to the **Grottes de Bétharram** (Ⓦwww.grottes-de-bethrarram.com; guided tours only late March to late Oct daily 9am–noon & 1.30–5.30pm; early Feb to late March groups only Mon–Fri 2.30–4pm; €9.50) at St-Pé-de-Bigorre, just off the D937 between Pau and Lourdes, 14km from the latter. Part of the eighty-minute tour around its spectacular stalactites and stalagmites takes place in a barge on an underground lake; the remaining kilometre is by miniature railway.

In the opposite (northwest) direction from Pau lies tourist-board-dubbed **Béarn des Gaves**, so called because several *gaves* – de Pau, de Oloron, the Seleys and the Saison – slant across the landscape before mingling with each other or, ultimately, the Adour. The four major destinations here duly have strategic riverside locations, and three were traditional stops on the **Chemin de St-Jacques**, though the main variant of the modern GR65 route traces a course across the southeast of the territory.

Orthez

Thirty kilometres northwest of Pau, **ORTHEZ** was the original capital of Béarn, its wealth due in large part to its beautiful and still-surviving thirteenth-century **fortified bridge**, which controlled the most important commercial route across the Gave de Pau for English and Flemish textiles, Aragonese wool, olive oil and wine. The town also serves as a gateway to Haute Soule in the Pays Basque: SNCF **buses** run from Puyôo, 12km west, to Salies-de-Béarn, Sauveterre-de-Béarn and Mauléon.

The **tourist office** (July & Aug Mon–Sat 9am–12.30pm & 2–7pm, Sun 9.30am–12.30pm; Sept–June Mon–Sat 9am–noon & 2–6pm; Ⓣ05.59.69.37.50) occupies the sixteenth-century Maison Jeanne d'Albret on rue du Bourg-Vieux, which also hosts a **Musée Jeanne d'Albret** on the second floor (Mon–Sat 10am–noon & 2–6pm; €2.50), tracing the history of local Protestantism. Other fine old houses can be found in the town centre, especially along **rue Moncade**, the continuation of rue du Bourg-Vieux, where the five-sided Tour Moncade is all that remains of Orthez's castle. The **church of St-Pierre**, close to the tourist office, still has some interesting Gothic sculptures, though it was badly damaged when the town was sacked by Jeanne d'Albret's Protestant general Montgomery in 1569. Should you need to **stay** overnight, your best option is the historic, en-suite *Hôtel Restaurant Au Temps de la Reine Jeanne*, opposite the tourist office at 44 rue du Bourg-Vieux (Ⓣ05.59.67.00.76, Ⓦwww.reine-jeanne.fr; ❸; closed late Feb to early March), with a traditional-fare restaurant (menus from €18). The municipal **campsite**, *Camping de la Source* is on boulevard Charles-de-Gaulle (Ⓣ05.59.69.04.81, Ⓦwww.camping-orthez.com; April–Oct).

Salies-de-Béarn to Navarrenx

Fifteen kilometres west from Orthez (TPR bus from Pau), **SALIES-DE-BÉARN** is a typical Béarnais village of winding lanes and flower-decked houses with brightly painted woodwork. The River Saleys, hardly more than a stream here, runs through the middle of it, separating the old village from the nineteenth-century development that sprang up to exploit the powerful saline spring for which it has long been famous. You can try the curative waters yourself at the wonderful nineteenth-century **thermal baths** (Ⓦwww.thermes-de-salies.com), in place Jardin Public, starting from €8 for a plunge in the outdoor, 32°C pool (daily May–Sept). The **tourist office** is 150m around the corner on rue des Bains (mid-June to mid-Sept Mon–Sat 9.30am–12.30pm & 2.30–7pm, Sun 9.30am–12.30pm; mid-Sept to mid-June Mon–Sat 9.30am–noon & 2–6pm; Ⓣ05.59.38.00.33, Ⓦwww.bearn-gaves.com).

Accommodation includes the the economical but en-suite *Au Petit Béarn* (Ⓣ05.59.38.17.42, Ⓕ05.59.65.01.75; ❷; closed 2 weeks in Feb, restaurant closed Fri eve & Sat noon Oct–Feb) on rue Bellecave, off the road to Sauveterre. A plusher but good-value option is the *Helios Golf* (Ⓣ05.59.38.37.59, Ⓦwww.golf.salies.com; ❹), on the northeastern outskirts of town, by the twelve-hole course. The closest local **campsite** is *Mosqueros*, 1km from the *thermes* (Ⓣ05.59.38.12.94; mid-March to Oct).

Heading south, the D933 winds over hilly farming country to **SAUVETERRE-DE-BÉARN**, another pretty country town beautifully sited on an escarpment high above the Gave d'Oloron, just before it mingles with the Saison. From the terrace by the thirteenth-century **church of St-André**

– over-restored but still retaining a fine west-portal relief of Christ in Glory – you look down over the river and the remains of fortified, half-ruined **Pont de la Légende**, while at the west end of the compact *cité médiévale* stand the ruins of a **château** built by Gaston Fébus. A pedestrian-only lane leads down to the bridge and river, full of bathers on hot days despite its murky greenness; many come from the adjacent, tent-friendly *Camping du Gave* (ⓣ05.59.38.53.30; mid-April to mid-Oct). Surviving indoor **accommodation** comprises *Auberge du Saumon* (ⓣ05.59.38.53.20; closed mid-Jan to mid-Feb & Sat low season; ❷), an old coaching inn across the river on the road south out of town, and less remote *La Maison de Navarre* in quartier St-Marc (ⓣ05.59.38.55.28, ⓦwww.lamaisondenavarre.com; closed Feb, restaurant closed Sun eve low season & Wed; ❹), a converted garden-set mansion.

Just across the river, the D936 bears southeast along the flat valley bottom to **NAVARRENX**, 20km away on the Pau–Mauléon bus route, a sleepy, old-fashioned market town built as a *bastide* in 1316 and still surrounded by its medieval **walls**; having crossed the medieval **bridge**, you enter from the west by the fortified **Porte St-Antoine**. The *Hôtel du Commerce* just inside on place des Casernes makes an agreeable place to **stay** (ⓣ05.59.66.50.16, ⓦwww.hotel-commerce.fr; ❸; closed mid-Dec to Jan; excellent restaurant with menus from €18). GR 65 hikers have two pilgrims' **gîtes** to choose from: the spartan *Communal* on place du Forail, housed in a medieval arsenal (ⓣ05.59.66.02.67, all year, 35 places, €10 pp) or the higher-standard *Charbel* some way out on chemin du Moulin (ⓣ05.59.66.07.25, ⓦwww.etapecharbel.com; April–Oct; 20 places; €13pp, includes 6 double rooms), set in a parkland with a pond. There's also a riverside **campsite**, the *Beau Rivage*, in allée des Marronniers southwest of the ramparts (ⓣ05.59.66.10.00, mid-March to mid-Oct).

Lourdes and around

LOURDES, 37km southeast of Pau by either of two routes, has just one function. Over seven million Catholic pilgrims arrive here each year, and the town is totally given over to looking after and exploiting them. Lourdes was hardly more than a village before 1858, when Bernadette Soubirous, 14-year-old daughter of a poor local miller, had the first of eighteen visions of the Virgin Mary in the Grotte de Massabielle by the Gave de Pau. Since then, Lourdes has become one of the biggest attractions in this part of France, many of its visitors hoping for a miraculous cure for conventionally intractable ailments.

The first large-scale **pilgrimage** took place in 1873, organized by a fundamentalist Catholic movement called the Assomptionistes, whose avowed purpose was to stem the advancing tide of republicanism and rationalism. They took over the management of Lourdes, shoving aside the local clergy who had wanted to organize the pilgrimages themselves. Adroit propagandists and agitators, the Assomptionistes sought to promote their cause by publishing a cheap mass-circulation paper called *La Croix*, aimed at the poor and uneducated.

Practically every shop is given over to the sale of unbelievable (in all senses) religious kitsch: Bernadette and/or the Virgin in every shape and size, adorning barometers, thermometers, plastic tree trunks, key rings, empty bottles that you can fill with holy Lourdes water, bellows, candles, sweets and illuminated plastic grottoes. There's even a waxworks museum, the **Musée Grévin**, at 87 rue de la Grotte (daily: Easter to mid-July & late Aug to Oct daily 9am–noon & 1.45–6.30pm; mid-July to Aug 9am–6.30pm; €6), with over a hundred life-

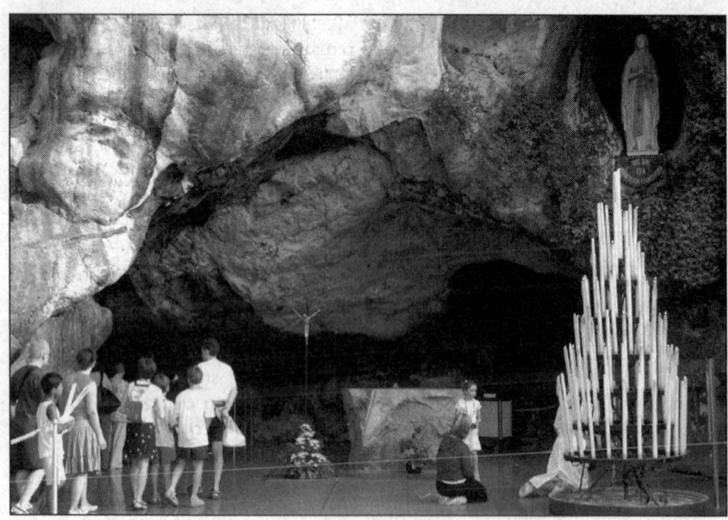

△ Grotte de Massabielle, Lourdes

size figures illustrating the lives of Bernadette and Christ. Clustered around the miraculous grotto are the churches of the Domaine de la Grotte, an annexe to the town proper that sprang up in the century following Bernadette's visions. The first to be built was an underground crypt in 1866, followed by the flamboyant double **Basilique du Rosaire et de l'Immaculée Conception** (1871–1883), and then in 1958 by the massive subterranean **Basilique St-Pie-X**, which claims to be able to fit in 20,000 people at a time. The **Grotte de Massabielle** itself is the focus of the pilgrimages – a moisture-blackened overhang by the riverside with a marble statue on high of the Virgin, where pilgrims queue to circumambulate, stroking the grotto wall with their left hand. To one side are taps for filling souvenir containers with the holy spring water; to the other are the *bruloirs* or rows of braziers where enormous votive candles burn, to prolong the prayers of supplicants.

Musée Pyrénéen

Lourdes' only secular attraction is its **château**, poised on a rocky bluff east of the Gave de Pau, guarding the approaches to the valleys and passes of the central Pyrenees. Briefly an English stronghold in the late fourteenth century, it later became a state prison. Inside, it houses the surprisingly excellent **Musée Pyrénéen** (1hr guided visits daily: April to mid-July & mid-Aug to Sept 9am–noon & 1.30–6.30pm; mid-July to mid-Aug 9am–6.30pm; Oct–March 9am–noon & 2–5/6pm; last tour 1hr before closing; €5). Its collections include Pyrenean fauna, all sorts of fascinating pastoral and farming gear, and an interesting section on the history of Pyrenean mountaineering.

Practicalities

Tarbes-Ossun-Lourdes **airport** receives only charters (for summer pilgrims) at the moment, but a no-frills airline may serve it in the near future; there's no shuttle bus at present, and a taxi the 11km into Lourdes costs an inflated €22.

Lourdes' **gare SNCF** is on the northeast edge of the town centre, at the end of avenue de la Gare; the **gare routière** is in the central place Capdevieille, and the not terribly helpful **tourist office** is in place Peyramale (Easter–June & Sept to mid-Oct Mon–Sat 9am–7pm, Sun 11am–6pm; July & Aug Mon–Sat 9am–7pm, Sun 10am–6pm; mid-Oct to Easter Mon–Sat 9am–noon & 2–6pm; Ⓣ05.62.42.77.40, Ⓦwww.lourdes-infotourisme.com).

Lourdes has more **hotels** than any city in France outside Paris, mostly modest establishments concentrated in the streets around the castle. A comfortable hotel, opposite the food *halles*, some 300m south of place Peyramale, is the two-star *Hôtel d'Albret* (Ⓣ05.62.94.75.00, Ⓔalbret.taverne.lourdes@libertysurf.fr; ❸; closed mid-Nov to mid-March), with the affiliated *Taverne de Bigorre* on the ground floor offering a range of menus (€19 gets you three hearty courses). The nearest **campsite** is the cramped *Poste*, 26 rue de Langelle, just south of the *gare SNCF* (Ⓣ05.62.94.40.35; April to mid-Oct).

Tarbes

Twenty minutes away by train to the north, **TARBES** is a relatively dull town dominated by its history as a military stronghold, but useful for visiting Lourdes or launching into the mountains to the south. Tarbes' only real highlight is the Napoleonic stud farm, **Les Haras**, entered from chemin de Mauhourat (Ⓦwww.haras-nationaux.fr; 1hr guided visits by appointment only: tours depart July & Aug Mon–Fri half-hourly 10–11am & 2–5pm, rest of year Mon–Fri 10am, 11am, 2pm, 3pm & 4pm; also some Sun half-hourly 2.30–4pm; Ⓣ05.62.56.30.80; €6), best known for the *cheval Tarbais*, bred from English, Basque and Arabian stock as a cavalry horse. You can watch them drilling at 3.15pm except February to July when the horses are out to stud.

The **gare SNCF** is on avenue Maréchal-Joffre, about 500m north of the centre, and the **gare routière** on the other side of town on place au Bois, off rue Larrey. The **tourist office** is near the central place de Verdun, at 3 cours Gambetta (Mon–Sat 9am–12.30pm & 2–7pm; Ⓣ05.62.51.30.31, Ⓦwww.tarbes.com). Tarbes has some reasonably priced **hotels** in the vicinity of the station, the best of these being *Hôtel Isard*, 70 av Maréchal-Joffre (Ⓣ05.62.93.06.69, Ⓕ05.62.93.99.55; ❷); there's also a **HI hostel** at 88 av Alsace-Lorraine (Ⓣ05.62.38.91.20, Ⓔaj.tarbes@orange.fr). Most people will probably only stop long enough for a meal, so luckily there's more choice in **restaurants**. A bit out of the way, but worth the trek east of the Jardin Massey, is *Chez Patrick* at 6 rue Adolphe-d'Eichtal, a cheery working-class institution that fills by 12.30pm and features a sustaining five-course menu (including wine and coffee). Rues Bertrand-Barère and parallel Victor-Hugo in particular are good hunting grounds for everything from Moroccan to local cooking, but the town's best is indisputably *L'Ambroiserie* occupying an old mansion at 48 rue Abbé-Tornee near the Préfecture, the *département*'s only Michelin-starred restaurant. There's garden seating on fine days, and an affordable weekday lunch menu, but budget €85 à la carte otherwise.

The valleys of the Aspe and Ossau

The parallel north to south valleys of the **Aspe** and **Ossau** present the central Pyrenees at their most undeveloped, especially in the Aspe valley, because inappropriate topography and unreliable snow conditions have precluded ski-resort construction – but what tourism has failed to do, a major road-building scheme threatens to achieve (see box below). To see the best of the region you should get out a large-scale map and walk perpendicular to the line of the valleys, using the handful of refuges or camping in permitted areas along the way.

Oloron-Ste-Marie

The valley of the Aspe begins at the grey town of **OLORON-STE-MARIE**, around 45km west of Lourdes and only 33km southwest of Pau, where the mountain streams of the Aspe and Ossau meet to form the Gave d'Oloron. It's served by train from Pau as well as by CITRAM buses, with daily SNCF buses continuing up the valley to Urdos, a few of these continuing as far as Canfranc in Spain. Oloron was long famous as the manufacturing centre for the famous woollen pancake-shaped *beret basque*, once the standard headgear for all French men but now seldom seen; the single surviving factory has had to branch out into more fashionable hats.

There is little here to detain the visitor other than the **Cathédrale Ste-Marie** across the Gave d'Aspe, with its beautiful Romanesque west portal in Pyrenean marble. In the upper arch, the elders of the Apocalypse play violins and rebecs, while in the second arch scenes from medieval life – a cooper, the slaying of

The Vallée d'Aspe autoroute

Since the early 1990s, the **Vallée d'Aspe** has been the focus of bitter controversies between mainly out-of-area environmentalists, and official planners plus local boosters of a multi-lane **autoroute** through the valley. This was part of a wider campaign for two or more tunnels under the middle of the range, a strategy with stronger advocacy in Spain, keen to export its heavy and/or perishable goods – paving stones, manufactured goods, farm produce – as quickly and cheaply as possible to northern Europe.

In the case of the Aspe, an all-weather tunnel was finally opened in 2003 under the Col du Somport at the head of the valley, after being delayed some years by cost overruns and design changes required by the environmental litigants, many of them part of the organization CSAVA, based at Cette-Eygun. Locals at first bitterly resented now-defunct CSAVA and its flamboyant chief Eric Pétetin, seeing increased north–south communication as the only hope of keeping valley communities from dying on the vine, but since the tunnel has opened and the next phase of the project looms, there's been a change of heart as implications sink in. The slopes of the Aspe would be blasted and engineered to accommodate a six-lane highway carrying hundreds of articulated lorries daily, blighting the villages which were supposed to be rejuvenated by the project. Everywhere in the area you'll see bumper stickers with a terse "NON" and the silhouette of a truck in the middle of the "O".

As a condition of the tunnel's construction, provision was supposed to have been made to rehabilitate the long-abandoned trans-frontier railway to carry freight as well as passengers; although EU funding has been approved "in principle", the only sign of rehabilitation is the current restoration of Canfranc station, just over the border, as a hotel and convention centre in expectation of increased traffic. Ironically, two factors are conspiring to make the Somport tunnel obsolete within a few years of opening: spiralling costs will soon make the mega-motorway unfeasible, and the low-wage economies of the EU's newest Central European members will render Spanish exports uneconomical in comparison. The likely outcome may instead be massive expansion of port facilities around Perpignan and Bayonne at each end of the range, to take pressure off the hopelessly lorry-congested motorways there.

a wild boar, fishing for salmon – are represented. The gallant knight on horseback over the outer column on the right is Gaston IV, Count of Béarn, who commissioned the portal on his return from the first Crusade at the beginning of the twelfth century – hence the inclusion of Saracens in chains among the sculptures. The magnificent studded doors were a present from Henri IV. Inside, well away from the main area of worship, stands a stoup reserved for use by the Cagots, a stark reminder of centuries-long persecution and segregation of this mysterious group of people, thought by some to have been lepers and by others to have been of Visigothic origin. Across the river in Oloron, hilltop **Sainte-Croix** is one of the oldest Romanesque structures in Béarn, its unusual interior vaulting created by thirteenth-century Spanish stonemasons in imitation of the Great Mosque in Córdoba.

Oloron's **tourist office** lies west of the Aspe in the Villa Bourdeu (July & Aug Mon–Sat 9am–7pm, Sun 10am–1pm; Sept–June Mon–Sat 9am–12.30pm & 2–6.30pm; ⓣ05.59.39.98.00, ⓦwww.ot-oloron-ste-marie.fr). **Accommodation** nearby includes the *Hôtel Bristol* at 9 rue Carréot (ⓣ05.59.39.43.78, ⓕ05.59.39.08.19; ❸) with a restaurant (menus from €18; closed Sun lunch), or the *Hôtel de la Paix* at 24 av Sadi-Carnot opposite the train station (ⓣ05.59.39.02.63; ❸), quiet despite the location and with easier parking. The closest **campsite** is *Camping du Stade*, on the D919 Arrette road (ⓣ05.59.39.11.26; May–Sept). Independent **restaurants** are not especially numerous; try cheap and cheerful *La Cour des Miracles* at 13 place de la Cathédrale, opposite the Romanesque portal, or *Samia*, a late-serving Moroccan eatery in Oloron on place Amédée-Gabe.

Along the Aspe valley

The narrow enclosed world of the valley proper, an important variant of the Chemin de St-Jacques, begins south of Oloron at the village of **Escot**. South of there, the road follows the river through a narrow defile, past the attractive riverside village of **SARRANCE**, where the **Ecomusée du Vallée d'Aspe** (July–Sept daily 10am–noon & 2–7pm; Oct–June Sat & Sun 2–6pm; €4), devoted to local history, is less interesting than the ancient **monastic church of Notre-Dame-de-la-Pierre**, particularly its wonderfully rustic cloister with wood columns and pyramidal roofs over the upper gallery.

Some 7km further south is **BEDOUS**, the largest settlement in the upper valley, with a miniature château, an arcaded *mairie* and the *gîte d'étape Le Mandragot* (ⓣ05.59.34.59.33), all on or near place de l'Église. Just outside town on the minor road east to Aydius is the **Moulin d'Orcun**, the last surviving stone-grinding flour mill in the area, now run as a museum (guided visits July–Aug daily 11am, 3pm, 4pm, 5pm 6pm; Sept–June by appointment only on ⓣ05.59.34.74.91).

Lescun and its cirque

Six steep kilometres southwest of the N134 and valley floor at L'Estanguet, the ancient stone-and-stucco houses of **LESCUN** huddle together on the north-east slopes of a huge and magnificent green **cirque**. The floor of the cirque and the lower slopes, dimpled with vales and hollows, have been gently shaped by generations of farming, while to the west it's overlooked by the great grey molars of **Le Billare**, Trois Rois and Ansabère, beyond which is the storm-lashed bulk of the **Pic d'Anie** (2504m). Over 1km below the village by the stream draining the cirque, the grassy *Camping Le Lauzart* (ⓣ05.59.34.51.77; May–Sept) must be one of the best sites anywhere, with an unimpeded view of

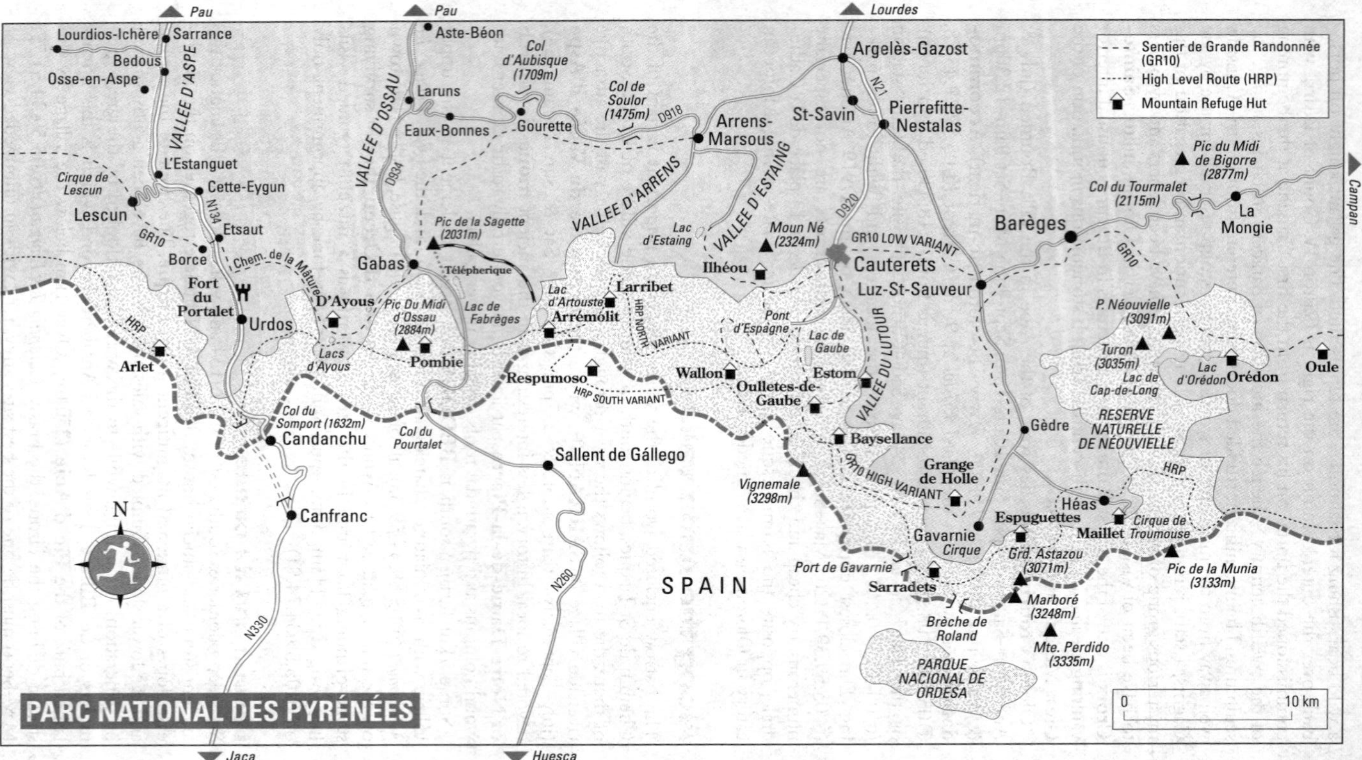
PARC NATIONAL DES PYRÉNÉES
Sentier de Grande Randonnée (GR10)
High Level Route (HRP)
Mountain Refuge Hut
0
10 km
N
Pau
Pau
Lourdes
Campan
La-Pierre-St-Martin
Jaca
Huesca
Lourdios-Ichère
Sarrance
Bedous
Osse-en-Aspe
VALLEE D'ASPE
L'Estanguet
Cirque de Lescun
Lescun
Cette-Eygun
N134
Etsaut
GR10
Borce
Chem. de la Mâture
Fort du Portalet
Urdos
HRP
Arlet
Col du Somport (1632m)
Candanchu
Canfranc
N330
Aste-Béon
Laruns
Eaux-Bonnes
VALLEE D'OSSAU
D934
Col d'Aubisque (1709m)
Gourette
Col de Soulor (1475m)
D918
Pic de la Sagette (2031m)
Téléphérique
Gabas
D'Ayous
Lacs d'Ayous
Pic Du Midi d'Ossau (2884m)
Pombie
Lac de Fabrèges
Col du Pourtalet
Sallent de Gállego
N260
SPAIN
Arrens-Marsous
VALLEE D'ARRENS
VALLEE D'ESTAING
Lac d'Estaing
Lac d'Artouste
Larribet
Arrémolit
HRP NORTH VARIANT
Respumoso
HRP SOUTH VARIANT
Ilhéou
Moun Né (2324m)
Pont d'Espagne
Wallon
Oulletes-de-Gaube
Lac de Gaube
Estom
VALLEE DU LUTOUR
Baysellance
Vignemale (3298m)
Argelès-Gazost
St-Savin
N21
Pierrefitte-Nestalas
D920
GR10 LOW VARIANT
Cauterets
Luz-St-Sauveur
GR10 HIGH VARIANT
Grange de Holle
Gavarnie
Cirque
Port de Gavarnie
Sarradets
Brèche de Roland
Espuguettes
Grd. Astazou (3071m)
Marboré (3248m)
Mte. Perdido (3335m)
PARQUE NACIONAL DE ORDESA
Gèdre
Héas
Maillet
Cirque de Troumouse
Pic de la Munia (3133m)
HRP
RESERVE NATURELLE DE NÉOUVIELLE
Barèges
GR10
Col du Tourmalet (2115m)
Pic du Midi de Bigorre (2877m)
La Mongie
P. Néouvielle (3091m)
Turon (3035m)
Lac de Cap-de-Long
Lac d'Orédon
Orédon
Oule

the peaks. Lescun itself has a lovely old antique-furnished **hotel**, the *Pic d'Anie* (Ⓣ05.59.34.71.54, Ⓕ05.59.34.53.22; ❸; April–Sept), with a decent restaurant and a *gîte d'étape* opposite (same number).

The obvious **walk** in the area is along the GR10 in the direction of La-Pierre-St-Martin. From Lescun, the path keeps close to a minor road as far as the abandoned Refuge de Labérouat – around a ninety-minute walk – then crosses meadows before entering beech forest beneath the organ-pipe crags of **Les Orgues de Camplong**, with fantastic views of the pine-stippled ridges of Billare. It emerges above the tree line in a long, hanging valley by the primitive **Cabane d'Ardinet**, reaching the shepherds' hut at **Cap de la Baigt** (1689m) in a further ninety minutes. From there you can either continue on the GR towards La-Pierre-St-Martin, or swing south for the Col des Anies and the Pic d'Anie itself – a good two and a half hours to the summit.

Cette-Eygun south to the border

A couple of kilometres beyond the turn-off for Lescun, **CETTE-EYGUN** offers, in its upper Cette quarter, the excellent, welcoming *Au Château d'Arance* (Ⓣ05.59.34.75.50, Ⓦwww.auchateaudarance.com; ❹), a converted twelfth-century manor made very contemporary with Wi-Fi access in the modern rooms; meals (pricy at €26 menu) and leisurely breakfast (7.30–11am) are served on a terrace with unbeatable views, whilst co-managed, 2006-built *chambres d'hôtes* (❸) occupy a nearby house, next to the swimming pool.

Some 3.5km southeast at **ETSAUT**, there's a **Maison du Parc** (May to mid-Sept daily 10am–noon & 1.30–6.30pm; Ⓣ05.59.34.88.30) in the old *gare SNCF*. There's a **gîte d'étape** beyond the church, *Auberge La Garbure* (Ⓣ05.59.34.88.98, Ⓦwww.garbure.net; €12pp), and a **hotel** on the square, *Des Pyrénées* (Ⓣ05.59.34.88.62, Ⓕ05.59.34.86.96; ❷; closed mid-Dec to mid-Jan) with a restaurant, though you may find the welcome warmer across the *place* at *Bar Tabac Le Randonneur*, which does *plats du jour* in the bar or full meals in the attractive diner upstairs, as well as offering Wi-Fi **Internet** access (€1 donation). If you're not travelling with a laptop, the post office has Internet access for slightly higher rates.

BORCE, a more attractive medieval village 1km away on the west flank of the valley, is home to more **gîtes**: *La Communal* (Ⓣ05.59.34.86.40; 18 places; €10pp) in the centre, above the bar-*épicerie*, plus the historic *Hospitalet de Borce* (no phone; 6 places) on the north outskirts, next to the original pilgrims' church which is now an annexe of the Ecomusée in Sarrance.

Further upstream at one of the narrowest, rockiest, steepest points of the Aspe – a serious challenge to would-be motorway builders (see box, p.790) – squats the menacing **Fort du Portalet** (privately owned), which served as a prison for 1930s Socialist premier Léon Blum under Pétain's Vichy government, and then for Pétain himself after the liberation of France. Just before the fort, the GR10 threads east along the **Chemin de la Mâture**, an eighteenth-century mule path hacked out of the precipitous rock slabs that form the sides of a dizzy ravine, facilitating the transport of tree trunks felled for use as ships' masts. The really spectacular part – which however, has minimal exposure and attracts lots of young families – ends after about 45min from the upper parking area (1hr from the lower car park at Pont de Cebers south of Etsaut); the GR10 continues to the **Lacs d'Ayous refuge** (see p.796) opposite the Pic du Midi d'Ossau in five-plus hours, but by careful study of *Carte de Randonée* no. 3, "Béarn", it's easy to form a three-hour loop hike returning you to the Pont de Cebers area on local trails.

Less than 2km south of the fort, **URDOS** is the last village on the French side of the frontier, and has arguably the best hotel-restaurant in the valley: *Hôtel des Voyageurs* (T05.59.34.88.05, Ehotel.voyageurs.urdos.@orange.fr; 3) – with an annexe across the road known as the *Hôtel Somport* – which serves a wonderful, four-course set dinner menu (€26). They also keep a basic pilgrims' *gîte* (€10pp). From here, you can continue through the tunnel under the **Col de Somport** and on to Canfranc in Spain, the terminus for trains from Jaca, though in fine weather the far more scenic old road over the pass is not that strenuous a drive.

Along the Ossau valley

The **Ossau valley** is notable mainly for its distinctive **Pic du Midi**, around which are some beautiful lakes set in rugged country; the usual base for visiting is tiny **Gabas** hamlet. The main valley market town of **Laruns** is pleasant enough, and the route east via the spa of **Eaux-Bonnes** and the ski resort of **Gourette** has its appeal. Pic Bus runs two daily **bus services** in summer and winter peak seasons to the top of the valley via Laruns and Gabas, calling once in each direction at the trailhead for the most visited lakes, whilst CITRAM provides service most of the year to Eaux-Bonnes and Gourette.

Pau to Laruns

Between Pau and Laruns, there are only a couple places worth stopping. First is **ARUDY**, for its **Maison d'Ossau** (July & Aug 10am–noon & 3–6pm; rest of year Mon 10am–noon, Tues, Thurs & Sat 2.30–5pm, Sun 3–6pm; €3), which offers a comprehensive account of the prehistoric Pyrenees and an exhibition of the flora and fauna of the *parc national*. Some 7km upvalley from here, **ASTE-BÉON** is home to **La Falaise aux Vautours** (Wwww.falaise-aux-vautours.com; May & Sept daily 2–6pm; June–Aug daily 10.30am–12.30pm & 2–6.30pm; rest of year school vacations only daily 2–5pm; €6), a vulture-watching installation where over a hundred breeding pairs and their chicks are observable nesting naturally.

LARUNS, on the valley bottom just before steep wooded heights rise towards the border, comes alive for its August 15–16 festival, with revellers in trad dress and live music. Otherwise it's undistinguished but with ample facilities. The **tourist office** on the main place de la Mairie (Mon–Sat 9am–12.30pm & 2–6.30pm, Sun 9am–noon & 2–6pm; T05.59.05.31.41) stands back-to-back with a **Maison du Parc** (mid-June to mid-Sept daily 10am–1pm & 2–6.30pm/no phone). **Accommodation** includes the central *Hôtel d'Ossau* (T05.59.05.30.14; 3), with a restaurant out front, or the characterful *Hôtel de France*, at the eastern end of town opposite the disused *gare SNCF* (T05.59.05.33.71; 3). There's also *Chalet-Refuge L'Embaradère* (T05.59.05.41.88; 28 places; cheap meals offered; closed Mon–Tues low season), more or less opposite the *Hôtel de France*. The nearest all-year **campsites** are *Ayguebere* (T05.59.05.38.55) and *Pont Lauguère* (T05.59.05.35.99), both in Le Pon quarter. Two of the few independent **restaurants** are found on rue du Bourguet off the square: *L'Arrégalet* at no. 37 (closed lunch Mon & Tues), strong on local recipes, and *Auberge Bellevue* at no.55 (closed Mon eve & all Tues low season), with three varied menus and brasserie grub available between main-meal hours.

Eaux-Chaudes and Gabas

The road to Gabas, 13km south, winds steeply into the upper reaches of the Gave d'Ossau valley, through dozy **EAUX-CHAUDES** spa, whose one bright spot is the excellent ★ *Auberge La Caverne* (ⓣ05.59.05.36.40, ⓦauberge.lacaverne.free.fr; all year), run by a hard-working couple who offer both dorms (€12 pp) and doubles (❶) in an atmospheric old building, as well as very salubrious *table d'hôte* meals (€12 includes house wine and coffee).

Primarily a base for climbers and walkers, there's little to **GABAS** beyond a minuscule chapel and abundant **accommodation** – which fills quickly in summer. Most comfortable of this, near the south end of "town", is *Le Chalet des Pyrénées* (ⓣ05.59.05.30.51, ⓕ05.59.05.33.64; closed Nov; ❸), with vast common areas including a lawn garden, tennis court and restaurant, with the best small but en-suite rooms facing the river. At Gabas' north entrance, *Hôtel Chez Vignau* (ⓣ05.59.05.34.06, ⓕ05.59.05.46.12; all year; ❷) has basic rooms with toilets down the hall, but a good restaurant across the road, though the best independent **restaurant** is *Du Pic du Midi* up the road (menus €12–22). There's also the well-run CAF *Chalet-Refuge* (ⓣ05.59.05.33.14; 46 places in dorms; open June–Sept & winter weekends except mid-Oct to mid-Nov; €8.20pp) 700m above Gabas, with unusually good food.

Pic du Midi d'Ossau

The **Pic du Midi d'Ossau**, with its craggy, mitten-shaped summit (2884m), is a classic Pyrenean landmark, visible for kilometres around. From Gabas, it's a steep 4.5-kilometre climb on the D231 road (1 daily morning bus) to the artificial **Lac de Bious-Artigues**, so named because it flooded the *artigue* or "mountain pasture" that formerly existed beside the infant *gave*. Drivers will be directed by park wardens to one of two car parks, the higher one just above the dam. There are no longer any facilities of note here (though a refuge will supposedly be built in 2008), so come prepared.

A hiking circuit of the peak, excluding the summit – the **Tour du Pic du Midi** – takes about six hours. It can be broken by a **stay** at the CAF *Refuge de Pombie* (ⓣ05.59.05.71.78; open June–Sept, weekends May & Oct), below the southeast flank of the mountain. From Bious-Artigues, follow the GR10, initially a broad track, along the *gave*; at the turning right to the Lacs d'Ayous (see below), instead cross the Pont de Bious, following a signpost indicating "Pombie Par Peyreget", and continue upstream across an expanse of flat meadow. There follows a steepish zigzagging climb on a path to the junction with the HRP route, which takes you (1hr 30min from the dam) to the tiny **Lac de Peyreget**. Once over the **Col de Peyreget** (2320m), you descend east – with great views – to *Refuge de Pombie* (about 3hr 30min along). The path continues north via the **Col de Suzon** – where the standard semi-technical ascent of the *pic* begins – then finally west back to Bious-Artigues.

The Tour des Lacs

Starting again from the Bious-Artigues trailhead, the **loop around the lakes** of Ayous, Bersau and Castérau is another, very popular classic, in some ways more impressive than circling the Pic du Midi d'Ossau itself, especially if you spend the night above the lakes to get the quintessential dawn view of the peak silhouetted against the rising sun and reflected in the slaty waters of Lac Gentau.

Begin walking as for the Tour du Pic du Midi, but instead of crossing the Pont de Bious, bear right onto the GR10 – a sign says "Lacs d'Ayous 1hr 30min" – to climb through woods of pine and beech, with ever-widening views of the valley scattered with herds of livestock. Near the top, you reach three small lakes, the third and largest of which is **Lac Gentau**; on its banks there's an expanse of flat, soft meadow for camping, permitted here as you're just outside the PNP.

Above looms the 2002-rebuilt *Refuge d'Ayous* (1982m; ⓣ05.59.05.37.00; 47 places; mid-June to mid-Sept).

Continue south on the obvious path to **Lac Bersau**, dominated by the peaks – both nearly 2400m high – of Larry and Hourquette; it's a favourite picnicking spot and irresistible for a swim on a hot day. A col (circa. 2150m) just south is the high point of the Tour des Lacs, which now turns east under the shadow of **Pic Castérau** (2227m) to pass the eponymous lake and begins a sharp descent, with full-on views of the Pic du Midi. After passing some shepherds' *cabanes* – a path short cuts the 4WD tracks serving them – you follow the *gave* northeast to the Pont de Bious and the car park. The circuit's basically four hours' walking, but allow six with stops; many people reverse these directions so as to have lunch at the refuge.

Lac d'Artouste and Le Petit Train

Some 6.5km out of Gabas, the Pourtalet road passes the dammed **Lac de Fabrèges**, with an access drive around the east shore leading to a burgeoning ski-chalet complex, among which is concealed the *billeterie* for a *télécabine*. This attains the base of **Pic de la Sagette** (2031m) to connect with **Le Petit Train**, a miniature rail line running 10km southeast through the mountains to the **Lac d'Artouste**. Built in the 1920s to service a hydroelectric project which raised the lake level 25m, it was later converted for tourist purposes. Weather permitting, the train starts operating in late May and keeps going until late September (June & Sept 10am–3pm, July & Aug 9am–5pm; reserve on ⓣ05.59.05.36.99 or ⓦwww.train-artouste.com). It's a beautiful trip, lasting about four hours, including the *télécabine*; you've time to walk down to the lake and back (and to *Refuge Arrémoulit*, ⓣ05.59.05.31.79; around 40 places) if you set a brisk pace, but allow a half-hour for the *télécabine* (first departure 8.30–9.30am). Prices start at €18 return; walkers may be able to negotiate one ways. In **winter** the same lift gives access to the small beginner to intermediate downhill **ski centre** on the northeast side of the Col de la Sagette.

Eaux-Bonnes, Gourette and the road to the Gave de Pau

The only way of reaching the Gave de Pau by road without going back towards Pau is via the minor D918 east over the Col d'Aubisque, via Eaux-Bonnes and **Gourette**, 12km east of Laruns and the favourite **ski centre** of folk from Pau. The base development is ugly but the skiing, on 28 north-facing runs from a top point of 2400m, is more than respectable. You can of course stay here, but the Second Empire spa village of **EAUX-BONNES**, 8km below Gourette, is more elegant and pleasant. Here the old-fashioned *Hôtel de la Poste* on the central park-square (ⓣ05.59.50.33.06, ⓕ05.59.50.43.03; closed late April & mid-Oct to Christmas; ❸) represents excellent value, especially at half-board rates with a four-course *table d'hôte* supper.

The **Col d'Aubisque** itself (1709m), a grassy saddle with a souvenir stall/café on top, usually sees the Tour de France come through, making the pass an irresistible challenge to any French cyclist worth his salt. Once over the next, lower Col de Soulor, the route descends, 18km in all, to attractive **ARRENS-MARSOUS**, at the head of the Val d'Azun. Despite being another gateway to the PNP, with **information** from the Maison du Val d'Azun (ⓣ05.62.97.49.49, ⓦwww.valdazun.com; Mon–Sat 9am–noon & 3–6/7pm), **accommodation** is limited to *Gîte Camélat*, in a fine, rambling house from 1887 just off the central *place* (ⓣ05.62.97.40.94, ⓔgite-camelat@orange.fr; 50 places; all year) with both doubles (❸) and dorm space (€15pp). More comfort is available 3km northeast at **AUCUN**, where 2004-built *Hôtel le Picors* (Ⓣ05.62.97.40.90, Ⓦwww.hotel-picors.com; open May–Sept, Christmas & mid-Feb to mid-March; ❸) represents excellent value with a popular on-site restaurant and covered pool.

The Gave de Pau and around

From its namesake city, the **Gave de Pau** forges southeast towards the mountains, bending sharply south at Lourdes and shortly fraying into several tributaries: the **Gave d'Azun**, the **Gave de Cauterets**, the **Gave de Gavarnie** (draining the eponymous cirque) and the **Gave de Bastan**, dropping from the Col du Tourmalet. All four of these valleys, and the holiday bases in them, are served by SNCF buses from Lourdes or Argelès-Gazost. **Cauterets**, 30km due south of Lourdes, and **Gavarnie** 37km southeast of Argelès, are busy, established resorts on the edge of the PNP, but the countryside they give access to is so spectacular that you forgive their deficiencies. If you want a smaller, more manageable base, then either **Barèges**, up a side valley from the spa resort of **Luz-St-Sauveur**, or Luz itself, are better bets. But if you pick your season – or even the time of day – right, you can still enjoy the most popular sites in relative solitude. At Gavarnie few people stay the night, so it's quiet early or late, and the **Cirque de Troumouse**, which is just as impressive in its way (though much harder to get to without a car), has very few visitors. The spa-town of **Bagnères-de-Bigorre**, just east of the *gave* within striking distance of Lourdes, is fairly dull, primarily a gateway to the Vallée de Campan.

St-Savin

Between Lourdes and Cauterets, some 3km southeast of the congested town of Argelès-Gazost, pleasant, sleepy **ST-SAVIN** merits a stop for its twelfth-century **abbey-church**, with later fortifications and a fine Romanesque portal. The interior (daily 9am–7pm) offers an amusing organ cabinet carved with grotesque faces – supposedly those of damned souls – that were designed to grimace as the unbearable (for them) heavenly music played. The **treasury** (daily: April–June 2.30–6.30pm; July & Aug 10.30am–12.30pm & 2.30–6.30pm; €2), installed in the vaulted former chapterhouse, is home to a particularly interesting piece, a twelfth-century "black Madonna" which tradition holds was carried back from Syria by Crusaders. Also worth a visit is the little eleventh-century hilltop chapel of **Notre-Dame-de-Piétat** (Sun year-round 2.30–6pm, otherwise July–Aug Sun–Fri 2.30–6pm, spring/autumn 3–6pm; free), 1km south of the village, which has an elaborately painted ceiling, where birds perch on floral motifs covering every available space.

Cauterets and around

CAUTERETS is a pleasant if unexciting little spa town that owes its fame and its rather elegant Neoclassical architecture (especially on bd Latapie-Flurin) to its waters. In modern times, it has also become one of the main Pyrenean ski and mountaineering centres.

Its origins as a spa began with Count Raymond de Bigorre's grant of land to the monks of St-Savin in 945 AD. In the seventeenth century, Marguerite d'Angoulême came to take the waters and wrote her *Heptameron* here. The eighteenth and nineteenth centuries were its heyday, especially the latter with its

Romantic worship of mountains. Hugo visited, as did Chateaubriand, Baudelaire, Debussy, Sarah Bernhardt, Edward VII and many other celebrities.

The modern town is small enough to present no difficulties in orientation; most of it is still squeezed between the steep wooded heights that close the mouth of the Gave de Cauterets valley. Next door to the **gare routière** on the north edge of the centre, where SNCF coaches stop, the **Maison du Parc** (daily 9.30am–noon & 3.30–7pm; ⓣ05.62.92.52.56) has a small display of flora and fauna. In the centre, five minutes' walk distant, you'll find the **tourist office** in place Maréchal-Foch (Mon–Sat: July & Aug 9am–12.30pm & 2–7pm; Sept–June 9am–noon & 2–6pm; ⓣ05.62.92.50.50, ⓦwww.cauterets.com); the nearby Bureau des Guides at 5 place Clemenceau (mid-June to mid-Sept daily 10am–noon & 4.30–7.30pm; ⓣ05.62.92.62.02), organizes adventure activities.

Inexpensive **hotels** include *Le Grum* at 4 rue Victor-Hugo, off rue de la Raillère (ⓣ05.62.92.53.01, ⓕ05.62.92.64.99; closed mid-Oct to mid-Dec; ❷), with a mix of rooms en suite and not; and *Le Pas de l'Ours*, 21 rue de la Raillère (ⓣ05.62.92.58.07, ⓦwww.lepasdelours.com; all year; ❸), which also runs a **gîte** (€17pp). There's another *gîte* around the corner: *Le Beau Soleil*, at 25 rue Maréchal-Joffre (ⓣ05.62.92.53.52, ⓔgite.beau.soleil@orange.fr; open ski season to mid-Oct; €21ppB&B). Several well-equipped **campsites** line the road north of town, the closest being *La Prairie* (ⓣ05.62.92.54.28; June–Sept).

For a more upmarket hotel, try the atmospheric *Lion d'Or* at 12 rue Richelieu (ⓣ05.62.92.52.87, ⓦwww.hotel-lion-dor.net; closed Oct to mid-Dec & mid-May; ❺), or the underrated *Asterides-Sacca* at 11 bd Latapie-Flurin (ⓣ05.62.92.50.02; closed mid-Oct to mid-Dec; ❹).

As many hotels require half-board in peak season, independent **restaurants** are thin on the ground: the *Giovanni Pizzeria* at 5 rue de la Raillère and *Casa Bodega Manolo*, with Spanish-style tapas, nearby at no. 11 are pretty much it.

Hikes around Cauterets

Most classic excursions around Cauterets begin up the Val de Jéret from the **Pont d'Espagne** 7km south, where the Gave de Gaube and Gave du Marcadau hurtle together in a boiling spume of spray, before rushing down to Cauterets over a series of spectacular waterfalls. In season there are six daily *navettes* from the town centre to the giant visitor centre and car park (€4–6 per vehicle) here; purists can walk there in about two hours along an attractive, streamside trail, known first as the "Avenue Demontzey" and, once past the satellite spa of **La Raillère**, as the "Chemin des Cascades".

From Pont d'Espagne (1420m), you can proceed southwest some two hours up the **Marcadau valley** to the *Refuge Wallon* (1886m; ⓣ05.62.92.64.28; 115 places; open mid-May to Oct), poised between the HRP and GR10, and the base for numerous walks – the most popular being the five-hour loop north, then east, then back to the refuge via the **lakes of Nère, Pourtet and de l'Embarrat**.

Alternatively, head due south up into the alpine valley of the Gave de Gaube, with picturesque **Lac de Gaube** (1725m) backed by the snowy north face of **Vignemale** (3298m). There's even a combined *télécabine/télésiège* (June–Sept; €6.70 return) to spare you most of the ascent from Pont d'Espagne. Beyond the lake, the path continues to the *Refuge Oulettes-de-Gaube* at the base of Vignemale (ⓣ06.64.45.41.46 or 05.62.92.62.97; 2151m; 120 places; open May–Oct 15; 3hr from Pont d'Espagne), from where you can return to La Raillère via one of two routes.

The HRP from *Refuge Oulettes* goes over a high (2734m) pass to the *Refuge de Bayssellance* (ⓣ05.62.92.40.25; 58 places; open June–Sept; weekends April & Oct weather permitting) and then loops broadly around to the *Refuge d'Estom*

(Ⓣ05.62.92.74.86; 1804m; open June–Sept) in the beautiful and quieter **Lutour valley**; alternatively you can omit *Bayssellance* and head straight to *Estom* over the lower (2583m) Col d'Arraillé, and then to La Raillère. Even with bus and *télécabine* rides at the start and using this lower route, you should allow eight hours for the walking day; if you take in the high country around *Bayssellance*, it's best to schedule an overnight at one of the three refuges.

A less-frequented walk from Cauterets is to the **Lac d'Ilhéou** along the **GR10** (about 3hr). To avoid the initial steep climb you can take another combined *télécabine/télésiege* (July–Aug only; €8 one way, €9.50 return; discount for users of those at Pont d'Espagne and vice versa), up to the 2300-metre contour under the Crêtes du Lys. From there's it's a 45-minute descent to the popular but expensive *Refuge d'Ilhéou* (1988m; Ⓣ05.62.92.52.38; open June–Sept) beside its lake – very pretty in June, with snow still on the surrounding peaks and ice floes drifting on its still surface. From the refuge, you can either descend the Gave d'Ilhéou back to Cauterets or, more ambitiously, pop over the Col de la Haugade (2311m) into the Marcadau valley and thence back to Cauterets via the Val de Jéret.

Luz-St-Sauveur and Gèdre

The only road approach to Gavarnie and Troumouse, best known of the Pyrenean cirques, is through **LUZ-ST-SAUVEUR**, astride the GR10 and a regular SNCF bus route from Lourdes. Like Cauterets, this was a nineteenth-century spa, patronized by Napoléon III and Eugénie, and the left-bank St-Saveur quarter owes its elegant Neoclassical facades to this period. The principal sight, at the top of Luz's medieval, right-bank quarter, is the **church of St-André** (daily May 15–Sept 30 3–6pm; €2). Built in the late twelfth century, it was fortified in the fourteenth by the Knights of St John with a crenellated outer wall and two stout towers. The north entrance, beneath one of the towers, sports a handsome portal surmounted by a Christ in Majesty carved in fine-grained local stone.

The **tourist office** (all year minimum hours Mon–Sat 9am–7.30pm, Sun 9am–12.30pm & 4.30–7.30pm; Ⓣ05.62.92.30.30, Ⓦwww.luz.org), edges the central place du Huit-Mai, by the crossroads for Gavarnie or Barèges. Two worthwhile central **hotels**, both under new management in 2006, are the fully en-suite *Les Templiers* (Ⓣ05.62.92.81.52, Ⓦwww.hotellestempliers.com; closed April or May; ❸), opposite the church with half-board offered and the pricier rooms with view, and partly en-suite *Les Cimes* (Ⓣ05.62.92.83.03; ❷), 70m downhill on the same lane. Best of two **campsites**, also with a *gîte* on site, is *Les Cascades* (Ⓣ05.62.92.94.14; Dec–Sept), uphill from the church. **Restaurants** aren't numerous; two reliable ones are *La Tasca* on place St-Clement, tops for Spanish tapas and seafood, and *Chez Christine* (closed late autumn & early spring) near the post office, specializing in own-made pasta and desserts plus locally sourced meat and trout.

Eleven kilometres south, just before the turning for the Cirque de Troumouse, is tiny **GÈDRE**. This can offer a comfortable **hotel**, *La Brèche de Roland* (Ⓣ05.62.92.48.54, Ⓦwww.pyrenees-hotel-breche.com; HB only, ❻; May–Sept plus winter weekends/hols), with a reasonable restaurant – plus two highly rated **gîtes d'étape** nearby: *Le Saugué* (Ⓣ05.62.92.48.73; May–Oct; 25 places; €12pp), and *L'Escapade* (Ⓣ05.69.92.49.37, Ⓦwww.gite-escapade.com; 28 places; all year; €13pp).

Gavarnie and its cirque

A further 8km up the ravine from Gèdre, **GAVARNIE** is connected with Luz-St-Sauveur by two daily **bus services** (July & Aug only; otherwise just 3 weekly, or a taxi from Luz), though you can walk it on the higher variant of the

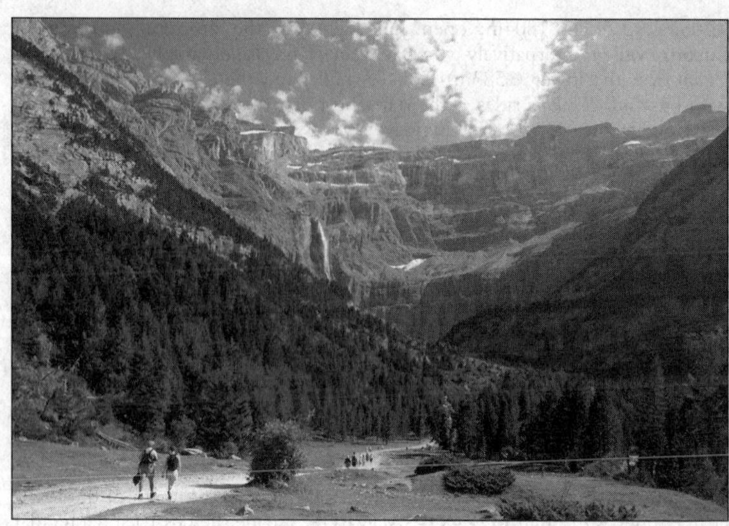

△ Cirque de Gavarnie

GR10 from Cauterets in two days. If you drive in, a parking fee (8am–5pm; €4) is charged during peak summer season; otherwise there is plenty of free parking around the shops and hotels. Once poor and depopulated, Gavarnie has found the attractions of mass tourism – much of it the excursion trade from Lourdes – too seductive to resist, and is now an unattractive mess of pricey accommodation, souvenir shops and mediocre snack bars. Like other overly popular sites, the key is to visit in shoulder season and/or before 9am or after 5pm, to avoid the bus-borne hordes.

However, the **cirque** itself – Victor Hugo called it "Nature's Colosseum" – is magnificent, a natural amphitheatre scoured out by glaciers. Over 1500m high, it consists of three sheer bands of rock streaked by seepage and waterfalls, and separated by sloping ledges covered with snow and glacier remnants. To the east, it's dominated by the jagged peaks of **Astazou** and **Marboré**, both over 3000m. In the middle, a corniced ridge sweeps round to the **Brèche de Roland**, a curious vertical slash, 100m deep and about 60m wide, said to have been hewn from the ridge by Roland's sword, Durandal. In winter, there's good **skiing** for beginners and intermediates at the nearby, 24-run resort of **Gavarnie-Gèdre**, with great views of the cirque from the top point of 2400m.

Practicalities

La Bergerie (Ⓣ05.62.92.48.41; mid-May to Oct), on the east bank of the *gave* on the cirque side of the village, must be one of the most stunningly located **campsites** in the Pyrenees, with views right into the cirque compensating for exceedingly basic, tent-only facilities. The other campsite, *Le Pain de Sucre* (Ⓣ & Ⓕ05.62.92.47.55; June–Sept & mid-Dec to mid-April), 3km north of the village, is really meant for camper-caravans.

In terms of **hotels**, good-value options include en-suite *Le Taillon* (Ⓣ05.65.92.48.20, Ⓦwww.letaillon.com; closed Nov to mid-Dec; ③), with a competent restaurant, and the smallish *Hôtel Compostelle* by the church (Ⓣ05.62.92.49.43, Ⓦwww.compostellehotel.com; closed Oct to Christmas; ③), with most rooms facing the cirque. You can park by or close to both but note the village is closed to traffic in high season 10am–6pm. Most idyllically set, by the *gave*, is non-en-suite *La Chaumière* (Ⓣ05.62.92.48.08, Ⓔam.garcie@orange.fr; closed Oct–Christmas; ❷).

Otherwise, dorm-type accommodation comprises the high-standard *Gîte Auberge Le Gypaëte* (Ⓣ05.62.92.40.61; 45 places; all year; €10pp), below the main car park, and the CAF *Chalet Refuge La Grange de Holle*, 2km above Gavarnie on the Port de Gavarnie road (Ⓣ05.62.92.48.77; 50 places; closed Oct to mid-Dec; €13–16pp). The best independent **restaurant** is *Les Cascades*, next to the Maison du Parc (Mon–Sat 9am–noon & 1.30–6.30pm; Ⓣ05.62.92.42.48) on the north side of the village; other **information** sources include the tourist office by the car parks (daily summer 9am–7pm; Ⓣ05.62.92.49.10, Ⓦwww.gavarnie.com), and the CRS mountain rescue unit opposite *La Bergerie*, for accurate snow and weather reports.

The cirque and around

It's an easy walk from Gavarnie into the cirque, using either the main east-bank track or the longer, steeper west-bank trail beside the *gave* draining it. Luckily, the scale of the place is sufficient to dwarf humans, but for a bit of serenity it's still best to use the west-bank path, or go up before 10am or after 5pm, when the grandeur and silence are almost alarming. The broad track ends after 45 minutes at the *Hôtel du Cirque et de la Cascade*, once a famous meeting place for mountaineers and now a popular, surprisingly reasonable snack bar in summer. To get to the foot of the cirque walls, you face a steeper, final half-hour on a dwindling, increasingly slippery path which ends in a spray-bath at the base of the **Grande Cascade**, at 423m the highest waterfall in Europe. This plummets and fans out in three stages down the rock faces – a fine sight in sunny weather, with rainbows in the wind-teased plumes.

If you don't want to retrace your steps, an enjoyable and not too demanding walk back to Gavarnie runs via the path from the *Hôtel du Cirque* up the east flank of the Gavarnie valley to the **Refuge des Espuguettes** (2030m; Ⓣ05.62.92.40.63; 60 places; daily May–Sept, weekends Easter & Oct; 2hr). It's a beautiful path, cut into rocky, pine-shaded slopes, with fine views of the cirque and the Brèche de Roland; at the top, you emerge into open meadows tilting up to the refuge. Those staying overnight here may want to bag **Piméné** (2801m; 3hr 30min return), the bare peak above you, for unbeatable views over the Cirque d'Estaubé, and Monte Perdido in Spain. To return to Gavarnie, turn right (north) at the signposted trail fork below the refuge (allow 90min from there).

La Brèche de Roland

La Brèche de Roland is *the* walk to do around Gavarnie. It's high, and involves crossing a glacier, which means being properly equipped with ice-axe and crampons. It is, however, extremely popular in summer, so there's a good chance of being able to team up with someone more experienced. The *brèche* is about forty minutes above the refuge cited below, with the glacier crossing occupying the final moments.

There are three approaches to the *brèche*, all converging on the **Refuge des Sarradets/Brèche de Roland** (2587m; Ⓣ06.83.38.13.24; 60 places; open June–Sept, weekends in Oct); for which reservations are always necessary in high season. The easiest route is from the end of the road to the Port de Boucharo, where a clear path climbs under the north face of Le Taillon to join the footpath coming directly from Gavarnie (1hr-plus). The latter path starts beside the church, climbs steadily up the valley of Pouey Aspé, then zigzags steeply up to join the first-cited path on the flank of Sarradets peak (2hr 45min). From the junction of these two paths, it's about half an hour to the refuge. The third route (4hr 30min from Gavarnie to the hut) is via the **Échelle des Sarradets/HRP** path above the *Hôtel du Cirque*, better than it appears from depiction on IGN maps, though scrambling sections, slippery surfaces and cable-holds are found at several points.

The Cirque de Troumouse

A vast, wild place, much bigger than Gavarnie and, in bad weather, rather intimidating, the **Cirque de Troumouse** lies up a desolate valley whose only habitations are the handful of farmsteads and pilgrimage chapel that make up the hamlet of **HÉAS** – one of the loneliest outposts in France before the road in was constructed. The only **rooms** and **meals** in Héas proper are at *Auberge de la Munia* (ⓣ05.62.92.48.39, ⓦwww.aubergedelamunia.com; HB only ❺). As you reach the head of the valley there's a **tollgate** (9am–5pm; €4 per car), after which the road climbs in tight hairpins 4km to the *Auberge du Maillet* (ⓣ05.62.92.48.97; mid-May to mid-Dec; ❸), beside a small tarn. After this the road climbs again, even more steeply over 3km, beneath bare shining crags, to a car park. Nearby, a prominent statue of the Virgin Mary crowns a grassy knoll amidst enough moorland pasture for thousands of animals, enclosed by the wide sweeping walls of the cirque. Beneath the eastern walls of the cirque are scattered a half-dozen blue glacial lakelets, the **Lacs des Aires**. A *parc national* path does the circuit from Héas (no toll for walkers, 4hr).

The Vallée de Bastan

Luz-St-Sauveur marks the start of the eighteen-kilometre climb east along the D918 through the **Vallée de Bastan**, culminating in the **Col du Tourmalet** (2115m), one of the major torments of the Tour de France and the fulcrum of a giant **skiing** *domaine*. North of the pass rises the landmark **Pic du Midi de Bigorre** (2877m), with its observatory usually reached by funicular.

The only major village in between is **BARÈGES**, 7km along, linked with Lourdes by SNCF bus (change at Pierrefite-Nestalas). An attractive if one-street town, Barèges has been a popular spa since 1677, when it was visited by Madame de Maintenon with her infant charge, the seven-year-old Duc de Maine, son of Louis XIV. A military hospital opened here in 1744, as its waters became renowned for the treatment of gunshot wounds, and a low-key army connection endures – a mountain warfare training centre and an R&R facility stand opposite each other. But today it's primarily a skiing, mountaineering and paragliding centre, and the most congenial, low-key resort around the Gave de Pau.

The central **tourist office** (July & Aug Mon–Sat 9am–12.30pm & 2–7pm, Sun 10am–noon & 4–6pm; Sept–June shorter afternoon hours; ⓣ05.62.92.16.00, ⓦwww.bareges.com) can supply accommodation lists and ski-lift plans. The through road is lined with a half-dozen **hotels**, all fairly similar in standards, opening season (May–Oct) and price (typically ❹); best value among these is *Hôtel Le Central* (ⓣ05.62.92.68.05, ⓦwww.central-tourmalet.com), with a pool, Wi-Fi Internet access and extensive common areas. More distinctive are two high-quality, English-run *chambres d'hôtes Les Sorbiers* on the main street (ⓣ05.62.92.86.68, ⓦwww.lessorbiers.co.uk; ❸; closed late April to mid-May, Oct & Nov), offering

Skiing and hiking around Barèges

With its links to the adjacent, equal-sized *domaine* of **La Mongie** over 10km east on the far side of the Col du Tourmalet, Barèges offers access to the largest **skiing** area in the French Pyrenees, including downhill pistes totalling 125km (1850–2400m) and 31km of cross-country trails running through the wooded Lienz plateau (1350–1700m). The beginners' runs finishing in Barèges village are much too low (1250m) to retain snow, so all skiers usually have to start from the areas of Tournaboup or Tourmalet. Since the millennium, high-speed, state-of-the-art chair lifts are the rule at Barèges, and runs have been regraded to make the resort more competitive, but La Mongie over the hill, despite its hideous purpose-built development, offers even higher, longer pistes. For more information consult Ⓦwww.bareges-tourmalet.com.

The **GR10** passes through Barèges on its way southeast into the lake-filled **Néouvielle Massif**, part of France's oldest (1935) natural reserve, and highly recommended as a hiking area. The best trailhead for **day-hikes**, with limited parking, lies 3km east at **Pont de la Gaubie** (1538m), from where the classic loop takes in the Vallée des Aygues Cluses plus the lakes and peak of Madamète, followed by a descent via Lac Nère and Lac dets Coubous back to Gaubie. For those **traversing** with full packs, a seven-hour walking day from Barèges via either the Col de Madamète or the Horquette d'Aubert brings you into the Néouvielle reserve for an overnight at either the mammoth, modernized *Chalet du Lac d'Orédon* (Ⓣ05.62.23.05.72.60; mid-June to mid-Sept; doubles ❸ & dorms), or the *Chalet-Hôtel de l'Oule* (Ⓣ05.62.98.48.62; 28 places; open early June to mid-Sept & ski season).

vegetarian meals on request, and *Mountain Bug* (Ⓣ05.62.92.16.39, Ⓦwww.mountainbug.com; ❹) behind the butcher's, a superbly restored eighteenth-century farmhouse with modern bathrooms and tasteful wood-floored common areas; proprietors Robert and Emma are certified guides offering local walking holidays.

There are also two **gîtes d'étape**, both open year-round except April and October: *L'Hospitalet* (Ⓣ05.62.92.68.08; €13pp), at the southern edge of town on the hillside, somewhat institutional owing to its past as a military hospital, and the welcoming, Anglo–French-run *L'Oasis*, right behind the spa (Ⓣ05.62.92.69.47, Ⓦwww.gite-oasis.com; 40 places, €13pp); both offer evening meals and reasonable half-board rates.

The Col du Tourmalet and the Pic du Midi de Bigorre

Some 3km out of Barèges, the D918 begins climbing in earnest over denuded slopes to the **Col du Tourmalet**, at 2115m the highest motorable pass in the French Pyrenees. Even in summer it's apt to be desolate and windy, flanked by a café-restaurant on the far side and a sleeker replacement of the rough-hewn, anatomically correct original cyclist-statue, commemorating the first passage of the Tour through here in 1910. By the statue, a dirt road meanders off in the direction of the **Pic du Midi**, though you can no longer use this to drive to the observatory up top, but must visit either on foot or by **téléphérique** (June–Sept daily 9am–4.30pm; sporadic, complicated schedule otherwise; €23, includes admission to museum) from La Mongie. The venerable observatory, continuously staffed since opening in 1880 and still a serious research facility, long resisted commercialization but has bowed to the inevitable with an on-site **astronomical museum**, solar observatory, observation deck and restaurant.

From the col the road (summer only) descends past La Mongie ski centre, down into the gentle green Vallée de Campan.

Bagnères-de-Bigorre and the Vallée de Campan

BAGNÈRES-DE-BIGORRE, nearly equidistant from Tarbes and Lourdes, is yet another pleasant if nondescript Pyrenean spa town which has managed to burnish its somewhat faded image with **Aquensis** (daily: school hols 10.30am–9pm, otherwise 10.30am/1pm–8pm; ⓦwww.aquensis-bagneres.com), certainly the most striking thermal baths in the Pyrenees with the central pool overarched by a forest of cantilevered wood beams. The town is served by frequent SNCF buses from Tarbes, which call at the **gare SNCF** on avenue de Belgique, 400m north of the town centre. The **tourist office** is at 3 allée Tournefort (July & Aug daily 9am–12.30pm & 2–7pm, Sept–June Mon–Sat 9/9.30am–noon & 2–6pm; ⓣ05.62.95.50.71, ⓦwww.hautebigorre.com), close to pedestrianized, central **place de Strasbourg** with its cafés and nearby *halles*.

Many hotels can be fusty and/or overpriced. Better-value choices include, just north of the *halles* on rue de l'Horloge 3bis, the old-fashioned *Hôtel l'Horloge* (ⓣ05.62.91.00.20; March–Nov; ❶); the well-kept *Hôtel de la Paix* (ⓣ05.62.95.20.60, ⓦwww.hotel-delapaix.com; closed mid-Dec to Jan; ❸), with a decent restaurant and room facing away from the noisy avenue; and (especially for drivers) the rambling *Hôtel Tivoli* (ⓣ05.62.91.07.13, ⓕ05.62.91.15.20; all year; ❸), in its own grounds southwest of the centre on avenue du Salut. **Restaurants** aren't Bagnères' strong point: try *Le Bigourdan* (closed Mon) at 14 rue Victor-Hugo, corner rue de l'Horloge, with a €25 supper menu encompassing *cèpes*, monkfish and varied desserts, or cheap-and-cheerful *Crêperie d' l'Horloge* next door at no. 12, better for sweet or savoury crêpes, salads and cider than the perfunctory *plats du jour*.

The Vallée de Campan

Upstream from Bagnères, regular daily summer buses serve the meadowy **Vallée de Campan**, whose architecture is quite distinct from the valleys to the west. Farm roofs are still slate, but house and barn are built in line as one building, with the balconied living quarters always to the right as you face the sun. The valley's "capital" is **CAMPAN**, with its interesting sixteenth-century covered market, old houses and another curious-looking fortified church with a presumed Cagot door in the west wall. **STE-MARIE-DE-CAMPAN**, 6.5km further along, has less character as a village but better **accommodation** and **eating** choices in *Hôtel les Deux Cols* (ⓣ05.62.91.85.60, ⓕ05.62.91.85.31; closed mid-Oct to mid-Dec; ❶) and the pricey *Gîte L'Ardoisière* (ⓣ05.62.91.88.88; shut Nov-Christmas; doubles ❸ & dorms), both offering half-board. If you're planning on driving or cycling on towards the Pic du Midi and Barèges, remember that the Col du Tourmalet is only reliable from late May/early June until the first snowdrifts (late November).

The Comminges

Stretching from **Luchon** almost as far as Toulouse, the **Comminges** is an ancient feudal county encompassing the upper valley of the River Garonne. It also hosts one of the finest buildings in the Pyrenees, the magnificent cathedral of **St-Bertrand-de-Comminges**, built over three distinct periods. The mountainous southern part is what you want to reach; access is via the unprepossessing little town of Montréjeau, from where there are daily bus and train services to Luchon.

Valcabrère

The village of **VALCABRÈRE** lies a short way south of Montréjeau, itself on the main Bayonne–Toulouse rail line. It can be reached by SNCF bus (direction "Luchon") to the hamlet of Labroquère, by the Garonne, and then a short stroll across the river. It's a sleepy place of rough stone barns and open lofts for drying hay, with an exquisite Romanesque church, **St-Just** (daily 9am–noon & 2–7pm; €2), whose square tower rises above a cemetery full of cypress trees. The north portal is girded by four elegant full-length sculptures and overtopped by a relief of Christ in Glory borne heavenward by angels. Between the altar and apse with its blind arches stands a carved Gothic shrine once containing saintly relics, which pilgrims could mount by means of the now off-limits stone staircase. Both interior and exterior are full of recycled masonry from the old Roman settlement of **Lugdunum Convenarum**, whose remains are visible at the crossroads just beyond the village. Founded by Pompey in 72 BC, this was a town of some 60,000 inhabitants in its prime, making it one of the most important in Roman Aquitaine. Josephus, the Jewish first-century AD historian, says it was the place of exile of Herod Antipas and his wife Herodias, who had John the Baptist beheaded. Destroyed by Vandals in the fifth century and again by Burgundians in the sixth century, it remained deserted until Bishop Bertrand, the future saint, appeared toward the end of the eleventh century.

St-Bertrand-de-Comminges and around

Further southwest 2km is **St-Bertrand-de-Comminges**, whose grey fortress-like **Cathedral** (Feb–April & Oct Mon–Sat 10am–noon & 2–6pm, Sun 2–6pm; May Mon–Sat 9am–6pm, Sun 2–6pm; June–Sept Mon–Sat 9am–7pm, Sun 2–7pm; Nov–Jan Mon–Sat 10am–noon & 2–5pm, Sun 2–5pm; Oct admission to cloister and choir €4) commands the plain from the knoll ahead, the austere white-veined facade and heavily buttressed nave totally subduing the clutch of fifteenth- and sixteenth-century houses huddled at its feet. To the right of the west door a Romanesque twelfth-century cloister with carved capitals looks out across a green valley to the foothills, haunt of Resistance fighters during World War II. In the aisleless interior, the church's great attraction is the central choir, built by Toulousain craftsmen and installed 1523–1535. The 66 elaborately carved stalls, each one the work of a different craftsman, are a feast of virtuosity, mingling piety, irony and malicious satire – though sadly roped off-limits and difficult to see in detail even from a metre away. Each of the gangways dividing the misericords has a representation of a cardinal sin on top of the end partition. By the middle gangway on the south side, for example, Envy is represented by two monks, faces contorted with hate, fighting a furious tug-of-war over the abbot's baton of office. The armrest south of the (locked) rood-screen entrance depicts the abbot birching a monk, while the bishop's throne has a particularly fine back panel in marquetry, depicting St Bertrand himself and St John. In the ambulatory a fifteenth-century shrine depicts scenes from St Bertrand's life, with the church and village visible in the background of the top right panel.

Practicalities

The former peak-season ban on **cars** in the village appears to have been suspended, but **parking** is restricted to two car parks at the south and southwest outskirts. During July and August the cathedral and St-Just in Valcabrère, both with marvellous acoustics, host the musical **Festival du Comminges** (Ⓦwww.festival-du-comminges.com). The **tourist office** is installed in the nineteenth-century Olivétain chapel and monastery on the cathedral square (Mon–Sat 10/11am–5/6/7pm, Ⓣ05.61.88.32.00 or 05.61.98.45.35 and also doubles as an adjunct festival box office.

Staying overnight is an attractive proposition, at least outside peak season. Opposite the cathedral, the friendly *Hôtel du Comminges* (Ⓣ05.61.88.31.43, Ⓕ05.61.94.98.22; April–Sept; ❷) makes a fine, slightly old-fashioned option, though only breakfast is served (outside in fine weather). The *Hôtel L'Oppidum* (Ⓣ05.61.88.33.50, Ⓕ05.61.95.94.04; mid-March to mid-Nov; ❸), north of the cathedral on rue de la Poste, has variable but engaging en-suite rooms, though if you're not staying you're made to feel distinctly unwelcome at their restaurant. Other **eating** options in and around St-Bertrand aren't up to much, so if you have transport, strike out 6km east to **BARBAZAN**, where *Hôtel-Restaurant Le Rocher* (Ⓣ05.61.89.58.56, Ⓦwww.hotelducrocher.com; closed Wed eve; ❷) offers better value (menu from €17) and less snootiness. The nearest **campsite** – shady and well laid out – is *Es Pibous* (Ⓣ05.61.94.98.20; May–Sept), north of the road to St-Just.

The Grottes de Gargas

About 6km from St-Bertrand in the direction of St-Laurent, the **Grottes de Gargas** (45-minute guided tours daily: July & Aug 10am–12.30pm & 2.30–7pm; rest of year by prior arrangement, but reservations almost always necessary Ⓣ05.62.39.72.39, Ⓦwww.gargas.org; last tour 45min before stated closing time; €7) are renowned for their 231 prehistoric painted hand-prints. Outlined in black, red, yellow or white, they mostly seem deformed – perhaps the result of leprosy, frostbite or ritual mutilation, though no one really knows why. There are representations of large animals as well.

Luchon and around

There's none of the usual spa-town fustiness about **LUCHON** (formerly known as Bagnères de Luchon), long one of the focuses of Pyrenean exploration. The main street, **allées d'Étigny**, lined with cafés and brasseries, has a metropolitan elegance and bustle. There is not, however, much to see, apart from the **Musée du Pays de Luchon** (daily 9am–noon & 2–6pm; €1.60) next to the tourist office, which has an extraordinarily eclectic collection of engravings and travel posters, ancient climbing or skiing gear, and strange rural impedimenta, and the nineteenth-century **baths** (March–Oct Mon–Sat 7.30–11.45am, also Wed & Sat 5–7pm) at the end of allées d'Étigny behind the **Parc des Quinconces**. Luchon is best considered as a comfortable base for exploring the surrounding mountains in summer, and for **skiing** at the nearby centres of Superbagnères and Peyragudes in winter. Because of the peculiar local topography, the valley here is also one of the major French centres for **paragliding** and **light aviation**. A long-dormant **tunnel** campaign has been re-activated locally, advocating a bore from somewhere between the Pont de Jouéu and the Hospice de France (see p.808) to emerge in Spain's Val de Benasque, but it won't happen before 2012 – if ever.

The area west of town, en route to the Col de Peyresourde along the D618, is also home to three Romanesque churches. The most accessible of these is **St-Aventin**, in the eponymous village 5km west of Bagnères. The south portal is completely surrounded by fine relief carving, including a fine Christ in Majesty, a Virgin and Child and the beheading of St-Aventin, followed by a bull discovering his grave. There are more carvings, and frescoes inside; a key can be borrowed from the *mairie* (Mon–Fri 9am–noon & 2–5pm).

Practicalities

The **gare SNCF**, also the **gare routière**, is in avenue de Toulouse across the River One in the northern part of the town. The **tourist office** is at 18 allée d'Étigny (daily: July–Aug & peak ski season 8.30am–7pm, rest of year same hours but closes over lunch; ⓣ05.61.79.21.21, ⓦwww.luchon.com), who stock leaflets detailing currently operating activity outfitters.

You're best off forsaking the obvious **accommodation** on allées d'Étigny itself for better value in the quieter side streets. Possibilities there include *Hôtel des Deux Nations* to the west at 5 rue Victor-Hugo (ⓣ05.61.79.01.71, ⓦwww.hotel-des2nations.com; ❶–❸), a popular en suite with a busy downstairs restaurant and the best rooms on the lower two floors; *Hôtel des Sports*, 12 av Maréchal-Foch (ⓣ05.61.79.97.80, ⓦwww.hotel-des-sports.net; ❸), quiet, non-smoking and with secure bike parking; or, east of the main street, *Hôtel la Petite Auberge*, 15 rue Lamartine (ⓣ05.61.79.02.88, ⓕ05.61.79.30.03; ❷), in a *belle-époque* mansion, with ample parking and a *table d'hôte* restaurant. Perhaps the most appealing option is romantically sited *Hôtel Le Jardin des Cascades*, above the church in Montauban-de-Luchon, 2km east (ⓣ05.61.79.83.09, ⓕ05.61.79.79.16; closed mid-Oct to early April; ❸; HB obligatory peak season), with just a half-dozen peaceful, wood-decor rooms in a lovely spot backed by a wild, hilly garden nurtured by the falls of the name. There's no *gîte* or hostel in town, but there are ten **campsites** in the vicinity; least cramped, and with the best amenities, is *Camping La Lanette* (ⓣ05.61.79.00.38, ⓦwww.camping-la-lanette.com; open mid-Dec to Oct), 1.5km east over the Pique (down rue Lamartine) near Montauban-de-Luchon.

As with lodging, the best **eating-out** prospects are some distance away from the allée d'Etigny, with the exception of *L'Arbesquens* at no. 47 (closed Sun eve & Wed), tops for fondue and grilled meat. Alternatively, the shaded terrace restaurant at *Le Jardin des Cascades* (directions and phone same as hotel, above) serves creative gourmet food, and offers sweeping views west and good service; there are cheaper lunch menus, but normally budget €35 per person, and mandatory reservations. With transport, try *L'Auberge de Castel-Vielh*, 2.5km south on the D125 (April–Oct daily; Nov–March weekends only; closed Wed; menus from €20), in a converted country house, serving excellent game and regional dishes, including snails, offal and trout; or – 7km west in **Billière** village – *La Ferme d'Espiau* (book on ⓣ05.61.79.69.69; 5 menus; closed Mon–Wed low season), which excels at local meat or game and foie gras served amidst antique rustic decor.

Hiking and skiing around Luchon

There are several classic hikes south and southwest of Luchon, though there's no public transport to most of the various trailheads. The exception, 14km south-west of Luchon, is **Granges d'Astau**, jump-off point for the **Lac d'Oô**, and served by three daily shuttle buses (July–early Sept). Here, you'll find the *Auberge d'Astau* (ⓣ05.61.79.35.63, ⓦwww.astau-pyrenees.com; May–Sept; ❷), with a restaurant (menus €11–16), though many hikers like *Le Mailh d'Astau* next door for meals. From the car park here a busy section of the GR10 climbs an hour to the dammed lake, where the pricey *Refuge-Auberge du Lac d'Oô* (1504m; ⓣ05.61.79.12.29, ⓦwww.refuge-lac-oo.com; 26 places; €18pp; May–Oct) perches beyond the west end of the dam. The onward path leads to the *Refuge d'Espingo* exactly an hour above Oô, just below the Col d'Espingo. This hut

(1967m; ⓣ05.61.79.20.01; 70 places; June–Oct 15) overlooks the beautiful, undammed **Lac d'Espingo**, and the frontier ridge; most day-trippers stop here, as beyond nearby Lac Saussat the grade stiffens considerably. You can also get to the lakes by taking the *télécabine* from Luchon up to Superbagnères (daily April to mid-Oct 1.30–5pm, also July–Aug 9.45am–12.15pm; €11 return, €7 one way), then continuing west on the GR10 to the *Refuge d'Espingo* (4hr 30min total).

Another possible walking route from Luchon involves following the Pique valley south 11km, partly on the D125, to the derelict **Hospice de France** (1385m), originally founded by the Knights of St John, from where a signposted path climbs a steep, narrow valley to the **Boums du Port** (2hr with daypack), four small, scenic lakes; beside the highest sits the small but welcoming *Refuge de Vénasque* (ⓣ05.61.79.26.46; late May to early Oct), which serves unusually good meals well into the afternoon. Suitably fortified, you can tackle the short, sharp path-climb to the notch on the frontier ridge known as the **Port de Vénasque** (3hr from Hospice de France), with superb views of the **Maladeta massif** and the **Pico d'Aneto**, highest summit of the Pyrenees (3404m). Return the same way, or fashion a classic loop taking in the frontier ridge to the east, then a descent of the Vallée de la Frèche back to the Hospice.

Luchon has two downhill **ski resorts** within striking distance, of which **Peyragudes** (ⓦwww.peyragudes.com) 15km west of Luchon overlooking each approach to Peyresourde, is much better. Its 43 runs, mostly of intermediate calibre and broad by Pyrenean standards, start from 2400m, with superb views of the frontier ridge and a decent lift system. Lower-altitude **Superbagnères** (ⓦwww.luchon.com), right above the town and accessible by a 15-kilometre road or the *téléphérique* (included in ski pass), has 24 mostly beginnner-to-intermediate pistes lamentably exposed to morning sun and thus often mushy.

The Eastern Pyrenees

The dominant climatic influence of the **Eastern Pyrenees**, excepting the misty Couserans region, is the Mediterranean; with more annual days of sunshine than the west, the climate is hotter, the landscape more arid. Dry-weather plants like cistus, broom and thyme make their appearance, and the lower foothills are planted with vines. The proximity of Spain is evident, too, and much of the region belongs to historical Catalonia, definitively incorporated into France only in 1659. As with the rest of the Pyrenees, the countryside is spectacular, and densely networked with hiking trails. Historical sights, with the exception of the painted cave of **Niaux** and the Cathar castle of **Montségur**, are concentrated towards the coast in French Catalonia, comprising Roussillon and La Cerdagne (Rosilló and La Cerdanya in Catalan).

The Ariège valley

Whether you're coming from the western Pyrenees or heading south from the major transport hub of Toulouse, the **Valley of the Ariège** marks the start of

Walking in France

France is quite simply a walker's paradise. It has some 60,000km of long-distance footpaths, known as GRs (*sentiers de grande randonnée*), not to mention thousands of shorter routes (PRs, or *sentiers de promenade et de randonnée*), all well maintained and signposted. They take you through the best of France's beautiful and varied landscape, including the majestic Alps in the east, the volcanic plugs of the Massif Central and the lofty Pyrenees in the south.

▲ Ibex in the Parc National de la Vanoise

The Alps

For sheer mountain grandeur the **northern Alps** are unbeatable. The area has over a hundred peaks topping 3000m – including the highest, Mont Blanc (4807m) – glaciers, soaring pinnacles, high Alpine meadows and rich flora and fauna. The two main areas for walking are the Chamonix valley, which offers plenty of impressive views of Mont Blanc, and the Parc National de la Vanoise, created to protect the wild ibex; you'll stand a good chance of seeing these wild goats on one of the spectacular high-level hikes through the park.

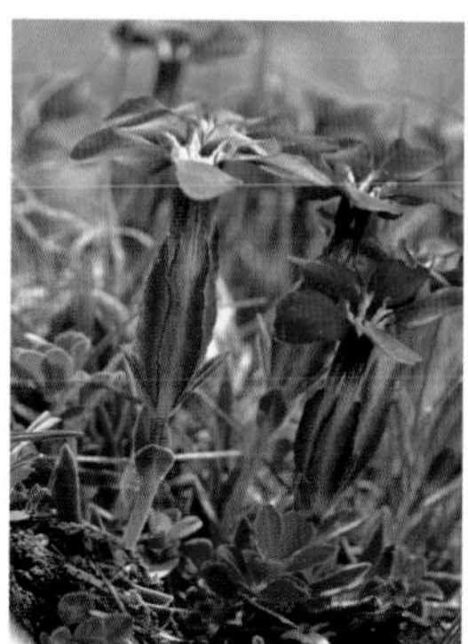

▲ Gentians in the Parc Naturel Régional du Vercors

Generally speaking the peaks of the **southern Alps** are more accessible to less experienced walkers and don't require mountaineering equipment and skills. A good introduction to the area is the Parc Naturel Régional du Vercors, criss-crossed with around 2850km of waymarked paths. At its heart is the impressive Vercors plateau, edged with craggy limestone cliffs and riven with deep gorges. On the lower slopes beech, fir and scots pine forests thrive, and in spring gentians, yellow wild tulips and lilies bloom. More Mediterranean in appearance is the more southerly Parc Naturel Régional du Queyras, with its scrub-covered mountains and meadows of violets, orchids and pinks.

▼ Cirque de Gavarnie, Pyrenees

The Pyrenees

Generally less formidable than the Alps, the Pyrenees are still serious mountains, with a number of peaks topping 3000m, and offer some of France's finest walking. The classic long-distance path is the GR10, which traverses the whole range from west to east and is about 800km long. There are plenty of shorter walks too, the best of which are to be found in the central Ariège region, characterized by steep lush-green valleys, meadows full of wild flowers and abundant wildlife, including vultures – lammergeiers and griffon vultures – and marmots.

▲ Salers cattle in the Auvergne

The Auvergne

At the heart of France, well away from any coast, sparsely populated and little touched by industry, the Auvergne region of the Massif Central is well and truly *France profonde*. It's wild and rugged terrain, formed by three volcanic mountain chains, the Monts-Dore, Monts du Cantal and the smaller Monts-Dômes: much of the landscape consists of deep-cut wooded valleys and wide-open treeless uplands, grazed by red Salers cattle. The biggest draw for walkers is the jagged Puy de Sancy (1885m), the highest peak and source of the Dordogne River.

The Cévennes

Just south of the Auvergne, the hilly Cévennes region is equally isolated, though more Mediterranean in feel. The landscape is a picturesque one of deep valleys clothed with chestnut trees, high limestone plateaux and soft rounded granite peaks. It's fairly easy walking country, and a number of long-distance paths wind their way through the area, the best known of which is the GR70, the route famously described by R. L. Stevenson in his book *Travels with a Donkey*; you can even hire a donkey for the really authentic experience (ⓦwww.chemin-stevenson.org).

Provence

This most beguiling region, with its lovely warm light and Mediterranean colours and scents, has numerous walking possibilities. You could hike through the dramatic and vast Gorges du Verdon, Europe's largest gorge, or ramble among the gentle hills and lavender fields of the Luberon. Towards the Italian border is the Parc National du Mercantour, an unspoilt Alpine wilderness, sheltering chamois, golden eagles and and rare species of flowers.

▼ Lavender field, Provence

Corsica

The Mediterranean island of Corsica offers some of the most varied and adventurous walking in France. Scores of footpaths give access to spectacular coastline, rocky gorges and mountainous peaks. It also boasts the most challenging long-distance trail in the country, if not in Europe – the GR20, a breathtaking high ridge path which crosses the island's mountains from north to south. If you're not quite up to this you could try the more straightforward Mare e Monti Nord, a ten-day hike taking in beauty spots such as the Spelunca Gorges and the Scandola bird reserve.

Ten top walks in France

- Northern Alps: the Alpine section of the Routes des Grandes Alpes (GR5), especially the two-day walk from Le Brévent to Sixt via the Lac d'Anterne. See p.987.
- The Chemin de Saint-Jacques, the ancient pilgrimage route that starts in Le-Puy-en-Velay and ends at Santiago de Compostela in Spain (see p.950). To hike the whole thing would take weeks, but you could do just a section, such as the six-day stretch between Figeac and Moissac through the Lot valley, one of the most picturesque parts of the walk.
- A two-day loop walk above Cauterets in the Pyrenees: Pont d'Espagne–Vallée du Gaube–Vallée de Lutour–Pont d'Espagne. See p.798.
- The Crête d'Iparla, one of the best ridge walks in the Pyrenees (a day-hike along the GR10). See p.774.
- Corsica's two hundred-kilometre-long GR20, possibly Europe's most testing walk. See p.1226.
- The Côte de Granit Rose (see p.433). This attractive stretch of Brittany coast is dotted with pink granite rocks sculpted into weird and wonderful shapes by the weather. One of the best stretches is from Trégastel to Tréguier (a three-day hike) along the GR34.
- The ninety-minute walk up and down the rocky headlands from Cassis, on the Côte d'Azur, to the Calanque d'En Vau, with its beautifully secluded beach. See p.1136.
- The circuit of the southern Alps' Parc National des Écrins (along the GR54), hard to beat for the grandeur of its scenery. See p.1017.
- The Canyon du Verdon: the seven-hour walk from La Maline to the Point Sublime is by far the best way to explore the canyon. See p.1106.
- The GR70 "Stevenson trail", which takes about a fortnight to walk, passing through the rugged Gévaudan highlands and the bare hilltops of Mont Lozère. See p.941.

the transition to the Mediterranean zone. The river valley, extending from high peaks along the Andorran border around the spa of **Ax-les-Thermes** down to agricultural plains north of **Foix**, forms the main axis of the eponymous *département*. In between lie a wealth of **caves**, most notably near **Tarascon** and **Mas d'Azil**. Transport is no problem as long as you stick to the valley, but for side trips into the **Couserans** region on the west you really need a car or cycle.

Foix and around

Administrative centre of the *département* of Ariège, and France's smallest provincial capital, **FOIX** lies 82km south of Toulouse on the Toulouse–Barcelona train line and the N20 road to Ax-les-Thermes and the Spanish border. It's an agreeable country town of narrow alleys and sixteenth- to seventeenth-century half-timbered houses, with an attractive old quarter squeezed between the rivers Ariège and Arget.

Dominating all are the three distinctive hilltop towers of the **Château des Comtes de Foix**, which contains a dull handful of themed exhibits (May, June & Sept daily 9.45am–noon & 2–6pm; July & Aug daily 9.30am–6.30pm; Oct–April Wed–Sun 10.30am–noon & 2–5.30pm; €4.20) – though the views are worth the climb. Determined opponents of the territorial ambitions of the Capetian kings of France and stout defenders of Catharism, the counts of Foix attracted the wrath of Simon de Montfort, who four times laid unsuccessful siege to the castle, though he did capture the town in 1211. Their resistance was finally broken in 1229 when Count Roger-Bernard was obliged to accept the suzerainty of the French king. Foix's age of glory came in 1290 when its counts married into the house of Béarn and subsequently transferred their court to Orthez in the fourteenth century. This was the beginning of a powerful Pyrenean mini-state, whose influence lasted three centuries and came to include the kingdom of Navarre, leading finally to the throne of France with the accession of Henri IV in 1589.

The **gares SNCF and routière** are together on avenue de la Gare, off the N20 on the right bank of the Ariège; except on Sundays, there's a daily **bus** service east via Lavelanet to Quillan and four buses a day west to St-Girons. The **tourist office** is on rue Théophile-Delcasse (July & Aug Mon–Sat 9am–7pm, Sun 10am–noon & 2–6pm; Sept–June Mon–Sat 9am–noon & 2–6pm; ⓣ05.61.65.12.12, ⓦwww.ot-foix.fr).

Most **accommodation** is found in the old town, on the west bank of the Ariège, though little of it is inspiring. The quietest and most comfortable option is three-star *Hôtel Lons*, on 6 place Duthil, near the Pont-Vieux (ⓣ05.61.65.52.44, ⓔhotel-lons-foix@orange.fr; ❹; closed late Dec to early Jan), with a respected restaurant. The *Eychenne* at 11 rue Noël-Peyrevidal (ⓣ05.61.65.00.04; ⓕ05.61.65.56.63; ❸) has been upgraded to fully en-suite status, with a busy ground-floor café (but no restaurant). Opposite at no. 16, the *Auberge Léo Lagrange* (ⓣ05.61.65.09.04, ⓔleolagrange-foix@orange.fr; €16pp) offers hostel-style accommodation (72 bunks in doubles or quads), plus economical weekday lunches in its downstairs *foyer*. The municipal **campsite**, *Lac de Labarre* (ⓣ05.61.65.11.58; all year), is 3km down the N20 towards Toulouse.

A prime area for **eating** is rue de la Faurie, the old blacksmiths' bazaar at the heart of the old town. At no. 17, *Le Jeu de l'Oie* does classic French country-bistro fare – *cassoulet*, duck dishes, *terrines*, offal, good desserts – at friendly prices (*formules* from under €10), which guarantees a lunch-time crush – though service doesn't suffer unduly. Also popular is *Les Quatres Saisons* at no. 11 (menus from €13.50–16; closed Sun–Thurs eve low season), whose specialty is *pierrade* – hot ceramic plates at your table to grill fish and meat.

Labouiche and Mas d'Azil

Six kilometres northwest of Foix, the **underground river** at **Labouiche** (April–June & Sept daily 10–11.15am & 2–5.15pm; July & Aug daily 9.30am–5.15pm; Oct–Nov 11 weekends/hols 10am–11.15 & 2–4.30pm, expect a 15-minute wait; €7.50) is the longest navigable subterranean river in Europe. The visit consists of a barge trip lasting one and a quarter hours, along 1km of the river, 60m underground, to admire its stalactites and stalagmites.

Twenty-five kilometres west of Foix, the **Mas d'Azil** was one of the first prehistoric caves to yield evidence of human habitation, but its most impressive feature is a magnificent 500-metre-long natural tunnel, scoured by the River Arize, which now carries the main road (the D119) from here towards Pamiers. Without transport it's not easy to reach as it lies 12km north of the Foix–St-Girons bus route: get off at Ségalas after La-Bastide-de-Sérou and take the D15 – over two hours on foot.

Secondary caves leading off the river-cavern are the focus of historical interest; they were inhabited in prehistoric periods for more than 20,000 years and used as a refuge by Cathars and Protestants in more recent times. The most important galleries are sealed off, though this hasn't stopped damage from road pollution, and those caves you can visit are interesting mainly for their sheer size (March, Oct & Nov Sun 2–6pm; April–May Mon–Fri 2–6pm, Sun 10am–noon & 2–6pm; June & Sept daily 10am–noon & 2–6pm; July & Aug daily 10am–6pm; €6.10, including museum entry).

A few animal bones and other artefacts found during excavation remain on view in glass cases in the caves, but the best pieces are now on display in the attractive, sleepy village of **LE MAS-D'AZIL**, 1km to the north, in the **Musée de la Préhistoire** (same hours and ticket as the cave). Among other engraved tools and weapons, the museum's most outstanding exhibit is the beautiful carved antler known as *le faon aux oiseaux* (fawn with birds), perhaps used as a spear-thrower. There's just one surviving **hotel** here, the *Hôtel Gardel* (Ⓣ05.61.69.90.05, Ⓕ04.61.69.70.27; ❷; closed mid-Nov to mid-March), as well as a municipal **campsite** (Ⓣ05.61.69.71.37; mid-June to mid-Sept) a twenty-minute walk away. The best place to eat is *Le Jardin de Cadettou* (closed Sat lunch time, Sun eve & Mon; Ⓣ05.61.69.95.23), a homely restaurant with excellent menus of regional cuisine from €23; they also rent rooms (❸). Other accommodation in the area includes British-run *chambre d'hôtes La Baquette* (Ⓣ & Ⓕ 05.61.96.37.67; April to mid-Oct; ❷; *table d'hôte* supper €15) at **LESCURE** hamlet, near La Baure and the junction of the D119 and D117.

Tarascon and around

TARASCON-SUR-ARIÈGE lies 17km south of Foix, where the N20 crosses the Ariège (a bypass diverts the worst of the traffic). Once a centre for the now-defunct iron-mining industry, it's a hot, unexciting little town enclosed by high wooded ridges. However, Tarascon is useful as a base for visiting the nearby prehistoric caves, and more pleasant than first impressions suggest. From the east bank of the Ariège, where riverside cafés provide vantage points, narrow **rue de Barri** leads to St-Michel church in the old quarter, presiding over a partly arcaded square. Two parts of the mostly razed medieval walls survive: the **Tour St-Michel**, and the **Porte-d'Espagne**.

The combined **gare SNCF/halte routière** is a few minutes' walk north from the centre, on the west bank. The **tourist office** is also just west of the bridge in the Centre Multimédia François Mitterrand (Mon–Sat 9am–1pm & 2–6pm, also Sun 9.30am–1pm peak summer/ski season; Ⓣ05.61.05.94.94, Ⓦwww.paysdetarascon.com). **Accommodation** options include quiet *Hôtel Confort* on riverside quai Armand-Sylvestre (Ⓣ & Ⓕ05.61.05.61.90; closed Jan; ❷), with some rooms facing a courtyard; for rooms facing the river, try *Hostellerie de la Poste* (Ⓣ05.61.05.60.41, Ⓦwww.hostellerieposte.com; all year; ❸), three doors down from the post office on the main street. This also has the best **restaurant** (closed Nov 15–Dec 15) in town, with summer seating facing a lawn-garden and four menus (including one vegetarian) at €14–35. There's also a **campsite**, *Pré Lombard* (Ⓣ05.61.05.61.94), on the left bank of the river, ten minutes' walk upstream from the bridge.

Niaux and other prehistoric caves

Just south of Tarascon, the D8 cuts up right into the green valley of Vicdessos; the hamlet of **NIAUX** lies in the valley bottom, 4km further on. The tiny settlement has an interesting **Musée Pyrénéen** (daily: July & Aug 9am–8pm; Sept–June 10am–noon & 2–6pm; €8), with an unrivalled collection of tools, furnishings, and old photos illustrating the vanished traditions of peasant Ariège.

But the real reason people descend on this little hamlet is for the **Grotte de Niaux**, a huge cave complex under an enormous rock overhang 2km north of the hamlet (45min guided tours: July & Aug daily 9.15am–5.30pm, English tours at 9.30am & 1pm; Sept daily 10am–5.30pm, English at 1pm; Oct–June Tues–Sun, tours at 11am, 2.30pm & 4pm; €9.40; max group size 20, advance reservations mandatory on Ⓣ05.61.05.88.37, Ⓦwww.sesta.org). There are about 4km of galleries in all, with paintings of the Magdalenian period (circa 11,000 BC) scattered throughout, although tours see just a fraction of the complex. The paintings you're allowed to see are in a vast chamber, a slippery 900-metre walk from the entrance of the cave along a subterranean riverbed. No colour is used to depict the subjects – horses, ibex, stags and bison – just a dark outline and shading to give body to the drawings, executed with a "crayon" made of bison fat and manganese oxide. They present an extraordinary mix of bold impressionistic strokes and delicate attention to detail: nostrils, pupils and tendons are all drawn in.

The village of **ALLIAT**, right across the valley from Niaux, is home to the Grotte de la Vache (1hr 30min guided tours: April–June, Sept & school hols 2.30–4pm; July & Aug daily 10am–5.30pm; otherwise by arrangement; Ⓣ05.61.05.95.06 Ⓦwww.grotte-de-la-vache.org; €9), a relatively rare example of an inhabited cave where you can observe hearths, embossed bones, tools and other remnants *in situ*. The area's third cave, the **Grotte de Bédeilhac** (same tour length and schedule as de la Vache, plus all Sun at 3pm; €8) above **BÉDEILHAC** village is reached by a different road out of Tarascon, the D618 towards Saurat; after 5km, the cave entrance yawns in the Soudour ridge. Inside are examples of every known technique of Paleolithic art; though not as immediately powerful as at Niaux, its diversity – including modelled stalagmites and mud reliefs of beasts – compensates.

Ax-les-Thermes

Twenty-six kilometres east of Tarascon, still on the banks of the Ariège, the spa town of **AX-LES-THERMES** is completely hemmed in by shaggy mountains, for which it's a good exploration base; Ax is the last place of any size before the Andorran and Spanish frontiers.

The town itself is small and agreeable enough, but there's little to see once you've wandered a couple of streets in the quarter west of the N20, which (until the bypass road is completed) forms the main through road, avenue Delcassé. Rue de l'École and rue de la Boucarie offer a few medieval buildings, and above place du Breilh, the **church of St-Vincent** retains a Romanesque tower. On place du Breilh you can dangle your feet for free in the **Bassin des Ladres**, a pool of hot sulphurous water – one of forty local *sources* – which is all that remains of the hospital founded in 1260 by St Louis for soldiers wounded in the Crusades.

The **gare SNCF** is off avenue Delcassé on the northwest side of town. The **tourist office** (July & Aug daily 9am–1pm & 2–7pm; Sept–June 9am–noon & 2–6pm; ⓣ05.61.64.60.60, ⓦwww.vallees-ax.com) is halfway through town on the north side of the main road. In terms of **accommodation**, a good if resolutely old-fashioned cheapie at part-pedestrianized 6 place du Marché is *Hôtel Le Plaza* (ⓣ05.61.64.22.01; ❷). Next niche up in standards is occupied by *Hôtel Restaurant Le Grillon* on rue St-Udaut, 300m southeast of place du Breilh (ⓣ05.61.64.31.64, ⓦwww.hotel-le-grillon.com; closed Easter to late May; ❸). But much the best deal in town is *Hôtel Restaurant Le Chalet* at 4 av Turrel, opposite the *thermes* (ⓣ05.61.64.24.31, ⓦwww.le-chalet.fr; ❸), managed by a friendly, energetic young couple and thoroughly overhauled in 2006. All the airy rooms over two wings are unique, but all have parquet floors and plasma TV, and most have balconies overlooking the river. There's also a **campsite**, *Le Malazéou* (ⓣ05.61.64.09.14; closed Nov), on the riverbank 500m downstream from the *gare SNCF*.

Eating out, you'll do best for full meals at *Le Grillon* (€18 weekday menu, otherwise à la carte), or at the riverside diner of *Le Chalet* (menus €16–40). However there's more of a buzz to **drinking** at *Le Grand Café*, on avenue Delcassé, and *Brasserie Le Club*, on place Roussel, which occasionally hosts live jazz.

Into the Couserans

Back at Niaux, the road continues along the valley bottom, beneath the romantically pinnacled ruins of the **Château of Miglos** (unrestricted access), to Vicdessos and Auzat, the latter with an unsightly aluminium works. From Vicdessos, the stunning, summer-only D18 climbs the lush, largely abandoned **Vallée de Suc** to the pass at the **Port de Lers** (1517m) – from November to May only the D618, via Massat, is kept open. On the far side of the *port*, cattle graze the alpine meadows down to the Étang de Lers. Then the road climbs again to another col overlooking the head of the **Vallée du Garbet**, luxuriant with beeches; directly south looms a high-walled crenellated cirque underlined by wedges of snow lying beneath their sheerest faces. From here west lies the **Pays de Couserans**, one of the poorest, least developed and most depopulated regions of the Pyrenees. Its villages, **Aulus-les-Bains** in particular, were once renowned for their bear-trainers, who – driven by poverty – toured the lowland towns with their performing beasts.

Aulus-les-Bains

Once in the Garbet valley, the road drops quickly west to **AULUS-LES-BAINS**, a remote spa-village surrounded by fragrant meadows and dramatic peaks; remote though it feels, Aulus has daily (Mon–Sat) bus links with St-Girons. Like other such spots, Aulus enjoyed its moment of glory and fell again into rustic somnolence, from which it is trying to resurrect itself once more. There's not much to do other than enjoy (and walk through) the scenery; the classic hike here involves heading south on a local path to the **Étang de Guzet** and then east to the **Cascade d'Ars** on a bit of the GR10, then returning to Aulus via the stream draining from it (round trip about 5hr). The **thermal baths** themselves are undergoing phased renovation but remain open (early May to early Oct Mon–Sat 8.30am–noon & 4–8pm; rest of year Sat & Sun only same hours except daily winter holidays & Easter).

For summer bike rental and information on other activities, consult the **tourist office** in allée des Thermes (daily: July & Aug 10am–1pm & 2–7pm; Sept–June 10am–noon & 2–6pm; ⓣ05.61.96.01.79). Among various **accommodations**, two friendly, good-value choices are *Hôtel L'Oustalet* (ⓣ05.61.96.00.90, ⓦwww.hotel-ariege-loustalet.com; ❶–❷), its **restaurant** in particular a tasty slice of old-fashioned France (weekday lunch menu €12 gets 4 hearty courses plus wine; otherwise €15–23.50; closed Sun eve & Mon, & Nov), and turreted *Les Oussaillès* (ⓣ05.61.96.03.68, ⓔjcharrue@free.fr; all year; ❸), with more modern rooms, English-speaking staff and a competent restaurant (by arrangement in winter), with menus from €14 and wider choice in summer. The better of two **gîtes d'étape**, at the rear of the old casino, is *La Goulue* (ⓣ05.61.66.53.01; all year; 16 places, some doubles ❶), offering meals and bike storage. *Le Couledous* (ⓣ05.61.96.02.26; all year), 500m west along the river, is the local **campsite**.

St-Girons

With numerous SNCF buses a day from Boussens on the main Tarbes–Toulouse rail line, and ordinary bus connections on to Aulus, Ustou, Massat and Seix, **ST-GIRONS** may be your first taste of the Couserans. Apart from its long association with cigarette-paper manufacture – one pulp plant at the outskirts just survives – the most striking things about St-Girons are its reddish-pink marble paving stones on many pavements. And although there are no other memorable sights, it's a far from unpleasant town, with a lively July **music festival**.

The simplest point for orientation is the **Pont-Vieux**, just below picturesque rapids on the River Salat; the bridge points you into the old commercial centre of the town on the right bank, whose old-fashioned shops have alas largely succumbed to modern competitors. To the right, past the tiny cathedral, lies the typically provincial **place des Poilus**, ringed by elegantly faded period-pieces. Beyond this square, along the river, the asphalted **Champ de Mars** – shaded by plane trees – hosts general markets on the second and fourth Mondays of every month, plus every Saturday morning: herbs, honey, clothes, produce and Africana.

Buses arrive at place des Capots on the left bank of the river. The well-stocked **tourist office** is inside the Maison de Couserans (July & Aug Mon–Sat 9am–7pm, Sun 10am–1pm; Sept–June Mon–Sat 9am–noon & 2–6pm; ⓣ05.61.96.26.60, ⓦwww.ville-st-girons.fr), on the right bank, just downriver from the cathedral. If you want to **stay**, a good economical option is *Hôtel Restaurant La Flamme Rouge* (ⓣ05.61.66.12.77, ⓦwww.hotel-la-flamme-rouge.com; ❸) on the west bank at 15 av Galliéni, with simple but cheerful rooms facing a rear garden, pool and secure parking. For more comfort, choose the *Domaine de Beauregard* at the edge of St-Girons on the road to Seix, comprising two affiliated hotel-restaurants sharing a pool and parkland; the better value of these is ⁂ *Château de Beauregard* (ⓣ05.61.66.66.66, ⓦwww.domeainedebeauregard.com; closed March; ❹–❺), 2006-renovated rooms in a nineteenth-century manor – upstairs units have bathrooms in the turrets. Their restaurant, *L'Auberge d'Antan* (eves only; closed Wed/Thurs low season) offers a weekly-changing, five-course menu for €30. The other recommendable local eatery, *Les Nourritures Terrestres* (closed Sat lunch, Sun lunch) specializing in cheese-based dishes, is in the far northwest of town at 17 av Fernand-Loubet.

St-Lizier

ST-LIZIER, 2km and a short drive downstream along the Salat, totally outclasses St-Girons in the tourism stakes. Full of history on a hilltop, it's walled, arcaded, cobbled, cathedraled, half-timbered, pretty, and utterly lifeless outside of summer.

Architecturally the most interesting building in town is the **Cathédrale de St-Lizier** (May–Oct daily 9am–noon & 2–7pm; Nov–April Mon–Sat 10am–noon & 2–6pm; free), with its distinctive octagonal tower posing photogenically against the mountains to the south. Inside are some twelfth-century frescoes faded almost to invisibility, and a fine Romanesque cloister, also twelfth century, with an array of unique, sculpted column capitals. The building only comes into its own when used as a venue for the late-July to mid-August **classical music festival**. A second cathedral, **Notre-Dame-de-Sède**, within the grounds of the bishop's palace, is closed indefinitely for renovation, though the palace is also home to the **Musée Départemental de l'Ariège** on the first floor (April, May, Sept & Oct Tues–Sun 2–5.30pm; June daily 10am–noon & 2–6pm; July & Aug daily 10am–6.30pm; €4), which contains a permanent ethnographic collection devoted to the Vallée du Bethmale, not really worth the admission fee. It is, however, worth walking up to the palace for views over St-Lizier, and continuing on around the old **ramparts**.

The helpful **tourist office** is located by the lower cathedral (same hours as at St-Girons; ⓣ05.61.96.77.77). There's just one place to **stay**, the *Hôtel de la Tour* (ⓣ05.61.66.38.02, ⓔhoteldelatour09@orange.fr; ❸–❹), in a remodelled old building down by the River Salat on rue du Pont, with the pricier rooms overlooking the water. The on-site **restaurant** has four seafood-strong menus, but reports indicate quality varies. You'll have a consistently better feed 600m northwest, just over the municipal boundary in **LORP-SENTARAILLE**, at ⁂ *La Petite Maison* (closed Mon & Tues; menus €16–46) on the main road, whose blank facade belies pleasant garden seating; the cuisine is *minceur* but highly creative.

The Pays de Sault

The Pays de Sault – a magnificent upland bounded by the rivers Ariège and Aude, and the D117 road from Foix to Quillan – marks the start of "Cathar country" if you're approaching from the west. The first of their former strongholds encountered is **ROQUEFIXADE**, roughly 19km east of Foix on the D117 (or a bit less on the minor D9a); the ruinous (free, unenclosed) eleventh-century castle towers above the eponymous village, a thirteenth-century *bastide* with a quality *gîte d'étape* (ⓣ05.61.03.01.36; all year; 15 places) which does meals. The region's main town, **LAVELANET**, is a nondescript but not unattractive place on the banks of the River Touyre, 28km from Foix and

35km from Quillan. However, offers little beyond bus connections – including north to **Mirepoix**, covered below for convenience though not strictly in the *pays* – and a **tourist office** (July & Aug Mon–Sat 9am–noon & 2–7pm, Sun 9am–noon; Sept–June Mon–Sat 9am–noon & 2–7pm; ⓣ05.61.01.22.20).

Montségur

From Lavelanet, there's no public transport south towards Montségur, so whether you approach via Montferrier (12km) or via Bélesta and Fougax-et-Barrineuf (21km in all) is a matter of taste. The **village** of **MONTSÉGUR** is arrayed in long terraces at the foot of its castle-rock, a modified version of a *bastide* (the original settlement was up at the foot of the castle). Depopulated now except as a second-home venue, the place comes to life only with the influx of tourists, most of them day-trippers. It's worth having a glance at the one-room **museum** (daily: May–Sept 10am–noon & 2–7pm, Oct–April 2–5pm; free), with its collection of bits and pieces from around the castle, before going up there.

A footpath from the top of the village shortens the way up to the saddle of the hill and the Prats des Cramats, the field where the Cathar martyrs (see below) were burnt. From here it's a steep twenty-minute climb to the **Château** (daily: Feb 10.30am–4pm; March 10am–5pm; April & Sept–Oct 9.30am–6pm; May–Aug 9am–7.30pm; Nov 10am–5.30pm; Dec 10.30am–4.30pm; €4), of which all that remain are the stout, now truncated curtain walls and keep. The space within is terribly cramped, and one can easily imagine the sufferings of the besieged. The walls are off-limits, though from the keep you can access the west *donjon* to gaze out over kilometres of forested hills and snowy peaks.

There's a seasonal **tourist office** in the village (July–Sept daily 10am–1pm & 2–6pm; ⓣ05.61.03.03.03, ⓦwww.citaenet.com/montsegur). Several **accommodation** options fill quickly in (and even out of) season; least expensive is the old-fashioned, partly en-suite *Hôtel Café Couquet* (ⓣ05.61.01.10.28; ❷), a rambling pension fronted by pollarded lime trees and with an unsigned restaurant on the first floor (3 courses *table d'hôte* supper with wine €15). An even homier option is *Maison d'Hôtes L'Oustal* at the north end of the village

The fall of Montségur

Between 1204 and 1232, Montségur's castle was reconstructed by Guilhabert de Castres as a strongpoint for the **Cathars** (see p.821). By 1232 it – and the village at the base of the *pog* or rock pinnacle – had become the effective seat of the beleaguered Cathar Church under the protection of a garrison commanded by Pierre-Roger de Mirepoix, with a population of some five hundred, clergy as well as ordinary believers on the run from the persecution of the Inquisition.

Provoked by de Mirepoix's raid on Avignonet in May 1242, in which the eleven chief Inquisitors were hacked to pieces, the forces of the Catholic Church and the king of France laid siege to the castle in May 1243. By March 1244, Pierre-Roger, despairing of relief, agreed to terms. At the end of a fortnight's truce, the 225 Cathar civilians who still refused to recant their beliefs were burnt on a communal pyre on March 16.

Four men who had escaped Montségur unseen on the night of March 15 recovered the Cathar "treasure", hidden in a cave for safekeeping since the preceding Christmas, and vanished. Two of them later reappeared in Lombardy, where these funds were used to support the refugee Cathar community established there for another 150 years. More recent New-Agey speculations, especially in German writings, identify this "treasure" as the Holy Grail, and the Cathars themselves with the Knights of the Round Table.

(Ⓣ05.61.02.80.70, Ⓔserge.germa@orange.fr; ❸), with extrovert hosts Serge and Annick laying on a superb, four-course supper (€16); the four rooms, mostly triples/quads, share baths but there are extensive common areas. If Montségur is full and you've transport, consider another excellent *chambre d'hôte* 8km downhill in **FOUGAX-ET-BARRINEUF**, opposite the post office: English/Canadian-run *Tindleys* (Ⓣ05.61.01.34.87, Ⓦwww.tindleys.com; ❸), with three restored rooms, a copious breakfast and supper (€15) on request.

The Gorges de la Frau

From either Montségur or Fougax-et-Barrineuf, you can take an impressive half-day walk through the **Gorges de la Frau**, emerging at Comus hamlet in the heart of the Pays de Sault. The route from Montségur initially follows the "Sentier Cathare" until linking up with the **GR107** (formerly the GR7B) at Pelail in the valley of the Hers river, which has carved out the gorge. Starting from Fougax, just follow the minor D5 south along the Hers until, past Pelail, tarmac dwindles to a rough, steep track as you enter the *gorges* proper, where thousand-metre-high cliffs admit direct sunlight only at midday. The canyon bottom is densely wooded with beech, ash, cornelian and fir, though it is in fact a major pastoral-migratory route; each mid-October hundreds of cattle who've summered on the Sault plateau are driven down en masse. The defile ends some 3.5km before Comus, where the track broadens and the grade slackens. **COMUS** itself has a good *gîte d'étape* in the former school (Ⓣ04.68.20.33.69, Ⓦwwwgites-comus.com; 38 places, some doubles ❶); here you're just 2.5km shy of the D613 road between Ax-les-Thermes and Quillan, with a daily bus to the latter.

Mirepoix and Camon

Heading north from Lavelanet in the direction of Carcassonne, it's definitely worth stopping in at **MIREPOIX**, a late thirteenth-century *bastide* built around one of the loveliest surviving arcaded market squares – **Les Couverts** – in the country. The square is bordered by houses dating from the thirteenth to the fifteenth centuries, and a relatively harmonious modern *halle* on one side, but its highlight is the medieval **Maison des Consuls** (council house), whose rafter-ends are carved with dozens of unique portrayals of animals, monsters, and caricatures of medieval social groups and professions, as well as ethnic groups from across the world. Just south of Les Couverts, the early Gothic cathedral of **St-Maurice** is claimed to have the largest undivided nave in France, supported only by airy rib vaulting.

There's a **tourist office** in the main square (Mon–Sat 9.15am–12.15pm & 2–6pm; Ⓣ05.61.68.83.76, Ⓦwww.ot-mirepoix.fr). If you're feeling extravagant, **stay** at the four-star *Hôtel Relais Royal* at the edge of the *bastide* on 8 rue Maréchal-Clauzel (Ⓣ05.61.60.19.19, Ⓦwww.relaisroyal.com; ❾), a meticulously restored eighteenth-century palace. Allow €100 à la carte at its in-house restaurant *Le Ciel de Or* (though there is a €30 menu), but the best-value **eating** – and thus you often have to reserve – is at modest but salubrious *Hôtel-Restaurant Le Commerce*, 20 cours Docteur-Chabaud by the cathedral (Ⓣ05.61.68.10.29, Ⓦwww.chez.com/lecommerce; ❸), where three generous, expertly prepared à la carte courses (*salad chèvre chaud*, *filets de rougets*, sorbet) plus house wine won't much top €24. Falling between these two on the scale, at no. 6 of the arcaded square, is the *Maison des Consuls* (Ⓣ05.61.68.81.81, Ⓦwww.maisondeconsuls.com; all year; ❺–❼), its plushly furnished units just above the carved rafters. There's a municipal **campsite** on the Limoux road (Ⓣ05.61.01.55.44; closed mid-Sept to mid-June).

△ Market square, Mirepoix

If you've transport, there's another **accommodation** option 13km southeast in the medieval village of **CAMON**, easiest reached off the D625 Lavelanet-Mirepoix road. Here the twelfth- to fourteenth-century **fortified Benedictine abbey** at the summit of things has been transformed by new English owners into *chambres d'hôtes* with a difference, *L'Abbaye-Château de Camon* (Ⓣ05.61.60.31.23, Ⓦwww.chateaudecamon.com; closed early Jan to mid-March; ❼, breakfast extra). There's a large pool, part of the original cloister, eighteenth-century canvases in the lounge, a frescoed chapel, plus all the echoing galleries and spiral staircases you could want; the competent restaurant is open to all for supper (€30 *table d'hôte*).

Along the Aude

South of Carcassonne, the D118 road and the rail line both climb steadily up the twisting valley of the **Aude**, between scrubby hills and vineyards, past river-straddling **Limoux** and sleepy **Alet-les-Bains**, before reaching **Quillan** where the topography changes. Beyond here, the route squeezes through a series of awesome gorges either side of **Axat** before emerging once again towards the river's headwaters on the Capcir plateau, east of the Carlit Massif in the high Pyrenees. It's a magnificent drive or slightly hair-raising cycle-ride; buses run to isolated **Quérigut** three times a week.

Limoux

The first stop 24km south of Carcassonne, **LIMOUX** is served several times daily by either **SNCF trains or buses**; those arriving by car will find free **parking** on the riverbanks by the picturesque old bridge. The town straddles

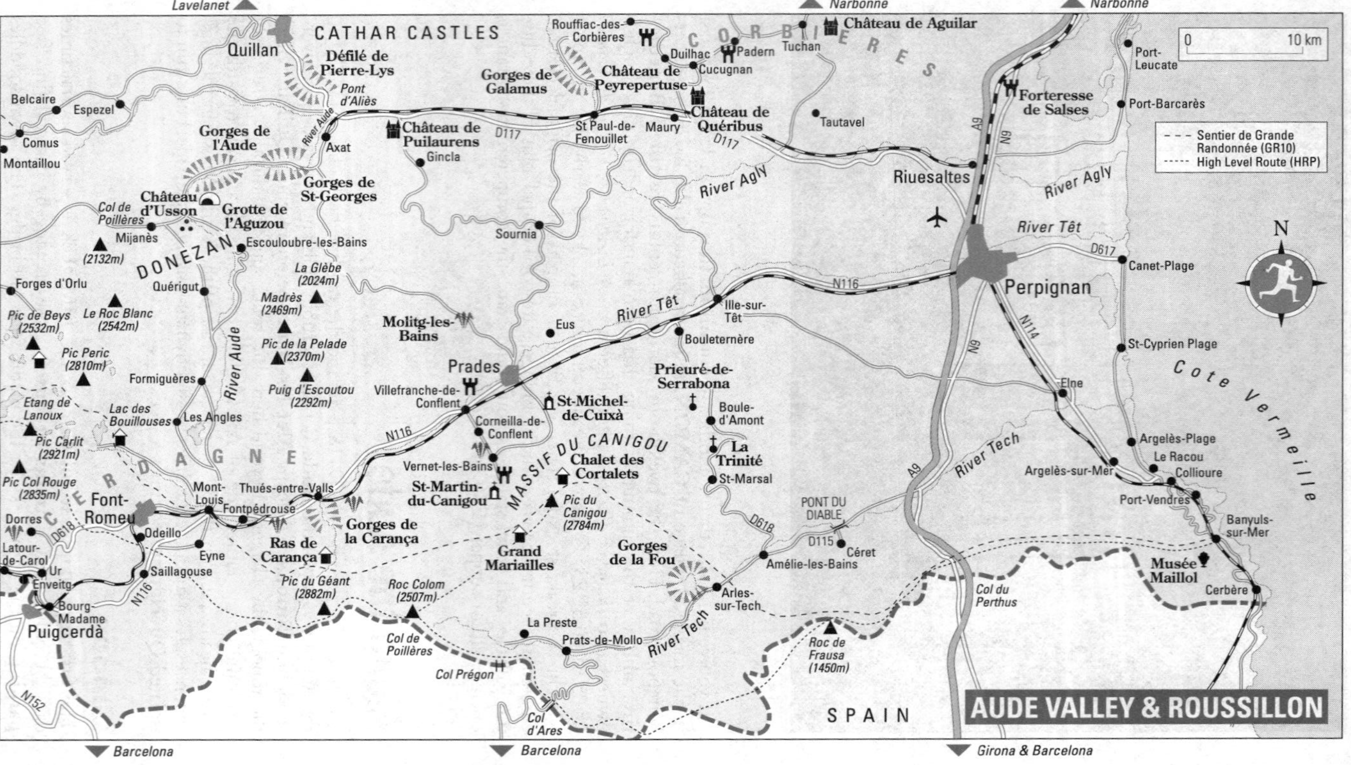
AUDE VALLEY & ROUSSILLON
CATHAR CASTLES
0 10 km
Sentier de Grande Randonnée (GR10)
High Level Route (HRP)
N
Lavelanet
Narbonne
Narbonne
Montségur
Ax-les-Thermes
Barcelona
Barcelona
Girona & Barcelona
Quillan
Défilé de Pierre-Lys
Pont d'Aliès
River Aude
Axat
Belcaire
Espezel
Comus
Montaillou
Gorges de l'Aude
Gorges de St-Georges
Château de Puilaurens
D117
Gincla
Château d'Usson
Grotte de l'Aguzou
Col de Poillères
Mijanès
(2132m)
DONEZAN
Escouloubre-les-Bains
Quérigut
Forges d'Orlu
Le Roc Blanc (2542m)
Pic de Beys (2532m)
Pic Peric (2810m)
La Glèbe (2024m)
Madrès (2469m)
Pic de la Pelade (2370m)
Puig d'Escoutou (2292m)
Formiguères
Etang de Lanoux
Lac des Bouillouses
Les Angles
Pic Carlit (2921m)
Pic Col Rouge (2835m)
CERDAGNE
Mont-Louis
Font-Romeu
Dorres
D618
Odeillo
Latour-de-Carol
Ur
Enveitg
Eyne
Saillagouse
N116
Bourg-Madame
Puigcerdà
N152
Thués-entre-Valls
Fontpédrouse
Ras de Carança
Gorges de la Carança
Pic du Géant (2882m)
Roc Colom (2507m)
Col de Poillères
Col Prégon
Col d'Ares
Rouffiac-des-Corbières
Gorges de Galamus
Château de Peyrepertuse
Duilhac
Padern
Cucugnan
Tuchan
Château de Aguilar
CORBIÈRES
St Paul-de-Fenouillet
Maury
Château de Quéribus
D117
Tautavel
Sournia
River Agly
Molitg-les-Bains
Eus
River Têt
Prades
Villefranche-de-Conflent
N116
Corneilla-de-Conflent
Vernet-les-Bains
St-Martin-du-Canigou
St-Michel-de-Cuixà
MASSIF DU CANIGOU
Chalet des Cortalets
Pic du Canigou (2784m)
Grand Mariailles
Ille-sur-Têt
Bouleternère
Prieuré-de-Serrabona
Boule-d'Amont
La Trinité
St-Marsal
D618
Gorges de la Fou
Arles-sur-Tech
River Tech
La Preste
Prats-de-Mollo
Amélie-les-Bains
PONT DU DIABLE
D115
Céret
Roc de Frausa (1450m)
SPAIN
Col du Perthus
Riuesaltes
Forteresse de Salses
A9
N9
River Agly
River Têt
Perpignan
D617
N114
Port-Leucate
Port-Barcarès
Canet-Plage
St-Cyprien Plage
Elne
Cote Vermeille
River Tech
Argelès-Plage
Argelès-sur-Mer
Le Racou
Collioure
Port-Vendres
Banyuls-sur-Mer
Musée Maillol
Cerbère

the Aude, which for much of the year is a powerful brownish-green flood of snowmelt. Life revolves around the pretty **place de la République** in the heart of the old town, with its Friday market, brasseries and cafés, and the nineteenth-century **promenade du Tivoli**, in effect a bypass road to the west. Known in the past for its woollens and the tanning of hides brought down from the mountains, the town's claim to fame today is the production of its excellent sparkling wine, Blanquette de Limoux, cheaper than champagne.

The **tourist office**, at promenade du Tivoli 32 (July & Aug daily 9am–7pm; Sept–June Mon–Fri 9am–noon & 2–6pm, Sat & Sun 10am–noon & 2–5pm; ⓣ04.68.31.11.82), shares a building with the **Musée Petiet** (same hours; €3), a collection of not very distinguished local nineteenth-century paintings. **Accommodation** choices include the overpriced *Hôtel Modern & Pigeon* just west of place de la République, opposite the *halles* (ⓣ04.68.31.00.25, ⓔhotelmodernepigeon@orange.fr; ❺; restaurant closed Wed), and the humbler but better-value *Hôtel Les Arcades*, north of St-Martin church at 96 rue St-Martin (ⓣ04.68.31.02.57, ⓕ04.68.31.66.42; closed Dec 15–Jan 1 & Wed; ❷). The municipal **campsite** (ⓣ04.68.31.13.63; mid-May to Oct) is on the east bank of the river, south of the old bridge.

The best independent **restaurant** is *Maison de la Blanquette*, at 46bis promenade du Tivoli, which purveys regional dishes and wines (closed Tues & Wed; menus from €15.95; ⓣ04.68.31.01.63); otherwise head to one of the hotels above. Menus at the *Modern & Pigeon* (closed Sun noon & Mon) start at €29.50, probably more interesting than the merely sustaining fare (menus from €15) in *Les Arcades'* time-warped diner overlooking St-Martin church. If you're interested in buying local **wine**, the best place to go is the co-operative, Aimery-Sieur d'Arques, in avenue du Mauzac (daily 9am–noon & 2.30–7pm).

Alet-les-Bains and Rennes-le-Château

South of Limoux, the next place to halt is the thermal resort of **ALET-LES-BAINS**; the spa on the outskirts is incidental to the lovely half-timbered houses and arcaded *place* inside the fortifications. There's also a ruined Romanesque abbey, next to the tourist office which has the keys (daily: 10am–noon & 2.30–6pm), and an excellent **hotel**, the *Hostellerie de l'Évêché* (ⓣ04.68.69.90.25, ⓦwww.hotel-eveche.com; April–Oct; ❹), by the abbey in its own vast park-like grounds. They've a restaurant, but meals are for guests only.

With transport, it's worth taking a detour south of Alet, following the D52 as it climbs 4.5km out of Couiza towards the mountain-top village of **RENNES-LE-CHÂTEAU**. The views alone repay the effort, but the primary reason for the jaunt is the mysterious **parish church** run by Abbé Bérenguer Saunière from 1885 until 1910, when he was defrocked by the bishop of Carcassonne for failing to explain how he financed his comfortable lifestyle and the lavish redecoration of the fifteenth-century church (free admission). This is supposedly full of veiled symbols and secret codes, which – say some (others will see merely lavish kitsch) – indicate that he had discovered the lost treasure of Solomon, brought here by the Visigoths in the fifth century. This and a host of other theories are explored in the **Musée Presbytère de l'Abbé** (daily: March–April & mid-Sept to Oct 11am–5.30pm; May to mid-Sept 10am–7pm, Nov–Feb 10am–5pm; ⓦwww.rennes-le-chateau.fr; €4.25) comprising Saunière's Villa Béthania – where he lived openly with his mistress Marie Denardaud – and its gardens.

Quillan and Axat

Back on the main road, **QUILLAN**, 28km upstream from Limoux, is a pleasant little town, useful as a staging post on the way south into the mountains or east to the Cathar castles (see opposite) – it has daily bus connections with Perpignan via St-Paul-de-Fenouillet. The only monument of interest is the ruined castle, burnt by the Huguenots in 1575 and partly dismantled in the eighteenth century. The **gare SNCF** and **gare routière** sit together on the main bypass road, whilst the **tourist office** (June–Sept Mon–Sat 8am–noon & 2–7pm, Sun 9am–noon; Oct–May Mon–Fri 9am–noon & 2–6pm, Sat 9am–1pm; ⓣ04.68.20.07.78, ⓦwww.ville-quillan.com) stands opposite in the former Art Deco public baths. **Accommodation** options on the same (noisy) boulevard include the *Canal* at no. 36 (ⓣ04.68.20.08.62; ❷) and the *Cartier*, at no. 31 (ⓣ04.68.20.05.14, ⓦwww.hotelcartier.com; ❷–❸; restaurant closed mid-Dec to mid-March & Sat low season). A good independent **restaurant** is *Pizzeria des Platanes* at 2 av Pasteur, towards the river by the cinema, with seating outdoors under the namesake trees. The *Sapinette* **campsite** is at 21 rue René-Delpech (ⓣ04.68.20.13.52; April–Oct).

Beyond Quillan, the road heads southeast 11km, through the narrow **Défilé de Pierre-Lys**, to **Pont d'Aliès**, where there's another campsite and a clutch of **river-rafting** outfitters, the Aude being a major venue for water sports. Just 1km south of the *pont* is **AXAT**, again covering both banks of the river; you can **stay** at *Auberge La Petite Ourse* (ⓣ04.68.20.59.20; ❹), at no. 89 on the main highway, or the *Hôtel Axat* at no. 99 (no phone; ❸). Otherwise, Axat is the westerly terminus of the Train du Pays Cathare et du Fenouillèdes (see p.822), and the last town of any size before entering the rocky canyons to the south.

The Aude gorges and Grotte de l'Aguzou

On its first 20km south of Axat, the D618 threads hazardously through two consecutive canyon systems: the **Gorges de St-Georges** and the **Gorges de l'Aude**. Beyond the second set of narrows is a magnificent cave, the **Grotte de l'Aguzou**. It's expensive to visit, but – accoutred like a pro – as near to real speleology as you can get without being a caver. Visits require a week's advance notice, and there's a minimum of four people (contact Philippe Moreno, ⓣ04.68.20.45.38, ⓔgrotte.aguzou@orange.fr; €30 half-day, €60 full day). The closest indoor **accommodation** is 8km up the Aude at **ESCOULOUBRE-LES-BAINS**, where *Chambres d'Hôtes Maison Roquelaure* (ⓣ04.68.20.47.29, ⓔdaniel.bilot@orange.fr; ❷), in the old thermal establishment, makes evening meals for hikers and cyclists, and still has an on-site hot spring.

The Donezan: Usson, Mijanès and Quérigut

Upstream, the road divides just after abandoned Usson-les-Bains (the easterly fork goes to Escouloubre-les-Bains). On a shaggy bluff between the arms of the fork, dwarfed in turn by the heights either side, stand the forlorn ruins of the **Château d'Usson** (complicated, limited hours low season, July & Aug daily 10am–1pm & 3–7pm; €3.50), allegedly the hiding place of the "Cathar treasure" after the siege of Montségur (see box, p.815). This is the gateway to the **Donezan** region, beautifully forested but the poorest, most neglected and depopulated corner of the Ariège. Passing the castle's base, the westerly road winds up to the attractive tiered houses of **MIJANÈS** – where there's a good **hotel-restaurant**, the *Relais de Pailhères* (ⓣ04.68.20.46.97; ❷), which should be reserved as it's the only facility in the area comparable in quality to *Maison Roquelaure*.

From Mijanès a road heads 8km up-valley to **QUÉRIGUT**, last settlement before the border with Roussillon and end of the summer bus line. The high, chilly village is guarded by the ruined **Château de Donezan**, last refuge of Cathars who held out for eleven years after the fall of Montségur. There's a single, central, simple **hotel-restaurant**, *Du Donezan* (Ⓣ04.68.20.42.40, Ⓕ04.68.20.47.06; ❷), plus a **campsite** below the village. Beyond Quérigut, it's 14km south through forest and meadowland on the D16 to Formiguères, chief village of the Capcir, and as much again to Mont-Louis in the Cerdagne, with more facilities and public transport.

The Cathar castles

Romantic and ruined, the medieval fortresses which pepper the hills to the west and north of Perpignan have become known as the **Cathar castles**, though in fact many were built either before or after the Cathar era. The south of France, especially Roussillon, Languedoc and the eastern Ariège, was this twelfth-century sect's power-base; their name derives from the Greek word for "pure", *katharon*, as they abhorred the materialism and worldly power of the established Church, were initially pacifist and denied the validity of feudal vows or allegiances. Although Cathars probably never accounted for more than ten percent of the population, they included many members of the nobility and mercantile classes, which alarmed the powers that were.

Once disputational persuasion by the ecclesiastical hierarchy proved fruitless, Pope Innocent III anathemized the Cathars as heretics in 1208 and persuaded the French king to mount the first of many "Albigensian" crusades, so called after Albi, a Cathar stronghold. Predatory northern nobles, led for a decade by the notoriously cruel Simon de Montfort, descended on the area with their forces, besieging and sacking towns, massacring Cathar and Catholic civilians alike, laying waste or seizing the lands of local counts. The effect of this brutality was to unite both the Cathars and their Catholic neighbours in southern solidarity against the barbarous north. Though military defeat became inevitable with the capitulation of Toulouse in 1229 and the fall of the castle of Montségur (see box, p.815) in 1244, it took the informers and torturers of the Holy Inquisition another 180 years to root out Catharism completely.

The best of the castles stud the arid, herb-scented hills of the **Corbières** which separate Roussillon from Languedoc. **Walking** is the most direct way to experience them, and the **GR36**, crossing from Carcassonne to St-Paul-de-Fenouillet, and the **Sentier Cathare**, crossing east to west from Port La-Nouvelle to

Intersite Pass

If you're planning on visiting several of the Cathar-related and other medieval sites in the Aude, consider purchasing an **Intersite Pass**, available for €4 at any of the eighteen participating monuments in the *département*. The card (valid 1 year) gives €1 off adult admission, and free child tickets, for the ramparts of Carcassonne, Lastours, Saissac, Caunes-Minervois, St-Hilaire, Lagrasse, Fontfroide, Puilaurens, Usson, Peyrepetuse, Queribus, Aguilar and other sites.

Foix, together pass most of the sites. The Sentier Cathare is described in *Sentier Cathare* Topo-guide (Rando Éditions), available in local bookstores.

Without transport or walking boots, the best way to tackle the castles is from the south, as the most spectacular ones are close to the **Quillan–Perpignan road**. This route is served by bus, but a better option is the narrow-gauge **Train du Pays Cathare et du Fenouillèdes** (ⓣ04.68.59.96.18, ⓦwww.tpcf.fr) which runs from Rivesaltes, just north of Perpignan, to Axat, stopping at the main towns along the way. The service (sometimes only St-Paul-de-Fenouillet to Axat) runs on weekends in May, June, September and October, daily in July & August (adult fare €8–17 depending on direction and distance).

Puilaurens and Gincla

The westernmost of the Fenouillèdes Cathar castles can be reached by road from Quillan or rail from Axat, from the Lapradelle station of the seasonal train noted on above. Lapradelle, 6km east of Axat, is in turn 2km north of the turnings for dramatically sited **Château de Puilaurens** (daily: April–June & Sept 10am–5.30pm; July & Aug 9am–7.30pm; Oct–March 10am–4.30pm, but closed Nov 16–Jan 31 & weekdays Feb/March; €3.50). You can either drive up a 1500-metre side road starting 500m south of Puilaurens hamlet, or there's a shorter and fairly gentle path up from the hamlet. The castle perches atop a wooded hill at 700m, its fine crenellated walls sprouting organically from the rock outcrops. Originally the site of a Visigothic citadel, it was fortified to its present extent in the early thirteenth century, when it passed from the king of France to the count of Roussillon, and then to the king of Aragón. It sheltered many Cathars up to 1256, when Chabert de Barbera, the region's *de facto* ruler, was captured and forced to hand over his citadel here and at Quéribus further east to secure his release. The castle remained strategically important – being close to the Spanish border – until 1659, when France annexed Roussillon and the frontier was pushed south. Highlights of a visit are the **west donjon** and **southeast postern gate**, where you're allowed briefly on the curtain wall for views, and the **Tour de la Dame Blanche**, with a rib-vaulted ceiling.

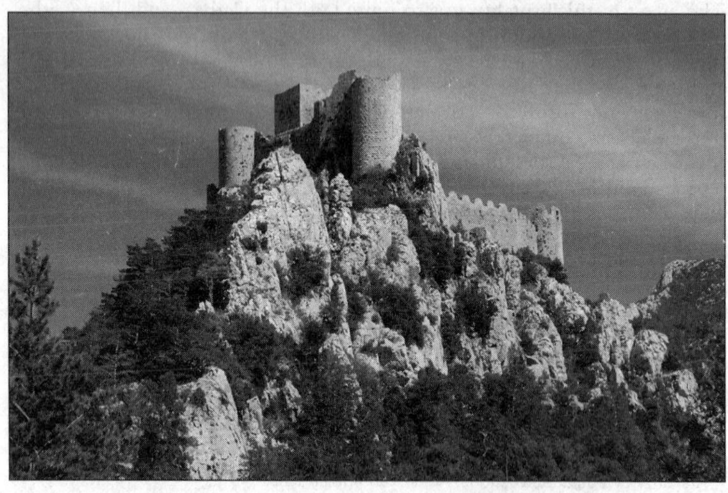

△ Château de Puilaurens

Six kilometres south of Puilaurens village in the centre of sleepy **GINCLA** is the *Hostellerie du Grand Duc* (Ⓣ04.68.20.55.02, Ⓦwww.host-du-grand-duc.com; closed Nov–March; ❺), a converted manor house with an equally pricey restaurant, though they also manage *chambres d'hôtes* (❸).

Quéribus, Cucugnan and Duilhac

The **Château de Quéribus** (Jan Sat, Sun & school hols 10am–5pm; Feb daily 10am–5.30pm; March, Nov & Dec daily 10am–6pm; April–June & Sept daily 9.30am–7pm; July & Aug daily 9am–8pm; Oct daily 10am–6.30pm; €5), 30km further east towards Perpignan, overlooks the vine-ringed village of Cucugnan (see below) from the ridge which marked the French-Spanish border until 1659. Spectacularly situated above the Grau de Maury pass 6km north of the Quillan–Perpignan road, the castle balances on a storm-battered pillar of rock above sheer cliffs – access is forbidden in bad weather.

Because of the cramped topography, the space within the walls is stepped in terraces, linked by a single stairway and dominated by the polygonal keep. High point, in all senses, is the so-called **Salle de Palmier**, whose vaulted ceiling is supported by a graceful pillar sprouting a canopy of intersecting ribs. More steep stairs lead to the roof and fantastic views in every direction, including northwest to the next Cathar castle, Peyrepertuse.

The history of Quéribus is similar to that of Puilaurens, holding out until 1255 or 1256; never reduced by siege, its role as their sanctuary ended with the capture of the luckless Chabert, though the Cathar garrison escaped to Spain.

A popular base for visiting Quéribus (and Peyrepertuse) is the small village of **CUCUGNAN**, in the valley roughly halfway between the two, and its popularity is such that in season you must **park** vehicles at the outskirts. There's plenty of **accommodation**, including *Chambres d' Hôtes L'écuri de Cucunan* at 10 rue Achille-Mir (Ⓣ04.68.33.37.42, Ⓔecurie.cucugnan@orange.fr; ❹ B&B); fully fledged hotels include the central *Auberge du Vigneron* at 2 rue Achille-Mir (Ⓣ04.68.45.03.00, Ⓔauberge.vigneron@ataraxie.fr; ❸; restaurant, menus from €19, closed Sun eve & Mon, also mid-Nov to March), and the *Auberge de Cucugnan* (Ⓣ04.68.45.40.84, Ⓕ04.68.45.01.52; closed Wed & Jan to mid-March; ❸), downhill from the church (which supposedly contains a statue of a pregnant Virgin), with a restaurant known for its hearty servings of game (from €16; closed on Wed Sept–June). The nearest other rooms are in **DUILHAC**, about 4km away just below Peyrepertuse (see below), at the unstaffed *Auberge du Vieux Moulin de la Source* (contact *Auberge du Vigneron*).

Peyrepertuse, Rouffiac, Gorges de Galamus and Aguilar

If you only have time for one of the Cathar castles, let it be the **Château de Peyrepertuse** (Feb, March & Nov to early Jan 10am–5pm; April–June & Sept daily 10am–7pm, later closing Easter week; July & Aug daily 9am–8.30pm; Oct daily 10am–6pm; closed 3 weeks in Jan; €5), not only for its unbeatable site and stunning views, but also because the complex is unusually well preserved, staying in use until 1789. The 3.5-km access road starts in Duilhac or, alternatively, you can walk up from Rouffiac des Corbières village to the north via the GR36 – a tough, hot climb of over an hour. But either way the effort is rewarded, for Peyrepertuse is one of the most awe-inspiring castles anywhere in Europe, draped the length of a jagged rock-spine with sheer drops at most points. Access is banned during fierce summer thunderstorms, when (as at Quéribus) the ridge makes an ideal lightning target.

Tickets are sold by the southerly car park, but you then walk fifteen minutes through thickets of box to the entrance on the north side. The bulkiest fortifications enclose the lower, eastern end of the ridge, with a keep and barbican controlling the main gate. Things get increasingly airier as you progress west along the ridge past and through various cisterns, chapels and bastions, culminating in a stairway of over a hundred steps carved into the living rock, which leads to a keep, tower and **chapel of San Jordi** at the summit. The views – some of the most sweeping in southern France – are as you'd expect; the castle was obtained by treaty with the Kingdom of Aragón in 1258, and most of the existing fortifications were built afterwards.

In sleepy **ROUFFIAC-DES-CORBIÈRES,** 3km north, there's a **hotel**, the *Auberge de Peyrepertuse* (☎04.68.45.40.40; closed Dec 15–Jan 15, plus Tues; €43), with a hearty restaurant (menus €14 & €18) and well-appointed en-suite rooms. For hikers, there's a rudimentary shop; the Sentier Cathare heads west-southwest towards Puilaurens, or generally east via the castles of Quéribus, Padern and Aguilar.

Moving on from Rouffiac by car or bike, you can return to St-Paul-de-Fenouillet, initially via the villages of Soulatgé and Cubières-sur-Cinoble, through the **Gorges de Galamus**, a short but impressive defile worn through the limestone ridge by the River Agly. From Cubières, a perilously narrow corniche road threads the gorge, with a limited number of turnouts and car parks, from one of which a path lead downs to the bottom via the eagle's-nest **Ermitage de St-Antoine** (daily 10am–6pm) on the east flank of the ravine. This is a popular canyoning venue, though most just swim in river-pools below the *ermitage*.

Alternatively, the drive, cycle or hike east from Rouffiac offers more castles, including one at **Padern** village and the especially fine, isolated **Château d'Aguilar** (April to mid-June & mid-Sept to mid-Nov 11am–5pm; mid-June to mid-Sept 11am–7pm, closed mid-Nov to March; €3.50), a hexagonal thirteenth-century citadel with six towers just east of Tuchan, overlooking the Côtes de Roussillon-Villages wine *domaine*.

Roussillon

The area comprising the eastern fringe of the Pyrenees and the lowlands down to the Mediterranean coast is known as **Roussillon**, or **French Catalonia**. Catalan power first emerged in the tenth century under the independent counts of Barcelona, who then became kings of Aragón as well in 1162. They attempted to unify with Occitania under the counts of Toulouse, but that ended unhappily with the death of Pere II of Aragón at the battle of Muret in 1213, fighting with Raymond VI of Toulouse against anti-Cathar crusader Simon de Montfort. The Catalan zenith was reached during the thirteenth and fourteenth centuries, when the Franco-Catalan frontier traced the Corbières hills north of

As in the Aude region (see p.821), there's an **Intersite Pass** scheme for Roussillon, with the same rules and discounts. The 38 participating attractions include the abbeys of St-Martin-du-Canigou and St-Michel-de-Cuixà, the Palais des Rois de Majorque, the art museum in Céret and the cloister at Elne.

Perpignan. But Jaume I of Aragón and Valencia made the mistake of dividing his kingdom between his two sons at his death in 1276. The Roussillonais part became the kingdom of Mallorca under Jaume II with its mainland capital at Perpignan, but – coveted by the rival brother, King Pere III of Aragón – it immediately allied itself with the French kings, who saw this as a splendid opportunity to expand their southern territories, thus ensuring continuous see-saw battles and annexations that were only ended by the Treaty of the Pyrenees, negotiated by Louis XIV and the Spanish king in 1659.

After the treaty, the French began a ruthless process of Frenchification, more successful in Perpignan where the bourgeoisie tended to identify their commercial interest with a central power. The Pyrenean hinterland, however, was largely unaffected until the late nineteenth century, when the collapse of traditional agriculture, the introduction of compulsory education and the devastation of the vineyards by phylloxera combined to depopulate the mountains – a still on-going process.

Although there's no real separatist impetus among French Catalans today, their sense of identity remains strong: the language is very much alive (not least in bilingual place-signage), and the national red-and-yellow flag is ubiquitous. The **Pic du Canigou**, which completely dominates Roussillon despite its modest (2784m) elevation, shines as a powerful beacon of Catalan nationalism, attracting hordes of Catalans from across the border to celebrate St John's Eve (June 23–24). At its feet the little town of **Prades**, place of exile from Franco's Spain of cellist Pau Casals, served as a focus of Catalan resistance until 1975.

Most of the region's attractions are easily reached from Roussillon's capital, **Perpignan**. The coast and foothills between it and the Spanish frontier are beautiful, especially at **Collioure**, though predictably crowded and in most places overdeveloped. You'll find the finest spots in the **Tech** and **Têt valleys** which slice southwest towards the high peaks, among them the Romanesque monasteries of **Serrabona**, **St-Michel-de-Cuixà** and **St-Martin-du-Canigou**, Vauban's fortress town of **Villefranche-de-Conflent**, the world-class modern art museum at **Céret** and **Mont Canigou** itself, lapped by foothill orchards of peaches and cherries.

Perpignan

So far south, climate and geography alone would ensure a palpable Spanish influence. But aside from this, a good part of **PERPIGNAN**'s population is of Spanish origin – refugees from the Civil War and their descendants. The southern influence is further augmented by a substantial contingent of North Africans, including both Arabs and white French settlers repatriated after Algerian independence in 1962.

Perpignan's glory days were the late thirteenth and early fourteenth centuries, when the kings of Mallorca held court here, and most of its historical interest derives from this period. Yet there are surprisingly few memorable and visitable monuments, and the city won't necessarily make a good first impression; street life ranges from the lively – flamenco buskers and such – to downright dirty and shabby, with numerous boarded-up business premises evidence of hard contemporary times. Few will want to stay more than a day or two before taking advantage of the good public transport links in every direction; if you've your own transport, you may prefer to base yourself somewhere in the surrounding area.

Arrival, information and accommodation

From the **airport** at Rivesaltes, 6km north (daily flights from London Stansted with Ryanair), there are up to six daily shuttle buses into town (€5), which call at

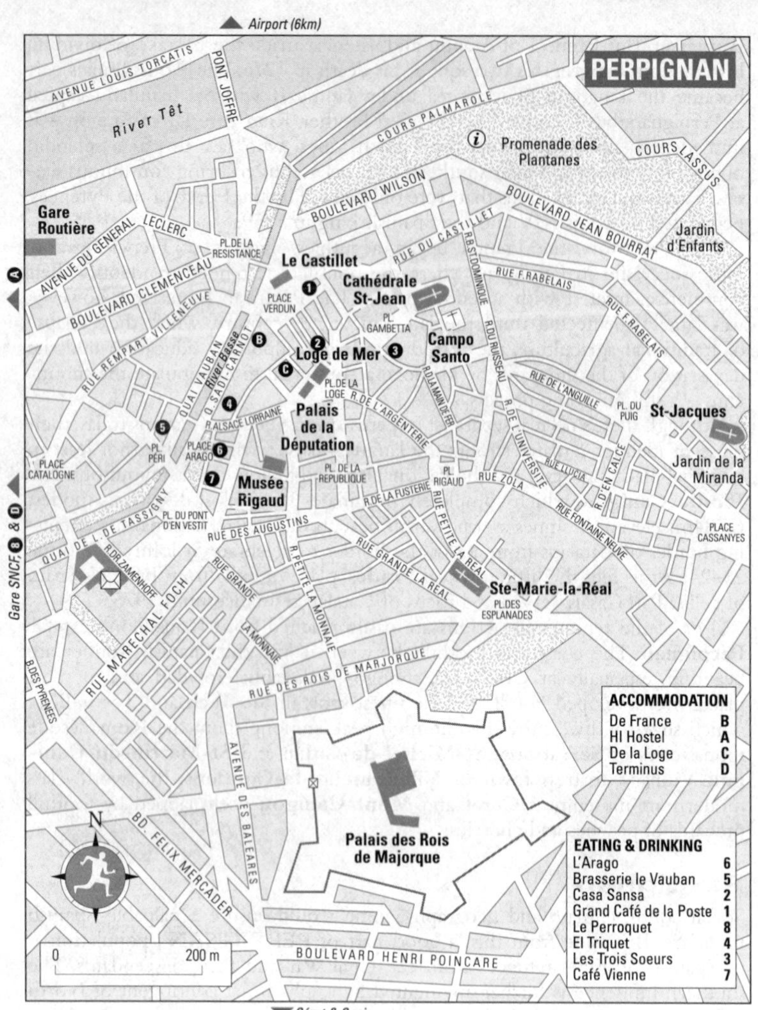

the **gare routière** just off avenue Général-Leclerc, near the Pont Arago; a taxi will run about three times as much. The **gare SNCF** is on avenue Général-de-Gaulle in the west of town. Both stations are a fifteen-minute walk from the **municipal tourist office** in the Palais des Congrès at the end of boulevard Wilson (mid-June to mid-Sept Mon–Sat 9am–7pm, Sun 10am–4pm; rest of year Mon–Sat 9am–6pm, Sun 9am–noon; ⓣ04.68.66.30.30, ⓦwww.perpignantourisme.com). For information and tickets for **city buses**, visit Kiosque CTP (Mon–Sat 9am–noon & 1.45–6.15pm) on place Péri, near the regional tourist office.

There's cheap **accommodation** near the *gare SNCF*, the best standard being the *Hôtel Terminus*, 2 av Général-de-Gaulle (ⓣ04.68.34.32.54, ⓕ04.68.35.48.16; ❷), right opposite the station. However, you're generally better off in the town centre, where the best value is offered by *Hôtel de la Loge* at 1 Fabriques d'en Nabot (Ⓣ04.68.34.41.02, Ⓦwww.hoteldelaloge.fr; ③), a well-renovated medieval mansion with a central courtyard, on a quiet alley. Next comfort-notch up is occupied by the three-star *Hôtel de France* at 26 quai Sadi-Carnot (Ⓣ04.68.34.92.81, Ⓔfrancehotel@orange.fr; ④), a well-kept nineteenth-century building at the edge of the old quarter, overlooking the canalized Basse River. In addition, there is a welcoming, if somewhat traffic-noisy, **HI hostel** (Ⓣ04.68.34.63.32; closed late Dec to late Jan), behind the public gardens of La Pépinière by Pont Arago (entrance from avenue de Grande-Bretagne), and the closer of two **campsites**, *La Garrigole* (Ⓣ04.68.54.66.10), on rue Maurice-Lévy (take bus #19), 5km northwest.

The City

The best place to begin your exploration of Perpignan is at **Le Castillet**, built as a gateway in the fourteenth century and now home to the **Casa Païral** (Wed–Mon: May–Sept 10am–7pm; Oct–April 11am–5.30pm; €4), an interesting museum of Roussillon's Catalan rural culture and the anti-French rebellions of 1661–74, when the tower held captured Catalan insurgents. A short distance down rue Louis-Blanc you come to the **place de la Loge**, focus of the pedestrianized heart of the old town, with a voluptuous Venus statue by Aristide Maillol (see p.830) in the centre. Dominating the three cafés and brasseries of the narrow square is Perpignan's most interesting building, the 1397-vintage Gothic **Loge de Mer**. Designed to hold the city's stock exchange and maritime court, it features gargoyles, lancet windows and lacy balustrades up top. Side by side next door are the sixteenth-century **Hôtel de Ville**, with its magnificent wrought-iron gates and another Maillol (*La Méditerranée*) in the courtyard, and the fifteenth-century **Palais de la Députation**, once the parliament of Roussillon.

From place de la Loge, rue St-Jean leads northeast to the fourteenth-century **Cathédrale St-Jean** on place Gambetta (Mon & Wed–Sat 10am–noon & 2–5pm, Tues & Sun 2–5pm; free), its external walls built of alternating bands of river stones and brick. The dimly lit interior is most interesting for its elaborate Catalan altarpieces and for the fourteenth-century, Rhenish polychrome Crucifixion, known as the *Dévôt Christ*; it's in the fifth side chapel along the north wall, probably brought from the Low Countries by a travelling merchant. Out the side door, a few steps on the left is the entrance to the **Campo Santo**, a vast enclosure that's one of France's oldest cemeteries, now used for summer concerts (otherwise May & Sept Tues–Sun noon–7pm; Oct–April Tues–Sun 11am–5pm).

South of the cathedral, rue de la Révolution-Française and rue de l'Anguille lead into the teeming, dilapidated maze of the **Maghrebian and Romany quarters**, where women congregate on the secluded inner lanes but are seldom seen on the busier thoroughfares. Here you'll find North African shops and cafés, especially on rue Llucia, and a daily market on place Cassanyes. Uphill and north from this stands the elegant church of **St-Jacques** (Tues–Sun 11am–5pm) dating from around 1200, on the edge of **La Miranda gardens** (daily: June–Sept 8–11.45am & 2–5.45pm; Oct–May 8–11am & 3.30–6pm), laid out on a section of the old city walls.

A twenty-minute walk southwest through place des Esplanades brings you to the main entrance of the **Palais des Rois de Majorque** (daily: June–Sept 10am–6pm; Oct–May 9am–5pm; €4), crowning the hill that dominates the southern part of the old town. Although Vauban's walls surround it now, the two-storey palace and its great arcaded courtyard date originally from the late thirteenth century. Thanks to the Spanish influence, there's a sophistication and finesse about the Gothic-Moorish architecture and detailing – for instance in the beautiful marble porch to the lower of the two chapels – that you don't often find in heavier northern styles.

Finally, at 16 rue de l'Ange near place Arago, you'll find the **Musée Rigaud** (Wed–Mon: May–Sept noon–7pm, Oct–April 11am–5.30pm; €4), dedicated to the work of locally born portraitist Hyacinthe Rigaud, who became official painter to the court of Versailles in the late seventeenth century. The collection also includes works by Dufy, Maillol, Picasso, Tapiès and Appel.

Eating, drinking and entertainment

Full-service **restaurants** are thin on the ground in central Perpignan. A budget choice is popular *Le Perroquet*, near the station at 1 av de Gaulle, with a good selection of reasonably priced Catalan dishes (closed Wed Sept–April; dinner menus from €20). For something smarter, head for *Casa Sansa*, 3 rue Fabriques-Couvertes, founded in 1846 and serving traditional Catalan cuisine amidst bullfight posters and old photos. Continuing the Iberian theme, *El Triquet* at 9 rue Lazare (closed Sun & Mon) gives good-value and decent-sized portions of both tapas and local dishes.

You'll have better luck with **brasserie** fare or at **cafés**. Favourites include *L'Arago* (open daily until late), with big portions, and *Café Vienne*, on palm-shaded place Arago, or the Art Deco *Brasserie le Vauban* across the River Basse at 29 quai Vauban. On place Verdun, in front of Le Castillet, the *Grand Café de la Poste* is a great place to watch the world go by, and it's here, too, that on summer evenings you see the Catalan dance, the *sardana*, being performed by anyone whom the spirit moves.

The most reliable central **bar** is *Les Trois Sœurs*, 2 rue Fontfroide, with tapas to nibble on during novelty acts and dedicated evenings (eg Sun "tea dance" at 6.30pm, Wed jazz night, "hen nights" with male live acts). There's also **live street theatre and music** in the city centre every Thursday night during July and August (the tourist office has details). The Palais des Rois de Majorque is the venue for the Trobades festival (22–24 June), plus **jazz** concerts every Friday in July. But Perpignan's best-known spectacle is **La Procession de la Sanch**, the Maundy Thursday procession of red-hooded penitents that goes from the church of St-Jacques to the cathedral between 3 and 5pm.

Around Perpignan

CANET-PLAGE, 12km due east, is the closest place near Perpignan for a dip in the Mediterranean, although there's nothing to recommend the place, except that its beach is wide and sandy and the sea is wet; take a CTP bus #1 from place Catalogne. Perhaps more interesting, 15km north and served by regular trains, is the **Forteresse de Salses** (daily: June–Sept 9.30am–7pm; Oct–May 10am–12.15pm & 2–5pm; €6.50). Built by the Catalans during the early fifteenth century, it was one of the first forts to be designed with a ground-hugging profile to protect it from artillery fire, though higher up it exhibits the traits of a pre-cannon-age château.

Another place, with not so much to see but interesting from an anthropological point of view, is the vine-girt village of **Tautavel**, 25km northwest off the St-Paul-de-Fenouillet road. In 1971 the remains of the oldest known European human being – dated to around 450,000 BC – were discovered near the village, and a reconstruction of the skull is on display in the village's **Musée de la Préhistoire** (April–June & Sept daily 10am–12.30pm & 2–6.30pm; July & Aug daily 10am–7pm; Oct–March 10am–12.30pm &

2–5.30pm; Ⓦ www.tautavel.com; €7). Also on show are other finds from the cave where the skull was unearthed, the **Caune d'Arago**, a few kilometres north, which can itself be visited (daily: July & Aug 10am–noon & 12.30–5.30pm; Sept–June by arrangement).

Fourteen kilometres southeast of Perpignan, on the way to the resorts of the Côte Vermeille (see below), lies the town of **ELNE**. This small place once had the honour of seeing Hannibal camp below its walls en route to Rome, and used to be the capital of Roussillon. It was only eclipsed by Perpignan when the latter became the seat of the kings of Mallorca; Elne's decline accelerated in 1602 when the bishopric moved to Perpignan. Today, it's worth a stop for its fortified, partially Romanesque **cathedral of Ste-Eulalie** and extremely beautiful **cloister** (daily: April & May 9.30am–5.45pm, June–Sept 9.30am–7pm, Oct 9.30am–12.30pm & 2–5.45pm, Nov–March 9.30am–12.30pm & 2–4.45pm; €4). The four colonnades of the cloister ably demonstrate a gradual transition from Romanesque to Gothic styles, clockwise from the south bay (twelfth century) to the east bay (fourteenth), intricately carved with biblical and secular scenes, plus mythical creaures. It's the best possible introduction to Roussillon Romanesque, especially if you're planning to visit Serrabona and St-Michel-de-Cuixà further west. Around the cathedral are the strollable lanes of the old town, and a certain amount of **accommodation**, including very pricey, 2006-renovated *Hôtel Restaurant Cara Sol* at 10 bd Illibéris (Ⓣ 04.68.22.10.42, Ⓦ www.hotelcarasol.com; ❻); their somewhat more reasonable, competent restaurant has unbeatable view seating on the ramparts outside.

The Côte Vermeille

The Côte Vermeille, where the Pyrenees meet the sea, is the last patch of French shoreline before Spain, its seaside villages once so remote that the Fauvist painters of the early 1900s hid out here. Mass tourism has put paid to any sense of exclusivity or unspoiltness, but in low season at least they remain attractive, and well served by buses and trains from Perpignan. **Argèles-Plage** is the first resort beyond Elne, but you're best off bypassing it in favour of the ports of **Collioure** and **Banyuls-sur-Mer**.

Argelès and Collioure

ARGELÈS, with the last of the broad sandy beaches on this stretch of coast, is lively and friendly but packed out mostly with foreign tourists. **Argelès-Plage** resort is now rather bigger than its older inland parent, **Argelès-sur-Mer**. Short **stays** are frowned on during summer season; one more flexible place in the inland *ville* might be *Hôtel Clair Logis* at 78 Route Nationale (Ⓣ 04.68.81.03.27; all year; ❸).

Five kilometres southeast, **COLLIOURE** is achingly picturesque – and achingly expensive. Palm trees line the curving main beach of Port d'Avall, while slopes of vines and olives rise to ridges crowned with ruined forts and watchtowers. Its setting and monuments inspired Henri Matisse and André Derain to embark in 1905 on their explosive Fauvist colour experiments; you can follow the chemin de Fauvisme, with reproductions of twenty of their works fixed to walls around the town. Collioure is dominated by the **Château-Royal** (daily: June–Sept 10am–6/7pm; Oct–May 9am–5pm; €4), founded by the Templars in the twelfth century and subject to later alterations at the hands of the kings of Mallorca and Aragón, and again after the Treaty of the Pyrenees gave Collioure to France. Sadly, the mediocre permanent "collection" inside scarcely merits the entrance fee; attend instead a concert in the courtyard.

Collioure's other landmark is the distinctive round belfry of the seventeenth-century **church of Notre-Dame-des-Anges** (daily 9am–noon & 2–6pm), formerly the harbour lighthouse. Behind it two small **beaches** (the northerly one naturist) are divided by a causeway leading to the **chapel of St-Vincent**, built on what used to be an islet, while west from here a concrete path follows the rocky shore to the bay of **Le Racou**.

Just north of the château lies the **old harbour**, still home to a bare handful of brightly painted lateen-rigged fishing boats – now more likely used as pleasure craft – all that remains of Collioure's traditional fleet. Beyond this, the stone houses and sloping lanes of the **Mouré** or old quarter are the main focus of interest. The **tourist office** is here on place de 18-Juin (July & Aug daily 9am–8pm; Sept–June Tues–Sat 9am–noon & 2–6.30pm; Ⓣ04.68.82.15.47, Ⓦwww.collioure.com).

The most central place to **stay** is the atmospheric *Hostellerie des Templiers* (Ⓣ04.68.98.31.10, Ⓦwww.hotel-templiers.com; closed Jan; 3 annexes, 4 main bldg) at 12 av Camille-Pelletan, crammed with artwork and housing overflow in various annexes. With a car (central **parking** is nightmarish) and/or desire for a sea view, opt instead for *Hôtel Triton*, Port d'Avall beach (Ⓣ04.68.98.39.39, Ⓔhoteltriton@orange.fr; all year; ❸–❹) or the remoter *Hôtel Caranques* (Ⓣ04.68.82.06.68, Ⓔles-caranques@little-france.com; ❸–❹) at the east side of the bay on route de Port-Vendres, overpriced but very friendly and with direct access to a lido from the terraced gardens. The best **campsite** is seaside, caravan-free *La Girelle* (Ⓣ04.68.81.25.56; April–Sept), at plage d'Ouille, west of town on the coastal path to Le Racou. Rue Camille-Pelletan and its perpendicular lanes have some cafés and **restaurants**, but – except at *Crêperie Bretonne* at 8 rue Camille-Pelletan – you'll usually fork out well over the odds for listless grub. Get, at least, what you pay for at *Amphytrion* on Port d'Avall, crowded even off season for the sake of good-sized seafood-based menus from €20.

Port-Vendres and Banyuls-sur-Mer

Port-Vendres, 3km further down the coast along the minor D914, is by contrast a functional place, with no special sights. Although the harbour has declined from its heyday during the century-plus after 1830, when it provided the main link with North Africa, it still lands more **fish** than any other port on this coast. The boats arrive between about 4.30 and 6pm every day except Sunday; you can watch them unload and auction the catch on the dock at the far end of the harbour, and maybe tuck into a seafood meal afterwards at a quayside restaurant.

South towards **BANYULS-SUR-MER**, 7km further on, the main highway winds through attractive vineyards, with the Albères hills rising steeply on the right. The town itself, built round a broad sweep of pebble beach, is pleasant (and is where the GR10 meets the Mediterranean) but lacks the overt charm of Collioure. There are, however, several things to see and do in Banyuls. One is the seafront **aquarium** of the Laboratoire Arago (daily: July & Aug 9am–1pm & 2–9pm; Sept–June 9am–noon & 2–6.30pm; €4), run by the Sorbonne's marine biology department, whose tanks contain a comprehensive collection of the region's submarine life; this is protected in a nearby *réserve marine*, France's best, which can be explored with local **scuba outfitters**. Also worth a look are the works of sculptor **Aristide Maillol** (1861–1944), who was born near Banyuls; they are best seen at the **Musée Maillol** (daily: May–Sept 10am–noon & 4–7pm; Oct–April 10am–noon & 2–5pm; Ⓦwww.museemaillol.com; €3.50), 4km outside the town in the Vallée de Roume, where he is buried under his statue *La Pensée*. You might also sample the dark, full-bodied Banyuls dessert **wine**, an *appellation* which applies only to the vineyards of the Côte Vermeille.

The **tourist office** stands diagonally opposite the *mairie* on the seafront (July & Aug daily 9.30am–12.30pm & 2.30–7pm; Sept–June Mon–Sat 9am–noon & 2–7pm; ⓣ04.68.88.31.58, ⓦwww.banyuls-sur-mer.com). Of the cheaper **hotels**, best is *Le Manoir*, 20 rue de Maréchal-Joffre (ⓣ04.68.88.32.98; ❷), while with a bit more to spend try *Al-Fanal* (ⓣ04.68.88.00.81; ❹) overlooking the yacht port. This also has its own seafood **restaurant**, but perhaps the best value in town – on an otherwise touristy street – is provided by *La Casa Miguel* at 3 rue St-Pierre, purveying abundant, savoury tapas; inside are original Maillol lithrographs and photos of old Banyuls.

Céret and the valley of the Tech

The first tempting stop on the D115, the main road which follows the **Tech valley** inland all the way up to the Spanish border just past Prats-de-Mollo, is **CÉRET**, capital of the Vallespir region, and served like the rest of the valley by regular buses from Perpignan. It's a delightful place, with a wonderfully shady old town overhung by huge plane trees; central streets are narrow and winding, opening onto small squares like the **Plaça de Nou Reigs** ("Nine Spouts" in Catalan), named after its central fountain. There's a large and varied Saturday **market**, which spills out of place Pablo-Picasso into the main street, avenue d'Espagne, where two remnants of the medieval walls, the **Porte de France** and **Porte d'Espagne**, are visible. In summer, Céret is also a big centre for cherries from surrounding orchards, *corridas* (bullfights) and Pamplona-style running of bulls. Other annual events include the Easter Sunday procession of the Resurrected Christ, and an international *sardana* jamboree at the end of August.

Céret's main sight, however, is the remarkable **Musée d'Art Moderne** (July to mid-Sept daily: 10am–7pm; rest of year daily except Tues 10am–6pm; ⓦwww.musee-ceret.com; €5.50), just off boulevard Maréchal-Joffre. Between about 1910 and 1935, Céret's charms – coupled with the residence here of the Catalan artist and sculptor Manolo – drew a number of avant-garde artists to the town, including Matisse and Picasso, who personally dedicated a number of pictures to the museum; it also contains work by Chagall, Miró, Pignon and Dufy, among others. The Picassos include a marvellous series of ceramic bowls illustrating bullfighting scenes, executed over just five days in April 1953.

Get current information on festival dates from the **tourist office** on avenue Clemenceau (July & Aug Mon–Sat 9.30am–12.30pm & 2–7pm; Sept–May Mon–Fri 9am–noon & 2–5pm, Sat 9.30am–12.30pm; ⓣ04.68.87.00.53, ⓦwww.ceret.fr). There's no better **accommodation** than friendly *Hôtel Vidal* at 4 place Soutine (ⓣ04.68.87.00.85, ⓦwww.hotelvidalceret.com; closed Nov; ❸), a tastefully converted episcopal palace with variable-sized but salubrious en-suite rooms. Full-service **restaurant** options aren't abundant but include the Vidal's very own *El Bisbe* (closed Tues & Wed low season), with gourmet if *minceur* menus at €28; *Pizzeria Quattrocento* on Plaça de Nou Reigs; and *Le P'tit Grill* at 47 rue St-Ferréol down from the museum, exactly as described, economical and thus hugely popular (reserve on ⓣ06.13.56.73.35).

Arles-sur-Tech and Gorges de la Fou

West of Céret, past the leaping single span of its fourteenth-century **Pont du Diable**, the view opens west towards the towering eminence of the Canigou massif. Once past the congested spa of Amélie-les-Bains (8km), it's 4km further to **ARLES-SUR-TECH**, a more interesting proposition. The Carolingian origins of its Romanesque **Abbaye de Ste-Marie** (July & Aug 9am–7pm; Sept–June Mon–Sat 9am–noon & 2–6pm; also Sun April–Oct 2–5pm; €3.50) are thought to account for the back-to-front alignment of altar at the west end and entrance at the east. Entry is now via the thirteenth-century cloister, pleasant enough though it can't remotely compare in merit to Elne's or St-Michel-de-Cuixà's. The unique and compelling feature of the massive church interior is a band of still-vividly coloured twelfth-century **fresco** high up in the apse of the eastern antichapel dedicated to St-Michel, appropriately featuring the archangel.

Outside next to the east facade – surmounted by an impressive Romanesque relief of Christ and the Tetramorphs — stands a very ancient (fourth- or fifth-century) sarcophagus, known as the **Sainte-Tombe**, which has the scientifically inexplicable habit of slowly filling with very pure water. Every year, on July 30, when Arles celebrates its *fête* dedicated to SS Abdon and Sennen (two Roman martyrs whose bones used to lodge in the sarcophagus), the water is siphoned out and distributed after Mass to the pilgrims who have come to worship. The town's other festivals include the probably prehistoric **Fête de l'Ours**, designed to exorcize human fear of awakening bears, traditionally held at the end of February when hibernation ended; there's also a torchlight **Procession de la Sanch** at Easter. Arles is also an important stage on the **GR10**, which from here heads northwest towards the Canigou massif or southeast towards Las Illas.

The **tourist office** (Mon–Sat 9am–noon & 2–6pm, Sun 2–6pm; ⓣ04.68.39.11.99, ⓦwww.villes-arles-sur-tech.fr) also serves as the abbey ticket office. **Accommodation** is limited to the *Hôtel les Glycines* on rue du Jeu-de-Paume (ⓣ04.68.39.10.09, ⓔhotelglycines@orange.fr; ❸), with a terrace restaurant (from €18), and *Chambres d'Hôtes La Couvent Sana* (ⓣ04.68.83.92.90; ❸), on the edge of town. There's also a **campsite**, *Riuferrer* (ⓣ04.68.39.11.06), on the west side of town.

Just west of Arles, on the road to Prats-de-Mollo, is the entrance to the **Gorges de la Fou**, some 2km in length, very narrow and up to 250m deep (ⓣ04.68.39.16.21; April–Nov daily 10am–6pm weather permitting; €5). It's spectacular, but inevitably a tourist trap, with a car park, snack stalls and a metal catwalk all along the bottom of the gorge.

Prats-de-Mollo and the Spanish frontier

Beyond the gorge, the D115 climbs steadily, between valley sides thick with walnut, oak and sweet chestnut, 19km to **Prats-de-Mollo**, end of the bus line. Prats is the last French town before the Spanish frontier, 13km beyond at Col d'Ares, but it has none of the usual malaise of border towns and is much the most attractive place in the valley since Céret. Hub of the newer quarter is **El Firal**, the huge square in use for markets since 1308; the walled and gated **ville haute** just south makes for a wonderful wander, with steep cobbled streets and a weathered grey church with marvellous ironwork on the door under the porch. The old town's walls were rebuilt in the seventeenth century after the suppression of a local revolt against onerous taxation imposed by Louis XIV on his new, post-Treaty of the Pyrenees holdings. Vauban's **Fort Lagarde** (April–June & Sept–Oct Tues–Sun 2–5.30pm; July & Aug daily 11am–1pm & 5–7pm; €3.50), on the heights above the town, also dates from this period, built to intimidate the local population as much as to keep the Spanish out.

There's plenty of good-quality **accommodation**, which makes Prats a good base or transit stopover; in the walled quarter, go for *Hostellerie Le Relais* at 3 place Josep de la Trinxeria (ⓣ04.68.39.71.30, ⓦwww.hostellerie-le-relais.com;

❸), with cheerful pastel-hued rooms and a south-facing garden restaurant. Just outside, overlooking El Firal, is *Hôtel Le Bellevue* (ⓣ04.68.39.72.48, ⓦwww.lebellevue.fr.st; closed Dec to mid-Feb; ❸), with more old-fasioned rooms but a creditable restaurant (menu from €19). Alternatively, pamper yourself with affordable luxury 8km west at **La Preste spa** and its associated *Grand Hôtel Thermal* (ⓣ04.68.87.55.00, ⓦwww.sante-eau.com; April to early Nov; ❹).

Les Aspres: Trinité and Serrabona

The only direct route between the **valleys of the Tech and the Têt**, best covered with a small car or cycle, is the D618 from Amélie-les-Bains to Bouleternère, across the eastern spurs of Canigou. It's 44 slow kilometres of mountain road, twisting through alternating hillside meadows and magnificent woods, past isolated *masies* (Catalan farmsteads), many now tenanted by foreigners or veteran French *soixante-huitard* idealists drawn to **Les Aspres**, as this region is known. The only amenities en route, 20km along, are in the tiny village of **ST-MARSAL** with its broad vistas, at *Hôtel Auberge de Saint-Marsal* (ⓣ04.68.39.42.68, ⓦwww.saintmarsal.net; ❷), a converted *mas*. Some 5km further, the Romanesque **Chapelle de la Trinité** stands by the road, opposite the *mairie* of Prunet-Belpuig. Inside (usually open) is a fine, serene *majestat*, the particularly Catalan wood-carved Crucifixions of the eleventh or twelfth centuries; most of the Spanish examples were destroyed in 1936.

From here the D618 descends into the Boulès River valley, through the pretty hamlet of **Boule d'Amont**, before reaching the steep D84 side road climbing 4km to the remarkable, bluff-top **Prieuré de Serrabona** (formerly Serrabonne; daily except major holidays 10am–6pm; €3). One of the finest examples – arguably *the* finest – of Roussillon Romanesque, the interior of the church (consecrated 1151) is starkly plain, making the beautifully carved column-capitals of its rib-vaulted tribune even more striking: lions, centaurs, griffins and human figures with Asiatic faces and hairstyles – motifs brought back from the Crusades – executed in pink marble from Villefranche-de-Conflent. The altar is made of the same stone, as are the pillars and equally elaborate capitals of the cloister, set to one side of the church on a high terrace. Despite the rigours of monastic life here – long abandoned – the settlement was well developed, and the monks' cultivation terraces and irrigation systems have been partly adapted to support a lush botanical garden.

The valley of the Têt and Canigou

The upper part of the **Têt valley**, known as the **Pays de Conflent**, is utterly dominated by the **Pic du Canigou**. The valley bottoms are lush with fields and orchards, but the mountain presides over all, vast and uncompromising. As you continue upstream, the valley narrows and steepens until you emerge onto the Cerdagne plateau.

Prades and St-Michel-de-Cuixà

Chief valley town is **Prades**, easily accessible by train and bus on the Perpignan–Villefranche–Latour-de-Carol route, and the obvious starting point for all excursions in the Canigou region. Although there are no great sights beyond the **church of St-Pierre** in central place de la République, the town enjoys a status out of proportion to its size or economic power. This is largely thanks to Catalan cellist Pau (Pablo) Casals, who set up home here as an exile and fierce opponent of the Franco regime in Spain. In 1950 he instituted the internationally renowned **chamber music festival** (ⓦwww.prades-festival-casals.com), held annually from late July to mid-August, the usual venue being the abbey of St-Michel-de-Cuixà (see below). Prades (or Prada) also hosts a Catalan university in mid-August and the first Catalan-language primary school in France.

The **tourist office** is at 4 rue des Marchands (July & Aug Mon–Sat 9am–12.30pm & 2–7pm, Sun 9am–noon; Sept–June Mon–Fri 9am–noon & 2–6pm; ⓣ04.68.05.41.02, ⓦwww.prades-tourisme.com). Prades has two central hotels, but both have seen better days, and currently the best **accommodation** lies just west of town on chemin de la Llitera: *Chambres d'Hôtes Castell Rose* (ⓣ04.68.96.07.57, ⓦwww.castellrose-prades.com; ❺–❻), in a converted manor house set in extensive grounds with a pool and tennis court. If that's beyond your budget, and you've transport, make for the delightful, welcoming *Hôtel St Joseph*, 7km west across the river in gorge-set **MOLITG-LES-BAINS** (ⓣ04.68.05.02.11, ⓔgerard.pommerol6yahoo.fr; all year; rooms ❷, studios ❸), which has an excellent restaurant (copious *table d'hôte* suppers €12). The municipal **campsite** (ⓣ04.68.96.29.83; April–Sept) is by the river on the road to Molitg. Back in Prades, the newest, freshest independent **restaurant** is *La Meridienne* at 20 rue des Marchands, with a properly trained chef and menus/ *formules* at €12 and €15.

Three kilometres south of Prades stands one of the loveliest abbeys in France, originally eleventh-century **St-Michel-de-Cuixà** (May–Sept Mon–Sat 9.30–11.50am & 2–6pm, Sun 2–6pm; Oct–April Mon–Sat 9.30–11.50am & 2–5pm, Sun 2–5pm; €4). Although mutilated after the Revolution it is still beautiful, with its crenellated tower (there were two until the 1830s) silhouetted against the wooded – sometimes snowy – slopes of Canigou. You enter via the labyrinthine, vaulted crypt, with a round central chamber, before proceeding to the church with its strange Visigothic-style "keyhole" arches. But the glory of the place is the **cloister** and its twelfth-century column capitals. Although most of the north and east bays were taken to the Cloisters Museum in New York early in the twentieth century, the remaining west and south series rival Serrabona and Elne for virtuosity. Carved in the same rose marble used at Serrabona, they depict highly stylized figures strongly reminiscent of Sumerian, Assyrian or Persian relief art: often monsters, either alone or being grappled by human keepers displaying an array of Asiatic beards, headgear and corpulent anatomies.

Vernet-les-Bains and St-Martin-du-Canigou

A not unpleasant little hillside spa, **VERNET-LES-BAINS**, 12km along the minor, foothill-skimming D27 from the abbey, can make a useful base for picking up provisions to climb the Pic du Canigou. It has a **tourist office** in place de la Mairie (Mon–Fri 9am–noon & 2–6pm; ⓣ04.68.05.55.35, ⓦwww.ot-vernet-les-bains.fr). Several two-star **hotels** offer a range of amenities: two of the best are the spa hotel itself, *Les Sources* (ⓣ04.68.05.52.84, ⓦwww.thermes-vernet.com; ❷), and the *Princess*, rue de Lavandiers (ⓣ04.68.05.56.22, ⓦwww.hotel-princess,com; ❸). There are two **campsites** outside Vernet and a **gîte d'étape** (ⓣ04.68.05.51.30) next to the municipal pool. For a **meal**, try roast-meat specialist *Le Cortal* (closed Oct, Nov & Mon), at the top of the old quarter behind the church.

A half-hour mandatory walk (no car access) above the hamlet of Casteil, itself 2.5km south of Vernet, is the stunning abbey of **St-Martin-du-Canigou**, founded in 1001. Resurrected from ruins between 1902 and 1982, and now occupied by a working religious community, the monastery at over 1000m altititude occupies a narrow promontory of rock surrounded by chestnut and oak woods, while above it rise the precipitous slopes and eroded pinnacles of

Canigou. Below, the ground drops sheerly into the ravine of the Cady stream that rushes down from the Col de Jou. The place is visitable in French-narrated tours (year-round Mon–Sat 10am, 11am, 2pm, 3pm, 4pm; also noon & 5pm June–Sept; Sun/hols 10am & 12.30pm rather than 10am, 11am, noon; closed Jan & Mon low season; €4). What you see is a beautiful little garden and cloister overlooking the ravine, a low dark atmospheric chapel beneath the church and the church itself.

From the reception building, a **path** leads up to a rocky viewpoint from which most photographs of the monastery are taken. This trail continues to meet the GR10 at the Col de Segalès on the GR10, and from there to the staffed *Refuge Grand Mariailles* (1718m; ⓣ04.68.92.22.90 or 04.68.04.49.86; 55 bunks; late May to early Oct) on Canigou's west flank. For a **day-loop** walk back to Casteil, another path drops down into the Cady ravine just at the start of the monastery buildings.

The Pic du Canigou

You can get at least part of the way up the **Pic du Canigou** by vehicle, although given the roughness of the road you may not want to risk your own buggy. Sturdy **cars** (preferably 4WD) can get as far as the *Chalet des Cortalets* refuge either by the track from Clara-Villerach, near Taurinyà, or the even steeper and rougher mining road that begins by the *Al Pouncy* **campsite** near Fillols. Both routes take about an hour at the wheel. Alternatively, you could **rent a jeep** and driver from Ria (ⓣ04.68.05.27.08) or Corbières Grand Raid (ⓣ04.68.05.24.24) in Prades, plus Garage Villaceque (ⓣ04.68.05.66.58) or Jean-Paul Bouzan (ⓣ04.68.05.62.28) in Vernet-les-Bains. For **walkers**, the standard ascent is from Vernet on a path that begins about 700m along the road to Fillols, joining up with the **GR10** at the Refuge de Bonaigua (about 3hr) which you leave (about 1hr later) below the **Pic Joffre** to follow an HRP variant up the ridge to the summit (about 1hr). It's not for faint hearts or the inexperienced (some have fallen to their deaths), because the final ascent is rather exposed. There's an easier five-hour alternative, starting from Casteil, passing the aforementioned *Refuge Grand Marialles*, then following the HRP for the last stretch via the unstaffed Arago hut.

From the *Chalet des Cortalets* (2150m; ⓣ04.68.96.36.19; 111 places; mid-May to late Oct; doubles plus two grades of dorm bunk, restaurant from €13), it's an easy ninety-minute walk to the top. Strike west through the last trees, past a little lake, with a magnificent view into the cirque below the summit, round the back of the Pic Joffre, and up the long stony Crête de Barbet to the cross and Catalan flag that crown the summit.

Although the **ascent** by this route is straightforward in good weather, you should be properly equipped and have a good map. On the night of June 23, Catalans for kilometres around, including half the population of Barcelona, head for the top to light the bonfire from which a flame is carried to kindle all the *focs de Sant Joan* of the Catalan villages – though the scene around the refuge can be pretty horrendous, with tents, boom-boxes and litter galore.

Villefranche-de-Conflent and the Petit Train Jaune

A medieval garrison town suffering from arrested development, **VILLEFRANCHE-DE-CONFLENT**, 6km up the Têt from Prades and a similar distance below Vernet-les-Bains, lives off its tweeness but nevertheless merits a stop. Founded in 1092 by the counts of Cerdagne to block incursions from rivals in Roussillon, then remodelled by Vauban in the seventeenth century after annexation by France, its streets and fortifications have remained untouched by subsequent events. Worth a look is the **church of St-Jacques**, with a primitively carved thirteenth-century baptismal font just inside the door; you can also walk the perimeter of the **walls** (daily: Feb–May & Oct–Dec 10.30am–12.30pm & 2–5/6pm; June & Sept 10am–7pm; July & Aug 10am–8pm; closed Jan; €4.50). If you do, you'll see why in 1681 Vauban constructed the **Château-Fort Libéria** on the heights overlooking the town to protect it from "aerial" bombardment. Getting up there (daily: June–Sept 9am–8pm; Oct–May 10am–6pm; €5.80) involves taking the free minibus leaving from near the town's main gate; you can return to Villefranche by descending a subterranean stairway of a thousand steps, which debouches at the end of rue St-Pierre.

The **tourist office** (Feb–Dec daily 10am–12.30pm & 2–5.30pm; ⓣ04.68.96.22.96, ⓦwww.conflent.com) is in place d'Église. There is no **accommodation** in the walled town, but just north near the train station are the welcoming, comfortable *Chambres d'Hôtes Mireille Pena* (ⓣ04.68.96.52.35, ⓔmpebafain@aol.com; ❹). The best-value local **restaurant**, in the old town at 31 rue St-Jean, is *La Casa de la Nine* (all year closed Sun eve & Mon, Oct–March also closed Tues & all eves except Fri/Sat, all Feb) English-run but well respected by locals.

Villefranche is the terminus for main-line trains from Perpignan. From here up to La Tour-de-Carol on the Spanish frontier, transport is by SNCF bus, or – far nicer – the narrow-gauge, year-round **Petit Train Jaune**, which climbs along the Têt at a pace that allows you a walker's or cyclist's proximity to the scenery, especially in summer when some of the carriages are open-air (ⓣ04.68.96.56.62, ⓦwww.ter-sncf.com/trains_touristiques/train_jaune.htm). The summertime frequency of the trains (up to 7 daily) makes it practical to hop off and on, allowing you to explore the areas around the smaller, isolated stations, many of them *haltes facultatifs* (ask to be set down).

The upper Têt

Some 17km southwest of Villefranche on the south side of the main valley, the wild wooded canyon of the **Gorges de Carança** cuts south through the mountains towards Spain. A clear path, with catwalks, follows the gorge to the GR10 at the basic *Refuge Ras de Carança* (3–4hr; 1831m; ⓣ04.68.04.13.18; 30 places; June–Sept 15), while as much walking again brings hikers to the HRP on the frontier. **THUÈS-ENTRE-VALLS** is the closest village to the canyon, with a *halte facultatif* on the Petit Train Jaune, and Luk & Micheline Peters' unsigned **gîte** *Mas de Bordes* (ⓣ04.68.97.05.00; all year; doubles ❷, dorm €12, evening meal €13), up the single lane from the train line. This also offers a camping meadow, and an on-site **hot spring** (free, 40-degrees) a 25-minute tough but scenic walk distant.

At **FONTPÉDROUSE**, 4km beyond Thuès, there's one of the better **restaurants** in the valley – *Pyrénéen*, with Antillean influences – and a minor side road veering south across the river and up a grassy spur above the River Aigues towards the village of Prat-Balaguer. Bearing right instead at a fork leads, 3km from Fontpédrouse station, to the organized **Bains de St-Thomas** (daily 10am–7.40pm, last admittance 8.40pm July/Aug; closed Nov 14–Dec 5; €4–4.50), with open pools at a pleasant 37–38°C.

The Cerdagne

Another 10km up the N116 road from Fontpédrouse, or three stops on the train, brings you onto the wide, grassy **plateau of the Cerdagne**, whose once-powerful counts controlled lands from Barcelona to Roussillon. It's an area that has never been sure whether it is Spanish or French. After the French annexation of Roussillon, it was partitioned, with Spain retaining – as it still does – the enclave of Lliva. The Petit Train Jaune snakes its way laboriously across the entire plateau, though stations aren't always convenient for the settlements they nominally serve.

Easterly gateway to the region is the little garrison town of **MONT-LOUIS**, built by Vauban in 1679–82; the top citadel is still a training school for paratroops and marines. There isn't much to see other than the **ramparts** (Mon–Sat 10am–noon & 2–5/6pm, also Sun July–Aug; €4.50), but it is a far pleasanter place to stay than the monstrous ski resort of **Font-Romeu** just up the road, far from the best locally (that title is shared between Les Angles and Formiguères in the nearby Capcir). There's a **tourist office** (July & Aug daily 9.30am–noon & 2–7pm; Sept–June Tues–Sat 10am–noon & 2–6pm; ⓣ04.68.04.21.97, ⓦwww.mont-louis.net), while the best **accommodation** is *Chambres d'Hôtes La Volute* (ⓣ04.68.04.27.21, ⓦwww.lavolute.monsite.orange.fr; ④), a B&B set in the seventeenth-century former governor's mansion, with a lawn-garden atop a section of the ramparts.

The Têt ultimately has its source in the Carlit massif, which looms above the dammed **Lac des Bouillousses**, 13km northwest of Mont-Louis by the D60 and very crowded in summer. Car access along this road is limited to a *navette* during peak season, or you can hike in along the GR10 from Mont-Louis in under four hours. On arrival you'll find a triple choice of **accommodation**; best of the three, east of the dam, is *Auberge du Carlit* (ⓣ04.68.04.22.23; all year), with rooms (⑤ HB) and a 32-bunk *gîte* in a separate building (€27pp HB).

The Petit Train Jaune carries on past Mont-Louis, though the drama of the ride is diminished compared to the lower Têt valley. A good intermediate spot to alight and seek shelter and food is **SAILLAGOUSE**, where the dead-central *Hôtel Planotel* (ⓣ04.68.04.72.08, ⓦwww.planotel.fr) offers rooms in the 1895-built *vieille maison* (③) or a nearby modern annexe (④), and excellent-value meals either in its brasserie (€14) or the full-on restaurant. Ur-les-Escaldes is the closest (5km) station to more hot springs in **DORRES**, the **Bains Romans** (daily 8.30am–8.15pm; €3.90), with open-air granite pools (39–40° C) at their best in ski season. End of the line is **LATOUR-DE-CAROL** with its fine old quarter 1km northwest of Enveitg station; on the main road the *Auberge Catalane* (ⓣ04.68.04.80.66, ⓦwww.auberge-catalane.fr; ③) has been going since 1929, with soundproofed rooms and a well-attended restaurant where menus encompass fish, foie gras, *gesiers* and *boudin noir*.

Travel details

Trains

Bayonne to: Biarritz (14 daily; 10min); Bordeaux (6–12 daily; 1hr 40min–2hr 10min); Boussens (7–8 daily; 3hr); Cambo-les-Bains (4–5 daily; 25min); Hendaye (14 daily; 35min); Lourdes (5–8 daily; 1hr 45min–2hr); Orthez (5–6 daily; 45min–1hr); Pau (7–8 daily; 1hr 15min); St-Gaudens (7–8 daily; 2hr 45min); St-Jean-de-Luz (16–20 daily; 25min); St-Jean-Pied-de-Port (4–5 daily; 1hr); Tarbes (7–8 daily; 2hr); Toulouse (7–12 daily; 3hr–3hr 30min).

Foix to: Ax-les-Thermes (11–13 daily, some on SNCF bus; 55min); Barcelona (3–4 daily; 5hr 15min–6hr); Latour-de-Carol (7 daily, some on SNCF bus; 1hr 45min–2hr); Tarascon-sur-Ariège (11–13 daily; 15–20min); Toulouse (11–13 daily; 1hr 20min–1hr 45min).

Luchon to: Montréjeau (8 daily; usually SNCF coach; 45–55min).

Pau to: Bordeaux (5–7 daily; 1hr 15min–2hr); Oloron-Ste-Marie (6–9 daily; 35min); Orthez (5–6 daily; 20min).

Perpignan to Argelès-sur-Mer (8–12 daily; 20min); Banyuls-sur-Mer (8–12 daily; 30min); Cerbère (8–12 daily; 40min); Collioure (8–12 daily; 25min); Elne (8–12 daily; 10min); Narbonne (10–13 daily;

35–50min); Prades (5–8 daily; 45min); Salses (7–9 daily; 15min); Toulouse (10–12 daily; 2hr 30min–3hr); Villefranche-de-Conflent (5–8 daily; 55min).
Quillan to: Carcassonne (4–5 daily, mostly SNCF coach; 55min–1hr 15min); Limoux (6–7 daily, mostly SNCF coach; 30–40min).
St-Girons to: Boussens (6–8 daily on SNCF coach; 45min).
Tarbes to: Bordeaux (6–9 daily; 3hr 15min); Dax (6–9 daily; 1hr 50min); Lourdes (11–14 daily; 15min); Orthez (3–5 daily; 1hr 10min).
Villefranche-de-Conflent to Latour-de-Carol (4–7 daily; 2hr 45min); Mont–Louis (5–8 daily; 1hr 35min).

Buses

Bayonne to: Biarritz (local transport; 15–20min); Cambo-les-Bains (several daily; 30–40min); Orthez (3 daily; 50min); Pau (2–3 daily; 1hr 10min); San Sebastian (2 daily Mon–Sat; 1hr 45min); St-Jean-de-Luz (5–7 daily; 40min).
Biarritz to: Hendaye (5–7 daily; 35min); Orthez (2–3 daily; 1hr 45min); Pau (2–3 daily; 2hr 30min); St-Jean-de-Luz (11–16 daily; 25min); Salies-de-Béarn (2 daily; 1hr 20min).
Foix to: Lavelanet (2–3 daily; 30min); Mirepoix (2–3 daily; 45min); Quillan (1 daily; 1hr 30min).
Laruns to: Bious-Oumette trailhead (1 daily in morning, summer only; 40min); Fabrèges (2 daily summer and winter ski seasons; 55min); Gabas (2 daily summer and winter ski seasons; 25min).
Lourdes to: Bagnères-de-Bigorre (2–3 daily; 45min); Barèges, usually changing at Pierrefite-Nestalas (6–7 daily on SNCF coach or SALT bus; 1hr 10min); Cauterets, changing at Pierrefitte-Nestalas (4–7 daily; 50min); Gavarnie, changing at Luz-St-Sauveur (July & Aug 2 daily, otherwise 3 weekly; 1hr 15min); Luz-St-Sauveur (5–7 daily; 45min); Pau (4–8 daily; 1hr 15min).
Oloron-Ste-Marie to: Bedous (4–6 daily on SNCF coach; 30min); Urdos (4–6 daily; 50min).
Pau to: Agen (1–2 daily; 3hr); Bayonne (3–4 daily on TPR; 2hr 15min); Biarritz (2–3 daily on TPR; 2hr 30min); Eaux-Bonnes (3 daily on CITRAM; 1hr 15min); Gourette (2 daily on CITRAM; 1hr 30min); Laruns (5–8 daily via Buzy; 1hr 10min); Oloron-Ste-Marie (2–3 daily on CITRAM; 45min); Orthez (2–3 daily; 45min); Salies-de-Béarn (3 daily; 1hr 10min).
Perpignan to: Argelès (3 daily; 30min); Arles-sur-Tech (6 daily; 1hr 15min); Axat (2 daily, 1hr 40min); Banyuls-sur-Mer (3 daily; 1hr 10min); Céret (14 daily; 55min); Collioure (3 daily; 45min); Latour-de-Carol (2–3 daily; 3hr); Mont-Louis (4 daily; 2hr 15min); Port-Vendres (3–6 daily; 55min); Prades (7 daily; 1hr); Prats-de-Molló (6 daily; 1hr 40min); La Preste (3 daily; 2hr 5min); Villefranche-le-Conflent (7 daily; 1hr 15min).
Quillan to: Axat (2 daily; 20min); Carcassonne (2 daily; 1hr 20min); Comus (1–2 daily; 1hr 5min); Perpignan (1 daily; 1hr 30min); Quérigut (3 weekly in summer; 1hr 30min).
St-Girons to: Aulus-les-Bains (Mon–Sat 1–2 daily; 45min); Boussens (Mon–Sat 7 daily, Sun 5 on SNCF coach; 40min); Foix (4 daily; 1hr); Toulouse (2–3 daily; 2hr).
St-Jean-de-Luz to: Cambo-les-Bains (2–4 daily; 45min); Espelette (2 daily; 35min); Hendaye (9–17 daily; 20min); Sare (2–3 daily; 30min).
Tarbes to: Auch (2–6 daily; 1hr 40min); Bagnères-de-Bigorre (4–6 daily by SNCF coach; 40min); Lourdes (hourly; 30min); Luz-St-Sauveur (5–7 daily on SALT bus; 1hr); Pau (6 daily; 1hr).

Languedoc

UNITED KINGDOM
BELGIUM
GERMANY
LUX.
ENGLISH CHANNEL
SWITZERLAND
ATLANTIC
OCEAN
ITALY
N
SPAIN
MEDITERRANEAN
SEA
0
250 km
1
2
3
4
5
6
7
8
9
10
11
12
13
14
15
16

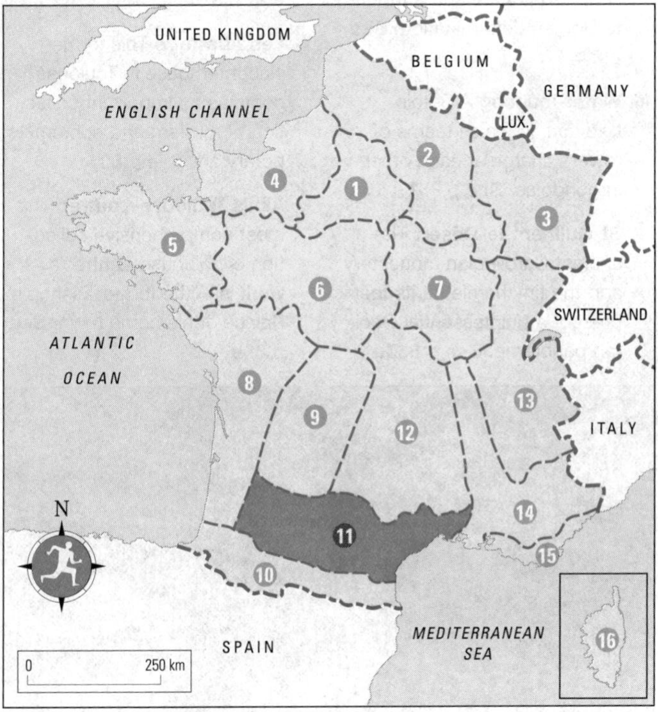

CHAPTER 11

Highlights

* **Bulls** Whether in the ring or on your plate as a succulent *boeuf à la gardienne*, the *taureaux* of the plains of Languedoc are famous. See p.845

* **Pont du Gard** This graceful aqueduct is an emblem of southern France and a tribute to Roman determination. See p.848

* **Water-jousting** A Setois tradition, in which teams of rowers charge at each other in gondolas. See p.857

* **St-Guilhem-le-Désert** The ancient Carolingian monastery and the tiny hamlet at its feet present a quintessential Occitan panorama. See p.860

* **Carcassonne** The Middle Ages come alive in this walled fortress town. See p.872

* **The Canal du Midi** Cycling, walking or drifting along this tree-shaded canal is the most atmospheric way of savouring France's southwest. See p.874

* **Les Abattoirs** This former slaughterhouse in Toulouse contains an important collection of modern and contemporary art. See p.884

* **Albi's Toulouse-Lautrec** The most comprehensive collection of Toulouse-Lautrec's work is in the former Bishop's Palace of his home town. See p.890

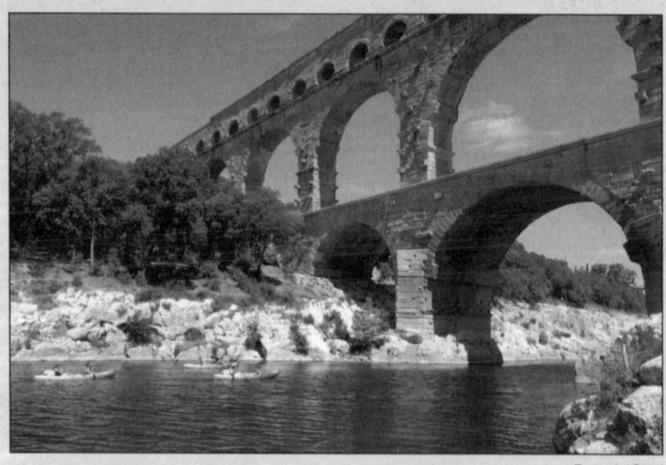

△ Pont du Gard

11

Languedoc

Languedoc is more an idea than a geographical entity. The modern *région* covers only a fraction of the lands where Occitan or the *langue d'oc* – the language of *oc*, the southern Gallo-Latin word for *oui* – once dominated. These stretched south from Bordeaux and Lyon into Spain and northwest Italy.

The heartland today is the Bas Languedoc – the coastal plain and dry, stony vine-growing hills between Carcassonne and Nîmes. It's here that the **Occitan** movement has its power base, demanding recognition of its linguistic and cultural distinctiveness. A good part of its character derives from resentment of political domination by remote and alien Paris, aggravated by the area's traditional poverty. In recent times this has been focused on Parisian determination to drag the province into the modern world, with massive tourist development on the coast and the drastic transformation of the cheap wine industry. It is also mixed up in a vague collective folk memory with the brutal repression of the Protestant Huguenots around 1700, the thirteenth-century massacres of the Cathars and the subsequent obliteration of the brilliant *langue d'oc* troubadour tradition. It is a hostility that has made an essentially rural and conservative population vote traditionally for the Left – at least until the elections of 2002, which saw wide support for Le Pen's resurgent Front National. Although a sense of Occitan identity remains strong in the region, it has very little currency as a spoken or literary language, despite the popularity of university-level language courses and the foundation of Occitan-speaking elementary schools.

Toulouse, the cultural capital of medieval and modern Languedoc, lies outside the administrative *région* but is included in this chapter and is a high point among numerous other attractions. There are great stretches of dramatic landscape and river gorges, from the **Cévennes** foothills in the east to the **Montagne Noire** and **Corbières** hills in the west. There's ecclesiastical architecture in **Albi** and **St-Guilhem-le-Désert**, and medieval towns at **Cordes** and **Carcassonne**, which also provides access to the unforgettably romantic Cathar castles to the south. **Nîmes** has extensive Roman remains, and there are great swathes of **beach** where – away from the major resorts – you can still find a kilometre or two to yourself.

Eastern Languedoc

Heading south from Paris via Lyon and the Rhône valley, you can go one of two ways: east to Provence and the Côte d'Azur – which is what most people

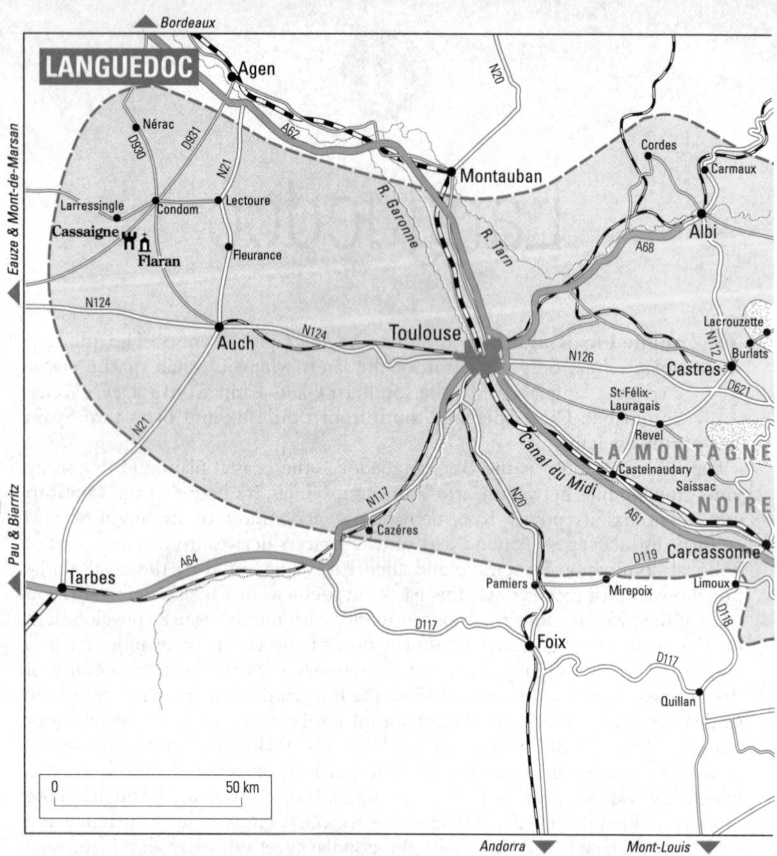

do – or west to **Nîmes**, **Montpellier** and the comparatively untouched northern Languedoc coast. Nîmes itself, while not officially part of the modern administrative *région*, makes for a good introduction to the area, a hectic modern town impressive both for its Roman past and for some scattered attractions – the **Pont du Gard** for one – nearby. Montpellier is also worth a day or two, not so much for any historical attractions as for a heady vibrancy and ease of access to the ancient villages, churches and fine scenery of the upper **Hérault valley**. This was the part of Languedoc most affected by the spread of Protestantism in the sixteenth century, an experience that has marked the region's character more than any other. The Protestants, with their attachment to rationality and self-improvement, espoused the cause of French over Occitan, supported the Revolution and the Republic, fought Napoléon III's coup against the 1848 Revolution and adhered to the anticlerical and socialist movement under the Third Republic. They dominated the local textile industry in the nineteenth century and were extremely active in the Resistance to the Nazis.

They also suffered a great deal for their cause, as did the whole region. After the Revocation of the Edict of Nantes in 1685 – the treaty which had granted religious toleration at the end of the sixteenth century – persecution drove their

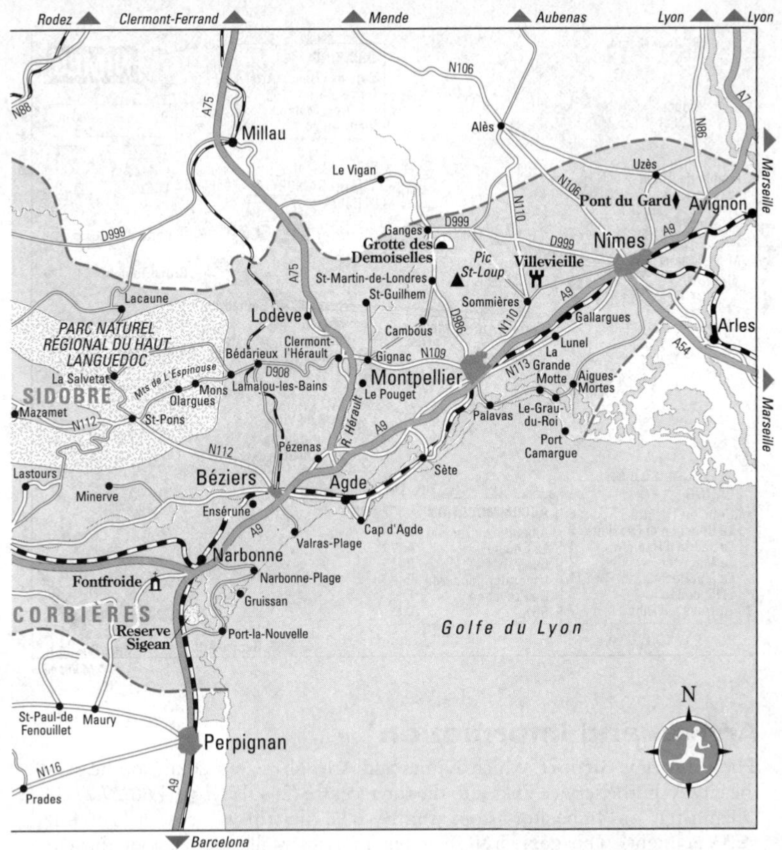

most committed supporters, especially in the Cévennes to the north, to form clandestine *assemblées du Désert*, and finally, in 1702, to take up arms in the first guerrilla war of modern times, La Guerre des Camisards, conflicts which still resonate in the minds of both Huguenot and Catholic families.

Nîmes and around

On the border between Provence and Languedoc, the name of **NÎMES** is inescapably linked to two things – denim and Rome. The latter's influence resulted in some of the most extensive Roman remains in Europe, while the former (*de Nîmes*), equally visible on the backsides of the populace, was first manufactured in the city's textile mills, and exported to the southern USA in the nineteenth century to clothe slaves. The city is worth a visit, in part for the ruins but also to experience its new-found energy and direction, having enlisted the services of a galaxy of architects and designers – including Norman Foster, Jean Nouvel and Philippe Starck – in a to-date futile bid to wrest southern supremacy from neighbouring Montpellier.

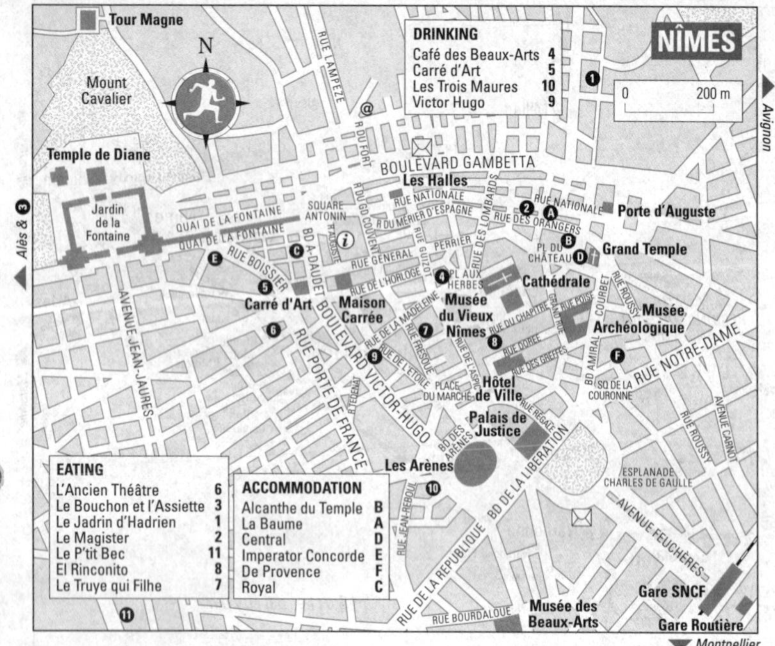

Arrival and information

The Camargue **airport**, which Nîmes and Arles share, lies 20km southeast of the city. A shuttle service links it to the town centre (2–4 daily; ⓣ04.66.29.27.29; "Gambetta" or "Imperator" stop; €5). By taxi, the trip will cost at least €28 (€33 at night). The **gare SNCF** is ten minutes' walk southeast of the city centre at the end of avenue Feuchères, which leads down from Esplanade Charles-de-Gaulle, with the **gare routière** (ⓣ04.66.29.52.00) just behind in rue Ste-Félicité (access through the train station). The main **tourist office** is at 6 rue Auguste, by the Maison Carrée (Easter–Sept Mon–Fri 8am–7/8pm, Sat 9am–7pm, Sun 10am–6pm; Oct–Easter Mon–Fri 8.30am–7pm, Sat 9am–7pm, Sun 10am–5pm; ⓣ04.66.58.38.00, ⓦwww.ot-nimes.fr).

Accommodation

There are several decent **hotels** in Nîmes, located in two main zones: a cluster north of the train station and in the old city. An attractive **HI hostel** with tent space can be found on chemin de la Cigale, 2km northwest of the centre (ⓣ04.66.68.03.20, ⓦwww.hinimes; July & Aug membership required; Sept–June no curfew; €9); take bus #2 direction "Alès/ Villeverte" from the *gare SNCF* to stop "Stade" – the last bus goes at 8pm. The municipal **campsite** (ⓣ04.66.62.05.82, ⓦwww.camping-nimes.com; year-round) is on route de Générac, 5km south of the city centre, beyond the modern Stade Costières and the autoroute.

Alcanthe du Temple 1 rue Charles Babout ⓣ04.66.67.54.61, ⓦwww.hotel-du-temple.com. A clean and economical hotel, with friendly staff, good amenities and 24-hour access. This is one of the old town's best bargains. Closed Jan. ❸

La Baume 21 rue Nationale ⓣ04.66.76.28.42, ⓦwww.new-hotel.com. Set in a renovated mansion, with a courtyard dining area, and appointed with tasteful restraint. The best in the mid-range, with excellent location and price (and off-season reductions). 6

Central 2 place du Château ⓣ04.66.67.27.75, ⓦwww.hotel-central.org. Set on the edge of the historic centre in an eighteenth-century building, this hotel is excellent value for money. 2

Imperator Concorde quai de la Fontaine ⓣ04.66.21.90.30, ⓦwww.hotel-imperator.com. The city's finest choice, and a favourite of Hemingway's, located by the Jardin de la Fontaine. The luxuriously appointed rooms have a/c and satellite TV, the service is excellent and there is private parking. 9

De Provence 5/7 square de la Couronne ⓣ04.66.76.04.92, ⓦwww.hoteldeprovence.net. Friendly, well kept and set in an eighteenth-century house, with excellent amenities – such as cable TV – for its price. 3

Royal 3 bd Alphonse-Daudet ⓣ04.66.67.32.89, ⓕ04.66.21.90.30. Atmospheric mid-market hotel near the Maison Carrée, equipped with all mod cons. Also has a good restaurant, with an excellent selection of tapas. 4

The City

Most of what you'll want to see is contained within the boulevards de la Libération, Amiral-Courbet, Gambetta and Victor-Hugo, and there's much pleasure to be had from just wandering the narrow lanes that they enclose, discovering unexpected squares with fountains and cafés.

Les Arènes

The focal point of the city is a first-century Roman arena, known as **Les Arènes** (March & Oct 9.30am–5.30pm; April, May & Sept 9am–6pm; June–Aug 9am–7pm; Nov–Feb 9.30am–4.30pm; closed during special events; €7.70), which lies at the junction of boulevards de la Libération and Victor-Hugo. One of the best-preserved Roman arenas in the world, its arcaded two-storey facade conceals massive interior vaulting, riddled with corridors and supporting raked tiers of seats with a capacity of more than 20,000 spectators, whose staple fare was the blood and guts of gladiatorial combat. When Rome's sway was broken by the barbarian invasions, the arena became a fortress and eventually a slum, home to an incredible 2000 people when it was cleared in the early

The bullfight

Nîmes' great passion is **bullfighting**, and its *ferias* are acknowledged and well attended by both aficionados and fighters at the highest level. The wildest and most famous is the Feria de Pentecôte, which lasts five days over the Whitsun weekend. A couple of million people crowd into the town (hotel rooms need to be booked a year in advance), and seemingly every city native opens a bodega at the bottom of the garden for dispensing booze. There are *corridas*, which end with the killing of the bull, *courses* where *cocards* are snatched from the bulls head, and semi-amateur *courses libres* when a small posse of bulls is run through the streets and the daring try to snatch the *cocards* from their heads. In 1996, Nîmes witnessed the acclamation of the first-ever woman matador, Cristina Sanchez, though she took an early retirement in 1999, blaming the machismo of the profession. In recent years events have been frequently marked by small but vocal protests and in 2006 several organizers of the local tauromachie world were injured by letter bombs. Two other *ferias* take place: one at carnival time in February, when the inflatable roof of the Arènes is pulled over for protection from the weather; the other in the third week of September at grape-harvest time, the Feria des Vendanges. The **tourist office** can supply full details and advise you about accommodation if you want to visit at *feria* time.

1800s. Today it has recovered something of its former role, with the passionate summer crowds still turning out for some real-life blood-letting – Nîmes has the premier European bullfighting scene outside Spain.

The Maison Carrée and Porte d'Auguste

Behind the arena, through the beautiful little place du Marché, rue Fresque leads towards the city's other famous landmark, the **Maison Carrée** (March & Oct 9am–6pm; April, May & Sept 9am–7pm; June–Aug 9am–8pm; Nov–Feb 10am–5pm; €4.50), a neat, jewel-like temple celebrated for its integrity and harmonic proportions. Built in 5 AD, it's dedicated to the adopted sons of Emperor Augustus – all part of the business of inflating the imperial personality cult. No surprise, then, that Napoleon, with his love of flummery and tendency to ennoble his cronies to boost his own legitimacy, should have taken it as the model for the church of the Madeleine in Paris. The temple stands in its own small square opposite rue Auguste, where the Roman forum used to be, with pieces of Roman masonry scattered around. On the north side of place de la Maison Carrée, there's a gleaming example of French architectural boldness, the **Carrée d'Art**, by British architect Norman Foster. In spite of its size, this box of glass, aluminium and concrete sits modestly among the ancient roofs of Nîmes, its slender portico echoing that of the Roman temple opposite. Light pours in through the walls and roof, giving it a grace and weightlessness that makes it not in the least incongruous. Housed within the Carrée d'Art is the excellent **Musée d'Art Contemporain** (Tues–Sun 10am–6pm; €4.90), containing an impressive collection of French and Western European art from the last four decades. There's a roof-terrace café at the top, overlooking the Maison Carrée.

Though already a prosperous city on the Via Domitia, the main Roman road from Italy to Spain, Nîmes did especially well under Augustus. He gave the city its walls, remnants of which surface here and there, and its gates, as the inscription on the surviving **Porte d'Auguste** at the end of rue Nationale – the Roman main street – records. The emperor is also responsible for the chained crocodile, which figures on Nîmes' coat of arms. The device was copied from an Augustan coin struck to commemorate his defeat of Antony and Cleopatra after he settled veterans of that campaign on the surrounding land.

The Cathédrale Notre-Dame-et-St-Castor and around

Running back east into the old quarter from the Maison Carrée, **rue de l'Horloge** leads to the delightful **place aux Herbes**, with two or three cafés and bars and a fine twelfth-century house on the corner of rue de la Madeleine. In the former bishop's palace, the **Musée du Vieux Nîmes** (Tues–Sun 10am–6pm; free) has displays of Renaissance furnishings and decor and documents to do with local history. Opposite, the **Cathédrale Notre-Dame-et-St-Castor** sports a handsome sculpted frieze on the west front, illustrating the story of Adam and Eve, and a pediment inspired by the Maison Carrée. It's practically the only existing medieval building in town, as most were destroyed in the turmoil that followed the Michelade, the St Michael's Day massacre of Catholic clergy and notables by Protestants in 1567. Despite brutal repression in the wake of the Camisard insurrection of 1702, Nîmes was, and remains, a doggedly Protestant stronghold. Apart from that, the cathedral is of little interest, having been seriously mutilated in the Wars of Religion and significantly altered in the nineteenth century. The author Alphonse Daudet was born in its shadow, as was Jean Nicot – a doctor, no less – who introduced tobacco into France from Portugal in 1560 and gave his name to the world's most widely consumed drug.

Banned from public office, the Protestants put their energy into making money. The results of their efforts can be seen in the seventeenth- and eighteenth-century *hôtels* they built in the streets around the cathedral – rues de l'Aspic, Chapitre, Dorée and Grande-Rue, among others. Their church is the serious-looking **Grand Temple** on boulevard Amiral-Courbet, a short walk south of Porte d'Auguste. On the same street, the **Musée Archéologique** and **Muséum d'Histoire Naturelle** (Tues–Sun 10am–6pm; €4.90 for both), housed in a seventeenth-century Jesuit chapel at no. 13, are full of Roman bits and bobs and stuffed animals. There's another museum, the **Musée des Beaux-Arts**, south of the Arènes in rue de la Cité-Foulc (Tues–Sun 10am–6pm; €4.90), which prides itself on a huge Gallo-Roman mosaic showing the Marriage of Admetus, but is otherwise pretty ordinary. If you're planning on making the rounds of the museums, opt for the Billet Global museum passes (available at the tourist office; €9.50, for the Roman ruins, €9 for the museums), which give one-time access to the four sites (including the Musée d'Art Contemporain) listed above.

The interior of the **Hôtel de Ville**, between rue Dorée and rue des Greffes, has been redesigned by the architect Jean-Michel Wilmotte to combine high-tech design with classical stone. Most of the other major examples of revolutionary building are out on the southern edge of town: Jean Nouvel's pseudo-Mississippi-steamboat housing project off the Arles road behind the *gare SNCF*, named **Nemausus** after the deity of the local spring that gave Nîmes its name; and the magnificent sports stadium, the **Stades des Costières**, by Vittorio Gregotti, close to the autoroute along the continuation of avenue Jean-Jaurès.

Jardin de la Fontaine

Perhaps the most refreshing thing you can do in Nîmes is head northwest of the centre to the **Jardin de la Fontaine**, France's first public garden, created in 1750. Behind the formal entrance, where fountains, nymphs and formal trees enclose the **Temple de Diana**, steps climb the steep wooded slope, adorned with grottoes and nooks and artful streams, to the **Tour Magne** (July & Aug daily 9am–7pm; Sept–June daily 10am–5pm; €2.70). The 32-metre tower, left over from Augustus' city walls, gives terrific views out over the surrounding country – as far, it is claimed, as the Pic du Canigou on the edge of the Pyrenees. At the foot of the slope flows the gloriously green and shady **Canal de la Fontaine**, built to supplement the rather unsteady supply of water from the *fontaine*, the Nemausus spring, whose presence in a dry, limestone landscape gave Nîmes its existence.

Eating and drinking

The best places to hang out for **coffee and drinks** are the numerous little squares scattered through the old town: place de la Maison-Carrée, place du Marché and place aux Herbes (breakfast here early at the *Café des Beaux-Arts* to watch the sun creep up behind the cathedral tower). *Les Trois Maures*, in boulevard des Arènes, is a classic Nîmes café. For a quiet evening, you can head to *Carrée d'Art* piano bar on rue Gaston-Bossier, near the canal and the post-modern place d'Assas, while the *Victor Hugo*, a music-bar at 36 bd Victor-Hugo attracts a younger, livelier crowd.

For **eating**, boulevard de la Libération and boulevard Amiral-Courbet harbour a stock of reasonably priced brasseries and pizzerias, and the squares are full of possibilities.

Restaurants

L'Ancien Théâtre 4 rue Racine ☎04.66.76.26.30. A short stroll from the Maison Carrée, offering zippy Mediterrranean cuisine from €13. Closed Mon out of season.

Le Bouchon et l'Assiette 5bis rue de Sauve, ☎04.66.62.02.93. Serves up elaborate *gastronomique* variations on traditional Tarnaise themes, with menus from €15 to €44. Closed Tues & Wed.

Le Jardin d'Hadrien 111 rue Enclos-Rey ☎04.66.21.86.65. Inventive southeastern Gardoise cuisine with both fish and beef-based *plats* such as *boeuf à la gardienne* at reasonable prices. Menus at €17–26.

Le Magister 5 rue Nationale ☎04.66.76.11.00. Affordable and daringly *gastronomique* restaurant, with a €30 menu and a pricier *carte*. Closed Sat noon & Sun.

Le P'tit Bec 87bis rue de la République ☎04.66.38.05.83. The best mid-range place for typical Gardoise cuisine (from €18), such as *boeuf à la gardienne*. Closed Sun, Mon & Wed eve.

El Rinconcito 7 rue des Marchands ☎04.66.76.17.30. Friendly Chilean restaurant which provides a welcome break from the local fare (lunch menu from €8.50). Closed Sun & Mon.

La Truye qui Filhe 9 rue Fresque. Attractive self-service, where you can eat for around €9. Lunchtimes only, closed Sun & Aug.

The Pont du Gard and Uzès

Some twenty kilometres northeast from Nîmes, the **Pont du Gard** is the greatest surviving stretch of a fifty-kilometre-long Roman aqueduct built in the middle of the first century AD to supply fresh water to the city. With just a seventeen-metre difference in altitude between start and finish, the aqueduct was quite an achievement, running as it does over hill and dale, through a tunnel, along the top of a wall, into trenches and over rivers; the Pont du Gard carries it over the River Gardon. Today the bridge is a UNESCO World Heritage Site and something of a tourist trap, but is nonetheless a supreme piece of engineering and a brilliant combination of function and aesthetics: it made the impressionable Rousseau wish he'd been born Roman.

Three tiers of **arches** span the river, with the covered water conduit on the top, rendered with a special plaster waterproofed with a paint apparently based on fig juice. A visit here used to be a must for French journeymen masons on their traditional tour of the country, and many of them have left their names and home towns carved on the stonework. Markings made by the original builders are still visible on individual stones in the arches, such as "FR S III – frons sinistra", front side left no. 3. The Pont du Gard has recently undergone a massive restoration programme and now features an extensive multimedia complex, the **Site de Pont du Gard**, which includes a state-of-the-art **musuem** (daily May–Sept 9.30am–7pm; Oct–April 9.30am–5pm; €6), botanical **gardens** (April to mid-Oct daily 9.30am–6pm; €4), and a range of regular activities aimed at children. With the swimmable waters of the Gardon and ample picnic possibilities available as well, you could easily spend a day here.

Uzès

Seventeen kilometres further on, near the start of the aqueduct and served by daily buses from Nîmes, **UZÈS** is a lovely old town perched on a hill above the River Alzon. Half a dozen medieval towers – the most fetching is the windowed Pisa-like **Tour Fenestrelle**, tacked onto the much later cathedral – rise above its tiled roofs and narrow lanes of Renaissance and Neoclassical houses. The latter were the residences of the seventeenth- and eighteenth-century local bourgeoisie, who had grown rich, like their fellow Protestants in Nîmes, on textiles. From the mansion of Le Portalet, with its view out over the valley, walk past the Renaissance church of **St-Étienne** and into the medieval place aux Herbes, where there's a Saturday morning market, and up the arcaded rue de la République. The Gide family used to live off the square, the young André spending summer vacations with his granny there. To the right of rue de la République is the **castle of Le Duché** (1hr 30min guided tours: mid-June to mid-Sept 10am–1pm & 2–6.30pm; mid-Sept to mid-June 10am–noon & 2–6pm; €12), still inhabited by the same family a thousand years on, and dominated by its original keep, the **Tour Bermonde** (tower only €7). Today, there are guided tours around the castle building and exhibits of local history and vintage cars. Opposite, the courtyard of the eighteenth-century **Hôtel de Ville** holds summer concerts.

For details of these and other summer events, including more bull-running, consult the **tourist office** in place Albert-1er on boulevard Gambetta (June–Sept Mon–Fri 9am–6/7pm, Sat & Sun 10am–noon & 1–5pm; Oct–May Mon–Fri 9am–12.30pm & 2–6pm, Sat 10am–1pm; ⓣ04.66.22.68.88, ⓦwww.uzes-tourisme.com). The **gare routière** (ⓣ04.66.22.00.58) is further west on avenue de la Libération. Should you need **accommodation**, head for the friendly *Hostellerie Provençal* in two old row houses at 1 rue Grand Bourgade, south of the church of St-Étienne (ⓣ04.66.22.11.06, ⓦwww.hostellerieprovencale.com; ❺), or the attractively renovated *La Taverne* (ⓣ04.66.22.13.10, ⓔlataverne.uzes@orange.fr; ❹) a small and welcoming hotel with good amenities (including Wi-Fi) set behind the tourist office at 4 rue Xavier-Sigalon, and with a good *terroir* restaurant up the road at no. 7 (€20). The town's deluxe option is the *General d'Entraigues*, 8 rue de la Calade (ⓣ04.66.22.32.68, ⓦwww.hoteldentraigues.com; ❹–❾), in a converted fifteenth-century mansion opposite the cathedral. Alternatively, there's a municipal **campsite** off avenue Maxime-Pascal (mid-June to mid-Sept; ⓣ04.66.22.11.79) on the Bagnols-sur-Cèze road running northeast of town.

The Via Domitia and Sommières

About 25km west of Nîmes, off the Sommières road out of Lunel and close to the A9 autoroute, the Roman **Via Domitia** crosses the vineyards from the village of Gallargues to the bank of the River Vidourle, where one isolated arch of the original **Roman bridge** remains. On the west bank, a fine stretch of the old **cobbled way** is visible climbing the slopes of the former Roman settlement of **Ambrussum**, a fortified staging post on the road. From the top of the hill you can look down on the modern international traffic still passing the same way on the autoroute and parallel rail line.

About 10km to the north, 28km from Nîmes and still on the Vidourle, the little medieval town of **SOMMIÈRES**, with a much-modified Roman bridge, is where author Lawrence Durrell spent the last years of his life. The town itself boasts no major sights, though it's well preserved and atmospheric. However, a visit to the **castle of Villevieille** (May & June daily 2–7pm; July–Sept daily 2–8pm; Oct–April school hols only 2–7pm; €7), on the hillside 3km above Sommières, should not be missed. Owned by the same family for nearly eight hundred years, the castle is full of exquisite antique furniture. There are daily **buses** to Sommières from Nîmes; for **accommodation**, try the *L'Estelou* (ⓣ04.66.77.71.08, ⓦwww.hoteldelestelou.com; ❸), an arty hotel set in the town's old *gare*, or the *chambre d'hôte, La Mas Fontclaire* in 8 av Émile-Jamais (ⓣ & ⓕ04.66.77.78.69; English spoken; ❹). There's also a municipal **campsite** on rue Eugène-Rouch.

Montpellier

A thousand years of trade and intellectual activity have made **MONTPELLIER** a teeming, energetic city. Benjamin of Tudela, the tireless

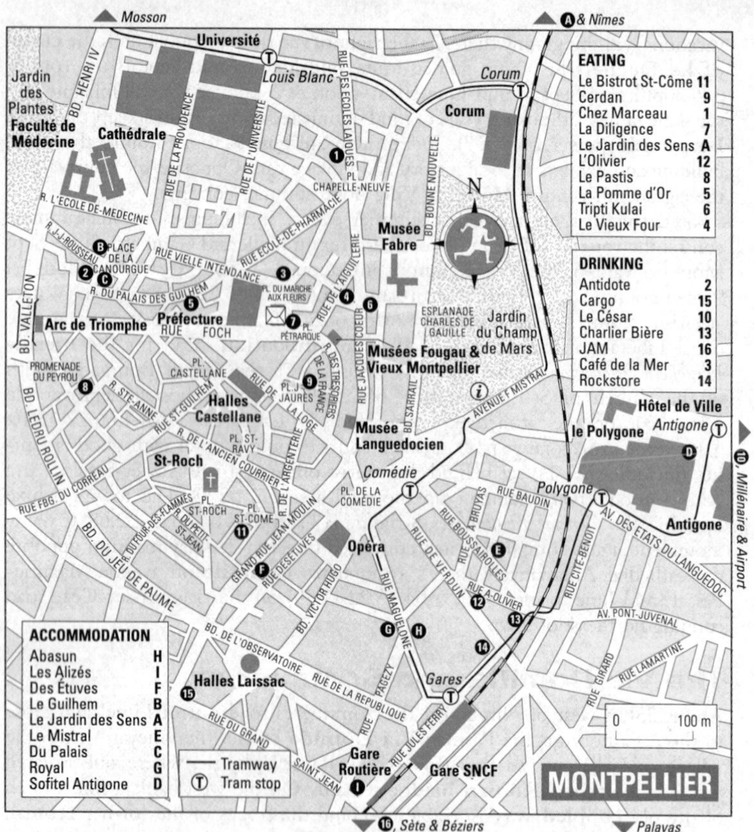

twelfth-century Jewish traveller, reported its streets crowded with traders from every corner of Egypt, Greece, Gaul, Spain, Genoa and Pisa. After the king of Mallorca sold it to France in 1349 it became an important university town in the 1500s, counting the radical satirist François Rabelais among its alumni. Periodic setbacks, including almost total destruction for its Protestantism in 1622, and depression in the wine trade in the early years of the twentieth century – have done little to dent this progress. Today it vies with Toulouse for the title of the most dynamic city in the south. The reputation of its university especially, founded in the thirteenth century and most famous for its medical school, is a long-standing one: more than 60,000 students still set the intellectual and cultural tone of the city – the average age of whose residents is said to be just 25.

Montpellier is renowned for its **cultural life**, and hosts a number of annual festivals. Le Printemps des Comédiens (mid-June to mid-July) is a theatre festival; Montpellier Danse (late June to mid-July) is a festival of dance. There's also a music festival, Le Festival de Radio-France et de Montpellier, held in the second half of July, and the Festival du Cinéma Méditerranéen, in the second half of October and early November. The tourist office provides information about programmes and booking.

Arrival and information

The **gare SNCF** (ⓣ04.99.74.15.10) and **gare routière** (ⓣ04.67.92.01.43) are next to each other at the opposite end of rue Maguelone from the central place de la Comédie. The **airport**, Montpellier-Méditerranée (ⓣ04.67.20.85.00, ⓦwww.montpellier.aeroport.fr), is 8km to the southeast beside the Étang de Mauguio; from here a **navette** (timed for flights; 15min €5) runs to the stop on rue de Crète (by the Léon Blum tramstop); it will cost you €12–30 by **taxi** depending on the time of day and traffic conditions. Much of the city centre is pedestrianized, but you can street park outside of the centre and there are many well-signalled municipal garages.

The **tourist office** (daily: Mon–Fri 9am-6.30pm, Sat 10am–6pm, Sun & public hols 10am–1pm & 2–5pm; ⓣ04.67.60.60.60, ⓦwww.ot-montpellier.fr), which has money exchange facilities, lies at the east end of place de la Comédie, opposite the Polygone shopping centre. They also sell the one-, two- and three-day City Card, which includes public transport, free admission to many sites and other discounts. TAM **city buses** run between the stations and outer districts (as far as coastal Palavas), while the Petibus crosses the city centre – tickets cost €1.30 (day ticket for €3.20) and cover both services for one hour, including transfers. The green transport policies of Montpellier have also resulted in the construction of a **tramway**, sweeping across town from northwest to southeast, as well as over 120km of **bike paths** running throughout the city and as far as the sea – information can be found at the tourist office.

Accommodation

Most hotel **accommodation** is conveniently concentrated in the streets between the train station and place de la Comédie, or in the nearby centre of the old town. There's a well-equipped **hostel** in a renovated old building in impasse Petite Corraterie, off rue des Écoles Laïques (closed mid-Dec to mid-Jan; ⓣ04.67.60.32.22, ⓔmontpellier@fuaj.org; bus #6 "Ursulines"; ❶), plus several **campsites** around Montpellier, particularly in nearby Palavas (bus #28); the most central and expensive is *L'Oasis Palavasienne* (ⓣ04.67.15.11.61; April to mid-Oct), just south of town on the D21 (to Palavas; bus #28).

Hotels

Abasun 13 rue Maguelone ⓣ04.67.58.36.80, ⓦwww.abasunhotelmontpelliercentre.com. On a busy street a stone's throw from the train station, this recently renovated hotel is clean, if somewhat basic – a good option for budget-conscious travellers. ❷

Les Alizés 14 rue Jules-Ferry ⓣ04.67.12.85.35, ⓦwww.hotel-alizes.com. Perhaps overpriced, but convenient, with a station-side location. Amenities include en-suite bath, satellite TV in every room, and a restaurant serving from 5am–1am. ❺

Des Étuves 24 rue des Étuves ⓣ04.67.60.78.19, ⓦwww.hoteldesetuves.fr. Simple, spotless rooms in the old city, all with en-suite bathrooms and TV. ❸

Le Guilhem 18 rue J.J.-Rousseau ⓣ04.67.52.90.90, ⓦwww.leguilhem.com. Beautifully restored sixteenth-century town house whose cheerful rooms mostly overlook quiet gardens, with a sunny breakfast terrace. ❺

Le Jardin des Sens 11 av St-Lazare ⓣ04.67.79.63.38, ⓦwww.jardindessens.com. The best of the upmarket hotels and the epitome of restrained and tasteful luxury, *Le Jardin* boasts a swimming pool, elegant rooms and one of the region's most acclaimed restaurants. ❾

Le Mistral 25 rue Boussairolles ⓣ04.67.58.45.25, ⓦwww.hotel-le-mistral.com. Decent, comfortable hotel, offering satellite TV and garage parking (€5 extra). ❸

Du Palais 3 rue du Palais ⓣ04.67.60.47.38, ⓦwww.hoteldupalais-montpellier.fr. Tastefully renovated eighteenth-century mansion on the west side of the old town. Cosy rooms, most with en-suite facilities. ❺

Royal 8 rue Maguelone ⓣ04.67.92.13.36, ⓦwww.hotel.royal-34.com. Good amenities in this three-star hotel between the Comédie and the *gare*, although its old-world ambience does not come cheap. ⑥

Sofitel Antigone 1 rue des Pertuisanes ⓣ04.67.99.72.72, ⓦwww.sofitel-montpellier.com. Suitably futuristic design, with a somewhat cold predominance of concrete over glass, set in the city's flagship Antigone development. Four-star service and amenities including a pool. ⑨

The City

Montpellier's city centre – the **old town** – is small, compact, architecturally homogeneous, full of charm and teeming with life, except in July and August when the students are on holiday and everyone else is at the beach. And the place is almost entirely pedestrianized, so you can walk the narrow streets without looking anxiously over your shoulder.

Place de la Comédie and the old town

At the hub of the city's life, joining the old part to its newer additions, is **place de la Comédie**, or "L'Oeuf" ("the egg") to the initiated. This colossal, oblong square, paved with cream-coloured marble, has a fountain at its centre and cafés either side. One end is closed by the **Opéra**, an ornate nineteenth-century theatre; the other opens onto the **Esplanade**, a beautiful tree-lined promenade that snakes it's way to the Corum **concert hall**, dug into the hillside and topped off in pink granite, with splendid views from the roof. South of the Corum, the city's most trumpeted museum, the **Musée Fabre**, has closed for major renovation. Visitors may have to wait until 2008 to view its large and historically important collection of seventeenth- to nineteenth-century European painting, including works by Delacroix, Raphael, Jan van Steen and Veronese.

From the north side of L'Oeuf, **rue de la Loge** and **rue Foch**, opened in the 1880s in Montpellier's own Haussmann-izing spree, slice through the heart of the old city. Either side of them, a maze of narrow lanes slopes away to the encircling modern boulevards. Few buildings survive from before the 1622 siege, but the city's busy bourgeoisie quickly made up for the loss, proclaiming their

△ Place de la Comédie, Montpellier

financial power through austere seventeenth- and eighteenth-century mansions. Known as "Lou Clapas" (rubble), the area is rapidly being restored and gentrified. It's a pleasure to wander through and come upon secretive little squares like place St-Roch, place St-Ravy and place de la Canourgue.

First left off rue de la Loge is **Grande-Rue Jean-Moulin**, where Moulin, hero of the Resistance, lived at no. 21. To the left, at no. 32, the present-day Chamber of Commerce is located in one of the finest eighteenth-century *hôtels*, the Hôtel St-Côme, originally built as a demonstration operating theatre for medical students. On the opposite corner, rue de l'Argenterie forks up to **place Jean-Jaurès**. This square is a nodal point in the city's student life: on fine evenings between 6 and 7pm you get the impression that the half of the population not in place de la Comédie is sitting here and in the adjacent place du Marché-aux-Fleurs. Through the Gothic doorway of no. 10, place Jean-Jaurès, is the so-called palace of the kings of Aragon, named after the city's thirteenth-century rulers. Close by is the **Halles Castellane**, a graceful, iron-framed market hall.

A short walk from place Jean-Jaurès, the Hôtel de Varenne, on place Pétrarque, houses two local history museums of somewhat specialized interest and a rather paltry range of artefacts; the **Musée du Vieux Montpellier** (Tues–Sat 10.30am–12.30pm & 1.30–6pm; €1.50) concentrates on the city's history, and the more interesting, private **Musée Fougau** on the top floor (Wed & Thurs 3–6pm; free), deals with the folk history of Languedoc and things Occitan. Off to the right, the lively little rue des Trésoriers-de-France has one of the best seventeenth-century houses in the city, the **Hôtel Lunaret**, at no. 5, while round the block on rue Jacques-Coeur you'll find the **Musée Languedocien** (Mon–Sat 2/2.30–5/5.30pm; €6), which houses a very mixed collection of Greek, Egyptian and other antiquities.

Jardin des Plantes and around

On the hill at the end of rue Foch, from which the royal artillery bombarded the Protestants in 1622, the formal gardens of the **Promenade du Peyrou** look out across the city and away to the Pic St-Loup, which dominates the hinterland behind Montpellier, with the distant smudge of the Cévennes beyond. At the farther end a swagged and pillared water tower marks the end of an eighteenth-century aqueduct modelled on the Pont du Gard. Beneath the grand sweep of its double tier of arches is a daily fruit and veg market and a huge Saturday **flea market**. At the city end of the promenade, the vainglorious **Arc de Triomphe** shows Louis XIV as Hercules, stomping on the Austrian eagle and the English lion, forcefully reminding the locals of his victory over their Protestant "heresy".

Lower down the hill, on boulevard Henri-IV, the lovely but slightly run-down **Jardin des Plantes** (July & Aug daily noon–8pm; Sept–June daily 2–5pm; free), with avenues of exotic trees, was founded in 1593 and is France's oldest botanical garden. Across the road is the long-suffering **cathedral**, with its massive porch, sporting a patchwork of styles from the fourteenth to the nineteenth centuries. Inside is a memorial to the bishop of Montpellier, who sided with the half-million destitute vine-growers who came to demonstrate against their plight in 1907 and were fired on by government troops. Above the cathedral, in the university's prestigious medical school on rue de l'École-de-Médecine, the **Musée Atger** (Mon, Wed & Thurs 1.30–5.45pm; free) has a distinguished academic collection of French and Italian drawings, while the macabre **Musée d'Anatomie** (daily 2.30–5pm; free) displays all sorts of revolting things in bottles.

Close by is the pretty little place de la Canourgue, and, beyond, down rue d'Aigrefeuille, the old university quarter, with some good academic bookshops on rue de l'Université.

Antigone

South of place de la Comédie stretches the controversial quarter of **Antigone**, a chain of post-modern squares and open spaces designed to provide a mix of fair-rent housing and offices, aligned along a monumental axis from the place du Nombre-d'Or, through place du Millénaire, to the glassed-in arch of the Hôtel de la Région. It's more interesting in scale and design than most attempts at urban renewal, but it has failed to attract the crowds away from the place de la Comédie and is often deserted. The enclosed spaces in particular work well, with their theatrical references to classical architecture, like oversized cornices and columns supporting only sky. The more open spaces are, however, disturbing, with something totalitarian and inhuman about their scale and blandness.

Eating, drinking and entertainment

Montpellier's year-round vitality supports a variety of **restaurants** and **bars** to suit all budgets and tastes. **Cafés** line every square while some of the more expensive restaurants use the city's ancient interiors to stunning effect. And Montpellier's youthful population ensures an energetic bar and **nightclub** scene right through to the early hours.

There's always plenty of **drinking** activity in the place de la Comédie, place du Marché-aux-Fleurs and place Jean-Jaurès, and two very different options are *Charlier Bière*, a grungy beer bar at 22 rue Olivier, and *Antidote*, a snappy cocktail joint on place de la Canourgue, which attracts the arty set. The *Café de la Mer*, at 5 place de Marché-aux-Fleurs, is a popular, gay-friendly establishment with a busy terrace. The old perennial for late-night dancing and live gigs is the *Rockstore*, near the station at 20 rue de Verdun (☎04.67.58.70.10), while *JAM*, at 100 rue Ferdinand-Lesseps, and *Cargo*, on place St-Denis, offer jazz and blues respectively. In addition to its clubs, bars and live music, Montpellier has a very lively **theatre scene**, as well as a tradition of engaging *café-littéraires* on a variety of themes; *Le César* at 17 place Nombre-d'Or (☎04.67.20.27.02) hosts two such gatherings, the *café des femmes* and the *café des arts* – check for days and times. For what's on at the various venues, look for posters around town or check the free weekly listings magazines, *Le Sortir* and *Olé*. The best central food **markets** are Halles Castellane, on rue de la Loge, and Laissac, place A. Laissace (daily 7.30am–1pm).

Restaurants and cafés

Le Bistrot St-Côme 2 place St-Côme. The best of a phalanx of open-air eateries dominating the south side of place St-Côme, offering a range of menus and standard but dependable French fare (€12–22). Service from noon till 11.30pm.

Cerdan 8 rue Collot ☎04.67.60.86.96. High-quality cuisine combining Norman and Algerian specialties, just off of the place de la Comédie. Lunch from €10 and dinners €14–27. Closed Sun & noon Mon.

Chez Marceau 7 place de la Chapelle Neuve ☎04.67.66.08.09. Excellent-value Languedocian cuisine (both inland and coastal varieties) with a wonderful shaded terrace. The *pâtés de canard* are particularly delicious. Menus €12 at lunch and €18 at dinner. Closed Sun & Wed in the off season.

La Diligence 2 place Pétrarque ☎04.67.66.12.21. *La Diligence* boasts an atmospheric, vaulted medieval setting perfect for a good-value dip into the finest French cuisine. Menus from €18–60. Closed Sat lunch, Sun & Mon lunch.

Le Jardin des Sens 11 av St-Lazaire ☎04.67.79.63.38. Located just north of Le Corum and run by the Pourcel twins, scions of a local vinter family renowned for their *gastronomique* creativity, this is one of the highest-rated restaurants in Languedoc. The ever-changing *carte* features excellent *terroir*-based creations ranging from pigeon pie to stuffed squid, served in elegant surroundings. Menus €50–190. Closed Sun, Mon, Tues & Wed lunch.

L'Olivier 12 rue Aristide-Olivier ☎04.67.92.86.28. Pretty little restaurant north of the station offering excellent-value traditional French cuisine. Menus at €32–47. Closed Sun, Mon and Aug.

Le Pastis 3 rue Terral ☎04.67.02.78.59. Great southern French cooking in a fine old mansion. Lunch menu at €14, dinner from €26. Closed Sat.

La Pomme d'Or 23 rue du Palais des Guilhem ☎04.67.52.82.62. Arty restaurant-bar with a predominantly gay clientele. A very wide selection of inventive menus at €18.

Tripti Kulai 20 rue Jacques-Coeur. Quirky, friendly women-run vegetarian restaurant. Dishes with oriental-influenced flair, including a good choice of salads, start at €9. Closed Sun.

Le Vieux Four 59 rue de l'Aiguillerie ☎04.67.60.55.95. Meat-eaters should head for this cosy, candlelit place specializing in *grillades au feu de bois*. Menus from €14–25. Eves only; closed Sun in summer.

Listings

Bike rental Bikes can be rented at Vill'a Vélo at the *gare routière* (☎04.67.92.92.67).

Books English books at: As You Like It, 8 rue du Bras de Fer; Book Shop, 4 rue de l'Université. Travel books at: Les Cinq Continents, 20 rue Jacques-Coeur.

Internet There are lots of cybercafés around town; try *Cybersurf*, 22 place du Millénaire in Antigone (Mon–Fri 8am–9pm, Sat & Sun 10am–6pm).

Medical emergency ☎04.67.22.81.67 or ☎15; Centre Hospitalier de Montpellier, 555 rte de Ganges (☎04.67.33.93.02) – take bus #16 from the gare to "Route de ganges" or the tram to "Hôpital Lapeyronie" and walk.

Post office The main office is on place Rondelet, 34000 Montpellier (Mon–Fri 9am–7pm, Sat 9am–noon).

Shopping The most convenient place is the Polygone mall, which contains a FNAC and Galeries Lafayette.

Swimming The nearest beaches for a dip are at Palavas (tram direction "Odysseum" to Port Marianne, then bus #28), but the best are slightly to the west of the town.

The coast: Aigues-Mortes to Agde

On the face of it, the **Languedoc coast** isn't particularly enticing, lined with bleak beaches and treeless strands, often irritatingly windswept and cut off from the sea by marshy *étangs* (lagoons). The area does, however, have long hours of sunshine, 200km of only sporadically populated sand and relatively unpolluted water. Resorts – mostly geared towards families who settle in for a few weeks at a time – have sprung up, sometimes engulfing once quiet fishing towns, but there's still enough unexploited territory to make this coast a good getaway from the crowds, and many of the old towns have managed to sustain their character and traditions despite the summer onslaught.

La Grande-Motte, Le Grau-du-Roi and Aigues-Mortes

The oldest of the new resorts, on the fringes of the Camargue, **LA GRANDE-MOTTE** is a 1960s vintage beach-side Antigone – a "futuristic" planned community which has aged as gracefully as the bean bag and eight-track tape. In summer, its seaside and streets are crowded with semi-naked bodies; in winter, it's a depressing, wind-battered place with few permanent residents. If you plan on **staying**, both *Camping Louis Pibols* (☎04.67.56.50.08; April–Oct) and *Camping le Garden* (☎04.67.56.50.09; March–Oct) offer excellent facilities and are just a couple of minutes' walk from the beach. The most appealing among the town's dozen or so near-identical **hotels** is the *Azur Bord du Mer* (Ⓣ04.67.56.56.00, Ⓦwww.hotelazur.net; ⑤); set out dramatically on the extremity of the town's quay.

A little way east are Port-Camargue, with a sprawling, modern marina, and **LE GRAU-DU-ROI**, which manages to retain something of its character as a working fishing port. Tourist traffic still has to give way every afternoon at 4.30pm when the swing bridge opens and lets in the trawlers to unload the day's catch onto the quayside, from where it's whisked off to auction – *la criée* – conducted today largely by electronic means rather than the harsh-voiced shouting of former times. For a reasonable place to **stay**, try the *Bellevue et d'Angleterre*, quai Colbert (closed Jan; Ⓣ04.66.51.40.75, Ⓦwww.hotelbellevueetdangleterre.com; ③), or the huge *Camping L'Eden* (April–Oct; Ⓣ04.66.51.49.81, Ⓦwww.campingeden.fr), just east of town.

Eight kilometres inland lies the appealingly named town of **AIGUES-MORTES** ("dead waters"), built as a fortress port by Louis IX in the thirteenth century for his departure on the Seventh Crusade. Its massive walls and towers remain virtually intact. Outside the ramparts, amid drab modern development, flat salt pans lend a certain otherworldly appeal, but inside all is geared to the tourist. If you visit, consider a climb up the **Tour de Constance** on the northwest corner of the town walls (daily: May–Aug 10am–7pm; Sept–April 10am–5pm; €6.50), where Camisard women were imprisoned (Marie Durand was incarcerated for 38 years), and a walk along the wall, where you can gaze out over the weird mist-shrouded flats of the Camargue.

Palavas and Maguelone

A dozen kilometres south of the city by road, **PALAVAS** is the bathing station for the citizens of Montpellier – a concrete sprawl with little to recommend it apart from the presence of the sea, though there's plenty of summertime activity in the discos and the rip-off quayside bars and restaurants. The best place to swim and sunbathe is a little way to the west off the long flat strand that borders the marsh, where some of Europe's few flamingos feed, and herons, egrets and other sea birds squabble and dive. The **Cathédrale de Maguelone** (daily 9am–7pm), dating mainly from the twelfth century, stands pale, grey and fortress-like on an island of vines and pines in the middle of the marsh. In the Middle Ages there was a thriving town here, and its cathedral was declared by Urban II to be "second only to that of Rome" in spiritual importance. However, the cathedral is all that remains of the settlement, which was largely destroyed by Louis XIII because of its Protestant leanings. Cavernous and cool, the strong, simple church interior serves as the venue for a sacred music festival in the second half of June.

Sète

Some 28km southeast of Montpellier, twenty minutes away by train, **SÈTE** has been an important port for three hundred years. The upper part of the town straddles the slopes of the Mont St-Clair, which overlooks the vast Bassin de Thau, a breeding ground of mussels and oysters, while the lower part is intersected by waterways lined with tall terraces and seafood restaurants. It has a lively workaday bustle in addition to its tourist activity, at its height during the summer *joutes nautiques* (see box opposite).

Arrival, information and accommodation

The **gare routière** is awkwardly placed on quai de la République, and the **gare SNCF** further out still on quai Maréchal-Joffre – though it is on the

Joutes nautiques

Water-jousting is a venerable coastal tradition which pits boat-borne jousting teams against each other in an effort to unseat their opponents. Two sleek boats, each manned by eight oarsmen and bearing a lance-carrying jouster, charge at each other on a near head-on course. As the boats approach, the jousters attempt to strike their adversary from his mount. There are about a dozen *sociétés des joutes* in Sète itself, and you can see them in action all through the summer.

main bus route, which circles Mont St-Clair (last bus about 7pm). **Ferries** for Morocco (1–2 weekly) and Mallorca (1–3 weekly) depart from the *gare maritime* at 4 quai d'Alger (Ⓣ04.67.46.68.00). Be warned that **hitching** out of Sète is horribly difficult; you're better off taking a train or bus to the nearest town and trying from there. The **tourist office**, at 60 Grand'Rue Mario-Roustan (April–June Mon–Fri 9.30am–6pm, Sat & Sun 9.30am–12.30pm & 2–5.30pm; July & Aug daily 9.30am–7.30pm; Sept–March Mon–Fri 9.30am–6pm, Sat & Sun 9.30am–12.30pm & 2–5.30pm; Ⓣ04.67.74.71.71, Ⓦwww.ot-sete.fr), has a good array of English-language information.

For **accommodation**, try the decaying but funky *Grand Hôtel de Paris* (Ⓣ04.67.74.98.10; May–Sept; ❸) at 2 rue Fréderic-Mistral. For somewhere more comfortable, there's the *belle-époque* splendour of the *Grand Hôtel,* 17 quai de Lattre-de-Tassigny (Ⓣ04.67.74.71.77, Ⓦwww.legrandhotelsete.com; ❺), and *L'Orque Bleu* at 10 quai Aspirant-Herber (Ⓣ04.67.74.72.13, Ⓔlorque-bleue@orange.fr; ❸). The **HI hostel** (mid-Jan to Nov; Ⓣ04.67.53.46.68, Ⓦwww.fuaj.org; ❶ – €20 half-pension only) is high up in the town on rue Général-Revest. Campers should ask the tourist office for details of the numerous campsites in the area.

The Town

Sète's crowded and vibrant pedestrian streets are scattered with café tables. A short climb up from the harbour is the **cimetière marin**, the sailors' cemetery, where poet Paul Valéry is buried. A native of the town, he called Sète his "singular island", and the **Musée Paul Valéry**, in rue Denoyer (July & Aug daily 10am–noon & 2–6pm; Sept–June Wed–Sun 10am–noon & 2–6pm; €3), opposite the cemetery, has a room devoted to him, as well as a small but strong collection of modern French paintings. If you're feeling energetic, you can continue through the pines to the top of the hill for a view that's fabulous when it's not engulfed in sea mist. Below the sailors' cemetery, and neatly poised above the water, is Vauban's **Fort St-Pierre**, now home to an open-air theatre.

Over on the west side of the hill, George Brassens, associate of Sartre and the radical voice of a whole French generation, is buried in the Cimetière le Py, in spite of his song *Plea to be Buried on the Beach at Sète*. In **Éspace Brassens** (June & Sept daily 10am–noon & 2–6pm; July & Aug daily 10am–noon & 2–7pm; Oct–May Tues–Sun 10am–noon & 2–6pm; €5), overlooking the cemetery, the locally-born singer-songwriter lives again through his words and music, narrating his life-story (in French only) on the museum's headsets. Closer to the centre of town you'll find the quirky new **Musée International des Arts Modestes** (July & Aug daily 10am–noon & 2–6pm; Sept–June daily except Tues 10am–noon & 2–6pm) at 23 quai Maréchal-Lattre, containing a collection of art made from cast-off goods and spinning on popular culture themes.

Eating and drinking

There's a barrage of **restaurants** along quai Général-Duran, from the Pont de la Savonnerie right down to the fish market at the mouth of the pleasure port, all offering seafood in the €15–30 bracket. Local favourite *La Palangrotte* (ⓣ04.67.74.80.35; closed Sun lunch & Mon & Wed off season) at 1 rampe Paul-Valéry, is famous for its mussels and bouillabaisse (€23–36) and solid wine list. Another good choice is *La Galinette*, 26 place des Mouettes (closed Jan–June & Sun eve, Fri lunch & Sat lunch Sept–Dec; ⓣ04.67.51.16.77), on the north side of town.

Agde and around

Midway between Sète and Béziers, at the western end of the Bassin de Thau, **AGDE** is the most interesting of the coastal towns. Originally Phoenician, and maintained by the Romans, it thrived for centuries on trade with the Levant. Outrun as a seaport by Sète, it later degenerated into a sleepy fishing harbour.

Today, it's a major tourist centre with a good deal of charm, notably in the narrow back lanes between rue de l'Amour and the riverside, where fishing boats tie up. The town's most distinctive and surprising feature is its colour – which comes from the black volcanic stone of the Mont St-Loup quarries. There are few sights apart from the impressively fortified **cathedral**, though the **waterfront** is attractive, and by the bridge you can watch the Canal du Midi slip modestly into the River Hérault on the very last leg of its journey from Toulouse to the Bassin de Thau and Sète.

The **tourist office** is in place Molière near the bridge (daily 9am–noon & 2–6pm; ⓣ04.67.94.29.68, ⓦwww.ville-agde.fr). The pick of the town's **hotels** is *La Galiote* (ⓣ04.67.94.45.58, ⓦwww.lagaliote.fr; ➎), located in the old bishop's palace on place J.-Jaurès, with its excellent service and restrained elegance while *Le Donjon* (ⓣ04.67.94.12.32, ⓦwww.hotelledonjon.com; ➎) in another atmospheric old building next door, comes a close second. For cheaper but still comfortable rooms, try *Hôtel des Arcades* (ⓣ04.67.94.21.64; ➌), in an old convent at 16 rue Louis-Bages. Aside from the numerous places to **eat** around La Promenade, a good bet is *La Fine Fourchetté* (ⓣ04.67.94.49.56) at 2 rue du Mont-Saint-Loup, featuring a delightful *carte* (menus from €9.45) with imaginative culinary combinations. One of the area's best restaurants is at *Le Jardin de Beaumont* (04.67.21.19.23), set in a wine *domaine* 3km north of town, where you can dine on tapas and excellent wines indoors or out (about €30).

An hourly **bus service** operates between the town and the sea at **Cap d'Agde** (see below); you can pick it up at the *gare SNCF* at the end of avenue Victor-Hugo, at the bridge and on La Promenade. Should you want to explore the Canal du Midi, **boat trips** are organized by Bateaux du Soleil, 6 rue Chassefières (ⓣ04.67.94.08.79).

Cap d'Agde

CAP D'AGDE lies to the south of Mont St-Loup, 7km from Agde. The largest (and by far the most successful) of the newer resorts, it sprawls out from the volcanic mound of St-Loup in an excess of pseudo-traditional modern buildings that offer every type of facility and entertainment – and are all expensive. It is perhaps best known for its colossal **quartier naturiste**, one of the largest in France, with the best of the beaches, space for 20,000 visitors, and its own restaurants, banks, post offices and shops. Access is possible if you're not actually staying there (€9 per car, €2.80 on foot; both until 8pm only).

If you have time to fill, head for the **Musée de l'Éphèbe** (daily 9am–noon & 2–6pm; €4), which displays antiquities discovered locally, many of them from the sea. Alternatively, the **Fort de Brescou** (mid-June to early Sept; €3), which dates back to 1680, lies on a rocky, seagull-infested island just offshore; it can be reached by ferries departing from the centre port at Cap d'Agde (Sarl Croisières: July & Aug Thurs–Mon 10.30am, 2.30 & 6.30pm; €6) or le Grau d'Agde (Ile de Brescou: July & Aug 2.30 & 4.30pm; €7).

Inland from Montpellier

For getting out into the country of the Bas Languedoc, there are two good routes from Montpellier, both served by regular buses: the D986 to **Ganges** and the N109 to **Lodève**. This out-of-the-way corner of Languedoc is best for its relatively untouristed villages, as well as excellent hiking and rafting opportunities.

The Ganges route

The Ganges road weaves north across the Plateau des Garrigues, a landscape of scrubby trees, thorns and fragrant herbs cut by torrent beds. The plateau is dominated by the high limestone ridge of the **Pic St-Loup** until you reach the first worthwhile stopping place, **ST-MARTIN-DE-LONDRES**, 25km on, whose name derives from the old Celtic word for "swamp". It's a lovely little town of arcaded houses and cobbled passageways set around the roadside place de la Fontaine. The pride of the place is an exceptionally handsome early Romanesque **church**, reached through a vaulted passage just uphill from the square. The honey-coloured stone is simply decorated with Lombard arcading, the plain rounded porch with a worn relief of St Martin on horseback, while the interior has an unusual clover-shaped ground plan. For accommodation, there is an excellent and welcoming **chambre d'hôte**, *De ci…De là!* (Ⓣ04.67.86.36.83, Ⓦwww.decidela.fr; ❹) on the edge of town at 6 rte des Cévennes. The **campsite**, *Pic de Loup* (Ⓣ04.67.55.00.53, Ⓔcamping-pic@tourisme.com; April–Sept), is just east on the main road.

About 6km south, off the Gignac road near Viols-le-Fort (on the main Clermont–Montpellier bus route) and the Château de Cambous, the marvel-

The Camisards

By issuing the Revocation of the Edict of Nantes in 1685, Louis XIV ended religious freedom in France, outlawing the Calvinist Protestantism of the Hugenots. Some five hundred thousand chose to flee the country, including many merchants and textile workers, while those who remained were subjected to **oppression**; some feigned conversion, some were deported to the colonies, and others fled to the "desert" – the wild and isolated hills of the Cévennes. It was here that they staged the **Camisard** revolt, so-called for the shirts they wore as a sign of recognition (from "chemise", French for "shirt)".

In July 1702, the parish priest of Chayla arrested a small group of fugitive Protestants, and was killed in the ensuing struggle. Knowing that retribution would be swift and cruel, Protestants across the Cévennes began a guerrilla war which pitted their forces, numbering between three and five thousand, against some thirty thousand royal troops. Unable to conclude the struggle militarily against the rebel guerrillas, the French army succeeded in bribing one of the leaders to change sides, precipitating the defeat of the movement in 1704.

lous **prehistoric village** of **Cambous** (May, June & Sept–Nov Sat & Sun 2–6pm; July & Aug Tues–Sun 2–7pm; €2.50) dates from 2500 BC and was only discovered in 1967. The site consists of a group of cabins, each about 20m long, their outlines clearly delineated, with the holes for the roof supports and door slabs still in place. A reconstruction shows them to have been much like the sheep stalls in the old *bergeries* that dot the plateau.

Further north, through dramatic river gorges almost as far as Ganges, you reach the **Grotte des Demoiselles** (March & Oct daily 10–11am & 2–4.30pm; April–June & Sept daily 10am–5.30pm; July & Aug daily 10am–6pm; Nov–Feb Mon–Fri 2–4pm, Sat & Sun 10–11am & 2–4pm; Ⓦwww.demoiselles.com; €8), the most spectacular of the region's many caves: a set of vast cathedral-like caverns hung with stalactites descending with millennial slowness to meet the limpid waters of eerily still pools. Located deep inside the mountain, it's reached by funicular (hourly departures).

Ganges

GANGES itself, 46km from Montpellier and connected by regular buses (which continue to Le Vigan on the southern edge of the Cévennes), is a rather nondescript but busy market town (Friday's the day), whose old quarter is notable for its vaulted alleys, designed for defence in the Wars of Religion. This, too, was a Protestant town, peopled by refugees from the plains, who made it famous for its silk stockings. It was here that the last-ditch revolt of the Camisards (see box, p.859) earned its name; the rebels sacked and pillaged a shirt factory and went off wearing the shirts (*chemises/camises*). Heading north from Ganges on your own steam will lead you deeper into Protestant territory, to the Huguenot villages around Le Vigan (see p.944).

The **tourist office** (Mon–Sat 10am–noon & 2–6pm, plus July & Aug Sun 10am–noon; Ⓣ04.67.73.00.56, Ⓦwww.ot-cevennes.com) is on plan de l'Ormeau. On the same square you'll find the basic *De la Poste* (Ⓣ04.67.73.85.88, Ⓦwww.hoteldelaposteganges.com; closed Jan; ❷), the best overnight choice in town. West of town, on the road towards Navacelles, is the splendid *Château de Madières* (closed Nov–March; Ⓣ04.67.73.84.03, Ⓦwww.chateau-madieres.fr; ❾), a renovated fourteenth-century castle. The municipal **campsite** (mid-June to Aug; Ⓣ04.67.57.92.97), along the river at the southern end of town, has the only laundry. You'll find an excellent, homely Lyonnais **restaurant** here, *Le Melodie* (Ⓣ04.67.73.66.02; closed Wed; menus €9 at lunch, €14 at dinner), at 4 place Fabre-d'Olivet.

The Lodève route

The second inland route runs due west from Montpellier, passing **Gignac** – the turn-off for the spectacular **Gorges de l'Hérault** and **St-Guilhem-le-Désert** – before reaching **Clermont-l'Hérault**, a transport hub from where you can access the Haut Languedoc to the west or the old cathedral town of **Lodève** further north.

St-Guilhem-le-Désert and around

The small town of **Gignac** lies amid vineyards 30km west of Montpellier. It is here that buses turn off for the glorious abbey and village of **ST-GUILHEM-LE-DÉSERT,** which lies in a side ravine, 6km further north up the Hérault beyond the famed medieval Pont du Diable. A ruined castle spikes the ridge above, and the ancient tiled houses of the village ramble down the banks of the rushing Verdus, which is everywhere channelled into carefully tended gardens. The grand focus

△ St-Guilhem-le-Désert

is the tenth- to twelfth-century **abbey church**, founded at the beginning of the ninth century by St Guilhem, comrade-in-arms of Charlemagne. The church is a beautiful and atmospheric building, though architecturally impoverished by the dismantling and sale of its cloister – now in New York – in the nineteenth century. It stands on place de la Liberté, surrounded by honey-coloured houses and arcades with traces of Romanesque and Renaissance domestic styles in some of the windows. The interior of the church is plain and somewhat severe compared to the warm colours of the exterior, best seen from rue Cor-de-Nostra-Dama/Font-du-Portal, where you get the classic view of the perfect apse.

There are a couple of easy and worthwhile **walks** you can make from here – up the valley of the Verdus into the red-stained walls of the **Cirque du Bout-du-Monde** (from place de la Liberté, take rue du Bout-du-Monde out of the village and continue for about 30min), or up the zigzagging path of the GR74, through the sweet-scented shrubs and flowers towards the castle ridge (also about 30min). From the crest of the ridge the view down onto the village is magnificent. The path divides here: one branch leads back right to the ruins of the castle, while the other continues along the GR74 to the Ermitage Notre-Dame-de-Belle-Grâce (1hr 30min), and on to join the GR7 at St-Maurice-Navacelles on the Causse de Larzac.

In season the village is on every tour operator's route, making early mornings and late afternoons the best times for visiting. The best **hotel** is *Le Guilhaume d'Orange* (Ⓣ04.67.57.24.53, Ⓦwww.guilhaumedorange.com; ❺), while budget travellers should head to the English-speaking *Gîte de la Tour* (Ⓣ & Ⓕ04.67.57.34.00; ❶). The nearest **campsite** is *Le Moulin de Siau* (Ⓣ04.67.57.51.08, Ⓦwww.camping-moulin-de-siau.com; June–Aug), near Aniane on the road back down to Gignac. Nearby, cave enthusiasts will enjoy the **Grotte de Clamouse** (daily: June, Sept & Oct 10am–6pm; July & Aug 10am–7pm; Nov–May noon–5pm; €8). This extensive and beautiful stalactite cave is entered along a subterranean river and opens up into three expansive grottoes.

Clermont-l'Hérault and around

Eight kilometres west of Gignac, the market town of **CLERMONT-L'HÉRAULT** – accessible by bus from Montpellier – is a rather dull little cantonal capital, whose only recommendation is that it is a good jumping-off point for visiting the area around **Lac Salagou** to the west, an attractive man-made reservoir sited amidst striking iron-rich terrain. The sole interesting site in town is a thirteenth-century **church**, fortified in the fourteenth century to defend it against the English.

The **tourist office** (Mon–Fri 9am–12.30pm & 2–7pm, Sat 9am–noon & 2–5/6pm; plus July & Aug Sun 10am–noon; ⓣ04.67.96.23.86, ⓦwww.ot-clermont-l-herault.com) is at 9 rue René-Gosse, close to the cathedral. By far the best **place to stay** is *Le Terminus*, on allées Roger-Salengro near the old station (ⓣ04.67.88.45.00, ⓔleterminus@orange.fr; ❷). If you're **camping**, head for the year-round site *Le Salagou* (ⓣ04.67.96.13.13), northwest of Clermont near the lake. Reasonable **meals** can be had at Clermont-l'Hérault at *L'Arlequin*, tucked under the south wall of the church on place St-Paul (closed Sun & Mon; menus from €14).

Around Clermont-l'Hérault

Three kilometres west from Clermont-l'Hérault, along the main road to Bédarieux, lies **VILLENEUVETTE**. This model factory and workers' settlement was created in the seventeenth century for the production of high-quality wool for sale in the Mediterranean. Initially successful, the factory eventually closed down in 1954, but the settlement still boasts 85 inhabitants. There's a very nice, if somewhat pricey, **hotel** tacked on to the village walls – *La Source* (closed Jan to mid-Feb & late Nov; ⓣ04.67.96.05.07, ⓦwww.hoteldelasource.com; English spoken; ❺), with a good restaurant (€18–30), pool and garden. Eight kilometres further west just off the Bédarieux road, in the picturesque little village of **MOURÈZE**, you'll find an alternative hotel, *Les Hauts de Mourèze* (ⓣ04.67.96.04.84, ⓕ04.67.96.25.85; closed Nov–March; ❹). Further accommodation options are available about 4km west in Salasc, at the *Auberge Campagnard* (ⓣ04.67.96.15.62, ⓦwww.aubergedusalagou.fr; ❸ with breakfast), and at *Octon in La Calade* (ⓣ04.67.96.19.21, ⓦwww.hotel-lacalade.com; March to mid-Dec; ❸), a comfortable old hotel in the village centre (closed Tues & Wed out of season; menus from €15).

Three other interesting and little-visited places west of Clermont are only feasible if you have a car. The first is a very fine **dolmen** on the end of a low ridge overlooking the D32 – best reached from the village of **LE POUGET**, 7km to the southwest, where it is signposted. Continuing along the D139, you come within sight of the pale grey ruins of the keep and chapel of the **Château d'Aumelas**, romantically silhouetted on the edge of the *causse* (limestone plateau). To reach it by road – you'll need to take a rather long and steep detour (about 6km in total) – bear right onto the D114 and then take a dirt track opposite a farm. It's a beautiful and silent place, and the chapel is in near-perfect condition. Two kilometres further along the D114, down an unsigned and bumpy track leading right onto the *causse*, there is a marvellous and remote silvery chapel, **St-Martin-de-Cardonnet**, built in the twelfth century – all that remains of an ancient priory.

On to Lodève

Heading north from Clermont to **LODÈVE**, 19km away, the swift A75 autoroute brings heavy traffic down from Clermont-Ferrand. It passes through countryside further scarred by uranium mining – the area around the village of St-Martin-du-Bosc has some of the highest soil concentration of radioactivity in the world.

Lodève, entirely enclosed by vine-terraced hills at the confluence of the Lergues and Soulondres rivers, is almost in the shadow of the **Causse de**

Larzac. There are no real sights here, but it's a pleasant, old-fashioned place to pause on your way up to Le Caylar or La Couvertoirade on the *causse*. The **cathedral** – a stop on the pilgrim route to Santiago de Compostela – is worth a look, as is the unusual World War I **Monument aux Morts**, in the adjacent park, by local sculptor Paul Dardé. This spooky *mise en scène* of civilians mourning a soldier fall on the field is a departure from the usual stiff commemorations of the "Morts pour la France". More of his work is on display at the town **museum** in the Hôtel Fleury (Tues–Sun 9.30am–noon & 2–6pm; €3.20, €6 during special exhibitions) and the **Halle Dardé** (daily 9am–7pm; free) in the place du Marché. With a bit of organizing it's also possible to visit the **Atelier National de Tissage de Tapis** (Tues–Thurs 1.30–3.30pm; €3.20; call ahead, ⓣ04.67.96.40.40), on the outskirts of Lodève, where priceless Gobelins tapestries are woven.

The **tourist office** is at 7 place de la République (Mon–Fri 9am–noon & 2–6pm, Sat 9.30am–noon; ⓣ04.67.88.86.44, ⓦwww.lodeve.com), next door to the **gare routière**, where you can catch buses to Montpellier, Béziers, Millau, Rodez and St-Afrique. The best place to **stay** in town is the *Hôtel du Nord* (ⓣ04.67.44.92.78, ⓦwww.hotellodeve.com; ❷) at 18 bd de la Liberté, or the family-run *Hôtel de la Paix* (ⓣ04.67.44.07.46, ⓦwww.hotel-dela-paix.com; ❸; closed Jan & Feb) on 11 bd Montalangue. There's a big **market** on Saturdays, and local farmers bring in their produce three times a week in summer.

Southern Languedoc

Southern Languedoc presents an exciting and varied landscape, its coastal flats stretching south from the mouth of the Aude towards Perpignan, interrupted by occasional low, rocky hills. Just inland sits **Béziers**, its imposing cathedral set high above the languid River Orb, girded in the north by the amazingly preserved Renaissance town of **Pézenas** and in the south by the pre-Roman settlement of the **Ensérune**. It's also a gateway to the spectacular uplands of the **Monts de l'Espinouse** and the **Parc Naturel Régional du Haut Languedoc**, a haven for ramblers. Just south of Béziers, the ancient Roman capital of **Narbonne** guards the mouth of the Aude. Following the course of this river, which is shadowed by the historic **Canal du Midi**, you arrive at the quintessential medieval citadel, the famous fortress-town of **Carcassonne**. Once a shelter for renegade **Cathar** heretics, Carcassonne is also a fine departure point for the Cathar castles – a string of romantically ruined castles covered on pp.821–824.

Béziers and around

Though no longer the rich city of its nineteenth-century heyday, **BÉZIERS** has risen out of its recent dreariness with admirable panache. The town is the capital of the Languedoc **wine** country and a focus for the **Occitan** movement, as well as being the birthplace of Resistance hero **Jean Moulin**. The fortunes of the movement and the vine have long been closely linked; Occitan activists have helped to organize the militant local vine-growers, and there were ugly events during the mid-1970s, when blood was shed in confrontations with the authorities over the import of cheap foreign wines and the low prices paid for the essentially poor-grade local product. Things are calmer now, the conservatism of Languedoc farmers giving way to more modern attitudes in the face of public demand for something better than the traditional table wine. As a result, some of the steam has also gone out of the movement; interest today is more in the culture than in anti-Paris separatist feelings. The town is also home to two great Languedocian adopted traditions: English **rugby** and the Spanish **corrida**, both of which are followed with a passion. The best time to visit is during the mid-August **feria**, a raucous four-day party that can be enjoyed even if bull-fighting isn't to your taste.

The City

The finest view of the old town is from the west, as you come in from Carcassonne: crossing the willow-lined River Orb by the Pont-Neuf, you can look upstream at the sturdy arches of the **Pont-Vieux**, above which rises a steep-banked hill crowned by the **Cathédrale St-Nazaire** which, with its crenellated towers, resembles a castle more than a church. The best approach to the cathedral is up the medieval lanes at the end of Pont-Vieux, rue Canterelles and passage Canterellettes. Its architecture is mainly Gothic, the original building having been burnt in 1209 during the sacking of Béziers, when Armand Amaury's crusaders massacred some seven thousand people at the church of the Madeleine for refusing to hand over about twenty Cathars. "Kill them all", the pious abbot is said to have ordered, "God will recognize his own!"

From the top of the cathedral **tower**, there's a superb view out across the vine-dominated surrounding landscape. Next door, you can wander through the ancient **cloister** (free) and out into the shady **bishop's garden** overlooking the river. In the adjacent **place de la Révolution**, a monument commemorates the people who died resisting Napoléon III's coup d'état in 1851 and their leader, Mayor Casimir Péret, who was shipped off to Cayenne where he drowned in a Papillon-style escape attempt. Also on the square, the Hôtel Fabrégat houses a **Musée des Beaux-Arts** (Tues–Sun: July & Aug 10am–6pm; Sept–June 9/10am–noon & 2–5/6pm; €2.45) which, apart from an interesting collection of Greek Cycladic vases, won't keep you long. Nearby, **Hôtel Fayet**, at 9 rue Capus (same hours and ticket), has been pressed into service as an annexe to the museum, though it's as much of interest for its period interiors as its collection of nineteenth- and early twentieth-century art and works by local sculptor Jean-Antoine Injalbert.

The city's other museum, the **Musée du Biterrois** (Tues–Sun: July & Aug 10am–6pm; Sept–June 9/10am–noon & 2–5/6pm; €2.45), in the old St-Jacques barracks on avenue de la Marne near the train station, displays a variety of entertaining exhibits, ranging from Greek amphorae and nineteenth-century door knockers to distilling manuals, clogs and winepresses. You might also take a look at the modest remains of the **Roman amphitheatre** two streets to the north of the museum off of rue St-Jacques, which at the time of writing was being developed as an open-air museum. It once had a capacity of over 13,000 spectators, and its stones were used to construct the medieval walls.

Away from the medieval streets round the cathedral, the centre of life in Béziers is the **allées Paul-Riquet**, a broad, leafy esplanade lined with cafés, crêpe stalls, restaurants, banks and shops; it's named after the seventeenth-century tax collector who lost health and fortune in his obsession with building the Canal du Midi to join the Atlantic and the Mediterranean. Laid out in the last century, the *allées* runs from an elaborate nineteenth-century theatre on place de la Victoire to the gorgeous little park of the **Plateau des Poètes**, whose ponds, palms and lime trees were laid out in the so-called English manner by the man who created the Bois de Boulogne in Paris.

Practicalities

From the **gare SNCF** on boulevard Verdun, the best way into town is through the landscaped gardens of the Plateau des Poètes opposite the station entrance and up the allées Paul-Riquet. The **gare routière** is in place de Gaulle, at the northern end of the *allées*, while the **tourist office** is in the new Palais des Congrès at 29 av Saint-Saëns (July & Aug Mon–Sat 9am–7pm, Sun 9.30am–12.30pm; Sept–June Mon–Sat 9am–noon/12.30pm & 1.30/2–6pm; ⓣ04.67.76.47.00, ⓦwww.ville-beziers.fr).

For a central place to **stay**, try the *Hôtel des Poètes*, 80 allées Paul-Riquet (ⓣ04.67.76.38.66, ⓦwww.hoteldespoetes.net; ❸), at the southern end overlooking the gardens, the smarter *Hôtel du Théâtre*, 13 rue Coquille (ⓣ04.67.49.13.43 ⓔhoteldutheatre.beziers@9online.com; ❷), right beside the municipal theatre, or the new *France* (ⓣ04.67.28.44.72, ⓦwww.hotel2france.com; ❹) at 36 rue Boiëdieu. The town's deluxe option, *Hôtel Imperator* (ⓣ04.67.49.02.25, ⓦwww.hotel-Imperator.fr; ❹), at 28 allées Paul-Riquet, is a notch above the rest but won't break the bank. There's no **campsite** in Béziers, but you can head to *Les Berges du Canal* (ⓣ04.67.39.36.09, ⓦwww.lesbergesducanal.com; mid-April to mid-Sept) in nearby Villeneuve-lès-Béziers, about 4km southeast of the town centre, or 6km east to *Clariac* (ⓣ04.67.76.78.97; April–Sept).

A string of **restaurants** with patios are lined along the west side of allées Paul-Riquet, serving the usual *steak-frites*-type menus for about €12. Better fare can be found in the old quarter; rue Viennet has a good choice of places. The best choice is probably *Le Cep d'Or*, at no. 7, a bistro with a charming old-fashioned air, serving mostly seafood (menus from €13–20; closed Sun eve & Mon out of season), while *Les Deux Lombard*, at no. 32, is more upmarket, with menus from €30. Lighter fare can be found at *La Table Bretonne* (closed Mon), at no. 21, an airy crêperie with a large street-side patio where savoury or sweet pancakes start at €9. *L'Ambassade* (closed Sun & Mon; ⓣ04.67.76.06.24), at 22 bd de Verdun is one of the town's best places.

Béziers has one of the star **rugby** clubs in France, A.S.B.H., based at the Stade de la Méditerranée in the eastern suburbs (ⓣ04.67.11.03.76, ⓦwww.asbh.net). If you fancy pottering along the Canal du Midi, you can rent **bikes** at La Maison du Canal (ⓣ04.67.62.18.18) beside the Pont-Neuf, south of the *gare SNCF*.

Pézenas

PÉZENAS lies 18km east of Béziers on the old N9. Market centre of the coastal plain, it looks across to rice fields and shallow lagoons, hazy in the heat and dotted with pink flamingos. The town was catapulted to glory when it became the seat of the parliament of Languedoc and the residence of its governors in 1465, and reached its zenith in the late seventeenth century when the prince Armand de Bourbon made it a "second Versailles". The legacy of this illustrious past can be seen in the town's exquisite array of fourteenth- to seventeenth-century mansions.

The town also plays up its association with **Molière**, who visited several times with his troupe in the mid-seventeenth century, when he enjoyed the patronage of Prince Armand. He put on his own plays at the **Hôtel d'Alfonce** on rue Conti, including the first performance of *Le Médecin Volant*, according to local tradition. The building is now privately owned, but in summer you can visit the courtyard that served as **Molière's theatre** (July & Aug Mon–Fri 10am–noon & 2–6pm; €2). When in town, he lodged at the Maison du Barbier-Gély in the unspoiled **place Gambetta**, today occupied by the **tourist office** (July & Aug Mon, Tues, Thurs & Sat 9am–7pm, Wed & Fri 9am–10pm, Sun 10am–7pm; Sept–June Mon–Sat 9am–noon & 2–6pm, Sun 10am–noon & 2–5pm; ⓣ04.67.98.36.40, ⓦwww.ot-pezenas-valdherault.com). Although Molière features in the eclectic **Musée Vulliod St-Germain** (Mon–Sat 10am–noon & 2–5pm, Sun 2–5pm; €2), housed in a sixteenth-century palace just off the square, it's the grand salon, with its Aubusson tapestries and collection of seventeenth- and eighteenth-century furniture, that steals the show.

The tourist office distributes a guide to all the town's eminent houses, taking in the former **Jewish ghetto** on rue des Litanies and rue Juiverie, but you can just as easily follow the explanatory plaques posted all over the centre, starting at the east end of rue François-Outrin where it leaves the town's main square, place du 14-Juillet.

Practicalities

The **gare routière** is on the opposite side of the square on the riverbank, with buses to Montpellier, Béziers and Agde, while an enormous **market** takes place each Saturday on cours Jean-Jaurès, a five-minute walk away.

There are two **hotels** in old Pézenas: *Genieys*, at 9 rue Aristide-Briand (ⓣ04.67.98.13.99, ⓦwww.logis-de-france.fr; ❸), and the splendid *Molière*, 18 place du 14-Juillet (ⓣ04.67.98.14.00, ⓦwww.hotel-le-moliere.com; ❻). There are plenty of **restaurants** to choose from, most with menus for under €18. *Le Pomme d'Amour* (March–Dec; closed Mon eve & Tues in winter), on rue Albert-Paul-Alliés, has good duck dishes and *Le Conti*, 27 rue Conti (closed Sun & out of season Mon), is a popular pizzeria. The best spot, however, is *Les Palmiers* on 50 rue de Mercière (ⓣ04.67.09.42.56; June–Sept only), a beautiful and welcoming establishment featuring inventive Mediterranean-style cuisine from about €28. For those with a sweet tooth, there are two local delicacies to sample: flavoured sugar-drops called *berlingots*, and *petits pâtés* – bobbin-shaped pastries related to mince pies, reputedly introduced by the Indian cook in the household of Clive of India, who stayed in Pézenas in 1770.

Narbonne and around

On the Toulouse–Nice main train line, 25km west of Béziers, is **NARBONNE**, once the capital of Rome's first colony in Gaul, Gallia Narbonensis, and a thriving port in classical times and the Middle Ages. Plague, war with the English and the silting-up of its harbour finished it off in the fourteenth century, though a tentative prosperity returned in the late nineteenth century with the birth of the modern wine industry. Today, despite the ominous presence of the Malvesi nuclear power plant just 5km out of town, it's a pleasant provincial city with a small but well-kept old town, dominated by the great truncated choir of its cathedral and bisected by a grassy esplanade on the banks of the Canal de la Robine.

In the early 1990s Narbonne acquired notoriety as a flash point in France's continuing problems with its ethnic minorities, as the Harkis – Algerians who had enlisted in the French forces and fought with them against their own people in the Algerian war of independence in the late 1950s – began angrily to protest official neglect of their community. The discontent has rumbled on, and the Harkis have organized a political group, the Mouvement Harki, to counter the city's far-right municipal administration.

The Town

One of the few Roman remnants in Narbonne is the **Horreum**, at the north end of rue Rouget-de-l'Isle (April–Sept 9.30am–noon & 2–6pm; Oct–March 10am–noon & 2–5pm), an unusual underground grain store divided into a series of small chambers leading off a rectangular passageway. At the opposite end of the same street, close to the attractive tree-lined banks of the **Canal de la Robine**, is Narbonne's other principal attraction, the enormous Gothic **Cathédrale St-Just-et-St-Pasteur**. With the Palais des Archevêques and its forty-metre high keep, it forms a massive pile of masonry that completely dominates the restored lanes of the old town, and – like the cathedral of Béziers – can be seen for kilometres around. In spite of its size, it's actually only the choir of a much more ambitious church, whose construction was halted to avoid wrecking the city walls. The immensely tall interior has some beautiful fourteenth-century stained glass in the chapels on the northeast side of the apse and imposing Aubusson tapestries – one of the most valuable tapestries is kept in the **Salle du Trésor** (April–Sept 9.30am–noon & 2–6pm; Oct–March 10am–noon & 2–5pm; €2.20), along with a small collection of ecclesiastical treasures.

The adjacent **place de l'Hôtel-de-Ville** is dominated by the great towers of St-Martial, the Madeleine and Bishop Aycelin's keep. From there the passage de l'Ancre leads through to the **Palais des Archevêques** (Archbishops' Palace), housing a fairly ordinary **museum of art** and a good **archeology museum** (both museums have the same hours and ticket as the Horreum), whose interesting Roman remains include a massive 3.5-metre wood and lead ship's rudder, and a huge mosaic. Across into the southern part of the town, beyond the bisecting Canal de la Robine and the built-over Pont des Marchands, the small early Christian crypt of the church of **St-Paul**, off rue de l'Hôtel-Dieu (Mon–Sat 9am–noon & 2–6pm & Sun 9am–noon; free), is worth a quick look, as is the deconsecrated church of **Notre-Dame-de-Lamourguié,** which now houses a collection of Roman sculptures and epigraphy (same hours and cost as the Horreum).

Practicalities

The **gare routière** and the **gare SNCF** are next door to each other on avenue Carnot on the northwest side of town. The **tourist office** is on place Salengro, next to the cathedral (mid-June to mid-Sept Mon–Sat 9am–7pm, Sun 9.30am–12.30pm; rest of year Mon–Sat 8.30am–noon & 2–6pm, plus Sun 9.30am–12.30pm May & June only; Ⓣ04.68.65.15.60, Ⓦwww.mairie-narbonne.fr).

The best budget **accommodation** is the modern and friendly *MJC Centre International de Séjour*, in place Salengro (Ⓣ04.68.32.01.00, Ⓦwww.cis-narbonne.com; ❶ €25). Two of the more reasonable hotels are *Will's Hotel*, 23 av Pierre-Sémard (Ⓣ04.68.90.44.50, Ⓦwww.willshotel-narbonne.com; ❸), a homely backpackers' favourite near the station, and the spruce *Hôtel de France*, 6 rue Rossini (Ⓣ04.68.32.09.75, Ⓦwww.hotelnarbonne.com; ❸), beside the attractive market hall. A fancier option is the plush *La Résidence*, 6 rue du 1er-Mai (Ⓣ04.68.32.19.41, Ⓦwww.hotelresidence.fr; ❹), in a nineteenth-century renovated house, but best is *Grand Hôtel du Languedoc***,** 22 bd Gambetta,

Ⓣ04.68.65.14.74, Ⓦwww.hoteldulanguedoc.com; ❹), set in a dignified nineteenth-century house. The nearest **campsite** is *Les Folralys* (Ⓣ04.68.32.65.65, Ⓦwwww.lesfloralys.com), on the route de Gruissan to the south of town (take bus #2 from the Hôtel de Ville).

As for **food**, you'll find a string of alfresco snack bars and brasseries along the terraces bordering the Canal de la Robine in the town centre, while *L'Estagnol* (Ⓣ04.68.65.09.27; closed Sun & Mon eve; menus €10–28), across the canal on Cours Mirabeau, attracts the crowds with its simple, good-value fare. For something a little fancier, try *Aux Trois Caves*, at 4 rue Benjamin-Crémieux (menus €10–22), with *terroir* dining in a medieval cellar. *L'Alsace*, at 2 av Pierre-Sémard (Ⓣ04.68.65.10.24; closed Tues & Wed) is Narbonne's best restaurant, hands down, featuring mammoth servings of excellent *terroir* and northeastern French dishes as well as local seafood dishes at €10–29 – the baked sea wolf is a house speciality.

Fontfroide and the Étang de Bages

For a side trip from Narbonne – only 15km southwest, but nigh impossible without transport of your own – the lovely **abbey** of **FONTFROIDE** enjoys a beautiful location, tucked into a fold in the dry cypress-clad hillsides. The extant buildings go back to the twelfth century, with some elegant seventeenth-century additions in the entrance and courtyards, and were in use from their foundation until 1900, first by Benedictines, then Cistercians. It was one of the Cistercian monks, Pierre de Castelnau, whose murder as papal legate set off the Albigensian Crusade against the Cathars in 1208.

Visits to the restored abbey are only possible on a **guided tour** (daily: 10am–noon & 2–4pm on the hour; €9). Star features include the cloister, with its marble pillars and giant wisteria, the church itself, some fine ironwork and a rose garden. The stained glass in the windows of the lay brothers' dormitory consists of fragments from churches in north and eastern France damaged in World War I.

Just south of Narbonne, the **Étang de Bages et de Sigean** forms a large lagoon frequently visited by flamingos. A scenic drive leads out over the *étang* to the village of **Bages**. It's a notably arty community, and some houses feature unusually decorous ceramic drainpipes. From Bages the road continues south along the edge of the *étang* to **PEYRIAC-DE-MER** and the **Réserve Africaine Sigean** (9am–4/6.30pm – check website for closing times; €22; Ⓦwww.reserveafricainesigean.fr). This immense (and better than average) drive-through park (no motorcycles) contains over 150 species from Africa and the rest of the world.

The coast: Valras to Gruissan

The coast close to Béziers and Narbonne enjoys the same attributes – and problems – as the rest of the Languedoc shoreline: fantastic sand but not a stitch of shade, and endless tacky development buffeted by a wind that would rip the shell off a tortoise.

For a quick escape from Béziers, you can take a thirty-minute bus ride across the flat vine-covered coastal plain to **VALRAS**, at the mouth of the River Orb, whose old-fashioned family resort status is still just discernible. Further south, St-Pierre and Narbonne-Plage (reachable by bus from Narbonne) are uninspiring, modern resorts, and the only redeeming feature of this stretch of coast is the mini-landscape of the **Montagne de la Clape**, a former island, pine-covered and craggy, and not more than 200m above sea level, despite its name. At its far end the fishing village of **GRUISSAN**, 13km from Narbonne (there are buses), built in concentric rings around the hub of the Tour Barberousse, is the only real place of character left, and it, too, is under assault from developers. Out along the beach, *plages des chalets*, is a section of houses originally built on stilts to keep them clear of the sea, but since the danger of flooding has receded many have now added ground floors.

The one really worthwhile thing to visit near Gruissan is the **Chapelle Notre-Dame-des-Auzils**. It's about 4km up a winding lane into the Montagne and stands in a quiet and highly atmospheric spot in the pine woods. All along the road leading to it are moving **memorials** to the people of Gruissan lost at sea in merchant ships, trawlers and warships, from Haiti to the Greek island of Skiros. If the chapel's open, take a peek inside at the *ex votos* offered by grateful seamen and their families, many of them now painted onto the walls, the originals having been stolen in the 1960s.

Parc Naturel Régional du Haut Languedoc

Embracing Mont Caroux in the east and the Montagne Noire in the west, the **Parc Naturel Régional du Haut Languedoc** is the southernmost extension of the Massif Central. The west, above Castres and Mazamet, is Atlantic in feel and climate, with deciduous forests and lush valleys, while the east is dry, craggy and calcareous. Except in high summer you can have it almost to yourself. Buses serve the **Orb valley** and cross the centre of the park to **La Salvetat** and **Lacaune**, but you really need transport of your own to make the most of it.

Bédarieux to St-Pons: the valleys of the Orb and Jaur

Some 34km north of Béziers, the pleasant if unremarkable town of **BÉDARIEUX** lies on the edge of the park. Served by buses from both Béziers and Montpellier, and by train from Béziers, it makes a good base for entering the park, especially as the bus service continues along the Orb and Jaur valleys to St-Pons beneath the southern slopes of the Monts de l'Espinouse.

The best part of town is to the east of the river, where the tall, crumbly old houses are redolent of a rural France long since vanished in more prosperous areas. You'll find the **tourist office** on place aux Herbes (June–Sept Mon–Sat 9am–noon & 2–6pm, Sun 3–6pm; Oct–May Mon–Fri 9am–noon & 2–6pm, Sat 2–6pm, Sun 3–6pm; ⓣ04.67.95.08.79, ⓦwww.bedarieux.fr). The town's only **hotel**, *Hôtel de l'Orb* (ⓣ04.67.23.35.90, ⓦwww.hotel-orb.com; ❷) is on route de St-Pins, near the station, and there's a municipal **campsite** on boulevard Jean-Moulin (ⓣ04.67.23.30.19; closed Oct to mid-June). The best **restaurant** deal can be had at *Le Rapier*, by the Hôtel de Ville on rue de la République, where a four-course meal including dessert, coffee and wine runs to around €17.

The Orb valley and Mons

Continuing west, the D908 (on the Bédearieux bus route) moves through spectacular scenery, with the peaks of the Monts de l'Espinouse rising up to 1000m on your right. The spa town of **LAMALOU-LES-BAINS**, 8km on, is notably livelier than neighbouring settlements, boasting the attraction of **recuperative springs** where the likes of André Gide and crowned heads of Spain and Morocco soothed their aches and pains. At the west end of the town by the main road, the **cemetery** is an untypically grand necropolis crowned with ornate mausoleums, while the ancient **church** on the north side of town contains carvings left by Mozarab (Christian) refugees from Moorish Spain.

At the village of Colombières, 5km to the west, a path leaves the road to take you up into the **Gorges de Madale**. Here it joins the GR7, which crosses the southern part of the park to Labastide-Rouairoux beyond St-Pons.

Seven or eight kilometres further along the D908 is **MONS**, which features a comfortable B&B, *Manoir le Trivalle* (ⓣ04.67.97.85.56, ⓦwww.monslatrivalle.com; ❺). Some 2km away on the D14, there's a municipal **campsite** mid-April to mid-Sept; ⓣ04.67.97.71.50). From Mons a road climbs 5km up the dramatic Gorges d'Héric to the hamlet of Héric, with the Gorges de l'Orb winding their way southwards back to Béziers along the D14.

Olargues and St-Pons-de-Thomières

Five kilometres after Mons, you reach the medieval village of **OLARGUES**, scrambling up the south bank of the Jaur above its thirteenth-century single-span bridge. The steep twisting streets, presumably almost unchanged since the bridge was built, lead up to a thousand-year-old belfry crowning the top of the hill. With the river and gardens below, the ancient and earth-brown farms on the infant slopes of Mont Caroux beyond, and swifts swirling round the tower in summer, you get a powerful sense of age and history. There's a tiny **tourist office** on rue de la Place near the church (July & Aug daily 9am–1pm & 4–7pm; Sept–June Mon, Tues & Thurs–Sat 9am–noon & 2–5pm; ⓣ04.67.97.71.26, ⓦwww.olargues.org), as well as an old train station now served only by SNCF **buses**. There is a deluxe country **hotel**, the *Domaine de Rieumégé* (ⓣ04.67.97.73.99. ⓦwww.domainederieumege.com; ❻) just outside of town on the St-Pons road, but a better deal the homely *Les Quatr' Farceurs* in rue de la Comporte (ⓣ04.67.97.81.33, ⓦwww.olargues.co.uk; ❸), which also serves huge meals with free-flowing wine for €20. **Campers** should head for *Camping Le Baous*, down by the river (mid-April to mid-Sept; ⓣ04.67.97.71.50).

ST-PONS-DE-THOMIÈRES, 18km further west, is a little larger and noisier: it's on the Béziers–Castres and Béziers–La Salvetat bus routes, as well as the Bédarieux–Mazamet route. This is the "capital" of the park, with the **Maison du Parc** housed in the local **tourist office** (July & Aug Mon–Sat 9.20am–1pm & 2–7pm & Sun 9.30am–1pm; Sept–June Tues–Sat 10am–noon & 2–6pm; ⓣ04.67.97.06.65, ⓦwww.saint-pons-tourisme.com) on place du Forail. Sights include the **cathedral** – a strange mix of Romanesque and classical – and a small and reasonably interesting **Musée de la Préhistoire** (mid-June to Oct daily 10am–noon & 2.30–6pm; Nov to mid-June Wed, Sat & Sun 10am–noon & 2–5pm; €3.50), across the river from the tourist office.

If you need to **stay**, try the basic *Le Somail* (ⓣ04.67.97.00.12, ⓕ04.67.97.05.84; ❷). The municipal **campsite** (ⓣ04.67.97.34.85) is on the main road east to Bédarieux. Deluxe accommodation can be found at the *Bergeries de Ponderach* 1km east of town (ⓣ04.67.97.02.57, ⓦbergeries-ponderach.com; ❽), a luxurious seventeenth-century country estate with a fine **restaurant**. Head north up the D907 and you'll reach the Col du Cabaretou and the stunningly situated *Relais du Cabaretou* (ⓣ04.67.95.31.62, ⓦwww.lecabaretou.com; ❸; closed mid-Jan to mid-Feb), with a *terroir* restaurant serving menus starting at €30. North of here the D907 leads to La Salvetat in the heart of the park.

The park's uplands

The uplands of the park are a wild and little-travelled area, dominated by the towering peak of **Mont Caroux** and stretching west along the ridge of the **Monts de l'Espinouse**. This is prime hiking territory, where thick forest of stunted oak alternates with broad mountain meadows, opening up on impressive vistas. Civilization appears again to the west in the upper Agout valley, where **Fraïsse** and **La Salvetat** have become thriving bases for outdoor recreation, and to the north, at the medieval spa town of **Lacaune**. There's no transport crossing the uplands, but the D180 takes you from Le Poujol-sur-Orb, 2km west of Lamalou-les-Bains, to Mont Caroux and L'Espinouse.

Into the Agout valley

The D180 is the most spectacular way to clinb into the park. Soon after leaving the main highway, you'll pass the **Forêt des Écrivains-Combattants**, named after the French writers who died in World War I. Just above the hamlet of Rosis, the road levels out in a small mountain valley, whose slopes are brilliant yellow with broom in June. Continuing north, the D180 climbs another 12km above deep ravines, offering spectacular views to the summit of **L'Espinouse**. The Col de l'Ourtigas is a good place to stretch your legs and take in the grandeur surrounding you. Here the landscape changes from Mediterranean cragginess to marshy moor-like meadow and big conifer plantations, and the road begins to descend west into the valley of the River Agout. It runs through tiny Salvergues, with plain workers' cottages and a striking fortress-church; Cambon, where the natural woods begin; postcard-pretty **FRAÏSSE-SUR-AGOUT** – where you can **stay** at the homely *Auberge de l'Espinouse* (Ⓣ04.67.95.40.46; Ⓦaubergespinouse.net; ❸) which also has a good *terroir* **restaurant** (May–Nov; menu €17).

Next, you'll reach **LA SALVETAT-SUR-AGOUT**, another attractive mountain town built on a hill above the river, with car-wide streets and houses clad in huge slate tiles, situated between the artificial lakes of La Raviège and Laouzas. It's usually half-asleep except at holiday time, when it becomes a busy outdoor activities centre. With several **campsites**, including *La Blaquière* (June–Aug; Ⓣ04.67.97.61.29, Ⓦwww.blaquiere.fr.st) on allée St-Étienne de Cavall just north of the centre, and the friendly, English-owned *La Pergola* hotel (Ⓣ04.67.97.60.57, Ⓕ04.67.97.56.76; ❷), it's a convenient stopover for the centre of the park. There's a **tourist office** in place des Archers at the top of the hill (Mon–Fri 9am–noon & 2–6pm, Sat & Sun 10am–noon & 2–5pm, Sept–June closed Sun; Ⓣ04.67.97.64.44, Ⓦwww.lasalvetatot.com).

Lacaune

Twenty kilometres further north, **LACAUNE** makes another agreeable stop if you're heading for Castres. Surrounded by rounded wooded heights that stand around the 1000m mark, it's very much a mountain town, one of the centres of Protestant Camisard resistance at the end of the seventeenth century, when its inaccessibility made the region ideal for clandestine worship.

The air is fresh, and the town, though somewhat grey in appearance because of the slates and greyish stucco common throughout the region, is cheerful enough. For a place to **stay**, try *Fusiés*, an erstwhile coaching inn opposite the church on rue de la République (Ⓣ05.63.37.02.03, Ⓦwww.hotelfusies.fr; ❸), offering an old-fashioned class, or the simpler *Hôtel Calas*, a little way up the hill (Ⓣ05.63.37.03.28, Ⓦwww.pageloisirs.com/calas; ❷; closed mid-Dec to mid-Jan), which has a good **restaurant** (menus €11–35). There are **bus** connections most days – not at very convenient times, usually afternoon or very early morning – to Castres, Albi and Bédarieux.

From here to Castres the most agreeable route is along the wooded **Gijou valley**, following the now defunct train track, past minuscule Gijounet and **LACAZE**, where a nearly derelict **château** strikes a picturesque pose in a bend of the river.

Carcassonne and around

Right on the main Toulouse–Montpellier train link, **Carcassonne** couldn't be easier to reach. For anyone travelling through this region it is a must – one of the most dramatic, if also most-visited, towns in the whole of Languedoc. Carcassonne owes its division into two separate "towns" to the wars against the Cathars. Following Simon de Montfort's capture of the town in 1209, its people tried in 1240 to restore their traditional ruling family, the Trencavels. In reprisal King Louis IX expelled them from the **Cité**, only permitting their return on condition they built on the low ground by the River Aude – what would become the **ville basse**.

Arrival and information

Arriving by **train**, you'll find yourself in the *ville basse* on the north bank of the Canal du Midi at the northern limits of the town. To reach the **centre** from the

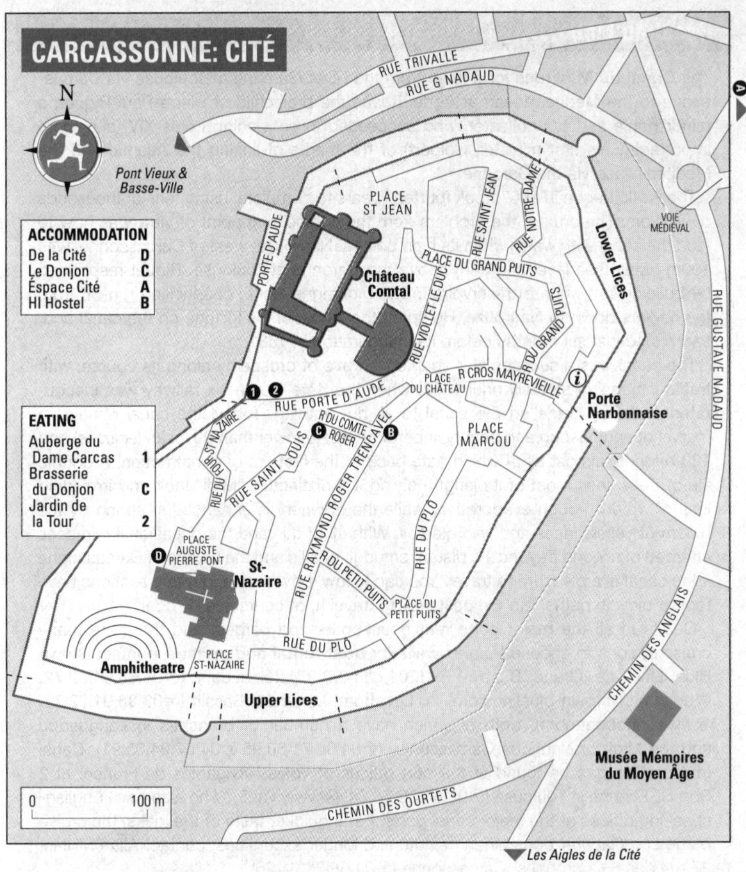

train station, cross the canal bridge by an oval lock, pass the Jardin Chénier and follow rue Clemenceau, which will take you through the central **place Carnot** and out to the exterior boulevard on the southern side of town (a fifteen-minute walk). The **gare routière** (in fact a series of bus stops with no actual building) is on boulevard de Varsovie on the northwest side of town, south of the canal, while the **airport** (ⓣ04.68.71.96.46, ⓦwww.carcassonne.cci.fr) lies just west of the city. An hourly service (15min; €5) leaves from outside the terminal and stops in town at the *gare SNCF*, square Gambetta and the Cité; a taxi to the centre will cost €8–15. If you are planning on visiting other medieval sites in the vicinity of Carcassonne (including the Cathar castles), you might purchase the Intersite Card, which gives you a discounted admission price to many castles and monuments (see p.821 for details).

The **tourist office** is at 15 bd Camille-Pelletan (July, Aug daily 9am–7pm; Sept–June Mon–Sat 9am–6pm, Sun 9am–noon; ⓣ04.68.10.24.30, ⓦwww.carcassonne-tourisme.com), at the end of square Gambetta, where the main road from Montpellier enters the town across the Pont-Neuf and the River Aude. There's also an annexe (daily: June–Sept 9am–6/7pm; Oct–May 9am–5pm) just inside the main gate to the medieval Cité, Porte Narbonnaise. For

Canal du Midi

The **Canal du Midi** runs for 240km from the River Garonne at Toulouse via Carcassonne to the Mediterranean at Agde. It was the brainchild of Pierre-Paul Riquet, a minor noble and tax collector, who succeeded in convincing Louis XIV (and more importantly, his first minister, Colbert) of the merits of linking the Atlantic and the Mediterranean via the Garonne.

The work, begun in 1667, took fourteen years to complete, using tens of thousands of workers. The crux of the problem from the engineering point of view was how to feed the canal with water when its high point at Naurouze, west of Carcassonne, was 190m above sea level and 58m above the Garonne at Toulouse. Riquet responded by building a system of reservoirs in the Montagne Noire, channelling run-off from the heights down to Naurouze. He spent the whole of his fortune on the canal and, sadly, died just six months before its inauguration in 1681.

The canal was a success and sparked a wave of prosperity along its course, with traffic increasing steadily until 1857, when the Sète–Bordeaux railway was inaugurated, reducing trade on the canal to all but nothing. Today, the canal remains a marvel of engineering and beauty, incorporating no fewer than 99 locks (*écluses*) and 130 bridges, almost all of which date back to the first era of construction. A double file of trees lines most of its length, giving it a distinctive "Midi" look and impeding loss of water through evaporation, while the greenery is enhanced in spring by the bloom of yellow irises and wild gladioli. With all of this and the occasional glimpses afforded of a world beyond – a distant smudge of hills and the towers of Carcassonne – the canal is a pleasure to travel. You can follow it by road, and many sections have foot or bicycle paths, but the best way to travel it, of course, is by boat.

Outfits in all the major ports rent houseboats and barges, and there are many cruise options to choose from as well. For **boat rental and cruises**, contact Crown Blue Line, Le Grand Bassin, BP1201, 11492 Castelnaudary (ⓣ04.68.94.52.72, ⓔboathols@crown-blueline.com), or Locaboat, Le Grand Bassin (ⓣ03.86.91.72.72, ⓦwww.locaboat.com), both of which have a number of branches in Languedoc and the Midi; or Nautic in Carcassonne (ⓣ04.68.71.88.95,ⓕ04.67.94.05.91). Canal **information** can be found at the port offices of Voies Navigables de France, at 2 Port St-Étienne in Toulouse (ⓣ05.61.36.24.24, ⓦwww.vnf.fr), who also have English-speaking offices at the major canal ports. For a quicker taste of the locks, the cruise barge *Lou Gabaret* does ninety-minute and longer excursions; contact Allan Millian, 27 rue des 3 Couronnes, Carcassonne (ⓣ04.68.71.61.26).

information on the **Cathars**, consult the Centre National d'Études Cathares, 53 rue de Verdun (ⓣ04.68.47.24.66), while local bookshops offer plenty of Cathar literature and souvenir picture books, some in English.

Accommodation

With the exception of the modern, clean, but frequently booked-up **HI hostel** on rue Trencavel (ⓣ04.68.25.23.16, ⓔcarcassonne@fuaj.org), which offers beds for €14, the price of staying in the Cité can be high. If you don't mind paying, the *Hôtel de la Cité* (ⓣ04.68.71.98.71, ⓦwww.hoteldelacite.com; ❾) offers rooms and suites in the opulent surroundings of a medieval manor house, with a heated swimming pool and stunning views from the battlemented walls. *Le Donjon*, 2 rue Comte-Roger (ⓣ04.68.11.23.00, ⓦwww.hotel-donjon.fr; ❻), is more economical, but still luxurious. *Hôtel Espace Cité*, just outside the main gate at 132 rue Trivalle (ⓣ04.68.25.24.24, ⓦwww.hotel.espacecite.fr; ❸), has all mod cons and efficient service at reasonable prices.

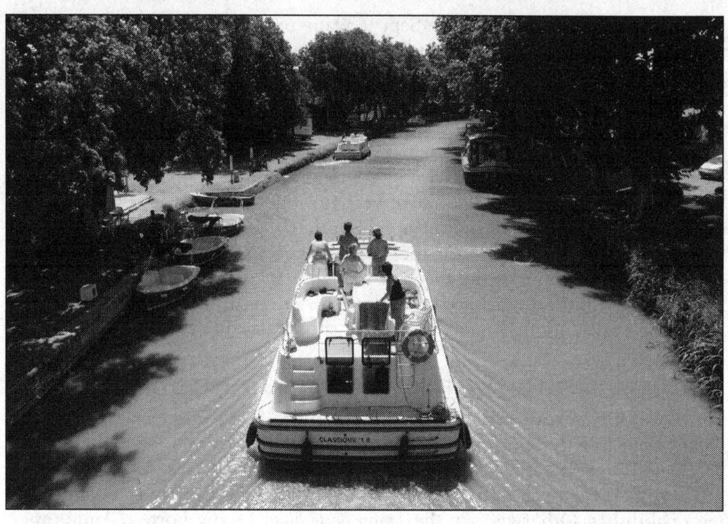

△ Canal du Midi

There are, however, some very well-priced hotels in the *ville basse*. Pride of place goes to the *Hôtel du Soleil Terminus*, at 2 av de Maréchal-Joffre (Ⓣ04.68.25.25.00, Ⓕ04.68.75.53.09; ⑤; closed Dec–Feb), a station-side hotel of decaying steam-age luxury, with a splendid *fin-de-siècle* facade. The *Montségur*, 27 allée d'Iéna (Ⓣ04.68.25.31.41, Ⓦwww.hotelmontsegur.com; ③), is a comfortable nineteenth-century town house, with ample-size rooms, but is not very close to the Cité. A good economy option is the surprisingly well-equipped *La Bastide*, at 81 rue de la Liberté (Ⓣ04.68.71.96.89, Ⓕ04.68.71.36.28; ②).

There's a **campsite**, *Camping de la Cité*, on route St-Hilaire (Ⓣ04.68.25.11.17, Ⓦwww.campeoles.fr; mid-March to Oct), with good shady sites, a shop and some bungalows. Tucked off among parkland to the south of town, it can be reached by local bus (line 8) or by foot (about 20min) from the Cité.

The Cité

The attractions of the well-preserved and lively *ville basse* notwithstanding, what everybody comes for is the **Cité**, the double-walled and turreted fortress that crowns the hill above the River Aude. From a distance it's the epitome of the fairy-tale medieval town. Viollet-le-Duc rescued it from ruin in 1844, and his "too-perfect" restoration has been furiously debated ever since. It is, as you would expect, a real tourist trap. Yet, in spite of the chintzy cafés, arty-crafty shops and the crowds, you'd have to be a very stiff-necked purist not to be moved at all.

To reach the Cité from the *ville basse*, take bus #2 from outside the station, or a *navette* from square Gambetta. Alternatively, you can walk it in under thirty minutes, crossing the Pont-Vieux and climbing rue Barbacane, past the church of St-Gimer to the sturdy bastion of the **Porte d'Aude**. This is effectively the back entrance – the main gate is **Porte Narbonnaise**, round on the east side.

There is no charge for admission to the streets or the grassy *lices* – "lists" – between the walls, though cars are banned from 10am to 6pm. However, to see the inner fortress of the **Château Comtal** and walk the walls, you'll have to join a **guided tour** (daily April–Sept 9.30am–6pm, Oct–March 9.30am–5pm; 35–40min; €6.50). These – including several per day in English from June to September – assume some knowledge of French history, and point out the various phases in the construction of the fortifications, from Roman and Visigothic to Romanesque and the post-Cathar adaptations of the French kings.

In addition to wandering the narrow streets, don't miss the beautiful **church of St-Nazaire** (mid-June to mid-Sept Mon–Fri 9–11.45am & 1.45–6pm, Sun 9–10.45am & 2–4.30pm; rest of year closes at 5pm), towards the southern corner of the Cité at the end of rue St-Louis. It's a serene combination of nave with carved capitals in the Romanesque style and a Gothic choir and transepts, along with with some of the loveliest stained glass in Languedoc. In the south transept is a tombstone believed to belong to Simon de Montfort. You can also climb the **tower** (same hours; €1.50), for spectacular views over the Cité.

Eating, drinking and entertainment

With over fifty **restaurants** within its walls, the Cité is a good place to look for somewhere to eat, though it tends to be expensive. First choice is the *Auberge de Dame Carcas*, 3 place du Château (☎04.68.71.23.23; closed Sun eve, Mon lunch & Feb; menu at €13.50), a traditional bistro offering cassoulet and other regional dishes. Otherwise try the *Jardin de la Tour*, 11 rue Porte d'Aude (open eves only Tues–Sat; closed Nov), with outside tables, or the smart *Brasserie du Donjon*, in the hotel of the same name; both serve *terroir* menus from €20.

There's a much greater variety of affordable places in the *ville basse*: among these *Le Petit Couvert*, at 18 rue de l'Aigle d'Or, has good cheap menus (closed Sun & Mon & March; from €11) and a small street-side terrace. Nearby, at 29 bd Jean-Jaurès, the *Divine Comédie* serves a varied menu of pasta, pizzas and regional dishes in generous portions (closed Sun; from €12). For something more sophisticated, try *L'Écurie* (☎04.68.72.04.04) at 43 bd Barbès, offering local cuisine with adventurous touches, such as roast lamb with thyme and garlic (menus €15–28; closed Sun eve & Wed). For picnic provisions, head for the market on place Carnot (Tues, Thurs & Sat mornings).

Carcassonne hosts two major festivals: the month-long **Festival de la Cité** in July, with dance, theatre and music, the highpoint of which is the mammoth fireworks display on Bastille Day (July 14); and the elaborate medieval pageant, **Les Médiévales**, held in the first fortnight of August.

Castelnaudary

Thirty-six kilometres west of Carcassonne, on the main road from Toulouse, **CASTELNAUDARY** is one of those innumerable French country towns that boast no particular sights but are nonetheless a real pleasure to spend a couple of hours in, having coffee or shopping for a picnic in the market. Today it serves as an important commercial centre for the rolling Lauragais farming country hereabouts, as it once was for the traffic on the Canal du Midi. In fact, the most flattering view of the town is still that from the canal's **Grand Bassin**, which makes it look remarkably like a Greek island town, with its ancient houses climbing the hillside from the water's edge.

In town you'll find some fine old **mansions**, a restored **windmill** and an eighteenth-century **semaphore** tower. However, Castelnaudary's chief claim to fame is as the world capital of **cassoulet**, which, according to tradition, must be made in an earthenware pot from Issel (a *cassolo*) with beans grown in Pamiers or Lavelanet, and cooked in a baker's oven fired with rushes from the Montagne Noire. To try it, go to the **Grand-Hôtel Fourcade**, 14 rue des Carmes

Ⓣ04.68.23.02.08, Ⓔhotelfourcade@ataraxie.fr; closed Jan; ❷), where you can gorge yourself for €15, then sleep off the after-effects by taking a room upstairs. More attractive alternatives for spending the night are the modern *Hôtel du Canal*, 2 av Arnaut-Vidal (Ⓣ04.68.94.05.05, Ⓦwww.hotelducanal.com; ❸), in a shady position beside the canal just west of the Grand Bassin, and the *Hôtel du Centre et du Lauragais* (Ⓣ04.68.23.25.95, Ⓕ04.68.94.01.66; ❹; closed Jan to mid-Feb), a converted nineteenth-century house that's centrally located at 31 cours de la République, close to the post office. The **tourist office** is in Castelnaudary's central Halle aux Grains (April–June & Sept Mon–Sat 9am–12.30pm & 2–6pm; July & Aug Mon–Sat 9am–1pm & 2–7pm, Sun 10am–12.30pm & 3–6pm; Ⓣ04.68.23.05.73).

Minerve

The village of **MINERVE** lies a dozen kilometres north of the Canal du Midi, halfway between Carcassonne and Béziers in the middle of the Minervois wine country. Its location is extraordinary, isolated on an island of rock between the gorges of the Briant and Cesse rivers, the latter of which has cut its course through two enormous tunnels in the rock known as the Ponts Naturels.

The village turned Cathar at the beginning of the thirteenth century, which made it a target for Simon de Montfort's crusade. On July 22, 1210, after a seven-week siege, he took the castle and promptly burnt 180 *parfaits* (or "purified souls"). Nothing remains of the castle save for the ruins of a wall, but there's a memorial to the *parfaits* by the **church** – and, inside, one of the most ancient altars in Gaul, dated 456 AD. If you are looking to stay, head to the *Relais Chantovent* (Ⓣ04.68.91.14.18, Ⓕ04.68.91.81.99; ❹), which is also one of the better places in town to get a meal (menus from €18); alternatively, there's free **camping** in the valley bottom by the cemetery. The **tourist office** (July & Aug daily 10am–noon & 2–6pm; Ⓣ04.68.91.81.43) has information about other accommodation possibilities in the area.

The Montagne Noire

There are two good routes from Carcassonne north into the **Montagne Noire**, which forms the western extremity of the Parc Naturel Régional du Haut Languedoc: Carcassonne–Revel and Carcassonne–Mazamet by the valley of the Orbiel. Neither is served by public transport, but both offer superlative scenery.

The Revel route

The **Revel route** follows the N113 out of Carcassonne, then the D629 through Montolieu (17km) and Saissac. **MONTOLIEU**, semi-fortified and built on the edge of a ravine, has set itself the target of becoming France's secondhand book capital (a conscious imitation of Wales's Hay-on-Wye), with shops overflowing with dog-eared and antiquarian tomes. Drop in at the Librairie Booth, by the bridge over the ravine, for English titles.

SAISSAC, 8km further on, is much more an upland village. Conifers and beech wood, interspersed with patches of rough pasture, surround it, and gardens are terraced down its steep slopes. Remains of towers and fortifications poke out among the ancient houses, and on a spur below the village stand the romantic ruins of its castle and the church of St-Michel.

If you wish to **stay** in the area, try the rather aged *Montagne Noire* (Ⓣ04.68.24.46.36, Ⓕ04.68.24.46.20; ❸) on the road through Saissac. To eat, head to *Au Beau Site* (Ⓣ04.68.24.40.37; closed Sat & Sun Sept–June) in the town below, which has good views and menus from €30. More idyllic accommodation is available north of town at *Domaine du Lampy-Neuf* (Ⓣ04.68.24.46.07, Ⓦwww.domainedulampy-neuf.com; ❸), a *chambre d'hôte* by the banks of the Bassin du Lampy, which also functions as a *gîte*. If you have your own transport, the best **campsite** hereabouts, and an experience in itself, is the *Camping du Bout du Monde* (Ⓣ04.68.94.20.92; all year round), at a beautiful tumbledown farm near Verdun-en-Lauragais, 5km west of Saissac. You camp among the broom at the edge of the woods.

Some 14km west of Saissac on the D103 (or just a few kilometres south-west of the *Bout du Monde* campsite), the ancient village of **ST-PAPOUL**, with its walls and Benedictine **abbey**, makes for a gentle side trip. The abbey is best known for the sculpted corbels on the exterior of the nave, executed by the "Master of Cabestany". These can be viewed at any time without charge, although the interior of the church and its pretty fourteenth-century cloister (daily April–June, Sept, Oct 10–11.30am & 2–5.30pm; July & Aug 10am–6.30pm; Nov–March Sat, Sun & hols 10–11.30am & 2–6.30pm; €3.50) are also worth a peek.

Back on the "main" D629, the road winds down through the forest, past the Bassin de St-Férréol, constructed by Riquet to supply water to the Canal du Midi, and on to **REVEL**. Revel is a *bastide* dating from 1342, featuring an attractive arcaded central square with a superb wooden-pillared medieval *halle* in the middle. Now a prosperous market town (Saturday is market day), it makes an agreeably provincial stopover. The *Auberge du Midi* at 34 bd Gambetta (closed late Nov to early Dec; Ⓣ05.61.83.50.50, Ⓦwww.logis-de-france.fr; ❷) is set in a refined old nineteenth-century mansion, and also has the town's best restaurant (menus €29–43). Close by at 7 rue de Taur, you'll find the *Commanderie Hôtel* (05.34.66.11.24; closed part Feb, part June, part Sept; ❸), a good second choice, with an old timber-frame facade and a remodelled interior.

Lastours and the valley of the Orbiel

The alternative route from Carcassonne into the Montagne Noire takes you through the region known as the **Cabardès**. Cut by the deep ravines of the Orbiel and its tributary streams, it's covered with Mediterranean scrub lower down and forests of chestnut and pine higher up. The area is extremely poor and depopulated, with rough stone villages and hamlets crouching in the valleys. Until relatively recently, its people lived off beans and chestnut flour and the meat from their pigs, and worked in the region's copper, iron, lead, silver and gold mines. Nothing now remains of that tradition save for the gold mine at Salsigne, a huge and unsightly open pit atop a bleak windswept plateau.

The most memorable site in the **Orbiel valley** is the **Châteaux de Lastours** (Feb, March, Nov & Dec Sat, Sun & hols 10am–5pm; April–June & Sept daily 10am–6pm; July & Aug daily 9am–8pm; Oct daily 10am–5pm; €4), the most northerly of the Cathar castles (see p.821), 16km north of Carcassonne. As the name suggests, there is more than one castle – four in fact, their ruined keeps jutting superbly from a sharp ridge of scrub and cypress that plunges to rivers on both sides. The two oldest castles, Cabaret (mid-eleventh century) and Surdespine (1153), fell into de Montfort's hands in 1211, after their lords had given shelter to the Cathars. The other two, Tour Régine and Quertinheux, were added after 1240, when the site became royal property, and a garrison was maintained here as late as the Revolution. Today, despite their ruined state, they look as impregnable and beautiful as ever. A path winds up from the roadside, bright in early summer with iris, cistus, broom and numerous other flowers.

About 7km upriver from Lastours, the road and river divide. The left fork leads to the village of **Mas-Cabardès**, hunkered down defensively in the river bottom. The right goes to **Roquefère**, whose ancient château hosts summertime theatre. From here a steep, serpentine road winds up through magnificent scenery to the tiny hamlet of **Cupservies**, balanced on the edge of a sudden and deep ravine where the Rieutort stream drops some 90m into the bottom. A couple of kilometres further, by the crossroads at **Caninac**, there's a tenth-century chapel, **St-Sernin**, in the middle of the woods. To get here without transport, there's a marked footpath from Roquefère, which then returns via Labastide-Esparbairenque (a 4hr 30min round trip).

Toulouse and western Languedoc

With its sunny, cosmopolitan charms, **Toulouse** is a very accessible kick-off point for any destination in the southwest of France. Of the immediately surrounding places, **Albi**, with its highly original cathedral and comprehensive collection of Toulouse-Lautrec paintings is the number-one priority. Once you've made it that far, it's worth the extra hop to the well-preserved medieval town of **Cordes**. West of Toulouse the land opens up into the broad plains of the **Gers**, a sleepy and rather dull expanse of wheat fields and rolling hills. Those in search of a solitary little-visited France will enjoy its uncrowded monuments, especially lovers of rich *terrines* and Armagnac.

Toulouse

TOULOUSE, with its beautiful historic centre, is one of the most vibrant and metropolitan provincial cities in France. This is a transformation that has come about since World War II, under the guidance of the French state, which has poured in money to make Toulouse the think-tank of high-tech industry and a sort of premier trans-national Euroville. Long an **aviation** centre – St-Exupéry and Mermoz flew out from here on their pioneering airmail flights over Africa and the Atlantic in the 1920s – Toulouse is now home to Aérospatiale, the driving force behind Concorde, Airbus and the Ariane space rocket. The national Space Centre, the European shuttle programme, the leading aeronautical schools, the frontier-pushing electronics industry – it's all happening in Toulouse, whose 110,000 students make it second only to Paris as a **university** centre. But it's not to the burgeoning suburbs of factories, labs, shopping and housing complexes that all these people go for their entertainment, but to the old **Ville Rose** – pink not only in its brickwork, but also in its politics.

This is not the first flush of pre-eminence for Toulouse. From the tenth to the thirteenth centuries the counts of Toulouse controlled much of southern

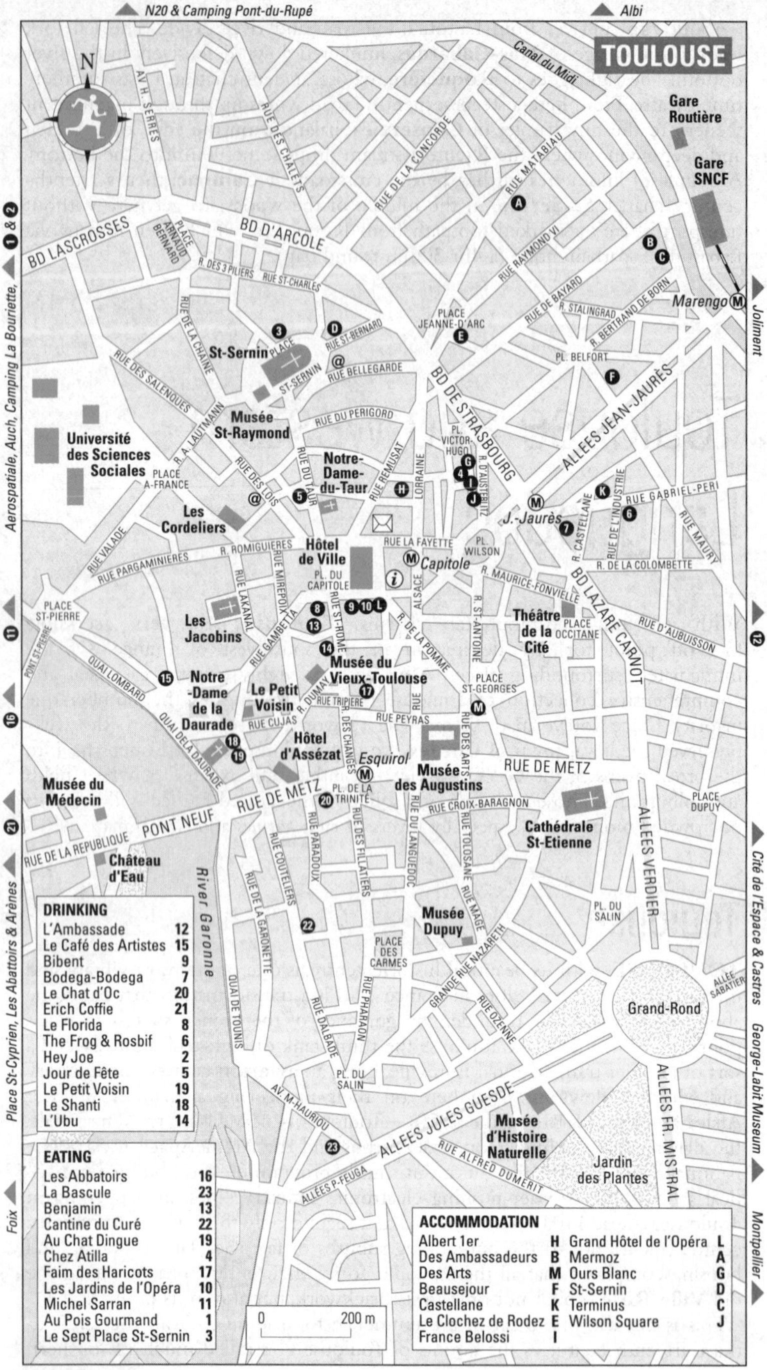

TOULOUSE
N20 & Camping Pont-du-Rupé
Albi
Aerospatiale, Auch, Camping La Bouriette, 1 & 2
Jolimont
12
Cité de l'Espace & Castres
George-Labit Museum
Montpellier
Foix
Place St-Cyprien, Les Abattoirs & Arènes
11
16
21
Canal du Midi
Gare Routière
Gare SNCF
Marengo
BD LASCROSSES
BD D'ARCOLE
PLACE ARNAUD BERNARD
AV H. SERRES
RUE DES CHALETS
RUE DE LA CONCORDE
RUE MATABIAU
RUE RAYMOND VI
RUE DE BAYARD
R. STALINGRAD
R. BERTRAND DE BORN
PLACE JEANNE-D'ARC
PL. BELFORT
ALLEES JEAN-JAURÈS
BD DE STRASBOURG
R. DES 3 PILIERS
RUE ST-CHARLES
RUE DE LA CHAINE
RUE DES SALENQUES
St-Sernin
PLACE ST-SERNIN
RUE ST-BERNARD
RUE BELLEGARDE
RUE DU PERIGORD
Musée St-Raymond
Université des Sciences Sociales
R. A. LAUTMANN
PLACE A-FRANCE
RUE DES LOIS
RUE DU TAUR
Notre-Dame-du-Taur
RUE REMUSAT
LORRAINE
PL. VICTOR-HUGO
R. D'AUSTERLITZ
J.-Jaurès
R. CASTELLANE
RUE DE L'INDUSTRIE
RUE GABRIEL-PERI
RUE MAURY
R. DE LA COLOMBETTE
Les Cordeliers
RUE VALADE
RUE PARGAMINIERES
R. ROMIGUIERES
Hôtel de Ville
RUE LA FAYETTE
PL. WILSON
Capitole
PL. DU CAPITOLE
ALSACE
RUE MIREPOIX
RUE LAKANAL
PLACE ST-PIERRE
Les Jacobins
RUE GAMBETTA
RUE ST-ROME
R. DE LA POMME
R. MAURICE-FONVIELLE
R. ST-ANTOINE
Théâtre de la Cité
PLACE OCCITANE
BD LAZARE CARNOT
RUE D'AUBUISSON
PONT ST-PIERRE
QUAI LOMBARD
Notre-Dame de la Daurade
Le Petit Voisin
Musée du Vieux-Toulouse
R. DUMAY
RUE TRIPIERE
RUE CUJAS
RUE PEYRAS
PLACE ST-GEORGES
QUAI DE LA DAURADE
Hôtel d'Assézat
R. DES CHANGES
Esquirol
Musée des Augustins
RUE DES ARTS
RUE DE METZ
Musée du Médecin
PONT NEUF
PL. DE LA TRINITÉ
RUE CROIX-BARAGNON
PLACE DUPUY
ALLEES VERDIER
RUE DE LA REPUBLIQUE
Château d'Eau
River Garonne
RUE COUTELIERS
RUE PARADOUX
RUE DES FILLATIERS
RUE DU LANGUEDOC
RUE TOLOSANE
Cathédrale St-Etienne
RUE DE LA GARONETTE
RUE MAGE
Musée Dupuy
PL. DU SALIN
PLACE DES CARMES
GRANDE RUE NAZARETH
RUE OZENNE
QUAI DE TOUNIS
RUE DALBADE
RUE PHARAON
Grand-Rond
ALLEE SABATIER
AV. M-HAURIOU
PL. DU SALIN
ALLEES JULES GUESDE
Musée d'Histoire Naturelle
RUE ALFRED DUMERIT
Jardin des Plantes
ALLEES FR. MISTRAL
ALLÉES P-FEUGA
0 200 m
DRINKING
L'Ambassade 12
Le Café des Artistes 15
Bibent 9
Bodega-Bodega 7
Le Chat d'Oc 20
Erich Coffie 21
Le Florida 8
The Frog & Rosbif 6
Hey Joe 2
Jour de Fête 5
Le Petit Voisin 19
Le Shanti 18
L'Ubu 14
EATING
Les Abbatoirs 16
La Bascule 23
Benjamin 13
Cantine du Curé 22
Au Chat Dingue 19
Chez Atilla 4
Faim des Haricots 17
Les Jardins de l'Opéra 10
Michel Sarran 11
Au Pois Gourmand 1
Le Sept Place St-Sernin 3
ACCOMMODATION
Albert 1er H
Des Ambassadeurs B
Des Arts M
Beausejour F
Castellane K
Le Clochez de Rodez E
France Belossi I
Grand Hôtel de l'Opéra L
Mermoz A
Ours Blanc G
St-Sernin D
Terminus C
Wilson Square J

France. They maintained the most resplendent court in the land, renowned especially for its troubadours, the poets of courtly love, whose work influenced Petrarch, Dante and Chaucer and thus the whole course of European poetry. The arrival of the hungry northern French nobles of the Albigensian Crusade put an end to that; in 1271 Toulouse became crown property.

Arrival and information

The **gare SNCF** (better known to locals as **gare Matabiau**), and **gare routière** (ⓣ05.61.61.67.67), stand side by side in boulevard Pierre-Sémard on the bank of the tree-lined Canal du Midi. This is where you might find yourself if you arrive by air as well – the **airport shuttle** (every 20min; 20min; €4) puts you down at the bus station (with stops in allées Jean-Jaurès and at place Jeanne-d'Arc). It's also the best spot to aim for if you're in a car: leave the **boulevard périphérique** at exit 15.

To reach the city centre from the train station takes just five minutes by **métro** to Capitole (€1.30, covering one hour's transport by métro and Tisseo-Connex city buses within the city centre), or twenty minutes on foot. Turn left out of the station, cross the canal and head straight down allées Jean-Jaurès, through place Wilson and on into place du Capitole, the city's main square. Just before it lie the shady and much-frequented gardens of the square Charles-de-Gaulle, where the main **tourist office** (June–Sept Mon–Sat 9am–7pm, Sun 10am–1pm & 2–6.15pm; Oct–May Mon–Fri 9am–6pm, Sat 9am–12.30pm & 2–6pm, Sun 10am–12.30pm & 2–5pm; ⓣ05.61.11.02.22, ⓦwww.ot-toulouse.fr) is housed in a sixteenth-century tower that has been restored to look like a castle keep; the Capitole métro stop is right outside.

The top guides to **what's on** in and around the city – and usually there is a lot, from opera to cinema – are the weekly listings magazines *Toulouse Hebdo* (€0.50) and *Flash* (€1). More highbrow interests are covered in the free monthly *Toulouse Culture*, available from the tourist office, among other places.

Accommodation

The best place to **stay** is in the city centre, where there are a number of excellent-value hotels, as well as many more upmarket establishments. The area around the train station, though charmless and still retaining some of its red-light seediness, has a few acceptable options. There's no hostel, but there are a number of accommodation centres for visitors who plan on staying for more than a few days: the CRIJ (ⓣ05.61.21.20.20, ⓔcrij-tlse.org) can provide details. The closest **campsite** is *Camping de Rupé*, chemin du Pont du Rupé (ⓣ05.61.70.07.35; bus #59, stop "Rupé").

Hotels

Albert 1er 8 rue Rivals ⓣ05.61.21.17.91, ⓦwww.hotel-albert1.com. This small, comfortable and good-value establishment is set in a quiet side street just off the Capitole and close to the central market in place Victor-Hugo. Special weekend deals are sometimes available. ❺

Des Ambassadeurs 68 rue Bayard ⓣ05.61.62.65.84, ⓦwww.hotel-des-ambassadeurs.com. Very friendly little hotel run by a young couple, just down from the station. All rooms have TV, en-suite bath and phone – a surprisingly good deal given the price. ❷

Des Arts 1bis rue Cantegril ⓣ05.61.23.36.21, ⓕ05.61.12.22.37. On a corner diagonally opposite the Augustins museum, this is a top choice in the lower price range, with large, quirky rooms (some with a fireplace) in a superb old building. ❷

Beausejour 4 rue Caffarelli ⓣ & ⓕ05.61.62.77.59. Basic, but dirt-cheap and with a great copper-balconied facade and soundproofed rooms. This is the best of the hotels in the slightly dodgy but engagingly gritty neighbourhood around place de Belfort. ❶

Castellane 17 rue Castellane ⓣ05.61.62.18.82, ⓦwww.castellanehotel.com. A cheerful hotel with a wide selection of room types and sizes – most of which are bright and quiet. One of the few wheelchair-accessible hotels in this price range. ❹

Le Clochez de Rodez 14 de Jeanne-d'Arc ⓣ05.61.62.42.92, ⓦwww.leclochezderodez.com. Comfortable and central, with secure parking and all mod cons. Despite its size, it exudes a very personal hospitality. ❺

France Belossi 5 rue d'Austerlitz ⓣ05.61.21.88.24, ⓦwww.hotel-france-toulouse.com. One of the better options in the rue d'Austerlitz/place Wilson area. Clean rooms with cable television and air conditioning. ❸

Grand Hôtel de l'Opéra 1 place du Capitole ⓣ05.61.21.82.66, ⓦwww.grand-hotel-opera.com. The grand dame of Toulouse's hotels presides over the place du Capitole in the guise of a seventeenth-century convent. The rich decor, peppered with antiques and artwork, underlines the atmosphere of sophistication. Has a fitness centre for working off that second helping of foie gras. ❾

Mermoz 50 rue de Matabiau ⓣ05.61.63.04.04, ⓦwww.hotel-mermoz.com. Immaculate, comfortable rooms in a 1930s Art Deco-style hotel close to the station. Also has wheelchair access and a parking garage. ❼

Ours Blanc 25 place de Victor-Hugo ⓣ05.61.21.62.40, ⓦwww.hotel-ours-blanc.fr. Right by the covered market and steps from the Capitole, this welcoming hotel is one of the city's better bargains. The entire building has recently been redecorated and each room has TV, a/c, Wi-Fi and telephone, as well as a private bath. ❹

St-Sernin 2 rue St-Bernard ⓣ05.61.21.73.08, ⓕ05.61.22.49.61. Well-renovated old hotel in one of the best districts of the old town, around the basilica – close to all the action, but far enough away to provide peace in the evening. ❸

Terminus 13 bd Bonrepos ⓣ05.61.62.44.78, ⓦwww.terminus31.com. This old three-star station-side hotel has large, reconditioned rooms that make it worth the price, and there are special room prices for off-season weekends. Parking and buffet breakfast (€8) available, the only drawback being that the hotel is rather far from the sights. ❹

Wilson Square12 rue d'Austerlitz ⓣ05.61.21.67.57, ⓦwww.hotel-wilson.com. Clean and well-kept place at the top end of rue Austerlitz, with TV, air conditioning and a lift. Also has a great patisserie on street level. ❹

The City

The part of the city you'll want to see forms a rough hexagon clamped round a bend in the wide, brown River Garonne and contained within a ring of nineteenth-century boulevards, including Strasbourg, Carnot and Jules-Guesde. The Canal du Midi, which here joins the Garonne on its way from the Mediterranean to the Atlantic, forms a further ring around this core. Old Toulouse is effectively quartered by two nineteenth-century streets: the long shopping street, **rue d'Alsace-Lorraine/rue du Languedoc**, which runs north–south; and **rue de Metz**, which runs east–west onto the Pont-Neuf and across the Garonne. It's all very compact and easily walkable, and the city's métro is of little use for getting to sites of interest.

In addition to the general pleasure of wandering the streets, there are three very good museums and some real architectural treasures in the churches of St-Sernin and Les Jacobins and in the magnificent Renaissance town houses – *hôtels particuliers* – of the merchants who grew rich on the woad-dye trade. This formed the basis of the city's economy from the mid-fifteenth to the mid-sixteenth century, when the arrival of indigo from the Indian colonies wiped it out.

Place du Capitole is the centre of gravity for the city's social life. Its smart cafés throng with people at lunchtime and in the early evening, when the dying sun flushes the pink facade of the big town hall opposite. This is the scene of a mammoth Wednesday **market** for food, clothes and junk, and a smaller organic food market on Tuesday and Saturday mornings. From place du Capitole, a labyrinth of narrow medieval streets radiates out to the town's other squares, such as place Wilson, the more intimate place St-Georges, the delightful triangular place de la Trinité and place St-Étienne, in front of the cathedral.

For green space, you have to head for the sunny banks of the Garonne or the lovely formal gardens of the **Grand-Rond** and **Jardin des Plantes** in the southeast corner of the centre. A less obvious but attractive alternative is the towpath of the Canal du Midi; the best place to join it is a short walk southeast of the Jardin des Plantes, by the neo-Moorish pavilion of the Georges-Labit Museum, which houses a good collection of Egyptian and Oriental art.

The Capitole and the hôtels particuliers

Occupying the whole of the eastern side of the eponymous square, the **Capitole** has been the seat of Toulouse's city government since the twelfth century. In medieval times it housed the *capitouls*, who made up the oligarchic and independent city council from which its name derives. This institution, under the name of *consulat*, was common to other Languedoc towns and may have been the inspiration for England's first parliamentary essays, often attributed to Simon de Montfort, son of the general who became familiar with these parts in the course of his merciless campaigns against the Cathar heretics in the early 1200s. Today, these medieval origins are disguised by an elaborate pink and white classical facade (1750) of columns and pilasters, from which the flags of Languedoc, the Republic and the European Union are proudly flown. If there are no official functions taking place, you can have a peek inside (Mon–Fri 9am–5pm, Sat 9am–1pm; free) at the Salle des Illustres and a couple of other rooms covered in flowery, late nineteenth-century murals and some more subdued Impressionist works by Henri Martin.

Many of the old *capitouls* built their **hôtels** in the dense web of now mainly pedestrianized streets round about. The material they used was almost exclusively the flat Toulousain brick, whose rosy colour gives the city its nickname of *Ville Rose*. It is an attractive material, lending a small-scale, detailed finish to otherwise plain facades, and setting off admirably any wood- or stonework. Although many of the *hôtels* survive, they are rarely open to the public, so you have to do a lot of nonchalant sauntering into courtyards to get a look at them. The best known, open to visitors thanks to its very handsome Bemberg collection of paintings, is the **Hôtel d'Assézat**, at the river end of rue de Metz (Tues–Sun 10am–6pm, Thurs until 9pm; €4.60, plus €3 for temporary exhibits, Ⓦwww.fondation-bemberg.fr). Started in 1555 under the direction of Nicolas Bachelier, Toulouse's most renowned Renaissance architect, and never finished, it is a sumptuous palace of brick and stone, sporting columns of the three classical orders of Doric, Ionic and Corinthian, plus a lofty staircase tower surmounted by an octagonal lantern. The paintings within include works by Cranach the Elder, Tintoretto and Canaletto as well as moderns like Pissarro, Monet, Gauguin, Vlaminck, Dufy and a roomful of Bonnards. From April to October there's also a *salon de thé* in the covered entrance gallery.

Other fine houses exist just to the south: on rue Pharaon, in place des Carmes, on rue du Languedoc and on rue Dalbade, where the Hôtel Clary (also known as de Pierre) at no. 25 is unusual for being built of stone. To the north, it's worth wandering along rue St-Rome, rue des Changes, rue de la Bourse and rue du May, where the Hôtel du May at no. 7 houses the **Musée du Vieux-Toulouse** (Tues–Sun 10am–12.30pm & 1.30–6pm; €2.20), a rather uninspiring museum of the city's history.

The Musée des Augustins, the cathedral and the riverside

Right at the junction of rue de Metz and rue d'Alsace-Lorraine stands the **Musée des Augustins** (Thurs–Tues 10am–6pm, Wed 10am–9pm; Ⓦwww.augustins.org; €3). Outwardly unattractive, the nineteenth-century building incorporates two surviving cloisters of an Augustinian priory (one now restored as a monastery garden) and contains outstanding collections of Romanesque and medieval sculpture, much of it saved from the now-vanished churches of Toulouse's golden age. Many of the pieces form a fascinating, highly naturalistic display of contemporary manners and fashions: merchants with forked beards touching one another's arms in a gesture of familiarity, and the Virgin represented as a pretty, bored young mother looking away from the Child who strains to escape her hold.

To the south of the museum, just past the Chambre de Commerce, the pretty **rue Croix-Baragnon**, full of smart shops and galleries, opens at its eastern end onto the equally attractive **place St-Étienne**, which boasts the city's oldest fountain, the Griffoul (1546). Behind it stands the lopsided **cathedral of St-Étienne**, whose construction was spread over so many centuries that it makes no architectural sense at all. But there's ample compensation in the quiet and elegant streets of the quarter immediately to the south, and in the **Musée Paul-Dupuy**, a few minutes' walk away along rue Tolosane and rue Mage at 13 rue de la Pléau (daily 10am–5pm; June–Sept until 6pm; €3), which has a beautifully displayed and surprisingly interesting collection of clocks, watches, clothes, pottery and furniture from the Middle Ages to the present day, as well as a good display of religious art.

If you follow the rue de Metz westward from the Musée des Augustins, you come to the **Pont-Neuf** – begun in 1544, despite its name – where you can cross over to the **St-Cyprien quarter** on the left bank of the Garonne. At the end of the bridge on the left, an old water tower, erected in 1822 to supply clean water to the city's drinking fountains, now houses the **Galerie Municipale du Château d'Eau** (Tues–Sun 1–7pm; free), a small but influential photography exhibition space and information centre, with frequently changing exhibitions. Next door in the old hospital buildings, there's a small **medical museum** (Mon–Sat 2–6pm; free), housing a selection of surgical instruments and pharmaceutical equipment.

But the star of the left bank is undoubtedly Toulouse's new contemporary art gallery, **Les Abattoirs**, at 76 allées Charles-de-Fitte (Tues–Sun 11am–7pm; €8, free first Sun of month; Ⓦ www.lesabattoirs.org). This splendid venue is not only one of France's best contemporary art museums, but an inspiring example of urban regeneration, constructed in a vast brick abattoir complex dating from 1828. The space itself is massive, with huge chambers perfectly suited to display even the largest canvases. The collection comprises over 2000 works (painting, sculpture, mixed- and multimedia) by artists from 44 countries, but the most striking piece is undoubtedly Picasso's massive 14m by 20m theatre backdrop, *La dépouille du Minotaure en costume d'Arlequin*, painted in 1936 for Romain Rolland's *Le 14 Juillet*, which towers over the lower gallery.

The churches of Les Jacobins and St-Sernin

A short distance west of place du Capitole, on rue Lakanal, you can't miss the **church of the Jacobins**. Constructed in 1230 by the Order of Preachers (Dominicans) which St Dominic had founded here in 1216 to preach against Cathar heretics, the church is a huge fortress-like rectangle of unadorned brick, buttressed – like Albi cathedral – by plain brick piles, quite unlike what you'd normally associate with Gothic architecture. The interior is a single space divided by a central row of ultra-slim pillars from whose minimal capitals spring an elegant splay of vaulting ribs – 22 from the last in line – like palm fronds. Beneath the altar lie the bones of the philosopher St Thomas Aquinas. On the north side, you step out into the calming hush of a **cloister** with a formal array of box trees and cypress in the middle, and its adjacent art **exhibition hall** (daily 10am–7pm; €3). Nearby, at the corner of rue Gambetta and rue Lakanal, poke your nose into the stone-galleried courtyard of the **Hôtel de Bernuy**, one of the city's most elaborate Renaissance houses.

From the north side of place du Capitole, **rue du Taur** leads past the belfry wall of **Notre-Dame-du-Taur**, whose diamond-pointed arches and decorative motifs represent the acme of Toulousain bricklaying skills, to place St-Sernin. Here you're confronted with the largest Romanesque church in France, the **basilica of St-Sernin**, begun in 1080 to accommodate the passing hordes of Santiago pilgrims, and one of the loveliest examples of its genre. Its most striking external features are the octagonal brick belfry with rounded and pointed arches, diamond lozenges, colonnettes and mouldings picked out in stone, and the apse with nine radiating chapels. Entering from the south, you pass under the Porte Miégeville, whose twelfth-century carvings launched the influential Toulouse school of sculpture. Inside, the great high nave rests on brick piers, flanked by double aisles of diminishing height, surmounted by a gallery running right around the building. The small fee for the **ambulatory** (daily 10am–6pm; €2) is well worth it for the exceptional eleventh-century marble reliefs on the end wall of the choir and for the extraordinary wealth of reliquaries in the spacious **crypt**.

Right outside St-Sernin is the city's archeological museum, **Musée St-Raymond** (June–Sept 10am–6pm; Oct–May 10am–5pm; €3), housed in what remains of the block built for poor students of the medieval university and containing a large collection of objects ranging from prehistoric to Roman, as well as an excavated necropolis in the basement. On Sunday mornings the whole of place St-Sernin turns into a marvellous, teeming **flea market**.

The suburbs

To see something of the modern face of Toulouse, it's necessary to venture out into the suburbs, where you can visit a high-tech amusement park and a very specialized but surprisingly interesting aircraft assembly plant. The first of these is the **Cité de l'Espace** (early-Feb to late April daily 9am–5/6pm; late April–Aug daily 9am–5/6/7pm; Sept to early Jan Tues–Sun 9am–5/6pm; Ⓦwww.cite-espace.com; €18.50, children under 5 €12), beside exit 17 of the A612 *périphérique* on the road to Castres, or take bus #19 from place Marengo (school hols only). The theme is space and space exploration, including satellite communications, space probes and, best of all, the opportunity to walk inside a mock-up of the Mir space station – fascinating, but absolutely chilling. Many of the exhibits are interactive and, though it's a bit on the pricey side, you could easily spend a half-day here, especially if you've got children in tow.

In 1970 Toulouse became home to **Aérospatiale**, which, along with the aerospace industries of Germany, Britain and Spain, now manufactures Airbus passenger jets. The planes are assembled, painted and tested in a vast hangar, L'Usine Clément Ader, before taking their maiden flights from next-door Blagnac airport. Members of the public are allowed inside the plant on a highly informative guided tour (July & Aug contact the tourist office, Sept–June call Ⓣ05.61.18.06.01, Ⓦwww.taxiway.fr; €14; normally in French), but you need to apply at least two weeks before with your passport details, or a few days before for citizens of EU-member countries. After a brief bus tour round the site and a short PR film, you climb high above the eerily quiet assembly bays where just one hundred people churn out five planes a week, ably assisted by scores of computerized robots. Look out for the latest Airbus, the A380, a two-storey superliner which dwarfs even the Jumbo.

Eating, drinking and entertainment

Regular daytime **café-lounging** can be pursued around the popular student-arty hangout of place Arnaud-Bernard, while place du Capitole is the early evening meeting place. Place St-Georges remains popular, though its clientele is no longer convincingly bohemian, and place Wilson also has its enthusiasts.

There are several good areas to look for a place to **eat**. One of the most attractive and fashionable, with a wide choice, is the rue de la Colombette, in the St-Aubin district just across boulevard Carnot. Another is place Arnaud-Bernard and the tiny adjacent place des Tiercerettes, just north of St-Sernin. Rue du Taur has a number of Vietnamese places and sandwich bars, and the narrow rue du May has a crêperie, pasta place and restaurant. For lunch, however, there is no surpassing the row of five or six small restaurants jammed in line on the mezzanine floor above the gorgeous **food market** in place Victor-Hugo, off boulevard de Strasbourg. They only function at lunchtime, are all closed on Monday, and cost as little as €12 for market-fresh menus. Both food and atmosphere are perfect.

Cafés

Le Café des Artistes place de la Daurade. Lively young café overlooking the Garonne. A perfect spot to watch the sun set on warm summer evenings, as floodlights pick out the brick buildings along the *quais*.

Bibent 5 place du Capitole. On the south side of the square, this is Toulouse's most distinguished café, with exuberant plasterwork, marble tables and cascading chandeliers.

Le Florida 12 place du Capitole. Relaxed café with a retro air. One of the most pleasant places to hang out on the central square.

Jour de Fête 43 rue de Taur. Trendy tearoom and brasserie with a small street-side patio. Friendly service and a young university-set crowd.

Le Shanti 21 rue Peyrolières. A funky "Indian" tea house where you can enjoy a narghile (Arab water-pipe).

Restaurants

Les Abbatoirs 97 allée Charles-de-Fitte ⓣ05.61.42.04.95. Family-run for two generations, this is one of the last of the traditional slaughter-house-side meat emporia, with a reputation for top-of-the-line intestinal delicacies, such as calves' brains and pig's feet. Menus from €18. Closed Sun, Mon & Aug.

La Bascule 14 av Maurice-Hauriou ⓣ05.61.52.09.51. A Toulouse institution. Its chromey interior is pure Art Deco and the food well preprared and presented. The menu includes regional dishes like cassoulet, *foie de canard* and oysters from the Bay of Arcachon. Menus from €20. Closed Sun.

Benjamin 7 rue des Gestes ⓣ05.61.22.92.66. A long-standing institution for economical *terroir* food; service is pleasant and professional, although the atmosphere is somewhat anonymous. The wide selection of duck-based lunch and dinner menus are €11–23. Open daily.

Cantine du Curé 2 rue H.-de-Grosse. Cosy *terroir* restaurant, housed in a small but atmospheric old building, complete with wooden beams, by the entrance to the Dalbade church. One of the two tiny dining areas has a fireplace. Evening menu from €28. Closed Sun eve & Mon.

Au Chat Dingue 40bis rue Peyrolières. Small, hip bistro with cool blue decor across from the *Petit Voisin* bar. The selection is not overly imaginative, with a solid southern French base and occasional Italian incursions (usually in the form of pasta). Menus are €18–22, but considerably more à la carte. Closed Sun.

Chez Atilla in the market at place Victor-Hugo. The best of the market restaurants, this no-nonsense lunchtime establishment is also one of Toulouse's best options for seafood – their Spanish *zarzuela* stew is a fish-lover's dream. Menus from €12. Closed Mon & part Aug.

Faim des Haricots 3 rue de Puits Vert ⓣ05.61.22.49.25. Toulouse's newest vegetarian option, with generous all-you-can-eat salad and dessert buffets (both €9), bottomless bowls of soup and a *plat du jour*. Open Mon–Sat lunch & Thurs–Sat dinner; closed first half Aug.

Les Jardins de l'Opéra 1 place du Capitole ⓣ05.61.21.05.56. The *Grand Hôtel*'s restaurant is Toulouse's best and most luxurious. If you fancy a splurge you will pay for it – a basic menu starts at €40 – but the food is outstanding. Closed Sun & Mon lunch & part Aug.

 **Michel Sarran** 21 bd Armand-Duportal ⓣ05.61.12.32.32. Justifiably renowned

gastronomique restaurant, a fifteen-minute walk from the place du Capitole (follow rue des Lois and rue des Salenques to the end, and turn left). Imaginative dishes with a strong Mediterranean streak are served with style and warmth. Menus from €45 at lunch and €95 at dinner. Closed part Aug.

Au Pois Gourmand 3 rue Émile-Heybrard ⓣ05.61.31.95.95. Great location in a riverside nineteenth-century house with a beautiful patio. The quality French cuisine does not come cheap here (menus €22–64), but is of a predictably high standard, and the *carte* presents a pleasant departure from purely regional dishes. Bus #66 or #14 from métro St-Cyprien-République. Closed Sat lunch & Sun.

Le Sept Place St-Sernin 7 place St-Sernin ⓣ05.62.30.05.30. A small house behind the basilica conceals a lively and cheerful restaurant serving inventive and original cuisine with a constantly changing *carte*, followed by dazzling desserts. Menus €18–45. Closed Sat lunch & Sun.

Bars and clubs

L'Ambassade 22 bd de la Gare. Downbeat club where funk and soul rule. Live jazz on Sunday nights. Mon–Fri 7pm–2am, Sat & Sun 7pm–5am.

Bodega-Bodega 1 rue Gabriel-Péri. The old Telegraph newspaper building makes a superb venue for this bar-restaurant, with its hugely popular disco after 10pm. Daily 7pm–2am, till 4am on Sat.

Le Chat d'Oc 7 rue de Metz. Hip bar near the Garonne, attracting a mixed crowd which gets younger as the night progresses. Nightly animations include DJs and occasional live acts. Mon–Fri 7am–2am, Sat 9am–5am.

Erich Coffie 9 rue Joseph-Vié ⓣ05.61.42.04.27. Just west of the river in the quartier St-Cyprien, this is one of the city's liveliest and most enjoyable music bars (food available), with an eclectic music policy. Live bands most evenings. Open Tues–Sat from 10pm.

The Frog & Rosbif 14 rue de l'Industrie. Stop by this friendly British pub, just off boulevard Lazare-Carnot, for a pint of Darktagnan stout, or one of their other excellent home-brews. Quiz nights, football and fish and chips draw a surprisingly international crowd. Mon–Fri & Sun 5.30pm–2am, Sat 2pm–4am. Closed part Aug.

Hey Joe place Héraclès. Popular disco with theme nights on Thursdays. Men pay €8, women get in free; happy hour midnight–1am. Open daily 11pm–5am.

Le Petit Voisin 37 rue Peyrolières. A neighbourhood place, just like the name says, laid-back during the day, and with DJs at night. Open Mon–Fri 7.30am–2am, Sat 8am–4am. Closed mid-Aug.

L'Ubu 16 rue St-Rome ⓣ05.61.23.26.75. Longstanding pillar of the city's dance scene, which remains as popular as ever. Mon–Sat 11pm till dawn.

Film, theatre and live music

Drinking and dancing aside, there's plenty to do at night in Toulouse. Several **cinemas** regularly show *v.o.* films, including: ABC, 13 rue St-Bernard (ⓣ05.61.29.81.00); Cinémathèque, 68 rue de Taur (ⓣ05.62.30.30.10, ⓦwww.lacinemathequedetoulouse.com); Cratere, 95 Grande-Rue St-Michel (ⓣ05.61.52.50.53); and Utopia, 24 rue Montardy (ⓣ05.61.23.66.20, ⓦwww.cinemas-utopia.org). There's also an extremely vibrant **theatre** culture here. The tourist office can give you a full list of venues, which range from the official Théâtre de la Cité, 1 rue Pierre-Baudis (ⓣ05.34.45.05.05, ⓦwww.tnt-cite.com), to the workshop Nouveau Théâtre Jules-Julien, 6 av des Écoles-Jules-Juliens (Mon–Fri 9am–noon & 2–5pm; ⓣ05.61.25.79.92). The larger venues, such as Odyssud, 4 av du Parc Blagnac (ⓣ05.61.71.75.15; bus #66), feature both theatre and **opera**, while the Orchestre National du Capitole has its base in the Halle aux Grains on place Dupuy (ⓣ05.61.99.78.00, ⓦwww.onct.mairie-toulouse.fr). The city's biggest **concert venue** (9000 seats), specializing in rock, is Zénith, at 11 av Raymond Badiou (ⓣ05.62.74.49.49; métro Arènes), while Cave-Poesie at 71 rue de Taur (ⓣ05.61.23.62.00) is home to literary workshops and gatherings of a decidedly bohemian spirit.

Listings

Airport Aéroport Toulouse-Blagnac ⓣ05.61.42.44.00 and 05.24.61.80.00, ⓦwww.toulouse.aeroport.fr; for shuttle bus information ⓣ05.34.60.64.00.

Bicycle rental The municipal bike co-op Movimento (Mon–Fri 8am–7pm, Sat & Sun 10am–7pm; ⓦ movimento.coop), has branches at square Charles-de-Gaulle (opposite the tourist office) and 5 Port Saint-Saveur. Holiday Bikes, 9 bd des Minimes (ⓣ 05.34.25.79.62, ⓔ toulouse@holiday-bikes.com) also has scooters and motorcycles.
Books For English-language books, Books and Mermaides, 3 rue Mirepoix, specializes in secondhand tomes and will exchange, while The Bookshop, 17 rue Lakanal, stocks new titles. There are book markets on Thursday mornings in place Arnaud-Bernard, and all day Saturday in place St-Étienne.
Car rental A2L, 81 bd Déodat-de-Séverac ⓣ 05.61.59.33.99; Avis, *gare SNCF* ⓣ 05.61.63.71.71; Budget, 49 rue Bayard ⓣ 05.61.63.18.18; Europcar, 15 bd Bonrepos ⓣ 05.61.62.52.89; Hertz, *gare SNCF* ⓣ 05.61.62.94.12.
Consulates Canada, 10 rue Jules de Resseguier ⓣ 05.61.52.19.06, ⓔ consulat.canada.toulouse@orange.fr; USA, 25 allées Jean-Jaurès ⓣ 05.34.41.36.50, ⓦ www.amb-usa.fr; the closest British Consulate is in Bordeaux at 353 bd Wilson (ⓣ 05.57.22.21.10).
Gay and lesbian For information contact the gay and lesbian students' group Jules et Julies (Comité des Étudiants, Université du Mirail, 5 allée Machado, 31058) or Gais et Lesbiennes en Marche (ⓣ 06.11.87.38.81, ⓔ gelem@altern.org).
Internet Cyber Media-Net, 19 rue de Lois (Mon–Fri 9am–11.30pm, Sat 10am–midnight), or @fterbug, 12 place St-Sernin (Mon–Fri noon–2am, Sat noon–5am, Sun 2.30–10.30pm).
Pharmacy The Pharmacie de Nuit, 70–76 allées Jean-Jaurès (entry on rue Arnaud-Vidal) is open 8pm–8am.
Police 23 bd de l'Embouchure ⓣ 05.61.12.77.77.
Taxi Capitole ⓣ 05.34.25.02.50; Taxi Radio Toulousain ⓣ 05.61.42.38.38. For taxis to the airport call ⓣ 05.61.30.02.54.

Albi and around

ALBI, 77km and an hour's train ride northeast of Toulouse, is a small industrial town with two unique sights: a museum containing the most comprehensive collection of Toulouse-Lautrec's work (Albi was his birthplace); and one of the most remarkable Gothic cathedrals you'll ever see. Its other claim to fame comes from its association with Catharism; though not itself an important centre, it gave its name – Albigensian – to both the heresy and the crusade to suppress it.

The town hosts three good **festivals** over the course of the year: jazz in May, theatre at the end of June and beginning of July, and classical music at the end of July and beginning of August. During July and August there are also free organ recitals in the cathedral (Wed 5pm & Sun 4pm).

The Town

The **Cathédrale Ste-Cécile** (daily: June–Sept 9am–6.30pm; Oct–May 9am–noon & 2.30–6.30pm; free; entry to choir €1, to treasury €3), begun about 1280, is visible from miles around, dwarfing the town like some vast bulk carrier run aground, the belfry its massive superstructure. The comparison sounds unflattering, and this is not a conventionally beautiful building; it's all about size and boldness of conception. The sheer plainness of the exterior is impressive on this scale, and it's not without interest: arcading, buttressing, the contrast of stone against brick – every differentiation of detail becomes significant. Entrance is through the south portal, by contrast the most extravagant piece of flamboyant-Gothic sixteenth-century frippery. The interior, a hall-like nave of colossal proportions, is dominated by a huge mural of the Last Judgement, believed to be the work of Flemish artists in the late fifteenth century. Above, the vault is covered in richly colourful paintings of sixteenth-century Italian workmanship, while a rood screen, delicate as lace, shuts off the choir: Adam makes a show of covering himself, Eve strikes a flaunting model's pose beside the central doorway, and the rest of the screen is adorned with countless statues.

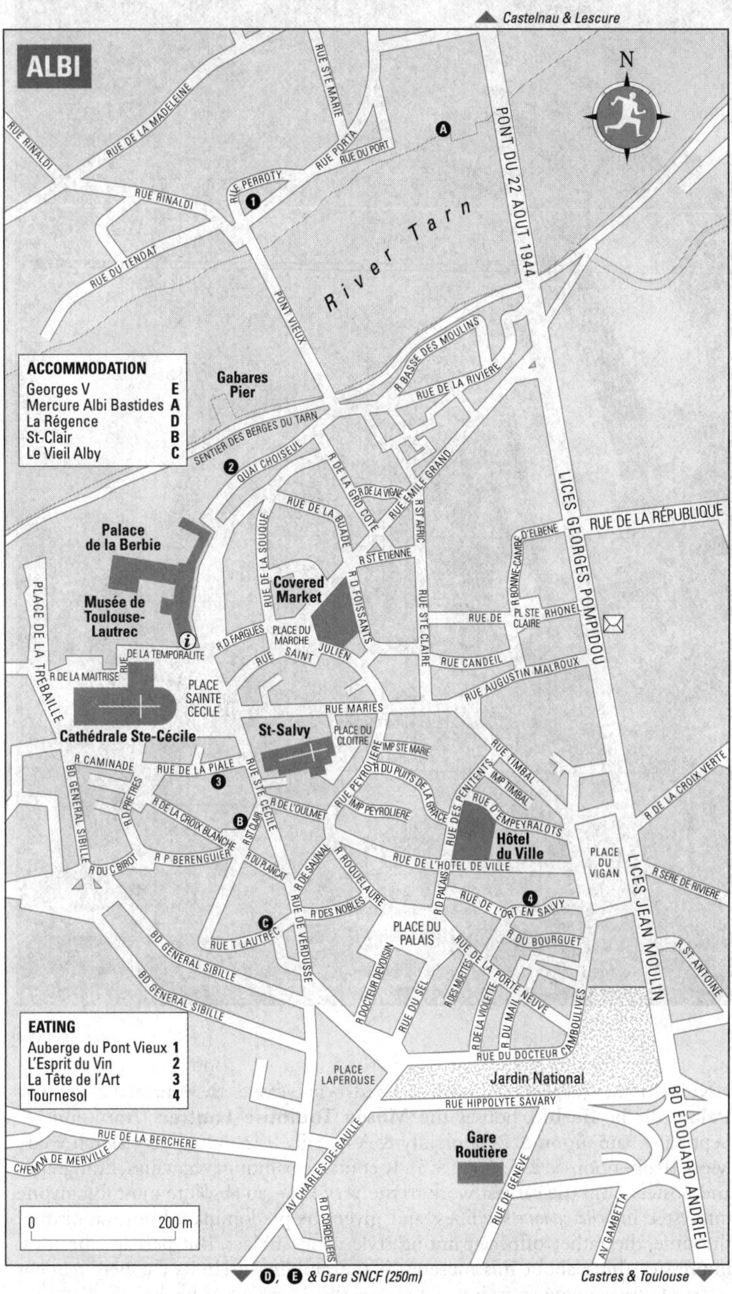
Castelnau & Lescure
ALBI
N
ACCOMMODATION
Georges V E
Mercure Albi Bastides A
La Régence D
St-Clair B
Le Vieil Alby C
EATING
Auberge du Pont Vieux 1
L'Esprit du Vin 2
La Tête de l'Art 3
Tournesol 4
River Tarn
Gabares Pier
Palace de la Berbie
Musée de Toulouse-Lautrec
Covered Market
Cathédrale Ste-Cécile
St-Salvy
Hôtel du Ville
Jardin National
Gare Routière
PLACE DE LA TREBAILLE
PLACE SAINTE CECILE
PLACE DU MARCHE
PLACE DU CLOITRE
PL STE CLAIRE
PLACE DU VIGAN
PLACE DU PALAIS
PLACE LAPEROUSE
RUE RINALDI
RUE DE LA MADELEINE
RUE STE MARIE
RUE PORTA
RUE DU PORT
RUE PERROTY
RUE DU TENDAT
PONT VIEUX
PONT DU 22 AOUT 1944
R BASSE DES MOULINS
RUE DE LA RIVIERE
SENTIER DES BERGES DU TARN
QUAI CHOISEUL
R DE LA GRD COTE
R DE LA VIGNE
RUE EMILE GRAND
R ST AFRIC
RUE DE LA BUADE
RUE DE LA SOUQUE
R ST ETIENNE
R D FOISSANTS
RUE STE CLAIRE
LICES GEORGES POMPIDOU
RUE DE LA RÉPUBLIQUE
R D'ELBENE
R BONNE-CAMBE
RUE DE RHONEL
RUE CANDEIL
RUE AUGUSTIN MALROUX
R D FARGUES
RUE SAINT JULIEN
RUE DE LA TEMPORALITE
R DE LA MAITRISE
RUE MARIES
R CAMINADE
RUE DE LA PIALE
RUE STE CECILE
IMP STE MARIE
RUE PEYROLIERE
R DU PUITS DE LA GRACE
IMP PEYROLIERE
RUE TIMBAL
IMP TIMBAL
RUE DES PENITENTS
RUE D'EMPEYRALOTS
R DE LA CROIX VERTE
BD GENERAL SIBILLE
R D PRETRES
R DE LA CROIX BLANCHE
R ST CLAIR
R DE L'OULMET
R P BERENGUIER
R DU C BIROT
R DU PLANCAT
R DE SAUNAL
RUE ROQUELAURE
RUE DE L'HOTEL DE VILLE
R SERE DE RIVIERE
LICES JEAN MOULIN
R D PALAIS
RUE DE L'ORT EN SALVY
R DES NOBLES
RUE DE VERDUSSE
RUE T LAUTREC
R DU BOURGUET
R ST ANTOINE
RUE DE LA PORTE NEUVE
R DOCTEUR DEVOISIN
RUE DU SEL
R DES MUETTES
R DE LA VIOLETTE
R DU MAIL
RUE CAMBOULIVES
RUE DU DOCTEUR CAMBOULIVES
RUE HIPPOLYTE SAVARY
BD EDOUARD ANDRIEU
RUE DE LA BERCHERE
CHEMIN DE MERVILLE
AV CHARLES-DE-GAULLE
R D CORDELIERS
RUE DE GENEVE
AV GAMBETTA
0 200 m
D, E & Gare SNCF (250m)
Castres & Toulouse

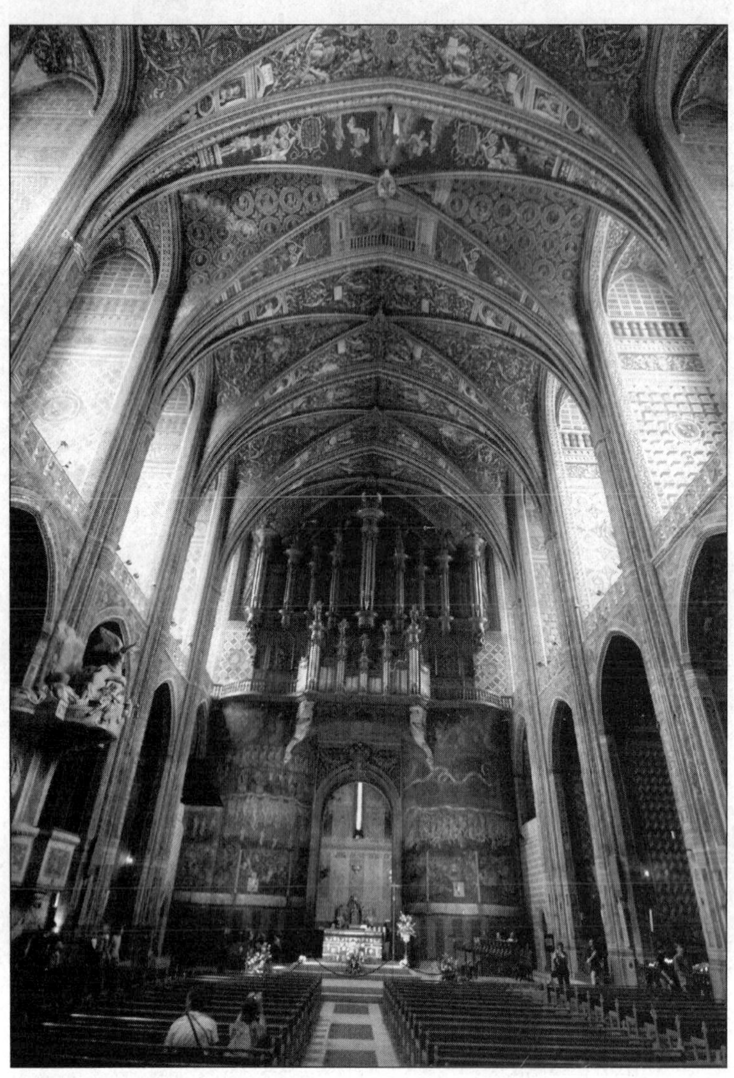

△ Albi Cathedral

Next to the cathedral, a powerful red-brick castle, the thirteenth-century **Palais de la Berbie**, houses the **Musée Toulouse-Lautrec** (April–June & Sept daily 9am–noon & 2–6pm; July & Aug daily 9am–6pm; Oct–March Wed–Mon 10am–noon & 2–5/6pm; €5). It contains paintings, drawings, lithographs and posters from the earliest work to the very last – an absolute must for anyone interested in *belle-époque* seediness and, given the predominant Impressionism of the time, the rather offbeat painting style of its subject. But perhaps the most impressive thing about this museum is the building itself, its parapets, gardens and walkways giving stunning views over the river and its bridges.

Opposite the east end of the cathedral, rue Mariés leads into the shopping streets of the old town, most of which has been impeccably renovated and restored. The little square and covered passages by the **church of St-Salvy** are worth a look as you go by. Eventually you come to the broad **Lices Georges Pompidou**, the main thoroughfare of modern Albi, which leads down to the river and the road to Cordes. Less touristy, this is the best place to look for somewhere to eat and drink.

Practicalities

From the **gare SNCF** on place Stalingrad it's a ten-minute walk into town along avenues Maréchal-Joffre and de-Gaulle; you'll see the **gare routière** on your right in place Jean-Jaurès as you reach the limits of the old town. The **tourist office** is in one corner of the Palais de la Berbie (July & Aug Mon–Sat 9am–7pm, Sun 10am–12.30pm & 2.30–5pm; Sept–June Mon–Sat 9am–12.30pm & 2–6pm, Sun 10am–12.30pm & 2.30–5pm; Ⓣ05.63.49.48.80, Ⓦwww.albi-tourisme.fr); ask for a copy of their English-language leaflet describing three walking tours round Albi.

There are two attractive **hotels** near the station on avenue Maréchal-Joffre: *La Régence*, at no. 27 (Ⓣ05.63.54.01.42, Ⓦwww.hotellaregence.com; ❶), and the slightly more expensive *Georges V*, at no. 29 (Ⓣ05.63.54.24.16, Ⓦwww.hotelgeorgev.com; ❷). On the opposite side of the town, on the north bank of the river, you'll find the luxurious *Mercure Albi Bastides* (Ⓣ05.63.47.66.66, Ⓔmercure.albi@orange.fr; ❺) at 41 rue Porta. In the heart of old Albi near the cathedral, the *Hôtel St-Clair*, 8 rue St-Clair (Ⓣ05.63.54.25.66, Ⓔmichelandrieu@hotmail.com; ❷) is a good bargain, but *Le Vieil Alby*, 25 rue Toulouse-Lautrec (Ⓣ05.63.54.15.69, Ⓕ05.63.54.96.75; ❸) is a real find – cheap and comfortable, with a friendly owner and excellent home-cooked food available. Otherwise, there's a municipal **campsite** (Ⓣ05.63.60.37.06; closed mid-Oct to March) in the Parc de Caussels, about 2km east on the D999 Millau road.

Albi's cuisine is predominantly *terroir* – local cooking notable only for *lou tastou*, the local version of tapas. One of the best *terroir* **restaurants** is *Auberge du Pont Vieux*, at 98 rue Porta (Ⓣ05.63.77.61.73; closed Oct–May & Wed lunch & Thurs outside midsummer; from €16), on the north bank of the Tarn. *La Tête de l'Art*, 7 rue de la Piale (Ⓣ05.63.38.44.75; Tues & Wed off season & Aug; from €14), is set apart by unrestrained atmosphere and wacky decor, while *L'Esprit du Vin*, 11 quai Choiseul (Ⓣ05.63.54.60.44; closed Sun eve, all Mon & mid-Feb to May; from €42), has imaginative *gastronomique* cuisine. *Tournesol*, off place du Vigan (Ⓣ05.63.38.44.60; closed Sun & Mon, lunch only), is Albi's vegetarian option (from €15).

Cagnac-les-Mines and Cordes

The country between Albi and Carmaux, 16km to the north, has long been a coal-mining and industrial area, associated in particular with the political activity of Jean Jaurès, father figure of French socialism. Elected deputy for Albi in 1893, after defending the striking miners of Carmaux, he then championed the glassworkers in 1896 in a strike that led to the setting up of a pioneering workers' co-operative, La Verrerie Ouvrière, which still functions today. The tourist office in Albi can provide a list of interesting industrial sites in the area, including the pit at **CAGNAC-LES-MINES**, just north of Albi, where the Musée Mine de Cagnac (May, June, Sept & Oct daily 10am–noon & 2–6pm, July & Aug daily 10am–7pm, Nov–April Tues–Sat 10am–noon & 2–5pm, Sun

10am–noon & 2–6pm; €7), presents a vivid recreation of the world of the coal mine, and is undoubtedly the region's most original museum.

Of more conventional tourist interest is the town of **CORDES**, perched on a conical hill 24km northwest of Albi, from which it's a brief trip by train (as far as Cordes-Vindrac, 5km away, with bike rental from the station) or bus (daily except Sun). Founded in 1222 by Raymond VII, Count of Toulouse, Cordes was a **Cathar** stronghold, and the ground beneath the town is riddled with tunnels for storage and refuge in time of trouble. As one of the southwest's oldest and best-preserved *bastides*, complete with thirteenth- and fourteenth-century houses climbing steep cobbled lanes, Cordes is inevitably a major tourist attraction: medieval banners flutter in the streets and artisans practise their crafts. The **Musée Charles-Portal** (Easter–June & Sept–Oct Sun & hols 3–6pm; July & Aug daily 11am–1pm & 3–7pm; €2.30) depicts the history of the town. Also of interest is the **Musée d'Art Moderne et Contemporain** (Feb–March & Nov–Dec 2–5pm; April–May & Oct 11.30am–12.30pm & 2–6.30pm; June–Sept 11am–12.30pm & 2–7pm; €4), which features works by the figurative painter Yves Brayer, who lived in Cordes from 1940. The best **hotel** in town is the splendid *Grand Écuyer* (Ⓣ05.63.53.79.50, Ⓦwww.thuries.fr; closed mid-Oct to Easter; ❻–❾) – from its gargoyle-studded facade to the ponderous stone of the interior, this former palace of Count Raymond VII of Toulouse is an evocative combination of medieval atmosphere and modern amenities. Just down the street, the *Vieux Cordes* (closed Jan; Ⓣ05.63.53.79.20, Ⓦwww.thuries.fr; ❸) is housed in a medieval building. There's also a **campsite** (Ⓣ & Ⓕ05.63.56.11.10; closed Oct–March) 1km southeast down the Gaillac road.

Castres and around

In spite of its industrial activities, **CASTRES**, 40km south of Albi and 55km east of Toulouse, has kept a lot of its charm, in the streets on the right bank of the Agout and, in particular, the riverside quarter where the old tanners' and weavers' houses overhang the water. The centre is a bustling, businesslike sort of place, with a big morning **market** on Saturdays on place Jean-Jaurès. By the rather unremarkable old cathedral, the former bishop's palace holds the Hôtel de Ville and Castres' **Musée Goya** (July & Aug daily 9am–noon & 2–6pm; Sept–June Tues–Sun 9am–noon & 2–5/6pm; €2.30), home to the biggest collection of Spanish paintings in France outside the Louvre. Goya is represented by some lighter political paintings and a large collection of engravings, and there are also works by other famous Iberian artists, like Murillo and Velázquez.

Castres' other specialist museum is the **Musée Jean-Jaurès** (same hours as Musée Goya; €1.50), dedicated to its famous native son. It's located in place Pélisson, and getting to it takes you through the streets of the old town, past the splendid seventeenth-century **Hôtel Nayrac**, on rue Frédéric-Thomas. The museum was opened in 1988 by President Mitterrand – appropriately enough, because Mitterrand's Socialist Party is the direct descendant of Jaurès' SFIO, founded in 1905, which split at the Congress of Tours in 1920, when the "Bolshevik" element left to form the French Communist Party. The slightly hagiographic museum nonetheless pays well-deserved tribute to one of France's boldest and best political writers, thinkers and activists of modern times. Jaurès supported Dreyfus, founded the newspaper *L'Humanité*, campaigned against the death penalty and colonialism, and was murdered for his courageous pacifist stance at the outbreak of World War I – oddly enough by a man called Villain.

There could be no better epitaph than his own last article in *L'Humanité*, in which he wrote: "The most important thing is that we should continue to act and to keep our minds perpetually fresh and alive … That is the real safeguard, the guarantee of our future."

Practicalities

Arriving from Toulouse by train, you'll find the **gare SNCF** a kilometre southwest of the town centre on avenue Albert-1er. The **gare routière** is on place Soult, with bus services to Mazamet and Lacaune. The **tourist office** stands beside the Pont Vieux at 3 rue Milhau-Ducommun (July & Aug daily 9.30am–12.30pm & 1.30–6.30pm; otherwise Mon–Sat 9.30am–12.30pm & 2–6pm; ⓣ05.63.62.63.62, ⓦwww.ville-castres.fr).

Castres has two marvellous seventeenth-century mansions converted into luxurious but affordable **hotels**; the marginally more deluxe *Renaissance* is at 17 rue Victor-Hugo (ⓣ05.63.59.30.42, ⓦwww.hotelrenaissance.fr; ❹), while *L'Europe*, is up the same street, at no. 5 (ⓣ05.63.59.00.33, ⓦwww.hotelrenaissance.fr; ❹). Otherwise, the *Rivière*, 10 quai Tourcaudière (ⓣ05.63.59.04.53, ⓔhotelriviere@orange.fr; ❷), has pleasant views over the Agout and helpful staff, and the very friendly and clean *Le Périgord*, 22 rue Zola (ⓣ& ⓕ05.63.59.04.74; ❷), is a bargain. The municipal **campsite** (ⓣ05.63.59.72.30; closed Oct–March) is in a riverside park 2km northeast of town on the road to Roquecourbe, which you can also reach by river-taxi (round trip €4).

For simple, inexpensive **meals**, you can't beat the upstairs dining room in the *Brasserie des Jacobins*, on place Jean-Jaurès. In the evening, the best bet is the *Renaissance* or *L'Europe* (see above) both of which offer all-you-can eat buffets for €10.

Le Sidobre and Lacrouzette

Just east of Castres rises the westernmost extremity of the Parc Naturel Régional du Haut Languedoc, cut by deep river valleys and covered with marvellous woods. This is **Le Sidobre**, an area renowned for its granite: huge boulders litter the woods, often carved by the millennia into zoomorphic or other shapes – Les Trois Fromages and L'Oie, for example – that give them commercial value in the eyes of the tourist industry. Exploration is best done on foot: the **GR36** footpath passes this way.

LACROUZETTE, 15km from Castres, is the main town and capital of the granite industry. The demand for tombstones being impervious to recession, the town continues to prosper, though it's not the most beautiful place. If you're on your way up the Agout and Gijou valleys to Lacaze and Lacaune, head for the *chambres d'hôtes* of the luxurious fourteenth- to sixteenth-century castle in **Burlats**, 10km northeast of Castres (ⓣ05.63.35.29.20, ⓔle.castel.de-burlats@orange.fr; ❹).

The Gers

West of Toulouse, the *département* of **Gers** lies at the heart of the historic region of Gascony. In the long struggle for supremacy between the English and the French in the Middle Ages it had the misfortune to form the frontier zone between the English base at Bordeaux and the French at Toulouse – hence the large number of fortified villages, or *bastides*, dominating the hilltops.

The attractive if unspectacular rolling agricultural land is dotted with ancient, honey-stoned farms. Settlement is sparse and – with the exception of **Auch**, the capital – major monuments are largely lacking, which keeps it well off the beaten tourist trails, although the gently varied topography and tranquillity make it an ideal region for biking and hiking.

The region's traditional sources of renown are its stout-hearted mercenary warriors – of whom Alexandre Dumas' d'Artagnan and Edmond Rostand's Cyrano de Bergerac are the supreme literary exemplars – its rich cuisine and its **Armagnac**. The food and brandy still flourish: Gers is the biggest producer of **foie gras** in the country. Other traditional dishes are *magret de canard*, Henri IV's *poulet au pot* (the chicken that he promised to provide for every peasant's Sunday dinner), confit of duck and goose, thick *garbure* soup and *daube de por*. Then there's *croustade*, a tart of apple and Armagnac, the speciality of Gascon *pâtissiers*. The red wines of Madiran, Buzet and St-Mont and the whites of Pacherenc du Vic-Bilh wash it all down.

Auch

The sleepy provincial capital of the Gers, **AUCH** is most easily accessible by rail from Toulouse, 78km to the east. The old town, which is the only part worth exploring, stands on a bluff overlooking the tree-lined River Gers, with the cathedral towering dramatically over the town.

It is this building – the **Cathédrale Ste-Marie** – which makes a trip to Auch worthwhile. Although not finished until the latter part of the seventeenth century, it is built in broadly late Gothic style, with a classical facade. Of particular interest are the choir stalls (daily: April–June & Sept 8.30am–noon & 2–6pm; July & Aug 8.30am–6.30pm; Oct–March 8.30am–noon & 2–5pm; €1.50) and the stained glass; both were begun in the early 1500s, though the windows are of clearly Renaissance inspiration, while the choir remains Gothic.

Armagnac

Armagnac is a dry, golden brandy distilled in the district extending into the Landes and Lot and Garonne *départements*, divided into three distinct areas: Haut-Armagnac (around Auch), Ténarèze (Condom) and Bas-Armagnac (Éauze), in ascending order of output and quality. Growers of the grape like to compare brandy with whisky, equating malts with the individualistic, earthy Armagnac distilled by small producers, and blended whiskies with the more consistent, standardized output of the large-scale houses. Armagnac grapes are grown on sandy soils and, importantly, the wine is distilled only once, giving the spirit a lower alcohol content but more flavour. Aged in local black oak, Armagnac matures quickly, so young Armagnacs are relatively smoother than corresponding Cognacs.

Distilled originally for medicinal reasons, Armagnac has many claims made for its efficacy. Perhaps the most optimistic are those of the priest of Éauze de St-Mont, who held that the eau de vie cured **gout** and hepatitis. More reasonably, he also wrote that it "stimulates the spirit if taken in moderation, recalls the past, gives many joy above all else, conserves youth. If one retains it in the mouth, it unties the tongue and gives courage to the timid."

Many of the producers welcome visitors and offer tastings, whether you go to one of the bigger *chais* of Condom or Éauze, or follow a faded sign at the bottom of a farm track. For more **information**, contact the Bureau National Interprofessionnel de l'Armagnac, place de la Liberté, 32800 Éauze (ⓣ05.62.08.11.00, ⓦwww.cognacnet.com/armagnac).

The stalls are thought to have been carved by the same craftsmen who executed those at St-Bertrand-de-Comminges, and show the same extraordinary virtuosity and detail. The eighteen windows, unusual in being a complete set, parallel the scenes and personages depicted in the stalls. They are the work of a Gascon painter, Arnaud de Moles, and are equally rich in detail.

Immediately south of the cathedral, in the tree-filled place Salinis, is the forty-metre-high **Tour d'Armagnac**, which served as an ecclesiastical court and prison in the fourteenth century. Descending from here to the river is a **monumental stairway** of 234 steps, with a statue of d'Artagnan gracing one of the terraces. From place de la République, in front of the cathedral's main west door, rue d'Espagne connects with rue de la Convention and what is left of the narrow medieval stairways known as the **pousterles**, which give access to the lower town. On the north side of place de la République, the tourist office inhabits a splendid half-timbered fifteenth-century house on the corner with rue Dessoles, a pedestrianized street boasting an array of fine buildings. Just down the steps to the east of rue Dessoles, on place Louis-Blanc, the former convent, now the **Musée des Jacobins** (May–Sept daily 10am–noon & 2–6pm; rest of the year Tues–Sun 10am–noon & 2–5pm; €3) houses one of the best collections of pre-Columbian and later South American art in France, left to the town by an adventurous son, M. Pujos, who had lived in Chile in the last years of the nineteenth century. Also of interest is its small collection of traditional Gascon furniture, religious artefacts and Gallo-Roman remains.

Practicalities

The **tourist office** (mid-July to mid-Aug Mon–Sat 9.30am–6.30pm & Sun 10am–12.15pm & 3–6.15pm; mid-Aug to mid-July Mon–Sat 9.15am–noon & 2–6/6.30pm; also open Sun 10am–12.15pm May–Oct; ⓣ05.62.05.22.89, ⓦwww.mairie-auch.fr) stands at the corner of place de la République and rue Dessoles. West of here, place de la Libération leads to the allées d'étigny, with the **gare routière** off to the right.

In terms of accommodation, the only choice in the centre is the relatively luxurious *Hôtel de France* at 2 place de la Libération (ⓣ05.62.61.71.71, ⓦwww.hoteldefrance-auch.com; ❺), right by the *mairie* and only a few minutes' walk west of the cathedral. The only other alternative is the more economical *Hôtel de Paris*, 38 av de la Marne (ⓣ05.62.63.26.22, ⓕ05.62.60.04.27; ❸; closed Nov). To get there from the **gare SNCF**, turn right on avenue de la Gare, follow it to the end, then turn left. Otherwise, the municipal **campsite** (ⓣ05.62.05.00.22; mid-April to mid-Sept) is beside the river on the south side of town.

Avenue d'Alsace, in the lower town, is the best place to look for inexpensive places to **eat**. Alternatively, up by the cathedral, place de la République and place de la Libération boast a fair selection of cafés and brasseries; try *Café Daroles* by the fountain (menus from €16 or €10.50 at lunch). For something traditional, *La Table d'Oste*, off rue Dessoles at 7 rue Lamartine, offers good Gascon fare from €16 (closed Sat–Mon, depending on season). The well-regarded restaurant of the *Hotel de France* has menus from €11.50, although à la carte will set you back considerably more.

Around Auch

Outside Auch are a couple of quiet country towns, **Lectoure** and **Condom**, with no great sights, but which, along with the surrounding countryside, make for a lazy taste of French provincial life. They are all connected by bus from

Auch, but away from the main roads – the N21 for Fleurance and Lectoure, and the D930 for Condom – you'll be stuck without your own transport.

Lectoure

Thirty-five kilometres north of Auch sits **LECTOURE**, the smallest and prettiest of the surrounding towns, built along a narrow escarpment looking out over the surrounding farmland. Capital of the colony of Novempopulania in Roman times and of the counts of Armagnac until their demise at the hands of Louis XI in 1473, it's now renowned for its melons. In the middle of the main street, the **Cathédrale de St-Gervais-et-de-St-Protais** raises its enormous tower above the town, while down the rue Fontelié, behind the tourist office, among scarcely altered medieval houses, you come to the unremarkable thirteenth-century vaulted Gothic **Fontaine de Diane**. The real reason for stopping here is the **Musée Lapidaire** (10am–noon & 2–6pm, closed Tues Oct–Feb; €3), in the basement of the *mairie* (the former wine cellar of the bishops' palace). Here you'll find some impressive rarities including a collection of Roman funerary stones, testament to the once popular local oracular cult of the bull, and various Merovingian-era decroated clothing clasps.

The **tourist office** is on place de la Cathédrale (Jan & Feb Tues & Thurs–Sat 3–6pm; mid-June to mid-Sept 10am–1pm & 3–7pm; rest of year Tues, Wed, Fri & Sat 10am–noon & 3–6pm, Sun 10am–noon; ⓣ05.62.68.76.98, ⓦwww.lectoure.fr). Close by is the superb but unfortunately named *Hôtel de Bastard* in rue Lagrange (ⓣ05.62.68.82.44, ⓦwww.hotel-de-bastard.com; ❸; closed late Dec to Jan; menus from €40), while the *Auberge des Bouviers*, at 8 rue Montebello near the central market hall, makes for an atmospheric place to eat (from €20). Heading on to Condom with your own transport, stop in at La Romieu, halfway between the two towns, where the badly weathered **collegiate church**, once a stop on the Santiago trail, contains a sacristy with worn but notable fourteenth-century murals. (May–Sept Mon–Sat 10am–6.30/7pm & Sun 2–6.30/7pm; Oct–May Mon–Sat 10am–noon & 2–6pm, Sun 2–6pm; €4.50).

Condom

Some 43km north of Auch and 21km west of Lectoure lies the town of **CONDOM**. Contrary to what one might assume, there's no connection between the place and the device. Unremarkable in every other field, Condom is nonetheless good for a quick visit or an overnight stop, and makes an ideal base for exploring several interesting sights in the neighborhood. With its uniformly honey-brown houses, the old town retains some atmosphere, but the sixteenth-century cathedral, completed just in time to be ravaged by the Wars of Religion, is badly damaged and nondescript. Armagnac drinkers will be interested in the **Musée de l'Armagnac**, 2 rue Jules-Ferry (Wed–Sun: April–Sept 10am–noon & 3–6pm; Oct–March 2–5pm; €2.20), and the Chais Ryst-Duperon, where the spirit is aged (July & Aug daily 10am–noon & 2–6pm; Sept–June Wed–Sun 10am–noon & 2–5pm; free). For other places to taste and buy Armagnac, ask the tourist office in place Bossuet (July & Aug Mon–Sat 9am–7pm, Sun 10.30am–12.30pm; Sept–Oct Mon–Sat 9am–noon & 2–6pm; ⓣ05.62.28.00.80, ⓦwww.tourisme-teneraze.com).

The cheapest place to **stay** is the *Relais de la Ténaréze*, at 20 av d'Aquitaine (ⓣ05.62.28.02.54, ⓦwww.logisdefrancegers.com; ❸). Two more appealing options, both with pools, are the *Hôtel des Cordeliers*, in rue de la Paix (ⓣ05.62.28.03.68, ⓦwww.logisdescordeliers.com; ❸), and, if you want to treat yourself, the *Hôtel des Trois Lys* (ⓣ05.62.28.33.33, ⓦwww.lestroislys.com; ❼;

closed Feb; restaurant from €40). For a straightforward place to **eat**, try *Pizzéria l'Origan*, at 4 rue Cadéot in the town centre (closed Sun & Mon) or *Café des Sports*, on rue Charron by the cathedral, which also does pizzas and a reasonable menu at €18. A more upmarket alternative is *Le Moulin du Petit Gascon* (☎05.62.28.28.42; closed Dec–Feb, also Sun eve & Mon; menus from €18), out of town by the campsite, and attractively sited beside a canal lock.

Around Condom

The sights around Condom can be visited in a morning by car, but are equally accessible (time permitting) by bicycle or hiking trail. Just 5km west of Condom, the tiny twelfth-century village of **LARRESSINGLE** was once home to Condom's bishops, who lived in fortified splendour away from the hoi polloi. The compact village is girded by a moat and walls and contains the bishop's keep and stout church. It is best visited in low and shoulder seasons, preferably before 10am or after 7pm; it's now an obligatory stop on local tours and one busload is enough to dissipate its considerable charms.

Just off the main road to Condom sits the abbey of **FLARAN** (July & Aug 9.30am–7pm, Sept–June 9.30am–12.30pm & 2–6pm; €4). This Cistercian monastery dates back to 1151, and although compact maintains the key elements of the monastic house: the weighty and austere Romanesque church, a cloister, a beautiful chapterhouse, luxurious pre-Revolution monks' apartments and a refectory. All the more remarkable is the tale of its reconstruction after a member of the family who owned Flaran set fire to the monastery as part of an insurance scam in 1972. Justice was served, the culprit was imprisoned and the local authorities impounded the site and converted it into public patrimony.

Travel details

Trains

Béziers to: Agde (18 daily; 45min); Arles (10–14 daily; 2hr 10min); Avignon (4–10 daily; 2hr); Bédarieux (4–8 daily; 40min); Carcassonne (22 daily; 15min); Clermont-Ferrand (3 daily; 6–7hr); Marseille (8 daily; 3hr 10min); Millau (4–6 daily; 2hr); Montpellier (26 daily; 45min); Narbonne (18 daily; 14min); Nîmes (20 daily; 1hr 15min); Paris (30 daily; 4hr 30min–12hr); Perpignan (18 daily; 40min–1hr); Sète (23 daily; 25min).

Carcassonne to: Arles (4–8 daily; 2hr 40min–3hr 30min); Béziers (22 daily; 45min); Bordeaux (18–22 daily; 3hr 20min–4hr 30min); Limoux (16 daily; 25min); Marseille (12–18 daily; 3hr 20min–5hr 30min); Montpellier (18 daily; 1hr 30min–4hr); Narbonne (22 daily; 35min); Nîmes (26 daily; 2hr 5min–3hr 10min); Quillan (6 daily; 1hr 15min); Toulouse (22 daily; 45min–1hr).

Montpellier to: Arles (10–14 daily; 1hr 20min); Avignon (22 daily; 1hr 15min–2hr); Béziers (18 daily; 40min); Carcassonne (22 daily; 1hr 15min); Lyon (18 daily; 1hr 40min–3hr 30min); Marseille (18–22 daily; 2hr 20min); Mende (18 daily; 3hr 40min–4hr 30min); Narbonne (26 daily; 45min–1hr 15min); Paris (16 daily; 3hr 15min—6hr); Perpignan (12 daily; 2hr 15min); Sète (22 daily; 15–20min); Toulouse (18 daily; 2hr 15min–2hr 55min).

Narbonne to: Arles (18–22 daily; 2hr); Avignon (4–8 daily; 2hr 10min); Béziers (18 daily; 14min); Bordeaux (18–22 daily; 3hr 45min–6hr); Carcassonne (22 daily; 35min); Cerbère (12–16 daily; 1hr–1hr 30min); Marseille (20 daily; 2hr 40min–3hr 30min); Montpellier (26 daily; 45min–1hr 15min); Nîmes (20 daily; 1hr 45min); Perpignan (24 daily; 36–45min); Sète (23 daily; 45min); Toulouse (18 daily; 1hr 30min).

Nîmes to: Arles (22 daily; 30–40min); Avignon (14–18 daily; 30min); Béziers (36 daily; 1hr 15min); Carcassonne (26 daily; 2hr 5min–3hr 10min); Clermont-Ferrand (12–16 daily; 5–6hr); La Bastide-St-Laurent (6–8 daily; 1hr 45min–2hr 40min); Marseille (20 daily; 40min–1hr 15min); Montpellier (26 daily; 30min); Narbonne (20 daily; 1hr 45min); Paris (23 daily; 3–9hr 30min); Perpignan (12 daily; 2hr 45min); Sète (22 daily; 48min);.

Toulouse to: Albi (17 daily; 1hr); Auch (18–20 daily; 1hr 15min–2hr 30min); Ax-les-Thermes

(6 daily; 1hr 55min); Bayonne (18–22 daily; 2hr 25min–3hr 45min); Bordeaux (18–22 daily; 2hr 30min); Castres (11 daily; 1hr 5min); Foix (13 daily; 47min–1hr 15min); La-Tour-de-Carol (6 daily; 2hr 30min) Lourdes (8–16 daily; 1hr 40min); Lyon (14–18 daily; 4–6hr); Marseille (22 daily; 3hr 30min–6hr); Mazamet (11 daily; 1hr 30min–1hr 55min); Pamiers (13 daily; 50min – 1hr 10min); Paris (13 daily; 5hr 20min–6hr 45min); Pau (6–10 daily; 2hr–2hr 30min); Tarascon-sur-Ariège (13 daily; 1hr 20min); Tarbes (6–13 daily; 1hr 45min).

Buses

Albi to: Cordes-sur-Ciel (2 daily; 35min).
Auch to: Agen (6–10 daily; 1hr 30min); Bordeaux (1 daily; 3hr 40min); Condom (1–2 daily; 40min); Lectoure (4–8 daily; 40min); Montauban (0–3 daily; 2hr); Tarbes (3–4 daily; 2hr); Toulouse (1–4 daily; 1hr 30min).
Bédarieux to: Olargues (1–2 daily; 40min); St-Pons-de-Thomières (3 daily; 1hr 20min).
Béziers to: Agde (2 daily & 4–6 in summer; 25min); Bédarieux (0–2 daily; 1hr); Castres (2 daily; 2hr 50min); La Salvetat (0–2 daily; 2hr 10min) Mazamet (2 daily; 2hr); Pézenas (4–11 daily; 32min); St-Pons-de-Thomières (4 daily; 1hr 20min).
Carcassonne to: Castelnaudary (3–5 daily; 45min); Quillan (2 daily; 1hr 20min).
Montpellier to: Aigues-Mortes (2–4 daily; 1hr); Bédarieux (3–4 daily; 1hr 35min); Clermont-l'Hérault (3–4 daily; 1hr); Ganges (4–5 daily; 1hr 15min); Gignac (for St-Guilhem: 6–8 daily; 40min); La Grande-Motte (8–12 daily; 1hr 5min; hourly in summer); Grau-du-Roi (4–8 daily; 1hr 10min); Le Vigan (3–5 daily; 1hr 40min); Lodève (4 daily; 1hr 15min); Millau (2–8 daily; 2hr 20min); Palavas (local service); Rodez (1–3 daily; 3hr 55min); St-Martin-de-Londres (2–4 daily; 50min); St-Pons-de-Thomières (1–3 daily; 2hr 55min); Viols-le-Fort (2–9 daily; 40min).
Narbonne to: Gruissan (3–6 daily; 45min); Narbonne-Plage (2–8 daily; 45min).
Nîmes to: Aigues-Mortes (17 daily; 55min); Ganges (2–3 daily; 1hr 30min); La Grande-Motte (2–9 daily; 1hr 30min); Le Grau-du-Roi (12–18 daily; 1hr 15min); Le Vigan (3–5 daily; 1hr 50min) Pont du Gard (8 daily; 45min); Sommières (8 daily; 45min); Uzès (8–12 daily; 30min–1hr).
Sète to: Montpellier (3–15 daily; 1hr 5min).
Toulouse to: Albi (12–16 weekly; 2hr 40min); Carcassonne (1 daily; 2hr 20min); Castres (8–12 weekly; 1hr 40min–2hr); St-Girons (3 daily; 2hr 30min).

12

The Massif Central

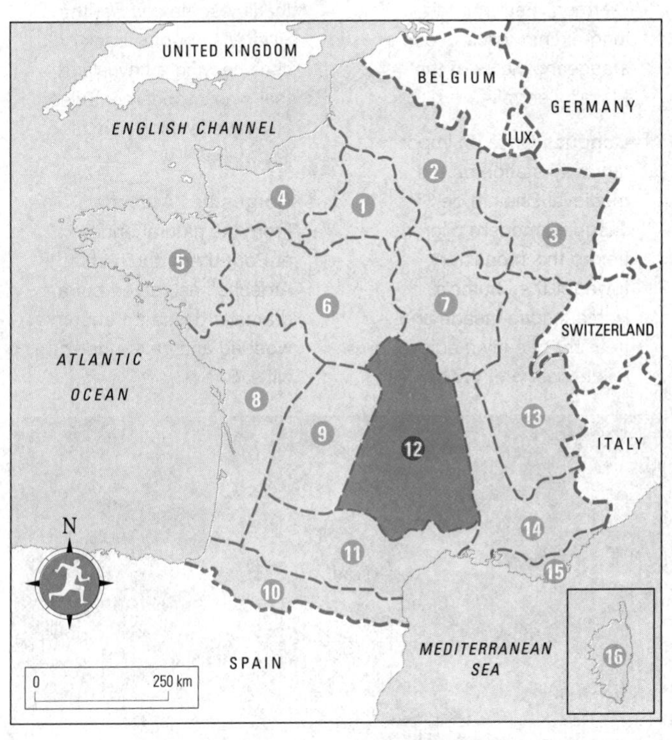

CHAPTER 12

Highlights

- **Cheese** The pasture lands of France's central region produce some of its best cheeses: Roquefort, Laguiole and St. Nectaire. See p.903
- **Puy de Dôme** Four hundred metres above Clermont-Ferrand, this long-extinct volcano offers staggering vistas of the Massif Central. See p.909
- **Conques** Once an important way-station on the medieval Chemin de St-Jacques, modern pilgrims trek to this monastery town for the church's Romanesque facade and treasury of early medieval reliquaries. See p.929
- **Canoeing** The river gorges of the Tarn, Lot and Ardèche provide near limitless opportunities for kayaking and canoeing. See pp.938 & 947
- **Cirque de Navacelles** Cutting 150m down into the limestone *causse*, the River Vis doubles back on itself, leaving a tiny island that was capped centuries ago by a farming hamlet. See p.944
- **Gorges de l'Ardèche** From the natural bridge at Pont d'Arc, the rushing Ardèche has carved out a dramatic descent through wooded and cave-riddled cliffs. See p.947

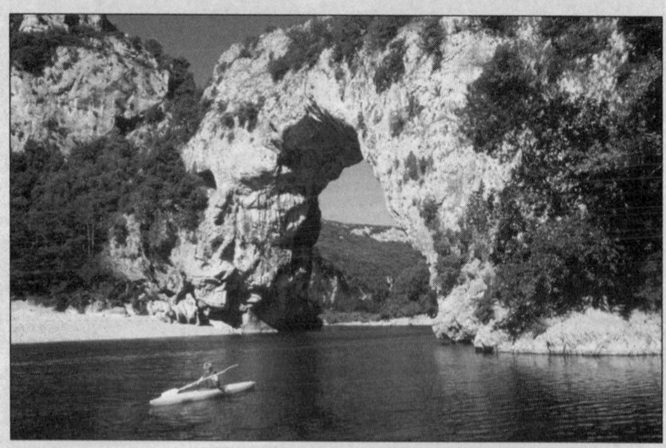

△ Pont d'Arc, Gorges de l'Ardèche

12

The Massif Central

One of the loveliest spots on earth . . . a country without roads, without guides, without any facilities for locomotion, where every discovery must be conquered at the price of danger or fatigue . . . a soil cut up with deep ravines, crossed in every way by lofty walls of lava, and furrowed by numerous torrents.

Thus one of George Sand's characters described the Haute-Loire, the central *département* of **the Massif Central**, and it's a description that could still be applied to some of the region. Thickly forested and sliced by numerous rivers and lakes, these once volcanic uplands are geologically the oldest part of France and culturally one of the most firmly rooted in the past. Industry and tourism have made few inroads here, and the people remain rural and somewhat taciturn, with an enduring sense of regional identity.

The Massif Central takes up a huge portion of the centre of France, but only a handful of towns have gained a foothold in its rugged terrain: **Le Puy**, spiked with theatrical pinnacles of lava, is the most compelling, with its steep streets and majestic cathedral; the spa town of **Vichy** has an antiquated elegance and charm; even heavily industrial **Clermont-Ferrand**, the capital, has a certain cachet in the black volcanic stone of its historic centre and its stunning physical setting beneath the **Puy de Dôme**, a 1464-metre-high volcanic plug. There is pleasure, too, in the unpretentious provinciality of **Aurillac** and in the untouched medieval architecture of smaller places like **Murat**, **Besse**, **Salers**, **Orcival**, **Sauveterre-de-Rouergue**, **La Couvertoirade** and in the hugely influential abbey of **Conques**. But, above all, this is a country where the sights are landscapes rather than towns, churches and museums.

The heart of the region is the **Auvergne**, a wild and unexpected scene of extinct volcanoes (*puys*), stretching from the grassy domes and craters of the **Monts-Dômes** to the eroded skylines of the **Monts-Dore**, and deeply ravined **Cantal mountains** to the rash of darkly wooded pimples surrounding Le Puy. It's one of the poorest regions in France and has long remained outside the main national lines of communication: much of it is above 1000m in height and snowbound in winter. However, the Clermont–Montpellier autoroute is now near completion, providing a convenient means of travel from the capital to the gorges of the Tarn and Ardèche. There's little arable land in the region, just thousands of acres of upland pasture, traditionally grazed by sheep brought up from the southern lowlands for the summer. Nowadays, cows far outnumber the sheep, some raised for beef and some still for the production of Auvergne's four great cheeses (see box, p.903). The **population** has emigrated for generations, especially to Paris, where the café and restaurant trade has long been in

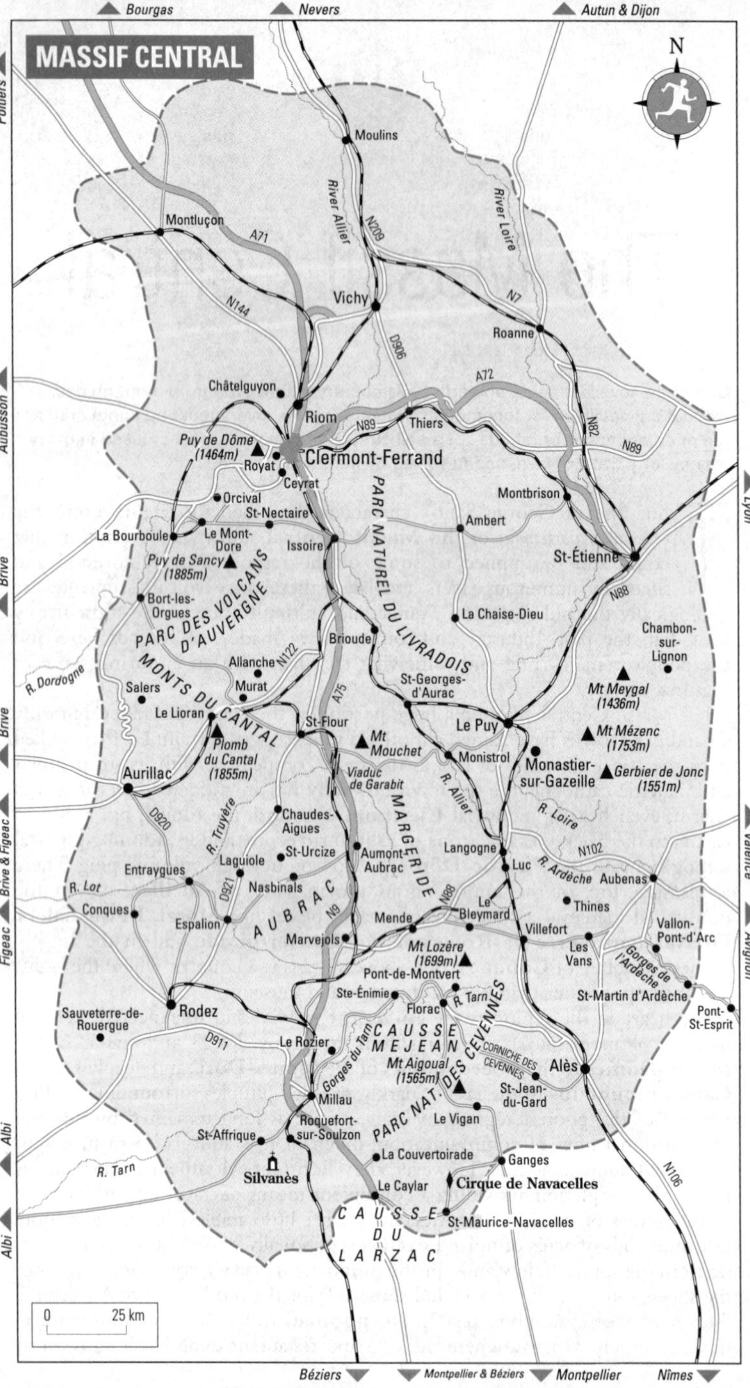
MASSIF CENTRAL
N
Bourgas
Nevers
Autun & Dijon
Poitiers
Aubusson
Brive
Brive
Brive & Figeac
Figeac
Albi
Albi
Lyon
Valence
Avignon
Béziers
Montpellier & Béziers
Montpellier
Nîmes
Moulins
River Allier
N209
River Loire
Montluçon
A71
N144
Vichy
N7
Roanne
D906
A72
Châtelguyon
Riom
N89
Thiers
N82
N89
Puy de Dôme (1464m)
Royat
Clermont-Ferrand
Ceyrat
PARC NATUREL DU LIVRADOIS
Orcival
St-Nectaire
Montbrison
Ambert
La Bourboule
Le Mont-Dore
Issoire
St-Étienne
Puy de Sancy (1885m)
PARC DES VOLCANS D'AUVERGNE
Bort-les-Orgues
La Chaise-Dieu
N88
Brioude
Chambon-sur-Lignon
R. Dordogne
Allanche
N122
MONTS DU CANTAL
Murat
St-Georges-d'Aurac
Mt Meygal (1436m)
Salers
Le Lioran
A75
Le Puy
St-Flour
Mt Mézenc (1753m)
Mt Mouchet
Plomb du Cantal (1855m)
Monistrol
Monastier-sur-Gazeille
Gerbier de Jonc (1551m)
Aurillac
Viaduc de Garabit
R. Allier
MARGERIDE
R. Loire
D920
R. Truyère
Chaudes-Aigues
Langogne
N102
St-Urcize
Aumont-Aubrac
Luc
R. Ardèche
Aubenas
Laguiole
Entraygues
Nasbinals
D921
R. Lot
AUBRAC
N88
Thines
Conques
N9
Le Bleymard
Espalion
Mende
Villefort
Vallon-Pont-d'Arc
Marvejols
Les Vans
Mt Lozère (1699m)
Gorges de l'Ardèche
Pont-de-Montvert
St-Martin d'Ardèche
Ste-Énimie
R. Tarn
Florac
Rodez
Pont-St-Esprit
Sauveterre-de-Rouergue
CAUSSE MEJEAN
Gorges du Tarn
D911
Le Rozier
CORNICHE DES CEVENNES
Alès
Mt Aigoual (1565m)
PARC NAT. DES CEVENNES
St-Jean-du-Gard
Millau
Le Vigan
Roquefort-sur-Soulzon
St-Affrique
La Couvertoirade
R. Tarn
Ganges
Silvanès
Cirque de Navacelles
N106
Le Caylar
CAUSSE DU LARZAC
St-Maurice-Navacelles
0
25 km

The food of the Massif Central

Don't expect anything very refined from the cuisine of the Auvergne and Massif Central: it's solid peasant fare as befits a poor and rugged region. The best-known dish is **potée auvergnate**, basically a kind of cabbage soup. It's easy to make and very nourishing. The ingredients – potatoes, pork or bacon, cabbage, beans, turnips – though added at different intervals, are all boiled up together. Another popular cabbage dish is **chou farci**, cabbage stuffed with pork and beef and cooked with bacon.

Two potato dishes are very common – **la truffade** and **l'aligot**. For *truffade*, the potatoes are sliced and fried in lard, then fresh Cantal cheese is added; for an *aligot*, the potatoes are puréed and mixed with cheese. Less palatable for the squeamish, **tripoux**, usually a stuffing of either sheep's feet or calf's innards, cooked in a casing of stomach lining. **Fricandeau**, a kind of pork pâté, is also wrapped in sheep's stomach.

By way of dessert, **clafoutis** is a popular fruit tart in which the fruit is baked with a batter of flour and egg simply poured over it. The classic fruit ingredient is black cherries, though pears, blackcurrants or apples can also be used.

The Auvergne and the Ardèche in the east produce some wines, though these are not of any great renown. **Cheese**, however, is a different story. In addition to the four great cow's milk cheeses – St-Nectaire (see p.917), Laguiole, Cantal, Fourme d'Ambert and Bleu d'Auvergne – this region also produces the prince of all cheeses, **Roquefort**, made from sheep's milk at the edge of the Causse du Larzac (see p.937).

the hands of Auvergnats. The same flight of population has affected the equally infertile but beautiful and more Mediterranean southern part of the region: the hills and valleys of the **Cévennes**, where Robert Louis Stevenson and his donkey made one of the more famous literary hikes in 1878.

Many of France's greatest rivers rise in the Massif Central: the **Dordogne** in the Monts-Dore, the **Loire** on the slopes of the Gerbier de Jonc in the east, and in the Cévennes the **Lot** and the **Tarn**. It is these last two rivers which create the distinctive character of the southern parts of the Massif Central, dividing and defining the special landscapes of the *causses*, or limestone plateaux, with their stupendous gorges. This is territory tailor-made for walkers and lovers of the **outdoors**, and everywhere you go tourist offices will supply ideas and routes for walks and bike rides.

The Parc des Volcans d'Auvergne

The **Parc Naturel Régional des Volcans d'Auvergne** encompasses the whole of the western edge of the Massif Central, from **Vichy** in the north to **Aurillac** in the south. It consists of three groups of extinct volcanoes – the

Dômes, the **Monts-Dore** and the **Monts du Cantal** – linked by the ıux of Artense and the Cézallier. It's big, wide-open country, sparsely and with largely treeless pasture grazed by the cows whose milk .es Cantal and St-Nectaire cheese.

.ne park organization, whose headquarters are at the **Maison du Parc**, Château de Montlosier, 20km southwest of Clermont-Ferrand just off the Mont-Dore road (May–Oct Mon–Fri 8.30am–12.30pm & 1–5pm; ⓣ04.73.65.64.00, ⓦwww.parc-volcans-auvergne.com), oversees various subsidiary *maisons du parc*, each a kind of museum devoted to different themes or activities: fauna and flora, shepherd life, peat bogs and so on.

The best way to understand the park, its landscapes and activities is to walk or bike around it. Four **GR footpaths** cross or make circuits within the park. The **GR40** runs from north to south. The **GR441** makes a circuit round the Monts-Dômes, called the **Tour de la Chaîne des Puys**. The **GR400** encircles the Cantal mountains, and the **GR30** the lakes of the Artense plateau and Cézallier, under the title of the **Tour des Lacs d'Auvergne**. There are also lots of shorter walks; ask at local tourist offices for more information, and for details of mountain bike rental.

If only because of the practicalities of transport, you will likely pass through **Clermont-Ferrand**, the capital of the *département*. Given its rather dramatic historical associations – it was the site of Pope Urban II's speech which launched the Crusades in 1095 – the city may disappoint, but nonetheless the town is worth an afternoon of rambling. Otherwise, the towns in the area are few and of secondary interest, although **Orcival**, **Murat** and **Salers** are unexpectedly attractive; **St-Nectaire** contains an exceptionally beautiful small church in the distinct Auvergne version of Romanesque; and **St-Flour** and **Aurillac** have an agreeable provincial insularity.

Clermont-Ferrand and around

CLERMONT-FERRAND lies at the northern tip of the Massif Central. Although its situation is magnificent, almost encircled by the wooded and grassy volcanoes of the **Monts-Dômes**, it has for over a century been a typical smokestack industrial centre, the home base of Michelin tyres, which makes it a rather incongruous capital for the rustic, even backward province of the Auvergne.

Its roots, both as a spa and a communications and trading centre, go back to Roman times. It was just outside the town, on the plateau of Gergovia to the south, that the Gauls under the leadership of **Vercingétorix** won their only victory against Julius Caesar's invading Romans. In the Middle Ages, the rival towns of Clermont and Montferrand were ruled respectively by a bishop and the count of Auvergne. Louis XIII united them in 1630, but it was not until the rapid industrial expansion of the late nineteenth century that the two really became indistinguishable.

Michelin came into being thanks to the inventions of Charles Mackintosh, the Scotsman of raincoat fame. His niece married Edouard Daubrée, a Clermont sugar manufacturer, and brought with her some ideas about making rubber goods that she had learnt from her uncle. In 1889, the company became Michelin and Co, just in time to catch the development of the automobile and the World War I aircraft industry. The family ruled the town and employed 30,000 of its citizens until the early 1980s, when the industry went into decline. In

the years since, the workforce has been halved, causing rippling unemployment throughout Clermont's economy.

As in many other traditional industrial towns hit by recession and changing global patterns of trade, Clermont has had to struggle to reorientate itself, turning to service industries and the creation of a university of 34,000 students. Nonetheless, many people have moved elsewhere in search of work, reducing the population by nearly a tenth. The town has changed physically, too, as many of the old factories have been demolished. Despite all of this, the old centre has a surprisingly hip and youthful feel, with pavement bars packed out in the evenings as the boutiques and galleries which have sprung up wind down for the day.

Arrival and information

The **gare SNCF** is on avenue de l'Union Soviétique, from where it is a ten-minute bus journey to place de Jaude, at the western edge of the cathedral hill. The **gare routière** (ⓣ04.73.35.05.62) is on boulevard François-Mitterrand, with a city transport information kiosk called Boutique T2C at 24 bd Charles-de-Gaulle (ⓣ04.73.28.70.00). The city **airport** (ⓣ04.73.62.71.00, ⓦwww.clermont-fd.cci.fr) is at Aulnat, 7km east, with daily flights to and from Paris internal destinations, as well as to London during the summer. A one way) connects the airport with both the train and bus station. **tourist office** is opposite the cathedral in place de la Victoire pt Mon–Fri 9am–7pm, Sat & Sun 10am–7pm; Oct–April Mon–Fri opm, Sat 10am–1pm & 2–6pm, Sun 9.30am–12.30pm & 2–6pm; 04.73.98.65.00, www.ot-clermont-ferrand.fr), and there's another conveniently placed annexe immediately to the left outside the train station exit (June–Sept Mon–Sat 9.15–11.30am & 12.15–5pm; Oct–May closed Sat; 04.73.91.87.89). At the main office you can pick up a *Passe Découverte* (€10) which will admit you once to each of the town's museums. The **departmental office** is on place de la Bourse (04.73.42.22.50, planetepuydedome.com), and the **regional office** at 44 av des États-Unis (04.73.29.49.49, www.crt-auvergne.fr). Specific hiking or mountain-bike information is available from Chamina, 5 rue Pierre-le-Vénérable (04.73.92.81.44). Bikes are available from the SNCF, at the main station and at a central office at 20 place Remoux (04.73.14.12.36). For **Internet** access your best bet is CyberFrag at 3 rue de la Boucherie near the cathedral (Mon–Sun 11am–11pm; 04.73.91.51.64) or closer to the train station there is CyberStrike at 31 av de Grande-Bretagne (Mon–Sat 10am–2am, Sun noon–2am, 04.73.92.96.78)

Accommodation

Most of Clermont's **hotels** are concentrated just off the lively place de Jaude, close to the town's main shops, and around the rather characterless station area. There's not a tremendous choice, but they are generally good value. Campers will find municipal **campsites** at Royat (*L'Oclède*), 4km to the southwest (04.73.35.97.05; closed Nov–March; bus #41); Ceyrat (*Le Chanset*), 5km to the south (04.73.61.30.73; bus #4C & #41, stop "Preguille"); and Cournon (*Le Pré des Laveuses*), 10km to the east, on the River Allier (04.73.84.81.30; bus #3, stop "Plaine de jeux").

Albert Elisabeth 37 av Albert-Elisabeth 04.73.92.47.41, www.hotel-albertelisabeth.com. Well-run family hotel, with pastel-decorated rooms; handy for the train station. 3

Des Deux Avenues 4 av de la République 04.73.92.37.52, hotel.2avenues@wanadoo.fr Located a few minutes walk from place Delille. This funky place is the best option in town and offers clean airy rooms at budget rates; about five minutes' walk from the station. 1

Foch 22 rue Maréchal-Foch 04.73.93.48.40, www.hotel-foch-clermont.com. Tucked away down a side street off place de Jaude, this is a good-value budget hotel, with bright, summery rooms. 2

Lyon 16 place de Jaude 04.73.17.60.80, hotel.de.lyon@wanadoo.fr. Tastefully furnished, though the lively bar and brasserie below can get a little noisy at night (*plats* around €8.50). 3

Des Puys d'Arverne 16 place Delille 04.73.91.92.06, www.hoteldespuys.com. A modern, top-of-the-range hotel, offering spacious rooms, some with balconies. Its first-rate gourmet restaurant has splendid views of the town and Le Puy de Dôme (menus from €14.50–44). 5

Ravel 8 rue de Maringues 04.73.91.51.33, hotelravel63@wanadoo.fr. Opposite the old Marché St-Joseph, this friendly hotel offers attractive rooms, with sunny Mediterranean decor and good value for money. The proximity to the train and bus stations makes it specially convenient for travellers passing through. Closed Jan. 2

Regina 14 rue Bonnabaud 04.73.93.44.76, www.hotel-foch-clermont.com. Looks a little grubby from the outside, but inside an elegant spiral staircase leads up to fresh, clean rooms. 3

The City

The most dramatic and flattering approach to Clermont is from the Aubusson road or along the scenic rail line from Le Mont-Dore, both of which cross the chain of the Monts-Dômes just north of the Puy de Dôme. This way you descend through the leafy western suburbs with marvellous views over the town, dominated by the black towers of the cathedral sitting atop the volcanic stump that forms the hub of the old town.

The Cathédrale Notre-Dame and around

Clermont's reputation as a *ville noire* becomes immediately understandable when you enter the appealing medieval quarter, clustered in a characteristic muddle around the cathedral. The colour is due not to industrial pollution but to the black volcanic rock used in the construction of many of its buildings. The **Cathédrale Notre-Dame** stands at the centre and highest point of the old town; Freda White evocatively described its sombre grey-black-stone lava from the quarries at nearby Volvic as being "like the darkest shade of a pigeon's wing". Begun in the mid-thirteenth century, it was not finished until the nineteenth, under the direction of Viollet-le-Duc, who was the architect of the west front and those typically Gothic crocketed spires, whose too methodically cut stonework at close range betrays the work of the machine rather than the mason's hand. The interior is swaddled in gloom, illuminated all the more startlingly by the brilliant colours of the rose windows in the transept and the stained-glass windows in the choir, most dating back to the fourteenth century. Remnants of medieval frescoes survive, too: a particularly beautiful Virgin and Child adorns the right wall of the Chapelle Ste-Madeleine and an animated battle scene between the crusaders and Saracens unfolds on the central wall of the Chapelle St-Georges.

If the day is fine, it's worth climbing the **Tour de la Bayette** (Mon–Fri 10am–5.15pm, Sun 3–6pm; €1.50) by the north transept door: you look back over the rue des Gras to the Puy de Dôme looming dramatically over the city, with white morning mist retreating down its sides like seaweed from a rock.

Northeast of the cathedral, down the elegant old rue du Port, stands Clermont's other great church, the Romanesque **Basilique Notre-Dame-du-Port** – a century older than the cathedral and in almost total contrast both in style and substance, built from softer stone in pre-lava-working days and consequently corroding badly from exposure to Clermont's polluted air. For all that, it's a beautiful building in pure Auvergnat Romanesque style, featuring a Madonna and Child over the south door in the strangely stylized local form, both figures stiff and upright, the Child more like a dwarf than an infant. Inside, it exudes the broody mysteriousness so often generated by the Romanesque style. Put a coin in the slot and you can light up the intricately carved ensemble of leaves, knights and biblical figures on the church's pillars and capitals. It was here in all probability that Pope Urban II preached the First Crusade in 1095 to a vast crowd who received his speech with the Occitan cry of *Dios lo volt* (God wills it) – a phrase adopted by the crusaders in justification of all subsequent massacres.

For general animation, shopping, drinking and eating, the streets between the cathedral and place de Jaude are best, with the main morning market taking place in the conspicuously modern **place St-Pierre** just off rue des Gras. **Place de Jaude** remains another monument to planners' deviation in spite of the shops, the cafés well placed to take in the morning sun and an attempt to make it more attractive with trees and a fountain. Smack in the middle of the traffic, the Romantic equestrian statue of Vercingétorix stands vigil, his sword raised dramatically in salute of the Puy de Dôme.

Outside the city centre

Away from these central streets, there are a few concrete sights to tempt the pedestrian. Among these are **rue Ballainvilliers**, whose eighteenth-century

…all the sombre elegance of Edinburgh and lead to the **Musée Bargoin** …0am–noon 1–5pm, Sun 2–7pm; €4), with displays of archeological …nclude an array of fascinating domestic bits: Roman shoes, baskets, …d fruit, glass and pottery, as well as a remarkable burial find from nearby …s-de-Veyre dating back to the second century AD. There is also a diverse …ollection of tapestries and textiles. Though not of great interest, the **Musée Lecoq**, directly behind the Musée Bargoin (May–Sept Tues–Sat 10am–noon & 2–6pm, Sun 2–6pm; Oct–April 10am–noon & 2–5pm; €4), is devoted mainly to natural history – and named after the gentleman who also founded the public garden full of beautiful trees and formal beds just across the street.

Clermont-Ferrand's most impressive museum, the **Musée d'Art Roger-Quillot** (Tues–Sun 10am–6pm; €4), is situated on place Louis-Deteix in **Monteferrand**, some 2.5km northeast of the centre (bus #1, #9 or #16 from place de Jaude). Housed in a daringly renovated eighteenth-century Ursuline convent, this museum holds a broad collection of over two thousand works of art from the medieval to the contemporary. Notable pieces include a collection of carved capitals and a stunning enamelled reliquary of Thomas Becket. Montferrand is today little more than a suburb of larger Clermont, standing out on a limb to the north – if you journey out for the museum you should take time to stroll around. Built on the *bastide* plan, its principal streets, rue de la Rodade and rue Jules-Guesde (the latter named after the founder of the French Communist Party, as Montferrand was home to many of the Michelin factory workers), are still lined with the fine town houses of its medieval merchants and magistrates.

Eating and drinking

For a daytime drink, *Le Suffren*, on the corner of place de Jaude, is one of the most popular places to hang out. More unusual is *Les Goûters de Justine, a salon de thé*, tucked away in old rue Pascal and furnished with antique chairs, old sofas and oriental carpets. At night one of the most fashionable places is *Le Magma Café* on place de la Vicotoire, while young rockers head for the suburban village of Orcines, beneath the Puy de Dôme, to long-standing *Phidias*, aka *Boudu's*, on route de la Baraque (℡04.73.62.18.34; until 5am; closed Sun & Mon).

Restaurants

Auvergnat 27 av de l'Union Soviétique. Possibly the best option in the station area: the restaurant is oak-beamed and rustic-looking. The menu includes standard Auvergne dishes such as *truffade*.

Le Bistrot Vénitie 36 rue des Gras. Serves good pizza and pasta from €15. Closed Sun.

Le Bougnat 29 rue des Chaussetiers. Offers local regional cuisine at affordable prices; from €12. Closed Sun & Mon eve, Tues lunch.

Hôtel des Commerçants opposite the station. Inexpensive and very friendly, with a terrace at the back (menus from €9.80).

Crêperie 1513 3 rue des Chaussetiers. Sited opposite the cathedral, this is the best of the cheaper places and very popular. The restaurant occupies a superb Renaissance mansion built in 1513. Lunchtime menu €9.

Aux Délices de la Treille 33 rue de la Treille ℡04.73.91.26.90. A well-known and quirky place where customers pack into the tiny and flamboyant dining room or eat in the narrow street: €12 at lunchtime, otherwise €16 plus.

Gérard Anglard 17 rue Lamartine, off place de Jaude ℡04.73.93.52.25. Provides a specialized gastronomic experience, with refined and inventive cooking. The lunchtime menu starts at €18. Closed Sun & first two weeks Aug.

La Goulette 12 rue St-Esprit. Offers excellent and cheap North African *briques* for as little as €3.50.

Mai Lan 41 bd Trudaine. Serves first-class Vietnamese cooking for around €20. Closed Sun & Mon lunch.

Pescajoux 13 rue du Port. A good place for a quick snack with a lunch crêpe-menu starting from €9.

Petit Bonneval 5km southeast off the N9 Issoire road at Pérignat-lès-Sarliève ℡04.73.79.11.11. A delicious stop for dinner on a summer evening; menus from €19. Closed Sun eve.

Around Riom

From Riom SNCF buses run to **MOZAC**, on the edge of town, with a twelfth-century **abbey church** whose Romanesque sculpture is as beautiful as you'd expect, and continue to the bourgeois spa resort of **CHÂTEL-GUYON** in around twenty minutes. With thirty different **hot springs**, great views over the surrounding countryside and *puys*, and a couple of well-equipped **campsites**, this is as good a place as any if you want to rest up for a night. For an easy stroll from here, you can wander out along the leafy **valleys of the Sardon and Prades**.

The little town of **VOLVIC** is also close by, renowned for its spring water and the quarries that furnished the black rock for Clermont's cathedral, as well as so many other Auvergnat buildings. Its **Maison de la Pierre**, on rue Viallard (closed for refurbishment at time of writing), features a surprisingly engaging display about the use of lava rock, including a historical and geological explanation, as well as a tour of the disused quarries – a warm jacket is advised.

Vichy

VICHY is famous for two things: its World War II puppet government under Marshal Pétain, and its curative sulphurous springs, which attract thousands of ageing and ailing visitors, or *curistes*, every year. There's no mention of Pétain's government in town, but the fact that Vichy is one of France's foremost spa resorts colours everything you see here. The town is almost entirely devoted to catering for its largely elderly, genteel and rich population, which swells severalfold in summer; they come here to drink the water, wallow in it, inhale its steam or be sprayed with it. An attempt is now being made to rejuvenate the image of Vichy by appealing to a younger, more fitness-conscious generation.

The Town

All of this makes Vichy seem unappealing, and yet it has a certain element of charm. There's a real *fin-de-siècle* atmosphere about the place and a curious fascination in its continuing function. The town revolves around the **Parc des Sources**, a stately tree-shaded park that takes up most of the centre. At its north end stands the **Hall des Sources**, an enormous iron-framed greenhouse in which people sit and chat or read newspapers, while from a large tiled stand in

Volvic to Laschamp walk

For a good day's walk and a thorough exploration of the *puys*, take the train from Clermont to Volvic-Gare. Follow the D90 road beside the train line for about 1km until you join up with the **GR441** path, where the road turns right under the track. Keep along your side of the train track for a few minutes longer and follow the GR441 round to the left, almost doubling back southwest along the line of the wooded Puys Nugères, Jumes and Coquille to the northern foot of the Puy de Chopine (2–3hr). Here you join up with the **GR4** and follow the combined GR4–441 across the Orcines–Pontgibaud road to the summit of the Puy de Dôme (about 2hr 30min from the road). From the Puy, descend to the Col de Ceyssat in half an hour (good chance of a lift back to Clermont), or continue to **Laschamp** (50min), where there is a **gîte d'étape** (7–8hr, though a fit walker could do it in 6hr).

You should not set off without either the relevant section of the GR4 Topo-guide or, preferably, the IGN 1:25,000 map, the *Chaîne des Puys*, which also marks the GR441 from Volvic-Gare. If you don't feel up to a walk, there's a really beautiful train ride from Clermont to the town of Le Mont-Dore, which follows the chain of the *puys*.

the middle the various waters emerge from their spouts, beside the just-visible remains of the Roman establishment. The *curistes* line up to get their prescribed cupful, and for a small fee you can join them. The Célestins is the only one of the springs that is bottled and widely drunk: if you're into a taste experience, try the remaining five. They are progressively more sulphurous and foul, with the Source de l'Hôpital, which has its own circular building at the far end of the park, an almost unbelievably nasty creation. Each of the springs is prescribed for a different ailment and the tradition is that, apart from the Célestins, they must all be drunk on the spot to be efficacious – a dubious but effective way of drawing in the crowds.

Although all the springs technically belong to the nation and treatment is partially funded by the state, they are in fact run privately for profit by the Compagnie Fermière, first created in the mid-nineteenth century to prepare for a visit by the Emperor Napoléon III, whose interest in the waters brought Vichy to public notice. The Compagnie not only has a monopoly on selling the waters but also runs the casino and numerous hotels – even the chairs conveniently dotted around the Parc des Sources are owned by it.

Directly behind the Hall des Sources, on the leafy **Esplanade Napoléon III**, is the enormous, Byzantine-style **Grand Établissement Thermal**, the former thermal baths, decorated with Moorish arches, gold-and-blue domes and blue ceramic panels of voluptuous mermaids. All that remains inside of the original baths is the grand entrance hall, with its fountain and two beautiful murals, *La Bain* and *La Source*, painted by Osberd in 1903. The arcades leading off either side of the hall, once the site of gyms and treatment rooms, now house expensive boutiques.

To provide distraction for the *curistes*, a grand **casino** and **opera house** were built at the southern end of the Parc des Sources. From May to September the opera house is the venue for regular concerts and opera productions, while lighter music oompahs out from the open-air bandstand in the park behind it.

After the waters, Vichy's curiosities are limited. There's a pleasant, wooded riverside in the **Parc de l'Allier**, also created for Napoléon III. And, not far from here, the old town boasts the strange **church of St-Blaise**, actually two churches in one, with a 1930s Baroque structure built onto the original Romanesque one – an effect that sounds hideous but is rather imaginative. Inside, another Auvergne Black Virgin, Notre-Dame-des-Malades, stands surrounded by plaques offered by the grateful healed who stacked their odds with both her and the sulphur.

Practicalities

Vichy's **gare SNCF** is about a ten-minute walk from the centre, on the eastern edge of the city centre at the end of rue de Paris. The **gare routière** sits on the corner of rue Doumier and rue Jardet, by the central place Charles-de-Gaulle, and there's a public transport information line on ⓣ04.70.30.17.30. The building that used to house the wartime Vichy government at 19 rue du Parc is now home to the **tourist office** (April–June & Sept Mon–Sat 9am–12.30pm & 1.30–7pm, Sun 9.30am–12.30pm & 3–7pm; July & Aug 9am–7pm, Sun 9.30am–12.30pm & 3–7pm; Oct–March Mon–Fri 9am–noon & 1.30–6pm, Sat 9am–noon & 2–6pm, Sun 2.30–5.30pm; ⓣ04.70.98.71.94, ⓦwww.vichy-tourisme.com). Internet access is available at Echap Internet Café (12 rue Source de l'Hôpital, Tues–Sat noon–midnight, Sun 2pm–midnight).

There is an abundance of hotels and finding a place to stay is not difficult. You'll find several around the station, but more pleasant are the friendly, grand neo-Baroque *Midland*, 4 rue de l'Intendance, in a quiet street off rue de Paris

(ⓣ04.70.97.48.48, ⓦwww.hotel.midland.com; ❹–❺; closed mid-Oct to mid-April; good restaurant with menus from €17), and the *Hôtel Londres*, 7 bd de Russie, behind the casino (ⓣ04.70.98.28.27, ⓦwww.hoteldelondres.fr; ❷–❺; closed Nov to Feb), which was the secret meeting place for Jean Moulin and fellow Resistance fighters in 1941. There's a municipal **campsite**, *La Gravière*, at the Centre Omnisports (ⓣ04.70.59.21.00; closed Oct to late-May).

For **eating**, apart from the hotel-restaurants listed above, the simplest solution is to head for the area around the junction of rue Clemenceau and rue de Paris, where there are several brasseries and cafés. To do so, however, would be to miss out on the best that Vichy has to offer – a surprising range of top-notch restaurants. Two of the best include the frenetically eclectic *Jacques Decoret* on 7 av de Gramont (ⓣ04.70.97.65.06; closed Tues & Wed & Aug), which has menus drawing on flavours from places as jarringly diverse as Oaxaca and Marseille from €40–95, and the more affordable and less daring *La Table d'Antoine* at 8 rue Burnol (ⓣ04.70.98.99.71; closed Sun lunch & Mon; from €21).

The Monts-Dore

The **Monts-Dore** lie about 50km southwest of Clermont. Also volcanic in origin – the main period of activity was around five million years ago – they are much more rugged and more obviously mountainous than their gentler, younger neighbours, the Monts-Dômes. Their centre is the precipitous, plunging valley of the River Dordogne, which rises on the slopes of the **Puy de Sancy**, at 1885m the highest point in the Massif Central, just above the little town of **Le Mont-Dore**.

In spite of their relative ruggedness, there are few crags or rock faces and their upper slopes, albeit steep, are grassy and treeless for miles and miles. They are known as *montagnes à vaches* – mountains for cows – as they traditionally provided summer pasture land for herds of cows, raised above all for their milk and the production of **St-Nectaire** cheese. The herdsmen who milked them and made the cheese set up their primitive summer homes in the dozens of (now mainly ruined) stone huts, or *burons*, that scatter the landscape.

Although these traditional activities still continue, many of the upland herds are now beef cattle being fattened for the autumn sales, often for export to Italy, Germany and Spain. And tourism has become an important part of the local economy, although mostly unobtrusive and low-key, with mainly walkers in summer and cross-country skiers in winter.

Le Mont-Dore and the Puy de Sancy

Squeezed out along the narrow wooded valley of the infant Dordogne, grey-slated **LE MONT-DORE**, 50km southwest of Clermont, is a long-established spa resort, with Roman remnants testifying to just how old it is. Its popularity goes back to the eighteenth century, when metalled roads replaced the old mule paths and made access possible, but reached its apogee with the opening of the rail line around 1900. It is an altogether wholesome and civilized sort of place.

The **Établissement Thermal** – the baths, which give the place its *raison d'être* – are in the middle of town and are certainly worth visiting (30min guided tours Mon–Sat: mid-May to mid-Oct on the hour; €2). Early every morning, the *curistes* stream into its neo-Byzantine halls – an extravaganza of tiles, striped columns and ornate ironwork – hoping for a remedy in this self-proclaimed "world centre for treatment of asthma". For many Parisians, of all ages and walks of life, this is their annual mecca: whiling away their days sniffing sulphur from bunsen burner tubes, and sitting in thick steam.

Walkers also frequent the town, the principal attraction being the **Puy de Sancy** (1885m), whose jagged skyline blocks the head of the Dordogne valley, 3km away (mid-May to Sept; 4 buses daily from the tourist office; €3.10). Accessible by *téléphérique* (€6.50 return) since the 1930s, it's one of the busiest tourist sites in the country. As a result, the path from the *téléphérique* station to the summit has had to be railed and paved with baulks of timber to prevent total erosion. Combined with the scars of access tracks for the ski installations, this has done little for its beauty.

However, with a little sweat and effort you can escape to wilder areas of the mountain. The **GR30** passes this way and on down to La Bourboule, giving a good sense of the typical landscape: long views over meadows full of gentians and violets, grazed by sheep and cows. Start out along the summit path and at the first intermediate peak, take a right and go downhill. The GR30 is signposted. It follows the western ridge of the Dordogne valley for about an hour and a half, before turning ninety degrees left, away from the valley. Keep straight ahead at this point, go down a gravelly track, with the rocky dome of **Le Capucin**, above Le Mont-Dore, directly in front of you. The track enters the woods to the left of this bump by a ruined house. Five minutes later, on the right, just past a concrete water-pipe junction, a path drops steeply down through beech trees to Le Capucin *funiculaire* station and down again to Le Mont-Dore (3hr).

Practicalities

Without a car, Le Mont-Dore is most easily accessible by train from Clermont. The **train** and **bus stations** are at the entrance to the town. A ten-minute walk down avenue Michelet takes you to the centre, where the **tourist office** sits in the park on avenue de la Libération (May & June Mon–Sat 9am–12.30pm & 2–6.30pm; July & Aug Mon–Sat 9am–1pm & 2–7pm, Sun 9am–noon & 2–6pm; Ⓣ04.73.65.20.21, Ⓦwww.sancy.com); the helpful staff will advise about other walking and cycling possibilities (VTT rental), as well as day bus excursions to some otherwise rather inaccessible places in the area. Internet access can be found at Sancyber at 4 rue Georges-Lagaye (Mon–Sun 10am–midnight).

Accommodation is not hard to come by, as the town is brimming with hotels. Close to the baths, at 8 rue Favart, *Hôtel aux Champs d'Auvergne* (Ⓣ04.73.65.00.37, Ⓦwww.auxchampsdauvergne.com; ❶; closed Nov to mid-Dec; restaurant from €12) is very welcoming and serves copious breakfasts, while the elegant *Hôtel de la Paix*, nearby on rue Rigny (Ⓣ04.73.65.00.17, Ⓦwww.hotel-de-la-paix.info; ❸), has comfortable, clean rooms and an excellent restaurant (menus €19–49). One of the best deals, with mod cons at a bargain price, is the *Beau Site* at 17 rue des Déportés (Ⓣ04.73.65.05.51, Ⓕ04.73.65.26.88; ❶–❸; closed mid-Oct to Dec & mid-March to April; restaurant from €13), beside the main baths. There's an efficient modern **hostel** on the Puy de Sancy road, with a stunning view of the mountains (Ⓣ04.73.65.03.53, Ⓔle-mont-dore@fuaj.org; closed Nov), and a very cheap *gîte*, *Les Hautes Pierres* (Ⓣ04.73.65.25.65, Ⓦwww.gite-les-hautes-pierres.com; Jan–Oct or by request) on chemin de Vergnes. The municipal **campsite**, *Les Crouzets* (Ⓣ & Ⓕ04.73.65.21.60; closed mid-Oct to mid-Dec), is nearby, opposite the station. The other municipal campsite is *L'Esquiladou* (Ⓣ04.73.65.23.74; closed Nov–April), off to the right on the road to La Bourboule.

As far as **eating** is concerned, there are large numbers of brasseries and cafés in the centre offering *plats* for €6.50–8. A particularly pleasant place is rustic *Le Bougnat*, 23 av Clemenceau, which serves various Auvergnat traditional dishes, as well as *raclette* and fondue (Ⓣ04.73.65.28.19; closed Mon; menus from €15). A great place for a **drink** is the atmospheric, 1940s-style *Café de Paris*, located on rue Jean-Moulin.

La Bourboule

LA BOURBOULE is just 7km down the road from Le Mont-Dore. Known as the sister to Le Mont-Dore, it's another traditional spa – the "capital of allergies" – but with a more open feel and, because of its lower altitude, temperatures are a degree or two warmer. The big **casino**, the domed **Grands Thermes baths** and several other *belle-époque* buildings which once housed privately run baths are ornate, gilded and wonderfully vulgar, with a faded, permanently off-season look to them, though the town has a certain Parisian flair that sets it apart from the smaller more provincial towns in the region. All in all, it's a cool, tranquil place to unwind: as the tourist office's leaflet says, "You will be able to put your vital node to rest in La Bourboule".

Behind the Hôtel de Ville, the large wooded **Parc Fenestre** has a *télécabine* taking you right up to **Plateau de Charlannes** (1300m), where it's possible to stroll in the woods or ski in winter; the **tourist office** in the Hôtel de Ville on place de la République (April–June & Sept daily 9.30am–noon & 1.30/2–6pm; July & Aug Mon–Sat 9am–7pm & Sun 9am–6pm; Oct–March Mon–Sat 9.30am–noon & 1.30–5.30pm, Sun 9.30am–12.30pm; Ⓣ04.73.65.57.71, Ⓦwww.sancy.com) sells a booklet of local walks.

Hotels here are plentiful, three good bargains being the *Aviation Hôtel*, in rue de Metz (Ⓣ04.73.81.32.32, Ⓦwww.avaition.fr; ④; closed Oct–Dec 20; restaurant from €15), with indoor pool; the welcoming, Art Deco-style *Le Pavillon*, 209 av d'Angleterre (Ⓣ04.73.65.50.18, Ⓔhotel.lepavillon@wanadoo.fr; ③; closed Oct–March; restaurant from €16); and the more basic *Les Fleurs* on avenue de Mussy (Ⓣ04.73.81.09.44, Ⓦwww.hotellesfleurs.com; ③; closed Nov & Dec; vegetarian restaurant from €11–26). There's also a good selection of **campsites**, with the *camping municipal* on avenue Maréchal Lattre-de-Tassigny (Ⓣ04.73.81.10.20), and another at Murat-le-Quaire, 4km away, along the Mont-Dore road (Ⓣ04.73.65.54.81).

Orcival

Twenty-seven kilometres southwest of Clermont and about 20km north of Le Mont-Dore, lush pastures and green hills punctuated by the abrupt eruptions

Walking and skiing around La Bourboule

Fit and serious walkers may want to conquer the **Puy de Sancy**, a six-hour hike south of La Bourboule on the GR30–41, passing after about two hours the two fine waterfalls of the **Cascade de la Vernière** and **Plat à Barbe** – themselves a satisfying destination. For the summit of Puy de Sancy, see the account of Le Mont-Dore, p.913. An easier walk out of La Bourboule is to the summit of the **Banne d'Ordanche** (1500m): pick up the GR path to the east of the town where it crosses the D130 road and the train line, then take the signposted GR41 where it diverges from the GR30. During winter months, both Le Mont-Dore and La Bourboule double as ski resorts – centres of a **ski-de-fond** (cross-country) network of circular pistes, some over 20km long, and there is limited downhill skiing as well, although at a maximum of 1150m this is not a resort for enthusiasts. Skiable paths also connect La Bourboule to other ski centres in the locality – Sancy, Besse, Chastreix and Picherande.

of the *puys* enclose the small village of **ORCIVAL**, the home town of ex-President Valéry Giscard d'Estaing. A pretty, popular, place, founded by the monks of La Chaise-Dieu in the twelfth century, it makes a suitable base for hiking in the region.

Orcival is dominated by the stunning Romanesque **church of Notre-Dame** (daily 8am–noon & 2–7pm), built of the same dark-grey volcanic stone as the cathedral in Clermont and topped with a spire and fanned with tiny chapels. Once a major parish, it counted no less than 24 priests in the mid-1200s, and the ironwork on the north door, with its curious forged human head motif, dates from that era. Inside, attention focuses on the choir, neatly and harmoniously contained by the semicircle of pillars defining the ambulatory. Mounted on a stone column in the centre is the celebrated **Virgin of Orcival**, a gilded and enamelled twelfth-century statue in typical Romance style; the object of a popular cult since the Middle Ages and still carried through the streets on Ascension Day.

There's no public transport to Orcival itself; the nearest **bus station** is at Rochefort-Montagne, 6km away, served by buses from Clermont-Ferrand. There is, however, a helpful **tourist office** (July & Aug daily 10am–noon & 2–7pm; rest of year holiday periods only Tues–Sat 2–5pm; ⓣ04.73.65.89.78), just below the church. Modest **accommodation** can be found at the *Hôtel des Touristes* (ⓣ04.73.65.82.55, ⓕ04.73.65.97.37; ❷; closed mid-Nov to mid-Feb; restaurant from €12) near the church. There's a lakeside **campsite**, *Camping de l'Étang de Fléchat* (ⓣ04.73.65.82.96; closed mid-Sept to April), 2km outside Orcival, but a better bet is the municipal site at St-Bonnet, 5km to the north of the village (ⓣ04.73.65.83.32; closed Oct–April), set on a hillside with wonderful views of the surrounding mountains.

St-Nectaire and around

ST-NECTAIRE lies some way to the southeast of Orcival, midway between Le Mont-Dore and Issoire. It comprises the tiny spa of **St-Nectaire-le-Bas**, whose main street is lined with grand but fading *belle-époque* hotels, which was

Walks around Orcival

Walking possibilities from Orcival include trips to **Lac de Servières** and **Lac de Guéry**. The first takes two and a half hours, the second some five hours. For Lac de Servières, follow the **GR141–30** south through the woods above the valley of the Sioule. The lake is a beauty; it's 1200m up, with gently sloping shores surrounded by pasture and conifers. You can either head southeast to the **gîte d'étape** at Pessade (ⓣ04.73.79.31.07), or continue to the larger Lac de Guéry, lent a slightly eerie air by the black basalt boulders strewn across the surrounding meadows, where there's a romantically situated lakeside hotel, the *Lac de Guéry* (ⓣ04.73.65.02.76, ⓦwww.auberge-lac-guery.fr; ❸; closed mid-Oct to mid-Jan; restaurant from €16).

If you're driving to Le Mont-Dore, only 9km further on from here, just before the Lac de Guéry, the road takes you round the head of the **Fontsalade valley**, where two prominent rocks composed of banks of basalt organ-pipes rise spectacularly from the woods: the **Roche Tuilière** and the **Roche Sanadoire**. A footpath takes you on a two-hour walk round the valley, starting from the roadside belvedere overlooking Sanadoire. A little higher up, on the bare slopes of the **Puy de l'Aiguiller**, a roadside memorial commemorates some English airmen killed in an accident while making a parachute drop to the maquis in March 1944.

A detailed *Topo-guide* to the region is available from both the Orcival and Bourboule tourist offices (€6).

St-Nectaire cheese

St-Nectaire is an *appellation contrôlée*, to which only cheeses made from herds grazing in a limited area to the south of the Monts-Dore are entitled. It is made in two stages. First, a white creamy cheese or *tomme* is produced. This is matured for two to three months in a cellar at a constant temperature, resulting in the growth of a mould on the skin of the cheese which produces the characteristic smell, taste and whitish or yellowy-grey colour.

There are two kinds: St-Nectaire **fermier** and St-Nectaire **laitier**. The *fermier* is the strongest and tastiest and some of it is still made entirely on the farm. Increasingly, however, individual farmers make the *tomme* stage, but then sell it on to wholesalers for the refining. The *laitier* is much more an "industrial" product, made from the milk of lots of different herds, sold onto a co-operative or cheese manufacturer for all its stages.

added on to the old village of **St-Nectaire-le-Haut**, overlooked by a magnificent Romanesque **church** (daily 9am–7pm). Like the church in Orcival and Notre-Dame-du-Port in Clermont, this is one of the most striking examples of the Auvergne's Romanesque architecture. The carved capitals around the apse retain the tantalizing hues of the paint which once covered the whole interior, while the church's treasures are guarded in the north transept and include a magnificent gilded bust of St Baudime (the third-century missionary of the Auvergne and parish-founder), a polychrome *Virgin in Majesty*, and two enamelled plaques, all dating from the twelfth century. Among the town's other curiosities are a couple of caverns, the spa (a two-hour basic session from €12), and the **Maison du Saint-Nectaire** where you'll find an exhibition on the cheese-making process and a chance to visit a cheese-ripening cellar. The surrounding countryside is notable for its menhirs and other pre-historic megaliths; the tourist office has information on how to find them.

The **tourist office** (July & Aug Mon–Sat 9.30am–12.15pm & 2–6.45pm, Sun 9.30am–12.15pm & 2–4.45pm; Sept–June Mon–Sat 9.30–11.45am & 2–4.45pm; ⓣ04.73.88.50.86, ⓦwww.ville-saint-nectaire.fr) is located in the "Grandes Thermes" complex on the main road and has information on six different circuit walks of various lengths that take from two to five hours to complete. For a **place to stay**, *Hotel de la Paix*, situated at the base of the GR30 footpath below the church, offers comfortable rooms and a reasonably priced restaurant (ⓣ04.73.88.49, ⓔhotelpaix63710@aol.com; ❸; menus from €13; April–Oct). Greater comfort can be found at the *Mercure*, near the town centre, a converted spa renovated as a hotel (ⓣ04.73.88.57.00, ⓔH1814@accor-hotels.com; ❻; closed Nov, Dec & part Jan & March), also with a fine restaurant (menu €21). The best-value campsite is the *Clé des Champs* (ⓣ04.73.88.52.33, ⓦwww.campingcledeschamps.com) located on the D996 on the right when heading in the direction of Champeix. For walkers, the GR30 heads north from here to Lac Aydat in five hours, or west to the forest-girt **Lac Chambon** in three hours via Murol. There's a *gîte* on the way at Phialeix (ⓣ04.73.79.32.43; closed Nov–March).

For shorter walks out of St-Nectaire, take the D150 past the church through the old village towards the **Puy de Mazeyres** (919m), and turn up a path to the right for the final climb to the summit (1hr), where you get a superb aerial view of the surrounding country. Alternatively, follow the D966 along the Couze de Chambon valley to **SAILLANT**, where the stream cascades down a high lava rock face in the middle of the village.

Murol

MUROL, 6km west of St-Nectaire by road (July & Aug twice-daily bus to Clermont) or 5.5km by footpath, is an attractive, sleepy little place best known for its powerful medieval **château**, dramatically situated on top of a basalt cone commanding the approaches for kilometres around (April–June & Sept daily 10am–noon & 1.30–6pm; July & Aug daily 10am–7pm; Oct–March Sat, Sun & hols 2–5pm; €4). In summer, a local organization re-enacts the medieval life of the castle in costume (€7.50).

There are several small family-run **hotels** here. Try the *Hôtel des Pins*, on rue de Levat (Ⓣ04.73.88.60.50, Ⓕ04.73.88.60.29; ❷; closed Oct to May; restaurant from €10), or the *Hôtel de Paris*, on place de l'Hôtel-de-Ville (Ⓣ04.73.88.60.09, Ⓔplaneix.hotelparis.murol@wanadoo.fr; ❷; closed Nov to Easter). Of the **campsites**, the best value is the *Ribeyre*, a short distance away at **JASSAT** (Ⓣ04.73.88.64.29, Ⓦlaribeyre.free.fr; closed mid-Sept to April).

Besse

Eleven kilometres due south of Murol, **BESSE** is one of the prettiest and oldest villages in the region. Its fascinating winding streets of noble lava-built houses – some fifteenth-century – sit atop the valley of the Couze de Pavin, with one of the original fortified town **gates** still in place at the upper end of the village.

Its wealth was due to its role as the principal market for the farms on the eastern slopes of the Monts-Dore, and its co-operative is still one of the main producers of St-Nectaire cheese (see p.917). The annual **festivals** of the Montée and Dévalade, marking the ascent of the herds to the high pastures in July and their descent in autumn, are still celebrated by the procession of the Black Virgin of Vassivière from the **church of St-André** in Besse to the chapel of **La Vassivière**, west of **Lac Pavin**, and back again in autumn (July 2 & first Sun after Sept 21).

Lac Pavin lies 5km west of the village, on the way to the purpose-built downhill ski resort of **SUPER-BESSE** (both are connected to Besse by an hourly *navette*). It's a perfect volcanic lake, filling the now wooded crater. The **GR30** goes through, passing by the **Puy de Montchal**, whose summit (1407m) gives you a fine view over several other lakes and the rolling plateau south towards **ÉGLISENEUVE-D'ENTRAIGUES**, 13km by road, where the Parc des Volcans' **Maison du Fromage** gives a detailed account of the making of the different cheeses of Auvergne (daily: mid-May to June & Sept 2–6pm; July & Aug 10am–12.30pm & 2.30–7pm; €3.50).

Besse's **tourist office** is next to the church on place du Dr-Pipet (July & Aug Mon–Sat 9–7pm, Sun 10am–noon & 2–6pm; Sept–June Mon–Sat 10am–noon & 2–6pm, Sun 10am–noon 2–4pm; Ⓣ04.73.79.52.84, Ⓦwww.sancy.com), and will provide information and advice about walking, mountain biking and skiing. Good, simple fare can be had next door at the *Le Sancy*, which has a *plat du jour* for €6.50. For a place to **stay**, there's none better than the attractive old *Hostellerie du Beffroi*, 24 rue Abbé-Blot (Ⓣ04.73.79.50.08, Ⓕ04.73.79.57.87; ❸–❻), whose good restaurant serves up a range of local specialities from €20.

The Monts du Cantal

The **Cantal Massif** forms the most southerly extension of the Parc des Volcans. Still nearly 80km in diameter and once 3000m in height, it is one of the world's largest (albeit extinct) volcanoes, shaped like a wheel without a rim. The hub is formed by the three great conical peaks that survived the erosion of the original single cone: **Plomb du Cantal** (1855m), **Puy Mary** (1787m) and **Puy de Peyre-Arse** (1686m).

From this centre a series of deep-cut wooded valleys radiates out like spokes. The most notable are the **valley of Mandailles** and the **valleys of the Cère and Alagnon** in the southwest, where the road and rail line run, and in the north the **valleys of Falgoux and the Rhue**. Between the valleys, especially on the north side, are huge expanses of gently sloping grassland, including the **Plateau du Limon**, and it's these which for centuries have been the mainstay of life in the Cantal: summer pasture for the cows whose milk makes the firm yellow Cantal cheese, pressed in the form of great crusty drums. But this traditional activity has long been in serious decline; as elsewhere, many of the herds are now beef cattle. And tourism is on the increase, in particular walking, horse-riding and skiing.

The main walking routes are the fairly arduous **GR400**, which does a circuit of the whole massif, and the **GR4**, which crosses it from the north to the southeast. There are also more than fifty shorter routes, details of which are obtainable through Chamina Publications (see p.906). The two main summits, Plomb du Cantal and Puy Mary, are – for better or worse – accessible to all: the former by *téléphérique* from Super-Lioran, the latter by a veritable highway of a footpath from the road at Pas de Peyrol. The best section of the GR4–400 for an experienced hiker with limited time is the three-hour stretch between Super-Lioran and the Puy Mary, with the possibility of taking in a couple of extra summits on the way. For motorists, there's the long, sinuous **Route des Crêtes**, which does a rather wider circuit than the GR400. But, be warned, if you hit a period of bad weather, you'll drive a long way seeing no more than white banks of mist illumined by your headlights.

The main centres within the massif lie on the N122 between Murat and Aurillac: **LE LIORAN**, where the road and rail tunnels begin, and **SUPER-LIORAN**, the downhill and cross-country ski centre, with many hotels, including the rustic and comfortable *Rocher de Cerf* (Ⓣ04.71.49.50.14, Ⓕ04.71.49.54.07; ❹; half-*pension* normally required, otherwise ❷) and several *gîtes d'étape*, as well as a tourist office (Mon–Sat: July & Aug 9.30am–12.30pm & 2–6.30pm; Sept–June 8.30am–12.30pm & 1.30–6pm; Ⓣ04.71.49.50.08, Ⓦwww.lelioran.com). **THIEZAC**, 10km south, also has a tourist office (July & Aug daily 9.30am–12.30pm & 3.30–7pm; Sept–June Tues–Sat 9.30am–12.30pm & 2–5pm; Ⓣ04.71.47.03.50, as well as the *Hôtel La Belle Vallée* (Ⓣ04.71.47.00.22, Ⓦwww.elanceze.com; ❸; closed Nov–Dec 20; restaurant €14–28), three *gîtes d'étape* and a municipal campsite, *La Bedisse* (Ⓣ04.71.47.00.41; closed mid-Sept to May). Further south at **VIC-SUR-CÈRE** there's a tourist office (July & Aug daily 9.30am–12.30pm & 2.30–7.30pm; June & Sept daily 9.30–noon & 2–6pm; Ⓣ04.71.47.50.68), and accommodation at the *Hôtel des Bains*, 9 av de la Promenade (Ⓣ04.71.47.50.16, Ⓦwww.cantal-logis.com/vicsurcere/hoteldesbains; ❸; closed Oct–April; restaurant from €20), and the riverside municipal **campsite** (Ⓣ04.71.47.54.18; closed mid-Sept to March).

Aurillac

AURILLAC, the provincial capital of the Cantal, lies on the west side of the mountains, 98km east of Brive and 160km from Clermont-Ferrand. In spite of its good main-line train connections and the fact that its population has almost doubled in the last forty years to around 30,000, it remains one of the most out-of-the-way French provincial capitals. It was until recently a major manufacturer of umbrellas, though that seems doomed to eventual extinction, like its older traditional lace-making and tanning industries. It is now mainly an administrative and commercial centre, with important cattle markets in the suburb of Sistrières on Mondays. Although there are no important sights, it makes a pleasant and unpretentious place to stop over on your way into the Massif Central from the west.

The most interesting part of town is the kernel of old streets, now largely pedestrianized and full of good shops, just to the north of the central **place du Square**. **Rue Duclaux** leads through to the attractive **place de l'Hôtel-de-Ville**, where the big Wednesday and Saturday markets are held in the shadow of the handsome grey-stone **Hôtel de Ville**, built in restrained Republican-classical style in 1803. Beyond it, the continuation of **rue des Forgerons** leads to the beautiful little **place St-Géraud**, with a round twelfth-century fountain overlooked by a Romanesque house that was probably part of the original abbey guesthouse, and the externally rather unprepossessing **church of St-Géraud**, which nonetheless has a beautifully ribbed late Gothic ceiling.

At the back of the church, past a delightful small garden, **rue de la Fontaine** comes out on the riverbank by the Pont du Buis, with a shady walk back along cours d'Angoulême on the other side to the Pont-Rouge and **place Gerbert**, where there is an ancient *lavoir*, or washing place. On a steep bluff overlooking this end of town towers the eleventh-century keep of the Château St-Étienne, containing the town's only worthwhile museum, the **Muséum des Volcans** (Tues-Sat: mid-June to mid-Sept 10am–6.30pm; mid-Sept to mid-June 2-6pm; €4), with a good section on volcanoes and a splendid view over the mountains to the east.

Southeast of the town towards Aubrac, the road leads through **Carlat**, once an important feudal fiefdom, as well as the particularly attractive villages of **Mur-de-Barrez**, **Brommat** and **Albinhac**, with some lovely old houses and curious churches in the latter two villages.

Practicalities

The **gare SNCF** and **gare routière** are together on place Sémard, a ten-minute walk from the central place du Square along avenue de la République and rue de la Gare. The **tourist office** occupies a small kiosk on the downhill side of place du Square (April–June & Sept Mon–Sat 9am–noon & 2–6.30pm, Sun 10am–noon & 2–5pm; July & Aug daily 9am–7pm; Oct–March Mon–Sat 9am–noon & 2–6.30pm; ⓣ04.71.48.46.58), with a number of guidebooks and maps on sale, as well as a money-changing facility when the banks are closed. There's **Internet** access at the Faisan Doré cyber café, 8 place d'Aurigues.

For a **place to stay** in the centre of town, try the smart and comfortable *Le Square*, 15 place du Square (ⓣ04.71.48.24.72, ⓦwww.cantal-hotel.com; ❸), with a restaurant whose stuffed cabbage has won several prizes (from €15). Rather more deluxe accommodation can be found at the *Grand Hotel de Bordeaux* at 2 av République (ⓣ04.71.48.01.84, ⓦwww.hotel-de-bordeaux.fr; ❹), set in a nineteenth-century mansion.

There are a number of **restaurants** where you can sample Auvergnat specialities. Two of the most popular are the atmospheric *Le Terroir du Cantal*, 5 rue du Buis (closed Sun pm & Mon; from €15), with its rough-stone walls and wooden benches, and *Poivre et Sel*, 4 rue du 14-Juillet (closed Sun & Mon; menus from €11), featuring classic dishes such as *magret de canard*. The pretty, riverside *Birdland*, by the Pont-Rouge, done out in the French version of pub style, serves pizzas for around €8.50 and menus for €17 (closed Sun); if you're looking for **nightlife**, the *L'Aventure* disco is part of the same establishment (Thurs–Sun 11pm–4/5am; €10). Finally, Aurillac's most unexpected event is an annual international **street theatre festival** (Ⓦwww.aurillac.net) during the last full week in August, which attracts performers from all over Europe and fills the town with rather more exotic characters than are normally to be seen in these provincial parts.

Salers

SALERS lies 42km north of Aurillac, at the foot of the northwest slopes of the Cantal and within sight of the Puy Violent. Scarcely altered in size or aspect since its sixteenth-century heyday, it remains an extraordinarily homogeneous example of the architecture of that time. If things appear rather grand for a place so small, it's because the town became the administrative centre for the highlands of the Auvergne in 1564 and home of its magistrates. Exploiting this past is really all it has left, but Salers still makes a very worthwhile visit.

If you arrive by the Puy Mary road, you'll enter town by the **church**, which is worth a look for the super-naturalistic statuary of the *Entombment of Christ* (1496), hidden in a side chapel near the entrance. In front of you, the cobbled **rue du Beffroi** leads uphill, under the massive clock tower, and into the central **place Tyssandier-d'Escous**. It is a glorious little square, surrounded by the fifteenth-century mansions of the provincial aristocracy with pepper-pot turrets, mullioned windows and carved lintels, among them the sturdy **Maison du Bailliage**, and, nearby, the **Maison des Templiers**, housing the small Musée de Salers (mid-April to Sept daily 10.30am–noon & 2–7.30pm, closed Tues except July & Aug; €3). Though the museum itself is rather dull, with exhibitions on the Salers cattle breed, traditional costumes and the local cheese-making industry, it's worth having a look at the vaulted ceiling of the entrance passageway, with its carved lions and heads of saints, such as St John the Baptist, framed by wild flowing hair. Before you're done, be sure to make your way to the **Promenade de Barrouze** for the view out across the surrounding green hills and the Puy Violent.

The **tourist office** is in place Tyssandier-d'Escous (July & Aug 10am–7pm; Sept–June Tues–Sun 10am–noon & 2–6pm; Ⓣ04.71.40.70.33, Ⓦwww.pays-de-salers.com). If you want to **stay**, try the *Hôtel des Remparts*, near the Promenade de Barrouze (Ⓣ04.71.40.70.33, Ⓦwww.salers-hotel-remparts.com ❸; closed mid-Oct to mid-Dec), whose restaurant specializes in Auvergnat cuisine (from €13), or the more luxurious *Le Gerfaut* in route du Puy-Mary (Ⓣ04.71.40.75.75, Ⓦwww.salers-hotel-gerfaut.com; ❸; closed Nov–Easter). There's a municipal **campsite,** *Le Mouriol*, on the Puy Mary road (Ⓣ04.71.40.73.09, Ⓣ04.71.40.72.33 off season; closed mid-Oct to mid-May).

Murat

MURAT, on the eastern edge of the Cantal, is the closest town to the high peaks and a busy little place, its cafés and shops bustling uncharacteristically for the region. It is also the easiest to access, lying on the N122 road and main train line, about 12km northeast of Le Lioran. Rather than any particular sight, it's the ensemble of grey-stone houses that attracts, many dating from the fifteenth and sixteenth centuries. Crowded together on their medieval lanes, they make a magnificent sight, especially as you approach from the St-Flour road, with the backdrop of the steep basalt cliffs of the **Rocher Bonnevie**, once the site of the local castle and now surmounted by a huge white statue of the Virgin Mary. Facing the town, perched on the distinctive mound of the **Rocher**

Bredons, on your left as you approach, there's the lovely Romanesque **Église de Bredons** (July & Aug daily 10am–noon & 2.30–6.30pm; free), containing some fine eighteenth-century altarpieces. One of the finest of the old houses is now open to the public as the **Maison de la Faune** (July & Aug Mon–Sat 10am–12.30 & 2–7pm, Sun 10am–noon & 3-7pm; Sept–June Mon–Sat 10am–noon & 2–5pm, Sun 2–5pm; €4), full of stuffed animals and birds illustrating the wildlife of the Parc des Volcans.

The **monument** to deportees on place de l'Hôtel-de-Ville and the name of the **avenue des 12-et-24-Juin-1944**, opposite the tourist office, both commemorate one of the blackest days in Murat's recent history. On June 12, 1944, a local Resistance group interrupted a German raid on the town and killed a senior SS officer. In reprisal, the Germans burnt several houses down on June 24 and arrested 120 people, 80 of whom died in deportation. Near the river, below the Rocher Bredons, a stone with an inscription marks the spot where the villagers were assembled before being deported.

Practicalities

The **tourist office** is at 2 rue du Faubourg Notre-Dame (July & Aug Mon–Sat 9am–12.30pm & 1.30–6.30pm, Sun 9.30am–12.30pm & 2.30–6.30pm; Sept–June Mon–Sat 9am–noon & 2–6pm; ⓣ04.71.20.09.47, ⓦwww.paysdemurat.fr/tourisme), and you can rent **mountain bikes** from La Godille, opposite, or from Bernard Escure, in place Gandilhon-Gens-d'Armes. The **gare SNCF** is on the main road, avenue du Dr-Mallet, where there are also some good **places to stay**. The most comfortable is the *Hôtel des Breuils*, a handsome, ivy-covered bourgeois house at no. 34 (ⓣ04.71.20.01.25, ⓔhostellerie.les.breuils@wanadoo.fr; ❹; closed Nov–Christmas & April), with a heated outdoor pool, while at no. 22 there is the equally friendly and simple *Les Globe-Trotters* (ⓣ04.71.20.07.22, ⓕ04.71.20.16.88; ❶; closed mid-Oct to mid-Nov). A few doors down at no. 18, *Les Messageries* (ⓣ04.71.20.04.04, ⓕ04.71.20.02.81; ❸) has somewhat clinical rooms, but the restaurant (from €12–25) serves up good hearty cooking, including home-made terrines and fruit tarts. The town's **campsite**, *Les Stalapos*, is southwest of the centre in rue du Stade (ⓣ04.71.20.01.83, ⓔville-de-murat@wanadoo.fr; closed Oct–April).

St-Flour and the Margeride

Seat of a fourteenth-century bishopric, **ST-FLOUR** stands dramatically on a cliff-girt basalt promontory above the River Ander, 92km west of Le Puy and 92km south of Clermont-Ferrand. Prosperous in the Middle Ages because of its strategic position on the main road from northern France to Languedoc and the proximity of the grasslands of the Cantal whose herds provided the raw materials for its tanning and leather industries, it fell into somnolent decline in modern times, only partially reversed in the last thirty-odd years.

While the lower town that has grown up around the station is of little interest, the wedge of old streets that occupies the point of the promontory surrounding the cathedral has considerable charm. The best time to come is on a Saturday morning when the old town is filled with market stalls selling sausages, cheese and other local produce. If you're in a car, leave it in the car park in the chestnut-shaded square, **Les Promenades**. One end of the square is dominated by the **memorial** to Dr Mallet, his two sons and other hostages and assorted citizens executed in reprisals by the Germans during World War II.

The narrow streets of the old town lead off from here and converge on the **place d'Armes**, where the fourteenth-century **Cathédrale St-Pierre** stands, backing onto the edge of the cliff, with a terrace giving good views out over the countryside. From the outside, the plain grey volcanic rock of the cathedral makes for a rather severe and uninspiring appearance; it's an impression that is partly mitigated inside by the fine vaulting of the ceiling and the presence of a number of works of art, most notably a carved, black-painted walnut figure of Christ with a strikingly serene expression, dating from the thirteenth century.

Facing the cathedral on the place d'Armes are some attractive old buildings, housing a couple of cafés under their arcades, while at the north and south extremities of the square stand the town's two museums. At the north end, the fine fourteenth-century building that was once the headquarters of the town's consuls contains the **Musée Alfred Douët**'s somewhat ragbag collections of furniture, tapestries and paintings (mid-April to mid-Oct daily 9am–noon & 2–6pm; mid-Oct to mid-April closed Sun; €3.30, joint ticket with Haute-Auvergne museum €3.40); the view from the cliffs behind the museum gives a sense of the impregnable position of the town. At the south end of the square, the current Hôtel de Ville, formerly the bishop's palace built in 1610, houses the more interesting **Musée de la Haute-Auvergne** (mid-April to mid-Oct daily 10am–noon & 2–6pm; mid-Oct to mid-April closed Sun; same prices as above), whose collections include some beautifully carved Auvergnat furniture and exquisitely made traditional musical instruments, such as the *cabrette*, a kind of accordion peculiar to the Auvergne.

Practicalities

The **gare SNCF** is on avenue Charles-de-Gaulle in the lower town. A few trains from Clermont-Ferrand and Aurillac stop here, but most journeys involve changing at Neussargues onto a SNCF bus, which can drop you off on the Promenades in the old town, saving you the walk up. The **tourist office** is on the Promenades, opposite the memorial (April–June & Sept–Oct Mon–Sat 9am–6pm, Sun 3.30–5.30pm; July & Aug Mon–Sat 9am–8pm, Sun 10am–12.30pm & 3–7pm; Nov–March Mon–Sat 9am–6pm; ⓣ04.71.60.22.50, ⓦwww.saint-flour.com). **Internet** access can be found at Cg-Net on rue Marchande (daily 9.30am–9pm).

The best deal for **accommodation** in the atmospheric upper town is the magnificent, old-style *La Maison des Planchettes* at 7 rue des Planchettes (ⓣ04.71.60.10.08, ⓦwww.maison-des-planchettes.com; ❶) which has half-*pensions* for as low as €30 and a *terroir* restaurant with menus from €12. Another great option is the *Hotel de France*, 28 rue de Lacs (ⓣ04.71.60.04.75, ⓔle-france3@wanadoo.fr; ❶), a welcoming, family-run establishment. The town's municipal **campsite**, *Les Orgues*, is off avenue des Orgues in the old town (ⓣ04.71.60.44.01; closed mid-Sept to mid-May). The best place for both local cuisine and *gastronomique* is *Le Nautilus* on 23 av Charles-de-Gaulle (ⓣ04.71.60.11.36; closed Oct–Easter) with menus from €15–55. For a delicious snack visit the famous *La Fouac L'Roux* patisserie on rue des Lacs.

The Margeride

South and east of St-Flour stretch the wild, rolling, sparsely populated wooded hills of the **Margeride**, one of the strongholds of the wartime Resistance groups. If you have your own transport, the D4 makes a slow but spectacular route east (92km) to Le Puy, crossing the forested heights of **Mont Mouchet**, at 1465m the highest point of the Margeride. A side turning, the D48 (signposted), takes you to the national Resistance **monument** by the woodman's hut that served as HQ to the local Resistance commander during the June 1944 battle to delay German reinforcements moving north to strengthen resistance to the D-day landings in Normandy. There's an **eco-museum** here (La Tour, Ruynes-en-Margeride; May to mid-Sept daily 9.30am–noon & 2–7pm; mid-Sept to mid-Oct Mon–Fri 9.30am–noon & 2–7pm, Sat & Sun 10am–noon & 2–6pm; Ⓦwww.ecomusee-margeride.org; €4), sketching the progression of the Resistance movement in the area. The views back west from these heights to the Cantal are superb.

Further south, the modern autoroute crosses the gorge of the River Truyère beside the delicate steel tracery of the **Viaduc de Garabit**, built by Gustave Eiffel (of Tower fame) in 1884 to carry the newly constructed rail line; experience he put to important use in the Tower. Not far away, about 20km south of St-Flour and perched above the waters of the lake created by the damming of the Truyère for hydroelectric power, are the romantic ruins of the keep of the **Château d'Alleuze**, stronghold in the 1380s of one Bernard de Garlan, a notorious leader of lawless mercenaries employed by the English in the Hundred Years War to sow panic and destruction in French-held parts of the country.

The southwest: Aubrac and Rouergue

In the southwest corner of the Massif Central, the landscapes start to change and the mean altitude begins to drop. The wild, desolate moorland of the **Aubrac** is cut and contained by the savage gorges of **the Lot and Truyère rivers**. To the south of them, the arid but more southern-feeling plateaux of the *causses* form a sort of intermediate step to the lower hills and coastal plains of Languedoc. And they in turn are cut by the dramatic trenches formed by the **gorges of the Tarn**, **Jonte** and **Dourbie**, along with the spectacular caves of the **Aven Armand** and **Dargilan**. These are places best avoided at the height of the holiday season, when they turn into overcrowded outdoor playgrounds for amateur canoeists, parties of schoolchildren, motorists and campers.

The bigger towns, like **Rodez** and **Millau** in the old province of the **Rouergue**, also have much more of a southern feel. Both are worth a visit, although their attractions need not keep you for more than half a day. Rodez has a fine cathedral and Millau is worth considering as a base for exploring the *causses* and river gorges of the Tarn and Jonte.

The two great architectural draws of the area are **Conques**, with its medieval village and magnificent abbey, which owes its existence to the Santiago pilgrim route (now the GR65), and the perfect little *bastide* town of **Sauveterre-de-Rouergue**.

The mountains of Aubrac

The **Aubrac** lies to the south of St-Flour, east of the valley of the River Truyère and north of the valley of the Lot. It's a region of bleak, windswept uplands with long views and huge skies, dotted with glacial lakes and granite villages hunkered down out of the weather. The highest points are between 1200m and 1400m, and there are more cows up here than people; you see them grazing the boggy, peaty pastures, divided by dry-stone walls and turf-brown streams. There are few trees: a scatter of willow and ash and the occasional stand of hardy beeches on the tops, and only abandoned shepherds' huts testify to more populous times. It's an area that's invisible in bad weather, but which, in good conditions, has a bleak beauty, little disturbed by tourism or modernization.

Aumont-Aubrac and Aubrac

The waymarked **Tour d'Aubrac** footpath does a complete circuit of the area in around ten days, starting from the town of **AUMONT-AUBRAC**, where you'll find *Chez Camillou* at 10 rue Languedoc (Ⓣ04.66.42.80.22, Ⓔcamillou@clubinternet.fr; ❸; restaurant from €16; periodic closings mid-Nov to mid-Feb), the *Relais de Peyre*, across the street at no. 9 (Ⓣ04.66.42.85.88, Ⓕ04.66.42.90.08; ❷; closed Jan; restaurant €14.50–23.50), and a municipal **campsite** (Ⓣ04.66.42.80.02). The **tourist office** is on a small side street to the right of the town hall (Mon–Sat 9am–12.30pm & 2–7pm, Sun 9.30am–12.30pm & 3–6pm). There is also a daily train connection on the Millau–St-Flour line.

The marathon **GR65** from Le Puy to Santiago de Compostela in Spain also crosses the area from northeast to southwest en route to Conques. In fact, the tiny village of **AUBRAC**, which gave its name to the region, owes its existence to this Santiago pilgrim route; around 1120, a way-station was opened here for the express purpose of providing shelter for the pilgrims on these inhospitable heights. Little remains of it today, beyond the windy **Tour des Anglais**, into which is incorporated the friendly *Hôtel de la Dômerie* (Ⓣ05.65.44.28.42, Ⓕ05.65.44.21.47; ❸; closed mid-Nov to April; restaurant €18–37).

St-Urcize and Nasbinals

This is the wildest and most starkly beautiful part of the Aubrac. The close-huddled village of **ST-URCIZE**, 13km north of the town of Aubrac, hangs off the side of the valley of the River Lhère, with a lovely Romanesque church at its centre and a World War I **memorial**, with so many names on it you wouldn't have thought it possible such a small place could furnish so much cannon fodder. The village is ghostly out of season, with most of the unspoiled granite houses owned by people who live elsewhere. Should you wish to **stay**, there's a campsite and the welcoming *Hôtel Remise* (Ⓣ04.71.23.20.02, Ⓕ04.71.23.20.02; ❷; excellent food for around €15; closed Jan). On the other hand, if you can afford it, it would be a shame to pass up *Guy Prouhèze*, on 2 rte de Languedoc (Ⓣ04.66.42.80.07, Ⓦwww.prouheze.com; closed Nov–March; ❺), a hotel featuring a famed *gastronomique* restaurant (menus €31–89; closed Sun noon & Mon). Those on a budget can enjoy a gourmet experience at *L'Ousta Bas* (Ⓣ04.66.42.87.44; closed off season Tues & Wed and weekdays Nov–March), which has *terroir* menus from €14.50.

NASBINALS, 8km to the southeast, is rather bigger and livelier, and something of a cross-country ski resort in winter. It, too, has a beautiful small-scale **church** of the twelfth century, joined onto the adjacent house with a round fortified tower incorporated in the transept wall by the entrance. Just above the building, the *Hôtel de La Route d'Argent* (ⓣ04.66.32.50.03, ⓕ04.66.32.56.77; ❷) provides comfortable accommodation and good food (from €18). The friendly English- and German-speaking village **tourist office** is on the other side of the road (July & Aug Mon–Sat 9.30am–noon & 2.30–6pm, Sun 10am–noon; Sept–June Mon & Wed–Sat 10am–noon & 2–5pm; ⓣ04.66.32.55.73. For Internet access there's a computer at *Café Du Foirail* on place du Foirail on the edge of town. A **campsite** (ⓣ04.66.32.50.17) and **gîte d'étape** (ⓣ04.66.32.50.65; meals available) are located on the St-Urcize road.

Laguiole

Seventeen kilometres west of St-Urcize and 24km north of Espalion, **LAGUIOLE** passes for a substantial town in these parts. Derived from the Occitan word for "little church", it's a name which now stands for knives and cheese. The **knives**, which draw hordes of French to the town's many shops, are characterized by a long, pointed blade and bone handle that fits the palm; the genuine article should bear the effigy of a bee stamped on the clasp that holds the blade open. It's an industry that started in the nineteenth century, then moved to industrial Thiers, outside Clermont-Ferrand, before returning to Laguiole in 1987, when the Société Laguiole (the only outlet for the genuine article) opened a factory designed by Philippe Starck on the St-Urcize road, with a giant knife projecting from the roof of the windowless all-aluminium building. They have a shop on the main through-road, on the corner of the central marketplace (ⓦwww.forge-de-laguiole.com). Laguiole's **cheese-making** tradition dates back to the twelfth century; unpasteurized cow's milk is formed into massive cylindrical cheeses, and aged up to eighteen months. The hard, tangy result is a world apart from neighbouring Roquefort; to sample or buy, the factory outlet on the north edge of town is the best bargain.

There's nothing of great significance to see in the village, though the **Musée du Haut-Rouergue** (irregular hours; free), with its collection of objects illustrative of the pastoral life, might be of interest. Nonetheless, it is a relatively metropolitan base for exploring round about.

The **tourist office** is in place du Mairie (Mon–Sat 10am–12.30pm & 2–7pm, Sun 10.30am–12.30pm & 2–5pm; ⓣ05.65.44.35.94, ⓦwww.laguiole-online.com). For first-class **accommodation**, *Michel Bras*, a highly rated hotel (ⓣ05.65.51.18.20, ⓦwww.michel-bras.fr; ❾) with one of the country's finest restaurants (menus €49–143) is located just outside of town on the route d'Auibrac. For the more budget conscious there are several hotels on the main street. Try the *Aubrac* opposite the marketplace (ⓣ05.65.44.32.13, ⓦwww.hotel-aubrac.fr; ❷; restaurant from €9.70), or the *Grand Hôtel Auguy* (ⓣ05.65.44.31.11, ⓦwww.hotel-auguy.fr; ❹), 2 allée de l'Amicale, with a good restaurant with menus at €28–72. For more alternative accommodation try the tiny *Hotel Noù 4* on rue Bardière, a cosy cross between a café-restaurant, boutique and hotel (ⓣ05.65.51.68.30, ⓦwww.nou4.com; ❷).

Out of town, there's a sort of *chambre d'hôte* at Le Combaïre, in a quiet rural setting 3km west on the D42 (ⓣ05.65.44.33.26, ⓕ05.65.44.37.38; ❷); *gîtes d'étape* at Le Vayssaire (ⓣ05.65.48.44.69) and Soulages-Bonneval (ⓣ05.65.44.42.18, ⓕ05.65.44.42.80; meals available), 5km away on the D54; and a municipal **campsite** (ⓣ05.65.44.39.72; closed mid-Sept to mid-May) on the St-Urcize road. Communications, however, are not good, and if you don't have a car your only chance of getting in or out is the daily bus to Rodez.

Marvejols

MARVEJOLS lies at the southeast extremity of the Aubrac, on the main N9 road and the Paris–Béziers train line. The country changes drastically as you approach. The bare, granite-strewn plateau opens into a wide deep basin, wooded with pines and punctuated by the erosion-formed table-topped pinnacles known hereabouts as *trucs*. It's a small, undeveloped and unpretentious country town, whose ancient streets are contained within surviving medieval gates, and there's little to do beyond savouring the atmosphere.

The **tourist office** is in the main gateway on the main road (June–Sept Mon–Sat 9am–noon & 2–7pm, Sun 10am–noon; Oct–May Mon–Sat 9am–noon & 2–6pm; ⓣ04.66.32.02.14, ⓦwww.ville-marvejols.fr). Should you need to **stay**, the pleasant *Hôtel les Rochers* (ⓣ04.66.32.10.58, ⓔhotel.rocher@worldonline.fr; ❷; good restaurant at €14–30), is opposite the *gare SNCF*, which is 800m uphill to the right off the N9 in the direction of Chirac. The *Domaine de Carrière* (ⓣ04.66.32.28.14, ⓕ04.66.32.49.60; ❹) an eighteenth-century mansion on the edge of town also offers rooms, as well as excellent dining (from €22). There's a **campsite** beside a tributary stream on the other side of the River Colagne from the town.

Rodez and the upper valley of the Lot

A particularly beautiful and out-of-the-way stretch of country lies on the southwestern periphery of the Massif Central, bordered roughly by the valley of the **River Lot** in the north and the **Viaur** in the south. The upland areas are open and wide, with views east to the mountains of the Cévennes and south to the Monts de Lacaune and the Monts de l'Espinouse. **Rodez**, capital of the Rouergue, with a fine cathedral, is the only place of any size, accessible on the main train and bus routes. But the most dramatic places are in the river valleys, in particular the great abbey of **Conques** and the small towns of **Entraygues** and **Estaing**.

Wolves and the Bête du Gévaudan

In Marvejols, at the junction of the bridge across the Colagne and the N9, there stands a hideous, flattened-out bronze statue of a semi-wolf, which represents the terrible legendary **Bête du Gévaudan**, supposedly the culprit of a series of horrific attacks in the eighteenth century. Between 1764 and 1767, the whole area between here and Le Puy was terrorized, and 25 women, 68 children and 6 men were slain. The king sent his dragoons, then his best huntsman, who eventually found and killed an enormous wolf, but the mysterious deaths continued until one Jean Chastel shot another wolf near Saugues.

It has never been established if a wolf was really guilty of these deaths – a wolf that attacked women and children almost exclusively, that moved about so rapidly, that never touched a sheep – and the question remains whether it was perhaps a human psychopath.

If you would like reassurance about the temperament of real wolves, visit the **Parc Zoologique du Gévaudan** in the hamlet of Ste-Lucie just off the N9, 9km north of Marvejols, where more than a hundred wolves live in semi-liberty (ⓦwww.loupsdu-gevaudan.com; guided visits roughly every one and a half hours: daily 10am–6pm; €6.50), the first to do so in France since the beginning of the last century.

Rodez

Until the 1960s, **RODEZ** and the Rouergue were synonymous with back-country poverty and underdevelopment. Today it's an active and prosperous provincial town with a charming, renovated centre, even though the approach, through spreading commercial districts, is uninspiring.

Built on high ground above the River Aveyron, the **old town**, dominated by the massive red-sandstone **Cathédrale Notre-Dame**, is visible for kilometres around. No matter from what direction you approach, you'll find yourself in the **place d'Armes**, where the cathedral's plain, fortress-like west front and the seventeenth-century bishop's palace sit side by side – both buildings were incorporated into the town's defences. The Gothic cathedral, its plain facade relieved only by an elaborately flowery rose window, was begun in 1277 and took three hundred years to complete. Towering over the square is the cathedral's 87-metre **belfry**, decorated with pinnacles, balustrades and statuary almost as fantastical as that of Strasbourg cathedral. The impressively spacious interior, architecturally as plain as the facade, is adorned with a magnificently extravagant seventeenth-century walnut organ loft and choir stalls that were crafted by André Sulpice in 1468.

Leaving by the splendid south porch, you find yourself in the tiny place Rozier in front of the fifteenth-century **Maison Cannoniale**, whose courtyard is guarded by jutting turrets. From the back of the cathedral to the north and the south, a network of well-restored medieval streets connects place de-Gaulle, place de la Préfecture and the attractive place du Bourg, with its fine sixteenth-century houses. In place Foch, just south of the cathedral, the Baroque chapel of the old **lycée** is worth a look for its amazing painted ceiling, while in place Raynaldy, the modern **Hôtel de Ville** and the **médiathèque** are interesting examples of attempts to graft modern styles onto old buildings.

Practicalities

The **tourist office** is situated on place Foch, just off boulevard Gambetta and the place d'Armes, near the cathedral (June & Sept Mon–Sat 9am–12.30pm & 1.30–6.30pm; July & Aug Mon–Sat 9am–12.30pm & 1.30–6.30pm & Sun 10am–noon; Oct–May Mon 2.30–6pm, Tues–Fri 9am–12.30pm & 1.30–6pm, Sat 9.30am–12.30pm & 2.30–6pm; ⓣ05.65.75.76.77, ⓦwww.ot-rodez.fr). The **gare routière** is on avenue V.-Hugo (ⓣ05.65.68.11.13), and the **gare SNCF** on boulevard Joffre, on the northern edge of town.

For reasonable, if somewhat charmless, hotel **accommodation**, try the *Hôtel des Voyageurs* at 22 av Maréchal-Joffre (ⓣ05.65.42.08.41; ⓕ05.65.78.90.23; ❶), or the better *Hôtel du Clocher*, off the east end of the cathedral at 4 rue Séguy (ⓣ05.65.68.10.16; ❷). More upmarket is *La Tour Maje*, on boulevard Gally behind the tourist office (ⓣ05.65.68.34.68, ⓦwww.hotel-tour-maje.fr; ❸), a modern building tacked onto a medieval tower. *Hotel Le Broussy*, recognizable by its beautiful Art Deco facade on avenue Victor-Hugo next to the cathedral, provides stylish accommodation and a leisurely *terrasse* restaurant (ⓣ05.65.68.18.71; ❸; menus €10).

Budget accommodation is available at the **HI hostel** in **ONET-LE-CHÂTEAU**, 3km to the north at 26 bd des Capucines, *Quatre-Saisons* (ⓣ05.65.77.51.05, ⓔfjt-aj-rodez@wanadoo.fr; bus #1 or #3, direction "Quatre Saisons", stop "Marché d'Oc/Les Rosiers/Capucine"), with a good canteen serving local specialities for around €7. Rodez' municipal **campsite** (ⓣ05.65.67.09.52; closed Oct–May) is on the riverbank in the quartier Layoule, about 1km from the centre.

As for **eating**, one of the best places to sample local cuisine is *La Taverne*, 23 rue de l'Embergue (closed Sun; menus from €10.50), with an attractive terrace at the back, while the place to go for more gourmet food is the classy *Goûts et Couleurs*, 38 rue Bonald (closed Sun & Mon), where menus range from €26 to €60. *Le Bistroquet*, 17 rue du Bal, off place d'Olmet (closed Sun & Mon), does good salads and grills for around €11. For a **drink**, head for the *Café de la Paix*, on place Jean-Jaurès, or *Au Bureau*, in the Tour Maje. The most central **Internet** access, Resolument Plus Net, is at 11 rue Béteille (Ⓣ05.65.75.66.87, Tues–Thurs 11am–10pm, Fri–Sat 11am–midnight).

Sauveterre-de-Rouergue and the gorges of the Viaur

Forty kilometres southwest of Rodez and 6.5km northwest of Naucelle, **SAUVETERRE-DE-ROUERGUE** makes the most rewarding side trip in this part of the Rouergue. It is a perfect, otherworldly *bastide*, founded in 1281, with a large, wide central square, part cobbled, part gravelled, and surrounded by stone and half-timbered houses built over arcaded ground floors. Narrow streets lead off to the outer road, lined with stone-built houses the colour of rusty iron. On summer evenings, *pétanque* players come out to roll their *boules* beneath chestnut and plane trees, while swallows and swifts swoop and dive overhead.

In summer, a **bus** runs once a weekday here in the late afternoon from Rodez. The **tourist office** is in the main square (June–Sept Mon–Sun 10am–1pm & 2.30–7pm, Fri until 9pm; Ⓣ05.65.72.02.52. There are several agreeable **hotels**, including the cheap and charming *Hôtel La Grappe d'Or*, on the outer road (Ⓣ05.65.72.00.62; ❷), whose restaurant (closed Oct–April) offers an excellent menu at €13.50, with dishes like *gésiers chauds*, *tripoux*, cheese, ice cream and *fouace* (a kind of sweet cake). More upmarket is the *Sénéchal*, at the entrance to the village (Ⓣ05.65.71.29.00, Ⓦwww.senechal.net; ❼; closed Jan to late March), with an indoor pool and an excellent restaurant (closed Mon plus Tues lunch; menus €24–99). There's also a **campsite**, just off the D997 (Ⓣ05.65.47.05.32).

The country round about, known as the **Ségala**, is high (around 500m) and wide, cut by sudden and deep river valleys full of lush greenery. The most spectacular of these is the valley of the **River Viaur** to the south and west of Sauveterre, where a car is essential. If you're heading west towards Najac, there's a marvellous backcountry route through La Salvetat, crossing the Viaur at Bellecombe and again at Moulin-de-Bar, where there's a riverside **campsite**, *Le Gomvassou*. The wartime Resistance was very active hereabouts and there are numerous memorials to the Resistance fighters who lost their lives in the aftermath of the D-day landings. There is a particularly interesting one beside the tiny church in **Jouqueviel**, further downstream, dedicated to a unit of Polish volunteers and 161 escaped Soviet POWs.

Conques

CONQUES, 37km north of Rodez, is one of the great villages of southwest France. It occupies a spectacular position on the flanks of the steep, densely wooded gorge of the little **River Dourdou**, a tributary of the Lot. For all its glory, Conques is not easy to get to. The only public transport to the village is a seasonal bus that runs up the Tarn valley from Entreaygues via Vieillevie and as far as St-Geniez d'Olt. The shuttle makes one run in each direction (June & Sept Mon; July–Aug Tues, Thurs & Sat; confirm departure times with the tourist office at Conques), allowing you to visit Conques and return the same day.

It's the abbey which brought the village into existence. Its origins go back to a hermit called Dadon who settled here around 800 AD and founded a community of Benedictine monks, one of whom pilfered the relics of the martyred girl, Ste Foy, from the monastery at Agen. Known for her ability to cure blindness and liberate captives, Ste Foy's presence brought the pilgrims flocking to Conques in ever-increasing numbers, which earned the abbey a prime place on the pilgrimage route to Compostela.

The abbey church

At the village's centre, dominating the landscape, stands the renowned Romanesque **church of Ste-Foy**, whose giant pointed towers are echoed in those of the medieval houses that cluster tightly about it. Begun in the eleventh century, its plain fortress-like facade rises on a small cobbled square beside the tourist office and pilgrims' fountain, the slightly shiny silver-grey schist prettily offset by the greenery and flowers of the terraced gardens.

In startling contrast to this plainness, the elaborately sculpted *Last Judgement* in the **tympanum** above the door admonishes all who see it to espouse virtue and eschew vice (ask at the tourist office for guided tours of the tympanum and the tribunes; 45min; €3.30). Christ sits in judgement in the centre, with the chosen on his right hand, among them Dadon the hermit and the emperor Charlemagne, while his left hand directs the damned to Hell, as usual so much more graphically and interestingly portrayed with all its gory tortures than the boring bliss of Paradise, depicted in the bottom left panel.

The **inside** of the church was designed to accommodate the large numbers of pilgrims and channel them down the aisles and round the ambulatory. From here they could contemplate Ste Foy's relics displayed in the choir, encircled by a lovely wrought-iron screen, still in place. There is some fine carving on the capitals, especially in the triforium arches, too high up to see from the nave: you need to climb to the organ loft, which gives you a superb perspective on the whole interior. This is also a good place to admire the windows, designed by the Abstract artist Pierre Soulages, which consist of plain plates of glass that subtly change colour with the light outside.

The unrivalled asset of this church is the survival of its medieval treasure of extraordinarily rich, bejewelled **reliquaries**, including a gilded statue of Ste Foy, bits of which are as old as the fifth century, and one known as the *A of Charlemagne*, because it is thought to have been the first in a series given as presents by the emperor to monasteries he founded. Writing in 1010, a cleric named Bernard d'Angers gave an idea of the effect of these wonders on the medieval pilgrim: "The crowd of people prostrating themselves on the ground was so dense it was impossible to kneel down. … When they saw it for the first time [Ste Foy], all in gold and sparkling with precious stones and looking like a human face, the majority of the peasants thought that the statue was really looking at them and answering their prayers with her eyes." The treasure is kept in a room adjoining the now ruined cloister (daily: April–Sept 9.30am–12.30pm & 2–6.30pm; Oct–March 10am–noon & 2–6pm; €6); the second part of the Conques museum, displayed on three floors of a house on the cathedral square, consists of a miscellany of sixteenth-century and later tapestries, furnishings and assorted bits of medieval masonry.

By far the best way to experience the beauty of Conques is by visiting the church at around 9.30pm on a summer evening for the **Nocturne des Tribunes**. The church is opened to the public and is beautifully illuminated while an organist or pianist fills it with music (€5).

△ Abbey church of Ste-Foy, Conques

The village

The **village** of Conques is very small, largely depopulated and mainly contained within the medieval **walls**, parts of which still survive, along with three of its **gates**. The houses date mainly from the late Middle Ages. The whole ensemble of cobbled lanes and stairways is a pleasure to stroll through. There are two main streets, the old **rue Haute**, or "upper street", which was the route for the pilgrims coming from Estaing and Le Puy and passing onto Figeac and Cahors through the **Porte de la Vinzelle**; and the lane, now **rue Charlemagne**, which leads steeply downhill through the **Porte de Barry** to the river and the ancient **Pont Romain**, with the little **chapel of St-Roch** off to the left, from where you get a fine view of the village and church. Better still: climb the road on the far side of the valley. The rather grandiose-sounding **European centre for medieval art and civilization**, hidden in a bunker right at the top of the hill (9am–noon & 2–6pm), sometimes has exhibitions and displays. Throughout August, the village hosts a prestigious **classical music festival**, most of the concerts taking place at the abbey church; contact the tourist office for more information.

Walkers can use sections of the **GR65** and **GR62**, both of which pass through the village; the tourist office will provide information about shorter local walks.

Practicalities

The **tourist office** is on the square beside the church (daily: April–Sept 9.30am–12.30pm & 2–6.30pm; Oct–March 10am–noon & 2–6pm; ⓣ08.20.82.08.03, ⓦwww.conques.fr; Internet access available). For somewhere central to **stay**, the *Auberge St-Jacques* (ⓣ05.65.72.86.36, ⓦwww.aubergestjacques.fr; ❸), near the church, provides good-value, old-fashioned accommodation and also has a popular restaurant, with menus from €15 and *plats du jour* at €8–11. A good alternative is the *Auberge du Pont Romain*, on the main road below the hill on which Conques stands (ⓣ05.65.69.84.07, ⓕ05.65.69.85.12; ❷; closed first two weeks Nov; menus from €13) – it's a twenty-minute walk from here to the church. A little way upstream, the attractive *Moulin de Cambelong* (ⓣ05.65.72.84.77, ⓦwww.moulin-de-cambelong.com; ❼) offers more comfort – some rooms have spacious wooden balconies with great views of the river – and a first-rate restaurant, specializing in duck dishes (à la carte from €45).

There are several **campsites** in Conques: try *Beau Rivage* (ⓣ05.65.69.82.23; closed Oct–March), on the banks of the Dourdou, just below the village, *St-Cyprien-sur-Dourdou* (ⓣ05.65.72.80.52), 7km to the south, or *Le Moulin* (ⓣ05.65.72.87.28; closed Nov–March), at Grand-Vabre, 5km downstream.

The upper valley: Grand-Vabre to Entraygues

The most beautiful stretch of the **Lot Valley** is the 21.5km between the bridge of Coursavy, below **Grand-Vabre**, just north of Conques, and **Entraygues**: deep, narrow and wild, with the river running full and strong, as yet unaffected by the dams higher up, with scattered farms and houses high on the hillsides among long-abandoned terracing. The shady, tree-tunnelled road is level and not heavily used, making it ideal for cycling.

There are two hotels 6.5km east in **VIEILLEVIE**, where canoe rental is also available: the *Hôtel de la Terrasse* (ⓣ04.71.49.94.00, ⓔhotel-de-la-terrasse@wanadoo.fr; ❸; closed mid-Nov to April; restaurant €16–32) and the ramshackle but homely *Le Cantou* (ⓣ04.71.49.98.82; ❷; restaurant from €13.50). A further possibility is the delightful *Auberge du Fel*, some 10km further on, high on the north slopes of the valley in the hamlet of **LE FEL** (ⓣ05.65.44.52.30, ⓦwww.auberge-du-fel.com; ❹; closed mid-Nov to March; excellent restaurant with menus from €18–36), which by an unexpected quirk of climate produces a little local wine. There is also a beautifully sited municipal **campsite** high on the hillside (ⓣ05.65.44.51.86; closed Oct–May).

Entraygues and around

ENTRAYGUES, with its riverside streets and attractive grey houses, has an airy, open feel that belies its mountain sleepiness. It lies right in the angle of the junction of the Lot with the equally beautiful River Truyère. The brown towers of a thirteenth-century **château** overlook the meeting of the waters, and a magnificent four-arched **bridge** of the same date crosses the Truyère a little way upstream, alongside the ancient tanners' houses.

The **tourist office** is on place de la République (July & Aug Mon–Sat 9.30am–12.30pm & 3–7pm, Sun 10am–12.30pm; Sept–June Mon 2–6pm, Tues–Fri 10am–12.15pm & 2–6pm, Sat 10am–12.15pm & 2–5pm; Ⓣ05.65.44.56.10). It frequently remains open outside of its official hours and will provide information about walking, mountain biking and canoeing in the area. Reasonable **places to stay** include the *Hôtel Le Centre*, on the main street (Ⓣ05.65.44.51.19, Ⓕ05.65.48.63.09; ❷; menus €11–29), and the *Lion d'Or*, on the corner of the main street and the bank of the Lot (Ⓣ05.65.44.50.01, Ⓕ05.65.44.55.43; ❸), with a covered swimming pool and garden and attached restaurant (from €15). There's also a **campsite**, *Le Val-de-Saures* (Ⓣ05.65.44.56.92; closed Oct–April), and two *gîtes d'étape* – Mme Galan (Ⓣ05.65.44.58.44) and *Le Battedou* (Ⓣ05.65.48.61.62) – on the GR65 at **GOLINHAC**, about 7km south of Entraygues on the other side of the Lot. There is a **bus** to Aurillac (Tues–Fri 12.50pm from the post office) in the north and Rodez (Mon–Sat) to the south.

There are further accommodation options at **ESTAING**, another beautiful village huddled round a rocky bluff and castle in a bend of the Lot about 10km beyond Golinhac. The *Hôtel aux Armes d'Estaing*, named after the family who occupied the castle for five hundred years, offers attractive rooms and very good food in the centre of the village (Ⓣ05.65.44.70.02, Ⓔremi.catusse@wanadoo.fr; ❷; closed mid-Nov to mid-March; restaurant from €14–35). There's also a municipal **campsite** (Ⓣ05.65.44.72.77; closed Oct–April) and **gîte d'étape** on the GR65 (Ⓣ05.65.44.71.74). A date to watch out for is the first Sunday in July when the place fills up with people, many in medieval dress, who come to honour the relics of **St Fleuret**, bishop of Clermont, who died here in 621 AD and is buried in the fifteenth-century church by the castle.

Espalion

The substantial little town of **ESPALION** lies in a mild, fertile opening in the valley of the Lot, 10km from Estaing and 32km northeast of Rodez. It was the "first smile of the south" to the muleteers, pilgrims and other travellers coming down from the rude heights of the Massif Central and places north. Home town of Benoît Rouquayrol and Auguste Denayrouze, inventors of diving suits, Espalion is best known in France for its exiles, in particular its countless sons and daughters who set up in the café business in Paris from the 1850s onwards.

The only interesting part of town is the **riverside quarter**, with its galleried and balconied old houses, once used as tanneries, hanging over the water. The finest view of the area is from the Pont Neuf, where the main road to Rodez crosses the Lot, as just upstream there's a lovely red sandstone packhorse **bridge** with the domed and turreted château dating from 1572 right behind it.

Surprisingly, there's an interesting museum dedicated principally to the life of the region: **Musée Joseph Vaylet**, in an old medieval church, on the main road, boulevard Poulenc (daily July–Sept 10am–noon & 2–7pm; Oct–June Wed–Sat & Sun 2–6pm; €4) contains mainly furniture and domestic objects. Here you will also find the **Musée du Scaphandre** which showcases the diving gear invented by the two Espalionnais mentioned above as well as other objects of a sub-aquatic nature (Ⓦwww.musee-scaphandre.com).

Don't miss the glorious little twelfth-century Romanesque **church of St-Hilarion de Perse**, built on the spot, so the story goes, where, in the reign of Charlemagne, the Saracens lopped off the head of St Hilarion. It sits on the edge of the cemetery, about fifteen minutes' walk to the left of the bridge on the château side of the river, past the campsite. Built in red sandstone, with a wall belfry and wide porch with sculpted tympanum and dozens of figures adorning the corbel ends of the apse, it's a delight.

Also well worth a visit is the **Château de Calmont d'Olt** (July & Aug daily 9am–noon & 2–7pm; €6.75; Ⓦwww.chateaucalmont.org), for its unbeatable views of the town and the country beyond. It's a rough and atmospheric old fortress dating from the eleventh century, on the very peak of an abrupt bluff, 535m high and a stiff 1km climb above the town on the south bank. Particularly good for children is a regular programme of activities throughout the day (afternoon only out of season), including demonstrations of medieval siege engines and artillery.

Practicalities

The **tourist office** is just across the Pont Vieux in rue St-Antoine (June & Sept Mon–Fri 9am–noon & 2–6pm & Sat 10am–noon & 2.30–5.30pm; July & Aug Mon–Fri 10am–1pm & 2–7pm, Sat 10am–1pm & 2–6pm, Sun 10am–12.30pm; Oct–May Tues–Fri 9am–noon & 2–6pm, Sat 10am–noon & 2.30–5.30pm; Ⓣ05.65.44.10.63, Ⓦwww.ot-espalion.fr). For **accommodation**, there's no better place to stay than the *Hôtel Moderne* on the crossroads in the middle of town at 27 bd de Guizard (Ⓣ05.65.44.05.11, Ⓦwww.hotelmoderne12.com; ❷; closed mid-Nov to mid-Dec). The rooms are comfortable but, more importantly, its restaurant is first-rate, especially for river fish (menus from €12–45). There's also a municipal **gîte** (Ⓣ06.77.58.53.08) at 5 rue St-Joseph. A riverside **campsite**, Roc de l'Arche, sits behind the château (Ⓣ05.65.44.06.79; closed Sept to mid-April), but better if you have the time and the means, is the prettier, simpler and cheaper riverside *Belle Rive* (Ⓣ05.65.44.05.85; closed Oct to mid-May) in the attractive village of **ST-CÔME D'OLT**, another 4km upstream, where there's also a **gîte d'étape** in a beautiful old house on rue St-Joseph (Ⓣ05.65.51.10.30, Ⓔmairie-espalion@wanadoo.fr; closed Nov–Feb) where you'll find the GR65, GR6 and GR620.

Espalion has a second superb **restaurant**, *Méjane*, by the old bridge (Ⓣ05.65.48.22.37; closed Sun eve, & Mon lunch & Wed in July & Aug; menus €16–53), specializing in regional cuisine with a post-*nouvelle* influence, while for uncomplicated eating, there are several brasseries on the main through-street.

Millau, Roquefort and the Gorges du Tarn

MILLAU, sub-prefecture of the Aveyron *département* and second town after Rodez in the old province of Rouergue, occupies a beautiful site in a bend of the River Tarn at its junction with the Dourbie. It's enclosed on all sides by impressive white cliffs, formed where the rivers have worn away the edges of the

△ Grand Viaduc du Millau

causses, especially on the north side, where the spectacular table-top hill of the **Puech d'Andan** stands sentinel over the town. From medieval until modern times, thanks to its proximity to the sheep pastures of the *causses*, the town was a major manufacturer of leather goods, especially gloves. Although outclassed by cheaper producers in the mass market and suffering serious unemployment as a result, Millau still leads in top-of-the-range goods.

In recent years the town hit the headlines with the construction of the astonishing **Grand Viaduc du Millau** in 2004, a 2.5-kilometre bridge supported by seven enormous pillars that, at times, puncture through the cloud level (the tallest is 326m high, taller than the Eiffel tower). Designed by British architects Foster and Partners (of Sir Norman Foster fame), French engineer Michel Virbgeux (whose previous credits include the wonderful Pont de Normandie) and Eiffage, a construction firm that traces its heritage back to Gustave Eiffel, it is as much a work of art as it is a way of getting traffic to the Côte d'Azur from Paris faster than of old.

Arrival, information and accommodation

From the **bus and train stations** it's about a ten-minute walk down rue Alfred-Merle to the main square, place du Mandarous. The **tourist office** is on place du Beffroi in the centre of the old town (July & Aug Mon–Sun 9am–7pm; Sept–June Mon–Fri 9am–12.30pm & 2–6.30pm, Sat 9am–6.30pm, Sun 9.30am–4pm; ⓣ05.65.60.02.42, ⓦwww.ot-millau.fr). **Bikes and outdoor equipment** can be rented from Roc et Canyon, 55 av Jean-Jaurès.

For an overnight **stay**, try the good-value *Hôtel du Commerce*, 8 place du Mandarous (ⓣ05.65.60.00.56, ⓕ05.65.47.66.01; ❶), with clean, well-furnished rooms; those at the back are best to avoid any noise from the square. A bit more expensive, but with more character, is *Des Causses*, in an attractive building on the N9 at 56 av Jean-Jaurès (Ⓣ05.65.60.03.19; ❶–❹), which has a reasonable restaurant (from €30). Even more evocative is the *Emma Calvé* at 28 rue Jean-Jaurès (Ⓣ05.65.60.13.49, Ⓦemmacalve.ifrance.com; ❺), once home of the popular nineteenth-century singer of that name and with decor and furnishings evocative of the old bourgeousie. Though modern and characterless, *Hotel de la Capelle* (Ⓣ05.65.60.14.72; ❶) is a good-value option with its clean rooms and pleasant location, overlooking the Puech d'Andan at 7 place de la Fraternité. There are several **gîtes**, and scattered round about are several **campsites**: one of the best is *Cureplat* (Ⓣ05.65.60.15.75; closed Oct–March) at 121 av de Millau Plage, on the left bank of the Tarn, north of the confluence with the Dourbie – take the bridge at the end of avenue Gambetta. For Internet access, Cyber-café at 5 rue Droite is the most central option (Mon–Sat 10am–8pm).

The Town

Millau is a very pleasant, lively provincial town whose clean and well-preserved old streets have a summery, southern charm. It owes its original prosperity to its position on the ford where the Roman road from Languedoc to the north crossed the Tarn, marked today by the truncated remains of a medieval **bridge** surmounted by a watermill jutting out into the river beside the modern bridge.

Whether you arrive from north or south, you'll find yourself sooner or later in **place du Mandarous**, the main square, where avenue de la République, the road to Rodez, begins. South of here, the **old town** is built a little way back from the river to avoid floods and contained within an almost circular ring of shady boulevards. The rue Droite cuts through the centre, linking the three squares: place Emma-Calvé, place des Halles and place Foch. The prettiest by far is **place Foch**, with its cafés, shaded by two big plane trees and bordered by houses supported on stone pillars; some are twelfth century. In one corner, the **church of Notre-Dame** is worth a look for its octagonal Toulouse-style belfry, originally Romanesque. In the other, there's the very interesting **Musée de Millau** (May–Sept daily 10am–noon & 2–6pm; July & Aug 10am–6pm; Oct–March closed Sun; €5), housed in a stately eighteenth-century mansion. Its collections revolve around the bizarre combination of archeology and gloves, and include the magnificent red pottery of the Graufesenque works (see below), as well as a complete 180-million-year-old plesiosaurus. Millau's other two squares have been the subject of some rather questionable attempts at reconciling old stones and Richard Rogers-inspired contemporary urban design. Off one of these squares, place Emma-Calvé, the **clock tower** (June & Sept Mon–Sat 10–11.30am & 3–5.30pm; July & Aug daily 10am–noon & 3.30–6pm; €3.50) is worth a climb for the great all-round view. Take a look also in the streets off the square – rue du Voultre, rue de la Peyrollerie and their tributaries – for a sense of the old working-class and bourgeois districts.

Clear evidence of the town's importance in Roman times is to be seen in the **Graufesenque pottery works** archeology museum, just upstream on the south bank (Tues–Sun: May & Sept 10am–noon & 2–6pm; July & Aug 10am–12.30pm & 2.30–7pm; Oct–April 9am–noon & 2–5pm; €4), whose renowned red terracotta ware (*terra sigillata*) was distributed throughout the Roman world.

Millau has some of the best conditions in France for **paragliding** due to the constant currents of warm air that blow down the *causse*. To try it yourself arrange a tandem flight with the professional pilots at challeng'Air (06.33.43.08.63, www.challeng-air.com; English speaking; €65), a friendly family-run company located across the River Tarn on route de Millau-Plage next to *Le Golf* café.

Eating and drinking

If you're just looking for a quick **meal**, you'll find numerous brasseries and cafés on place du Mandarous. For something more traditional, dine in the magnificent surroundings of *La Mustardière* at 34 av de la République (05.65.60.20.63; closed Dec–Feb; €33–50) which serves excellent *gastronomique* and *terroir* specialities, or the less upmarket *La Braconne*, on place Foch (05.65.60.30.93; closed Sun eve & Mon; from €17), offering high-calorie fare such as stuffed goose and pork with juniper berries. Alternatively, head for boulevard de la Capelle on the northeast side of the old town, where two good establishments spread their tables under the trees: *La Mangeoire*, at no. 8 (05.65.60.13.16; closed Mon; menu from €18–45), which serves grilled fish, meat and game dishes; and next door, *La Marmite du Pêcheur*, featuring menus from €18, including *aligot*. A popular place for a **drink** is *La Locomotive*, at 33 av Gambetta (till 2am), which has live music on summer evenings.

Roquefort-sur-Soulzon and the Abbey of Silvanès

Twenty-one kilometres south of Millau, the little village of **ROQUEFORT-SUR-SOULZON** has nothing to say for itself except cheese, and almost every building is devoted to the cheese-making process. What gives the cheese its special flavour is the fungus, *penicillium roqueforti*, that grows exclusively in the fissures in the rocks created by the collapse of the sides of the valley on which Roquefort now stands. Legend has it that once upon a time a local shepherd one day forgot his lunch of bread and cheese, and found it some months later, covered with mould. He bit tentatively and discovered to his surprise that instead of ruining the cheese, the mould had much improved its taste.

While the sheep's milk used in the making of the cheese comes from different flocks and dairies as far afield as the Pyrenees, the crucial fungus is grown here, on bread. Just 2g of powdered fungus are enough for 4000 litres of milk, which in turn makes 330 Roquefort cheeses; they are matured in Roquefort's many-layered cellars, first unwrapped for three weeks and then wrapped up again. It takes three to six months for the full flavour to develop.

Two of the cheese manufacturers have organized visits: **Société** (daily: July & Aug 9.30am–6.30pm; Sept–June 9.30am–noon & 1.30–5.30pm; €3) and **Papillon** (April–June & Sept daily 9.30–11.30am & 1.30–5.30pm; July & Aug daily 9.30am–6.30pm; Oct–March Mon–Fri 9.30–11.30am & 1.30–4.30pm; free). Each visit consists of a short film, followed by a tour of the cellars and tasting – not, in fact, very interesting.

Some 25km further south, deep in the isolation of the *causses*, squats the twelfth-century **Cistercian Abbey of Silvanès** (daily 9.15am–12.30pm & 2–6pm; €2), founded in 1137 and the first Cistercian house in the region. Having largely survived the depredations of war and revolution, the abbey serves today as an important religious and cultural centre. Although you'll have to manage your own transport, it's worth visiting not only for the evocative setting, but also for the excellently preserved thirteenth-century church as well as the surviving monastic buildings, including a refectory and scriptorium dating back to the 1100s. There are a couple of **hotels** in the village by the abbey, but only 4km from the monastery you can stay at the magnificent sixteenth-century *Château de Gissac* (Ⓣ05.65.98.14.60, Ⓦwww.sylvanes.com; ❻) which also offers half and full *pensions.*

The Gorges du Tarn

Jampacked with tourists in July and August, but absolutely spectacular nonetheless, the **Gorges du Tarn** cuts through the limestone plateaux of the Causse de Sauveterre and the Causse Méjean in a precipitous trench 400–500m deep and 1000–1500m wide. Its sides, cloaked with woods of feathery pine and spiked with pinnacles of eroded rock, are often sheer and always very steep, creating within them a microclimate in sharp distinction to the inhospitable plateaux above. The permanent population is tiny, though there's plenty of evidence of more populous times in abandoned houses and once-cultivated terraces. Because of the press of people and the subsequent overpricing of **accommodation**, the best bet, if you want to stay along the gorge, is to head up onto the Causse Méjean, where there are several small family-run hotels and *chambres d'hôte*, among which is the attractively sited *Auberge de la Cascade* in St-Chély-du-Tarn (Ⓣ04.66.48.52.82, Ⓦwww.aubergecascade.com; ❸; closed Nov–March; restaurant from €15).

The most attractive section of the gorge runs northeast for 53km from the pretty village of **LE ROZIER**, 21km northeast of Millau, to **ISPAGNAC**. If you want to stay in Le Rozier, good accommodation can be found at the *Grand Hôtel Voyageurs* (Ⓣ05.65.62.60.09, Ⓦwww.hotelvoyageurs.com; ❷; menu from €17; closed Nov–Easter) and there's a municipal **campsite** (Ⓣ05.65.62.63.98, Ⓕ05.65.62.60.83; closed Oct–April). A better bet, however, is *Le Vallon* (Ⓣ04.66.44.21.24, Ⓦwww.hotel-vallon.com; ❶) in Ispagnac, a small hotel with an excellent *terroir* restaurant (from €16) and which has family-size rooms and good-value half-pensions.

A narrow and very twisty road follows the right bank of the river from Le Rozier, but it's not the best way to see the scenery. For the car-borne, the best views are from the road to St-Rome-de-Dolan above Les Vignes, and from the roads out of La Malène and the attractive **STE-ÉNIMIE**, where you'll find a well-informed **tourist office** (Easter–June & Sept–Oct Mon–Fri 9.30am–12.30pm & 1.30–5.30pm, Sat 9am–12.30pm & 2–5.30pm; July & Aug Mon–Sat 9am–7pm & Sun 9am–12.30pm; Nov–Easter Mon–Fri 9.30am–12.30pm & 1.30–5.30pm; Ⓣ04.66.48.53.44, Ⓦwww.gorgesdutarn.net). La Malène has a municipal **campsite** (Ⓣ04.66.48.58.55; closed mid-Oct to March) and *La Blanquière* site (Ⓣ04.66.48.54.93, Ⓔcamping.blaquière@wanadoo.fr; closed mid-Sept to May), which is beautifully sited on the main road towards Les Vignes some 6km from town.

But it's best to walk if possible, or follow the river's course by boat or canoe – there are dozens of places to rent canoes (€15 per person for 2–3hr, plus pick-up). For walkers, the **GR6a**, a variant of the GR6 which crosses the *causses*, climbs steeply out of Le Rozier between the junction of the Tarn with the equally spectacular gorges of the River Jonte onto the Causse Méjean, then follows the rim of the Tarn gorge for a while before descending to rejoin the GR6 at Les Vignes (4–5hr).

Also eminently worth seeing are two beautiful **caves** about 25km up the Jonte from Le Rozier. **Aven Armand** (daily: 10am–noon, 1.30–5pm; May–Sept opens at 9.30am, Ⓦwww.aven-armand.com; €8.30), on the edge of the Causse Méjean, which is fitted with a funicular, claims the world's tallest stalagmite towering 30m above the cave floor. The **Grotte de Dargilan** (daily: April–June & Sept 10am–noon & 2–5.30pm; July & Aug 10am–6.30pm; Oct 10am–noon & 2–4.30pm; Ⓦwww.grotte-dargilan.com; €8.30), on the south side of the river on the edge of the Causse Noir, known as the "pink cave" from the colour of its rock, is known as one of the country's most beautiful stalactite caverns. **HYELZAS**, near the Aven Armand cave, has a *gîte d'étape* (Ⓣ04.66.45.66.56).

The Cévennes and Ardèche

The **Cévennes** mountains and River **Ardèche** form the southeastern defences of the Massif Central, overlooking the Rhône valley to the east and the Mediterranean littoral to the south. The bare upland landscapes of the inner or western edges are those of the central Massif. The outer edges, Mont Aigoual and its radiating valleys and the tributary valleys of the Ardèche, are distinctly Mediterranean: deep, dry, close and clothed in forests of sweet chestnut, oak and pine.

Remote and inaccessible country until well into the twentieth century, the region has bred rugged and independent inhabitants. For centuries it was the most resolute stronghold of Protestantism in France, and it was in these valleys that the persecuted Protestants put up their fiercest resistance to the tyranny of Louis XIV and Louis XV. In World War II, it was heavily committed to the Resistance, while in the aftermath of 1968, it became the promised land of the hippies – *zippies*, as the locals called them; they moved into the countless abandoned farms and hamlets, whose native inhabitants had been driven away by hardship and poverty. The odd hippy has stuck it out, true to the last to the alternative life. In more recent times, it has been colonized by Dutch and Germans.

The author Robert Louis Stevenson crossed it in 1878 with Modestine, a donkey he bought in miserable Le Monastier-sur-Gazeille near the astounding town of **Le Puy** and sold at journey's end in the former Protestant stronghold of **St-Jean-du-Gard**, a now-famous route described in *Travels with a Donkey* (see p.1329).

The Parc National des Cévennes

The **Parc National des Cévennes** was created in 1970 to protect and preserve the life, landscape, flora, fauna and architectural heritage of the Cévennes. North to south, it stretches from **Mende** on the Lot to **Le Vigan** and includes both **Mont Lozère** and **Mont Aigoual**. Access, to the periphery at least, is surprisingly easy, thanks to the Paris–Clermont–Alès–Nîmes train line and the Montpellier–Mende link.

Numerous walking routes crisscross the area: **GRs 6**, **7** and **60** cross all or part of the range, and other paths complete various circuits. The **GR66** does the tour of Mont Aigoual in 78.5km, the **GR68** of Mont Lozère in 110km. Another good route is the 130-kilometre **Tour des Cévennes** on the **GR67**. If you do go off hiking, remember that these are proper mountains for all their southerly latitude. You need good hiking boots, warm and weatherproof clothing, emergency shelter, adequate food, maps and guidebooks. The current weather situation is obtainable on: ⓣ07.08.36.68.02 (Ardèche); ⓣ08.36.68.02.30 (Gard); ⓣ08.36.68.02.48 (Lozère).

The **main information office** for the park is at Florac (see p.942). It publishes numerous leaflets on the flora, fauna and traditions of the park, plus activities and routes for walkers, cyclists, canoeists and horse riders. It also provides a list of **gîtes d'étape** in the park and can provide information for those following Stevenson's route, including where to hire a donkey. In July and August, it's wise to book ahead for accommodation; otherwise you could find yourself sleeping out.

Mende and Mont Lozère

Capital of the Lozère *département*, **MENDE** lies well down in the deep valley of the Lot at the northern tip of the Parc des Cévennes, 28km east of Marvejols and 40km north of Florac, with train and bus links to the Paris–Nîmes and Clermont–Millau lines. It's an attractive southern town, though much of its charm is lost in the newly commercialized streets of the city centre. What Mende lacks in authenticity it makes up for in practicality: it's a great place to purchase last-minute supplies before you head off to the mountains.

Standing against the haze of the mountain background, the town's main landmark, the **cathedral**, owes its construction to Pope Urban V, who was born locally and wished to give something back to his native soil. Although work began in 1369, progress was hampered by war and natural disasters and the building wasn't completed until the end of the nineteenth century. The most obvious signs of its patchy construction are the two unequal towers that frame the front entrance, from where there's a fine view back along the pine-clad Lot valley. Inside is a handsome choir, and, suspended from the clerestory, eight great Aubusson tapestries, depicting the life of the Virgin. She's also present in one of the side chapels of the choir in the form of a statue made from olive wood, thought to have been brought back from the Middle East during the crusades.

Aside from the cathedral, most pleasure resides in a quiet wander in the old town's minuscule squares and narrow medieval streets, with their houses bulging outwards, as though buckling under the weight of the upper storeys. In **rue Notre-Dame**, which separated the Christian from Jewish quarters in medieval times, the thirteenth-century house at no. 17 was once a synagogue. If you carry on down to the river, you'll see the medieval packhorse bridge, the **Pont Notre-Dame**, with its worn cobbles.

Twenty-two kilometres east of Mende, route 901 passes through a tunnel under the impressive ruins of the twelfth-century Château du Tournel. A footpath leads 500 twisting metres up above the motorway to the ruins. From this height, especially at dusk, the dark towers have an eerie looming presence above the surrounding hills giving a strong sense of its defensive advantage over the region.

Practicalities

The **tourist office** is on place du Foirail located at the southern end of boulevard Henri-Bourrillon, the ring road that encircles the city centre (July & Aug Mon–Sat 9am–12.30pm & 2–7pm, Sun 10am–noon & 3–5pm; Sept–June Mon–Fri 9am–12.30pm & 2–6pm, Sat 9am–noon; ⓣ04.66.94.00.23, ⓦwww.ot-mende.fr). The **gare SNCF** (ⓣ04.66.49.00.39) lies across the river, north of the centre. **Buses** depart from either the station or place du Foirail.

For a place to **stay**, best choice is the *Lion d'Or* at 12–14 bd Britexte (Ⓣ04.66.49.16.46, Ⓦwww.liondor-mende.com; ❸), set in a beautiful, renovated old building and featuring an excellent *terroir* restaurant (from €18). Another good choice is the pretty *Hôtel de France* on boulevard Lucien-Arnault, the northern part of the inner ring road (Ⓣ04.66.65.00.04, Ⓦwww.hoteldefrance-mende.com; ❸; closed Dec & Jan; menu from €12). Slightly further out of town, on the river at 2 av du 11-Novembre, the classy *Hôtel Pont-Roupt* (Ⓣ04.66.65.01.43, Ⓦwww.hotel-pont-roupt.com; ❹) offers such luxuries as an indoor pool, terrace and good restaurant: dishes include *truite au lard* and *salade au Roquefort* (menus €24–52). For budget travellers there's the basic and slightly dingy *Hôtel Du Gévaudan* (Ⓣ04.66.65.14.74; ❶) on rue d'Aigues Passes where you can take a room for as little as €18. The best **restaurant** in town is *La Safranière* in Chabrits (Ⓣ04.66.49.31.54), which daringly blends *terrior* and *gastronomique* styles (menus €20–44). Another good choice is *Le Mazel* (Ⓣ04.66.65.05.33; closed Mon eve & Tues; from €14), though the setting – in the only modern square in the old town – is a little disappointing. More atmospheric, *Les Voutes*, in a renovated medieval building at 13 rue d'Aigues-Passes, specializes in pizzas and *plats du jour* (from €7).

Mont Lozère

Mont Lozère is a windswept and desolate barrier of granite and yellow grassland, rising to 1699m at the summit of **Finiels**, still grazed by herds of cows, but in nothing like the numbers of bygone years when half the cattle in Languedoc came up here for their summer feed. Snowbound in winter and wild and dangerous in bad weather, it has claimed many a victim among lost travellers. In some of the squat granite hamlets on the northern slopes, like Servies, Auriac and Les Sagnes, you can still hear the bells, known as *clochers de tourmente*, that tolled in the wind to give travellers some sense of direction when the cloud was low.

If you're travelling by car from Mende, the way to the summit is via the village of **LE BLEYMARD**, about 30km to the east on the bank of the infant River Lot, with accommodation in the form of the comfortably rustic *Hôtel La Remise* (Ⓣ04.66.48.65.80, Ⓦwww.hotel-laremise.com; ❷; *terroir* restaurant from €16). From here, the D20 winds 7km up through the conifers to another country-style hotel/*gîte* and restaurant, the *Chalet-Hotel du Mont Lozère* (Ⓣ04.68.48.62.84, Ⓦwww.chalet-mt-lozere.fr; ❷), where it's joined by the GR7, which has taken a more direct route from Le Bleymard. This is the route that Stevenson took, waymarked as the "Tracé Historique de Stevenson". Road and footpath run together as far as the **Col de Finiels**, where the GR7 strikes off on its own to the southeast. The source of the River Tarn is about 3km east of the col, the summit of Lozère 2km to the west. From the col, the road and Stevenson's route drop down in tandem, through the lonely hamlet of **FINIELS** to the pretty but touristy village of **LE PONT-DE-MONTVERT**.

At Le Pont, a seventeenth-century **bridge** crosses the Tarn by a stone tower that once served as a tollhouse. In this building in 1702, the Abbé du Chayla, a priest appointed by the Crown to reconvert the rebellious Protestants enraged by the revocation of the Edict of Nantes, set up a torture chamber to coerce the recalcitrant. Incensed by his brutality, a group of them under the leadership of one Esprit Séguier attacked and killed him on July 23. Reprisals were extreme; nearly 12,000 were executed, thus precipitating the Camisards' guerrilla war against the state (see p.859).

At the edge of the village, there's also an *écomusée* on the life and character of the region, the **Maison du Mont Lozère** (May–Sept daily 10.30am–12.30pm

& 2.30–6.30pm; €3.50). If you're tempted to **stay**, there's the small and atmospheric *Auberge des Cévennes* (Ⓣ04.66.45.80.01; ❶; closed mid-Nov to March; restaurant from €15), overlooking the bridge. There's also a *gîte d'étape* in the Maison du Mont Lozère (Ⓣ04.66.45.80.10 or 04.66.45.80.73; closed Jan & Feb; reservations obligatory).

Florac and Mont Aigoual

Situated 39km south of Mende, **FLORAC** lies in the bottom of the trench-like valley of the Tarnon just short of its junction with the Tarn. Behind the village rises the steep wall that marks the edge of the Causse Méjean. When you get here, you will have already passed the frontier between the northern and Mediterranean landscapes; the dividing line seems to be the **Col de Montmirat** at the western end of Mont Lozère. Once you begin the descent, the scrub and steep gullies and the tiny abandoned hamlets, with their eyeless houses oriented towards the sun, speak clearly of the south.

The village, with some 2000 inhabitants, is strung out along the left bank of the Tarnon and the main street, **avenue Jean-Monestier**. There's little to see, though the close lanes of the village up towards the valley side have their charms, especially the plane-shaded **place du Souvenir**. It is worth visiting on a Thursday during summer for the **market**, when you'll find the tiny streets packed with merchants and local produce. A red-schist castle stands above the village, housing the **Centre d'Information du Parc National des Cévennes** (Easter–Oct daily 9.30am–12.30pm & 2–6pm; Oct–Easter Mon–Fri 9.30am–12.30pm & 2–6pm; Ⓣ04.66.49.53.01, Ⓔpnc@bsi.fr). The **tourist office** is on avenue Jean-Monestier (Mon–Fri 9am–12.30pm & 2–7pm, Sat 9.30am–12.30pm & 2–6pm, Sun 10am–1pm; Ⓣ04.66.45.01.14, Ⓦwww.mescevennes.com); they provide details on the year-round "Festival of Nature" programme, with guided treks around the national park. **Mountain bike rental** is available from Cévennes Evasion, in place Boyer (Ⓣ04.66.45.18.31).

The **accommodation** on offer is not fantastic. The best place is the *Grand Hôtel du Parc* on avenue Jean-Monestier (Ⓣ04.66.45.03.05, Ⓦwww.grandhotelduparc.fr; ❸; closed Dec to March; restaurant €15–30), with pleasant gardens and a pool. *Les Gorges du Tarn* at 48 rue de Pecheur (Ⓣ04.66.45.00.63, Ⓔgorges-du-tarn.adonis@wanadoo.fr; ❹) is the most comfortable option, while *Au 21 Esplanade*, a restaurant in the middle of the Esplanade, has six simple rooms (Ⓣ04.66.32.83.46, ❶). Local **gîtes d'étape** include *La Carline*, 18 rue du Pêcher (Ⓣ04.66.45.24.54, Ⓦwww.causses-cevennes.com/lagrave.htm; closed mid-Nov to Jan) and the *gîte d'etape communal*, 1 rue du Four (Mme Rives: Ⓣ04.66.45.14.93, Ⓔmairie@ville-florac.fr; closed Dec). The best-value **campsite** is the municipal one at Le Pont-du-Tarn out on the road towards Ispagnac (Ⓣ04.66.45.18.26; closed mid-Oct to March).

Florac's Esplanade is a good place to look for somewhere to **eat**, otherwise the *Adonis* restaurant in the *Les Gorges* hotel serves high-quality local cuisine (menus €17–35; closed Sun lunch), while another good choice is the riverside *La Source du Pêcher* at 1 rue de Rémuret in the old town (Ⓣ04.66.45.03.01; menus from €15–30; closed Nov–Easter). **Internet** access can be found on rue du Pêcher at Florac-Online (Tues–Sat 9.30am–12.30pm & 3–7pm).

Mont Aigoual

It's 24km by road up the beautiful valley of the Tarnon to the **Col de Perjuret**, where a right turn will take you on to the **Causse Méjean** and to the strange rock formations of **Nîmes-le-Vieux**, and a left turn along a rising ridge a further 15km to the 1565-metre summit of **Mont Aigoual** (GR6, GR7, GR66). From the latter, it is said that you can see a third of France, from the Alps to the Pyrenees, with the Mediterranean coast from Marseille to Sète at your feet. It's not a craggy summit, although the ground drops away pretty steeply into the valley of the River Hérault on the south side, but the view and the sense of exposure to the elements is dramatic enough. At the summit is an **observatory** which has been in use for over a century. A small but interesting **exhibition** (May–Sept daily 10am–6pm; free) shows modern weather-forecasting techniques alongside displays of old barometers and weather vanes. The observatory also harbours a CAF refuge and *gîte d'étape* (Ⓣ04.67.82.62.78; closed Oct–April).

The descent to Le Vigan by the valley of the Hérault is superb; a magnificent twisty road follows the deepening ravine through dense beech and chestnut woods, to come out at the bottom in rather Italianate scenery, with tall, close-built villages and vineyards beside the stream. The closest accommodation to the summit is the *Hôtel du Touring* (Ⓣ04.67.82.60.04, Ⓕ04.67.82.65.09; ❷; restaurant menus €11–20; closed April & Nov to mid-Dec) at **L'ESPÉROU**, a rather soulless mountain resort just below the summit. Better to go down to the charming village of **VALLERAUGUE**, with its brown-grey schist houses and leafy riverside setting. There are a number of hotels here, including the welcoming *Petit Luxembourg* (Ⓣ04.67.82.20.44, Ⓕ04.67.82.24.66; ❷; menus €15–30).

The Causse du Larzac

In the 1970s, the **Causse du Larzac** was continually in the headlines over sustained political resistance to the high-profile presence of the French military. Originally there was a small military camp outside the village of **LA CAVALERIE** on the N9, long tolerated for the cash its soldiers brought in. But in the early 1970s the army decided to expand the place and use it as a permanent strategic base, expropriating a hundred or so farms. The result was explosive. A federation was formed – Paysans du Larzac – which attracted the support of numerous ecological, left-wing and Occitan groups in a protracted campaign of resistance under the slogan "Gardarem lo Larzac" ("Let's protect Larzac"). Successful acts of sabotage were committed, and three huge peace festivals were held here, in 1973, 1974 and 1977. The army's plans were scotched by Mitterrand when he came to power in 1981, but you still find Larzac graffiti from here to Lyon, shorthand for opposition to the army, the state and the Parisian central government, and in favour of self-determination and independence for the south.

The best way to immerse yourself in the empty, sometimes eerie atmosphere of Larzac is to walk: **GRs 7**, **71** and **74** cross the plateau, though you shouldn't attempt them without a Topo-guide. If you have no time for anything else, the area between La Couvertoirade, Le Caylar and Ganges in the foothills of the Cévennes will give you a real sense of life on the *causse*.

LA COUVERTOIRADE lies 5km off the main road (parking €3). Billed as a perfect "Templar" village, its present remains postdate the dissolution of that Order in the late thirteenth century. Anomalies aside, it is a striking site, still completely enclosed by its towers and walls and almost untouched by renovation. Its forty remaining inhabitants live by tourism, and you have to pay to walk around the **ramparts** (daily: March–June & Sept to mid-Nov 10am–noon & 2–5/6pm; July & Aug 10am–7pm; €5, including a video presentation; English audio-guide available). Just outside the walls on the south side is a *lavogne*, a paved water hole of a kind seen all over the *causse* for watering the flocks, whose milk is used for Roquefort cheese. If you want to stay, there's the municipal **gîte d'étape** (☎05.65.58.17.75 or 06.12.50.09.86; ❶) in the far corner from the entrance, serving the GR71 and GR71C. A bus from Millau (Mon, Wed & Fri) serves the village during July & August. Half a dozen kilometres south, the closest point served by regular public transport, the village of **LE CAYLAR** clusters in similar fashion at the foot of a rocky outcrop, the top of which has been fashioned into a fortress – worth clambering up for the aerial view of the surrounding *causse*.

St-Maurice-Navacelles and the Cirque de Navacelles

If you've got your own transport and a good map, the back road from here, via St-Michel to **ST-MAURICE-NAVACELLES**, is strongly recommended. Wild box grows along the lanes, often meticulously clipped into hedges. Here and there among the scrubby oak and thorn or driving along the road at milking time, you pass flocks of sheep. Occasional farmhouses materialize, like Les Besses – one of the few still in use – huge, self-contained and fortress-like, with the living quarters upstairs and the sheep stalls down below. St-Maurice-Navacelles, on the GR7 and GR74, is a small and sleepy hamlet with a fine World War I memorial by Paul Dardé at its centre. Its services include a summer-only shop and a *gîte* (04.76.44.62.55) which also does meals. There's no official **campsite**, but if you ask they'll direct you to a grassy place by the cemetery, where a traditional *glacière* – a stone-lined pit for storing snow for use as ice before the days of refrigerators – has been restored. Its chief advantage is as a base for visiting the **Cirque de Navacelles**, 10km north on the D130 past the beautiful ruined seventeenth-century sheep farm of La Prunarède. The cirque is a widening in the 150-metre deep trench of the Vis *gorges*, formed by a now dry loop in the river that has left a neat pyramid of rock sticking up in the middle like a wheel hub. An ancient and scarcely inhabited hamlet survives in the bottom – a bizarre phenomenon in an extraordinary location, and you get literally a bird's-eye view of it from the edge of the cliff above. Both road and GR7 go through. Continuing to Le Vigan or Ganges via Montdardier, you pass a prehistoric **stone circle** on the left of the road, a silent and evocative place, especially in a close *causse* mist.

Le Vigan and the Huguenot strongholds

Only 64km from Montpellier and 18km from Ganges, **LE VIGAN** makes a good starting point for exploring the southern part of the Cévennes. It's a leafy, cool and thoroughly agreeable place, at its liveliest during the **Fête d'Isis** at the beginning of August and the colossal fair that takes over the Parc des Châtaigniers on September 9 and 22.

The prettiest part of the town is around the central **place du Quai**, shaded by lime trees and bordered by cafés and brasseries. From here it's only a two-minute walk south, down rue Pierre-Gorlier, to reach the gracefully arched **Pont Vieux**. Beside it stands the **Musée Cévenol** (April–Oct daily except Tues

10am–noon & 2–6pm; Nov–March Wed only 10am–noon & 2–6pm; €4.50), a well-presented look at traditional rural occupations in the area, including the woodcutter, butcher, shepherd and wolf-hunter. There's also a room devoted to the area's best-known twentieth-century writer, André Chamson, noted for his novels steeped in the traditions and countryside of the Cévennes. Interestingly, Coco Chanel also features in the museum: she had local family connections and it seems found inspiration for her designs in the *cévenol* silks.

The **tourist office** occupies a modern block in the centre of the place du Marché, at the opposite end of the place du Quai from the church (July & Aug Mon–Sat 8.30am–12.30pm & 1.30–7pm, Sun 10am–1pm; Sept–June Mon–Fri 9am–12.30pm & 2–6pm, Sat 8.30am–1pm; Ⓣ04.67.81.01.72). For somewhere to **stay**, try the simple but attractive *Hôtel du Commerce*, with its wisteria-covered balcony and little garden, at 26 rue des Barris (Ⓣ04.67.81.03.28, Ⓔsarreboubee.serge@wanadoo.fr; ❶; closed mid-Oct to mid-Nov). The best alternative is a couple of kilometres out of town, south towards Montdardier on the D48: the handsome old *Auberge Cocagne* in the village of **AVÈZE** (Ⓣ04.67.81.02.70, Ⓔauberge-cocagne@wanadoo.fr; ❶; closed mid-Nov to mid-Feb; restaurant from €13). There are also **campsites** in Avèze (Ⓣ04.67.81.95.01; closed mid-Sept to mid-June), or 2km upriver from Le Vigan, on the opposite bank, is the well-shaded riverside Val de l'Arre (Ⓣ04.67.81.02.77, Ⓦwww.valdelarre.com/valdelarre; closed Oct–March). There's a **gîte d'étape** at 1 rue de la Carrierrasse (Ⓣ04.67.81.01.71). One of the best places to eat in Le Vigan is *Le Jardin* (closed Mon), in place du Terral, just off the main square; menus start at €18 and feature French classics with a local twist, such as *filet mignon* with a chestnut sauce. A good alternative is *Le Chandelier* (closed Mon), housed in a converted cellar on rue du Pouzadou; the €13 menu includes *confit de canard* and a choice of delicious desserts.

From Le Vigan, or more particularly from the Pont de l'Hérault bridge, a beautiful lane (D153) slowly winds around 45km northeast through typical south Cévennes landscape – deep valleys thick with sweet chestnut and thinly peopled with isolated farms half-buried in greenery – from Sumène to St-Jean-du-Gard.

St-Jean-du-Gard and around

Thirty-two kilometres west of Alès, **ST-JEAN-DU-GARD** was the centre of Protestant resistance during the Camisard war in 1702–04 (see below). It straggles along the bank of the River Gardon, crossed by a graceful, arched eighteenth-century bridge, with a number of picturesque old houses still surviving in the main street, **Grande-Rue**. One of them contains the splendid **Musée des Vallées Cévenoles** (April–Oct daily 10am–12.30pm & 2–7pm; July & Aug 10am–7pm; Nov–March Tues–Sat 9am–noon & 2–6pm, Sun 2–6pm; €4), a museum of local life with displays of tools, trades, furniture, clothes, domestic articles and a fascinating collection of pieces related to the silk industry. The work of spinning the silk was done by women in factories and lists of regulations and rules on display give some idea of the tough conditions in which they had to work.

The **tourist office** is just off the main street by the post office (July & Aug Mon & Wed–Fri 9am–1pm & 3–6pm, Tues & Sat 9am–7pm, Sun 10am–noon; Sept–June Mon–Fri 9am–12.30pm & 1.30–5pm, Sat 10am–12.30pm; Ⓣ04.66.85.32.11, Ⓦotsi.st.jeandugard.free.fr). They can advise you about the times of the **steam train** that operates between St-Jean and Anduze (April to mid-Sept daily; mid-Sept to Oct Tues–Sun; €11 return). There's a big **market** all along Grande-Rue on Tuesday mornings.

The best bet for **accommodation** is *Auberge du Peras* on route de Nîmes (☎04.66.85.35.94, Ⓦwww.aubergeduperas.com; ❸; good restaurant from €13). There's a *gîte d'étape* 3km north on the D907 at **LE MOULINET**; contact Mme Laurtay on ☎04.66.85.10.98.

The Musée du Désert

Signposts at St-Jean direct you to the museum at **MAS SOUBEYRAN**, a minuscule hamlet of beautiful rough-stone houses in a gully above the village of Mialet, about 12km east. The **Musée du Désert** (daily: March–June & Sept–Nov 9.30am–noon & 2–6pm; July & Aug 9.30am–7pm; €4.50) is in the house that once belonged to Rolland, one of the Camisards' self-taught but most successful military leaders, and it remains much the same as it would have been in 1704, the year of his death. It catalogues the appalling sufferings and sheer dogged heroism of the Protestant Huguenots in defence of their freedom of conscience; and the "desert" they had to traverse between the Revocation of the Edict of Nantes in 1685 and the promulgation of the Edict of Tolerance in 1787, which restored their original rights (full emancipation came with the Declaration of the Rights of Man in the first heady months of the Revolution in 1789). During this period, they had no civil rights, unless they abjured their faith. They could not bury their dead, baptize their children or marry. Their priests were forced into exile on pain of death. The recalcitrant were subjected to the infamous *dragonnades*, which involved the forcible billeting of troops on private homes at the expense of the occupants. As if this were not enough, the soldiers would beat their drums continuously for days and nights in people's bedrooms in order to deprive them of sleep. Protestants were also put to death or sent to the galleys for life and their houses were destroyed.

Not surprisingly, such brutality led to armed rebellion, inspired by the prophesying of the lay preachers who had replaced the banished priests, calling for a holy war. The rebels were hopelessly outnumbered and the revolt was ruthlessly put down in 1704 (see box, p.859). On display are documents, private letters and lists of those who died for their beliefs, including the names of five thousand who died as galley slaves (*galériens pour la foi*) and the women who were immured in the Tour de Constance prison in Aigues-Mortes. Also on show are the chains and rough uniform of a *galérien*.

Prafrance and the Mine Témoin

Twelve kilometres southeast of St-Jean in the direction of Anduze, **PRAFRANCE** is noteworthy for **La Bambouseraie** (March to mid-Nov daily 9.30am–closing time dependent on season and weather; €7.50), an extraordinary and appealing garden consisting exclusively of bamboos of all shapes and sizes; the project was started in 1855 by local entrepreneur Eugène Mazel. An easy way to get here is to take the steam train (see p.945) from St-Jean-du-Gard; it takes just ten minutes.

If you want to leave the area by main-line train, the place to head for is **ALÈS** on the Nîmes–Paris line. This was a major coal-mining centre, though 25,000 jobs have been lost and all but two open-cast pits closed in the last four decades. Today, it has a superb museum on the history and techniques of coal-mining, known as the **Mine Témoin**, in the underground workings of a disused mine on chemin de la Cité Ste-Marie in the Rochebelle district (French-only guided tours daily: June 10am–7pm; July & Aug 9am–6pm; Sept–May 9.30am–12.30pm & 2.30–5.30pm; €6.70; last visit 1hr 30min before closing).

Aubenas and the northern Cévennes

A small but prosperous and surprisingly industrial town of around 12,000, **AUBENAS** sits in the middle of the southern part of the Ardèche *département*, high up on a hill overlooking the middle valley of the River Ardèche. Located 91km southeast of Le Puy and 42km west of Montélimar, the town, with a character and non-tourist-dependent economy of its own, makes a much better base than overly crowded places further downstream around Vallon-Pont-d'Arc.

The central knot of streets with their cobbles and bridges, occupying the highest point of town around **place de l'Hôtel-de-Ville**, have great charm, particularly towards place de la Grenette and place 14-Juillet. Place de l'Hôtel-de-Ville is dominated by the eleventh-century **château**, from which the local *seigneurs* ruled the area right up until the Revolution (90-min guided tours: April–June & Sept Tues & Thurs–Sat 10.30am & 2pm; July & Aug daily 11am, 2pm & 5pm; Oct & Dec–March Tues, Thurs & Sat 2pm; closed on hols; €3.50). Other sights include the heavily restored thirteenth-century **St-Laurent church**, which has an elaborate fifteenth-century chapel (July & Aug Mon–Fri 5pm; €3.50), and the curious seventeenth-century hexagonal **Dôme Bênoit chapel** (July & Aug Mon–Fri 5pm; €3.50). There's a magnificent view of the Ardèche snaking up the valley from under an arch beside the castle, as there is from the end of boulevard Gambetta 200m downhill, where the **tourist office** is located on the (July & Aug Mon–Sat 9am–12.30pm & 1.30–7pm; Sept–June Mon–Sat 9am–noon & 2–6pm; ⓣ04.75.89.02.03, ⓦwww.aubenasvals.com). To use the **Internet** go to Espace Informatique at 10 bd Saint-Didier (Mon noon–7pm, Tues–Sat 10am–7pm).

For somewhere to **stay**, the budget choice is the old-fashioned *Hôtel des Négociants*, right next to the château on place de l'Hôtel-de-Ville (ⓣ04.75.35.18.74; ❶; closed Oct), which does nourishing meals from €9. *Hotel Le Provence* on boulevard de Vernon is another cheap option (ⓣ04.75.35.28.43, ❶) with clean simple rooms. At the top end of the scale the 5-room *La Bastide du Soleil* (ⓣ04.75.36.91.66, ⓦwww.chateauxhotels.com/bastidesoleil; ❻–❽; closed Dec–Jan) offers a splendid blend of antique charm and modern convenience (restaurant from €30). There are many campsites to choose from in between Aubenas and Vallon. Cafés and brasseries line boulevard de Vernon on the south side of town; the best place for both food and atmosphere is *Le Fournil*, 34 rue du 4-Septembre, set in a fifteenth-century house at the end of Béranger-de-la-Tour, in the heart of the old town (closed Sun eve & Mon; from €18–33), or *Le Coyote*, 13 bd Jean-Mathon (ⓣ04.75.35.01.28; menus from €16.50), whose specialities are fish and foie gras.

The Gorges de l'Ardèche

The **Gorges de l'Ardèche** begin at the **Pont d'Arc**, a very beautiful arch that the river has cut for itself through the limestone, just downstream from **VALLON**, itself 39km south of Aubenas. They continue for about 35km to **ST-MARTIN-D'ARDÈCHE** in the valley of the Rhône.

The fantastic gorges wind back and forth, much of the time dropping 300m straight down in the almost dead-flat scrubby Plateau des Gras. Unfortunately they are also an appalling tourist trap; the road following the rim, with spectacular viewpoints marked out at regular intervals, is jammed with traffic in summer. The river, down in the bottom, which is where you really want to be to appreciate the grandeur of the canyon, is likewise packed with canoes in high season. It is walkable, depending on the water level, but you would need to bivouac midway at either Gaud or Gournier. Generally speaking, if you can't go out of season, you're better off giving it a miss.

The plateau itself is riddled with caves. **Aven Marzal**, a stalactite cavern north of the gorge (daily 11am–5.30pm; €8, joint ticket with zoo €13.80), has a prehistoric **zoo**, which consists of reconstructions of dinosaurs and friends (Feb, March, Oct & Nov Sun & school hols 10.30am–6pm; April–Sept daily 11.30am–5pm; €8), but the frequency of visits to the cave depends on the number of visitors waiting – they are approximately every twenty minutes in July and August, falling to four per day in other months. Best of the area's caves is the **Aven Orgnac**, to the south of the gorge (90-min tour daily: Feb, March, Nov & Dec hols 10.30am–4.45pm; April, June & Sept 9.30am–5.30pm; July & Aug 9.30am–6.30pm; Oct 9.30am–5.15pm; €9.40), one of France's most spectacular and colourful stalactite formations. In addition to the normal tours, you can also opt for the "visites spéléologiques" hard-core caving tours; they last three and eight hours respectively and it's best to reserve two weeks ahead (ⓣ04.75.38.65.10). There's also a very good prehistory **museum** (daily: March–June & Sept to mid-Nov 10am–noon & 2–6pm; July & Aug 10am–6pm; €5, joint ticket €9.20).

Further upstream near Vallon-Pont-d'arc, a complex series of cave paintings was discovered in December 1994, after being left untouched for 30,000 years, making the **Chauvet-Pont d'Arc** cave the oldest-known decorated cave in the world. The cave system is currently being investigated by archeologists and causing a major rethink about the history of art. The paintings depict woolly rhinos, bison, lions and bears, and display a remarkable mastery of perspective. It's unlikely that Chauvet-Pont d'Arc will ever be open to the public. However, there is a small but rewarding **exhibition** on the cave complex at Vallon, behind the *mairie*. The highlight is a video taken inside the caves, showing many of the paintings close up (Tues–Sun: mid-March to May & Sept to mid-Nov 10am–noon & 2–5.30pm; June–Aug 10am–1pm & 3–8pm; €4).

Practicalities

Accommodation in the area can be a problem during the high season. By far the best is *Le Manoir du Raveyron*, rue Henri-Barbusse (ⓣ04.75.88.03.59, ⓔle.manoir.du.raveyron@wanadoo.fr; ❹; closed Oct to mid-March), with a good restaurant from €20, while another good option is the *Hôtel du Tourisme*, on rue du Miarou in Vallon (ⓣ04.75.88.02.12, ⓦwww.hotel-tourisme-pont-darc.com; closed Dec–Feb; ❹). The river is lined with **campsites**, the cheapest being the municipal one (ⓣ04.75.88.04.73; closed Oct–March). There's a **gîte d'étape** on place de la Mairie (ⓣ04.75.88.07.87), and a **tourist office** on the south side of town (April & Oct Mon–Sat 9am–noon & 2–5pm, Sat closed at 4pm; May, June & Sept Mon–Sat 9am–noon & 2–6pm, Sat closed at 5pm, Sun 9.30am–12.30pm; July & Aug Mon–Sat 9am–1pm & 3–7pm, Sun 9.30am–12.30; Nov–March Mon–Fri 9am–noon & 2–5pm, Sat 9am–noon ⓣ04.75.88.04.01, ⓦwww.vallon-pont-darc.com). Eight kilometres upstream is a well-priced municipal **campsite** at **RUOMS** (ⓣ04.75.93.99.16; closed Oct to mid-May).

The valley of the Chassezac and the Corniche du Vivarais

Between Aubenas and Les Vans, 27km to the southwest, several wild mountain streams flow out of the northern part of the Cévennes to join the Ardèche. One of the most beautiful is the **Chassezac**, which rises north of Villefort and carves a dry, twisting ravine covered with pine, bracken and sweet chestnut down to **LES VANS**.

The centre of the town is occupied by the wide and cheerful **place Léopold-Ollier**. Nearby you'll find the comfortable *Viverais* (Ⓣ04.75.37.22.73, Ⓦwww.le-vivarais-hotel.com; ❷; closed mid-Sept to April), which has a *terroir* restaurant (menus €13) and offers full *pensions*. Worth seeking out, however, is the beautifully renovated former convent, *Le Carmel*, at 7 montée Carmel (Ⓣ04.75.94.99.60, Ⓦwww.le-carmel.com; ❹; closed mid-Dec to Feb), home to one of the area's best restaurants (€25). You must book either place well in advance in high season. Other attractions are the remains of the old town and, just outside, the bizarre rock formations of the **Bois de Paiolive**. There's a **gîte d'étape** across the river at Chambonas (Ⓣ04.75.37.24.99).

Thines to the Col de Meyrand

THINES is a dozen twisting kilometres up the Chassezac from Les Vans, past isolated farms, abandoned terracing and numerous tumbling streams, then a further 5km or so up a side valley. The lane that leads to it is no wider than a car, and nature encroaches on either side. Traces remain of the old mule road, and in the torrent bed stand the stumps of packhorse bridges long since carried away. Tourists are to leave their vehicles in a car park about 500m from Thines (be sure to lock up and take your valuables with you as the isolated location of the parking lot makes it a prime target for thieves). The village itself is at the end of the road high on a spur, looking back down the valley: just a handful of squat, grey-stone houses tightly grouped around a very lovely twelfth-century **church**, decorated with bands of red and white stone, the faces of its sculptures smashed during the Wars of Religion. At the top of the village, where the **GR4** and the local **GRP** enter from the scrubby heights behind, there is a strange **rock-cut relief** commemorating Resistance people killed here in August 1943. There's also a **gîte**, *Chez Estelle* (Ⓣ04.75.36.94.33; closed Oct–March). If you call and make a reservation you can have a meal at the tiny *ferme auberge*, *Chez Chantal* (Ⓣ04.75.36.94.47, closed mid-Nov to Easter).

If your car is reasonably robust, you can get up onto the D4 on the 1000m ridge above Thines by a track that starts just above the bridge over the stream below the village. This is the so-called **Corniche du Vivarais Cévenol**, which you would otherwise have to make a long detour to reach. **SABLIÈRES**, another desolate Cévennes village, lies in the valley of the Drobie down to your right.

The landscape changes completely up here. The Mediterranean influence is left behind; it's windswept moorland, with natural beechwoods and mountain ash around the few bleak farms and plantations of conifers on the tops. The land rises steadily to over 1400m above the **Col de Meyrand**, itself at 1370m, from where it's possible to head back down to the main road and train line at **LUC**, 18km to the west.

Le Puy-en-Velay and the northeast

Right in the middle of the Massif Central, 78km from St-Étienne and 132km from Clermont, **LE PUY-EN-VELAY**, often shortened to Le Puy, is one of the most remarkable towns in the whole of France, with a landscape and architecture that are totally theatrical. Slung between the higher mountains to

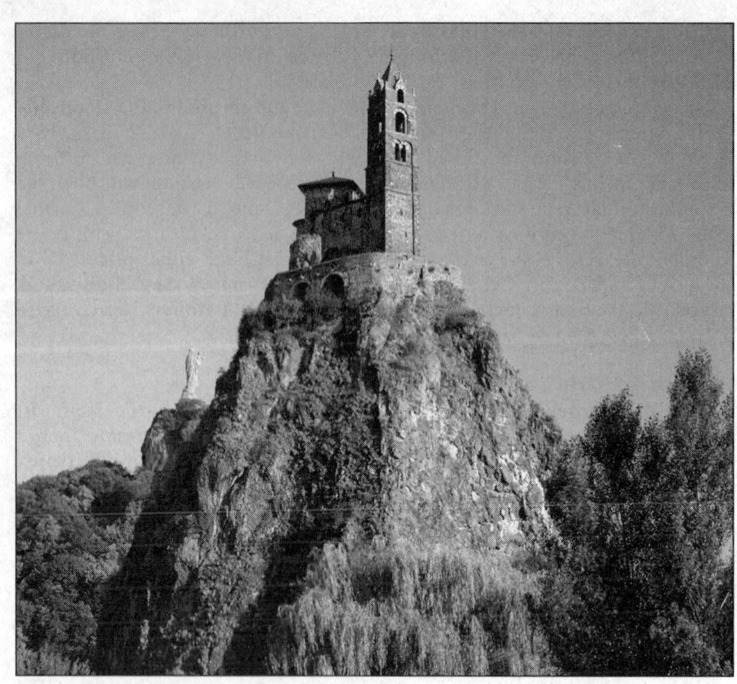

△ Church of St-Michel, Le Puy-en-Velay

east and west, the countryside erupts in a chaos of volcanic acne: everywhere is a confusion of abrupt conical hills, scarred with dark outcrops of rock and topknotted with woods. Even in the centre of the town, these volcanic thrusts burst through.

In the past, Le Puy enjoyed influence and prosperity because of its ecclesiastical institutions, which were supported in part by the production of the town's famous green lentils. It was – and in a limited way, still is – a centre for pilgrims embarking on the 1600-kilometre trek to Santiago de Compostela. The specific starting point is place du Plot (also the scene of a lively Saturday market) and rue St-Jacques. History has it that Le Puy's Bishop Godescalk, in the tenth century, was the first pilgrim to make the journey. During the Wars of Religion the town managed to resist the Protestant fervour of much of the Massif Central. Recently, however, it has fallen somewhat on hard times, and its traditional industries – tanning and lace – have essentially gone bust. Even today Le Puy is somewhat inaccessible for the capital of a *département*: the three main roads out all cross passes more than 1000m high, which causes problems in winter.

Arrival, information and accommodation

If you arrive at the **gare SNCF** or **gare routière** (ⓣ04.71.09.25.60), facing each other in place Maréchal-Leclerc, you'll find yourself barely a ten-minute walk from the central place du Clauzel and the **tourist office** (Easter–June & Sept–Oct Mon–Sat 8.30am–noon & 1.30–6.15pm, Sun 9am–noon & 2–6pm; July & Aug daily 8.30am–7.30pm; Nov–Easter Mon–Sat 8.30am–noon & 1.30–

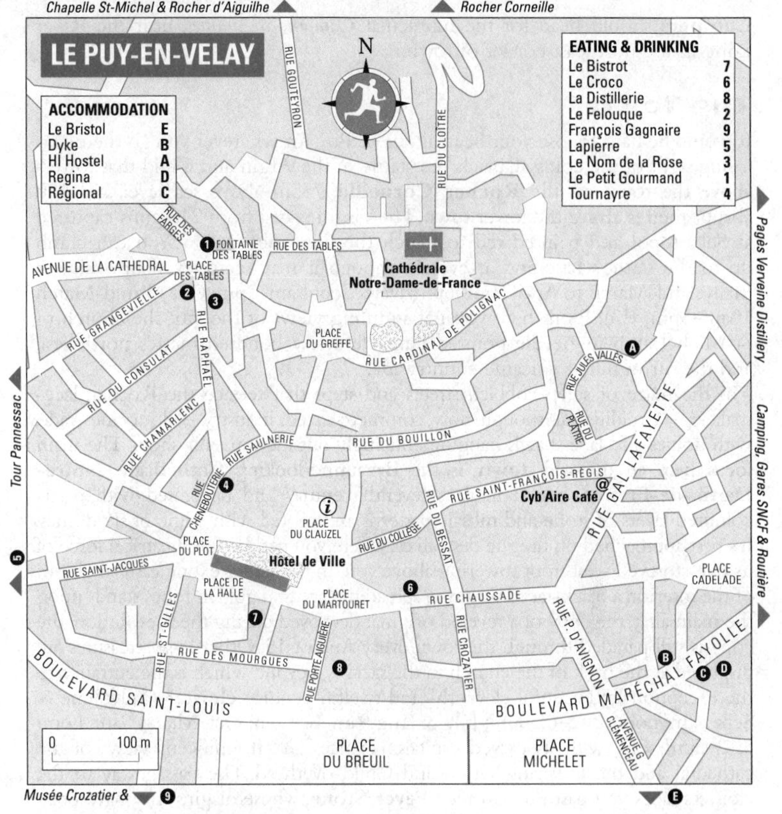

6.15pm, Sun 10am–noon; ⓣ04.71.09.38.41, ⓦwww.ot-lepuyenvelay.fr). The town hall at 1 place Monsiegneur de Galard is home to the **Comité Départemental du Tourisme** (June–Aug Mon–Sat 8.30am–7.30pm, Sun 9am–noon & 2–6pm; Sept–May Mon–Sat 8.30am–noon & 2–6pm; ⓣ04.71.07.41.54, ⓦwww.mididelauvergne.com). Here you'll find information useful for venturing into the countryside. There are quite a few places to access the **Internet**, the best option being Cyb'Aire at 17 rue Général-Lafayette.

Le Puy doesn't have a superabundance of **hotels**, so it's wise to book ahead in peak season. The budget options include the clean and pleasant *Dyke Hôtel*, at no. 37 (ⓣ04.71.09.05.30, ⓕ04.71.02.58.66; ②), and the basic *Régional*, at no. 36 (ⓣ04.71.09.37.74; ①), both on boulevard Maréchal-Fayolle, the main boulevard connecting the station and place du Clauzel. On the same street but more luxurious is the renovated old mansion, at no. 34 (ⓣ04.71.09.14.71, ⓦwww.hotelrestregina.com; ③–⑥; restaurant €15–35). Best of all is *Le Bristol*, 7 av Foch (ⓣ04.71.09.13.38, ⓦwww.hotelbristol-lepuy.com; ③), set in one of the area's oldest buildings, a former pilgrim's hostel, with a restaurant offering an excellent regional set menu from €10. For those on a tight budget, there's a good **HI hostel**, the attractive *Centre Pierre-Cardinal* at 9 rue Jules-Vallès (ⓣ04.71.05.52.40, ⓔauberge.jeunesse@mairie-le-puy-en-velay.fr; closed weekends Oct–March), just off rue Lafayette, in the heart of the old town.

Campers should head for the municipal *Camping d'Audinet*, near the River Loire in the northeast corner of town.

The Town

It would be hard to lose your bearings in Le Puy, for wherever you go there's no losing sight of the colossal, brick-red statue of the Virgin and Child that towers above the town on the **Rocher Corneille**, 755m above sea level and 130 abrupt metres above the lower town. The Virgin is cast from 213 guns captured at Sebastopol and painted red to match the tiled roofs below. You can climb up to the statue's base and, irreverent though it may seem, even up inside it (daily: mid-March to April 9am–6pm; May–Sept 9am–7pm; Oct to mid-March 10am–5pm; €3). From here you get stunning views of the city, the church of St-Michel atop its needle-pointed pinnacle a few hundred metres northwest, and the surrounding volcanic countryside.

In the maze of steep cobbled streets and steps that terrace the Rocher, lace-makers – a traditional, though now commercialized, industry – do a fine trade, with doilies and lace shawls hanging enticingly outside souvenir shops. The main focus here, in the **old town**, is the Byzantine-looking **Cathédrale Notre-Dame-de-France**, begun in the eleventh century and decorated with parti-coloured layers of stone and mosaic patterns and roofed with a line of six domes. It's best approached up the rue des Tables, where you get the full theatrical force of its five-storeyed west front towering above you. In the rather exotic eastern gloom of the interior, a black-faced Virgin in spreading lace and golden robes stands upon the main altar, the copy of a revered original destroyed during the Revolution; the copy is still paraded through the town every August 15. Other lesser treasures are displayed at the back of the church in the sacristy, beyond which is the entrance to the exceptionally beautiful eleventh- and twelfth-century **cloister** (daily: June & Sept 9am–noon & 2–6.30pm; July & Aug 9am–6.30pm; Oct–March 9am–noon & 2–5pm; €5), with its carved capitals, cornices and magnificent views of the cathedral and the towering Virgin and Child overhead. The passageway to the cloisters takes you past the so-called **Fever Stone**, whose origins may have been as a prehistoric dolmen and which was reputed to have the power of curing fevers. The surrounding ecclesiastical buildings and the **place du For**, on the south side of the cathedral, all date from the same period and form a remarkable ensemble.

It's a ten-minute walk from the cathedral to the **church of St-Michel** (sign-posts lead the way), perched atop the 82-metre needle-pointed lava pinnacle of the **Rocher d'Aiguilhe**. The little Romanesque church, built on Bishop Godescalk's return from his pilgrimage and consecrated in 962, is a beauty in its own right, and its improbable situation atop this ridiculous needle of rock is quite extraordinary – it's a long haul up 265 steps to the entrance (daily: Feb to mid-March 2–5pm; mid-March to April & Oct to mid-Nov 9.30am–noon & 2–5.30pm; May–Sept 9am–6.30pm; €2.75).

The new town and Pagès Verveine distillery

In the new part of town, beyond the squat **Tour Pannessac**, which is all that remains of the city walls, **place de Breuil** joins **place Michelet** and forms a social hub backed by the spacious Henri Vinay public gardens, where the **Musée Crozatier** (May–Sept daily 10am–noon & 2–6pm, but closed Tues & Sun afternoons mid-June to mid-Sept; Oct–April Mon & Wed–Sat 10am–noon & 2–4pm, €3.20) is best known for its collections relating to the region's traditional lace-making activities. Busy boulevard Maréchal-Fayolle converges with place Cadelade, where there's another of Le Puy's crazier aspects: the extraordinary bulbous tower of what used to be the **Pagès Verveine distillery**. The *verveine* (verbena) plant is normally used to make *tisane* (herb tea), but in this region provides a vivid green, powerful digestive liqueur instead. Production has now moved to a distillery 5km outside Le Puy, which is open for guided tours and tasting (March–June & Sept-Dec Tues–Sat 10am–noon & 1.30–6.30pm, July–Aug daily 10am–12.30pm & 1.30–6.30pm; €5.80). To get there take the N88 and exit at the *zone industrielle* Blavozy.

Eating and drinking

For a city its size, Le Puy has an impressive array of fine yet economical **restaurants**, so there is little need to resort to the row of anonymous brasseries on the main street. The best of the eateries is the creative cuisine of the *François Gagnaire Restaurant* at 4 av Charbonnier (T 04.71.02.75.55, W www.francois-gagnaire-restaurant.com; closed Sun eve, Mon and Tues lunch, July & Aug closed Sun, Mon, Tues lunch; menus €23–75); try the *Saint-Jacques* with green lentils. Other good choices include *Restaurant Tournayre*, set in a seventeenth-century building at 12 rue Chènebouterie (T 04.71.09.58.94; closed Sun & Wed eve, Mon & Jan), specializing in the regional fare (menus €21–65), and the *gastronomique Lapierre* at 6 rue Capucins (T 04.71.09.08.44; closed Dec & Jan, Sun out of season & Sat) with menus from €24. Two cheaper establishments, both on rue Raphaël beginning at the bottom of rue des Tables, are the *Nom de la Rose*, at no. 48 (closed Mon), offering Mexican food, with menus from €14.60, and *La Felouque*, at no. 49 (closed Feb & Sept–May and Tues year round; menus €8–20), which serves Middle Eastern dishes and excellent grilled salmon. Try the local green lentil beer which is also available in many of Le Puy's pubs. For salads and crêpes, *Le Croco* on 5 rue Chaussade is a local favourite (closed Sun, menus from €13).

For a **drink** or light snack, the terrace of *Le Petit Gourmande*, at the bottom of rue des Tables, makes a pleasant stop in summer (closed Wed; *galettes* for €5, à la carte from €13). Though lacking atmosphere, the large *La Distillerie* pub on place du Breuil has an impressive selection of regional speciality beers and liqueurs. *Le Bistrot* at 7 place de la Halle is a lively place for an evening drink.

North of Le Puy

North of Le Puy, the D906 crosses a vast and terminally depopulated area of pine-clad uplands – now the Parc Naturel Régional Livradois-Forez – and continues all the way to Vichy, via the historic town of **La Chaise-Dieu** and the old industrial centres of **Ambert** and **Thiers**.

La Chaise-Dieu

After 42km you come to the little town of **LA CHAISE-DIEU**, renowned for the **abbey church of St-Robert** (daily: June–Sept 9am–noon & 2–7pm; Oct–May 10am–noon & 2–5pm; €3), whose square towers dominate the town. Founded in 1044 and restored in the fourteenth century at the expense of Pope Clement VI, who had served as a monk here, the church was destroyed by the Huguenots in 1562, burnt down in 1692, and remained unfinished when the Revolution brought a wave of anticlericalism. It was only really finished in the twentieth century. Its interior contains the tomb of Clement VI, some magnificent Flemish tapestries of Old and New Testament scenes hanging in the choir, which also boasts some fine Gothic stalls, and a celebrated fresco of the **Danse Macabre**, depicting Death plucking at the coarse plump bodies of 23 living figures, representing the different classes of society (open May–Oct; €3.70 or €1.80 for treasury only). "It is yourself", says the fifteenth-century text below, as indeed it might easily have been in an age when plague and war were rife.

Nearby on the place de l'Echo, the **Salle de l'Echo** (10am–6pm, until 5pm Nov–April; free) is another product of the risk of contagion – if not from plague, then from leprosy. For in this room, once used for hearing confession from the sick and dying, two people can turn their backs on each other, stand in opposite corners and still have a perfectly audible conversation just by whispering.

A **classical music festival** takes place here in late August and early September, details of which are available from the **tourist office**, on place de la Mairie (Easter–June & Sept Tues–Sun 10am–noon & 2–6pm; July & Aug daily 9am–12.30pm & 1.30–7pm; Oct–March Tues–Sat 10am–noon & 2–6pm; Ⓣ04.71.00.01.16, Ⓦwww.tourisme.fr/lachaisedieu). The *Hôtel Monastère et Terminus*, on avenue de la Gare (Ⓣ04.71.00.00.73, Ⓦwww.hotel-monastere-terminus.com; ❷; closed Nov–March; menus at €12–22), and *De La Casadei* in place l'Abbaye (Ⓣ04.71.00.00.58, Ⓔcasadei@es-conseil.com; ❷; restaurant from €14), offer reasonable comfort for a night's stay. There's also a municipal **campsite**, *Les Parades*, on the Vichy side of the D906 (Ⓣ04.71.00.07.88; closed Oct–May).

Ambert

Twenty-five kilometres north of La Chaise-Dieu, the little town of **AMBERT** was, from the fourteenth to eighteenth centuries, the centre of papermaking in France. It especially supplied the printers of Lyon, a connection that brought the region into contact with new ideas, in particular the revolutionary teachings of the Reformed Church. Although those small-scale operations have long since been sidelined, there is still a **paper mill** in operation at Richard-de-Bas just east of the town, with its **Musée Historique du Papier** (daily: July & Aug 9am–8pm; Sept–June 9am–noon & 2–6pm; €5), featuring exhibits and explanations from papyrus to handmade samples from medieval days. In the town itself, there's a small **museum** (July & Aug daily 9am–noon & 2–7pm; Sept–June Tues & Thurs–Sat 9am–noon & 2.30–7pm; €4) devoted to the manufacture of the soft blue Fourme d'Ambert cheese, the region's speciality. An old diesel *train panoramique* runs between Ambert and **Sembadel** stopping at La Chaise-Dieu on the way (€13 return); a leisurely way to see the region. There is also an authentic steam train named "Picasso" that will take you from Ambert to **Arlanc** (€11 return).

Thiers

THIERS, another 49km to the north, has an illustrious industrial history as the country's greatest manufacturer of knives. In spite of serious decline, especially since decolonization and the loss of such huge captive markets, it still accounts for some seventy percent of French production. It's an interesting little town, built over the steep slopes of the valley of the Durolle, whose water power drove the forges and blade-makers' wheels for centuries. There's the **Maison des Couteliers**, devoted to local knife-crafting, at 58 rue de la Coutellerie in the centre (July & Aug daily 10am–12.30pm & 1.30–6.30pm; Sept–June Tues–Sun 10am–noon & 2–6pm; €4.75), while all along the deep valley bottom you can see where the old workshops were. You probably wouldn't want to stay overnight – there are frequent trains from Clermont-Ferrand (30min).

East of Le Puy

East of Le Puy lies the barrier of the mountains of the Vivarais, rounded and wooded with beech, pine and fir, interspersed with open cow pastures. The highest points are the **Gerbier de Jonc** (1551m) and **Mont Mézenc** (1753m), with long views west across the whole of the Massif Central.

The Gerbier is a curious wooded mound rising out of the otherwise flattish surrounding uplands, about 50km southeast of Le Puy, with the River Loire rising on its upper slopes – home to a bucolic and still-isolated countryside. To get out there, take the D535 through **MONASTIER-SUR-GAZEILLE**, where R. L. Stevenson bought his donkey and started his famous journey. Although the village is pretty, with a particularly lovely church, there's something forlorn and unfriendly about it. The rather bleak *Hôtel Le Provence* above the village would do for a night's stay (Ⓣ04.71.03.82.37, Ⓔinfo@le-provence.fr; ❷; restaurant €11–21). The riverside municipal **campsite** (Ⓣ04.71.03.82.24; closed Oct–May) and **gîte d'étape** (Ⓣ04.71.03.82.24) are more welcoming. From here, thirty kilometres of winding lanes lead to the summit itself.

St-Étienne

ST-ÉTIENNE, 78km northeast of Le Puy, was until recently a particularly bland town. Almost unrelievedly industrial, it was a major armaments manufacturer, enclosed for kilometres around by mineworkings, warehouses and factory chimneys. Like so many other industrial centres, it fell on hard times, and the demolition gangs have moved in to raze its archaic industrial past. Only in recent years has an equilibrium been restored thanks to a concerted programme to revitalize the town.

The centre is now quite cheerful, bouyed by a collection of small new museums, the best of which is the **Musée d'Art Moderne** at La Terrasse (La Terrasse station is served by frequent trains from St-Étienne's central station, Châteaucreux), in the north of the city (daily except Tues 10am–6pm; €4.50). This justifies a detour for anyone with an interest in twentieth-century art – a quite unexpected treasure house of contemporary work, both pre- and post-World War II, with a good modern American section, in which Andy Warhol and Frank Stella figure prominently, along with work by Rodin, Matisse, Léger and Ernst, and rooms filled entirely with French art, imaginatively laid out to exciting effect. The **Musée d'Art et d'Industrie**, 2 place Louis-Comte, is also good on St-Étienne's industrial background, including the development of the revolutionary Jacquard loom, and an impressive exhibition of arms and armour (daily except Tues 10am–6pm, closed on Mon 12.30–2.30pm; €4.40).

St-Étienne's small airport (Ⓣ04.77.55.71.71, Ⓦwww.saint-etienne.aeroport.fr) is mainly used for internal flights to and from Paris. The **tourist office** on 16 av de la Liberation (April–Sept Mon–Sat 9am–7pm & Sun 9am–noon; Oct–March Mon–Sat 9am–6pm & Sun 10am–noon; Ⓣ08.92.70.05.42, Ⓦwww.tourisme-st-etienne.com) is around ten minutes' walk from Châteaucreux train station along avenue D.-Rochereau. If you decide to stay, try *Hôtel de la Tour*, 1 rue Mercière (Ⓣ04.77.32.28.48, Ⓔhoteldelatour@libertysurf.fr; ❶), *Le Cheval Noir*, 11 rue François-Gillet (Ⓣ04.77.33.41.72, Ⓦwww.hotel-chevalnoir.com; ❸), or *Hôtel Terminus du Forez*, 29-31 av D.-Rochereau (Ⓣ04.77.32.48.47, Ⓔhotel.forez@wanadoo.fr; ❹). For a truly fine meal dine at *La Bouche Pleine* at 2 place Chavanelle (Ⓣ04.77.33.92.47; closed Sat & Sun in Aug; menus from €20).

Travel details

Trains

Alès to: Nîmes (6–9 daily; 35min); Villefort (6–8 daily; 1hr).
Aurillac to: Brive (4 daily; 1hr 40min); Le Lioran (3–5 daily; 40min); Murat (3–5 daily; 50min); Neussargues (3–5 daily; 1hr); Toulouse (3–7 daily; 2hr 40min); Vic-sur-Cère (3–5 daily; 15min).
Clermont-Ferrand to: Aurillac (4–6 daily; 2hr 30min–5hr); Béziers (3 daily; 6–7hr); La Bourboule (4 daily; 1hr 20min); Brive (3 daily; 3hr 40min); Limoges (4 daily; 3hr 30min–4hr); Le Lioran (3–4 daily; 2–4hr); Le Mont-Dore (4 daily; 1hr 30min); Lyon (12–18 daily; 2hr 45min–3hr 30min); Marvejols (4 daily; 2hr 15min–3hr); Millau (1 daily; 4hr 15min); Murat (5–7 daily; 1hr 40min); Neussargues (12–14 daily; 1hr 30min–3hr 30min); Nîmes (12–16 daily; 5–6hr); Paris (5–10 daily; 2–5hr); Riom (12–14 daily; 10min); St-Étienne (2–3 daily; 2hr 10min) St-Flour (4 daily; 1hr 20min–2hr); Thiers (6 daily; 35min); Vic-sur-Cère (5–7 daily; 2hr 15min); Vichy (12–14 daily; 40min); Volvic (5 daily; 24min).
Le Puy to: St-Étienne (8 daily; 1hr 20min).
Mende to: La Bastide-Puylaurent (2–3 daily; 50min); Marvejols (3–5 daily; 40min); Montpellier (16–20 daily; 3hr–4hr 30min); Nîmes (16–20 daily; 2hr 30min–4hr); St-Flour (1–2 daily; 1hr 40min).
Millau to: Aumont-Aubrac (4 daily; 1hr 30min); Béziers (3 daily; 2hr); Marvejols (5 daily; 1hr 10min); Paris (2 daily direct; 8hr–9hr 30min).
Rodez to: Millau (7 daily; 1hr 10min–2hr 30min).
St-Étienne to: Clermont-Ferrand (3–6 daily; 2hr 40min); Lyon (3 daily; 45min); Paris (3 daily; 2hr 50min); St-Germain-des-Fosses (2 daily; 3hr).
St-Flour to: Neussargues (2–3 daily; 25min).
Vichy to: Clermont-Ferrand (12–14 daily; 40min); Nîmes (12–16 daily; 7–9hr); Paris (4 daily; 3hr 30min).

Buses

Ambert to: St-Étienne (1 daily; 2hr).
Aubenas to: Alès (2–3 daily; 2hr 10min); Entraygues (1–4 daily; 1hr); Les Vans (4 daily; 1hr 10min); Valence (7 daily; 2hr); Vallon-Pont-d'Arc (1–2 daily; 45min); Les Vans (4 daily; 1hr 10min).
Aurillac to: Brommat, changing at Mur-de-Barrez (3 weekly; 2hr); Carlat (3–4 daily; 30min); Entraygues (1 daily; 1hr 30min); Mandailles (1 daily; 1hr 20min); Murat (1 daily; 1hr 40min); St-Flour (1 daily; 2hr 10min); Super-Lioran (1 daily; 1hr 20min); Vic-sur-Cère (2–3 daily; 40min).
Clermont-Ferrand to: Ambert (1–2 daily; 1hr 40min); Aydat (1–2 daily; 40min); Besse (July & Aug 2 daily; 1hr 35min); La Chaise-Dieu (1 Mon; 2hr); Lyon (daily; 4hr); Mauriac (1–2 daily; 2hr 45min); Moulins (4 daily; 2hr 30min); Murol (July & Aug 2 daily; 1hr 10min); Le Puy (1 daily; 2hr 15min); Riom (2 daily; 40min); St-Flour (2 weekly; 2hr); St-Nectaire (July & Aug 2 daily; 1hr); Superbesse (July & Aug 2 daily; 1hr 45min); Thiers (several daily; 1hr); Vichy (5 daily; 1hr 45min).
Conques to: Entraygues (June & Sept Tues, July & Aug Tues, Thurs & Sat 1 daily; 35min); Espalion (June & Sept Tues, July & Aug Tues, Thurs & Sat 1 daily; 1hr 20min); Najac (June & Sept Tues, July & Aug Tues & Fri 1 daily; 2hr 30min); St-Geniez-d'Olt (June & Sept Tues, July & Aug Tues, Thurs & Sat 1 daily; 2hr 15min).
La Bourboule to: Le Mont-Dore (3–5 daily; 10min); Le Sancy (3–5 daily; 35min).
Le Puy to: Aubenas (2 weekly; 3hr 15min); La Chaise-Dieu (2 daily; 1hr); Clermont-Ferrand (1 daily; 3hr); St-Étienne (4 daily; 2hr 10min).
Le Vigan to: Ganges (1–6 daily; 25min); Montpellier (3 daily; 2hr); Nîmes (3–5 daily; 1hr 50min); Valleraugue (July & Aug 1 daily; 30min).
Mende to: Le Puy (2 daily; 2hr); Marvejols (3 daily; 50min); St-Chély (1 daily; 1hr 10min); St-Étienne (1 daily; 3hr).
Millau to: Aven Armand (July & Aug daily; 1hr 45min); Le Caylar (2–6 daily; 40min); Le Rozier (1–4 daily; 40min); Montpellier (3–8 daily; 2hr 20min); Rodez (4 daily; 1hr 30min); Roquefort (July & Aug 3 weekly; 30min); St-Affrique (3–6 daily; 45min); Ste-Énimie (July & Aug daily; 2hr 25min); Toulouse (2 daily; 4hr).
Neussargues to: Allanche (2–3 daily; 20min); Condat (2–3 daily; 30min); Riom-ès-Montagnes (2–3 daily; 1hr 15min); St-Flour (2 daily; 30min).
Riom to: Volvic (4–8 daily; 25min).
Rodez to: Albi (3 daily; 2hr); Conques (1 daily; 1hr); Entraygues (1–2 daily; 2hr); Espalion (3–4 daily; 45min); Laguiole (1 daily; 1hr 45min); Le Caylar (1–4 daily; 2hr 40min); Mende (1 daily; 3hr 30min); Millau (3–8 daily; 1hr 40min); Montauban (1 daily; 3hr 15min); Montpellier (1–4 daily; 3hr 55min); Mur-de-Barrez (1 daily; 2hr 45min); Sauveterre-de-Rouergue (5 weekly; 55min); Séverac-le-Château (several daily; 45min); Toulouse (2–4 daily; 3hr 30min); Villefranche-de-Rouergue (1–2 daily; 1hr 30min).
St-Chély-d'Aubrac to: Espalion (1 daily; 30min).
St-Flour to: Laguiole (Tues, Thurs & Sat 1 daily; 3hr).
St-Martin-d'Ardèche to: Avignon (1 daily; 1hr 40min); Pont St-Esprit (2 daily; 15min); Vallon-Pont-d'Arc (2 daily; 1hr 10min).
Vichy to: Ambert (4 daily; 2hr 10min); La Chaise-Dieu (daily; 2hr 45min); Thiers (several daily; 40min).
Villefranche-de-Rouergue to: Conques (July & Aug Tues & Fri 1 daily; 2hr); Najac (July & Aug Tues & Fri 1 daily; 30min).

13

The Alps and Jura

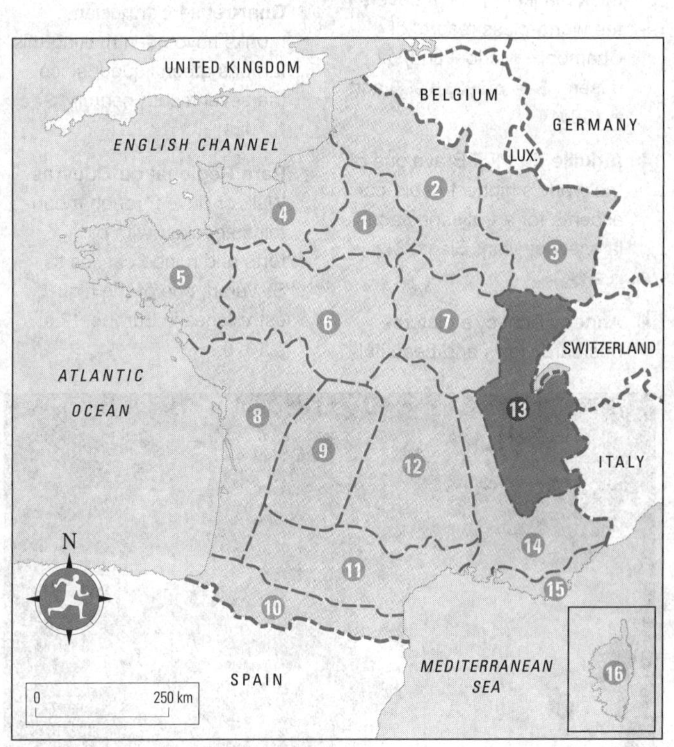

CHAPTER 13

Highlights

* **Lake Geneva** Enjoy the sedate pleasures of the spa towns on the French side of this huge lake, or hop on one of the frequent ferries to Switzerland. See p.975

* **Skiing and snowboarding** From December to April a thick blanket of snow covers the world-class resorts of Chamonix, Méribel and Val d'Isère. See p.983, p.996 and p.1000

* **Aiguille du Midi** Brave one of the world's highest cable-car ascents for a truly spectacular view of Mont Blanc. See p.986

* **Annecy** Annecy's picture-postcard views and beautiful lake more than make up for the crowds and commercialism. See p.988

* **Grenoble** The "Capital of the Alps" is a modern, thriving city, offering lively nightlife and fine museums. See p.1003

* **Chartreuse** Carthusian monks have been making this famous green liqueur since the seventeenth century. See p.1011

* **Parc Régional du Queyras** Walk or drive through mountains specked with old forts and ruined castles to St-Véran, one of the highest villages in Europe. See p.1020

△ Aiguille du Midi

13

The Alps and Jura

"I need torrents, rocks, firs, dark woods, mountains, steep roads to climb or descend, abysses beside me to make me afraid"; so wrote Rousseau in his *Confessions*, and he certainly found what he was looking for in the Alps. Formed by the collision of two continental plates two hundred million years ago, the range contains some of France's most dramatic landscapes, with roads, rail lines and population confined to the deep valley floors. To get the best out of this region you have to walk – or in winter, ski (the box on p.981 has a short roundup of the resorts). There are seven **national** or **regional parks** in the area covered by this chapter – Vanoise, Chartreuse, Bauges, Écrins, Queyras, Vercors and Haut Jura – all with round-the-park trails, requiring one to two weeks' walking. The classic long-distance **Tour of Mont Blanc** path is of similar length. Then there is the transalpine **Route des Grandes Alpes**, which crosses all the major massifs from Thonon-les-Bains on Lake Geneva to Menton.

All these routes are clearly marked, equipped with refuge huts and *gîtes d'étape*, and described in Topo-guides (see Basics, p.61). The Bureau Info Montagne office in Grenoble will provide information on all **GR paths**, and in addition local tourist offices often produce detailed maps of walks in their own areas. The Alps are also an ideal place for **rock climbing**, since many of the best faces are already bolted. You can find plenty of **day walks** from bases in or close to the parks; and there are some spectacular road routes, too. The **Vercors**, **Chartreuse**, **Aravis**, **Faucigny** and **Chablais** areas are the gentlest and quietest introductions to Alpine walking.

As for **accommodation**, you can camp freely on the fringes of the parks, but once inside you're supposed to pitch only in an emergency and move on after one night. Hotels are often seasonal (closed in late spring and late autumn), overbooked and overpriced – if you're on a budget but don't want to carry camping equipment, using *gîtes* and refuges is a better solution. The Alps are almost as **crowded** in midsummer as they are in winter (the Chamonix-Mont Blanc area is the worst black spot), but you're more or less obliged to go in high season if you want to walk: unreliable weather aside, anywhere above 2000m may be snowbound until the beginning of July. Drivers should remember that some high passes such as the Col du Galibier and the Col de l'Iseran in the east of the region can remain closed well into June, requiring long detours or excursions into Italy via expensive Alpine tunnels.

THE ALPS AND JURA
Mulhouse
N19
Vesoul
Ronchamp
Belfort
A36
Rhône-Rhine Canal
Basel
FRANCHE-COMTÉ
Montbéliard
Audincourt
D437
Dijon
N57
St-Hippolyte
A38
Besançon
R. Doubs
A6
N57
JURA MOUNTAINS
Saut de Doubs
Ornans
Villers-le-Lac
Dole
Morteau
A36
N
Neuchâtel
BERN
Arbois
D472
Pontarlier
River Doubs
Levier
Chateau de Joux
Lac de Neuchâtel
Poligny
A1
Champagnole
SWITZERLAND
Lons-le-Saunier
Cascades du Herisson
A6
N78
St-Laurent
N1
A12
Lausanne
Clairvaux-les-Lacs
Morez
Les Rousses
PARC HAUT JURA
A39
Lake Geneva (Lac Leman)
St-Claude
N5
Évian
St-Gingolph
A40
Col de la Faucille
Yvoire
Thonon
N5
D21
Dijon
A40
Bourg
D902
Abondance
N9
River Ain
Annemasse
Morzine
Bourg-en-Bresse
Geneva
Nantua
Cluses
Martigny
Samoëns
N83
A40
La-Roche-sur-Foron
Sixt
Le Buet
Flaine
River Rhône
La Clusaz
N506
A41
Chamonix
N504
Gorges du Fier
Lac du Bourget
Annecy
St Gervais
Megève
Mont Blanc Tunnel
Lac d'Annecy
Menthon-St-Bernard
N212
Mont Blanc 4807 m
A42
Talloires
Courmayeur
D925
Abbaye de Hautecombe
Crêt de Châtillon
Duingt
N508
Lyon
Ugine
Petit St-Bernard
Aosta, Milan & Turin
A432
Doussard
Albertville
Aix-les-Bains
PARC DES BAUGES
Bourg-St-Maurice
Séez
A43
Mt Revard
N90
ITALY
SAVOIE
Aime
N90
Chambéry
A43
R. Isère
N90
D902
La Plagne
PARC DE CHARTREUSE
N75
A41
A43
Moûtiers
Val d'Isère
Méribel
Col de l'Iseran
Grande Chartreuse Monastery
St-Laurent-du-Port
N6
Bonneval-sur-Arc
N6
Voiron
PARC DE LA VANOISE
Bessans
La Tornette
St-Pierre-de-Chartreuse
A48
MASSIF DE LA CHARTREUSE
R. Arc
Lanslebourg
St-Michel
Pic Blanc (3330m)
Modane
Lans-en-Vercors
Grenoble
Valloire
Col du Galibier
Col d'Echelle
Fréjus Tunnel
Villard-de-Lans
Alpe d'Huez
D902
Turin & Milan
D531
N91
La Grave
Névache
PARC VERCORS
A49
Le Bourg-d'Oisans
N91
Col du Lautaret
Vallée de la Clarée
La Chapelle
D530
Le Monêtier-les-Bains
D994
Serre Chevalier
DAUPHINE
Les Deux-Alpes
Mt Peloux (3946m)
Col de Montgenèvre
Ailefroide
D204
Briançon
Vassieux-en-Vercors
D518
Vallouise
Château-Ville-Vieille
Col d'Izoard
N85
D902
Col de Rousset
Clelles
PARC DES ECRINS
Argentières
L'Échalp
Valence
Die
Mont Dauphin
D93
St-Véran
Guillestre
Châtillon
N75
Lac de Serre-Ponçon
N94
PARC DU QUEYRAS
0
25 km
Gap
Embrun
ITALY
Savines-le-Lac
R. Durance
Sisteron, Marseille & Cannes

Food and drink in the Alps and Jura

Alpine cuisine overall is heavy, its obvious intent being to line the stomach in cold weather, while the drink is light and often disappointing. One of the best regional items is the rock-hard cured **sausage**, or *saucisson*, which is exported from here to butchers shops all over the country, and can be found in large quantities in the weekly morning markets held in every town.

In the *départements* of **Savoie** and **Haute Savoie**, many restaurants serve **fish** from local lakes, as well as lots of **cheese**, from the familiar fondue to the lesser-known *raclette* and *tartiflette*, both cheese-based dishes with ham and potatoes. In Savoie the main cheeses are Roblochon (for the *tartiflette*), Emmental, Chèvre (often in a form that's good for melting), Comté and Beaufort – in the *fromagerie* make sure to ask for the Beaufort d'Été, which is more flavourful since it's made when the cows have better access to grass and flowers. In the **Hautes-Alpes** near Briançon, food takes a more Provençal turn – expect desserts to be accompanied by honey, and *saucisson* to be surrounded by or filled with flavourful herbs. For more interesting and creative food head to **Grenoble**, where chefs are more likely to take the local ingredients and turn them into something new.

In the **Jura** the Ognon and Doubs rivers provide a plentiful supply of fish, particularly salmon, and the forests are a good source of game. Other specialities include *brési* (cured beef in thin slices) and *poulet au vin jaune* (chicken and morels in a creamy sauce flavoured with the local wine).

As for **drink**, as early as lunchtime you'll start to see the ever-present *pastis*, the regional rosé, and the local **red wine** that is so magenta that it resembles rosé. These wines are light and fruity, and most are without much complexity. In contrast the white **vin jaune** from the Jura is a potent, golden wine, made from Sauvignon grapes with a fermentation process similar to that of sherry – it remains in the cask for 6–10 years before being bottled. You may not see many people drinking the **génépy**, a local mountain liqueur, but you may be able to taste it as a sauce in your dessert or as a *parfum* in a local ice cream.

The **towns** in the Alps offer good facilities for campers and hikers, and often provide attractions of their own. **Grenoble** is the economic and intellectual capital of the region, and has a lively cultural scene; **Chambéry** and picturesque **Annecy** are good bases for expeditions into the Parc des Bauges and Massif de Chartreuse, and the countryside around the **Lac d'Annecy** respectively; and **Briançon**, the highest town in Europe, is close to the Écrins and Queyras parks. The websites Ⓦwww.rhonealpes-tourisme.com and Ⓦwww.alpes-guide.com are useful introductions to the region.

The **Jura mountains** – gentle in the west, precipitous in the east, with wide, high-forested plateaux in between – cover most of the old county of **Franche-Comté**, once part of the realms of the Grand Dukes of Burgundy, but properly French only since the late seventeenth century. Within its four *départements* – the Territoire de Belfort, the Haute-Saône, the Doubs and, largest of all, the Jura – the towns, especially the capital **Besançon**, are beautiful and tranquil, with the River Doubs flowing through, and some of the villages are exceptionally pretty. Otherwise, what there is to see is countryside – hundreds of square kilometres of woodland, lake and pasture that are hard to reach without a car – but are best explored once you're there on foot or by bicycle. There are several GR **footpaths** in the area, including the marathon GR5 from the Netherlands to the Mediterranean, and the GR9, which snakes its way through the Parc Régional du Haut-Jura.

Belfort and around

Nestled in the gap between the southern reaches of the Vosges and the northern outliers of the Jura mountains – the one natural chink in France's eastern geological armour and the obvious route for invaders – **BELFORT** is assured of a place in French hearts for its deeds of military daring. Its name is particularly linked with the 1870 Prussian War, when its long resistance to siege spared it the humiliating annexation to Germany suffered by much of neighbouring Alsace-Lorraine. The commanding officer at the time, Colonel Denfert-Rochereau (the "Lion of Belfort"), earned himself the honour of numerous street names as well as that of a Parisian square and métro station. These days it's an interesting town with mixed Franco-German influences in architecture and cuisine. Belfort is also a good base for exploring the towns of **Ronchamp, Montbéliard**, the northeastern corner of the **River Doubs** and for organizing treks into the southern Vosges (see "Hiking in the southern Vosges" box, p.319).

The Town

Finding your way around Belfort is easy enough. The town is sliced in two by the River Savoureuse: the **new town** to the west is the commercial hub; to the east lies the quieter **old town**, laid out below the massive red **château**. Built by the ubiquitous fortress architect Vauban on the site of a medieval fort, it now houses the **Musée d'Art et d'Histoire** (May–Sept daily 10am–7pm; Oct–April daily except Tues 10am–noon and 2–5pm; ⓣ03.84.54.25.51/52; €2.90, or €3.20 including entry to the viewing platform at the lion – see opposite), containing works by Dürer, Doré and Rodin. The other collections include military objects from Belfort's centuries of conflicts, and Bronze and Iron Age artefacts, including painted pottery, jewellery and tools, found in the funeral cave 5km north at Cravanche in 1876. Vauban is also responsible for the fortifications surrounding Belfort, which created a five-sided old town whose street plan is still largely unchanged.

Belfort's other museum, the **Donation Maurice Jardot** (daily except Tues 10am–6pm; €4), is a ten-minute walk away from the tourist office down rue de Mulhouse, at no. 8, and will be of interest to fans of Cubism. Jardot was an associate of Daniel-Henry Kahnweiler, one of the great twentieth-century art dealers: his collection, left to the town of Belfort on his death in 1997, contains 110 works of art, including some by Braque, Léger and Picasso.

The most famous and photographed phenomenon in town is the eleven-metre-high red sandstone **lion** carved out of the rock-face that you pass on the way up to the castle, Bartholdi's monument to commemorate the 1870 siege. From the **viewing platform** at the front paw of the lion (€1, or €3.20, combined ticket to the Musée d'Art et d'Histoire), you get some stunning views over the town and surrounding countryside.

Practicalities

The **gare SNCF** and departure point for local **buses** are at the end of Faubourg-de-France, the main pedestrianized shopping drag in the new town. The **tourist office** (mid-June to mid-Sept Mon–Sat 9am–7pm; mid-Sept to mid-June Mon–Sat 9am–12.30pm & 1.45–6pm; ⓣ03.84.55.90.90, ⓦwww.ot-belfort.fr) is at 2bis rue Clemenceau, a ten-minute walk from the station down Faubourg-de-France as far as the river, then left along quai Charles-Vallet until you reach rue Clemenceau; the castle houses a tourist information annexe during the summer (July & Aug daily 10am–12.30pm and 2–6.30pm).

There is an excellent choice of **hotels**: the *Au Relais d'Alsace*, 5 av de la Laurencie (Ⓣ03.84.22.15.55, Ⓦwww.arahotel.com; ❸), is where out-of-town musicians stay when they perform in Belfort, and the staff will be happy to advise you about what's happening in the region. Other options include the *Hôtel Vauban*, 4 rue du Magasin (Ⓣ03.84.21.59.37, Ⓦwww.hotel-vauban.com; ❺), where the artist-owner's paintings brighten the individually decorated rooms, and the rather more impressive *Grand Hôtel du Tonneau d'Or*, 1 rue Reiset (Ⓣ03.84.58.57.56, Ⓦwww.tonneaudor.fr; ❼), though the columns and architraves that adorn the lobby are more impressive than the functional but clean rooms. Belfort's **hostel**, *Résidence Madrid*, is 1km west of the railway line at 6 rue de Madrid (Ⓣ03.84.21.39.16, Ⓔfjt.belfort@wanadoo.fr), and its **campsite**, *Camping International de l'Étang des Forges*, is on rue du Général-Béthouart, north of the old town (Ⓣ03.84.22.54.92, Ⓦwww.campings-belfort.com; May to mid-Oct).

Inexpensive **places to eat** can be found in the place d'Armes and place de la République, while rue de la Porte de France, linking the two squares, is lined with antique shops and old-fashioned grocery stores such as l'Épicerie de Lion. *Boeuf-Carottes*, 14 rue Lecourbe (Ⓣ03.84.21.15.40; closed Sun eve & Mon), is a good option, with menus at €17–22. *Café Théâtre*, behind the theatre on place Corbis, has outdoor tables by the river and is a pleasant place for a coffee, while *La Poudrière*, place de l'Arsenal (closed late July & Aug), is the best place for **live music**.

Ronchamp

Before taking to the hills, there is one day-trip from Belfort worth undertaking – to the mining town of **RONCHAMP**, 20km west (connected by train and bus), where the architect Le Corbusier built one of his most enduring and atypical masterpieces in the 1950s, the **Chapelle de Notre-Dame-du-Haut** (daily 9.30am–6.30pm; €2; Ⓦwww.chapellederonchamp.com). Visible from miles away and white, reflective and all in concrete, it stands above the town

Cross-country skiing and mountain biking in the Jura

The nature of the Jura's terrain – its high plateaux guaranteeing winter snow but without excessively steep gradients – has made it France's most popular destination for **cross-country skiing**, or *ski de fond*. The goal of any superfit *fondeur* is the 210-kilometre Grande Traversée du Jura (GTJ), which roughly follows the long-distance GR5 footpath across the high plateau from Villers-le-Lac to Hauteville-Lompnes.

The same gentle topography and established infrastructure that enable cross-country skiing have made this region an ideal high-summer venue for **mountain biking**, with hundreds of waymarked cross-country skiing pistes used out of season as trails for adventuresome mountain bikers. The 300-kilometre **GTJ–VTT**, starting near Montbéliard, has become the greatest long-distance challenge in the area. Many people cycle on the road; there aren't that many cars, so if you can handle the hills, go for it.

The headquarters of the departmental tourist board, the **Comité Départemental du Tourisme de Jura** (Ⓣ03.84.87.08.88, Ⓦwww.jura-tourism.com), can supply plenty of information, maps and literature – in English – on outdoor leisure opportunities of all kinds in the Jura.

on the top of a wooded hill, with its aerodynamic tower and wave-curved roof cutting into the sky beyond. Inside, the rough-textured walls are pierced with unequal embrasures, several closed by patterns of primary glass, whose reds, blues and yellows stain the dipping floor. With its pared-down crucifix and steel altar rail, it's highly atmospheric.

The **tourist office** is on place 14-Juillet (daily 9am–noon and 2–7pm; ⓣ03.84.63.50.82). If it's getting late and you're worried about a place to **stay**, try *La Pomme d'Or*, 34 rue le Corbusier, alongside the train line (ⓣ03.84.20.62.12; ❸). Hostellers can take another twenty-minute train ride west to **Vesoul**, where there's a **HI hostel** by the Lac de Vesoul-Vaivre (ⓣ03.84.76.48.55; bus #1, stop "Peugeot"), but check the train timetables: there are not many trains to or from either Belfort or Vesoul.

Montbéliard and around

MONTBÉLIARD, 16km south of Belfort, thrives mainly thanks to the Peugeot factory in its southern suburb of Audincourt (see below), the second car production plant to be created in Europe. There are some unexpected features to Montbéliard, however: the town has been part of France only since 1793, so the architecture of the old town has a strong Germanic look. The imposing **Château des Ducs de Wurtemburg** (daily except Tues 10am–noon & 2–6pm; €1.50), constructed during the fifteenth and sixteenth centuries, has been restored to house various exhibitions: there's always a specialist international exhibition as well as the permanent display of the collection of famous French zoologist Georges Cuvier, who was born in Montbéliard and whose work paved the way for Darwin. Also on display are some Gallo-Roman objects found nearby at the remains of the huge **Roman theatre** at Mandeure, just off the D437 8km south of Montbéliard. The old houses around the château have been repainted in their original colours. Note the circular stairwells, always at the back of the house – this architectural curiosity developed in the days when space was taxed as part of an elaborate tax-avoidance scheme. The **Bourg des Halles** covered market was built in the sixteenth century, and is another fine Germanic building. An outdoor Christmas **market**, Lumières de Noël, is held annually around the St-Martin church, and there's also a three-kilometre labyrinth at the **Parc du Près-la-Rose**.

The **tourist office** is at 1 rue Henri-Mouhot (Mon 1.30–6pm, Tues–Sat 9am–noon & 1.30–7pm; mid-Sept to mid-June also Sun 10am–noon and 2–4pm; ⓣ03.81.94.45.60, ⓦwww.ot-pays-de-montbeliard.fr). For **accommodation**, the choice is better in Belfort, but you could try the *Hôtel de la Balance*, 40 rue de Belfort (ⓣ03.81.96.77.41, ⓦwww.hotel-la-balance.com; ❼), in the old town, which also has a restaurant with menus at €12–22. There are plenty of outdoor **cafés** in the old town area: *Café de la Paix*, 12 rue des Febvres, near Les Halles, is a great place to relax. Both Belfort and Montbéliard have some good music and art **festivals** – to find out details, pick up the free cultural magazine *Atmosphere*, or *Montbéliard Magazine*, available in tourist offices.

The Doubs valley

The River Doubs runs a course like a series of hairpins, doubling back on itself repeatedly, with its most dramatic change of course at **AUDINCOURT**, where the chief sight is the modern **church of Sacré-Coeur**, which has windows and a tapestry by Fernand Léger. Just north of Audincourt, **Sochaux**, another

Montbéliard suburb, is home to the **Musée Peugeot** (daily 10am–6pm; €7), which displays the products of over a century of automotive manufacturing, from the Bey of Tunis's one-off quadricycle to contemporary rally winners and concept cars.

From Audincourt, southwards and upstream, the D437 follows the valley of the Doubs, winding and climbing steadily between steep, wooded banks to the bridging point at **ST-HIPPOLYTE**, where you'll find the riverside *Hôtel Bellevue* (Ⓣ03.81.96.51.53, Ⓕ03.81.96.52.40; ❺) and a **campsite** (May–Sept). Seven kilometres west along the D39, the *Auberge de Moricemaison*, in Valoreille (Ⓣ03.81.64.01.72, Ⓦwww.moricemaison.fr; ❷), offers rustic simplicity and wholesome evening meals from €15.

A less congested scenic route from Besançon follows the D464 south of the river, but without a car you'd have to hitch all this – manageable but slow. Beyond St-Hippolyte the road climbs onto a wide plateau at an altitude of around 850m, with grassy cattle pastures encompassed by fir-clad ridges and dotted with broad-roofed farms and barns. Once up here, cycling is easy enough. Alternatively, it's a lovely but long hike of well over 50km along the **GR5 footpath** from St-Hippolyte across the plateau and up the Doubs valley to the plunging waterfall of the **Saut du Doubs** outside Villers-le-Lac – the beginning of the **GTJ** marathon cross-country ski piste. To reach the fall, it's a four-kilometre walk from the last houses above the north end of the lake in **VILLERS** along a track through the woods.

By road, Villers is 47km south of St-Hippolyte along the D437, which turns east at **MORTEAU**, a village with nothing more than a much-altered, thirteenth-century priory church to recommend it. The D437 is part of the Route du Comté, so if you like cheese, it's worth the detour. There is **accommodation** up on the plateau at the welcoming *Hôtel des Montagnards* (Ⓣ03.81.67.08.86, Ⓦwww.hotel-les-montagnards.newfr.net; ❸; closed Sun out of season).

Besançon and around

The capital of Franche-Comté, **BESANÇON** is an ancient and attractive grey-stone town at the northern edge of the Jura mountains, enclosed in a loop of the River Doubs, whose lugubrious meanders define the layout of the old town. The tongue of land on which it sits has been protected since Roman times, when it lay on a major trading route; the indefatigable Vauban added the still-extant fortifications and a citadelle to guard the natural breach in the river. Once a major centre of French clock-making, Besançon was also the birthplace of artificial silk – or rayon – in 1890. It counts among its native sons both the pioneering Lumière brothers and epic novelist Victor Hugo.

The **River Doubs** rises on the high plateau 100km to the south of here, making a diversion far to the northeast of the town, gathering tributaries and broadening as it briefly crosses the Swiss border before entering Besançon. A lazy journey upstream to **Pontarlier** can make a rewarding excursion over a couple of days. From Pontarlier a direct return north to Besançon can be made by following the **River Loue**'s steep descent through its heavily wooded valley past the pretty mill town of **Ornans**. To the west, the former regional capital of **Dole** was the birthplace of the chemist Louis Pasteur.

Arrival, information and accommodation

The **gare SNCF** is at the end of avenue Maréchal-Foch, while the **gare routière** is at 9 rue Proudhon off rue de la République; buses for Pontarlier and Ornans leave from here. The best way to reach the town centre from the *gare SNCF* is to take the underground passage (next to the monument in front of the station) and cut across the park down to the *quais* – the old town is on the other side of the river. The **tourist office** is upstream on the right bank by the Pont de la République on place de la Première Armée-Française (Mon–Sat 10am–7pm, Sun 10am–5pm; ⓣ03.81.80.92.55, ⓦwww.besancon.com). On the other side of the Pont de la République from the tourist office is the departure point for the **bateaux-mouches** (daily April–Oct; €10), which tour round the outer limits of the town centre.

Hotels include the comfortable and friendly family-run *Granvelle*, 13 rue Lecourbe, close to the citadelle (ⓣ03.81.81.33.92, ⓦwww.hotel-granvelle.fr; ❹); the central *Regina*, with rooms around a quiet court on 91 Grande-Rue (ⓣ03.81.81.50.22, ⓦwww.besancon-regina.fr; ❹); the *Hôtel de Paris*, 33 rue des Granges (ⓣ03.81.81.36.56, ⓦwww.hotel-deparis.com; ❺), in an old town house with free parking for guests; and the *Hôtel du Nord*, at 8–10 rue de Moncey in the centre (ⓣ03.81.81.34.56, ⓦwww.hotel-du-nord-besancon.com; ❹), with large rooms. For something more upmarket, the *Castan*, 6 square Castan (ⓣ03.81.65.02.00, ⓦwww.hotelcastan.fr; ❾) is housed in a beautiful seventeenth-century town house and offers supreme comfort. Besançon's **hostel**, *Les Oiseaux*, is a couple of kilometres northeast of the train station at 48 rue des Cras (ⓣ03.81.40.32.00, ⓔfjtlesoiseaux@yahoo.fr; bus #7, stop "Les Oiseaux"; ❷, or €15.70 for a bed in a small dorm). **Camping** is at *Camping de Chalezeule*, 5km out on the Belfort road (ⓣ03.81.88.04.26; April–Oct; bus #1 towards Palente).

The Town

Once you're in the old town, getting around is simple. Rue de la République leads from the river to the central **place du 8-Septembre** and the sixteenth-century **Hôtel de Ville**. The principal street, **Grande-Rue**, cuts across the square along the line of an old Roman road. At its northwestern end – the livelier part of town with shops and cafés – is the place de la Révolution and the excellent **Musée des Beaux-Arts** (daily except Tues 9.30am–noon & 2–6pm; €3.20, free Sun), with some good nineteenth- and twentieth-century works, two magnificent Bonnards and a wonderful clock collection. Midway down Grande-Rue, the fine sixteenth-century **Palais Granvelle** (Wed–Sun 1–7pm; €3, free Sat) contains an interactive museum paying homage to the town's history of clock-making, the Musée du Temps. Continuing up the street, you pass place Victor-Hugo (he was born at no. 140) and arrive at the **Porte Noire**, a second-century Roman triumphal arch spanning the street and partially embedded in the adjoining houses. Beside it, in the shady little square Archéologique A.-Castan, are the remains of a **nymphaeum**, a small reservoir of water fed by an aqueduct. Beyond the arch is the pompous eighteenth-century **Cathédrale St-Jean** (closed Tues) which houses the nineteenth-century **Horloge Astronomique** (hourly guided visits in French: Feb, March & Oct–Dec Mon & Thurs–Sun 9.50–11.50am & 2.50–5.50pm; April–Sept daily except Tues same hours; closed Jan; €2.50), detailing over a hundred terrestrial and celestial positions and containing some 30,000 parts.

The spectacular **citadelle** (daily: April–June & Sept to mid-Nov 9am–6pm; July & Aug 9am–7pm; mid-Nov to April 10am–5pm; €7.80) is a steep fifteen-minute climb from the cathedral, and has a crow's-nest view of the town and the noose-like bend in the river that contains it. It houses many worthwhile museums (all times as citadelle): there's the **Musée d'Histoire Naturelle** for animal lovers, with aquarium, insectarium and zoo; the **Musée Comtois**, with pottery, furniture and a good collection of nineteenth-century marionettes, as well as some marvellous old farming implements; the **Espace Vauban**, devoted to the military architect; and – best of all – the **Musée de la Résistance et de la Déportation**, a superb aid to understanding postwar France's political consciousness (English audio commentary available).

Eating, drinking and entertainment

There are plenty of lively and inexpensive **restaurants**, **cafés** and **bars** by the Doubs near place Battant, particularly along the little streets running parallel to the river. The busy *Brasserie du Commerce*, 31 rue des Granges, has rather grand decor, an impressive wine list and a traditional quality brasserie menu served by attentive waiters, while the *Brasserie du Palais Granvelle*, in a lovely shady park next door to the Palais Granvelle, is the best place for breakfast and coffee. For a substantial meal try: the century-old *Restaurant au Petit Polonais*, 81 rue des Granges (ⓣ03.81.81.23.67; closed Sat eve & Sun; menus from €12), which serves regional food; or *Le Poker d'As*, 14 square St-Amour (ⓣ03.81.81.42.49; closed Sun eve & Mon; menus from €21), a touch old-fashioned but one hundred percent reliable. For lunch, there's the superb *Le Café-Café*, 5bis rue Luc-Breton (ⓣ03.81.81.15.24; Mon–Sat lunch only; *plats* from €10); or the trendy *La Femme du Boulanger*, 6 rue Morand (ⓣ03.81.82.86.93; Mon–Sat 7.30am–8pm, Sun 9am–7pm), where fresh salads cost around €11.

The two biggest **cultural events** of the year in Besançon are Jazz en Franche-Comté, which takes place in June and July, and an international young conductors' competition in the first two weeks of September.

Pontarlier and around

Sixty kilometres southeast of Besançon lies **PONTARLIER**, one of the bigger Jura towns, and not very interesting in itself except as a transit point and recreational base. Just south of town, though, past a divinely aromatic chocolate factory, a steep road to the left ascends for 11km to **Le Grand Taureau**, whose 1328-metre summit is just a short walk from the road's end and offers a view over the whole Jura Massif and across Switzerland to the Alps. A couple of kilometres further south of Pontarlier, the **Château de Joux** (French guided tours daily: Jan–June & Sept–Oct 10am, 11.30am, 2pm & 3.30pm; July & Aug every 30min 9am–4.30pm; closed Nov & Dec; €5.80; ⓦwww.chateaudejoux.com) stands over the defile known as La Cluse et Mijoux, the ancient Franco-Swiss frontier. It was originally constructed in the eleventh century, and Vauban had a hand in remodelling and modernizing it, but most of what you see today is less than a century old. The fort's history and impressive appearance are of more interest than its collection of military uniforms.

Pontarlier's **tourist office**, 14bis rue de la Gare (Mon–Sat 9am–noon & 2–6pm; June–Sept also Sun 10.30am–noon & 5.30–7pm; ⓣ03.81.46.48.33, ⓦwww.pontarlier.org), has some good hiking and VTT maps. If you need **accommodation** in town, try the *Hôtel de Morteau*, 26 rue Jeanne-d'Arc, near the river (ⓣ03.81.39.14.83, ⓦwww.hoteldemorteau.com; ❸), which has an excellent restaurant. There's also an HI hostel at 2 rue Jouffroy, near the station (ⓣ03.81.39.06.57, ⓔpontarlier@fuaj.org); plus a municipal **campsite** in rue de Toulombief. For places to **eat**, try the rue de Besançon, which is full of cafés and brasseries, or, for a fuller meal, the *Brasserie de la Poste*, 55 rue de la République. Good-quality **mountain bikes** can be rented from Cycles Pernet, 15–23 rue de la République (Ⓣ03.81.46.48.00).

Ornans and the valley of the Loue

Some 17km north of Pontarlier, the D67 splits west off the N57 and plunges precipitously into the **valley of the Loue**. A couple of kilometres above the village of Ouhans lies the source of the river, issuing from an enormous rock beneath a tiered cliff, in winter entirely fringed with icicles. From this point you can continue on foot along the **GR595 footpath** down the valley bounded by densely wooded limestone cliffs, a descent no less dramatic by road, passing through a string of pretty villages.

Roughly halfway between Pontarlier and Besançon, **ORNANS** is the prettiest village of all, an archetypal Franche-Comté town that has become the touristic focal point of the valley. The Loue here is an abrupt trench, the river washing the foundations of ancient balconied houses, and the town is easily appreciated from its numerous footbridges. Pierre Vernier, inventor of the eponymous gauge, and the painter Gustave Courbet were both born here: the latter's house is now the **Musée de la Maison Natale de Gustave Courbet** (April–June, Sept & Oct daily 10am–noon & 2–6pm; July & Aug daily 10am–6pm; Nov–March daily except Tues 10am–noon & 2–6pm; €3, €6 during summer exhibitions; Ⓦwww.musee-courbet.com), displaying some of his drawings, sculpture and locally painted scenes. The **tourist office** is at 7 rue Pierre-Vernier (April–June, Sept, Oct & school hols Mon–Sat 9.30am–noon and 2–6pm; July & Aug Mon–Sat 9am–7pm, Sun 10am–noon & 3–6pm; Nov–March Mon–Fri 10am–noon & 3–5pm; Ⓣ03.81.62.21.50). There's **accommodation** in the form of the simple riverside *Hôtel Restaurant La Table de Gustave*, 11 rue Jacques-Gervais (Ⓣ03.81.62.16.79, Ⓕ03.81.62.19.10; ❸). There are **campsites** and *gîtes d'étape* dotted around the countryside between Ornans and the village of Vuillifans, 8km southeast.

Dole

Halfway between Besançon and Dijon, on the edge of the flat and fertile valley of the Saône, **DOLE** is a quiet and provincial town. The medieval capital of the Comté region until Louis XI ordered its destruction in 1479, it's a peaceful place to pause, and attractive enough in a subdued way. Grey-stone houses with barred ground-floor windows stand on narrow streets around the vast, stolid **collegiate of Notre-Dame**, with its lofty belfry (July & Aug guided visits roughly three times a week; check with the tourist office for the days and times; €4) – worth climbing for the view. Inside the church, there are beautiful windows and a wonderful Rococo organ. The Rhône–Rhine **canal** washes the feet of the town, and along its bank below the church runs the narrow rue Pasteur, birthplace of the French biologist and chemist **Louis Pasteur**. The son of a tanner, he is best known for discovering the rabies virus (and its cure), and is commemorated in the process of "pasteurization", another of his discoveries. His house, like those of his father's tanner workmates, backs onto a pretty waterside walkway leading to an island. The house is now a **museum** (April–June, Sept & Oct Mon–Sat 10am–noon and 2–6pm, Sun 2–6pm; July & Aug Mon–Sat 10am–6pm, Sun 2–6pm; Nov–March Sat 10am–noon and 2–5pm, Sun 2–5pm; €3). Whatever happens in Dole happens between the Grande-Rue – the street leading to the main bridge over the Doubs – and place Grévy. At the top of Grande-Rue is the delightful place aux Fleurs, with a fountain and amusing bronze **sculpture** of *Les Trois Commères* ("The Three Gossips").

Dole's **gare routière** is next to the **gare SNCF**, a ten-minute walk northeast of the Collegiate Notre-Dame down avenue A.-Briand. The **tourist office** is on the northern side of place Grévy at no. 6 (June Mon–Fri 9am–6pm, Sat 9am–noon & 2–6pm; July & Aug Mon–Fri 8.30am–6.30pm, Sat 9am–noon & 2–6pm; Sept–May Mon 2–6pm, Tues–Fri 9am–noon & 2–6pm, Sat 9am–noon; Ⓣ03.84.72.11.22, Ⓦwww.dole.org). There are some reasonable **hotels** in Dole, including *Le Grand Cerf*, 6 rue Arney, near place Grévy (Ⓣ03.84.72.11.68; ❷). For more comfort and prices to match, try *La Chaumière*, across the river on avenue Maréchal-Juin (Ⓣ03.84.70.72.40, Ⓕ03.84.79.25.60; ❺). The cheapest rooms, as usual, are at the **HI hostel**, *St-Jean*, place Jean-XXIII (Ⓣ03.84.82.36.74, Ⓔlestjean@wanadoo.fr); take bus #1, direction "Mesnils-Poiset", stop "Les Paters". The local **campsite**, *Camping du Pasquier*, is down by the river (Ⓣ03.84.72.02.61; mid-March to mid-Oct). For **food**, there are various pizzerias and crêperies – such as *La Demi-Line*, 39 rue Pasteur, and place Grévy is good for cafés. Real gourmands though should try *Le Bec Fin*, 67 rue Pasteur (Ⓣ03.84.82.43.43), for the contemporary haute cuisine of laid-back chef Romuald Fassenet (menus €21–65).

Lons-le-Saunier to Arbois

Around fifty kilometres southeast of Dole, at the base of the central plateau's west-facing rim and set picturesquely astride rivers and in the midst of fertile soils, are a number of towns that have supported centuries of agriculture and have more recently accommodated the small, specialist industries so typical of the Jura. The spa town and departmental capital of **Lons-le-Saunier** is a tranquil place, with fireworks on July 14, and on July 31 for St-Désiré, and outdoor music concerts throughout the summer. North of the town a string of vineyards traces the plateau's edge to just beyond **Arbois**, the Jura's wine-making capital. This is the eighty-kilometre **Route des Vins du Jura**, where the region's distinctive wines – such as the sherry-like *vin jaune* – are cultivated and manufactured from a variety of vines. South of Arbois at **Poligny**, more wines and the long-refined Comté cheese, produced in the Jura since the thirteenth century, are available for sampling at the Maison du Comté.

Lons-le-Saunier

Once the site of a Neolithic settlement, **LONS-LE-SAUNIER** was all but destroyed by a fire in the early seventeenth century. Most buildings today date from this era, and a wander around some of the older examples is an agreeable way to fill half a day.

The central **place de la Liberté** is a good place to start. Should you happen to be in the square on the hour, the **theatre clock** at the eastern end will chime a familiar half-dozen notes from *La Marseillaise* to honour Lons' most famous son, Rouget de Lisle, the anthem's composer. Just north of the square is the attractive, colonnaded thoroughfare of **rue du Commerce**, where some of Lons' oldest buildings line the street in which de Lisle was born. Continuing north through the place de la Comédie and past the ancient **salt well**, Le Puits Salé, you arrive at the **Musée Municipal d'Archéologie**, 25 rue Richebourg (Mon & Wed–Fri 10am–noon & 2–6pm, Sat & Sun 2–5pm; €2). It presents some absorbing prehistoric displays, including a touching Neolithic family scene circa

△ Lons-le-Saunier

4000 BC, a dug-out canoe found locally and a life-size replica of a 210-million-year-old plateosaurus, France's oldest-known dinosaur. The museum, which also mounts various temporary exhibitions, is housed in the old Bel cheese factory, whose enduringly popular *La Vache Qui Rit* ("Laughing cow") cheese spread is now produced in larger premises near the station. Returning south along rue Richebourg to avenue Jean-Moulin, you come to the inevitable **statue** of Rouget de Lisle, designed by Frédéric Bartholdi, the sculptor who went on to refine de Lisle's stirring pose on a much grander scale in the Statue of Liberty. A left turn here leads to the pleasant **Parc Edouard Guenon**, where you'll find the **Salines**, or mineral baths (☎03.84.24.20.34 for admission details), with their ornate *fin-de-siècle* exterior, which are lavishly equipped with a sauna, Turkish bath and Jacuzzi. The saline immersions not only soothe the usual aches and pains, but are also renowned for their ability to cure juvenile bed-wetting.

Practicalities

Lons' **gare SNCF** is a ten-minute walk south of place de la Liberté. The **tourist office** is in the same building as the theatre (Mon–Fri 8am–noon & 2–6pm, Sat 8am–noon & 2–5pm; ⓣ03.84.24.65.01, ⓦwww.ville-lons-le-saunier.fr). For information about the Jura region, the **Comité Départemental du Tourisme** is at 8 rue Louis-Rousseau (Mon–Fri: April–Nov 8.30am–12.30pm and 2–6pm; Dec–March 8.30am–6pm; ⓣ03.84.87.08.88). Two good **hotels** are the smart *Terminus*, 37 av Aristide-Briand, by the *gare SNCF* (ⓣ03.84.24.41.83, ⓦwww.hotel-terminus-lons.com; ❹), and the cosy *Nouvel Hôtel*, 50 rue Lecourbe (ⓣ03.84.47.20.67, ⓦwww.nouvel-hotel-lons.fr; ❹), just west of place de la Liberté. There's a **campsite**, *Camping de la Marjorie* (ⓣ03.84.24.26.94; April to mid-Oct), on the northeast edge of town. For a truly inspired **meal** in a charming setting, pay a visit to the *Bistrot des Marronniers*, 22 rue de Vallière, west off rue St-Désiré (closed Sun; à la carte from €11), and for a coffee or drink, head for the *Grand Café de Strasbourg*, next to the theatre and boasting a beautiful interior.

Poligny and Arbois

North of Lons along the Route des Vins du Jura, the attractive medieval town of **POLIGNY**, at the southern end of the Culée de Vaux valley, is noteworthy for its well-preserved, early Romanesque buildings, including the **church of St-Hippolyte**, which features the characteristic bell-like tower seen all over Franche-Comté. But the town's principal attraction is the hallowed **Maison du Comté** (July & Aug daily 1hr guided tours at 10am, 11am, 2pm, 3.30pm & 4.30pm; ⓣ03.84.37.23.51; €2) on avenue de la Résistance, which leads south from the central place des Deportés, an old *fromagerie* that now forms the headquarters of the Comité Interprofessional du Gruyère du Comté, France's favourite cheese.

The town's attractive medieval houses and other sites of interest are indicated on the blue *Walking Through the Old Town* leaflet available from the friendly **tourist office** at 20 place des Déportés (July & Aug Mon–Fri 9am–12.30pm & 1.30–6.30pm, Sat 9am–12.30pm & 2–6pm, Sun 9am–12.30pm; Sept–June Mon–Fri 9am–12.30pm & 2–6pm, Sat 9am–noon and 2–5pm; ⓣ03.84.37.24.21, ⓦwww.ville-poligny.fr). There are a handful of hotels in Poligny but Arbois has a better choice.

Arbois

There's no mistaking that **ARBOIS**, 10km to the north, is the capital of this region's viticulture. Glittering wine emporia line the central place de la Liberté, entreating you to sample the unusual local wines. Of these, the sweet *vin de paille* is the rarest; it's so called because its grapes are dried on beds of straw, giving the wine a strong aftertaste. Chocolatier M. Hirsinger has developed chocolates to eat with wines, especially the Jura's own *vin jaune*, a wine flavoured with walnuts. A visit to the Hirsinger chocolate shop on place de la Liberté is a must, especially for its delicious ice cream.

Louis Pasteur lived in Arbois after his family moved from Dole, and his boyhood home, the **Maison de Louis Pasteur** on avenue Pasteur, is open to the public (guided visits daily: April, May & Oct hourly 2.15–5.15pm; June–Sept hourly 9.45–11.45am & every 30min 2.15–6.15pm; €5.50). In the basement of the tourist office (see p.972) is the **Musée de la Vigne et du Vin** (March–June, Sept & Oct daily except Tues 10am–noon & 2–6pm; July & Aug daily 10am–12.30pm & 2–6pm; Nov–Feb daily except Tues 2–6pm; €3.20), which details the development and production of wine in the Jura.

The **tourist office** is at 10 rue de l'Hôtel-de-Ville (July & Aug Mon–Sat 9am–12.30pm & 2–6.30pm, Sun 10am–noon & 2–5pm; Sept–June Mon 3–6pm, Tues–Sat 9am–noon & 2–6pm; ⓣ03.84.66.55.50 ⓦwww.arbois.com); If you're **staying** overnight in town, try *Les Messageries* (ⓣ03.84.66.15.45, ⓦwww.hoteldesmessageries.com; ❷) a large, old stone town house with character and atmosphere, up from the Maison Pasteur. There's a **campsite**, *Camping Municipal Les Vignes*, on avenue Général-Leclerc (ⓣ03.84.66.14.12, ⓕ03.84.66.25.50; April–Sept), 1km east of the centre. For a **meal**, head to *La Balance*, 47 rue de Courcelles (ⓣ03.84.37.45.00), where a range of interesting menus (€23–55) has been concocted to complement the local wines.

The Central Plateau and the Haut Jura

On the broad upland plateau, the Jura landscape unrolls, stretches and rises in increasingly abrupt steps to the mountains bordering the Swiss frontier. With its lakes and pine forests, small farming communities and – at the higher altitudes – huge ski resorts enveloping tiny villages, semi-deserted in summer, this is the most beautiful area of the Jura and, as you might expect – despite trains linking **Champagnole**, **Morez** and **St-Claude** with Arbois and Pontarlier – best appreciated with your own transport.

Champagnole, Nozeroy and the Forêt de la Joux

Situated at a major crossroads on the plateau, **CHAMPAGNOLE**, an industrial town largely rebuilt after a major fire in 1798, holds little intrinsic interest for the passing visitor, with the exception of an **archeological museum**, 26 rue Baronne-Delfort (July & Aug daily except Tues 2–6pm; €2), above the tourist office, which displays an interesting array of Gallic and Roman artefacts found in the vicinity. However, the town does serve as a useful base for exploring the surrounding countryside, in particular the Forêt de la Joux, to the northeast.

The **tourist office** is in an annexe of the *mairie* at 26 rue Baronne-Delfort (Mon–Fri 9am–noon & 2–6pm, Sat 9am–noon & 2–5pm; ⓣ03.84.52.43.67), and provides lots of information about exploring the surrounding forests and lakes, including hiking and mountain biking kits for €5 each. For central **accommodation**, try the *Hôtel de la Londaine*, 31 rue du Général-Leclerc (ⓣ03.84.52.06.69; ❷) or, for some old-style glitz, the *Grand Hôtel Ripotot*, 54 rue Maréchal-Foch (ⓣ03.84.52.15.45, ⓕ03.84.52.09.11; ❹), which is definitely the nicest hotel in town. The **campsite**, *Camping de Boyse*, is on rue Georges-Vallery (ⓣ03.84.52.00.32; ⓦwww.camping.champagnole.com; June to mid-Sept).

A couple of kilometres north at the source of the River Ain, spread over a small hill surrounded by pastures, is the old walled village of **NOZEROY**, ancestral home of the Chalon family, who dominated regional politics in feudal times. The town preserves much of its medieval charm today, with the **Porte de l'Horloge** – once part of the town's fortifications – framing the beginning of the Grande-Rue. This thoroughfare, lined with many ancient houses, ends at the place des Annonciades and the ruins of the thirteenth-century **castle**.

Forêt de la Joux

North of Nozeroy, on the other side of the D471 Champagnole–Pontarlier road, the **Forêt de la Joux** is considered one of the most beautiful of France's native pine forests. It's crisscrossed by a net of narrow fire roads – paths cut into the forest to prevent the spread of wild fires – but if you don't have a car, you can use the Gare de la Joux, in the heart of the forest on the Champagnole–Pontarlier train line, from where you can explore further on foot or by bicycle. There are many well-marked walking trails through the forest: the most popular area is the **Sapins de la Glacière**. The **Route des Sapins** is the approved tourist drive, signposted for 50km from the D471 to the village of Levier, passing lookouts and the 45-metre-high **Sapin Président** (a two-hundred-year-old fir tree) along the way. But the less regimented can just as easily enjoy getting mildly disorientated by following any number of lesser, unmarked roads and discovering the wonder of the forest for themselves.

The Région des Lacs

South of Champagnole, the flattened plateau, unable to shed the Haut Jura's winter run-off, collects the meltwaters in a series of natural and not-so-natural lakes known as the **Région des Lacs**, or Lake District, loosely strung along the valley of the River Ain. Here the ground begins to crumple upward to the eastern summits, gorges and waterfalls highlighting each successive step, and the views down to the tiny villages, each huddled around its characteristic mosaic-domed church, become more impressive with each bend. Some of the lakes charge parking fees during the day, but after 6pm, when the crowds and swimming supervisors go home, the lakes are deserted and peaceful – perfect for an evening picnic watching the sun set.

Clairvaux-les-Lacs and the Cascades du Hérisson

The region's main resort town is **CLAIRVAUX-LES-LACS**. It's here that the northern tip of the serpentine **Lac de Vouglans**, dammed 25km downstream, reverts to the River Ain that feeds it. The **Grand Lac**, just south of town, is the focus of summer resort activity, with a beach area and watersports facilities. It's calm and scenic, in spite of all the camping activity going on around it. The **Office du Tourisme du Pays des Lacs**, 36 Grande-Rue (Mon–Fri 9am–noon & 2–6pm, Sat 9am–noon; July & Aug also Sun 10am–noon; ⓣ03.84.25.27.47, ⓦwww.juralacs.com), is the place to find information about the region and outdoor activities such as boat and bike rental. For **hiking**, the *63 Circuits de Petite Randonnée* (€7 from the tourist office) has maps and descriptions of the circuits. Simple, reasonably priced **accommodation** can be found on the Grand Lac, at the *Chaumière du Lac* (ⓣ03.84.25.81.52, ⓕ03.83.25.24.54; ❷; closed Oct–March).

Surrounded by hills, **Lac de Chalain**, 16km north of Clairvaux and near the village of **DOUCIER**, has a much more impressive setting. It's also a very popular spot for **camping**, hence the prices can be high, especially in midsummer. Of the five campsites in town the jointly run *Fayolan* and *Le Grand Lac*, both on the lake (ⓣ03.84.25.26.19, ⓦwww.campingfayolan.com; May to mid-Sept), are the nicest.

By far the most interesting sight around here – and one of the Jura's best-known natural spectacles – is the **Cascades du Hérisson**, a septet of waterfalls descending nearly 300m in just 3km. Well-marked from either end of the gorge, the easiest walk, accessible by road via Val-Dessous southeast of Doucier, leads to the best-known and prettiest of the falls, the **Éventail**. A ten-minute stroll from the car park leads to the cascade, which spreads out in ever-widening tiers, giving it the fan-like appearance after which it is named. Continuing upstream, you'll shake off most casual spectators and pass through the woods of wild oak and springtime daffodils to the dramatic **Grand Saut**, with its clear drop of sixty metres; the pathway passes behind the waterfall – an alarmingly windy spot to shower in. A steep climb leads to smaller springs feeding the odd swimming-hole, past a drinks kiosk – at the intersection of another path which leads south to the village of Bonlieu – to the uppermost **Saut Girard**, 3km up from the Éventail and close to the village of **ILAY**. There's a choice of restaurants in Ilay, but only one **hotel**, the *Auberge du Hérisson*, 5 rue des Lacs (Ⓣ03.84.25.58.18, Ⓦwww.herisson.com; ❸; closed Nov–Jan; restaurant menus €15–40); they'll also be able to provide some tourist information.

A short drive up the N78 east of Ilay leads to a lookout atop **Pic de l'Aigle**: at nearly 1000m high, this is one of the best spots from which to view the Jura's topography. On fine days, the views extend as far as Mont Blanc to the east, and west to the plain of the Saône.

Up to Morez and Les Rousses

The main trans-Jura route into Switzerland, the N5, begins its ascent to the frontier around **St-Laurent-en-Grandvaux**, which is great as a base for cross-country skiing but unmemorable apart from the picturesque **Lac de l'Abbaye**, 4km south of town on the D437. The Arbois–St-Claude train passes this way, stopping at **MOREZ**, 12km southeast of St-Laurent-en-Grandvaux. Squeezed along the narrow valley floor, the town is noted for the manufacture of watches and spectacles. Its **tourist office** is in the central place Jaurès (mid-July to mid-Aug Mon–Sat 9am–noon & 2–6pm, Sun 10am–noon; rest of year Mon 2–6pm, Tues–Fri 9am–noon & 2–6pm, Sat 10am–noon; Ⓣ03.84.33.08.73, Ⓦwww.haut-jura.com), along with the **gare routière**, from where buses depart for La Cure on the Franco–Swiss border. Once on the Swiss side, you can catch trains down to Nyon on Lac Léman and to Geneva itself.

A couple of kilometres before the frontier, **LES ROUSSES** exists purely for skiing – downhill and especially cross-country – but just before it a lane leads down to a very attractive **HI hostel** in an old, red-shuttered farmhouse by a stream, 2km away at Bief-de-la-Chaille (Ⓣ03.84.60.02.80, Ⓔles-rousses@fuaj.org; closed mid-April to mid-May & Oct to mid-Dec); from here you can see the eerie spheres of the satellite-tracking station on the summit of La Dôle (1677m), the Jura's highest peak, just over the Swiss border. The **GR9 footpath** passes through here, beginning a magnificent hiking section all along the crest of the ridge to the Col de la Faucille and beyond.

There are plenty of **hotels** in Les Rousses itself: the *Hôtel le France*, 323 rue Pasteur (Ⓣ03.84.60.01.45, Ⓕ03.84.60.04.63; ❹), is the town's best, but less extravagant lodgings can be found at the *Du Gai Pinson*, 1465 rte Blanche (Ⓣ03.84.60.02.15; Ⓦwww.hotelgaipinson.com; ❹), or *Le Village*, 344 rue Pasteur (Ⓣ03.84.34.12.75; ❹) both of which are chalet-style buildings with cosy wood-clad rooms. For a **meal** try the *Restaurant Les P'Losses* (Ⓣ03.84.60.06.68; à la carte from €10), in the winter sports centre on the Geneva road southwest of town. There are also plenty of cafés and pizzerias.

St-Claude and beyond

From Morez, the train line leaves the N5 and heads along the Gorges de la Bienne to the industrial town of **ST-CLAUDE** to the southwest, hemmed in by even higher mountains than those around Morez. It's famous for pipes (the smoking kind) and diamonds and other cut stones, with a museum, the **Musée des Pipiers, Diamantaires et Lapidaires** (Jan–April & Oct Mon–Sat 2–6pm; May, June & Sept daily 9.30am–noon & 2–6.30pm; July & Aug daily 9.30am–6.30pm; closed Nov & Dec; €4), dedicated to the makers of all three, opposite the fortified cathedral of St-Pierre on rue du Marché. The **tourist office**, 1 av de Belfort (Mon–Sat 9am–noon & 2–6pm; July & Aug also open Sun 10am–1pm; ⓣ03.84.45.34.24), distributes a free leaflet in English, *The City's Discovery Tour*, which gives a florid description of a two-hour walk around town.

Should you wish to **stay** here, try the *Hôtel de la Poste*, on rue Reybert (ⓣ03.84.45.52.34; ❸). Plusher accommodation can be found at the *Jura Hôtel*, 40 av de la Gare (ⓣ03.84.45.24.04, ⓕ03.84.45.58.10; ❺), or *Le Joly* (ⓣ03.84.45.12.36; ❹) in Le Martinet, 3km southeast of town on the Col de la Faucille road, right next to a **campsite** (ⓣ03.84.45.00.40). Wholesome, inexpensive food is served at the **restaurant** of *Hôtel St-Hubert* on the place St-Hubert and at *Brasserie le Lacuzon*, at 5 rue Victor-Hugo.

What gives purpose to the rest of the onward route from either St-Claude or Les Rousses are the superb views from the crest of the great fir-clad ridge that overlooks Lac Léman to the east. The N5 crosses the ridge at the **Col de la Faucille** (1323m). If it's clear, the view is unbelievably dramatic from the Col or the GR footpath; the whole range of the western Alps stretches out before you, dominated by Mont Blanc, with the steely cusp of Lac Léman at your feet. There's an even better view from the top of nearby **Mont Rond** (1534m), accessible by chair lift. Of course, if it's not clear, the journey will have been in vain, but if you're carrying on south of Geneva, 30km away, it's downhill all the way – with the thought of some revitalizing bars of Swiss chocolate at the day's end.

Lake Geneva

The dolphin-shaped expanse of **Lake Geneva** (Lac Léman to the French) forms a natural border with Switzerland. Over 70km long, 14km wide and an amazing 310m deep, the lake is fed and drained by the Rhône. It's a real inland sea, subject to violent storms, as Byron and Shelley discovered to their discomfort in 1816. On a calm day, though, sailing slowly across its silky-smooth surface is a serene experience. The largest town on the French side, **Thonon-les-Bains**, is far less touristy than its surrounding neighbours, the world-famous spa town of **Évian** and ancient, picturesque **Yvoire**, and makes a good base for exploring the lakeside and the surrounding Chablais region.

Thonon-les-Bains

Though the town itself is only of minor interest, **THONON-LES-BAINS**' position overlooking the lake is stunning. It's also the starting point of the 700-kilometre-long **Route des Grandes Alpes**, a popular, signposted tourist route which winds its way through the mountains to Menton, on the Mediterranean coast (ⓦwww.routedesgrandesalpes.com).

The waterfront, connected to the upper town by **funicular railway** (daily every 2–4min: April–June & Sept 8am–9pm; July & Aug 8am–11pm; €1.80 round trip), is a pleasant place to while away a summer afternoon, with its tiny fishermen's cottages, cafés, restaurants and snack kiosks. Running northwards, the flower-decked lakefront promenade, the quai de Ripaille, leads past the marina and the fantastic public **swimming pools** (daily May–Sept 9am–7pm; €3.50) to the **Château de Ripaille** (guided tours daily: Feb, March, Oct & Nov 3pm; April–June & Sept 11am, 2.30pm & 4pm; July & Aug 11am & on the half-hour 2.30–5pm; €6; ⓦwww.ripaille.fr). The château was built in the fifteenth century by Amédée VIII, the colourful first duke of Savoie, who later served ten years as anti-pope before retiring from the post to become Bishop of Geneva. In fact, despite its turrets it looks more like a lovely country manor than a castle, due in part to major restoration in the late nineteenth century, which left a rich legacy of Art Nouveau interiors. The vineyard attached to the property produces one of the region's best-regarded wines, which are available to taste and buy at the château on weekdays.

Practicalities

From the **gare SNCF**, avenue de la Gare leads to place des Arts, from which rue des Granges takes you to the port via the **tourist office** on place du Marché (Mon–Fri 9am–12.30pm & 1.30–6.30pm; Sat 10am–12.30pm & 1.30–6.30pm; ⓣ04.50.71.55.55, ⓦwww.thononlesbains.com). There's also a summertime tourist office kiosk at the harbour (July & Aug daily 10.30am–12.30pm & 2–6.30pm; ⓣ04.50.26.19.94). As Thonon is itself compact, its **hotels** are modest but pleasant two-star affairs. Try the lakeside *Le Port*, 1 quai de Ripaille (ⓣ04.50.26.01.62; ④), or the basic but comfortable *Le Comte Rouge*, 10 bd du Canal (ⓣ04.50.71.06.04, ⓕ04.50.81.93.49; ③), near the *gare SNCF* and the town centre. There's a **campsite**, *Le Saint-Disdille* (April–Sept ⓣ04.50.71.14.11, ⓦwww.disdille.com) on the eastern edge of town just off the avenue de St-Disdille. One of Thonon's best **restaurants** is *Le Scampi*, 1 av du Léman, which specializes in fresh fish from the lake, with menus starting at €18 (ⓣ04.50.71.10.04). A less expensive option is the Chinese *Royal Thonon*, 3 rue des Ursules (ⓣ04.50.71.92.03).

Yvoire

Some 16km to west of Thonon lies the pretty medieval village of **YVOIRE**, famous for its extravagant flower displays, which seem to drip in profusion from every building in summer, when the narrow cobbled lanes are frequently choked with hordes of day-trippers. The main attraction is the lovely **Labyrinthe-Jardin des Cinq Sens**, off rue du Lac (April to mid-May daily 11am–6pm; mid-May to mid-Sept 10am–7pm; mid-Sept to Oct 1–5pm; €8), a spread of immaculate formal gardens laid out with a huge variety of plants, and designed to appeal to each of the five senses. The **tourist office** is on place de la Mairie (April–Oct daily 10am–12.30pm & 1.30–5pm; Nov–March closed Sat & Sun; ⓣ04.50.72.80.21, ⓦwww.yvoiretourism.com). Finding a **room** in the village can be difficult, especially in high season, though you could try *Hôtel le Pré de la Cure* on place de la Mairie (ⓣ04.50.72.83.58, ⓦwww.pre-delacure.com; closed mid-Nov to March; ⑤); the tourist office may also be able to help locate a room. Finding somewhere to **eat** is rather easier, with several harbour-side restaurants serving up fresh fish dishes to the tourist crowds.

Évian

Moving eastwards, **ÉVIAN**, or Évian-les-Bains as it is known officially, is a pleasant and peaceful spa resort, though there isn't a great deal to see or do other than simply enjoy the serenity of the waterfront, or take leisurely trips on the lake. The mineral water for which the town is famous is now bottled at Amphion, 3km along the lakeside (reserve at the tourist office for one of the four daily tours; ⓣ04.50.26.80.29; €1.70), but the **Source Cachat** on avenue des Sources still gushes away behind the Évian company's Art Nouveau offices in rue Nationale, providing unlimited free and refreshing water round the clock. There's a funicular that begins from just above the **casino**; though the views are underwhelming, it has the advantage of being free (mid-May to mid-Sept 10am–7pm; every 20min).

The waterfront is elegantly laid out with squares of billiard-table grass, brilliant flower-beds and exotic trees, mini-golf, water slides and other peaceful ways of amusing oneself. There are **ferries** to explore other towns around the lake, including Lausanne (12 daily; €40.30 return) and Geneva (2 daily; €38.50 return) in Switzerland and Yvoire (3 daily; €25.80 return) and Thonon-les-Bains (4 daily; €15.80 return) on the French side. CGN Ferries also runs a number of sightseeing **cruises** (Ⓦwww.cgn.ch), which do circuits of the lake, stopping at picturesque spots; enquire at the tourist office for details. The tourist office also reserves spaces on a boat that goes to **Les Pré-Curieux** water gardens, picturesque lakeside gardens, each organized around a water-based ecosystem. The tour includes a visit to a colonial house that contains educational exhibitions on the wetlands (open May–Sept; reserve at the tourist office or email Ⓔinfo@precurieux.com).

Practicalities

The **tourist office** is on place d'Allinges (May–Sept Mon–Fri 8.30am–noon & 2–7pm, Sat 9am–noon & 3–7pm, Sun 10am–noon & 3–6pm; Oct–April Mon–Fri 8.30am–noon & 2–7pm; Ⓣ04.50.75.04.26, Ⓦwww.eviantourism.com). The town has a few top-notch four-star **hotels** if you're after some full-on luxury, but there are many more affordable options available too, the best of which is the *Hôtel Continental*, 65 rue Nationale (Ⓣ04.50.75.37.54, Ⓦwww.continental-evian.com; ❹), in the centre of town, with rooms on the top floor that have a view of the lake. The nearby *Bourgogne*, place Charles-Cottet (Ⓣ04.50.75.01.05, Ⓦwww.hotel-evian-bourgogne.com; ❻), offers large rooms and a higher standard of comfort, while the *Terminus*, at 32 av de la Gare (Ⓣ04.50.75.15.07, Ⓦwww.hotel-terminus-evian.com; ❹), is a basic option directly across from the *gare SNCF*. On the waterfront, the *Savoy*, 17 quai Besson (Ⓣ04.50.83.15.00, Ⓦwww.savoy-hotel.com; ❻), provides comfortable, contemporary rooms, some of which overlook the lake, without breaking the bank. There's also a private **hostel**, *Côté Lac Evian,* on avenue de Neuvecelle (Ⓣ04.50.75.35.87, Ⓦwww.cotelacevian.com; ❶) – the D21 towards Abondance – and four-star **camping** at *De la Plage*, 304 rue de la Garenne (Ⓣ04.50.70.00.46; Ⓦwww.camping-dela-plage.com; closed Oct–April), less than 1km from the town centre. There are plenty of **places to eat**: at the cheaper end, try *Le Siam*, 5 rue Clermont, with good Thai food starting at €10, or some of the pizzerias on the east end of rue Nationale. The restaurants at the *Bourgogne* and the *Savoy* hotels offer more upmarket menus, with prices starting at €16.

Lake Geneva to Mont Blanc: Chablais, Faucigny and Aravis

Softer, greener and a lot less crowded than the mighty ranges further south, the Northern pre-Alps climb up in steps from the shores of Lake Geneva. The first of the mountainous regions is the **Chablais**, whose sleepy farming hamlets of **Morzine** and **Les Gets** spring into life both during the ski season from December to April, and increasingly in July and August for mountain bikers. South over **Mont Buet** lies the **Faucigny** and the pretty village of **Samoëns**, a contrast with its neighbour the purpose-built 1960s ski village of **Flaine**. And to the east is the **Aravis,** divided from the Chablais and the Faucigny by a deep U-shaped valley created during the last Ice Age. This cut has provided a route through the mountains since Roman times and is now shared by the Autoroute Blanche, railway lines and heavy industry around the valley towns along the river Arve. To the south, and just west of Mont Blanc, **Mégève** is one of the most upmarket of French ski resorts.

Morzine and the Chablais region

From Thonon the D902 winds south through a narrow gorge cut by the raging River Dranse. As the road climbs higher the cliffs and tunnels disappear, replaced by the lush fields and charming hamlets of the **Chablais**. At the head of the valley sits **MORZINE**, a market town made rich through tourism. Despite the heavy development of skiing and biking, the village, with its narrow streets and wooden chalets, has retained much of its original character. A handful of older farmhouses and prospectors' cottages date back to 1734 when **slate mining** began in the Prodains valley 2km east of Morzine. Mining by hand continues to this day and the mines can be visited: contact Franck Buet (Ⓣ04.50.79.12.21, Ⓦwww.ardoise-morzine.com), a young slate worker who offers weekly guided tours. Agriculture also plays an important part in the local economy, and tomme, Réblochon and Abondance cheeses are all produced locally; Nicolas Baud at the Fruitière de Morzine, l'Alpage (Ⓣ04.50.79.12.39; Wed & Thurs 9am; free) gives visitors the chance to take part in the **cheese-making** process.

In the winter season (Dec–April) the town's ski lifts link into the Portes du Soleil area, which stretches across the border into Switzerland, making it one of the largest areas in the world. The Super Morzine *télécabine* and the *téléphérique* at Prodains take you to the purpose-built resort of **Avoriaz** above Morzine, while the Pleney and Nyon lifts head towards **Les Gets**. During the summer season (July & Aug) several of the main lifts remain open to mountain bikers, walkers and paragliders.

Practicalities

Morzine's **tourist office**, on the place de l'Office du Tourisme (daily 9am–12.30pm & 3.30–6.30pm; Ⓣ04.50.74.72.72, Ⓦwww.morzine.com), offers helpful hiking maps, with mountain refuge phone numbers listed. There are a mass of **ski hire** shops in the village; try Starski on route du Téléphérique. The École de Ski Français on the same road (Ⓣ04.50.79.13.13, Ⓦwww.esf-morzine.com) is one of five **ski schools** organizing instructors for individual private lessons or group lessons.

Accommodation, mainly in small, chalet-style hotels and guesthouses, is not cheap, especially in high season, and must be booked in advance. Try the central *Le Sporting Hotel*, rond-point de Joux Plane (Ⓣ04.50.79.15.03, Ⓦwww.hotelsporting-morzine.com; compulsory half-board ❺); or the rustic *Farmhouse*, in a 1771 *grand manoir* overlooking the village on chemin de la Coutettaz (Ⓣ04.50.79.08.26; Ⓦwww.thefarmhouse.co.uk; closed Oct & Nov; summer ❽, winter compulsory half-board ❾). Catered chalets operate during the main winter and summer season: try *Chilly Powder*, Les Prodains (Ⓣ04.50.74.75.21, Ⓦwww.chillypowder.com; winter season €495–995 per person per week chalet board, rest of year ❹). In summer, there's the option of **camping** at *Les Marmottes*, 3km north in Essert Romand (Ⓣ04.50.75.74.44; closed Oct, Nov & May).

Most local **restaurants** serve pizzas and cheese-based dishes; *Café Chaud* (Ⓣ04.50.79.03.31) is the best. Up in the mountains, *La Pointe de Nyon*, accessible from the *téléphérique de Nyon* 1.5km south, is worth the trek, with panoramic views of the Plateaux de Nyon (ⓣ04.50.79.11.74; à la carte from around €15); Pascal's team serve delicious mountain cuisine, including wild mushroom risotto. **Nightlife** in town centres around the Taille de Mas Pleney, just by the tourist office, where revellers spill out of the many bars and crowd onto the pavement.

Samoëns and the Faucigny

A fine place to absorb the region's atmosphere is the gentle and attractive village of **SAMOËNS**, south of Morzine on the main Geneva–Chamonix Autoroute Blanche lying at the foot of the Aiguille de Criou (2207m) with the tall peak of Mont Buet (3099m) in the distance. The village's architectural claim to fame is its sixteenth-century **Gothic church**, Notre-Dame de l'Assomption, built on Romanesque foundations, with a doorway with crouching lions. The village is also known as the birthplace of Marie-Louise Cognacq-Jay, who left to seek her fortune in Paris at the age of 15 in 1853, and found it as the founder of the famous French department store, La Samaritaine. There's also a beautiful **botanical garden** (daily: summer 8am–noon & 1–7pm; winter 8am–noon & 1.30–5.30pm; free), on the slope above the old part of the village, created by Madame Jay and planted with specimens of mountain flora from all over the world. Despite its low altitude, Samoëns is becoming more popular with **skiers** thanks to a short transfer time from Geneva and a new *télécabine*, the Express du Grand Massif, 2km south of the village, which links it to the main ski area.

Buses arrive at place de l'Autogare, opposite the **tourist office** (ⓣ04.50.34.40.28, ⓦwww.samoens.com), which has excellent walking and

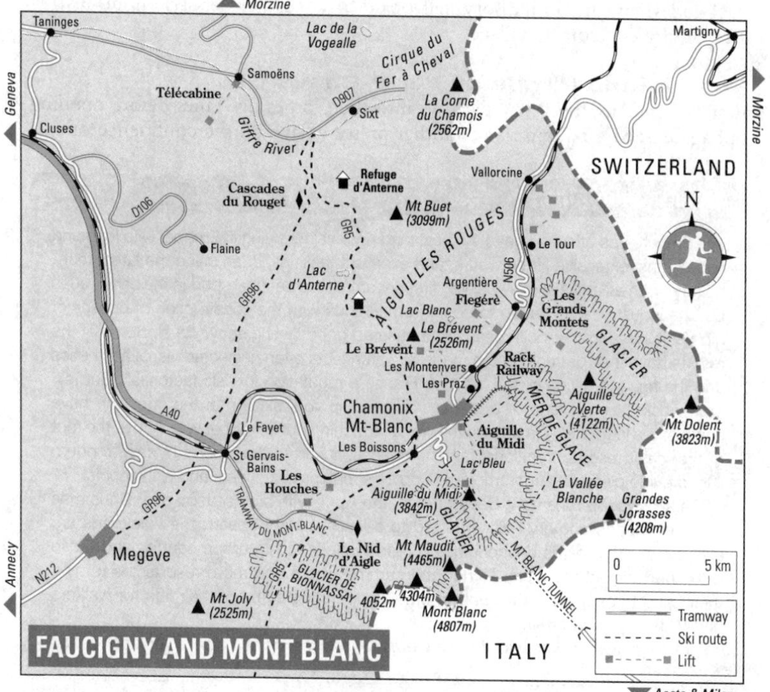

VTT maps of the surrounding area, and sells ski passes (which are also available at the *télécabine*). There are dozens of **sports shops** both in town and around the base of the ski lift that rents ski equipment; try Anthonioz Ski on avenue Cognac-Jaÿ, which also rents out VTT bikes during summer months. Next door the ESF (ⓣ04.50.34.43.12, ⓦwww.esfsamoens.com) is one of four ski schools in the village offering instruction for both adults and children. For **accommodation**, try *Hotel Les Drugères* (ⓣ04.50.34.43.84, ⓦhotel.lesdrugeres.com; ❺; closed May & Nov) or *Hotel Les Glaciers* (ⓣ04.50.34.40.06, ⓦwww.hotel-les-glaciers.com; closed May, June & Sept to mid-Dec; ❽). Both hotels have restaurants and good-sized, comfortable rooms; the latter also has an indoor and outdoor pool. The most beautiful option in town are the *chambres d'hôtes* at *La Maison de Fifine* (ⓣ04.50.34.10.29, ⓦwww.fifine.com; ❺), a rustic and cosy old farmhouse converted with a contemporary touch, while at the other end of the scale there's a municipal **campsite**, *Le Giffre* (ⓣ04.50.34.41.92, ⓦwww.camping-samoens.com) by the River Giffre.

Flaine

South of Samoëns, **FLAINE** is the second major resort making up the local ski area. Built at 1600m in the late 1960s by the eminent Bauhaus architect Marcel Breuer, the proposed fusion between man, mountains and art became more of a monument to concrete, its four arcaded tower blocks surrounding a square, which has at its centre Picasso's *La Tête de Femme* sculpture. The resort is only open during the winter (Dec–April) and summer (July & Aug) seasons, and **accommodation** is principally in apartments; contact the **tourist office** on Galerie Marchande Forum (ⓣ04.50.90.80.01, ⓦwww.flaine.com) for information. An alternative is the *Chalet La Cascade* (ⓣ04.50.90.87.66, ⓦwww.lacascade-flaine.fr; compulsory half-board ❾) a cosy, chalet-style hotel-restaurant on the edge of the village.

Sixt and the Cirque du Fer-à-Cheval

East of Samoëns, the valley narrows into the Gorges des Tines before opening out again at **SIXT**, 7km away, another pretty village on the confluence of two

Skiing in the Alps

The French Alps offers some of the best (and best-value) skiing in Europe, with long and varied runs, extensive lift networks, and excellent facilities, often using the latest technology, such as artificial snow. Skiing first became a recreational sport in the early 1900s but the industry really began to boom in the 1960s with the construction of dozens of high-altitude, purpose-built resorts that ensured good lasting snow cover. Some of the resorts have their detractors: the modernist architects often neglected visual aesthetics and the need for living space, earning France a reputation for "ski factories". But few can knock their efficiency – at many, you can clip your skis on at the door and have some of the largest ski circuses in the world stretching out in front of you. And at the foot of the major resorts, traditional farming villages, linked to the resorts by fast, modern lifts, provide plenty of accommodation options, equipment outlets and ski schools.

The ski **season** runs from December to late April, with high season over Christmas and New Year, February half-term and to a lesser extent Easter; the weekends are also busy with crowds descending on resorts close to big urban centres and those with short airport transfers. During the summer more and more resorts are turning their hand to catering for **mountain bikers**, operating some of their lifts for walkers and VTT (*velo tout terrain*).

For information on where to ski, see the "Alpine ski resorts at a glance" box opposite.

Alpine ski resorts at a glance

Resort name	Altitude	Towns	Round-up	Km of Piste	Cross-country	Ski-lifts	Six-day pass	Page
Chamonix Valley	1000–3842m	Chamonix, Argentière, Les Houches	Six unconnected areas, strung along a traffic-ridden valley, ascending to high mountains and spectacular off-piste for advanced skiers. Popular year round with tourists, the town's hip bars filled with gnarly mountaineers and dreadlocked skiers.	155km	45km	47	€186	987
Megève	1000–2350m	Megève, St-Gervais	The Monaco of skiing: poodles with fur coats, giant chalets and gentle intermediate skiing amongst stunning scenery.	300km	76km	82	€216	983
Massif des Aravis	1200–2600m	La Clusaz, Le Grand Bornand	Pretty traditional villages with a very French feel a short transfer away from Geneva. Good value but limited nightlife. Family-oriented resorts with intermediate skiing amongst beautiful mountains covered in fir trees but may be a bit low so snow is less certain.	220km	70km	98	€156	982
Grand Massif	900–2480m	Samoëns, Flaine	The very pretty, low-altitude village of Samoëns has plenty of bars and even a market but no direct ski access while the soulless, concrete, high mountain blocks of Flaine provide ski-in-ski-out apartments and hotels linking into the intermediate and beginner-suited area.	265km	110km	75	€174	979
Portes du Soleil	900–2350m	Morzine, Avoriaz, Châtel-les-Gets	Pretty, low-altitude, traditional family resorts of Morzine and Les Gets link into the modern, purpose-built Avoriaz situated an the top of a cliff via a tenuous link. Avoriaz is popular with pro snowboarders, and has bars to match. Area provides excellent skiing for all levels.	650km	130km	260	€184	978
Trois Vallées	1300–3195m	Méribel, Courchevel, Val Thorens	A favourite with Brits, this massive area is suitable for all abilities but is a veritable soulless factory of skiing. Be prepared for queuing and overcharging, and the scenery is disappointing.	580km	130km	200	€215	996
Paradiski	1250–3250m	Les Arcs, La Plagne	These areas were recently joined in order to compete with other super-size French resorts. Purpose-built village lacks charm or planning but there's good skiing for all abilities.	425km	115km	165	€229	998
Espace Killy	1550–3656m	Val d-Isère, Tignes	A high snow-shore Mecca for advanced skiers, this harsh environment is difficult to get to. Resorts are butt-ugly but the nightlife is excellent.	300km	44km	100	€198	1000
Les Deux-Alpes	1600–3568m	Les Deux-Alpes, La Grave	Intermediate slopes of Deux-Alpes are popular with snowboarders and at weekends are filled to bursting with students from nearby Grenoble. Best nightlife in France to match. While La Grave is for hardcore skiers and mountaineers, it's very dangerous – ski with guide only.	200km	20km	63	€169	1013
Alpe d'Huez	1500–3330m	Alpe d'Huez	Purpose-built, sunny resort, good skiing for all levels. Extensive and still very French.	220km	50km	85	€187	1012
Serre Chevalier	1400–2830m	Serre Chevalier	Pretty village, beautiful scenery and good skiing for all abilities, but low, unsatisfactory ski links between the different areas often break down because of lack of snow.	250km	35km	72	€160	1015

branches of the Giffre: the Giffre-Haut, which comes down from Salvagny; and the Giffre-Bas, which rises in the Cirque du Fer-à-Cheval.

The cirque begins about 6km from Sixt – there's a footpath along the left bank of the Giffre-Bas. It's a vast semicircle of rock walls, up to 700m in height and 4–5km long, blue with haze on a summer's day and striated with the long chains of white water from the waterfalls. The left-hand end of the cirque is dominated by a huge spike of rock known as La Corne du Chamois (The Goat's Horn). At its foot the valley of the Giffre bends sharply north to its source in the glaciers above the Fond de la Combe. The bowl of the cirque is thickly wooded except for a circular meadow in the middle where the road ends.

There's a **tourist office** and a park office in the centre of Sixt (both Mon–Sat 9am–noon & 2–7pm; ⓣ04.50.34.49.36, ⓦwww.sixtferacheval.com). The park office produces a useful and well-illustrated folder of walks in the region. Sixt also has three *gîtes d'étape* and a **hotel**, *Le Petit Tetras* (ⓣ04.50.34.42.51, ⓦwww.le-petit-tetras.fr; ❺; closed mid-Sept to Dec), a modern chalet with an outdoor pool.

La Clusaz and the Aravis Mountains

The other side of the Cluses valley and the Autoroute Blanche, in the Aravis range of mountains, the old farming community of **LA CLUSAZ** was one of the first to turn its hand to skiing, and the **ski museum** at 23 route de l'Étale (ⓣ06.62.89.21.76; mid-June to mid-Sept & late Dec to April daily except Sat 4–7.30pm; €2.50) tells the story of a hundred years of winter sports in the area. The **tourist office**, 161 place de l'Église (ⓣ04.50.32.65.00, ⓦwww.laclusaz.com; daily except Sun 9am–noon & 2–6pm), sells lift tickets, has information on ski schools and rental shops and also provides excellent walking and cycling maps. For chalet **accommodation** try *Chalet Maxim*, 1/37 rte de la Piscine (ⓣ06.15.04.25.18, ⓦwww.chaletmaxim.com; winter €650–970 per person per week chalet board) while the beautiful *Ferme de Vanille* (ⓣ04.50.09.08.32, ⓦwww.lafermedevanille.com; compulsory half-board ❻), 11km north in Le Grand Bornand provides wonderful *chambres d'hôtes* in a chalet that dates back to 1708.

Megève

Stunning views of Mont Blanc and an old-world charm make **MEGÈVE**, 30km south of La Clusaz, one of the most beautiful French resorts, and exclusive hotels, designer boutiques and smart ski-rental shops lend it a jet-set feel. The traffic-free place de l'Église, surrounded by carefully restored old buildings, lies at the heart of the village. In winter, outside the fine medieval church, a queue of brightly painted sleigh-taxis driven by local farmers takes visitors on village tours.

The **tourist office** is on place de l'Église (Mon–Sat 9am–12.30pm & 2–6.30pm; ⓣ04.50.21.27.28 ⓦwww.megeve.com). Upmarket **hotels** include the luxurious *Les Fermes de Maries* (ⓣ04.50.93.03.10, ⓦwww.fermesdemarie.com; ❾), whose individual chalets are linked by underground passages so as not to disturb the beauty of the snow outside, and *Le Mont Blanc* (ⓣ04.50.21.20.02, ⓦwww.hotelmontblanc.com; ❽); both hotels offer spa treatments and fireplaces in some of the suites. Budget accommodation in the centre is hard to find and many options insist on week-long stays, but it's worth trying the plain but comfortable *Hotel le Prairie*, rue Charles-Feige (ⓣ04.50.21.48.55, ⓦwww.hotellaprairie.com; closed June and Sept–Nov; ❺), which often lets you book rooms per night at the last minute. For **eating**, *Les Enfants Terribles* at the

Mont Blanc Hotel offers excellent Savoyard cuisine (Ⓣ04.50.58.76.69; à la carte from €24).

Mont Blanc

Sixty kilometres south of Évian on the Swiss and Italian borders looms **Mont Blanc** (4807m), Western Europe's highest peak, right on the Italian border. First climbed in 1786, this mountain is the biggest tourist draw in the Alps, but its grandeur is undiminished by the hordes of visitors, and if you're walking in the area, you can soon get away from the crowds. The closest airport is in Geneva, but if you're coming from France then Annecy (see p.988) is the easiest city from which to approach the mountain, and, of the two road routes, the one east via the Megève is the more interesting. The two main approach roads to Mont Blanc come together at Le Fayet, a village just outside **St-Gervais-les-Bains**, where the **tramway du Mont Blanc** begins its 75-minute haul to the **Nid d'Aigle**, a vantage point on the northwest slope (€23.50 return). From here it's an easy one-hour round-trip walk to the Glacier de Bionnassay. The remainder of Mont Blanc activities are based from around **Chamonix-Mont Blanc**, the French base camp for all Mont Blanc activities, just 20km from St-Gervais.

Chamonix-Mont Blanc

Bustling, cosmopolitan **CHAMONIX**, with its rash of restaurants and flashy boutiques, may have long since had its village identity submerged in a sprawl of tourist development, but the stunning backdrop of glaring snowfields, eerie blue glaciers and ridges of shark-toothed aiguilles surrounding Mont Blanc are more than ample compensation.

Arrival and information

The **gare SNCF**, **gare routière** and main car park are a short walk east of place du Triangle-de-l'Amitié, where the **tourist office**, at no. 85 (daily: July & Aug 8.30am–7.30pm; Sept–June 8.30am–12.30pm & 2–7pm; Ⓣ04.50.53.00.24, Ⓦwww.chamonix.com), offers up-to-the minute walking and climbing information, and publishes a map of summer walks in the area (€4). The Chamonix multipass (see p.986) and other mountain lift passes can also be purchased here, as well as at the foot of each cable-car ascent. The **websites** Ⓦwww.chamonix.net and Ⓦwww.chamonixexperience.com are also good sources of information on the town. Near the tourist office, the Maison de la Montagne houses the Compagnie des Guides (daily: 8.30am–noon and 3.30–7.30pm; Ⓣ04.50.53.00.88, Ⓦwww.chamonix-guides.com) for those who don't want to ski off-piste or hike unaccompanied; the guides also run rock- and ice-climbing schools. Also enclosed in the Maison are the Office de Haute Montagne (daily: July to mid-Aug 9am–noon & 3–6pm; Ⓣ04.50.53.22.08, Ⓦwww.ohm-chamonix.com), which gives advice on *refuges* as well as a meteorological service (Ⓣ04.50.53.22.08). There's an **Internet** café at CyBar, 80 rue des Moulins (daily 11am–midnight), though if you can stand it the terminals at the *McDonald's* on avenue Michel-Croz are less expensive.

Accommodation

One of the biggest headaches in and around Chamonix is finding a bed, especially if, as a walker or climber, you're having to sit out bad weather while waiting to get into the hills. All hotels need booking in advance and tend to be expensive;

CHAMONIX

ACCOMMODATION	
Auberge du Bois Prin	H
La Bagna	B
Le Belvédère	C
Crémerie Balmat	A
Les Crêtes Blanches	F
Hostel	I
Red Mountain Lodge	E
La Tapia	D
Le Touring	G

EATING AND DRINKING	
Arbate	8
Atmosphère	5
Cantina	3
MBC	1
Munchies	2
Osteria la Dolce Vita	7
La Poêle	9
La Terrace	4
Valentino	6

however, there's also a good supply of hostel and *gîte* accommodation. **Campsites** are numerous, though in high season there may only be room for a small mountain tent. Two convenient sites are *Camping de la Mer de Glace*, less than 2km north of town, close to Les Praz (ⓣ04.50.53.44.03, ⓦwww.chamonix-camping.com; closed mid-Sept to May), and *Les Rosières* off the route des Praz (ⓣ04.50.53.10.42, ⓦwww.campinglesrosieres.com; year-round; €14 tent and two people).

High **season** in Chamonix is February to March and July and August, with the summer season being less expensive than the winter; many establishments close in May and October. Over New Year, though, prices nearly double – expect to pay €100 for a room that costs only €65 for the rest of high season.

Auberge du Bois Prin 69 chemin de l'Hermine ⓣ04.50.53.33.51, ⓦwww.boisprin.com. Ultra-swish, this deluxe hotel has a romantic wooded location in the suburb of Les Moussoux, 1km south of the town centre. ❾

La Bagna 337 rte des Gaudenays ⓣ04.50.53.62.90, ⓦwww.la-bagna.com. A simply converted eighteenth-century farmhouse with cosy wooden rooms in the village of Les Praz, 2km north of Chamonix near the golf course and at the foot of 3754-metre Mont Dru. ❹

Le Belvédère 501 rte du Plagnolet, Argentière ⓣ04.50.54.02.59, ⓦwww.gitebelvedere.com. Simple rooms in a town house at the foot of the Grands Montes ski area, 6km north of Chamonix. ❸

Crémerie Balmat 749 promenade des Crémeries ⓣ04.50.53.24.44, ⓕ04.50.53.29.42. Basic but cheap hotel 1.5km north of the town centre just off route du Bouchet in a quiet spot surrounded by pine forests and with views to Mont Blanc. ❸

Les Crêtes Blanches 16 impasse du Génépy ⓣ04.50.53.05.62, ⓦwww.cretes-blanches.com. A 1960s wood-clad block; the interior has been decorated as an old town house with lots of wood, stone and a cosy roaring fire. ❺

Hostel 127 montée Jacques-Balmat, Les-Pèlerins-en-Haut ⓣ04.50.53.14.52, ⓔchamonix@fuaj.org. Modern, comfortable hostel in the western part of town. Bus towards Les Houches and get off at "Pèlerins École" – the hostel is signposted from there. Closed for one week in mid-May & Nov to mid-Dec. €16.70 for a bed in a small dorm.

Red Mountain Lodge 435 rue Joseph-Vallot ⓣ04.50.53.94.79, ⓔredmountainlodge@yahoo.com. A good-value chalet whose living room has an open fire and comfy sofas. run by extraordinarily friendly, English-speaking staff. Meals provided *gîte*-style. Open May–Oct. ❹

La Tapia 152 rte de la Frasse, Les Mouilles ⓣ04.50.53.18.19, ⓦwww.latapia.com. Located in a small quiet village 1.5km northeast of Chamonix, this *gîte* has basic bunk-bed rooms for 2–6 people and wonderful views. ❶

Le Touring 95 rue Joseph-Vallot ⓣ04.50.53.59.18, ⓦwww.hoteltouring-chamonix.com. A pretty, traditional hotel with antique furniture in a very central spot; street-facing rooms may be noisy. ❺

The Town

The mountains provide the main sights and activities, but on days when the bad weather sets in, there are a few things to do in town. The **Musée Alpin**, off avenue Michel-Croz in the town centre (daily: 2–7pm; €5), will interest mountaineers, but its collection of equipment and documents is a bit disappointing. Its star exhibit is Jacques Balmat's account of his first ascent of Mont Blanc in 1786. The **Richard Bozon Sports Centre** on avenue de la Plage has ice-skating, a pool, sauna and hamam, climbing wall and tennis courts (hours vary; ⓣ04.50.53.09.07). Across the street, the **library** contains a good selection of English-language books.

Eating, drinking and nightlife

The choice **restaurants** and bars reflect not only Chamonix's geographical location, with influences from Switzerland and Italy, but also the tastes of the cosmopolitan mix of visitors. Vietnamese, fusion and hamburger places share the food scene with more traditional Savoyard restaurants, pizzerias and *haute* French cuisine. Rue Joseph-Vallot has plenty of gourmet **food shops** with local cheeses and other Alpine delicacies, and there are several well-stocked supermarkets in town for making a picnic. If you're after a **drink**, rue des Moulins is packed from end to end with English-speaking bars and clubs.

Restaurants

Atmosphère 123 place Balmat ☎04.50.55.97.97. High-quality dining in a cosy setting; in summer an outside balcony terrace overhangs the river. Elaborate dishes from €21.

Munchies 87 rue des Moulins ☎04.50.53.45.41. Ultra-hip hangout offering French-Japanese-Thai fusion including authentic sushi; mains start at €16.

Osteria La Dolce Vita 78 rue de Lyret ☎04.50.53.91.29. Italian wine bar specializing in bruschetta, focaccia, as well as all manner of generously filled panini (around €6). Cosy, fun atmosphere with delicious smells emanating from the wood-burning oven.

La Poêle 79 av de l'Aiguille-du-Midi ☎04.50.55.96.13. Good-value restaurant with simple home-cooked cuisine; try one of the excellent omelettes. À la carte €7.80–20.

La Terrace 43 place Balmat ☎04.50.53.09.95. Soak up the sun and admire the views from the 1920s Art Deco-style balcony, sit out on the square next to the river or dine beneath the grand ceilings inside. Simple bistro food served from 4.30pm, and late-night there's music – rock most nights, house on Thurs.

Valentino 30 place Balmat ☎04.50.53.67.72. An excellent, cheap and centrally located pizzeria, which also serves a good cappuccino. Around €11 for a pizza and beer.

Cafés and bars

Arbate 80 chemin du Sapi ☎04.50.53.44.43. A favourite après-ski bar with British and Scandinavian *seasonaires*. The atmosphere is festive on rock, house and pop nights despite the barn-like wooden decor and feeble lighting.

Cantina 37 impasse des Rhododendrons ☎04.50.53.83.80. A small authentic Mexican cantina with a popular downstairs nightclub playing host to DJs, live bands and dancing most nights from 6pm–2am.

MBC (Micro Brasserie de Chamonix) 350 rte du Bouchet ☎04.50.53.61.59. Five beers are brewed on the premises at this laid-back bar, and fermented in large vessels on view behind the bar, Open daily 4pm–2am, with American-style food served 7–11pm.

Around Chamonix

There are a number of exhilarating excursions around Chamonix that are worth experiencing – it may be worth getting a **multipass** that covers all the lifts in the area (starting at €52 for 36 hours or €66 for two non-consecutive days).

The most famous excursion is the very expensive, and often very crammed, **téléférique** (May–Sept 7.30am–5pm, mid-Dec to April 8.30am–4pm; €36 return, advance reservations €2, call ☎08.92.68.00.67) to the **Aiguille du Midi** (3842m), one of the longest cable-car ascents in the world, rising no fewer than 3000m above the valley floor in two impossibly steep stages. Penny-pinching by buying a ticket only as far as the Plan du Midi, which is used principally by climbers heading up to the routes on the Aiguilles du Chamonix, is a waste of money: go all the way or not at all. If you do go up, make the effort to be on your way before 9am, as the summits tend to cloud over towards midday, and huge crowds may force you to wait for hours if you try later. Take warm clothes – even on a summer's day it'll be below zero at the top – and suntan lotion is also advisable to protect against the glare off the snow. You need a steady head, too: the drop beneath the little bubble of steel and glass is terrifying.

The Aiguille is an exposed granite pinnacle on which a restaurant and the *téléférique* dock are precariously balanced. The view is incredible. At your feet is the snowy plateau of the **Col du Midi**, with the glaciers of the Vallée Blanche and Géant crawling off left at their millennial pace. To the right a steep snowfield leads to the easy ridge route to the summit of Mont Blanc with its cap of ice. Away to the front, rank upon rank of snow- and ice-capped monsters recede into the distance. Most impressive of all, spanning the horizon to your left, from the east to south, is a mind-blowing cirque of needle-sharp peaks and precipitous cliffs: the Aiguille Verte, Triollet and the Jorasses, with the Matterhorn and Monte Rosa visible in the far distance across a glorious landscape of rock, snow and cloud-filled valleys – the lethal testing ground of all climbers.

From the Aiguille you can continue to **Pont Helbronner** on a ski lift above the Glacier du Géant, and from there descend to **Italy**, from where a bus will take you back through the Mont Blanc tunnel to Chamonix (€54 including the Aiguille du Midi ascent, not included on the multipass).

An alternative to descending all the way from the Aiguille by cable car is to get off at the midway station at **Plan de l'Aiguille** and hike to Lac Bleu (1hr round trip), or take a two-and-a-half hour hike along the Plan de l'Aiguille-Montvers traverse to the top of the **Montenvers rack railway** (May–Sept 8.30am–5.30pm; Oct to mid-Nov & mid-Dec to April 10am–4pm; €16 return). At the top you have the option of taking a short cable-car ride down into an **ice cave** carved out of the Mer de Glace every summer (an additional €6.60). A cheaper way, however, to view a glacier is to take the chair lift from the village of Les Bosson, 2km south of Chamonix, up to the **Glacier des Bossons** (daily: July & Aug 8am–6pm; €9.50), where you can see the biggest precipice in Europe (a drop of 3500m), as well as the Alps' lowest ice face. A nature trail at the top, along with the spectacular views, makes for a good half-day outing.

Hiking and climbing in the Chamonix valley

Opposite Mont Blanc, the north side of Chamonix valley is enclosed by the lower but nonetheless impressive **Aiguilles Rouges**, with another *téléférique* to **Le Brévent** (15min; €20 return), the 2526-metre peak directly above the town. Classic walks this side of the valley include the **Lac Blanc**, starting from Les Praz and the Flégère *téléférique* (20min; €18 return), or walking to the top of the Flégère lift via the lovely lunch stop *La Floria* on the trail of the same name. The **Grand** and **Petit Balcon Sud** trails traverse the Aiguilles Rouges (from the top of Flégère to the top of Planpraz is a relatively easy two hours), and at points the trails open up to spectacular views of Mont Blanc. A highly recommended two-day hike is the **GR5** stage north from Le Brévent to the village of Sixt via **Lac d'Anterne**, with a night at the *Refuge d'Anterne*. The classic long-distance route is the two-week **Tour du Mont Blanc** (TMB), described in a Topo-guide, Andrew Harvey's *Tour of Mont Blanc and Chamonix-Mont Blanc: A Walker's Guide*. The famous **Haute Route** from Chamonix to Zermatt can be done on foot in summer in eight days, or on touring skis in winter in six days. The trail rarely falls below 2500m and despite the crowded huts and paths it is a fantastic adventure for the scenery alone. **Climbing Mont Blanc** should not be undertaken lightly. It is a semi-technical climb and quickly changing conditions mean that a guide is essential. There are several different routes, the most popular being the Gouter ridge route (three days). The Cosmiques route offers a safer, shorter but more technical alternative (two days).

Skiing in the Chamonix valley

Despite its fame, Chamonix is not the most user-friendly of ski resorts and access to the slopes depends on shuttle buses or car. For advanced skiers, however, it's probably one of the best places in the Alps since it offers an impressive range of challenging runs and off-piste itineraries. It's not so much a single resort as a chain of unconnected ski areas set along both sides of the Chamonix valley and dominated by Mont Blanc. The sunny **Brévent** and **Flégère** areas on the southern slopes have jaw-dropping scenery in fine weather and good spots for lunch, while **Argentière–Les Grands Montets** and L'Aiguille du Midi, departure point for the famous Vallée Blanche, are cold, north-facing areas suited to advanced skiers. The intermediate areas of **Le Tour** and **Les Houches** can be found at the northern and southern ends of the valley, with their tree level slopes facing east and west. These areas are both good options in nasty weather conditions as the trees give definition to an otherwise white landscape.

Annecy and around

Sixty kilometres south of Geneva, at the northern tip of the turquoise Lac d'Annecy, and bounded to the east by the turreted peaks of La Tournette and to the west by the long wooded ridge of Le Semnoz, **ANNECY** is one of the most beautiful and popular resort towns of the French Alps, though the tourist traffic can get a bit wearing in high season. Historically, it enjoyed a brief flurry of importance in the early sixteenth century, when Geneva opted for the Reformation and the fugitive Catholic bishop decamped here with a train of ecclesiastics and a prosperous, cultivated elite. The main attractions, however, are not historic, but scenic; surrounded by picturesque mountains Annecy resembles a fairy-tale city, and is replete with a castle on a hill and an island prison.

Arrival, information and accommodation

The **gare SNCF** and **gare routière** complex is northwest of the centre, five minutes' walk north of the rue Royale. The road's continuation is the arcaded rue Pâquier, which contains the modern shopping precinct of Centre Bonlieu, housing the **tourist office** (Mon–Sat 9am–12.30pm & 1.45–6pm; July & Aug also open Sun same times; ⓣ04.50.45.00.33, ⓦwww.annecytourisme.com). For **Internet** in the old town try L'Emailerie, 6 place aux Bois. There's **bike rental** from Roul' ma poule at 4 rue des Marquisats (ⓣ04.50.27.86.83).

Annecy has a number of good **hotels**. Reserve well in advance in high season, or you can chance it on one of the quirky no-star hotels on the far side of the *gare SNCF*. The municipal **campsite**, *Le Belvédère* (ⓣ04.50.45.48.30), is situated off boulevard de la Corniche – turn right up the lane opposite chemin du Tillier; it's on the left past the *Hôtel Belvédère*. There are other sites all around the shore of the lake.

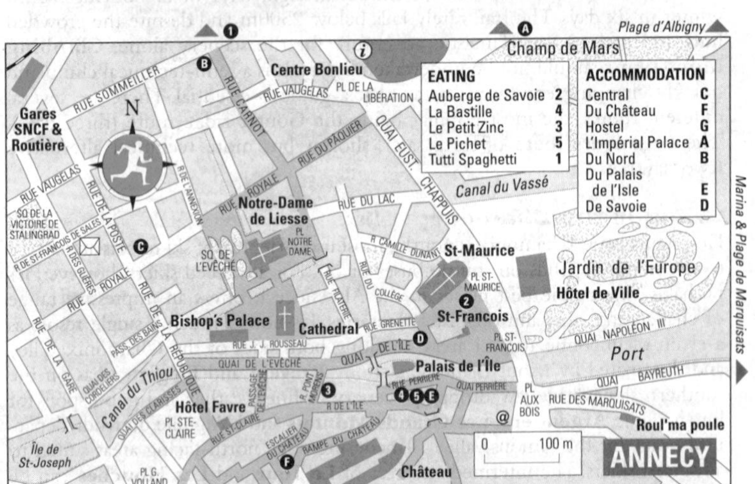

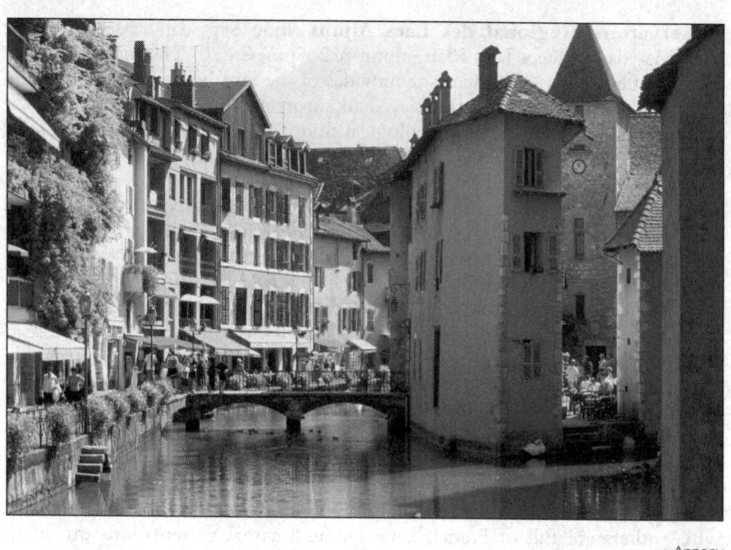

△Annecy

Central 6 rue Royale ⓣ04.50.45.05.37, ⓦwww.hotelcentralannecy.com. One of the cheapest hotels in the centre of town. Small and serviceable, with basic but clean and modern rooms in an old building whose balconies are swathed in plants. ❸

Du Château 16 rampe du Château ⓣ04.50.45.27.66, ⓦwww.annecy-hotel.com. A homely hotel just uphill from the madding crowds with a terrace overlooking the town. ❹

Hostel 4 rte du Semnoz ⓣ04.50.45.33.19, ⓔannecy@fuaj.org. A short distance east from the centre, just uphill past the Centre Hospitalier; in the summer take summer bus marked "ligne d'été", or follow the signs to Semnoz. Closed Dec to mid-Jan. €15.70 for a bed in a small dorm.

L'Impérial Palace 32 av d'Albigny ⓣ04.50.09.30.00, ⓦwww.imperial-annecy.com. A luxurious four-star, in a beautiful mansion on the northeast bank of the lake beside the casino. ❾

Du Nord 24 rue Sommeiller ⓣ04.50.45.08.78, ⓦwww.annecy-hotel-du-nord.com. Modern and functional a/c rooms, close to the lake and the train station. ❹

Du Palais de l'Isle 13 rue Perrière ⓣ04.50.45.86.87, ⓦwww.hoteldupalaisdelisle.com. One of the more upmarket options in the heart of the medieval town, with light and airy rooms, some with views of the canal and lake. ❺

De Savoie 1 place St-François ⓣ04.50.45.15.45, ⓦwww.hoteldesavoie.fr. Very pretty old building facing a cobbled square on one side and the canal on the other. Inside the furniture and floral decor are a bit passé but it still has plenty of character. ❺

The Town

The most picturesque part of Annecy, the old town lies at the foot of the castle hill, a warren of lanes, passages and arcaded houses, below and between which flow branches of the **Canal du Thiou**, draining the lake into the River Fier. The houses, ringed by canalside railings overflowing with geraniums and petunias, are incredibly beautiful, though most of the shops now sell souvenirs.

From rue de l'Île on the canal's south bank, the narrow rampe du Château leads up to the **château**, former home of the counts of Genevois and the dukes of Nemours, a junior branch of the house of Savoy. There has been a castle on this site from the eleventh century but the Nemours, finding the old fortress too rough and unpolished for their taste, added living quarters in the sixteenth century, which now house the collections of the **Musée-Château** and

Observatoire Régional des Lacs Alpins (June–Sept daily 10.30am–6pm; Oct–May daily except Tues 10am–noon & 2–5pm; €4.70). The main attraction is the castle itself, and the views it provides of the lake below, but some of the exhibits are also of interest. Displayed in surprisingly modern and high-tech fashion, objects range from archeological finds from around the lake to Savoyard popular art and woodwork; there's also an aquarium with lake fish and an informative exhibition on the geography of the Alps.

At the base of the château is **rue Ste-Claire**, the main street of the old town, with arcaded shops and houses. At no. 18 is the **Hôtel Favre**, where in 1606 Antoine Favre, an eminent lawyer, and Bishop de Sales founded the literary-intellectual Académie Florimontane "because the Muses thrive in the mountains of Savoie". At the west end of the street is its original medieval gateway. Parallel to rue Ste-Claire, on the other side of the canal, rue J.-J.-Rousseau passes the seventeenth-century former **bishop's palace** and the unremarkable **cathedral**, where Rousseau once sang as a chorister.

Nearby, to the east, you'll find the picture-perfect **Palais de l'Île**, a tiny twelfth-century fort which served in turn as palace, mint, court and prison (the latter as late as World War II). It now houses a **Centre for Urban Interpretation** (June–Sept daily 10.30am–6pm; Oct–May daily except Tues 10am–noon & 2–5pm; €3.10). One room on the ground floor relates the building's history, while others are full of French-language audiovisual presentations on urban environments in the region.

A few steps to the north, the fifteenth-century **church of St-Maurice** conceals some excellent fifteenth- and sixteenth-century religious art. Across the square to the east of the church, the **Hôtel de Ville** backs onto shady public gardens, from where a bridge crosses a canal to the lakeside lawns of the extensive **Champ de Mars**.

From the Hôtel de Ville a stroll south on rue des Marquisats and past the **marina** leads along the lake to the free grassy **plage de Marquisats**, while a slightly longer walk in the other direction around the lake past the casino reaches the **plage d'Albigny**. In recent years in hot weather there have been cases of "swimmers itch" (*puces de canard*) from swimming in the lake; if cases have been noted, make sure to shower straight after swimming.

Eating and drinking

Annecy's **restaurants** churn out rather unimaginative fare to feed the tourist crowds. You'll find a string of inexpensive places to eat overlooking the canal along quai Perrière and rue Ste-Claire.

Auberge de Savoie place St-François ⓣ04.50.45.03.05. One of the better options on the north side of the canal, serving Savoyard specialities and fish from the lake. Menus €24–50; closed Wed.

La Bastille 3 quai des Vieilles Prison ⓣ04.50.45.09.37. Savoyard fare in a pretty setting by the canal overlooking the old prison. Menus €11–20.

Le Petit Zinc 11 rue Pont-Morens ⓣ04.50.51.12.93. This place manages to rise above the surrounding mediocrity, serving hearty local dishes in a warm interior. Lunch from €14, dinner €16–26.

Le Pichet 13 rue Perrière ⓣ04.50.45.32.41. Served on a large terrace, fare here is dependable and includes local dishes. Menus from €18.

Tutti Spaghetti 84 rue Carnot ⓣ04.50.67.42.32 Wide choice of pasta dishes and salads (from €8) at this popular place – seating can get a bit tight when the terrace is not in use.

Around Annecy

While Annecy's high-season crowds may be bearable for only a day or two, the town's environs offer a number of agreeable excursions. As well as **boat tours**,

cycling is an enjoyable means of appreciating Lac d'Annecy. The 40km road circuit of the lake is a very popular Sunday morning activity among sporty Annéciens and a traffic-free cycle route follows the west shore of the lake. The surrounding hills offer walking and mountain-biking excursions (as well as more specialized pursuits) to suit all. Experienced walkers should enjoy the relatively undemanding ascent of **La Tournette** on the eastern side of the lake, while gentler walks and cycle routes are to be found in the forested **Semnoz mountains** on the lake's west side.

Ten kilometres west of Annecy, the **Gorges du Fier** and nearby Château de Montrottier combine both natural and historical spectacle within a short distance of each other; and, if you're leaving Annecy to the north, the **Pont de la Caille** also deserve a look.

Around the lake

Although a very busy road rings Lake Annecy, a far more tranquil way of appreciating the lakeside is aboard one of the frequent **boats** that depart from Annecy's canalside port; you also have the option of stopping over or returning later in the day. Trips stopping off at various points on the lake are offered by Compagnie de Navigation (Ⓦwww.annecy-croisieres.com) on place aux Bois, beside quai Bayreuth – a full circuit costs €13.30.

On the east shore of the lake, signposted out of the village of **MENTHON-ST-BERNARD**, is the grand, turreted **Château de Menthon** (May, June & Sept Fri–Sun & hols 2–6pm; July & Aug daily noon–6pm; €6, €7 for weekend medieval costume shows). Inhabited since the twelfth century and birthplace of St Bernard, the patron saint of mountaineers, the fortress was extensively renovated in the nineteenth century in the romantic Gothic revival style and possesses a fine collection of period furniture, as well as views across the lake back to Annecy. You can **eat** here at the lakeside *Buvette du Port*, which offers *plats du jour* for around €10, while for a place to **stay**, try *Le Saint-Bernard* in the centre of the village (Ⓣ04.50.60.01.55, Ⓦwww.hotelstbernard.com; ❹), which also has a good restaurant. A few kilometres down the road is the lovely lakeside village of **TALLOIRES**, whose eleventh-century Benedictine abbey has been converted into the luxurious *Hôtel de l'Abbaye de Talloires* on chemin des Moines (Ⓣ04.50.60.77.33, Ⓦwww.abbaye-talloires.com; ❾; closed Nov to mid-April).

On the west side of the lake, the village of **DUINGT** occupies a peninsula where there are two more thousand-year-old **châteaux**, one in ruins and the other partly rebuilt. Like Menthon-St-Bernard and Talloires, it has a small beach, with the opportunity to rent pleasure craft. The village has a few good-value **hotels**, among them the *Auberge du Roselet* (Ⓣ04.50.68.67.19, Ⓦwww.hotel-restaurant-leroselet.com; ❹). For a more tranquil overnight stay, head 7km south to the village of **DOUSSARD**, where the *Hôtel Arcalod* at Grand Parc (Ⓣ04.50.44.30.22, Ⓦwww.hotelarcalod.com; closed Oct–Feb; ❻) offers lakeside accommodation and a swimming pool.

La Tournette and the Semnoz mountains

Experienced hill-walkers wanting a stiff but straightforward mountain ascent could tackle **La Tournette** (2351m), which dominates the east side of the lake with its patchy snowfields and crenellated summits. A road just north of Talloires crosses the **Col de la Forclaz**, doubles back to the left before the hamlet of Montmin, and ends in a steep but drivable track up to the **Col de l'Aulp**, less than 1000m from the summit. From the col, the climb is immediate, steep and clear, leading to a **refuge**, where snow and increasing exposure demand extra care. Some scrambling (with fixed chains and handrails) is required to take you up to a broad, exposed shoulder on the way to the summit. To the east, the Chaîne des Aravis stretches before the snowbound massif of Mont Blanc on the horizon, just 50km away, while in the other direction the turquoise lake and Annecy itself lie at your feet.

Facing La Tournette on the lake's opposite shore, the wooded ridges of the **Semnoz mountains** offer less radical hiking. From the village of Duingt, a four-hour walk leads southwards up the Taillefer ridge, involving just over 300m of ascent to the 765-metre summit of **Taillefer** itself. From the town church follow the signs for **Grotte de Notre Dame du Lac**, a steep walk up the ridge, and follow the red and yellow markers thereafter. Towards the summit of Taillefer, there's some scrambling, but nothing too difficult, and 1500m after the peak the path turns round and returns north via the hamlet of Les Maisons.

The highest peak in the Semnoz is the **Crêt de Châtillon**, 16km directly south of Annecy along the D41. At 1699m it offers panoramic views, most impressively east past La Tournette towards Mont Blanc. A twenty-minute walk across meadows from the road's highest point leads to the cross on the summit and an orientation table pointing out the surrounding features.

The Gorges du Fier and Pont de la Caille

West of Annecy, the River Fier, which trickles out of the lake through Annecy's picturesque canals, has cut a narrow crevice through the limestone rock at the **Gorges du Fier** (daily: mid-March to mid-June & mid-Sept to mid-Oct 9am–noon & 2–6pm; mid-June to mid-Sept 9am–7pm; €4.50). Signposted off the D14 at Lovagny, a footpath leads down into the 300-metre-long gorge, which is traversed along an impressive high-level walkway pinned to the gorge side. On the way to the *gorges* you'll catch glimpses of the **Château de Montrottier** (mid-March to May & Sept daily except Tues 9am–1pm and 2–6pm; June–Aug daily 9am–1pm & 2–7pm; Oct daily 2–5pm; €7), which can be reached by continuing along the road for another three kilometres. The castle, which dates from the thirteenth century, possesses an eclectic collection of furniture, earthenware and lace as well as exotic objects from former French colonies in West Africa and the Far East, amassed during the nineteenth century by one Léon Mares.

Chambéry and around

Chambéry, 44km south of Annecy, lies in a valley separating the Chartreuse Massif (see p.1011) from the Bauges mountains, historically an important strategic position since it commands the entrance to the big Alpine valleys leading toward the passes into Italy. Around 13km north of town is the spa resort of **Aix-les-Bains**, with its famous thermal baths, just a few kilometres from the magnificent **Lac du Bourget**, the largest natural lake in France.

Chambéry

CHAMBÉRY grew up around the château built by Count Thomas of Savoie in 1232, and became the Savoyard capital, enjoying a golden age in the fourteenth and fifteenth centuries. Although superseded as capital by Turin in 1562, it remained an important commercial and cultural centre. The philosopher Rousseau spent some of his happiest years in the town during the 1730s. Only incorporated into France in 1860, modern Chambéry is a bustling provincial town with a wealth of grand Italianate architecture and a strong sense of its regional identity – look out for the "Savoie Libre" bumper stickers throughout the town and the Haute Savoie *départements*.

Arrival, information and accommodation

The **gare SNCF** is on rue Sommeiller, 500m north of the old town, with the **gare routière** just outside in place de la Gare. Five minutes' walk away at no. 24 boulevard de la Colonne, where all the **city buses** stop, is the **tourist office** (July & Aug Mon–Sat 9am–noon & 1.30–7pm, Sun 9.30am–12.30pm; Sept–June Mon–Sat 9am–noon & 1.30–6pm, Sun 9.30am–noon; ⓣ04.79.33.42.47, ⓦwww.chambery-tourisme.com). If you're planning on exploring the Vanoise (see p.995), the Maison du Parc, 135 rue Docteur-Juilland (ⓣ04.79.62.30.54), to the west of town can help with maps and information.

There's plenty of inexpensive **accommodation** scattered about the centre of Chambéry. One budget option is *Le Savoyard*, 35 place Monge (ⓣ04.79.33.36.55, ⓔsavoyard@noos.fr; ❸), conveniently located southeast of the cathedral, while *Hôtel des Princes* at 4 rue de Boigne (ⓣ04.79.33.45.36, ⓦwww.interhotel desprinces.com; ❺), has larger and creatively decorated rooms. For a bit of rural tranquillity and a lovely view, head for *Hôtel aux Pervenches*, 600 chemin des Charmettes (ⓣ04.79.33.34.26, ⓔemauvray@wanadoo.fr; ❺), in the village of Les Charmettes, Rousseau's summertime home, 2km south of the centre; it also has a good restaurant serving menus from €14.50.

The Town

Halfway down the broad, leafy boulevard de la Colonne is Chambéry's most famous monument, the splendidly extravagant and somewhat off-scale **Fontaine des Éléphants**, erected in homage to the Comte de Boigne, a native son who amassed a fortune working as a mercenary in India in the eighteenth century, and who used much of his vast wealth to fund major urban developments in his home town. **Musée Savoisien** on nearby square de Lannoy-de-Bissy (Mon & Wed–Sun 10am–noon & 2–6pm; €3), chronicles the history of Savoie from the Bronze Age onwards. The first floor houses paintings, including a finely executed fifteenth-century work showing the Annunciation, and painted wooden statues from various churches in the region; on the second floor, there's a collection of tools, carts, hay-sledges, and some fine furniture from a house in Bessans in the Vanoise, with a fascinating kitchen range made of wood and lined with *lauzes* (slabs of schist). Extremely rare thirteenth-century wall paintings from Cruet, housed in their own temperature-regulated room, depict secular scenes of frenzied battles and images of elegant court life.

Next to the museum, in the enclosed place Métropole, is the **cathedral**, its interior painted in elaborate nineteenth-century trompe l'oeil, imitating the twisting shapes and whorls of the high Gothic style (Sat only 3–6pm; free). From here a passage leads to **rue de la Croix-d'Or**, and numerous restaurants, from which after 100m a right turn brings you to the long, rectangular **place St-Léger**, home in 1735 to Rousseau and Mme de Waren. The square has a fountain and more cafés, where street musicians perform on summer evenings.

In the northeast corner of the square the smart **rue de Boigne**, leads back to the Fontaine des Éléphants, but if you turn left the road leads to the **Château des Ducs de Savoie**. A massive and imposing structure, it was once the main home of the dukes of Savoie, and is now occupied by the prefecture; the interior is only accessible by guided tours, which begin from the office across the street (May, June & Sept daily 2.30pm; July & Aug Mon–Sat 10.30am, 2.30, 3.30 and 4.30pm, Sun afternoons only; €4). A short walk north from the castle exit along promenade Veyrat is the **Musée des Beaux-Arts** (Mon

& Wed–Sat 10am–noon & 2–6pm; €3), which is largely devoted to works by lesser-known sixteenth- to eighteenth-century Italian artists, though the pride of the collection is Uccello's *Portrait of a Young Man*, and there are also a few minor Titian cartoons.

Two kilometres south of town on the rustic chemin des Charmettes is Rousseau's other Chambéry address, the country cottage **Les Charmettes**, now home to the **Musée Jean-Jacques Rousseau** (April–Sept daily except Tues 10am–noon & 2–6pm; Oct–March daily except Tues 10am–noon & 2–4.30pm; €3). Furnished in the style of the day, it includes the philosopher's writing desk and chaise longue, and outside a lovely formal garden and apple orchard alongside.

Eating and drinking

Good food at decent prices is not hard to come by in Chambéry, and mid-priced Savoyard **restaurants** abound – many specializing in lake and river fish. The best value of these are *La Chaumière*, 14–16 rue Denfert-Rochereau, with menus starting at €13 (Ⓣ04.79.33.16.26; by reservation only on Sun) and *Le Savoyard* in the hotel of the same name. For a lighter, vegetarian meal, try *Le Bar @ Thym*, 22 place Monge, which serves ethically sourced produce in a modern style – try the Bolivian organic hot chocolate (Ⓣ04.79.70.96.40, closed Sun & Mon). If you fancy a splurge, truly exceptional cuisine can be found at *Le St-Real*, in a converted seventeenth-century church at 86 rue St-Real (Ⓣ04.79.70.09.33; closed Sun), one of the best restaurants in the *département*, but pricey at €30–73.20 for gastronomic set menus.

Aix-les-Bains and the Lac du Bourget

AIX-LES-BAINS, 13km north of Chambéry, has been one of France's premier spa resorts since the eighteenth century. It boasts a wealth of elegant architecture, recalling the town's *belle-époque* heyday, when high society from across Europe dropped by to relax and take the waters: Queen Victoria, calling herself the "Countess of Balmoral", made several incognito visits, commemorated by a statue to her on the left side of avenue Charles-de-Gaulle as you walk up the hill. These days, Aix-les-Bains is a sedate and genteel place, populated mostly by French pensioners, who descend on the town en masse throughout the year for state-funded thermal treatments. Unless you're after a mud-bath or a glass of sulphurous water, the main draw today is the beautiful **Lac du Bourget**. Rising above Aix is Mont Revard (1550m), a vast plateau, made up of gentle meadows and forests, offering a range of trails for ramblers and cyclists – it is also one of France's finest cross-country skiing areas.

The Town

The town centres around place Maurice-Mollard, where you'll find the original monstrous Art Deco Thermes Nationaux at **Thermes Pellegrini**, accessible only with a French doctor's note. Just across from the baths is the *mairie*, which is built right into a Roman temple. And in front of the *thermes* is another grand Roman remnant, the **Arc de Campanus**, a rare funerary monument from the first century BC. A short walk north from here is the uber-modern spa centre **Les Thermes d'Aix-les-Bains** (Mon, Fri & Sat 2–8pm, Tues–Thurs 2–6pm, Sun 10am–8pm, Ⓦwww.thermaix.com; €15 per day), one of the best places to experience the healing qualities of the local sulphurous water. Also north of the *place*, at 10 bd Côtes, is the charming **Musée Faure** (daily except Tues 10am–noon & 1.30–6pm; €4), an elegant house with a small but impressive collection of nineteenth-century art on display, including a room of Rodins, paintings from the best-known Impressionists, and some lovely Degas pastels. South of place Maurice-Mollard lies the compact warren of pedestrianized streets that make up the old town.

Practicalities

The **gare SNCF** is on the western edge of town, just off boulevard Président-Wilson, from where it's a brief stroll up avenue Charles-de-Gaulle to the town centre. The **tourist office** is to the right of the Thermes Nationaux (daily: June–Aug 9am–6.30pm; Sept–May 9am–noon & 2–6pm; Ⓣ04.79.88.68.00, Ⓦwww.aixlesbains.com). Several **Internet** cafés line rue de Chambéry, the road that descends diagonally from the Parc Thermal.

Aix-les-Bains has almost a hundred **hotels**, though they bustle year-round with pensioners so advance bookings are advisable. For a taste of real *fin-de-siècle* elegance, try the *Astoria*, 7 place des Thermes (Ⓣ04.79.35.12.28, Ⓦwww.hotelastoria.fr; closed Dec; ❻), or for a cheaper but equally comfortable option head to the more modern *Agora*, rue de Chambéry (Ⓣ04.79.34.20.20, Ⓦwww.hotel-agora.com; ❹). The basic *Beaulieu*, 29 av Charles-de-Gaulle (Ⓣ04.79.35.01.02, Ⓦwww.hotel-beaulieu.fr; ❸), is handy for the *gare SNCF*, or, if you want to be nearer the lake, the friendly *Davat*, 21 chemin des Bateliers (Ⓣ04.79.63.40.40, Ⓦwww.davat.fr; ❹), is a good choice. There are four **campsites** near the Lac du Bourget, the best of which is *International du Sierroz* on boulevard Barrier (Ⓦwww.aixlesbains.com/campingsierroz)

There's an equally broad range of **restaurants**. One of the best is *Le Manoir*, 37 rue Georges-1er (Ⓣ04.79.61.44.00), with excellent gourmet menus at €25–49. The restaurants that line rue des Bains are more central and less expensive; try the pizzeria *Le Passe* at 6 rue du Dauphin, just off rue des Bains, with menus starting at €12. One of the most relaxing places to enjoy a coffee or an aperitif is *La Rotonde*, a very pleasant outdoor café in the Parc Thermal.

Lac de Bourget

Around 3km west of the centre of Aix, along avenue du Grand Port, lies the **Lac du Bourget**. Connected to the River Rhône by the Canal de Savières, it's a place of great beauty, a protected wildlife reserve and home to the now scarce European beaver. "Nowhere could one find such perfect concord between water, mountains, earth and sky", enthused the French writer Balzac, and it's clear what attracted him, and so many other poets and artists to this place. The lake's "Côte Sauvage" rises precipitously above the sparkling blue water on its west bank, dominated at its southern end by the looming presence of the Dent du Chat (1390m). There are daily sightseeing **cruises** on the lake between March and November, as well as more expensive lunch, dinner and evening cruises (contact the Bateaux du Lac du Bourget office at the port in Aix-les-Bains; Ⓣ04.79.88.92.09, Ⓦwww.gwel.com; from €12).

On the western side of the lake, close to the village of St-Pierre de Curtille is the picturesque **Abbaye d'Hautecombe** (daily audioguide tours 10–11.15am & 2–5pm), the final resting place of many members of the royal house of Savoie, including the last king and queen of Italy, Umberto II de Savoie and his wife Marie-José. The town, just off the D18, is accessible by road or boat.

The Isère valley and the Vanoise

The **Vanoise**, the rugged massif rising up to the southeast of Albertville, and over to the Italian border is a superb area for skiing and hiking. The dramatic range, whose highest peaks rise to altitudes in excess of 3500 metres, is roughly diamond-shaped, hemmed in by the valley of the **Isère** to the northeast, where **Bourg-St-Maurice** is the best base for exploration, and the **Arc valley** in the southwest. The glacier-capped southeast quadrant of the Vanoise, where both of these great rivers have their source, has been incorporated in the **Parc National de la Vanoise**, across which lonely and spectacular GR trails offer unparalleled opportunities for seasoned hikers. Easiest road access to the region is from Chambéry or Grenoble, although driving the winding and precipitous old highways from Annecy or Chamonix is an adventure in itself.

The Isère valley

The A43 from Chambéry cuts between the Massif des Bauges to the north and the Vanoise to the south, following the path of the lower **Isère River** as it flows down from the industrial town Albertville. Following the river by road from here involves a 180-kilometre journey south, north and south again back to its source high in the mountains near the **Col de l'Iseran**, close to the Italian frontier. From Albertville, whose edge-of-town hypermarkets make it a useful place for stocking up, the N90 climbs southeast along the bends of the Isère River for 50km to Moûtiers, the turn-off for the massive **Les Trois Vallées** ski region. Here the river course swings northeast, passing Aime, whose main Grande-Rue presents a pretty and little-spoilt succession of buildings. Six kilometres further up the valley is **Bourg-St-Maurice**, the midpoint of the upper Isère valley, known as the Tarentaise. At Séez, a short distance east the road heads south again along the D902 through dramatic scenery to the famous resort of **Val d'Isère**.

Méribel and Les Trois Vallées

Just off the N90, south of the industrial town of Moûtiers, **Les Trois Vallées** (Ⓦwww.les3vallees.com) is one of the world's largest linked skiing areas, with an ingenious lift network that makes skiing from village to village easy, and near endless off-piste possibilities awaiting the intrepid. There are several component resorts: expensive and luxurious Courchevel (Ⓦwww.courchevel.com); ugly and family-oriented Les Menuires (Ⓦwww.lesmenuires.com), which has a number of cheap hotels; and lively Val Thorens (Ⓦwww.valthorens.com), popular with younger crowds and the snowboard set. The main focus of interest, right at the hear of Les Trois Vallées however is traditionally British-dominated **MÉRIBEL** (Ⓦwww.meribel.net), established in 1938 by Scotsman Colonel Peter Lindsay, and offering a good range of cheap accommodation and après-ski activities. Despite its pubs, *Pizza Express* and other British imports, it retains a traditional Savoyard feel with small wooden chalets topped with slate roofs climbing the east side of the valley. At the valley bottom is the large **Olympic Ice Rink** (Dec–April, July & Aug daily 3–7pm, until 9.30pm Tues & Thurs; €4.60) and the departure point for the main ski lifts.

Practicalities

Méribel's **tourist office** (daily 9am–noon & 3–7pm; Ⓣ04.79.08.60.01), at the top of the route de la Monte in the village centre, provides information on mountain biking and walking in summer, as well as **Internet** access. Espace Gliss Skiset, in Bâtiment l'Eterlou opposite the ice rink, is one of dozens of ski shops that sell and rent skis and snowboards and mountain bikes in summer, while the ESF ski school office is in the Maison du Tourisme (Ⓣ04.79.08.60.31). Next door, the Bureau des Guides organizes rock climbing, walking and VTT expeditions.

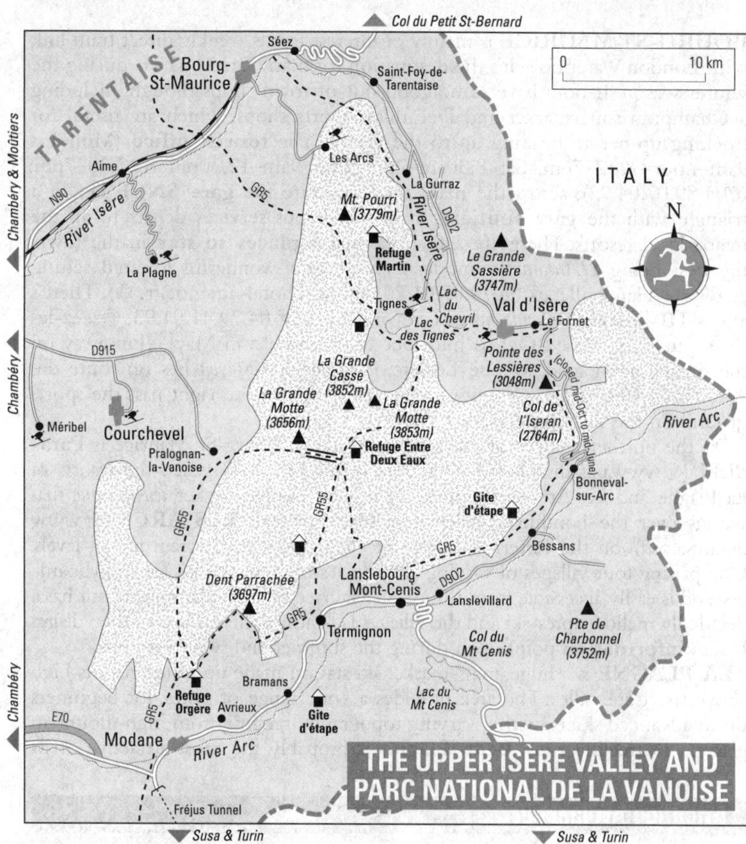

Though most local **accommodation** centres around British tour companies with Saturday to Saturday fixed packages, there are a few independent guest-houses and hotels offering more flexibility, the most central of which is *Hôtel Doron* (Ⓣ04.79.08.60.02; ⑥), a lively hotel with a young clientele and fairly basic rooms but close to the bars, nightlife and pistes. For traditional chalet-style holidays try *Chalet Raphael* in Le Raffort, 2km away on the western slope of the valley (Ⓣ04.79.00.45.69, Ⓦwww.skimeribelchalet.com; winter €385–959 per person per week chalet board, rest of the year ④).

Restaurants include the smart *Le Grain de Sel* (Ⓣ04.79.06.12.17; €25 for two courses) in the Méribel Mottaret district, or for cheap eats and good après-ski try the snack bar *Rond Point*, towards the Altiport at the top of town, which has a big terrace hosting DJs and lively barbecues during the main seasons. For **nightlife** head to *Jack's Bar* on route de Mussillon near the tourist office and serving strong Mutzig beer, followed by *Dick's T-Bar*, further down the same road, whch is open till 4am.

Bourg-St-Maurice and around

An unremarkable town situated in the shadow of the Tarentaise mountains on the roaring confluence of the Isère and Chapieux rivers, sleepy, grey

BOURG-ST-MAURICE is mainly of interest for its weekly direct train link with London Waterloo – it's the destination for many British skiers during the winter season. It does have some good out-of-town shops though, including a Champion supermarket and Decathlon sports shops, which are useful for stocking up before heading up to the resorts. The **tourist office** (Mon–Fri 9am–noon & 2–7pm, Sat 8.30am–7pm, Sun 9am–12.30pm & 3.30–7pm; Ⓣ04.79.07.04.92), across the main road opposite the **gare SNCF** lies in a triangle with the **gare routière**, from which bus services depart to all the major local resorts. There are a few reasonable **places to stay** in the town, the best being *L'Autantic*, a modern chalet in a wonderful forested setting at 69 rte Hauteville (Ⓣ04.79.07.01.70, Ⓦwww.hotel-autantic.fr; ❹). There's also a **HI hostel**, *La Verdache*, just beyond Séez (Ⓣ04.79.41.01.93, Ⓔseez-les-arcs@fuaj.org; closed Oct to mid-Dec & two weeks in May), 4km away on the dreary main road, avenue Leclerc. *Camping le Versoyen* lies on route des Arcs (Ⓣ04.79.07.03.45, Ⓦwww.leversoyen.com), on the right past the sports ground on the Val d'Isère road.

On the northern slopes of the mountains above Bourg-St-Maurice is **Paradiski** (Ⓦwww.paradiski.com), a ski area formed in 2003 when the resorts of La Plagne and Les Arcs were joined by a giant double-decker *téléphérique* that swings over the Ponthurin valley in a single bound. **LES ARCS** (Ⓦwww.lesarcs.com), on the eastern side, has excellent snow and terrain for all levels. Comprising four villages of varying altitude, it's high on the list for snowboarders, and is easily accessible from Bourg-St-Maurice by funicular railway, but has a decidedly mellow après-ski and the villages lack atmosphere. Each of the villages has an **information** point open during the summer and winter seasons.

LA PLAGNE is a huge, mass-market ski station made up of ten resorts high above the Isère valley. The area provides a wide range of pistes, for beginners up to advanced skiers, with a varying topography ranging from high mountain glaciers to treeline runs. **Belle Plagne** is probably the most attractive of its

Attention Avalanche!

There are few places on earth where **global warming** is more noticeable than in the Alps, and as a consequence of climate change tree levels are rising, glaciers are retreating and devastating rock falls and **avalanches** are much more frequent. Although greater understanding of avalanches has led to the introduction of safety measures, including tunnels, fencing and the use of dynamite to dislodge unstable snow, dozens of people are still killed every year, usually because they haven't heeded warnings. In resorts the avalanche risk is announced through signs and coloured flags, often found at ticket kiosks:

Yellow=low risk
Black/yellow checked = risk
Black = severe risk

You should also check up-to-date weather information (Ⓦwww.meteofrance.com) and ensure that you have sufficient **insurance** (see p.74) – bear in mind that even if policies cover skiing, this may not include unguided off-piste. If in doubt purchase a Carte Neige (Ⓦwww.ffs.fr/carteneige), available at most resorts with your lift ticket. **Mountain rescue** is carried out by resort ski patrol teams known as *pisteurs*, but for more serious incidents the PGHM (Ⓦwww.pghm-chamonix.com), a branch of the Gendarmerie Nationale specialized in mountain rescue are used. For more information, see "Basics", p.70.

purpose-built resorts, with an attempt made to construct the apartments in a more sympathetic style using wood and slate as opposed to concrete. Accommodation though is still dominated by apartments, and nightlife is minimal. Of the four linked lower villages, **Montchavin** is the most traditional and a rural smell still hangs in the air around its paved streets, working farms and slate roofs. The best **place to stay** is *Le Chalet du Friolin* in neighbouring Les Coches (Ⓣ04.79.07.45.84, Ⓦwww.lechaletdufriolin.com; Dec–April; ❾ half-board), a small and beautiful chalet with bar and restaurant right on the pistes. For apartments contact the Centre de Reservation (Ⓣ04.79.09.79.79) or the **tourist office** in La Plagne Centre (Ⓣ04.79.09.79.79; Ⓦwww.la-plagne.com), which can also provide information on rental shops, ski schools, restaurants and activities available in summer, including mountain bike trail maps.

Bourg-St-Maurice to Val d'Isère

Beyond Bourg-St-Maurice the N90 continues to wind upwards for a further 5km to the village of Séez, where it forks. The right turn takes you onto the D902, following the path of the Isère as it climbs towards Val d'Isère (see p.1000) and the perilous **Routes des Pierres Fortes de Savoie**, while the N90 continues to climb steeply towards the **Col du Petit St-Bernard**, following the path of the ancient Roman Way, now a classic touring route into the Italian Val d'Aosta. The pass, at a height of 2188m, has couple of barrack-like buildings and a row of statues of St Bernard, who built a hostel for mountain travellers here in the twelfth century. With its Swiss twin, the Grand St-Bernard, it was the only route around the Mont Blanc massif until the Mont Blanc tunnel was opened in 1965.

The Routes des Pierres Fortes de Savoie clings to the eastern side of the valley, leading to the relatively new resort of **SAINTE-FOY-DE-TARENTAISE**. Though it only has three chair lifts and a handful of chalets, it still manages some excellent off-piste skiing. Seven kilometres beyond Sainte-Foy, a right-hand turn off the D902, marked La Planche, winds a further 3km up the west-facing slope (an hour's walk from the road) to the tiny summer *alpage* villages of **La Savinaz** and **La Gurraz**, whose creamy **church tower** is a landmark for miles around. High above, though looking ominously close, are the blue ice cliffs that terminate the Glacier de la Gurraz decending from the northern face of **Mont Pourri** (3779m). The area is untouched by tourism. La Gurraz's dozen old houses have wide eaves and weathered balconies spread with sweet drying hay, and firewood stacked outside. The houses are all sited in the lee of a knoll for protection against the avalanches that come thundering off the glacier above. There are no provisions available, so bring your own. From La Gurraz, a signposted path climbs to *Refuge de la Martin* in an hour and a half. It zigzags up the slope behind La Savinaz, onto a spur by a ruined chalet, where a right-hand path goes up the rocks overhead to the edge of the glacier. The *refuge* path continues left along the side of a deep gully, crosses a ferocious torrent by a plank bridge and follows a mule track up to the mountain pastures by the *refuge*. The Mont Pourri glaciers are directly above. Opposite is the big Glacier de la Sassière and up to your right Val d'Isère, with the Col de l'Iseran behind.

Back on the D902, continuing south brings you to the artificial **Lac de Chevril**. The hydroelectric dam dominates the pretty hamlet of Tignes Les Brévières cowering beneath it. The right turn over the *barrage* takes you under a series of avalanche tunnels to the purpose-built ski resort of **Tignes**, while continuing past the dam, along the lake will bring you to into Val d'Isère. Tignes is not attractive, and in summer has little to offer aside from foot access to the Parc National de la Vanoise (see box p.1002) and a handful of lifts open for glacier skiing. But in winter, the bowl around the resort, in the shadow of the 3656-metre **Grand Motte**, becomes a desolate white ski wilderness; 130km of pistes link over the mountain to the village of Val d'Isère (see below) to form the **Espace Killy**, named after French downhill legend Jean-Claude Killy, creating one of the best ski areas in the world. The resort's inaccessibility means that it is usually filled with package-holidayers, but independent travellers can try the **hostel** *Les Clarines* (Ⓣ04.79.41.01.93, Ⓔtignes@fuaj.org; €15.50 for a bed in a small dorm). Alternatively, apartments can be booked through the **tourist office** (Ⓣ04.79.40.04.40, Ⓦwww.tignes.net).

Val d'Isère

Once a tiny mountain village, **VAL D'ISÈRE** is now a hideous agglomeration of cafés, supermarkets, apartments and chalets. Because it is so hard to get to, the resort really does close down in the off season, with only one hotel of the many in town open in May. In the summer it makes a convenient centre for walking, and you can ski year-round on the glacier – details are available from the **tourist office** (daily 8.30am–7.30pm; Ⓣ04.79.06.06.60, Ⓦwww.valdisere.com). Ski shops litter the village: try the cool Misty Fly shop opposite the tourist office, a local institution with snowboarders, freestyle-skiers and mountain bikers. Misty Fly also operate one of the best of Val d'Isère's twelve **ski schools**.

The **skiing** around Val d'Isère is varied and demanding; many international experts never ski anywhere else. Of the three areas, **Le Fornet** is the most traditional and undeveloped, with old lifts and narrow, unkept pistes, while the **Solaise** provides easily accessible sheltered skiing between larch trees during bad weather, and has two free beginner's lifts near its swimming pool and ice skating complex. **Le Rocher de Bellevard** is home to the Olympic downhill and has notoriously dangerous off-piste on its northern face; behind it are a snow park for snowboarders and gentle, wide intermediate runs down to La Daille.

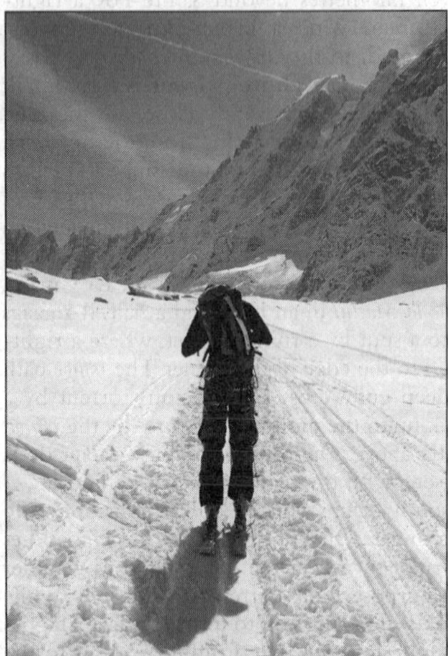

△ Val d'Isère

Staying here will certainly lighten your wallet. One of the cheapest options is *Séracs* (Ⓣ04.79.06.03.61, Ⓦwww.seracs.net; ❷), or try *Sakura* apartments (Ⓣ04.79.06.04.08, Ⓦwww.sakura7.com; €410–840 per week for two people), while there's a **campsite** nearby on the edge of the resort at Le Laisinant. The resort's **eateries** are geared towards the mainly British clientele, as a result of which prices are high and quality low. *Bananas* near the bottom of the pistes has a choice of Tex-Mex style dishes in a cosy, atmospheric bar, while the *Billabong Café*, on the main drag, avenue Olympic, is a American-style diner popular with *seasonaires*. *Folie Douce*, at the top of La Daille *télécabine*, is the most lively of the mountain restaurants with barbecues and booming music on the terrace when the weather is good. Après-ski centres around the cheesy **nightclub**, *Dicks T-Bar*, while *Café Face*, *Le Danois* and *L'Aventure* provide a welcome alternative to the school-disco music.

The Col de l'Iseran

From Val d'Isère, both the **D902** and the **GR5** veer south from the river, climbing towards the **Col de l'Iseran**. Despite the dangers of weather and the arduous climb, the pass has been used for centuries, being by far the quickest route between the remote upper valleys of the Isère and Arc. The volume of traffic was too small to disturb the nature of the tiny communities that eked out an existence on the approaches, but twentieth-century roads and the development of winter sports have changed all that. From October to June, the pass is blocked by snow, but in summer, being the highest pass in the Alps (2770m), it's a must-see sight for tourists with cars.

The GR5 reaches its zenith at the **Pointe des Lessières**, where on a clear day you have views of the Italian side of Mont Blanc and the whole of the frontier chain of peaks. Whether you head back or continue on to Bonneval (see below), the walk is a solid two and a half hours. If you continue south, a clear day will afford splendid views of the glaciers at the head of the Arc. As you descend along the Lenta stream through masses of anemones blooming in the stony ground, the riverbed winds through a desolate cirque, before dropping through a narrow defile towards the town.

The Arc valley

The **Arc valley** is wide and light below the Col de l'Iseran, though the treeless landscape can be more forbidding than joyous, especially under a stormy sky. Bare crags hang above the steep meadows on the north flanks; glaciers threaten to the south and east. Descending through meadows and patches of cultivation into the valley bottom with the lighter foliage of larches gracing the mountainsides you pass through humble hamlets of squat, rough, grey-stone houses – the homes of people who have had to struggle to wring a living from harsh weather and unyielding soil. It's surprising at first to find such a wealth of exuberant **Baroque art** in the outwardly simple **churches** in small villages like Avrieux, Bramans, Termignon, Lanslevillard and **Bessans**. But probably it's precisely because of the harshness and poverty of their lives that the mountain people sought to express their piety with such colourful vitality. Schools of local artists flourished, particularly in the seventeenth and eighteenth centuries, inspired and influenced by itinerant Italian artists who came and went across the adjacent frontier.

Bonneval-sur-Arc and Bessans

The first settlement of any size as you descend into the valley is **BONNEVAL-SUR-ARC**, 1835m above sea level, at the foot of the Col de l'Iseran, which looks out on the huge glaciers of the Sources de l'Arc to the east. Better preserved and more obviously picturesque than other towns of the valley, Bonneval stops a lot of tourists on their way to and from the col. It's in danger of becoming twee, with its houses clustered tightly around the church, and only the narrowest of lanes between them. You sense how very isolated these places were until only a few years ago, cut off for months by heavy snow, forced in upon their own resources. Several graves in the churchyard record deaths by avalanche.

From here the valley descends to **BESSANS**, which retains its village character better than most. Its squat dwellings are built of rough stone with tiny windows,

The Parc National de la Vanoise

The **Parc National de la Vanoise** (Ⓦwww.vanoise.com) occupies the eastern end of the Vanoise Massif. It's extremely popular, with over 500km of marked paths, including the **GR5**, **GR55** and **GTA** (Grande Traversée des Alpes), and numerous refuges along the trails. For information on the spot, the tourist offices in Modane, Val d'Isère and Bourg-St-Maurice are helpful. The Maison du Parc in Chambéry (see p.993) also gives advice and sells maps.

To cross the park, take the **GR5** from the northern edge of the transpontine section of Modane. When the trail splits, continue north on the **GR55**. From here the path leads to Pralognan, over the **Col de la Vanoise** and right across the park to the Lac de Tignes – a tremendous walk. An alternative is to stick with the GR5 (past the *Refuge de l'Orgère* from where a path north similarly joins up with the **GR55** and the previous route), which keeps east of La Dent Parrachée mountain, and follows a great loop up towards the **Refuge d'Entre-Deux-Eaux** before turning south and continuing up the north flank of the Arc valley and over the Col de l'Iseran to Val d'Isère.

and roofed with heavy slabs to withstand the long hard winters. Most have south-facing balconies to make the most of the sun and galleries under deep eaves for drying *grebons*, the bricks of cow dung and straw used locally for fuel. The **church** has a collection of seventeenth-century painted wooden statues and a retable, signed by Jean Clappier, a member of a local family who produced several generations of artists. On the other side of the small cemetery, the **chapel of St-Antoine** has exterior murals of the Virtues and Deadly Sins and inside, some fine sixteenth-century frescoes. Two kilometres beyond Bessans you pass the **chapel of Notre-Dame-des-Grâces** on the left, with another *ex voto* by Clappier. There's a small **tourist office** in the centre of Bessans (Ⓣ04.79.05.96.52, Ⓦwww.bessans.com), and some **accommodation**, including the *Hôtel Le Mont-Iseran* (Ⓣ04.79.05.95.97, Ⓦwww.montiseran.com; closed mid-April to mid-June & Oct–Jan; ❻ half-board), with old-fashioned wood-clad rooms, and the more modern *Hôtel La Vanoise* (Ⓣ04.79.05.96.79, Ⓦwww.hotel-vanoise.com; ❸), in a pretty, white building with magnificent views to the Vanoise.

Lanslebourg

In **LANSLEBOURG**, some 25km downstream from Bonneval, Haute Maurienne Information, in the town's old church (daily except Sat 3–7pm; Ⓣ04.79.05.91.57, Ⓦwww.hautemaurienne.com), organizes **tours** of village churches along the Arc valley. Lanslebourg is also the start of the climb to the **Mont Cenis pass** over to Susa in Italy, another ancient transalpine route; last stop before the perils of the trek, it was once a prosperous and thriving town. Relief at finishing the climb from the French side was tempered by an alarming descent *en ramasse*, a sort of crude sledge, which shot downhill at breakneck speed, much to the alarm of travellers: "So fast you lose all sense and understanding", a terrified merchant from Douai recounted in 1518. Lanslebourg has a municipal **campsite** (Ⓣ04.79.05.82.83, Ⓦwww.camping-les-balmasses.com) and a **HI hostel** with a fantastic view and good rooms (Ⓣ04.79.05.90.96, Ⓔval-cenis@fuaj.org; closed April–May & mid-Sept to mid-Oct); alternatively, try the comfortable, rustic *Hôtel de la Vieille Poste* (Ⓣ04.79.05.93.47, Ⓦwww.lavieilleposte.com; ❸; closed Nov–June).

Modane

MODANE, 20km downstream from Lanslebourg, is where the Arc valley starts to cut down dramatically through the high plateau down towards Chambéry. It's a dreary little place, destroyed by Allied bombing in 1943 and now little more than a rail junction. Nonetheless, it's a good kicking-off point for walkers on the south side of the **Vanoise Massif**, the area contained between the upper valleys of the Isère and Arc rivers. It's easily accessible by train from Chambéry and has a **tourist office**, in place Sommeiller (Mon–Sat 9am–noon & 2–6pm; ⓣ04.79.05.28.58, ⓦwww.canton-de-modane.com), which will give advice on walks in the surrounding area. If you want to **stay**, try the simple but clean *Hôtel Le Commerce*, 20 place Sommeiller (ⓣ04.79.05.00.78; ③), or the well-sited grassy municipal **campsite**, *Les Combes* (ⓣ04.79.05.00.23), just up the road to the Fréjus tunnel (which leads to Bardonecchia in Italy).

Grenoble

Beautifully situated on the Drac and Isère rivers, and surrounded by mountains, **GRENOBLE**, the self-styled "capital of the Alps", is a lively, modern city,

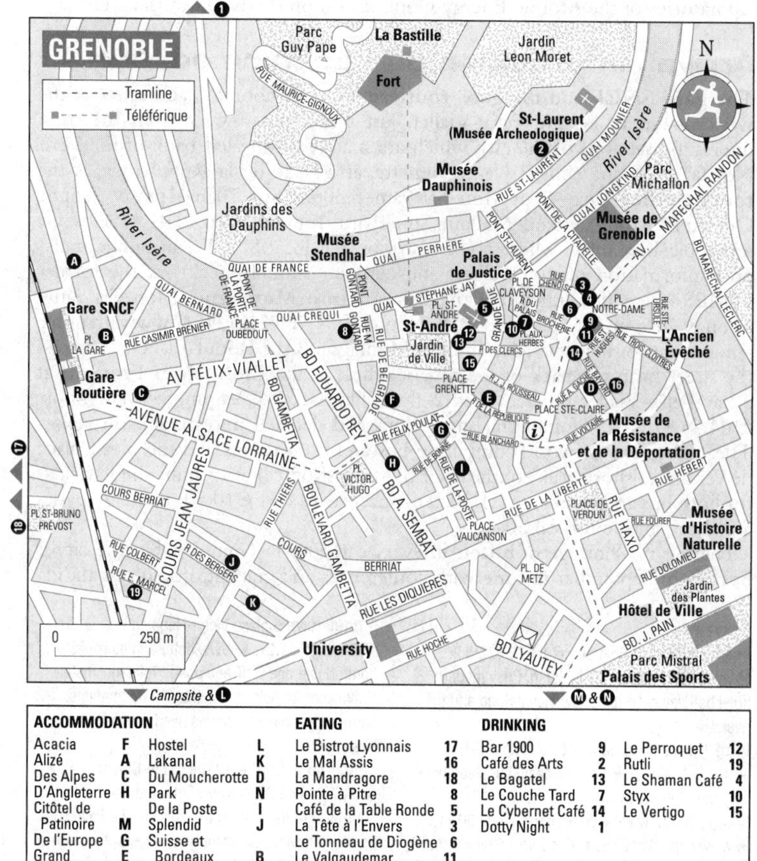

City passes

Many of the city museums no longer charge admission fees, but it still may be worth it to buy a **city pass** from the tourist office (one-day pass €12). This will allow you a guided tour of the old town, admission to one of the fee-charging museums (such as the Musée de Grenoble), a return trip on the *téléférique* and a ride on the little tourist train.

home to several universities and more than 50,000 students. In the Middle Ages, the princes of Dauphiné held court here, until the province was annexed by France in the fourteenth century, and the city is also famous for the Journée des Tuiles, a local uprising in 1788 which is held to be the first act of the French Revolution. Grenoble's prosperity was originally founded on glove-making, but in the nineteenth century its economy diversified to include mining, cement, paper milling, hydroelectric power and metallurgy. Its international profile was boosted in 1968, when it hosted the Winter Olympics, and today it's a centre of the chemical and electronics industries and nuclear research, with the big, new laboratories of the Atomic Energy Commission on the banks of the Drac.

Arrival, information and accommodation

The **gare SNCF** and the **gare routière** are next door to each other at the western end of avenue Félix-Viallet, just ten minutes' walk from the most interesting sections of the city, which are mainly on the left bank of the Isère. Not far from the central place Grenette, at 14 rue de la République, is the **tourist office** (May–Sept Mon–Sat 9am–6.30pm, Sun 10am–1pm & 2–5pm; Oct–April Mon–Sat 9am–6.30pm, Sun 10am–1pm; Ⓣ04.76.42.41.41, Ⓦwww.grenoble-isere.info), where you'll also find the local SNCF and public transport information offices. Walkers and climbers should check out the former CIMES office, now known as the **Bureau Info Montagne** (Mon–Fri 9am–noon & 2–6pm, Sat 10am–noon & 2–5pm; Ⓣ04.76.42.45.90, Ⓦwww.grenoble-montagne.com), in the Maison de la Montagne, 3 rue Raoul-Blanchard, across the street from the back of the tourist office, or the **Club Alpin Français** at 32 av Félix-Viallet (Tues & Wed 2–6pm, Thurs & Fri 2–8pm, Sat 9am–noon; Ⓣ04.76.87.03.73) for hiking suggestions and detailed information on *refuges*. The **transport** network, combining bus and tram routes, has the bleak place de Verdun (a short walk southeast of the tourist office) as its hub. Single tickets for both bus and tram cost €1.30, ten-ticket strips cost €10.50, and daily passes are also available for €3.50.

There is no shortage of **hotels** in every category in Grenoble, but the city is busy from September to June with conferences and graduations, so call ahead.

Hotels

Acacia 13 rue de Belgrade Ⓣ04.76.87.29.90, Ⓦwww.hotelacaciagrenoble.com. Cosy modern hotel halfway between place Victor-Hugo and the river. ❸

Alizé 1 place de la Gare Ⓣ04.76.43.12.91, Ⓕ04.76.47.62.79. Extremely basic but clean hotel very near the *gare SNCF*. ❶

Des Alpes 45 av Félix-Viallet Ⓣ04.76.87.00.71, Ⓦwww.hotel-des-alpes.fr. Good-value, family-run hotel near the *gare SNCF*, with small plain rooms. ❸

D'Angleterre 5 place Victor-Hugo Ⓣ04.76.87.37.21, Ⓦwww.hotel-angleterre.fr. Comfortable and well-equipped "Tulip Inn" hotel, convenient for both the sights and the stations. Some rooms have balconies overlooking the square. ❹

Citôtel de Patinoire 12 rue Marie-Chamoux Ⓣ04.76.44.43.65, Ⓦwww.hotel-patinoire.com. Southeast of the city centre, close to the Palais des Sports, this is an excellent mid-range option with a generous breakfast at €6.50. ❸

De l'Europe 22 place Grenette ⓣ04.76.46.16.94, ⓦwww.hoteleurope.fr. Well-maintained and hospitable place smack on Grenoble's liveliest square. ❸
Grand 5 rue de la République ⓣ04.76.44.49.36, ⓦwww.grand-hotel-grenoble.com. Smart nineteenth-century hotel in the centre of town, not far from the tourist office. ❺
Lakanal 26 rue des Bergers ⓣ04.76.46.03.42, ⓕ04.76.17.21.24. The cheapest beds in town, and it's not hard to see why, as they are dingy, dark and out of the way, but this budget option often has space when others are full. A little off the beaten path, a 10min walk southwest of place Victor-Hugo, near the tram stop "Gambetta". ❷
Du Moucherotte 1 rue Auguste-Gaché, near place Ste-Claire ⓣ04.76.54.61.40, ⓕ04.76.44.62.52. Surprisingly opulent decor and high ceilings accompany the peeling paint and wallpaper in this small, conveniently located hotel in the popular student quarter. ❷
Park 10 place Paul-Mistral ⓣ04.76.85.81.23, ⓦwww.park-hotel-grenoble.fr. Luxury four-star hotel, with a magnificent facade looking out onto one of the old town's liveliest squares, west of Parc Mistral. ❾
De la Poste 25 rue de la Poste ⓣ & ⓕ04.76.46.67.25. Tiny, friendly and rather old-fashioned establishment beginning on the third floor of an apartment building and located on a pedestrian street, off place Vaucanson. ❷
Splendid 22 rue Thiers ⓣ04.76.46.33.12, ⓦwww.splendid-hotel.com. The walls are all painted with different pastel-style murals in this all-en-suite two-star. It's a quiet, mid-range hotel, a 10min walk from the commercial centre. ❹
Suisse et Bordeaux 6 place de la Gare ⓣ04.76.47.55.87, ⓦwww.hotel-sb-grenoble.com. Friendly and clean hotel across from the *gare SNCF*. ❸

Hostel and campsite

Hostel 10 av de Gresivaudan ⓣ04.76.09.33.52, ⓔgrenoble@fuaj.org. Modern and recently renovated hostel 5km south of the city in Echirolles. Take bus #1 to "Quinzaine," or tram A to "La Rampe." €15.70 including breakfast, non-members €2.90 extra.
Camping des Trois Pucelles 58 rue des Allobroges, in Seyssins on the left bank of the Drac, 4km west of town ⓣ04.76.96.45.73, ⓦwww.camping-trois-pucelles.com. Take tram A to "Albert 1er", and change to bus #5 for "Mas des Iles," or take bus #23.

The City

The best way to start your tour is to take the **téléférique** (opening times are complex but approximately daily: April–Sept 10am–midnight; Nov–March 11am–6.30pm; ⓣ04.76.44.33.65, ⓦwww.bastille-grenoble.com) from the riverside quai Stéphane-Jay to **Fort de la Bastille** on the steep slopes above the north bank of the Isère. The ride is hair-raising, as you're whisked steeply and swiftly into the air in a sort of transparent egg, which allows you to see very clearly how far you would fall in the event of an accident. If you don't like the sound of the cable car, you can climb the steep but pleasant footpath from the St-Laurent church or from the Musée Dauphinois (see p.1007).

Although the fort is of little interest, the **view** is fantastic. At your feet the Isère flows under the old bridges which join the St-Laurent quarter, colonized by Italian immigrants in the nineteenth century, to the nucleus of the medieval town, whose red roofs cluster tightly around the church of St-André. To the east, snowfields gleam in the gullies of the Belledonne massif (2978m). Southeast is Taillefer and south-southeast the dip where the Route Napoléon passes over the mountains to Sisteron and the Mediterranean – this is the road Napoleon took after his escape from Elba in March 1815 on his way to rally his forces for the campaign that led to his final defeat at Waterloo. To the west are the steep white cliffs of the Vercors massif; the highest peak, dominating the city, is Moucherotte (1901m). The jagged summits at your back are the outworks of the Chartreuse massif. Northeast on a clear day you can see the white peaks of Mont Blanc up the deep glacial valley of the Isère, known as La Grésivaudan. It was in this valley that the first French hydroelectric project went into action in 1869. For heading back into town, a path down through the public gardens offers an alternative to the cable car.

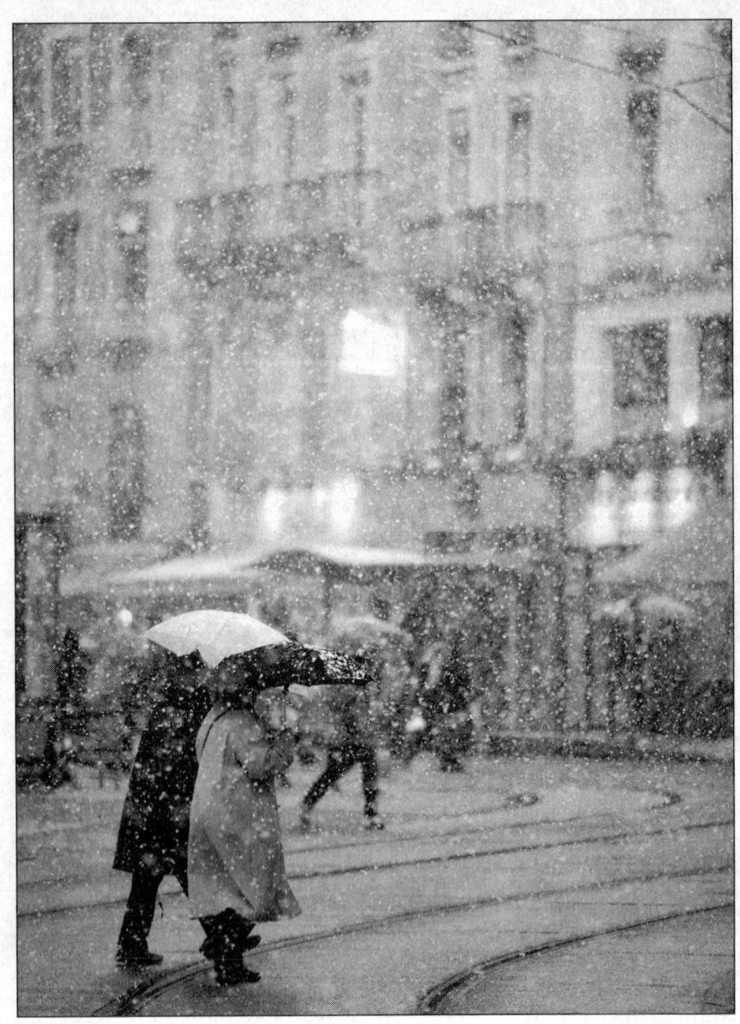

△ Grenoble

Upstream from the *téléférique* station is the sixteenth-century **Palais de Justice** (open to the public), with place St-André and the **church of St-André** behind. Built in the thirteenth century, the church once served as the palace chapel of the princes of Dauphiné, though it has been heavily restored since, and today is of little architectural interest. Meanwhile, the narrow streets leading towards places Grenette, Vaucanson and Verdun pass through the liveliest and most colourful quarter of the city. Life focuses on a chain of little squares – aux Herbes, Claveyson, de Gordes, Grenette and Notre-Dame – where people congregate at the numerous cafés and restaurants. The small produce **market** (Tues–Sun 6am–1pm) on place aux Herbes is a great place to stock up on inexpensive local produce.

Close to place St-André, in the former town hall at 1 rue Hector-Berlioz, in the corner of the Jardin de Ville gardens, is the **Musée Stendhal** (mid-July to mid-Sept Tues–Sat 9am–noon & 2–6pm; mid-Sept to mid-July Tues–Sat 2–6pm; closed all hols; free), with a couple of rooms containing family portraits and manuscripts associated with the much-revered author, who was born in Grenoble as Marie-Henri Beyle. You can also visit his grandfather's house, **La Maison Stendhal**, where he spent his childhood, at 20 Grande-Rue, just off place Grenette (same hours as the Musée (mid-July to mid-Sept 9am–noon & 2–6pm; mid-Sept to mid-July Tues–Sat 10am–noon; free).

Near the bustling place Notre-Dame, on the riverbank at 5 place de Lavalette, is the **Musée de Grenoble** (daily except Tues 10am–6.30pm; €5), an enormous modern complex housing a gallery of mainly contemporary art. The building itself is impressive, and many major schools of painting are represented, including a few works by Rubens and Canaletto, though the collection is uneven. The best rooms are those of nineteenth- and twentieth-century artists including Gauguin, Chagall and Matisse. Directly on the east side of place Notre-Dame is **L'Ancien Évêché** (daily except Sun 9am–6pm, Sun 10am–7pm; free). Housed in the old bishop's palace, the museum offers a brisk tour through Grenoble's history from the Stone Age to the twentieth century. The remains of the Roman town walls and a fifth-century **baptistry** are on show in the basement, while among the prized exhibits upstairs are Neolithic jade jewellery, Bronze Age weapons and a wealth of Roman artefacts, including a colourful mosaic floor panel, decorated with a pair of parrots.

On the opposite bank of the Isère, the **Musée Archéologique Église St-Laurent**, on place St-Laurent (closed until mid-2007 for renovation – check ⓦwww.musee-archeologique-grenoble.com for new opening times) gives a fascinating insight into the history of the city, as you descend through various stages of excavations in this former church, passing through an early Christian necropolis, an eighth-century crypt and a high medieval cloister. A few minutes to the west, lying up a steep cobbled path opposite the St-Laurent footbridge, the **Musée Dauphinois**, 30 rue Maurice-Gignoux (May–Oct daily except Tues 10am–7pm; Nov–April 10am–6pm; free), housed in the former convent of Ste-Marie-d'en-Haut, is largely devoted to the history, arts and crafts of the province of Dauphiné. There are exhibits on the lives of the rugged and self-sufficient mountain people, including mock-ups of the modest rustic homes that they shared with their animals during the seven-month long winters. There's also an exhibition illustrating the history of skiing, and, in the basement, a splendid Baroque chapel, with grey and gold wall paintings depicting episodes from the New Testament and scenes from the life of St-François-de-Sales, who founded the convent in the seventeenth century.

Wedged between the park and the old town at 14 rue Hébert is the **Musée de la Résistance et de la Déportation de l'Isère** (daily except Tues: July & Aug 10am–7pm; Sept–June 9am–6pm; free), with a touching and high-tech exhibition of photographs, video footage and memorabilia from the brutal Nazi occupation of the Dauphiné, with all captions translated into English. Two blocks south, standing among the fine trees of the Jardin des Plantes at 1 rue Dolomieu is the **Muséum d'Histoire Naturelle** (Mon–Fri 9.30am–noon & 1.30–5.30pm, Sat, Sun and hols 2–6pm; €3.80). It has a marvellous collection, ranking second after the Paris museum for sheer depth and breadth – it includes, amongst many other things, all the Alpine birds of prey and an aquarium.

Eating, drinking and nightlife

Eating in Grenoble is a pleasure; it's less expensive than nearby Lyon but just as creative. There are a wide variety of **restaurants** catering to all budgets and tastes – a call ahead is recommended for most of the places listed below, especially in the evenings. For those with a knowledge of French, it's useful to pick up a copy of the *Guide Dahu* in local *tabacs* – a restaurant and nightlife guide compiled by local students (€2.50).

Interesting, atmospheric places to drink are also easy to find, with places Grenette, St-André and Notre-Dame full of **café-bars**, though the more interesting ones are usually on the streets between those squares. On place Notre-Dame, try *Bar 1900* or *Le Shaman Café*, which also has good food, while on place St-André, *Le Bagatel* and *Le Perroquet* are particularly popular. If you're looking for a local bohemian hangout, try the *Café des Arts* over the bridge at 36 rue St-Laurent or *Le Cybernet Café* at 3 rue Bayard, which despite its name has no Internet access, while on place Claveyson you could also drop into *Styx*, an atmospheric little cocktail bar in a nineteenth-century wine cellar. The popular **gay** establishment, *Rutli*, is west of the old town at 9 rue Étienne-Marcel (daily 6pm–1am). Grenoble's student population keeps the **nightlife** hopping, with clubs like *Le Vertigo*, 18 Grande-Rue (Wed–Sat 10.30pm–5.30am), one of the liveliest venues. *Dotty Night*, 56 rte de Lyon (daily except Mon 11pm–5.30am), 500m north of the Pont de la Porte de France, caters for a slightly older crowd and *Le Couche Tard* (☎04.76.44.18.79; 8pm–2am) in between place aux Herbes and place du Tribunal is the most anglicized bar, buzzing with exchange students.

Restaurants

Le Bistrot Lyonnais 168 cours Berriat ☎04.76.21.95.33. It's worth the walk behind the *gare SNCF* to try the food from this charming restaurant's truffle-infused menu. Menus from €30 for lunch, €39 dinner. Closed Sat, Sun and three weeks in Aug.

Le Mal Assis 9 rue Bayard ☎04.76.54.75.93. A small and elegant traditional family-run restaurant, serving dishes with a Provençal flavour and an excellent wine *carte*; à la carte from around €16. Closed Sun, Mon and mid-July to Aug.

La Mandragore 11 rue Marx-Dormoy ☎04.76.96.18.95. Terrific vegetarian restaurant, serving extraordinarily creative and tasty green cuisine. The menu changes daily, and even meat-eaters will leave satisfied. Vegan meals can be supplied upon request. Lunch *plat du jour* €12. Near the St Bruno stop (one stop west of the train station on tram lines A or B). Closed Sat night plus all day Sun & Mon.

Pointe à Pitre 2 rue Marius-Gontard ☎04.76.47.26.10. Extremely friendly restaurant serving up specialities from the French Caribbean at reasonable prices, though it's à la carte only, with *plats* from €10. Daily 7pm–1am.

Café de la Table Ronde 7 place St-André ☎04.76.44.51.41. While not famous for its food – local fare which never quite rises above average quality – this is an atmospheric place, notable for being the second oldest restaurant in France (1739), numbering among its clients Rousseau and Léon Blum. Menus from €22 to €34.

La Tête à l'Envers 10 rue Chenoise ☎04.76.51.13.42. It's a one-man show in this tiny restaurant. What it lacks in size it makes up in sheer creativity – a new menu every other day includes a plate of four appetizers (€9.50), entrées served with eight different vegetables (from €11.50), and a plate of six desserts (€9.50) – guess the flavourings of five of the six and win a free coffee or *digestif*. Closed Sun, Mon and Aug.

Le Tonneau de Diogène place Notre-Dame ☎04.76.42.38.40. A cheap standby, with uninspiring *steak-frites*-type cuisine, but incredibly popular with tourists and a good place to meet fellow travellers. Meals from under €15. Closed Sun eve and Mon lunch.

Le Valgaudemar 2 rue St-Hugues ☎04.76.51.38.85. Referred to affectionately by students as Le Valgo, this cosy, rustic-styled haven in the heart of Grenoble serves traditional specialities of the Hautes-Alpes. Lunch from €11 and dinner from €17. Closed Sun and Mon, Tues and Wed eve, and Aug.

Listings

Bike rental Cycle des Arts, 14 rue des Arts ☎04.76.47.18.83; Veloparc Gare, 1 place de la Gare ☎04.76.85.08.94; Metrovelo Gare, 1 place de la Gare ☎08.20.22.38.38.

Bookshop Arthand, 23 Grande-Rue, sells some English-language books.
Car rental ADA, 1 place de la Gare ⓣ04.76.43.00.36; Avis, *gare SNCF* ⓣ04.76.47.11.33 & 22 cours Jean-Jaurès ⓣ04.76.86.62.50; Budget, 30 rue Émile-Gueymard ⓣ04.76.46.66.90; Europcar, *gare SNCF* ⓣ04.76.86.27.81; Hertz, *gare SNCF* ⓣ04.76.86.55.80; Self Car, 24 rue Émile-Gueymard ⓣ04.76.50.96.96.
Internet Neptune, 2 rue de la Paix (Mon–Sat 9am–10pm, Sun 1–8pm); Pl@net On-Line, 1 place Vaucanson (Mon–Sat 10am–1am, Sun 1–10pm).
Medical emergencies Centre Hospitalier Universitaire ⓣ04.76.76.75.75; ambulance Alp'Azur ⓣ04.76.21.11.11.
Pharmacy Pharmacie Bethalet, 8 place Victor-Hugo; Pharmacie du Château d'Eau, 6 place Grenette; late-night and hols call ⓣ04.76.63.42.55 for the *pharmacie de garde*.
Police 36 bd Maréchal-Leclerc ⓣ04.76.60.40.40.
Taxi 14 rue République, 24hr radio taxi service ⓣ04.76.54.42.54.

The Vercors and Chartreuse massifs

The **Vercors massif** and **Chartreuse massif** are very close to Grenoble, particularly the Vercors, which stretches out to the southwest of the city, parallel to the River Drac on the west side of the N75. Chartreuse is north of the city, running up the west bank of the River Isère towards Chambéry.

Both ranges are relatively gentle, making them ideal practice for less experienced walkers. The Grenoble **Bureau Info Montagne** (BIM) office (see p.1004) publishes route descriptions. Neither massif is heavily populated, and the lack of industry makes them authentic and unspoilt Alpine destinations, popular with all types of energetic outdoor enthusiasts from cavers to mountain bikers.

The Vercors massif

The limestone plateau of ridges and valleys that comprise the **Vercors massif** is a beautiful oasis of undeveloped tranquility teeming with wildlife, including chamois, mouflon and marmots. The area's proximity to Grenoble is reflected in restaurants and hotel prices, however, and there is often congestion on the little mountain roads. The #5100 **bus** leaves from the *gare routière* in Grenoble for the park's larger towns several times a day. BIM leaflets detail a number of walks of varying difficulty around the area from the simplest and most accessible to St-Nizier, detailed below, to other good but more strenuous walks, such as Villard-de-Lans to Claix, near Grenoble (1700m descent; 7hr), and the circuit of Mont Aiguille, starting from Clelles (1hr by train south of Grenoble; 6hr 30min–9hr).

St-Nizier-du-Moucherotte

The easiest of the CIMES walks is a four-hour circular walk to **ST-NIZIER-DU-MOUCHEROTTE**, just over the rim of the Vercors massif, with a fantastic view of the whole area. Start by taking bus #5 from place Victor-Hugo in Grenoble and get off in Seyssinet village by the school. The path starts about 200m uphill from the school on the right. For most of the way you follow GR9 with its red-and-white waymarks. It's not difficult, but the path crosses the D106 a few times, and the continuation is not always obvious, so it's worth getting the leaflet. It's about two and a half hours to St-Nizier (return the same way) through beautiful thick woods with long views back over Grenoble to the mountains beyond. The lovely purplish martagon lily blooms in the woods in early July. It's a further three and a half hours (there and back) to the top of Moucherotte on GR91.

Villard-de-Lans to La Chapelle

The D531 winds up to the park from Sassenage, emerging onto a plateau of hay meadows before the village of **VILLARD-DE-LANS** a good base for exploring the Vercors. There's a **tourist office** (daily 9am–12.30pm & 2–7pm; ⓣ04.76.95.10.38, ⓦwww.villarddelans.com) with information about walks and skiing. **Accommodation** in town includes: the welcoming and neat *Villa Primerose*, 147 av des Bains (ⓣ04.76.95.13.17, ⓦwww.hotel-villa-primerose.com; closed Nov; ❸), with self-catering facilities available in a communal kitchen; and the smart *Hôtel Le Christiania*, 220 av Professeur-Nobécourt (ⓣ04.76.95.12.51, ⓦwww.hotel-le-christiania.fr; ❻; closed May, Oct & Nov). There's **camping** at *L'Oursière*, just north of town (ⓣ04.76.95.14.77, ⓦwww.camping-oursiere.fr).

Beyond Villard-de-Lans are the **Gorges de la Bourne** where the road cuts in under the rocks almost shutting out the sky above. A left turn (signposted St-Martin) brings you to **LA CHAPELLE**, where you can stay at the friendly, reasonably priced *Hôtel des Sports* (ⓣ04.75.48.20.39, ⓦwww.hotel-des-sports.com; ❸), which also offers advice on local cycling routes. From La Chapelle the road climbs again to the wide dry plateau of Vassieux, bordered to the east by a rocky ridge rising from thick pine forest and to the west by low hills covered with scrubby vegetation. Nearby are the **Grottes de Choranche**, beautiful caves which contain gigantic stalactites. Part of the complex, the Grotte de Coufin, can be visited by guided tour (April & Oct every 30min 10am–noon & 1.30–6pm; May, June & Sept every 30min 9.30am–noon & 1.30–6pm; July & Aug every 20min 9.30am–6.30pm; Nov–March hourly 10.30am–4.30pm; €7.70).

Vassieux-en-Vercors

It was around the village of **VASSIEUX-EN-VERCORS**, 10km south of La Chapelle, that the fighters of the Vercors maquis suffered a bloody and bitter defeat at the hands of the SS in July 1944. During 1942–43 they had been gradually turning the Vercors into a Resistance stronghold, to the annoyance of the Germans and the French militia. The Germans finally, in June 1944, decided to wipe them out. They encircled and attacked the *maquisards* with vastly superior forces and parachuted an SS division into Vassieux. The French appealed in vain for Allied support and were very bitter about the lack of response. The Germans took vicious reprisals and, despite their attempts to disperse into the woods, 700 *maquisards* and civilians were killed and several villages razed. The Germans' most ferocious act was to murder the wounded, along with their nurses and doctors, in the **Grotte de la Luire** (April–Oct), a cave off the La Chapelle–Col de Rousset road.

Vassieux itself, a dull little village now rebuilt, has a memorial cemetery and small museum, the **Memorial de la Résistance du Vercors** (April–Sept daily 10am–6pm; Oct–March 10am–5pm; €5), with documents, photos and other memorabilia to do with the maquis and the battle. In the field outside are the remains of two gliders used by the German paratroops. Also near the town, is the **Musée de la Préhistoire** (same times and price), built over the site of a 4000-year-old flint mine and axe works; it contains various tools and relics that have been found there. If you want to **stay**, try the comfortable *Auberge du Tétras Lyre* in rue Abbé-Gagnol (ⓣ04.75.48.28.04, ⓦwww.tetraslyre.com; ❸; restaurant with menus from €15).

Die to Châtillon

From Vassieux, the **Col de Rousset** road winds south through 8km of woods of pine and fir before taking the final steep twisting descent of 10km to Die, with terrific views of the white crags and pinnacles of the southeast end of the massif. Although it's an attractive little place, **DIE** is worth no more than a brief stop to sample the local *crémant* (sparkling white wine), Clairette de

Die, which can be tasted and bought in the *caves* surrounding the town. **La Cave de Die Jaillance** on avenue de la Clairette offers a free tour and tasting (ⓣ04.75.22.30.15; daily: July–Aug 9am–7pm; Sept–June 9am–12.30pm & 2–6.30pm). There's a **tourist office** on rue des Jardins (July & Aug Mon–Sat 9am–7pm; Sept–June Mon–Sat 9am–noon & 2–6pm, Sun 9.30am–12.30pm; ⓣ04.75.22.03.03, ⓦwww.diois-tourisme.com). If you plan to **stay** the night here, try the modest but comfortable *Hôtel St-Dominique*, 44 rue Camille-Buffardel (ⓣ04.75.22.03.08, ⓕ04.75.22.24.48; ❸). There are also five **campsites**, the cheapest being the *Camping de Justin* in the quartier du Pont Rompu (ⓣ04.75.22.14.77, ⓦwww.camping-die.com; closed Oct–Dec) on the edge of town. *La Dolce Vita* **restaurant** on place de l'Horloge serves Italian-influenced menus from €11–29, including pizzas.

Six kilometres south along the River Drôme at the Pont de Quart the road forks left for **CHÂTILLON**, a lovely village lying in a narrowing valley bottom and surrounded by apple and peach orchards, vineyards, walnut trees and fields of lavender. You can stay at the *Hôtel du Dauphiné* on place Dévoluy (ⓣ04.75.21.13.13, ⓔhoteldudauphine@wanadoo.fr; ❸), which has eight clean and simple rooms; alternatively, there are three campsites nearby.

The Chartreuse massif and Grande Chartreuse monastery

The Chartreuse massif, designated in 1995 as the **Parc Naturel Régional de Chartreuse** (ⓦwww.parc-chartreuse.net), stretches north from Grenoble towards Chambéry and, like Vercors, is not easy to visit without your own vehicle. The landscape, however, is spectacular and very different to that of the Vercors: precipitous limestone peaks, mountain pastures and thick forest.

Grande Chartreuse Monastery

The massif's main local landmark is the **Grande Chartreuse Monastery**, situated up the narrow Gorges des Guiers Morts, southeast of St-Laurent-du-Pont, and some 35km from Grenoble, one of nineteen Carthusian monasteries still functioning worldwide. The Carthusian Order, dating from the eleventh century, was the last great monastic reform movement, and was founded in answer to the degeneration of the Cistercian Order. Practising a strictly hermit-like existence, its members live in cells and meet only for Mass and a weekly communal meal, eaten in silence. Since 1605, however, the Carthusians have been better known as the producers of **Chartreuses** – powerfully alcoholic herbal elixirs, ranging from the better-known green and yellow variants to a number of gentler fruit liqueurs. The monastery is not open to the public, but near the village of **ST-PIERRE-DE-CHARTREUSE**, 5km back on the Grenoble road, you can visit the **Musée de la Grande Chartreuse**, formerly La Correrie monastery, which illustrates the life of the Carthusian Order (daily: April & Oct 10am–noon & 2–6pm; May, June & Sept 9.30am–noon & 2–6.30pm; July & Aug 9.30am–6.30pm; €4; ⓦwww.musee-grande-chartreuse.fr).

Voiron

For those less interested in religious austerity and more interested in that mysterious green liqueur, a visit to **VOIRON**, 30km west of the park and on the train line from Grenoble to Lyon, is in order. The **Caves de la Chartreuse** on boulevard Edgar-Kofler (April–June & Sept–Oct daily 9–11.30am & 2–6.30pm; July & Aug daily 9am–6.30pm; Nov–March Mon–Fri 9–11.30am & 2–5.30pm; free) are where the "elixir of life" is now bottled. The tour is good fun – it takes visitors through the world's largest liqueur cellars, and includes a rather corny 3-D film on the history of the monastery and a tasting of one of the monks' alcoholic beverages. The town's **tourist office** is at 30 cours Becquart-Castelbon (Mon–Sat 9am–noon & 2–6pm; Ⓣ04.76.05.00.38; Ⓦwww.paysvoironnais.info). There's not much else to see in Voiron, which is best known as the home of the Rossignol ski factory, but if you're looking for a **hotel**, try the small but comfortable *La Chaumière* (Ⓣ04.76.05.16.24, Ⓕ04.76.05.13.27; ❸).

Grenoble to Briançon

Connecting Grenoble to Briançon, the **N91** twists through the precipitous valley of the Romanche and over the **Col du Lautaret** (2058m), which is kept open all year round and served regularly by the Grenoble–Briançon bus. As well as being an exciting foretaste of the high mountain scenery to come, this route offers the opportunity for some worthwhile detours, including the climb across the **Col du Galibier** to **Valloire** and some fine mountain hikes above the modern ski resort of **L'Alpe d'Huez**, which is perched on the northern slopes of the Romanche valley above the attractive town of **Le Bourg-d'Oisans**. On the southern slopes is the sprawling village of **Les Deux-Alpes**, which has been wholly subsumed by the skiing industry, while close to Briançon another modern resort, **Serre Chevalier**, has been created around five farming hamlets.

Le Bourg-d'Oisans

The first major settlement on the route, **LE BOURG-D'OISANS**, 20km southeast of Grenoble, is of no great interest in itself, but it's a good place to catch your breath. You can pick up information from the **tourist office**, on quai Girard, by the river in the middle of town (July & Aug 9am–7pm; Sept–June Mon–Sat 9am–noon & 2–6pm; Ⓣ04.76.80.03.25, Ⓦwww.oisans.com), and the **Maison du Parc National des Écrins** on rue Gambetta (July & Aug 8am–noon & 3–7pm; Sept–June Mon–Fri 8am–noon & 2–5.30pm; Ⓣ04.76.80.00.51). There are some good-value **hotels** here, among them *L'Oberland*, on avenue de la Gare (Ⓣ04.76.80.24.24, Ⓦwww.hoteloberland.com; ❹), and the *Hôtel Le Florentin* at 8 rue Thiers (Ⓣ04.76.80.01.61, Ⓦwww.le-florentin.com; ❸). There's also a municipal **campsite** on rue Humbert near the town centre and a concentration of sites across the river on the Alpe d'Huez road. If you like the idea of cycling in vigorous mountain air, **bikes** can be rented from Cycles d'Oisans on rue Viennois – not such a crazy undertaking as you might think if you keep to the valley bottoms where the gradients aren't too fearsome.

L'Alpe d'Huez and around

One place you're unlikely to be cycling to is the ski resort of **L'ALPE D'HUEZ**, signposted just outside Le Bourg. It's situated more than a vertical kilometre above the valley floor, and the eleven-kilometre road, which crawls up the valley side, is often used as a stage in the Tour de France. As you ascend through the 21 hairpins, there's a fine view of the acutely crumpled strata of rock exposed by passing glaciers on the south side of the Romanche valley. Undoubtedly a skier's paradise in winter, the purpose-built resort itself has little character in July and August.

L'Alpe d'Huez became famous during the 1968 Olympics for its melting bobsleigh, and was also the birthplace of the ski lift when in 1936 Jean

Pomagalski invented the first toe, a rope attached to a modified tractor engine which pulled skiers up the slope. Beginner toes, now known as *Pomas* the world over, radiate out from the village's sunny south-facing slopes. Beyond these, an extensive network of *télécabines* and *téléphériques* whisk skiers to the **Pic Blanc** (3330m), at the bottom of the Chaîne des Rousses ridge, from which two mammoth black runs, over two kilometres in length, descend; skiing is possible here is summer too. As well as skiing, the *télécabines* can also be used to undertake some superb **high mountain walks**. Two recommended ones (details from the tourist office – see below), are the eight-kilometre Lac Blanc and *Refuge de la Fare* walk, which winds through the bleak wilderness past the lakes encircling the Dôme des Petites Rousses to the east of the glacier-clad *chaîne*, and the less exposed ten-kilometre hike to the gorges of the Sarennes valley, to the east of the resort along the **GR54**.

Practicalities

L'Alpe d'Huez's **tourist office** in the Maison de l'Alpe, in place Paganon (May–Nov daily 9am–12.30pm & 2.30–6pm, Dec–April daily 9am–7pm; ⓣ04.76.11.44.44, ⓦwww.alpedhuez.com), provides detailed walking and mountain biking maps; the Maison also houses the ESF **ski school** office (ⓣ04.76.80.31.69, ⓦwww.esf-alpedhuez.com). Good places to stay, both in Huez en Oisans below the main village, include *chambres d'hôtes* at *Florineige* (ⓣ04.76.80.94.89, ⓦwww.hebergement-florineige.com; ❸), and *Hôtel L'Ancolie* (ⓣ04.76.11.13.13, same website; ❻). Yves, who runs both establishments with his wife Sylvie, is a ski instructor in winter and a mountain guide in summer, so a very useful host.

Les Deux-Alpes

Five kilometres beyond Le Bourg-d'Oisans on the N91 begins the ascent up to the **Gorges de l'Infernet**. The slate-black valley walls close around you before broadening out again as you cross the Barrage du Lac du Chambon. Here the road divides; the N91 continues around the lake towards La Grave and the Col du Lautaret, while a right turn leads to the resort of **Les Deux-Alpes,** on a high hanging valley.

A consequence of a massive tourism drive, the two farming communities that once made up Les Deux-Alpes have been now buried beneath a blanket of unplanned urban sprawl. The resort is a favourite with young **skiers**, particularly students, from across Europe, as well from nearby Grenoble, who come as much for its lively weekend après-ski as for its high, gentle slopes, ideal for **snowboarding**. It's definitely not for everyone, with its burgeoning snow parks pumping out rap music around jumps adorned with graffiti, but it does offer some useful facilities – in summer thousands of **mountain bikers** and **parapante** gliders descend on the resort to make use of its ski lifts and thermal currents. The high glacier on Dôme de Puy Salé, accessed via the Jandri ski lift, has a **grotte de glace** (€20), with impressive sculptures carved out of its ice walls, as well as three summer skiing slopes.

The **tourist office**, situated between the Jandri ski lifts on place des Deux-Alpes (ⓣ04.76.79.22.00, ⓦwww.les2alpes.com), has lists of self-catering apartments for rent, and gives information on local activities. Cheap **accommodation** options include an HI hostel (ⓣ04.76.79.22.80, ⓔles-deux-alpes@fuaj.org), where beds in a small dorm cost €11, and *Alpenzym*, 8 rue Ste-Luce (ⓣ04.76.79.08.38, ⓦwww.alpenzym.fr; open year-round; €36 per person half-board in 4 to 10-person bunk-bedded rooms), a 32-bed hostel on the slopes behind the ESF ski school office on avenue de la Muzelle.

La Grave and the Col du Lautaret

Continuing on the N91 towards La Grave you'll pass two waterfalls issuing from the north side of the valley: early summer run-off enhances the slender, 300-metre plume of the **Cascade de la Pisse**, while, 6km further on, the near-vertical fall of churning white water called the **Saut de la Pucelle** ("the virgin's leap") is a breathtaking sight.

LA GRAVE, 18km on from the Barrage du Lac du Chambon, lies at the foot of the Col du Lautaret, facing the majestic glaciers of the north side of **La Meije**. The small collection of stone buildings that make up the village are a Mecca to climbers and extreme skiers. It's a good base for walking: the **GR54** climbs up to Le Chazelet on the slopes northwest of the village and continues to the **Plateau de Paris** and the **Lac Noir**, with breathtaking views of La Meije (3984m). An easier way to appreciate the stunning vistas is to take the *télécabine*, which rises sharply from the centre of the village to the 3200-metre summit of **Le Rateau**, just west of La Meije (mid-June to early Sept & late Dec to early May; €18 return), a 35-minute ride that's very good value for money when you consider that the view of the barely accessible interior of the Écrins (see opposite) is normally seen only by the most intrepid mountain walkers. The lift also provides access to acres of off-piste skiing, and the freezing conditions of the mountain's northerly face make it ideal for ice climbing. The **tourist office**, near the *télécabine* (ⓣ04.76.79.90.05, ⓦwww.lagrave-lameije.com) has plenty of information about guides and routes, while for **accommodation** make for the *chambres d'hôtes* at *La Roche Meane*, 3km east in Villar d'Arène (ⓣ04.76.79.91.43, ⓦwww.rochemeane.com; ⑥). This wonderful old stone farmhouse has been converted by mountain guide Xavier and his wife into a friendly guesthouse with colourful rooms, exposed stone walls and plenty of character.

From La Grave it's only 11km to the top of the **Col du Lautaret**, a pass that's been in use for centuries. The Roman road from Milan to Vienne crossed it, and its name comes from the small temple (*altaretum*) the Romans built to placate the deity of the mountains. Around the col is a huge expanse of meadow long known to botanists for its glorious variety of Alpine flowers, seen at their best in mid-July. You'll also find **Le Jardin Botanique Alpin du Lautaret**, founded in 1899 and maintained by the University of Grenoble (June–Sept daily 10am–6pm; €4); it displays plants from mountain ranges throughout the world.

The Col du Galibier and Valloire

Turn north at Lautaret and you're on your way to the even higher **Col du Galibier** (no public transport), which is closed by snow from mid-October to mid-June – sometimes the snow lingers longer, making life for riders in the Tour de France yet more hellish. The road to the pass is a tremendous haul up to 2556m, utterly bare and wild, with the huge red-veined peak of the Grand Galibier rearing up on the right and a fearsome spiny ridge blocking the horizon beyond. A monument on the south side of the col commemorates Henri Desgranges, founder of the Tour de France. Crossing the col is one of the most gruelling stages in the race, with a long, brutal ascent and terrifying descent at breakneck speed. The road loops down in hairpin after hairpin, through **VALLOIRE**, a sizeable ski resort, whose church is one of the most richly decorated in Savoie, then over the **Col du Télégraphe** (1570m) and down into the deep wooded valley of the Arc, known as **La Maurienne**, with the Massif de la Vanoise rising abruptly behind. Valloire has pleasant, reasonably priced **hotels** in *Le Tatami* (ⓣ04.79.59.06.08, ⓦwww.letatami.com; €525–630 per person per week compulsory half-board) and the *Christiania Hôtel* (ⓣ04.79.59.00.57, ⓦwww.christiania-hotel.com; ⑤; restaurant from €15).

Le Casset

LE CASSET, back on the Briançon road about 12km beyond the Col du Lautaret, is a hamlet of dilapidated old houses clustered around a church with a bulbous dome. There's nothing to see in the town but the site is superb, with the Glacier du Casset dazzling above the green of the larches. Parking here makes it easy to access the **GR54**; a good day's walk is to follow the path out of the village as far as the **Col d'Arsine** (about 3hr), from which point you can either turn back or go on down to La Grave on the north side of the park, making an overnight stop at the CAF *Refuge del'Alpe/Villar d'Arène* (ⓣ04.76.79.94.66), below the col.

Serre Chevalier

Strung out along the N91 as it follows the bottom of the Guisanne valley and just 9km west of Briançon, the skiing area of **SERRE CHEVALIER** is the collective name given to five traditional farming hamlets whose old wooden chalets have now been surrounded by small hotels and holiday homes. Saint-Chaffrey and Chantemerle form Serre Chevalier 1350 (at an altitude of 1350m), Villeneuve and La-Salle-les-Alpes make up Serre Chevalier 1400, and Le Monêtier-les-Bains is Serre Chevalier 1500. Each area is linked by a series of **ski lifts** and pistes which climb and descend the north-facing slopes of the valley, and there are ESF ski school offices in all three areas (ⓦwww.esf-serrechevalier.com), as well as plenty of shops from which to rent equipment. Of all the villages, **Le Monêtier-les-Bains** is the prettiest, its narrow streets weaving between old stone houses and rickety wooden balconies. The village has been a thermal spa since Roman times, with two hot-water springs, one at 34°C and one at 38°C, and baths which are currently under renovation and scheduled to open by the end of 2007.

The **tourist office** is in the centre ofVilleneuve (ⓣ04.92.24.98.98, ⓦwww.serre-chevalier.com), while the smartest **hotels** are in Le Monêtier-les-Bains; these include *Hôtel Alliey*, a modern boutique hotel with spa and pool (ⓣ04.92.24.44.20, ⓦwww.alliey.com; closed May & mid-Sept to mid-Dec; winter half-board ❾, summer ❻) and the more traditional *L'Auberge du Choucas* (ⓣ04.92.24.42.73, ⓦwww.aubergeduchoucas.com; closed May & Nov; ❻), which has an excellent gourmet restaurant serving menus between €29 and €60. *Les Marmottes* in Chantemerle (ⓣ04.92.24.11.17, ⓦperso.orange.fr/chalet.marmottes; ❹), a renovated farmhouse offering *chambres d'hôtes* is another good option. There's also a very nice **hostel** at Le Bez, 500m from the centre of Serre Chevalier 1400 (ⓣ04.92.24.74.54, ⓔserre-chevalier@fuaj.org), where a bed in a dorm costs €11.50.

The Hautes-Alpes: Briançon, the Écrins and the Queyras

The **Hautes-Alpes** are an area of high mountains between Savoie and the Vanoise to the north and the Alpes de Provence to the south. East is the Italian border and to the west, the River Drac and Grenoble. The region is sliced in two by the Durance valley with the **Parc National des Écrins** to the west and the **Parc Naturel Régional du Queyras** to the east. At the head of the Durance valley, where the Guisane and Durance rivers converge, the ancient fortified city of **Briançon** makes an excellent base for exploring the surrounding region.

Briançon

Located 100km east of Grenoble along the N91, **Briançon** is the capital of the Écrins and Europe's highest town. An imposing citadel, it looms on the cusp of a rocky outcrop, high above the Durance and Guisane valleys. Fortified originally by the Romans to guard the Mons Matrona from Milan to Vienne, the town is encircled by lofty ramparts and sheer walls constructed by Vauban in the seventeenth century. Today, despite its apparent remoteness, the town is a lively mix of students, military personnel and international tourists, with a surprisingly cosmopolitan feel.

The steep, narrow streets of the **ville haute**, high above the urban spread of the modern town, are the main focus of interest. There are four **gates**: portes Dauphine and Pignerol lie to the north, porte d'Embrun to the southwest and porte de la Durance to the east. If you come by car the best thing is to park at the **Champ de Mars** at the top of the hill and to enter the town through the porte Pignerol. From here the narrow main street – known as the *grande gargouille* because of the "gurgling" stream running down the middle – tips steeply downhill, bordered by mostly eighteenth-century houses. To the right is the sturdy plain **collegiate church**, designed under the supervision of Vauban, again with an eye to defence. Beyond it, there's a fantastic **view** from the walls, especially on a clear starry night, when the snows on the surrounding barrier of mountains give off a silvery glow.

Vauban's **citadelle**, above the porte Pignerol – the highest point of the fortifications – can be visited for free in July and August, and by guided tour from just inside the northern gate the rest of the year (usually 3pm; €4.50). The fortified keep, designed by Vauban, looks over the strategic intersection of five valleys and guards the start of the climb to the desolate and windswept **Col de Montgenèvre**, one of the oldest and most important passes into Italy.

Down in the *ville basse*, the **télécabine du Prorel** shoots up from avenue René-Froger and links Briançon with the Serre Chevalier skiing resort area. It also provides a head start to mountain walkers (€5.30).

Practicalities

The **gare SNCF** is along avenue de la République in the *ville basse*, 1.5km south of the old city. Local **buses** #1, #2 and #3 link the station and the Champ de Mars. Briançon's **tourist office** is in the place du Temple close to the porte Pignerol gateway (Mon–Sat 8.30am–noon & 1.30–6.30pm, Sun 10am–12.30pm & 2.30–6pm; ⓣ04.92.21.08.50, ⓦwww.briancon.com). The mountain guides' office is in Parc Chancel (summer daily 9.30am–noon & 3–7pm; ⓣ04.92.20.15.73), and the Maison du Parc National des Écrins is in place Médecin-Général-Blanchard (ⓣ04.92.21.42.15, ⓦwww.les-ecrins-parc-national.fr).

One of the least expensive **hotels** in Briançon is the *Pension des Remparts*, in the citadelle itself at 14 av de Vauban (ⓣ & ⓕ04.92.21.08.73; ❸; closed Nov), or try the slightly nicer *Auberge de la Paix* (ⓣ04.92.21.37.43, ⓦwww.auberge-de-la-paix.com; ❸) nearby at 3 rue Porte Méane. A more comfortable option is the chain-run *Hôtel Mercure* on avenue du Dauphiné (ⓣ04.92.20.02.00, ⓦwww.mercure.com; ❼), a large, modern place in the centre of the *ville basse* with a sauna and swimming pool. The nearest **campsite** is *Camping des Cinq Vallées* at St-Blaise (ⓣ04.92.21.06.27, ⓦwww.camping5vallees.com; open June–Sept), 2km from town. There are a number of *gîtes d'étape*, including the cosy *Le Petit Phoque*, 2km along the Montgenèvre road at Le Fontenil (ⓣ04.92.20.07.27, ⓦwww.lepetitphoque.com; closed first two weeks in Nov; €12).

The *ville haute* is full of wonderful Italian **cafés** serving delicious cakes and pizzas, and there are plenty of reasonably priced **restaurants**, such as *Les Templiers*, which has a patio on the place du Temple (beside the tourist office), and cheap, solid menus for around €15. If you'd rather escape the *tartiflette*, there's reasonable Indian food from €13 at *Palais de Jaipur*, 8 place Général-Eberle (ⓣ04.92.21.09.18).

The Parc National des Écrins

Some 50km southeast of Grenoble and 20km west of Briançon, the **Parc National des Écrins** (ⓦwww.les-ecrins-parc-national.fr) covers 230,000 acres of Alpine terrain, its highest peaks rising to 4102m in the **Massif de Pelvoux** in the north of the park. The Écrins is the second most popular place for climbing in the country (Mont Blanc being the first), and with its sunny weather, mazy rivers, and impressive wild flowers it's hard not to regard the park as a big playground. Not only are many of the massifs bolted for sport **climbing**, but plenty have actually been turned into ropes courses, or *Via Ferrata* – the wires and ladders are already built in so that inexperienced climbers can strap on a harness and spend a day climbing (pick up the *Via Ferrata en Grand Briançonnais* brochure at any of the tourist offices). The small towns in the park are of little interest in themselves, especially in comparison with the architecture and culture of the Queyras and the nightlife in Chamonix, but the Écrins is worth a trip for the sheer variety of sports that it offers in a much less crowded setting than Mont Blanc.

The easiest route into the park is from **Argentières**, an unattractive former mining town 16km south of Briançon (for tours of the town's silver mines call ⓣ04.92.23.02.94 in advance). From here a small road cuts west into the valley towards **Vallouise**, with the ice-capped monster of Mont Pelvoux itself (3946m) rearing in front of you all the way.

La Bâtie and Les Vigneaux

The first place you come to on the road into the park from Argentières is **LA BÂTIE**, where there are remains of the so-called **Mur des Vaudois**. The origins of the wall are uncertain: it was probably built either to keep out companies of marauding soldiers-turned-bandits, or to control the spread of plague in the fourteenth century. Despite its name, the wall actually has nothing to do with the Valdois, a sect prominent in this part of the country (see box, p.1018).

A couple of kilometres beyond La Bâtie on the right is the lovely village of **LES VIGNEAUX**, surrounded by apple orchards and backed by the fierce crags of Montbrison. The village **church** has a fine old door and lock under a vaulted porch. Beside it on the exterior wall of the church are two bands of paintings depicting the Seven Deadly Sins. A man carrying a leg of mutton and drinking wine from a flask represents Gluttony, while a woman with rouged cheeks, green stockings and an enticing expanse of thigh on display represents Lust. In the lower band they are all getting their comeuppance, writhing in the agonies of hellfire.

Vallouise

VALLOUISE lies under a steep wooded spur at the junction of two rivers, the Gyronde (which combines the Gyr and the Onde, smaller rivers north of town) and the Gérendoine, about 10km from Argentière. The great glaciered peaks visible up the latter valley are called Les Bans; up in front is Mont Pelvoux. The nucleus of the old village – narrow lanes between sombre stone chalets

– is again its **church**, fifteenth-century with a sixteenth-century porch on pink marble pillars. A fresco of the Adoration of the Magi adorns the tympanum above the door, itself a magnificent object, with carved Gothic panels along the top and an ancient lock-and-bolt with a chimera's head. Inside are some more frescoes, and a collection of naive wooden statues.

The **GR54**, which does the circuit of the Écrins park, passes through Vallouise: the stage on from here to Le Monetier via Lac de l'Eychauda is one of the best. Another good walk is to the hamlet of **PUY AILLAUD**, high on the west flank of the Gyr valley. The path starts just to the right of the church and zigzags up the steep slope behind it with almost aerial views of the valley beneath.

There's a **tourist office** in place de l'Église (May–Sept daily 9am–noon & 3–7pm; Oct–April daily 9am–noon & 2.30–6.30pm ⓣ08.10.00.11.12, ⓦwww.paysdesecrins.com), and a Bureau des Guides hut in the main car park (ⓣ04.92.23.32.29, ⓦwww.guides-ecrins.com). The Maison du Parc des Écrins provides hiking information (ⓣ04.92.23.32.31). There's a **minibus** service as far as Ailefroide in summer, starting from the bar next to the *Edelweiss* hotel (see below); to walk takes two hours or so. Vallouise has a **campsite**, some **gîtes** and a handful of **hotels**: the *Edelweiss* is the least expensive (ⓣ04.92.23.38.58, ⓕ04.92.23.33.46; ❷; closed mid-April to mid-June & mid-Sept to mid-Dec), or for apartment accommodation try *Alpbase*, a series of self-catered chalets rented out by a British couple for short periods (ⓣ04.92.23.45.69, ⓦwww.alpbase.com). All rooms in the village are likely to be full in July and August unless you book. For **food** try the microbrewery *Brasserie AlpHand* on place du Village (ⓣ04.92.23.20.00; closed May to mid-June).

Ailefroide

The six-kilometre drive beyond Vallouise to **AILEFROIDE** is absolutely spectacular; the village cowers beneath the daunting ridges, peaks and glaciers of Pelvoux. Ailefroide is really no more than a huge **campsite** (ⓣ04.92.23.46.43, ⓦwww.ailefroide.com) with a couple of shops and a climbing centre: not quite wilderness (it can get quite crowded in August) but a long drive from the nearest city. Beyond Ailefroide, however, towards the end of the road at the Pré du Madame Carle and the old *Refuge Cézanne*, you'll be rewarded with some magnificent scenery.

This is the start of the steep climb to the CAF *Refuge du Glacier Blanc* (ⓣ04.92.23.50.24), right beside the beetling glacier. Quieter, but a good deal

The Valdois

The **Valdois** ("Waldensians" in English) were a heretical sect founded in the late twelfth century by Pierre Valdo, a merchant from Lyon, who preached against worldly wealth and the corruption of the clergy and, practising as he preached, gave his wealth to the poor. Excommunicated in 1186, the Valdois came more and more to deny the authority of the Church, and sought refuge from persecution in the remote mountain valleys of Pelvoux, especially in the area around Vallouise and Argentières.

There was a crop of executions for sorcery in the early fifteenth century, and many of the victims were probably Valdois, burnt to death in wooden cabins built for this purpose. In 1488, Charles VIII launched a full-scale crusade against them. There's a spot west of Ailefroide known as Baume Chapelue where they were smoked out by the military and butchered. In 1562 they joined the growing Huguenot cause, but after the Revocation of the Edict of Nantes, they were finally exterminated in the eighteenth century, when 8000 troops went on the rampage, creating total desolation and "leaving neither people nor animals".

longer, is the approach to the CAF *Refuge du Sélé* (Ⓣ04.92.23.39.49) and the Pointe du Sélé, due west of Ailefroide; bear in mind that this is a difficult trek for experienced hikers, not an afternoon stroll.

Briançon to Queyras

The direct route from Briançon to Queyras, crossing the 2360m **Col d'Izoard**, is a beautiful trip, but, with no buses covering the distance, you need a car to do it. Leaving Briançon, the D902 begins to climb the steep Cerveyrette valley, the seemingly endless series of switchbacks entering an ever denser forest until it arrives at **Le Laus**, a cluster of old stone houses with long, sloping, wooden roofs set in meadows beside the stream. Soon you reach the tree line and cross the Col d'Izoard to the **Casse Déserte**, a wild, desolate region with huge screes running down off the peaks and weirdly eroded orangey rocks. From the top the view extends over many kilometres of mountain landscape, and it's from here that the vertiginous descent commences, entering another river valley, which is lined by a succession of tiny hamlets, **Brunissard**, **La Chalp** and, finally, larger **ARVIEUX**, lying in a high valley surrounded by fields and meadows, just 6km from Château-Queyras. A splendidly ornate Baroque church, dedicated to St Thomas Becket, stands guard at the entrance to the village. The **GR5** passes through, running a parallel route from Briançon; if you started out late and can't reach Arvieux by nightfall, there is also a **gîte**, *Les Bons Enfants* (Ⓣ04.92.46.73.85, Ⓔlesbonsenfants@free.fr) in Brunissard higher up in the valley. Or, once in Arvieux, you can try the apartments rented out by *La Casse Déserte* (Ⓣ04.92.46.72.91; ❷).

Mont-Dauphin and Embrun

If the Col d'Izoard is closed, or if you don't like slow, winding, high roads, then the Queyras can be reached from the north or the south on the N94. From Briançon, the River Durance meanders leisurely through a wide valley, following the N94, until some 27km later it passes **MONT-DAUPHIN**, a formidably **bastioned village**, and one of the many Alpine fortifications designed by Vauban in the seventeenth century, commanding the entrance to the valley of the Guil. There's a **tourist office** (Mon–Sat 9am–noon & 3–6pm; Ⓣ04.92.45.17.80), a **gîte**, *Le Glacier Bleu* (Ⓣ04.92.45.18.47, Ⓦwww.leglacierbleu.fr; ❸), and several restaurants inside the walled perimeter.

Twenty kilometres further along its course the river reaches **EMBRUN**, a beautiful little town of narrow streets on a rocky bluff above the Durance and an important base for both the Parc du Queyras and the Parc des Écrins. It has been a fortress town for centuries. Hadrian made it the capital of the Maritime Alps, and from the third century to the Revolution it was the seat of an important archbishopric. The chief sight is its twelfth-century cathedral that inspired numerous imitators throughout the region. The **tourist office**, in a former chapel of the Cordeliers on place Général-Dosse (July & Aug Mon–Sat 9am–7.30pm, Sun 9.30am–noon & 4–7pm; Sept–June Mon–Sat 9am–noon & 2–6.30pm; Ⓣ04.92.43.72.72, Ⓦwww.ot-embrun.fr), is next door to the bureau for **mountain guides**, which organizes a daily programme of walks in the surrounding mountains. There's an **Internet** café, Omnis Cyberspace, 30 rue de la Liberté, just down the street. The park zones and the area south of Embrun have extensive facilities for outdoor activities ranging from rafting to sailing and climbing (enquire at the tourist office).

There are two very agreeable **hotels** by the central place de la Mairie: the simple, but delightful *Hôtel du Commerce*, just off the square in rue St-Pierre

(Ⓣ04.92.43.54.54, Ⓕ04.92.43.81.89; ❷), with an excellent restaurant serving menus from €14; and the flower-decked *Hôtel de la Mairie* on the square itself (Ⓣ04.92.43.20.65, Ⓦwww.hoteldelamairie.com; ❸; closed Oct–Nov), also with a good restaurant (closed Mon & Sun eve in winter; from €15) serving tasty local specialities. There are several **campsites** as well: two reasonably priced ones are *Le Moulin* (Ⓣ04.92.43.00.41; closed mid-Sept to Jan), on the left after the bridge on the Gap road (N94), and *La Tour*, on route de la Madeleine close to the Durance off the D994 (Ⓣ04.92.43.17.66; closed Sept to late June).

Just a few kilometres past Embrun is **Lac de Serre-Ponçon**, the largest man-made lake in Europe, created in the 1950s by damming and taming the wild Durance. A **hostel** overlooks the lake 10km from Embrun at **SAVINES-LE-LAC** (Ⓣ04.92.44.20.16, Ⓔsavines@fuaj.org; closed mid-Sept to April), a town that was moved from what is now the bottom of the lake to its current location.

Parc Régional du Queyras

The **Parc Régional du Queyras** (Ⓦwww.queyras.com), spreading southeast of Briançon to the Italian border, is much more Mediterranean in appearance than the mountains to the north, with low scrub covering the mountainsides, poor shallow soil, white friable rock and a huge variety of flora. The open land along the park's rolling roads makes it particularly enjoyable to spend a few hours driving along them up to **St-Véran**, an Alpine village near the Italian border. The park has some good walking opportunities, with the **GR58** path making a circuit of the park, running through St-Véran and L'Échalp, and the **GR5** crossing through Ceillac and Arvieux on its way from Briançon towards Embrun.

Guillestre

The road into the Queyras park follows the River Guil from Mont-Dauphin. First stop is **GUILLESTRE**, a pretty mountain village that only really comes to life in summer. Its houses, in typical Queyras style, have open granaries on the upper floors and its church has a lion-porch in emulation of the cathedral at Embrun. The village lies at the foot of the long climb southwards to the **Col de Vars** (2111m), which gives access to the remote and beautiful walking country of the upper Ubaye valley; it's six hours, via Lac Miroir, Lac Ste-Anne and the Col Girardin, to the CAF *Refuge de Maljasset* (Ⓣ04.92.84.34.04; closed Jan & mid-May to mid-June).

Château-Ville-Vieille and around

The road route into the park from Guillestre strikes northeast through the narrow gorge of the **Combe du Queyras**, scarcely more than a claustrophobic crack between walls up to 400m high. Far below the road, the clear stream bubbles down over red and green rocks. It was only in the twentieth century that road-building techniques became sufficiently sophisticated to cope with these narrows – previously they had to be circumvented by a detour over the adjacent heights.

At the upper end of the Combe, the valley broadens briefly, and ahead you see the fortifications of **Château-Queyras** barring the way so completely that there's scarcely room for the road to squeeze around its base – Vauban at work again, though the original fortress was medieval. There is an exhibit on the geological conditions that created the Alps in the crypt of the castle's chapel (daily: May & Sept 10am–6pm; June–Aug 9am–7pm; €3.50). Just beyond is **CHÂTEAU-VILLE-VIEILLE**, where the road for St-Véran branches right

over the Guil and up the ravine of the Aigue Blanche torrent. A smaller place than Guillestre, it has only a few old houses still intact and a **church** with its square tower and octagonal steeple flanked by four short triangular pinnacles – a style characteristic of this corner of the Alps. The road continues along the Guil through the villages of Aiguilles, Abriès and L'Échalp (all with *gîtes d'étape*), to the **Belvédère du Viso**, close to the Italian border and the **Monte Viso**, at 3841m the highest peak in the area.

St-Véran

Seven kilometres south of Château-Ville-Vieille lies **ST-VÉRAN**, which at 2042m claims to be the highest permanently inhabited village in Europe. As with most high Alpine villages, traditional terrace farming has now practically died out and today the principal economic activity is entertaining tourists.

St-Véran's houses are part stone and part timber, and there are several refurbished old drinking fountains, made entirely of wood. The stone **church** stands prettily on the higher of the two "streets", its white tower silhouetted against the bare crags across the valley. Just south of the village, the **GR58**, waymarked and easy to follow, turns right down to the river, beside which there are some good spots for **camping sauvage**. The path continues up the left bank through woods of pine and larch as far as the chapel of Notre-Dame-de-Clausis. There, above the treeline, it crosses to the right bank of the stream and winds up damp grassy slopes to the **Col de Chamoussière**, about three and a half hours from St-Véran. The ridge to the right of the col marks the frontier with Italy. In the valley below, you can see the *Refuge Agnel*, about an hour away, with the **Pain de Sucre** (3208m) behind it. In early July, there are glorious flowers – violets, Black Vanilla orchids, pinks and gentians – in the meadows leading up to the col.

St-Véran's very accommodating **tourist office** is halfway down the main high street (ⓣ04.92.45.82.21, ⓦwww.saintveran.com; Mon–Sat 9am–12.30pm & 2–5.30pm; also open Sun in high season). The nicest **accommodation** option is *Chalet Auberge L'Estoilies*, a beautifully converted rustic wooden farmhouse in Le Raux, a kilometre below the main village (ⓣ04.92.45.82.65, ⓦwww.estoilies.com; ③).

Travel details

Trains

Annecy to: Aix-les-Bains (frequent; 30–40min); Chambéry (frequent; 45min); Grenoble (several daily; 2hr); Lyon (several daily; 2hr); Paris (frequent; 4hr 30min); St-Gervais (9–10 daily; 1hr 35min–2hr).
Annemasse, near Geneva to: Annecy, changing at La-Roche-sur-Foron (4–5 daily; 1hr 30min); Évian (frequent; 35min); Paris (1 daily; 8hr).
Belfort to: Besançon (10 daily; 1hr–1hr 15min); Dole (5 daily; 1hr 30min); Montbéliard (hourly; 20min), Paris-Est (2 daily; 5hr); Ronchamp (12 daily; 5min).
Besançon to: Bourg-en-Bresse (4–5 daily; 2hr 30min); Dijon (10 daily; 1hr); Dole (10 daily; 30min); Morez (4 daily; 2hr 10min–2hr 30min); Paris-Lyon (up to 6 daily; 2hr 30min); St-Claude (4 daily; 2hr 30min–3hr); St-Laurent (4 daily; 1hr 40min–2hr).
Briançon to: Marseille (3 daily; 4hr 30min); Grenoble (4 daily; 4hr).
Chambéry to: Aix-les-Bains (frequent; 10min); Annecy (frequent; 45min); Bourg-St-Maurice (5 daily; 2hr); Geneva (several daily; 1hr 30min); Grenoble (several daily; 1hr); Lyon (frequent; 1hr 30min–2hr 30min); Modane (frequent; 1hr 20min); Paris (frequent; 5hr 30min).
Évian to: Geneva (7 daily; 1hr); Thonon-les-Bains (frequent; 15min).
Grenoble to: Annecy (several daily; 2hr); Briançon, changing at Veynes-Dévoluy (1–2 daily; 4hr); Chambéry (several daily; 1hr); Lyon (frequent; 1hr 30min–1hr 45min); Paris-Lyon (several daily; 3hr 10min–7hr 15min).
St-Gervais to: Chamonix (5–7 daily; 45min).

Buses

Annecy to: Albertville (4 daily; 50min); Évian (4 daily; 1hr 30min); Lyon (2 daily; 2hr 30min); Talloires (6 daily; 50min).
Belfort to: Ronchamp (1 daily; 45min).
Besançon to: Ornans (4 daily; 30min); Pontarlier (4 daily; 1hr).
Bourg-St-Maurice to: Aosta (1 daily July & Aug; 2hr 30min); Val d'Isère (1–2 daily; 50min–1hr 20min).
Briançon to: Mont-Dauphin (3–5 daily; 1hr 15min).
Chambéry to: Aix-les-Bains (several daily; 20min); Annecy (several daily; 1hr); Grenoble (several daily; 1hr).
Chamonix to: Annecy, via La-Roche-sur-Foron (3 daily; 3hr); Annecy, via Megève (1 daily; 3hr); Geneva (1 daily; 2hr 30min); Grenoble (1 daily; 3hr 30min).
Grenoble to: L'Alpe d'Huez (2 daily; 45min); Le Bourg-d'Oisans (4–6 daily; 1hr 20min); Briançon (several daily; 2hr); Chambéry (several daily; 1hr); Col du Lautaret (1 daily; 2hr); La Grave (1 daily; 1hr 40min); Le Monêtier-les-Bains (1 daily; 2hr 25min); St-Pierre-de-Chartreuse (at least 1 daily; 1hr); Villard-de-Lans and other towns in the Vercors (at least 1 daily; 45min).
Mont-Dauphin to (summer only): Ceillac (2 daily; 35min); Guillestre (2–3 daily; 5min); St-Véran (2–3 daily; 1hr 30min); Vars (2 daily; 50min); Ville-Vieille (2–3 daily; 1hr 5min).
Thonon-les-Bains to: Évian (frequent; 25min); Yvoire (3–4 daily; 20min).
Valloire to (summer only): St-Michel-de-Maurienne (2 daily; 45min).

14

The Rhône valley and Provence

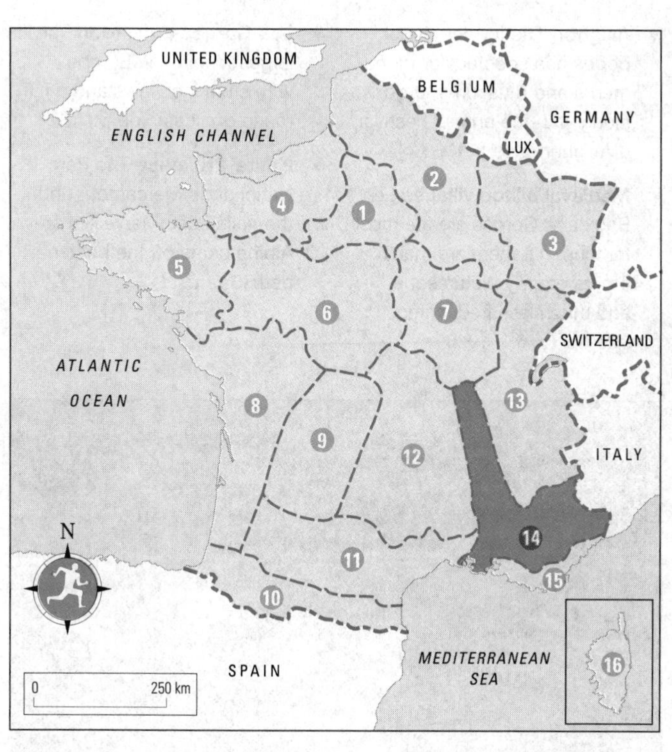

CHAPTER 14

Highlights

* **Lyon** *Traboulez* through the Renaissance quarter and savour the culinary genius of some of France's top chefs. See p.1037

* **Roman remains** Impressive arenas in Vienne, Orange and Arles host summer festivals and concerts. See pp.1044, 1052 & 1079

* **Avignon** The former city of popes has spectacular monuments and museums to go along with the annual Festival d'Avignon. See p.1060

* **Medieval hilltop villages** Les Baux and Gordes are the most famous, but there are many others equally picturesque, and much less frequented. See pp.1076 & 1090

* **La Camargue** The marshland of the Rhône delta is home to white horses, flamingos and unearthly landscapes. See p.1083

* **Aix** The most beautiful of Provence's major cities is a wonderful place for café idling and has the region's most vibrant markets. See p.1094

* **Les Gorges du Verdon** The largest canyon in Europe, with stunning views and a full range of hikes. See p.1104

* **Haute-Provence** The Parc National du Mercantour and the Vallée des Merveilles are Alpine gems off the beaten path. See p.1113

△ Camargue

14

The Rhône valley and Provence

Of all the areas of France, **Provence** is the most irresistible. Geographically it ranges from the snow-capped mountains of the **southern Alps** to the delta plains of the **Camargue**, and it boasts the greatest European canyon, the **Gorges du Verdon**. Fortified towns guard its old borders; countless villages perch defensively on hilltops; and its great cities – **Aix-en-Provence** and **Avignon** – are full of cultural glories. The sensual inducements of Provence include warmth, food and wine, and the perfumes of Mediterranean vegetation. Along with its coast – which is covered in the following chapter – it has attracted the rich and famous, the artistic and reclusive, and countless arrivals who have found themselves unable to conceive of life elsewhere.

In appearance, despite the throngs of foreigners and French from other regions, **inland Provence** remains remarkably unscathed. The history of its earliest known natives, of the Greeks, then Romans, raiding Saracens, schismatic popes, and shifting allegiances to different counts and princes, is still in evidence. Provence's complete integration into France dates only from the nineteenth century and, though the Provençal language is only spoken by a small minority, the accent is distinctive even to a foreign ear. In the east the rhythms of speech become clearly Italian.

Unless you're intending to stay for months, the main problem with Provence is choosing where to go. In the west, along the **Rhône valley**, are the Roman cities of **Orange**, **Vaison-la-Romaine**, **Carpentras** and **Arles**, and the papal city of **Avignon**, with its fantastic summer festival. **Aix-en-Provence** is the mini-Paris of the region and was home to Cézanne, for whom the **Mont Ste-Victoire** was an enduring subject; Van Gogh's links are with **St-Rémy** and Arles. The Gorges du Verdon, **the Parc National du Mercantour** along the Italian border, **Mont Ventoux** northeast of Carpentras, and the flamingo-filled lagoons of the **Camargue** are just a selection of the diverse and stunning landscapes of this region.

Before you reach Provence from the north there are the **vineyards of the Rhône valley** and, before them, the French centre of gastronomy and second largest city of the country, **Lyon**. With its choice of restaurants, clubs, culture and all the accoutrements of an affluent and vital Western city, it stands in opulent contrast to the medieval hilltop villages of Provence.

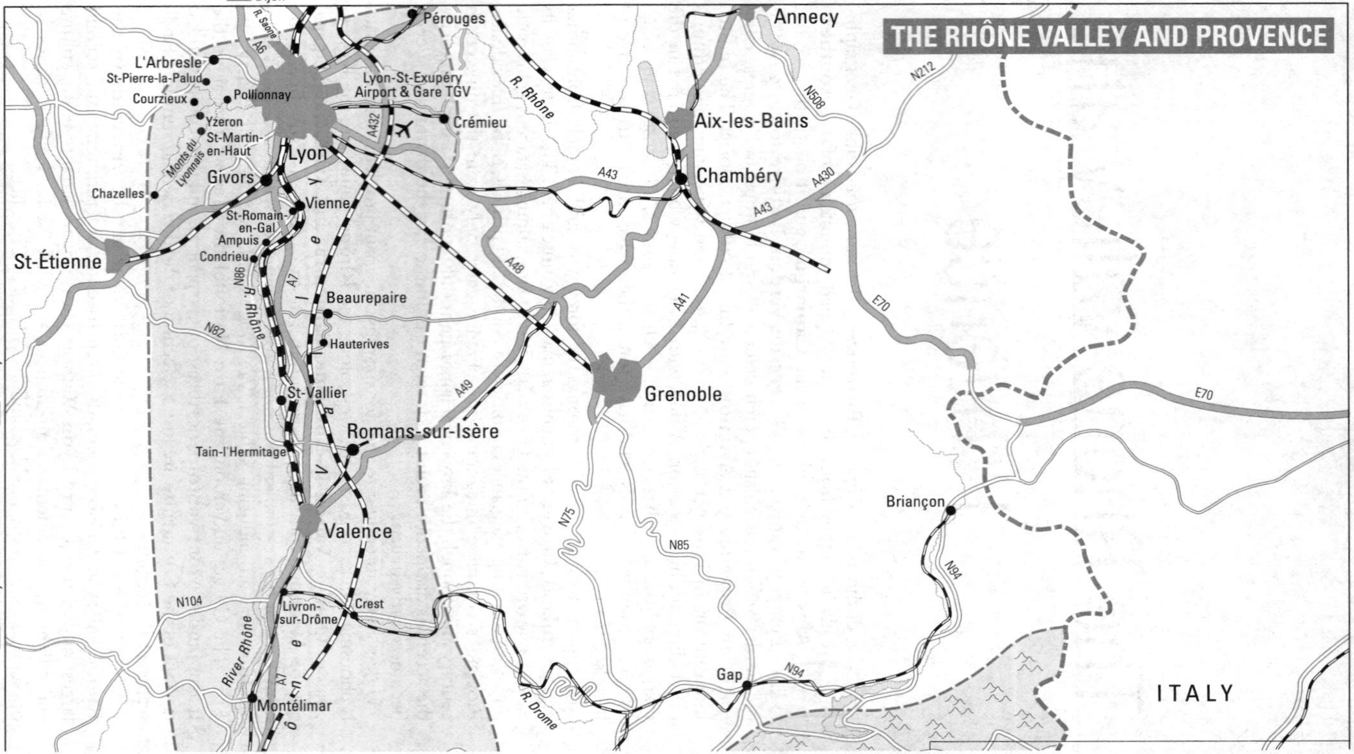

THE RHÔNE VALLEY AND PROVENCE

Dijon
Geneva
Turin
Le Puy & Clermont-Ferrand
Le Puy & Clermont-Ferrand
Annecy
Pérouges
L'Arbresle
St-Pierre-la-Palud
Pollionnay
Courzieux
Yzeron
St-Martin-en-Haut
Monts du Lyonnais
Lyon
Lyon-St-Exupéry Airport & Gare TGV
Crémieu
Givors
Chazelles
Vienne
St-Romain-en-Gal
Ampuis
Condrieu
St-Étienne
Beaurepaire
Hauterives
St-Vallier
Romans-sur-Isère
Tain-l'Hermitage
Valence
Livron-sur-Drôme
Crest
Montélimar
Aix-les-Bains
Chambéry
Grenoble
Briançon
Gap
ITALY
R. Saone
R. Rhône
River Rhône
R. Drome
Vallée du Rhône
A6
A7
A41
A43
A48
A49
A430
A432
E70
N82
N85
N86
N75
N94
N104
N212
N508

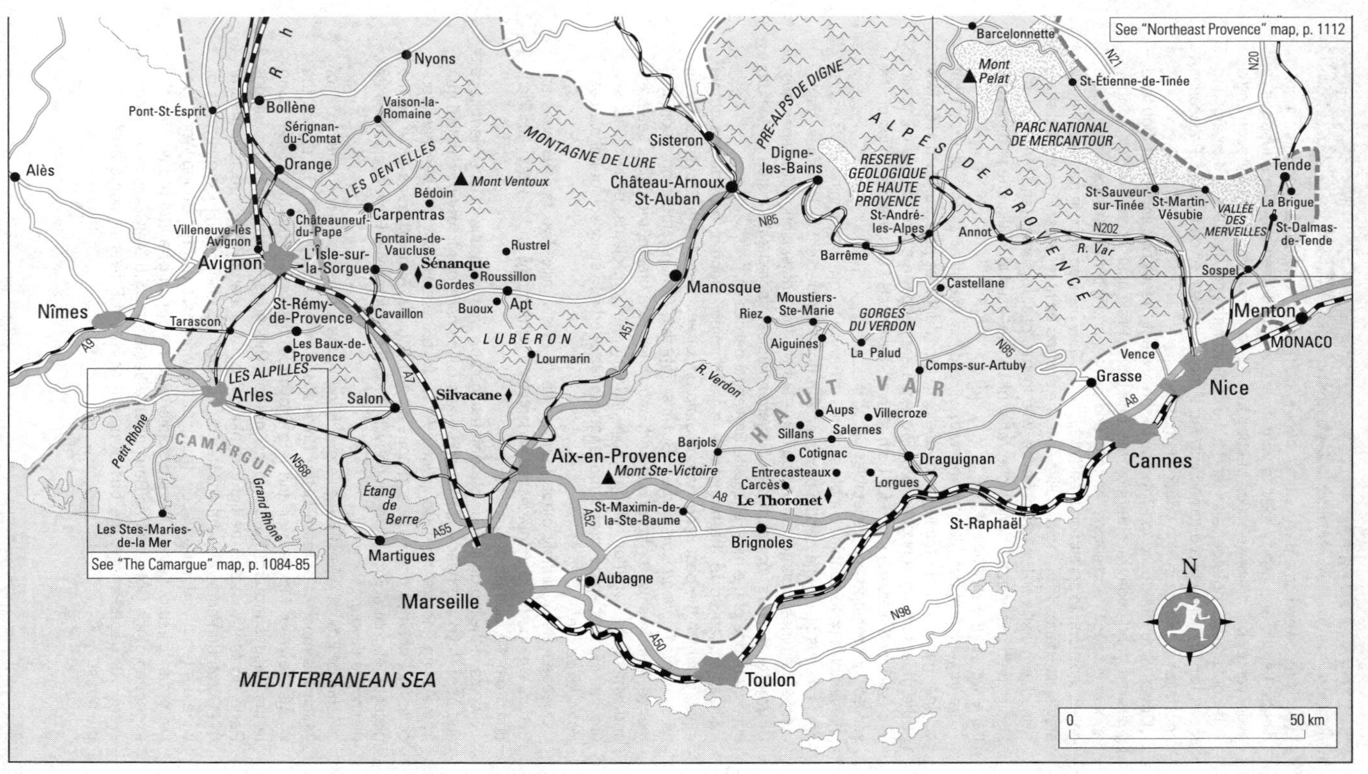
See "Northeast Provence" map, p. 1112
Barcelonnette
Mont Pelat
St-Étienne-de-Tinée
N21
N20
PARC NATIONAL DE MERCANTOUR
ALPES DE PROVENCE
PRE-ALPS DE DIGNE
RESERVE GEOLOGIQUE DE HAUTE PROVENCE
Tende
La Brigue
St-Sauveur-sur-Tinée
St-Martin-Vésubie
VALLÉE DES MERVEILLES
St-Dalmas-de-Tende
Sospel
Menton
MONACO
Nice
Vence
Grasse
A8
Cannes
St-Raphaël
N202
R. Var
Annot
St-André-les-Alpes
Barrême
Digne-les-Bains
Castellane
N85
Sisteron
Château-Arnoux St-Auban
Manosque
A51
MONTAGNE DE LURE
Nyons
Vaison-la-Romaine
Bollène
Pont-St-Ésprit
Sérignan-du-Comtat
Orange
LES DENTELLES
Mont Ventoux
Bédoin
Carpentras
Châteauneuf-du-Pape
Villeneuve-lès-Avignon
Avignon
Alès
Fontaine-de-Vaucluse
L'Îsle-sur-la-Sorgue
Rustrel
Sénanque
Roussillon
Gordes
Apt
Buoux
Cavaillon
St-Rémy-de-Provence
Les Baux-de-Provence
Nîmes
A9
Tarascon
LES ALPILLES
Arles
LUBERON
Lourmarin
Salon
A7
Silvacane
Petit Rhône
CAMARGUE
N568
Grand Rhône
Les Stes-Maries-de-la Mer
See "The Camargue" map, p. 1084-85
Étang de Berre
A55
Martigues
Marseille
Aix-en-Provence
Mont Ste-Victoire
R. Verdon
Moustiers-Ste-Marie
Riez
GORGES DU VERDON
Aiguines
La Palud
Comps-sur-Artuby
HAUT VAR
Aups
Villecroze
Sillans
Salernes
Barjols
Cotignac
Draguignan
Entrecasteaux
Carcès
Lorgues
Le Thoronet
A8
St-Maximin-de-la-Ste-Baume
A52
Brignoles
Aubagne
N98
A50
Toulon
MEDITERRANEAN SEA
N
0
50 km

Food of Provence and the Rhône valley

Lyon is renowned as a gastronomic centre, combining southern and northern ingredients. Its rich and hearty food is very meat- and offal-oriented, with **sausages** of every variety and a fine selection of **cheeses**. A Lyonnais salad includes bacon and a soft-cooked egg; potatoes also tend to be cooked with egg, cheeses and cream; and meat, fish and cheese are turned into fat, filling *quenelles*, or dumplings. Patisseries specialize in extremely rich chocolate **gâteaux**.

Olives were introduced to Provence by the ancient Greeks two and a half thousand years ago and today accompany the traditional Provençal aperitif of *pastis*; they appear in sauces and salads, on tarts and pizzas, and mixed with capers in a paste called *tapenade* to spread on bread or biscuits. They are also used in traditional meat stews, like *daube Provençale*. Olive oil is the starting point for most Provençal dishes; spiced with chillis or Provençal **herbs** (wild thyme, basil, rosemary and tarragon), it's also poured over pizzas, sandwiches and, of course, used in vinaigrette and mayonnaise with all the varieties of salad.

The ingredient most often mixed with olive oil is the other classic of Provençal cuisine: **garlic**. Whole markets are dedicated to strings of pale purple garlic. Two of the most famous concoctions of Provence are *pistou*, a paste of olive oil, garlic and basil, and aïoli, the name for both a garlic mayonnaise and the dish in which it's served with salt cod and vegetables.

Vegetables have double or triple seasons in Provence, often beginning while northern France is still in the depths of winter. **Ratatouille** ingredients – tomatoes, capsicum, aubergines, courgettes and onions – are the favourites, along with asparagus. **Courgette flowers**, or *fleurs de courgettes farcies*, stuffed with *pistou* or tomato sauce, are one of the most exquisite Provençal delicacies.

Sheep, taken up to the mountains in the summer months, provide the staple meat, of which the best is *agneau de Sisteron*, often roasted with Provençal herbs as *a gigot d'agneau aux herbes*. But it's **fish** that features most on traditional menus, with freshwater trout, salt cod, anchovies, sea bream, monkfish, sea bass and whiting all common, along with wonderful seafood: clams, periwinkles, sea urchins, oysters, spider crabs and langoustines piled into spiky sculptural *plateaux de fruits de mer*.

Cheeses are invariably made from goat's or ewe's milk. Two famous ones are Banon, wrapped in chestnut leaves and marinated in brandy, and the aromatic Picadon, from the foothills of the Alps.

Sweets of the region include **chocolates**, notably from Valrhona in Tain l'Hermitage and from Puyricard near Aix, almond sweets called *calissons* from Aix, candied fruit from Apt and nougat from Montélimar. As for fruit, the melons, white peaches, apricots, figs, cherries and Muscat grapes are unbeatable. **Almond trees** grow on the plateaux of central Provence, along with lavender, which gives Provençal **honey** its distinctive flavour.

Some of France's best **wine** is produced in the Côtes du Rhône vineyards, of which the most celebrated is the Crozes-Hermitage *appellation*. Once past the nougat town of Montélimar and into Provence, the best wines are to be found in the villages around the Dentelles, notably Gigondas, and at Châteauneuf-du-Pape. To the west are the light, drinkable, but not particularly special wines of the Côtes du Ventoux and the Côtes du Lubéron *appellations*. Huge quantities of wine are produced in Provence, many of the vineyards planted during World War I in order to supply every French soldier with his ration of a litre a day. With the exception of the Côteaux des Baux around Les Baux, and the Côtes de Provence in the Var *département*, the best wines of southern Provence come from along the coast.

The Rhône valley

The **Rhône valley**, the north–south route of ancient armies, medieval traders and modern rail and road, is now as industrialized as the least attractive parts of the north. Though the river is still a means of transport, its waters now also cool the reactors of the Marcoule and Tricastin nuclear power station between **Montélimar** and Avignon and act as a dumping ground for the heavy industries along its banks. Following the River Rhône holds few attractions, with the exceptions of the scenic stretch of **vineyards** and fruit orchards between the Roman city of **Vienne** and the distinctly southern city of **Valence**. But the big magnet is, of course, the gastronomic paradise of **Lyon**, with hundreds of sophisticated bars and restaurants.

Lyon and around

LYON is physically the second biggest city in France, a result of its uncontrolled urban sprawl. Viewed at high speed from the Autoroute du Soleil, the impression it gives is of a major confluence of rivers and roads, around which only petrochemical industries thrive. In fact, from the sixteenth century right up until the postwar dominance of metalworks and chemicals, silk was the city's main industry, generating the wealth which left behind a multitude of Renaissance buildings. But what has stamped its character most on Lyon is the commerce and banking that grew up with its industrial expansion. It is this that gives the city its affluent, self-confident air.

The city is now busy forging a role for itself within a new Europe, with international schools and colleges, the new HQ for Interpol, a recently inaugurated eco-friendly tram system, a second TGV station with links to the north that bypass Paris, and high-tech industrial parks for international companies, making it a modern city *par excellence*. More so than any other French city, it has embraced the monetarist vision of the European Union and is acting, with some success, as a post-modern city-state within it.

Most French people would find themselves in Lyon for business rather than for recreation: it's a get-up-and-go place, not a lie-back-and-rest one, with an almost Swiss sense of cleanliness, order and efficiency. But as a wonderfully manageable slice of urban France, Lyon certainly has its charms. Foremost among these is **gastronomy**; there are more restaurants per Gothic and Renaissance square metre of the old town than anywhere else on earth, and the city could form a football team with its superstars of the international chef circuit. While the **textile museum** is the second famous reason for stopping here, Lyon's nightlife, cinema and theatre (including the famous Lyonnais puppets), its antique markets, music and other cultural festivities might tempt you to stay at least a few days. As if that weren't enough, Lyon's distinctive older quarters and its winding, secret *traboules* are an urban explorer's paradise.

Lyon is organized into arrondissements, of which there are nine. A visit to the city will necessarily take you into the Presqu'île (1er and 2e arrondissements), the area between the rivers Saône and Rhône, and you're likely to spend some time

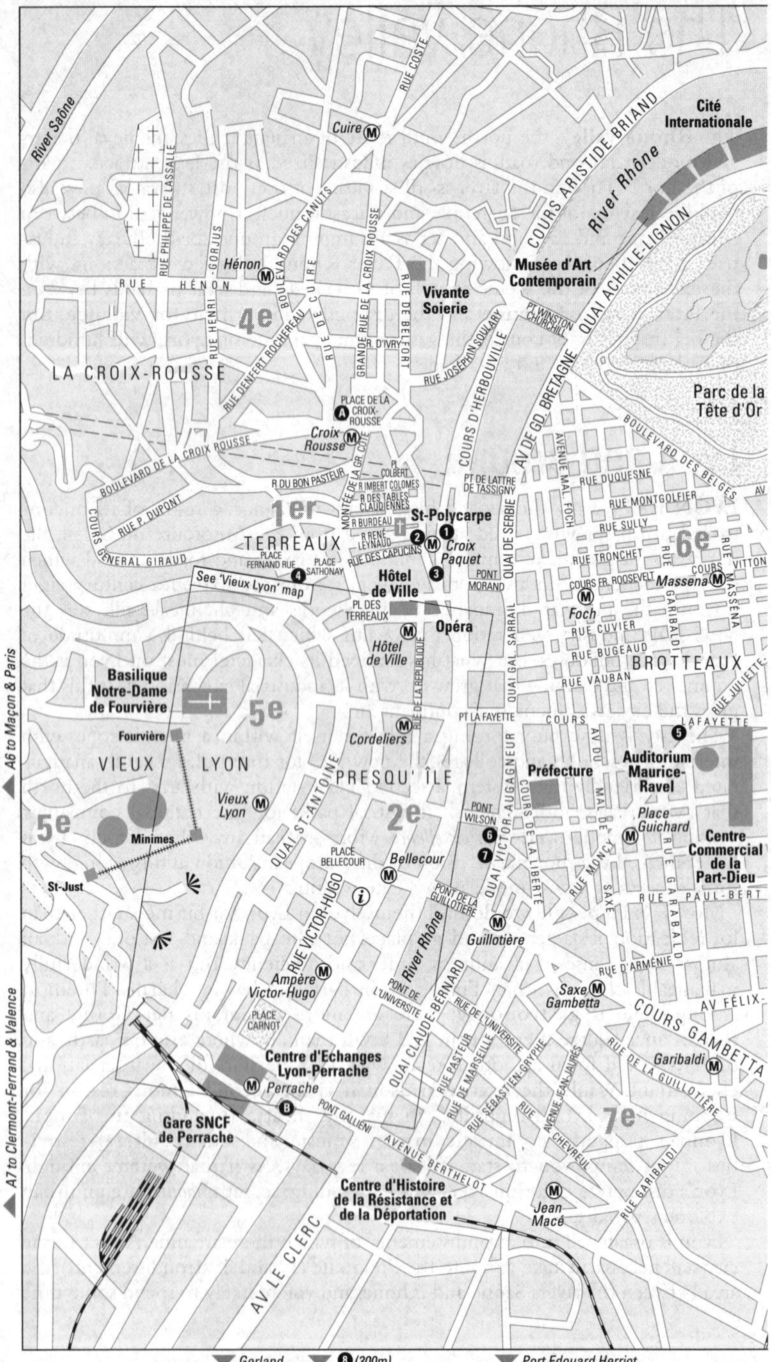
River Saône
RUE COSTE
Cuire
Cité Internationale
COURS ARISTIDE BRIAND
River Rhône
QUAI ACHILLE-LIGNON
Musée d'Art Contemporain
RUE PHILIPPE DE LASSALLE
RUE GORJUS
BOULEVARD DES CANUTS
RUE DE LA CROIX ROUSSE
Hénon
RUE HÉNON
RUE HENRI
RUE DE CUIRE
GRANDE RUE DE LA CROIX ROUSSE
RUE DE BELFORT
Vivante Soierie
4e
RUE DENFERT ROCHEREAU
R. D'IVRY
RUE JOSÉPHIN SOULARY
PT WINSTON CHURCHILL
COURS D'HERBOUVILLE
AV DE GD. BRETAGNE
LA CROIX-ROUSSE
PLACE DE LA CROIX-ROUSSE
Parc de la Tête d'Or
Croix Rousse
BOULEVARD DE LA CROIX ROUSSE
MONTÉE DE LA GR. CÔTE
PL COLBERT
R DU BON PASTEUR
R IMBERT COLOMES
R DES TABLES CLAUDIENNES
BOULEVARD DES BELGES
PT DE LATTRE DE TASSIGNY
AVENUE MAL. FOCH
RUE DUQUESNE
RUE MONTGOLFIER
RUE P. DUPONT
COURS GENERAL GIRAUD
1er
R BURDEAU
R RENÉ LEYNAUD
St-Polycarpe
Croix Paquet
RUE SULLY
6e
TERREAUX
RUE DES CAPUCINS
QUAI DE SERBIE
RUE TRONCHET
COURS VITTON
PLACE FERNAND RUE
PLACE SATHONAY
Hôtel de Ville
PONT MORAND
COURS FR. ROOSEVELT
Masséna
RUE MASSÉNA
See 'Vieux Lyon' map
PL DES TERREAUX
Foch
Opéra
RUE CUVIER
RUE GARIBALDI
Hôtel de Ville
RUE BUGEAUD
BROTTEAUX
QUAI GAL. SARRAIL
RUE VAUBAN
Basilique Notre-Dame de Fourvière
5e
RUE DE LA RÉPUBLIQUE
PT LA FAYETTE
COURS LAFAYETTE
RUE JULIETTE
Fourvière
Cordeliers
Auditorium Maurice-Ravel
VIEUX LYON
QUAI ST-ANTOINE
PRESQU'ÎLE
Préfecture
QUAI VICTOR-AUGAGNEUR
AV DU MAL DE SAXE
Vieux Lyon
2e
COURS DE LA LIBERTÉ
Place Guichard
5e
Minimes
PONT WILSON
Centre Commercial de la Part-Dieu
PLACE BELLECOUR
Bellecour
RUE MONCY
St-Just
RUE PAUL-BERT
PONT DE LA GUILLOTIÈRE
River Rhône
Guillotière
RUE VICTOR-HUGO
RUE D'ARMÉNIE
Ampère Victor-Hugo
PONT DE L'UNIVERSITÉ
QUAI CLAUDE-BERNARD
RUE DE L'UNIVERSITÉ
Saxe Gambetta
COURS GAMBETTA
AV FÉLIX-
PLACE CARNOT
Centre d'Echanges Lyon-Perrache
RUE PASTEUR
RUE DE MARSEILLE
RUE SÉBASTIEN-GRYPHE
AVENUE JEAN-JAURÈS
Garibaldi
RUE DE LA GUILLOTIÈRE
Perrache
PONT GALLIENI
RUE CHEVREUL
7e
Gare SNCF de Perrache
AVENUE BERTHELOT
RUE GARIBALDI
Centre d'Histoire de la Résistance et de la Déportation
Jean Macé
AV LE CLERC
A6 to Maçon & Paris
A7 to Clermont-Ferrand & Valence
Gerland
8 (300m)
Port Edouard Herriot

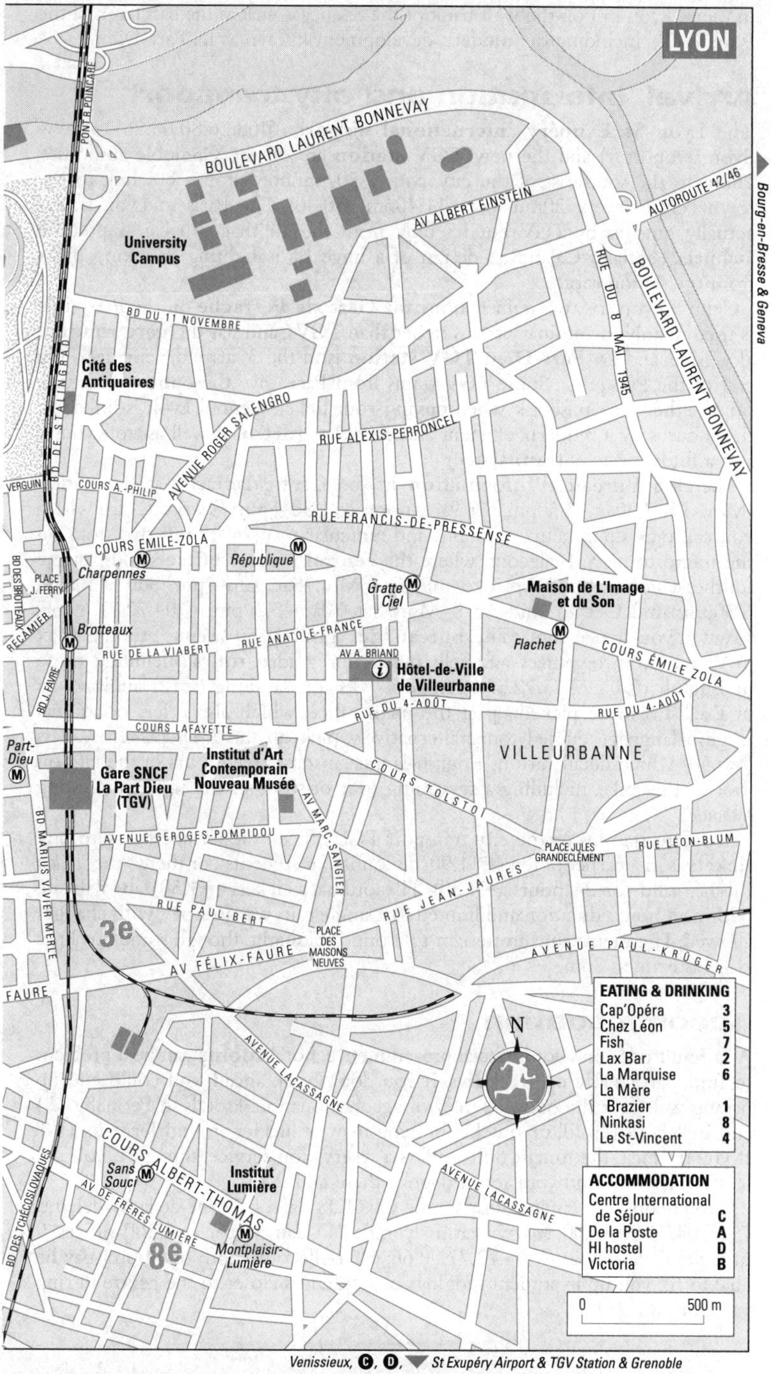

LYON
Bourg-en-Bresse & Geneva
BOULEVARD LAURENT BONNEVAY
PONT R. POINCARE
AV ALBERT EINSTEIN
AUTOROUTE 42/46
University Campus
BD DU 11 NOVEMBRE
RUE DU 8 MAI 1945
BOULEVARD LAURENT BONNEVAY
BD DE STALINGRAD
Cité des Antiquaires
AVENUE ROGER SALENGRO
RUE ALEXIS-PERRONCEL
VERGUIN
COURS A.-PHILIP
RUE FRANCIS-DE-PRESSENSÉ
COURS EMILE-ZOLA
Charpennes
République
BD DES BROTTEAUX
PLACE J. FERRY
Gratte Ciel
Maison de L'Image et du Son
RECAMIER
Brotteaux
RUE ANATOLE-FRANCE
Flachet
RUE DE LA VIABERT
AV A. BRIAND
Hôtel-de-Ville de Villeurbanne
COURS ÉMILE ZOLA
BD J. FAVRE
RUE DU 4-AOÛT
RUE DU 4-AOÛT
COURS LAFAYETTE
Part-Dieu
Institut d'Art Contemporain Nouveau Musée
VILLEURBANNE
Gare SNCF La Part Dieu (TGV)
COURS TOLSTOI
AV MARC-SANGIER
BD MARIUS VIVIER MERLE
AVENUE GEROGES-POMPIDOU
PLACE JULES GRANDCLÉMENT
RUE LÉON-BLUM
RUE JEAN-JAURES
RUE PAUL-BERT
3e
PLACE DES MAISONS NEUVES
AV FÉLIX-FAURE
AVENUE PAUL-KRÜGER
FAURE
EATING & DRINKING
Cap'Opéra 3
Chez Léon 5
Fish 7
Lax Bar 2
La Marquise 6
La Mère Brazier 1
Ninkasi 8
Le St-Vincent 4
N
AVENUE LACASSAGNE
COURS ALBERT-THOMAS
Sans Souci
Institut Lumière
BD DES TCHECOSLOVAQUES
AV DE FRERES LUMIERE
AVENUE LACASSAGNE
ACCOMMODATION
Centre International de Séjour C
De la Poste A
HI hostel D
Victoria B
8e
Montplaisir-Lumière
0 500 m
Venissieux, C, D, St Exupéry Airport & TGV Station & Grenoble

in Vieux Lyon (5e) on the west bank of the Saône, as well as the east bank of the Rhône (3e), including the modern development known as La Part-Dieu.

Arrival, information and city transport

The **Lyon-St Exupéry international airport** (Ⓣ08.26.80.08.26, Ⓦwww.lyon.aeroport.fr) and the new **TGV station** are off the Grenoble autoroute, 25km to the southeast of the city, with a 50-minute Satobus bus link to the town centre (every 20min 6am–11.40pm; €8.40). The Paris to Lyon trip is actually quicker by TGV, but it's only from the air that you can appreciate architect Santiago Calatrava's design of a huge bird alighting or taking flight from the station roof.

Central Lyon has two train stations: the **Gare de Perrache** on the Presqu'île is used mainly for ordinary trains rather than TGVs, and has the **gare routière** alongside; and **La Part-Dieu TGV station** is in the 3e arrondissement to the east of the Presqu'île. Some TGV trains from Paris give the option of getting off at either station, so ask when buying your ticket. Central Lyon is linked to the suburbs by a modern, efficient and driverless **métro**, as well as trolleybuses and a futuristic new **tram** system.

There's a **Bureau d'Information** in the Centre Perrache at the station (Mon–Fri 7.30am–6.30pm, Sat 9am–noon & 1.30–5pm; Ⓦwww.tcl.fr), where you can pick up a métro, tram, bus and funicular map; or it's just two stops on the métro to place Bellecour, where the **central tourist office** stands on the southeast corner (mid-April to mid-Oct Mon–Sat 9am–7pm, Sun 9.30am–6.30pm; mid-Oct to mid-April Mon–Sat 10am–5.30pm; Ⓣ04.72.77.69.69, Ⓦwww.lyon-france.com). The **bureau des guides**, on avenue Adolph-Max in Vieux Lyon, organizes and sells tickets for guided **tours**, including those in English (Ⓣ04.72.77.72.33). Half-day (€8) or day-long (€12) audio tours in English can be picked up at the main office, which also offers occasional English-language guided tours; alternatively, pick up the *Lyon Balades* leaflets (€0.50) which detail various English-language self-guided tours of the city on foot and by bike, including a rewarding tour of some of the more interesting *traboules*.

At métro stations or the city transport TCL offices, the cheapest way to buy **tickets** is in a carnet of ten (€11.90, discounts for students), or there's the *Ticket Liberté*, valid for 24 hours (€4.30). The ordinary tickets (€1.50) are flat-rate within an hour's duration and limited to a single one-way journey, with changes allowed. The métro runs from 5am to around midnight, though some bus lines close as early as 8pm.

Accommodation

As a result of Lyon's commercial pre-eminence, hotel **rooms** can be a problem to find, particularly on weekdays. If you don't book ahead, you could end up paying well over the odds for inferior accommodation. Hotels in Perrache (2^e) and Bellecour (2^e) fill up quickly, but you may be luckier around Terreaux (1er). If you're stuck, the tourist office offers a reservation service, though if you use it you'll have to find your room deposit there and then.

If you're on a real budget, stop by the CROUS offices, 59 rue de la Madeleine, 7e (Ⓣ04.72.80.13.00, Ⓦwww.crous-lyon.fr; M° Jean-Macé), or CRIJ offices, 9 quai des Celestins, 2e (Ⓣ04.72.77.00.66; M° Bellecour), both of whom may be able to fix you up in student lodgings or residences closer to the centre during vacation time.

Hotels

D'Ainay 14 rue des Remparts d'Ainay, 2e ⓣ04.78.42.43.42, ⓔhotel.ainay@wanadoo.fr; Mº Ampère Victor-Hugo. Situated in a pleasant, lively quarter, this place is preferable to its many cheap neighbours because of its decent-sized rooms, but it does fill fast. ❸

Alexandra 49 rue Victor-Hugo, 2e ⓣ04.78.37.75.79, ⓕ04.72.40.94.34; Mº Ampère Victor-Hugo. Well-run old hotel overlooking place Ampère, a lively pedestrian zone. Parking available. ❸

College 5 place St-Paul, 5e ⓣ04.72.10.05.05, ⓦwww.college-hotel.com; Mº Vieux-Lyon. Stylish three-star boutique hotel in a great Vieux Lyon location. ❻

Cour des Loges 2–8 rue du Boeuf, 5e ⓣ04.72.77.44.44, ⓦwww.courdesloges.com; Mº Vieux-Lyon. Lyon's finest hotel, set in a seventeenth-century former Jesuit college, with a stunning dining area in the glazed atrium. ❾

Globe et Cécil 21 rue Gasparin, 2e ⓣ04.78.42.58.95, ⓦwww.globeetcecilhotel.com; Mº Bellecour. Attractive, central and upmarket place with good service and a touch of originality in the decor. ❻

De la Marne 78 rue de la Charité, 2e ⓣ04.78.37.07.46, ⓔhoteldelamarnelyon@wanadoo.fr; Mº Perrache. Convenient and pleasant, with cheerful, newly refurbished rooms and smart marble bathrooms. ❸

De la Poste 1 rue Victor-Fort, 4e ⓣ & ⓕ04.78.28.62.67; Mº Croix-Rousse. A clean, acceptable old-fashioned cheapie near place Croix-Rousse. ❶

St-Pierre-des-Terreaux 8 rue Paul-Chenavard, 1er ⓣ04.78.28.24.61, ⓕ04.72.00.21.07; Mº Hôtel-de-Ville. A convenient if rather charmless establishment in a good location. ❸

St-Vincent 9 rue Pareille, 1er ⓣ04.78.27.22.56, ⓦwww.hotel-saintvincent.com; Mº Hôtel-de-Ville. Atmospheric old hotel near the Saône and the St-Vincent footbridge. Some rooms have exposed beams, stone walls and marble fireplaces. ❸

Du Théâtre 10 rue de Savoie, 2e ⓣ04.78.42.33.32, ⓦwww.hotel-du-theatre.fr; Mº Bellecour. A comfortable hotel with some character, well run by a pleasant young couple. ❺

La Tour Rose 22 rue du Boeuf, 5e ⓣ04.78.92.69.10, ⓦwww.tour-rose.com; Mº Vieux-Lyon. Swirling Lyon silks decorate twelve suites in a fifteenth-century house with garden courtyards. ❾

Vaubecour 28 rue Vaubecour, 2e ⓣ04.78.37.44.91, ⓔhotelvaubecour@wanadoo.fr; Mº Ampère Victor-Hugo. One block from the Saône, on the second floor of a grand nineteenth-century building. A bit shabby, but friendly and comfortable for the price. ❸

Victoria 3 rue Delandine, 2e ⓣ04.78.37.57.61, ⓦwww.hotelvictorialyon.com; Mº Perrache. A reasonable two-star near the Perrache station. ❸

Hostels and campsite

Centre International de Séjour de Lyon 103 bd États-Unis, 8e ⓣ04.37.90.42.42, ⓦwww.cis-lyon.com. Not far from the Vénissieux hostel, but a bit more expensive; the advantage is that it's out of earshot of the main ring road. It costs €15.70 for a dorm bed, and doubles are also available. Take bus #32 from Perrache or #36 from Part-Dieu, stop "États-Unis-Beauvisage". Check-in from 2.30pm. Open 24hr. ❶

HI hostel 51 rue Roger-Salengro, Vénissieux ⓣ04.78.76.39.23, ⓔlyon-sud@fuaj.org; Mº Gare de Vénissieux. Excellent hostel 4km southeast of the centre, with a full range of facilities. Beds in both doubles and dorms are €12. Take bus #36 from the métro, stop "J Curie – Auberge de Jeunesse".

HI hostel (Vieux Lyon) 41–45 montée du Chemin Neuf, 5e ⓣ04.78.15.05.50, ⓔlyon@fuaj.org; Mº Vieux-Lyon/Minimes. Modern hostel, with great views over Lyon and access to the Internet. Set in a steep part of the old town, the nearest métro station is Vieux-Lyon, but if you want to avoid the climb, get the funicular to Minimes and walk down the montée du Chemin Neuf. Beds are €18.60.

Camping Porte de Lyon Dardilly ⓣ04.78.35.64.55, ⓦwww.camping-lyon.com. North along the A6 from Lyon or by bus #89 (stop "Camping International") from the gare de Vaise. Alternatively #3 from Hôtel de Ville. Pleasant though expensive, with a tourist information bureau. €17.64 for a tent and two people.

The City

The centre of Lyon is the **Presqu'île**, or "peninsula", the tongue of land between the rivers Saône and Rhône, just north of their confluence. Most of it lies within the 2e arrondissement, but it's known by its *quartiers*, which include **Bellecour**, around the central square, and **Perrache**, around the station. At the top end of the Presqu'île, as the Saône veers west, is the 1er arrondissement,

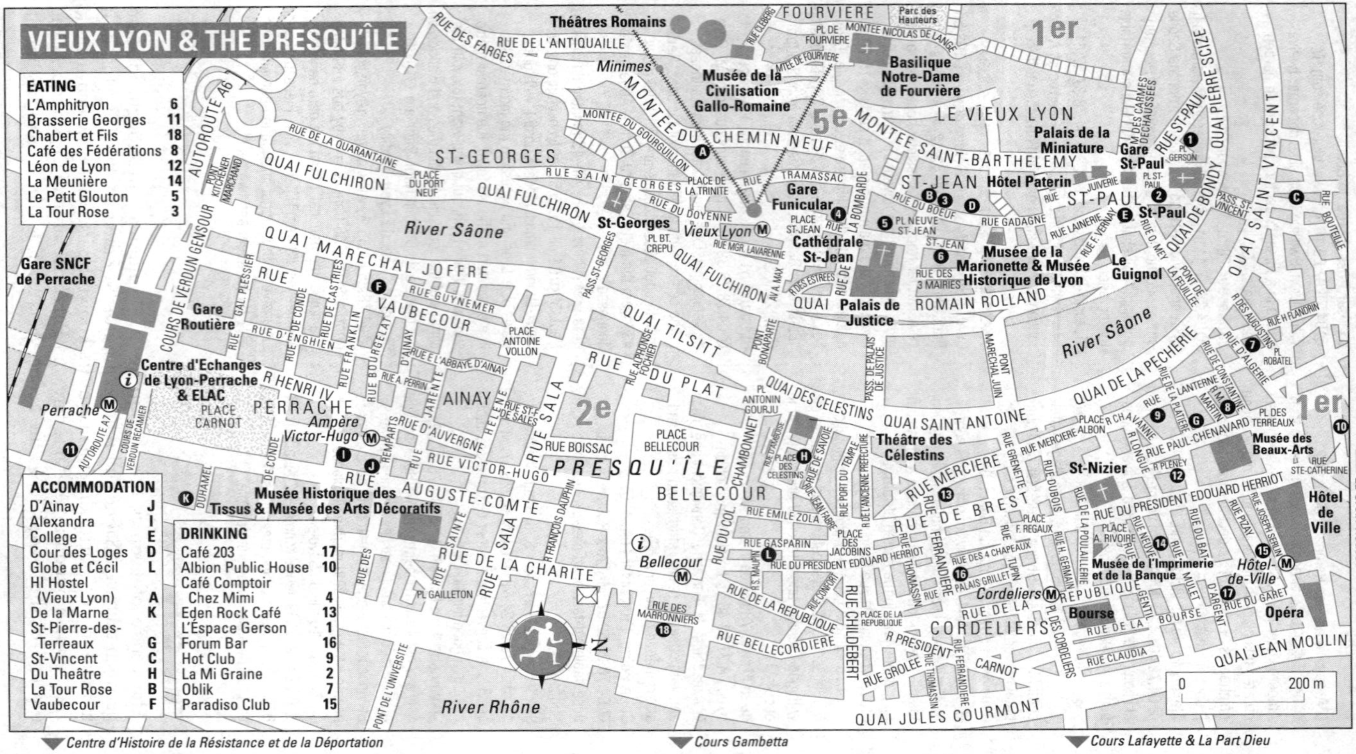
VIEUX LYON & THE PRESQU'ÎLE
EATING
L'Amphitryon 6
Brasserie Georges 11
Chabert et Fils 18
Café des Fédérations 8
Léon de Lyon 12
La Meunière 14
Le Petit Glouton 5
La Tour Rose 3
ACCOMMODATION
D'Ainay J
Alexandra I
College E
Cour des Loges D
Globe et Cécil L
HI Hostel (Vieux Lyon) A
De la Marne K
St-Pierre-des-Terreaux G
St-Vincent C
Du Théâtre H
La Tour Rose B
Vaubecour F
DRINKING
Café 203 17
Albion Public House 10
Café Comptoir Chez Mimi 4
Eden Rock Café 13
L'Espace Gerson 1
Forum Bar 16
Hot Club 9
La Mi Graine 2
Oblik 7
Paradiso Club 15
Théâtres Romains
Musée de la Civilisation Gallo-Romaine
Basilique Notre-Dame de Fourvière
Minimes
FOURVIERE
Parc des Hauteurs
1er
5e
2e
LE VIEUX LYON
ST-GEORGES
ST-JEAN
ST-PAUL
Palais de la Miniature
Gare St-Paul
St-Paul
Hôtel Paterin
Gare Funicular
Cathédrale St-Jean
Palais de Justice
Musée de la Marionette & Musée Historique de Lyon
Le Guignol
St-Georges
Vieux Lyon
River Saône
Gare SNCF de Perrache
Perrache
Gare Routière
Centre d'Echanges de Lyon-Perrache & ELAC
PLACE CARNOT
PERRACHE
Ampère Victor-Hugo
AINAY
Musée Historique des Tissus & Musée des Arts Décoratifs
PLACE BELLECOUR
PRESQU'ÎLE
BELLECOUR
Bellecour
Théâtre des Célestins
St-Nizier
Musée des Beaux-Arts
Hôtel de Ville
Hôtel-de-Ville
Musée de l'Imprimerie et de la Banque
Cordeliers
Bourse
Opéra
CORDELIERS
River Rhône
QUAI FULCHIRON
QUAI MARECHAL JOFFRE
QUAI ROMAIN ROLLAND
QUAI TILSITT
QUAI DES CELESTINS
QUAI SAINT ANTOINE
QUAI DE LA PECHERIE
QUAI SAINT VINCENT
QUAI PIERRE SCIZE
QUAI DE BONDY
QUAI JEAN MOULIN
QUAI JULES COURMONT
RUE DE LA REPUBLIQUE
RUE DU PRESIDENT EDOUARD HERRIOT
RUE VICTOR-HUGO
RUE AUGUSTE-COMTE
RUE DE LA CHARITE
RUE MERCIERE
RUE DE BREST
MONTEE DU CHEMIN NEUF
MONTEE SAINT-BARTHELEMY
AUTOROUTE A6
AUTOROUTE A7
COURS DE VERDUN GENSOUR
0 200 m
La Croix-Rousse
Centre d'Histoire de la Résistance et de la Déportation
Cours Gambetta
Cours Lafayette & La Part Dieu

Lyon City Card and Discovery Weekend

The **Lyon City Card** (€18, €28 or €38 for one, two or three days) grants unlimited access to the métro, bus and tramway, nineteen museums (including the Roman ruins in St-Romain-en-Gal), guided city tours and several short boat trips. The card is available from the tourist office and the major TCL (public transit) offices.

The **Discovery Weekend** (from €120 per person) includes two nights in a two-, three- or four-star hotel, the City Card, and lunch at a local *bouchon*. The package is available online through the tourist office website.

known as **Terreaux**, centred on place des Terreaux and the Hôtel de Ville. On the west bank of the Saône is the old town, or **Vieux Lyon**, at the foot of Fourvière, on which the Romans built their capital of Gaul, Lugdunum. Vieux Lyon is made up of three villages: St-Paul, St-Jean and St-Georges, and forms the eastern end of the 5ᵉ arrondissement. The 9ᵉ lies to its north.

To the north of the Presqu'île is the old silk-weavers' district of **La Croix-Rousse**, the 4ᵉ arrondissement. **Modern Lyon** lies east of the Rhône, with the 7ᵉ and 8ᵉ arrondissements to the south, the 3ᵉ arrondissement in the middle, with **La Part-Dieu TGV station** amidst an assertive cultural and commercial centre, and the 6ᵉ arrondissement, known as **Brotteaux**, to the north. North of Brotteaux is Lyon's main open space, the **Parc de la Tête d'Or**. The district of **Villeurbanne**, home to the university and the Théâtre National Populaire, lies east of the 6ᵉ and the park.

The Presqu'île

The pink gravelly acres of **place Bellecour** were first laid out in 1617, and today form a focus on the peninsula, with views up to the looming bulk of Notre-Dame-de-Fourvière. The square is vast, dwarfing even the central statue of Louis XIV in the guise of a Roman emperor. Running south, **rue Auguste-Comte** is full of antique shops selling heavily framed eighteenth-century art works, and **rue Victor-Hugo** is a pedestrian precinct that continues north of place Bellecour on rue de la République all the way up to the back of the Hôtel de Ville below the area of La Croix-Rousse.

South of place Bellecour on rue de la Charité is Lyon's best museum, the **Musée Historique des Tissus** (Tues–Sun 10am–5.30pm; €5), housed in the eighteenth-century former town palace of the Duke of Villeroy. It doesn't quite live up to its claim to cover the history of decorative cloth through the ages, but it does have brilliant collections from certain periods, notably third-century Greek-influenced and sixth-century Coptic tapestries, woven silk and painted linen from Egypt. The fragment of woven wool *aux poissons* ("with fish"; second to third century AD) has an artistry unmatched in European work until at least the eighteenth century. There are silks from Baghdad and carpets from Iran, Turkey, India and China. The stuff produced in Lyon itself reflects the luxurious nature of the silk trade: seventeenth- to nineteenth-century hangings and chair covers, including hangings from Marie-Antoinette's bedroom at Versailles, from Empress Josephine's room at Fontainebleau and from the palaces of Catherine the Great of Russia. Sadly, there's almost nothing from the period of the Revolution, but there are some lovely twentieth-century pieces – including Sonia Delaunay's *Tissus Simultanés* – and couture creations from Worth to Mariano Fortuny, Paco Rabanne and Christian Lacroix. The **Musée des Arts Décoratifs** next door (Tues–Sun 10am–noon & 2–5.30pm; same ticket as Musée des Tissus) displays faïence, porcelain, furniture and a couple of eighteenth-century rooms removed from old houses in the Presqu'Île, plus a room-sized nineteenth-century panorama of Lyon and a collection of superb modern silverware by noted architects, including Richard Meier and Zaha Hadid.

To the south, the station area around Perrache is of little interest, but over the Rhône, across the adjacent pont Gallieni, at 14 av Berthelot, is the **Centre d'Histoire de la Résistance et de la Déportation** (Wed–Sun 9am–5.30pm; €3.80; M° Perrache/Jean-Macé). In addition to a library of books, videos, memoirs and other documents recording experiences of resistance, occupation and deportation to the camps, there's an exhibition space housed over the very cellars and cells in which Klaus Barbie, the Gestapo boss of Lyon, tortured and murdered his victims. Barbie was brought back from Bolivia and tried in Lyon in 1987 for crimes against humanity; the principal "exhibit" is a moving and unsettling 45-minute video (five shows daily; French only) of the trial in which some of his victims recount their terrible ordeal.

To the north of place Bellecour at the top of quai St-Antoine is the **quartier Mercière**, the old commercial centre of the town, with sixteenth- and seventeenth-century houses lining rue Mercière, and the **church of St-Nizier**, whose bells used to announce the nightly closing of the city's gates. In the silk-weavers' uprising of 1831 (see box opposite), workers fleeing the soldiers took refuge in the church, only to be massacred. Today, traces of this working-class life are almost gone, edged out by bars, restaurants and designer shops, the latter along rue du Président Edouard-Herriot and the long pedestrian rue de la République in particular. Close to St-Nizier, at 13 rue de la Poulaillerie, is the **Musée de l'Imprimerie et de la Banque** (Wed–Sun 9.30am–noon & 2–6pm; €3.80); unfortunately, its collection is unattractively displayed, which is a pity, for Lyon was both a leading publishing and banking centre in Renaissance times.

Further north, the monumental nineteenth-century **fountain** in front of the even more monumental **Hôtel de Ville** on place des Terreaux symbolizes rivers straining to reach the ocean. It was designed by Bartholdi, of Statue of Liberty fame, although the rows of watery leaks that sprout up unexpectedly across the rest of the square are a modern addition. Opposite is the large bulk of the **Musée des Beaux-Arts** (Mon–Thurs, Sat & Sun 10am–6pm; Fri 10.30am–6pm; €6), housed in a former Benedictine abbey and whose collections are second in France only to those in the Louvre. The museum is organized roughly by genre, with nineteenth- and twentieth-century sculpture, represented by Canova, Barye and Rodin's *Temptation of St Anthony* in the ex-chapel on the ground floor. There's a fine collection of medieval French, Dutch, German and Italian woodcarving on the first floor along with antiquities, coins and *objets d'art*. The representation of twentieth-century painting was strengthened in 1998 by the donation of Lyon-born actress Jaqueline Delubac's collection, including works by Picasso and Matisse. There are also Braques, a brace of typically domestic Bonnards and a gory Francis Bacon. The nineteenth century is represented by the Impressionists and their forerunners, Corot and Courbet; there are works by the Lyonnais artists Antoine Berjon and Fleury Richard, and from there you can work your way back through Rubens, Zurbarán, El Greco, Tintoretto and a hundred others.

Behind the Hôtel de Ville, on the edge of several linked squares, stands Lyon's **opera house** (tours Sat at 1pm; €9, book through the tourist office on place Bellecour). Radically redesigned in 1993 by the architect Jean Nouvel, its original Neoclassical elevations are now topped by a huge glass Swiss roll of a roof, and the interior is now entirely black with silver stairways climbing into the darkness.

La Croix-Rousse

La Croix-Rousse is the old silk-weavers' district and spreads up the steep slopes of the hill above the northern end of the Presqu'île. It's still a working-class area, but barely a couple of dozen people operate the modern high-speed computerized looms that are kept in business by the restoration and maintenance of France's palaces and châteaux. You can see an authentic silk worker's atelier at the **Soierie Vivante**, 21 rue Richan (Tues 2–6.30pm, Wed–Sat 9am–noon & 2–6.30pm, M° Croix-Rousse; €3), while at **Passage Thiaffait** on rue Réné-Leynaud one of the original **traboules** – alleyways and tunnelled passages originally built to provide shelter from the weather for the silk-weavers as they moved their delicate pieces of work from one part of the manufacturing process to another – has been refurbished to provide premises for young couturiers.

The streets running down from **boulevard de la Croix-Rousse**, as well as many across the river in Vieux Lyon, are intersected by these *traboules*. Normally hidden by plain doors, they are impossible to distinguish from normal entryways; hence they proved an indispensable escape network for prewar gangsters, wartime Resistance fighters and, more recently, for anarchists, who used them in thwarting police efforts to capture them during the 2005 riots, forcing the authorities to resort to temporary curfews. Try going up past the right of St-Polycarpe on **rue Réné-Leynaud** above place Terreaux, then take rue Pouteau. Turn right into **rue des Tables Claudiennes**, and enter no. 55 emerging opposite 29 rue Imbert-Colomes. Climb the stairs into 14bis, cross three more courtyards, including the spectacular cour des Voraces, and you finally emerge at **place Colbert**.

Officially the *traboules* of La Croix-Rousse and Vieux-Lyon are public thoroughfares during daylight hours – one of the tourist office's *Lyon Balades* guides explores them – but you may find some closed today for security reasons, especially as the area is gradually being gentrified. The long climb up the part-pedestrianized **Montée de la Grande Côte**, however, still gives an idea of

The silk strike of 1831

Though the introduction of the Jacquard loom of 1804 made it possible for one person to produce 25cm of silk in a day instead of taking four people four days, **silk workers**, or *canuts* – whether masters and apprentices, or especially women and child workers – were badly paid whatever their output. Over the three decades following the introduction of the Jacquard, the price paid for a length of silk fell by over fifty percent. Attempts to regulate the price were ignored by the dealers, even though hundreds of skilled workers were languishing in debtors' jails. On November 21, 1831, the *canuts* called an all-out **strike**. As they processed down the Montée de la Grande Côte with their black flags and the slogan "Live working or die fighting", they were shot at and three people died. After a rapid retreat uphill they built barricades, assisted by half the National Guard, who refused to fire cannon at their "comrades of Croix-Rousse". For three days the battle raged on all four banks, the silk workers using sticks, stones and knives to defend themselves, and the bourgeoisie running scared, with only the area between the rivers, place des Terreaux and just north of St-Nizier still under their control. Unfortunately for the *canuts*, their employers were able to call on outside aid, and 30,000 extra troops arrived to quash the rebellion. Some 600 people were killed or wounded, and in the end the silk industrialists were free to pay whatever pitiful fee they chose, but the uprising was one of the first instances of organized labour taking to the streets during the most revolutionary fifty years of French history.

what the *quartier* was like in the sixteenth century, when the *traboules* were first built. Take a look at the pretty **place Sathonay** at the bottom, where a public garden and a lively local café are overlooked by Croix-Rousse Mairie, and, if you have enough energy left, come down by the **rue Joséphin-Soulary**, which looks more like a lane in a country village and will bring you down a long flight of steps to the pont Winston-Churchill.

Vieux Lyon

Reached by one of the three *passerelles* (footbridges) crossing the Saône from Terreaux and the Presqu'île, **Vieux Lyon** is made up of the three villages of St-Jean, St-Georges and St-Paul at the base of the hill overlooking the Presqu'île.

South of place St-Paul, the streets of Vieux Lyon, pressed close together beneath the hill of **Fourvière**, form a backdrop of Renaissance and medieval facades, bright night-time illumination and a swelling chorus of well-dressed Lyonnais in search of supper or a midday splurge. One of the most impressive buildings at the northern end is the sixteenth-century **Hôtel Paterin** at 4–6 rue Juiverie, a galleried mansion best viewed from the bottom of montée St-Barthélémy, just up from place St-Paul.

A short way south of the Hôtel Paterin, the **Musée Historique de Lyon**, on the ground floor of a fifteenth-century mansion on place du Petit-Collège, has a good collection of Nevers ceramics, but was closed for major refurbishment at the time of writing (check with tourist office for information). In any case, the **Musée de la Marionnette**, on the first floor, is a lot more entertaining, and features the eighteenth-century Lyonnais creations, Guignol and Madelon – the French equivalents of Punch and Judy. If you want to see them in action, check out the times of performances at **Le Guignol**, 2 rue Garrand, by quai de Bondy (Oct–May Wed, Sat & Sun 3pm; €8–13; for tickets and other puppet shows ⓣ04.78.28.92.57).

If you're *traboule*-hunting in Vieux Lyon, two of the best can be found on two streets leading south from place du Petit-Collège: the winding passage behind the door at 27 rue de Boeuf, and that at 28 rue St-Jean, which leads to the courtyard of a fifteenth-century palace. The central pedestrianized **rue St-Jean** ends at the twelfth- to fifteenth-century **Cathédrale St-Jean** (Mon–Fri 8am–noon & 2–7.30pm; Sat, Sun & holidays 8am–noon & 2–5pm). Though the west facade lacks most of its statuary as a result of various wars and revolutions, it's still impressive, and the thirteenth-century stained glass above the altar and in the rose windows of the transepts is in perfect condition. In the northern transept is a fourteenth-century astronomical clock, its mechanism cloaked by a beautiful Renaissance casing: it's capable of computing moveable feast days (such as Easter) till the year 2019, and most days on the strike of noon, 2pm, 3pm and 4pm, the figures of the Annunciation go through an automated set piece, heralded by the lone bugler at the top of the clock. The cathedral treasury is also worth a look for its religious artefacts, ranging from Byzantine to nineteenth-century (Wed–Sun 10am–noon & 2–6pm; free).

Just beyond the cathedral, opposite avenue Adolphe-Max and pont Bonaparte, is the **gare funicular** and the Vieux Lyon métro, from where you can ascend to the town's Roman remains (direction "St-Just", stop "Minimes"). The antiquities consist of two ruined **theatres** dug into the hillside (entrance at 6 rue de l'Antiquaille; mid-April to mid-Sept 9am–9pm; mid-Sept to mid-April 9am–7pm; free) – the larger of which was built by Augustus and extended in the second century by Hadrian to seat 10,000 spectators – and an underground museum of Lyonnais life from prehistoric times to 7 AD, the **Musée de la Civilisation Gallo-Romaine**, 17 rue Cléberg (Tues–Sun: March–Oct 10am–6pm;

Nov–Feb 10am–5pm; €3.80). Here, a unique pre-Roman bronze processional chariot heralds an imaginatively displayed collection. The fragments of a fine bronze engraving of a speech by the Lyon-born Emperor Claudius, as well as the sheer number and splendour of the mosaics here, serve to underline Roman Lyon's importance. Nowadays, the ancient theatres are the focal point for the **Nuits de Fourvière** music and film festival that takes place annually in June and July (Ⓣ04.72.32.00.00, Ⓦwww.nuitsdefourviere.fr).

From the museum, it's just a moment's walk to the **Basilique Notre-Dame de Fourvière**, a fussily ornamented wedding cake of a church built, like the Sacré-Coeur in Paris, in the aftermath of the 1871 Commune to emphasize the defeat of the godless socialists. And like the Sacré-Coeur, its hilltop position has become an almost defining element in the city's skyline. What makes a visit worthwhile is the magnificent view of the city, best appreciated from the top of the **Tour de l'Observatoire** (Wed–Sun 10.30am–noon & 2–6.30pm; €2), from which you can distinguish the different quarters and see how they have grown and been shaped by the Saône and Rhône over the centuries. The Basilique is also accessible direct from the Vieux Lyon funicular station: if you arrive by this route, it's worth walking down along the **montée St-Barthélémy** footpath, which winds back to Vieux Lyon through the hanging gardens below the church.

Modern Lyon

On the skyline from Fourvière, you can't miss the gleaming pencil-like skyscraper that belongs to Lyon's homegrown Crédit Lyonnais bank. This is the centrepiece of **La Part-Dieu**, a business-culture-commerce conglomerate which includes one of the biggest public libraries outside Paris, a mammoth concert hall and a busy shopping centre (M° Part-Dieu). The elegant tower aside, it's all rather lumpen and unfriendly to look at. Penetrate the forbidding exterior of the main market at 102 cours Lafayette, however, and you'll discover a gastronomic wonderland within, with superb seafood, poultry, cheese and charcuterie stalls (Mon–Thurs 7.30am–noon & 3–7pm; Fri & Sat 7.30am–7pm; Sun 7.30am–noon).

For a break from city buildings head north to the **Parc de la Tête d'Or** (M° to Masséna, then walk up rue Masséna), where there are ponds and rose gardens, botanical gardens, a small zoo and lots of amusements for kids. It's overlooked by the bristling antennae of the international headquarters of Interpol, part of a new **Cité Internationale**, which also includes luxury apartments and a new **Musée d'Art Contemporain**, at 81 quai Charles-de-Gaulle (Wed–Sun noon–7pm; Ⓦwww.moca-lyon.org; €3.80; Line B to M° Saxe-Gambetta or M° Place Guichard then bus #4, stop "Musée d'Art Contemporain"). The museum owns the largest public collection of installation art in the world, hosts excellent temporary exhibitions and is also one of the homes of the Lyon art biennial. Designed by Renzo Piano, it's a curious-looking structure with a 1930s Neoclassical facade on the park side and a pink concrete cinema tacked onto the riverside. The colour echoes the adjacent **Palais des Congrès** conference centre, whose front is masked by a glass screen curving up over the roof, reminiscent of Jean Nouvel's Institut du Monde Arabe in Paris. There are some screens, catwalks and companionways: the features that have become part of the currency of architectural language since the Pompidou Centre first shocked the world. But it looks good, if a little artificial and immaculate behind its security barriers. To the east, dividing the park and the university, is boulevard de Stalingrad, where antique-fanciers can browse in the **Cité des Antiquaires** arcades at no. 117 (Thurs, Sat & Sun 9.30am–12.30pm & 2.30–7pm; closed Sun afternoon in summer).

In Villeurbanne, not far to the east of Part-Dieu, is the **Institut d'Art Contemporain**, 11 rue Dr-Dolard (June–Sept Wed 1–8pm, Thurs–Sun 1–7pm; Oct–May Wed–Sun 1–6pm; Ⓦwww.i-art-c.org; €4; bus #1, stop "Cité/Nouveau Musée"), where thought-provoking and engaging exhibitions by contemporary artists question the function of art and architecture and their relation to society. It's also worth looking out for exhibitions at Villeurbanne's **Maison du Livre de l'Image et du Son**, to the east on avenue Émile-Zola (Mon 2–7pm, Tues–Fri 11am–7pm, Sat 10am–6pm; M° Flachet), which might feature anything from medieval illuminations to CD-ROMs.

Further south, on the edge of the 8e arrondissement, is the **Institut Lumière**, 25 rue du Premier-Film (Tues–Sun 11am–6.30pm; Ⓦwww.institut-lumiere.org; €6.50; M° Monplaisir-Lumière). The building was the home of Antoine Lumière, father of Auguste and Louis, who made the first films, and the exhibits feature early magic lanterns and the cameras used by the brothers, along with various art photographs. The Institut also shows several different films nightly; check their website for the schedule.

Right down in the south of the city, in the **Gerland quartier** (7e), is a newly developed area with a marina and a park on the Rhône's east bank, which provides an illusion of nature around the mirrored Institut Pasteur and the thrusting wings and arches of the École Normale Supérieure. Across the bridge from the southern tip of the Presqu'île, just off place Antonin-Perrin, squats the massive **Tony Garnier Hall** (M° Debourg), a former abbatoir, whose 17,000 cubic metres is completely free of roof-supporting columns. Its walls graced with contemporary murals, it is now the main host to Lyon's art biennial – a major European show of new art convened here every other year (Sept–Jan in odd-numbered years). On even-numbered years Lyon instead hosts the dance biennial which rocks the city through September with over 160 performances taking place at 23 different venues.

Eating, drinking and entertainment

You'll find **restaurants** offering dishes from every region of France and overseas in Lyon. Vieux Lyon is the area with the greatest concentration of eateries, though you'll find cheaper and less busy ones between place des Jacobins and place Sathonay at the top of the Presqu'île, with a particularly dense and atmospheric concentration in rue Mercière. The possibilities are endless, but on weekends booking ahead is always a good idea.

The **bouchon**, the traditional Lyonnais eating establishment, is the best place to eat *quenelles*, sausages, tripe and the like. Its name derives either from *bouchon* (cork), or *bouchonner* (to rub down). One popular theory has it that wine bottles were lined up as the evening progressed, and at the end of the night the bill was determined by measuring from the first cork to the last. Another explanation, however, is that inns serving wine would attach small bundles of straw to their signs, indicating that horses could be cared for (*bouchonnés*) while the coachmen went inside to have a drink.

Lyon is almost as good a place for **nightlife** and **entertainment** as it is for eating, with a good range of clubs, cinema, opera, jazz, classical music concerts and theatre. The best places to wander if you are looking for a **bar** are rue Mercière, the area around place des Terreaux and the Opéra (where most of Lyon's **lesbian and gay** scene is also found) and, most particularly, the streets of Vieux Lyon. Make a point of crossing the river by the *passerelles*; the whole district looks magnificent at night.

For **listings**, pick up a free copy of the weekly newspaper, *Le Petit Bulletin*, or the free monthly *…491* from tourist offices and outlets citywide. Alternatively

△ Lyon *bouchon*

buy a copy of the weekly *Lyon Poche*, available from newsagents (every Wed; €1), or look online at Ⓦwww.lyonpoche.com.

Restaurants

L'Amphitryon 33 rue St-Jean, 5ᵉ ⓣ04.78.37.23.68; Mº Vieux-Lyon. Usually packed restaurant serving Lyonnais specialities; menus from €15. Service till midnight.

Brasserie Georges 30 cours de Verdun, 2ᵉ ⓣ04.72.56.54.54; Mº Perrache. Vast Art Deco brasserie originally founded in 1836; *choucroutes* are the speciality. Menus at €19.50, €21.50 & €24.50.

Chabert et Fils 11 rue des Marronniers, 2ᵉ ⓣ04.78.37.01.94; Mº Bellecour. *Bouchon* offering the ubiquitous *quenelle* and *andouillette* (offal sausage) specialities, along with other first-rate dishes. Menus €16.50–33.

Chez Léon Halles de la Part-Dieu, 102 cours Lafayette, 3ᵉ ⓣ04.78.62.30.28; Mº Part-Dieu. Tiny, bustling oyster bar in the market halls. Around €19 for lunch. Closed outside the oyster season, which usually means May–Aug.

Café des Fédérations 8 rue du Major-Martin, 1ᵉʳ ⓣ04.78.28.26.00; Mº Hôtel-de-Ville. Typical *bouchon* serving the earthiest of Lyonnais specialities (marinated tripe, black pudding and fish quenelles) in an atmosphere to match: there's even sawdust on the floor. Menu at €23.50 for dinner. Closed Sat, Sun & Aug.

Léon de Lyon 1 rue Pléney, 1ᵉʳ ⓣ04.72.10.11.12; Mº Hôtel-de-Ville. Sophisticated and delicious food, with original culinary creations as well as traditional Lyonnais recipes in this upmarket brasserie. Menus from €105, but there's a lunch menu for €57. Closed first three weeks in Aug.

La Mère Brazier 12 rue Royale, 1ᵉʳ ⓣ04.78.28.15.49; Mº Croix-Paquet. A beautiful setting complements the excellent food at this restaurant, still run by Mme Brazier, the granddaughter of the couple who founded it in 1921. Menus at €46 and €55, but you can easily spend more. Closed Sat lunch, Sun, Tues & Aug.

La Meunière 11 rue Neuve, 1ᵉʳ ⓣ04.78.28.62.91; Mº Hôtel-de-Ville. Booking is essential in this excellent *bouchon*, but it's worth it, with menus of Lyonnais specialities from €15 to €27. Closed Sun, Mon & mid-July to mid-Aug.

Paul Bocuse 40 rue de la Plage, Collonges-au-Mont-d'Or ⓣ04.72.42.90.90. Lyon's most famous restaurant, named after its celebrity chef-owner, is 9km north of the city, on the west bank of the Saône. Traditional French gastronomy is the bill of fare, with bass *en croûte* or soup with black truffle. From €60 upwards.

Le Petit Glouton 56 rue St-Jean, 5ᵉ ⓣ04.78.37.30.10; Mº Vieux-Lyon. A small but airy and unpretentious bistro in the heart of Vieux Lyon. You can dine inside or on the small street-side terrace from €12.

Le St-Vincent 6 place Fernand-Rey 1ᵉʳ ⓣ04.72.07.70.43; Mº Hôtel-de-Ville. A dozen tables in a quiet arty square shaded by mimosas. Delicious foie gras or veal kidneys in Martini under an awning strung with coloured lights. Lunch €12.50, evening menu €21. Closed Sun.

La Tour Rose 22 rue du Boeuf, 5e ⓣ04.78.92.69.10; M° Vieux-Lyon. Gastronomic place with concoctions like asparagus with an oyster mousse or salad of lobster and spinach with a creamed truffle sauce. From €55. Closed Sun. Worth peeking at is the actual Tour Rose (the tower of a small Renaissance house) in the courtyard next door at nearby no.16.

Bars and clubs

Café 203 9 rue du Garet, 1er; M° Hôtel-de-Ville. Lively bar taking its name from the classic Peugeots parked out front. Cheap *plats du jour* all day. Daily 7am–1am, closed Sun lunch.

Albion Public House 12 rue Ste-Catherine, 1er; M° Hôtel-de-Ville. Oldest English-style pub in Lyon with draught beer and a good selection of whiskies. You can play darts, watch Premiership football or surf the Net. Regular live music and theme nights. Daily 5pm–3am; closed end July to early Aug.

Café Comptoir Chez Mimi 68 rue St-Jean, 5e; M° Vieux-Lyon. Tiny, convivial bistro which looks like it was decorated from a flea market, offering drinks, salads, and omelettes. Simple but good if you can get a seat. Wed–Sat noon–1am & 6.30-11.30pm, Sun noon–9pm.

Eden Rock Café 68 rue Mercière, 2e; M° Cordeliers. Massive bar, decorated with memorabilia and modern art from the States, with cheap beer and food served until 1am. Live music Wed–Sat with an accent on rock. Tues & Wed noon–1am, Thurs noon–2am, Fri & Sat noon–3am; closed part of Aug.

L'Éspace Gerson 1 place Gerson, 5e; M° Vieux-Lyon. Cool modern bar with frequent jazz and performance art, plus billiards. €7–15 entry normally. Mon–Sat 8pm–midnight.

Fish opposite 21 quai Augagneur, 3e; M° Guillotière. One of Lyon's hippest nightclubs, specializing in house. Admission €7–15, prices higher after midnight. Tues–Fri 10pm–5am, in summer from 7pm; Tues student night, Fri theme night.

Hot Club 26 rue du Lanterne, 1er ⓦwww.hotclubjazz.com; M° Hôtel-de-Ville. Jazz jam sessions and concerts of all varieties in a vaulted cellar. Tues–Sat 9pm–1am; closed Aug.

La Marquise opposite 20 quai Augagneur, 3e; M° Guillotière. Old barge with dance club below deck. DJs spin jungle, salsa and house. There is usually no cover unless it's a special guest DJ, in which case you'll pay €6–8. Wed–Sat from anytime between 8 & 11pm onwards.

La Mi Graine 11 place St-Paul, 5e; M° Vieux-Lyon. Welcoming small café with live music and/or DJs Thurs–Sat. Also serves meals. Open daily 11.30am–3am.

Ninkasi 267 rue Marcel Mérieux, 7e; M° Gerland. Lyon's own microbrewery, with salads and burgers upstairs, bar, DJs and live music downstairs. Outdoor film screenings Wed in summer. Mon–Thurs 10–1am; Fri & Sat 10–3am; Sun 4pm–midnight.

Paradiso Club 24 rue Pizay, 1er; M° Hôtel-de-Ville. Over-25s disco with regular Chippendales and singles' nights. €13 cover. Daily 10.30pm–dawn.

Lesbian and gay bars and clubs

Cap'Opéra 2 place Louis-Pradel, 1er; M° Hôtel-de-Ville. Trendy, officially "mixed" (but really mostly gay) DJ bar close to the opera house. Mon–Sat 2pm–3am.

Forum Bar 15 rue des Quatre-Chapeaux, 2e; M° Cordeliers. Convivial men's bar with bearish decor and clientele, tucked in an alley just north of the places des Jacobins and de la République. Mon–Thurs & Sun 5pm–2am, Fri & Sat 5pm–3am.

Lax Bar 2 rue Coysevox, 1er; M° Hôtel-de-Ville. As much a youth club as a bar, with Internet access, pool table and giant video screen. Mixed, but it tends to be gayer later. Open 4pm–3am.

Oblik 26 rue Hippolyte-Flandrin, 1er; M° Hôtel-de-Ville. Relaxed café/bar popular with gay men and lesbians. Regular exhibitions of work by young artists. Tues–Sat 5pm–1am.

Theatre, music and film

Look out for **stage productions** by the Théâtre National Populaire (TNP), 8 place Lazare-Goujon (ⓣ04.78.03.30.00; M° Gratte-Ciel), based across the street from Villeurbanne's town hall. Less radical stuff is shown at the city's gilded Théâtre des Célestins, in place des Célestins, 2e (ⓣ04.72.77.40.00, ⓦwww.celestins-lyon.org; M° Bellecour). The **opera house**, one of the best in France, is on place de la Comédie, 1er (ⓣ04.72.00.45.45, ⓦwww.opera-lyon.org; M° Hôtel-de-Ville), with cheap tickets sold just before performances begin. For avant-garde, classic and obscure **films**, usually in their original language, check the listings for the cinemas CNP Terreaux, Bellecour, Fourmi Lafayette, Opéra and Ambiance, as well as the Institut Lumière. Also, look out for the Lyon dance biennial, which brings in hundreds of artists and troupes from around the world (last three weeks of Sept in even-numbered years; Ⓦwww.biennale-de-lyon.org).

Listings

Bike rental Holiday Bikes, 199 rue Vendome, 3e Ⓣ04.78.60.11.10, Ⓦwww.holiday-bikes.com.
Boat trips Société Naviginter, 13bis quai Rambaud, 2e Ⓣ04.78.42.96.81. Leaving from quai des Célestins, boats run up the Saône or down to the confluence with the Rhône at the Île Barbe (April–June & Sept–Oct Tues–Sun, July & Aug daily; €7). The same company offers lunch and dinner cruises from €37.
Car rental Europcar, 40 rue de la Villette, 3e Ⓣ08.25.00.25.22; Hertz, 40 rue Villette, 3e Ⓣ04.72.33.89.89; Avis, Gare Part-Dieu, 3e Ⓣ04.72.33.37.19. All the above also have offices at the airport and at the Perrache centre.
Consulates Canada, 21 rue Bourgelat, 2e Ⓣ04.72.77.64.07; UK, 24 rue Childebert, 2e Ⓣ04.72.77.81.70; USA, 16 rue République, 2e Ⓣ04.78.38.36.88.
Disabled travellers For information on facilities for the disabled contact Délégation Départmentale APF, 73ter, rue Francis de Pressensé, Villeurbanne Ⓣ04.72.43.01.01, Ⓕ04.78.93.61.99.
Emergencies Samu – emergency medical attention Ⓣ15; Police Ⓣ17; SOS Médecins Ⓣ04.78.83.51.51. Hospitals: Croix-Rousse, (Ⓣ04.72.07.10.46); Hôpital Edouard-Herriot, place d'Arsonval, 3e (Ⓣ04.72.11.69.53). For house calls contact the medical referral centres (Ⓣ04.72.33.00.33).
Internet Planète Net Phone, 21 rue Romarin, 1er (Ⓦwww.cybercafe-planete-net-phone.com; Mon–Sat 10am–9pm), has plenty of terminals; Raconte Moi de la Terre, 38 rue Thomassin, 2e (Ⓦwww.raconte-moi.com; Mon–Sat 10am–7.30pm), is cheaper and also serves snacks.
Lesbian and gay info ARIS (Accueil Rencontres Informations Services), 16 rue Polycarpe Ⓣ04.78.27.10.10. Gay and lesbian centre organizing various activities and producing a useful scene guide. État d'Esprit, 19 rue Royale Ⓣ04.78.27.76.53, is a gay and lesbian bookstore that also holds cultural events. Forum Gai et Lesbien, 17 rue Romarin Ⓣ04.78.39.97.72, Ⓦwww.fgllyon.org. Lyon celebrates lesbian and gay pride in mid-June.
Money exchange AOC, 20 rue Gasparin (Mon–Sat 9.30am–6.30pm); AOC Opéra, 3 rue de la République (Mon–Fri 9am–6pm).
Pharmacy Blanchet, 5 place des Cordeliers, 2e Ⓣ04.78.42.12.42. Daily till midnight.
Police The main commissariat is on rue de la Charité, 2e Ⓣ04.78.42.26.56.
Post office PTT, place Antonin-Poncet, Lyon 69002.
Taxis Ⓣ04.78.28.23.23 or 04.78.27.31.31.

Around Lyon

Within easy reach of the city, the **Monts du Lyonnais** to the south and west of Lyon may not reach spectacular heights, but they offer quiet and solitude among steep, forested hills and unassuming villages surrounded by cherry orchards, the region's main source of income. Tourism is low-key, but food and accommodation in the hostels of the mountain villages are rarely a problem for visitors to the area's parks and museums. **Bus** services from the main *gare routière* and the western gare de Gorge du Loup (M° Gorge-du-Loup; 9e) to the larger villages are reasonably frequent, and to the east of Lyon, the medieval town of **Pérouges** can easily be reached by train from both stations. The mountains can be visited every Sunday from June until the middle of September by steam train, leaving from **L'Arbresle**, just west of Lyon (frequent trains from Lyon-Perrache; €9 return); it's a scenic service but not very useful for getting anywhere.

St-Pierre-la-Palud and St-Martin-en-Haut

Fifteen kilometres west of Lyon, the **Musée de la Mine** at **ST-PIERRE-LA-PALUD** (March–Nov Sat, Sun & hols 2–6pm; €4.60) is guaranteed to instill admiration for the endurance of the miners who put up with working conditions like those simulated in the reconstructed mine shaft which forms the main exhibit. Going down into the copper sulphate mine shaft while an ex-miner explains its workings in meticulous detail (2hr; in French) is not recommended if you're claustrophobic. Back on the surface, you move on to an exhibition about the former mining village and pit.

Although most of the villages in the Lyonnais mountains have a restaurant or two, finding a place to stay is somewhat more challenging. In **ST-MARTIN-EN-HAUT**, an hour's bus ride from the gare de Gorge du Loup in Lyon, is the hotel *Le Relais des Bergers* (ⓣ04.78.48.51.22; ❸), probably the best bet for the area. There's also a tourist office on place de l'Église (Tues–Sat 9am–noon & 2–6pm, Sun 10am–noon & 3–6pm; ⓣ04.78.48.64.32), and a municipal **campsite** just outside the village on the D122 (ⓣ04.78.48.62.16; all year).

Pérouges and Crémieu

Twenty-nine kilometres northeast of Lyon on the N84, **PÉROUGES** is a beautiful village of cobbled alleyways and ancient houses, some of them pleasing ruins. Its charm has not gone unnoticed by the French film industry – historical dramas like *The Three Musketeers* and *Monsieur Vincent* were filmed within its fortifications – nor by some of the residents, who have fought long and hard for preservation orders on its most interesting buildings. The result is an immaculate, if perhaps rather stifling, work of conservation.

Local traditional life is also thriving in the hands of a hundred or so workers who still weave locally grown hemp. No particular monument stands out, but the central square, the **place du Halle**, and its main street, the **rue du Prince**, have some of the best-preserved French medieval remains. The **lime tree** on place du Halle is a symbol of liberty, planted in 1792. The place both to **stay** and eat in Pérouges, if you can afford it, is the *Ostellerie du Vieux Pérouges* (ⓣ04.74.61.00.88, ⓦwww.ostellerie.com; ❾), in a medieval town house fronting the square; its **restaurant** serves traditional mountain dishes of rabbit and carp, with menus at €44 and €60.

CRÉMIEU, to the south on the D517, is less immediately compelling, despite its local sausages (*sabodet*), monumental architecture and eight hundred years of history. The town was once an important commercial centre, as signified by the fifteenth-century **market buildings** on rue du Lt-Col-Bel, the ruined château of the kingdom of Dauphiné and the site of the former mint. With whole streets of handsome fifteenth-, sixteenth- and seventeenth-century houses, it deserves further exploration. Several of the imposing medieval city gates also survive. The artisan boulangerie in a fifteenth-century house opposite the Hôtel de Ville makes a useful stop for picnic provisions.

Vienne and around

Heading south from Lyon on the A7, a twenty-kilometre stretch of oil refineries, steel, chemical and paper works, cement, fertilizer and textile factories, all spewing plumes of grey and orange pollution into the air, may well tempt you to make a bee-line for the lavender fields of Provence. However, a short detour off the autoroute brings you to **VIENNE**, which, along with **St-Romain-en-Gal**, across the river, makes for the most interesting stop on the Rhône before Orange.

With their riverside positions, Vienne and St-Romain prospered as Rome's major wine port and *entrepôt* on the Rhône, and many Roman monuments survive to attest to this past glory. Several important churches recall Vienne's medieval heyday as well: it was a bishop's seat from the fifth century and the

Vienne museum pass

The Théâtre Antique, Église and Cloître de St-André-le-Bas, Musée des Beaux-Arts et d'Archéologie and Église-Musée St-Pierre can be visited on a single ticket (€6), which can be picked up at any of the sites and is valid for 48 hours.

home town of twelfth-century Pope Calixtus II. Today, the compact old quarter is crisscrossed with pedestrian precincts which make for enjoyable menu-browsing around **rue des Clercs** and **place Charles-de-Gaulle**. And there's a feeling that despite the distant rumble of the autoroute calling you to sunnier climes, the town has maintained its character and sense of purpose.

The Town

Roman monuments are scattered liberally around the streets of Vienne, and it requires little effort to take in the magnificently restored **Temple d'Auguste et de Livie** on place du Palais, a perfect, scaled-down version of Nîmes' Maison Carrée, or the bulky remains of the **Théâtre de Cybèle**, off place de Miremont. The **Théâtre Antique**, off rue du Cirque at the base of Mont Pipet to the north (April–Aug daily 9.30am–1pm & 2–6pm; Sept & Oct Tues–Sun 9.30am–1pm & 2–6pm; Nov–March Tues–Sat 9.30am–12.30pm & 2–5pm, Sun 1.30–5.30pm; €2.20, or €6 combined ticket), is more of a haul but it's worth making the trip for the view of the town and river from the very top seats. The theatre is the venue of an **international jazz festival** for the first two weeks of July, when it pulls in some of the biggest names on the jazz and rock circuit. An **audioguide** (available in English, from the tourist office; half day €5, day €8) will give you more information on the city's glorious past at each of the main temples and ruins.

The **Église-Musée St-Pierre** (April–Oct Tues–Sun 9.30am–1pm & 2–6pm; Nov–March Tues–Fri 9.30am–12.30pm & 2–5pm, Sat & Sun 2–6pm; €2.20 or €6 combined ticket with other museums) stands on the site of one of France's first cathedrals. Since its origins in the fifth century, the building has suffered much reconstruction and abuse, including a stint as a factory in the nineteenth century, though the monumental portico of the former church is still striking. Today it has something of the atmosphere of an architectural salvage yard, housing substantial but broken chunks of Roman columns, capitals and cornice. Close by is the most prominent – and vaunted – of Vienne's monuments, the **Cathédrale St-Maurice** (daily 8am–6pm; free), whose unwieldy facade, a combination of Romanesque and Gothic, appears as if its upper half has been dumped on top of a completely alien building. The interior, with its ninety-metre-long vaulted nave, is impressive though, spare and elegant, with some modern stained-glass windows and traces of fifteenth-century frescoes.

The **Église** (visits by arrangement; enquire at the cloister) and **Cloître de St-André-le-Bas** (same hours and ticket as St-Pierre) on place du Jeu de Paume, a few streets north of the cathedral, date from the ninth and twelfth centuries. The back tower of the church, on rue de la Table Ronde, is a remarkable monument, studded with tiny carved stone faces, while the cloister, entered through a space where temporary exhibits are held, is a beautiful little Romanesque affair, whose walls are decorated with local tombstones, some dating from the fifth century.

The major museum in Vienne is the **Musée des Beaux-Arts et d'Archéologie** on place de Miremont (same hours and ticket as St-Pierre), with a preponderance of eighteenth-century French pottery, but also some attractive pieces of third-century Roman silverware. More enlightening is the small textile museum, the **Musée de la Draperie** (mid-April to mid-Sept Wed–Sun 2–6pm; €2.20), in the Espace St-Germain to the south of the centre off rue Vimaine, which, with the aid of videos, working looms and weavers, illustrates the complete process of cloth-making as it was practised in the city for over two hundred years.

Practicalities

The cours Brillier runs at right angles to the river, with the **tourist office** at no. 3, near quai Jean-Jaurès (Mon–Sat 9am–noon & 2–6pm; Sun 10am–noon & 2–5pm; ⓣ04.74.53.80.30, ⓦwww.vienne-tourisme.com), and the **gare SNCF** at the other end. Halfway up the cours, rue Boson leads up to the west front of the cathedral.

If you plan to **stay**, try the *Poste*, 47 cours Romestang (ⓣ04.74.85.02.04, ⓦwww.hotel-vienne.fr; ⑥), between the station and place de Miremont, which has good rooms overlooking the *cours*. One of the few budget options is the *Ibis*, by the *gare routière* in place Camille-Jouffray (ⓣ04.74.78.41.11, ⓦwww.ibishotel.com; ④), just down from the tourist office. The *Hotel Central* is well located, as the name implies, decent enough but rather gloomy (ⓣ04.74.85.18.38, ⓦwww.hotel-central-vienne.com; ⑥). If you have your own transport, however, you should stay at the *Château des Sept Fontaines*, 5km northwest on the N7 at **Seyssuel** (ⓣ04.74.85.25.70, ⓦwww.hotel7fontaines.com; ⑦; closed Dec–April), with a large garden and comfortable rooms. There's also an **HI hostel** on the other side of the park from the tourist office at 11 quai Riondet (ⓣ04.74.53.21.97, ⓕ04.74.31.98.93; reserve Fri–Sun mid-Sept to mid-May; €9.10 per person).

The old town has a number of promising **places to eat**, including a good selection of cheapies in rue de la Table Ronde (near St-André-le-Bas), among them *L'Estancot* at no. 4 (ⓣ04.74.85.12.09; closed Mon & Sun; €17.50) and *Au Petit Chez Soi* at no. 6 (ⓣ04.74.85.19.77; closed Sun evening & Mon), serving *moules-frites* for €16. Alternatively, classy and welcoming *Le Bec Fin*, 7 place St-Maurice (ⓣ04.74.85.76.72; closed Sun & Wed evening & Mon), offers filling menus of Lyonnais dishes at €20.50 and €56. However, if you fancy a splurge, head for the superlative restaurant in the hôtel *La Pyramide*, 14 bd Fernand-Point (ⓣ04.74.53.01.96; closed Sun & Mon), with menus from €95 to €140; going à la carte will cost you at least €80. For **drinking**, there are a number of bars in town, including *Les 12 Mesures* in rue des Clercs, *The Celtic House* in rue Allmer, and the gay-friendly *West Saloon*, with live blues at weekends, on rue de la Table Ronde. For **Internet** access, go to World of Gamers Cybercafé, 16 rue des Clercs (Mon–Fri 11am–8pm, Sat 2pm–midnight).

St-Romain-en-Gal

Facing Vienne across the Rhône, several hectares of Roman ruins constitute the site of **ST-ROMAIN-EN-GAL**, also the name of the modern town surrounding it. The excavations (still ongoing), just across the road bridge from Vienne, attest to a significant community dating from the first century BC to the third AD, and give a vivid picture of the daily life and domestic architecture of Roman France. You enter through the excellent modern **Musée Archéologique de St-Romain-en-Gal** (site & museum Tues–Sun: March–Oct 10am–6pm; Nov–Feb 10am–5pm; €3.80), which displays frescoes, superb mosaics and other objects recovered from the site, along with explanatory models. The ruins themselves are clearly laid out, with illuminating reconstructions and informative but not overly technical explanatory plaques in English – ideal for adults and children alike. Be sure to check out the Romans' lavishly decorated marble public toilets, by the entry ramp to the dig.

Between Vienne and Valence

Between Vienne and Valence are some of the oldest, most celebrated **vineyards** in France: the renowned Côte Rotie, Hermitage and Crozes-Hermitage *appellations*. If you've got any spare luggage space, it's well worth stopping to pick up a bottle from the local co-op; even their *vin ordinaire* is superlative and unbelievably cheap, considering its quality. Just south of Ampuis on the west bank, 8km south of Vienne, is the tiny area producing one of the most exquisite French white wines, Condrieu, and close by one of the most exclusive – Château-Grillet – an *appellation* covering just this single château (by appointment; ⓣ04.74.59.51.56).

Between **St-Vallier** and **Tain l'Hermitage**, the Rhône becomes quite scenic, and after Tain you can see the Alps. In spring you're more likely to be conscious of orchards everywhere rather than vines. Cherries, pears, apples, peaches and apricots, as well as bilberries and strawberries, are cultivated in abundance.

Tain-l'Hermitage and around

TAIN-L'HERMITAGE, accessible from both the N7 and the A7, is unpretentious and uneventful. The only reason to stay here is to drink wine and eat chocolate. You can sample a good selection of the renowned Hermitage and Crozes-Hermitage **wines** within walking distance of the *gare SNCF* at the vast Cave de Tain-l'Hermitage, 22 rte de Larnage (daily: 9am–noon & 2–6pm; July & Aug 9am–12.30pm & 1.30–7pm; ⓣ04.75.08.91.86), and if your visit happens to fall on the last weekend in February you can try out wines from 78 vineyards in the Foire aux Vins des Côtes du Rhône Septentrionales. The celebrated **chocolates** in question are made by Valrhona and available at their shop (Mon–Fri 9am–7pm, Sat 9am–6pm) on avenue du Président-Roosevelt (the RN7), past the junction with the RN95 as you're heading south.

The **tourist office** at place du 8-mai-1945 (Sept–May Mon–Sat 9am–noon & 2–6pm; June–Aug Mon–Sat 9am–7pm, Sun 9.30am–noon; ⓣ04.75.08.06.81, ⓦwww.tain-tourisme.com), on the RN7 further north, can provide you with lists of vineyard addresses. If you need to **stay**, try the inexpensive but rather tired *Hôtel de la Gare* at 19 av du Dr-Paul-Durand, (ⓣ06.13.48.37.47, ⓕ04.75.07.11.71; ②), or the smarter *Les 2 Côteaux*, 18 rue Joseph-Péala, directly across avenue Jean-Jaurès from place Taurobole next to the rather splendid pedestrian suspension bridge (ⓣ04.75.08.33.01, ⓦwww.hotel-les-2-coteaux.com; ④). For a cheap **meal** in Tain try the crêperie *La Récré*, 8 place Taurobole (€8 upwards), as an alternative to the stuffier establishments on avenue Jean-Jaurès. The town's best restaurant, *Jean-Marc Reynaud*, 82 av du Président-Roosevelt (ⓣ04.75.07.22.10; Sun evening & Mon à la carte only, closed one week Aug & two weeks Jan), has an excellent value €30 menu, with à la carte upwards of €50.

On the third weekend of September, the different wine-producing villages celebrate their cellars in the **Fête des Vendanges**. But at any time of the year you can go bottle-hunting along the N86 for some 30km north of Tain along the right bank, following the *dégustation* signs and then crossing back over between Serrières and Chanas.

Hauterives

HAUTERIVES, 25km northeast of Tain, is a small village with a remarkable creation – a manic, surreal **Palais Idéal** (daily: Jan & Dec 9.30am–12.30pm & 1.30–4.30pm; Feb, March, Oct & Nov 9.30am–12.30pm & 1.30–5.30pm; April–June & Sept 9am–12.30pm & 1.30–6.30pm; July & Aug 9am–12.30pm & 1.30–7.30pm; Ⓦwww.facteurcheval.com; €5.10) built by a local postman by the name of Ferdinand Cheval (1836–1912). The house is truly bizarre, a bubbling frenzy reminiscent of the *modernista* architecture of Spain, with features that recall Thai or Indian temples. The eccentric building took thirty years to carve, and Cheval designed an equally bizarre tombstone which can also be seen. Various Surrealists have paid homage to the building and psychoanalysts have given it much thought, but it defies all classification. The *palais* is a tourist magnet, reached along a lane cluttered with shops hawking assorted gewgaws. The rest of the village, however, is relatively unspoilt. If you want to **stay** here, you have the choice of the *Camping du Château* on the edge of town on the N538 (Ⓣ04.75.68.80.19, Ⓕ04.75.68.90.94; closed Oct–March) and a **hotel**, *Le Relais* (Ⓣ04.75.68.81.12, Ⓕ04.75.68.92.42; ❹; closed mid-Jan to Feb), opposite the village church.

Romans-sur-Isère

South of Hauterives and 15km east of the Rhône at Tain is **ROMANS-SUR-ISÈRE**. It's not the most exciting of towns but it does have a fascinating museum of shoemaking – the industry that has kept Romans going for the last five centuries. The extensive **Musée International de la Chaussure** is in the former Convent of the Visitation at 2 rue Ste-Marthe (May, June & Sept Tues–Sat 10am–6pm, Sun 2.30–6pm; July & Aug Mon–Sat 10am–6pm, Sun 2.30–6pm; Oct–April Tues–Sat 10am–5pm, Sun 2.30–6pm; €4.30, or joint ticket with Palais Idéal at Hauterives, see above, €6.80) and also includes a permanent exhibition on the Resistance. Your toes will curl in horror at the extent to which women have been immobilized by their footwear from ancient times to the present on every continent, while at the same time you can't help but admire the craziness of some of the creations. Romans is also a good place to buy shoes, with several factory shops in the town including Charles Jourdan, and a smart outlet centre to the east along avenue Gambetta.

The rather neglected old town has plenty of beautiful old corners to explore, and the region has two gastronomic specialities: a ringed spongy bread flavoured with orange water, known as a *pogne*, and *ravioles*, cornflour-based ravioli with an eggy, cheesy, buttery filling. You can sample these at *La Cassolette*, at 16 rue Rebatte in a beautiful old stone house off place Jacquemart (Ⓣ04.75.02.55.71; closed Sun, Mon & three weeks from last week in July; menus €13.50 & €36).

There's a **tourist office** on place Jean-Jaurès (April–Oct Mon–Fri 9am–7pm, Sat 9am–6pm, Sun 9.30am–12.30pm; Nov–March Mon–Sat 9am–6pm, Sun 9.30am–12.30pm; Ⓣ04.75.02.28.72 Ⓦwww.ville-romans.com), and several **hotels**, including *Des Balmes*, northwest of the town centre in the *quartier* of the same name (Ⓣ04.75.02.29.52, Ⓦwww.hoteldesbalmes.com; ❹), with an excellent and inexpensive restaurant (closed Sun eve out of season). Cheaper options include the *Magdeleine*, 31 av Pierre-Sémard (Ⓣ04.75.02.33.53, Ⓦwww.magdeleine-hotel.com ❸; closed Sun eve out of season), and the *Cendrillon*, 9 place Carnot, across from the train station (Ⓣ04.75.02.83.77; ❸). The municipal **campsite**, *Les Chasses* (Ⓣ04.75.72.35.27; closed Oct–April), is 1km off the N92 northeast of the city, next to the aerodrome.

Festive France

The French celebrate everything, from saints' days to cinema to wine. While summer is the prime festive season, even in winter you'll be able to track down some festival or other. Indeed, the calendar is packed so full of events, it's hard to know which to plump for. Below is a round-up of some of the best, the most famous and the relatively undiscovered. For websites – and further ideas – see Basics, pp.56–58.

▲ Fête de la Musique

Nationwide celebrations

France's independence day, **Bastille Day** (July 14), is celebrated with firework displays and dances countrywide. On the more formal side, there's a military parade in Paris and the president addresses the nation.

Music-lovers are in for a treat with the **Fête de la Musique** (June 21), which marks the summer solstice. All manner of musical events take place, including many free concerts, which may be amateur or professional, spontaneous or programmed. And it keeps getting bigger and better each year.

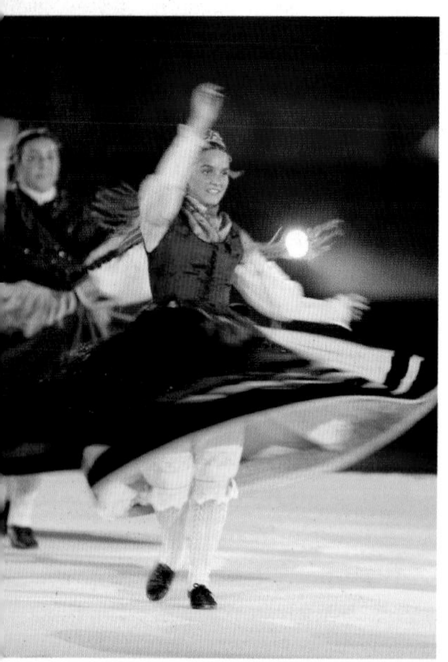
▲ Festival Inter-Celtic, Lorient

Religious and folk festivals

Catholicism is deeply ingrained in rural culture and **religious feast days** still bring people out in all their finery. Amongst the most famous are the Breton *pardons* (June–Sept), when processions to commemorate the dead wind through the countryside; the biggest takes place at Sainte-Anne d'Auray in the Morbihan (July 26).

Another annual event with deep historical roots is the great **gypsy gathering** at Les Stes-Maries-de-la-Mer in the Camargue (May 24 & 25) to honour their patron saint, the mysterious, black-faced Sara-la-Kâli. A jubilant crowd carries her statue from the church to the sea and back, to the sound of pealing bells. It's a unique and exhilarating spectacle.

One folk festival definitely worth attending is the **Festival Inter-Celtic** (early Aug), held at Lorient in Brittany. Thousands of musicians, dancers, writers and scholars from around the world – and some 650,000 spectators – gather to celebrate contemporary Celtic music and culture.

▼ Gypsy gathering, Les Stes-Maries-de-la-Mer

Music

Classical music-lovers will be hard pressed to choose from the tremendous variety of festivals on offer, from sacred music to comic opera, almost nonstop throughout the year. In the depths of winter, Nantes hosts La Folle Journée (late Jan), in which dozens of concerts take place over five packed days, with a different theme each year. If you've got the energy, there are also theatre performances, films and conferences. Prices are very affordable.

▲ Festival des Vieilles Charrues, Carhaix

▼ Jazz in Marciac

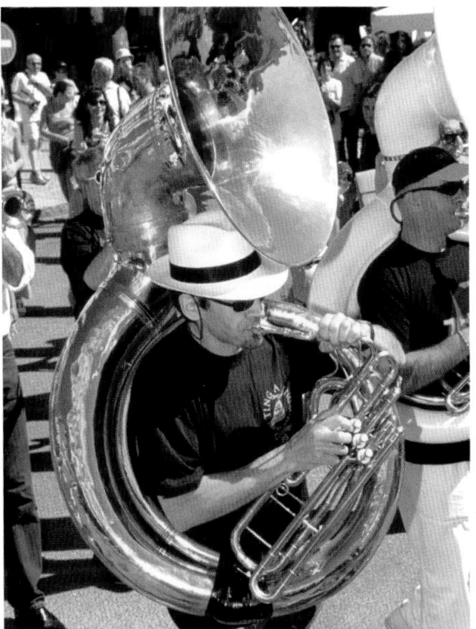

In July and August **jazz** fills the air of many French towns and villages. Fans flock to the big-name concerts at Jazz à Vienne (first two weeks of July), but there are plenty of more intimate events, too. Jazz in Marciac (early Aug), for example, set in a little market town in the heart of Gascony, still retains the atmosphere of a local fête.

Intimate is not how you'd describe the Festival des Vieilles Charrues, a **pop fest** held at Carhaix in Brittany (mid-July). This is one of France's largest annual bashes, attracting over 200,000 revellers to hear the likes of Johnny Hallyday and Madness, Iggy Pop and Charles Trenet play the massive open-air stages. Side events feature local Breton bands and electronic music. Truly eclectic.

Fest-Noz and Fest-Diez

Brittany boasts a particular rich and vibrant cultural calendar, with the most lively events being the hugely popular summer **dance festivals**, Fest-Noz (held at night) and Fest-Diez (in the daytime). These ancient folk festivals originally celebrated a marriage or the end of the harvest, but today they're just an excuse for partying; thousands of people gather to dance, eat, drink and make merry to the accompaniment of traditional Breton music. It's infectious stuff, played on bagpipes, *bombarde* (a high-pitched flute), and increasingly nowadays violins and other musical instruments. Dancers follow simple steps, usually linking hands to form a chain or circle – everyone is welcome to join in. Dates of upcoming events are listed on ⓦwww.fest-noz.net.

Performance arts

▲ Dancers outside the Palais des Papes, Avignon

Contemporary **performance arts** are alive and kicking in France. The highlight is probably Avignon's packed programme of avant-garde theatre, dance and music (July). Directed by a different guest artist each year, and featuring many new productions, it's a veritable showcase for up-and-coming talent, with performances taking place in the Pope's Palace as well as churches, school halls and even a stone quarry.

It's also worth catching one of the growing number of **street theatre** festivals. At Aurillac's four-day festival (mid-Aug), for example, some five hundred companies from around the world come together in a frenzy of creativity. You'll also find contemporary **circus** – acrobatic theatre rather than performing lions – well represented at the aptly named Festival Furies (early June) at Châlons-en-Campagne. Anarchic, provocative and endlessly entertaining, the Furies kicks off with a performance by the graduation class at Châlons' national school for circus arts.

France's oldest festival

The Chorégies d'Orange **opera festival** (July–Aug) dates from 1860, and is regarded as the oldest festival in France. The programme originally included Greek and Roman tragedies and contemporary French dramas along with opera, but after 1971 it dropped the extras and has become one of the world's most important lyric festivals, attracting in the past big-name stars such as Luciano Pavarotti and Barbara Hendricks and, more recently, Angela Gheorghiu and Roberto Alagna. The setting makes it even more spectacular: a perfectly preserved Roman theatre complete with its original stage wall – which means almost perfect acoustics. The theatre holds up to 9000 spectators but, with only one or two performances a week during the month-long festival, tickets often sell out months in advance.

Cinema

Everyone's heard of Cannes international film festival (May), of course, but the French passion for **cinema** is reflected in dozens of smaller events throughout the year.

▼ Cannes Film Festival

There's a festival of animated films at Annecy (June; ⓦwww.annecy.org), another devoted to women's film at Créteil (March; ⓦwww.filmsdefemmes.com), near Paris, even a festival of detective movies at Cognac (April; ⓦwww.festival.cognac.fr). And that's only scratching the surface.

Valence

At an indefinable point along the Rhône, there's an invisible sensual border, and by the time you reach **VALENCE**, you know you've crossed it. The quality of light is different and the temperature higher, bringing with it the scent of eucalyptus and pine, and the colours and contours suddenly seem worlds apart from the cold lands of Lyon and the north. Valence is the obvious place to celebrate your arrival in the **Midi** (as the French call the south), with plenty of good bars and restaurants in the old town, though little else.

Arrival, information and accommodation

If you come in on the autoroute, running along the Rhône's left bank, you exit onto avenue Gambetta, with the old town, its ramparts replaced by boulevards, on your left. To the southeast of the old town are the **gare routière**, the **gare SNCF** and the **tourist office** on parvis de la Gare (June–Aug Mon–Sat 9.30am–6.30pm, Sun 10am–1pm; Sept–May Mon–Fri 9.30am–12.30pm & 1.30–6pm, Sat 9.30am–12.30pm & 1.30–5pm; ⓣ08.92.70.70.99, ⓦwww.tourisme-valence.com). The new **TGV** station is 10km northeast, along the autoroute to Romans. There are regular shuttles and trains (daily 6.30am–10.50pm; €2.20) which connect the *gare TGV* with the *gare SNCF*.

Hotels

Europe 15 av Félix-Faure ⓣ04.75.82.62.65, ⓔhoteleurope.valence@wanadoo.fr. Has satellite TV and en-suite showers. ❸

De Lyon 23 av Pierre-Semard ⓣ04.75.41.44.66, ⓦwww.hoteldelyon.com. A decent two-star with Internet access, which has just been completely redone. White walls and bright colours give it a bit of a chain feel but it's good value and located just opposite the station. ❹

Les Négociants 27 av Pierre-Semard ⓣ04.75.44.01.86, ⓦwww.hotel-lesnegociantsvalence.com. Clean lines, minimalist furniture and probably an orchid on your bedside table. ❹

Pic 285 av Victor-Hugo ⓣ04.75.44.15.32, ⓦwww.pic-valence.com. Fifteen beautiful large and luxurious rooms in an old coach house, along with a gastronomic restaurant full of character (see p.1050). ❾

Yan's quartier Maninet, rote de Monteleger ⓣ04.75.55.52.52, ⓦwww.yanshotel.com. Spacious rooms in a stylish modern building with park and pool, southeast of the city on the route de Montéléger. ❻

The Town

Valance seems to have found a new lease of life: with the TGV has come new boulevards and parks, facades are being cleaned and restored and hotels and public buildings modernized. The focus of Vieux Valence, the **Cathédrale St-Apollinaire** (Mon 8am–6.30pm, Tues–Sat 8am–7pm, Sun 11.30am–6.30pm), was consecrated in 1095 by Pope Urban II (who proclaimed the First Crusade), and largely reconstructed in the seventeenth century after a local baron went on the rampage, avenging the execution of three Protestants during the Wars of Religion. More work was carried out later, including the horribly mismatched nineteenth-century tower, but the interior still preserves its original Romanesque grace – especially the columns around the ambulatory.

Between the cathedral and **Église de St-Jean** at the northern end of Grande-Rue, which has preserved its Romanesque tower and porch capitals, are some of the oldest and narrowest streets of Vieux Valence. They are known as **côtes**: côte St-Estève just northwest of the cathedral; côte St-Martin off rue du Petit-Paradis; and côte Sylvante off rue du Petit-Paradis' continuation, rue A.-Paré. Diverse characters who would have walked these steep and crooked streets include Rabelais, a student at the university founded here in 1452 and suppressed during the Revolution, and the teenage Napoleon Bonaparte, who began his military training as a cadet at the artillery school.

Though Valence lacks the cohesion of the medieval towns and villages further south, it does have several vestiges of the sixteenth-century city, most notably the Renaissance **Maison des Têtes** at 57 Grande-Rue. Be sure if you can to look at the ceiling in the passageway here (office hours only), where sculpted roses transform into the cherub-like heads after which the palace is named. Also worth a look is the **Maison Dupré-Latour**, on rue Pérollerie, which has a superbly sculptured porch and spiral staircase. By contrast the **Musée de Valence**, near the cathedral on place des Ormeaux (mid-June to Sept Tues–Sat 10am–noon & 2–6.45pm, Sun 2–6.45pm; Oct to mid-June 2–5.45pm; €3), contains a mishmash of unremarkable local art and archeological finds, and frankly is not worth the price of admission. On Sunday a **bric-a-brac market** fills the streets with stalls selling everything from underwear to oranges.

At sunset, or even better at dawn, Parc Jouvet is definitely the best place to be in the city – a tranquil oasis away from the town's bustle – with a bottle of Cornas or sparkling St-Peray from the vineyards across the water.

Eating and drinking

Le Bistrot des Clercs 48 Grande-Rue ⓣ04.75.55.55.15. An old-fashioned brasserie with a wide range of dishes and prices. À la carte from €19.

L'Épicerie 18 place Belat ⓣ04.75.42.74.46. One of the most congenial places to eat, with art hung on the fifteenth-century walls, jazz some nights and imaginative food on menus from €22 to €39. Closed Sat lunch, Sun & Aug.

Maurin Fils 17 av Pierre-Semard. A good bakery for sampling *pogne* from nearby Romans.

One Two Tea 37 Grande-Rue. Excellent *salon de thé*.

Père Joseph 9 place des Clercs ⓣ04.75.42.57.80. Serves excellent traditional food, with a menu at €23.

Pic 285 av Victor-Hugo ⓣ04.75.44.15.32. The city's top-notch restaurant: Quercy lamb with vegetable *confit* and tempura of dates, or roast veal with parsley gnocchi, lemon and anchovies are among the delights. Menu €115 (or €59 for a lunch weekday menu). Closed Sun eve & Mon, plus Tues Nov–March & three weeks in Jan.

Café Victor-Hugo 30 av Victor-Hugo ⓣ04.75.40.18.11. Grand 1920s Parisian-style café with high ceilings and smart waiters. À la carte from €10.

Montélimar

In **MONTÉLIMAR**, 40km south of Valence, every street proclaims the glory of the nougat that has been made here for centuries and is the town's chief *raison d'être*. It's a lively enough place with a pleasant *vieille ville* and a fascinating museum dedicated to miniaturization.

The main street of the old town, **rue Pierre-Julien**, runs from the one remaining medieval **gateway** on the nineteenth-century ring of boulevards at place St-Martin, south past the **church of Sainte-Croix** with its well-populated square, and onto place Marx-Dormoy. At no. 19, opposite the post office, is the **Musée de la Miniature** (July & Aug daily 10am–6pm; Sept–June Wed–Sun 2–6pm; €4.90), whose tiny exhibits, some so small you have to use a microscope, have been created by leading contemporary artists. There's a grain of rice bearing a portrait of Pushkin and one of his poems, and a table laid with a chess game is no bigger than a five-cent coin.

Leading off rue Pierre-Julien are many medieval lanes with sixteenth- and seventeenth-century town houses, though the facades and old arcades of **place**

du Marché serve chiefly nowadays as a backdrop to parked cars. Above the old town to the east is the impressive **Château des Adhémars** on rue du Château (April–June & Sept–Oct daily 9.30–11.30am & 2–5.30pm; July & Aug daily 9.30–11.30am & 2–6pm; Nov–March daily except Tues 9.30–11.30am & 2–5.30pm; €3.50). Originally belonging to the family after whom the town ("Mount of the Adhémars") was named, the castle is mostly fourteenth-century, but also boasts a fine eleventh-century chapel and twelfth-century living-quarters. If you wish to find out more about the town's famous **nougat** (the word is a contraction of a phrase meaning "you spoil us"), you can visit the Nougats Gerbe d'Or factory in **the Parc d'Activité Fortuneau**, south of the centre (daily 8.30am–noon & 2–6pm), where you will be shown around the plant and have a chance to sample (and buy) the end product.

Practicalities

The **gare SNCF** is a short way west of the old town across the Jardin Public, with the **tourist office** close by on the corner of allée Champs-de-Mars and boulevard Marre-Desmarais (July & Aug Mon–Sat 9am–7pm, Sun 10.30am–noon & 3–5.30pm; Sept–June Mon–Sat 9am–12.15pm and 2–6.30pm; ⓣ04.75.01.00.20, ⓦwww.montelimar-tourisme.com).

There are plenty of **hotels** around the boulevards, including the very pleasant *Sphinx*, in a seventeenth-century town house at 19 bd Marre-Desmarais (ⓣ04.75.01.86.64, ⓦwww.sphinx-hotel.fr; ❸; closed mid-Dec to mid-Jan), and *Du Printemps*, north of the old town at 8 chemin de la Manche (ⓣ04.75.46.03.14, ⓦwww.hotel-du-printemps.com; ❹), with a pool and garden. In the old town the *Pierre*, 7 place des Clercs (ⓣ04.75.01.33.16; ❸), is, despite the unpromising exterior, comfortable and very peaceful, apart from the nearby bell of Sainte-Croix tolling the hours. The **campsite**, *L'Île Blanc* (ⓣ04.75.51.20.05, ⓦwww.camping-montelimar.com; closed Oct–March), is at Montélimar-Ancône, 5km northwest of the town.

For good traditional **food**, head for the *Relais de l'Empereur*, 1 place Max-Dormoy (ⓣ04.75.01.29.00; closed Sun & mid-Nov to mid-Dec; menus from €20). Opposite is the standard café *La Bourse* dishing out large salads to its packed terrace for around €14; alternatively they offer an unextraordinary but good-value €9.20 menu. Montélimar's prime (and very pleasant) spot for **café** lounging is outside the old town on the stretch of boulevard between the tourist office and the Théâtre Municipal.

Western Provence

The richest area of Provence, the Côte d'Azur apart, is the **west**. Most of the large-scale production of fruit, vegetables and wine is based here in the low-lying plains beside the Rhône and the Durance rivers. The only heights are the rocky outbreaks of the **Dentelles** and the **Alpilles**, and the narrow east–west ridges of **Mont Ventoux**, the **Luberon** and the **Mont Ste-Victoire**. The two dominant cities of inland Provence, **Avignon** and **Aix**, both have rich histories and contemporary fame in their festivals of art; **Arles**, **Orange** and **Vaison-la-Romaine** have impressive Roman remains. Around the Rhône delta, the **Camargue** is a unique self-contained region, as different from the rest of Provence as it is from anywhere else in France.

Orange and around

ORANGE was the former seat of the counts of Orange, a title created by Charlemagne in the eighth century and passed to the Dutch crown in the sixteenth century. The family's most famous member was Prince William, who ascended the English throne with his consort Mary in the 1688 "Glorious Revolution". Today the town is best known for its spectacular **Roman theatre**, which hosts the important summer Chorégies **music festival**. While the rest of Orange is certainly attractive, there's not a lot to detain you once you've visited the theatre and adjacent museum and taken a quick look at the Roman triumphal arch at the northern approach to the town centre. Unfortunately, the victory of Le Pen's Front National in the municipal elections of 1995, and again in 2001, has forced the May strip-cartoon festival, which brought in all kinds of weird and wonderful entertainment, to be abandoned.

Arrival, information and accommodation

The **gare SNCF** is about 1.5km east of the centre, at the end of avenue Frédéric-Mistral. The nearest bus stop is at the bottom of rue Jean-Reboul, the first left as you walk away from the station. Bus #1, direction "Aygues", takes you to the Théâtre Antique, opposite which there's a **seasonal tourist office** (April–June & Sept Mon–Sat 10am–1pm & 2.15–6pm, Sun 10am–12.30pm & 2.30–6pm; July & Aug daily 10am–1pm & 2.15–8pm), from which it's a

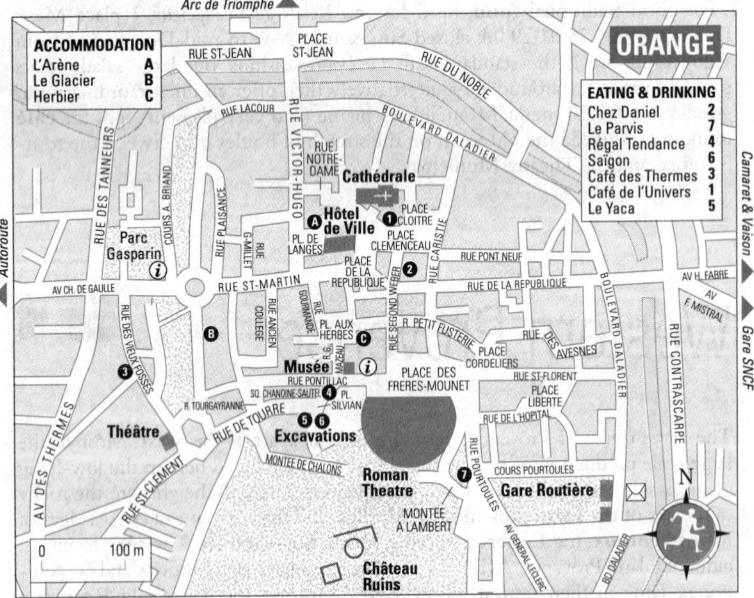

short distance on foot to the main **tourist office** on cours Aristide-Briand (April–June & Sept Mon–Sat 9.30am–7pm; July & Aug Mon–Sat 9.30am–7pm, Sun 10am–6pm; Oct–March Mon–Sat 10am–1pm & 2–5pm; ⓣ04.90.34.70.88, ⓦwww.provence-orange.com). The **gare routière** is close to the centre on boulevard Edouard-Daladier.

Of the **hotels**, good options include small, appealing and good-value *Herbier*, 8 place aux Herbes (ⓣ04.90.34.09.23, ⓦwww.lherbierdorange.com; ❷); *L'Arène*, on pretty place de Langes (ⓣ04.90.11.40.40, ⓦwww.hotel-arene.fr; ❻), with spacious rooms and all mod cons; and the very comfortable *Le Glacier*, 46 cours Aristide-Briand (ⓣ04.90.34.02.01, ⓦwww.le-glacier.com; ❸). Orange's **campsite**, *Le Jonquier*, rue Alexis-Carrel (ⓣ04.90.34.49.48, ⓦwww.campinglejonquier.com; closed Oct–March), to the northwest, is equipped with tennis courts and a pool. The price for two people and a tent is €22.80.

The Town

Days off in Orange circa 55 AD were most entertainingly spent from dawn to dusk watching farce, clownish improvisations, song and dance, and occasionally, for the sake of a visiting dignitary, a bit of Greek tragedy in Latin at the huge Roman **theatre** (daily: March & Oct 9am–6pm; April, May & Sept 9am–7pm; June–Aug 9am–8pm; Nov–Feb 9am–5pm; €7.70, including audioguide and combined ticket with museum), built into the hill which squats on the south side of the old town. The theatre was as much a way of disseminating Roman culture in the conquered provinces as a place of entertainment, and despite its impressive dimensions was by no means exceptional for a city of Orange's size. Its acoustics allowed a full audience of 9000 to hear every word. The hill of St-Eutrope, into which the seats were built, plus a vast awning strung from the top of the stage wall, protected the spectators from the weather. It is one of the best-preserved examples in existence, with its stage wall still standing 103m across and 36m high, and completely plain like some monstrous prison wall when you see it from outside. The interior, although missing much of its

△ Roman theatre, Orange

original decoration, has its central, larger-than-life-size statue of Augustus, and niches for lesser statues. Despite Augustus' overbearing swagger, the statue's creators prudently allowed for the head to be changed should the emperor's rule prove less enduring than his marble likeness.

The best view of the theatre in its entirety is from St-Eutrope hill. You can follow a path up the hill either from the top of cours Aristide-Briand (montée P. de Chalons) or from cours Pourtoules (montée Albert-Lambert) until you are looking directly down onto the stage. The ruins around your feet are those of the short-lived seventeenth-century castle of the princes of Orange. Louis XIV had it destroyed in 1673 and the principality of Orange was officially annexed to France forty years later.

The **municipal museum**, across the road from the theatre entrance (same hours and ticket as theatre), has documents concerning the Orange dynasty, including a suitably austere portrait of the founder of the Netherlands, William "the Silent". It also has Roman bits and pieces from the theatre and a collection rotated on a yearly basis containing diverse items such as the contents of a seventeenth-century pharmacy and an unlikely selection of works by Frank Brangwyn (1867–1956), the largely forgotten Bruges-born British Arts and Crafts painter whose figurative works adorn the House of Lords in London and the Rockefeller Center in New York.

If you've arrived by road from the north you'll have passed the town's second major Roman monument, the **Arc de Triomphe**, whose intricate frieze and relief celebrate imperial victories against the Gauls. It was built around 20 BC outside the town walls to recall the victories of the Roman Second Legion. Orange's old town is very small, hemmed in between the theatre and the River Meyne, featuring some pretty fountain-adorned squares and houses with ancient porticoes and courtyards.

Eating, drinking and entertainment

For **food**, cheap pizzas, pasta and more expensive seafood platters can be had at *Chez Daniel,* rue Segond-Weber (daily; evenings only Fri–Sun; pizzas from €8), while *Le Yaca*, 24 place Silvain (Ⓣ04.90.34.70.03; closed Tues eve, Wed off season & Nov), gives a generous choice of dishes for €22 in an old vaulted chamber. Kitchens close rather early in Orange, especially on Sundays, but one place that stays open late is the very acceptable Vietnamese-Chinese *Saïgon*, next to the theatre at 20 place Sylvain (Ⓣ04.90.34.18.19, menus from around €12). However, the best food you're likely to get in the city is at *Le Parvis*, 3 cours des Pourtoules (Ⓣ04.90.34.82.00; closed Sun evening & Mon), with a weekday lunch menu from €16.50. For **drinking**, head for place Clemenceau in the centre, where there's the *Café de l'Univers*, painted in Provençal yellow. On the other side of cours Aristide-Briand, the *Café des Thermes*, 29 rue des Vieux-Fossés, has pool, a good selection of beers and a youngish clientele. *Régal Tendance*, rue Madeleine-Roch (Ⓦwww.regal-tendance.com) boasts 55 flavours of possibly the most delicious home-made **ice cream** in all Provence.

Orange's main festival is the **Chorégies**, a programme of opera, oratorios and orchestral concerts in July – details and tickets from the Bureau des Chorégies, 18 place Silvain (Ⓣ04.90.34.24.24, Ⓦwww.choregies.asso.fr). The theatre is also used throughout the year for jazz, film, folk and rock concerts. Prices range from €4 to €180; details from the Service Culturel de la Ville, 14 place Silvain (Ⓣ04.90.51.57.57). Tickets for all events can be bought from FNAC shops in all big French cities, and at the theatre box office in Orange.

Sérignan-du-Comtat

The village of **SÉRIGNAN-DU-COMTAT**, 8km northeast of Orange (three buses daily from Orange and Avignon), was the final home of **Jean-Henri Fabre**, a remarkable self-taught scientist, famous for his insect studies, who also composed poetry, wrote songs and painted his specimens with artistic brilliance as well as scientific accuracy. In the 1860s he had to resign from his teaching post at Avignon because parents and priests thought his lectures on the fertilization of flowering plants were licentious, if not downright pornographic. His **house** – on the N976 towards Orange – which he named the *Harmas* – contains a jungle-like garden, his study – with his complete classification of the herbs of France – and, on the ground floor, a selection from his extraordinary watercolour series of the fungi of the Vaucluse. The house and garden were re-opened to the public in 2006 after over five years of meticulous renovation (mid-May to Oct Wed–Mon 10am–12.30pm & 2.30–6pm; €5). At the crossroads in the centre of the town there's a **statue** of Fabre in front of the red-shuttered buildings of the church and *mairie*.

Châteauneuf-du-Pape

If you're heading down to Avignon, the slower route through **CHÂTEAUNEUF-DU-PAPE** (1–2 buses daily from Orange) exerts a strong pull. The village takes its name from the summer palace of the Avignon popes, but neither the views down the Rhône valley towards Avignon from the ruins of the fourteenth-century **château** (freely accessible) nor the medieval streets around **place du Portail** – the hub of the village – give Châteauneuf its special appeal. Rather it's the wines produced by the local vineyards, warmed at night by the large pebbles that cover the ground and soak up the sun's heat during the day, that are its real attraction. The rich ruby red is one of France's most renowned, but the white, too, is exquisite.

The *appellation* Châteauneuf-du-Pape does not, alas, come cheap. For the uninitiated, the best place to taste a good selection from the scores of *domaines* before making an investment is at the boutique **La Maison des Vins**, at 8 rue du Maréchal-Foch (July & Aug daily 10am–7pm; Sept–June daily 10am–12.30pm & 2–6.30pm). For a more casual introduction, the Cave Père-Anselme on avenue Bienheureux-Pierre-de-Luxembourg has a **Musée du Vin** (daily July & Aug 9am–1pm & 2–7pm; Sept–June 9am–noon & 2–6pm; free), plus free tastings of its wines. Otherwise, the **tourist office** on place du Portail (July & Aug Mon–Sat 9.30am–7pm; Sept–June Mon–Sat 9.30am–12.30pm & 2–6pm; Ⓣ04.90.83.71.08), or the Fédération des Syndicats de Producteurs, 12 av Louis-Pasteur (Ⓣ04.90.83.72.21), can provide a complete list of producers, or you can visit an Association de Vignerons, such as Prestige et Tradition at 3 rue de la République (Aug & Sept Mon–Fri 7.30am–noon & 1.30–4pm), who bottle the wine of ten producers.

If your visit coincides with the first weekend of August you'll find free *dégustation* stalls throughout the village as well as parades, dances, equestrian contests, medieval entertainment and so forth, all to celebrate the reddening of the grapes in the **Fête de la Véraison**. As well as wine, a good deal of grape liqueur – *marc* – gets consumed.

Accommodation is confined to four very pleasant but small **hotels**: *La Garbure*, 3 rue Joseph-Ducos (Ⓣ04.90.83.75.08, Ⓦwww.la-garbure.com; ❹); the four-star *Hostellerie du Château des Fines Roches*, on route d'Avignon (Ⓣ04.90.83.70.23, Ⓦwww.chateaufinesroches.com; ❾); *La Mère Germaine*, on avenue Cdt-Lemaître (Ⓣ04.90.83.54.37, Ⓦwww.lameregermaine.com; ❺); and *La Sommellerie*, 3km north of the village on route de Roquemaure (Ⓣ04.90.83.50.00, Ⓦwww.hotel-la-sommellerie.com; ❻, closed Jan to mid-Feb).

You can **eat** well for around €15 at the brasserie *La Mule du Pape*, 2 rue de la République (restaurant closed Sun & evenings out of season), or pay a bit more at *La Mère Germaine* (see p.1055), with its well-crafted Provençal dishes, and much more at *La Sommellerie* (see above; closed Sun evening & Mon out of season; menus €29–78), where the cook is one of France's master chefs. Everything here is made on the premises, from the bread to the fine desserts, and meat is cooked on an outdoor wood fire.

Vaison-la-Romaine and around

VAISON-LA-ROMAINE lies 27km northeast of Orange and hit the headlines in 1992 when the River Ouvèze, which divides the medieval and eighteenth-century towns, burst its banks, destroying riverside houses, the modern road bridge and an entire industrial quarter. Though the town has recovered remarkably, its character has changed – it seems much more commercialized and less friendly.

It still, however, has the strong attractions of its immaculate medieval **haute ville**, with a ruined clifftop castle, a **Roman bridge** that held out against the floods, a cloistered former cathedral and the exceptional excavated remains of two **Roman districts**. Just south of Vaison there are sculptures in natural settings to be discovered at the **Crestet Centre d'Art**.

Arrival, information and accommodation

Buses to and from Carpentras, Orange and Avignon stop at the **gare routière** on avenue des Choralies near the junction with avenue Victor-Hugo, east of the town centre on the north side of the river. The **tourist office** is on place du Chanoine-Sautel (July & Aug Mon–Sat 9am–12.30pm & 2–6.45pm, Sun 9am–noon; Sept–June Mon–Sat 9am–noon & 2–5.45pm, Sun 9am–noon; Ⓣ04.90.36.02.11, Ⓦwww.vaison-la-romaine.com), between the two archeological sites in the north of the modern town.

There may be few hotels in Vaison but there are a couple of gems, the best being *Le Beffroi*, a sixteenth-century residence on rue de l'Évêché in the *haute ville* (Ⓣ04.90.36.04.71, Ⓦwww.le-beffroi.com; ❻; closed mid-Jan to March); and a little further up the same street there's an exquisite B&B, *L'Évêché* (Ⓣ04.90.36.13.46, Ⓦwww.eveche-vaison.com; ❺), where you breakfast on a terrace with wonderful views over the river and beyond. Back in the new town, the cool *Hotel Burrhus* (Ⓣ04.90.36.00.11, Ⓦwww.burrhus.com; ❸), on noisy place de Montfort, is decorated with an eclectic mix of retro furniture. *Fête en Provence*, a restaurant in the *haute ville* also rents out rooms (Ⓣ04.90.36.36.43, Ⓦwww.hotellafete-provence.com; ❹). For **campers**, there's the central *Camping du Théâtre Romain* on chemin du Brusquet, off avenue des Choralies, quartier des Arts (Ⓣ04.90.28.78.66, Ⓦwww.camping-theatre.com; closed mid-Nov to mid-March, €19 for two people and a tent).

The Town

The **haute ville** lies on the south side of the river, with **rue du Pont** climbing up towards place des Poids and the fourteenth-century **gateway** to the town. More steep zigzags take you past the Gothic gate and overhanging portcullis of the **belfry** and into the heart of this sedately quiet, uncommercialized and rich *quartier*.

On the north bank from the **Pont Romain**, a Roman bridge that has been patched up over the years, Grande-Rue leads up to the central streets of rue de la République and cours Henri-Fabre, after which it becomes avenue Général-de-Gaulle. The two excavated **Roman residential districts** lie to either side of this avenue: **Puymin** to the east (April & May 9.30am–6pm; June & Sept 9.30am–6pm; July & Aug 9.30am–6.45pm; Oct–March 10am–noon & 2–5pm) and **La Villasse** to the west (April & May Mon & Wed–Sun 10am–noon & 2.30–6pm; Tues 2.30–6pm; June & Sept 9.30am–12.30pm & 2–6pm; July & Aug 9.30am–12.30pm & 2–6.45pm; Oct–March 10am–noon & 2–5pm). The ticket for both plus Puymin museum and cathedral cloisters costs €7.50.

The Puymin excavations contain the theatre, several mansions and houses, a colonnade known as the *portique de Pompée* and the museum for all the items discovered. The excavations of La Villasse reveal a street with pavements and gutters with the layout of a row of arcaded shops running parallel, more patrician houses (some with mosaics still intact), a basilica and the baths. The houses require a certain amount of imagination, but the street plan of La Villasse, the colonnade with its statues in every niche, and the theatre, which still seats 7000 people during the July festival, make it easy to visualize a comfortable, well-serviced Roman town.

Most of the detail and decoration of the buildings are displayed in the **museum** in the Puymin district (same hours as Puymin archeological site). Tiny fragments of painted plaster have been jigsawed together with convincing reconstructions of how whole painted walls would have looked. There are mirrors of silvered bronze, lead water pipes, taps shaped as griffins' feet, dolphin door knobs, weights and measures, plus impressive busts and statues.

Tickets can be bought at the Puymin entrance just by the tourist office or in the cloisters of the former **Cathédrale Notre-Dame**, west down chemin Couradou, which runs along the south side of La Villasse. The apse of the cathedral is a confusing overlay of sixth-, tenth- and thirteenth-century construction, using pieces quarried from the Roman ruins. The **cloisters** are fairly typical of early medieval workmanship – pretty enough but not wildly exciting. The only surprising feature is the large inscription visible on the north wall of the cathedral, a convoluted precept for the monks.

Eating and drinking

The **restaurant** to head for is *Le Bateleur*, 1 place Théodore-Aubanel, downstream from the Pont Romain on the north bank (Ⓣ04.90.36.28.04; closed Mon, Thurs eve, Sat lunch out of season; closed Mon & Sat lunch July–Oct; menus €25 & €35, *plats* around €20); the lamb stuffed with almonds and the *rascasse* (scorpion fish) soufflé are highly recommended. Alternatively, *La Fontaine* at *Le Beffroi* on rue de l'Évêché in the medieval village (Ⓣ04.90.36.04.71; closed Nov–March) offers Provençal dishes in menus at €28–45. You can get crêpes and pizzas in the old town and brasserie fare on place de Montfort, the obvious **drinking** place to gravitate towards. For a more local atmosphere, try *Vasio Bar* on cours Taulignan.

Le Crestet and Mont Ventoux

South of Vaison, 3.5km down the Malaucène road, a turning to the right leads to the tiny hilltop village of **LE CRESTET** from where signs direct you the short distance to the Crestet Centre d'Art (free access), where modern sculptures have been placed, almost hidden, in an expanse of oak and pine woods. Though the Centre itself is now closed, there's a map in the lay-by above it, indicating the position of various artworks it is still possible to view dotted among the woods. Some of the sculptures are formed from the trees themselves, others are startling metal structures such as a mobile and a Meccano cage. **MONT VENTOUX**, whose outline repeatedly appears upon the horizon from the Rhône and Durance valleys, rises some 20km east of Vaison. White with snow, black with storm-cloud shadow or reflecting myriad shades of blue, the barren pebbles of the uppermost 300m are like a weathervane for all of western Provence. Winds can accelerate to 250km per hour around the meteorological, TV and military masts and dishes on the summit, but if you can stand still for a moment the view in all directions is unbelievable. A road, the D974, climbs all the way to the top, though no buses go there. The road up the northern face from Malaucène is wider, straighter, and better surfaced than the southern ascent.

If you want to make the ascent on foot, the best path is from Les Colombets or Les Fébriers, two hamlets off the D974, east of **BEDOIN**, whose **tourist office** on the espace M.-L.-Gravier (mid-June to Sept Mon–Sat 9am–12.30pm & 2–6pm, Sun 9.30am–12.30pm; Oct to mid-June Mon–Fri 9am–12.30pm & 2–6pm; ⓣ04.90.65.63.95) can give details of routes (including a once a week night-time ascent in July & Aug), plus addresses of campsites and *gîtes ruraux*. It also sells a guide to eleven walks on Mont Ventoux for €5.

Mont Ventoux is one of the challenges of the Tour de France, hence its appeal in summer for committed cyclists. Within sight of the stony summit is a memorial to the British cyclist Tommy Simpson, who died here from heart failure on one of the hottest days ever recorded in the race; according to race folklore his last words were "Put me back on the bloody bike."

The Dentelles and around

The **Dentelles**, a row of jagged limestone pinnacles, run across an arid, windswept and near-deserted upland area, the **Massif Montmirail-St-Amand**, just south of Vaison-la-Romaine. Their name refers to lace – the limestone protrusions were thought to resemble the contorted pins on a lace-making board – though the word's alternative connection with teeth (*dents* means "teeth") is equally appropriate.

The area is best known for its wines. On the western and southern slopes lie the wine-producing villages of **Gigondas**, **Beaumes-de-Venise**, **Sablet**, **Séguret**, **Vacqueyras** and, across the River Ouvèze, **Rasteau**. Each one carries the distinction of having its own individual *appellation contrôlée* within the Côtes du Rhône or Côtes du Rhône Villages areas: in other words, their wines are exceptional. In addition, some of the villages are alluringly picturesque, with Séguret super-conscious of its Provençal beauty.

The most reputed red **wine** in the Dentelles is made at Gigondas – it's strong with an aftertaste of spice and nuts. You can taste the produce from forty different *domaines* at the **Caveau du Gigondas** on place de la Mairie in the village (daily 10am–noon & 2–6.30pm). The most distinctive wine, and elixir for those who like it sweet, is the pale amber-coloured Beaumes-de-Venise muscat which you can buy from the Cave des Vignerons (Mon–Sat 8.30am–noon & 2–6pm, Sun 9am–12.30pm & 2–6pm) on the D7 just outside Beaumes.

Besides *dégustation* and bottle-buying, you can go for long walks in the Dentelles, stumbling upon mysterious ruins or photogenic panoramas of Mont

Ventoux and the Rhône valley. The pinnacles are favourite scaling faces for apprentice rock-climbers – though their wind-eroded patterns can be appreciated just as well without risking your neck on an ascent. Information on walking and climbing is available from Gigondas' **tourist office** on place du Portail (June–Sept Mon–Fri 10am–12.30pm & 2.30–6pm; Oct–May Mon–Fri 10am–noon & 2–5pm; ⓣ04.90.65.85.46), which also sells a local footpath map for €2.50.

Although it's possible to get to the villages by public transport from Vaison or Carpentras, your own vehicle is definitely an advantage. **Hotel** possibilities include, in Beaumes, the old-fashioned and quiet *Auberge St-Roch*, on avenue Jules-Ferry (ⓣ04.90.65.08.21, *demi-pension*; ❺; restaurant closed Wed out of season), and *Le Relais des Dentelles*, past the old village and over the river (ⓣ04.90.62.95.27; ❷; restaurant closed Sun evening, Mon & Jan). Gigondas has *Les Florets*, 2km from the village along the route des Dentelles (ⓣ04.90.65.85.01, ⓦwww.hotel-lesflorets.com; ❼, half-board obligatory in season), and the more upmarket *Hôtel Montmirail*, which you reach via Vacqueyras (ⓣ04.90.65.84.01, ⓦwww.hotelmontmirail.com; ❹; closed mid-Oct to mid-March). There are also **campsites** in Sablet (ⓣ04.90.46.82.55), Beaumes (ⓣ04.90.62.95.07) and Vacqueyras (ⓣ04.90.65.84.24, ⓕ04.90.65.83.28).

Besides the restaurants of the hotels mentioned above, places to stop to **eat** or drink are few and far between once you leave the villages. In Séguret *Le Bastide Bleue*, route de Sablet (ⓣ04.90.46.83.43; closed Tues & Wed out of season, plus Jan & Feb; menus €21–26), is renowned for its use of fresh local ingredients. In Gigondas, *L'Oustalet*, place Gabriel-Andéol (ⓣ04.90.65.85.30; closed Jan to mid-Feb plus Mon out of season; menus €27 and €42), has a pleasant shaded terrace and serves hearty home-style food; cheaper eats can be had at the *Café de la Poste* on rue Principale.

Carpentras

With a population of around 30,000, **CARPENTRAS** is a substantial city for this part of the world. It's also a very old one, its known history commencing in 5 BC as the capital of a Celtic tribe. The Greeks who founded Marseille came to Carpentras to buy honey, wheat, goats and skins, and the Romans had a base here. For a brief period in the fourteenth century, it became the papal headquarters and gave protection to Jews expelled from France.

Carpentras is currently in the throes of gradual refurbishment, so that immaculately restored squares and fountains alternate with gently decayed streets of seventeenth- and eighteenth-century houses, some forming arcades over the pavement. The local history museum – the **Musée Comtadin** on boulevard Albin-Durand (Wed–Sun: April–Oct 10am–noon & 2–6pm; Nov–March 10am–noon & 2–4pm; €2) – is dark and dour. The erotic fantasies of a seventeenth-century cardinal frescoed by Nicolas Mignard in the **Palais de Justice**, formerly the episcopal palace, were effaced by a later incumbent. The *palais* is attached to the dull **Cathédrale St-Siffrein**, behind which, almost hidden in the corner, stands a **Roman arch** inscribed with scenes of prisoners in chains. Fifteen hundred years after its erection, Jews – coerced, bribed or otherwise persuaded – entered the cathedral in chains to be unshackled as converted Christians. The door they passed through, the **Porte Juif**, is on the southern side and bears strange symbolism of rats encircling and devouring a globe. The **synagogue** (Mon–Thurs 10am–noon & 3–5pm, Fri 10am–noon & 3–4pm; closed Jewish feast days; free), near the Hôtel de Ville, is a seventeenth-century construction on fourteenth-century foundations, making it the oldest surviving place of Jewish worship in France.

Carpentras cheers up every Friday for the **market**, which from the end of November to early March specializes in truffles, and during **festival** time in the second half of July. It also makes a useful base for excursions into the Dentelles, Mont Ventoux and the towns and villages south towards Apt.

Buses (trains are freight only) arrive either on avenue Victor-Hugo or place Terradou, a short walk away from place Aristide-Briand, where the **tourist office** is located (June–Sept Mon–Sat 9.30am–12.30pm & 2–6pm; July & Aug Mon–Sat 9am–1pm & 2–7pm, Sun 9.30am–1pm; ⓣ04.90.63.00.78, ⓦwww.carpentras-ventoux.com). Central **accommodation** options include the basic but adequate *Univers*, 110 place A.-Briand (ⓣ04.90.63.00.05, ⓦwww.hotel-univers.com; ❸). For something grander with greater character, try *Le Fiacre*, 153 rue Vigne (ⓣ04.90.63.03.15, ⓦwww.hotel-du-fiacre.com; ❻), an eighteenth-century town house with lovely architectural features in many of the rooms, and a garden. A little way out of town, the *Safari Hotel*, 1 av J.-H.-Fabre (ⓣ04.90.63.35.35, ⓦwww.safarihotel.fr; ❺), is a bit characterless but has a pool and Internet connection. At the local **campsite**, *Lou Comtadou*, rhododendrons surround hard pitches, closed from November to March (ⓣ04.90.67.03.16).

The Friday market and seasonality influence the **restaurant** menus. In winter, sample the local truffles at *Franck Restaurant*, 30 place de l'Horloge (ⓣ04.90.60.75.00; closed Tues & Wed), which has modern gastronomic cuisine on a pretty terrace with menus from €26.50 and a €20 lunch. More traditional bistro fare is to be had at *Chez Serge*, 90 rue Cottier (ⓣ04.90.63.21.24; closed Sun; menu € 26.50 and a *plat du jour* from €10). *Aux Petites Ya-ya*, 41 rue Galonne (ⓣ04.90.63.24.11; closed Sun & Mon) offers home cooking on a small square with menus at €15–25. Once the sun goes down in Carpentras, the best place for café or **bar** crawling is place Aristide-Briand, where *Le Club* at no. 106 and the nearby *Pub Peter Polo* maintain a semblance of nightlife.

Avignon

AVIGNON, great city of the popes, and for centuries one of the major artistic centres of France, can be dauntingly crowded in summer and stiflingly hot. Away from the main tourist drag the old town is often remarkably unkempt and somewhat intimidating, with a laissez-faire approach to rubbish collection at odds with its UNESCO World Heritage status and an intrusive graffiti problem that leaves even the prettiest facades disfigured. But it's worth braving for its spectacular monuments and museums, countless impressively decorated buildings, ancient churches, chapels and convents. During the **Festival d'Avignon** in July and the beginning of August, it is *the* place to be.

Central Avignon is still enclosed by its medieval walls, built in 1403 by the antipope Benedict XIII, the last of nine **popes** who based themselves here throughout most of the fourteenth century. The first pope to come to Avignon was Clement V in 1309, who was invited over by the astute King Philippe le Bel ("the Good"), ostensibly to protect Clement from impending anarchy in Rome. In reality, Philip saw a chance to extend his power over the Church by keeping the pope in the safety of Provence, during what came to be known as the Church's "Babylonian captivity". Clement's successors were a varied group, from the villainous John XXII (of Umberto Eco's *Name of the Rose* fame), to the dedicated Urban V, and later Gregory XI, who managed to re-establish the

The Festival of Avignon

Unlike most provincial festivals of international renown, the **Festival d'Avignon** is dominated by theatre rather than classical music, though there's also plenty of that, as well as lectures, exhibitions and dance. It uses the city's great buildings as backdrops to performances, and takes place every year for three weeks from the second week in July. During festival time everything stays open late and everything gets booked up; there can be up to 200,000 visitors, and getting around or doing anything normal becomes virtually impossible.

Originally created in 1947 by actor-director **Jean Vilar**, over the years programmes have included theatrical interpretations as diverse as Molière, Euripides and Chekhov, performed by companies from across Europe. While big-name directors (Jacques Lasalle, Alain Françon) draw the largest crowds to the main venue, the Cour d'Honneur in the Palais des Papes, there's more than enough variety in all the smaller productions, dance performances and lectures to keep everyone sufficiently entertained. In addition to the introduction of new works staged by lesser-known directors and theatre troupes, each year the festival also spotlights a different culture, which in the past have ranged from showings of the Hindi epic *Ramayana* to the debut of THEOREM (Theatres from the East and from the West), a European cultural venture designed to bring together the two halves of Europe on the stage.

The main **festival programme**, with details of how to book, is available from the second week in May from the Bureau du Festival d'Avignon, 20 rue du portail Boquier, 84000 Avignon (Ⓦwww.festival-avignon.com), or from the tourist office. Ticket prices are reasonable (€5–36) and go on sale from the second week in June. As well as phone sales (9am–5pm; Ⓣ04.90.14.14.14), they can be bought from FNAC shops in all major French cities and via the FNAC website. During the festival, tickets are available until three hours before the performance. The Festival Off programme is available from mid-May from Avignon Public Off, 45 cours Jean-Jaurès (Ⓣ04.90.25.24.30, Ⓦwww.avignon-off.org). Ticket prices range from €10 to €19 and a *Carte Public Adhérent* for €10 gives you thirty percent off all shows.

papacy in Rome in 1378. However, this was not the end of the papacy here – after Gregory's death in Rome, dissident local cardinals elected their own pope in Avignon, provoking the Western Schism: a ruthless struggle for the control of the Church's wealth, which lasted until the pious Benedict fled Avignon for self-exile near Valencia in 1409.

As home to one of the richest courts in Europe, fourteenth-century Avignon attracted hordes of princes, dignitaries, poets and raiders, who arrived to beg from, rob, extort money from and entertain the popes. According to Petrarch, the overcrowded, plague-ridden papal entourage was "a sewer where all the filth of the universe has gathered". Burgeoning from within its low battlements, the town must have been a colourful, frenetic sight.

Arrival, information and accommodation

Both the **gare SNCF** on boulevard St-Roch and the adjacent **gare routière** (Ⓣ04.90.82.07.35) are close to Porte de la République, on the south side of the old city. In addition to the main *gare*, there's a new **TGV** station, which has cut travel to Paris down to two and a half hours, near the hospital 2km south of the city centre. Regular shuttles connect the TGV station with Avignon Centre (daily 6.14am–11.11pm; €1.10); passengers are picked up or dropped off next to the post office, a short walk from the main tourist office. The city's main **local bus** information centre can be found at 1 av de Lattre de Tassigny

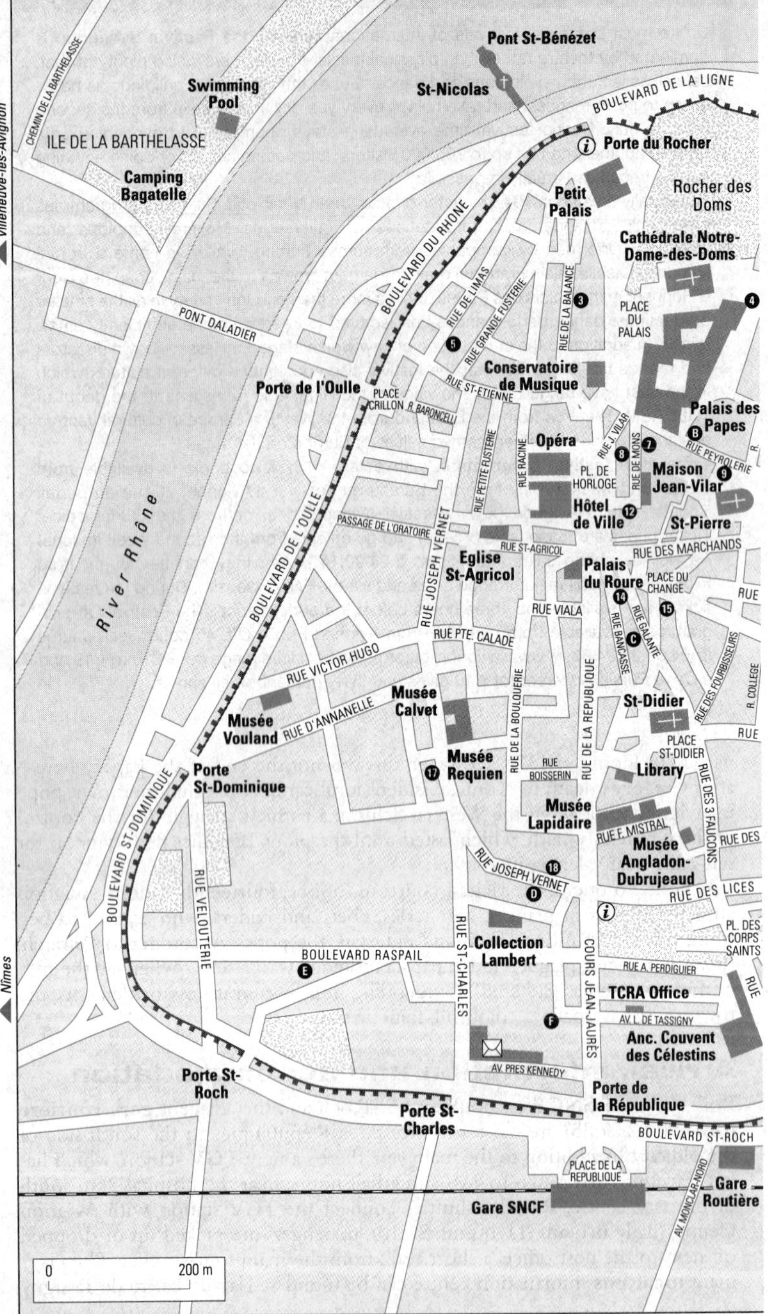
Other Campsites, A & 1
Pont St-Bénézet
St-Nicolas
Swimming Pool
CHEMIN DE LA BARTHELASSE
ILE DE LA BARTHELASSE
Camping Bagatelle
Villeneuve-lès-Avignon
BOULEVARD DE LA LIGNE
Porte du Rocher
Petit Palais
Rocher des Doms
Cathédrale Notre-Dame-des-Doms
BOULEVARD DU RHONE
RUE DE LIMAS
RUE GRANDE FUSTERIE
RUE DE LA BALANCE
PLACE DU PALAIS
PONT DALADIER
Conservatoire de Musique
RUE ST-ETIENNE
Porte de l'Oulle
PLACE CRILLON
R. BARONCELLI
Palais des Papes
RUE J. VILAR
Opéra
RUE DE MONS
RUE PEYROLERIE
PL. DE HORLOGE
Maison Jean-Vilar
RUE PETITE FUSTERIE
RUE RACINE
Hôtel de Ville
St-Pierre
PASSAGE DE L'ORATOIRE
RUE ST-AGRICOL
RUE DES MARCHANDS
Eglise St-Agricol
Palais du Roure
PLACE DU CHANGE
River Rhône
BOULEVARD DE L'OULLE
RUE JOSEPH VERNET
RUE VIALA
RUE BANCASSE
RUE GALANTE
RUE PTE. CALADE
RUE VICTOR HUGO
RUE DES FOURBISSEURS
R. COLLEGE
Musée Calvet
St-Didier
Musée Vouland
RUE D'ANNANELLE
RUE DE LA BOULQUERIE
RUE DE LA REPUBLIQUE
PLACE ST-DIDIER
Porte St-Dominique
Musée Requien
RUE BOISSERIN
Library
RUE DES 3 FAUCONS
Musée Lapidaire
RUE F. MISTRAL
Musée Angladon-Dubrujeaud
RUE JOSEPH VERNET
BOULEVARD ST-DOMINIQUE
RUE VELOUTERIE
RUE DES LICES
PL. DES CORPS SAINTS
RUE ST-CHARLES
Collection Lambert
BOULEVARD RASPAIL
COURS JEAN-JAURÈS
RUE A. PERDIGUIER
Nîmes
TCRA Office
AV. L. DE TASSIGNY
Anc. Couvent des Célestins
AV. PRES KENNEDY
Porte St-Roch
Porte de la République
Porte St-Charles
BOULEVARD ST-ROCH
PLACE DE LA REPUBLIQUE
AV. MONCLAR-NORD
Gare Routière
Gare SNCF
0
200 m
TGV Station

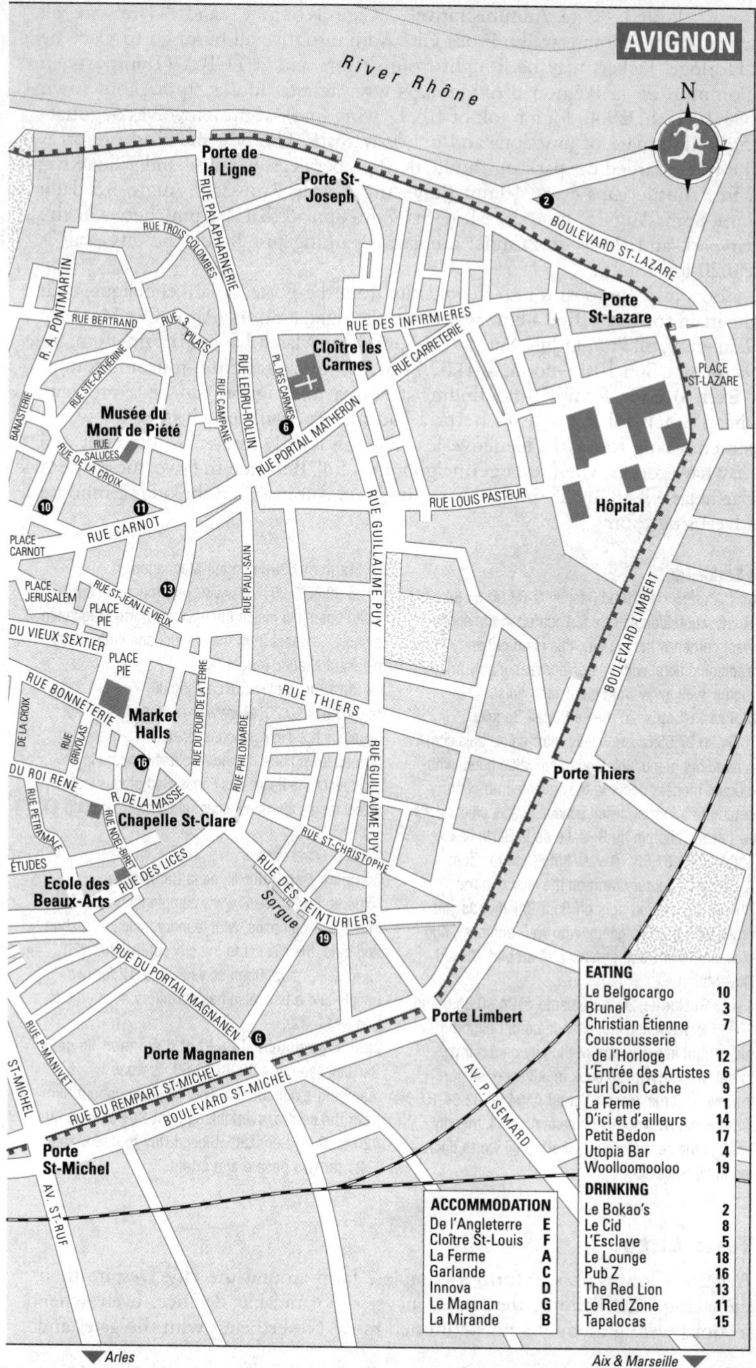
AVIGNON
River Rhône
Porte de la Ligne
Porte St-Joseph
Boulevard St-Lazare
Porte St-Lazare
Place St-Lazare
Rue Trois Colombes
Rue Palapharnerie
R. A. Pontmartin
Rue Bertrand
Rue 3 Pilats
Rue des Infirmieres
Cloître les Carmes
Pl. des Carmes
Rue Carreterie
Rue Ste-Catherine
Rue Campane
Rue Ledru-Rollin
Rue Portail Matheron
Banasterie
Musée du Mont de Piété
Rue Saluces
Rue de la Croix
Rue Louis Pasteur
Hôpital
Rue Carnot
Place Carnot
Rue Guillaume Puy
Place Jerusalem
Rue St-Jean le Vieux
Place Pie
Rue Paul-Sain
Du Vieux Sextier
Boulevard Limbert
Rue Bonneterie
Rue Thiers
Rue du Four de la Terre
Market Halls
De la Croix
Rue Grivolas
Rue Philonarde
Du Roi Rene
R. de la Masse
Porte Thiers
Rue Petramale
Rue Noel-Biret
Chapelle St-Clare
Rue St-Christophe
Études
Rue des Lices
Ecole des Beaux-Arts
Rue des Teinturiers
Sorgue
Rue du Portail Magnanen
Porte Limbert
Porte Magnanen
Rue P.-Manivet
St-Michel
Rue du Rempart St-Michel
Boulevard St-Michel
Av. P. Semard
Porte St-Michel
Av. St-Ruf
Orange & Carpentras
APT
Arles
Aix & Marseille
EATING
Le Belgocargo 10
Brunel 3
Christian Étienne 7
Couscousserie de l'Horloge 12
L'Entrée des Artistes 6
Eurl Coin Cache 9
La Ferme 1
D'ici et d'ailleurs 14
Petit Bedon 17
Utopia Bar 4
Woolloomooloo 19
DRINKING
Le Bokao's 2
Le Cid 8
L'Esclave 5
Le Lounge 18
Pub Z 16
The Red Lion 13
Le Red Zone 11
Tapalocas 15
ACCOMMODATION
De l'Angleterre E
Cloître St-Louis F
La Ferme A
Garlande C
Innova D
Le Magnan G
La Mirande B

(stops "Poste", "Cité Administrative", "Gare Routière" and "Gare" are all within a five-minute walk). From Cité Administrative all buses go to place de l'Horloge. Tickets may be bought from drivers and at TCRA (Transports en Commun de la Région d'Avignon; Ⓦwww.tcra.fr) kiosks throughout town (€1.10 each; €9.40 for a book of 10). Driving into Avignon involves negotiating a nightmare of junctions and one-way roads. The best **parking** option is the free, guarded car park on the Île de Piot, between Avignon and Villeneuve; a free shuttle runs every 10min (July–Aug 7 daily 7am–2am, Aug 8–15 daily 7am–8pm; Aug 15–June 30 Mon–Fri 7am–8pm & Sat 1–8pm) between the car park and Porte de l'Oulle; otherwise parking just inside the city wall is €0.20 for 45min.

Cours Jean-Jaurès runs into the old city from the Porte de la République, with the main **tourist office** a little way up on the right at no. 41 (April–Oct Mon–Sat 9am–6pm, till 7pm in July, Sun 10am–5pm; Nov–March Mon–Fri 9am–6pm, Sat 9am–5pm, Sun 10am–noon; Ⓣ04.32.74.32.74, Ⓦwww.avignon-tourisme.com).

Even outside festival time, finding a **room** in Avignon can be a problem: cheap hotels fill fast and it's never a bad idea to book in advance. It's worth remembering too that Villeneuve-lès-Avignon is only just across the river and may have rooms when its larger neighbour is full. Between the two, the Île de la Barthelasse is an idyllic spot for **camping**, and you may find the odd farmhouse advertising rooms.

Hotels

De l'Angleterre 29 bd Raspail Ⓣ04.90.86.34.31, Ⓦwww.hoteldangleterre.fr. Located in the south-west corner of the old city, this is an old and traditional hotel with some very reasonably priced rooms, well away from night-time noise. ❹

Cloître St-Louis 20 rue de Portail-Boquier Ⓣ04.90.27.55.55, Ⓦwww.cloitre-saint-louis.com. A large but personable and good-value hotel, with elegant modern decor in the seventeenth-century setting of a former Jesuit school. Air-conditioned. ❽

La Ferme chemin du Bois, Île de la Barthelasse Ⓣ04.90.82.57.53, Ⓦwww.hotel-laferme.com. A sixteenth-century farm on the island in the Rhône (signposted right off Pont Daladier as you cross over from Avignon), with well-equipped and pleasant rooms and greenery all around. Closed Nov–March. ❺

Garlande 20 rue Galante Ⓣ04.90.85.08.85 Ⓦwww.hoteldegarlande.com. Delightful place right in the centre of the city on a narrow street. Well known, so book in advance. ❼

Innova 100 rue Joseph-Vernet Ⓣ04.90.82.54.10, Ⓔhotel.innova@numericable.fr. A small, friendly hotel in the centre of town that's well worth booking in advance. ❸

Le Magnan 63 rue Portail-Magnanen Ⓣ04.90.86.36.51, Ⓦwww.hotel-magnan.com. Quiet hotel just inside the walls by Porte Magnanen a short way east from the station, and with a very pleasant shaded garden. ❺

La Mirande 4 place de La Mirande Ⓣ04.90.14.20.20, Ⓦwww.la-mirande.fr. The most luxurious hotel in Avignon is located in a grand historic town house facing a cobbled square in the shadow of the Palais des Papes. Sumptuous individual rooms surround a central courtyard garden. ❾

Campsites

Camping Bagatelle Île de la Barthelasse Ⓣ04.90.86.30.39, Ⓦwww.campingbagatelle.fr. Three-star campsite, with laundry facilities, a shop and café; the closest to the city centre. Bus #20 "Bagatelle" stop. Open all year. €17.12 for two people and a tent. Also has dormitory accommodation (€11–12).

Camping municipal du Pont d'Avignon Île de la Barthelasse Ⓣ04.90.80.63.50, Ⓦwww.camping-avignon.com. Four-star site, about 3km from the centre, overlooking Pont St-Bénézet. Bus #20 to stop "Bénézet". Closed Nov to late March. €21 for two people and a tent.

The City

Avignon's low walls still form a complete loop around the city. Despite their menacing crenellations, they were never a formidable defence, even when sections were girded by a now-vanished moat. Nevertheless with the gates and

Avignon Passion passports

The tourist offices in Avignon and Villeneuve-lès-Avignon distribute free **Avignon Passion passports**. After paying the full admission price for the first museum you visit, you and your family receive discounts of 20–50 percent on the entrance fees of all subsequent museums in Avignon. The pass also gives you discounts on tourist transport (such as riverboats and bus tours), and is valid for 15 days after its first use.

towers all restored, the old ramparts still give a sense of cohesion and unity to the old town, dramatically marking it off from the formless sprawl of the modern city beyond.

Rue de la République, the extension of cours Jean-Jaurès and the main axis of the old town, ends at **place de l'Horloge**, the city's main square. Beyond that is **place du Palais**, with the city's most imposing monument, the **Palais des Papes**, the **Rocher des Doms** park and the Porte du Rocher, overlooking the Rhône by the **pont d'Avignon**, or pont St-Bénézet as it's officially known.

The Palais des Papes and around

Rising high above the east side of place du Palais is the **Palais des Papes** (daily: mid-March to Oct 9am–7pm; Nov to mid-March 9.30am–5.45pm; last ticket 1hr before closing; €9.50, or €11.50 for palace and the Pont (€7.50 with the Avignon Passion passport, see box above); ticket includes an audioguide; guided tours on request). With its massive stone vaults, battlements and sluices for pouring hot oil on attackers, the palace was built primarily as a fortress, though the two pointed towers which hover above its gate are incongruously graceful. Close up it is simply too monstrous to take in all at once; cross to the northwestern side of the place du Palais as far as you can go to take in the wide-angle view, or follow rue Peyrollerie, rue Banasterie and the Escaliers Ste-Anne around the less familiar south and east sides for tantalizing, dramatic close-ups

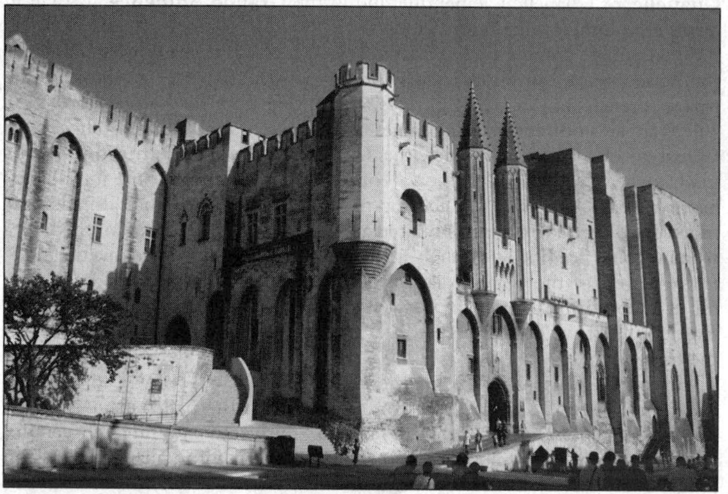

△ The Palais des Papes, Avignon

of the massive walls, the humble dimensions of the surrounding houses only adding to the impression of vastness. Inside the palace, so little remains of the original decoration and furnishings that you can be deceived into thinking that all the popes and their retinues were as pious and austere as the last official occupant, Benedict XIII. The denuded interior leaves hardly a whiff of the corruption and decadence of fat, feuding cardinals and their mistresses, the thronging purveyors of jewels, velvet and furs, musicians, chefs and painters competing for patronage, the riotous banquets and corridor schemings.

The visit begins in the **Pope's Tower**, otherwise known as the Tower of Angels. You enter the **Treasury** where the serious business of the church's deeds and finances went on. Four large holes found in the floor (covered over) of the smaller downstairs room served as safes. The same cunning storage device was used for the chamberlain who lived upstairs in the **Chambre du Camérier** (just off the Jesus Hall), where the safes have been revealed. As he was the Pope's right-hand man, the quarters would have been lavishly decorated, but successive occupants have left their mark, most recently military whitewash, and what is now visible is a confusion of layers. The other door in this room leads into the **Papal Vestiary**, where the Pope would dress before sessions in the consistory. He also had a small library here and could look out onto the gardens below.

A door on the north side of the Jesus Hall leads to the **Consistoire** of the **Vieux Palais**, where sovereigns and ambassadors were received and the canonizations examined and proclaimed. The room was damaged by fire in 1413, and the only decoration that remains are fragments of frescoes moved from the cathedral, and a nineteenth-century line-up of the popes, in which all nine look remarkably similar thanks to the artist using the same model for each portrait. The **kitchen** on this floor gives a hint of the scale of papal gluttony with its square walls becoming an octagonal chimneypiece for a vast central cooking fire. As you cross from the Vieux Palais to the **Palais Neuf**, Clement VI's bedroom and the Chambre du Cerf – his study – are further evidence of this pope's secular concerns, the walls in the former adorned with wonderful entwined oak and vine leaf motifs, the latter with superb hunting and fishing scenes. But austerity resumes in the cathedral-like proportions of the **Grande Chapelle**, or Chapelle Clementine, and in the **Grande Audience**, its twin in terms of volume on the floor below.

When you've completed the circuit, which includes a heady walk along the roof terraces, you can watch a glossy but informative film on the history of the palace (French only, but English version available from the palace shop, €15). There are also **concerts**: programmes are available from the ticket office.

Next to the Palais des Papes, the **Cathédrale Notre-Dame-des-Doms** might once have been a luminous Romanesque structure, but the interior has had a bad attack of Baroque, and the result is an incoherent mess. In addition, nineteenth-century maniacs mounted an enormous gilded Virgin on the belfry, which would look silly enough anywhere, but when dwarfed by the fifty-metre towers of the popes' palace is absurd. There's greater reward behind, in the **Rocher des Doms** park. As well as ducks and swans and views over the river to Villeneuve and beyond, it has a sundial in which your own shadow tells the time.

The **Petit Palais** (daily except Tues: June–Sept 10am–1pm & 2–6pm; Oct–May 9.30am–1pm & 2–5.30pm; €6), not far from the park's main entrance, contains a daunting collection of first-rate thirteenth- to fifteenth-century painting and sculpture, most of it by masters from northern Italian cities. As you progress through the collection, you can watch as the masters wrestle with and finally conquer the representation of perspective – a revolution from medieval art, where the size of figures depended on their importance rather than position. Highlight of the collection, in room XVI, Botticelli's sublime *Virgin and Child* depicts a tender Mary, playfully coddling a smiling infant.

Behind the Petit Palais, and well signposted, is the half-span of Pont St-Bénézet, or the **Pont d'Avignon** (same hours as Palais des Papes; €4, €11.50 combined ticket with Palais des Papes, audioguide in English included). The gatehouse now has a chamber dedicated to the famous song where for €5 you can record a video clip of your own version. One theory has it that the lyrics say "*Sous le pont*" (under the bridge) rather than "*Sur le pont*" (on the bridge), and refer to the thief and trickster clientele of a tavern on the Île de la Barthelasse (which the bridge once crossed on its way to Villeneuve) dancing with glee at the arrival of more potential victims. Keeping the bridge in repair from the ravages of the Rhône was finally abandoned in 1660, three and a half centuries after it was built, and only four of the original 22 arches remain. Despite its limited transportational use, the bridge remained a focus of river boatmen, who constructed a chapel to their patroness on the first of the bridge's bulwarks. And the bridge's failure over the centuries to withstand the rigours of its function didn't stop its builder, Bénézet, from becoming the patron saint of architects.

Around place de l'Horloge

The café-lined **place de l'Horloge**, frenetically busy most of the time, is the site of the city's imposing **Hôtel de Ville** and **clock tower**, and the **Opéra**. Around the square, on rues de Mons, Molière and Corneille, famous faces appear in windows painted on the buildings. Many of these figures from the past were visitors to Avignon, and of those who recorded their impressions of the city it was the sound of over a hundred bells ringing that stirred them most. On a Sunday morning, traffic lulls permitting, you can still hear myriad different peals from churches, convents and chapels in close proximity. The fourteenth-century **church of St-Agricol**, just behind the Hôtel de Ville (closed for restoration at the time of writing), is one of Avignon's best Gothic edifices.

To the south, just behind rue St-Agricol on rue Collège du Roure, is the beautiful fifteenth-century **Palais du Roure**, a centre of Provençal culture. The gateway and the courtyard are definitely worth a look; there may well be temporary art exhibitions, and if you want a rambling tour through the attics to see Provençal costumes, publications and presses, photographs of the Camargue in the 1900s and an old stagecoach, you need to turn up at 3pm on Tuesday (€4.60).

To the west of place de l'Horloge are the most desirable Avignon addresses – both now and three hundred years ago – and it's below the mellow stone facades along **rue Joseph-Vernet** and **rue Petite-Fusterie** that you'll find Avignon's most luxurious shops.

The Banasterie and Carmes quartiers

The **quartier de la Banasterie**, lying immediately east of the Palais des Papes, is almost solid seventeenth- and eighteenth-century, and the heavy wooden doors, with their highly sculptured lintels, today bear the nameplates of lawyers, psychiatrists and doctors. Here, tourist-oriented commercialism is kept in check, and at night in particular this is an atmospheric and beautiful part of the city.

Between Banasterie and **place des Carmes** are a tangle of tiny streets guaranteed to get you lost. Pedestrians have priority over cars on many of them, and there are plenty of tempting café or restaurant stops. At 6 rue Saluces, you'll find the peculiar **Musée du Mont de Piété**, an ex-pawnbroker's shop and now home to the town's archives (Mon 10am–noon & 1.30–5pm, Tues–Fri

8.30am–noon & 1.30–5pm; free). It has a small display of papal bulls and painted silk desiccators for determining the dry weight of what was the city's chief commodity.

Rue de la République to place Pie

Between the chainstore blandness of rue de la République and the hideous modern **market hall** on **place Pie** (mornings Tues–Sun) is the main pedestrian precinct, centring on **place de la Principale**. **Rue des Marchands** and **rue du Vieux-Sextier** have their complement of chapels and late medieval mansions, in particular the **Hôtel des Rascas** on the corner of rue des Marchands and rue Fourbisseurs, and the **Hôtel de Belli** on the corner of rue Fourbisseurs and rue du Vieux-Sextier. The Renaissance **church of St-Pierre** on place St-Pierre has superb doors sculpted in 1551, and a retable dating from the same period. More Renaissance art is on show in the fourteenth-century **church of St-Didier** (daily 8am–6.30pm), chiefly *The Carrying of the Cross* by Francesco Laurana, commissioned by King René of Provence in 1478. There are also fourteenth-century frescoes in the left-hand chapel.

Musée Calvet and around

The excellent **Musée Calvet**, 65 rue Joseph-Vernet (daily except Tues 10am–1pm & 2–6pm; €6), and the impressive eighteenth-century palace housing it, have been undergoing gradual restoration and transformation for the past few years. The collection begins with the **Galerie des Sculptures**. A better introduction to a museum couldn't be wished for, with a handful of languorous nineteenth-century marble sculptures, including Bosio's *Young Indian*, perfectly suited to this elegant space. The end of the gallery houses the Puech collection with a large selection of silverware, Italian and Dutch paintings and, more unusually, a Flemish curiosities cabinet, painted with scenes from the story of Daniel. Upstairs is a fine set of seasons by Nicolas Mignard, whilst Joseph Vernet sticks to representing the different times of the day. Further down, Horace Vernet donated the subtle *Death of Young Barra* by Jacques-Louis David as well as Géricault's *Battle of Nazareth*. On the way out don't miss the Victor Martin collection, including Vlaminck's *At the Bar*, Bonnard's *Winter Day* and the haunting *Downfall* by Chaïm Soutine.

Avignon's remaining museums are considerably less compelling. Next door to the Musée Calvet is the **Musée Requien** (Tues–Sat 9am–noon & 2–6pm; free); its subject is natural history and its sole advantage is in being free and having clean toilets. With little more to recommend it is the **Musée Lapidaire**, a museum of Roman and Gallo-Roman stones housed in the Baroque chapel at 27 rue de la République (daily except Tues 10am–1pm & 2–6pm; €2). Finally, at the **Musée Vouland**, at the end of rue Victor-Hugo near Porte St-Dominique (Tues–Sat: May–Oct 10am–noon & 2–6pm, Sun 2–6pm; Nov–April 2–6pm; €4), you can feast your eyes on the fittings, fixtures and furnishings that French aristocrats enjoyed both before and after the Revolution. There's also some brilliant Moustiers faïence, exquisite marquetry and Louis XV ink-pots with silver rats holding the lids. Just west of the tourist office, down rue Violette, is the **Collection Lambert** (Tues–Sun: July & Aug 11am–7pm; Sept–June 11am–6pm; €5.50), Avignon's first attempt at a contemporary art gallery, which leans heavily towards conceptual, installation and video art. Though it's not especially high powered, the permanent collection includes a few Nan Goldin photographs and works by Anselm Kiefer and Cy Twombly, and there are occasionally interesting temporary exhibitions.

Southeast: to rue des Teinturiers

Between rue de la République and place St-Didier, on rue Labourer, is the **Musée Angladon** (Wed–Sun 1–6pm, plus Tues in high season; €6), displaying the remains of the private collection of Jacques Doucet. Although the collection, which once contained works like Picasso's *Demoiselles d'Avignon* and Douanier Rousseau's *The Snakecharmer* (now in the Musée d'Orsay), has seen better days, it is still very much worth a look. The visit begins with a series of rooms furnished and decorated as coherent units, the first Renaissance and the remainder eighteenth-century (including an orientalist room). The paintings which remain are alone worth the admission price, and include Foujita's *Portrait of Mme Foujita* and a *Self-Portrait*, Modigliani's *The Pink Blouse*, various Picassos and Van Gogh's *The Railroad Cars*, the only painting from Van Gogh's stay in Provence to be on permanent display in the region.

Through the park by the tourist office (where there's an old British red phone box) you come to **place des Corps-Saints**, a lively area of cafés and restaurants whose tables fill the square. Just to the north, rue des Lices runs eastwards, past the École des Beaux-Arts, to **rue des Teinturiers**, the city's most atmospheric street. Its name refers to the eighteenth- and nineteenth-century business of calico printing. The cloth was washed in the Sorgue canal which still runs alongside the street, turning the wheels of long-gone mills, and, although the water is fairly murky and sometimes smelly, this is still a great street for evening strolls, with a large number of cheap restaurants.

Eating and drinking

Reasonably priced midday **meals** are easy to come by in Avignon and eating well in the evening needn't break the bank. The large terraced café-brasseries on place de l'Horloge and rue de la République all serve quick, if not necessarily memorable, meals. Rue des Teinturiers is good if you're on a budget, and the streets between place Crillon and place du Palais are full of temptation if you're not.

Restaurants and cafés

Le Belgocargo 10 place des Châtaignes ⓣ04.90.85.72.99. A Belgian restaurant where the staunch royalist owner serves *moules-frites* and beer; lunch menu with drink for €11.80. Closed Sun out of season.

Brunel 46 rue Balance ⓣ04.90.85.24.83. Superb regional dishes, with evening menus from €30. Closed Sun & Mon, and first half of Aug.

Christian Étienne 10 rue de Mons ⓣ04.90.86.16.50. One of Avignon's best restaurants, housed in a fourteenth-century mansion and offering exotic combinations such as fennel sorbet with a saffron sauce plus some great seafood dishes. Menus €55–105. Closed Sun & Mon.

Couscousserie de l'Horloge 2 rue de Mons ⓣ04.90.85.84.86. Popular Algerian-run restaurant with a jovial atmosphere and excellent North African food. Try the delicious €14.50 *tagine aux prunes* and wash it down with an Algerian *coteaux de Mascara* red.

L'Entrée des Artistes 1 place des Carmes ⓣ04.90.82.46.90. Small, friendly bistro serving traditional French dishes; €25 weekday menu. Closed Sat, Sun & early Aug to early Sept.

Eurl Coin Cache 3 place du Cloître St-Pierre ⓣ04.90.82.07.31. Small funky café on a beautiful shaded square. A choice of home-made tarts which change daily.

La Ferme chemin du Bois, Île de la Barthelasse ⓣ04.90.82.57.53. A traditional farmhouse, serving well-prepared simple dishes, from €23. Closed Mon & Wed, plus Nov to mid-March.

D'ici et d'ailleurs 4 rue Galante ⓣ04.90.14.63.65. Tasteful modern surroundings, Provençal dishes from "here", international flavours from "there"; good and not expensive. Menus €15.50 and €19. Service until 11pm; closed Sun & Mon.

Petit Bedon 70 rue Joseph-Vernet ⓣ04.90.82.33.98. The "Potbelly" is a well-regarded and smart Provençal restaurant, though not quite the bargain it was. Lunch menu €23; otherwise regional dishes are from €19 à la carte. Closed Sun & Mon.

Utopia Bar 4 rue Escaliers Ste-Anne. In the shadow of the Palais des Papes, this elegant but slightly snooty café has changing exhibitions adorning the walls, live jazz some nights, and is just next door to a good cinema.

Woolloomooloo 16bis rue des Teinturiers ⓣ04.90.85.28.44. An old printshop with all the presses still in place. The cuisine is from just about everywhere, as are the teas. Menus at €13 & €18 (lunch) or €21. Occasional theme nights. Closed Mon.

Bars and clubs

Le Bokao's 9bis St-Lazare ⓣ04.90.82.47.95. Eclectic mix of music styles including house and techno at the weekends in a converted barn. Wed–Sat 10pm–5am.

Le Cid 11 place de l'Horloge ⓣ04.90.82.30.38 Trendy mixed gay/straight bar and terrace which stays open long after the rest of place de l'Horloge has closed for the night.

L'Esclave 12 rue du Limas ⓣ04.90.85.14.91. Avignon's gay and lesbian bar, with regular DJs, drag shows and karaoke nights. Tues–Sun from 11pm.

Le Lounge 83 rue Joseph-Vernet. Swanky modern cocktail bar with DJ Thurs–Sat. Open 6pm–1.30am.

Pub Z cnr rues Bonneterie & Artaud, close to Les Halles. Rock bar with black and white decor and DJs Fri and Sat. Open till 1.30am; closed Sun & last two weeks of Aug.

The Red Lion 21–23 rue St-Jean-le-Vieux ⓣ04.91.72.71.80. English-style pub with live music twice a week and regular theme evenings.

Le Red Zone 25 rue Carnot ⓣ04.90.27.02.44. Bar with DJs and weekly concerts. Daily 9pm–3am.

Tapalocas 15 rue Galante ⓣ04.90.82.56.84. Tapas at €2.20 a dish, happy hour on aperitifs between 6–7.30pm and Spanish music, sometimes live. Daily noon–1am.

Theatre, music and film

There's a fair amount of nightlife and cultural events in Avignon: the **Opéra**, on place de l'Horloge (ⓣ04.90.82.81.40), mounts a good range of productions; Le Chêne Noir, 8bis rue Ste-Catherine (ⓣ04.90.86.58.11), is a theatre company worth seeing, with mime, musicals or Molière on offer; and plenty of **classical concerts** are performed in churches, usually for free. Cinéma Utopia, at La Manutention, rue Escaliers Ste-Anne (ⓣ04.90.82.65.36), shows films in *version originale* (ie undubbed); the same complex houses the AJMI Jazz Club (ⓣ04.90.86.08.61), which hosts live jazz every Thursday night and features major acts and some adventurous new groups. The café *La Tache d'Encre*, rue Tarasque (ⓣ04.90.85.97.13; closed Sun), presents local theatre performances. To find out what's on, get hold of the tourist office's free monthly calendar *Rendez-Vous*. They may also have the arts, events and music magazine *César* (also free), which is otherwise found in arts centres.

Listings

Bike rental Holiday Bikes, 20 bd St-Roch ⓣ04.32.76.25.88; Provence Bike, 52 bd St-Roch ⓣ04.90.27.92.61 (also scooters and motorbikes).

Boat trips Grands Bateaux de Provence, allée de l'Oulle ⓣ04.90.85.62.25, ⓦavignon-et-provence.com/mireio. Offering year-round trips upstream towards Châteauneuf-du-Pape and downstream to Arles; two-week advance booking recommended.

Books Shakespeare, 155 rue Carreterie. English bookshop and *salon de thé*. Closed Sun, Mon & evenings.

Car rental National/Citer, *gare TGV* ⓣ04.90.27.30.07, *gare SNCF* bd St-Roch ⓣ04.90.85.96.47; Rent a Car, 130 av Pierre-Sémard ⓣ04.90.88.08.02; Sixt, 3 bd St-Ruf ⓣ04.90.86.06.61.

Emergencies Doctor/ambulance ⓣ15; hospital, Centre Hospitalier H.-Duffaut, 305 rue Raoul-Follereau ⓣ04.32.75.33.33; night chemist, call police ⓣ04.90.80.50.00 for addresses.

Internet CyberHighway, 30 rue des Infirmières; Webzone 3 rue St-Jean-le-Vieux/place Pie.

Laundry 9 rue du Chapeau-Rouge; 27 rue Portail-Magnanen; 113 av St-Ruf.

Money exchange Cie Avignonnaise de la Change, 19 rue de la République ⓣ04.90.16.04.04; Mondial Change, 34 rue de la Balance; post office, cours Kennedy.

Police 13ter quai St-Lazare (due to move in 2007) ⓣ08.00.00.84.00 or simply ⓣ17

Post office Poste, cours Président-Kennedy, Avignon 84000.

Swimming pool Piscine Olympique on the Île de la Barthelasse (mid-May to Aug 10am–7pm).

Taxis place Pie ⓣ04.90.82.20.20.

Villeneuve-lès-Avignon

VILLENEUVE-LÈS-AVIGNON rises up a rocky escarpment above the west bank of the Rhône, looking down upon its older neighbour from behind far more convincing fortifications. Historically, Villeneuve operated largely as a suburb of Avignon, with palatial residences constructed by the cardinals and a great monastery founded by Pope Innocent VI.

To this day, Villeneuve is technically a part of Languedoc and not Provence, and would score better in the hierarchy of towns to visit were it further from Avignon, whose monuments it can almost match for colossal scale and impressiveness. Despite the closeness of its relationship with Avignon it is, however, a very different – and really rather sleepy – kind of place, and as such retains a repose and a sense of timelessness that bustling Avignon inevitably lacks. In summer it provides venues for the Avignon Festival as well as alternatives for accommodation overspill, and it's certainly worth a day, whatever time of year you visit.

Arrival, information and accommodation

From Avignon's post office on cours Président-Kennedy, across the way from the *gare SNCF*, the half-hourly #11 bus (take care not to go in the direction "Les Angles–Villeneuve") runs direct to place Charles-David ("Office du Tourisme" stop) taking less than ten minutes, or five if you catch it from Porte d'Oulle. After 7.30pm you'll have to take a taxi or walk – it's only 3km. Place Charles-David is where you'll find both the **tourist office** (July daily 10am–7pm; Aug–June Mon–Sat 9am–12.30pm & 2–6pm; ⓣ04.90.25.61.33, ⓦwww.villeneuvelezavignon.fr/tourisme), and a food **market** on Thursday morning and bric-a-brac on Saturday morning. A little south of the square rue Farigoule runs west to rue de la République, the main street, which runs due north past place Jean-Jaurès. It's here you'll find what limited restaurant and bar life there is.

Hotels

L'Atelier 5 rue de la Foire ⓣ04.90.25.01.84, ⓦwww.hoteldelatelier.com. A sixteenth-century house around a central stone staircase bathed in light, with huge open fireplaces and a shady walled garden. ❺

Les Cèdres 39 av Pasteur ⓣ04.90.25.43.92, ⓦwww.lescedres-hotel.fr. An austere Louis XVIII country house with old-fashioned decor, a pool and restaurant. ❹

Les Écuries des Chartreux 66 rue de la République ⓣ04.90.25.79.93, ⓦwww.ecuries-des-chartreux.com. B&B in a light and airy rustic house with exposed stone walls and antique furniture. ❺

Jardin de la Livrée 4bis rue Camp de Bataille ⓣ04.90.26.05.05, ⓦwww.la-livree.oxatis.com. B&B in an old house in the centre of the village with comfortable rooms around a swimming pool, also has a good-value restaurant. ❺

Le Prieuré 7 place du Chapitre ⓣ04.90.15.90.15, ⓦwww.leprieure.fr. The first choice if money is no object. An old priory surrounded by a peacful garden full of flowers. The restaurant serves Provençal cuisine with a gourmet twist. ❽

Hostel and campsites

YMCA hostel 7bis chemin de la Justice ⓣ04.90.25.46.20, ⓦwww.ymca-avignon.com. Beautifully situated overlooking the river by Pont du Royaume, with balconied rooms for one to four people (€23 for dorm bed) and an open-air swimming pool (stop "Pont d'Avignon" on Avignon–Villeneuve bus or "Gabriel Péri" on the Villeneuve–Avignon bus).

Camping Municipal de la Laune chemin St-Honoré ⓣ04.90.27.49.40, ⓕ04.90.25.88.03. A three-star site off the D980, near the sports stadium and swimming pools. Closed mid-Oct to March.

The Town

For a good overview of Villeneuve – and Avignon – make your way to the **Tour Philippe-le-Bel** at the bottom of montée de la Tour (bus stop "Philippe-le-Bel").

This tower was built to guard the French end of Avignon's Pont St-Bénézet (or Pont d'Avignon), and a climb to the top (March–Nov Tues–Sun 10am–12.30pm & 2–6.30pm; €1.80) will be rewarded with stunning views.

Even more indicative of French distrust of its neighbours is the enormous **Fort St-André** (daily: April–Sept 10am–1pm & 2–6pm; Oct–March 10am–1pm & 2–5pm; €5), whose bulbous double-towered gateway and vast white walls loom over the town. Inside, refreshingly, there's not a hint of a postcard stall or souvenir shop – just tumbledown houses and the former **abbey**, with its gardens of olive trees, ruined chapels, lily ponds and dovecotes (Tues–Sun: July & Aug 10am–12.30pm & 2–6pm; Sept–June 10am–noon & 2–5pm; €4). Its cliff-face terrace is the classic spot for artists to aim their brushes, or photographers their cameras, over Avignon. You can reach the approach to the fortress, montée du Fort, from place Jean-Jaurès on rue de la République, or by the "rapid slope" of **rue Pente-Rapide**, a cobbled street of tiny houses leading off rue des Récollets on the north side of place Charles-David.

Almost at the top of rue de la République, on the right, allée des Muriers leads from place des Chartreux to the entrance of **La Chartreuse du Val de Bénédiction** (daily: April–Sept 9am–6.30pm; Oct–March 9.30am–5.30pm; €6.50). This Carthusian monastery, one of the largest in France, was founded by the sixth of the Avignon popes, Innocent VI (pope 1352–62), whose sharp profile is outlined on his tomb in the church. The buildings, which were sold off after the Revolution and gradually restored last century, are totally unembellished. With the exception of the Giovanetti frescoes in the chapel beside the refectory, all the paintings and treasures of the monastery have been dispersed, leaving you with a strong impression of the austerity of the Carthusian order. You're free to wander around unguided, through the three cloisters, the church, chapels, cells and communal spaces, which have little to see but plenty of atmosphere to absorb. It's one of the best venues in the Festival of Avignon.

Another festival venue is the fourteenth-century **Église Collègiale Notre-Dame** and its cloister on place St-Marc close to the *mairie* (April–Sept 10am–12.30pm & 2–6.30pm; Oct–March daily 10am–noon & 2–5pm; free). Notre-Dame's most important treasure is a rare fourteenth-century smiling Madonna and Child made from a single tusk of ivory, now housed, along with many of the paintings from the Chartreuse, in the **Musée Pierre-de-Luxembourg**, just to the north along rue de la République (same hours as Église Collègiale Notre-Dame; €3). The spacious layout includes a single room, with comfortable sofas and ample documentation, given over to the most stunning painting in the collection – *The Coronation of the Virgin*, painted in 1453 by Enguerrand Quarton as the altarpiece for the church in the Chartreuse.

Eating and drinking

Aubertin 1 rue de l'Hôpital ☎04.90.25.94.84. In the shade of the old arcades by the Collègiale Notre-Dame. Simple local dishes followed by delicious deserts: try the *soufflé aux marrons et au rhum avec glace à la vanille*. €36 menu. Closed Sun & Mon.

La Banaste 28 rue de la République ☎04.90.25.64.20. Serves plentiful *terroir* meals. Menus from €26. Closed Thurs.

Kream 9 rue de la République ☎06.13,55.02.42. Good ice cream, crêpes and milkshakes on the leafy main village square, place Jean-Jaurès, where you can also find Internet acess at Cyber Espace.

La Magnanerie 37 rue Camp de Bataille ☎04.90.25.11.11. For blowout posh nosh off rue de la République, with a menu for €49 (à la carte over €30).

Mon Mari Etait Pâtissier 3 av Pasteur ☎04.90.25.52.79. Popular restaurant where the chef has moved on from pastries to swordfish. Menus from €35. Closed Sun eve & Mon.

Le Prieuré 7 place du Chapitre ☎04.90.15.90.15. Luxurious restaurant that's part of Relais & Chateaux; subtly blended Mediterranean flavours dominate. Lunch menus from €36; dinner menu €60.

St-Rémy-de-Provence and the Alpilles

The watery and intensely cultivated scenery of the Petite Crau plain south of Avignon changes abruptly with the eruption of the **Chaîne des Alpilles**, whose peaks look like the surf of a wave about to engulf the plain. At their northern foot nestles **ST-RÉMY-DE-PROVENCE**, a dreamy place approached along long avenues of plane trees and whose busy boulevards contain an old town no more than half a kilometre in diameter. Outside this ring, the modern town is sparingly laid out, so for once you don't have to plough your way through dense developments to reach the centre. It's a beautiful place, as unspoilt as the villages around it.

The best time to visit St-Rémy is during the **Fête de Transhumance** on Whit Monday, when a 2000-strong flock of sheep, accompanied by goats and donkeys, does a tour of the town before being packed off to the Alps for the summer. Another good time to come is for the **Carreto Ramado**, on August 15, a harvest thanksgiving procession in which the religious or secular symbolism of the floats reveals the political colour of the various village councils, while a pagan rather than workers' **May Day** is celebrated with donkey-drawn floral floats on which people play fifes and tambourines.

Arrival, information and accommodation

There's no train station in St-Rémy; **buses** from Avignon, Aix and Arles drop you in place de la République, the main square abutting the old town on the east. The **tourist office**, at place Jean-Jaurès (Easter–Oct Mon–Sat 9am–12.30pm & 2–6.30pm, Sun 10am–noon & 3–6pm; Nov–Easter Mon–Sat 9am–noon & 2–6pm; ⓣ04.90.92.05.22, ⓦwww.saintremy-de-provence.com); they have excellent free guides to **cycling and walking routes** in and around the Alpilles and can provide addresses for renting **horses**. If you want to rent a **bike**, try Telecycles (ⓣ04.90.92.83.15). Without a car, it's difficult to get to Glanum or Les Baux except by foot or taxi (taxis ⓣ06.07.02.25.64 or 06.09.31.50.38).

St-Rémy has a fairly wide choice of **accommodation**, though bargains are hard to come by. In the old town, *Ville Verte*, on the corner of place de la

Nostradamus

Michel de Nostredame was born in St-Rémy in 1503, and, educated as a physician, he first received recognition for his innovative treatment of plague victims. It wasn't until the latter part of his life that his interest in astrology and the occult would lead to the publication of *The Prophecies of Michel Nostradamus*, a collection of 942 prophetic quatrains. Already well known in his own day, Nostradamus used a deliberately obscure and cryptic writing style for fear that he would be persecuted by the authorities were they to understand completely his **predictions**. The end result was some extremely ambiguous French verse, which has since been the subject of numerous forgeries, urban legends and some very liberal interpretations. Today he is most often given credit for predicting the rise of Napoleon and Hitler, and major catastrophes such as the Great Fire of London in 1666. While Nostradamus may or may not have been able to accurately foresee the future, his success as a writer remains undisputed: his collection of prophecies, now known as *Centuries*, has been kept in print continuously since its first publication in 1551. The tourist office in St-Rémy publishes an excellent leaflet, *Provence in the days of Nostradamus*, with **itineraries** leading from St-Rémy to Salon and back again, though the Nostradamus link is often tenuous.

République and avenue Fauconnet (Ⓣ04.90.92.06.14, Ⓦwww.hotel-villeverte.com; closed Jan; ❼), has a garden and a pool, and some rooms on the ground floor with kitchenettes. Outside the old town, try *Hostellerie du Chalet Fleuri*, 15 av Frédéric-Mistral (Ⓣ04.90.92.03.62, Ⓕ04.90.92.60.28; ❸), to the north, with parking, a restaurant and garden, or *Le Castellet des Alpilles*, 6 place Mireille (Ⓣ04.90.92.07.21, Ⓦ www.castelet-alpilles.com; ❹; closed Nov–March), to the south past the tourist office, which is small and friendly, and has some rooms with great views.

There are three functional and busy **campsites** near St-Rémy: the municipal *Le Mas de Nicolas*, 800m from the centre on a turning off the route de Mollèges (Ⓣ04.90.92.27.05; €15; closed mid-Oct to mid-March); *Monplaisir*, 1km from the centre on chemin de Monplaisir (Ⓣ04.90.92.22.70, Ⓦwww.camping-monplaisir.fr; €17.50; closed mid-Nov to Feb); and *Pegomas*, on avenue Jean-Moulin to the east of the boulevards (Ⓣ04.90.92.01.21, Ⓦwww.campingpegomas.com; €15.40; closed Nov–Feb).

The Town

To reach the old town from place de la République, take avenue de la Résistance, which runs alongside the town's imposing main church, the **Collégiale St-Martin** (organ recitals July–Sept Sat 5.30pm), and start wandering up the alleyways into immaculate, leafy squares. For an introduction to the region, a good first visit would be to the **Musée des Alpilles** on place Favier, housed in the Hôtel Mistral de Mondragon (daily: Feb–Nov 10am–noon & 2–6pm; Dec–Jan 2–5pm; €3). The museum features interesting displays on folklore, festivities and traditional crafts, plus some intriguing local landscapes, creepy portraits by Marshal Pétain's first wife and souvenirs of local boy Nostradamus.

The neighbouring **Musée Archéologique** in the Hôtel de Sade (daily: April–Aug 11am–6pm; Sept–March 11am–5pm; €6.50 includes entry to Glanum), displays finds from the archeological digs at the Greco-Roman town of Glanum. The hour or so which it takes to wander through the museum may be a bit much for the non-committed, but there are some stunning pieces, in particular the temple decorations.

In addition to the two fifteenth- to sixteenth-century hôtels that house the museums, you'll find more ancient stately residences as you wander through the old town, particularly along **rue Parage**. On rue Hoche is the birthplace of **Nostradamus**, though only the facade is contemporary with the savant, and the house is not open for visits. The Hôtel d'Estrine, 8 rue Estrine, houses the **Centre d'Art Présence Van Gogh** (April to mid-Oct Tues–Sun 10.30am–1pm & 3–7pm; mid-Oct to Dec Tues–Sun 10.30am–12.30pm & 2–6pm; €3.20), which hosts contemporary art exhibitions and has a permanent exhibition ofVan Gogh reproductions and extracts from letters, as well as audiovisual presentations on the painter.

Eating and drinking

You'll find plenty of **brasseries** and **restaurants** in and around old St-Rémy. There are a few good options on rue Carnot (leading from boulevard Victor-Hugo east through the old town to boulevard Marceau). The Provençal *La Gousée d'Ail'*, 6 bd Marceau (Ⓣ04.90.92.16.87; closed Thurs & Sat lunch, plus Feb), has a menu at €32 and occasional live jazz. *La Maison Jaune*, 15 rue Carnot (Ⓣ04.90.92.56.14; closed Mon & Tues lunch in summer, Mon & Sun evening in winter, plus Jan & Feb), has a menu at €34 and a fabulous *menu dégustation Provençal* for €52. Alternatively, *Le Jardin de Frédéric*, 8 bd Gambetta

(☎04.90.92.27.76; closed Sun & Mon lunch), with a €16 lunch menu, usually serves up some interesting dishes. For a scenic spot to dine on crêpes, try *Lou Planet*, 7 place Favier, by the Musée des Alpilles, and for brasserie fare go to *Le Bistrot des Alpilles*, 15 bd Mirabeau (open till midnight). Chic café-lounging is the theme at the rather elegant *Café des Arts*, 30 bd Victor-Hugo.

South of St-Rémy: Les Antiques, St-Paul-de-Mausole and Glanum

About 1.5km south of the old town, following avenue Pasteur, which becomes avenue Vincent-Van-Gogh, you'll come to **Les Antiques** (free access), a triumphal arch supposedly celebrating the Roman conquest of Marseille, and a mausoleum thought to commemorate two grandsons of Augustus. Save for a certain amount of weather erosion, the mausoleum is perfectly intact, while on the arch you can still make out the sculptures of fruits and leaves representing the fertility of "the Roman Province" (hence "Provence"), and the figures of chained captives, symbolizing Roman might.

The arch would have been a familiar sight to **Vincent Van Gogh**, who in 1889 requested that he be put under medical care for several months. He was living in Arles at the time, and the hospital chosen by his friends was in the old monastery **St-Paul-de-Mausole**, a hundred metres or so east of Les Antiques; it remains a psychiatric clinic today. Although the regime was more prison than hospital, Van Gogh was allowed to wander out around the Alpilles and painted prolifically during his twelve-month stay. *The Oliviers' Fields*, *The Reaper*, *The Enclosed Field* and *The Evening Stroll* are among the 150 canvases of this period. The **church** and **cloisters** can be visited (April–Oct Sun–Fri 9.45am–6.15pm & Sat 10.45am–5.15pm; Nov–March daily 10.30am–5pm; €3.80): take avenue Edgar-Leroy or allée St-Paul from avenue Vincent-Van-Gogh, go past the main entrance of the clinic and into the gateway on the left at the end of the wall.

Not very far beyond the hospital is a signposted farm called **Mas de la Pyramide** (daily: July & Aug 9am–noon & 2–7pm; Sept–June 9am–noon & 2–5pm; €4). It's an old troglodyte farm in the Roman quarries for Glanum with a lavender and cherry orchard surrounded by cavernous openings into the rock filled with ancient farm equipment and rusting bicycles. The farmhouse is part medieval and part Gallo-Roman, with pictures of the owner's family who have lived there for generations.

One of the most impressive ancient settlements in France, **Glanum**, 500m south of Les Antiques (daily: April–Aug 10am–6.30pm; Sept–March Tues–Sun 10.30am–5pm; €6.50), was dug out from alluvial deposits at the very foot of the Alpilles. The site was originally a Neolithic homestead; then, between the second and first centuries BC, the Gallo-Greeks, probably from Massalia (Marseille), built a city here, on which the Gallo-Romans, from the end of the first century BC to the third century AD, constructed yet another town.

Though Glanum is one of the most important archeological sites in France, it can be very difficult to get to grips with. Not only were the later buildings moulded onto the earlier, but the fashion at the time of Christ was for a Hellenistic style. You can distinguish the Greek levels from the Roman most easily by the stones: the earlier civilization used massive hewn rocks while the Romans preferred smaller and more accurately shaped stones. The leaflet at the admission desk is helpful, as are the attendants if your French is good enough.

The site is bisected by a road running from north to south, with several **Hellenic houses** to the northwest. East of here are the **Thermes**, a complex of furnaces, bathing chambers and pools, and beyond this the **Maison du**

Capricorne with some fine mosaics. A **forum** dating from Roman times is south of here, near a restored **theatre** and the superb sculptures on the Roman **Temples Geminées** (Twin Temples). The temples also have fragments of mosaics, fountains of both Greek and Roman periods and first-storey walls and columns. As the site narrows in the ravine at the southern end, you'll find a Grecian edifice around a **sacred spring** – the feature that made this location so desirable. Steps lead down to a pool, with a slab above for the libations of those too disabled to descend. An inscription records that Agrippa was responsible for restoring it in 27 BC and dedicating it to Valetudo, the Roman goddess of health.

Les Baux and the Val d'Enfer

At the top of the Alpilles ridge, 7km southwest of St-Rémy, lies the distinctly unreal fortified village of **LES BAUX-DE-PROVENCE**, where the ruined eleventh-century citadel is hard to distinguish from the edge of the plateau, whose rock is both foundation and part of the structure.

Once Les Baux lived off the power and widespread possessions in Provence of its medieval lords, who owed allegiance to no one. When the dynasty died out at the end of the fourteenth century, however, the town, which had once numbered 6000 inhabitants, passed to the counts of Provence and then to the kings of France. In 1632, Richelieu razed the feudal citadel to the ground and fined the population into penury for their disobedience. From that date until the nineteenth century, both citadel and village were inhabited almost exclusively by bats and crows. The discovery in the neighbouring hills of the mineral bauxite (whose name derives from "Les Baux") brought back some life to the village, and tourism has more recently transformed the place. Today the population stays steady at around 400, while the number of visitors exceeds 1.5 million each year. Day-tripping crowds thin rapidly in Les Baux after around 5pm so, depending on the season, it can be worthwhile turning up rather late and enjoying the splendid castle in relative peace.

The lived-in village has many very beautiful buildings. There are half a dozen museums, one of the best being the **Musée Yves Brayer** in the Hôtel des Porcelet (mid-Feb to March & Oct–Dec daily except Tues 10am–12.30pm & 2–5.30pm; April–Sept daily 10am–12.30pm & 2–6.30pm; €4), showing the paintings of the twentieth-century figurative artist whose work also adorns the seventeenth-century **Chapelle des Pénitents Blancs**. Changing exhibitions of contemporary Provençal artists' works are displayed in the **Hôtel de Manville** (10am–6pm; free). The museum of the **Fondation Louis Jou** in the fifteenth-century Hôtel Jean de Brion contains the presses, wood lettering blocks and hand-printed books of a master typographer (visits by reservation only; €3; ☎04.90.54.34.17), while the **Musée des Santons** in the old Hôtel de Ville (daily 8am–7pm; free) displays traditional Provençal Nativity figures.

Following the signs to the Château will bring you to the entrance to the now-abandoned **Citadelle de la Ville Morte**, the main reason for coming to Les Baux (daily: 9am–6pm; €7.50 audioguide in English available), and where you can find ruins and several more museums. The **Maison de la Famille de la Tour de Brau** in the vaulted space of Tour de Brau, at the entrance to the chateau, has a collection of archeological remains and models to illustrate the history from medieval splendour to bauxite works. The most impressive ruins are those of the feudal castle demolished on Richelieu's orders; there's also the partially restored **Chapelle Castrale** and the **Tour Sarrasine**, the cemetery, ruined houses half carved out of the rocky escarpment and some spectacular views, the best of which is out across the Grande Crau from beside the statue of Provençal poet Charloun Riev at the southern edge of the plateau where you will also find replicas of medieval catapults and battering rams.

The **tourist office** is at the beginning of Grande-Rue (daily: July & Aug 9am–7pm; Sept–June 9am–6pm; ⓣ04.90.54.34.39, ⓦwww.lesbauxdeprovence.com). You have to park – and pay – before entering the village. Nothing in Les Baux comes cheap, least of all **accommodation**. Try *Hostellerie de la Reine Jeanne*, by the entrance to the village (ⓣ04.90.54.32.06, ⓦwww.la-reinejeanne.com; ❸; closed mid-Nov to mid-Feb), with a good restaurant (menus from €22); alternatively B&B *Le Prince Noir*, in an artist's house on rue de l'Orme, has bags of characteur and is tastefully decorated (ⓣ04.90.54.39.57, ⓦwww.leprincenoir.com; ❻). If you're feeling rich and want to treat yourself, head for the luxurious hotel-restaurant *Oustau de Baumanière*, just below Les Baux to the west on the road leading down to the Val d'Enfer (ⓣ04.90.54.33.07, ⓦwww.oustaudebaumaniere.com; ❾).

The Val d'Enfer

Within walking distance of Les Baux, along the D27 leading northwards, is the valley of quarried and eroded rocks named the **Val d'Enfer** – the Valley of Hell. One quarry has been turned into an audiovisual experience under the title of the **Cathédrale des Images** (daily 10am–6pm; €7), signposted to the right downhill from Les Baux's car park. The projection is continuous, so you don't have to wait to go in. You're surrounded by images projected all over the floor, ceilings and walls of these vast rectangular caverns, and by music that resonates strangely in the captured space. The content of the show, which changes yearly, doesn't really matter (recent ones include the Egyptian city of Alexandria); it's an extraordinary sensation, wandering on and through the shapes and colours. As an erstwhile work site put to good use, it couldn't be bettered.

Arles

ARLES is a major town on the tourist circuit, its fame sealed by the extraordinarily well-preserved Roman arena, **Les Arènes**, at the city's heart, and backed by an impressive variety of other stones and monuments, both Roman and medieval. It was the key city of the region in Roman times, then, with Aix, main base of the counts of Provence before unification with France. For centuries it was Marseille's only rival, profiting from the inland trade route up the Rhône whenever the enemies of France were blocking Marseille's port. Arles declined when the railway put an end to this advantage, and it was an inward-looking depressed town that **Van Gogh** came to in the late nineteenth century. Today it's a staid and conservative place with an unmistakable small-town feel, but comes to life for the **Saturday market**, which brings in throngs

Museum passes

The **Pass Monuments** (€13.50) grants free admission to all of Arles' museums and monuments except the Fondation Vincent Van Gogh, and is available either from the tourist office or at the sites themselves.

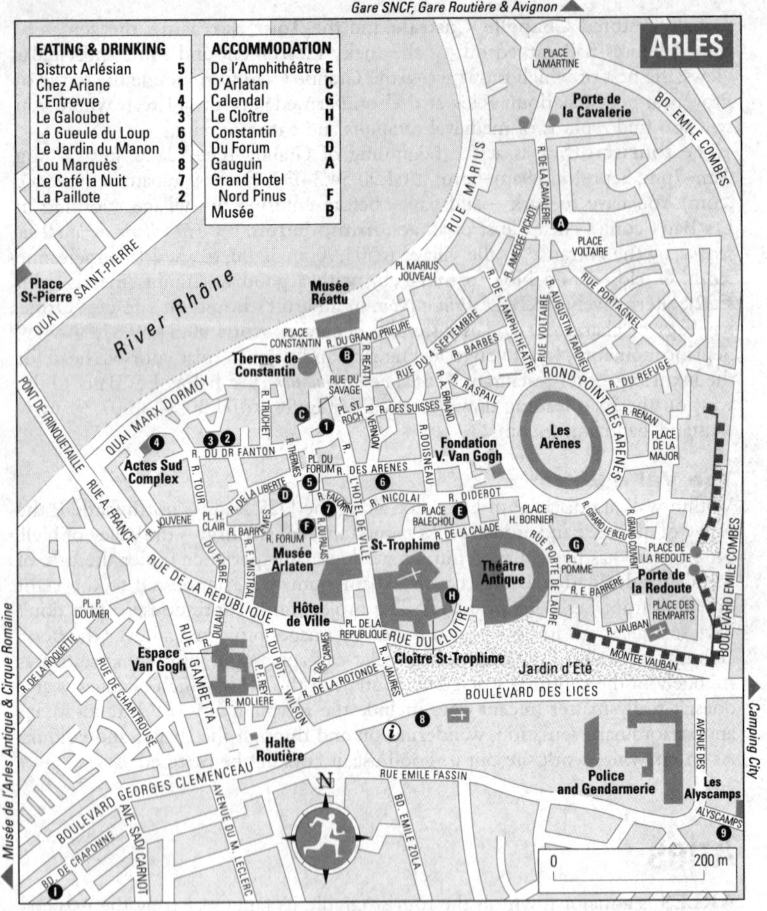

of farmers from the surrounding countryside, and during the various **festivals** of *tauromachie* between Easter and All Saints, when the town's frenzy for bulls rivals that of neighbouring Nîmes.

Arrival, information and accommodation

Arriving by train eases you gently into the city, with the **gare SNCF** conveniently located a few blocks to the north of the Arènes. Most buses also arrive here at the unstaffed adjacent **gare routière**, though some, including all local buses, stop on the north side of boulevard Georges-Clemenceau just east of rue Gambetta. Rue Jean-Jaurès, with its continuation rue Hôtel-de-Ville, is the main axis of old Arles. At the southern end it meets boulevard Georges-Clemenceau and boulevard des Lices, with the **tourist office** directly opposite (March–Sept daily 9am–6.45pm; Oct–April Mon–Sat 9am–4.45pm, Sun 10am–12.45pm; ⓣ04.90.18.41.20, ⓦwww.tourisme.ville-arles.fr); there's also an annexe in the *gare SNCF* (Mon–Sat 9am–1pm). You can rent **bikes** from Peugeot, 15 rue du Pont, or Europbike, 1 rue Philippe-Lebon, and **cars** from Europcar (T04.90.93.23.24), Eurorent (T04.90.93.50.14) or Hertz (T04.90.96.75.23), all on avenue Victor-Hugo. To connect to the **Internet**, head for Hexaworld, on rue 4-Septembre, near place Voltaire.

There's little shortage of **hotel** rooms at either end of the scale. The best place to look for cheap rooms is in the area around Porte de la Cavalerie near the station. If you get stuck, the tourist office will find you accommodation for a €1 fee.

Hotels

De l'Amphithéâtre 5–7 rue Diderot T04.90.96.10.30, W www.hotelamphitheatre.fr. Situated close to Les Arènes, this place has plenty of warm colours, tiles and wrought ironwork. 4

D'Arlatan 26 rue du Sauvage T04.90.93.56.66, W www.hotel-arlatan.fr. This may not be Arles' most expensive hotel, but it is probably the most luxurious, set in a beautiful old fifteenth-century mansion and decorated with antiques. Closed Jan. 6

Calendal 5 rue Porte de Laure T04.90.96.11.89, W www.lecalendal.com. Pleasant, welcoming hotel with generous, air-conditioned rooms overlooking a garden. Closed Jan. 5

Le Cloître 16 rue du Cloître T04.90.96.29.50, W www.hotelcloitre.com. A cosy hotel with some rooms giving views of St-Trophime. Closed Nov to mid-March. 3

Constantin 59 bd de Craponne, off bd Clemenceau T04.90.96.04.05, E hotelconstantin @wanadoo.fr. Pleasant, well-kept and comfortable hotel, with prices kept down by the proximity of the Nîmes highway (some traffic noise) and its location a little way from the centre. 3

Du Forum 10 place Forum T04.90.93.48.95, W www.hotelduforum.com. Spacious rooms in an old house in the ancient heart of the city, with a swimming pool in the garden. A bit noisy but very welcoming. Closed Nov–Feb. 5

Gauguin 5 place Voltaire T04.90.96.14.35, F04.90.18.98.87. Comfortable, cheap and well run. Advisable to book. 2

Grand Hotel Nord Pinus place du Forum T04.90.93.44.44, W www.nord-pinus.com. Twenty-six chic rooms in a grand old house, located at the head of a pretty square in the heart of the old town. 9

Musée 11 rue du Grand-Prieuré T04.90.93.88.88, W www.hoteldumusee.com.fr. Small, good-value family-run place in a quiet location opposite Musée Réattu, with a pretty, flower-filled terrace and air-conditioned rooms. 4

Hostel and campsites

Auberge de Jeunesse 20 av Foch T04.90.96.18.25, E arles@fuaj.org. Old-style hostel with dormitory accommodation only. Bus no. 4 from town, direction "Fourchon"; alight at stop "Fournier". €14.55 per bed Closed Jan.

La Bienheureuse 7km out on the N453 at Raphèles-les-Arles T04.90.98.48.06, W www.labienheureuse.com. Best of Arles' half-dozen campsites; the restaurant here is furnished with pieces similar to those displayed in the Musée Arlaten and full of pictures of popular Arlesian traditions. Regular buses from Arles. €14.50 for two people and a tent. Open all year.

Camping City 67 rte de Crau T04.90.93.08.86, W www.camping-city.com. The closest campsite to town on the Crau bus route. €16 for two people and a tent. Closed Oct–March.

The City

The centre of Arles fits into a neat triangle between boulevard E.-Combes to the east, boulevards Clemenceau and des Lices to the south, and the Rhône to the west. The **Musée de l'Arles Antique** is southwest of the expressway by the river, not far from the end of boulevard Clemenceau; **Les Alyscamps** is down across the train lines to the southeast. But these apart, all the **Roman and medieval monuments** are within easy walking distance in this very compact city centre.

Roman Arles

Roman Arles provided grain for most of the western empire and was one of the major ports for trade and shipbuilding. Under Constantine it became the capital

The bullfight

Bullfighting, or more properly *tauromachie* (roughly, "the art of the bull"), comes in two styles in Arles and the Camargue. In the local **courses camarguaises**, which are held at fêtes from late spring to early autumn (the most prestigious of which is Arles' Cocarde d'Or in early July), *razeteurs* run at the bulls in an effort to pluck ribbons and cockades tied to the bulls' horns, cutting them free with special barbed gloves. The drama and grace of the spectacle is in the stylish way the men leap over the barrier away from the bull, and in the competition for prize money between the *razeteurs*. In this gentler bullfight, people are rarely injured and the bulls are not killed.

More popular, however, are the brutal Spanish-style **corridas** (late April, early July & Sept, at Arles), consisting of a strict ritual leading up to the all-but-inevitable death of the bull. After its entry into the ring, the bull is subjected to the *bandilleros* who stick decorated barbs in its back, the *picadors*, who lance it from horseback, and finally, the *torero*, who endeavours to lead the bull through as graceful a series of movements as possible before killing it with a single sword stroke to the heart. In one *corrida* six bulls are killed by three *toreros*, for whom injuries (sometimes fatal) are not uncommon. Whether you approve or not, *tauromachie*, which has a history of some centuries here, is your best way of taking part in local life and of experiencing the Roman arena in Arles (€6 per seat). The tourist office, local papers and publicity around the arena will give you the details, or call the Bureau des Arènes ⓣ04.90.96.03.70.

△ Bullfighting at Les Arènes, Arles

of Gaul and reached its height as a world trading centre in the fifth century. Once the empire crumbled, however, Arles found itself isolated between the Rhône, the Alpilles and the marshlands of the Camargue – an isolation that allowed its Roman heritage to be preserved.

A good place to start any tour of Roman Arles is the **Musée de l'Arles Antique** (daily: March–Oct 9am–7pm, Nov–Feb 10am–5pm; €5.50), southwest of the town centre on the spit of land between the Rhône and the Canal de Rhône. It's housed in a resolutely contemporary building positioned on the axis of the second-century **Cirque Romaine**, an enormous chariot racetrack (the excavation of which has been temporarily halted due to lack of funding) that stretches 450m from the museum to the town side of the expressway. The museum is a treat – open-plan, flooded with natural light and immensely spacious. It covers the prehistory of the area, then takes you through the five centuries of Roman rule, from Julius Caesar's legionary base through Christianization to the period when spices and gems from Africa and Arabia were being traded here. Fabulous mosaics are laid out with walkways above; and there are numerous sarcophagi with intricate sculpting depicting everything from music and lovers to gladiators and Christian miracles.

Back in the centre of Arles, the most impressive Roman monument is the amphitheatre, known as **Les Arènes** (daily: March, April & Oct 9am–5.30pm, May–Sept 9am–6pm; Nov–Feb 10am–4.30pm; €5.50, or covered by Pass Monuments – see box, p.1077), dating from the end of the first century. To give an idea of its size, it used to shelter over two hundred dwellings and three churches built into the two tiers of arches that form its oval surround. This medieval quarter was cleared in 1830 and the Arènes was once more used for entertainment. Today, though missing its third storey and most of the internal stairways and galleries, it's still a very dramatic structure and a stunning venue for performances, seating 20,000 spectators. Although restoration work is scheduled until 2006, it continues to be open to the public.

The **Théâtre Antique** (daily: March, April & Oct 9–11.30am & 2–5.30pm; May–Sept 9am–6pm; Nov–Feb 10–11.30am & 2–4.30pm; €3), just south of the Arènes, comes to life during July, with the Fête du Costume in which local folk groups parade in traditional dress, and the Mosaïque Gitane Romany festival. The theatre is nowhere near as well preserved as the arena, with only one pair of columns standing, all the statuary removed and the sides of the stage littered with broken bits of stone.

At the river end of rue Hôtel-de-Ville, the **Thermes de Constantin** (daily: March, April & Oct 9–11.20am & 2–5.30pm; May–Sept 9am–noon & 2–6pm; Nov–Feb 10–11.30am & 2–4.30pm; €5.50), which may well have been the biggest Roman baths in Provence, are all that remain of the emperor's palace that extended along the waterfront. The Roman forum was up the hill on the site of **place du Forum**, still the centre of life in Arles. You can see the pillars of an ancient temple embedded in the corner of the *Nord-Pinus* hotel.

The Romans had their burial ground southeast of the centre, and it was used by well-to-do Arlesians well into the Middle Ages. Now only one alleyway, foreshortened by a train line, is preserved. To reach **Les Alyscamps** (daily: March, April & Oct 9–11.30am & 2–5.30pm; May–Sept 9am–6pm; Nov–Feb 10–11.30am & 2–4.30pm; €3.50), follow avenue des Alyscamps from the east end of boulevard des Lices. Sarcophagi still line the shaded walk, whose tree trunks are azure blue in Van Gogh's rendering. There are numerous tragedy masks, too, though any with special decoration have long since been moved to serve as municipal gifts, as happened often in the seventeenth century, or to reside in the museums. But there is still magic to this walk, which ends at the twelfth-century Romanesque St-Honorat's church, wonderfully simple and cool on a hot day.

The cathedral, museums and medieval Arles

The doorway of the **Cathédrale St-Trophime** on Arles' **central place de la République** is one of the most famous examples of twelfth-century Provençal stonecarving in existence. It depicts the Last Judgement, trumpeted by angels playing with the enthusiasm of jazz musicians while the damned are led naked in chains down to hell and the blessed, all draped in long robes, process upwards. The cathedral itself was started in the ninth century on the spot where, in 597 AD, St Augustine was consecrated as the first bishop of the English, and it was largely completed by the twelfth century. A font in the north aisle and an altar illustrating the crossing of the Red Sea in the north transept were both originally Gallo-Roman sarcophagi. The nave is decorated with d'Aubusson tapestries, while there is superlative Romanesque and Gothic stonecarving in the extraordinarily beautiful **cloisters**, accessible from place de la République to the right of the cathedral (daily: March–April & Oct 9am–5.30pm; May–Sept 9am–6pm; Nov–Feb 10am–4.30pm; €3.50).

Across place de la République from the cathedral stands the palatial seventeenth-century **Hôtel de Ville**, inspired by Versailles. You can walk through its vast entrance hall, with its flattened vaulted roof designed to avoid putting extra stress on the **Cryptoporticus du Forum** below. This is a huge, dark, dank and wonderfully spooky three-sided underground gallery, built by the Romans, possibly as a food store, possibly as a barracks for public slaves, but certainly to provide sturdy foundations for the forum above. Access is from rue Balze (daily: March–April & Oct 9–11.30am & 2–5.30pm; May–Sept 9am–noon & 2–6pm; Nov–Feb 10–11.30am & 2–4.30pm; €3.50).

In case you feel that life stopped in Arles, if not after the Romans, then at least after the Middle Ages, head for the **Musée Arlaten** on rue de la République (daily: April, May & Sept 9.30am–12.30pm & 2–6pm; June–Aug 9.30am–1pm & 2–6.30pm; Oct–March 9.30am–12.30pm & 2–5pm; €4). The museum was set up in 1896 by Frédéric Mistral, the Nobel Prize-winning novelist who was responsible for the turn-of-the-twentieth-century revival of interest in all things Provençal, and whose statue stands in place du Forum. The collections of costumes, documents, tools, pictures and paraphernalia of Provençal life are alternately tedious and intriguing. The evolution of Arlesian dress is charted in great detail for all social classes from the eighteenth century to World War I and there's a mouthwatering life-size scene of a bourgeois Christmas dinner.

Another must-see in Arles is the main collection of the **Musée Réattu** (daily: March, April & Oct 10am–noon & 2–5pm; May–Sept 10am–noon & 2–6.30pm; Nov–Feb 1–5pm; €5.50), housed in a beautiful fifteenth-century priory opposite the Roman baths. Much of it comprises tedious and rigid eighteenth-century works by the museum's founder and his contemporaries, but dotted round this are some good modern works: Zadkine's study in bronze for the two Van Gogh brothers, Mario Prassinos' monochrome studies of the Alpilles, César's *Compression 1973* and, best of all, Picasso's *Woman with Violin* sculpture and 57 ink-and-crayon sketches made in Arles between December 1970 and February 1971. Amongst the split faces and clowns is a beautifully simple portrait of his mother.

Van Gogh in Arles

At the back of the Réattu museum, lanterns line the river wall where **Van Gogh** used to wander, wearing candles on his hat, watching the night-time light: *The Starry Night* is the Rhône at Arles. Much of the riverfront and its bars and bistros were destroyed during World War II. Another casualty of the bombing was the "Yellow House" on place Lamartine, where the artist lived before entering the hospital at St-Rémy. However, the café painted in *Café de Nuit* still stands in place du Forum, and the distinctive Pont Langlois drawbridge painted by the artist in March 1888 can be seen on the southern edge of the town (poorly signposted off the D35). Van Gogh had arrived by train in February 1888 to be greeted by snow and a bitter mistral wind. But he started painting straight away, and in this period produced such celebrated canvases as *The Sunflowers*, *Van Gogh's Chair*, *The Red Vines* and *The Sower*. Van Gogh found few kindred souls in Arles and finally managed to persuade Gauguin to join him in mid-autumn. Although the two were to influence each other substantially in the following weeks, their relationship quickly soured as the increasingly bad November weather forced them to spend more time together indoors. According to Gauguin, Van Gogh, feeling threatened by his friend's possible departure, finally succumbed to a fit of psychosis and attacked first Gauguin and then himself. He was packed off to the Hôtel-Dieu hospital on rue du Président-Wilson down from the Musée Arlaten, now the **Espace Van Gogh**, an academic and cultural centre with arty shops in its arcades and courtyard flower beds re-created according to Van Gogh's painting and descriptions of the hospital garden.

Arles has none of the artist's works but the **Fondation Vincent Van Gogh** (April–June daily 10am–6pm; July–Sept daily 10am–7pm; Oct–March Tues–Sun 11am–5pm; €7), facing the Arènes at 26 rond-point des Arènes, exhibits works by contemporary artists inspired by Van Gogh, including Francis Bacon, Jasper Johns, Hockney and Lichtenstein, and sunflower-drenched photographs by the likes of Cartier-Bresson and Doisneau.

Eating and drinking

Arles has a good number of excellent-quality and cheap **restaurants**, and if you're looking for quick meals, or just want to watch the world go by, there's a wide choice of brasseries on the main boulevards. Place du Forum is the centre of **café** life; here you'll find *Le Café la Nuit*, immaculately re-created à la Van Gogh and open late, and the young and noisy *Bistrot Arlésien*. Nevertheless, don't be surprised to discover that most of Arles packs up for the night around 10.30pm.

Chez Ariane 2 rue Dr-Fanton ⓣ04.90.52.00.65. Specializes in organic wine and hearty home cooking. A blackboard displays à la carte dishes from €9 which change daily according to what's on offer at the market. Closed Mon.

L'Entrevue place Nina-Berberova ⓣ04.90.93.37.28. Hip Moroccan/Provençal café with an attached hamam and a terrace next to the river. Menu €27. Closed Sun lunch.

Le Galoubet 18 rue du Dr-Fanton ⓣ04.90.93.18.11. Pleasant, vine-covered terrace and elegant dining room in which to taste the modern Provençal cuisine on a good-value €25 menu. Closed Sun and Mon lunch.

La Gueule du Loup 39 rue des Arènes ⓣ04.90.96.96.69. Cosy restaurant serving traditional dishes, with menus from €26. Closed Mon lunch.

Le Jardin du Manon 14 av des Alyscamps ⓣ04.90.93.38.68. Hospitable Provençal restaurant serving elaborate regional dishes and delicious desserts, which you can enjoy in a small patio garden. €16–36. Closed Tues night & Wed.

Lou Marquès *Hôtel Jules-César*, bd des Lices ⓣ04.90.52.52.52. The top gourmet palace in the top grand hotel. The specialities, which include *baudroie* (monkfish), langoustine salad and Camargue rice cake, are all served with the utmost pomposity. Menus from €27. The other restaurant in the hotel, *Le Cloître*, has a lunch menu at around €20. *Lou Marquès* closed Sat & Mon lunch, *Le Cloître* Wed & Sun evening, both closed Nov & Dec.

La Paillote 28 rue Dr-Fanton ⓣ04.90.96.33.15. Very friendly place with a good €15 menu. Closed Wed.

The Camargue

The boundaries of the **CAMARGUE** are not apparent until you come upon them. Its shimmering horizons are infinite because land, lagoon and sea share the same horizontal plain. Both wild and human life have traits peculiar to this drained, ditched and now protected delta land. Today, the whole of the Camargue is a Parc Naturel Régional, with great efforts made to keep an equi-

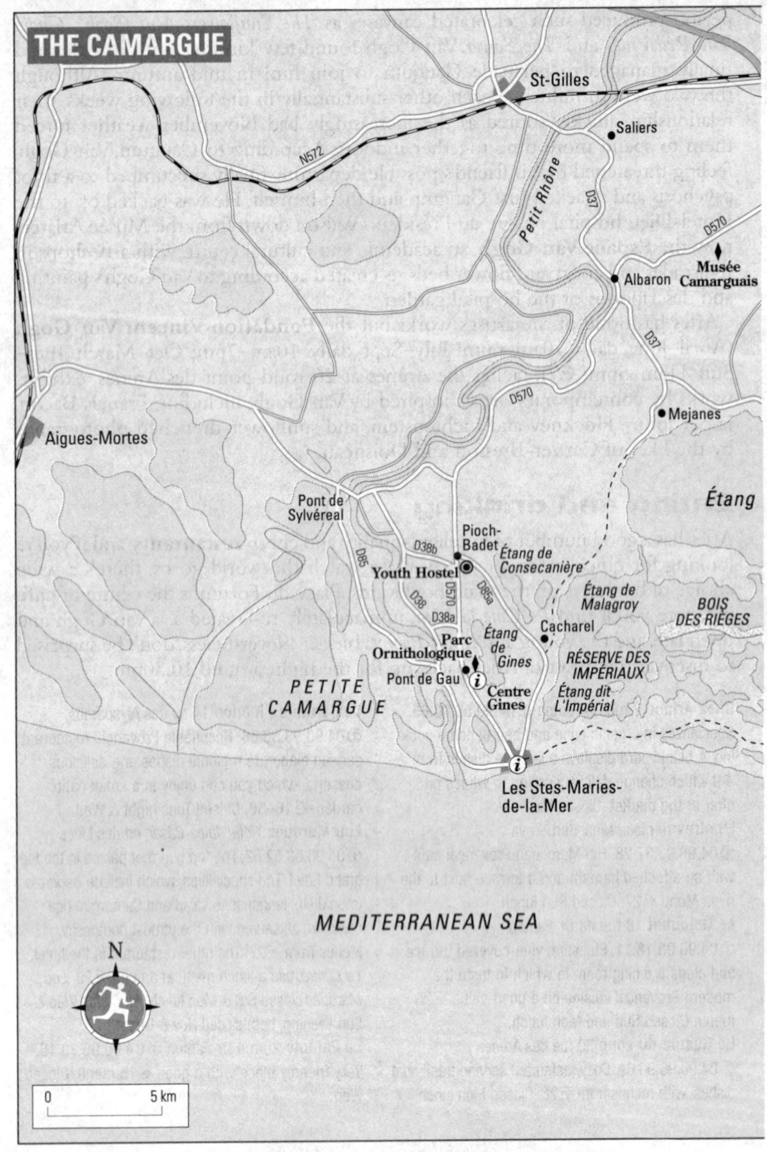

librium between tourism, agriculture, industry and hunting on the one hand, and the indigenous ecosystems on the other.

The Camargue is home to the **bulls** and to the **white horses** that the region's *gardiens*, or herdsmen, ride. Neither beast is truly wild, though both run in semi-liberty. The Camargue horse, whose origin is unknown, remains a distinct breed, born dark brown or black and turning white around its fourth year. It is

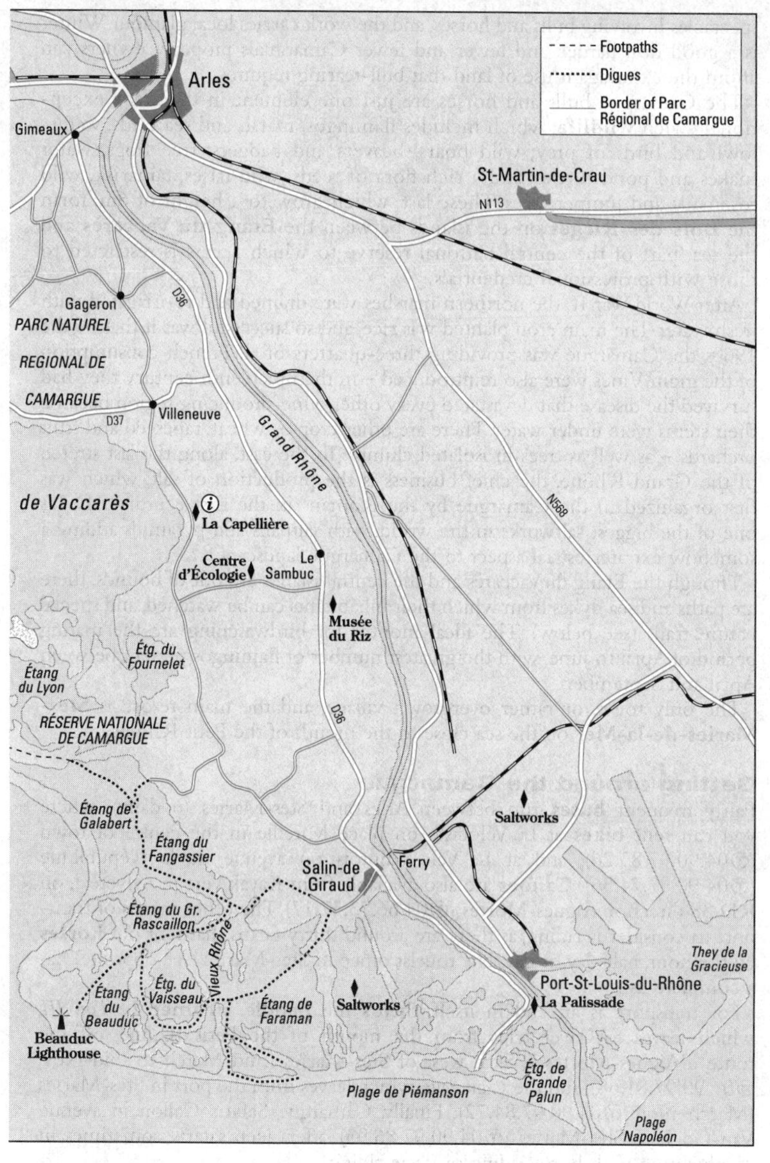

never stabled, surviving the humid heat of summer and the wind-racked winter cold outdoors. The *gardiens* likewise are a hardy community. Their traditional homes, or *cabanes*, are thatched and windowless one-storey structures, with bulls' horns over the door to ward off evil spirits. They still conform, to some extent, to the popular cowboy myth, and play a major role in guarding Camarguais traditions. Throughout the summer they're kept busy in every village arena with spectacles involving bulls and horses, and the work carries local glamour. Winter is a good deal harder, and fewer and fewer Camarguais property owners can afford the extravagant use of land that bull-rearing requires.

The Camargue bulls and horses are just one element in the area's exceptionally rich **wildlife**, which includes flamingos, marsh and sea birds, waterfowl and birds of prey; wild boars, beavers and badgers; tree frogs, water snakes and pond turtles; and a rich flora of reeds, wild irises, tamarisk, wild rosemary and juniper trees. These last, which grow to a height of 6m, form the **Bois des Rièges** on the islands between the **Étang du Vaccarès** and the sea, part of the central national reserve to which access is restricted to those with professional credentials.

After World War II, the northern marshes were drained and re-irrigated with fresh water. The main crop planted was rice, and so successful was it that by the 1960s the Camargue was providing three-quarters of all French consumption of the grain. Vines were also reintroduced – in the nineteenth century they had survived the disease that devastated every other wine-producing region because their stems were under water. There are other crops – wheat, rapeseed and fruit orchards – as well as trees in isolated clumps. To the east, along the last stretch of the Grand Rhône, the chief business is the production of salt, which was first organized in the Camargue by the Romans in the first century AD. It's one of the biggest saltworks in the world, with saltpans and pyramids adding a somehow extraterrestrial aspect to the Camargue landscape.

Though the Étang du Vaccarès and the central islands are out of bounds, there are paths and sea dykes from which their inhabitants can be watched, and special nature trails (see below). The ideal months for birdwatching are the mating period of April to June, with the greatest number of flamingos present between April and September.

The only town, or rather overgrown village, and the main resort, is **Stes-Maries-de-la-Mer** on the sea close to the mouth of the Petit Rhône.

Getting around the Camargue

Fairly frequent **buses** run between Arles and Stes-Maries (6 daily), where you can rent **bikes** at Le Vélociste on place Mireille in the centre of town (Ⓣ04.90.97.83.26), and at Le Vélo Saintois on avenue de la République (Ⓣ04.90.97.74.56). **Canoes** are also available from Kayak Vert in Sylvéréal, on RD 38 direction Aigues-Mortes (Ⓣ04.66.73.57.17). The other means of transport to consider is riding, as there are around thirty farms that rent out **horses** by the hour, half-day or day. The tourist office in Stes-Maries (see opposite) has a complete list.

For transport as an end in itself, there's the **paddle steamer** *Le Tiki III*, which leaves for river trips from the mouth of the Petit Rhône, off the route d'Aigues-Mortes, 2.5km west of Stes-Maries (mid-March to mid-Nov; Ⓣ04.90.97.81.68), and the *Camargue*, which leaves from the port in Stes-Maries (March–Nov; Ⓣ04.90.97.84.72). Finally, Camargue Safaris Gallon in avenue Van-Gogh in Stes-Maries (Ⓣ04.90.97.86.93) offers jeep safaris, sometimes in combination with horse-riding or cycle riding.

Be wary of taking your car or bike along the **dykes**: although maps and road signs show which routes are closed to vehicles and which are accessible only at low tide, they don't warn you about the road surface. The other problem is **theft** from cars. There are well-organized gangs of thieves with a particular penchant for foreign licence plates.

There are three main walking **trails** around the protected central area of the Camargue. You can skirt the Réserve des Impériaux along a drovers' path, the *draille de Cacharel*, between Cacharel, 4km north of Ste-Maries, and *Méjanes*, just south of the D37. Another trail, with one of the best observation points for flamingos, follows the dyke between the Étangs du Fangassier and Galabert, starting near Faraman, a few kilometres west of Salin-de-Giraud. Between these two is the *Digue à la Mer* running just back from the beach of Stes-Maries' bay.

If you're walking in the area, be warned that **mosquitoes** are rife from March through to November; keeping right beside the sea will be OK, but otherwise you'll need serious chemical weaponry. Biting flies are also prevalent and can take away much of the pleasure of this hill-less land for bicycling. The other problem is the **winds**, which in autumn and winter can be strong enough to knock you off your bike. Conversely, in summer the weather can be so hot and humid that the slightest movement is an effort. There's really no ideal time for visiting the area.

Les Stes-Maries-de-la-Mer

LES STES-MARIES-DE-LA-MER is best known for its annual festival on May 24–25, when the town is swamped with Romanies asking favours from their patron Ste-Sarah. The rest of the time it's unmistakably and unashamedly a holiday resort: unobtrusive white houses with tiled roofs line a tidy grey sandy beach with countless bucket-and-spade shops, fish restaurants with neon signs and ice-cream parlours. It's a good base from which to explore the Camargue, with plenty of reasonably priced accommodation and restaurants.

On the way there you could drop in on the **Musée de la Camargue** (April–June & Sept daily 9.15am–5.45pm; July & Aug 9.15am–6.45pm; Oct–March daily except Tues 10.15am–4.45pm; €5), halfway between Gimeaux and Albaron, which documents the traditions and livelihoods of the Camarguais

The legend of Sarah

Sarah was the servant of Mary Jacobé, Jesus' aunt, and Mary Salomé, mother of two of the apostles, who, along with Mary Magdalene and various other New Testament characters, are said to have been driven out of Palestine by the Jews and put on a boat without sails or oars.

The boat apparently drifted to an island in the mouth of the Rhône, where the Egyptian god Ra was worshipped. Here Mary Jacobé, Mary Salomé and Sarah, who was herself Egyptian, settled to carry out conversion work, while the others headed off for other parts of Provence. In 1448 their relics were "discovered" in the fortress church of Stes-Maries on the erstwhile island, around the time that the Romanies were migrating to western Europe from the Balkans and from Spain.

Romanies have been making their **pilgrimage** to Stes-Maries since at least the sixteenth century. It's a time for weddings and baptisms, as well as music, dancing and fervent religious observance. After Mass on May 24, the shrines of the saints are lowered from the high chapel to an altar where the faithful stretch out their arms to touch them. Then the statue of Black Sarah is carried by the Romanies to the sea. On the following day the statues of Mary Jacobé and Mary Salomé, sitting in a wooden boat, follow the same route, accompanied by the mounted *gardiens* in full Camargue cowboy dress, Arlesians in traditional costume, and spectators. The sea, the Camargue, the pilgrims and the Romanies are blessed by the bishop from a fishing boat, before the procession returns to the church with much bell-ringing, guitar-playing, tambourines and singing. Another ceremony in the afternoon sees the shrines lifted back up to their chapel.

people through the centuries, in the old sheep barn of a working farm. At Pont de Gau, just 4km short of Stes-Maries, the **Maison du Parc** (April–Sept daily 10am–6pm; Oct–March daily except Fri 9.30am–5pm; ⓣ04.90.97.86.32; free) has exhibitions on the local environment and is the place to go for detailed maps of paths and dykes. Just down the road is the engrossing **Parc Ornithologique** (daily: April–Sept 9am–sunset; Oct–March 10am–sunset; €6.50), with some of the less easily spotted birds kept in aviaries, plus trails across a twelve-hectare marsh and a longer walk with vantage points, all with ample signs and information. The village livens up on Monday and Friday mornings for the **market** on place des Gitans.

Arrival, information and accommodation

There's good, secure parking on the seafront in Stes-Maries at the Police Municipale, close to the **tourist office** on avenue Van-Gogh, which will happily weigh you down with information detailing all the town's festivals and events (daily: Jan, Feb, Nov & Dec 9am–5pm; March & Oct 9am–6pm; April–June & Sept 9am–7pm; July & Aug 9am–8pm; ⓣ04.90.97.82.55, ⓦwww.saintesmaries.com).

From April to October **rooms** in Stes-Maries should be booked in advance, and for the Romany festival, several months before. Prices go up considerably during the summer and at any time of the year are more expensive than at Arles. Outlying *mas* (farmhouses) renting out rooms tend to be quite expensive. **Camping** on the beach is not officially tolerated, but even at Stes-Maries people sleeping beneath the stars rarely get told to move on. The fifteen-kilometre seaside plage de Piemanson, also known as the plage d'Arles, south of Salin-de-Giraud, 10km east of Stes-Maries, is a favoured venue for *camping sauvage* in summer.

Hotels

Camille 13 av Maurice-Challe (ex av de la Plage) ⓣ04.90.97.80.26, ⓦwww.hotel-camille.camargue.fr. Fairly plain but decent modern cheapie with a sea view; some rooms have balconies. Closed mid-Nov to mid-March. ③

Le Fangassier rte de Cacharel ⓣ04.90.97.85.02, ⓦwww.fangassier.camargue.fr. Pleasant though basic hotel fairly close to the centre of town, with friendly staff. ③

Hostellerie du Pont de Gau rte d'Arles, Pont de Gau, 4km north of Stes-Maries, between the Maison du Parc and the Parc Ornithologique ⓣ04.90.97.81.53, ⓦwww.pontdegau.camargue.fr. Old-fashioned Camarguais decor, pleasant rooms and a good restaurant. Closed Jan to mid-Feb. ③

Mangio Fango rte d'Arles ⓣ04.90.97.80.56, ⓦwww.hotelmangiofango.com Situated 600m from Stes-Maries, overlooking the Étang des Launes. Vibrantly coloured carpets and hangings, simple modern art and tropical plants surround the pool and patios. Closed Nov & Dec. ⑥

Des Rièges rte de Cacharel ⓣ04.90.97.85.07, ⓦwww.hoteldesrieges.com. An upmarket hotel in a cluttered old farmhouse, with swimming pool and garden. Down a track signed off the D85a at the edge of Stes-Maries. Closed mid-Nov to mid-Feb. ⑤

Les Vagues 12 av Théodore-Aubane ⓣ & ⓕ04.90.97.84.40. A low-priced modern option above a smart restaurant, overlooking the marina on the rte d'Aigues-Mortes. ③

Hostel and campsites

Hostel on the Arles–Stes-Maries bus route, 10km north of Stes-Maries in the hamlet of Pioch-Badet ⓣ04.90.97.51.72, ⓕ04.90.97.54.88. Bike rental, horse rides and other excursions. Open all year, but you must make reservations. €27.30 (half-board only).

Camping La Brise rue Marcel-Carrière ⓣ04.90.97.84.67, ⓕ04.90.97.72.01. A three-star site, with a pool and laundry facilities, and tents, mobile homes or bungalows for rent. On the Arles–Stes-Maries bus route, on the east side of the village (stop "La Brise"). Closed Nov. €21 for two people and a tent.

Camping Le Clos du Rhône at the mouth of the Petit Rhône, 2km west of the village on the rte d'Aigues-Mortes ⓣ04.90.97.85.99, ⓕ04.90.97.78.85. A busy four-star site with a pool, laundry and shop. Only two of the Arles–Stes-Maries buses continue to here (stop "Clos du Rhône"). Closed Oct–March. €23.60 for two people and tent.

The Town

Stes-Maries is a neat and pleasant, if excessively commercialized town, in size scarcely more than a large village. Its open streets of plain, low houses are quite unlike the Provençal norm, and the grey-gold Romanesque church, with its strange outline of battlements and watchtower, is really the only distinctive monument. It exploits its monopoly as the only Camargue resort and every leisure activity is catered for, to excess. There are kilometres of **beach**; a pleasure port with boat trips to the lagoons; horses or bikes to ride; watersports; the *arènes* for bullfights, cavalcades and other entertainment (events are posted on a board outside); and flamenco guitarists playing on the restaurant and café terraces – it can all be very good fun.

As for sights, the fortified **church of Stes-Maries** allows a look at Sarah's tinselled and sequinned statue, which is carried into the sea each year (see box, p.1087). It's at the back of the crypt on the right, and always surrounded by candles and abandoned crutches and callipers from the miraculously cured. The church itself has beautifully pure lines and fabulous acoustics. During the time of the Saracen raids it provided shelter for all the villagers and even has its own freshwater well. The church **tower** (March–June & Sept–Oct 10am–12.30pm & 2–6.30pm, Sun 10am–7pm; July–Aug daily 10am–8pm; Nov–Feb Wed, Sat & Sun 10am–noon & 2–5pm; €2) has one of the best possible views over the Camargue; it's the tallest thing for miles.

A few steps south of the church on rue Victor-Hugo, the **Musée Baroncelli** (currently closed for renovation, check with tourist office; €1.50) is named after the man who, in 1935, was responsible for initiating the Romanies' procession down to the sea with Sarah. This was motivated by a desire to give a special place in the pilgrimage to the Romanies. The museum covers this event, other Camarguais traditions and the region's fauna and flora.

Eating and drinking

Few of the **restaurants** in Stes-Maries are bargains, though there are plenty to choose from, and out of season the quality improves and prices come down. Right by the marina, the restaurant at *Les Vagues* on rue T.-Aubanel (Ⓣ04.90.97.84.40) serves pleasant fish dishes on a range of menus at €16–31.50. Or try the tapas and bargain wine at *Kahlua Bodéga Pub*, 1 rue Jean-Roche (Ⓣ04.90.97.98.41; closed Jan, Tues out of season; tapas €3.50 each). The best places to try local fish specialities, however, are at the beach hut restaurants *Chez Juju* and *Chez Marc et Mireille* in **Beauduc**, over the dykes on the spit of sand on the opposite side of the bay from Stes-Maries. They're not easy to get to, but if you're hiking or cycling in the area, it's worth the extra mile. By car it's a good thirty minutes from Salin-de-Giraud.

From Avignon to Gordes

If you're heading east from Avignon towards Apt and the Luberon, two worthwhile stops are romantic **Fontaine-de-Vaucluse** and the picturesque **Gordes**, close to the **Abbaye de Sénanque**. Between Gordes and Apt are the old ochre-quarrying villages of **Roussillon** and **Rustrel**. Visiting all these places without your own transport is not that easy; Fontaine is accessible by bus from Avignon or from L'Isle-sur-la-Sorgue's *gare SNCF* 6km away, Gordes from Cavaillon, 24km southwest of Avignon, and Roussillon only infrequently from Apt.

Fontaine-de-Vaucluse

The source of the Sorgue, the stream that runs alongside rue des Teinturiers in Avignon, is at **FONTAINE-DE-VAUCLUSE**, 29km southeast of Avignon, and is one of the most powerful natural springs in the world. At the top of the gorge above the village is a mysterious tapering fissure deeper than the sheer 230-metre cliffs that barricade its opening. This is where the waters of the Sorgue appear, sometimes in spectacular fashion, bursting down the gorge (in March and April normally), at other times – when you might wonder what the fuss is about – seeping stealthily through subterranean channels to meet the riverbed further down. The best time to admire it is in the early morning before the crowds arrive.

Fontaine-de-Vaucluse was once a rustic backwater where the fourteenth-century poet Petrarch pined for his Laura. It remains a somewhat romantic place despite its hordes of visitors and the attendant tourist clutter. If you're intrigued by the source of the river, visit the **L'Écomusée du Gouffre** (hourly 45-minute tours in French: Feb–May & Oct–Nov 9.30am–noon & 2–6pm; June–Sept 9.30am–7.30pm; closed Dec & Jan; €5) at the *rond point* at the start of the chemin de la Fontaine, the path to the source. Nearby you'll find the rather dull **Musée du Santon** (April–June & Sept 10am–7pm; July & Aug 10am–8pm; Oct–March 10am–6pm; €4), displaying an unremarkable collection of Provençal Nativity figures. A short way up the path on the riverside you'll find the Vallis Clausa paper mill, whose products are geared to the fine art market.

Further up the path there's also the impressive **Musée d'Histoire 1939–1945** (March–May daily except Tues 10am–noon & 2–6pm; June–Sept daily except Tues 10am–6pm; Oct daily except Tues 10am–noon & 2–5pm; Nov–Feb Sat & Sun 10am–noon & 2–5pm; €3.50), portraying life under the Vichy regime and commemorating the Resistance. Across the river, through an alleyway just past the bridge, is the much more interesting **Musée de Pétrarque** (daily except Tues: March–May 10am–noon & 2–6pm; June–Sept 9.30am–noon & 2–6.30pm; first two weeks Oct 10am–noon & 2–6.30pm; mid-Oct to Dec 10am–noon & 2–5pm; €3.50), with beautiful books dating back to the fifteenth century and pictures of Petrarch, his beloved Laura and of Fontaine, where he passed sixteen years of his unrequited passion.

The **tourist office** is on chemin de la Fontaine (Tues–Sat 9.30am–1pm & 1.30–6pm; ⓣ04.90.20.32.22). The most characterful hotel in the village itself is the *Hôtel les Sources* (ⓣ04.90.20.31.84, ⓦwww.hoteldessources.com; ❹), with a whole variety of *vieille France* rooms. On the road out towards Saumane de Vaucluse, 3km from the village, is a budget hotel worth trying, *Font de Lauro* (ⓣ & ⓕ04.90.20.31.49; ❷). There's also a **hostel** on chemin de la Vignasse, 1km south on the road to Lagnes (ⓣ04.90.20.31.65, ⓔfontaine@fuaj.org; closed mid-Nov to Jan; €15.40 per bed), and a **campsite**, *Les Prés* (ⓣ04.90.20.32.38; all year), 500m downstream from the village, with tennis courts and swimming pool. For **food**, you have a choice of several reasonably priced restaurants in town, including *Château* (ⓣ04.90.20.31.54; menus €29 and up) and *Lou Fanau* (ⓣ04.90.20.31.90; closed Wed; menus €15.90–24.60), both of which serve solid regional food.

Gordes and around

GORDES, just 5km east of Fontaine as the crow flies, but 18km by road, is a picturesque Provençal village much favoured by Parisian media personalities, film directors, artists and the like. This might prompt you to give it a miss – and it is an expensive place – but there are good reasons for its popularity with the rich and famous, for it's a spectacular sight. You climb winding roads past buildings of ancient stone before arriving at the summit, where a church and houses surround a mighty twelfth- to sixteenth-century **château**, housing the contemporary paintings of the Flemish artist Pol Mara (daily 10am–noon & 2–6pm; €4).

The **tourist office** is in the château (Mon–Sat 9am–noon & 2–6pm, Sun 10am–noon & 2–6pm; Ⓣ04.90.72.02.75, Ⓦwww.gordes-village.com). If you're looking for somewhere to **stay**, the most reasonably priced hotel within the village is *Le Provençal* (Ⓣ04.90.72.10.01, Ⓕ04.90.72.04.20; ④), while *Les Romarins* (Ⓣ04.90.72.12.13, Ⓦwww.hoteldesromarins.com; ⑥), overlooking the village on the route de Sénanque, is an old country house with comfortable, traditionally styled rooms. For luxury head to *La Bastide de Gordes* in the old village (Ⓣ04.90.72.12.12, Ⓦwww.bastide-de-gordes.com; ⑨), built into the old ramparts; some of the rooms have vaulted ceilings and the terrace boasts impressive views. The best **eating** place in town is *Les Cuisines du Château* on place du Château (Ⓣ04.90.72.01.31; closed Mon & Jan–Feb), always full of Parisians in summer, and serving à la carte dishes from €21. *L'Arlegal* (Ⓣ04.90.72.02.54; closed Sun evening, Mon & Feb) on place Genty-Pantaly is a bit less expensive, and offers good Provençal standards, with lunchtime *plats* around €14.

Around Gordes

Four kilometres north of **Gordes**, set amidst lavender fields in a deep cleft in the hills, stands the twelfth-century Cistercian **Abbaye de Sénanque** (visits by 1hr guided tour only; Ⓣ04.90.72.05.72 or enquire at abbey shop; €6). It's still in use as a monastery and you can visit the church, cloisters and all the main rooms of this substantial and austere building; a shop sells the monks' produce, including a liqueur, as well as honey and lavender essence.

The other historical site of note near Gordes is the **Village des Bories** (daily 9am–sunset; €5.50), 3.5km east off the D2 to Cavaillon, a strange collection of dry-stone dwellings with peculiar geometric shapes that suggest prehistoric pedigree. In fact most were built in the eighteenth century and inhabited up until a hundred years ago.

The best and most surreal detour in the vicinity is to the old **ochre mines** between Gordes and Apt. The houses in the village of **ROUSSILLON**, 5km east of Gordes, radiate all the different shades of the seventeen ochre tints once quarried here; a well-signed footpath leads from the car park and **tourist office** (Ⓣ04.90.05.60.25) on place de la

△ Abbaye de Sénanque

Poste to the old workings. More dramatic quarries, known as the **Colorado Provençal**, are signed off the D22 towards Gignac, just before you reach **RUSTREL**, about 10km northeast of Apt. Various paths lead you to an amphitheatre of coffee, vanilla and strawberry ice cream whipped into pinnacles and curving walls.

The Luberon

After its descent from the Alps, the River Durance makes a wide curve to the west before joining the Rhône, skirting the massive rock-fold known as the **Luberon** that runs for 50km between Cavaillon and Manosque. The Luberon has long been escape country for well-heeled Parisians, Dutch and British, but has also attracted a good number of artists; the main attraction is the countryside itself and the tiny, immaculately preserved villages.

The Luberon's northern face is damper, more alpine in character than the southern face, extremely cold in winter, and dotted with tiny villages clinging stubbornly to the foothills. The southern slopes, by contrast, are Mediterranean in scent and feel. It's almost all wooded, except for the summer sheep pastures at the top, and there's just one main route across it, through the Combe de Lourmarin.

Apt

The sole town base for exploring the Luberon is **APT**, though in itself it's not much of a town for sightseeing, nor is it renowned for the charm and friendliness of its people. Its large confectionery factory spews mucky froth into the concrete-channelled River Coulon and, as late as early spring, when mimosa is blossoming down on the coast, the temperature around Apt can drop to well below freezing. It cheers up, however, every Saturday for the weekly market when cars are barred from the town centre to allow artisans and cultivators from all the surrounding countryside to set up stalls. As well as featuring every imaginable Provençal edible, the **market** is accompanied by barrel organs, jazz musicians, stand-up comics, aged hippies and assorted freaks.

Arriving by bus – Apt's *gare SNCF* is freight-only – you'll be dropped at **place de la Bouquerie**, the main square lined with cafés and restaurants, or at the **gare routière** on avenue de la Libération at the eastern end of the town on avenue Saignon (ⓣ04.90.74.20.21). The **tourist office** is at 20 av Philippe-de-Girard (May, June & Sept Mon–Sat 9am–noon & 2–6pm, Sun 9.30am–12.30pm; July & Aug 9am–7pm, 9.30am–12.30pm; Oct–April Mon–Sat 9am–noon & 2–6pm; ⓣ04.90.74.03.18, ⓦwww.luberon-apt.fr), just up to the left from place de la Bouquerie as you face the river.

Accommodation

There's a good choice of **places to stay** in Apt; in the more scenic hilltop villages, rooms tend to be reserved months before the summer season.

In Apt

L'Aptoi 289 cours Lauze de Perret ⓣ04.90.74.02.02, ⓦwww.aptois.fr.st. A friendly family hotel on the southeastern edge of the town centre. ❹

Auberge du Luberon 8 place du Faubourg du Ballet ⓣ04.90.74.12.50, ⓦwww.auberge-luberon-peuzin.com. A traditional French hotel just across the river, with pleasant rooms and a good restaurant. ❻

Le Palais 24 place Gabriel-Péri ⓣ04.90.04.89.32, ⓔhotel-le-palais@wanadoo.fr. Basic but very central with the market right outside; closed mid-Nov to March. ❸

Camping Les Cèdres Ave de Viton Ⓣ & Ⓕ04.90.74.14.61. Across the bridge from place St-Pierre within easy walking distance of the town. €10.20 for two people and a tent. Closed Dec to mid-Feb.

Outside Apt

Auberge du Presbytère Place de la Fontaine in the village of Saignon, on a hillside 4km southeast of Apt Ⓣ04.90.74.11.50, Ⓦwww.auberge-presbytere.com. Simple tasteful Provençal rooms. Closed mid-Nov to mid-Feb. ❺

Auberge des Seguins Near Buoux, a village 10km south of Apt Ⓣ04.90.74.16.37, Ⓦwww.lesseguins.com. A labyrinth of rooms occupies a welcoming old stone house, tucked away in a spectacular canyon. Half-board only ❺

Bastide St-Joseph rte de Banon in Rustrel, 10km north east of Apt Ⓣ04.90.04.97.80 Ⓦwww.bastide-saint-joseph.com. A tastefully renovated eighteenth-century *bastide* with a pool. ❽

Relais de Roquefure Le Chêne, 6km from Apt on the N100 towards Avignon Ⓣ04.90.04.88.88, Ⓦwww.relaisderoquefure.com. Individual rooms decorated in shades of ochre. The grand stone country house overlooks an inviting swimming pool. ❹

Eating

If you haven't stuffed yourself with chocolates and candied fruit (Apt's speciality), you can get cheap and decent **meals** at the *Grand Café Grégoire* on place de la Bouquerie (open till 10pm; *plats* from €15). Further out on the Avignon road, at Le Chêne, there's real *gourmandise* to be had at *Bernard Mathys* (Ⓣ04.90.04.84.64; eve only, closed Tues & Wed; menus from €48).

The Parc Naturel Régional du Luberon

A large area of the Luberon has been designated **the Parc Naturel Régional du Luberon** (Ⓦwww.parcduluberon.com), with the aim of conserving the natural fauna and flora and limiting development. The park is administered by the **Maison du Parc**, 60 place Jean-Jaurès in Apt (April–Sept Mon–Sat 8.30am–noon & 1.30–7pm; Oct–March Mon–Fri 8.30am–noon & 1.30–6pm; Ⓣ04.90.04.42.00), which is the place to go for information about every aspect of the Luberon. The centre also houses a small **Musée de la Paléontologie** (€1.50), which is specifically designed to amuse children and is fun. A submarine-type "time capsule" door leads down to push-button displays that include magnified views of insect fossils and their modern descendants.

Given the region's general dearth of public transport, the only practical and pleasurable way to explore the park without a car is by hiking or cycling. The organization **Vélo Loisir en Luberon** (Ⓣ04.92.79.05.82, Ⓦwww.veloloisirluberon.com) is a consortium of hotels, campsites and cycle hire and repair shops which promotes cycle tourism throughout the region and can provide transfers to airports or rail stations, guided cycle tours, forward transport of luggage, suggested itineraries and technical assistance and repairs. In Apt, bikes can be hired from Sport 2000, 699 av Victor-Hugo (Ⓣ04.90.04.30.00).

The Abbaye de Silvacane

If you're heading for Aix-en-Provence from Apt, you'll pass close to another ancient Cistercian abbey contemporary with Sénanque, 29km south of Apt, just across the Durance. After a long history of abandonment and evictions, the **Abbaye de Silvacane** (June–Sept daily 10am–6pm; Oct–May daily except Tues 10am–1pm & 2–5pm; €6.10) is once again a monastic institution. Isolated from the surrounding villages on the bank of the Durance, its architecture has hardly changed over the last 700 years; you can visit the stark, pale-stoned splendour of the church, its cloisters and surrounding buildings.

Aix-en-Provence and around

AIX-EN-PROVENCE would be the dominant city of central Provence were it not for the great metropolis of Marseille, just 25km away. Historically, culturally and socially, the two cities are moons apart and the tendency is to love one and hate the other. Aix is complacently conservative and a stunningly beautiful place, its riches based on landowning and the liberal professions. The youth of Aix are immaculately dressed; hundreds of foreign students, particularly Americans, come to study here; and there's a certain snobbishness, almost of Parisian proportions.

From the twelfth century until the Revolution, Aix was the capital of Provence. In its days as an independent county, its most mythically beloved ruler, "Good" King René of Anjou (1409–80), held a brilliant court renowned for its popular festivities and patronage of the arts. René was an archetypal Renaissance man, a speaker of many languages (including Greek and Hebrew), a scientist, poet and economist; he also introduced the muscat grape to the region – today he stands in stone in picture-book medieval fashion, a bunch of grapes in his left hand, looking down the majestic seventeenth-century cours Mirabeau.

Arrival, information and accommodation

Cours Mirabeau, which replaced the town's old southern fortifications, is the main thoroughfare of Aix, with the multi-fountained place Général-de-Gaulle, or La Rotonde, at its west end, the main point of arrival. The **gare SNCF** is on rue Gustavo-Desplace at the end of avenue Victor-Hugo, the avenue leading south from the square; the **gare routière** is on avenue de l'Europe, at the end of avenue des Belges (Ⓣ08.91.02.40.25). The **TGV** station is 10km to the southwest of Aix; regular shuttles connect the station with the *gare routière* (every 30 min: daily 4.45am–10.30pm; €3.70). **Driving** into Aix can be confusing: the entire ring of boulevards encircling the old town is essentially one giant roundabout, circulating anticlockwise; hotels are signposted off this ring in yellow. Parking in Aix isn't easy; the ring is probably the best bet for on-street parking as the old town is pretty nightmarish; there are also some good, modern underground car parks, notably at the Centre de Congrès (€1 for 40min). The busy **tourist office** is located on the *rond point* at the western end of cours Mirabeau at 2 place Général-de-Gaulle (June & Sept daily 8.30am–8pm; July & Aug 8.30am–9pm; Sept–May Mon–Sat 8.30am–7pm, Sun 10am–1pm & 2–6pm; Ⓣ04.42.16.11.61, Ⓦwww.aixenprovencetourism.com), between avenue des Belges and avenue Victor-Hugo.

From mid-June to the end of July (festival time) your chances of getting a **hotel** room are pretty slim unless you've reserved a couple of months in advance at least. Outside this time, there is a decent range of accommodation to choose from.

Visa pass

The **Visa Pour Aix et le Pays D'Aix** grants a 20–50 percent discount on selected museums in and around Aix, in addition to a reduced rate at concerts and on local buses and half-price guided tours. It can be purchased at the tourist office or museums for €2.

Hotels

Des Arts 69 bd Carnot ⓣ04.42.38.11.77, ⓕ04.42.26.77.31. Very welcoming, though slightly noisy hotel, with the cheapest rooms to be found in the centre of Aix. You can't book, so turn up early. Quieter, more expensive rooms are at the back. ❸

La Caravelle 29 bd Roi-René ⓣ04.42.21.53.05, ⓦwww.lacaravelle-hotel.com. By the boulevards to the southeast of the city. The more expensive (renovated) rooms overlook courtyard gardens. ❹

Cardinal 22–24 rue Cardinale ⓣ04.42.38.32.30, ⓔhotel-cardinal@wanadoo.fr. Clean, peaceful and welcoming establishment; great value. ❹

De France 63 rue Espariat ⓣ04.42.27.90.15, ⓦwww.hoteldefrance-aix.com. Right in the centre and with very comfortable rooms. ❹

Le Manoir 8 rue d'Entrecasteaux ⓣ04.42.26.27.20, ⓦwww.hotelmanoir.com. Comfortable and characterful old hotel in a central but discreet location with parking. Breakfast is taken in the sixteenth-century cloister. ❹

Number One 10 cours des Minimes ⓣ04.42.64.45.01, ⓕ04.42.64.45.01. Fairly basic and it's on a busy road, but this is one of the cheapest options in Aix. ❷

Paul 10 av Pasteur ⓣ04.42.23.23.89, ⓦwww.aix-en-provence.com/hotelpaul. Good value for Aix, with a garden. Rooms have private shower and phone and there are also some for three and four people. ❷

Des Quatre-Dauphins 54 rue Roux-Alphéran ⓣ04.42.38.16.39, ⓕ04.42.38.60.19. Old-world charm in the quartier Mazarin. ❺

St-Christophe 2 av Victor-Hugo ⓣ04.42.26.01.24, ⓦwww.hotel-saintchristophe.com. Comfortable, air-con 1920s-style place above a popular brasserie, close to both the station and cours Mirabeau. ❺

Hostels and campsites

Airotel Camping Chantecler rte de Nice, Val St-André ⓣ04.42.26.12.98, ⓕ04.42.27.33.53. 3km from the centre on bus #3 or #10, Expensive site in a big park surrounding a Provençal country house. €18.30 for two people and a tent. Open all year.

Camping Arc-en-Ciel rte de Nice, Pont des Trois Sautets ⓣ04.42.26.14.28, ⓦcampingarcenciel.free.fr. Located 3km southeast of town on bus #3, this is not a particularly cheap site but has very good facilities. €17.20 for two people and a tent. Closed Oct–March.

HI hostel 3 av Marcel-Pagnol ⓣ04.42.20.15.99, ⓕ04.42.59.36.12. Located 2km west of the centre, this hostel has small dorm rooms (€17), a restaurant, baggage deposit, tennis and volleyball courts, as well as sought-after parking. However they operate a midnight curfew and there are no cooking facilities. Take bus #4, direction "La Mayanelle", stop "Vasarély". Closed Christmas–Feb.

CROUS Cité Universitaire des Gazelles, 38 av Jules-Ferry ⓣ04.42.93.47.70. This student organization can sometimes find cheap rooms on one of Aix's two main campuses during July & Aug. Take bus #5, direction "Moulin de Testas", stop "Moulin de Testas". ❶

△ Market produce, Aix-en-Provence

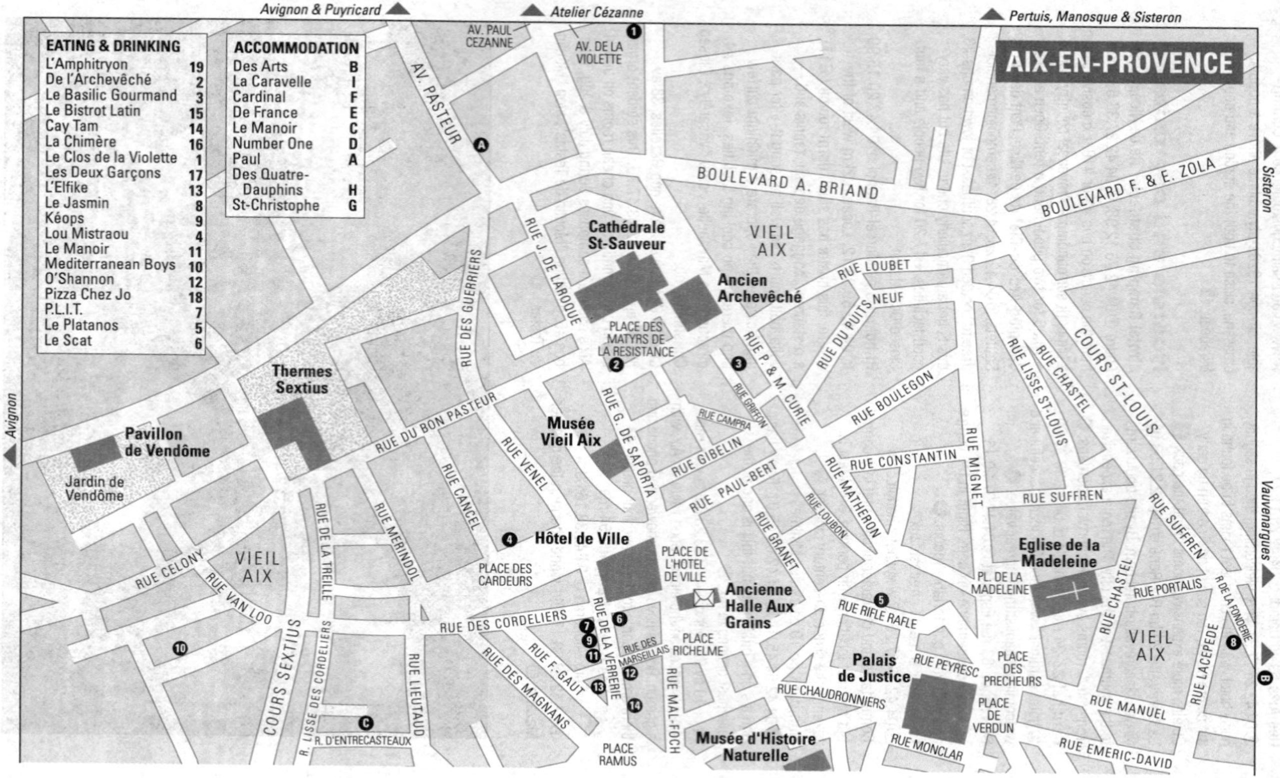

AIX-EN-PROVENCE

EATING & DRINKING	
L'Amphitryon	19
De l'Archevêché	2
Le Basilic Gourmand	3
Le Bistrot Latin	15
Cay Tam	14
La Chimère	16
Le Clos de la Violette	1
Les Deux Garçons	17
L'Elfike	13
Le Jasmin	8
Kéops	9
Lou Mistraou	4
Le Manoir	11
Mediterranean Boys	10
O'Shannon	12
Pizza Chez Jo	18
P.L.I.T.	7
Le Platanos	5
Le Scat	6

ACCOMMODATION	
Des Arts	B
La Caravelle	I
Cardinal	F
De France	E
Le Manoir	C
Number One	D
Paul	A
Des Quatre-Dauphins	H
St-Christophe	G

Avignon & Puyricard
Atelier Cézanne
Pertuis, Manosque & Sisteron
Sisteron
Vauvenargues
Avignon
AV. PAUL CEZANNE
AV. DE LA VIOLETTE
AV. PASTEUR
BOULEVARD A. BRIAND
BOULEVARD F. & E. ZOLA
VIEIL AIX
Cathédrale St-Sauveur
Ancien Archevêché
RUE LOUBET
RUE DU PUITS NEUF
COURS ST-LOUIS
RUE CHASTEL
RUE LISSE ST-LOUIS
RUE J. DE LAROQUE
RUE DES GUERRIERS
PLACE DES MATYRS DE LA RESISTANCE
RUE P. & M. CURIE
RUE GRIFFON
RUE CAMPRA
RUE BOULEGON
Thermes Sextius
RUE DU BON PASTEUR
Musée Vieil Aix
RUE G. DE SAPORTA
RUE GIBELIN
RUE CONSTANTIN
RUE MIGNET
Pavillon de Vendôme
Jardin de Vendôme
RUE VENEL
RUE CANCEL
RUE PAUL-BERT
RUE MATHERON
RUE LOUBON
RUE GRANET
RUE SUFFREN
Hôtel de Ville
PLACE DE L'HOTEL DE VILLE
Eglise de la Madeleine
PL. DE LA MADELEINE
RUE PORTALIS
R DE LA FONDERIE
RUE CELONY
RUE VAN LOO
RUE DE LA TREILLE
RUE MERINDOL
PLACE DES CARDEURS
Ancienne Halle Aux Grains
RUE RIFLE RAFLE
RUE DES CORDELIERS
RUE DE LA VERRERIE
RUE DES MARSEILLAIS
PLACE RICHELME
RUE LACEPEDE
Palais de Justice
RUE PEYRESC
PLACE DES PRECHEURS
RUE F.-GAUT
RUE DES MAGNANS
RUE CHAUDRONNIERS
PLACE DE VERDUN
RUE MANUEL
COURS SEXTIUS
R. LISSE DES CORDELIERS
RUE LIEUTAUD
R. D'ENTRECASTEAUX
PLACE RAMUS
RUE MAL-FOCH
Musée d'Histoire Naturelle
RUE MONCLAR
RUE EMERIC-DAVID

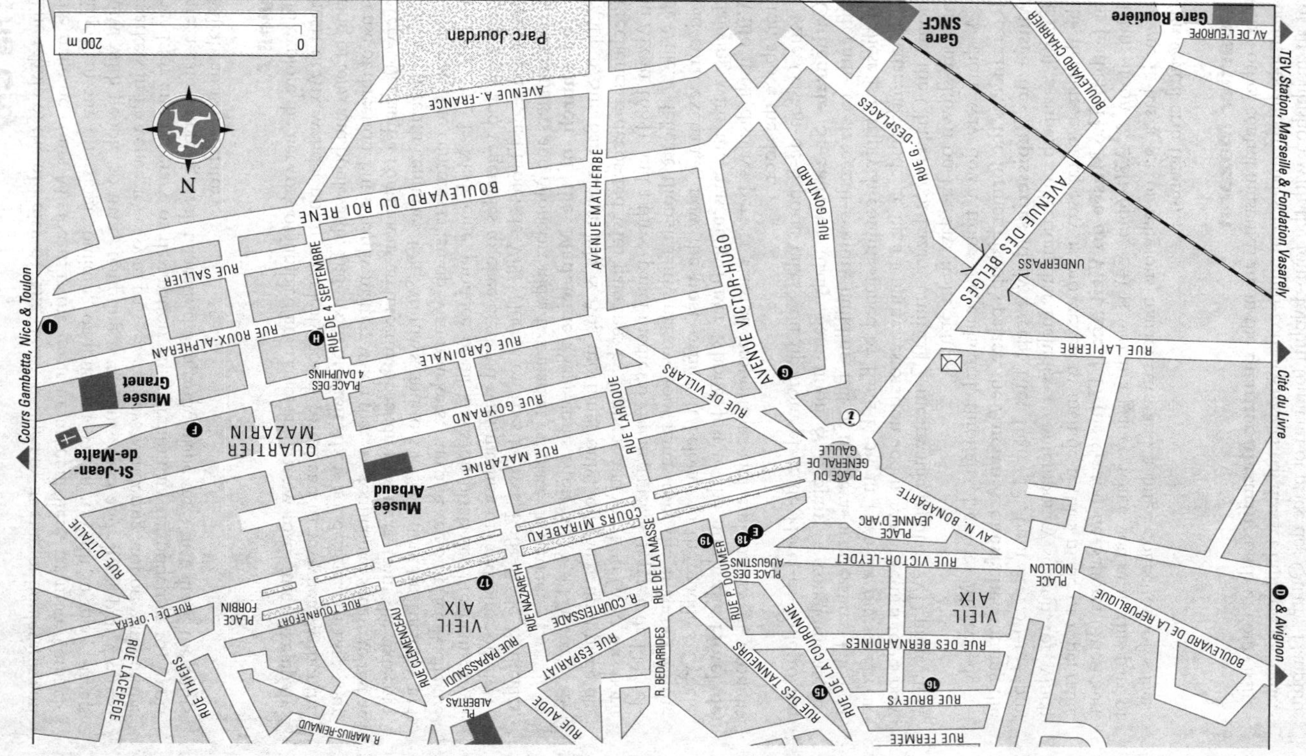
Cours Gambetta, Nice & Toulon
TGV Station, Marseille & Fondation Vasarely
Cité du Livre
& Avignon
0
200 m
N
Parc Jourdan
Gare SNCF
Gare Routière
AV. DE L'EUROPE
BOULEVARD CHARRIER
AVENUE A.-FRANCE
BOULEVARD DU ROI RENE
AVENUE MALHERBE
RUE G.-DESPLACES
AVENUE DES BELGES
UNDERPASS
RUE GONTARD
AVENUE VICTOR-HUGO
RUE LAPIERRE
RUE SALLIER
RUE DE 4 SEPTEMBRE
RUE ROUX-ALPHERAN
RUE CARDINALE
PLACE DES 4 DAUPHINS
Musée Granet
QUARTIER MAZARIN
St-Jean-de-Malte
RUE GOYRAND
RUE MAZARINE
Musée Arbaud
RUE LAROQUE
RUE DE VILLARS
PLACE DU GENERAL DE GAULLE
AV N. BONAPARTE
PLACE JEANNE D'ARC
RUE VICTOR-LEYDET
PLACE NIOLLON
BOULEVARD DE LA REPUBLIQUE
VIEIL AIX
RUE DES BERNARDINES
RUE BRUEYS
RUE FERMEE
COURS MIRABEAU
RUE DE LA MASSE
PLACE DES AUGUSTINS
RUE P. DOUMER
RUE DE LA COURONNE
RUE DES TANNEURS
R. BEDARRIDES
R. COURTEISSADE
RUE ESPARIAT
RUE AUDE
RUE NAZARETH
VIEIL AIX
RUE CLEMENCEAU
RUE PAPASSAUDI
PL. ALBERTAS
RUE TOURNEFORT
PLACE FORBIN
RUE DE L'OPERA
RUE D'ITALIE
RUE THIERS
RUE LACEPEDE
R. MARIUS-REINAUD

The City

The whole of the **old city of Aix**, clearly defined by its ring of boulevards and the majestic cours Mirabeau, is the great monument here, far more compelling than any one single building or museum within it. With so many streets alive with people, so many tempting restaurants, cafés and shops, plus the best markets in Provence, it's easy to pass several days wandering around without the need for any itinerary or destination. As a preliminary introduction to Aixois life, a café-stopping stroll beneath the gigantic plane trees that shade the cours Mirabeau is mandatory.

Vieil Aix

To explore the network of jumbled little lanes and narrow roads that make up the heart of Aix, wander north from leafy **cours Mirabeau** to anywhere within the ring of *cours* and boulevards. The layout of **Vieil Aix** is not designed to assist your sense of direction, but it hardly matters when there's a fountained square to rest at every 50m and a continuous architectural backdrop of treats from the sixteenth and seventeenth centuries. On Saturdays, and to a lesser extent on Tuesdays and Thursdays, the centre is taken up with **markets**: fruit and veg on place Richelme and place de la Madeleine; produce of all kinds on place des Prêcheurs, from fresh fruit and vegetables to cheeses, dried wild mushrooms and olive oil; flowers on place de l'Hôtel-de-Ville; clothes on rues Peyresc, Rifle-Rafle, Bouteilles, Chaudronniers and Monclar; and a flea market on place de Verdun.

The **church of the Madeleine** (Sept–June Mon–Sat 8–11.30am & 3–5.30pm, Sun 8am–noon; July & Aug mornings only), on the central place des Prêcheurs, is decorated with paintings by Rubens and Van Loo (who was born in Aix in 1684), and a three-panel medieval *Annunciation*. On place de l'Hôtel-de-Ville, a delicate though fairly massive foot hangs over the architrave of the old corn exchange, now the **post office**. It belongs to the goddess Cybele, dallying with the masculine River Rhône. Just to the north, the **Hôtel de Ville** itself displays perfect classical proportions and embroidery in wrought iron above the door.

Rue Gaston-de-Saporta takes you up from place de Hôtel-de-Ville to the **Cathédrale St-Sauveur** (daily: 8am–noon & 2–6pm), a conglomerate of fifteenth- to sixteenth-century building, full of medieval art treasures. The best of these is a triptych commissioned by King René in 1475, *Le Buisson Ardent*. It is currently undergoing a lengthy restoration and may not return to its new home, the Chapel of St Lazare, until 2007; meanwhile regular DVD projections of it are shown on Tuesdays from 3pm.

A short way down from the cathedral, through place des Martyrs-de-la-Résistance, is the former bishop's palace, the **Ancien Archevêché**, housing the **Musée des Tapisseries** (daily except Tues 10am–12.30pm & 1.30–6.45pm; €2.50), a superb collection that includes a contemporary section, for which the definition of tapestry is broadened to include textiles made of rope, raffia or feathers. The **Musée du Vieil Aix** at 17 rue Gaston-de-Saporta (Tues–Sun: 10am–noon & 2.30–6pm; €4) is worth a glance while you're in this part of town. It has a set of religious marionettes and a huge collection of *santons* (Provençal crib figures).

Quartier Mazarin

Aix's other central museums are in the **quartier Mazarin**, south of cours Mirabeau, a beautiful mid-seventeenth-century residential district built on the orders of an archbishop, with the four-dolphin fountain of place des Quatre-Dauphins at its heart. On place St-Jean-de-Malte the most substantial of all Aix's museums, the **Musée Granet** (Wed–Mon 11am–6pm; €10), covers art and archeology. It exhibits the finds from the Oppidum d'Entremont (see below), a Celtic-Ligurian township 3km north of Aix, which flourished for about a hundred years, along with the remains of the Romans who routed them in 124 BC and established their city of Aquae Sextiae, the future Aix. The museum's paintings are a mixed bag – Italian, Dutch, French, mostly seventeenth to nineteenth century. The museum was re-opened in 2006 after two years of renovation to accommodate an exhibition marking 100 years since the death of the most famous Aixois painter, **Paul Cézanne.** Though the exhibition hosted over 100 works loaned from galleries around the world, those left on permanent display are a less impressive handful of minor canvases such as *Bathsheba, The Bathers* and *Portrait of Madame.* There are also two of his student drawings from when he studied on the ground floor of the building, at that time the art school Granet.

Beyond the centre

Cézanne used many studios in and around Aix but he finally had a house built for the purpose in 1902 at what is now 9 av Paul-Cézanne, overlooking Aix from the north. It was here that he painted the *Grandes Baigneuses*, the *Jardinier Vallier* and some of his greatest still lifes. The **Atelier Cézanne** (April–June & Sept 10am–noon & 2–6pm; July & Aug daily 10am–6pm; Oct–March 10am–noon & 2–5pm; €5.50; bus #20, stop "P. Cézanne") is exactly as it was at the time of his death in 1906: coat, hat, wineglass and easel, the objects he liked to paint, his pipe, a few letters and drawings … everything save the pictures he was working on.

Collective cultural life is the basis of the **Cité du Livre** in the old matchmaking factory at 8–10 rue des Allumettes, a short way southwest from the tourist office (Tues, Thurs & Fri noon–6pm, Wed & Sat 10am–6pm; free). Entered by doorways in the form of giant books leaning together as if on a shelf, it includes libraries, a cinema, theatre space, a *videothèque d'art lyrique* (where you can watch just about any French opera performance) and all manner of exhibitions. Since 1996 the complex has been the home base for the internationally renowned modernist dance company, Ballet Preljocaj.

For a totally different experience, both visually and conceptually, you can escape the sometimes cloying grandeur of seventeenth-century Aix by visiting the **Fondation Vasarély** on avenue Marcel-Pagnol in Jas-de-Bouffan, 4km west of the city centre (Mon–Sat: July & Aug 11am–1pm & 2–7pm; Sept–June 10am–1pm & 2–6pm; €7; bus #4, stop "V. Vasarély"). There are innumerable sliding showcases, showing images related to all the themes of architect/artist Vasarély's work, including his "plastic alphabet" and designs for apartment buildings. But the seven hexagonal spaces on the ground floor, each hung with six huge designs, is where you'll get the immediate impact of this extraordinary man's work.

And finally, 3km north of the city, the **Oppidum d'Entremont** (daily except Tues 9am–noon & 2–6pm; free; take bus #20 from cours Sextius) is the excavated site of the Gallic settlement which preceded the foundation of the town, predating the Roman conquest by more than 200 years. You'll find the remains of a fortified enclosure, spectacularly sited, as well as excavations of the residential and commercial quarters of the town.

Eating, drinking and entertainment

Aix is stuffed full of **restaurants** of every price and ethnic origin. Place des Cardeurs, just northwest of the Hôtel de Ville, is nothing but restaurant, brasserie and café tables, while rue de la Verrerie running south from the Hôtel de Ville and place Ramus have an immense variety of Indian, Chinese and North African restaurants. Rue des Tanneurs is a good street for low budgets. The café-brasseries on cours Mirabeau are also tempting, and in between them you'll find cheaper snackeries. More expensive are Aix's soft biscuits, the elliptical candied-fruit and almond-flavoured *calissons.* They're very good with a strong dark espresso. Local gourmet chocolatier Puyricard has a shop at 7 rue Rifle-Rafle.

Aix is too pretty to have gritty, urban **nightlife**. Instead students congregate around the fountains and cafés near cours Mirabeau until midnight when the bars on rue Verrerie get going. For **jazz, rock & funk** there's *Le Scat* at no.11 (Ⓦwww.lescatclub.aix.free.fr). If you'd rather a more mainstream **disco**, head for *P.L.I.T.* at no. 24 (Ⓣ06.12.58.86.79). For **pubs** with live music or DJs, try *Le Manoir* and *O'Shannon* at nos. 25 and 30 respectively. **Heavy rock** booms out next door at no. 32, at *l'Elfike*, Aix's Goth venue. Aix's **gay** bar is *Mediterranean Boys*, 6 rue de la Paix, while another great jazz venue is *Hot Brass*, chemin d'Eguilles-Celony (Ⓣ04.42.23.13.12, Ⓦwww.hotbrassaix.com).

Cafés and restaurants

L'Amphitryon 2–4 rue Paul-Doumer Ⓣ04.42.26.54.10. Eclectic cuisine with market-fresh ingredients, served on a flower-drenched terrace in historical old Aix. An excellent restaurant which won't break the bank. Menu from €26. Closed Sun, Mon & second half Aug.

De l'Archevêché place des Martyrs-de-la-Résistance Ⓣ04.42.21.43.57. Smart lunch spot with good midday pasta, tapas, tagines and salads from around €10.

Le Basilic Gourmand 6 rue du Griffon Ⓣ04.42.96.08.58. Classic Provençal food, à la carte only from €14. Amiable staff, bric-a-brac decor and occasional live music. Closed Sun & Mon.

Le Bistrot Latin 18 rue Couronne Ⓣ04.42.38.22.88. Superbly presented scallop and tapenade profiteroles and honey and garlic rabbit are two of the top dishes here. Lunch menu €16, evening from €21. Closed Sat, Sun & Mon lunch out of season.

Cay Tam 29 rue Verrerie Ⓣ04.42.27.28.11. The best East Asian cooking in Aix. Vietnamese dishes are the main feature, but dim sum is also available. Menus from €15.50. Closed Mon & Tues, lunch Wed & Fri.

La Chimère 15 rue Brueys Ⓣ04.42.38.30.00. New spin on French standards, with dishes like salad of octopus with Provençal herbs or roast sea bream with lemon, *tian* of vegetables and *sauce vierge.* Menu €26.50. Closed Sun.

Le Clos de la Violette 10 av de la Violette Ⓣ04.42.23.30.71. Aix's most renowned restaurant serves dishes that might not sound very seductive, like stuffed lamb's feet, but are in fact gastronomic delights. More obviously alluring are the puddings: a *clafoutis* of greengages and pistachios with peach sauce and a tart of melting dark chocolate. Lunch menu €54, otherwise menus start at €130 and if you're going à la carte the *plats* alone start around €40. Closed Sun & Mon & Wed lunch & middle 2 weeks Aug.

Les Deux Garçons 53 cours Mirabeau. The erstwhile haunt of Camus is done up in faded 1900s style and still attracts a motley assortment of literati. Good brasserie food, but not cheap (from €27.80). Service daily till midnight.

Le Jasmin 6 rue de la Fonderie Ⓣ04.42.38.05.89. Tasty and distinctive Persian food for around €16.50. For dessert try the traditional Iranian *choleh zard*, a rice dish with saffron, spices and nuts. Closed Sun.

Kéops 28 rue de la Verrerie Ⓣ04.42.96.59.05. Egyptian cuisine featuring falafel, stuffed pigeon and gorgeous milk-based desserts. Menu €10. Closed Wed lunch.

Lou Mistraou 38 place des Cardeurs Ⓣ04.42.96.98.69. Provençal restaurant with a €25 veggie menu, though watch out for the anchovies. Closed Sun & Mon in winter, plus Jan.

Pizza Chez Jo/Bar des Augustins place des Augustins Ⓣ04.42.26.12.47. This place is usually packed for its cheap pizzas and traditional *plats du jour.* From €12. Closed Sun.

Le Platanos 13 rue Rifle-Rafle Ⓣ04.42.21.33.19. Very cheap and popular Greek place with €10 lunch menu. Closed Sun & Mon.

Festivals

During the annual **music festivals**, Aix en Musique (world music, jazz, experimental and classical; June; Ⓣ04.42.21.69.69) and the Festival International d'Art

Lyrique (opera and classical concerts; last two weeks of July; ⓣ04.42.17.34.34), the alternative scene – of street theatre, rock concerts and impromptu gatherings – turns the whole of Vieil Aix into one long party. Tickets for events range from €12 to €185 and can be obtained, along with programmes, from La Boutique du Festival at Espace Forbin, 11, rue Gaston de Saporta (ⓣ04.42.17.34.34, ⓦwww.festival-aix.com). Details of the Danse à Aix international dance festival (two weeks in mid-July) are available from 1 place Rewald off cours Gambetta (ⓣ04.42.96.05.01).

Listings

Bike rental Cycles Zammit, 27 rue Mignet ⓣ04.42.23.19.53.
Books Paradox Bookstore, 15 rue du 4-Septembre, or Book in Bar, 1bis rue Cabassol, for English books; Vents du Sud, 7 rue Maréchal-Foch, is the best French bookshop.
Car rental ADA Location, 1 av Henri-Mouret ⓣ04.42.52.36.36; Avis, 11 bd Gambetta ⓣ04.42.21.64.16; Europcar, 55 bd de la République ⓣ04.42.27.83.00; Rent a Car, 35 rue de la Molle ⓣ04.42.38.58.29.
Cinema The Cézanne, rue Marcel-Guillaume, sometimes screens English or American films in *version originale*, ie with the original soundtrack.
Emergencies Centre Hospitalier, av des Tamaris ⓣ04.42.33.90.28; SOS Médecins ⓣ04.42.26.24.00; for a late-night pharmacy, ring the *gendarmerie* on ⓣ04.42.26.31.96.
Internet Le Hublot, 17 rue Paul-Bert; Progamers, 14 Forum des Cardeurs; Virtualis, 40 rue des Cordeliers; Cyber@Vanloo, 20 rue Van Loo.
Laundry 15 rue Jacques de la Roque; 5 rue de la Fontaine; 60 rue Boulegon; 36 cours Sextius.
Money exchange L'Agence, 15 cours Mirabeau; Change Nazareth, 7 rue Nazareth; La Poste, 2 rue Lapierre.
Police place Niollon ⓣ04.42.91.91.11.
Post office 2 rue Lapierre.
Taxis ⓣ04.42.21.61.61; ⓣ04.42.27.71.11 (24hr).

Mont Ste-Victoire

Mont Ste-Victoire, a rough pyramid whose apex has been pulled off-centre, lies 10km east of Aix. Ringed at its base by the dark green and orange-brown of pine woods and cultivated soil, the limestone rock reflects light, turning blue, grey, pink or orange. In the last years of his life **Cézanne** painted and drew Ste-Victoire more than fifty times, and, as part of his childhood landscape, it came to embody the incarnation of life within nature.

You may, however, be more interested in climbing Mont Ste-Victoire and in the view from it, though hiking on the Mont, and many other summits in the area, is forbidden from July to mid-September. The southern face has a sheer 500-metre drop, but from the north the two-hour walk requires nothing more than determination. The **GR9**, also called the Chemin des Venturiers, leaves from a small car park on the D10 just before **VAUVENARGUES**, 14km east of Aix. Having reached the 945-metre ridge, marked by a monumental nineteenth-century cross that doesn't figure in any of Cézanne's pictures, you can follow the path east along the ridge to the summit of the massif and then descend south to **PUYLOUBIER** (about 15km from the cross; reckon on four and a half hours). Bring plenty of water and protection against the fierce sun if walking in hot weather. Much of the walk was badly affected by forest fires in 1989 and consequently, to guard against erosion, you're urged to stick to the path.

At Vauvenargues (several buses daily from the Aix *gare routière*), a perfect weather-beaten, red-shuttered fourteenth-century **château** (definitely not open to the public) stands just outside the village, with nothing between it and the slopes of Ste-Victoire. **Picasso** bought the château in 1958, lived there until his death and now lies buried in the gardens, his grave adorned with his sculpture *Woman with a Vase*. There is a friendly, good-value hotel in the village, *Au Moulin de Provence*, 33 rue de Maquisards (☎04.42.66.02.22; ❸), whose owners speak English.

Eastern Provence

In **eastern Provence**, it's the landscapes not the towns that dominate. The gentle hills and villages of the **Haut-Var**, the northern half of the Var *département*, make for happy exploration by car or bike, before the foothills of the Alps gradually close in, eventually reaching heights of over 3000m in the far north-eastern corner, around **Barcelonnette**. Winter visitors are almost exclusively skiers, while the summer brings a variety of dedicated hikers, birdwatchers, botanists and climbers. The **Parc National du Mercantour** is a conservation area in this mountainous terrain, but the most exceptional geographical feature is the **Gorges du Verdon** – Europe's answer to the Grand Canyon – in the heart of Provence.

Between Valence and Montélimar, the River Drôme joins the Rhône at **Livron-sur-Drôme**. Following the Drôme upstream by train towards Sisteron, or by road towards **Sisteron** or Barcelonnette, is one of the most dramatic ways of entering eastern Provence.

Haut-Var villages and Aups

Between **ST-MAXIMIN-DE-LA-STE-BAUME**, 35km east of Aix and famous for its supposed possession of the relics of Mary Magdalene, and **DRAGUIGNAN**, an unremarkable military town except for the wonderful *Les Milles Colonnes* restaurant in place aux Herbes, a network of small roads wind through farmland, vineyards and woods and alongside streams and lakes, linking a dozen villages, all of which are ideal for Provençal-style loafing. The only problem is the general scarcity of accommodation.

East of the **Lac de Carcès**, between Cabasse and Carcès, off the D19, lies the last of the three great Cistercian monasteries of Provence. Even more so than Silvacane and Sénanque, the **Abbaye du Thoronet** (April–Sept Mon–Sat 10am–6.30pm, Sun 10am–noon & 2–6.30pm; Oct–March Mon–Sat 10am–1pm & 2–5pm, Sun 10am–noon & 2–5pm; €6.50) has been unscathed by the vicissitudes of time, and during the Revolution was kept intact as a remarkable monument of history and art; today it is occasionally used for concerts. It was first restored in the 1850s, while a more recent campaign has brought it to clear-cut perfection. As with the other two abbeys, its interior spaces, delineated by walls of pale rose-coloured stone, are inspiring.

LORGUES, further east, has a serious gourmet stop in the **restaurant** *Chez Bruno* on route de Vidauban (☎04.94.85.93.93; closed Mon & Sun evening out of season; seasonal truffle menu at €120, à la carte around €59), where the truffle reigns supreme, appearing in myriad forms, even in desserts. There's a Terre des Truffes shop in an annexe to the main building, and space to land your helicopter. Heading 13km northwest, **ENTRECASTEAUX** has an ancient stone **laundry** by the river that's still used, and a very beautiful **château** (guided tours daily except Sat at 4pm; ⓣ04.94.04.43.95; €7).

COTIGNAC, 9km west of Entrecasteaux, is the Haut-Var village *par excellence*, with a shaded main square for *pétanque* and passages and stairways bursting with begonias, jasmine and geraniums leading through a cluster of medieval houses. More gardens sprawl at the foot of the bubbly rock cliff that forms the back wall of the village, threaded with troglodyte walkways.

North of Cotignac, **SILLANS-LA-CASCADE** has a beautiful walk, signposted off the main road, to an immense waterfall and aquamarine pool (about 20min). **SALERNES**, 6km east of Sillans, makes tiles and pottery and has the old-fashioned *Relais de la Belle Époque* **hotel** and restaurant on route de Sillans (ⓣ04.94.70.60.30, ⓦwww.lerelaisdelabelleepoque.com; menus €25; ④). **VILLECROZE** and **TOURTOUR** to the northeast are both suitably picturesque. The Norwegian-owned *Auberge des Lavandes*, on place du Général-de-Gaulle in Villecroze (ⓣ04.94.70.76.00, ⓕ04.94.70.56.45; ④), is one of the best-value hotels in the region, while in Tourtour, on route de Flayosc, you can shelter in total luxury at *La Bastide de Tourtour* (ⓣ04.98.10.54.20, ⓦwww.verdon.net/tourtour; ⑨). A second option in Tourtour, which won't break the bank, is *La Petite Auberge* (ⓣ04.98.10.26.16, ⓦwww.petiteauberge.net; ⑥). Between the two villages is a highly reputed **restaurant**, *Les Chênes Verts* (ⓣ04.94.70.55.06; closed Tues eve & Wed), with a menu *dégustation* at €55.

Aups

As a base for visiting the villages of Haut-Var or the Gorges du Verdon, the small town of **AUPS** is ideal, as long as you have your own transport. It has a lot of charm and still depends to a large extent on agriculture rather than tourism. Scarcely more than a village itself, its speciality is truffles and, if you're here on a Thursday between November and mid-March, you can witness the **truffle market**.

On **place Martin-Bidauré**, which, along with **place Frédéric-Mistral** (Wed & Sat market), makes up the leafy open space before the start of the old town, a rare monument commemorates the town's citizens who died in 1851 defending the republic and its laws. The year was that of Louis Napoléon's coup d'état and establishment of the Second Empire. Peasant and artisan resistance was strongest in Provence, and the defeat of the insurgents was followed by a bloody massacre of men and women. This might explain the enormous *République Française, Liberté, Egalité, Fraternité* sign on the **church of St-Pancrace**, proclaiming it as state property. The church was designed by an English architect 400 years ago, and has recently had its doors restored by two local British carpenters.

Surprisingly for such a small place, Aups has a museum of modern art, the **Musée Simon Segal** in the former chapel of a convent on avenue Albert-1er (July & Aug daily 10am–noon & 4–7pm; €2.30). The best works are those by the Russian-born painter Simon Segal, but there are interesting local scenes in the other paintings, such as the Roman bridge at Aiguines, now drowned beneath the artificial lake of Sainte-Croix. Just outside Aups, 3.5km along the Tourtour road, is a sculpture park by local artist Maria de Faykod (daily except Tues: June 2–7pm; July & Aug 10am–noon & 3–7pm; Sept, Oct & Dec–May 2–6pm; closed Nov; €6), with dramatic human forms in marble.

Practicalities

The **tourist office** is part of the *mairie* on place Frédéric-Mistral (June Mon–Sat 9am–12.30pm & 2.30–5.30pm; July & Aug daily 9am–12.30pm &

3–6.30pm; Sept–May Mon–Sat 9am–12.30pm & 2–5.30pm; ⓣ04.94.84.00.69, ⓦmembres.lycos.fr/otsiaups). All the hotels are good value: *Le Provençal* on place Martin-Bidauré (ⓣ04.94.70.00.24, ⓕ04.94.84.06.25; ❸) and the *Grand Hôtel* on place Duchâtel (ⓣ04.94.70.10.82, ⓦwww.grand-hotel-aups.com; closed March; ❸) are both good inexpensive options. There are two **campsites** close to town: the two-star *Camping Les Prés*, to the right off allée Charles-Boyer towards Tourtour (ⓣ04.94.70.00.93, ⓕ04.94.70.14.41; open all year; €12), with bikes to rent nearby, and the three-star *Saint Lazare,* 2km along the Moissac road (ⓣ04.94.70.12.86, ⓕ04.94.70.01.55; closed Oct–March; €11.60), which has a pool.

For **meals**, your first choice should be the hotel-restaurant *St-Marc* (ⓣ04.94.70.06.08, ⓦwww.lesaintmarc.com ❸; closed three weeks in November). Serving local dishes, truffles and boar in season, it offers menus at €16–30 (Sept–June closed Tues & Wed). For snacks, try the boulangerie-patisserie *À la Claire Fontaine* on place Général-Giraud or the *Boulanger Arpsoise* at 12 rue M.- Foch.

The Gorges du Verdon and around

From Aups, the road north leads to the western end of the **Gorges du Verdon**. A more dramatic approach crosses the vast military terrain of the Camp de Canjuers from Comps-sur-Artuby. The road runs west through 16km of deserted heath and hills, with each successive horizon higher than the last. When you reach the canyon, it's as if a silent earthquake had taken place during your journey.

This vantage point, known as the **Balcons de la Mescla**, is a memorable *coup de théâtre*, with the view withheld until you are almost upon it. You look down 250m to the base of the V-shaped, 21km-long gorge incised by the River Verdon through piled strata of limestone. Ever changing in its volume and energy, the river falls from Rougon at the top of the gorge, disappearing into tunnels, decelerating for shallow, languid moments and finally exiting in full, steady flow at the **Pont de Galetas**. The huge artificial **Lac de Sainte-Croix**, filled by the Verdon as it leaves the gorge, is great for swimming when the water levels are high; otherwise the beach becomes a bit sludgy. West from the Balcons runs the **Corniche sublime**, the D71, built expressly to give the most breathtaking and hair-raising views crossing the 182-metre Pont de l'Artuby. On the north side, the **Route des Crêtes**, the D952 is even more dramatic – not least because on some of the highest stretches there's nothing to stop you driving straight off into the abyss – but it's not so consistently scenic, even though at some points you look down a sheer 800m drop to the sliver of water below. The mid-section of the Route des Crêtes is one way (westbound only), so if you want to do it all you'll have to start from the more scenic eastern end. It closes each winter from November 15 to March 15.

The entire circuit around the gorge is 130km long and it's cycling country solely for the preternaturally fit. Even for drivers it's hard work, as the hidden bends and hairpins in the road are perilous and, in July and August, so is the traffic.

Public transport around the canyon is less than comprehensive. There's just one bus in each direction between Aix, Moustiers, La Palud, Rougon and Castellane on Monday, Wednesday and Saturday from July to mid-September and just once a week on a Saturday during the rest of the year.

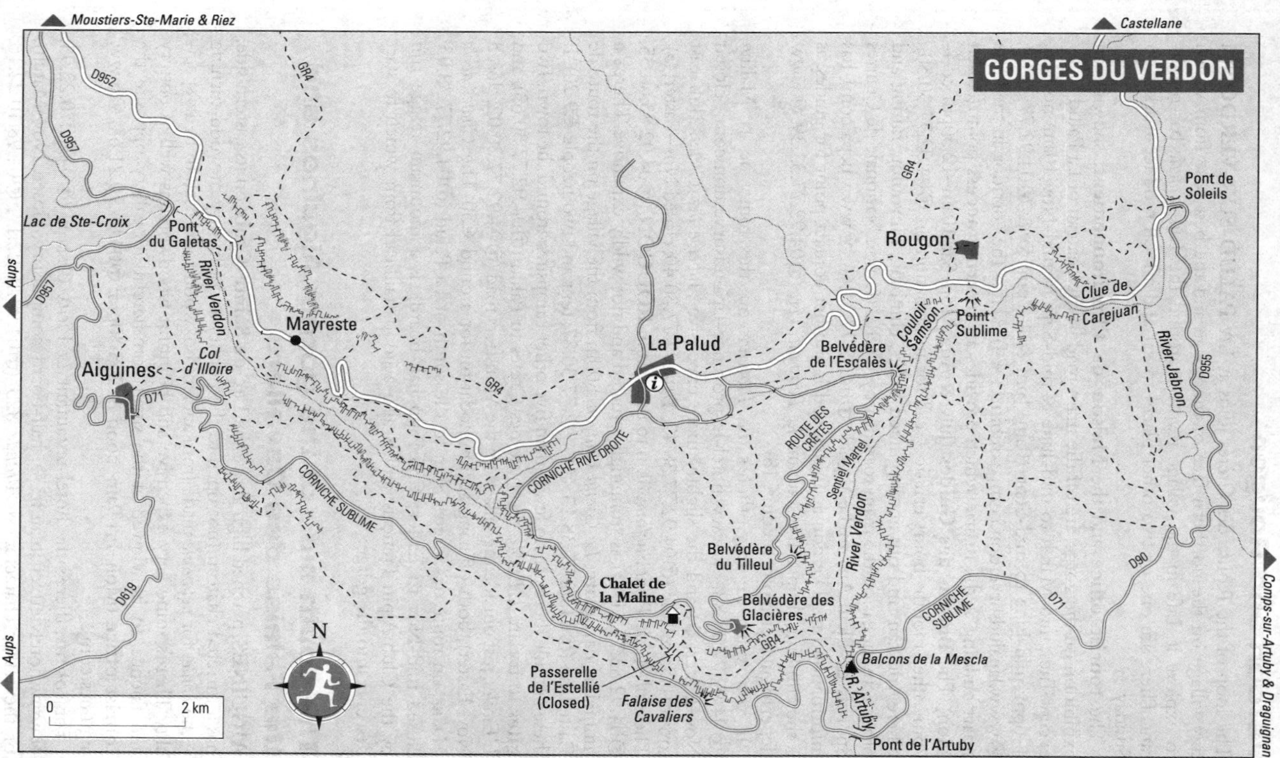
GORGES DU VERDON
Moustiers-Ste-Marie & Riez
Castellane
Comps-sur-Artuby & Draguignan
Aups
Aups
D952
D957
D957
D619
D71
D71
D90
D955
GR4
GR4
GR4
GR4
Lac de Ste-Croix
Pont du Galetas
River Verdon
Col d'Illoire
Aiguines
Mayreste
La Palud
Rougon
Pont de Soleils
Clue de Carejuan
River Jabron
Point Sublime
Couloir Samson
Belvédère de l'Escalès
ROUTE DES CRÊTES
Sentier Martel
River Verdon
CORNICHE RIVE DROITE
CORNICHE SUBLIME
CORNICHE SUBLIME
Belvédère du Tilleul
Belvédère des Glacières
Chalet de la Maline
Passerelle de l'Estellié (Closed)
Falaise des Cavaliers
Balcons de la Mescla
R. Artuby
Pont de l'Artuby
N
0
2 km

The north side of the gorge: La Palud-sur-Verdon and Rougon

The loop of the Route des Crêtes joins at **LA PALUD-SUR-VERDON**, a tiny village on the northern face of the gorge and the best base from which to explore it. Life in the village revolves around the *Lou Cafetie* bar-restaurant. There are one or two other places to eat and a local produce market on Sunday.

The **tourist office** and the **Maison de l'Environnement,** showing an exhibition on the gorge, are off the main road in the château of La Palud (daily except Tues: mid-March to mid-June & mid-Sept to mid-Nov 10am–noon & 4–6pm; mid-June to mid-Sept 10am–1pm & 4–7pm; ⓣ & ⓕ04.92.77.32.02, ⓦwww.lapaludsurverdon.com; exhibition €4). Across the corridor, in the same smart building, is the mairie which provides an **Internet access** point (closed Mon). The **Bureau des Guides** (July & Aug Mon–Sat 10am–12.30pm & 4–7pm; other months hours erratic – call for information on ⓣ04.92.77.30.50), where you can find out about guided walks, climbing, canyoning, rafting and other activities, is on the main road nearby. UCPA (Union Nationale de Centres Sportifs de Plein Air) in Le Vignal (ⓣ04.92.77.31.66, ⓦwww.ucpa.com) has information on all Verdon activities, and is another contact point for guides, as is the climbing shop and restaurant *Le Perroquet Vert* (ⓣ04.92.77.33.39, ⓦwww.leperroquetvert.com; menu €18).

If you want to **stay**, there's *Le Provence* on the route de la Maline (ⓣ04.92.77.38.88, ⓦwww.hotel-le-provence-lapaludsurverdon.com; closed Nov–Easter; ④) and the slightly more expensive *Auberge des Crêtes*, 1km east towards Castellane (ⓣ04.92.77.38.47, ⓕ04.92.77.30.40; closed Nov–Easter; ④). The *Auberge du Point Sublime*, 8km to the east in **ROUGON** (ⓣ04.92.83.60.35, ⓕ04.92.83.74.31; ③), is stunningly situated and not wildly expensive. There's a municipal **campsite**, *Le Grand Canyon*, 800m from the village on the route de Castellane (ⓣ04.92.77.38.13, ⓕ04.92.77.30.87; tent and two people €9.20). If these are full, there are no fewer than five other campsites around the town. Two **gîtes** to try are *L'Étable*, on route des Crêtes in Palud (ⓣ04.92.77.30.63), and *L'Escales*, just outside the village on the Moustiers road (ⓣ04.92.77.30.02; closed Nov–Easter), both offering accommodation for around €30. The *Chalet de la Maline*, on route des Crêtes 8km to the south of La Palud (ⓣ04.92.77.38.05; closed mid-Nov to Easter; €35.15pp half-board), is a mountain refuge run by the Club Alpin Français, and is also a good trailhead from which to start descents into the gorge.

The south side of the gorge: Aiguines and the Falaise des Cavaliers

AIGUINES, perched high above the **Lac de Sainte-Croix** on its eastern side, has a turreted château (not open to the public) and a history of wood-turning – the *boules* for *pétanque* made from ancient boxwood roots used to be its speciality. There's some very expensive and beautiful woodwork, as well as pottery and faïence, to be viewed at the small commercial art gallery opposite the **tourist office** (Mon–Fri 9am–noon & 2–5.30pm; ⓣ04.94.70.21.64, ⓦwww.aiguines.com).

For **rooms**, there's the hotel-restaurant *Le Vieux Château* (ⓣ04.94.70.22.95, ⓦwww.hotelvieuxchateau.fr; ④, half-board compulsory; closed Nov–March), or the rather characterless *Altitude 823* (ⓣ04.98.10.22.17, ⓕ04.98.10.22.16; €54pp half-board compulsory; closed Nov–March). Of the seven **campsites** in the vicinity, *Le Galetas* (Ⓣ04.94.70.20.48; closed mid-Oct to March; €12) is almost within diving distance of the lake, a long way down from the village. However, the best place to stay on the south side – as long as you don't suffer from vertigo – is the *Hôtel du Grand Canyon du Verdon* by the dramatic precipice of the Falaise des Cavaliers (Ⓣ04.94.76.91.31, Ⓕ04.94.76.92.29; ❼; closed Nov–Easter) on the Corniche Sublime, a good 20km from Aiguines, with stunning views. The restaurant serves reasonable food.

West of the gorge: Moustiers-Ste-Marie, Riez and Quinson

The complex traffic management and long lines of parked cars on the approach to **MOUSTIERS-STE-MARIE** tell you all you need to know about the summer popularity of the place: once you reach the village, it's little more than a picturesque setting for a shopping expedition, since almost every house seems to be selling the pastel, pretty Moustiers faïence. But it is *very* picturesque, almost absurdly so: the backdrop of sheer cliffs and the single star suspended high above the village being the sort of view that launched a thousand calendars. You can best escape the shoppers by making the steep ascent to the appropriately named **church of Notre Dame de Beauvoir**, and it's all rather more appealing out of season. Just below the village is celebrity chef Alain Ducasse's luxurious **hotel-restaurant** *La Bastide de Moustiers* (Ⓣ04.92.70.47.47, Ⓦwww.bastide-moustiers.com; ❾), set in a seventeenth-century country house, with menus from €75. It's idyllic, except perhaps when the helicopter pad is in use. A more down-to-earth but just as lovely option is the *chambre d'hôte Clerissy* (Ⓣ04.92.74.62.67, Ⓦwww.clerissy.fr; ❸), place du Chevalier de Blacas, in the centre of the village, which also has a colourful restaurant with a €15 menu.

A more unspoilt village is low-key **RIEZ**, 15km west of Moustiers, where the main business is derived from the lavender fields that cover this corner of Provence. Just over the river on the road south is a lavender distillery making essence for the perfume industry. At the other end of the town, 1km along the road to Digne, is the **Maison de l'Abeille** (House of the Bee), a research and visitors' centre (June–Sept daily 10am–12.30pm & 2.30–7.30pm; Oct–May Tues–Sat 2–6pm; free). Visitors can buy various honeys (including the local speciality, lavender honey) and hydromel – the honey alcohol of antiquity made from nectar – and, if you show interest, you'll get an enthusiastic tour.

In size, Riez is more village than town, but it soon becomes clear that it was once more influential than it is now. Some of the houses on **Grande-Rue** and **rue du Marché** – the two streets above the main allées Louis-Gardiol – have rich Renaissance facades, and the **Hôtel de Ville** on place Quinquonces is a former episcopal palace. The scant remains of the sixth-century **cathedral** (freely visited), which was abandoned 400 years ago, have been excavated just across the river from allées Louis-Gardiol. Much more impressive is the **baptistry** across the road (mid-June to mid-Sept Mon, Tues, Fri & Sat 3–7pm; €2), restored in the nineteenth century but originally constructed, like the cathedral, around 600 AD. If you recross the river and follow it downstream, you'll find the even older and much more startling relics of four **Roman columns** standing in a field.

A rather more strenuous walk, heading first for the clock tower above Grande-Rue and then taking the path past the cemetery and on uphill (leaving the cemetery to your left), brings you to a cedar-shaded platform on the hilltop where the pre-Roman Riezians lived. The only building now occupying the site is the eighteenth-century Chapelle Ste-Maxime, with a gaudily patterned interior.

The **tourist office** is on place de la Marie (July & Aug Mon–Sat 9am–1pm & 3–7pm, Sun 9am–1pm; Sept–June Mon–Fri 8.30am–12.30pm & 1.30–6pm; ⓣ04.92.77.99.09, ⓦwww.ville-riez.fr). For **accommodation**, there's an executive-style hotel on the other side of the river, the *Hôtel Carina* (ⓣ04.92.77.85.43, ⓕ04.92.77.85.44; ❹; closed Nov–Easter), with views and comfort to make up for its lack of character. Alternatively head out of town on the route de Valensole, where 1km off the main road you'll find the excellent-value *Château de Pontfrac* (ⓣ04.92.77.78.77, ⓦwww.chateaudepontfrac.com; ❺), with a swimming pool and access to facilities such as riding stables (bring your own horse). If you want to **eat** in the village and aren't in a rush, try *Le Rempart* on 17 rue du Marché, next to the bell tower (ⓣ04.92.77.89.54); the Provençal and Italian dishes are superb, and a two- to three-hour meal for most diners seems to be the norm. Lunch menus start at €13, dinners from €21.

Some 21km south of Riez along the D11, the village of **QUINSON** marks the start of the Basses Gorges du Verdon, which if you haven't seen the upper gorge will probably strike you as dramatically scenic. The chief attraction here, however, is the **Musée du Préhistoire des Gorges du Verdon**, route de Montmeyan (Feb, March & Oct–Dec daily except Tues 10am–6pm; April–June & Sept daily except Tues 10am–7pm; July & Aug daily 10am–8pm; €7), designed by the British architect Sir Norman Foster in a clean and sympathetic modern style, so that despite its immense size it does not dominate the village. It's the largest museum of human prehistory in Europe, using the latest audio-visual techniques to chart one million years of human habitation in Provence. In addition to the museum itself, there's a themed path leading past reconstructed prehistoric homes to the **cave of Baume Bonne** (guided visits by arrangement), the most important of the sixty or so archeological sites around Quinson. Excavations here have traced human habitation back 400,000 years.

Castellane

Few towns can have as dramatic a setting as **CASTELLANE**, east of the gorge, 12km upstream from La Palud on the Route Napoléon (see opposite), and sitting at the foot of an immense rock face topped by a chapel, **Notre Dame du Roc**. Billed as the "gateway" to the Gorges du Verdon, Castellane's chief business is the servicing of activity-based tourism. Houses in the old part of town huddle together as if seeking protection from the sheer violence of the landscape, with some lanes barely shoulder-wide. There's not a lot to see, so you might as well climb up to the chapel – thirty minutes from behind the modern church. The gorge itself is out of sight, but the view is still worth the trouble.

The **tourist office**, at the top of rue Nationale (July & Aug Mon–Sat 9am–12.30pm & 2–7pm, Sun 10am–12.30pm; Sept–June Mon–Fri 9am–noon & 2–6pm; ⓣ04.92.83.61.14, ⓦwww.castellane.org), can provide a full list of the many **hotels** and campsites in the village and its environs. The *Auberge Bon Accueil* on place Marcel-Sauvaire (ⓣ04.92.83.62.01, ⓦwww.auberge-du-bon-accueil.com; ❸; closed mid-Oct to mid-March) is one of the cheapest, while the three-star *Hôtel du Commerce* on place de l'Église (ⓣ04.92.83.61.00, ⓦwww.hotel-fradet.com; ❹; closed Nov–Feb) is the swanky option, and has a beautiful garden **restaurant** serving amazing Provençal menus from €20 up. The eleven switch-back bends to *Chambres d'Hôtes Chasteuil* (ⓣ04.92.83.72.45, ⓦwww.gitedechasteuil.com; ❸), in a small village by the same name 9km west of Castellane, are well worth it: the six rooms in the old stone school house all have views down the gorge. The closest **campsite** to town, a mere hundred metres off place Marcel-Sauvaire on boulevard Frédéric-Mistral, is *Le Frédéric Mistral* (ⓣ04.92.83.62.27, closed mid-Nov to Feb). Castellane is full of adventure activity specialists offering everything from **canyoning** to **canoeing** on the Lac de Castellane and the Gorges du Verdon. For information, go to Aqua Verdon at 8 rue Nationale (☎04.92.83.72.75), or try Aboard Rafting (☎04.92.83.76.11) on place de l'Église, or Aqua Viva Est (☎04.92.83.75.74) on boulevard de la République, both of which also rent out mountain **bikes**.

The Route Napoléon to Sisteron

North of Castellane, the **Route Napoléon** passes through the barren scrubby rocklands of some of the most obscure and empty parts of Provence. The road was built in the 1930s to commemorate the great leader's journey north through Haute-Provence on return from exile on Elba in 1815, in the most audacious and vain recapture of power in French history. Using mule paths still deep with winter snow, Napoleon and his 700 soldiers forged ahead towards **Digne-les-Bains** and **Sisteron** on their way to Grenoble – a total of 350km – in just six days. One hundred days later, he lost the battle of Waterloo and was permanently incarcerated on the island of St Helena.

At Barrème, the road is joined by the narrow-gauge **Chemin de Fer de la Provence** (see box, p.1179), also known as the Train des Pignes, which runs between Nice and Digne-les-Bains. Other stations on the line are Annot and St-André-les-Alpes; though neither has bus connections with Castellane, the town is connected to both Nice and Marseille by bus. Local tourist offices will have timetables.

Digne-les-Bains

The spa town of **DIGNE-LES-BAINS** is the chief town of the Alpes-de-Haute-Provence *département*, and lies in a superb position between the Durance valley and the start of the real mountains. A retirement town, it bustles by day but is rather lifeless in the evening. The surrounding area has particular attractions for geologists and admirers of Tibet. Covering over 150,000 hectares to the north and east of Dignes, the **Réserve Naturelle Géologique de Haute-Provence** is the largest geological reserve in Europe, with fossils dating back 300 million years. The starting point is the **Musée-Promenade** (April–Oct daily 9am–noon & 2–5.30pm, closes Fri 4.30pm; Nov–March Mon–Fri 9am–noon & 2–5.30pm; €4.60; ☎04.92.36.70.70) just north of the city, down to the left after the bridge across the Bléone on the Barles road, with extremely good videos, workshops and exhibitions on the reserve, and a new gallery of fossilized insects. Themed walks fan out from the museum. A couple of kilometres further along the Barles road you can see, on a bank to your left, a wall of ammonites.

The town's connection with Tibet is through the explorer Alexandra David-Neel, who managed to spend two months in the forbidden city of Lhasa disguised as a beggar in 1924. She spent the last years of her long life in Digne, dying there at the age of 101, and her house, Samten Dzong, at 27 av du Maréchal-Juin, is now home to the **Musée Alexandra David-Neel** (guided visits only; July–Sept at 10am, 2pm, 3.30pm & 4.30pm; Oct–June at 10am, 2pm & 4pm; free), devoted to her memory. The Dalai Lama himself has visited the place twice. Also a cut above the normal is the town's recently renovated municipal museum, the **Musée Gassendi** at 64 bd Gassendi (daily except Tues: April–Sept 11am–7pm; Oct–March 1.30–5.30pm; €4), with some great sixteenth- to nineteenth-century paintings and homages to local seventeenth-century mathematician and savant Pierre Gassendi.

The **tourist office** is on the rond-point du 11-Novembre-1918 (June–Sept Mon–Sat 8.45am–12.30pm & 2–6.30pm, Sun 10am–noon; Oct–May Mon–Sat 8.45am–noon & 2–6pm; ⓣ04.92.36.62.62, ⓦwww.ot-dignelesbains.fr), with the **gare routière** adjacent. The **gare Chemins de Fer de la Provence** is to the west over the river on avenue Pierre-Sémard; there are no longer any passenger trains from the adjacent *gare SNCF*. A very cheap **hotel** option is *Origan*, 6 rue Pied-de-Ville (ⓣ & ⓕ04.92.31.62.13, ⓦwww.origan.fr; ❷), with an excellent **restaurant** which has menus starting at €18 (closed Mon). *Le Grand Paris*, 19 bd Thiers (ⓣ04.92.31.11.15, ⓦwww.hotel-grand-paris.com; ❼; closed Dec–Feb), is considerably more luxurious and also has a good, though expensive, restaurant (closed midday Mon & Tues out of season; €25 lunchtime menu Mon–Sat, otherwise from €41).

Sisteron

The Route Napoléon leads eventually to **SISTERON**, 25km northwest of Digne as the crow flies, and the most important mountain gateway to Provence. The site has been fortified since time immemorial and even now, half destroyed by the Anglo-American bombardment of 1944, its citadel stands as a fearsome sentinel over the city and the solitary bridge across the River Durance.

A visit to the **citadelle** (April–Nov daily 9am–dusk; €5) is highly rewarding, with 360-degree views from the upper rampart, while far below a superbly atmospheric subterranean passage leads down 280 steps to another vantage point, though the door at the bottom is frequently locked. There is a leaflet in English but no guides, just recordings in French attempting to re-create historic moments, such as Napoleon's march, of course, and the imprisonment in 1639 of Jan Kazimierz, the future king of Poland. Most of the extant defences were constructed after the Wars of Religion, and added to a century later by Vauban when Sisteron was a front-line fort against neighbouring Savoy. The eleventh-century castle was destroyed in the mid-thirteenth century during a pogrom against the local Jewish population.

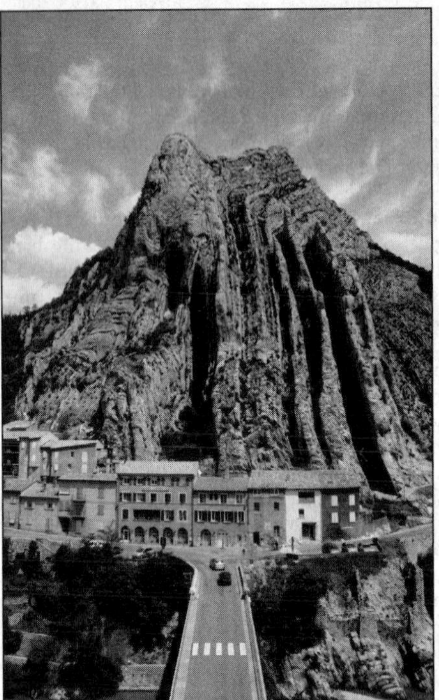

△ Sisteron

In July and August, the festival known as Nuits de la Citadelle has open-air performances of music, drama and dance in the citadel grounds. There is also a small **historical museum** with a room dedicated to Napoleon, and temporary art exhibitions in the vertiginous late-medieval chapel, **Notre-Dame-du-**

Château, restored to its Gothic glory and given very beautiful subdued stained-glass windows in the 1970s.

Back in Sisteron's old town, you'll see three huge **towers**, which belonged to the ramparts built in 1370. Beside them is the **Cathédrale Notre-Dame-des-Pommiers** (daily 3–6pm), a well-proportioned twelfth-century church whose entryway is flanked by marble columns, but whose interior contains nothing of interest. From the cathedral, rue Deleuze leads to **place de l'Horloge**, where the Wednesday and Saturday **market** is held and which, on the second Saturday of every month, hosts a fair. If you fancy a **swim**, there's a large artificial lake between the allée de Verdon and the river.

Practicalities

Arriving by train at Sisteron, turn right out of the **gare SNCF** along avenue de la Libération until you reach place de la République, where you'll find the **tourist office** (July & Aug Mon–Sat 9am–7pm, Sun 10am–noon & 2–5pm; Sept–June Mon–Sat 9am–noon & 2–6pm; Ⓣ04.92.61.12.03, Ⓦwww.sisteron.com) and the **gare routière**. The genteel and old-fashioned *Grand Hôtel du Cours* on allée de Verdon (Ⓣ04.92.61.04.51, Ⓔhotelducours@wanadoo.fr; ❹; closed mid-Nov to mid-March), is the best **hotel** in town. For cheaper rooms, head for *La Citadelle* (see below). Sisteron's four-star **campsite** is across the river and 3km along the D951 (Ⓣ04.92.61.19.69; closed Nov–Feb; €13 for two people and a tent).

The food in Sisteron's **restaurants** is nothing special, though the view down the valley from the terrace of the *Hôtel-Restaurant de la Citadelle*, 126 rue Saunerie, certainly is (Ⓣ06.82.67.80.76, Ⓕ04.92.61.06.39; ❷; menus from €14). *Le Cours*, on the allée de Verdon (Ⓣ04.92.61.00.50), serves copious meals, with the renowned *gigot d'agneau de Sisteron* included on a €20 menu, and you'll find plenty of eating places along rue Saunerie and on the squares around the clock tower. *Le Mondial* **bar**, on the left at the top of rue Droite, stays open late, as does *L'Horloge* on place de l'Horloge.

Northeast Provence

Depending on the season, the **northeastern corner of Provence** is two different worlds. In winter, the sheep and shepherds find warmer pastures, leaving the snowy heights to horned mouflons, chamois and the perfectly camouflaged ermine. The villages where shepherds came to summer markets are battened down for the long, cold haul, while modern conglomerations of Swiss-style chalet houses, sports shops and discotheques come to life around the ski lifts. From November to May many of the mountain road passes are closed, cutting off the dreamy northern town of **Barcelonnette** from its lower neighbours.

In spring, the fruit trees in the narrow valley orchards blossom, and melting waters swell the Vésubie, the Tinée and the Roya, sometimes flooding villages and carrying whole streets away. In summer and early autumn you move from the valleys to the snow-capped peaks through groves of chestnut and olive trees,

NORTHEAST PROVENCE

The Parc National du Mercantour

The **Parc National du Mercantour** is a long, narrow band of mountainland running for 75km close to the Italian border, from south of the town of Barcelonnette almost as far as Sospel, 16km north of the Mediterranean. The area is a haven for wildlife, with colonies of chamois, mouflon, ibex and marmots, breeding pairs of golden eagles and other rare birds of prey, great spotted woodpeckers and hoopoes, blackcocks and ptarmigan. In recent years grey wolves have begun returning to the area from neighbouring Italy, since disappearing in the 1930s. The flora too is very special, with many unique species of lilies, orchids and Alpine plants, including the rare multi-flowering saxifrage.

The park is crossed by numerous paths, including the GR5 and GR52, with *refuge* huts providing basic food and bedding for hikers. For more detailed information, contact the **Maisons du Parc** in Barcelonnette, St-Étienne-de-Tinée or St-Martin-Vésubie, which can provide maps and accommodation details as well as advice on footpaths and weather conditions. Camping, lighting fires, picking flowers, playing radios or doing anything that might disturb the delicate environment is strictly outlawed.

then pine forests edged with wild raspberries and bilberries, up to moors and grassy slopes covered with Alpine flowers.

An uninhabited area of 68,500 hectares along the Italian border has been designated the **Parc National du Mercantour** (see box above). It can be explored from the small towns of **St-Étienne-de-Tinée**, **St-Martin-Vésubie, St-Sauveur-sur-Tinée** and from the **upper Roya valley**, but all the countryside in this mountainous region is breathtaking. To the south, the Italianate town of Sospel is a real delight.

Transport other than by foot or vehicle is a problem. Apart from the Turin–Nice train line down the Roya valley, there are regular bus connections going out from Barcelonnette or from Sospel but they don't meet, and there are only infrequent buses between villages on market days.

Barcelonnette

BARCELONNETTE, at the centre of the **Vallée de L'Ubaye**, is a place of immaculate charm, with snow-capped mountains visible at every turn. It's not very big, and a more ideal spot for doing nothing would be hard to find. The central square, **place Manuel**, has café tables from which to gaze at the blue sky or at the white clock tower commemorating the centenary of the 1848 Revolution. It's close to several ski resorts and to the northern edge of the Parc du Mercantour.

The **Maison du Parc** for the Mercantour (summer only: June 15–30 & Sept 1–15 daily 3–6pm; July & Aug 10am–noon & 3–7pm; ⓣ04.92.81.21.31, ⓦwww.parc-mercantour.com) shares premises at 10 av de la Libération with the **Musée de la Vallée** (June & Sept Tues–Sat 3–6pm; July & Aug 10am–noon & 2.30–7pm; Oct–May groups by arrangement; €3.20), which details the popular emigration to Mexico during the nineteenth century. Barcelonnette is full of Mexican connections (many came back with fortunes); during the August Mexican festival, the **Maison du Mexique**, opposite the Musée de la Vallée, puts on films and exhibitions.

Barcelonnette's **tourist office** is on place Frédéric-Mistral (July & Aug daily 9am–8pm; Sept–June Mon–Sat 9am–noon & 2–6pm; ⓣ04.92.81.04.71, ⓦwww.barcelonnette.com). The best place to **stay** is the Mexican-style

Azteca on rue François-Arnaud (Ⓣ04.92.81.46.36, Ⓦwww.hotel-azteca.fr.st; ❹), closely followed by the *Grande Épervière*, 18 rue des Trois-Frères-Arnaud (Ⓣ04.92.81.00.70, Ⓦwww.hotel-grande-eperviere.com; ❹). *Le Cheval Blanc*, 12 rue Grenette (Ⓣ04.92.81.00.19; ❸), is one of the cheaper options and its restaurant has a menu with local trout for €48. There are three **campsites**, the closest being the three-star *Du Plan* at 52 av E.-Aubert (Ⓣ04.92.81.08.11, Ⓦwww.campingduplan.com; closed late Sept to mid-May; €11.16 for two people and a tent).

The best **restaurant** in the area is 9km east in Jausiers: *Villa Morella* (Ⓣ04.92.84.67.78, Ⓦwww.villa-morelia.com) is a Mexican place serving nouvelle cuisine (menu €60). Back in Barcelonnette, and continuing the South American theme, try the small and atmospheric *L'Argentine* at 4 place St-Pierre (Ⓣ06.22.81.44.35; à la carte from €15) for grilled meats. Be sure also to sample the local juniper liquor, *Genepy*, produced by the distiller La Maison Rousseau at La Fresquière, 10km from Barcelonnette, but generally available in the town on market days. **Nightlife** is limited to the bars *St-Tropez* and *Chocas* on place Manuel. For **Internet** access head to *Le Cyber Truc*, rue Saint-Dominique (Ⓣ04.92.81.57.50).

Barcelonnette to Sospel

The road across the Cime de la Bonette pass (the D64 from Barcelonnette), claimed to be the highest in Europe, reaches over 2800m and gives a feast of high-altitude views, winding past a string of desolate and abandoned bunkers and military outposts. It's only open for three months of the year, from the end of June until September. The air is cold even in summer and the green and silent spaces of the approach to the summit, circled by barren peaks, are magical. There's no transport over the pass, but from Barcelonnette you can take a bus (July & Aug Wed & Fri) to Jausiers at the route's north end, and hike or hitch from there to St-Étienne, from where you can then connect to Nice and points between.

Once over the pass, you descend into the Tinée valley and its highest town, **ST-ÉTIENNE-DE-TINÉE**, which comes to life only during its sheep fairs, held twice every summer, and the Fête de la Transhumance at the end of June. On the west side of the town off boulevard d'Auron, a cable car then chair lift climb to the summit of **La Pinatelle** (€6.90), linking the village to the ski resort of **AURON**. In **summer** a handful of the lifts are open to hikers and mountain bikers (July & Aug; €8.30 day) while in **winter** the 21 lifts and 135km of trails are used by skiers (Dec–April; €26.30 day). Georges Sports 2000 in St-Étienne-de-Tinée (Ⓣ04.93.02.45.95) **rents** bikes in summer and ski equipment in winter.

There are two welcoming **hotel-restaurants** on offer: the *Regalivou*, boulevard d'Auron (Ⓣ & Ⓕ04.93.02.49.00; ❹), and *Des Amis*, 1 rue Val-Gélé (Ⓣ & Ⓕ04.93.02.40.30; ❹). On the edge of the village, you'll find a small **campsite** (summer only, from June 5; Ⓣ04.93.02.41.57) adjacent to the **Maison du Parc** (July & Aug daily 9.30am–noon & 2–6pm; Sept–June Mon, Tues, Thurs & Fri 8.30am–noon, Wed, Sat & Sun 2–6pm; Ⓣ04.93.01.42.27).

The next stretch downstream from St-Étienne has nothing but white quartz and heather, with only the silvery sound of crickets competing with the water's roar before reaching **Isola**, an uneventful village at the bottom of the climb to the purpose-built ski resort of **ISOLA 2000** (Ⓦwww.isola2000.com), a jumble of concrete apartment blocks high in the mountain, built to accommodate skiers using the 22 lifts and 120km of piste (Dec–April; €26.30 day).

After Isola, the road – now the D2205 – and river turn south through the **Gorges de Valabre** to **ST-SAUVEUR-SUR-TINÉE**, a pleasantly sleepy place, with a useful, if pricey, boulangerie on place de la Mairie selling general provisions (daily except Tues 1–4pm). Shifting east to the Vésubie valley, you come to the lovely little town of **ST-MARTIN-VÉSUBIE** where a cobbled, narrow street with a channelled stream runs through the old quarter beneath the overhanging roofs and balconies of Gothic houses. Of the four **hotels**, try *La Bonne Auberge* (Ⓣ04.93.03.20.49, Ⓦwww.labonneauberge06.fr; ❷) or *Edward's et la Châtaigneraie* (Ⓣ04.93.03.21.22, Ⓕ04.93.03.33.99; ❸; closed Oct–May), both on the allées de Verdon. The closest **campsite** is the *Ferme St-Joseph* (Ⓣ04.93.03.20.14; all year), on the route de Nice by the lower bridge over La Madone. The most pleasant **restaurant** in St-Martin is *La Trappa* on place du Marché (closed Dec & Jan; menus €17–22), which serves local dishes. The **tourist office** on place Félix-Faure (July–Aug daily 9am–7pm; Sept–June Mon–Sat 9am–noon & 2.30–6pm, Sun 10am–noon; Ⓣ04.93.03.21.28, Ⓦwww.saintmartinvesubie.fr) provides details on walks and *gîtes/refuges* in the vicinity as well as information on **Alpha** (Ⓦwww.alpha-loup.com; daily 10am–5pm; €9) a wolf reserve, which despite its lack of information and signage in English makes an interesting visit, particularly in spring when you can see newborn puppies from three observation points.

Sospel and the Roya valley

The D2566 from the Vésubie valley crosses the dramatic col de Turini, forming part of the Routes des Grandes Alpes, to join the **Roya valley** at **SOSPEL**, a dreamy Italianate town spanning the gentle River Bévéra. You may find it over-tranquil after the excitements of the high mountains or the flashy speed of the Côte d'Azur, but it can make a pleasant break.

The main street, **avenue Jean-Médecin**, follows the river on its southern bank. The central bridge, the **Vieux Pont**, was built in the eleventh century to link the town centre on the south bank with its suburb across the river. The best approach to the old town is from the eastern place St-Pierre, along the gloomy, deeply shadowed rue St-Pierre. Suddenly it opens up into **place St-Michel**, one of the most beautiful series of peaches-and-cream Baroque facades in all Provence, made up of the **Église St-Michel**, two chapels and several arcaded houses. The road behind the church, rue de l'Abbaye, reached by steps between the chapels, leads up to an ivy-covered **castle** ruin, from which you get a good view of the town. An even better view can be had from the **Fort St-Roch**, part of the ignominious interwar Maginot Line, along chemin de St-Roch, which houses the **Musée de la Résistance**, illustrating the courageous local Resistance movement during World War II (April–June & Oct Sat & Sun 2–6pm; July–Sept Tues–Sun 2–6pm; €5).

The **gare SNCF** is southeast of the town on avenue A.-Borriglione, which becomes avenue des Martyrs-de-la-Résistance, before leading down to the park on place des Platanes opposite place St-Pierre. The **tourist office**, 19 av Jean-Médecin (Mon 2.30–5.30pm, Tues–Sat 9.30am–12.30pm & 2.30–5.30pm, Sun 9.30am–12.30pm; Ⓣ04.93.04.15.80, Ⓦwww.sospel-tourisme.com). If you want to **stay**, the *Hôtel de France*, 9 bd de Verdun (Ⓣ04.93.04.00.01, Ⓕ04.93.04.20.46; ❹), and the *Auberge Provençale*, on route du Col de Castillon, 1500m uphill from the town (Ⓣ04.93.04.00.31, Ⓦwww.aubergeprovencale.fr; ❼), offer comparable quality, the latter with a pleasant garden and terrace from which to admire the town. There are three **campsites** around Sospel, the closest of which is *Le Mas Fleuri* in quartier La Vasta (Ⓣ04.93.04.03.48, Ⓦwww.camping-mas-fleuri.com;

all year; €14.50 for two people and a tent), with its own pool, 2km along the D2566 to Moulinet, following the river upstream.

There are various **eating** places along avenue Jean-Médecin. Alternatively, try *Relais du Sel*, 3 bd de Verdun (ⓣ04.93.04.00.43; closed Thurs & Nov), just across the eastern bridge, where you can eat for €20–30 on a terrace above the river.

The upper Roya valley

One of the strangest sights in the Provençal Alps is best approached from **ST-DALMAS-DE-TENDE** in the upper Roya valley, three stops on the train from Sospel. The first person to stumble upon the lakes and tumbled rocks of the **Vallée des Merveilles**, on the western flank of Mont Bego, was a fifteenth-century traveller who had lost his way. He described it as "an infernal place with figures of the devil and thousands of demons scratched on the rocks": a pretty accurate description, except that some of the carvings are of animals, tools, people working and mysterious symbols, dated to some time in the second millennium BC.

The easiest route into the valley is the ten-kilometre hike (5–7hr there and back) that starts at *Les Mesches Refuge*, about 8km west of St-Dalmas-de-Tende, on the D91. The engravings are beyond the *Refuge des Merveilles*. Note that certain areas are out of bounds unless accompanied by an official guide – and remember that blue skies and sun can quickly turn into violent hailstorms and lightning, so go prepared, properly shod and clothed, and take your own food and water. **Guided walks** depart from the *refuge* and last between 2hr 30min and 3hr 30min (June, Sept & Oct weekends only, 8am & 1pm; July–Aug daily 8am, 11am, 1pm, 3pm; €8; contact Maison du Parc in Tende ⓣ04.93.04.67.00 or local tourist offices; one guide speaks English).

St-Dalmas is the nearest town to the Vallée des Merveilles and has a reasonably priced **hotel** on rue des Martyrs-de-la-Résistance, the *Terminus* (ⓣ04.93.04.96.96, ⓦwww.hoterminus.fr; ❸), named after the large abandoned station opposite, built by Mussolini to transport salt from the mountains.

LA BRIGUE, one stop up the line from St-Dalmas-de-Tende, is a good base for the Vallée des Merveilles, with some good-value hotels. While you're here, make the trip 4km east of town to the sanctuary of **Notre-Dame-des-Fontaines**, whose frescoes were executed by one Jean Canavéso at around the same time as the anonymous fifteenth-century traveller was freaking out about the demons of the Vallée des Merveilles. The frescoes, which cover the entire building, are akin to an arcade of video nasties. The goriest detail is a devil extracting Judas's soul from his disembowelled innards. The chapel is open in the summer (June–Sept daily except Tues 10am–noon & 2–5.30pm; closed Thurs afternoon; €1.50), and in the winter you can visit it with a guide from the **tourist office** on place St-Martin (summer daily 9am–12.30pm & 1.30–5pm; winter Tues–Sat 9.30am–12.30pm & 1.30–4.30pm; ⓣ04.93.04.60.04, ⓦwww.labrigue-tourisme.org; closed mid-Jan to mid-Feb). The three **hotels** in La Brigue are: *Le Mirval*, rue Vincent-Ferrier (ⓣ04.93.04.63.71, ⓦwww.lemirval.com; ❹); *Auberge St-Martin* (ⓣ04.93.04.62.17, ⓦwww.auberge-st-martin.fr; closed mid-Nov to Feb; ❸) and the *Fleurs des Alpes* (ⓣ04.93.04.61.05, ⓕ04.93.04.59.68; ❸), both on place St-Martin.

One more stop north on the train line brings you to **TENDE**, where the French spoken has a distinctly Italian accent. If you've missed the Vallée des Merveilles engravings you can see them reproduced outside the beautifully designed **Musée des Merveilles** on avenue du 16-Septembre-1947 (May to mid-Oct daily 10am–6.30pm; mid-Oct to April daily except Tues 10am–5pm;

€4.57), a very contemporary museum covering the wildlife, prehistory and geology of the region. That apart, the old town is fun to wander through, looking at the symbols of old trades on the door lintels, the overhanging roofs and multiple balconies. The **tourist office** is at 103 16-Septembre-1947 (May–Sept Mon–Sat 9am–12.30pm & 2–6pm; Oct–April Mon–Sat 9am–noon & 2–5.30pm; ⓣ04.93.04.73.71, ⓦwww.tendemerveilles.com). For **accommodation**, there's the basic *Du Centre* on place de la République (ⓣ04.93.04.62.19; ❷; closed Nov–March). Tende has plenty of shops and restaurants, though nothing very special on the gourmet front.

Travel details

Trains

Aix-en-Provence to: Briançon (2–3 daily; 3hr 40min); Marseille (every 30min; 30–45min); Sisteron (3–4 daily; 1hr 20min).

Aix-en-Provence TGV to: Avignon TGV (15 daily; 25min); Lille-Europe (3 daily; 5hr); Lyon (10 daily; 1hr 25min); Marseille (12 daily; 15min); Paris (10 daily; 3hr); Paris CDG Airport (3 daily; 3hr 20min); Valence TGV (6 daily; 1hr).

Arles to: Avignon (11–16 daily; 20min); Avignon TGV (4 daily; 40min); Lyon (9 daily; 2hr 45min); Marseille (frequent; 45min–1hr).

Avignon to: Arles (hourly; 20–45min); Cavaillon (9–14 daily; 30min); Lyon (8–11 daily; 2hr 20min); Marseille (4–13 daily; 1hr 20min); Orange (every 15min–1hr; 15–25min); Valence (half-hourly at peak times; 1hr 25min).

Avignon TGV to: Aix-en-Provence TGV (9 daily; 25min); Lille-Europe (5 daily; 4hr 30min); Lyon (13 daily; 1hr 30min); Marseille (12 daily; 30min); Paris (8 daily; 2hr 40min); Paris CDG Airport (6 daily; 3hr 30min); Valence TGV (9 daily; 30–40min).

Digne to: Nice (4 daily; 3hr 20min).

Lyon (La Part-Dieu or Perrache) to: Annecy (8 daily; 2hr 15min); Arles (9 daily; 2hr 45min); Avignon (11 daily; 2hr 20min); Avignon TGV (13 daily; 1hr 30min); Bourg-en-Bresse (8–14 daily; 50min–1hr 15min); Clermont-Ferrand (5–8 daily; 3hr); Dijon (13–18 daily; 2hr); Grenoble (16–21 daily; 1hr 15min–2hr); Lille-Europe (9 daily; 3hr 10min); Marseille (every 2hr; 2hr 10min–3hr 45min); Montélimar (9 daily; 1hr 35min); Orange (8 daily; 2hr 5min); Paris (hourly; 2hr); Paris CDG Airport (8 daily; 2hr 10min); Roanne (hourly; 1hr 30min); St-Étienne (hourly, more frequent at peak times; 45min–1hr); Tain l'Hermitage (hourly; 1hr); Valence (hourly; 1hr 5min); Valence TGV (11–18 daily; 35min); Vienne (frequent; 20min).

Lyon St-Exupéry TGV to: Paris (5 daily; 1hr 50min).

Sospel to: La Brigue (1–3 daily; 40min); Nice (5–6 daily; 50min); St-Dalmas-de-Tende (3 daily; 40min); Tende (3 daily; 50min).

Valence to: Briançon (3–4 daily; 4hr); Die (3–5 daily; 1hr 10min); Gap (3–5 daily; 2hr 30min); Grenoble (18–20 daily; 1hr 15min–1hr 40min); Lyon (hourly; 1hr 5min); Montélimar (frequent: approx hourly at peak times; 30min), Tain l'Hermitage (frequent; 12min).

Valence TGV to: Aix-en-Provence TGV (6 daily; 1hr); Avignon TGV (9 daily; 35min); Lyon (11–18 daily; 35min); Marseille (13 daily; 1hr 10min); Paris (9 daily; 2hr 10min).

Vienne to: Lyon (frequent; 20–30min); Valence (frequent; 50min).

Buses

Aix-en-Provence to: Apt (2 daily; 1hr 55min); Arles (6 daily; 1hr 30min); Avignon (10 daily; 1hr 15min); Barcelonnette (1 daily; 3hr 5min); Carpentras (2 daily; 1hr 40min); Cavaillon (2 daily; 1hr); Draguignan (2 daily; 2hr 55min); Les Baux (1 daily; 1hr 10min); Marseille (frequent; 30–50min); Sisteron (2–4 daily; 2hr); Vauvenargues (2–7 daily; 30min).

Arles to: Aix (5 daily; 1hr 15min); Avignon (5 daily; 50min); Avignon TGV (5 daily; 35–40min); Cavaillon (3 daily; 1hr 15min); Stes-Maries-de-la-Mer (6 daily; 50min); St-Rémy (3 daily; 25–30min).

Aups to: Aiguines (2 daily; 35min); Cotignac (1 daily; 20–25min); Draguignan (1 daily; 40min–1hr).

Avignon to: Aix (10 daily; 1hr 15min); Apt (6 daily; 1hr 10min–1hr 30min); Arles (5 daily; 50min); Carpentras (frequent; 35–45min); Cavaillon (frequent; 35min); Châteauneuf-du-Pape (3 daily; 30–45min); Digne (3–4 daily; 3hr 10min);

Fontaine-de-Vaucluse (10 daily; 55min); L'Isle-sur-la-Sorgue (19 daily; 40min); Les Baux (8 daily; 45min); Orange (Mon–Fri every 30–45min, Sun 5 trains; 45min); St-Rémy (10 daily; 40min); Vaison (10 daily; 1hr 25min).
Barcelonnette to: Digne (1 daily; 1hr 45min); Gap (3 daily; 1hr 20min); Marseille (4 daily; 3hr 50min).
Carpentras to: Aix (2–3 daily; 1hr 25min–1hr 50min); Avignon (frequent; 35–45min); Beaumes (1 daily; 20min); Cavaillon (2–4 daily; 45min); Gigondas (1 daily; 30min); L'Isle-sur-la-Sorgue (2–3 daily; 20min); Marseille (3 daily; 1hr 15min–2hr 5min); Orange (4–5 daily; 40–45min); Sablet (1 daily; 35min); Vacqueyras (1 daily; 30min); Vaison (2–3 daily; 45min).
Cavaillon to: Gordes (3–4 daily; 25–30min).
Digne to: Aix (4 daily; 2hr); Aups (2 daily; 30–40min); Avignon (3 daily; 3hr 15min); Barcelonnette (1 daily; 1hr 30min); Castellane (1 daily; 1hr 10min); Grenoble (1 daily; 4hr 50min); Marseille (4 daily; 2hr–2hr 30min); Moustiers-Ste-Marie (1daily; 1hr 20min); Nice (4 daily; 3hr–3hr 15min); Sisteron (1 daily; 45–50min).
Draguignan to: Aups (2–3 daily; 1hr 10min); Nice airport (4 daily; 1hr).
Gordes to: Cavaillon (3 daily; 30–35min).
Lyon to: St-Martin-en-Haut (2–9 daily; 55min); Vienne (2 daily; 40min–1hr 20min).
Orange to: Avignon (Mon–Sat hourly; Sun 5 trains; 50min); Carpentras (4–5 daily; 40–45min); Châteauneuf-du-Pape (1–5 daily; 25min); Sablet (1–3 daily; 35min); Seguret (2 daily; 40min); Sérignan (3 daily; 20min); Vaison (2 daily; 40–50min).
St-Rémy to: Les Baux (2 daily; 15–20min).
Sospel to: Menton (9 daily; 40–45min).

15

The Côte d'Azur

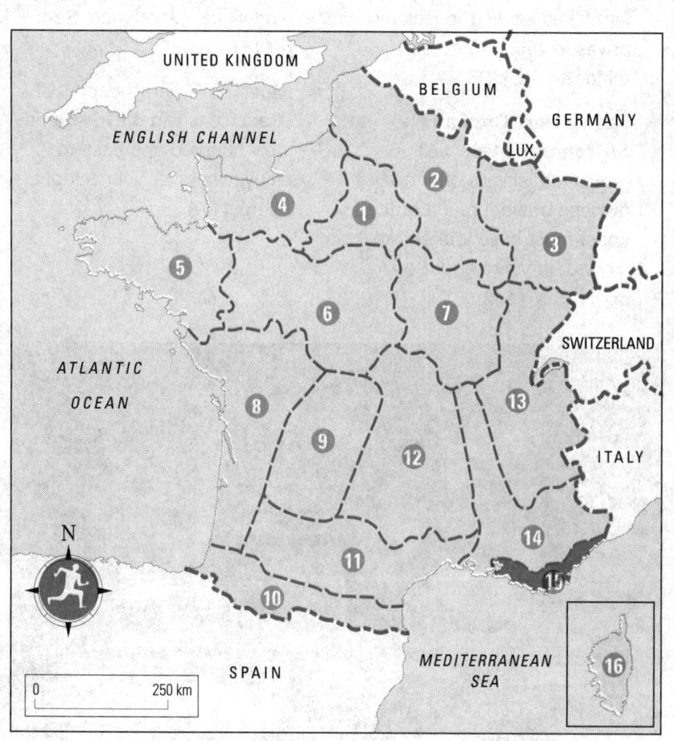

CHAPTER 15

Highlights

* **Vieux Port, Marseille** The gritty port, with its bars, cafés and restaurants, attracts the most colourful characters in southern France. See p.1127

* **Les Calanques** The limestone cliffs between Marseille and Cassis make for excellent hikes leading to isolated coves in which to go swimming. See p.1136

* **Îles de Port-Cros and St-Honorat** These well-preserved islands offer a glimpse of what much of the coast must have looked like a hundred years ago. See pp.1145 & 1168

* **Massif des Maures** This undeveloped range of hazy coastal hills is a world apart from the glitz and glamour of the Côte. See p.1148

* **Fondation Maeght** Modern art, architecture and landscape fuse to create a stunning visual experience. See p.1177

* **Nice** The Riviera's capital of street life is laid back, surprisingly cultured and easy to enjoy, whatever your budget. See p.1178

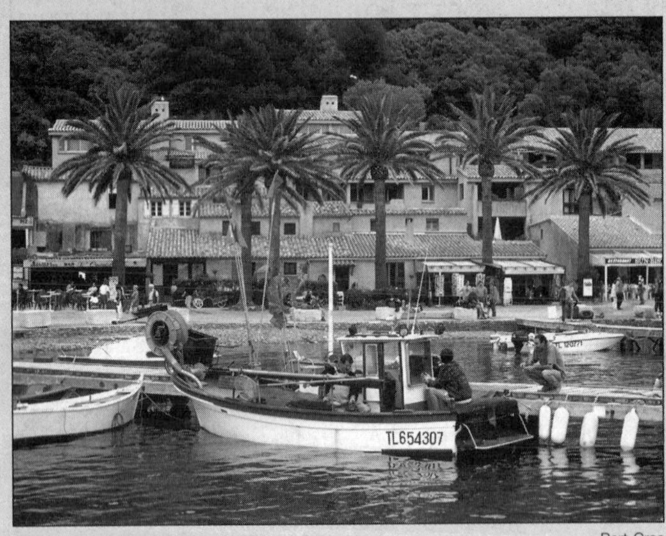

△ Port-Cros

15

The Côte d'Azur

The **Côte d'Azur** polarizes opinions like few other places in France. For some, it is the quintessential Mediterranean playground – the glamour queen of the coast – while for others, it has become almost a parody of its image, an overdeveloped and expensive victim of its own hype. But in the gaps between the uncontrolled and often eclectic developments, and on the offshore islands, in the remarkable beauty of the hills, the scent of the plant life, the mimosa blossom in February and the impossibly blue water after which the coast is named, the Côte d'Azur remains undeniably captivating. The chance to

Food and wine of the Côte d'Azur

The **Côte d'Azur**, as part of Provence, shares its culinary fundamentals of olive oil, garlic and the herbs that flourish in dry soil, its gorgeous vegetables and fruits, plus Menton's lemons, the goat's cheeses and, of course, the predominance of fish.

The fish soups of **bouillabaisse**, famous in Marseille, and **bourride**, served with a garlic and chilli-flavoured mayonnaise known as *rouille*, are served all along the coast, as are **fish** covered with Provençal herbs and grilled over an open flame. **Seafood** – from spider crabs to clams, sea urchins to crayfish, crabs, lobster, mussels and oysters – are piled onto huge *plateaux de mer*, which don't necessarily represent Mediterranean harvest, more the luxury associated with this coast.

The **Italian influence** is even stronger on the coast than it is inland, particularly in Nice, with delicate ravioli stuffed with asparagus, prawns, wild mushrooms or *pistou*, pizzas with wafer-thin bases and every sort of pasta as a vehicle for anchovies, olives, garlic and tomatoes. **Nice** has its own specialities, such as *socca*, a chickpea flour pancake, *pissaladière*, a tart of fried onions with anchovies and black olives, *salade niçoise* and *pan bagnat*, which combines egg, olives, salad, tuna and olive oil, and *mesclum*, a salad of bitter leaves including dandelion: consequently, Nice is about as good a spot to enjoy cheap street food as you'll find. *Petits farcies* – stuffed aubergines, peppers or tomatoes – are a standard feature on Côte d'Azur menus, as well as in inland Provence.

The Italian **dessert** tiramisu, made of mascarpone cheese, chocolate and cream, appears in Nice, while St-Tropez has its own sweet speciality in the sickly *tarte Tropezienne*. The sweet chestnuts that grow in the Massif des Maures are candied or turned into purée. Outlets for ice cream and sorbets are ubiquitous.

As for **wine**, the rosés of Provence might not have great status in the viniculture hierarchy, but for baking summer days they are hard to beat. The best of the Côte wines come from Bandol: Cassis too has its own *appellation*, and around Nice the Bellet wines are worth discovering. Fancy cocktails are a Côte speciality, and *pastis* is the preferred thirst quencher at any time of the day.

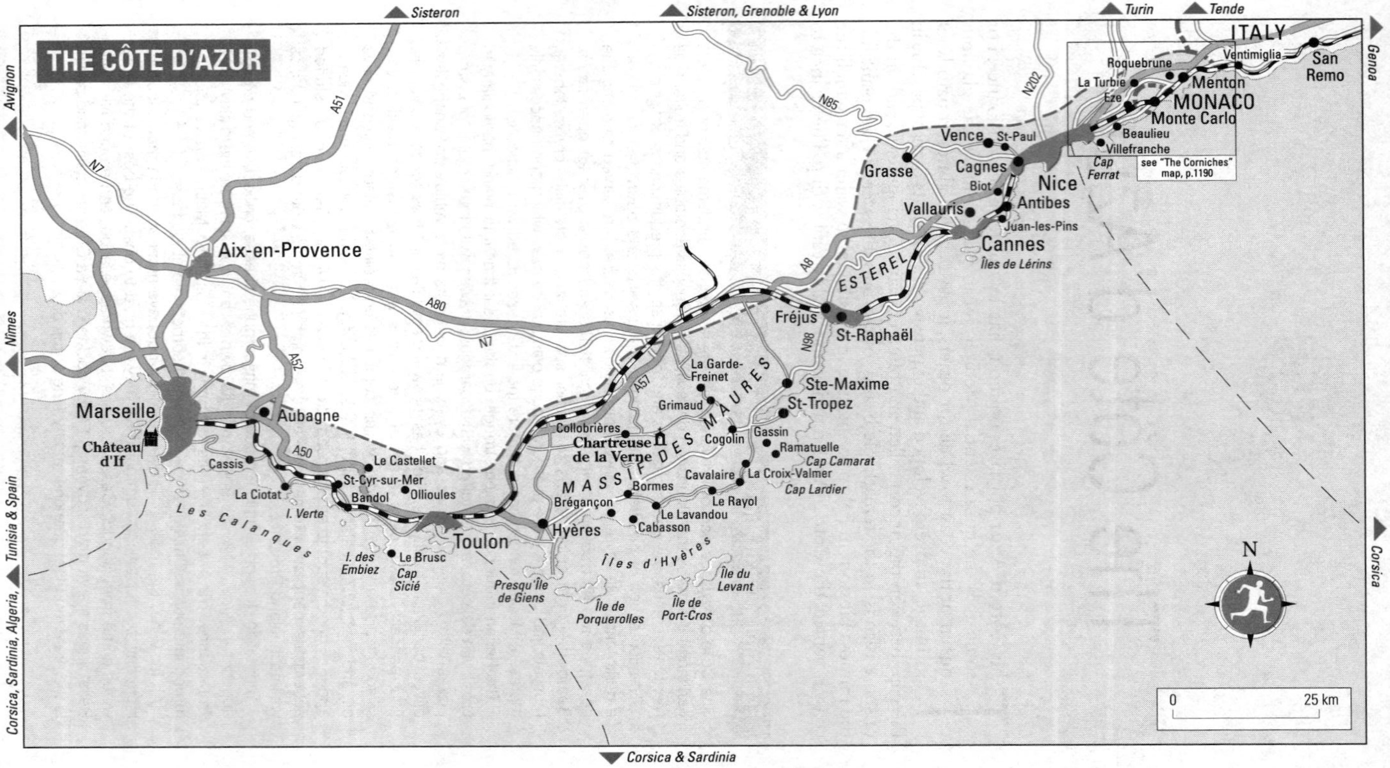

THE CÔTE D'AZUR

Sisteron
Sisteron, Grenoble & Lyon
Turin
Tende
Genoa
Avignon
Nîmes
Corsica, Sardinia, Algeria, Tunisia & Spain
Corsica & Sardinia
Corsica
ITALY
Ventimiglia
San Remo
Roquebrune
La Turbie
Menton
Èze
MONACO
Monte Carlo
Beaulieu
Villefranche
Cap Ferrat
see "The Corniches" map, p.1190
Vence
St-Paul
Grasse
Cagnes
Nice
Biot
Antibes
Vallauris
Juan-les-Pins
Cannes
Îles de Lérins
ESTEREL
N85
N202
A51
N7
A80
A8
A52
A57
A50
N98
Aix-en-Provence
Fréjus
St-Raphaël
Ste-Maxime
St-Tropez
La Garde-Freinet
Grimaud
MASSIF DES MAURES
Collobrières
Chartreuse de la Verne
Cogolin
Gassin
Ramatuelle
Cap Camarat
Cavalaire
La Croix-Valmer
Cap Lardier
Bormes
Le Rayol
Brégançon
Le Lavandou
Cabasson
Marseille
Aubagne
Château d'If
Cassis
Le Castellet
St-Cyr-sur-Mer
La Ciotat
Bandol
Ollioules
Les Calanques
I. Verte
Toulon
Hyères
I. des Embiez
Le Brusc
Cap Sicié
Presqu'Île de Giens
Îles d'Hyères
Île de Porquerolles
Île de Port-Cros
Île du Levant
N
0
25 km

see the works of innumerable artists seduced by the land and light also justifies the trip: Cocteau in **Menton** and **Villefranche**, Matisse and Chagall in **Nice** and **Vence**, Léger in **Biot**, Picasso in **Antibes** and **Vallauris**, and collections of Fauvists and Impressionists at St-Tropez and Hauts-de-Cagnes. And it must be said that **Monaco** and **Cannes**, places you either love or hate, certainly have an entertainment value, while the two great cities of **Marseille** and Nice possess their own special magnetism.

The months to try to avoid are July and August, when hotels are booked up, overflowing campsites become health hazards, the locals get short-tempered, and the vegetation is at its most barren, and November, when many museums, hotels and restaurants close and the weather is wet.

From Marseille to Toulon

From the vast and wonderful scruffiness of **Marseille** to the utilitarian naval base of **Toulon**, this stretch of the Mediterranean is not what most people think of as the Côte d'Azur. There is no continuous corniche, few villas are in the grand style, and work is geared to an annual rather than summer cycle. **Cassis** is the exception, but the overriding attraction here is Marseille – a city that couldn't be confused with any other.

Marseille

The most renowned and populated city in France after Paris, **MARSEILLE** has prospered and been ransacked over the centuries. It has lost its privileges to sundry French kings and foreign armies, recovered its fortunes, suffered plagues, religious bigotry, republican and royalist Terror and had its own Commune and Bastille-storming. It was the presence of so many Marseillaise revolutionaries marching from the Rhine to Paris in 1792 that gave the *Hymn of the Army of the Rhine* its name of *La Marseillaise*, later to become the national anthem.

In recent years Marseille has undergone something of a renaissance, shaking off much of its old reputation for sleaze and danger – the crime rate is actually lower than in Nice – to attract a wider range of visitors. The TGV link has made it more accessible to weekending northerners, who can be seen picking up their hire cars at the *gare St-Charles* on Friday nights. Slowly, the splendid facades along La Canebière are getting scrubbed, and the shops in the streets to the south are increasingly trendy or elegant. But the march of progress is not relentless: too often last year's prestige civic project becomes this year's broken, bottle-strewn fountain. A detachment of the city's prostitutes and vagrants has colonized the intersection of rue St-Saëns and rue Glandevès, a few paces from the elegant opera house and the touristy restaurants of the Vieux Port. But that's Marseille. If you don't like your cities gritty, it may not be for you. See past its occasional squalor though, and chances are you will warm to this down-to-earth, cosmopolitan, vital metropolis.

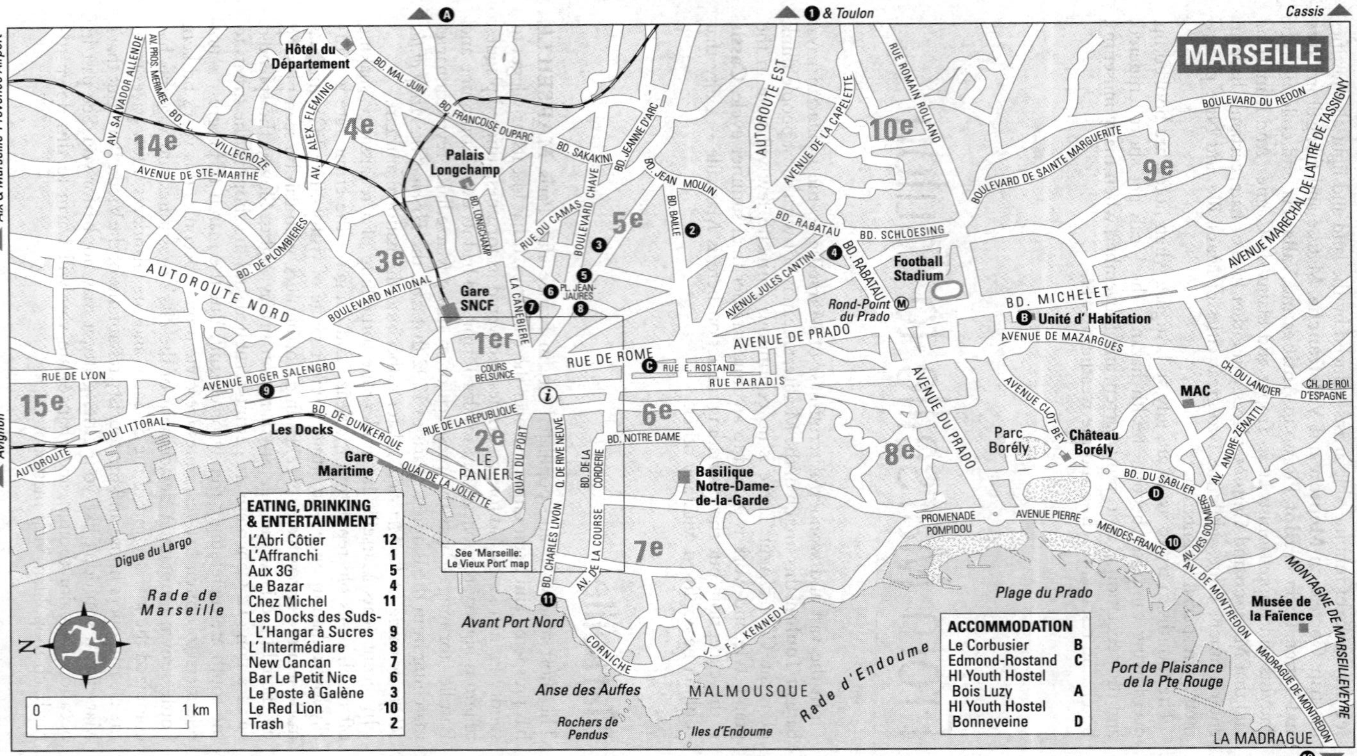
MARSEILLE
Cassis
1 & Toulon
A
Aix & Marseille-Provence Airport
Avignon
12
Hôtel du Département
Palais Longchamp
Gare SNCF
Gare Maritime
Les Docks
Football Stadium
Rond-Point du Prado
Unité d' Habitation
MAC
Parc Borély
Château Borély
Basilique Notre-Dame-de-la-Garde
Musée de la Faïence
LE PANIER
Plage du Prado
Port de Plaisance de la Pte Rouge
Avant Port Nord
Anse des Auffes
MALMOUSQUE
Rade d'Endoume
Rochers de Pendus
Iles d'Endoume
Rade de Marseille
Digue du Largo
LA MADRAGUE
See 'Marseille: Le Vieux Port' map
1er
2e
3e
4e
5e
6e
7e
8e
9e
10e
14e
15e
AUTOROUTE NORD
AUTOROUTE EST
AVENUE DU PRADO
AVENUE DE PRADO
RUE DE ROME
RUE PARADIS
BD. MICHELET
AVENUE DE MAZARGUES
LA CANEBIÈRE
BOULEVARD NATIONAL
BOULEVARD CHAVE
RUE DU CAMAS
BD. LONGCHAMP
BD. FRANCOISE DUPARC
BD. SAKAKINI
BD. JEANNE D'ARC
BD. JEAN MOULIN
BD. BAILLE
BD. RABATAU
BD. SCHLOESING
AVENUE JULES CANTINI
AVENUE DE LA CAPELETTE
RUE ROMAIN ROLLAND
BOULEVARD DE SAINTE MARGUERITE
BOULEVARD DU REDON
AVENUE MARECHAL DE LATTRE DE TASSIGNY
CH. DU LANCIER
CH. DE ROI D'ESPAGNE
AVENUE CLOT BEY
AV. ANDRE ZENATTI
BD. DU SABLIER
AV. DES GOUMIERS
AVENUE PIERRE MENDES-FRANCE
PROMENADE POMPIDOU
AV. DE MONTREDON
MADRAGUE DE MONTREDON
MONTAGNE DE MARSEILLEVEYRE
J. - F. - KENNEDY
CORNICHE
AV. DE LA COURSE
BD. CHARLES LIVON
Q. DE RIVE NEUVE
BD. DE LA CORDERIE
BD. NOTRE DAME
QUAI DU PORT
RUE DE LA REPUBLIQUE
COURS BELSUNCE
RUE E. ROSTAND
PL. JEAN-JAURES
QUAI DE LA JOLIETTE
BD. DE DUNKERQUE
AVENUE ROGER SALENGRO
RUE DE LYON
DU LITTORAL
AUTOROUTE
BD. DE PLOMBIERES
AVENUE DE STE-MARTHE
VILLECROZE
BD. L.
AV. ALEX. FLEMING
BD. MAL. JUIN
AV. PROS. MERIMEE
AV. SALVADOR ALLENDE
N
0
1 km
EATING, DRINKING & ENTERTAINMENT
L'Abri Côtier 12
L'Affranchi 1
Aux 3G 5
Le Bazar 4
Chez Michel 11
Les Docks des Suds-L'Hangar à Sucres 9
L' Intermédiare 8
New Cancan 7
Bar Le Petit Nice 6
Le Poste à Galène 3
Le Red Lion 10
Trash 2
ACCOMMODATION
Le Corbusier B
Edmond-Rostand C
HI Youth Hostel Bois Luzy A
HI Youth Hostel Bonneveine D

The Grand Mosque

Immediately following his re-election in 2001 as the mayor of Marseille, **Jean-Claude Gaudin** promised the construction of a **Grande Mosquée and Islamic Cultural Centre** for the Muslim community, who account for approximately one quarter of the city's inhabitants. The proposal was long overdue; requests for an official mosque dated back to Gaudin's initial election in 1995, and the places of worship that currently existed for Muslims were often nothing more than simple prayer rooms in suburban housing projects. Although Gaudin was not always supportive of the idea – he once replied that he was definitely in favour of the construction of the mosque, "but in Marrakech" – an almost equally intractable obstacle proved to be the lack of unity in the Muslim population, who come from backgrounds as culturally and geographically diverse as Algeria and Comoros, and who are divided between various moderate and radical factions. For want of any consensus, the grand mosque plan was shelved. Gaudin's stance changed during his second term of office, and finally, in July 2006 the Conseil Municipal voted with near unanimity to grant a 99-year lease on a site in the 15e arrondissement for the Grand Mosque, which will be capable of accommodating 5000 worshippers.

Arrival, information and city transport

The city's **airport**, the Aéroport de Marseille-Provence (Ⓣ04.42.14.14.14, Ⓦwww.marseille.aeroport.fr), is 20km northwest of the city centre, linked to the *gare SNCF* by a shuttle bus service (every 20min 6am–10.50pm; later buses meet flights; €8.50). The **gare SNCF St-Charles** is on the northern edge of the 1er arrondissement on esplanade St-Charles (Ⓣ08.91.02.40.25) with the new **gare routière** alongside it at 3 rue Honnorat (Ⓣ08.91.02.40.25). From the *gare SNCF*, a monumental Art Deco staircase leads down to boulevard d'Athènes and thence to La Canebière, Marseille's main street. The **tourist office** is at 4 La Canebière (Mon–Sat 9am–7pm, Sun & public hols 10am–5pm; Ⓣ04.91.13.89.00, Ⓦwww.marseille-tourisme.com), down by the Vieux Port.

Marseille has an efficient **bus** and **métro** network, supplemented by two new **tram** lines scheduled to open during 2007. The métro runs from 5am until 9pm on weekdays and until after midnight at weekends; night buses run from 9.30pm to around 12.45am. You can get a plan of the transport system from RTM at 6 rue des Fabres (Mon–Fri 8.30am–6pm, Sat 9am–12.30pm & 2–5.30pm; Ⓦwww.rtm.fr), one street north of La Canebière near the Bourse, the city's stock exchange. **Tickets** are flat rate for buses, trams and the métro and can be used for journeys combining all three as long as they take less than one hour. You can buy individual tickets (€1.70) from bus and tram drivers, and from métro ticket offices, or **multi-journey** *Cartes Libertés* (in increments of €6 and €12), which are valid for five and ten journeys respectively; these can be bought from métro stations, RTM kiosks and shops displaying the RTM sign. You should also consider the good-value one-day *Carte Journée* (€4.50) or three-day *Carte 3 Jours* (€6). Tickets must be punched in the machines on the bus, on tramway platforms or at métro gates.

Accommodation

Since Marseille is not a great tourist city, **finding a room** in July or August is no more difficult than at any other time. Hotels are plentiful, though if you get stuck the tourist office offers a same-day **accommodation hotline**, Allotel (Ⓣ08.26.88.68.26; premium rates apply). The cheapest options are the city's **hostels**, both quite a way from the centre.

Hotels

Alizé 35 quai des Belges, 1er ⓣ04.91.33.66.97, ⓦwww.alize-hotel.com. Comfortable, bright, soundproofed rooms; the more expensive ones look out onto the Vieux Port. Public areas are a little gloomy, however. ❺

Athènes 37 bd d'Athènes, 1er ⓣ04.91.90.03.83. Right next to the train and bus stations; thin on charm but with rock-bottom prices, and a few rooms have balconies. ❶

Le Béarn 63 rue Sylvabelle, 6e ⓣ04.91.37.75.83, ⓦwww.hotel-bearn.com. Comfortable, friendly, inexpensive and close to the centre, if a bit shabby. ❷

Bellevue 34 quai du Port, 2e ⓣ04.96.17.05.40, ⓕ04.96.17.05.41. Boutique-style hotel on the port, with chic modern decor and good prices but no lift. ❻

Le Corbusier Unité d'Habitation, 280 bd Michelet, 8e ⓣ04.91.16.78.00, ⓦwww.hotel-lecorbusier.com. Stylish hotel on the third floor of the renowned architect's iconic high-rise; book in advance. ❹

Edmond-Rostand 31 rue Dragon, 6e ⓣ04.91.37.74.95, ⓦwww.hoteledmondrostand.com. Helpful management, great charm and atmosphere, and well known, so you should book in advance. ❹

Etap Hotel Vieux Port 46 rue Sainte, 1er ⓣ08.92.68.05.82, ⓦwww.etaphotel.com. Big branch of the comfortable budget chain in a superb location close to the Vieux Port. ❸

Lutétia 38 allée Léon-Gambetta, 1er ⓣ04.91.50.81.78, ⓦwww.hotelmarseille.com. Right in the thick of things with pleasant, soundproofed and a/c rooms. ❹

Du Palais 26 rue Breteuil 6e ⓣ04.91.37.78.86, ⓦwww.hotelmarseille.com. Very smart three-star in a great location a short walk from the Vieux Port. ❺

St Ferréol 19 rue Pisançon, cnr rue St-Ferréol, 1er ⓣ04.91.33.12.21, ⓦwww.hotel-stferreol.com. Pretty decor and marble baths with Jacuzzis, in a central pedestrianized area. Popular with gay visitors. ❻

Tonic 43 quai des Belges, 1er ⓣ04.91.55.67.46, ⓦwww.tonichotel.com. Smart and modern with a great port-side location close to the restaurants. ❼

Hostels

HI Youth Hostel 76 allée des Primevères, 12e ⓣ04.91.49.06.18, ⓦwww.fuaj.org. Bus #8 from Centre Bourse (direction "St-Julien", stop "Bois Luzy"). Cheap, clean youth hostel in a former château a long way out from the centre. Curfew 11pm. Reception 7.30–noon & 5–10.30pm. Dormitory bed €9.50.

HI Youth Hostel Bonneveine impasse Bonfils, av J.-Vidal, 8e ⓣ04.91.17.63.30, ⓦwww.fuaj.org. Mo Rd-Pt-du-Prado, then bus #44 (direction "Roy d'Espagne", stop "Place Bonnefon") or night bus #583 from Vieux Port. Recently renovated hostel just 200m from the beach, with Internet access. Reception 7am–1am, curfew at 1am. Closed mid-Dec to mid-Jan.

The City

Marseille is divided into fifteen arrondissements which spiral out from the focal point of the city, the **Vieux Port**. Due north lies the old town, **Le Panier**, site of the original Greek settlement of Massalia, and beyond that the rapidly regenerating area of **Les Docks**. The wide boulevard leading from the head of the Vieux Port, La Canebière is the central east–west axis of the town. The **Centre Bourse** and the little streets of **quartier Belsunce** border it to the north, while the main shopping streets lie to the south. The main north–south axis is **rue d'Aix**, becoming cours Belsunce then rue de Rome, avenue du Prado and finally boulevard Michelet. The lively, youngish quarter around place Jean-Jaurès and the trendy cours Julien lies to the east of rue de Rome. From

Marseille City Pass

If you're going to be visiting several of Marseille's museums it may be worth considering the **Marseille City Pass**, which for €18 or €25 for one or two days respectively includes free admission to museums, city guided tours, entry to the Château d'If and free use of the métro and bus system.

the headland west of the Vieux Port, the **corniche** heads south past the city's most favoured residential districts towards the **beaches** and promenade night-life of the **Plage du Prado**.

The Vieux Port

The cafés around the east end of the **Vieux Port** indulge the sedentary pleasures of observing street life, despite the fumes of exhausts and of fish sold straight off the boats on quai des Belges. Prime afternoon café lounging spot is the north (Le Panier) side, where the terraces are sunnier and the streets cleaner. The seafood restaurants on the pedestrianized streets between the southern quay and cours d'Estienne-d'Orves ensure that the Vieux Port remains the centre of city life in the evening too.

Two **fortresses** guard the harbour entrance. **St-Jean**, on the north side, dates from the Middle Ages when Marseille was an independent republic, and is now only open when hosting exhibitions; its imposing Tour Carré du Roy René is currently undergoing conversion to create a new national Musée des Civilisations d'Europe et de la Méditerranée. The Fort St-Jean's enlargement in 1660 and the construction of **St-Nicolas** on the south side of the port, represent the city's final defeat as a separate entity. Louis XIV ordered the new fort to keep an eye on the city after he had sent in an army, suppressed the city's council, fined it, arrested all opposition and – in an early example of rate-capping – set ludicrously low limits on Marseille's subsequent expenditure and borrowing. The best view of the Vieux Port is from the **Palais du Pharo**, on the headland beyond Fort St-Nicolas, or, for a wider angle, from **Notre-Dame-de-la-Garde** (daily: summer 7am–7pm; winter 7.30am–5.30pm; bus #60 or tourist train from Vieux Port), the city's Second Empire landmark atop the hill south of the harbour. Crowned by a monumental gold Virgin that gleams to ships far out at sea, it's the most distinctive of all Marseille landmarks. Inside, model ships hang from the rafters while the paintings and drawings displayed are by turns kitsch, unintentionally comic or deeply moving, as they depict the shipwrecks, house fires and car crashes from which the Virgin has supposedly rescued grateful believers.

A short way inland from the Fort St-Nicolas, above the Bassin de Carénage, is Marseille's oldest church, the **Basilique St-Victor** (daily 9am–7pm; €2 entry to crypt). Originally part of a monastery founded in the fifth century on the burial site of various martyrs, the church was built, enlarged and fortified – a vital requirement given its position outside the city walls – over a period of 200 years from the middle of the tenth century. It looks and feels like a fortress, with some of the walls almost 3m thick, and it's no conventional beauty, though the interior has an austere power and the **crypt** is a fascinating, crumbling warren containing several sarcophagi, including one with the remains of St Maurice.

Le Panier and les Docks

To the north of the Vieux Port is the oldest part of Marseille, **Le Panier**, where, up until the last war, tiny streets, steep steps and houses of every era formed a *vieille ville* typical of the Côte. In 1943, however, with Marseille under German occupation, the quarter became an unofficial ghetto for *Untermenschen* of every sort, including Resistance fighters, Communists and Jews. The Nazis gave the 20,000 inhabitants one day's notice to quit; many were deported to the camps. Dynamite was laid, and everything from the waterside to rue Caisserie was blown sky-high, except for three old buildings that appealed to the fascist aesthetic: the seventeenth-century **Hôtel de Ville**, on the quay; the **Hôtel de Cabre**, on the corner of rue Bonneterie and Grande-Rue; and the

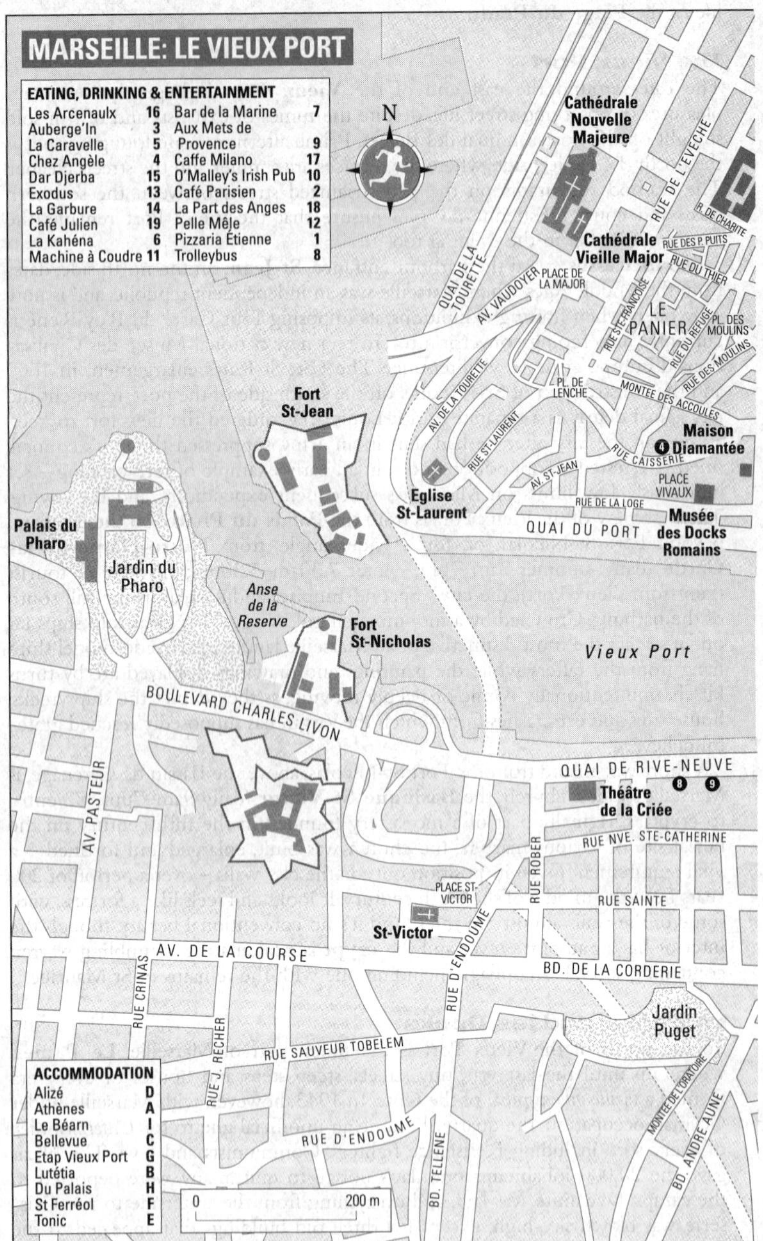
MARSEILLE: LE VIEUX PORT
EATING, DRINKING & ENTERTAINMENT
Les Arcenaulx 16
Auberge'In 3
La Caravelle 5
Chez Angèle 4
Dar Djerba 15
Exodus 13
La Garbure 14
Café Julien 19
La Kahéna 6
Machine à Coudre 11
Bar de la Marine 7
Aux Mets de Provence 9
Caffe Milano 17
O'Malley's Irish Pub 10
Café Parisien 2
La Part des Anges 18
Pelle Mêle 12
Pizzaria Étienne 1
Trolleybus 8
N
Cathédrale Nouvelle Majeure
Cathédrale Vieille Major
QUAI DE LA TOURETTE
AV. VAUDOYER
PLACE DE LA MAJOR
RUE DE L'EVECHE
R. DE CHARITE
RUE DES P. PUITS
RUE DU THIER
LE PANIER
RUE STE-FRANCOISE
RUE DU REFUGE
PL. DES MOULINS
RUE DES MOULINS
PL. DE LENCHE
MONTEE DES ACCOULES
AV. DE LA TOURETTE
RUE ST-LAURENT
AV. ST-JEAN
RUE CAISSERIE
Maison Diamantée
PLACE VIVAUX
RUE DE LA LOGE
QUAI DU PORT
Musée des Docks Romains
Fort St-Jean
Eglise St-Laurent
Palais du Pharo
Jardin du Pharo
Anse de la Reserve
Fort St-Nicholas
Vieux Port
BOULEVARD CHARLES LIVON
QUAI DE RIVE-NEUVE
Théâtre de la Criée
RUE NVE. STE-CATHERINE
RUE SAINTE
RUE ROBER
AV. PASTEUR
PLACE ST-VICTOR
St-Victor
RUE D'ENDOUME
AV. DE LA COURSE
BD. DE LA CORDERIE
RUE CRINAS
Jardin Puget
RUE SAUVEUR TOBELEM
RUE J. RECHER
MONTEE DE L'ORATOIRE
BD. ANDRE AUNE
BD. TELLENE
ACCOMMODATION
Alizé D
Athènes A
Le Béarn I
Bellevue C
Etap Vieux Port G
Lutétia B
Du Palais H
St Ferréol F
Tonic E
0
200 m

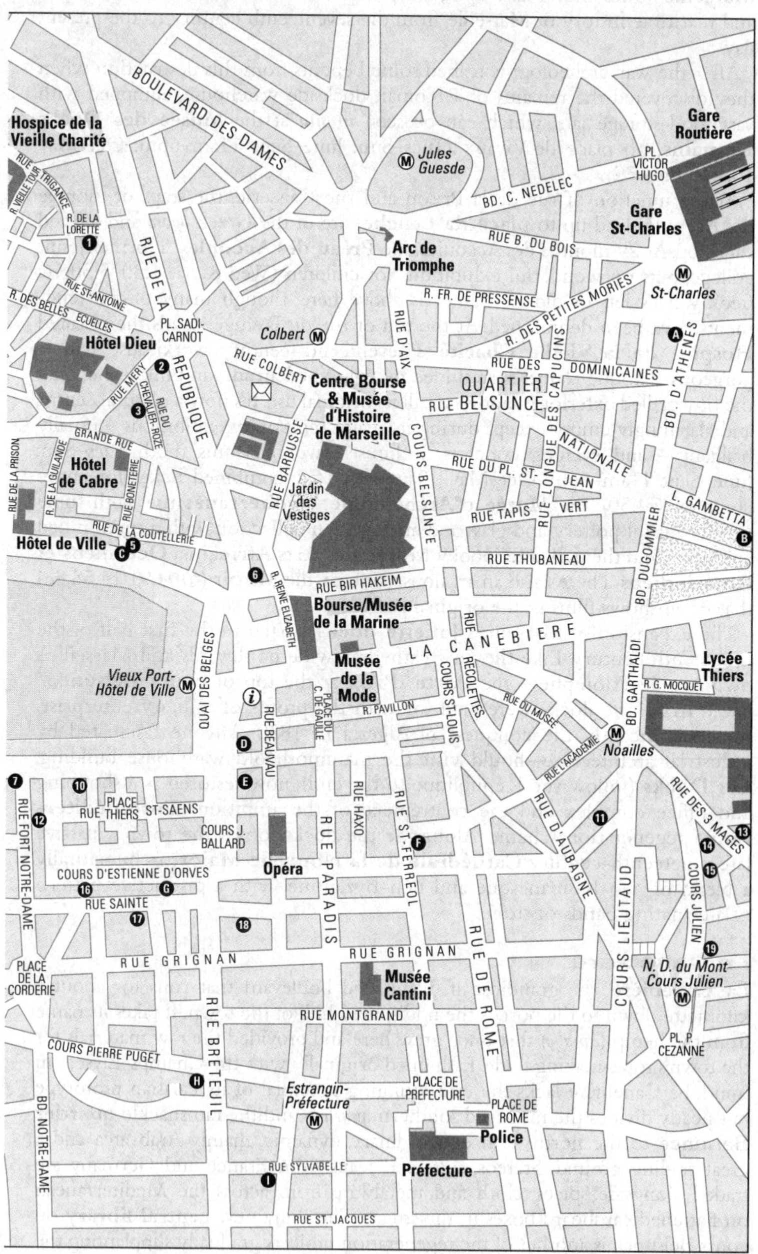

15

THE CÔTE D'AZUR

Maison Diamantée, on rue de la Prison, which houses the **Musée de Vieux Marseille** (Tues–Sun 10am–5pm; €3), whose collections cover the lifestyles and maritime history of Marseille from the seventeenth century to the present day.

After the war, archeologists reaped some benefits from this destruction when they discovered the remains of a Roman dockside warehouse, equipped with vast food-storage jars, which can be seen *in situ* at the **Musée des Docks Romains**, on place de Vivaux (Tues–Sun: June–Sept 11am–6pm; Oct–May 10am–5pm; €2).

At the junction of rue de la Prison and rue Caisserie, the steps of montée des Accoules lead up to **place de Lenche**, site of the Greek *agora* and a good café stop. At 29 montée des Accoules, the **Préau des Accoules**, a former Jesuit college, puts on wonderful exhibitions for children (Wed & Sat 1.30–5.30pm; free). What's left of old Le Panier is above here, though many of the tenements have been demolished. At the top of rue du Réfuge stands the restored **Hospice de la Vieille Charité**, a seventeenth-century workhouse with a gorgeous Baroque chapel surrounded by columned arcades in pink stone; only the tiny grilled exterior windows recall its original use. It's now a cultural centre, and alarmingly empty except during its major temporary exhibitions – usually brilliant – and evening concerts. It houses two museums (both Tues–Sun: June–Sept 11am–6pm; Oct–May 10am–5pm; €2; combined ticket for entire complex €4.50): the **Musée d'Archéologie Méditerranéenne** with some very beautiful pottery and glass and an Egyptian collection with a mummified crocodile; and the dark and spooky **Musée des Arts Africains, Océaniens et Amérindiens**. There's also an art house cinema, the **Miroir** (Ⓣ04.91.14.58.88) that often shows films in the original language.

The expansion of Marseille's **Joliette docks** started in the first half of the nineteenth century. Like the new cathedral, wide boulevards and Marseille's own Arc de Triomphe – the **Porte d'Aix** at the top of **cours Belsunce**/ rue d'Aix – the docks were paid for with the profits of military enterprise, most significantly the conquest of Algeria in 1830. Anyone fascinated by industrial architecture should visit the mammoth old warehouse building, **Les Docks** (follow rue République to the end), now restored as a shopping and office complex and the centrepiece of the ambitious **Euroméditerranée** regeneration scheme. Alongside the docks looms the town's massive late nineteenth-century **Cathédrale de la Nouvelle Major**, architecturally a blend of neo-Romanesque and neo-Byzantine, with a distinctive pattern of alternating bands of stone.

La Canebière

La Canebière, the grandiose if dilapidated boulevard that runs for about a kilometre down to the port, is the undisputed hub of the town. It takes its name from the hemp (*canabé*) that once grew here and provided the raw materials for the town's rope-making trade. Fashioned originally with the Champs-Élysées in mind, La Canebière lacks the café-lounging potential of its Parisian prototype but neatly divides the moneyed southern *quartiers* and the ramshackle **quartier Belsunce** to the north – an extraordinary, dynamic, mainly Arab area and a great trading ground. Stereos, suits and jeans from France and Germany are traded alongside spices, cloth and metalware from across the Mediterranean on flattened cardboard boxes in the streets. The shiny new **central library** on cours Belsunce is another of the regeneration projects gradually supplanting the dilapidated tenements, its slick modernity softened by a beaux-arts portal that recalls the old Alcazar music hall that it replaced - where the likes of Tino Rossi and Yves Montand once performed.

Immediately west of cours Belsunce, the fiendishly ugly **Centre Bourse** provides a stark contrast – useful, nevertheless, for mainstream shopping. Behind it is the **Jardin des Vestiges**, where the ancient port extended, curving northwards from the present quai des Belges. Excavations have revealed a stretch of the Greek port and bits of the **city wall** with the bases of three square towers and a gateway, dated to the second or third century BC. Within the Centre Bourse, the **Musée d'Histoire de Marseille** (Mon–Sat noon–7pm; €2) presents the rest of the finds, including a third-century wreck of a Roman trading vessel. Back at the Vieux Port end of La Canebière is the **Musée de la Marine** (daily 10am–6pm; €2), housed on the ground floor of the grandiose, Neoclassical stock exchange and with a superb collection of shipbuilders' models, including the legendary 1930s liner *Normandie* and Marseille's own prewar queen of the seas, the *Providence*. A bit further up at no. 11, the **Musée de la Mode** (Tues–Sun: June–Sept 11am–6pm, Oct–May 10am–5pm; €3) displays fashion and swimwear from 1945 to the present day.

The Palais Longchamp and the Hôtel du Département

The **Palais Longchamp**, 2km east of the port at the end of boulevard Longchamp (bus #8, or M° Longchamp–Cinq-Avenues), forms the grandiose conclusion of an aqueduct that brought water from the Durance to the city. Although the aqueduct is no longer in use, water is still pumped into the centre of the colonnade connecting the two palatial wings.

The palace's north wing is the city's **Musée des Beaux-Arts** (currently closed for renovation), a hot and slightly stuffy place, but with a fair share of delights, including works by Rubens, Jordaens, Corot and Signac. The nineteenth-century satirist from Marseille, Honoré Daumier, has a whole room for his cartoons. Plans for the city, sculptures and the famous profile of Louis XIV by Marseille-born Pierre Puget are on display along with graphic contemporary canvases of the plague that decimated the city in 1720. The other wing is taken up with the **Musée d'Histoire Naturelle** (Tues–Sun 10am–5pm; €4), and its collection of stuffed animals and fossils. Opposite the palace, at 140 bd Longchamp, is the **Musée Grobet-Labadi** (Tues–Sun: June–Sept 11am–6pm; Oct–May 10am–5pm; €2) an elegant late-nineteenth-century bourgeois town house filled with exquisite objets d'art.

Northeast of the Palais Longchamp, at the end of boulevard Mal-Juin, stands the vast, ultramodern and very blue **Hôtel du Département** (M° St-Just; visits by appointment, Mon–Fri 9.30am & 2.30pm; ⓣ04.91.21.29.77). Deliberately set away from the centre of town in the run-down St-Just–Chartreux *quartier*, the seat of local government for the Bouches-du-Rhône *département* was the biggest public building to be erected in the French provinces in the twentieth century. It was designed by the English architect Will Alsop.

South of La Canebière

The prime shopping district of Marseille is encompassed by three streets running **south from La Canebière**: rue Paradis, rue St-Ferréol and **rue de Rome**. Some of the smaller, intervening streets close to La Canebière are pretty seedy, with prostitutes on every corner day and night, but the atmosphere is usually friendly. Between rues St-Ferréol and Rome, on rue Grignan, is the city's most important art museum, the **Musée Cantini** (Tues–Sun: June–Sept 11am–6pm; Oct–May 10am–5pm; €3), with Fauvists and Surrealists well represented, plus works by Matisse, Léger, Picasso, Ernst, Le Corbusier, Miró and Giacometti.

A few blocks east of rue de Rome is one of the most pleasant places to idle in the city, **cours Julien** (M° Notre-Dame-du-Mont–Cours-Julien), with pools, fountains, pavement restaurant tables and enticing boutiques, populated by Marseille's arty and bohemian crowd and its diverse immigrant community, all of it buried under copious quantities of graffiti. Streets full of bars and music shops lead east to **place Jean-Jaurès**, locally known as "la Pleine", where the market is a treat, particularly on Saturdays.

The corniche, beaches and Parc Borély

The most popular stretch of sand close to the city centre is the **plage des Catalans**, a few blocks south of the Palais du Pharo. This marks the beginning of Marseille's **corniche**, avenue J.-F.-Kennedy, which follows the cliffs past the dramatic statue and arch that frames the setting sun of the **Monument aux Morts des Orients**. South of the monument, steps lead down to an inlet, **Anse des Auffes**, which is the nearest Marseille gets to being picturesque. Small fishing boats are beached on the rocks, the dominant sound is the sea, and narrow stairways and lanes lead nowhere. The corniche then turns inland, bypassing the **Malmousque peninsula**, whose coastal path gives access to tiny bays and beaches – perfect for swimming when the mistral wind is not inciting the waves. You can see along the coast as far as Cap Croisette and, out to sea, the abandoned monastery on the Îles d'Endoume and the Château d'If (see below).

The corniche ends at the **Plage du Prado**, the city's main sand beach, where the water is remarkably clean. A short way up **avenue du Prado**, avenue du Park-Borély leads into the city's best green space, the **Parc Borély**, with a boating lake, rose gardens, palm trees and a botanical garden (daily 6am–9pm; free; regular guided tours €4) The quickest way to the park and the beaches is by bus #44 from métro Rd-Pt-du-Prado; for the corniche, take bus #83 from the Vieux Port.

The Château d'If

The **Château d'If** (Jan–March Tues–Sun 9am–5pm; April & May daily 9am–5pm; June–Sept 9.30am–6.30pm; Sept–Dec Tues–Sun 9.30am–5pm; €5) on the tiny island of If is best known as the penal setting for Alexandre Dumas' *The Count of Monte Cristo*. Having made his watery escape after fourteen years of incarceration as the innocent victim of treachery, the hero of the piece, Edmond Dantès, describes the island thus: "Blacker than the sea, blacker than the sky, rose like a phantom the giant of granite, whose projecting crags seemed like arms extended to seize their prey". The reality, for most prisoners, was worse: they went insane or died (and sometimes both) before reaching the end of their sentences. Only the nobles living in the less fetid upper-storey cells had much chance of survival. The sixteenth-century castle and its cells are horribly well preserved, and the views back towards Marseille are fantastic. **Boats** for If leave regularly from the quai des Belges in the Vieux Port (hourly in summer; five daily in winter; €10), with the last boat back timed to coincide with the château's closing time; the journey takes twenty minutes.

The Musée de la Faïence, MAC and the Cité Radieuse

From the plage du Prado the promenade continues all the way to the subur of **Montredon**, where the nineteenth-century Château Pastré, set in a hu park, contains the **Musée de la Faïence** (Tues–Sun: June–Sept 11am–6p Oct–May 10am–5pm; €2). The eighteenth- and nineteenth-century cera ics, most produced in Marseille, are of an extremely high quality, and a sm collection of novel modern and contemporary pieces is housed on the tc floor. The entrance to the park (free) is at 157 ave de Montredon (bus #19 from M° Rd-Pt-du-Prado, stop "Montredon-Chancel"). Along the coast from here are easily accessible *calanques* (rocky inlets), ideal for evening swims and supper picnics as the sun sets.

Between Montredon and **boulevard Michelet**, the main road out of the city, is the contemporary art museum, **MAC** (Tues–Sun: June–Sept 11am–6pm; Oct–May 10am–5pm; €3), at 69 av d'Haïfa (bus #23 or #45 from M° Rd-Pt-du-Prado, stop "Haïfa" or "Marie-Louise"). The permanent collection includes works from the 1960s to the present day by Buren, Christo, Klein, Niki de Saint-Phalle, Tinguely and Warhol, as well as Marseillais artists César and Ben.

△ The Unité d'Habitation, Marseille

Set back just west of boulevard Michelet stands a building that broke the mould, Le Corbusier's seventeen-storey block of flats, the **Unité d'Habitation**, designed in 1946 and completed in 1952. The Cité Radiense, as it's also known, only fails to amaze now because so many architects the world over have tried to imitate Le Corbusier's revolutionary model, but up close the difference in quality between this and what followed is apparent. At ground level the building is decorated with Le Corbusier's famous human figure, the Modulor; on the third floor there is a hotel (see p.1126) and café. Not all of the iconic rooftop recreation area can be visited, though a circuit of the running track is essential. To reach the Unité, take bus #21 from M° Rd-Pt-du-Prado to "Le Corbusier".

Eating and drinking

Fish and **seafood** are the mainstay of Marseille's diet, and the superstar of dishes is the city's own expensive invention, **bouillabaisse**, a saffron- and garlic-flavoured soup with bits of fish, croutons and *rouille* thrown in; theories conflict s to which fish should be included, but one essential is the *rascasse* or scorpion ish. The other speciality is *pieds et paquets* – mutton or lamb belly and trotters.

Good **restaurant** hunting grounds include cours Julien or place Jean-Jaurès nternational options), the Vieux Port (touristy and fishy), the Corniche and f age du Prado (glitzy and pricey) or Le Panier (snacks and old-time bistros). Rue i inte is good for smart, fashioniable dining close to the opera and Vieux Port; C lls on cours Belsunce sell chips and sandwiches for under €3. On Sunday pickv gs are slim, and many Marseille restaurants also take long summer breaks.

Cafés and bars

Aux 3G 3 rue St-Pierre, 5e. Marseille's most popular lesbian bar, regularly packed at weekends. Open Thurs & Sun 7pm–midnight, Fri & Sat until 2am.

Bar de la Marine 15 quai de Rive-Neuve, 1er. A favourite bar for Vieux Port lounging, and inspiration for Pagnol's celebrated Marseille trilogy. Open daily.

O'Malley's Irish Pub 9 quai de Rive Neuve, 1er. A wildly popular Vieux Port boozer with the usual "Irish" trimmings, including Beamish and Guinness, and live music on Thurs.

Café Parisien 1 place Sadi-Carnot, 2e. Very stylish mix of old elegance and modern chic, with pasta dishes from around €11 and meat mains from €14 up. Closed Sun.

Bar Le Petit Nice 26 place Jean-Jaurès, 1er. The place to head for on Saturday morning during the market, with an interesting selection of beers. Open Mon–Sat from 6.30am.

Le Red Lion 231 av Pierre-Mendès-France, 8e. Large, raucous, British-style pub close to plage Borély, with eleven beers on draught. Open until 4am Fri & Sat.

Trash 28 rue du Berceau, 5e. Slick, cruisy gay men's bar with DJ, live entertainment and plenty of dark corners. Open weekdays 9pm–2am, later at weekends.

Restaurants

L'Abri Côtier bd des Baigneurs, plage du Fortin 8e ⓣ04.91.72.27.29. Smart beachside restaurant in Montredon, serving fish, meat and pizzas. It's a block or so down from the boulevard and a little tricky to find, despite the many signs. Menus from €28. Closed Oct–March.

Les Arcenaulx 25 cours d'Estienne-d'Orves, 1er ⓣ04.91.59.80.40. Lovely, atmospheric intellectual haunt that is also a bookshop and *salon de thé*; the €22.50 lunch menu is good value, otherwise €29.50 and €52. Last orders 11pm. Closed Sun.

Auberge'In 25 rue du Chevalier-Roze, 2e ⓣ04.91.90.51.59. Health-food shop and restaurant on the edge of Le Panier, with a vegetarian *menu fixe* for €13.50. Open for lunch Mon–Sat, dinner Fri & Sat only.

Chez Angèle 50 rue Caisserie, 2e ⓣ04.91.90.63.35. Packed Le Panier local, dishing up fresh pasta and pizza. Closed lunchtimes Sat & Sun.

Chez Michel 6 rue des Catalans, 7e ⓣ04.91.52.30.63. There's no debate about the bouillabaisse ingredients here. A basket of five fishes, including the elusive and most expensive one, the *rascasse*, is presented to the customer before the soup is made – and this is quite simply the place to eat this dish. Expect to pay €58 per person for the bouillabaisse alone. Closed last two weeks of Feb.

Dar Djerba 15 cours Julien, 6^e^ ⓣ04.91.48.55.36. Excellent Tunisian restaurant with beautiful tiling, friendly service and a €22.90 menu. Closed Mon.

La Garbure 9 cours Julien, 6e ⓣ04.91.47.18.01. Rich specialities from southwest France, including Bresse chicken. Menus around €24. Closed Sat midday & Sun.

La Kahena 2 rue de la République, 2e ⓣ04.91.90.61.93. Popular Tunisian restaurant near the Vieux Port, with grills and couscous from €8.50. Open daily.

Aux Mets de Provence 18 quai de Rive-Neuve, 7e ⓣ04.91.33.35.38. A Marseille institution with authentic Provençal cooking at the top of a steep staircase. Lunch menu at €40, otherwise €60 including wine. Closed lunchtime Sat–Mon.

Caffe Milano 43 rue Sainte, 1er ⓣ04.91.33.14.33. Sleek, sophisticated and hugely popular Italian. Meat-based *plats* around €14, pasta dishes around €10. Closed Sat lunch & Sun.

La Part des Anges 33 rue Sainte, 1er ⓣ04.91.33.55.70. Wonderful *cave de vins* serving hearty food to mop up the classy alcohol; *plats* around €12. Open daily.

Pizzaria Étienne 43 rue Lorette, 2e. An old-fashioned Le Panier pizzeria; hectic, cramped and crowded.

Nightlife and entertainment

Marseille's **nightlife** has something for everyone, with plenty of live rock and jazz, nightclubs and discos, as well as theatre, opera and classical concerts. Theatre is particularly innovative and lively in Marseille. The Virgin Megastore at 75 rue St-Ferréol, the book- and record shop FNAC in the Centre Bourse and the tourist office's ticket bureau are the best places to go for **tickets and information**. Virgin also stocks English books and has a café, open, like the rest of the store, Monday to Saturday until 9pm and on Sundays until 8pm. There is a free weekly **listings** mag, *Ventilo*, and a couple of monthlies, *César* and *Marseille In Situ*, which you can pick up from FNAC, Virgin, tourist offices, museums and cultural centres.

Live music and clubs

L'Affranchi 212 bd de St-Marcel, 11e ⓣ04.91.35.09.19. Venue in the eastern suburbs with a varied programme of clubs and live gigs, including rap, hip-hop and reggae. Open 8.30pm when concerts on, mostly on Sat.

Le Bazar 90 bd Rabatau, 8e ⓣ04.91.79.08.00. Big, mainstream disco playing house and occasionally hosting big-name international DJs. Open Thurs–Sun.

La Caravelle 34 quai du Port, 2e. Prewar cabaret on the first floor of the *Hôtel Bellevue* with portside views. Free plates of tapas 6–9.30pm; live jazz weekends. Daily till 2am.

Les Docks des Suds – le Hangar à Sucres 12 rue Urbain V, 3e ⓣ04.91.99.00.00. Vast warehouse that serves as the venue for Marseille's annual Fiesta des Suds world-music festival.

Exodus 9 rue des Trois Mages, 1e ⓣ04.91.42.02.39. Small performance space between cours Julien and place Jean-Jaurès, presenting world music and theatre with a strong focus on Africa and Asia. Live events usually start at 8.30pm.

L'Intermédiare 63 place Jean-Jaurès, 6e ⓣ04.91.47.01.25. Loud, hip, smoky bar with a variety of live bands, from rock to jazz and world music, plus old-skool DJ nights. Mon–Sat 6.30pm–2am.

Café Julien 39 cours Julien, 6e ⓣ04.91.24.34.10. Lively bar with mixed clientele, part of the Espace Julien. Regular live rock and reggae music; performances start 8.30–9pm.

Machine à Coudre 6 rue Jean-Roque, 1e ⓣ04.91.55.62.65. Music café hosting alternative rock and reggae acts. €4–7 entry charge depending on act. Open Thurs–Sat.

New Cancan 3 rue Sénac, 1er ⓣ04.91.48.59.76. Cheesy, dated and expensive, but the *New Cancan* is nevertheless Marseille's best-known and longest running gay disco. Open Thurs–Sun 11pm–dawn.

Pelle Mêle 8 place aux Huiles, 1er ⓣ04.91.54.85.26. Intimate, smart and lively jazz bistro and piano bar. Open 6pm–2am daily.

Le Poste à Galène 103 rue Ferrari, 5e ⓣ04.91.47.57.99. Live pop, rock and electro plus 80s nights and a bar. Open at 8 or 8.30pm, depending on event.

Trolleybus 24 quai de Rive-Neuve, 7e ⓣ04.91.54.30.45. Disco in a series of vaulted rooms; house, pop, electro, hip-hop and techno. Closed Sun–Wed.

Film, theatre and concerts

Alhambra 2 rue du Cinéma, 16e ⓣ04.91.03.84.66. Art house cinema occasionally showing undubbed English-language films (*v.o*).

Ballet National de Marseille 20 bd Gabès, 8e ⓣ04.91.32.72.72. The home venue of the famous dance company, founded in 1972 by Roland Petit.

La Friche la Belle de Mai 41 rue Jobin, 3e ⓣ04.95.04.95.04. Interdisciplinary arts complex occupying a former industrial site in the north of the city, hosting theatre, dance, live music and arts exhibitions.

Le Miroir 2 rue de la Charité, 2e ⓣ04.91.14.58.88. Art house films in comfortable surroundings at the Vieille Charité, often undubbed in *v.o.*

Opéra 2 rue Moliére, 1er ⓣ04.91.55.11.10. Symphony concerts and operas in a magnificent setting, part Neoclassical, part Art Deco.

Théâtre National la Criée 30 quai de Rive-Neuve, 7e ⓣ04.96.17.80.00. Home of the Théâtre National de Marseille and Marseille's best theatre.

Les Variétés 37 rue Vincent Scotto, 1er ⓣ08.36.68.20.15. Downtown cinema offering *v. o.* films.

Listings

Airlines Air France, 14 La Canebière, 1er ⓣ08.20.82.08.20; Cathay Pacific, 41 La Canebière, 1er ⓣ04.91.91.14.69.

Bike rental Cycles Ulysse, 3 av du Parc Borély; ⓣ04.91.77.14.51; Tandem, 16 av du Parc Borély ⓣ04.91.22.64.80.

Bookstore Virgin, 75 rue St-Ferréol, 1er, has an English books section; Maupetit, 140 La Canebière, 1er, is a good general French bookshop.

Car hire Avis, Gare St-Charles ⓣ08.20.61.16.36; Budget, 40 bd de Plombières ⓣ04.91.64.40.03; National Citer, 20 bd Schloessing, 8e ⓣ04.91.83.05.05; Europcar, 59 allées Léon Gambetta, 1er ⓣ08.25.82.56.80; Hertz, 21 bd Maurice-Bourdet, 1er ⓣ04.91.14.04.24. All also have head offices at the airport.

Consulates UK, 24 av du Prado, 6e ⓣ04.91.15.72.10; USA, place Varian Fry/12 bd Paul-Peytral, 6e ⓣ04.91.54.92.00.

Emergencies Ambulance ⓣ15; SOS Médecins ⓣ04.91.52.91.52; 24hr casualty departments at La Conception, 144 rue St-Pierre, 5e ⓣ04.91.38.36.52; and SOS Voyageurs, Gare St-Charles, 3e ⓣ04.91.62.12.80.

Ferries SNCM (61 bd des Dames ⓣ32.60, ⓦwww.sncm.fr), runs ferries to Corsica, Tunisia and Algeria.

Internet Info-Café, 1 quai du Rive Neuve, 1er ☎04.91.33.74.98.
Lost property 18 rue de la Cathédrale, 2e ☎04.91.90.99.37.
Pharmacy Syndicat des Pharmaciens ☎04.91.15.72.61
Police Commissariat Central, 2 rue Antoine-Becker, 2e (24hr; ☎04.91.39.80.00).
Post office 1 place de l'Hôtel-des-Postes, 1er.
Taxis Marseille Taxi ☎04.91.02.20.20; Taxi Blanc Bleu ☎04.91.51.50.00; Eurotaxi (multilingual drivers) ☎04.91.05.31.98; disabled facilities ☎06.11.54.99.99.

Cassis, La Ciotat and Bandol

Hard as it is to picture now, chic little **Cassis** once had a busy industrial harbour, while at **La Ciotat** ships were built right up until 1989. La Ciotat is probably the friendliest of all the resorts between Marseille and Toulon, and has the distinction of being the birthplace of film-making. Tucked in a cove between La Ciotat and Toulon, **Bandol** is a rarity on the Côte d'Azur, a family resort which has managed to maintain something of an unhurried air.

Cassis

A lot of people rate **CASSIS** the best resort this side of St-Tropez – its inhabitants most of all. Hemmed in by high cliffs, its modern development has been modest. Portside posing and drinking aside, there's not much to do except sunbathe and look up at the ruins of the town's medieval **castle**, built in 1381 and refurbished by Monsieur Michelin, the authoritarian boss of the family tyres and guides firm.

The favoured pastime, though, is to take a boat trip to the **calanques** (from around €8) – long, narrow, deep fjord-like inlets that have cut into the limestone cliffs. Several companies operate from the port, but check if they let you off or just tour in and out, and be prepared for rough seas. If you're feeling energetic, you can take the well-marked footpath from the route des Calanques behind the western beach; it's about ninety minutes' walk to the furthest and best *calanque*, **En Vau**, where you can climb down rocks to the shore. The water is deep blue and swimming between the vertical cliffs is an experience not to be missed. From July until the second Saturday in September you have to stick to the coastal path or the sea from 11am until 4pm because of the risk of fire.

Les Sports Loisirs Nautiques (☎04.42.01.80.01) by the beach next to the port hires out windsurfing and watersports equipment. The spectacular clifftop **route des Crêtes** links Cassis with La Ciotat; regular belvederes allow you to stop and take the perfect shot of distant headlands receding into the sunset – vertigo permitting. The route is closed during high winds.

The Cosquer Cave

In 1991, **Henri Cosquer**, a diver from Cassis, discovered paintings and engravings of animals, painted handprints and finger tracings in a cave between Marseille and Cassis, whose sole entrance is a long, sloping tunnel that starts 37m under the sea. The cave would have been accessible from dry land no later than the end of the last ice age, and carbon dating has shown that the oldest work of art here was created around 27,000 years ago. For safety reasons it's not possible to visit the cave, though **diving schools** in Cassis organize dives in the bay and the *calanques*.

Practicalities

Buses from Marseille arrive at rond-point du Gendarmerie from where it's a couple of minutes' walk to the port and the beach. The **gare SNCF** is 3km from town, connected to it by a bus (Mon–Fri & Sat am) which takes around 15 minutes. The **tourist office** is on the port at quai des Moulins (March–June, Sept & Oct Mon–Fri 9am–12.30pm & 2–6pm, Sat 9.30am–12.30pm & 2–5.30pm, Sun 10am–12.30pm; July & Aug Mon–Fri 9am–7pm, Sat & Sun 9.30am–12.30pm & 3–6pm; Nov–Feb Mon–Fri 9.30am–12.30pm & 2–5.30pm, Sat 10am–12.30pm & 2–5pm, Sun 10am–12.30pm; ⓣ08.92.25.98.92, ⓦwww.cassis.fr).

Cassis is a small place, so demand for cheaper **rooms** in high season is intense. The least expensive are at *Le Commerce*, 1 rue St-Clair (ⓣ04.42.01.09.10, ⓕ04.42.01.14.17; ❸, closed mid-Nov to mid-Jan), and *Le Provençal*, 7 av Victor-Hugo (ⓣ04.42.01.72.13, ⓕ04.42.01.39.58; ❸), close to the port. For a little more money, and a view over the port, try *Le Golfe*, place du Grand-Carnot (ⓣ04.42.01.00.21, ⓦwww.hotel-le-golfe-cassis.com; ❺; closed Nov–March). Further out, there's also *Le Joli Bois*, route de la Gineste (ⓣ04.42.01.02.68; ❷), just off the Marseille road, 3km from Cassis and with few amenities. Far more isolated is the gorgeously scenic **hostel**, *La Fontasse*, in the hills above the *calanques* west of Cassis (ⓣ04.42.01.02.72, ⓦwww.fuaj.org; mid-March to Dec; €9.50 per night. reception 8–10.30am & 5–9pm); by car from Cassis, take the D559 for 4km then turn left. The Cassis–Marseille bus stops on the D559 (bus stop "Les Calanques"). It's 2.5km walk from the centre of Cassis, towards the Col de la Gardiole; take avenue des Calanques from the port. Facilities are basic – there are no showers, and power and water are rationed. If you're **camping**, *Les Cigales* (ⓣ04.42.01.07.34; closed mid-Nov to mid-March; €18.60 for car, tent and two people), is just off the D559 from Marseille before avenue de la Marne turns down into Cassis.

Restaurants are abundant along the port. The ratatouille and fresh fish at *Chez Gilbert*, 19 quai Baux (ⓣ04.42.01.71.36; menu €27; closed Tues eve & Wed), are hard to beat. *El Sol*, at no. 23 (ⓣ04.42.01.76.10; closed Mon all day & Tues lunch), with *terroir* fare, costs a bit less. In the backstreets, *Le Clos des Arômes* at 10 rue Abbé Paul-Mouton (ⓣ04.42.01.71.84, closed Mon, Tues & Wed lunch; menu €25) is well regarded and has a pretty garden.

La Ciotat

Cranes still loom over the little port of **LA CIOTAT**, where vast oil tankers were once built. Today, the town's economy relies on property development, tourism and yachting, yet it remains a pleasantly unpretentious place. La Ciotat is not a town for museum-visiting or monument-spotting. It's a relaxing place with excellent beaches and a lively waterfront with plenty of places to eat and drink.

In 1895, **August and Louis Lumière** filmed the first moving pictures here, including the arrival of a train at the *gare SNCF*, which had Parisians jumping out of their seats in fright when it was premiered there. The world's oldest movie house, the **Eden Cinema**, still stands on the corner of boulevard A.-France and boulevard Jean-Jaurès, though it awaits restoration; the main venue for the annual film festival in June is the modern Cinéma Lumière on place Evariste-Gras. The brothers are commemorated by a solid 1950s monument on plage Lumière.

The streets of the old town, apart from rue Poilus, are uneventful, though the increasing numbers of boutiques and *immobiliers* reflect the change from working shipyard to pleasure port. Both Vedette Voltigeur (Ⓣ04.42.83.11.44) and Vedette Monte Cristo (Ⓣ04.42.71.53.32) make the crossing to the islet of Île Verte daily, while Catamaran Le Citharista (Ⓣ06.09.35.25.68) runs trips to the *calanques* of Cassis and Marseille (€17–23) from quai Ganteaume.

Alternatively, take a walk through the **Parc du Mugel** (daily: April–Sept 8am–8pm; Oct–March 9am–6pm; bus #30, stop "Mugel"), with its strange cluster of rock formations on the promontory beyond the shipyards. A path leads up through overgrown vegetation to a narrow terrace overlooking the sea. If you continue on bus #30 to Figuerolles you can reach the **Anse de Figuerolles** *calanque* down the avenue of the same name, and its neighbour, the **Gameau**.

Practicalities

The **gare SNCF** is 5km from the town but bus #21 is frequent at peak times and gets you to the Vieux Port in around twenty minutes. The old town and port look out across the Baie de la Ciotat, whose inner curve provides the beaches and resort lifestyle of La Ciotat's modern extension, **La Ciotat-Plage**. The **gare routière** is at the end of boulevard Anatole-France by the Vieux Port right beside the **tourist office** (June–Sept Mon–Sat 9am–8pm, Sun 10am–1pm; Oct–May Mon–Sat 9am–noon & 2–6pm; Ⓣ04.42.08.61.32, Ⓦwww.tourisme-laciotat.com). **Bikes** can be hired from Cycle Lleba at 3b av F.-Mistral (Ⓣ04.42.83.60.30).

For **hotels**, the best cheapies are *La Marine*, 1 av Fernand Gassion (Ⓣ & Ⓕ04.42.08.35.11; ❷), and *La Rotonde*, 44 bd de la République (Ⓣ04.42.08.67.50, Ⓦlarotonde.littoralmedia.com; ❸), both on the fringes of the old town. In La Ciotat-Plage, *Miramar*, 3 bd Beaurivage (Ⓣ04.42.83.33.79; Ⓦwww.miramarla-ciotat.com; ❼), is right on the palm-fringed seafront, while across the bay, on Corniche du Liouquet, you can stay in little villas in a park at *Ciotel Le Cap* (April–Nov; Ⓣ04.42.83.90.30, Ⓦwww.leciotel.com; ❽). La Ciotat has five campsites, three of them by the sea, of which *St-Jean*, 30 av St-Jean (Ⓣ04.42.83.13.01, Ⓦwww.asther.com/stjean; €23 for two people and a tent; closed Oct–May), is the closest to the centre (bus #40, stop "St-Jean Village").

La Ciotat's best **restaurant** is *La Fresque*, 18 rue des Combattants (Ⓣ04.42.08.00.60; closed Sun eve & Mon), with the likes of duck stuffed with foie gras and menus from €18. Otherwise, *Coquillages Franquin*, 13 bd Anatole-France (Ⓣ04.42.83.59.50), serves fish on a €16.50 menu, and there are plenty of cafés and brasseries around the Vieux Port and along boulevard Beaurivage in La Ciotat Plage.

Bandol and around

Across La Ciotat bay are the fine sand and shingle beaches and unremarkable family resort of **LES LECQUES**, an offshoot of the old inland town of **St-Cyr-Sur-Mer**, to which it is fused by a belt of modern suburbia. The **train station** is in St-Cyr, but the tourist office (July & Aug Mon–Sat 9am–7pm, Sun 10am–1pm & 4–7pm; June & Sept Mon–Sat 9am–6pm; Oct–May Mon–Fri 9am–6pm, Sat 9am–noon & 2–6pm; Ⓣ04.94.26.73.73, Ⓦwww.saintcyrsurmer.com) is on the place de l'Appel du 18 Juin, on the seafront in Les Lecques. St-Cyr has the cheapest **accommodation**, such as the basic but serviceable *Auberge Le Clos Fleuri* (Ⓣ04.94.26.27.46; ❶), near the station on avenue Général-de-Gaulle, but there's more choice in Les Lecques. A ten-kilometre **coastal path** (signposted) runs from the east end of Les Lecques' beach through a stretch of secluded beaches and *calanques* to the unpretentious resort of **BANDOL**, while inland *dégustation* signs announce the the *appellation* Bandol, whose **vineyards** produce some of the best wines on the Côte. The reds are the most reputed.

In Bandol there are several reasonable **hotels** near the centre, including *Hôtel Florida*, 26 impasse de Nice (ⓣ04.94.29.41.72; ❸; half board ❻) obligatory May–Sept), and *La Cigale Bleue* on avenue de la Gare (ⓣ04.94.29.41.40; ❸). The very pleasant *Golf Hotel* (ⓣ04.94.29.45.83, ⓦwww.golfhotel.fr; open mid-March to mid-Nov; ❺) is right on Rénecros beach, west of the town centre. The **tourist office**, on allée Vivien by the quayside (late June & early Sept 9am–noon & 2–6pm; July & Aug daily 9am–7pm; Sept–June Mon–Fri 9am–noon & 2–6pm, Sat 9am–noon; ⓣ04.94.29.41.35, ⓦwww.bandol.fr), will help if you're stuck during the high season.

The other stretch of **coastal path** this side of Toulon is along the southern edge of the **Sicié peninsula** from Le Brusc. The path climbs up to the sturdy clifftop chapel of Notre-Dame-du-Mai, once a primitive lighthouse, which affords fantastic views of the coast and hinterland. The chapel is only open in May, on the first Saturday morning of the month from October to April, and on certain special dates (Easter Monday, Aug 15, and for the pilgrimage on Sept 14).

Toulon

Never the loveliest of cities, **TOULON** was half destroyed in the last war and brutally rebuilt. It's still dominated by the military: the arsenal that Louis XIV created remains one of the major employers of southeast France, and the port is home to the French Navy's Mediterranean fleet. Up until the eighteenth century, slaves and convicts still powered the king's galleys; after the Revolution convicts were sent to Toulon with iron collars round their necks for sentences of hard labour.

Today, heavy traffic crawls through the centre, the old town is fringed by forbidding 1960s architecture, and the damage done to Toulon's reputation by a period of overtly racist National Front control – which ended in 2001 – will take decades to repair. And yet the city is fighting back. The splendid **Opéra** has been refurbished, the impressive **Hôtel des Arts** in the former Conseil Général building on boulevard Maréchal-Leclerc (Tues–Sun 11am–6pm; free) pulls in touring exhibitions of modern art from Paris, and everywhere there's an orgy of repaving, replanting and general beautification. A certain seediness lingers, but given the high standards and low prices of some of Toulon's accommodation it makes a logical stopover if you're passing this way. While you're here, it's worth taking the *téléphérique* to the top of **Mont Faron** (bd Amiral Vence; daily 9.30am–7.30pm weather permitting; €6.10; bus #40 from bd de Strasbourg in central Toulon) for the views over Toulon's magnificent natural harbour. Back in town, naval buffs will find the **Musée de la Marine** on place Monsenergue (daily except Tues 10am–5pm; €5) engrossing – particularly the dramatic photographs of the French fleet scuttled in Toulon harbour in 1942, in order to keep it from falling into German hands.

Practicalities

The **gare SNCF**, on place de l'Europe, and the adjacent **gare routière**, lie northeast of the town centre. There's a **tourist office** (June & Sept Mon & Wed–Sat 9am–6pm, Tues 10am–6pm, Sun 10am–noon; July & Aug Mon & Wed–Sat 9am–8pm, Tues 10am–8pm, Sun 10am–noon; Oct–May Mon &

Wed–Sat 9.30am–5.30pm, Tues 10.30am–5.30pm; ⓣ04.94.18.53.00, ⓦwww.toulontourisme.com) at 334 av de la République on the **port**: head down rue Vauban, cross place d'Armes and follow the busy avenue that runs parallel to the coast, which becomes avenue de la République.

There's plenty of budget **accommodation**: the basic but cheap *Hôtel des Allées*, 18 allées Amiral-Courbet (ⓣ04.94.91.10.02; ❶); the modern and comfortable *Trois Dauphins*, 9 place des 3 Dauphins (ⓣ04.94.92.65.79, ⓕ04.94.09.09.17; ❷); or its sister hotel, the bright and more upmarket *Little Palace*, directly opposite the *Trois Dauphins* at 6–8 rue Berthelot (ⓣ04.94.92.65.79, ⓦwww.hotel-littlepalace.com; ❸) – all very central. There are innumerable brasseries and **cafés** lining the port and a cluster of **restaurants** around the Opéra.

The central resorts and islands

Out of season, the coast between **Hyères** and **Fréjus/ St-Raphaël** and its backdrop of wooded hills hold their own against the cynicism engendered by tourist brochure overkill. The magic lies in the scented Mediterranean vegetation, silver beaches glimpsed between purple cliffs, secluded islands and medieval hilltop villages.

Hyères, which preserves a certain air of gentility, flashy St-Raphaël and historic Fréjus are the only significant towns, though the urban sprawl around the erstwhile fishing villages of **Le Lavandou**, **Cavalaire-sur-Mer** and **Ste-Maxime** keeps any sense of wilderness at bay. But there are moments when it's almost possible to imagine the coastline of old: near the **Cap de Bregançon** south of **Bormes**, between **Le Rayol** and Cavalaire, in the **Domaine de Rayol gardens**, and around the southern tip of the **St-Tropez peninsula**. Out to sea, on the **Îles d'Hyères** (often called the Îles d'Or), you can experience unspoilt landscapes with some of the best fauna and flora in Provence. **La Croix-Valmer** is probably the most pleasant of the resorts, and **St-Tropez** is a must – for a day-trip anyway. Inland, amidst the dense wooded hills of the **Massif des Maures**, are the gorgeous villages of **Collobrières** and **La Garde Freinet**.

Sheer expense aside, **transport** is the one big problem. There is a regular bus service along the coast, but there are no trains, traffic is extremely slow in high season, and cycling doesn't get you very far unless you're Tour de France material.

Hyères

HYÈRES is the oldest resort on the Côte, listing Queen Victoria and Tolstoy among its early admirers, but the lack of a central seafront meant the town lost out when the foreign rich switched from winter convalescents to quayside strollers, and today it has the rare distinction of not being totally dependent on the summer influx; in addition it exports cut flowers and exotic plants, the most important being the date palm, which graces every street. Hyères is also a garrison town, the home of the French army's 54th artillery regiment.

Arrival, information and accommodation

The **gare SNCF** is on place de l'Europe, 1.5km south of the town centre, with frequent buses (#29, #39 or #67) to the **gare routière** on place Mal-Joffret, two blocks south of the entrance to the old town (ⓣ08.25.00.06.50, ⓦwww.reseaumistral.com). The modern Hyères-Toulon **airport** is between Hyères and Hyères-Plage, 3km from the centre (ⓣ08.25.01.83.87, ⓦwww.toulon-hyeres.aeroport.fr), to which it's connected by an infrequent bus service. The **tourist office** is at the Forum du Casino, 3 av Ambroise Thomas (July & Aug daily 8.30am–7.30pm; Sept–June Mon–Fri 9am–6pm, Sat 10am–4pm; ⓣ04.94.01.84.50, ⓦwww.ot-hyeres.fr); there is another office close to rond-point Henri-Petit at the western entrance to the town. **Bikes** and **mopeds** can be hired from Holiday Bikes, 10 rue Jean d'Agrève, near port Saint-Pierre (ⓣ04.94.38.79.45, ⓦwww.holiday-bikes.com).

Hotels in the old town include the *Hôtel du Soleil*, on rue du Rempart (ⓣ04.94.65.16.26, ⓦwww.hoteldusoleil.com; ➎), in a renovated house at the foot of the parc St-Bernard, and the smaller *Le Portalet*, 4 rue de Limans (ⓣ04.94.65.39.40, ⓦwww.hotel-portalet.com; ➌). Overlooking the port at Ayguade is *La Reine Jane* (ⓣ04.94.66.32.64, ⓦwww.reinejane.com; ➎).

There are plenty of **campsites** on the coast. Two smaller ones are *Camping-Bernard*, a two-star in Le Ceinturon (ⓣ04.94.66.30.54, ⓕ04.94.66.48.30; closed Oct–Easter), and *Clair de Lune*, avenue du Clair de Lune (ⓣ04.94.58.20.19, ⓦwww.campingclairedelune.com; closed mid-Nov to Jan; €18), a three-star one on the Presqu'Île de Giens.

The Town

Walled and medieval **old Hyères** perches on the slopes of Casteou hill, 5km from the sea; below it lies the **modern town**, with avenue Gambetta the main north–south axis. At the coast, the **Presqu'Île de Giens** is leashed to the mainland by an isthmus, known as **La Capte**, and a parallel sand bar enclosing the salt marshes and a lake. Le Ceinturon, Ayguade and Les Salins d'Hyères are the villages-cum-resorts along the coast northeast from Hyères-Plages; L'Almanarre is to the west where the sand bar starts.

From place Clemenceau, a medieval gatehouse, the **Porte Massillon**, opens into the old town on rue Massillon, lined with tempting shops selling fruit and vegetables, chocolate, soaps, olive oil and wine. It ends at **place Massillon**, a perfect Provençal square with terraced cafés overlooking the twelfth-century **Tour des Templiers**, the remnant of a Knights Templar fort elegantly converted into exhibition space for contemporary art (April–Oct daily except Tues 10am–noon & 4–7pm; Nov–March Wed–Sun 10am–noon & 2–5.30pm; free). Behind the tower, rue Ste-Catherine leads uphill to place St-Paul, from which you have a panoramic view over the Golfe de Giens.

Wide steps fan out from the Renaissance door of the former collegiate **church of St-Paul** (closed for renovation at the time of writing; normally May–Sept daily except Tues 10am–noon & 4–7pm; Oct–April Wed–Sun 10am–noon & 2–5.30pm), whose distinctive belfry is pure Romanesque, as is the choir, though the simplicity of the design is masked by the collection of votive offerings hung inside. Today, the church is only used for special services – the main place of worship is the mid-thirteenth-century former monastery **church of St-Louis**, on place de la République.

To the right of St-Paul, a Renaissance house bridges rue St-Paul, its turret supported by a pillar rising beside the steps. Through this arch you can head up rue Ste-Claire to the entrance of **Parc Ste-Claire** (daily 8am–dusk; free), the exotic gardens around **Castel Ste-Claire**, once home to the American writer and interior designer Edith Wharton and now the offices of the Parc National de Port-Cros. Cobbled paths lead up the hill towards the **Parc St-Bernard** (daily 8am–dusk; free), full of almost every Mediterranean flower known. At the top, above montée des Noailles (which by car you reach from cours Strasbourg and avenue Long), is the **Villa Noailles**, a Cubist mansion enclosed within part of the old citadel walls, designed by Mallet-Stevens in the 1920s and a home to all the luminaries of Dada and Surrealism. It now hosts contemporary art exhibitions (July–Sept daily except Tues 10am–12.30pm & 4–7.30pm, Fri until 10pm; Oct–June Wed–Sun 10am–noon & 2–6pm; free). To the west of the park and further up the hill are the immaculate remains of the eleventh-century **castle**, whose keep and ivy-clad towers give stunning views out to the Îles d'Hyères and east to the Massif des Maures.

The switch from medieval to eighteenth- and nineteenth-century Hyères at **avenue des Îles-d'Or** and its continuation, **avenue Général-de-Gaulle**, is abrupt, with wide boulevards, opulent villas and palms creating a spa town atmosphere. If you're keen on the ancient history of this coast, the **Site Archéologique d'Olbia** in Almanarre (April–Sept Tues & Sat 3–6pm, Thurs & Fri 9.30am–12.30pm & 3–6pm; €4.60) is worth a visit: the remains of the fortified Greek trading post are supplemented by later Roman and medieval remains, including those of the abbey of Saint-Pierre de l'Almanarre. An alternative pastime is to wander around the spectacular array of cacti and palms in the **Jardins Olbius-Riquier**, just to the southeast of avenue Gambetta (daily 7.30am–dusk; free). It has a small zoo and miniature train to keep kids happy.

Eating and drinking

For **eating and drinking**, place Massillon is the obvious place: filled with restaurant tables and with an unmistakably Mediterranean atmosphere in the evening. Of its restaurants *Le Bistrot de Marius*, 1 place Massillon (☎04.94.35.88.38; closed Mon in July & Aug), is perhaps the most tempting, with plenty of fish on its €26–32 menus. In the new town, *Les Jardins de Bacchus*, 32 av Gambetta (☎04.94.65.77.63; menus from €32; closed Sat lunch, Sun dinner & Mon), serves novel concoctions with panache, while *Les Jardins de Saradam*, 35 av de Belgique (☎04.94.65.97.53, closed Sun eve & Mon out of season), is a reliable North African restaurant with a pretty garden and filling couscous and tagines from around €11. Hyères' **cafés**, though numerous – especially around place Clemenceau – are rather unprepossessing.

Around Hyères

Hyères's coastal suburbs have plenty of beaches, but can be subject to mosquito plagues in spring and summer. **L'Almanarre**, about 5km south of town, hosts windsurfing championships in June and has a narrow crescent of sand from which you can swim. **La Capte** is rather built-up, but offers warmer, shallow water and a long sandy beach. Alternatively, take the route du Sel (closed mid-Nov to mid-April) to the **Presqu'Île de Giens** for a glimpse of the saltworks and the flamingos on the adjoining lake. Besides the peculiarity of its attachment to the mainland (last broken by storms in 1811), **Giens** is fairly nondescript. There are, however, some fine cliffs facing the sea, and in rough weather you can understand why so many wrecks have been discovered here. **La Tour Fondue**, a Richelieu construction on the eastern side of Giens, overlooks the small port that serves the Îles d'Hyères.

Traffic fumes and the proximity to the airport make the beaches between Hyères-Plage and Le Ceinturon/Ayguade rather undesirable. Best to head further up the coast to the fishing port of **Les Salins d'Hyères**. East of Les Salins, where the coastal road finally turns inland, you can follow a path between abandoned salt flats and the sea to a secluded beach.

The Îles d'Hyères

A haven from tempests in ancient times, then the peaceful home of monks and farmers, the **Îles d'Hyères** became, from the Middle Ages onwards, the target of piracy and coastal attacks. The three main islands, **Porquerolles**, **Port-Cros** and **Levant**, are covered in half-destroyed, rebuilt or abandoned forts, dating from the sixteenth century, when François I started a trend of under-funded fort building, up to the twentieth century, when the German gun positions on Port-Cros and Levant were put out of action by the Americans. Porquerolles and Levant are not yet free of garrisons, thanks to the knack of the French armed forces for securing prime beauty sites for their bases. Their presence has helped prevent development and, in the non-military areas, the islands' very fragile environment is protected by the Parc National de Port-Cros and the Conservatoire Botanique de Porquerolles. Sheer pressure of visitor numbers has nevertheless created problems, so in 2004 the authorities announced plans to limit visitor numbers to 5000 daily on Porquerolles and 1500 daily on Port-Cros. Ferry operators must turn away further bookings once the daily total has been reached.

Ferries to the Îles d'Hyères

Departures from:

Bandol quai d'Honneur (Ⓣ04.94.32.51.41, Ⓦwww.atlantide1.com). To Porquerolles July & Aug only.

La Tour Fondue Presqu'Île de Giens (Ⓣ04.94.58.21.81, Ⓦwww.tlv-tvm.com). The closest port to Porquerolles; all year round to Porquerolles, plus summer two-island trip to Porquerolles and Port Cros.

Le Lavandou gare maritime (Ⓣ04.94.71.01.02, Ⓦwww.vedettesilesdor.fr). The closest port to Port-Cros and Levant; year-round daily services to Levant and Port-Cros; thrice-weekly service April–Sept to Porquerolles (daily July & Aug). The same line runs less frequent seasonal services from Cavalaire to Levant, Port Cros and Porquerolles and also from La Croix Valmer.

La Londe Port Miramar (Ⓣ04.94.05.21.14, Ⓦwww.bateliersсotedazur.com) Porquerolles and Port Cros, April–Sept only.

Port d'Hyères Hyères-Plage (Ⓣ04.94.57.44.07, Ⓦwww.tlv-tvm.com). Services to Port-Cros and Levant all year.

St-Raphaël quai Nomy, Vieux Port (Ⓣ04.94.95.17.46, Ⓦwww.tmr-saintraphael.com). Services to Port-Cros Fri only July & Aug.

Toulon Batelier de la Rade (Ⓣ04.94.46.24.65). Excursions to Porquerolles, Port Cros and Le Levant.

The islands' wild, scented greenery and fine sand beaches are a reminder of what much of the mainland was like forty years ago. To **stay** on them, the only reasonable option is Levant, though you must book months in advance. Accommodation on Porquerolles is limited, expensive and needs reserving in advance; on Port-Cros it's almost non-existent. All visitors should observe signs forbidding smoking (away from the ports), flower-picking and littering.

Île de Porquerolles

The most easily accessible of the islands is **Porquerolles**, whose permanent village, also called **PORQUEROLLES**, has a few hotels and restaurants, plenty of cafés, a market and interminable games of *boules*. It dates from a nineteenth-century military settlement, and the village still focuses around the central **place d'Armes**, the erstwhile military exercise ground. In summer its population explodes to over 10,000, but there is some activity all year round. This is the only cultivated island of the three, with a few olive groves and three Côtes de Provence *domaines* that can be visited.

Porquerolles is big enough to find yourself alone amid its stunning landscapes. The **lighthouse** (June–Sept 11am–noon & 2.30–4.30pm weather permitting), due south of the village, and the **calanques** to its east make good destinations for an hour's walk, though don't even think of swimming on this side of the island, unless you fancy cliff diving. The southern shoreline is all cliffs, with scary paths meandering close to the edge through heather and exuberant maquis scrub. Just off the path to the lighthouse at the southern end of the village is the **Maison du Parc** (Mon–Fri & Sun: July & Aug 9.30am–12.30pm & 2.30–6.15pm; April–June, Sept & Oct 9.30am–12.30pm & 1.30–5.15pm) with a garden of palms from around the world, information on the national park's activities and tours of the nearby Mediterranean botanic garden of **Le Hameau**. The longest beach is the **plage Notre-Dame**, 3km northeast of the village just before the *terrain militaire* on the northern tip. The nearest beach to the village is the **plage d'Argent**, 1km away (continue west from the port past the Arche de Noë and take the first, well-signed right). This 500–metre strip of white sand fringes a curving bay backed by pine forests, and has a pleasant **restaurant**, *La Plage d'Argent* (☎04.94.58.32.48; closed Sept–March; lunchtime *plat du jour* €13–24).

△ Plage d'Argent, Île de Porquerolles

Practicalities

There's a small **information centre** by the harbour (daily: April–Sept 9am–5.30pm; Oct–March 9am–12.30pm; ⓣ04.94.58.33.76, ⓦwww.porquerolles.com) where you can get basic maps. You can hire **bikes** from several outlets: La Bécane (ⓣ04.94.58.37.94) and L'Indien (ⓣ04.94.58.30.39) are both on place d'Armes. Expect to pay upwards of €100 a night for **hotel** accommodation in Porquerolles in season; marginally cheaper is the *Relais de la Poste*, place d'Armes (ⓣ04.98.04.62.62, ⓦwww.lerelaisdelaposte.com; ❻; closed Oct–March). Otherwise, you might try *Les Mèdes*, rue de la Douane (ⓣ04.94.12.41.24, ⓦwww.hotel-les-medes.fr; ❽; closed Jan to mid-March & early Nov to late Dec), or *Villa Sainte-Anne*, on place d'Armes (ⓣ04.98.04.63.00, ⓦwww.sainteanne.com; ❾; closed early Nov to mid-Feb), which has the most character. There's no campsite and *camping sauvage* is strictly forbidden, so don't miss the last ferry to the mainland. Most of the cafés and **restaurants** in the village are pure tourist fodder, though *L'Oustaou* on place d'Armes (ⓣ04.94.58.30.13, closed mid-Nov to Jan) does more ambitious fare – tuna, *pave de rumsteak* or *andouillettes* – from around €12.50. You can buy sandwiches and *pan bagnat* on the place d'Armes for around €4, and there's a supermarket and an excellent fruit and vegetable stall.

Île de Port-Cros

The dense vegetation and mini-mountains of **Port-Cros** (ⓦwww.portcrosparcnational.fr) make its exploration much tougher than Porquerolles, though it's less than half the size. Aside from ruined forts and the handful of buildings around the port, the only intervention is the classification labels on some of the plants and the extensive network of paths; you're not supposed to stray from these and it would be difficult to do so given the thickness of the undergrowth. The entire island is a protected zone, and has the richest fauna and flora of all the islands. Kestrels, eagles and sparrowhawks nest here; there are shrubs that flower and bear fruit at the same time, and more common species like broom, lavender, rosemary and heather flourish. One kilometre from the port (and a 45min walk) is the nearest beach, **plage de la Palud**; it takes rather longer to reach Mont Vinaigre, the island's highest point, via the **Vallon de la Solitude** – a three-hour round trip. From here there are views over the island's south coast and the islet of Gabinière. There are some 30 kilometres of paths on Port Cros, though all except those to the beaches are liable to closure during times of high fire risk.

The only **hotel**, *Le Manoir d'Hélène* (ⓣ04.94.05.90.52, ⓦmonsite.orange.fr/hotelmanoirportcros; ❾ half-board; closed Oct to mid-April; menus from €43), has few vacancies; there are five half-board rooms at the restaurant, *Hostellerie Provençale* (ⓣ04.94.05.90.43; closed Nov–Easter; ❾). Almost as expensive is dining in the few **restaurants** around the port, though you can get a sandwich or a slice of pizza. Once you leave the village, however, there's nothing; at the very least, walkers should be sure they carry enough water. Again, camping is forbidden.

Île du Levant

The **Île du Levant** – ninety percent military reserve – is almost always humid and sunny. Cultivated plant life goes wild, with the result that giant geraniums and nasturtiums climb three-metre hedges, overhung by gigantic eucalyptus trees and yuccas. The tiny bit of the island spared by the military is the **nudist colony** of **HELIOPOLIS,** set up in the 1930s. About sixty people live here all year round, joined by thousands who come for the summer, and by tens of thousands of day-trippers, who are treated as voyeurs; if you **stay**, even for one night, you'll receive a friendlier reception. The most reasonable **hotels** are *Chez Valéry* (ⓣ04.94.05.90.83, ⓕ04.94.05.92.95; ❺; closed Oct–March) and *Gaëtan* (ⓣ04.94.05.91.78, ⓦwww.hotelgaetan.com; ❸; closed Oct–March). There are two **campsites**: *Le Colombero* (ⓣ04.94.05.90.29; closed Oct–March) and *La Pinède* (ⓣ04.94.05.92.81, ⓦwww.campingdulevant.free.fr).

Levant has a better choice of **restaurants** than the other islands, though price and quality still don't match. The restaurant of the *Hôtel Gaëtan* is reasonable, with a €24 menu.

The Corniche des Maures

The Côte really gets going with the resorts of the **Corniche des Maures**, as multi-million-dollar residences lurk increasingly in the hills, luxurious yachts moor in the bays, and seafront prices become alarming. Douglas Fairbanks Jr, the late Grand Duke of Luxembourg and sundry other titled names have pushed this coastline into legend.

The Corniche des Maures has beaches that shine silver (from the mica crystals in the sand), tall dark pines, oaks and eucalyptus to shade them, glittering rocks of purple, green and reddish hue and chestnut-forested hills keeping winds away.

Bormes-les-Mimosas and around

Seventeen kilometres east of Hyères, chic **BORMES-LES-MIMOSAS** is medieval in flavour, with a ruined but restored **castle** at the summit of its hill, protected by spiralling lines of pantiled houses backing onto immaculately restored flights of steps. The mimosas here, and all along the Côte d'Azur, are no more indigenous than the people passing in their Porsches: the tree was introduced from Mexico in the 1860s, but the town still has some of the most luscious climbing flowers of any Côte town, and in summer, the displays of bougainvillea and oleander are impressive.

To the southwest of Bormes is one of those rare unbuilt-up stretches of coast around **BREGANÇON** and **CABASSON**, good wine-growing terrain, harbouring a presidential residence in the castle at **Cap de Bregançon**. Unfortunately, access to the sea is heavily controlled, with three **beaches** charging hefty parking fees (€7) and a small fee to cyclists and walkers. The beach by the castle past Cabasson is the best.

Practicalities

Two **hotels** worth trying in old Bormes are the rather plain and old-fashioned *Bellevue*, on place Gambetta (ⓣ04.94.71.15.15, ⓦbellevuebormes.fr.st; ❸; closed mid-Nov to Jan) or the fancier *Hostellerie du Cigalou* opposite (ⓣ04.94.41.51.27, ⓦwww.hostellerieducigalou.com; ❼) In Cabasson, the attractive and peaceful *Les Palmiers*, 240 chemin du Petit-Fort (ⓣ04.94.64.81.94, ⓦwww.hotellespalmiers.com; ❾; closed Dec–Jan; half-board compulsory in summer), has its own path to the beach. All **campsites** are just below the main road or in La Favière, closer to Le Lavandou than to Bormes. One of the best is *Clau-Mar-Jo* at 895 rte de Bénat (ⓣ04.94.71.53.39; €26 for two people; closed mid-Oct to mid-March). The **tourist office** in Bormes is on place Gambetta (April–Sept daily 9am–12.30pm & 2.30–6.30pm; Oct–March Mon–Sat 9am–12.30pm & 2–6pm; ⓣ04.94.01.38.38, ⓦwww.bormeslesmimosas.com).

Good **restaurants** include *La Tonnelle* on place Gambetta (ⓣ04.94.71.34.84; closed Nov; lunch menus from €27), specializing in local recipes including *daube de boeuf*; *La Cassole* at 1 ruelle du Moulin (ⓣ04.94.71.14.86; menus from €26) which serves Provençal specialities in unpretentious surroundings and *Pâtes…et Pâtes*, on place du Bazar (ⓣ04.94.64.85.75; closed Tues & Thurs lunchtimes), which serves the best pasta in town from around €12.50.

Le Lavandou to La Croix-Valmer

LE LAVANDOU, a few kilometres east of Bormes, is a pleasantly unpretentious seaside town known for its good, sandy beaches. Its name derives from *lavoir* or "wash-house" rather than "lavender". From the central promenade of quai Gabriel-Péri the sea is all but invisible thanks to the pleasure boats moored at the three harbours, and it's only demand from restaurateurs that keeps the dozen or so fishing vessels, from a fleet that once numbered fifty, still in business. If you want to indulge in watersports or nightlife, the **tourist office** on quai Gabriel-Péri (May–Sept daily 9am–12.30pm & 2.30–7pm; Nov–March Mon–Sat 9am–noon & 2.30–6pm; ⓣ04.94.00.40.50, ⓦwww.lelavandou.com) will happily advise. For **accommodation**, try the *Hôtel L'Oustaou*, 20 av Général-de-Gaulle (ⓣ04.94.71.12.18, ⓦwww.lavandou-hotel-oustaou.com; ❸), a clean, family-run place in the town centre.

The town beach at Le Lavandou is quite broad and sandy, but if you're after the fabled silver beaches you need to head out of town and east along the corniche to **Cavalière**, **Pramousquier**, **Le Canadel** and **Le Rayol**. It's hardly countryside, but you can explore the Pointe du Layet headland just east of Cavalière, follow the sinuous D27 up to the **Col du Canadel** for breathtaking views and beautiful cork-oak woodland, and, in **Le Rayol**, visit a superb garden, the **Domaine de Rayol** (daily: summer 9.30am–7.30pm; winter 9.30am–5.30pm; €7) with plants from differing parts of the world that share the Mediterranean climate.

Beyond Le Rayol the corniche climbs away from the coast through 3km of open countryside, scarred almost every year by fires. As abruptly as this wilderness commences, it ends with the sprawling, bland family resort of **Cavalaire-sur-Mer**. From here another exceptional stretch of coastline, dressed only in its natural covering of rock and woodlands, is visible across the Baie de Cavalaire. This is the **Domaine de Cap Lardier**, a wonderful coastal conservation area around the southern tip of the St-Tropez peninsula, easily accessible from **LA CROIX-VALMER**. The resort's centre is 2.5km from the sea, but this only adds to its charm, since some of the land in between is taken up by vineyards producing a very decent Côte de Provence.

La Croix-Valmer's **tourist office** is at les Jardins de la Gare (mid-June to mid-Sept Mon–Sat 9.15am–12.30pm & 2.30–7pm, Sun 9am–1pm; mid-Sept to mid-June Mon–Fri 9.15am–noon & 2–6pm, Sat & Sun 9.15am–noon; ⓣ04.94.55.12.12, ⓦwww.lacroixvalmer.fr), just up from the junction of the D559 and D93. A good-value **hotel** is *La Bienvenue* on rue L.-Martin (ⓣ04.94.17.08.08, ⓦwww.hotel-la-bienvenue.com; ❸; closed Nov–Feb) in the village centre. One of the cheapest options near the beach is the family-run *Hostellerie La Ricarde*, plage du Débarquement (ⓣ04.94.79.64.07, ⓦwww.golfe-infos.com/la-ricarde; ❸; closed Oct–March), whilst at the other end of the scale is *Le Château de Valmer*, on route de Gigaro (ⓣ04.94.55.15.15, ⓦwww.chateauvalmer.com; ❾; closed mid-Oct to mid-April), a luxurious old mansion within walking distance of the sea. You can **camp** at the four-star *Sélection*, on boulevard de la Mer (ⓣ04.94.55.10.30, ⓦwww.selectioncamping.com;

€31.50 per tent; closed mid-Oct to mid-March; booking advisable), 400m from the sea and with excellent facilities. Good pizzas are guaranteed (€10 up) at *L'Italien* (☎04.94.79.67.16) on plage de Gigaro, just before the conservation area. Two other good but expensive **restaurants** on this beach are *La Brigantine* and *Souleïas*.

The Massif des Maures

The secret of the Côte d'Azur is that however grossly vulgar the coast, Provence is still just behind – sparsely populated, village-oriented and dependent on the land for produce, not real estate. The most bewitching hinterland is the **Massif des Maures**, stretching from Hyères to Fréjus. The highest point of these hills stops short of 800m, but the quick succession of ridges, the sudden drops and views, and the curling, looping roads, are pervasively mountainous. Where the lie of the land allows, vines are grown. Elsewhere the hills are thickly forested, with Aleppo and umbrella pines, holly, cork oaks and sweet chestnut trees. In spring, the sombre forest is enlivened by millions of wild flowers, and the narrow, tortuous upland roads are busy with cyclists; in winter, this is the haunt of hunters. Amidst the brush lope the last of the Hermann's tortoises which once could be found along the whole of the northern Mediterranean coast.

Much of the Massif is inaccessible even to walkers. However, the **GR9 footpath** follows the highest and most northerly ridge from Pignans on the N97 past Notre-Dame-des-Anges, La Sauvette, **La Garde-Freinet** and down to the head of the Golfe de St-Tropez. If you're **cycling**, the D14 that runs for 42km through the middle, parallel to the coast, from Pierrefeu-du-Var, north of Hyères, to **Cogolin** near St-Tropez, is manageable and stunning, climbing from 150m to 411m above sea level.

Collobrières and La Chartreuse de la Verne

At the heart of the Massif is the ancient village of **COLLOBRIÈRES**, reputed to have been the first place in France to learn from the Spanish that a certain tree plugged into bottles allows a wine industry to grow. From the

The forest fires of 2003

The summer of 2003 was not a happy one for Provence. A terrorist bomb in Nice was quickly forgotten in the face of the worst **forest fires** for a generation. A dry spring was followed by a long heatwave coupled with high mistral winds, which conspired to create tinderbox conditions, leading to fires in much of the region, from Salon de Provence to the Riviera. Worst affected was the Massif des Maures, where fires came closer to the coastal resorts than many could remember and 20,000 residents and holidaymakers were evacuated. People too frightened to return to their homes took to the beach at Les Issambres, near Ste-Maxime, while two holidaymakers died trying to flee flames near La Garde Freinet. The authorities introduced stop and search procedures as it became clear some of the fires had been started deliberately. But most of the fires probably started naturally or through carelessness, which sparked a wider debate about the wisdom of planting so many non-native pine trees. On the D14 between Collobrières and Grimaud a lovely belvedere acts as a memorial to the three *sapeurs-pompiers* from La-Seyne-sur-Mer who died here while fighting the fires.

Middle Ages until very recent times, cork production has been the major business of the village. However, the sweet chestnut tree is the mainstay of the local economy nowadays. The church, the *mairie* and the houses don't seem to have been modernized for a century, but the **Confiserie Azurienne** on boulevard Koenig (9.30am–12.30pm & 1.30–7.15pm) exudes efficiency and modern business skill in the manufacture of all things chestnut: ice cream, jam, nougat, purée and *marrons glacés*. There's a small outdoor café there where you can enjoy the delicious ice cream.

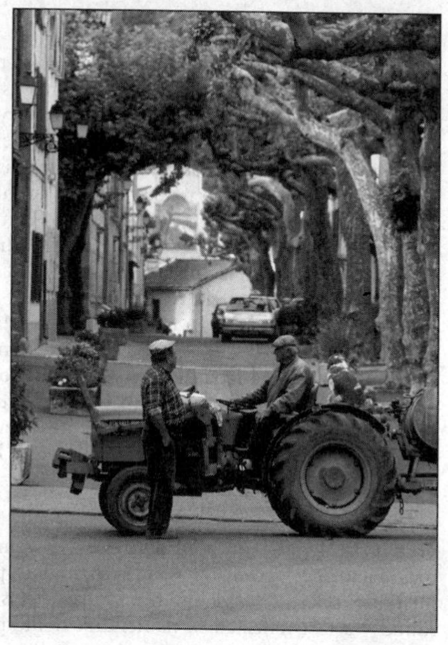

△ Collobrières

Collobrières' **tourist office** on boulevard Charles-Caminat (July & Aug Mon–Fri 10am–12.30pm & 3–7pm, Sat & Sun 10am–12.30pm & 3.30–7pm; Sept–June Tues–Sat 8.30am–noon & 2–5.30pm, Sat 8.30am–noon; ⓣ04.94.48.08.00, ⓦwww.collobrieres.fr; not always open during its published opening hours) can supply details of walks in the surrounding hills. There are two **hotels**: *Notre-Dame*, 15 av de la Libération (ⓣ04.94.48.07.13, ⓕ04.94.48.05.95; ❶; closed mid-Dec to mid-Feb), and the equally excellent-value *Hôtel des Maures*, 19 bd Lazare Carnot (ⓣ04.94.48.07.10, ⓕ04.94.48.02.73; ❶, and ❷ per person full board). There are also two great **chambres d'hôtes**: *L'Atelier*, Colette Brésis' ceramic studio at Le Vallon des Fées, 2km west of the village along the D14 and with just one double room (ⓣ04.94.48.05.92; ❸; closed Nov–March); and Loïc and Andrée de Saleneuve's *La Bastide de La Cabrière*, 6km in the direction of Gonfaron on the D39 (ⓣ04.94.48.04.31, ⓦwww.saleneuve.com; ❺). A municipal **campsite**, the St-Roch, south of the village near place Charles-de-Gaulle, is open in July and August (ⓣ04.94.28.15.72; bookings through the tourist office). *Camping sauvage* is forbidden; one stray spark and you could be responsible for a thousand acres of burnt forest.

For food other than chestnuts, the **restaurant** *La Petite Fontaine*, 6 place de la République (ⓣ04.94.48.00.12; closed Sun eve & Mon), is congenial and affordable, with menus from €24, but books up fast. If you want to buy some local **wines**, visit Les Vignerons de Collobrières close to the *Hôtel Notre-Dame* at the western entrance to the village. Local **market** days are Thursday and Sunday.

Hidden in the forest, 12km from Collobrières on a minor road off the D14 towards Grimaud, is a huge and now largely restored twelfth-century monastery, **La Chartreuse de la Verne** (daily except Tues: Feb–May & Oct–Dec 11am–5pm; June–Sept 11am–6pm; €5), abandoned at the time of the Revolution. If anything, the ongoing restoration work has left it looking a little too pristine, though there's no denying the wonder of its setting. The access road deteriorates into a rutted track for the last 500m.

Grimaud

GRIMAUD, 25km east of Collobrières along the twisting D14 and more easily reached from St-Tropez or La Croix Valmer, is a film set of a *village perché*. The cone of houses enclosing the eleventh-century church and culminating in the ruins of a medieval castle appears as a single, perfectly unified entity, though the effect of timelessness is undermined by the glass lift that whisks visitors up into the village from the main road. The most vaunted street is the arcaded **rue des Templiers**, which leads up to the pure Romanesque **Église de St-Michel** and a house of the Knights Templar, while the view from the **castle** ruins is superb. There's a **tourist office** at 1 bd des Aliziers just off the main road passing the village (Mon–Sat: April–June & Sept 9am–12.30pm & 2.30–6.15pm; July & Aug 9am–12.30pm & 3–7pm; Oct–March Mon–Sat 9am–12.30pm & 2.15–5.30pm; ⓣ04.94.55.43.83, ⓦwww.grimaud-provence.com) and a little folk museum, the **Musée des Arts et Traditions** (Tues–Sat 2.30–5.50pm; free) close by. Great-value **menus** from €45 are offered at *Le Coteau Fleuri*, place des Pénitents (ⓣ04.94.43.20.17, ⓦwww.coteaufleuri.fr; closed Tues all day, Mon & Fri lunch, plus Nov & early Dec), which also has a few **rooms** (❺).

Cogolin

COGOLIN, just south of Grimaud, is remarkable for its traditional craft manufacturing – reeds for wind instruments, pipes for smoking, wrought-iron furniture, silk yarn and knotted wool carpets. The town is animated all year round – a fact reflected in its fiendish traffic problem and even more fiendish traffic control measures.

Visits to some of the **craft factories** can be arranged and are free. The **tourist office** on place de la République (March–June & Sept–Oct Mon–Fri 9am–12.30pm & 2–6.30pm, Sat 9am–12.30pm; July & Aug Mon–Sat 9am–1pm & 2–6.30pm; Nov–Feb Mon–Fri 9am–12.30pm & 2–6pm, Sat 9.30am–12.30pm; ⓣ04.94.55.01.10, ⓦwww.cogolin-provence.com) will provide you with a complete list of addresses and times, and help with making appointments. Or you can just wander down **avenue Georges-Clemenceau** and pop into the retail outlets. Pipes made from briar wood are on show in Courrieu at no. 58 (daily 9am–noon & 2–6pm), and the Manufacture de Tapis, just off the avenue on boulevard Louis-Blanc, re-creates designs by famous artists such as Léger and Mondrian (exhibition room open Mon–Thurs 8.30am–noon & 2–5.30pm, Fri until 5pm). World-famous musicians get their reeds from Rigotti, on rue Barbusse; visits are restricted however to musicians and groups only.

From place Bellevue, at the top of the town away from the bustling centre, you can see across the St-Tropez peninsula to Gassin, Ramatuelle and St-Tropez itself. Having taken in that view and seen enough of Cogolin's manufacturing businesses, try the local **wines**: the Cave des Vignerons is on rue Marceau, just before the junction with the N98 heading westwards (daily: mid-June to mid-Sept 2.30–7.30pm; mid-Sept to mid-June 8.30am–12.30pm & 2–6pm). There are a couple of **hotels** in Cogolin that make viable bases for trips into St-Tropez: amiable, comfortable *Coq Hôtel*, place de la République (ⓣ04.94.54.13.71, ⓕ04.94.54.03.06; ❻); and trendy boutique hotel *Bliss*, next door (ⓣ04.94.54.15.17, ⓕ04.94.54.42.78; ❼). Both, however, are in somewhat noisy, central locations.

La Garde-Freinet

The attractive village of **LA GARDE-FREINET**, 10km northwest of Grimaud, was founded in the late twelfth century by people from the nearby villages of Saint Clément and Miremer. The original fortified settlement sat further up the hillside, and the foundations of the fortress are still visible above the village beside the ruins of a fifteenth-century castle (take the path from La Planette car park at the western end of the village). These days a note of St-Tropez trendiness is creeping in, but it still feels that it belongs to the locals, thanks in part to the regeneration of forestry business around cork and chestnut. It also has medieval charm; easy walks to stunning panoramas; markets twice a week (Wed & Sun); a chestnut cooperative on the northern approach to the village; tempting food shops like La Voute, selling organic produce and good local wines; and very reasonable accommodation. The **tourist office** operates from the Chapelle St Jean, on place de la Mairie (Easter–Oct Mon–Sat 9.30am–1pm & 4–6.30pm, Sun 10am–12.30pm; Nov–Easter Mon–Sat 10am–12.30pm & 2–5pm; ⓣ04.94.43.67.41, ⓦwww.lagardefreinet-tourisme.com), and will provide details for the entire Maures region, including suggesting **walks** and hikes such as the spectacular 21-kilometre GR9 route des Crêtes. The danger of forest fires is particularly high here; the current risk level is posted up outside the tourist office. Next door is the **Conservatoire du Patrimoine** (Tues–Sat 10am–12.30pm & 3–6pm; €2) which organizes guided walks on various local topics and has exhibits on local sericulture, a model of the old fortress.

For **rooms**, *La Claire Fontaine* on place Vieille (ⓣ & ⓕ04.94.43.63.76; ❸) and *Le Fraxinois* on place Neuve (ⓣ04.94.43.62.84, ⓕ04.94.43.69.65; ❹) are incredibly good value. There's also a campsite, *La Ferme de Bérard*, 5km along the D558 towards Grimaud (ⓣ04.94.43.21.23, ⓕ04.94.43.32.33; €11.20 for two adults, car and tent; closed Nov–Feb).

The place to be of an evening is *Le Carnotzet* bar, art gallery and **restaurant**, on the exquisite place du Marché (ⓣ04.94.43.62.73; menu from €20; occasional live jazz). *La Colombe Joyeuse*, on place Vieille (ⓣ04.94.43.65.24; closed Tues in winter; €15 menu), has pigeon as its à la carte speciality, whilst *La Faucado*, on the main road to the coast (ⓣ04.94.43.60.41; closed Tues in winter; à la carte around €60), is overpriced, but serves some beautiful dishes from local produce in a pretty garden setting.

St-Tropez and its peninsula

The origins of **ST-TROPEZ** are unremarkable: a fishing village that grew up around a port founded by the Greeks of Marseille, which was destroyed by the Saracens in 739 and finally fortified in the late Middle Ages. Its sole distinction was its inaccessibility: stuck on a small peninsula that never warranted proper roads, St-Tropez could only easily be reached by boat. This held true as late as the 1880s, when the novelist Guy de Maupassant sailed into the port during his final high-living binge before the onset of syphilitic insanity.

Soon after, the painter Paul Signac was sailing down the coast when bad weather forced him to moor in St-Tropez. He promptly decided to build a house there, to which he invited his friends. Matisse was one of the first to accept, with Bonnard, Marquet, Dufy, Dérain, Vlaminck, Seurat and Van Dongen following suit, and by the eve of World War I St-Tropez was an established hangout for bohemians. The 1930s saw a new influx, of writers as much as painters: Cocteau, Colette and Anaïs Nin, whose journal records "girls riding bare-breasted in the back of open cars". In 1956, Roger Vadim arrived to film Brigitte Bardot in *Et Dieu Créa la Femme*, the international cult of Tropezian

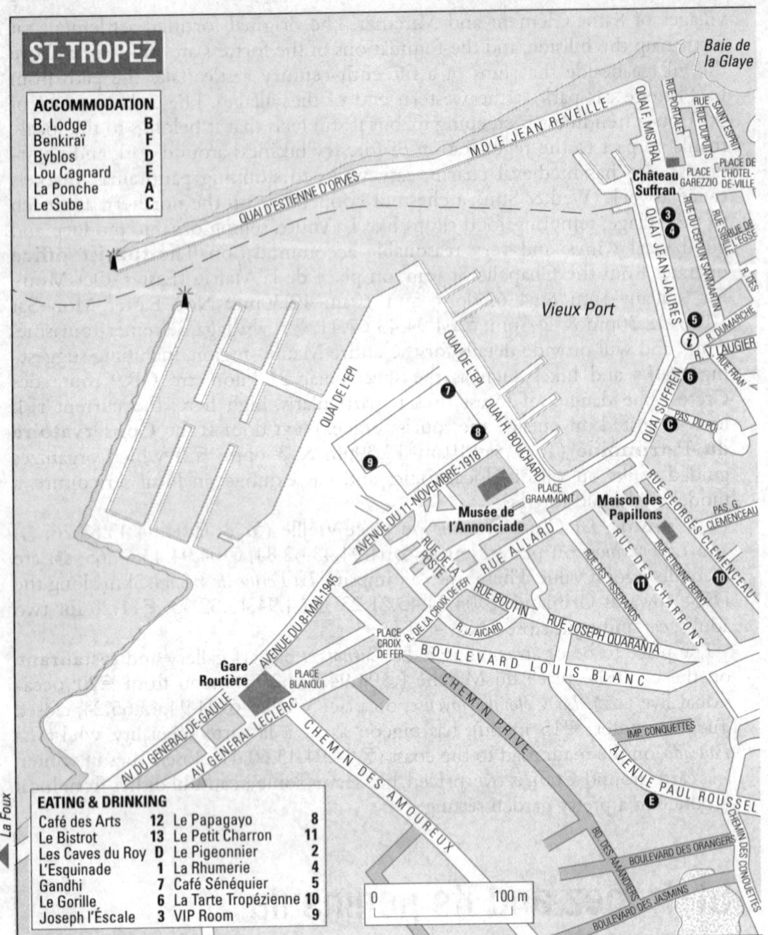

sun, sex and celebrities promptly took off and the place has been groaning under the weight of impossible numbers of visitors ever since.

As the summer playground of Europe's youthful rich and famous, St-Tropez remains undeniably glamorous, its oversize yachts and infamous champagne "spray" parties creating an air of hedonistic excess. Unless you have the holiday budget of a supermodel or Formula One racing driver, however, it can feel like a party you're not invited to.

Arrival, information and accommodation

Buses run between the main coast road at **La Foux** and St-Tropez, 5.5km away, every thirty minutes to an hour or so in season (rather less frequently at other times), dropping you at the **gare routière** on avenue Général-de-Gaulle. From here it's a short walk along avenue du 8-Mai-1945 to the **Vieux Port**,

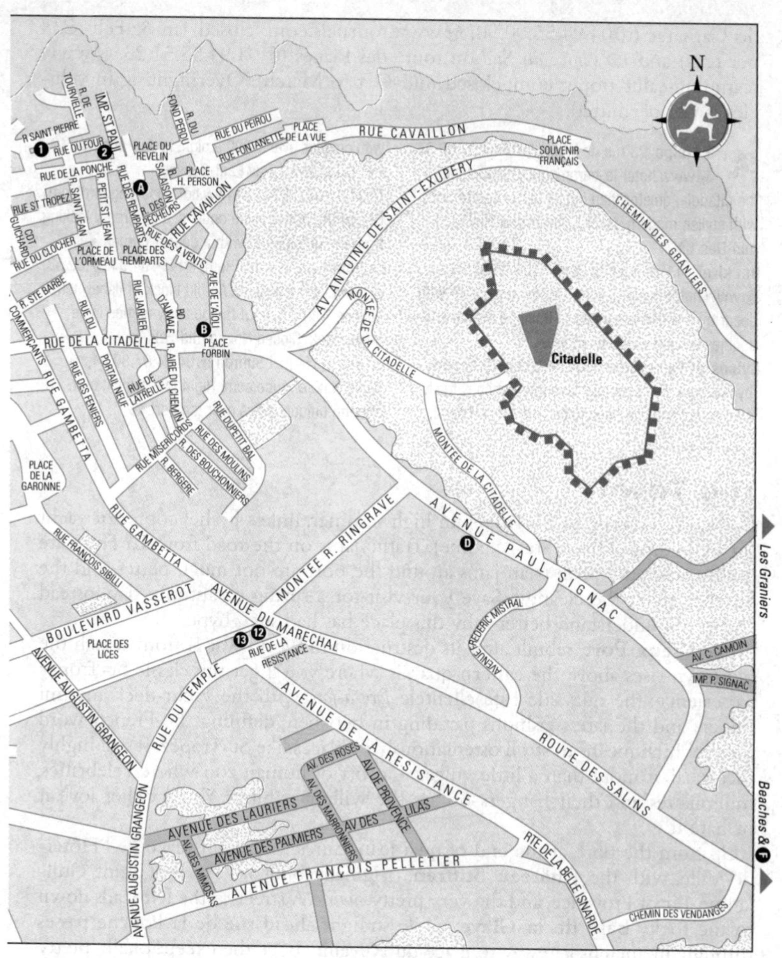

where you'll find the **tourist office** on quai Jean-Jaurès (daily: April–June & Sept 9.30am–12.30pm & 2–7pm; July & Aug 9.30am–8pm; Oct–March 9.30am–12.30pm & 2–6pm; ⓣ04.94.97.45.21, ⓦwww.ot-saint-tropez.com). **Bikes** and **motorbikes** can be rented at Holiday Bikes at 12 av G.-Leclerc (ⓣ04.94.97.09.39, ⓦwww.holiday-bikes.com).

Accommodation is a problem; between April and September you'll be lucky to find a room unless you've booked in advance or are prepared to pay exorbitant prices. The tourist office can help with reservations, but, transport permitting, you might be better off staying in La Croix-Valmer or La Garde-Freinet. Many hotels close out of season. **Camping** near St-Tropez can be expensive, with many sites more geared towards chalet lets than providing emplacements for tents. The nearest sites are the two on the plage du Pampelonne, which charge extortionate rates and are massively crowded in high summer. Otherwise, within a three-kilometre radius of Ramatuelle are *Les Tournels* on route de Camarat (T 04.94.55.90.90, W www.tournels.com; closed Jan & Feb, €38 per tent) and *La Croix du Sud* on route des Plages (T 04.94.55.51.23, W www.camping-saint-tropez.com; closed mid-Oct to March). Overnighting in vehicles is not permitted.

B.Lodge 23 rue de l'Aïoli T 04.94.97.06.57, W www.hotel-le-baron.com. Overlooking the citaddle, quieter than hotels in the centre and with stylish modern decor; closed mid-Nov to mid-Dec. 4

Benkiraï 11 chemin du Pinet T 04.94.97.04.37, W www.hotel-benkirai.com. Trendy newcomer with decor by a young associate of Philippe Starck and doubles around €450 in summer. 9

Byblos av Paul-Signac T 04.94.56.68.00, W www.byblos.com. The perennial favourite if money really is no object and you need to be with the in-crowd, with doubles over €500 a night in July and Aug. 9

Lou Cagnard 18 av Paul-Roussel T 04.94.97.04.24, W www.hotel-lou-cagnard.com. One of the better value options, a bit dreary looking from the outside but with a decent garden. 4

La Ponche 3 rue des Remperts T 04.94.97.02.53, W www.laponche.com. An old block of fishermen's houses with a host of famous arty names in its guest book. Closed Nov to mid-Feb. 9

Le Sube 15 quai Suffren T 04.94.97.30.04, W www.hotel-sube.com. Right in the thick of it, offering unique views over the port. 8

The Town

Beware of coming to St-Tropez in high summer, unless by helicopter or yacht (or by hydrofoil from Ste-Maxime). Traffic jams on the road from La Foux are nightmarish, the pedestrian jams around the port are not much better, and the beaches aren't the cleanest. Save your visit for a spring or autumn day instead and you'll understand better why this place has had such hype.

The **Vieux Port**, rebuilt after its destruction in World War II from which the old town rises above the eastern quay, is where you'll get the classic St-Tropez experience: the quayside café clientele *face-à-face* with the yacht-deck martini sippers and the latest fashions parading in between, defining the French word *frimer*, which means to stroll ostentatiously in places like St-Tropez. It's all highly theatrical, if more than a little vulgar – a sort of human zoo where celebrities, millionaires and their hangers-on are the willing exhibits. You'll either love it or hate it.

Up from the port, at the end of quai Jean-Jaurès, you enter place de l'Hôtel-de-Ville, with the **Château Suffren**, originally built in 980 by Count Guillaume 1er of Provence, and the very pretty *mairie*. A street to the left leads down to the rocky **baie de la Glaye**, while straight ahead rue de la Ponche passes through an ancient gateway to place du Revelin above the exceptionally pretty **fishing port** and its tiny beach. Turning inland and upwards, struggling past continuous shopfronts, stalls and café tables, you finally reach the open space around the sixteenth-century **citadelle**. It houses a local history **museum** (closed for renovation but scheduled to reopen during 2007; usually daily: April–Oct 10am–8pm; Nov–March 10am–6.30pm; summer nocturnes in high season until 10pm Wed–Sat; €5.50) which occasionally hosts art exhibitions. The walk round the ramparts (closed for restoration) has the best views of the gulf and the back of the town – views that haven't changed all that much since their translations in oil onto canvas before the war.

Some of these paintings you can see at the marvellous **Musée de l'Annonciade**, in the deconsecrated sixteenth-century chapel on place Georges-Grammont, right on the port (daily except Tues: Jan–June & Dec 10am–noon & 2–6pm; July–Oct 10am–1pm & 3–7pm; summer nocturnes until 10pm Wed & Fri; €5.50). It was originally Signac's idea to have a permanent exhibition space for the neo-Impressionists and Fauvists who painted here, though it was not until 1955 that the collections of various individuals were put together. The Annonciade features works by Signac, Matisse and most of the other artists who worked here: grey, grim, northern views of Paris, Boulogne and Westminster, and then local, brilliantly sunlit scenes by the same brush – a real delight and unrivalled outside Paris for the 1890–1940 period of French art. Just inland from the port at 9 rue Etienne Berny is the **Maison des Papillons** (April–Oct Mon–Sat 2.30–6pm; €3), a butterfly museum housing 4500 specimens including many rare and endangered species.

The other pole of St-Tropez's life, south of the Vieux Port, is **place des Lices**. The café-brasseries have – like those on the port – become a bit too Champs-Elysées in style, but you can still sit on benches in the shade of decayed but surviving plane trees and watch the *boules* games.

The beaches

The beach within easiest walking distance is **Les Graniers**, below the citadelle just beyond the port des Pêcheurs along rue Cavaillon. From there, a path follows the coast around the **baie des Canebiers**, with its small beach, to Cap St-Pierre, Cap St-Tropez, the very crowded **Les Salins** beach and right round to Tahiti-Plage, about 11km away.

Tahiti-Plage is the start of the almost straight, five-kilometre north–south **Pampelonne** beach, famous bronzing belt of St-Tropez and world initiator of the topless bathing cult. The water is shallow for 50m or so, and the beach is exposed to the wind, and sometimes scourged by dried sea vegetation, not to mention more distasteful garbage. But spotless glitter comes from the unending line of **beach bars** and restaurants, all with patios and sofas, serving cocktails and gluttonous ice creams (as well as full-blown meals). *Le 55* on boulevard Patch (☎04.94.97.55.55) is the original and most famous; *La Voile Rouge*, boulevard Patelli, chemin des Moulins (☎04.94.79.84.34) is where topless bathing first became the norm; and *Maison Ocoa*, boulevard Patch (☎04.94.79.89.80) is *über*-trendy – almost a nightclub on the beach. Though you'll stumble across people in the nude on all stretches of the beach, only some of the bars welcome people carrying wallets and nothing else.

Transport from St-Tropez to the beaches is provided by a frequent **minibus** service (June–Sept only) from place des Lices to Salins, or the infrequent bus service #105 to Ramatuelle which runs along the route de Pampelonne. If you're driving, you'll be forced to pay high parking charges at all the beaches, or to leave your car or motorbike some distance from the sea and easy prey to thieves.

Eating and drinking

Restaurants in St-Tropez obsess as much over how stylish they (and their customers) look as over the quality of the food they offer, and budget offerings – while not unknown – are distinctly in the minority. Whatever the category of restaurant, you should reckon on paying quite a bit more than in comparable places in other resorts in the Var.

Café des Arts place des Lices ☎04.94.97.02.25. The number-one brasserie on the square, where Mick and Bianca Jagger held their wedding reception in 1971; lunchtime *plats du jour* €16, evenings €16 and upwards.

Le Bistrot 3 place des Lices ☎04.94.97.11.33. Leather seating and chic decor for traditional preening and excellent but expensive eats; midday *formule* €14, otherwise from €32. Closed Wed in winter.

Gandhi 3 quai de l'Epi ☎04.94.97.71.71. Curries and tandoori, with a good selection of fish and shellfish on the menu. Lunch menu from €18.50 and dinner from €30. Closed all day Wed out of season, Wed lunch in April & Oct.

Le Gorille 1 quai Suffren. Straightforward steak and burger fare on the port, for around €15. July & Aug open 24hr.

Joseph l'Escale 9 quai Jean-Jaurès ⓣ04.94.97.00.63. Slick quayside restaurant that is rather more affordable than its sister restaurant around the corner, with main course fish dishes from around €17 and a menu at €37.

Le Papagayo Résidence du Port ⓣ04.94.79.29.50. Enormous bar/restaurant/club in a strategic location right on the port, with a big terrace and sushi on the menu.

Le Petit Charron 6 rue des Charrons ⓣ04.94.97.73.78. Tiny terrace and dining room serving beautifully cooked Provençal specialities. *Plats du jour* from around €18. Closed Sun out of season.

La Rhumerie quai Jean-Jaurès ⓣ04.94.97.31.58. Just about the cheapest proper meals on the port, with pasta dishes from €8.60 and *plats du jour* around €14.

Café Sénéquier 90 quai Jean-Jaurès. The top quayside café, open from breakfast; vast and expensive – horribly so for drinks – but it sells sensational nougat (also on sale from the shop in place aux Herbes at the back).

La Tarte Tropezienne 36 rue G.-Clemenceau. Patisserie claiming to have invented the rather sickly sponge and cream custard cake, though you no longer have to come to St-Tropez to sample it – the company has evolved into quite a large chain with branches the length of the Côte d'Azur.

Nightlife

In season St-Tropez stays up late. You can spend the evening trying on fancy clothes in the couturier shops; the *boules* games on place des Lices continue until well after dusk; and the portside spectacle doesn't falter till the early hours. If you're rich or mad enough to want to pay to see – and be seen with – the **nightlife** creatures of St-Tropez, clubs include: *Les Caves du Roy*, in the flashy *Hôtel Byblos* on rue Paul-Signac (the most expensive and exclusive); *L'Esquinade*, on rue du Four, which has been going strong since Bardot was young; and the *VIP Room* on the Nouveau Port. There's also a gay club, *Le Pigeonnier*, in rue de la Ponche.

Gassin and Ramatuelle

Though the coast of the **St-Tropez peninsula** sprouts second residences like a cabbage patch gone to seed, the interior is almost uninhabited, thanks

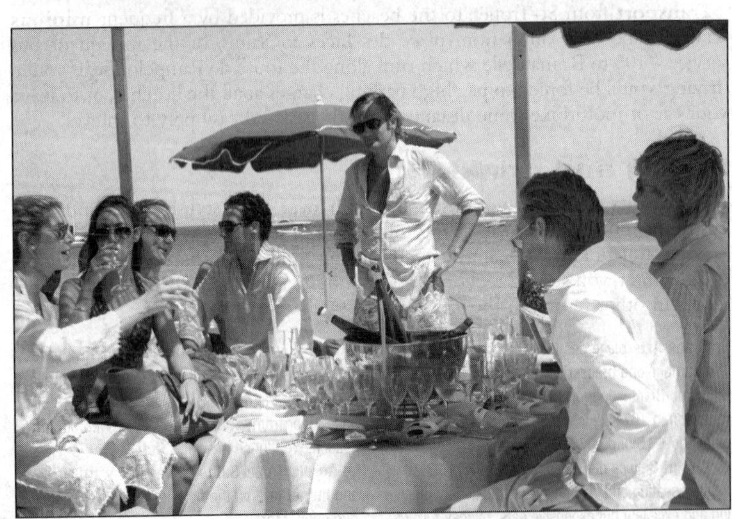

△ St-Tropez

to government intervention, complex ownerships and the value of some local wines. The best view of this richly green and flowering countryside is from the hilltop village of Gassin, its lower neighbour Ramatuelle, or the tiny road between them, the dramatic route des Moulins de Paillas, where three ruined windmills could once catch every wind.

GASSIN is the shape and size of a small ship perched on a summit; once an eighth-century Muslim stronghold, it is now, of course, highly chic, and best known as the birthplace of soccer idol David Ginola. It's an excellent place for a blowout dinner, sitting outside by the village wall with a spectacular panorama east over the peninsula. Of the handful of **restaurants**, *Bello Visto*, 9 place des Barrys (Ⓣ04.94.56.17.30, Ⓕ04.94.43.45.36; closed Tues lunch), has very acceptable Provençal specialities on a €27 menu, plus nine rooms at excellent prices for this brilliant setting (❹).

RAMATUELLE is bigger than its neighbour, though just as old, and is surrounded by some of the best Côte de Provence vineyards. The twisting, arcaded streets are full of arts and crafts of dubious talent, but it's all very pleasant. The most beautiful French actor ever to have appeared on screen, Gérard Philippe (1922–59), is buried in Ramatuelle's **cemetery**. His ivy-covered tomb, shaded by a rose bush, is set against the wall on the right as you look down. Hotels worth trying are the fairly basic *Chez Tony*, 31 rue Clemenceau (Ⓣ04.94.79.20.46; ❸), and the more attractive *Lou Castellas*, route des Moulins (Ⓣ04.94.79.20.67, Ⓦwww.lecurieducastellas.com; ❻). For **food**, great pasta dishes are to be had at *Au Fil à la Pâte*, 7 rue Victor-Léon (Ⓣ04.94.79.16.40; closed Nov–Feb), with good *plats du jour* at €12.

Port Grimaud

At the head of the Golfe de St-Tropez, just north of La Foux on the main coast road, the ultimate Côte d'Azur property development half stands and half floats. **PORT GRIMAUD** was created in the 1960s as a private community, with waterways for roads and yachts parked at the bottom of every garden. It's very well done, with all the houses in exquisitely tasteful old Provençal style, though the village is surrounded by vast car parks rather than vineyards or fields of lavender and there's a certain theme-park artificiality about the place. The well-heeled inhabitants include a certain Joan Collins.

The main visitors' entrance is 800m up the well-signed road off the N98. You don't have to pay to get in, but you can't explore all the islands without hiring a boat (€20 for 30min) or joining a crowded boat tour (€4). Even access to the church tower for views is controlled by an automatic barrier (€1). However, if you want to **eat and drink**, there are rows upon rows of brasseries, restaurants and cafés, clearly designed for the visiting public rather than the residents, and not particularly good value (though affordable enough).

Ste-Maxime and around

Facing St-Tropez across its gulf, **STE-MAXIME** is the perfect Côte stereotype: palmed corniche and enormous pleasure-boat harbour, beaches crowded with confident bronzed windsurfers and water-skiers, and estate agents outnumbering any other businesses by something like ten to one. It sprawls a little too much – merging with its northern neighbours to create a continuous suburban strip all the way to Fréjus. But the appeal of the water's edge is hard to deny, and though it's hardly as colourful as St-Tropez, it's a good deal less pretentious and the beaches are cleaner.

If your budget denies you the pleasures of water-skiing, wet-biking and windsurfing, you might find Ste-Maxime a little lacking in diversions. You can, at least, eat at reasonable cost, since there are plenty of crêperies, *glaciers* and snack places along the central avenue Charles-de-Gaulle.

For the spenders, the east-facing plage de la Nartelle, 2km east from the centre towards Les Issambres, is the strip of sand to head for. Here, at **Barco Beach** and its seven neighbours, you'll pay for shaded cushioned comfort, you can enter the water on a variety of different vehicles, eat grilled fish, have drinks brought to your mattress and listen to a piano player as dusk falls. A kilometre or so further on, **plage des Éléphants** recalls the town's link to Jean de Brunhoff, creator of Babar the elephant, who had a holiday home in Ste-Maxime. Sainte Maxime also has a **gay beach**, Havana Plage, in front of the casino in the town centre.

Ste-Maxime's *vieille ville* has several good **markets**: a covered flower and food market on rue Fernand-Bessy (June–Sept daily 7am–noon & 4–8pm; Oct–May every morning except Mon); a Thursday morning food market on and around place du Marché; bric-a-brac every Friday morning on place Jean-Mermoz; and arts and crafts in the pedestrian streets (mid-June to mid-Sept daily 5–11pm).

High up in the Massif des Maures on the road to Le Muy, some 10km north of Ste-Maxime, the marvellous **Musée du Phonographe et de la Musique Mécanique**, in the parc St-Donat (Easter–June & Sept Wed–Sun 10am–noon; July & Aug Wed–Sun 10am–noon & 4–6.30pm; €3), is the result of one amazing woman's forty-year obsession with collecting audio equipment, amassing a wide selection of automata, musical boxes and pianolas, plus one of Thomas Edison's "talking machines" dating from 1878.

Practicalities

Buses into town stop outside the **tourist office** on the promenade Simon-Lorière (June & Sept Mon–Sat 9am–noon & 2–7pm; July & Aug Mon–Sat 9am–8pm, Sun 10am–noon & 4–7pm; Oct–May Mon–Sat 9am–noon & 2–6pm; ⓣ04.94.55.75.55, ⓦwww.ste-maxime.com), which can give you information on trips and advice on hotel vacancies – once again, rare in summer. If you're heading for St-Tropez from Ste-Maxime, an alternative to the bus, at not much greater cost, is to go by **boat**; the twenty-minute service from Ste-Maxime's *gare maritime* on the port (€11.50 return) runs from April to early January, with more frequent crossings in July and August. Bikes can be rented at **Holiday Bikes**, 10 rte du Plan de la Tour (ⓣ04.94.43.90.19, ⓦwww.holiday-bikes.com).

Finding accommodation in Ste-Maxime can be a nightmare in high season: if you're coming in July or August, call well in advance to make a reservation. The best of the cheaper **hotels** is the good-value and welcoming *Auberge Provençale*, 19 rue Aristide-Briand (ⓣ04.94.55.76.90, ⓕ04.94.55.76.91; ❸), with its own restaurant; or there's the small *Castellamar*, 8 av G.-Pompidou (ⓣ04.94.96.19.97; ❸; closed Oct–March), on the west side of the river but still close to the centre and the sea. For more comfortable surroundings, try the central *Hôtellerie de la Poste*, 11 bd Frédéric-Mistral (ⓣ04.94.96.18.33, ⓦwww.hotelleriedusoleil.com; ❼), a modern but attractive hotel with very nice rooms; or the small and unobtrusive *Marie-Louise*, 2km west in the Hameau de Guerre-Vieille (ⓣ04.94.96.06.05, ⓦwww.hotel-marielouise.com; ❹), tucked away in greenery but in sight of the sea. For camping, *Les Cigalons*, in quartier de la Nartelle, is the two-star seaside option (Ⓣ04.94.96.05.51, Ⓦwww.campingcigalon.com; closed mid-Oct to March; €19). It also rents holiday bungalows.

For non-beach **eating**, the *Hostellerie de la Belle Aurore*, 5 bd Jean-Moulin (Ⓣ04.94.96.02.45; closed Wed outside high season & mid-Oct to March; weekday menu €38), offers gourmet food on a sea-view terrace; or, less expensively, there's classic French cuisine at *La Table des Gémeaux*, 33 rue des Maures (Ⓣ04.94.49.16.54; menus starting at €26).

Fréjus and St-Raphaël

The major conurbation of **St-Raphaël** on the coast and Fréjus, 3km inland, has a history dating back to the Romans. Fréjus was established as a naval base under Julius Caesar and Augustus, St-Raphaël as a resort for its veterans. The ancient port at Fréjus, or Forum Julii, had 2km of quays and was connected by a walled canal to the sea, which was considerably closer then. After the battle of Actium in 31 BC, the ships of Antony and Cleopatra's defeated fleet were brought here.

The area between Fréjus and the sea is now the suburb of **Fréjus-Plage** with a vast 1980s marina, **Port-Fréjus**. Both Fréjus and Fréjus-Plage merge with St-Raphaël, which in turn merges with **Boulouris** to the east.

Despite the obsession with facilities for the seaborne rich – there were already two pleasure ports at St-Raphaël before Port-Fréjus was built – this is no bad place for a stopover. There's a wide range of hotels and restaurants in St-Raphaël, reasonable sandy beaches, good transport links and some interesting sightseeing to be done in Fréjus.

Fréjus

The population of **FRÉJUS**'s *vieille ville*, which lies within the Roman perimeter, was greater in the first century BC than it is today. Little remains of the Roman walls that once circled the city, and the harbour that made Fréjus an important Mediterranean port silted up early on and was finally filled in after the Revolution. It's the **medieval centre**, as much as the classical remnants, that evokes the antiquity of this ancient town.

Arrival, information and accommodation

Up to sixteen eastbound and nine westbound trains a day stop at Fréjus' **gare SNCF**, just five to eight minutes away from St-Raphaël. Trains to St-Raphaël itself are much more common, and it's usually easiest to alight there and then take the #1,#3,#4, #5, #6 or #7 Agglobus, which run frequently between the two towns. The **gare routière** is on the east side of the town centre on place Paul-Vernet (Ⓣ04.94.53.78.46), opposite which is the **tourist office**, at 325 rue Jean-Jaurès (Mon–Sat 9.30am–noon & 2–6pm, Sun & public hols 10am–noon & 3–6pm; Ⓣ04.94.51.83.83, Ⓦwww.frejus.fr). If you're planning to visit most of Fréjus's sights it may be worth getting a **Frejus'Pass** (€4.60), which is valid for seven days and includes access to the amphitheatre, Roman theatre and Musée Archéologique. You can pick up the pass at the sights themselves. Cycles Patrick Béraud at 337 rue de Triberg (Ⓣ04.94.51.20.20), and Holiday Bikes, 238 av de Verdun (Ⓣ04.94.40.16.62, Ⓦwww.holiday-bikes.com), have **bikes** for rent. To connect to the **Internet**, head for Espace Bureaucratique, 58 rue de Grisolle (Ⓣ04.94.17.15.70).

If you're looking to stay the night in Fréjus, three central **hotels** worth trying are the plush *Aréna*, 145 rue de Général-de-Gaulle (Ⓣ04.94.17.09.40, Ⓦwww

.arena-hotel.com; ⑦), with pretty, if rather small rooms and a pool; *Le Bellevue*, place Paul-Vernet (Ⓣ04.94.17.12.20; ②), fairly basic but in a convenient though not particularly quiet location; and *La Riviera*, 90 rue Grisolle (Ⓣ04.94.51.31.46, Ⓕ04.94.17.18.34; ②), very small and not very modern, but clean and perfectly acceptable. There's an **HI hostel** 2km northeast from the centre of Fréjus at 675 chemin du Counillier (Ⓣ04.94.53.18.75, Ⓦwww.fuaj.org; reception 8–11am & 5.30–8.30pm); bus #10 from St Raphaël *gare routière*. Beds are €13. There are many **campsites** in the Fréjus area, mostly west of the town, some of them extremely large. One of the more moderate-sized sites is *Les Acacias*, 370 rue Henri-Giraud (Ⓣ04.94.53.21.22, Ⓦwww.acacias.net; April–Oct, €21 for tent, car & two people), 2.5km from the centre.

The Roman town

A tour of the Roman remains will give you a good idea of the extent of Forum Julii, but they are scattered throughout and beyond the town centre and take a full day to get around. Turning right out of the *gare SNCF* and then right down boulevard Severin-Decuers brings you to the **Butte St-Antoine**, against whose east wall the waters of the port would have lapped, and which once was capped by a fort. It was one of the port's defences, and one of the ruined **towers** may have been a lighthouse. A path around the southern wall follows the quayside (some stretches are visible) to the medieval **Lanterne d'Auguste**, built on the Roman foundations of a structure marking the entrance of the canal into the ancient harbour.

In the other direction from the station, past the Roman **Porte des Gaules** and along rue Henri-Vadon, you come to the **amphitheatre** (Tues–Sun: May–Oct 9.30am–12.30pm & 2–6pm; Nov–April 9.30am–12.30pm & 2–5pm; €2, or covered by the Fréjus'Pass, see p.1159), smaller than those at Arles and Nîmes, but still able to seat around 10,000. Today it's used for bullfights and concerts. Its upper tiers have been reconstructed in the same greenish local stone used by the Romans, but the vaulted galleries on the ground floor are largely original. The Roman **theatre** (same hours and prices) is north of the town, along avenue du Théâtre-Romain, its original seats long gone, though again it's still used for shows in summer. Northeast of it, in the parc Aurelienne at the far end of avenue du XVème-Corps-d'Armée, six arches are visible of the forty-kilometre **aqueduct**, once as high as the ramparts. Closer to the centre, on rue des Moulins, are the arcades of the **Porte d'Orée**, positioned on the former harbour's edge alongside what was probably a **bath complex**.

The medieval town

The **Cité Episcopale**, or cathedral close, takes up two sides of **place Formigé**, the marketplace and heart of both contemporary and medieval Fréjus. It comprises the cathedral, flanked by the fourteenth century bishop's palace (now the Hôtel de Ville), the baptistry, chapterhouse, cloisters and archeological museum. Visits to the cloisters and baptistry are guided (June–Sept daily 9am–6.30pm; Oct–May Tues–Sun 9am–noon & 2–5pm; €5); access to the main body of the cathedral is free (8am–noon & 2.30–7pm).

The oldest part of the complex is the **baptistry**, built in the fourth or fifth century and so contemporary with the decline of the city's Roman founders. Its two doorways are of different heights, signifying the enlarged spiritual stature of the baptized. Bits of the early Gothic **cathedral** may belong to a tenth-century church, but its best features, apart from the bright diamond-shaped tiles on the spire, are Renaissance: the choir stalls, a wooden crucifix on the left of the entrance and the intricately carved doors with scenes of a Saracen massacre, protected by a wooden cover and only opened for the guided tours. Far the most beautiful and engaging component of the whole ensemble, however, are the **cloisters**. In a small garden of scented bushes around a well, slender marble columns, carved in the twelfth century, support a fourteenth-century ceiling of wooden panels painted with apocalyptic creatures. The treasures of the **Musée Archéologique** on the upper storey of the cloisters (same hours and prices as amphitheatre) include a complete Roman mosaic of a leopard and a copy of a double-headed bust of Hermes.

Eating, drinking and entertainment

One of the best **restaurants** in the old town is the tiny *Les Potiers*, 135 rue des Potiers (ⓣ04.94.51.33.74, eves only July & Aug except Sun), with menus of fresh seasonal ingredients from €23. The rather more expensive restaurant at *L'Aréna* hotel is excellent for fish and seafood, with a €25 lunch menu and evening menus at €40 and up. Cheaper eats can be found on place Agricola, place de la Liberté and the main shopping streets. *Cadet Rousselle*, at the top of place Agricola (ⓣ04.94.53.36.92), is a crêperie with a €12.50 menu that includes three crêpes. Equally good value are the massive salads at the *Brasserie Hermès* (ⓣ04.94.17.26.02) opposite the cathedral at 15 place Formigé. At Fréjus-Plage there's a string of eating options, though menus are monotonously alike, with more upmarket *plateau des fruits de mer* outlets at Port-Fréjus. The *Bar du Marché*, on the place de la Liberté, is a good establishment for a bit of café lounging. The main **market days** are Wednesday and Saturday. If you happen to be in town during the August **Féria**, you can take in a Spanish-style **bull-fight**, plus the associated entertainment – flamenco and the like.

Around Fréjus

Unlikely remnants of the more recent past come in the shape of a Vietnamese pagoda, and an abandoned mosque, both built by French colonial troops. The **Mosquée Missiri de Djenné** is on the left off the D4 to Bagnols, in the middle of an army camp 2km from the RN7 junction. A strange, guava-coloured, fort-like building, it's a replica of a Sudanese mosque in Mali, decorated inside with fading murals of desert journeys gracefully sketched in white on the dark pink walls. Sadly it's fenced off, though much of the interior is visible from outside. The **pagoda Hong Hien** (daily: summer 9am–7pm; winter 9am–5pm; €2), still maintained as a Buddhist temple, is on the crossroads of the RN7 to Cannes and the D100, about 2km out of Fréjus. Alongside the pagoda is the massive, and rather moving, memorial to the dead of the Indo-Chinese wars of the 1940s and 1950s (daily except Tues 10am–5.30pm). Much in the manner of the US Vietnam memorial, it is inscribed with the name of every fallen Frenchman; the sheer length of the lists suggesting the years 1950–54 were the most bloody. Just off the RN7 at La Tour de Mare is the last of Jean Cocteau's artistic landmarks, the chapel of **Notre-Dame-de-Jerusalem** (same hours and prices as amphitheatre). Conceived as the church for a failed artistic community, the octagonal building was not completed until after Cocteau's death in 1963, and the interior was completed to Cocteau's plans by Edouard Dermit. The Last Supper scene inside includes a self portrait of Cocteau; the building's exterior is covered in elegantly simple mosaics and its floors with vibrant blue tiles.

If **mountain biking** tempts you, there are a number of trails which start in the Base Nature, just west of Port-Fréjus along the coast, and head up into the forested hills of the **Massif de l'Esterel** to the northeast of the town. The trails range from a flat, five-kilometre ride around a marsh to more serious 35-kilometre rides in the massif. The tourist office in St Raphaël sells a map and guide to the Esterel for €8.50, or call the Point Accueil VTT for more information (Ⓣ04.94.51.91.10).

For children, there's a **zoo** in Le Capitou, close to exit 38 on the D4 heading north (daily: March–May & Sept–Oct 10am–5pm; June–Aug 10am–6pm; Nov–Feb 10.30am–4.30pm; €12, children aged 3–9 €8; bus #2), and a water amusement park, **Aqualand** (daily: June & Sept 10am–6pm; July & Aug 10am–7pm; €23, children under 12 €18; bus #9), off the RN98 to St-Aygulf.

St-Raphaël

A large resort and now one of the richest towns on the Côte, **ST-RAPHAËL** became fashionable at the turn of the twentieth century. Its seafront *belle-époque* mansions and hotels, flattened by bombardments in World War II, have mostly been rebuilt, while the **old town** beyond place Carnot on the other side of the railway line is pleasantly low-key, no longer the commercial focus of the town but a good place to stroll and browse. On rue des Templiers a crumbling fortified Romanesque church has fragments of the Roman aqueduct that brought water from Fréjus in its courtyard along with a local history and underwater archeology **museum** (July & Aug Tues, Wed, Fri & Sat 10am–12.30pm & 2.30–7pm, Thurs 10am–12.30pm & 2.30–6pm; Sept–June Tues–Sat 9am–12.30pm & 2–5.30pm; entry to church and museum free).

The **beaches** stretch between the newly laid out Jardin Bonaparte at the entrance to the old port and the modern **Marina Santa Lucia**, with opportunities for every kind of watersport. You can also take boat trips to St-Tropez, the Îles d'Hyères and the much closer *calanques* of the Esterel coast from the quai Nomy on the south side of the Vieux Port. When you're tired of sea and sand you can lose whatever money you have left on slot machines or blackjack at the **casino** on Square de Gand overlooking the Vieux Port (daily 10am–dawn), or there are plenty of snooty discotheques.

Practicalities

St-Raphaël's **gare SNCF**, in the centre of town, is the main station for the Marseille–Ventimiglia line; the **gare routière** is on square du Dr-Régis, across the rail line behind the *gare SNCF*. Information on the surrounding region is available from the **tourist office**, facing the Vieux Port at quai Albert-1er (July & Aug daily 9.30am–7.30pm; Sept–June Mon–Sat 9am–12.30pm & 2–6pm; Ⓣ04.94.19.52.52, Ⓦwww.saint-raphael.com). Car hire outlets cluster around the gare SNCF. **Bikes** can be rented from Patrick Moto, 280 av Général-Leclerc (Ⓣ04.94.53.65.99).

Seafront **accommodation** in St-Raphaël is available on promenade René-Coty at the *Beau Séjour* (Ⓣ04.94.95.03.75, Ⓦwww.hotelbeausejour.fr; ❺; closed Nov–March), one of the cheaper hotels along here, with a pleasant terrace; or at the elegant old *Excelsior* (Ⓣ04.94.95.02.42, Ⓦwww.excelsior-hotel.com; ❽), whose rooms are luxurious and well equipped. *Bellevue*, 22 bd Félix-Martin (Ⓣ04.94.19.90.10, Ⓔhotel.bellevue@wanadoo.fr; ❸), is good value for its central location; and the *Provencal*, 195 rue de la Garonne (Ⓣ04.98.11.80.00, Ⓦwww.hotel-provencal.com; ❺), is a smart two-star hotel close to the old port. East of the centre, the *Hôtel du Soleil*, 47 bd du Domaine du Soleil, off boulevard Christian-Lafon (Ⓣ04.94.83.10.00, Ⓦperso.wanadoo.fr/hotel.du.soleil; ❺), is a small, pretty villa with its own garden. There's a two-star **campsite** close to the beach, *Camping de L'Ile d'Or*, on the N98 in Boulouris (Ⓣ & Ⓕ04.94.95.52.13), is open from late March until the end of October.

Food markets are held every day on place Victor-Hugo and place de la République. You'll find reasonably priced cafés and brasseries around these, and plenty of pizzerias, crêperies and restaurants of varying quality around the Vieux Port, Port Santa Lucia and along the promenades. Of the more expensive establishments, one of the best is *Le Sirocco*, 35 quai Albert-1er (ⓣ04.94.95.39.99), a smart restaurant specializing in fish (menus €18.50–39.50) with a view of the port; alternatively, try *Charius* at 45 rue de la République in the old town (ⓣ04.94.82.29.16; closed Mon all year & Sun out of season), with Provençal menus from €14 featuring the likes of *daube de boeuf, pieds et paquets* and grilled fish.

For **drinking**, try the selection of beers at the *Blue Bar* on promenade René-Coty, plage du Veillat (open till 4am in summer); *Aux Ambassadeurs*, a brasserie in the Casino complex that attracts a young crowd (till midnight); the *Coco-Club* at Port Santa Lucia (till 5am) for more expensive cocktails; or one of the beachfront discos like *La Réserve* on promenade René Coty or *L'Odysée* or *La Playa* in Fréjus-Plage. If you're staying outside the centre though, note that late-night taxis are almost impossible to come by in this part of the world.

The Riviera

The **Riviera**, the seventy-odd kilometres of coast between **Cannes** and **Menton** by the Italian border, was once an inhospitable shore with few natural harbours, its tiny communities preferring to cluster round feudal castles high above the sea. It wasn't until the nineteenth century that the first foreign aristocrats began to winter in the region's mild climate. In the interwar years the aristocrats were gradually supplanted by new elites – film stars, artists and writers – and the democratization of the Riviera began when French workers were granted paid holidays by Léon Blum's socialist government in 1936. But the real transformation came in the 1950s and after, as films like Alfred Hitchcock's *To Catch a Thief* and Roger Vadim's *...et Dieu Créa la Femme* generated an image of elegance and excitement. Nowadays, it's an almost uninterrupted promenade, lined by palms and megabuck hotels, with speeding sports cars on the corniche roads and yachts like ocean liners moored at each resort.

Attractions, however, still remain, most notably in the legacies of the artists who stayed here: Picasso, Léger, Matisse, Renoir and Chagall. **Nice**, too, has real substance as a major city.

Museums passport

The **Carte Musées Côte d'Azur** allows unlimited access to 65 of the most important art and history museums, monuments and gardens in the Riviera region. A one-day pass costs €10, a three-day pass costs €17 and a seven-day pass €27. Passes are available at participating museums and principal tourist offices.

Cannes and around

If you've got it, **CANNES** is as good a place as any in the south of France to flaunt it. Superficial it may be, but it's the definitive Riviera resort of popular fantasy, with its immaculate seafront hotels and exclusive beach concessions, glamorous yachts and designer boutiques. It's a place where appearances count,

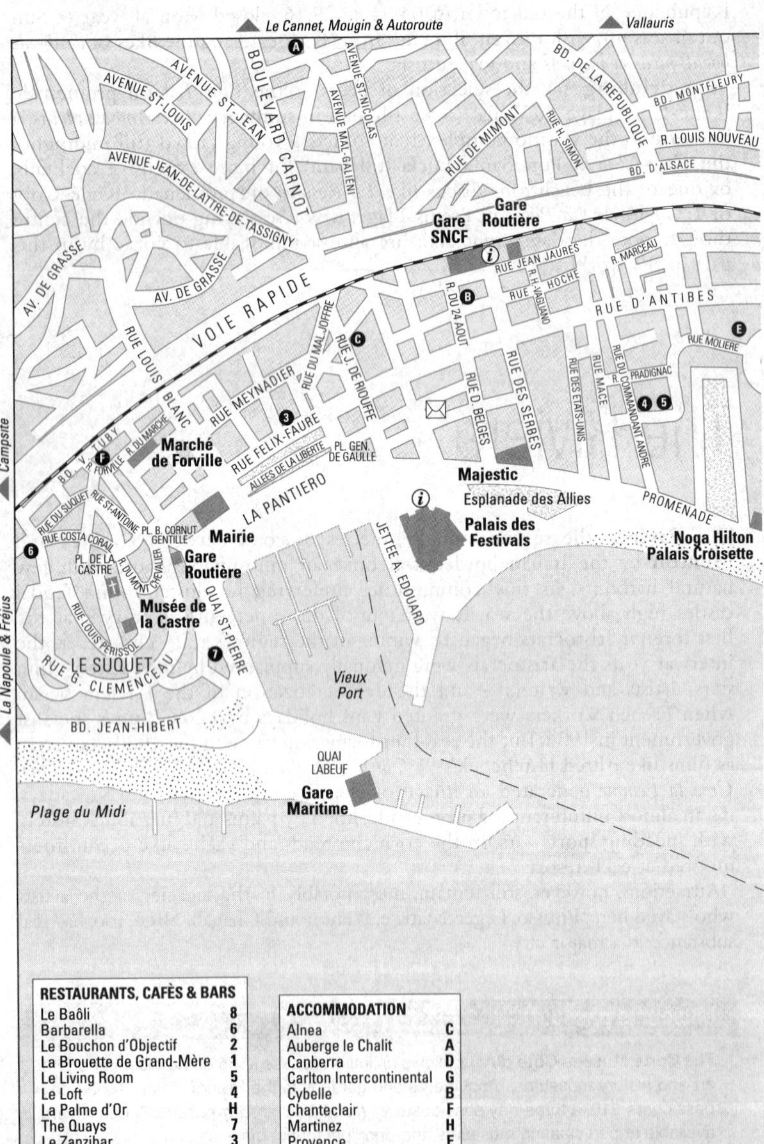

especially during the film festival in May, when the orgy of self-promotion reaches its annual peak. The vast seafront Palais des Festivals is the heart of the film festival but also hosts conferences, tournaments and trade shows throughout the year. Despite its glittery reputation Cannes works surprisingly well as a big seaside resort, since there are good, sandy public beaches away from the famed plage de la Croisette, and if it all gets too much the **Îles de Lérins**, a

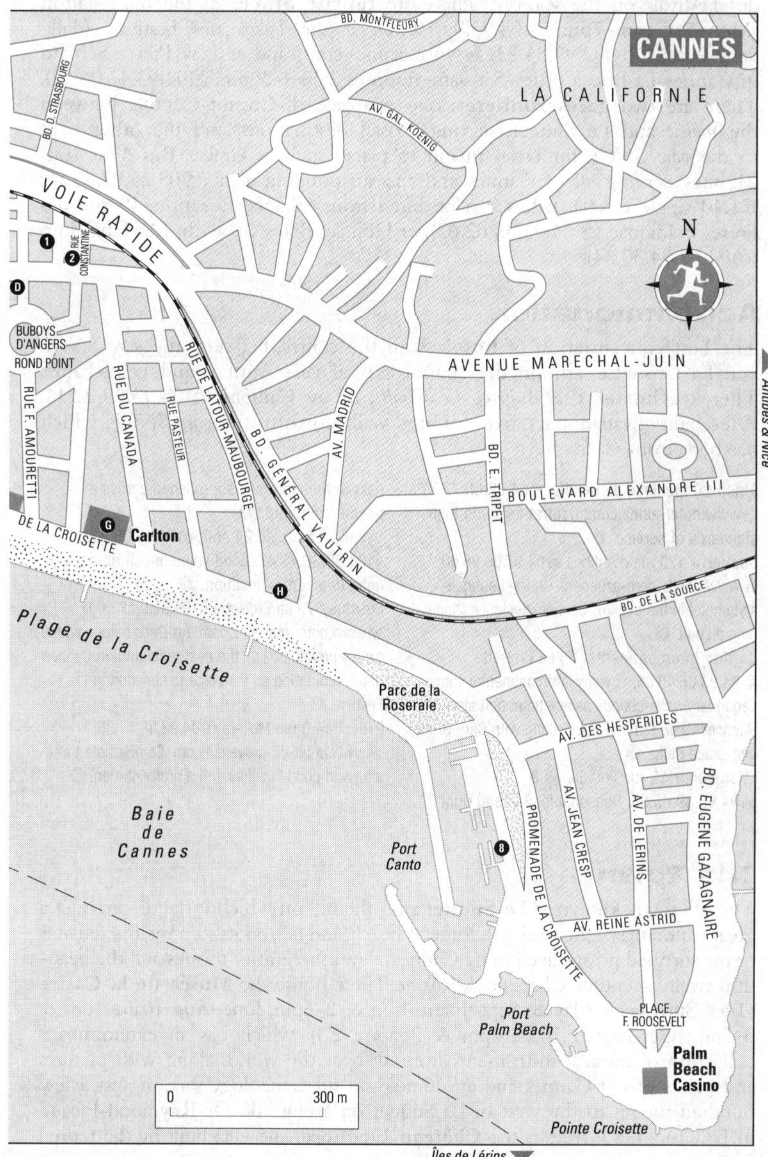

short boat ride offshore, offer a sublime contrast. As an alternative, visitors can escape the glitz of present-day Cannes by exploring the nineteenth-century glitz of La Croix des Gardes and La Californie, the aristocratic suburbs once populated by Russian and British royals.

Arrival, information and transport

The **gare SNCF** is on rue Jean-Jaurès, five blocks north of the concrete Palais des Festivals on the seafront. There are **tourist offices** at the train station (Mon–Sat 9am–7pm; ⓣ04.93.99.19.77); at the Palais des Festivals (daily 9am–7pm; ⓣ04.92.99.84.22, ⓦwww.cannes.com) and at 1 av Pierre-Sémard in Cannes-La Bocca (Tues–Sat 9am–noon & 2.30–6.30pm; ⓣ04.93.47.04.12). There are two **gares routières**: one on place B.-Cornut-Gentille between the *mairie* and Le Suquet, serving coastal destinations; and the other next to the *gare SNCF* for buses inland to places such as Grasse. Bus Azur runs 21 lines, serving all of Cannes and the surrounding area (ⓣ08.25.82.55.99; €1.40 single ticket). **Bikes** can be hired from Alliance Location, 19 rue des Frères Pradignac (ⓣ04.93.38.62.62), or Holiday Bikes, 32 av du Maréchal-Juin (ⓣ04.93.94.30.34).

Accommodation

The best concentration of **hotels** is in the centre, between the *gare SNCF* and La Croisette, around the central axis of rues Antibes and Félix-Faure. There's a **hostel**, the *Auberge Le Chalit*, 27 av Galliéni (ⓣ04.93.99.22.11, ⓔle-chalit@wanadoo.fr), five minutes' walk north of the *gare SNCF*, which has beds from €16.

Alnea 20 rue Jean de Riouffe ⓣ04.93.68.77.77, ⓦwww.hotel-alnea.com. Central and with high standards of service. ❺

Canberra 120 rue d'Antibes ⓣ04.97.06.95.00, ⓦwww.hotels-ocre-azur.com. Classy boutique-style hotel in the thick of Cannes' designer shopping district. ❼

Carlton Intercontinental 58 La Croisette ⓣ04.93.06.40.06, ⓦwww.intercontinental.com. Legendary *belle-époque* palace hotel that starred in Hitchcock's *To Catch a Thief*, along with Cary Grant and Grace Kelly. ❾

Chanteclair 12 rue Forville ⓣ & ⓕ04.93.39.68.88. Reasonable cheapie, right next to the old town, approached across a private courtyard. ❸

Cybelle 14 rue du 24 Août ⓣ04.93.38.31.33, ⓕ04.93.38.43.47. Good value, much renovated hotel in a central location. ❺

Martinez 73 La Croisette ⓣ04.92.98.73.00, ⓦwww.hotel-martinez.com. Art Deco palace with a trendy private beach, the best restaurant in Cannes and a reputation as *the* place to stay during the Festival. ❾

Provence 9 rue Molière ⓣ04.93.38.44.35, ⓦwww.hotel-de-provence.com. Comfortable three star with good facilities and a pretty garden. ❺

The Town

The old town, known as **Le Suquet** after the hill on which it stands, provides a great panorama of the twelve-kilometre beach, and has, on its summit, the remains of the fortified priory lived in by Cannes' eleventh-century monks and the beautiful twelfth-century Chapelle Ste-Anne. These house the **Musée de la Castre** (Tues–Sun; April, May & Sept 10am–1pm & 2–6pm; June–Aug 10am–1pm & 3–7pm; Oct–March 10am–1pm & 2–5pm; €3), which has an extraordinary collection of musical instruments from all over the world, along with pictures and prints of old Cannes and an ethnology and archeology section. Just a few hundred metres to the west of Le Suquet on avenue du Dr-Raymond-Picaud in La Croix des Gardes is the **Château Eléonore**, the villa built by the retired

△ *Carlton Hotel*, Cannes

British Chancellor Lord Brougham after his enforced stay in the then-unknown village of Cannes in 1834; he couldn't reach Nice because of a cholera epidemic but, liking what he found in Cannes, he built his villa here and laid the foundations for Cannes' development as an aristocratic resort.

You'll find the non-paying **beaches** to the west of Le Suquet towards the suburb of **La Bocca** along the **plages du Midi**, though there's also a tiny public section of beach on **La Croisette**, just east of the Palais des Festivals. La Croisette is certainly the sight to see, with its palace hotels on one side and private beaches on the other. It's possible to find your way down to the beach without paying, but not easy (you can of course walk along it below the rows of sun beds). The beaches, owned by the deluxe *palais-hôtels* – the *Martinez*, *Carlton* and *Noga Hilton* – are where you're most likely to spot a face familiar in celluloid or a topless hopeful, especially during the film festival, though you'll be lucky to see further than the sweating backs of the paparazzi. Alternative entertainment can be had buying your own food in the **Forville covered market** two blocks behind the *mairie*, or by wandering through the day's flower shipments on the allées de la Liberté, just back from the Vieux Port.

Eating, drinking and nightlife

Cannes has hundreds of **eateries** catering for every budget. Rue Meynadier, Le Suquet and quai St-Pierre are good places to look. For menus under €18, try *Le Bouchon d'Objectif*, 10 rue de Constantine (☎04.93.99.21.76). *La Brouette de Grand-Mère*, 9bis rue d'Oran (☎04.93.39.12.10; closed Sun) has a single, very filling €35 menu including wine. If you'd just won a film festival prize the place to celebrate would be *La Palme d'Or* in the *Hôtel Martinez*, 73 La Croisette (☎04.92.98.74.14; menus at €75, €98 and €145). *Barbarella,* 16 rue Saint Dizier in Le Suquet (☎04.92.99.17.33; Tues–Sun, eves only except during festival; menus from €29), is rather more affordable but still stylish and fun, with a Japanese-influenced fusion menu.

Cannes abounds with trendy, exclusive **bars** and **clubs,** especially in the grid of streets bounded by rue Macé, rue V. Cousin, rue Dr G.-Monod and rue des Frères Pradignacs. Smart, trendy bars to try include *Le Loft* and *Le Living Room*, both on rue Dr-Gérard-Monod and open until 2.30am; if you want to rub shoulders with celebrities the place to head is *Le Baôli* at Port Pierre Canto (Nov–April Fri & Sat 8pm–5am), an exotic outdoor disco/restaurant with palms, tented pavilions and Asian food. For something more straightforward, *The Quays*, 17 quai St-Pierre, is the inevitable Irish pub, open until well after midnight. Cannes has one of the oldest **gay** bars in France, *Le Zanzibar*, 85 rue Félix-Faure (6pm–4am).

Îles de Lérins

The **Îles de Lérins** would be lovely anywhere, but at fifteen minutes' ferry ride from Cannes, they're not far short of paradise facing purgatory. **Boats** for both islands leave from the quai des Îles at the seaward end of the quai Max-Laubeuf. **St-Honorat** is served by Compagnie Planaria (Ⓣ04.92.98.71.38, Ⓦwww.abbayedelerins.com; summer 10 daily; winter 7 daily; €11): the last boat back to Cannes leaves at 5pm in winter & 6pm in summer). There are regular services to **Ste-Marguerite** run by two companies, S.A.R.L. Horizon (hourly; winter 9am–4.15pm, spring months 9am–5.15pm, summer until 6.15pm; Ⓣ04.92.98.71.36, €11), and Trans Côte d'Azur (Ⓣ04.92.98.71.30, Ⓦwww.trans-cote-azur.com; up to 16 departures 9am–5pm; €11): the last boats back to Cannes leave Ste-Marguerite at 5.15pm, 6pm or 7pm, depending on the operator and season. Taking a picnic is a good idea, particularly out of season, as the handful of restaurants on the islands are overpriced – though there are reasonably-priced snack stalls on Ste-Marguerite during the summer months.

Ste-Marguerite

Ste-Marguerite is more touristy than its peaceful neighbour, St-Honorat. It's still beautiful, though, and large enough for visitors to find seclusion by following the trails that lead away from the congested port, through the Aleppo pines and woods of evergreen oak that are so thick they cast a sepulchral gloom. The western end is the most accessible, but the lagoon here is brackish, so the best points to swim are the rocky southern shore, reached most easily along the **allée des Eucalyptus**. The channel between Ste-Marguerite and St-Honorat is however a popular anchorage for motor yachts, so you're unlikely to find real solitude.

The dominating structure of the island is the **Fort Ste-Marguerite** (April to mid-June & mid- to late Sept Tues–Sun 10.30am–1.15pm & 2.15–5.45pm; mid-June to mid-Sept daily 10.30am–5.45pm; Oct–March Tues–Sun 10.30am–1.15pm & 2.15–4.45pm; €3), a Richelieu commission that failed to prevent the Spanish occupying both of the Lérin islands between 1635 and 1637. Later, Vauban rounded it off, presumably for Louis XIV's *gloire* – since the strategic value of greatly enlarging a fort facing your own mainland without upgrading the one facing the sea is pretty minimal. There are cells to see, including the one in which Dumas' *Man in the Iron Mask* is supposed to have been held, and the **Musée de la Mer** (same hours and ticket as fort), containing mostly Roman local finds but also remnants of a tenth-century Arab ship.

Ste-Honorat

Owned by monks almost continuously since its namesake and patron founded a monastery here in 410 AD, **St-Honorat**, the smaller southern island, was home to a famous bishops' seminary, where St Patrick trained before setting out for Ireland. The present **abbey** buildings date mostly from the nineteenth century, though some vestiges of the medieval and earlier constructions remain in the austere church and the cloisters. You can visit the church, but there is no access to the residential part of the monastery unless you're staying there on a spiritual retreat. A shop sells the sought-after white wine and liqueurs produced by the 28 Cistercian brothers of the monastic community. Behind the cloisters on the sea's edge stands the eleventh-century fortified monastery.

There's one small restaurant near the landing stage (open April–Oct only), and there are no bars, hotels or cars: just vines, lavender, herbs and olive trees mingled with wild poppies and daisies, and pine and eucalyptus trees shading the paths beside the white rock shore mixing with the scents of rosemary, thyme and wild honeysuckle.

Vallauris

Pottery and Picasso are the twin attractions of **VALLAURIS**, an otherwise unremarkable town in the hills above Golfe-Juan, 6km east of Cannes. It was here that Picasso first began to use clay, thereby reviving one of the traditional crafts of this little town. Today the main street, **avenue Georges-Clemenceau**, sells nothing but pottery, much of it garish bowls or figurines that could feature in souvenir shops anywhere. Picasso used to work in the **Madoura workshop** on avenue des Ancien-Combattants-d'AFN, to the left as you ascend avenue Georges-Clemenceau; it still has sole rights on reproducing his designs, which it sells, at a price, in the shop (Mon–Fri 10am–12.30pm & 3–6pm; closed Sat, Sun & Nov).

The bronze statue of **Man with a Sheep**, Picasso's gift to the town, stands in the main square, place Paul Isnard, beside the church and castle. The local authorities also suggested he should decorate the deconsecrated early medieval **chapel** in the castle courtyard (daily except Tues: mid-June to mid-Sept 10am–12.15pm & 2–6pm; mid-Sept to mid-June 10am–12.15pm & 2–5pm; €3.20), which he finally did in 1952: his subject was war and peace. The space is tiny, with the architectural simplicity of an air-raid shelter, and at first it's easy to be unimpressed by the painted panels covering the vault – as many critics still are – since the work looks mucky and slapdash, with paint-runs on the plywood panel surface. But stay a while and the passion of this violently drawn display of pacifism slowly emerges. The ticket for the chapel also gives admission to the **Musée de la Céramique/Musée Magnelli** in the castle (same hours and ticket), which exhibits Picasso's and other ceramics.

Regular buses from Cannes and from Golfe-Juan SNCF arrive at the rear of the château. The **tourist office** is at the bottom of avenue Georges-Clemenceau on square du 8-Mai-1945 (July & Aug daily 9am–7pm; Sept–June Mon–Sat 9am–12.15pm & 1.45–6pm; ⓣ04.93.63.82.58, ⓦwww.vallauris-golfe-juan.fr), which is where you'll also find the main tourist **car park**.

Grasse

GRASSE, 16km inland from Cannes and with some stunning views over the Côte, is the world capital of *parfumiers* and has been for almost 300 years. These days it promotes a perfumed image of a medieval hill town surrounded by scented flowers, though in truth its outskirts sprout boxy suburban villas with rather more luxuriance. Making perfumes is presented as a mysterious process, an alchemy, turning the soul of the flower into a liquid of luxury and desire, and the industry is at pains to keep quiet about modern innovations and techniques. Grasse is the official starting point of the Route Napoléon but is equally easy to visit as a day-trip from the coast.

The Town

Even when Grasse was part of the aristocratic tourist boom of the late nineteenth century, the desirable addresses, Queen Victoria's among them, were all east of **Vieux Grasse**, and in recent years the pretty *vieille ville* degenerated into little more than a picturesque slum. But after years of peeling into oblivion, Vieux Grasse is now changing rapidly as an energetic programme of restoration – and, inevitably, of gentrification – kicks in.

Place aux Aires, at the top of the town, is the main meeting point and the venue for the daily flower and vegetable **market**. It's ringed by arcades of different heights and the elegant wrought-iron balcony of the *Hôtel Isnard* at no. 33, and at one time was the exclusive preserve of the tanning industry. At the opposite end of Vieux Grasse lie the **cathedral** – containing various paintings, including one by local boy Jean-Honoré Fragonard, three by Rubens and a wondrous triptych by the sixteenth-century Niçois painter Louis Bréa – and the **bishop's palace**, now the Hôtel de Ville, both built in the twelfth century.

Grasse has several engrossing small museums. The **Musée d'Art et d'Histoire de Provence**, 2 rue Mirabeau (June–Sept daily 10am–6.30pm; Oct & Dec–May Wed–Mon 10am–12.30pm & 2–5.30pm; €3), is housed in a luxurious town house commissioned by Mirabeau's sister as a place to entertain. As well as all the gorgeous fittings and an eighteenth-century kitchen, the collections are highly eclectic and include eighteenth- to nineteenth-century faïence from Apt and Le Castellet, Mirabeau's death mask, a tin bidet and six prehistoric bronze leg bracelets. The fascinating **Musée International de la Parfumerie**, 8 place du Cours (closed for reconstruction until 2008, usually same hours and prices as Musée d'Histoire), displays perfume bottles from the ancient Greeks via Marie-Antoinette to the present, and has a reconstruction of a perfume factory.

You can see more works by Jean-Honoré Fragonard in the **Villa-Musée Fragonard** at 23 bd Fragonard (same hours and price as Musée d'Histoire). The celebrated Rococo painter returned to live in this villa after the Revolution. The staircase has impressive wall paintings by his son Alexandre-Evariste, while the salon is graced by copies of *Love's Progress in the Heart of a Young Girl*, which Jean-Honoré painted for Madame du Barry.

The perfume factories

There are thirty-odd **parfumeries** in and around Grasse, most of them making not perfume but essences-plus-formulas which are then sold to Dior, Lancôme, Estée Lauder and the like, who make up their own brand-name perfumes. One litre of pure rose essence can cost as much as €19,000; perfume contains twenty percent essence (eau de toilette and eau de Cologne considerably less). The major cost in this multi-billion-dollar business is marketing. The grand Parisian couturiers, whose clothes, on strictly cost-accounting grounds, serve simply to promote the perfume, go to inordinate lengths to sell their latest fragrance, spending millions of euros a year on advertising alone.

The ingredients that the "nose" – as the creator of the perfume's formula is known – has to play with include resins, roots, moss, beans, bark, civet (extract of cat genitals), ambergris (intestinal goo from whales), bits of beaver and musk from Tibetan goats. If that hasn't put you off, you can visit the various **showrooms**, with overpoweringly fragrant shops and free guided tours, in English, of the traditional perfume factory set-up (the actual working industrial complexes are strictly out of bounds). These visits are free and usually open daily without interruption in summer; a few to choose from are: **Fragonard**, 20 bd Fragonard (Feb–Oct daily 9am–6pm; Nov–Jan Mon–Sat 9am–12.30pm & 2–6.30pm; Ⓦwww.fragonard.com); **Galimard**, 73 rte de Cannes (guided visits daily: summer 9am–6.30pm; winter 9am–noon & 2–6pm; Ⓦwww.galimard.com); and **Molinard** at 60 bd Victor-Hugo (March–Sept daily Mon–Fri 9am–6pm; Oct–Feb Mon–Sat 9am–12.30pm & 2–6pm; Ⓦwww.molinard.com).

Practicalities

Grasse's **gare routière** is to the north of the old town at the Parking Notre-Dame-des-Fleurs. Head downhill on avenue Thiers, which becomes boulevard du Jeu de Ballon (where there's an annexe of the tourist office) and you'll find the major museums fronting place du Cours, with the main **tourist office** on cours Honoré-Cresp (July–Sept Mon–Sat 9am–7pm, Sun 9am–1pm & 2–6pm; Oct–June Mon–Sat 9am–12.30pm & 2–6pm; Ⓣ04.93.36.66.66, Ⓦwww.grasse-riviera.com).

One possible **hotel** at the cheaper end of the market is *Les Palmiers*, 17 av Y.-Baudoin (Ⓣ & Ⓕ04.93.36.07.24; ❹), a *chambres d'hôte* with good views of the surrounding countryside and down to the coast. More expensive, the *Panorama*, on place du Cours (Ⓣ04.93.36.80.80, Ⓦwww.hotelpanorama-grasse.com; closed Jan; ❹), offers rooms with views and all mod cons. Even more comfortable, if less well located, is the *Charme Hôtel du Patti*, place du Patti (Ⓣ04.93.36.01.00, Ⓦwww.hotelpatti.com; ❺), with pretty, Provençal-style rooms including three adapted for for wheelchair users.

Compared with the coastal towns Grasse isn't terribly well endowed with **restaurants**. The best in town is *La Bastide Saint Antoine*, 48 rue Henri-Dunant (Ⓣ04.93.70.94.94), which serves *cuisine gourmande* with a Provençal twist (lunch menus €55; otherwise menus from €140). Alternatively, *Lou Fassum*, 5 rue de Fabreries (Ⓣ04.93.42.99.69, closed Sun & Mon, menu €32), is a traditional Provençal restaurant serving specialities from the pays de Grasse. For drinks, the bars on place aux Aires are friendly. At *Maison Venturini*, 1 rue Marcel-Journet (Ⓣ04.93.36.20.47; closed Sun & Mon), you can buy fabulous sweet *fougassettes* – a local pastry, flavoured with the Grasse speciality of orange blossom – to take away.

Antibes and around

Graham Greene, who lived in **Antibes** for more than twenty years, considered it the only place on this stretch of coast to have preserved its soul. And whilst Antibes and its twin, **Juan-les-Pins**, have not completely escaped the overdevelopment that blights much of this region, they have avoided its worst excesses. Antibes itself is a pleasing old town, extremely animated, with one of the finest **markets** on the coast and the best **Picasso collection** in its ancient seafront castle; and the southern end of the Cap d'Antibes still has its woods of pine, in which some of the most exclusive mansions on the Riviera hide.

Lording it over the Antibes ramparts and the sea, the sixteenth-century **Château Grimaldi** is a beautifully cool, light space, with hexagonal terracotta floor tiles, windows over the sea and a terrace garden with sculptures by Germaine Richier, Miró, César and others. In 1946, Picasso was

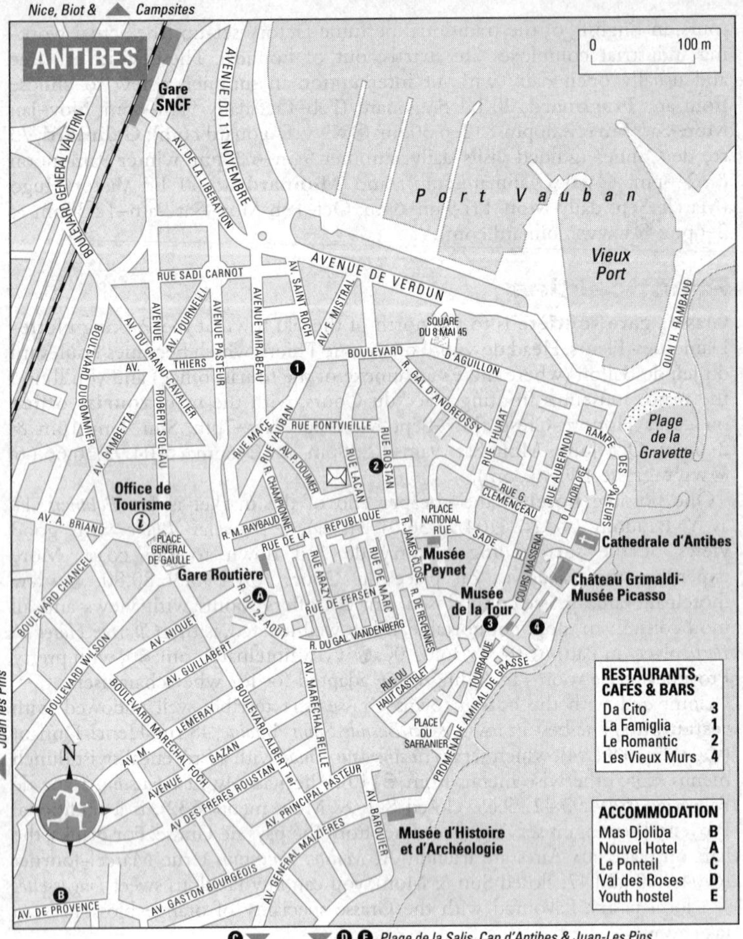

offered the dusty building – by then already a museum – as a studio. Several extremely prolific months followed before he moved to Vallauris, leaving all his Antibes output to what is now the **Musée Picasso** (closed until summer 2007 for renovation; check with tourist office for further information). Although Picasso donated other works later on, the bulk of the collection belongs to this one period. Picasso himself is the subject of works here by other painters and photographers, including Man Ray, Hans Hartung and Bill Brandt; there are also several anguished canvases by Nicolas de Staël, who stayed in Antibes for a few months from 1954 to 1955. Alongside the castle is the **cathedral**, built on the site of an ancient temple. The choir and apse survive from the Romanesque building that served the city in the Middle Ages while the nave and stunning ochre facade are Baroque. Inside, in the south transept, is a sumptuous medieval altarpiece surrounded by immaculate panels of tiny detailed scenes.

One block inland, the morning **covered market** on cours Masséna overflows with Provençal goodies and a profusion of cut **flowers**, the traditional and still-flourishing Antibes business (June–Aug daily 6am–1pm; Sept–May Tues–Sun 6am–1pm). In the afternoons, a **craft market** (Easter–Sept Thurs–Sun; Oct–Easter Thurs–Sat) takes over from about 3pm (4.30pm on Sat), and when the stalls pack up, café tables take their place.

Cap d'Antibes

Plage de la Salis, the longest Antibes beach, runs along the eastern neck of Cap d'Antibes, with no big hotels owning mattress exploitation rights – an amazing rarity on the Riviera. To the south, at the top of chemin du Calvaire, you have superb views from the **Chapelle de la Garoupe** (daily 10am–noon & 2.30–7pm), which contains Russian spoils from the Crimean War and hundreds of *ex votos*. To the west, on boulevard du Cap between chemins du Tamisier and G.-Raymond, you can wander around the **Jardin Thuret** (Mon–Fri: summer 8am–6pm, winter 8.30am–5.30pm; free; groups by appointment, €1.50 per person; ☎04.97.21.25.00), botanical gardens belonging to a national research institute. Back on the east shore, further south, lies a second public beach, **plage de la Garoupe**. From here a footpath follows the shore to join the chemin des Douaniers. At the southern end of the Cap d'Antibes, on avenue L.D. Beaumont, stands the grandiose **Villa Eilenroc** (gardens Tues & Wed 9am–5pm, free; villa out of season Wed 9am–noon & 1.30–5pm, closed in summer; free), designed by Charles Garnier, architect of the casino at Monte Carlo, and surrounded by lush gardens. There are more sandy coves and little harbours along the western shore, where you'll also find the **Musée Napoléonien** (Tues–Sat: mid-June to mid–Sept 10am–6pm; mid-Sept to mid-June 10am–4.30pm; €3), at the end of avenue J.-F.-Kennedy. This documents the great return from Elba along with the usual Bonaparte paraphernalia of hats, cockades and signed commands. Much of the southern tip of the *cap* is a warren of private roads, including the area around the fabled *Hotel du Cap Eden Roc* and the so-called "bay of millionaires".

Juan-les-Pins

JUAN-LES-PINS, less than 2km from the centre of Antibes, is another of those mystical Côte d'Azur names. It had its heyday in the interwar years, when the summer season on the Riviera first took off and the resort was the haunt of film stars like Charlie Chaplin, Maurice Chevalier and Lilian Harvey, the polyglot London-born 1930s musical star who lingered here until 1968, long after her fame had faded. Juan-les-Pins isn't as glamorous as it once was either, though it still has a casino and a certain cachet, the beaches are sand, and there are haunting reminders of its glory days, including the Art Deco bulk of the derelict **Hotel Provençal,** which looms over the town from the eastern side of boulevard Baudoin.

Juan's **international jazz festival** – known simply as Jazz à Juan – takes place in the middle two weeks of July. It's the best in the region and is held in the central pine grove, the **Jardin de La Pinède** (known simply as La Pinède), and **square Gould** above the beach by the casino. A Hollywood-style walk of fame immortalizes various jazz greats.

Practicalities

Antibes' **gare SNCF** lies to the north of the old town at the top of avenue Robert-Soleau. Turn right out of the station and three minutes' walk along avenue R.-Soleau will bring you to place de Gaulle. The **tourist office** is on this square, at no. 11 (July & Aug daily 9am–7pm; Sept–June Mon–Fri 9am–

12.30pm & 1.30–6pm, Sat 9am–noon & 2–6pm; ⓣ04.97.23.11.11, ⓦwww.antibesjuanlespins.com). The **gare routière** is east of here on place Guynemer with frequent buses to and from the *gare SNCF*. Bus #2 goes to Cap d'Antibes, bus #3 to Juan-les-Pins and #10 to Biot. **Bikes** can be hired from Midi Location Service, Galerie du Port, rue Lacan (ⓣ04.93.34.48.00), and Holiday Bikes, 122 bd Wilson in Juan les Pins (ⓣ04.93.61.51.51). Rue de la République leads into the heart of Vieux Antibes around place Nationale, from where rue Sade leads to cours Masséna, beyond which lie the cathedral, the castle and the sea.

The most economical **hotel** in the centre of Antibes, *Le Nouvel Hôtel*, 1 av du 24-Août (ⓣ04.93.34.44.07, ⓕ04.93.34.44.08; ❹), is a stone's throw from the *gare routière*; avenue de l'Estérel and around in Juan-les-Pins is another good place to try for cheap hotels. For greater comfort, try the *Mas Djoliba*, 29 av de Provence (ⓣ04.93.34.02.48, ⓦwww.hotel-djoliba.com; closed Nov–Jan; ❼), between the old town and the beach, or *Le Ponteil*, 11 impasse Jean-Mensier (ⓣ04.93.34.67.92, ⓦwww.leponteil.com; ❼; half-board obligatory in high season), in a quiet location at the end of a cul-de-sac close to the sea. For something secluded and elegant, it's worth trying *Val des Roses*, an upmarket **chambres d'hôte** on chemin des Lauriers just off the plage de la Salis (ⓣ06.85.06.06.29, ⓦwww.val-des-roses.com; ❾).

There's a **hostel** on Cap d'Antibes, the *Relais International de la Jeunesse* on boulevard de la Garoupe (ⓣ04.93.61.34.40, ⓦwww.clasjud.fr; closed Oct–April; €15; bus #2 stops right outside), which needs booking well in advance. All of Antibes' **campsites** are 3–5km north of the city in the *quartier* of La Brague (bus #10 or one train stop to "Gare de Biot"). The three-star *Logis de La Brague* (ⓣ04.93.33.54.72; ⓦwww.camping-logisbrague.com; closed Oct–April) is closest to the station, while the two-star *Idéal-Camping* (ⓣ04.93.74.27.07; closed Oct–April) is south of the station; both are on the route de Nice and close to the sea.

Place Nationale and cours Masséna are lined with **cafés**; rue James-Close is nothing but **restaurants** and rue Thuret and its side streets also offer numerous menus to browse. For pizzas, there's *Da Cito* in the covered market, and *La Famiglia*, a cheap family-run outfit at 34 av Thiers (closed Wed, Sat & Sun lunch). *Le Romantic*, 5 rue Rostan (ⓣ04.93.34.59.39; closed Mon & Tues lunch), lives up to its name and offers menus from €22, although in the evening the *terroir*-dominated *carte* will take the bill higher. *Les Vieux Murs*, near the castle at avenue Amiral-de-Grasse (ⓣ04.93.34.06.73, closed Mon lunch in season, all day Mon rest of year; lunch menu €29, otherwise €42 or €60) serves very classy food, such as king crab with *niçois* ratatouille or scallops with orange butter in a perfect setting on the ramparts.

La Passagère at the *Hotel Belles Rives* (ⓣ04.93.61.02.79) serves up modern Mediterranean delights in lovely, restored Art Deco surroundings, with menus at €45 for lunch, and €95 at other times. The terrace has wonderful views over the bay. That apart, Juan-les-Pins is not blessed with particularly memorable restaurants, so take pot luck from the countless menus on offer on the boulevards around La Pinède. *Le Café de la Plage*, at 1 bd Edouard-Baudouin (ⓣ04.93.61.37.61; lunchtime *plats* €12), is a good bet, serving seafood, cocktails and ice cream in a pleasant seafront spot, while *Helios Plage*, promenade du Soleil (ⓣ04.93.61.85.77; open mid-April to end Sept) is about the smartest of the beach concessions, with *plats* from around €22.

Juan-les-Pins still cuts a dash in the nightlife stakes. The fads and reputations of the different **discos** may change, but in general opening hours are midnight to dawn, and you can count on searching appraisal of your attire and on paying around €16 for entrance plus your first drink. Some of the current hotspots include *Whisky a Gogo*, on rue Jacques-Leonetti, *Le Milk* on avenue G.-Gallice and *Minimal* on avenue

Guy-de-Maupassant. The perennially popular **live music** venue *Le Pam-Pam*, 137 bd Wilson, often has Brazilian bands, but you'll need to go early to get a seat.

Finally, if you've run out of reading material, head for Heidi's English Bookshop at place Audiberti in Antibes, the cheapest English **bookshop** on the coast.

Biot

Frequent buses connect Antibes with the village of **BIOT**, 8km to the north, where Fernand Léger lived for a few years at the end of his life. A stunning collection of his intensely life-affirming works, created between 1905 and 1955, can be seen at the **Musée Fernand Léger**, built especially to display them (daily except Tues: July–Sept 10.30am–6pm; Oct–June 10am–12.30pm & 2–5.30pm; €4.50). The museum is just east of the village on the chemin du Val de Pome, stop "Fernand Léger" on the Antibes bus, or a rather unpleasant and dangerous thirty-minute walk from Biot's *gare SNCF*.

The village itself is extremely beautiful (if rather self-consciously so) and oozes with art in every form – architectural, sculpted, ceramic, jewelled, painted and culinary. The **tourist office**, 46 rue Saint Sebastien, at the western entrance to the village (July & Aug Mon–Fri 10am–7pm, Sat & Sun 2.30–7pm; Sept–June Mon–Fri 9am–noon & 2–6pm, Sat & Sun 2–6pm; Ⓣ04.93.65.78.00, Ⓦwww.biot.fr) can provide lists of art galleries and glassworks – the traditional industry that brought Léger here, and which produces the famous hand-blown **bubble glass**. If you book well in advance you could stay at the very reasonable *Hôtel des Arcades*, 16 place des Arcades (Ⓣ04.93.65.01.04, Ⓕ04.93.65.01.05; ❸), full of old-fashioned charm and with huge rooms in the medieval centre of the village. Its **café-restaurant**, which also doubles as an art gallery, serves delicious traditional Provençal food (closed Sun eve & Mon; *plats du jour* around €16), or try the delightful *salon de thé*, *Le Mas Des Orangers*, at 3 rue des Roses.

Above the Baie des Anges

Between Antibes and Nice, the **Baie des Anges** laps at a long stretch of fairly undistinguished twentieth-century resorts. At Villeneuve-Loubet-Plage the vast concrete sails of the Marina Baie des Anges – an unmissable landmark along the entire length of this coast – give the landscape a controversial and defiantly modernist stamp. Harder to forgive is the strip-mall squalor of drive-in restaurants, furniture stores and car dealerships that represents what passes for a townscape here.

The old towns and softer visual stimulation lie inland. **Cagnes** is another artists' town – associated in particular with Renoir – as is **St-Paul-de-Vence**, which houses the wonderful modern art collection of the Fondation Maeght. Vence has a small chapel decorated by Matisse, and is a relaxing place to stay, if quiet in the evenings.

Cagnes

CAGNES is a confusing agglomeration, made up of a seaside district known as Cros-de-Cagnes, the immaculate medieval village of Haut-de-Cagnes overlooking the town from the northwest, and Cagnes-sur-Mer, the traffic-choked town centre wedged between the two. The three busy coastal roads slicing through the town don't add to its appeal.

At the top of place de-Gaulle, the main square in **Cagnes-sur-Mer**, avenue Auguste-Renoir runs right and crosses the road to La Gaude. A short way further on, chemin des Collettes leads off to the left up to **Les Collettes**, the house that Renoir had built in 1908 and where he spent the last twelve years of his life. It's now a **memorial museum** (daily except Tues: May–Sept 10am–noon & 2–6pm; Oct & last week in Nov to April 10am–noon & 2–5pm; €3), and you can wander around the house and through the olive and rare orange groves that surround it. One of the two studios in the house – north-facing to catch the late afternoon light – is arranged as if Renoir had just popped out. Albert André's painting, *A Renoir Painting*, shows the ageing artist hunched over his canvas, plus there's a bust of him by Aristide Maillol, and a crayon sketch by Richard Guido. Bonnard and Dufy were also visitors to Les Collettes; Dufy's *Hommage à Renoir*, transposing a detail of *Le Moulin de la Galette*, hangs here. Renoir's own work is represented by several sculptures, some beautiful water-colours and ten paintings from his Cagnes period.

Haut-de-Cagnes is a favourite haunt of successes in the contemporary art world, as well as those of decades past, and it lives up to everything dreamed of in a Riviera *village perché*. The ancient village backs up to a crenellated feudal **château** (May–Sept daily 10am–noon & 2–6pm; Oct–April daily 10am–noon & 2–5pm; €3; shuttle bus from bus station June–Sept, or by foot, the steep ascent along rue Général-Bérenger and montée de la Bourgade), with a stunning Renaissance interior, housing museums of local history, olive cultivation, the **donation Solidor** – a diverse collection of paintings of the famous cabaret artist Suzy Solidor – and exhibition space for **contemporary art**.

Practicalities

The **gare SNCF** Cagnes-sur-Mer (one stop from the *gare SNCF* Cros-de-Cagnes) is southwest of the centre alongside the autoroute; turn right on the northern side of the autoroute along avenue de la Gare to head into town. The sixth turning on your right, rue des Palmiers, leads to the **tourist office** at 6 bd Maréchal-Juin (June & Sept Mon–Sat 9am–noon & 2–7pm; July & Aug Mon–Sat 9am–7pm, Sun 9am–noon & 3–7pm; Oct–May Mon–Sat 9am–noon & 2–6pm; ⓣ04.93.20.61.64, ⓦwww.cagnes-tourisme.com). Bus #42 runs from the *gare SNCF* to the **gare routière** on square Bourdet.

Cros de Cagnes has the largest choice of **hotels** but also plenty of traffic: you might try *Beaurivage*, 39 bd de la Plage on the seafront (ⓣ04.93.20.16.09, ⓦwww.beaurivage.biz; ❹), which has very pleasant rooms with views of the sea, or there's *Le Turf*, 13 rue des Capucines (ⓣ04.93.20.64.00, ⓕ04.93.73.92.64; ❹), set back slightly from the seafront. If you're feeling extremely flush, you could try rue Sous Barri (ⓣ04.93.20.73.21, ⓦwww.le-cagnard.com; ❾), the ancient guard room for the castle, with a top-notch restaurant. **Campsites** are plentiful, and mostly in wooded locations inland. Try the three-star *Le Todos*, 4km north of Cros-de-Cagnes at 159 chemin Vallon des Vaux (ⓣ04.93.31.20.05, ⓦwww.letodos.fr; €19.20 per tent; closed Oct–March), with a pool, bar and restaurant.

The best places to **eat** are in Haut-de-Cagnes, and for café lounging, place du Château or place Grimaldi, to either side of the castle, are the obvious spots. *Fleur de Sel* at no 85 montée de la Bourgade (ⓣ04.92.20.33.33; closed Wed & Tues lunch), serves octopus salad and *pieds et paquets* on a €23 lunch menu. *Le Cagnard* hotel has a predictably smart restaurant (ⓣ04.93.20.73.21; menus from €55; closed mid-Nov to mid-Dec), or there's *Josy-Jo*, 2 rue du Planastel (ⓣ04.93.20.68.76; around €25; closed Sat lunch, Sun & mid-Nov to late Dec), with Provençal delicacies dished up in the space that served as Soutine's workshop in the interwar years.

In summer there are free **jazz concerts** on place du Château and, at the end of August, a bizarre **square boules** competition takes place down montée de la Bourgade.

St-Paul-de-Vence: the Fondation Maeght

Further into the hills, the fortified village of **ST-PAUL-DE-VENCE** is home to yet another artistic treat, and one of the best in the whole region: the remarkable **Fondation Maeght**, created in the 1950s by Aimé and Marguerite Maeght, art collectors and dealers who knew all the great artists who worked in Provence (daily: July–Sept 10am–7pm; Oct–June 10am–12.30pm & 2.30–6pm; €11). The Nice–Vence **bus** has two stops in St-Paul: the Fondation is signposted from the second, and is approximately 1km from the old town, a few hundred metres up a steep hill from the main D7 road through the village. By **car** or **bike**, follow the signs just before you reach the village, off the D7 from La-Colle-sur-Loup or the D2 from Villeneuve.

Once through the gates, any idea of dutifully seeing the catalogue of priceless museum pieces crumbles; this, instead, is a sublime fusion of art, modern architecture and landscape. Alberto Giacometti's *Cat* is sometimes stalking along the edge of the grass; Miró's *Egg* smiles above a pond and his totemed *Fork* is outlined against the sky. It's hard not to be bewitched by the Calder mobile swinging over watery tiles, by Léger's *Flowers, Birds and a Bench* on a sunlit rough stone wall, or by the clanking tubular fountain by Pol Bury. The building itself is a superb piece of architecture: multi-levelled and flooded with daylight, and the collection it houses of works by Braque, Miró, Chagall, Léger and Matisse, along with more recent artists and the young up-and-comings, is fabulous. Not all the works are exhibited at any one time, and during the summer, when the main annual exhibition is mounted, none are on show, apart from those that make up the decoration of the building.

The other famous sights are in the extremely busy but beautiful *vieux village*. The hotel-restaurant **La Colombe d'Or** on place du Général-de-Gaulle (Ⓣ04.93.32.80.02, Ⓦwww.la-colombe-dor.com; ❾; *plats du jour* from around €20, closed Nov to late Dec) is celebrated not for its food but for the art on its walls, donated in lieu of payment for meals by the then-impoverished Braque, Picasso, Matisse and Bonnard in the lean years following World War I. Rather fewer visitors make the pilgrimage to the simple grave of **Marc Chagall** on the right-hand side of the little **cemetery** (summer 7.30am–8pm; winter 8am–5pm) at the southern end of the village, running the gauntlet of the many boutiques and art galleries on rue Grande to get there.

Vence

A few kilometres north, with abundant water and the sheltering pre-Alps behind, **VENCE** has always been a town of some significance. The old town is blessed with numerous ancient houses, gateways, fountains, chapels and a **cathedral** containing Roman funeral inscriptions and a Chagall mosaic. In the 1920s it became yet another haven for painters and writers: André Gide, Raoul Dufy, D.H. Lawrence (who died here in 1930 whilst being treated for tuberculosis contracted in England) and Marc Chagall were all long-term visitors, along with **Matisse** whose work is the reason most people come.

Towards the end of World War II, Matisse moved to Vence to escape the Allied bombing of the coast, and his legacy is the town's most famous and exciting building, the **Chapelle du Rosaire**, at 466 av Henri-Matisse, off the road to St-Jeannet which leaves the town from carrefour Jean-Moulin at the top of avenue des Poilus (Mon, Wed & Sat 2–5.30pm, Tues & Thurs 10–11.30am & 2–5.30pm; Sunday Mass 10am; additional openings during school hols, check with the tourist office; closed mid-Nov to mid-Dec; €2.60). The chapel was his last work – consciously so – and not, as some have tried to explain, a religious conversion.

"My only religion is the love of the work to be created, the love of creation, and great sincerity", he said in 1952 when the five-year project was completed.

The drawings on the chapel walls – black outline figures on white tiles – were executed by Matisse with a paintbrush fixed to a two-metre long bamboo stick specifically to remove his own stylistic signature from the lines. He succeeded in this to the extent that many people are bitterly disappointed, not finding the "Matisse" they expect. Yet it is a total work – every part of the chapel is Matisse's design – and one that the artist was content with.

Vieux Vence has all the chic boutiques and arty restaurants worthy of an *haut-lieu* of the Côte aristocracy, but it also has an everyday feel about it, with ordinary people and run-of-the-mill cafés. On place du Frêne, by the western gateway, the fifteenth-century **Château de Villeneuve Fondation Emile Hugues** (Tues–Sun: summer 10am–6pm; winter 10am–12.30pm & 2–6pm; €5) provides a beautiful temporary exhibition space for the works of artists such as Matisse, Dufy, Dubuffet and Chagall.

Practicalities

Arriving by bus, you'll be dropped near place du Frêne at the **gare routière** on place du Grand-Jardin, where you'll find the **tourist office** (mid-June to mid-Sept Mon–Sat 9am–7pm, Sun 10am–6pm; mid-Sept to mid-June Mon–Sat 9am–6pm; ⓣ04.93.58.06.38, ⓦwww.ville-vence.fr). You can rent **bikes** at Vence Motos on avenue Henri Isnard, just behind the tourist office.

Vence is a real town, with affordable **places to stay**. If you're on a tight budget, your best bet is the soundproofed, very central *La Victoire*, on place du Grand Jardin (ⓣ & ⓕ04.93.24.21.15; ❸); otherwise try the welcoming and peaceful *La Closerie des Genêts*, 4 impasse Maurel, off avenue M.-Maurel to the south of the old town (ⓣ04.93.58.33.25, ⓕ04.93.58.97.01; ❸), and *Le Provence*, 9 av M.-Maurel (ⓣ04.93.58.04.21, ⓦwww.hotelleprovence.com; ❸), with a pleasant garden. A little more luxury, including a pool, is available at *La Villa Roseraie*, 51 av Henri-Giraud (ⓣ04.93.58.02.20, ⓦwww.villaroseraie.com; ❻). There's a **campsite**, *La Bergerie* (€20 for two people and a tent), 3km west off the road to Tourettes-sur-Loup (ⓣ04.93.58.09.36, ⓦwww.camping-domainedelabergerie.com; closed mid-Oct to late March).

For a special, excellent-value **meal**, try *La Farigoule*, 15 av Henri-Isnard (ⓣ04.93.58.01.27; menus from €29.50). The fabled chef Jacques Maximin has opened a gourmet palace in Vence: *Jacques Maximin Restaurant Table des Amis*, 689 chemin de la Gaude (ⓣ04.93.58.90.75; closed Mon & Tues), prepares exquisite fare, with the cheapest menu starting at €50 and rising rapidly in price and indulgence. For more run-of-the-mill fare, try the astounding choice of pizzas from €7.50 at *Le Pêcheur du Soleil*, 1 place Godeau. You'll find plenty of cafés in the squares of Vieux Vence. *Le Clemenceau*, on place Clemenceau, is the big café-brasserie-glacier, but you might find *Henry's Bar*, on place de Peyra, more congenial. *La Régence*, on place du Grand-Jardin, serves excellent coffee to sip beneath its stylish parasols.

Nice

The capital of the Riviera and fifth largest city in France, **NICE** lives off a glittering reputation, its former glamour now gently faded. First popularized by English aristocrats in the eighteenth century, Nice reached its zenith in the *belle-époque* of the late nineteenth century, an era that left the city with several

Chemin de Fer de Provence

The **Chemin de Fer de Provence** runs one of France's most scenic and fun railway routes, from the Gare de Provence on rue Alfred-Binet (4 daily; 3hr 12min). The line runs up the Var valley into the hinterland of Nice to Digne-les-Bains, and climbs through some spectacular scenery as it goes. The return fare to Digne is €35.30 (for more information call ⓣ04.97.03.80.80 or check online at ⓦwww.trainprovence.

extraordinary architectural flights of fancy. Today, more than a quarter of Nice's permanent residents are over 60, their pensions and investments contributing to the high ratio of per capita income to economic activity.

Far too large to be considered simply a beach resort, Nice nevertheless manages to be a delightful, vibrant Mediterranean metropolis with all the advantages and disadvantages its city status brings: superb cultural facilities, wonderful street life and excellent shopping, eating and drinking, but also a high crime rate, graffiti and – in summer – horrendous traffic. Yet somehow things never seem as bad as they might be: the sun shines, the sea sparkles and a thousand sprinklers keep the lawns and flowerbeds lush.

Nice's easy-going charm, however, is at odds with its reactionary **politics**. For decades municipal power was the monopoly of a dynasty whose corruption was finally exposed in 1990, when Mayor Jacques Médecin fled to Uruguay, only to be extradited and jailed. From his prison cell, Médecin backed Jacques Peyrat, the former Front National member and close friend of Jean-Marie Le Pen, in the 1995 local elections. Peyrat won with ease and has been mayor ever since, while the Front National retains significant support in the city.

Nice has retained its historical styles almost intact: the medieval rabbit warren of **Vieux Nice**, the Italianate facades of **modern Nice** and the rich exuberance of **fin-de-siècle residences** dating from when the city was Europe's most fashionable winter retreat. It has also retained mementos from its ancient past, when the Romans ruled the region from here, and earlier still, when the Greeks founded the city. Nice's many museums are a treat for art lovers: within France the city is second only to Paris for art.

Of late the city has been smartening up its act with extensive **refurbishment** of its public spaces and the construction of a new **tramway**. Conservative it may be, but this is not a place that rests on its laurels.

Arrival and information

From the **airport**, two fast buses connect with the city: – #99 goes to the **gare SNCF** on avenue Thiers (14–28min; €4 day pass required) and #98 to the **gare routière** (14–34min; €4 day pass) on boulevard Jean-Jaurès. The regular bus #23 (40min; €1.30) also serves the *gare SNCF* from the airport. It continues up to place Général-de-Gaulle, a couple of blocks from the **Gare de Provence** on rue A.-Binet. **Taxis** are plentiful at the airport and will cost about €20–28 into town.

The main **tourist office** is beside the *gare SNCF* on avenue Thiers (June–Sept Mon–Sat 8am–8pm, Sun 9am–7pm; Oct–May Mon–Sat 8am–7pm, Sun 10am–5pm; ⓣ08.92.70.74.07, ⓦwww.nicetourisme.com). It's one of the most helpful in the region – though it can be a nightmare trying to get through by phone – and has annexes at 5 promenade des Anglais (June–Sept Mon–Sat 8am–8pm, Sun 9am–6pm; Oct–May Mon–Sat 9am–6pm), and at terminal 1 of the airport (June–Sept daily 8am–9pm; Oct–May Mon–Sat 8am–9pm).

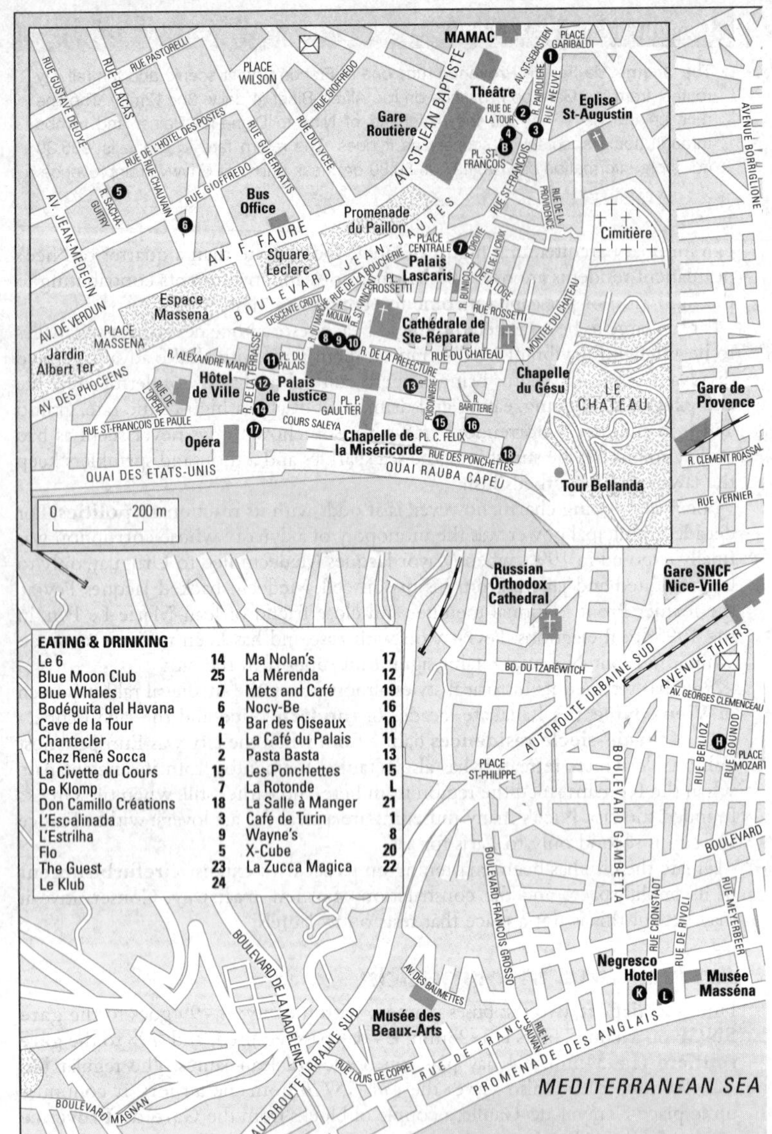

EATING & DRINKING

Le 6	14	Ma Nolan's	17
Blue Moon Club	25	La Mérenda	12
Blue Whales	7	Mets and Café	19
Bodéguita del Havana	6	Nocy-Be	16
Cave de la Tour	4	Bar des Oiseaux	10
Chantecler	L	La Café du Palais	11
Chez René Socca	2	Pasta Basta	13
La Civette du Cours	15	Les Ponchettes	15
De Klomp	7	La Rotonde	L
Don Camillo Créations	18	La Salle à Manger	21
L'Escalinada	3	Café de Turin	1
L'Estrilha	9	Wayne's	8
Flo	5	X-Cube	20
The Guest	23	La Zucca Magica	22
Le Klub	24		

Airport, Musée Anatole Jakovsky, Phoenix Parc Floral de Nice & Musée des Artes Asiatiques

Buses are frequent and run until early evening (roughly 7.30–9pm), after which four Noctambus night buses serve most areas from place Masséna until 11.10pm. Fares are flat rate and you can buy a single ticket (€1.30), a Multi+ carnet of seventeen tickets (€20), or a day pass (€4) on the bus; a ten-journey multipass (€10) and seven-day passes (€15) are available from *tabacs*, kiosks, newsagents and from Ligne d'Azur, the transport office, at 10 av Félix-Faure,

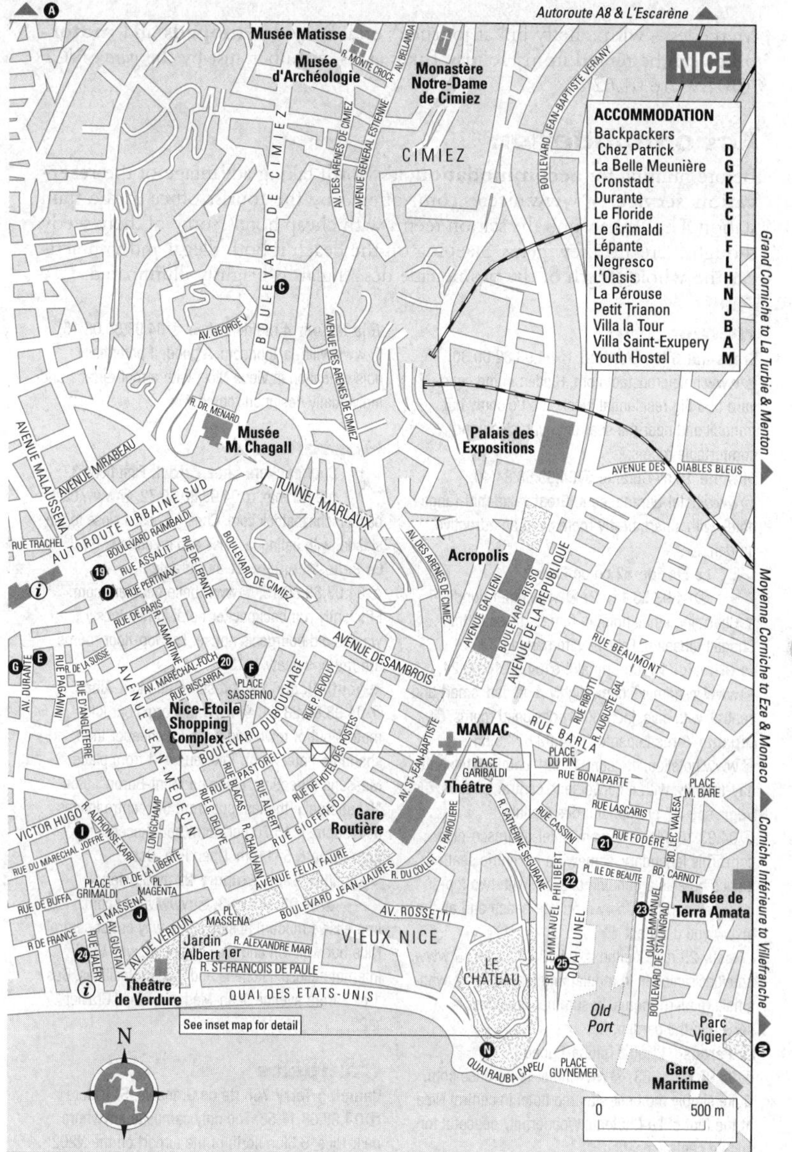

where you can also pick up a free route map. A new **tramway** system was scheduled to begin operation during 2007.

Taxis around town are scarce, and cost €1.56 per kilometre by day; night rates (7pm–7am and all day at weekends) are €2.08 per kilometre. There are various surcharges. There are also scams: if you allow a restaurant or bar to call a cab for you, you may enjoy a luxurious ride home in a top of the range

Mercedes – with a hefty bill at journey's end. **Bicycles**, **mopeds** and **motorbikes** can be rented from Holiday Bikes at 34 av Auber, just by the *gare SNCF* (Ⓣ04.93.16.01.62).

Accommodation

Before hunting for **accommodation**, it's worth taking advantage of the **reservation service** (Ⓦwww.niceres.com) offered by the tourist office at the train station. The area around the station teems with cheap hotels, some of them seedy, though there are a few gems. Sleeping on the beach is both illegal and impractical: the whole length of the promenade des Anglais is brightly illuminated.

Hotels

Cronstadt 3 rue Cronstadt Ⓣ04.93.82.00.30, Ⓦwww.hotelcronstadt.com. Hidden in the courtyard of a big residential block, a bit gloomy but tranquil and near the seafront, with clean and comfortable rooms. ⑤

Durante 16 av Durante Ⓣ04.93.88.84.40, Ⓦwww.hotel-durante.com. Great value mid-range hotel, with smart, pretty rooms and an attractive garden. ⑤

Le Floride 52 bd de Cimiez Ⓣ04.93.53.11.02, Ⓦwww.hotel-floride.fr. Charming small hotel in Cimiez, close to the Chagall museum. Free private parking. ④

Le Grimaldi 15 rue Grimaldi Ⓣ04.93.16.00.24, Ⓦwww.le-grimaldi.com. Highly regarded, smart and central, with chic, individually designed rooms. ⑥

Lépante 6 rue Lépante Ⓣ04.93.62.20.55, Ⓦwww.hotellepante.com. Smart, comfortable and gay-friendly, with a convenient, central location. ⑤

Negresco 37 promenade des Anglais Ⓣ04.93.16.64.00, Ⓦwww.hotel-negresco-nice.com. This legendary, somewhat eccentric seafront palace hotel is a genuine one-off, with two top-class restaurants, its own private beach and all the luxury you'd expect. ⑨

L'Oasis 23 rue Gounod Ⓣ04.93.88.12.29, Ⓦwww.hoteloasis-nice.fr. In a quiet and leafy setting, with small, modern rooms. In summer breakfast is served in the garden. ④

La Pérouse 11 quai Rauba-Capeu Ⓣ04.93.62.34.63, Ⓦwww.hotel-la-perouse.com. Quite simply the best-situated hotel in central Nice, at the foot of Le Château. Wonderfully peaceful for such a central location. ⑨

Petit Trianon 11 rue Paradis Ⓣ04.93.87.50.46, Ⓔhotel.nice.lepetittrianon@wanadoo.fr. Cheerful if basic hotel close to place Masséna and the *vieille ville*, with free Internet access and beach towels. ②

Villa la Tour 4 rue de la Tour Ⓣ04.93.80.08.15, Ⓦwww.villa-la-tour.com. A good, if potentially noisy, location in Vieux Nice, with a roof terrace and individually designed rooms. ⑤

Hostels

Backpackers Chez Patrick First floor, 32 rue Pertinax Ⓣ04.93.80.30.72, Ⓦwww.backpackerschezpatrick.com. Cheerful hostel close to the station, with eating facilities and no curfew. €21.

La Belle Meunière 21 av Durante Ⓣ04.93.88.66.15, Ⓦwww.bellemeuniere.com. Efficiently run backpacker hotel in fabulously wasted old bourgeois house. The top-floor rooms are rather sweaty. €15.

HI Youth Hostel rte Forestière du Mont-Alban Ⓣ04.93.89.23.64, Ⓦwww.fuaj.org. Four kilometres out of town and not a lot cheaper than sharing a hotel room. Take bus #14 from place Masséna (direction "place du Mont-Boron", stop "L'Auberge"); the last bus from the centre leaves at 7.50pm. €15.70 per dorm bed. Reception 7am–noon & 5–11pm. Open Feb–Oct.

Villa Saint-Exupery 22 av Gravier Ⓣ04.93.84.42.83, Ⓦwww.vsaint.com. Impressive modern hostel, some way out of central Nice but well run and well equipped, with Wi-Fi Internet access, kitchens and laundry facilities. Bus 1 or 2 from avenue Jean-Médecin, stop "Gravier". €22.

Campsite

Camping Terry 768 rte de Grenoble, St-Isidore Ⓣ04.93.08.11.58. The only campsite anywhere near Nice, 6.5km north of the airport on the N202; take the #59 bus from the *gare routière* to "La Manda" stop (or ask the driver to drop you at the site), or the Chemins de Fer de la Provence train to "Bellet-Tennis des Combes".

The City

It doesn't take long to get a feel for the layout of Nice. Shadowed by mountains that curve down to the Mediterranean east of its port, it still breaks up more

Museum charges

Formerly free, most of Nice's **museums** now charge for admission, with free entry now limited to the first and third Sunday of each month. To prevent entrance charges piling up, it makes sense to buy the **Carte Passe-Musée** (€7), which is valid for seven days and covers all municipal museums. It excludes the Musée Chagall and Musée Départmental des Arts Asiatiques, which are administered separately.

or less into old and new. **Vieux Nice**, the old town, groups about the hill of **Le Château**, its limits signalled by **boulevard Jean-Jaurès**, built along the course of the River Paillon. Along the seafront, the celebrated **promenade des Anglais** runs a cool 5km until forced to curve inland by the sea-projecting runways of the airport. The central square, **place Masséna**, is at the bottom of the modern city's main street, **avenue Jean-Médecin**, while off to the north is the exclusive hillside suburb of **Cimiez**.

The château and Vieux Nice

For initial orientation, with fantastic sea and city views, fresh air and the scent of Mediterranean vegetation, the best place to make for is the **Château park** (daily: April, May & Sept 8am–7pm; June–Aug 8am–8pm; Oct–March 8am–6pm). It's where Nice began as the ancient Greek city of Nikea, hence the mosaics and stone vases in mock Grecian style. There's no château as such, but the real pleasure lies in looking down on the scrambled rooftops and gleaming mosaic tiles of Vieux Nice and along the sweep of the promenade des Anglais. To reach the park, you can either take the lift by the Tour Bellanda (€0.80) at the eastern end of quai des États-Unis, or climb the steps from rue de la Providence or montée du Château in the old town.

Vieux Nice has been greatly gentrified in recent years, but the expensive shops, smart restaurants and art galleries still coexist with little hardware stores selling brooms and bottled gas, tiny cafés full of men in blue overalls, and washing strung between the tenements. Its dark and mysterious alleys are resistant to over-prettification and away from the showpiece squares a certain shabbiness lingers. Tourism now dominates Vieux Nice: throbbing with life day and night in August, much of it seems deserted in November. Its streets are too narrow for buses and are best explored on foot.

The central square is **place Rossetti**, where the soft-coloured Baroque **Cathédrale de Ste-Réparate** (Mon–Sat 9am–noon & 2–6pm, Sun 3–6pm) just manages to be visible in the concatenation of eight narrow streets. There are two cafés to relax in, with the choice of sun or shade, and a magical ice-cream parlour, *Fenocchio*, with an extraordinary choice of flavours. The real magnet of the old town, though, is **cours Saleya** and the adjacent place Pierre-Gautier and place Charles-Félix. These are wide-open, sunlit spaces alongside grandiloquent municipal buildings and Italianate chapels and the site of the city's main **market**. Every day except Monday from 6am to 1.30pm there are gorgeous displays of fruit, vegetables, cheeses and sausages, plus cut flowers and potted roses, mimosa and other scented plants displayed till 5.30pm (except Sunday afternoons); on Monday the stalls sell bric-a-brac and secondhand clothes (7.30am–6pm). Café and restaurant tables fill the *cours* on summer nights.

To feast your eyes on Baroque splendour, pop into the **chapels** and **churches** of Vieux Nice: La Chapelle de la Miséricorde, on cours Saleya (Tues 2.30–5pm); L'Église du Gesu, on rue Droite (open Thurs pm, Sat am & Sun eve); or L'Église

St-Augustin, on place St-Augustin (Tues–Sun 9am–noon & 2–5pm), which also contains a fine pietà by Louis Bréa. For contemporary graphic and photographic art, check out the best **art galleries** in Vieux Nice, which include: Galerie Espace Ste-Réparate, 4 rue Ste-Réparate; Galerie Municipale Renoir, 8 rue de la Loge; and Galerie du Château, 14 rue Droite.

Also on rue Droite is the **Palais Lascaris** (daily except Tues 10am–6pm; free), a seventeenth-century palace built by the Duke of Savoy's Field-Marshal, Jean-Paul Lascaris, whose family arms, engraved on the ceiling of the entrance hall, bear the motto "Not even lightning strikes us". It's all very sumptuous, with frescoes, tapestries and chandeliers, along with a collection of porcelain vases from an eighteenth-century pharmacy.

Place Masséna and around

The stately **place Masséna** is the hub of the new town, built in 1835 across the path of the River Paillon, with good views north past fountains and palm trees to the mountains. A balustraded terrace and steps on the south of the square lead to Vieux Nice; the new town lies to the north. It's a spacious, handsome expanse, more for passing through than lingering. A short walk to the west lie the **Jardins Albert 1er**, where the Théâtre de Verdure occasionally hosts concerts.

The covered course of the Paillon north of place Masséna is the site of the city's more recent prestige projects. Most appealing of these is the marble **Musée d'Art Moderne et d'Art Contemporain**, or MAMAC (Tues–Sun 10am–6pm; €4; Ⓦwww.mamac-nice.org), with rotating exhibitions of avant-garde French and American movements from the 1960s to the present. New Realism (smashing, burning, squashing and wrapping the detritus or mundane objects of everyday life) and Pop Art feature strongly with works by Warhol, Klein, Lichtenstein, César, Arman and Christo.

Running north from place Masséna, **avenue Jean-Médecin** is the city's nondescript main shopping street. You'll find all the mainstream clothes and household accessory chains at the revamped Nice-Étoile **shopping complex**, between rue Biscarra and boulevard Dubouchage; there are branches of FNAC and Virgin nearby for books, CDs and concert tickets. **Couturier** shops are to be found west of place Masséna on rue du Paradis and rue Alphonse Karr. Both these streets intersect with the pedestrianized **rue Masséna** and the end of **rue de France** – true holiday territory, all hotels, ice-cream parlours and big brasseries, and always crammed with strolling tourists.

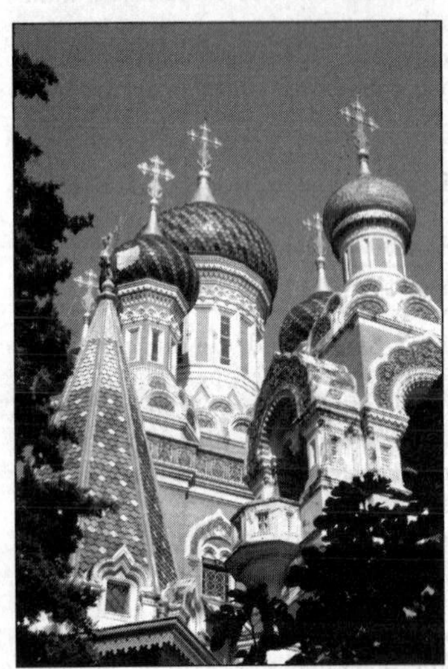

△ Russian Orthodox Cathedral, Nice

The chief interest in western Nice is in the older architecture: eighteenth- and nineteenth-century Italian Baroque and Neoclassical, florid *belle-époque* and unclassifiable exotic aristo-fantasy. The trophy for the most gilded, exotic and elaborate edifice goes to the **Russian Orthodox Cathedral**, at the end of avenue Nicolas-II, which runs off boulevard Tsaréwitch (daily except Sun morning: mid-Feb to April & Oct 9.15am–noon & 2.30–5.30pm; May–Sept 9am–noon & 2.30–6pm; Nov to mid-Feb 9.30am–noon & 2.30–5pm; €3), reached by bus #14 or #17 (stop Tzaréwitch).

The promenade des Anglais and the beaches

The point where the Paillon flows into the sea marks the beginning of the world-famous **promenade des Anglais**, created by nineteenth-century English residents for their afternoon's sea-breeze stroll along the Mediterranean sea coast. Today it's more or less a permanent traffic jam, still bordered by some of the most fanciful turn-of-the-twentieth-century architecture on the Côte d'Azur. At nos. 13–15, the Palais de la Méditerranée is once again a luxurious casino, though the splendid Art Deco facade is all that remains of the legendary 1930s original.

Most celebrated of all is the opulent and vaguely eccentric **Negresco Hotel** at no. 37, built in 1906, and filling up the block between rues de Rivoli and Cronstadt. Though they will try to stop you if you are not deemed to be wearing *tenue correcte* (especially in the evenings), you can try wandering in to take a look at the Salon Louis XIV and the Salon Royale. The first, on the left of the foyer, has a seventeenth-century painted oak ceiling and mammoth fireplace, plus royal portraits, all from various French châteaux. The Salon Royale, in the centre of the hotel, is a vast domed oval room, decorated with 24-carat gold leaf and the biggest carpet ever to have come out of the Savonnerie workshops. The chandelier is one of a pair commissioned from Baccarat by Tsar Nicholas II – the other hangs in the Kremlin.

Just before the *Negresco*, with its entrance at 65 rue de France, stands the **Musée Masséna**, the city's art and history museum. Closed indefinitely for major renovations, only its unexceptional but shady gardens are open to the public (daily 9am–5pm).

A kilometre or so down the promenade and a couple of blocks inland at 33 av des Baumettes lies the **Musée des Beaux-Arts** (Tues–Sun 10am–6pm; €4, bus #38, stop "Chéret"), where the chief glory is the collection of 28 works by Raoul Dufy, who is intimately connected with the visual image of Nice. Continuing southwest along the promenade des Anglais towards the airport, you'll find the **Musée International d'Art Naïf Anatole Jakovsky** (daily except Tues 10am–6pm; €4), home to a refreshingly different and surprisingly good collection of over six hundred pieces of amateur art from around the world.

The **beach** below the promenade des Anglais is all pebbles and mostly public, with showers provided. It's not particularly clean and you need to watch out for broken glass. There are twenty private beaches, clustering at the more scenic, eastern end of the bay close to Vieux Nice. If you don't mind rocks, you might want to try the string of coves beyond the port that starts with the **plage de la Réserve**, opposite Parc Vigier (bus #20 or #30). Further up, past **Coco Beach** (bus #30 only, stop "Villa La Côte"), rather smelly steps lead down to a coastal path which continues around the headland. Towards dusk this becomes a gay pick-up place.

On the far side of the castle sits the **old port**, flanked by gorgeous red to ochre eighteenth-century buildings and headed by the Neoclassical Notre-Dame du Port; it's full of yachts but has little quayside life despite the restaurants along quai Lunel. On the hill to the east, prehistoric life in the region has been reconstructed on the site of an excavated fossil beach in the well-designed **Musée de Terra Amata**, 25 bd Carnot (Tues–Sun 10am–6pm, €4, bus 81 or 100, stop "Gustavin").

Cimiez

The northern suburb of **Cimiez** has always been posh. The approach up boulevard de Cimiez is punctuated by vast *belle-époque* piles, many of them former hotels: at the foot of the hill stands the gargantuan *Majestic,* while the summit is dominated by the equally vast *Hôtel Régina*, built for a visit by Queen Victoria. The heights of Cimiez were the social centre of the local elite some 1700 years ago, when the town was capital of the Roman province of Alpes-Maritimae. Part of a small amphitheatre still stands, and excavations of the **Roman baths** have revealed enough detail to distinguish the sumptuous and elaborate facilities for the top tax official and his cronies, the plainer public baths and a separate complex for women. All the finds, plus an illustration of the town's history up to the Middle Ages, are displayed in the impressive, modern **Musée d'Archéologie**, 160 av des Arènes (daily except Tues 10am–6pm; €4; bus #15, #17 or #22, stop "Arènes").

The seventeenth-century villa between the excavations and the arena is the **Musée Matisse** (daily except Tues 10am–6pm; €4; closed until June 2007 for renovation; Ⓦwww.musee-matisse-nice.org). Matisse spent his winters in Nice from 1916 onwards, staying in hotels on the promenade – from where *A Storm at Nice* was painted – and then from 1921 to 1938 renting an apartment overlooking place Charles-Félix. It was here that he painted his most sensual, colour-flooded canvases of odalisques posed against exotic draperies. As well as the Mediterranean light, Matisse loved the cosmopolitan aspect of Nice and the presence of fellow artists Renoir, Bonnard and Picasso in neighbouring towns. He died in Cimiez in November 1954, aged 85.

The Roman remains and the Musée Matisse back onto an old olive grove, one of the best open spaces in Nice and venue for the July **jazz festival**. At its eastern end are the sixteenth-century buildings and exquisite gardens of the **Monastère Notre-Dame de Cimiez** (Mon–Sat 10am–noon & 3–6pm; free); the oratory has brilliant murals illustrating alchemy, while the church houses three masterpieces of medieval painting by Louis and Antoine Bréa. Adjoining the monastery is the Musée Franciscain.

At the foot of Cimiez hill, just off boulevard Cimiez on avenue du Docteur-Menard, **Chagall's Biblical Message** is housed in a **museum** built specially for the work and opened by the artist in 1972 (daily except Tues: July–Sept 10am–6pm; Oct–June 10am–5pm; €6.50, €7.70 during temporary exhibitions, bus #15, stop "Musée Chagall"). The rooms are light, white and cool, with windows allowing you to see the greenery of the garden beyond the indescribable shades between pink and red of the *Song of Songs* canvases. The seventeen paintings are all based on the Old Testament and complemented with etchings and engravings.

The Phoenix Parc Floral de Nice

Right out by the airport is a vast tourist attraction, the **Phoenix Parc Floral de Nice**, 405 promenade des Anglais (daily: April–Sept 9.30am–7.30pm; Oct–March 9.30am–6pm; €2; exit St-Augustin from the highway or bus #9, #10 or #23 from Nice). It's a cross between botanical gardens, a bird and insect zoo and a tacky theme park: automated dinosaurs and mock Mayan temples along with alpine streams, ginkgo trees, butterflies and cockatoos.

The best reason to make the trip out to the park is Nice's newest museum, the **Musée Départemental des Arts Asiatiques** (daily except Tues: May to mid-Oct 10am–6pm; mid-Oct to April 10am–5pm; €4.50; Ⓦwww.arts-asiatiques.com), housed in a beautiful building designed by Japanese architect Kenzo Tange. It houses a collection of ethnographic artefacts, including silk goods and pottery, as well as traditional and contemporary art.

Eating, drinking and entertainment

Nice is a great place for **eating**, whether you're picnicking on market fare, snacking on Niçois specialities or dining in the palace hotels. The Italian influence is strong, with pasta on every menu; seafood is also a staple. For **snacks**, many of the cafés sell sandwiches with typically Provençal fillings such as fresh basil, olive oil, goat's cheese and *mesclum*, the unique green salad mix of the region. If you want to buy the best bread or croissants in town, seek out Espuno, 35 rue Droite, in the old town.

Despite the usual fast-food chains and tourist traps dotted around, most areas of Nice have plenty of reasonable restaurants. Vieux Nice has a dozen on every street catering for a wide variety of budgets; the port quaysides have very good, but pricey, fish restaurants. In summer it's wise to book tables or turn up before 8pm, especially in Vieux Nice.

Vieux Nice is also the centre of Nice's lively **pub** and **club** scene. A good place to set out is along rue Central in the old town, where many pubs have early evening happy hours. Many Vieux Nice bars boast huge selections of beers and spirits and offer regular live music. As for Niçois nightclubs, bouncers judging your wallet or exclusive membership lists are the rule.

Nice's **lesbian and gay** nightlife scene is surprisingly active given the city's reactionary politics, and for lesbian and gay visitors the city has a relaxed feel. The annual Pink Parade takes place in early June.

For festivals, the **Mardi Gras Carnival** opens the year's events in Nice in February (Ⓦ www.nicecarnaval.com), with the last week of July taken up by the **Nice Jazz Festival** in the Parc de Cimiez (Ⓣ 08.92.70.75.07, Ⓦ www.nicejazzfest.com for info, or contact the main tourist office in May/June).

Cafés

Cave de la Tour 3 rue de la Tour Ⓣ 04.93.80.03.31. Local *bar à vins* that serves wine from the bottle, or for the more daring, straight from huge vats.

Nocy-be 2 rue Jules-Gilley. This New-Agey tea house has a cushioned interior which evokes a Bedouin tent. Countless varieties of teas and infusions. Mon–Sat until 12.30am.

Le Café du Palais place du Palais. A prime al-fresco lounging spot on the handsome square by the Palais de Justice.

Les Ponchettes and **La Civette du Cours** cours Saleya. At Le Château end of the marketplace, neighbouring cafés with cane seats fanning out a good 50m from the doors. Open late in summer.

Restaurants

Chantecler and **La Rotonde** *Hôtel Negresco*, 37 promenade des Anglais Ⓣ 04.93.16.64.00. The *Chantecler* is the best restaurant in Nice, seriously expensive à la carte, but chef Bruno Turbot provides a lunchtime menu, including wine and coffee, for €55, which will give you a good idea of how sublime Niçois food is at its best. At *La Rotonde* you can taste less fancy but still mouth-watering dishes on the €25 menu. Closed Mon, Tues & Jan 7–Feb 7.

Chez René Socca 2 rue Miralhéti, off rue Pairolière Ⓣ 04.93.85.95.67. The cheapest meal in town: you can buy helpings of *socca*, *pissaladière*, stuffed peppers, pasta or calamares at the counter and eat with your fingers; the bar opposite serves the drinks. Closed Mon & Jan.

Don Camillo Créations 5 rue des Ponchettes Ⓣ 04.93.85.67.95. Elegant modern restaurant with contemporary Niçois/Italian cooking on a €36 menu. Closed Mon lunch & Sun.

L'Escalinada 22 rue Pairolière Ⓣ 04.93.62.11.71. Good Niçois specialities on a €23 menu – *pissaladière* to start, then you help yourself to chickpea salad from a huge pot. The location is pretty, at the foot of a stepped sidestreet. Open daily.

L'Estrilha 13 rue de l'Abbaye Ⓣ 04.93.62.62.00. Reservations essential in summer for this popular restaurant that serves *bourride, civet de lapin* and *daube niçoise. Plats* around €12.50.

Flo 4 rue Sacha-Guitry Ⓣ 04.93.13.38.38. Wonderful Parisian-style serving *choucroute, confit de canard*, seafood and great *crème brûlée* in the Art Deco surroundings of a theatre where Mistinguett and Piaf performed. Lunch menu €22.50, evening €29.50. Last orders midnight. Open daily.

La Mérenda 4 rue de la Terrasse. Courgette fritters, *tripe à la niçoise* and the like from Dominic le

Stanc, former chef at *Chantecler*. À la carte only, around €25. No phone, no smoking, no credit cards. Closed Sat, Sun & two weeks in Aug.

Mets and Café 28 rue Assalit ⓣ04.93.80.30.85. Good value, busy budget brasserie close to many of the backpacker hostels, with a €9 menu and no shortage of custom. Closed Sun.

Pasta Basta 18 rue de la Préfecture ⓣ04.93.80.03.57. Excellent fresh pasta from €4.40 plus a bewildering variety of sauces from €2.40 – and they hand you the block of parmesan to grate yourself.

La Salle à Manger 7 rue Fodéré ⓣ04.93.56.00.94 Tiny, brightly modern gay-lesbian-friendly restaurant north of the port, with *amuse bouches* and a welcome glass of kir on the €23 menu. Eves only, closed Mon.

Café de Turin 5 place Garibaldi ⓣ04.93.62.29.52. Queues around the block for the spectacular seafood at this restaurant on the edge of Vieux Nice. *Plateaux de fruits de mer* from just under €20. There are seafood stalls in the street outside if you get tired of waiting. Closed Wed.

La Zucca Magica 4bis quai Papacino ⓣ04.93.56.25.27. Long-established, homely Italian vegetarian restaurant on the port, with a sound reputation but a tendency to overdo the cheese. Around €25, no credit cards. Closed Sun & Mon.

Bars, clubs and live entertainment

Blue Moon Club 26 quai Lunel. Bar and mainstream disco. Entrance free until midnight, then €10 and finally €16 with *conso*.

Blue Whales 1 rue Mascoïnat. Intimate venue with a friendly atmosphere and live music on Fridays. Open daily till 2.30am.

Bodéguita del Havana 14 rue Chauvain. Wildly popular Cuban salsa bar with DJs and live music. Open Tues–Sun until 2.30am. Smart dress required.

De Klomp 6 rue Mascoïnat. Dutch-style brown café with twelve beers on draught, sixty whiskies and regular live music. Mon–Sat 5.30pm–2.30am.

The Guest 5 quai des Deux-Emmanuel. Very stylish (and expensive) portside bar with a dance floor, attracting a slightly older crowd. Cocktails from €9.50.

Ma Nolan's 2 rue St-François de Paul. Vast, slick Irish pub with regular live music, televised Irish and British sport plus Murphy's and Guinness on draught. Popular with a younger crowd.

Bar des Oiseaux 5 rue St-Vincent. Eccentric cabaret bar named for the birds that fly down from their nests in the loft and the pet parrot and screeching myna bird that perch by the door. Live jazz, bossa nova, *chanson* and flamenco. Open Tues–Sun until 1am.

Wayne's 15 rue de la Préfecture. Big, popular rock bar on the edge of Vieux Nice, still the lynchpin of the area's nightlife despite its vaguely Neanderthal sexual politics. Regular live British bands plus theme nights including quizzes, ladies' and student nights. Open daily.

Lesbian and gay clubs and bars

Le 6 6 rue de la Terrasse. Smart lesbian and gay music bar, with regular live entertainment including drag, rai (Algerian funk/rap music) and karaoke. Tues–Sun from 10pm.

Le Klub 6 rue Halévy. Nice's largest and best gay club attracts a young, stylish crowd including women and some heteros. Wed–Sun from midnight.

X-Cube 13 av Maréchal Foch. Slick, stylish minimalist gay men's lounge bar attached to a sex shop and cruising club. Daily until 2.30am.

Listings

Airlines Aer Lingus ⓣ01.70.20.00.72; Air France ⓣ36.54; Air Transat ⓣ08.25.12.02.48; BMI Baby ⓣ08.90.71.00.81; British Airways ⓣ08.25.82.54.00; British Midland ⓣ01.41.91.87.04; Delta ⓣ08.11.64.00.05; Easyjet ⓣ08.99.70.00.41; United ⓣ0810.72.72.72.

Airport information ⓣ08.20.42.33.33, ⓦwww.nice.aeroport.fr.

Books The Cat's Whiskers, 30 rue Lamartine, sells English-language books.

Car rental Major firms have offices at the airport and/or at the *gare SNCF* on av Thiers. Try also: Avis, 2 av Phocéens ⓣ04.93.80.63.52; Europcar, 3 av Gustave-V ⓣ04.92.14.44.50; or Hertz, 9 av Gustav-V ⓣ04.93.87.11.87.

Cinema Cinéma Mercury, 16 place Garibaldi (ⓣ08.36.68.81.06), Cinémathèque de Nice, 3 Esplanade Kennedy (ⓣ04.92.04.06.66), UGC Rialto, 4 rue de Rivoli (ⓣ08.92.68.00.41), all show subtitled films in the original language (*v.o.*).

Consulates Canada, 10 rue Lamartine ⓣ04.93.92.93.22; UK, 22 av Notre Dame ⓣ04.93.62.94.95; USA, 7 av Gustave-V, 3rd floor ⓣ04.93.88.89.55.

Disabled access Transport for people with reduced mobility ⓣ04.93.96.09.99.

Emergencies SAMU ☎15; SOS Médecins ☎08.10.85.01.01; Riviera Medical Services (English speaking doctors) ☎04.93.26.12.70; Hôpital St-Roch, 5 rue Pierre-Dévoluy ☎04.92.03.33.75; SOS Dentaire ☎04.93.80.77.77.
Ferries SNCM *gare maritime*, quai du Commerce ☎04.93.13.66.66, Ⓦwww.sncm.fr; Corsica Ferries, quai Amiral-Infernet ☎08.25.09.50.95.
Internet Internet Café, 30 rue Pertinax; Taxi Phone Internet, 10 rue de Belgique and at 25 rue Paganini.
Laundry Best One, 16 rue Pertinax; Lavomatique, 11 rue du Pont-Vieux and at cnr of rue Lamartine and Pertinax; du Mono, 8 rue de Belgique.
Lost property 1 rue Raoul Bosio ☎04.97.13.44.10.
Money exchange American Express, 11 promenade des Anglais; Change Or, 7 av Thiers; Thomas Cook, 12 av Thiers.
Pharmacy 7 rue Masséna ☎04.93.87.78.94; 66 av Jean Médecin ☎04.93.62.54.44.
Police Commissariat Central de Police, 1 av Maréchal Foch ☎04.92.17.22.22.
Post office 21 av Thiers.
Taxis ☎04.93.13.78.78.
Trains General information and reservations ☎36.35; for information on the Chemin de Fer de Provence, go to 4bis rue Alfred-Binet ☎04.97.03.80.80.
Youth information Centre Information Jeunesse, 19 rue Gioffredo ☎04.93.80.93.93.

The Corniches

Three **corniche roads** run east from Nice to the independent principality of Monaco and to Menton, the last town of the French Riviera. Napoleon built the **Grande Corniche** on the route of the Romans' Via Julia Augusta, and the **Moyenne Corniche** dates from the first quarter of the twentieth century, when aristocratic tourism on the Riviera was already causing congestion on the lower, coastal road, the **Corniche Inférieure**. The upper two are the classic location for car commercials, and for movie car crashes. Real deaths occur too – most notoriously Princess Grace of Monaco, who died as she descended from La Turbie to the Moyenne Corniche – a bitter irony, since the corniches had been the backdrop to one of her greatest film successes, *To Catch a Thief*.

Buses take all three routes; the **train** follows the lower corniche, and all three are superb means of seeing the most mountainous stretch of the Côte d'Azur. **Hotel** rooms between Nice and Menton are relatively scarce and frequently expensive; it probably makes more sense to base yourself in Nice.

The Corniche Inférieure

The characteristic Côte d'Azur mansions that represent the stylistically incompatible fantasies of their original owners parade along the **Corniche Inférieure**.

VILLEFRANCHE-SUR-MER is just over the other side of Mont Alban from Nice, and marks the beginning of one of the most picturesque and unspoiled sections of the Riviera, though the cruise liners attracted by the deep-water anchorage in Villefranche's beautiful bay ensure a steady stream of tour buses climbing the hill from the port. But as long as your visit doesn't coincide with shore excursions, the old town, with its active fleet of fishing boats, sixteenth-century citadelle and its covered medieval rue Obscure running beneath the houses, is a tranquil and charming place to while away an afternoon.

The tiny fishing harbour is overlooked by the medieval **Chapelle de St-Pierre** (Tues–Sun: spring 10am–noon & 3–7pm; summer 10am–noon & 4–8pm; autumn & winter 10am–noon & 2–6pm; €2), decorated by Jean Cocteau in 1957 in shades he described as "ghosts of colours". The drawings portray

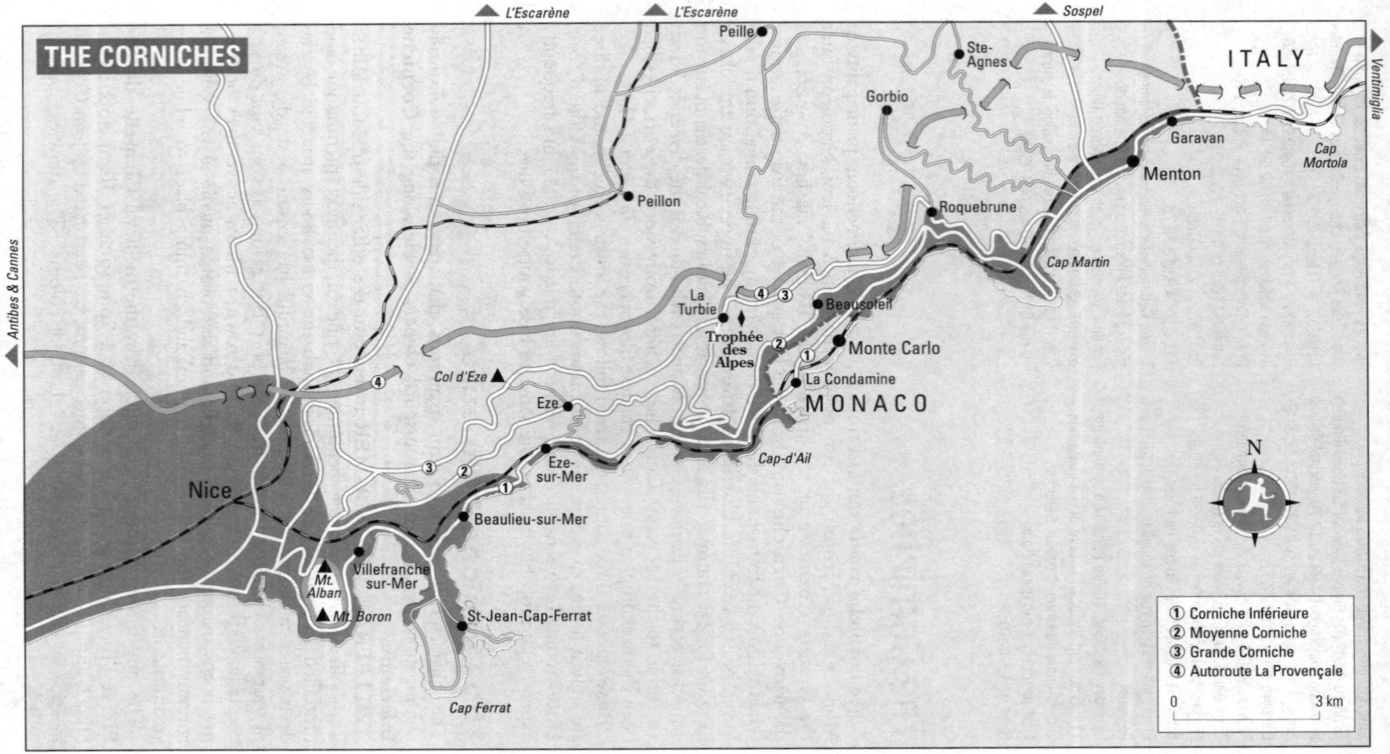

THE CORNICHES

L'Escarène
L'Escarène
Sospel
Ventimiglia
Antibes & Cannes
ITALY
Peille
Ste-Agnes
Gorbio
Peillon
Garavan
Menton
Cap Mortola
Roquebrune
Cap Martin
La Turbie
Trophée des Alpes
Beausoleil
Monte Carlo
La Condamine
MONACO
Cap-d'Ail
Col d'Eze
Eze
Eze-sur-Mer
Nice
Beaulieu-sur-Mer
Villefranche-sur-Mer
Mt. Alban
Mt. Boron
St-Jean-Cap-Ferrat
Cap Ferrat
N

① Corniche Inférieure
② Moyenne Corniche
③ Grande Corniche
④ Autoroute La Provençale

0 3 km

scenes from the life of St Peter and homages to the women of Villefranche and to the gypsies. The chapel is used just once a year, on June 29, when local fishermen celebrate the feast day of St Peter and St Paul with a Mass.

On the main road along the neck of the **Cap Ferrat peninsula**, between Villefranche and Beaulieu, stands the **Villa Éphrussi** (Feb–June & Sept to early Oct daily 10am–6pm; July & Aug daily 10am–7pm; Nov–Jan Mon–Fri 2–6pm, Sat & Sun 10am–6pm; last entry 30min before closing; €9.50, €2 extra to visit first-floor collections). Built in 1912 for a Rothschild heiress, it overflows with decorative art, paintings, sculpture and artefacts ranging from the fourteenth to the nineteenth centuries, and from European to Far Eastern origins. The villa is surrounded by elaborate gardens.

Attractive, *belle-époque* **BEAULIEU** overlooks the pretty Baie des Fourmis and is sheltered by a ring of hills that ensure some of the highest temperatures on the Côte. Its main point of interest is the **Villa Kérylos** (Jan to mid-Feb & early Nov to Dec Mon–Fri 2–6pm, Sat & Sun 10am–6pm; mid-Feb to June & Sept to early Nov 10am–6pm; July & Aug 10am–7pm; €8), a near-perfect reproduction of an ancient Greek villa, just east of the casino on avenue Gustav-Eiffel. Théodore Reinach, the archeologist who had it built in 1900, lived here for twenty years, eating, dressing and acting like an Athenian citizen, taking baths with his male friends and assigning separate suites to women. However perverse the concept, it's a visual knockout, with faithfully reproduced mosaics and vases and lavish use of marble and alabaster. The villa is only five minutes' walk from the **gare SNCF**. For those tempted to **stay** overnight, two economical options are the family-run *Hôtel Riviera* at 6 rue Paul Doumer, right in the centre near the sea (Ⓣ04.93.01.04.92, Ⓦwww.hotel-riviera.fr; ❹), and the *Select*, 1 place Général-de-Gaulle (Ⓣ04.93.01.05.42, Ⓔselect.beaulieu@wanadoo.fr; ❹), which is basic but clean, comfortable and excellent value for this part of the world.

The Moyenne Corniche

Of the three roads, the **Moyenne Corniche** is the most photogenic, a real cliff-hanging, car-chase highway. Eleven kilometres from Nice, the medieval village of **EZE** winds round its conical rock just below the corniche. No other *village perché* is more infested with antique dealers, pseudo-artisans and other caterers to rich tourists, and it requires a major mental feat to recall that the labyrinth of tiny vaulted passages and stairways was designed not for charm but from fear of attack. At the summit, a cactus garden, the **Jardin Exotique** (July & Aug daily 9am–10pm; Sept–June 9am–6/7pm; €5), covers the site of the former castle.

From place du Centenaire, just outside the old village, you can reach the shore through open countryside via the **sentier Frédéric-Nietzsche**. The philosopher is said to have conceived part of *Thus Spoke Zarathustra*, his shaggy dog story against believing answers to ultimate questions, on this path. You arrive at the Corniche Inférieure at the eastern limit of Eze-sur-Mer (coming upwards, it's signposted to La Village).

The Grande Corniche

At every other turn on the **Grande Corniche**, you're invited to park your car and enjoy a *belvédère*. At certain points, such as **Col d'Eze**, you can turn off upwards for even higher views. Eighteen stunning kilometres from Nice, you reach the village of **LA TURBIE** and its **Trophée des Alpes**, a huge monument raised in 6 BC to celebrate the subjugation of the tribes of Gaul. Originally a statue of Augustus Caesar stood on the 45-metre plinth, which was pillaged, ransacked for building materials and blown up over the centuries. Painstakingly restored in the 1930s, it now stands statueless, 35m high, and, viewed from a distance, still looks imperious. If you want a closer inspection, you'll have to buy a ticket (Tues–Sun: mid-May to mid-Sept 9.30am–1pm & 2.30–6.30pm; mid-Sept to mid-May 10am–1.30pm & 2.30–5pm; €5). Several buses a day run from here to Monaco and Nice, from Monday to Saturday.

As the corniche descends towards Cap Martin, it passes the eleventh-century castle of **ROQUEBRUNE**, its village nestling round the base of the rock. The **castle** (daily: Jan, Nov & Dec 10am–12.30pm & 2–5pm; Feb, March & Oct 10am–12.30pm & 2–6pm; April–June & Sept 10am–12.30pm & 2–6.30pm; July & Aug 10am–12.30pm & 3–7.30pm; €3.50) has been kitted out enthusiastically in medieval fashion, while the tiny vaulted passages and stairways of the village are almost too good to be true. One thing that hasn't been restored is the vast millennial **olive tree** that lies just to the east of the village on the chemin de Menton. To get to the *vieux village* from the **gare SNCF**, turn east and then right up avenue de la Côte d'Azur, then first left up escalier Corinthille, across the Grande Corniche and up escalier Chanoine-J.-B.-Grana. The best **hotel** in the old village is *Les Deux Frères*, place des Deux-Frères (Ⓣ04.93.28.99.00, Ⓦwww.lesdeuxfreres.com; ❼), which is worth booking in advance to try to get one of the rooms with the awesome view.

Southeast of the old town and the station is the peninsula of **Cap Martin**, with a **coastal path**, giving you access to a wonderful shoreline of white rocks, secluded beaches and wind-bent pines. The path is named after **Le Corbusier**, who spent several summers in Roquebrune and died by drowning off Cap Martin in 1965. His grave – designed by himself – is in the **cemetery** (square J near the flagpole), high above the old village on promenade 1er-DFL.

A gourmet treat here is the panoramic **restaurant** *Le Vistaero*, on the Grande Corniche (Ⓣ04.92.10.40.00), with lunch menus at €40 and €55.

Monaco

Viewed from a distance, there's no mistaking the thick cluster of towers that is **MONACO**. Rampant development in the 1960s and 1970s rescued the tiny principality from postwar decline but elbowed aside much of its former Italianate prettiness, leaving it looking like nowhere else on the Riviera. Not for nothing was **Prince Rainier**, who died in 2005, known as the Prince Bâtisseur ("Prince Builder").

Though it may have lost its looks, this tiny state, no bigger than London's Hyde Park, retains its comic opera independence. It has been in the hands of the ruling Grimaldi family since the thirteenth century, and in theory Monaco would once again become part of France were the royal line to die out. The current ruler, Prince Albert II, is the one constitutionally autocratic ruler left in Europe, under whose nose every French law is passed for approval prior to being applied to Monaco.

Phoning Monaco

Monaco phone numbers have only eight digits and no -04 French area code. If you are phoning from France you must dial Monaco's international code, 00377–, then the number (leaving out the first 0).

Along with its great wealth, Monaco latterly acquired an unwelcome reputation for wheeler-dealer **sleaze**. On his accession in 2005, the US-educated Albert declared he no longer wished Monaco to be known – in the words of Somerset Maugham – as "a sunny place for shady people". He set about trying to get the principality off an OECD list of uncooperative tax havens. Monaco now levies tax on the interest income of EU citizens resident there. Even so, it remains home to 6000 British expats – including Roger Moore and Shirley Bassey – out of a total population of 32,000.

One time to avoid Monaco – unless you're a motor-racing enthusiast – is the end of May, when racing cars burn around the port and casino for the Formula 1 **Monaco Grand Prix**. Every space in sight of the circuit is inaccessible without a ticket, making casual sightseeing – or sneaky free views of the race – out of the question.

The Principality

The oldest part of the two-kilometre-long state is **Monaco-Ville**, around the palace on the high rocky promontory, with the new suburb and marina of **Fontvieille** in its western shadow. **La Condamine** is the old port quarter on the other side of the promontory; **Larvotto**, the rather ugly bathing resort with artificial beaches of imported sand, reaches to the eastern border; and **Monte-Carlo** is in the middle.

Monte-Carlo

Monte-Carlo is the area of Monaco where the real money is flung about, and its famous **casino** (Ⓦwww.casinomontecarlo.com; bus #1, #2 #4 or #6) demands to be seen. Entrance is restricted to over-18s and you may have to show your passport; dress code is rigid, with shorts and T-shirts frowned upon, though most visitors are scarcely the last word in designer chic. Skirts, jackets and ties are obligatory for the more interesting sections. Bags and large coats are checked at the door.

The first gambling hall is the **Salons Européens** (open from 2pm; €10) where slot machines surround the American roulette, craps and blackjack tables, the managers are Vegas-trained, the lights low and the air oppressively smoky. Above this slice of Nevada, however, the decor is *fin-de-siècle* Rococo extravagance, while the ceilings in the adjoining Pink Salon Bar are adorned with female nudes smoking cigarettes. The heart of the place is the **Salons Privés** (Mon–Fri from 4pm, Sat & Sun from 3pm), through the Salles Touzet. To get in, you have to look like a gambler, not a tourist (no cameras), and

△ Casino, Monte-Carlo

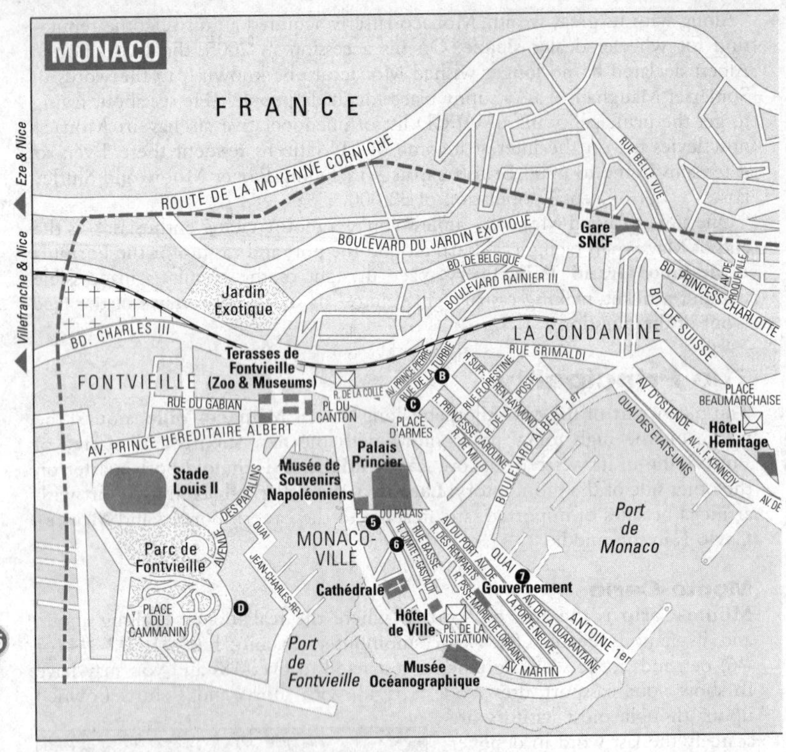

dispense with €20 at the door. Rather larger and more richly decorated than the European Rooms, its early-afternoon or out-of-season atmosphere is that of a cathedral. No clinking coins, just sliding chips and softly-spoken croupiers.

Adjoining the casino is the gaudy **opera house**, and around the palm-tree-lined place du Casino are more casinos plus the city's palace-hotels and *grands cafés*. The American Bar of the **Hôtel de Paris** is *the* place for the elite to meet, while the turn-of-the-twentieth-century **Hermitage** has a beautiful Gustave Eiffel iron-and-glass dome.

Monaco-Ville, Fontvieille and Larvotto

After the casino, the amusements of **Monaco-Ville** (bus #1 or #2), where it seems every other shop sells junky souvenirs, are less exciting, though the glacé-iced old town is the one part of the principality to have been spared the developer's worst. You can take a self-guided tour around the Lilliputian splendour of the **Palais Princier** (April 10.30am–6pm; May–Sept 9.30am–6.30pm; Oct 10am–5.30pm; €7); look at Napoleonic relics and items from the palace's historical archives at the **Musée des Souvenirs Napoléoniens et Collection des Archives Historiques du Palais**, place du Palais (Jan–March Tues–Sun 10.30am–12.30pm & 2–5pm; April daily 10.30am–6pm; May–Sept daily 9.30am–6.30pm; Oct 10am–5.30pm; Dec 10.30am–5pm; €4); see the tombs of Prince Rainier and Princess Grace in the rather dull nineteenth-century **cathedral** (summer daily 9.30am–7pm; winter daily 9.30am–6pm) on rue

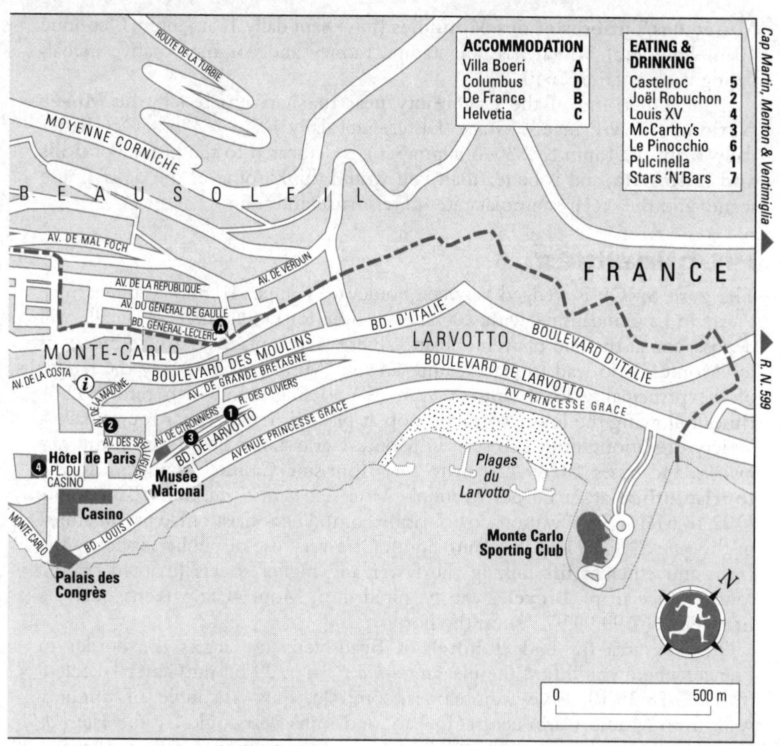

Colonel; and even watch Monaco the movie, at the **Monte-Carlo Story**, parking des Pecheurs (Jan–June & Sept–Oct 2–5pm; July & Aug 2–6pm; €7).

If you've had your fill of Grimaldis, check out the **Musée de la Chapelle de la Visitation** on place de la Visitation (Tues–Sun 10am–4pm; €3), displaying part of Barbara Piasecka Johnson's collection of religious art This small but exquisite collection includes works by Zurbarán, Rivera, Rubens, and Vermeer.

One of Monaco's best sights is the aquarium in the imposing **Musée Océanographique** (April–June & Sept 9.30am–7pm; July & Aug 9.30am–7.30pm; Oct–March 10am–6pm; €11), where the fishy beings outdo the weirdest Kandinsky or Hieronymus Bosch creations. Less exceptional but still peculiar, cactus equivalents can be viewed in the **Jardin Exotique**, on boulevard du Jardin Exotique high above Fontvieille (mid-May to mid-Sept 9am–7pm; mid-Sept to mid-May 9am–6pm or dusk; €6.90; bus #2).

There are yet more museums in **Fontvieille**, below the rock of Monaco-Ville. They include: the **Collection de Voitures Anciennes de SAS le Prince de Monaco** (daily 10am–6pm; €6), an enjoyable miscellany of old and not-so-old cars, both prestigious and humble – there's everything from a 1928 Hispano-Suiza worthy of Cruella de Ville to Princess Grace's elegant 1959 Renault Florida Coupé; the **Musée Naval** (daily 10am–6pm; €4), containing 250 model ships; the **zoo** (March–May 10am–noon & 2–6pm; June–Sept 9am–noon & 2–7pm; Oct–Feb 10am–noon & 2–5pm; €4), with exotic birds, a black panther and a white tiger; and the museum of stamps and coins, the

Musée des Timbres et des Monnaies (July–Sept daily 10am–6pm; Oct–June 10am–5pm; €3), which has rare stamps, money and commemorative medals dating back as far as 1640.

At the other end of the principality near the Larvotto beach, the **Musée National**, 17 av Princesse Grace (Easter–Sept daily 10am–6.30pm; Oct–Easter daily 10am–12.15pm & 2.30–6.30pm; €6), is dedicated to the history of **dolls and automata**, and is better than you would think: some of the dolls' house scenes and the creepy automata are quite surreal and fun.

Practicalities

The **gare SNCF** is wedged between boulevard Rainier III and avenue Prince Pierre in La Condamine, with several exits: signs for Le Rocher-Fontvieille will deposit you at the end of avenue Prince Pierre above place d'Armes; directions for Monte-Carlo lead to place Sainte Dévote. Municipal buses ply the length of the principality from 7am to 9pm (€1.50 single; four-trip card €3.50). Buses following the lower corniche stop at place d'Armes; other routes have a variety of stations; most also stop in Monte-Carlo. Local bus #4 from the *gare routière*, and buses #1 & #2 run to the "Tourisme-Casino" stop, close to the **tourist office** at 2a bd des Moulins (Mon–Sat 9am–7pm, Sun 10am–noon; ⓣ92.16.61.16, ⓦwww.monaco-tourisme.com). The tourist office has an annex in the *gare SNCF* (Tues–Sat 9am–5pm). One very useful public service is the clean and efficient **lift** linking the lower and higher streets (marked on the tourist office map). **Bicycles** can be hired from Monte-Carlo-Rent, quai des États-Unis (ⓣ99.99.97.79) on the port.

The best area for budget **hotels** is Beausoleil, just across the border in France, where you'll find the pleasant *Villa Boeri* at 29 bd du Général-Leclerc (ⓣ04.93.78.38.10, ⓦwww.hotelboeri.com; ❹), only a couple of minutes' walk from Monte-Carlo centre. In La Condamine you could try the *Hôtel de France*, at 6 rue de la Turbie (ⓣ93.30.24.64, ⓦwww.monte-carlo.mc/france; ❺). Another reasonable option is *Helvetia*, 1bis rue Grimaldi (ⓣ93.30.21.71, ⓕ92.16.70.51; ❹), a small and comfortable old hotel with optional air conditioning and most rooms en suite. If you want luxury but don't want to pay the steep prices at the palace hotels, *Columbus*, 23 av des Papalins (ⓣ92.05.90.00, ⓦwww.columbushotels.com; ❾), is a stylish modern boutique hotel in Fontvieille with sea views. Monaco has no campsite, and caravans are illegal – as are bathing costumes, bare feet and bare chests once you step off the beach. Camper vans have to be parked at the Parking des Écoles, in Fontvieille, and even then not overnight.

La Condamine and the old town are replete with **restaurants**, but good food and reasonable prices don't exactly match. Menu prices near casino can reach absurd levels, and not just in the palace hotels. The best-value cuisine is Italian, notably *Le Pinocchio*, at 30 rue Comte-F.-Gastaldi (ⓣ93.30.96.20; closed mid-Dec to early Jan), with *plats du jour* from €11, and *Pulcinella*, 17 rue du Portier in Monte-Carlo (ⓣ93.30.73.61); menu at €28, *plats* from €13. Alternatively, try *Castelroc*, in the old town on place du Palais (ⓣ93.30.36.68; closed Mon & mid-Dec to late Jan), which has a generous €21 menu. It's really not worth going upmarket in Monaco unless you're prepared to pay €90 and more per head, in which case Monaco has some worthy places to splash out: Alain Ducasse's *Louis XV* (ⓣ92.16.29.76; closed Tues, Wed, Dec & second half Feb) in the *Hôtel de Paris*, or the *Restaurant Joël Robuchon* at the *Hotel Métropole*, 4 av de la Madone (ⓣ93.15.15.10), where the cooking is under the aegis of one of France's most respected chefs.

Your best bet for non-casino **nightlife** is the large *Stars 'N' Bars* on the quai Antoine 1er, packed out on Fridays and Saturdays, with a lively club upstairs, or the ubiquitous Irish pub, *McCarthy's*, 7 rue du Portier, for Guinness and occasional live music.

Menton

Of all the Côte d'Azur resorts, **MENTON** – the warmest and most Italianate, being right on the border – is the one that retains an atmosphere of aristocratic tourism. It got its first boost as a resort in 1861 when a British doctor, James Henry Bennet, published a treatise on the benefits of Menton's mild winter climate to tuberculosis sufferers, and soon thousands of well-heeled invalids were flocking to the town in the vain hope of a cure. Menton glories chiefly in its climate and year-round lemon crops. It's ringed by protective mountains, so hardly a whisper of wind disturbs this suntrap of a city; you'll notice the difference in winter, when you'll need a change of clothes between here and the exposed central resorts.

Arrival and information

Roquebrune and Cap Martin merge into Menton along the three-kilometre shore of the Baie du Soleil. The modern town is arranged around three main streets parallel to the promenade du Soleil. The **gare SNCF** is on the top one, boulevard Albert-1er, from which a short walk to the left as you come out brings you to the north–south avenue de Verdun and avenue Boyer divided by the Jardins Biovès – central location for citrus sculptures during February's **Fête du Citron**. The **tourist office** is at 8 av Boyer (mid-June to mid-Sept daily 9am–7pm; mid-Sept to mid-June Mon–Sat 8.30am–12.30pm & 2–6pm; ⓣ04.92.41.76.76, ⓦwww.villedementon.com), in the Palais de l'Europe; the building was once a casino, but now hosts various cultural activities and art exhibitions.

The **gare routière** and the **urban bus station** are between the continuation of the two avenues north of the train line on the avenue de Sospel. All the local bus lines (€1) pass through the *gare routière*. The district of **Garavan**, further east again, is the most exclusive residential area and overlooks the marina.

Accommodation

Menton is no less popular than the other major resorts, so in summer you should reserve **accommodation** in advance. The tourist office won't make reservations for you, though they will tell you where there are rooms free.

Hotels

L'Aiglon 7 av de la Madonne ⓣ04.93.57.55.55, ⓦwww.hotelaiglon.net. Spacious rooms in a nineteenth-century residence surrounded by a large garden. ❼

Beauregard 10 rue Albert-1er ⓣ04.93.28.63.63, ⓕ04.93.28.63.79. Traditionally furnished rooms and a relaxed atmosphere. ❸

Moderne 1 cours George-V ⓣ04.93.57.20.02, ⓦwww. hotel-moderne-menton.com. Good-value modern, central hotel; many rooms have balconies. ❹

M. Paul Gazzano 151 rte de Castellar ⓣ04.93.57.39.73. *Chambres d'hôte* 2km from Menton; a delightful house with a terrace looking down over the wooded slopes to the sea. ❹

Napoléon 29 porte de France, Garavan ⓣ04.93.35.89.50, ⓦwww.napoleon-menton.com. Elegantly modern seafront hotel with pool and garden. Mountain or sea views from the rooms. ❼

Hostel and campsite

HI hostel plateau St-Michel ⓣ04.93.35.93.14, ⓦwww.fuaj.org. Up a gruelling flight of steps (signposted Camping St-Michel) from the northern side of the railway to the east of the station, or take bus #6 from the *gare routière* (stop "*Camping St-Michel*"). 10pm curfew. Reception 7–10am & 5–10pm. Closed Nov–Jan. €15.60.

Camping St-Michel rte des Ciappes ⓣ04.93 .35.81.23, ⓕ04.93.57.12.35. Reasonably priced campsite in the hills above the town, with plenty of shade and good views; follow directions for youth hostel. Closed Nov–March except for Fête du Citron. €17.75 per tent.

The Town

The **promenade du Soleil** runs along the pebbly beachfront of the Baie du Soleil, stretching from the quai Napoléon-III past the casino towards Roquebrune. The most diverting building on the front is a seventeenth-century fort by the quai Napoléon-III south of the old port, now the **Musée Jean Cocteau** (daily except Tues 10am–noon & 2–6pm; €3), set up by the artist himself. It contains pictures of his Mentonaise lovers in the *Inamorati* series, a collection of delightful *Fantastic Animals* and the tapestry of *Judith and Holofernes* telling the sequence of seduction, assassination and escape. There are also photographs, poems, ceramics and a portrait by his friend Picasso.

As the *quai* bends around the western end of the Baie de Garavan from the Cocteau museum, a long flight of black-and-white pebbled steps leads up into the **vieille ville** to the **Parvis St-Michel**, an attractive Italianate square hosting concerts during the summer and giving a good view out over the bay. The frontage of the **Église St-Michel** (Mon–Fri 10am–noon & 3–5.15pm) proclaims its Baroque supremacy in perfect pink-and-yellow proportions, and a few more steps up to another square will reward you with the beautiful facade of the **chapel of the Pénitents-Blancs** (Mon & Wed 3–5pm) in apricot-and-white marble, with pastel campaniles and disappearing stairways between long-lived houses. The **cemetery**, at the top of the old town on the site once occupied by the town's château, is hauntingly sad – many of the young foreign tuberculosis sufferers who ended their days in Menton are buried here – but also bewitchingly beautiful, with imposing, crumbly tombs and lovely views along the coast into Italy.

In the middle of the modern town, the **Salles des Mariages** (Mon–Fri 8.30am–12.30pm & 2–5pm; €1.50) or registry office, forms part of the **Hôtel de Ville** on place Ardoiono and was decorated in inimitable style by Jean Cocteau in 1957.

On avenue de la Madone, at the other end of the modern town, an impressive collection of paintings from the Middle Ages to the twentieth century can be seen in the **Palais Carnolès** (daily except Tues 10am–noon & 2–6pm; free; bus #3), the old summer residence of the princes of Monaco. Of the early works, the *Madonna and Child with St Francis* by Louis Bréa is exceptional. The most recent include canvases by Graham Sutherland, who spent some of his last years in Menton.

If it's cool enough, the gardens of **Garavan**'s villas make a change from shingle beaches. The best is **Les Colombières**, just north of boulevard de Garavan, but it's privately owned (check for information on occasional guided visits with the tourist office). Designed by the artist Ferdinand Bac between 1918 and 1927, there are staircases screened by cypresses, balustrades to lean against for the soaring views through pines and olive trees out to sea, fountains, statues and a frescoed swimming pool. Alternatively, try the **Jardin Exotique Val Rameh** (daily except Tues: April–Sept 10am–12.30pm & 3.30–6.30pm; Oct–March 10am–12.30pm & 2–5pm; €5) below boulevard de Garavan or **Fontana Rosa** (guided visits Friday at 10am, €5) on avenue Blasco-Ibañez, the former home of the Spanish author Vincente Blasco-Ibañez and bright with ceramic decoration. From here it's a short walk up rue Webb-Ellis and chemin Wallaya behind the Garavan *gare SNCF* to the villa **Isola Bella**, the former home of author Katherine Mansfield, though it is not open to the public.

Eating and drinking

Menton's **restaurants** tend towards the informal and touristy; the pedestrianized rue St-Michel is promising ground for cheap eats. Much fancier is the modern Mediterranean fare at the *Hotel Ambassadeurs*' elegant *restaurant gastronomique*, *Le Louvre* (2 rue du Louvre; ⓣ04.93.28.75.75), with a €35 lunch menu. Down on the port at 15 quai Bonaparte, *La Lyre* (ⓣ04.93.35.38.16) serves excellent calamares and other Italian dishes from around €11.50. Menton also has an excellent Moroccan restaurant, *Le Darkoum*, 23 rue St-Michel (ⓣ04.92.07.34.72), offering *plats* from around €12.

Travel details

Trains

Cannes to: Antibes (approx. every 20min peak time; 10–15min); Biot (every 40–50min; 18min); Cagnes-sur-Mer (every 25–50min; 20min); Cros-de-Cagnes (every 40–50min; 30min); Golfe Juan-Vallauris (every 40–50min; 7min); Juan-les-Pins (every 25–50min; 11min); Marseille (approx. every 30min–1hr; 2hr); Nice (approx. every 20min peak time; 40min); St-Raphaël (every 30min–1hr; 35min–1hr 5min); Villeneuve-Loubet-Plage (every 40–50min; 22min).

Marseille to: Aix (approx. every 30min–1hr; 40min); Arles (16–22 daily; 50min); Avignon (8–13 daily; 1hr 15min); Bandol (17–30 daily; 37–42 min); Cannes (15–21 daily; 2hr 5 min–2hr 20min); Cassis (16–29 daily; 22min); Cavaillon (2–4 daily; 55min–1hr 15min); Hyères (1–4 daily; 1hr 15min–1hr 30min); L'Estaque (10–20 daily; 10–20min); La Ciotat (18–31 daily; 30min); La Seyne-Six Fours (16–27 daily; 52min); Les Arcs-Draguignan (8–16 daily; 1hr 20min–2hr); Lyon (5–12 daily; 3hr 30min); Menton (1–2 daily; 3hr 20min); Nice (14–20 daily; 2hr 20min–2hr 45min); Ollioules-Sanary (16–27 daily; 50min); Paris (TGV: 10–22 daily; 3hr 15min); St-Cyr/Les Lecques (16–27 daily; 35min); St-Raphaël (14–21 daily; 1hr 30min–1hr 45min); Salon (2–3 daily; 45–55min); Tarascon (2 daily; 1hr); Toulon (every 20min at peak times; 40min–1hr 3min).

Nice to: Annot (4 daily; 1hr 55min); Beaulieu (every 15–30min; 12min); Breil-sur-Roya (6 daily; 1hr 5min); Cannes (every 10–35min; 25–40min) Cap d'Ail (every 35min–1hr; 20min); Cap Martin–Roquebrune (every 35 min–1hr; 30min); Digne (4 daily; 3hr 16min); Entrevaux (4 daily; 1hr 35min); Èze-sur-Mer (every 35min–1hr; 15min); L'Escarène (6 daily; 40min); Marseille (6 daily; 2hr 24min); Menton (every 15–35min; 25–40min); Monaco (every 15–35min; 20–25min); Peillon (6 daily; 25min); Puget-Théniers (4 daily; 1hr 26min); St-Raphaël (frequent; 1hr–1hr 20min); Sospel (6 daily; 50min); Tende (3 daily; 1hr 50min); Touét-sur-Var (4 daily; 1hr 14min); Villars-sur-Var (4 daily; 1hr 5min); Villefranche (every 15–55min; 9min).

St-Raphaël to: Boulouris (approx every 1–2hr; 4min); Cannes (every 10min–1hr 5min; 30–45min); Nice (every 10min–1hr 5min; 45min–1hr 22min).

Toulon to: Hyères (9 daily; 20–25min); Marseille (every 20min–1hr; 40min–1hr); Paris (3 daily; 3hr 50min).

Buses

Antibes to: Biot (hourly; 35–40min); Cannes (every 20min; 30–35min); Juan-les-Pins (every 20–30min; 8min); Nice (every 20min; 45min–1hr 10min); Nice Airport (every 20min; 20–45min.

Cannes to: Antibes (every 20min; 25–35min); Cagnes (every 20min; 50min–1hr); Grasse (every 20min; 40–50min); La Napoule (every 15–45min; 40min); Nice (every 20min; 1hr 20min–1hr 35min); Nice Airport (every 20min; 1hr 5min–1hr 15min); St Raphaël (summer only: 7 daily, 1hr 10min); Vallauris (every 30min; 15min).

Grasse to: Cagnes (every 30–50min; 50min); Cannes (every 15–45min; 40min–1hr); Nice (every 30–50min; 1hr 25min); Vence (3 daily; 50–55min).

Hyères to: Bormes (approx hourly; 25min); La Croix-Valmer (8 daily; 1hr 15min); Le Lavandou

(approx. hourly; 35min); Le Rayol (8 daily; 55min); St-Tropez (8 daily; 1hr 35min–1hr 45min); Toulon (every 15–45min; 35min–1hr 10min).
Le Lavandou to: Bormes (13 daily; 8–10min); Hyères (15 daily; 30min); La Croix-Valmer (8 daily; 45min); Le Rayol (8 daily; 20min); St-Tropez (8 daily; 1hr 15min); Toulon (15 daily; 1hr 5min–1hr 15min).
Marseille to: Aix (every 5min at peak times; 30–50min); Apt (1–2 daily; 2hr 15min); Barcelonnette (1–3 daily; 3hr 50min–4hr 50min); Carpentras (2–3 daily; 1hr 35min–2hr 20min); Cassis (7–14 daily; 40–50min); Digne (3–5 daily; 2hr 20min–2hr 50min); Grenoble (1 daily; 3hr 55min); La Ciotat (15 daily; 30–45min); Manosque (8–13 daily; 1hr 5min–1hr 30min); Salon (6 daily; 1hr 10min); Sisteron (3–5 daily; 2hr 10min–2hr 25min).
Menton to: Monaco (every 15min; 35min); Nice (every 15min; 1hr 30min); Sospel (3–5 daily; 35–45min).
Monaco to: Èze (every 15min; 17min); La Turbie (3–6 daily; 30min); Menton (every 15min; 45min); Nice (every 15min; 55min).
Nice to: Aix (3–5 daily; 2hr 15min–4hr 10min); Beaulieu (every 15min; 10–15min); Cagnes-sur-Mer (every 20min; 35–40min); Cannes (every 20 min; 1hr 25 min–1hr 55min); Cap d'Ail (every 15min; 30min); Digne (2 daily; 2hr 50min–3hr 25min); Èze-Village (14 daily; 20min); Grasse (every 30–45 min; 1hr 10min–1hr 35min); Grenoble (1 daily; 7hr 15min); La Turbie (5 daily; 40min); Marseille (5 daily; 2hr 45min–4hr 30min); Menton (every 15min; 1hr 25min); Monaco (every 15min; 30–40min); Roquebrune (every 15min; 1hr); St-Paul (every 35–40min; 55min); Sisteron (2 daily; 3hr 30min–4hr 10min); Toulon (2 daily; 2hr 30min); Vence (every 20–35min; 1hr–1hr 10min); Villefranche (every 15min; 10min).
St-Raphaël to: Cannes (summer only 7 daily; 1hr 10min); Cogolin (6 daily; 1hr 25min); Draguignan (3 daily; 1hr–1hr 20min); Fréjus (frequent; 20–30min); Grimaud (6 daily; 1hr–1hr 15min); La Foux (14 daily; 1hr 20min–1hr 35min); Nice Airport (4 daily; 1hr 15min); Ste-Maxime (15 daily; 40–50min); St-Tropez (14 daily; 1hr 30min–1hr 50min).
St-Tropez to: Bormes (6 daily; 1hr 5min–1hr 40min); Cogolin (4–5 daily; 20min); Gassin (2 weekly; 25min); Grimaud (5 daily; 30–40min); Hyères (8 daily; 1hr 30min–2hr); Hyères airport (1–2 daily; 1hr); La Croix-Valmer (9 daily; 20–25min); La Garde-Freinet (2 daily; 45min); Le Lavandou (9 daily; 55min–1hr 25min); Ramatuelle (4 daily; 37min); Ste-Maxime (approx hourly; 40–55min); St-Raphaël (approx hourly; 55min–2hr 10min); Toulon (9 daily; 2hr 5min–2hr 30min).
Toulon to: Aix (5 daily; 1hr 15min); Hyères (every 15min–1hr; 50min–1hr 10min); La Croix-Valmer (8 daily; 1hr 50min–2hr 5min); Le Lavandou (15 daily; 1hr–1hr 25min); Nice (2 daily; 2hr 30min); St-Tropez (8 daily; 1hr 55min–2hr 15min).
Vence to: Cagnes (every 20–30min; 15–35min); Nice (every 15–30min; 50min); St-Paul-de-Vence (approx every 20min–1hr; 5–10min)

Ferries

For Îles d'Hyères and Îles de Lérins services, see box on p.1143 & p.1168.
Marseille to: Corsica (1–5 daily; 12–14hr).
Nice to: Corsica (summer 2–8 daily; winter 1 weekly; 3hr–5hr 30min).
Toulon to: Corsica (1–2 daily 5hr 45min–10hr).

16

Corsica

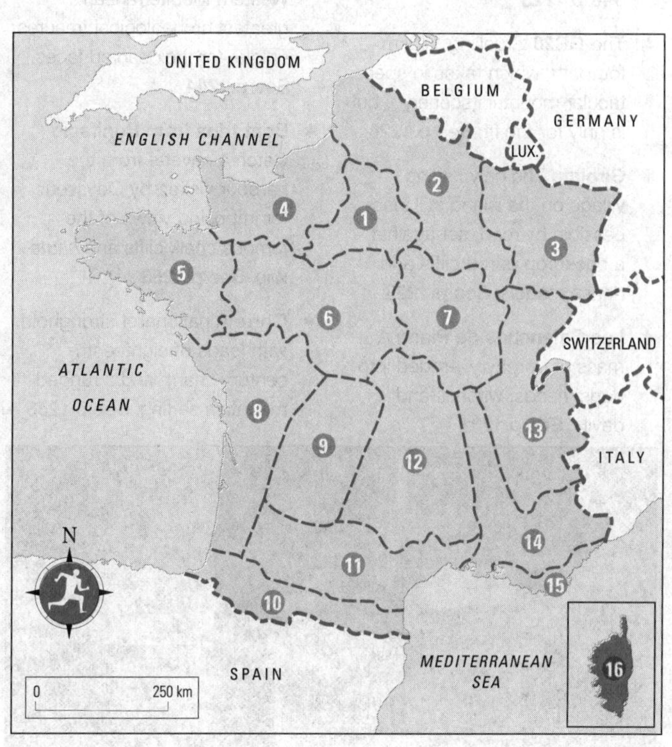
UNITED KINGDOM
BELGIUM
GERMANY
LUX.
ENGLISH CHANNEL
SWITZERLAND
ATLANTIC
OCEAN
ITALY
N
0
250 km
SPAIN
MEDITERRANEAN
SEA
1
2
3
4
5
6
7
8
9
10
11
12
13
14
15
16

CHAPTER 16

Highlights

* **Plage de Saleccia** Soft white shell sand, turquoise water and barely a building in sight. See p.1220

* **Calvi** Corsica's hallmark resort, framed by snow peaks and a spectacular blue gulf. See p.1223

* **The GR20** Gruelling 170km footpath, which takes in spectacular mountain scenery – but is only for the fit. See p.1226

* **Girolata** The only fishing village on the island still inaccessible by road, set against a backdrop of red cliffs and dense maquis. See p.1228

* **Les Calanches de Piana** A mass of porphyry, eroded into dogs' heads, witches and devils. See p.1231

* **Apéritif at L'Hôtel Les Roches Rouges** Sublime sea views and a *fin-de-siècle* ambience make this the perfect spot for a *muscat corse*. See p.1232

* **Filitosa menhirs** Among the Western Mediterranean's greatest archeological treaures, unique for their carved faces. See p.1244

* **Boat trips from Bonifacio** Catch a navette from the harbour visited by Odysseus for imposing views of the famous chalk cliffs and *haute ville*. See p.1253

* **Corte** A nationalist stronghold, with loads of eighteenth-century charm and a rugged mountain setting. See p.1258

△ Calvi

16

Corsica

Over two million people visit **Corsica** each year, drawn by the mild climate and by some of the most diverse landscapes in all Europe. Nowhere in the Mediterranean has beaches finer than the island's perfect half-moon bays of white sand and transparent water, or seascapes more dramatic than the red porphyry Calanches of the west coast. Even though the annual visitor influx now exceeds the island's population seven or eight times over, tourism hasn't spoilt the place: there are a few resorts, but overdevelopment is rare and high-rise blocks are confined to the main towns.

Bastia, capital of the north, was the principal Genoese stronghold, and its fifteenth-century citadelle has survived almost intact. Of the island's two large towns, this is the more purely Corsican, and commerce rather than tourism is its main concern. Also relatively undisturbed, the northern Cap Corse harbours inviting sandy coves and fishing villages such as **Macinaggio** and **Centuri-Port**. Within a short distance of Bastia, the fertile region of the Nebbio contains a scattering of churches built by Pisan stoneworkers, the prime example being the cathedral of Santa Maria Assunta at the appealingly chic little port of **St-Florent**.

To the west of here, **L'Île-Rousse** and **Calvi**, the latter graced with an impressive citadelle and fabulous sandy beach, are major targets for holiday-makers. The spectacular **Scandola nature reserve** to the southwest of Calvi is most easily visited by boat from the tiny resort of **Porto**, from where walkers can also strike into the wild **Gorges de Spelunca**. **Corte**, at the heart of Corsica, is the best base for exploring the mountains and gorges of the interior which form part of the **Parc Naturel Régional** that runs almost the entire length of the island.

Sandy beaches and rocky coves punctuate the west coast all the way down to **Ajaccio**, Napoleon's birthplace and the island's capital, where pavement cafés and palm-lined boulevards are thronged with tourists in summer. Slightly fewer make it to nearby **Filitosa**, greatest of the many prehistoric sites scattered across the south. **Propriano**, the town perhaps most transformed by the tourist boom, lies close to stern **Sartène**, former seat of the wild feudal lords who once ruled this region and still the quintessential Corsican town.

More megalithic sites are to be found south of Sartène on the way to **Bonifacio**, a comb of ancient buildings perched atop furrowed white cliffs at the southern tip of the island. Equally popular **Porto-Vecchio** provides a springboard for excursions to the amazing beaches of the south. The eastern plain has less to boast of, but the Roman site at **Aléria** is worth a visit for its excellent museum.

The food of Corsica

It's the herbs – thyme, marjoram, basil, fennel and rosemary – of the maquis (the dense, scented scrub covering lowland Corsica) that lend the island's cuisine its distinctive aromas.

You'll find the best **charcuterie** in the hills of the interior, where pork is smoked and cured in the cold cellars of village houses – it's particularly tasty in Castagniccia, where wild pigs feed on the chestnuts which were once the staple diet of the locals. Here you can also taste chestnut fritters (*fritelli a gaju frescu*) and chestnut porridge (*pulenta*) sprinkled with sugar or eau de vie. **Brocciu**, a soft mozzarella-like cheese made with ewe's milk, is found everywhere on the island, forming the basis for many dishes, including omelettes and cannelloni. *Fromage corse* is also very good – a hard **cheese** made in the sheep- and goat-rearing central regions, where *cabrettu à l'istrettu* (kid stew) is a speciality.

Game – mainly stews of hare and wild boar but also roast woodcock, partridge and wood pigeon – features throughout the island's mountain and forested regions. Here blackbirds (*merles*) are made into a fragrant pâté, and eel and trout are fished from the unpolluted rivers. **Sea fish** like red mullet (*rouget*), bream (*loup de mer*) and a great variety of shellfish is eaten along the coast – the best crayfish (*langouste*) comes from around the Golfe de St-Florent, whereas oysters (*huîtres*) and mussels (*moules*) are a speciality of the eastern plain.

Corsica produces some excellent, and still little-known, **wines**, mostly from indigenous vinestocks that yield distinctive, herb-tinged aromas. Names to look out for include: Domaine Torraccia (Porto-Vecchio); Domaine Fiumicicoli (Sartène); Domaine Saparale (Sartène); Domaine Gentille (Patrimonio); Domaine Leccia (Patrimomio); and Venturi-Pieretti (Cap Corse). In addition to the usual whites, reds and rosés, the latter also makes the sweet muscat for which Cap Corse was renowned in previous centuries. Another popular aperitif is the drink known as Cap Corse, a fortified wine flavoured with quinine and herbs. Note that **tap water** is particularly good quality in Corsica, coming from the fresh mountain streams.

Some history

Set on the western Mediterranean trade routes, Corsica has always been of strategic and commercial appeal. Greeks, Carthaginians and Romans came in successive waves, driving native Corsicans into the interior. The Romans were ousted by Vandals, and for the following thirteen centuries the island was attacked, abandoned, settled and sold as a nation-state, with generations of islanders fighting against foreign government. In 1768 France bought Corsica from Genoa, but over two hundred years of French rule have had a limited effect and the island's Baroque churches, Genoese fortresses, fervent Catholic rituals and a Tuscan-influenced indigenous language and cuisine show a more profound affinity with Italy.

Corsica's uneasy relationship with the mainland has worsened in recent decades. Economic neglect and the French government's reluctance to encourage Corsican language and culture spawned a nationalist movement in the early 1970s, whose clandestine armed wing – the FLNC (Fronte di Liberazione Nazionale di a Corsica) – has been engaged ever since in a bloody conflict with the central government. The violence seldom affects tourists but signs of the "troubles" are everywhere, from the graffiti-sprayed roadsigns to the bullet holes plastering public buildings.

Relations between the island's hard-line nationalists and Paris may be perennially fraught, but there's little support among ordinary islanders for the armed struggle, and still less for total independence. Corsica is bankrolled by $480

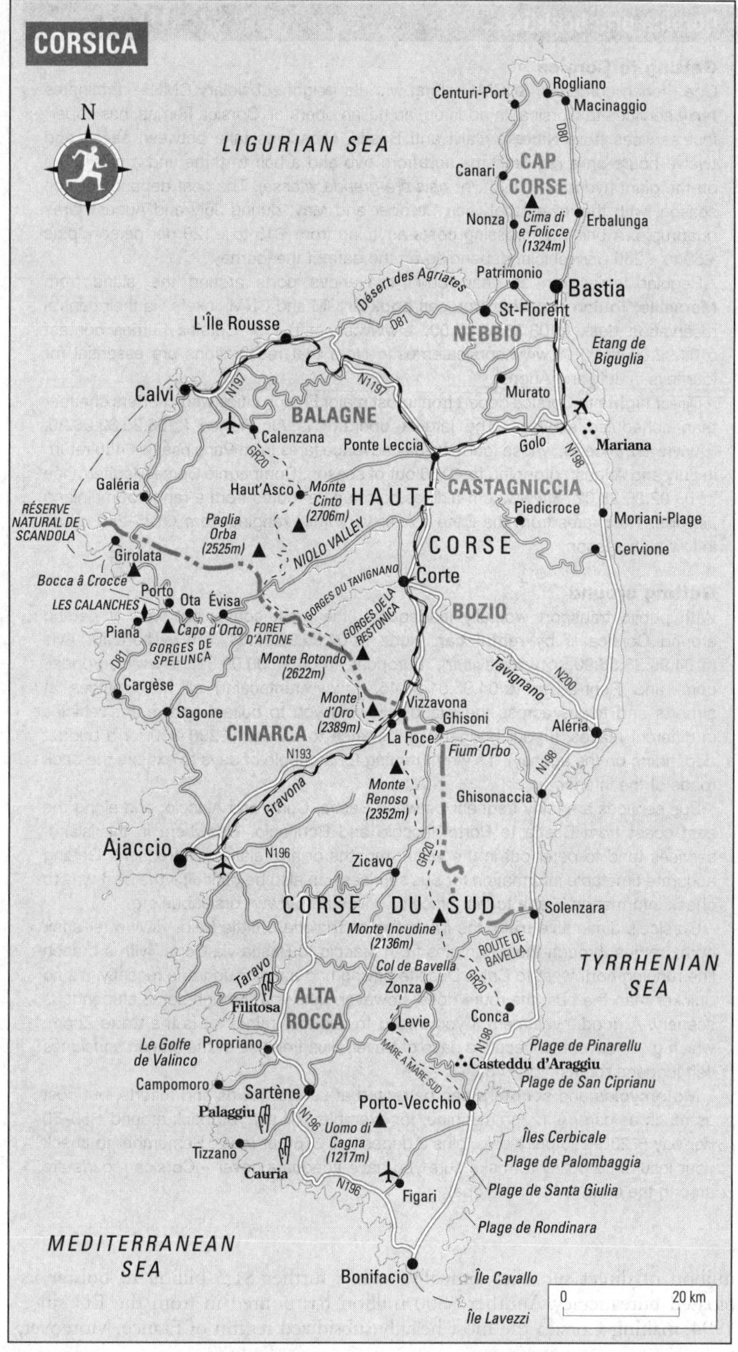

CORSICA
N
LIGURIAN SEA
Centuri-Port
Rogliano
Macinaggio
D80
Canari
CAP
CORSE
Nonza
Cima di
e Folicce
(1324m)
Erbalunga
Patrimonio
Bastia
Désert des Agriates
St-Florent
L'Île Rousse
D81
NEBBIO
Etang de
Biguglia
N1197
N197
Calvi
Murato
BALAGNE
Calenzana
GR20
Ponte Leccia
Golo
Mariana
N198
Galéria
Haut'Asco
Monte
Cinto
(2706m)
HAUTE
CASTAGNICCIA
Piedicroce
Moriani-Plage
RÉSERVE
NATURAL DE
SCANDOLA
Paglia
Orba
(2525m)
NIOLO VALLEY
CORSE
Cervione
Girolata
Bocca â Crocce
Porto
Ota
Évisa
LES CALANCHES
Piana
Capo d'Orto
GORGES DE
SPELUNCA
FORET
D'AITONE
GORGES DU TAVIGNANO
GORGES DE LA
RESTONICA
Corte
BOZIO
Monte Rotondo
(2622m)
Tavignano
N200
Cargèse
Monte
d'Oro
(2389m)
Vizzavona
Ghisoni
Sagone
CINARCA
La Foce
Aléria
Fium'Orbo
N193
N198
Gravona
Monte
Renoso
(2352m)
Ghisonaccia
Ajaccio
N196
Zicavo
GR20
CORSE DU SUD
Solenzara
Monte Incudine
(2136m)
ROUTE DE
BAVELLA
Col de Bavella
TYRRHENIAN
SEA
Taravo
Zonza
ALTA
ROCCA
Filitosa
Levie
Conca
Le Golfe
de Valinco
Propriano
MARE A MARE SUD
Plage de Pinarellu
Casteddu d'Araggiu
Campomoro
Plage de San Ciprianu
Sartène
Porto-Vecchio
Palaggiu
Uomo di
Cagna
(1217m)
Îles Cerbicale
Tizzano
Plage de Palombaggia
Cauria
N196
Figari
Plage de Santa Giulia
Plage de Rondinara
MEDITERRANEAN
SEA
Bonifacio
Île Cavallo
Île Lavezzi
0
20 km

Corsica practicalities

Getting to Corsica

One French company, SNCM – along with its freight subsidiary CMN – dominates **ferry** services to Corsica. In addition, an Italian operator, Corsica Ferries, has super-fast services from **Nice** to Calvi and Bastia. Crossings take between seven and twelve hours on a regular ferry, and from two and a half to three and a half hours on the giant hydrofoil ("NGV", or *navire à grande vitesse*). The cost depends on the season, with the lowest between October and May; during July and August fares quadruple. A one-way crossing costs anything from €15 to €120 per person, plus €50 to €250 per vehicle, depending on the date of the journey.

Regular ferries run all year round to various ports around the island from **Marseille**, **Toulon** and **Nice**. You can **book** SNCM and CNM tickets via their central reservation desk (Ⓣ08.36.67.95.00, Ⓦwww.sncm.fr). For Corsica Ferries contact Ⓣ04.92.00.42.93, Ⓦwww.corsicaferries.fr. Note that reservations are essential for journeys in July and August.

Direct **flights** to Corsica depart from most major French cities with charters cheaper than scheduled services. The largest operator is Air France (Ⓣ08.20.82.08.20, Ⓦwww.airfrance.fr), whose fourteen-day advance fares from Paris rise to €450 return in July and August, dropping to €160 out of season. Compagnie Corse Méditerranée (Ⓣ08.02.80.28.02, Ⓦwww.ccm-airlines.com) offers routes from a range of mainland airports. Their fares from the Côte d'Azur vary little: ranging from €125–260 return in low/high season.

Getting around

With public transport woefully inadequate, the most convenient way of getting around Corsica is by **rental car**. Hertz (Ⓣ04.95.23.57.04, Ⓦwww.hertz.fr), Avis (Ⓣ04.95.23.56.90, Ⓦwww.avis.fr), Europcar (Ⓣ04.95.30.09.50, Ⓦwww.europcar.com) and Rent-a-Car (Ⓣ04.95.51.34.45, Ⓦwww.rentacar.fr) all have offices at airports and towns across the island, allowing you to collect and return vehicles in different places. If your budget won't stretch to a week (€200–350 for a budget depending on the agency), it's worth renting for a couple of days to explore the back roads of the interior.

Bus services are fairly frequent between Bastia, Corte and Ajaccio, and along the east coast from Bastia to Porto-Vecchio and Bonifacio. Elsewhere in the island, services tend to peter out in the winter months or are relatively infrequent. Getting accurate timetable information for bus services can also be difficult – the best way to check information is at a tourist office or online at Ⓦwww.corsicabus.org.

Corsica's diminutive **train**, the *Micheline* or *Trinighellu* (little train; Ⓦwww.ter-sncf.com), rattles through the mountains from Ajaccio to Bastia via Corte, with a branch line running northwest to Calvi. Despite having had a major upgrade recently, it's no quicker than the bus; the route does, however, take you through some stupendous scenery. A good investment if you intend to use the train a lot is the Carte Zoom, which gives seven consecutive days of travel, plus free use of the station *consignes* (left luggage rooms), for €48.

Motorcycles and **scooters** can be rented at several towns and resorts, but cost as much as cars. A 125cc machine, for example, will set you back around €50–60 per day (€230–275 per week), plus a deposit of €750 or more. Remember to check your insurance policy to make sure you have adequate cover – Corsican roads are among the most lethal in Europe.

million of direct subsidies annually, with a further $1.3 billion to bolster its bloated bureaucracy. Another $800 million has poured in from the EU since 1994, making Corsica the most heavily subsidized region of France. Moreover,

Corsicans are exempt from social security contributions and the island as a whole enjoys preferential tax status, while one third of the permanent population is an employee of the state. Increasingly, nationalist violence is seen as biting the hand that feeds it. Opinion, however, remains divided on the best way forward for Corsica. In 2003, an end to the troubles seemed tantalizingly close as Chirac's administration, despite strong opposition from the Gaullist Right, proposed a new package of devolutionary measures and placed them before the island in a referendum. But the initiative was narrowly defeated, a setback many commentators have attributed less to lack of support for greater autonomy than to the PR bungle that followed the arrest of Corsica's most wanted terrorist on the eve of the vote. The triumphalist tone adopted by Paris following the capture of Yvan Colonna, wanted for the murder of the island's former governor, provoked a patriotic backlash that may well have been decisive.

Interior Minister Nicholas Sarkozy responded by condemning the result as a "wasted opportunity", and promptly ordered a crackdown on corruption and organized crime on the island. Among the highest profile casualties has been the nationalist paramilitary honcho, **Charles Pieri** who, along with 21 associates (including the president of Bastia's premiership football club, SCB), was alleged to have managed a huge extortion and money-laundering racket.

Pieri's arrest provoked a predictably angry reponse from the FLNC-U (currently the most potent paramilitary force on the island). The rate of bombings, machine gun and rocket attacks on State symbols and second homes soared through 2004 and 2005, as Corsica seemed to return to the bad old days of the mid-1990s.

More recently, a strike called by the French transport union to oppose government plans to privatize the ailing SNCM ferry company made national headlines after Corsican sailors commandeered a ferry, the *Pascal Paoli*, to publicize their objections. Special forces were called in to reclaim the vessel, amid riots and strikes on the dockside. Eventually, to avert further civil unrest, Sarkosy capitulated and released the sailors without charge, prompting widespread jubilation across the island.

The administration's policy regarding the long-term future of Corsica, meanwhile, remains more rudderless than ever.

Bastia and around

The dominant tone of Corsica's most successful commercial town, **BASTIA**, is one of charismatic dereliction, as the city's industrial zone is spread onto the lowlands to the south, leaving the centre of town with plenty of aged charm. The old quarter, known as the Terra Vecchia, comprises a tightly packed network of haphazard streets, flamboyant Baroque churches and lofty tenements, their crumbling golden-grey walls set against a backdrop of maquis-covered hills. Terra Nova, the historic district on the opposite side of the old port, is a tidier area that's now Bastia's trendy quarter.

The city dates from Roman times, when a base was set up at Biguglia to the south, beside a freshwater lagoon, or *étang*. Little remains of the former colony, but the site merits a day-trip for the well-preserved pair of Pisan churches at Marana, rising from the southern fringes of Poretta airport. Bastia began to thrive under the Genoese, when wine was exported to the Italian mainland from Porto Cardo, forerunner of Bastia's Vieux Port, or Terra Vecchia. Despite the fact that in 1811 Napoleon appointed Ajaccio capital of the island, initiating

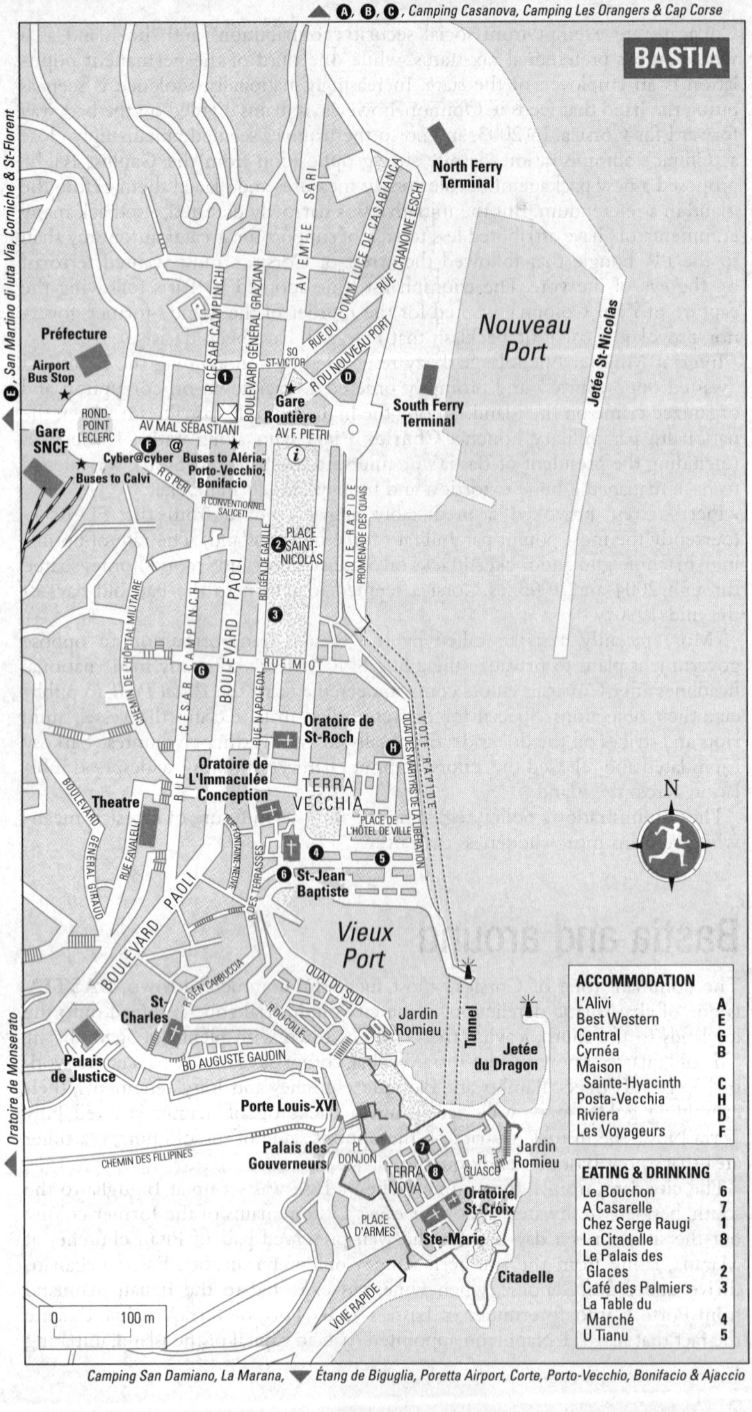

A, B, C, Camping Casanova, Camping Les Orangers & Cap Corse

BASTIA

North Ferry Terminal
Nouveau Port
Jetée St-Nicolas
South Ferry Terminal
Préfecture
Airport Bus Stop
Gare SNCF
Rond-Point Leclerc
Av Mal Sébastiani
Cyber@cyber
Buses to Calvi
Buses to Aléria, Porto-Vecchio, Bonifacio
Gare Routière
Av F. Pietri
Sq St-Victor
R du Nouveau Port
Rue du Comm Luce de Casabianca
Rue Chanoine Leschi
Av Emile Sari
Boulevard Général Graziani
R César Campinchi
R G Peri
R Conventionnel Saliceti
Place Saint-Nicolas
Bd Gén de Gaulle
Voie Rapide
Promenade des Quais
Boulevard Paoli
Rue César Campinchi
Chemin de l'Hôpital Militaire
Rue Miot
Rue Napoleon
Oratoire de St-Roch
Oratoire de L'Immaculée Conception
Terra Vecchia
Quai des Martyrs de la Libération
Place de l'Hôtel de Ville
Theatre
Boulevard Général Giraud
Rue Favalelli
Rue Fontaine-Neuve
R des Terrasses
St-Jean Baptiste
Vieux Port
Quai du Sud
R Gen Carbuccia
R du Colle
St-Charles
Bd Auguste Gaudin
Palais de Justice
Jardin Romieu
Tunnel
Jetée du Dragon
Porte Louis-XVI
Chemin des Fillipines
Palais des Gouverneurs
Pl Donjon
Terra Nova
Pl Guasco
Jardin Romieu
Oratoire St-Croix
Place d'Armes
Ste-Marie
Citadelle
Voie Rapide
0 100 m
N

E, San Martino di luta Via, Corniche & St-Florent

Oratoire de Monserato

ACCOMMODATION	
L'Alivi	A
Best Western	E
Central	G
Cyrnéa	B
Maison Sainte-Hyacinth	C
Posta-Vecchia	H
Riviera	D
Les Voyageurs	F

EATING & DRINKING	
Le Bouchon	6
A Casarelle	7
Chez Serge Raugi	1
La Citadelle	8
Le Palais des Glaces	2
Café des Palmiers	3
La Table du Marché	4
U Tianu	5

Camping San Damiano, La Marana, Étang de Biguglia, Poretta Airport, Corte, Porto-Vecchio, Bonifacio & Ajaccio a rivalry between the two towns which exists to this day, Bastia soon established a stronger trading position with mainland France. The Nouveau Port, created in 1862 to cope with the increasing traffic with France and Italy, became the mainstay of the local economy, exporting chiefly agricultural products from Cap Corse, Balagne and the eastern plain.

Arrival, information and accommodation

Bastia's Poretta **airport** (ⓣ04.95.54.54.54, ⓦwww.bastia.aeroport.fr) is 16km south of town, just off the Route Nationale (N193). **Shuttle buses** into the centre coincide with flights, dropping passengers at the north side of the main square, place St-Nicolas, and terminating at the train station for €8 (one way). **Taxis** from the airport cost €40–45. **Ferries** arrive at the **Nouveau Port**, just a five-minute walk from the centre of town. Bastia doesn't have a proper bus station, which can cause confusion, with services arriving and departing from different locations around the north side of the main square. **Buses** from Bonifacio, Porto-Vecchio and the east coast stop outside the travel agents opposite the post office (PTT) on avenue Maréchal-Sébastiani, whereas those coming from Calvi pull in further up the same street outside the **train station** (ⓣ04.95.32.80.61). Services from Ajaccio, Corte, St-Florent and Cap Corse work out of a small square, north of avenue Maréchal-Sébastiani – which, confusingly, is referred to as the *gare routière*, even though it's little more than a roadside stop. A summary of bus times and departure points is available at the **tourist office**, at the north end of place St-Nicolas (June to mid-Sept daily 8am–8pm; mid-Sept to May Mon–Sat 8am–6pm, Sun 9am–1pm; ⓣ04.95.54.20.40, ⓦwww.bastia-tourisme.com).

Although you're usually guaranteed to find somewhere to stay in Bastia, the choice of **hotels** is not great, particularly at the budget end the scale. Most of the classier places line the road to Cap Corse north of the port; the more basic ones are found in the centre of town, within striking distance of place St-Nicolas. Wherever you plan to stay, it's essential to reserve well in advance.

There's also a handful of **campsites** located outside the town. The most convenient if you're relying on public transport are at Miomo, 5km north (buses every 30min Mon–Sat, hourly Sun, until 7.30pm, from the top of place St-Nicolas opposite the tourist office).

Hotels

L'Alivi rte du Cap, Ville Pietrabugno ⓣ04.95.55.00.00, ⓦwww.hotel-alivi.com. Large three-star, 3km north of the city, with a pool, car park and private access to the beach. The rooms are light, spacious and sea-facing with glorious views from their terraces. ❺

Best Western av Zuccarelli ⓣ04.95.55.05.10, ⓦwww.bestwestern-corsica-hotels.com. Hardly the most characterful option, but rates are highly competitive, the location (on the hill above town) attractive, and rooms spacious for the price. Central a/c. ❺

Central 3 rue Miot ⓣ04.95.31.82.40, ⓦwww.centralhotel.fr. Just off the south-west corner of place St-Nicolas. Attractively decorated rooms, a welcoming *patronne* and the smell of fresh bread wafting from the boulangerie next door make this by far the most pleasant and best-value place to stay in the centre. ❹

Cyrnéa Pietranea ⓣ04.95.31.41.71, ⓕ04.95.31.72.65. Congenial little two-star, 4km out of town. All rooms are en suite, but only some overlook the water. You also get the run of a little garden strewn with sun loungers, which leads to a secluded pebble beach. ❺

Maison Sainte-Hyacinth 8km up the eastern Cape (3km inland from Miomo) ⓣ04.95.33.28.29. Bright, modern, comfortable en-suite rooms (€45–60, or bunk-bedded "box" dorms from €13) in a convent staffed by three friendly Polish nuns and their helpers. There's also a relaxing café-bar and refectory offering simple, inexpensive meals, all set in three acres of attractively landscaped gardens. Complimentary shuttle bus from Bastia available if you book in advance. Open June–Sept. ❶–❸

Posta-Vecchia quai-des-Martyrs-de-la-Libération ⓣ04.95.32.32.38, ⓦwww.hotel-postavecchia.com. The only hotel in the Vieux Port, and good value, with views across the sea from its (pricier) rooms at the front. Smaller, cheaper options are in the old block across the lane. ❹

Riviera 1bis rue du Nouveau-Port ⓣ04.95.31.07.16, ⓦwww.corsehotelriviera.com. Basic, and a bit noisy but convenient for the harbour. ❹

Les Voyageurs 9 av Maréchal-Sébastiani ⓣ04.95.34.90.80, ⓦwww.hotel-lesvoyageurs.com. Swish three-star opposite the post office, done out in pale yellow and with two categories of rooms: the larger, pricier ones have baths instead of showers. ❺

Campsites

Casanova Miomo, 5km north along the rte du Cap ⓣ04.95.33.91.42. Larger and greener than its neighbour, but fractionally more expensive, and with a bar. Open April–Oct.

Les Orangers Miomo, 5km north along the rte du Cap ⓣ04.95.33.24.09. Tiny site crammed onto narrow terraces, just off the main road. The cheaper of the pair in this suburb. Open April–Oct.

San Damiano Pineto, 10km south of Bastia ⓣ04.95.33.68.02, ⓦwww.campingsandamiano.com. Huge, pricey site 5km south of the city and right behind the beach, with top facilities. Hourly buses run out here from the *gare routière* in season. Open April–Oct.

The Town

Bastia is not especially large, and all its sights can easily be seen in a day without the use of a car. The spacious **place St-Nicolas** is the obvious place to get your bearings: open to the sea and lined with shady trees and cafés, it's the main focus of town life. Running parallel to it on the landward side are boulevard Paoli and rue César-Campinchi, the two main shopping streets, but all Bastia's historic sights lie within **Terra Vecchia**, the old quarter immediately south of place St-Nicolas, and **Terra Nova**, the area surrounding the Citadelle. Tucked away below the imposing, honey-coloured bastion is the much-photographed **Vieux Port**, with its boat-choked marina and crumbling eighteenth-century tenement buildings. By contrast, the **Nouveau Port**, north of the *place*, is bland and modern, with little of note other than restaurants, bars and a self-service laundry.

Terra Vecchia

From place St-Nicolas the main route into Terra Vecchia is **rue Napoléon**, a narrow street with some ancient offbeat shops and a pair of sumptuously decorated chapels on its east side. The first of these, the **Oratoire de St-Roch**, is a Genoese Baroque extravagance, reflecting the wealth of the rising bourgeoisie. Built in 1604, it has walls of finely carved wooden panelling and a magnificent gilt organ.

A little further along stands the **Oratoire de L'Immaculée Conception**, built in 1611 as the showplace of the Genoese in Corsica, who used it for state occasions. Overlooking a pebble mosaic of a sun, the austere facade belies the flamboyant interior, where crimson velvet draperies, a gilt and marble ceiling, frescoes and crystal chandeliers create the ambience of an opera house.

Just behind the oratoire, the place de l'Hôtel-de-Ville is commonly known as **place du Marché** after the lively farmers' market that takes place here each morning, from around 7am until 2pm. Dominating the south end of the square is the **church of St-Jean-Baptiste**, an immense ochre edifice that dominates the Vieux Port. Its twin campaniles are Bastia's distinguishing feature, but the interior is less than impressive. Built in 1636, the church was restored in the eighteenth century in a hideous Rococo overkill of multicoloured marble. Decorating the walls are a few unremarkable Italian paintings from Napoleon's uncle, Cardinal Fesch, an avid collector of Renaissance art.

Around the church extends the oldest part of Bastia, a secretive zone of dark alleys, vaulted passageways and seven-storey houses. By turning right outside and following rue St-Jean you'll come to rue Général-Carbuccia, the heart of Terra Vecchia. Corsican independence leader Pascal Paoli once lived here, at no. 7, and Balzac stayed briefly at no. 23 when his ship got stuck in Corsica on the way to Sardinia. Set in a small square at the end of the road is the **church of St-Charles**, a Jesuit chapel whose wide steps provide an evening meeting place for the locals; opposite stands the **Maison de Caraffa**, an elegant house with a strikingly graceful balcony.

The **Vieux Port** is easily the most photogenic part of town: soaring houses seem to bend inwards towards the water and peeling plaster and boat hulls glint in the sun, while the south side remains in the shadow of the great rock that supports the citadelle. Site of the original Roman settlement of *Porto Cardo*, the Vieux Port later bustled with Genoese traders, but since the building of the ferry terminal and commercial docks to the north it has become a backwater. The most atmospheric time to come here is early evening, when huge flocks of swifts swirl in noisy clouds above the harbour. Things liven up after sunset, with the glow and noise from the waterside bars and restaurants, which continue round the north end of the port along the wide **quai des-Martyrs-de-la-Libération**, where live bands clank out pop covers for the tourists in summer.

Terra Nova

The military and administrative core of old Bastia, **Terra Nova** (or the citadelle) has a distinct air of affluence, its lofty apartments now colonized by Bastia's yuppies. The area is focused on **place du Donjon**, which gets its name from the squat round tower that formed the nucleus of Bastia's fortifications and was used by the Genoese to incarcerate Corsican patriots – Sampiero Corso (the nationalist hero who mounted an insurrection against the Genoese in 1657) was held in the dungeon for four years in the early sixteenth century.

Facing the place du Donjon is the impressive fourteenth-century **Palais des Gouverneurs**. With its great round tower, arcaded courtyard and pristine peach-coloured paintwork, this building has a distinctly Moorish feel and was built for the governor and local bishop during the town's Genoese heyday. When the French transferred the capital to Ajaccio it became a prison, then was destroyed during a British attack of 1794 (in which an ambitious young captain named Horatio Nelson played a decisive part). The subsequent rebuilding was not the last, as parts of it were blown up by American B-52s in 1943 – on the day after Corsica's liberation, when thousands of Bastiais were celebrating in the streets. Extensive restoration work – due for completion in 2007 – has regained something of the building's former grandeur. Part of the palace is given over to the **Musée d'Ethnographie** (daily: June 9am–6.30pm; July & Aug 9am–8pm; Sept–May 9am–noon & 2–6pm; last entry 45min before closing time; admission around €5), which presents the history of Corsica from prehistoric times to the present day. Its vaulted chambers contain some fascinating historical titbits, including a diminutive Roman sarcophagus decorated with hunting scenes, busts of famous Corsicans and an original 1755 Flag of Independence, with its distinctive Moorish emblem.

Back in place du Donjon, if you cross the square and follow rue Notre-Dame you come out at the **Église Ste-Marie**. Built in 1458 and overhauled in the seventeenth century, it was the cathedral of Bastia until 1801, when the bishopric was transferred to Ajaccio. Inside, the church's principal treasure is a small silver statue of the Virgin (housed in a glass case on the right wall as you face the altar), which is carried through Terra Nova and Terra Vecchia on August 15, the Festival of the Assumption. Immediately behind Ste-Maire in rue de l'Évêché stands the **Oratoire Sainte-Croix**, a sixteenth-century chapel decorated in Louis XV style, with lashings of rich blue paint and gilt scrollwork. It houses another holy item, the *Christ des Miracles*, a blackened oak crucifix much venerated by Bastia's fishermen, which in 1428 was discovered floating in the sea surrounded by a luminous haze. A festival celebrating the miracle takes place in Bastia on May 3, when local fishing families carry it around Terra Nova. Beyond the church, the narrow streets open out to the secluded **place Guasco**, where a few benches offer the chance of a rest before descending back into the fray.

L'Oratoire de Monserato

One of Bastia's most extraordinary monuments, the **Oratoire de Monserato,** lies a pleasant two-kilometre walk from the town centre. From Terra Nova, leave the citadelle through its main (northern) gateway next to the Palais des Gouverneurs and follow the chemin des Fillipines (a stepped lane starting on the opposite side of the main road) uphill for ten minutes. When you reach a road at the top turn left and keep going for another 300m until you see a lane leading left to the Oratoire. The building itself looks unremarkable from the outside, but its interior houses the much revered **Scala Santa**, a replica of the Holy Steps of the Basilica of Saint John of Lateran in Rome. Penitents who ascend it on their knees as far as its high altar may be cleansed, or so it is believed, of all sins, without the intercession of a priest. Only Rome, Lourdes and Fatima enjoy such a privilege, an anomaly dating from the First Empire when bishops and other prominent clerics who refused to accede to Napoleon's Concordat of 1801 were imprisoned in the citadelle. The townsfolk of Bastia complained bitterly about this rough treatment of such high-ranking clergy and were granted permission to host the priests in their own homes instead. Following Napoleon's demise, the liberated clergy then petitioned Rome to grant the town a special favour in recognition of its generosity, whence the Scala Santa.

The beaches

Crowded with schoolchildren in the summer, the pebbly **town beach** in Bastia is only worth visiting if you're desperate for a swim. To reach it, go left at the flower shop on the main road south out of town, just beyond the citadelle. A more salubrious alternative is the long beach of **L'Arinella** at Montesoro, a further 1km along the same road, the beginning of a sandy shore that extends along the whole east coast. A bus to L'Arinella leaves from outside *Café Riche* on boulevard Paoli every twenty minutes; just get off at the last stop and cross the train line to the sea. There are a couple of sailing and windsurfing clubs here, and a bar.

Eating and drinking

Numerous pizza vans are scattered about town, evidence of a strong Italian influence that's also apparent in the predominance of **pizzerias** and pasta places in the Nouveau Port area. The town also boasts some excellent inexpensive **restaurants** serving Corsican specialities: the posh places on the quai des Martyrs do the best *aziminu*, a Corsican version of *bouillabaisse*. Most of the good restaurants are to be found around the Vieux Port and on the quai des Martyrs, with a sprinkling in the citadelle.

Drinking is a serious business in Bastia, with the Casanis *pastis* factory on the outskirts in Lupino making the town's favourite drink. There are many bars and cafés all over town, varying from the stark and brightly lit bars of Terra Vecchia, which are the haunt of old men, to the elegant, dimly lit cafés on place St-Nicolas, which entertain a younger, more lively clientele. For a more sedate atmosphere, boulevard Paoli and rue Campinchi are lined with chi-chi *salons de thé* offering elaborate creamy confections, local chestnut cake and doughnuts.

Bars and cafés

Le Bouchon 4bis rue St-Jean, Vieux Port. Occupying a prime position on the quayside, this easy-going wine bar serves local and continental French wines by the glass (€4–6), as well as variously priced gastro-tapas on slate platters. Closed Wed & Sun.

Chez Serge Raugi 2bis rue Capanelle, off bd Général Graziani. Arguably Corsica's greatest ice-cream maker, with tables on a cramped pavement terrace or upstairs on an even smaller mezzanine floor. In winter, they also do a legendary chickpea tart to take away.

Café des Palmiers place St-Nicolas. One of the few cafés along this stretch, with delicious fresh pastries, attentive service and comfy wicker chairs that catch the sun at breakfast time.

Restaurants

A Casarelle 6 rue Sainte-Croix ⓣ04.95.32.02.32. Innovative Corsican-French cuisine served on a terrace on the edge of the citadelle. The chef's specialities are traditional dishes of the Balagne, such as *casgiate* (nuggets of fresh cheese baked in fragrant chestnut leaves) or the rarely prepared *storzapreti* (balls of *brocciu*, spinach and herbs in tomato sauce). €25 per head for lunch, €33 for dinner. Closed Sat & Sun lunchtimes.

La Citadelle 6 rue du Dragon ⓣ04.95.31.44.70. One of the finest places to eat on the island, in the heart of Terra Nova. Sumptuous French cuisine served in a cellar with mellow lighting and an old olive press in the corner. Prices are high (€35 for the three-course *menu fixe*, or around €45 per head à la carte without wine), but you get what you pay for.

Le Palais des Glaces place St-Nicholas ⓣ04.95.35.05.01. One of the few dependable lunch spots on the main square, frequented as much by Bastiais as visitors. Their good value €24 menu, served under swish awnings beneath the plane trees, often includes the house favourite: fish *bruschettas*.

La Table du Marché place du Marché ⓣ04.95.31.64.25. Elegant, old-fashioned lunch venue on the atmospheric market square, serving a popular €24 *menu regional* featuring local crayfish, east coast oysters and filets of St Pierre. Get there around midday for a seat on the terrace.

U Tianu 4 rue Rigo ⓣ04.95.31.36.67. Tiny, unpretentious, family-run restaurant with lots of atmosphere hidden in a narrow backstreet behind the Vieux Port. Their limited but excellent-value menus (€19–23) change daily but feature typical country dishes such as *figatellu* pâté, blackbird terrine, chickpeas with anchovies, sardines stuffed with *brocciu*, and *fiadone* soaked in home-made eau de vie.

Listings

Bicycle and motorbike rental Locacycles, behind the Palais de Justice (ⓣ04.95.32.30.64), rents bicycles by the day (€17) or for longer periods, as does Objectif Nature, rue Notre-Dame-de Lourdes (ⓣ04.95.32.54.34, ⓦobj-nature.ifrance.com). The only place in Bastia offering motorbike rental is Toga Location, Port Toga, at the north side of the Nouveau Port (ⓣ04.95.31.49.01), which has bikes from 125cc to 660cc. Rates range from €60 to €120 per day depending on the size of the machine.

Car rental ADA, 35 rue César-Campinchi ⓣ04.95.31.48.95, airport ⓣ04.95.54.55.44; Avis (Ollandini), 40 bd Paoli ⓣ04.95.31.95.64, airport ⓣ04.95.54.55.46; Europcar, 1 rue du Nouveau-Port ⓣ04.95.31.59.29, airport ⓣ04.95.30.09.50; Hertz, square St-Victor ⓣ04.95.31.14.24, airport ⓣ04.95.30.05.00; Rent-a-Car, Poretta airport ⓣ04.95.54.55.11.

Ferries Corsica Ferries, 5bis, rue Chanoine-Leschi ⓣ04.95.32.95.95, or at the *gare maritime* ⓣ04.95.32.95.94; Mobylines, Sarl Colonna D'Istria & Fils, 4 rue Luce de Casablanca, just behind the Nouveau Port ⓣ04.95.34.84.94; SNCM, Nouveau Port, BP 57 ⓣ04.95.54.66.99.

Internet Cyber@Cyber, near the post office on av Mar. Sébastiani; or CyberTaz South off the place St-Nicholas on cours Pierre-Angeli. Both charge around €3.50/hr.

Left Luggage At the time of writing, left luggage *consignes* at the ferry terminals and train stations were closed as a security precaution.

Post office av Maréchal-Sébastiani. Mon–Fri 8am–7pm, Sat 8am–noon.

La Marana, Mariana and the Étang de Biguglia

Traditionally the summer haunt of prosperous Bastia families, the sixteen-kilometre littoral known as **LA MARANA** lies a few kilometres south of Bastia.

The beach here offers shady pine woods, restaurants and bars, though the sea is quite polluted. The whole of this part of the coast is divided into holiday residences or sections of beach attached to bars, the latter freely open to the public.

Fed by the rivers Bevinco and Golo, the **Étang de Biguglia** is the largest lagoon in Corsica, and one of its best sites for rare migrant birds. In summer, reed and Cetti's warblers nest in the reeds, while in winter, Biguglia supports a resident community of grey herons, kingfishers, great-crested grebes, little grebes, water rails and various species of duck.

The Roman town of **MARIANA**, just south of Étang de Biguglia, can be approached by taking the turning for Poretta airport, 16km along the N193, or the more scenic coastal route through **La Marana**. It was founded in 93 BC as a military colony, but today's houses, baths and basilica are too ruined to be of great interest. It's only the square baptistry, with its remarkable mosaic floor decorated with dancing dolphins and fish looped around bearded figures representing the four rivers of paradise, that is worth seeking out.

Adjacent to Mariana stands the **church of Santa Maria Assunta**, known as **La Canonica**. Built in 1119 close to the old capital of Biguglia, it's the finest of around three hundred churches built by the Pisans in their effort to evangelize the island. Modelled on a Roman basilica, the perfectly proportioned edifice is decorated outside with Corinthian capitals plundered from the main Mariana site and with plates of Cap Corse marble, their delicate pink and yellow ochre hues fusing to stunning effect.

Marooned amid muddy fields about 300m to the south of La Canonica is another ancient church, **San Parteo**, built in the eleventh and twelfth centuries over the site of a pagan burial ground. A smaller edifice than La Canonica, it displays some elegant arcading and fine sculpture – on the south side, the door lintel is supported by two writhing beasts reaching to a central tree, a motif of oriental origins.

Cap Corse

Until Napoléon III had a coach road built around **Cap Corse** in the nineteenth century, the promontory was effectively cut off from the rest of the island, relying on Italian maritime traffic for its income – hence its distinctive Tuscan dialect. Many Capicursini later left to seek their fortunes in the colonies of the Caribbean, which explains the distinctly ostentatious mansions, or *palazzi*, built by the successful émigrés (nicknamed "les Américains") on their return. For all the changes brought by the modern world, Cap Corse still feels like a separate country, with wild flowers in profusion, vineyards and quiet, traditional fishing villages.

Forty kilometres long and only fifteen across, the peninsula is divided by a spine of mountains called the Serra, which peaks at Cima di e Folicce, 1324m above sea level. The coast on the east side of this divide is characterized by tiny ports, or *marines*, tucked into gently sloping rivermouths, alongside coves which become sandier as you go further north. The villages of the western coast are sited on rugged cliffs, high above the rough sea and tiny rocky inlets that can be glimpsed from the corniche road.

The main villages on Cap Corse are connected to Bastia's *gare routière* by **bus**. Services are fairly frequent during the summer, but drop off considerably between October and May. Running up the east coast to Rogliano and Macinaggio, the

Bastia municipal bus company, SAB (Ⓣ04.95.31.06.65, Ⓦwww.bastiabus.com), lay on between two and three services Monday–Saturday from June–Sept, the first departing at 7pm from Bastia and arriving 1hr 15min later in Macinaggio. In winter, one bus per day runs on Monday, Wednesday and Friday. For Nonza and Canari, on the western cape, Transports Saoletti's Wednesday bus (Ⓣ04.95.37.84.05) departs Bastia's *gare routière* at 4pm.

Erbalunga

Built along a rocky promontory 10km north of Bastia, the small port of **ERBALUNGA** is the highlight of the east coast, with aged, pale buildings stacked like crooked boxes behind a small harbour and ruined Genoese watchtower. A little colony of French artists lived here in the 1920s, and the village has drawn a steady stream of admirers ever since. It attracts a fair number of tourists throughout the year, and come summer it's transformed into something of a cultural enclave, with concerts and art events adding a spark to local nightlife. The town is most famous, however, for its Good Friday procession, known as the **Cerca** (Search), which evolved from an ancient fertility rite. Hooded penitents, recruited from the ranks of a local religious brotherhood, form a spiral known as a *Granitola*, or snail, which unwinds as the candlelit procession moves into the village square.

A port since the time of the Phoenicians, Erbalunga was once a more important trading centre than Bastia or Ajaccio. In the eleventh century, with the increasing exportation of wine and olive oil, it became the capital of an independent village-state, ruled by the da Gentile family, who lived in the **palazzu** that dominates place de-Gaulle.

The one **hotel**, the gorgeous *Castel Brando* (Ⓣ04.95.30.10.30, Ⓦwww.castelbrando.com; April to mid-Oct; ❺), stands at the entrance to the *place*, shaded by a curtain of mature date palms, like the backdrop to a classic Visconti movie. It's an elegant, old, stone-floored *palazzu* with a lovely pool and its own car park. Period furniture and antique Corsican engravings fill the rooms and apartments, which are all air-conditioned; those on the top floor have great views. Pick of the harbourside **restaurants** is the renowned *Le Pirate* (Ⓣ04.95.33.24.20; Easter–Oct) for whose *cuisine gastronomique* well-heeled Bastias flock here throughout the year. Seafood delicacies – such as local lobster with wild asparagus – dominate their menu, but vegetarians are well catered for with entrées from the *carte*. The house set menu costs around €35/55 for lunch/dinner; à la carte courses range from €22–65. A less expensive option is *A Piazzetta* (Ⓣ04.95.33.28.69), in the tiny square behind the harbour, which does excellent *moules-frites*, a range of tasty pasta dishes from €18–28, and superb sorbets.

Macinaggio (Macinaghju) and around

A port since Roman times, well-sheltered **MACINAGGIO**, 20km north of Erbalunga, was developed by the Genoese in 1620 for the export of olive oil and wine to the Italian peninsula. The Corsican independence leader, Pascal Paoli, landed here in 1790 after his exile in England, whereupon he kissed the ground and uttered the words "O ma patrie, je t'ai quitté esclave, je te retrouve libre" ("Oh my country, I left you as a slave, I rediscover you a free man") – a plaque commemorating the event adorns the wall above the ship chandlers. There's not much of a historic patina to the place nowadays, but with its boat-jammed **marina** and its line of colourful seafront awnings, Macinaggio has a certain appeal, made all the stronger by its proximity to some of the best beaches on Corsica. Daily **boat trips** from the marina on board the *San Paulu* (Ⓣ04.95.35.07.09; €18) transport visitors to some of the best of them, as well as the remote islands off the north coast of the cape. Another reason to linger is to sample the superb **Clos Nicrosi** wines, grown in the terraces below Rogliano. Of all Corsica's top AOC labels, it's perhaps the hardest to find, but at their little shop on the north side of the Rogliano road, opposite the *U Ricordu* hotel, you can taste the *domaine*'s famously crisp white wine and heavily scented muscat.

The least expensive **place to stay** is the recently renovated *Hôtel des Îles*, opposite the marina (Ⓣ04.95.35.43.02, Ⓕ04.95.35.47.05; open April–Oct; ❷), which also has a serviceable restaurant on its ground floor. All the tiny rooms have showers and toilets; those at the front of the building overlook the port but get noisy at night, being above the most popular bar in the resort, so if you're a light sleeper ask for a room at the back. Otherwise try the more modern *U Libecciu*, down the lane leading from the marina to the Plage de Tamarone (Ⓣ04.95.35.43.22, Ⓦwww.u-libecciu.com; April–Oct, obligatory half-board July & Aug; ❸); it's a modern building with no view to speak of, but the rooms are spacious and particularly good value in shoulder season. The three-star *U Ricordu*, on the south side of the road to Rogliano (Ⓣ04.95.35.40.20, Ⓦwww.hotel-uricordu.com; March–Sept, with obligatory half board Aug; ❺), is the most luxurious option hereabouts, with a swimming pool, sauna, tennis courts and over-the-top tariffs. Macinaggio's only **campsite**, *U Stazzu*, lies 1km north of the harbour and is signposted from the Rogliano road (Ⓣ04.95.35.43.76; May–Oct). The ground is like rock, but it's cheap and there's ample shade and easy access to the nearby beach; particularly good breakfasts are also served in the site's little café.

Besides the hotel **restaurants** above, commendable places to eat in Macinaggio include the *Pizzeria San Columbu*, at the end of the port facing out to sea. For a taste of local seafood, you won't do better than the *Osteria di u Portu* (Ⓣ04.95.35.40.49; open April–Sept), facing the marina. The other established favourite is *Les Îles*, also on the quayside, whose good-value €18.50 *menu fixe* features *soupe de poisson*, grilled *daurade* (gilt head) and *pâtisserie maison*.

North of the town lie some beautiful stretches of white sand and clear sea. A marked footpath, known as **Le Sentier des Douaniers** because it used to be patrolled by customs officials, threads its way across the hills and coves along the coast, giving access to an area that cannot by reached by road. The **Baie de Tamarone**, 2km along this path, has deep clear waters, making it a good place for diving and snorkelling. Just behind the beach, the road forks, and if you follow the left-hand track for twenty minutes you'll come to a stunning arc of turquoise sea known as the **rade de Santa Maria**, site of the isolated Romanesque **Chapelle Santa-Maria**. Raised on the foundations of a sixth-century church, the building comprises two chapels, one tenth- the other twelfth-century, merged into one, hence the two discrepant apses. The bay's other principal landmark is the huge **Tour Chiapelle**. Dramatically cleft in half and entirely surrounded by water, the ruined three-storeyed tower was one of three built on the northern tip of the cape by the Genoese in the sixteenth century (the others are at Tollare and Barcaggio) as lookout posts against the increasingly troublesome Moorish pirates. As Macinaggio grew in importance, the *torri* began to be used also by health and customs officers, who controlled the maritime traffic with Genoa. Pascal Paoli established his garrison here in 1761, having been unsuccessful in his attempt to take Macinaggio, and contemplated building a rival port. The **tourist office** in Macinaggio will furnish you with a free **map** and route description of the path. Otherwise get hold of a copy of IGN #4347 OT; which covers the entire route to Centuri-Port (7–8hrs).

Centuri-Port

When Dr Johnson's biographer, James Boswell, arrived here from England in 1765, the former Roman settlement of **CENTURI-PORT** was a tiny fishing village, recommended to him for its peaceful detachment from the dangerous turmoil of the rest of Corsica. Not much has changed since Boswell's time: Centuri-Port exudes tranquillity despite a serious influx of summer residents, many of them artists who come to paint the fishing boats in the slightly prettified harbour, where the grey-stone wall is highlighted by the green serpentine roofs of the encircling cottages, restaurants and bars. The only drawback is that you'll find the small beach disappointingly muddy and not ideal for sunbathing (although it is an excellent spot for snorkelling).

Centuri-Port has more **hotels** than anywhere else on Cap Corse. *Hôtel-Restaurant du Pêcheur* (Ⓣ04.95.35.60.14; Easter to mid-Nov; ❹), the pink building in the harbour, is among the most pleasant and has a popular restaurant. If it's full, try *Hôtel La Jetée*, to the left on the road as you arrive in Centuri (Ⓣ04.95.35.64.46, Ⓕ04.95.35.64.18; April–Sept; ❸), whose rooms are ordinary and for the most part without sea views, but the cheapest in the village during high season. The *Vieux Moulin* (Ⓣ04.95.35.60.15, Ⓦwww.le-vieux-moulin.net; March–Oct; ❺), opposite, is the most stylish option: a converted *maison d'Américain* with a wonderful terrace and attractively furnished en-suite rooms. For **campers**, choice is limited to the rather scruffy *Camping l'Isolettu*, 400m south along the D35 (Ⓣ04.95.35.62.81, Ⓕ04.95.35.63.63; May–Oct).

Nonza

Set high on a black rocky pinnacle that plunges vertically into the sea, the village of **NONZA**, 18km south of Centuri, is one of the highlights of the Cap Corse shoreline. It was formerly the main stronghold of the da Gentile family, and the remains of their **fortress** are still standing on the furthest rocks on the overhanging cliff.

The village is also famous for **St Julia**, patron saint of Corsica, who was martyred here in the fifth century. The story goes that she had been sold into slavery at Carthage and was being taken by ship to Gaul when the slavers docked here. A pagan festival was in progress, and when Julia refused to participate she was crucified; the gruesome legend relates that her breasts were then cut off and thrown onto a stone, from which sprang two springs, now enshrined in a chapel by the beach. To get there, follow the sign on the right-hand side of the road before you enter the square, which points to **La Fontaine de Ste-Julia**, down by the rocks. Reached by a flight of six hundred steps, Nonza's long grey **beach** is discoloured as a result of pollution from the now disused asbestos mine up the coast. This may not inspire confidence, but the locals insist it's safe (they take their own kids there in summer), and from the bottom you do get the best view of the tower, which looks as if it's about to topple into the sea.

The village has two **accommodation** options: a stylish little B&B called *Casa Maria* (Ⓣ04.95.37.80.95; ❺), in an restored schist house above the square; and the *Auberge Patrizi* (Ⓣ04.95.37.82.16; ❹) an attractively converted stone house five minutes' walk down a steep flight of steps towards the beach. The best room in the latter has a gorgeous terrace with sweeping views across the gulf to the Désert des Agriates.

The Nebbio (U Nebbiu)

Taking its name from the thick mists that sweep over the region in winter, the **Nebbio** has for centuries been one of the most fertile parts of the island, producing honey, chestnuts and some of the island's finest wine. Tourism, however, has so far made little impact on this depopulated area, which comprises the amphitheatre of rippled hills, vineyards and cultivated valleys that converge on St-Florent, a handful of kilometres due west of Bastia. Aside from EU subsidies, the major money earner here is viticulture: some of the island's wines are produced around the commune of **Patrimonio**, and *caves* offering wine tastings are a feature of the whole region.

A bishopric until 1790, **St-Florent** is a chic coastal resort at the base of Cap Corse. It remains the Nebbio's chief town, and is the obvious base for day-trips to the beautifully preserved Pisan church of Santa Maria Assunta, just outside the town, and the **Désert des Agriates**, a wilderness of parched maquis-covered hills whose rugged coastline harbours one of Corsica's least accessible, but most beautiful, beaches.

The principal **public transport** serving the Nebbio is the twice-daily bus from Bastia to St-Florent, operated by Transports Santini (Ⓣ04.95.37.02.98) which leaves the *gare routière* at 10.30am and 5.30pm between June and September, and at 11am and 6pm during the rest of the year (except Oct–May Wed & Sat, when they leave at noon & 5.30pm).

St-Florent and around

Viewed from across the bay, **ST-FLORENT** (San Fiurenzu) appears as a bright line against the black tidal wave of the Tenda hills, the pale stone houses seeming to rise straight out of the sea, overlooked by a squat circular citadelle. It's a relaxing town, with a decent beach and a good number of restaurants, but the key to its success is the **marina**, which is jammed with expensive boats throughout the summer. Neither the tourists, however, nor indeed St-Florent's proximity to Bastia, entirely eclipse the air of isolation conferred on the town by its brooding backdrop of mountains and scrubby desert.

In Roman times, a town called Cersunam – referred to as Nebbium by chroniclers from the ninth century onwards – existed a kilometre east of the present village. Few traces remain of the settlement, and in the fifteenth century it was eclipsed by the port that developed around the new Genoese citadelle. St-Florent, as it became known, prospered as one of Genoa's strongholds, and it was from here that Paoli set off for London in 1796, never to return.

Place des Portes, the centre of town life, has café tables facing the sea in the shade of plane trees, and in the evening fills with strollers and pétanque players. In rue du Centre, which runs west off the square, parallel to the seafront and marina, you'll find some restaurants, a few shops and a couple of wine-tasting places – be sure to sample the sweet, maquis-scented muscat made around here. The fifteenth-century circular **citadelle** can be reached on foot from place Doria at the seafront in the old quarter. Destroyed by Nelson's bombardment in 1794, it was renovated in the 1990s and affords superb views from its terrace.

Just a kilometre to the east of the town off a small road running off place des Portes, on the original site of Cersanum, the **church of Santa Maria Assunta** – the so-called "cathedral of the Nebbio" – is a fine example of Pisan Romanesque architecture. Built of warm yellow limestone, the building has a distinctly barn-like appearance – albeit a superlatively elegant one. Gracefully symmetrical blind arcades decorate the western facade, and at the entrance twisting serpents and wild animals adorn the pilasters on each side of the door. The interior, too, appears deceptively simple. Carved shells, foliage and animals adorn the capitals of the pillars dividing the nave where, immediately to the right, you'll see a glass case containing the mummified figure of St Flor, a Roman soldier martyred in the third century.

Practicalities

Bus times vary a little from year to year, but can be checked at the **tourist office**, at the top of the village in the same building as the **post office**, 100m north of place des Portes (July & Aug Mon–Fri 8.30am–12.30pm & 2–7pm, Sat & Sun 9am–noon & 3–6pm; Sept–June Mon–Fri 9am–noon & 2–5pm, Sat 9am–noon; Ⓣ & Ⓕ04.95.37.06.04). There's a small **cyber café** just off the square, on the left (north) side of the road leading to Santa Maria Assunta. It charges by the minute at a rate of €5 per hour.

St-Florent is a popular resort, and **hotels** fill up quickly, especially at the height of summer when prior booking is essential. The *De l'Europe* in place des Portes (Ⓣ04.95.37.00.33, Ⓦwww.hotel-europe2.com; ❹) is the most attractive option in town – and the only one open in winter. Otherwise, try *Du Centre*, just up the road from the *Europe* (Ⓣ04.95.37.00.68, Ⓕ04.95.37.41.01; ❸; closed Nov–April), which has tiny rooms but is the cheapest place in town, or the more modern and swisher *Maxime*, just off place des Portes (Ⓣ04.95.37.05.30, Ⓕ04.95.37.13.07; ❹; closed Nov–April). A couple of kilometres northeast on the Bastia road, *Le Maloni* (Ⓣ04.95.37.14.30, Ⓦwww.malonihotel.com; ❷) is a friendly, popular, budget choice close to the beach and offering simple en-suite rooms opening onto a leafy garden.

A fair number of **campsites** are dotted about the coast, but are packed in August and closed out of season. *Camping Kallisté*, route de la Plage (Ⓣ04.95.37.03.08, Ⓦwww.camping-kalliste.com; closed Oct–May) is the closest to town and most congenial.

St-Florent is renowned for the seafood from its gulf and there's no better location to enjoy it than down on the quayside, where a handful of swish gourmet places stand alongside standard pizzerias and tourist **restaurants**. With menus from €21–35, *La Rascasse* (Ⓣ04.95.37.06.99) has become renowned for its imaginative spins on local seafood: cream of ray's wing, mussel and chestnut fritters, and lobster sautéed in cured ham with tartlets of warm *brocciu*. In a similar price bracket is the nearby *La Gaffe* (Ⓣ04.95.37.00.12; closed Tues, except in July & Aug), where you can order sumptuous devilfish stew on a bed of tagliatelle, with menus at €28 and €40.

Patrimonio (Patrimoniu)

Leaving St-Florent by the Bastia road, the first village you come to, after 6km, is **PATRIMONIO**, centre of the first Corsican wine region to gain *appellation contrôlée* status. Apart from the renowned local muscat, which can be sampled in the village or at one of the *caves* along the route from St-Florent, Patrimonio's chief asset is the sixteenth-century **church of St-Martin**, occupying its own little hillock and visible for kilometres around. The colour of burnt sienna, it stands out vividly against the rich green vineyards. In a garden 200m south of the church stands a limestone **statue-menhir** known as U Nativu, a late megalithic piece dating from 900–800 BC. A carved T-shape on its front represents a breastbone, and two eyebrows and a chin can also be made out.

△ Patrimonio

The Désert des Agriates

Extending westwards from the Golfe de St-Florent to the mouth of the Ostriconi River, the **Désert des Agriates** is a vast area of uninhabited land, dotted with clumps of cacti and scrub-covered hills. It may appear inhospitable now, but during the time of the Genoese this rocky moonscape was, as its name implies, a veritable breadbasket (*agriates* means "cultivated fields"). In fact, so much wheat was grown here that the Italian overlords levied a special tax on grain to prevent any build-up of funds that might have financed an insurrection. Fires and soil erosion eventually took their toll, however, and by the 1970s the area had become a total wilderness.

Numerous crackpot schemes to redevelop the Désert have been mooted over the years – from atomic weapon test zones to concrete Club-Med-style resorts – but during the past few decades the government has gradually bought up the land from its various owners (among them the Rothschild family) and designated it as a protected nature reserve. Nevertheless, species such as the Agriates' rare wild boar remain under threat, mainly from trigger-happy hunters and bush fires.

A couple of rough *pistes* wind into the desert, but without some kind of 4WD vehicle the only feasible way to explore the area and its rugged coastline, which includes two of the island's most beautiful **beaches**, is by foot. From St-Florent, a pathway winds northwest to **plage de Perajola**, just off the main Calvi highway (N1197), in three easy stages. The first takes around five hours, 30 minutes, and leads past the famous **Martello tower** and much-photographed **plage de Loto** to **plage de Saleccia**, a huge sweep of soft white sand and turquoise sea that was used as a location for the invasion sequences in the film *The Longest Day*. There's a seasonal **campsite** here, *U Paradisu* (Ⓣ04.95.37.82.51; mid-June to Sept only). From plage de Saleccia, it takes around three hours to reach the second night halt, **plage de Ghignu**, where a simple *gîte d'étape* (Ⓣ04.95.37.09.86) provides basic facilities for €10 per night. The last stretch to Perajola can be covered in under six hours.

Note that the only water sources along the route are at Saleccia and Ghignu, so take plenty with you. It's also worth knowing that between May and October, **excursion boats**, leaving throughout the day from the jetty in St-Florent marina (€12 return, or €6 one way), ferry passengers across the gulf to and from plage de Loto. If you time your walk well, you can pick one up for the return leg back to town.

The Balagne (A Balagna)

The **Balagne**, the region stretching west from the Ostriconi valley as far as the red-cliffed wilderness of Scandola, has been renowned since Roman times as "Le Pays de l'Huile et Froment" (Land of Oil and Wheat). Backed by a wall of imposing, pale grey mountains, the characteristic outcrops of orange granite punctuating its spectacular coastline shelter a string of idyllic beaches, many of them sporting ritzy marinas and holiday complexes. These, along with the region's two honeypot towns, **L'Île Rousse** and **Calvi**, get swamped in summer, but the scenery more than compensates. In any case, Calvi, with its cream-coloured citadelle, breathtaking white-sand bay and mountainous backdrop, should not be missed.

Year-round **transport** in the Balagne is limited to the *Micheline* train, which descends the Ostriconi valley and runs west along the coast as far as Calvi, and a bus connection with Bastia, via Ponte Leccia. In July and August, you can also travel to Calvi from Porto by bus, and between Calvi and L'Ile Rousse on hourly tram-trains.

L'Île Rousse

Developed by Pascal Paoli in the 1760s as a "gallows to hang Calvi", the port of **L'ÎLE ROUSSE** (Isula Rossa) simply doesn't convince as a Corsican town, its palm trees, smart shops, neat flower gardens and colossal pink seafront hotel creating an atmosphere that has more in common with the French Riviera. Pascal Paoli had great plans for his new town on the Haute-Balagne coast, which was laid out from scratch in 1758 as a port to export the olive oil produced in the region. A large part of the new port was built on a grid system, featuring lines of straight parallel streets quite at odds with the higgledy-piggledy nature of most Corsican villages and towns. Thanks to the busy trading of wine and oil, it soon began to prosper and, two and a half centuries later, still thrives as a successful port. These days, however, the main traffic consists of holiday-makers, lured here by brochure shots of the nearby beaches. This is officially the hottest corner of the island, and the town is thus deluged by German and Italian sun-worshippers in July and August. Given the proximity of Calvi, and so much unspoilt countryside, it's hard to see why you should want to stop here for more than a couple of hours.

Arrival, information and accommodation

The **train station** (☎04.95.60.00.50) is on route du Port, 500m south of where the ferries arrive. The Bastia–Calvi **bus** stops just south of place Paoli in the town's main thoroughfare, avenue Piccioni. The SNCM office is on avenue J.Calizi (☎04.95.60.09.56), and the **tourist office** on the south side of place Paoli (April–June & Sept–Oct Mon–Fri 9am–noon & 2–5pm; July & Aug daily 9am–1pm & 2.30–7.30pm; ☎04.95.60.04.35, Ⓦwww.ot-ile-rousse.fr). For **Internet** access, go to Movie Stores (Mon–Sat 10am–2am; €5 per hour), diagonally opposite the supermarket on the crossroads where the Route Nationale cuts through the centre of town.

L'Île Rousse fills up early in the year and it can be difficult to find a **hotel** at any time from May to October. Most places are modern buildings, more functional than personable. The town has two main **campsites**: *Les Oliviers*, 1km east (Ⓣ04.95.60.19.92), and *Le Bodri* (Ⓣ04.95.16.19.70, Ⓦwww.campinglebodri.com), 3km west off the main Calvi road. The latter site, which is slap on the beach, can be reached direct by rail – ask for "l'arrêt Bodri".

Hotels

Le Grillon 10 av Paul-Doumer Ⓣ04.95.60.00.49, Ⓕ04.95.60.43.69. The best cheap hotel in town, just 1km from the centre on the St-Florent/Bastia road. Nothing special, but quiet and immaculately clean. April–Oct. ❸

De la Puntella rte du Port Ⓣ04.95.60.04.34, Ⓕ04.95.60.40.87. Smart little "studios" (rooms with four beds, kitchenette and bathroom), which are usually booked on a weekly basis during August; particularly good value for families. Ample parking too. ❹

Santa Maria rte du Port Ⓣ04.95.63.05.05, Ⓦwww.hotelsantamaria.com. Next to the ferry port, this is one of the larger and best-value three-star places. Their recently refurbished, air-conditioned rooms have small balconies or patios opening onto a garden and pool, and there's exclusive access to a tiny pebble beach. ❼

Splendid 4 bd Valéry-François Ⓣ04.95.60.00.24, Ⓦwww.le-splendid-hotel.com. Well-maintained, 1930s-style building with a small swimming pool and some sea views from upper floors; very reasonable tariffs, given the location. April to mid-Nov. ❺

The town and beaches

All roads in L'Île Rousse lead to **place Paoli**, a shady square that's open to the sea and has as its focal point a fountain surmounted by a bust of "U Babbu di u Patria" (Father of the Nation), one of many local tributes to Pascal Paoli. There's a Frenchified covered **market** at the entrance to the square, which hosts a popular artisan-cum-antiques sale on Saturday mornings, while on the west side rises the grim facade of the **church of the Immaculate Conception**.

To reach the **Île de la Pietra**, the islet that gives the town its name, continue north, passing the station on your left. Once over the causeway connecting the islet to the mainland, you can walk through the crumbling mass of red granite as far as the lighthouse at the far end, from where the view of the town is spectacular, especially at sundown, when you get the full effect of the red glow of the rocks.

Immediately in front of the promenade, the **town beach** is a crowded Côte d'Azur-style strand, blocked by ranks of sun loungers and parasols belonging to the row of lookalike café-restaurants behind it. With your own transport, you're better off heading 3km west up the N197, where a signpost pointing right off the main road (next to the turning for *Camping Bodri*) leads 300m downhill to a fee-charging municipal car park (€5 for the day; no shade) from where you can walk to two of the most beautiful beaches on the north coast. To your right as you face the sea, **plage de Botri** is the more sheltered, backed by soft white dunes in which is nestled a smart but overpriced *paillote* (beach bar). The sand is clean and the water crystal clear, but from late June onwards this normally isolated cove is swamped by campers from the nearby campsite. A short walk further west around the rocky Punta di Ginebre, **Baie de Giunchetu** is a larger, though less picturesque beach. Note that you can reach both of these by train: just behind plage de Botri is a little request stop at which you can ask to be dropped by any of the services running between L'Île Rousse and Calvi.

Eating and drinking

Though there's an abundance of mediocre **eating** places in the narrow alleys of the old town, a few restaurants do stand out, some offering classic gourmet menus and others serving superb fresh seafood. The best cafés are found under the plane trees lining the southern side of place Paoli.

L'Escale rue Notre Dame ⓣ04.95.60.10.53. Giant fresh mussels, prawns and crayfish from the east coast *étangs* are the thing here, served in various *formules* and menus (€13–25) on a spacious terrace looking across the *micheline* line to the bay. Brisk, courteous service, copious portions and for once the house white (by the glass or *pichet*) is palatable. The *menu pêcheur* (a mixed platter) is especially good value.

L'Ostéria place Santelli ⓣ04.95.60.08.39. On a quiet backstreet in the old quarter, this established Corsican speciality restaurant offers an excellent set menu (€18), featuring delicious courgette fritters, *soupe de nos villages*, tarragon-scented *gratin d'aubergines*, stuffed sardines and fresh pan-fried prawns. You can sit in a vaulted room adorned with farm implements or on the shaded terrace.

A Pasturella On the square, Monticello ⓣ04.95.60.06.65. Stylish gastro-Corsican restaurant, up in one of the Balagne's prettiest *villages perchés*. Only ten minutes' drive from town, but the views, and cooking, are of the highest order. There's an unusually international flavour to the menu (tandoori fish, prawns in satay sauce), and some imaginative gourmet takes on local classics (such as devilfish and saffron ragout). Menus at €29–60.

A Quadrera 6 rue Napoléon ⓣ04.95.60.44.52. Sunny Mediterranean salads, quality charcuterie and imaginative seafood dishes, stylishly served inside an eighteenth-century town house with exposed stone walls. Their €17.50 menu offers great value for money, as does the legendary "*salade de M.Jo-Jo*", featuring local *panzetta* ham.

Calvi

Seen from the water, **CALVI** is a beautiful spectacle, with its three immense bastions topped by a crest of ochre buildings, sharply defined against a hazy backdrop of mountains. Twenty kilometres west along the coast from L'Île Rousse, the town began as a fishing port on the site of the present-day *ville basse* below the citadelle, and remained just a cluster of houses and fishing shacks until the Pisans conquered the island in the tenth century. Not until the arrival of the Genoese, however, did the town become a stronghold when, in 1268, Giovaninello de Loreto, a Corsican nobleman, built a huge citadelle on the windswept rock overlooking the port and named it Calvi. A fleet commanded by Nelson launched a brutal two-month attack on the town in 1794, when Nelson lost the sight in his eye; he left saying he hoped never to see the place again.

The French concentrated on developing Ajaccio and Bastia during the nineteenth century, and Calvi became primarily a military base, used as a point for smuggling arms to the mainland in World War II. A hangout for European glitterati in the 1950s, the town these days has the ambience of a slightly kitsch Côte d'Azur resort, whose glamorous marina, souvenir shops and fussy boutiques jar with the down-to-earth villages of its rural hinterland. It's also an important base for the French Foreign Legion's crack parachute regiment, the 2e REP, and immaculately uniformed legionnaires are a common sight around the bars lining avenue de la République.

Arrival, information and accommodation

Ste-Catherine airport lies 7km south of Calvi (ⓣ04.95.65.88.88, ⓦwww.calvi.aeroport.fr); the only public transport into town is by **taxi**, which shouldn't cost more than €16–18 weekdays (or €20–22 on weekends). The **train station** (ⓣ04.95.65.00.61) is on avenue de la République, close to the marina, where you'll find the **tourist office** on quai Landry (mid-June to Sept daily 9am–7pm; Oct to mid-June Mon–Fri 9am–noon & 2–5.30pm, Sat 9am–noon; ⓣ04.95.65.16.67, ⓦwww.tourisme.fr/calvi). **Buses** from Bastia and towns along the north coast stop outside the train station on place de la Porteuse d'Eau, whereas those from Porto pull in behind the marina.

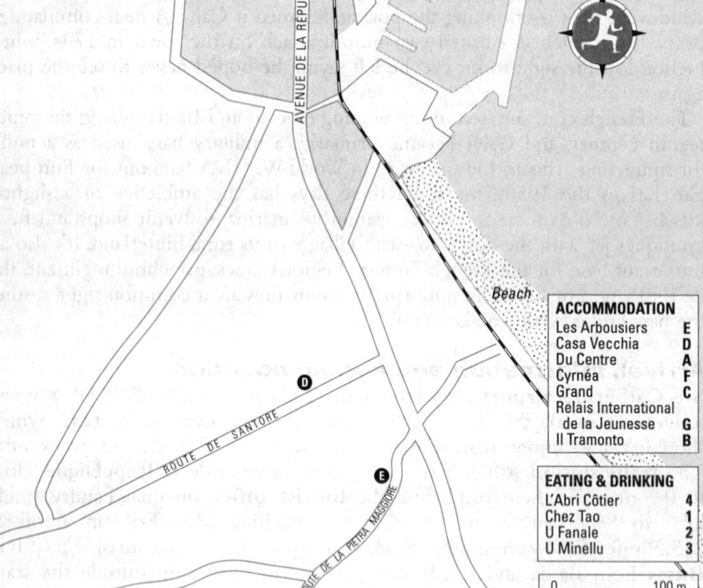
CALVI
ST-FRANÇOIS
Anse de Fontanaccia
La Maison Colomb
CITADELLE
R. COLOMB
Cathédrale St-Jean-Baptiste
Oratoire St-Antoine
Caserne Sampiero
Port
Marseille & Toulon
AVE SAINT-FRANÇOIS
PLACE DE L'OMBRE
RUE DE L'URUGUAY
PLACE CHRISTOPHE COLOMB
QUAI LANDRY
B, 2, Galéria & Punta de la Revellata
Garage d'Angeli
VILLAS SAINT-ANTOINE
VILLE BASSE
AVENUE NAPOLEON
BOULEVARD WILSON
R ALSACE-LORRAINE
R CLEMENCEAU
Tour du Sel
Port de Commerce
Hôtel de Ville
Ste-Marie-Majeure
Nice & Genoa
AVENUE GERARD MARCHE
PL ST-CHARLES
RUE CLEMENCEAU
QUAI LANDRY
Boat excursions to Girolata
Beaux Voyages Buses
PL DE LA PORTEUSE D'EAU
RUE JOFFRE
Gare SNCF
AVENUE SANTA MARIA
AVENUE DE LA REPUBLIQUE
Marina
N
Beach
ROUTE DE SANTORE
ROUTE DE LA PIETRA MAGGIORE
ACCOMMODATION
Les Arbousiers E
Casa Vecchia D
Du Centre A
Cyrnéa F
Grand C
Relais International de la Jeunesse G
Il Tramonto B
EATING & DRINKING
L'Abri Côtier 4
Chez Tao 1
U Fanale 2
U Minellu 3
0 100 m
F, G, Ste-Catherine Airport, L'Île Rousse& Camping Bella Vista

Ferries, including NGV hydrofoils, dock at the Port de Commerce at the foot of the citadelle. Tramar (aka "CCR"), agents for **SNCM,** are on the quai Landry (Ⓣ04.95.65.01.38); Corsica Ferries' office is over in the Port de Commerce (Ⓣ04.95.65.43.21). You can **rent bicycles** from Garage d'Angeli, rue Villa-Antoine, on the left just west of place Christophe-Colomb (Ⓣ04.95.65.02.13, Ⓦwww.garagedangeli.com) for €15–17 per day. Take along your credit card or passport, which they'll need to secure the €150 deposit.

Accommodation is easy to find in Calvi except during the jazz festival (third week of June). Hotels range from inexpensive pensions to luxury piles with pools and sweeping views of the bay. If you're on a tight budget, take your pick from the town's two excellent **hostels**, or the dozen **campsites** within walking distance of the centre.

Hotels

Les Arbousiers rte de Pietra-Maggiore Ⓣ04.95.65.04.47, Ⓕ04.95.65.26.14. Large, fading pink place set back from the main road, with rooms ranged around a quiet courtyard. Particularly good deal mid-and low season. ❸

Casa Vecchia rte de Santore Ⓣ04.95.65.09.33, Ⓦwww.hotel-casa-vecchia.com. A dependable budget option with small chalets set in a leafy garden, 500m south of town, and 200m from the beach. Advance booking essential. May–Sept. ❹

Du Centre 14 rue Alsace-Lorraine Ⓣ04.95.65.02.01. Old-fashioned *pension*, with a welcoming owner, occupying a former police barracks in a narrow, pretty street near Église Ste-Marie-Majeure and harbourside. Its rooms are large for the price, but plain with shared WC. The cheapest option in town by a long chalk: from €32 per double June/Sept, rising to a mere €45 in July and August. Open June–Oct. ❷

Cyrnéa rte de Bastia Ⓣ04.95.65.03.35, Ⓦwww.hotelcyrnea.com. Large budget hotel, 20min walk south of town or 300m from the beach. Good-sized rooms for the price, all with bathrooms and balconies (ask for one with a "vue montagne" to the rear). Outstanding value for money, even in high season. April–Nov. ❹

Grand 3 bd Wilson Ⓣ04.95.65.09.74, Ⓦwww.grand-hotel-calvi.com. Wonderful old luxury hotel in the centre of town, with original *fin-de-siècle* furniture and fittings. The rooms, though somewhat dowdy and in need of a lick of paint, are huge, and many have good views (as does the breakfast salon, which looks over the rooftops of the old quarter). Smaller-than-average tariff increases in high season. April–Oct. ❺

Il Tramonto rte de Porto Ⓣ04.95.65.04.17, Ⓦwww.hotel-iltramonto.com. Another excellent little budget hotel, with clean, comfortable and light rooms. Definitely try for one with "vue mer", which have little terraces and superb views over Punta de la Revellata. ❸

Hostels and campsites

Relais International de la Jeunesse "U Carabellu" 4km from the centre of town on rte Pietra-Maggiore Ⓣ04.95.65.14.16, Ⓕ04.95.80.65.33. Follow the N197 for 2km, turn right at the sign for Pietra-Maggiore, and the hostel – two little houses with spacious, clean dormitories at €13 per bed (or €24 with breakfast), looking out over the gulf – is in the village another 2km further on (along a track that's impassable for cars). Phone ahead to make sure it's open. May–Oct.

Camping Bella Vista rte de Pietra-Maggiore, 1km southeast of the centre (700m inland from the beach) Ⓣ04.95.65.11.76, Ⓦwww.camping-bellavista.com. The best option for backpackers as it's much closer to the centre of town than the competition – though you pay a couple of euros per night extra for the privilege. Plenty of shade, nice soft ground and clean toilet blocks. Closed Nov–March.

The town and citadelle

Social life in Calvi focuses on the restaurants and cafés of the **quai Landry**, a spacious seafront walkway linking the marina and the port. This is the best place to get the feel of the town, but as far as sights go there's not a lot to the *ville basse*. At the far end of the quay, under the shadow of the citadelle, stands the sturdy **Tour du Sel**, a medieval lookout post once used to store imported salt. If you head up through the narrow passageways off quai Landry, you'll come to rue Clemenceau, where restaurants and souvenir shops are packed into every available space. In a small square giving onto the street stands the pink-painted **Église Ste-Marie-Majeure**, built in 1774, whose spindly bell tower rises elegantly above the cafés on the quay but whose interior contains nothing of interest. From the church's flank, a flight of steps connects with boulevard Wilson, a wide modern high street which rises to place Christophe-Colomb, point of entry for the *haute ville*, or **citadelle**.

Beyond the ancient gateway to the citadelle, with its inscription of the town's motto ("Civitas Calvis Semper Fidelis" – always faithful), you come immediately to the enormous **Caserne Sampiero**, formerly the governor's palace. Built in the thirteenth century, when the great round tower was used as a dungeon, the castle is currently used for military purposes, and therefore closed to the public. The best way of seeing the rest of the citadelle is to follow the ramparts, which connect the three immense bastions. From each bastion the views across the sea, the Balagne and the Cinto Massif are magnificent.

Within the walls the houses are tightly packed along tortuous stairways and narrow passages that converge on the diminutive place d'Armes. Dominating the square is the **Cathédrale St-Jean-Baptiste**, set at the highest point of the promontory and sitting uncomfortably amid the ramshackle buildings. This chunky ochre edifice was founded in the thirteenth century, but was partly destroyed during the Turkish siege of 1553 and then suffered extensive damage twelve years later, when the powder magazine in the governor's palace exploded. It was rebuilt in the form of a Greek cross. The church's great treasure is the **Christ des Miracles**, housed in the chapel on the right of the choir;

The GR20

Winding some 170km from Calenzana (12km from Calvi) to Conca (22km from Porto-Vecchio), the **GR20** is Corsica's most demanding long-distance footpath. Only one third of the estimated 17,000 hikers who start it each season complete all sixteen stages (*étapes*), which can be covered in ten to twelve days if you're in good physical shape – if you're not, don't even think about attempting this route. Marked with red-and-white splashes of paint, it comprises a series of harsh ascents and descents, sections of which exceed 2000m and become more of a climb than a walk, with stanchions, cables and ladders driven into the rock as essential aids. The going is made tougher by the necessity of carrying a sleeping bag, all-weather kit and two or three days' food with you. That said, the rewards more than compensate. The GR20 takes in the most spectacular mountain terrain in Corsica and along the way you can spot the elusive mouflon (mountain sheep), glimpse lammergeier (a rare vulture) wheeling around the crags, and swim in ice-cold torrents and waterfalls.

The first thing you need to do before setting off is get hold of the Parc Régional's indispensable **Topo-guide**, published by the Fédération Française de la Randonnée Pédestre, which gives a detailed description of the route, along with relevant sections of IGN contour maps, lists of refuges and other essential information. Most good bookshops in Corsica stock them, or call at the park office in Ajaccio (see p.1237). More detailed coverage of the route (in English) is featured in David Abram's *Corsica Trekking: the GR20* book (see p.1336).

The route can be undertaken in either **direction**, but most hikers start in the north at Calenzana, tackling the most demanding *étapes* early on. The hardship is alleviated by extraordinary mountainscapes as you round the Cinto massif, skirt the Asco, Niolo, Tavignano and Restonica valleys, and scale the sides of Monte d'Oro and Rotondo. At Vizzavona on the main Bastia–Corte–Ajaccio road, roughly the halfway mark, you can call it a day and catch a bus or train back to the coast, or press on south across two more ranges to the needle peaks of Bavella. With much of the forest east of here this crucifix was brandished at marauding Turks during the 1553 siege, an act which reputedly saved the day.

To the north of place d'Armes in rue de Fil stands **La Maison Colomb**, the shell of a building which Calvi believes – as the plaque on the wall states – was Christopher Columbus's birthplace, though the claim rests on pretty tenuous, circumstantial evidence. The house itself was destroyed by Nelson's troops during the siege of 1794, but as recompense a statue was erected in 1992, the 500th anniversary of Columbus's "discovery" of America; the date of this historic landfall, October 12, is now a public holiday in Calvi.

Calvi's outstanding **beach** sweeps right round the bay from the end of quai Landry, but most of the first kilometre or so is owned by bars which rent out sun loungers for a hefty price. To avoid these, follow the track behind the sand which will bring you to the start of a more secluded stretch. The sea might not be as sparklingly clear as at many other Corsican beaches, but it's warm, shallow and free of rocks. You can also sunbathe, and swim off the rocks, at the foot of the citadelle, which has the added attraction of fine views across the bay.

Eating and drinking

Eating is a major pastime in Calvi, and you'll find restaurants and snack bars on almost every street. Fish restaurants predominate in the marina, where – at a price – you can eat excellent seafood fresh from the bay. **Cafés**, fronted with fashionable parasols and teak furniture, line the marina, becoming more expensive the nearer they are to the Tour du Sel.

blackened by fire, hikers in recent years have been leaving the GR20 at Zonza, below the Col de Bavella (served by daily buses to Ajaccio and Porto-Vecchio), and walking to the coast along the less arduous Mare a Mare Sud trail.

Accommodation along the route is provided by **refuges**, where, for around €10, you can take a hot shower, use an equipped kitchen and bunk down on mattresses. Usually converted *bergeries*, these places are staffed by wardens during the peak period (June–Sept). Advance reservation is not possible; beds are allocated on a first-come-first-served basis, so be prepared to bivouac if you arrive late. Another reason to be on the trail soon after dawn is that it allows you to break the back of the *étape* before 2pm, when clouds tend to bubble over the mountains and obscure the views.

The **weather** in the high mountains is notoriously fickle. A sunny morning doesn't necessarily mean a sunny day, and during July and August violent storms can rip across the route without warning. It's therefore essential to take good wet-weather gear with you, as well as a hat, sunblock and shades. In addition, make sure you set off on each stage with adequate **food** and **water**. At the height of the season, many refuges sell basic supplies (*alimentation*), but you shouldn't rely on this service; ask hikers coming from the opposite direction where their last supply stop was and plan accordingly (basic provisions are always available at the main passes of Col de Vergio, Col de Vizzavona, Col de Bavella and Col de Verde). The refuge wardens (*gardiens*) will be able to advise you on how much water to carry at each stage.

Finally a word of **warning**: each year, injured hikers have to be air-lifted to safety off remote sections of the GR20, normally because they strayed from the marked route and got lost. Occasionally, fatal accidents also occur for the same reason, so always keep the paint splashes in sight, especially if the weather closes in – don't rely purely on the many cairns that punctuate the route, as these sometimes mark more hazardous paths to high peaks.

Cafés and bars

Chez Tao rue St-Antoine, in the citadelle ⓣ04.95.65.00.73. Legendary nightclub, opened in the wake of the Bolshevik Revolution by a Muslim White Russian, and long the haunt of the Riviera's glitterati. Now turned into a pricey piano bar serving fussy nouvelle cuisine and local fish dishes, costing around €30 à la carte. June–Sept 7pm–midnight.

Restaurants

L'Abri Côtier On quai Landry, but entrance on rue Joffre ⓣ04.95.65.12.76. Mostly seafood dishes (such as sea bass with fennel) and pizzas (from €10), served on a lovely terrace looking out to sea. Their set menus (€20, 28 & 35) and *suggestions du jour* are invariably the best deals.

U Fanale rte de Porto, just outside the centre of town on the way to Punta de la Revellata ⓣ04.95.65.18.82. Worth the walk out here for their delicious, beautifully presented Corsican specialities – mussels or lamb simmered in ewe's cheese and white wine, a fine *soupe Corse*, and melt-in-the-mouth *fiadone* (traditional flan). Menus €24 plus a full à la carte choice, and pizzas from €10. You can dine outside in the garden or inside their *salle panoramique*, with views across the bay to Punta de la Revellata.

U Minellu Off bd Wilson, nr Ste-Marie-Majeure. Wholesome Corsican specialities served in a narrow stepped alley, or on a shady terrace with pretty mosaic tables. Their menu features baked lamb, *cannelloni al brocciu*, spider crab dressed "à la Calvaise", and a cheese platter – good value at €20.

The Réserve Naturel de Scandola and Girolata

The **Réserve Naturel de Scandola** takes up the promontory dividing the Balagne from the Golfe de Porto, its name derived from the wooden tiles (*scandules*) that cover many of the island's mountain houses. But the area's roof-like rock formations are only part of its amazing geological repertoire: its stacked slabs, towering pinnacles and gnarled claw-like outcrops were formed by Monte Cinto's volcanic eruptions 250 million years ago, and subsequent erosion has fashioned shadowy caves, grottoes and gashes in the rock. Scandola's colours are as remarkable as the shapes, the hues varying from the charcoal grey of granite to the incandescent rusty purple of porphyry.

The headland and its surrounding water were declared a nature reserve in 1975 and now support significant colonies of sea birds, dolphins and seals, as well as 450 types of seaweed and some remarkable fish such as the grouper, a species more commonly found in the Caribbean. In addition, nests belonging to the rare Audouin's gull are visible on the cliffs, and you might see the odd osprey – there used to be only seven pairs here, but careful conservation has increased this number to 24.

Scandola is off-limits to hikers and can be viewed only by **boat** (Colombo Lines ⓣ04.95.62.32.10, ⓦwww.colombo-line.com), which means taking one of the daily excursions from Calvi or Porto. These leave from Calvi at 9.15am and 2pm, and from Porto at various intervals throughout the daytime and early evening (April–Oct), the first two stopping for two hours at Girolata (see below) and returning in the late afternoon. It's a fascinating journey and well worth the €40 fare, although it's a good idea to take a picnic, as the restaurants in Girolata are very pricey.

Girolata

Connected by a mere mule track to the rest of the island (1hr 30min on foot from the nearest road), the tiny fishing haven of **GIROLATA**, immediately east of Scandola, has a dreamlike quality that's highlighted by the vivid red of the surrounding rocks. A short stretch of stony beach and a few houses are dominated by a stately watchtower, built by the Genoese later in the seventeenth century in the form of a small castle on a bluff overlooking the cove. For most of the year, this is one of the most idyllic spots on the island, with only the odd yacht and party of hikers to threaten the settlement's tranquillity. From June through September, though, daily boat trips from Porto and Calvi ensure the village is packed during the middle of the day, so if you want to make the most of the scenery and peace and quiet, walk here and stay a night in one of the *gîtes*.

The head of the Girolata trail is at **Bocca â Crocce** (Col de la Croix), on the Calvi–Porto road, from where a clear path plunges downhill through dense maquis and forest to a flotsam-covered cove known as **Cala di Tuara** (30min). The more rewarding of the two tracks that wind onwards to Girolata is the more gentle one running left around the headland, but if you feel like stretching your legs, follow the second, more direct route uphill to a pass.

In Girolata, *La Cabane du Berger* (Ⓣ04.95.20.16.98; May–Oct; €32 per person for dorm bed, half-board) offers a choice of **accommodation** in dorms or small wood cabins in the garden behind (these accommodate two people); you can also put your tent up here. Meals are served in their quirky wood-carved bar, but the food isn't up to much. The same is true of the other *gîte*, *Le Cormorant*, among the houses at the north end of the cove (Ⓣ04.95.20.15.55; July & Aug; €32; half-board obligatory), which has eighteen dorm spaces and a small restaurant overlooking the boat jetty. Unless you're staying at one of the *gîtes*, you'll be better off paying a little extra to eat at one of the two restaurants just up the steps. With a terrace overlooking the beach, *Le Bel Ombra* is the pricier of the pair, offering local seafood specialities, including fresh Scandola lobster. *Le Bon Espoir*, next door, is marginally cheaper, with menus from €20 to €31. Note that neither restaurant accepts credit cards.

Porto (Portu) and around

The overwhelming proximity of the mountains, combined with the pervasive eucalyptus and spicy scent of the maquis, give **PORTO**, 30km south of Calvi, a uniquely intense atmosphere that makes it one of the most interesting places to stay on the west coast. Except for a watchtower built here by the Genoese in the second half of the sixteenth century, the site was only built upon with the onset of tourism since the 1950s; today the village is still so small that it can become claustrophobic in July and August, when overcrowding is no joke. Off season, the place becomes eerily deserted, so you'd do well to choose your times carefully; the best months are May, June and September.

The crowds and traffic jams tend to be most oppressive passing the famous **Calanches**, a huge mass of weirdly eroded pink rock just southwest of Porto, but you can easily sidestep the tourist deluge in picturesque **Piana**, which overlooks the gulf from its southern shore, or by heading inland from Porto through the **Gorges de Spelunca**. Forming a ravine running from the sea to the watershed of the island, this spectacular gorge gives access to the equally grandiose **Forêt d'Aïtone**, site of Corsica's most ancient Laricio pine trees and a deservedly popular hiking area. Throughout the forest, the river and its tributaries are punctuated by strings of *piscines naturelles* (natural swimming pools) – a refreshing, tranquil alternative to the beaches hereabouts, which tend to be crammed in peak season. If you're travelling between Porto and Ajaccio, a worthwhile place to break the journey is the clifftop village of **Cargèse** where the two main attractions are the Greek church and spectacular beach.

Arrival and information

Buses from Calvi, via Galéria, and from Ajaccio, via Cargèse, pull into the junction at the end of route de la Marine, opposite the Banco supermarket, en route to the marina. Timetables are posted at the stops themselves, and at the **tourist office**, down in the marina (May, June & Sept daily 9am–6pm; July & Aug daily 9am–7pm; Oct–April Mon–Fri 9am–5pm; ⓣ04.95.26.10.55, ⓦwww.porto-tourisme.com), where you can buy *Topoguides* and brochures for hikes in the area. Timetable information and tickets for the **boat excursions** to Scandola, the Calanches and Girolata are available in advance from the operators at their counters around the marina.

Accommodation

Competition between **hotels** is more cut-throat in Porto than in any other resort on the island. During slack periods towards the beginning and end of the season, most places engage in a full-on price war, pasting up cheaper tariffs than their neighbours – all of which is great for punters. In late July and August, however, the normal sky-high rates prevail. Photos of all the hotels listed below are posted on the local tourist office website (see "Arrival and information", above).

Hotels

Le Belvédère Porto marina ⓣ04.95.26.12.01, ⓦwww.hotel-le-belvedere.com. This three-star is the smartest of the hotels overlooking the marina, with great views from its comfortable rooms and terraces of Capo d'Orto. Reasonable rates given the location. ❸–❺

Brise de Mer On the left of rte de la Marine as you approach tower from the village, opposite the telephone booths ⓣ04.95.26.10.28, ⓦwww.brise-de-mer.com. A large, old-fashioned place with very friendly service and a congenial terrace restaurant. Rooms at the back have the best views. April to mid-Oct. ❸

Le Colombo At the top of the village opposite the turning for Ota ⓣ04.95.26.10. ⓦwww.hotellecolombo.com. An informal, sixteen-room hotel overlooking the valley, imaginatively decorated in sea-blue colours with driftwood and flotsam sculpture. ❺–❻

Le Golfe At the base of the rock in the marina ⓣ04.95.26.13.33. Small, cosy and unpretentious; every room has a balcony with a sea view. Among the cheapest at this end of the village. May–Oct. ❸

Le Maquis At the top of the village just beyond the Ota turning ⓣ04.95.26.12.19, ⓦwww.hotel-lemaquis.com. A perennially popular, well-maintained budget hotel; rooms are basic, but comfortable enough, and they give good off-season discounts. Advance booking recommended; half-board obligatory July and Aug. ❷–❸

Campsites

Camping Les Oliviers ⓣ04.95.26.14.49, ⓦwww.camping-oliviers-porto.com. Top-notch two-star site, boasting a huge multi-layered pool. April–Nov.

Camping Sol e Vista At the main road junction near the supermarkets ⓣ04.95.26.15.71, ⓦwww.camping-sol-e-vista.com. A superb location on shady terraces ascending a steep hillside with a small café at the top. Great views of Capo d'Orto cliffs opposite, and immaculate toilet blocks. April–Nov.

The Town

Eucalyptus-bordered **route de la Marine** links the two parts of the resort. The village proper, known as **Vaïta**, comprises a strip of supermarkets, shops and hotels 1km from the sea, but the main focus of activity is the small **marina**, located at the avenue's end. Overlooking the entrance to the harbour is the much-photographed **Genoese Tower** (May–Sept daily 9am–8.45pm; €3, or €7 for combined entry with the aquarium, see opposite), a square chimney-shaped structure that was cracked by an explosion in the seventeenth century, when it was used as an arsenal. An awe-inspiring view of the crashing sea and maquis-shrouded mountains makes it worth the short climb. Occupying a converted powder house down in the square opposite the base of the tower is the newly established **Aquarium de la Poudrière** (June–Aug daily 10am–10pm, Sept–May Mon–Sat 10am–7pm; €5.50, or €7 for combined ticket with the tower), where you can view the various species of sealife that inhabit the gulf, including grouper, moray eels and sea horses.

The **beach** consists of a pebbly cove south beyond the shoulder of the massive rock supporting the tower. To reach it from the marina, follow the little road that skirts the rock, cross the wooden bridge which spans the River Porto on your left, then walk through the car park under the trees. Although it's rather rocky and exposed, and the sea very deep, the great crags overshadowing the shore give the place a vivid, wild atmosphere.

Eating and drinking

The overall standard of restaurants in Porto is pitiably poor, with overpriced food and indifferent service the norm, particularly during high season. There are, however, a handful of exceptions.

Le Maquis In the hotel of the same name. Honest, affordable home cooking served either in a warm bar or on a tiny terrace that hangs over the valley. Their good-value €24 menu includes delicious scorpion fish in mussel sauce.

La Mer Opposite the tower ☎04.95.26.11.27. One of the finest seafood restaurants in the area, with fish fresh from the gulf, imaginatively prepared and served in an ideal setting. Menus from €18.50. Reserve early for a seat with a view.

Le Sud Along the walkway leading from the square to the marina ☎04.95.26.14.11. Arguably the best restaurant in Porto, thanks to their strict policy of serving nothing except the freshest local food. Simple and delicious cooking from around the Mediterranean ("*cuisine de tous les suds*") served on a stylish terrace overlooking the marina. À la carte only (dishes €18–25) plus wine from a definitive list.

The Calanches

The UNESCO-protected site of the **Calanches**, 5km southwest of Porto, takes its name from *calanca*, the Corsican word for creek or inlet, but the outstanding characteristics here are the vivid orange and pink rock masses and pinnacles which crumble into the dark blue sea. Liable to unusual patterns of erosion, these tormented rock formations and porphyry needles, some of which soar 300m above the waves, have long been associated with different animals and figures, of which the most famous is the Tête de Chien (Dog's Head) at the north end of the stretch of cliffs. Other figures and creatures conjured up include a Moor's head, a monocled bishop, a bear and a tortoise.

One way to see the fantastic cliffs of the Calanches is by boat from Porto; excursions leave daily in summer, cost €22 and last about an hour. Alternatively, you could drive along the corniche road which weaves through the granite archways on its way to Piana. Eight kilometres along the road from Porto, the *Roches Bleues* café is a convenient landmark for walkers.

Piana

Picturesque **PIANA** occupies a prime location overlooking the Calanches, but for some reason does not suffer the deluge of tourists that Porto endures. Retaining a sleepy feel, the village comprises a cluster of pink houses ranged around an eighteenth-century church and square, from the edge of which the panoramic views over the Golfe de Porto are sublime.

Calanches walks

The rock formations visible from the road are not a patch on what you can see from the waymarked **trails** winding through the Calanches, which vary from easy ambles to strenuous stepped ascents. An excellent leaflet highlighting the pick of the routes is available free from tourist offices. Whichever one you choose, leave early in the morning or late in the afternoon to avoid the heat in summer, and take plenty of water.

The most popular walk is the one to the **Château Fort** (1hr), which begins at a sharp hairpin in the D81, 700m north of the *Café Roches Rouges* (look for the car park and signboard at the roadside). Passing the famous **Tête de Chien**, it snakes along a ridge lined by dramatic porphyry forms to a huge square chunk of granite resembling a ruined castle. Just before reaching it there's an open platform from where the views of the gulf and Paglia Orba, Corsica's third highest mountain, are superb – one of the best sunset spots on the island – but bring a torch to help find the path back.

For a more challenging extension to the above walk, begin instead at the **Roches Rouges café**. On the opposite side of the road, two paths strike up the hill: follow the one on your left nearest the stream (as you face away from the café), which zigzags steeply up the rocks, over a pass and down the other side to rejoin the D81 in around 1hr 15min. A hundred and fifty metres west of the spot where you meet the road is the trailhead for the Château Fort walk, with more superb views.

A small Oratory niche in the cliff by the roadside, 500m south of *Café Roches Rouges*, contains a Madonna statue, Santa Maria, from where the wonderful **sentier muletier** (1hr) climbs into the rocks above. Before the road was blasted through the Calanches in 1850, this old paved path, an extraordinary feat of workmanship supported in places by dry-stone banks and walls, formed the main artery between the villages of Piana and Ota. After a very steep start, the route contours through the rocks and pine woods above the restored mill at Pont de Gavallaghiu, emerging after one hour back on the D81, roughly 1.5km south of the starting point. Return by the same path.

If you want to **stay**, head straight for the *Les Roches Rouges* (Ⓣ04.95.27.81.81, Ⓦwww.lesrochesrouges.com; April–Oct; ❺), an elegant old *grand hôtel* rising from the eucalyptus canopy on the outskirts. Having lain empty for two decades, the turn-of-the-century building was restored with most of its original fittings and furniture intact, and possesses loads of *fin-de-siècle* style. The rooms are huge and light, with large shuttered windows, but make sure you get one facing the water. Non-residents are welcome to drop in for a sundowner on the magnificent terrace, or for a meal in the fresco-covered restaurant, whose *menus gastronomiques* (€28, €32 and €64), dominated by local seafood delicacies, are as sophisticated as the ambience. A cheaper alternative is the *Continental*, an old house with high wooden ceilings, stripped wood floors and a leafy garden, on the right as you leave Piana for Porto (Ⓣ04.95.27.89.00, Ⓦwww.continentalpiana.com; ❸–❹).

The Gorges de Spelunca

Spanning the 2km between the villages of Ota and Évisa, a few kilometres inland from Porto, the **Gorges de Spelunca** are a formidable sight, with bare orange granite walls, 1km deep in places, plunging into the foaming green torrent created by the confluence of the rivers Porto, Tavulella, Onca, Campi and Aïtone. The sunlight, ricocheting across the rock walls, creates a sinister effect that's heightened by the dark jagged needles of the encircling peaks. The most dramatic part of the gorge can be seen from the road, which hugs the edge for much of its length.

ÉVISA's bright orange roofs emerge against a lush background of chestnut forests about 10km from Ota, on the eastern edge of the gorge, and the village makes the best base for hiking in the area. Situated 830m above sea level, it caters well for hikers and makes a pleasant stop for a taste of mountain life – the air is invariably crisp and clear, and the food particularly good.

The best **place to stay** is the rambling *La Châtaigneraie*, on the west edge of the village on the Porto road (Ⓣ04.95.26.24.47, Ⓦwww.hotel-la-chataigneraie.com; April–Oct; ❷–❸). Set amid chestnut trees, this traditional schist and granite building has a dozen smart, cosy rooms (with and without toilets) in an annexe around the back of the main building. On the front side, a pleasant little restaurant serves mountain cooking such as wild boar stew with *pulenta* made from local chestnuts. The young *patronne* is American, so English is spoken. At the other end of the village, *L'Aïtone* (Ⓣ04.95.26.20.04, Ⓦwww.hotel-aitone.com; ❷–❻) is a large country hotel with a wide range of differently priced rooms, a swimming pool and relaxing bar-restaurant that enjoys a reputation both for gastronomic prowess and for its fine views. For **campers**, the *Camping Acciola* (Ⓣ04.95.26.23.01), a small site with a café-bar and great views of the mountains, lies roughly 3km out of Evisa: take the D84 for 2km, and turn right at the T-junction towards Cristinacce; the site lies another 400m on your left.

Forêt d'Aïtone

Thousands of soaring Laricio pines, some of them as much as 50m tall, make up the **Forêt d'Aïtone**, just a few kilometres east of Évisa. The most beautiful forest in Corsica, it extends over ten square kilometres between Évisa and the Col de Verghio (1477m), the highest point in Corsica traversable by road. Well-worn tourist paths cross the forest at various points, but local wildlife still thrives here.

Some of the oldest pines in the forest are approaching five hundred years old. Fine-grained, strong and very resistant to weathering, the Laricio was highly valued by the Genoese for ships' masts and furniture, and it was they who first built a road down the valley to the coast, later upgraded by the French using convict labour. Throughout the nineteenth century, forests all over Corsica were regularly decimated, as the island has the very best specimens of this species, which only grows in forests higher than 1000m. When the British artist and poet Edward Lear came here in the 1860s, he noted with regret "the ravages of [the] hatchets: here and there on the hillside are pale patches of cleared ground, with piles of cut and barked pines ... everywhere giant trees lie prostrate".

One of the most popular short **walks** goes to the **Belvédère**, a great natural balcony giving magnificent views across the copper-tinted rocks of the Spelunca gorge. To reach it, look for the wide lay-by on the left-hand side of the road, 5km northeast of Evisa. A signpost pointing left indicates the well-trodden route through the forest. Following the unsurfaced forest track that peels left a little further up the main road, you can also drop down to the **piscine naturelle d'Aïtone**, one of the more accessible bathing spots in the forest, where the river crashes through a series of idyllic pools and falls.

Cargèse (Carghjese)

Sitting high above a deep blue bay on a cliff scattered with olive trees, **CARGÈSE**, 20km southwest of Porto, exudes a lazy charm that attracts hundreds of well-heeled summer residents to its pretty white houses and hotels. The full-time locals, half of whom are descendants of Greek refugees who fled the Turkish occupation of the Peloponnese in the seventeenth century, seem to accept with nonchalance this inundation – and the proximity of a large Club Med complex – but the best times to visit are May and late September, when Cargèse is all but empty.

Two churches stand on separate hummocks at the heart of the village, a reminder of the old antagonism between the two cultures (resentful Corsican patriots ransacked the Greeks' original settlement in 1715 because of the newcomers' refusal to take up arms against their Genoese benefactors). The **Roman Catholic church** was built for the minority Corsican families in 1828 and is one of the latest examples of Baroque with a trompe l'oeil ceiling, though this can't really compete with the view from the terrace outside. The **Greek church**, however, is the more interesting of the two: a large granite neo-Gothic edifice built in 1852 to replace a building that had become too small for its congregation. Inside, the outstanding feature is an unusual iconostasis, a gift from a monastery in Rome, decorated with uncannily modern-looking portraits. Behind it hang icons brought over from Greece with the original settlers – the graceful Virgin and Child, to the right-hand side of the altar, is thought to date as far back as the twelfth century.

The best beach in the area, **plage de Pero**, is 2km north of the village – head up to the junction with the Piana road and take the left fork down to the sea. Overlooked by a Genoese tower, this white stretch of sand has a couple of bars and easily absorbs the crowds that descend on it in August. **Plage du Chiuni**, a further 2km along the same road, is much busier thanks to its windsurfing facilities and the presence of Club Med. A more secluded spot is **plage du Monachi**, 1km south of the village; this small, sandy cove is reached by climbing down the track at the side of the road past the little chapel on the cliffside.

Practicalities

There's a **tourist office** on rue Dr-Dragacci (daily: July–Sept 9am–noon & 4–7pm; Oct–June 3–5pm; ⓣ04.95.26.41.31, ⓦwww.cargese.net), which can help find accommodation and sells tickets for summer boat trips to the Calanches, costing about €40. **Buses** for Ajaccio and Porto stop outside the tiny main square in the centre of the village.

The least expensive of the **hotels** in Cargèse is the *De France*, on rue Colonel-Fieschi (ⓣ04.95.26.41.07, ⓦwww.infocorse.com/defrance; ❷), whose rooms are a bit dark and noisy (the front rooms open on to the main road), but unbelievably cheap, even in August. Overlooking the crossroads at the top of the village, two comfortable midscale options are *Le Continental* (ⓣ04.95.26.42.24; ❺) and *St Jean* (ⓣ04.95.26.46.68, ⓦwww.lesaintjean.com; ❺). Better still, head down the lane dropping from opposite these last two places to the wonderful plage de Pero beach, where you'll find the beautifully situated *Les Lentisques* (ⓣ04.95.26.42.34, ⓦwww.leslentisques.com; ❹), a congenial, family-run three-star with a large, breezy breakfast hall and ten simple rooms (fully en suite and sea-facing). The nearest **campsite**, *Camping Torraccia* (ⓣ04.95.26.42.39), is 4km north of Cargèse on the main road.

A fair number of **restaurants** are scattered about the village, as well as the standard crop of basic pizzerias, but the most tempting places to eat are down in the harbour. On a raised deck overlooking the jetty, *Le Cabanon de Charlotte* serves local seafood in a wooden cabin, with menus at €19–32, or you can go for their fresh fish of the day.

Ajaccio (Aiacciu)

Edward Lear claimed that on a wet day it would be hard to find so dull a place as **AJACCIO**, a harsh judgement with an element of justice. The town has none of Bastia's sense of purpose and can seem to lack a definitive identity of its own, but it is a relaxed and good-looking place, with an exceptionally mild climate, and a wealth of cafés, restaurants and shops.

Although it's an attractive idea that Ajax, hero of the Trojan War, once stopped here, the name of Ajaccio actually derives from the Roman *Adjaccium* (place of rest), a winter stop-off point for shepherds descending from the mountains to stock up on goods and sell their produce. This first settlement, to the north of the present town in the area called Castelvecchio, was destroyed by the Saracens in the tenth century, and modern Ajaccio grew up around the citadelle that was founded in 1492. **Napoleon** gave the town international fame, but though the self-designated *Cité Impériale* is littered with statues and street names related to the Bonaparte family, you'll find the Napoleonic cult has a less dedicated following in his home town than you might imagine. The emperor is still considered by many Ajacciens as a self-serving Frenchman rather than as a Corsican, and his impact on the townscape of his birthplace isn't enormous.

Since the early 1980s, the town has gained an unwelcome reputation for nationalist violence. The most infamous terrorist atrocity of recent years was the murder, in February 1998, of the French government's most senior official on the island, Claude Erignac, who was gunned down as he left the opera. However, separatist violence rarely (if ever) affects tourists, and for visitors Ajaccio remains memorable for the things that have long made it attractive – its battered old town, relaxing cafés and the encompassing view of its glorious bay.

Arrival, information and accommodation

Ajaccio's Campo dell'Oro **airport** (Ⓣ04.95.23.56.56; Ⓦwww.ajaccio.aeroport.fr) is 6km south of town; shuttle buses (three per hour 6.30am–10.45pm; Ⓣ04.95.23.29.41) provide an inexpensive link with the centre, stopping on cours Napoléon, the main street – tickets cost €5 one way, and the journey takes around twenty minutes. Heading in the other direction, the best place to pick up buses to the airport is the car park adjacent to the main **bus station** (*terminal routière*), a five-minute walk north of the centre (Ⓣ04.95.51.55.45). Ferries also dock nearby, and the SNCM office is directly

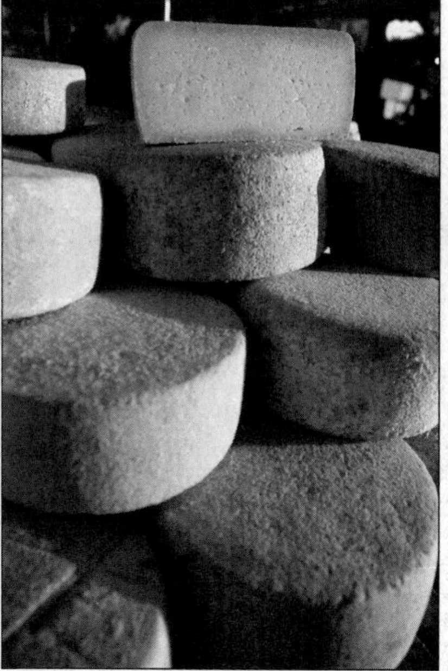

△ *Fromage corse*

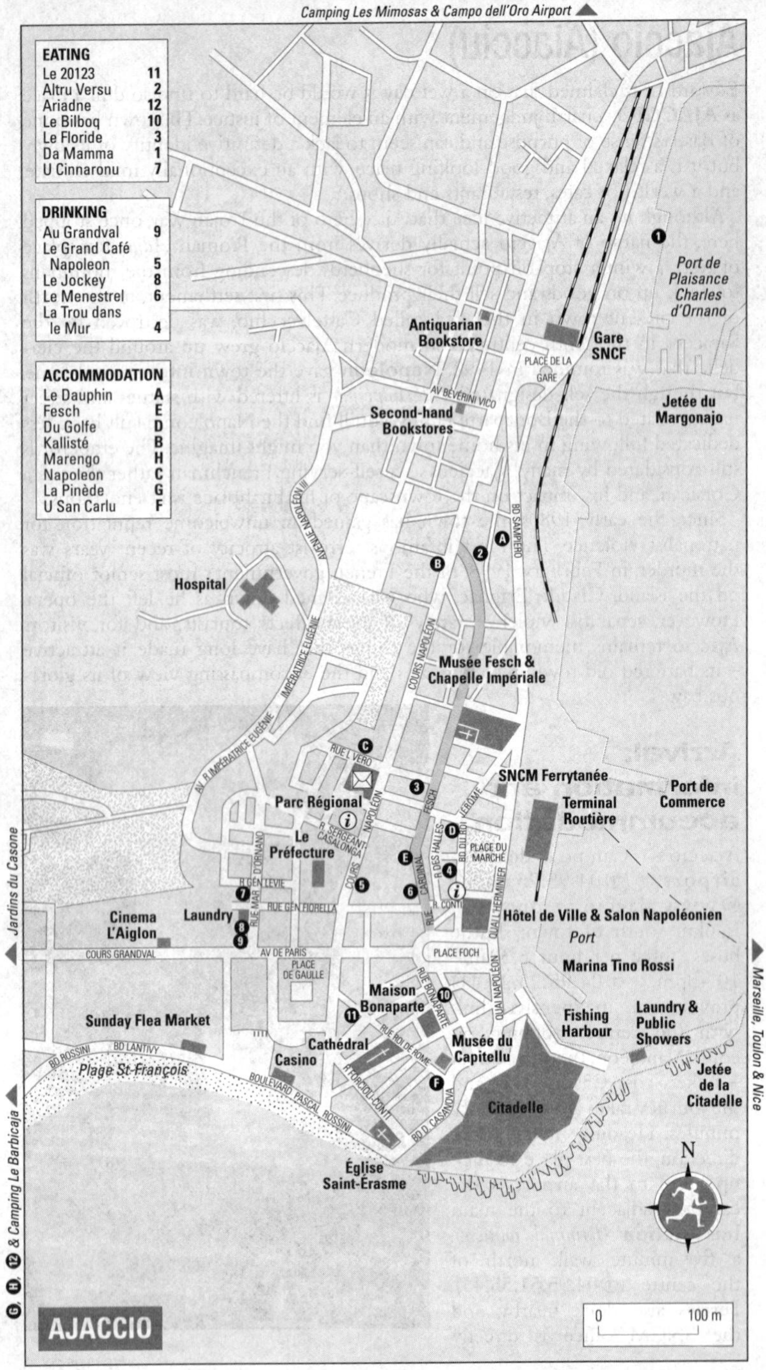

Camping Les Mimosas & Campo dell'Oro Airport

EATING

Le 20123	11
Altru Versu	2
Ariadne	12
Le Bilboq	10
Le Floride	3
Da Mamma	1
U Cinnaronu	7

DRINKING

Au Grandval	9
Le Grand Café Napoleon	5
Le Jockey	8
Le Menestrel	6
La Trou dans le Mur	4

ACCOMMODATION

Le Dauphin	A
Fesch	E
Du Golfe	D
Kallisté	B
Marengo	H
Napoleon	C
La Pinède	G
U San Carlu	F

Port de Plaisance Charles d'Ornano
Antiquarian Bookstore
Gare SNCF
Place de la Gare
Av Bévérini Vico
Jetée du Margonajo
Second-hand Bookstores
Avenue Napoléon III
Bd Sampiero
Hospital
Impératrice Eugénie
Cours Napoléon
Musée Fesch & Chapelle Impériale
Av R. Impératrice Eugénie
Rue L'Vero
SNCM Ferrytanée
Port de Commerce
Terminal Routière
Parc Régional
R. Sergeant Casalonga
Jérôme
Le Préfecture
R. des Halles
R. du Roi
Place du Marché
Cardinal Fesch
R. Gén Levie
Rue Mar d'Ornano
Quai l'Herminier
R. Conti
Rue Gén Fiorella
Cinema L'Aiglon
Laundry
Hôtel de Ville & Salon Napoléonien
Port
Cours Grandval
Av de Paris
Place Foch
Place de Gaulle
Marina Tino Rossi
Jardins du Casone
Marseille, Toulon & Nice
Maison Bonaparte
Rue Bonaparte
Quai Napoléon
Sunday Flea Market
Fishing Harbour
Laundry & Public Showers
Bd Rossini
Bd Lantivy
Cathédral
Rue Roi de Rome
Musée du Capitellu
Casino
Plage St-François
Jetée de la Citadelle
Boulevard Pascal Rossini
R. Forcioli-Conti
Bd D. Casanova
Citadelle
Église Saint-Érasme
G, H, 12 & Camping Le Barbicaja
N
0 100 m

AJACCIO

opposite at quai l'Herminier (ⓣ04.95.29.66.99). The **gare SNCF** lies almost a kilometre north along boulevard Sampiero (ⓣ04.95.23.11.03; ⓦwww.ter-sncf.com/corse), a continuation of the quai l'Herminier.

The **tourist office** on the place du Marché, behind the Hôtel de Ville (April–June & Sept Mon–Sat 8am–7pm, Sun 9am–1pm; July & Aug Mon–Sat 8am–8.30pm, Sun 9am–1pm & 4–7pm; Oct–March Mon–Fri 8.30am–6pm, Sat 8.30am–noon; ⓣ04.95.51.53.03, ⓦwww.ajaccio-tourisme.com) hands out large free glossy maps and posts transport timetables for checking departure times. Anyone planning a long-distance hike should head for the office of the national parks association, the **Parc Naturel Régional de Corse**, 2 rue Sergeant-Casalonga, around the corner from the *préfecture* on cours Napoléon (Mon–Fri 8am–noon & 2–6pm; ⓦwww.parc-naturel-corse.com; ⓣ04.95.51.79.00), where you can buy Topo-guides, maps, guidebooks and leaflets. Cars can be rented from: Rent-a-Car, at the *Hôtel Kallisté*, 51 cours Napoléon (ⓣ04.95.51.34.45), and the airport (ⓣ04.95.23.56.36); Avis-Ollandini, 1 rue Colonna d'Istria (ⓣ04.95.23.92.50) and the airport (ⓣ04.95.21.28.01); and Hertz-Locasud, 8 cours Grandval (ⓣ04.95.21.70.94) and the airport (ⓣ04.95.23.57.04). **Internet access** is free in the lobby of the *Hotel Kallisté* on cours Napoléon.

Ajaccio suffers from a dearth of inexpensive **accommodation**, but there are a fair number of mid- and upscale places. Whatever your budget, it's essential to **book ahead**, especially for weekends between late May and September, when beds are virtually impossible to come by at short notice.

Hotels

Le Dauphin 11 bd Sampiero ⓣ04.95.21.12.94, ⓦwww.ledauphinhotel.com. No-frills place above a bar, opposite the port de Commerce. Some rooms are on the grotty side for the price, but their budget options in an adjacent building (with shared showers and toilets) are among the cheapest beds in town. Includes breakfast. ❹

Fesch 7 rue Cardinal-Fesch ⓣ04.95.51.62.62, ⓦwww.hotel-fesch.com. One of the oldest-established hotels in Ajaccio, and famous as the site of a (bloodless) armed siege in 1980, when it was occupied by fugitive nationalist guerrillas and their French secret service hostages. Following a recent refit, all rooms are bright and modern with a/c and TVs; balconies cost extra. ❹–❺

Du Golfe 5 bd du Roi-Jérôme ⓣ04.95.21.47.64, ⓦwww.hoteldugolfe.com. Large, well-appointed three-star whose slightly pricier (soundproofed) front rooms overlook the market square and bay. Reasonable value given the location, and handy for ferry port, bus and train stations. ❺

Kallisté 51 cours Napoléon ⓣ04.95.51.34.45, ⓦwww.hotel-kalliste-ajaccio.com. Revamped three-storey hotel right in the centre, with plenty of parking space. Soundproofed rooms for up to four people, all with cable TVs and bathrooms. Internet facilities in lobby, and the staff speak English. The best choice in this category. ❹

Marengo 12 bd Mme-Mère ⓣ04.95.21.43.66, ⓦwww.hotel-marengo.com. A ten-minute walk west of the centre, up a quiet side street off bd Mme-Mère. Slightly boxed in by tower blocks, but it's a secluded, quiet and pleasant small hotel (with only 16 rooms) away from the city bustle. Open mid-March to mid-Nov. ❹

Napoleon 4 rue Lorenzo-Vero ⓣ04.95.51.54.00, ⓦwww.hotelnapoleonajaccio.com. Dependable mid-scale hotel slap in the centre of town, up a side road off cours Napoléon, in a recently revamped Second Empire style. Comfortable, very welcoming and good value for the location. ❺

La Pinède rte des Sanguinaires ⓣ04.95.52.00.44, ⓦwww.la-pinede.com. Most secluded and peaceful of the swish hotels, 4km west of the town centre. It's 300m from the beach (up a narrow lane signposted right off the main road as you head out of town), but with great views of the gulf, a large pool and tennis court. ❼–❽

U San Carlu 8 bd Danielle-Casanova ⓣ04.95.21.13.84, ⓦwww.hotel-sancarlu.com Sited opposite the citadelle and close to the beach, this three-star hotel is the poshest option in the old town. Well-appointed rooms, private parking facilities, and a special room for disabled guests in the basement. ❻

Napoleon and Corsica

Napoleon Bonaparte was born in Ajaccio in 1769, a year after the French took over the island from the Genoese. They made a thorough job of it, crushing the Corsican leader Paoli's troops at Ponte Nuovo and driving him into exile. Napoleon's father Carlo, a close associate of Paoli, fled the scene of the battle with his pregnant wife in order to escape the victorious French army. But Carlo's subsequent behaviour was quite different from that of his former leader – he came to terms with the French, becoming a representative of the newly styled Corsican nobility in the National Assembly, and using his contacts with the French governor to get a free education for his children.

At the age of nine, Napoleon was awarded a scholarship to the **Brienne military academy**, an institution specially founded to teach the sons of the French nobility the responsibilities of their status, and the young son of a Corsican Italian-speaking household used his time well, leaving Brienne to enter the exclusive **École Militaire** in Paris. At the age of sixteen he was commissioned into the artillery. When he was twenty the Revolution broke out in Paris and the scene was set for a remarkable career.

Always an ambitious opportunist, he obtained leave from his regiment, returned to Ajaccio, joined the local Jacobin club and – with his eye on a colonelship in the Corsican militia – promoted enthusiastically the interests of the Revolution. However, things did not quite work out as he had planned, for Pascal Paoli had also returned to Corsica.

Carlo Bonaparte had died some years before, and Napoleon was head of a family that had formerly given Paoli strong support. Having spent the last twenty years in London, **Paoli** was pro-English and had developed a profound distaste for revolutionary excesses. Napoleon's French allegiance and his Jacobin views antagonized the older man, and his military conduct didn't enhance his standing at all. Elected second-in-command of the volunteer militia, Napoleon was involved in an unsuccessful attempt to wrest control of the citadelle from royalist sympathizers. He thus took much of the blame when, in reprisal for the killing of one of the militiamen, several people were gunned down in Ajaccio, an incident which engendered eight days of civil war. In June 1793, Napoleon and his family were chased back to the mainland by the Paolists.

Napoleon promptly renounced any special allegiance he had ever felt for Corsica. He Gallicized the spelling of his name, preferring Napoléon to his baptismal Napoleone. And, although he was later to speak with nostalgia about the scents of the Corsican countryside, he put the city of his birth fourth on the list of places he would like to be buried.

Campsites

Le Barbicaja 4.5km west along the rte des Sanguinaires ⓣ04.95.52.01.17. Crowded site, but close to the beach and easier to reach by bus (#5 from place de Gaulle) than *Les Mimosas*. Open April–Oct.

Les Mimosas 3km northwest of town ⓣ04.95.20.99.85, ⓕ04.95.10.01.77. A shady and well-organized site with clean toilet blocks, friendly management and fair rates. It's a long trudge if you're loaded with luggage so take a taxi (around €15). Open May–Oct.

The Town

The core of the **old town** holds the most interest in Ajaccio: a cluster of ancient streets spreading north and south of **place Foch**, which opens out to the seafront by the port and the marina. Nearby, to the west, **place de Gaulle** forms the town centre and is the source of the main thoroughfare, **cours Napoléon**, which extends parallel to the sea almost 2km to the northeast. West of place de Gaulle stretches the modern part of town fronted by the **beach**, overlooked at its eastern end by the citadelle.

If you're intending to work your way around all of the town's museums and galleries, it's worth investing in a **Passemusée**. Costing €10, the pass covers all the museums (except A Bandera) and is valid for seven days from the time of your first visit; you can buy them at the tourist office and at the admission desks of the museums themselves.

Around place de Gaulle and the new town

Place de Gaulle (otherwise known as place du Diamant, after the Diamanti family who once owned much of the property in Ajaccio) is the most useful point of orientation, even if it's not much to look at – just a windy concrete platform surrounded by a shopping complex. The only noteworthy thing on the square is the huge, bronze equestrian statue, a pompous lump commissioned by Napoléon III in 1865 showing the first Napoleon in Roman attire, surrounded by his four brothers.

Devotees of Napoleon should take a stroll 1km up **cours Grandval**, the wide street rising west of place de Gaulle and ending in a square, the **Jardins du Casone**, where gaudily spectacular son et lumière shows and costumed re-enactments take place throughout the tourist season. An impressive monument to Napoleon dominates the square, standing atop an appropriately huge, proto-Fascist pedestal inscribed with the names of his battles. Behind the monument lies a graffiti-bedaubed cave where Napoleon is supposed to have frolicked as a child.

Place Foch

Once the site of the town's medieval gate, **place Foch** lies at the heart of old Ajaccio. A delightfully shady square sloping down to the sea and lined with cafés and restaurants, it gets its local name – place des Palmiers – from the row of palms bordering the central strip. Dominating the top end, a fountain of four marble lions provides a mount for the inevitable statue of Napoleon, this one by Ajaccien sculptor Maglioli. A humbler effigy occupies a niche high on the nearest wall – a figurine of Ajaccio's patron saint, **La Madonnuccia**, dating from 1656, a year in which Ajaccio's local council, fearful of infection from plague-struck Genoa, placed the town under the guardianship of the Madonna in a ceremony conducted on this spot.

At the northern end of place Foch is the **Hôtel de Ville** of 1826, with its prison-like wooden doors. The first-floor **Salon Napoléonien** (mid-June to mid-Sept Mon–Sat 9–11.45am & 2–5.45pm; mid-Sept to mid-June Mon–Fri 9–11.45am & 2–4.45pm; €2.80) contains a replica of the ex-emperor's death mask in pride of place, along with a solemn array of Bonaparte family portraits and busts. A smaller medal room has a fragment from Napoleon's coffin and part of his dressing case, plus a model of the ship that brought his body back from St Helena, and a picture of the house where he died.

South of place Foch

The south side of place Foch, standing on the former dividing line between the poor district around the port and the bourgeoisie's territory, gives access to **rue Bonaparte**, the main route through the latter quarter. Built on the promontory rising to the citadelle, the secluded streets in this part of town – with their dusty buildings and hole-in-the-wall restaurants lit by flashes of sea or sky at the end of the alleys – retain more of a sense of the old Ajaccio than anywhere else.

Napoleon was born in what's now the colossal **Maison Bonaparte**, on place Letizia (May–Sept Mon 2–6pm, Tues–Fri 9am–noon & 2–6pm, Sat 9–11.45am & 2–6pm, Sun 9am–noon; Oct–April Mon 2–6pm, Tues–Sat 10am–noon & 2–5pm, Sun 10am–noon; €4), off the west side of rue Napoléon. The house passed to Napoleon's father in the 1760s and here he lived, with his wife and family, until his death. But in May 1793, the Bonapartes were driven from the house by Paoli's partisans, who stripped the place down to the floorboards. Requisitioned by the English in 1794, Maison Bonaparte became an arsenal and a lodging house for English officers until Napoleon's mother Letizia herself funded its restoration. Owned by the state since 1923, the house now bears few traces of the Bonaparte family's existence.

One of the few original pieces of furniture left in the house is the wooden sedan chair in the hallway – the pregnant Letizia was carried back from church in it when her contractions started. Upstairs, there's an endless display of portraits, miniatures, weapons, letters and documents. Amongst the highlights of the first room are a few maps of Corsica dating from the eighteenth century, some deadly "vendetta" daggers and two handsome pairs of pistols belonging to Napoleon's father. The next-door Alcove Room was, according to tradition, occupied by Napoleon in 1799 when he stayed here for the last time, while in the third room you can see the sofa upon which the future emperor first saw the light of day on August 15, 1769. Adjoining the heavily restored long gallery is a tiny room known as the Trapdoor Room, whence Letizia and her children made their getaway from the marauding Paolists.

Napoleon was baptized in 1771 in the **cathedral** (Mon–Sat 8am–1.30pm & 2.30–6pm; no tourist visits on Sun), around the corner in rue Forcioli-Conti. Modelled on St Peter's in Rome, it was built in 1587–93 on a much smaller scale than intended, owing to lack of funds – an apology for its diminutive size is inscribed in a plaque inside, on the wall to the left as you enter. Inside, to the right of the door, stands the font where he was dipped at the age of 23 months; his sister, Elisa Baciochi, donated the great marble altar in 1811. Before you go, take a look in the chapel to the left of the altar, which houses a gloomy Delacroix painting of the Virgin.

A left turn at the eastern end of rue Forcioli-Conti brings you onto boulevard Danielle-Casanova. Here, opposite the citadelle, an elaborately carved capital marks the entrance to the **Musée du Capitellu** (May–Oct Mon–Sat 10am–noon & 2–6pm, Sun 10am to noon; €4), a tiny museum mainly given over to offering a picture of domestic life in nineteenth-century Ajaccio. The house belonged to a wealthy Ajaccien family, the Baciochi, who were related to Napoleon through his sister's marriage. Amid the watercolour landscapes and marble busts, the glass display cases hold the most fascinating exhibits, including a rare edition of the first history of Corsica, written by Agostino Giustiniani, a bishop of the Nebbio who drowned in 1536, and the 1769 Code Corse, a list of laws set out by Louis XV for the newly acquired Corsica.

Opposite the museum, the restored **citadelle**, a hexagonal fortress and tower stuck out on a wide promontory into the sea, is occupied by the military and usually closed to the public. Founded in the 1490s, the fort wasn't completed until the occupation of Ajaccio by Sampiero Corso and the powerful Marshal Thermes in 1553–58. The building overlooks the town **beach**, plage St-François, a short curve of yellow sand which faces the expansive mountain-ringed bay. Several flights of steps lead down to the beach from boulevard Danielle-Casanova.

A little further along the promenade, the car park in front of the municipal sports centre hosts a weekly **flea market** each Sunday morning, starting at around 9am. For the nicest beach within easy walking distance of the town, press on past the exercise area and gendarmerie to **plage Trottel**, which is larger and much cleaner than plage St-François.

North of place Foch

The dark narrow streets backing onto the port to the north of place Foch are Ajaccio's traditional trading ground. Each weekday and Saturday morning (and on Sundays during the summer), the square directly behind the Hôtel de Ville hosts a small **fresh produce market** – a rarity in Corsica – where you can browse and buy top-quality fresh produce from around the island, including myrtle liqueur, wild-boar sauces, ewe's cheese from the Niolo valley and a spread of fresh vegetables, fruit and flowers.

Behind here, the principal road leading north is **rue Cardinal-Fesch**, a delightful meandering street lined with boutiques, cafés and restaurants. Halfway along the street, set back from the road behind iron gates, stands Ajaccio's best gallery, the **Musée Fesch** (July & Aug Mon 1.30–6pm, Tues–Thurs 9am–6.30pm, Fri & Sat 10.30am–12.15pm, Sun 10.30am–6pm; Sept–June Mon 1–5.15pm, Tues–Sun 9.15am–12.15pm & 2.15–5.15pm; €5.30). Cardinal Joseph Fesch was Napoleon's step-uncle and bishop of Lyon, and he used his lucrative position to invest in large numbers of paintings, many of them looted by the French armies in Holland, Italy and Germany. His bequest to the town includes seventeenth-century French and Spanish masters, but it's the Italian paintings that are the chief attraction: Raphael, Titian, Bellini, Veronese and Botticelli all have a place here.

You'll need a separate ticket for the **Chapelle Impériale** (same hours; €1.50), which stands across the courtyard from the museum. With its gloomy monochrome interior the chapel itself is unremarkable, and its interest lies in the crypt, where various members of the Bonaparte family are buried. It was the cardinal's dying wish that all the Bonaparte family be brought together under one roof, so the chapel was built in 1857 and the bodies – all except Napoleon's – subsequently ferried in.

Eating, drinking and nightlife

At mealtimes, the alleyways and little squares of Ajaccio's old town become one large, interconnecting **restaurant** terrace lit by rows of candles. All too often, however, the breezy locations and views of the gulf mask indifferent cooking and inflated prices. With the majority of visitors spending merely a night or two here in transit, only those places catering for a local clientele attempt to provide real value for money. **Bars** and **cafés** jostle for pavement space along cours Napoléon, generally lined with people checking out the promenaders, and on place de Gaulle, where old-fashioned cafés and *salons de thé* offer a still more sedate scene. If you fancy a view of the bay, try one of the flashy cocktail bars that line the seafront on boulevard Lantivy, which, along with the casino, a few cinemas and a handful of overpriced clubs, comprise the sum total of Ajaccio's **nightlife**.

Bars and cafés

Le Grand Café Napoleon 10 cours Napoléon, opposite the *préfecture*. Allegedly the oldest café in town, with Second Empire decor and a *troisième âge* clientele. The bar inside was the scene of a famous shootout during World War II, when a cell of key Resistance members was disturbed by the Italian *caribinieri* and forced to flee, guns blazing. The €16 lunch menu ranks among the best midday meal deals in town.

Au Grandval 4 rue Maréchal-Ornano. Lively neighbourhood bar that's famous for its collection of antique photos of Ajaccio (mostly evocative portraits). Only a couple of doors down from *Le*

Jockey, which stays open later.

Le Jockey 1 rue Maréchal-Ornano. An Ajaccien institution, renowned above all for its extraordinary list of wines, which you can order by the glass or bottle: Saint Amar, Cantemerle, Morgon, Sancerre, Chasse-Spleen, Châteauneuf du Pâpe and all the local stars. The decor's a quirky but cosy hotch-potch of ephemera and old memorabilia, with a soundtrack to match.

Le Menestrel 5 rue Cardinal-Fesch. Dubbed "*le rendez-vous des artistes*" because local musicians play here most evenings after 7pm; café jazz, traditional mandolin and guitar tunes, with the odd chanson singalong number. Popular with bus parties of pensioners.

Le Trou dans le Mur square César-Campinchi. During the hot summer months this workaday café monopolizes the shade along the side of the market place, and serves as a popular chill-out spot for bleary-eyed clubbers on Sunday mornings.

Restaurants

Le 20123 2 rue Roi-de-Rome ⓣ04.95.21.50.05. Decked out like a small hill village, complete with *fontaine* and parked Vespa, the decor here's a lot more frivolous than the food: serious Corsican gastronomy featured on a single €29 menu. Top-notch cooking, and organic AOC wine. Closed Mon, except in July & Aug.

Altru Versu 2 rue Jean-Baptiste Marcaggi ⓣ04.95.50.05.22. Classy Corsican speciality place hosted by one of the island's top young chefs. The menu's a mouthwatering array of traditional fare given a gourmet twist: seabass soufflé with *brocciu* and fresh mint, clams in flaky pastry and Muscat sauce, chestnut tagliatelle. À la carte only (count on €40–45 per head, plus wine). Live Corsican music on Fri & Sat. Closed Sun.

Ariadne rte des Sanguinaires, near *Barbicaja* campsite ⓣ04.95.52.09.63. The oldest and most cheerful of Ajaccio's many beachside *paillotes*, with a terrace opening straight on to the sand. World cuisine dominates the menu and there's usually live music (salsa/reggae/soukous) from 8.30pm. Most main courses €15–20. Open Easter–Oct Tues–Sun. You can get there from place de Gaulle on bus #5.

Le Bilboq ("Chez Jean-Jean") av des Glacis, just off place Foch ⓣ04.95.51.35.40. The eponymous *patron* (a former fisherman and boxer) of this legendary seafood joint is Ajaccio's undisputed "lobster king", and there's no point in coming here to eat anything but local *langouste*, served grilled with spaghetti. You can dine al fresco on a narrow alley terrace, or inside, regaled by Tino Rossi music (which, unlike the lobster, is definitely an acquired taste). Count on €30 per head for three courses, plus wine.

Da Mamma passage Guinghetta ⓣ04.95.21.39.44. Tucked away down a narrow passageway connecting cours Napoléon and rue Cardinal-Fesch. Authentic but affordable Corsican cuisine – such as *cannelloni al brocciu*, roast kid and seafood – on set menus from €17 to €29.50, served either in a stone-walled dining room or under a rubber tree in a tiny courtyard.

Le Floride port de Plaisance Charles-d'Ornano ⓣ04.95.22.67.48. Sublime local seafood, stylishly prepared and served in an airy dining hall overlooking the marina. Weekday lunchtimes are dominated by business clients, but the suits and mobile phones peter out in the evenings. If your budget can stretch to it, go for their €39 *menu poisson frais*. Closed Sat & Sun lunchtimes.

U Cinnaronu rue Maréchal-Ornano ⓣ04.95.21.49.37. Small backstreet restaurant that's a Mecca for charcuterie enthusiasts across the island. You won't eat better *figatellu*, *lonzu* or *coppa* anywhere, and they also do pizzas and succulent *grillades*. Closed Sun.

Le Golfe de Valinco

From Ajaccio, the vista of whitewashed villas and sandy beaches lining the opposite side of the gulf may tempt you out of town when you first arrive. On closer inspection, however, **Porticcio** turns out to be a faceless string of leisure settlements for Ajaccio's smart set, complete with tennis courts, malls and flotillas of jet-skis. Better to skip this stretch and press on south along the Route Nationale (RN194) which, after scaling the **Col de Celaccia**, winds down to the stunning **Golfe de Valinco**. A vast blue inlet bounded by rolling, scrub-covered hills, the gulf presents the first dramatic scenery along the coastal highway. It also marks the start of militant and Mafia-ridden south Corsica, more closely associated with vendetta, banditry and separatism than any other part of the island. Many of the mountain villages glimpsed from the roads hereabouts are riven with age-old divisions, exacerbated in recent years by the spread of organized crime and nationalist violence. But the island's seamier side is rarely discernible to the hundreds of thousands of visitors who pass through each summer, most of whom stay around the small port of **Propriano**, at the eastern end of the gulf. In addition to offering most of the area's tourist amenities, this busy resort town lies within easy reach of the menhirs at **Filitosa**, one of the western Mediterranean's most important prehistoric sites, and the secluded fishing village of **Campomoro**, on the opposite shore of the gulf, from where you can strike out south on foot to explore one of Corsica's wildest stretches of coast.

The Golfe de Valinco region is reasonably well served by public **transport**, with buses running four times per day between Ajaccio and Bonifacio, via Propriano and Sartène. Note, however, that outside July and August there are no services along this route on Sundays.

Propriano (Pruprià)

Tucked into the narrowest part of the Golfe de Valinco, the small port of **PROPRIANO**, 57km southeast of Ajaccio, centres on a fine natural harbour that was exploited by the ancient Greeks, Carthaginians and Romans, but became a prime target for Saracen pirate raids in the eighteenth century, when it was largely destroyed. Redeveloped in the 1900s, it now boasts a thriving marina, and handles ferries to Toulon, Marseille and Sardinia. The town around the port has also grown in importance, largely under the direction of a powerful coalition of nationalist-backed politicians and shady Mafia figures, which has held at bay the kind of power struggles that have undermined other resorts of comparable size.

Propriano's underworld connections, however, in no way deter the tourists, who come here in droves for the area's **beaches**. The nearest of these, **plage de Lido**, lies 1km west, just beyond the Port de Commerce; it's patrolled by lifeguards during the summer and is much safer and more appealing than the grubby **plage de Baracci**, 1km north of town, where the undertow is precariously strong. Just 3km beyond the Baracci beach, the D157 branches off to the left and continues along the coast, which is built up with hotels and package-tour holiday blocks until **Olmeto plage**, 10km west, where an abundance of campsites are on offer (see below). You can reach Olmeto on the three daily buses from Propriano to Porto.

Practicalities

Ferries from the mainland and Sardinia dock in the Port de Commerce, ten minutes' walk from where the **buses** stop at the top of rue du Général-de-Gaulle, the town's main street. The SNCM office is on quai Commandant-L'Herminier (ⓣ04.95.76.04.36), while the **tourist office** is down in the harbour master's office in the marina (June & Sept Mon–Sat 9am–noon & 3–7pm; July & Aug daily 8am–8pm; Oct–May Mon–Fri 9am–noon & 2–6pm; ⓣ04.95.76.01.49, ⓦwww.propriano.net).

There's a reasonable choice of **hotels** in the centre of town, including the high-tech *Loft*, 3 rue Camille-Pietri (ⓣ04.95.76.17.48, ⓕ04.95.76.22.04; ❸), directly behind the port; and the *Bellevue* on avenue Napoléon (ⓣ04.95.76.01.86, ⓕ04.95.76.38.94; ❹), overlooking the marina and with the cheapest central rooms. If you have a car, one other place worth trying is the *Arcu di Sole*, 3km northeast on the route de Baracci (ⓣ04.95.76.05.10, ⓦwww.arcudisole.fr.st; ❹), which has a pool and gourmet restaurant.

Campers are well provided for, although the best sites are well out of town: for the best facilities go to *Camping Colomba* (Ⓣ04.95.76.06.42, Ⓦwww.camping-colomba.com), 3km north along route de Baracci, which has a swimming pool.

Cafés and **restaurants** are concentrated along the marina's avenue Napoléon. For fresh seafood, though, you can't beat *L'Hippocampe* (Ⓣ04.95.76.11.01), tucked away behind the port on rue Pandolphi, where the good-value €18.50 and €32 menus are served indoors or on a flower-filled pavement terrace. On the opposite side of town, behind the marina, *Le Tout Va Bien* (Ⓣ04.95.76.12.14) is Propriano's classiest seafood restaurant, offering *haute gastronomie* on a terrace jutting over the marina. It's far from cheap, but they do offer affordable *formules* (€21–28) at lunchtime; otherwise, count on €55–65 à la carte, plus wine.

Filitosa

Set deep in the countryside of the fertile Vallée du Taravo, the extraordinary **Station Préhistorique de Filitosa** (Easter–Oct 9am–sunset, out of season by arrangement only; Ⓣ04.95.74.00.91; €5), 17km north of Propriano, comprises a wonderful array of statue-menhirs and prehistoric structures encapsulating some eight thousand years of history. Vehicles can be left in the small car park in the hamlet of Filitosa, where you pay the entrance fee; from here it's a five-minute walk to the entrance, where you'll find a café, a small museum and a workshop producing reproduction prehistoric ceramics. There's no public transport to the site.

Filitosa was settled by Neolithic farming people who lived here in rock shelters until the arrival of navigators from the east in about 3500 BC. These invaders were the creators of the menhirs, the earliest of which were possibly phallic symbols worshipped by an ancient fertility cult. When the seafaring people known as the Torréens (after the towers they built on Corsica) conquered Filitosa around 1300 BC, they destroyed most of the menhirs, incorporating the broken stones into the area of dry-stone walling surrounding the site's two *torri*, or towers, examples of which can be found all over the south of Corsica. The site remained undiscovered until a farmer stumbled across the ruins on his land in the late 1940s.

Filitosa V looms up on the right shortly after the main entrance to the site. The largest statue-menhir on the island, it's an imposing sight, with clearly defined facial features and a sword and dagger outlined on the body. Beyond a sharp left turn lies the *oppidum* or central monument, its entrance marked by the **eastern platform**, thought to have been a lookout post. The cave-like structure sculpted out of the rock is the only evidence of Neolithic occupation and is generally agreed to have been a burial mound. Straight ahead, the Torréen **central monument** comprises a scattered group of menhirs on a circular walled mound, surmounted by a dome and entered by a corridor of stone slabs and lintels. Nobody is sure of its exact function.

Nearby **Filitosa XIII** and **Filitosa IX**, implacable lumps of granite with long noses and round chins, are the most impressive of the menhirs. Filitosa XIII is typical of the figures made just before the Torréen invasion, with its vertical dagger carved in relief – **Filitosa VII** also has a clearly sculpted sword and shield. **Filitosa VI**, from the same period, is remarkable for its facial detail. On the eastern side of the central monument stand some vestigial Torréen houses, where fragments of ceramics dating from 5500 BC were discovered; they represent the most ancient finds on the site, and some of them are displayed in the museum.

The **western monument**, a two-roomed structure built underneath another walled mound, is thought to have been some form of Torréen religious building. A flight of steps leads to the foot of this mound, where a footbridge opens onto a meadow that's dominated by five statue-menhirs arranged in a semicircle beneath a thousand-year-old olive tree. A bank separates them from the quarry from which the megalithic sculptors hewed the stone for the menhirs – a granite block is marked ready for cutting.

The **museum** is a downbeat affair, but the artefacts themselves are fascinating. The major item here is the formidable **Scalsa Murta**, a huge menhir dating from around 1400 BC and discovered at Olmeto. Like other statue-menhirs of this period, this one has two indents in the back of its head, which are thought to indicate that these figures would have been adorned with headdresses. Other notable exhibits are **Filitosa XII**, which has a hand and a foot carved into the stone, and **Trappa II**, a strikingly archaic face.

At the time of writing, work was nearing completion on a digital sound and light show, scheduled to open for business in 2007. Details of ticket prices and timings will be available from the tourist office in Propriano (see p.1243); or telephone the site direct on ⓣ04.95.74.00.91.

Campomoro

Isolated at the mouth of the Golfe de Valinco, **CAMPOMORO**, 17km southwest of Propriano, ranks among the most congenial seaside villages on the island. The main attraction here is a two-kilometre-long **beach**, overlooked by an immense and well-preserved Genoese watchtower. In late July and August, it's swamped by Italian families from the adjacent campsites, but for the rest of the year Campomoro remains a tranquil enough place, with barely enough permanent residents to support a post office.

Another incentive to venture out here is the wild and windswept stretch of coast south of Campomoro, which is punctuated by outlandish rock formations and a string of empty pebble beaches. The absence of a road into the area, recently designated a **regional nature reserve**, means the only way to explore it is by boat or on foot, via the waymarked coastal path that begins below Campomoro's watchtower. From here, the path is easy to follow for the first eighty minutes or so as it threads through a series of dramatic granite outcrops, eroded into phantasmagorical shapes. However, once you hit the **anse d'Eccia**, a sandy bottle-necked cove, the going gets tougher. Determined, well-equipped hikers can walk all the way to **Tizzano**, 20km down the coast, via the much-photographed Senetosa Tower, but to do so it's essential to take along a detailed map, plenty of fresh water and camping equipment in case you get lost. For additional route advice, contact the owner of Big Blue boat trips at his caravan near the tourist office in Propriano (ⓣ04.95.76.35.27, ⓦwww.propriano.net/bigblue). He takes customers to anse d'Eccia by catamaran, and provides photographs to help you follow the trail back to Campomoro; the cost of this half-day trip is around €25.

Practicalities

There are no bus services to Campomoro, but hitching is fairly reliable once you've turned off the main Propriano–Bonifacio road. The village possesses a couple of campsites and two **hotels**: *Le Ressac*, about 100m behind the chapel (ⓣ04.95.74.22.25; April–Oct; ❺–❼), a friendly family-run place with excellent views across the bay, is generally a better option than the more expensive, more formal *Le Campomoro*, overlooking the beach at the tower end of the village (Ⓣ04.95.74.20.89, Ⓕ04.95.74.20.89; ⑤). Of the two **campsites**, *Camping Peretto Les Roseaux*, 300m from the post office towards the tower (Ⓣ04.95.74.20.52; May–Oct), is the more peaceful. For **food**, try the popular *La Mouette* café opposite the church (Ⓣ04.95.74.22.26), which serves a selection of filling salads for around €10 on its beachside terrace. More sophisticated Corsican cooking is served at *Le Ressac*'s restaurant, which offers Corsican standards such as *cannelloni al brocciu*, squid, and lamb stew on a good-value €19 menu;. they also do pizzas (€7–9.50).

Sartène (Sartè) and around

Prosper Mérimée famously dubbed **SARTÈNE** "*la plus corse des villes corses*" (the most Corsican of Corsican towns), but the nineteenth-century German chronicler Gregorovius put a less complimentary spin on it when he described it as a "town peopled by demons". Sartène hasn't shaken off its hostile image, due in large part to a heavy presence of wealthy-looking godfather types. On the other hand it's a smart, clean place, noticeably better groomed than many small Corsican towns, its principal income coming from Sartène wine, the best on the island. The main square doesn't offer many diversions once you've explored the enclosed old town and prehistory museum, and the only time of year Sartène teems with tourists is at Easter for **U Catenacciu**, a Good Friday procession that packs the main square with onlookers.

Close to Sartène are some of the island's best-known **prehistoric sites**, most notably Filitosa, the megaliths of **Cauria** and the **Alignement de Palaggiu** – Corsica's largest array of prehistoric standing stones.

The Town

Place Porta – its official name, place de la Libération, has never caught on – forms Sartène's nucleus. Once the arena for bloody vendettas, it's now a well-kept square opening onto a wide terrace that overlooks the rippling green valley of the Rizzanese. Flanking the south side of place Porta is the **church of Ste-Marie**, built in the 1760s but completely restored to a smooth granitic appearance. Inside the church, the most notable feature is the weighty wooden cross and chair carried through the town by hooded penitents during the Easter **Catenacciu** procession.

A flight of steps to the left of the **Hôtel de Ville**, formerly the governor's palace, leads past the post office to a ruined **lookout tower**, which is all that remains of the town's twelfth-century ramparts. This apart, the best of the old town is to be found behind the Hôtel de Ville in the **Santa Anna** district, a labyrinth of constricted passageways and ancient fortress-like houses that rarely give any signs of life. Featuring few windows and often linked to their neighbours by balconies, these houses are entered by first-floor doors which would have been approached by ladders – dilapidated staircases have replaced these necessary measures against unwelcome intruders. To the left of rue des Frères-Bartoli are the strangest of all the vaulted passageways, where outcrops of rock block the paths between the ancient buildings. Just to the west of the Hôtel de Ville, signposted off the tiny place Maggiore, you'll find the **impasse Carababa**, a remarkable architectural puzzle of a passageway cut through the awkwardly stacked houses.

Sartène's only other cultural attraction is **Musée de la Préhistoire Corse** (closed at time of writing, pending a move to new premises across town; check with tourist office), Corsica's centre for archeological research. The museum contains a rather dry collection of mostly Neolithic and Torréen pottery fragments, with some bracelets from the Iron Age and painted ceramics from the thirteenth to sixteenth centuries.

Practicalities

Arriving in Sartène by **bus**, you'll be dropped either at the top of avenue Gabriel-Péri or at the end of cours Général-de-Gaulle. The **tourist office**, on cours Soeur Amélie (summer only Mon–Fri 9am–noon & 2.30–6pm; ⓣ04.95.77.15.40), can help find accommodation in the area if the hotels listed below are full.

The only **hotel** in Sartène itself is *Les Roches* on avenue Jean-Jaurès, a large family-run place just below the old town (ⓣ04.95.77.07.61, ⓦwww.sartenehotel.fr; ❹); it commands panoramic views of the Vallée du Rizzanese and has a restaurant that serves hearty Corsican food. Otherwise try the *Villa Piana*, 1km out of town on the Propriano road (ⓣ04.95.77.07.04, ⓦwww.lavillapiana.com; ❻), an upmarket place, with a pool and tennis court, overlooking the Golfe de Valinco, or the even swankier, Swiss-owned *U San Damianu* (ⓣ04.95.70.55.41, ⓦwww.sandamianu.fr; ❼), just across the bridge from the *vielle ville*, beneath the convent of the same name. A three-star occupying a plum spot with spectacular views over the town, it offers all the comforts and amenities you'd expect for a hotel in this class, although it's a bit bland. The nearest **campsite**, *U Farrandu*, lies 1km down the main Propriano road (ⓣ04.95.73.41.69; closed Nov–April).

As for **restaurants**, a dependable choice is the *Restaurant du Cours ("Chez Jean")* at 20 cours Soeur Amélie (ⓣ04.95.77.19.07), which serves wholesome, honest *cuisine sartenaise* (pork stews, stuffed courgettes and local liver sausage grilled over an open fire), as well as inexpensive pizzas, in a stone-walled inn. The house menus are priced around €20. For more refined local gastronomy, head down the mountainside to the *Auberge Santa Barbara* (ⓣ04.95.77.09.66), 2km out of town on the Propriano road, where you can enjoy fine, authentic Sartenais dishes from both the coast and interior, served in a lovely garden. Seafood lovers should try the bream with aubergine caviar or cuttlefish in red wine; and leave room for the *flan grandemère.* **Cafés** cluster around place Porta, and are great places for crowd-watching.

The megalithic sites

Sparsely populated today, the rolling hills of the southwestern corner of Corsica are rich in prehistoric sites. The megaliths of **Cauria**, standing in ghostly isolation 10km southwest from Sartène, comprise the Dolmen de Fontanaccia, the best-preserved monument of its kind on Corsica, while the nearby alignments of **Stantari** and **Renaggiu** have an impressive congregation of statue-menhirs.

More than 250 menhirs can be seen northwest of Cauria at **Palaggiu**, another rewardingly remote site. Equally wild is the coast hereabouts, with deep clefts and coves providing some excellent spots for diving and secluded swimming.

The only public transport in this region is the twice-daily Ajaccio–Bonifacio bus.

Cauria

To reach the **Cauria megalithic site**, you need to turn off the N196 about 2km outside Sartène, at the Col de l'Albitrina (291m), taking the D48 towards

Tizzano. Four kilometres along this road a left turning brings you onto a winding road through maquis, until eventually the **Dolmen de Fontanaccia** comes into view on the horizon, crowning the crest of a low hill amidst a sea of maquis. A blue sign at the parking space indicates the track to the dolmen, a fifteen-minute walk away.

Known to the locals as the **Stazzona del Diavolu** (Devil's Forge), a name that does justice to its enigmatic power, the Dolmen de Fontanaccia is in fact a burial chamber from around 2000 BC. This period was marked by a change in burial customs – whereas bodies had previously been buried in stone coffins in the ground, they were now placed above, in a mound of earth enclosed in a stone chamber. What you see today is a great stone table, comprising six huge granite blocks nearly 2m high, topped by a stone slab that remained after the earth eroded away.

The twenty "standing men" of the **Alignement de Stantari**, 200m to the east of the dolmen, date from the same period. All are featureless, except two which have roughly sculpted eyes and noses, with diagonal swords on their fronts and sockets in their heads where horns would probably have been attached.

Across a couple of fields to the south is the **Alignement de Renaggiu**, a gathering of forty menhirs standing in rows amid a small shadowy copse, set against the enormous granite outcrop of Punta di Cauria. Some of the menhirs have fallen, but all face north to south, a fact that seems to rule out any connection with a sun-related cult.

Palaggiu

To reach the **Alignement de Palaggiu**, the largest concentration of menhirs in Corsica, regain the D48 and head southwards past the Domaine la Mosconi vineyard (on your right, 3km after the Cauria turn-off), 1500m beyond which a green metal gate on the right side of the road marks the turning. From here a badly rutted dirt track leads another 1200m to the stones, lost in the maquis, with vineyards spread over the hills in the half-distance. Stretching in straight lines across the countryside like a battleground of soldiers, the 258 menhirs include three statue-menhirs with carved weapons and facial features – they are amidst the first line you come to. Dating from around 1800 BC, the statues give few clues as to their function, but it's a reasonable supposition that proximity to the sea was important – the famous Corsican archeologist Roger Grosjean's theory is that the statues were some sort of magical deterrent to invaders.

Bonifacio (Bonifaziu)

BONIFACIO enjoys a superbly isolated location at Corsica's southernmost point, a narrow peninsula of dazzling white limestone creating a town site unlike any other. The much-photographed **haute ville**, a maze of narrow streets flanked by tall Genoese tenements, rises seamlessly out of sheer cliffs that have been hollowed and striated by the wind and waves, while on the landward side the deep cleft between the peninsula and the mainland forms a perfect natural harbour. A haven for boats for centuries, this inlet is nowadays a chic marina that attracts yachts from around the Med. Separated from the rest of the island by a swathe of dense maquis, Bonifacio has maintained a certain temperamental detachment from the rest of Corsica, and is distinctly more Italian than French in atmosphere. The town retains Renaissance features found only here, and its inhabitants have their own dialect based on Ligurian, a legacy of the days when this was practically an independent Genoese colony.

Such a place has its inevitable drawbacks: exorbitant prices, overwhelming crowds in August and a commercial cynicism that's atypical of Corsica as a whole. However, the old town forms one of the most arresting spectacles in the Mediterranean, easily transcending all the tourist frippery that surrounds it, and warrants at least a day-trip. If you plan to come in peak season, try to get here early in the day before the bus parties arrive at around 10am.

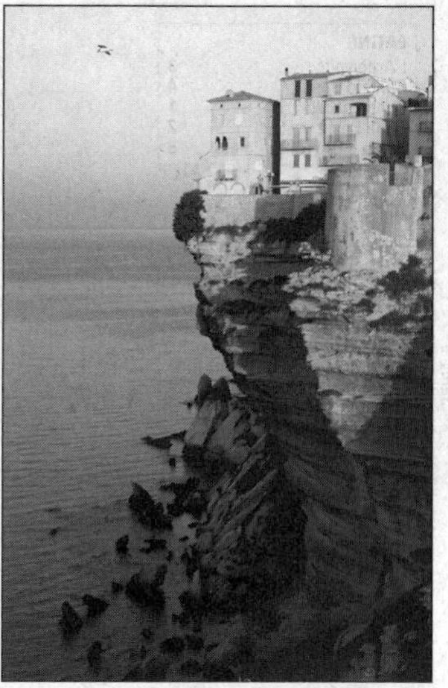

△*Haute ville*, Bonifacio

Arrival, information and accommodation

Figari **airport**, 17km north of Bonifacio (Ⓣ04.95.71.10.10), handles flights from mainland France and a few charters from the UK. There's a seasonal **bus** service operated by Transports Rossi (Ⓣ04.95.71.00.11) that in theory should meet incoming flights, stopping at Bonifacio en route to Porto-Vecchio; otherwise, your only option is to take a taxi into town – around €45–50. If you're coming by bus from other parts of the island you'll be dropped at the car park by the marina, close to most of the hotels. The **tourist office** is up in the *haute ville*, in the Fort San Nicro at the bottom of rue F. Scamaroni (July–Sept daily 9am–8pm; Oct–June Mon–Fri 9am–12.30pm & 2–5.15pm; Ⓣ04.95.73.11.88, Ⓦwww.bonifacio.fr); they can check for you which hotels have vacancies. **Cars** may be rented from Avis, quai Banda del Ferro Ⓣ04.95.73.01.28; Citer, quai Noel-Beretti Ⓣ04.95.73.13.16; Hertz, quai Banda del Ferro Ⓣ04.95.73.06.41. All of the above also have branches at the airport. If you need to change money, note that Bonifacio's only **ATM**, at the Société Générale on the quai J. Comparetti, frequently runs out of cash, so get there early in the day or you'll be at the mercy of the rip-off bureaux de change dotted around the town. *Bomiboom.com*, also on quai Comparetti, offers pricey **Internet** access (€0.15/min).

Finding a **place to stay** can be a chore, as Bonifacio's hotels are quickly booked up in high season; for a room near the centre, reserve well in advance. Better still, save yourself the trouble, and a considerable amount of money, by finding a room somewhere else and travelling here for the day; tariffs in this town are the highest on the island. The same applies to the large campsites dotted along the road to Porto-Vecchio, which can get very crowded.

Hotels

La Caravelle 35 quai J. Comparetti Ⓣ04.95.73.00.03, Ⓦwww.hotel-caravelle-corse.com. Long-established place in prime location on the quayside, whose standard rooms are on the small side for the price. ❼

Centre Nautique on the marina Ⓣ04.95.73.02.11, Ⓦwww.centre-nautique.com. Chic but relaxed hotel on the waterfront, fitted out with mellow wood and nautical charts. All rooms are tastefully furnished and consist of two storeys connected with a spiral staircase. The best upmarket option in town. ❼–❽

Des Étrangers 4 av Sylvère-Bohn Ⓣ04.95.73.01.09, Ⓕ04.95.73.16.97. Simple rooms (the costlier ones have TV and a/c) facing

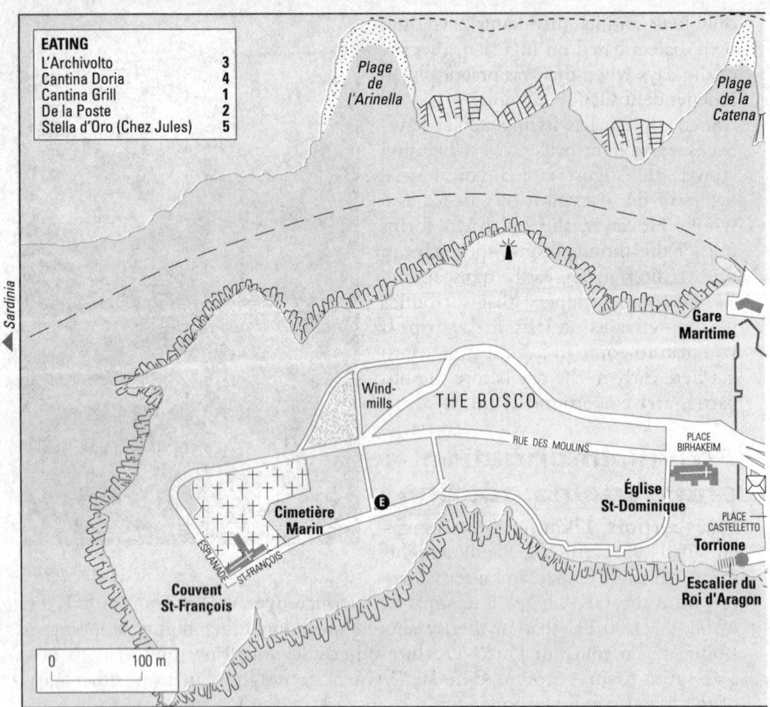

the main road, just up the main Porto-Vecchio road from the port. Nothing special, but pretty good value for Bonifacio. April–Oct. ❺

Le Roy d'Aragon 13 quai J. Comparetti ⓣ04.95.73.03.99, ⓦwww.royaragon.com. A pleasant three-star with contemporary furnishings overlooking the marina. Some of the rooms are small, but the pricier ones have sunny interconnecting terraces looking across the port; and they do better than average off-season discounts. ❻

Santa Teresa quartier Saint-François ⓣ04.95.73.11.32, ⓦwww.hotel-santateresa.com. Large three-star on the clifftop overlooking Cimetière Marin, worth a mention for its stupendous views across the straits to Sardinia. Not all the rooms are sea-facing though, so ask for "*vue mer avec balcon*" when you book. ❼

Campsites

L'Araguina av Sylvère-Bohn ⓣ04.95.73.02.96. Closest place to town, but unwelcoming, cramped in season, and with inadequate washing and toilet facilities. Avoid unless desperate. That said, it's undoubtedly the most convenient if you're backpacking. April–Sept.

Campo di Liccia 3km north towards Porto-Vecchio, ⓣ04.95.73.03.09. Well shaded and large, so you're guaranteed a place. April–Oct.

Pian del Fosse 4km out of town on the rte de Santa Manza ⓣ04.95.73.16.34. Big three-star site that recently had a makeover. Very peaceful and quiet in June and September, and well placed for the beaches. April to mid-Oct.

The Town

Apart from the cafés, hotels and restaurants of **quai Comparetti**, the only attraction in the **ville basse** is the marina's **aquarium** (daily: May, June, Sept & Oct 10am–8pm, July & Aug 10am–midnight; €4), where a solitary blue lobster is the star attraction. At the far end lies the **port** where ferries leave for Sardinia

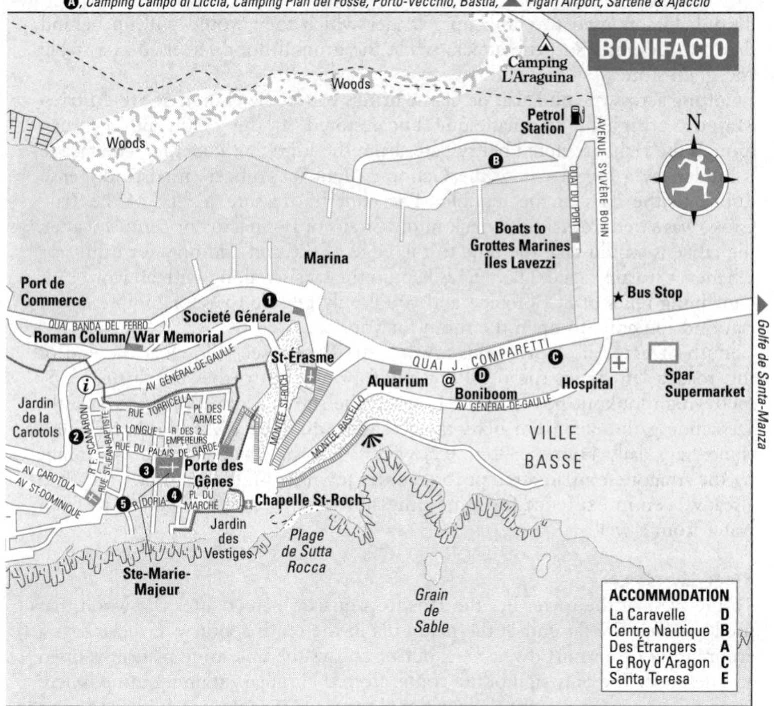

and, in between, a cluster of restaurants and shops lies at the foot of **Montée Rastello**, the steps up to the **haute ville**. In the *haute ville* many of the houses are bordered by enormous battlements which, like the houses themselves, have been rebuilt many times – the most significant modifications were made by the French during their brief period of occupation following the 1554 siege, after they had reduced the town walls to rubble.

From the top of the montée Rastello steps you can cross avenue Général-de-Gaulle to **montée St-Roch**, which gives a stunning view of the white limestone cliffs and the huge lump of fallen rock-face called the Grain de Sable. At the **Chapelle St-Roch**, built on the spot where the last plague victim died in 1528, more steps lead down to the tiny beach of **Sutta Rocca**.

At the top of the montée St-Roch steps stands the drawbridge of the great **Porte des Gênes**, once the only entrance to the *haute ville*. Through the gate, in place d'Armes, you can see the **Bastion de l'Étendard** (April–June & Sept Mon–Sat 11am–5.30pm; July & Aug daily 10am–9pm; €2.50), sole remnant of the fortifications destroyed during the siege of 1554. A few paces further lies **rue des deux Empereurs**, where no. 4 features the flamboyant marble escutcheon of the Cattacciolo family, one of many such adornments on the houses of this quarter. Opposite stands the house in which Napoleon resided for three months in 1793.

Nearby **rue du Palais de Garde** is one of the handsomest streets in Bonifacio, with its closed arcades and double-arched windows separated by curiously stunted columns. The oldest houses along here did not originally have doors;

the inhabitants used to climb up a ladder which they would pull up behind them to prevent a surprise attack, while the ground floor was used as a stable and grain store.

Cutting across rue du Palais de Garde brings you to the church of **Ste-Marie-Majeure**, originally Romanesque but restored in the eighteenth century, though the richly sculpted belfry dates from the fourteenth century. The facade is hidden by a loggia where the Genoese municipal officers used to dispense justice in the days of the republic. The church's treasure, a relic of the True Cross, was saved from a shipwreck in the Straits of Bonifacio; for centuries after, the citizens would take the relic to the edge of the cliff and pray for calm seas whenever storms raged. The relic is kept in the sacristy, along with an ivory cask containing relics of St Boniface, and you'll only be able to get a glimpse if you can find someone to open the room for you.

South of here, rue Doria leads towards the Bosco (see below); at the end of this road a left down rue des Pachas will bring you to the **Torrione**, a 35-metre-high lookout post built in 1195 on the site of Count Bonifacio's castle. Descending the cliff from here, the **Escalier du Roi d'Aragon**'s 187 steps (June–Sept daily 11am–5.30pm; €2) were said to have been built in one night by the Aragonese in an attempt to gain the town in 1420, but in fact they had already been in existence for some time and were used by the people to fetch water from a well.

The Bosco

To the west of the tower lies the **Bosco**, a quarter named after the wood that used to cover the far end of the peninsula in the tenth century. In those days a community of hermits dwelt here, but nowadays the limestone plateau is open and desolate. The only sign of life comes from the military training camp where young Corsicans sweat out their national service. The entrance to the Bosco is marked by the **church of St-Dominique**, a rare example of Corsican Gothic architecture – it was built in 1270, most probably by the Templars, and later handed over to the Dominicans.

Beyond the church, rue des Moulins leads on to the ruins of three **mills** dating from 1283, two of them decrepit, the third restored. Behind them stands a memorial to the 750 people who died when a troopship named *Sémillante* ran aground here in 1855, on its way to the Crimea, one of the many disasters wreaked by the notoriously windy straits.

The tip of the plateau is occupied by the **Cimetière Marin**, its white crosses standing out sharply against the deep blue of the sea. Open until sundown, the cemetery is a fascinating place to explore, with its flamboyant mausoleums displaying a jumble of architectural ornamentations: stuccoed facades, Gothic arches and classical columns. Next to the cemetery stands the **Couvent St-François**, allegedly founded after St Francis sought shelter in a nearby cave – the story goes that the convent was the town's apology to the holy man, over whom a local maid had nearly poured a bucket of slops. Immediately to the south, the **Esplanade St-François** commands fine views across the bay to Sardinia.

Eating, drinking and nightlife

Eating possibilities in Bonifacio might seem unlimited, but it's best to avoid the chintzy restaurants in the marina, few of which merit their exorbitant prices – the places in the *haute ville* are less pretentious. For a snack, try the boulangerie-patisserie Faby, 4 rue St-Jean-Baptiste in the *haute ville*, a tiny local bakery serving Bonifacien treats such as *pain des morts* (sweet buns with walnuts and raisins), *fugazzi* (*galettes* flavoured with eau de vie, orange, lemon and aniseed) and *migliacis* (buns made with fresh ewe's cheese), in addition to the usual range of spinach and *brocciu bastelles*, baked here in the traditional way – on stone. For a scrumptious Bonifacien breakfast you can buy a *pain de morts* warm out of the oven at the *Patisserie Sorba* (follow the smell of baking bread to the bottom of the Montée Rastello steps) and take it to *Bar du Quai* a couple of doors down.

The **bars** and **cafés** further along quai Comparetti are the social focus for the town and what little nightlife there is revolves around the terraces here. Bonifacio's only nightclub was blown up by nationalist bombers a couple of years back, so for a real *nuit blanche* you'll have to head for Porto-Vecchio.

Restaurants

L'Archivolto rue de l'Archivolto ⓣ04.95.73.17.48. With its candlelit, antique- and junk-filled interior, this would be the most commendable place to eat in the *haute ville* were the cooking a little less patchy and the prices fairer. But it still gets packed out – advance reservation is recommended. Lunch menus around €15; evening à la carte only, around €28–30 for three courses. Open Easter–Oct.

Cantina Doria 27 rue Doria ⓣ04.95.73.50.49. Down-to-earth Corsican specialities at down-to-earth prices. Their popular three-course €15 menu – which includes the house speciality, aubergines *à la bonifacienne* – offers unbeatable value for the *haute ville*, though you'll soon bump up your bill if you succumb to the temptations of the excellent wine selection.

Cantina Grill quai Banda del Ferro ⓣ04.95.70.49.86. Same *patron* as the popular *Cantina Doria* in the citadelle, but down in the marina and with a better choice of seafood (octopus risotto, swordfish steaks, fish soup). They also do succulent *grillades* with a selection of different sauces. The food is dependably fresh, well prepared and presented, and the prices great value.

De la Poste 6 rue F. Scamaroni. A cheap and cheerful pizza place serving oven-baked lasagne, spaghetti *al brocciu*, stuffed mussels and delicious pizzas (€10).

Stella d'Oro (Chez Jules) 7 rue Doria, near église St-Jean-Baptiste. À la carte place with stone walls and wood beams, whose top-notch Corsican dishes include the definitive *merrizzane* (stuffed aubergine) – the local speciality. They also do a famous spaghetti in lobster sauce and ravioli *brocciu*. Midday menu at €22; count on €35 à la carte.

Around Bonifacio

There are impressive views of the citadelle from the **cliffs** at the head of the montée Rastello (reached via the pathway running left from the top of the steps), but they're not a patch on the spectacular panorama to be had from the sea. Throughout the day, a flotilla of excursion **boats** ferries visitors out to the best vantage points, taking in a string of caves and other landmarks only accessible by water en route, including the **Îles Lavezzi**, the scattering of small islets where the troop ship *Sémillante* was shipwrecked in 1855, now designated as a nature reserve. The whole experience of bobbing around to an amplified running commentary is about as touristy as Bonifacio gets, but it's well worth enduring just to round the mouth of the harbour and see the *vieille ville*, perched atop the famous chalk cliffs. The Lavezzi islets themselves are surrounded by wonderfully clear seawater, offering Corsica's best snorkelling. On your way back, you skirt the famous **Île Cavallo**, or "millionaire's island", where the likes of Princess Caroline of Monaco and other French and Italian glitterati have luxury hideaways. The boats leave from the east side of the marina: tickets cost €10–12 for trips to the caves, and around €20–25 for the longer excursions to Lavezzi.

The **beaches** along this part of the coast are generally smaller and less appealing than most in southern Corsica, although those fringing the **Golfe de Santa Manza**, to the north, are set amid some fine scenery. On the southernmost tip of the island, reached via a narrow but easily motorable road, a trio of small coves are the most popular beaches within easy reach of town. The first, **plage de Pianterella**, 7km east of Bonifacio, is also the dullest, backed by an unsavoury swamp. Walk south around the headland for fifteen minutes and you'll reach the more pleasant **plage de Sperone**, a pearl-white cove with calm, shallow water that's ideal for kids. However, this beach gets jam-packed in the summer and you may want to venture further along the coast to **Calalonga**, where you stand a better chance of escaping the crowds. To get there, head east out of town on the D58, and take the first turning right, after around 3km.

By far the most photogenic beach in this area is **Rondinara**, a perfect shell-shaped cove of turquoise water enclosed by dunes and a pair of twin headlands. Thankfully, it's well off the beaten track, although the recent appearance of a surfaced road all the way to the beach could well change that. To see it at its emptiest, get here early in the morning. The turning for Rondinara is signposted 10km north along the N198.

Porto-Vecchio and around

Set on a hillock overlooking a beautiful deep blue bay, **PORTO-VECCHIO**, 25km north of Bonifacio, was rated by James Boswell as one of "the most distinguished harbours in Europe". It was founded in 1539 as a second Genoese stronghold on the east coast, Bastia being well established in the north. The site was perfect: close to the unexploited and fertile plain, it benefited from secure high land and a sheltered harbour, although the mosquito population spread malaria and wiped out the first Ligurian settlers within months. Things began to take off mainly thanks to the cork industry, which still thrived well into the twentieth century. Today most revenue comes from tourists, the vast majority of them well-heeled Italians who flock here for the fine outlying **beaches**: spectacular stretches of shoreline lie to the south, with Palombaggia the most popular and Golfe de Santa Giulia coming a close second, while to the north, the deep inlet of the Golfe de Porto-Vecchio boasts some fine pine-backed strands. To the northwest, the little town of **Zonza** makes a good base for exploring the dramatic forest that surrounds the **route de Bavella**.

Around the centre of town there's not much to see, apart from the well-preserved **fortress** and the small grid of **ancient streets** backing onto the main place de la République. East of the square you can't miss the **Porte Génoise**, which frames a delightful expanse of sea and salt pans and through which you'll find the quickest route down to the modern marina, lined with cafés and restaurants.

Practicalities

Porto-Vecchio doesn't have a **bus** station; instead, the various companies who come here stop and depart outside their agents' offices on the edge of the old town. Coming from Bastia or the eastern plain, you'll be dropped at the Corsicatours office on 7 rue Jean-Jaurès; services to and from Ajaccio via Bonifacio, Sartène and Propriano stop outside the Trinitours office on rue Pasteur, just north of the citadelle; finally, the minibus connecting Porto-Vecchio with Ajaccio, via the chief villages of Bavella and Alta Rocca, pulls in at Île de Beauté Voyages, at 13 rue Général-de-Gaulle, near the post office. From here it's a five-minute walk to the main square, place de l'Hôtel-de-Ville, site of the efficient **tourist office** (June & Sept Mon–Sat 9am–1pm & 3–6pm; July & Aug

Mon–Sat 9am–8pm, Sun 9am–1pm; Oct–May Mon–Fri 9am–noon & 2–6pm, Sat 9am–noon; ⓣ04.95.70.09.58, ⓦwww.accueil-portovecchio.com), where you can consult timetables for local buses.

Accommodation is easy to come by except in high summer. One of the least expensive places is the *Panorama*, 12 rue Jean-Nicoli, just above the old town (ⓣ04.95.70.07.96, ⓕ04.95.70.46.78; ❸), which isn't all that well maintained but offers the cheapest beds in the centre of town. Moving up a bracket, the *San Giovanni* (ⓣ04.95.70.22.55, ⓦwww.hotel-san-giovanni.com; ❺), a couple of kilometres south of Porto-Vecchio on the D659 towards Arca, has thirty comfortable chalet-style rooms set in landscaped gardens, with a pool and tennis courts. It's well run, peaceful and good value for money.

Of the many **campsites** in the area, *Matonara* (ⓣ04.95.70.37.05, ⓦwww.lamatonara.com), just north of the centre at the Quatre-Chemins intersection, is the most easily accessible. Lying within easy reach of the 'Hyper U' supermarket, it's large and shaded by stands of cork trees. Otherwise, try the better-equipped *Arutoli* on route de l'Ospédale, 2km northwest of town along the D368 (ⓣ04.95.70.12.73, ⓦwww.arutoli.com), which has an enormous pool.

For quality local **food**, try *U Sputinu*'s copious *grande assiette* – a selection of quality charcuterie, cheese, spinach pasties (*chaussons herbes*), savoury fritters (*migliacciu*) and mint omelettes (€14) – served on rustic wooden tables in the little square in front of the church. *L'Antigu* (ⓣ04.95.70.39.33), on rue Borgo is a more gastronomic Corsican place with a wonderful *terrasse panoramique* surveying the gulf. It offers three menus (at €17, €21 and €35) of refined regional dishes using only locally sourced ingredients. Plenty of other places to eat are clustered around the marina and *port de commerce*, but none can rustle up pizzas more delectable than those served at *U Corsu* (ⓣ04.95.70.13.91). Reserve early for a sea view on their *pieds dans l'eau* terrace.

Nightlife in Porto-Vecchio centres on the main square in the old town where, in the summer, hordes of Italians strut their stuff. The only bona fide club in the area is *Via Notte* (ⓣ04.95.72.02.12, ⓦwww.vianotte.com), a glitzy Italian-oriented place that stages top Euro DJs in July and August (when admission charges and drink prices go through the roof).

Golfe de Porto-Vecchio

Much of the coast of the **Golfe de Porto-Vecchio** and its environs is characterized by ugly development and hectares of swampland, yet some of the clearest, bluest sea and whitest beaches on Corsica are also found around here. The most frequented of these, Palombaggia and Santa Giulia, can be reached by **bus** from the town in summer, timetables for which are posted in the tourist office (see opposite); at other times you'll need your own transport. The same applies to the **Casteddu d'Araggiu**, one of the island's best-preserved Bronze Age sites, which stands on a ledge overlooking the gulf to the north of town.

Heading south of Porto-Vecchio along the main N198, take the turning signposted for **Palombaggia**, a golden semicircle of sand edged by short twisted umbrella pines that are punctuated by fantastically shaped red rocks. This might be the most beautiful beach on the island were it not for the crowds, which pour on to it in such numbers that a wattle fence has had to be erected to protect the dunes. A few kilometres further along the same road takes you to **Santa Giulia**, a sweeping sandy bay backed by a lagoon. Despite the presence of several holiday villages and facilities for windsurfing and other, noisier watersports, crowds are less of a problem here, and the shallow bay is an extraordinary turquoise colour.

North of Porto-Vecchio, the first beach worth a visit is **San Ciprianu**, a half-moon bay of white sand, reached by turning left off the main road at the Elf petrol station. Carry on for another 7km, and you'll come to the even more picturesque beach at **Pinarellu**, an uncrowded, long sweep of soft white sand with a Genoese watchtower and, like the less inspiring beaches immediately north of here, benefiting from the spectacular backdrop of the Massif de l'Ospédale.

The coast between Porto-Vecchio and Solenzara is also strewn with **prehistoric monuments**. The most impressive of these, Casteddu d'Araggiu, lies 12km north along the D759. From the site's car park (signposted off the main road), it's a twenty-minute stiff climb through maquis and scrubby woodland to the ruins. Built in 2000 BC and inhabited by a community that lived by farming and hunting, the *casteddu* consists of a complex of chambers built into a massive circular wall of pink granite, splashed with vivid green patches of lichen, from the top of which the views over the gulf are superb.

The route de Bavella

Starting from the picture-postcard-pretty mountain village of **ZONZA**, 40km northwest of Porto-Vecchio, and running northeast towards the coast, the D268 – known locally as the **route de Bavella** – is perhaps the most dramatic road in all Corsica. Well served by buses, it also affords one of the simplest approaches to the spectacular landscapes of the interior. The road penetrates a dense expanse of old pine and chestnut trees as it rises steadily to the **Col de Bavella** (1218m), where a towering statue of **Notre-Dame-des-Neiges** marks the windswept pass itself. An amazing panorama of peaks and forests spreads out from the col: to the northwest the serrated granite ridge of the Cirque de Gio Agostino is dwarfed by the pink pinnacles of the Aiguilles de Bavella; behind soars Monte Incudine.

Just below the pass, the seasonal hamlet of **BAVELLA** comprises a handful of congenial cafés, corrugated-iron-roofed chalets and hikers' hostels from where you can follow a series of waymarked **trails** to nearby viewpoints. Deservedly the most popular of these is the two-hour walk to the **Trou de la Bombe**, a circular opening that pierces the Paliri crest of peaks. From the car park behind the *Auberge du Col* (see below), follow the red-and-white waymarks of GR20 for 800m, then head right when you see orange splashes. Those with a head for heights should climb right into the hole for the dizzying panorama down the sheer 500m cliff on the other side. Even more amazing views may be had from the summit of the adjacent peak, **Calanca Murata**, which you can scale after a steep forty-minute haul from the head of the ravine just below Trou de la Bombe. Small stone cairns mark the route. At no stage do you need to climb, but the views, which take in the entire Bavella massif to the west and a huge sweep of the eastern plains, are on a par with those from any of the island's major peaks.

From Bavella, it's a steep descent through what's left of the **Forêt de Bavella**, which was devastated by fire in 1960 but still harbours some huge Laricio pines. The winding road offers numerous breathtaking glimpses of the Aiguilles de Bavella and plenty of places to pull over for a swim in the river.

The best **place to stay** locally is Zonza, which has a cluster of hotels, all with more than decent restaurants, such as *Le Tourisme*, set back on the west side of the Quenza road north of the village (Ⓣ04.95.78.67.72, Ⓦwww.hoteldutourisme.fr; ❹–❺; April–Oct), or *L'Aiglon* in the village centre (Ⓣ04.95.78.67.72, Ⓦwww.aiglonhotel.com; ❹; April–Dec). For hikers, clean and comfortable dormitory accommodation is available at the *Auberge du*

Col (Ⓣ04.95.72.09.87, Ⓕ04.95.72.16.48; ❶; April–Oct), the best set-up of the small *gîtes d'étapes* at Bavella. Regular **buses** run to Zonza from Ajaccio, Propriano, Sartène and Porto-Vecchio; for the current timetables ask at a tourist office.

Aléria

Built on the estuary at the mouth of the River Tavignano on the island's east coast, 40km southeast of Corte along the N200, **ALÉRIA** was first settled in 564 BC by a colony of Greek Phoceans as a trading port for the copper and lead they mined and the wheat, olives and grapes they farmed. After an interlude of Carthaginian rule, the Romans arrived in 259 BC, built a naval base and re-established its importance in the Mediterranean. Aléria remained the east coast's principal port right up until the eighteenth century. Little is left of the historic town except Roman ruins and a thirteenth-century Genoese fortress, which stands high against a background of chequered fields and green vineyards. To the south, a strip of modern buildings straddling the main road makes up the modern town, known as **Cateraggio**, but it's the village set on the hilltop just west of here that holds most interest. Aléria/Cateraggio can be reached on any of the daily **buses** running between Bastia and the south of the island via the east coast.

To sample the famous Nustale oysters hauled fresh each day from the nearby Étang de Diane lagoon, head 1.2km north and look for a signboard on the right (east) side of the road pointing the way down a surfaced lane to the *Aux Coquillages de Diane* **restaurant** (Ⓣ04.95.57.04.55). Resting on stilts above the water, it serves a great-value €21 seafood platter, featuring clams, mussels and a terrine made from dried mullet's eggs called *poutargue* – the kind of food one imagines the Romans must have feasted on when they farmed the *étang* two millennia ago.

The site

Before looking around the ruins of the ancient city, set aside an hour for the **Musée Jerôme Carcopino** (mid-May to Sept daily 8am–noon & 2–7pm; Oct to mid-May Mon–Sat 8am–noon & 2–5pm; €2), housed in the Fort Matra. It houses remarkable finds from the **Roman site**, including Hellenic and Punic coins, rings, belt links, elaborate oil lamps decorated with Christian symbols, Attic plates and a second-century marble bust of Jupiter Ammon. Etruscan bronzes fill another room, with jewellery and armour from the fourth to the second century BC.

A dusty track leads from here to the Roman site itself (closes 30min before museum; same ticket), where most of the excavation was done as recently as the 1950s, even though the French novelist Prosper Merimée had noticed signs of the Roman settlement during his survey of the island in 1830. Most of the site still lies beneath ground and is undergoing continuous digging, but the balneum (bathhouse), the base of Augustus's triumphal arch, the foundations of the forum and traces of shops have already been unearthed.

First discovered was the arch, which formed the entrance to the governor's residence – the praetorium – on the western edge of the forum. In the adjacent balneum, a network of reservoirs and cisterns, the caldarium bears traces of the underground pipes that would have heated the room, and a patterned mosaic floor is visible inside the neighbouring chamber. To the north of the site lie the foundation walls of a large house, while at the eastern end of the forum the foundations of the temple can be seen. At its northern edge, over a row of column stumps, are the foundations of the apse of an early Christian church.

Some traces of the **Greek settlement**, comprising the remains of an acropolis, have been discovered further to the east. It's believed that the main part of the town would have extended from the present site over to this acropolis and down to the Tavignano estuary. The port was located to the east of the main road, where the remnants of a second-century bathhouse have been found.

Corte (Corti)

Stacked up the side of a wedge-shaped crag against a spectacular backdrop of granite mountains, **CORTE** epitomizes *l'âme corse*, or "Corsican soul" – a small town marooned amid a grandiose landscape, where a spirit of dogged defiance and patriotism is never far from the surface. Corte has been the home of Corsican nationalism since the first National Constitution was drawn up here in 1731, and was also where **Pascal Paoli**, "U Babbu di u Patria" (Father of the Nation), formed the island's first democratic government later in the eighteenth century. Self-consciously insular and grimly proud, it can seem an

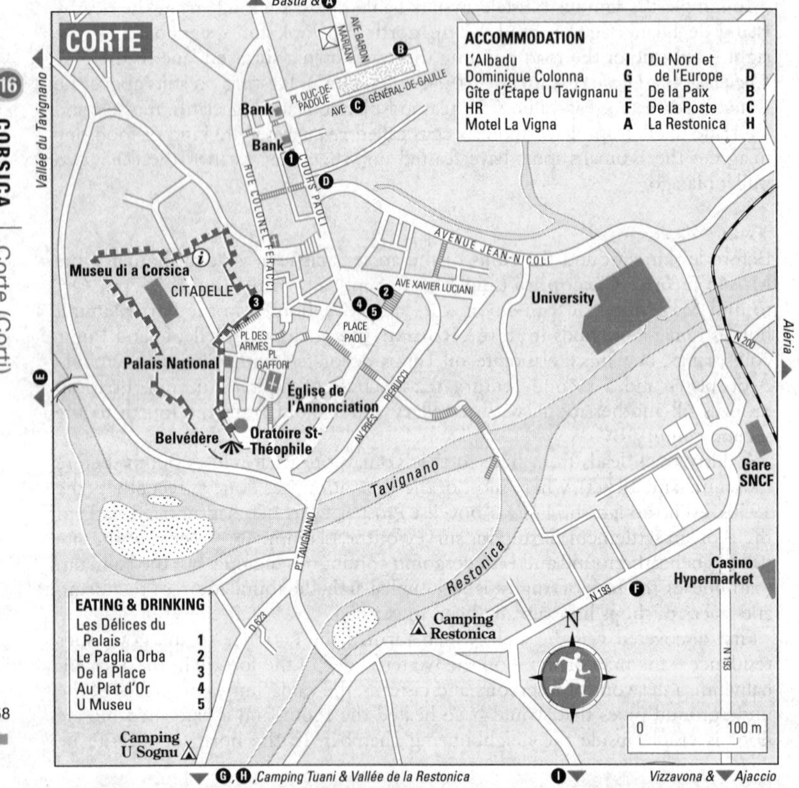

inhospitable place at times, although the presence of the island's only university lightens the atmosphere noticeably during term-time, when the bars and cafés lining its long main street fill with students. For the outsider, Corte's charm is concentrated in the tranquil *haute ville*, where the forbidding **citadelle** – site of the island's premier **museum** – presides over a warren of narrow, cobbled streets. Immediately behind it, the Restonica and Tavignano gorges afford easy access to some of the region's most memorable mountain scenery, best enjoyed from the marked trails that wind through them.

Arrival, information and accommodation

Buses from Ajaccio and Bastia stop in the centre of town on avenue Xavier-Luciani; the **gare SNCF** (ⓣ04.95.46.00.97) is at the foot of the hill near the university, a ten-minute walk from the centre and campsites. If you're driving, the best place to **park** is at the top of avenue Jean-Nicoli, the road which leads into town from Ajaccio. Corte's **tourist office** is situated just inside the main gates of the citadelle, near the museum (Jan–May & Oct–Dec Mon–Fri 9am–noon & 2–6pm, plus Sat in May; June & Sept Mon–Sat 9am–1pm & 2–7pm; July & Aug daily 9am–8pm; ⓣ04.95.46.26.70, ⓦwww.corte-tourisme.com). In the same building is the information office of the **Parc Régional** (same hours and phone number).

Finding a **place to stay** can be a problem from mid-June until early September, when it's advisable to book in advance. With three **campsites** in the town, and a couple a short drive away, tent space is at less of a premium, although the sites across the river get crowded in high season.

Hotels

L'Albadu ancienne rte d'Ajaccio, 2.5km southwest of town ⓣ04.95.46.24.55, ⓕ04.95.46.13.08. Simply furnished rooms with showers (shared toilets) on a working farm-cum-equestrian centre. Warm family atmosphere, beautiful horses, fine views and top Corsican speciality food. Advance reservation essential. ❷

Dominique Colonna vallée de la Restonica, 2km south of town ⓣ04.95.45.25.65, ⓦwww.dominique-colonna.com. The more modern of this pair of jointly owned luxury *auberges* (see below) set amid pine woods next to the stream. With less character than its neighbour (see *La Restonica* below), but smart and efficient and with all the mod cons you'd expect of a three-star. Closed Nov to mid-March. ❺–❽

HR allée du 9-Septembre ⓣ04.95.45.11.11, ⓦwww.hotel-hr.com. This converted concrete-block *gendarmerie*, 200m southwest of the *gare SNCF*, looks grim from the outside, but its 125 rooms are comfortable enough and its rates rock-bottom; bathroom-less options are the best deal. No credit cards. ❷–❸

Motel La Vigna chemin de Saint-Pancrace ⓣ04.95.46.02.19. Tucked away on the leafy edge of town, this small but rather swish students' hall of residence is vacated between early June and the end of September and converted into a motel. The rooms are simple and lacking character by Corte standards, but clean and all en suite, with balconies. Open June–Sept. ❸

Du Nord et de l'Europe 22 cours Paoli ⓣ04.95.46.00.33, ⓦwww.hoteldunord-corte.com. Pleasant, clean place right in the centre. Despite recent renovation, the building has oodles of charm and the (variously priced) rooms are large for the tariffs. Reception in the *Café du Cours* next door. ❻

De la Paix 1 av Général-de-Gaulle ⓣ04.95.46.06.72, ⓔsocoget@orange.fr. Large, smart and central, in an elegant part of town. Their pricier rooms have large balconies and TVs. No credit cards. ❹

De la Poste 2 place du Duc-de-Padoue ⓣ04.95.46.01.37. The cheapest rooms in the centre, in a huge old building that opens onto a quiet square just off the main drag. Comfortable enough, but on the gloomy side. ❷

La Restonica vallée de la Restonica, 2km southwest from town ⓣ04.95.46.09.58, ⓦwww.aubergerestonica.com. Sumptuous comfort in a wood-lined riverside hotel set up by a former French national footballer, Dominique Colonna, who bought it after winning the lottery. There's a large pool and garden terrace. Good value in summer, but not such a great deal in winter, since rates are the same year round. ❺

Hostels and campsites

L'Albadu 2.5km southwest of town ⓣ04.95.46.24.55. Perfect little *camping à la ferme*, situated on a hillside above Corte. Basic, but much nicer than any of the town sites, and well worth the walk.

Gîte d'Étape U Tavignanu ("Chez M. Gambini") behind the citadelle ⓣ04.95.46.16.85. Run-of-the-mill hikers' hostel with small dorms and a relaxing garden terrace that looks over the valley. Peaceful, secluded, and the cheapest place to stay after the campsites. Follow the signs for the Tavignano trail (marked with orange spots of paint) around the back of the citadelle. €17 per bed (includes breakfast).

Restonica 500m south of the town centre. Middle-sized site on the riverside, close to town, with terraces close to the water plenty of shade and its own café-bar.

Tuani vallée de la Restonica, 7km south-east ⓣ04.95.46.11.62. Too far up the valley without your own car, but the wildest and most atmospheric of the campsites around Corte, overlooking a rushing stream, deep in the woods. Ideally placed for an early start on Monte Rotondo. Basic facilities, although they do have a cheerful little café serving good *bruschettas* and other hot snacks.

U Sognu rte de la Restonica ⓣ04.95.46.09.07. At the foot of the valley, a 15min walk from the centre. Has a good view of the citadelle, plenty of poplar trees for shade, and toilets in a converted barn. There's also a small bar and restaurant (in summer).

The Town

Corte is a very small town whose centre effectively consists of one street, **cours Paoli**, which runs from place Paoli at the southern end, a tourist-friendly zone packed with cafés, restaurants and market stalls, to **place du Duc-de-Padoue**, an elegant square of *fin-de-siècle* buildings.

The old **haute ville** is next to the cours Paoli, reached by climbing one of the cobbled ramps on the west side of the street or by taking the steep rue Scoliscia from place Paoli. **Place Gaffori**, the hub of the *haute ville*, is dominated by a statue of General Gian-Pietru Gaffori pointing vigorously towards the church. On its base a bas-relief depicts the siege of the Gaffori house by the Genoese, who attacked in 1750 when the general was out of town and his wife Faustina was left holding the fort. Their house stands right behind, and you can clearly make out the bullet marks made by the besiegers.

Opposite the house is the **church of the Annunciation**, built in 1450 but restored in the seventeenth century. Inside, there's a delicately carved pulpit and a hideous wax statue of St Theophilus, patron of the town, on his deathbed. The saint's birthplace – behind the church in place Théophile – is marked by the **Oratoire St-Théophile**, a large arcaded building which commands a magnificent view across the gorges of Tavignano and Restonica.

For the best view of the citadelle, follow the signs uphill to the viewing platform, the **Belvédère**, which faces the medieval tower, suspended high above the town on its pinnacle of rock and dwarfed by the immense crags behind. The platform also gives a wonderful view of the converging rivers and encircling forest – a summer bar adds to the attraction.

Just above the place Gaffori, left of the gateway to the citadelle, stands the **Palais National**, a great, solid block of a mansion that's the sole example of Genoese civic architecture in Corte. Having served as the seat of Paoli's government for a while, it became the Università di Corsica in 1765, offering free education to all (Napoleon's father studied here). In the spirit of the Enlightenment, Franciscan monks taught the contemporary social thought of philosophers such as Rousseau and Montesquieu as well as traditional subjects like theology, mathematics and law. The university closed in 1769 when the French took over the island after the Treaty of Versailles, not to be resurrected until 1981. Today several modern buildings have been added, among them the Institut Universitaire d'Études Corses, dedicated to the study of Corsican history and culture.

The Museu di a Corsica and citadelle

The monumental gateway just behind the Palais National leads from place Poilu into Corte's Genoese citadelle, whose lower courtyard is dominated by the modern buildings of **Museu di a Corsica** (April–June 19 & Sept 20–Oct daily except Tues 10am–6pm; June 20–Sept 19 daily 10am–8pm; Nov–March Tues–Sat 10am–6pm; €5.30), a state-of-the-art museum inaugurated in 1997 to house the collection of ethnographer Révérend Père Louis Doazan, a Catholic priest who spent 27 years amassing a vast array of objects relating to the island's traditional transhumant and peasant past. Gifted to the state in 1972, the three thousand pieces he collected remained in storage for nearly a quarter of a century until a suitable site could be found to exhibit them. The austere building certainly makes the most of its historically significant location at the heart of the island, but ultimately upstages the lacklustre selection of old farm implements, craft tools and peasant dress inside it.

The museum's entrance charge also admits you to Corte's principal landmark, the **citadelle**. The only such fortress in the interior of the island, the Genoese structure served as a base for the Foreign Legion from 1962 until 1984, but now houses a pretty feeble exhibition of nineteenth-century photographs. It's reached by a huge staircase of Restonica marble, which leads to the medieval tower known as the **Nid d'Aigle** (Eagle's Nest). The fortress, of which the tower is the only original part, was built by Vincentello d'Istria in 1420, and the barracks were added during the reign of Louis-Philippe (1830–48). These were later converted into a prison, in use as recently as World War II, when the Italian occupiers incarcerated Corsican Resistance fighters in tiny cells. Adjacent to the cells is a former **watchtower** which at the time of Paoli's government was inhabited by the hangman.

Eating and drinking

Corte has only three **restaurants** worthy of note, plus the usual handful of pizzerias and crêperies. As a rule of thumb, avoid anywhere fronted by gaudy food photographs and multilingual menus; their dishes may be cheap, but they offer poor value for money – for not much more you'll eat a lot better in one of the places listed below.

Cafés and bars

Les Délices du Palais cours Paoli. Frilly little crêperie-cum-*salon-de-thé* whose bakery sells a selection of delicious Corsican patisserie: try their *colzone* (spinach pasties), or *brocciu* baked in flaky chestnut-flour pastry.

De la Place place Paoli. On the shady side of the main square, this is the place to hole up for a spot of crowd-watching over a *barquettes de frites* (a pile of chips) and draught Pietra.

Restaurants

U Museu rampe Ribanelle in the *haute ville* at the foot of the citadelle, 30m down rue Colonel-Feracci ☎04.95.61.08.36. Congenial and well-situated place. Try the €15 *menu corse*, featuring lasagne in wild boar sauce, trout, and *tripettes* (imaginatively translated as "trips"). Their hot goat's cheese (*chèvre chaud*) salad, filling enough for two, comes on a groaning bed of richly flavoured potatoes. Great value for money, atmospheric terrace and the house wines are local AOC.

Le Paglia Orba 1 av Xavier-Luciani ☎04.95.61.07.89. Quality Corsican cooking at very reasonable prices, served on a raised terrace overlooking the street. Most people come for their succulent pizzas (€6–8), but they also offer plenty of choice à la carte, particularly for vegetarians. Pan-fried veal served with *stozapreti* (nuggets of *brocciu* and herbs) is their *plat de résistance*. Menus from €16.

Au Plat d'Or place Paoli ☎04.95.46.27.16. The classiest option in Corte: Corsican specialities made from locally produced ingredients, and served under awnings on the shady side of place Paoli. Meat and seafood dishes are their forte, but they also do pizzas, pastas and home-made desserts. Menu for €23 (four courses). Closed Sun.

Central Corsica

Central Corsica is a nonstop parade of stupendous scenery, and the best way to immerse yourself in it is to get onto the region's ever-expanding network of trails and forest tracks. The ridge of granite mountains forming the spine of the island is closely followed by the epic **GR20** footpath, which can be picked up from various villages and is scattered with refuge huts, most of them offering no facilities except shelter. For the less active there also are plenty of roads penetrating deep into the **forests** ofVizzavona, La Restonica and Rospa Sorba, crossing lofty passes that provide exceptional views across the island.

The most popular attractions in the centre, though, are the magnificent **gorges** of La Restonica and Tavignano, both within easy reach of Corte.

Gorges du Tavignano

A deep cleft of ruddy granite beginning 5km to the west of Corte, the **Gorges du Tavignano** offers one of central Corsica's great walks, marked in yellow paint flashes alongside the broad cascading River Tavignano. You can pick up the trail from opposite the Chapelle Sainte-Croix in Corte's *haute ville* and follow it as far as the Lac de Nino, 30km west of the town, where it joins the GR20. There's a refuge, *A Sega*, 15km along the route.

From the trailhead in Corte, the old mule track steadily climbs the steep left bank of the river across a bare hillside scarred with the remains of old farming terraces. Massive rocks border the river below, which you can scramble down to in places for a secluded swim. Some 5km into the walk, the gorge proper begins and the scenery becomes wilder, with rock faces surging up on each side. Passing through patches of dense maquis interspersed with evergreen oak and chestnut trees, you gradually rejoin the river, crossed at the Passarelle de Rossolino footbridge after around two and a half hours. Once on the right bank, the mountainside grows steeper as the path skirts the Ravin de Bruscu, swathed in forest that was severely damaged by fire in 2000, then winds gently above the stream to the refuge, reached after five and a half hours from Corte.

Gorges de la Restonica

The glacier-moulded rocks and deep pools of the **Gorges de la Restonica** make the D936 running southwest from Corte the busiest mountain road in Corsica – if you come in high summer, expect to encounter traffic jams all the way up to the car park at the **Bergeries de Grotelle**, 15km from Corte. **Minibuses** run from Corte to the Bergeries, costing €12; taxis charge around €35. The gorges begin after 6km, just beyond where the route penetrates the **Forêt de la Restonica**, a glorious forest of chestnut, Laricio pine and the tough maritime pine endemic to Corte. Not surprisingly, it's a popular place to walk, picnic and bathe in the many pools fed by the cascading torrent of the River Restonica, easily reached by scrambling down the rocky banks.

From the *bergeries*, a well-worn path winds along the valley floor to a pair of beautiful glacial lakes. The first and larger, **Lac de Melo**, is reached after an easy hour's hike through the rocks. One particularly steep part of the path has been fitted with security chains, but the scramble around the side of the passage is perfectly straightforward, and much quicker. Once past Lac de Melo, press on for another forty minutes along the steeper marked trail over a moraine to the second lake, **Lac de Capitello**, the more spectacular of the pair. Hemmed in by vertical cliffs, the deep turquoise-blue pool affords fine views of the Rotondo massif on the far side of the valley, and in clear weather you can spend an hour or two exploring the surrounding crags, the haunt of rock pipits. Beyond here, the trail climbs higher to meet the GR20, and should only be attempted by well-equipped mountain-walkers.

Vizzavona and its forest

Monte d'Oro dominates the route south of Corte to **VIZZAVONA**, about 10km away. Shielded by trees, the village is invisible from the main road, so keep your eyes peeled for a turning on the right signposted for the train station. With its handful of *gîtes d'étape* and restaurants, Vizzavona is an ideal place to spend a few days walking in the forest, although it gets crowded in summer when it fills with hikers taking a break from the GR20, which passes nearby. The glorious **forest** of beech and Laricio pine surrounding the hamlet is among the most popular walking areas in Corsica, thanks to the easy access by main road or train. A lot of people come here to tackle the ascent of 2389-metre-high **Monte d'Oro**, but there are many less demanding trails to follow, among them the busy route to the **Cascade des Anglais**, connected to Vizzavona by the red-and-white waymarks of the GR20.

Among the **accommodation** options here, top of the range is *I Laricci* (Ⓣ04.95.47.21.12, Ⓦwww.ilaricci.com; ❹; closed Nov–March) an old-fashioned alpine-style hotel with pitched roofs and charming Moroccan carpets decorating the walls of its dining room. In addition to comfortable en-suite rooms, they also have beds in dorms for walkers (€30 half board). A cheaper option is *Resto-Refuge-Bar "De la Gare"* (Ⓣ & Ⓕ04.95.47.22.20; €13.50 per dorm bed; May–Oct), directly opposite the station. When full, the dormitories here are stuffy and cramped; half board (€33) isn't obligatory, which is just as well as the food isn't up to much, either. For more atmosphere, head 3km further south along the main road to the hamlet of **LA FOCE**, where the venerable old *Monte d'Oro* (Ⓣ04.95.47.21.06, Ⓦwww.monte-oro.com; ❸–❺) occupies a prime spot overlooking the valley – with its period furniture and fittings, *fin-de-siècle* feel and magnificent terrace looking out onto the mountain, it ranks among the most congenial hotels in Corsica. Adjacent to the *Monte d'Oro*, on the main road, is a little *gîte d'étape* (Ⓣ04.95.45.25.27; ❷) that's nowhere near as gloomy as it looks and makes a handy fallback if the places down in the village are fully booked. The nearest bona fide **campsite** is the *Savaggio*, 4km north of Vizzavona (Ⓣ04.95.47.22.14; open year round); note that the train will make a special request stop at the site if you give the conductor plenty of warning.

Travel details

Note that the details apply to June–Sept only; during the winter both train and bus services are considerably scaled down.

Trains

Ajaccio to: Bastia (4 daily; 3hr 45min–4hr); Calvi (2 daily; 4hr 25min–5hr); Corte (4 daily; 1hr 45min–2hr); L'Île Rousse (2 daily; 4hr); Vizzavona (4 daily; 1hr).
Bastia to: Ajaccio (2–4 daily; 3hr 10min–3hr 40min); Biguglia (2–4 daily; 20min); Calvi (2 daily; 3hr 15min); Corte (2–4 daily; 2hr); L'Île Rousse (2 daily; 2hr 30min); Ponte Leccia (2–4 daily; 1hr); Vizzavona (2–4 daily; 2hr 10min).
Calvi to: Ajaccio (2 daily; 5hr 10min); Bastia (2 daily; 3hr 30min); Corte (2 daily; 3hr 15min); L'Île Rousse (2–10 daily; 30min).
Corte to: Ajaccio (4 daily; 2hr); Bastia (4 daily; 1hr 50min); Calvi (2 daily; 2hr 30min); L'Île Rousse (2 daily; 2hr 30min); Vizzavona (4 daily; 50min).

L'Île Rousse to: Ajaccio (2 daily; 4hr 30min); Bastia (2 daily; 2hr 50min); Corte (2 daily; 2hr 40min).
Vizzavona to: Ajaccio (4 daily; 55min); Bastia (4 daily; 3hr); Corte (4 daily; 1hr); Ponte Leccia (4 daily; 1hr 40min).

Buses

Ajaccio to: Bastia (2 daily; 3hr); Bonifacio (3 daily; 4hr); Cargèse (2–3 daily; 1hr 10min); Corte (2 daily; 1hr 45min); Évisa (1–3 daily; 2hr); Porto (1–2 daily; 2hr 10min); Porto-Vecchio (2–5 daily; 3hr 10min–3hr 45min); Propriano (2–6 daily; 1hr 50min); Sartène (2–6 daily; 2hr 15min); Vizzavona (2 daily; 1hr); Zonza (3 daily; 2hr 15min–3hr).
Aléria to: Bastia (2 daily; 1hr 30min); Corte (3 weekly; 1hr 25min); Porto-Vecchio (2 daily; 1hr 20min).
Bastia to: Ajaccio (2 daily; 3hr); Bonifacio (2–4 daily; 3hr 50min); Calvi (2 daily; 2hr 20min); Centuri (3 weekly; 2hr); Corte (2–3 daily; 1hr 15min); Erbalunga (hourly; 30min); L'Île Rousse (2 daily; 1hr 40min); Porto-Vecchio (2 daily; 3hr); St-Florent (2 daily; 1hr).
Bonifacio to: Ajaccio (2 daily; 3hr 30min–4hr); Bastia (2–4 daily; 3hr 35min); Porto-Vecchio (1–4 daily; 30min); Propriano (2–4 daily; 1hr 40min–2hr 10min); Sartène (2 daily; 1hr 25min–2hr).
Calvi to: Bastia (1 daily; 2hr 15min); L'Île Rousse (2 daily; 40min); Porto (1 daily; 2hr 30min); St-Florent (1 daily; 1hr 20min).
Cargèse to: Ajaccio (1–2 daily; 1hr 10min); Porto (2–3 daily; 1hr).
Corte to: Ajaccio (2 daily; 2hr); Bastia (2 daily; 1hr 15min); Évisa (4 daily; 2hr); Porto (4 daily; 2hr 30min).
Évisa to: Ajaccio (1–3 daily; 1hr 45min).
Porto to: Ajaccio (1–2 daily; 2hr); Calvi (1 daily; 3hr); Cargèse (2–3 daily; 1hr 15min).
Porto-Vecchio to: Ajaccio (2–4 daily; 3hr 30min); Bastia (2 daily; 3hr); Bonifacio (1–4 daily; 30min); Propriano (2–4 daily; 2hr 10min); Sartène (2–4 daily; 40min).
Propriano to: Ajaccio (2–4 daily; 1hr 35min–1hr 50min); Bonifacio (2–4 daily; 2hr 15min); Porto-Vecchio (2–4 daily; 2hr 10min); Sartène (2–4 daily; 20min).

Ferries

Marseille to: Ajaccio (3–7 weekly; 11hr overnight, or 4hr 35min NGV); Bastia (1–3 weekly; 10hr); L'Île Rousse (1–3 weekly; 11hr 30min overnight); Porto-Vecchio (1–3 weekly; 14hr 30min overnight); Propriano (1 weekly; 12hr overnight).
Nice to: Ajaccio (1–6 weekly; 12hr overnight); Bastia (1–12 weekly; 6hr, or 2hr 30min NGV); Calvi (2–5 weekly; 2hr 45min NGV); L'Île Rousse (1–3 weekly; 7hr overnight, or 2hr 45min NGV).
Toulon to: Ajaccio (1–4 weekly; 10hr overnight); Bastia (1–3 weekly; 8hr 30min overnight).

Contexts

Contexts

History..1267–1290

Art 1291–1304

Architecture...1305–1312

Cinema..1313–1327

Books..1328–1337

History

As a major European power, France has had a long and colourful history, exerting influence around the world, and what follows is necessarily a brief account of major events in the country's past. For more in-depth coverage see the choices given in "Books", p.1329.

Early civilizations

Traces of human existence are rare in France until about 50,000 BC. Thereafter, beginning with the stone tools of the Neanderthal "Mousterian civilization", they become ever more numerous, with an especially heavy concentration of sites in the Périgord region of the Dordogne, where, near the village of Les Eyzies, remains were discovered in 1868 of a late Stone Age people, subsequently dubbed "Cro-Magnon". Flourishing from around 25,000 BC, these cave-dwelling hunters seem to have developed quite a sophisticated culture, the evidence of which is preserved in the beautiful paintings and engravings on the walls of the region's caves.

By 10,000 BC, human communities had spread out widely across the whole of France. The ice cap receded, the climate became warmer and wetter, and by about 7000 BC, **farming and pastoral communities** had begun to develop. By 4500 BC, the first **dolmens** (megalithic stone tombs) showed up in Brittany, while dugout canoes dating back to the same epoch have been unearthed in Paris. Around 2000 BC, copper made its appearance; and by 1800 BC, the **Bronze Age** had arrived in the east and southeast of the country, and trade links had begun with Spain, central Europe and southern Britain.

Significant population shifts occurred, too, at this time. Around 1200 BC the **Urnfield people**, who buried their dead in sunken urns, began to make incursions from the east. By 900 BC, they had been joined by the **Halstatt people** who worked with iron and settled in Burgundy, Alsace and Franche-Comté near the principal ore **deposits**. At some point around 450 BC, the first Celts made an appearance in the region.

Pre-Roman Gaul

There were about fifteen million people living in **Gaul**, as the Romans called what we know as France (and parts of Belgium), when Julius Caesar arrived in 58 BC to complete the Roman conquest.

The southern part of this territory – more or less equivalent to modern **Provence** – had been a colony since 118 BC and exposed to the influences of Italy and Greece for much longer. **Greek colonists** had founded Massalia (Marseille) as far back as 600 BC. But even the inhabitants of the rest of the country, what the Romans called "long-haired Gaul", were far from shaggy barbarians. Though the economy was basically rural, the **Gauls** had established large **hilltop towns** by 100 BC, notably at Bibracte near Autun, where archeologists have identified separate merchants' quarters.

The Gauls also invented the barrel and soap and were skilful manufacturers. By 500 BC, they were capable of making metal-wheeled carts, as was proved by the "chariot tomb" of **Vix**, where a young woman was found buried lying on a cart with its wheels removed and propped against the wall. She was wearing rich gold jewellery and next to her were Greek vases and black figure pottery, dating the burial at around 500 BC and revealing the extent of commercial relations. Interestingly, too, the Gauls' money was based on the gold staters minted by Philip of Macedon, father of Alexander the Great.

Romanization

Gallic **tribal rivalries** made the Romans' job much easier, and when at last they were able to unite under **Vercingétorix** in 52 BC, the occasion was their total and final defeat by **Julius Caesar** at the battle of **Alésia**.

This event was one of the major turning points in the history of France. **Roman victory** fixed the frontier between Gaul and the Germanic peoples at the Rhine. It saved Gaul from disintegrating because of internal dissension and made it a Roman province. During the five centuries of peace that followed, the Gauls farmed, manufactured and traded, became urbanized and educated – and learnt Latin. Roman victory at Alésia laid the foundations of modern French culture and established them firmly enough to survive the centuries of chaos and destruction that followed the collapse of Roman power.

Lugdunum (Lyon) was founded as the capital of Roman Gaul as early as 43 BC, but it was the emperors **Augustus** and **Claudius** who really set the process of **Romanization** going. Augustus founded numerous cities – including Autun, Limoges and Bayeux – built roads, settled Roman colonists on the land and reorganized the entire administration. Gauls were inducted into the Roman army and given citizenship; Claudius made it possible for them to hold high office and become members of the Roman Senate, blurring the distinction and resentment between colonizer and colonized. Vespasian secured the frontiers beyond the Rhine, thus ensuring a couple of hundred years of peace and economic expansion.

Serious **disruptions** of the Pax Romana only began in the third century AD. Oppressive aristocratic rule and an economic crisis turned the destitute peasantry into gangs of marauding brigands – precursors of the medieval *jacquerie*. But most devastating of all, there began a series of incursions across the Rhine frontier by various restless **Germanic tribes**, the first of which, the Alemanni, pushed down as far as Spain, ravaging farmland and destroying towns.

In the fourth century the reforms of the emperor **Diocletian** secured some decades of respite from both internal and external pressures. Towns were rebuilt and fortified, an interesting development that foreshadowed feudalism and the independent power of the nobles since, due to the uncertainty of the times, big landed estates or *villae* tended to become more and more self-sufficient – economically, administratively and militarily.

By the fifth century, however, the Germanic invaders were back: **Alans**, **Vandals** and **Suevi**, with **Franks** and **Burgundians** in their wake. While the Roman administration assimilated them as far as possible, granting them land in return for military duties, they gradually achieved independence from the empire. Many Gauls, by now thoroughly Latinized, entered the service of the **Burgundian court of Lyon** or of the **Visigoth kings of Toulouse** as skilled administrators and advisers.

The Franks and Charlemagne

By 500 AD, the **Franks**, who gave their name to modern France, had become the dominant invading power. Their most celebrated king, **Clovis**, consolidated his hold on northern France and drove the Visigoths out of the southwest into Spain. In 507 he made the until-then insignificant little trading town of Paris his capital and became a Christian, which inevitably hastened the **Christianization** of Frankish society.

Under the succeeding **Merovingian** dynasty the kingdom began to disintegrate until in the eighth century the Pepin family, who were the Merovingians' chancellors, began to take effective control. In 732, one of their most dynamic scions, **Charles Martel**, reunited the kingdom and saved western Christendom from the northward expansion of Islam by defeating the Spanish Moors at the **battle of Poitiers**.

In 754 Charles's son, Pepin, had himself crowned king by the pope, thus inaugurating the **Carolingian dynasty** and establishing for the first time the principle of the divine right of kings. His son was **Charlemagne**, who extended Frankish control over the whole of what had been Roman Gaul, and far beyond. On Christmas Day in 800, he was crowned emperor of the **Holy Roman Empire**, though again, following his death, the kingdom fell apart in squabbles over who was to inherit various parts of his empire. At the Treaty of Verdun in 843, his grandsons agreed on a division of territory that corresponded roughly with the extent of modern France and Germany.

Charlemagne's administrative system had involved the royal appointment of counts and bishops to govern the various provinces of the empire. Under the destabilizing attacks of Norsemen/Vikings (who evolved into the Normans) during the ninth century, Carolingian kings were obliged to delegate more power and autonomy to these **provincial governors**, whose lands, like **Aquitaine** and **Burgundy**, already had separate regional identities as a result of earlier invasions – the Visigoths in Aquitaine, the Burgundians in Burgundy.

Gradually the power of these governors overshadowed that of the king, whose lands were confined to the Île-de-France. When the last Carolingian died in 987, it was only natural that they should elect one of their own number to take his place. This was Hugues Capet, founder of a dynasty that lasted until 1328.

The rise of the French kings

The years 1000 to 1500 saw the gradual extension and consolidation of the power of the **French kings**, accompanied by the growth of a centralized administrative system and bureaucracy. These factors also determined their foreign policy, which was chiefly concerned with restricting papal interference in French affairs and checking the English kings' continuing involvement in French territory. While progress towards these goals was remarkably steady and single-minded, there were setbacks, principally in the seesawing fortunes of the conflict with the English.

Surrounded by vassals much stronger than themselves, **Hugues Capet** and his successors remained weak throughout the eleventh century, though they made the most of their feudal rights. As dukes of the French, counts of Paris and anointed kings, they enjoyed a prestige their vassals dared not offend – not least because that would have set a precedent of disobedience for their own lesser vassals.

At the beginning of the twelfth century, having successfully tamed his own vassals in the Île-de-France, Louis VI had a stroke of luck. **Eleanor**, daughter of the powerful duke of Aquitaine, was left in his care on her father's death, so he promptly married her off to his son, the future Louis VII.

Unfortunately, the marriage ended in divorce and immediately, in 1152, Eleanor married Henry of Normandy, shortly to become **Henry II** of England. Thus the **English** crown gained control of a huge chunk of French territory, stretching from the Channel to the Pyrenees. Though their fortunes fluctuated over the ensuing three hundred years, the English rulers remained a perpetual thorn in the side of the French kings, with a dangerous potential for alliance with any rebellious French vassals.

Philippe Auguste (1179–1223) made considerable headway in undermining English rule by exploiting the bitter relations between Henry II and his three sons, one of whom was Richard the Lionheart. But he fell out with Richard when they took part in the **Third Crusade** together. Luckily, Richard died before he was able to claw back Philippe's gains, and by the end of his reign Philippe had recovered all of Normandy and the English possessions north of the Loire.

For the first time, the royal lands were greater than those of any other French lord. The foundations of a systematic administration and civil service had been established in **Paris**, and Philippe had firmly and quietly marked his independence from the papacy by refusing to take any interest in the crusade against the heretic Cathars of Languedoc. When Languedoc and Poitou came under royal control in the reign of his son Louis VIII, France was by far the greatest power in western Europe.

The Hundred Years War

In 1328 the Capetian monarchy had its first succession crisis, which led directly to the ruinous **Hundred Years War** with the English. Charles IV, last of the line, had only daughters as heirs, and when it was decided that France could not be ruled by a queen, the English king, **Edward III**, whose mother was Charles's sister, claimed the throne of France for himself.

The French chose **Philippe, Count of Valois**, instead, and Edward acquiesced for a time. But when Philippe began whittling away at his possessions in Aquitaine, Edward renewed his claim and embarked on war. With its population of about twelve million, France was a far richer and more powerful country, but its army was no match for the superior organization and tactics of the English. Edward won an outright victory at **Crécy** in 1346 and seized the port of Calais as a permanent bridgehead. Ten years later, his son, the Black Prince, actually took the French king, Jean le Bon, prisoner at the **battle of Poitiers**.

Although by 1375 French military fortunes had improved to the point where the English had been forced back to Calais and the Gascon coast, the strains of war and administrative abuses, as well as the madness of Charles VI, caused other kinds of damage. In 1358 there were **insurrections** among the Picardy peasantry (the *jacquerie*) and among the townspeople of Paris under the leadership of Étienne Marcel. Both were brutally repressed, as were subsequent risings in Paris in 1382 and 1412.

When it became clear that the king was mad, two rival camps began to vie for power: the **Burgundians**, led by the king's cousin and Duke of Burgundy, Jean sans Peur, and the **Armagnacs**, who gathered round the Duke of Orléans, Charles' brother. The situation escalated when Jean sans Peur had Orléans assassinated, and when fighting broke out between the two factions, they both called on the English for help. In 1415 Henry V of England inflicted another crushing defeat on the French army at **Agincourt**. The Burgundians seized Paris, took the royal family prisoner and recognized Henry as heir to the French throne. When Charles VI died in 1422, Henry's brother, the duke of Bedford, took over the government of France north of the Loire, while the young French heir, the Dauphin Charles, ineffectually governed the south from his refugee capital at Bourges.

At this point **Jeanne d'Arc** (Joan of Arc) arrived on the scene. In 1429 she persuaded Charles to launch an aggressive campaign, helped raise the English siege of the crucial town of Orléans and had the Dauphin crowned at Reims as Charles VII. Joan fell into the hands of the Burgundians, who sold her to the English, resulting in her being tried and burnt as a heretic. But her dynamism and martyrdom raised French morale and tipped the scales against the English: except for a toehold at Calais, they were finally driven from France altogether in 1453.

By the end of the century, **Dauphiné**, **Burgundy**, **Franche-Comté** and **Provence** were under royal control, and an effective standing army had been created. The taxation system had been overhauled, and France had emerged from the Middle Ages a rich, powerful state, firmly under the centralized authority of an absolute monarch.

The Wars of Religion

After half a century of self-confident but inconclusive pursuit of military glory in Italy, brought to an end by the **Treaty of Cateau-Cambrésis** in 1559, France was plunged into another period of devastating internal conflict. The **Protestant** ideas of Luther and Calvin had gained widespread adherence among all classes of society, despite sporadic brutal attempts by François I and Henri II to stamp them out.

Catherine de Médicis, acting as regent for her son, later Henri III, implemented a more tolerant policy, provoking violent reaction from the ultra-Catholic faction led by the **Guise** family. Their massacre of a Protestant congregation coming out of church in March 1562 began a civil **War of Religion** that, interspersed with ineffective truces and accords, lasted for the next thirty years.

Well organized and well led by the Prince de Condé and Admiral Coligny, the **Huguenots** – French Protestants – kept their end up very successfully, until Condé was killed at the battle of Jarnac in 1569. Three years later came one of the blackest events in the memory of French Protestants, even today: the **massacre of St Bartholomew's Day**. Coligny and three thousand Protestants who had gathered in Paris for the wedding of Marguerite, the king's sister, to the Protestant Henri of Navarre were slaughtered at the instigation of the Guises, and the bloodbath was repeated across France, especially in the south and west where the Protestants were strongest.

In 1584 Henri III's son died, leaving his brother-in-law, **Henri of Navarre**, heir to the throne, to the fury of the Guises and their Catholic league, who seized Paris and drove out the king. In retaliation, Henri III murdered the Duc de Guise, and found himself forced into alliance with Henri of Navarre, whom the pope had excommunicated. In 1589 Henri III was himself assassinated, leaving Henri of Navarre to become Henri IV of France. It took another four years of fighting and the abjuration of his faith for the new king to be recognized. "Paris is worth a Mass," he is reputed to have said.

Once on the throne, Henri IV set about reconstructing and reconciling the nation. By the **Edict of Nantes** of 1598, the Huguenots were accorded freedom of conscience, freedom of worship in certain places, the right to attend the same schools and hold the same offices as Catholics, their own courts and the possession of a number of fortresses as a guarantee against renewed attack, the most important being La Rochelle and Montpellier.

Kings, cardinals and absolute power

The main themes of the seventeenth century, when France was largely ruled by just two kings, **Louis XIII** (1610–43) and **Louis XIV** (1643–1715), were, on the domestic front, the strengthening of the centralized state embodied in the person of the king; and in external affairs, the securing of frontiers in the Pyrenees, on the Rhine and in the north, coupled with the attempt to prevent the unification of the territories of the Habsburg kings of Spain and Austria. Both kings had the good fortune to be served by capable, hard-working ministers dedicated to these objectives. Louis XIII had **Cardinal Richelieu** and Louis XIV had cardinals **Mazarin** and **Colbert**. Both reigns were disturbed in their early years by the inevitable aristocratic attempts at a coup d'état.

Having crushed revolts by Louis XIII's brother Gaston, Duke of Orléans, Richelieu's commitment to extending royal absolutism brought him into renewed conflict with the Protestants. Believing that their retention of separate fortresses within the kingdom was a threat to security, he attacked and took La Rochelle in 1627. Although he was unable to extirpate their religion altogether, Protestants were never again to present a military threat.

The other important facet of Richelieu's domestic policy was the promotion of economic self-sufficiency – **mercantilism**. To this end, he encouraged the growth of the luxury craft industries, especially textiles, in which France was to excel right up to the Revolution. He built up the navy and granted privileges to companies involved in establishing **colonies** in North America, Africa and the West Indies.

In pursuing his foreign policy objectives, Richelieu adroitly kept France out of actual military involvement by funding the Swedish king and general, Gustavus Adolphus, to make war against the Habsburgs in Germany. When in 1635, the French were finally obliged to commit their own troops, they made significant gains against the Spanish in the Netherlands, Alsace and Lorraine, and won Roussillon for France.

The Sun King

Richelieu died just a few months before Louis XIII in 1642. As Louis XIV was still an infant, his mother, Anne of Austria, acted as regent, served by Richelieu's protégé, **Cardinal Mazarin**, who was hated just as much as his predecessor by the traditional aristocracy and the *parlements*. They considered him an upstart and were anxious that their privileges, including the collection of taxes, would be curtailed. Spurred by these grievances, which were in any case exacerbated by the ruinous cost of the Spanish wars, various groups in French society combined in a series of revolts, known as the **Frondes**.

The first Fronde, in 1648, was led by the *parlement* of Paris, which resented royal oversight of tax collection. It was quickly followed by an aristocratic Fronde, supported by various peasant risings round the country. All were suppressed easily enough. These were not so much revolutionary movements but, rather, the attempts of various groups to preserve their privileges in the face of the growing power of the state.

In 1659 Mazarin successfully brought the Spanish wars to an end. Two years later, **Louis XIV** reached his majority, declaring that he would rule without a first minister. He embarked on a long struggle to modernize the administration. The war ministers, Le Tellier and his son Louvois, provided Louis with a well-equipped and well-trained professional army that could muster some 400,000 men by 1670. But the principal reforms were carried out by **Colbert**, who set about streamlining and improving the state's finances and tackling bureaucratic corruption. He set up a free-trade area in northern and central France, continued Richelieu's mercantilist economic policies, established the French East India Company, and built up the navy and merchant fleets with a view to challenging the world commercial supremacy of the Dutch.

These were all policies that the hard-working king was involved in and approved of. But in addition to his love of an extravagant court life at **Versailles**, which earned him the title of the **Sun King**, he had another obsession, ruinous to the state – the love of a prestigious military victory. His campaigns were even more ruinously expensive than his lifestyle. They were, however, fairly successful. He embarked on a war against the Dutch in 1672, which ultimately resulted in the acquisition of Franche-Comté and a swathe of Flanders including the city of Lille. In 1681 he simply grabbed Strasbourg, and got away with it.

In 1685, under the influence of his very Catholic mistress, Madame de Maintenon, the king removed all privileges from the **Huguenots** by revoking the Edict of Nantes. The result was devastating. Many of France's most skilled artisans, its wealthiest merchants and its most experienced soldiers were Protestants, and they fled the country in huge numbers – over 200,000 by some estimates. The Huguenots took their talents with them to Protestant countries, who promptly combined under the auspices of the League of Augsburg to fight the French. Another long and exhausting war followed, ending, most unfavourably for the French, in the **Peace of Rijswik** (1697).

No sooner was this concluded than Louis became embroiled in the question of who was to succeed the moribund Charles II of Spain as ruler of the Hapsburg domains in Europe. William of Orange, now king of England as well as ruler of the Dutch United Provinces, organized a Grand Alliance against Louis. The so-called **War of the Spanish Succession** broke out and went badly for the French. A severe winter in 1709 compounded the hardships with famine and riots at home, causing Louis to seek negotiations. The terms were too harsh for him and the war dragged on until 1713, leaving the country totally impoverished. The Sun King, finally, was eclipsed. He died in 1715, after ruling for 72 years over a country that had grown to dominate Europe, and had become unprecedentedly prosperous, largely because of colonial trade. Louis XIV's power and control, however, had masked growing tensions between central government and traditional vested interests.

Louis XV and the parlements

Louis XIV had outlived both his son and grandson. His successor, **Louis XV**, was only 5 when his great-grandfather died. During the **Regency**, the traditional aristocracy and the *parlements*, who for different reasons hated Louis XIV's advisers, scrambled – successfully – to recover a lot of their lost power and prestige. An experiment with government by aristocratic councils failed, and attempts to absorb the immense national debt by selling shares in an overseas trading company ended in a huge collapse. When the prudent and reasonable **Cardinal Fleury** came to prominence upon the regent's death in 1726, the nation's lot began to improve. The Atlantic seaboard towns grew rich on trade with the American and Caribbean colonies, though industrial production did not improve much and the disparity in wealth between the countryside and the growing towns continued to increase.

In mid-century there followed more disastrous military ventures, including the **War of Austrian Succession** and the **Seven Years War**, both of which were in effect contests with England for control of the colonial territories in America and India – contests that France lost. The need to finance the wars led to the introduction of a new tax, the Twentieth, which was to be levied on everyone. The *parlement*, which had successfully opposed earlier taxation and fought the Crown over its religious policies, dug its heels in again. This led to renewed conflict over Louis' pro-Jesuit religious policy. The Paris *parlement* staged a strike, was exiled from Paris, then inevitably reinstated. Disputes about its role continued until the *parlement* of Paris was actually abolished in 1771, to the outrage of the privileged groups in society, which considered it the defender of their special interests.

The division between the *parlements* and the king and his ministers continued to sharpen during the reign of **Louis XVI**, which began in 1774. Attempts by the enlightened finance minister Turgot to cooperate with the *parlements* and introduce reforms to alleviate the tax burden on the poor produced only short-term results. The national debt trebled between 1774 and 1787. Ironically, the one radical attempt to introduce an effective and equitable tax system led directly to the Revolution. Calonne, finance minister in 1786, tried to get his proposed tax approved by an **Assembly of Notables**, a device that had not been employed for more than a hundred years. His purpose was to bypass the *parlement*, which could be relied on to oppose any radical proposal. The attempt backfired. He lost his position, and the *parlement* ended up demanding a meeting of the **Estates-General**, representing the nobles, the clergy and the bourgeoisie, as being the only body competent to discuss such matters. The town responded by exiling and then recalling the *parlement* of Paris several times. As law and order began to break down, it gave in and agreed to summon the Estates-General on May 17, 1789.

Revolution

Against a background of deepening economic crisis and general misery, exacerbated by the catastrophic harvest of 1788, controversy focused on how the **Estates-General** should be constituted, and whether they should meet separately as on the last occasion in 1614. This was the solution favoured by the *parlement* of Paris, a measure of its reactionary nature: separate meetings would make it easy for the privileged, namely the clergy and nobility, to outvote the

Third Estate, the bourgeoisie. The king ruled that they should hold a joint meeting, with the Third Estate represented by as many deputies as the other two Estates combined, but no decisions were made about the order of voting.

On June 17, 1789, the Third Estate seized the initiative and declared itself the National Assembly. Some of the lower clergy and liberal nobility joined them. Louis XVI appeared to accept the situation, and on July 9 the Assembly declared itself the National Constituent Assembly. However, the king then tried to intimidate it by calling in troops, which unleashed the anger of the people of Paris, the *sans-culottes* (literally, "without trousers").

On July 14 the *sans-culottes* stormed the fortress of the **Bastille**, symbol of the oppressive nature of the *ancien régime* (old regime). Similar insurrections occurred throughout the country, accompanied by widespread peasant attacks on landowners' châteaux and the destruction of records of debt and other symbols of their oppression. On the night of August 4, the Assembly abolished the feudal rights and privileges of the nobility – a momentous shift of gear in the Revolutionary process, although in reality it did little to alter the situation. Later that month they adopted the **Declaration of the Rights of Man**. In December church lands were nationalized, and the pope retaliated by declaring the Revolutionary principles impious.

Bourgeois elements in the Assembly tried to bring about a compromise with the nobility, with a view to establishing a constitutional monarchy, but these overtures were rebuffed. Émigré aristocrats were already working to bring about foreign invasion to overthrow the Revolution. In June 1791 the king was arrested trying to escape from Paris. The Assembly, following an initiative of the wealthier bourgeois **Girondin** faction, decided to go to war to protect the Revolution.

On August 10, 1792, the *sans-culottes* set up a **Revolutionary Commune** in Paris and imprisoned the king. The Revolution was taking a radical turn. A new National Convention was elected and met on the day the ill-prepared Revolutionary armies finally halted the Prussian invasion at Valmy. A major rift swiftly developed between the more moderate **Girondins** and the **Jacobins** and *sans-culottes* over the abolition of the monarchy. The radicals carried the day. In January 1793, Louis XVI was executed. By June, the Girondins had been ousted.

Counter-Revolutionary forces were gathering in the provinces and abroad. A Committee of Public Safety was set up as chief organ of the government. Left-wing popular pressure brought laws on general conscription and price controls and a deliberate policy of de-Christianization, and **Robespierre** was pressed onto the Committee as the best man to contain the pressure from the streets.

The **Terror** began. As well as ordering the death of the hated queen, Marie-Antoinette, Robespierre felt strong enough to guillotine his opponents on both Right and Left. But the effect of so many rolling heads was to cool people's faith in the Revolution; by mid-1794, Robespierre himself was arrested and executed, and his fall marked the end of radicalism. More conservative forces gained control of the government, decontrolled the economy, repressed popular risings, limited the suffrage, and established a five-man executive Directory (1795).

Napoleon

In 1799, **General Napoleon Bonaparte**, who had made a name for himself as commander of the Revolutionary armies in Italy and Egypt, returned to

France and took power in a coup d'état. He was appointed First Consul, with power to choose officials and initiate legislation. He redesigned the tax system and created the Bank of France, replaced the power of local institutions by a corps of *préfets* answerable to himself, made judges into state functionaries – in short, laid the foundations of the modern French administrative system.

Though Napoleon upheld the fundamental reforms of the Revolution, the retrograde nature of his regime became more and more apparent with the proscription of the Jacobins, granting of amnesty to the émigrés and restoration of their unsold property, reintroduction of slavery in the colonies, recognition of the Church and so on. Although alarmingly revolutionary in the eyes of the rest of Europe, his Civil Code worked essentially to the advantage of the bourgeoisie. In 1804 he crowned himself **emperor** in the presence of the pope.

Decline, however, came with military failure. After 1808, Spain – under the rule of Napoleon's brother – rose in revolt, aided by the British. This signalled a turning of the tide in the long series of dazzling military successes. The nation began to grow weary of the burden of unceasing war.

In 1812, Napoleon threw himself into a **Russian campaign**, hoping to complete his European conquests. He reached Moscow, but the long retreat in terrible winter conditions annihilated his veteran Grande Armée. By 1814, he was forced to abdicate by a coalition of European powers, who installed **Louis XVIII**, brother of the decapitated Louis XVI, as monarch. In a last effort to recapture power, Napoleon escaped from exile in Elba and reorganized his armies, only to meet final defeat at **Waterloo** on June 18, 1815. Louis XVIII was restored to power.

Restorations and revolutions

The years following Napoleon's downfall were marked by a determined campaign, including the **White Terror**, on the part of those reactionary elements who wanted to wipe out all trace of the Revolution and restore the *ancien régime*. **Louis XVIII** resisted these moves and was able to appoint a moderate royalist minister, Decazes, under whose leadership the liberal faction that wished to preserve the Revolutionary reforms made steady gains. This process, however, was wrecked by the assassination of the Duc de Berry in an attempt to wipe out the Bourbon family. In response to reactionary outrage, the king dismissed Decazes. An attempted liberal insurrection was crushed and the four Sergeants of La Rochelle were shot by firing squad. Censorship became more rigid and education was once more subjected to the authority of the Church.

In 1824, Louis was succeeded by the thoroughly reactionary **Charles X**, who pushed through a law indemnifying émigré aristocrats for property lost during the Revolution. When the opposition won a majority in the elections of 1830, the king dissolved the Chamber and restricted the already narrow suffrage.

Barricades went up in the streets of Paris. Charles X abdicated and parliament was persuaded to accept **Louis-Philippe**, Duc d'Orléans, as king. On the face of it, divine right had been superseded by popular sovereignty as the basis of political legitimacy. The **1814 Charter**, which upheld Revolutionary and Napoleonic reforms, was reaffirmed, censorship abolished, the tricolour restored as the national flag, and suffrage widened.

However, the **Citizen King**, as he was called, had somewhat more absolutist notions about being a monarch. In the 1830s his regime survived repeated challenges from both attempted coups by reactionaries and some serious labour unrest in Lyon and Paris. The 1840s were calmer under the ministry of **Guizot**, the first Protestant to hold high office, and it was at this time that **Algeria** was colonized.

Guizot, however, was not popular. He resisted attempts to extend the vote to enfranchise the middle ranks of the bourgeoisie. In 1846, economic crisis brought bankruptcies, unemployment and food shortages. Conditions were appalling for the growing urban working class, whose hopes of a more just future received a theoretical basis in the **socialist writings** and activities of Blanqui, Fourier, Louis Blanc and Proudhon, among others.

1848 and the Second Republic

When the government banned an opposition *banquet* – the only permissible form of political meeting – in February 1848, workers and students took to the streets. When the army fired on a demonstration and killed forty people, civil war appeared imminent. The Citizen King fled to England, a provisional government was set up and a **republic** proclaimed. The government issued a right-to-work declaration, set up national workshops to relieve unemployment and extended the vote to all adult males – an unprecedented move for its time.

All was not plain sailing, though. By the time elections were held in April, a new tax designed to ameliorate the financial crisis had antagonized the countryside. A massive conservative majority was re-elected, to the dismay of the radicals. Three days of bloody street fighting at the barricades followed, when General Cavaignac, who had distinguished himself in the suppression of Algerian resistance, turned the artillery on the workers. More than 1500 were killed and 12,000 arrested and exiled.

A reasonably democratic constitution was drawn up and elections called to choose a president. To everyone's surprise, Louis-Napoléon, nephew of the emperor, romped home. In spite of his liberal reputation, he restricted the vote again, censored the press and pandered to the Catholic Church. In 1852, following a coup and further street fighting, he had himself proclaimed Emperor Napoléon III.

Empire and Commune

Through the 1850s, **Napoléon III** ran an authoritarian regime whose most notable achievement was a rapid growth in industrial and economic power. Foreign trade trebled, the rail system grew enormously, and the first investment banks were established. In 1858, in the aftermath of an attempt on his life by an Italian patriot, the emperor suddenly embarked on a policy of **liberalization**, initially of the economy, which alienated much of the business class. Reforms included the right to form trade unions and to strike, an extension of public education, lifting of censorship and the granting of ministerial "responsibility" under a government headed by the liberal opposition.

Disaster, however, was approaching in the shape of the **Franco–Prussian** war. Involved in a conflict with Bismarck and the rising power of Germany, Napoléon III declared war. The French army was quickly defeated and the emperor himself taken prisoner in 1870. The result at home was a universal demand for the proclamation of a **third republic**. The German armistice agreement insisted on the election of a national assembly to negotiate a proper peace treaty. France lost Alsace and Lorraine and was obliged to pay hefty war reparations.

Outraged by the monarchist majority re-elected to the new Assembly and by the attempt of its chief minister, Thiers, to disarm the National Guard, the people of Paris created their own municipal government known as the **Commune**. However, it had barely existed two months before it was savagely crushed. On May 21, the "*semaine sanglante*" began in which government troops fought with the Communards street by street, massacring around 25,000, the last of them lined up against the wall of Père Lachaise cemetery and shot. It was a brutal episode that left a permanent scar on the country's political and psychological landscape.

The Third Republic

In the wake of the Commune, competing political factions fought it out for control. Legitimists supported the return of a Bourbon to the throne, while Orléanists supported the heir of Louis-Philippe. Republicans, of course, would have none of either. Thanks in part to the intransigence of the Comte de Chambord, the Bourbon claimant who refused to accept a constitutional role – and in part to a corruption scandal surrounding the first President of the Third Republic, himself a monarchist – it was the Radicals and Socialists who came out on top. Minister Jules Ferry set out laws for free, secular education in 1881 and 1882, and the Crown Jewels were sold off in 1885.

From 1894, the **Dreyfus Affair** dramatically widened the split between right and left. Captain Dreyfus was a Jewish army officer convicted of spying for the Germans and shipped off to the penal colony of Devil's Island. It soon became clear that he had been framed – by the army itself – yet they refused to reconsider his case. The affair immediately became an issue between the anti-Semitic, Catholic Right and the Republican Left, with Radical statesman Clemenceau, Socialist leader Jean Jaurès and novelist Émile Zola coming out in favour of Dreyfus. Charles Maurras, founder of the fascist Action Française – precursor of Europe's Blackshirts – took the part of the army.

Dreyfus was officially rehabilitated in 1904, but in the wake of the affair the more radical element in the Republican movement began to dominate the administration, bringing the army under closer civilian control and dissolving most of the religious orders. In 1905 the Third Republic affirmed its anticlerical roots by introducing a law on the **separation of church and state**.

In the years preceding **World War I**, the country enjoyed a period of renewed prosperity. Yet the conflicts in the political fabric of French society remained unresolved. With the outbreak of war in 1914, France found itself swiftly overrun by Germany and its allies, and defended by its old enemy, Britain. The cost of the war was even greater for France than for the other participants because it was fought largely on French soil. Over a quarter of the eight million men called up were either killed or injured; industrial production fell to sixty percent of the prewar level. This – along with memories of the Franco-Prussian war of 1870 – was the reason that the French were more aggressive than either the British or the Americans in seeking war reparations from the Germans.

In the **postwar struggle for recovery** the interests of the urban working class were again passed over, save for Clemenceau's eight-hour-day legislation in 1919. An attempted general strike in 1920 came to nothing, and the left's strength was again undermined by the irreversible split in the Socialist Party at the 1920 Congress of Tours – the pro-Lenin majority forming the newly named **French Communist Party**. As the **Depression** deepened in the 1930s and Nazi power across the Rhine became more menacing, fascist thuggery and antiparliamentary activity increased in France, culminating in a pitched battle outside the Chamber of Deputies in February 1934. The effect of this fascist activism was to unite the Left, including the Communists, in the **Front Populaire** – which won the 1936 elections with a handsome majority. **Léon Blum** became France's first socialist and first Jewish Prime Minister.

Frightened by the apparently revolutionary situation, the major employers signed the **Matignon Agreement** with Blum, which provided for wage increases, nationalization of the armaments industry and partial nationalization of the Bank of France, a forty-hour week, paid annual leave and collective bargaining on wages. These **reforms** were pushed through parliament, but when Blum tried to introduce exchange controls to check the flight of capital, the Senate threw the proposal out and he resigned. The Left remained out of power, with the exception of coalition governments, until 1981. Most of the Front Populaire's reforms were promptly undone.

World War II

The agonies of **World War II** were compounded for France by the additional traumas of **occupation**, **collaboration** and **Resistance** – in effect, a civil war.

After the lightning defeat of the Anglo-French forces in May–June 1940, **Maréchal Pétain**, a cautious and conservative veteran of World War I, emerged from retirement to sign an armistice with Hitler and head the collaborationist **Vichy government**, which ostensibly governed the southern part of the country, while the Germans occupied the strategic north and the Atlantic coast. Pétain's prime minister, Laval, believed it was his duty to adapt France to the new authoritarian age heralded by the Nazi conquest of Europe.

There has been endless controversy over who collaborated, how much and how far it was necessary in order to save France from even worse sufferings. One thing at least is clear: Nazi occupation provided a good opportunity for out-and-out French fascists to track down Communists, Jews, Resistance fighters, freemasons – all those who they considered "alien" bodies in French society.

While some Communists were involved in the **Resistance** right from the start, Hitler's attack on the Soviet Union in 1941 freed the remainder from ideological inhibitions and brought them into the movement on a large scale. Resistance numbers were further increased by young men taking to the hills to escape conscription as labour in Nazi industry. General de Gaulle's radio appeal from London on June 18, 1940 resulted in the Conseil National de la Résistance, unifying the different Resistance groups in May 1943.

Although British and American governments found him irksome, **de Gaulle** was able to impose himself as the unchallenged spokesman of the Free French, leader of a government in exile, and to insist that the voice of France be heard as an equal in the Allied councils of war. Even the Communists accepted his leadership. Thanks to his persistence, representatives of his provisional government moved into liberated areas of France behind the Allied advance after D-Day, thereby saving the country from localized outbreaks of civil war. It was also thanks to de Gaulle that Free French units, notably General Leclerc's Second Armoured Division, were allowed to perform the psychologically vital role of

△ General de Gaulle at Bayeux, June 14, 1944

being the first Allied troops to enter Paris, Strasbourg and other emotionally significant towns in France.

The aftermath of war

France emerged from the war demoralized, bankrupt and bomb-wrecked. Almost half its population were peasants, living off the land, and its industry was in ruins. The only possible provisional government in the circumstances was de Gaulle's **Free French** and the Conseil National de la Résistance, which meant a coalition of Left and Right. As an opening move to deal with the mess, coal mines, air transport and Renault cars were nationalized. But a new constitution was required and elections, in which **French women** voted for the first time, resulted in a large Left majority in the new Constituent Assembly – which, however, soon fell to squabbling over the form of the new constitution. De Gaulle resigned in disgust. If he was hoping for a wave of popular sympathy, he didn't get it.

The constitution finally agreed on, with little enthusiasm in the country, was not much different from the discredited Third Republic. In the shadow of Vichy, the presidency was a weak institution, and the new **Fourth Republic** began its life with a series of short-lived coalitions. Nevertheless, the foundations for welfare were laid, banks nationalized and trade union rights extended. And thanks in part to American aid in the form of the Marshall Plan, France achieved enormous industrial **modernization and expansion** in the 1950s, its growth rate even rivalling that of West Germany at times. In foreign policy

France opted to remain in the US fold, but at the same time aggressively and independently pursued **nuclear technology**, finally detonating its own atom bomb in early 1960. France also took the lead in promoting closer **European integration**, a process culminating in 1957 with the creation of the European Economic Community.

Colonial wars

In its **colonial policy**, on the other hand, the Fourth Republic seemed firmly committed to nineteenth-century imperialism, despite the cosmetic reform of renaming the Empire the French Union.

On the surrender of Japan to the Allies in 1945, **Vietnam**, the northern half of the French Indochina colony, came under the control of Ho Chi Minh and his Communist organization Vietminh. Attempts to negotiate were bungled, and there began an eight-year armed struggle which ended with French defeat at Dien Bien Phu and partition of the country at the Geneva Conference in 1954 – at which point the Americans took over in the south, with well-known consequences.

In that year the government got embroiled in the **Algerian war of liberation**. The situation was complicated from the French viewpoint by the legal fiction that Algeria was a *département*, an integral part of France, and by the fact that there were a million or so settlers, or *pieds noirs*, claiming to be French, plus there was oil in the south. But by 1958, half a million troops, most of them conscripts, had been committed to the war. It was a bloody and brutal affair, characterized by torture and terrorism on both sides, and horrific loss of life. The Algerian government estimates the number of dead at almost a million, the French at roughly a third of that number.

When it began to seem in 1958 that the government would take a more liberal line towards Algeria, the hard-line Rightists among the settlers and in the army staged a putsch and threatened to declare war on France. General de Gaulle, waiting in the wings to resume his mission to save France, let it be known that in its hour of need and with certain conditions – ie stronger powers for the president – the country might call upon his help. Thus, on June 1, 1958, the National Assembly voted him full powers for six months and the Fourth Republic came to an end.

De Gaulle's presidency

As prime minister, then president of the **Fifth Republic** – with powers as much strengthened as he had wished – **de Gaulle** wheeled and dealed with the *pieds noirs* and Algerian rebels, while the war continued. In 1961, a General Salan staged a military revolt and set up the OAS (Secret Army Organization) to prevent a settlement. When his coup failed, his organization made several attempts on de Gaulle's life – thereby strengthening the feeling on the mainland that it was time to be done with Algeria.

An episode in the same year – covered up and censored until the 1990s – when between seventy and two hundred French Algerians were killed by the police in Paris, reinforced this feeling. This "**secret massacre**" began with a peaceful demonstration in protest against police powers to impose a curfew on any place in France frequented by North Africans. The police, it seems, went mad – shooting at crowds, batoning protesters and then throwing their bodies into the Seine. For weeks corpses were recovered, but the French media remained silent.

Eventually in 1962, a referendum gave an overwhelming yes to **Algerian independence**, and *pieds noirs* refugees flooded into France. Most of the rest of the French colonial empire had achieved independence by this time also, and the succeeding years were to see a resurgence of fascist and racist activity, among both the French "returnees" and the usual insular, anti-immigrant sectors. From the mid-1950s to the mid-1970s a French labour shortage led to massive recruitment campaigns for workers in North Africa, Portugal, Spain, Italy and Greece. People were promised housing, free medical care, trips home and well-paid jobs. When they arrived in France, however, these **immigrants** found themselves paid half as much as their French co-workers, accommodated in prison-style hostels and sometimes poorer than they had been at home. They had no vote, no automatic permit renewal, were subject to frequent racial abuse and assault and were forbidden to form their own organizations.

De Gaulle's leadership was haughty and autocratic in style, more concerned with *gloire* and grandeur than the everyday problems of ordinary lives. His quirky strutting on the world stage greatly irritated France's partners. He blocked British entry to the EC, cultivated the friendship of the Germans, rebuked the US for its imperialist policies in Vietnam, withdrew from NATO, refused to sign a nuclear test ban treaty and called for a "free Québec". If this projection of French influence pleased some, the very narrowly won presidential election of 1965 (in which Mitterrand was his opponent) showed that a good half of French voters would not be sorry to see the last of the general.

May 1968

Notwithstanding a certain domestic discontent, the sudden explosion of **May 1968** took everyone by surprise. Beginning with protests against the paternalistic nature of the education system by students at the University of Nanterre, the movement of revolt rapidly spread to the Sorbonne and out into factories and offices.

On the night of May 10, barricades went up in the streets of the Quartier Latin in Paris, and the CRS (riot police) responded by wading into everyone, including bystanders and Red Cross volunteers, with unbelievable ferocity. A **general strike** followed, and within a week more than a million people were out, with many factory occupations and professionals joining in with students and workers to march under radical slogans. Rather than demanding specific reforms, there was a general feeling that all French institutions – French society itself – needed overhauling.

De Gaulle seemed to lose his nerve and on May 27 he vanished from the scene. It turned out he had gone to assure himself of the support of the commander of the French army of the Rhine. On his return he appealed to the nation to elect him as the only effective barrier against left-wing dictatorship, and dissolved parliament. The frightened silent majority voted massively in his favour.

There were few radical changes as a result of May 1968, except perhaps in education. By and large, the formal, paternalistic and often authoritarian structures and institutions of France remained in place. But the failure of *les événements* – "the events", as they were called – to bear fruit didn't kill off French radicalism. For the next forty years, groups from feminists and ecologists to film-makers and outright anarchists would look back to May 1968 with mixed feelings of bitterness and inspiration. Many believe that the legacy of *les événements* is still being played out in French politics today.

Pompidou and Giscard

Having petulantly staked his presidency on the outcome of yet another referendum (on a couple of constitutional amendments) and lost, de Gaulle once more took himself off to his country estate and retirement. He was succeeded as president by his business-oriented former prime minister, **Georges Pompidou**.

The new regime was devotedly capitalist, and Pompidou hoped to eradicate the memory of 1968 in the creation of wealth, property and competition. His visions, however, had little time to attain reality. Having survived an election in 1972, Pompidou died, suddenly. His successor – and the 1974 presidential election winner by a narrow margin over the socialist François Mitterrand – was the former finance minister **Valéry Giscard d'Estaing**.

Having announced that his aim was to make France "an advanced liberal society", Giscard opened his term of office with some spectacular media coups, inviting Parisian trash collectors to breakfast, visiting prisons in Lyon and addressing the nation on television from his living room every evening. But, aside from reducing the voting age to 18 and liberalizing divorce laws, the advanced liberal society did not make a lot of progress. In the wake of the 1974 oil crisis the government introduced economic austerity measures. Giscard fell out with his ambitious prime minister, **Jacques Chirac**, who set out to challenge the leadership with his own RPR Gaullist party. And in addition to his superior, monarchical style, Giscard further compromised his popularity by accepting diamonds from the (literally) child-eating emperor of the Central African Republic, Bokassa, and by involvement in various other scandals.

The Left seemed well placed to win the coming 1978 elections, when the fragile union between the Socialists and Communists cracked, the latter fearing their roles as the coalition's junior partners. The result was another right-wing victory, with Giscard able to form a new government, with the grudging support of the RPR. Law and order and immigrant controls were the dominant features of Giscard's second term.

The Mitterrand Era, 1981–95

When **François Mitterrand** won the presidential elections over Giscard in 1981, inaugurating the first Socialist government for decades, hopes and expectations were sky high. The government pledged to increase state control over industry, introduce higher taxes for the rich, devolve more power to local government, raise the living standards of the least well-off and pursue European integration. By 1984, however, the flight of capital, inflation and budget deficits had forced a complete turnaround. Prime minister **Laurent Fabius** presided over a cabinet of centrist to conservative "socialist" ministers, clinging desperately to power. The 1986 parliamentary election saw the Right, under Jacques Chirac, winning a clear majority in parliament, so beginning *cohabitation* – the head of state and head of government belonging to opposite sides of the political fence. As Prime Minister, Chirac embarked on a policy of privatization and monetary control.

The 1980s ended with the most absurd blow-out of public funds ever – the **bicentennial celebrations of the French Revolution**. They symbolized a culture industry spinning mindlessly around the vacuum at the centre of the French vision for the future. And they highlighted the contrast between the unemployed and homeless begging on the streets and the limitless cash available for prestige projects.

During this period, Jean-Marie Le Pen, extreme right-winger and leader of the racist Front National, began to attract support. In 1991, Mitterrand sacked Socialist prime minister Michel Rocard, and appointed **Édith Cresson** as France's first woman prime minister. Her brand of left-wing nationalist rhetoric combined with centrist pragmatism made her highly unpopular at home and abroad.

In 1992, Mitterand staked his reputation on the **Maastricht referendum** on creating closer political union in Europe, as well as economic. The vote was carried by a narrow margin in favour. On the whole, poorer rural areas voted "No" while rich urbanites and political parties voted "Yes". Only the extreme end of the political spectrum, the Communists and the Front National remained determinedly anti-Europe.

Scandals over cover-ups and corruption culminated in the rout of the Socialists in the 1993 parliamentary elections, and the mysterious suicide a few months later of their last prime minister, **Pierre Bérégovoy**. Ushering in another period of *cohabitation*, **Edouard Balladur**, a fresh and fatherly face from the Right, was appointed prime minister. His government carried out a new privatization programme but soon lost the respect of its natural supporters after a series of U-turns following demonstrations by Air France workers, teachers, farmers, fishermen and school pupils, and the state's rescue of the Crédit Lyonnais bank after spectacular losses.

Mitterrand tottered on to the end of his presidential term, looking less and less like the nation's favourite uncle. Two months after Bérégovoy's suicide, Réné Bousquet, head of police in the Vichy government and responsible for the rounding up of Jews in 1942, was murdered. A personal friend of Mitterrand's, he was thought to have carried shady secrets about the president to his grave. A biography of Mitterrand, *Le Grand Secret*, stirred up further controversy about the president's war record as an official in the Vichy regime before he joined the Resistance.

Allegations of **corruption** against politicians and leading figures in industry were becoming an almost weekly occurrence. Several mayors ended up in jail, but it seemed as if the Paris establishment was above the law. Meanwhile, the country's profile abroad was also suffering. In 1994, France sent troops into **Rwanda**, whose previous murderous government they had supported and armed. French troops were accused of giving protection to French-speaking Hutus responsible for the genocide, and of acting too late to save any of the English-speaking Tutsis.

By the time Mitterrand finally stepped down, he had been the French head of state for fourteen years, during a period when crime rose and increasing numbers of people found themselves excluded from society by racism, poverty and homelessness. Corruption scandals touched the president, politicians of all parties and business chiefs and, as faith in old left-wing certainties foundered, support for extreme Right policies propelled the Front National from a minority faction to a serious electoral force. Despite this, when he died in January 1996, Mitterrand was genuinely mourned as a man of culture and vision, a supreme political operator, and an unwavering supporter of a united Europe.

Chirac's presidency

Elected as president in 1995 and winning a second mandate in 2002, Chirac has shown himself every bit as astute a politician as Mitterand, and no less prone to scandal and controversy. One of the first decisions he took on election in 1995 was to delay signing the Nuclear Non-Proliferation Treaty until France had carried out a new series of **nuclear tests** in the South Pacific – provoking almost universal condemnation.

On the home front, Chirac's Prime Minister, Alain Juppé, introduced **austerity measures**, designed to prepare France for European monetary union. Reforms to pensions and healthcare spending provoked a series of damaging strikes in 1995 and 1996, and led to growing popular disenchantment with the idea of closer European integration. The **Front National** played up their image of standing up for the small man against the corrupt political establishment, and at municipal elections in June 1995 gained control of three towns, including the major port of Toulon. The **Algerian bomb attacks** which rocked Paris in the mid-1990s – designed to punish France for supporting Algeria's anti-Islamist military government – further played into the hands of the far Right and diminished public confidence in the government as guardian of law and order. The interior minister, **Charles Pasqua**, tapped into the general feelings of insecurity and stepped up anti-immigration measures. As a result, around 250,000 people living and working in France had their legal status revoked.

Feeling increasingly beleaguered and unable to deliver on the economy, Chirac called a snap parliamentary election in May 1997. His gamble failed spectacularly as he saw the Right trounced by the Socialists. Chirac was forced into a weak *cohabitation* with the Socialists, headed by **Lionel Jospin**, who promptly introduced the 35-hour working week, a 50:50 gender quota for representatives of political parties and, in 1999, the **Pacs** or Pacte Civile de Solidarité, a contract giving cohabiting couples, particularly gay couples, almost the same rights as married people.

Jospin's government was soon hit by a series of scandals, however, including the resignation of internationally respected finance minister Dominique Strauss-Kahn over his alleged involvement in a party-funding scandal, though he was later acquitted. In 1999, Mitterrand-era cabinet ministers went on trial for involvement in the **tainted blood** scandal of the mid-1980s, in which four thousand transfusion recipients contracted AIDS. The court doled out acquittals and suspended sentences for the three main defendants, prompting outrage from the victims and their families, and ever-growing public cynicism.

Skeletons in the mayoral cupboard

The most persistent **corruption scandals**, however, have dogged the Right, rather than the Left, focusing on the finances of the Paris town hall dating back to the 1980s. In 1995 it was revealed that Alain Juppé had rented a luxury flat in Paris for his son at below-market rates, and in 1998 the conservative Paris mayor **Jean Tiberi** was implicated in a scandal involving subsidized real-estate and fake town-hall jobs – with real salaries – for party activists and relatives. The prosecutors edged ever closer to Chirac himself. In 2001 the president was accused of using some three million francs in cash from illegal sources to pay for luxury holidays, and in 2003 it was revealed that in eight years in office as mayor of Paris he and his wife had run up grocery bills of 2.2 million euros – over half of which had been reimbursed in cash. When investigating magistrates tried to question Chirac he claimed presidential immunity, a position that was upheld by France's highest court, though only as long as he remained in office.

What will happen when **Chirac stands down**, in 2007, is uncertain. An ominous note was sounded in 2004 when his right-hand man, **Alain Juppé**, was convicted of involvement in the town hall fake jobs scam. He was banned from office for ten years. In September 2006, critics accused Chirac of taking out insurance after he appointed his former legal adviser, Laurent de Mesle, as Paris's chief public prosecutor. The job will give De Mesle the task of deciding whether or not to press corruption charges when Chirac's presidential immunity finally ends.

The election earthquake

In the run-up to the **presidential elections of 2002**, everyone in France assumed that the race was between Jacques Chirac and his Socialist rival, Lionel Jospin. Other candidates were dismissed as marginal figures. The far left was as divided as ever, while the far-right vote had been damagingly split since 1996, when Bruno Mégret, the ambitious lieutenant of Front National leader **Jean-Marie Le Pen**, had formed a breakaway party. Le Pen himself had lost much support for punching a woman Socialist candidate in 1998.

Lionel Jospin's hopes had been bolstered by the election of Socialist **Bertrand Delanoë** as Mayor of Paris in March 2001 – the first time that the Socialists had won control of the capital since the bloody uprising of the Paris Commune in 1871. In the run-up to the elections, however, Jospin's lead over Chirac dwindled. The economy began to falter, unemployment was once more on the rise and fears over crime were widespread. Jospin was also hampered by his dowdy image. The backslapping, high-living Chirac, on the other hand, despite his scandal-mired background and poor record of achievement, had lost none of his ability to charm.

It was with utter shock that the country heard the announcement on the evening of April 21 that Jospin had been beaten into third place by Le Pen – leaving Chirac and Le Pen to stand against each other in the final run-off in May. The result, widely referred to as an "earthquake", sent shockwaves throughout the country and abroad. Widespread **voter apathy** and disillusionment were blamed. Many voters had abstained or voted for marginal candidates as a way of protesting against the mainstream parties. It was also felt that Chirac unwittingly helped Le Pen by campaigning on immigration and law and order, thus giving credibility to the very issues which formed the core of Le Pen's manifesto. Le Pen himself had fought a canny campaign, toning down his racist rhetoric and making capital out of the mainstream parties' sleaze and remoteness from ordinary people.

It was a wake-up call to the nation. On May 1, 800,000 people packed the boulevards of Paris to protest against Le Pen and his anti-immigration policies, in the biggest **demonstration** the capital had seen since the student protests of 1968. Chirac's victory in the next round was assured, with the Socialists calling on their supporters to vote for Chirac in order to keep Le Pen out. Chirac duly swept the board, winning by an unprecedented 82 percent. With the **parliamentary elections** still to come, Chirac's supporters rallied round to create an umbrella grouping of right-wing parties, called the **Union for a Presidential Majority**, to try and win for Chirac the majority in parliament that he'd failed to secure in 1997. The Socialists, severely shaken by Jospin's earlier defeat, were no match and the Right swept to power with 369 of the 577 seats in the

National Assembly. In an attempt to address widespread concerns about lack of representation and government accountability, one of Chirac's first measures was a **devolution** bill, giving more power to 26 regional assemblies and ending centuries of central government steadily accruing power to itself.

Iraq, Muslims and climate change

In 2003, a reinvigorated Chirac thrust himself into the international spotlight by adopting a remarkably intransigent stance over the **Iraq war**. As self-appointed spokesman for the no-sayers, Chirac declared in early March that he would wield France's Security Council veto if the US tried to table a resolution that contained an ultimatum leading to war. It was a bravura performance to an approving domestic crowd, the nationalist Right admiring Chirac's Gaullist flexing of France's international muscles and the Left reluctantly applauding his jaw-jutting opposition to American imperialism. Internationally, some interpreted France's stance as a principled defence of the UN and international law, others saw it as a test of the EU's diplomatic clout, and an assertion of France's power within Europe. Others still saw Chirac's actions as cynical political posturing.

Whether blamed on US bullishness or French pig-headedness, the result was an almighty farmyard scrap that left the US-led "coalition of the willing" exposed in Iraq without the diplomatic cover of definitive UN sanction. On either side of the Atlantic, the cherished Franco-American relationship suffered its worst spat ever. In France, American tourist numbers plummeted, and the nation indulged itself in an orgy of anti-Americanism.

One thing France's tough stance wasn't based on was any particularly pro-Arab or pro-Islamic bias, despite the presence of 5 million or more **Muslims** in France – the largest community in Europe. During 2003, Chirac presided over a government setting expulsion targets for illegal immigrants and enacting a hugely controversial bill – though it was backed by almost two thirds of the population and passed in parliament by 494 votes to 36 – banning "ostensibly religious" signs, notably Islamic headscarves, from schools and hospitals. Proposing the measure in December 2003, Chirac avowed that "Secularity is one of the republic's great achievements...We must not allow it to be weakened."

In 2003 **climate change** also bludgeoned its way onto the headlines, by indirectly causing the deaths of some 15,000 people over the norm. In Paris, temperatures in the first half of August were the hottest ever recorded, regularly topping 40°C (104°F) – more than ten degrees above the average maximum for that time of year. The authorities blamed lack of air-conditioning and the duration of the heatwave; the opposition blamed an ill-prepared health ministry. No one seemed willing to take responsibility for doing anything about it.

Reform and revolt

Faced with an ageing population, unemployment flatlining at around ten percent and a budget deficit persistently exceeding the eurozone's three-percent ceiling, the newly confident Right decided it would take on the public sector once and for all. Dubbed Agenda 2006, the **reform programme**'s targets were loathed by economic liberalizers and loved by most of the French public in equal measure. First to go under the knife would be the state's generous pensions and unemployment benefits, then worker-friendly hiring and firing rights, and finally the world-leading health service.

The government of Prime Minister **Jean-Pierre Raffarin** insisted that there simply wasn't enough money to go round. But most of France saw the programme less as prudent milk-rationing and more as getting their sacred cow ready to be sent off to slaughter. In the spring of 2003 the country suffered wave after wave of public-sector strikes and marches rolled through the streets. By mid-May, two million workers were out on strike; and on May 26 half a million protested in the streets of Paris. And this was only in defence of pensions, never mind the health service.

By 2004, the government had curbed its ambitions, while still insisting that reform was essential. The slick and ambitious new finance minister, **Nicolas Sarkozy**, set out a programme of privatizations and public-sector parsimony. The health-care budget would be trimmed, but so would the defence budget, and the electorate would be further mollified by consumer-focused tax breaks. The public response was unequivocal. In the regional elections of March 2004 just one of the 22 mainland regional councils remained in the control of the centre-right. Overnight, the electoral map had turned a furious pink.

The electorate's anger was not aimed solely at the Right. In the referendum of May 2005, 55 percent of French voters rejected the proposed new EU constitution when the major political parties had all urged them to vote "Yes". Former Socialist leader Laurent Fabius was even expelled from his party for joining an alliance of Greens, far-leftists and extreme right-wingers to campaign for a "No" vote. Opponents of the draft constitution saw it as wedding France to an "Anglo-Saxon" Europe after the neoliberal economic model. Many were voting against globalization or political paternalism as much as against the constitution itself.

In the wake of his government's defeat, Chirac's popularity plummeted to new depths, but he survived by sacking Raffarin as Prime Minister and replacing him with the intellectual-minded **Dominique de Villepin**, the architect of France's oppostion to war in Iraq. Nicolas Sarkozy – who had meantime got himself elected by a landslide as the new leader of Chirac's UMP party – was appointed Interior Minister. Both men were jockeying for position as Chirac's successor. And by the end of 2006, both men would have their reputations seriously undermined.

Civil unrest

Nicolas Sarkozy's test came with the wave of **civil unrest** that swept France's urban areas in November 2005. The initial cause was the accidental deaths of two teenagers, on 27 October. They were electrocuted in an electricity substation in Clichy-sous-Bois, a run-down area in the Paris *banlieue*, while running away from police they believed were chasing them. "The suburbs" doesn't begin to translate this word, *banlieue*. Great swathes of estates outlying the centre of major French cities suffer from poverty, social exclusion and government neglect on a scale unimaginable in bourgeois France.

Local anger led to numerous **car-burnings** and confrontations with police on three successive nights. By the fourth and fifth night, unrest had spread to other Parisian suburbs, and before a week was out localized rioting had spread to Dijon, Rouen and Marseille. Night after night, youths torched first cars, then buses, schools and police and power stations – anything associated with the state. The notorious, hardline response of "Sarko", as the Interior Minister was now dubbed, was to call the rioters *racailles* (a rabble) and to demand the neighbourhoods were cleaned with power-hoses. A state of emergency was declared and after three weeks, the banlieue seemed to have burned itself out. Almost 9000 vehicles and property worth €200 million had gone up in smoke, right across France, and almost over 2900 people had been arrested.

The causes of the unrest were hotly debated. A complete breakdown of relations between disaffected young people and the police was certainly the major factor. Right-wingers tried to blame Muslim radicals but this idea was quickly, and comprehensively, discredited. Young people who actually lived in the *cités* saw the main causes as anger at **racism** and exclusion from society, including exclusion from employment. Many of the worst-affected areas are home to communities of largely African or North-African origin, where youth unemployment runs as high as fifty percent – double the already high average among young people.

Youth and the CPE

Dominique de Villepin came out of the civil unrest with his career in better shape than that of his rival, Nicolas Sarkozy. But the issue of **youth employment** would soon put de Villepin, too, to the test. As part of his government's

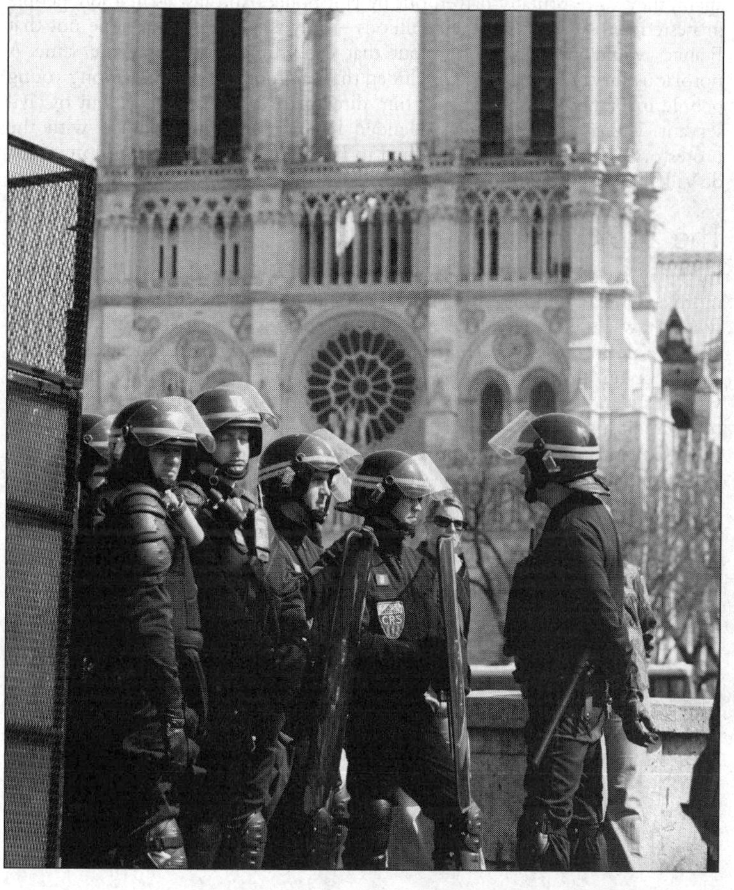

△ Riot police during the CPE riots, Paris, April 7, 2006

attempt to tackle France's stagnant growth and stubborn budget deficit, he launched new legislation giving small companies the right to dismiss new employees – those with under two years' service – without having to give cause. Labour-market flexibility was the goal. Such measures are by no means uncommon, but from the historical perspective of France's hard-won struggle for labour rights, they looked like an attack on the cherished **French exception** – the political status quo whereby the state protects workers' rights, the national agricultural and industrial base, and French culture generally, eschewing neoliberal or "Anglo-Saxon" capitalism. On 5 October, 2005, a million workers across the country marched against the new labour law, and polls showed that three-quarters of the population supported them.

In 2006, the laws were to be extended to all companies employing workers under the age of 26, as part of the Contrat première embauche (**CPE**), or first employment contract. The law was supposed to encourage firms to hire young people. Students and the young, however, saw it differently: why should they, uniquely, be denied the rights their elders took for granted? In March, students in Paris **occupied the Sorbonne**, in conscious imitation of May 1968. Once again, they were brutally driven out by riot police. And just as in 1968, people protested across France in their millions – only this time in the hope not that France would radically change, but that everything would stay the same. A notorious survey at this time concluded that the most desired job among young people in France was not that of film director or political activist, but of civil servant. *Casseurs*, or hooligans, blended in and sometimes clashed with the protestors – who seemed determined to back down. On April 10, Dominique de Villepin withdrew the law.

The 2007 presidential election

In the wake of the CPE debacle, Nicolas Sarkozy edged into the lead once more as **Chirac's likely successor**. De Villepin's fortunes took a further blow when newspapers alleged he had instructed judges to investigate Sarkozy's alleged role in the **Clearstream scandal**, in which French officials were said to have taken bribes as part of a 1991 deal to sell frigates to Taiwan. Sarkozy vigorously and successfully defended himself, even suggesting there was a plot to discredit him.

As it turns out, the ambitions of both men may yet come to nothing. Since 2002, the far-right candidacy of Le Pen cannot be discounted – and his popularity grew after the riots of 2005 and 2006. And as the elections approached, a new potential winner emerged: **Ségolène Royal**, of the opposition Socialist Party. Her campaign occupied a Blairite centre ground previously rare in French politics. On the one hand she promoted an anti-chauvinist agenda, while on the other she criticized the 35-hour week, and talked tough on law and order, thus edging into traditionally right-wing territory. It remains to be seen whether France – where women only got the vote in 1944 – is ready to accept its first female President.

Art

Since the Middle Ages, France has held – with occasional gaps – a leading position in the history of European painting, with Paris, above all, attracting artists from the whole continent. The story of French painting is one of richness and complexity, partly due to this influx of foreign painters and partly due to the capital's stability as an artistic centre.

Beginnings

In the late Middle Ages, the itinerant life of the nobles led them to prefer small and transportable works of art; splendidly **illuminated manuscripts** were much praised and the best painters, usually trained in Paris, continued to work on a small scale until the fifteenth century. In spite of the small size of the illuminated image, painters made startling steps towards a realistic interpretation of the world and in the exploration of new subject matters.

Many of these illuminators were also panel painters, foremost of whom was **Jean Fouquet** (c.1420–1481), born in Tours in the Loire valley and the central artistic personality of fifteenth-century France. Court painter to Charles VIII, Fouquet drew from both Flemish and Italian sources, utilizing the new fluid oil technique that had been perfected in Flanders, and concerning himself with the problem of representing space convincingly, much like his Italian contemporaries. Through this he moulded a distinct personal style, combining richness of surface with broad, generalized forms and, in his feeling for volume and ordered geometric shapes, laying down principles that became intrinsic to French art for centuries to come, from Poussin to Seurat and Cézanne.

Two other fifteenth-century French artists are worthy of brief mention, principally for the broad range of artistic expression they embody. **Enguerrand Quarton** (c.1410–c.1466) was the most famous Provençal painter of the time; his art, profoundly religious in subject as well as feeling, already shows the impact of the Mediterranean sun in the strong light that pervades his paintings. His *Pietà* in the Louvre is both stark and intensely poignant, while the *Coronation of the Virgin* that hangs at Villeneuve-lès-Avignon is a vast panoramic vision not only of heaven but also of a very real earth, in what ranks as one of the first city/landscapes in the history of French painting: Avignon itself is faithfully depicted and the Mont Ste-Victoire, later to be made famous by Cézanne, is recognizable in the distance.

The **Master of Moulins**, active in the 1480s and 1490s, was noticeably more northern in temperament, painting both religious altarpieces and portraits commissioned by members of the royal family or the fast-increasing bourgeoisie.

Mannerism and Italian influence

At the end of the fifteenth and the beginning of the sixteenth centuries, the French invasion of Italy brought both artists and patrons into closer contact with the Italian Renaissance.

The most famous of the artists who were lured to France was **Leonardo da Vinci**, spending the last three years of his life (1516–19) at the court of François 1er. From the Loire valley, which until then had been his favourite residence, the French king moved nearer to Paris, where he had several palaces decorated. Italian artists were once again called upon, and two of them, **Rosso** and **Primaticcio**, who arrived in France in 1530 and 1532 respectively, were to shape the artistic scene in France for the rest of the sixteenth century.

Both artists introduced to France the latest Italian style, **Mannerism**, a sometimes anarchic derivation of the High Renaissance of Michelangelo and Raphael. Mannerism, with its emphasis on the fantastic, the luxurious and the large-scale decorative, was eminently compatible with the taste of the court, and it was first put to the test in the revamping of the old Château de Fontainebleau.

There, a horde of French painters headed by the two Italians came to form what was subsequently called the **School of Fontainebleau**. Most French artists worked at Fontainebleau at some point in their career, or were influenced by its homogeneous style, but none stands out as a personality of any stature, and for the most part the painting of the time was dull and fanciful in the extreme.

Antoine Caron (c.1520–1600), who often worked for Catherine de Médicis, the widow of Henri II, contrived complicated allegorical paintings in which elongated figures are arranged within wide, theatre-like scenery packed with ancient monuments and Roman statues. Even the Wars of Religion, raging in the 1550s and 1560s, failed to rouse French artists' sense of drama, and representations of the many massacres then going on were detached and fussy in tone.

Portraiture tended to be more inventive. The portraits of **Jean Clouet** (c.1485–1541) and his son **François** (c.1510–72), both official painters to François 1er, combined sensitivity in the rendering of the sitter's features with a keen sense of abstract design in the arrangement of the figure, conveying with great clarity social status and giving clues to the sitter's profession. Though influenced by sixteenth-century Italian and Flemish portraits, their work remains, nonetheless, very French in its general sobriety.

The seventeenth century

In the **seventeenth century**, Italy continued to be a source of inspiration for French artists, most of whom were drawn to Rome – at that time the most exciting artistic centre in Europe, dominated by Italian painters such as Michelangelo Merisi da Caravaggio and Annibale Carracci.

Some French painters like **Moise Valentin** (c.1594–1632) worked in Rome and were directly influenced by Caravaggio; others, such as the great painter from Lorraine, **Georges de la Tour** (1593–1652), benefited from his innovations at one remove, gaining inspiration from the Utrecht Caravaggisti who were active at the time in Holland. Starting with a descriptive realism in which naturalistic detail made for a varied painted surface, La Tour gradually simplified both forms and surfaces, producing deeply felt religious paintings in which figures appear to be carved out of the surrounding gloom by the magical light of a candle. Sadly, his output was very small – just some forty or so works in all.

Lowlife subjects and attention to naturalistic detail were also important aspects of the work of the **Le Nain brothers**, especially **Louis** (1593–1648), who depicted with great sympathy, but never with sentimentality, the condition of the peasantry. He chose moments of inactivity or repose within the lives of the peasants, and his paintings achieve timelessness and monumentality by their very stillness. The other Italian artist of influence, the Bolognese **Annibale Carracci** (d. 1609), impressed French painters not only with his skill as a decorator but, more tellingly, with his ordered, balanced landscapes, which were to prove of prime importance for the development of the classical landscape in general, and in particular for those painted by **Claude Lorrain** (1604/5–82).

Claude, who started work as a pastry cook, was born in Lorraine, near Nancy. He left France for Italy to practise his trade, and worked in the household of a landscape painter in Rome, somehow persuading his master, who painted landscapes in the classical manner of Carracci, to let him abandon pastry for painting. Later he travelled to Naples, where the beauty of the harbour and bay made a lasting impression on him, the golden light of the southern port, and of Rome and its surrounding countryside, providing him with endless subjects of study, which he drew, sketched and painted for the rest of his life. Claude's landscapes are airy compositions in which religious or mythological figures are lost within an idealized, Arcadian nature, bathed in a luminous, transparent light which, golden or silvery, lends a tranquil mood.

Landscapes, harsher and even more ordered, but also recalling the Arcadian mood of antiquity, were painted by the other French painter who elected to make Rome his home, **Nicolas Poussin** (1594–1665). Like Claude, Poussin selected his themes from the rich sources of Greek, Roman and Christian myths and stories; unlike Claude, however, his figures are not subdued by nature but rather dominate it, in the tradition of the masters of the High Renaissance, such as Raphael and Titian, whom he greatly admired. During the working out of a painting Poussin would make small models, arrange them on an improvised stage and then sketch the puppet scene – which may explain why his figures often have a still, frozen quality. Poussin only briefly returned to Paris, called by the king, Louis XIII, to undertake some large decorative works quite unsuited to his style or character. Back in Rome he refined a style that became increasingly classical and severe.

Many other artists visited Italy, but most returned to France, the luckiest to be employed at the court to boost the royal images of Louis XIII and XIV and the egos of their respective ministers, Richelieu and Colbert. **Simon Vouet** (1590–1649), **Charles Le Brun** (1619–90) and **Pierre Mignard** (1612–95) all performed that task with skill, often using ancient history and mythology to suggest flattering comparisons with the reigning monarch.

The official aspect of their works was paralleled by the creation of the new **Academy of Painting and Sculpture** in 1648, an institution that dominated the arts in France for the next few hundred years, if only by the way artists reacted against it. **Philippe de Champaigne** (1602–74), a painter of Flemish origin, alone stands out at the time as remotely different, removed from the intrigues and pleasures of the court and instead strongly influenced by the teaching and moral code of Jansenism, a purist and severe form of the Catholic faith. The apparent simplicity and starkness of his portraits hides an unusually perceptive understanding of his sitters' personalities. But it was the more courtly, fun-loving portraits and paintings by such artists as Mignard that were to influence most of the art of the following century.

The early eighteenth century

The semi-official art encouraged by the foundation of the Academy became more frivolous and light-hearted in the **eighteenth century**. The court at

Versailles lost its attractions, and many patrons now were to be found among the hedonistic bourgeoisie and aristocracy living in Paris. History painting, as opposed to genre scenes or portraiture, retained its position of prestige, but at the same time the various categories began to merge and many artists tried their hands at landscape, genre, history or decorative works, bringing aspects of one type into another. **Salons**, at which painters exhibited their works, were held with increasing frequency and bred a new phenomenon in the art world – the art critic. The philosopher **Diderot** was one of the first of these arbiters of taste, doers and undoers of reputations.

Possibly the most complex personality of the eighteenth century was **Jean-Antoine Watteau** (1684–1721). Primarily a superb draughtsman, Watteau's use of soft and yet rich, light colours reveals how much he was struck by the great seventeenth-century Flemish painter Rubens. The open-air scenes of flirtatious love painted by Rubens and by the fifteenth/sixteenth-century Venetian Giorgione provided Watteau with precedents for his own subtle depictions of dreamy couples (sometimes depictions of characters from the Italian Commedia dell'Arte) strolling in delicate, mythical landscapes. In some of these *Fêtes Galantes* and in pictures of solitary musicians or actors (*Gilles*), Watteau conveyed a mood of melancholy, loneliness and poignancy that was largely lacking in the works of his many imitators and followers (Nicolas Lancret, J.-B. Pater).

The work of **François Boucher** (1703–70) was probably more representative of the eighteenth century: the pleasure-seeking court of Louis XV found the lightness of morals and colours in his paintings immensely congenial. Boucher's virtuosity is seen at its best in his paintings of women, always rosy, young and fantasy-erotic.

Jean-Honoré Fragonard (1732–1806) continued this exploration of licentious themes but with an exuberance, a richness of colour and a vitality (*The Swing*) that was a feast for the eyes and raised the subject to a glorification of love. Far more restrained were the paintings of **Jean-Baptiste-Siméon Chardin** (1699–1779), who specialized in homely genre scenes and still lifes, painted with a simplicity that belied his complex use of colours, shapes and space to promote a mood of stillness and tranquillity. **Jean-Baptiste Greuze** (1725–1805) chose stories that anticipated reaction against the laxity of the times; the moral, at times sentimental, character of his paintings was all-pervasive, reinforced by a stage-like composition well suited to cautionary tales.

Neoclassicism

This new seriousness became more severe with the rise of **Neoclassicism**, a movement for which purity and simplicity were essential components of the systematic depiction of edifying stories from the classical authors. Roman history and legends were the most popular subjects, and though **Jacques-Louis David** (1748–1825), a pupil of an earlier exponent of Neoclassicism, J.M. Vien, conformed to that to a certain extent, he was different in that he was also keenly sensitive to the changing mood and philosophies of his time and to the reaction against frivolity and self-indulgence. Many of his paintings are reflections of republican ideals and of contemporary history, from the *Death of Marat* to events from the life of Napoleon, who was his patron. For the emperor and his family, David painted some of his most successful portraits – *Madame Recamier* is not only an exquisite example of David's controlled use of shapes and space and his debt to antique Rome, but can also be seen as a paradigm of Neoclassicism.

Two painters, **Jean-Antoine Gros** (1771–1835) and **Baron Gérard** (1770–1837), followed David closely in style and in themes (portraits, Napoleonic history and legend), but often with a touch of softness and heroic poetry that pointed the way to Romanticism.

Jean-Auguste-Dominique Ingres (1780–1867) was a pupil of David; he also studied in Rome before coming back to Paris to develop the purity of line that was the essential and characteristic element of his art. His effective use of it to build up forms and bind compositions can be admired in conjunction with his recurrent theme of female nudes bathing, or in his magnificent and stately portraits that depict the nuances of social status.

Romanticism

Completely opposed to the stress on drawing advocated by Ingres, two artists created, through their emphasis on colour, form and composition, pictures that look forward to the later part of the nineteenth century and the Impressionists. **Théodore Géricault** (1791–1824), whose short life was still dominated by the heroic vision of the Napoleonic era, explored dramatic themes of human suffering in such paintings as *The Raft of the Medusa*, while his close contemporary, **Eugène Delacroix** (1798–1863), epitomized the **Romantic movement** – its search for emotions and its love of nature, power and change.

Delacroix was deeply aware of tradition, and his art was influenced, visually and conceptually, by the great masters of the Renaissance and the seventeenth and eighteenth centuries. In many ways he may be regarded as the last great religious and decorative French painter, but through his technical virtuosity, freedom of brushwork and richness of colours, he can also be seen as the essential forerunner of the Impressionists. For Delacroix there was no conflict between colour and design: David and Ingres saw these elements as separate aspects of creation, but Delacroix used colours as the basis and structure of his designs. His technical freedom was partly due to his admiration for two English painters, John Constable and his close friend, Richard Parkes Bonington, with whom he shared a studio for a few months. Bonington especially had a freshness of approach to colour and a free handling of paint, both of which had a strong impact on Delacroix. His numerous themes ranged from intimate female nudes, often with mysterious and erotic Middle Eastern overtones, to studies of animals and hunting scenes. Ancient and contemporary history supplied him with some of his most harrowing and dramatic paintings: *The Massacre at Chios* was based on an event that took place during the Greek War of Independence against the Turks, and *Liberty Guiding the People* was painted to commemorate the Revolution of 1830. Both paintings were his personal response to contemporary events and the human tragedies they entailed.

Other painters working in the Romantic tradition were still haunted by the Napoleonic legends, as well as by North Africa (Algeria) and the Middle East, which had become better known to artists and patrons alike during the Napoleonic wars. These were the subjects of paintings by **Horace Vernet** (1789–1863), **Jean-Louis-Ernest Meissonier** (1815–91) and **Théodore Chassériau** (1819–56).

Among their contemporaries was **Honoré Daumier** (1808–79): very much an isolated figure, influenced by the boldness of approach of caricaturists, he was content to depict everyday subjects such as a laundress or a third-class rail car – caustic commentaries on professions and politics that work as brilliant observations of the times.

Landscape painting and realism

Some painters of the first part of the **nineteenth century** were fascinated by other themes. Nature, in its true state, unadorned by conventions, became a subject for study, and running parallel to this was the realization that painting could be the visual externalization of the artist's own emotions and feelings. These two aspects, which until this time had only been very tentatively touched upon, were now more fully explored and led directly to the innovations of the Impressionists and later painters.

Jean-Baptiste-Camille Corot (1796–1875) started to paint landscapes that were fresh, direct and influenced as much by the unpretentious and realistic country scenes of seventeenth-century Holland as by the balanced compositions of Claude. His loving and attentive studies of nature were much admired by later artists, including Monet.

At the same time, a whole group of painters developed similar attitudes to landscape and nature, helped greatly by the practical improvement of being able to buy oil paint in tubes rather than as unmixed pigments. Known as the **Barbizon School** after the village on the outskirts of Paris around which they painted, they soon discovered the joy and excitement of *plein-air* (open-air) painting.

Théodore Rousseau (1812–67) was their nominal leader, his paintings of forest undergrowth and forest clearings displaying an intimacy that came from the immediacy of the image. **Charles-François Daubigny** (1817–78), like Rousseau, often infused a sense of drama into his landscapes.

Jean-François Millet (1814–75) is perhaps the best-known associate of the Barbizon group, though he was more interested in the human figure than simple nature. Landscapes, however, were essential settings for his figures; indeed, his most famous pictures are those exploring the place of people in nature and their struggle to survive. *The Sower*, for instance, was a typical Millet theme, suggesting the heroic working life of the peasant. As is so often the case for painters touching on new themes or on ideas that are uncomfortable to the rich and powerful, Millet enjoyed little success during his lifetime, and his art was only widely recognized after his death.

The moralistic and romantic undertone in Millet's work was something that **Gustave Courbet** (1819–77) strove to avoid. Courbet was a socialist and his frank, outspoken attitude led to his being accused of taking part in the destruction of the column in Paris's Place Vendôme after the outbreak of the Commune and, eventually, to his exile. After an initial resounding success in the Salon exhibition of 1849, he endured constant criticism from the academic world and patrons alike: scenes of ordinary life, such as the *Funeral at Orléans*, which he often chose to depict, were regarded as unsavoury and deliberately ugly.

But Courbet had a deep admiration for the old masters, especially for Rembrandt and the Spanish painters of the seventeenth and eighteenth centuries. This link with tradition was probably one of the underlying themes of his large masterpiece, *The Studio*, which was emphatically rejected by the jury of the 1855 Exposition Universelle, and in which Courbet portrayed himself, surrounded by his model, his friends, colleagues and admirers, among them the poet Baudelaire. Courbet subsequently decided to hold a private exhibition of some forty of his works, writing at the same time a manifesto explaining his intentions of being true to his vision of the world and of creating "living art". Writing the word **Realism** in large letters on the door leading to the exhibition, he stated his intentions and gave a label to his art.

Impressionism

Like Courbet, **Edouard Manet** (1832–83) was strongly influenced by Spanish painters, whose works had become more easily accessible to artists when a large collection belonging to the Orléans family was confiscated by the state in 1848. Unlike Courbet, though, he never saw himself as a socialist or indeed as a rebel or avant-garde painter, yet his technique and interpretation of themes was quite new and shocked as many people as it inspired. Manet used bold contrasts of light and very dark colours, giving his paintings a forcefulness that critics often took for a lack of sophistication. And his detractors saw much to decry in his reworking of an old subject originally treated by the sixteenth-century Venetian painter, Giorgione, *Le Déjeuner sur l'Herbe*. Manet's version was shocking because he placed naked and dressed figures together, and because the men were dressed in the costume of the day, implying a pleasure party too specifically contemporary to be "respectable".

Manet was not interested in painting moral lessons, however, and some of his most successful pictures are reflections of ordinary life in bars and public places, where respectability, as understood by the late nineteenth-century bourgeoisie, was certainly lacking. To Manet, painting was to be enjoyed for its own sake and not as a tool for moral instruction – in itself an outlook on the role of art that was quite new, not to say revolutionary, and marked a definite break with the paintings of the past. With Manet, the basis of our present expectations and understanding of modern art was established.

From the 1870s, Manet began to adopt the **Impressionist** techniques of painting out-of-doors, and his work became lighter and freer. Although it is doubtful whether Manet either wanted or expected to assume the role of leader, he found himself a much-admired member of that group of painters, one of whom was **Claude Monet** (1840–1926). Born in Le Havre, Monet came into contact with **Eugène Boudin** (1824–98), whose colourful beach scenes anticipated the way the Impressionists approached colour. He then went to Paris to study under Charles Gleyre, a respected teacher in whose studio he met many of the people with whom he formulated his ideas. Monet soon discovered that, for him, light and the way in which it builds up forms and creates an infinity of colours was the element that governed all representations. Under the impact of Manet's bright hues and his unconventional attitude ("art for art's sake"), Monet soon began using pure colours side by side, blended together to create areas of brightness and shade.

In 1874, a group of thirty artists exhibited together for the first time. Among them were some of the best-known names of this period of French art: Degas, Monet, Renoir, Pissarro. One of Monet's paintings was entitled *Impression: Sun Rising*, a title that was singled out by the critics to ridicule the colourful, loose and unacademic style of these young artists. Overnight they became, derisively, the "**Impressionists**".

Camille Pissarro (1830–1903) was slightly older than most of them and seems to have played the part of an encouraging father-figure, always keenly aware of any new development or new talent. Not a great innovator himself, Pissarro was a very gifted artist whose use of Impressionist technique was supplemented by a lyrical feeling for nature and its seasonal changes. But it was really with **Monet** that Impressionist theory ran its full course: he studied endlessly the impact of light on objects and the way in which it reveals colours. To understand this phenomenon better, Monet painted the same motif again and again under different conditions of light, at different times of the day, and in different seasons, producing whole series of paintings such as *Grain Stacks*, *Poplars* and, much later, his *Waterlilies*. In the late 1870s and the early 1880s many other artists helped formulate the new style, though few remained true to its principles for very long.

Auguste Renoir (1841–1919), who started life as a painter of porcelain, was swept up by Monet's ideas for a while, but soon felt the need to look again at the old masters and to emphasize the importance of drawing to the detriment of colour. Renoir regarded the representation of the female nude as the most taxing and rewarding subject that an artist could tackle. Like Boucher in the eighteenth century, Renoir's nudes are luscious, but rarely, if ever, erotic. They have a healthy, uncomplicated quality that was, in his later paintings, to become cloyingly, almost overpoweringly, sickly and sweet. Better were his portraits of women fully clothed, both for their obvious and innate sympathy and for their keen sense of design.

Edgar Degas (1834–1917) was yet another artist who, although he exhibited with the Impresssionists, did not follow their precepts very closely. The son of a rich banker, he was trained in the tradition of Ingres: design and drawing were an integral part of his art, and, whereas Monet was fascinated mainly by light, Degas wanted to express movement in all its forms. His pictures are vivid expressions of the body in action, usually straining under fairly exacting circumstances – dancers and circus artistes were among his favourite subjects, as well as more mundane depictions of laundresses and other working women.

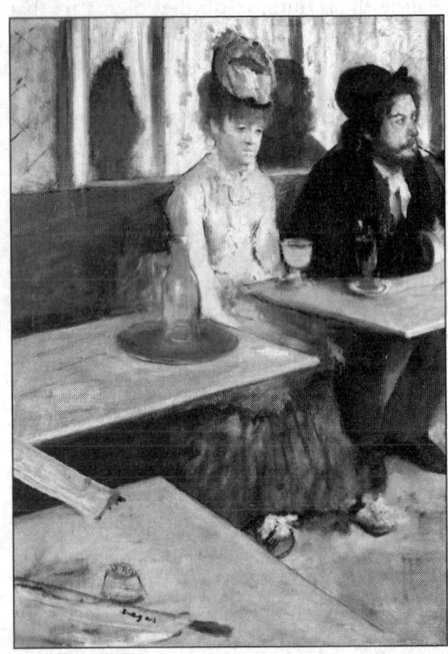

△ Degas' *L'Absinthe*

Like so many artists of the day, Degas had his imagination fired by the discovery of **Japanese prints**, which could for the first time be seen in quantity. These provided him with new ideas of composition, not least in their asymmetry of design and the use of large areas of unbroken colour. **Photography**, too, had an impact, if only because it finally liberated artists from the task of producing accurate, exacting descriptions of the world.

Degas' extraordinary gift as a draughtsman was matched only by that of the Provençal aristocrat **Henri de Toulouse-Lautrec** (1864–1901). Toulouse-Lautrec, who had broken both his legs as a child, was unusually small, a physical deformity that made him particularly sensitive to free and vivacious movements. A great admirer of Degas, he chose similar themes: people in cafés and theatres, working women and variety dancers all figured large in his work. But, unlike Degas, Toulouse-Lautrec looked beyond the body, and his work is scattered with social comment, sometimes sardonic and bitter. In his portrayal of Paris prostitutes, there is sympathy and kindness; to study them better he lived in a brothel, revealing in his paintings the weariness and sometimes gentleness of these women.

Post-Impressionism

Though a rather vague term, as it's difficult to date exactly when the backlash against Impressionism took place, **Post-Impressionism** represents in many ways a return to more formal concepts of painting – in composition, in attitudes to subject and in drawing.

Paul Cézanne (1839–1906), for one, associated only very briefly with the Impressionists and spent most of his working life in relative isolation, obsessed with rendering, as objectively as possible, the essence of form. He saw objects as basic shapes – cylinders, cones, and so on – and tried to give the painting a unity of texture that would force the spectator to view it not so much as a representation of the world but rather as an entity in its own right, as an object as real and dense as the objects surrounding it. It was this striving for pictorial unity that led him to cover the entire surface of the picture with small, equal brush strokes which made no distinction between the textures of a tree, a house or the sky.

The detached, unemotional way in which Cézanne painted was not unlike that of the seventeenth-century artist Poussin, and he found a contemporary parallel in the work of **Georges Seurat** (1859–91). Seurat was fascinated by current theories of light and colour, and he attempted to apply them in a systematic way, creating different shades and tones by placing tiny spots of pure colour side by side, which the eye could in turn fuse together to see the colours mixed out of their various components. This **pointillist** technique also had the effect of giving monumentality to everyday scenes of contemporary life.

While Cézanne, Seurat and, for that matter, the Impressionists sought to represent the outside world objectively, several other artists – the **Symbolists** – were seeking a different kind of truth, through the subjective experience of fantasy and dreams. **Gustave Moreau** (1840–98) represented, in complex paintings, the intricate worlds of the romantic fairy tale, his visions expressed in a wealth of naturalistic details. The style of **Puvis de Chavannes** (1824–98) was more restrained and more obviously concerned with design and the decorative. And a third artist, **Odilon Redon** (1840–1916), produced some weird and visionary graphic work that especially intrigued Symbolist writers; his less frequent works in colour belong to the later part of his life.

The subjectivity of the Symbolists was of great importance to the art of **Paul Gauguin** (1848–1903). He started life as a stockbroker who collected Impressionist paintings, a Sunday artist who gave up his job in 1883 to dedicate himself to painting.

During his stay in Pont-Aven in Brittany, Gauguin worked with a number of artists who called themselves the **Nabis**, among them **Paul Sérusier** and **Émile Bernard**. He began exploring ways of expressing concepts and emotions by means of large areas of colour and powerful forms, and developed a unique style that was heavily indebted to his knowledge of Japanese prints and of the tapestries and stained glass of medieval art. His search for the primitive expression of primitive emotions took him eventually to the South Sea islands and Tahiti, where he found some of his most inspiring subjects and painted some of his best-known canvases.

A similar derivation from Symbolist art and a wish to exteriorize emotions and ideas by means of strong colours, lines and shapes underlies the work of **Vincent Van Gogh** (1853–90), a Dutch painter who came to live in France. Like Gauguin, with whom he had an admiring but stormy friendship, Van Gogh started painting relatively late in life, lightening his palette in Paris under the influence of the Impressionists, and then heading south to Arles where, struck by the harshness of the Mediterranean light, he turned out such frantic expressionistic pieces as *The Reaper* and *Wheatfield with Crows*. In all his later pictures the paint is thickly laid on in increasingly abstract patterns that follow the shapes and tortuous paths of his deep inner melancholy.

Both Gauguin and Van Gogh saw objects and colours as means of representing ideas and subjective feelings. **Édouard Vuillard** (1868–1940) and **Pierre Bonnard** (1867–1947) combined this with Cézanne's insistence on unifying the surface and texture of the picture. The result was, in both cases, paintings of often intimate scenes in which figures and objects are blended together in a series of complicated patterns. In some of Vuillard's works, people dressed in checked material, for example, merge into the flowered wallpaper behind them, and in the paintings of Bonnard, the glowing design of the canvas itself is as important as what it's trying to represent.

Fauvism, Cubism, Surrealism

The **twentieth century** kicked off to a colourful start with the **Fauvist** exhibition of 1905, an appropriately anarchic beginning to a century which, in France above all, was to see radical changes in attitudes towards painting. The painters who took part in the exhibition included, most influentially, **Henri Matisse** (1869–1954), **André Derain** (1880–1954), **Georges Rouault** (1871–1958) and **Albert Marquet** (1875–1947), and they were quickly nicknamed the Fauves (Wild Beasts) for their use of bright, wild colours that often bore no relation whatsoever to the reality of the object depicted. Skies were just as likely to be green as blue since, for the Fauves, colour was a way of composing, of structuring a picture, and not necessarily a reflection of real life. Raoul Dufy (1877–1953) used Fauvist colours in combination with theories of abstraction to paint an effervescent industrial age.

Fauvism was just the beginning: the first decades of the twentieth century were times of intense excitement and artistic activity in Paris, and painters and sculptors from all over Europe flocked to the capital to take part in the liberation from conventional art that individuals and groups were gradually instigating. This loose, cosmopolitan grouping of artists gradually became known as the **Ecole de Paris**, though it was never a "school" as such. **Pablo Picasso** (1881–1973) was one of the first to arrive in Paris – from Spain, in 1900. He soon started work on his first Blue Period paintings, which describe the sad and squalid life of itinerant actors in tones of blue. Later, while Matisse was experimenting with colours and their decorative potential, Picasso came under the sway of Cézanne and his organization of forms into geometrical shapes. He also learned from "primitive", and especially African, sculpture, and out of these studies came a painting that heralded a definite new direction, not only for Picasso's own style but for the whole of modern art – *Les Demoiselles d'Avignon*. Executed in 1907, this painting combined Cézanne's analysis of forms with the visual impact of African masks.

It was from this semi-abstract picture that Picasso went on to develop the theory of **Cubism**, inspiring artists such as **Georges Braque** (1882–1963) and **Juan Gris** (1887–1927), another Spaniard, and formulating a whole new movement. The Cubists' aim was to depict objects not so much as they saw them but rather as they knew them to be: a bottle and a guitar were shown from the front, from the side and from the back as if the eye could take in all at once every facet and plane of the object. Braque and Picasso first analysed forms into these facets (analytical Cubism), then gradually reduced them to series of colours and shapes (synthetic Cubism), among which a few recognizable symbols such as letters, fragments of newspaper and numbers appeared. The complexity of different planes overlapping one another made the deciphering of Cubist paintings sometimes difficult, and the very last phase of Cubism tended increasingly towards abstraction.

Spin-offs of Cubism were many: such movements as **Orphism**, headed by **Robert Delaunay** (1885–1941) and **Francis Picabia** (1879––1953), who experimented not with objects but with the colours of the spectrum, and **Futurism**, which evolved first in Italy, then in Paris, and explored movement and the bright new technology of the industrial age. **Fernand Léger** (1881–1955), one of the main exponents of the so-called School of Paris, had also become acquainted with modern machinery during **World War I**, and he exploited his fascination with its smoothness and power to create geometric and monumental compositions of technical imagery that were indebted to both Cézanne and Cubism.

The war, meanwhile, had affected many artists: in Switzerland, **Dada** was born out of the scorn artists felt for the petty bourgeois and nationalistic values that had led to the bloodshed, a nihilistic movement that sought to knock down all traditionally accepted ideas. It was best exemplified in the work of the Frenchman **Marcel Duchamp** (1887–1968), who selected everyday objects ("ready-mades") and elevated them, without modification, to the rank of works of art simply by taking them out of their ordinary context and putting them on display – his most notorious piece was a urinal which he called *Fontaine* and exhibited in New York in 1917. His conviction that art could be made out of anything was to have a huge influence on later twentieth-century artists, especially conceptual artists, for whom "art as idea" was key.

Dada was a literary as well as an artistic movement, and through one of its main poets, André Breton, it led to the inception of **Surrealism**. It was the unconscious and its dark unchartered territories that interested the Surrealists: they derived much of their imagery from Freud and even experimented in words and images with free-association techniques. Strangely enough, most of the "French" Surrealists were foreigners, primarily the German **Max Ernst** (1891–1976) and the Spaniard **Salvador Dalí** (1904–89), though Frenchman **Yves Tanguy** (1900–55) also achieved international recognition. Mournful landscapes of weird, often terrifying images evoked the landscape of nightmares in often very precise details and with an anguish that went on to influence artists for years to come. **Picasso**, for instance, shocked by the massacre at the Spanish town of Guernica in 1936, drew greatly from Surrealism to produce the disquieting figures of his painting of the same name.

Towards Nouveau Réalisme

World War II knocked Paris from its position at the pinnacle of world art. At the outbreak of World War II many artists emigrated to the US, where the economic climate was more favourable. France was no longer the artistic melting pot of Europe, though Paris itself remained full of vibrant new work. Sculptors like the Romanian **Brancusi** (1876–1957) and the Swiss **Giacometti** (1886–1966) lived most of their lives in city. Reacting against the rigours of Cubism, many French artists of the 1940s and 50s opened themselves instead to the language and methods of American Abstract Expressionism, emanating from a vibrant New York. French painters such as **Pierre Soulages** (b.1919) and **Jean Dubuffet** (1901–1985) pursued **Tachisme**, also known as **l'Art informel**. Dubuffet was heavily influenced by **Art Brut** – that is, works created by children, prisoners or the mentally ill. He produced thickly textured, often childlike paintings, pioneering the depreciation of traditional artistic materials and methods, fashioning junk, tar, sand and glass into the shape of human beings. His work (which provoked much outrage) influenced both the French-born American, **Arman** (1928–2005), and **César** (1921–1998), both of whom made use of scrap metals – their output ranging from presentations of household debris to towers of crushed and compressed cars. Even more controversially, the Swiss **Daniel Spoerri** (b.1930) used the remnants – including the crockery – of his dinners and glued them onto a canvas.

These artists, among others, began to constitute what would be seen as the last coherent French art movement of the century: **Nouveau Réalisme**. A phenomenon largely of the late 1950s and 1960s, this movement rejected traditional materials and artistic genres, and concentrated instead on the distortion of the objects and signs of contemporary culture. It is often compared to Pop Art. Nouveau Réaliste sculpture is best represented by the works of the Swiss **Jean Tinguely** (1925–91), whose work was concerned mainly with movement and the machine, satirizing technological civilization. His most famous work, executed in collaboration with **Niki de Saint-Phalle** (1926–2002), is the exuberant fountain outside the Pompidou Centre, featuring fantastical birds and beasts shooting water in all directions.

Loosely associated with the Nouveaux Réalistes, though resisting all classification, **Yves Klein** (1928–1962) laid the foundations for several currents in contemporary art. He is seen as a precursor of Minimalism thanks to his exhibition "Le Vide" in 1958, in which he redefined the void and the immaterial as having a pure energy. He was fascinated by the colour blue, which he considered to possess a spiritual quality. He even patented his own colour, International Klein Blue, a deep and luminous blue which he used to execute a series of monochromes. He also used the colour in a series of "body prints", in which he covered female models with paint and got them to leave their imprints on paper, prefiguring body and performance art.

Conceptual and contemporary

The chief legacy of Surrealism in 1960s France was the way avant-garde artists regularly banded together – and often quickly disbanded – around ideological or conceptual manifestos. These groups were not art schools as such, more conscious experiments in defining and limiting what art could be, in the search for political or theoretical meaning – in search, some would say, of coherence. One of the first such self-constituted groups of the 1960s, **GRAV** (Groupe de recherche d'art visuel) played with abstraction in the form of mirrors, visual tricks and **kinetic art** – which had a strong heritage in France from Duchamp and Alexander Calder. Among the leading figures were **François Morellet** (b.1926), who focused on geometric works, and the Argentine-born **Julio Le Parc** (b.1928). GRAV's goal, as its 1963 *Manifesto* declared, was to demystify art by tricking the spectator into relaxing in front of the artwork.

Perhaps the most significant group launched itself in January 1967, when Daniel Buren, Olivier Mosset, Michel Parmentier and Niele Toroni removed their own works from the walls of the Salon de la Jeune Peinture, in protest against the reactionary nature of painting itself – and, paradoxically, to reaffirm the relevance of painting as an art form existing in itself, without interpretation. It was an early taste of the politics of 1968. The works of **BMPT** – the name was taken from the four men's surnames – focused on abstract colour, often in regular patterns. The best-known of the four, **Daniel Buren** (b.1938), caused a furore in 1985–6 with his installation in the courtyard of the Palais Royal consisting of numerous black-and-white, vertically striped columns of differing heights. Now, however, the one-time *enfant terrible* of the art world has become one of France's most respected living artists – a status confirmed by a one-man show at the Pompidou Centre in 2002.

Following BMPT's lead, the geometrically abstract **Supports-Surfaces** group emerged in Nice in 1969, founded by the likes of **Daniel Dezeuze** (b.1942), **Jean-Pierre Pincemin** (1944–2005) and **Claude Villat** (b.1936). The group stressed the importance of the painting as object – as paint applied to a surface. As Viallat put it, "Dezeuze painted stretchers without canvases, I painted canvases without stretchers".

The 1977 opening of the Musée Nationale d'Art Moderne, in Paris's Pompidou Centre, was a sign of the increased state support that French contemporary art was beginning to attract – a support that would be hugely boosted in the early 1980s by the active buying policy of the Socialist government. The landmark Pompidou exhibition of 1979, *Tendances de l'art en France*, showed artists in three groupings. The first was broadly abstract, the second, figurative. It was the third, however, which would look most prophetic of future directions; it focused on **conceptual artists**, many of them working with unconventional materials. This third group included the BMPT iconoclasts, along with three artists who would become landmark figures in French contemporary art: **Christian Boltanski** (b.1944) and **Annette Messager** (b.1943) – who were then husband and wife – and **Bertrand Lavier** (b.1949). All three work with found objects: Boltanski's often harrowing work has even employed personal property lost in public places, while Messager has drawn on toys and needlework to create unsettling works, often challenging perceptions of women. Lavier, meanwhile, is best-known for playing with art and reality – principally by applying paint to industrial objects.

A quintessentially French reaction to minimalist and conceptual art emerged in 1981 with **Figuration Libre**, a movement which absorbed comic-strip art and graffitti in an explosion of punk creativity. Among the key figures were **Jean-Charles Blais** (b.1956), **Robert Combas** (b.1957), **Francois Boisrond** (b.1959) and **Herve di Rosa** (b.1959). Despite such breakout movements, the juggernaut of conceptual art continued to roll on through the last two decades. Large-scale installation has become important, particularly in the works of **Jean-Marc Bustamante** (b.1952) and **Jean-Luc Vilmout** (b.1952), who have been known to co-opt buildings themselves, resulting in a blurring of the aesthetic and the functional. Artists crossing and recrossing generic boundaries is another ongoing theme. Bustamente, for example, also works with photography, and in the early 1980s he collaborated for three years with the sculptor Bernard Bazile (b.1952) under the name **Bazile Bustamante.**

A new generation of artists is using non-traditional media, including video, photography, electronic media and found objects. Recent work could hardly be more diverse, but a common thread seems to be the use of films and installations which explore the relationships between reality and fiction, between interiority and the exterior world. The current star of the scene is **Pierre Huyghe** (b.1962) who in 2005–06 had solo exhibitions at London's Tate Gallery and Paris's Musée de l'Art Moderne de la Ville de Paris. Huyghe is often associated with – and has worked with – the Algerian-born **Philippe Parreno** (b.1964), who in 2006 released a feature film which followed the footballer Zinédine Zidane for ninety minutes of relentless close-up. Two other associated artists are **Dominique Gonzalez-Foerster** (b.1965), who works with films, photographs, installations and even métro stations and shop windows to create worlds where fantasy and reality seem to overlap, and **Claude Closky** (b.1963), whose "books" and videos restructure everyday flotsam and jetsam. Closky has declared "My work bears on all that daily life has made banal, on things that are never called into question". He won the Marcel Duchamp prize in 2006. Similarly eclectic in his choice of media is **Fabrice Hybert** (b.1961), who has created the world's largest-ever bar of soap (at 22 tons) and a working television studio. His playful, interactive work taps into what he describes as the "enormous reservoir of the possible". **Sophie Calle** (b.1953) blends texts and photographs; among her most publicized works have been her intimate documentations of the lives of both strangers and – after she asked her mother to hire a private detective for the purpose – Calle herself.

In such a multimedia milieu, some critics have claimed that actual painting is moribund in France. In 2006, however, the Lyonnais painter **Marc Desgrandchamps** (b.1960), who has worked with traditonal oil paints in recent years, was recognized with a solo exhibition in the Pompidou Centre. Another key contemporary figure whose work bucks the conceptual trend is the French-born American sculptor **Louise Bourgeois** (b.1911). Now in her nineties, but still prolific, she draws on the Surrealist heritage to create disturbing and sometimes erotic works, often with a powerfully feminist theme.

Architecture

France's architectural legacy is rich and important, reflecting the power and personality of successive kings, the Church and the state, vying to outdo their peers with bold, lavish statements in brick and stone. Many architectural trends filtered into France from Italy – Romanesque, Renaissance and Baroque – but they have been refined and developed by the French. Rococo grew from Baroque, Neoclassicism came from the Renaissance, and Art Nouveau was a brilliant, confused jumble of Baroque features combined with the newly developed cast-iron industry. Architecture in the twentieth century produced two great names – Auguste Perret and Le Corbusier – but France's contemporary scene is still thriving, with a host of new developments throughout the country.

The Romans

The south of France was colonized by the **Romans** by around 120 BC in order to expand their trading operations, and they set up substantial settlements at Marseille, Narbonne, Orange, Arles, Fréjus, Glanum near St-Rémy, and Nice, with a network of roads linking them.

The Romans were fine town-planners, linking complexes of buildings with straight roads punctuated by decorative fountains, arches and colonnades. They built essentially in the Greek style, and their large, functional buildings were concerned more with strength and solidity than aesthetics. A number of substantial Roman building works survive: in **Nîmes** you can see the Maison Carrée, the best-preserved Roman temple still standing, and the Temple of Diana, one of just four vaulted Roman temples in Europe. Gateways remain at **Autun**, **Orange**, **Saintes** and **Reims**, and largely intact amphitheatres can be seen at Nîmes and **Arles**. The **Pont du Gard** aqueduct outside Nîmes is still a magnificent and ageless monument of civil engineering, built to carry the town's fresh water over the gorge, and Orange has its massive theatre, with Europe's only intact Roman facade. There are excavated archeological sites at **Glanum** near St-Rémy, **Vienne**, **Vaison-la-Romaine** and **Lyon**.

Carolingian and Romanesque

The **Carolingian dynasty** of Charlemagne attempted a revival of the symbols of civilized authority by recourse to Roman or "**Romanesque**" (ninth to twelfth centuries) models. Of this era, practically nothing remains visible, though the motifs of arch and vault are carried on in their simplest forms, and the semicircular apse and the basilican plan of nave and aisles persist as the basis of the succeeding phases of Christian architecture. An interesting anomaly is the plan of the **church of St-Front** at Périgueux, a copy of St Mark's in Venice, brought by trading influence west along the Garonne in the early twelfth century.

Elsewhere development may be divided roughly north–south of the Loire. Southern Romanesque is naturally more Roman, with stone barrel vaults, aisleless naves and domes. **St-Trophime** at Arles (1150) has a porch directly derived from Roman models and, with the church at St-Gilles nearby, exhibits a delight in carved ornament peculiar to the south at this time. The cathedral at **Angoulême** typifies the use of all these elements.

The south, too, was the readiest route for the introduction of new cultural developments, and it's here that the pointed arch and vault first appear – from Spanish Muslim sources – in churches such as **Notre-Dame** at Avignon, the cathedral at **Autun** and **Ste-Madeleine** at Vézelay (1089–1206), which contains the earliest pointed cross vault in France.

In the north of the country, the nave with aisles is more usual, together with the development of twin western towers to mask the end of the aisles. The **Abbaye aux Hommes** at Caen (1066–77) is typical. It contains the elements later developed as "Gothic", in piers, pillars, buttresses, arcades, ribbed vaults and spires. The best examples are found in Normandy, and it's from here, with the introduction of the pointed arch from the south, that the Gothic style developed.

Gothic

The reasons behind the development of the **Gothic style** (twelfth to sixteenth centuries) lie in the pursuit of the sublime; to achieve great height without apparent great weight would seem to imitate religious ambition. Its development in the north is partly due to the availability of good building stone and soft stone for carving, but perhaps more to the growth of royal aspiration and power based in the Île de France, which, allied with the papacy, stimulated the building of the great **cathedrals** of Paris, Bourges, Chartres, Laon, Le Mans, Reims and Amiens in the twelfth and thirteenth centuries.

The Gothic phase began with the building of the choir of the **abbey of St-Denis** near Paris in 1140, and ran through to the end of the fifteenth century. Architecturally, it encompasses the development of wider, traceried windows of coloured glass, filling the wall spaces liberated by the refinement of vertical structure; the "rose" or wheel is an early and especially French feature in window tracery. The glass at Chartres shows better than anywhere the concerted architectural effect of these developments. Another distinctive element is the flying buttress outside the walls to resist the outward push of the vaulting.

In the south, as at Albi and Angers, the great churches are generally broader and simpler in plan and external appearance, with aisles often almost as high as the nave. Many secular buildings survive – some of the most notable in their present form being the work of Viollet-le-Duc, the pre-eminent nineteenth-century restorer – and even whole towns, for example **Carcassonne** and **Aigues Mortes**; **Avignon** has the bridge and the papal palace.

Castles, of necessity, lent themselves less to the disappearing walls of the Gothic style. The **Château de Pierrefonds**, as restored by Viollet, may be taken as typical. The walls of many others disappeared by force, not whim, as gunpowder made them obsolete and a more settled and subjugated order led to the development of château-palaces, such as **Châteaudun** and **Blois**. The **Château de Josselin** in Brittany is a marvellous example of the smaller fortresses that became common towards the end of the Gothic period. In addition, a series of colonial settlements, the **bastides**, or fortified towns, of the English occupation, remain in the Dordogne region and are a refreshing antidote to triumphal French bombast.

Renaissance

French military adventures in Italy in the early sixteenth century hastened the arrival of a new style borrowing heavily from the Italian **Renaissance**. Coupled with the persistence of Gothic traditions and the necessity of steep roofs and tall chimneys in the French climate, it appears immediately "Frenchified" rather than in its pure imported form. The châteaux of kings and courtiers in the area round Paris and in the Loire valley, such as **Blois**, **Chambord** and **Chenonceau**, exemplify this style, with their wholly un-Italian concentration of interest on the skyline and an elaboration of detail in the facades at the expense of the clear modelling of form. The wing of the **Château de Blois** containing the famous staircase designed for François 1er in 1515 shows a characteristic new emphasis on horizontal lines, but the many Italian motifs are still overlaid on a basically Gothic form. With the passing of time, however, the dominant style in France became more purely classical; an adjacent wing at Blois, designed by **Mansart** in 1635, is still distinctively French, but much more true to classical principles. Above all, the **Louvre** embodies the whole history of the classical style in France, having been worked over by all the grand names of French architecture from Lescot in the early sixteenth century, via François Mansart and Claude Perrault in the seventeenth, to the later years of the nineteenth century.

It's unfortunate that the Renaissance style in France is chiefly seen in giant structures such as the Louvre and Versailles, which because of their scale can scarcely be experienced as buildings. That this is the case is largely due to the developing despotism and concentration of power under Louis XIII and Louis XIV. But there was a lighter side. François Mansart, at Blois and **Maisons Lafitte** (1640), shows a certain suavity and elegance, attitudes that appear again in the eighteenth century in the town houses of the Rococo period. On the other hand, **Claude Perrault** (1613–88), who designed the great colonnaded east front of the Louvre, gives an austere face to the official architecture of despotism, magnificent but far too imperial to be much enjoyed by common mortals. The high-pitched roofs, which had been almost universal until then, are replaced here by the classical balustrade and pediment, the style grand but cold and supremely secular. Art and architecture were at the time organized by boards and academies, including the Académie Royale d'Architecture, and style and employment were strictly controlled by royal direction. Between 1643 and 1774 France was governed by two monarchs who both ruled by the same maxim – absolute power. With such a limitation of ideas at the source of patronage, it's hardly surprising that there was a certain dullness to the era.

Baroque

In a similar way to the preceding century, the churches of the **seventeenth and eighteenth centuries** have a coldness quite different from the German, Flemish and Italian **Baroque**. When the Renaissance style first appeared in the early sixteenth century, there was no great need for new church building, the country being so well endowed from the Gothic centuries. **St-Étienne-du-Mont** (1517–1620) and **St-Eustache** (1532–89), both in Paris, show how old forms persisted with only an overlay of the new style.

It was with the Jesuits in the seventeenth century that the Church embraced the new style to combat the forces of rational disbelief. In Paris the churches of the **Sorbonne** (1653) and **Val-de-Grâce** (1645) exemplify this, as do a good number of other grandiose churches in the **Baroque** style, through **Les Invalides** at the end of the seventeenth century to the **Panthéon** of the late eighteenth century. Here is the Church triumphant, rather than the state, but no more beguiling.

The architect of Les Invalides was **Jules Hardouin Mansart**, a product of the Académie Royale d'Architecture, which harked back to the ancient, classical tradition. Mansart also greatly extended the palace of **Versailles** and so created the Cinemascope view of France with that seemingly endless horizon of royalty. As an antidote to this pomposity, the **Petit Trianon** at Versailles is as refreshing now as it was to Louis XV, who had it built in 1762 as a place of escape for his mistress. This is even more true of that other pearl formed of the grit of boredom in the enclosed world of Versailles – **La Petite Ferme**, where Marie-Antoinette played at being a milkmaid, which epitomizes the Arcadian and "picturesque" fantasy of the painters Boucher and Fragonard.

The lightness and charm that was undermining official grandeur with Arcadian fancies and **Rococo** decoration was, however, snuffed out by the Revolution. There's no real Revolutionary architecture, as the necessity of order and authority soon asserted itself and an autocracy every bit as absolute returned with Napoleon, drawing on the old grand manner but with a stronger trace of the stern old Roman. One architect, **Claude Ledoux**, was highly original and influential, both in England and Germany. And the visionary millennialist **Boullée** could also be said to be a child of Revolutionary times, though it's likely that such men were inspired as much by the rediscovered plainness of the Greek Doric order as by radical politics.

In Paris it was not the democratic Doric but the imperial Corinthian order that re-emerged triumphant in the church of the **Madeleine** (1806) and, with the **Arc de Triomphe** like some colossal paperweight, reimposed the authority of academic architecture in contrast to the fancy-dress structures of contemporary Regency England.

The nineteenth century

The restoration of legitimate monarchy after the **fall of Napoleon** stimulated a revival of interest in older Gothic and early Renaissance styles, which offered a symbol of dynastic reassurance not only to the state but also to the newly rich. So in the private and commercial architecture of the nineteenth century these earlier styles predominate – in mine-owners' villas and bankers' headquarters.

This traditional style was also favoured by **Baron Haussmann** (1809–1891), the architect who transformed Paris over a period of twenty years. He got rid of the city's narrow streets and cramped medieval buildings, and replaced them with wide boulevards, large squares and imposing edifices, largely creating the modern city we see today.

By the mid-nineteenth century, a neo-Baroque strain had established itself, a style exemplified by Charles Garnier's Opéra in Paris (1861–74), which, under the heading of Second Empire and with its associations of voluptuous good living, seductive painting and general "ooh-la-la", provides probably the most persistent image of France among the non-French.

In addition to the correct, official Classicism and the robust, exuberant and commercial Baroque, there is a third strand running through the nineteenth century that was ultimately more fruitful. The rational engineering approach, embodied in the official **School of Roads and Bridges** and invigorated by the teaching of Viollet-le-Duc, who reinterpreted Gothic style as pure structure, led to the development of new techniques out of which "modern" architectural style was born. Iron was the first significant new material, often used in imitation of Gothic forms and destined to be developed as an individual architectural style in America. In the **Eiffel Tower** (1889), France set up a potent symbol of things to come.

A more significantly French development was in the use of reinforced concrete towards the end of the century, most notably by **Auguste Perret**, whose 1903 apartment house at 25 rue Franklin in Paris turns the concrete structure into a visible virtue and breaks with conventional facades. Changes in the patterns of work and travel were making the need for new urban planning very acute in such cities as Paris. Perret and other **modernists** were all for the high-rise buildings that were going to better the haphazard layouts in America by a rational integration to new street systems. Some of their designs for gigantic skyscraper avenues and suburban rings now look like totalitarian horror-movie sets. But it was tradition, not charity, that blocked their projects at the time.

The twentieth century and beyond

The greatest proponent of the super New York scale, who also had genuine if mistaken concern for how people lived, was **Le Corbusier**, the most famous **twentieth-century** French architect. His stature may now appear diminished by the ascendancy of a blander style in concrete boxing, as well as by the significant technical and social failures of his buildings and his total disregard for historic streets and monuments.

But while his manifesto, *Vers une architecture moderne*, sounds like a call to arms for a new and revolutionary movement, Le Corbusier should perhaps be more fairly assessed as the original, inimitable and highly individual artist he undoubtedly was. You should try to see some of his work – there's the Cité **Radieuse** in Marseille and plenty of examples in Paris – to make up your own mind about the man largely responsible for changing the face and form of buildings throughout the world.

△ Von Spreckelsen's Grande Arche de la Défense, Paris

One respect in which Paris at the turn of the century lagged behind London, Glasgow, Chicago and New York was in **underground transport**. First proposed in the 1870s, it took twenty years of furious debate before the Paris métro was finally realized in 1900. The design of the entrances was as controversial as every other aspect of the system, but the first commission went to **Hector Guimard**, renowned for his variations on the then-current fashion in style. The whirling metal railings, Art Nouveau lettering and bizarre antennae-like orange lamps were his creation. Conservatives were less amused when it came to sites such as the Opéra. **Charles Garnier**, architect of that edifice, demanded classical marble and bronze porticoes for every station, and his line was followed, on a less grandiose scale, wherever the métro steps surfaced by a major monument, putting Guimard out of a job. Some of the early ones remain (**Place des Abbesses** is one), as do some of the white-tiled interiors, replaced after World War II in central stations by bright paint with matching seats and display cases.

Art Nouveau designs also found their way onto buildings – the early department stores in Paris, such as Printemps and La Samaritaine, are the best examples – but the new materials and simple geometry of the modern or International Style favoured the **Art Deco** look; again, you're most likely to come across them in the capital.

The miserable 1950s and 1960s buildings found all over the country are probably best skipped over. From the 1970s onwards, however, France again established itself as one of the most exciting patrons of international **contemporary architecture**. The **Pompidou Centre**, by **Renzo Piano** and **Richard Rogers**, derided, adored and visited by millions, maximizes space by putting the service elements usually concealed in walls and floors on the outside. The visible ducts, cables and pipes are painted in accordance with the colour code of architectural plans. You might think the whole thing is a professional in-joke, but the Pompidou Centre is one of the great contemporary buildings in western Europe – for its originality, popularity and practicality.

Paris was the focus of more innovative and exciting architecture in the 1980s with President Mitterand's *grands projets* ("grand projects"). One of his most ambitious projects was to extend the grand axis from the Louvre to the Arc de Triomphe westwards with the **Grande Arche de la Défense**, symbol of the new La Défense business district. Designed by Von Spreckelsen, the Grande Arche isn't really an arch but a huge hollow cube aligned with the Arc de Triomphe and conceived as an open gateway or window to the world. Mitterand also left his stamp at the other end of the grand axis with Ieoh Ming Pei's glass **pyramid** in the Cour Napoléon, the main entrance to the Louvre. Hugely controversial at first, it's now widely accepted and admired. The pyramid was just one part of a bigger project, the "Grand Louvre", designed to free up more exhibition space. As part of the reorganization, the **Ministry of Finance** moved out of their coveted offices, thus clearing the Richelieu wing of the Louvre for museum use. The Ministry decamped to a new building in **Bercy** designed by Paul Chemetov and nicknamed the "steamboat" because of its titanic length and its anchoring in the Seine. It's just one of many new buildings that have recently gone up in Bercy, formerly full of wine warehouses and now extensively redeveloped. The district's centrepiece is the Parc de Bercy, lined with neo-Haussmanian buildings and containing Frank Gehry's (architect of Bilbao's Guggenheim Museum) free-form, exuberant American Centre.

One of Mitterand's pet projects was the **Opéra Bastille**, intended as a "modern and popular" alternative to the Opéra Garnier. It was built by the young Uruguayan Carlos Ott, who was selected because his design seemed to make best use of the quirkily shaped site. The resulting building, divided into simple volumes, the most visible of which is the cylindrical extension housing the 2700-seat auditorium, met with mixed responses however, and was thought by many to be too large for the space. The building hasn't weathered particularly well either: bits of the facade's sheathing have started coming away and are being temporarily held in place with unsightly netting. The auditorium does have good acoustics however, nearly all the seats have frontal views of the stage and it's packed most nights.

Rather more successful is the **Cité de la Musique**, commissioned from acclaimed architect Christian de Portzamparc. The complex, which includes a grand concert hall, music conservatoire and museum, is designed, metaphorically, like a symphony, made up of many instruments and sounds to create a harmonious ensemble. The Cité is the finishing touch to the **Parc de la Villette** complex which was built under Giscard d'Estaing on the site of an old abattoir, and which also houses the Cité des Sciences and Bernard Tschumi's 21 "*folies*" of urban life. Perhaps the most outstanding of Mitterand's grands travaux is the **Institut du Monde Arabe** by **Jean Nouvel**, France's most eminent contemporary architect, with a design which ingeniously marries high-tech architecture and motifs from traditional Arabic culture. In a reference to the decorative wooden sunscreens used in Islamic countries, the facade is patterned with geometric metal screens punctured with apertures that are supposed to work a bit like a camera lens, opening and closing in response to the amount of sunlight received (though, in fact, the computer-operating system is unreliable).

Mitterand's last project was the **Bibliothèque Nationale**. Designed by Dominique Perrault, it's made up of four L-shaped tower blocks, resembling four open books, set around an inaccessible sunken garden. This apparently facile design is made up for by the complexity (and expense) of the detail. The aluminium shutters are covered in rare *oukoumé* reddish wood, which contrasts with the grey *ipé* and yellow *doussié* wood, to give the impression from a distance that the towers are bookshelves containing different bound volumes. Two-thirds of the library's 11 million books are stored in the basement; indeed, Perrault has likened his design to an iceberg, with much of its volume invisible beneath the towers. The Bibliothèque forms a central part of the **Paris Rive Gauche** project, a huge-scale redevelopment of the formerly industrial southern part of the 13e arrondissement, alongside the Seine. The scheme is edging towards completion, with the University Paris 7 soon to be installed in the massive **Grands Moulins de Paris** and **Halle aux Farines**, and a new school of architecture – appropriately enough – about to take up residence in the handsomely arched, late nineteenth-century **SUDAC** building. The futuristically twisting double-ribbon of the **Passarelle Bercy-Tolbiac**, meanwhile, already bridges the Seine opposite the library.

Outside Paris, the latest state-funded projects confirm French seriousness about innovative design. In Marseille there's Will Alsop's mammoth seat of regional government, while the first cathedral to be built in France since the nineteenth century, the **Cathédrale d'Évry**, masterminded by Swiss Mario Botta and finished in 1995, is a huge cylindrical red-brick tower which, besides being a place of worship, houses an art centre, concert hall and cinema screen. Its roof is slanted at 45 degrees to receive more light, and is crowned by 24 trees emulating the laurel wreaths of Roman emperors Hadrian and Augustus. Its stained-glass window is at the foot of the building and symbolizes the roots of a tree. The new **European Parliament** building in Strasbourg, designed by the Architecture Studio group, was finished in 1997, and is a huge boomerang-shaped structure with a glass dome and metal tower. It sits across the river from the eccentric, high-tech Richard Rogers-designed **European Court of Human Rights**.

Museums continue to attract innovative architects. In Nîmes, Norman Foster's **Carré d'Art** modern art museum (1993), is characterized by its simple transparent design, while his **Musée de Préhistoire des Gorges du Verdon** (2001) in Provence uses local materials – part of the museum is folded into the landscape and blends on one side into an existing stone wall, while the entrance hall resembles the very caves the museum celebrates. Jean Nouvel's curving, light-filled **Quai Branly** museum (2006), on the banks of the Seine beside the Eiffel Tower, is set in a lush garden designed by Gilles Clément, who landscaped the Parc André Citroën.

In **housing**, new styles and forms are to be seen in city suburbs and vacation resorts, many of them disastrous and visually unappealing, but interesting to look at when you don't have to live there. One of the largest projects of recent years is the Neoclassical **Antigone** development in Montpellier, laid out by the Catalan architect **Ricardo Bofill**.

The country's ever-advancing transport network has provided sites for some of the most high-tech office buildings with state-of-the-art engineering in Europe, as in **Roissy**, around the Charles-de-Gaulle airport, and especially at **Euralille**, the large urban complex around Lille's TGV/Eurostar station, masterminded by Dutch architect Rem Koolhaas.

The French are also very good at preserving the past – too good, some would say. A passion for restoring "*la patrimoine*" results in many fine old buildings being practically rebuilt – the dominant restoration theory in France is to restore to perfection rather than halt decay. More often than not, restoration is carried out by the **Maisons de Compagnonage**, the old craft guilds, which have maintained traditional building skills, handing them down as of old from master to apprentice (and never to women), while also taking on new industrial skills.

Cinema

The first (satisfied) cinema audience in the world was French. Screened to patrons of the Grand Café, on Paris's boulevard des Capucines, in December 1895, Louis **Lumière**'s single-reelers may have been jerky documentaries, but they were light-years ahead of anything that had come before. Soon after, Georges Méliès' magical-fantastical features were proving a big hit with theatre audiences, and the twin cinematic poles of Realism and Surrealism had been established. France took to cinema with characteristic enthusiasm and seriousness. Ciné-clubs were formed all over the country, journals were published, critics made films and film-makers became critics. The avant-garde wing of French cinema acquired the moniker of **French Impressionism**, a genre characterized by experimental directors such as Louis Delluc, Jean Epstein and Abel Gance, who used experimental, highly visual techniques to express altered states of consciousness. It was only a short step from here to the all-out **Surrealism** of the artist-polymath Jean Cocteau, and the Spanish director Luis Buñuel.

Towards the end of the 1920s, histrionic adaptations of novels, epic historical dramas and broad comedies attracted mass audiences, but the silent heyday ended abruptly with the advent of sound in 1929. Most silent stars faded into obscurity, but a number of directors successfully made the transition, notably Jean Renoir, the son of the painter, René Clair, Julien Duvivier, Jean Gremillon and Abel Gance. Among the newcomers were Jean Vigo, who died young in 1934, and Marcel Carné, who worked with the powerful scripts of the poet Jacques Prévert. The film-makers of the 1930s developed a bold new style, dubbed **Poetic Realism** for its pessimism, powerful visual aesthetic – high-contrast, often nocturnal – and devotion to "realistic", usually working-class, settings.

In 1936 the collector Henri Langlois set up the **Cinémathèque Française**, devoted to the preservation and screening of old and art films – an indication of the speed with which the "*septième art*" had found its niche within the pantheon of French culture. Langlois played an important role in saving thousands of films from destruction during the war, but the Occupation had surprisingly little effect on the industry. Renoir and Clair sought temporary sanctuary in Hollywood, and domestic production dipped, but hundreds of films continued to be made in Vichy France at a time when audiences sought the solace and comfort of the cinema in record numbers.

Post-war and pre-television, the late 1940s and early 1950s was another boom time for French cinema. Poetic Realism morphed into **film noir**, whose emphasis on darkness and corruption gave birth in turn to the thriller, a genre exemplified by the films of Henri-Georges Clouzot and Jean-Pierre Melville. During this period the mainstream cinema industry became highly organized and technically slick, older directors such as Clair, Renoir and Jacques Becker making superbly controlled masterpieces spanning genres as diverse as thrillers, comedies and costume dramas.

The first shot of the coming revolution – a warning shot only – was fired by the acerbic young critic François Truffaut, writing in the legendary film magazine, **Les Cahiers du cinéma**, in the mid-1950s. In opposition to what he and fellow critics dubbed *la tradition de qualité*, Truffaut envisaged a new kind of cinema based on the independent vision of a writer-director, an *auteur* (author), who would make films in a purer and and more responsive manner. Directors such as Melville and Louis Malle – who made his first film with the diver Jacques Cousteau – were beginning to make moves in this direction, but Truffaut's vision was only fully realized towards the end of the decade, when the **Nouvelle Vague** ("New Wave") came rolling in. Claude Chabrol's *Les Cousins*, Truffaut's own *Les Quatre-cents Coups*, Eric Rohmer's *Le Signe du Lion*, Alain Resnais' *Hiroshima Mon Amour* and Jean-Luc Godard's *À Bout de Souffle* were all released in 1959. The trademark freedom of these *auteur*-directors' films – loosely scripted, highly individualistic and typically shot on location – ushered in the modern era.

The 1960s was the heyday of the *auteur*. Truffaut established his pre-eminent status by creating an extraordinary oeuvre encompassing science fiction, thriller, autobiography and film noir, all his films characteristically elegant and excitingly shot. But the "new wave" hadn't carried all before it: René Clément, Henri-Georges Clouzot and even Jean Renoir were still working throughout the decade, Jean-Pierre Melville continued shooting his characteristically noir **films policiers** (crime-thrillers), and the Catholic director Robert Bresson carried on making films on his favourite theme of salvation. And Jacques Tati, the maverick genius behind the legendary comic character M. Hulot, made two of his greatest and most radical quasi-silent films, *Playtime* and *Trafic*, at either end of the 1960s.

The 1970s is probably the least impressive decade in terms of output, but a shot in the arm was delivered in the 1980s by the **Cinéma du Look**, a genre epitomized in the films of Jean-Jacques Beineix, Luc Besson and Leos Carax. Stylish, image-conscious and postmodern, films such as *Diva* or *Betty Blue* owed much to the look of American pulp cinema and contemporary advertising. Meanwhile, throughout the 1980s and into the 1990s, high-gloss costume dramas – historical or adaptations of novels – were the focus of much attention. Often called **Heritage Cinema**, the best films of this genre are the superbly crafted creations of Claude Berri, though Jean-Pierre Rappeneau's *Cyrano de Bergerac* is probably the internationally recognized standard-bearer. At the other end of the scale lies **cinéma beur**: naturalistic, socially responsible and low-budget films made by French-born film-makers of North African origin – *les beurs* in French slang. The newest trends in contemporary art cinema follow a related path of social realism. In recent years, a number of younger directors, notably Mathieu Kassovitz, have made films set in the deprived suburbs (*la banlieue*), creating a number of sub-genres that have been acclaimed variously as **New Realism**, **cinéma de banlieue** and **le jeune cinéma** ("young cinema").

Today, France remains the second-largest exporter of films in the world. The industry's continued health is largely due to the intransigence of the French state, which continues to protect and promote domestic cinema as part of its policy of **l'exception culturelle** – despite the complaints of the free-marketeers who would have the French market "liberalized". Half of the costs of making a feature film in France are paid for by state subsidies, levied on television stations, box-office receipts and video sales. Currently, American-made films capture around 50 percent of the French market, while home-grown productions make up around 40 percent. But the future looks promising: recent years have seen the number of films made in France rise to almost two hundred a year, most of them domestically funded.

Note that the **films reviewed below** are only intended to give an overview of the landmarks of French cinema; we can't review every Godard film or every much-loved classic, nor cover every significant director. Alternative English titles are given for those films renamed for the main foreign release. Films marked are highly recommended.

The classic era

Silent films

Lumière and Méliès Early Lumière films such as *L'Arrivé d'un train en gare* (1895) don't have the same impact now as when they made audiences jump with fright, but *L'Arroseur arrosé* (1896) works around a tight narrative that is still entertaining – a boy plays a prank on a gardener doing the watering and is chased and punished. By contrast with Lumière's documentary approach, Méliès's early short films, such as *Le Voyage dans la lune* (1902), used studio sets to create groundbreaking magical-surreal effects.

Paris qui dort/The Crazy Ray René Clair, 1924. Clair's first feature was heavily indebted to Surrealism. An inventor activates a ray that suspends time across the entire city of Paris – giving Clair plenty of opportunities to try out trick photography. Only a few Parisians are unaffected, including the watchman on top of the Eiffel Tower. Liberated from their inhibitions, they go on a criminal rampage.

Nana Jean Renoir, 1926. Second son of the painter Auguste Renoir, the greatest of France's early directors began his career making silent movies, of which the best is this ambitious and complex adaptation of Zola's novel, *Nana*. Fans of Renoir's later work may find the film's style surprisingly mannered, especially the performance of his wife Catherine Hessling, which owes a lot to Expressionist cinema.

Un Chapeau de paille d'Italie René Clair, 1927. As the film opens, the hero's horse eats the straw hat (*chapeau de paille*) of a young woman in the Bois de Boulogne, thus setting in motion a fast-paced and farcical chain of events as he attempts to find a replacement hat while simultaneously trying to get to his own wedding.

Napoléon vu par Abel Gance/Napoleon Abel Gance, 1927. This five-hour masterpiece is often called the greatest silent flick ever made, and not just because of its length. A histrionic thread of nationalism runs throughout, but the epic scale and use of experimental techniques such as split screen, superimposition and horseback-mounted camerawork – for chase scenes – make this one of the most ambitious films ever made.

La Passion de Jeanne d'Arc Carl Dreyer, 1927. Restricting himself to the events of Jeanne's trial and execution, Danish director Dreyer focuses on both the saint's physical and spiritual anguish at the hands of the intractable church authorities. Amidst bleached-out interiors, the slow tracking shots and unflinching close-ups – in particular of Renée Falconetti's extraordinarily expressive face – create an atmosphere of almost unbearable intensity.

Un Chien andalou/An Andalusian Dog Luis Buñuel, 1929. Made in collaboration with Salvador Dali, this short opens with a woman's eye being cut into with a razorblade. While it doesn't get any less weird or shocking for the rest of its twenty-minute length, it's surprisingly watchable – when it came out, it was a big hit at Paris's Studio des Ursulines cinema. Buñuel further developed his Surrealist techniques in the feature-length talkie *L'Age d'or* (1930), which was banned shortly after its first screening at Montmartre's Studio 38.

Le Sang d'un poète/Blood of a Poet Jean Cocteau, 1930. A response to Buñuel's *L'Age d'or*, this early, dreamy short by the poet-director mixes autobiographical events and documentary footage with mind-grabbing Surrealist images, leaving the viewer as unsure as the hero about what is real and what is fantasy. Indelibly stamped with Cocteau's hallmark camp morbidness.

Poetic Realism

Le Million René Clair, 1931. In 1930 Clair had made the first great French talkie, *Sous les toits de Paris*, using a montage of songs, sounds and images, but it wasn't until *Le Million* that the true musical film was born – there's more singing than dialogue. A hunt for a lost winning lottery ticket provides plenty of opportunity for madcap comedy, suspense and romance. Not exactly a Poetic Realist film, but essential 1930s viewing anyway.

L'Atalante Jean Vigo, 1934. Aboard a barge, a newly married couple struggle to reconcile themselves to their new situation. Eventually, the wife, Juliette, tries to flee, but is brought back by the unconventional deck-hand, Père Jules, superbly portrayed by the great Michel Simon. This sensual and naturalistic portrait of a relationship was made just before Vigo died, and is his only feature film.

La Belle équipe/They Were Five Julien Duvivier, 1936. A group of unemployed workers wins the lottery and sets up a cooperative restaurant. The result depends on which version you see – the one with an upbeat conclusion that was such a hit with contemporary audiences, or the darker ending preferred by Duvivier himself. Jean Gabin stars as the defeated hero, as in Duvivier's other greats, *La Bandéra* (1935) and the cult classic, *Pépé-le-Moko* (1937).

La Bête humaine Jean Renoir, 1938. This dark adaptation of Zola's powerful story of erotic passion, violence and revenge was scripted by Renoir himself in just two weeks. Jean Gabin is superbly cast in the role of the homicidal engine driver, but the real hero is the steam train itself, which is thrillingly shot, especially in the classic five-minute opening sequence. A classic of the Poetic Realist genre, along with Renoir's *Le Crime de Monsieur Lange* (1936) and *La Grande illusion* (1937).

Le Jour se lève/Daybreak Marcel Carné, 1939. This brooding classic from the Poetic Realist stable has Jean Gabin, the greatest star of the era, playing another of his iconic working-class hero roles. After shooting his rival, the villainous old music-hall star Valentin, François (Gabin) is holed up in a hotel bedroom. In the course of the night, he recalls the events that led up to the murder. Tragedy comes with the daybreak. Also stars the great female idol of the 1930s, Arletty, and a superb script by the poet Jacques Prévert. Carné's *Hôtel du Nord* (1938) and *Quai des brumes* (1938) are in a similar vein.

La Règle du jeu/The Rules of the Game Jean Renoir, 1939. Now hailed as the foremost masterpiece of the prewar era, this was a complete commercial failure when it was released. The Marquis de la Chesnaye invites his wife, mistress and a pilot friend to spend a weekend hunting and partying in the countryside. Matching the four are a group of four servants with similarly interweaved love lives. Renoir himself plays Octave, who moves between the two groups. A complex, almost farcical plot based around misunderstanding and accusations of infidelity moves inexorably towards disaster.

Le Ciel est à vous/The Woman Who Dared Jean Grémillon, 1944. Praised for its positive outlook by Pétain and the Resistance alike, "The Sky is Yours" is an inspiring and moving portrait of a heroically determined but otherwise ordinary woman, played by Madeleine Renaud, who discovers a passion for flight. Grémillon's career peaked with this film, and his post-war work is relatively disappointing.

Les Enfants du Paradis Marcel Carné, 1945. Probably the greatest of the collaborations between Carné and the poet-scriptwriter, Jacques Prévert, this film is set in the low-life world of the popular theatre of 1840s Paris. Beautiful and worldly actress Garance (the great Arletty) is loved by arch-criminal Lacenaire, ambitious actor Lemaître, and brilliant, troubled mime Baptiste – unforgettably played by the top mime of the 1940s, Jean-Louis Barrault. The outstanding character portrayals and romantic, humane ethos are reminiscent of a great nineteenth-century novel.

Post-war cinema

La Belle et la bête/Beauty and the Beast Jean Cocteau, 1946. Cocteau's theatrical rendition of the "Beauty and the Beast" tale teeters on the edge of the surreal. The sets are laden with self-referential symbols – clocks, mirrors, magical lamps – and the acting highly stylized, but the pace is as compelling as any thriller. *Orphée* (1950) is more widely considered to be Cocteau's masterpiece, a surreal retelling of the Orpheus tale in a setting strongly redolent of wartime France.

Les Vacances de Monsieur Hulot/Mr Hulot's Holiday Jacques Tati, 1951. The slapstick comic mime Jacques Tati created his most memorable character in Hulot, the unwitting creator of chaos and nonchalant hero of this gut--wrenchingly funny film. So full of brilliantly conceived and impeccably timed sight gags that you hardly notice the innovative absence of much dialogue or plot. Groundbreaking cinema, and superlative entertainment. The later *Mon oncle* (1958) has an edgier feel, adopting a distinctly critical attitude to modern life.

Casque d'or/Golden Marie Jacques Becker, 1952. Becker's first great film depicts an overwhelming and ultimately tragic romance between a gang-member, Manda, and the beautiful, golden-haired prostitute Marie, nicknamed Casque d'or ("golden helmet") – portrayed with legendary seductiveness by Simone Signoret. Underneath the love story, however, lies the murkiness and moral corruption of a brilliantly recreated turn-of-the-century Paris. Becker went on to make the seminal crime thriller, *Touchez pas au grisbi/Honour Among Thieves* (1953).

Les Jeux interdits René Clément, 1952. A small Parisian girl loses her parents and her dog in a Stuka attack on a column of refugees, and is rescued and befriended by a peasant boy. Together, they seek solace from the war by building an animal cemetery in an abandoned barn. This moving meditation on childhood and death extracted two remarkable performances from the child actors.

Le Salaire de la peur/The Wages of Fear Henri-Georges Clouzot, 1953. This is the tensest, most suspense-driven of all the films made by the "French Hitchcock", focusing on four men driving an explosive-laden lorry hundreds of miles to a burning, third-world oil field. Tight and shatteringly sustained right up to the magnificent finale.

Un Condamné à mort s'est échappé/A Man Escaped Robert Bresson, 1956. A prisoner, Fontaine (François Leterrier), calmly plans his escape from prison, working with a painstaking slowness that is brilliantly matched by the intensely absorbed, magnificent camerawork – a hymn to the close up. The sparing, precisely realistic sound creates an incredibly intense mood, even before there's any real action. Working with real locations and amateur actors, Bresson echoed the work of the Italian Neo-realists, and foreshadowed the work of the Nouvelle Vague directors. Sometimes entitled *Le Vent souffle où il veut.*

Et ... Dieu créa la femme/And God Created Woman Roger Vadim, 1956. This film should be called "And Roger Vadim created Brigitte Bardot", as its chief interest is not its harmless plot – love and adultery in St-Tropez – but its scantily clad main actress, who spends most of the time sunbathing and dancing in front of fascinated males. Deemed "obscene" by the moralizing authorities of the time, it helped liberate the way the body was represented in film.

Ascenseur pour l'échafaud/Elevator to the Gallows/Frantic Louis Malle, 1957. This thriller is Louis Malle's remarkable debut. Two lovers (Jeanne Moreau and Maurice Ronet) murder the woman's husband but get trapped by a series of unlucky coincidences. Beautifully shot – especially when Jeanne Moreau wanders through the streets of Paris, accompanied by Miles Davis' superb original score – and as breathtaking as any Hitchcock film.

The modern era

The Nouvelle Vague

Les Cousins/The Cousins Claude Chabrol, 1959. The Balzac-inspired plot centres around Charles (Gérard Blain), an earnest provincial student, who comes to live in Neuilly with his glamorous cousin Paul (Jean-Claude Brialy). Despite its disappointing ending, the film is highly watchable as a near-caricature of the Nouvelle Vague - idle students in the Quartier Latin, extravagant parties, convertible cars and exciting music.

Les Quatre-Cents coups/The 400 Blows François Truffaut, 1959. A young *cinéphile* and critic turned filmmaker, François Truffaut triumphed at the 1959 Cannes film festival with this semi-autobiographical film, showing a Parisian adolescent (Jean-Pierre Léaud) trying to escape his lonely, loveless existence, and slowly drifting towards juvenile delinquency. Léaud's poignant performance, and Truffaut's sensitive, sympathetic observation, make this one of the most lovable films of the Nouvelle Vague.

A bout de souffle/Breathless Jean-Luc Godard, 1959. This is the film that came nearest to defining the Nouvelle Vague: insolent charm, cool music and sexy actors. Jean-Paul Belmondo is a petty criminal, Michel, while Jean Seberg plays Patricia, his American girlfriend. The film's revolutionary style, with its jerky, unconventional narrative, abrupt cuts and rough camerawork, proved one of the most influential of the twentieth century.

Hiroshima, mon amour Alain Resnais, 1959. On her last days of shooting a film in

Hiroshima, a French actress (Emmanuelle Riva) falls in love with a Japanese architect (Eiji Okada). Gradually, she reveals the story of her affair with a German soldier during the Occupation, and her subsequent disgrace. Based on an original script by Marguerite Duras, Resnais' first film masterfully weaves together past and present in a haunting story of love and memory.

Jules et Jim François Truffaut, 1962. Jules (Oskar Werner) and Jim (Henri Serre) love the same woman, the fascinating Katherine (Jeanne Moreau), who proves unable to choose between them. This tragic story of impossible love spanning over twenty years contains some beautiful moments of pure *joie de vivre*, expressing Truffaut's yearning for a lost paradise of innocence and harmony.

Cléo de Cinq à Sept/Cleo from 5 to 7 Agnès Varda, 1962. In real time – the camera only leaves her twice – this visually impressive film documents ninety minutes in the life of a young and beautiful pop singer. While waiting for a hospital report, Cléo (Corinne Marchand) goes on a journey through the streets of Paris, where she encounters various friends and meets a conscript bound for the Algerian war. A subtle portrait of a woman moving from vanity and self-obsession to love, by the only female filmmaker of the Nouvelle Vague.

Les Biches/The Does/The Girlfriends Claude Chabrol, 1968. In this classic exposition of French cinema's obsession with the ménage-à-trois, wealthy, sophisticated Frédérique (Stéphane Audran) picks up drifting young artist Why (Jacqueline Sassard) in a Paris street and takes her back to her bohemian home in St-Tropez. When local architect Paul (Jean-Louis Trintignant) comes between the two, it sets in motion a Hitchcockian nightmare of psychosis.

Ma nuit chez Maude/My Night at Maud's Eric Rohmer, 1969. Rohmer's career-long obsessions with sexuality, conversation, existential choices and the love triangle are given free rein in this moody, lingering portrait of a flirtation. Jean-Louis Trintignant plays a handsome egotist who, during the course of one long night, is drawn into a strange and inconclusive relationship with his friend's friend, the hypnotically attractive Maude (Françoise Fabian).

Le Rayon Vert/The Green Ray Eric Rohmer, 1986. It is summer, and a restless, lonely and undeniably flaky Delphine (Marie Rivière) has no one to go on holiday with. Using subtle, improvisatory techniques, Rohmer – who stayed true to the principles of the Nouvelle Vague throughout his career – masterfully lays the ground for the gently explosive finale.

Comedies

Belle de jour Luis Buñuel, 1966. At first sight, this is a far cry from Buñuel's prewar collaborations with Dalí though as the action progresses, the film moves away from the initial acerbic comedy towards a bizarre surrealism where fantasy and reality merge. The subject matter is perfectly apt: Catherine Deneuve plays Séverine, who lives out her sexual fantasies and obsessions in a brothel – thus (almost) fulfilling the fantasy of half the male cinemagoing population.

Playtime Jacques Tati, 1967. Tati once more plays Hulot, cinema's most radical slapstick creation, but with a newly profound sense of purpose. From a simple premise – he is showing a group of tourists round a futuristic Paris – he creates an intimately observed and perfectly controlled farce. Just as the city has somehow been transformed into a refined and faceless world of glass and steel. Tati's comedy has become infinitely subtle and reflective.

Zazie dans le métro/Zazie Louis Malle, 1960. In one of his few comedies, Malle successfully rendered novelist Raymond Queneau's verbal experiments by using cartoon-like visual devices. Twelve-year-old Catherine Demongeot is perfect as the delightfully rude little girl driving everybody mad; and the film offers some great shots of Paris, climaxing in a spectacular scene at the top of the Eiffel Tower.

La Grande vadrouille Gérard Oury, 1966. Head and shoulders the biggest blockbuster in French cinema history, "The Big Jaunt" stars Bourvil and Louis de Funès as a conductor and a decorator. Set in wartime Paris, the comic plot sees three Allied soldiers parachuting down on the hapless pair. In their desperation to be rid of the parachutists, they end up leading them to the free zone.

La Cage aux folles/Birds of a Feather Edouard Molinaro, 1978. Renato runs a cabaret nightclub at which his boyfriend, Albin, is the headlining drag act. When Renato's son, Laurent, decides to get married, the couple are drawn into an escalating farce as they try to present themselves as a conventional mother-and-son couple to Laurent's conservative in-laws. A supremely camp international hit.

Trois Hommes et un couffin Coline Serreau, 1985. "Three Men and a Cradle" was a giant box-office success even before it was trashily remade in Hollywood as *Three Men and a Baby*. In Serreau's film, the three friends live together in Paris when a bombshell arrives in the shape of the baby daughter of one of their ex-girlfriends. Cue lots of gender gags, along with a farcical sub-plot involving a nappy-hidden cache of heroin.

Les Visiteurs/The Visitors Jean-Marie Poiré, 1993. A medieval knight and his squire are transported to present-day France, where they discover their castle has been turned into a country hotel by their descendants. The earthily comic encounters between time-travellers and modern middle-classes make for an extremely funny comedy of manners. French audiences so loved being sent up that this became the third most successful film in French history.

Gazon maudit/French Twist Josiane Balasko, 1995. "Cursed Lawn" – as the title translates literally – is a lesbian sex-comedy turned massive mainstream hit. It successfully milks the comic potential of butch urban lesbian Marijo's explosive entry into a *ménage à trois* with a hitherto straight, provincial couple. The resulting confusion of gender and sexual roles is a very watchable blend of slapstick and gentler social comedy.

Le Dîner de cons/The Dinner Game Francis Veber, 1998. In this light-hearted, straight-up farce, a group of friends compete as to who can invite the most ridiculous person to dinner. Inevitably, and hilariously, the tables are turned. Bravura performances from Thierry Lhermitte as the smug publisher whose life falls apart in front of Jacques Villeret, his buffoon-like guest.

Le Fabuleux destin d'Amélie Poulain/Amélie Jean-Pierre Jeunet, 2001. Known as plain *Amélie* outside

France, this sentimental, feel-good portrait of a youthful ingenue wandering around a romanticized Montmartre was a worldwide hit. Amélie (Audrey Tatou) is on a mission to help the world find happiness; her own is harder to fix up. Filmed on location, though it looks edible enough to be an idealized set.

Les Triplettes de Belleville/ Belleville Rendez-vous Sylvain Chomet, 2003. Jacques Tati was clearly a major influence on this cheeky but thoughtful animation. A champion cyclist is kidnapped by the Mafia before the big race and carted off to the nightmarish city of Belleville; it is up to his grand-mother, her dog and the singing Belleville sisters to rescue him. Acclaimed (or decried) as a satire on America, Chomet targets France just as acutely.

Thrillers/films policiers

Pierrot-le-fou Jean-Luc Godard, 1965. Godard's fascination with American pulp fiction is most brilliantly exploited in this highly charged and deeply sophisticated thriller. Accidentally caught up in a murderous gangland killing, Ferdinand (Jean-Paul Belmondo) flees with his babysitter (Godard's then-wife, Anna Karina) to the apparent safety of a Mediterranean island. The bizarre and tragic denouement is one of the great scenes of French cinema.

Le Samouraï/The Samurai Jean-Pierre Melville, 1967. The main attraction of this modern-day film noir is Alain Delon, who gives a brilliantly impassive yet stylish performance as Jef Costello, an ice-cold hit man on the run. Hunted by both the police and his own employers, he responds with brilliant ingenuity and violence. One of the all-time great *films policiers*.

L'Armée des ombres/The Army in the Shadows Jean-Pierre Melville, 1969. A small group of Resistance fighters, played by Yves Montand, Simone Signoret and Jean-Pierre Meurisse, are betrayed, questioned and then released, free to enact their revenges and to continue their subversive activities. This is one of the most remarkable depictions of the Resistance in French cinema: the tight, minimalist style creates a suffocating tension that culminates in the unforgettable conclusion.

Le Boucher/The Butcher Claude Chabrol, 1969. A young schoolteacher in a tiny southwest village lives in an apartment above her school. Her loneliness is eased by a surprising fledgling romance with the local butcher – a kindly yet sinister figure – until a sequence of schoolgirl murders sows doubt in her mind. This would be gripping as a portrayal of village life even without the underlying tension and lurking violence.

z/The Anatomy of a Political Assassination Costa-Gavras, 1969. In this stunningly filmed offering from Greek director Costa-Gavras, Yves Montand, an activist in a fascist-run country (Greece, though it's unnamed) is assassinated after giving an inflammatory speech. The great Jean-Louis Trintignant plays the rigorous investigating judge unravelling a complex police conspiracy. Won an Oscar for Best Foreign Film and single-handedly created a new genre, the political thriller.

Coup de Torchon/Clean Slate Bertrand Tavernier, 1981. The setting is colonial West Africa, 1938. Ineffective, humiliated police chief Cordier (Philippe Noiret) decides to take murderous revenge on his wife, her lover, his mistress's husband and the locals he views as uniformly corrupt. As much an extremely black comedy as a true thriller.

Monsieur Hire Patrice Leconte, 1989. A slow-moving, unsettlingly erotic psychological thriller based on a novel by Georges Simenon. Michel Blanc plays the spookily impassive Monsieur Hire, a voyeur who always watches his neighbour, Alice, undressing. One day he sees her boyfriend commit a murder. He becomes the prime suspect in the police's investigation, and is slowly drawn into Alice's world, with tragic consequences.

Irréversible Gaspar Noé, 2002. This is surely one of the most disturbing films ever made, and not just for the nightmarish – and infamous – anal rape scene but for the way it eviscerates the most terrifying elements of the male sexual psyche. A giddy, swooping camera traces the events of one horrific night backwards in time from a brutal murder in a gay sex dungeon to a post-coital couple (Vincent Cassel and Monica Bellucci) getting ready for a party.

36 Quai des Orfèvres Olivier Marchal, 2004. Two elite police squads, under rivals Vrinks (Daniel Auteuil) and Klein (Gérard Dépardieu), are in pursuit of a violent gang of bank robbers. This would be merely one of the best thrillers to come out of France recently – if it wasn't taken to another level by the revenge drama that emerges as the film's real theme.

Caché/Hidden Michael Haneke, 2005. The smooth bourgeois life of literary TV presenter Georges (Daniel Auteuil) and his wife Anne (Juliette Binoche) is disrupted when they receive a chillingly innocuous videotape of their own home under surveillance. In what has been widely read as a metaphor for France's attitude to its own colonial past, Georges is forced to confront a childhood friend, Majid (Maurice Bénichou), and his own troubled conscience.

Films d'amour

Les Parapluies de Cherbourg/The Umbrellas of Cherbourg Jacques Demy, 1964. Demy's most successful film also gave Catherine Deneuve one of her first great roles. It is an extraordinarily stylized musical, shot in bright, artificial-looking colours, and entirely sung rather than spoken. Demy disturbingly twists the traditional cheerfulness of the musical genre to give a dark, bitter ending to this story of love and abandonment, set during the Algerian war.

Un Homme et une femme/A Man and a Woman Claude Lelouch, 1966. An actress-widow (Anouk Aimée) and a racing-driver-widower (Jean-Louis Trintignant) meet by chance while visiting their children at a boarding school. Slowly and uncertainly at first, their relationship develops past the initial misunderstandings and things not said. A bittersweet but lyrical film about falling in love a second time, with a rapturous score.

Baisers Volés/Stolen Kisses François Truffaut, 1968. The third of Truffaut's five-part semi-autobiographical sequence, which began with *Les Quatre-cents coups*, is probably the simplest and most delightful. Returning from military service, idealistic young Antoine Doinel (Jean-Pierre Léaud), mooches about Paris while working variously as a hotel worker, private detective and TV repairman. Through various amorous and bizarre adventures he slowly finds his way back towards the girl he loved and left behind.

La Maman et la putain/The Mother and the Whore Jean Eustache, 1972. Years after the revolutionary "events" of May 1968, Alexandre (Jean-Pierre Léaud) is still living the left-wing café life in St-Germain. He has an older girlfriend, but soon takes up with a young, unstable nurse, who also moves in. The tensions – sexual, emotional, political – between the three of them are explored at an excruciating pace and pitch. Eustache's penultimate feature reprises many of the themes of the original "new wave".

Le Dernier métro/The Last Metro François Truffaut, 1980. This huge commercial success stars Catherine Deneuve and Gérard Depardieu as two actors who fall in love while rehearsing a play during the German Occupation. Wartime Paris is evoked through lavish photography and a growing feeling of imprisonment inside the confined space of the theatre. Swept the Césars that year, for Best Film, Director, Actor and Actress.

Loulou Maurice Pialat, 1980. In this tale of an "inappropriate" love affair Isabelle Huppert plays Nelly, a woman who abandons her husband and middle-class life to shack up with Loulou, a pleasure-loving slob played with great relish by Gérard Depardieu. Add the apparently improvised dialogue, and Pialat seems to have stumbled into Eric Rohmer territory, but this is a much less gentle world with an edge of violence and sexual obsessiveness that is never far from the surface.

L'Ami de mon amie/Boyfriends and Girlfriends Eric Rohmer, 1987. This is Rohmer at his most beguiling and apparently superficial, featuring a strangely symmetrical plot and a script that loads a seemingly inconsequential dialogue with emotional nuance. Two glossy young women in a flashy new town outside Paris – Cergy-Pontoise – become friends. Whle Blanche is away, Léa falls in love with Blanche's boyfriend Alexandre; when Blanche comes back, she in turn falls in love with Léa's boyfriend, Fabien. Behind the light comedy lurks a profound film about love and free will.

Le Mari de la coiffeuse/The Hairdresser's Husband Patrice Leconte, 1990. Leconte's film about a man who grows up obsessed with hairdressers, and ends up marrying one, epitomizes the best in French romantic film-making. A quirky, subtle and engagingly twisted portrait of an obsessive relationship.

La Belle Noiseuse Jacques Rivette, 1991. Based loosely on a Balzac short story, "the beautiful troublemaker" originally stretched to four hours, though the more commonly screened "Divertimento" cut is half that length. A washed-out painter (the splendidly stuttering Michel Piccoli) lives in the deep south with his wife (Jane Birkin). An admiring younger painter offers his beautiful girlfriend (Emmanuelle Béart) as a nude model. Her fraught sittings become the catalyst for all the latent tensions in the two relationships to slowly, quietly explode.

Un Coeur en hiver/A Heart in Winter/A Heart of Stone Claude Sautet, 1992. In this thoughtful, fresh *ménage à trois* scenario, violinist Camille (Emmanuelle Béart) is paired first with Maxime (André Dussolier), a violin shop owner, and then with loner Stéphane (Daniel Auteuil), the chief craftsman. As the title "A Heart in Winter" suggests, this is a moody but ultimately sentimental film about love, and the fear of love.

Trois Couleurs: Rouge/Three Colours: Red Krzysztof Kieslowski, 1994. The final part of Polish-born director's Kieslowski's

△ Still from *The Beat that My Heart Skipped*

"tricolore" trilogy is perhaps the most satisfying, though to get the most out of the powerful denouement, in which all the strands are pulled together through a series of chances and accidents, you really need to have watched *Bleu* and *Blanc* as well. A young model, Valentine (Irène Jacob), runs over a dog and traces its owner, a reclusive retired judge (Jean-Louis Trintignant) who assuages his loneliness by tapping his neighbours' phone calls. The film's "colour" is expressed through presiding red-brown tones and the theme of *fraternité*, the third principle of the French Republic.

De battre mon coeur s'est arrêté/The Beat that My Heart Skipped Jacques Audiard, 2005. Romain Duris gives a compellingly intense performance as a young man struggling to escape his violent, semi-criminal life in Paris by retraining as a concert pianist. Despite being a remake of the 1978 film, *Fingers*, it won eight awards at the 2006 Césars, including Best Film.

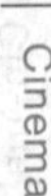

Heritage cinema

Jean de Florette Claude Berri, 1986. This masterful adaptation of Marcel Pagnol's novel began a new trend in French cinema, that of the rose-tinted *cinema du patrimoine*. It drew on an idealized heritage – in this case, the gorgeous, rugged setting of inland, prewar Provence. Gérard Depardieu plays Jean, a bookish and deformed refugee from the city who is struggling to create a self-sufficient rural utopia. He is opposed by the shrewd peasant Papet (Yves Montand), who wants to create a lucrative orchard, and the simpleton Ugolin (Daniel Auteuil), who dreams of giant fields of carnations. The excellent sequel, *Manon des Sources* (1987), launched the stellar career of the improbably pouting Emmanuelle Béart.

Au Revoir les enfants/Goodbye, Children Louis Malle, 1987. Malle's autobiographical tale is one of the finest film portraits of the war, and of school life in general. It is minutely observed, and desperately moving without being unduly sentimental. Three Jewish boys are hidden among the pupils at a Catholic boys' boarding school. Eventually, the Gestapo discover the ruse.

La Vie et rien d'autre/Life and Nothing But Bertrand Tavernier, 1989. The master of high-gloss heritage cinema here turns his hand to a grim film set in the aftermath of World War I. Philippe Noiret plays an army major charged with finding the right candidate for the memorial to the Unknown Soldier, under the Arc de Triomphe. During his search, he meets a rich Parisian woman who is trying to find her husband. They find consuming love amid the ashes.

Cyrano de Bergerac Jean-Paul Rappeneau, 1990. It's hard to know what's finest about this extravagantly romantic film: Rostand's original story, set in seventeenth-century France, or Gérard Depardieu's landmark performance as the large-nosed swashbuckler-poet, Cyrano, who hopelessly loves the brilliant and beautiful Roxanne. The film's panache is made all the more magnificent by the ease with which the cast deliver the verse dialogue – brilliantly rendered into English subtitles by Anthony Burgess. Hilarious, exciting and, ultimately, sublimely weepy.

Indochine Régis Warnier, 1991. This sweeping colonial melodrama stars the mature Catherine Deneuve as a ruthlessly independent and sexually emancipated rubber baroness in prewar French Indochina (Vietnam). As the colony begins to crumble, so does her relationship with her adopted daughter, a scion of the Indochinese royal family.

Cinéma du Look

Diva Jean-Jacques Beineix, 1980. *Diva*'s glossy yet quirky feel established the presiding tone of the *cinéma du look*. Like many conventional crime thrillers, the story is set in motion by an accident: moped-riding postman Jules mixes up two tapes – a bootleg recording of an opera singer and a message from a prostitute linking a detective with a vice ring. But the film is much more about style than suspense, its beguiling depiction of a sexy, bohemian and youthful Paris contrasting with the operatic soundtrack.

Subway Luc Besson, 1985. The favoured urban-nocturnal setting of the *cinéma du look* is given its coolest expression in *Subway*. Like Diva, the action focuses on one man in possession of something he shouldn't have – in this case it's shock-headed Christophe Lambert, with a cache of documents. Hunted by police and criminals alike, he hides out in the Paris métro where he manages to form a rock band with a crowd of various low-lifes – before being found by Isabelle Adjani. Film noir meets MTV.

37°2 le matin/Betty Blue Jean-Jacques Beineix, 1986. Pouty Béatrice Dalle puts on a compellingly erotic performance as Betty, a free-thinking girl who lives in a beach house with struggling writer Zorg. The film opens in romantic mood with a sustained and passionate sex scene but rapidly spirals towards its disturbing ending. The film's intense and sometimes weird stylishness, along with its memorable score, made it an international hit.

Nikita Luc Besson, 1990. More of a hit abroad than at home, *Nikita* is a sci-fi thriller buzzing with edgy cool. After killing a policeman in a gang shoot-out, the eponymous heroine is remanded to the Kafkaesque "Centre" where she is trained as a government assassin and sent on missions of dubious morality. Glossy on the surface, but underpinned by themes of anarchy versus fascism, and the tension between female star and male director/spectator. *Leon* (1994) finds a similar vein.

Delicatessen Jean-Pierre Jeunet/Marc Caro, 1991. Set in a crumbling apartment block in a dystopian fantasy city – Occupation Paris meets comic book – a grotesque local butcher murders his assistants and sells them as human meat, until his daughter falls in love with the latest butcher boy and the subterranean vegetarian terrorists find out. Hilarious and bizarre in equal measure, with superb cameos from the neighbours.

Les Amants du Pont-Neuf Léos Carax, 1991. Homeless painter Michèle (Juliette Binoche) is losing her sight. One day, on Paris's Pont-Neuf, she meets an indigent, fire-eating acrobat (Denis Lavant), and they tumble together into a consuming love, madly played out against the background of their life on the streets. An intense and beautiful film.

New Realism: Beur, Banlieue and Jeune

Le Thé à la menthe Abdelkrim Bahloul, 1984. In this funny and ultimately touching film, an Algerian immigrant living in the Barbès quarter of northern Paris writes home to his mother to let her know how successful he has become in his new life. In fact, he struggles to get by on minor scams and chancey ventures. When his mother makes a surprise visit, he foolishly tries to carry on the pretence – to great comic effect.

Le Thé au harem d'Archimède/Tea In The Harem Mehdi Charef, 1985. A concrete housing wasteland is the harsh setting for this somewhat meandering story of a friendship between two young *zonards* from the Paris banlieue. Despite their different ethnicity – Madjid is a *beur* (French-born, of North African origin), Pat is white French – the two friends share much: delinquent habits, poverty and futile but potent dreams. Slow as buddy flicks go, but fascinating.

Hexagone Malik Chibane, 1991. Shooting in just 24 days, and using amateur actors, Chibane somehow pulled off exactly what he planned: to raise the profile of the new generation of *beurs*. The story is a simple enough rite-of-passage tale focused on five young friends who get in trouble, but the recurring motif of the sacrifice of Abraham gives it a thoughtful twist. The street-slang peppered script and cinematography – strong on handheld shots of the inner city landscape – are superb.

Bye-Bye Karim Dridi, 1995. Two North African brothers living in France are told by their father that they must return to the family home in the Maghreb. Mouloud refuses, and drifts into delinquency, while Ismaël gets a job in a Marseille shipyard, where he has an affair with a white workmate's girlfriend. Ultimately, the brothers decide to leave France anyway. Sympathetic characterization leavens the downbeat subject matter, and the raï and French hip-hop soundtrack is superb.

La Haine/Hate Mathieu Kassovitz, 1995. The flagship film of the *cinéma de banlieue*, films of the tough suburbs, centres on three friends: Hubert, of black African origin; Saïd, a *beur* (from North Africa); and Vinz, who has white

Jewish roots – and a gun. They spend a troubled night wandering Paris before heading back to the *banlieue* and a violent homecoming. Brilliantly treads the line between gritty realism and street cool – the fact that it's shot in black-and-white helps, as does the soundtrack from French rapper MC Solaar, among others.

Y aura-t-il de la neige à Noël?Will It Snow For Christmas? Sandrine Veysset, 1996. This moving, sometimes painful depiction of a rural childhood comes in three separate sections – summer, autumn and winter. Veysset depicts the lives of seven children who work on a southern farm owned by their menacing, exploitative father. The unwaveringly realistic tone is a great antidote to the old cinematic clichés of the rural idyll, but fairytale moments of childish joy break through.

La Ville est tranquille/The Town Is Quiet Robert Guédiguian, 2000. Notwithstanding its title, this harrowing film describes the dysfunctional society of a far-from-quiet city – Marseille – focusing on the hardships of Michèle (Ariane Ascaride), a 40-year-old woman working in a fish factory while fighting to save her heroin-addict daughter. After a series of light, happy tales, Robert Guédiguian magnificently turns here to a more realistic and political tone.

Comme une image/Look at Me Agnès Jaoui, 2004. Agnès Jaoui manages to be both sensitive and hard-hitting in this exploration of the dysfunctional relationship between a self-conscious, under-confident daughter (Marilou Berry) and her monstrously egotistical, literary lion of a father – a role played superbly by Jean-Pierre Bacri, who co-wrote the script with Jaoui.

Documentaries

Être et Avoir/To Be and To Have Nicolas Philbert, 2002. A low-budget documentary that became an international hit, this film follows the progress of a handful of children in a one-class primary school in a strikingly remote area in the Auvergne. The star is Georges Lopez, their soft-spoken but inspirational teacher who guides his charges with apparently effortless simplicity and endless patience.

James McConnachie and Eva Lœchner

Books

Publishers are detailed below in the form of British publisher/American publisher, where both exist. Where books are published in one country only, UK or US follows the publisher's name. Books marked 🏃 are highly recommended. Abbreviations: o/p (out of print); UP (University Press).

Travel

Julian Barnes *Something to Declare* (Picador/Knopf, 2002). This journalistically highbrow collection of essays on French culture – films, music, the Tour de France, and of course Flaubert – wears its French-style intellectualism on its sleeve, but succeeds in getting under the skin anyway.

🏃 **Walter Benjamin** *The Arcades Project* (Harvard, 2002). An all-encompassing portrait of Paris from 1830 to 1870, in which the passages are used as a lens through which to view Parisian society. Never completed, Benjamin's magnum opus is a kaleidoscopic assemblage of essays, notes and quotations, gathered under such headings as "Baudelaire", "Prostitution", "Mirrors" and "Idleness".

James Boswell *An Account of Corsica* (OUP, 2006). Typically robust and witty account of encounters with the Corsican people.

🏃 **Dorothy Carrington** *Granite Island* (Penguin, 2004, o/p). By far the best study of Corsica ever written in English. A fascinating and immensely comprehensive book, combining the writer's personal experiences with an evocative portrayal of historical figures and events.

Stephen Clarke *A Year in the Merde* (Black Swan/Bloomsbury, 2006). In this semi-autobiographical comic novel of cultural miscomprehension, a young English entrepreneur moves to Paris – where he finds that everything is crap. Some find it hilarious, others crude and objectionable.

Julien Green *Paris* (Marion Boyars, 2005). A collection of very personal sketches and impressions of the city, by an American who has lived all his life in Paris, writes in French, and is considered one of the great French writers of the century. Bilingual text.

Richard Holmes *Fatal Avenue* (Pimlico/Trafalgar Square, o/p). The phrase is de Gaulle's, used to describe France's northeast frontier whose notorious topographical vulnerability has made it the natural route for invaders since time began. An exciting and informative read.

Richard Holmes *Footsteps* (Flamingo, 2004/Vintage, 1996). A marvellous mix of objective history and personal account, such as the tale of the author's own excitement at the events of May 1968 in Paris, which led him to investigate and reconstruct the experiences of the British in Paris during the 1789 Revolution.

Michael de Larrabeiti *French Leave* (Robert Hale, 2003). In the summer of 1949, aged just 15, Michael de Larrabeiti set off on his own by bicycle to Paris from the UK. This book provides a wonderfully evocative testimony to his love of

France as he looks back over fifty years working and travelling throughout the country.

Laurence Sterne *A Sentimental Journey Through France and Italy* (Hackett, 2006). Rambling tale by the eccentric eighteenth-century author of *Tristram Shandy* who, despite the title, never gets further than Versailles.

Robert Louis Stevenson *Travels with a Donkey* (Penguin/Echo, 2006). Mile-by-mile account of Stevenson's twelve-day trek in the Haute Loire and Cévennes uplands with the donkey Modestine. Devotees of Stevenson's footpaths – and there are a surprising number in France – might be interested in his first book, *Inland Voyage*, on the waterways of the north.

Freda White *Three Rivers of France* (Pavilion/Faber, o/p), *West of the Rhone* (Faber, US, o/p), *Ways of Aquitaine* (Faber, o/p). Freda White spent a great deal of time in France in the 1950s before tourism came along to the backwater communities that were her interest. These are all evocative books, slipping in the history and culture painlessly, if not always too accurately.

History

General

Alfred Cobban *A History of Modern France* (3 vols: 1715–99, 1799–1871 and 1871–1962; o/p). Complete and very readable account of the main political, social and economic strands in French history, from the death of Louis XIV to mid-de Gaulle.

Alistair Horne *Seven Ages of Paris* (Pan, 2003/Vintage, 2004). Compelling and thoroughly readable account of the city's history, focusing on seven key ages, from the twelfth century to de Gaulle.

Andrew Hussey *Paris, The Secret History* (Penguin, 2007). An entertaining book that delves into some fascinating and little-known aspects of Paris's history, including occultism, freemasonry and the seedy underside of the city. Hussey is concerned above all with ordinary Parisians and shows how in large part the history of Paris is shaped by its citizens' suffering and frequent clashes with authority.

Colin Jones *The Cambridge Illustrated History of France* (CUP, 1999). A political and social history of France from prehistoric times to the mid-1990s, concentrating on issues of regionalism, gender, race and class. Good illustrations and a friendly, non-academic writing style.

Colin Jones *Paris: Biography of a City* (Penguin, 2006). Jones focuses tightly on the actual life and growth of the city, from the Neolithic past to the future. Five hundred pages flow by easily, punctuated by thoughtful but accessible "boxes" on characters, streets and buildings whose lives were especially bound up with Paris's, from the Roman arènes to Zazie's métro. The best single book on the city's history.

Robert Tombs & Isabelle Tombs *That Sweet Enemy: The British and the French from the Sun King to the Present* (Pimlico/Arrow, 2007). A fascinating, original and mammoth study of a strangely intimate relationship. The authors are a French woman and her English husband, and they engage in lively debate between themselves. Covers society, culture and personalities, as well as politics.

France in literature

Listed below is a highly selective recommendation of works – mostly novels – that are rooted in the various French regions, and which would make good holiday reading.

△Marcel Proust

Paris and around

Honoré de Balzac *Old Goriot*
Steven Barclay (ed) *A Place in the World Called Paris*
Charles Baudelaire *Baudelaire's Paris*, trans Laurence Kitchen
André Breton *Nadja*
Blaise Cendrars *To the End of the World*
Didier Daeninckx *Murder in Memoriam*
Charles Dickens *A Tale of Two Cities*
Gustave Flaubert *A Sentimental Education*
André Gide *The Counterfeiters*
Ernest Hemingway *A Moveable Feast*
Victor Hugo *Les Misérables*
Jack Kerouac *Satori in Paris*
Henry Miller *Quiet Days in Clichy, Tropic of Cancer, Tropic of Capricorn*
Anaïs Nin *Journals 1917–1974*
George Orwell *Down and Out in Paris and London*
Daniel Penac *Monsieur Malaussène*
Georges Perec *Life: A User's Manual*
Marcel Proust *Remembrance of Things Past*
Raymond Queneau *Zazie dans le Métro*
Paul Rambali *French Blues*
Jean Rhys *Quartet, Good Morning Midnight*
Jean-Paul Sartre *Roads to Freedom* trilogy
Georges Simenon Any Maigret thriller
Michel Tournier *The Golden Droplet*
Émile Zola *Nana, L'Assommoir, La Bête Humaine, La Curée, Le Ventre de Paris*

The north

Sebastian Faulks *Birdsong*
Julien Gracq *A Balcony in the Forest, The Opposing Shore*
Émile Zola *Germinal, La Débâcle, La Terre*

Alsace, Franche-Comté and Jura

John Berger *Pig Earth*
Bernard Clavel *The Spaniard*
Colette *My Mother's House*
Pierre Gascar *Women and the Sun*
Stendhal *Scarlet and Black*

Theodore Zeldin *A History of French Passions: 1848–1945* (OUP, 1993). Brilliant and original set of books tackling French history by theme. Volume 1 covers Ambition and Love, Volume 2 Intellect and Pride, and so on. Highly readable and unusually stimulating.

The Middle Ages

Natalie Zemon Davis *The Return of Martin Guerre* (Harvard UP, 1984). A vivid account of peasant life in the sixteenth century and a perplexing and titillating hoax in the Pyrenean village of Artigat.

Normandy and Brittany

Honoré de Balzac *Les Chouans, Modeste Mignon*
Colette *Ripening Seed*
Gustave Flaubert *Madame Bovary*
André Gide *Strait is the Gate*
Pierre Loti *Pêcheur d'Islande*
Guy de Maupassant *Selected Short Stories*
Jean Rouard *Fields of Glory, Of Illustrious Men*
Jean-Paul Sartre *La Nausée*

The Loire

Honoré de Balzac *Eugénie Grandet*
Alain Fournier *Le Grand Meaulnes*
Joanne Harris *Five Quarters of the Orange*
Rabelais *Gargantua and Pantagruel*
George Sand *The Devil's Pool*

Burgundy

Gabriel Chevallier *Clochemerle, Atlantic Coast*
François Mauriac *Thérèse*

The Pyrenees

Pierre Loti *Ramuntcho*

Languedoc

Hannah Closs *High Are the Mountains*

Rhône valley and Provence

Lawrence Durrell *The Avignon Quintet*
Jean Giono *The Horseman on the Roof, The Man Who Planted Trees, Joy of Man's Desiring*
Marcel Pagnol *Jean de Florette, Manon des Sources*
Émile Zola *Fortune of the Rougons*

Côte d'Azur

Colette *Collected Stories*
Alexandre Dumas *The Count of Monte Cristo*
F. Scott Fitzgerald *Tender is the Night*
Graham Greene *Loser Takes All, May We Borrow Your Husband?*
Katherine Mansfield *Selected Short Stories*
Françoise Sagan *Bonjour Tristesse*

Corsica

Prosper Mérimée *Colomba*

J. H. Huizinga *The Waning of the Middle* Ages (Dover, 1999). Primarily a study of the culture of the Burgundian and French courts – but a masterpiece that goes far beyond this, building up meticulous detail to re-create the whole life and mentality of the fourteenth and fifteenth centuries.

R. J. Knecht *Renaissance Warrior and Patron: The Reign of Francis I* (CUP, 1996). Fascinating account of one of the great Renaissance kings by a leading academic.

Emmanuel Le Roy Ladurie *Montaillou* (Penguin, 1989). Village gossip on who's sleeping with whom, tales of trips to Spain and details of work, all extracted by the Inquisition from Cathar peasants of the eastern Pyrenees in the fourteenth century, and stored away until recently in the Vatican archives. Though academic and heavy going in places, most of this book reads like a novel.

Nancy Mitford *Madame de Pompadour* (Penguin, 1995/New York Review, 2001). Mitford's unashamedly biased admiration for Pompadour – Louis XV's mistress and France's greatest art patron – makes this a fascinating read.

Stephen O'Shea *The Perfect Heresy* (Profile, 2001/Walker, 2000). Lively but partisan non-academic account of the history of the Cathars and their faith and the Catholic campaign mounted to wipe them out.

Barbara Tuchman *A Distant Mirror* (o/p). The history of the fourteenth century – plagues, wars, peasant uprisings and crusades – told through the life of a sympathetic French nobleman whose career takes him through England, Italy and Byzantium and finally ends in a Turkish prison.

Marina Warner *Joan of Arc* (UCal Press, 2000). The most illuminating and erudite of all the books on Joan, placing her within a historical, spiritual and intellectual tradition and attempting to tease out the nuances of her historical context.

Eighteenth and nineteenth centuries

Rupert Christiansen *Paris Babylon* (Pimlico, 2003/Penguin, 2006). The compulsive and irresistible story of Paris in the last years of the Second Empire and the physical and social upheavals of the Prussian siege and the Commune. It combines a serious historical overview with tabloid-style detail.

Vincent Cronin *Napoleon* (Harper-Collins UK, 1990). Enthusiastic and accessible biography.

Christopher Hibbert *The French Revolution* (Penguin, 1982/Harper, 1999). Well-paced and entertaining narrative treatment by a master historian.

Alistair Horne *The Fall of Paris* (Pan, 2002). A very readable and humane account of the extraordinary period of the Prussian siege of Paris in 1870 and the ensuing struggles of the Commune.

Philip Mansel *Paris Between Empires* (Orion, 2003/St Martin's Press, 2003). Passionate and meticulous account of Parisian politics and society in the fragile, revolution-bedevilled period between the end of Napoleon's empire and the beginning of Napoléon III's.

Lucy Moore *Liberty: The Lives and Times of Six Women in Revolutionary France* (HarperCollins, 2006). This utterly engaging and original book follows the lives of six influential – and very different women – through the Revolution. Moore conjures the fervid atmosphere of the times superbly, taking in everything from sexual scandal to revolutionary radicalism. The book has a serious edge to it, too, exploring how the ideals of liberty and equality were betrayed – for women, at least.

Simon Schama *Citizens* (Penguin, 2004). Bestselling and highly tendentious revisionist history of the Revolution, which pretty well takes the line that the ideologues of the Revolution were a gang of fanatics who simply failed to see how good the *ancien régime* was. It reveals as much about the intellectual climate of conservative America in the 1980s as it does about 1789, but it's a well-written, racy and provocative book.

Ruth Scurr *Fatal Purity: Robespierre And The French Revolution* (Chatto & Windus/Metropolitan, 2006). This myth-busting biography of the "remarkably odd" figure of the man they called The Incorruptible, and who went on to orchestrate the notorious Terror, ends up being one of the best books on the Revolution in general.

Chantal Thomas *The Wicked Queen: The Origins of the Myth of Marie-Antionette* (Zone, 2001). Scholarly but lively review of the muckraking of France's most infamous queen, orginally published in French in 1989. Draws in a host of colourful characters of aristocratic and revolutionary Paris, and contains translations of the sensationalist pamphlets which were written against the queen.

Twentieth century

Marc Bloch *Strange Defeat* (Norton, 1999). Moving personal study of the reasons for France's defeat and subsequent caving-in to fascism. Found among the papers of this Sorbonne historian after his death at the hands of the Gestapo in 1942.

Geoff Dyer *The Missing of the Somme* (Weidenfeld, 2001). Structured round the author's visits to the war graves of northern France, this is a highly moving meditation on the trauma of World War I and the way its memory has been perpetuated.

Robert Gildea *France Since 1945* (OUP, 2002). Pithy but serious contemporary history, with a particular interest in France's national self-image.

Julian Jackson *The Fall of France: The Nazi Invasion of 1940* (OUP, 2004). Fascinating and balanced account of May and June 1940, skilfully unpicking the cultural, political and military reasons behind France's speedy defeat.

H. R. Kedward *In Search of the Maquis: Rural Resistance in South France 1942–44* (Clarendon, 1994/OUP, 1995). Slightly dry style, but full of fascinating detail about the brave and often mortal struggle of the countless ordinary people across France who fought to drive the Germans from their country.

François Maspero *Cat's Grin* (o/p). Semi-autobiographical novel about a young teenager in Paris during the war with his brother in the Resistance, his parents taken to concentration camps as Paris is liberated, and everyone else busily collaborating. An intensely moving and revealing account of the war period.

Irène Nemirovsky *Suite Française* (Vintage, 2007/Knopf, 2006). The author was transported to Auschwitz, where she died. Before she left, she deposited the notebooks containing these two extraordinary novellas with her daughter. They were only published in 2004. The part details the flight from Paris in June 1940; the second depicts life in a provincial town under German occupation.

Ian Ousby *Occupation: The Ordeal of France 1940–1944* (Pimlico, 1999/Cooper Square, 2000). Revisionist 1997 account which shows how relatively late resistance was, how widespread collaboration was, and why. Good mix of salient events and how it felt to live through these times.

Barbara Tuchman *The Proud Tower* (Ballantine, 1996). A portrait of England, France, the US, Germany and Russia in the years

1890–1914. Written in Tuchman's inimitable and readable style, it includes superb chapters on the extraordinary passions and enmities of the Dreyfus Affair, and on the different currents in the socialist movement in the run-up to World War I.

Paul Webster *Pétain's Crime: The Full Story of French Collaboration in the Holocaust* (Pan, 2001). The fascinating and alarming story of the Vichy regime's more than willing collaboration with the Holocaust and the bravery of those, especially the Communist resistance in occupied France, who attempted to prevent it.

Society and politics

John Ardagh *France in the New Century: Portrait of a Changing Society* (Penguin, 2000). Long-time writer on France gets to grips with the 1980s and 90s. Attempts to be a comprehensive survey, but gets rather too drawn into party politics and statistics.

Roland Barthes *Mythologies* (Vintage, 1993; Hill & Wang, 1972). *Mythologies* is a brilliant and witty structuralist critique on the socio-historical importance of myth and its signs in France today, based on a series of quirky examples.

Jean Baudrillard *Selected Writings* (Polity, 2001/Stanford UP, 2001). Essential reading to get an overview of the most interesting contemporary French philosopher and artist.

Simone de Beauvoir *The Second Sex* (Vintage, 1997/Everyman, 1993). One of the prime texts of Western feminism, written in 1949, covering women's inferior status in history, literature, mythology, psychoanalysis, philosophy and everyday life. The style is dry and intellectual, but the subject matter easily compensates.

Denis Belloc *Slow Death in Paris* (o/p). A harrowing account of a heroin addict in Paris. Not recommended holiday reading but, if you want to know about the seedy underbelly of the city, this is the book.

Mary Blume *A French Affair: The Paris Beat 1965–1998* (Plume, 2000). Incisive and witty observations on contemporary French life by the *International Herald Tribune* reporter who was stationed there for three decades.

Émilie Carles *Wild Herb Soup* (Orion UK, 1996). A moving and inspiring autobiography of a girl born and raised in a remote Alpine valley in the early twentieth century.

Jonathan Fenby *On the Brink* (Abacus, 2002/Arcade, 2000). While France isn't perhaps quite as endangered as the title suggests, this provocative book takes a long, hard look at the problems facing contemporary France.

Mark Girouard *Life in the French Country House* (Knopf, 2000). Girouard meticulously re-creates the social and domestic life that went on between the walls of French châteaux, starting with the great halls of early castles and ending with the commercial marriage venues of the twentieth century.

Faïza Guène *Just Like Tomorrow* (Chatto & Windus/Harvest, 2006). A simple, touching tale of a shy 15-year old Muslim girl in the Paris housing projects trying to make good. Published in the US with a literal translation of the original French title: *Kiffe Kiffe Tomorrow*.

Gisèle Halimi *Milk for the Orange Tree* (Quartet, 1991). A gutsy autobiographical story of a woman who was born in Tunisia, the daughter of an Orthodox Jewish family, and who ran away to Paris to become a lawyer, and defender of women's rights, Algerian FLN fighters and all unpopular causes.

Bernard Henri-Lévy *Adventures on the Freedom Road: The French Intellectuals in the 20th Century* (o/p). Huge, clever and complex essays by the contemporary celebrity philosopher. Mercilessly analyses the response of all the great French thinkers, of Left and Right, to the key events of the century. Easy to dip into, surprisingly readable and very provocative.

Tim Moore *French Revolutions: Cycling the Tour De France* (Vintage, 2002/St Martin's, 2003). A whimsical bicycle journey along the route of the Tour by a genuinely hilarious writer. Lots of witty asides on Tour history and French culture.

Jim Ring *Riviera: the Rise and Rise of the Cote d'Azur* (John Murray, 2005). A fascinating portrait of France's most anomalous region, taking in its discovery by aristocratic pleasure-seekers in the nineteeth century, the golden years of the 1920s when it was the playgroud of artists, film stars and millionaires, and the inevitable fall from grace.

Gillian Tindall *Célestine: Voices from a French Village* (Minerva UK, 1996). Intrigued by some nineteenth century love letters left behind in the house she has bought in Chassignolles, Berry, Tindall researches the history of the village back to the 1840s. She produces a meticulous, thoughtful and moving portrait of rural French life and its slow but dramatic transformation. A brilliant piece of social history.

Eugen Weber *My France* (Harvard, 1992). A collection of essays, fascinating and offbeat, about numerous aspects of French culture and politics. Some prior knowledge of mainstream French history is needed to make the most of them.

Theodore Zeldin *The French* (Harvill UK, 1997). A wise and original book that attempts to describe a country through the prism of the author's intensely personal conversations with a fascinating range of French people. Chapter titles include "How to be chic" and "How to appreciate a grandmother".

Art and poetry

John Berger *The Success and Failure of Picasso* (Vintage UK, 1993). The success is self-explanatory; the failure (and the tragedy) lies in Picasso's poverty of subject matter – or so Berger argues in this brief and highly persuasive book. Perhaps the best one-volume study of Picasso in English.

Brassaï *The Secret Paris of the Thirties* (Thames & Hudson UK, 2001). Extraordinary photos of the capital's nightlife in the 1930s – brothels, music halls, street-cleaners, transvestites and the underworld – each one a work of art and a familiar world (now long since gone) to Brassaï and his mate, Henry Miller, who accompanied him on his nocturnal expeditions.

André Chastel *French Art* (Flammarion, France 1995–96). Authoritative, three-volume study by one of France's leading art historians.

Discusses individual works of art in some detail in an attempt – from architecture to tapestry, as well as painting – to locate the Frenchness of French art. With glossy photographs and serious-minded but readable text.

Kenneth J. Conant *Carolingian and Romanesque Architecture, 800–1200* (Yale, 1992). Good European study with a focus on Cluny and the Santiago pilgrim route.

John Richardson *The Life of Picasso: Vol 1 1881–1906* (Pimlico, 1992/Random House, 1996) and *Vol 2 1907–17* (Pimlico, 1997/Random House, 1996). No twentieth-century artist has ever been subjected to as much scrutiny as Picasso receives in Richardson's exhaustive and brilliantly illustrated biography. The author has taken many years to complete the first two volumes, and there's a risk he'll never reach the end, but the mould-breaking years have now been covered. Volumes 3 and 4 are in the pipeline.

Stephen Romer (editor) *20th-Century French Poems* (Faber, 2002). A collection of around 150 French poems spanning the whole of the century. Although there's no French text, many of the translations are works of art in themselves, consummately rendered by the likes of Samuel Beckett, T.S. Eliot and Paul Auster. An equally enjoyable read for the novice and those already familiar with modern French poetry.

Vivian Russell *Monet's Garden* (Frances Lincoln, 1995). Sumptuous colour photographs by the author, old photographs of the artist and reproductions of his paintings. Includes a detailed description of the garden's evolution and seasonal cycle that will delight serious gardeners.

Gertrude Stein *The Autobiography of Alice B Toklas* (Penguin UK, 2001). The goings-on at Stein's famous salon in Paris. The most accessible of her works, written from the point of view of Stein's long-time lover, gives an amusing account of the Paris art and literary scene of the 1910s and 1920s.

Guides

David Abram *Corsica Trekking GR20* (Trailblazer, 2007). Trailblazer's guide to the island's long-distance footpaths covers the GR20, Mare a Mare Nord & Sud and Mare e Monti Nord routes. Written by the author of our Corsica chapter, this is the most comprehensive book of its kind, with lively route descriptions, 67 hand-drawn maps and a full-colour field guide to Corsican flora.

James Bromwich *The Roman Remains of Southern France* (Routledge, 1996). The only comprehensive guide to the subject – detailed, well illustrated and approachable. In addition to accounts of the famous sites, it will lead you off the map to little-known discoveries.

Glynn Christian *Edible France* (Interlink, 1998). A guide to food rather than restaurants: regional produce, local specialities, markets and best shops for buying goodies to bring back home.

Cicerone Walking Guides (Cicerone, UK). Neat, durable guides with detailed route descriptions. Titles include *Tour of Mont Blanc*; *Chamonix-Mont Blanc*; *Tour of the Oisans* (GR54); *French Alps* (GR5); *The Way of Saint James* (GR65); *Tour* *of the Queyras*; *The Pyrenean Trail* (GR10); *Walks and Climbs in the Pyrenees*; *Walking in the Alps*.

Elizabeth David *French Provincial Cooking* (Penguin, 1998). A classic cookery book, written in 1960 by the English expert on French food. The recipes are in fine prose rather than manual speak, with excellent detail and warnings about tricky processes or the need for particular skills; and they work, even with non-French ingredients.

David Hampshire *Living and Working in France* (Survival Books, 2007). An invaluable guide for anyone considering residence or work in France; packed with ideas and advice on job hunting, bureaucracy, tax, health and so on. Usually updated every two years.

W. Lippert *Fleurs des Montagnes, Alpages et Forêts* (Nathan, France, 1991). Best palm-sized colour guide if you want something to pack away with your gear in the mountains.

Douglas Streatfeild-James & others *Trekking in the Pyrenees* (Trailblazer UK, 2005). The best English-language guide to the GR10 and its variants, also including choice bits of the Camino de Santiago and most of the GR11. Easy-to-use sketch maps, and plenty of practical details.

Patricia Wells *The Paris Cookbook* (Kyle Cathie, UK, 2003). American journalist and long-time resident of the capital, Patricia Wells takes her inspiration for these sophisticated recipes from her favourite Parisian restaurants, shops and markets.

Language

Language

Phrasebooks and courses 1341

Pronunciation 1341

Basic words and phrases 1342

Food and dishes 1346

Glossary 1354

French

French can be a deceptively familiar language because of the number of words and structures it shares with English. Despite this, it's far from easy, though the bare essentials are not difficult to master and can make all the difference. Even just saying "Bonjour Madame/Monsieur" and then gesticulating will usually get you a smile and helpful service. People working in tourist offices, hotels and so on, almost always speak English and tend to use it when you're struggling to speak French – be grateful, not insulted.

Phrasebooks and courses

The Complete Merde! The Real French You Were Never Taught at School (HarperCollins). More than just a collection of swearwords, this book is a passkey into the French people actually use. As such, it's an inspiring resource for anyone wishing to break out of school-level French, and get a window into French culture.

Breakthrough French (Palgrave Macmillan). One of the best teach-yourself courses, with three levels to choose from. Each comes with a book and CD-ROM.

Get Into French Course Pack (BBC Worldwide). Comes with an audio CD, a book and a CD-ROM which allows you to set up your own role-play situations. The BBC offers a whole range of French learning products – see ⓦwww.bbc.co.uk/languages/french, which also offers a basic "Quick Fix", with free mp3 downloads, and a free, 24-part, online audio course: "French Steps".

Harrap's French Mini Dictionary (Harrap). This relatively comprehensive French–English and English–French dictionary also has a brief grammar and pronunciation guide.

Rough Guide French Phrasebook (Rough Guides). Mini dictionary-style phrasebook with both English–French and French–English sections, along with cultural tips and a menu reader.

Pronunciation

One easy rule to remember is that **consonants** at the ends of words are usually silent: the most obvious example is Paris, pronounced "Paree", while the phrase *pas plus tard* (not later) sounds something like "pa-plu-tarr". The exception is when the following word begins with a vowel, in which case you run the two together: *pas après* (not after) becomes "pazaprey". Otherwise, consonants are much as in English, except that: *ch* is always "sh", *c* is "s", *h* is silent, *th* is the same as "t", *ll* is like the "y" in yes, *w* is "v", and *r* is growled (or rolled).

Vowels are the hardest sounds to get exactly right, but they rarely differ enough from English to make comprehension a problem. The most obvious differences are that *au* sounds like the "o" in "over"; *aujourd'hui* (today) is thus pronounced "oh-jor-dwi". Another one to listen out for is *oi*, which sounds like "wa"; *toi* (to you) thus sounds like "twa". Lastly, adding "m" or "n" to a vowel, as in *en* or *un*, adds a nasal sound, as if you said just the vowel with a cold.

Basic words and phrases

French nouns are divided into masculine and feminine. This causes difficulties with adjectives, whose endings have to change to suit the nouns they qualify – you can talk about *un château blanc* (a white castle), for example, but *une tour blanche* (a white tower). If you're not sure, stick to the simpler masculine form – as used in this glossary.

Essentials

merci	thank you
bonjour	hello (morning or afternoon)
bonsoir	hello (evening)
bonne nuit	good night
au revoir	goodbye
s'il vous plaît	please
pardon/Je m'excuse	sorry
pardon	excuse me
oui	yes
non	no
d'accord	OK/agreed
au secours!	help!
ici	here
là	there
ceci	this one
celà	that one
ouvert	open
fermé	closed
grand	big
petit	small
plus	more
moins	less
un peu	a little
beaucoup	a lot
bon marché	cheap
cher	expensive
bon	good
mauvais	bad
chaud	hot
froid	cold
avec	with
sans	without
entrée	entrance
sortie	exit
un homme	man
une femme	woman (pronounced "fam")

Numbers

un	1
deux	2
trois	3
quatre	4
cinq	5
six	6
sept	7
huit	8
neuf	9
dix	10
onze	11
douze	12
treize	13
quatorze	14
quinze	15
seize	16
dix-sept	17
dix-huit	18
dix-neuf	19
vingt	20
vingt-et-un	21
vingt-deux	22

trente	30	**cent**	100
quarante	40	**cent-et-un**	101
cinquante	50	**deux cents**	200
soixante	60	**trois cents**	300
soixante-dix	70	**cinq cents**	500
soixante-quinze	75	**mille**	1000
quatre-vingts	80	**deux milles**	2000
quatre-vingt-dix	90	**cinq milles**	5000
quatre-vingt-quinze	95	**un million**	1,000,000

Time

aujourd'hui	today	**maintenant**	now
hier	yesterday	**plus tard**	later
demain	tomorrow	**à une heure**	at one o'clock
le matin	in the morning	**à trois heures**	at three o'clock
l'après-midi	in the afternoon	**à dix heures et demie**	at ten-thirty
le soir	in the evening	**à midi**	at midday

Days and dates

janvier	January	**dimanche**	Sunday
février	February	**lundi**	Monday
mars	March	**mardi**	Tuesday
avril	April	**mercredi**	Wednesday
mai	May	**jeudi**	Thursday
juin	June	**vendredi**	Friday
juillet	July	**samedi**	Saturday
août	August	**le premier août**	August 1
septembre	September	**le deux mars**	March 2
octobre	October	**le quatorze juillet**	July 14
novembre	November	**le vingt-trois novembre**	November 23
décembre	December	**deux mille sept**	2007

Talking to people

When addressing people a simple *bonjour* is not enough; you should always use *Monsieur* for a man, *Madame* for a woman, *Mademoiselle* for a young woman or girl. This isn't as formal as it seems, and it has its uses when you've forgotten someone's name or want to attract someone's attention.

Parlez-vous anglais?	Do you speak English?	**...irlandais[e]**	...Irish
Comment ça se dit en français?	How do you say it in French?	**...écossais[e]**	...Scottish
Comment vous appelez-vous?	What's your name?	**...gallois[e]**	...Welsh
Je m'appelle...	My name is...	**...américain[e]**	...American
Je suis...	I'm...	**...australien[ne]**	...Australian
...anglais[e]	...English	**...canadien[ne]**	...Canadian
		...néo-zélandais[e]	...a New Zealander
		...sud-africain[e]	...South African

Je comprends	I understand	**Je ne sais pas**	I don't know
Je ne comprends pas	I don't understand	**Allons-y**	Let's go
S'il vous plaît, parlez moins vite	Can you speak slower?	**À demain**	See you tomorrow
Comment allez-vous?/Ça va?	How are you?	**À bientôt**	See you soon
Très bien, merci	Fine, thanks	**Fichez-moi la paix!**	Leave me alone (aggressive)
		Aidez-moi, s'il vous plaît	Please help me

Finding the way

autobus/bus/car	bus
gare routière	bus station
arrêt	bus stop
voiture	car
train/taxi/ferry	train/taxi/ferry
bâteau	boat
avion	plane
navette	shuttle
gare (SNCF)	train station
quai	platform
Il part à quelle heure?	What time does it leave?
Il arrive à quelle heure?	What time does it arrive?
un billet pour…	a ticket to…
aller simple	single ticket
aller retour	return ticket
compostez votre billet	validate your ticket
valable pour	valid for
vente de billets	ticket office
combien de kilomètres?	how many kilometres?
combien d'heures?	how many hours?
autostop	hitchhiking
à pied	on foot
Vous allez où?	Where are you going?
Je vais à …	I'm going to…
Je voudrais descendre à …	I want to get off at…
la route pour…	the road to…
près/pas loin	near
loin	far
à gauche	left
à droite	right
tout droit	straight on
à l'autre côté de	on the other side of
à l'angle de	on the corner of
à côté de	next to
derrière	behind
devant	in front of
avant	before
après	after
sous	under
traverser	to cross
pont	bridge
centre ville	town centre
toutes directions	all through roads (road sign)
autres directions	other destinations (road sign)
ville haute/haute ville	upper town
ville basse/basse ville	lower town
vieille ville	old town

Questions and requests

The simplest way of asking a question is to start with *s'il vous plaît* (please), then name the thing you want in an interrogative tone of voice. For example:

S'il vous plaît, la boulangerie?	Where is there a bakery?
S'il vous plaît, la route pour la tour Eiffel?	Which way is it to the Eiffel Tower?

Similarly with requests:

S'il vous plaît, une chambre pour deux?	Can we have a room for two
S'il vous plaît, un kilo d'oranges?	Can I have a kilo of oranges?

Question words

où?	where?
comment?	how?
combien?	how many/how much?
quand?	when?
pourquoi?	why?
à quelle heure?	at what time?
quel est?	what is/which is?

Accommodation

une chambre pour une/deux personne(s)	a room for one/two persons
un lit double	a double bed
une chambre avec douche	a room with a shower
une chambre avec salle de bain	a room with a bath
pour une/deux/trois nuits	for one/two/three nights
Je peux la voir?	Can I see it?
une chambre sur la cour	a room on the courtyard
une chambre sur la rue	a room over the street
premier étage	first floor
deuxième étage	second floor
avec vue	with a view
clef	key
repasser	to iron
faire la lessive	do laundry
draps	sheets
couvertures	blankets
calme	quiet
bruyant	noisy
eau chaude	hot water
eau froide	cold water
Est-ce que le petit déjeuner est compris?	Is breakfast included?
Je voudrais prendre le petit déjeuner	I would like breakfast
Je ne veux pas de petit déjeuner	I don't want breakfast
chambre d'hôte	bed and breakfast
On peut camper ici?	Can we camp here?
camping/terrain de camping	campsite
tente	tent
emplacement	tent space
foyer	hostel
auberge de jeunesse	youth hostel

Driving

garage	service station
service	service
garer la voiture	to park the car
un parking	car park
défense de stationner/ stationnement interdit	no parking
poste d'essence	petrol/gas station
essence	fuel
sans plomb	unleaded
super	leaded
gazole	diesel
faire le plein	(to) fill it up
huile	oil
ligne à air	air line
gonfler les pneus	put air in the tyres
batterie	battery
la batterie est morte	the battery is dead
bougies	plugs
tomber en panne	to break down
bidon	gas can
assurance	insurance
carte verte	green card
feux	traffic lights
feu rouge	red light
feu vert	green light

Health matters

médecin	doctor	**règles**	period
Je ne me sens pas bien	I don't feel well	**douleur**	pain
médicaments	medicines	**ça fait mal**	it hurts
ordonnance	prescription	**pharmacie**	chemist/pharmacist
Je suis malade	I feel sick	**hôpital**	hospital
J'ai mal à la tête	I have a headache	**préservatif**	condom
mal à l'estomac	stomach ache	**pilule du lendemain**	morning-after pill

Other needs

boulangerie	bakery	**camping gaz**	camping gas
alimentation	food shop	**tabac**	tobacconist
charcuterie, traiteur	delicatessen	**timbres**	stamps
pâtisserie	cake shop	**banque**	bank
fromagerie	cheese shop	**argent**	money
supermarché	supermarket	**toilettes**	toilets
manger	to eat	**police**	police
boire	to drink	**téléphone**	telephone
dégustation	tasting, eg wine tasting	**cinéma**	cinema
		théâtre	theatre
		réserver	to reserve/book

Food and dishes

Basic terms

l'addition	bill/check	**lait**	milk
beurre	butter	**moutarde**	mustard
bio or biologique	organic	**oeuf**	egg
bouteille	bottle	**offert**	free
chauffé	heated	**pain**	bread
couteau	knife	**pimenté**	spicy
cru	raw	**plat**	main course
cuillère	spoon	**poivre**	pepper
cuit	cooked	**salé**	salted/savoury
emballé	wrapped	**sel**	salt
à emporter	takeaway	**sucre**	sugar
formule	lunchtime set menu	**sucré**	sweet
fourchette	fork	**table**	table
fumé	smoked	**verre**	glass
huile	oil	**vinaigre**	vinegar

Snacks

un sandwich/une baguette	a sandwich	**panini**	toasted Italian sandwich
au jambon	with ham	**tartine**	buttered bread or open sandwich, often with jam
au fromage	with cheese	**oeufs**	eggs
au saucisson	with sausage	**au plat**	fried
au pâté (de campagne)	with pâté (country-style)	**à la coque**	boiled
croque-monsieur	grilled cheese and ham sandwich	**durs**	hard-boiled
croque-madame	grilled cheese and bacon, sausage, chicken or egg sandwich	**brouillés**	scrambled
pain bagnat	bread roll with egg, olives, salad, tuna, anchovies and olive oil	**omelette**	omelette
		nature	plain
		aux fines herbes	with herbs
		au fromage	with cheese
		salade de tomates	tomato salad
		salade vert	green salad

Pasta (pâtes), pancakes (crêpes) and flans (tartes)

nouilles	noodles	**panisse**	thick chickpea flour pancake
pâtes fraîches	fresh pasta	**pissaladière**	tart of fried onions with anchovies and black olives
raviolis	pasta parcels of meat or chard à Provençal	**tarte flambée**	thin pizza-like pastry topped with onion, cream and bacon or other combinations
crêpe au sucre /aux oeufs	pancake with sugar /eggs		
galette	buckwheat pancake		
socca	thin chickpea flour pancake		

Soups (soupes)

baudroie	fish soup with vegetables, garlic and herbs	**potage**	thick vegetable soup
bisque	shellfish soup	**potée auvergnate**	cabbage and meat soup
bouillabaisse	soup with five fish	**rouille**	red pepper, garlic and saffron mayonnaise served with fish soup
bouillon	broth or stock	**soupe à l'oignon**	onion soup with rich cheese topping
bourride	thick fish soup	**velouté**	thick soup, usually fish or poultry
consommé	clear soup		
garbure	potato, cabbage and meat soup		
pistou	parmesan, basil and garlic paste added to soup		

Starters (hors d'œuvres)

assiette anglaise	plate of cold meats
assiette composée	mixed salad plate, usually cold meat and veg
crudités	dressed raw vegetables
hors d'oeuvres	combination of the above often with smoked or marinated fish

Fish (poisson), seafood (fruits de mer) and shellfish (crustaces or coquillages)

aiglefin	small haddock or fresh cod
anchois	anchovies
anguilles	eels
barbue	brill
baudroie	monkfish or anglerfish
bigourneau	periwinkle
brème	bream
bulot	whelk
cabillaud	cod
calmar	squid
carrelet	plaice
claire	type of oyster
colin	hake
congre	conger eel
coques	cockles
coquilles	scallops St-Jacques
crabe	crab
crevettes grises	shrimp
crevettes roses	prawns
daurade	sea bream
éperlan	smelt or whitebait
escargots	snails
favou(ille)	tiny crab
flétan	halibut
friture	assorted fried fish
gambas	king prawns
hareng	herring
homard	lobster
huîtres	oysters
langouste	spiny lobster
langoustines	saltwater crayfish (scampi)
limande	lemon sole
lotte de mer	monkfish
loup de mer	sea bass
maquereau	mackerel
merlan	whiting
moules (marinière)	mussels (with shallots in white wine sauce)
oursin	sea urchin
palourdes	clams
poissons de roche	fish from shoreline rocks
praires	small clams
raie	skate
rouget	red mullet
saumon	salmon
sole	sole
thon	tuna
truite	trout
turbot	turbot
violet	sea squirt

Fish dishes and terms

aïoli	garlic mayonnaise served with salt cod and other fish
anchoïade	anchovy paste or sauce
arête	fish bone
assiette de pêcheur	assorted fish
beignet	fritter
darne	fillet or steak
la douzaine	a dozen
frit	fried
friture	deep-fried small fish
fumé	smoked
fumet	fish stock

L

LANGUAGE | Food and dishes

gigot de mer large fish baked whole
grillé grilled
hollandaise butter and vinegar sauce
à la meunière in a butter, lemon and parsley sauce
mousse/mousseline mousse
pané breaded
poutargue mullet roe paste
raïto red wine, olive, caper, garlic and shallot sauce
quenelles light dumplings
thermidor lobster grilled in its shell with cream sauce

Meat (viande) and poultry (volaille)

agneau (de pré-salé) lamb (grazed on salt marshes)
andouille pork and tripe sausage
andouillette tripe sausage
bavette French cut of beef equivalent to flank
bifteck steak
boeuf beef
boudin blanc sausage of white meats
boudin noir black pudding
caille quail
canard duck
caneton duckling
contrefilet sirloin roast
coquelet cockerel
dinde/dindon turkey
entrecôte rib steak
faux filet sirloin steak
foie liver
foie gras (duck/goose) liver
gibier game
gigot (d'agneau) leg (of lamb)
grenouilles (cuisses de) frogs' (legs)
grillade grilled meat
hâchis chopped meat or mince hamburger
langue tongue
lapin/lapereau rabbit/young rabbit
lard/lardons bacon/diced bacon
lièvre hare
merguez spicy, red sausage
mouton mutton
museau de veau calf's muzzle
oie goose
onglet French cut of beef that makes a prime steak
os bone
poitrine breast
porc pork
poulet chicken
poussin baby chicken
rillettes pork mashed with lard and liver
ris sweetbreads
rognons kidneys
rognons blancs testicles
sanglier wild boar
steak steak
tête de veau calf's head (in jelly)
tournedos thick slices of fillet
tripes tripe
tripoux mutton tripe
veau veal
venaison venison

Meat and poultry dishes and terms

aïado roast shoulder of lamb stuffed with garlic and other ingredients
aile wing
au feu de bois cooked over wood fire
au four baked
baeckoffe Alsatian hotpot of pork, mutton and beef baked with potato layers
blanquette, daube, estouffade, hochepôt, navarin, ragoût types of stew

blanquette de veau	veal in cream and mushroom sauce
boeuf bourguignon	beef stew with Burgundy, onions and mushrooms
canard à l'orange	roast duck with an orange and wine sauce
canard pâté de périgourdin foie gras	roast duck with prunes and truffles
carré	best end of neck, chop or cutlet
cassoulet	casserole of beans, sausages and duck/goose
choucroute	pickled cabbage with peppercorns, sausages, bacon and salami
civet	game stew
confit	meat preserve
côte	chop, cutlet or rib
cou	neck
coq au vin	chicken slow-cooked with wine, onions and mushrooms
cuisse	thigh or leg
épaule	shoulder
en croûte	in pastry
farci	stuffed
garni	with vegetables
gésier	gizzard
grillade	grilled meat
grillé	grilled
hâchis	chopped meat or mince hamburger
magret de canard	duck breast
marmite	casserole
médaillon	round piece
mijoté	stewed
pavé	thick slice
pieds et paques	mutton or pork tripe and trotters
poêlé	pan-fried
poulet de Bresse	chicken from Bresse
râble	saddle
rôti	roast
sauté	lightly fried in butter
steak au poivre (vert/rouge)	steak in a black peppercorn sauce (green/red peppercorn)
steak tartare	raw chopped beef, topped with a raw egg yolk
tagine	North African casserole
tournedos rossini	beef fillet with foie gras and truffles
viennoise	fried in egg and breadcrumbs

Terms for steaks

bleu	almost raw
saignant	rare
à point	medium rare
bien cuit	well done
très bien cuit	very well done/ruined
brochette	kebab

Garnishes and sauces

américaine	sauce of white wine, cognac and tomato
arlésienne au porto	with tomatoes, onions, aubergines, potatoes and rice in port
auvergnat	with cabbage, sausage and bacon
béarnaise	sauce of egg yolks, white wine, shallots and vinegar
beurre blanc	sauce of white wine and shallots, with butter
bonne femme	with mushroom, bacon, potato and onions
bordelaise	in a red wine, shallot and bone-marrow sauce
boulangère	baked with potatoes and onions

bourgeoise	with carrots, onions, bacon, celery and braised lettuce
chasseur	sauce of white wine, mushrooms and shallots
châtelaine	with artichoke hearts and chestnut purée
diable	strong mustard seasoning
forestière	with bacon and mushroom
fricassée	rich, creamy sauce
mornay	cheese sauce
pays d'auge	cream and cider
périgourdine	sauce with foie gras and possibly truffles
piquante	with gherkins or capers, vinegar and shallots
provençale	sauce of tomatoes, garlic, olive oil and herbs
savoyarde	with gruyère cheese
véronique	sauce of grapes, wine and cream

Vegetables (légumes), grains (grains), herbs (herbes) and spices (épices)

ail	garlic
anis	aniseed
artichaut	artichoke
asperge	asparagus
avocat	avocado
basilic	basil
betterave	beetroot
blette/bette	Swiss chard
cannelle	cinnamon
capre	caper
cardon	cardoon, a beet related to artichoke
carotte	carrot
céleri	celery
champignons, cèpes, ceps, girolles, chanterelles, pleurotes	mushrooms
chou (rouge)	(red) cabbage
choufleur	cauliflower
concombre	cucumber
cornichon	gherkin
échalotes	shallots
endive	chicory
épinard	spinach
estragon	tarragon
fenouil	fennel
férigoule	thyme (in Provençal)
fèves	broad beans
flageolets	flageolet beans
gingembre	ginger
haricots	beans
verts	green beans
rouges	kidney beans
beurres	yellow snap beans
laurier	bay leaf
lentilles	lentils
maïs	maize (corn)
menthe	mint
moutarde	mustard
oignon	onion
panais	parsnip
pélandron	type of string bean
persil	parsley
petits pois	peas
piment rouge/vert	red/green chilli pepper
pois chiche	chickpeas
pois mange-tout	mange-tout
pignons	pine nuts
poireau	leek
poivron (vert, rouge)	sweet pepper (green, red)
pommes de terre	potatoes
primeurs	spring vegetables
radis	radish
riz	rice
safran	saffron
sarrasin	buckwheat
tomate	tomato
truffes	truffles

Vegetable dishes and terms

alicot	puréed potato with cheese
allumettes	very thin chips
à l'anglaise	boiled
beignet	fritter
duxelles	fried mushrooms and shallots with cream
farci	stuffed
feuille	leaf
fines herbes	mixture of tarragon, parsley and chives
gratiné	browned with cheese or butter
à la grecque	cooked in oil and lemon
jardinière	with mixed diced vegetables
mousseline	mashed potato with cream and eggs
à la parisienne	sautéed potatoes, with white wine and shallot sauce
parmentier	with potatoes
petits farcis	stuffed tomatoes, aubergines, courgettes and peppers
râpée	grated or shredded
sauté	lightly fried in butter
à la vapeur	steamed
en verdure	garnished with green vegetables

Fruit (fruit) and nuts (noix)

abricot	apricot
acajou	cashew nut
amande	almond
ananas	pineapple
banane	banana
brugnon, nectarine	nectarine
cacahouète	peanut
cassis	blackcurrant
cérise	cherry
citron	lemon
citron vert	lime
datte	date
figue	fig
fraise (de bois)	strawberry (wild)
framboise	raspberry
fruit de la passion	passion fruit
grenade	pomegranate
groseille	redcurrant
mangue	mango
marron	chestnut
melon	melon
mirabelle	small yellow plum
myrtille	bilberry
noisette	hazelnut
noix	walnuts; nuts
orange	orange
pamplemousse	grapefruit
pastèque	watermelon
pêche	peach
pistache	pistachio
poire	pear
pomme	apple
prune	plum
pruneau	prune
raisin	grape
reine-claude	greengage

Fruit dishes and terms

agrumes	citrus fruits
beignet	fritter
compôte	stewed fruit
coulis	sauce of puréed fruit
crème de marrons	chestnut purée
flambé	set aflame in alcohol
fougasse	bread flavoured with orange-flower water or almonds (can be savoury)
frappé	iced

Desserts (desserts or entremets) and pastries (pâtisserie)

bombe	moulded ice-cream dessert
brioche	sweet breakfast roll
calisson	almond sweet
charlotte	custard and fruit in lining of almond fingers
chichi	doughnut shaped into a stick
clafoutis	heavy custard and fruit tart
crème Chantilly	vanilla-flavoured and sweetened whipped cream
crème fraîche	sour cream
crème pâtissière	thick, eggy pastry-filling
crêpe suzette	thin pancake with orange juice and liqueur
fromage blanc	cream cheese
gaufre	waffle
glace	ice cream
Île flottante /oeufs à la neige	whipped egg-white floating on custard
macaron	macaroon
madeleine	small sponge cake
marrons Mont Blanc	chestnut purée and cream on a rum-soaked sponge cake
mousse au chocolat	chocolate mousse
omelette norvégienne	baked alaska
palmier	caramelized puff pastry
parfait	frozen mousse, sometimes ice cream
petit-suisse	a smooth mixture of cream and curds
petits fours	bite-sized cakes/ pastries
poires belle hélène	pears and ice cream in chocolate sauce
tarte Tatin	upside-down apple tart
tarte tropezienne	sponge cake filled with custard cream, topped with nuts
yaourt/yogourt	yoghurt

Glossary

alimentation food

appellation (d'origine) contrôlée government certification guaranteeing the quality of a French wine or cheese; often written AOC

arrondissement city borough

autoroute motorway/freeway

boulangerie baker's

boulevard périphérique ring road

causse limestone plateau

centre ville town centre

chais warehouses

chambre d'hôte B&B accommodation in someone's house

charcuterie butcher's

confiserie shop selling sweets, chocolate and sometimes ice cream

département administrative division of France, roughly equivalent to an English county

dégustation tasting, as in wine tasting or gourmet food menu

formule lunchtime set menu

foyer residential hostel for young workers and students

fromagerie cheese shop

gare station

gare routière bus station

gare SNCF train station

gîte (d'étape) country cottage rentable by the week, or hikers' accommodation

grands projets series of large-scale architectural projects initiated by Mitterrand in the 1980s

halles market

Hôtel de Ville town hall

mairie town hall

maquis French World War II Resistance movement, taking its name from the thick shrub found in coastal areas of the Mediterranean which provided cover for members

navette shuttle service

patisserie cake shop

plage beach

plats du jour daily specials

pont bridge

puy mountain formed from a volcano

quartier district in a town or city

rue street

tabac tobacconist's, also selling bus/métro tickets and phone cards

table d'hôte a communal dining table in a restaurant

traiteur delicatessen

Architectural terms

These are either terms you'll come across in the Guide, or come up against while travelling around.

abbaye abbey

ambulatory passage round the outer edge of the choir of a church

apse semicircular termination at the east end of a church

Baroque High Renaissance period of art and architecture, distinguished by extreme ornateness

basse ville lower town

bastide walled town

Carolingian dynasty (and art, sculpture etc) named after Charlemagne; mid-eighth to early tenth centuries

château mansion, country house, castle

château fort castle

chevet east end of a church

choir the eastern part of a church between the altar and nave, used by the choir and clergy

Classical architectural style incorporating Greek and Roman elements: pillars, domes, colonnades, etc, at its height in France in the seventeenth century and revived, as Neoclassical, in the nineteenth century

clerestory upper storey of a church, incorporating the windows

donjon castle keep

église church

flamboyant florid form of Gothic

Gallo-Roman from the Roman era in France

haute ville upper town

hôtel particulier mansion or town house

Merovingian dynasty (and art etc), ruling France and parts of Germany from sixth to mid-eighth centuries

narthex entrance hall of church

nave main body of a church

porte gateway

Renaissance art/architectural style developed in fifteenth-century Italy and imported to France in the early sixteenth century

retable altarpiece

Roman Romanesque (easily confused with Romain-Roman)

Romanesque early medieval architecture distinguished by squat, rounded forms and naive sculpture, called Norman in Britain

stucco plaster used to embellish ceilings etc

tour tower

transepts transverse arms of a church

tympanum sculpted panel above a church door

voussoir sculpted rings in arch over church door

Travel store

www.roughguides.com

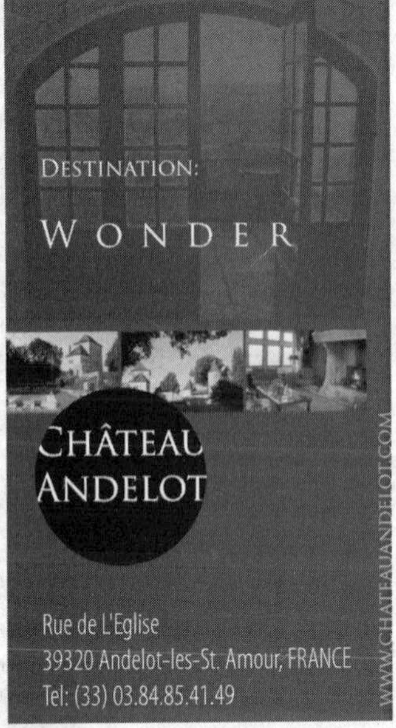
DESTINATION:
WONDER
CHÂTEAU
ANDELOT
Rue de L'Eglise
39320 Andelot-les-St. Amour, FRANCE
Tel: (33) 03.84.85.41.49
WWW.CHATEAUANDELOT.COM

Small print and

Index

A Rough Guide to Rough Guides

Published in 1982, the first Rough Guide – to Greece – was a student scheme that became a publishing phenomenon. Mark Ellingham, a recent graduate in English from Bristol University, had been travelling in Greece the previous summer and couldn't find the right guidebook. With a small group of friends he wrote his own guide, combining a highly contemporary, journalistic style with a thoroughly practical approach to travellers' needs.

The immediate success of the book spawned a series that rapidly covered dozens of destinations. And, in addition to impecunious backpackers, Rough Guides soon acquired a much broader and older readership that relished the guides' wit and inquisitiveness as much as their enthusiastic, critical approach and value-for-money ethos.

These days, Rough Guides include recommendations from shoestring to luxury and cover more than 200 destinations around the globe, including almost every country in the Americas and Europe, more than half of Africa and most of Asia and Australasia. Our ever-growing team of authors and photographers is spread all over the world, particularly in Europe, the USA and Australia.

In the early 1990s, Rough Guides branched out of travel, with the publication of Rough Guides to World Music, Classical Music and the Internet. All three have become benchmark titles in their fields, spearheading the publication of a wide range of books under the Rough Guide name.

Including the travel series, Rough Guides now number more than 350 titles, covering: phrasebooks, waterproof maps, music guides from Opera to Heavy Metal, reference works as diverse as Conspiracy Theories and Shakespeare, and popular culture books from iPods to Poker. Rough Guides also produce a series of more than 120 World Music CDs in partnership with World Music Network.

Visit www.roughguides.com to see our latest publications.

Rough Guide travel images are available for commercial licensing at www.roughguidespictures.com

Rough Guide credits

Text editors: Edward Aves, Sarah Eno, James Smart, Helena Smith and Lucy White
Layout: Ajay Verma
Cartography: Jai Prakash Mishra
Picture editor: Harriet Mills
Production: Katherine Owers
Proofreaders: Karen Parker, Madhavi Singh and Punita Singh
Cover design: Chloë Roberts
Photographers: David Abram, Jean-Christophe Godet, Michelle Grant, James McConnachie and Greg Ward

....

Editorial: **London** Kate Berens, Claire Saunders, Ruth Blackmore, Polly Thomas, Richard Lim, Alison Murchie, Karoline Densley, Andy Turner, Keith Drew, Edward Aves, Nikki Birrell, Alice Park, Sarah Eno, Lucy White, Jo Kirby, Samantha Cook, James Smart, Natasha Foges, Roisin Cameron, Joe Staines, Duncan Clark, Peter Buckley, Matthew Milton, Tracy Hopkins, Ruth Tidball; **New York** Andrew Rosenberg, Steven Horak, AnneLise Sorensen, Amy Hegarty, April Isaacs, Ella Steim, Anna Owens, Joseph Petta, Sean Mahoney
Design & Pictures: **London** Scott Stickland, Dan May, Diana Jarvis, Mark Thomas, Jj Luck, Harriet Mills, Chloë Roberts, Nicole Newman; **Delhi** Umesh Aggarwal, Ajay Verma, Jessica Subramanian, Ankur Guha, Pradeep Thapliyal, Sachin Tanwar, Anita Singh, Madhavi Singh
Production: Katherine Owers, Aimee Hampson
Cartography: **London** Maxine Repath, Ed Wright, Katie Lloyd-Jones; **Delhi** Jai Prakash Mishra, Rajesh Chhibber, Ashutosh Bharti, Rajesh Mishra, Animesh Pathak, Jasbir Sandhu, Karobi Gogoi, Amod Singh, Alakananda Bhattacharya, Athokpam Jotinkumar
Online: **New York** Jennifer Gold, Kristin Mingrone; **Delhi** Manik Chauhan, Narender Kumar, Rakesh Kumar, Amit Kumar, Amit Verma, Rahul Kumar, Ganesh Sharma, Debojit Borah
Marketing & Publicity: **London** Liz Statham, Niki Hanmer, Louise Maher, Jess Carter, Vanessa Godden, Anna Paynton, Rachel Sprackett; **New York** Geoff Colquitt, Megan Kennedy, Katy Ball; **Delhi** Reem Khokhar
Special Projects Editor: Philippa Hopkins
Manager India: Punita Singh
Series Editor: Mark Ellingham
Reference Director: Andrew Lockett
Publishing Coordinator: Megan McIntyre
Publishing Director: Martin Dunford
Commercial Manager: Gino Magnotta
Managing Director: John Duhigg

Publishing information

This tenth edition published May 2007 by **Rough Guides Ltd**,
80 Strand, London WC2R 0RL
345 Hudson St, 4th Floor,
New York, NY 10014, USA
14 Local Shopping Centre, Panchsheel Park,
New Delhi 110017, India
Distributed by the Penguin Group
Penguin Books Ltd,
80 Strand, London WC2R 0RL
Penguin Group (USA)
375 Hudson Street, NY 10014, USA
Penguin Group (Australia)
250 Camberwell Road, Camberwell,
Victoria 3124, Australia
Penguin Books Canada Ltd,
10 Alcorn Avenue, Toronto, Ontario,
Canada M4V 1E4
Penguin Group (NZ)
67 Apollo Drive, Mairangi Bay, Auckland 1310,
New Zealand

Cover concept by Peter Dyer.
Typeset in Bembo and Helvetica to an original design by Henry Iles.
Printed in Italy at LegoPrint

1396pp includes index
A catalogue record for this book is available from the British Library
ISBN: 978-1-84353-797-7

1 3 5 7 9 8 6 4 2

Help us update

We've gone to a lot of effort to ensure that the tenth edition of **The Rough Guide to France** is accurate and up to date. However, things change – places get "discovered", opening hours are notoriously fickle, restaurants and rooms raise prices or lower standards. If you feel we've got it wrong or left something out, we'd like to know, and if you can remember the address, the price, the time, the phone number, so much the better. We'll credit all contributions, and send a copy of the next edition (or any other Rough Guide if you prefer) for the best letters. Everyone who writes to us and isn't already a subscriber will receive a copy of our full-colour thrice-yearly newsletter. Please mark letters: "**Rough Guide France Update**" and send to: Rough Guides, 80 Strand, London WC2R 0RL, or Rough Guides, 4th Floor, 345 Hudson St, New York, NY 10014. Or send an email to **mail@roughguides.com**
Have your questions answered and tell others about your trip at
www.roughguides.atinfopop.com

Acknowledgements

Andrew Benson: Many thanks to Anna Trigona for her Mediterranean hospitality in a very un-Mediterranean city; to David Muller for all his help and support; and to all my friends in Alsace and Lorraine, locals and non-locals.

Brian Catlos thanks Elena Aznar, Caroline Berland (OT Montpellier), Lysiane Boissy d'Anglas (CDT Gard), Mélissa Buttelli (OT Toulouse), John Dagenais (UCLA), Myriam Journet-Fillaquier (CDT Aude), Patricia de Pouzilhac (CRT LR), Núria Silleras-Fernández, Valérie Crouineau (CDT Ariège) and Mélissa Buttelli (OT Toulouse).

Belinda Dixon: Huge thanks go to Ed and Lucy at Rough Guides; Amanda Monroe at Raileurope and to every tourist information officer, guesthouse owner, wine-maker and excellent chef (of which there are many) in Burgundy.

Marc Dubin would like to thank: Rob and Rachel Williamson in Barèges, Katie and Peter Lawton in Camon, and Luk and Micheline Peters at Thuès-entre-Valls for their hospitality and assistance; Peter Derbyshire in Luz-St-Sauveur for the usual inside tips; and Carol Coulter at Skycars for travel facilities.

Neville Walker thanks Geoff Hinchley and Kathryn Walker.

Nick Woodford wishes to thank La Maison de France and local tourist offices, in particular Brignoles, as well as Ed Aves for his editing guidance on the Alps and Louise Armstrong for proving that the Med isn't always a calm ocean.

Readers' letters

Thanks to all the readers who have taken the time to write in with comments and suggestions (and apologies if we've inadvertently omitted or misspelt anyone's name):

Alf Anderson, Stephen Bach, Alice Bailey and Stuart Gadsden, Iain Baird, Philip Barstow, Tony Bellworthy, Fiona Bennett, Dr Berger, Jenny Blackie, Graham Block, Caroline Bowden, Don Broadley, Brendan and Marc, Diana Brooke, Neville Browne, Clare and Gerald Chapman, Tim Claridge, Judith Cole and Nick Church, Stuart Connell, Olivier Couraud, Andrew Davidson, Peter Day, Thierry Desaga, Hans Deseure, Noemie and Cedric Dewavrin, John Fletcher, Margaret Gallery, Amanda Garrett and Holly Blue, Martin Gilges and Anja Plemper, Andrew Gillett, Jen Gold, Bill Goldman, Jenny Green, Roger Gregory, Barbara Guyon, Paul Hagman, Anne Hansen, Janie and Patrick Hapur, Sam Hardie, Dr Val Harris, Lisa Hartmann, P.L. Herlevi, Alan Hickey, Peter Hill, Imogen Hobbis, Annette Hope, Edo Huber, Cecile Hubert, Malcolm James, Ken Jones, Susan Kagan, Panu Kalmi, Rory Kelleher, Elizabeth, Malcolm and Rosina Lanyon, Katie Lawton, John and Carole LeBrun, Marcus Loxton, Jonas Ludvigsson, Martin, Sue Martin, B. Marzen, John McCann, John Medforth, Peter Meijer, Alana Michael, Richard Mills, Lisa Muran, Martyn Nappleby, Anthony Nichols and Yves Jatteau, James Nitram, Timothy Nodder, Sarah Ottaway, Sally Pabst, David Pack, Kathy Parker, Charlie & Doug Pearman, Nik Petrovic, Philip Pool, Gwerfyl Price, Rupert Price, Steve and Gill Price, Mark Radnan, Steve Rock, Kevin Rogers, Eric and Sally Rowland, James Seidler, Rebecca Shtasel and Andy Player, Ben Siegel, Trevor Smith, Keith Spittlehouse, Philip Stanley and Baerbel Menke, Nicola Roberts, Yvonne Rogers, Tim Salmon, Veronica Simpson, Jan Smith, Jonathon Snicker, Anthony Steele, Vivienne Stott, J. Sweeney, Paul and Anne Taylor, Esther Thompson, Peter Thompson, Nancy Trasande, Mike Turner, Catherine Van de Wiele, Saija Vuola and Suvi Vainiomäki, Pam Walker, J. Wells, Matt Wiles, Tori Woodward, Chris Woollacott, Andrew Young.

Photo credits

All photos © Rough Guides except the following:

Introduction

p.1 Spectators at the Tour de France © Stefano Rellandini/Reuters
p.8 St-Cirque Lapopie, Lot valley © David Noton/Taxi/Getty Images
p.10 Camargue horses © J.P. De Manne/ Robert Harding
p.11 Hôtel de Ville, Carentan © Edward Aves
p.12 View from Roquelbrune towards Nice © DK Images

Things not to miss

01 Harvesting grapes, Bordeaux © Peter Horree/Alamy
03 Fireworks, Bastille Day, Paris © Peter Turnley/Corbis
05 Pont d'Avignon and Palais des Papes © John Miller/Robert Harding
07 Amiens cathedral © DK Images
08 Final stage of the Tour de France, Paris © Reuters
10 *The Concert of Angels* from the Issenheim Altarpiece © Musee d'Unterlinden, Colmar/ Giraudon/Bridgeman Art Library
13 Château de Chambord © James McConnachie
15 The GR20, Corsica © David Abram
16 Boats in the Calanque d'En Vau, near Cassis © Dylan Reisenberger
18 War cemetery at Ryes © Edward Aves
19 Fontenay Abbey © Roger Day/Alamy
20 Bayeux tapestry detail: King Harold II at sea © Gianni Dagli Orti/Corbis
21 Rock-climbing, Puy-de-Dôme © Agence Images/Alamy
22 Gordes © DK Images
23 Monpazier © Patrick Ward/Alamy
25 Café, Aix-en-Provence © Ian Dagnall/ Alamy
26 Dom Perignon statue at Moët & Chandon champagne *maison* © Jack Sullivan/Alamy
27 Strasbourg cathedral © Geoff Renner/ Robert Harding
28 Château de Peyrepertuse © Agence Images/Alamy
30 Skiing in the Alps © Agence Images/Alamy
31 Pont d'Arc © John Mottershaw/Alamy
32 Palais de l'Île, Annecy © John Miller/ Robert Harding

Festive France colour section

Fireworks, Menton © Sergio Pitamitz/Robert Harding
Anna Torres performs at the Fête de la Musique, Paris © Amel Pain/Reuters/Corbis
Scottish dancers at the Inter-Celtic Festival, Lorient © Valery Hache/AFP/Getty Images
Camargue horse riders at the gypsy gathering, Les Stes-Maries-de-la-Mer © Cristian Baitg Reportage/Alamy
Vieilles Charrues music festival, Carhaix © Andre Durand/AFP/Getty Images
Marciac Jazz Festival © Tor Eigeland/Alamy
Dancers perform outside the Palais des Papes, Avignon © AP Photo/Claude Paris/ EMPICS
Eva Herzigova at the 59th Cannes Film Festival © Eric Gaillard/Reuters

Walking In France colour section

Climbing Mont Blanc, Alps © Nick Woodford
Ibex in the Parc National de la Vanoise © Cyril Ruoso/JH Editorial/Minden Pictures/FLPA
Gentians in the Parc Naturel de Vercors © Richard Becker/FLPA
Path to the Cirque de Gavarnie © Ian Cumming/Axiom
Cattle in the Monts du Cantal, Auvergne © Cephas Picture Library/Alamy
Stone house in a lavender field, Bonnieux, Provence © Gallo/Getty Images
Climbing down from Monte Cinto, Corsica © Ian Cumming/Axiom

Black and whites

p.202 Statue of Louis XVI, Basilique St-Denis © DK Images
p.212 Hall of Mirrors, Versailles © DK Images
p.218 Lutyens' Memorial to the Missing, Thiepval © DK Images
p.234 Nausicáa, Boulogne © Robert Haines/ Alamy
p.240 Boat near St-Valery-sur-Somme © Images of France
p.249 Grand'Place, Lille © Axiom
p.260 Vimy Ridge © Peter Titmuss/Alamy
p.282 Troyes © DK Images
p.294 Hôtel de Ville, Nancy © Robert Harding/Alamy
p.306 Bierstub, Strasbourg © Stockfolio/ Alamy

p.314 Barbary macaque, La Montagne des Singes, Kintzheim © Morales/Superstock
p.320 Bugatti at Schlumpf Automobile National Museum, Mulhouse © Mark Zylber/Alamy
p.329 The river Moselle at Metz © Robert Harding/Corbis
p.490 Château du Plessis-Bourré © James McConnachie
p.505 Along the river Loire at Gien © James McConnachie
p.526 Cyclists, Forêt de Chambord © James McConnachie
p.538 Formal gardens at Villandry © J.P. De Mann © Robert Harding
p.546 Saumur weekly market © Michael Juno/Alamy
p.562 Fontenay Abbey © Malcolm Park/Alamy
p.578 Castle and the Pont Joly, Semur-en-Auxois © Simon Batley/Alamy
p.597 Church of Notre-Dame from rue de la Musette, Dijon © Hemis/Alamy
p.616 River Sèvres near Coulon © Michael Busselle/Robert Harding
p.633 Vieux port, La Rochelle © Ruth Tomlinson/Robert Harding
p.651 Cognac distillery cellar © Peter Horree/Alamy
p.664 Place de Parlement, Bordeaux © Ray Roberts/Images of France
p.708 River Dordogne at Domme © Hugh Clancy
p.756 Prehistoric cave art at Niaux © Jean-Marc Charles/Sygma/Corbis
p.817 Mirepoix © Michael Busselle/Robert Harding
p.900 Pont d'Arc © Images of France
p.909 Puy de Dôme © Brian Harris/Alamy
p.931 Conques © DK Images
p.935 Grand Viaduc du Millau © Photolibrary.com
p.950 Church of St-Michel, Le Puy-en-Velay © Travel Library/Robert Harding
p.958 View from Aiguille du Midi towards Grand Jorasses and Aiguille du Géant © Johanna Huber/4 Corners
p.970 Vineyards near Lons-le-Saunier © Michael Busselle/Robert Harding
p.989 Footbridge over the Thiou, Annecy © Ruth Tomlinson/Robert Harding
p.1000 Cross-country skiing, Val d'Isere © Nick Woodford
p.1006 Place Grenette, Grenoble © Jon Arnold Images/Alamy
p.1024 Flamingos, La Camargue © DK Images
p.1041 Bouchon, rue Mercière, Lyon © Hemis/Alamy
p.1080 Bullfight, Arles © mediacolor's/Alamy
p.1095 Market produce, Aix © DK Images
p.1120 Port-Cros © DK Images
p.1133 Le Corbusier's Unité d'Habitation, Marseille © Jack Hobhouse/Alamy
p.1149 Collobrières © DK Images
p.1280 Charles de Gaulle and crowd at Bayeux, 14 June 1944 © Bettmann/Corbis
p.1289 Riot police near Notre-Dame cathedral after student demonstrations against the CPE youth jobs law, Paris, April 2006 © Charles Platiau/Reuters
p.1298 Edgar Degas, *L'Absinthe* (c.1875–76; oil on canvas) © Musée d'Orsay, Paris, France/Giraudon/Bridgeman Art Library
p.1309 Grande Arche de la Défense, Paris © DK Images
p.1324 Still from *De Battre Mon Coeur S'est Arrêté* ("The Beat That My Heart Skipped") © Why Not Productions/Ronald Grant Archive
p.1330 Portrait of Marcel Proust © Private Collection/Archives Charmet/Bridgeman Art Library

Index

Map entries are in colour.

A

Abbeville 240
Abense-de-Haut 779
Abri du Cap Blanc 702
accommodation 45–50
addresses in France 44
adventure sports 63
Agde 858
Agen 752
Agincourt, battle of 238, 1271
Aigues-Mortes 856
Aiguille du Midi 986
Aiguilles Rouges 987
Aiguines 1106
Ailefroide 1018
Ainhoa 772
airlines 32
Aix-en-Provence 22, 1094–1101
Aix-en-Provence 1096–1097
Aix, Île d' 642
Aix-les-Bains 994
Ajaccio 1235–1242
Ajaccio 1236
Alain-Fournier 527
Albert 262
Albi 888–891
Albi 889
Albinhac 920
Alençon 400
Aléria 1257
Alès 946
Alésia 576
Alésia, battle of 1268
Alet-les-Bains 819
Algeria 1281, 1282, 1285
Alise-Ste-Reine 576
Alliat 811
Alps, the 975–1022
Alps, the 960
Alsace 298–322
Alsace 296–297
Alsatian language 302
Ambert 954
Amboise 534–537
Amiens 16, 241–244
Amiens 242
Amnéville 331
ancien régime ... 1275, 1276
Angers 549–554
Angers 550
Anglet 767
Angoulême 653–656
Angoulême 654
Annecy .... 24, 988–990, *Festive France* colour section
Annecy 988
Antibes 1171–1175
Antibes 1172
Anzy-le-Duc 613
Apt 1093
Aquitaine 657–677
Aquitaine 618
Arbois 971
Arc valley 1001–1003
Arcachon 675
Arçais 629
architecture 1305–1312, 1354
Ardennes, the 289–291
Argelès 829
Argentière-Les Grand Montets 987
Argentières 1016
Ariège valley .... 808–812, *Walking in France* colour section
Arles 1077–1083
Arles 1078
Arles-sur-Tech 832
Armagnac 894
Arman 1302
Arnac-Pompadour 726
Arras 258
Arrens-Marsous 796
Arromanches 377
art 1291–1304
Arudy 794
Arvieux 1019
Ascain 772
Aspe valley 789–794
Aste-Béon 794
ATMs 76
au pair work 66
Aubenas 947
Aubeterre-sur-Dronne ... 690
Aubrac, the 924–927
Aubusson 721
Auch 894
Aucun 797
Aude gorges 820
Aude valley 818
Audierne 453
Audinghen 232
Auguste, Philippe 1270
Augustus, Caesar 1268
Aulnay 651
Aulus-les-Bains 812
Aumont-Aubrac 925
Aups 1103
Aurillac .... 919–921, *Festive France* colour section
Auron 1114
Autoire 731
Autun 587–590
Autun 588
Auvers-Sur-Oise 204
Auxerre 568–570
Auxerre 568
avalanches 998
Avallon 580–582
Avallon 581
Aven Armand 938
Aven Marzal 948
Aven Orgnac 948
Aveyron, River 744–747
Avèze 945
Avignon .... 16, 1060–1070, *Festive France* colour section
Avignon 1062–1063
Avoriaz 978
Avranches 389
Axat 820
Ax-les-Thermes 811
Azay-le-Rideau 539
Azincourt 238

B

Bages 868
Bagnères-de-Bigorre 804
Bagnoles-de-l'Orne 401
Baie des Anges 1175
Baie des Trépassés 451
Baker, Josephine 706
Balagne, the 1221–1228
Balladur, Edouard 1284
Balleroy 381
Bandol 1139
Banyuls-sur-Mer 830
Barbazan 806
Barbie, Klaus 1036
Barbizon 205, 1296
Barcelonnette 1113

Barèges 802
Barfleur 385
Barnenez, Cairn du 436
Baroque architecture .. 1307
Barr 312
Bastia 1207–1213
Bastia 1208
bastides 21, 695, 1306
Bastille Day .. 15, 200, *Festive France* colour section
Bastille, the storming of 1275
Batz, Île de 441
Baume Bonne 1108
Bavella 1256
Bayeux ... 20, 375, 378–381
Bayeux 378
Bayonne 760–764
Bayonne 761
Bazas 674
Bazile, Bernard 1304
Béarn des Gaves 785
Beau Rivage 463
Beaugency 501
Beaujolais, the 611
Beaulieu 1191
Beaulieu-les-Loches 518
Beaulieu-sur-Dordogne .. 712
Beaumes-de-Venise ... 1058
Beaumont-Hamel 263
Beaumont-le-Roger 394
Beaune 602–604
Beaune 602
Beauvais 244
Becket, Thomas ... 566, 571
bed and breakfast 47
Bédarieux 869
Bédeilhac 811
Bedoin 1058
Bedous 791
Béhérobie 777
Belfort 962
Belle-Île (Brittany) 470
Belvès 706
Benedictine Distillery 348
Bénodet 458
Bérégovoy, Pierre 1284
Bergerac 692–694
Bergerac, Cyrano de 693
Bergheim 315
Bernard, Émile 1299
Besançon 965–967
Bessans 1001
Besse 918
Besson, Luc 1314
Bête du Gévaudan, the .. 927
Beuvron-en-Auge 396
Beynac-et-Cazenac 707
Béziers 863–865
Biarritz 764–767
Biarritz 765
Bibracte 590
Biguglia, Étang de 1214
Bidarray 774
Binic 431
Biot 1175
Biriatou 771
Biron 696
bistros .... *Cafés, bistros and brasseries* colour section
Blais, Jean-Charles 1303
Blaye 670
Bligny 281
Blois 519–522
Blois 520
Blum, Léon 1279
BMPT 1303
Bocage, the 402–405
Bofill, Ricardo 1312
Boisrond, François 1303
Boltanski, Christian 1303
Bonifacio 1248–1253
Bonifacio 1250–1251
Bonnard, Pierre 1300
Bonneval-sur-Arc 1001
books 1328–1337, 1341
Borce 793
Bordeaux 18, 657–666
Bordeaux 658–659
Bordeaux wine region 667–675
Bories, Village des 1091
Bormes-les-Mimosas ... 1146
Boschaud, abbaye de .. 691
Botta, Mario 1311
Boucher, François 1294
Boudin, Eugène 1297
Boule d'Amont 833
boules 61
Boulogne-sur-Mer 232–235
Boulogne-sur-Mer 233
Bourdeilles 689
Bourg-Charente 653
Bourg-en-Bresse 609
Bourgeois, Louise 1304
Bourges 508–512
Bourg-St-Maurice 997
Bourré 515
Boyardville 645
Bracieux 526
Brancusi 1302
Brantôme 689
Braque, Georges 1301
brasseries .... *Cafés, bistros and brasseries* colour section
Bregançon 1146
Bréhat, Île de 432
Brest 445–447
Bretenoux 712
Breton language 412
Brévent 987
Briançon 1016
Briare 507
Brignogan-Plage 442
Brionne 394
Brissac-Quincé 555
Brittany 407–487
Brittany 410
Brive-la-Gaillarde 724
Brommat 920
Brou 608
Brouage 643
Bruniquel 747
Bugeat 723
bullfighting ... 61, 845, 1080
Buñuel, Luis 1313
Buren, Daniel 1303
Burgundy 561–614
Burgundy 564
buses to France 31, 34
buses within France 38
Bustamante, Jean-Marc 1303

C

Cabardès, the 878
Cabasson 1146
Cabourg 369
Cabrerets 744
Cadouin, abbaye de 705
Caen 370–374
Caen 370
Caesar, Julius 576, 1268
cafés .... 19, *Cafés, bistros and brasseries* colour section
Cagnac-les-Mines 891
Cagnes 1175
Cahors 733–736
Cahors 734
Calais 226–229
Calais 226
Calanches, the .. 1231, 1232
calanques, the .... 19, 1136, *Walking in France* colour section
Calle, Sophie 1304
Calvi 1223–1228
Calvi 1224
Calvin, John 271
Camaret 449
Camargue, the .. 1083–1089

Camargue, the...1084–1085
Cambo-les-Bains 772
Cambous.........................860
Cambrai 256
Camembert 397
Camisards, the 859
Camon.............................817
Campagne 701
Campan...........................804
camping 49
Campomoro 1245
canal trips 43
Canal de Bourgogne........573–579
Canal du Midi 15, 874
Cancale 425
Candes-St-Martin 549
Canet-Plage....................828
Caninac 879
Cannes.......... 1164–1168, *Festive France* colour section
Cannes............1164–1165
canoeing.........64, 709, 737
Cap Corse 1214–1217
Cap d'Agde 858
Cap d'Antibes.............1173
Cap Ferret 676
Capet, Hugues 1269
car rental 42
carbon offsetting 29
Carcassonne.. 24, 872–876
Carcassonne: cité 873
Carcassonne: ville basse 872
Cardaillac.......................742
Carennac 712
Cargèse.........................1233
Carhaix ....462, *Festive France* colour section
Carlat...............................920
Carnac 16, 472–475
Carnac 472
Carolingian dynasty.... 1269
Caron, Antoine 1292
Carpentras....................1059
Carracci, Annibale.....1293
Carrouges 401
Cars 723
Carsac 699
Casals, Pau (Pablo) 833
Cascades du Hérisson..973
Casernes 779
Casse Déserte............1019
Cassel 225
Cassis...... 1136, *Walking in France* colour section
Casteddu d'Araggiu ... 1255
Castellane.....................1108
Castelnaudary 876
Castres 892
Cateraggio....................1257
Cateau-Cambrésis, Treaty of 1271
Cathar castles, the......22, 821–824
Cathars..................815, 874
Caudebec-en-Caux 354
Caurel 463
Cauria............................1247
Causse de Gramat 731
Causse du Larzac 943
Cauterets... 797, *Walking in France* colour section
cave art, prehistoric....24, 701–703, 744, 811, 948
caves, troglodyte (Loire valley) 543, 545, 547
caving 63
Cazals.............................732
Célé, River.....................743
cellphones 78
Centuri-Port.................1217
Cerdagne, the...............836
Céret 831
Cerisy 381
César 1302
Cette-Eygun 793
Cévennes, Parc National des ..939–943, *Walking in France* colour section
Cézanne, Paul..1099, 1101, 1299
Chablais, the 977
Chablis 571
Châlons-en-Champagne.........*Festive France* colour section
Chalon-sur-Saône 604
Châlus 719
Chambéry............992–994
Chambord 18
chambres d'hôtes 47
Chamonix ....983–986, *Walking in France* colour section
Chamonix......................984
Champagne........271–288
Champagne 220–221
champagne....22, 273, 276, 279
Champagnole 972
Champaigne, Philippe de.............................1293
Channel Tunnel..29, 30, 34, 231
Chantilly 206
Chardin, Jean-Baptiste-Siméon 1294
Charente, the 648–657
Charente, the...............618
Charlemagne..............1269
Charles I 523
Charles VII ...359, 504, 508, 543
Charles VIII 538
Charles X 1276
Charleville-Mézières 289
Charollais, the 613
Charolles 613
Charter of 1814, the...1276
Chartres 213–215
Chartres 214
Chartreuses 1011
Chassenon 719
Chassériau, Théodore..1295
Chassezac, River..........948
chateaux
- Abbadie, d'.......................770
- Aguillar, d' 824
- Alleuze, d' 924
- Ancy-le-Franc, d' 574
- Beauregard 524
- Bonaguil..........................737
- Brézé 548
- Brissac 555
- Bussy-Rabutin 577
- Castelnau-Bretenoux 712
- Castelnaud......................707
- Châlucet..........................720
- Chambord 18, 525
- Chaumont 523
- Chenonceau 512
- Cheverny 523
- Clos-de-Vougeot 604
- Fayrac 707
- Ferté-St-Aubin 502
- Fougères 524
- Hautefort 692
- If, d' 1132
- Joux 967
- Langeais 538
- Marqueyssac...................707
- Meung 501
- Monbazillac 694
- Monbrun..........................719
- Montaigne 694
- Montrottier 992
- Moulin 527
- Peyrepertuse...................823
- Plessis-Bourré 555
- Puyguilhem 691
- Quéribus..........................823
- Queyras.........................1020
- Roche-Jagu 434
- Serrant 555
- Tanlay 575
- Ussé, d' 540
- Usson, d'.........................820
- Valençay 516
- Villandry 537

INDEX

châteaux, visiting..500, 530
Château-Chinon...........586
Châteaulin....................462
Châteauneuf-du-Pape..1055
Château-Ville-Vieille....1020
châteaux of the Loire..513
Châtel-Guyon..............911
Châtillon.........................1011
Châtillon-sur-Siene.......575
Chatou, Île de...............204
Chaumont.....................286
Chauvet-Pont d'Arc......948
Chauvigny.....................624
Chavannes, Puvis du..1299
cheese.....17, 52, 224, 341, 397, 494, 563, 579, 760, 903, 917, 961, 978, 1028, 1204
Chemin de Fer de la Provence........1109, 1179
Chemin de la Mâture....793
Chemin de Saint-Jacques..775, 785, *Walking in France* colour section
Cher, the...............512–519
Cherbourg 382–385
Cherbourg....................382
children, travelling with...69
Chinon 541–544
Chinon...........................542
Chirac, Jacques...89, 124, 130, 148, 212, 723, 1283, 1285–1290
Ciboure..........................769
cinema ....1313–1327, *Festive France* colour section
Ciran..............................503
Circuit de Souvenir, the..263
Cirque de Gavarnie......801
Cirque de Navacelles...944
Cirque de Troumouse...802
Clairiére de l'Armistice..270
Clairvaux-les-Lacs........973
Clamecy.........................584
Claudius, Emperor......1268
Clearstream scandal, the...........................1290
Clécy.............................399
Clermont-l'Hérault........861
Clermont-Ferrand............904–908
Clermont-Ferrand........905
climate............................12
climate change.....29, 1287
climbing..................62, 987
Closky, Claude...........1304
Clos-Lucé.....................536
Clouet, François.........1292
Clouet, Jean..............1292
Clovis the Frank.........1269
Cluny............................610
Cocteau, Jean..1198, 1313
Cognac..........651, *Festive France* colour section
Cogolin........................1150
Col d'Aubisque............796
Col d'Izoard...............1019
Col de l'Iseran............1001
Col de la Faucille.........975
Col de Vars.................1020
Col du Galibier...........1014
Col du Lautaret...........1014
Col du Midi..................986
Col du Tourmalet.........803
Colbert, Cardinal.......1272, 1273
Colleville-sur-Mer........375
Collioure......................829
Collobrières................1148
Collonges-la-Rouge.....726
Colmar 316–318
Colmar..........................316
Colombey-les-Deux-Églises.......................287
colonial wars..............1281
Combas, Robert.........1303
Combe du Queyras....1020
Comminges, the..804–808
Commune, the...........1278
Communism...............1279
Compiégne.........288–271
Comus.........................816
Concarneau........459–461
Concarneau.................459
conceptual art...........1303
Conches-en-Ouche......394
Condom.......................896
Confolens...................657
Conques.............929–932
consulates....................73
contraception...............68
Cordes.........................892
Corniche des Maures.........1146–1148
Corniches, the (Côte d'Azur)..........1189–1191
Corniches, the (Côte d'Azur)....................1190
Corot, Jean-Baptiste-Camille.....................1296
corridas......................1080
Corsica...........1201–1264
Corsica.......................1205
Corte..............1258–1261
Corte..........................1258
Cosquer Cave............1136
costs...............................70
Côte Basque, the..760–771
Côte d'Albâtre.....346–350
Côte d'Argent......675–677
Côte d'Azur, the...............1119–1200
Côte d'Azur...............1122
Côte d'Émeraude........430
Côte d'Opale................231
Côte d'Or............601–604
Côte de Goëlo.............431
Côte de Granit Rose..433–435, *Walking in France* colour section
Côte Vermeille, the..................829–831
Cotentin Pensinsula, the..................381–389
Cotignac.....................1103
Coucy-le-Château-Auffrique.................267
Coulon.........................628
Courbet, Gustave........968, 1296
Courceau.....................577
Cour-Cheverny........... 524
courses camarguaises..........1080
courses, language......1341
Cousteau, Jacques....1314
Coutances...................387
CPE riots....................1290
Crécy.................238, 1270
credit cards 76
Crémieu......................1044
Cresson, Édith...........1284
Crêt de Châtillon.........992
Crête d'Iparla.....*Walking in France* colour section
Créteil........*Festive France* colour section
Crèvecoeur-en-Auge....396
crime.............................70
Crozon peninsula, the..................447–449
Crozon peninsula, the.. 447
Cubism.......................1301
Cucugnan....................823
Cupservies...................879
currency exchange........76
Cuzals.........................743
cycling 43, 59, 62, 495, 963, 991

INDEX

D

Dada 1301
Dalí, Salvador 1301
Dambach-la-Ville 314
Daoulas 448
Daubigny, Charles-François 1296
Daumier, Honoré 1295
David, Jacques-Louis 1294
David-Neel, Alexandra 1109
D-Day beaches .. 374–378, 386
D-Day beaches 374
Deauville 368
debit cards 76
Degas, Edgar 1298
Delacroix, Eugène 1295
Delanoë, Bertrand 1286
Delaunay, Robert 1301
Dénezé-sous-Doué 548
Dentelles, the .. 1058–1060
Depression, the 1279
Derain, André 1300
Désert des Agriates 1220
Desgrandchamps, Marc 1304
Dezeuze, Daniel 1303
Die 1010
Dieppe 342–346
Dieppe 343
Dignes-les-Bains 1109
Dijon 593–600
Dijon 594–595
Dinan 425–428
Dinan 426
Dinard 429
Diocletian 1268
disabled travellers 71
discount cards 76
Disneyland Paris..207–209
Dives 369
Dol-de-Bretagne 419
Dole 968
Domfront 402
Domme 709
Dordogne, the 683–713
Dordogne, Limousin and the Lot 682
Dorres 837
Douai 254
Douarnenez 450
Douaumont 335
Doubs, River 964
Doucier 973
Doussard 991
Drauguignan 1102
Dreyfus, Alfred....320, 1278
drink .....10, 14, 22, 52–54, 224, 273, 276, 279, 298, 311, 348, 411, 494, 563, 601, 648, 651, 667, 668, 894, 953, 961, 1011, 1121, *Cafés, bistros and brasseries* colour section
driving in France.... 39–43, 1345
driving to France 30
Dronne valley 688–691
drugs 71
Dubuffet, Jean 1302
Duchamp, Marcel 1301
Duilhac 823
Duingt 991
Dumas, Alexandre 1132
Dune du Pyla 676
Dunkerque 222–224

E

Eaux-Bonnes 796
Eaux-Chaudes 794
École de Paris, the 1300
Ecomusée de Marquèze 677
Écrins, Parc National des ...... 1016, *Walking in France* colour section
Edict of Nantes....485, 655, 1272
Edward III, King 1270
Egletons 723
Égliseneuve-d'Entraigues 918
Eleanor of Aquitaine ... 402, 501, 548, 632, 711, 1270
electricity 72
Elne 829
embassies 73
Embrun 1019
emergency phone numbers 71
Entraygues 933
Entrecasteaux 1103
Entre-Deux-Mers 672
entry requirements 72
Eperlecques 230
Épernay 22, 279–281
Époisses 578
Erbalunga 1215
Ermitage de St-Antoine 824
Ernst, Max 1301
Erquy 430
Escalles 231
Escolives-Ste-Camille 573
Escouloubre-les-Bains 820
Espace Killy 999
Espagnac-Ste-Eulalie 743
Espalion 933
Espelette 773
Estaing 933
Estérençuby 776
Étaples 237
etiquette ....67, *Cafés, bistros and brasseries* colour section
Étretat 349
Etsaut 793
Eurostar 29, 246
Eurotunnel 30, 34, 231
Évian 976
Évisa 1233
Évreux 394
Eymoutiers 724
Eze 1191

F

Fabius, Laurent 1283
Fabre, Jean-Henri 1055
Falaise 398
Faucigny, the 979–983
Faucigny, the 979
Fauvism 1300
Faviéres 239
feast days....*Festive France* colour section
Fécamp 348
Fenioux 650
fermes auberges .....*Cafés, bistros and brasseries* colour section
Fermont, Fort de 334
ferries from the UK and Ireland 31, 34
ferries within France 39
festivals ......56–58, *Festive France* colour section
Fifth Republic, the 1281
Figeac ... 740–742, *Walking in France* colour section
Figuration Libre movement 1303
Filitosa 1244
film ......1313–1327, *Festive France* colour section
Finiels 941
Finistère 436–461
fishing 64
Flaine 980
Flaran 897

Flégère ... 987
Fleury ... 335
Fleury, Cardinal ... 1274
flights
- to France from Australia, New Zealand and South Africa ... 28
- to France from the UK and Ireland ... 27
- to France from the US and Canada ... 28
- within France ... 39

Florac ... 942
Foissac ... 742
Foix ... 809
Fondation Maeght ... 1177
Fontainebleau ... 211
Fontainebleau, School of ... 1292
Fontaine-de-Vaucluse .. 1090
Fontenay abbaye de ... 19, 576
Fontevraud, abbaye de .. 548
Fontfroide ... 868
Fontpédrouse ... 836
Font-Romeu ... 837
food ... 10, 17, 50–52, 1346–1353, *Cafés, bistros and brasseries* colour section
- in Alsace ... 298
- in Brittany ... 411
- in Burgundy ... 563
- in Champagne ... 224
- in Corsica ... 1204
- in French Flanders ... 224
- in Normandy ... 341
- in Périgord ... 684
- in Provence ... 1028
- in the Alps and Jura ... 961
- in the Basque country ... 760
- in the Côte d'Azur ... 1121
- in the Loire valley ... 494
- in the Massif Central ... 903
- in the Rhône valley ... 1028

football ... 59
Forêt d'Aïtone ... 1233
Forêt d'Iraty ... 778
Forêt de Chinon ... 544
Forêt de Compiégne ... 270
Forêt de la Joux ... 972
Forêt de Paimpont ... 416
Forêt des Écrivains-Combattants ... 871
Foster, Sir Norman ... 846, 935, 1108, 1312
Foucault, Léon ... 136
Fouesnant ... 459
Fougax-et-Barrineuf ... 816
Fougéres ... 417
Fouquet, Jean ... 1291
Fouras ... 642
Fourth Republic, the ... 1280
Fragonard, Jean-Honoré ... 1294
Fraïsse-sur-Agout ... 871
François I ... 512, 514, 521, 536
Franco–Prussian war, the ... 1277
Franks, the ... 1269
Fréjus ... 1159–1161
French language ... 1339–1353
French Revolution .. 88, 128, 1274
Frondes, the ... 1273
Front Populaire, the ... 1279
Fuissé ... 609
Futurism ... 1301
Futuroscope ... 623, 624

G

Gabas ... 795
Gance, Abel ... 1313
Ganges ... 860
Garabit, Viaduc de ... 924
Garnier, Charles ... 1310
Gassin ... 1157
Gaudin, Jean-Claude . 1125
Gauguin, Paul ... 1299
Gaul, ancient ... 1267
Gaulle, General Charles de .. 148, 249, 1279–1282
Gavarnie ... 799–801
Gave de Pau ... 797
Gavrinis ... 479
gay travellers ... 73
Gèdre ... 799
general strike (1968) ... 1282
Gênets ... 389
Gérard, Baron ... 1295
Géricault, Théodore ... 1295
Germigny-des-Près 503
Gers ... 893–897
Gévaudan, Parc Zoologique du ... 927
Giacometti ... 1302
Gien ... 505
Gigondas ... 1058
Gimel ... 728
Gincla ... 823
Girolata ... 1228
Girondins, the ... 1275
Giscard d'Estaing, Valéry ... 1283
gîtes ... 48
gîtes d'étape ... 49
Giverny ... 364
Glanum ... 1075
global warming ... 29
glossary ... 1354
Godard, Jean-Luc ... 1314
golf ... 64
Golfe de Morbihan ... 479–481
Golfe de Morbihan ... 479
Golfe de Porto-Vecchio ... 1255–1256
Golfe de Valinco ... 1242–1246
Golinhac ... 933
Gollet, Katell (Katherine the Damned) ... 438
Gonzalez-Foerster, Dominique ... 1304
Gordes ... 20, 1090
Gorges d'Ehujarré ... 780
Gorges d'Holzarte ... 779
Gorges de Carança ... 836
Gorges de Galamus ... 824
Gorges de Kakuetta ... 779
Gorges de l'Ardèche ... 23, 947
Gorges de l'Infernet ... 1013
Gorges de la Fou ... 832
Gorges de la Frau ... 816
Gorges de la Restonica ... 1262
Gorges de Madale ... 870
Gorges de Spelunca .. 1232, *Walking in France* colour section
Gorges du Fier ... 992
Gorges du Tarn ... 938
Gorges du Tavignano .. 1262
Gorges du Verdon ... 17, 1104–1107, *Walking in France* colour section
Gorges du Verdon ... 1105
Gothic architecture ... 1306
Gouffre de Padirac ... 730
Gourdon ... 731
Gourette ... 796
Goya, Francisco ... 892
GR20 .. 18, 1226, *Walking in France* colour section
Grace of Monaco, Princess ... 1189, 1194, 1195
Grand Viaduc du Millau .. 935
Grand-Vabre ... 932
Granges d'Astau ... 807
Granville ... 388
Grasse ... 1169–1171
Grenoble ... 1003–1009

Grenoble 1003
Greuze, Jean-Baptiste..1294
Gréville-Hague.............387
Grimaud......................1150
Gris, Juan 1301
Gros, Jean-Antoine 1295
Grotte de Bédeilhac.....811
Grotte de Clamouse.....861
Grotte de Dargilan........939
Grotte de Font-de-Gaume.........................701
Grotte de la Luire 1010
Grotte de Lascaux..24, 704
Grotte de Niaux............811
Grotte de Notre Dame du Lac..........................992
Grotte de Pech-Merle...743
Grotte de Villars 691
Grotte des Combarelles..702
Grotte des Demoiselles..860
Grotte du Grand Roc....703
Grottes de Bétharram...785
Grottes de Choranche................1010
Grottes de Cougnac.....732
Grottes de Gargas........806
Groupe de recherche d'art visuel (GRAV)..........1303
Gruissan 869
Guérande 481
Guesclin, Bertrand du..415, 427
guidebooks.................1336
Guillestre....................1020
Guimard, Hector.........1310
Guimiliau 438
Guise family, the.........1271
Guizot 1277

H

Haig, Sir Douglas 262
Haussmann, Baron 89, 1308
Haute Soule.........777–780
Hautecombe, abbaye d'...................995
Hauterives 1048
Haut Languedoc, Parc Naturel Régional du......869–872
Haut-Var villages 1102
health 73
Héas 802
Heliopolis (Île du Levant)....................1145
Hendaye 770
Hennessy Cognac Company 652
Henri II 512, 536
Henri III 521
Henri of Navarre (Henri IV)..................1271
Henry II, King......711, 1270
Henry V, King..............1271
Henry, Young King..711, 729
Hergé 524
Hesdin 238
hiking *see* walking
history.............1267–1290
Hoëdic 471
Holy Roman Empire ...1269
Honfleur 365–368
Honto............................775
horse riding 63
hostels 48
hotels 45
Houat 471
Houlgate 369
Huelgoat 462
Hugo, Victor 129
Huguenots........1271, 1273
Hunawihr 315
Hundred Years War 496, 1270
Huyghe, Pierre............1304
Hybert, Fabrice...........1304
Hyères............. 1140–1142
Hyères, Îles de 1143–1146

I

Ilay 974
Île Cavallo..................1253
Île d'Aix 642
Île d'Oléron 644
Île d'Ouessant 443, 444
Île de Batz 441
Île de Bréhat 432
Île de Chatou 204
Île de Molène 443, 444
Île de Noirmoutier....... 630
Île de Porquerolles......1144
Île de Port-Cros..........1145
Île de Ré 638
Île de Sein 453
Île du Levant...............1145
Îles d'Hyères ... 1143–1146
Îles de Lérins 1168
Îles Lavezzi.................1253
illuminated manuscripts............1291
Impressionism 1297
Ingres, Jean-Auguste-Dominique 1295
insurance, car.....39, 42, 74
Inter-Celtic Festival .....468, *Festive France* colour section
Internet access 75
invasion beaches, Normandy..374–378, 386
invasion beaches, Normandy 374
Irancy 573
Iraq war 1287
Isère valley........ 996–1001
Isère valley, the upper..997
Isola 1114
Ispagnac........................938
Itxassou 773

J

Jacobins 1275
Jardins d'Eyrignac.........700
Jarnac 653
Jaurès, Jean 892
Joan of Arc..275, 359, 361, 496, 498, 502, 504, 543, 1271
Joigny 567
Josephine, Empress.....215
Jospin, Lionel 1285
Josselin 464
Jouqueviel 929
Juan-les-Pins 1173
Julius Caesar......576, 1268
Jumiéges 354
Juppé, Alain......1285, 1286
Jura, the 963–975
Jura, the 960

K

Kassovitz, Mathieu 1314
Kaysersberg 315
Kermaria-an-Isquit........431
Kernascléden................463
kinetic art....................1303
Kintzheim.....................314
Klein, Yves..................1302
Koolhaas, Rem 1312

L

L'Aber-Wrac'h 442
L'Almanarre 1142
L'Alpe d'Huez 1012

L'Epau, abbaye de 560
L'Espérou.....................943
L'Espinouse 871
L'Île Rousse..... 1221–1223
La Bambouseraie 946
La Bâtie 1017
La Baule 482
La Bourboule.................915
La Brèche de Roland ...801
La Brée-les-Bains 645
La Brigue 1116
La Bussière 506
La Capte.......................1142
La Cavalerie..................943
La Chaise-Dieu 953
La Chapelle 1010
La Chapelle-Aubareil 704
La Chapelle-sur-Vire.... 404
La Ciotat.....................1137
La Clusaz......................982
La Cotiniére 645
La Coupole 230
La Couvertoirade..........943
La Croix-Valmer...........1147
La Ferriére-sur-Risle 394
La Ferté-Fresnel 398
La Foce........................1263
La Forêt-Fouesnant......459
La Garde-Freinet 1150
La Grande Motte 855
La Grave.....................1014
La Gurraz......................999
La Hague 387
La Maline .... *Walking in France* colour section
La Marana 1213
La Maurienne..............1014
La Pallice 639
La Palmyre 647
La Palud-sur-Verdon .. 1106
La Plagne 998
La Réole 673
La Rhune......................771
La Roche Maurice 439
La Rochelle 631–638
La Rochelle 632
La Roque St-Christophe 703
La Roque-Gageac 707
La Rouchefoucauld 656
La Salvetat-sur-Agout .. 871
La Sauve-Majeure 673
La Savinaz....................999
La Targette 261
La Tournette 991
La Turbie.....................1191
Labouiche.....................810
Lac Bersau 796
Lac d'Anterne.....*Walking in France* colour section
Lac d'Artouste.............796
Lac d'Espingo 808
Lac d'Ilhéou.................799
Lac d'Oô.......................807
Lac de Bious-Artigues..795
Lac de Chalain 973
Lac de Fabrèges 796
Lac de Serre-Ponçon . 1020
Lac des Bouillousses ...837
Lac du Bourget.............995
Lac Gentau...................795
Lacaune........................871
Lacaze 872
Lacrouzette...................893
Laguiole 926
Lake Geneva 975–977
Lamalou-les-Bains 869
Lamarque 669
Lamartine, Alphonse ...607
Lamotte-Beuvron 528
Lampaul 444
Lampaul-Guimiliau 438
Landévennec 448
Langeais 538
Langres 287
language.......... 1339–1355
language courses.. 66, 1341
Languedoc 839–898
Languedoc 842–843
Lannion 436
Lanslebourg................1002
Laon 265–267
La-Pierre-St-Martin 780
Larrau 778
Larressingle 897
Laruns...........................794
Lascaux 24, 704
Lassay-sur-Croisne 527
Lastours........................878
Latour-de-Carol............837
laundry 75
Lauzerte........................749
Lavelanet 814
Lavezzi, Îles 1253
Lavier, Bertrand 1303
Le Bec-Hellouin 393
Le Bleymard 941
Le Bourg 432
Le Bourg-d'Oisans 1012
Le Bourget 210
Le Brévent.....987, *Walking in France* colour section
Le Brun, Charles.........1293
Le Casset 1015
Le Cateau-Cambrésis ..257
Le Caylar 944
Le Château 645
Le Conquet 442
Le Corbusier.... 1133, 1192, 1309
Le Crestet...................1057
Le Creusot 590
Le Croisic 483
Le Crotoy......................239
Le Faou 448
Le Faouët 463
Le Fel............................932
Le Gouffre.....................434
Le Grand Taureau.........967
Le Grau-du-Roi 856
Le Havre 350–353
Le Havre 351
Le Laus........................1019
Le Lavandou................1147
Le Lioran.......................919
Le Mans 556–560
Le Mans 557
Le Mas d'Azil................810
Le Monêtier-les-Bains..1015
Le Mont-Dore 913
Le Moulinet...................946
Le Nain, Louis 1292
Le Palais 470
Le Parc, Julio..............1303
Le Pen, Jean-Marie 1286
Le Pont-de-Montvert....941
Le Pouget 862
Le Puy-en-Velay..949–953, *Walking in France* colour section
Le Puy-en-Velay 951
Le Rozier 938
Le Sidobre 893
Le Struthof concentration camp 313
Le Teich 676
Le Thot 704
Le Touquet 236
Le Tour.........................987
Le Tréport 346
Le Val-Hulin 548
Le Vigan.......................944
Lectoure 896
Ledoux, Claude 1308
Léger, Fernand 1301
Lérins, Îles de 168
Les Andelys 363
Les Antiques...............1075
Les Arcs........................998
Les Arques 732
Les Aspres 833
Les Baux-de-Provence.................1076
Les Deux-Alpes 1013
Les Épesses 631
Les Eyzies-de-Tayac 700

INDEX

Les Gets....................978
Les Goupillières.............540
Les Haras...................789
Les Hautes-Rivières.....291
Les Houches...............987
Les Landes..................677
Les Lecques..............1138
Les Milandes...............706
Les Rousses................974
Les Sables-d'Olonne....629
Les Salins d'Hyères....1143
Les Stes-Maries-de-la-Mer...1087–1089, *Festive France* colour section
Les Trois Vallées...........996
Les Vans......................949
Les Vigneaux.............1017
lesbian travellers............73
Lescun.........................791
Leszczynski, Stanislas..325
Levant, Île du.............1145
Lewarde.......................255
Licq..............................779
Lille 246–253
Lille 247
Limeuil.........................700
Limoges..............713–717
Limoges 714
Limousin, the 713–728
Limousin, the..............682
Limoux.........................817
Lisieux 395
Livarot.........................397
living in France 65
Loches 517
Locmariaquer 475
Locronan 450
Lodève.........................862
Logibar 779
Loire châteaux 513
Loire valley, the... 489–560
Loire valley, the.... 492–493
Longueval 264
Lons-le-Saunier............969
Lorgues......................1102
Lorient...........467, *Festive France* colour section
Lorp-Sentaraille............814
Lorrain, Claude...........1293
Lorraine 322–336
Lorraine 296–297
Lot valley, the...... 728–754
Lot valley............. 738–739
Loti, Pierre 641
Loue, River 968
Louis VII 501
Louis XI 523
Louis XIII 285, 525
Louis XIII....................1272
Louis XIV 148, 209, 212, 486, 514, 768, 1272, 1273
Louis XV 212, 325, 1274
Louis XVI 1274
Louis XVIII 1276
Louis-Philippe 131, 212, 536, 1276
Lourdes...............787–789
Luberon ... 1092, *Walking in France* colour section
Luc...............................949
Luchon.........................806
Luçon 629
Lugdunum Convenarum.............805
Lumière, August and Louis.............1137, 1313
Lutour valley 799
Luzech 737
Luz-St-Sauveur 799
Lyon 1029–1043
Lyon................1030–1031
Lyon and the Presqu'Île, Vieux.......................1034

M

Maastricht referendum..............1284
Macinaggio 1215
Mâcon 607
Mâconnais, the ... 609–611
magazines 55
Maginot Line 334
mail 75
Mailly-le-Château 573
Malestroit 465
Malle, Louis 1313
Malmaison.................. 215
Malo-les-Bains 224
Manet, Edouard.........1297
mannerism................ 1291
Mansart, François.......1307
Mansart, Jules Hardouin................1308
maps 75
Marais Poitevin 628
Marcadau valley 798
Marciac........*Festive France* colour section
Marcilhac-sur-Célé.......743
Marennes 644
Margaux 669
Margeride, the 923
Mariana......................1214
Marquay 699
Marquenterre Bird Sanctuary 238
Marquet, Albert...........1300
Marseille......... 1123–1136
Marseille....................1124
Marseille, Le Vieux Port............... 1128–1129
Martel 711
Martel, Charles 1269
Marvejois 927
Mas de la Pyramide ... 1075
Mas Soubeyran 946
Mas-Cabardès 879
Massif Central, the 899–956
Massif Central, the 902
Massif de l'Esterel......1161
Massif des Maures......... 1148–1151
Massif Montmirail-St-Armand.................1058
Master of Moulins, the..........................1291
Matignon Agreement..1279
Matisse, Henri..1177, 1186, 1300
Mazarin, Cardinal 1272
media 55, 58
Médicis, Catherine de.. 512, 514, 521, 523, 1271
Médoc, the 667
megalithic sites..474, 1244, 1247
Megève........................982
Meissonier, Jean-Louis-Ernest 1295
Méliès, Georges 1313
Mende 940–941
Menthon-St-Bernard....991
Menton 1197–1199
mercantilism 1272
Mercantour, Parc National du.......... 1113, *Walking in France* colour section
Mercantour, Parc National du 1112
Méribel.........................996
Merovingian dynasty .. 1269
Messager, Annette......1303
Metz 327–331
Metz 328
Meudon 205
Meymac.......................722
Meyssac 727
Michelin 904
Mignard, Pierre..........1293
Mijanès 820
Millau 934–937
Millet, Jean-François..1296

Millevaches 721–724
Minerve 877
Mirepoix 816
Mitterand, François 115, 580, 586, 653, 1283, 1310
mobile phones 78
Modane 1002
Moissac ..... 750, *Walking in France* colour section
Molene, Île de 443, 444
Molière 865
Molitg-les-Bains 834
Monaco 1192–1197
Monaco 1194–1195
Monastier-sur-Gazeille.. 955
Monet, Claude 114, 204, 364, 1297
money 70, 76
Monflanquin 740
Monpazier 21, 694–696
Mons (Languedoc) 870
Mont Aigoual 942
Mont Blanc .... 983–988, *Walking in France* colour section
Mont Blanc 979
Mont d'Huisnes 375
Mont de Marsan 677
Mont Lozère .. 941, *Walking in France* colour section
Mont Rond 975
Mont Ste-Victoire 1101
Mont St-Michel 15, 389–392
Mont Ventoux 1058
Montagne de la Clape.. 868
Montagne Noire .. 877–879
Montauban 748
Montbéliard 964
Montcaret 694
Montceaux-l'Étoile 613
Mont-Dauphin 1019
Monte d'Oro 1263
Monte-Carlo 1193
Montélimar 1050
Monthermé 290
Montignac 703
Montigny-Sous-Chatillon 281
Mont-Louis 837
Montolieu 877
Montpellier 849–855
Montpellier 850
Montreuil-sur-Mer 237
Montrichard 514
Monts du Cantal, the ... 918–924, *Walking in France* colour section
Monts du Lyonnais 1043
Montsauche 586
Monts-Dore .... 913–918, *Walking in France* colour section
Montségur 815
Montsoreau 549
Moreau, Gustave 1299
Morellet, François 1303
Morez 974
Morgat 448
Morlaix 437
Morteau 965
Morvan, Parc Régional du 586
Morzine 978
motorbikes 44
Moulin, Jean 863
mountain biking 963
Mourèze 862
Moustiers-Ste-Marie... 1107
Moux 586
Mozac 911
Mulhouse 319–322
Munster 318
Mur des Vaudois 1017
Murat 921
Mur-de-Barrez 920
Murol 918
Musée de Plein Air du Quercy 743
Muslims in France 1287

N

Nabis, the 1299
Najac 746
Nancy 323–327
Nancy 324
Nantes .... 483–487, *Festive France* colour section
Nantes 484
Nantes–Brest Canal 461–466
Napoleon Bonaparte 88, 215, 516, 1238, 1239, 1240, 1275, 1276
Napoléon III ... 89, 327, 577, 1277
Narbonne 866–868
Nasbinals 925
Navarrenx 787
Nebbio, the 1218–1221
Neuville-St-Vaast 262
Nevers 591
newspapers 55
Nexon 719
Niaux 811
Nice 1179–1189
Nice 1180–1181
Nietzsche, Friedrich 1191
Nîmes 843–848
Nîmes 844
Niort 627
Niou 444
Nive, River 772–777
Noirmoutier-en-l'Île 630
Nolette 240
Nonza 1217
Normandy 337–405
Normandy 340
Normandy, Battle of 398, 403
north, the 219–292
north, the 220–221
Nostradamus 1073
Nouveau Réalisme 1302
Nouvel, Jean 1311, 1312
Noyers-sur-Serein 572
Noyon 270
Nozeroy 972

O

Obernai 311
ochre mines 1091
Oger 281
Olargues 870
Oléron, Île de 644
Oloron-Ste-Marie 790
Omonville-la-Petite 387
Onet-le-Château 928
opening hours 77
Operation Dynamo 223
Oradour-sur-Glane 717
Orange .... 1052–1054, *Festive France* colour section
Orange 1052
Orb valley 869
Orbec 397
Orbiel valley 878
Orcival 915
Orglandes 375
Orléans 495–501
Orléans 496
Ornans 968
Orphism 1301
Orthez 786
Ossau valley 794–797
Ouistreham 376
Ouessant, Île d' 443, 444
outdoor activities ... 20, 23, 61–64, 319, 936, *Walking in France* colour section

oysters 643

P

Paimpol 431
Paimpont 417
Paiolive, Bois de 949
Palaggiu 1248
Palavas 856
Paradiski 998
paragliding 936
Paray-le-Monial 612
PARIS 83–201
Paris 86–87
- accommodation 99–106
- airports 90
- Arc de Triomphe, the 111
- arrival in Paris 89
- Auteuil 154
- bars 165–177
- Bastille 131
- Bastille 126–127
- Beauborg 124
- Beauborg 122
- Beaux Quartiers 153
- Belleville 161
- Bercy 163
- Bibliothéque Nationale ... 121, 153
- boat trips 98, 99
- Bois de Boulogne 154
- Bois de Vincennes 164
- buses 96
- cabaret 182
- cafés 164–177
- campsites 106
- Canal St-Martin 159
- catacombs 151
- Cathédrale de Notre-Dame 108
- Centre Georges Pompidou 123, 1310
- Champs-Élysées 110–114
- Champs-Élysées 110–111
- children's Paris 193
- cinema 188
- Cinémathéque 163
- circus 194
- Cité des Enfants 160, 193
- Cité des Sciences et de l'Industrie 159
- city transport 93
- classical music 184
- clubs 183
- concert venues 184
- Conciergerie 108
- crypte archéologique 109
- dance 190
- department stores 196
- disabled travellers 97
- drinking 164–180
- driving 97
- eating 164–180
- Eiffel Tower 146
- ethnic restaurants 178
- Eurostar 89, 91
- festivals 185, 200
- film 188
- funfairs 194
- Galeries nationales 113
- gay Paris 185–187
- gourmet restaurants 179
- Goutte d'Or 158
- Grand Palais 113
- hostels 105
- Hôtel de Ville 124
- hotels 100–105
- Île de la Cité 107–110
- Île St-Louis 131
- Île St-Louis 126–127
- information 199
- Institut du Monde Arabe .. 133, 1311
- Jardin d'Acclimatation 193
- Jardin des Plantes 137
- Jardin du Luxembourg 21, 141
- Jewish quarter 128
- kids' Paris 193
- kilométre zero 109
- La Voie Triomphale 110–111
- Le Mémorial de la Déportation 109
- Les Halles 122–124
- Les Halles 122
- Les Invalides 148
- lesbian Paris 185–187
- listings 199
- Louvre, the 23, 115–119, 1307, 1310
- Madeleine, the 120
- Marais, the 124
- Marais, the 126–127
- markets 198
- Mémorial de la Shoah 130
- Ménilmontant 161
- metro, the 96
- métro, the 94–95
- Montmartre 155–160
- Montmartre 156
- Montparnasse 150
- mosque 137
- Moulin Rouge 155, 182
- Musée Carnavalet 125
- Musée d'Orsay 141
- Musée de l'Armée 148
- Musée de l'Erotisme 158
- Musée de l'Histoire de France 125
- Musée du Louvre 12, 115–119, 1307, 1310
- Musée du Quai Branly 147
- Musée Jacquemart-André 112
- Musée Maillol 149
- Musée National d'Art Moderne 123
- Musée National du Moyen-Âge 133
- Musée Picasso 128
- Musée Rodin 149
- Muséum National d'Histoire Naturelle 137
- museum pass 92
- music 180–185
- nightlife 180–185
- Observatoire 151
- opera 185
- Opéra District 119–122
- Opéra-Bastille 131, 185, 1310
- Opéra-Garnier 120
- Orangerie 114
- Palais de Chaillot 143
- Palais de Justice 108
- Palais de Tokyo 143
- Palais Royal 121
- Panthéon 136
- Parc de la Villette 159
- Parc des Buttes-Chaumont 160
- Parc Floral 194
- Parc Zoologique 194
- parking 97
- passages 120
- Pére-Lachaise cemetery .. 161
- Pére-Lachaise cemetery .. 162
- Pigalle 158
- place de la Concorde 113
- place des Abbesses 155
- place des Vosges 129
- place du Tertre 156
- place Vendôme 121
- Pompidou Centre ... 123, 1310
- Pont-Neuf 107
- Promenade Plantée 163
- public transport 93
- Quartier Latin 132–137
- Quartier Latin 134–135
- restaurants 164–180
- Sacré-Coeur 157
- Sainte-Chapelle 108
- shopping 194–199
- Sorbonne 133
- sports 191
- St-Étienne-du-Mont 136
- St-Germain 137
- St-Germain 138–139
- St-Ouen flea market 157
- St-Séverin church 132
- student accommodation .. 105
- student restaurants 176
- taxis 96
- theatre 189
- tourist information 92
- trains 89
- Trocadéro 144–145
- Tuileries 114
- Union Centrale des Arts Décoratifs 119
- vegetarian restaurants 175
- youth hostels 105

Paris, around 201–216
Paris, around 201
parlements, the 1274
Parnay 548
Parreno, Philippe 1304

INDEX

Parthenay 626
Pasqua, Charles 1285
Pasteur, Louis.......968, 971
Patrimonio 1219
Pau 782–785
Pau 782
Pauillac 669
Pays Basque, the..758–780
Pays d'Auge, the ..395–399
Pays de Sault, the 814–817
Peace of Rijswik.........1273
Pegasus Bridge 377
Pei, I.M. 1310
pelota 61
Penne 747
Penne-d'Agenais..........739
people 11
Pepin 1269
perfume (Grasse)........1170
Périgord 683–710
Périgord 682
Périgord Noir 697
Périgueux 684–688
Périgueux 685
Pérols-sur-Vézère 723
Péronne 264
Pérouges 1044
Perpignan 825–828
Perpignan.....................826
Perrault, Claude..........1307
Perret, Auguste...351, 1309
Perros-Guirec 434
Pétain, Maréchal.........1279
pétanque 61
pets, travelling with 31
Peyragudes 808
Peyriac-de-Mer............868
Peyrusse-le-Roc...........742
Pézenas........................865
Philippe, Count of Valois 1270
phones 77
Piana...........................1231
Piano, Renzo 1310
Pic Blanc 1013
Pic Castérau.................796
Pic de la Sagette..........796
Pic du Canigou.............835
Pic du Midi d'Ossau.....795
Picabia, Francis..........1301
Picasso, Pablo...128, 1101, 1171, 1300, 1301
Pierrefonds 270
Pinceman, Jean-Pierre..1303
Pineau des Charentes..648
Pissarro, Camille 1297
Plouescat 441
Plougrescant 434
Plouha 431
Ploumanac'h 434
Point Sublime.....*Walking in France* colour section
Pointe des Lessières..1001
Pointe du Grouin..........424
Pointe du Raz 451
Poitiers 619–623
Poitiers 620
Poitiers, battle of 1269, 1270
Poitou 619–631
Poitou-Charentes..615–678
Poitou-Charentes 618
police 70
Poligny 971
Pompidou, Georges ...1283
Pont d'Arc 23, 947
Pont d'Espagne............798
Pont d'Ouilly 400
Pont du Diable.............831
Pont du Gard...............848
Pontarlier 967
Pont-Audemer 393
Pont-Aven 461
Pontigny 570
Pontivy 464
Pontorson 392
popes, Avignon 1060
Porquerolles, Île de.....1144
Portalet, Fort du 793
Port Grimaud..............1157
Port-Clos 432
Port-Cros, Île de.........1145
Porto 1229–1231
Porto-Vecchio............1254
Portsall 442
Port-Vendres 830
post offices 75
Post-Impressionism....1299
Pouilly 609
Poussin, Nicolas.........1293
Poziéres 264
Prades 833
Prafrance 946
Prats-de-Mollo 832
Presqu'Île de Giens 1142
Presqu'île de Quiberon..468
Presqu'île de Rhuys 481
Prieuré de Serrabona ...833
Primaticcio.................1292
Prissé 609
Propriano 1243
Provence 1051–1118
Provence..........1026–1027
Provence, northeast ..1112
public holidays 77
Puilaurens....................822
Pujols...........................739
Puy Aillaud.................1018
Puy de Dôme...............909
Puy de Pariou..............909
Puy de Sancy ....914, *Walking in France* colour section
Puy-l'Évêque 737
Puyloubier 1101
Pyrenees, the 755–838
Pyrenees, the.......758–759
Pyrénées, Parc National des.............................781
Pyrénées, Parc National des.............................792

Q

Quarton, Enguerrand..1291
Quénécan Forest..........463
Quéribus 823
Quérigut.......................820
Queyras, Parc Régional du.......... 1020, *Walking in France* colour section
Queyras, Parc Régional du 1021
Quiberon 468–470
Quillan 820
Quimper 454–458
Quimper 455
Quinéville 386
Quinson 1108

R

racism 71
radio 55
Raffarin, Jean-Pierre...1288
rail passes 30, 38
rail routes, France ... 36–37
rail travel to France 29–31, 34
rail travel within France 35–39
Rainbow Tribe, the 706
Rainier of Monaco, Prince 1192, 1194
Ramatuelle..................1157
Rappeneau, Jean-Pierre 1314
Rasteau 1058
Ré, Île de 638
Realism (in art)...........1296
Redon 466
Redon, Odilon 1299

refuge huts 49
Regency, the.............. 1274
Région des Lacs (Haut Jura).................. 973–975
Reims 272–279
Reims 272
religious wars 1271
Renaissance architecture............. 1307
Rennes 413–417
Rennes 413
Rennes-le-Château 819
Renoir, Jean............... 1313
Renoir, Pierre-Auguste .. 142, 205, 1176, 1298
Resistance, the........... 1279
restaurants............... *Cafés, bistros and brasseries* colour section
Revel............................ 878
Revin 291
Revolution, the French .. 88, 128, 1274
Rhône valley, the 1029–1051
Rhône valley, the 1026–1027
Ribeauvillé 315
Ribérac 690
Richard the Lionheart .. 363, 548, 711, 1270
Richelieu, Cardinal 1272
Richemont 653
Rièges, Boise des 1086
Riez........................... 1107
Rigny-Ussé.................. 540
Rimbaud, Arthur 289
Riom 910
Rioux 651
Riquewihr..................... 315
river trips 43
Riviera, the French........... 1163–1199
Rixheim........................ 322
Robespierre, Maximilien................ 1275
Rocamadour 728–730
Rochechouart.............. 718
Rochefort 640–642
Rochefort-en-Terre....... 465
Rochemenier 547
Rocher Bonnevie.......... 921
Rocher Bredons 922
Rodez 928
Rodin, Auguste 149, 205
Rogers, Richard .. 1310, 1312
Rohmer, Eric............... 1314
Roman architecture 1305
Romanesque architecture............. 1305
Romans-sur-Isère....... 1048
Romanticism (art) 1295
Romorantin-Lanthenay .. 527
Ronchamp 963
Roquebrune............... 1192
Roquefère.................... 879
Roquefixade 814
Roquefort-sur-Soulzon.. 937
Rosa, Henri di 1303
Roscoff 439
Rosheim 312
Rosso 1292
Rouault, Georges 1300
Roubaix 253
Rouen 355–363
Rouen.......................... 356
Rouffiac-des-Corbières... 824
Rougon....................... 1106
Rousse, Île de... 1221–1223
Rousseau, Jean-Jacques 994
Rousseau, Théodore .. 1296
Roussillon........... 824–837
Roussillon 818
Roussillon ......(village) 1091
Route des Grandes Alpes...... 975, *Walking in France* colour section
Route des Sapins......... 973
Route du Vin 311–315
Route Napoléon 1109
Routes des Pierres Fortes de Savoie................. 999
Roya valley 1115–1117
Royal, Ségolène 1290
Royan 645–647
Rue 239
rugby 60
Rustrel 1092
Rwanda 1284
Ryes 375

S

Sablet 1058
Sablières..................... 949
Sabres 677
safety 70, 71
Saillac 727
Saillagouse 837
Saillant......................... 917
Saint-Phalle, Niki de... 1302
Sainte-Foy-de-Tarentaise 999
Saintes 648–650
Saintes 649
Saissac 877
Salernes..................... 1103
Salers.......................... 921
Salies-de-Béarn........... 786
Samoëns 979
Sancerre 507
sans-culottes, the....... 1275
Saône valley, the .. 604–609
Sare 772
Sarkozy, Nicolas........ 1288
Sarlat 697–700
Sarlat 698
Sarran 724
Sarrance 791
Sartène 1246
Sartre, Jean-Paul......... 353
Sarzeau 481
Saulieu 585
Saumur 544–547
Saunière, Abbé Bérenguer................ 819
Sauternes 674
Sauveterre-de-Béarn.... 786
Sauveterre-de-Rouergue................... 929
Sauzon 470
Saverne 308–310
Savines-le-Lac........... 1020
Scandola, Réserve Naturel de .... 1228, *Walking in France* colour section
School of Roads and Bridges 1309
scooters 44
Second Republic, the.. 1277
secret massacre (Algerians) 1281
Sedan 291
Ségala, the 929
Séguret 1058
Sein, Île de.................. 453
Sélestat 313
self-catering 47
Semnoz mountains....... 992
Semur-en-Auxois 578
Sénanque, Abbaye de.. 1091
Sens 565–567
Senta 780
Sérignan-du-Comtat .. 1055
Serre Chevalier 1015
Sérusier, Paul............. 1299
Sète 856–858
Seurat, Georges 1299
Seven Years War 1274
Sèvres 210
shopping 68,
Sillans-la-Cascade 1103
Silvacane, abbaye de. 1093

Silvanès, abbaye de 937
Sisteron 1110
Sixt ..... 980, *Walking in France* colour section
skiing 23, 62, 803, 808, 915, 963. 980, 981, 987, 1013
smoking 67
snowboarding 62
Soissons 267
Solignac 719
Sologne, the 526–528
Solutré-Pouilly 609
Somme battlefields 260–264
Somme estuary 239
Sommières 849
Sorges 692
Sospel 1115
Souillac 710
Soulages, Pierre 1302
Souville, Fort de 334
Spoerri, Daniel 1302
sports 59–64
St Bartholomew's Day, massacre of 1271
Stade de France 205
St-Aignan 515
St-André-des-Arques 733
St-Antonin-Noble-Val 747
St-Armand-de-Coly 705
St-Benoît-sur-Loire 504
St-Bertrand-de-Comminges 805
St-Brieuc 430
St-Brisson 586
St-Céré 731
St-Cirque-Lapopie 736
St-Claude 974
St-Cosme 533
St-Dalmas-de-Tende 1116
St-Denis 202–206
St-Denis 203
St-Émilion 671
St-Estèphe 670
St-Étienne 955
St-Étienne-de-Baïgorry 774
St-Étienne-de-Tinée 1114
St-Florent 1218
St-Flour 922
St-Gelven 463
St-Georges-sur-Loire 555
St-Germain 210
St-Germain-de-Confolens 657
St-Girons 813
St-Guilhem-le-Désert 860
St-Hippolyte 965
St-Honorat 1168
St-Jacques 481
St-Jean-de-Côle 691
St-Jean-de-Luz 767–769
St-Jean-du-Gard 945
St-Jean-le-Thomas 389
St-Jean-Pied-de-Port 775
St-Junien 718
St-Laurent-de-Médoc 670
St-Laurent-en-Grandvaux 974
St-Léger-sous-Beauvray 589
St-Léonard-de-Noblat 720
St-Léon-sur-Vézère 704
St-Lizier 814
St-Lô 403
St-Macaire 673
St-Malo 420–424
St-Malo 420
St-Marcel 465
St-Marsal 833
St-Martin 639
St-Martin-d'Ardèche 947
St-Martin-de-Londres 859
St-Martin-du-Canigou 834
St-Martin-en-Haut 1044
St-Martin-Vésubie 1115
St-Maurice-Navacelles 944
St-Maximin-de-la-Ste-Baume 1102
St-Mihiel 335
St-Nectaire 916
St-Nizier-du-Moucherotte 1009
St-Omer 229
St-Papoul 878
St-Paul-de-Mausole 1075
St-Paul-de-Vence 1177
St-Père 583
St-Pierre-de-Chartreuse 1011
St-Pierre (Île d'Oléron) 645
St-Pierre-la-Palud 1043
St-Point 610
St-Pol-de-Léon 441
St-Pons-de-Thomières 870
St-Quay-Portrieux 431
St-Raphaël 1162
St-Rémy-de-Provence 1073–1075
St-Romain-en-Gal 1046
St-Sauveur-en-Puisaye 568
St-Sauveur-sur-Tinée 1115
St-Savin (Poitou) 625
St-Savin (Pyrenees) 797
St-Thégonnec 438
St-Tropez 1151–1156
St-Tropez 1152–1153
St-Urcize 925
St-Vaast-la-Hougue 386
St-Valéry-en-Caux 347
St-Valéry-sur-Somme 239
St-Véran 1021
St-Viâtre 528
St-Wandrille 354
Ste-Anne d'Auray ..... *Festive France* colour section
Ste-Engrâce 780
Ste-Énimie 938
Ste-Marguerite 1168
Ste-Marie-de-Campan 804
Ste-Marie-du-Mont 386
Ste-Maxime 1157–1159
Stevenson, R.L. ..... 939, 941, 955, *Walking in France* colour section
Strasbourg 22, 299–308
Strasbourg 300
student accommodation 48
studying in France 66
Sully-sur-Loire 504
Superbagnères 808
Super-Besse 918
Super-Lioran 919
Supports-Surfaces group 1303
surfing 63
Surrealism 1301
swimming 63
Symbolists, the 1299

T

Tachisme 1302
Taillefer 992
Tain-l'Hermitage 1047
Taizé 611
Talleyrand, Prince de 516
Talloires 991
Talmont 647
Tamniès 704
Tanguy, Yves 1301
Tapestry of the Apocalypse 551
Tarbes 789
Tati, Jacques 1314
Tautavel 828
Tavant 544
teaching English 65
Tech valley 831
telephones 77
television 58
Tende 1116
Terror, the 1275
Tesse-Madeleine 402
theft 70

Thiepval 264
Thiers 954
Thiezac 919
Thines 949
Third Estate, the 1275
Third Republic, the 1277–1279
Thiviers 691
Thonac 704
Thonon-les-Bains 975
Thoronet, Abbaye du.. 1102
Thuès-entre-Valls 836
Thury-Harcourt 399
Tiberi, Jean 1285
Tignes 999
time 79
Tinguely, Jean 1302
Tintin 524
tipping 67
toilets 67
Tonnerre 573
Tonneville 387
Torigni-sur-Vire 404
Toulon 1139
Toulouse 879–888
Toulouse 880
Toulouse-Lautrec, Henri 890, 1298
Tour de France.. 16, 59, 191
Tour des Cévennes 939
Tour du Mont Blanc 987
Tour, Georges de la 1292
tour operators 33
tourist offices 79
Tournus 606
Tours 528–534
Tours 529
Tourtour 1103
train passes 30, 38
train routes, France.. 36–37
trains to France.. 29–31, 34
trains within France 35–39
Trascon-sur-Ariège 810
travel agents 33
Treasure of Vix 575
Trébeurden 435
Trégastal .... 435, *Walking in France* colour section
Tréguier...... 434, *Walking in France* colour section
Treignac 723
Trémazan 442
Trouville 368
Troyes 281–286
Truffaut, François 1313
Tulle 727
Turenne 726
Turquant 548

U

Urdos 794
Urrugne 769
Ussel 722
Utah Beach 386
Uzerche 725
Uzès 848
Uzeste 674

V

Vacqueyras 1058
Vaison-la-Romaine 1056
Val d'Enfer, the 1077
Val d'Isère 1000
Valance 1049
Valcabrère 805
Valdois, the 1018
Valentin, Moise 1292
Vallauris 1169
Valleraugue 943
Valloire 1014
Vallon 947
Vallouise 1017
Valras 868
Van Gogh, Vincent 204, 1075, 1082, 1300
Vannes 476–478
Vannes 476
Vanoise, Parc National de la.......... 1002, *Walking in France* colour section
Vanoise, Parc National de la 997
Varengeville 347
Vassieux-en-Vercors... 1010
Vauvenargues 1101
Vauville 387
Vaux 573
Vaux, Fort de 335
Vaux-le-Vicomte 209
vegetarian food 52, 175
Venarey-les-Laumes..... 576
Vence 1177
Vendée, the 629–631
Vercingétorix 904, 1268
Vercors massif..1009–1011, *Walking in France* colour section
Verdun 332–336
Verne, Jules 243
Vernet, Horace 1295
Vernet-les-Bains 834
Vernier, Pierre 968
Versailles ... 211–213, 1273
Vézelay 582–584
Vézère valley, the... 700–705
Via Domitia 849
Viam 723
Viaud, Julien 641
Vichy 911–913
Vichy government, the... 1279
Vic-sur-Cère 919
Vieillevie 932
Vienne.. 1044–1046, *Festive France* colour section
Vietnam war 1281
Vigo, Jean 1313
Vilar, Jean 1061
Villa Kérylos 1191
Villandraut 674
Villards-de-Lans 1009
Villars 691
Villat, Claude 1303
Villecroze 1103
Villedieu-les-Poêles 404
Villefranche 611
Villefranche-de-Conflent 835
Villefranche-de-Rouergue.......... 744–746
Villefranche-sur-Mer ... 1189
Villeneuve-lès-Avignon ... 1071
Villeneuve-sur-Lot 738
Villeneuvette 862
Villepin, Dominique de 1288, 1289
Villers 965
Villers-Bretonneux 264
Vilmout, Jean-Luc 1303
Vimoutiers 397
Vimy Ridge 260
Vincelottes 573
Vinci, Leonardo da 536, 1292
Vinzelles 609
Vire 404
visas 72
Vitrac 699
Vitré 418
Vix 575, 1268
Vizzavona 1263
Voie Sacrée, La ("Sacred Way") 335
Voiron 1011
Volcans d'Auvergne, Parc Régional des ... 903–924
voltage 72
Volvic 911
Vosges mountains .... 308–31[illegible]
Vouet, Simon .... 129[illegible]
Vuillard, Édouard .... 13[illegible]

W

walking ....61, 291, 319, 527, 775, 798, 803, 807, 904, 911, 915, 916, 987, 991, 1232, *Walking in France* colour section
war cemeteries....240, 259, 263, 375
war memorials 19, 261, 264, 335, 373, 375
War of Austrian Succession.............1274
War of the Spanish Succession.............1273
Wars of Religion ...88, 485, 536, 632, 1271
water sports 63
water-jousting...............857
Waterloo, battle of......1276
Watteau, Jean-Antoine..1294
weather 12
websites 79
White Terror, the 1276
William the Conqueror 398
windsurfing 63
wine 14, 52, 224, 273, 276, 279, 298, 311, 411, 494, 563, 571, 572, 601, 609, 611, 667, 668, 684, 694, 760, 961, 1028, 1055, 1058, 1204
wine bars......*Cafés, bistros and brasseries* colour section
winter sports 23
Wissant 231
Wissembourg 310
women travellers 68
working in France 65
World War I..256–264, 270, 327, 332–336, 1278
World War II......223, 259, 262, 313, 373, 374–378, 398, 403, 445, 586, 1279
Wright, Wilbur.......558, 559

Y

Yonne, River 572
youth hostels..................48
Yvoire...........................976

Z

Zola, Émile....................647
Zonza..........................1256